# 2 0 0 0
# WRITER'S
# MARKET

## 8,000 EDITORS WHO BUY WHAT YOU WRITE

EDITOR
## KIRSTEN C. HOLM

ASSISTANT EDITOR
## DONYA DICKERSON

**WRITER'S DIGEST BOOKS**
CINCINNATI, OHIO

# Praise for *Writer's Market*

"This volume is a freelancer's working tool, as important as the basic computer or typewriter."
—*The Bloomsbury Review*

"The writer's bible and best friend. If you're serious about selling what you write and if you submit material regularly, you need a new copy every year."
—*Freelance Writer's Report*

"Each year the editor's of *Writer's Market* continue to improve this already indispensable resource."
—*Writer's Write*

# Praise for *Writer's Market*— *The Electronic Edition*

"Writer's Digest Books goes digital, bringing its invaluable resources for writers to CD-ROM."
—*PC Magazine*

"The unpublished writer's best friend, and a published writer's best revenue lead."
—*We Compute*

"Writer's Market—The Electronic Edition brings what has always been the bible for serious writers into the computer age. It provides the road map on the writer's road to success."
—*ComputerEdge*

Managing Editor, Annuals Department: Cindy Laufenberg
Supervisory Editor: Barbara Kuroff
Production Editor: Anne Bowling

Writer's Digest Website: http://www.writersdigest.com

Library of Congress Catalog Number 31-20772
International Standard Serial Number 0084-2729
International Standard Book Number 0-89879-911-2
International Standard Book Number 0-89879-916-3 (Electronic Edition)

*Special thanks to SRDS for allowing us to use their editorial descriptions for publications that did not respond to our request for information.*

**Attention Booksellers:** This is an annual directory of F&W Publications. Return deadline for this edition is December 31, 2000.

# contents at a glance

# Contents

## Getting Published

### Before Your First Sale  5
*The basics of writing for publication.* **Bill Henderson**, *writer, editor and publisher of The Pushcart Press and The Pushcart Prize, takes on technology and the negative impact computers have on writing and how writers write on* **page 7**. *"All writers need," he says, "is a pencil, a piece of paper, a brain and a soul."*

### Six Secrets to Successful Submissions, by Kelly Milner Halls  18
*An accomplished full-time freelancer shares six winning tips she learned the hard way that make her submissions stand out from the crowd.*

### How to Study a Printed Magazine Article, by Gordon Burgett  21
*Close reading can give you clues as to why an article was published—and how you can follow suit with your own article.*

### Query Letter Clinic, by Don Prues  22
*Eight new, real-life examples of queries that succeeded and queries that failed, with plenty of comments to help you understand why. A quick checklist of items a good query should contain is also included.*

### Crafting a Successful Synopsis, by Evan Marshall  33
*A literary agent shows you how to craft a winning proposal that shows your novel to its best advantage.*

## Personal Views

### Jane Smiley: The All-True Result of Loving to Write, by Paula Deimling  37
*Novelist Jane Smiley talks about finding joy in writing and mastering the self-confidence to suspend judgmental thoughts and let the book develop itself. Every first draft is a perfect draft, she says, because all it has to do is exist. Revision means analyzing that draft to uncover the real answers to the writer's questions.*

# The Business of Writing

# Literary Agents

*Looking for a literary agent? Here's where to start your search, with 60 reputable literary agents that are open to new and previously published writers. This year we've also listed 20 WGA Signatory script agents.*

## How to Find (and Keep) the Right Agent, by Lori Perkins *91*

*An insider's look at what agents do . . . and how to get one to do it for you.*

## Literary Agents: The Listings *98*

### Literary Agents Subject Index *122*

# The Markets

## Book Publishers *128*

*From A&B Publishers to Zondervan, hundreds of places to sell your book ideas. The introduction to this section helps you refine your approach to publishers.*

## Canadian Book Publishers *355*

*The introduction to this section covers how to submit your work to international markets.*

## Small Presses *374*

*Companies publishing three or fewer books per year are listed here. Small presses often have narrowly tailored subjects—be sure to read each listing closely.*

## Book Producers *389*

*Book producers, or packagers as they are sometimes called, assemble the elements of books (writers, editors, designers and illustrators) for publishers.*

## Consumer Magazines *393*

*This section offers plentiful opportunities for writers with hundreds of listings for magazines on nearly every subject under the sun.*

## Trade, Technical & Professional Journals  797

*Magazines listed in this section serve a wide variety of trades and professions. The introduction tells
how to break in and establish yourself in the trades.*

## Scriptwriting  913

*Markets for film and television scripts and stageplays are listed here. Novelist, screenwriter and TV
producer **Robert Ward** discuses the different demands of each career jump on **page 946**.*

## Syndicates 960

*Newspaper syndicates distribute writers' works around the nation and the world. The introduction offers advice for breaking into this market.*

## Greeting Cards & Gift Ideas 968

*Greeting card and gift markets provide outlets for a wide variety of writing styles. The introduction to this section tells you how to approach these companies professionally.*

## Contests & Awards 975

*Contests and awards offer many opportunities for writers, and can launch a successful writing career. Playwright and contest winner **Claudia Haas** talks about the benefits of entering contests on **page 977**.*

# Resources

## Publications 1048

## Websites 1050

## Organizations 1054

## Glossary 1057

### Book Publishers Subject Index 1061

## General Index 1085

---

## COMPLAINT PROCEDURE

If you feel you have not been treated fairly by a listing in **Writer's Market**, we advise you to take the following steps:

• First try to contact the listing. Sometimes one phone call or a letter can quickly clear up the matter.

• Document all your correspondence with the listing. When you write to us with a complaint, provide the details of your submission, the date of your first contact with the listing and the nature of your subsequent correspondence.

• We will enter your letter into our files and attempt to contact the listing to resolve the situation if you wish.

• The number and severity of complaints will be considered in our decision whether or not to delete the listing from the next edition.

# From the Editors

On January 1, 2000 this book will be up and running, just as it was December 31, 1999. The market listings won't disappear, replaced by meaningless binary code. The queries you've sent won't suddenly backdate themselves to 1899. The power grid connecting Consumer Magazines to Trade Journals won't fail (and cause a blackout with widespread looting of "Women's" by the residents of "Advertising, Marketing & PR").

Well, it might not happen overnight, but technology has changed and will continue to change some things about writing. Certainly working on computers, sending electronic queries and delivering manuscripts via e-mail, and researching on and writing for the Internet has a major impact. But in the end, good writing doesn't depend that much on the time it was written. Good writing does depend, however, on the time it took to write it.

And that's one thing that has come through clearly in talking to many of the writers interviewed for *2000 Writer's Market*. The necessity of first drafts and subsequent revision, taking the time to write and rewrite, is stressed over and over.

For **Jane Smiley**, the first draft of a work is an end in itself. Once the whole arc of the story is out in the open, she can analyze the connections that have developed. Her methods have differed from one book to another, but the key thought, she says, must be not to judge the work but to analyze it, discovering the hidden answers or missing elements to be added or enhanced in the next revision.

In her writing and teaching **Julia Cameron** stresses freedom and creativity, counseling writers to write a first draft "that throws it at the page." Many writers will create a first draft that comes close to the final version if they are able to suspend judgment and enter fully into writing, she says. Trying to write the final draft from the outset creates an artificial, analytical distance that can cripple the work.

When **Russell Banks** is writing a first draft he limits his vision, "thinking only about the sentence in front of me." He works to make each paragraph clear and precise and only after the story is set down goes back to revise. You won't know how all the parts fit in until that point, he says.

**Bill Henderson** abhors the ease computers have brought to writing. The unthinking facility of putting words down on the page leads to bloated writing which is rarely revised, and belies the difficulty of writing. Writing is tough, he says, but there is value in the struggle. Real wisdom takes time and effort to get to.

Come January you may be leafing through this book by kerosene lamplight, gnawing on a piece of freeze-dried beef jerky, your bank account registering zero (a strong motivator to find a publisher for your manuscript). With the arctic wind howling around your darkened home, keep in mind what Bill Henderson firmly believes: "All a writer needs is a pencil and a piece of paper and a brain and a soul. That's all they need, nothing else."

Wishing you the best of luck and a successful year,

*Kirsten Campbell Holm*

Kirsten Campbell Holm, Editor
writersmarket@fwpubs.com

*Donya Dickerson*

Donya Dickerson, Assistant Editor
literaryagents@fwpubs.com

# Using Your *Writer's Market* to Sell Your Writing

*Writer's Market* is here to help you decide where and how to submit your writing to appropriate markets. Each listing contains information about the editorial focus of the market, how it prefers material to be submitted, payment information and other helpful tips.

## WHAT'S NEW?

*Writer's Market* has always given you the important information you need to know in order to approach a market knowledgeably. We've continued to search out improvements to help you access that information more efficiently.

**Symbols.** Scanning through the listings to find the right publisher for your book manuscript just got easier. The key symbol ( ⚭ ) quickly sums up a publisher's interests, along with information on what subjects are currently being emphasized or phased out. In Consumer Magazines the ⚭ zeroes in on what areas of that market are particularly open to freelancers to help you break in. Other symbols let you know, at a glance, whether a listing is new, a book publisher accepts only agented writers, comparative pay rates for a magazine, and more. A key to the symbols appears on the front and back inside covers.

**Literary agents.** Recognizing the increasing importance of literary agents in the book publishing field, we've researched and included 60 literary and 20 script agents at the beginning of the listings on page 98. All of these agents have indicated a willingness to work with new, previously unpublished writers as well as more established authors. Most are members of the Association of Authors' Representatives (AAR), or the Writers Guild of America (WGA).

**More names, royalty rates and advances highlighted.** In the U.S. Book Publishers section we identify acquisition editors with the word **Acquisitions** to help you get your manuscript to the right person. Royalty rates and advances are highlighted in boldface, as well as important information on the percentage of first-time writers, unagented writers, the number of books published and manuscripts received.

**Names, pay rates and percentage freelance-written highlighted.** Can you send an editor a query by e-mail? This year we asked editors if they accept e-queries as well as by mail, fax or phone. In Consumer Magazines, who to send your article to at each magazine is identified by the boldface word **Contact**. In addition, the percentage of a magazine that is freelance written, the number of articles and pay rates for features, columns and departments, and fillers are also highlighted, quickly identifying the information you need to know when considering whether or not to submit your work.

**New articles.** Be sure to check out the new articles geared to more experienced writers in Minding the Details. In Sell It Again Sam, Gordon Burgett offers valuable tips on how to boost your income by selling reprints and rewrites. Take advantage of the expertise of hundreds of freelance writers recently surveyed for our annual guide to pay ranges in How Much Should I Charge? by Lynn Wasnak. Michael Ray Taylor and Anthony Tedesco let you in on how—and where—to sell your writing on the Web. And Clifton Dowell introduces three freelancers who have successfully used their writing skills in less obvious ways.

**Interviews with bestselling authors.** Personal Views offers interviews with bestselling authors on writing and success. Jane Smiley, Caroline Alexander, Russell Banks and Julia Cameron offer insights into their writing life and advice for yours.

As always, all of the listings have been checked and verified, with more e-mail addresses and websites added.

# IF *WRITER'S MARKET* IS NEW TO YOU . . .

A quick look at the Table of Contents will familiarize you with the arrangement of *Writer's Market*. The three largest sections of the book are the market listings of Book Publishers; Consumer Magazines; and Trade, Technical & Professional Journals. You will also find other sections of market listings for Scriptwriting, Syndicates, Greeting Cards and Contests & Awards. The section introductions contain specific information about trends, submission methods and other helpful resources for the material included in that section.

The articles in the first section, Getting Published, are included with you in mind. Kelly Milner Halls lets you in on six secrets that will help your submissions stand out. Gordon Burgett walks you through how to analyze a printed article to uncover why it was successful. Query Letter Clinic showcases "good" and "bad" letters with comments straight from the editors' mouths about what attracted and what distracted. And literary agent Evan Marshall offers his practiced advice on how to put together a winning novel synopsis.

## Narrowing your search

After you've identified the market categories you're interested in, you can begin researching specific markets within each section.

Book Publishers are categorized, in the Book Publishers Subject Index, according to types of books they are interested in. If, for example, you plan to write a book on a religious topic, simply turn to the Book Publishers Subject Index and look under the Religion subhead in Nonfiction for the names and page numbers of companies that publish such books.

Consumer Magazines and Trade, Technical & Professional Journals are categorized by subject to make it easier for you to identify markets for your work. If you want to publish an article dealing with some aspect of retirement, you could look under the Retirement category of Consumer Magazines to find an appropriate market. You would want to keep in mind, however, that magazines in other categories might also be interested in your article (for example, women's magazines publish such material as well). Keep your antennae up while studying the markets: less obvious markets often offer the best opportunities.

## Interpreting the markets

Once you've identified companies or publications that cover the subjects you're interested in, you can begin evaluating specific listings to pinpoint the markets most receptive to your work and most beneficial to you.

In evaluating an individual listing, first check the location of the company, the types of material it is interested in seeing, submission requirements, and rights and payment policies. Depending upon your personal concerns, any of these items could be a deciding factor as you determine which markets you plan to approach. Many listings also include a reporting time, which lets you know how long it will typically take for the publisher to respond to your initial query or submission. (We suggest that you allow an additional month for a response, just in case your submission is under further review or the publisher is backlogged.)

Check the Glossary at the back of the book for unfamiliar words. Specific symbols and abbreviations are explained in the key appearing on the front and back inside covers. The most important abbreviation is SASE—self-addressed, stamped envelope. Always enclose one when you send unsolicited queries, proposals or manuscripts. This requirement is not included in most of the individual market listings because it is a "given" that you must follow if you expect to receive a reply.

A careful reading of the listings will reveal that many editors are very specific about their needs. Your chances of success increase if you follow directions to the letter. Often companies do not accept unsolicited manuscripts and return them unread. Read each listing closely, heed the tips given, and follow the instructions. Work presented professionally will normally be given more serious consideration.

Whenever possible, obtain writer's guidelines before submitting material. You can usually obtain them by sending a SASE to the address in the listing. Magazines often post their guidelines on their website as well. You should also familiarize yourself with the company's publications. Many of the listings contain instructions on how to obtain sample copies, catalogs or market lists. The more research you do upfront, the better your chances of acceptance, publication and payment.

## Additional help

The book contains many articles on a variety of helpful topics. Insider Reports—interviews with writers, editors and publishers—offer advice and an inside look at publishing. Some listings contain editorial comments, indicated by a bullet (●), that provide additional information discovered during our compilation of this year's *Writer's Market*. E-mail addresses and websites have been included for many markets. Publications in the Resources section includes some, but by no means all, trade magazines, directories and sources of information on writing-related topics. The Websites section points you to writing-related material on the Web.

Newer or unpublished writers should be sure to read Before Your First Sale. Minding the Details offers valuable information about rights, taxes and other practical matters. There is also a helpful section titled How Much Should I Charge? that offers guidance for setting your freelance fees.

---

### Important Listing Information

- Listings are based on editorial questionnaires and interviews. They are not advertisements; publishers do not pay for their listings. The markets are not endorsed by *Writer's Market* editors. F&W Publications, Inc., Writer's Digest Books and its employees go to great effort to ascertain the validity of information in this book. However, transactions between users of the information and individuals and/or companies listed herein are strictly between those parties.
- All listings have been verified before publication of this book. If a listing has not changed from last year, then the editor told us the market's needs have not changed and the previous listing continues to accurately reflect its policies. We require documentation in our files for each listing.
- *Writer's Market* reserves the right to exclude any listing.
- When looking for a specific market, check the index. A market may not be listed for one of these reasons:
    1. It doesn't solicit freelance material.
    2. It doesn't pay for material.
    3. It has gone out of business.
    4. It has failed to verify or update its listing for the 2000 edition.
    5. It was in the middle of being sold at press time, and rather than disclose premature details, we chose not to list it.
    6. It hasn't answered *Writer's Market* inquiries satisfactorily. (To the best of our ability, and with our readers' help, we try to screen out fraudulent listings.)
    7. It buys few manuscripts, constituting a very small market for freelancers.
- Individual markets that appeared in last year's edition but are not listed in this edition are included in the General Index, with a notation giving the basis for their exclusion.

# Getting Published
## Before Your First Sale

Many writers new to the craft feel that achieving publication—and getting paid for their work—is an accomplishment so shrouded in mystery and magic that there can be little hope it will ever happen to *them*. Of course, that's nonsense. All writers were newcomers once. Getting paid for your writing is not a matter of insider information or being handed the one "key" to success. There's not even a secret handshake.

Making money from your writing will require three things of you:
- Good writing
- Knowledge of writing markets (magazines and book publishers) and how to approach them professionally
- Persistence

Good writing without marketing know-how and persistence might be art, but who's going to know if it never sells? A knowledge of markets without writing ability or persistence is pointless. And persistence without talent and at least a hint of professionalism is simply irksome. But a writer who can combine the above-mentioned virtues stands a good chance of not only selling a piece occasionally, but enjoying a long and successful writing career.

You may think a previously unpublished writer has a difficult time breaking into the field. As with any profession, experience is valued, but that doesn't mean publishers are closed to new writers. While it is true some editors prefer working with established writers, most are open to professional submissions and good ideas from any writer, and quite a few magazine editors like to feature different styles and voices.

In nonfiction book publishing, experience in writing or in a particular subject area is valued by editors as an indicator of the author's ability and expertise in the subject. As with magazines, the idea is paramount, and new authors break in every year with good, timely ideas.

As you work in the writing field, you may read articles or talk to writers and editors who give conflicting advice. There are some norms in the business, but they are few. You'll probably hear as many different routes to publication as writers you talk to.

The following information on submissions has worked for many writers, but it's not the *only* method you can follow. It's easy to get wrapped up in the specifics of submitting (should my name go at the top left or right of the manuscript?) and fail to consider weightier matters (is this idea appropriate for this market?). Let common sense and courtesy be your guides as you work with editors, and eventually you'll develop your own most effective submission methods.

## DEVELOP YOUR IDEAS, THEN TARGET THE MARKETS

Writers often think of an interesting story, complete the manuscript and then begin the search for a suitable publisher or magazine. While this approach is common for fiction, poetry and screenwriting, it reduces your chances of success in many other writing areas. Instead, try choosing categories that interest you and study those sections in *Writer's Market*. Select several listings that you consider good prospects for your type of writing. Sometimes the individual listings will even help you generate ideas.

Next, make a list of the potential markets for each idea. Make the initial contact with markets using the method stated in the market listings. If you exhaust your list of possibilities, don't give up. Reevaluate the idea or try another angle. Continue developing ideas and approaching markets with them. Identify and rank potential markets for an idea and continue the process.

As you submit to the various periodicals listed in *Writer's Market*, it's important to remember that every magazine is published with a particular slant and audience in mind. Probably the number one complaint we hear from editors is that writers often send material and ideas that are completely wrong for their magazines. The first mark of professionalism is to know your market well. That knowledge starts here in *Writer's Market*, but you should also search out back issues of the magazines you wish to write for and learn what specific subjects they have published in past issues and how those subjects have been handled. Websites can be an invaluable source. Not only do many magazines post their writer's guidelines on their site, many publish some or all of the current issue, as well as an archive of past articles. This will give you clues as to what they're interested in and what they've already published.

Prepare for rejection and the sometimes lengthy wait. When a submission is returned, check your file folder of potential markets for that idea. Cross off the market that rejected the idea and immediately mail an appropriate submission to the next market on your list. If the editor has given you suggestions or reasons as to why the manuscript was not accepted, you might want to incorporate these when revising your manuscript.

*About rejection*. Rejection is a way of life in the publishing world. It's inevitable in a business that deals with such an overwhelming number of applicants for such a limited number of positions. Anyone who has published has lived through many rejections, and writers with thin skin are at a distinct disadvantage. The key to surviving rejection is to remember that it is not a personal attack—it's merely a judgment about the appropriateness of your work for that particular market at that particular time. Writers who let rejection dissuade them from pursuing their dream or who react to each editor's "No" with indignation or fury do themselves a disservice. Writers who let rejection stop them do not publish. Resign yourself to facing rejection now. You will live through it, and you will eventually overcome it.

## QUERY AND COVER LETTERS

A query letter is a brief but detailed letter written to interest an editor in your manuscript. It is a tool for selling both nonfiction magazine articles and nonfiction books. With a magazine query you are attempting to interest an editor in buying your article for her periodical. A book query's job is to get an editor interested enough to ask you for either a full proposal or the entire manuscript. (Note: Some book editors accept proposals on first contact. Refer to individual listings for contact guidelines.) Some beginners are hesitant to query, thinking an editor can more fairly judge an idea by seeing the entire manuscript. Actually, most nonfiction editors prefer to be queried.

There is no query formula that guarantees success, but there are some points to consider when you begin. Queries should:

- Be limited to one page, single-spaced, and address the editor by name (Mr. or Ms. and the surname).
- Grab the editor's interest with a strong opening. Some magazine queries begin with a paragraph meant to approximate the lead of the intended article.
- Indicate how you intend to develop the article or book. Give the editor some idea of the work's structure and content.
- Let the editor know if you have photos available to accompany your magazine article (never send original photos—send photocopies or duplicates).
- Mention any expertise or training that qualifies you to write the article or book. If you've published before, mention it; if not, don't.
- End with a direct request to write the article (or, if you're pitching a book, ask for the go-ahead to send in a full proposal or the entire manuscript). Give the editor an idea of the expected length and delivery date of your manuscript.

## insider report

# Unplugging for the new millennium

In 1994, Bill Henderson, publisher of Pushcart Press, and a respected editor and writer, got something off his chest. In March of that year, on its op-ed page, *The New York Times* published Henderson's manifesto for a homegrown association he called the Lead Pencil Club. His gripe was this: Technology, and computers in particular, had assumed a status in our lives that was undeserved, overhyped and destructive. The electronic "revolution," backed by big business and driven by the twin motives of greed and speed, was, in Henderson's words, "a disaster."

**Bill Henderson**

"The god of our godless age is speed," the manifesto began. "Driven by our obsession to compete, we have embraced this electronic god with a frenzy." In the fashion of the astute little boy who made so bold as to point out the emperor's nudity, Henderson's essay skewered this generation's unthinking preoccupation with its beeping and blinking gadgetry and technology's headlong rush to nowhere. His tone was serious, but not without humor. "The Lead Pencil Club warns that we have gone Gizmo Gaga," Henderson wrote. "We ask where are we zapping to on this highway? . . . Speed Kills. Where's the Fire? Haste Makes Waste. Back to Basics. Not So Fast!" Henderson was opting out of the computer revolution, and his manifesto was an open invitation for like-minded "Leadites" to join him.

The *New York Times* piece drew thousands of letters from sympathizers all over the world, correspondents who shared Henderson's consternation with the empty promises of the digital age. He heard from reporters, teachers, students, writers, office workers—each with an ax to grind and happy to have found Henderson's sympathetic ear. The club's ranks swelled.

Two years later, in 1996, Henderson published *Minutes of the Lead Pencil Club*, offering a collection of essays, letters and commentary on how readers could "pull the plug on the electronic revolution" and why they might want to. A paperback edition of *Minutes* was published by W.W. Norton in 1997. A follow-up, *Unplug!: Letters to the Lead Pencil Club*, a collection culled from some 4,000 letters Henderson has received since the publication of *Minutes*, is forthcoming.

---

**BILL HENDERSON**

*Editor*
*Pushcart Press*, Pushcart Prize

The computer, Henderson says, has wrought changes on the publishing and writing business from top to bottom. For instance, online booksellers, he says, have played a part in the dwindling number of independent bookstores. "So it's goodbye to the community bookstore," says Henderson, "a store where you knew the owner and the owner knew you and what you liked, and he would suggest books to you and order books for you and such. Now people sit in their rooms and order books from Amazon.com, which, hilariously, has not made a dime yet."

Nearer to the writer's art, the computer has changed the way writers work, and, in Henderson's view, the change has not been a good one. For one thing, gone is the manuscript trail that all writers used to leave in their wake before the age of word processing. "All my writer friends tell me it's easier to write on a computer, because you can move stuff around fast," he says. "I refuse to do that. I just triple space on my typewriter, then I can make changes later on the page, and I can see the changes I've made. If you're working on a computer, you wipe out your changes and you can't tell where you've been when you're revising. You used to have these wonderful things called manuscripts; you can look at Hemingway's or Dickens' and see how they made their changes and what was going through their minds. There is a record there. Now, all you have is a printout—you don't see the mind of the writer at work."

Henderson, whose most recent book was banged out on a seven-dollar manual Olivetti purchased at a yard sale, says the older technology also forces writers to work more slowly and thus invites a more studied approach to the writing process. "It's so easy to write on a computer that everything is about 1,000 pages when it should probably be about 200," he says. Pair this bloated output with the vanity "publishing" capabilities of the World Wide Web, and Henderson sees a recipe for artistic mayhem. "I think the real danger for writers is that they think, 'I won't even try to get this published. I'll just blast this off over the Internet, and I'll be published right away.' What they're calling publishing is not publishing at all. They never bother to revise, they probably never get much feedback. It's just too damn easy to kiss it off into the wind and think that all these millions of people around the world are reading it. Well, they're not. It's just joining the rest of the garbage stream.

"Writing is tough, and getting published is tough," Henderson says. There is value in the struggle, though, and he advises writers not to seek the easy way out. "The fact that it's tough is often good for a writer, because your first effort, your first adolescent go, is usually crap. You have to go back and think about it some more. You have to work at it; you have to live and feel and think. Kids growing up today might think the only things of value are speed and convenience. If you think that, then you're going to live a very empty existence. I mean there are real struggles that have happened in this world, and there is real wisdom, but they've taken time and effort to get to."

Today's writers are as awash in information as everyone else. But they must strive to simplify and maintain their focus on their art. "The information revolution is a fraud," Henderson says. "Most people want less information. We can't digest what we've got now. And we certainly can't find any wisdom in it, which is what great writing is supposed to be about. You're supposed to learn something from it, but if all you've got is raw data, it's just a cesspool of stuff that's coming at you at lightning speed. I don't know when you're supposed to get time to think about it."

At its root, the message of the Lead Pencil Club is best summed up in the one-word exhortation of its "founder emeritus," Henry David Thoreau: "Simplify."

"All writers need," Henderson says, "is a pencil and a piece of paper and a brain and a soul. That's all they need, nothing else. They don't need an office, they don't need a computer, they don't need a typewriter. They just need to be thinking, caring people."

—*Mark Garvey*

Some writers state politely in their query letters that after a specified date (slightly beyond the listed reporting time), they will assume the editor is not currently interested in their topic and will submit the query elsewhere. It's a good idea to do this only if your topic is a timely one that will suffer if not considered quickly.

A brief single-spaced cover letter enclosed with your manuscript is helpful in personalizing a submission. If you have previously queried the editor on the article or book, the cover letter should be a brief reminder, not a sales pitch. "Here is the piece on goat herding, which we discussed previously. I look forward to hearing from you at your earliest convenience."

If you are submitting to a market that considers unsolicited complete manuscripts, your cover letter should tell the editor something about your manuscript and about you—your publishing history and any particular qualifications you have for writing the enclosed manuscript.

Once your manuscript has been accepted, you may offer to get involved in the editing process, but policy on this will vary from magazine to magazine. Most magazine editors don't send galleys to authors before publication, but if they do, you should review the galleys and return them as soon as possible. Book publishers will normally involve you in rewrites whether you like it or not.

The Query Letter Clinic on page 22 presents several specific real-life query letters, some that worked (and some that didn't), along with editors' comments on why the letter was successful or where the letter failed to garner an assignment.

For more information about writing query letters, read *How to Write Irresistible Query Letters*, by Lisa Collier Cool, or *How To Write Attention-Grabbing Query & Cover Letters*, by John Wood (both Writer's Digest Books).

## Querying for fiction

Fiction is sometimes queried, but most fiction editors don't like to make a final decision until they see the complete manuscript. Most editors will want to see a synopsis and sample chapters for a book, or a complete short story manuscript. Consult individual listings for specific fiction guidelines. If a fiction editor does request a query, briefly describe the main theme and story line, including the conflict and resolution. For more information on what goes into a novel synopsis, see Crafting a Successful Synopsis, by Evan Marshall, on page 33, excerpted from *The Marshall Plan for Novel Writing*, or *Your Novel Proposal: From Creation to Contract*, by Blythe Camenson and Marshall J. Cook (both by Writer's Digest Books).

## BOOK PROPOSALS

Most nonfiction books are sold by book proposal, a package of materials that details what your book is about, who its intended audience is, and how you intend to write it. Most fiction

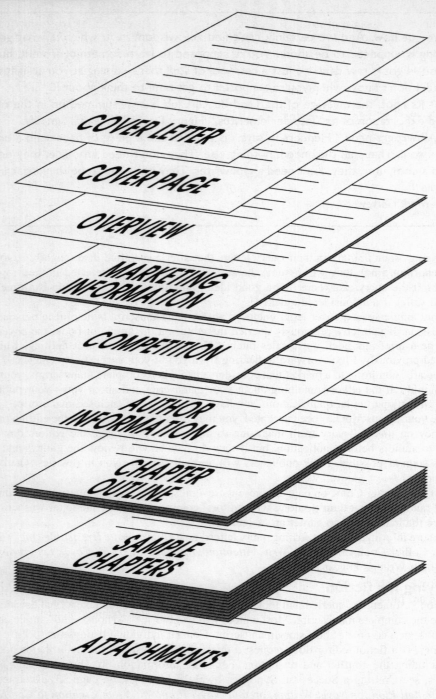

COVER LETTER

COVER PAGE

OVERVIEW

MARKETING INFORMATION

COMPETITION

AUTHOR INFORMATION

CHAPTER OUTLINE

SAMPLE CHAPTERS

ATTACHMENTS

A nonfiction book proposal will usually consist of the elements illustrated above. Their order is less important than the fact that you have addressed each component.

is sold either by complete manuscript, especially for first-time authors, or by two or three sample chapters. Take a look at individual listings to see what submission method editors prefer.

The nonfiction book proposal includes some combination of a cover or query letter, an overview, an outline, author's information sheet and sample chapters. Editors also want to see information about the audience for your book and about titles that compete with your proposed book.

If a listing does not specify, send as much of the following information as you can.

- The cover or query letter should be a short introduction to the material you include in the proposal.
- An overview is a brief summary of your book. For nonfiction, it should detail your book's subject and give an idea of how that subject will be developed. If you're sending a synopsis of a novel, cover the basic plot.
- An outline covers your book chapter by chapter. The outline should include all major points covered in each chapter. Some outlines are done in traditional outline form, but most are written in paragraph form.
- An author's information sheet should—as succinctly and clearly as possible—acquaint the editor with your writing background and convince her of your qualifications to write about the subject.
- Many editors like to see sample chapters, especially for a first book. In fiction it's essential. In nonfiction, sample chapters show the editor how well you write and develop the ideas from your outline.
- Marketing information—i.e., facts about how and to whom your book can be successfully marketed—is now expected to accompany every book proposal. If you can provide information about the audience for your book and suggest ways the book publisher can reach those people, you will increase your chances of acceptance.
- Competitive title analysis is an integral part of the marketing information. Check the *Subject Guide* to *Books in Print* for other titles on your topic. Write a one- or two-sentence synopsis of each. Point out how your book differs and improves upon existing titles.

For more detailed information on what your book proposal should contain, see *How to Write a Book Proposal*, by Michael Larsen (Writer's Digest Books).

## A WORD ABOUT AGENTS

Recognizing the importance of literary agents in publishing today, we've included a section of 75 agents, 50 handling books and 25 handling scripts, beginning on page 98. We've selected agents who describe themselves as open to both previously published and newer writers and who do not charge a fee to look at work. The literary agents belong to the Association of Authors' Representatives (AAR), a voluntary professional organization. We've also included a few who are not members of AAR but have come to agenting after a notable career in editing and publishing. The script agents are all signatory agencies of The Writers Guild of America.

An agent represents a writer's work to buyers, negotiates contracts, follows up to see that contracts are fulfilled and generally handles a writer's business affairs, leaving the writer free to write. Effective agents are valued for their contacts in the publishing industry, their savvy about which publishers and editors to approach with which ideas, their ability to guide an author's career, and their business sense. In How to Find (and Keep) The Right Agent on page 91, literary agent Lori Perkins offers an inside look at how an agent works and how to find one that will go to work for you.

While most book publishers listed in *Writer's Market* publish books by unagented writers, some of the larger ones are reluctant to consider submissions that have not reached them through a literary agent. Companies with such a policy are noted by a symbol ( $) at the beginning of the listing, as well as in the submission information within the listing.

For more information about finding and working with a literary agent, as well as 500 listings of literary and script agents, see *Guide to Literary Agents* (Writer's Digest Books). The *Guide* offers listings similar to those presented here, as well as a wealth of informational articles on the author-agent relationship and publishing processes.

## PROFESSIONALISM AND COURTESY

Publishers are as crunched for time as any other business professional. Between struggling to meet deadlines without exceeding budgets and dealing with incoming submissions, most editors find that time is their most precious commodity. This state of affairs means an editor's communications with new writers, while necessarily a part of his job, have to be handled efficiently and with a certain amount of bluntness.

But writers work hard, too. Shouldn't editors treat them nicely? Shouldn't an editor take the time to point out the *good* things about the manuscript he is rejecting? Is that too much to ask? Well, in a way, yes. It *is* too much to ask. Editors are not writing coaches; much less are they counselors or therapists. Editors are in the business of buying workable writing from people who produce it. This, of course, does not excuse editors from observing the conventions of common business courtesy. Good editors know how to be polite (or they hire an assistant who can be polite for them).

The best way for busy writers to get along with (and flourish among) busy editors is to develop professional business habits. Correspondence and phone calls should be kept short and to the point. Don't hound editors with unwanted calls or letters. Honor all agreements, and give every assignment your best effort. Pleasantness, good humor, honesty and reliability will serve you as well in publishing as they will in any other area of life.

You will occasionally run up against editors and publishers who don't share your standard of business etiquette. It is easy enough to withdraw your submissions from such people and avoid them in the future.

## WRITING TOOLS

*Typewriters and computers*. For many years, *the* tool of the writer's trade was the typewriter. While many writers continue to produce perfectly acceptable material on their manual or electric typewriters, more and more writers have discovered the benefits of writing on a computer. Editors, too, have benefited from the change; documents produced on a computer are less likely to present to the editor such distractions as typos, eraser marks or globs of white correction fluid. That's because writing composed on a computer can be corrected before it is printed out.

If you think computers are not for you, you should reconsider. A desktop computer, running a good word processing program, can be the greatest boon to your writing career since the dictionary. For ease of manipulating text, formatting pages and correcting spelling errors, the computer handily outperforms the typewriter. Many word processing programs will count words for you, offer synonyms from a thesaurus, construct an index and give you a choice of typefaces to print out your material. Some will even correct your grammar (if you want them to). When you consider that the personal computer is also a great way of tracking your submissions and staying on top of all the other business details of a writing career—and a handy way to do research if you have a modem—it's hard to imagine how we ever got along without them.

Many people considering working with a computer for the first time are under the mistaken impression that they face an insurmountable learning curve. That's no longer true. While learning computer skills once may have been a daunting undertaking, today's personal computers are much more user-friendly than they once were. And as prices continue to fall, good systems can be had for under $1,000.

Whether you're writing on a computer or typewriter, your goal should be to produce pages of clean, error-free copy. Stick to standard typefaces, avoiding such unusual styles as script or italic. Your work should reflect a professional approach and consideration for your reader. If you are printing from a computer, avoid sending material printed from a low-quality dot-matrix printer, with hard-to-read, poorly shaped characters. Many editors are unwilling to read these manuscripts.

New laser and ink jet printers, however, produce high-quality pages that *are* acceptable to editors. Readability is the key.

*Electronic submissions.* Many publishers are accepting or even requesting that final manuscript submissions be made on computer disk. This saves the magazine or book publisher the expense of having your manuscript typeset, and can be helpful in the editing stage. The publisher will simply download your finished manuscript into the computer system they use to produce their product. Be sure to mention if you are able to submit the final manuscript on disk. The editors will let you know what computer format they use and how they would like to receive your material.

Some publishers who accept submissions on disk also will accept electronic submissions by modem. Modems are computer components that can use your phone line to send computerized files to other computers with modems. It is an extremely fast way to get your manuscript to the publisher. However, you must work out submission information with the editor *before* you send something via modem. Causing the editor's system to crash, or unwittingly infecting his system with a virus, does not make for a happy business relationship.

*Fax machines and e-mail.* Fax machines transmit copy across phone lines. E-mail addresses are for receiving and sending electronic mail over a computer network, most commonly the Internet. Those publishers who wanted to list their fax machine numbers and e-mail addresses have done so.

Between businesses, the fax has come into standard daily use for materials that have to be sent quickly. Fax machines are in airports, hotels, libraries and even grocery stores. Many libraries, schools, copy shops and even "cyber cafés" offer computer time for free or for a low hourly rate. However, do not fax or e-mail queries, proposals or entire manscripts to editors unless they indicate they are willing to receive them. A proposal on shiny fax paper curling into itself on the editor's desk makes an impression—but not the one you want. If your proposal is being considered, it will probably be routed to a number of people for their reactions. Fax paper won't stand up well to that amount of handling. Writers should continue to use traditional means for sending manuscripts and queries and use the fax number or e-mail address we list only when an editor asks to receive correspondence by this method.

Letters and manuscripts sent to an editor for consideration should be neat, clean and legible. That means typed (or computer-printed), double spaced, on 8½ × 11 inch paper. Handwritten materials will most often not be considered at all. The typing paper should be at least 16 lb. bond (20 lb. is preferred).

The first impression an editor has of your work is its appearance on the page. Why take the chance of blowing that impression with a manuscript or letter that's not as appealing as it could be?

You don't need fancy letterhead for your correspondence with editors. Plain bond paper is fine. Just type your name, address, phone number and the date at the top of the page—centered or in the right-hand corner. If you want letterhead, make it as simple and businesslike as possible. Keep the cute clip art for the family newsletter. Many quick print shops have standard typefaces and can supply letterhead stationery at a relatively low cost. Never use letterhead for typing your manuscripts. Only the first page of queries, cover letters and other correspondence should be typed on letterhead.

## MANUSCRIPT FORMAT

When submitting a manuscript for possible publication, you can increase its chances of making a favorable impression by adhering to some fairly standard matters of physical format. Many professional writers use the format described here. Of course, there are no "rules" about what a manuscript must look like. These are just guidelines—some based on common sense, others more a matter of convention—that are meant to help writers display their work to best advantage. Strive for easy readability in whatever method you choose and adapt your style to your own personal tastes and those of the editors to whom you submit.

Most manuscripts do not use a cover sheet or title page. Use a paper clip to hold pages together, not staples. This allows editors to separate the pages easily for editing. Scripts should be submitted with plain cardstock covers front and back, held together by Chicago or Revere screws.

The upper corners of the first page of an article manuscript contain important information about you and your manuscript. This information should be single-spaced. In the upper *left* corner list your name, address and phone number. If you are using a pseudonym for your byline, your legal name still should appear in this space. In the upper *right* corner, indicate the approximate word count of the manuscript, the rights you are offering for sale and your copyright notice (© 1999 Ralph Anderson). A handwritten copyright symbol is acceptable. (For more information about rights and copyright, see Minding the Details on page 50.) For a book manuscript include the same information with the exception of rights. Do not number the first page of your manuscript.

Center the title in capital letters one-third of the way down the page. Set the spacing to double-space. Type "by" and your name or pseudonym centered one double-space beneath that.

After the title and byline, drop down two double-spaces, paragraph indent, and begin the body of your manuscript. Always double-space your manuscript and use standard paragraph indentations of five spaces. Margins should be about 1¼ inches on all sides of each full page of the manuscript.

On every page after the first, type your last name, a dash and the page number in either the upper left or right corner. The title of your manuscript may, but need not, be typed on this line or beneath it. Page number two would read: Anderson—2. Follow this format throughout your manuscript.

If you are submitting novel chapters, leave the top one-third of the first page of each chapter blank before typing the chapter title. Subsequent pages should include the author's last name, the page number, and a shortened form of the book's title: Anderson—2—Skating. (In a variation on this, some authors place the title before the name on the left side and put the page number on the right-hand margin.)

When submitting poetry, the poems should be typed single-spaced (double-space between stanzas), one poem per page. For a long poem requiring more than one page, paper clip the pages together. You may want to write "continued" at the bottom of the page, so if the pages are separated, editors, typesetters and proofreaders won't assume your poem ends at the bottom of the first page.

For more information on manuscript formats, see *Formatting & Submitting Your Manuscript*, by Jack and Glenda Neff and Don Prues (Writer's Digest Books).

## ESTIMATING WORD COUNT

Many computers will provide you with a word count of your manuscript. Your editor will count again after editing the manuscript. Although your computer is counting characters, an editor or production editor is more concerned with the amount of space the text will occupy on a page. Several small headlines, or subheads, for instance, will be counted the same by your computer as any other word of text. An editor may count them differently to be sure enough space has been estimated for larger type.

For short manuscripts, it's often quickest to count each word on a representative page and multiply by the number of pages. You can get a very rough count by multiplying the number of pages in your manuscript by 250 (the average number of words on a double-spaced typewritten page). Do not count words for a poetry manuscript or put the word count at the top of the manuscript.

To get a more precise count, add the number of characters and spaces in an average line and divide by six for the average words per line. Then count the number of lines of type on a representative page. Multiply the words per line by the lines per page to find the average number of words per page. Then count the number of manuscript pages (fractions should be counted as fractions, except in book manuscript chapter headings, which are counted as a full page). Multiply the number of pages by the number of words per page you already determined. This will give you the approximate number of words in the manuscript.

## PHOTOGRAPHS AND SLIDES

The availability of good quality photos can be a deciding factor when an editor is considering a manuscript. Many publications also offer additional pay for photos accepted with a manuscript. Check the magazine's listing when submitting black & white prints for the size an editor prefers to review. The universally accepted format for transparencies is 35mm; few buyers will look at color prints. Don't send any transparencies or prints with a query; wait until an editor indicates interest in seeing your photos.

On all your photos and slides, you should stamp or print your copyright notice and "Return to:" followed by your name, address and phone number. Rubber stamps are preferred for labeling photos since they are less likely to cause damage. You can order them from many stationery or office supply stores. If you use a pen to write this information on the back of your photos, be careful not to damage the print by pressing too hard or by allowing ink to bleed through the paper. A felt tip pen is best, but you should take care not to put photos or copy together before the ink dries.

Captions can be typed on adhesive labels and affixed to the back of the prints. Some writers, when submitting several transparencies or photos, number the photos and type captions (numbered accordingly) on a separate 8½×11 sheet of paper.

Submit prints rather than negatives or consider having duplicates made of your slides or transparencies. Don't risk having your original negative or slide lost or damaged when you submit it.

## PHOTOCOPIES

Make copies of your manuscripts and correspondence before putting them in the mail. Don't learn the hard way, as many writers have, that manuscripts get lost in the mail and that publishers sometimes go out of business without returning submissions. You might want to make several good quality copies of your manuscript while it is still clean and submit them while keeping the original manuscript as a file copy.

Some writers include a self-addressed postcard with a photocopied submission and suggest in the cover letter that if the editor is not interested in the manuscript, it may be tossed out and a reply returned on the postcard. This practice is recommended when dealing with international markets. If you find that your personal computer generates copies more cheaply than you can pay to have them returned, you might choose to send disposable manuscripts. Submitting a disposable manuscript costs the writer some photocopy or computer printer expense, but it can save on large postage bills.

## MAILING SUBMISSIONS

No matter what size manuscript you're mailing, always include a self-addressed, stamped envelope (SASE) with sufficient return postage that is large enough to contain your manuscript if it is returned. The website for the U.S. Postal Service, http://www.usps.gov, and the website for the Canadian Postal Service, http://www.canadapost.ca, both have handy postage calculators if you are unsure of how much you'll need.

A manuscript of fewer than six pages may be folded in thirds and mailed as if it were a letter using a #10 (business-size) envelope. The enclosed SASE can be a #10 folded in thirds or a #9 envelope which will slip into the mailing envelope without being folded. Some editors also appreciate the convenience of having a manuscript folded into halves in a 6×9 envelope. For manuscripts of six pages or longer, use 9×12 envelopes for both mailing and return. The return SASE may be folded in half.

A book manuscript should be mailed in a sturdy, well-wrapped box. Enclose a self-addressed mailing label and paper clip your return postage to the label. Unfortunately, new mailing restrictions make it more difficult to mail packages of 12 ounces and over, causing some publishers to discontinue returning submissions of this size.

Always mail photos and slides First Class. The rougher handling received by standard mail could damage them. If you are concerned about losing prints or slides, send them certified or registered mail. For any photo submission that is mailed separately from a manuscript, enclose a short cover letter of explanation, separate self-addressed label, adequate return postage and an envelope. Never submit photos or slides mounted in glass.

To mail up to 20 prints, you can buy photo mailers that are stamped "Photos—Do Not Bend" and contain two cardboard inserts to sandwich your prints. Or use a $9 \times 12$ manila envelope, write "Photos—Do Not Bend" and make your own cardboard inserts. Some photography supply shops also carry heavy cardboard envelopes that are reusable.

When mailing a number of prints, say 25-50 for a book with illustrations, pack them in a sturdy cardboard box. A box for typing paper or photo paper is an adequate mailer. If, after packing both manuscript and photos, there's empty space in the box, slip in enough cardboard inserts to fill the box. Wrap the box securely.

To mail transparencies, first slip them into protective vinyl sleeves, then mail as you would prints. If you're mailing a number of sheets, use a cardboard box as for photos.

## Types of mail service

- **First Class** is an expensive way to mail a manuscript, but many writers prefer it. First Class mail generally receives better handling and is delivered more quickly. Mail sent First Class is also forwarded for one year if the addressee has moved, and is returned automatically if it is undeliverable.
- **Priority mail** reaches its destination within two to three days. To mail a package of up to 2 pounds costs $3.20, less than either United Parcel Service or Federal Express. First Class mail over 11 ounces is classified Priority. Confirmation of delivery is an additional 35¢.
- **Standard mail** rates are available for packages, but be sure to pack your materials carefully because they will be handled roughly. To make sure your package will be returned to you if it is undeliverable, print "Return Postage Guaranteed" under your address.
- **Certified Mail** must be signed for when it reaches its destination. If requested, a signed receipt is returned to the sender. There is a $1.35 charge for this service, in addition to the required postage, and a $1.10 charge for a return receipt.
- **Registered Mail** is a high-security method of mailing where the contents are insured. The package is signed in and out of every office it passes through, and a receipt is returned to the sender when the package reaches its destination. The cost depends on the weight, destination and whether you obtain insurance.
- If you're in a hurry to get your material to your editor, you have a lot of choices. In addition to fax and computer technologies mentioned earlier, overnight and two-day mail services are provided by both the U.S. Postal Service and several private firms. More information on next day service is available from the U.S. Post Office or check your Yellow Pages under "Delivery Services."

## Other correspondence details

Use money orders if you are ordering sample copies or supplies and do not have checking services. You'll have a receipt, and money orders are traceable. Money orders for up to $700 can be purchased from the U.S. Postal Service for an 85 cents service charge. Banks, savings and loans, and some commercial businesses also carry money orders; their fees vary. *Never* send cash through the mail for sample copies.

Insurance is available for items handled by the U.S. Postal Service but is payable only on typing fees or the tangible value of the item in the package—such as typing paper—so your best insurance when mailing manuscripts is to keep a copy of what you send. Insurance is 75 cents for $50 or less and goes up to a $45.70 plus postage maximum charge for $5,000.

When corresponding with publishers in other countries, International Reply Coupons (IRCs) must be used for return postage. Surface rates in other countries differ from those in the U.S., and U.S. postage stamps are of use only within the U.S.

U.S. stamps can be purchased online with a credit card at http://www.usps.gov or by calling 1-800-STAMP24. Non-U.S. residents can call (816)545-1000 or (816)545-1011 to order stamps. Canadian postage can be purchased online at http://www.canadapost.ca.

Because some post offices don't carry IRCs (or because of the added expense), many writers dealing with international mail send photocopies and tell the publisher to dispose of them if the manuscript is not appropriate. When you use this method, it's best to set a deadline for withdrawing your manuscript from consideration, so you can market it elsewhere.

International money orders are also available from the post office for a charge of $3 or $7.50, depending on the destination.

## RECORDING SUBMISSIONS

Once you begin submitting manuscripts, you'll need to manage your writing business by keeping copies of all manuscripts and correspondence, and by recording the dates of submissions.

One way to keep track of your manuscripts is to use a record of submissions that includes the date sent, title, market, editor and enclosures (such as photos). You should also note the date of the editor's response, any rewrites that were done, and, if the manuscript was accepted, the deadline, publication date and payment information. You might want to keep a similar record just for queries.

Also remember to keep a separate file for each manuscript or idea along with its list of potential markets. You may want to keep track of expected reporting times on a calendar, too. Then you'll know if a market has been slow to respond and you can follow up on your query or submission. It will also provide you with a detailed picture of your sales over time.

# Six Secrets to Successful Submissions

BY KELLY MILNER HALLS

When I first made the jump from part-time writer to full-time freelancer, it took me six years to go from rank beginner to editorial asset. During those years, I discovered six techniques that made my submissions more successful. These six "secrets" can do the same for you–and you won't have to spend years learning them the hard way.

## SECRET 1: STUDY THE GUIDELINES

For the price of a self-addressed stamped envelope (SASE), most publications will mail writer's guidelines—rules and focal points to help would-be contributors understand just what the magazine is hoping to communicate and how. My first step was to request guidelines from each publication that appealed to me. (You can often find them at magazines' websites and more than 1,000 of them are collected at *Writer's Digest*'s website, http://www.writersdigest.com.) And according to *U\*S\*Kids* editor and 17-year freelance veteran Jeff Ayers, following those guidelines was my first step toward success.

"Using writer's guidelines is essential to narrowing the focus of what a freelancer should write about," Ayers says. "You'd think that would be a pretty obvious first step. But I'd estimate 80 percent of the submissions I get aren't related to the mission and normal content of *U\*S\*Kids*."

It's like flossing, says *Guideposts for Kids* editor Mary Lou Carney. "Nobody wants to do it, but it's terribly necessary. Nothing puts you on the inside track of a magazine like its guidelines. Magazines exist because they have distinctive editorial voices and biases. Don't think you can skim over the marketing process and hope to score sales."

## SECRET 2: READ THE MAGAZINE

After I'd studied the writer's guidelines, I sat down with several recent issues (most editors suggest at least six), and read them cover to cover. As I read, I asked myself questions: Is the writing conversational or academic? Is slang part of the editorial makeup, or is the style formal? Are there illustrations? What kinds of advertising surround the articles? Those questions helped me get to know the publications.

"My best advice is to really read the publication," says *FamilyFun* senior editor Deb Geigus Berry. "If you haven't read *FamilyFun* in a year, even six months, you've probably missed something important." *Guideposts for Kids*'s Carney agrees. "Learn all you can about the magazines you want to sell to. Look for the distinctive edge or slant that will make an editor say, 'Now that's just right for us.'"

"But don't pretend you've seen a publication if you really haven't," warns Jessica Solomon, former editor of Chicago-based *curiocity for kids* and *Brainstorm*. "I can't count the number of times a writer will regurgitate something they've seen in a description of our publication as

**KELLY MILNER HALLS** *has been a full-time freelance writer for nearly a decade, contributing frequently to the* Chicago Tribune, *the* Atlanta Journal Constitution, *the* Denver Post, FamilyFun, Teen People, High-lights for Children *and dozens of other publications. She has four books of nonfiction in various stages, and her fifth,* I Bought a Baby Chick, *will be published by Boyds Mills Press in Spring 2000. She lives as a single mother in Spokane, with two daughters, four cats, two dogs and a ferret.*

evidence that they're familiar with our magazine. I write the descriptions; I know what they say. I'd rather a writer tell me they're unfamiliar with the publication, but they have a great story idea."

## SECRET 3: CRAFT QUERIES WITH PUNCH

Getting a clear fix on writing an effective query was my next step—and it was a doozy. Even the concept was intimidating: one shot to convince the editor my story idea was worth paying for and that I was the best writer for the job. It took me months to figure out what most editors could explain over a cup of coffee.

"Even after 17 years, the secret of the query was something I didn't fully understand until I wound up on this side of the desk," says *U*S*Kids*'s Ayers. "As an editor, I came to appreciate the beauty of a very brief pitch letter." According to Ayers, if the query is concise and to the point, the writer is more likely to handle an assignment the same way. "There seems to be a connection between the level of professionalism and the strength of that short pitch," he says. "The best queries come in at just under a page."

With less than a page to win a professional ally, it's important to start strong. "I get at least ten queries a day," says Solomon. "If a writer doesn't grab me in the first paragraph or two, they're not going to make it. If they can't grab me with their query's lead, how are they going to grab the reader with the lead of their story?"

Make that first paragraph count. Start with the one thing an editor wants most—a well-written, publication-specific story idea. Once your concept is on the page, briefly explain why you're qualified to write the piece. Confidence is fine, but avoid idle boasting. "I shy away from writers who insist they'll be the best thing that ever happened to me," says *Chicago Tribune KidNews* editor Devin Rose.

Finally, proofread your query *before* you submit. As Solomon says, "A writer loses credibility real fast if they spell my name or the name of the publication wrong. If you're unsure, call the office. If someone can't take a couple of minutes to double-check the spelling of the editor's or the publication's name, how can I trust they're going to double-check the facts in their story?"

## SECRET 4: RESEARCH FROM THE TOP DOWN

Writing for *Highlights for Children* was one of my first goals as a freelancer. But for months I couldn't seem to hit the mark. Finally, associate editor Rob Crisell made what turned out to be one of the most important suggestions of my career. "Don't be timid when researching your subjects," he said. "When you want to get the facts, go straight to the top."

Editors don't want and can't use the same details found in other publications. They need fresh ideas, freshly stated. Before I wrote the June 1997 *U*S*Kids* cover story on dolphin therapy for disabled kids, I studied what was already in print, then focused my interviews on details the other articles had overlooked.

The same goes for sources who've been quoted everywhere. While you're looking for over-looked details, keep an eye out for important sources other writers have missed.

## SECRET 5: REMEMBER THE ART

One often-overlooked detail that can mean the difference between "sold" and "sorry" is photo availability. It's a key factor (apart from strong, accurate writing) in securing follow-up assignments—and that's the freelancer's primary objective. (Regular bylines pay the bills.) Any service you can provide that might make you part of an editor's regular team is worth the time invested.

"A good editor never forgets the impact of a great photo," says Carney at *Guideposts for Kids*. "So, after good copy, good photo research is the best thing a writer can deliver."

It's not essential to take photos yourself. In fact, many editors prefer to use professional photographers. "What's really valuable," Carney says, "are the names and numbers of people who may have suitable photos (newspapers that have featured this person, organizations that sponsor/photograph him). Busy editors remember which writers are thorough when it comes to photo details, and give them assignments again and again."

But don't send original artwork until you're asked. "I love it when a freelancer lets me know that photos are available," says Ayers. "It's particular handy if they send photocopies so I'm aware of what the visuals are. But I hate it when people send photographs I haven't requested because then I'm charged with returning them safely. It almost never works out and it's a red flag for lack of professionalism."

## SECRET 6: REMEMBER WHAT THE AUDIENCE—AND THE EDITOR—EXPECT

I started to sell with consistency the moment I learned to sit back and listen to what editors and audiences really want. You can't hit the mark with the wrong ammunition. Staying current when it comes to the trends and interests that impact your publication's readership is crucial.

"If a freelancer wants to write for us, she must focus in on our purpose," says *FamilyFun*'s Berry. "We look for and cover activities for families to do *with* their kids. If a writer queries about romantic getaways parents can take *without* their kids, clearly she's missing the point."

Now you know my six secrets for successful submissions. If I'd stumbled across an article like this when I was first getting started, I could have saved myself years in the school of hard knocks. Take the lessons I've learned and use them to become a successful freelancer—in a lot fewer than the six years it took me.

## How to Study a Printed Magazine Article

1. Read closely each article in recent issues of the magazine to which you are trying to sell. Most contain an answer to a basic working question. Identify that question. How does the article answer it? Which of the "5 Ws and H of journalism" does it use: who, what, why, where, when and how?

2. Now read the entry for that publication in *Writer's Market* to find out what that magazine was seeking. Put yourself in the writer's shoes. How did the writer slant the subject to appeal to the magazine's readers? Why did the editor buy it? Study its structure, length, illustrations and artwork.

3. To see how the writer carries the main theme through the article, underline each word that relates directly to that theme, then outline the entire piece. Study the writer's use of facts, quotes and anecdotes. What is the ratio between them? How is humor used? Is it spread and balanced to the same degree throughout? Do other articles in this issue use facts, quotes, anecdotes and humor in roughly the same way and in the same proportion?

4. List every source used, including direct references and quotations. Where would the writer find the facts, opinions and quotes that are not clearly identified by source in the article? If you are uncertain, indicate where you would find the material—or where you would go to find out.

5. Focus on the quotations. Why is each used? How do they carry the theme forward? Note how the sources of the quotations are introduced, and how much the reader must know about those sources to place them and what is said in perspective.

6. Is the article written in first person (*I*), second (*you*) or third (*he, she, it* or "Mr. Smith")? How does that point of view strengthen the article? Does the point of view change? Why or why not? Are most articles in the same issue written in the same person?

7. Concentrate on the lead. How long is it, in words or sentences? Does it grab your interest? Does it make you want to read more? Why? How does it compare with other leads in that issue?

8. Most articles begin with a short lead followed by a longer second paragraph that ties the lead to the body of the article. Called the "transitional paragraph," it tells where you are going and how you will get there. It bridges the attention-grabbing elements to the body by setting direction, tone and pace. Find the transitional paragraph and study it.

9. Now underline the first sentence in each paragraph. They should form a chain that will pull you through the piece. Note how the writer draws the paragraphs together with transitional words and phrases. Circle the words that perform this linking function. Often the same words or ideas will be repeated in the last sentence of one paragraph and the first sentence of the next.

10. Earlier you outlined the article. Now look at the transitional words and the underlined first sentences and see how the structure ties the theme together. Is the article structured chronologically, developmentally, by alternating examples, point-by-point? How did the writer build the organizational structure to answer the article's question?

11. How does the article end? Does it tie back to the lead? Does it repeat an opening phrase or idea? The conclusion should reinforce and strengthen the direction the article has taken. Does it? How?

12. Finally, look at the title. It may have been changed or rewritten by the editor. Nonetheless, does it correctly describe the article that follows? Does it tease, quote, pique one's curiosity, state facts? What technique does it use to make the reader want to read the article?

—*Gordon Burgett*

# Query Letter Clinic

BY DON PRUES

The most indispensable companion to an unsold piece of writing is its query letter. Whether you're trying to sell a 100-word sidebar, a 4,000-word feature article, a 60,000-word nonfiction book or a 100,000-word novel, you need a darn good query letter to go with it. Period.

The *Writer's Encyclopedia* defines a query letter as "a sales letter to an editor that is designed to interest him in an article or book idea." With so many submissions to evaluate, editors tend to make fast judgments. So you must pitch a tight and concise query that explains the gist of your piece, why readers will want to read it, and why you're the perfect person to write it.

## PRE-QUERY PROVISIONS

Identifying what to omit and what to include in your query can mean the difference between earning a sale or receiving a rejection so take precautions before submitting.

Trust the editor and suppress your paranoia. Some writers exclude important information from a query fearing the editor will "steal" their idea. Bad move. Editors aren't thieves, and leaving important information out of your query will only increase your chances of keeping yourself out of print. As will mentioning fees in your query; it will send your query straight to the can. If you're an unpublished writer, don't mention that either. Finally, never include a separate cover letter with your query letter. The query is your cover letter, your letter of inquiry, and your letter of intent—all packed into one tightly-wrapped, single-spaced page.

While some rules are meant to be broken, the rule of keeping a query to one page remains intact. If you can't explain your idea in less than a page, you're probably not too clear about the idea itself.

Just because a query is simply one page don't assume it is simple to compose. A saleable query demands you include all the right information in a small space. Addressing your query to the appropriate editor is most important. Ensure this by calling the editorial office and asking who handles the type of material you're submitting. If you want to write a travel piece for a magazine, call and ask for the name and title of the travel editor. That's it. Don't ask to speak with the travel editor; merely get the correct spelling of his name. Always type or word process your query and put it on simple letterhead—editors want good ideas, not fancy fonts and cute clip art. Make your salutation formal; no "Dear Jim" or "Hello" (just today I saw two queries with these exact salutations!). And always offer an estimated word count and delivery date.

## COMPOSING THE QUERY

You're ready to write your letter. Introduce your idea in a sentence or two that will make the editor curious, such as an interesting fact, an intriguing question, or maybe something humorous. Then state your idea in one crisp sentence to grab the editor's attention. But don't stop there. Reel in the editor with one or two paragraphs expounding upon your idea. Walk through the

---

**DON PRUES** *is the co-author of* Formatting & Submitting Your Manuscript *(Writer's Digest Books).*

| The Ten Query Commandments | The Ten Query Sins |
|---|---|
| Each query letter must be: | No query letter must ever be: |

| The Ten Query Commandments | The Ten Query Sins |
|---|---|
| 1. Professional (includes SASE, is error-free, is addressed to the right editor, etc.). | 1. Wordy (text rambles; length exceeds one-and-a-half pages). |
| 2. New (idea is fresh, set off, and up front). | 2. Sketchy (idea isn't fleshed out enough). |
| 3. Provocative (lead pulls you in). | 3. Presumptuous (tone is too cocky). |
| 4. Creative (presentation is offbeat). | 4. Egotistical (topic is yourself). |
| 5. Focused (story is narrowed down, length is kept to one page). | 5. Reluctant (lame reason why you're doing it). |
| 6. Customized (slanted to that magazine). | 6. Loose-lipped (article is offered on spec). |
| 7. Multifaceted (offers several options on how it could be done). | 7. Stubborn (prior rejects from same editor haven't given you the hint). |
| 8. Realistic (instills confidence that you're reliable and the project's doable). | 8. Intrusive (phone call precedes or supplants query). |
| 9. Accredited (includes your clips, credits, and qualifications). | 9. Inappropriate (clips don't match the idea). |
| 10. Conclusive (confirms that you're the best and only writer to do it). | 10. Careless (faults are mentioned or major gaffe is made). |

*From *How To Write Attention-Grabbing Query & Cover Letters*, by John Wood (Writer's Digest Books)

steps of your project and explain why you're the perfect person to write what you're proposing. List your sources, particularly if you have interviews lined up with specialists on your topic, as this will help establish the credibility of your work.

The tone of your writing is also important. Create a catchy query laden with confidence but devoid of cockiness. Include personal information only if it will help sell your piece, such as previous writing experience with the topic and relevant sample clips. And never forget a SASE. (Before sending your queries, use Andrew Scheer's Query Letter Checklist on page 32.)

Most questions about queries revolve around whether to send simultaneous submissions. Sending simultaneous queries to multiple editors is typically okay if you inform all editors you're doing so. But some editors refuse to read simultaneous queries (*Writer's Market* listings indicate an editor is not receptive to them) because they want an exclusive option to accept or reject your submission. This can be a problem if editors do not respond quickly; it keeps you from submitting to other markets. The two clear advantages to sending simultaneous queries are that you have many lines in the water at once and it prompts a rapid reply—an editor excited by your query will be more apt to get back to you knowing the competition could get to you first.

## WHAT THE CLINIC SHOWS YOU

Unpublished writers wonder how published writers break into print. It's not just a matter of luck; published writers construct compelling queries. What follows are eight actual queries submitted to editors (names and addresses have been altered). Four queries are strong; four are not. Detailed comments from the editors show what the writer did and did not do to secure a sale. As you'll see, there's no such thing as a boilerplate "good" query; every winning query works its own magic.

# Precious ⊠ Pages Inc

*This looks a little silly. "Cute" doesn't indicate respect for the juvenile market.*

May 17, 1999   (Bad)

Marcia Marshall
Executive Editor
Atheneum Books for Young Readers
New York, New York 10020

*Don't assume editor is married.*

Dear Mrs. Marshall,

I write for children, and I call my stories Precious Pages. Although I not yet a published writer, I do have thirty stories finished and I think each of them would make a great book. All of them together would make a great line of its own, called Precious Pages.

*Too much irrelevant personal information. Relatives aren't valid critics.*

I am a mother of three young children, two twin girls (age 4) and a boy (age 7). Over the years I've been concocting stories and telling them to my kids, sometimes when we're on long car trips, sometimes when we're waiting in line at the check out stand, and most often when I'm trying to put them to bed. My boy doesn't get as drawn into my stories as my daughters do. But they just love them and often ask me to repeat stories I already told them. They'll say, "Mommy tell us the story about the unicorn again." That's when I realized I have a knack for creating precious stories, ones that really appeal to young girls. My husband suggested I write them down and find a publisher.

*Vague. No specifics. I don't know what one of these stories is actually about. Moralizing is not a story.*

Most of the Precious Pages stories teach good moral lessons, such as how to love yourself, how to forgive your those who harm you (brothers!), how to be a good grandchild, how to respect those who know better than you (parents!), and the like. My stories are kind of like "Veggie Tales" but the main characters are unicorns, not vegetables.

*Please do not send illustrations! We prefer to use illustrators of our own choosing.*

I have teamed up with a local illustrator and she's done a marvelous job adding wonderful colors and images to the stories. She's created a trademark unicorn that looks like no other. I will be glad to send a few illustrations to you.

Looking forward to hearing from you.

*This sounds overwhelming and non-professional rather than necessary.*

Best,

*There is no criteria to choose from in requesting the ms. This query letter is too broad and unfocused.*

Sarah Sosorry

Comments provided by Marcia Marshall, executive editor of Atheneum Books for Young Readers

8 January 1999

Ms. Caitlyn Dlouhy, Senior Editor
Atheneum Books for Young Readers
Simon & Schuster Children's Publishing Division
1230 Avenue of the Americas
New York, NY 10022

Dear Caitlyn,

Mummies—the mummified remains of human corpses—have fascinated kids
for centuries. It's as if the dearly departed have been frozen in time, captured
in an odd state of human limbo. They're dead, but not quite as dead as most,
from a kid's unique perspective.

*True, kids do love them.*

MY MUMMY'S A KID will profile ten different mummies, but with a twist.
These people died and were physically preserved prior to their 18th birthdays.
These mummies were kids.

*Intriguing.*

Each chapter will explore how a child lived his or her life, how and why they
died, what mummification process preserved their body, what artifacts were
found with them, and who made the scientific discovery.

*Good specifics.*

I propose a text-light, illustration-heavy book to entertain AND educate, using
a timeless hook—life and mummified death.

After nearly ten years as a full-time freelance writer, I feel confident I can
research and write this book. I have written hundreds of articles for the *Chicago
Tribune*, *KidNews*, the *Atlanta Journal Constitution News for Kids*, *Boys' Life*,
*Highlights for Children*, *Fox Kids* and many other high profile publications
(clips included). I have also written books for John Wiley & Sons, John Muir
Publications and Publishers International Inc.

*Credentials make sense for this project.*

*Books more important than magazine work. Shows ability to sustain interest in subject.*

Beyond my own experience, I have recruited Susan Harnessi, a children's writer
with a degree in anthropology. While I have final say over the submission,
she will be co-writer (entitled to half of any contractual benefits). I have also
researched a follow up book, MY MUMMY'S A BEAST—about mummified
animals.

*Added expert helps.*

*Nice practical follow-up suggestion. Not a pie-in-the-sky dream of a multiple book series.*

Thanks for your help. I look forward to your response.

Best wishes,

Kelly Awesome Query
KAQwrites@aol.com
(330)999-5555

Comments provided by Marcia Marshall, executive editor of Atheneum Books for Young Readers

This kind of commentary is ineffective and unprofessional. Every writer feels his or her project is "really good". Also, the first paragraph of a query should offer something intriguing and informative about the book itself—something sorely lacking here.

Although it's helpful to include education and professional writing experience, the author doesn't include relevant information. This might be of interest as background information; if the author has an expertise in the subject matter of the book, that is also worth noting.

The description of the book and its genre should be coherent and concise. The author suggests the book resembles science fiction—a genre that I don't handle, as he might have discovered with a bit more research—but he fails to say what the book is about. This rambling, off-the-cuff narrative is both dizzying and unfocused.

(Bad)

Russell Outrageous
654 Try Again Rd.
Goodluck Nextime, CA 90015

Dear Literary Agent:

As impersonal as they come! Tells me the author hasn't done a scrap of research on me, the kind of books I handle, or my tastes and qualifications. He's taking a "throw a hundred query letters against the wall and see what sticks" approach—not the mark of someone who has thought carefully about whether his novel would be a good fit with any particular agent.

   Hi—My name is Russell Outrageous, and I've written a book. I actually wrote it a few years ago but didn't have any luck pitching it to agents, I think because I came off like a used car salesman. Its been sitting on the shelf for three years, and today I picked up the manuscript and read it. I'm kind of scared—I think it might be really good. I have a good bit of rewriting to do, now that I have some perspective on what doesn't work and what the book has going for it.

   I should tell you its only about 60,000 words, but it's the kind of thing that should be short. If the length prohibits its being considered, please make a note of that on the form letter so I can know where I stand. Otherwise I think we really have something here. I start graduate school in Art History in the fall, I'm 26, so I'm already a bit of a writer. I'm really good with theoretical ideas, and the book is packed with them, but always in a larger context. In fact it was my mission as an undergrad to turn critical writing into an art form, and some would say I succeeded. The book is called *Nearly Human*. It has few of the usual science fiction tools—no made up words or technology, except where they're being satirized. The gadgets are all psychological, and metaphysical, so the characters themselves become the gadgets. The reading goes from dense explanation to slapstick—and takes turns around some crooked corners.

   The book has all the elements of a regular science fiction story—superhero, mad scientist, average Joe and his girlfriend save the world type of thing, only it reads like its warped by a doppler effect. The setup is simple—a mutant superman appears and behaves like you'd expect Superman to behave, a little camped up, only he's actually a twisted bad guy. The story deals with the very odd ways in which the world reacts, in addition to the love story and the guy trying to save his girlfriend from the evil genius who has tampered with his mind. It's about the way we evolve, what choices we have, what our contribution really is.

   *Nearly Human* may not be for kids—it's certainly not for everyone—but it is strange and original enough to be important to science fiction. I think it would be worth your while to look it over. In fact, the original version I made into a copy-store-bound manu-book, and I have several copies. It would be no trouble at all to send you one over. A friend of mine drew a color cover featuring a monkey at a typewriter and an alien with a laptop facing each other. You get the drift.

Thanks for your time,

To suggest that the author's publishing history (of lack thereof) "won't matter—promise," is a bit presumptuous. How does the author know whether it will matter? Some agents won't even consider novels by previously unpublished authors; also, an author's publishing history can directly affect the saleability of a given project. Not that an unpublished author can't get published—but information of this nature usually is important to the agent, so it's best not to treat it as an afterthought.

(P.S.—No, I haven't published before, but it won't matter. Promise.)

Comments provided by Theresa Park, agent with Sanford J. Greenburger Associates, Inc.

*This letter was initially addressed to Diane Cleaver, an agent at Sanford J. Greenburger Associates, without the knowledge that Diane had passed away three months earlier. The letter was passed on to me.*

July 5, 1995

(Great Query)

Dear Ms. Cleaver,

I would like to introduce you to my second literary novel entitled *The Notebook*.

My first novel, *Wokini*, in which I collaborated with William Mills, was published by Orion Books, a division of Random House in 1994. An inspirational work, it was characterized by Al Neuharth, founder and former chairman of *USA Today*, as "a powerful picture on the meaning of life," while Peter Ueberroth called it "overwhelming and insightful." A moderate commercial success, by May 1995, it had sold over 56,000 copies.

This novel, *The Notebook*, is a love story inspired by two special people who recently passed away after sixty years of marriage. They were no one you would know, but there was a grand romance between them, an underlying passion and understanding that had taken a lifetime to develop. In this day and age, the unconditional love they felt for one another makes for a wonderful story, one that is all to rare and much too beautiful to let die without being told.

Like *Romeo and Juliet* or *The Bridges of Madison County* however, all great love stories need tragedy and separation, as well as love, to fully touch the reader, and their story was no exception. Alzheimers became part of their lives during their final years together and my most vivid memories are those of my grandfather sitting by a bedside and reading to his wife of sixty years, a woman who no longer remembered him. Seeing them this way nearly broke my heart, but never once did he bemoan his plight. "In my mind," he used to tell me, "she's the young woman I married long ago and nothing will ever change that." This story is their story, a story of love, the most faithful love I have ever seen.

*The Notebook* is a tender novel set in the deep South, a love story written in lyric prose. Like most Southern literary novels, *The Notebook* envelopes all that is special about the region and its people; tradition, loyalty, kindness, love and remembrance. Yet, this novel stands alone in two important ways. First, it is one of the few passionate love stories written about the elderly, and it reveals a rare but dignified portrait of a couple struggling with the ultimate reality that their lives will be ending soon. Even more importantly, however, *The Notebook* is the first novel that describes the heart-wrenching effects of Alzheimers disease on two people who had loved each other all their lives. The result is a moving eulogy to old age itself—a story of love and grief which pretty much sums up the notable context of most lives.

As a young writer in South Carolina, I am looking for an experienced agent based in New York and your reputation is impeccable. your varied experiences as an editor at Doubleday, Straight Arrow, Scribner's and Simon & Schuster are impressive, and it would be an honor to work with you on this novel.

I have included a short biography for your review. The novel is 52,000 words and fully complete. May I send you a copy of the manuscript? I look forward to hearing from you soon.

Sincerely,

*An extremely important postscript—here the author tells me who the potential market for this book is, and why it might be particularly attractive to a publisher, from a marketing perspective.*

Nicholas Sparks

P.S. Because 22% of the people in this country (40 + million) are over 52 years old and 4.5 million people suffer from Alzheimers, this book is unique and marketable to a wide audience. In addition, at 52,000 words, it is short enough not to be cost-prohibitive to most publishing houses.

Comments provided by Theresa Park, agent with Sanford J. Greenburger Associates, Inc.

*Provides important information about writing history—lists publication dates, publisher and notable reviews.*

*Summarizes the "hook" of the novel. Who could resist this description of the author's faithful grandfather, reading to a wife who no longer remembers him?*

*Very important to point out what distinguishes this book from the thousands of others while still making a strong case for the universality of its appeal. Shows how this book is different, yet familiar enough for everyone to relate to.*

*Though I wasn't the intended recipient of this letter (there's no way he could have known of her recent death), that he had done significant research on her and had chosen her for specific reasons, impressed me.*

*A brief biography is a good idea—educational background, publications (if any), anything else relevant to your profile as an author.*

Bad

There is no description of who Hannes Keller is nor what his role in diving might be, making it tough to decide if the subject is worth exploring. By lower casing the subject's first name, the writer shows his concern for the person he plans to interview. Such name dropping indicates the correspondent may make other assumptions about what constitutes commonly shared knowledge, then file a story rife with jargon and unexplained details, contrary to Immersed's style of explaining everything no matter how mundane. Proposing an interview story demonstrates a lack of awareness of the magazine's content. Immersed publishes a personality profile in each issue, but not question and answer interviews.

Date: Mon, 19 Apr 1999 12:26:46-0400
From: BBQ@compuserve.com
Subject: Imersed
Sender: BBQ@compuserve.com
To: Bob Sterner, bsterner@prodigy.net

This query gets off to a bad start with the misspelling of the magazine's title, Immersed.

Interview with hannes Keller

Project 'Beyond the Blue' Wolds Deepest Sink hole

Interested???

Bobby Bad Query

Additional points are lost with the second query by noting "deepest" as the site's main feature. While the leading edge of scuba diving is the very heart of Immersed's editorial coverage, the emphasis is always on the knowledge that is gained from the experience and the safety factors that mitigate the dangers of gaining this knowledge. By focusing on the hazardous aspect of the dive this correspondent comes off as an egotistical thrill seeker. Also, so many misspellings in such a short phrase does not bode well for this writer's language skills. Beyond the Blue should be in full quotes if it's a proper title or none at all if it's not. Wolds no doubt should be World's, and sinkhole is one word.

There is no indication of what, if any, artwork would be available to support either of these manuscripts, an important detail in choosing stories for a full-color glossy magazine. There is no means of contacting this writer other than via e-mail, a substantial inconvenience. A telephone number would allow for a quick conversation to nail down deadlines and points to be included in the stories, sparing a lot of work for writer and editor alike. Providing a mailing address would ease sending out a contract. Not surprisingly, this correspondent does not mention any previous story sales nor any other credentials that would demonstrate a capability to file a viable story within a set time frame.

Interested??? No Way!

Comments provided by Bob Sterner, publisher of Immersed magazine.

From: David Diver
PADI DM #82825
123 Winning Query Rd.
Published, CA 91111
(310)333-5555
Fax: (310)333-4444

*Writer quickly establishes his diving credentials by providing his Dive Master certification number from the Professional Association of Diving Instructors.*

*Providing an address and telephone number eases contacting the writer.*

Date: August 25, 1998

To: Bob Sterner
Immersed
(718)545-1325, fax (718)545-3889

re: query/Farallon Islands Article

*The purpose of the correspondence is quickly defined.*

*A quick description of writing and diving credentials lets me know this writer is capable of writing and filing a story on time.*

Dear Mr. Sterner,

I have been writing professionally since 1989. With regard to diving, my areas of moderate expertise include: spearfishing (on SCUBA and free-diving), wilderness diving and Pacific Coast Species identification. Since 1992, I have contributed occasionally to *California Diving News*. In the last few months, I have placed two articles with *Western Diver* and one with *The Undersea Journal*. Both editors have requested further submissions.

*Tells the content of what is readily available. Quickly acknowledges how the subject matter might be off-target for Immersed's focus by not being especially "technical." However, he provides a tie-in that is paramount to safe diving—risk management. —a hook that appeals to Immersed readers.*

I've nearly completed a 2,000-word piece on the recent history of recreational diving in the Farallon Islands. The article begins with risk-management analysis, continues with a diver's-eye-view of the extraordinary natural history of these islands and concludes with a great white shark encounter. Tangentially, the piece addresses the issue of resource management in the National Marine Sanctuary.

Since it's hardly hi-tech stuff, it may not interest you at all. On the other hand, the story does involve a group of cool-headed and adventurous divers, who carefully weighed the risks of diving without cages in the heart of great white shark country. Their solutions to the risk-management problem are surprisingly simple and, to date, effective.

I have some pictures of a 1997 trip. I am in the process of gathering more recent photos, including some great white shark shots. I'm now fact-checking the piece; should be able to deliver it within a week. The pictures may take a bit longer. If you want to review this text, please let me know ASAP.

*Noting the availability of photos puts this higher in the in-basket, and it's great to read that the correspondent already is fact-checking the manuscript.*

Sincerely,


David Diver

Comments provided by Bob Sterner, publisher of *Immersed* magazine.

*The Tuesday is a bit much—HOW is a bimonthly magazine, not a daily newspaper!*

*No salutation, indicating this is a mass-mailed form letter. The exclamation point is a bit much.*

*punctuation error*

*It's ironic that he's pitching tips from another author—he slammed marketing authors in the previous sentence. And the following tips aren't even useful.*

*The use of "you" in this paragraph is confusing, changing the focus and tone of the letter.*

*This pitch is too little, too late. It's clear that he hasn't asked for our writer's guidelines—word counts, timetables and payment price aren't mentioned. He doesn't clarify who will be writing the article (here's a surprise, it's not him!) until the next paragraph. I want contact with the person who's going to write the article, not her public-relations rep.*

Bad

Tuesday, March 9, 1999

Tom Poorquery
123 Sorry Lane
Cloudy, CA 94100

Query: You Don't Need A Marketing Plan!   *unnecessary*

    With an abundance of marketing resources out there directed at small and medium sized businesses, it's easy to wonder if there's anything left to say about marketing. Books, workshops, consultants, audio cassettes, and marketing programs cover almost every nook and cranny on the subject of marketing a small business. But even though there is a ocean of marketing knowledge available, it's ironic that many small businesses never achieve the one desired result—getting clients now and consistently throughout the life of their businesses.

    It's easy to think there is a secret to successful marketing and sales. It's tempting to keep spending money on books and workshops in search of the magic key that will open the door to abundant clients. According to business coach A.B. Sell, author of "Market Like Crazy!" most marketing techniques, however; don't apply to small businesses, for a variety of reasons:   *awkward word choice*

• Most advice is too complex or irrelevant. One person businesses need something simple and straight forward. Instead of lofty statements like "increase market share," small businesses need specific action items like "interview 20 former and current clients to find out why they chose us—by Oct. 31"

• For small businesses, marketing can be overwhelming. There are just too many ideas to consider and too many choices to make. Struck by "analysis paralysis," many people start and stop, sit and stew, or just do nothing.

• The small business owner needs to stay motivated With no boss looking over your shoulder, it's easy to avoid marketing and sales. When you don't see immediate results, you get discouraged. When someone rejects your sales pitch, it's hard not to take it personally. It's so tempting just to wait for the phone to ring, and blame your lack of business on the economy, the weather, or the time of year.

    I would like to propose an article on "Doing Away with That Tired Marketing Plan!" for HOW. This article will outline simple processes that demystify marketing while providing a framework for immediate and effective action.

    As a marketing consultant for Ms. Sell, I can discuss this idea with you and provide an outline of the article upon request. Because Ms. Sell will author the article upon your acceptance, I have included her credentials and previously published articles. I have included a SASE for your response.

Interested?   *This ending is rude and unprofessional.*

Tom Poorquery

*Take another look at the letter and notice that HOW's target audience—graphic designers—aren't even mentioned. Boilerplate letters lead to boilerplate articles.*

Comments provided by Ann Weber, senior editor of *HOW* magazine.

*Good*

January 23, 1998

Ed Strongquery
5432 Inprint Rd.
Sunny, CA 93000

Ph: (805)569-999
Fax: (805)569-8888

*The opening paragraph offers a teaser on the topic and grabbed my attention.*

Dear Ms. Weber:

"Pro bono client"—does the term make designers run for the hills, or step forward and volunteer? Well, it depends . . .

As a graphic designer, I am interested in writing on topics related to the field. Enclosed is a copy of a book review which I am submitting as a writing sample. The review has been accepted for publication by *Letter Arts Review*.

The article I am now working on is about designers' efforts to do pro-bono work, specifically for non-profit organizations. These areas will be covered:
1. Rationale and motivation for the designer: desire to help the community; feeling an obligation to perform a professional duty; seeing a chance to do projects which would not otherwise be available; using the experience as a public relations device, etc.
2. Perceptions among the non-profits: most of them don't know what designers do; many non-profits don't see their own shortcomings in the areas of design quality, sophistication, and consistency; many non-profits believe that professional design is always expensive; at training workshops, non-profits are often advised that they can do their own design, etc.
3. Risks for the designer: the non-profit client may perceive an outsider as a threat to their turf; may have a personal attachment to a name, logo, or project; may have another volunteer (a non-designer) who is providing "design"; may be resistant to changing the ways things are done; may expect/require the designer to "work with" others; or may be unwilling to give up any creative control, etc.
4. Tips for the designer/choosing a non-profit: try to find out how it currently handles its design needs; who is responsible for designed items; how it is organized (board of directors, officers, etc.); what other local firms donate services or products; if it has previous or current experience in working with a designer, etc.
5. The benefits: public recognition of donated talent and time; new contacts in the community; a wider audience for your work; contacts among vendors who may be a source of information and/or clients; personal satisfaction; enhanced business skills; chance to meet people from other fields (who will get to know you in a non-selling environment), etc.

If you have any interest in this material I will be glad to send the completed article. I am also submitting this idea to other design publications. Thank you for your consideration; I will look forward to hearing from you.

Cordially,

*This letter led directly to publication, as well as many other HOW assignments. Two details that would have made this letter even better: 1. What design firms will be covered in this article? 2. What artwork can be used to highlight points in the story?*

Ed Strongquery

*The writer details his (limited) writing experience and shows he has first-hand knowledge of the graphic design field. But I would've liked more information on his design background.*

*The letter contains a few grammatical and punctuation errors. Always proofread query letters before sending them.*

*Breakdowns like this really convey what the article will cover, demonstrating the author knows what he's talking about.*

*I like this writer already! These points show that he knows our magazine and that HOW articles offer lots of concrete advice that readers can use.*

*This sentence is a little disconcerting—most magazines want an "exclusive." But I appreciate his honesty and straightforward approach.*

Comments provided by Ann Weber, senior editor of *HOW* magazine.

## ANDREW SCHEER'S QUERY LETTER CHECKLIST

### CONTENT
1. Working title (to help editors grasp your idea quickly)
2. Summary of topic or theme
3. Intended reader application (takeaway value)
4. Approximate article length (e.g., 800 words, 1,500 words)
5. Sample paragraph: lead or key segment (a big help in assessing your writing)
6. Paragraph summarizing key supporting material (e.g., anecdotes, interviews)
7. Your qualifications to write on this topic (incl. writing experience, if applicable)

### MECHANICS
1. Current magazine title
2. Current magazine address
3. Correct editor (when in doubt, ask first)
4. Correct spelling of editor's name
5. Neat, error-free typing
6. One page, single-spaced
7. Self-addressed, stamped envelope (SASE) (hint: fold it in thirds)
8. Mailed in #10 business envelope

### INFORMATION ABOUT YOU
1. Your name
2. Your title (Miss, Ms., Mrs., Mr., Dr., etc.)
3. Your address
4. Your day phone number (fax, e-mail if available)

### INFORMATION ABOUT YOUR ARTICLE
1. Approximate article length (e.g., 500 words, 1,200 words)
2. When article is available (e.g., immediately, in 4 weeks)
3. Rights available (first, one-time, or reprint)

### OPTIONAL (in descending order of potential usefulness)
1. Samples (include only if applicable/impressive to this publication)
2. Reply Postcard
3. Letterhead (avoid unconventional stock or too many dingbats)
4. Business Card

### DON'TS
1. Phone or fax (unless urgent article, e.g., L.A. earthquake story on 1/18/95)
2. Unrealistic deadline ("If I don't hear from you in one week . . .")
3. Query for a topic that's just been given major coverage
4. Confess unfamiliarity with the magazine
5. Request guidelines as part of your query
6. "Dear Editor"/"Occupant" letter
7. Long or vague letter
8. Bad attitude (antagonistic, defeatist)
9. Query for type of articles the magazine doesn't print

There's no special format that results in a yes; let it reflect you and the nature of your topic.

Andrew Scheer is the managing editor of *Moody Magazine*.

# Crafting a Successful Synopsis

## BY EVAN MARSHALL

Your novel is finished and ready to mail to an agent or editor. You shoot off a query letter. The agent or editor asks to see your manuscript, *or* she asks to see a proposal: three chapters and a synopsis, or one chapter and a synopsis, or just a synopsis.

A *what*? A synopsis, a brief narrative summary of your novel. It's a vital marketing tool for a novelist, because it often has to do the entire job of enticing an agent or editor enough to want to read your novel. Think of the synopsis as a sales pitch for your book.

A synopsis has other uses, too. Later, when you sell your novel, your editor may ask you for a synopsis to be used as the basis for jacket or cover copy for your book. Other departments in the publishing house, such as Art or Sales or Publicity, may want to read your synopsis to get a quick idea of your story.

Even later, when it's time to sell your next novel, you'll be able to secure a contract solely on the basis of a synopsis and a few chapters, or just a synopsis. (The only time you should have to finish a book before selling it is the first time.) As you can see, the synopsis performs a number of important functions. It therefore deserves as careful attention as you've given the novel itself.

## SYNOPSIS MECHANICS

The synopsis is formatted much like your manuscript. Use Courier or Times Roman type; double-space all text; set your left, right and bottom margins at 1¼″, your top margin at ½″. Justify the left margin only.

On every page except the first, type against the top and left margins a slugline consisting of your last name, a slash, your novel's title in capital letters, another slash and the word *Synopsis*, like this: Price/UNDER SUSPICION/Synopsis. Number the pages consecutively in the upper right-hand corner of the page, against the top and right margins. The first line of text on each page should be about ¾″ below the slugline and page number.

On the first page of your synopsis, against the top and left margins, type single-spaced your name, address and telephone number. Against the top and right margins, type single-spaced your novel's genre, its word count and the word *Synopsis*. (The first page of the synopsis is not numbered, though it is page 1.)

Double-space twice, center your novel's title in capital letters, double-space twice again, and begin the text of your synopsis.

See the next page for how the synopsis of Sara Bradford's story would begin.

**EVAN MARSHALL** *is the president of The Evan Marshall Agency, a leading literary agency that specializes in representing fiction writers. A former book editor and packager, he has contributed articles on writing and publishing to* Writer's Digest *and other magazines. He is the author of* Eye Language *and a forthcoming series of mystery novels. This article is excerpted from* The Marshall Plan for Novel Writing *copyright © 1998 Evan Marshall. Used with permission of Writer's Digest Books, a division of F&W Publications, Inc. For credit card orders phone toll free 1-800-289-0963.*

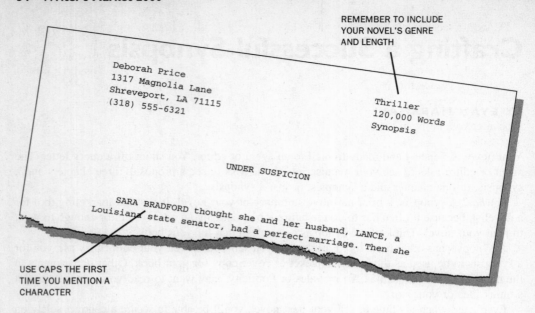

REMEMBER TO INCLUDE
YOUR NOVEL'S GENRE
AND LENGTH

Deborah Price
1317 Magnolia Lane
Shreveport, LA 71115
(318) 555-6321

Thriller
120,000 Words
Synopsis

UNDER SUSPICION

SARA BRADFORD thought she and her husband, LANCE, a
Louisiana state senator, had a perfect marriage. Then she

USE CAPS THE FIRST
TIME YOU MENTION A
CHARACTER

## SYNOPSIS BASICS

Before we get to the subtleties of writing the synopsis, be aware of a few basic rules.

1. The synopsis is always written in the present tense (called the historical present tense).

2. The synopsis tells your novel's *entire* story. It doesn't leave out what's covered by the sample chapters submitted with it. Nor does it withhold the end of the story—for example, "who done it" in a murder mystery—in order to entice an agent or editor to want to see more. The synopsis is a miniature representation of your novel; to leave anything out is to defeat the purpose of the synopsis.

3. The synopsis should not run too long. An overlong synopsis also defeats its purpose. My rule is to aim for one page of synopsis for every 25 pages of manuscript. Thus a 400-page manuscript calls for a 16-page synopsis. If you run a page or two over or under, don't worry.

4. To achieve this conciseness, write as clean and tight as you can. Cut extra adverbs and adjectives. Focus on your story's essential details. Let's say, for example, you have a section in which your lead meets another character for dinner at a chic French bistro to try to convince her to lend him some money. We don't need to know where they had dinner or what they ate or even exactly what was said. We need something on the order of "Ray meets Lenore for dinner and tries to convince her to lend him the money. Lenore refuses." Actual dialogue is rarely, if ever, needed in the synopsis.

5. Don't divide your synopsis by chapters; write one unified account of your story. You can use paragraphing to indicate a chapter or section break.

## HOW TO MAKE YOUR SYNOPSIS SIZZLE

Now, keeping all of the above in mind, translate your manuscript into synopsis. Begin with your lead and her crisis as the hook of your synopsis. Then tell how your lead intends to solve the crisis (what is her story goal?). For example:

BARBARA DANFORTH has never been especially fond of her brother-in-law, GRA-HAM, but she would never have murdered him. Yet all the clues point to her as Graham's killer. She'll have to prove her innocence if she doesn't want to end up as dead as Graham.

PATRICK WARMAN, founder and director of Philadelphia's Friendship Street Shelter for runaway children, has always been careful to maintain a professional distance from the young people he helps. That's why he is especially horrified to realize he has fallen in love with

PEARL, a teenage girl in his care. If he can't come to terms with these forbidden feelings, he'll lose everything he's worked for. Yet he can't bear to lose 16-year-old Pearl.

RITA RAYMOND is delighted when an employment agency sends her to work as a companion to a man recovering from an accident. She would never have accepted the job if she had known the man was her ex-husband, AARON. And damn if she isn't falling in love with him again. Yet Aaron was the cause of everything wrong in her life.

Soon after your problem hook, give the vital details about your lead: age, occupation, marital status (if you haven't already), as well as details of time (the present? the past?) and place.

Barbara, single at 38, has lived quietly in Rosemont, Texas, working as a stenographer and generally minding her own business. When her sister TRISH invited her to a party to celebrate the tenth anniversary of Trish's marriage to Graham, Barbara balked. She'd never liked Graham. But she accepted—her first mistake. Agreeing to let Graham take her for a moonlit walk around the couple's lavish estate was her second. . . .

Patrick, 28, has been married to MARIANNE for 9 years, but although she helps at the shelter, their marriage is in name only. . . .

At 29, Rita has made peace with her life as a divorcée. She earns enough money as a high school teacher to support herself and her seven-year-old daughter, ALLEGRA, though Allegra's severe asthma has been an emotional and financial strain. Even so, life these past five years without Aaron has been better than life was *with* him. . . .

Now continue telling your story, keeping to the main story points. Remember that the synopsis is not necessarily meant to convey the circumstances of *how* something happens; the happenings themselves are the concern here.

Most important, remember that *motivation and emotion are things that happen*; they are plot points, as important as any physical action a character might perform. Some of the worst synopses I've seen from would-be clients are dry and lifeless because these aspects have been left out.

Don't just tell us that Brandon tells Carla he's accepted the job in Sydney and that the next morning Carla has coffee at her friend Tanya's house and tells her the news. Tell us that when Brandon tells Carla he's accepted the job in Sydney, Carla sees her happy life collapsing around her. Devastated, the next morning over coffee she pours her heart out to Tanya.

Don't just tell us that Jake Hammond stomps into the bank and dumps a sack of money on the president's desk, announcing he's repaying his loan. Tell us that Jake, full of angry self-righteousness at how the bank has treated his sister, stomps into the bank and dumps the money on the president's desk.

The agents and editors who will read and evaluate your synopsis are looking for the same things as your eventual readers: emotion and human drama. Bear down on these life-breathing aspects of your story and you can't go wrong.

Indicate other characters' story lines in your synopsis by beginning a new paragraph and describing the character's actions. Sometimes transitions such as "Meanwhile" or "Simultaneously" or "At the hotel" can help ground the reader in time and place.

As you write the synopsis, think of it as your novel in condensed form, and present events in the same order that they occur in the novel itself. Also, reveal information at the same points you do so in your novel.

Stay "invisible" in your synopsis; by this I mean several things. First, don't use devices that emphasize the mechanics of storytelling. One of these is the use of such headings as "Background," "Setting" and "Time" at the beginning of your synopsis. All of these elements should be smoothly woven into the narrative. Another such device is the use of character sketches or descriptions at the beginning or end of the synopsis. For one thing, they go into more detail than is appropriate for a synopsis. Second, they make it difficult for the agent or editor to follow your story: If he reads the synopsis first, it's meaningless because he has no information about the characters. If he reads the character sketches first, they are equally meaningless because the characters are not presented in the context of the story. Characters and story do not exist independently of each other. Give any important facts or background when you introduce a character.

In the text, type a character's name in capital letters the first time you use it—a technique borrowed from film treatments. Also, to avoid confusion, always refer to a character the same way throughout the synopsis (not "Dr. Martin" in one place, "the doctor" somewhere else and "Martin" somewhere else).

Another way to stay invisible is to avoid referring to the structural underpinnings of your story. When I was a kid, we used to go to an amusement park with a scary jungle ride which went through a dark tunnel where a native jumped out and scared us silly. One day as we floated through the tunnel and the native jumped out, I noticed that the figure of the native had come loose from its metal support. I could see ugly gray metal and a tangle of electrical wires. The ride was never the same after that.

That's how I feel when I can see the scaffolding of a synopsis—for example, "In a flashback, Myron. . . ." Better to simply say "Myron remembers. . . ." Don't write "At the darkest moment of her Point of Hopelessness . . ."; just tell what happens. Avoid "As the story begins . . ." or "As the story ends . . ."; just tell the story.

As you near the end of the synopsis and your story's resolution, quicken the pace by using shorter paragraphs and shorter sentences. A staccato effect increases the suspense.

Above all, never in your synopsis review your story, as "In a nerve-jangling confrontation . . ." or "In a heart-wrenching confession. . . ." This kind of self-praise is amateurish and inappropriate in a synopsis, which presents "just the (story) facts, ma'am"; let your story's attributes speak for themselves.

Once your synopsis is finished, polish, polish, polish! In many cases your synopsis will be your foot in the door, and many agents and editors will judge your storytelling and writing style from this selling piece alone. When I receive a synopsis containing misspellings, poor grammar and sloppy presentation, I do not ask to see the manuscript. I assume it will contain the same kinds of errors.

One final word of advice: Don't try to write your synopsis from your section sheets. It's not impossible, but you'll make your life more difficult than necessary. The section sheets contain too great a level of detail; if you translate them, you're likely to find your synopsis running too long. Work from your manuscript, reading each section or chapter and then retelling it briefly, as you might if you were telling your story to a friend.

Writing the synopsis is an art you should become proficient in. A masterful synopsis starts selling your novel to an agent or editor before she even looks at your manuscript. In fact, a few times during my career I have read a synopsis so well crafted that later I felt I had read the book! That's real magic.

## KEYS TO A SUCCESSFUL SYNOPSIS

- A well-written synopsis is a vital marketing tool for your novel, both before and after it's sold.
- Follow correct manuscript format.
- Write the synopsis in the present tense.
- Tell the entire story, with events in the same order as in the novel.
- Aim for a length of 1 synopsis page for every 25 manuscript pages.
- Focus on story essentials.
- Start with a problem-and-story-goal hook.
- Include characters' motivations and emotions.
- Don't let story mechanics show.

# Jane Smiley: The All-True Result of Loving to Write

### BY PAULA DEIMLING

There is usually a degree of angst that surfaces in any interview with an author—either complaints about editors or reviews, or complaints about not having enough hours in the day. But talking with Jane Smiley, you sense that the joy of writing is always there. There's a calmness in her speaking voice, a self-confidence that you unknowingly might attribute to her having won the Pulitzer Prize for *A Thousand Acres* (Knopf) or having written 11 novels, but she is adamant: the Pulitzer didn't change her life or her writing.

**Jane Smiley**

The day before this interview had been a long one—Smiley flying into Cincinnati from the West Coast and signing books until nine o'clock that evening. On the day of this interview, she was heading to Louisville, Kentucky. Her novel-in-progress, *Horse Heaven* (Knopf), is about thoroughbreds, and a Breeders' Cup race is scheduled that weekend. She has work to do.

## WRITING REGIMEN

In 1996, after two decades of teaching literature and creative writing, Smiley moved to northern California to write fulltime and pursue her new "second job," horse breeding. She owns 12 horses, 3 of them stabled on the property where she lives.

Smiley writes for about two to three hours every day, usually in the mornings. "At the moment, I'm trying to write four [double-spaced] pages a day, but my normal pace is about three. I spend the majority of the day riding horses, taking care of kids, doing errands." Most authors have lives, she points out; writing is just one part of that life.

"I can't write all day—never did, couldn't do it," she says. "But I have to write every day. The result of that kind of schedule is that all my novels have a certain deliberate pace. Most of them are written in *adagio* rather than *allegro*."

When starting a new book, Smiley sets aside the tendency to judge or analyze it. Her goal is to get the whole arc of the story on paper, and then to see the connections between the disparate elements. "Every first draft is perfect because all the first draft has to do is exist. It's perfect in its existence," she says. "The only way it could be imperfect would be not to exist."

So how does Smiley create such realistic scenes, like the swell of people coping on a river boat en route to the Kansas Territory in 1855 in *The All-True Travels and Adventures of Lidie Newton*? "Part of the answer is that it's illusory," she says. "I try to give enough details—visual or sensory—so the reader has something concrete to hang on to. That's become almost second nature now, what things look like, what they sound like, and knowing how long you let those lines hang before you come back in with more."

---

**PAULA DEIMLING** *is a full-time writer, and former editor of* Writer's Market. *She is one of the authors of* The Writer's Essential Desk Reference *(Writer's Digest Books). Past interviews have included Isaac Asimov, Peter Davidson, Molly Peacock and William Zinsser.*

Again the casual self-confidence surfaces in the conversation, but her novels—as they explore how people interact with one another—are anything but casual. "If you're interested in the process and what's coming out, as opposed to what it's going to get you, then you're always going to be confident because you're not afraid," she says. "Writing is a process that's endlessly fascinating to me to see what comes out, to see how things mesh. Why invest it with defensiveness or anxiety?"

But it's not as if everything always goes her way. Smiley was not accepted into the Iowa Writers' Workshop on her first application. While in the University of Iowa's graduate English program on the third floor, she'd go upstairs to the fourth floor workshop and read the stories of students in the program. Was she discouraged? "No," she says. "I just wanted to do it." She re-applied again, and in the autumn of 1974, entered the program.

At a fiction reading last year, Smiley told her audience about posting rejection slips on the window over the sink to read while doing dishes. "A rejection slip is a business letter, not a personal letter," she says. Still, she acknowledges, "rejection slips last a long time." To put rejection in perspective, Smiley believes it's important for writers to understand the difference between career and work. "You can't experience your career. You can experience your work all the time. The real center of your existence is within your work."

As a writing professor, Smiley encouraged writers to care only about the work. "It has to do with the idea of your writing not being a possession of your ego. You don't have to feel you need to defend it or promote it, that it's more interesting than that."

## 'ONLY THE WORK MATTERS'

Anxiety about writing, Smiley observes, is a kind of performance anxiety relating to how the writer will look after committing to a particular performance. "But the paradox is that you can't commit yourself until you get rid of your performance anxiety. And the only way you can commit yourself to something is to become so interested in it that all ego considerations disappear and you can feel yourself fully engaged. That's the state in which all your best writing is done. You have to give up the anxiety in order to commit yourself, but you have to commit yourself in order to give up your anxiety. It's a paradox until it happens, then it's easy."

To learn any discipline, from writing to riding a horse, a person must be able to observe himself with a degree of detachment or the person can't fully learn. That doesn't mean detachment, though, from one's subject matter, Smiley says.

Generally, in the writing courses she has taught, Smiley found that writers fell into two groups. One group would write purely from their own feelings and experiences without having read extensively or having learned to communicate. Another group, which had done considerable reading, needed to gain a sense of the importance of their own experiences and to add authenticity to their work. "They both had different things they had to learn," she says.

What is the worst writing advice she has received as a writer? " 'Write what you know.' That's wrong. 'Know what you write' is the right answer."

Writers can come to know their subjects in many ways: talking with people, gossiping, having a particular experience, reading, researching, seeing a place. "There are a lot of ways of knowing things," says Smiley. "There are things you know or suspect. Then there are things you haven't thought about, and they come up again on the page, but it's still something you know because it has a feel of authenticity."

Part of her work process is showing passages of a work-in-progress to people who can point out inaccuracies or inconsistencies. That was one of her goals in going to Louisville as she was writing *Horse Heaven*—to seek out what she calls 'informants.' "You, the writer, are flooded with your own picture of your novel, she says. "You write from that picture." With this latest novel timed to coincide with the Kentucky Derby in May 2000, she wanted the details about racing to be accurate, to have that "feeling of authenticity."

# THE ART OF REVISING

"For the real revision to begin, it is essential for the writer to push all the way to the end of the first draft, no matter how awkward the draft seems, for hidden in the rough draft are all the answers to the writer's questions about the material," writes Smiley in a recent Associated Writing Programs *Chronicle* article about revision. Revising, she has learned over the years, is different for every book. "Every novel asks a different thing of you," she says. "Your key thought is that you're not there to judge your work, only there to analyze it."

When she wrote *Duplicate Keys* (Knopf) in the early 1980s, Smiley created cards listing each chapter's contents and characters, and what was needed in the book. The cards became an informational analysis of how the plot was progressing. When she revised *Moo* (Knopf), she took the first draft apart and looked at it on two levels. First, she isolated the sections about each character and read each section in order, re-editing the book for continuity. This process made it easier to see what was missing about each character, and what needed to be added. Next, she re-ordered and re-edited *Moo* for continuity of plot.

In editing the first draft of *Lidie Newton*, Smiley noticed how Lidie's character would disappear in the descriptions of historical incidents. It was difficult to make the historical parts personal. Smiley found a remedy, related to the pre-Civil War era depicted in the novel: "You have to sift it through her consciousness instead of having her tell it like a book; you have to have her tell it by gossip," Smiley says. "In those days, the only media were gossip, so that was something I had to remember all the time."

In developing Lidie's character, Smiley says, she didn't have a particular strategy. "She [Lidie] started talking, and her voice took over. If the reader doesn't accept the protagonist's voice, the reader won't accept the book at all. So you do your research and think about it and prepare and then it comes. It's not a case of you constructing it; otherwise it would be too laborious and it would look laborious. The author has to come up with the particular voice to tell the story—the author's voice is filtered through the narrator's."

# PLANNING THE JOURNEY OF A NOVEL

For Smiley, planning a novel is like making any plan—a dinner party, she mentions as an example. She tries to be eagerly receptive to the possibilities. "If you try to make everything fit your plan, then you're not open to the larger thing." Allowing the unexpected to intervene is important for a writer. "If you think you know the end and how to get there word for word, then the wonderful things aren't going to happen," she says. "As I write more and more, I find myself allowing what seem to not be good ideas on the page."

For instance, Smiley recalls a chapter she'd just written and adored; the chapter had seemed easy to write. The next chapter, about two characters falling in love, demanded a significant change in pace and tone. When she'd completed this latter chapter, she was sweating. "It had been an effort." Initially, she didn't know how an image of a pony fit into the scene. She didn't want to write it, but persisted. At the end, this wonderful image surfaced. "I had worked hard to get that. That image was a real gift. Who was the giver? I don't know. But every writer recognizes there's a gift. No one writes alone. The gift is coming from literature, the Jungian mind, God, the muse, your friends. The real gift in that sense is receptivity itself."

Sometimes, when an image surfaces in a first draft, "all sorts of judgmental thoughts come up, and eventually you learn your biggest thrill is the wonder of 'where did that come from?' " Smiley says. "The image comes in the course of five minutes. If you'd gone on to something else, you may not have received that image. You may have aborted your own process."

The last thing Smiley says she learned as a writer was the full and profound realization that she wasn't writing the book; rather, she was "letting the book develop in its own way. It has taken me 11 novels to get to that point. The last skill I mastered was backing off." For instance, she says, letting Lidie tell her story or letting *Horse Heaven* develop in its own way.

And how does a writer get to this point? "Writing," she says, matter-of-factly.

# Interview With an Adventurer: Caroline Alexander

## BY JOANNE MILLER

Nonfiction author Caroline Alexander was introduced to the breadth of the world at an impressionable age. As a girl, she experienced a wide variety of cultures, habitats, and adventures in the course of her British-born mother's work as a traveling teacher and translator. Since that early exposure, Alexander has parlayed her lifelong love of adventure into a writing career marked by the publication of four nonfiction books, including her most recent and bestselling work, *The Endurance* (Knopf), which chronicles the trials of the crew of a ship trapped on Antarctic ice floes for a grueling winter season.

Caroline Alexander

© 1999 Elizabeth Iannuzzi

"I always knew I was going to be a writer," says Alexander, who also contributes to such notable periodicals as *Smithsonian, National Geographic* and *Condé Nast Traveler.* "It was an accepted fact in my family."

As an undergraduate at the University of Florida, Alexander tested herself with continued adventures, honing skills ascribed to the ideal warrior: fencing, shooting, riding, swimming and running, "the pursuits of a pentathlete." She was accepted into the U.S. Olympic Training Center, and trained there until she left to further her education at Oxford, applying for the prestigious Rhodes Scholarship. "It celebrated good grades, manly outdoor activities, and leadership—a truly colonial viewpoint," Alexander says. Like the pentathlon, the scholarship was available only to men until the year Alexander applied. After completing her studies in Great Britain, she sought work as a teacher in Africa: "I was willing to go anywhere; I literally had a list of every college-level school on the continent, and I typed letters to them, one by one." She was hired by the University of Malawi to teach classics, and stayed there for three years.

A year later, while studying for her Ph.D. at Columbia University, Alexander realized a childhood ambition and began writing. "During the hiatus between Oxford and Columbia, a friend and I had gone to Borneo to collect diseased insects. It was a lark, really, but we had the support of the Oxford Department of Virology," she recalls. "At Columbia, the story of that adventure bubbled up, and I was seized with a desire to write about it. A fairy godmother helped me along—my dissertation supervisor. I wrote the piece, she critiqued it and arranged for me to meet the person who became my agent." That story, "North Borneo Expedition," was published in *The New Yorker.*

Alexander's first book, also conceived and written while she attended Columbia, was the result of reading a book written in 1895 by Mary Kingsley chronicling her adventures in Gabon, Africa. Alexander recalls thinking, "What a wonderful journey to retrace." With the help of her agent, she targeted Alfred A. Knopf, which bought her idea, negotiated a book deal and advance,

**JOANNE MILLER** *is author of the comprehensive guides* Pennsylvania Handbook *(Moon Publications) and* Maryland-Delaware Handbook *(Moon Publications, Spring 2000). Her interviews with Arthur Golden and the editors of* Sunset Magazine *appeared in the 1999 edition of* Writer's Market.

and sent Alexander off once again to Africa, this time to write *One Dry Season: In the Footsteps of Mary Kingsley*.

Her next book was sparked by a discussion of the ideal exotic destination. "It made me think of Coleridge's *Xanadu*; I knew that this poem, which was written in an opium trance, was based on real places Coleridge had read about. I researched his sources—travel books about north Florida, Inner Mongolia, the mountains of Kashmir, and Mt. Abora—and wrote *The Way to Xanadu*."

Alexander followed that book with *Battle's End*, which followed the lives of young men she had tutored while in college. "The advances I received for these books—both part of a two-book deal with Knopf—and related articles made it possible for me to be a full-time writer."

In 1996, Alexander wrote a children's book, *Mrs. Chippy's Last Expedition*. That story, the tale of a cat which belonged to the ship's carpenter on The Endurance, was later placed at HarperCollins and propelled Alexander into her fourth book, *The Endurance*. Publication of that book coincided with a photographic exhibition of the expedition at the Museum of Natural History in New York. The book, written in a narrative style with quotes from diaries of the participants, tells of the ill-fated expedition of Sir Ernest Shackleton and his men to Antarctica in 1915. Their ship, The Endurance, was destroyed by sea ice; the men were forced to test body and spirit during a harrowing winter spent on the floes of the Weddell Sea. To reach help before another winter overtook them, Shackleton and a few companions set out on a near-impossible voyage in a small open boat 800 miles across the south Scotia Sea—a classic tale of steadfast strength in the face of overwhelming adversity.

Here Alexander talks with *Writer's Market* about the inspiration for her work, researching her nonfiction subjects, and what has given *The Endurance* its enduring appeal.

### How did you become interested in the classics? Did your training in that discipline shape your writing?

When I was young, I read *The Iliad* in translation; I was enamored. I wanted to read the original. Studying the classics was an ideal background for me; I suppose I have old-fashioned tastes in literature. The discipline of translating long passages of Greek and Latin is excellent desk training for a writer, in general. There are no shortcuts. Both languages exist between the spoken word and your imagination—shadow languages. I loved the intimacy of translation. The classics taught me shades of meaning and instilled an obsession with finding the exact right word in my own writing.

### Does your writing stem from your adventures?

My writing falls into the adventure genre, but what interests me most are stories about things past. *The Endurance* was about my fascination with Shackleton and the others as people rather than Antarctica, the place.

My third book, *Battle's End*, was a departure from my usual writing, though it proves the point about my interest in people and their stories. The title is taken from the University of Florida fight song. When I was training as a pentathlete, I tutored University football players in remedial English. Most read at a sixth-grade level; with few exceptions, though, these young men were very bright. They had a wonderful, spontaneous sense of humor. The book grew from my desire to follow up on them 12 years after they'd graduated. I didn't want to speak for them; I wanted to let each speaker assess his own experience as to why he ended up in my remedial class in the first place and what he had gone on to do after leaving the university.

### Which came first, the exhibition at the Museum of Natural History or your book, The Endurance?

Because of my interest in Mrs. Chippy, I saw the work of Frank Hurley, who had kept a photographic record of the expedition. My partner, a photographer, was struck by the quality of

Hurley's work. We were surprised that Hurley hadn't been exhibited much outside of his native Australia, so I decided to mount an exhibition.

When I contacted the Museum of Natural History, they wanted a more extensive exhibit—and a book. My editor at Knopf, almost as a favor, accepted *The Endurance* as the book to fulfill my contract. The book came out before the exhibit purely by accident because the museum was forced to postpone the exhibit. We were worried the book would fail because we saw it as an adjunct to the exhibit, rather than as an independent entity. Happily, we were proven wrong.

### Why do you think *The Endurance* has gained such popularity? Is it the contrast between our anxious-but-comfortable modern lives and Shackleton's real survival challenges? Or is it Shackleton's famous line, "Optimism is true moral courage"?

Both those ideas are factors—and the book is riding on a wave of interest in true adventure stories. But what *The Endurance* offers, I believe, is a set of values that are rare today. Perhaps there is a sort of end-of-the-millennium nostalgia for the way we once were. Shackleton's party survived because each worked together for the survival of all; all were accepted, whether weak or strong; and everyone subordinated himself to "The Boss." Their continued existence was based on real character, an attitude of personal honor and responsibility—things that appear to have gone by the wayside.

Today, quiet sublimation seems unlikely, and individualism leads to mutiny. Shackleton's attitude saved them all. He believed he would make it and his men would make it with him. And they did.

### Is that attitude what drew you to the story of the Endurance?

The Endurance touched me because I saw it as an embodiment of my old favorite, *The Iliad*. Homer wrote a swift-moving epic adventure in simple and uncomplicated language. The characters remained very human throughout the book, and the story ends, not with the great battle, but with Achilles contemplating his own mortality. I modeled *The Endurance* after *The Iliad* in many ways, including the straightforward style; that's also why I continued the story of the crewmen of the Endurance after they had been rescued. I wanted to show that their fierce fight for survival in the Antarctic, their "great battle," was only one thing that happened to them—that they, too, had to live on after this cataclysmic event. I felt it was more real and honest, and more affecting to those who read it. These men weren't superheroes; they were ordinary people in extraordinary circumstances.

### You did considerable research for *Mrs. Chippy's Last Expedition, The Endurance*, and the exhibit. How did you know what to look for and when to stop?

My total research time for all three projects was about two and a half years. The initial research for *Mrs. Chippy's* was all done out-of-pocket, as I hadn't placed the story yet. After I read all the available books on the expedition, I visited the Scott Polar Research Institute in Cambridge, England. There, I read several diaries written by expedition members while they were aboard The Endurance and got to know them as individuals. Later, when I researched the exhibit, tracing objects for the museum lead to unusual sources; word got out, people volunteered information, I was introduced to family members. They were incredibly generous, and often, their generosity was brought out by the mention of Mrs. Chippy, who had indeed captured the hearts of the Endurance shipmates. The expedition was a significant point of pride in the history of these families.

In England, class distinction still reigns; institutes and archives focus on the privileged leaders, while the families of other participants must keep their own unique memories alive. I'd still like to locate the descendants of the sailors who were inadvertently made members of the expedition because of the ship's entrapment in sea ice. I'd love to hear their stories, but few records are left that give clues to where these men lived. I believe that writers have an instinct as to when the story is in them (rather than in sources) and it's time to deliver. And then there are deadlines.

### Do you write the body of the book or article while you're researching, or do you take notes and wait until you've laid a foundation?

I write continuously. Something new is always coming up in the research, so I also edit continuously. On day one, I'll write something, and on day two, I'll edit what I've written on day one, and write something more to edit on day three. When I get to the end, the book is usually done, though I might change the opening.

### What advice would you give to other writers?

Read, read, read! I get most of my story ideas poking about in library stacks, on the lookout for books that interest me. An article I wrote for *The New Yorker*, "White Goddess of Wongora," came about because of a book I found, written by an actress in the early days of film. It chronicled her adventures on location in West Africa; she had a wonderful story to tell. Reading is serendipitous. The past is there to be mined, and the quirky stories are the ones to pursue.

### Lately, you've been involved in several projects that go beyond the printed word. Do you intend to branch out?

No. I have a specific book project in mind, but I won't talk about it—talking dissipates creative energy. I backed out of being a full-time producer for the documentary to avoid becoming overly involved in that world [Alexander co-produced a two-hour feature on the Endurance for the TV show *Nova*. The film will be released to theaters around January 2000]. The other project, for IMAX, will be completed by the autumn of 2000. Its goal is to simulate Shackleton's experience as much as possible. The film crew will make several trips to the Antarctic, visiting the sites in the book. I hope to accompany them on at least one trip.

### Still seeking adventure?

I'm always curious, but I suppose so are most writers.

# Russell Banks: Seeing Is the Goal

**BY PAULA DEIMLING**

In the mornings, about six days a week, novelist Russell Banks heads out to his studio. To the right, in the warmer months, is a meadow of wildflowers; on the left, large rocks reminiscent of New England. It's a short walk, down a hill, to an old remodeled sugar shack that overlooks a river. *His* studio. "Splendid rural isolation," Banks calls it.

**Russell Banks**

This land in upstate New York in the Adirondack Mountains is very much connected to Banks's work, especially his latest novel, *Cloudsplitter* (HarperCollins). The burial site of abolitionist John Brown, one of the main characters of *Cloudsplitter*, is about 12 miles away; so is a view of Brown's favorite mountain, Tahawus, so named Cloudsplitter by the Iroquois Indians.

"The mornings are the real work time for me," Banks says. He writes on a laptop computer, sometimes in longhand, and later types the words. There is no particular pattern to this work process, Banks says—whatever feels right that day. He works four to five hours a day on the novel. Around lunch time, he heads back to the house and spends the afternoon on various projects, or hikes around the property—the latter activity, perhaps, the inspiration for the vivid descriptions of landscapes and skies in his writing.

"I believe and have always believed that before all else I want my readers to see," says Banks, quoting Joseph Conrad. "He meant literally visualize, not understand. That's the ambition for me as a writer, too—so that my readers can see the world or themselves or other human beings in the world a little differently, a little more clearly." When Banks takes the train through Westchester County to New York City, he says he can't see the passing suburbs in the same way he might have had he not read author John Cheever. "I see the men with their hats and briefcases differently. I see them with more compassion, with more understanding, more patience; I don't stereotype them as easily. A good book makes you see them differently. As a reader, the mark of a good book is that after having finished, I'm a slightly different person. I think a little differently, I see the world a little differently, than before I read that book."

## THE UNFORSEEABLE FUTURE

Banks' life today—with 13 published books—is quite different from the one he imagined in his early 20s when he started writing stories. He never expected to earn a living or support a family solely on his writing income, or to achieve commercial success as a literary novelist. "I prepared for that by giving myself over to a teaching career."

Over the years, Banks has taught at Sarah Lawrence College, Columbia University, New York University and Princeton University. In 1998—after about 16 years teaching in Princeton's Creative Writing Program—he moved to upstate New York and began writing fulltime, heading to his studio "almost as if I had a real job."

---

**PAULA DEIMLING** *is a full-time writer, and former editor of* Writer's Market. *She is one of the authors of* The Writer's Essential Desk Reference (*Writer's Digest Books*). *Past interviews have included Isaac Asimov, Peter Davidson, Molly Peacock and William Zinsser.*

The turning point in his career was the publication of the novel *Continental Drift* (HarperCollins), in 1985. He was 45 then. The 6 published books to his credit hadn't sold more than 10,000 to 12,000 in hardcover. "The novel is an absorbing and powerful book that ambitiously attempts to 'speak' to the times," wrote a critic in the *New York Review of Books* of *Continental Drift*, which dealt with immigration at a time of widespread curiosity and anxiety on the issue. "One of the things that mattered in gaining a wider audience was that it was set in a world that mattered to people," says Banks.

Ironically, Banks doesn't deliberately seek out a subject or theme just to sell books. "I'm following my own curiosity and anxieties and concerns and obsessions, I suppose, without regard to how widely they may be shared," he says. "If it turns out they are widely shared, well and good, and if it turns out they're not, then I can live with that. But I have to be faithful to myself and my own intuitions."

His current novel-in-progress is a contemporary story set in West Africa—quite a contrast, at first thought, from the historical *Cloudsplitter*, and the 1850s American Civil War issues. But this next book most likely will deal with the themes of civil war in Liberia. Will Banks's treatment of the events in West Africa say something about life in middle America? "I can just smell it— I don't know how or why; I'll have to write the book to find out," he says. "The valuable writer, poet or storyteller is the one who can name the source of a pervasive cultural anxiety that hasn't yet got a name. A writer can dramatize that in a way to make it articulate to himself or herself and to the readers."

The next major "continental drift" in Banks's career has perhaps been Hollywood's awareness of Banks's work. *The Sweet Hereafter*, based on his 1991 novel, was a Grand Prix winner at the 1997 Cannes Film Festival. The film also earned Academy Award nominations for Best Director and Best Screenplay Adaptation. In 1999, actor James Coburn won an Oscar for Best Supporting Actor in *Affliction*, a film based on Banks's 1989 novel of the same name. Additional film projects based on Banks's novels are in development.

For a literary novelist to find filmmakers "attracted to the work whose visions overlap my own is very rare. Makes me nervous when you have that much luck," says Banks.

## WHEN WRITING FICTION

For Banks, it's important to get the first draft written before attempting to revise or enhance it. You don't know at that point how certain parts will fit in. "When I'm writing fiction, I'm really only thinking about the sentence in front of me."

A paragraph in a Banks novel can sometimes carry such emotional intensity for the reader and such life-changing consequences for the characters. How does he decide when a paragraph is completed? "If it feels right and has the weight and emotional depth, is clear and precise, then you're free to move on."

It's important for Banks to envision and understand whom the listener will be in a novel that he's writing. Keep in mind, he points out, that people speak differently, depending on whether the listener is a friend, lover or family member. "I try to avoid feeling as if I'm speaking through the character. I want to be sure I'm listening to that character." For instance, with *Cloudsplitter*, Banks imagined himself to be Miss Mayo "listening" to Owen Brown's account of the events surrounding the Harpers Ferry siege. In the novel, Brown remarks, "As I have said, we each will have very different uses for it [inscription of John Brown's history] anyhow, uses shaped by those to whom we each imagine we are telling our respective tales."

Early in 1999, Banks went on a ten-city tour to promote the paperback version of *Cloudsplitter* and the film *Affliction*. He's not able to write when he's on the road—too many interruptions, he says. But there is one benefit: "It re-affirms something you know in a theoretical way— readers take stories into their lives in a personal, intimate way."

The range of readers he meets on tour can vary greatly. In Cincinnati, he gave a lecture, "The Voice of History," to 200 people at the private Mercantile Library where Ralph Waldo Emerson,

Herman Melville and William Thackeray once lectured. And earlier that day, Banks met with small groups of high school students. One student had asked "how to avoid the middle part of a writer's life"—the time between the decision to write and the checks coming in. Ninety-nine percent of a writer's time, Banks answered, is spent alone in a room, writing—not giving lectures or promoting one's books.

"Sometimes, it's the reader who takes the book personally and the critic who knows more about the book than the writer," he says. A surprising observation, especially the latter. But the reader knows how the book applies to his or her own life, and the critic knows how the book applies to the whole of literature, Banks says. "A book is always in a lineage, one would hope, just as a writer participates in a tradition or has a lineage too; some of it's very conscious and some of it's not that conscious."

## CONTRASTING FICTION AND NONFICTION

When Banks is in the midst of writing a novel, he's careful not to take on projects that put additional deadlines in his path. Like essays, for instance. When he does find time to write nonfiction, he can spend many more hours in one stretch—sometimes 12 to 15 hours a day. For him, writing nonfiction seems less draining. "Nonfiction doesn't seem to draw from the same well."

What will the writer of nonfiction encounter when trying to write a novel? "The main difference is when you write fiction, you enter another world, the fictional world, and when you write nonfiction, you don't; you stay in your own world and you work with the materials in front of you. It's a completly different mindset, a different level of intensity. Writing fiction is a little bit like hallucinating or out-of-body travel."

Some of the same techniques are used but for very different ends. In nonfiction, those techniques are used to build an argument, win a case, make a point, he says. "In fiction you're using those techniques to build a fictional alternative world to the one you or the reader lives in."

Reading is the best way to know the differences, he points out. "All you have to do is examine your own reading process and what is going on when you're reading a novel. You're having visual and oral hallucinations—you're seeing things and you're hearing things. Dialogue is an oral hallucination. Exposition and description create visual hallucinations. . . . I think of fiction as a controlled hallucination. That kind of hallucination is something I'm conscious of trying to induce."

When Banks, at age 22, decided to write a novel, he says he was "trying to imitate what I was reading." After seven or eight years, "I realized I could reach a certain level of competence, at least that. I didn't know if I could reach a level of artistry that I could perceive in other works."

When does a writer reach a satisfactory level of artistry? "You really don't know that, even if the critics praise you; even then you really don't know. Every writer I admire has that kind of self-doubt at bottom. And even when you look back over your own career, you still don't know."

A writer must remain faithful to his origins, Banks says, and yet at the same time must go out of familiar territory into other people's lives. That doesn't necessarily mean moving to a place with a literary reputation. Splendid isolation will do just fine, with occasional forays.

The late novelist Nelson Algren, Banks's mentor, taught him by example never to confuse one's writing career with the actual work of writing. The work, Banks stresses, must come "first and foremost and solely—only." No matter where.

# Julia Cameron: Take the Risk of Writing

BY ANNE BOWLING

As a career writer, Julia Cameron is a bit of a maverick, and the advice she gives those looking for publication is equally noncon-formist. Author of the million-selling creativity guide *The Artist's Way* (Tarcher/Putnam), Cameron advises freelance writers to fol-low their creative impulses first and find the market once the work is done.

**Julia Cameron**

"I believe if we get people writing, we will get people selling," Cameron says. "I know so, from experience. I have written many plays, movies and books, almost all of them without contracts. If I want to write something, I go ahead and write it, and then say, 'Would you like to buy it?' I've run my whole career that way."

And Cameron's has been a productive career. In her 25 years of writing, she has published poetry, plays, fiction and essays. Cameron also has an award-winning journalist's career to her credit, with work published in *The New York Times*, *Rolling Stone*, *The Washington Post*, *The Village Voice* and others.

"Some people say they won't write on spec? I find it much more difficult to write on assign-ment," Cameron says. "I've had some wonderful collaborations with editors, where they trusted me, and I'd say, 'I think I'd like to write about this,' and they'd say, 'Go ahead,' which is a lovely position to be in. But I really do know that if people continue to take the risk of writing, they will end up publishing."

The philosophical basis for Cameron's advice is spelled out in her most recent creativity title *The Right to Write* (Tarcher/Putnam). In a series of essays and exercises, Cameron invites readers to write as a way of life, debunks negative stereotypes around the writing life, and offers solid instruction for writers facing perennial problems such as writer's block. She also strikes a blow for the notion that the best writing is writing that arises organically, rather than that which is created to fill a market need. "We've got our thinking greatly reversed," Cameron says. "For example, *The Artist's Way* has sold more than a million books. When I wrote it, my agent said, 'There is absolutely no market for this book. No one will want to read it, why don't you just go back to writing movies?' Which tells us we don't know what the market is. Sometimes a market doesn't appear to exist for something just because the item has never existed."

With *The Artist's Way*, Cameron designed a spiritual process of "creative self-recovery," which includes "morning pages" of daily writing exercises and a weekly "artist's date," de-signed to replenish creative resources. *The Right to Write* outlines a step-by-step process for readers looking for an introduction to the writing life, as well as for pros hoping to regain a sense of joy in their work.

---

**ANNE BOWLING** *is production editor for* Writer's Market *and a frequent contributor to* Writer's Digest Books. *Previous interviews include Anna Quindlen, Ann Beattie, Jay McInerney, Scott Turow, Terry McMil-lan and Alice McDermott.*

"All of my advice circles back to write every day, write in whatever form interests you, walk through every door that opens," Cameron says. "I think Joseph Campbell was very right when he said when we follow our bliss, there are a thousand unseen helping hands. You don't need to strategize your career—you need to experiment, knock on doors and see what opens."

Here Cameron talks with *Writer's Market* about her philosophies on the writing life, and offers her advice for the trail.

**It's obvious *The Right to Write* can help initiate those who don't write into the writing life, but can the book also be used as a tool to improve craft for commercial writers?**

Oh, absolutely. The questions I deal with in *The Right to Write* are the questions that any working writer deals with all the time. I believe the book will help many people who have not been writing to be able to write. But it's also a support tool for writers at any place in their careers, in the sense that sometimes we need to be reminded of what we know. And I think the book is effective at doing that.

**Why do you think writers do better work on spec than on assignment?**

It takes the heart out of writing to ask people to envision the work they haven't done yet. I think a lot of times you have to tell writers go ahead and write it. That's the story on most of my books. The idea is actually embedded in creation, as you create the ideas come.

People say, "Julia, what are the odds of selling an original screenplay?" And the answer is, "A lot higher if you write it." I sold nine in a row before somebody told me the odds. It's sort of like the odds don't matter. I think we need to be willing to bet on ourselves more.

**Is writer's block the same in origin and form for writers no matter what they're writing—essays, fiction, nonfiction—and if so, are the tools to overcome it the same?**

Yes. Essentially writer's block is a feeling of powerlessness, constriction and self-conciousness. And the cure is to have tools that make you unself-concious, more free, more self-nurturing, more involved with process than with product. These tools allow you to forget yourself so that, ironically, you can remember how to write. And those will work regardless of what form you're working in.

I would say the bedrock tool for any writer just in terms of freeness of expression would still be the three pages of daily morning writing called the morning pages. The morning pages miniaturize the censor and let you move freely onto the page. And a weekly artist's date puts images back into your image bank, keeps you from overfishing your pond as a writer, and is pivotal to ease in writing, particularly when you're on deadline.

Somebody will say to me, 'Julia, I was writing brilliantly, why did it dry up?' The answer is it dried up because you were writing brilliantly. In other words we have a finite number of images in our inner reservoir and we must treat ourselves like an ecosystem. And that's true whether you're doing technical writing, a novel, a play, a screenplay or journalism. All of us need to learn how to get freely onto the page and how to use our critical thinking as second draft.

**You've described creativity as festive and hydra-headed, and I wondered how you advise writers to control that spirit when working within the confines of deadline.**

I don't believe in controlling it very much. I think people need to write a first draft that throws it at the page. And if we can get out of our own way, there is a real wisdom that is subconcious and organic to whatever we're trying to write. Very often if you can teach people to write rough drafts, those rough drafts come out very close to final draft, whereas if people try to write final drafts, they get so cerebral and analytical that the piece doesn't have its own organic shape. This is how *The Right to Write* can support writers at any level.

I wish it were true that we had beginning writing problems and advanced writing problems, but I've been writing for 35 years, and the problems are the same. Am I on the page today? Am I on the page freely? Is it rich or is it shallow? Those problems don't change. You confront the same monsters. You get a little more practiced—"Oh, it's just the monster." The difference is, for the beginning writer, it's, "My God, a monster!" When you're a little further down the road, it's, "There *you* are again."

That's the internal censor saying, "Who do you think you are? This isn't any good, you're not original, this has been done before, you've fooled everybody so far, no one will like it." There are 15 or so things that show up, and they always say the same thing.

### What practical steps do you offer writers to get beyond the censor?

Start at a really bedrock level, and write everyday. So that's morning pages. The second thing is try whatever you think you like. The third thing is try not to let the market tell you what to write. It's a very interesting thing—a lot of times young writers are focused on how do they get an agent and how do they place their work. And I think we do people a real disservice if we emphasize that aspect over doing the work. People will want to write a treatment to sell a book. Well, in my experience, it's sometimes a lot harder to write a treatment, and you waste nine months waiting to hear back on it and you could have written the book.

### Would you encourage professional writers to write for personal exploration as a separate activity and if so, why?

Oh, absolutely. Because we are the origin of our work. I think people really need to learn their own field, and I don't mean the field of writing—I mean their own creative acreage. I totally think the most advantageous writing you do is the morning writing, which clears your decks, prioritizes your day and points you toward new directions. I think for a writer to only write professionally, and not do that work with turning on the inner lights, so to speak, means that you could drift pretty far from your own authentic impulses. You might be writing a great deal, but not too happily.

Again, we're much more talented than we think we are. People are able to pull off a lot more than they believe they're able to. And one of the things that happens when you're doing morning writing is something will repeatedly tap at your conciousness until you listen, and it may be a direction that you'd never thought of going. You know, the novelist might be urged to write essays, the technical writer might be urged to try a play, and at first blush you think, "This is nuts." But the idea will keep coming back, and when you surrender to trying it, it very often has an enormous amount of vigor, and passion, and real brilliance to it. And I think that without doing the morning writing you run the risk of making it difficult for your soul or your writing heart to break through your business and get your attention. You need to give it a place to contact you.

### You spend time in *The Right to Write* dispelling myths about writers—they're broke, addicted, suffering, crazy and so on. Why is it important to dispel these myths?

Because people are afraid to write. People really believe that writing brings with it a cartload of misery. So you start saying to people if you write, you'll probably sell your work, eventually. If you write, you're going to be happier than if you don't write. If you write and write well, you're going to be more comfortable in your intimate relationships. It begins to make it a less threatening arena for people to enter. Admittedly we lose some of the high drama and some of the cherished images, but I do think people need to know it is possible to write in a nontortured way. It's a skill that can be learned, and I think the tools are pragmatic, step-by-step tools to move people into greater creative ease.

### Is there any parting advice you'd like to share with writers?

I think the pivotal thing is simply for people to lay track. I believe the more we write, the more easily we write.

# The Business of Writing
## Minding the Details

Writers who have had some success in placing their work know that the effort to publish requires an entirely different set of skills than does the act of writing. A shift in perspective is required when you move from creating your work to selling it. Like it or not, successful writers—*career* writers—have to keep the business side of the writing business in mind as they work.

Each of the following sections discusses a writing business topic that affects anyone selling his writing. We'll take a look at contracts and agreements—the documents that license a publisher to use your work. We'll consider your rights as a writer and sort out some potentially confusing terminology. We'll cover the basics of copyright protection—a topic of perennial concern for writers. And for those of you who are already making money with your writing, we'll offer some tips for keeping track of financial matters and staying on top of your tax liabilities.

Our treatment of the business topics that follow is necessarily limited. Look for complete information on each subject at your local bookstore or library—both in books (some of which we mention) and periodicals aimed at writers. Information is also available from the federal government, as indicated later in this article.

## CONTRACTS AND AGREEMENTS

If you've been freelancing even a short time, you know that contracts and agreements vary considerably from one publisher to another. Some magazine editors work only by verbal agreement; others have elaborate documents you must sign in triplicate and return before you begin the assignment. As you evaluate any contract or agreement, consider carefully what you stand to gain and lose by signing. Did you have another sale in mind that selling all rights the first time will negate? Does the agreement provide the publisher with a number of add-ons (electronic rights, advertising rights, reprint rights, etc.) for which they won't have to pay you again?

In contract negotiations, the writer is usually interested in licensing the work for a particular use but limiting the publisher's ability to make other uses of the work in the future. It's in the publisher's best interest, however, to secure rights to use the work in as many ways as possible, both now and later on. Those are the basic positions of each party. The negotiation is a process of compromise and capitulation on questions relating to those basic points—and the amount of compensation to be given the writer for his work.

A contract is rarely a take-it-or-leave-it proposition. If an editor tells you that his company will allow *no* changes on the contract, you will then have to decide how important the assignment is to you. But most editors are open to negotiation, and you should learn to compromise on points that don't matter to you while maintaining your stand on things that do.

When it's not specified, most writers assume that a magazine publisher is buying first rights. Some writers' groups can supply you with a sample magazine contract to use when the publisher doesn't supply one, so you can document your agreement in writing. Members of The Authors

Guild are given a sample book contract and information about negotiating when they join. For more information about contracts and agreements, see *Business and Legal Forms for Authors & Self-Publishers*, by Tad Crawford (Allworth Press, 1990); *From Printout to Published*, by Michael Seidman (Carroll & Graf, 1992) or *The Writer's Guide to Contract Negotiations*, by Richard Balkin (Writer's Digest Books, 1985), which is out of print but should be available in libraries.

## RIGHTS AND THE WRITER

A creative work can be used in many different ways. As the originator of written works, you enjoy full control over how those works are used; you are in charge of the rights that your creative works are "born" with. When you agree to have your work published, you are giving the publisher the right to use your work in one or more ways. Whether that right is simply to publish the work for the first time in a periodical or to publish it as many times as he likes and in whatever form he likes is up to you—it all depends on the terms of the contract or agreement the two of you arrive at. As a general rule, the more rights you license away, the less control you have over your work and the more money you should be paid for the license. We find that writers and editors sometimes define rights in different ways. For a classification of terms, read Types of Rights, below.

Sometimes editors don't take the time to specify the rights they are buying. If you sense that an editor is interested in getting stories but doesn't seem to know what his and the writer's responsibilities are regarding rights, be wary. In such a case, you'll want to explain what rights you're offering (preferably one-time or first serial rights only) and that you expect additional payment for subsequent use of your work.

You should strive to keep as many rights to your work as you can from the outset, otherwise, your attempts to resell your writing may be seriously hampered.

The Copyright Law that went into effect January 1, 1978, said writers were primarily selling one-time rights to their work unless they—and the publisher—agreed otherwise in writing. Book rights are covered fully by the contract between the writer and the book publisher.

## TYPES OF RIGHTS

- **First Serial Rights**—First serial rights means the writer offers a newspaper or magazine the right to publish the article, story or poem for the first time in any periodical. All other rights to the material remain with the writer. The qualifier "North American" is often added to this phrase to specify a geographical limit to the license.

    When material is excerpted from a book scheduled to be published and it appears in a magazine or newspaper prior to book publication, this is also called first serial rights.
- **One-Time Rights**—A periodical that licenses one-time rights to a work (also known as simultaneous rights) buys the *nonexclusive* right to publish the work once. That is, there is nothing to stop the author from selling the work to other publications at the same time. Simultaneous sales would typically be to periodicals without overlapping audiences.
- **Second Serial (Reprint) Rights**—This gives a newspaper or magazine the opportunity to print an article, poem or story after it has already appeared in another newspaper or magazine. Second serial rights are nonexclusive—that is, they can be licensed to more than one market.
- **All Rights**—This is just what it sounds like. If you license away all rights to your work, you forfeit the right to ever use it again. If you think you'll want to use the material later, you must avoid submitting to such markets or refuse payment and withdraw your material. Ask the editor whether he is willing to buy first rights instead of all rights before you agree to an assignment or sale. Some editors will reassign rights to a writer after a given period, such as one year. It's worth an inquiry in writing.
- **Electronic Rights**—These rights cover usage in a broad range of electronic media, from

online magazines and databases to CD-ROM magazine anthologies and interactive games. The magazine contract should specify if—and which—electronic rights are included. The presumption is that unspecified rights are kept by the writer.

- **Subsidiary Rights**—These are the rights, other than book publication rights, that should be covered in a book contract. These may include various serial rights; movie, television, audiotape and other electronic rights; translation rights, etc. The book contract should specify who controls these rights (author or publisher) and what percentage of sales from the licensing of these sub rights goes to the author.
- **Dramatic, Television and Motion Picture Rights**—This means the writer is selling his material for use on the stage, in television or in the movies. Often a one-year option to buy such rights is offered (generally for 10 percent of the total price). The interested party then tries to sell the idea to other people—actors, directors, studios or television networks, etc. Some properties are optioned over and over again, but most fail to become dramatic productions. In such cases, the writer can sell his rights again and again—as long as there is interest in the material. Though dramatic, TV and motion picture rights are more important to the fiction writer than the nonfiction writer, producers today are increasingly interested in nonfiction material; many biographies, topical books and true stories are being dramatized.

## SELLING SUBSIDIARY RIGHTS

The primary right in the world of book publishing is the right to publish the book itself. All other rights (such as movie rights, audio rights, book club rights, electronic rights and foreign rights) are considered secondary, or subsidiary, to the right to print publication. In contract negotiations, authors and their agents traditionally try to avoid granting the publisher subsidiary rights that they feel capable of marketing themselves. Publishers, on the other hand, typically hope to obtain control over as many of the sub rights as they can. Philosophically speaking, subsidiary rights will be best served by being left in the hands of the person or organization most capable of—and interested in—exploiting them profitably. Sometimes that will be the author and her agent, and sometimes that will be the publisher.

Larger agencies have experience selling foreign rights, movie rights and the like, and many authors represented by such agents prefer to retain those rights and let their agents do the selling. Book publishers, on the other hand, have subsidiary rights departments, which are responsible for exploiting all sub rights the publisher was able to retain during the contract negotiation.

That job might begin with a push to sell foreign rights, which normally bring in advance money which is divided among author, agent and publisher. Further efforts then might be made to sell the right to publish the book as a paperback (although many book contracts now call for hard/soft deals, in which the original hardcover publisher buys the right to also publish the paperback version).

Any other rights which the publisher controls will be pursued, such as book clubs and magazines. Publishers usually don't control movie rights to a work, as those are most often retained by author and agent.

The marketing of electronic rights to a work, in this era of rapidly expanding capabilities and markets for electronic material, can be tricky. With the proliferation of electronic and multimedia formats, publishers, agents and authors are going to great pains these days to make sure contracts specify exactly *which* electronic rights are being conveyed (or retained).

Compensation for these rights is a major source of conflict between writers and publishers, as many book publishers seek control of them and many magazines routinely include electronic rights in the purchase of all rights, often with no additional payment. Alternative ways of handling this issue include an additional 15 percent added to the amount to purchase first rights to a royalty system or a flat fee for use within a specified time frame, usually one year.

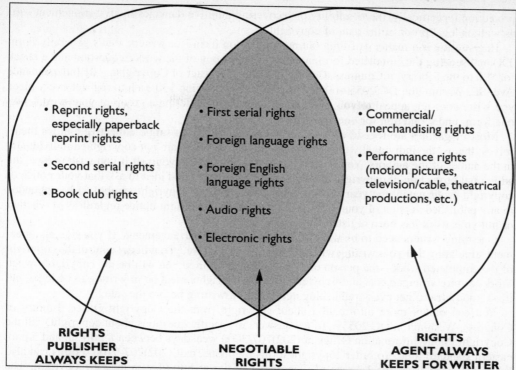

**RIGHTS PUBLISHER ALWAYS KEEPS**
- Reprint rights, especially paperback reprint rights
- Second serial rights
- Book club rights

**NEGOTIABLE RIGHTS**
- First serial rights
- Foreign language rights
- Foreign English language rights
- Audio rights
- Electronic rights

**RIGHTS AGENT ALWAYS KEEPS FOR WRITER**
- Commercial/ merchandising rights
- Performance rights (motion pictures, television/cable, theatrical productions, etc.)

Some subsidiary rights are always granted to the publisher. Some should always be retained by the author. The remainder are negotiable, and require knowledgeable advice from a literary agent or attorney in deciding whether it is more advantageous to grant them to the publisher or reserve them.

## COPYRIGHT

Copyright law exists to protect creators of original works. It is engineered to encourage creative expression and aid in the progress of the arts and sciences by ensuring that artists and authors hold the rights by which they can profit from their labors.

Copyright protects your writing, unequivocally recognizes you (its creator) as its owner, and grants you all the rights, benefits and privileges that come with ownership. The moment you finish a piece of writing—whether it is a short story, article, novel or poem—the law recognizes that only you can decide how it is to be used.

The basics of copyright law are discussed here. More detailed information can be obtained from the Copyright Office and in the books mentioned at the end of this section.

Copyright law gives you the right to make and distribute copies of your written works, the right to prepare derivative works (dramatizations, translations, musical arrangements, etc.—any work based on the original) and the right to perform or publicly display your work. With very few exceptions, anything you write today will enjoy copyright protection for your lifetime plus 70 years. Copyright protects "original works of authorship" that are fixed in a tangible form of expression. Titles, ideas and facts can *not* be copyrighted.

Some people are under the mistaken impression that copyright is something they have to send away for, and that their writing is not properly protected until they have "received" their copyright from the government. The fact is, you don't have to register your work with the Copyright Office in order for your work to be copyrighted; any piece of writing is copyrighted the moment it is put to paper. Registration of your work does, however, offer some additional protection (specifically, the possibility of recovering punitive damages in an infringement suit) as well as legal proof of the date of copyright.

Registration is a matter of filling out an application form (for writers, that's generally Form TX) and sending the completed form, a nonreturnable copy of the work in question and a check for $30 to the Library of Congress, Copyright Office, Register of Copyrights, 101 Independence Ave. SE, Washington DC 20559-6000. If the thought of paying $30 each to register every piece you write does not appeal to you, you can cut costs by registering a group of your works with one form, under one title for one $30 fee.

Most magazines are registered with the Copyright Office as single collective entities themselves; that is, the individual works that make up the magazine are *not* copyrighted individually in the names of the authors. You'll need to register your article yourself if you wish to have the additional protection of copyright registration. It's always a good idea to ask that your notice of copyright (your name, the year of first publication, and the copyright symbol ©) be appended to any published version of your work. You may use the copyright notice regardless of whether or not your work has been registered.

One thing writers need to be wary of is "work for hire" arrangements. If you sign an agreement stipulating that your writing will be done as work for hire, you will not control the copyright of the completed work—the person or organization who hired you will be the copyright owner. Work for hire arrangements and transfers of exclusive rights must be in writing to be legal, but it's a good idea to get every publishing agreement in writing before the sale.

You can obtain more information about copyright from the Copyright Office, Library of Congress, Washington DC 20559. To get answers to specific questions about copyright, call the Copyright Public Information Office at (202)707-3000 weekdays between 8:30 a.m. and 5 p.m. eastern standard time. To order copyright forms by phone, call (202)707-9100. Forms can also be downloaded from the Library of Congress website at http://lcweb.loc.gov/copyright. The website also includes information on filling out the forms, general copyright information and links to other websites related to copyright issues. A thorough (and thoroughly enjoyable) discussion of the subject of copyright law as it applies to writers can be found in Stephen Fishman's *The Copyright Handbook: How to Protect and Use Written Works* (Nolo Press, 1994). A shorter but no less enlightening treatment is Ellen Kozak's *Every Writer's Guide to Copyright & Publishing Law* (Henry Holt, 1990).

## FINANCES AND TAXES

As your writing business grows, so will your obligation to keep track of your writing-related finances and taxes. Keeping a close eye on these details will help you pay as little tax as possible and keep you apprised of the state of your freelance business. A writing business with no systematic way of tracking expenses and income will soon be no writing business at all. If you dislike handling finance-related tasks, you can always hire someone else to handle them for a fee. If you do employ a professional, you must still keep the original records with an eye to providing the professional with the appropriate information.

If you decide to handle these tasks yourself—or if you just want to know what to expect of the person you employ—consider these tips:

Accurate records are essential, and the easiest way to keep them is to separate your writing income and expenses from your personal ones. Most professionals find that separate checking accounts and credit cards help them provide the best and easiest records.

Get in the habit of recording every transaction (both expenses and earnings) related to your writing. You can start at any time; you don't need to begin on January 1. Because you're likely to have expenses before you have income, start keeping your records whenever you make your first purchase related to writing—such as this copy of *Writer's Market*.

Any system of tracking expenses and income will suffice, but the more detailed it is, the better. Be sure to describe each transaction clearly—including the date; the source of the income (or the vendor of your purchase); a description of what was sold or bought; whether the payment was by cash, check or credit card; and the amount of the transaction.

The other necessary component of your financial record-keeping system is an orderly way to store receipts related to your writing. Check stubs, receipts for cash purchases, credit card receipts and similar paperwork should all be kept as well as recorded in your ledger. Any good book about accounting for small business will offer specific suggestions for ways to track your finances.

Freelance writers, artists and photographers have a variety of concerns about taxes that employees don't have, including deductions, self-employment tax and home office credits. Many freelance expenses can be deducted in the year in which they are incurred (rather than having to be capitalized, or depreciated, over a period of years). For details, consult the IRS publications mentioned later.

There also is a home office deduction that can be claimed if an area in your home is used *exclusively* and *regularly* for business and you have no other fixed location where you conduct substantial activities for your business. Contact the IRS for information on requirements and limitations for this deduction. If your freelance income exceeds your expenses, regardless of the amount, you must declare that profit. If you make $400 or more after deductions, you must pay Social Security tax and file Schedule SE, a self-employment form, along with your Form 1040 and Schedule C tax forms.

While we cannot offer you tax advice or interpretations, we can suggest several sources for the most current information.

- Check the IRS website, http://www.irs.ustreas.gov/. Full of helpful tips and information, the site also provides instant access to important IRS forms and publications.
- Call your local IRS office. Look in the white pages of the telephone directory under U.S. Government—Internal Revenue Service. Someone will be able to respond to your request for IRS publications and tax forms or other information. Ask about the IRS Tele-tax service, a series of recorded messages you can hear by dialing on a touch-tone phone. If you need answers to complicated questions, ask to speak with a Taxpayer Service Specialist.
- Obtain the basic IRS publications. You can order them by phone or mail from any IRS office; most are available at libraries and some post offices. Start with *Your Federal Income Tax* (Publication 17) and *Tax Guide for Small Business* (Publication 334). These are both comprehensive, detailed guides—you'll need to find the regulations that apply to you and ignore the rest. There are many IRS publications relating to self-employment and taxes; Publication 334 lists many of these publications—such as *Business Use of Your Home* (Publication 587) and *Self-Employment Tax* (Publication 533).
- Consider other information sources. Many public libraries have detailed tax instructions available on tape. Some colleges and universities offer free assistance in preparing tax returns. And if you decide to consult a professional tax preparer, the fee is a deductible business expense on your tax return.

# Sell It Again Sam: Selling Reprints and Rewrites

BY GORDON BURGETT

Selling an article once is a major accomplishment, at least while you're earning your spurs. Selling the same article again and again, or other articles derived from the same research, is utter delight.

Showing you how that is done is the purpose of this article.

For clarification, let's distinguish between the two major means of reselling. The first, called "reprints," is in its simplest form the selling of the same article, as is, repeatedly to different markets. The second, called "rewrites," is the taking of the same facts, quotes and anecdotes and reshuffling, expanding and rewriting them into new forms, each a different article using some or much of the same material.

## REPRINTS

A traditional reprint sale follows the original sale of an article to an editor who purchased first rights. That editor bought the right to use your words, that article, in print first. When those words appeared in print, the rights automatically reverted back to you, and your rights relationship with that editor ended.

What remained were second rights, which are also called reprint rights. (Second and reprint rights mean the same thing; the terms are interchangeable.)

Once your article has appeared in print from a first-rights sale, you can immediately offer that very same article, without change, to any other editor you think might buy it. It couldn't be more straightforward.

*Writer's Market* tells you what rights editors buy and whether they buy reprints, or the editor will tell you when you receive a go-ahead to your query. It also tells whether the magazine pays on acceptance or publication.

Who buys second or reprint rights? Mostly editors who pay on publication, plus a few, whose readers would not likely have read your words in the first publication, who pay on acceptance.

How much do they pay? What they can get it for, or normally pay, since editors buying reprints have no idea what you originally received. Alas, those paying on publication often aren't high rollers, and those paying on acceptance for a piece already used will recognize that you will sell for less (since you've already been paid for putting the research and words in final form), so figure a third to one-half of what the original purchaser paid, then consider it a boon if you make more.

The best thing about reprints is that through diligent and creative marketing, you can resell the same piece many times. So when the final tally is made, you might have earned more money for churning the same winning prose repeatedly than you made for selling the original.

Using dollars to illustrate the point, if the original article took you 8 hours to sell, research and write and paid you $450, that is a gross profit of $56.25 an hour. If you resell the same

**GORDON BURGETT** *is the author of* Sell & Resell Your Magazine Articles, The Travel Writer's Guide, Publishing the Niche Market *and* How to Sell More than 75% of Your Writing. *He lives in Santa Maria, California.*

article 3 times, each paying $200 and taking 45 minutes apiece to find the market, prepare a copy of the article, reprint the cover letter and get it in the mail, that is an additional $600, or $267 an hour. (You can substitute your own prep time and payment rates.)

Mind you, nobody has ever sold a reprint before he sold the original article, so the hard work—the idea finding, market picking, querying, editor studying, researching, writing, editing, rechecking and submitting—is done first. Reprints sold later are very tasty dessert to a hard-won meal.

So how do you get editors to buy reprints?

## The reprint selling process

Sometimes editors feverishly seek you out, begging you to let them reuse a masterpiece you already sold—you name the price. (Or so I've heard from writers whose imaginations vastly exceed their credibility.)

Yet it does happen, on a far lesser scale. *Reader's Digest* and *Utne Reader* are two well-known magazines that do seek high-quality reprints to use (sometimes rewritten in a condensed form) on their pages. You can shorten their searches by sending copies of a particularly strong article with a cover letter suggesting they may wish to consider that recently published work for their pages.

There is no choice with the rest of the editors who might consider reusing your bought prose. You must find them, approach them in a sensible manner through a reprint cover letter and include a copy of the article in question and an SASE.

## Finding the most likely reprint buyers

Common sense guides this search. Since you want to sell the reprint without change, comb *Writer's Market* to find other publications similar to that which originally printed your article. Check in the same subject category, or those with similar readerships. Start with the Table of Contents. Read carefully about every publication that might even be remotely similar or use a topic like yours, as is or redirected to a different market or from a different setting.

Now create two columns on a sheet of paper. In the first column, write the title of every magazine that might use the article exactly as it is. Note the page number of the reference next to it, for easy finding later.

In the second column, write the title of every magazine that might use the subject if you rewrote or redirected it. Next to the name write down how you would have to rewrite the article to make it buyable: "for women: change examples, approach from female perspective," "wants history, focus on subject in early 1990s," "uses bullets: extract key points, create bullets," "change the setting to France, use French examples." Also include the page number for reference.

Let's focus on column one here, since the changes needed to rewrite the piece are obvious in column two.

You'll most likely want to contact the editors of all of the publications in column one, whether they pay on publication or acceptance. Once you've created a master reprint cover letter, computers make it quick to customize the address and salutation and insert a personalized reference in the text. The potential of a resale, even slight, outweighs the small amount of time, copying and postage required to get your article and letter before a healthy scattering of eyes.

Do not send the reprint cover letter and article copy to those magazine editors paying on acceptance who already rejected your query, or to those major magazines that never buy second rights. Sometimes there are reprint buyers that are flat-out foes of each other. Submit to one first (the most likely to use it or pay the most), and the second if the first says no. (Years back I sold to the *Air California* and *PSA* magazines, both fierce competitors. While I was within my rights to simultaneously offer reprints to both, since reprint sales are nonexclusive, if both had bought the reprint and used it on their pages, I would have lost two good clients forever!)

Once you have identified your marketing targets, you'll need a clear copy of the article you want to sell as a reprint. If the article is exactly one page long and includes only your copy, great. Copy and send it as is. But when there is adjacent, nonrelated copy next to the text or the prose trickles onto later pages, you'll want to cut your article out and paste it up. Include the photos or illustrations you also wish to sell. If the name of the publication and date of the issue aren't in the copy, add them to every page. And number the pages in consecutive order.

Then head to the quick copy shop to have as many copies reproduced as you will need, collated and stapled.

Just make certain the final copies you will send to the editors are clear, easy to read and include everything you want to be seen.

## The reprint cover letter

It's not enough just to have names and addresses plus copies of what you want the editor to buy. You must sell the prospective buyer through a one-page cover letter accompanying the reproduced copy of the article.

Your cover letter must do five things:

1. It must make the topic come alive before the editor ever reads a word of the actual article.
2. It must tell what you are offering and the rights involved.
3. It must describe any additional items or services you can provide.
4. It must tell how the manuscript will reach that editor.
5. By far the least important, it might talk a bit about you and your credentials.

Let's look at each of these areas.

The editor doesn't know you, already gets too much mail, and has too little time to waste on an unexpected and probably unpromising letter with an article also enclosed. So your first (and probably second) paragraph has to make the subject of the article jump off the page. It has to make the editor say, "Wow!" or, "I'd be a fool not to want to read this article," or, at the least, "Looks interesting. I'd better read that." This is where you show the editor you can write, discuss the topic on which you have focused your obvious talents and why (by inference or statement) that topic would find high favor with her readers. This gets the editor to pick up the article and read it through.

The next paragraph is short and falls after the point where you've stirred the editor's interest. It tells what you are offering and what rights are available. You must tell who bought the first rights, when the piece was in print and what rights you are selling. I usually get right to the point, since I don't want to dally here: "As you can see by the article attached, first rights were bought by (publication) and appeared in print on (date). I am offering second rights." (I could say reprint rights as well.)

In the following paragraph you will want to tell of other items beyond the words that you are also offering.

These could be photos. Since photos are almost always bought on a one-time rights basis, you can offer the photos the editor sees in the article or any of the rest that weren't bought. You can offer to send slides or prints for the editor's selection, if interested.

They could be line drawings, charts, graphs or any other artwork that either appears in the printed article or that you could prepare to add to the piece.

You could also offer a box or sidebar that you prepared but wasn't bought by the first editor—or one you could produce. (If the text exists, you might send it along with the copy of the article to expedite the sale and show the reprint editor precisely how it reads.)

Somewhere in the reprint cover letter you must tell the editor what format you will be sending the manuscript in. If you say nothing, the editor will assume that you expect the copy of the article to be retyped or scanned, neither exciting prospects. You enhance the reprint sale by offering either to send the original text double-spaced in manuscript form or on a computer disk, mailed or sent by e-mail. Electronic submissions are by far the most appealing.

As for what to say about yourself, the article alone will speak volumes, and the quality of the reprint cover letter will probably fill in as many gaps as the editor needs. There are three areas you may wish to expand upon, if it isn't done in the bio slug with the article:
- If you have many publishing credits, particularly in this field,
- If you have a related book in print or are an acknowledged expert in the field, and
- If the work described in the article offers some element of original, unique knowledge or research.

In other words, inject more biographical information only if that significantly increases the importance of the article or why the editor should use it. Otherwise, the editor knows the most important information already: that another editor thought your writing was good enough to buy and use. The rest the editor can probably deduce from reading the text. If not, supplement.

Finally, don't forget to include either an SASE or a self-addressed postcard for a reply. Otherwise you'll never know that the editor didn't want to buy your words for reuse.

The reprint cover letter is a sales letter, on one exciting page. Spelling, punctuation, grammar all count. Make the topic come alive and shout to be used on the editor's pages. Keep the rest businesslike, forthright, easy to understand and compelling. It's a letter from one businessperson to another, one who has space to fill, another with space fillers to sell.

## Modified reprints

What if an editor wants to use your article but insists upon changes? Fine. But is it a reprint or a rewrite? That depends upon how much change the editor wants and who will write it.

If the changes are major, treat it like a rewrite, which will be discussed next.

But sometimes an editor just wants to squeeze the piece a bit, dropping a few words here, an example later. Or use his own photo. He will make all of the changes.

No problem. You might ask to see the final copy before it is printed, to make sure the changes make sense.

Or the editor may want you to tie the topic to his locale, adding in a quote or two, some local examples or even a sidebar that offers local specifics. He wants to use the reprint as the core, with modifications by you.

The more labor you put into it, the more you might want to negotiate the price. Find out what the editor intends to pay for the reprint, then try to get that increased to compensate you for the additional research and writing.

## REWRITES

A rewrite, in the least complicated terms, is an article based on an earlier article and uses most or all of the first article's information. It is rewritten to create a different article that has its own sales life.

Let's say you write an article about training in long jumping for the Olympics. You follow the usual format: complete a feasibility study, query, receive a go-ahead, do the research, write the text and edit it. The article is printed. Then you find two other, smaller magazines that pay on publication that are interested in the same topic, so you send their editors a reprint cover letter, copy of the published article and a return postcard. One buys a reprint.

But why end there? Why not go back to that first article and see how you can reuse most or all of your research to create other solid, saleable articles?

For example, why not an article for the high school athlete called "So You Want to Be in the Olympics?" From the original, you develop a long-range focus and training program for any athlete in any field, perhaps using long jumping as the example—or tying in several examples, including long jumping.

Or an article based on three or four athletes each from a different country showing the paths they followed to the Olympics, with tips from each for the reading hopeful. If all four are long jumpers, you have less research but probably less saleability as well.

Or four U.S. Olympians from widely varying fields, including long jumping, to show their reflections on having competed: Was it worth the effort? What benefits have they received? In retrospect what would they do differently? What do they advise the readers thinking of following their Olympic paths?

By now the process is clear: Extract something from the original article and build on it for a subsequent article. The more you can use from your original research, the less time you need at the feasibility, querying and researching stages.

The trick is equally as obvious: You need a clearly different article, one that has its own angle or slant, reason for being, message and structure.

Rewrites need their own titles, leads, quotes and conclusions built around a different frame. You can use the same facts, quotes and anecdotes but in a different way and for a different purpose.

Once you've designed a different article, it must pass through the same selling phases we've described: the feasibility questions, the query, the go-ahead, the additional research, the new writing, the editing and publication in a different magazine.

Since rewrites have their own legal existence, you can even sell reprints of rewrites. You can even rewrite rewrites, then sell reprints of rewrites of rewrites. That's just a name game. The editor buying a rewrite calls it an article, an original work created for that magazine and its readers. He doesn't want to know, and you don't want to reveal, that it's a spin-off of earlier research. Does it have its own legs? Does it stand on its own merits? If so, the term "rewrite" has sense only to you, as part of the developmental chronology and evolution of an idea put to print.

Further discussion of rewrites falls squarely under the general discussion about how you create and sell copy. Since a rewrite is based on an idea that already sold and comes from research that has passed the test of acceptability, it simply has an edge on the competing articles—if it is worth using in its own right.

## A SUMMARY OF REPRINTS AND REWRITES

The difference is best seen from the rights perspective.

A reprint is an article sold on a first-rights basis that is being sold again (and again). The original buyer purchased the right to use that article on his pages first. Once used, the rights reverted to the writer. Following the protocol described, the writer then contacts other editors offering the resale of that original piece, on a reprint or second-rights, nonexclusive basis. The copy is the same or includes few changes.

A rewrite is a different article based on a previously written article and all the research that involved. It's a rewrite only in the mind of the writer. To the buyer it must be completely different from the work sold, since first rights to those words have already been purchased and is not being marketed as second or reprint rights.

Reprints and rewrites require attention to publishing proprieties. If they are done improperly, you can lose more goodwill, and future earnings, than you earn at the outset. The most important element of those proprieties is honesty—defining in your own mind whether the piece is a reprint or a rewrite.

If in doubt, discuss it with the interested editors. They don't bite; they just hold their purse strings tightly.

# How Much Should I Charge?

BY LYNN WASNAK

If you are reading this article with serious intent, chances are you agree with Dr. Samuel Johnson when he said, "No man but a blockhead ever wrote except for money." He knew in the 1700s what we have to remind ourselves en route to the millennium—while it is not at all easy to get rich being a writer, it is definitely possible to earn a living freelancing. You may not be able to afford that vacation home you dreamed of or the 30-foot yacht. But every year, real people not much different from you put food on the table, a roof overhead and even pay for the kids' dental bills with their freelance writing income.

This is said despite the well-established reality that writers in general are underpaid and, according to surveys conducted by the Author's Guild and others, writer's wages on the whole are stagnant or declining. Most recent information from the National Writers Union says only 15 percent of working writers make more than $30,000 annually. There is no doubt this is a problem, and writers need to band together through organizations such as the NWU, American Society of Journalists and Authors and others to rattle corporate cages everywhere and give professional writers more respect and more cash.

But we take the glass-is-half-full side of the argument here, because there is data from *Writer's Market*'s newest survey of freelance income that shows a substantial number of writers earn $30,000 to $40,000 and more (sometimes well into 6 figures) by freelance writing activities.

So how are some writers able to "make it" while others are stewing in credit card juice? The money-making writers have certain traits in common. Most are solid, experienced writers who spent some time learning their craft, either independently or as employees in PR departments, ad agencies, magazines, newspapers or book publishers. They have talent, they are reliable professionals who respect deadlines, and most of the better earners specialize in subjects or types of writing in which they have developed "insider" knowledge and expertise. There appears to be more money for more writers in business and technology markets (including advertising and PR) than there is in magazine or book publishing/editing, though some writers prefer the variety and/or prestige offered in traditional publishing arenas. For most freelancers, newspapers are not the way to go if income is a priority. However, they may be useful as a source of initial clips to promote work in better-paying markets, and they may be helpful to specialists or self-publishers who benefit from the publicity.

But the real difference between the haves and the have-nots among freelancers is sheer, unglamorous business savvy. In short, the money-earning freelancer puts effort into developing and refining all small business skills, especially the key element: marketing. There is reason to argue that writers' pay in general is low partly because so few writers care much about the business aspects of this occupation. In this, freelance writing is similar to other creative fields. Hobby artists, photographers, potters and musicians love what they're doing and get paid "hobby" rates, if at all. Professionals in those fields, if they also have good business sense, earn a living with what they do.

So let's assume you are an aspiring freelancer with fairly well-developed writing skills, or

**LYNN WASNAK** *has been a full-time freelancer for more than 20 years. She is intimately acquainted with the peaks, valleys and sinkholes of this fascinating business, and looks forward to making more mistakes (and learning from them) as time goes on.*

an active freelancer who wants to earn more or break into new areas. We'll also assume you would like to be (sooner rather than later) in that giddy realm of the NWU's top 15 percent who earn more than $30,000. The meat of this article is in the rates that follow (gleaned, as previously mentioned, from our survey participants and other writing income analysis). But before you get to the meat, let's tackle the bread-making ingredients of the freelance business.

## WHERE THE JOBS ARE

Where do freelancers find their jobs? According to our survey participants, the top job-getter is a toss-up between networking with fellow writers and prior contact with the editor/writing buyer. Both score high. Other strong job leads come from e-mail and/or hard-copy queries, networking with businesses (through Chambers of Commerce and specialized industry meetings), and of course, *Writer's Market*, *Writer's Digest* and topic-specific publications such as *The Travelwriter Marketletter*. Some writers send samples and résumés out cold to potential clients, or do cold-calling on the phone to set up interviews or present samples. (Cold-calling is more acceptable among general business and technology firms than in magazine and book publishing.) Some writers have used direct mail self-promotions successfully, though others said they found it a waste of money.

Obviously, you'll want to stay abreast of developments in the particular industries that you focus on (or would like to enter). Book writers/editors find *Publishers Weekly* a must-read, and business writers of most every stripe will find possible stories or clients in *The Wall Street Journal*. (Both publications and many others have classified want ads that sometimes seek writing or creative talent.) If you have access to press events or conferences where editors and writers mingle, by all means take full advantage. Don't forget to carry a few samples along with your nicely printed brochure and business cards (you *do* have them, don't you?)

But whether or not you have access to the editorial party scene, don't miss the newest wave of writers' marketing opportunities on the Internet. If your freelance activities don't yet include a computer (you need this ASAP, plus fax machine, organized file cabinets etc.), visit your local library, log on and take a peek at websites such as http://www.inkspot.com. This site and several others provide information on both contract (freelance) and staff jobs for writers.

But by far, the most credible referrals for future jobs come about when a past client tells someone you're a top-notch writer. So as you do each assignment, even the most tedious, give your absolute best effort. That person you're writing for might become the best job recruiter you've ever had!

## HOW TO CHOOSE YOUR OWN SALARY

Can you really choose your own salary? As an independent business person, unlike an employee, you not only can, you *must* set your own goals. That includes income. You may also set a time frame in which you either expect to meet or exceed these goals—or rethink your business plan. (And yes, it's a very good idea to set down a written plan for your freelancing activity. It doesn't have to be as formal as the business plan for a bank or a retail store, but if you want to earn money, you have to figure out what writing skills you have to sell, who might want them and how you will persuade them that you are the best writer for the job.)

To determine your income requirements, start off with your required annual income and add 30 percent for current expenses and the additional expenses you may have to incur as a new freelancer. Don't forget to figure in approximately another 30 percent for health insurance, social security, retirement and other benefits that may be paid in whole or in part by your present employer. (If you need to get health insurance, check out some of the writers' organizations which offer insurance as a membership option.) This number is your basic income requirement.

Next, figure a standard hourly rate, or rate range. Some business plans suggest arriving at an hourly rate by dividing the basic income requirement above by 2,080 (the number of hours in a 40-hour work week, 52 weeks a year). But this calculation is not too helpful for freelance

## Figuring an Hourly Rate

$$\frac{\text{required annual income} + 30\% \text{ (expenses)} + 30\% \text{ (benefits)}}{\text{billable hours worked per year}}$$

For example,

$$\frac{\$30,000 + \$9,000 + \$9,000}{1,500 \text{ hours}} = \$32/\text{hour}$$

writers, most of whom are set up as sole proprietorships, unless you plan to work more hours. That's because, as a sole proprietor, you are not likely to bill clients for 40 hours each week, unless you put in a lot of overtime. Full-time freelancers may bill as few as 800 hours annually, because running a writing business means doing it *all*. Researching markets, preparing samples, interviewing prospective clients, putting together proposals, creating your webpage, networking—all these vital tasks eat up time. (Occasionally the office needs a good vacuuming, too. Without a helpful partner, the crumbs will stay unless *you* sweep them up.) Few writers have secretaries to do their filing, or accountants to handle the routine jobs of invoicing and check writing. (Many writers do employ outside accountants to handle their taxes, including the somewhat cumbersome Business Schedule C. These suppliers may also serve as on-the-fly financial consultants and an accountant might be a useful critic for your business plan.) Most of us who freelance also want a few days of vacation here or there. So subtract these nonbillable hours to get a more realistic number. Divide the realistic billable number into your income goal to come up with a basic hourly rate that will allow you to hit your income target.

When you look at that rate, it may seem extremely high. Maybe it is, maybe it isn't. Your next step is to study the rate guidelines that follow this introduction to see if your hourly fee is in the ballpark. Then do more job-specific research on your own. Ask other writers in your locale (or those who work for the same kind of organization, if it is elsewhere) what they charge. You'll need to factor the competitive rate into your personal equation.

If you follow the job hunting and income guidelines, with a little luck you will be asked to bid on a job. Nearly every one of the freelancers who were earning adequate income stressed the requirement: "Don't sell yourself short!" Most professional freelancers suggest starting your estimate somewhere in the middle range, and being willing to negotiate. They say it is far easier to negotiate your fee downward than the reverse.

## HOW LONG DOES IT TAKE?

Hourly rates are a good place to start your process of estimates and billing, but sometimes it's hard to get a handle on how long a project will take. In our survey, we asked participants to estimate the time it takes them to complete various writing assignments. The results pointed out, once again, what wide variables there are among writers, both in the type of work they commonly produce and in the speed of their writing.

This is not a scientific sample by any means, but it may give you some clues to the amount of work time to expect. Of course the best way to figure your own hours once you're active is to keep a detailed work log per project—and don't omit any part of it. (If you have to have

## Project Time Guidelines

(Writing time estimates, assuming research at hand)
**4-page brochure:**
Extremes: 2 hours, low/15 days, high; Typical: 1-2 days
**700-word technical article:**
Extremes: 45 minutes, low/6 weeks, high; Typical: 2-4 hours
**Feature article (2,000 words):**
Extremes: 2 hours, low/12 weeks, high; Typical: 10 hours to 1 week
**2-page PR release:**
Extremes: 20 minutes, low/1 week, high; Typical: 2-4 hours
**Speech for corporate executive:**
Extremes: 2 hours, low/3 weeks, high; Typical: 3-5 days
**8-page newsletter:**
Extremes: 4 hours, low/5 weeks, high; Typical: 2-4 days

"thinking time," put that on the log, even if you don't bill the client the full amount.) By keeping good time records of specific project types, before too long you will be able to discern a pattern. Some writers use this pattern to determine their "per project" fees, multiplying their usual hours times their hourly rate (often adding a cushion to cover extraordinary circumstances). Writers who prefer "project fees" may gain speed with experience, and thereby earn higher hourly rates without the client feeling any pain.

Again, the following work times are given as a very rough guideline, not gospel. You've got to take the time it takes you to do the job properly, while keeping the market rates in mind.

## TIPS FROM FREELANCING PROS

To conclude this introduction to rate guidelines, here are a few helpful suggestions and warnings we received from our survey participants:

### On writing contracts and proposals

"My proposals have a section with (a) what happens if I can't finish and (b) what happens if the client pulls a project. Obviously they pay a lot more if they kill the project. If I ever had to back out, my clients would only pay for 'substantially complete and usable' work."
—*Elena Westerbrook of Fairview, Texas*

"Try to avoid bidding on lump sum (flat fee) projects unless you are very sure of the scope of the project. It's easy to get caught in a situation where the scope has changed but the client wants you to stick to the original estimate. As a newbie, you might not have the confidence to say 'no.' "
—*Winifred Day of Ontario, California*

"I now ask for half on any book with an expert. This is how I make a living, but people sometimes try to give me a hard time. If there are two experts working together, I still get half. (If I wrote for the seven dwarfs, would I get offered an eighth?)"
—*D.B. of New York City*

"Ask for more and negotiate. Freelance writing may be the only business in which one party (a writer) accepts whatever is offered. What an irony—the conglomerates writers do business with negotiate fees for every other aspect of their business! It's possible to routinely boost fees by 10 to 30 percent, simply by asking."
—*S.S., who reported earnings over $148,000 last year writing for business and technology*

"Don't accept verbal agreements, not even from 'friends.' Get it in writing."
—*Carol Jose of Florida*

## On clients and negotiating

"All clients are different. Some make up for smaller fees in volume or pleasant relationships. Some clients are so unpleasant that no amount of money is worth their bad attitude. Building good relationships with enjoyable projects is better than being paid handsomely to work for jerks."
—*Jeff Kurtti of California*

"Assume good faith on everyone's part, but be prepared for trouble."
—*Anonymous*

"Be professional. Don't compromise. Don't sound desperate. Express thanks and be courteous about all dealings."
—*Karen O'Connor of California*

"Try to get them to mention money first. Then repeat the amount slowly, with a questioning voice. Then decide if you'll take it or ask for more."
—*S.J. of California*

"Build an inventory of stock negotiating phrases. For example, if I want some negotiating room on rates, I say, 'I charge in the neighborhood of . . .' to avoid a take-it-or-leave-it stance. If a client's offer is not acceptable, I usually say, 'I'm not comfortable working for that amount, but I hope we can come closer together.' I may also point out, 'We both want my best efforts, and I don't believe I could deliver a satisfactory product for that rate.' "
—*Joseph T. Straub of Orlando, Florida*

## On slow payment

"Be a persistent, pleasant pest. It works."
—*John Behreus of New York*

"Money is not an ugly subject. You should have a healthy interest in getting yours. Don't be meek. Staffers would flip out if they went unpaid an extra week."
—*Claudia Lapin*

"If I do not receive a fee, I call or e-mail the managing editor to check on it. Sometimes it's just a matter of their not having my social security number or the payment date is later than I thought. It's important to keep a file of your contracts to make it easy to check dates, etc."
—*Doris Larson of Kent, Ohio*

(A number of freelancers mentioned using the collection assistance of NWU and ASJA before taking the last resort: small claims court.)

## AND FINALLY . . .

"Do your best. Don't take things personally. Cherish the triumphs. Disregard the disappointments and keep forging forward."
—*Nancy Jackson of California*

## ADVERTISING, COPYWRITING & PR

**Advertising copywriting:** $400 low, $1,000 mid-range, $2,000 high/full page ad depending on the size and kind of client; $50 low, $75 mid-range, $100 high/hour; $250 and up/day; $500 and up/week; $1,000-2,000 as a monthly retainer. In Canada, rates range from $40-80/hour.

**Advertorials:** $25-35/hour; up to $1/word or by flat fee ($300/700 words is typical). In Canada, 40-80¢/word; $35-75/hour.

**Book jacket copywriting:** $100-600/front cover jacket plus flaps and back jacket copy summarizing content and tone of the book.

**Campaign development or product launch:** $3,500 low, $7,000 mid-range, $12,000 high/project.

**Catalog copywriting:** $25-$45/hour or $85 and up/project.

**Copyediting for advertising:** $25-35/hour.

**Direct mail copywriting:** $25-45/hour; $75 and up/item or $400-800/page.

**Direct mail packages:** This includes copywriting direct mail letter, response card and advertising materials. $50 low, $75 mid-range, $115 high/hour; $2,500-10,000/project, depending on complexity. Additional charges for production such as desktop publishing, addressing, etc.

**Direct mail response card for a product:** $250-500/project.

**Direct mail production (DTP):** $50-60/hour.

**Event promotions/publicity:** $40 low, $60 mid-range, $70 high/hour; $500-750/day.

**Fundraising campaign brochure:** $50-75 for research (20 hours) and copywriting (30 hours); up to $5,000 for major campaign brochure, including research, writing and production (about 50 hours of work).

**High-tech marketing materials:** $85 low, $125 mid-range, $250 high/hour.

**New product release:** $20-35/hour or $300-500/release.

**News release:** *See Press/news release.*

**Political campaigns, public relations:** Small town or state campaigns, $10-50/hour; congressional, gubernatorial or other national campaigns, $25-100/hour or up to 10% of campaign budget.

**Promotion for events:** $20-30/hour. For conventions and longer events, payment may be per diem or a flat fee of $500-2,500. *See also Press/news release.*

**Press kits:** $50 low, $70 mid-range, $125 high/hour; $1,000-5,000/project.

**Press/news release:** $40 low, $70 mid-range, $150 high/hour; $150 low, $350 mid-range, $500 high/project.

**Print advertisement:** $200-500/project. In Canada, $100-200/concept. *See also Advertising copywriting.*

**Product information:** $30-60/hour; $400-500/day or $100-300/page. *See also Sales and services brochures and fliers.*

**Promotion for tourism, museums, art shows, etc.:** $20-$50 and up/hour for writing or editing promotion copy. Additional charges for production, mailings, etc.

**Public relations for businesses:** $250-600/day plus expenses average—more for large corporations.

**Public relations for government:** $25-50/hour or a monthly retainer based on number of hours per period. Lower fees for local government agencies, higher for state-level and above.

**Public relations for organizations or nonprofits:** $15-35/hour. If working on a monthly retainer, $100-500/month.

**Public relations for schools or libraries:** $15-20/hour for small districts or libraries; up to $35/ hour for larger districts.

**Public relations monthly retainers:** $500 low, $800 mid-range, $1,000 high (fee includes press releases, modest events etc.).

**Radio advertisement:** $50 low, $75 mid-range, $125 high/hour; $400 low, $750 mid-range, $2,000 high/spot; $200-400/week for part-time positions writing radio ads, depending on the size of the city (and market).

**Sales and services brochures and fliers:** $30 low, $65 mid-range, $100 high/hour; $500 low, $1,000 mid-range, $2,500 high/4-page project depending on size and type of business (small nonprofit organization to a large corporation), the number of pages (usually from 1-16) and complexity of the job.

**Sales letters:** $2/word; $40 low, $70 mid-range, $125 high/hour; $400 low, $750 mid-range, $2,000 high/project.

**Speech editing or evaluation:** $50 low, $90 mid-range, $125/high, $200 very high/finished minute. In Canada, $75-125/hour or $70-100/minute of speech.

**Speechwriting (general):** $50 low, $90 mid-range, $125 high, $200 very high/finished minute. In Canada, $75-125/hour or $70-100/minute of speech.

**Speechwriting for business owners or executives:** Up to $80/hour or a flat fee of about $100 for a short (6- or 7-minute speech); $500-3,000 for up to 30 minutes. Rates also depend on size of the company and the event.

**Speechwriting for government officials:** $4,000/20 minutes plus up to $1,000 for travel and expenses.

**Speechwriting for political candidates:** $250 and up for local candidates (about 15 minutes); $375-800 for statewide candidates and $1,000 or more for national congressional candidates.

**TV commercial:** 30 second spot: $950-1,500. In Canada, $60-130/minute of script (CBC pays Writers Guild rates, CTV pays close to that and others pay less. For example, TV Ontario pays $70-100/script minute).

## AUDIOVISUALS & ELECTRONIC COMMUNICATIONS

(See Technical for computer-related services)

**Audiocassette scripts:** $10-50/scripted minute, assuming written from existing client materials, with no additional research or meetings; otherwise $85-100/minute, $750 minimum.

**Audiovisuals:** For writing, $250-350/requested scripted minute; includes rough draft, editing conference with client, and final shooting script. For consulting, research, producing, directing, soundtrack oversight, etc. $400-600/day plus travel and expenses. Writing fee is sometimes 10% of gross production price as billed to client. Some charge flat fee of $1,500-2,100/package.

**Book summaries for film producers:** $50-100/book. *Note: You must live in the area where the business is located to get this kind of work.*

**Business film scripts (training and information):** $50 low, $85 mid-range, $200 high/hour; $75 low, $100 mid-range, $175 high/finished minute.

**Copyediting audiovisuals:** $20-25/hour.

**Educational/training film scripts:** $50 low, $85 mid-range, $200 high/hour; $100/finished minute.

**Industrial product film:** $125-150/minute; $500 minimum flat fee.

**Novel synopsis for film producer:** $150-300/5-10 pages typed, single spaced.

**Options (feature films):** $1,500 low, $15,000 mid-range, $50,000 high, $400,000 very high/project.

**Radio continuity writing:** $5/page to $150/week, part-time. In Canada, $40-80/minute of script; $640/show for a multi-part series.

**Radio copywriting:** *See Advertising, Copywriting & PR.*

**Radio documentaries:** $258/60 minutes, local station.

**Radio editorials:** $10-30/90-second to 2-minute spots.

**Radio interviews:** For National Public Radio, up to 45 seconds, $25; 2 minutes and longer, $62/minute. Small radio stations would pay approximately 50% of the NPR rate; large stations, double the NPR rate.

**Script synopsis for business:** $40/hour.

**Script synopsis for agent or film producer:** $75/2-3 typed pages, single-spaced.

**Scripts for nontheatrical films for education, business, industry:** Prices vary among producers, clients, and sponsors and there is no standardization of rates in the field. Fees include $75-120/minute for one reel (10 minutes) and corresponding increases with each successive reel; approximately 10% of the production cost of films that cost the producer more than $1,500/release minute.

**Screenwriting:** $6,000 and up/project.

**Slide presentation:** Including visual formats plus audio, $150-600/10-15 minutes.

**Slide/single image photos:** $75 flat fee.

**Slide/tape script:** $50 low, $75 mid-range, $100 high/hour; $100 low, $300 high/finished minute; $1,500-3,000/finished project.

**TV commercial:** *See Advertising, Copywriting & PR.*

**TV documentary:** 30-minute 5-6 page proposal outline, $1,839 and up; 15-17 page treatment, $1,839 and up; less in smaller cities. In Canada research for a documentary runs about $6,500.

**TV editorials:** $35 and up/1-minute, 45 seconds (250-300 words).

**TV filmed news and features:** From $10-20/clip for 30-second spot; $15-25/60-second clip; more for special events.

**TV information scripts:** Short 5- to 10-minute scripts for local cable TV stations, $10-15/hour.

**TV, national and local public stations:** For programs, $35-100/minute down to a flat fee of $5,000 and up/30- to 60-minute script.

**TV news film still photo:** $3-6 flat fee.

**TV news story/feature:** $60 low, $95 mid-range, $140 high.

**TV scripts: (non-theatrical):** $50 low, $75 mid-range, $85 high/hour; $300 per finished minute; $3,000/project.

**TV scripts: (Teleplays/mow):** $15,000/30-minute sitcom.

# BOOK PUBLISHING

**Abstracting and abridging:** $40 low, $60 mid-range, $85 high/hour; $30-35/hour for reference and professional journals; $600/5,000 word book summary.

**Anthology editing:** Variable advance plus 3-15 percent of royalties. Advance should cover reprint fees or fees are handled by the publisher. Flat-fee-per-manuscript rates range from $500-5,000 and up.

**Book jacket copywriting:** *See Advertising, Copywriting & PR.*

**Book proposal consultation:** $20-75/hour or a flat rate of $100-250.

**Book proposal writing:** 50¢/word; $45 low, $65 mid-range, $85 high/hour: $2,000-3,500/project, depending on length and whether the client provides full information or the writer must do research, and whether a sample chapter is required.

**Book query critique:** $50 for critique of letter to the publisher and outline.

**Book summaries for book clubs:** $50-100/book.

**Book writing (own):** $20 low, $40 mid-range, $50 high/hour; (advances) $15 low, $35 mid-range, $45 high/hour.

**Content editing (scholarly):** $14 low, $22 mid-range, $32 high, $100 very high/hour.

**Content editing (textbook):** $14 low, $35 mid-range, $65 high, $100 very high/hour.

**Content editing (trade):** $30 low, $60 mid-range, $100 high/hour; $800 low, $1,200 mid-range, $6,000 high/project.

**Copyediting:** $17 low, $30 mid-range, $50 high, $75 very high/hour; $3-5/page. Lower-end rates charged for light copyedit (3-10 pages/hour) of general, trade material. Higher-end rates charged for substantive copyediting or for textbooks and technical material (2-5 pages/hour).

**Ghostwriting, as told to:** This is writing for a celebrity or expert either for a self-published book or for a publisher. Author gets full advance plus 50 percent of royalties, typically $15,000 low, $25,000 high/project plus a percentage of ownership and 'with' credit line. Hourly rates for subjects who are self-publishing are $25 low, $55 mid-range, $85 high/hour; $125 low, $175 high/book page. In Canada, author also gets full advance and 50 percent of royalties or $10,000-20,000 flat fee per project. Research time is charged extra.

**Ghostwriting, no credit:** Projects may include writing for an individual planning to self publish or for a book packager, book producer, publisher, agent or corporation. Rates range from $5,000 very low, $15,000 low, $25,000 mid-range, $50,000 high/project (plus expenses); packagers pay flat fee or combination of advance plus royalties. For self-published clients, ask for one-fourth down payment, one-fourth when book is half-finished, one-fourth at the three-quarters mark and one-fourth upon completion.

**Indexing:** $15 low, $25 mid-range, $40 high, $95 very high/hour; charge higher hourly rate if using a computer index program that takes fewer hours. Also can charge $2-6/indexable page; 40-70¢/line of index or a flat fee of $250-500 depending on length.

**Manuscript evaluation and critique:** $150-200/outline and first 20,000 words; $300-500/up to 100,000 words. Also $15-35/hour for trade books, slightly less for nonprofits. Page rates run from $1.50-2.50/page.

**Movie novelization:** $3,500-15,000 depending on writer's reputation, amount of work to be done and amount of time writer is given.

**Novel synopsis for a literary agent:** $150/5-10 pages typed, single-spaced.

**Page layout (desktop publishing/camera-ready copy):** $25 low, $40 mid-range, $50 high/hour. Higher per-page rates may be charged if material involves complex technical material and graphics.

**Production editing/project management:** $15 low, $30 mid-range, $75 high, $150 very high/hour. This is overseeing the production of a project, coordinating editing and production stages, etc.

**Proofreading:** $15 low, $30 mid-range, $55 high/hour; $4-6/page. High-end rates are charged for technical, scientific and reference material.

**Research for writers or book publishers:** $20-40/hour and up; $150 and up/day plus expenses. A flat rate of $300-500 may be charged, depending on complexity of the job.

**Rewriting:** $18-50/hour; $5-7/page. Some writers receive royalties on book projects.

**Summaries for book clubs/catalogues:** $20 low, $40 mid-range, $75 high/hour.

**Textbooks:** $20 low, $40 mid-range, $60 high/hour.

**Translation (literary):** 10¢/word, $30-35/hour; also $95-125/1,000 English words.

**Typesetting:** $20-45/hour or $5-10/page.

# BUSINESS

**Annual reports:** A brief report with some economic information and an explanation of figures, $35 low, $70 mid-range, $100 high, $150 very high/hour; $300 low, $600 high/page; $500/day; $3,000 low, $6,000 mid-range, $12,000 high/project if extensive research and/or writing is involved in a large project. A report that must meet Securities and Exchange Commission (SEC) standards and reports requiring legal language could bill $75-150/hour. Bill separately if desktop publication (typesetting, page layout, etc.) is involved (some smaller firms and nonprofits may ask for writing/production packages).

**Associations and organizations (writing for):** $15-25/hour for small organizations; up to $50/hour for larger associations or a flat fee depending on the length and complexity of the project. For example, $500-1,000 for an association magazine article (2,000 words) or $1,000-1,800 for a 10-page informational booklet.

**Audiovisuals/audiocassette scripts:** *See Audiovisuals & Electronic Communications.*

**Book summaries for businesses:** $25-50/page or $20-35/hour.

**Brochures, fliers, booklets for business:** $25-40/hour for writing or from $500-$4,000 and up/project (12-16 pages and more). Additional charges for desktop publishing, usually $20-40/hour; $20-30/page or a flat fee per project. *See also Copyediting for business or Manuscript editing/evaluation for trade journals.*

**Business editing (general):** $25 low, $40 mid-range, $85 high/hour.

**Business letters:** $25 low, $65 mid-range, $100 high/hour, depending on the size of the business and the length/complexity of the material, or $2/word.

**Business plan:** $1/word; $200/manuscript page or up to $1,500/project. High-end rates are charged if extensive research is involved. Sometimes research is charged separately per hour or per day.

**Business writing (general):** $30-80/hour. In Canada, $1-2/word or $50-100/hour. *See other entries in this section and in Advertising, Copywriting & PR for specific projects such as* *brochures, copywriting, speechwriting, brochures or business letters. For business film script-writing see Audiovisuals & Electronic Communications.*

**Business writing seminars:** $500 for a half-day seminar, plus travel expenses or $1,000-5,000/ day. Rates depend on number of participants as well as duration. Average per-person rate is $50/person for a half-day seminar. *See also Educational and Literary Services.*

**Catalogs for business:** $25-40/hour or $25-600/printed page; more if tables or charts must be reworked for readability or consistency. Additional charges for desktop publishing ($20-40/ hour is average).

**Collateral materials for business:** *See individual pieces (brochures, catalogs, etc.) in this section and in Advertising, Copywriting & PR.*

**Commercial reports for business, insurance companies, credit agencies:** $6-15/page.

**Consultation on communications:** $25 low, $50 mid-range, $85 high/hour; $600 low, $2,000 high/day (includes travel). Lower-end fees charged to nonprofits and small businesses.

**Consumer complaint letters (answering):** $25-30/letter.

**Copyediting for business:** $20-40/hour or $20-50/manuscript page, up to $40/hour for business proposals. Charge lower-end fees ($15-25/hour) to nonprofits and very small businesses.

**Corporate histories:** $30 low, $70 mid-range, $100 high/hour; $500/day; $7,500/project.

**Corporate periodicals, editing:** $20 very low, $40 low, $60 mid-range, $85 high/hour.

**Corporate periodicals, writing:** $25 very low, $40 low, $70 mid-range, $120 high/hour, depending on size and nature of the corporation. Also $1-3/word. In Canada, $1-2/word or $40-90/ hour.

**Corporate profile:** $1,250-2,500 flat fee for up to 3,000 words or charge on a per word basis, up to $1/word.

**Financial presentation:** $1,500-4,500 for a 20-30 minute presentation.

**Fundraising campaign brochure:** *See Advertising, Copywriting & PR.*

**Ghostwriting for business (usually trade magazine articles or business columns):** $25-100/ hour; $200 or more/day plus expenses (depending on amount of research involved, length of project).

**Government research:** $35-50/hour.

**Government writing:** $30-50/hour. In Canada, $50-80/hour.

**Grant proposal writing for nonprofits:** $30-100/hour or flat fee.

**Indexing for professional journals:** $20-40/hour.

**Industrial/service business training manual:** $25-40/hour; $50-100/manuscript page or a flat fee, $1,000-4,000, depending on number of pages and complexity of the job.

**Industry training film scripts:** *See Business film scripts in Audiovisuals & Electronic Communications.*

**Industrial product film script:** *See Audiovisuals & Electronic Communications.*

**Job application letters:** $20-40/letter.

**Manuals/documentation:** $25-60/hour. *See also Computers, Scientific & Technical.*

**Manuscript editing/evaluation for trade journals:** $20-40/hour.

**Market research survey reports:** $25-50/hour or $500-1,500/day; also flat rates of $500-2,000/ project.

**Newsletters, abstracting:** $30/hour.

**Newsletters, desktop publishing/production:** $25 low, $40 mid-range, $85 high/hour. Higher-end rates for scanning photographs, advertising layout, illustration or design. Editing charged extra.

**Newsletters, editing:** $25 low, $45 mid-range, $85 high/hour; $200-500/issue; $2/word. Higher-end fees charged if writing or production is included. Editors who produce a regular newsletter on a monthly or quarterly basis tend to charge per month or per issue—and find them easier to do after initial set up.

**Newsletters, writing:** $35 low, $50 mid-range, $100 high/hour; $500 low, $1,350 mid-range,

$2,500 high/project; $200 and up/page. In Canada, $45-70/hour.

**Nonprofit editing:** $15 low, $30 mid-range, $55 high/hour.

**Nonprofit writing:** $15 very low, $25 low, $50 mid-range, $70 high/hour.

**Programmed instruction consultation fees:** *See Educational & Literary Services.*

**Programmed instruction materials for business:** *See Educational & Literary Services.*

**Proofreading for business:** $15-50/hour; low-end fees for nonprofits.

**Public relations:** *See Advertising, Copywriting and PR.*

**Résumé writing:** $30 low, $55 mid-range, $100 high.

**Retail newsletters for customers:** Charge regular newsletter rates or $175-300/4-page project. Additional charges for desktop publishing.

**Sales brochures, fliers, letters, other advertising materials:** *See Advertising, Copywriting & PR.*

**Scripts for business/training films:** *See Audiovisuals & Electronic Communications.*

**Translation, commercial:** $30-45/hour; $115-125/1,000 words. Higher-end fees for non-European languages into English.

**Translation for government agencies:** $30-45; up to $125/1,000 words. Higher-end fees for non-European languages into English.

**Translation through translation agencies:** Agencies pay 33⅓% average less than end-user clients and mark up translator's prices by as much as 100% or more.

**Translation, technical:** $30-45/hour; $125 and up/1,000 words, depending on complexity of the material.

## COMPUTER, SCIENTIFIC & TECHNICAL

**Abstracting, CD-ROM:** $50/hour.

**Abstracting, online:** $40/hour.

**Computer documentation, general (print):** $35 low, $60 mid-range, $100 high/hour; $100-150/page. *See also Software manual writing.*

**Computer documentation (online):** $20 low, $50 mid-range, $85 high/hour.

**Demonstration software:** $70 and up/hour.

**Legal/government editing:** $15 very low, $25 low, $50 mid-range, $65 high/hour.

**Legal/government writing:** $15 very low, $30 low, $50 mid-range, $65 high/hour.

**Medical and science editing:** $20 low, $60 mid-range, $85 high/hour, depending on the complexity of the material and the expertise of the editor.

**Medical and science proofreading:** $15-30/hour.

**Medical and science writing:** $35 low, $70 mid-range, $150 high/hour; $1-3/word, depending on the complexity of the project and the writer's expertise.

**Online editing:** $25 low, $40 mid-range, $68 high/hour.

**Software manual writing:** $15 low, $50 mid-range, $100 high/hour for research and writing.

**Technical editing:** $20-60/hour or $150-1,000/day.

**Technical typesetting:** $4-7/page; $25-35/hour; more for inputting of complex material.

**Technical writing:** $30-75/hour; $20-30/page. *See also Computer documentation and Software manual writing.*

**Technical translation:** *See item in Business.*

**Webpage design:** $50 low, $85 mid-range, $125 high/hour..

**Webpage writing/editing:** $50 low, $85 mid-range, $125 high/hour; $170 mid-range, $500 high/page.

## EDITORIAL/DESIGN PACKAGES

**Business catalogs:** *See Business.*

**Desktop publishing:** For 1,000 dots-per-inch type, $5-15/camera-ready page of straight type; $30/camera-ready page with illustrations, maps, tables, charts, photos; $100-150/camera-ready page for oversize pages with art. Also $25-50/hour depending on graphics, number of photos, and amount of copy to be typeset. Packages often include writing, layout/design, and typesetting services.

**Greeting cards ideas (with art included):** Anywhere from $30-300, depending on size of company.

**Newsletters:** *See Desktop publishing (this section) and Newsletters (Business).*

**Picture editing:** $20-40.

**Photo brochures:** $700-15,000 flat fee for photos and writing.

**Photo research:** $15-30/hour.

**Photography:** $10-150/b&w photo; $25-300/color photo; also $800/day.

## EDUCATIONAL & LITERARY SERVICES

**Business writing seminars:** *See Business.*

**Consultation for individuals (in business):** $250-1,000/day.

**Consultation on communications:** *See Business.*

**Developing and designing courses for business or adult education:** $250-$1,500/day or flat fee.

**Editing for individual clients:** $10-50/hour or $2-7/page.

**Educational consulting and educational grant and proposal writing:** $250-750/day or $30-75/hour.

**Lectures at national conventions by well-known authors:** $2,500-20,000 and up, plus expenses; less for panel discussions.

**Lectures at regional writers' conferences:** $300 and up, plus expenses.

**Lectures to local groups, librarians or teachers:** $50-150.

**Lectures to school classes:** $25-75; $150/day; $250/day if farther than 100 miles.

**Manuscript evaluation for theses/dissertations:** $15-30/hour.

**Poetry manuscript critique:** $25/16-line poem.

**Programmed instruction consultant fees:** $300-1,000/day, $50-75/hour.

**Programmed instruction materials for business:** $50/hour for inhouse writing and editing; $500-1,000/day plus expenses for outside research and writing. Alternate method: $2,000-5,000/hour of programmed training provided depending on technicality of subject.

**Public relations for schools:** *See Advertising, Copywriting & PR.*

**Readings by poets, fiction writers:** $25-600 depending on author.

**Scripts for nontheatrical films for education:** *See Audiovisuals & Electronic Communications.*

**Short story manuscript critique:** 3,000 words, $40-60.

**Teaching adult education course:** $15 low, $45 mid-range, $125 high/hour; $1,750-2,500/continuing education course; fee usually set by school, not negotiated by teachers.

**Teaching adult seminar:** $20 low, $40 mid-range, $60 high/hour; $750-1,000/3-day course. In Canada, $35-50/hour.

**Teaching business writing to company employees:** *See Consultation on communications in Business.*

**Teaching college course or seminar:** $15-70/class hour.

**Teaching creative writing in school:** $15-70/hour of instruction, or $1,500-2,000/12-15 week semester; less in recessionary times.

**Teaching elementary and middle school teachers how to teach writing to students:** $75-150/1- to 1½ hour session.

**Teaching home-bound students:** $5-15/hour.

**Tutoring:** $25/1- to 1½ hour private session.

**TV instruction taping:** $150/30-minute tape; $25 residual each time tape is sold.

**Workshop instructing:** $25 low, $50 mid-range, $75 high/hour; $2,500-3,500/13-week course.

**Writer-in-schools:** Arts council program, $130/day; $650/week. Personal charges plus expenses vary from $25/day to $100/hour depending on school's ability to pay.

**Writer's workshop:** Lecturing and seminar conducting, $50-150/hour to $750/day plus expenses; local classes, $35-50/student for 10 sessions.

**Writing for individual clients:** $25-100/hour, depending on the situation. *See also Business writing in Business.*

**Writing for scholarly journals:** $75/hour.

## MAGAZINES & TRADE JOURNALS

**Abstracting:** $20-30/hour for trade and professional journals; $20 low, $30 mid-range, $60 high/hour for scholarly journals.

**Advertorial:** $650 low, $1,000 high/printed page.

**Article manuscript critique:** $40/3,000 words.

**Arts reviewing:** $35-100 flat fee or 20-30¢/word, plus admission to events or copy of CD (for music).

**Book reviews:** $22 low, $50 mid-range, $175 high, $750 very high/piece; 25¢-$1/word.

**Consultation on magazine editorial:** $1,000-1,500/day plus expenses.

**Copyediting magazines:** $16-30/hour.

**Editing:** General, $25-500/day or $250-2,000/issue; religious publications, $200-500/month or $15-30/hour.

**Fact checking:** $26 low, $50 mid-range, $75 high/hour.

**Feature articles:** Anywhere from 20¢-$4/word; or $150-2,750/1,500 word article, depending on size (circulation) and reputation of magazine.

**Ghostwriting articles (general):** Up to $2/word; or $300-3,000/project.

**Indexing:** $15-40/hour.

**Magazine, city, calendar of events column:** $50-150/column.

**Magazine column:** 25¢ low, $1.50 mid-range, $4 high/word; $25 low, $200 mid-range, $2,500 high/piece. Larger circulation publications pay fees related to their regular word rate.

**Magazine copyediting:** $15 low, $25 mid-range, $50 high, $100 very high/hour.

**Magazine editing:** $15 low, $30 mid-range, $60 high/hour.

**Magazine research:** $20 low, $40 mid-range, $75 high/hour.

**Manuscript consultation:** $25-50/hour.

**Manuscript criticism:** $40-60/article or short story of up to 3,000 words. Also $20-25/hour.

**Picture editing:** *See Editorial/Design Packages.*

**Permission fees to publishers to reprint article or story:** $75-500; 10-15¢/word; less for charitable organizations.

**Production editing:** $15-30/hour.

**Proofreading:** $12-25/hour.

**Research:** $20-25/hour.

**Rewriting:** Up to $80/manuscript page; also $100/published page.

**Science writing for magazines:** $2,000-5,000/article. *See also Computer, Scientific & Technical.*

**Special news article:** For a business's submission to trade publication, $250-500/1,000 words. In Canada, 25-45¢/word.

**Stringing:** 20¢-$1/word based on circulation. Daily rate: $150-250 plus expenses; weekly rate: $900 plus expenses. Also $10-35/hour plus expenses; $1/column inch.

**Trade journal ad copywriting:** *See Advertising, Copywriting & PR.*

**Trade journal feature article:** For business client, $400-1,000. Also $1-2/word.

## NEWSPAPERS

**Ads for small business:** $25/small, one-column ad, or $10/hour and up. *See also Advertising, Copywriting & PR.*

**Arts reviewing:** For weekly newspapers, $15-50 flat fee; for dailies, $50 and up; for Sunday supplements, $100-400. Also admission to event or copy of CD (for music).

**Book reviews:** For small newspapers, byline and the book only; for larger publications, $35-200 and a copy of the book.

**Column, local:** $40 low, $125 mid-range, $300 high/hour, depending on circulation.

**Copyediting:** $10-30/hour; up to $40/hour for large daily paper.

**Copywriting:** *See Advertising, Copywriting & PR.*

**Dance criticism:** $25-400/article.

**Drama criticism:** Local, newspaper rates; non-local, $50 and up/review.

**Editing/manuscript evaluation:** $25/hour.

**Fact checking:** *See Magazines & Trade Journals.*

**Feature:** $25 low, $200 mid-range, $500 high/piece, depending on circulation. In Canada, $15-40/word, but rates vary widely.

**Obituary copy:** Where local newspapers permit lengthier than normal notices paid for by the funeral home (and charged to the family), $15-25. Writers are engaged by funeral homes.

**Picture editing:** *See Editorial/Design Packages.*

**Proofreading:** $16-20/hour.

**Reporting:** $25 low, $45 mid-range, $100 high/piece (small circulation); $60 low, $175 high/ per piece (large circulation).

**Science writing for newspapers:** *See Computer, Scientific & Technical.*

**Stringing:** $10 low, $25 mid-range, $40 high/piece; $1/column inch, sometimes with additional mileage payment.

**Syndicted column, self-promoted:** $5-10 each for weeklies; $10-25/week for dailies, based on circulation.

## MISCELLANEOUS

**Comedy writing for nightclub entertainers:** Gags only, $5-25 each. Routines, $100-1,000/ minute. Some new comics may try to get a 5-minute routine for $150; others will pay $2,500 for a 5-minute bit from a top writer.

**Comics writing:** $35-50/page and up for established comics writers.

**Contest judging:** Short manuscripts, $10/entry; with one-page critique, $15-25. Overall contest judging: $100-500.

**Corporate comedy skits:** $300-800/half-hour skit (used at meetings, conventions).

**Craft ideas with instructions:** $50-200/project.

**Encyclopedia articles:** Entries in some reference books, such as biographical encyclopedias, 500-2,000 words; pay ranges from $60-80/1,000 words. Specialists' fees vary.

**Family histories:** Fees depend on whether the writer edits already prepared notes or does extensive research and writing; and the length of the work, $500-15,000.

**Institutional (church, school) history:** $200-1,000/15-50 pages, or $20-35/hour.

**Manuscript typing:** Depending on manuscript length and delivery schedule, $1.25-2/page with one copy; $15/hour.

**Party toasts, limericks, place card verses:** $1.50/line.

**Research for individuals:** $5-30/hour, depending on experience, geographic area and nature of work.

**Special occasion booklet:** Family keepsake of a wedding, anniversary, Bar Mitzvah, etc., $120 and up.

# Eyes Open for Opportunity

## BY CLIFTON DOWELL

"Any writer who's out on his own is an entrepreneur, whether he uses that word or not," says Terri Lonier, business expert and author of *Working Solo* (John Wiley & Sons, Inc., 1994). "When you look back to the founding of our country, we had the butcher, the baker, the candlestick maker. Now we have the freelance writer and the web designer."

Writers could do worse than thinking of themselves as entrepreneurs, particularly when it comes to sizing up potential markets. A talented entrepreneur is adept at recognizing opportunity.

"To think of yourself as just one type of writer is focusing too narrowly," Lonier says. "Writers are essentially communicators, which means they have the ability to take ideas, clarify them and share them with the world. These days, that may mean that instead of doing a freelance article for a magazine, you may be creating web content, doing speech writing or writing creative briefs."

And the list goes on. To get an idea of just how many ways there are to sell your writing— and your editorial expertise—leaf through the How Much Should I Charge? section of this book. Pay particular attention to listings you may have ignored in the past, perhaps those for "Advertising, Copywriting & PR," "Business" or "Educational & Literary Services." An experienced writer might find a dozen new careers on those pages, not to mention several dozen sidelines. For the freelancer who likes to mix and match, the possibilities are virtually endless.

"Content is king," Lonier says. "Writing is such a broad skill, and there's such a demand for it these days. More than ever before, writers have great opportunities—if they can harness not only their skills, but also their business acumen."

Many freelance writers say the market is as wide as the net you cast. With hard work and a little luck, you can find ways to use the skills you've already developed as a writer to make money in ways you've never considered. There's nothing stopping you from putting together a profitable editorial enterprise that combines all the things you enjoy.

## Virginia Holman

### *Redbook, Self, DoubleTake*

Virginia Holman has seen the publishing business from both sides. Before launching her freelance writing career, she worked as chief copyeditor for a publishing house and ran her own freelance trade and academic copyediting business. With publications ranging from literary essays to technical manuals on the intricacies of AC drive motors, Holman is familiar with the diversity of the marketplace. Here are some of the ways she's found to apply her skills:

*Manuscript critique*: "I'm part of a manuscript critique service offered through the local writers' network. People send in their manuscripts and, for a real reasonable fee, get relatively expert one-on-one feedback. It's especially useful for people who don't have a writing group."

© 1999 MJ Sharp

**Virginia Holman**

---

**CLIFTON DOWELL** *is a journalist and communications consultant in Chapel Hill, North Carolina, and copublisher of* Dream/Girl, *an arts magazine that encourages creative genius in girls 11-15 years old.*

*Technical writing*: "It was awful. Technical writing can probably be really fascinating if you enjoy it, but I found it horribly dull—even the high pay couldn't sway me to pursue it. Would I ever do it again? It depends—if you've got to feed the kids, you've got to feed the kids. I didn't particularly enjoy copyediting either, but, you know, it's a way to make a living."

*Manuscript marketing*: "A woman who was in one of my classes asked me to help her send her book around. I was familiar with the short story market, and she wasn't. I also had contacts in New York."

*Workshop teaching*: "I've taught fiction writing to undergraduates and teens. I've taught essay writing and classes about publishing, as well as classes on personal narratives. Early on, I took teaching jobs to get the income and experience. Now, I teach when I can because I like it. You don't get paid a whole lot of money in most cases, but you get more out of it than the money. Every time I teach a class, the students teach me how to write."

*Words to the Wise*: "This is not the business to be in just for money. A freelance business of any sort is a lifestyle choice. You're doing it because you want something for yourself—you want to be happy, or you want to be free, or whatever. You've got to be true to yourself throughout the whole process or there's no point.

"My personal philosophy is, 'Do what you're interested in.' When I started trying to make the transition from freelance book editing to freelance writing, one of my first assignments wasn't something I really wanted to be doing. It was $35 an hour, but I was miserable and backed out of the job. There was my issue: Did I want money or did I want happiness? I wanted both, so I made a promise to myself to try to write only what I was interested in. I started pursuing those topics with vigor, and it paid off. And, I'm happy."

## Bridgette A. Lacy

*Southern Living, Victoria, Attaché*

Bridgette A. Lacy makes use of her journalism experience to provide a stable foundation for her freelance career. As a part-time newspaper feature writer, she has reliable access to both income and ideas.

"The problem is that freelancing is kind of feast or famine," Lacy says. "With a part-time job, I know I have a certain amount of pay I can factor in. It allows me more flexibility, and I don't always have to be running around trying to find an assignment."

Lacy says a related part-time job can enhance a writing career, but finding one can be tricky. Luckily, there's more than one way for enterprising writers to make money:

**Bridgette A. Lacy**

*Radio commentary*: "I've sold commentaries to the local NPR station. That came about because I was listening to NPR while making my dinner one night. I heard a commentary and I thought, 'I could do that.' I called the station and learned what it was you had to do."

*Legal publicity*: "I've written press releases for a lawyer. The lawyer knew my work from the newspaper and found out I was a freelancer. He wanted to send press releases about two of his cases to newspapers and get them interested in the stories. He used a lot of jargon, and I was able to break down, in more human terms, what the case was about."

*Media escort*: "I've driven touring authors around the area when they fly in for readings and book signings. It came about because I was broke one day and thought it would be a nice way to make money, as well as another way to talk to established authors about the craft. Basically, I called a bookstore owner, and she passed my name on to publicists."

*Words to the Wise*: "It's endless what you can do. Always look for an opportunity. You have these skills and you can execute them differently, depending on what is called for. I think you want to have the skill set and say, 'Today I'll use it this way, tomorrow I'll use it that way.' You do these other things so you can do what you love, to support your passion. But I'm lucky. I've liked all the jobs I've done."

## Ginny Turner

**Ginny Turner**

*Travel & Leisure*, *Westways*, *Endless Vacation*
Ginny Turner knows plenty about freelancing and about taking the entrepreneurial approach to markets. In fact, one of her side ventures worked so well she found a new career. She's now the editorial director of Creative Development Group and finds herself hiring freelancers.

"I didn't anticipate becoming a full-time book editor," Turner says, "but I'm finding it more satisfying than I had thought. I don't have much time to query for articles anymore—I do it occasionally, but it's rare. Now, I describe myself as a book editor who has published 200 magazine articles."

Turner attributes her success, both as a magazine writer and an editor, to her readiness to take advantage of the opportunities that presented themselves. Of course, enterprising writers can influence how frequently opportunities arise:

*Entrepreneurial efforts*: "Don't be shy. It's important to say what you do. I was riding my bike in the neighborhood and met a man who asked what I did. When I told him I was a writer and an editor, he responded by saying he had written a manuscript. I later spent five hours helping him rearrange the material and rewriting some of it. I got $125. You never know."

*Networking*: "I can't emphasize enough that you have to pay attention to the people around you. Be interested in their work and try to find out how they're related to other people in the community. Spread your cards around. Tell everybody you know that you're a writer. Volunteer to do writing jobs for the groups you belong to—certainly the ones with a wide range of individuals. That's how you meet people, and volunteer work can yield things.

"Talk to anybody who has done any kind of production of words on paper. Check out the bulletin board at the copy shop. Be open all the time, and keep your ears up. Stay on good terms with anyone you know even remotely related to publishing. They may have something for you someday; if not there, perhaps at the next place they work."

*Words to the Wise*: "It's never a matter of choosing what to do, it's a matter of looking out for opportunities. There's never enough money and there's never enough work. You can't risk passing up a job that might lead to a big client or a steady stream of money. You have to take everything."

# Write for the Web—and Sell!

BY MICHAEL RAY TAYLOR

In the past few years, freelance assignments have taken me to some interesting places: I've hiked the steaming caldera of a Hawaiian volcano, snorkeled the world's deepest spring, rappelled into an Alabama cave, and held a piece of ALH 84001, the famous rock from Mars. I've written about these adventures at the average rate of a dollar per word.

What's unusual in my case (but quickly getting to be the norm) is that none of the stories I wrote about these adventures ever appeared on a printed page. They were published on the World Wide Web, in *The Discovery Channel Online (DCOL)* and *ABCNews.com*. And as such professionally produced, well-funded electronic magazines like these proliferate, print writers can expect to find a lucrative and growing market on the electronic frontier.

It's a mistake to assume, however, that editors of web-based media want the same material you'd produce for that quaint wood-pulp-based medium you're reading at the moment. As Marshall McLuhan famously said, "The medium is the message." The Web is still in its infancy; so far no one has figured out exactly what message its audience wants. But what has become increasingly clear is that the online audience doesn't want to read traditional magazine articles thrown across a computer screen.

What follows, then, are a few evolving guidelines for the online freelancer. Keep in mind that the key word is evolving: Since my first article was posted in July 1995, hundreds of magazines have appeared online. Hundreds have vanished. The few long-term survivors have changed their basic look and content, on average, every three to four months. This means that any print-based information for specific markets (including information in this book) may be out of date by the time you read it. So the trick is learning how to analyze the ever-morphing markets on your own, and how to sell to a particular site once you've pinned it down for the moment.

## STUDY THE MARKETS

Even though the medium is new, my first point of advice isn't. As with freelancing in print, you can't expect to sell professional writing to a magazine you've never read. In order to break into a given website, study every available screen of content. (This means that to sell to the online magazines, you must have regular access to a personal computer loaded with Netscape Navigator, Microsoft Internet Explorer or some other Internet browser, as well as Internet access.) Use the "Magazine" listings on such search engines as Yahoo!, Excite or AOL Find to browse the marketplace.

Look at current issues, and call up past screens from archives (which virtually all sites maintain). Notice such things as number and type of advertisers. With most online magazines, the ads are narrow bars (called banners) at the top of the page. Clicking on these will usually lead you through several pages of information. Studying the organization of these advertising pages will tell you a great deal about the demographics of the magazine's audience.

If there are no advertisers, chances are there is no available money to pay freelancers, unless

**MICHAEL RAY TAYLOR** *is the author of* Dark Life, *published on bleached wood pulp by Scribner in 1999. He teaches online and old-fashioned journalism at Henderson State University in Arkadelphia, Arkansas.*

the website is sponsored by a large private organization, such as a national environmental organization.

Pay attention to regular departments, or slots, especially those featuring the bylines of a number of different authors—a sure sign that the slot is open to freelancers. Observe the use of photos, audio and video, as well as the number of screens of print devoted to particular articles.

You may be able to find market information for sites that interest you in the "Online Markets" section of this book, in the Markets section of *Writer's Digest* online at http://www.writersdigest.com or in *Online Markets for Writers*, by Anthony Tedesco (Owl Books/Henry Holt, Spring 2000), online at http://www.marketsforwriters.com. With print magazines, prospective writers often send a SASE for writer's guidelines, which they usually receive a few weeks later. But many online magazines post guidelines on their site, although you may have to navigate around for a while to find them.

Usually, if you click on a magazine's logo or the phrase "About Us," you'll get a mission statement describing the editorial slant and the intended audience, a masthead listing staff members, and guidelines for freelance submissions. Some sites will include brief bios of specific editors in the masthead, letting them describe in their own words the sections they edit and their particular tastes—invaluable information for the freelancer.

Even more useful are the editors' e-mail addresses. Virtually all correspondence with online magazines, from your initial query letter through final revisions and corrections of your published article, will be handled via e-mail. If you don't have the editor's e-mail address (and, obviously, if you don't have an e-mail address yourself), you have little hope for making a sale.

If the site you want to sell to doesn't list e-mail addresses for editors, usually a "Feedback" button will allow you to e-mail the editorial offices. If editors names are listed, but no e-mail address is given, you may be able to track down the proper address through Bigfoot, WhoWhere or one of the other Internet e-mail directories. (At many websites, especially those tied to television networks, the editors are called "producers," but they assign articles and edit text in exactly the same was as other websites' editors.)

When you've picked out a likely magazine, one that interests you and uses (and clearly pays for!) freelance material, and you've found an e-mail address for an appropriate editor at that magazine, you're ready for the next step: selling the piece. I use a process that I've shortened to the acronym SELL: **S**lots; **E**litist hipster attitude; **L**ong equals bad; and **L**inks, links, links.

## SLOTS

As with print magazines, most online markets separate main features and cover stories from shorter, regular departmental pieces. And as with print, the best way to break in is to pitch an appropriate, well-honed slot idea to the appropriate editor. The best-known, highest paying sites—places like *DCOL*, *Salon*, *HotWired*, *Slate* and *Women's Wire*—use well-known authors and journalists for big features, but are all surprisingly receptive to freelance contributors in their smaller slots. (The obvious exceptions are columns contracted to individual writers, such as the science columns written by Les Dye at *ABCNews.com* or Hannah Holmes at *DCOL*.)

Slots are often difficult for editors to fill because each week or month they have to find an idea that fits the format without duplicating a piece already posted. For example, early in my online career, I sold several essays to a slot at *DCOL* called Gone, which was published weekly in the Exploration department, edited by Greg Henderson. Every essay that ran in the slot was entitled "Gone . . ." followed by a type of adventurous destination: "Gone . . . to the Volcano," "Gone . . . to the Cave Carnival," "Gone . . . Searching for Aliens" and so on. The essays were always written in first-person, about 750 words long and described what Henderson called "a single scene from the midst of an adventure." Any writer who read several of these in a row could easily come up with a personal experience—or perhaps even a piece already written for print—that could be shaped to the demands of the Gone slot.

I refer to Gone in the past tense because this slot, as often happens with ever-shifting online

## IN YOUR MANUSCRIPT . . .

**Single-space**. Use two hard returns between paragraphs. Do not indent paragraphs.

**Show some ID**. Begin your message with your name, byline (if different), phone number, and street and e-mail addresses. For attached files, give the file name and application.

**Ditch the styles**. Italics, boldface or font changes can get lost in transition. If a passage must run in italics, type [ITALICS] on either side of it.

**Make links**. Underline *only* to indicate a link. After your article's text, retype the link above the intended sidebar (internal links), or the URL (external links).

**Send the facts**. Include fact-check material (phone numbers of quoted sources and published material consulted for the piece). If you have ideas for photos or graphics, append those as well.

---

markets, is now gone for good. But other slots took its place: I've become a frequent contributor of science news briefs to the *Discovery Online* News section. Virtually every department of every online magazine has several "regular" slots, which usually enjoy a run of several months to a year between redesigns.

## ELITIST HIPSTER ATTITUDE

From its beginning in the fall of 1996, my "Writing for New Media" course (which focuses mainly on the Internet) has required students to give periodic oral reports on particular sites. One student discovered, in the writer's guidelines for *Charged*, a youth-targeted spinoff of *Outside Online*, a phrase that the class embraced as mantra, with great success: "The pieces we're looking for," a *Charged* editor wrote, "show elitist hipster attitude."

None of us quite knew what the phrase meant. But we grokked that it described the esthetic of many of the sites we'd studied. We even shortened the phrase to EHA, and in many of our workshops one writer would say to another, "This piece could work if it just had more EHA." Like the web surfers who spend time reading online, online writing is informal, smart, often irreverent, occasionally profane, unafraid to use the verb *grok* (which means "to understand," from a classic sci-fi novel) or to drop references to, say, the TV show *Friends*, Robert Heinlein, hip-hop, and Immanuel Kant within the space of a paragraph.

In short, online writing is playfully cool.

Whenever I sit down to write a web piece, I imagine I'm sending a casual e-mail to a well-read friend, rather than addressing a Mass Audience as an Electronic Journalist. I do the same careful reporting I'd do for print, of course. I gather accurate facts, arresting quotes and vivid scenic detail. I just keep in mind that the level of diction evolving for this medium is far more relaxed, if also a bit more self-conscious, than the diction of *Consumer Reports* or *The Atlantic Monthly*.

Such writing doesn't always come naturally. But if you can master it, beginning with the e-mail correspondence by which you introduce yourself to editors, you'll have come a long way toward adopting the prevalent culture of the Web. Even the fairly straightforward news items at *ABCnews.com* indulge in puns and pop culture analogies in ways that would make Peter Jennings bristle.

Perhaps the best mainstream example of EHA can be found in the articles and essays of *Salon* and *HotWired*. These web magazines assume their readers are informed on current technology, current events and the media, and that they really enjoy their fun. And have retained at least a few bytes of whatever classical education they were once exposed to. And aren't particularly offended by sentence frags, unexplained computer terms, or lines ending in prepositions.

## LONG EQUALS BAD

The little glowing window of even a high-resolution monitor requires type to be much larger than what readers tolerate on a magazine page, and the window is made even smaller than the screen by the order imposed by a web browser. So from type size alone, even a fairly short and snappy magazine piece can appear dreary and endless on a computer screen. A typical 3,000 word feature from *Glamour* or *Sports Illustrated* becomes Joyce's *Ulysses* online, unless broken into discrete nuggets on separate screens.

Writing and pictures must work together with entirely different constraints than those imposed on a magazine page, and some websites also toss audio and even video into the mix. Whenever you put a story online, your readers are never more than a mouse-click away from arcade shoot-outs and nude celebrities. Every line must grab attention.

The first article I sold to an online market was a 2,500-word feature with all sorts of internal hypertext links and sidebars and video clips, which ran in July 1995, during the inaugural week of *DCOL*. Thousands of readers clicked onto the story's spectacular opening photo—which took a frustrating amount of time for older PCs to download—and many read the opening screen of text. But fewer than ten percent bothered to navigate through the many screens of the entire piece. Now, at *DCOL* as at most other sites, the longest a single piece ever gets is about 1,000 words. Big features, such as a dinosaur dig in Mongolia or an expedition to retrieve a Mercury space capsule from the ocean floor, appear in the form of several separate articles, each posted on different days in serial fashion.

Online readers may read several related pieces of 700 to 1,000 words, but they just don't have the patience for very long features; very few online magazines will now consider anything longer. And there are many shorter pieces, in the range of 300-500 words. It's not so much that Internet readers have short attention spans (although that may be true of many), but the physical act of reading on a screen and scrolling with a mouse is simply more effort to most people than the comparable act of thumbing through a magazine on the couch or in bed. Therefore, the material must move faster, and deliver knowledge and entertainment more quickly.

Length is a consideration at all levels of your writing. Within a piece, paragraphs are typically much shorter than those in print magazines. If a paragraph can't fit into a single browser window, it probably needs to be broken into two or three. Sentences, like paragraphs, need to be short online. Words, too—short ones are better than long ones.

## LINKS, LINKS, LINKS

The final key to successful online writing is to take full advantage of the medium by providing readers (and your editor) with both internal and external hot links. A *link* is an underlined word or phrase that appears on the computer screen in a different color than the surrounding text. Clicking on an internal link takes you to a sidebar or elsewhere in an article. Clicking on an external link takes you out of the article and into some other domain—usually another website with useful information on the underlined topic.

For example, if a travel piece contained the line, "We drove north from Rome past the ancient town of Viterbo," clicking on the word "Viterbo" might bring to a reader to an internal link comparing three reasonably priced hotels in Viterbo. Or it might just as well take the reader to an external website maintained by an Italian company that runs tours to Viterbo's famous hot springs. Because an external site might lure a reader away from an article (and the magazine's advertisers), most sites use them sparingly, often saving them for the end of the article or a separate "Links" button. But nearly all sites use internal links. They provide a way of making the main article—which is always too long—a little shorter.

In your initial query, it is thus wise to suggest one to three internal links for the average factual article (links are not as common in personal essays, which are usually fairly linear). You should also suggest four or five external links, not only as possible uses for the proposed piece, but as a means for the editor to seek more information on your proposed topic, if the editor wants it. And if the site employs still images, video or audio, you might also suggest links to external sites that might serve as willing sources for such material.

## SELL IT

If you can become familiar with the aspects of web journalism, you'll quickly find that the markets are more responsive than most print magazines. The medium is new enough that editors haven't yet been overwhelmed with thousands of bad queries and jam-smeared religious short stories. You'll often receive a quick response to your query (anywhere from minutes to a few days, as opposed to the weeks you'll wait for answers from the slicks). In those instances where you don't receive a quick response, follow-up emails are easy to send and in fact often expected by editors. And when you do make a sale, you'll almost certainly be asked to contribute additional stories to the site.

I don't think the Web will replace bleached wood pulp within my lifetime. I still have ideas for long, in-depth pieces that I dream of selling to *Harper's* or *The New Yorker*. But writers write and professionals write for money.

I've learned that online articles are more than a great way to earn a few dollars: They've helped me grow as a writer, by forcing me to adopt an economy of style that the printed page didn't always demand. They've helped me grow as a reader, by immersing me in a creative medium I might otherwise have ignored. I've received instantaneous feedback from readers' e-mail and my articles stay "in print" for as long as the website maintains it archives—usually a year or two.

In other words, I feel like a real writer, as opposed to a virtual one.

---

### IN YOUR ELECTRONIC QUERY . . .

**Be salutation savvy**. Address the editor as "Dear Mr. Smith:" or "Dear Ms. Jones:" If gender can't be determined, use the full name ("Dear Terry Jones"). As soon as you receive a personal response, you can address that editor by first name.

**Single-space**. Use two hard returns between paragraphs.

**Use electronic clips**. If you've published in other professional online markets (or if you have a good sample posted by a nonpaying market), include one or two URLs for sites where your work appears.

**Keep it short**. An e-query should never run more than a single page, no matter how complex the story. If you're querying about a very short slot, send just a few lines, or submit the piece on spec.

# Online Writing Markets: A Love Story

BY ANTHONY TEDESCO

I'm not suggesting you run out and marry an online market, but let's face it, they're pretty darn attractive right now. Sort of the sweet, bright-eyed siblings of stodgy old print markets. They're fetchingly easy and affordable to approach, forsaking paper, envelopes and postage for short e-mails with electronic clips attached. And once queried, online markets don't act aloof, gracing you with a response in a few months. They're considerate/enabled enough to get right back to you within a week or two, often within only a few days. The best part? Despite their empowering allure, most online markets are sheepishly more receptive than print markets. The Internet medium is still so new that there's less competition, fewer writers vying for their attention. Endearing, isn't it? Online markets don't even know how attractive they are.

If my wannabe-cupid routine has got you curious about writing online, you're in luck. Finding online markets that make your heart flutter can be as easy as saying, "Anthony, you've beaten this love-market metaphor way beyond literary decorum." With such a multitude of markets already online—consumer magazines, corporate sites seeking customer-entertaining content, e-mail newsletters, etc.—you're sure to engage partner publications which share your most idiosyncratic of interests. Michael Ray Taylor's article on page 78 can help you find and woo potential online markets, as can my book, *Online Markets for Writers: Where and How to Sell Your Writing on the Internet* (Owl Books/Henry Holt & Co.), my website at http://www.markets forwriters.com, and did I mention my book?

Just so you know I care: To help with your own—book or book-free—search for Ms./Mr. Right Markets, I've brought over a few potential online publications you might be interested in meeting, as well as one final/superfluous metaphor because, who knows, you may just find online-writing love at first sight.

## ONLINE MARKETS

**CYBERTIMES**, http://www.nytimes.com/yr/mo/day/cyber/index.html
The New York Times on the Web, 1120 Avenue of the Americas, New York NY 10036. (212) 597-8023. Fax: (212) 597-8014. E-mail: cybertimes@nytimes.com. **Contact**: John Haskins, CyberTimes Editor. **60-70% freelance written**. *CyberTimes* is *The New York Times*'s interactive daily newspaper focusing on the social, cultural, political and economic implications of the Internet. Estab. 1996. Circ. 200,000 visits/month. Pays on publication. Byline given. Buys all world rights, print and electronic, in perpetuity. Accepts electronic submissions via e-mail to cybertimes@nytimes.com. Reports in 1 day on queries; 1-3 days on mss.
**Nonfiction:** News, news features, exposé, interview/profile, historical/nostalgic. Query, or query with published clips. Length: 600-800 words. **Pays $400-500**. Pays expenses of writers on assignment.
**Photos:** State availability of photos with submission. Negotiates payment individually. Captions, identification of subjects required. Buys one-time electronic rights, permanently archived.
**Tips:** "*CyberTimes*, a web-only technology section of *The New York Times*, is the interactive daily newspaper of cyberspace. We are looking for features and news articles that place computer and Internet technologies in a human and

**ANTHONY TEDESCO** *is author of* Online Markets for Writers: Where and How to Sell Your Writing on the Internet *(Owl Books/Henry Holt & Co., Spring 2000) and online publisher of the writer resource, Markets for Writers, at http://www.marketsforwriters.com. He welcomes questions/comments, direct/dis-counted book orders and flowery love letters to anthony@marketsforwriters.com.*

social context and describe new dimensions of the networked experience, from simple fun to the most serious endeavors in science, politics and culture. Keep in mind that this is a *New York Times* publication. *CyberTimes* adheres to the same journalistic standards and most of the style dictates of the print edition of the newspaper."

**[N] FEED MAGAZINE**, http://www.feedmag.com

225 Lafayette St., Suite 606. New York, NY 10012. (212)343-3510. E-mail: alex@feedmag.com, Alex Abramovich, editor. Steven Johnson, editor-in-chief. "*FEED* is a web-only magazine of culture, politics and technology. We are most frequently compared with magazines like *The New Republic*, *Harper's* and *Wired*. Our contributors range in social and political attitudes from John Perry Barlow and Katha Pollitt to Laura Ingraham and Senator Exon. Estab. 1995. Circ. 250,000 visits/month. Pays within 60 days after publication. Byline given. Buys electronic and print rights for specified periods of time. Editorial lead time ranges from a week to a month. Accepts simultaneous submissions and electronic submissions. Reports in 2 weeks on queries and manuscripts.

**Nonfiction:** Book excerpts, essays, exposé, general interest, technical, opinion. "All submissions should contain writing of high caliber, with thoughtful analysis of relevant ideas." Query with or without published clips. Length: 1,000-3,000 words. **Pays $400-1,500.** Sometimes pays expenses of writers on assignment.

**Columns/Departments:** Daily: (500 words); Essay (1,200-2,000 words); Deep Read (2,200-2,800 words); Document (annotation of book passage, graphics, etc.); Dialog (panel members discuss an issue in 3 rounds of commentary, of at least 300 words each); Interviews; BottomFEEDer (funny interviews with people behind the scenes at well-known, often media-related jobs).

**Tips:** "A query familiar with our format, and our sensibility, is always welcome. Proposals by e-mail are preferred. If you have other work online, please provide the URLs. If you're writing about a well-known cultural, political or technological phenomenon it is important to have a new take on the subject, to risk being a little offbeat. Ideas for relevant links are helpful, but not at all required. Writing and analysis of the highest caliber is all we ask. No reprints."

**[N] INKLINGS: Inkspot's Newsletter for Writers**, http://www.inkspot.com/inklings/

E-mail: submissions@inkspot.com. **Contact:** Debbie Ridpath Ohi, editor-in-chief. **75% freelance written.** *Inklings* is a free, biweekly electronic newsletter for writers. Its focus is on the craft and business of writing. Estab. 1995. Circ. over 45,000 subscribers. Pays on publication. Byline given. Purchases first-time, exclusive, one-time rights, plus nonexclusive archiving rights (back issues of *Inklings* are kept online). Editorial lead time 3 months. Accepts simultaneous submissions (if informed) and electronic submissions only. Reports in 2 weeks on queries, 1 month on manuscripts.

**Nonfiction:** How-to, interview. Query with published clips. Word length: 250-1000 (average: 800). **Pays 5-10 ¢/word for assigned articles; 5¢/word for unsolicited articles**.

**Tips:** Guidelines are available by autoresponder: guidelines@inkspot.com.

**[N] NEWYORK.SIDEWALK**, http://www.newyork.sidewalk.com

Microsoft, 825 Eighth Ave., 18th Floor, New York NY 10019. (212)621-7091. Fax: (212)246-3398. E-mail: kateo@micro soft.com. **Contact:** Kate O'Hara, features producers. **85% freelance written.** *NewYork.Sidewalk* is a guide to arts, entertainment and shopping in New York City. Estab. 1997. **Pays on acceptance**. Byline given. Buys all rights. Editorial lead time 3 weeks. Accepts simultaneous submissions. Reports in 1 week on queries and mss.

**Nonfiction:** Contact: Kate O'Hara, features producer. Reviews/previews of NYC events. Query with published clips. Length: 25-100 words. Pays flat weekly rate for contributors. Sometimes pays expenses of writers on assignment.

**Photos:** Contact: Brian Colby, creative director. Send photos with submission. Reviews contact sheets, transparencies, prints. Negotiates payment. Captions, model releases, identification of subjects required. Buys all, universal rights.

**Columns/Departments:** What to Buy, Shop Talk, The A-list, City Survival Guide, Lengths 75-200 words.

**[N] PARENT SOUP**, http://www.parentsoup.com

iVillage, 170 Fifth Ave., New York NY 10010. Fax: (212)604-9133. **Contact:** Linda Osborne, programming director. **10% freelance written.** *Parent Soup* is the #1 online community for parents. Articles are generally 1,500 words or less and focus on information for parents of all ages, from expecting parents to grandparents. Estab. 1996. Circ. 2 million visits/month. **Pays on acceptance**. Byline given. Buys negotiated rights. Accepts simultaneous submissions, previously published submissions and electronic submissions via e-mail to PSeditor@mail.ivillage.com. Reports in 2 weeks on queries and mss.

**Nonfiction:** Book excerpts, humor, personal experience, essays, inspirational, interview/profile, historical/nostalgic. Query with published clips or send complete ms. Length: 200-1,500 words. Negotiates payment individually.

**Tips:** "Please be familiar with *Parent Soup* before submitting article ideas. We are interested in either humor or educating parents about all things concerning the family, including but not limited to health, education, activities, finance, sports, parenting styles, entertainment, technology, holidays, and the ages and stages of children."

**[N] SALON MAGAZINE**, http://www.salon.com

Salon Internet, Inc., 706 Mission St., 2nd Floor, San Francisco, CA. 94103. E-mail: salon@salon.com. **Contact**: Laura Miller, New York editorial director. **50% freelance written.** "Every day, *Salon* publishes stories about books, arts, entertainment, politics and society. Featuring original reviews, interviews, and commentary on topics ranging from technology and travel to parenting and sex." Estab. 1995. Circ. 300,000 visits/month. Pays on publication. Byline given. Purchases exclusive rights for 60 days from the date of the initial publication, unless otherwise negotiated. Editorial lead time varies. Accepts electronic submissions via e-mail to salon@salon.com. Reports on mss in 3 weeks.

**Nonfiction:** Book excerpts, health, family, academia, humor, personal experience, essays, exposé, interview/profile, religious, general interest, technical, opinion, travel, high-tech, politics, media, news-related, book reviews, music reviews. Query with published clips. Length: 500-2,000 words. **Pays $100-1,000 for assigned articles.** Sometimes pays expenses of writers on assignment.

**Photos:** State availability of photos with submission. Reviews prints. **Pays $25-75/photo.** Captions, model releases, identification of subjects required. Buys one-time rights.

**Columns/Departments:** Wanderlust (travel column); 21st (technology); Media Circus (critical updates); NewsReal (national and international stories). Length: under 1,000 words.

**Tips:** "Submit a query or pitch letter to the general e-mail box. It will be forwarded to the appropriate editor. Additional information on how to query or submit articles is available at http://www.salon.com/contact/submissions/. For subjects covered, visit that page on the site and check out the masthead to find out what we publish and who edits it. *Salon* is in perpetual flux, with new sections starting and others being cut all the time."

**N WORD**, http://www.word.com

Zap Corp., 1700 Broadway, 9th Floor, New York NY 10019. **Contact**: Michelle Golden, managing editor. **80% freelance written.** "*Word* is an intelligent, witty, general-interest publication for men and women in their 20s and 30s which features primarily what we call 'creative nonfiction.' *Word* doesn't publish reviews, celebrity or lifestyle stories, or anything self-consciously trendy. *Word* does publish irreverent and insightful personal essays and eccentric humor pieces." Estab. 1995. Circ. 80,000 visits/month. **Pays on acceptance.** Byline given. Buys exclusive electronic rights for 60 days, nonexclusive thereafter. Editorial lead time varies, but generally 1-3 months. Accepts simultaneous submissions, previously published submissions, electronic submissions via email to word_editor@word.com. Reports in 2 weeks on queries; 6 weeks on mss.

**Nonfiction:** Book excerpts, humor, personal experience, essays, inspirational, photo feature, exposé, interview/profile, religious, general interest, historical/nostalgic, opinion, travel. "We *do not want* straight journalism, reviews, celebrity stories, stories about the media, product reviews, or stories about the Internet or digital media." Query with or without published clips or send complete ms. Length: 400-3,000 words. **Pays $200-1,500 for assigned articles; $100-1,000 for unsolicited articles.**

**Photos:** State availability of photos with submission. Reviews contact sheets. Negotiates payment individually. Buys exclusive electronic rights for 60 days, nonexclusive thereafter.

**Columns/Departments:** Work column (people talking about their jobs); Money column (real-life situations involving the drama of money); both 1,500 words.

**Fiction:** "We only publish fiction by well-known writers."

**Tips:** "For aspiring *Word* writers, we have two pieces of advice: 1) Read the magazine before you submit a query, and 2) Don't write in a typical, glib, 'professional' magazine voice—we hate that. *Word* has a very particular 'voice,' and many different subject areas are permissible, as long as they're written in the right kind of voice. Written material is best submitted through e-mail or on disk (but note that disks or hard copy cannot be returned). Please try to keep text submissions under 2,000 words. Photos, video and audiocassettes, and other art pieces should include a SASE if you want us to return them. Our official submissions page is at http://word.com/info/submit.html."

**N WOMEN.COM**, http://women.com

WOMEN.COM Networks, Inc., 1820 Gateway Dr., Suite 100, San Mateo CA 94404. **Contact:** Lisa Stone, director of programming. **30% freelance written.** Women.com is a leading network for women. It includes 20 channels, including Career, Entertainment, Money, Small Business, Travel, Weddings, plus 12 magazine sites, including *Cosmopolitan*, *Redbook* and *Prevention*. Updated daily. Estab. 1995. Audience: 4 million people/month. **Pays on acceptance.** Byline given sometimes. Buys all rights. Editorial lead time 1-3 months. Accepts electronic submissions via e-mail to editor@wo men.com. Reports in a few weeks on queries. No unsolicited mss.

**Nonfiction:** Personal experience (first person OP/EDs), essays, general interest (features). "We don't want long articles." Query with published clips. Length: 300-1,000 words. Negotiates payment individually.

**Tips:** "Be sure to visit the website before you make any queries. See what kinds of things are featured already. When pitching an idea, make web-specific suggestions, i.e., about how you'd lay it out or illustrate it, how it's interactive. Think very visually about your piece. Note that unsolicited manuscripts are not accepted. And note that Women.com is flooded with inquiries; editors look for published writers who have written for national publications and who have web experience, great clips and original ideas."

# Publishers and Their Imprints: A Breakdown

Keeping up with the heavy wave of buying, selling, merging, consolidating and dissolving among publishers and their imprints over the last few years can leave even the most devout *Publishers Weekly* reader dizzy. To help curious writers sort it out, we offer this breakdown of major publishers, who owns whom, and which imprints are under which umbrella. Remember, this list is just a snapshot of how things are shaped at our press time—due to the dynamic nature of the publishing world, it's subject to change at any moment.

## RANDOM HOUSE, INC. (Bertelsmann Book Group)

### The Ballantine Publishing Group
Ballantine Books
Columbine
Del Rey
Fawcett (Crest, Gold Medal, Juniper)
House of Collectibles
Ivy
Library of Contemporary Thought
One World

### Bantam Dell Publishing Group
Bantam Classics
Bantam Crime Line
Bantam Fanfare
Bantam Spectra
Delacorte Press
Dell Books
Delta Books
Dial Press
DTP
Island Books
Laurel Books

### Doubleday Broadway Publishing Group
Broadway Books
Currency
Doubleday
Doubleday Religious Publishing
Image Books
Main Street Books
Nan A. Talese
WaterBrook Press

### The Crown Publishing Group
Bell Tower
Clarkson Potter
Crown Publishers Inc.
Custom Publishing
Harmony Books
Living Language
Park Lane Press
Three Rivers Press

### Fodor's Travel Publications

### Knopf Publishing Group
Everyman's Library
Alfred A. Knopf Inc.
Pantheon Books
Schocken Books
Vintage Anchor Publishing
    Anchor
    Vintage

### Random House Audio Publishing Group
BDD House Audio Publishing
Random House Audio Publishing

## Random House Children's Publishing

Bantam Books for Young Readers
Crown Books for Young Readers
CTW Publishing
Delacorte Press Books for Young Readers
Doubleday Books for Young Readers
Dragonfly Books
First Choice Chapter Books
Knopf Books for Young Readers
Knopf Paperbacks
Laurel Leaf
Picture Yearling
Random House Children's Media
Random House Children's Publishing
Random House Entertainment
Skylark
Starfire
Yearling

## Random House Diversified Publishing Group

Children's Classics
Crescent Books
Derrydale
Gramercy Books
Gramercy Park Gift & Stationery
JellyBean Press
Random House Large Print Publishing
Wings Books

## Random House International

Bantam Doubleday Dell of Canada
Knopf
Knopf Canada
Random House of Canada
Random House UK

## Random House New Media

## Random House Trade Group

The Modern Library
Random House Adult Trade Books
Villard Books

## Random House Information Group

Discovery Books
Princeton Review
Random House Reference & Information
    Publishing
Sierra Club Adult Books
Times Books
        Times Business Books

# SIMON & SCHUSTER (Viacom, Inc.)

## Pocket Books

Archway Paperbacks
Minstrel Books
MTV Books
Pocket Books Hardcover
Pocket Books Trade Paperbacks
Sonnet
Washington Square Press

## Simon & Schuster Children's Publishing

Aladdin Paperbacks
Atheneum Books for Young Readers
Little Simon
Margaret K. McElderry Books
Simon & Schuster Books for Young Readers
Simon Spotlight
Simon & Schuster Interactive

## Simon & Schuster Audio

## Simon & Schuster Trade

Fireside
The Free Press
Scribner
        Lisa Drew Books
        Rawson Associates
Simon & Schuster
Simon & Schuster Editions
Simon & Schuster Libros en Espanol
Touchstone

# PENGUIN PUTNAM INC. (Pearson)

## Penguin USA

### Viking Penguin
Penguin
Penguin Studio
Viking

### Dutton Signet
DAW Books
Dutton
Mentor
Meridian
New American Library (NAL)
Obelisk
Onyx
Pelham
Plume
ROC
Signet
Topaz

## The Putnam Berkley Group
Ace
Berkley Books
Berkley Prime Crime
Boulevard
HP Books
Jove
Perigee
Price Stern Sloan, Inc.
G.P. Putnam's Sons
Riverhead
Jeremy P. Tarcher

## Penguin Putnam Books for Young Readers Group
Dial Books for Young Readers
Dutton Children's Books
Phyllis Fogelman Books
Grosset & Dunlap
Philomel Books
Planet Dexter
Price Stern Sloan, Inc.
Puffin
   PaperStar
G.P. Putnam's Sons
Viking Children's Books
Frederick Warne
Wee Sing

# HARPERCOLLINS (Rupert Murdoch)

Cliff Street Books
HarperAudio
HarperBusiness
HarperCollins
HarperCollins Children's Books
HarperEdge
HarperEntertainment
HarperEntertainment Children's Books
HarperFlamingo
HarperHorizon
HarperPaperbacks
HarperPerennial
HarperPrism
HarperResource

HarperSanFrancisco
HarperTaste
HarperTrophy
HarperVoyager
Regan Books
Zondervan Publishing House

HarperCollinsAustralia
HarperCollinsCanada
HarperCollinsUK

• *At press time, HarperCollins
   acquired Avon and William
   Morrow from the Hearst Corporation.*

# TIME WARNER

## Warner Books

Mysterious Press
Warner Aspect
Warner Romance
Warner Vision

## Time Life Inc.

## Time Warner Audiobooks

## Little, Brown and Company

Back Bay Books
Bullfinch Press
Little, Brown Books for Children and
    Young Adults

# HOLTZBRINCK

## Farrar Straus & Giroux

Faber & Faber Inc.
Farrar Straus & Giroux Books for Young
    Readers
        Aerial Fiction
        Francis Foster Books
        Mirasol/Libros Juveniles
        R and S Books
        Sunburst Paperbacks
Hill and Wang
Noonday Press
North Point Press
Sunburst Books

## Henry Holt & Co.

Henry Holt & Co. Books for Young Readers
    Edge Books
    Red Feather Books
Henry Holt Reference Books
John Macrae Books
Bill Martin Jr. Books
Metropolitan Books
Owl Books
Marian Wood Books

## St. Martin's

Bedford Books
Buzz Books
Dead Letter
Tom Doherty Associates, Inc.
    TOR
    Forge
Thomas Dunne Books
Griffin
Let's Go
Picador
St. Martin's Paperbacks
St. Martin's Press
St. Martin's Scholarly & Reference
Stonewall Inn
Truman Talley Books

# HEARST BOOKS

## Avon

Avon Eos
Avon Flare
Bard
Camelot
Mass Market
Spike
Tempest
Trade Paperback
Twilight
WholeCare

## William Morrow

Beech Tree Books
Eagle Brook
Greenwillow Books
Lothrop, Lee & Shepard Books
William Morrow Books
Morrow Junior Books
Mulberry Books
Quill Trade Paperbacks
Tupelo Books
Rob Weisbach Books

# Literary Agents

The publishing world is never static. There's the quiet ebb and flow of imprints expanding and editors moving, and then there's the cataclysmic explosion when two publishing giants collide to become one. Through it all, the literary agent has become an increasingly important mediator, connecting writers, ideas and publishers to form new books.

With an increasing emphasis on profit margins, many of the larger publishers have eliminated the entry level editorial assistants primarily responsible for reading manuscripts sent in by writers—"over the transom" to the "slush pile," in the jargon. As a result, agents have taken over some of this task, separating the literary wheat from the chaff and forwarding the promising manuscripts on to possible publishers. Most publishers remain open to receiving at least query letters directly from authors, but some of the largest publishers accept agented submissions only.

As you look through the Book Publishers section of *Writer's Market*, you will see the symbol Ⓐ at the beginning of some listings. This symbol denotes publishers that accept submissions only from agents. If you find a book publisher that is a perfect market for your work but only reads agented manuscripts, contacting an agent is your next logical step.

Finding an agent is *not* easier than finding a publisher. It may even be harder, since there are far fewer agents than publishing companies. However, if you do secure representation, your "reach" into the publishing world has extended to include everyone that agent knows.

## CHOOSING AND USING AN AGENT

Literary agents, like authors, come in all shapes and sizes, with different areas of interest and expertise. It's to your advantage to take the time and choose an agent who is most closely aligned to your interests and your manuscript's subject.

The agents listed in this section have all indicated that they are open to working with new, previously unpublished writers as well as published writers. None of the agents listed here charge a "reading fee," which is money paid to an agent to cover the time and effort in reading a manuscript or a few sample chapters. While there is nothing wrong with charging a reading fee (after all, agents have to make a living too), we encourage writers to first try agents that do not.

Most of the agents listed here are members of AAR, the Association of Authors' Representatives. The AAR is a voluntary professional organization, whose members agree to abide by a strict code of ethics that prohibits charging fees for reading a manuscript or editorial services or receiving "consideration fees" for successful referrals to third parties.

We've also added a small section of script agents, all members of the Writers' Guild of America (WGA). WGA signatory agencies are prohibited from charging fees from WGA members; most do not charge fees of nonmembers, as well.

Literary agent Lori Perkins's article, How to Find (and Keep) the Right Agent, will arm you with the basics of choosing and using a literary agent. From query protocol to typical activities in her day, she outlines what you can expect in seeking representation and what to do after you've secured it.

The listings that follow Perkins's article contain the information you need to determine if an agent is suitable for your work. Read each listing carefully to see if an agency specializes in your subject areas. Or go straight to the Literary Agent Subject Index found after the listings to compile a list of agencies specifically interested in the subjects you write. We've broken the Subject Index into three main categories: Nonfiction, Fiction and Scripts.

# How to Find (and Keep) the Right Agent

BY LORI PERKINS

I have always wanted to get published.

Before I became an agent, I was a journalist, and before that I was an aspiring writer. After nearly two decades of working with words for a living, I am finally the author of two books of my very own. I can honestly say that I would not be published, and published well, without the guidance of my agent. So I write this article from both sides of the fence.

Before I became a literary agent, I used to think New York literary agents were mystical beings who would change my life with one phone call, if only they would respond to my query letters. When I finally left the news business and became an agent, I was honestly surprised to find that agents were mere mortals with no super powers, only high-powered rolodexes and a nearly insane desire to get people published.

Now that I'm on the other side, I know that a literary agent with a good reputation receives at least a thousand query letters a month. Your work as a writer has to be exceptional (and professional) from the beginning, because the competition is fierce, and the publishing world is changing rapidly.

As someone who has been on the outside looking in and now as an insider looking out, I write this article to give you an insider's view on how to get and keep the right agent for you.

## WHAT IS AN AGENT?

You'd be surprised at the number of writers who think an agent is their editor, business manager, lawyer, publicist, banker, therapist, groupie, mother, new best friend, fairy god-mother—the list is endless.

A synonym for agent is "author's representative," and that really is a perfect definition of the agent's role. An agent is your representative to the publishing industry, whom you hire to negotiate in your best interests. What each agent does can vary slightly from agent to agent, but it generally falls into the following basic tasks (assuming your material is ready for submission):

- knowing which editors to send your work to;
- helping you choose the right publisher/editor (should more than one be interested);
- negotiating the terms of your contract;
- representing the foreign and subsidiary rights to your book (film, magazine, audio, elec-tronic, etc.);
- making sure your publisher keeps you informed of your book's progress before and after publication;
- preparing your next project for submission and negotiating those terms;

**LORI PERKINS** *is the founding partner in Perkins, Rubie & Associates, a New York literary agency. She has been a literary agent for 15 years. She is currently team-teaching a class on agenting at NYU's Center for Publishing. Prior to becoming an agent, she was the publisher of* The Uptown Dispatch, *a Manhattan newspaper. She is the author of* The Insider's Guide to Finding and Keeping an Agent *(Writer's Digest Books) and* The Cheapskate's Guide to Entertaining: How to Throw Fabulous Parties on a Modest Budget *(Carol Publishing).*

- keeping on top of the financial and legal matters related to your books after publication;
- giving you career guidance, for both the long and short term, along the way.

## DO YOU REALLY NEED AN AGENT?

You may now be saying to yourself, that's all very nice, but do I really need an agent? Couldn't I do all that myself? Look at the list of things an agent does and tell me you have the time, ability and inclination to handle it all without making mistakes that could set back your career in ways you can't even imagine. Or let me put it to you another way: only a fool has himself for a client.

That's not to say authors don't sell books themselves, but there's much more to being an agent than making a sale. Often, when an author sells his own book, the editor will refer him to an agent to guide him through the contract and production process and fill him in on all the publishing details the editor doesn't have the time to explain. Editors edit.

Agents know what the industry norms are (such as how much the industry is paying right now for certain kinds of books, what rights are selling, where a house is flexible on contract terms, etc.); they know the history of the publisher with your kind of book, as well as the strengths and weaknesses of your editor, and the industry gossip on which publishing houses are about to merge.

And agents have clout. When your publisher (and editor) does a deal with your agent, the entire agency roster is on your side. They don't want to upset your agent because it might affect another book they have under contract or their chances of getting one of your agent's really hot writers when their next book comes up.

But that's not the only reason you need an agent. When I entered the publishing business, I was stunned at the sheer number of books published every year (about 65,000 in 1997). Only someone who eats (we lunch professionally), sleeps, and schmoozes books for a living could possibly keep up with who's buying what for how much and why. Writers write. If you're spending the amount of time necessary to keep up with the publishing business, than you are either working for *Publishers Weekly* or not as serious about writing as you should be.

## WHAT DOES AN AGENT REALLY DO?

When I go to writers' conferences, authors are always amazed that I don't read manuscripts in the office and that I read at the same speed they do. One author actually thought I had some special ability to read manuscripts at super-human speed. Most of the time, we don't even read the query letters sent to us. We have assistants who read queries and manuscripts for us.

Most of the people who act as the first screening level in an agent's office are young, and do not have much editorial experience. They are instructed to reject at least 90 percent of the material that comes into the office. But they are usually eager to find new talent, and may one day grow into agents or editors themselves.

It is very rare for an established agent to take on a writer from the unsolicited manuscripts, which those in publishing affectionately call "the slush pile," (or just "slush,") or the "unsolicit-eds." This happens so rarely nowadays, that when it does, it makes the news.

What agents do in the office is talk on the phone, mostly to editors. They "pitch" the books they are currently trying to sell, follow-up on submissions they've already made, negotiate terms for books that an editor has made an offer on, and guide their clients through the shaping process in putting together their next book.

They also over-see an assortment of assistants who photocopy, collate, staple (and sometimes mutilate) the material they've pitched to the editors, as well as give reader's reports on manuscripts and cull through the slush.

The way I work, which is similar to many agents I am friendly with, is I make three to five copies of a novel and ten copies of a nonfiction proposal. It takes about two weeks to get a response on the average nonfiction proposal. I hope to hear from editors of fiction within a month, but it often takes longer because it's a holiday season or the editor isn't really looking for new fiction or the market is tight. I spend a lot of time following up on my submissions. I usually have 20 projects on submission at one time.

I negotiate contracts too, making sure there are no onerous clauses that entitle the publisher to the writer's first book, and first born child, as well. I also chase down writers' payments.

## A DAY IN THE LIFE OF AN AGENT

The best way to tell you what agents really do is to describe a typical work day. I start at 10:00 a.m. because editors straggle into their office late, and I work until 6:00 p.m. The first thing I do is call all the editors who have promised to respond to me by that day and check up on projects on submission. Most of the time I leave a message, and the editors get back to me after lunch.

I then prepare the day's multiple submissions, which includes writing pitch letters, calling all the editors and pitching the book, and then getting everything packaged by 5:00 p.m. for UPS.

Lunch is an extremely important part of my business. It's where I get to know an individual editor's taste, learn what they and their publishing house are buying right now, hear industry gossip, and pitch my agency for future projects. A good, productive lunch can net me up to ten book sales over a year. I rarely remember what I've eaten, but I always remember what the editor is interested in. Lunch is therefore sacred, and I do it seriously. I usually have lunch at 12:30 p.m., which means I leave my office at noon to travel. Lunch lasts about two hours, and I'm always back at my desk by 3:00 p.m. I tell you this because you should never call an agent between noon and 3:00 New York time, unless you just want to leave a message. We should be out to lunch, and if we are in our office answering phone calls, we're not doing our job.

I keep a 16-page client list, which describes the past and present work of all the agency's authors. I give this to every editor I have lunch with, and I tell them to look it over carefully when they get back to the office and to let me know if there are clients or titles that interest them. I suggest they make copies and share it with other editors. This client list is a very valuable calling card, but one I only give out face to face. I cannot tell you the number of deals that have come about as a result of leaving this list with editors.

During the afternoon I call back editors who have returned my calls, go through the mail, perhaps read over a contract or prepare a foreign mailing (I have 11 foreign agents who represent my books throughout the world and I send them monthly bulletins about my books along with a mailing).

From 5:00 to 6:00 p.m., I call my authors because I don't have to worry about being interrupted by editors since their work day is over. I can devote my full attention to my authors this way. I also return phone calls from the West Coast at this time, because they are just returning from their lunches.

I get home, have dinner, put my son to sleep, unwind, and try to read at least an hour each weeknight and five hours over the weekend. I average about one novel and four or five proposals a week.

I represent about 50 writers, each of whom writes at least 1 book a year; some write as many as 4. I have one author who wrote 10 books this year, but he's an exception. My stable of writers takes up most of my reading time. The same is true of my business partner, Peter Rubie. We recently brought on a new agent, June Clark, so she is the one who is going through the unsoliciteds and taking on new clients. After 6 months, she has about 20 clients now. She will have about 50 by the end of next year.

Most agents represent between 50 and 75 writers. If an agent is established, she is quite busy with the authors she has already made a commitment to and will relegate responding to query letters as a lesser priority. As I mentioned, most agents assign this task to the lowliest person in their office or wait until the pile is so high you can cut through it with a scythe.

Right now, we receive about 1,000 query letters a month, so it takes a while to respond to all the mail. Our new associate sifts through the agency's unsolicited mail. If there is something intriguing that she is not interested in taking on herself, she will call our attention to those letters that fit our tastes. My partner and I then read through this material when we have a free moment, which is very rare. This is why it often takes up to three months to get a form rejection in your self-addressed stamped envelope (SASE). This is also why it's so important for you to include that SASE in your mailing.

## THE CHANGING PUBLISHING INDUSTRY

Right now, book publishing is going through major changes that will affect how books are published and how they are sold in the 21st century. While many in publishing feel that the sky is about to fall, I think it is really a time of great transition, similar to that in the early '90s when music recording went from LPs to CDs.

There have been two dramatic changes in publishing in the last three years. The first is the conglomeration of publishing and entertainment companies, which has resulted in approximately 65 percent of the publishing industry being owned by 2 giant companies. The second major change is the advent of book sales through the Internet. What this means is that there are fewer major publishers to buy and publish your books, while there are more ways for the reader to buy books.

What this will mean for the writer is that it will become harder to sell your book to the big publishers (even with an agent), but new, smaller publishing companies will emerge from the field, especially since the demand for product (well-written books) will continue to grow as it becomes easier for more and more readers to buy books. It means that for the right writers, it's a whole new ballgame.

Just as the publishing market has changed, a good agent changes her taste and skills with the market. While agents will always be selling to the major publishers, they will be the writer's guide to these new publishers and technologies.

Although I represent both fiction and nonfiction, nearly all the agency's clients have been, or still are, journalists. So when one market declines, we often move a client into another area of that market (from adult to young adult fiction or to nonfiction) while their genre is in a slump, so they can continue to publish (and pay their mortgages).

Because my partner and I were both journalists before we became agents, we can also come up with ideas for our clients when their own ideas don't sell. We've received quite a reputation for coming up with book ideas from editors, and now editors often call us with books that they're looking for. We represent the author, not just the book. About a third of our business is now done this way.

## HOW DO I FIND THE RIGHT AGENT?

The best way to get an agent is to be informed, and that doesn't mean clipping the *USA Today* article about how much John Grisham got for his latest book. It means buying a book like this one, using a specialized directory such as the *Guide to Literary Agents* (Writer's Digest Books) or going to the library, or getting online, and doing a little research. You will quickly learn that there are about 1,000 literary agents throughout the country and, just like writers, they are all different.

You could do a mass mailing to all agents listed, but that's not a wise investment. The best thing to do is to narrow your field of submission by finding out what areas the agents specialize in and matching them to your type of book.

All books fall into a category or genre, and "fiction," "nonfiction," "mainstream," or "bestseller" are not specific enough. All agents specialize in some area of publishing. It's impossible nowadays to be a generalist, although most of us are open to new areas as they open up.

For instance, my areas of expertise are in dark fiction, which includes horror, thrillers and some literary fiction, as well as nonfiction about popular culture. My partner specializes in literate science fiction and fantasy, mysteries, crime novels and narrative nonfiction. Recently, the adult horror market crashed, but the young adult horror market has boomed, so many of my former adult horror writers are now writing for the young adult and middle grade market.

Another area of niche publishing that has recently opened up is serious books about popular science, such as *The Science of Star Wars* (St. Martin's Press) or *Cybertrek: The Computers of Star Trek* (Basic Books). Both of these titles were written by authors who had published both science fiction and nonfiction.

The single most frequent reason I reject query letters is because I don't handle the material I am being queried on. You can save yourself postage and aggravation if you do this research ahead of time.

Once you know the kind of book you are writing, you should join the professional organization that supports those writers. All genres have associations (Romance Writers of America, Science Fiction Writers of America, etc.), as do professions (The Society of Journalists and Authors). Many of these organizations compile a list of agents representing their kind of book. Some charge nonmembers for access to this list, others do not.

## HOW DO I GET THE RIGHT AGENT TO REPRESENT ME?

Don't try to dazzle or impress a prospective agent with gimmicks. Be direct. In a one-page query letter, tell me what your book is about and who you are. Let your work speak for itself. Don't tell me how your wife, kids, aunt and high school English teacher think you are the next Stephen King. I only want to know if you were a high school track star or Honda Salesman of the Year if it relates directly to your book. The only background information I want in a query letter is your relevant publishing history, educational information (writing workshops, who you've studied with/under, etc.), and maybe some biographical information that relates directly to your book (such as the fact that you're a doctor and you've written a medical thriller).

Don't overwhelm me. If you've been writing unpublished for 16 years and have 17 novels in the closet, don't try to pitch all of them to me at once. Just send a query about the one you think is best, with a brief line about how you have other completed manuscripts, should I be interested in seeing something else. Show me that you've done some research. If you took the time to go to *Writer's Market*, and chose me from that listing, tell me so in your letter. You might even want to start your letter off that way. It will definitely get my attention.

If you've joined a writer's organization, tell me. If they gave you my name, tell me that. If you got my name from one of my clients, definitely tell me that, because if a client of mine asks me to look at something from a new writer, it moves to the top of my pile. If you think your book is similar to a book you know I've represented, tell me that as well.

Below is a basic example of a query letter that would grab my interest:

"Dear Ms. Perkins:
I read your article on agents in the *2000 Writer's Market* and I thought you might be interested in seeing an outline and sample chapters of my novel, (title). It's about (brief description).
For your information, I am a member of (professional organization) and I have attended (University writing program). My short stories have appeared in (publications).
I've enclosed an SASE for your response."

The only other thing you should do is to make sure your presentation to me is professional. That means typed, double-spaced on 8½ × 11 nonerasable paper with a SASE with the proper postage. Your query letter should be free of typographical and grammatical errors.

Because of the sheer volume of queries our agency receives and the hours it takes to go through everything, I prefer to receive a simple query letter first and additional material only if I ask for it. The less material you send, the sooner someone will respond to you.

Many agents are now on the Internet and some welcome e-mail queries, though we do not accept queries this way. You can also fax a query letter, especially if the book you want to write is timely, but you may not get any response at all from an e-mail or fax query, which is why I prefer an SASE. Do not query about sending a query letter. Do not send disks unsolicited. Never send your whole novel, even over the Internet.

## HOW DOES THE AGENT/WRITER RELATIONSHIP WORK?

Okay, let's assume you receive a letter from me requesting sample chapters and an outline. Take your time and send me the most polished material you can. Send me the first three chapters of your novel or representative chapters of nonfiction, or published articles about that topic.

Then be patient. I will endeavor to get back to you within six weeks, but life often gets in the way. For instance, things slow down over the Thanksgiving to New Year's holiday season, as well as in the summer. If you haven't heard from me in six weeks, feel comfortable in giving me a polite phone call asking me for an estimate of when I should be able to get to your work. Don't e-mail me or fax me.

Let's assume I like what you've sent and I've read the whole novel or proposal. I might ask you to make some changes that I feel will help sell the book or make it more commercial. Trust my judgment. I don't get paid until I sell your work, and that's the only reason I am asking for these changes.

You send me the work, and we agree it's ready to go out. You then become my client with a verbal handshake over the phone.

Some literary agencies have agency contracts, but I do not. When I sell a book, the publishing contract includes a clause that insures I am the agent of record for that title until the rights revert. That's all I need.

I then go over the terms of our representation, which are pretty standard. Most agents today take a 15 percent commission on domestic sales, 20 percent on foreign sales (because they split this with foreign agents). The older (established prior to 1975) and bigger agencies take a 10 percent commission, and some agencies charge for expenses such as phone calls, faxes, postage, etc., but most also charge for copying.

Your material is then sent out to multiple editors and we wait. A sale can be made in a week (more likely for nonfiction) and it has taken me up to 3 years to sell a novel (rejected by 33 publishers).

If your work is under submission and you haven't heard from me in six weeks, by all means give me a call to ask what's happening. However, if you haven't heard from me it means that no one has gotten back to me, or I've only had rejections. You will definitely hear from me if I've got an offer for your book. Sometimes, I send an author copies of relevant rejection letters (maybe the editor had something to say that was thought-provoking), but it's not a regular procedure, unless you request it.

Once I have an offer for your book, I go over it with you. We discuss everything from how much money you get and how you get it to when you will deliver the manuscript. Once the terms of the agreement are made, I usually get you and your editor together over the phone.

It usually takes four to six weeks for me to receive the contract, which I go over with the publisher's contracts department and then send on to you for your signature. You return it to me, and we wait another four to six weeks for the signing payment.

You then write the book, or make the changes that the editor requested. All editorial matters go directly to your editor, but you should keep me informed of your progress on the book, especially if you are having problems with your editor.

Sometimes I have to interfere on your behalf.

Let's say you deliver your manuscript and your editor loves it. I then write a letter requesting your delivery and acceptance payment, and we wait at least another six weeks for that.

I then begin asking you about your next book. You draw up an outline and sample chapters (whether it's fiction or nonfiction), and I send it to your editor. We then wait for her response.

## TIPS TO IMPROVE THE AUTHOR/AGENT RELATIONSHIP

**Be mindful of your agent's schedule**. Don't call during lunch hours. Don't call more than once a day. Remember that during the summer, publishers and agents close at noon on Fridays.

**Be mindful of your agent's workload**. Remember that we have many clients (and many books to read). If we don't get to something right away, it is not a comment on our love for you or your work. It just means we are overwhelmed.

**Say "Thank you" once in awhile**. You can't imagine how nice it is to hear those words or see them in a letter or a card. Yes, it's my job, but it's nice to know that you think I did it well.

# Literary & Script Agents: The Listings

This section consists of 80 individual agency listings, followed by a Subject Index of nonfiction and fiction book and script categories which list the names of agencies that have expressed an interest in manuscripts on that subject. We've included listings for both literary and script agents. Literary agents are interested in nonfiction and fiction book manuscripts while script agents read only television and movie scripts.

You can approach the information listed here in two ways. You can skim through the listings and see if an agent stands out as particularly right for your manuscript and proceed from there. Or you can check the Subject Indexes that follow these listings to focus your search more narrowly. Cross-referencing categories and concentrating on those agents interested in two or more aspects of your manuscript might increase your chances of success.

Either way, it is important to carefully read the information contained in the listing. Each agency has different interests, submission requirements and response times. They'll tell you what they want, what they don't want, and how they want to receive it. Try to follow their directions as closely as possible. For these agents in particular, time is extremely important, and wasting theirs won't help your case.

There are several sections to each listing. The first paragraph lists the agency's name, address and contact information. It also includes when the agency was established, how many clients it represents and what percentage of those clients are new/previously unpublished writers. It offers the agency's self-described areas of specialization and a breakdown of the different types of manuscripts it handles (nonfiction, fiction, movie scripts, etc.).

The first subsection is **Members Agents**, which lists the individuals who work at the agency. The next is **Handles**, which outlines the different nonfiction and fiction categories an agency will look at. **How to Contact** specifies how agents want to receive material and how long you should wait for their response. **Needs** identifies subjects they are particularly interested in seeing, as well as what they definitely do not handle and will not look at. **Recent Sales** is pretty self-explanatory. **Terms** offers information on the commission an agent takes (domestic and foreign), if a written contract is offered, and whether and what miscellaneous expenses are charged to an author's account. **Writers' Conferences** identifies conferences that agent attends. And **Tips** presents words of advice an agent might want to give prospective authors.

## FOR MORE ON THE SUBJECT . . .

The *Guide to Literary Agents* (Writer's Digest Books) offers 550 agent listings and a wealth of informational articles on the author/agent relationship and other related topics.

## LITERARY AGENTS

**[N] BETSY AMSTER LITERARY ENTERPRISES**, P.O. Box 27788, Los Angeles CA 90027-0788. **Contact:** Betsy Amster. Estab. 1992. Member of AAR. Represents over 50 clients. 40% of clients are new/unpublished writers. Currently handles: 75% nonfiction books; 25% novels.

●  Prior to opening her agency, Ms. Amster was an editor at Pantheon and Vintage for 10 years and served as editorial director for the Globe Pequot Press for 2 years. "This experience gives me a wider perspective on the business and the ability to give focused editorial feedback to my clients."

**Represents:** Nonfiction books, novels. **Considers these nonfiction areas:** biography/autobiography; business; child guidance/parenting; cyberculture; ethnic/cultural interests; gardening; health/medicine; history; how-to; money/finance/

economics; popular culture; psychology; self-help/personal improvement; sociology; women's issues/women's studies. **Considers these fiction areas:** detective/police/crime; ethnic; literary; mystery/suspense.

**How to Contact:** For fiction, send query and first page. For nonfiction, send query only. For both, "include SASE or no response." Reports in 1 month on queries; 2 months on mss.

**Needs:** Actively seeking "outstanding literary fiction (the next Jane Smiley or Wally Lamb) and high profile self-help/psychology." Does not want to receive poetry, children's books, romances, westerns, science fiction. Obtains new clients through recommendations from others, solicitation, conferences.

**Recent Sales:** *Esperanza's Box of Saints* (Scribner); *Chicana Falsa and Other Stories of Death, Identity, and Oxnard*, by Michele M. Serros (Riverhead); *Darkest Desire: The Wolf's Own Tale* (Ecco); *Baby Minds: Recognizing and Fostering Your Infant's Intellectual Development in the Critical First Years* (Bantam); *The Highly Sensitive Person in Love* (Broadway).

**Terms:** Agent receives 15% commission on domestic sales. Offers written contract, binding for 1-2 years. 60 days notice must be given to terminate contract. Charges for photocopying, postage, long distance phone calls, messengers and galleys and books used in submissions to foreign and film agents and to magazines for first serial rights.

**Writers' Conferences:** Maui Writers Conference; Pacific Northwest Conference; San Diego Writers Conference; UCLA Writers Conference.

**LORETTA BARRETT BOOKS INC.**, 101 Fifth Ave., New York NY 10003. (212)242-3420. Fax: (212)691-9418. E-mail: lbarbooks@aol.com. President: Loretta A. Barrett. **Contact:** Kirsten Lundell or Loretta A. Barrett. Estab. 1990. Member of AAR. Represents 70 clients. Specializes in general interest books. Currently handles: 25% fiction; 75% nonfiction.

● Prior to opening her agency, Ms. Barrett was vice president and executive editor at Doubleday for 25 years.

**Represents: Considers all areas of nonfiction. Considers these fiction areas:** action/adventure; cartoon/comic; confessional; contemporary issues; detective/police/crime; ethnic; experimental; family saga; fantasy; feminist; gay; glitz; historical; humor/satire; lesbian; literary; mainstream; mystery/suspense; psychic/supernatural; religious/inspirational; romance; sports; thriller/espionage.

**How to Contact:** Query first with SASE. Reports in 6 weeks on queries.

**Recent Sales:** Sold about 20 titles in the last year. Prefers not to share information on specific sales.

**Terms:** Agent receives 15% commission on domestic sales; 20% on foreign sales. Offers written contract. Charges for shipping and photocopying.

**Writers' Conferences:** San Diego State University Writer's Conference; Maui Writer's Conference.

**[N] PAM BERNSTEIN & ASSOCIATES, INC.**, 790 Madison Ave., Suite 310, New York NY 10021. (212)288-1700. Fax: (212)288-3054. **Contact:** Pam Bernstein or Donna Downing. Estab. 1992. Member of AAR. Represents 50 clients. 20% of clients are new/previously unpublished writers. Specializes in commercial adult fiction and nonfiction. Currently handles: 60% nonfiction books; 40% fiction.

● Prior to becoming agents, Ms. Bernstein served as vice president with the William Morris Agency; Ms. Downing was in public relations.

**Represents: Considers these nonfiction areas:** child guidance/parenting; cooking/food/nutrition; current affairs; government/politics/law; health/medicine; how-to; New Age/metaphysics; popular culture; psychology; religious/inspirational; self-help/personal improvement; sociology; true crime/investigative; women's issues/women's studies. **Considers these fiction areas:** contemporary issues; detective/police/crime; ethnic; historical; mainstream; mystery/suspense; romance (contemporary); thriller/espionage.

**How to Contact:** Query. Reports in 2 weeks on queries; 1 month on mss. Include postage for return of ms.

**Needs:** Obtains new clients through referrals from published authors.

**Recent Sales:** Sold 25 titles in the last year. *Tempest Rising*, by Diane McKinney-Whetstone (William Morrow); *The Misdiagnosed Child*, by Janice and Demitri Papolos (Broadway).

**Terms:** Agent receives 15% commission on domestic sales; 20% on foreign sales. Offers written contract, binding for 3 years, with 30 day cancellation clause. 100% of business is derived from commissions on sales. Charges for postage and photocopying.

**CURTIS BROWN LTD.**, 10 Astor Place, New York NY 10003-6935. (212)473-5400. Member of AAR; signatory of WGA. Perry Knowlton, chairman & CEO. Peter L. Ginsberg, president.

**Member Agents:** Laura Blake Peterson; Ellen Geiger; Emilie Jacobson, vice president; Maureen Walters, vice president; Virginia Knowlton; Timothy Knowlton, COO (film, screenplays, plays); Marilyn Marlow, executive vice president; Ed Wintle (film, screenplays, plays); Jennifer MacDonald; Andrew Pope; Clyde Taylor; Mitchell Waters; Dave Barber (translation rights).

**Represents:** Nonfiction books, juvenile books, novels, novellas, short story collections, poetry books. **All categories of nonfiction and fiction considered.**

**How to Contact:** No unsolicited mss. Query first with SASE. Reports in 3 weeks on queries; 5 weeks on mss (only if requested).

**Needs:** Obtains new clients through recommendations from others, solicitation, at conferences and query letters.

**Recent Sales:** Prefers not to share information on specific sales.

**Terms:** Offers written contract. Charges for photocopying, some postage.

**Also Handles:** Movie scripts (feature film), TV scripts (TV MOW), stage plays. Considers these script subject areas:

action/adventure; comedy; detective/police/crime; ethnic; feminist; gay; historical; horror; lesbian; mainstream; mystery/suspense; psychic/supernatural; romantic comedy and drama; thriller; westerns/frontier.

**SHEREE BYKOFSKY ASSOCIATES, INC.**, 16 W. 36th St., 13th Floor, New York NY 10018. Website: http://www.users.interport.net/~sheree. **Contact:** Sheree Bykofsky. Estab. 1984. Incorporated 1991. Member of AAR, ASJA, WNBA. Represents "a limited number" of clients. Specializes in popular reference nonfiction. Currently handles: 80% nonfiction; 20% fiction.
- Prior to opening her agency, Ms. Bykofsky served as executive editor of The Stonesong Press and managing editor of Chiron Press. She is also the author or co-author of more than 10 books.
**Represents:** Nonfiction, commercial and literary fiction. **Considers all nonfiction areas,** especially biography/autobiography; business; child guidance/parenting; cooking/foods/nutrition; current affairs; ethnic/cultural interests; gay/lesbian issues; health/medicine; history; how-to; humor; music/dance/theater/film; popular culture; psychology; inspirational; self-help/personal improvement; true crime/investigative; women's issues/women's studies. "I have wide-ranging interests, but it really depends on quality of writing, originality, and how a particular project appeals to me (or not). I take on very little fiction unless I completely love it—it doesn't matter what area or genre."
**How to Contact:** Query with SASE. No unsolicited mss or phone calls. Reports in 1 week on short queries; 1 month on solicited mss.
**Needs:** No poetry, children's, screenplays. Obtains new clients through recommendations from others.
**Recent Sales:** Sold 50 titles in the last year. *Falling Flesh Just Ahead*, by Lee Potts (Longstreet); *Tripping*, by Charles Hayes (Viking); and *The Magic of Christmas Miracles* and *Mother's Miracles*, by Jamie Miller, Jennifer Basye Sander and Laura Lewis (Morrow).
**Terms:** Agent receives 15% commission on domestic sales; 15% on foreign sales. Offers written contract, binding for 1 year "usually." Charges for postage, photocopying and fax.
**Writers' Conferences:** ASJA (NYC); Asilomar (Pacific Grove CA); Kent State; Southwestern Writers; Willamette (Portland); Dorothy Canfield Fisher (San Diego); Writers Union (Maui); Pacific NW; IWWG; and many others.
**Tips:** "Read the agent listing carefully and comply with guidelines."

**C G & W ASSOCIATES**, 252 Stanford Ave. (or P.O. Box 7613), Menlo Park CA 94025-6328. (650)854-1020. Fax: (650)854-1020. E-mail: sallyconley@msn.com. **Contact:** Sally Conley. Estab. 1996. Represents 11 clients. 72% of clients are new/unpublished writers. Specializes in literary and commercial mainstream fiction. Currently handles: 18% nonfiction books; 82% novels.
- Prior to opening her agency, Ms. Conley spent 20 years as co-owner of The Guild Bookstore (Menlo Park, CA) and was a Peace Corps volunteer for women in development from 1993-96.
**Represents:** Nonfiction books, novels. **Considers these nonfiction areas:** biography/autobiography; current affairs; ethnic/cultural interests; women's issues/women's studies. **Considers these fiction areas:** action/adventure; confessional; contemporary issues; detective/police/crime; ethnic; family saga; glitz; historical; literary; mainstream; mystery/suspense; regional; romance (contemporary, historical); thriller/espionage; young adult.
**How to Contact:** Query with first 50 pages and SASE large enough to return pages. Reports in 1 week on queries; 1 month on mss.
**Needs:** Actively seeking "writers with a highly original voice."
**Recent Sales:** New agency with no reported sales at press time. Clients include Karl Luntta.
**Terms:** Agent receives 15% commission on domestic sales; 20% on foreign sales. Offers written contract. 30 days written notice must be given to terminate contract.

**RUTH COHEN, INC. LITERARY AGENCY**, P.O. Box 7626, Menlo Park CA 94025. (650)854-2054. **Contact:** Ruth Cohen or associates. Estab. 1982. Member of AAR, Authors Guild, Sisters in Crime, Romance Writers of America, SCBWI. Represents 75 clients. 20% of clients are new/previously unpublished writers. Specializes in "quality writing in mysteries; juvenile fiction; adult women's fiction." Currently handles: 15% nonfiction books; 40% juvenile books; 45% novels.
- Prior to opening her agency, Ms. Cohen served as directing editor at Scott Foresman & Co. (now HarperCollins).
**Represents:** Adult novels, juvenile books. **Considers these nonfiction areas:** ethnic/cultural interests; juvenile nonfiction; women's issues/women's studies. **Considers these fiction areas:** detective/police; ethnic; historical; juvenile; literary; mainstream; mystery/suspense; picture books; romance (historical, long contemporary); young adult.
**How to Contact:** *No unsolicited mss.* Send outline plus 2 sample chapters; must include SASE. Reports in 1 month on queries.
**Needs:** Does not want to receive poetry or scripts. Obtains new clients through recommendations from others.
**Recent Sales:** Prefers not to share information on specific sales.
**Terms:** Agent receives 15% commission on domestic sales; 20% on foreign sales, "if a foreign agent is involved." Offers written contract, binding for 1 year "continuing to next." Charges for foreign postage and photocopying for submissions.
**Tips:** "A good writer cares about the words she uses—so do I. If no SASE is included, material will not be read."

**COLUMBIA LITERARY ASSOCIATES, INC.**, 7902 Nottingham Way, Ellicott City MD 21043-6721. (410)465-1595. **Contact:** Linda Hayes. Estab. 1980. Member of AAR, IACP, RWA, WRW. Represents 30 clients. 10% of clients are new/previously unpublished writers. Specializes in women's commercial contemporary fiction (mainstream/genre),

commercial nonfiction, especially cookbooks. Currently handles: 40% nonfiction books; 60% novels.
**Represents:** Nonfiction books, novels. **Considers these nonfiction areas:** cooking/food/nutrition; health/medicine; self-help. **Considers these fiction areas:** mainstream; commercial women's fiction; suspense; contemporary romance; psychological/medical thrillers.
**How to Contact:** Reports in 1 month on queries; 2 months on mss; "rejections faster."
**Recent Sales:** Sold 20-30 titles in the last year. *Second Sight*, by Beth Amos (HarperPaperbacks); *Legend MacKinnon*, by Donna Kauffman (Bantam); *Wente Vineyards Cookbook*, by Kimball Jones and Carolyn Wente (Ten Speed).
**Terms:** Agent receives 15% commission on domestic sales. Offers single- or multiple-book written contract, binding for 6-month terms. "Standard expenses are billed against book income (e.g., books for subrights exploitation, toll calls, UPS)."
**Writers' Conferences:** Romance Writers of America; Int'l. Association of Culinary Professionals; Novelists, Inc.
**Tips:** "CLA's list is very full; we're able to accept only a rare few top-notch projects." Submission requirements: "For fiction, send a query letter with author credits, narrative synopsis, first chapter or two, manuscript word count and submission history (publishers/agents); self-addressed, stamped mailer mandatory for response/ms return. (When submitting romances, note whether manuscript is mainstream or category—if category, say which line(s) manuscript is targeted to.) Same for nonfiction, plus include table of contents and note audience, how project is different and better than competition (specify competing books with publisher and publishing date.) Please note that we do *not* handle: historical or literary fiction, westerns, science fiction/fantasy, military books, poetry, short stories or screenplays."

**ROBERT CORNFIELD LITERARY AGENCY**, 145 W. 79th St., New York NY 10024-6468. (212)874-2465. Fax: (212)874-2641. E-mail: rbcbc@aol.com. **Contact:** Robert Cornfield. Estab. 1979. Member of AAR. Represents 60 clients. 20% of clients are new/previously unpublished writers. Specializes in film, art, literary, music criticism, food, fiction. Currently handles: 60% nonfiction books; 20% scholarly books; 20% novels.
● Prior to opening his agency, Mr. Cornfield was an editor at Holt and Dial Press.
**Represents:** Nonfiction books, novels. **Considers these nonfiction areas:** animals; anthropology/archaeology; art/architecture/ design; biography/autobiography; cooking/food/nutrition; history; language/literature/criticism/ music/dance/theater/film. **Considers literary fiction.**
**How to Contact:** Query. Reports in 3 weeks on queries.
**Needs:** Obtains new clients through recommendations.
**Recent Sales:** Sold 15-20 titles in the last year. *Mixed Signals*, by Richard Barrios (Routledge); *Multiple Personalities*, by Joan Acorella (Jossey-Bass).
**Terms:** Agent receives 10% commission on domestic sales; 20% on foreign sales. No written contract. Charges for postage, excessive photocopying.

**N. RICHARD CURTIS ASSOCIATES, INC.**, 171 E. 74th St., New York NY 10021. (212)772-7363. Fax: (212)772-7393. E-mail: ltucker@curtisagency.com. Website: http://www.curtisagency.com. **Contact:** Pam Talvera. Estab. 1969. Member of AAR, RWA, MWA, WWA, SFWA, signatory of WGA. Represents 100 clients. 5% of clients are new/previously unpublished writers. Specializes in general and literary fiction and nonfiction, as well as genre fiction such as science fiction, women's romance, horror, fantasy, action-adventure. Currently handles: 50% nonfiction books; 50% novels.
● Prior to opening his agency, Mr. Curtis was an agent with the Scott Meredith Literary Agency for 7 years and has authored over 50 published books.
**Member Agents:** Amy Victoria Meo, Laura Tucker, Richard Curtis.
**Represents:** Nonfiction books, scholarly books, novels. **Considers all nonfiction and fiction areas.**
**How to Contact:** "We do not accept fax or e-mail queries, conventional queries (outline and 3 sample chapters) must be accompanied by SASE." Reports in 1 month on queries; 1 month on mss.
**Needs:** Obtains new clients through recommendations from others, solicitations and conferences.
**Recent Sales:** Sold 100 titles in the last year. *Courtney Love: The Real Story*, by Poppy Z. Brite (Simon & Schuster); *Darwin's Radio*, by Greg Bear (Del Rey/Random House); *Expendable*, by James Gardner (Avon). Other clients include Dan Simmons, Jennifer Blake, Leonard Maltin, Earl Mindell and Barbara Parker.
**Terms:** Agent receives 15% commission on domestic sales; 20% on foreign sales. Offers written contract, binding on a "book by book basis." Charges for photocopying, express, fax, international postage, book orders.
**Writers' Conferences:** Romance Writers of America; Nebula Science Fiction Conference.

**DARHANSOFF & VERRILL LITERARY AGENTS**, 179 Franklin St., 4th Floor, New York NY 10013. (212)334-5980. Estab. 1975. Member of AAR. Represents 100 clients. 10% of clients are new/previously unpublished writers. Specializes in literary fiction. Currently handles: 25% nonfiction books; 60% novels; 15% short story collections.
**Member Agents:** Liz Darhansoff, Charles Verrill, Leigh Feldman.
**Represents:** Nonfiction books, novels, short story collections. **Considers these nonfiction areas:** anthropology/archaeology; biography/autobiography; current affairs; health/medicine; history; language/literature/criticism; nature/environment; science/technology. **Considers literary and thriller fiction.**
**How to Contact:** Query letter only. Reports in 2 weeks on queries.
**Needs:** Obtains new clients through recommendations from others.
**Recent Sales:** *Cold Mountain*, by Charles Frazier (Atlantic Monthly Press); *At Home in Mitford*, by Jan Karon (Viking).

**N: JOAN DAVES AGENCY**, 21 W. 26th St., New York NY 10010. (212)685-2663. Fax: (212)685-1781. **Contact:** Jennifer Lyons, director. Estab. 1960. Member of AAR. Represents 100 clients. 10% of clients are new/previously unpublished writers. Specializes in literary fiction and nonfiction, also commercial fiction.

**Represents:** Nonfiction books, novels. **Considers these nonfiction areas:** biography/autobiography; gay/lesbian issues; popular culture; translations; women's issues/women's studies. **Considers these fiction areas:** ethnic, family saga; gay; literary; mainstream.

**How to Contact:** Query. Reports in 3 weeks on queries; 6 weeks on mss.

**Needs:** Obtains new clients through editors' and author clients' recommendations. "A few queries translate into representation."

**Recent Sales:** *Fire on the Mountain*, by John Maclean (William Morrow); *Dancing with Cats*, by Burton Silver (Chronicle).

**Terms:** Agent receives 15% commission on domestic sales; 20% on foreign sales. Offers written contract, on a per book basis. Charges for office expenses. 100% of business is derived from commissions on sales.

**DH LITERARY, INC.**, P.O. Box 990, Nyack NY 10960-0990. (212)753-7942. E-mail: dhendin@aol.com. **Contact:** David Hendin. Estab. 1993. Member of AAR. Represents 50 clients. 20% of clients are new/previously unpublished writers. Specializes in trade fiction, nonfiction and newspaper syndication of columns or comic strips. Currently handles: 60% nonfiction books; 10% scholarly books; 20% fiction; 10% syndicated material.

● Prior to opening his agency, Mr. Hendin served as president and publisher for Pharos Books/World Almanac as well as senior vp and COO at sister company United Feature Syndicate.

**Represents:** Nonfiction books, novels, syndicated material. **Considers these nonfiction areas:** animals; anthropology/archaeology; biography/autobiography; business; child guidance/parenting; current affairs; education; ethnic/cultural interests; government/politics/law; health/medicine; history; how-to; language/literature/criticism; military/war; money/finance/economics; music/dance/theater/film; nature/environment; popular culture; psychology; science/technology; self-help/personal improvement; true crime/investigative; women's issues/women's studies. **Considers these fiction areas:** literary; mainstream; mystery; thriller/espionage.

**How to Contact:** Reports in 6 weeks on queries.

**Needs:** Obtains new clients through referrals from others (clients, writers, publishers).

**Recent Sales:** *Nobody's Angels*, by Leslie Haynesworth and David Toomey (William Morrow); *Backstab*, by Elaine Viets (Dell); *The Created Self*, by Robert Weber (Norton); *The Books of Jonah*, by R.O. Blechman (Stewart, Tabori and Chang); *Eating the Bear*, by Carole Fungaroli (Farrar, Straus & Giroux); *Miss Manners Basic Training: Eating*, by Judith Martin (Crown); *Do Unto Others*, by Abraham Twerski, M.D. (Andrews & McMeel).

**Terms:** Agent receives 15% commission on domestic sales; 20% on foreign sales. Offers written contract, binding for 1 year. Charges for out of pocket expenses for postage, photocopying manuscript, and overseas phone calls specifically related to a book.

**Tips:** "Have your project in mind and on paper before you submit. Too many writers/cartoonists say 'I'm good . . . get me a project.' Publishers want writers with their own great ideas and their own unique voice. No faxed submissions."

**SANDRA DIJKSTRA LITERARY AGENCY**, 1155 Camino del Mar, #515, Del Mar CA 92014. (619)755-3115. **Contact:** Sandra Zane. Estab. 1981. Member of AAR, Authors Guild, PEN West, Poets and Editors, MWA. Represents 100 clients. 30% of clients are new/previously unpublished writers. "We specialize in a number of fields." Currently handles: 60% nonfiction books; 5% juvenile books; 35% novels.

**Member Agents:** Sandra Dijkstra.

**Represents:** Nonfiction books, novels. **Considers these nonfiction areas:** anthropology; biography/autobiography; business; child guidance/parenting; nutrition; current affairs; ethnic/cultural interests; government/politics; health/medicine; history; literary studies (trade only); military/war (trade only); money/finance/economics; nature/environment; psychology; science/technology; self-help/personal improvement; sociology; sports; true crime/investigative; women's issues/women's studies. **Considers these fiction areas:** contemporary issues; detective/police/crime; ethnic; family saga; feminist; literary; mainstream; mystery/suspense; thriller/espionage.

**How to Contact:** Send "outline/proposal with sample chapters for nonfiction, synopsis and first 50 pages for fiction and SASE." Reports in 6 weeks on queries and mss.

**Needs:** Obtains new clients primarily through referrals/recommendations, but also through queries and conferences and often by solicitation.

**Recent Sales:** *The Mistress of Spices*, by Chitra Divakaruni (Anchor Books); *The Flower Net*, by Lisa See (HarperCollins); *Outsmarting the Menopausal Fat Cell*, by Debra Waterhouse (Hyperion); *Verdi*, by Janell Cannon (children's, Harcourt Brace); *The Nine Secrets of Women Who Get Everything They Want*, by Kate White (Harmony).

**Terms:** Agent receives 15% commission on domestic sales; 20% on foreign sales. Offers written contract, binding for 1 year. Charges for expenses from years we are *active* on author's behalf to cover domestic costs so that we can spend time selling books instead of accounting expenses. We also charge for the photocopying of the full manuscript or nonfiction proposal and for foreign postage."

**Writers' Conferences:** "Have attended Squaw Valley, Santa Barbara, Asilomar, Southern California Writers Conference, Rocky Mountain Fiction Writers, to name a few. We also speak regularly for writers groups such as PEN West and the Independent Writers Association."

**Tips:** "Be professional and learn the standard procedures for submitting your work. Give full biographical information on yourself, especially for a nonfiction project. Always include SASE with correct return postage for your own protection of your work. Query with a 1 or 2 page letter first and always include postage. Nine page letters telling us your life story, or your book's, are unprofessional and usually not read. Tell us about your book and write your query well. It's our first introduction to who you are and what you can do! Call if you don't hear within a reasonable period of time. Be a regular patron of bookstores and study what kind of books are being published. READ. Check out your local library and bookstores—you'll find lots of books on writing and the publishing industry that will help you! At conferences, ask published writers about their agents. Don't believe the myth that an agent has to be in New York to be successful—we've already disproved it!"

**N THE JONATHAN DOLGER AGENCY**, 49 E. 96th St., Suite 9B, New York NY 10128. (212)427-1853. President: Jonathan Dolger. **Contact:** Dee Ratteree. Estab. 1980. Member of AAR. Represents 70 clients. 25% of clients are new/unpublished writers. Writer must have been previously published if submitting fiction. Prefers to work with published/established authors; works with a small number of new/unpublished writers. Specializes in adult trade fiction and nonfiction, and illustrated books.
• Prior to opening his agency, Mr. Dolger was vice president and managing editor for Simon & Schuster Trade Books.
**Represents:** Nonfiction books, novels, illustrated books.
**How to Contact:** Query with outline and SASE.
**Recent Sales:** Sold 15-20 titles in the last year. Prefers not to share info on specific sales.
**Terms:** Agent receives 15% commission on domestic and dramatic sales; 25% on foreign sales. Charges for "standard expenses."

**N DONADIO AND OLSON, INC.**, 121 W. 27th St., Suite 704, New York NY 10001. (212)691-8077. Fax: (212)633-2837. **Contact:** Neil Olson. Estab. 1970. Member of AAR. Represents approximately 100 clients. Specializes in literary fiction and nonfiction. Currently handles: 40% nonfiction; 50% novels; 10% short story collections.
**Member Agents:** Edward Hibbert (literary fiction); Neil Olson; Ira Silverberg; Peter Steinberg.
**Represents:** Nonfiction books, novels, short story collections.
**How to Contact:** Query with 50 pages and SASE.
**Recent Sales:** Sold over 15 titles in the last year. Prefers not to share information on specific sales.
**Terms:** Agent receives 15% commission on domestic sales; 20% on foreign sales.

**N JANIS A. DONNAUD & ASSOCIATES**, 5 W. 19th St., 9th Floor, New York NY 10011. (212)620-0910. Fax: (212)352-1196. E-mail: jdonnaud@aol.com. **Contact:** Janis A. Donnaud. Also: Donnaud & Rennert, 584 Castro, Suite 114, SL, San Francisco CA 94114. Phone/fax: (415)552-7444. E-mail: arennert@pacbell.net. **Contact:** Amy Rennert. Member of AAR. Signatory of WGA. Represents 40 clients. 10% of clients are new/unpublished writers. Specializes in health, medical, cooking, humor, pop psychology, narrative nonfiction, photography, art, literary fiction, popular fiction. "We give a lot of service and attention to clients." Currently handles: 85% nonfiction books; 5% juvenile books; 10% novels.
• Prior to opening her agency, Ms. Donnaud was vice president, associate publisher, Random House Adult Trade.
**Member Agents:** Janis Donnaud; Amy Kennert (literary fiction and narrative nonfiction).
**Represents:** Nonfiction books, novels. **Considers these nonfiction areas:** animals; art/architecture/design; biography/autobiography; business; child guidance/parenting; cooking/food/nutrition; current affairs; ethnic/cultural interests; gay/lesbian issues; health/medicine; history; how-to; humor; interior design/decorating; language/literature/criticism; money/finance/economics; music/dance/theater/film; nature/environment; photography; popular culture; psychology; science/technology; self-help/personal improvement; sociology; sports; true crime/investigative; women's issues/women's studies. **Considers these fiction areas:** cartoon/comic; contemporary issues; erotica; ethnic; feminist; gay/lesbian; historical; humor/satire; literary; mainstream; psychic/supernatural; sports; thriller/espionage.
**How to Contact:** Query with SASE. Reports in 2 weeks on queries; 1 month on mss.
**Needs:** Actively seeking serious narrataive nonfiction; literary fiction; commercial fiction; cookbooks; health and medical. Does not want to receive poetry, mysteries, juvenile books, romances, science fiction, young adult, religious, fantasy. Obtains new clients through recommendations from other clients.
**Recent Sales:** Sold 36 titles in the last year. *Nancy Silverton's Mornings at the La Brea Bakery*, by Nancy Silverton (Random House); *A Year of Weddings*, by Maria McBride-Mellinger (HarperCollins); *The Raji Jallepalli Cookbook*, by Raji Jallepalli (HarperCollins).
**Terms:** Agent receives 15% commission on domestic sales; 20% on foreign sales. Offers written contract. 30 days notice must be given to terminate contract. Charges for messengers, photocopying, purchase of books.
**Writer's Conferences:** Palm Springs Writers Conference (Amy Rennert, spring).

**JANE DYSTEL LITERARY MANAGEMENT**, One Union Square West, New York NY 10003. (212)627-9100. Fax: (212)627-9313. Website: http://www.dystel.com. **Contact:** Miriam Goderich, Todd Keithley. Estab. 1994. Member of AAR. Represents 200 clients. 50% of clients are new/previously unpublished writers. Specializes in commercial and literary fiction and nonfiction plus cookbooks. Currently handles: 65% nonfiction books; 25% novels; 10% cookbooks.
• Prior to opening her agency, Ms. Dystel was a principal agent in Acton, Dystel, Leone and Jaffe.
**Member Agents:** Jane Dystel, Jessica Jones, Stacey Glick, Todd Keithley, Jo Fagan, Miriam Goderich, Charlotte Ho (foreign rights).
**Represents:** Nonfiction books, novels, cookbooks. **Considers these nonfiction areas:** animals; anthropology/archaeol-

ogy; biography/autobiography; business; child guidance/parenting; cooking/food/nutrition; current affairs; education; ethnic/cultural interests; gay/lesbian issues; government/politics/law; health/medicine; history; humor; military/war; money/finance/economics; New Age/metaphysics; popular cultures; psychology; religious/inspirational; science/technology; true crime/investigative; women's issues/women's studies. **Considers these fiction areas:** action/adventure; contemporary issues; detective/police/crime; ethnic; family saga; gay; lesbian; literary; mainstream; thriller/espionage.
**How to Contact:** Query. Reports in 3 weeks on queries; 6 weeks on mss.
**Needs:** Obtains new clients through recommendations from others, solicitation, at conferences.
**Recent Sales:** *No Physical Evidence*, by Gus Lee (Knopf); *The Sparrow*, by Mary Russell (Villard); *Lidia's Italian Table*, by Lidia Bastianich (William Morrow); *The World I Made for Her*, by Thomas Moran (Riverhead).
**Terms:** Agent receives 15% commission on domestic sales; 19% of foreign sales. Offers written contract on a book to book basis. Charges for photocopying. Galley charges and book charges from the publisher are passed on to the author.
**Writers' Conferences:** West Coast Writers Conference (Whidbey Island WA, Columbus Day weekend); University of Iowa Writer's Conference; Pacific Northwest Writer's Conference; Pike's Peak Writer's Conference; Santa Barbara Writer's Conference.

**FELICIA ETH LITERARY REPRESENTATION**, 555 Bryant St., Suite 350, Palo Alto CA 94301-1700. (650)375-1276. Fax: (650)375-1277. E-mail: feliciaeth@aol.com. **Contact:** Felicia Eth. Estab. 1988. Member of AAR. Represents 25-35 clients. Works with established and new writers. Currently handles: 85% nonfiction; 15% adult novels.
**Represents:** Nonfiction books, novels. **Considers these nonfiction areas:** animals; anthropology; biography; business; child guidance/parenting; current affairs; ethnic/cultural interests; gay/lesbian issues; government/politics/law; health/medicine; history; nature/environment; popular culture; psychology; science/technology; sociology; true crime/investigative; women's issues/women's studies. **Considers these fiction areas:** ethnic; feminist; gay; lesbian; literary; mainstream; thriller/espionage.
**How to Contact:** Query with outline. Reports in 3 weeks on queries; 1 month on proposals and sample pages.
**Recent Sales:** Sold 8 titles in the last year. *An Unburdened Heart*, by Mariah Nelson (HarperCollins); *Hand Me Down Dreams*, by Mary Jacobsen (Crown Publishers); *Java Joe & the March of Civilization*, by Stewart Allen (Soho Press); *The Charged Border*, by Jim Nolman (Henry Holt & Co.).
**Terms:** Agent receives 15% commission on domestic sales; 20% on dramatic sales; 20% on foreign sales. Charges for photocopying, express mail service—extraordinary expenses.
**Writers' Conferences:** Independent Writers of (LA); Conference of National Coalition of Independent Scholars (Berkeley CA); Writers Guild.
**Tips:** "For nonfiction, established expertise is certainly a plus, as is magazine publication—though not a prerequisite. I specialize in provocative, intelligent, thoughtful nonfiction on a wide array of subjects which are commercial and high-quality fiction; preferably mainstream and contemporary. I am highly selective, but also highly dedicated to those projects I represent."

**JEANNE FREDERICKS LITERARY AGENCY, INC.**, 221 Benedict Hill Rd., New Canaan CT 06840. Phone/fax: (203)972-3011. E-mail: jflainc@ix.netcom.com. **Contact:** Jeanne Fredericks. Estab. 1997. Member of AAR. Represents 70 clients. 10% of clients are new/unpublished writers. Specializes in quality adult nonfiction by authorities in their fields. Currently handles: 98% nonfiction books; 2% fiction.
• Prior to opening her agency, Ms. Fredericks was an agent and acting director with the Susan P. Urstadt Inc. Agency.
**Represents:** Nonfiction books. **Considers these nonfiction areas:** animals; anthropology/archeaology; art/architecture; biography/autobiography; business; child guidance/parenting; cooking/food/nutrition; crafts/hobbies; current affairs; education; health/medicine; history; horticulture; how-to; interior design/decorating; money/finance/economics; nature/environment; New Age/metaphysics; photography; psychology; science/technology; self-help/personal improvement; sports; women's issues/women's studies. **Considers these fiction areas:** family saga; historical; literary.
**How to Contact:** Query first with SASE, then send outline/proposal or outline and 1-2 sample chapters with SASE. Reports in 3 weeks on queries; 6 weeks on mss.
**Needs:** Obtains new clients through referrals, submissions to agency, conferences.
**Recent Sales:** *Classic Garden Structures*, by Michael and Jan Gettley (Taunton); *The Office Romance*, by Dennis Powers, Esq. (Amacom).
**Terms:** Agent receives 15% commission on domestic sales; 20% on foreign sales; 25% with foreign co-agent. Offers written contract, binding for 9 months. 2 months notice must be given to terminate contract. Charges for photocopying of whole proposals and mss, overseas postage, priority mail and Federal Express.
**Writers' Conferences:** PEN Women Conference (Williamsburg VA, February); Connecticut Press Club Biennial Writers' Conference (Stamford CT, April); ASJA Annual Writers' Conference East (NY, May); BEA (Chicago, June).
**Tips:** "Be sure to research the competition for your work and be able to justify why there's a need for it. I enjoy building an author's career, particularly if s(he) is professional, hardworking, and courteous. Aside from eight years of agenting experience, I've had ten years of editorial experience in adult trade book publishing that enables me to help an author polish a proposal so that it's more appealing to prospective editors. My MBA in marketing also distinguishes me from other agents."

**Ⓝ SARAH JANE FREYMANN LITERARY AGENCY**, 59 W. 71st St., New York NY 10023. (212)362-9277. Fax: (212)501-8240. **Contact:** Sarah Jane Freymann. Member of AAR. Represents 100 clients. 20% of clients are new/previously unpublished writers. Currently handles: 75% nonfiction books; 2% juvenile books; 23% novels.

**Represents:** Nonfiction books, novels, lifestyle-illustrated. **Considers these nonfiction areas:** animals; anthropology/archaeology; art/architecture/design; biography/autobiography; business; child guidance/parenting; cooking/food/nutrition; current affairs; ethnic/cultural interests; gay/lesbian issues; health/medicine; history; interior design/decorating; nature/environment; psychology; religious/inspirational; self-help/personal improvement; women's issues/women's studies. **Considers these fiction areas:** contemporary issues; ethnic; literary; mainstream; mystery/suspense; thriller/espionage.

**How to Contact:** Query with SASE. Reports in 2 weeks on queries; 6 weeks on mss.

**Needs:** Obtains new clients through recommendations from others.

**Recent Sales:** *Just Listen*, by Nancy O'Hara (Broadway); *Flavors*, by Pamela Morgan (Viking); *Silent Thunder*, by Katherine Payne (Simon & Schuster); *The Wisdom of Depression*, by Dr. Jonathan Zuess (Crown).

**Terms:** Agent receives 15% commission on domestic sales; 20% on foreign sales. Offers written contract. Charges for long distance, overseas postage, photocopying. 100% of business is derived from commissions on ms sales.

**Tips:** "I love fresh new passionate works by authors who love what they are doing and have both natural talent and carefully honed skill."

**N THE GISLASON AGENCY**, 219 Main St. SE, Suite 506, Minneapolis MN 55414-2160. (612)331-8033. Fax: (612)331-8115. E-mail: gislasonbj@aol.com. Attorney/Agent: Barbara J. Gislason. Estab. 1992. Member of Minnesota State Bar Association, Internet Committee, Art & Entertainment Law Section (Former Chair), Minnesota Intellectual Property Law Association Copyright Committee (Former Chair), SFWA, MWA, RWA, Sisters In Crime, University Film Society (Board Member). 50% of clients are new/previously unpublished writers. Specializes in fiction. "The Gislason Agency represents published and unpublished mystery, science fiction, fantasy, romance and law-related works and is seeking submissions in all categories." Currently handles: 10% nonfiction books; 90% fiction.

• Ms. Gislason became an attorney in 1980, and continues to practice Art & Entertainment Law and has been recognized as a leading attorney in a variety of publications.

**Member Agents:** Patti Anderson (mystery); Jocelyn Pihlaja (romance); Deborah Sweeney (fantasy); Sally Morem (science fiction).

**Represents:** Fiction. **Considers these fiction areas:** fantasy; law related; mystery/suspense; romance; science fiction.

**How to Contact:** Query with synopsis and first 3 chapters. SASE required. Reports in 1 month on queries, 3 months on mss.

**Needs:** Do not send personal memoirs, poetry or children's books. Obtains half of new clients through recommendations from other authors and editors and contacts made at conferences and half from *Guide to Literary Agents*, *Literary Market Place* and other reference books.

**Recent Sales:** *Night Fires* (3 book deal), by Linda Cook (Kensington); *A Deadly Shaker Spring* (3 book deal), by Deborah Woodworth (Avon). Clients include Robert Kline, Paul Lake, Joan Verba, Marjorie DeBoer and Candace Kohl.

**Terms:** Agent receives 15% commission on domestic sales; 20% on foreign sales. Offers written contract, binding for 1 year with option to renew. Charges for photocopying and postage.

**Writers' Conferences:** Dark & Stormy Nights; Boucheron; Minicon; Romance Writers of America; Midwest Fiction Writers; University of Wisconsin Writer's Institute.

**Tips:** "Cover letter should be well written and include a detailed synopsis of the work, the first three chapters and author information. Appropriate SASE required. The Gislason Agency is looking for a great writer with a poetic, lyrical or quirky writing style who can create intriguing ambiguities. We expect a well-researched imaginataive and fresh plot that reflects a familiarity with the applicable genre. Do not send us a work with ordinary writing, a worn-out plot or copycat characters. Scenes with sex and violence must be intrinsic to the plot. Remember to proofread, proofread, proofread. If the work was written with a specific publisher in mind, this should be communicated. In addition to owning an agency, Ms. Gislason practices law in the area of Art and Entertainment and has a broad spectrum of entertainment industry contacts."

**SANFORD J. GREENBURGER ASSOCIATES, INC.**, 55 Fifth Ave., New York NY 10003. (212)206-5600. Fax: (212)463-8718. **Contact:** Heide Lange. Estab. 1945. Member of AAR. Represents 500 clients.

**Member Agents:** Heide Lange, Faith Hamlin, Beth Vesel, Theresa Park, Elyse Cheney, Dan Mandel.

**Represents:** Nonfiction books, novels. **Considers all nonfiction areas. Considers these fiction areas:** action/adventure; contemporary issues; detective/police/crime; ethnic; family saga; feminist; gay; glitz; historical; humor/satire; lesbian; literary; mainstream; mystery/suspense; psychic/supernatural; regional; sports; thriller/espionage.

**How to Contact:** Query first. Reports in 3 weeks on queries; 2 months on mss.

**Needs:** Does not want to receive romances or westerns.

**Recent Sales:** Sold 200 titles in the last year. Prefers not to share information on specific sales. Clients include Andrew Ross, Margaret Cuthbert, Nicholas Sparks, Mary Kurcinka, Edy Clarke and Peggy Claude Pierre.

**Terms:** Agent receives 15% commission on domestic sales; 20% on foreign sales. Charges for photocopying, books for foreign and subsidiary rights submissions.

**N REECE HALSEY NORTH**, 98 Main St., #704, Tiburon CA 94920. (415)789-9191. Fax: (415)789-9177. **Contact:** Kimberley Cameron. Estab. 1957. Member of AAR, signatory of WGA. Represents 40 clients. 30% of clients are new/previously unpublished writers. Specializes mostly in books/excellent writing. Currently handles: 30% nonfiction books; 60% novels; 10% movie scripts.

• The Reese Halsey Agency has an illustrious client list largely of established writers, including the estate of Aldous

Huxley and has represented Upton Sinclair, William Faulkner and Henry Miller. Ms. Cameron has recently opened a Northern California office and all queries should be addressed to her at the Tiburon office.

**Member Agents:** Kimberley Cameron.

**Represents:** Nonfiction books, novels. **Considers these nonfiction areas:** biography/autobiography; current affairs; history; language/literature/criticism; memoirs; popular culture; true crime/investigative; women's issues/women's studies. **Considers these fiction areas:** action/adventure; contemporary issues; detective/police/crime; ethnic; family saga; historical; literary; mainstream; mystery/suspense; science fiction; thriller/espionage; women's fiction.

**How to Contact:** Query with SASE. Reports in 3 weeks on queries; 3 months on mss.

**Terms:** Agent receives 15% commission on domestic sales of books, 10% commission on script sales. Offers written contract, binding for 1 year. Requests 6 copies of ms if representing an author.

**Writers' Conferences:** ABA and various writer conferences, Maui Writers Conference.

**Tips:** Obtains new clients through recommendations from others and solicitation. "Always send a well-written query and include a SASE with it!"

**▣ JOHN HAWKINS & ASSOCIATES, INC.**, 71 W. 23rd St., Suite 1600, New York NY 10010. (212)807-7040. Fax: (212)807-9555. E-mail: jhawkasc@aol.com. **Contact:** John Hawkins, William Reiss. Estab. 1893. Member of AAR. Represents over 100 clients. 5-10% of clients are new/previously unpublished writers. Currently handles: 40% nonfiction books; 20% juvenile books; 40% novels.

**Member Agents:** Warren Frazier, Anne Hawkins, Moses Cardona, Elly Sidel.

**Represents:** Nonfiction books, juvenile books, novels. **Considers all nonfiction areas** except computers/electronics; religion/inspirational; translations. **Considers all fiction areas** except confessional; erotica; romance.

**How to Contact:** Query with outline/proposal. Reports in 1 month on queries.

**Needs:** Obtains new clients through recommendations from others.

**Recent Sales:** *Eddie's Bastard*, by William Kowalski (HarperCollins); *Hart's War*, by John Katzenbach (Ballantine); and *House of Leaves*, by Mark Danielewski (Pantheon).

**Terms:** Agent receives 15% commission on domestic sales; 20% on foreign sales. Charges for photocopying.

**HEACOCK LITERARY AGENCY, INC.**, 1523 Sixth St., Suite #14, Santa Monica CA 90401-2514. (310)393-6227. **Contact:** Rosalie Grace Heacock. Estab. 1978. Member of AAR, Author's Guild, SCBWI. Represents 60 clients. 10% of clients are new/previously unpublished writers. Currently handles: 90% nonfiction books; 10% novels.

**Represents:** Adult nonfiction and fiction books, children's picture books. **Considers these nonfiction areas:** anthropology; art/architecture/design; biography (contemporary celebrity); business; child guidance/parenting; cooking/food/nutrition; crafts/hobbies; ethnic/cultural interests; health/medicine (including alternative health); history; how-to; language/literature/criticism; money/finance/economics; music; nature/environment; popular culture; psychology; religious/inspirational; science/technology; self-help/personal improvement; sociology; spirituality/metaphysics; women's issues/women's studies. Considers limited selection of top children's book authors; no beginners.

**How to Contact:** "No multiple queries, please." Query with sample chapters. Reports in 3 weeks on queries; 2 months on mss.

**Needs:** Does not want to receive scripts. Obtains new clients through "referrals from present clients and industry sources as well as mail queries."

**Recent Sales:** Prefers not to share information on specific sales.

**Terms:** Agent receives 15% commission on domestic sales; 25% on foreign sales, "if foreign agent used; if sold directly, 15%." Offers written contract, binding for 1 year. Charges for actual expense for telephone, postage, packing, photocopying. We provide copies of each publisher submission letter and the publisher's response." 95% of business is derived from commission on ms sales.

**Writers' Conferences:** Maui Writers Conference; Santa Barbara City College Annual Writer's Workshop; Pasadena City College Writer's Forum; UCLA Symposiums on Writing Nonfiction Books; Society of Children's Book Writers and Illustrators.

**Tips:** "Take time to write an informative query letter expressing your book idea, the market for it, your qualifications to write the book, the 'hook' that would make a potential reader buy the book. Always enclose SASE; we cannot respond to queries without return postage. Our primary focus is upon books which make a contribution."

**THE JEFF HERMAN AGENCY LLC**, 332 Bleecker St., New York NY 10014. (212)941-0540. E-mail: jherman@ix. net.com. Website: http://www.WritersGuide.com. **Contact:** Jeffrey H. Herman. Estab. 1985. Member of AAR. Represents 100 clients. 10% of clients are new/previously unpublished writers. Specializes in adult nonfiction. Currently handles: 85% nonfiction books; 5% scholarly books; 5% textbooks; 5% novels.

**Member Agents:** Deborah Levine (vice president, nonfiction book doctor).

**Represents: Considers these nonfiction areas:** business, computers; health; history; how-to; politics; popular psychology; popular reference; recovery; self-help; spirituality.

**How to Contact:** Query. Reports in 2 weeks on queries; 1 month on mss.

**Recent Sales:** *Joe Montana On The Magic of Making Quarterback*, by Joe Montana (Henry Holt); *The Aladdin Factor*, by Jack Canfield and Mark Victor Hansen (Putnam); *The I.Q. Myth*, by Bob Sternberg (Simon & Schuster); *All You Need to Know About the Movie and TV Business*, by Gail Resnick and Scott Trost (Fireside/Simon & Schuster).

**Terms:** Agent receives 15% commission on domestic sales. Offers written contract.

**[N] JAMES PETER ASSOCIATES, INC.**, P.O. Box 772, Tenafly NJ 07670-0751. (201)568-0760. Fax: (201)568-2959. E-mail: bertholtje@compuserve.com. **Contact:** Bert Holtje. Estab. 1971. Member of AAR. Represents 72 individual authors and 5 corporate clients (book producers). 15% of clients are new/previously unpublished writers. Specializes in nonfiction, all categories. "We are especially interested in general, trade and academic reference. Currently handles: 100% nonfiction books.

  • Prior to opening his agency, Mr. Holtje was a book packager, and before that, president of an advertising agency with book publishing clients.

**Represents:** Nonfiction books. **Considers these nonfiction areas:** anthropology/archaeology; art/architecture/design; biography/autobiography; business; child guidance/parenting; current affairs; ethnic/cultural interests; gay/lesbian issues; government/politics/law; health/medicine; history; language/literature/criticism; memoirs (political or business); military/war; money/finance/economics; music/dance/theater/film; popular culture; psychology; self-help/personal improvement; travel; women's issues/women's studies.

**How to Contact:** Send outline/proposal and SASE. Reports in 1 month on queries.

**Needs:** Actively seeking "good ideas in all areas of adult nonfiction." Does not want to receive "children's and young adult books, poetry, fiction." Obtains new clients through recommendations from other clients and editors, contact with people who are doing interesting things, and over-the-transom queries.

**Recent Sales:** Sold 51 titles in the last year. *The Business Travelers World Guide*, by Philip Seldon (McGraw-Hill); *Dictionary of American Folklore*, by H. Oster and A. Axelrod (Penguin Viking); *The Hypericum Handbook*, by Carol Turkington (M. Evans).

**Terms:** Agent receives 15% commission on domestic sales; 20% on foreign sales. Offers written contract on a per book basis.

**Tips:** "Phone me! I'm happy to discuss book ideas any time."

**[N] KIRCHOFF/WOHLBERG, INC., AUTHORS' REPRESENTATION DIVISION**, 866 United Nations Plaza, #525, New York NY 10017. (212)644-2020. Fax: (212)223-4387. Director of Operations: John R. Whitman. **Contact:** Lisa Pulitzer-Voges. Estab. 1930s. Member of AAR, AAP, Society of Illustrators, SPAR, Bookbuilders of Boston, New York Bookbinders' Guild, AIGA. Represents 50 authors. 10% of clients are new/previously unpublished writers. Specializes in juvenile through young adult trade books and textbooks. Currently handles: 5% nonfiction books; 80% juvenile books; 5% novels; 5% novellas; 5% young adult.

**Member Agents:** Liza Pulitzer-Voges (juvenile and young adult authors).

**Represents:** "We are interested in any original projects of quality that are appropriate to the juvenile and young adult trade book markets. But, we take on very few new clients as our roster is full."

**How to Contact:** "Send a query that includes an outline and a sample; SASE required." Reports in 1 month on queries; 2 months on mss. Please send queries to the attention of Liza Pulitzer-Voges.

**Needs:** "Usually obtains new clients through recommendations from authors, illustrators and editors."

**Recent Sales:** Sold over 50 titles in the last year. Prefers not to share information on specific sales.

**Terms:** Agent receives standard commission "depending upon whether it is an author only, illustrator only, or an author/illustrator book." Offers written contract, binding for not less than 1 year.

**Tips:** Kirchoff/Wohlberg has been in business for over 50 years."

**[N] LINDA KONNER LITERARY AGENCY**, 10 W. 15th St., Suite 1918, New York NY 10011-6829. (212)691-3419. E-mail: 103113.3417@compuserve.com. **Contact:** Linda Konner. Estab. 1996. Member of AAR and ASJA. Signatory of WGA. Represents 50 clients. 5-10% of clients are new/unpublished writers. Specializes in health, self-help, how-to. Currently handles: 100% nonfiction books.

**Represents:** Nonfiction books (adult only). **Considers these nonfiction areas:** business; child care/parenting; diet/nutrition; gay/lesbian issues; health/medicine; how-to; personal finance; popular culture; psychology; relationships; self-help/personal improvement; women's issues.

**How to Contact:** Query. Send outline or proposal with sufficient return postage. Reports in 1 month.

**Needs:** Obtains new clients through recommendations from others and occasional solicitation among established authors/journalists.

**Recent Sales:** *How to Help Your Man Get Healthy*, by Jonas and Kassberg (Avon); *Special Siblings*, by Mary McHugh (Hyperion); *All Men are Jerks (Until Proven Otherwise)*, by Daylle Deanna Schwartz (Adams Media); *Toxic Friends, True Friends*, by Florence Isaacs (Morrow).

**Terms:** Agent receives 15% commission on domestic sales; 30% on foreign sales. Offers written contract. Charges $75 one-time fee for domestic expenses; additional expenses may be incurred for foreign sales.

**Writers' Conferences:** American Society of Journalists and Authors (New York City, May).

**BARBARA S. KOUTS, LITERARY AGENT**, P.O. Box 560, Bellport NY 11713. (516)286-1278. **Contact:** Barbara Kouts. Estab. 1980. Member of AAR. Represent 50 clients. 10% of clients are new/previously unpublished writers. Specializes in adult fiction and nonfiction and children's books. Currently handles: 20% nonfiction books; 60% juvenile books; 20% novels.

**Represents:** Nonfiction books, juvenile books, novels. **Considers these nonfiction areas:** biography/autobiography; child guidance/parenting; current affairs; ethnic/cultural interests; health/medicine; history; juvenile nonfiction; music/dance/theater/film; nature/environment; psychology; self-help/personal improvement; women's issues/women's studies.

**Considers these fiction areas:** contemporary issues; family saga; feminist; historical; juvenile; literary; mainstream; mystery/suspense; picture book; young adult.

**How to Contact:** Query. Reports in 1 week on queries; 6 weeks on mss.

**Needs:** Obtains new clients through recommendations from others, solicitation, at conferences, etc.

**Recent Sales:** *Dancing on the Edge*, by Han Nolan (Harcourt Brace); *Cendrillon*, by Robert San Souci (Simon & Schuster).

**Terms:** Agent receives 10% commission on domestic sales; 20% on foreign sales. Charges for photocopying.

**Tips:** "Write, do not call. Be professional in your writing."

**MICHAEL LARSEN/ELIZABETH POMADA LITERARY AGENTS**, 1029 Jones St., San Francisco CA 94109-5023. (415)673-0939. E-mail: larsonpoma@aol.com. Website: http://www.Larsen-Pomada.com. **Contact:** Mike Larsen or Elizabeth Pomada. Estab. 1972. Members of AAR, Authors Guild, ASJA, NWA, PEN, WNBA, California Writers Club. Represents 100 clients. 40-45% of clients are new/unpublished writers. Eager to work with new/unpublished writers. "We have very diverse tastes. We look for fresh voices and new ideas. We handle literary, commercial and genre fiction, and the full range of nonfiction books." Currently handles: 70% nonfiction books; 30% novels.

● Prior to opening their agency, both Mr. Larsen and Ms. Pomada were promotion executives for major publishing houses. Mr. Larsen worked for Morrow, Bantam and Pyramid (now part of Berkley), Ms. Pomada worked at Holt, David McKay, and The Dial Press.

**Member Agents:** Michael Larsen (nonfiction), Elizabeth Pomada (fiction, books of interest to women).

**Represents:** Adult nonfiction books, novels. **Considers these nonfiction areas:** anthropology/archaeology; art/architecture/design; biography/autobiography; business; cooking/food/nutrition; current affairs; ethnic/cultural interests; futurism; gay/lesbian issues; government/politics/law; health/medicine; history; how-to; humor; interior design/decorating; language/literature/criticism; memoirs; money/finance/economics; music/dance/theater/film; nature/environment; New Age/metaphysics; parenting; photography; popular culture; psychology; religious/inspirational; science/technology; self-help/personal improvement; sociology; sports; travel; true crime/investigative; women's issues/women's studies. **Considers these fiction areas:** action/adventure; contemporary issues; detective/police/crime; ethnic; experimental; family saga; fantasy; feminist; gay; glitz; historical; horror; humor/satire; lesbian; literary; mainstream; mystery/suspense; psychic/supernatural; religious/inspirational; romance (contemporary, gothic, historical, regency).

**How to Contact:** Query with synopsis and first 10 pages of completed novel. Reports in 2 months on queries. For nonfiction, "please read Michael's book *How to Write a Book Proposal* (Writer's Digest Books) and then mail or e-mail the title of your book and 1 page promotion plan." Always include SASE. Send SASE for brochure and title list.

**Needs:** Actively seeking commercial and literary fiction. "Fresh voices with new ideas of interest to major publishers. Does not want to receive children's books, plays, short stories, screenplays, pornography.

**Recent Sales:** *Black Raven* (10th book in the Deverry Series), by Katharine Kerr (Bantam/Spectra); *A Crack In Forever*, by Jeannie Brewer (Simon & Schuster/Avon); *The Emerald Tablet: Message for the Millenium*, by Dennis William Hauck (Penguin).

**Terms:** Agent receives 15% commission on domestic sales; 15% on dramatic sales; 30% on foreign sales. May charge writer for printing, postage for multiple submissions, foreign mail, foreign phone calls, galleys, books, and legal fees.

**Writers' Conferences:** BEA; Santa Barbara Writers Conference; Maui Writers Conference; ASJA.

**LEVANT & WALES, LITERARY AGENCY, INC.**, 108 Hayes St., Seattle WA 98109-2808. (206)284-7114. Fax: (206)284-0190. E-mail: bizziew@aol.com. **Contact:** Elizabeth Wales or Adrienne Reed. Estab. 1988. Member of AAR, Pacific Northwest Writers' Conference, Book Publishers' Northwest. Represents 65 clients. We are interested in published and not-yet-published writers. Especially encourages writers living in the Pacific Northwest, West Coast, Alaska and Pacific Rim countries. Specializes in mainstream nonfiction and fiction, as well as narrative nonfiction and literary fiction. Currently handles: 60% nonfiction books; 40% novels.

● Prior to becoming an agent, Ms. Wales worked at Oxford University Press and Viking Penguin.

**Represents:** Nonfiction books, novels. **Considers these nonfiction areas:** animals; biography/autobiography; business; child guidance/parenting; current affairs; education; ethnic/cultural interests; gardening; gay/lesbian issues; health; language/literature/criticism; lifestyle; memoirs; nature; New Age; popular culture; psychology; science; self-help/personal improvement; women's issues/women's studies—open to creative or serious treatments of almost any nonfiction subject. **Considers these fiction areas:** cartoon/comic/women's; ethnic; experimental; feminist; gay; lesbian; literary; mainstream (no genre fiction).

**How to Contact:** Query first with cover letter, writing sample (no more than 30 pages) and SASE. Reports in 3 weeks on queries; 6 weeks on mss.

**Recent Sales:** Sold 15 titles in the last year. *How Close We Come: A Novel*, by Susan S. Kelly (Warner Books); *Can I Get A Witness?: For Sister When The Blues Is More Than A Song*, by Julia A. Boyd (Dutton); *Savage Love*, by Dan Savage (Dutton); *Animals As Guides For The Soul*, by Susan Chernak McElroy (Ballantine).

**Terms:** Agent receives 15% commission on domestic sales. "We make all our income from commissions. We offer editorial help for some of our clients and help some clients with the development of a proposal, but we do not charge for these services. We do charge, after a sale, for express mail, manuscript photocopying costs, foreign postage and outside USA telephone costs."

**Writers' Conferences:** Pacific NW Writers Conference (Seattle, July).

**ELLEN LEVINE LITERARY AGENCY, INC.**, 15 E. 26th St., Suite 1801, New York NY 10010. (212)889-0620. Fax: (212)725-4501. **Contact:** Ellen Levine, Elizabeth Kaplan, Diana Finch, Louise Quayle Estab. 1980. Member of AAR. Represents over 100 clients. 20% of clients are new/previously unpublished writers. "My three younger colleagues at the agency (Louise Quayle, Diana Finch and Elizabeth Kaplan) are seeking both new and established writers. I prefer to work with established writers, mostly through referrals." Currently handles: 55% nonfiction books; 5% juvenile books; 40% fiction.
**Represents:** Nonfiction books, juvenile books, novels, short story collections. **Considers these nonfiction areas:** anthropology; biography; current affairs; health; history; memoirs; popular culture; psychology; science; women's issues/women's studies; books by journalists. **Considers these fiction areas:** literary; mystery; women's fiction, thrillers.
**How to Contact:** Query. Reports in 3 weeks on queries, if SASE provided; 6 weeks on mss, if submission requested.
**Needs:** Obtains new clients through recommendations from others.
**Recent Sales:** *The Day Diana Died*, by Christopher Anderson (William Morrow); *Maxing Out: Why Women Sabotage Their Financial Security*, by Colette Dowling (Little, Brown).
**Terms:** Agent receives 15% commission on domestic sales; 20% on foreign sales. Charges for overseas postage, photocopying, messenger fees, overseas telephone and fax, books ordered for use in rights submissions.

**WENDY LIPKIND AGENCY**, 165 E. 66th St., New York NY 10021. (212)628-9653. Fax: (212)628-2693. **Contact:** Wendy Lipkind. Estab. 1977. Member of AAR. Represents 60 clients. Specializes in adult nonfiction. Currently handles: 80% nonfiction books; 20% novels.
**Represents:** Nonfiction, novels. **Considers these nonfiction areas:** biography; current affairs; health/medicine; history; science; social history, women's issues/women's studies. **Considers these fiction areas:** mainstream and mystery/suspense. No mass market originals.
**How to Contact:** For nonfiction, query with outline/proposal. For fiction, query with SASE only. Reports in 1 month.
**Needs:** Usually obtains new clients through recommendations from others.
**Recent Sales:** *The Explosive Child*, by Ross Greene (HarperCollins); *How To Snag a Baseball in a Major League Park*, by Zack Hample (Simon & Schuster).
**Terms:** Agent receives 15% commission on domestic sales; 20% on foreign sales. Sometimes offers written contract. Charges for foreign postage, messenger service, photocopying, transatlantic calls and faxes.
**Tips:** "Send intelligent query letter first. Let me know if you sent to other agents."

**LOWENSTEIN ASSOCIATES, INC.**, 121 W. 27th St., Suite 601, New York NY 10001. (212)206-1630. Fax: (212)727-0280. President: Barbara Lowenstein. Estab. 1976. Member of AAR. Represents 150 clients. 20% of clients are new/unpublished writers. Specializes in multicultural books (fiction and nonfiction), medical experts, commercial fiction, especially suspense, crime and women's issues. "We are a full-service agency, handling domestic and foreign rights, film rights, and audio rights to all of our books." Currently handles: 60% nonfiction books; 40% novels.
**Member Agents:** Barbara Lowenstein (president); Nancy Yost (agent); Eileen Cope (agent); Norman Kurz (business affairs); Deborah Cateiro (associate agent).
**Represents:** Nonfiction books, novels. **Considers these nonfiction areas:** animals; anthropology/archaeology; art/architecture/design; biography/autobiography; business; child guidance/parenting; craft/hobbies; current affairs; education; ethnic/cultural interests; gay/lesbian issues; government/politics/law; health/medicine; history; how-to; humor; language/literature/criticism/; memoirs; money/finance/economics; music/dance/theater/film; nature/environment; New Age/metaphysics, popular culture; psychology; religious/inspirational; science/technology; self-help/personal improvement; sociology; sports; travel; true crime/investigative; women's issues/women's studies. **Considers these fiction areas:** contemporary issues; detective/police/crime; erotica; ethnic; feminist; gay; historical; humor/satire; lesbian; literary mainstream; mystery/suspense; romance (contemporary, historical, regency); medical thrillers.
**How to Contact:** Send query with SASE, "otherwise will not respond." For fiction, send outline and 1st chapter. *No unsolicited mss.* Reports in 6 weeks on queries.
**Needs:** Obtains new clients through referrals, journals, magazines, media, solicitations and a very few conferences.
**Recent Sales:** Sold approximately 75 titles in the last year. *Awakening the Buddha Within*, by Lama Surya Das (Broadway); *The Mozart Effect*, by Don Campbell (Avon); *Invasion of Privacy*, by Perri O'Shaughnessy (Dell). Other clients include Gina Barkhordar Nahai, Ishmael Reed, Lee Upton, Kevin Young and Myrlie Evers Williams.
**Terms:** Agent receives 15% commission on domestic sales; 20% on foreign sales; 20% on dramatic sales. Offers written contract on a book-by-book basis. Charges for large photocopy batches and international postage.
**Writer's Conference:** Malice Domestic; Bouchercon.
**Tips:** "Know the genre you are working in and READ!"

**CAROL MANN AGENCY**, 55 Fifth Ave., New York NY 10003. (212)206-5635. Fax: (212)675-4809. **Contact:** Carol Mann. Estab. 1977. Member of AAR. Represents over 100 clients. 25% of clients are new/previously unpublished writers. Specializes in current affairs; self-help; psychology; parenting; history. Currently handles: 70% nonfiction books; 30% novels.
**Member Agents:** Gareth Esersky (contemporary nonfiction); Jim Fitzgerald (literary, cinematic, Internet projects).
**Represents:** Nonfiction books. **Considers these nonfiction areas:** anthropology/archaeology; art/architecture/design; biography/autobiography; business; child guidance/parenting; current affairs; ethnic/cultural interests; government/politics/law; health/medicine; history; money/finance/economics; psychology; self-help/personal improvement; sociology; women's issues/women's studies. **Considers literary fiction.**

**How to Contact:** Query with outline/proposal and SASE. Reports in 3 weeks on queries.

**Needs:** Actively seeking "nonfiction: pop culture, business and health; fiction: literary fiction." Does not want to receive "genre fiction (romance, mystery, etc.)."

**Recent Sales:** *The Making of a Classic: Hitchcock's Vertigo*, by Dan Aviler (St. Martin's); *Radical Healing*, by Rudolph Ballentine, M.D. (Harmony); *Hand to Mouth*, by Paul Auster (Holt); *Stopping Cancer Before It Starts*, by American Institute for Cancer Research (Golden). Other clients include Dr. William Julius Wilson, Barry Sears (*Mastering The Zone*), Dr. Judith Wallerstein, Lorraine Johnson-Coleman (*Just Plain Folks*), Pulitzer Prize Winner Fox Butterfield and James Tobin, NBCC Award Winner for *Ernie Pyle* (Free Press).

**Terms:** Agent receives 15% commission on domestic sales; 20% on foreign sales. Offers written contract.

**Tips:** No phone queries. Must include SASE for reply.

**N MANUS & ASSOCIATES LITERARY AGENCY, INC.**, 417 E. 57th St., Suite 5D, New York NY 10022. (212)644-8020. Fax: (212)644-3374. **Contact:** Janet Wilkens Manus. Also: 375 Forest Ave., Palo Alto CA 94301. (650)470-5151. Fax: (650)470-5159. E-mail: manuslit@vpvp.com. **Contact:** Jillian Manus. Estab. 1985. Member of AAR. Represents 75 clients. 15% of clients are new/previously unpublished writers. Specializes in quality fiction, mysteries, thrillers, true crime, health, pop psychology. "Our agency is unique in the way that we not only sell the material, but we edit, develop concepts, and participate in the marketing effort. We specialize in large, conceptual fiction and nonfiction and always value a project that can be sold in the TV/feature film market." Currently handles: 60% nonfiction books; 10% juvenile books; 30% novels (sells 40% of material into TV/film markets).

• Prior to becoming agents, Jillian Manus was associate editor of 2 national magazines and director of development at Warner Brothers and Universal Studios; Janet Manus has been a literary agent for 20 years.

**Represents:** Nonfiction books, novels. **Considers these nonfiction areas:** biography/autobiography; business; child guidance/parenting; current affairs; ethnic/cultural interests; health/medicine; how-to; memoirs; nature/environment; popular culture; pop-psychology; self-help/personal improvement; dramatic nonfiction; women's issues/women's studies. **Considers these fiction areas:** contemporary issues; detective/police/crime; ethnic; family saga; feminist; mainstream; mystery/suspense; thriller/espionage; women's.

**How to Contact:** Send outline and 2-3 sample chapters with SASE. Reports in 3 weeks on queries; 6 weeks on mss.

**Needs:** Actively seeking high concept, thrillers, commercial, literary fiction, celebrity biographies, memoirs, multicultural fiction, caper mysteries, pop-health, women's empowerment. Does not want to receive horror, science fiction, romance, westerns, fantasy, young adult. Obtains new clients through recommendations from others, at conferences, and from editors.

**Recent Sales:** *Jitterjoint*, by Howard Swindle; *The Last City Room*, by Al Martinez; *Sole Survivor*, by Derek Hansen; *False Accusations*, by Alan Jacobson; *Stop Screaming at the Microwave*, by Mary Loverde (Fireside).

**Terms:** Agent receives 15% commission on domestic sales; 20% on foreign sales. Offers written contract, binding for 2 years, with 45-day cancellation clause. 100% of business is derived from commissions on sales.

**Writer's Conferences** San Diego Writers Conference (January); Maui Writers Conference (September); Jack London Conference (San Jose, March); Columbus Writer's Conference (Columbus, Ohio, September); Mendocini Writers Conference; Willamette Writers Conference.

**THE DENISE MARCIL LITERARY AGENCY, INC.**, 685 West End Ave., New York NY 10025. (212)932-3110. **Contact:** Denise Marcil. Estab. 1977. Member of AAR. Represents 70 clients. 40% of clients are new/previously unpublished authors. Specializes in women's commercial fiction, business books, popular reference, how-to and self-help. Currently handles: primarily nonfiction.

• Prior to opening her agency, Ms. Marcil served as an editorial assistant with Avon Books and as an editor with Simon & Schuster.

**Represents:** Nonfiction books, novels. **Considers these nonfiction areas:** business; child guidance/parenting; ethnic/cultural interests; nutrition; alternative health/medicine; how-to; inspirational; money/finance/economics; psychology; self-help/personal improvement; spirituality; women's issues/women's studies. **Considers these fiction areas:** mystery/suspense; romance (contemporary).

**How to Contact:** Query with SASE *only*! Reports in 3 weeks on queries. *No unsolicited mss.*

**Needs:** Actively seeking "big, commercial books with solid plotting, in-depth characters, and suspense. Cyberthrillers may be the next hot topic." Does not want to receive "cozies or British-style mysteries." Obtains new clients through recommendations from other authors. "35% of my list is from query letters!"

**Recent Sales:** Sold 67 titles in the last year. *Good News For Bad Days*, by Father Paul Keenan (Warner Book); *Stepping Out With Attitude: Sister Sell Your Dream*, by Anita Bunkley (HarperCollins); *His Flame*, by Arnette Lamb (Pocket Books); *Getting Rich in America*, by Dr. Richard McKenzie and Dr. Dwight Lee (HarperCollins).

**Terms:** Agent receives 15% commission on domestic sales; 20% on foreign sales. Offers written contract, binding for 2 years. Charges $100/year for postage, photocopying, long-distance calls, etc. 100% of business is derived from commissions on ms sales.

**Writers' Conferences:** Maui Writers Conference (August); Pacific Northwest Writers Conference; RWA.

**Tips:** "Only send a one-page query letter. I read them all and ask for plenty of material; I find many of my clients this way. *Always* send a SASE."

**ELAINE MARKSON LITERARY AGENCY**, 44 Greenwich Ave., New York NY 10011. (212)243-8480. Fax: (212)691-9014. **Contact:** Yael Adler. Estab. 1972. Member of AAR and WGA. Represents 200 clients. 10% of clients are new/unpublished writers. Specializes in literary fiction, commercial fiction, trade nonfiction. Currently handles: 35% nonfiction books; 55% novels; 10% juvenile books.

**Member Agents:** Geri Thoma, Sally Wofford-Girand, Elizabeth Sheinkman, Elaine Markson.

**Represents:** Quality fiction and nonfiction.

**How to Contact:** Query with outline (must include SASE). SASE is required for the return of any material.

**Recent Sales:** *The First Horseman*, by John Case (Ballantine); *Life, the Movie*, by Neal Gabler (Knopf); *The Hidden Jesus*, by Donald Spoto (St. Martins).

**Terms:** Agent receives 15% commission on domestic sales; 20% on foreign sales. Charges for postage, photocopying, foreign mailing, faxing, long-distance telephone and other special expenses. "Please make sure manuscript weighs no more than one pound."

**N** **THE EVAN MARSHALL AGENCY**, 6 Tristam Place, Pine Brook NJ 07058-9445. (973)882-1122. Fax: (973)882-3099. E-mail: evanmarshall@erols.com. Website: http://www.thenovelist.com. **Contact:** Evan Marshall. Estab. 1987. Currently handles: 50% nonfiction books; 50% novels.

• Prior to opening his agency, Mr. Marshall served as an editor with New American Library, Everest House, and Dodd, Mead & Co., and then worked as a literary agent at The Sterling Lord Agency.

**Represents:** Nonfiction books, novels. **Considers these nonfiction areas:** animals; biography/autobiography; business; child guidance/parenting; cooking/food/nutrition; crafts/hobbies; current affairs; government/politics/law; health/medicine; history; how-to; humor; interior design/decorating; language/literature/criticism; military/war; money/finance/economics; music/dance/theater/film; nature/environment; New Age/metaphysics; psychology; religious/inspirational; science/technology; self-help/personal improvement; true crime/investigative; women's issues/women's studies. **Considers these fiction areas:** action/adventure; contemporary issues; detective/police/crime; erotica; ethnic; family saga; glitz; historical; horror; humor/satire; literary; mainstream; mystery/suspense; psychic/supernatural; religious/inspirational; romance; (contemporary, gothic, historical, regency); science fiction; thriller/espionage; westerns/frontier.

**How to Contact:** Query. Reports in 1 week on queries; 2 months on mss.

**Needs:** Obtains many new clients through referrals from clients and editors.

**Recent Sales:** *Cause for Alarm*, by Erica Spindler (Mira); *Maybe Tomorrow*, by Joan Hohl (Kensington); *A Gift of Sanctuary*, by Candace Robb (St. Martin's); *Sympathy for the Devil*, by Jerrilyn Farmer (Avon); *Going Out in Style*, by Joyce Christmas (Fawcett).

**Terms:** Agent receives 15% on domestic sales; 20% on foreign sales. Offers written contract.

**N** **MARGRET MCBRIDE LITERARY AGENCY**, 7744 Fay Ave., Suite 201, La Jolla CA 92037. (619)454-1550. Fax: (619)454-2156. Estab. 1980. Member of AAR, Authors Guild. Represents 50 clients. 15% of clients are new/unpublished writers. Specializes in mainstream fiction and nonfiction.

• Prior to opening her agency, Ms. McBride served in the marketing departments of Random House and Ballantine Books and the publicity departments of Warner Books and Pinnacle Books.

**Represents:** Nonfiction books, novels, audio, video film rights. **Considers these nonfiction areas:** biography/autobiography; business; child guidance/parenting; cooking/food/nutrition; current affairs; ethnic/cultural interests; gay/lesbian issues; government/politics/law; health/medicine; history; how-to; money/finance/economics; music/dance/theater/film; popular culture; psychology; religious/inspirational; science/technology; self-help/personal improvement; sociology; sports; true crime/investigative; women's issues/women's studies. **Considers these fiction areas:** action/adventure; detective/police/crime; ethnic; historical; humor; literary; mainstream; mystery/suspense; thriller/espionage; westerns/frontier.

**How to Contact:** Query with synopsis or outline. No unsolicited mss. Reports in 6 weeks on queries.

**Needs:** No screenplays.

**Recent Sales:** *Freeing Fauziya*, by Fauziya Kasinga with Layli Miller Bashir; *The Unimaginable Life*, by Kenny and Julia Loggins; *The Golden Door Cookbook*, by Michele Stroot; *Ain't Gonna Be The Same Fool Twice*, by April Sinclair; *Weddings*, by Collin Cowel.

**Terms:** Agent receives 15% commission on domestic sales; 10% on dramatic sales; 25% on foreign sales charges for overnight delivery and photocopying.

**N** **DORIS S. MICHAELS LITERARY AGENCY, INC.**, 1841 Broadway, Suite #903, New York NY 10023. (212)265-9474. **Contact:** Doris S. Michaels. Estab. 1994. Member of WNBA, AAR. Represents 30 clients. 50% of clients are new/previously unpublished writers. Currently handles: 40% nonfiction books; 60% novels.

• Prior to opening her agency, Ms. Michaels was an editor for Prentice-Hall, consultant for Prudential-Bache, and an international consultant for the Union Bank of Switzerland.

**Represents:** Nonfiction books, novels. **Considers these nonfiction areas:** biography/autobiography; business; current affairs; ethnic/cultural interests; health; history; how-to; money/finance/economics; music/dance/theater/film; nature/environment; self-help/personal improvement; sports; women's issues/women's studies. **Considers these fiction areas:** action/adventure; contemporary issues; family saga; feminist; historical; literary; mainstream.

**How to Contact:** Query with SASE. No phone calls or unsolicited mss. Reports ASAP on queries with SASE; no answer without SASE.

**Needs:** Obtains new clients through recommendations from others, solicitation and at conferences.

**Recent Sales:** Sold 25 titles in the last year. *How to Become CEO*, by Jeffrey J. Fox (Hyperion); *The Neatest Little Guide to Personal Finance*, by Jason Kelly (Plume); *Swimming Lessons*, by Lynne Hugo and Anna Tuttle Villegas

(William Morrow). Other clients include Maury Allen, Wendy Rue, Karin Abarbanel and Eva Shaw.

**Terms:** Agent receives 15% commission on domestic sales; 20% on foreign sales. Offers written contract, binding for 1 year, with 30 day cancellation clause. Charges for office expenses including deliveries, postage, photocopying and fax. 100% of business is derived from commissions on sales.

**Writers' Conferences:** BEA (Chicago, June); Frankfurt Book Fair (Germany, October); London Book Fair; Society of Southwestern Authors; San Diego State University Writers' Conference; Willamette Writers' Conference; International Women's Writing Guild; American Society of Journalists and Authors.

**N THE CRAIG NELSON COMPANY**, 77 Seventh Ave., Suite 8F, New York NY 10011-6621. (212)929-0163. E-mail: litagnt@aol.com. Website: http://members.aol.com/litagnt. **Contact:** Craig Nelson. Estab. 1997. Member of AAR, signatory of WGA. Represents 50 clients. 50% of clients are new/unpublished writers. Currently handles: 75% nonfiction books; 25% novels.

● Prior to becoming an agent, Mr. Nelson was an executive editor for 20 years at Random House and HarperCollins.

**Represents:** Nonfiction books, novels. **Considers these nonfiction areas:** animals; anthropology/archaeology; biography/autobiography; business; computers/electronics; current affairs; ethnic/cultural interests; gay/lesbian issues; health/medicine; history; how-to; humor; money/finance/economics; music/dance/theater/film; nature/environment; popular culture; psychology; science/technology; self-help/personal improvement; true crime/investigative. **Considers these fiction areas:** contemporary issues; ethnic; gay/lesbian; horror; humor/satire; literary; mainstream; suspense; thriller/espionage.

**How to Contact:** Query with SASE. "Prefer e-mail queries. Absolutely no fax or web submissions." Reports in 1 month on queries; 6 weeks on mss.

**Needs:** Actively seeking "page-turning thrillers, eye-opening journalism, original literary fiction."

**Recent Sales:** Sold 15 titles in the last year. *Untitled Memoirs*, by Steve Wozniak (Pocket); *The Deal*, by Joe Hutsko (Forge); *Tiger in My Salad*, by Martine Colette (HarperCollins); *How to Win Friends*, by Lynne Russell (St. Martin's).

**Terms:** Agent receives 15% commission on domestic sales; 20% on foreign sales. Offers written contract, binding for 30 days. 30 days notice must be given to terminate contract.

**N NEW ENGLAND PUBLISHING ASSOCIATES, INC.**, P.O. Box 5, Chester CT 06412-0645. (203)345-READ and (203)345-4976. Fax: (203)345-3660. E-mail: nepa@nepa.com. **Contact:** Elizabeth Frost-Knappman, Edward W. Knappman. Estab. 1983. Member of AAR. Represents over 100 clients. 15% of clients are new/previously unpublished writers. Specializes in adult nonfiction books of serious purpose.

**Represents:** Nonfiction books. **Considers these nonfiction areas:** biography/autobiography; business; child guidance/parenting; government/politics/law; health/medicine; history; language/literature/criticism; military/war; money/finance/economics; nature/environment; psychology; science/technology; personal improvement; sociology; true crime/investigative; women's issues/women's studies. "Occasionally represents crime fiction."

**How to Contact:** Send outline/proposal. Reports in 3 weeks on queries; 5 weeks on mss.

**Recent Sales:** *Eudora Welty*, by Ann Waldron (Doubleday); *Cigars, Whiskey and Winning*, by Al Kaltman (Prentice Hall); *The Woman's Migraine Survival Handbook*, by Christina Peterson and Christine Adamec; *Dictionary of Art*, by Nancy Frazier (Penguin); *The Prettiest Feathers* (crime fiction), *Stalemate* (true crime), by John Philpin (Bantam); *Susan Sontag*, by Carl Rollyson and Lisa Paddock.

**Terms:** Agent receives 15% commission on domestic sales; 20% foreign sales (split with overseas agent). Offers written contract, binding for 6 months.

**Writers' Conferences:** ABA (Chicago, June); ALA (San Antonio, January); ALA (New York, July).

**Tips:** "Send us a well-written proposal that clearly identifies your audience—who will buy this book and why."

**ALICE ORR AGENCY, INC.**, 305 Madison Ave., Suite 1166, New York NY 10165. (718)204-6673. Fax: (718)204-6023. E-mail: orragency@aol.com. Website: http://www.romanceweb.com/aorr/aorr.html. **Contact:** Alice Orr. Estab. 1988. Member of AAR. Represents over 20 clients. Specializes in commercial ("as in nonliterary") fiction and nonfiction. Currently handles: 5% nonfiction books; 5% juvenile books; 90% novels.

● Prior to opening her agency, Ms. Orr was editor of mystery-suspense and romance fiction; national lecturer on how to write and get that writing published; and is a published popular fiction novelist.

**Represents:** Considers commercial nonfiction. **Considers these fiction areas:** mainstream; romance (contemporary, historical); mystery/suspense.

**How to Contact:** Send SASE for synopsis/proposal guidelines. "Send nonfiction proposal prepared according to this agency's guidelines only." For fiction, send synopsis and first 3 chapters. Reports in 2 months.

**Needs:** Actively seeking "absolutely extraordinary, astounding, astonishing work." Does not want to receive "science fiction and fantasy, horror fiction, literary nonfiction, literary fiction, poetry, short stories, children's or juvenile fiction and nonfiction." Obtains new clients through recommendations from others, writer's conferences, meetings with authors and submissions.

**Terms:** Agent receives 15% commission on domestic sales; 20% on foreign and film sales. No written contract.

**Recent Sales:** Sold over 20 titles in the last year. Prefers not to share information on specific sales.

**Writers' Conferences:** Edgar Allen Poe Awards Week; Novelists Ink Conference; International Women's Writing Guild Skidmore College Conference & Retreat; Romance Writers of America National Convention; Romantic Times Booklovers Convention.

**FIFI OSCARD AGENCY INC.**, 24 W. 40th St., New York NY 10018. (212)764-1100. **Contact:** Ivy Fischer Stone, Literary Department. Estab. 1956. Member of AAR, signatory of WGA. Represents 108 clients. 5% of clients are new/unpublished writers. "Writer must have published articles or books in major markets or have screen credits if movie scripts, etc." Specializes in literary novels, commercial novels, mysteries and nonfiction, especially celebrity biographies and autobiographies. Currently handles: 40% nonfiction books; 40% novels; 5% movie scripts; 10% stage plays; 5% TV scripts.
**Represents:** Nonfiction books, novels, movie scripts, stage plays.
**How to Contact:** Query with outline. Reports in 1 week on queries if SASE enclosed. No unsolicited mss please.
**Recent Sales:** *The Return*, by William Shatner (Pocket Books); *Calendar of Wisdom*, by Leo Tolstoy, translated by Peter Sekirin (Scribner); *Autopsy On An Empire*, by Jack Matlock, Jr. (Random House).
**Terms:** Agent receives 15% commission on domestic sales; 10% on dramatic sales; 20% on foreign sales. Charges for photocopying expenses.

**PERKINS, RUBIE & ASSOCIATES**, (formerly Perkins, Rabiner, Rubie & Associates), 240 W. 35th St., New York NY 10001. (212)279-1776. Fax: (212)279-0937. **Contact:** Lori Perkins, Peter Rubie, June Clark. Estab. 1997. Member of AAR, HWA. Represents 130 clients. 15% of clients are new/previously unpublished writers. Perkins specializes in horror, dark thrillers, literary fiction, pop culture, Latino and gay issues (fiction and nonfiction). Rubie specializes in crime, science fiction, fantasy, off-beat mysteries, history, literary fiction, dark thrillers, narrative nonfiction. Currently handles: 60% nonfiction books; 40% novels.
● Lori Perkins is the author of *The Cheapskate's Guide to Entertaining; How to Throw Fabulous Parties on a Budget* (Carol Publishing) and *How to Get and Keep the Right Agent for You* (Writer's Digest Books). Prior to becoming an agent, she taught journalism at NYU. Mr. Rubie is the author of *The Elements of Storytelling* (John Wiley) and *Story Sense* (Writer's Digest Books).
**Represents:** Nonfiction books, novels. **Considers these nonfiction areas:** art/architecture/design; current affairs; commercial academic material; ethnic/cultural interests; music/dance/theater/film; science; "subjects that fall under pop culture—TV, music, art, books and authors, film, current affairs etc." **Considers these fiction areas:** detective/police/crime; ethnic; fact-based historical fiction; fantasy; horror; literary; mainstream; mystery/suspense; psychic/supernatural; science fiction; dark thriller.
**How to Contact:** Query with SASE. Reports in 6 weeks on queries with SASE; 10 weeks on mss.
**Needs:** Obtains new clients through recommendations from others, solicitation, at conferences, etc.
**Recent Sales:** *Big Rock Beat*, by Greg Kihn (Forge); *Piercing the Darkness: Uncovering the Vampires in America Today*, by K. Ramsland (Harper); *The Science of the X-Files*, by Jeanne Cavelos (Berkley); *Keeper*, by Gregory Rucka (Bantam); *Witchunter*, by C. Lyons (Avon); *How the Tiger Lost Its Stripes*, by C. Meacham (Harcourt Brace).
**Terms:** Agent receives 15% commission on domestic sales; 20% on foreign sales. Offers written contract, only "if requested." Charges for photocopying.
**Tips:** "Sometimes I come up with book ideas and find authors (*Coupon Queen*, for example). Be professional. Read *Publishers Weekly* and genre-related magazines. Join writers' organizations. Go to conferences. Know your market and learn your craft."

**STEPHEN PEVNER, INC.**, 248 W. 73rd St., 2nd Floor, New York NY 10023. (212)496-0474 or (323)464-5546. Fax: (212)496-0796. E-mail: spevner@aol.com. **Contact:** Stephen Pevner. Estab. 1991. Member of AAR, signatory of WGA. Represents under 50 clients. 50% of clients are new/previously unpublished writers. Specializes in motion pictures, novels, humor, pop culture, urban fiction, independent filmmakers. Currently handles: 25% nonfiction books; 25% movie scripts; 25% novels; TV scripts; stage plays.
**Represents:** Nonfiction books, novels, movie scripts, TV scripts, stage plays. **Considers these nonfiction areas:** art/architecture/design; biography/autobiography; business; cooking/food/nutrition; current affairs; ethnic/cultural interests; gay/lesbian issues; government/politics/law; history; humor; language/literature/criticism; memoirs; money/finance/economics; music/dance/theater/film; New Age/metaphysics; photography; popular culture; religious/inspirational; sociology; travel. **Considers these fiction areas:** cartoon/comic; contemporary issues; detective/police/crime; erotica; ethnic; experimental; gay; glitz; horror; humor/satire; lesbian; literary; mainstream; psychic/supernatural; science fiction; thriller/espionage; urban.
**How to Contact:** Query with outline/proposal. Reports in 2 weeks on queries; 1 month on mss.
**Needs:** Actively seeking urban fiction, popular culture, screenplays and film proposals. Obtains new clients through recommendations from others.
**Recent Sales:** Sold 6 titles in the last year. *In the Company of Men*, by Neil LaBute (Faber and Faber); *The Cross-Referenced Guide to the Baby Buster Generations Collective Unconscious*, by Glenn Gaslin and Rick Porter (Putnam/Berkley); *The Lesbian Brain*, by The Five Lesbian Brothers (Simon & Schuster).
**Terms:** Agent receives 15% commission on domestic sales; 20% on foreign sales. Offers written contract, binding for 1 year, with 6 week cancellation clause. 100% of business is derived from commissions on sales.
**Represents: Writer/directors:** Richard Linklater (*Slacker, Dazed & Confused, Before Sunrise*); Gregg Araki (*The Living End, Doom Generation*); Tom DiCillo (*Living in Oblivion*); Genvieve Turner/Rose Troche (*Go Fish*); Todd Solondz (*Welcome to the Dollhouse*); Neil LaBute (*In the Company of Men*).
**Terms:** Agent receives 10% commission on domestic sales; 10% on foreign sales. Charges for postage, long distance phone calls and photocopying.
**Also Handles:** Feature film, documentary, animation; TV MOW, miniseries, episodic drama; theatrical stage plays.

Considers these script subject areas: action/adventure; comedy; contemporary issues; detective/police/crime; gay; glitz; horror; humor; lesbian; mainstream; mystery/suspense; romantic comedy and drama; science fiction; teen; thriller.
**Writers' Conferences:** Sundance Film Festival, Independent Feature Market.
**Tips:** "Be persistent, but civilized."

**PINDER LANE & GARON-BROOKE ASSOCIATES, LTD.,** (formerly Jay Garon-Brooke Assoc. Inc.), 159 W. 53rd St., Suite 14E, New York NY 10019-6005. (212)489-0880. Vice President: Jean Free. Member of AAR, signatory of WGA. Represents 80 clients. 20% of clients are new/previously unpublished writers. Specializes in mainstream fiction and nonfiction. "With our literary and media experience, our agency is uniquely positioned for the current and future direction publishing is taking." Currently handles: 25% nonfiction books; 75% novels.
**Member Agents:** Nancy Coffey, Dick Duane, Robert Thixton.
**Represents:** Nonfiction books, novels. **Considers these nonfiction areas:** biography/autobiography; child guidance/parenting; gay/lesbian issues; health/medicine; history; memoirs; military/war; music/dance/theater/film; psychology; self-help/personal improvement; true crime/investigative. **Considers these fiction areas:** contemporary issues; detective/police/crime; family saga; fantasy; gay; literary; mainstream; mystery/suspense; romance; science fiction.
**How to Contact:** Query with SASE. Reports in 3 weeks on queries; 2 months on mss.
**Needs:** Does not want to receive screenplays, TV series teleplays or dramatic plays. Obtains new clients through referrals and from queries.
**Recent Sales:** Sold 15 titles in the last year. *Nobody's Safe*, by Richard Steinberg (Doubleday); *The Kill Box*, by Chris Stewart (M. Evans); *Return to Christmas*, by Chris Heimerdinger (Ballantine); *All I Desire*, by Rosemary Rogers (Avon).
**Terms:** Agent receives 15% on domestic sales; 30% on foreign sales. Offers written contract, binding for 3-5 years.
**Tips:** "Send query letter first giving the essence of the manuscript and a personal or career bio with SASE."

**AARON M. PRIEST LITERARY AGENCY**, 708 Third Ave., 23rd Floor, New York NY 10017. (212)818-0344.
**Contact:** Aaron Priest or Molly Friedrich. Member of AAR. Currently handles: 25% nonfiction books; 75% fiction.
**Member Agents:** Lisa Erbach Vance, Paul Cirone, Wendy Sherman.
**Represents:** Nonfiction books, fiction.
**How to Contact:** Query only (must be accompanied by SASE). Unsolicited mss will be returned unread.
**Recent Sales:** *Absolute Power*, by David Baldacci (Warner); *Three to get Deadly*, by Janet Evanovich (Scribner); *How Stella Got Her Groove Back*, by Terry McMillan (Viking); *Day After Tomorrow*, by Allan Folsom (Little, Brown); *Angela's Ashes*, by Frank McCourt (Scribner); *M as in Malice*, by Sue Grafton (Henry Holt).
**Terms:** Agent receives 15% commission on domestic sales. Charges for photocopying, foreign postage expenses.

**HELEN REES LITERARY AGENCY**, 123 N. Washington St., 5th Floor, Boston MA 02114. (617)723-5232. **Contact:** Joan Mazmanian. Estab. 1981. Member of AAR. Represents 50 clients. 50% of clients are new/previously unpublished writers. Specializes in general nonfiction, health, business, world politics, autobiographies, psychology, women's issues. Currently handles: 60% nonfiction books; 40% novels.
**Represents:** Nonfiction books, novels. **Considers these nonfiction areas:** biography/autobiography; business; current affairs; government/politics/law; health/medicine; history; money/finance/economics; women's issues/women's studies. **Considers these fiction areas:** contemporary issues; detective/police/crime; glitz; historical; literary; mainstream; mystery/suspense; thriller/espionage.
**How to Contact:** Query with outline plus 2 sample chapters. Reports in 2 weeks on queries; 3 weeks on mss.
**Needs:** Obtains new clients through recommendations from others, solicitation, at conferences, etc.
**Recent Sales:** *The Mentor*, by Sebastian Stuart (Bantam); *Managing the Human Animal*, by Nigel Nicholson (Times Books); *Breaking the Silence*, by Dr. William Beardslee (Little, Brown); *Stalin*, by Richard Louie (Counterpoint Press).
**Terms:** Agent receives 15% commission on domestic sales; 20% on foreign sales.

**THE DAMARIS ROWLAND AGENCY**, 510 E. 23rd St., #8-G, New York NY 10010-5020. (212)475-8942. Fax: (212)358-9411. **Contact:** Damaris Rowland or Steve Axelrod. Estab. 1994. Member of AAR. Represents 40 clients. 10% of clients are new/previously unpublished writers. Specializes in women's fiction. Currently handles: 75% novels, 25% nonfiction.
**Represents:** Nonfiction books, novels. **Considers these nonfiction areas:** animals; cooking/food/nutrition; health/medicine; nature/environment; New Age/metaphysics; religious/inspirational; women's issues/women's studies. **Considers these fiction areas:** detective/police/crime; historical; literary; mainstream; psychic/supernatural; romance (contemporary, gothic, historical, regency).
**How to Contact:** Send outline/proposal. Reports in 6 weeks.
**Needs:** Obtains new clients through recommendations from others, at conferences.
**Recent Sales:** *The Perfect Husband*, by Lisa Gardner (Bantam); *Soul Dating To Soul Mating, On The Path To Spiritual Partnership*, by Basha Kaplan and Gail Prince (Putnam Books); *My Dearest Enemy*, by Connie Brockway (Dell).
**Terms:** Agent receives 15% commission on domestic sales; 20% on foreign sales. Offers written contract, with 30 day cancellation clause. Charges only if extraordinary expenses have been incurred, e.g., photocopying and mailing 15 ms to Europe for a foreign sale. 100% of business is derived from commissions on sales.
**Writers' Conferences:** Novelists Inc. (Denver, October); RWA National (Texas, July), Pacific Northwest Writers Conference.

**PESHA RUBINSTEIN LITERARY AGENCY, INC.**, 1392 Rugby Rd., Teaneck NJ 07666-2839. (201)862-1174. Fax: (201)862-1180. E-mail: peshalit@aol.com. **Contact:** Pesha Rubinstein. Estab. 1990. Member of AAR, RWA, MWA, SCBWI. Represents 35 clients. 25% of clients are new/previously unpublished writers. Specializes in commercial fiction, romance, and children's books. Currently handles: 30% juvenile books; 70% novels.
   • Prior to opening her agency, Ms. Rubenstein served as an editor at Zebra and Leisure Books.
**Represents:** Commercial fiction, juvenile books, picture book illustration. **Considers these nonfiction areas:** child guidance/parenting. **Considers these fiction areas:** detective/police/crime; ethnic; glitz; humor; juvenile; mainstream; mystery/suspense; picture book; psychic/supernatural; romance (contemporary, historical); spiritual adventures.
**How to Contact:** Send query, first 10 pages and SASE. Reports in 2 weeks on queries; 6 weeks on requested mss.
**Needs:** Does not want to receive poetry or westerns.
**Recent Sales:** Sold 25 titles in the last year. *A is for Salad*, by Mike Lester (Grosset); *Tree of Hope*, by Amy Littlesugar (Philomel); untitled book, by Niki Rivers (Harlequin); *The Banned and the Banished*, by James Clemens (Del Rey); *Frontiers*, by Michael Jensen (Pocket).
**Terms:** Agent receives 15% commission on domestic sales; 20% on foreign sales. Offers written contract. Charges for photocopying and overseas postage. No weekend or collect calls accepted.
**Tips:** "Keep the query letter and synopsis short. Please send first ten pages of manuscript rather than selected chapters from the manuscript. I am a stickler for correct grammar, spelling and punctuation. The work speaks for itself better than any description can. Never send originals. A phone call after one month is acceptable. Always include a SASE covering return of the entire package with the material."

**RUSSELL & VOLKENING**, 50 W. 29th St., #7E, New York NY 10001. (212)684-6050. Fax: (212)889-3026. **Contact:** Joseph Regal or Jennie Dunham. Estab. 1940. Member of AAR. Represents 140 clients. 10% of clients are new/previously unpublished writers. Specializes in literary fiction and narrative nonfiction. Currently handles: 40% nonfiction books; 15% juvenile books; 2% short story collections; 40% novels; 2% novellas; 1% poetry.
**Member Agents:** Timothy Seldes (nonfiction, literary fiction); Joseph Regal (literary fiction, thrillers ,nonfiction); Jennie Dunham (literary fiction, nonfiction, children's books).
**Represents:** Nonfiction books, juvenile books, novels, novellas, short story collections. **Considers these nonfiction areas:** anthropology/archaeology; art/architecture/design; biography/autobiography; business; cooking/food/nutrition; current affairs; education; ethnic/cultural interests; gay/lesbian issues; government/politics/law; health/medicine; history; juvenile nonfiction; language/literature/criticism; military/war; money/finance/economics; music/dance/theater/film; nature/environment; photography; popular culture; psychology; science/technology; sociology; sports; true crime/investigative; women's issues/women's studies. **Considers these fiction areas:** action/adventure; detective/police/crime; ethnic; juvenile; literary; mainstream; mystery/suspense; picture book; sports; thriller/espionage; young adult.
**How to Contact:** Query. Reports in 1 week on queries; 1 month on mss.
**Recent Sales:** *A Patchwork Planet*, by Anne Tyler (Knopf); *The House Gun*, by Nadine Gordimer (Farrar, Straus & Giroux); *Truman Capote*, by George Plimpton (Doubleday); *Cookie Count*, by Robert Sabuda (Little Simon).
**Terms:** Agent receives 10% commission on domestic sales; 20% on foreign sales. Charges for "standard office expenses relating to the submission of materials of an author we represent, e.g., photocopying, postage."
**Tips:** "If the query is cogent, well-written, well-presented and is the type of book we'd represent, we'll ask to see the manuscript. From there, it depends purely on the quality of the work."

**VICTORIA SANDERS LITERARY AGENCY**, 241 Avenue of the Americas, New York NY 10014-4822. (212)633-8811. Fax: (212)633-0525. **Contact:** Victoria Sanders and/or Diane Dickensheid. Estab. 1993. Member of AAR, signatory of WGA. Represents 75 clients. 25% of clients are new/previously unpublished writers. Currently handles: 50% nonfiction books; 50% novels.
**Represents:** Nonfiction, novels. **Considers these nonfiction areas:** biography/autobiography; current affairs; ethnic/cultural interests; gay/lesbian issues; govenment/politics/law; history; humor; language/literature/criticism; music/dance/theater/film; popular culture; psychology; translations; women's issues/women's studies. **Considers these fiction areas:** action/adventure; contemporary issues; family saga; feminist; gay; lesbian; literary; thriller/espionage.
**How to Contact:** Query and SASE. Reports in 1 week on queries; 1 month on mss.
**Needs:** Obtains new clients through recommendations, "or I find them through my reading and pursue."
**Recent Sales:** *Bebe's by Golly Wow*, by Yolanda Joe (Doubleday); *Santa & Pete*, by Christopher Moore and Pamela Johnson (Simon & Schuster); and *The Forbidden Zone*, by Michael Harker (Simon & Schuster).
**Terms:** Agent receives 15% commission on domestic sales; 20% on foreign sales. Offers written contract binding at will. Charges for photocopying, ms, messenger, express mail and extraordinary fees. If in excess of $100, client approval is required.
**Tips:** "Limit query to letter, no calls and give it your best shot. A good query is going to get a good response."

**IRENE SKOLNICK**, 22 W. 23rd St., 5th Floor, New York NY 10010. (212)727-3648. Fax: (212)727-1024. E-mail: sirene35@aol.com. **Contact:** Irene Skolnick. Estab. 1993. Member of AAR. Represents 45 clients. 75% of clients are new/previously unpublished writers.
**Represents:** Adult nonfiction books, adult fiction. **Considers these nonfiction areas:** biography/autobiography; current affairs. **Considers these fiction areas:** contemporary issues; historical; literary.
**How to Contact:** Query with SASE, outline and sample chapter. No unsolicited mss. Reports in 1 month on queries.
**Recent Sales:** *An Equal Music*, by Seth Vikram; *Kaaterskill Falls*, by Allegra Goodman; *Taking Lives*, by Pye.

**Terms:** Agent receives 15% commission on domestic sales; 20% on foreign sales. Sometimes offers criticism service. Charges for international postage, photocopying over 40 pages.

**ROBIN STRAUS AGENCY, INC.**, 229 E. 79th St., New York NY 10021. (212)472-3282. Fax: (212)472-3833. E-mail: springbird@aol.com. **Contact:** Robin Straus. Estab. 1983. Member of AAR. Specializes in high-quality fiction and nonfiction for adults. Currently handles: 65% nonfiction books; 35% novels.
- Prior to becoming an agent, Robin Straus served as a subsidiary rights manager at Random House and Doubleday and worked in editorial at Little, Brown.

**Represents:** Nonfiction, novels. **Considers these nonfiction areas:** animals; anthropology/archaeology; art/architecture/design; biography/autobiography; child guidance/parenting; cooking/food/nutrition; current affairs; ethnic/cultural interests; government/politics/law; health/medicine; history; language/literature/criticism; music/dance/theater/film; nature/environment; popular culture; psychology; science/technology; sociology; women's issues/women's studies. **Considers these fiction areas:** contemporary issues; family saga; historical; literary; mainstream; thriller/espionage.
**How to Contact:** Query with sample pages. No e-mail inquiries. SASE ("stamps, not metered postage") required. Reports in 1 month on queries and mss.
**Needs:** Most new clients obtained through recommendations from others.
**Recent Sales:** Prefers not to share information.
**Terms:** Agent receives 15% commission on domestic sales; 20% on foreign sales. Offers written contract when requested. Charges for "photocopying, UPS, messenger and foreign postage, etc. as incurred."

**N** **TOAD HALL, INC.**, RR 2, Box 16B, Laceyville PA 18623. (717)869-2942. Fax: (717)869-1031. E-mail: toad.hall @prodigy.com. Website: http://www.toadhallinc.com. **Contact:** Sharon Jarvis, Anne Pinzow. Estab. 1982. Member of AAR. Represents 35 clients. 10% of clients are new/previously unpublished writers. Specializes in popular nonfiction, some category fiction. Prefers New Age, paranormal, unusual but popular approaches. Currently handles: 50% nonfiction books; 40% novels; 5% movie scripts; 5% ancillary projects.
- Prior to becoming an agent, Ms. Jarvis was an acquisitions editor.

**Member Agents:** Sharon Jarvis (fiction, nonfiction); Anne Pinzow (TV, movies); Roxy LeRose (unpublished writers).
**Represents:** Nonfiction books. **Considers these nonfiction areas:** animals; anthropology/archaeology; business; child guidance/parenting; cooking/food/nutrition; crafts/hobbies; health/medicine; how-to; nature/environment; New Age/metaphysics; popular culture; religious/inspirational; self-help/personal improvement. **Considers these fiction areas:** historical; mystery/suspense; romance (contemporary, historical, regency); science fiction.
**How to Contact:** Query. "No fax or e-mail submissions considered." Reports in 3 weeks on queries; 3 months on mss. For scripts, send outline/proposal with query. "We only handle scripts written by our clients who have published material agented by us." Reports in 3 weeks on queries; 3 months on mss.
**Also Handles:** Feature film; TV MOW, episodic drama. Considers these script areas: action/adventure; comedy; contemporary issues; detective/police/crime; ethnic; family saga; fantasy; feminist; historical; horror; juvenile; mainstream; mystery/suspense; romantic comedy; science fiction.
**Needs:** Does not want to receive poetry, short stories, essays, collections, children's books. Obtains new clients through recommendations from others, solicitation, at conferences.
**Recent Sales:** Sold 6 titles in the last year. *The Face of Time*, by Camille Bacon-Smith (DAW); *Against All Odds*, by Barbara Riefe (TOR); *Herbal Medicine*, by Mary Atwood (Sterling); *Blood on The Moon* by Sharman DiVono (movie option to ABC).
**Terms:** Agent receives 15% commission on domestic sales; 10% on foreign sales. Offers written contract, binding for 1 year. Charges for photocopying and special postage (i.e., express mail).
**Tips:** "Pay attention to what is getting published. Show the agent you've done your homework!"

**SUSAN ZECKENDORF ASSOC. INC.**, 171 W. 57th St., New York NY 10019. (212)245-2928. **Contact:** Susan Zeckendorf. Estab. 1979. Member of AAR. Represents 35 clients. 25% of clients are new/previously unpublished writers. "We are a small agency giving lots of individual attention. We respond quickly to submissions." Currently handles: 50% nonfiction books; 50% fiction.
- Prior to opening her agency, Ms. Zeckendorf was a counseling psychologist.

**Represents:** Nonfiction books, novels. **Considers these nonfiction areas:** art/architecture/design; biography/autobiography; child guidance/parenting; health/medicine; history; music/dance/theater/film; psychology; science; sociology; true crime/investigative; women's issues/women's studies. **Considers these fiction areas:** action/adventure; contemporary issues; detective/police/crime; ethnic; family saga; glitz; historical; literary; mainstream; mystery/suspense; thriller/espionage.
**How to Contact:** Query. Reports in 10 days on queries; 3 weeks mss. Obtains new clients through recommendations, listings in writer's manuals.
**Needs:** Actively seeking mysteries, literary fiction, mainstream fiction, thrillers, social history, parenting, classical music, biography. Does not want to receive science fiction, romance.
**Recent Sales:** *Scents of the Wight*, by Una-Mary Parker (Headline); *Fifth Avenue: The Best Address*, by Jerry Patterson (Rizzoli).
**Terms:** Agent receives 15% commission on domestic sales; 20% on foreign sales. Charges for photocopying, messenger services.
**Writers' Conferences:** Central Valley Writers Conference; the Tucson Publishers Association Conference; Writer's

Connection; Frontiers in Writing Conference (Amarillo, TX); Golden Triangle Writers Conference (Beaumont TX); Oklahoma Festival of Books (Claremont OK); Mary Mount Writers Conference.

# SCRIPT AGENTS

**⟦N⟧ THE ARTISTS AGENCY**, 10000 Santa Monica Blvd., Suite 305, Los Angeles, CA 90035. (310)277-7779. Fax: (310)785-9338. **Contact:** Merrily Kane. Estab. 1974. Signatory of WGA. Represents 80 clients. 20% of clients are new/previously unpublished writers. Currently handles: 50% movie scripts; 50% TV scripts.
**Represents:** Movie scripts (feature film), TV scripts (TV MOW). **Considers these script subject areas:** action/adventure; comedy; contemporary issues; detective/police/crime; mystery/suspense; romantic comedy and drama; thriller.
**How to Contact:** Query. Reports in 2 weeks on queries.
**Needs:** Obtains new clients through recommendations from others.
**Recent Sales:** Prefers not to share information.
**Terms:** Agent receives 10% commission. Offers written contract, binding for 1-2 years, per WGA.

**⟦N⟧ THE MARSHALL CAMERON AGENCY**, 19667 NE 20th Lane, Lawtey FL 32058. Phone/fax: (904)964-7013. E-mail: marshall_cameron@hotmail.com. **Contact:** Margo Prescott. Estab. 1986. Signatory of WGA. Specializes in feature films. Currently handles: 100% movie scripts.
**Member Agents:** Margo Prescott; Ashton Prescott.
**Represents:** Movie scripts (feature film). No longer represents books. **Considers these script subject areas:** action/adventure; comedy; detective/police/crime; drama (contemporary); mainstream; thriller/espionage.
**How to Contact:** Query. No phone queries. Query by letter with SASE or by e-mail. Reports in 1 week on queries; 1-2 months on mss.
**Recent Sales:** Prefers not to share information.
**Terms:** Agent receives 10% commission on domestic sales; 20% on foreign sales. Offers written contract, binding for 1 year.
**Tips:** "Often professionals in film will recommend us to clients. We also actively solicit material. Always enclose SASE with your query."

**⟦N⟧ DOUROUX & CO.**, 445 S. Beverly Dr., Suite 310, Beverly Hills CA 90212-4401. (310)552-0900. Fax: (310)552-0920. E-mail: douroux@relaypoint.net. Website: http://www.relaypoint.net/~douroux. **Contact:** Michael E. Douroux. Estab. 1985. Signatory of WGA, member of DGA. 20% of clients are new/previously unpublished writers. Currently handles: 50% movie scripts; 50% TV scripts.
**Member Agents:** Michael E. Douroux (chairman/CEO); Tara T. Thiesmeyer (associate).
**Represents:** Movie scripts (feature film); TV scripts (TV MOW, episodic drama, sitcom, animation). **Considers these script subject areas:** action/adventure; comedy; detective/police/crime; family saga; fantasy; historical; mainstream; mystery/suspense; romantic comedy and drama; science fiction; thriller/espionage; westerns/frontier.
**How to Contact:** Query.
**Recent Sales:** Prefers not to share information on specific sales.
**Terms:** Agent receives 10% commission. Offers written contract, binding for 2 years. Charges for photocopying only.

**⟦N⟧ EPSTEIN-WYCKOFF AND ASSOCIATES**, 280 S. Beverly Dr., #400, Beverly Hills CA 90212-3904. (310)278-7222. Fax: (310)278-4640. **Contact:** Karin Wakefield. Estab. 1993. Signatory of WGA. Represents 20 clients. Specializes in features, TV, books and stage plays. Currently handles: 1% nonfiction books; 1% novels; 60% movie scripts; 30% TV scripts; 2% stage plays.
**Member Agents:** Karin Wakefield (literary); Craig Wyckoff (talent); Gary Epstein (talent).
**Represents:** Movie scripts (feature film), TV scripts (TV MOW, miniseries, episodic drama, sitcom, animation, soap opera), stage plays. **Considers these script subject areas:** action/adventure; comedy; contemporary issues; detective/police/crime; erotica; family saga; feminist; gay; historical; juvenile; lesbian; mainstream; mystery/suspense; romantic comedy and drama; teen; thriller.
**How to Contact:** Query with SASE. Reports in 1 week on queries; 1 month on mss, if solicited.
**Needs:** Obtains new clients through recommendations, queries.
**Recent Sales:** Sold 10 projects in the last year. Prefers not to share information on specific sales.
**Terms:** Agent receives 15% commission on domestic sales of books, 10% on scripts; 20% on foreign sales. Offers written contract, binding for 1 year. Charges for photocopying.
**Also Handles:** Nonfiction books, novels.
**Writers' Conferences:** BEA.

**⟦N⟧ THE BARRY FREED CO.**, 2040 Ave. of the Stars, #400, Los Angeles CA 90067. (310)277-1260. Fax: (310)277-3865. E-mail: blfreed@aol.com. **Contact:** Barry Freed. Signatory of WGA. Represents 15 clients. 95% of clients are new/unpublished writers. Highly qualified small roster of writers who write comedy, action adventure/thrillers, adult drama, romantic comedy. Currently represents: 100% movie scripts.
● Prior to opening his agency, Mr. Freed worked for ICM.

**Represents:** Feature film, TV MOW. **Considers these script subject areas:** action/adventure; comedy; contemporary issues; detective/police/crime; ethnic; family saga; horror; mainstream; mystery/suspense; science fiction; sports; teen; thriller/espionage.

**How to Contact:** Query. Reports immediately on queries; in 3 moths on mss.

**Needs:** Actively seeking adult drama, comedy, romantic comedy, science fiction. Does not want to receive period, westerns. Obtains new clients through recommendations from others.

**Recent Sales:** Prefers not to share information on specific sales.

**Terms:** Offers written contract binding for 2 years.

**N: ROBERT A. FREEDMAN DRAMATIC AGENCY, INC.**, 1501 Broadway, Suite 2310, New York NY 10036. (212)840-5760. President: Robert A. Freedman. Vice President: Selma Luttinger. Estab. 1928. Member of AAR, signatory of WGA. Prefers to work with established authors; works with a small number of new authors. Specializes in plays, movie scripts and TV scripts.

 • Robert Freedman has served as vice president of the dramatic division of AAR.

**Represents:** Movie scripts, TV scripts, stage plays.

**How to Contact:** Query. No unsolicited mss. Usually reports in 2 weeks on queries; 3 months on mss.

**Terms:** Agent receives 10% on dramatic sales; "and, as is customary, 20% on amateur rights." Charges for photocopying.

**Recent Sales:** "We will speak directly with any prospective client concerning sales that are relevant to his/her specific script."

**N: SAMUEL FRENCH, INC.**, 45 W. 25th St., New York NY 10010-2751. (212)206-8990. Fax: (212)206-1429. Editors: William Talbot and Lawrence Harbison. Estab. 1830. Member of AAR. Represents plays which it publishes for production rights.

**Member Agents:** Pam Newton; Brad Lohrenze.

**Represents:** Stage plays (theatrical stage play, musicals, variety show). **Considers these script subject areas:** comedy; contemporary issues; detective/police/crime; ethnic; experimental; fantasy; horror; mystery/suspense; religious/inspirational; thriller.

**How to Contact:** Query or send entire ms. Replies "immediately" on queries; decision in 2-8 months regarding publication. "Enclose SASE."

**Recent Sales:** Prefers not to share information.

**Terms:** Agent usually receives 10% professional production royalties; variable amateur production royalties.

**N: WILLIAM KERWIN AGENCY**, 1605 N. Cahuenga, Suite 202, Hollywood CA 90028. (323)469-5155. **Contact:** Al Wood and Bill Kerwin. Estab. 1979. Signatory of WGA. Represents 5 clients. Currently handles: 100% movie scripts.

**Represents: Considers these script subject areas:** mystery/suspense; romance; science fiction; thriller/espionage.

**How to Contact:** Query. Reports in 1 day on queries; 1 month on mss.

**Needs:** Obtains new clients through recommendations and solicitation.

**Recent Sales:** HBO or TMC film *Steel Death*, starring Jack Scalia.

**Terms:** Agent receives 10% commission on domestic sales; 10% on foreign sales. Offers written contract, binding for 1-2 years, with 30 day cancellation clause. Offers free criticism service.

**Tips:** "Listen. Be nice."

**N: MONTEIRO ROSE AGENCY**, 17514 Ventura Blvd., #205, Encino CA 91316. (818)501-1177. Fax: (818)501-1194. E-mail: monrose@ix.netcom.com. **Contact:** Milissa Brockish. Estab. 1987. Signatory of WGA. Represents over 50 clients. Specializes in scripts for animation, TV and film. Currently handles: 40% movie scripts; 20% TV scripts; 40% animation.

**Member Agents:** Candace Monteiro (literary); Fredda Rose (literary); Milissa Brockish (literary).

**Represents:** Movie scripts (feature film, animation), TV scripts (TV MOW, episodic drama, animation). **Considers these script subject areas:** action/adventure; cartoon/animation; comedy; contemporary issues; detective/police/crime; ethnic; family saga; fantasy; historical; juvenile; mainstream; mystery/suspense; psychic/supernatural; romantic comedy and drama; science fiction; teen; thriller; western/frontier.

**How to Contact:** Query with SASE. Reports in 1 week on queries; 2 months on mss.

**Needs:** Obtains new clients through recommendations from others in the entertainment business and query letters.

**Recent Sales:** Prefers not to share information.

**Terms:** Agent receives 10% commission on domestic sales. Offers standard WGA 2 year contract, with 120-day cancellation clause. Charges for photocopying. 100% of business is derived from commissions.

**Tips:** "It does no good to call and try to speak to an agent before they have read your material, unless referred by someone we know. The best and only way, if you're a new writer, is to send a query letter with a SASE. If an agent is interested, they will request to read it. Also enclose a SASE with the script if you want it back."

**N: PANDA TALENT**, 3721 Hoen Ave., Santa Rosa CA 95405. (707)576-0711. Fax: (707)544-2765. **Contact:** Audrey Grace. Estab. 1977. Signatory of WGA, SAG, AFTRA, Equity. Represents 10 clients. 80% of clients are new/ previously unpublished writers. Currently handles: 5% novels; 40% TV scripts; 50% movie scripts; 5% stage plays.

**Story Readers:** Steven Grace (science fiction/war/action); Vicki Lima (mysterious/romance); Cleo West (western/true stories).

**Represents:** Feature film, TV MOW, episodic drama, sitcom. **Considers these script subject areas:** action/adventure; animals; comedy; detective/police/crime; ethnic; family saga; military/war; mystery/suspense; romantic comedy and drama; science fiction; true crime/investigative; westerns/frontier.

**How to Contact:** Query with treatment. Reports in 3 weeks on queries; 2 months on mss. Must include SASE.

**Recent Sales:** Prefers not to share information.

**Terms:** Agent receives 10% commission on domestic sales; 10% on foreign sales.

**[N] BARRY PERELMAN AGENCY**, 9200 Sunset Blvd., #1201, Los Angeles CA 90069. (310)274-5999. Fax: (310)274-6445. **Contact:** Chris Robert. Estab. 1982. Signatory of WGA, DGA. Represents 40 clients. 15% of clients are new/previously unpublished writers. Specializes in motion pictures/packaging. Currently handles: 4% nonfiction books; 60% movie scripts; 10% novels; 25% TV scripts; 1% stage plays.

**Member Agents:** Barry Perelman (motion picture/TV/packaging/below-the-line); Chris Robert (motion picture/TV).

**Represents:** Movie scripts. **Considers these script subject areas:** action/adventure; biography/autobiography; contemporary issues; detective/police/crime; historical; horror; mystery/suspense; romance; science fiction; thriller/espionage.

**How to Contact:** Send outline/proposal with query. Reports in 1 month.

**Needs:** Obtains new clients through recommendations and query letters.

**Recent Sales:** Prefers not to share information.

**Terms:** Agent receives 10% commission on domestic sales; 10% on foreign sales. Offers written contract, binding for 1-2 years. Charges for postage and photocopying.

**[N] JIM PREMINGER AGENCY**, 1650 Westwood Blvd., Suite 201, Los Angeles CA 90024. (310)475-9491. Fax: (310)470-2934. E-mail: rls@loop.com. **Contact:** Ryan L. Saul. Estab. 1980. Signatory of WGA, DGA. Represents 55 clients. 20% of clients are new/unpublished writers. Specializes in representing showrunners for television series, writers for television movies, as well as, directors and writers for features. Currently represents 47% movie scripts; 1% novels; 50% TV scripts; 1% nonfiction books; 1% stage plays.

**Member Agents:** Jim Preminger (television and features); Dean Schramm (features and television); Ryan L. Saul (features and television).

**Represents:** Feature film, episodic drama, TV MOW, sitcom, miniseries.

**How to Contact:** Query with SASE. Reports in 2 months on queries; 3 months on mss. "No unsolicited material."

**Needs:** Obtains new clients through recommendations.

**Recent Sales:** Prefers not to share information on specific sales.

**Terms:** Agent receives 10% commission on domestic sales; 10% on foreign sales. Offers written contract.

**[N] SILVER SCREEN PLACEMENTS**, 602 65th St., Downers Grove IL 60516-3020. (630)963-2124. Fax: (630)963-1998. E-mail: levin29@idt.net. **Contact:** William Levin. Estab. 1991. Signatory of WGA. Represents 9 clients. 100% of clients are new/previously unpublished writers. Currently handles: 10% juvenile books, 10% novels, 80% movie scripts.

• Prior to opening his agency, Mr. Levin did product placement for motion pictures/TV.

**Represents:** Movie scripts (feature film). **Considers these script subject areas:** action/adventure; comedy; contemporary issues; detective/police/crime; family saga; fantasy; historical; juvenile; mainstream; mystery/suspense; science fiction; thriller/espionage; young adult.

**How to Contact:** Brief query with outline/proposal and SASE. Reports in 1 week on queries; 6-8 weeks on mss.

**Needs:** Actively seeking "screenplays for young adults, 17-30." Does not want to receive "horror/religious/X-rated." Obtains new clients through recommendations from other parties, as well as being listed with WGA and *Guide to Literary Agents*.

**Recent Sales:** Sold 2 projects in the last year. Prefers not to share information on specific sales. Clients include Jean Hurley, Rosalind Foley, Charles Geier, Robert Smola, Sherri Fullmer.

**Terms:** Agent receives 10% commission on screenplay/teleplay sales; 15% on foreign and printed media sales. Offers written contract, binding for 2 years.

**Also Handles:** Juvenile books, novels. Considers these nonfiction areas: education; juvenile nonfiction; language/literature/criticism. Consider these fiction areas: action/adventure; cartoon/comic; contemporary issues; detective/police/crime; family saga; fantasy; historical; humor/satire; juvenile; mainstream; mystery/suspense; science fiction; thriller/espionage; young adult.

**Tips:** "Advise against 'cutsie' inquiry letters."

**[N] STANTON & ASSOCIATES LITERARY AGENCY**, 4413 Clemson Dr., Garland TX 75042-5246. (214)276-5427. Fax: (214)276-5426. E-mail: preston8@onramp.net. Website: http://rampages.onramp.net/~preston8. **Contact:** Henry Stanton, Harry Preston. Estab. 1990. Signatory of WGA. Represents 36 clients. 90% of clients are new screenwriters. Specializes in screenplays. Currently handles: 50% movie scripts; 40% TV scripts; 10% books.

• Prior to joining the agency, Mr. Preston was with the MGM script department and an author and screenwriter for 40 years.

**Represents:** Movie scripts (feature film), TV scripts (TV MOW). **Considers these script subject areas:** action/adventure; comedy; romance (comedy and drama); thriller.

**How to Contact:** Query. Reports in 1 week on queries; 1 month on screenplays (review).

**Needs:** Does not want to see science fiction, fantasy or horror. Obtains new clients through WGA listing, *Hollywood Scriptwriter*, word of mouth (in Dallas).

**Recent Sales:** *A Tale Worth Telling* (*The Life of Saint Patrick*), (Angelic Entertainment); *Chipita* (uprize Productions); *Today I will Nourish My Inner Martyr* (Prima Press); *Barbara Jordan, The Biography* (Golden Touch Press).

**Terms:** Agent receives 15% commission on domestic sales. Offers written contract, binding for 2 years on individual screenplays. Returns scripts with reader's comments.

**Tips:** "We have writers available to edit or ghostwrite screenplays and books. Fees vary dependent on the writer. All writers should always please enclose a SASE with any queries."

**[N] WARDEN, WHITE & ASSOCIATES**, 8444 Wilshire Blvd., 4th Floor, Beverly Hills CA 90211-3200. Estab. 1990. Signatory of WGA, DGA. Represents 100 clients. 10% of clients are new/previously unpublished writers. Specializes in film. Currently handles: 85% movie scripts; 15% TV scripts.

**Member Agents:** David Warden, Steve White.

**Represents:** Feature film, episodic drama, TV MOW. **Considers these script subject areas:** action/adventure; comedy; contemporary issues; fantasy; mystery/suspense; romance (comedy and drama); science fiction; thriller; westerns/frontier.

**How to Contact:** Query letters with SASE welcomed. Reports in 2 months on queries.

**Needs:** Does not accept TV writers; only feature writers. Obtains new clients only through referrals.

**Recent Sales:** *TV scripts*: *X Files* and *Viper*. "Also sold *Sleepless in Seattle* and *Wild Things* and represents authors of *Batman* and *Enemy of the State*.

**Terms:** Agent receives 10% commission on domestic sales; 10% on foreign sales. Offers written contract, binding for 2 years. Charges for photocopying.

**[N] WARDLOW AND ASSOCIATES**, 1501 Main St., Suite 204, Venice CA 90291. (310)452-1292. Fax: (310)452-9002. E-mail: wardlowagc@aol.com. Estab. 1980. Signatory of WGA. Represents 30 clients. 5% of clients are new/previously unpublished writers. Currently handles: 50% movie scripts; 50% TV scripts.

**Member Agents:** David Wardlow (literary, packaging).

**Represents:** Movie scripts (feature film); TV scripts (TV MOW, miniseries, episodic drama, sitcom). **Considers all script subject areas,** particularly: action/adventure; contemporary issues; detective/police/crime; family saga; fantasy; gay; horror; humor; mainstream; mystery/suspense; romance; science fiction; thriller; western/frontier.

**How to Contact:** Query with SASE. Replies only to queries which they are interested in unless accompanied by SASE.

**Needs:** Obtains new clients through recommendations from others and solicitation. Does not want to receive "new sitcom/drama series ideas from beginning writers."

**Recent Sales:** Prefers not to share information on specific sales.

**Terms:** Agent receives 10% commission on domestic sales; 10% on foreign sales. Offers written contract, binding for 1 year.

**[N] PEREGRINE WHITTLESEY AGENCY**, 345 E. 80 St., New York NY 10021. (212)737-0153. Fax: (212)734-5176. **Contact:** Peregrine Whittlesey. Estab. 1986. Signatory of WGA. Represents 30 clients. 50% of clients are new/previously unpublished writers. Specializes in playwrights who also write for screen and TV. Currently handles: 20% movie scripts, 80% stage plays.

**Represents:** Movie scripts, stage plays.

**How to Contact:** Query. Reports in 1 week on queries; 1 month on mss.

**Needs:** Obtains new clients through recommendations from others.

**Recent Sales:** *The Stick Wife* and *0 Pioneers!*, Darrah Cloud (Dramatic Publishing); *Alabama Rain*, by Heather McCutchen (Dramatic Publishing).

**Terms:** Agent receives 10% commission on domestic sales; 15% on foreign sales. Offers written contract, binding for 2 years.

**[N] THE WRIGHT CONCEPT**, 1811 W. Burbank Blvd., Burbank CA 91506-1314. (818)954-8943. (818)954-9370. E-mail: mrwright@www.wrightconcept.com. Website: http://www.wrightconcept.com. **Contact:** Marcie Wright. Estab. 1985. Signatory of WGA, DGA. Specializes in TV comedy writers and feature comedy writers. Currently handles: 50% movie scripts; 50% TV scripts.

**Member Agents:** Marcie Wright (TV/movie).

**Represents:** Movie scripts (feature film, animation); TV scripts (TV MOW, episodic drama, sitcom, variety show, animation, syndicated material). **Considers these script subject areas:** action/adventure; teen; thriller. Also handles CD-ROM games.

**How to Contact:** Query with SASE. Reports in 2 weeks.

**Needs:** Obtains new clients through recommendations and queries.

**Recent Sales:** Sold over 25 projects in the last year. *Movie/TV MOW script(s) optioned/sold:* *Mickey Blue Eyes* (Castlerock); *The Pentagon Wars* (HBO); *Shot Through the Heart* (HBO).

**Terms:** Agent receives 10% commission on sales. Offers written contract, binding for 1 year, with 90 day cancellation clause. 100% of business is derived from commissions on sales.

**Writers' Conferences:** Speaks at UCLA 3-4 times a year; Southwest Writers Workshop (Albuquerque, August);

*Fade-In Magazine* Oscar Conference (Los Angeles, May); *Fade-In Magazine* Top 100 People in Hollywood (Los Angeles, August); University of Georgia's Harriett Austin Writers Conference; Houston Film Festival.

**N ANN WRIGHT REPRESENTATIVES**, 165 W. 46th St., Suite 1105, New York NY 10036-2501. (212)764-6770. (212)764-6770. Fax: (212)764-5125. **Contact:** Dan Wright. Estab. 1961. Signatory of WGA. Represents 23 clients. 30% of clients are new/unpublished writers. Prefers to work with published/established authors; works with a small number of new/unpublished authors. "Eager to work with any author with material that we can effectively market in the motion picture business worldwide." Specializes in "book or screenplays with strong motion picture potential." Currently handles: 50% novels; 40% movie scripts; 10% TV scripts.

• Prior to becoming an agent, Mr. Wright was a writer, producer and production manager for film and television (alumni of CBS Television).

**Represents:** Feature film, TV MOW, episodic drama, sitcom. **Considers these script subject areas:** action/adventure; comedy; detective/police/crime; gay; historical; horror; lesbian; mainstream; mystery/suspense; psychic/supernatural; romantic comedy and drama; sports; thriller; westerns/frontier.

**How to Contact:** Query with outline and SASE. Does not read unsolicited mss. Reports in 3 weeks on queries; 4 months on mss. "All work must be sent with a SASE to ensure its return."

**Needs:** Actively seeking "strong competitive novelists and screen writers." Does not want to receive "fantasy or science fiction projects at this time."

**Recent Sales:** Sold 7 projects in the last year.

**Also Handles:** Novels. Considers these fiction areas: action/adventure; detective/police/crime; feminist; gay; humor/satire; lesbian; literary; mainstream; mystery/suspense; romance (contemporary, historical, regency); sports; thriller/espionage; westerns/frontier.

**Terms:** Agent receives 10% commission on domestic sales; 10% on dramatic sales; 15-20% on foreign sales; 20% on packaging. Offers written contract, binding for 2 years. Critiques only works of signed clients. Charges for photocopying expenses.

**Tips:** "Send a letter with SASE. Something about the work, something about the writer."

**Terms:** Agent receives 10% commission on domestic sales; 15% on foreign sales. 100% of business is derived from commissions on sales.

**Tips:** Obtains new clients through recommendations from others or cold submissions. "Don't write a novel based on the suffering of you or your family."

**FOR LISTINGS OF OVER 500** literary and script agents, consult the *Guide to Literary Agents* (Writer's Digest Books).

# Subject Index

## LITERARY AGENTS/FICTION

**Action/Adventure:** Barrett Books, Loretta; CG&W Assoc.; Dystel, Jane; Greenburger Assoc., Sanford J.; Halsey North, Reece; Hawkins & Assoc., John; Larsen/Elizabeth Pomada, Michael; Marshall, Evan; McBride, Margret; Michaels, Doris S.; Pevner, Stephen; Russell & Volkening; Sanders, Victoria; Zeckendorf Assoc., Susan

**Cartoon/comic:** Barrett Books, Loretta; Donnaud & Assoc., Janis A.; Hawking & Assoc., John; Levant & Wales; Pevner, Stephen

**Confessional:** Barrett Books, Loretta; CG&W Assoc.

**Contemporary issues:** Barrett Books, Loretta; Bernstein & Assoc., Pam; CG&W Assoc.; Dijkstra, Sandra; Donnaud & Assoc., Janis A.; Dystel, Jane; Freymann, Sarah Jane; Greenburger Assoc., Sanford J.; Halsey North, Reece; Hawkins & Assoc., John; Kouts, Barbara S.; Larsen/Elizabeth Pomada, Michael; Lowenstein Assoc.; Manus & Assoc.; Marshall, Evan; Michaels, Doris S.; Nelson, Craig; Pevner, Stephen; Pinder Lane & Garon-Brooke Assoc.; Rees, Helen; Sanders, Victoria; Skolnick, Irene; Straus, Robin; Zeckendorf Assoc., Susan

**Detective/police/crime:** Amster, Betsy; Barrett Books, Loretta; Bernstein & Assoc., Pam; CG&W Assoc.; Cohen, Literary Agency, Ruth; Dijkstra, Sandra; Dystel, Jane; Greenburger Assoc., Sanford J.; Halsey North, Reece; Hawkins & Assoc., John; Larsen/Elizabeth Pomada, Michael; Lowenstein Assoc.; Manus & Assoc.; Marshall, Evan; McBride, Margret; Perkins, Rubie & Assoc.; Pevner, Stephen; Pinder Lane & Garon-Brooke Assoc.; Rees, Helen; Rowland, Damaris; Rubenstein, Pesha; Russell & Volkening; Zeckendorf Assoc., Susan

**Erotica:** Donnaud & Assoc., Janis; Lowenstein Assoc.; Marshall, Evan; Pevner, Stephen

**Ethnic:** Amster, Betsy; Barrett Books, Loretta; Bernstein & Assoc., Pam; CG&W Assoc.; Cohen, Ruth; Daves, Joan; Dijkstra, Sandra; Donnaud & Assoc., Janis; Dystel, Jane; Eth, Felicia; Freymann, Sarah Jane; Greenburger Assoc., Sanford J.; Halsey North, Reece; Hawkins & Assoc., John; Larsen/Elizabeth Pomada, Michael; Levant & Wales; Lowenstein Assoc.; Manus & Assoc.; Marshall, Evan; McBride, Margret; Nelson, Craig; Perkins, Rubie & Assoc.; Pevner, Stephen; Rubenstein, Pesha; Russell & Volkening; Sanders, Victoria; Zeckendorf Assoc., Susan

**Experimental:** Barrett Books, Loretta; Hawkins & Assoc., John; Larsen/Elizabeth Pomada, Michael; Levant & Wales; Pevner, Stephen

**Family saga:** Barrett Books, Loretta; CG&W Assoc.; Daves, Joan; Dijkstra, Sandra; Dystel, Jane; Fredericks, Jeanne; Greenburger Assoc., Sanford J.; Halsey North, Reece; Hawkins & Assoc., John; Kouts, Barbara S.; Larsen/Elizabeth Pomada, Michael; Manus & Assoc.; Marshall, Evan; Michaels, Doris S.; Pinder Lane & Garon-Brooke Assoc.; Sanders, Victoria; Straus, Robin; Zeckendorf Assoc., Susan

**Fantasy:** Barrett Books, Loretta; Gislason Agency, The; Hawkins & Assoc., John; Larsen/Elizabeth Pomada, Michael; Perkins, Rubie & Assoc.; Pinder Lane & Garon-Brooke Assoc.

**Feminist:** Barrett Books, Loretta; Dijkstra, Sandra; Eth, Felicia; Gislason Agency, The; Greenburger Assoc., Sanford J.; Hawkins & Assoc., John; Kouts, Barbara S.; Larsen/Elizabeth Pomada, Michael; Levant & Wales; Lowenstein Assoc.; Manus & Assoc.; Michaels, Doris S.; Sanders, Victoria

**Gay:** Barrett Books, Loretta; Daves, Joan; Donnaud & Assoc., Janis; Dystel, Jane; Eth, Felicia; Greenburger Assoc., Sanford J.; Hawkins & Assoc., John; Larsen/Elizabeth Pomada, Michael; Levant & Wales; Lowenstein Assoc.; Nelson, Craig; Perkins, Rubie & Assoc.; Pevner, Stephen; Pinder Lane & Garon-Brooke Assoc.; Sanders, Victoria

**Glitz:** Barrett Books, Loretta; CG&W Assoc.; Greenburger Assoc., Sanford J.; Hawkins & Assoc., John; Larsen/Elizabeth Pomada, Michael; Marshall, Evan; Pevner, Stephen; Rees, Helen; Rubenstein, Pesha; Zeckendorf Assoc., Susan

**Historical:** Barrett Books, Loretta; Bernstein & Assoc., Pam; CG&W Assoc.; Cohen, Literary Agency, Ruth; Donnaud & Assoc., Janis; Fredericks, Jeanne; Greenburger Assoc., Sanford J.; Halsey North, Reece; Hawkins & Assoc., John; Kouts, Barbara S.; Larsen/Elizabeth Pomada, Michael; Lowenstein Assoc.; Marshall, Evan; McBride, Margret; Michaels, Doris S.; Perkins, Rubie & Assoc.; Rees, Helen; Rowland, Damaris; Skolnick, Irene; Straus, Robin; Toad Hall; Zeckendorf Assoc., Susan

**Horror:** Hawkins & Assoc., John; Larsen/Elizabeth Pomada, Michael; Marshall, Evan; Nelson, Craig; Perkins, Rubie & Assoc.; Pevner, Stephen

**Humor/satire:** Barrett Books, Loretta; Donnaud & Assoc., Janis; Greenburger Assoc., Sanford J.; Larsen/Elizabeth

Pomada, Michael; Lowenstein Assoc.; Marshall, Evan; McBride, Margret; Nelson, Craig; Pevner, Stephen; Rubenstein, Pesha

**Juvenile:** Cohen, Literary Agency, Ruth; Hawkins & Assoc., John; Kirchoff/Wohlberg, Inc., Authors' Representation Division; Kouts, Barbara S.; Rubenstein, Pesha; Russell & Volkening

**Lesbian:** Barrett Books, Loretta; Dystel, Jane; Eth, Felicia; Greenburger Assoc., Sanford J.; Hawkins & Assoc., John; Larsen/Elizabeth Pomada, Michael; Levant & Wales; Lowenstein Assoc.; Perkins, Rubie & Assoc.; Pevner, Stephen; Sanders, Victoria

**Literary:** Amster, Betsy; Barrett Books, Loretta; CG&W Assoc.; Cohen, Literary Agency, Ruth; Cornfield, Robert; Darhansoff & Verrill; Daves, Joan; DH Literary; Dijkstra, Sandra; Donnaud & Assoc., Janis; Dystel, Jane; Eth, Felicia; Fredericks, Jeanne; Freymann, Sarah Jane; Greenburger Assoc., Sanford J.; Halsey North, Reece; Hawkins & Assoc., John; Kouts, Barbara S.; Larsen/Elizabeth Pomada, Michael; Levant & Wales; Levin, Ellen; Lowenstein Assoc.; Mann, Carol; Markson, Elaine; Marshall, Evan; McBride, Margret; Michaels, Doris S.; Nelson, Craig; Perkins, Rubie & Assoc.; Pevner, Stephen; Pinder Lane & Garon-Brooke Assoc.; Rees, Helen; Rowland, Damaris; Russell & Volkening; Sanders, Victoria; Skolnick, Irene; Straus, Robin; Zeckendorf Assoc., Susan

**Mainstream:** Barrett Books, Loretta; Bernstein & Assoc., Pam; CG&W Assoc.; Cohen, Literary Agency, Ruth; Columbia Literary Assoc.; Daves, Joan; DH Literary; Dijkstra, Sandra; Donnaud & Assoc., Janis; Dystel, Jane; Eth, Felicia; Freymann, Sarah Jane; Greenburger Assoc., Sanford J.; Halsey North, Reece; Hawkins & Assoc., John; Kouts, Barbara S.; Larsen/Elizabeth Pomada, Michael; Levant & Wales; Lipkind, Wendy; Lowenstein Assoc.; Manus & Assoc.; Markson, Elaine; Marshall, Evan; McBride, Margret; Michaels, Doris S.; Nelson, Craig; Orr, Alice; Perkins, Rubie & Assoc.; Pevner, Stephen; Pinder Lane & Garon-Brooke Assoc.; Rees, Helen; Rowland, Damaris; Rubenstein, Pesha; Russell & Volkening; Straus, Robin; Zeckendorf Assoc., Susan

**Mystery/suspense:** Amster, Betsy; Barrett Books, Loretta; Bernstein & Assoc., Pam; CG&W Assoc.; Cohen, Literary Agency, Ruth; DH Literary; Dijkstra, Sandra; Freymann, Sarah Jane; Gislason Agency, The; Greenburger Assoc., Sanford J.; Halsey North, Reece; Hawkins & Assoc., John; Kouts, Barbara S.; Larsen/Elizabeth Pomada, Michael; Levin, Ellen; Lipkind, Wendy; Lowenstein Assoc.; Manus & Assoc.; Marcil, Denise; Marshall, Evan; McBride, Margret; Nelson, Craig; Perkins, Rubie & Assoc.; Pinder Lane & Garon-Brooke Assoc.; Rees, Helen; Rubenstein, Pesha; Russell & Volkening; Toad Hall; Zeckendorf Assoc., Susan

**Open to all fiction categories:** Brown, Curtis; Bykofsky Assoc., Sheree; Curtis Assoc., Richard

**Picture book:** Cohen, Literary Agency, Ruth; Hawkins & Assoc., John; Heacock Literary Agency; Kouts, Barbara S.; Rubenstein, Pesha; Russell & Volkening

**Psychic/supernatural:** Barrett Books, Loretta; Donnaud & Assoc., Janis A.; Greenburger Assoc., Sanford J.; Hawkins & Assoc., John; Larsen/Elizabeth Pomada, Michael; Marshall, Evan; Perkins, Rubie & Assoc.; Pevner, Stephen; Rowland, Damaris; Rubenstein, Pesha

**Regional:** CG&W Assoc.; Greenburger Assoc., Sanford J.; Hawkins & Assoc., John

**Religious/inspiration:** Barrett Books, Loretta; Hawkins & Assoc., John; Larsen/Elizabeth Pomada, Michael; Marshall, Evan

**Romance:** Barrett Books, Loretta; Bernstein & Assoc., Pam; CG&W Assoc.; Cohen, Literary Agency, Ruth; Columbia Literary Assoc.; Gislason Agency, The; Larsen/Elizabeth Pomada, Michael; Lowenstein Assoc.; Marcil, Denise; Marshall, Evan; Orr, Alice; Pinder Lane & Garon-Brooke Assoc.; Rowland, Damaris; Rubenstein, Pesha; Toad Hall

**Science fiction:** Gislason Agency, The; Halsey North, Reece; Hawkins & Assoc., John; Marshall, Evan; Perkins, Rubie & Assoc.; Pevner, Stephen; Pinder Lane & Garon-Brooke Assoc.; Toad Hall

**Sports:** Barrett Books, Loretta; Donnaud & Assoc., Janis; Greenburger Assoc., Sanford J.; Hawkins & Associates, Inc., John; Russell & Volkening

**Thriller/espionage:** Barrett Books, Loretta; Bernstein & Assoc., Pam; CG&W Assoc.; Columbia Literary Assoc.; Darhansoff & Verrill; DH Literary; Dijkstra, Sandra; Donnaud & Assoc., Janis; Dystel, Jane; Eth, Felicia; Freymann, Sarah Jane; Greenburger Assoc., Sanford J.; Halsey North, Reece; Hawkins & Assoc., John; Levin, Ellen; Lowenstein Assoc.; Manus & Assoc.; Marshall, Evan; McBride, Margret; Nelson, Craig; Perkins, Rubie & Assoc.; Pevner, Stephen; Rees, Helen; Russell & Volkening; Sanders, Victoria; Straus, Robin; Zeckendorf Assoc., Susan

**Westerns/frontier:** Hawkins & Assoc., John; Marshall, Evan; McBride, Margret

**Young adult:** CG&W Assoc.; Cohen, Literary Agency, Ruth; Kirchoff/Wohlberg, Inc., Authors' Representation Division; Kouts, Barbara S.; Russell & Volkening

# LITERARY AGENTS/NONFICTION

**Agriculture/horticulture:** Amster, Betsy; Fredericks, Jeanne; Hawkins & Assoc., John; Levant & Wales

**Animals:** Cornfield, Robert; DH Literary; Donnaud & Assoc., Janis; Dystel, Jane; Eth, Felicia; Fredericks, Jeanne; Freymann, Sarah Jane; Hawkins & Assoc., John; Levant & Wales; Lowenstein Assoc.; Marshall, Evan; Nelson, Craig; Rowland, Damaris; Straus, Robin; Toad Hall

**Anthropology:** Cornfield, Robert; Darhansoff & Verrill; DH Literary; Dijkstra, Sandra; Dystel, Jane; Eth, Felicia; Fredericks, Jeanne; Freymann, Sarah Jane; Hawkins & Assoc., John; Heacock Literary Agency; James Peter Assoc.; Larsen/ Elizabeth Pomada, Michael; Levin, Ellen; Lowenstein Assoc.; Mann, Carol; Nelson, Craig; Russell & Volkening; Straus, Robin; Toad Hall

**Art/architecture/design:** Cornfield, Robert; Donnaud & Assoc., Janis; Fredericks, Jeanne; Freymann, Sarah Jane; Hawkins & Assoc., John; Heacock Literary Agency; James Peter Assoc.; Larsen/Elizabeth Pomada, Michael; Lowenstein Assoc.; Mann, Carol; Perkins, Rubie & Assoc.; Pevner, Stephen; Russell & Volkening; Straus, Robin; Zeckendorf Assoc., Susan

**Biography/autobiography:** Amster, Betsy; Bykofsky Assoc., Sheree; CG&W Assoc.; Cornfield, Robert; Darhansoff & Verrill; Daves, Joan; DH Literary; Dijkstra, Sandra; Donnaud & Assoc., Janis; Dystel, Jane; Eth, Felicia; Fredericks, Jeanne; Freymann, Sarah Jane; Halsey North, Reece; Hawkins & Assoc., John; Heacock Literary Agency; James Peter Assoc.; Kouts, Barbara S.; Larsen/Elizabeth Pomada, Michael; Levant & Wales; Levin, Ellen; Lipkind, Wendy; Lowenstein Assoc.; Mann, Carol; Manus & Assoc.; Marshall, Evan; McBride, Margret; Michaels, Doris S.; Nelson, Craig; New England Publishing Assoc.; Pevner, Stephen; Pinder Lane & Garon-Brooke Assoc.; Rees, Helen; Russell & Volkening; Sanders, Victoria; Skolnick, Irene; Straus, Robin; Zeckendorf Assoc., Susan

**Business:** Amster, Betsy; Bykofsky Assoc., Sheree; DH Literary; Dijkstra, Sandra; Donnaud & Assoc., Janis; Dystel, Jane; Eth, Felicia; Fredericks, Jeanne; Freymann, Sarah Jane; Hawkins & Assoc., John; Heacock Literary Agency; Herman Agency, Jeff; James Peter Assoc.; Konner, Linda; Larsen/Elizabeth Pomada, Michael; Levant & Wales; Lowenstein Assoc.; Mann, Carol; Manus & Assoc.; Marcil, Denise; Marshall, Evan; McBride, Margret; Michaels, Doris S.; Nelson, Craig; New England Publishing Assoc.; Pevner, Stephen; Rees, Helen; Russell & Volkening; Toad Hall

**Child guidance/parenting:** Amster, Betsy; Bernstein & Assoc., Pam; Bykofsky Assoc., Sheree; DH Literary; Dijkstra, Sandra; Donnaud & Assoc., Janis; Dystel, Jane; Eth, Felicia; Fredericks, Jeanne; Freymann, Sarah Jane; Hawkins & Assoc., John; Heacock Literary Agency; James Peter Assoc.; Konner, Linda; Kouts, Barbara S.; Larsen/Elizabeth Pomada, Michael; Levant & Wales; Lowenstein Assoc.; Mann, Carol; Manus & Assoc.; Marcil, Denise; Marshall, Evan; McBride, Margret; New England Publishing Assoc.; Pinder Lane & Garon-Brooke Assoc.; Rubenstein, Pesha; Straus, Robin; Toad Hall; Zeckendorf Assoc., Susan

**Computers/electronics:** Herman Agency, The Jeff; Nelson, Craig

**Cooking/food/nutrition:** Bernstein & Assoc., Pam; Bykofsky Assoc., Sheree; Columbia Literary Assoc.; Cornfield, Robert; Dijkstra, Sandra; Donnaud & Assoc., Janis; Dystel, Jane; Fredericks, Jeanne; Freymann, Sarah Jane; Hawkins & Assoc., John; Heacock Literary Agency; Konner, Linda; Larsen/Elizabeth Pomada, Michael; Marshall, McBride, Margret; Pevner, Stephen; Rowland, Damaris; Russell & Volkening; Straus, Robin Toad Hall

**Crafts/hobbies:** Fredericks, Jeanne; Hawkins & Assoc., John; Heacock Literary Agency; Lowenstein Assoc.; Marshall, Evan; Toad Hall

**Current affairs:** Bernstein & Assoc., Pam; Bykofsky Assoc., Sheree; CG&W Assoc.; Darhansoff & Verrill; DH Literary; Dijkstra, Sandra; Donnaud & Assoc., Janis; Dystel, Jane; Eth, Felicia; Fredericks, Jeanne; Freymann, Sarah Jane; Halsey North, Reece; Hawkins & Assoc., John; James Peter Assoc.; Kouts, Barbara S.; Larsen/Elizabeth Pomada, Michael; Levant & Wales; Levin, Ellen; Lipkind, Wendy; Lowenstein Assoc.; Mann, Carol; Manus & Assoc.; Marshall, Evan; McBride, Margret; Michaels, Doris S.; Nelson, Craig; Perkins, Rubie & Assoc.; Pevner, Stephen; Rees, Helen; Russell & Volkening; Sanders, Victoria; Skolnick, Irene; Straus, Robin

**Education:** DH Literary; Dystel, Jane; Fredericks, Jeanne; Levant & Wales; Lowenstein Assoc.; Russell & Volkening

**Ethnic/cultural interests:** Amster, Betsy; Bykofsky Assoc., Sheree; CG&W Assoc.; Cohen, Literary Agency, Ruth; DH Literary; Dijkstra, Sandra; Donnaud & Assoc., Janis; Dystel, Jane; Eth, Felicia; Freymann, Sarah Jane; Hawkins & Assoc., John; Heacock Literary Agency; James Peter Assoc.; Kouts, Barbara S.; Larsen/Elizabeth Pomada, Michael; Levant & Wales; Lowenstein Assoc.; Mann, Carol; Manus & Assoc.; Marcil, McBride, Margret; Michaels, Doris S.; Nelson, Craig; Perkins, Rubie & Assoc.; Pevner, Stephen; Russell & Volkening; Sanders, Victoria; Straus, Robin

**Gay/Lesbian issues:** Bykofsky Assoc., Sheree; Daves, Joan; Donnaud & Assoc., Janis; Dystel, Jane; Eth, Felicia; Freymann, Sarah Jane; Hawkins & Assoc., John; James Peter Assoc.; Konner, Linda; Larsen/Elizabeth Pomada, Michael; Levant & Wales; Lowenstein Assoc.; McBride, Margret; Nelson, Craig; Perkins, Rubie & Assoc.; Pevner, Stephen; Pinder Lane & Garon-Brooke Assoc.; Russell & Volkening; Sanders, Victoria

**Government/politics/law:** Bernstein & Assoc., Pam; DH Literary; Dijkstra, Sandra; Dystel, Jane; Eth, Felicia; Hawkins & Assoc., John; Herman Agency, Jeff; James Peter Assoc.; Larsen/Elizabeth Pomada, Michael; Lowenstein Assoc.; Mann, Carol; Marshall, Evan; McBride, Margret; New England Publishing Assoc.; Pevner, Stephen; Rees, Helen; Russell & Volkening; Sanders, Victoria; Straus, Robin

**Health/medicine:** Amster, Betsy; Bernstein & Assoc., Pam; Bykofsky Assoc., Sheree; Columbia Literary Assoc.; Darhansoff & Verrill; DH Literary; Dijkstra, Sandra; Donnaud & Assoc., Janis; Dystel, Jane; Eth, Felicia; Fredericks, Jeanne;

Freymann, Sarah Jane; Hawkins & Assoc., John; Heacock Literary Agency; Herman Agency, Jeff; James Peter Assoc.; Konner, Linda; Kouts, Barbara S.; Larsen/Elizabeth Pomada, Michael; Levant & Wales; Levin, Ellen; Lipkind, Wendy; Lowenstein Assoc.; Mann, Carol; Manus & Assoc.; Marcil, Denise; Marshall, Evan; McBride, Margret; Michaels, Doris S.; Nelson, Craig; New England Publishing Assoc.; Pinder Lane & Garon-Brooke Assoc.; Rees, Helen; Rowland, Damaris; Russell & Volkening; Straus, Robin; Toad Hall; Zeckendorf Assoc., Susan

**History:** Amster, Betsy; Bykofsky Assoc., Sheree; Cornfield, Robert; Darhansoff & Verrill; DH Literary; Dijkstra, Sandra; Donnaud & Assoc., Janis; Dystel, Jane; Eth, Felicia; Fredericks, Jeanne; Freymann, Sarah Jane; Halsey North, Reece; Hawkins & Assoc., John; Heacock Literary Agency; Herman Agency, Jeff; James Peter Assoc.; Kouts, Barbara S.; Larsen/Elizabeth Pomada, Michael; Levin, Ellen; Lipkind, Wendy; Lowenstein Assoc.; Mann, Carol; Marshall, Evan; McBride, Margret; Michaels, Doris S.; Nelson, Craig; New England Publishing Assoc.; Pevner, Stephen; Pinder Lane & Garon-Brooke Assoc.; Rees, Helen; Russell & Volkening; Sanders, Victoria; Straus, Robin; Zeckendorf Assoc., Susan

**How-to:** Amster, Betsy; Bernstein & Assoc., Pam; Bykofsky Assoc., Sheree; DH Literary; Donnaud & Assoc., Janis; Fredericks, Jeanne; Heacock Literary Agency; Herman Agency, Jeff; Konner, Linda; Larsen/Elizabeth Pomada, Michael; Lowenstein Assoc.; Manus & Assoc.; Marcil, Denise; Marshall, Evan; McBride, Margret; Michaels, Doris S.; Nelson, Craig; Toad Hall

**Humor:** Bykofsky Assoc., Sheree; Donnaud & Assoc., Janis; Dystel, Jane; Larsen/Elizabeth Pomada, Michael; Lowenstein Assoc.; Marshall, Evan; Nelson, Craig; Pevner, Stephen; Sanders, Victoria

**Interior design/decorating:** Donnaud & Assoc., Janis; Fredericks, Jeanne; Freymann, Sarah Jane; Hawkins & Assoc., John; Larsen/Elizabeth Pomada, Michael; Marshall, Evan

**Juvenile nonfiction:** Cohen, Literary Agency, Ruth; Hawkins & Assoc., John; Kirchoff/Wohlberg, Inc., Authors' Representation Division; Kouts, Barbara S.; Rubenstein, Pesha; Russell & Volkening

**Language/literature/criticism:** Cornfield, Robert; Darhansoff & Verrill; DH Literary; Dijkstra, Sandra; Donnaud & Assoc., Janis; Halsey North, Reece; Hawkins & Assoc., John; Heacock Literary Agency; James Peter Assoc.; Larsen/Elizabeth Pomada, Michael; Levant & Wales; Lowenstein Assoc.; Marshall, Evan; New England Publishing Assoc.; Pevner, Stephen; Russell & Volkening; Sanders, Victoria; Straus, Robin

**Memoirs:** James Peter Assoc.; Larsen/Elizabeth Pomada, Michael; Levant & Wales; Levin, Ellen; Lowenstein Assoc.; Manus & Assoc.; Pevner, Stephen; Pinder Lane & Garon-Brooke Assoc.; Zeckendorf Assoc., Susan

**Military/war:** DH Literary; Dijkstra, Sandra; Dystel, Jane; Hawkins & Assoc., John; James Peter Assoc.; Marshall, Evan; New England Publishing Assoc.; Pinder Lane & Garon-Brooke Assoc.; Russell & Volkening

**Money/finance/economics:** Amster, Betsy; DH Literary; Dijkstra, Sandra; Donnaud & Assoc., Janis; Dystel, Jane; Fredericks, Jeanne; Hawkins & Assoc., John; Heacock Literary Agency; James Peter Assoc.; Konner, Linda; Larsen/Elizabeth Pomada, Michael; Lowenstein Assoc.; Mann, Carol; Marcil, Denise; Marshall, Evan; McBride, Margret; Michaels, Doris S.; Nelson, Craig; New England Publishing Assoc.; Pevner, Stephen; Rees, Helen; Russell & Volkening

**Music/dance/theater/film:** Bykofsky Assoc., Sheree; Cornfield, Robert; DH Literary; Donnaud & Assoc., Janis; Hawkins & Assoc., John; Heacock Literary Agency; James Peter Assoc.; Kouts, Barbara S.; Larsen/Elizabeth Pomada, Michael; Lowenstein Assoc.; Marshall, Evan; McBride, Margret; Michaels, Doris S.; Nelson, Craig; Perkins, Rubie & Assoc.; Pevner, Stephen; Pinder Lane & Garon-Brooke Assoc.; Russell & Volkening; Sanders, Victoria; Straus, Robin; Zeckendorf Assoc., Susan

**Nature/environment:** Darhansoff & Verrill; DH Literary; Dijkstra, Sandra; Donnaud & Assoc., Janis; Eth, Felicia; Fredericks, Jeanne; Freymann, Sarah Jane; Hawkins & Assoc., John; Heacock Literary Agency; Kouts, Barbara S.; Larsen/Elizabeth Pomada, Michael; Levant & Wales; Lowenstein Assoc.; Manus & Assoc.; Marshall, Evan; Michaels, Doris S.; Nelson, Craig; New England Publishing Assoc.; Rowland, Damaris; Russell & Volkening; Straus, Robin; Toad Hall

**New age/metaphysics:** Bernstein & Assoc., Pam; Dystel, Jane; Fredericks, Jeanne; Hawkins & Assoc., John; Heacock Literary Agency; Larsen/Elizabeth Pomada, Michael; Levant & Wales; Lowenstein Assoc.; Marshall, Evan; Pevner, Stephen; Rowland, Damaris; Toad Hall

**Open to all nonfiction categories:** Barrett Books, Loretta; Brown, Curtis; Bykofsky Assoc., Sheree; Curtis Assoc., Richard; Greenburger Assoc., Sanford J.

**Photography:** Donnaud & Assoc., Janis; Fredericks, Jeanne; Hawkins & Assoc., John; Larsen/Elizabeth Pomada, Michael; Pevner, Stephen; Russell & Volkening

**Popular culture:** Amster, Betsy; Bernstein & Assoc., Pam; Bykofsky Assoc., Sheree; Daves, Joan; DH Literary; Donnaud & Assoc., Janis; Dystel, Jane; Eth, Felicia; Halsey North, Reece; Heacock Literary Agency; James Peter Assoc.; Konner, Linda; Larsen/Elizabeth Pomada, Michael; Levant & Wales; Levin, Ellen; Lowenstein Assoc.; Manus & Assoc.; McBride, Margret; Nelson, Craig; Orr, Alice; Perkins, Rubie & Assoc.; Pevner, Stephen; Russell & Volkening; Sanders, Victoria; Straus, Robin; Toad Hall

**Psychology:** Amster, Betsy; Bernstein & Assoc., Pam; Bykofsky Assoc., Sheree; DH Literary; Dijkstra, Sandra; Donnaud & Assoc., Janis.; Dystel, Jane; Eth, Felicia; Fredericks, Jeanne; Freymann, Sarah Jane; Hawkins & Assoc., John; Heacock Literary Agency; Herman Agency, Jeff; James Peter Assoc.; Konner, Linda; Kouts, Barbara S.; Larsen/Elizabeth Pomada,

Michael; Levant & Wales; Levin, Ellen; Lowenstein Assoc.; Mann, Carol; Manus & Assoc.; Marcil, Denise; Marshall, Evan; McBride, Margret; Nelson, Craig; New England Publishing Assoc.; Pinder Lane & Garon-Brooke Assoc.; Russell & Volkening; Sanders, Victoria; Straus, Robin; Zeckendorf Assoc., Susan

**Religious/inspirational:** Bernstein & Assoc., Pam; Bykofsky Assoc., Sheree; Dystel, Jane; Freymann, Sarah Jane; Heacock Literary Agency; Larsen/Elizabeth Pomada, Michael; Lowenstein Assoc.; Marcil, Denise; Marshall, Evan; McBride, Pevner, Stephen; Rowland, Damaris; Toad Hall

**Science/technology:** Artists Agency, The; Darhansoff & Verrill; DH Literary; Dijkstra, Sandra; Donnaud & Assoc., Janis; Dystel, Jane; Epstein-Wyckoff & Assoc.; Eth, Felicia; Fredericks, Jeanne; Frency, Samuel; Hawkins & Assoc., John; Heacock Literary Agency; Larsen/Elizabeth Pomada, Michael; Levant & Wales; Levin, Ellen; Lipkind, Wendy; Lowenstein Assoc.; Marshall, Evan; McBride, Margret; Monteiro Rose; Nelson, Craig; New England Publishing Assoc.; Perkins, Rubie & Assoc.; Pevner, Stephen; Russell & Volkening; Silver Screen Placements; Straus, Robin; Wardlow & Assoc.; Zeckendorf Assoc., Susan

**Self-help/personal improvement:** Amster, Bernstein & Assoc., Pam; Bykofsky Assoc., Sheree; Columbia Literary Assoc.; DH Literary; Dijkstra, Sandra; Donnaud & Assoc., Janis; Fredericks, Jeanne; Freymann, Sarah Jane; Hawkins & Assoc., John; Heacock Literary Agency; Herman Agency, Jeff; James Peter Assoc.; Konner, Linda; Kouts, Barbara S.; Larsen/Elizabeth Pomada, Michael; Levant & Wales; Lowenstein Assoc.; Mann, Carol; Manus & Assoc.; Marcil, Denise; Marshall, Evan; McBride, Margret; Michaels, Doris S.; Nelson, Craig; New England Publishing Assoc.; Pinder Lane & Garon-Brooke Assoc.; Toad Hall

**Sociology:** Amster, Betsy; Bernstein & Assoc., Pam; Dijkstra, Sandra; Donnaud & Assoc., Janis; Eth, Felicia; Hawkins & Assoc., John; Heacock Literary Agency; Larsen/Elizabeth Pomada, Michael; Lipkind, Wendy; Lowenstein Assoc.; Mann, Carol; McBride, Margret; New England Publishing Assoc.; Pevner, Stephen; Russell & Volkening; Straus, Robin; Zeckendorf Assoc., Susan

**Sports:** Dijkstra, Sandra; Donnaud & Assoc., Janis; Fredericks, Jeanne; Hawkins & Assoc., John; Larsen/Elizabeth Pomada, Michael; Lowenstein Assoc.; McBride, Margret; Michaels, Doris S.; Russell & Volkening

**Travel:** Hawkins & Assoc., John; James Peter Assoc.; Larsen/Elizabeth Pomada, Michael; Lowenstein Assoc.; Pevner, Stephen

**Translations:** Daves, Joan; Sanders, Victoria

**True crime/investigative:** Bernstein & Assoc., Pam; Bykofsky Assoc., Sheree; DH Literary; Dijkstra, Sandra; Donnaud & Assoc., Janis; Dystel, Jane; Eth, Felicia; Halsey North, Reece; Larsen/Elizabeth Pomada, Michael; Lowenstein Assoc.; Marshall, Evan; McBride, Margret; Nelson, Craig; New England Publishing Assoc.; Pinder Lane & Garon-Brooke Assoc.; Russell & Volkening; Zeckendorf Assoc., Susan

**Women's issues/women's studies:** Amster, Betsy; Bernstein & Assoc., Pam; Bykofsky Assoc., Sheree; CG&W Assoc.; Cohen, Literary Agency, Ruth; Daves, Joan; DH Literary; Dijkstra, Sandra; Donnaud & Assoc., Janis; Dystel, Jane; Eth, Felicia; Fredericks Literary Agency, Inc., Jeanne; Freymann, Sarah Jane; Halsey North, Reece; Hawkins & Assoc., John; Heacock Literary Agency; James Peter Assoc.; Konner, Linda; Kouts, Barbara S.; Larsen/Elizabeth Pomada, Michael; Levant & Wales; Levin, Ellen; Lipkind, Wendy; Lowenstein Assoc.; Mann, Carol; Manus & Assoc.; Marcil, Denise; Marshall, Evan; McBride, Margret; Michaels, Doris S.; New England Publishing Assoc.; Rees, Helen; Rowland, Damaris; Russell & Volkening; Sanders, Victoria; Straus, Robin; Zeckendorf Assoc., Susan

# SCRIPT AGENTS SUBJECT INDEX

**Action/Adventure:** Artists Agency, The; Cameron, Marshall; Douroux & Co.; Epstein-Wyckoff & Assoc.; Freed, Barry; Monteiro Rose; Panda Talent; Perelman, Barry; Silver Screen Placements; Stanton & Assoc.; Warden, White & Assoc.; Wardlow & Assoc.; Wright Concept, The; Wright Representatives, Ann

**Animation:** Douroux & Co.; Epstein-Wyckoff & Assoc.; Monteiro Rose; Panda Talent; Wright Concept, The

**Biography/autobiography:** Perelman, Barry

**Cartoon/animation:** Monteiro Rose

**Comedy:** Artists Agency, The; Cameron, Marshall; Douroux & Co.; Epstein-Wyckoff & Assoc.; Freed, Barry; Frency, Samuel; Monteiro Rose; Panda Talent; Silver Screen Placements; Stanton & Assoc.; Warden, White & Assoc.; Wright Concept, The; Wright Representatives, Ann

**Contemporary issues:** Freed, Barry; Perelman, Barry; Warden, White & Assoc.

**Detective/police/crime:** Artists Agency, The; Cameron, Marshall; Douroux & Co.; Epstein-Wyckoff & Assoc.; Freed, Barry; Frency, Samuel; Monteiro Rose; Panda Talent; Perelman, Barry; Silver Screen Placements; Wardlow & Assoc.; Wright Representatives, Ann

**Episodic drama:** Douroux & Co.; Epstein-Wyckoff & Assoc.; Monteiro Rose; Panda Talent; Preminger, Jim; Wardlow & Assoc.; Wright Concept, The; Wright Representatives, Ann

**Erotica:** Epstein-Wyckoff & Assoc.; Freed, Barry; Frency, Samuel; Monteiro Rose; Panda Talent

**Experimental:** Frency, Samuel

**Family saga:** Douroux & Co.; Epstein-Wyckoff & Assoc.; Freed, Barry; Monteiro Rose; Panda Talent; Silver Screen Placements; Wardlow & Assoc.

**Fantasy:** Douroux & Co.; Frency, Samuel; Monteiro Rose; Silver Screen Placements; Warden, White & Assoc.; Wardlow & Assoc.

**Feature film:** Artists Agency, The; Cameron, Marshall; Douroux & Co.; Epstein-Wyckoff & Assoc.; Freed, Barry; Monteiro Rose; Panda Talent; Preminger, Jim; Silver Screen Placements; Stanton & Assoc.; Warden, White & Assoc.; Wardlow & Assoc.; Whittlesey, Peregrine; Wright Concept, The; Wright Representatives, Ann

**Feminist:** Epstein-Wyckoff & Assoc.

**Gay:** Epstein-Wyckoff & Assoc.; Wardlow & Assoc.; Wright Representatives, Ann

**Glitz:** Epstein-Wyckoff & Assoc.

**Historical:** Douroux & Co.; Epstein-Wyckoff & Assoc.; Monteiro Rose; Perelman, Barry; Silver Screen Placements; Wright Representatives, Ann

**Horror:** Freed, Barry; Frency, Samuel; Perelman, Barry; Wardlow & Assoc.; Wright Representatives, Ann

**Juvenile:** Epstein-Wyckoff & Assoc.; Monteiro Rose; Silver Screen Placements

**Lesbian:** Epstein-Wyckoff & Assoc.; Wright Representatives, Ann

**Mainstream:** Cameron, Marshall; Douroux & Co.; Epstein-Wyckoff & Assoc.; Freed, Barry; Monteiro Rose; Silver Screen Placements; Wardlow & Assoc.; Wright Representatives, Ann

**Movie of the week:** Artists Agency, The; Douroux & Co.; Epstein-Wyckoff & Assoc.; Freed, Barry; Monteiro Rose; Panda Talent; Preminger, Jim; Stanton & Assoc.; Wardlow & Assoc.; Wright Concept, The; Wright Representatives, Ann

**Mystery/suspense:** Artists Agency, The; Douroux & Co.; Epstein-Wyckoff & Assoc.; Freed, Barry; Frency, Samuel; Kerwin, William; Monteiro Rose; Panda Talent; Perelman, Barry; Silver Screen Placements; Warden, White & Assoc.; Wardlow & Assoc.; Wright Representatives, Ann

**Open to all categories:** Wardlow & Assoc.

**Psychic/supernatural:** Monteiro Rose; Wright Representatives, Ann

**Religious/inspirational:** Frency, Samuel

**Romance:** Kerwin, William; Panda Talent; Perelman, Barry; Stanton & Assoc.; Warden, White & Assoc.; Wardlow & Assoc.

**Romantic comedy:** Artists Agency, The; Douroux & Co.; Epstein-Wyckoff & Assoc.; Monteiro Rose; Panda Talent; Stanton & Assoc.; Warden, White & Assoc.; Wright Representatives, Ann

**Romantic drama:** Artists Agency, The; Douroux & Co.; Epstein-Wyckoff & Assoc.; Monteiro Rose; Panda Talent; Stanton & Assoc.; Warden, White & Assoc.; Wright Representatives, Ann

**Science fiction:** Douroux & Co.; Freed, Barry; Kerwin, William; Monteiro Rose; Panda Talent; Perelman, Barry; Silver Screen Placements; Warden, White & Assoc.; Wardlow & Assoc.

**Sitcom:** Douroux & Co.; Epstein-Wyckoff & Assoc.; Panda Talent; Preminger, Jim; Wardlow & Assoc.; Wright Concept, The; Wright Representatives, Ann

**Soap opera:** Epstein-Wyckoff & Assoc.; Freed, Barry; Wright Representatives, Ann

**Teen:** Epstein-Wyckoff & Assoc.; Freed, Barry; Monteiro Rose; Wright Concept, The

**Theatrical stage play:** Epstein-Wyckoff & Assoc.; Frency, Samuel; Whittlesey, Peregrine

**Thriller/espionage:** Artists Agency, The; Cameron, Marshall; Douroux & Co.; Epstein-Wyckoff & Assoc.; Freed, Barry; Frency, Samuel; Kerwin, William; Monteiro Rose; Perelman, Barry; Silver Screen Placements; Stanton & Assoc.; Warden, White & Assoc.; Wardlow & Assoc.; Wright Concept, The; Wright Representatives, Ann

**Variety show:** Frency, Samuel; Wright Concept, The

**Western frontier:** Douroux & Co.; Monteiro Rose; Panda Talent; Warden, White & Assoc.; Wardlow & Assoc.; Wright Representatives, Ann;

# The Markets

## Book Publishers

The book business, for the most part, runs on hunches. Whether the idea for a book comes from a writer, an agent or the imagination of an acquiring editor, it is generally expressed in these terms: "This is a book that I *think* people will like. People will *probably* want to buy it." The decision to publish is mainly a matter of the right person, or persons, agreeing that those hunches are sound.

### THE PATH TO PUBLICATION

Ideas reach editors in a variety of ways. They arrive unsolicited every day through the mail. They come by phone, sometimes from writers but most often from agents. They arise in the editor's mind because of his daily traffic with the culture in which he lives. The acquisitions editor, so named because he is responsible for securing manuscripts for his company to publish, sifts through the deluge of possibilities, waiting for a book idea to strike him as extraordinary, inevitable, profitable.

In some companies, acquisitions editors possess the authority required to say, "Yes, we will publish this book." In most publishing houses, though, the acquisitions editor must prepare and present the idea to a proposal committee made up of marketing and administrative personnel. Proposal committees are usually less interested in questions of extraordinariness and inevitability than they are in profitability. The editor has to convince them that it makes good business sense to publish this book.

Once a contract is signed, several different wheels are set in motion. The author, of course, writes the book if he hasn't done so already. While the editor is helping to assure that the author is making the book the best it can be, promotion and publicity people are planning mailings of review copies to influential newspapers and review periodicals, writing catalog copy that will help sales representatives push the book to bookstores, and plotting a multitude of other promotional efforts (including interview tours and bookstore signings by the author) designed to dangle the book attractively before the reading public's eye.

When the book is published, it usually receives a concerted promotional push for a month or two. After that, the fate of the book—whether it will "grow legs" and set sales records or sit untouched on bookstore shelves—rests in the hands of the public. Publishers have to compete with all of the other entertainment industries vying for the consumer's money and limited leisure time. Successful books are reprinted to meet the demand. Unsuccessful books are returned from bookstores to publishers and are sold off cheaply as "remainders" or are otherwise disposed of.

### THE STATE OF THE BUSINESS

The book publishing industry is beginning to recover from the difficulties experienced in the last few years. Publishers sell their products to bookstores on a returnable basis, which means the stores usually have 120 days to either pay the bill or return the order. With independent bookstores continuing to close and superstores experiencing setbacks as well, many publishers were hit with staggering returns. This has slowed somewhat, but continues to be a concern. While there are many more outlets to *buy* books, including online bookstores such as Amazon.com,

Borders.com and Barnesandnoble.com, this doesn't necessarily translate into more books being *bought*. Some feel the superstore phenomenon has proved a mixed blessing. The greater shelf area means there are more materials available, but also drives a need for books as "wallpaper" that is continually refreshed by returning older books and restocking with newer ones.

But that's not to say publishers are rushing to bring esoteric or highly experimental material to the marketplace. The blockbuster mentality—publishing's penchant for sticking with "name brand" novelists—still drives most large publishers. It's simply a less risky venture to continue publishing authors whom they know readers like. On the other hand, the prospects for nonfiction authors are perhaps better than they have been for years. The boom in available shelf space has provided entree to the marketplace for books on niche topics that heretofore would not have seen the light of day in most bookstores. The superstores position themselves as one-stop shopping centers for readers of every stripe. As such, they must carry books on a wide range of subjects.

The publishing community as a whole is stepping back from the multimedia hype and approaching the market more cautiously, if not abandoning it entirely. While the possibilities offered by CD-ROM technology still exist, publishers realize that marrying format and content are crucial for a successful, profitable product. Online publishing seems to offer promise, if only publishers can figure out how to make money from this new and different format.

## HOW TO PUBLISH YOUR BOOK

The markets in this year's Book Publishers section offer opportunities in nearly every area of publishing. Large, commercial houses are here as are their smaller counterparts; large and small "literary" houses are represented as well. In addition, you'll find university presses, industry-related publishers, textbook houses and more.

The Book Publishers Subject Index is the place to start. You'll find it in the back of the book, before the General Index. Subject areas for both fiction and nonfiction are broken out for the over 1,150 total book publisher listings. Not all of them buy the kind of book you've written, but this Index will tell you which ones do.

When you have compiled a list of publishers interested in books in your subject area, read the detailed listings. Pare down your list by cross-referencing two or three subject areas and eliminating the listings only marginally suited to your book. When you have a good list, send for those publishers' catalogs and any manuscript guidelines available or check publishers' websites, which often contain catalog listings, manuscript preparation guidelines, current contact names and other information helpful to prospective authors. You want to make sure your book idea is in line with a publisher's list but is not a duplicate of something already published. Visit bookstores and libraries to see if their books are well represented. When you find a couple of books they have published that are similar to yours, write or call the company to find out who edited these books. This last, extra bit of research could be the key to getting your proposal to precisely the right editor.

Publishers prefer different kinds of submissions on first contact. Most like to see a one-page query with SASE, especially for nonfiction. Others will accept a brief proposal package that might include an outline and/or a sample chapter. Some publishers will accept submissions from agents only. Virtually no publisher wants to see a complete manuscript on initial contact, and sending one when they prefer another method will signal to the publisher "this is an amateur's submission." Editors do not have the time to read an entire manuscript, even editors at small presses who receive fewer submissions. Perhaps the only exceptions to this rule are children's picture book manuscripts and poetry manuscripts, which take only as much time to read as an outline and sample chapter anyway.

In your one-page query, give an overview of your book, mention the intended audience, the competition (check *Books in Print* and local bookstore shelves), and what sets your book apart.

Detail any previous publishing experience or special training relevant to the subject of your book. All of this information will help your cause; it is the professional approach.

Only one in a thousand writers will sell a book to the first publisher they query, especially if the book is the writer's first effort. Make a list of a dozen or so publishers that might be interested in your book. Try to learn as much about the books they publish and their editors as you can. Research, knowing the specifics of your subject area, and a professional approach are often the difference between acceptance and rejection. You are likely to receive at least a few rejections, however, and when that happens, don't give up. Rejection is as much a part of publishing, if not more, than signing royalty checks. Send your query to the next publisher on your list. Multiple queries can speed up the process at this early stage.

Personalize your queries by addressing them individually and mentioning what you know about a company from its catalog or books you've seen. Never send a form letter as a query. Envelopes addressed to "Editor" or "Editorial Department" end up in the dreaded slush pile.

If a publisher offers you a contract, you may want to seek advice before signing and returning it. An author's agent will very likely take 15% if you employ one, but you could be making 85% of a larger amount. Some literary agents are available on an hourly basis for contract negotiations only. For more information on literary agents, contact the Association of Authors' Representatives, 10 Astor Place, 3rd Floor, New York NY 10003, (212)353-3709. Also check the current edition of *Guide to Literary Agents* (Writer's Digest Books). Attorneys will only be able to tell you if everything is legal, not if you are getting a good deal, unless they have prior experience with literary contracts. If you have a legal problem, you might consider contacting Volunteer Lawyers for the Arts, 1 E. 53rd St., 6th Floor, New York NY 10022, (212)319-2787.

## AUTHOR-SUBSIDY PUBLISHER'S LISTINGS ELIMINATED

*Writer's Market* is a reference tool to help you sell your writing, and we encourage you to work with publishers that pay a royalty. Subsidy publishing involves paying money to a publishing house to publish a book. The source of the money could be a government, foundation or university grant, or it could be the author of the book. Publishers offering nonauthor-subsidized arrangements have been included in the appropriate section. If one of the publishers listed here offers you an author-subsidy arrangement (sometimes called "cooperative publishing," "co-publishing" or "joint venture"), asks you to pay for all or part of the cost of any aspect of publishing (printing, advertising, etc.) or to guarantee the purchase of any number of the books yourself, we would like you to let us know about that company immediately.

Sometimes newer publishers will offer author-subsidy contracts to get a leg up in the business and plan to become royalty-only publishers once they've reached a firm financial footing. Some publishers feel they must offer subsidy contracts to expand their lists beyond the capabilities of their limited resources. This may be true, and you may be willing to agree to it, but we choose to list only those publishers paying a royalty without requiring a financial investment from the author. In recent years, several large subsidy publishers have suddenly gone out of business, leaving authors without their money, their books, and in some cases, without the copyright to their own manuscripts.

## WHAT'S NEW

We've added several features to make *Writer's Market* even more helpful in your search for the right publisher for your work, features you won't find in any other writer's guide.

### The "key" to successful submissions

You may have written the most wonderful historical romance to ever grace the page. But if you submit it to a publisher of history textbooks, you're not likely to get too far. To help you quickly skim the listings for the right publisher, we've added a key symbol ( 🔑 ) with a brief summary of what that publisher does produce, as well as areas of interest they are currently emphasizing and areas they are de-emphasizing.

## Information at a glance

Most immediately noticeable, we've added a number of symbols at the beginning of each listing to quickly convey certain information at a glance. In the Book Publisher sections, these symbols identify new listings ( 🅽 ), "opportunity" markets that buy at least 50 percent from unagented or first-time writers ( ✪ ), and publishers that accept agented submissions only ( 🅂 ). Different sections of *Writer's Market* include other symbols; check the front and back inside covers for an explanation of all the symbols used throughout the book.

## How much money? What are my odds?

We've also highlighted important information in boldface, the "quick facts" you won't find in any other market guide but should know before you submit your work. This includes: how many manuscripts a publisher buys per year; how many from first-time authors; how many from unagented writers; the royalty rate a publisher pays; and how large an advance is offered.

## Publishers, their imprints and how they are related

In this era of big publishing—and big mergers—the world of publishing has grown even more intertwined. A "family tree" on page 86 lists the imprints and often confusing relationships of the largest conglomerate publishers.

In the listings, "umbrella" listings for these larger houses list the imprints under the company name. Imprint names in boldface indicate a separate, individual listing, easily located alphabetically, which provides much more detailed information about that imprints specific focus, needs and contacts.

Each listing includes a summary of the editorial mission of the house, an overarching principle that ties together what they publish. Under the heading **Acquisitions:** we list many more editors, often with their specific areas of expertise. We have also increased the number of recent titles to help give you an idea of the publishers' scope. We have included the royalty rates for those publishers willing to disclose them, but contract details are closely guarded and a number of larger publishers are reluctant to publicly state these terms. Standard royalty rates for paperbacks generally range from 7½ to 12½ percent, for hardcovers from 10 to 15 percent. Royalty rates for children's books are often lower, generally ranging from 5 to 10 percent.

Finally, we have listed a number of publishers who only accept agented submissions. This benefits the agents who use *Writer's Market*, those writers with agents who use the book themselves, and those as yet unagented writers who want to know more about a particular company.

**For a list of publishers according to their subjects of interest, see the nonfiction and fiction sections of the Book Publishers Subject Index. Information on book publishers and producers listed in the previous edition of *Writer's Market* but not included in this edition can be found in the General Index.**

**A&B PUBLISHERS GROUP**, 1000 Atlantic Ave., Brooklyn NY 11238. (718)783-7808. **Acquisitions:** Maxwell Taylor, editor. Estab. 1992. Publishes hardcover originals and trade paperback originals and reprints. **Publishes 12 titles/year. Receives 120 queries and 150 mss/year. 30% of books from first-time authors; 30% from unagented writers. Pays 5-12% royalty on net price. Offers $500-2,500 advance.** Publishes book 12-18 months after acceptance of ms. Accepts simultaneous submissions. Reports in 2 months on queries and proposals, 5 months on mss. Book catalog free.
    O━ The audience for A&B Publishers Group is children and adult African-Americans.
**Nonfiction:** Children's/juvenile, coffee table book, cookbook, illustrated book. Subjects include cooking/foods/nutrition, history. Query. Reviews artwork/photos as part of ms package. Send photocopies.
**Fiction:** "We have published no fiction but may start in fall 2000." Query.
**Tips:** "Read, read, read. The best writers are developed from good reading. There is not enough attention to quality."

⊘ **ABBEVILLE PRESS**, Abbeville Publishing Group, 22 Cortland St., New York NY 10007. *No unsolicited mss.*

**ABBOTT, LANGER & ASSOCIATES**, 548 First St., Crete IL 60417-2199. (708)672-4200. **Acquisitions:** Dr. Steven Langer, president. Estab. 1967. Publishes trade paperback originals, loose-leaf books. **Publishes 25 titles/year, mostly prepared inhouse. Receives 25 submissions/year. 10% of books from first-time authors; 90% of books from unagented writers. Pays 10-15% royalty. Offers advance.** Publishes book 18 months after acceptance. Book catalog for 6×9 SAE with 2 first-class stamps. Reports in 1 month on queries, 3 months on mss.
   O─ Abbott, Langer & Associates publishes books for human resource directors, wage and salary administrators, sales/marketing managers, security directors, etc. Currently emphasizing "a very limited number (3-5) of books dealing with specialized topics in the field of human resource management, wage and salary administration, sales compensation, recruitment, selection, etc."
**Nonfiction:** How-to, reference, technical on some phase of human resources management, security, sales management, etc. Query with outline. Reviews artwork/photos.
**Recent Title(s):** *Fire Safety & High Rise Buildings*, by Harry Azoni.
**Tips:** "A writer has the best chance selling our firm a how-to book in human resources management, sales/marketing management or security management."

**ABC-CLIO, INC.**, 501 S. Cherry St., Suite 350, Denver CO 80246. (303)333-3003. Fax: (303)333-4037. Subsidiaries include ABC-CLIO Ltd. **Acquisitions:** Gary Kuris, editorial director; Alicia Merritt, senior acquisitions editor (history, law, mythology); Todd Hallman, senior acquisitions editor (social sciences, folklore, multicultural studies); Kristi Ward, senior acquisitions editor (science, literature); Marie Ellen Larcada, senior acquisitions editor (history, environment, education). Estab. 1955. Publishes hardcover originals. **Publishes 45 titles/year. Receives 500 submissions/year. 20% of books from first-time authors; 95% from unagented writers. Pays royalty on net receipts. Offers advance.** Publishes ms 10 months after acceptance. Reports in 2 months on queries. Book catalog and ms guidelines free.
   O─ ABC-CLIO publishes "easy-to-use, authoritative sources on high-interest topics for the high school, undergraduate and public library audience. Currently emphasizing social sciences, science and folklore."
**Nonfiction:** Reference. Subjects include art/architecture, education, environmental issues, government/politics, history, literary studies, multicultural studies, mythology, science, women's issues/studies. No monographs or textbooks. Query or submit outline and sample chapters.
**Recent Title(s):** *Encyclopedia of the Vietnam War*, by Spencer C. Tucker.

**THE ABERDEEN GROUP**, 426 S. Westgate St., Addison IL 60101. (630)543-0870. Fax: (630)543-3112. Website: http//www.tagbookstore.com. **Acquisitions:** Mark DiCicco, publisher; Carolyn Schierhorn, acquisitions editor. Estab. 1956. **Publishes 6 titles/year. Receives 75 queries and 12 mss/year. 10% of books from first-time authors; 100% from unagented writers. Pays 6-18% royalty on retail price. Offers $1,000-2,000 advance.** Publishes book 6 months after acceptance of ms. Accepts simultaneous submissions. Reports in 1 month on queries and proposals, 2 months on mss. Book catalog free.
   O─ The Aberdeen Group seeks to strengthen and grow the concrete and masonry industries worldwide. "We strive to be the world's foremost information provider for these industries."
**Nonfiction:** How-to, technical (primarily in the concrete and masonry fields.) Subjects include architecture, construction, general engineering and construction business. Query with outline, 2-3 sample chapters, definition of topic, features, market analysis.
**Recent Title(s):** *Excavator Handbook*, by Rienar Christian.

**ABINGDON PRESS**, The United Methodist Publishing House, 201 Eighth Ave. S., Nashville TN 37203. (615)749-6000. Fax: (615)749-6512. Website: http://www.abingdon.org. President/Publisher: Neil M. Alexander. Vice President/Editorial Director: Harriett Jane Olson. **Acquisitions:** Ulrike Guthrie, senior editor (academic books); Robert Ratcliff, senior editor (professional clergy); Peg Augustine, editor (children's); Joseph A. Crowe, editor (general interest). Estab. 1789. Publishes hardcover and paperback originals; church supplies. **Publishes 120 titles/year. Receives 3,000 queries and 250 mss/year. Few books from first-time authors; 85% of books from unagented writers. Pays 7½% royalty on retail price.** Publishes book 2 years after acceptance. Book catalog free. Manuscript guidelines for SASE. Reports in 2 months.
   O─ Abingdon Press, America's oldest theological publisher, provides an ecumenical publishing program dedicated to serving the Christian community—clergy, scholars, church leaders, musicians and general readers—with quality resources in the areas of Bible study, the practice of ministry, theology, devotion, spirituality, inspiration, prayer, music and worship, reference, Christian education and church supplies.
**Imprint(s):** Dimensions for Living, Cokesbury.
**Nonfiction:** Religious-lay and professional, gift book, reference, children's religious books, academic texts. Query with outline and samples only.
**Recent Title(s):** *Celtic Praise*, by Van de Weyer (gift).

**ABIQUE**, 1700 Amelia Court, #423, Plano TX 75075. E-mail: abique@lycosmail.com. Website: http://www.cmpu.net/public/abique. **Acquisitions:** Tom Kyle, editorial director. Publishes hardcover and trade paperback originals. **Publishes 20 titles/year. Pays 10% royalty on retail price.** Publishes book 6 months after acceptance of ms. Accepts simultaneous submissions. Reports in 1 month on queries.

O→ "We are somewhat like a university press in that we seek books with too narrow an audience for other publishers to consider." Currently emphasizing history, local interest. De-emphasizing fiction, illustrated and photo books.

**Nonfiction:** Reference, technical, academic disciplines. Subjects include anthropology/archaeology, government/politics, health/medicine, history, nature/environment, philosophy, science, sociology. Query first with SASE. Reviews artwork/photos as part of the ms package. Send photocopies.

**Recent Title(s):** *America's Worst Train Disaster*, by Don Moody (nonfiction); *Poems, Poems, Poems*, by Eli Herd (poetry).

**Tips:** "We specialize in books aimed directly at a small specialized audience. Our authors are experts who write for a limited audience. We rely on them to direct us to that audience and to know what that audience wants to read. We want authors who will work to promote their book."

**HARRY N. ABRAMS, INC.**, La Martinière Groupe, 100 Fifth Ave., New York NY 10011. (212)206-7715. President/Publisher/Editor-in-Chief: Paul Gottlieb. Executive Editor: Susan Randol. **Acquisitions:** Margaret Chace, managing editor. Estab. 1949. Publishes hardcover and "a few" paperback originals. **Publishes 100 titles/year. Pays royalty. Offers variable advance.** Publishes book 2 years after acceptance of ms. Reports in 3 months. Book catalog for $5.

O→ "We publish *only* high-quality illustrated art books, i.e., art, art history, museum exhibition catalogs, written by specialists and scholars in the field."

**Nonfiction:** Art, nature and science, outdoor recreation. Requires illustrated material for art and art history, museums. Submit outline, sample chapters and illustrations. Reviews artwork/photos as part of ms package.

**Tips:** "We are one of the few publishers who publish almost exclusively illustrated books. We consider ourselves the leading publishers of art books and high-quality artwork in the U.S. Once the author has signed a contract to write a book for our firm the author must finish the manuscript to agreed-upon high standards within the schedule agreed upon in the contract."

**ABSEY & CO.**, 5706 Root Rd., Suite #5, Spring TX 77389. (281)257-2340. E-mail: abseyandco@aol.com. Website: http://www.absey.com. **Acquisitions:** Trey Hall, editor-in-chief. Publishes hardcover, trade paperback and mass market paperback originals. **Publishes 6-10 titles/year. 50% of books from first-time authors; 50% from unagented writers. Royalty and advance vary.** Publishes book 1 year after acceptance of ms. No e-mail submissions. Reports in 3 months on queries, 9 months on mss. Manuscript guidelines for #10 SASE or on website.

O→ "Our goal is to publish original, creative works of literary merit." Currently emphasizing educational, young adult literature. De-emphasizing self-help.

**Nonfiction:** Educational subjects and language arts, as well as general nonfiction. Query with SASE.

**Fiction:** "Since we are a small, new press, we are looking for book-length manuscripts with a firm intended audience." Query with SASE.

**Poetry:** Publishes the "Writers and Young Writers Series." Interested in thematic poetry collections of literary meit. Query with SASE.

**Recent Title(s):** *The Legacy of Roxaboxen*, by Alice McLerran (nonfiction); *Dragonfly*, by Alice McLerran (fiction); *Where I'm From*, by George Ella Lyon (poetry).

● Two Absey books, *Just People* and *Poetry After Lunch* were named 1998 Best Books for Young Adults by the American Library Association.

**Tips:** "We work closely and attentively with authors and their work."

**ACE SCIENCE FICTION AND FANTASY**, The Berkley Publishing Group, Penguin Putnam Inc., 375 Hudson St., New York NY 10014. (212)366-2000. Website: http//www.penguinputnam.com. **Acquisitions:** Anne Sowards, editor. Estab. 1953. Publishes hardcover, paperback and trade paperback originals and reprints. **Publishes 75 titles/year.** Reports in 6 months. Manuscript guidelines for #10 SASE.

O→ Ace publishes exclusively science fiction and fantasy.

**Fiction:** Science fiction, fantasy. *Agented submissions only.* Query first with SASE.

**Recent Title(s):** *The Night Watch*, by Sean Stewart.

**ACTA PUBLICATIONS**, 4848 N. Clark St., Chicago IL 60640-4711. Fax: (773)271-7399. E-mail: gfapierce@aol .com. **Acquisitions:** Gregory F. Augustine Pierce. Estab. 1958. Publishes trade paperback originals. **Publishes 10 titles/year. Receives 50 queries and 15 mss/year. 50% of books from first-time authors; 90% from unagented writers. Pays 10-12% royalty on wholesale price.** Publishes book 1 year after acceptance of ms. Reports in 2 months on proposals. Book catalog and author guidelines for SASE.

O→ Acta publishes non-academic, practical books aimed at the mainline religious market.

**Nonfiction:** Religion. Submit outline and 1 sample chapter. Reviews artwork/photos. Send photocopies.

**Recent Title(s):** *Protect Us from All Anxiety: Meditations for the Depressed*, by William Burke (self-help).

**Tips:** "Don't send a submission unless you have read our catalog or one of our books."

**ACTIVE PARENTING PUBLISHERS, INC.**, 810-B Franklin Court, Marietta GA 30067. Fax: (770)429-0334. E-mail: cservice@activeparenting.com. Website: http://www.activeparenting.com. **Acquisitions:** Gloriela Rosas, editorial manager. **Publishes 4 titles/year.**

O→ "Our aim is to develop human potential by producing quality programs and training which provide value to our customers and offer creative solutions to their needs."

**Nonfiction:** Self-help, textbook, educational. Subjects include child guidance/parenting, psychology, loss, self-esteem. Nonfiction work; mainly parent education and family issues. Query with SASE. *No unsolicited mss.*
**Recent Title(s):** *Parenting Your 1- to 4-Year-Old*, by Michael H. Popkin, Ph.D.; contributing authors: Betsy Gard, Ph.D. and Marilyn Montgomery, Ph.D. (self-help).

**ADAMS MEDIA CORPORATION**, 260 Center St., Holbrook MA 02343. (781)767-8100. Fax: (781)767-0994. Website: http://www.adamsmedia.com. Editor-in-Chief: Edward Walters. **Acquisitions:** Anne Weaver; Pam Liflander; Jere Calmes, senior business editor; Cheryl Kimball. Estab. 1980. Publishes hardcover originals, trade paperback originals and reprints. **Publishes 100 titles/year. Receives 1,500 queries and 500 mss/year. 25% of books from first-time authors; 25% from unagented writers. Pays standard royalty or makes outright purchase. Offers variable advance.** Publishes book 1 year after acceptance of ms. Accepts simultaneous submissions. Reports in 3 months.
O-π Adams Media publishes commercial nonfiction, not scholarly or literary material, including career titles, innovative business and self-help books.
**Nonfiction:** Biography, cookbook, gift book, how-to, humor, illustrated book, reference, self-help. Subjects include Americana, animals, business/economics, child guidance/parenting, cooking/foods/nutrition, gardening, government/politics, health/medicine, history, hobbies, language/literature, military/war, money/finance, nature/environment, psychology, regional, science, sports, women's issues/studies. Submit outline. Does not return unsolicited materials.
**Recent Title(s):** *The U.S.S. Essex*, by Frances Diane Robotti and James Vescovi (history).

**ADAMS-BLAKE PUBLISHING**, 8041 Sierra St., Fair Oaks CA 95628. (916)962-9296. Website: http//www.adams-blake.com. Vice President: Paul Raymond. **Acquisitions:** Monica Blane, senior editor. Estab. 1992. Publishes trade paperback originals and reprints. **Publishes 10-15 titles/year. Receives 150 queries and 90 mss/year. 90% of books from first-time authors; 90% from unagented writers. Pays 15% royalty on wholesale price.** Publishes book 6 months after acceptance of ms. Accepts simultaneous submissions. Reports in 1 month on mss. *Writer's Market* recommends allowing 2 months for reply.
O-π Adams-Blake Publishing is looking for business, technology and finance titles as well as data that can be bound/packaged and sold to specific industry groups at high margins. "We publish technical and training material we can sell to the corporate market. We are especially looking for 'high ticket' items that sell to the corporate market for prices between $100-300." Currently emphasizing technical, computers, technology. De-emphasizing how-to.
**Nonfiction:** How-to, technical. Subjects include business/economics, computers/electronics, health/medicine, money/finance, software. Query with sample chapters or complete ms. Reviews artwork/photos as part of ms package. Send photocopies.
**Recent Title(s):** *Success From Home*, by Alan Canton.
**Tips:** "We will take a chance on material the big houses reject. Since we sell the majority of our material directly, we can publish material for a very select market. This year we seek niche market material that we can Docutech™ and sell direct to the corporate sector. Author should include a marketing plan. Sell us on the project!"

**ADDAX PUBLISHING GROUP, INC.**, 8643 Hauser Dr., Suite 235, Lenexa KS 66215. (913)438-5333. Fax: (913)438-2079. E-mail: addax1@gvi.net. **Acquisitions:** Submissions Editor. Estab. 1992. Publishes hardcover and trade paperback originals. **Publishes 20 titles/year. 50% of books from first-time authors; 75% from unagented writers. Pays royalty. No advance.** Publishes book 1 year after acceptance of ms. Accepts simultaneous submissions.
O-π Addax Publishing Group publishes sports books on and with athletes and teams in both professional and college sports. "In addition, we publish children's books for holidays, goal-oriented children's books with sports themes, select inspiration, motivation, how-to, and humor books. Our titles have both regional and national emphasis."
**Nonfiction:** Biography, children's/juvenile, coffee table book. Subjects include sports. Submit completed ms.
**Recent Titles:** *Blood on the Horns*, by Roland Lazenby (sports).
**Tips:** "We have a fairly tightly defined niche in sports-related areas."

**ADDICUS BOOKS, INC.**, P.O. Box 45327, Omaha NE 68145. (402)330-7493. **Acquisitions:** Rod Colvin, president. E-mail: addicusbks@aol.com Website: http://www.AddicusBooks.com. Estab. 1994. Publishes trade paperback originals. **Publishes 8-10 titles/year. 70% of books from first-time authors; 60% from unagented writers. Pays royalty on retail price.** Publishes book 9 months after acceptance of ms. Accepts simultaneous submissions. Reports in 1 month on proposals. Guidelines for #10 SASE.
O-π Addicus Books, Inc. seeks mss with strong national or regional appeal.
**Nonfiction:** How-to, self-help. Subjects include Americana, business/economics, health/medicine, psychology, regional, true-crime. Query with outline and 3-4 sample chapters.
**Recent Title(s):** *Understanding Parkinson's Disease*, by Daivd Cram, M.D. (health).
**Tips:** "We are looking for quick-reference books on health topics. Do some market research to make sure the market is not already flooded with similar books. We're also looking for good true crime manuscripts, with an interesting story, with twists and turns, behind the crime."

**AEGIS PUBLISHING GROUP**, 796 Aquidneck Ave., Newport RI 02842-7246. (401)849-4200. Fax: (401)849-4231. E-mail: aegis@aegisbooks.com. Website: http//www.aegisbooks.com. **Acquisitions:** Robert Mastin, publisher. Estab.

1992. Publishes trade paperback originals and reprints. **Publishes 6 titles/year. Pays 12% royalty on net sales. Offers $1,000-4,000 advance.** Reports in 2 months on queries.

  ○┱ "Our specialty is telecommunications books targeted to small businesses, entrepreneurs and telecommuters—how they can benefit from the latest telecom products and services. Our goal is to become the primary publisher of nontechnical telecommunications books for small organizations, end users, new entrants to the industry and telecom managers."

**Nonfiction:** Reference, business. Subjects include telecommunications, data networking. "Author must be an experienced authority in the subject, and the material must be very specific with helpful step-by-step advice." Query with outline and SASE.

**Recent Title(s):** *Telecom & Networking Glossary*, edited by Robert Mastin.

**AHA PRESS**, American Hospital Association, One N. Frankin, Chicago IL 60606. (312)893-6800. Fax: (312)422-4516. E-mail: hill@aha.org. Website: http://www.ahapress.com. **Acquisitions:** Editorial Director. Estab. 1979. Publishes hardcover and trade paperback originals. **Publishes 35-40 titles/year. Receives 150-200 submissions/year. 20% of books from first-time authors; 100% from unagented writers. Pays 10-12% royalty on net sale. Offers $1,000 average advance.** Publishes book 1 year after acceptance. Reports in 3 months. Book catalog and ms guidelines for 9×12 SAE with 7 first-class stamps.

  ○┱ AHA Press publishes books on health care administration primarily for senior and middle management of health care institutions, as well as for trustees and other community leaders. Currently emphasizing comprehensive reference works and hand books. De-emphasizing monographs.

**Nonfiction:** Reference, technical, textbook. Subjects include business/economics (specific to health care institutions); health/medicine (never consumer oriented). Need field-based, reality-tested responses to changes in the health care field directed to hospital CEO's, planners, boards of directors, or other senior management. No personal histories, untested health care programs or clinical texts. Query with SASE.

**Recent Title(s):** *100 Faces of Health Care*; *Patient Care Redesign*.

**Tips:** "The successful proposal demonstrates a clear understanding of the needs of the market and the writer's ability to succinctly present practical knowledge of demonstrable benefit that comes from genuine experience that readers will recognize, trust and accept."

**AKTRIN FURNITURE INFORMATION CENTER**, 164 S. Main St., P.O. Box 898, High Point NC 27261. (336)841-8535. Fax: (336)841-5435. E-mail: aktrin@aktrin.com. Website: http://www.aktrin.com. **Acquisitions:** Carlene Damba, director of operations. Estab. 1985. Publishes trade paperback originals. **Publishes 8 titles/year. Receives 5 queries/year. 20% of books from first-time authors; 20% from unagented writers. Makes outright purchase of $1,500 minimum. Offers $300-600 advance.** Publishes book 2 months after acceptance. Accepts simultaneous submissions. Reports in 1 month. *Writer's Market* recommends allowing 2 months for reply. Book catalog free.

  ○┱ AKTRIN is a full-service organization dedicated to the furniture industry. "Our focus is on determining trends, challenges and opportunities, while also identifying problems and weak spots."

**Imprint(s):** AKTRIN Furniture Information Center-Canada (151 Randall St., Oakville, Ontario L6J 1P5 Canada. (905)845-3474. Contact: Stefan Wille).

**Nonfiction:** Reference. Business/economics subjects. "Have an understanding of business/economics. We are writing only about the furniture industry." Query.

**Recent Title(s):** *The American Demand for Household Furniture and Trends*, by Thomas McCormick (in-depth analysis of American household furniture market).

**Tips:** Audience is executives of furniture companies (manufacturers and retailers) and suppliers and consultants to the furniture industry.

**ALBA HOUSE**, 2187 Victory Blvd., Staten Island NY 10314-6603. (718)761-0047. **Acquisitions:** Edmund C. Lane, S.S.P., editor. Estab. 1961. Publishes hardcover, trade paperback and mass market paperback originals. **Publishes 24 titles/year. Receives 300 queries and 150 mss/year. 20% of books from first-time authors; 100% from unagented writers. Pays 7-10% royalty. No advance.** Publishes book 9 months after acceptance of ms. Reports in 1 month on queries and proposals, 2 months on mss. Book catalog and ms guidelines free.

  ○┱ Alba House is the North American publishing division of the Society of St. Paul, an International Roman Catholic Missionary Religious Congregation dedicated to spreading the Gospel message.

**Nonfiction:** Reference, textbook. Religious subjects. Manuscripts which contribute, from a Roman Catholic perspective, to the personal, intellectual and spiritual growth of individuals in the following areas: Scripture, theology and the Church, saints-their lives and teachings, spirituality and prayer, religious life, marriage and family life, liturgy and homily preparation, pastoral concerns, religious education, bereavement, moral and ethical concerns, philosophy, psychology. Reviews artwork/photos as part of ms package. Send photocopies.

**Recent Title(s):** *Living The Truth In Love*, by Benedict Ashley, O.P. (moral theology textbook).

**THE ALBAN INSTITUTE**, 7315 Wisconsin Ave., Suite 1250 W., Bethesda MD 20814-3211. (301)718-4407. Fax: (301)718-1958. **Acquisitions:** David Lott, managing editor (multicultural/diversity; faith & health). Beth Gaede, acquisitions editor (women's issues; congregational size issues; faith, money & lifestyle). Estab. 1974. Publishes trade paperback originals. **Publishes 12 titles/year. Receives 100 submissions/year. 100% of books from unagented writers. Pays 7-10% royalty on books;** makes outright purchase of $50-100 on publication for 450-2,000 word articles relevant to congregational life—practical—ecumenical. Publishes book 1 year after acceptance. Reports in 4 months. Book catalog and ms guidelines for 9×12 SAE with 3 first-class stamps.

O— "Our publications have a focus on practical, how-to materials, usually based on extensive research, that reaches an ecumenical and sometimes interfaith audience without a particular theological slant." Emphasizing multiculturalism; faith & health; mission & purpose; technology. De-emphasizing sexuality issues; pastoral searches; geriatrics.

**Nonfiction:** Religious—focus on local congregation—ecumenical. Must be accessible to general reader. Research preferred. Needs mss on the task of the ordained leader in the congregation, the career path of the ordained leader in the congregation, problems and opportunities in congregational life, and ministry of the laity in the world and in the church. No sermons, biblical studies, devotional, children's titles, novels, inspirational or prayers. Query for guidelines. Proposals only, no unsolicited mss.

**Recent Title(s):** *Letters to Lee: Mentoring the New Minister,* by Paul C. Clayton (nonfiction).

**Tips:** "Our audience is comprised of intelligent, probably liberal mainline Protestant and Catholic clergy and lay leaders, executives and seminary administration/faculty—people who are concerned with the local church at a practical level and new approaches to its ministry. We are looking for titles on congregations, the clergy role, calling and career; visions, challenges, how-to's; and the ministry of the laity in the church and in the world."

**ALBURY PUBLISHING,** P.O. Box 470406, Tulsa OK 74147. **Acquisitions:** Elizabeth Sherman, editorial development manager. Publishes hardcover and trade paperback originals and reprints. **Publishes 20 titles/year. Receives 200 queries and 45 mss/year. 1% of books from first-time authors; 80% from unagented writers. Pays royalty or makes outright purchase.** Publishes book 1 year after acceptance of ms. Reports in 6 months on proposals. Book catalog for 9×12 SAE and 5 first-class stamps. Manuscript guidelines for #10 SASE.

O— "We are a Christian publisher with an upbeat presentation."

**Nonfiction:** Bible teaching, humor, self-help, compilations of historic Christian leaders and devotionals. "Most of our authors are established ministers and friends of the house. In order to break into our market, writers must exhibit a clearly defined, professionally presented proposal that shows they know and understand our market." Submit outline, 3 sample chapters and author bio with SASE.

**Recent Title(s):** *God's Pathway to Healing Menopause,* by Dr. Reginald Cherry.

**ALEF DESIGN GROUP,** Torah Aura Productions, 4423 Fruitland Ave., Los Angeles CA 90058. (213)585-7312. Website: http://www.torahaura.com. **Acquisitions:** Jane Golub. Estab. 1990. Publishes hardcover and trade paperback originals. **Publishes 25 titles/year; imprint publishes 10 titles/year. Receives 30 queries and 30 mss/year. 80% of books from first-time authors; 100% from unagented writers. Pays 10% royalty.** Publishes book 3 years after acceptance of ms. Accepts simultaneous submissions. Reports in 6 months on mss. Book catalog for 9×12 SAE and 10 first-class stamps..

O— The Alef Design Group publishes books of Judaic interest only. Currently de-emphasizing picture books.

**Nonfiction:** Children's/juvenile, textbook. Subjects include language/literature (Hebrew), religion (Jewish). Query with SASE. Reviews artwork/photos as part of ms package. Send photocopies.

**Fiction:** Juvenile, religious, young adult. "We publish books of Judaic interest only." Query with SASE.

**Recent Title(s):** *Scripture Windows,* by Peter Pitzele (nonfiction); *The Road to Exile,* by Didier Nebot (fiction).

**ALGONQUIN BOOKS OF CHAPEL HILL,** Workman Publishing, P.O. Box 2225, Chapel Hill NC 27515-2225. (919)967-0108. Fax: (919)933-0272. Website: http://www.algonquin.com. Editorial Director: Shannon Ravenel. **Acquisitions:** Editorial Department. Estab. 1982. "We're a very small company that tries to give voice to new writers." Publishes hardcover originals, trade paperback originals and reprints of own titles. **Publishes 24 titles/year.** Query by mail. No e-mail queries of submissions.

O— Algonquin Books publishes quality literary fiction and nonfiction.

**N ★ ALLISON PRESS,** Star Rising Publishers, 2946 Maple Dr., Camp Verde AZ 86322. (520)567-5176. Fax: (520)567-8912. E-mail: robinmay@kachina.net. Website: http://www.homestead.com/starrisingpublishers. **Acquisitions:** Robin May, publisher (New Age, metaphysical); Kristen B. May, editor (poetry, fiction). Publishes trade paperback originals. **Publishes 5-6 titles/year; imprints publish 2-3 titles/year. Receives 100 queries and 75 mss/year. 90% of books from first-time authors; 90% from unagented writers. Pays 10-20% royalty on retail price or makes outright purchase of $500-5000. No advance.** Publishes book 18 months after acceptance of ms. Accepts simultaneous submissions. Reports in 1 month on queries and proposals, 4 months on mss. Book catalog and ms guidelines for #10 SASE or on website.

**Imprint(s):** Allison (contact Robin May), Star Rising (contact Kristen May).

**Nonfiction:** How-to, self-help. Subjects include creative nonfiction, philosophy, religion, spirituality, astrology, New Age, channeling, metaphysical. Submit complete ms. *Writer's Market recommends query with SASE first.*

**Fiction:** Fantasy, occult, poetry, religious, short story collections, spiritual. Submit complete ms. *Writer's Market recommends query with SASE first.* "We are looking for 'new writers' with that creative flow and uninhibited expression."

**Poetry:** Submit complete ms. *Writer's Market recommends query with SASE first.*

**Recent Title(s):** *Sirius Eleven,* by Leondra (channeling); *In Times Past,* by Leondra (general).

**Tips:** "Be creative and don't judge your work too harshly. Free up the creativity that we all possess."

**ALLWORTH PRESS**, 10 E. 23rd St., Suite 210, New York NY 10010-4402. Fax: (212)777-8261. E-mail: pub@allwort h.com. Website: http://www.allworth.com. **Acquisitions:** Tad Crawford, publisher; Nicole Porter, editor. Estab. 1989. Publishes hardcover and trade paperback originals. **Publishes 26 titles/year.** Reports in 1 month on queries and proposals. Book catalog and ms guidelines free on request.

    O→ Allworth Press publishes business and self-help information for artists, designers, photographers, authors and film and performing artists, as well as books about business, money and the law for the general public. The press also publishes the best of classic and contemporary writing in art and graphic design. Currently emphasizing photography, film, video and theater.

**Nonfiction:** How-to, reference. Subjects include the business aspects of art, design, photography, performing arts, writing, as well as business and legal guides for the public. Query.

**Recent Title(s):** *Design Literacy*, by Steven Heller.

**Tips:** "We are trying to give ordinary people advice to better themselves in practical ways—as well as helping creative people in the fine and commercial arts."

**ALLYN & BACON**, Pearson Education Group, 160 Gould St., Needham Heights MA 02194-2310. (781)455-1200. Website: http://www.abacon.com. **Acquisitions:** Nancy Forsyth, editorial director. *Education:* Arnis Burvikovs, editor (educational technology, reading/emergent literacy, language arts, children's literature, ESL/bilingual methods, education administration, vocational-ed methods); Norris Harrell, editor (C&I, social studies, curriculum, multicultural ed, math & science, early childhood); Paul Smith, editor (ed psych); Virginia Lanigan, editor (special ed, counseling); Steve Dragin, editor (special-path, aud, deaf study/ed, higher ed, foundations of education). *English:* Joe Opiela, editor (English comp plus developmental, authors with last name A-K and all developmental authors); Eben Ludlow, editor (English comp, authors with last name L-Z). *Communication:* Karen Bowers, editor (mass communication, speech communication, journalism, drama). *Psychology:* Becky Pascal, editor (psych, clinical, abnormal, statistics, human sexuality); Jeff Lasser, editor (psych, developmental); Carolyn Merrill, editor (intro, physio, social, cognitive); Joe Burns, editor (health, phys ed, dance, human sexuality). *Sociology:* Karen Hanson, editor (sociology/intro, crime, criminal justice); Judy Fifer, editor (social work, family therapy); Sarah Kelbaugh, editor (advanced sociology, anthropology). Publishes hardcover and trade paperback originals. **Publishes 300 titles/year. 5-10% of books from first-time authors; 95% from unagented writers. Pays 10-15% royalty on net price. Advance varies.** Publishes book 1-3 years after acceptance of ms. Accepts simultaneous submissions. Reports in 2 months on queries. Book catalog and ms guidelines free or on website.

    O→ Allyn & Bacon publishes college texts, freshman through graduate level, and professional reference books, in the areas of education, the humanities and the social sciences.

**Nonfiction:** Reference, technical, textbook; primarily college texts; some titles for professionals. Subjects include education, health, psychology, sociology, criminal justice, social work, speech, mass communication. Query with outline, 2-3 sample chapters, table of contents, author's vita and SASE. Reviews artwork/photos as part of ms package. Send photocopies.

**Recent Title(s):** *Social Psychology: Unraveling the Mystery*, by Kenrick Douglas, Steven Neubug and Robert Cialdini.

**Tips:** "We focus on a few areas and cover them thoroughly; publishing vertically, from freshman level through graduate level. We also publish a number of titles within each discipline, same area but different approach. So, just because we have titles in an area already, it doesn't mean we aren't interested in more."

◪ **ALYSON PUBLICATIONS, INC.**, 6922 Hollywood Blvd., Suite 1000, Los Angeles CA 90028. (323)860-6065. Fax: (323)467-0152. **Acquisitions:** Attn. Editorial Dept.; Scott Brassart, associate publisher (fiction, science); Angela Brown, associate editor (women's fiction, arts). Estab. 1979. Publishes trade paperback originals and reprints. **Publishes 40 titles/year. Receives 1,500 submissions/year. 40% of books from first-time authors; 70% from unagented writers. Pays 8-15% royalty on net price. Offers $1,500-15,000 advance.** Publishes book 18 months after acceptance. Reports in 2 months. Book catalog and ms guidelines for 6×9 SAE with 3 first-class stamps.

    O→ Alyson Publications publishes books for and about gay men and lesbians from all economic and social segments of society, and explores the political, legal, financial, medical, spiritual, social and sexual aspects of gay and lesbian life, and contributions to society. They also consider bisexual and transgender material. Emphasizing medical, legal and financial nonfiction titles. De-emphasizing first fiction.

**Imprint(s):** Alyson Wonderland, Alyson Classics Library.

**Nonfiction:** Gay/lesbian subjects. "We are especially interested in nonfiction providing a positive approach to gay/ lesbian/bisexual issues." Accepts nonfiction translations. Submit 2-page outline with SASE. No dissertations. Reviews artwork/photos as part of ms package.

**Fiction:** Gay novels. Accepts fiction translations. No short stories, poetry. Submit 1-2 page synopsis with SASE.

**Recent Title(s):** *Gay Lesbian Online*, by Jeff Dawson (nonfiction); *Salt Water*, by Barbara Wilson (fiction).

**Tips:** "We publish many books by new authors. The writer has the best chance of selling to our firm well-researched, popularly written nonfiction on a subject (e.g., some aspect of gay history) that has not yet been written about much. With fiction, create a strong storyline that makes the reader want to find out what happens. With nonfiction, write in a popular style for a nonacademic audience. We also look at manuscripts aimed at kids of lesbian and gay parents."

◪ **AMACOM BOOKS**, American Management Association, 1601 Broadway, New York NY 10019-7406. (212)903-8081. Fax: (212)903-8083. Website: http://www.amanet.org. Managing Director: Weldon P. Rackley. Publisher: Hank Kennedy. **Acquisitions:** Adrienne Hickey, executive editor (management, human resources development, training);

Ellen Kadin, senior acquisitions editor (marketing, sales, customer service, personal development); Ray O'Connell, senior acquisitions editor (manufacturing, finance, project management); William Hicks, senior acquisitions editor (management, organization development); Jacquie Flynn, acquisitions editor (information technology, training). Estab. 1923. Publishes hardcover and trade paperback originals, professional books in various formats, multimedia and self-study courses. **Publishes 75 titles/year. Receives 500 submissions/year. 40% of books from first-time authors; 70% from unagented writers. Pays 10-15% royalty on net receipts by the publisher. Publishes book 9 months after acceptance. Reports in 2 months. Book catalog and proposal guidelines free.**

☞ Amacom is the publishing arm of the American Management Association, the world's largest training organization for managers and executives. Amacom publishes books on business issues, strategies and tasks to enhance organizational and individual effectiveness.

**Nonfiction:** Publishes business books of all types, including management, marketing, training, technology applications, finance, career, professional skills for retail, direct mail, college and corporate markets. Query or submit outline/synopsis, sample chapters, résumé.

**Recent Title(s):** *Semper Fi*, by Dan Carrison and Rod Walsh.

**N ▨ AMBER BOOKS PUBLISHING**, 1334 E. Chandler Blvd., Suite 5-D67, Phoenix AZ 85048. (602)460-1660. Fax: (602)283-0991. E-mail: amberbk@aol.com. Website: http://www.amberbooks.qpg.com. **Acquisitions:** Tony Rose, publisher (self help/African-American entertainment bios). Tenny Iuony, editor (African-American fashion, style). Estab. 1997. Publishes trade paperback and mass market paperback originals. **Publishes 5-10 titles/year. Receives 30 queries and 15 mss/year. 100% of books from first-time authors; 100% from unagented writers. Pays 10-15% royalty on wholesale price. No advance.** Publishes book 2 months after acceptance of ms. Accepts simultaneous submissions. Reports in 1 month. Book catalog free on request or on website.

☞ Amber Books publishes entertainment bios on the latest African-American rappers and singers, self-help, finance, credit and how-to books.

**Nonfiction:** Biography, children's/juvenile, how-to, self-help. Subjects include multicultural, sports. Submit completed ms. Reviews artwork/photos as part of ms package. Send photocopies.

**Fiction:** Comic books, erotica, humor, romance (Black), sports. Submit completed ms.

**Recent Titles:** *Is Modeling For You? The Handbook and Guide for the Aspiring Black Model*, by Vonne Rose and Tony Rose (self help nonfiction).

**Tips:** The goal of Amber Books is to build a strong catalog comprised of "self-help" books, celebrity bio books, and children's books, in print and on software, along with computer games which pertain to, about, and for the African-American population.

**▨ AMERICA WEST PUBLISHERS**, P.O. Box 2208, Carson City NV 89702-2208. (775)585-0700. Fax: (877)726-2632. E-mail: global@hidlink.com. **Acquisitions:** George Green, president. Estab. 1985. Publishes hardcover and trade paperback originals and reprints. **Publishes 20 titles/year. Receives 150 submissions/year. 90% of books from first-time authors; 90% from unagented writers. Pays 10% on wholesale price. Offers $300 average advance.** Publishes book 6 months after acceptance. Accepts simultaneous submissions. Reports in 1 month. Book catalog and ms guidelines free.

☞ America West seeks the "other side of picture," political cover-ups and new health alternatives.

**Imprint(s):** Bridger House Publishers, Inc.

**Nonfiction:** Subjects include economic, health/medicine (holistic self-help), political (including cover-up), UFO—metaphysical. Submit outline/synopsis and sample chapters. Reviews artwork/photos as part of ms package.

**Recent Title(s):** *One World Order.*

**Tips:** "We currently have materials in all bookstores that have areas of UFOs; also political and economic nonfiction."

**AMERICAN ASTRONAUTICAL SOCIETY**, Univelt, Inc., Publisher, P.O. Box 28130, San Diego CA 92198. (760)746-4005. Fax: (760)746-3139. Website: http://univelt.staigerland.com. **Acquisitions:** Robert H. Jacobs, editorial director. Estab. 1970. Publishes hardcover originals. **Publishes 8 titles/year. Receives 12-15 submissions/year. 5% of books from first-time authors; 5% from unagented writers. Pays 10% royalty on actual sales.** Publishes book 4 months after acceptance. Accepts simultaneous submissions. Reports in 1 month. *Writer's Market* recommends allowing 2 months for reply. Book catalog and ms guidelines for 9×12 SAE with 3 first-class stamps.

☞ "Our books must be space-oriented or space-related. They are meant for technical libraries, research establishments and the aerospace industry worldwide."

**Nonfiction:** Proceedings or monographs in the field of astronautics, including applications of aerospace technology to Earth's problems. Call first, then submit outline and 1-2 sample chapters. Reviews artwork/photos as part of ms package.

**Recent Title(s):** *Space Cooperation in the 21st Century*, edited by Peter M. Bainum, et al.

**AMERICAN ATHEIST PRESS**, P.O. Box 5733, Parsippany NJ 07054-6733. (908)259-0700. Fax: (908)259-0748. E-mail: editor@atheists.org. Website: http://www.atheists.org. **Acquisitions:** Frank Zindler, editor. Estab. 1959. Publishes trade paperback originals and reprints. **Publishes 12 titles/year. Receives 200 submissions/year. 40-50% of books from first-time authors; 100% from unagented writers. Pays 5-10% royalty on retail price.** Publishes book 2 years after acceptance. Accepts simultaneous submissions. Reports in 4 months on queries. Book catalog for 6½×9½ SAE. Writer's guidelines for 9×12 SAE.

☞ "We are interested in books that will help Atheists gain a deeper understanding of Atheism, improve their ability to critique religious propaganda, and assist them in fighting to maintain the 'wall of separation between state and church.' " Currently emphasizing the politics of religion, science and religion. De-emphasizing biblical criticism (but still doing some).

**Imprint(s):** Gustav Broukal Press.

**Nonfiction:** Biography, reference, general. Subjects include history (of religion and atheism, of the effects of religion historically); philosophy and religion (from an atheist perspective, particularly criticism of religion); politics (separation of state and church, religion and politics); atheism (particularly the lifestyle of atheism; the history of atheism; applications of atheism). "We would like to see more submissions dealing with the histories of specific religious sects, such as the L.D.S., the Worldwide Church of God, etc." Submit outline and sample chapters. Reviews artwork/photos.

**Fiction:** Humor (satire of religion or of current religious leaders); anything of particular interest to atheists. "We rarely publish any fiction. But we have occasionally released a humorous book. No mainstream. For our press to consider fiction, it would have to tie in with the general focus of our press, which is the promotion of atheism and free thought." Submit outline/synopsis and sample chapters.

**Recent Title(s):** *The Altar Boy Chronicles*, by Tony Pasquarello (autobiography).

**Tips:** "We will need more how-to types of material—how to argue with creationists, how to fight for state/church separation, etc. We have an urgent need for literature for young atheists."

**AMERICAN BAR ASSOCIATION BOOK PUBLISHING**, 750 N. Lake Shore Dr., Book Publishing 8.1, Chicago IL 60611. Fax: (312)988-6030. E-mail: jweintraub@staff.abanet.org. Website: http://www.abanet.org/abapubs/. **Acquisitions:** J. Weintraub, director of publishing; Jane L. Johnston, executive editor. Estab. 1878. Publishes hardcover and trade paperback originals. **Publishes 100 titles/year. Receives 50 queries/year. 20% of books from first-time authors; 95% from unagented writers. Pays 5-15% royalty on wholesale or retail price.** Publishes book 18 months after acceptance of ms. Accepts simultaneous submissions. Reports in 1 months on queries and proposals, 3 months on mss. Book catalog for $5.95. Manscript guidelines free.

O-¬ "We are interested in books that will help lawyers practice law more effectively whether it's help in handling clients, structuring a real estate deal or taking an antitrust case to court."

**Nonfiction:** How-to (in the legal market), reference, technical. Subjects include business/economics, computers/electronics, money/finance, software, legal practice. "Our market is not, generally, the public. Books need to be targeted to lawyers who are seeking solutions to their practice problems. We rarely publish scholarly treatises." Query with SASE.

**Recent Title(s):** *Freedom of Speech in the Public Workplace* (municipal law).

**Tips:** "ABA books are written for busy, practicing lawyers. The most successful books have a practical, reader-friendly voice. If you can build in features like checklists, exhibits, sample contracts, flow charts, and tables of cases, please do so." The Association also publishes over 50 major national periodicals in a variety of legal areas. Contact Susan Yessne, executive editor, at the above address for guidelines.

**N: AMERICAN CHEMICAL SOCIETY**, 1155 16th St. NW, Washington DC 20036. (202)872-4564. Fax: (202)452-8913. E-mail: a_wilson@acs.org. **Acquisitions:** Anne Wilson, senior product manager. Estab. 1876. Publishes hardcover originals. **Publishes 35 titles/year. Pays royalty.** Accepts simultaneous submissions. Submissions not returned. Reports in 2 months on proposals. Book catalog free on request.

O-¬ American Chemical Society publishes symposium-based books for chemistry.

**Nonfiction:** Technical, semi-technical. Subjects include science. "Emphasis is on meeting-based books."

**Recent Nonfiction Title(s):** *Tailored Polymeric Materials for Controlled Delivery Systems*, edited by McCulloch and Shalaby.

**AMERICAN COLLEGE OF PHYSICIAN EXECUTIVES, (ACPE PUBLICATIONS)**, 4890 W. Kennedy Blvd., Suite 200, Tampa FL 33609. (813)287-2000. E-mail: wcurry@acpe.org. Website: http://www.acpe.org. **Acquisitions:** Wesley Curry, managing editor. Estab. 1975. Publishes hardcover and trade paperback originals. **Publishes 12-15 titles/ year. Receives 6 queries and 3 mss/year. 80% of books from first-time authors; 100% from unagented writers. Pays 10-15% royalty on wholesale price or makes outright purchase of $1,000-4,000.** Publishes book 8 months after acceptance of ms. Reports in 1 month on queries and ms, 2 months on proposals. Book catalog and ms guidelines free.

O-¬ "Our books are aimed at physicians in their roles as managers within the health care delivering and financing system."

**Nonfiction:** Technical, textbook. Subjects include business/economics, health/medicine. Query and submit outline. Reviews artwork/photos as part of ms package. Send photocopies.

**Recent Title(s):** *The Economics of Health Care as Seen by a Practicing Physician*, by Richard L. Johnson.

**AMERICAN CORRECTIONAL ASSOCIATION**, 4380 Forbes Blvd., Lanham MD 20706. (301)918-1800. Fax: (301)918-1896. E-mail: afins@aca.org. Website: http://www.corrections.com/aca. **Acquisitions:** Alice Fins, managing editor. Estab. 1870. Publishes hardcover and trade paperback originals. **Publishes 18 titles/year. Receives 40 submissions/year. 90% of books from first-time authors; 100% from unagented writers. Pays 10% royalty on net sales.** Publishes book 1 year after acceptance. Reports in 4 months. Book catalog and ms guidelines free.

O-¬ American Correctional Association provides practical information on jails, prisons, boot camps, probation, parole, community corrections, juvenile facilities and rehabilitation programs, substance abuse programs and other areas of corrections.

**Nonfiction:** How-to, reference, technical, textbook, correspondence courses. "We are looking for practical, how-to texts or training materials written for the corrections profession. No autobiographies or true-life accounts by current or former inmates or correctional officers, theses, or dissertations." No fiction. No poetry. Query with SASE. Reviews artwork/photos as part of ms package.

**Recent Title(s):** *No Time to Play: Youthful Offenders in Adult Correctional Systems*, by Barry Glick, Ph.D., William Sturgeon with Charles Venator-Santiago.

**Tips:** Authors are professionals in the field and corrections. "Our audience is made up of corrections professionals and criminal justice students. No books by inmates or former inmates." This publisher advises out-of-town freelance editors, indexers and proofreaders to refrain from requesting work from them.

**AMERICAN COUNSELING ASSOCIATION**, 5999 Stevenson Ave., Alexandria VA 22304-3300. (703)823-9800. **Acquisitions:** Carolyn C. Baker, director of publications. Estab. 1952. Scholarly paperback originals. **Publishes 10-15 titles/year. Receives 200 queries and 125 mss/year. 5% of books from first-time authors; 90% from unagented writers. Pays 10-15% royalty on net sales.** Publishes book within 7 months after acceptance of final draft. Accepts simultaneous submissions. Reports in 2 months on queries and proposals, 4 months on mss. Manuscript guidelines free.

    O➥ The American Counseling Association is dedicated to promoting public confidence and trust in the counseling profession.

**Nonfiction:** Reference, textbooks for professional counselors. Subjects include education, gay/lesbian, health/medicine, psychology, religion, sociology, women's issues/studies. ACA does not publish self-help books or autobiographies. Query with proposal package, including outline, 2 sample chapters and vitae and SASE.

**Recent Title(s):** *Cross-Cultural Counseling: A Case Book*, by Clemmont Von Hess, et. al.

**Tips:** "Target your market. Your books will not be appropriate for everyone across all disciplines."

**AMERICAN EAGLE PUBLICATIONS INC.**, P.O. Box 1507, Show Low AZ 85901. Phone/fax: (520)537-5512. E-mail: ameagle@whitemtns.com. **Acquisitions:** Mark Ludwig, publisher. Estab. 1988. Publishes scholarly hardcover and trade paperback originals and reprints. **Publishes 8 titles/year. 50% of books from first-time authors; 100% from unagented writers. Pays 7-15% royalty on retail price. Offers $1,000 average advance.** Publishes book 6 months after acceptance of ms. Accepts simultaneous submissions. Reports in 2 months. Catalog for #10 SASE.

    ● American Eagle is not interested in seeing military or other autobiographies.

**Nonfiction:** Historical biography, technical. Subjects include computers/electronics (security), military/war and science (computers, artificial intelligence). "We have recently established a line of patriot/political books. Writers should write and discuss what they have first." Query. Reviews artwork/photos as part of freelance ms package. Send photocopies.

**Recent Title(s):** *The Debt Bomb*, by Thomas McAuliffe.

**Tips:** Audience is "scholarly, university profs (some used as textbooks), very technical programmers and researchers, military, very international. No autobiographies."

**AMERICAN FEDERATION OF ASTROLOGERS**, P.O. Box 22040, Tempe AZ 85285. (480)838-1751. Fax: (480)838-8293. E-mail: afa@msn.com. **Acquisitions:** Kris Brandt Riske, publications manager. Estab. 1938. Publishes trade paperback originals and reprints. **Publishes 10-15 titles/year. Receives 10 queries and 20 mss/year. 50% of books from first-time authors; 100% from unagented writers. Pays 10% royalty.** Publishes book 10 months after acceptance of ms. Accepts simultaneous submissions. Reports in 6 months on mss. Book catalog for $2. Manuscript guidelines free.

    O➥ American Federation of Astrologers publishes only astrology books, calendars, charts and related aids.

**Nonfiction:** Astrology. Submit complete ms.

**Recent Title(s):** *The Astrologer's Forecasting Workbook*, by Lloyd Cope.

**AMERICAN INSTITUTE OF CERTIFIED PUBLIC ACCOUNTANTS**, Harborside Financial Center, 201 Plaza Three, Jersey City NJ 07711-3881. Fax: (201)938-3780. E-mail: mbareille@aicpa.org. Website: http://www.aicpa.org. Senior Manager: Marie Bareille. **Acquisitions:** Laura Inge (CPA firm management); Murray Schwartzberg (taxes, personal finance planning); Olivia Lane (computer technology and management accounting). Estab. 1959. Publishes hardcover and trade paperback originals and CD-ROM. **Publishes 104 titles/year. Receives 5 queries/year; 3 mss/year. 10% of books are from first-time authors; 100% from unagented writers. Pays 10-15% royalty on retail price. Offers $500-2,000 advance.** Publishes book 5 months after acceptance of ms. Reports in 1 month on queries, 3 months on proposals and mss. Book catalog and ms guidelines free.

    O➥ American Institute of Certified Public Accountants produces high-quality, advanced or cutting edge information for financial professionals. "Our books help business professionals make sense of a changing and complex world." Currently emphasizing consulting.

**Nonfiction:** Technical. Subjects include business/economics, computers/electronics, accounting, taxation, personal financial planning. "We are interested in expanding in topics for corporate accountants, consultants and computers." Submit proposal package including table of contents and outline.

**Recent Title(s):** *What Every CPA Needs to Know About the New IRAs; Solving the Year 2000 Dilemma*, by Sandi Smith (computer technology).

**Tips:** Audience is CPAs in public accounting firms and corporate accountants.

**AMERICAN NURSES PUBLISHING**, American Nurses Foundation, an affiliate of the American Nurses Association, 600 Maryland Ave. SW, #100 West, Washington DC 20024-2571. (202)651-7213. Fax: (202)651-7003. **Acquisitions:** Luanne Crayton, editor/project manager; Rosanne O'Connor, publisher. Publishes professional and trade paperback originals and reprints. **Publishes 15-20 titles/year. Receives 40 queries and 10 mss/year. 75% of books from first-time authors; 100% from unagented writers. Pays 10% royalty on retail price.** Publishes book 4 months after acceptance of ms. Reports in 4 months on proposals and mss. Catalog and ms guidelines free.

O—¬ American Nurses publishes books designed to help professional nurses in their work and careers. Through the publishing program, the Foundation fulfills one of its core missions—to provide nurses in all practice settings with publications that address cutting-edge issues and form a basis for debate and exploration of this century's most critical health care trends.

**Nonfiction:** Reference, technical and textbook. Subjects include advanced practice, computers, continuing education, ethics, human rights, health care policy, managed care, nursing administration, psychiatric and mental health, quality, research, workplace issues, key clinical topics. Submit outline and 1 sample chapter. Reviews artwork/photos as part of ms package. Send photocopies.

**Recent Title(s):** *Managed Care and Capitation: Issues in Nursing*, by Teri Britt, Cheryl Schrader and Paul Shelton.

**AMERICAN PRESS**, 520 Commonwealth Ave., Boston MA 02215-2605. (617)247-0022. **Acquisitions:** Jana Kirk, editor. Estab. 1911. Publishes college textbooks. **Publishes 25 titles/year. Receives 350 queries and 100 mss/year. 50% of books from first-time authors; 90% from unagented writers. Pays 5-15% royalty on wholesale price.** Publishes book 9 months after acceptance of ms. Reports in 3 months. Book catalog free.

**Nonfiction:** Technical, textbook. Subjects include agriculture/horticulture, anthropology/archaeology, art/architecture, business/economics, education, government/politics, health/medicine, history, music/dance, psychology, science, sociology, sports. "We prefer that our authors actually teach courses for which the manuscripts are designed." Query or submit outline with tentative table of contents. No complete mss.

**Recent Title(s):** *Basic Communications Course Annual 1999*, edited by Lawrence W. Hugenberg.

**THE AMERICAN PSYCHIATRIC PRESS, INC.**, 1400 K St. NW, Washington DC 20005. (202)682-6231. **Acquisitions:** Carol C. Nadelson, editor-in-chief. Estab. 1981. Publishes hardcover and trade paperback originals and reprints. **Publishes 50 titles/year. Receives 200 queries/year. 25% of books from first-time authors; 90% from unagented writers. Pays 10-15% royalty on net sales. Offers $3,000 advance.** Publishes book 1 year after acceptance of ms. Accepts simultaneous submissions, but this must be mentioned in the submission. Reports in 1 month on queries, 2 months on proposals. Book catalog, author questionnaire and proposal guidelines free.

O—¬ American Psychiatric Press publishes professional, authoritative reference books and general nonfiction on psychiatry only, including behavioral and social science material.

**Nonfiction:** Reference (psychiatry), textbook (psychiatry), handbooks, manuals, study guides, assessment/interview booklets, clinical and research aspects. All psychiatry-related. "Projects with significant clinical applications in psychiatry will be given the highest priority. We are also interested in authoritative books that interpret the scientific and medical aspects of serious mental illness for the lay public. Request and submit a completed author questionnaire. Do not submit an entire manuscript. American Psychiatric press prefers to consider proposals." Submit outline and 1 sample chapter and proposal package, including Author Questionnaire, table of contents, author's curriculum vitae with SASE. Reviews artwork/photos as part of the proposal package. Send photocopies.

**Recent Title(s):** *A Women's Guide to Menopause and Hormone Replacement Therapy*, by Lorraine Dennerstein and Julia Shelley.

**Tips:** "Primary audience is psychiatrists and other mental health professionals. Secondary audience is primary care physicians and other health care professionals."

**AMERICAN SOCIETY OF CIVIL ENGINEERS PRESS**, 1801 Alexander Bell Dr., Reston VA 20191-4400. (703)295-6275. Fax: (703)295-6278. E-mail: lehmer@asce.org. Website: http://www.asce.org. **Acquisitions:** Joy E. Chau, acquisitions editor: . Estab. 1988. **Publishes 15-20 titles/year. 50% of books from first-time authors; 100% from unagented writers. Pays 10% royalty. No advance.** Accepts simultaneous submissions. Request proposal guidelines.

O—¬ ASCE Press publishes volumes, technical in nature (primarily) that are useful to both practicing civil engineers and undergraduate and graduate level civil engineering students. "We publish books by individual authors to advance the civil engineering profession." Currently emphasizing geotechnical, hydrology, architectural engineering and bridge engineering. De-emphasizing highly specialized areas (e.g., numerical modeling) with narrow scope.

**Nonfiction:** Civil engineering. "We are looking for topics that are useful and instructive to the engineering practitioner." Query with outline, sample chapters and cv.

**Recent Title(s):** *Hydraulics of Open Channel Flow*, by Sergio Montes.

**Tips:** "ASCE Press is an extension of the publishing activities of ASCE and produces competitively prized professional books on a tight budget. All proposals and manuscripts undergo a vigorous review process. We have increased the number of new books produced by about 50%."

**AMERICAN WATER WORKS ASSOCIATION** 6666 W. Quincy Ave., Denver CO 80235. (303)794-7711. **Acquisitions:** Colin Murcray, senior acquisitions editor; Mindy Burke, senior technical editor. Estab. 1881. Publishes hardcover and trade paperback originals. **Publishes 100 titles/year. Receives 200 queries and 35 mss/year. 30% of books from first-time authors; 100% from unagented writers. Pays 15% royalty on wholesale or retail price. No advance.** Publishes book 1 year after acceptance of ms. Book catalog and manuscript guidelines free.

○━ AWWA strives to advance and promote the safety and knowledge of drinking water and related issues to all audiences—from kindergarten through post-doctorate.

**Nonfiction:** Subjects include nature/environment, science, software, drinking water-related topics. Query or submit outline, 3 sample chapters and author biography. Reviews artwork/photos as part of ms package. Send photocopies.

**Recent Title(s):** *The Changing Water Utility*, by Garret P. Westerhoff, et al.

**AMHERST MEDIA, INC.**, 155 Rano St., Suite 300, Buffalo NY 14207. (716)874-4450. Fax: (716)874-4508. E-mail: amherstmed@aol.com. **Acquisitions:** Craig Alesse, publisher. Estab. 1974. Publishes trade paperback originals and reprints. **Publishes 30 titles/year. Receives 50 submissions/year. 80% of books from first-time authors; 100% from unagented writers. Pays 6-8% royalty on retail price.** Publishes book 1 year after acceptance. Accepts simultaneous submissions. Reports in 2 months. Book catalog and ms guidelines free.

○━ Amherst Media publishes how-to photography books.

**Nonfiction:** Photography how-to. "Looking for well-written and illustrated photo books." Query with outline, 2 sample chapters and SASE. Reviews artwork/photos as part of ms package.

**Recent Title(s):** *The Freelance Photographer's Handbook*, by Cliff Holtenbeck (nonfiction).

**Tips:** "Our audience is made up of beginning to advanced photographers. If I were a writer trying to market a book today, I would fill the need of a specific audience and self-edit in a tight manner."

**THE AMWELL PRESS**, P.O. Box 5385, Clinton NJ 08809-0385. (908)537-6888. President: James Rikhoff. **Acquisitions:** Monica Sullivan, vice president. Corporate Secretary: Genevieve Symonds. Estab. 1976. Publishes hardcover originals. **Publishes 4 titles/year.** Publishes book 18 months after acceptance. Reports in 2 months on queries.

○━ The Amwell Press publishes hunting and fishing nonfiction, but not how-to books on these subjects.

**Nonfiction:** Hunting and fishing stories/literature (not how-to). No fiction. Mostly limited editions. Query with SASE.

**Recent Title(s):** *Wind Knots and Near Misses*, by Jack Samson.

**ANCESTRY INCORPORATED**, 266 W. Center St., Orem UT 84057. (801)426-3500. Fax: (801)426-3501. E-mail: rthorstenson@ancestry-inc.com. Book Editor: Rebekah Thorstenson. *Ancestry* magazine Editor: Jennifer Utley. **Acquisitions:** Loretto Szucs, executive editor. Estab. 1983. Publishes hardcover, trade and paperback originals and *Ancestry* magazine. **Publishes 12-20 titles/year. Receives over 100 submissions/year. 70% of books from first-time authors; 100% from unagented writers. Pays 8-12% royalty or makes outright purchase. No advance.** Publishes book 1 year after acceptance of ms. Accepts simultaneous submissions. Reports in 2 months. Book catalog for 9×12 SAE with 2 first-class stamps.

○━ "Our publications are aimed exclusively at the genealogist. We consider everything from short monographs to book length works on immigration, migration, record collections and heraldic topics."

**Nonfiction:** How-to, reference, genealogy. Subjects include Americana, historical methodology and genealogical research techniques. No mss that are not genealogical or historical. Query, or submit outline/synopsis and sample chapters with SASE. Reviews artwork/photos.

**Recent Title(s):** *Printed Sources*, by Kory L. Meyerink.

**Tips:** "Genealogical and historical reference, how-to, and descriptions of source collections have the best chance of selling to our firm. Be precise in your description. Please, no family histories or genealogies."

**[N] [A] ANCHOR PUBLISHING MARYLAND**, Box 2630, Landover Hills MD 20784. (301)459-0738. Fax: (301)552-0225. E-mail: tomantion@aol.com. Website: http://www.antion.com. **Acquisitions:** Tom Antion, president. Estab. 1988. Publishes trade paperback originals. **Publishes 5-10 titles/year. Receives 100 queries and 30 mss/year. 0% of books from first-time authors; 0% from unagented writers. Makes outright purchase of $500-1,000. No advance.** Publishes book 1 year after acceptance of ms. Reports in 3 months mss.

**Nonfiction:** How-to, humor. Subjects include business/economics. *Agented submissions only.*

**Recent Title(s):** *Wake Em Up Business Presentation.*

**▟ ANCHORAGE PRESS, INC.**, P.O. Box 8067, New Orleans LA 70182-8067. (504)283-8868. Fax: (504)866-0502. **Acquisitions:** Orlin Corey, editor. Publishes hardcover originals. Estab. 1935. **Publishes 10 titles/year. Receives 450-900 submissions/year. 50% of books from first-time authors; 80% from unagented writers. Pays 10-15% royalty on retail price. Playwrights also receive 50-75% royalties.** Publishes book 1-2 years after acceptance. Reports in 1 month on queries, 4 months on mss. Book catalog and ms guidelines free.

○━ "We are an international agency for plays for young people. First in the field since 1935."

**Nonfiction:** Textbook, plays. Subjects include education, language/literature, plays. "We are looking for play anthologies; and texts for teachers of drama/theater (middle school and high school.)" Query. Reviews artwork/photos.

**Plays:** Plays of juvenile/young people's interest. Query.

**Recent Title(s):** *The Theater of Aurand Harris*, by Lowell Swortzell.

**WILLIAM ANDREW, INC.**, Plastics Design Library, 13 Eaton Ave., Norwich NY 13815. (607)337-5000. Fax: (607)337-5090. E-mail: publishing@williamandrew.com. Website: http://www.williamandrew.com. **Acquisitions:**

George Wypych, editorial director (plastics, additives); William Woishnis, editor (welding); Sasha Gurke, vice president technology (CD-ROM, Web software). Estab. 1989. Publishes hardcover originals. **Publishes 11 titles/year. Receives 100 queries and 20 mss/year. 40% of books from first-time authors; 100% from unagented writers. Pays 8-15% royalty on wholesale price or uses in-house authors. Offers $1,000-5,000 advance.** Publishes book 6 months after acceptance of ms. Accepts simultaneous submissions. Reports in 1 month on queries, 2 months on proposals and mss. Book catalog and ms guidelines free.

> O⟶ William Andrew, Inc. specializes in technical information, both for printed and electronic publishing. "We supply the global community of engineers and scientists with a comprehensive collection of date intensive books, software and online products to expand their technical knowledge base." Currently emphasizing plastics/ chemicals.

**Imprint(s):** Plastics Design Library, (Bill Woishnis, publisher); Rover (Chris Forbes, president).
**Nonfiction:** Reference, technical, textbook. Subjects include science, engineering, materials science. Submit outline and SASE. Reviews artwork/photos as part of ms package. Send photocopies.
**Recent Title(s):** *Medical Plastics*, by George Wypych (all reference).

**Ⓐ ANDREWS McMEEL UNIVERSAL**, 4520 Main St., Kansas City MO 64111-7701. (816)932-6700. **Acquisitions:** Christine Schillig, vice president/editorial director. Estab. 1973. Publishes hardcover and paperback originals. **Publishes 300 titles/year. Pays royalty on retail price. Offers advance.**

> O⟶ Andrews McMeel publishes general trade books, humor books, miniature gift books, calendars, greeting cards, and stationery products.

**Nonfiction:** General trade, humor, how-to, pop culture. Also produces gift books, posters and kits. Query only. *Agented submissions only.*
**Recent Title(s):** *Confessions to My Mother*, by Cathy Guisewite.

**ANGELINES™ PUBLISHING**, (formerly AngeLines™ Productions), Multiple Corporation, 361 Post Rd. W., Suite 210, Wesport CT 06880. **Acquisitions:** J. Weber, editor-in-chief. Publishes trade paperback originals. **Publishes 6 titles/ year. Receives 200 queries and 100 mss/year. 10% of books from first-time authors; 75% from unagented writers. Royalty on retail price varies. No advance.** Publishes book 1 year after publication of ms. Accepts simultaneous submissions, if so noted. Reports in 2 months on proposals. Manuscript guidelines for #10 SASE.

> O⟶ AngeLines publishes books for metaphysically and spiritually aware adults. "We aim to be the premier publisher of channeled and psychic material from the most reputable channels and psychics." Currently emphasizing unique comprehensive material for advanced metaphysicians. De-emphasizing beginner, intro, "me-too" books.

**Nonfiction:** Self-help, self-actualization. Subjects include money/finance, psychology, metaphysics, spirituality. "We currently are producing a 14-volume series of articles, *ACP Oracles*™, by psychic/channel Amie Angeli. Most of our books published/contracted are channeled material." Submit proposal, chapter outline and 1-3 sample chapters with SASE. Reviews artwork/photos as part of the ms package. Send photocopies.
**Recent Title(s):** *The Numbers in Our Lives*, by Amie Angeli.
**Tips:** "Our ideal author is an advanced metaphysician with journalist experience, previously published; international experience is a real plus—our books are sold internationally."

**Ⓝ APDG PUBLISHING, INC.**, 4736 Shady Greens Dr., Fuguay-Varina NC 27526. Phone/fax: (919)557-2260. E-mail: jobriant@apdg-inc.com. Website: http://www.apdg-inc.com. **Acquisitions:** Judith Rourke-O'Briant, publishing director; Nancy Campbell, project manager. Estab. 1995. Publishes hardcover and trade paperback originals. **Publishes 5-7 titles/year. Receives 25-30 queries and 1-5 mss/year. 85% of books from first-time authors; 85% from un-agented writers. Pays 5-15% royalty on retail price. No advance.** Publishes book 18 months after acceptance of ms. Reports in 6 months on proposals, 9 months on mss. Book catalog on website. Manuscript guidelines free on request.

> O⟶ APDG supplies expertise and services to telecommunications and consumer electronics companies not only through publishing but consulting, research, training and techno-media as well.

**Nonfiction:** Technical. Subjects include telecommunications. Query with SASE. Reviews artwork/photos as part of ms package. Send photocopies.
**Recent Titles:** *Comprehensive Guide to Wireless Technologies*, by Harte (telecommunications).

**APPALACHIAN MOUNTAIN CLUB BOOKS**, 5 Joy St., Boston MA 02108. (617)523-0636. Fax: (617)523-0722. Website: http://www.outdoors.org. **Acquisitions:** Mark Russell, acquisitions. Estab. 1897. Publishes trade paperback originals. **Publishes 6-10 titles/year. Receives 200 queries and 20 mss/year. 30% of books from first-time authors; 90% from unagented writers. Pays 6-10% royalty on retail price. Offers modest advance.** Publishes book 10 months after acceptance of ms. Accepts simultaneous submissions. Reports in 3 months on proposals. Book catalog for 8½×11 SAE with 4 first-class stamps. Manuscript guidelines for #10 SASE.

> O⟶ Appalachian Mountain Club publishes hiking guides, water-recreation guides (non-motorized), nature, conservation and mountain-subject guides for America's Northeast. "We connect recreation to conservation."

**Nonfiction:** How-to, guidebooks. Subjects include history (mountains, Northeast), nature/environment, recreation, regional (Northeast outdoor recreation). Writers should avoid submitting: proposals on Appalachia (rural southern mountains); not enough market research; too much personal experience—autobiography." Query. Reviews artwork/ photos as part of ms package. Send photocopies and transparencies "at your own risk."
**Recent Title(s):** *Classic Northeast Whitewater Guide.*

**Tips:** "Our audience is outdoor recreationalists, conservation-minded hikers and canoeists, family outdoor lovers, armchair enthusiasts. Our guidebooks have a strong conservation message."

**A-R EDITIONS, INC.**, 801 Deming Way, Madison WI 53717. (608)836-9000. Fax: (608)831-8200. Website: http://www.areditions.com. **Acquisitions:** Paul Corneilson, managing editor, Recent Researches music editions; James L. Zychowicz, managing editor, Computer Music and Digital Audio Series. Estab. 1962. **Publishes 25 titles/year. Receives 40 queries and 24 mss/year. 50% of books from first-time authors; 100% from unagented writers. Pays royalty or honoraria.** Reports in 1 month on queries, 3 months on proposals and 6 months on mss. Book catalog and newsletter free. Manuscript guidelines free (check website).

    ○┬ A-R Editions publishes modern critical editions of music based on current musicological research. Each edition is devoted to works by a single composer or to a single genre of composition. The contents are chosen for their potential interest to scholars and performers, then prepared for publication according to the standards that govern the making of all reliable, historical editions.

**Nonfiction:** Historical music editions, computers and electronics, software; also titles related to computer music and digital audio. Query or submit outline with SASE.

**Recent Title(s):** *Selected Keyboard and Chamber Music, 1937-1994*, by Lou Harrison.

**ARABESQUE**, BET Books, 850 Third Ave., 16th Floor, New York NY 10022. (212)407-1500. Website: http://www.arabesque.com. **Acquisitions:** Karen Thomas, senior editor. Publishes mass market paperback originals. **Publishes 60 titles/year. 30-50% of books from first-time authors; 50% from unagented writers. Pays royalty on retail price, varies by author. Advance varies by author.** Publishes book 18 months after acceptance of ms. Accepts simultaneous submissions. Reports in 3 months on mss. Book catalog for #10 SASE.

    ○┬ Arabesque publishes contemporary romances about African-American couples.

**Fiction:** Multicultural romance. Query with synopsis and SASE. *No unsolicited mss.*

**Recent Title(s):** *Until There Was You*, by Francis Ray.

**ARCADE PUBLISHING**, 141 Fifth Ave., New York NY 10010. (212)475-2633. **Acquisitions:** Cal Barksdale, senior editor; Coates Bateman, editor; Richard Seaver, publisher/editor-in-chief; Jeannette Seaver, publisher/executive editor. Estab. 1988. Publishes hardcover originals, trade paperback originals and reprints. **Publishes 40 titles/year. 5% of books from first-time authors. Pays royalty on retail price. Offers $3,000-50,000 advance.** Publishes book within 18 months after acceptance of ms. Reports in 3 months on queries.

    ○┬ Arcade prides itself on publishing top-notch commercial nonfiction and literary fiction, with an emphasis on foreign writers.

**Nonfiction:** Biography, cookbook, general nonfiction. Subjects include cooking/foods/nutrition, government/politics, history, nature/environment and travel. *Agented submissions only.* Reviews artwork/photos. Send photocopies.

**Fiction:** Ethnic, historical, humor, literary, mainstream/contemporary, mystery, short story collections, suspense. *Agented submissions only.*

**Recent Title(s):** *Sons & Brothers: The Days of Jack and Bobby Kennedy*, by Richard Mahoney (nonfiction); *The Queen's Bastard*, by Robin Maxwell.

**ARCADIA PUBLISHING**, Tempus Publishing, 2-A Cumberland St., Charleston SC 29401. (843)853-2070. Fax: (843)853-0044. E-mail: arcadia@charleston.net. Website: http://www.arcadiaimages.com. **Acquisitions:** Mark Berry, Christine Riley, Katie White (southern subjects); Allison Carpenter (western subjects); Patrick Catel, Tessa Hellbusch (midwestern subjects); Heather Gunsalas, Pamela O'Neil, Amy Sutton (northeastern subjects). Query with SASE. Publishes mass market paperback originals. **Publishes 800 titles/year; imprint publishes 350 titles/year. Receives 100 queries and 20 mss/year. 80% of books from first-time authors; 95% from unagented writers. Pays 10% royalty.** Accepts simultaneous submissions. Reports in 1 month on queries. Book catalog on website. Manuscript guidelines for #10 SASE.

    ○┬ Arcadia is the publisher of the Images of America series, which chronicles the history of diverse communities from the beaches of Wells, Maine, to the Spanish moss-draped oaks of Mobile, Alabama. The series celebrates an individual town or region with over 200 b&w photographs, bringing life to people, places and events that have defined that community since the birth of photography.

**Nonfiction:** Coffee table book. Subjects include pictorial history, local history, African-American history, postcard history, sports history, college history, oral history, Civil War history. Local, national and regional publications. Query with SASE. Reviews artwork/photos as part of ms package. Send photocopies.

**Recent Title(s):** *Atlanta Scenes*, by Atlanta History Center (pictorial history).

**Tips:** "Writers should know that we only publish history titles. The majority of our books are on a city or region, and are pictorial in nature. We are beginning new series, including oral histories, sports histories, black histories and college histories."

**ARCHWAY PAPERBACKS**, Pocket Books for Young Readers, Simon & Schuster, 1230 Avenue of the Americas, New York NY 10020. (212)698-7669. Website: http://www.simonsayskids.com. Vice President/Editorial Director: Patricia MacDonald. **Acquisitions:** send all submissions Attn: Manuscript Proposals. Publishes mass market paperback originals and reprints. **Publishes approximately 100 titles/year. Receives over 1,000 submissions/year. Pays 6-8% royalty on retail price.** Publishes book 2 years after acceptance. Reports in 3 months.

**O—** Archway Paperbacks publishes fiction and current nonfiction for young adult readers ages 12-18.
**Nonfiction:** Young adult, ages 12-18. Subjects include current popular subjects or people, sports. Query with outline/synopsis, 2 sample chapters and SASE. SASE for all material necessary or query not answered. Reviews artwork/photos as part of ms package. Send photocopies.
**Fiction:** Young adult horror, mystery, suspense thrillers, contemporary fiction, romances for YA, ages 12-18. Query with outline/synopsis, sample chapters and SASE.
**Recent Title(s):** *Buffy the Vampire Slayer* and *Dawson's Creek* (TV-tie-in titles).

**ARDEN PRESS INC.**, P.O. Box 418, Denver CO 80201-0418. (303)697-6766. **Acquisitions:** Susan Conley, publisher. Estab. 1980. Publishes hardcover and trade paperback originals and reprints. 95% of books are originals; 5% are reprints. **Publishes 4-6 titles/year. Receives 600 submissions/year. 20% of books from first-time authors; 80% from unagented writers. Pays 8-15% royalty on wholesale price. Offers $2,000 average advance.** Publishes book 6 months after acceptance. Accepts simultaneous submissions. Reports in 2 months on queries. Manuscript guidelines free.
**O—** Arden Press publishes nonfiction on women's history and women's issues. "We sell to general and women's bookstores as well as public and academic libraries. Many of our titles are adopted as texts for use in college courses."
**Nonfiction:** Subjects include women's issues/studies. No personal memoirs or autobiographies. Query with outline/synopsis and sample chapters.
**Recent Title(s):** *Women Gardeners: A History*, by Yvonne Cuthbertson.
**Tips:** "Writers have the best chance selling us nonfiction on women's subjects. If I were a writer trying to market a book today, I would learn as much as I could about publishers' profiles *then* contact those who publish similar works."

**ARKANSAS RESEARCH**, P.O. Box 303, Conway AR 72033. (501)470-1120. Fax: (501)470-1120. E-mail: desmond @ipa.net. **Acquisitions:** Desmond Walls Allen, owner. Estab. 1985. Publishes hardcover originals and trade paperback originals and reprints. **Publishes 20 titles/year. 90% of books from first-time authors; 100% from unagented writers. Pays 5-10% royalty on retail price. Offers no advance.** Publishes book 2 months after acceptance of ms. Reports in 1 month. Book catalog for $1. Manuscript guidelines free.
**O—** "Our company opens a world of information to researchers interested in the history of Arkansas."
**Imprint(s):** Research Associates.
**Nonfiction:** How-to (genealogy), reference, self-help. Subjects include Americana, ethnic, history, hobbies (genealogy), military/war, regional, all Arkansas-related. "We don't print autobiographies or genealogies about one family." Query with SASE. Reviews artwork/photos as part of ms package. Send photocopies.
**Recent Title(s):** *Life & Times from The Clay County Courier Newspaper Published at Corning, Arkansas, 1893-1900.*

**JASON ARONSON, INC.**, 230 Livingston St., Northvale NJ 07647-1726. (201)767-4093. Fax: (201)767-4330. Website: http://www.aronson.com. Editor-in-chief: Arthur Kurzweil. **Acquisitions:** Arthur Kurzweil, (Judaica), vice president/editor-in-chief; Ann Marie Dooley, editor (psychotherapy). Estab. 1967. Publishes hardcover and trade paperback originals and reprints. **Publishes 250 titles/year. 50% of books from first-time authors; 95% from unagented writers. Pays 10-15% royalty on retail price. Offers advance.** Publishes book an average of 1 year after acceptance. Reports in 1 month. *Writer's Market* recommends allowing 2 months for reply. Catalog and ms guidelines free.
**O—** "We are looking for high quality, serious, scholarly books in two fields: psychotherapy and Judaica."
**Nonfiction:** Subjects include history, philosophy, psychology, religion translation. Query or submit outline and sample chapters. Reviews artwork/photos as part of ms packages. Send photocopies.
**Recent Title(s):** *The Candle of God*, by Adin Steinsaltz (Judaica).

**ART DIRECTION BOOK COMPANY, INC.**, 456 Glenbrook Rd., Glenbrook CT 06096-1800. (203)353-1441. Fax: (203) 353-1371. **Acquisitions:** Don Barron, editorial director. Estab. 1959. Publishes hardcover and paperback originals. **Publishes 8 titles/year. Pays 10% royalty on retail price. Offers average $1,000 advance.** Publishes book 1 year after acceptance. Reports in 3 months. Book catalog for 6×9 SASE.
**O—** Art Direction Book Company is interested in books for the professional advertising art field—books for art directors, designers, etc.; also entry level books for commercial and advertising art students in such fields as typography, photography, paste-up, illustration, clip-art, design, layout and graphic arts.
**Imprint(s):** Infosource Publications.
**Nonfiction:** Commercial art, ad art how-to and textbooks. Query with outline and 1 sample chapter. Reviews artwork/photos as part of ms package.

**ARTE PUBLICO PRESS**, University of Houston, Houston TX 77204-2174. (713)743-2841. Fax (713)743-2847. **Acquisitions:** Nicolas Kanellos, editor. Estab. 1979. Publishes hardcover originals, trade paperback originals and reprints. **Publishes 36 titles/year. Receives 1,000 queries and 500 mss/year. 50% of books from first-time authors; 80% from unagented writers. Pays 10% royalty on wholesale price. Offers $1,000-3,000 advance.** Publishes book 2 years after acceptance of ms. Accepts simultaneous submissions. Reports in 1 month on queries and proposals; 4 months on mss. Book catalog free. Manuscript guidelines for #10 SASE.
**O—** "We are a showcase for Hispanic literary creativity, arts and culture. Our endeavor is to provide a national forum for Hispanic literature."

**Imprint(s): Pinata Books.**
**Nonfiction:** Children's/juvenile, reference. Subjects include ethnic, language/literature, regional, translation, women's issues/studies. "Nonfiction is definitely not our major publishing area." Query with outline/synopsis, 2 sample chapters and SASE. "Include cover letter explaining why your manuscript is unique and important, why we should publish it, who will buy it, etc."
**Fiction:** Ethnic, literary, mainstream/contemporary. Query with synopsis, 2 sample chapters and SASE.
**Poetry:** Submit 10 sample poems.
**Recent Title(s):** *Chicano! The History of the Mexican American Civil Rights Movement*, by F. Arturo Rosales (history/nonfiction); *Project Death*, by Richard Bertematti (novel/mystery); *I Used to Be a Superwoman*, by Gloria Velasquez (poetry collection/inspirational).

**ARTEMIS CREATIONS PUBLISHING**, 3395 Nostrand Ave., 2-J, Brooklyn NY 11229. E-mail: artemispub@aol.com. President: Shirley Oliveira. Imprints are FemSuprem, Matriarch's Way. Publishes trade paperback and mass market paperback originals. **Publishes 4 titles/year. Pays 5-10% royalty on retail price or makes outright purchase of $300 minimum (30,000 words). No advance.**
○⊸ "Our publications explore femme supremacy, matriarchy, sex, gender, relationships, etc. Masochism (male only)."
**Nonfiction:** Subjects include women's issues/studies. "Strong feminine archetypes, subjects only." Query or submit outline, 3 sample chapters, author bio, marketing plan and SASE. Recent title(s): *Gospel of Goddess*, by Bond and Suffield (metaphysical).
**Fiction:** Erotica, experimental, fantasy, feminist, gothic, horror, mystery, occult, religious, science fiction. Query or submit synopsis and 3 sample, marketing plan and SASE.
**Recent title(s):** *Lady Killer: Tale of Horror and the Erotic*, by Tony Malo.
**Tips:** "Our readers are looking for strong, powerful feminie archetypes in fiction and nonfiction. Graphic sex and language are OK."

**ASA, AVIATION SUPPLIES & ACADEMICS**, 7005 132nd Place SE, Newcastle WA 98059. (425)235-1500. Director of Operations: Mike Lorden. Editor: Jennifer Trerise. **Acquisitions:** Fred Boyns, controller; Jacqueline Spanitz, curriculum director and technical advisor (pilot and aviation educator). **Publishes 25-40 titles/year. 100% of books from unagented writers.** Publishes book 9 months or more after acceptance. Book catalog free.
○⊸ ASA is an industry leader in the development and sales of aviation supplies, publications, and software for pilots, flight instructors, flight engineers and aviation technicians. All ASA products are developed by a team of researchers, authors and editors.
**Nonfiction:** How-to, technical, education. All subjects must be related to aviation education and training. "We are primarily an aviation publisher. Educational books in this area are our specialty; other aviation books will be considered." Query with outline. Send photocopies.
**Recent Title(s):** *The Savvy Flight Instructor: Secrets of the Successful CFI*, by Greg Brown (nonfiction).
**Tips:** "Two of our specialty series include ASA's *Focus Series*, and ASA *Aviator's Library*. Books in our *Focus Series* concentrate on single-subject areas of aviation knowledge, curriculum and practice. The *Aviator's Library* is comprised of titles of known and/or classic aviation authors or established instructor/authors in the industry, and other aviation specialty titles."

**ASIAN HUMANITIES PRESS**, Jain Publishing Co., P.O. Box 3523, Fremont CA 94539. (510)659-8272. Fax: (510)659-0501. E-mail: mail@jainpub.com. Website: http://www.jainpub.com. **Acquisitions:** M.K. Jain, editor-in-chief. Estab. 1989. Publishes hardcover and trade paperback originals and reprints. **Publishes 6 titles/year. Receives 200 submissions/year. 100% of books from unagented authors. Pays up to 15% royalty on net sales. Offers occasional advance.** Publishes book 1-2 years after acceptance. Reports in 3 months on mss if interested. Book catalog and ms guidelines on website.
○⊸ Asian Humanities Press publishes in the areas of Asian religions, philosophies, languages and literature. Currently emphasizing undergraduate-level textbooks.
**Nonfiction:** Reference, textbooks, general trade books. Subjects include Asian classics, language/literature (Asian), philosophy/religion (Asian and East-West), psychology/spirituality (Asian and East-West), art/culture (Asian and East-West). Submit proposal package, including vita, list of prior publications. Reviews artwork/photos as part of ms package. Send photocopies. Does not return proposal materials.
**Recent Title(s):** *Windows Into the Infinite: A Guide to the Hindu Scriptures*, by Barbara Powell (textbook).

**⊞ ASSOCIATION FOR SUPERVISION AND CURRICULUM DEVELOPMENT**, 1703 N. Beauregard St., Alexandria VA 22311. (703)578-9600. **Acquisitions:** John O'Neil, acquisitions director. Estab. 1943. Publishes trade paperback originals. **Publishes 24-30 titles/year. Receives 100 queries and 100 mss/year. 50% of books from first-time authors; 100% from unagented writers. Pays negotiable royalty on actual monies received or makes outright purchase. Offers advance.** Publishes book 1 year after acceptance of ms. Accepts simultaneous submissions. Reports in 6 months on proposals. Book catalog and ms guidelines free.
○⊸ Publishes professional books for educators.
**Nonfiction:** How-to, professional books for education field. Education subjects. Submit outline and 2 sample chapters. Reviews artwork/photos as part of the ms package. Send photocopies.

**Recent Titles:** *Teaching with the Brain in Mind*, by Eric Jensen.

**ASTRAGAL PRESS**, P.O. Box 239, Mendham NJ 07945. (973)543-3045. **Acquisitions:** Lisa Pollak, president. Estab. 1983. Publishes hardcover and trade paperback originals and reprints. **Publishes 4-6 titles/year. Receives 50 queries/year. Pays 10% royalty on net sales.** Publishes book 1 year after acceptance of ms. Reports in 1 month. Book catalog and ms guidelines free.
**Nonfiction:** Books on early tools, trades or technology. Query. Reviews artwork/photos as part of ms package. Send photocopies.
**Recent Title(s):** *A Price Guide to Antique Tools*, by Herbert Kear.
**Tips:** "We sell to niche markets. We are happy to work with knowledgeable amateur authors in developing titles."

**ASTRO COMMUNICATIONS SERVICES**, 5521 Ruffin Rd., San Diego CA 92123. (619)492-9919. Fax: (619)492-9917. E-mail: maritha@astrocom.com. Website: http://www.astrocom.com. **Acquisitions**: Maritha Pottenger, editorial director. Publishes trade paperback originals and reprints and mass market paperback originals and reprints. **Publishes 4-5 titles/year. Receives 100 queries and 15 mss/year. 20% of books from first-time authors; 95% from unagented writers. Pays 10-15% royalty.** Publishes book 1 year after acceptance of ms. Accepts simultaneous submissions. Reports in 3 months on queries and proposals, 6 months on mss. Book catalog and ms guidelines for 9×12 SAE with 3 first-class stamps.
  O→ ACS publishes astrology titles for professionals, serious students and general public interested in astrology, as well as people who want to improve themselves and their lives.
**Nonfiction:** Astrology only. Query with SASE. Reviews artwork/photos as part of ms package. Send photocopies.
**Recent Title(s):** *Millennium Fears, Fantasies & Facts*, foreword by Marion March.
**Tips:** "Make sure the publisher does work such as you're submitting. (Send to the right firms!) We do *astrology* only and emphasize personal responsibility and power."

**ATHENEUM BOOKS FOR YOUNG READERS**, Simon & Schuster, 1230 Avenue of the Americas, New York NY 10020. (212)698-2715. Associate Publisher/Vice President/Editorial Director: Jonathan J. Lanman. **Acquisitions:** Marcia Marshall, executive editor (nonfiction, fantasy); Anne Schwartz, editorial director, Anne Schwartz Books; Caitlyn Dlouhy, senior editor. Estab. 1960. Publishes hardcover originals. **Publishes 70 titles/year. Receives 15,000 submissions/year. 8-12% of books from first-time authors; 50% from unagented writers. Pays 10% royalty on retail price. Offers $2,000-3,000 average advance.** Publishes book 18 months after acceptance. Reports within 3 months. Manuscript guidelines for #10 SASE.
  O→ Atheneum Books for Young Readers publishes books aimed at children from pre-school age, up through high school.
**Nonfiction:** Biography, history, science, humor, self-help, all for juveniles. Subjects include: Americana, animals, art, business/economics, health, music, nature, photography, politics, psychology, recreation, religion, sociology, sports and travel. "Do remember, most publishers plan their lists as much as two years in advance. So if a topic is 'hot' right now, it may be 'old hat' by the time we could bring it out. It's better to steer clear of fads. Some writers assume juvenile books are for 'practice' until you get good enough to write adult books. Not so. Books for young readers demand just as much professionalism in writing as adult books. So save those 'practice' manuscripts for class, or polish them before sending them." *Query only for all submissions.*
**Fiction:** Adventure, ethnic, experimental, fantasy, gothic, historical, horror, humor, mainstream, mystery, science fiction, suspense, western, all in juvenile versions. "We have few specific needs except for books that are fresh, interesting and well written. Again, fad topics are dangerous, as are works you haven't polished to the best of your ability. (The competition is fierce.) Other things we don't need at this time are safety pamphlets, ABC books, coloring books and board books. In writing picture book texts, avoid the coy and 'cutesy,' such as stories about characters with alliterative names." *Query only for all submissions.* Send art samples under separate cover to Ann Bobco at the above address.
**Poetry:** "At this time there is a growing market for children's poetry. However, we don't anticipate needing any for the next year or two."
**Recent Title(s):** *Let My People Go*, by Patricia and Frederick McKissack (nonfiction); *The Paper Dragon*, by Marguerite W. Davol.

**ATL PRESS, INC.**, P.O. Box 4563, Shrewsbury MA 01545. (508)898-2290. Website: http://www.atlpress.com. **Acquisitions**: Paul Lucio, acquisitions manager. Estab. 1992. Publishes hardcover and trade paperback originals. **Publishes 8-12 titles/year. Receives 100 queries/year. 25% of books from first-time authors. Pays royalty on retail price.** Publishes book 3 months after acceptance of ms. Reports in 1-2 months on queries. Book catalog and ms guidelines for #10 SASE.
  O→ ATL specializes in science and technology publications for both the professional and the popular audience.
**Nonfiction:** Children's/juvenile, multimedia (CD-ROM), reference, technical, textbook. Subjects include business and economics, education, health/medicine, money/finance, nature/environment, science. "We look for well-written manuscripts in subjects with either broad, general interest topics of leading-edge professional topics. Avoid too narrow a focus." Submit outline and 3-4 sample chapters with SASE.
**Recent Title(s):** *New Technologies for Healthy Foods*, by M. Yalpani.
**Tips:** "Audience is educated, open-minded adults, juveniles, parents, educators, professionals. Realistically evaluate your manuscript against competition. We publish only titles for which there is an actual demand. We are committed to

produce authoritative and thought-provoking titles that are distinguished both in their content and appearance."

**AUGSBURG BOOKS**, Augsburg Fortress Publishers, P.O. Box 1209, Minneapolis MN 55440-1209. (612)330-3433. Director of Publications: Henry French. **Acquisitions:** Robert Klausmeier and Ronald Klug, acquisitions editors. Publishes trade and mass market paperback originals and reprints. **Publishes 30 titles/year. 2-3% of books from first-time authors. Pays royalty.** Publishes book 18 months after acceptance of ms. Reports in 3 months. Book catalog for 8½×11 SAE with 3 first-class stamps. Manuscript guidelines for #10 SASE.
- **⊶** Augsburg Book publishes for the mainline Christian market.
**Imprint(s):** Augsburg Books for Children & Families.
**Nonfiction:** Children's/juvenile, self-help. Subjects include religion, adult spirituality, healing/wholeness, interactive books for children and families, seasonal and picture books. Submit outline and 1-2 sample chapters if requested. Overstocked in children's book mss.
**Recent Title(s):** *Hello Night*, by Herbert Brokering.

**N** **AUSTIN & WINFIELD PUBLISHERS**, Imprint of Interscholars, 7831 Woodmont, #345, Bethesda MD 20814. (301)654-7335. Fax: (301)654-7336. E-mail: austinisp1@aol.com. Website: http://www.interscholars.com. **Acquisitions:** Robert West, publisher (law/criminal justice). Estab. 1992. Publishes hardcover originals and reprints. **Publishes 120 titles/year; imprint publishes 28 titles/year. Receives 300 queries and 180 mss/year. 60% of books from first-time authors; 100% from unagented writers. Pays 8-10% royalty on wholesale price. No advance.** Publishes book 10 months after acceptance of ms. Accepts simultaneous submissions. Reports in 1 month. Book catalog free for #10 SASE or on website. Manuscript guidelines free for #10 SASE.
- **⊶** Austin & Winfield is an international scholarly publisher specializing in law, criminal justice and legal policy. "We publish monographs and revised dissertations—this is what we are seeking."
**Nonfiction:** Reference, technical, textbook. Subjects include government/politics, philosophy, sociology. Submit proposal package, including outline, 2 sample chapters and résumé.
**Recent Titles:** *The Power*, by R. Randall Bridwell.
**Tips:** "Scholarly/library market is our main focus—we are like a university press in standards and expectations."

**AUTONOMEDIA**, P.O. Box 568, Williamsburgh Station, Brooklyn NY 11211. (718)963-2603. **Acquisitions:** Jim Fleming, editor (Semiotext(e)); Peter Lamborn Wilson, editor (New Autonomy). Estab. 1984. Publishes trade paperback originals and reprints. **Publishes 25 titles/year. Receives 350 queries/year. 30% of books from first-time authors; 90% from unagented writers. Pays variable royalty. Offers $100 advance.** Publishes book 6 months after acceptance of ms. Accepts simultaneous submissions. Reports in 2 months. Book catalog for $1.
- **⊶** Autonomedia publishes radical and marginal books on culture and politics.
**Imprint(s):** Semiotext(e); New Autonomy.
**Nonfiction:** Subjects include anthropology/archaeology, art/architecture, business/economics, gay/lesbian, government/politics, history, nature/environment, philosophy, religion, translation, women's issues/studies. Submit outline with SASE. Reviews artwork/photos as part of ms package. Send photocopies.
**Fiction:** Erotica, experimental, feminist, gay/lesbian, literary, mainstream/contemporary, occult, science fiction, short story collections. Submit synopsis with SASE.
**Poetry:** Submit sample poems.
**Recent Title(s):** *Pioneer of Inner Space*, by Donald Dulchinos (biography).

**AVALON BOOKS**, Thomas Bouregy & Co., Inc., 401 Lafayette St., New York NY 10003-7014. **Acquisitions:** Veronica Mixon, executive editor. Estab. 1950. **Publishes 60 titles/year. 10% of books from unagented writers. Pays royalty; contracts negotiated on an individual basis.** Publishes book 6 months after acceptance. Reports in 6 months. Manuscript guidelines for #10 SASE.
- **⊶** "We publish wholesome fiction. We're the 'Family Channel' of publishing. We try to make what we publish suitable for anybody in the family." Currently de-emphasizing romantic suspense.
**Fiction:** "We publish wholesome romances, mysteries, westerns. Our books are read by adults as well as teenagers, and their characters are all adults. All the romances and mysteries are contemporary; all the westerns are historical." Length: 40,000-50,000 words. Submit entire ms, a brief, but complete, summary of the book and SASE. "Manuscripts that are too long will not be considered."
**Recent Title(s):** *Death Flies on Final*, by Jackie Lewin (fiction).
**Tips:** "We are looking for love stories, heroines who have interesting professions, and we are actively seeking ethnic fiction. We do accept unagented manuscripts, and we do publish first novels. Right now we are concentrating on finding talented new mystery and romance writers with solid storytelling skills."

**AVANYU PUBLISHING INC.**, P.O. Box 27134, Albuquerque NM 87125. (505)266-6128. E-mail: brentric@aol.com. **Acquisitions:** J. Brent Ricks, president. Estab. 1984. Publishes hardcover and trade paperback originals and reprints. **Publishes 4 titles/year. Receives 40 submissions/year. 30% of books from first-time authors; 90% from unagented writers. Pays 8% maximum royalty on wholesale price.** Publishes book 1 year after acceptance. Reports in 2 months. Book catalog for #10 SASE.
- **⊶** Avanyu publishes highly-illustrated, history-oriented books and contemporary Indian/Western art.
**Nonfiction:** Biography, illustrated book, reference, Southwest Americana. Subjects include Americana, anthropology/

archaeology, art/architecture, ethnic, history, photography, regional, sociology. Query with SASE. Reviews artwork/photos as part of ms package.

**Recent Titles:** *Kachinas: Spirit Beings of the Hopi.*

**Tips:** "Our audience consists of libraries, art collectors and history students. We publish subjects dealing with modern and historic American Indian matters of all kinds."

**AVERY PUBLISHING GROUP, INC.**, 120 Old Broadway, Garden City Park NY 11040. (516)741-2155. Fax: (516)742-1892. Website: http://www.averypublishing.com. **Acquisitions:** Rudy Shur, publisher; Norman Goldfind, vice president, marketing and product development (health, alternative medicine). Estab. 1976. Publishes trade paperback originals. **Publishes 50 titles/year. Receives 3,000 queries and 1,000 mss/year. 70% of books from first-time authors; 90% from unagented writers. Pays royalty. Conservative advances offered.** Publishes book 1 year after acceptance of ms. Accepts simultaneous submissions. Reports in 2 weeks on queries, 3 weeks on proposals and manuscripts. *Writer's Market* recommends allowing 2 months for reply. Book catalog and ms guidelines free.

• Avery specializes in alternative medicine, natural medicine, health, healthy cooking, health reference, childcare and childbirth. Currently emphasizing health. De-emphasizing gardening.

**Nonfiction:** Cookbook, reference, self-help. Subjects include business/economics, child guidance/parenting, cooking, foods and nutrition, gardening, health/medicine, money/finance. "We generally do not publish personal accounts of health topics unless they outline a specific plan that covers all areas of the topic." Submit outline with proposal package, including cover letter, author biography, table of contents, preface with SASE.

**Recent Title(s):** *The No-Time-to-Cook Cookbook*, by Joanne Abrams and Marie Caratozzolo.

**Tips:** "Our mission is to enable people to improve their health through clear and up-to-date information."

**AVIATION PUBLISHERS**, Markowski International Publishers, 1 Oakglade Circle, Hummelstown PA 17036-9525. (717)566-0468. Fax: (717)566-6423. E-mail: avipub@aol.com. **Acquisitions:** Michael A. Markowski, editor-in-chief. Guidelines for #10 SASE with 2 first-class stamps.

• Aviation Publishers publishes books to help people learn more about aviation and model aviation through the written word.

**Nonfiction:** How-to and historical. Subjects include radio control, free flight, indoor models, electric flight, rubber powered flying models, micro radio control, aviation history, homebuilt aircraft, ultralights and hang gliders.

**Recent Title(s):** *Flying Models*, by Don Ross (model aviation how-to).

**Tips:** "Our focus is on books of short to medium length that will serve the emerging needs of the hobby. We want to help youth get started and enhance everyone's enjoyment of the hobby."

**AVIATION PUBLISHING, INC.**, P.O. Box 5674, Destin FL 32540-5634. (850)654-4696. Fax: (850)654-1542. E-mail: destina@cybertron.com. **Acquisitions:** Wallace Kemper, president (general aviation history). Publishes paperback originals. **Publishes 5-10 titles/year. Receives 20 queries/year. 50% of books from first-time authors; 90% from unagented writers. Pays 10% royalty on retail price.** Publishes book 6 months after acceptance of ms. Accepts simultaneous submissions. Reports in 1 month on queries. Book catalog and ms guidelines for #10 SASE.

• Aviation specializes in aviation-related nonfiction and fiction.

**Nonfiction:** General aviation history. Subjects include military/war, recreation. Query with SASE. Reviews artwork/photos as part of ms package. Send transparencies.

**Fiction:** In an aviation setting. Query with SASE.

**Recent Title(s):** *Worldwide Directory of Racing Aircraft*, by Don Berliner; *Ace*, by Nick Bloom (adventure fiction).

**Tips:** "Audience is older men who have pilots licenses and flew in World War II or Korea. Select a private aircraft of historical merit. Learn your subject and gather at least one illustration per page."

**AVISSON PRESS, INC.**, 3007 Taliaferro Rd., Greensboro NC 27408. **Acquisitions:** M.L. Hester, editor. Estab. 1994. Publishes hardcover originals and trade paperback originals and reprints. **Publishes 9-10 titles/year. Receives 600 queries and 400 mss/year. 5% of books from first-time authors; 90% from unagented writers. Pays 8-10% royalty on wholesale price. Offers occasional small advance.** Publishes book 15 months after acceptance of ms. Accepts simultaneous submissions, if so noted. Reports in 1 week on queries and proposals, 3 months on mss. Book catalog for #10 SASE.

• Avisson Press publishes helpful nonfiction for senior citizens, minority topics and young adult biographies (African-American, women).

**Nonfiction:** Biography, reference, self-help (senior citizens and teenagers), regional or North Carolina, textbook (creative writing text). Subjects include history (Southeast or North Carolina), language/literature, psychology, regional, sports, women's issues/studies. Query or submit outline and 1-3 sample chapters.

• Avisson Press no longer accepts fiction or poetry.

**Recent Title(s):** *Hunting the Snark*, by Robert Peters (criticism/textbook).

**Tips:** Audience is primarily public and school libraries.

**AVON BOOKS**, 1350 Avenue of the Americas, New York NY 10019. Website: http://www.avonbooks.com. Executive Managing Editor: Anne Marie Spagnuolo. **Acquisitions:** Editorial Submissions. Estab. 1941. Publishes hardcover, trade and mass market paperback originals and reprints. **Publishes 400 titles/year. Royalty and advance negotiable.** Publishes ms 2 years after acceptance of ms. Accepts simultaneous submissions. Reports in 3 months. Guidelines for SASE.

**Imprint(s): Avon Eos, Avon Flare, Avon Twilight**, Bard, **Camelot**, Post Road Press, Spike, WholeCare.
**Nonfiction:** How-to, popular psychology, self-help, health, history, war, sports, business/economics, biography, politics. No textbooks. Query only with SASE.
**Fiction:** Romance (contemporary, historical), science fiction, fantasy, men's adventure, suspense/thriller, mystery, western. Query only with SASE.
**Recent Title(s):** *Dr. Atkins' New Diet Revolution*, by Dr. Robert C. Atkins, M.D. (nonfiction); *What Looks Like Crazy on an Ordinary Day*, by Pearl Cleage (fiction).

**AVON EOS**, Avon Books, 1350 Avenue of the Americas, New York NY 10019. (212)261-6800. Website: http://www.avonbooks.com/eos. **Acquisitions:** Jennifer Brehl, executive editor; Diana Gill, associate editor. Publishes hardcover originals, trade and mass market paperback originals and reprints. **Publishes 55-60 titles/year. Receives 2,500 queries and 800 mss/year. 25% of books from first-time authors; 5% from unagented writers. Pays royalty on retail price, range varies.** Publishes book 18-24 months after acceptance of ms. Accepts simultaneous submissions, if so noted. Reports in 6 months. Manuscript guidelines for #10 SASE.
    ○─ "We are a 'small big company.' We can't be all things to all people. We put out a cutting-edge, literary, science fiction/fantasy line that appeals to people who want to read good books."
**Fiction:** Fantasy, science fiction. No horror or juvenile topics. "We look for original work that will break traditional boundaries of this genre." Query with full synopsis of book, 3 sample chapters and SASE.
**Recent Title(s):** *The Death of the Necromancer*, by Martha Wells (fantasy fiction).
**Tips:** "We strongly advise submitting via a literary agent. If you make an unsolicited, unagented submission, follow our guidelines (i.e., do not send an entire manuscript; send query, synopsis and sample chapters only)."

**AVON FLARE BOOKS**, Avon Books, 1350 Avenue of the Americas, New York NY 10019. (212)261-6800. Fax: (212)261-6895. Website: http://www.avonbooks.com. **Acquisitions:** Elise Howard, editor-in-chief; Ruth Katcher, senior editor. Publishes mass market paperback originals and reprints for young adults. **Publishes 24 new titles/year. 25% of books from first-time authors; 15% from unagented writers. Pays 6-8% royalty. Offers $2,500 minimum advance.** Publishes book 2 years after acceptance. Accepts simultaneous submissions. Reports in 4 months. Book catalog and ms guidelines for 8×10 SAE with 5 first-class stamps.
    ○─ Avon Flare publishes young adult books, primarily fiction.
**Nonfiction:** General. Submit outline/synopsis and sample chapters. "*Very* selective with young adult nonfiction."
**Fiction:** Adventure, ethnic, humor, mainstream, mystery, romance, suspense, contemporary. "Very selective with mystery." Manuscripts appropriate to ages 12-18. Query with sample chapters and synopsis.
**Recent Title(s):** *Making Out* series, by Katherine Applegate; *Enchanted Hearts*, by various authors.
**Tips:** "The YA market is not as strong as it was five years ago. We are very selective with young adult fiction. *Avon does not publish picture books,* nor do we use freelance readers."

**◨ AVON TWILIGHT**, Avon Books, 1350 Avenue of the Americas, New York NY 10019. (212)261-6800. Fax: (212)261-6895. Website: http://www.avonbooks.com/avon/mystery.html. **Acquisitions:** Jennifer Sawyer Fisher, senior editor (series detective mysteries). Publishes hardcover originals, trade paperback reprints, mass market paperback originals and reprints. **Publishes 60 titles/year. Pays 7½-15% royalty on retail price, depending on format.** Accepts simultaneous submissions.
    ○─ Avon Twilight publishes mainstream mystery novel series.
**Fiction:** Mystery. Query with synopsis, 2 sample chapters and SASE.
**Recent Title(s):** *The Ape Who Guards the Balance*, by Elizabeth Peters (mystery).
**Tips:** "Mystery series with a strong regional base are a plus."

**AZTEX CORP.**, P.O. 50046, Tucson AZ 85703-1046. (520)882-4656. Website: http://www.aztexcorp.com. **Acquisitions:** Elaine Jordan, editor. Estab. 1976. Publishes hardcover and paperback originals. **Publishes 10 titles/year. Receives 250 submissions/year. 100% of books from unagented writers. Pays 10% royalty.** Publishes book 18 months after acceptance. Reports in 3 months.
**Nonfiction:** "We specialize in transportation subjects (how-to and history)." Accepts nonfiction translations. Submit outline and 2 sample chapters. "Queries without return envelopes or postage are not responded to." Reviews artwork/photos as part of ms package.
**Tips:** "We look for accuracy, thoroughness and interesting presentation."

**BACKCOUNTRY PUBLICATIONS**, The Countryman Press, P. O. Box 748, Woodstock VT 05091-0748. (802)457-4826. Fax: (802)457-1678. E-mail: countrymanpress@wwnorton.com. Website: http://www.countrymanpress.com. **Acquisitions:** Ann Kraybill, managing editor. Estab. 1996. Publishes trade paperback originals. **Publishes 15 titles/year. Receives 1,000 queries and a few mss/year. 25% of books from first-time authors; 75% from unagented writers. Pays 7-10% royalty on retail price. Offers $1,500-2,500 advance.** Publishes book 18 months after acceptance of ms. Accepts simultaneous submissions. Returns submissions only with SASE. Reports in 2 months on proposals. Book catalog free. Ms guidelines for #10 SASE.

# Taking the mystery out of mysteries

Much to the delight of suspense lovers, Avon Books recently launched Avon Twilight, an imprint devoted to creating a recognizable title for their series mysteries. Looking to expand their established hold in the "cozy" market, Avon hopes its new imprint's wider range of authors and styles will broaden the publisher's readership. "We created an identity for our mysteries—one that reaches across the publishing avenues," says Avon Twilight senior editor Jennifer Sawyer Fisher. "We launched with four months worth of books, and so far all signs point toward success."

**Jennifer Sawyer Fisher**

Clearly this success was achieved not only through a distinct name and editorial philosophy, but through Fisher's own love of the genre. A seasoned member of the publishing community, she began at Kensington Books, describing it as a "great introduction to all the possibilities publishing can offer." From there Fisher went to Penguin USA where she focused on "women's fiction." She admits these two experiences were rewarding, but the chance to be a part of Avon was irresistible. "My true love has always been in the area of mystery and suspense—the kind of books I read and still read in my spare time. When the opportunity at Avon opened up, I was thrilled. It's both challenging and exciting with wonderful colleagues and great authors. What more could I ask for?"

Twilight's roster of authors includes Susan Rogers Cooper, Katy Munger and Jessica Speart, all of whose work Fisher describes as "edgy with a hint of violence." Also with Twilight are historical mystery writers Elizabeth Peters and Mark Graham. Fisher doubts that Avon Twilight will publish solely hardboiled mysteries, but will instead include a variety of books by authors such as G.M. Ford and Laura Lippman, who provide "a little something for everyone." Fisher's editorial expectations vary and she is reluctant to compare authors to one another. She is willing, however, to cite Lippman (who won an Edgar Award and is nominated again this year) as one example of a successful series writer. She also mentions Elizabeth Peters, who "sells well and receives enormous critical acclaim." Fisher is quick to add, "We consider all our series successes to one degree or another."

JENNIFER SAWYER FISHER

*Editor*
*Avon Twilight*

What exactly makes for a successful series? And how can budding authors ensure their submissions meet the criteria? Manuscripts that catch Fisher's eye are those with "an innate energy and enthusiasm which the author is able to portray through smart characters and intriguing settings." Fisher adds, "It's imperative that a mystery be at the heart of any book, not just stuffed into the cracks. The characters may be great, but without a clever mystery, readers won't come back for more." This rule is especially true for a series, a genre that depends on the narrative package to sustain the reader through several books. The key to planning a series, says Fisher, is to "establish primary characters and work with them over two or three books. Don't give away everything in the first book; hold something back for future stories." She warns, however, that authors "must wrap up the mystery in each story, or readers get frustrated or annoyed. Tease the reader, but be clear in your own mind where you're taking the characters over time."

Perhaps the greatest challenge is conveying a mystery's serial potential in the limited space of a query or synopsis. Fisher recommends that an author describe the sleuth in detail and suggest ways in which he will grow over time. "Highlighting the sleuth and showing how this individual will appear in future stories tells me this manuscript is meant to be the start of a series." Generally, queries should be short and sweet, and include "pertinent information such as sleuth, occupation, setting and any other hook to the series." She also suggests authors "position their work in terms of another published author" to give the editor a clearer idea of the manuscript. Synopses should be concise while still managing to map out all the plot elements, including the culprit. "I'm reading to see how the story fits together, to see what the nuts and bolts are. Ideally, I'd like to get a sense of the tone and atmosphere from the synopsis, but usually that's the job of the manuscript. The synopsis shows me you can in fact plot a mystery. And trust me, that's not to be overestimated!"

Fisher is clear about what *not* to do when submitting a manuscript. "*Never* end a synopsis without identifying the murderer. Lay out all the information, clues, red herrings, suspects and characters, and let me decide if the killer works or not. Don't end with 'And the killer is. . . . You'll have to read the manuscript to find out.' I have seen that, and it's simply not professional, nor is it cute." Other common mistakes include anything from poor grammar and spelling to major glitches in the story's logic. Fisher often sees writers "pulling the murderer out of the woodwork," and says this can be avoided by setting up "clues and a sequence of events in such a way that a clever reader can backtrack and figure out 'whodunit.' There's nothing worse than seeing an author box herself right into a corner and try to make her way out of it with some random and extraneous ending."

A desire to be trendy may also snare the unsuspecting author. Fisher notes that mysteries with a strong regional base, such as the work of Lauren Haney, which transports readers to a distant and exotic locale, or Beth Sherman, who focuses on small town life, are popular. These books depend on the author's love of time and place, Fisher says, a quality which "plays quite nicely to the mystery reader's experience." Rather than tailoring work to tap into a specific trend, Fisher recommends that authors cultivate and work from their own knowledge and passion. "Authors should never write a book because they perceive something as 'hot.' They must write because they are excited about the material. It's up to them to focus on whatever element gets them going and to make that the centerpiece of the book."

Although Fisher is not currently accepting unagented manuscripts, she encourages those wanting to submit to Avon Twilight to read and familiarize themselves with authors they are currently publishing, and to obtain an agent to represent their work. "It's a significant advantage to have an agent today. There's so much material being submitted on a daily basis that I naturally gravitate to those manuscripts that have been screened by someone I respect and/or know." But ultimately, Fisher suggests a more fulfilling road to publication: "Meeting and sharing with other authors is the best way to learn about the industry. Each book is a learning experience, whether you're published or not. Use all your resources to the utmost, and make them work for you."

—*Amanda Heele*

O→ Backcountry Publications publishes guidebooks that encourage physical fitness and appreciation for and understanding of the natural world, self-sufficiency and adventure.
**Nonfiction:** Subjects include nature/environment, outdoor, recreation: bicycling, hiking, canoeing, kayaking, fly fishing, walking, guidebooks and series. Query with outline, 50 sample pages and proposal package including market analysis and SASE.
**Recent Title(s):** *50 More Hikes in New Hampshire*, by Daniel Doan and Ruth Doan MacDougall (outdoor recreation).
**Tips:** "Look at our existing series of guidebooks to see how your proposal fits in."

**BAEN PUBLISHING ENTERPRISES**, P.O. Box 1403, Riverdale NY 10471-0671. (718)548-3100. Website: http://baen.com. **Acquisitions:** Jim Baen, editor-in-chief; Toni Weisskopf, executive editor. Estab. 1983. Publishes hardcover, trade paperback and mass market paperback originals and reprints. **Publishes 120 titles/year. Receives 5,000 submissions/year. 5% of books from first-time authors; 50% from unagented writers. Pays royalty on retail price.** Reports in 6-8 months on queries and proposals, 9-12 months on complete mss. Book catalog free. Manuscript guidelines for #10 SASE.
O→ "We publish books at the heart of science fiction and fantasy."
**Fiction:** Fantasy, science fiction. Submit outline/synopsis and sample chapters or complete ms.
**Recent Title(s):** *Echoes of Honor*, by David Weber.
**Tips:** "See our books before submitting. Send for our writers' guidelines."

**BAKER BOOK HOUSE COMPANY**, P.O. Box 6287, Grand Rapids MI 49516-6287. (616)676-9185. Fax: (616)676-2315. Website: http://www.bakerbooks.com.
**Imprint(s):** Baker Academic, **Baker Books**, Baker Bytes, **Chosen**, **Fleming H. Revell**, Spire, Wynwood.

**BAKER BOOKS**, Baker Book House Company, P.O. Box 6287, Grand Rapids MI 49516-6287. (616)676-9185. Fax: (616)676-9573. Website: http://www.bakerbooks.com. Director of Publications: Allan Fisher. **Acquisitions:** Rebecca Cooper, assistant editor. Estab. 1939. Publishes hardcover and trade paperback originals and trade paperback reprints. **Publishes 80 titles/year. 10% of books from first-time authors; 85% from unagented writers. Pays 14% royalty on net receipts.** Publishes book within 1 year after acceptance. Accepts simultaneous submissions, if so noted. Reports in 2 months on proposals. Book catalog for 8½×11 SAE with 6 first-class stamps or on website. Manuscript guidelines for #10 SASE or on website.
O→ "Baker Books publishes popular religious nonfiction and fiction, children's books, academic and reference books, and professional books for church leaders. Most of our authors and readers are evangelical Christians, and our books are purchased from Christian bookstores, mail-order retailers, and school bookstores."
**Imprint(s):** Hamewith, Hourglass, Labyrinth, Raven's Ridge, Spire Books.
**Nonfiction:** Anthropology, archaeology, biography, CD-ROM, children's/juvenile, contemporary issues, giftbook, illus-

trated book, parenting, psychology, reference, self-help, seniors' concerns, singleness, textbook, women's concerns, children's books, Christian doctrine, reference books, books for pastors and church leaders, textbooks for Christian colleges and seminaries. Query with proposal, including chapter summaries or outlines, sample chapters, résumé and SASE. Reviews artwork as part of ms package. Send 1-2 photocopies.

**Fiction:** Literary novels focusing on women's concerns, mainstream/contemporary, religious, mysteries, juvenile, picture books, young adult. Query with synopsis/outline, sample chapters, résumé and SASE.

**Recent Title(s):** *The Last Days According to Jesus*, by R.C. Sproul (theology); *Resting in the Bosom of the Lamb*, by Augusta Trobaugh (southern fiction).

**BALE BOOKS**, Bale Publications, 5121 St. Charles Ave., New Orleans LA 70115. **Acquisitions:** Don Bale, Jr, editor-in-chief. Estab. 1963. Publishes hardcover and paperback originals and reprints. **Publishes 10 titles/year. Receives 25 submissions/year. 50% of books from first-time authors; 90% from unagented writers. Offers standard 10-12½-15% royalty contract on wholesale or retail price; sometimes makes outright purchases of $500. No advance.** Publishes book 3 years after acceptance. Reports in 3 months. Book catalog for #10 SAE with 2 first-class stamps.

☞ "Our mission is to educate numismatists about coins, coin collecting and investing opportunities."

**Nonfiction:** Numismatics. "Our specialties are coin and stock market investment books; especially coin investment books and coin price guides." Submit outline and 3 sample chapters.

**Recent Title(s):** *Fabulous Collecting & Investing Potential of U.S. Copper Coins* (nonfiction).

**Tips:** "Most of our books are sold through publicity and ads in the coin newspapers. We are open to any new ideas in the area of numismatics. Write for a teenage through adult level. Lead the reader by the hand like a teacher, building chapter by chapter. Our books sometimes have a light, humorous treatment, but not necessarily. We look for good English, construction and content, and sales potential."

**BALLANTINE BOOKS**, Random House, Inc., 201 E. 50th St., New York NY 10022. (212)572-4910. Publishes hardcover and trade paperback originals. President: Gina Centrello. Editorial Coordinator: Betsy Flagler. **Acquisitions:** Leona Nevler, editor (all kinds of fiction and nonfiction); Peter Borland, executive editor (commercial fiction, pop culture); Elisa Wares, executive editor (romance, health, parenting, mystery); Joe Blades, associate publisher (mystery); Susan Randol, executive editor (business, narrative motivational, true medicine, true crime, mystery); Elizabeth Zack, editor (motivational, inspirational, women's sports, career, seasonal tie-ins); Joanne Wyckoff, senior editor (religion, spirituality, nature/pets, psychology); Andrea Schulz, editor (literary fiction, travel, women's studies, narrative nonfiction); Shauna Summers, senior editor (historical and contemporary romance, commercial women's fiction, general fiction, thrillers/suspense); Ginny Faber, senior editor (health, psychology, spirituality, travel, general nonfiction); Sarah Glazer, assistant editor (historical fiction, commercial fiction, arm-chair travel, animals). Estab. 1952. Publishes hardcover, trade paperback, mass market paperback originals.

☞ Ballantine Books publishes a wide variety of nonfiction and fiction.

**Nonfiction:** How-to, humor, illustrated book, reference, self-help. Subjects include animals, child guidance/parenting, cooking/foods/nutrition, health/medicine. Submit proposal and 100 ms pages with SASE. Reviews artwork/photos as part of ms package. Send photocopies.

**Fiction:** Historical fiction, women's mainstream, multicultural and general fiction.

**Recent Title(s):** *Rookery Blues*, by Jon Hassler (fiction); *Guilty By Reason of Insanity: A Psychiatrist Probes the Minds of Killers*, by Dorothy Otnow Lewis, M.D. (nonfiction).

**⒩ BANCROFT PRESS**, P.O. Box 65360, Baltimore MD 21209-9945. (410)358-0658. Fax: (410)764-1967. Website: http://www.bancroftpress.com. **Acquisitions:** Bruce Bortz, publisher (investments, politics, history, humor); Sarah E. Azizi, fiction editor (literary novels, poetry, mystery/thrillers). Publishes hardcover and trade paperback originals. **Publishes 4 titles/year. Pays various royalties on retail price.** Publishes book up to 3 years after acceptance of ms. Reports in 4 months on proposals. Book catalog for #10 SASE.

☞ Bancroft Press is a general trade publisher specializing in books by journalists. Currently emphasizing mystery and thriller fiction. De-emphasizing essay collections.

**Nonfiction:** Biography, how-to, humor, self-help. Subjects include business/economics, government/politics, health/medicine, money/finance, regional, sports, women's issues/studies, popular culture, essays. We advise writers to visit website www.bancroftpress.com." Submit proposal package, including outline, 2 sample chapters and competition/market survey.

**Fiction:** Literary, mystery, poetry, thrillers. Query with outline and 2 sample chapters.

**Recent Nonfiction Title(s):** *Live By the Sword: The Secret War Against Castro and the Death of JFK*, by Gus Russo (nonfiction); *Those Who Trespass*, by Bill O'Reilly (fiction).

**⒩ B&B PUBLISHING, INC.**, P.O. Box 96, Walworth WI 53184. Fax: (414)275-9530. **Acquisitions:** N. Kirschslager. Publishes hardcover and trade paperback originals. **Publishes 5-10 titles/year. Receives 1,000 queries and 100 mss/year. 10% of books from first-time authors; 90% from unagented writers. Usually contracts authors as work-for-hire.** Publishes book 1 year after acceptance. Accepts simultaneous submissions. Any submissions or queries without SASE will not be acknowledged. No unsolicited mss. Reports in 3 months. Book catalog and ms guidelines free.

☞ B&B Publishing seeks innovative supplementary educational materials, especially geography-based materials, for grades K-12. Also publishes a Southeastern Wisconsin quarterly tourism publication.

**Nonfiction:** Children's/juvenile, reference, Americana, trivia. Query with SASE. Reviews artwork/photos as part of ms package. Send photocopies.
**Recent Nonfiction Title(s):** *Serengeti Plain*, by Terri Wills.
**Tips:** Audience is interested in supplementary educational material.

**BANTAM BOOKS**, Bantam Dell Publishing Group, Random House, Inc., Dept. WM, 1540 Broadway, New York NY 10036. (212)354-6500. Senior Vice President/Deputy Publisher: Nita Taublib. **Acquisitions:** Toni Burbank, Ann Harris, executive editors. Estab. 1945. Publishes hardcover, trade paperback and mass market paperback originals, trade paperback; mass market paperback reprints and audio. **Publishes 350 titles/year.** Publishes book an average of 1 year after ms is accepted. Accepts simultaneous submissions from agents.
**Imprint(s):** Bantam Classics (reprints); Crime Line (Kate Miciak, associate publisher); **Fanfare** (Beth DeGuzman, Wendy McCurdy), **Spectra** (Pat LoBrutto, Anne Groell).
**Nonfiction:** Biography, how-to, humor, self-help. Subjects include Americana, business/economics, child care/parenting, diet/fitness, education, cooking/foods/nutrition, gay/lesbian, government/politics, health/medicine, history, language/literature, military/war, mysticism/astrology, nature, philosophy/mythology, psychology, religion/inspiration, science, sociology, spirituality, sports, true crime, women's studies. Query or submit outline/synopsis. *All unsolicited mss returned unopened.*
**Fiction:** Adventure, fantasy, feminist, gay/lesbian, historical, horror, literary, mainstream/contemporary, mystery, romance, science fiction, suspense. Query or submit outline/synopsis. *All unsolicited mss returned unopened.*

**BANTAM DOUBLEDAY DELL BOOKS FOR YOUNG READERS**, Random House Children's Publishing, Random House, Inc., 1540 Broadway, New York NY 10036. (212)782-9000. Fax: (212)782-9452. Website: http://www.rando mhouse.com/kids. Vice President/Associate Publisher/Editor-in-Chief: Beverly Horowitz. Editorial Director: Michelle Poploff. **Acquisitions:** Wendy Lamb, executive editor; Francoise Bui, executive editor; Lauri Hornik, senior editor; Karen Wojtyla, editor; Wendy Loggia, editor. Publishes hardcover, trade paperback and mass market paperback series originals, trade paperback reprints. **Publishes 300 titles/year. Receives thousands of queries/year. 10% of books from first-time authors; few from unagented writers. Pays royalty. Advance varies.** Publishes book 2 years after acceptance of ms. Reports in 2 months. Book catalog for 9 × 12 SASE.
  &#9758; "Bantam Doubleday Dell Books for Young Readers publishes award-winning books by distinguished authors and the most promising new writers."
**Imprint(s):** Delacorte Press Books for Young Readers, Doubleday Books for Young Readers, Laurel Leaf (ya), Picture Yearling, Skylark, Starfire, Yearling (middle grade).
  • The best way to break in to this market is through its two contests, the Marguerite de Angeli contest and the Delacorte Press Contest for a First Young Adult novel, listed in the Contests & Awards section of this book.
**Nonfiction:** "Bantam Doubleday Dell Books for Young Readers publishes a very limited number of nonfiction titles."
**Fiction:** Adventure, fantasy, humor, juvenile, mainstream/contemporary, mystery, picture books, suspense, young adult. Query with SASE. *No unsolicited material.*
**Recent Title(s):** *Lily's Crossing*, by Patricia Reilly Giff (Newbery Honor); *Beetle Boy*, by Lawrence David (picture book); *Burning Up*, by Caroline Cooney (fiction).

**N ⚡ BARBOUR PUBLISHING, INC.**, P.O. Box 719, Uhrichsville OH 44683. (740)922-6045. **Acquisitions:** Susan Johnson, senior editor (all areas); Rebecca Germany, managing editor (fiction). Estab. 1981. Publishes hardcover, trade paperback and mass market paperback originals and reprints. **Publishes 100 titles/year. Receives 520 queries and 625 mss/year. 75% of books from first-time authors; 95% from unagented writers. Pays 0-12% royalty on wholesale price or makes outright purchase of $500-5,000. Offers $500-1,500 advance.** Publishes book 2 years after acceptance of ms. Accepts simultaneous submissions. Reports in 1 month on queries, 3 months on proposals and mss. Book catalog for 9 × 12 SAE and 2 first-class stamps. Manuscript guidelines for #10 SASE.
  &#9758; Barbour Books publishes mostly devotional material that is non-denominational and evangelical in nature; Heartsong Presents publishes Christian romance. "We're a Christian evangelical publisher."
**Imprint(s):** Heartsong Presents (contact Rebecca Germany, managing editor), Promise Press (contact Susan Johnson, senior editor).
**Nonfiction:** Biography, children's/juvenile, cookbook, gift book, humor, illustrated book, reference. Subjects include child guidance/parenting, cooking/foods/nutrition, money/finance, religion (evangelical Christian), women's issues/studies. "We are always looking for biographical material for adults and children on heroes of the faith. Always looking for humor! Some writers do not explain their purpose for writing the book and don't specify who their audience is. Many proposals are sketchy, non-specific and difficult to understand. If I can't decipher the proposal, I certainly won't accept a manuscript." Submit outline and 3 sample chapters with SASE. Reviews artwork/photos as part of the ms package. Send photocopies. "Send sufficient postage if you want your materials returned."
**Fiction:** Historical, humor, mainstream/contemporary, religious, romance, short story collections, Western. "All of our fiction is 'sweet' romance. No sex, no bad language, etc. Audience is evangelical/Christian, and we're looking for wholesome material for young as well as old. Common writer's mistakes are a sketchy proposal, an unbelievable story and a story that doesn't fit our guidelines for inspirational romances." Submit synopsis and 3 sample chapters with SASE.
**Recent Title(s):** *God Is In the Small Stuff*, by Bruce Bickel and Stan Jantz (nonfiction); *Short Stories for Long Rainy Days*, by Katherine Douglas (fiction).

**Tips:** "Audience is evangelical/Christian conservative, non-denominational, young and old. We're looking for *great concepts*, not necessarily a big name author or agent. We want to publish books that will sell millions, not just 'flash in the pan' releases. Send us your ideas!"

**BARNEGAT LIGHT PRESS**, P.O. Box 607, Chatsworth NJ 08019-0607. (609)894-4415. Fax: (609)894-2350. **Acquisitions:** R. Marilyn Schmidt, publisher. Publishes trade paperback originals. **Publishes 8 titles/year. Receives 12 queries and 10 mss/year. 0% of books from first-time authors; 100% from unagented writers. Makes outright purchase.** Publishes book 6 months after acceptance of ms. Reports in 1 month. *Writer's Market* recommends allowing 2 months for reply. Book catalog free.
>   O—¬ "We are a regional publisher emphasizing the mid-Atlantic region. Areas concerned are gardening and cooking."

**Imprint(s):** Pine Barrens Press.
**Nonfiction:** Cookbook, how-to. Subjects include cooking/foods/nutrition, gardening, regional, travel, all New Jersey-oriented. Query.
**Recent Title(s):** *Exploring the Pine Barrens of New Jersey: A Guide*, by R. Marilyn Schmidt.

■ **BARRICADE BOOKS INC.**, 150 Fifth Ave., Suite 700, New York NY 10011-4311. (212)627-7000. Fax: (212)627-7028. **Acquisitions:** Carole Stuart, publisher. Estab. 1991. Publishes hardcover and trade paperback originals and trade paperback reprints. **Publishes 30 titles/year. Receives 200 queries and 100 mss/year. 80% of books from first-time authors; 50% from unagented writers. Pays 10-12% royalty on retail price for hardcover. Advance varies.** Publishes book 18 months after acceptance of ms. Reports in 1 month on queries. Book catalog for $3.
>   O—¬ "We look for nonfiction, mostly of the controversial type, and books we can promote with authors who can talk about their topics on radio and television and to the press."

**Nonfiction:** Biography, how-to, reference, self-help. Subjects include business/economics, ethnic, gay/lesbian, government/politics, health/medicine, history, nature/environment, psychology, sociology, women's issues/studies. Query with outline and 1-2 sample chapters with SASE or material will not be returned. Reviews artwork/photos as part of ms package. Send photocopies.
**Recent Title(s):** *The Animal in Hollywood*, by John L. Smith (crime/mafia).
**Tips:** "Do your homework. Visit bookshops to find publishers who are doing the kinds of books you want to write. Always submit to a *person*—not just 'editor.' *Always enclose SASE*."

**BARRON'S EDUCATIONAL SERIES, INC.**, 250 Wireless Blvd., Hauppauge NY 11788. Fax: (516)434-3217. Website: http://barronseduc.com. **Acquisitions:** Grace Freedson, managing editor/director of acquisitions. Estab. 1941. Publishes hardcover, paperback and mass market originals and software. **Publishes 400 titles/year. Reviews 2,000 queries and 1,000 mss/year. 40% of books from first-time authors; 75% from unagented writers. Pays 14-16% royalty on both wholesale and retail price or makes outright purchase of $2,500-5,000. Offers $2,500-5,000 advance.** Publishes book 2 years after acceptance of ms. Accepts simultaneous submissions. Reports in 1 month on queries, 8 months on ms. Book catalog free.
>   O—¬ Barron's tends to publish series of books, both for adults and children. "We are always on the lookout for creative nonfiction ideas for children and adults."

**Nonfiction:** Adult education, art, business, cookbooks, crafts, foreign language, review books, guidance, pet books, travel, literary guides, parenting, health, juvenile, young adult sports, test preparation materials and textbooks. Reviews artwork/photos as part of ms package. Query or submit outline/synopsis and 2-3 sample chapters. Accepts nonfiction translations.
**Fiction:** Juvenile, young adult. Submit complete ms.
**Recent Title(s):** *The Major Computer Major's Guide to the Real World*, by Alan Simon (career).
**Tips:** "Audience is mostly educated self-learners and hobbyists. The writer has the best chance of selling us a book that will fit into one of our series. SASE must be included for the return of all materials. Please be patient for replies."

**BATSFORD BRASSEY INC.**, (formerly Brassey's, Inc.), 4380 MacArthur Blvd., NW, 2nd Floor, Washington DC 20007. (202)333-2500. Fax: (202)333-5100. E-mail: brasseys@aol.com. Website: http://www.batsford.com. **Acquisitions:** Don McKeon, editorial director. Estab. 1984. Publishes hardcover and trade paperback originals and reprints. **Publishes 30 titles/year. Receives 900 queries/year. 30% of books from first-time authors; 80% from unagented writers. Pays 6-12% royalty on wholesale price. Offers $50,000 maximum advance.** Publishes book 1 year after acceptance of ms. Accepts simultaneous submissions. Reports in 2 months on proposals. Book catalog and ms guidelines for 9×12 SASE.
>   O—¬ Batsford Brassey specializes in national and international affairs, military history, biography, intelligence, foreign policy, defense and sports. "We are seeking to build our biography, military history and national affairs lists and have also created a new imprint, Brassey's Sports."

**Nonfiction:** Biography, coffee-table book, reference, textbook. Subjects include government/politics, national and international affairs, history, military/war, intelligence studies and sports. When submitting nonfiction, be sure to include sufficient biographical information (e.g., track records of previous publications), and "make clear in proposal how your work might differ from other such works already published and with which yours might compete." Submit proposal package, including outline, 1 sample chapter, bio, analysis of book's competition, return postage and SASE. Reviews artwork/photos as part of ms package. Send photocopies.

**Recent Title(s):** *Decision for Disaster: Betrayal at the Bay of Pigs*, by Grayston Lynch.
**Tips:** "Our audience consists of military personnel, government policymakers, and general readers with an interest in military history, biography, national/international affairs, defense issues, intelligence studies and sports." No fiction.

**BATTELLE PRESS**, Battelle Memorial Institute, 505 King Ave., Columbus OH 43201. (614)424-6393. Fax: (614)424-3819. E-mail: press@battelle.org. Website: http://www.battelle.org. **Acquisitions:** Joe Sheldrick. Estab. 1980. Publishes hardcover and paperback originals and markets primarily by direct mail. **Publishes 10 titles/year. Pays 10% royalty on wholesale price. No advance.** Publishes book 6 months after acceptance of ms. Accepts simultaneous submissions. Reports in 1 month. Book catalog free.
   **O–π** Battelle Press strives to be a primary source of books and software on science and the management of science.
**Nonfiction:** "We are looking for management, leadership, project management and communications books specifically targeted to engineers and scientists." Query. Reviews artwork/photos as part of ms package. Send photocopies. Returns submissions with SASE only by writer's request.
**Recent Title(s):** *Risk Communication, 2nd Edition*, by R. Lundgren.
**Tips:** Audience consists of engineers, researchers, scientists and corporate researchers and developers.

**BAYWOOD PUBLISHING CO., INC.**, 26 Austin Ave., Amityville NY 11701. (516)691-1270. Fax: (516)691-1770. E-mail: baywood@baywood.com. Website: http://www.baywood.com. **Acquisitions:** Stuart Cohen, managing editor. Estab. 1964. **Publishes 25 titles/year. Pays 7-15% royalty on retail price.** Publishes book within 1 year after acceptance of ms. Catalog and ms guidelines free.
   **O–π** Baywood Publishing publishes original and innovative books in the humanities and social sciences, including areas such as health sciences, gerontology, death and bereavement, psychology, technical communications and archaeology.
**Nonfiction:** Technical, scholarly. Subjects include anthropology/archaeology, computers/electronics, gerontology, imagery, labor relations, education, death/dying, drugs, nature/environment, psychology, public health/medicine, sociology, technical communications, women's issues/studies. Submit outline/synopsis and sample chapters.
**Recent Title(s):** *Eighteenth-Century British Aesthetics*, by Dabney Townsend.

**BEACHWAY PRESS**, 300 W. Main St., Suite A, Charlottesville VA 22903. Website: http://www.outside-america.com. **Acquisitions:** Scott Adams, publisher. **Publishes 10-15 titles/year. Pays 7½% royalty on wholesale price. Offers $2,500 advance.** Publishes book 1 year after acceptance of ms. Reports in 2 months on queries and proposals. Manuscript guidelines for #10 SASE.
   **O–π** Beachway Press publishes books designed to open up new worlds of experiences for those anxious to explore, and to provide the detailed information necessary to get them started.
**Nonfiction:** Innovative outdoor adventure and travel guidebooks. "We welcome ideas that explore the world of adventure and wonder; from day hikes to mountain bikes, from surf to skis." Query with outline, 2 sample chapters, methods of research and SASE. Reviews artwork/photos as part of ms package. Send proof prints.
**Recent Title(s):** *Mountain Bike America*™ (guidebook series).
**Tips:** "Someone interested in writing for us should be both an avid outdoors person and an expert in their area of interest. This person should have a clear understanding of maps and terrain and should enjoy sharing their adventurous spirit and enthusiasm with others."

**BEACON HILL PRESS OF KANSAS CITY**, Nazarene Publishing House, P.O. Box 419527, Kansas City MO 64141. Fax: (816)753-4071. E-mail: bjp@bhillkc.com. **Acquisitions:** Kelly Gallagher, director. Estab. 1912. Publishes hardcover and paperback originals. **Publishes 30 titles/year. Standard contract is 12% royalty on net sales for first 10,000 copies and 14% on subsequent copies. (Sometimes makes flat rate purchase.)** Publishes book within 1 year after acceptance. Reports within 3 months.
   **O–π** "Beacon Hill Press is a Christ-centered publisher that provides authentically Christian resources that are faithful to God's word and relevant to life."
**Nonfiction:** Applied Christianity, spiritual formation, leadership resources, contemporary issues. Doctrinally must conform to the evangelical, Wesleyan tradition. No fiction, autobiography, poetry, short stories or children's picture books. Contemporary issues acceptable. Accent on holy living; encouragement in daily Christian life. Query or proposal preferred. Average ms length: 30,000-60,000 words.
**Recent Title(s):** *Leading With Vision*, by Dale Galloway.

---

**MARKET CONDITIONS** are constantly changing! If this is 2001 or later, buy the newest edition of *Writer's Market* at your favorite bookstore or order directly from Writer's Digest Books.

**BEACON PRESS**, 25 Beacon St., Boston MA 02108-2892. (617)742-2110. Fax: (617)723-3097. E-mail: kdaneman@b eacon.org. Website: http://www.beacon.org/Beacon. Director: Helene Atwan. **Acquisitions:** Deborah Chasman, editorial director (African-American, Asian-American, Latino, Native American, Jewish and gay and lesbian studies, anthropology); Deanne Urmy, executive editor, (child and family issues, environmental concerns); Micah Kleit, editor (education, current affairs, philosophy, religion); Tisha Hooks, associate editor (cultural studies, Asian and Caribbean studies, women and spirituality); Amy Caldwell, assistant editor (poetry, gender studies, gay/lesbian studies and Cuban studies). Estab. 1854. Publishes hardcover originals and paperback reprints. **Publishes 60 titles/year. Receives 4,000 submissions/year. 10% of books from first-time authors. Pays royalty. Advance varies.** Accepts simultaneous submissions. Reports in 3 months.

○━ Beacon Press publishes general interest books that promote the following values: the inherent worth and dignity of every person; justice, equity, and compassion in human relations; acceptance of one another; a free and responsible search for truth and meaning; the goal of world community with peace, liberty and justice for all; respect for the interdependent web of all existence. Currently emphasizing innovative nonfiction writing by people of all colors. De-emphasizing poetry, children's stories, art books, self-help.

**Imprint(s):** Bluestreak Series (contact Deb Chasman, editor, innovative literary writing by women of color).

**Nonfiction:** General nonfiction including works of original scholarship, religion, women's studies, philosophy, current affairs, anthropology, environmental concerns, African-American, Asian-American, Native American, Latino and Jewish studies, gay and lesbian studies, education, legal studies, child and family issues, Irish studies. Query with outline/ synopsis, cv or résumé and sample chapters with SASE. *Strongly prefers agented submissions.*

**Recent Title(s):** *Five Thousand Days Like This One*, by Jane Brox (nonfiction); *The Healing*, by Gayl Jones (fiction).

**Tips:** "We probably accept only one or two manuscripts from an unpublished pool of 4,000 submissions per year. No fiction, children's book, or poetry submissions invited. Authors should have academic affiliation."

**BEAVER POND PUBLISHING**, P.O. Box 224, Greenville PA 16125. (724)588-3492. **Acquisitions**: Rich Faler, publications director. Estab. 1990. Publishes trade paperback originals and reprints. **Publishes 4 titles/year. Receives 30 queries and 20 mss/year. 50% of books from first-time authors; 100% from unagented writers. Pays 8% royalty on net sales or makes outright purchase.** Publishes book 1 year after acceptance of ms. Accepts simultaneous submissions. Reports in 1 month. Book catalog and ms guidelines free.

○━ Beaver Pond publishes primarily outdoor-oriented books and magazines.

**Nonfiction:** Outdoor how-to. Subjects include photography (outdoor), hunting, fishing. "We are actively seeking shorter length manuscripts suitable for 20-40 page booklets, in addition to longer length books. Don't offer too general a title with no 'meat.' " Query or submit outline and 2 sample chapters with SASE. Reviews artwork/photos as part of ms package.

**Recent Title(s):** *Deer Hunting Strategies for Whitetails*, by Terry Soderberg.

**Tips:** "Audience is active outdoor people that want to excel at their craft. Write the book that you would have wanted when you first began a specific outdoor activity. The manuscript needs to completely cover a narrow topic indepth."

**FREDERIC C. BEIL, PUBLISHER, INC.**, 609 Whitaker St., Savannah GA 31401. Phone/fax: (912)233-2446. E-mail: beilbook@beil.com. Website: http://www.beil.com. **Acquisitions:** Mary Ann Bowman, editor. Estab. 1982. Publishes hardcover originals and reprints. **Publishes 7 titles/year. Receives 1,500 queries and 7 mss/year. 80% of books from first-time authors; 100% from unagented writers. Pays 7½% royalty on retail price.** Publishes book 20 months after acceptance. Accepts simultaneous submissions. Reports in 1 month on queries. Book catalog free.

○━ Frederic C. Beil publishes in the fields of history, literature, biography, books about books, and the book arts.

**Imprint(s):** The Sandstone Press.

**Nonfiction:** Biography, general trade, illustrated book, juvenile, reference. Subjects include art/architecture, history, language/literature, book arts. Query. Reviews artwork/photos as part of ms package. Send photocopies.

**Fiction:** Historical and literary. Query.

**Recent Title(s):** *Civil War Savannah*, by Derek Smith (nonfiction); *The Aesculapian*, by Don Cloud (fiction).

**Tips:** "Our objectives are (1) to offer to the reading public carefully selected texts of lasting value; (2) to adhere to high standards in the choice of materials and in bookmaking craftsmanship; (3) to produce books that exemplify good taste in format and design; and (4) to maintain the lowest cost consistent with quality."

**Ⓝ BELLWETHER-CROSS PUBLISHING**, 18319 Highway 20 W., East Dubuque IL 61025. (815)747-6255 or (888)516-5096. Fax: (815)747-3770. E-mail: jcrow@shepherd.clrs.com. **Acquisitions:** Kennie Harris, senior developmental editor; Jill Crow, senior editor; Kate Jenkins, editor. Publishes trade paperback originals. **Publishes 12 titles/ year. Receives 20 queries and 25 mss/year. 80% of books from first-time authors; 100% from unagented writers. Pays 10-12% royalty on wholesale price. No advance.** Publishes book 8 months after acceptance of ms. No simultaneous submissions. Reports in 1 month. Manuscript guidelines free.

○━ Bellwether-Cross concentrates on environmental books, nontraditional textbooks with mainstream possibilities and cutting-edge computer books.

**Nonfiction:** Cookbook, textbook. Subjects include Americana, business/economics, computers/electronics, creative nonfiction, government/politics, nature/environment, philosophy, women's issues/women's studies. Submit proposal package, including cover letter explaining project and 3 sample chapters. Reviews artwork as part of ms package. Send photocopies.

**Recent Title(s):** *Experiences in Environmental Science*, by Barbara Krumhardt and Danielle Wirth (college textbook);

*FrameMaker 5.5 Made Easy*, by Gail Ryan.

**THE BENEFACTORY, INC.**, 1 Post Rd., Fairfield CT 06430. (203)255-7744. Fax: (203)255-6200. E-mail: benfactry @aol.com. **Acquisitions:** Cynthia A. Germain, senior manager, product development. Estab. 1990. Publishes hardcover and trade paperback originals and reprints. **Publishes 9 titles/year. 50% of books from first-time authors; 50% from unagented writers. Pays 3-5% royalty on wholesale price. Offers $3,000-5,000 advance.** Publishes book 1 year after acceptance of ms. Accepts simultaneous submissions. Reports in 2 months on queries and proposals, 4 months on mss. Book catalog and ms guidelines free.

○┉ The Benefactory's mission is to foster animal protection, motivate reading, teach core values and encourage children to become creative, responsible individuals.

**Nonfiction:** Children's/juvenile. Subjects include animals, nature/environment. "Each story must be a true story about a real animal and contain educational details. Both prose and verse are accepted." Submit outline and SASE. Reviews artwork/photos as part of ms package. Send photocopies.

**Recent Title(s):** *Caesar, On Deaf Ears*, by Loren Spiotta DiMare (nonfiction).

**BENTLEY PUBLISHERS**, (formerly Robert Bentley, Inc.), Automotive Publishers, 1734 Massachusetts Ave., Cambridge MA 02138-1804. (617)547-4170. **Acquisitions:** Michael Bentley, publisher. Estab. 1949. Publishes hardcover and trade paperback originals and reprints. **Publishes 15-20 titles/year. 20% of books are from first-time authors; 95% from unagented writers. Pays 10-15% royalty on net price or makes outright purchase. Advance negotiable.** Publishes book 1 year after acceptance. Reports in 6 weeks. Book catalog and ms guidelines for 9×12 SAE with 4 first-class stamps.

○┉ Bentley Publishers publishes books for automotive enthusiasts.

**Nonfiction:** How-to, technical, theory of operation, coffee table. Automotive subjects only; this includes motor sports. Query or submit outline and sample chapters. Reviews artwork/photos as part of ms package.

**Recent Title(s):** *Unbeatable BMW*, by Jeremy Walton.

**Tips:** "Our audience is composed of serious, intelligent automobile, sports car, and racing enthusiasts, automotive technicians and high-performance tuners."

**THE BERKLEY PUBLISHING GROUP**, Penguin Putnam, Inc., 375 Hudson St., New York NY 10014. (212)366-2000. Website: http://www.penguinputnam.com. **Acquisitions:** Denise Silvestro, senior editor (general nonfiction, business); Judith Stern Palais, senior editor (women's general, literary and romance fiction); Tom Colgan, senior editor (history, business, inspiration, biography, suspense/thriller, mystery, adventure); Gail Fortune, senior editor (women's fiction, romance, mystery); Martha Bushko, assistant editor (nonfiction, mystery, health); Kimberly Waltemyer, editor (adult western, romance, mystery); Lisa Considine, senior editor (nonfiction, literary fiction). Estab. 1954. Publishes paperback and mass market originals and reprints. **Publishes approximately 800 titles/year. Few books from first-time authors; 1% from unagented writers. Pays 4-15% royalty on retail price. Offers advance.** Publishes book 2 years after acceptance of ms. Reports in 6 weeks on queries.

○┉ The Berkley Publishing Group publishes a variety of general nonfiction and fiction including the traditional categories of romance, mystery and science fiction.

**Imprint(s): Ace Science Fiction**, Berkley, **Boulevard**, Jove, Prime Crime.

**Nonfiction:** Biography, reference, self-help, how-to. Subjects include business management, job-seeking communication, positive thinking, gay/lesbian, health/fitness, psychology/self-help, women's issues/studies, general commercial publishing. No memoirs or personal stories. Query with SASE. Prefers agented submissions.

**Fiction:** Mystery, romance, western, young adult. No adventure or occult fiction. Prefers agented material. Query with SASE.

**Recent Title(s):** *Tom Clancy's Rainbow Six*, by Tom Clancy (novel); *Meditations from Conversations with God*, by Neale Donald Walsch (inspiration).

◪ **BERKSHIRE HOUSE PUBLISHERS, INC.**, 480 Pleasant St., Suite #5, Lee MA 01238. (413)243-0303. Fax: (413)243-4737. President: Jean J. Rousseau. **Acquisitions:** Philip Rich, editorial director. Estab. 1989. **Publishes 12-15 titles/year. Receives 100 queries and 6 mss/year. 50% of books from first-time authors; 80% from unagented writers. Pays 5-10% royalty on retail price. Offers $500-5,000 advance.** Publishes book 18 months after acceptance. Accepts simultaneous submissions. Reports in 1 month on proposals. Book catalog free.

○┉ "We publish a series of travel guides, the Great Destinations™ Series, about specific U.S. destinations, guides to appeal to upscale visitors. We also specialize in books about our own region (the Berkshires in western MA), especially recreational activities in the area. We occasionally publish cookbooks related to New England or country living/country inns in general. We offer books of historical interest in our American Classics™ Series." Currently emphasizing guides to U.S. destinations of cultural interest. De-emphasizing cookbooks except those related to New England or country living and country inns.

**Nonfiction:** Subjects include US travel, Americana, history, nature/environment, recreation (outdoors), wood crafts, regional cookbooks. "To a great extent, we choose our topics then commission the authors, but we don't discourage speculative submissions. We just don't accept many. Don't overdo it; a well-written outline/proposal is more useful than a full manuscript. Also, include a cv with writing credits."

**Recent Title(s):** *The Charleston, Savannah & Coastal Islands Book: A Complete Guide*, by Cecily McMillan.

**Tips:** "Our readers are literate, active, prosperous, interested in travel, especially in selected 'Great Destinations' areas and outdoor activities and cooking."

**BETTERWAY BOOKS**, F&W Publications, 1507 Dana Ave., Cincinnati OH 45207. (513)531-2690. **Acquisitions:** William Brohaugh (genealogy, theater and the performing arts); Adam Blake (home decorating and remodeling, lifestyle (including home organization), woodworking, small business and personal finance, hobbies and collectibles). Estab. 1982. Publishes hardcover and trade paperback originals, trade paperback reprints. **Publishes 30 titles/year. Pays 10-20% royalty on net receipts. Offers $3,000-5,000 advance.** Accepts simultaneous submissions, if so noted. Publishes book an average of 18 months after acceptance. Reports in 1 month. Book catalog for 9×12 SAE with 6 first-class stamps.
   O─╖ Betterway books are instructional books that are to be *used.* "We like specific step-by-step advice, charts, illustrations, and clear explanations of the activities and projects the books describe."
**Nonfiction:** How-to, illustrated book, reference and self-help in 7 categories. "Genealogy and family traditions are topics that we're particularly interested in. We are interested mostly in original material, but we will consider republishing self-published nonfiction books and good instructional or reference books that have gone out of print before their time. Send a sample copy, sales information, and reviews, if available. If you have a good idea for a reference book that can be updated annually, try us. We're willing to consider freelance compilers of such works." No cookbooks, diet/exercise, psychology self-help, health or parenting books. Query with outline and sample chapters. Reviews artwork/photos as part of ms package.
**Recent Title(s):** *Organizing Your Family History Search*, by Sharon DeBartolo Carmack (genealogy).
**Tips:** "Keep the imprint name well in mind when submitting ideas to us. What is the 'better way' you're proposing? How will readers benefit *immediately* from the instruction and information you're giving them?"

**[N] [⊼] BICK PUBLISHING HOUSE**, 307 Neck Rd., Madison CT 06443. (203)245-0073. Fax: (203)245-5990. E-mail: bickpubhse@aol.com. **Acquisitions:** Dale Carlson, president (psychology); Hannah Carlson (special needs, disabilities); Irene Ruth (wildlife). Estab. 1994. Publishes trade paperback originals. **Publishes 4 titles/year. Receives 6-12 queries and mss/year. 55% of books from first-time authors; 55% from unagented writers. Pays 10% royalty on retail price. Offers $500-1,000 advance.** Publishes book 1 year after acceptance of ms. Reports in 1 month on queries, 2 months on proposals, 3 months on mss. Book catalog free. Manuscript guidelines for #10 SASE.
   O─╖ Bick Publishing House publishes step-by-step, easy-to-read professional information for the general adult public about physical, psychological and emotional disabilities or special needs, teenage psychology and also about wildlife rehabilitation.
**Nonfiction:** Subjects include animals (wildlife rehabilitation), health/medicine (disability/special needs), teen psychology. Submit proposal package, including outline, 3 sample chapters, résumé with SASE. Reviews artwork/photos as part of ms package. Send photocopies.
**Recent Title(s):** *Girls Are Equal Too: Teenage Girls Survival Book*, by Dale Carlson.

**[N] [⊼] BIOMED BOOKS**, 5801 Christie Ave., Suite 400, Emeryville CA 94608. (510)450-1657. Fax: (510)450-1336. E-mail: biocorp@aol.com. Website: http://www.biomedbooks.com. **Acquisitions:** Randy Malat, managing editor (health, medicine). Publishes trade paperback originals. **Publishes 5 titles/year. Receives 30 queries/year. 20% of books from first-time authors. Pays 5-10% royalty on retail price. May offer $2,000-5,000 advance.** Publishes book 3 months after acceptance of ms. Accepts simultaneous submissions. Reports in 1 month on queries.
   O─╖ Biomed Books is interested in scientifically sound coverage of health topics (e.g., nutrition, weight loss, women's health, cancer prevention, mind-body care and Internet medicine). Books are written by and geared toward licensed health professionals (e.g., nurses, physicians and dental hygienists).
**Nonfiction:** Books for continuing health education. Submit proposal package, including outline, 2 sample chapters and curriculum vitae. Reviews artwork/photos as part of ms package. Send photocopies.
**Recent Title(s):** *No Ordinary Pill: Vitamin E and Health*, *Complementary Medicine: A Practical Primer*, by Mary O'Brien, M.D.
**Tips:** "We sell primarily to health professionals. Books must be suitable for continuing education credits. We may expand into mass market sales by the year 2000."

**BIRCH BROOK PRESS**, P.O. Box 81, Delhi NY 13753. **Acquisitions:** Tom Tolnay, editor. Estab. 1982. Publishes hardcover and trade paperback originals. **Publishes 4-6 titles/year. Receives hundreds of queries and mss/year. 95% of books from unagented writers. Royalty varies. Offers modest advance.** Publishes book 1 year after acceptance of ms. Accepts simultaneous submission, if informed. Reports in 1 month on queries, 2 months on mss. Book catalog free. Manuscript guidelines for #10 SASE.
   O─╖ Birch Brook Press is a popular culture and literary publisher of handcrafted books and art, featuring letterpress editions produced at its own printing, typesetting and binding facility. Currently emphasizing anthologies.
**Imprint(s):** Birch Brook Impressions.
**Nonfiction:** Literary. Subjects include literature, books on books, baseball, fly fishing, opera. "We have a very limited nonfiction publishing program, mostly generated inhouse in anthologies." Query with SASE. Reviews artwork as part of ms package. Send photocopies to Frank C. Eckmair, art director.
**Fiction:** Literary, popular culture. "Mostly we do anthologies around a particular theme generated inhouse." Query with synopsis with sample chapter and SASE.
**Poetry:** Submit complete ms.

• This publisher recently took over the poetry publishing company Persephone Press.

**Recent Titles:** *The Derelict Genius of Martin M*, by Frank Fagan (fiction); *Waiting On Pentecost*, by Tom Smith (poetry).

**Tips:** "Audience is college educated, readers and collectors. Our books are mostly letterpress editions printed from metal type and therefore tend to be short with content suitable to antique printing methods."

**BIRCH LANE PRESS**, Carol Publishing, 120 Enterprise Ave., Secaucus NJ 07094. (201)583-6554. Fax: (201)271-7895. **Acquisitions:** Hillel Black, editorial director. Estab. 1989. Publishes hardcover and trade paperback originals. **Publishes 100 titles/year. 10% of books first-time authors; 10% from unagented writers. Pays 5-15% royalty on retail price. Offers $5,000-20,000 advance.** Publishes book 18 months after acceptance of ms. Accepts simultaneous submissions. Reports in 2 months on proposals.

○→ Birch Lane publishes general interest nonfiction for an adult audience.

**Nonfiction:** Subjects include business/economics, foods/nutrition, ethnic (African-American, Judaica), gambling, government/politics, history, humor, music/dance, New Age, popular culture. Query with outline, 2-3 sample chapters and SASE. Reviews artwork/photos as part of ms package. Send photocopies.

**Recent Title(s):** *The Financially Independent Woman*, by Barbara Lee (investment).

**N: BK MK PRESS**, University of Missouri-Kansas City, 5101 Rockhill Rd., Kansas City MO 64110-2499. (816)235-2558. Fax: (816)235-2611. E-mail: bkmk@umkc.edu. **Acquisitions:** Jim McKinley, executive editor (fiction/nonfiction); Michelle Boisseau, associate editor (poetry); Ben Furnish, managing editor. Estab. 1971. Publishes hardcover and trade paperback originals. **Publishes 5-6 titles/year. Receives 50-60 queries and 350 mss/year. 40% of books from first-time authors; 70% from unagented writers. Pays 10% royalty on wholesale price. No advance.** Publishes book 1 year after acceptance of ms. Accepts simultaneous submissions. Reports in 2 months on queries, 6 months on mss. Manuscript guidelines for #10 SASE.

○→ Bk Mk Press publishes fine literataure.

**Nonfiction:** Subjects include creative nonfiction. Query with SASE.

**Fiction:** Literary, poetry in translation, short story collections. Submit proposal package, including 50 pages, cover letter and SASE.

**Poetry:** Submit 10 sample poems.

**Recent Titles:** *Eyes Open in the Dark*, by Conger Beasley, Jr. (essays); *Body and Blood*, by Philip Russell (novel of linked stories); *Fall from Grace*, by Christopher Buckley (poetry).

**Tips:** "We skew toward readers of literature, particularly contemporary writing. Because of our limited number of titles published per year, we discourage apprentice writers or 'scattershot' submissions."

**BLACKBIRCH PRESS, INC.**, P.O. Box 3573, Woodbridge CT 06525. E-mail: staff@blackbirch.com. Website: http://www.blackbirch.com. **Acquisitions:** Bruce Glassman, editorial director. Estab. 1990. Publishes hardcover and trade paperback originals. **Publishes 30-40 titles/year. Receives 400 queries and 75 mss/year. 100% of books from unagented writers. Pays 4-8% royalty on wholesale price or makes outright purchase. Offers $1,000-5,000 advance.** Publishes book 1 year after acceptance of ms. Accepts simultaneous submissions. Replies only if interested. Manuscript guidelines free. "We cannot return submissions or send guidelines/replies without an enclosed SASE."

○→ Blackbirch Press publishes juvenile and young adult nonfiction and fiction titles.

**Nonfiction:** Children's/juvenile: biography, illustrated books, reference. Subjects include animals, anthropology/archeology, art/architecture, education, health/medicine, history, nature/environment, science, sports, travel, women's issues/studies. "No proposals for adult readers, please." Publishes in series—6-8 books at a time. Query with SASE. *No unsolicited mss or proposals. No phone calls.* Cover letters and résumés are useful for identifying new authors. Reviews artwork/photos as part of ms package. Send photocopies.

**Recent Title(s):** *Madeline Albright: U.S. Secretary of State*, by Rose Blue and Corrine J. Naden (biography); *Monsieur Thermidor*, by Richard Kidd (fiction).

**JOHN F. BLAIR, PUBLISHER**, 1406 Plaza Dr., Winston-Salem NC 27103-1470. (336)768-1374. Fax: (336)768-9194. **Acquisitions:** Carolyn Sakowski, editor. Estab. 1954. Publishes hardcover originals and trade paperbacks. **Publishes 15 titles/year. Receives 2,000 submissions/year. 20-30% of books from first-time authors; 90% from unagented writers. Royalty negotiable.** Publishes book 18 months after acceptance. Reports in 3 months. Book catalog and ms guidelines for 9×12 SAE with 5 first-class stamps.

○→ John F. Blair publishes in the areas of travel, history, folklore and the outdoors for a general trade audience, most of whom live or travel in the southeastern U.S.

**Nonfiction:** Especially interested in travel guides dealing with the Southeastern US. Also interested in Civil War, outdoors, travel and Americana; query on other nonfiction topics. Looks for utility and significance. Submit outline and first 3 chapters. Reviews artwork/photos as part of ms package.

**Fiction:** "We publish one work of fiction per year relating to the Southeastern U.S." No category fiction, juvenile fiction, picture books or poetry. *Writer's Market* recommends sending a query with SASE first.

**BLOOMBERG PRESS**, Bloomberg L.P., 100 Business Park Dr., P.O. Box 888, Princeton NJ 08542-0888. Website: http://www.bloomberg.com. **Acquisitions:** Jared Kieling, editorial director; Jacqueline Murphy, senior acquisitions editor (Bloomberg Professional Library). Estab. 1995. Publishes hardcover and trade paperback originals. **Publishes 12-**

**18 titles/year. Receives 90 queries and 17 mss/year. 45% of books from unagented writers. Pays negotiable, competitive royalty. Offers negotiable advance.** Publishes book 9 months after acceptance of ms. Accepts simultaneous submissions. Reports in 1 month on queries. Book catalog for 10×13 SAE with 5 first-class stamps.

> **○→** Bloomberg Press publishes professional books for practitioners in the financial markets and finance and investing for informed personal investors, entrepreneurs and consumers. "We publish commercially successful books of impressively high quality that stand out clearly from the competition by their brevity, ease of use, sophistication, and abundance of practical tips and strategies; books readers need, will use and appreciate."

**Imprint(s):** Bloomberg Personal Bookshelf, Bloomberg Professional Library, Bloomberg Small Business.

**Nonfiction:** How-to, reference, technical. Subjects include small business, current affairs, money/finance, personal finance and investing for consumers, professional books on finance, investment and financial services. "We are looking for authorities and experienced service journalists who know their subjects and beats cold. We are looking for original solutions to widespread problems and books offering fresh investment opportunities. Do not send us management books—we don't publish them—or unfocused books containing general information already covered by one or more well-established backlist books in the marketplace." Submit outline, sample chapters and SAE with sufficient postage.

**Recent Title(s):** *A Commonsense Guide to Your 401(k)*, by Mary Rowland (personal finance).

**Tips:** "*Bloomberg Professional Library:* Audience is upscale financial professionals—traders, dealers, brokers, planners and advisors, financial managers, money managers, company executives, sophisticated investors, such as people who lease a BLOOMBERG system. *Bloomberg Personal Bookshelf:* audience is upscale consumers and individual investors, as well as all categories listed for the Professional Library—readers of our magazine *Bloomberg Personal Finance*. Authors are experienced business and financial journalists and/or financial professionals nationally prominent in their specialty for some time who have proven an ability to write a successful book. Research Bloomberg and look at our specially formatted books in a library or bookstore, read *Bloomberg Personal Finance* and *Bloomberg* magazines and peruse our website."

**N. BLUE HERON PUBLISHING**, 1234 SW Stark St., Portland OR 97205. (503)221-6841. Fax: (503)221-6843. E-mail: bhp@teleport.com. Website: http://www.teleport.com/~bhp. **Acquisitions:** Dennis Stovall, president; Robyn Andersen, executive editor/associate publisher. Estab. 1985. Publishes trade paperback originals and reprints. **Publishes 6 titles/year.** Reports in 6 weeks. Book catalog for #10 SASE.

> **○→** Blue Heron Publishing publishes books on writing and the teaching of writing, young adult and adult literature, western outdoor photography, and leftwing novels of mystery and suspense. Now considering ethnic cookbooks. Currently emphasizing books on writing and the teaching of writing, mysteries. De-emphasizing young adult.

**Nonfiction:** Looking for books that sell in educational markets as well as the trade. Query with SASE.

**Recent title(s):** *The Sell-Your-Novel Tool Kit*, by Elizabeth Lyon.

**BLUE MOON BOOKS, INC.**, Avalon Publishing Group, 841 Broadway, New York NY 10003. (212)614-7880. Fax: (212)614-7887. E-mail: tmpress@aol.com. Website: http://www.bluemoonbooks.com. **Acquisitions:** Gayle Watkins, editor. Estab. 1987. Publishes trade paperback and mass market paperback originals. **Publishes 30-40 titles/year. Receives 1,000 queries and 500 mss/year. Pays 7½-10% royalty on retail price. Offers $500 and up advance.** Publishes book 1 year after acceptance of ms. Reports in 2 months. Book catalog free.

> **○→** "Blue Moon Books is strictly an erotic press; largely fetish-oriented material, B&D, S&M, etc."

**Nonfiction:** Trade erotic and sexual nonfiction. *No unsolicited mss.*

**Fiction:** Erotica. *No unsolicited mss.*

**Recent Title(s):** *Patong Sisters: An American Woman's View of the Bangkok Sex World*, by Cleo Odzer; *J and Seventeen*, by Kenzaburo Oe.

**BLUE POPPY PRESS**, 3450 Penrose Place, Suite 110, Boulder CO 80301. (303)447-8372. Fax: (303)245-8362. E-mail: bluepp@compuserve.com. Website: http://www.bluepoppy.com. **Acquisitions:** Bob Flaws, editor-in-chief. Estab. 1981. Publishes hardcover and trade paperback originals. **Publishes 9-12 titles/year. Receives 50-100 queries and 20 mss/year. 40-50% of books from first-time authors; 100% from unagented writers. Pays 10-15% royalty "of sales price at all discount levels."** Publishes book 1 year after acceptance of ms. Reports in 1 month. Book catalog and ms guidelines free.

> **○→** Blue Poppy Press is dedicated to expanding and improving the English language literature on acupuncture and Asian medicine for both professional practitioners and lay readers.

**Nonfiction:** Self-help, technical, textbook related to acupuncture and Oriental medicine. "We only publish books on acupuncture and Oriental medicine by authors who can read Chinese and have a minimum of five years clinical experience. We also require all our authors to use Wiseman's *Glossary of Chinese Medical Terminology* as their standard for technical terms." Query or submit outline, 1 sample chapter and SASE.

**Recent Title(s):** *Managing Menopause Naturally*, by Honora Wolfe.

**Tips:** Audience is "practicing acupuncturists, interested in alternatives in healthcare, preventive medicine, Chinese philosophy and medicine."

**THE BLUE SKY PRESS**, Scholastic Inc., 555 Broadway, New York NY 10012. (212)343-6100. Fax: (212)343-4535. Website: http://www.scholastic.com. Editorial Director: Bonnie Verburg. Associate Editor: Garen Thomas. **Acquisitions:** The Editors. Estab. 1982. Publishes hardcover originals. **Publishes 15-20 titles/year. Receives 2,500 queries/year. 1% of books from first-time authors; 75% from unagented writers. Pays 10% royalty on wholesale price, between**

**authors and illustrators.** Publishes book 2 1/2 years after acceptance of ms. Reports in 6 months on queries.

O╍ Blue Sky Press publishes primarily juvenile picture books—cutting edge, exciting books for children. Currently de-emphasizing historical fiction.

**Fiction:** Juvenile: adventure, fantasy, historical, humor, mainstream/contemporary, picture books, multicultural, folktales. Query with SASE.

● Because of a large backlog of books, The Blue Sky Press is not accepting unsolicited submissions.

**Recent Title(s):** *No, David!*, by David Shannon (fiction).

**BNA BOOKS,** The Bureau of National Affairs, Inc., 1250 23rd St. NW, Washington DC 20037-1165. (202)833-7470. Fax: (202)833-7490. E-mail: books@bna.com. Website: http://www.bna.com/bnabooks. **Acquisitions:** Tim Darby, new product director (labor and employment law, employee benefits); Jim Fattibene, acquisitions manager (legal practice, intellectual property, health law). Estab. 1929. Publishes hardcover and softcover originals. **Publishes 35 titles/year. Receives 200 submissions/year. 20% of books from first-time authors; 95% from unagented writers. Pays 5-15% royalty on net cash receipts. Offers $500 average advance.** Publishes book 1 year after acceptance of ms. Accepts simultaneous submissions. Reports in 3 months on queries. Book catalog and ms guidelines free.

O╍ BNA Books publishes professional reference books written by lawyers, for lawyers. Currently emphasizing health law. De-emphasizing environmental law.

**Nonfiction:** Legal reference, professional/scholarly. Subjects include labor and employment law, environmental law, legal practice, labor relations and intellectual property law. No fiction, biographies, bibliographies, cookbooks, religion books, humor or trade books. Submit detailed table of contents or outline.

**Recent Title(s):** *Patents and the Federal Circuit*, by Robert Harmon.

**Tips:** "Our audience is made up of practicing lawyers and business executives; managers, federal, state, and local government administrators; unions; and law libraries. We look for authoritative and comprehensive works that can be supplemented or revised every year or two on subjects of interest to those audiences."

**BOA EDITIONS, LTD.**, 260 East Ave., Rochester NY 14604. (716)546-3410. Fax: (716)546-3913. E-mail: boaedit@frontiernet.net. Website: http://www.boaeditions.org. **Acquisitions:** Steven Huff, publisher/managing editor; Tom Ward, editor. Estab. 1976. Publishes hardcover and trade paperback originals. **Publishes 10 titles/year. Receives 1,000 queries and 700 mss/year. 15% of books from first-time authors; 90% from unagented writers. Pays 7½-10% royalty on retail price. Advance varies, usually $500.** Publishes book 18 months after acceptance of ms. Accepts simultaneous submissions. Reports in 1 month on queries, 4 months on mss. Book catalog and ms guidelines free.

O╍ BOA Editions publishes distinguished collections of poetry and poetry in translation. "Our goal is to publish the finest American contemporary poetry and poetry in translation."

**Poetry:** Accepting mss for publication in 2001 and beyond. Query with full ms and SASE.

**Recent Title(s):** *Plus Shipping*, by Bob Hicok.

**Tips:** "Readers who, like Whitman, expect of the poet to 'indicate more than the beauty and dignity which always attach to dumb real objects . . . they expect him to indicate the path between reality and their souls,' are the audience of BOA's books."

**BONUS BOOKS, INC.**, Precept Press, 160 E. Illinois St., Chicago IL 60611. (312)467-0580. Fax: (312)467-9271. Website: http://www.bonus-books.com. Managing Editor: Andrea Rackel. **Acquisitions:** Jean Kang and Benjamin Strong, assistant editors. Estab. 1985. Publishes hardcover and trade paperback originals and reprints. **Publishes 30 titles/year. Receives 400-500 submissions/year. 40% of books from first-time authors; 60% from unagented writers. Royalties vary. Rarely offers advance.** Publishes book 8 months after acceptance. Accepts simultaneous submissions, if so noted. Reports in 2 months on queries. Book catalog for 9×11 SASE. Manuscript guidelines for #10 SASE.

O╍ Bonus Books is a publishing and audio/video company featuring subjects ranging from human interest to sports to gambling.

**Nonfiction:** Subjects include automotive/self-help, biography/current affairs, broadcasting, business/self-help, Chicago people and places, collectibles, cookbooks, education/self-help, fund raising, handicapping winners, home and health, humor, entertainment, regional, sports and women's issues/studies. Query with outline, sample chapters and SASE. Reviews artwork/photos as part of ms package. All submissions and queries must include SASE.

**Recent Title(s):** *Method Marketing*, by D. Hatch.

**BOOK WORLD, INC./BLUE STAR PRODUCTIONS**, (formerly Blue Star Productions), Bookworld, Inc., 9666 E. Riggs Rd., #194, Sun Lakes AZ 85248. (602)895-7995. Fax: (602)895-6991. E-mail: bkworld@aol.com. Website: http://www.bkworld.com. **Acquisitions:** Barbara DeBolt, editor. Publishes trade and mass market paperback originals. **Publishes 10-12 titles/year. Receives thousands of queries and mss/year. 75% of books from first-time authors; 90% from unagented writers. Pays royalty on wholesale or retail price. No advance for new authors.** Reports in 8 months on queries, 16 months on mss. Book catalog on website. Manuscript guidelines for #10 SASE or on website.

O╍ Book World, Inc. publishes mainstream and specialty books. Blue Star Productions focuses on UFOs, the paranormal, metaphysical, angels, psychic phenomena, visionary fiction, spiritual—both fiction and nonfiction.

**Nonfiction/Fiction:** UFO-related subjects, anything pertaining to the paranormal. "To save time and reduce the amount of paper submissions, we are encouraging e-mail queries and submissions (no downloads or attachments), or disk submissions formatted for Windows 95, using Word Perfect or Microsoft Word. Our response will be via e-mail so no SASE will be needed in these instances, unless the disk needs to be returned. For those without computer access, a

SASE is a must and we prefer seeing the actual manuscript or first three chapters vs. a query letter. *No phone queries.*"
**Recent Title(s):** *The Reindeer Boy*, by Christopher Harding; *Shadow of Time*, by Valerie Kirkwood.
**Tips:** "Know our guidelines. We are now accepting manuscripts on disk using WordPerfect 6.0 and higher."

**BOOKCRAFT, INC.**, 2405 W. Orton Circle, West Valley UT 84119. (801)908-3400. **Acquisitions:** Cory H. Maxwell, editorial manager. Estab. 1942. Publishes hardcover and trade paperback originals. **Publishes 75 titles/year. Receives 800-1,000 submissions/year. 20% of books from first-time authors; virtually 100% from unagented writers. Pays standard 7½-10-12½-15% royalty on net receipts. Rarely gives advance.** Publishes book 6 months after acceptance. Accepts simultaneous submissions. Reports in about 2 months. Book catalog and ms guidelines for #10 SASE.
  • "We publish well-written, accessible, inspirational books that help the reader understand, appreciate, and follow the principles of the Gospel of Jesus Christ."
**Imprint:** Parliament.
**Nonfiction:** "We publish for members of The Church of Jesus Christ of Latter-Day Saints (Mormons) and our books are closely oriented to the faith and practices of the LDS church, and we will be glad to review such mss. Those which have merely a general religious appeal are not acceptable. Ideal book lengths range from about 100-300 pages or so, depending on subject, presentation, and age level. We look for a fresh approach—rehashes of well-known concepts or doctrines not acceptable. Manuscripts should be anecdotal unless truly scholarly or on a specialized subject. We do not publish anti-Mormon works. We also publish short and moderate length books for children and young adults, and fiction as well as nonfiction. These reflect LDS principles without being 'preachy'; must be motivational. 50,000-100,000 words is about the right length, though good, longer manuscripts will be considered. We publish only 5 or 6 new juvenile titles annually. No poetry, plays, personal philosophizings, or family histories." Biography, childrens/juvenile, coffee table book, how-to, humor, reference, self-help. Subjects include: child guidance/parenting, history, religion. Query with full ms and SASE. *Writer's Market* recommends sending a query with SASE first. Reviews artwork/photos as part of ms package. Send photocopies.
**Fiction:** Should be oriented to LDS faith and practices. Adventure, historical, juvenile, literary, mainstream/contemporary, mystery, religious, romance, short story collections, suspense, western, young adult. Submit full ms with SASE. *Writer's Market* recommends sending a query with SASE first.
**Recent Title(s):** *A Convert's Guide to Mormon Life*, by Clark and Kathryn Kidd (nonfiction); *The Work and the Glory* Series, by Gerald N. Lund (historical fiction for adults).
**Tips:** "The competition in the area of fiction is much more intense than it has ever been before. We receive two or three times as many quality fiction manuscripts as we did even as recently as five years ago."

**[N] [◻] BOOKEDUP.COM**, P.O. Box 1539, New York NY 10021. E-mail: info@bookedup.com. Website: http://www.bookedup.com. **Acquisitions:** Richard Hurowitz. **Publishes 100 titles/year. Pays negotiable royalties. No advance.** Publishes book 3 months after acceptance of ms. Accepts simultaneous submissions. Reports in 1 month on queries. Book catalog and ms guidelines on website.
  • Bookedup.com publishes books in electronic form for purchase and download off the Internet.
**Nonfiction:** Biography, children's juvenile, coffee table book, cookbook, gift book, how-to, humor, illustrated book, multimedia (electronic), reference, self-help, technical, textbook. Subjects include agriculture/horticulture, Americana, animals, anthropology/archaeology, art/architecture, business/economics, child guidance/parenting, computers/electronics, cooking/foods/nutrition, creative nonfiction, education, ethnic, gardening, government/politics, health/medicine, history, hobbies, language/literature, memoirs, military/war, money/finance, multicultural, music/dance, nature/environment, philosophy, photography, psychology, recreation, regional, religion, science, sex, sociology, software, spirituality, sports, translation, travel, women's issues/studies. Query with SASE.
**Fiction:** Adventure, comic books, confession, erotica, ethnic, experimental, fantasy, feminist, gothic, hi-lo, historical, horror, humor, juvenile, literary, mainstream/contemporary, military/war, multicultural, multimedia, mystery, occult, picture books, plays, poetry, poetry in translation, regional, romance, science fiction, short story collections, spiritual, sports, suspense, translation, western, young adult. Query with SASE.
**Recent Titles:** *Shame*, by Sam Cohen (memoir); *Intimate Details*, by Robert Lieberman (short story collection).
**Tips:** "We are interested in quality manuscripts of all kinds. Our authors get global distribution over the Internet. Submissions should be made on a non-returnable floppy disk in word processor format. Our primary goal is to publish well-written books. We generally license only electronic rights so authors are free to find a print publisher as well."

**[N] [★] BOOKHOME PUBLISHING**, P.O. Box 5900, Navarre FL 32566. (850)936-4050. Fax: (850)939-4953. E-mail: bookhome@gte.net. Website: http://www.bookhome.com. **Acquisitions:** Scott Gregory, publisher (small business, relationships, lifestyles, self-help). Publishes hardcover and trade paperback originals. **Publishes 5 titles/year. Receives 100 queries and 100 mss/year. 50% of books from first-time authors; 50% from unagented writers. Pays 7-12% royalty on wholesale price. Offers $0-1,000 advance.** Publishes book 1 year after acceptance of ms. Accepts simultaneous submissions. Reports in 2 months on proposals. Book catalog for #10 SAE with 2 first-class stamps. Manuscript guidelines for #10 SASE.
  • "Our readers want to live better lives and build better businesses."
**Nonfiction:** How-to, self-help. Subjects include business/economics, child guidance/parenting, creative nonfiction, lifestyles, career. Submit proposal package, including outline, marketing plan, 2 sample chapters and SASE.
**Recent Title(s):** *Ten Commandments of Small-Business Success*, by Marguerite Kirk.
**Tips:** "Ask for our guidelines (include SASE) or review our guidelines at our website. Do your homework, then make

your proposal irresistible! Make sure a publicity plan is part of your proposal. We work hard to tell the world about our wonderful books, and we expect our authors to do the same."

**A** **BOULEVARD**, Penguin Putnam Inc., 375 Hudson St., New York NY 10014. (212)366-2000. Website: http://www.penguinputnam.com. **Acquisitions:** Elizabeth Beier, editorial director. Estab. 1995. Publishes trade paperback and mass market paperback originals and reprints. **Publishes 85 titles/year.** *Agented submissions only.*

**BOWLING GREEN STATE UNIVERSITY POPULAR PRESS**, Bowling Green State University, Bowling Green OH 43403-1000. (419)372-7866. Fax: (419)372-8095. Website: http://www.bgsu.edu/colleges/library/press/press.html. **Acquisitions:** (Ms.) Pat Browne. Estab. 1967. Publishes hardcover originals and trade paperback originals and reprints. **Publishes 25 titles/year. Receives 400 submissions/year. 50% of books from first-time authors; 100% from unagented writers. Pays 5-12% royalty on wholesale price or makes outright purchase.** Publishes book 9 months after acceptance of ms. Reports in 3 months. Book catalog and ms guidelines free.
**Nonfiction:** Biography, reference, textbook. Subjects include Americana, art/architecture, ethnic, history, language/literature, regional, sports, women's issues/studies. Submit outline and 3 sample chapters.
**Recent Title(s):** *Stephen King's America*, by Jonathan Davis.
**Tips:** "Our audience includes university professors, students, and libraries."

**BOYDS MILLS PRESS**, *Highlights for Children*, 815 Church St., Honesdale PA 18431-1895. (570)253-1164. Publisher: Kent L. Brown. **Acquisitions:** Beth Troop, manuscript coordinator; Larry Rosler, editorial director. Estab. 1990. Publishes hardcover originals and trade paperback originals and reprints. **Publishes 50 titles/year; imprint publishes 2-6 titles/year. Receives 10,000 queries and mss/year. 20% of books are from first-time authors; 20% from unagented writers. Pays 8-15% royalty on retail price. Advance varies.** Accepts simultaneous submissions. Reports in 1 month. Book catalog and ms guidelines for $2 postage and SAE.
　　○━ Boyds Mill Press, the book publishing arm of *Highlights for Children*, publishes a wide range of children's books of literary merit, from preschool to young adult. Currently emphasizing pre-school picture books, *not* board books.
**Imprint(s):** Wordsong (poetry).
**Nonfiction:** Juvenile subjects include agriculture/horticulture, animals, ethnic, history, hobbies, nature/environment, regional, religion, sports, travel. "Nonfiction should be accurate, tailored to young audience. Accompanying art is preferred, as is simple, narrative style, but in compelling, evocative language. Too many overwrite for the young audience and get bogged down in minutia. Boyds Mills Press is not interested in manuscripts depicting violence, explicit sexuality, racism of any kind or which promote hatred. We also are not the right market for self-help books or romances." Query with proposal package, including outline, 1 sample chapter, some art samples (photos, drawings), with SASE.
**Fiction:** Adventure, ethnic, historical, humor, juvenile, mystery, picture books, suspense, western, young adult. "Don't let a personal agenda dominate to the detriment of plot. In short, tell a good story. Too many writers miss the essence of a good story: beginning, middle, end; conflict and resolution because they're more interested in making a sociological statement." Submit outline/synopsis and 3 sample chapters for novel or complete ms for picture book.
**Poetry:** "Poetry should be appropriate for young audiences, clever, fun language, with easily understood meaning. Too much poetry is either too simple and static in meaning or too obscure." Submit 6 sample poems. Collections should have a unifying theme.
**Recent Title(s):** *Guess Whose Shadow*, by Stephen R. Swinburne (nonfiction); *Rusty, Trusty Tractor*, by Joy Cowley (fiction); *The Purchase of Small Secrets*, by David Harrison.
**Tips:** "Our audience is pre-school to young adult. Concentrate first on your writing. Polish it. Then—and only then—select a market. We need primarily picture books with fresh ideas and characters—avoid worn themes of 'coming-of-age,' 'new sibling,' and self-help ideas. We are always interested in multicultural settings. Please—no anthropomorphic characters."

**★** **BRANDEN PUBLISHING CO., INC.**, 17 Station St., Box 843, Brookline Village MA 02447. Fax: (617)734-2046. Website: http://www.branden.com. **Acquisitions:** Adolph Caso, editor. Estab. 1965. Publishes hardcover and trade paperback originals, reprints and software. **Publishes 15 titles/year. Receives 1,000 submissions/year. 80% of books from first-time authors; 90% from unagented writers. Pays 5-10% royalty on net. Offers $1,000 maximum advance.** Publishes book 10 months after acceptance. Reports in 1 month. *Writer's Market* recommends allowing 2 months for reply.
　　○━ Branden publishes books by or about women, children, military, Italian-American or African-American themes.
**Imprint(s):** International Pocket Library and Popular Technology, Four Seas and Brashear.
**Nonfiction:** Biography, illustrated book, juvenile, reference, technical, textbook. Subjects include Americana, art, computers, health, history, music, photography, politics, sociology, software, classics. Especially looking for "about 10 manuscripts on national and international subjects, including biographies of well-known individuals." No religion or philosophy. Paragraph query only with author's vita and SASE. *No unsolicited mss.* No telephone inquiries, e-mail or fax inquiries. Reviews artwork/photos as part of ms package.
**Fiction:** Ethnic (histories, integration); religious (historical-reconstructive). No science, mystery or pornography. Paragraph query only with author's vita and SASE. *No unsolicited mss.* No telephone, fax or e-mail inquiries.
**Recent Title(s):** *Straddling the Border*, by Martha Cummings (summer stay in Italy), *Snowball in Hell*, by Roland Hopkins (Nazi mystery).

**GEORGE BRAZILLER, INC.**, 171 Madison Ave., Suite 1103, New York NY 10016. (212)889-0909. Publisher: George Braziller. **Acquisitions:** Mary Taveras, production editor. Estab. 1955. Publishes hardcover originals, trade paperback originals and reprints. **Publishes 25 titles/year. Receives 300 queries and 60 mss/year. 2% of books from first-time authors; 80% from unagented writers. Pays standard royalty: 8% paperback, 10-15% hardcover.** Publishes book 10 months after acceptance of ms. Reports in 3 months on proposals. Book catalog and ms guidelines free.

**Nonfiction:** Art books. Subjects include art/architecture, history, language/literature. "We do very little nonfiction but, as we don't publish in specific categories only, we are willing to consider a wide range of subjects." Submit outline with 4 sample chapters and SASE. Reviews artwork/photos as part of ms package. Send photocopies.

**Fiction:** Ethnic, gay/lesbian, literary. "We rarely do fiction but when we have published novels, they have mostly been literary novels." Submit 4-6 sample chapters with SASE.

**Recent Title(s):** *Michelangelo: The Sistine Chapel Ceiling, Rome*, by Loren Partridge (art).

**BREVET PRESS, INC.**, P.O. Box 1404, Sioux Falls SD 57101. **Acquisitions:** Donald P. Mackintosh, publisher (business); Peter E. Reid, managing editor (technical); A. Melton, editor (Americana); B. Mackintosh, editor (history). Estab. 1972. Publishes hardcover and paperback originals and reprints. **Publishes 15 titles/year. Receives 40 submissions/year. 50% of books from first-time authors; 100% from unagented writers. Pays 5% royalty. Offers $1,000 average advance.** Publishes book 1 year after acceptance. Accepts simultaneous submissions. Reports in 2 months. Book catalog free.

O⌐ Brevet Books seeks nonfiction with "market potential and literary excellence."

**Nonfiction:** Specializes in business management, history, place names, and historical marker series. Subjects include Americana, business, history, technical books. Query with SASE. "After query, detailed instructions will follow if we are interested." Reviews artwork/photos as part of ms package. Send photocopies.

**Tips:** "Keep sexism out of the manuscripts."

**BREWERS PUBLICATIONS**, Association of Brewers, 736 Pearl St., Boulder CO 80302. (303)447-0816. Fax: (303)447-2825. E-mail: bp@aob.org. Website: http://beertown.org. **Acquisitions:** Toni Knapp, publisher. Estab. 1986. Publishes hardcover and trade paperback originals. **Publishes 8 titles/year. 50% of books from first-time authors; 50% from unagented writers. Pays royalty on net receipts. Advance negotiated.** Publishes book within 18 months of acceptance of ms. Accepts simultaneous submissions. Reports in 3 months. Book catalog free.

O⌐ Brewers Publications is the largest publisher of books on beer-related subjects.

**Nonfiction:** "We publish books on history, art, culture, literature, brewing and science of beer. In a broad sense, this also includes biographies, humor, cooking and suspense/mystery fiction." Query first with brief proposal and SASE.

**Fiction:** Suspense/mystery with a beer theme. Query.

**Recent Title(s):** *Sacred and Herbal Healing Beers: The Secrets of Ancient Fermentation*, by Stephen Buehner (New Age/health).

**Tips:** "We're moving into suspense fiction: Beer must be at the central theme and must 'educate'—as in other niche/ genre mystery fiction such as culinary, etc."

**BRIDGE WORKS PUBLISHING CO.**, Box 1798, Bridge Lane, Bridgehampton NY 11932. (516)537-3418. Fax: (516)537-5092. **Acquisitions:** Barbara Phillips, editor/publisher. Estab. 1992. Publishes hardcover originals and reprints. **Publishes 4-6 titles/year. Receives 1,000 queries and mss/year. 50% of books from first-time authors; 80% from unagented writers. Pays 10% royalty on retail price. Offers $1,000 advance.** Publishes book 1 year after acceptance of ms. Reports in 1 month on queries and proposals, 2 months on mss. Book catalog and ms guidelines for #10 SASE.

O⌐ "We are a very small press dedicated to quality fiction and nonfiction. We are not interested in mass market material, but look for writing that is original and inventive, as well as entertaining."

**Nonfiction:** Biography, history, language/literature, philosophy, psychology, sociology. "We *do not* accept multiple submissions. We prefer a query first." Query or submit outline and proposal package with SASE. Reviews artwork/ photos as part of ms package. Send photocopies.

**Fiction:** Historical, literary, mystery, short story collections. "Query with SASE before submitting ms. First-time authors should have manuscripts vetted by freelance editors before submitting. We do not accept or read multiple submissions." Query or submit synopsis and 2 sample chapters with SASE.

**Poetry:** "We publish only *one* collection every 5 years." Query and submit sample poems.

**Recent Title(s):** *Ending the War on Drugs: A Solution for America*, by Dirk Chase Eldredge (nonfiction); *The Road to the Island*, by Tom Hazuka (fiction).

**Tips:** "Query letters should be one page, giving general subject or plot of the book and stating who the writer feels is the audience for the work. In the case of novels or poetry, a portion of the work could be enclosed."

**BRIGHTON PUBLICATIONS, INC.**, P.O. Box 120706, St. Paul MN 55112-0706. (612)636-2220. Fax: (612)636-2220. **Acquisitions:** Sharon E. Dlugosch, editor. Estab. 1977. Publishes trade paperback originals. **Publishes 4 titles/year. Receives 100 queries and 100 mss/year. 50% of books from first-time authors; 100% from unagented writers. Pays 10% royalty on wholesale price.** Accepts simultaneous submissions. Reports in 3 months. Book catalog and ms guidelines for #10 SASE.

O⌐ Brighton Publications publishes books on celebration or seasonal how-to parties and anything that will help to give a better party such as activities, games, favors, and themes. Currently emphasizing games for meetings, annual parties, picnics, etc., celebration themes, and party/special event planning.

**Nonfiction:** How-to, games, tabletop, party themes. "We're interested in topics telling how to live any part of life well. Query. Submit outline and 2 sample chapters.

**Recent Title(s):** *Wedding Plans: 50 Themes for the Wedding of Your Dreams*, by Sharon Dlugosch.

**BRISTOL FASHION PUBLICATIONS**, P.O. Box 20, Enola PA 17025. **Acquisitions:** John Kaufman, publisher; Robert "Bob" Lollo, managing editor. Publishes hardcover and trade paperback originals. **Publishes 25 titles/year. Receives 50 queries and 40 mss/year. 50% of books from first-time authors; 100% from unagented writers. Pays 7-11% royalty on retail price. No advance.** Publishes books 2 months after acceptance of ms. Accepts simultaneous submissions, if so noted. Reports in 2 months. Book catalog for 9½×12 SAE and 99¢ postage. Ms guidelines for #10 SASE.

O— Bristol Fashion publishes books on boats and boating.

**Nonfiction:** Adventure, children's books, historical, how-to, reference and general interest relating to boats and boating. "We are interested in any title which relates to these fields for all age groups. Query with a list of ideas. Include phone number. This is a fast changing market. Our title plans rarely extend past 6 months, although we know the type and quantity of books we will publish over the next 2 years. We prefer good knowledge with simple to understand writing style containing a well-rounded vocabulary." Query first, including brief outline, writing samples, tearsheets or sample chapters with SASE. Reviews artwork/photos as part of the ms package. Send photocopies or JPEG files on disk.

**Fiction:** "We will publish a limited number of fiction titles over the next three years, possibly fifteen or so. The story line and characters must relate to boating, and include knowledge of boating and the sea. This should educate the reader as they enjoy a truly fine fictional work. The story should have a balance of adventure and character portrayal (not action packed) as the sea is rarely calm and seaman rarely understood."

**Recent Title(s):** *Racing the Ice to Cape Horn* (nonfiction); *Daddy and I Go Boating* (fiction).

**Tips:** "All of our staff and editors are boaters. As such, we publish what we would want to read relating to boats. Our audience is generally boat owners or expected owners who are interested in learning about boats and boating. Keep it easy and simple to follow. Use nautical terms where appropriate. Do not use complicated technical jargon, terms or formulas without a detailed explanation of same. Use experienced craftsmen as a resource for knowledge. Our publisher's favorite fiction writer is Clive Cussler with the character of Dirk Pitt. Others include Tom Clancy, Nelson Demille and Dick Francis. If your story line style is close to any of these styles, you have an excellent chance of being published but don't imitate."

**BRISTOL PUBLISHING ENTERPRISES**, 14692 Wicks Blvd., San Leandro CA 94577. (800)346-4889. (510)895-4461. **Acquisitions**: Carol M. Newman, managing editor. Estab. 1988. Publishes hardcover and trade paperback originals. **Firm publishes 18-30 titles/year; each imprint publishes 4-12 titles/year. Receives 50-75 queries/year. 50% of books from first-time authors; 100% from unagented writers. Pays 6% royalty on wholesale price or makes varying outright purchase.** Publishes book 6 months after acceptance of ms. Accepts simultaneous submissions. Reports in 4 months. Book catalog free. Manuscript guidelines for #10 SASE.

**Imprint(s):** Nitty Gritty cookbooks, The Best 50 Recipe Series.

**Nonfiction:** Cookbook, how-to. Subjects include cooking/foods/nutrition, entertaining. "Send a proposal or query first; editor will contact if interested in seeing manuscript. Most cookbooks are related to housewares products and/or hot culinary trends. Readers are novice cooks who want to know more about what is going on. Don't send family recipe collections; research our company before submitting." Query with outline and 1-2 samples chapters

**Recent Title(s):** *The Weekend Chef*, by Robin O'Neill.

**Tips:** "We encourage new authors. Sending a completed manuscript is useful but not necessary. A comprehensive outline, 6-10 sample recipes and writing sample is satisfactory. Our readers may not be very experienced or 'hip' to the current trends in cooking and entertaining, but are eager to learn. Our books educate without intimidating."

**BROADCAST INTERVIEW SOURCE, INC.**, Free Library, 2233 Wisconsin Ave., NW #301, Washington DC 20007. (202)333-4904. Fax: (202)342-5411. E-mail: davis@yearbooknews.com. Website: http://www.freelibrary.com. **Acquisitions:** Mitchell P. Davis, nonfiction editor; Randal Templeton, travel editor; Greg Daly, fiction editor/information-oriented titles. Estab. 1984. Publishes trade paperback originals and reprints. **Publishes 14 titles/year. Receives 750 queries and 110 mss/year. 20% of books from first-time authors; 40% from unagented writers. Pays 5-15% royalty on wholesale price or makes outright purchase of $2,000-10,000. Offers $2,000 advance, but rarely.** Publishes book 1 month after acceptance. Accepts simultaneous submissions. Reports in 1 month. Book catalog and ms guidelines free on request or on website.

O— Broadcast Interview Source develops and publishes resources for publicists and journalists.

**Nonfiction:** Biography, cookbook, gift book, how-to, humor, multimedia, reference, self-help, technical, textbook, catalogs, almanacs. Subjects include agriculture/horiticulture, Americana, business/economics, computers/electronics, education, history, hobbies, military/war, money/finance, psychology, recreation, religion, translation. Submit proposal package including outline and 3 sample chapters.

**Fiction:** Adventure, erotica, experimental, historical, humor, literary, mainstream/contemporary, military/war, plays, religious, translation, western. Submit proposal package, including synopsis and 2 sample chapters.

**Recent Titles:** *Family Words*, by Paul Dickson (dictionary of family pet-words).

**Tips:** "We expect authors to be available for radio interviews at www.radiotour.com."

**BROADMAN & HOLMAN PUBLISHERS**, 127 Ninth Ave. N., Nashville TN 37234. (615)251-2392. Publisher: Kenneth Stephens. **Acquisitions:** Richard Rosenbaum, editorial director. Estab. 1934. Publishes hardcover and paperback originals. **Publishes 48 titles/year. Pays negotiable royalty.** Reports in 2 months. Writer's guidelines for #10 SAE with 2 first-class stamps.

**Nonfiction:** Religion. "We are open to freelance submissions in all areas. Materials in these areas must be suited for an evangelical Christian readership." No poetry, biography, sermons, or art/gift books. Query with outline/synopsis and sample chapters with SASE.

   O⚬ Broadman & Holman publishes books that provide biblical solutions that spiritually transform individuals and cultures. Currently emphasizing inspirational/gift books and general Christian living. De-emphasizing men's books.

**Fiction:** Religious. "We publish a limited number of fiction titles. We want not only a very good story, but also one that sets forth Christian values. Nothing that lacks a positive Christian emphasis; nothing that fails to sustain reader interest." Query with SASE.

**Recent Title(s):** *Debt Proof Your Kids*, by Mary Hunt (nonfiction); *Murder on the Titanic*, by Jim Walker (fiction).

**Tips:** "Please study competing titles and be able to identify the unique, compelling features of your proposed book."

**A BROADWAY BOOKS**, Doubleday Broadway Publishing Group, Random House, Inc., 1540 Broadway, New York NY 10036. (800)223-6834. Website: http://www.broadwaybooks.com. Publisher/Editor-in-Chief: Robert Asahina. **Acquisitions:** Harriet Bell, executive editor (cookbooks); Lauren Marino, editor (pop culture, entertainment, spirituality); Suzanne Oaks, senior editor (business); Tracy Behar, associate publisher/senior editor (psychology/self-help, parenting, health); Charles Conrad, vice president and executive editor (general nonfiction). Estab. 1995. Publishes hardcover and trade paperback originals and reprints.

   O⚬ Broadway publishes general interest nonfiction and fiction for adults.

**Nonfiction:** General interest adult books. Subjects include biography/memoirs, business, child care/parenting, cookbooks, current affairs, diet/nutrition, health, history, illustrated books, New Age/spirituality, money/finance, politics, popular culture, psychology, women's studies, multicultural studies, gay and lesbian, sex/erotica, consumer reference, golf. *Agented submissions only.*

**Fiction:** Publishes commercial literary fiction.

**Recent Title(s):** *If Life is a Game, These Are the Rules*, by Cherie Carter-Scott; *Tomcat in Love*, by Tim O'Brien.

**BROOKLINE BOOKS**, P.O. Box 1047, Cambridge MA 02238. (617)868-0360. Fax: (617)868-1772. E-mail: brookline bks@delphi.com. Website: http://people.delphi.com/brooklinebks. **Acquisitions:** Milt Budoff, publisher/executive editor. Estab. 1984. Publishes trade and professional paperback originals and reprints. **Publishes 15-25 titles/year. Receives 50-100 queries and 30-50 mss/year. 30% of books from first-time authors; majority from unagented writers. Pays 10-15% royalty on wholesale price.** Publishes book 8 months after acceptance of ms. Accepts simultaneous submissions. Reports in 1 month on queries, 2 months on proposals and mss. Book catalog and ms guidelines free.

   O⚬ Brookline publishes books for parents, families and professionals whose lives were affected by disabilities, and the need for special education.

**Imprint(s):** Lumen Editions.

**Nonfiction:** Reference, technical, textbook, professional. Subjects include child guidance/parenting, education, health/medicine, language/literature, psychology, translation, special needs/disabilities. Query or submit outline, 3 sample chapters and SASE. Reviews artwork/photos as part of ms package. Send photocopies.

**Fiction:** First time translations of Latin American, European and Asian literary fiction and nonfiction. Query or submit synopsis, 3 sample chapters and SASE.

**Recent Title(s):** *New Voices*, by G. Dybwad and H. Bersani (self-advocacy among persons with mental retardation); *Urban Oracles*, by Mayra Santos-Febres (fictional stories of lives of Puerto Rican women).

**BRYANT & DILLON PUBLISHERS, INC.**, P.O. Box 39, Orange NJ 07050. (973)763-1470. Fax: (973)675-8443. **Acquisitions:** (Ms.) Gerri Dillon, editor (women's issues, film, photography). Estab. 1993. Publishes hardcover and trade paperback originals. **Publishes 8-10 titles/year. Receives 500 queries and 700 mss/year. 100% of books from first-time authors; 90% from unagented writers. Pays 6-10% royalty on retail price.** Publishes book 1 year after acceptance of ms. Accepts simultaneous submissions. Reports in 3 months on proposals.

   O⚬ Bryant & Dillon publishes books that speak to an African-American audience and others interested in the African-American experience.

**Nonfiction:** Biography, how-to, self-help. Subjects include Black studies, business/economics, education, ethnic, film, government/politics, history, language/literature, money/finance, women's issues/studies. "Must be on subjects of interest to African-Americans." Submit cover letter, author's information sheet, marketing information, outline and 3 sample chapters with SASE (envelope large enough for contents sent). "No faxes or phone calls!" No poetry or children's books.

**Recent Title(s):** *A Stranger in my Bed*, by Kevin Luttery.

**BUCKNELL UNIVERSITY PRESS**, Lewisburg PA 17837. (570)577-3674. Fax: (570)577-3797. E-mail: clingham@b ucknell.edu. Website: http://www.departments.bucknell.edu/univ_press. **Acquisitions:** Greg Clingham, director. Estab. 1969. Publishes hardcover originals. **Publishes 40-45 titles/year. Receives 400 inquiries and submissions/year. 20% of books from first-time authors; 99% from unagented writers. Pays royalty.** Publishes accepted works within 18 months of delivery of finished ms. Reports in 1 month on queries. Book catalog free.

    ○⟶ "In all fields, our criteria are scholarly excellence, critical originality, and interdisciplinary and theoretical expertise and sensitivity."

**Nonfiction:** English and American literary criticism, literary theory and cultural studies, historiography (including the history of law, medicine and science), art history, modern languages, classics, philosophy, anthropology, ethnology, psychology, sociology, religion, political science, cultural and political geography, and interdisciplinary combinations of the aforementioned. Series: Bucknell Studies in Eighteenth-Century Literature and Culture, Bucknell Studies in Latin American Literature and Theory, Bucknell Studies in Historiography, Bucknell Series in Contemporary Poetry; Biannual Journal: The Bucknell Review: A Scholarly Journal of Letters, Arts, and Sciences. Query with SASE.

**Recent Title(s):** *Cavendish: The Experimental Life*, by James McCormmach and Krista Jungnickel.

**Tips:** "An original work of high-quality scholarship has the best chance. We publish for the scholarly community."

**BULFINCH PRESS**, Little, Brown & Co., 3 Center Plaza, Boston MA 02108. (617)263-2797. Fax: (617)263-2857. Website: http://www.littlebrown.com. Publisher: Carol Judy Leslie. **Acquisitions:** Stacy Botelho, department assistant. Publishes hardcover and trade paperback originals. **Publishes 60-70 titles/year. Receives 500 queries/year. Pays variable royalty on wholesale price. Advance varies.** Publishes book 18 months after acceptance of ms. Accepts simultaneous submissions. Reports in 2 months on proposals.

    ○⟶ Bulfinch Press publishes large format art books.

**Nonfiction:** Style books, gift books, illustrated books. Subjects include art/architecture, gardening, photography. Query with outline, sample artwork and SASE. Send color photocopies or laser prints.

**Recent Title(s):** *Philippe Halsman: A Retrospective.*

**THE BUREAU FOR AT-RISK YOUTH**, P.O. Box 760, Plainview NY 11803-0760. **Acquisitions:** Sally Germain, editor-in-chief. Estab. 1988. **Publishes 25-50 titles/year. Receives hundreds of submissions/year. Most books from first-time authors; 100% from unagented writers. Pays royalty of 10% maximum on selling price. Advance varies.** Publication 1 year after acceptance of ms. Accepts simultaneous submissions. Reports in 1-8 months. Book catalog free if appropriate after communication with author.

    ○⟶ Publishes how-to prevention curriculum or short booklets, pamphlet series, curriculum and other educational materials on guidance topics for educators, parents, mental health and juvenile justice professionals.

**Nonfiction:** Educational materials for parents, educators and other professionals who work with youth. Subjects include child guidance/parenting, education. "The materials we publish are curriculum, book series, workbook/activity books or how-to-oriented pieces tailored to our audience. They are generally not single book titles and are rarely book length." Query.

**Recent Title(s):** *Teen Talk Prevention Pamphlets*, by Meredith Resnick, MSW, LCSW.

**Tips:** "Publications are sold exclusively through direct mail catalog. We do not publish book-length pieces. Writers whose expertise is appropriate to our customers should send query or proposal since we tailor everything very specifically to meet our audience's needs."

**BURFORD BOOKS**, P.O. Box 388, Short Hills NJ 07078. (973)258-0960. Fax: (973)258-0113. **Acquisitions:** Peter Burford, publisher. Estab. 1997. Publishes hardcover originals, trade paperback originals and reprints. **Publishes 25 titles/year. Receives 300 queries and 200 mss/year. 30% of books from first-time authors; 60% from unagented writers. Pays royalty on wholesale price.** Accepts simultaneous submissions. Publishes book 18 months after acceptance of ms. Reports in 1 month on queries and proposals, 2 months on mss. Book catalog and ms guidelines free.

    ○⟶ Burford Books publishes books on all aspects of the outdoors, from gardening to sports, practical and literary.

**Nonfiction:** How-to, illustrated book. Subjects include horticulture, animals, cooking/foods/nutrition, gardening, hobbies, military/war, nature/environment, recreation, sports, travel. Query with outline with SASE. Reviews artwork/photos as part of the ms package. Send photocopies.

**Recent Title(s):** *Three-Shot Golf for Women*, by Janet Coles.

**BUSINESS & LEGAL REPORTS, INC.**, 39 Academy St., Madison CT 06443-1513. (203)318-0000. Fax: (203)245-0483. E-mail: sromano@blr.com. Website: http://www.blr.com. **Acquisitions:** Sam Romano, editor-in-chief. Estab. 1978. Publishes loose leaf and soft cover originals. Averages 20 titles/year. **Receives 100 submissions/year. Pays 2½-5% royalty on retail price, or makes outright purchase for $1,000-5,000. Offers $3,000 average advance.** Publishes book an average of 6 months after acceptance of ms. Accepts simultaneous submissions. Book catalog free.

    ○⟶ Business & Legal Reports publishes administrative and management titles for business. Currently emphasizing "how-to" compliance guides.

**Nonfiction:** Reference. Human resources, management, safety, environmental management, training. Query.

**Recent Title(s):** *Seven Minute Safety Trainer.*

**BUSINESS McGRAW-HILL**, The McGraw Hill Companies, 11 W. 19th St., New York NY 10011. (212)337-4098. Fax: (212)337-5999. Publisher: Philip Ruppel. **Acquisitions:** Susan Barry, editorial director; Barbara Gilson (Schaum's Outline Series); Nancy Mikhail (trade reference); Betsy Brown, senior editor (self-help, communications). **Publishes 100 titles/year. Receives 1,200 queries and 1,200 mss/year. 30% of books from first-time authors; 60% from unagented writers. Pays 10-15% royalty on net price. Offers $5,000 advance and up.** Publishes book 6 months after acceptance of ms. Accepts simultaneous submissions. Reports in 3 months. Book catalog and ms guidelines free on request with SASE.

O→ "McGraw Hill's business division and trade reference is the world's largest business publisher, offering nonfiction trade and paperback originals in more than ten areas, including management, sales and marketing, careers, trade reference, self-help, training, finance and science."

**Nonfiction:** How-to, reference, self-help, technical. Subjects include business, money/finance. "Current, up-to-date, original ideas are needed. Good self-promotion is key." Submit proposal package, including outline, table of contents, concept.

**Recent Nonfiction Title(s):** *The 12 Simple Secrets of Microsoft Management*, by David Thielen; *Rethinking the Sales Force*, by Neil Rackham.

**BUTTE PUBLICATIONS, INC.**, P.O. Box 1328, Hillsboro OR 97123-1328. (503)648-9791. Fax: (503)693-9526. **Acquisitions**: M. Brink, president. Estab. 1992. **Publishes 6-8 titles/year. Receives 30 queries and 20 mss/year. 50% of books from first-time authors; 100% from unagented writers. Pays 8-12% royalty on net receipts.** Publishes book 1 year after acceptance of ms. Accepts simultaneous submissions. Reports in 1 month on queries, 4 months on proposals, 6 months on mss. Book catalog and ms guidelines free.

O→ Butte publishes books related to deafness and education. Currently emphasizing classroom materials. De-emphasizing fiction.

**Nonfiction:** Children's/juvenile, textbook. Subjects include education, all related to field of deafness and education. Submit proposal package, including author bio, synopsis, market survey and complete ms, if completed. Reviews artwork/photos as part of ms package (if essential to the educational value of the work). Send photocopies.

**Fiction:** Adventure, historical, mystery, young adult (deaf characters). All must deal with hearing loss or include deaf characters. Submit complete ms and SASE. *Writer's Market* recommends sending a query with SASE first.

**Recent Title(s):** *Language Issues in Deaf Education*, by Luetke-Stahlman (nonfiction); *Finding Abby*, by Scott.

**Tips:** "Audience is students, teachers, parents and professionals in the arena dealing with deafness and hearing loss."

**BUTTERWORTH-HEINEMANN**, Reed-Elsevier (USA) Inc., 225 Wildwood Ave., Woburn MA 01801-2041. Website: http://www.bh.com. **Acquisitions:** Karen Speerstra, publishing director (books on transforming business); Marie Lee, publisher (Focal Press); Phil Sutherland, publisher (Digital Press); Susan Pioli, publishing director (Medical); Laurel DeWolf, senior editor (Security Criminal Justice); Candy Hall, senior editor (Newnes). Estab. 1975. Publishes hardcover and trade paperback originals. **Publishes 150 titles/year. Each imprint publishes 25-30 titles/year. 25% of books from first-time authors; 95% from unagented writers. Pays 10-12% royalty on wholesale price. Offers modest advance.** Publishes book 9 months after acceptance of ms. Reports in 1 month on proposals. Book catalog and ms guidelines free.

O→ Butterworth-Heinemann publishes technical professional and academic books in technology, medicine and business; no fiction.

**Imprint(s):** Butterworth-Heinemann, Medical, Digital Press (computing), **Focal Press**, Medical, Newnes (electronics), Security & Criminal Justice.

**Nonfiction:** How-to (in our selected areas), reference, technical, textbook. Subjects include business, computers/electronics, health/medicine, photography, security/criminal justice, audio-video broadcast, communication technology. "Submit outline, 1-2 sample chapters, competing books and how yours is different/better, with SASE. Reviews artwork/photos as part of ms package. Send photocopies.

**Tips:** Butterworth-Heinemann has been serving professionals and students for over five decades. "We remain committed to publishing materials that forge ahead of rapidly changing technology and reinforce the highest professional standards. Our goal is to give you the competitive advantage in this rapidly changing digital age."

**CADENCE JAZZ BOOKS**, Cadence Building, Redwood NY 13679. (315)287-2852. Fax: (315)287-2860. **Acquisitions**: Bob Rusch, Carl Ericson. Estab. 1992. Publishes trade paperback and mass market paperback originals. **Publishes 15 titles/year. Receives 10 queries and 10 mss/year. 90% of books from first-time authors; 100% from unagented writers. Pays royalty or makes outright purchase.** Publishes book 6 months after acceptance of ms. Reports in 1 month.

O→ Cadence publishes jazz histories and discographies.

**Nonfiction:** Jazz music biographies, discographies and reference works. Submit outline and sample chapters and SASE. Reviews artwork/photos as part of ms package. Send photocopies.

**Recent Title(s):** *The Earthly Recordings of Sun Ra*, by Robert L. Campbell (discography).

**CAMBRIDGE EDUCATIONAL**, P.O. Box 2153, Charleston WV 25328-2153. (800)468-4227. Fax: (304)744-9351. Subsidiaries include: Cambridge Parenting and Cambridge Job Search. President: Edward T. Gardner, Ph.D. **Acquisitions:** Amy Pauley, managing editor. Estab. 1981. Publishes supplemental educational products. **Publishes 30-40 titles/year. Receives 200 submissions/year. 20% of books from first-time authors; 90% from unagented writers. Makes outright purchase of $1,500-4,000. Occasional royalty arrangement.** Publishes book 8 months after acceptance. Accepts simultaneous submissions.

O→ "We are known in the education industry for guidance-related and career search programs." Currently emphasizing social studies and science.

**Nonfiction:** Subjects include child guidance/parenting, cooking/foods/nutrition, education, health/medicine, money/

finance, career guidance, social studies and science. "We are looking for scriptwriters in the same subject areas and age group. We only publish books written for young adults and primarily sold to libraries, schools, etc. We do not seek books targeted to adults or written at high readability levels." Query or submit outline/synopsis and sample chapters. Does not respond unless interested. Reviews artwork/photos as part of ms package.

**Recent Title(s):** *Job Search Tactics.*

**Tips:** "We encourage the submission of high-quality books on timely topics written for young adult audiences at moderate to low readibility levels. Call and request a copy of all our current catalogs, talk to the management about what is timely in the areas you wish to write on, thoroughly research the topic, and write a manuscript that will be read by young adults without being overly technical. Low to moderate readibility yet entertaining, informative and accurate."

**CAMELOT BOOKS**, Avon Books, The Hearst Corp., 1350 Avenue of the Americas, New York NY 10019. (212)261-6800. Fax: (212)261-6895. **Acquisitions**: Elise Howard, editor-in-chief; Ruth Katcher, senior editor. Publishes hardcover and paperback originals and reprints. **Publishes 80 titles/year. Pays 6-8% royalty on retail price. Offers $2,000 minimum advance.** Publishes book 2 years after acceptance. Reports back in 4 months. Book catalog and ms guidelines for 8 × 10 SAE with 5 first-class stamps.

O➤ Camelot publishes fiction for children ages 8-12.

**Fiction:** Adventure, humor, juvenile (ages 8-12) mainstream, mystery, suspense. *No picture books.* Submit query letter *only.*

**Recent Title(s):** *The Key to the Indian*, by Lynne Reid Banks.

**CAMINO BOOKS, INC.**, P.O. Box 59026, Philadelphia PA 19102. (215)732-2491. Fax: (215)732-8288. Website: http://www.caminobooks.com. **Acquisitions**: E. Jutkowitz, publisher. Estab. 1987. Publishes hardcover and trade paperback originals. **Publishes 8 titles/year. Receives 500 submissions/year. 20% of books from first-time authors. Pays 6-12% royalty on net price. Offers $1,000 average advance.** Publishes book 1 year after acceptance. Reports in 2 weeks on queries. *Writer's Market* recommends allowing 2 months for reply.

O➤ Camino publishes nonfiction of regional interest to the Mid-Atlantic states.

**Nonfiction:** Biography, cookbook, how-to, juvenile. Subjects include agriculture/horticulture, Americana, art/architecture, child guidance/parenting, cooking/foods/nutrition, ethnic, gardening, government/politics, history, regional, travel. Query with outline/synopsis and sample chapters with SASE.

**Tips:** "The books must be of interest to readers in the Middle Atlantic states, or they should have a clearly defined niche, such as cookbooks."

**Ⓐ CANDLEWICK PRESS**, Walker Books Ltd. (London), 2067 Massachusetts Ave., Cambridge MA 02140. (617)661-3330. Fax: (617)661-0565. **Acquisitions:** Liz Bicknell, editor-in-chief (poetry, picture books, fiction); Mary Lee Donovan, senior editor (nonfiction/fiction); Gale Pryor, editor (nonfiction/fiction); Amy Ehrlich, editor-at-large (picture books); Liz Gavril, assistant editor; Kara LaReau, assistant editor; Cynthia Platt, assistant editor. Estab. 1991. Publishes hardcover originals, trade paperback originals and reprints. **Publishes 200 titles/year. Receives 1,000 queries and 1,000 mss/year. 5% of books from first-time authors; 20% from unagented writers. Pays 10% royalty on retail price. Advance varies.** Publishes book 3 years after acceptance of ms for illustrated books, 1 year for others. Accepts simultaneous submissions, if so noted. Reports in 10 weeks on mss.

O➤ Candlewick Press publishes high-quality, illustrated children's books for ages infant through young adult. "We are a truly child-centered publisher."

**Nonfiction:** Children's/juvenile. "Good writing is essential; specific topics are less important than strong, clear writing." *Agented submissions only.*

**Fiction:** Juvenile. *Agented submissions only.*

**Recent Title(s):** *Kennedy Assassinated!*, by Wilborn Hampton (nonfiction); *Fire, Bed, and Bone*, by Henrietta Branford (fiction); *Weslandia*, by Paul Fleischman, illustrated by Kevin Hawkes (picture book).

**C&T PUBLISHING**, 1651 Challenge Dr., Concord CA 94520. Fax: (510)677-0374. E-mail: ctinfo@ctpub.com. Website: http://www.ctpub.com. **Acquisitions:** Liz Aneloski, editor. Estab. 1983. Publishes hardcover and trade paperback originals. **Publishes 18-26 titles/year. Receives 80 submissions/year. 10% of books from first-time authors; 100% from unagented writers. Pays 5-10% royalty on retail price. Offers $1,000 average advance.** Accepts simultaneous submissions. Reports in 2 months. Free book catalog and proposal guidelines. No SASE required.

O➤ C&T publishes well-written, beautifully designed quilting and needlework books.

**Nonfiction:** Quilting books, primarily how-to, occasional quilt picture books, quilt-related crafts, wearable art, needlework, fiber and surface embellishments, other books relating to fabric crafting. "Please call or write for proposal guidelines." Extensive proposal guidelines are also available on their website.

**Recent Title(s):** *Through the Garden Gate: Quilters and Their Gardens*, by Jean and Valori Wells.

**Tips:** "In our industry, we find that how-to books have the longest selling life. Quiltmakers, sewing enthusiasts, needle artists and fiber artists are our audience. We like to see new concepts or techniques. Include some great examples and you'll get our attention quickly. Dynamic design is hard to resist, and if that's your forté, show us what you've done."

**CARDOZA PUBLISHING**, 132 Hastings St., Brooklyn NY 11235. Website: http://www.cardozapub.com. **Acquisitions:** Rose Swann, acquisitions editor. Estab. 1981. Publishes trade paperback originals, mass market paperback originals and reprints. **Publishes 15 titles/year. Receives 175 queries and 70 mss/year. 50% of books from first-time**

authors; **90% from unagented writers. Pays 5% royalty on retail price. Offers $500-2,000 advance.** Publishes book 6 months after acceptance of ms. Accepts simultaneous submissions. Reports in 2 months on queries.

○━ Cardoza is the world's foremost publisher of gaming and gambling books.

**Imprint(s):** Gambling Research Institute, Word Reference Library.

**Nonfiction:** How-to, reference. Subjects include gaming, gambling, health/fitness, publishing, reference/word, travel. "We are expanding into how-to books by qualified and knowledgeable writers. We're also actively seeking travel guides for our sister company Open Road Publishing, (32 Turkey Lane, Cold Spring Harbor, NY 11724) and multimedia and software titles on all subjects for our sister company, Cardoza Entertainment." Submit outline, table of contents and 2 sample chapters.

**Recent Title(s):** *How to Win at Gambling*, by Avery Cardoza.

**Tips:** "The books we put our name on must contain accurate information and be well written."

**THE CAREER PRESS, INC.**, Box 687, 3 Tice Rd., Franklin Lakes NJ 07417. (201)848-0310. Fax: (201)848-1727. President: Ronald Fry. **Acquisitions:** Betsy Sheldon, editor-in-chief. **Publishes 50 titles/year. Receives 100 queries and 200 mss/year. 50% of books from first-time authors; 50% from unagented writers. Pays royalty on retail price.** Publishes book 6 months after acceptance of ms. Accepts simlultaneous submissions. Reports in 2 months on queries, 3 months on mss. Book catalog and ms guidelines free.

○━ Career Press publishes primarily paperback and some hardcover nonfiction originals in the areas of job hunting and career improvement, including reference and education; as well as management philosophy titles for a small business and management audience. Career Press also offers a line of personal finance titles for a general readership.

**Nonfiction:** How-to, reference, self-help. Subjects include business/economics, money/finance, recreation, financial planning/careers. "Look through our catalog; become familiar with our publications. We like to select authors who are specialists on their topic." Query with outline, 1-2 sample chapters and SASE.

**Recent Title(s):** *Jerks at Work*, by Kenneth Lloyd (business).

**CAROL PUBLISHING**, 120 Enterprise Ave., Secaucus NJ 07094. (201)866-0490. Fax: (201)866-8159. Publisher: Steven Schragis. **Acquisitions:** Hillel Black (Birch Lane Press); Francine Hornberger (Citadel Press); Bob Berkel (Citadel Press and Birch Lane Press); Michael Lewis (Citadel Press); Gary Goldstein (Citadel Press); Carrie Cantor (Birch Lane Press). Estab. 1989. Publishes hardcover originals, trade paperback originals and mass market paperback reprints. **Publishes 180 titles/year. Receives 2,000 submissions/year. 10% of books from first-time authors; 10% from unagented writers. Pays 5-15% royalty on retail price. Offers $5,000-25,000 advance.** Publishes book 1 year after acceptance. Accepts simultaneous submissions. Reports in 2 months.

○━ Carol has a reputation for publishing celebrity biographies for a general audience.

**Imprint(s): Birch Lane Press**, **Citadel Press**, Lyle Stuart.

**Nonfiction:** Biography, cookbook, gift book, how-to, humor, self-help. Subjects include Americana, animals, art/architecture, business/economics, cooking/foods/nutrition, education ethnic, film, gay/lesbian, government/politics, health/medicine, history, hobbies, language/literature, military/war, money/finance, music/dance, nature/environment, philosophy, psychology, recreation, regional, science, sports, travel, women's issues/studies. Submit outline/synopsis, sample chapters and SASE. Reviews artwork as part of ms package. Send photocopies.

**Recent Title(s):** *Sinatra*, by J. Randy Taraborrelli.

**CAROLRHODA BOOKS, INC.**, Lerner Publications Co., 241 First Ave. N., Minneapolis MN 55401. (612)332-3344. Fax: (612)332-7615. Website: http://www.lernerbooks.com. **Acquisitions:** Rebecca Poole, submissions editor. Estab. 1969. Publishes hardcover originals. **Publishes 50-60 titles/year. Receives 2,000 submissions/year. 10% of books from first-time authors; 90% from unagented writers. Pays royalty on wholesale price, makes outright purchase or negotiates payments of advance against royalty. Advance varies.** Publishes book 18 months after acceptance. Accepts submissions from March 1-31 and October 1-31 *only*. Submissions received at other times of the year will be returned to sender. No phone calls.

○━ Carolrhoda Books is a children's publisher focused on producing high-quality, socially conscious nonfiction and fiction books with unique and well-developed ideas and angles for young readers that help them learn about and explore the world around them. Currently de-emphasizing picture books, biographies on more obscure figures.

**Nonfiction:** Children's/juvenile (pre-kindergarten to 6th grade). Subjects include biography, ethnic, nature/environment, science, sports. Carolrhoda Books seeks creative children's nonfiction "We are always interested in adding to our biography series. Books on the natural and hard sciences are also of interest." Query with SASE for return of ms. Reviews artwork/photos as part of ms package. Send photocopies.

**Fiction:** Juvenile, historical, picture books. "We only publish about one picture book per year. Not looking for folktales or anthropomorphic animal stories." Query with SASE, send complete ms for picture books.

**Recent Title(s):** *Revolutionary Poet: A Story about Phillis Wheatley* (Creative Minds Biography series), by Maryann N. Weidt; *Allen Jay and the Underground Railroad* (On My Own History series), by Marlene Targ Brill (fiction).

**Tips:** "Our audience consists of children ages four to eleven. We publish very few picture books. Nonfiction science topics, particularly nature, do well for us, as do biographies, photo essays, and easy readers. We prefer manuscripts that can fit into one of our series. Spend time developing your idea in a unique way or from a unique angle; avoid trite, hackneyed plots and ideas."

[A] **CARROLL & GRAF PUBLISHERS INC.**, Avalon Publishing Group, 19 W. 21st St., Suite 601, New York NY 10010. (212)627-8590. Fax: (212)627-8490. **Acquisitions:** Kent Carroll, publisher/executive editor. Estab. 1983. Publishes hardcover and trade paperback originals. **Publishes 120 titles/year. 10% of books from first-time authors. Pays 10-15% royalty on retail price for hardcover, 7½% for paperback. Offers $5,000-100,000 advance.** Publishes book 9 months after acceptance of ms. Reports in 1 month on queries. Book catalog free.

    O↝ Carroll and Graf Publishers offers quality fiction and nonfiction for a general readership. Carroll and Graf is one of the few remaining independent trade publishers and is therefore able to publish successfully and work with first-time authors and novelists.

**Nonfiction:** Biography, reference, self-help. Subjects include business/economics, history, contemporary culture, true crime. Publish general trade listings; are interested in developing long term relations with authors. Query. *Agented submissions only.*

**Fiction:** Erotica, literary, mystery, science fiction, suspense, thriller. Query. *Agented submissions only.*

**Recent Title(s):** *Faust's Metropolis: A History of Berlin,* by Alexandra Richie (history); *Master Georgie,* by Beryl Bainbridge (fiction).

**CARSTENS PUBLICATIONS, INC.**, Hobby Book Division, P.O. Box 700, Newton NJ 07860-0700. (973)383-3355. Fax: (973)383-4064. Website: http://www.carstens-publications.com. **Acquisitions:** Harold H. Carstens, publisher. Estab. 1933. Publishes paperback originals. **Averages 8 titles/year. 100% of books from unagented writers. Pays 10% royalty on retail price. Offers advance.** Publishes book 1 year after acceptance. *Writer's Market* recommends allowing 2 months for reply. Book catalog for SASE.

    O↝ Carstens specializes in books about railroads, model railroads and airplanes for hobbyists.

**Nonfiction:** Model railroading, toy trains, model aviation, railroads and model hobbies. "Authors must know their field intimately because our readers are active modelers. Writers cannot write about somebody else's hobby with authority. If they do, we can't use them. Our railroad books presently are primarily photographic essays on specific railroads." Query. Reviews artwork/photos as part of ms package.

**Recent Title(s):** *The Life and Times of a Locomotive Engineer,* by Charles Steffes.

**Tips:** "We need lots of good photos. Material must be in model, hobby, railroad and transportation field only."

**CARTWHEEL BOOKS**, Scholastic, Inc., 555 Broadway, New York NY 10012. (212)343-6100. Fax: (212)343-4444. Website: http://www.scholastic.com. Vice President/Editorial Director: Bernette Ford. **Acquisitions:** Grace Maccarone, executive editor; Sonia Black, editor; Kimberly Weinberger, editor; Liza Baker, acquisitions editor. Estab. 1991. Publishes hardcover originals. **Publishes 85-100 titles/year. Receives 250 queries/year; 1,200 mss/year. 1% of books from first-time authors; 50% from unagented writers. Pays royalty on retail price. Offers advance.** Publishes book 2 years after acceptance of ms. Accepts simultaneous submissions. Reports in 2 months on queries; 3 months on proposals; 6 months on mss/ Book catalog for 9×12 SAE. Manuscript guidelines free.

    O↝ Cartwheel Books publishes innovative books for children, ages 3-9. "We are looking for 'novelties' that are books first, play objects second. Even without its gimmick, a Cartwheel Book should stand alone as a valid piece of children's literature."

**Nonfiction:** Children's/juvenile. Subjects include animals, history, music/dance, nature/environment, recreation, science, sports. "Cartwheel Books publishes for the very young, therefore nonfiction should be written in a manner that is accessible to preschoolers through 2nd grade. Often writers choose topics that are too narrow or 'special' and do not appeal to the mass market. Also, the text and vocabulary are frequently too difficult for our young audience." *Agented submissions or previously published authors only.* Reviews artwork/photos as part of ms package.

**Fiction:** Humor, juvenile, mystery, picture books. "Again, the subject should have mass market appeal for very young children. Humor can be helpful, but not necessary. Mistakes writers make are a reading level that is too difficult, a topic of no interest or too narrow, or manuscripts that are too long." *Agented submissions or previously published authors only.*

**Recent Title(s):** *I Spy,* by Jean Marzollo and Walter Wick (picture book).

**Tips:** Audience is young children, ages 3-9. "Know what types of books the publisher does. Some manuscripts that don't work for one house may be perfect for another. Check out bookstores or catalogs to see where your writing would 'fit' best."

**CATBIRD PRESS**, 16 Windsor Rd., North Haven CT 06473-3015. (203)230-2391. **Acquisitions:** Robert Wechsler, publisher. Estab. 1987. Publishes hardcover and trade paperback originals and trade paperback reprints. **Publishes 4-5 titles/year. Receives 1,000 submissions/year. 5% of books from first-time authors; 90% from unagented writers. Pays 2½-10% royalty on retail price. Offers $2,000 average advance.** Publishes book 1 year after acceptance. Accepts simultaneous submissions, if so noted. Reports in 1 month on queries if SASE is included. *Writer's Market* recommends allowing 2 months for reply. Book catalog free. Manuscript guidelines for #10 SASE.

    O↝ Catbird publishes sophisticated, humorous, literary fiction and nonfiction with fresh styles and approaches.

**Imprint(s):** Garrigue Books (Czech works in translation).

**Nonfiction:** Humor, law, general. "We are looking for up-market prose humorists. No joke or other small gift books. We are also interested in very well-written general nonfiction that takes fresh, sophisticated approaches." Submit outline, sample chapters and SASE.

**Fiction:** Literary, humor, translations. "We are looking for writers of well-written literature who have a comic vision, take a fresh approach, and have a fresh, sophisticated style. No genre, wacky, or derivative mainstream fiction." Submit outline/synopsis, sample chapter and SASE.

**Recent Title(s):** *Coast to Coast*, by Frederic Raphael (fiction).

**Tips:** "First of all, we want writers, not books. Second, we are only interested in writing that is not like what is out there already. The writing should be highly sophisticated, but not obscure; the approach or, better, approaches should be fresh and humorous. If a writer is more interested in content than in style, that writer should look elsewhere."

**CATHOLIC UNIVERSITY OF AMERICA PRESS**, 620 Michigan Ave. NE, Washington DC 20064. (202)319-5052. Fax: (202)319-4985. E-mail: cua-press@cua.edu. Website: http://www.cua.edu/pubs/cupr. **Acquisitions:** Dr. David J. McGonagle, director. Estab. 1939. **Publishes 15-20 titles/year. Receives 100 submissions/year. 50% of books from first-time authors; 100% from unagented writers. Pays variable royalty on net receipts.** Publishes book 1 year after acceptance. Reports in 3 months. Book catalog for SASE.

    ○➤ The Catholic University of America Press publishes in the fields of history (ecclesiastical and secular), literature and languages, philosophy, political theory, social studies, and theology. "We have interdisciplinary emphasis on patristics, medieval studies and Irish studies. Our principal interest is in works of original scholarship intended for scholars and other professionals and for academic libraries, but we will also consider manuscripts whose chief contribution is to offer a synthesis of knowledge of the subject which may be of interest to a wider audience or suitable for use as supplementary reading material in courses."

**Nonfiction:** History, languages and literature, philosophy, religion, church-state relations, political theory. No unrevised doctoral dissertations. Length: 80,000-200,000 words. Query with outline, sample chapter, cv and list of previous publications.

**Recent Title(s):** *Hesburgh: A Biography*, by Michael O'Brien.

**Tips:** "Scholarly monographs and works suitable for adoption as supplementary reading material in courses have the best chance."

**CATO INSTITUTE**, 1000 Massachusetts Ave. NW, Washington DC 20001. (202)842-0200. **Acquisitions:** David Boaz, executive vice president. Estab. 1977. Publishes hardcover originals, trade paperback originals and reprints. **Publishes 12 titles/year. Receives 50 submissions/year. 25% of books from first-time authors; 90% from unagented writers. Makes outright purchase of $1,000-10,000.** Publishes book 9 months after acceptance. Accepts simultaneous submissions. Reports in 3 months. Book catalog free.

    ○➤ Cato Institute publishes books on public policy issues from a free-market or libertarian perspective.

**Nonfiction:** Public policy *only*. Subjects include foreign policy, economics, education, government/politics, health/medicine, monetary policy, sociology. Query.

**Ⓝ CAVE BOOKS**, 756 Harvard Ave., St. Louis MO 63130-3134. (314)862-7646. **Acquisitions:** Richard Watson, editor. Estab. 1980. Publishes hardcover and trade paperback originals and reprints. **Publishes 4 titles/year. Receives 20 queries and 10 mss/year. 75% of books from first-time authors; 100% from unagented writers. Pays 10% royalty on retail price.** Publishes book 18 months after acceptance. Accepts simultaneous submissions. Reports in 3 months on mss.

    ○➤ Cave Books publishes only books on caves, karst, and speleology.

**Nonfiction:** Biography, technical (science), adventure. Subjects are Americana, animals, anthropology/archaeology, history, nature/environment, photography, recreation, regional, science, sports (cave exploration), travel. Send complete ms. Reviews artwork/photos as part of ms package. Send photocopies.

**Recent Title(s):** *Caverns Measureless to Man*, by Sheck Exley (memoirs of the world's greatest cave diver).

**Fiction:** Adventure, historical, literary. "Must be realistic and centrally concerned with cave exploration. No gothic, science fiction, fantasy, romance, mystery or poetry. No novels that are not entirely about caves. The cave and action in the cave must be central, authentic, and realistic." Send complete ms.

**Tips:** "Our readers are interested only in caves, karst, and speleology. Please do not send manuscripts on other subjects. Query with outline and SAE first."

**◪ CAXTON PRESS**, (formerly The Caxton Printers, Ltd.), 312 Main St., Caldwell ID 83605-3299. (208)459-7421. Fax: (208)459-7450. Website: http://caxtonprinters.com. President: Gordon Gipson. **Acquisitions:** Wayne Cornell, managing acquisitions editor. Estab. 1907. Publishes hardcover and trade paperback originals. **Publishes 6-10 titles/year. Receives 250 submissions/year. 50% of books from first-time authors; 60% from unagented writers. Pays royalty. Offers advance.** Publishes book 18 months after acceptance. Accepts simultaneous submissions. Reports in 3 months. Book catalog for 9×12 SASE.

    ○➤ "Western Americana nonfiction remains our focus. We define Western Americana as almost any topic that deals with the people or culture of the west, past and present." Currently emphasizing Western narratives, outdoor oriented nonfiction. De-emphasizing "coffee table" or photographic intensive books.

**Nonfiction:** Americana, Western Americana. "We need good Western Americana, especially the Northwest, emphasis on serious, narrative nonfiction." Query. Reviews artwork/photos as part of ms package.

**Recent Title(s):** *Sidesaddles to Heaven: Women of the Rocky Mountain Mission.*

**Tips:** "Books to us never can or will be primarily articles of merchandise to be produced as cheaply as possible and to be sold like slabs of bacon or packages of cereal over the counter. If there is anything that is really worthwhile in this mad jumble we call the twentieth century, it should be books."

**CCC PUBLICATIONS**, 9725 Lurline Ave., Chatsworth CA 91311. (818)718-0507. **Acquisitions:** Cliff Carle, editorial director. Estab. 1983. Publishes trade paperback and mass market paperback originals. **Publishes 40-50 titles/year. Receives 1,000 mss/year. 25% of books from first-time authors; 25% of books from unagented writers. Pays 8-12% royalty on wholesale price.** Publishes book 6 months after acceptance. Accepts simultaneous submissions. Reports in 3 months. Catalog for 10×13 SAE with 2 first-class stamps.

○╾ CCC publishes humor that is "today" and will appeal to a wide demographic. Currently emphasizing "short, punchy pieces with *lots* of cartoon illustrations, or very well-written text if long form."

**Nonfiction:** Humorous how-to/self-help. "We are looking for *original, clever* and *current* humor that is not too limited in audience appeal or that will have a limited shelf life. All of our titles are as marketable five years from now as they are today. No rip-offs of previously published books, or too special interest manuscripts." Query or send complete ms with SASE. Reviews artwork/photos as part of ms package.

**Recent Title(s):** *In a Perfect World*, by Barry Dutter.

**Tips:** "Humor—we specialize in the subject and have a good reputation with retailers and wholesalers for publishing super-impulse titles. SASE is a must!"

**CELESTIAL ARTS**, Ten Speed Press, P.O. Box 7123, Berkeley CA 94707. (510)559-1600. Fax: (510)524-1052. **Acquisitions:** Veronica Randall, managing editor/interim publisher. Estab. 1966. Publishes hardcover and trade paperback originals, trade paperback reprints. **Publishes 40 titles/year. Receives 500 queries and 200 mss/year. 30% of books from first-time authors; 10% from unagented writers. Pays 15% royalty on wholesale price. Offers modest advance.** Publishes book 9 months after acceptance of ms. Accepts simultaneous submissions. Reports in 6 weeks. Book catalog and ms guidelines free.

○╾ Celestial Arts publishes nonfiction for a forward-thinking, open-minded audience interested in psychology, self-help, spirituality, health and parenting.

**Nonfiction:** Cookbook, how-to, reference, self-help. Subjects include child guidance/parenting, cooking/foods/nutrition, education, gay/lesbian, health/medicine, New Age, psychology, women's issues/studies. "We specialize in parenting, women's issues, health and family/parenting. On gay/lesbian topics, we publish nonfiction only. And please, no poetry!" Submit proposal package, including: outline, 1-2 sample chapters, author background and SASE. Reviews artwork/photos as part of ms package. Send photocopies.

**Recent Title(s):** *Uncommon Sense for Parents with Teenagers*, by Mike Riera.

**Tips:** Audience is fairly well-informed, interested in psychology and sociology related topics, open-minded, innovative, forward-thinking. "The most completely thought-out (developed) proposals earn the most consideration."

**CENTENNIAL PUBLICATIONS**, 256 Nashua Ct., Grand Junction CO 81503. (970)243-8780. **Acquisitions:** Dick Spurr, publisher. Estab. 1990. Publishes hardcover and trade paperback originals and reprints. **Publishes 4-5 titles/year. Receives 20 queries and 10 mss/year. 80% of books from first-time authors; 100% from unagented writers. Pays 8-10% royalty on retail price. Offers $1,000 average advance.** Publishes book 8 months after acceptance of ms. Reports in 1 week on queries, 2 weeks on proposals, 1 month on mss.

**Nonfiction:** Biography, how-to. Subjects include Americana, history, hobbies, fishing. "A phone call is easiest way to determine suitability of topic. No poorly researched topics." Submit proposal package, including outline and sample chapters. Reviews artwork/photos as part of the ms package. Send photocopies.

● Centennial Publications no longer publishes fiction.

**Recent Title(s):** *Bamboo Rod Restoration*, by Michael Sinclair (how-to).

**CENTERSTREAM PUBLICATIONS**, P.O. Box 17878, Anaheim Hills CA 92807. (714)779-9390. Fax: (714)779-9390. E-mail: centerstrm@aol.com. **Acquisitions:** Ron Middlebrook, Cindy Middlebrook, owners. Estab. 1980. Publishes hardcover and mass market paperback originals, trade paperback and mass market paperback reprints. **Publishes 12 titles/year. Receives 15 queries and 15 mss/year. 80% of books from first-time authors; 100% from unagented writers. Pays 10-15% royalty on wholesale price. Offers $300-3,000 advance.** Publishes book 8 months after acceptance of ms. Accepts simultaneous submissions. Reports in 3 months on queries. Book catalog and ms guidelines for #10 SASE.

○╾ Centerstream publishes music history and instructional books.

**Nonfiction:** Music history and music instructional book. Query with SASE.

**Recent Title(s):** *Essential Blues Guitar*, by Dave Celentano (music).

**CHANDLER HOUSE PRESS**, Rainbow New England Corp., 335 Chandler St., Worcester MA 01602. (508)756-7644. Fax: (508)756-9425. E-mail: databooks@tatnuck.com. Website: http://www.tatnuck.com. President: Lawrence J. Abramoff. **Acquisitions:** Richard J. Staron, publisher. Estab. 1993. Publishes hardcover and trade paperback originals and reprints. **Publishes 25 titles/year. Receives 200 queries and 50 mss/year. 50% of books from first-time authors; 70% from unagented writers. Pays royalty on net sales.** Publishes book 6-12 months after acceptance of ms. Accepts simultaneous submissions. Reports in 1 month. *Writer's Market* recommends allowing 2 months for reply. Book catalog and manuscript guidelines free.

○╾ Chandler House Press is a general interest nonfiction publisher. "We publish useful and timely books that are tools for living better personal and professional lives."

**Nonfiction:** Biography, gift book, how-to, illustrated book, reference, self-help. Subjects include regional Americana, business, regional history, parenting, personal finance, pets, recreation, relationships, sports, women's issues. Submit

outline, 1-3 sample chapters and SASE. Reviews artwork/photos as part of ms package. Send photocopies.
**Recent Title(s):** *The Women's Fix-It Book; Incredibly Simple Weekend Projects and Everyday Home Repair*, by Karen Dale Dustman (home repair).

**CHARIOT BOOKS**, Chariot Victor Publishing, 4050 Lee Vance View, Colorado Springs CO 80918. (719)536-3271. Fax: (719)536-3269. **Acquisitions:** Karen Artl, children's product manager; Jeannie Harmon, senior editor (nonfiction); Kathy Davis, senior editor (fiction). Publishes hardcover and paperback originals. **Publishes 40-50 titles/year. Receives 500-1,000 mss/year. Pays variable royalty on retail price or flat fee depending on the project.** Publishes book 18 months after acceptance of ms. Accepts simultaneous submissions if so noted. Reports in 4 months on queries. No fax or e-mail submissions. Book catalog on request. Manuscript guidelines for #10 SASE.

    ○━ Chariot Books publishes inspirational works for children, ages 1-12, with a strong underlying Christian theme or clearly stated biblical value.

**Nonfiction:** Biography, children's/juvenile; Bible stories, devotionals, picture books on nonfiction topics. Religious subjects. Send proposal with cover letter and SASE.

**Fiction:** Historical, juvenile, picture books, toddler books, religious. No teen fiction; currently overwhelmed with contemporary fiction. Accepts proposals with SASE from previously published authors or agented authors only.

**Recent Title(s):** *Devotions from the World of Sports*, by John & Kathy Hillman (nonfiction); *The Merchant & The Thief*, by Ravi Zacharias (fiction).

**CHARIOT/VICTOR PUBLISHING**, Cook Communications Ministries, 4050 Lee Vance View, Colorado Springs CO 80918. (719)536-3271. Fax: (719)536-3269. **Acquisitions:** Cindy Simon, administrative assistant. Estab. 1875. Publishes hardcover and trade paperback originals, both children's and adult, fiction and nonfiction. **Publishes 150 titles/year. 10% of books from first-time authors; 50% from unagented writers. Pays variable royalty on net price. Advance varies.** Publishes book 1-2 years after acceptance of ms. Accepts simultaneous submissions, if so noted. Reports in 2 months on queries. Manuscript guidelines for #10 SASE.

    ○━ Chariot/Victor publishes children's and family spiritual growth books. Books "must have strong underlying Christian themes or clearly stated Biblical value."

**Imprint(s): Chariot Books** (children), **Lion Publishing**, Rainfall (toys, media, games), Victor Adult Books.

**Nonfiction:** Biography, children's/juvenile. Child guidance/parenting, history, religion. Query with SASE.

    ● No longer publishing fiction.

**Recent Title(s):** *The Reflective Life*, by Ken Gire (nonfiction); *Loving a Prodigal*, by Norm Wright (family issues); *Dr. Laura: A Mother In America* (contemporary issues).

**Tips:** "All books must in some way be Bible-related by authors who themselves are evangelical Christians with a platform. Chariot Victor, therefore, is not a publisher for everybody. Only a small fraction of the manuscripts received can be seriously considered for publication. Most books result from contacts that acquisitions editors make with qualified authors, though from time to time an unsolicited proposal triggers enough excitement to result in a contract. A writer has the best chance of selling Chariot Victor a well-conceived and imaginative manuscript that helps the reader apply Christianity to her life in practical ways. Christians active in the local church and their children are our audience."

**THE CHARLES PRESS, PUBLISHERS**, 1314 Chestnut St., Suite 200, Philadelphia PA 19107. (215)545-8933. Fax: (215)545-89387. E-mail: mailbox@charlespresspub.com. Website: http://www.charlespresspub.com. **Acquisitions**: Lauren Meltzer, publisher. Estab. 1982. Publishes hardcover and trade paperback originals. **Publishes 12-16 titles/year. Estab. 1982. Receives 2,500 queries and 800 mss/year. Pays 7½-12% royalty. Offers $1,000-8,000 advance.** Publishes book 1 year after acceptance of ms. Accepts simultaneous submissions. Reports in 2 months on queries and proposals, 3 months on mss. Book catalog and ms guidelines free.

    ○━ Currently emphasizing true crime, criminology, psychology, suicide and violence.

**Nonfiction:** Subjects include biographies, child guidance/parenting, counseling, criminology, health/medicine, psychology, religion, sociology, spirituality, true crime. Query or submit proposal package, including description of book, intended audience, reasons people will buy it and SASE. Reviews artwork/photos as part of the ms package. Send photocopies or transparencies.

**Fiction:** Literary, mainstream/contemporary. No poetry. Query with synopsis and SASE.

**Recent Title(s):** *The Serial Killer Letters: A Penetrating Look Inside the Minds of Murderers*, edited by Jennifer Furio.

**CHARLESBRIDGE PUBLISHING**, Trade and School Divisions, 85 Main St., Watertown MA 02472. (617)926-0329. Fax: (617)926-5720. Estab. 1980. Publishes hardcover and trade paperback nonfiction (80%) and fiction for the trade and library markets, as well as school programs and supplementary materials. Senior Editor: Harold Underdown. **Acquisitions:** *Trade Division:* Submissions Editor. *School Division:* Elena Dworkin Wright, school division editorial director. **Publishes 20-24 trade books, 2-4 school titles plus school materials and curriculum. Receives 2,500 submissions/year. 10-20% from first-time authors; 80% from unagented writers.** Publishes books 2-4 years after acceptance of ms.

    ○━ The Trade Division is "always interested in innovative approaches to a difficult genre, the nonfiction picture book." No novels or nonfiction for older children. The School Division is "looking for fiction to use as literature in the math curriculum and kids activity books (not coloring)." Currently emphasizing nature, science, multiculturalism. De-emphasizing bedtime stories, "warm and fuzzy" fiction, poems.

**Imprint(s):** Talewinds (2 fiction titles/season for Trade Division).

**Nonfiction:** *Trade Division:* Strong interest in nature, environment, social studies and other topics for trade and library markets. Exclusive submissions only. *School Division:* School or craft books that involve problem solving, building, projects, crafts are written with humor and expertise in the field. Submit complete ms with cv and SASE.
**Fiction:** *Trade Division:* "Strong, realistic stories with enduring themes." Exclusive submissions only. *School Division:* Math concepts in non-rhyming story.
**Recent Title(s):** *Trade Division: Bugs for Lunch*, by Margery Facklam, illustrations by Sylvia Long; *School Division: Building a Wells Fargo Stagecoach*, by Richard Mansir (nonfiction).

**CHATHAM PRESS**, Box A, Old Greenwich CT 06870. Fax: (203)531-7755. **Acquisitions:** Jane Andrassi. Estab. 1971. Publishes hardcover and paperback originals, reprints and anthologies. **Publishes 10 titles/year. Receives 50 submissions/year. 25% of books from first-time authors; 75% from unagented writers. Nonauthor subsidy publishes 10% of books, mainly poetry or ecological topics. "Standard book contract does not always apply if the book is heavily illustrated. Average advance is low.** Publishes 6 months after acceptance. Reports in 2 months. Book catalog and ms guidelines for $6 \times 9$ SAE with 6 first-class stamps.
    O—π Chatham Press publishes "books that relate to the U.S. coastline from Maine to the Carolinas and which bring a new insight, visual or verbal, to the non-fiction topic."
**Nonfiction:** Illustrated books subjects include regional history (Northeast seaboard), natural history, nature/environment, recreation. Accepts nonfiction translations from French and German. Query with outline and 3 sample chapters. Reviews artwork/photos as part of ms package.
    • Press indicates its need for freelance material has lessened.
**Recent Title(s):** *Exploring Old Martha's Vineyard.*
**Tips:** "Illustrated New England-relevant titles have the best chance of being sold to our firm. We have a slightly greater (15%) skew towards cooking and travel titles."

**N: CHELSEA GREEN PUBLISHING COMPANY**, P.O. Box 428, #205 Gates-Briggs Bldg., White River Junction VT 05001-0428. (802)295-6300. Fax: (802)295-6444. Website: http://www.chelseagreen.com. **Acquisitions:** Jim Schley, editor-in-chief (environmentalism, ecology, nature, renewable energy, alternative building); Ben Watson, senior editor (organic gardening and farming). Estab. 1984. Publishes hardcover and trade paperback originals and reprints. **Publishes 16-20 titles/year; imprint publishes 3-4 titles/year. Receives 300-400 queries and 200-300 mss/year. 30% of books from first-time authors; 80% from unagented writers. Pays royalty on publisher's net. Offers $2,500-10,000 advance.** Publishes book 18 months after acceptance of ms. Reports in 1 month on queries, 2 months on proposals and mss. Book catalog and ms guidelines free on request or on website.
    O—π Chelsea Green publishes and distributes books relating to issues of sustainability with a special concentration on books about nature, the environment, independent living, organic gardening, renewable energy and alternative or natural building techniques. The books reflect positive options in a world of environmental turmoil.
**Imprint(s):** Real Goods Solar Living Book series.
**Nonfiction:** Biography, cookbook, how-to, reference, self-help, technical. Subjects include agriculture/horticulture, art/architecture, cooking/foods/nutrition, gardening, health/medicine, memoirs, money/finance, nature/environment, regional, forestry. Query with SASE or submit proposal package, including outline and 1-2 sample chapters. Reviews artwork/photos as part of ms package. Send "whatever is most representatiave and appropriate."
**Recent Titles:** *New Organic Grower*, by Eliot Coleman (gardening/farming).
**Tips:** "Our readers are passionately enthusiastic about ecological solutions for contemporary challenges in construction, energy harvesting, agriculture and forestry. Our books are also carefully and handsomely produced to give pleasure to bibliophiles of a practical bent. It would be very helpful for prospective authors to have a look at several of our current books, as well as our catalog and website. For certain types of book, we are the perfect publisher, but we are exceedingly focused on particular areas."

**CHEMICAL PUBLISHING COMPANY, INC.**, 192 Lexington Ave., Suite 1201, New York NY 10016-6823. (212)779-0090. Fax: (212)889-1537. E-mail: chempub@aol.com. Website: http://www.chemicalpublishing.com. **Acquisitions:** Ms. S. Soto-Galicia, publisher. Estab. 1966. Publishes hardcover originals. **Publishes 8 titles/year. Receives 20 queries/year. 50% of books from first-time authors; 100% from unagented writers. Pays 10% royalty on retail price or makes negotiable outright purchase. Offers negotiable advance.** Publishes book 8 months after acceptance of ms. Reports in 3 weeks on queries, 5 weeks on proposals, 2 months on mss. Book catalog and ms guidelines free.
    O—π Chemical publishes professional chemistry titles.
**Nonfiction:** How-to, reference, applied chemical technology. Subjects include agriculture, analytical methods, chemical technology, cosmetics, dictionaries, engineering, environmental science, food technology, formularies, industrial technology, medical, metallurgy, textiles. Submit outline and a few pages of 3 sample chapters and SASE. Reviews artwork/photos as part of ms package.
**Recent Title(s):** *Fireworks, Principles & Practice.*
**Tips:** Audience is professionals in various fields of chemistry, corporate and public libraries, college libraries.

**CHESS ENTERPRISES**, 107 Crosstree Rd., Caraopolis PA 15108-2607. Fax: (412)262-2138. E-mail: bgdudley@compuserve.com. **Acquisitions:** Bob Dudley, owner. Estab. 1981. Publishes trade paperback originals. **Publishes 10 titles/year. Receives 20 queries and 12 mss/year. 10% of books from first-time authors; 100% from unagented writers.**

**Makes outright purchase of $500-3,000. No advance.** Publishes book 4 months after acceptance of ms. Accepts simultaneous submissions. Reports in 1 month.

○━ Chess Enterprises publishes books on how to play the game of chess.

**Nonfiction:** Game of chess only. Query.

**Recent Title(s):** *Checkmate!*, by Koltanowsky and Finklestein.

**Tips:** "Books are targeted to chess tournament players, book collectors."

**CHICAGO REVIEW PRESS**, 814 N. Franklin, Chicago IL 60610-3109. (312)337-0747. Fax: (312)337-5985. E-mail: ipgbook@mcs.com. Website: http://www.ipgbook.com. **Acquisitions:** Cynthia Sherry, executive editor (general nonfiction, children's); Yuval Taylor, editor (African, African-American). Estab. 1973. Publishes hardcover and trade paperback originals and trade paperback reprints. **Publishes 30-35 titles/year. Receives 200 queries and 600 manuscripts/year. 50% of books from first-time authors; 50% from unagented writers. Pays 7-12½% royalty. Offers $1,500-3,000 average advance.** Publishes book 15 months after acceptance. Accepts simultaneous submissions. Reports in 3 months. Book catalog for $3.50. Manuscript guidelines for #10 SASE or on website.

○━ Chicago Review Press publishes intelligent nonfiction on timely subjects for educated readers with special interests.

**Imprint(s):** Lawrence Hill Books, A Capella Books (contact Yuval Taylor).

**Nonfiction:** Creative nonfiction, children's/juvenile (activity books only), cookbooks (specialty only), how-to. Subjects include art/architecture, child guidance/parenting/pregnancy, creative nonfiction, education, ethnic, gardening (regional), health/medicine, history, hobbies, memoirs, multicultural, music/dance, nature/environment, recreation, regional. Query with outline, toc and 1-2 sample chapters. Reviews artwork/photos.

**Recent Title(s):** *On Stage! Theater Games and Activities for Kids*, by Lisa Bany-Winters.

**Tips:** "Along with a table of contents and 1-2 sample chapters, also send a cover letter and a list of credentials with your proposal. Also, provide the following information in your cover letter: audience, market and competition—who is the book written for and what sets it apart from what's already out there."

**CHILD WELFARE LEAGUE OF AMERICA**, 440 First St. NW, Third Floor, Washington DC 20001. (202)638-2952. Fax: (202)638-4004. E-mail: books@cwla.org. Website: http://www.cwla.org. **Acquisitions:** Acquisitions Editor. Publishes hardcover and trade paperback originals. **Publishes 10-12 titles/year. Receives 60-100 submissions/year. 95% of books from unagented writers. 50% of books are nonauthor-subsidy published. Pays 0-10% royalty on net domestic sales.** Publishes book 1 year after acceptance of ms. Reports on queries in 3 months. Book catalog and ms guidelines free.

○━ CWLA is a privately supported, nonprofit, membership-based organization committed to preserving, protecting and promoting the well-being of all children and their families.

**Imprint(s):** CWLA Press (child welfare professional publications), Child & Family Press (children's books and parenting books for the general public).

**Nonfiction:** Subjects include children's books, child guidance/parenting, sociology. Submit outline and sample chapters; for children's books, send complete ms.

**Recent Title(s):** *Peace in the Streets: Breaking the Cycle of Gang Violence*, by Arturo Hernandez (gang and youth violence/education); *Sassafras*, by Audrey Penn (children's picture book on self-esteem/fiction).

**Tips:** "We are looking for positive, kid friendly books for ages 3-9. We are looking for books that have a positive message . . . a feel-good book."

**CHILDREN'S PRESS**, Grolier Publishing, 90 Sherman Turnpike, Danbury CT 06816. (203)797-6802. Fax: (203)797-6986. Website: http://www.grolier.com. Publisher: John Selfridge. **Acquisitions:** Mark Friedman, executive editor; Melissa Stewart, senior editor (science); Halley Gatenby, senior editor (geography). Estab. 1946. Publishes nonfiction hardcover originals. **Publishes 200 titles/year. Makes outright purchase for $500-1,000. No advance.** Publishes book 20 months after acceptance. Book catalog available.

○━ Children's Press publishes nonfiction for the school and library market. "Our books support textbooks and closely relate to the elementary and middle-school curriculum."

**Nonfiction:** Children's/juvenile. Subjects include animals, anthropology/archaeology, art/architecture, ethnic, health/medicine, history, hobbies, music/dance, nature/environment, science and sports. Query with SASE. "We publish nonfiction books that supplement the elementary school curriculum." No fiction, poetry, folktales, cookbooks or novelty books.

**Recent Title(s):** *Columbia*, by Marion Morison; *Mount Rushmore*, by Andrew Sandella; *Extraordinary Women of the West*, by Judy Alter.

**Tips:** Most of this publisher's books are developed inhouse; less than 5% come from unsolicited submissions. However, they publish several series for which they always need new books. Study catalogs to discover possible needs.

**CHINA BOOKS & PERIODICALS, INC.**, 2929 24th St., San Francisco CA 94110-4126. (415)282-2994. Fax: (415)282-0994. Website: http://www.chinabooks.com. **Acquisitions:** Greg Jones, editor (language study, health, history); Baolin Ma, senior editor (music, language study); Michael Rice, editor (language study, poetry, history). Estab. 1960. Publishes hardcover and trade paperback originals. **Averages 5 titles/year. Receives 300 submissions/year. 10% of books from first-time authors; 95% from unagented writers. Pays 6-8% royalty on net receipts. Offers $1,000**

**average advance.** Publishes book 1 year after acceptance. Accepts simultaneous submissions. Reports in 3 months on queries. Book catalog free. Manuscript guidelines for #10 SASE or on website.

> China Books is the main importer and distributor of books and magazines from China, providing an ever-changing variety of useful tools for travelers, scholars and others interested in China and Chinese culture. "We are looking for original book ideas, especially in the areas of language study, children's books, history and culture, all relating to China." Currently emphasizing language study. De-emphasizing art, fiction.

**Nonfiction:** "*Important: All* books *must* be on topics related to China or East Asia, or Chinese-Americans. Books on China's history, politics, environment, women, art/architecture; language textbooks, acupuncture and folklore." Query with outline and sample chapters. Reviews artwork/photos as part of ms package.

**Recent Titles:** *Flowing the Tai Chi Way*, by Peter Uhlmann (nonfiction); *Drinking with the Moon*, by Jeannette Faurat (poetry).

**Tips:** "We are looking for original ideas, especially in language study, children's education, adoption of Chinese babies, or health issues relating to traditional Chinese medicine."

**CHOSEN BOOKS PUBLISHING CO., LTD.**, Baker Book House Company, 3985 Bradwater St., Fairfax VA 22031-3702. (703)764-8250. Fax: (703)764-3995. E-mail: jecampbell@aol.com. Website: http://www.bakerbooks.com. **Acquisitions:** Jane Campbell, editor. Estab. 1971. Publishes hardcover and trade paperback originals. **Publishes 8 titles/ year. Receives 500 submissions/year. 15% of books from first-time authors; 99% from unagented writers. Pays royalty on net receipts.** Publishes book 18 months after acceptance. Accepts simultaneous submissions. Reports in 3 months. Manuscript guidelines for #10 SASE. Catalog not available.

> "We publish well-crafted books that recognize the gifts and ministry of the Holy Spirit, and help the reader live a more empowered and effective life for Jesus Christ."

**Nonfiction:** Expositional books on narrowly focused themes. "We publish books reflecting the current acts of the Holy Spirit in the world, books with a charismatic Christian orientation." No New Age, poetry, fiction, autobiographies, Bible studies, booklets, academic or children's books. Submit synopsis, chapter outline, résumé, 2 sample chapters and SASE. No response without SASE. No e-mail submissions; query only by e-mail. *No complete mss.*

**Recent Title(s):** *Kneeling On the Promises: Birthing God's Purposes Through Prophetic Intercession*, by Jim W. Goll.

**Tips:** "We look for solid, practical advice for the growing and maturing Christian from authors with professional or personal experience platforms. No conversion accounts or chronicling of life events, please. State the topic or theme of your book clearly in your cover letter."

**CHRISTIAN ED. PUBLISHERS**, P.O. Box 26639, San Diego CA 92196. (619)578-4700. Fax: (619)578-2431. E-mail: BibleClubs@cepub.com. Website: http://www.cepub.com. **Acquisitions:** Dr. Lon Ackelson, senior editor. **Publishes 64 titles/year. Makes outright purchase of 3¢/word.** Reports in 3 months on queries, 5 months on proposals. Book catalog for 9 × 12 SASE and 4 first-class stamps. Manuscript guidelines for #10 SASE.

> Christian Ed. Publishers is an independent, non-denominational, evangelical company founded nearly 50 years ago to produce Christ-centered curriculum materials based on the Word of God for thousands of churches of different denominations throughout the world. "Our mission is to introduce children, teens and adults to a personal faith in Jesus Christ and to help them grow in their faith and service to the Lord. We publish materials that teach moral and spiritual values while training individuals for a lifetime of Christian service." Currently emphasizing Bible curriculum for preschool through preteen ages.

**Nonfiction:** Bible Club curriculum. "All subjects are on assignment." Query with SASE.

**Fiction:** "All writing is done on assignment." Query with SASE.

**Recent Title(s):** *All-Stars for Jesus: Bible Curriculum for Primaries*.

**Tips:** "Read our guidelines carefully before sending us a manuscript. All writing is done on assignment only and must be age appropriate (preschool-6th grade)."

**CHRISTIAN LITERATURE CRUSADE**, 701 Pennsylvania Ave., P.O. Box 1449, Fort Washington PA 19034-8449. (215)542-1242. Fax: (215)542-7580. **Acquisitions:** E. Richard Brodhag, publications coordinator. Estab. 1941. Publishes mass market and trade paperback originals and reprints. **Publishes 6-8 titles/year. Receives 50-100 queries and 80-100 mss/year. 90% of books from first-time authors; 100% from unagented writers. Pays 5-10% on retail price.** Publishes book 1 year after acceptance of ms. Accepts simultaneous submissions. Reports in 3 months on proposals. Book catalog free. Manuscript guidelines for #10 SASE.

> Christian Literature Crusade publishes books which deal with the following areas: Evangelism, Discipleship, Deeper Spiritual Life and Mission. Our audience consists of 'Deeper Life' readers; missions, adults, and junior high students.

**Nonfiction:** Biography. Religious subjects. Query or submit outline with 3 sample chapters with SASE. Writers must query before submitting ms.

**Recent Title(s):** *Safe In the Arms of Jesus*, by C & S.A. Hearn (biography of Fanny Crosby); *Mountain Breezes*, by Amy Carmichael (poetry anthology).

**Tips:** "Publications are carefully selected to conform to our constitutional statement of only producing and distributing books which are true to the inerrant Word of God and the fundamentals of the faith as commonly held by all evangelical believers."

**CHRISTIAN PUBLICATIONS, INC.**, 3825 Hartzdale Dr., Camp Hill PA 17011. (717)761-7044. Fax: (717)761-7273. E-mail: editors@cpi-horizon.com. Website: http://www.cpi-horizon.com. Managing Editor: David E. Fessenden. **Acquisitions:** George McPeek, editorial director. Estab. 1883. Publishes hardcover originals; mass market and trade paperback originals and reprints. **Publishes 35 titles/year (about 50% are reprints of classic authors). Receives 1,000 queries and 1,000 mss/year. 50% of books from first-time authors; 80% from unagented writers. Pays 5-10% royalty on retail price or makes outright purchase. Advance varies.** Publishes book 18 months after acceptance of ms. Accepts simultaneous submissions; "We do *not* reprint other publishers' material." Reports in 2 months on queries, 3 months on proposals and mss. Book catalog for 9×12 SAE with 4 first-class stamps. Manuscript guidelines for #10 SASE.

    ○━ "Our purpose is to propagate the gospel of Jesus Christ through evangelistic, deeper life and other publishing, serving our denomination and the wider Christian community."

**Imprint(s):** Christian Publications, Inc., Horizon Books.

**Nonfiction:** Biography, gift book, how-to, humor, reference (reprints *only*), self-help, workbook. Subjects include religion (Evangelical Christian perspective), child guidance, parenting, history, spirituality. Submit proposal package, including chapter synopsis, 2 sample chapters (including chapter 1), audience and market ideas, author bio.

**Fiction:** Historical, humor, mainstream/contemporary, mystery, religious, spiritual, young adult. "All books must have an evangelical Christian slant. No poetry." *All unsolicited ms returned unopened.*

**Recent Title(s):** *Great Stories in American History*, by Rebecca Price Janney (nonfiction).

**Tips:** "We are owned by The Christian and Missionary Alliance denomination; while we welcome and publish authors from various denominations, their theological perspective must be compatible with The Christian and Missionary Alliance. We are especially interested in fresh, practical approaches to deeper life—sanctification with running shoes on. Readers are evangelical, regular church-goers, mostly female, usually leaders in their church. Take time with your proposal—make it thorough, concise, complete. Authors who have done their homework regarding our message and approach have a much better chance of being accepted. All submissions must reflect a Christian worldview, a clear understanding of scripture and an effort to integrate faith into daily living."

**CHRONICLE BOOKS**, Chronicle Publishing Co., 85 Second St., 6th Floor, San Francisco CA 94105. (415)537-3730. Fax: (415)537-4440. E-mail: frontdesk@chronbooks.com. Website: http://www.chroniclebooks.com. President: Jack Jensen. **Acquisitions:** Jay Schaefer, editor (fiction); Bill LeBlond, editor (cookbooks); Victoria Rock, editor (children's); Debra Lande, editor (ancillary products); (Mr.) Nion McEvoy, editor (general); Leslie Jonath, editor (lifestyle); Alan Rapp, (art and design); Sarah Malarky (popular culture). Estab. 1966. Publishes hardcover and trade paperback originals. **Publishes 250 titles/year. Receives 22,500 submissions/year. 20% of books from first-time authors. 15% from unagented writers.** Publishes book 18 months after acceptance. Accepts simultaneous submissions. Reports in 3 months on queries. Book catalog for 11×14 SAE with 5 first-class stamps. Guidelines available on website.

    ○━ "Chronicle Books specializes in high-quality, reasonably priced illustrated books for adults and children." Titles include best-selling cookbooks; fine art, design, photography, and architecture titles; full-color nature books; award-winning poetry and literary fiction; and gift and stationery items.

**Imprint(s):** Chronicle Books for Children, GiftWorks (ancillary products, such as stationery, gift books).

**Nonfiction:** Coffee table book, cookbook, architecture, art, design, gardening, gift, health, nature, nostalgia, photography, recreation. Query or submit outline/synopsis with artwork and sample chapters.

**Fiction:** Novels, novellas, short story collections. Submit complete ms and synopsis; do not query.

**Recent Title(s):** *Star Wars Chronicles*, by Deborah Fine and Aeon Inc. (film/popular culture); *Things Unspoken*, by Anita Sheen (novel).

**Ⓝ CHRONICLE BOOKS FOR CHILDREN**, Chronicle Books, 85 Second St., 6th Floor, San Francisco CA 94105. (415)537-3730. Fax: (415)537-4420. E-mail: frontdesk@chronbooks.com. Website: http://www.chroniclebooks.com/kids. **Acquisitions:** Victoria Rock, director of Children's Books (nonfiction/fiction); Amy Novesky, assistant managing editor (nonfiction/fiction plus middle grade and young adult). Publishes hardcover and trade paperback originals. **Publishes 40-50 titles/year. Receives 20,000 submissions/year. 5% of books from first-time authors; 25% from unagented writers. Pays 8% royalty. Advance varies.** Publishes book 18 months after acceptance of ms. Accepts simultaneous submissions if so noted. Reports in 2-18 weeks on queries; 5 months on mss. Book catalog for 9×12 SAE and 3 first-class stamps. Manuscript guidelines for #10 SASE.

    ○━ Chronicle Books for Children publishes an eclectic mixture of traditional and innovative children's books. "Our aim is to publish books that inspire young readers to learn and grow creatively while helping them discover the joy of reading. We're looking for quirky, bold artwork and subject matter." Currently emphasizing picture books, holiday titles. De-emphasizing young adult.

**Nonfiction:** Biography, children's/juvenile, illustrated book, nonfiction books for ages 8-12 years, and nonfiction picture books for ages up to 8 years. Subjects include animals, multicultural and bilingual, nature/environment, art, science. Query with outline and SASE. Reviews artwork/photos as part of the ms package.

**Fiction:** Fiction picture books, middle grade fiction, young adult projects. Mainstream/contemporary, multicultural, picture books, young adult, chapter books. Query with synopsis and SASE. Send complete ms for picture books.

**Recent Title(s):** *Games for Your Brain: Space and Ocean*, by Tina L. Seelig (nonfiction); *Manuelas's Gift*, by Kristyn Rehling Estes (fiction).

**Tips:** "We are interested in projects that have a unique bent to them—be it in subject matter, writing style, or illustrative technique. As a small list, we are looking for books that will lend our list a distinctive flavor. Primarily we are interested in fiction and nonfiction picture books for children ages up to eight years, and nonfiction books for children ages up to twelve years. We publish board, pop-up, and other novelty formats as well as picture books. We are also interested in early chapter books, middle grade fiction, and young adult projects."

**CIRCLET PRESS INC.**, 1770 Massachusetts Ave., #278, Cambridge MA 02140. (617)864-0492. Fax: (617)864-0663. E-mail: circlet-info@circlet.com. Website: http://www.circlet.com. **Acquisitions:** Cecilia Tan, publisher/editor. Estab. 1992. Publishes hardcover and trade paperback originals. **Publishes 6-10 titles/year. Receives 50-100 queries and 500 mss/year. 50% of stories from first-time authors; 90% from unagented writers. Pays 4-12% royalty on retail price or makes outright purchase (depending on rights); also pays in books if author prefers.** Publishes stories 12-18 months after acceptance of ms. Accepts simultaneous submissions. Reports in 1 month on queries, 6-18 months on mss. Book catalog and ms guidelines for #10 SASE.
  O─┐ "Circlet Press publishes science fiction/fantasy which is too erotic for the mainstream and to promote literature with a positive view of sex and sexuality, which celebrates pleasure and diversity. We also publish other books celebrating sexuality and imagination with our imprints—The Ultra Violet Library and Circumflex."
**Imprint(s):** The Ultra Violet Library (gay and lesbian science fiction and fantasy. "These books will not be as erotic as our others."); Circumflex (erotic and sexual nonfiction titles, how-to and essays).
**Fiction:** Erotic science fiction and fantasy short stories only. Gay/lesbian stories needed but all persuasions welcome. "Fiction must combine both the erotic and the fantastic. The erotic content needs to be an integral part of a science fiction story, and vice versa. Writers should not assume that any sex is the same as erotica." Submit full short stories up to 10,000 words between April 15 and August 31. Manuscripts received outside this reading period are discarded. Queries only via e-mail.
**Recent Title(s):** *A Taste of Midnight*, edited by Cecilia Tan.
**Tips:** "Our audience is adults who enjoy science fiction and fantasy, especially the works of Anne Rice, Storm Constantine, Samuel Delany, who enjoy vivid storytelling and erotic content. Seize your most vivid fantasy, your deepest dream and set it free onto paper. That is at the heart of all good speculative fiction. Then if it has an erotic theme as well as a science fiction one, send it to me. No horror, rape, death or mutilation! I want to see stories that *celebrate* sex and sexuality in a positive manner. Please write for our guidelines as each year we have a specific list of topics we seek."

**CITADEL PRESS**, Carol Publishing Group, 120 Enterprise, Secaucus NJ 07094. (201)866-0490. Fax: (201)271-7895. E-mail: info@citadelpublishing.com. Website: http://www.citadelpublishing.com. **Acquisitions:** Hillel Black, editorial director; Bob Berkel, Carrie Cantor, Francine Hornberger, Mike Lewis. Estab. 1945. Publishes paperback originals and reprints. **Publishes 60-80 titles/year. Receives 800-1,000 submissions/year. 7% of books from first-time authors; 50% from unagented writers. Pays 10% royalty on hardcover, 6-7½% on paperback. Offers average $7,000 advance.** Publishes book 1 year after acceptance. Accepts simultaneous submissions. Reports in 2 months. Book catalog for $1.
  O─┐ Citadel Press concentrates on biography, film, how-to, new age and gaming.
**Nonfiction:** Biography, film, psychology, humor, history. Also seeks "off-beat material, but no fiction, poetry, religion, politics." Accepts nonfiction translations. Query or submit outline/synopsis and 3 sample chapters. Reviews artwork/photos as part of ms package. Send photocopies with SASE.
**Recent Title(s):** *Making of Schindler's List*, by F. Palowski (Schindler and Spielberg's vision and how the film was made; rare photographs).

**[N] [★] CITY & COMPANY**, 22 W. 23rd St., New York NY 10010. (212)366-1988. Fax: (212)242-0412. E-mail: cityco@bway.net. **Acquisitions:** Helene Silver, publisher. Estab. 1994. Publishes hardcover and trade paperback originals. **Publishes 10 titles/year. Receives 75 queries and 10 mss/year. 50% of books from first-time authors; 75% from unagented writers. Pays 5-10% royalty on wholesale price. Offers advance.** Publishes book 6 months after acceptance of ms. Accepts simultaneous submissions. Reports in 3 months on queries. Book catalog and ms guidelines free.
  O─┐ City & Company specializes in single subject city guide books.
**Nonfiction:** Giftbook, illustrated book, reference, travel guidebooks. Subjects include child guidance/parenting, gardening, music/dance, nature/environment, recreation, regional, sports, travel, single subject city guide. Submit proposal package, including outline, 3 sample chapters and author bio. Reviews artwork/photos as part of ms package.

**CLEAR LIGHT PUBLISHERS**, 823 Don Diego, Santa Fe NM 87501-4224. (505)989-9590. E-mail: clpublish@aol.com. **Acquisitions:** Harmon Houghton, publisher. Estab. 1981. Publishes hardcover and trade paperback originals. **Publishes 18 titles/year. Receives 100 queries/year. 10% of books from first-time authors; 50% from unagented writers. Pays 10% royalty on wholesale price. Offers advance, a percent of gross potential.** Publishes book 1 year after acceptance of ms. Accepts simultaneous submissions. Reports in 3 months on queries. Book catalog free.
  O─┐ Clear Light publishes books that "accurately depict the positive side of human experience and inspire the spirit."
**Nonfiction:** Biography, coffee table book, cookbook. Subjects include Americana, anthropology/archaelogy, art/architecture, cooking/foods/nutrition, ethnic, history, nature/environment, philosophy, photography, regional (Southwest). Query with SASE. Reviews artwork/photos as part of ms package. Send photocopies (no originals).
**Recent Title(s):** *Children's Book of Yoga*, by Thia Luby; *Ancient Wisdom Living Traditions*, by Marcia Keegan; *Dee Brown's Civil War Anthology*, by Dee Brown and Stan Bahash.

**CLEIS PRESS**, P.O. Box 14684, San Francisco CA 94114-0684. Fax: (415)864-3385. **Acquisitions:** Frederique Delacoste. Estab. 1980. Publishes trade paperback originals and reprints. **Publishes 17 titles/year. 10% of books are from first-time authors; 90% from unagented writers. Pays variable royalty on retail price.** Publishes book 2 years after acceptance of ms. Accepts simultaneous submissions "only if accompanied by an original letter stating where and when ms was sent." Reports in 1 month. Book catalog for #10 SAE with 2 first-class stamps.

    O⊸ Cleis Press specializes in gay/lesbian fiction and nonfiction.

**Nonfiction:** Subjects include feminist, gay/lesbian and human rights. "We are interested in books by and about women in Latin America; on lesbian and gay rights; on sexuality; topics which have not already been widely documented. We do not want religious/spiritual tracts; we are not interested in books on topics which have been documented over and over, unless the author is approaching the topic from a new viewpoint." Query or submit outline and sample chapters.

**Fiction:** Feminist, gay/lesbian, literary. "We are looking for high quality fiction by women and men. No romances." Submit complete ms. *Writer's Market* recommends sending a query with SASE first.

**Recent Title(s):** *Gore Vidal: Sexually Speaking* (nonfiction); *The Woman Who Rode to the Moon*, by Bett Reece Johnson (fiction).

**Tips:** "Be familiar with publishers' catalogs; be absolutely aware of your audience; research potential markets; present fresh new ways of looking at your topic; avoid 'PR' language and include publishing history in query letter."

**CLEVELAND STATE UNIVERSITY POETRY CENTER**, R.T. 1813, Cleveland State University, Cleveland OH 44115-2440. (216)687-3986. Fax: (216)687-6943. E-mail: poetrycenter@popmail.csuohio.edu. Editors: David Evett, Ted Lardner, Ruth Schwartz and Leonard Trawick. Poetry Center Coordinator: Rita M. Grabowski. Estab. 1962. Publishes trade paperback and hardcover originals. **Publishes 4 titles/year. Receives 500 queries and 1,000 mss/year. 60% of books from first-time authors; 100% from unagented writers. 30% of titles subsidized by CSU, 20% by government subsidy. CSU Poetry Series pays one-time, lump-sum royalty of $200-400, plus 50 copies; Cleveland Poets Series (Ohio poets only) pays 100 copies. $1,000 prize for best full-length ms each year. No advance.** Accepts simultaneous submissions. Reports in 1 month on queries, 8 months on mss. Book catalog for $1. Manuscript guidelines for SASE. Manuscripts are not returned.

**Poetry:** No light verse, inspirational, or greeting card verse. ("This does not mean that we do not consider poetry with humor or philosophical/religious import.") Query; ask for guidelines. Submit only November-January. Charges $20 reading fee. Reviews artwork/photos only if applicable (e.g., concrete poetry).

**Recent title(s):** *Hammerlock*, by Tim Seibel.

**Tips:** "Our books are for serious readers of poetry, i.e. poets, critics, academics, students, people who read *Poetry*, *Field*, *American Poetry Review*, etc. Trends include movement away from 'confessional' poetry; greater attention to form and craftsmanship. Project an interesting, coherent personality; link poems so as to make coherent unity, not just a miscellaneous collection. Especially need poems with *mystery*, i.e., poems that suggest much, but do not tell all."

**CLIFFS NOTES, INC.**, IDG Books Worldwide, P.O. Box 80728, Lincoln NE 68501. (402)423-5050. Website: http://www.cliffs.com. **Acquisitions:** Gary Carey, senior editor (literature notes); Linnea Frederickson, managing editor (test preparation and course review). Estab. 1958. Publishes trade paperback originals. **Publishes 20 titles/year. 100% of books from unagented writers. Pays royalty on wholesale price. Buys majority of mss outright; "full payment on acceptance of ms."** Publishes book 1 year after acceptance. Reports in 1 month. "We provide specific guidelines when a project is assigned."

    O⊸ Cliffs Notes, Inc. publishes self-help study aids directed to junior high through graduate school audience. Publications include *Cliffs Notes*, *Cliffs Test Preparation Guides*, *Cliffs Quick Reviews* and other study guides.

**Nonfiction:** Self-help, textbook. "Most authors are experienced teachers, usually with advanced degrees. Some books also appeal to a general lay audience." Query.

**Recent Title(s):** *Cliffs Accounting Principles I Quick Review*; *Cliffs Notes on the Woman Warrior*.

**⒩ CLOUD PEAK**, P.O. Box 377, Dayton WY 82836. (307)655-3411. Fax: (307)265-6922. E-mail: phatwitz@isis-ihtl.com. **Acquisitions:** Paul Harwitz. Publishes hardcover originals and reprints, trade paperback originals and reprints, mass market paperback originals and reprints. **Publishes 36 titles/year. Receives 200 queries and 80 mss/year. 10% of books are from first-time authors; 50% from unagented writers. Pays 10% royalty for nonfiction, percentage for fiction varies on retail price. No advance.** Publishes book 1-2 years after acceptance of ms. Accepts simultaneous submissions. Reports back in 2 months on queries, 3 months on proposals, 2 months on mss. Book catalog and ms guidelines for #10 SASE or on website.

    O⊸ Cloud Peak is currently emphasizing nonfiction books about Indians, African-Americans, Asians, Hispanics and other "minorities" in the West.

**Nonfiction:** Biography, children's juvenile, how-to, humor. Subjects include Americana (Western), education, history, military/war, multicultural, sports, women's issues/women's studies. "Submissions to our 'Women of the West' line of nonfiction will receive special consideration." Query with SASE. *All unsolicited submissions returned unopened.* Reviews artwork/photos as part of ms package. Send photocopies, transparencies or computer files on 3½" floppy disk.

**Fiction:** Adventure, fantasy, historical, horror, humor, juvenile, military/war, multicultural, multimedia, mystery, poetry, science fiction, suspense, western, Native American. "Do everything you can to make the book a real 'page-turner,' Plots and sub-plots must be plausible and suited to the locale(s). Main and secondary characters must speak dialog which matches their respective personality traits. Blacks, Spanish-speaking people and other 'minorities' must *not* be portrayed stereotypically. Historical accuracy is important." Query with SASE. *All unsolicited mss returned unopened.*

**Poetry:** "We publish Western/cowboy/Indian poetry in single-author collections and multi-author anthologies." Query with 3 sample poems or send complete ms.

**Recent Title(s):** *Soldiers Falling Into Camp: The Battles at the Rosebud and Little Bighorn*, by Robert Kammen, Frederick Lefthand and Joe Marshall (military history); *The Watcher*, by Robert Kammen (Western/supernatural/ecological); *Riders of the Leafy Spurge*, by Bill Lowman (cowboy poetry).

**Tips:** "Buy, read and study the *Writer's Market* each year. Writing must flow. Imagine you are a reader visiting a bookstore. Write the first page of the book in such a way that the reader feels *compelled* to buy it. It helps a writer to work from an outline. When we solicit a manuscript for consideration, we like to receive both a hard copy and a floppy disk."

**N** ★ **COACHES CHOICE**, Sagamore Publishing, Inc., 804 N. Neil, Champaign IL 61820. (217)359-5940. Fax: (217)359-5975. E-mail: soutlaw@sagamorepub.com. Website: http://www.coacheschoice-pub.com. **Acquisitions:** Holly Kondras, general manager (sports); Tom Bast, director of acquisitions (sports); Sue Outlaw, director of operations (football, baseball, basketball). Publishes trade paperback originals and reprints. **Publishes 40 titles/year. Receives 100 queries and 60 mss/year. 50% of books from first-time authors; 95% from unagented writers. Pays 10-15% royalty. Offers $500-1,000 advance.** Publishes book 1 year after receipt of ms. Accepts simultaneous submissions. Reports in 2 months. Book catalog and ms guidelines free.

　　○➡ "We publish books for anyone who coaches a sport or has an interest in coaching a sport—all levels of competition."

**Nonfiction:** How-to, reference. Subjects include sports. Submit proposal package, including outline, 2 sample chapters. Reviews artwork/photos as part of ms package. Send photocopies and diagrams.

**Recent Title(s):** *101 Championship Drills*, by Glenn and Raissa Cecchini (baseball coach).

**COFFEE HOUSE PRESS**, 27 N. Fourth St., Suite 400, Minneapolis MN 55401. Fax: (612)338-4004. Publisher/Editor: Allan Kornblum. **Acquisitions:** Chris Fischbach, managing editor. Estab. 1984. Publishes hardcover and trade paperback originals. **Publishes 14 titles/year. Receives 5,000 queries and mss/year. 90% of books are from unagented writers. Pays 8% royalty on retail price.** Publishes book 18-24 months after acceptance. Reports in 1 month on queries or samples, 6 months on mss. Book catalog and ms guidelines for #10 SAE with 2 first-class stamps.

**Fiction:** Literary novels, short story collections. No genre. Query first with samples and SASE.

**Recent Title(s):** *The Cockfighter*, by Frank Manley (fiction); *Avalanche*, by Quincy Troupe (poetry).

**Tips:** "Look for our books at stores and libraries to get a feel for what we like to publish. No phone calls or faxes."

**N** ★ **COLLECTOR BOOKS**, Schroeder Publishing Co., Inc., 5801 Kentucky Dam Rd., P.O. Box 3009, Paducah KY 42002-3009. Publisher: Bill Schroeder. **Acquisitions:** Lisa Stroup, editor. Estab. 1974. Publishes hardcover and paperback originals. **Publishes 65 titles/year. 50% of books from first-time authors; 100% of books from unagented writers. Pays 5% royalty on retail price. No advance.** Publishes book 9 months after acceptance. Reports in 1 month. Book catalog for 9 × 12 SAE with 4 first-class stamps. Manuscript guidelines for #10 SASE.

　　○➡ Collector Books publishes books on antiques and collectibles.

**Nonfiction:** "We require our authors to be very knowledgeable in their respective fields and have access to a large representative sampling of the particular subject concerned." Query with outline and 2-3 sample chapters. Reviews artwork/photos as part of ms package.

**Tips:** "Common mistakes writers make include making phone contact instead of written contact and assuming an accurate market evaluation."

**COLLECTORS PRESS, INC.**, P.O. Box 230986, Portland OR 97281-0986. (503)684-3030. Fax: (503)684-3777. Website: http://www.collectorspress.com. **Acquisitions:** Lisa Perry, editor-in-chief. Estab. 1992. Publishes hardcover and trade paperback originals. **Publishes 8-10 titles/year. Receives 500 queries and 200 mss/year. 75% of books from first-time authors; 90% from unagented writers. Pays 2-10% royalty on wholesale price.** Publishes book 1 year after acceptance of ms. Reports in 1 month on proposals, 3 months on mss. Book catalog and ms guidelines free.

　　○➡ Collectors Press publishes art coffee table books on vintage 20th century collectibles and designers.

**Nonfiction:** Biography, coffee table book, gift book, illustrated book, reference. Art coffee table books: subjects include art/architecture, historical art, science fiction art, fantasy art, graphic design, photography. Submit proposal package, including market research, outline, 2 sample chapters and SASE. Reviews artwork/photos as part of ms package. Send transparencies or *very* clear photos.

**Fiction:** Fantasy, historical, mainstream/contemporary, mystery, picture books, science fiction.

---

**⟨$⟩ ⟨N⟩ ★ Ⓐ ▭ ▢ ∅ 🍁**

**FOR EXPLANATIONS OF THESE SYMBOLS, SEE THE INSIDE FRONT AND BACK COVERS OF THIS BOOK.**

**Recent Title(s):** *Pulp Culture: The Art of Fiction Magazines*, by Frank M. Robinson and Lawrence Davidson.
**Tips:** "Your professional package must be typed. No computer disks accepted."

**THE COLLEGE BOARD**, College Entrance Examination Board, 45 Columbus Ave., New York NY 10023-6992. (212)713-8000. Website: http://www.collegeboard.org. **Acquisitions:** Carolyn Trager, director of publications. Publishes trade paperback originals. **Publishes 30 titles/year; imprint publishes 12 titles/year. Receives 50-60 submissions/year. 25% of books from first-time authors; 50% from unagented writers. Pays royalty on retail price. Offers advance.** Publishes book 9 months after acceptance of ms. Reports in 2 months on queries. Book catalog free.
○┮ The College Board publishes guidance information for college-bound students.
**Nonfiction:** Education-related how-to, reference, self-help. Subjects include college guidance, education. "We want books to help students make a successful transition from high school to college." Query or send outline and sample chapters with SASE.
**Recent Title(s):** *The College Application Essay*, by Sarah Myers McGinty.

**COLLEGE PRESS PUBLISHING COMPANY**, P.O. Box 1132, Joplin MO 64802. (417)623-6280. Website: http://www.collegepress.com. **Acquisitions:** John Hunter, managing editor (New Testament, church history). Estab. 1959. Publishes hardcover and trade paperback originals and reprints. **Publishes 25-30 titles/year. Receives 400 queries and 300 mss/year. 25% of books from first-time authors; 90% from unagented writers. Pays 5-15% royalty on wholesale price. Offers $50-500 advance.** Publishes book 6 months after acceptance of ms. Accepts simultaneous submissions. Reports in 3 months on proposals. Book catalog for 9×12 SAE and 5 first-class stamps. Manuscript guidelines for #10 SASE.
○┮ "College Press is an organization dedicated to support the mission and work of the church. Its mission is the production and distribution of materials which will facilitate the discipling of the nations as commanded by our Lord Jesus Christ." Denomination affiliation with Christian churches/Churches of Christ.
**Nonfiction:** Textbook, Christian textbooks and small group studies. Subjects include religion, Christian Apologetics. "We seek textbooks used in Christian colleges and universities—leaning toward an Arminian and an amillennial mindset." Query with proposal package, including synopsis, author bio, 3 sample chapters with SASE.
**Recent Title(s):** *Yet Will I Trust Him*, by John Mark Hicks.
**Tips:** "Our core market is Christian Churches/Churches of Christ and conservative evangelical Christians. Have your material critically reviewed prior to sending it. Make sure that it is non-Calvinistic and that it leans more amillennial (if it is apocalyptic writing)."

**COMBINED BOOKS, INC.**, 476 W. Elm St., P.O. Box 307, Conshohocken PA 19428. (610)828-2595. Fax: (610)828-2603. **Acquisitions:** Kenneth S. Gallagher, senior editor. Estab. 1985. Publishes hardcover originals and trade paperback reprints. **Publishes 12-14 titles/year. 30% of books from first-time authors; 100% from unagented writers. Pays 8-10% royalty on wholesale price. Offers $1,000-1,500 advance.** Publishes book 1 year after acceptance of ms. Reports in 4 months. Book catalog free.
○┮ "We publish a series called Great Campaigns. Authors should be aware of the editorial formula of this series."
**Nonfiction:** Military history. Submit outline, 1 sample chapter and SASE. Reviews artwork/photos as part of ms package. Send photocopies only.
**Recent Title(s):** *Custer and His Wolverines*, by Edward Longacre.

**COMMUNE-A-KEY PUBLISHING**, P.O. Box 58637, Salt Lake City UT 84158. (801)581-9191. Fax: (801)581-9196. E-mail: keypublish@lgcy.com. **Acquisitions:** Caryn Summers, editor-in-chief. Estab. 1992. Publishes trade paperback originals. **Publishes 4-6 titles/year. 40% of books from first-time authors; 75% from unagented writers. Pays 7-8% royalty on retail price.** Publishes book 1 year after acceptance of ms. Accepts simultaneous submissions. Reports in 1 month on queries and proposals, 2 months on mss. Book catalog and ms guidelines with SASE.
○┮ Commune-A-Key's mission statement is: "Communicating the Key to Growth and Empowerment." Currently emphasizing gift books, inspirational. De-emphasizing women's studies.
**Nonfiction:** Gift book/inspirational, humor, self-help/psychology, spiritual. Subjects include health/medicine, psychology, men's or women's issues/studies, recovery, Native American. Query with SASE. Reviews artwork/photos as part of ms package. Send photocopies.
**Recent Title(s):** *Call to Connection*, by Carole Kammen and Jodi Gald (nonfiction).

**COMPANION PRESS**, P.O. Box 2575, Laguna Hills CA 92654. Fax: (949)362-4489. E-mail: sstewart@companionpress.com. **Acquisitions**: Steve Stewart, publisher. Publishes trade paperback originals. **Publishes 6 titles/year. Receives 50 queries and 25 mss/year. 50% of books from first-time authors; 100% from unagented writers. Pays 6-8% royalty on retail price or makes outright purchase. Offers $500-750 advance.** Publishes book 9 months after acceptance of ms. Reports in 1 month. *Writer's Market* recommends allowing 2 months for reply. Book catalog and ms guidelines for #10 SASE.
○┮ "We are interested in gay erotic books written for the general reader, rather than the academic. We only publish gay adult entertainment books for men." Currently emphasizing pornstar biographies. De-emphasizing novels.
**Fiction and Nonfiction:** Biographies, anthologies, photobooks, video guidebooks. Subjects niche: gay adult entertainment. Query. Reviews artwork/photos as part of ms package. Send photocopies.
**Recent Title(s):** *Hollywood Hardcore Diaries*, by Mickey Skee (gay erotic fiction).

**COMPASS AMERICAN GUIDES INC.**, Fodor's, Random House. 5332 College Ave., Suite 201, Oakland CA 94618. **Acquisitions:** Kit Duane, managing editor; Christopher Burt, creative director. Publishes trade paperback originals. **Publishes 10 titles/year. Receives 50 queries and 5 mss/year. 5% of books from first-time authors; 90% from unagented writers. Makes outright purchase of $5,000-10,000. Offers $1,500-3,000 advance.** Publishes book an average of 8 months after acceptance of ms. Accepts simultaneous submissions. Reports in 6 months. Book catalog for $1.

O—¬ Compass American Guides publishes guides to U.S. and Canadian states, provinces or cities.
**Nonfiction:** Travel guides. "We cannot guarantee the return of any submissions." Query this publisher about its specific format. Reviews artwork/photos as part of ms package. Photographers should send duplicate slides.

**CONARI PRESS**, 2550 Ninth St., Suite 101, Berkeley CA 94710. (510)649-7175. Fax: (510)649-7190. E-mail: conari @conari.com. Website: http://www.conari.com. **Acquisitions:** Claudia Schaab, managing editor. Estab. 1987. Publishes hardcover and trade paperback originals. **Publishes 30 titles/year. Receives 1,000 submissions/year. 50% of books from first-time authors; 50% from unagented writers. Pays 12-16% royalty on net price. Offers $5,000 average advance.** Publishes book 1-3 years after acceptance. Accepts simultaneous submissions. Reports in 3 months. Manuscript guidelines for 6×9 SASE.

O—¬ Conari Press seeks to be a catalyst for profound change by providing enlightening books on topics ranging from relationships, personal growth, and parenting to women's history and issues, social issues and spirituality. "We value integrity, process, compassion and receptivity, both in the books we publish and in our internal workings."
**Nonfiction:** Psychology, spirituality, women's issues, parenting. No poetry or fiction! Submit proposal and complete ms, attn: Claudia Schaab. Reviews artwork/photos as part of ms package.
**Recent Title(s):** *Stopping*, by David Kundtz.
**Tips:** "Writers should send us well-targeted, specific and focused manuscripts. No recovery issues. We have a commitment to publish quality books that contribute positively to society—books that reveal, explore, and incite us to grow spiritually and emotionally."

**CONCORDIA PUBLISHING HOUSE**, 3558 S. Jefferson Ave., St. Louis MO 63118-3968. (314)268-1000. Fax: (314)268-1329. E-mail: boverton@cphnet.org. Website: http://www.cph.org. **Acquisitions:** Rachel Hoyer, editor (adult and youth nonfiction and drama); Jane Wilke, associate editor (children's and teaching resources); Dawn Weinstock, managing editor (devotional collections). Estab. 1869. Publishes hardcover and trade paperback originals. **Publishes 150 titles/year. Receives 3,000 submissions/year. 10% of books from first-time authors; 95% from unagented writers. Pays royalty or makes outright purchase.** Publishes book 1 year after acceptance of ms. Simultaneous submissions discouraged. Reports in 3 months on queries. Manuscript guidelines for #10 SASE.

O—¬ Concordia publishes Protestant, inspirational, theological, family and juvenile material. All manuscripts must conform to the doctrinal tenets of The Lutheran Church—Missouri Synod. Currently emphasizing practical parenting books.
**Nonfiction:** Juvenile, adult. Subjects include child guidance/parenting (in Christian context), inspirational, how-to, religion. Query with SASE first.
**Fiction:** Juvenile. "We will consider preteen and children's fiction and picture books. All books must contain Christian content. No adult Christian fiction." Query with SASE first.
**Recent Title(s):** *Celebrate Home*, by Angie Peters (nonfiction); *Heads I Win, Tails You Lose*, by Paul Buchanan and Rod Randall (fiction).
**Tips:** "Our needs have broadened to include writers of books for lay adult Christians."

**N: ☆ CONFLUENCE PRESS, INC.**, Lewis-Clark State College, 500 Eighth Ave., Lewiston ID 83501-1698. (208)799-2336. Fax: (208)799-2324. **Acquisitions:** James R. Hepworth, publisher. Estab. 1975. Publishes hardcover originals and trade paperback originals and reprints. **Publishes 4-5 titles/year. Receives 500 queries and 150 mss/ year. 50% of books from first-time authors; 50% from unagented writers. Pays 10-15% royalty on net sales price. Offers $100-2,000 advance.** Publishes book 18 months after acceptance of ms. Accepts simultaneous submissions. Reports in 2 months on queries, 1 month on proposals, 3 months on mss. Book catalog and ms guidelines free.

O—¬ "We are increasingly moving toward strictly regional books by regional authors and rarely publish writers from outside the western United States." Currently emphasizing essay collections, biography, autobiography. De-emphasizing novels, short stories.
**Nonfiction:** Subjects include Americana, ethnic, history, language/literature, nature/environment, regional, translation. Query.
**Fiction:** Ethnic, literary, mainstream/contemporary, short story collections. Query.
**Poetry:** Submit 6 sample poems.
**Recent Title(s):** *A Little Bit of Wisdom: Conversations with a Nez Perce Elder* (nonfiction); *The Names of Time*, by Mary Ann Waters (poetry).

**CONSORTIUM PUBLISHING**, 640 Weaver Hill Rd., West Greenwich RI 02817-2261. (401)397-9838. Fax: (401)392-1926. **Acquisitions:** John M. Carlevale, chief of publications. Estab. 1990. Publishes trade paperback originals and trade paperback reprints. **Publishes 12 titles/year. Receives 150 queries and 50 mss/year. 50% of books from**

**first-time authors; 95% from unagented writers. Pays 10-15% royalty.** Publishes book 3 months after acceptance of ms. Reports in 2 months. Book catalog and ms guidelines for #10 SASE.

O→ Consortium publishes books for all levels of the education market.

**Nonfiction:** How-to, humor, illustrated book, reference, self-help, technical, textbook. Subjects include business/economics, child guidance/parenting, education, government/politics, health/medicine, history, music/dance, nature/environment, psychology, science, sociology, women's issues/studies. Query or submit proposal package, including table of contents, outline, 1 sample chapter and SASE. Reviews artwork/photos as part of ms package. Send photocopies.

**Recent Title(s):** *Teaching the Child Under Six, 4th edition*, by James L. Hymes, Jr. (education).

**Tips:** Audience is college and high school students and instructors, elementary school teachers and other trainers.

**N THE CONSULTANT PRESS**, 163 Amsterdam Ave., #201, New York NY 10023-5001. (212)838-8640. Fax: (212)873-7065. **Acquisitions:** Bob Persky, publisher. Estab. 1980. Publishes trade paperback originals. **Publishes 7 titles/year. Receives 25 submissions/year.** 20% of books from first-time authors; 75% from unagented writers. **Pays 7-12% royalty on receipts. Offers $500 average advance.** Publishes book 6 months after acceptance. Reports in 3 weeks. *Writer's Market* recommends allowing 2 months for reply. Book catalog free.

O→ "Our prime areas of interest are books on the business of art and photography."

**Imprint(s):** The Photographic Arts Center.

**Nonfiction:** How-to, reference, art/architecture, business/economics of the art world and photography. "Writers should check *Books In Print* for competing titles." Submit outline and 2 sample chapters.

**Recent Title(s):** *Art of Displaying Art*, by Lawrence B. Smith (displaying art in homes, offices and galleries).

**Tips:** "Artists, photographers, galleries, museums, curators and art consultants are our audience."

**CONSUMER PRESS**, 13326 SW 28 St., Suite 102, Ft. Lauderdale FL 33330. **Acquisitions**: Joseph Pappas, editorial director. Estab. 1989. Publishes trade paperback originals. **Publishes 2-5 titles/year. Receives 1,000 queries and 700 mss/year. 50% of books from first-time authors; 70% from unagented writers. Pays royalty on wholesale price or on retail price, as per agreement.** Publishes book 6 months after acceptance of ms. Accepts simultaneous submissions. Book catalog free.

**Imprint(s):** Women's Publications.

**Nonfiction:** How-to, self-help. Subjects include homeowner guides, building/remodeling, child guidance/parenting, health/medicine, money/finance, women's issues/studies. Query by mail with SASE.

**Recent Title(s):** *The Ritalin Free Child*, by Diana Hunter.

**COPPER CANYON PRESS**, P.O. Box 271, Port Townsend WA 98368. (360)385-4925. **Acquisitions:** Sam Hamill, editor. Estab. 1972. Publishes trade paperback originals and occasional clothbound editions. **Publishes 10 titles/year. Receives 1,500 queries/year and 500 mss/year.** 10% of books from first-time authors; 95% from unagented writers. **Pays 7-10% royalty on retail price.** Publishes book 18 months after acceptance of ms. Reports in 1 month. Book catalog free.

O→ Copper Canyon Press is dedicated to publishing poetry in a wide range of styles and from a full range of the world's many cultures.

**Poetry:** No unsolicited mss. "First and second book manuscripts are considered only for our Hayden Carruth Awards, presented annually." Send SASE for entry form in September of each year.

**Recent Title(s):** *East Window: The Asian Translations*, by W.S. Merwin; *The Shape of the Journey: Collected Poems*, by Jim Harrison; *Configurations: New & Selected Poems*, by Clarence Major; *Rave: Selected Poems*, by Olga Broumas.

**CORNELL MARITIME PRESS, INC.**, P.O. Box 456, Centreville MD 21617-0456. (410)758-1075. Fax: (410)758-6849. **Acquisitions:** Charlotte Kurst, managing editor. Estab. 1938. Publishes hardcover originals and quality paperbacks for professional mariners and yachtsmen. **Publishes 7-9 titles/year. Receives 150 submissions/year. 41% of books from first-time authors; 99% from unagented writers. "Payment is negotiable but royalties do not exceed 10% for first 5,000 copies, 12½% for second 5,000 copies, 15% on all additional.** Royalties for original paperbacks are invariably lower. Revised editions revert to original royalty schedule." Publishes book 1 year after acceptance. Reports in 2 months. Book catalog for 10×13 SAE with 5 first-class stamps.

O→ Cornell Maritime Press publishes books for the merchant marine and a few recreational boating books.

**Imprint:** Tidewater (regional history, folklore and wildlife of the Chesapeake Bay and the Delmarva Peninsula).

**Nonfiction:** Marine subjects (highly technical), manuals, how-to books on maritime subjects. Query first, with writing samples and outlines of book ideas.

**Recent Title(s):** *Marine Radionavigation and Communications*, by Jeffrey W. Monroe and Thomas L. Bushy.

**CORNELL UNIVERSITY PRESS**, Sage House, 512 E. State St., Ithaca NY 14850. (607)277-2338. Website: http://www.cornellpress.cornell.edu. **Acquisitions:** Frances Benson, editor-in-chief. Estab. 1869. Publishes hardcover and paperback originals. **Pays royalty. Offers $0-5,000 advance.** Publishes book 1 year after acceptance of ms. Sometimes accepts simultaneous submissions.

O→ Cornell Press is an academic publisher of nonfiction with particular strengths in anthropology, Asian studies, biological sciences, classics, history, labor and business, literary criticism, politics and international relations, psychology, women's studies, Slavic studies. Currently emphasizing sound scholarship that appeals beyond the academic community.

**Imprint(s):** Comstock (contact Peter J. Prescott, science editor), **ILR Press**.

**Nonfiction:** Biography, reference, textbook. Subjects include agriculture/horticulture, anthropology/archaeology, art/architecture, business and economics, education, ethnic, gay/lesbian, government/politics, health/medicine, history, language/literature, military/war, music/dance, philosophy, psychology, regional, religion, science, sociology, translation, women's issues/studies. Submit outline.

**Recent Title(s):** *Who Speaks for America.*

**Tips:** "Cornell University Press is the oldest university press in the country. From our beginnings in 1869, we have grown to be a major scholarly publisher, offering 150 new titles a year in many disciplines."

**CORWIN PRESS, INC.,** 2455 Teller Rd., Thousand Oaks CA 91320. (805)499-9734. Fax: (805)499-5323. E-mail: jay.whitney@corwinpress.com. **Acquisitions:** Jay Whitney, director of acquisitions (early childhood); Robb Clouse, editor (special education); Alice Foster, editor (curriculum and instruction). Estab. 1990. Publishes hardcover and paperback originals. **Publishes 70 titles/year. Pays 10% royalty on net sales.** Publishes book 7 months after acceptance of ms. Reports in 1 month on queries. Manuscript guidelines for #10 SASE.

    O─ Corwin Press, Inc. publishes leading-edge, user-friendly publications for education professionals.

**Nonfiction:** Curriculum activities and professional-level publications for administrators, teachers, school specialists, policymakers, researchers and others involved with early childhood-12 education. Seeking fresh insights, conclusions and recommendations for action. Prefers theory or research based books that provide real-world examples and practical, hands-on strategies to help busy educators be successful. No textbooks that simply summarize existing knowledge or mass-market books. Query.

**Recent Title(s):** *Sing Me a Story! Tell Me a Story!,* by Helda Jackman.

**COTTONWOOD PRESS, INC.,** 305 W. Magnolia, Suite 398, Fort Collins CO 80521. (800)864-4297. Fax: (970)204-0761. E-mail: cottonwod@cottonwoodpress.com. Website: http://www.verinet.com/cottonwood. **Acquisitions:** Cheryl Thurston, editor. Estab. 1965. Publishes trade paperback originals. **Publishes 2-8 titles/year. Receives 50 queries and 400 mss/year. 50% of books from first-time authors; 100% from unagented writers. Pays 10-12% royalty on net sales.** Publishes book 1 year after acceptance. Accepts simultaneous submissions, if so noted. Reports in 1 month on queries and proposals, 3 months on mss. Book catalog for 6×9 SAE with 2 first-class stamps. Manuscript guidelines for #10 SASE.

    O─ Cottonwood Press publishes creative and practical materials for English and language arts teachers, grades 5-12. "We believe English should be everyone's favorite subject."

**Nonfiction:** Textbook. Subjects include education, language/literature. Query with outline and 1-3 sample chapters. "We are always looking for truly original, creative materials for teachers."

**Recent Title(s):** *Abra Vocabra—The Amazingly Sensible Approach to Teaching Vocabulary.*

**Tips:** "We publish *only* supplemental textbooks for English/language arts teachers, grades 5-12, with an emphasis upon middle school and junior high materials. Don't assume we publish educational materials for all subject areas. We do not. Never submit anything to us before looking at our catalog. We have a very narrow focus and a distinctive style. Writers who don't understand that are wasting their time."

**[N] COUNCIL ON SOCIAL WORK EDUCATION,** 1600 Duke St., Alexandria VA 22314-3421. (703)683-8080. Fax: (703)683-8099. E-mail: publications@cswe.org. **Acquisitions:** Michael J. Monti, director of publications. Estab. 1952. Publishes trade paperback originals. **Publishes 4 titles/year. Receives 6 queries and 5 mss/year. 25% of books from first-time authors; 100% from unagented writers. Pays sliding royalty scale, starting at 10%. No advance.** Publishes book 1 year after acceptance of ms. Does not return submissions. Reports in 2 months on queries, 3 months on proposals and mss. Book catalog and ms guidelines free.

    O─ Council on Social Work Education produces books and nonprint media to enhance the quality of social work education.

**Nonfiction:** Books for social work and other educators. Subjects include education, sociology, social work. Query with proposal package, including cv, outline, 2 sample chapters and SASE. Reviews artwork/photos as part of ms package. Send photocopies.

**Recent Titles:** *Social Work in Rural Communities,* by Leon H. Ginsberg (textbook).

**Tips:** Audience is "Social work educators and students and others in the helping professions. Check areas of publication interest on website."

**[A] COUNTERPOINT,** Perseus Books Group, 1627 I St. NW, Suite 500, Washington DC 20006. (202)887-0363. Fax: (202)887-0562. **Acquisitions:** Jack Shoemaker, editor-in-chief. Estab. 1994. Publishes hardcover and trade paperback originals and reprints. **Publishes 20-25 titles/year. Receives 50 queries/week, 250 mss/year. 2% of books from first-time authors; 2% from unagented writers. Pays 7½-15% royalty on retail price.** Publishes book 18 months after acceptance of ms. Accepts simultaneous submissions. Reports in 3 months.

    O─ Counterpoint publishes serious literary work, with particular emphasis on natural history, science, philosophy and contemporary thought, history, art, poetry and fiction.

**Nonfiction:** Biography, coffee table book, gift book. Subjects include agriculture/horticulture, art/architecture, history, language/literature, nature/environment, philosophy, religion, science, translation. *Agented submissions only.*

**Fiction:** Historical, humor, literary, mainstream/contemporary, religious, short story collections. *Agented submissions only.*

**Recent Title(s):** *The Gary Snyder Reader*, by Gary Snyder (nonfiction); *The Autobiography of Joseph Stalin: A Novel*, by Richard Louric.

**THE COUNTRYMAN PRESS**, W.W. Norton, Inc., P.O. Box 748, Woodstock VT 05091-0748. (802)457-4826. Fax: (802)457-1678. E-mail: countrymanpress@wwnorton.com. Website: http://www.countrymanpress.com. Editor-in-Chief: Helen Whybrow. **Acquisitions:** Ann Kraybill, managing editor. Estab. 1973. Publishes hardcover originals, trade paperback originals and reprints. **Publishes 25 titles/year. Receives 1,000 queries/year. 30% of books from first-time authors; 70% from unagented writers. Pays 5-15% royalty on retail price. Offers $1,000-5,000 advance.** Publishes book 18 months after acceptance of ms. Accepts simultaneous submissions. Reports in 2 months on proposals. Book catalog free. Manuscript guidelines for #10 SASE.
　　O— Countryman Press publishes books that encourage physical fitness and appreciation for and understanding of the natural world, self-sufficiency and adventure.
**Imprint(s): Backcountry Publications.**
**Nonfiction:** How-to, guidebooks, general nonfiction. Subjects include gardening, nature/environment, recreation, New England, travel, country living. "We publish several series of regional recreation guidebooks—hiking, bicycling, walking, fly-fishing, canoeing, kayaking—and are looking to expand them. We're also looking for books of national interest on travel, gardening, rural living, nature and fly-fishing." Submit proposal package including outline, 3 sample chapters, market information, author bio with SASE. Reviews artwork/photos as part of ms package. Send photocopies.
**Recent Title(s):** *Nine Months to Gettysburg*, by Howard Coffin (history).

**CQ PRESS**, Congressional Quarterly, Inc., 1414 22nd St. NW, Washington DC 20037. (202)887-8500. Fax: (202)822-6583. E-mail: dtarr@cq.com. Website: http://www.books.cq.com. **Acquisitions:** David Tarr; Paul McClure (library/reference); Carrie Hutchisson (college/political science); Debra Mayberry (directory); Brenda Carter (CQ Press); acquisitions editors. Estab. 1945. **Publishes 50-70 hardcover and paperback titles/year. 95% of books from unagented writers. Pays college or reference royalties or fees. Sometimes offers advance.** Publishes book an average of 1 year after acceptance. Accepts simultaneous submissions. Reports in 3 months. Book catalog free.
　　O— CQ seeks "to educate the public by publishing authoritative works on American and international government and politics."
**Imprint(s):** CQ Press; College/Political Science, Library/Reference, Directory.
**Nonfiction:** All levels of college political science texts. "We are interested in American government, public administration, comparative government, and international relations." Academic reference books, information directories on federal and state governments, national elections, international/state politics and governmental issues. Submit proposal, outline and bio.
**Recent Title(s):** *Guide to Congress*.
**Tips:** "Our books present important information on American government and politics, and related issues, with careful attention to accuracy, thoroughness and readability."

**CRAFTSMAN BOOK COMPANY**, 6058 Corte Del Cedro, Carlsbad CA 92009-9974. (760)438-7828 or (800)829-8123. Fax: (760)438-0398. E-mail: ld_jacobs@msn.com. Website: http://www.craftsman-book.com. **Acquisitions:** Laurence D. Jacobs, editorial manager. Estab. 1957. Publishes paperback originals. **Publishes 12 titles/year. Receives 50 submissions/year. 85% of books from first-time authors; 98% from unagented writers. Pays 7½-12½% royalty on wholesale price or retail price.** Publishes book 2 years after acceptance. Accepts simultaneous submissions. Reports in 2 months. Book catalog and ms guidelines free.
　　O— Craftsman Book Company publishes manuals and estimating references for the construction industry. "Our books must be step-by-step instructions on topics for the professional builder. We do not sell to the do-it-yourselfer." Currently emphasizing cost estimating data.
**Nonfiction:** How-to, technical. All titles are related to construction for professional builders. Query with SASE. Reviews artwork/photos as part of ms package.
**Recent Title(s):** *Contractor's Guide to QuickBooks Pro.*, by Erwin Savage Mitchell (nonfiction).
**Tips:** "The book should be loaded with step-by-step instructions, illustrations, charts, reference data, forms, samples, cost estimates, rules of thumb, and examples that solve actual problems in the builder's office and in the field. The book must cover the subject completely, become the owner's primary reference on the subject, have a high utility-to-cost ratio, and help the owner make a better living in his chosen field."

**█N█ CREATION HOUSE**, Strang Communications, 600 Rinehart Rd., Lake Mary FL 32746. (407)333-3132. **Acquisitions:** Connie Gamb, submissions coordinator; Rick Norb, director of product development; Jerry Lenz, curriculum manager (children's curriculum). Publishes hardcover and trade paperback originals. **Publishes 40-50 titles/year. Receives 100 queries and 600 mss/year. 2% of books from first-time authors; 95% from unagented writers. Pays 4-18% royalty on retail price. Offers $1,500-5,000 advance.** Publishes book 9 months after acceptance of ms. Accepts simultaneous submissions. Reports in 2 months on proposals, 3 months on mss. Manuscript guidelines for #10 SASE.
　　O— Creation House publishes books for the Pentecostal/charismatic Christian market.
**Nonfiction:** Christian, spirit-filled interest, charismatic, cookbook, giftbook, health and fitness. Subjects include religion, spirituality (charismatic). Query with outline, 3 sample chapters, author bio and SASE.
**Recent Title(s):** *The Bible Cure*, by Dr. Reginald Cherry (health and spirit); *Thus Saith the Lord?*, by John Revere (charismatic interest).

**CREATIVE HOMEOWNER PRESS**, 24 Park Way, Upper Saddle River NJ 07458. (201)934-7100. Fax: (201)934-7541. E-mail: laurad@chp-publisher.com. **Acquisitions**: Mike McClintock, senior editor (home improvement/DIY); Neil Soderstrom, senior editor (gardening); Kathie Robits, editor (home decorating/design). Estab. 1978. Publishes trade paperback originals. **Publishes 12-16 titles/year. Receives dozens of queries and mss/year. 50% of books from first-time authors; 98% from unagented writers. Makes outright purchase of $8,000-35,000.** Publishes book 16 months after acceptance of ms. Reports in 6 months on queries. Book catalog free.

 O— Creative Homeowner Press is the one source for the largest selection of quality how-to books, booklets and project plans.

**Nonfiction:** How-to, illustrated book. Subjects include gardening, hobbies, home remodeling/building, home repairs, home decorating/design. Query or submit proposal package, including competitive books (short analysis) and outline and SASE. Reviews artwork/photos as part of ms package.

**Recent Title(s):** *Color in the American Home*, by Margaret Sabo Wills (home design).

**N CRICKET BOOKS**, Carus Publishing, 332 S. Michigan Ave., #1100, Chicago IL 60604. (312)939-1500. E-mail: cricketbooks@caruspub.com. Website: http://www.cricketmag.com. **Acquisitions**: Laura Tillotson, associate editor. Estab. 1999. Publishes hardcover originals. **Publishes 12 titles/year. Receives 300 queries and 600 mss/year. 33% of books from first-time authors; 33% from unagented writers. Pays 8-12½% royalty on retail price. Offers advance of $2,000-5,000.** Publishes book 18 months after acceptance. Accepts simultaneous submissions. Reports in 1 month on queries and proposals, 2 months on mss. Manuscript guidelines for #10 SASE.

 O— Cricket Books publishes chapter books and middle-grade novels for children ages 7-12.

**Fiction:** Juvenile. Submit complete ms. *Writer's Market* recommends sending query first.

**Recent Title(s):** *Oh No, It's Robert*, by Barbara Seuling (chapter book); *Two Suns in the Sky*, by Miriam Bat-Ami (young adult novel).

**Tips:** Audience is children ages 7-12. "Take a look at the fiction magazines we publish, *Spider* and *Cricket*, to see what sort of material we're interested in."

**CROSS CULTURAL PUBLICATIONS, INC.**, P.O. Box 506, Notre Dame IN 46556. (219)273-6526. Fax: (219)273-5973. E-mail: crosscult@aol.com. Website: http://www.crossculturalpub.com. **Acquisitions**: Cyriac Pullapilly, general editor. Estab. 1980. Publishes hardcover and softcover originals and hardcover and trade paperback reprints. **Publishes 5-20 titles/year. Receives 5,000 queries and 2,000 mss/year. 40% of books from first-time authors; 90% from unagented writers. Pays 10% royalty on wholesale price. No advance.** Publishes book 6 months after acceptance of ms. Accepts simultaneous submissions. Reports in 2 months on queries; 3 months on proposals, 4 months on mss. Book catalog and ms guidelines free on request or on website. *Writer's Market* recommends allowing 2 months for reply. Book catalog free.

 O— "We publish to promote intercultural and interfaith understanding."

**Nonfiction:** Biography, coffeetable book, cookbook, reference, textbook. Subjects include anthropology/archaeology, business/economics, ethnic, government/politics, history, memoirs multicultural, nature/environment/philosophy, psychology, religion, sociology, spirituality, translation, travel, women's issues/studies. Submit proposal package, including outline. "We publish scholarly books that deal with intercultural topics—regardless of discipline. Books pushing into new horizons are welcome, but they have to be intellectually sound and balanced in judgement."

**Fiction:** Historical, religious, romance, science fiction. "Should have a serious plot and message." Query with SASE or submit proposal package including synopsis.

**Poetry:** "Exceptionally good poetry with moving message." Query with sample poems or submit complete ms.

**Recent Title(s):** *Feminism and Love*, by Ruth Whitney, Ph.D. (nonfiction); *Night Autopsy Room*, by Yoshio Sakabe, MD (fiction); *Quester by the River*, by Aniyil Tharakan.

**THE CROSSING PRESS**, 97 Hangar Way, Watsonville CA 95019. (408)722-0711. Fax: (408)772-2749. Website: http://www.crossingpress.com. **Acquisitions**: Caryle Hirshberg, acquisitions editor; Elaine Goldman Gill, publisher. Estab. 1967. Publishes trade paperback originals. **Publishes 40-50 titles/year. Receives 2,000 submissions/year. 10% of books from first-time authors; 75% from unagented writers. Pays royalty.** Publishes book 18 months after acceptance of ms. Accepts simultaneous submissions. Reports in 2 months on queries. Book catalog free.

 O— The Crossing Press publishes titles on a theme of "tools for personal change" with an emphasis on health, spiritual growth, healing and empowerment.

**Nonfiction:** Natural and alternative health, spirituality, personal growth/transformation, empowerment, self-help, cookbooks. Submit detailed outline, sample chapter, market anaylsis, timetable and detailed vita.

**Recent Title(s):** *HMOs and the Patient's Bill of Rights*, by Molly Shapiro.

**Tips:** "Simple intelligent query letters do best. No come-ons, no cutes. It helps if you have credentials. Authors should research the press first to see what sort of books we currently publish."

**CROSSWAY BOOKS**, Good News Publishers, 1300 Crescent St., Wheaton IL 60187-5800. Fax: (630)682-4785. Editorial Director: Marvin Padgett. **Acquisitions**: Jill Carter. Estab. 1938. Publishes hardcover and trade paperback originals. **Publishes 75 titles/year. Receives 2,500 submissions/year. 2% of books from first-time authors; 75% from unagented writers. Pays negotiable royalty. Offers negotiable advance.** Publishes book 18 months after acceptance. Reports in up to 2 months. Book catalog for 9×12 SAE with 6 first-class stamps. Manuscript guidelines for #10 SASE.

O─π "With 'making a difference in people's lives for Christ' as its maxim, Crossway Books lists titles written from an evangelical Christian worldview."

**Nonfiction:** "Books that provide fresh understanding and a distinctively Christian examination of questions confronting Christians and non-Christians in their personal lives, families, churches, communities and the wider culture. The main types include: (1) Issues books that typically address critical issues facing Christians today; (2) Books on the deeper Christian life that provide a deeper understanding of Christianity and its application to daily life; and, (3) Christian academic and professional books directed at an audience of religious professionals. Be sure the books are from an evangelical Christian worldview. Writers often give sketchy information on their book's content." Query with SASE. No phone queries.

**Fiction:** "We publish fiction that falls into these categories: (1) Christian realism, or novels set in modern, true-to-life settings as a means of telling stories about Christians today in an increasingly post-Christian era; (2) Supernatural fiction, or stories typically set in the 'real world' but that bring supernatural reality into it in a way that heightens our spiritual dimension; (3) Historical fiction, using historical characters, times and places of interest as a mirror for our own times; (4) Some genre-technique fiction (mystery, western); and (5) Children's fiction. "We are not interested in romance novels, horror novels, biblical novels (i.e., stories set in Bible times that fictionalize events in the lives of prominent biblical characters), issues novels (i.e., fictionalized treatments of contemporary issues), and end times/prophecy novels. We do not accept full manuscripts or electronic submissions." Submit synopsis with 2 sample chaptes and SASE.

**Recent Title(s):** *A Living Hope*, by David Haney (nonfiction); *The Chairman*, by Harry Lee Kraus, Jr. (fiction).

**Tips:** "All of our fiction must have 'Christian' content—combine the Truth of God's Word with a passion to live it out. Writers often submit without thinking about what a publisher actually publishes. They also send full manuscripts without a synopsis. Without a synopsis, the manuscript does not get read."

**CUMBERLAND HOUSE PUBLISHING**, 431 Harding Industrial Dr., Nashville TN 37211. (615)832-1171. Fax: (615)832-0633. E-mail: cumbhouse@aol.com. **Acquisitions:** Ron Pitkin, president; Julia M. Pitkin (cooking/lifestyle). Estab. 1996. Publishes hardcover and trade paperback originals, and hardcover and trade paperback reprints. **Publishes 35 titles/year; imprint publishes 5 titles/year. Receives 1,000 queries and 400 mss/year. 30% of books from first-time authors; 80% from unagented writers. Pays 10-20% royalty on wholesale price. Offers $1,000-10,000 advance.** Publishes book an average of 8 months after acceptance. Accepts simultaneous submissions. Reports in 6 months on queries and proposals, 4 months on mss. Book catalog for 8 × 10 SAE and 4 first-class stamps. Manuscript guidelines free.

**Imprint(s):** Cumberland House Hearthside (contact Julia M. Pitkin, editor-in-chief).

**Nonfiction:** Cookbook, gift book, how-to, humor, illustrated book, reference. Subjects include Americana, cooking/foods/nutrition, government/politics, history, military/war, recreation, regional, sports, travel. Query or submit outline. Reviews artwork/photos as part of ms package. Send photocopies.

**Fiction:** Mystery. Writers should know "the odds are really stacked against them." Query.

**Recent Title(s):** *The Abbott & Costello Story*, by Stephen Cox and John Lofflin (entertainment); *Questionable Remains*, by Beverly Connor (mystery).

**Tips:** Audience is "adventuresome people who like a fresh approach to things. Writers should tell what their idea is, why it's unique and why somebody would want to buy it—but don't pester us."

**N: CUMMINGS & HATHAWAY**, 422 Atlantic Ave., East Rockaway NY 11518. (800)344-7579. **Acquisitions:** William Burke, director of publications. Estab. 1980. Publishes textbooks, paperback originals and reprints. Publishes 5-10 titles/year. **Receives 75-100 queries and 10-15 unsolicited mss/year. 99% of books from first-time authors; 99% from unagented writers. Pays 10-25% royalty on wholesale price. Rarely offers $500 maximum advance.** Publishes book 4 months after acceptance of ms. Reports in 1 month on queries. Manuscript guidelines free.

O─π "We are a 'teacher's publisher.' We are looking for manuscripts from college professors willing to use the book as a primary required text for their students."

**Nonfiction:** Biography, reference, technical, textbook. Subjects include anthropology/archaeology, business/economics, computers/electronics, education, ethnic, gay/lesbian, government/politics, health/medicine, history, language/literature, military/war, money/finance, music/dance, philosophy, psychology, regional, religion, sociology, women's issues/studies. "We publish texts for college courses controlled by the author and for which he/she can assure us of 100 copies sold within first year. Manuscript must be original. We do not publish collections requiring extensive permissions." Query. *No unsolicited mss.*

**Recent Title(s):** *Road Map of Head & Neck Anatomy*, by Rumy Hilloowala (textbook/reference); *Handbook of Public Speaking*, by Richard Letteri (textbook); *Macroeconomics in Brief*, by Peter M. Gutmann (textbook).

**Tips:** "Audience is college students."

**A: CURRENCY**, Doubleday Broadway Publishing Group, Random House, Inc., 1540 Broadway, New York NY 10036. (212)354-6500. Fax: (212)782-8911. **Acquisitions:** Roger Scholl, executive editor. Estab. 1989. **Pays 7½-15% royalty on retail price. Offers advance.** Publishes book 1 year after acceptance of ms.

O─π Currency publishes "business books for people who want to make a difference, not just a living."

**Nonfiction:** Business/economics subjects. *Agented submissions only.*

**Recent Title(s):** *The Dance of Change*, by Peter Senge et al., *Cyber Rules*, by Thomas Siebel and Pat House.

**CURRENT CLINICAL STRATEGIES PUBLISHING**, 27071 Cabot Rd., Suite 126, Laguna Hills CA 92653. E-mail: info@ccspublishing.com. Website: http://www.ccspublishing.com. **Acquisitions:** Camille deTonnancour, editor. Estab. 1988. Publishes trade paperback originals. **Publishes 20 titles/year. Receives 10 queries and 10 mss/year. 50% of books from first-time authors; 50% from unagented writers. Pays royalty.** Publishes book 6 months after acceptance of ms.

O→ Current Clinical Strategies is a medical publisher for healthcare professionals.

**Nonfiction:** Technical. Health/medicine subjects. Submit 6 sample chapters. *Physician authors only.* Reviews artwork/photos as part of ms package. Send file by e-mail only.

**Recent Title(s):** *Current Clinical Strategies, Gynecology and Obstetrics, 3rd ed.,* by Paul D. Chan and Christopher R. Winkle (medical reference).

**CYPRESS PUBLISHING GROUP**, 11835 ROE #187, Leawood KS 66211. (913)681-9875. Fax: (913)341-5158. Vice President Marketing: Carl Heintz. **Acquisitions:** William S. Noblitt, JoAnn Heinz. Publishes hardcover and trade paperback originals. **Publishes 10 titles/year. 80% of books from first-time authors; 90% from unagented writers. Pays 10-15% royalty on wholesale price.** Publishes book 8 months after acceptance of ms. Reports in 2 weeks on queries, 1 month on proposals and mss. *Writer's Market* recommends allowing 2 months for reply. Book catalog free. Manuscript guidelines for #10 SASE.

O→ "We are an innovative niche publisher with expertise in direct marketing."

**Nonfiction:** How-to, illustrated book, self-help, technical, textbook. Subjects include business/economics, computers/electronics (business related), hobbies (amateur radio, antique radio), money/finance, psychology (business related), software (business related). Query with proposal package, including outline, 1-3 sample chapters, overview of book. Send photocopies.

**Recent Title(s):** *The Edison Effect,* by Ron Ploof (adapting to technological change).

**Tips:** "We use America Online and CompuServe extensively. Our editorial plans change—we are always looking for outstanding submissions. Many writers fail to consider what other books on the topics are available. The writer must think about the fundamental book marketing question: Why will a customer *buy* the book?"

**DANTE UNIVERSITY OF AMERICA PRESS, INC.,** P.O. Box 843, Brookline Village MA 02147-0843. Fax: (617)734-2046. E-mail: danteu@usa1.com. Website: http://www.danteuniversity.org/dpress.html. **Acquisitions:** Adolph Caso, president. Estab. 1975. Publishes hardcover and trade paperback originals and reprints. **Publishes 5 titles/year. Receives 50 submissions/year. 50% of books from first-time authors; 50% from unagented writers. Pays royalty. Negotiable advance.** Publishes book 10 months after acceptance of ms. Reports in 2 months.

O→ "The Dante University Press exists to bring quality, educational books pertaining to our Italian heritage as well as the historical and political studies of America. Profits from the sale of these publications benefit the Foundation, bringing Dante University closer to a reality."

**Nonfiction:** Biography, reference, reprints, translations from Italian and Latin. Subjects include general scholarly nonfiction, Renaissance thought and letter, Italian language and linguistics, Italian-American history and culture, bilingual education. Query first with SASE. Reviews artwork/photos as part of ms package.

**Fiction:** Translations from Italian and Latin. Query first with SASE.

**Poetry:** "There is a chance that we would use Renaissance poetry translations."

**Recent Title(s):** *Trapped in Tuscany,* by Tullio Bertini (World War II nonfiction); *Rogue Angel,* by Carol Damioli (mystery).

**[N] DARLINGTON PRODUCTIONS, INC.,** P.O. Box 5884, Darlington MD 21034. (410)457-5400. E-mail: DPI14@aol.com. **Acquisitions:** Jeffrey D. McKaughan, president. Publishes hardcover originals, trade paperback originals and reprints. **Publishes 9 titles/year. Receives 20 queries/year. 75% of books published are from first-time writers; 100% from unagented writers. Pays 10% royalty on retail price and small bulk fee at time of release. No advance.** Publishes book 6 months after acceptance. Accepts simultaneous submissions. Reports in 1 month on queries and proposals, 3 months on mss. Book catalog and ms guidelines free.

O→ Darlington publishes military history/war reference and illustrated titles.

**Nonfiction:** Illustrated book, reference, technical. Military history/war subjects. Query with outline. Reviews artwork/photos as part of ms package. Send photocopies.

**Recent Nonfiction Title(s):** *U.S. Half-Tracks: Their Design & Development,* by David Haugh.

**MAY DAVENPORT, PUBLISHERS**, 26313 Purissima Rd., Los Altos Hills CA 94022. (415)948-6499. Fax: (650)947-1373. E-mail: robertd@whidbey.com. Website: http://www.maydavenportpublishers.com. **Acquisitions:** May Davenport, editor/publisher. Estab. 1976. Publishes hardcover and trade paperback originals. **Publishes 4 titles/year. Receives 1,500 submissions/year. 95% of books from first-time authors; 100% from unagented writers. Pays 15% royalty on retail price. No advance.** Publishes book 1 year after acceptance. Reports in 1 month. *Writer's Market* recommends allowing 2 months for reply. Book catalog and ms guidelines for #10 SASE.

O→ May Davenport publishes "literature for teenagers (before they graduate from high schools) as supplementary literary material in English courses nationwide." Looking particularly for authors able to write for the "teen internet" generation who don't like to read in-depth.

**Imprint:** md Books (nonfiction and fiction).

**Nonfiction:** Subjects include: Americana, language/literature, humorous memoirs for children/young adults. "For children ages 6-8: stories to read with pictures to color in 500 words. For preteens and young adults: exhibit your writing skills and entertain them with your literary tools." Query with SASE.

**Fiction:** Humor, literary. Novels: "We want to focus on novels junior and senior high school teachers can share with their reluctant readers in their classrooms."

**Recent Title(s):** *Magda Rose*, by Paul Luria; *Windriders*, by Blake F. Grant.

**Tips:** "We prefer books which can be *used* in high schools as supplementary readings in English or creative writing courses. Reading skills have to be taught, and novels by humorous authors can be more pleasant to read than Hawthorne's or Melville's novels, war novels, or novels about past generations. Humor has a place in literature. Since the TV-oriented youth in schools today do not like to read or to write, why not create books for that impressionable and captive audience? Great to work with talented writers especially when writers are happy and inspired within themselves."

**JONATHAN DAVID PUBLISHERS, INC.**, 68-22 Eliot Ave., Middle Village NY 11379-1194. (718)456-8611. Fax: (718)894-2818. E-mail: info@jonathandavidonline.com. Website: http://www.jonathandavidonline.com. **Acquisitions:** Alfred J. Kolatch, editor-in-chief. Estab. 1948. Publishes hardcover and trade paperback originals and reprints. **Publishes 20-25 titles/year. 50% of books from first-time authors; 90% from unagented writers. Pays royalty or makes outright purchase.** Publishes book 18 months after acceptance of ms. Reports in 2 months on queries. Book catalog for 6×9 SASE.

O➤ Jonathan David publishes "popular Judaica." Currently emphasizing projects geared toward children.

**Nonfiction:** Cookbook, how-to, reference, self-help. Submit outline, 1 sample chapter and SASE.

**Recent Title(s):** *Great African-American Women*, by Darryl Lyman.

**[N] DAVIS PUBLICATIONS, INC.**, 50 Portland St., Worcester MA 01608. (508)754-7201. Fax: (508)753-3834. **Acquisitions:** Claire Mowbray Golding, editorial director (grades K-8); Helen Ronan, editorial director (grades 9-12). Estab. 1901. **Publishes 5-10 titles/year. Pays 10-12% royalty.** Publishes book 1 year after acceptance of ms. Book catalog for 9×12 SAE with 2 first-class stamps. Authors guidelines for SASE.

O➤ Davis publishes art, design and craft books for the elementary and high school markets.

**Nonfiction:** Publishes technique-oriented art, design and craft books for the educational market, as well as books dealing with art and culture, and art history. "Keep in mind the intended audience. Our readers are visually oriented. All illustrations should be collated separately from the text, but keyed to the text. Photos should be good quality transparencies and black and white photographs. Well-selected illustrations should explain, amplify, and enhance the text. We average 2-4 photos/page. We like to see technique photos as well as illustrations of finished artwork, by a variety of artists, including students. Recent books have been on printmaking, clay sculpture, design, jewelry, drawing and watercolor painting." Submit outline, sample chapters and illustrations. Reviews artwork/photos as part of ms package.

**Recent Title(s):** *Careers in Art*, by Gerald F. Brommer and Joseph Gatto.

**DAW BOOKS, INC.**, Penguin Putnam Inc., 375 Hudson St., 3rd Floor, New York NY 10014-3658. Publishers: Elizabeth Wollheim and Sheila Gilbert. **Acquisitions:** Peter Stampfel, submissions editor. Estab. 1971. Publishes hardcover and paperback originals and reprints. **Publishes 60-80 titles/year. Pays in royalties with an advance negotiable on a book-by-book basis.** Sends galleys to author. Simultaneous submissions "returned unread at once, unless prior arrangements are made by agent." Reports in 6 weeks "or longer, if a second reading is required." Book catalog free.

O➤ DAW Books publishes science fiction and fantasy.

**Fiction:** "We are interested in science fiction and fantasy novels. We need science fiction more than fantasy right now, but we're still looking for both. We like character-driven books with attractive characters. We're not looking for horror novels, but we are looking for mainstream suspense thrillers. We accept both agented and unagented manuscripts. Long books are absolutely not a problem. We are not seeking collections of short stories or ideas for anthologies. We do not want any nonfiction manuscripts." Query with SASE first.

**Recent Title(s):** *Mountains of Black Glass*, by Tad Williams (science fiction).

**DAWN PUBLICATIONS**, 14618 Tyler Foote Rd., Nevada City CA 95959. (800)545-7475. Fax: (530)478-7541. E-mail: Dawnpub@oro.net. Website: http://www.dawnpub.com. **Acquisitions:** Victoria Covell, submissions editor. Estab. 1979. Publishes hardcover and trade paperback originals. **Publishes 6 titles/year. Receives 550 queries and 2,500 mss/ year. 35% of books from first-time authors; 100% from unagented writers. Pays royalty on wholesale price.** Publishes book 2 years after acceptance of ms. Accepts simultaneous submissions. Reports in 2 months. Manuscript guidelines for #10 SASE.

O➤ Dawn Publications' mission is to assist parents and educators to open the minds and hearts of children to the transforming influence of nature. Dawn Publications is dedicated to inspiring in children a sense of appreciation for all life on earth.

**Nonfiction:** Children's/juvenile. Nature awareness and inspiration. Query with SASE.

**Recent Title(s):** *Stickeen: John Muir & The Brave Little Dog*, by Donnell Rubay.

**Tips:** "All animals and art should appear as realistically as in nature."

**DAYBREAK BOOKS**, Rodale, 400 S. 10th St., Emmaus PA 18098. (610)967-7585. Fax: (610)967-8961. Website: http://www.rodalepress.com. **Acquisitions:** Neil Wertheimer, publisher. Publishes hardcover and trade paperback originals. **Publishes 6-9 titles/year. Pays 6-15% royalty on retail price.** Publishes book 12-18 months after acceptance of ms. Accepts simultaneous submissions. Reports in 1 month on queries, 2 months on proposals and mss. Book catalog and ms guidelines free; request from Sally Reith, acquisitions editor, Rodale Books.

**O**━ Daybreak Books explore all aspects of spirituality and humanity through a variety of voices, viewpoints and approaches.

**Nonfiction:** Spirituality, inspirational. Query with proposal package including outline, 1-2 sample chapters and author's résumé. Prefers agented submissions.

**Recent Title(s):** *Wisdom of Our Fathers*, by Joe Kita.

**N: DBS PRODUCTIONS**, P.O. Box 1894, Charlottesville VA 22903. (800)745-1581. Fax: (804)293-5502. E-mail: robert@dbs-sar.com. Website: http://www.dbs-sar.com. Estab. 1989. Publishes hardcover and trade paperback originals. **Publishes 6 titles/year. Receives 5 queries/year. 5% of books from first-time authors; 100% from unagented writers. Pays 5-20% royalty on retail price. No advance.** Publishes book 1 year after acceptance of ms. Reports in 2 months. Book catalog on request or on website. Manuscript guidelines for #10 SASE.

**O**━ dbs Productions produces search and rescue and outdoor first-aid related materials and courses. It offers a selection of publications, videotapes, management kits and tools and instructional modules.

**Nonfiction:** Technical, textbook. Subjects include health/medicine, search and rescue. Submit proposal package, including outline and 2 sample chapters. Reviews artwork/photos as part of ms package. Send photocopies.

**Recent Title(s):** *Law Enforcement Guide to the Lost Alzheimer's Subject.*

**A DEAD LETTER**, St. Martin's Press, 175 Fifth Ave., New York NY 10010. (212)674-5151. **Acquisitions:** Joe Veltre, editor. Publishes mass market paperback originals and reprints. **Publishes 36 titles/year. 15% of books from first-time authors; 0% from unagented writers. Pays variable royalty on net price. Advance varies.** Accepts simultaneous submissions. Book catalog and ms guidelines not available.

**O**━ Dead Letter publishes mysteries.

**Fiction:** Mystery. Query with synopsis, 3 sample chapters and SASE. *Agented submissions only.*

**Recent Title(s):** *A Stiff Risotto*, by Lou Jane Temple.

**DEARBORN FINANCIAL PUBLISHING, INC.**, 155 N. Wacker Dr., Chicago IL 60606-1719. (312)836-4400. Fax: (312)836-1021. Website: http://www.dearborn.com. **Acquisitions:** Cynthia Zigmund (finance); Jean Iversen, acquisitions editor (general business/management, consumer real estate); Robin Nominelli, product manager (entrepreneurship). Estab. 1959. Publishes hardcover and paperback originals. **Publishes 200 titles/year. Receives 200 submissions/year. 50% of books from first-time authors; 50% from unagented writers. Pays 1-15% royalty on wholesale price.** Publishes book 6 months after acceptance. Accepts simultaneous submissions. Reports in 1 month. Book catalog and ms guidelines free.

**O**━ The trade division of Dearborn publishes practical, solutions-oriented books for individuals and corporations on the subjects of finance, consumer real estate, business and entrepreneurship. Currently emphasizing finance, general business/management, consumer real estate. De-emphasizing small business.

**Imprint(s):** Upstart Publishing Co.

**Nonfiction:** How-to, reference, textbooks. Subjects include small business, real estate, insurance, banking, securities, money/finance. Query.

**Recent Title(s):** *The Handy Ma'am*, by Beverly DeJulio.

**Tips:** "People seeking real estate, insurance, broker's licenses are our audience; also professionals in these areas. Additionally, we publish for those interested in managing their finances or in starting and running a small business."

**IVAN R. DEE, INC.**, The Rowman & Littlefield Publishing Group, 1332 N. Halsted St., Chicago IL 60622-2637. (312)787-6262. Fax: (312)787-6269. E-mail: elephant@ivanrdee.com. Website: http://www.ivanrdee.com. **Acquisitions:** Ivan R. Dee, president. Estab. 1988. Publishes hardcover originals and trade paperback originals and reprints. **Publishes 40 titles/year. 10% of books from first-time authors; 75% from unagented writers. Pays royalty.** Publishes book 9 months after acceptance of ms. Reports in 1 month on queries. *Writer's Market* recommends allowing 2 months for reply. Book catalog free.

**O**━ Ivan R. Dee publishes serious nonfiction for general informed readers. Currently de-emphasizing literary criticism.

**Imprint(s):** Elephant Paperbacks, New Amsterdam Books.

**Nonfiction:** History, literature and letters, biography, politics, contemporary affairs, theater. Submit outline and sample chapters. Reviews artwork/photos as part of ms package.

**Recent Title(s):** *John Harmon McElroy*, (American beliefs); *Poems for the People*, by Carl Sandburg (poetry).

**Tips:** "We publish for an intelligent lay audience and college course adoptions."

**A DEL REY BOOKS**, Ballantine Publishing Group, Random House, Inc., 201 E. 50th St., New York NY 10022-7703. (212)572-2677. E-mail: delrey@randomhouse.com. Website: http://www.randomhouse.com/delrey/. Senior Editor: Veronica Chapman. **Acquisitions:** Veronica Chapman (fantasy); Shelley Shapiro, editorial director (science fiction). Estab. 1977. Publishes hardcover, trade paperback, and mass market originals and mass market paperback reprints. **Publishes 70 titles/year. Receives 1,900 submissions/year. 10% of books from first-time authors; 0% from unagented writers. Pays royalty on retail price. Offers competitive advance.** Publishes book 1 year after acceptance. Reports in 6 months, occasionally longer. Writer's guidelines for #10 SASE.

O— Del Rey publishes top level fantasy and science fiction.

**Fiction:** Fantasy ("should have the practice of magic as an essential element of the plot"), science fiction ("well-plotted novels with good characterization, exotic locales, and detailed alien cultures"). *Agented submissions only.*

**Recent Title(s):** *Bloom*, by Wil McCastley; *The Master Harper of Pern*, by Anne McCaffrey.

**Tips:** "Del Rey is a reader's house. Pay particular attention to plotting and a satisfactory conclusion. It must be/feel believable. That's what the readers like. In terms of mass market, we basically created the field of fantasy bestsellers. Not that it didn't exist before, but we put the mass into mass market."

**Ⓐ DELACORTE PRESS**, Bantam Dell Publishing Group, Random House, Inc., 1540 Broadway, New York NY 10036. (212)354-6500. Editor-in-Chief: Leslie Schnur. **Acquisitions:** (Ms.) Jackie Cantor (women's fiction); Tom Spain (commercial nonfiction and fiction). Publishes hardcover and trade paperback originals. **Publishes 36 titles/year.**

**Nonfiction and Fiction:** *Agented submissions only.*

**Recent Title(s):** *Why Not Me?*, by Al Franken (nonfiction); and *Be Cool*, by Elmore Leonard (fiction).

**Ⓐ DELL PUBLISHING ISLAND**, Bantam Dell Publishing Group, Random House, Inc., 1540 Broadway, New York NY 10036. (212)354-6500. **Acquisitions**: Maggie Crawford, editorial director. Publishes mass market paperback originals and reprints. Publishes bestseller fiction and nonfiction. **Publishes 12 titles/year.**

**Fiction:** Mystery, romance, suspense. *Agented submissions only.*

**Recent Title(s):** *The Runaway Jury*, by John Grisham (suspense).

**Ⓐ DELL TRADE PAPERBACKS**, Bantam Dell Publishing Group, Random House, Inc. 1540 Broadway, New York NY 10036. (212)354-6500. **Acquisitions**: Tom Spain, editorial director. Publishes trade paperback originals. **Publishes 36 titles/year.**

O— Dell Trade Paperbacks publishes light, humorous material and books on pop culture.

**Nonfiction:** Humor, self-help, pop culture. *Agented submissions only.*

**Recent Title(s):** *What Einstein Didn't Know*, by Robert Wolke.

**Ⓐ DELTA TRADE PAPERBACKS**, Bantam Dell Publishing Group, Random House, Inc., 1540 Broadway, New York NY 10036. (212)354-6500. **Acquisitions**: Tom Spain, editorial director. **Publishes 36 titles/year.**

O— Delta Trade Paperbacks publishes serious nonfiction and literary fiction.

**Nonfiction:** Biography, memoir. Subjects include ethnic, health/medicine, music. *Agented submissions only.*

**Fiction:** Literary, short story collections. *Agented submissions only.*

**Recent Title(s):** *Do They Hear You When You Cry*, by Fanziya Kassindja with Lagli Miller Zashir (nonfiction/women's studies); *Charming Billy*, by Alice McDermott (fiction).

**THE DENALI PRESS**, P.O. Box 021535, Juneau AK 99802-1535. (907)586-6014. Fax: (907)463-6780. E-mail: denalipr@alaska.net. Website: http://www.alaska.net/~denalipr/index.html. **Acquisitions:** Alan Schorr, editorial director; Sally Silvas-Ottumwa, editorial associate. Estab. 1986. Publishes trade paperback originals. **Publishes 5 titles/year. Receives 120 submissions/year. 50% of books from first-time authors; 80% from unagented writers. Pays 10% royalty on wholesale price or makes outright purchase.** Publishes book 1 year after acceptance of ms. Accepts simultaneous submissions. Reports in 1 month. *Writer's Market* recommends allowing 2 months for reply.

O— The Denali Press looks for reference works suitable for the educational, professional and library market. "Though we publish books on a variety of topics, our focus is most broadly centered on multiculturalism and Alaskana."

**Nonfiction:** Reference. Subjects include Americana, Alaskana, anthropology, ethnic, government/politics, history, recreation. "We need reference books—ethnic, refugee and minority concerns." Query with outline and sample chapters. All unsolicited mss are tossed. Author must contact prior to sending ms.

**Recent Title(s):** *Winning Political Campaigns: A Comprehensive Guide to Electoral Success*, by William S. Bike.

**T.S. DENISON & CO., INC.**, 9601 Newton Ave. S., Minneapolis MN 55431-2590. (612)888-6404. Fax: (612)888-6318. Director of Product Development: Sherrill B. Flora. **Acquisitions:** Danielle de Gregory, acquisitions editor. Estab. 1876. **Receives 1,500 submissions/year. 20% of books from first-time authors; 100% from unagented writers. No advance. Makes outright purchase.** Publishes book 2 years after acceptance of ms. Reports in 6 months. Book catalog and ms guidelines for 9 × 12 SASE with 3 first-class stamps.

O— T.S. Denison publishes supplemental educational materials; teacher aid materials; and a Christian line.

**Nonfiction:** Specializes in early childhood, elementary and middle school teaching aids. Submit complete ms. *Writer's Market* recommends query with SASE first. Reviews artwork/photos as part of ms package. Send prints if photos are to accompany ms.

**Recent Title(s):** *Cyberspace for Kids*, by The Mandel Family.

**Ⓝ ⭐ THE DESIGN IMAGE GROUP INC.**, 231 S. Frontage Rd., Suite 17, Burr Ridge IL 60521. (630)789-8991. Fax: (630)789-9013. E-mail: dig1956@aol.com. Website: http://www.designimagegroup.com. **Acquisitions:** Thomas J. Strauch, president (horror). Estab. 1984. Publishes trade paperback originals. **Publishes 6 titles/year. Receives 400 queries and 1,200 mss/year. 100% of books from first-time authors; 90% of books from unagented writers. Pays 7½-12% royalty on wholesale price. Offers $2,400-3,600 advance.** Accepts simultaneous submissions. Reports in 1 month on queries; 2 months on mss. Book catalog for $9 \times 12$ SAE with 3 first-class stamps. Manuscript guidelines for #10 SASE.

○━ The Design Image Group publishes "traditional supernatural, human form, monster-based horror fiction."
**Fiction:** Horror. Query. Submit 3 sample chapters and SASE. "Please, no complete ms. Absolutely no phone queries! Absolutely no fax queries!"
**Recent Titles:** *Carmilla: The Return,* by Kyle Marffin.
**Tips:** "Best advice to understand what we seek: send for our guidelines! They spell out quite clearly what we're looking for . . . and what we don't want to see. Horror is a small genre—only a fraction of the size of sci-fi or romance. Don't expect to ever get rich in this genre. Write horror because you love to do so. Show us something that's been rejected by the major New York trade publishers, and we might surprise you! Nontheless, we demand the same quality writing, suspenseful plotting and engaging characters any mass market publisher would; don't confuse the small press with amateur or experimental publishing. We seek mass market appeal for our smaller audience."

**DIAL BOOKS FOR YOUNG READERS**, Penguin Putnam Inc., 345 Hudson St., 3rd Floor, New York NY 10014. (212)366-2800. President/Publisher: Nancy Paulsen. Assistant Editor: Jocelyn Wright. **Acquisitions:** Submissions Editor. Publishes hardcover originals. **Publishes 50 titles/year. Receives 5,000 queries and submissions/year. 10% of books from first-time authors. Pays variable royalty and advance.** Reports in 4 months.

○━ Dial Books for Young Readers publishes quality picture books for ages 18 months-8 years, lively, believable novels for middle readers and young adults, and well-researched manuscripts for young adults and middle readers.
**Imprint(s):** Phyllis Fogelman Books.
**Nonfiction:** Juvenile picture books, middle grade and young adult books. Especially looking for "quality picture books and well-researched young adult and middle-reader manuscripts that lend themselves to attractive illustration." Not interested in alphabet books, riddle and game books, and early concept books. Responds to query letters outlining book and giving writer's credentials. Include SASE. *No unsolicited mss.*
**Fiction:** Juvenile picture books, middle grade readers, young adult books. Subjects include adventure, fantasy, historical, humor, mystery. Especially looking for "lively and well-written novels for middle grade and young adult children involving a convincing plot and believable characters. The subject matter or theme should not already be overworked in previously published books. The approach must not be demeaning to any minority group, nor should the roles of female characters (or others) be stereotyped, though we don't think books should be didactic, or in any way message-y. No topics inappropriate for the juvenile, young adult, and middle grade audiences. No plays." *Agented mss only.* Responds to query letter with SASE outlining book and author's credentials only. *No unsolicited mss.*
**Recent Title(s):** *Parts,* by Ted Arnold; *Jazmin's Notebook,* by Nikki Grimes.
**Tips:** "Our readers are anywhere from preschool age to teenage. Picture books must have strong plots, lots of action, unusual premises, or universal themes treated with freshness and originality. Humor works well in these books. A very well thought out and intelligently presented book has the best chance of being taken on. Genre isn't as much of a factor as presentation."

⬛ **DIAL PRESS**, Bantam Dell Publishing Group, Random House, Inc., 1540 Broadway, New York NY 10036. (212)354-6500. Fax: (212)782-9698. Website: http://www.bbd.com. **Acquisitions:** Susan Kamil, vice president, editorial director. Estab. 1924. **Publishes 6-12 titles/year. Receives 200 queries and 450 mss/year. 75% of books from first-time authors. Pays royalty on retail price. Offers advance.** Publishes book 18 months after acceptance of ms. Accepts simultaneous submissions.

○━ Dial Press publishes quality fiction and nonfiction.
**Nonfiction:** Biography, memoirs, serious nonfiction, cultural criticism. Subjects include Americana, art/architecture, government/politics, health/medicine, history, psychology, women's issues/studies. *Agented submissions only*; query by letter with SASE.
**Fiction:** General literary fiction. *Agented submissions only;* query with SASE.
**Recent Title(s):** *Kaaterskill Falls,* by Allegra Goodman (literary fiction); *Pack of Two,* by Caroline Knapp (memoir).

▨ ✪ **DIMEFAST LIMITED USA/UK**, P.O. Box 292375, Ft. Lauderdale FL 33329-2375. (954)894-6188. **Acquisitions:** Nancy Rosenberg (pet books, needlework); Rinaldo Matthews (science fiction, fantasy); R. Mathews-Danzer (mysteries, cookbooks). Publishes trade paperback originals. **Publishes 5 titles/year. Receives 3 queries and 3 mss/ year. 100% of books from first-time authors; 100% from unagented writers. Pays 8-15% royalty on wholesale price. No advance.** Publishes book 3 months after acceptance of ms. Reports in 1 month. Manuscript guidelines for #10 SASE.

○━ Dimefast publishes books for pet owners and breeders, exotic cookbooks and needlework design.
**Nonfiction:** Cookbook, how-to, self-help. Subjects include agriculture/horticulture, animal, cooking/foods/nutrition, needlework hobbies. Submit completed ms. Reviews artwork/photos as part of ms package. Send photocopies.
**Recent Titles:** *Planning an Aviary,* by R. Mathews-Danzer (pet).
**Tips:** "Research is key. Illustrations play to customer understanding. Diagrams must be easy to understand." This publisher plans to expand the titles published per year to 15-30.

**DIMI PRESS**, 3820 Oak Hollow Lane, SE, Salem OR 97302-4774. (503)364-7698. Fax: (503)364-9727. E-mail: dickbook@aol.com. Website: http://www.open.org/dicklutz/DIMI_PRESS.html. **Acquisitions:** Dick Lutz, president.

Publishes trade paperback originals. **Publishes 5 titles/year. Receives 100-150 queries and 20-25 mss/year. 80% of books from first-time authors; 90% from unagented writers. Pays 10% royalty on net receipts. No advance.** Publishes book 9 months after acceptance of ms. Accepts simultaneous submissions. Reports in 2 weeks on queries and proposals, 1 month on mss. Book catalog and ms guidelines for #10 SASE.

　　O┅ "We provide accurate information about unusual things in nature." Currently de-emphasizing self-help books.

**Nonfiction:** "Soliciting manuscripts on unusual things in nature, such as unusual animals or natural formations. Also natural disasters such as volcanic eruptions, earthquakes, or floods. Preferably of the world's 'worst.' Also related manuscripts on nature/travel/environment. No travel guides." Query with outline and 1 sample chapter and SASE, if answer is desired. Reviews artwork/photos as part of ms package. Send photocopies.

**Recent Title(s):** *Hidden Amazon*, by Lutz.

**Tips:** "Audience is adults who wish to learn something and are interested in unusual travel excursions. Please send for guidelines before submitting."

**N. DISCOVERY ENTERPRISES, LTD.**, 31 Laurelwood Dr., Carlisle MA 01741. (978)287-5401. Fax: (978)287-5402. **Acquisitions:** JoAnne W. Deitch, senior editor (American history and plays). Publishes trade paperback originals **Publishes 25 titles/year. Receives 50 queries and 20 mss/year. Publishes 5% from first-time authors; 90% from unagented writers. Pays 15-20% royalty on wholesale price or makes outright purchase of $500-1,000. No advance.** Publishes book 6 months after acceptance of ms. Accepts simultaneous submissions. Reports in 1 month. Book catalog for 6×9 SAE with 3 first-class stamps. No guidelines.

**Nonfiction:** Reference. Subjects include government/politics, history (American history, world history—primary source documents and analyses). Submit proposal package, including outline and cv.

**Plays:** "We're interested in 40-minute plays (reading time) for students in grades 5-9 on topics in U.S. history." Query about topics prior to sending completed play for review. Query with SASE, then submit complete ms.

**Recent Title(s):** *U.S. Space Program and American Society*, by Roger Laurius, Ph.D. (U.S. history); *The Drama of the Amistad*, by Susan B. Pickford (play).

**Tips:** "Call or send query letter on topic prior to sending manuscript for plays or proposals for American history books."

**DO-IT-YOURSELF LEGAL PUBLISHERS**, 60 Park Place, Suite 103, Newark NJ 07102. (973)639-0400. Fax: (973)639-1801. **Acquisitions:** Dan Benjamin, associate editor; Anne Torrey, editorial director. Estab. 1978. Publishes trade paperback originals. **Publishes 6 titles/year. Imprint publishes 2 titles/year. Receives 25 queries/year. Pays 15-20% royalty on wholesale price. No advance.** Publishes book 1 year after acceptance of ms. Accepts simultaneous submissions. Reports in 1 month on queries and proposals, 3 months on mss.

　　O┅ "The fundamental premise underlying our works is that the simplest problems can be effectively handled by anyone with average common sense and a competent guidebook."

**Imprint(s):** Selfhelper Law Press of America.

**Nonfiction:** How-to (law topics), self-help (law topics). Subject matter should deal with self-help law topics that instruct the lay person on how to undertake legal tasks without the use of attorney or other high cost experts. Query.

**Recent Title(s):** *The National Mortgage Reclamation Kit*, by Benji O. Anosike, Ph.D.

**DORAL PUBLISHING, INC.**, 8560 SW Salish Lane, #300, Wilsonville OR 97070-9612. (503)682-3307. Fax: (503)682-2648. E-mail: doralpub@easystreet.com. Website: http://www.doralpubl.com. **Acquisitions:** Alvin Grossman, publisher; Luana Luther, editor-in-chief (pure bred dogs); Mark Anderson, editor (general dog books). Estab. 1986. Publishes hardcover and trade paperback originals. **Publishes 7 titles/year. Receives 30 queries and 15 mss/year. 60% of mss from first-time authors, 85% from unagented writers. Pays 10% royalty on wholesale price.** Publishes book 6 months after acceptance of ms. *Writer's Market* recommends allowing 2 months for reply. Book catalog free. Manuscript guidelines for #10 SASE.

　　O┅ Doral Publishing publishes only books about dogs and dog-related topics, mostly geared for pure-bred dog owners and showing. Currently emphasizing breed books. De-emphasizing children's work.

**Nonfiction:** How-to, children's/juvenile, reference. Subjects must be dog-related (showing, training, agility, search and rescue, health, nutrition, etc.). "We are looking for new ideas. No flowery prose. Manuscripts should be literate, intelligent, but easy to read." Query first or submit outline and 2 sample chapters with SASE. Reviews artwork/photos as part of the ms package. Send photocopies.

**Fiction:** Children's/juvenile. Subjects must center around dogs. Either the main character should be a dog or a dog should play an integral role. Query with SASE.

**Recent Title(s):** *The Mastiff*; *The Welsh Terrier*.

**Tips:** "We are currently expanding and are looking for new topics and fresh ideas while staying true to our niche. While we will steadfastly maintain that market—we are always looking for excellent breed books—we also want to explore more 'mainstream' topics."

**DORCHESTER PUBLISHING CO., INC.**, 276 Fifth Ave., Suite 1008, New York NY 10001-0112. (212)725-8811. Fax: (212)532-1054. E-mail: dorchedit@dorchesterpub.com.

**Imprint(s):** Love Spell (romance), **Leisure Books**.

**A** **DOUBLEDAY ADULT TRADE**, Doubleday Broadway Publishing Group, Random House, Inc., 1540 Broadway, New York NY 10036. (212)782-9911. Fax: (212)782-9700. Website: http://www.bdd.com. Vice President/Editor-in-Chief: William Thomas. Estab. 1897. Publishes hardcover and trade paperback originals and reprints. **Publishes 200 titles/year. Receives thousands of queries and mss/year. 30% of books from first-time authors. Pays royalty on retail price. Advance varies.** Publishes book 1 year after acceptance of ms. Reports in 6 months on queries.

O─ Doubleday publishes high-quality fiction and nonfiction.

**Imprint(s):** Anchor Books; **Currency**; **Doubleday Religious Division**; **Image Books**; **Main Street**; **Nan A. Talese**;
**Nonfiction:** Biography, cookbook, gift book, how-to, humor, illustrated book, self-help. Subjects include agriculture/horticulture, Americana, animals, anthropology, art/architecture, business/economics, child guidance/parenting, computers/electronics, cooking/foods/nutrition, education, ethnic, gardening, gay/lesbian, government/politics, health/medicine, history, hobbies, language/literature, military/war, money/finance, music/dance, nature/environment, philosophy, photography, psychology, recreation, regional, religion, science, sociology, software, sports, translation, travel, women's issues/studies. *Agented submissions only.*
**Fiction:** Adventure, confession, erotica, ethnic, experimental, feminist, gay/lesbian, historical, horror, humor, literary, mainstream/contemporary, mystery, picture books, religious, short story collections, suspense. *Agented submissions only.*
**Recent Title(s):** *The Street Lawyer*, by John Grisham (fiction).

**A** **DOUBLEDAY RELIGIOUS DIVISION**, Doubleday Broadway Publishing Group, Doubleday, Random House, Inc., 1540 Broadway, New York NY 10036. (212)354-6500. Fax: (212)782-8911. Website: http://www.bdd.com. **Acquisitions**: Eric Major, vice president, religious division; Mark Fretz, senior editor; Trace Murphy, editor. Estab. 1897. Publishes hardcover originals and reprints, trade paperback originals and reprints. **Publishes 45-50 titles/year; each imprint publishes 12 titles/year. Receives 1,000 queries/year; receives 500 mss/year. 30% of books are from first-time authors; 3% from unagented writers. Pays 7½-15% royalty. Advance varies.** Publishes book 1 year after acceptance of ms. Accepts simultaneous submissions. Reports in 3 months on proposals. Book catalog for SAE with 3 first-class stamps.
**Imprint(s): Image Books**, Anchor Bible Commentary, Anchor Bible Reference, Galilee, New Jerusalem Bible.
**Nonfiction:** Biography, cookbook, gift book, reference, self-help. Subjects include child guidance/parenting, cooking/foods/nutrition, history, language/literature, memoirs, money/finance, religion, spirituality. *Agented submissions only.*
**Fiction:** Religious. *Agented submissions only.*
**Recent Title(s):** *The Left Hand of God*, by Shirley de Boulay (biography); *Christmas in My Heart*, by Joe Wheeler (fiction).

**DOVER PUBLICATIONS, INC.**, 31 E. 2nd St., Mineola NY 11501. **Acquisitions:** Paul Negri, editor-in-chief; John Grafton (math/science reprints). Estab. 1941. Publishes trade paperback originals and reprints. **Publishes 500 titles/year. Makes outright purchase.** Book catalog free.
**Nonfiction:** Biography, children's/juvenile, coffee table book, cookbook, how-to, humor, illustrated book, textbook. Subjects include agriculture/horticulture, Americana, animals, anthropology/archaeology, art/architecture, cooking/food/nutrition, health/medicine, history, hobbies, language/literature, music/dance, nature/environment, philosophy, photography, religion, science, sports, translation, travel. Publishes mostly reprints. Accepts original paper doll collections, game books, coloring books (juvenile). Query. Reviews artwork/photos as part of ms package.
**Recent Title(s):** *The Waning of the Middle Ages*, by John Huizenga.

**DOWLING PRESS, INC.**, 1110 17th Ave. S., #4, Nashville TN 37212. (615)340-0967. **Acquisitions:** Maryglenn McCombs. Publishes hardcover, trade paperback and mass market paperback originals. **Publishes 5 titles/year. Receives 150 queries and 100 mss/year. Pays 12% royalty on retail price. No advance.** Reports in 3 months on queries and proposals, 6 months on mss. Manuscript guidelines free.

O─ Dowling Press publishes books on pop culture, especially music and mysteries. Currently de-emphasizing self-help and biography.

**Nonfiction:** Humor. Subjects include hobbies, music/dance, women's issues/studies. Query with SASE.
**Fiction:** Mystery. Query.
**Recent Title(s):** *No Depression: An Introduction to Alternative Country Music (Whatever That Is)*, by Peter Blackstock and Grant Alden (nonfiction); *Hellhounds On Their Trail*, by Gary Patterson (fiction).
**Tips:** Audience is 18-40 year olds, middle class. "Please proofread! There is nothing worse than carelessness (especially in a cover letter). Don't call us a day after we've received the manuscript to ask what we think! Be patient."

**⊠** **DOWN EAST BOOKS**, Down East Enterprise, Inc., P.O. Box 679, Camden ME 04843-0679. Fax: (207)594-7215. E-mail: adevine@downeast.com. Senior Editor: Karin Womer. **Acquisitions:** Chris Cornell, editor (Silver Quill); Alice Devine, associate editor (general). Estab. 1967. Publishes hardcover and trade paperback originals, trade paperback reprints. **Publishes 20-24 titles/year. Receives 600 submissions/year. 50% of books from first-time authors; 90% from unagented writers. Pays 10-15% royalty on receipts. Offers $200 average advance.** Publishes book 1 year after acceptance. Accepts simultaneous submissions. Reports in 3 months. Manuscript guidelines for 9×12 SAE with 3 first-class stamps.

O─ Down East Books publishes books, calendars and videos which capture and illuminate the astonishing beauty and unique character of New England's people, culture, and wild places: the very aspects that distinguish New England from the rest of the United States.

**Imprint(s):** Silver Quill (fly fishing and wing-shooting market); Chris Cornell, editor, e-mail: ccornell@downeast.com)
**Nonfiction:** Books about the New England region, Maine in particular. Subjects include Americana, history, nature, guide books, crafts, recreation, field guides. "All of our regional books must have a Maine or New England emphasis." Query. Reviews artwork/photos as part of ms package.
**Fiction:** "We publish 1-2 juvenile titles/year (fiction and nonfiction), and 1-2 adult fiction titles/year." *Writer's Market* recommends sending a query with SASE first.
**Recent Title(s):** *Rockwell Kent's Forgotten Landscapes*, by Scott Ferris and Ellen Pearce (nonfiction); *Green Wood & Chloroform*, by Anthony Betts M.D. (fiction); *The Great New England Sea Monster*, by J.P. O'Neill.

**A LISA DREW BOOKS**, Simon & Schuster, 1230 Avenue of the Americas, New York NY 10020. (212)698-7000. **Acquisitions:** Lisa Drew, publisher. Publishes hardcover originals. **Publishes 10-14 titles/year. Receives 600 queries/ year. 10% of books from first-time authors. Pays royalty on retail price, varies by author and project. Advance varies.** Publishes book 1 year after acceptance of ms. Accepts simultaneous submissions, if so noted. Reports in 1 month on queries. Book catalog free through Scribner (same address).
  ○→ "We publish *reading* books; nonfiction that tells a story, not '14 ways to improve your marriage.' "
**Nonfiction:** Subjects include government/politics, history, women's issues/studies, law, entertainment. *Agented submissions only.* No unsolicited material.

**DUFOUR EDITIONS**, P.O. Box 7, Chester Springs PA 19425. (610)458-5005. **Acquisitions:** Thomas Lavoie, associate publisher. Estab. 1948. Publishes hardcover originals, trade paperback originals and reprints. **Publishes 5-6 titles/ year. Receives 100 queries and 15 mss/year. 20-30% of books from first-time authors; 50% from unagented writers. Pays 6-10% royalty on net receipts. Offers $500-1,000 advance.** Publishes book 18 months after acceptance of ms. Accepts simultaneous submissions. Reports in 3 months on queries and proposals, 6 months on mss. Book catalog and ms guidelines free.
  ○→ "We're a small literary house and distribute a number of quality fiction, poetry and nonfiction titles from the U.K. and Irish publishers as well."
**Nonfiction:** Biography. Subjects include history, translation. Query with SASE. Reviews artwork/photos as part of ms package. Send photocopies.
**Fiction:** Ethnic, historical, literary, short story collections. Query with SASE.
**Poetry:** Query.
**Recent Title(s):** *The Visitor's Guide to Northern Ireland*, by Rosemary Evans; *Undertow*, by Tom Foote (fiction).
**Tips:** "Audience is sophisticated, literate readers especially interested in foreign literature and translations, and a strong Irish-Celtic focus. Check to see if the publisher is really a good match for your subject matter."

**A DUMMIES TRADE PRESS**, IDG Books Worldwide, 645 N. Michigan Ave., Chicago IL 60611. (312)482-8460. Fax: (312)482-8561. E-mail: kwelton@idgbooks.com. Website: http://www.dummies.com. **Acquisitions:** Kathleen A. Welton, vice president/publisher. Publishes trade paperback originals. **Pays 10-15% royalty. Offers $0-25,000 advance.** Publishes book 3 months after acceptance of ms. Reports in 2 months. Manuscript guidelines free.
  ○→ "Dummies Trade Press dedicates itself to publishing innovative, high-quality "For Dummies℠" titles on the most popular business, self-help and general reference topics."
**Nonfiction:** Cookbook, gift book, how-to, illustrated book, reference, self-help. Subjects include animals, art/architecture, business/economics, child guidance/parenting, cooking/food/nutrition, diet/health/medical, gardening, government/ politics, hobbies, money/finance, music/dance, nature/environment, photography, recreation, sports, travel. *Agented submissions only.*
**Recent Title(s):** *Investing For Dummies*, by Eric Tyson.

**THOMAS DUNNE BOOKS**, St. Martin's Press, 175 Fifth Ave., New York NY 10010. (212)674-5151. **Acquistions:** Tom Dunne, publisher; Peter J. Wolverton, associate publisher; Ruth Cavin, associate publisher (mysteries). Publishes hardcover originals, trade paperback originals and reprints. **Publishes 90 titles/year. Receives 1,000 queries/year. 20% of books from first-time authors; less than 5% from unagented writers. Pays 10-15% royalty on retail price for hardcover, 7½% for paperback. Advance varies with project.** Publishes book 1 year after acceptance of ms. Accepts simultaneous submissions. Reports in 2 months on queries. Ms guidelines for #10 SASE.
  ○→ Thomas Dunne publishes a wide range of fiction and nonfiction.
**Nonfiction:** Biography. Subjects include government/politics, history, political commentary. "Author's attention to detail is important. We get a lot of manuscripts that are poorly proofread and just can't be considered." Query or submit outline and 100 sample pages with SASE. Reviews artwork/photos as part of ms package. Send photocopies.
**Fiction:** Mainstream/contemporary, thrillers, suspense, women's. Query or submit synopsis and 100 sample pages with SASE.
**Recent Title(s):** *An Ocean Apart*, by Robin Pilcher (commercial fiction).

**DUQUESNE UNIVERSITY PRESS**, 600 Forbes Ave., Pittsburgh PA 15282-0101. (412)396-6610. Fax: (412)396-5984. Website: http://www.duq.edu/dupress.html. **Acquisitions:** Susan Wadsworth-Booth, editor-in-chief. Estab. 1927. Publishes hardcover and trade paperback originals. **Publishes 8-12 titles/year. Receives 500 queries and 75 mss/year. 30% of books from first-time authors; 95% from unagented writers. Pays royalty on net price.** Publishes book 1 year after acceptance of ms. Reports in 1 month on proposals, 3 months on mss. Book catalog and ms guidelines free with SASE.

O⭢ Duquesne publishes scholarly monographs in the fields of literary studies (medieval & Renaissance), philosophy, ethics, religious studies and psychology. "We also publish a series, *Emerging Writers in Creative Nonfiction*, for first-time authors of creative nonfiction for a general readership."

**Nonfiction:** Creative nonfiction, scholarly/academic. Subjects include language/literature, philosophy, religion. "We look for quality of scholarship." For scholarly books, query or submit outline, 1 sample chapter and SASE. For creative nonfiction, submit 2 copies of ms.

**Recent Title(s):** *The Last Settlers*, by Jennifer Brice and Charles Mason.

**DUTTON CHILDREN'S BOOKS**, Penguin Putnam Inc., 345 Hudson St., New York NY 10014. (212)414-3700. **Acquisitions:** Lucia Monfried, editor-in-chief. Estab. 1852. Publishes hardcover originals. **Publishes 80 titles/year. 15% from first-time authors. Pays royalty on retail price.**

O⭢ Dutton Children's Books publishes fiction and nonfiction for readers ranging from preschoolers to young adults on a variety of subjects.

**Nonfiction:** For preschoolers to middle-graders; including animals/nature, U.S. history, science and photo essays. Query with SASE.

**Fiction:** Dutton Children's Books has a complete publishing program that includes picture books; easy-to-read books; and fiction for all ages, from "first-chapter" books to young adult readers. Send full picture book ms with SASE. For chapter books and novels, query with SASE.

**Recent Title(s):** *Hear These Voices: Youth at the Edge of the Millennium*, by Anthony Allison (nonfiction); *How Yussel Caught the Gefilte Fish*, by Charlotte Herman, illustrated by Katya Krenina (fiction).

**Ⓐ DUTTON PLUME**, Penguin Putnam Inc., 375 Hudson St., New York NY 10014. (212)366-2000. President: Clare Ferraro. **Acquisitions:** Lori Lipsky, publisher (business, mainstream fiction); Brian Tart, editor-in-chief (commercial fiction, self-help/spirituality); Elisa Petrini, executive editor (mainstream, literary and commercial fiction, biography, memoir, narrative and issue-oriented nonfiction, popular science, culture, history, sociology); Rosemary Ahern, senior editor (literary fiction, narrative nonfiction); Deb Brody, senior editor (narrative nonfiction, memoir, health, parenting, history, psychology, judaica); Laurie Chittenden, senior editor (multicultural and women's fiction, narrative nonfiction); Jennifer Dickerson, associate editor (women's commercial fiction, literary fiction, spirituality, self-help); Jennifer Moore, associate editor (narrative nonfiction, African-American history/politics/culture, memoir, self-help, pop culture, women's fiction); Kimberly Perdue, assistant editor (Gen-X fiction, humor, self-help). Estab. 1852. **Publishes 60 titles/year. Receives 20,000 queries and 10,000 mss/year. 30-40% of books from first-time authors; 2% from unagented writers. Advance negotiable.** Publishes book 18 months after acceptance. Reports in 6 months.

O⭢ Dutton publishes hardcover, original, mainstream, and contemporary fiction and nonfiction in the areas of biography, self-help, politics, psychology, and science for a general readership.

**Nonfiction:** Biography, gift book, how-to, humor, reference, self-help. Subjects include Americana, animals, anthropology/archaeology, art/architecture, business/economics, child guidance/parenting, cooking/foods/nutrition education, ethnic, gardening, gay/lesbian, government/politics, health/medicine, history, hobbies, language/literature, military/war, money/finance, music/dance, nature/environment, philosophy, photography, psychology, recreation, regional, religion, science, sociology, sports, translation, women's issues/studies. *Agented submissions only.*

**Fiction:** Adventure, erotica, ethnic, gay/lesbian, historical, literary, mainstream/contemporary, mystery, occult, short story collections, suspense. "We are looking for novelists who can write a book a year with consistent quality." *Agented submissions only.*

**Recent Title(s):** *Reaching to Heaven: A Spiritual Journey Through Life and Death*, by James Van Praagh (inspirational).

**Tips:** "Write the complete manuscript and submit it to an agent or agents. They will know exactly which editor will be interested in a project."

**EAGLE'S VIEW PUBLISHING**, 6756 N. Fork Rd., Liberty UT 84310. Fax: (801)745-0903. E-mail: eglcrafts@aol.com. **Acquisitions:** Denise Knight, editor-in-chief. Estab. 1982. Publishes trade paperback originals. **Publishes 4-6 titles/year. Receives 40 queries and 20 mss/year. 90% of books from first-time authors; 100% from unagented writers. Pays 8-10% royalty on net selling price.** Publishes book 1 year or more after acceptance of ms. Accepts simultaneous submissions. Reports in 1 year on proposals. Book catalog and ms guidelines for $3.

O⭢ Eagle's View publishes primarily how-to craft books with a subject related to historical or contemporary Native American/Mountain Man/frontier crafts. Currently emphasizing bead-related craft books. De-emphasizing earring books.

**Nonfiction:** How-to, Indian, mountain man and American frontier (history and craft). Subjects include anthropology/archaeology (Native American crafts), ethnic (Native American), history (American frontier historical patterns and books), hobbies (crafts, especially beadwork, earrings). "We are expanding from our Indian craft base to more general but related crafts." Submit outline and 1-2 sample chapters. Reviews artwork/photos as part of ms package. Send photocopies or sample illustrations. "We prefer to do photography in house."

**Recent Title(s):** *Hemp Masters: Ancient Hippie Secrets for Knotting Hip Hemp Jewelry*, by Max Lunger.

**Tips:** "We will not be publishing any new beaded earrings books for 1-2 years. We are interested in other craft projects using seed beads, especially books that feature a variety of items, not just different designs for one item."

**⬛ EAKIN PRESS/SUNBELT MEDIA, INC.**, P.O. Box 90159, Austin TX 78709-0159. (512)288-1771. Fax: (512)288-1813. **Acquisitions:** Edwin M. Eakin, editorial director; Virginia Messer, associate publisher. Estab. 1978. Publishes hardcover and paperback originals and reprints. **Publishes 50 titles/year. Receives 1,500 submissions/year. 50% of books from first-time authors; 90% from unagented writers. Pays 10-12-15% royalty on net sales.** Publishes book 18 months after acceptance. Accepts simultaneous submissions. Reports in 3 months. Book catalog for $1.25. Manuscript guidelines for #10 SASE.

○➔ Eakin specializes in Texana and Western Americana for adults and juveniles.

**Imprint(s): Eakin Press,** Nortex Press.

**Nonfiction:** Adult nonfiction: Western Americana, African American studies, business, sports, biographies, Civil War, regional cookbooks, Texas history, World War II. Juvenile nonfiction: includes biographies of historic personalities, prefer with Texas or regional interest, or nature studies; and easy-read illustrated books for grades 1-3. Query with SASE.

**Fiction:** No adult fiction. Juvenile fiction for grades 4-7, preferably relating to Texas and the Southwest or contemporary. Query or submit outline/synopsis and sample chapters.

**Recent Title(s):** *Willie Nelson Sings America*, by Steven Opdyke; *Jesse James Lived and Died in Texas*, by Betty Dorsett Duke.

**EASTERN NATIONAL**, (formerly Eastern National Association), 470 Maryland Dr., Fort Washington PA 19034. (215)283-6900. Fax: (215)283-6925. **Acquisitions:** Patti Plummer, production coordinator. Estab. 1948. Publishes trade paperback originals and reprints. **Publishes 50-60 titles/year. Receives 20 queries and 10 mss/year. 5% of books from first-time authors; 50% from unagented writers. Pays 1-10% royalty on retail price or makes outright purchase of $6,000 maximum.** Publishes book 2 years after acceptance of ms. Reports in 1 month on queries. *Writer's Market* recommends allowing 2 months for reply. Book catalog free.

○➔ "Our mission is to continue to strengthen our relationship with the National Park Service and other partners."

**Imprint(s):** Eastern Acorn Press.

**Nonfiction:** Biography, children's/juvenile. Subjects include Americana, history, military/war, nature/environment. "Requests for editorial plans are only accepted from member agencies." Query. *All unsolicited mss returned unopened.*

**Recent Title(s):** *National Parks on the Great Lakes*, by Ron Thomson.

**EASTLAND PRESS**, P.O. Box 99749, Seattle WA 98199. (206)217-0204. Fax: (206)217-0205. Website: http://www.eastlandpress.com. **Acquisitions:** John O'Connor, managing editor. Estab. 1981. Publishes hardcover and trade paperback originals. **Publishes 4-6 titles/year. Receives 25 queries/year. 30% of books from first-time authors; 90% from unagented writers. Pays 10-15% royalty on receipts. Offers $500-1,500 advance.** Publishes book 18 months after acceptance of ms. Accepts simultaneous submissions. Reports in 1 month. Book catalog free.

○➔ Eastland is interested in textbooks for practitioners of alternative medical therapies primarily Chinese and physical therapies and related bodywork.

**Nonfiction:** Reference, textbook, alternative medicine (Chinese and physical therapies and related bodywork). "We prefer that a manuscript be completed or close to completion before we will consider publication. Proposals are rarely considered, unless submitted by a published author or teaching institution." Submit outline and 2-3 sample chapters. Reviews artwork/photos as part of ms package. Send photocopies.

**Recent Title(s):** *Patterns & Practice in Chinese Medicine*, by Zhao Jingyi.

**THE ECCO PRESS**, HarperCollins, 10 E. 53rd St., New York NY 10022. (212)207-7000. Website: http://www.harpercollins.com. Editor-in-Chief: Daniel Halpern. **Acquisitions:** address queries to Submissions Editor. Estab. 1970. Publishes hardcover and trade paperback originals and reprints. **Publishes 60 titles/year. Receives 3,000 queries/year. Pays royalty. Offers advance.** Publishes book 1 year after acceptance of ms. Book catalog and ms guidelines free.

○➔ "The Ecco Press publishes finely crafted books of high literary merit, establishing a reputation as one of the most important literary publishers worldwide."

**Nonfiction:** Biography/autobiography, cookbook. Subjects include cooking/foods, literature, sports, translations. Query with SASE.

**Fiction:** Literary, short story collections. Query with SASE.

**Recent Title(s):** *Hare Brain, Tortoise Mind*, by Guy Claxton; *Letters to My Son On the Love of Books*, by Robert Cotroneo.

**⬛ ECS LEARNING SYSTEMS, INC.**, P.O. Box 791437, San Antonio TX 78279-1437. (830)438-4262. Fax: (830)438-4263. E-mail: ecslearn@gvtc.com or educyberstor@gvtc.com. **Acquisitions:** Lori Mammen, editor (educational material). Estab. 1982. **Publishes 15-25 titles/year. Receives 120 queries and 50 mss/year. 25% of books from first-time authors; 100% from unagented writers. Pays 10% royalty on wholesale price. No advance.** Publishes book 18 months after acceptance of ms. Reports in 2 months on queries, 4 months on proposals and mss. Book catalog and ms guidelines free.

○➔ ECS Learning Systems publishes practical educational material for teachers, parents and students including fun, motivating ideas to make children want to learn.

**Nonfiction:** Educational resource books for teachers, parents, students. Query with SASE. Reviews artwork/photos as part of ms package. Send photocopies.

**Recent Title(s):** *AlphaCapers*, by Debra Cavin Coltman (learning shapes and sounds of alphabet).

**Tips:** "Our audience breaks down into three groups—busy teachers looking for great, ready-to-use teaching ideas; supportive parents looking for ways to enhance their children's education; and discerning kids looking for learning activities/challenges outside the classroom. Submit practical, motivating material for learning. We are *not* interested in dry, theoretical material."

**N THE EDUCATION CENTER, INC.**, 3511 W. Market St., Suite 200, Greensboro NC 27403. Fax: (336)547-1590. Estab. 1973. **Publishes 50 titles/year. Receives 300 queries and 100 mss/year. Under 5% of books from first-time authors; 100% from unagented writers. Purchases ms with one-time payment or royalty. "Payment amount negotiated when contract signed."** Publishes book 1 year after acceptance of ms. Reports in 3 months on proposals.

  **O—** The Education Center publishes supplementary resource books for elementary teachers: preschool/grade 6. Currently emphasizing preschool books in a series.

**Nonfiction:** Teacher resource/supplementary materials. Subjects include education P/K-6, language/literature. Submit outline and 1 sample chapter.

**Recent Title(s):** *Busy Kids™ for Preschool-Kindergarten* series.

**Tips:** "We place a strong emphasis on materials that teach the basic language arts and math skills. We are also seeking materials for teaching science and literature-based activities. Technical, complex or comprehensive manuscripts (such as textbooks and theory/practice articles) are not accepted."

**EDUCATIONAL TECHNOLOGY PUBLICATIONS**, 700 Palisade Ave., Englewood Cliffs NJ 07632. (201)871-4007. E-mail: edtecpubs@aol.com. **Acquisitions:** Lawrence Lipsitz, publisher. Estab. 1969. Publishes hardcover and trade paperback originals. **Publishes 12-15 titles/year. Receives 100 queries and 50 mss/year. 33% of books from first-time authors; 100% from unagented writers. Pays 10-15% royalty on wholesale or retail price. No advance.** Publishes book 1 year after acceptance of ms. Reports in 1 month.

  **O—** Educational Technology publishes books on the use of technology in education.

**Nonfiction:** Technical, textbook, professional books on education technology. "No other topics, please. We are not a general purpose publisher." Query with outline and SASE. Reviews artwork/photos as part of ms package.

**Recent Title(s):** *Computer-Based Instruction: Design and Development*, by Andrew Gibbons & Peter Fairweather.

**Tips:** "Audience is sophisticated educators interested in all areas of technology in education. We desire only very expert authors, able to do high-level work—not P.R. 'flacks.' Only leading-edge, up-to-date material will be considered."

**EDUCATOR'S INTERNATIONAL PRESS, INC.**, 18 Colleen Rd., Troy NY 12180. (518)271-9886. **Acquisitions:** Sarah J. Biondello, publisher/acquisitions editor. Estab. 1996. Publishes hardcover and trade paperback originals and reprints. **Publishes 10-12 titles/year. Receives 50 queries and 50 mss/year. 50% of books from first-time authors; 98% from unagented writers. Pays 3-15% royalty on wholesale price.** Publishes book 1 year after acceptance of ms. Accepts simultaneous submissions. Reports in 2 months on queries and proposals, 3 months on mss. Book catalog and ms guidelines free.

  **O—** Educator's International publishes books in all aspects of education, broadly conceived, from pre-kindergarten to postgraduate. "We specialize in texts, professional books, videos and other materials for students, faculty, practitioners and researchers. We also publish a full list of books in the areas of women's studies, social and behavioral sciences, and nursing and health."

**Nonfiction:** Textbook, supplemental texts, conference proceedings. Subjects include education, gay/lesbian, health/medicine, language/literature, philosophy, psychology, software, women's issues/studies. Submit table of contents, outline, 2-3 chapters, résumé with SASE. Reviews artwork/photos as part of ms package.

**Recent Title(s):** *Awakening the Inner Eye: Intuition in Education*, by Noddings and Shore.

**Tips:** Audience is professors, students, researchers, individuals, libraries.

**EDUCATORS PUBLISHING SERVICES, INC.**, 31 Smith Place, Cambridge MA 02138-1089. (617)547-6706. Fax: (617)547-0412. Website: http://www.epsbooks.com. **Acquisitions:** Dorothy Miller, executive editor. Estab. 1952. **Publishes 26 titles/year. Receives 250 queries and 250 mss/year. 50% of books come from first-time authors; 100% from unagented writers. Pays 5-12% royalty on retail price.** Publishes book 8 months minimum after acceptance of ms. Accepts simultaneous submissions. Reports in 1 month on queries and 3 months on proposals and mss. Book catalog and ms guidelines free on request.

  **O—** EPS is looking for supplementary materials for the regular K-12 classroom. "We are particularly interested in workbook series, but will gladly consider any proposals for high-quality material that is useful to teachers and students."

**Nonfiction:** Workbooks (language arts and math) and some professional books. Language/literature subjects. Query. Reviews artwork/photos as part of ms package. Send photocopies.

**Recent Title(s):** *Ridgewood Analogies*, by Ridgewood New Jersey Public Schools.

**Tips:** Teacher, students (K-adult) audiences.

**EDUPRESS**, 1140-A Calle Cordillera, San Clemente CA 92673. (714)366-9499. **Acquisitions:** Kathy Rogers, production manager. Estab. 1979. Publishes trade paperback originals. **Publishes 40 titles/year. Receives 20 queries and 20 mss/year. 25% of books from first-time authors. Makes outright purchase.** Publishes book 1 year after acceptance of ms. Reports in 2 months on queries, 5 months on mss. Book catalog and ms guidelines free.

○━ Edupress publishes supplemental resources for classroom curriculum. Currently emphasizing more science, math, writing emphasis than in the past.

**Nonfiction:** Educational resources for pre-school through middle school. Submit proposal package, including ms copy, outline, 1 sample chapter and SASE. Reviews artwork/photos as part of ms package. Send photocopies. "We use inhouse artists but will consider submitted art."

**Recent Title(s):** *Space Exploration Activity Book*, by Mary Jo Keller.

**Tips:** Audience is classroom teachers and homeschool parents.

**EERDMANS BOOKS FOR YOUNG READERS**, William B. Eerdmans Publishing Co., 255 Jefferson Ave. SE, Grand Rapids MI 49503. (616)459-4591. Fax: (616)459-6540. **Acquisitions:** Judy Zylstra, editor. Publishes picture books and middle reader and young adult fiction and nonfiction. **Publishes 12-15 titles/year. Receives 3,000 submissions/year. Pays 5-7½% royalty on retail price.** Publishes middle reader and YA books 1 year after acceptance. Publishes picture books 2-3 years after acceptance. Accepts simultaneous submissions, if noted. Reports in 6 weeks on queries. Book catalog for SASE.

○━ "We publish books for children and young adults that deal with spiritual themes—but never in a preachy or heavy-handed way. Some of our books are clearly religious, while others (especially our novels) look at spiritual issues in very subtle ways. We look for books that are honest, wise and hopeful." Currently emphasizing general picture books (also picture book biographies), novels (middle reader and YA). De-emphasizing YA biographies, retellings of Bible stories.

**Nonfiction and Fiction:** Children's books. Picture books, middle reader, young adult fiction and nonfiction. Submit complete mss for picture books and middle readers under 200 pages with SASE. For longer books, send query letter and 3 or 4 sample chapters with SASE. "Do not send illustrations unless you are a professional illustrator." Send color photocopies rather than original art.

**Recent Title(s):** *A Traitor Among Us*, by Elizabeth Van Steenwyk.

**WILLIAM B. EERDMANS PUBLISHING CO.**, 255 Jefferson Ave. SE, Grand Rapids MI 49503. (616)459-4591. Fax: (616)459-6540. E-mail: sales@eerdmans.com. **Acquisitions:** Jon Pott, editor-in-chief; Charles Van Hof, managing editor (history); Judy Zylstra, children's book editor. Estab. 1911. Publishes hardcover and paperback originals and reprints. **Publishes 120-130 titles/year. Receives 3,000-4,000 submissions/year. 10% of books from first-time authors; 95% from unagented writers. Pays royalty.** Publishes book 1 year after acceptance. Accepts simultaneous submissions if noted. Reports in 6 weeks on queries. Book catalog free.

○━ "Approximately 80% of our adult publications are religious and most of these are academic or semi-academic in character (as opposed to inspirational or celebrity books), though we also publish books on the Christian life. Our nonreligious titles, most of them in regional history or on social issues, aim, similarly, at an educated audience."

**Imprint(s):** Eerdmans Books for Young Readers (Judy Zylstra, editor).

**Nonfiction:** Religious, reference, textbooks, monographs, children's books. Subjects include biblical studies, theology, ethics, literature, religious history, philosophy of religion, psychology, sociology, regional history. "We prefer that writers take the time to notice if we have published anything at all in the same category as their manuscript before sending it to us." Accepts nonfiction translations. Query with outline, 2-3 sample chapters and SASE for return of ms. Reviews artwork/photos.

**Recent Title(s):** *The Encyclopedia of Christianity*, edited by Fahlbusch et al.

**ELDER BOOKS**, P.O. Box 490, Forest Knolls CA 94933. (415)488-9002. E-mail: info@elderbooks.com. Website: http://www.elderbooks.com. **Acquisitions:** Carmel Sheridan, director. Estab. 1987. Publishes trade paperback originals. **Publishes 6-10 titles/year. Receives 200 queries and 50 mss/year. 50% of books from first-time authors; 50% from unagented writers. Pays 7% royalty on retail price. No advance.** Publishes book 9 months after acceptance of ms. Reports in 3 months on queries. Book catalog free.

○━ Elder Books is dedicated to publishing practical, hands-on guidebooks for family and professional caregivers of persons with Alzheimer's.

**Nonfiction:** Gift book, how-to, self-help. Subjects include parenting, education, health/medicine, money/finance, psychology, senior issues, Alzheimer's disease, women's issues/studies. Submit outline, 2 sample chapters. Reviews artwork/photos as part of ms package. Send photocopies.

**Recent Title(s):** *Coping With Caring: Daily Reflections for Alzheimer's Caregivers*, by Lyn Roche.

**Tips:** "Our books are written in a style that is user-friendly and nontechnical, presenting key information on caregiver concerns including: how to keep the person engaged through meaningful activities, prevent caregiver burnout, cope with wandering and organize a search in the event the person disappears, deal with difficult behaviors."

**N ELECTRIC WORKS PUBLISHING**, 605 Ave. C.E., Bismarck ND 58501. (701)255-0356. E-mail: editors@electricpublishing.com. Website: http://www.electricpublishing.com. **Acquisitions:** James R. Bohe, editor-in-chief. Publishes digital books. **Publishes 50 titles/year. Receives 30 queries and 250 mss/year. 60% of books from first-time authors; 99% from unagented writers. Pays 36-40% royalty on wholesale price. No advance.** Publishes book 2 months after acceptance of ms. Accepts simultaneous submissions. Reports in 2 months. Book catalog and ms guidelines on website.

**Nonfiction:** Biography, children's/juvenile, cookbook, how-to, humor, illustrated book, multimedia (CD-ROM, disk), reference, self-help, technical. Subjects include agriculture/horticulture, Americana, animals, anthropology/archaeology, art/architecture, business/economics, child guidance/parenting, computers/electronics, cooking/foods/nutrition, creative nonfiction, education, ethnic, gardening, government/politics, health/medicine, history, hobbies, language/literature, memoirs, military/war, money/finance, multicultural, music/dance, nature/environment, philosophy, photography, psychology, recreation, regional, religion, science, sociology, software, spirituality, sports, translation, travel, women's issues/women's studies. Submit proposal package, including outline. Reviews artwork/photos as part of ms package. Send files in JPEG or GIF format.

**Fiction:** Adventure, ethnic, experimental, fantasy, gothic, historical, horror, humor, juvenile, literary, mainstream/contemporary, military/war, multicultural, multimedia, mystery, occult, plays, poetry, poetry in translation, regional, religious, romance, science fiction, short story collections, spiritual, sports, suspense, translation, western, young adult. Submit complete ms electronically.

**Poetry:** Submit complete ms.

**Recent Title(s):** *Flight of the Forgotten*, by Mark A. Vance (historical nonfiction); *The Last Judgment*, by Albert E. Brewster (speculative fiction); *In the Green Grass*, by Lori Robinson.

**✦ ELEMENT BOOKS**, Element Books Ltd. (UK), 160 N. Washington St., 4th Floor, Boston MA 02114. (617)915-9400. Fax: (617)248-0909. E-mail: element@cove.com. **Acquisitions:** Roberta Scimone, editorial director. Estab. 1975. Publishes hardcover originals. **Publishes 15-20 titles/year. Receives 600 queries/year. 50% of books from first-time authors; 80% from unagented writers. Pays 15-20% royalty on retail price. Offers $3,000 average advance.** Publishes book 1 year after acceptance of ms. Accepts simultaneous submissions. Reports in 2 months on proposals. Book catalog and ms guidelines free.

⚬➤ Element Books publishes high-quality, accessible books on spiritual traditions, complimentary health and inner wisdom.

**Imprint(s):** One World (UK), Element Children's Books.

**Nonfiction:** Reference, self-help. Subjects include business/economics, health/medicine, philosophy, psychology, regional. Query with outline, 2-3 sample chapters, table of contents, author's bio and SASE. Reviews artwork/photos as part of ms package. Send photocopies.

**Recent Title(s):** *Little Stone*, by James Wanless (inspirational).

**EMC/PARADIGM PUBLISHING INC.**, EMC Corporation, 875 Montreal Way, St. Paul MN 55102. (651)290-2800. Fax: (651)290-2828. E-mail: educate@emcp.com. Website: http://www.emcp.com. **Acquisitions:** George Provol, publisher. Estab. 1980. **Publishes 50 titles/year. Receives 60 queries and 35 mss/year. 20% of books from first-time authors; 100% from unagented writers. Pays 6-10% royalty on net. Offers $1,000-2,500 advance.** Publishes book 1 year after acceptance of ms. Accepts simultaneous submissions. Reports in 2 months on proposals. Book catalog for 8×12 SAE with 4 first-class stamps. Manuscript guidelines free.

⚬➤ EMC/Paradigm focuses on textbooks for business and office, computer information systems, and allied health education marketed to proprietary business schools and community colleges.

**Nonfiction:** Textbook, multimedia. Subjects include business and office, communications, computers, psychology, allied health, accounting, keyboarding, staff development. Submit outline and 2 sample chapters.

**Recent Title(s):** *Word 2000*, by Nita Rutkosky.

**Tips:** "We are looking more seriously at materials for distributive education. Let us know what ideas you have."

**EMIS, INC.**, P.O. Box 1607, Durant OK 74702. President: Lynda Blake. Publishes trade paperback originals. **Publishes 4 titles/year. Pays 12% royalty on retail price.** Reports in 3 months. Book catalog and manuscript guidelines free.

⚬➤ "Our books are published as a medical text designed for physicians to fit in the lab coat pocket as a quick means of locating information." Currently emphasizing infectious diseases. De-emphasizing medical program management.

**Nonfiction:** Reference. Subjects include women's health/medicine and psychology. Submit 3 sample chapters with SASE.

**Recent Title(s):** *Managing Contraceptive Pill Patients*.

**Tips:** Audience is medical professionals and medical product manufacturers and distributors.

**⊞ ✦ ENCOUNTER BOOKS**, 116 New Montgomery St., Suite 206, San Francisco CA 94105-3640. (415)538-1460. Fax: (415)538-1461. E-mail: read@encounterbooks.com. Website: http://www.encounterbooks.com. **Acquisitions:** Peter Collier, publisher; Judy Hardin, operations manager. Hardcover originals and trade paperback reprints. **Publishes 12-20 titles/year. Receives 200 queries and 100 mss/year. 40% of books from first-time authors; 60% from unagented writers. Pays 7-10% royalty on retail price. Offers $2,000-25,000 advance.** Publishes book 14 months after acceptance of ms. Accepts simultaneous submissions. Reports in 1 month on queries, 2 months on proposals and mss. Book catalog and ms guidelines free or on website.

⚬➤ Encounter Books publishes serious nonfiction—books that can alter our society, challenge our morality, stimulate our imaginations. Currently emphasizing history, culture, social criticism and politics.

**Nonfiction:** Biography, reference. Subjects include anthropology/archaeology, business/economics, child guidance/parenting, creative nonfiction, education, ethnic, government/politics, health/medicine, history, language/literature, memoirs, military/war, money/finance, multicultural, nature/environment, philosophy, psychology, religion, science, sex,

sociology, spirituality, women's issues/studies, gender studies. Submit proposal package, including outline and 1 sample chapter.
**Recent Titles:** *Creating Equal: My Fight Against Race Preferences*, by Ward Connerly.

**ENSLOW PUBLISHERS INC.**, 40 Industrial Rd., Box 398, Berkeley Heights NJ 07922. (201)379-8890. Website: http://www.enslow.com. **Acquisitions:** Brian D. Enslow, editor. Estab. 1977. Publishes hardcover originals. **Publishes 120 titles/year. 30% require freelance illustration. Pays royalty on net price. Offers advance.** Publishes book 1 year after acceptance of ms. Reports in 1 month. *Writer's Market* recommends allowing 2 months for reply. Book catalog for $2 and 9×12 SAE with 3 first-class stamps. Writer's guidelines for SASE.
  ○━ Enslow publishes nonfiction for children and young adults in a variety of subjects including science, history, reference and biographies. Currently emphasizing ideas for series.
**Nonfiction:** Interested in nonfiction mss for young adults and children. Some areas of special interest are science, social issues, biography, reference topics, recreation. No fiction, fictionalized history or educational material. Query with information on competing titles and writer's résumé.
**Recent Title(s):** *Bizarre Insects*, by Margaret J. Anderson (science).

**EPICENTER PRESS, INC.**, P.O. Box 82368, Kenmore WA 98028. (425)485-6822. Fax: (425)481-8253. E-mail: epipress@aol.com. **Acquisitions:** Kent Sturgis, publisher. Estab. 1987. Publishes hardcover and trade paperback originals. **Publishes 10 titles/year. Receives 200 queries and 100 mss/year. 75% of books from first-time authors; 90% from unagented writers. Advance negotiable.** Publishes book 2 years after acceptance of ms. Reports in 2 months on queries. Book catalog and ms guidelines free.
  ○━ "We are a regional press founded in Alaska whose interests include but are not limited to the arts, history, environment, and diverse cultures and lifestyles of the North Pacific and high latitudes.
**Nonfiction:** Biography, coffee table book, gift books, humor. Subjects include animals, art/architecture, ethnic, history, nature/environment, photography, recreation, regional, travel, women's issues/studies. "Our focus is the Pacific Northwest and Alaska. We do not encourage nonfiction titles from outside Alaska and the Pacific Northwest, nor travel from beyond Alaska, Washington, Oregon and California." Submit outline and 3 sample chapters. Reviews artwork/photos as part of ms package. Send photocopies.
**Recent Title(s):** *Good Time Girls of the Alaska-Yukon Gold Rush*, by Lael Morgan.

**PAUL S. ERIKSSON, PUBLISHER**, P.O. Box 125, Forest Dale VT 05745-4210. (802)247-4210. Fax: (802)247-4256. **Acquisitions:** Paul S. Eriksson, publisher/editor; Peggy Eriksson, associate publisher/co-editor. Estab. 1960. Publishes hardcover and paperback trade originals, paperback trade reprints. **Publishes 5 titles/year. Receives 1,500 submissions/year. 25% of books from first-time authors; 95% from unagented writers. Pays 10-15% royalty on retail price. Offers advance if necessary.** Publishes book 6 months after acceptance of ms. *Writer's Market* recommends allowing 2 months for reply. Catalog for #10 SASE.
  ○━ "We look for intelligence, excitement and saleability."
**Nonfiction:** Americana, birds (ornithology), art, biography, business/economics, cooking/foods/nutrition, health, history, hobbies, how-to, humor, nature, politics, psychology, recreation, self-help, sociology, sports, travel. Query with SASE.
**Fiction:** Serious, literary. Query with SASE.
**Recent Title(s):** *The Year That Trembled*, by Scott Lax (novel).

**ESI INTERNATIONAL**, 4301 Fairfax Dr, #800, Arlington VA 22203. (703)558-3159. Fax: (703)558-3100. E-mail: aweaver@esi-intl.com. Website: http://www.esi-intl.com. **Acquisitions:** Angela Weaver, senior acquisitions editor (project management). Publishes hardcover and trade paperback originals, hardcover and trade paperback reprints. **Publishes 7-10 titles/year. Receives 100 queries and 50 mss/year. 10% of books from first-time authors; 100% from unagented writers. Pays 10-15% royalty on retail. No advance.** Publishes book 4 months after acceptance of ms. Accepts simultaneous submissions. Reports in 1 month. Book catalog and ms guidelines free on request or on website.
  ○━ ESI publishes practical, hands-on, how-to books for project managers, and other interested parties, who need proven techniques, tools, procedures, forms, systems, and ideas that will enable them to function more effectively in their day-to-day jobs. "We are always looking for practitioners who have found better ways of managing projects and who have the ability and interest in putting their findings in writing."
**Nonfiction:** How-to, reference, technical, textbook. Subjects include labor/management, business/economics. Submit proposal package, including outline. Reviews artwork/photos as part of ms package.
**Recent Title(s):** *Risk Management: Concepts & Guidance*, edited by Carl Pritchard.
**Tips:** "ESI International is actively looking for authors who believe they can make a contribution to the project management literature as a result of their practical experience. If you have published magazine articles, developed or delivered professional seminars, or solved important real-world problems in project management, you may be an excellent candidate for authorship."

**ETC PUBLICATIONS**, 700 E. Vereda Sur, Palm Springs CA 92262-4816. (760)325-5352. Fax: (760)325-8841. **Acquisitions:** Dr. Richard W. Hostrop, publisher (education and social sciences); Lee Ona S. Hostrop, editorial director (history and works suitable below the college level). Estab. 1972. Publishes hardcover and paperback originals. **Publishes**

6-12 titles/year. **Receives 100 submissions/year. 75% of books from first-time authors; 90% from unagented writers. Offers 5-15% royalty, based on wholesale and retail price.** Publishes book 9 months after acceptance. *Writer's Market* recommends allowing 2 months for reply.

    O→ ETC publishes works that "further learning as opposed to entertainment."

**Nonfiction:** Educational management, gifted education, futuristics, textbooks. Accepts nonfiction translations in above areas. Submit complete ms with SASE. *Writer's Market* recommends query first with SASE. Reviews artwork/photos as part of ms package.

**Recent Title(s):** *The Internet for Educators and Homeschoolers*, by Steve Jones, Ph.D.

**Tips:** "Special consideration is given to those authors who are capable and willing to submit their completed work in camera-ready, typeset form. We are particularly interested in works suitable for *both* the Christian school market and homeschoolers; e.g., state history texts below the high school level with a Christian-oriented slant."

**EVAN-MOOR EDUCATIONAL PUBLISHERS**, 18 Lower Ragsdale Dr., Monterey CA 93940-5746. (831)649-5901. Fax: (831)649-6256. E-mail: editorial@evan-moor.com. Website: http://www.evan-moor.com. **Acquisitions:** Marilyn Evans, senior editor. Estab. 1979. Publishes teaching materials. **Publishes 50-60 titles/year. Receives 50 queries and 100 mss/year. 1% of books from first-time authors; 100% from unagented writers. Makes outright purchase minimum of $1,000.** Publishes book 1 year after acceptance of ms. Accepts simultaneous submissions. Reports in 3 months. Book catalog and ms guidelines free or on website.

    O→ "Our books are teaching ideas, lesson plans, and blackline reproducibles for grades PreK-6 in all curriculum areas except music and bilingual." Currently emphasizing writing/language arts. De-emphasizing thematic materials.

**Nonfiction:** Teaching materials, grade PreK-6. Submit proposal package, including outline and 3 sample chapters.

**Recent Titles:** *Activities Using the World Wide Web*, by Jill Norris (technology resource book).

**Tips:** "Writers should know how classroom/educational materials differ from trade publications. They should request catalogs and submissions guidelines before sending queries or manuscripts."

**M. EVANS AND CO., INC.**, 216 E. 49th St., New York NY 10017-1502. Fax: (212)486-4544. **Acquisitions:** George C. deKay, editor-in-chief (general trade); Nancy Hancock (health). Estab. 1960. Publishes hardcover and trade paperback originals. Pays negotiable royalty. **Publishes 30-40 titles/year. 5% of books from unagented writers. Publishes book 8 months after acceptance.** Reports in 2 months. Book catalog for 9×12 SAE with 3 first-class stamps.

    O→ Evans has a strong line of health and self-help books but is interested in publishing quality titles on a wide variety of subject matters. "We publish a general trade list of adult nonfiction, cookbooks and semi-reference works. The emphasis is on selectivity, publishing commercial works with quality." Currently emphasizing health, pop-psych, commercial fiction. De-emphasizing literary fiction, westerns, children's material.

**Nonfiction:** "Our most successful nonfiction titles have been related to health and the behavioral sciences. No limitation on subject." Query. *No unsolicited mss.*

**Fiction:** "Our very small general fiction list represents an attempt to combine quality with commercial potential. We publish no more than one novel per season." Query. *No unsolicited mss.*

**Recent Title(s):** *Dr. Atkins' New Diet Revolution* (health); *The Kill Box*, by Chris Stewart (fiction).

**Tips:** "A writer should clearly indicate what his book is all about, frequently the task the writer performs least well. His credentials, although important, mean less than his ability to convince this company that he understands his subject and that he has the ability to communicate a message worth hearing. Writers should review our book catalog before making submissions."

**EXCALIBUR PUBLICATIONS**, P.O. Box 35369, Tucson AZ 85740-5369. **Acquisitions:** Alan M. Petrillo, editor. Publishes trade paperback originals. **Publishes 6-8 titles/year. Pays royalty or makes outright purchase.** Reports in 2 months on mss.

    O→ Excalibur publishes works on military history, strategy and tactics, history of battles, firearms, arms and armour.

**Nonfiction** Military history, strategy and tactics, as well as the history of battles, firearms, arms and armour. "We are seeking well-researched and documented works. Unpublished writers are welcome." Query with outline, first and any 2 additional consecutive chapters with SASE. Include notes on photos, illustrations and maps.

**Recent Title(s):** *Japanese Rifles of World War II*, by Duncan McCollum.

**EXCELSIOR CEE PUBLISHING**, P.O. Box 5861, Norman OK 73070. (405)329-3909. Fax: (405)329-6886. **Acquisitions:** J.C. Marshall. Estab. 1989. Publishes hardcover and trade paperback originals. **Publishes 8 titles/year. Receives 100 queries/year. Pays royalty or makes outright purchase (both negotiable). Offers no advance.** Publishes book 1 year after acceptance of ms. Accepts simultaneous submissions. Reports in 1 month. *Writer's Market* recommends allowing 2 months for reply. Book catalog for #10 SASE.

    O→ "All of our books speak to the reader through words of feeling—whether they are how-to, educational, humor or whatever genre, the reader comes away with feeling, truth and inspiration."

    ● In 1999, this publisher celebrated its 10th anniversary.

**Nonfiction:** Biography, coffee table book, how-to, humor, self-help, textbook. Subjects include Americana, education, history, hobbies, language/literature, women's issues/studies, writing. Query with SASE.

**Recent Title(s):** *Anyone Can Write—Just Let it Come Out*, by Jimmie Blaine Marshall.
**Tips:** "We have a general audience, book store browser interested in nonfiction reading. We publish titles that have a mass appeal and can be enjoyed by a large reading public. We publish very few unsolicited manuscripts, and our publishing calendar is 75% full up to 1 year in advance."

**N: EXECUTIVE EXCELLENCE PUBLISHING**, 1344 E. 1120 S., Provo UT 84606. (801)375-4060. Fax: (801)377-5960. E-mail: trentp@eep.com. Website: http://www.eep.com. **Acquisitions:** Ken Shelton, chairman/CEO (business management, personal leadership); Trent Price, editorial director (business, leadership, psychology/self-help). Estab. 1996. Publishes hardcover and trade paperback originals and trade paperback reprints. **Publishes 20-24 titles/ year. Receives 250 queries and 100 mss/year. 35% of books from first-time authors; 95% from unagented writers. Pays 10-15% on cash received and 50% of subsidiary rights proceeds. No advance.** Publishes book 6-9 months after acceptance of ms. Accepts simultaneous submissions. Reports in 1 month on queries and proposals, 3 months on mss. Book catalog free on request or on website.

O-- Executive Excellence publishes business and self-help titles. "We help you—the busy person, executive or entrepreneur—to find a wiser, better way to live your life and lead your organization." Currently emphasizing business innovations for general management and leadership (from the personal perspective). De-emphasizing technical or scholarly textbooks on operational processes and financial management or workbooks.

**Imprints:** Families Worldwide, Home/Work-The Family Connection, Novations Group, More Alike Than Different Publishing, Pacific Institute Publishing, Pressmark International.
**Nonfiction:** Self-help. Subjects include business/leadership, entrepreneurship, career, small business, relationships, lifestyle. Submit proposal package, including outline, 1-2 sample chapters and author bio, company information.
**Recent Title(s):** *Old Dogs, New Tricks*, by Warren Bennis.
**Tips:** "We have very little time to help authors who do not plan to *actively* participate in a highly collaborative marketing effort. We are small. We are not rich. But we, with you, can accomplish amazing things by working together. Be prepared to deliver *specific* marketing and promotional ideas (that do not require much expense)."

**FACTS ON FILE, INC.**, 11 Penn Plaza, New York NY 10001. (212)967-8800. Fax: (212)967-9196. E-mail: pkatzman.f actsonfile.com. Website: http://www.factsonfile.com. **Acquisitions:** Laurie Likoff, editorial director (science, music, history); Eleanora Von Dehsen (science, nature, multi-volume reference); Nicole Bowen, senior editor (American history, women's studies, young adult reference); James Chambers, trade editor (health, pop culture, sports); Pam Katzman, editorial assistant. Estab. 1941. Publishes hardcover originals and reprints. **Publishes 135 titles/year. Receives approximately 2,000 submissions/year. 25% of books from unagented writers. Pays 10-15% royalty on retail price. Offers $10,000 average advance.** Accepts simultaneous submissions. Reports in 2 months on queries. Book catalog free.

O-- Facts on File produces high-quality reference materials on a broad range of subjects for the school library market and the general nonfiction trade.

**Imprint(s):** Checkmark Books.
**Nonfiction:** Reference. Informational books on careers, education, health, history, entertainment, natural history, philosophy, psychology, recreation, religion, language, sports, multicultural studies, science, popular culture. "We publish serious, informational books for a targeted audience. All our books must have strong library interest, but we also distribute books effectively to the book trade. Our library books fit the junior and senior high school curriculum." No computer books, technical books, cookbooks, biographies (except YA), pop psychology, humor, fiction or poetry. Query or submit outline and sample chapter with SASE. No submissions returned without SASE.
**Recent Title(s):** *Smart Start*, by Marian Borden.
**Tips:** "Our audience is school and public libraries for our more reference-oriented books and libraries, schools and bookstores for our less reference-oriented informational titles."

**N: FAIRLEIGH DICKINSON UNIVERSITY PRESS**, 285 Madison Ave., Madison NJ 07940. Phone/fax: (973)443-8564. E-mail: fdupress@fdu.edu. **Acquisitions:** Harry Keyishian, director. Estab. 1967. Publishes hardcover originals. **Publishes 45 titles/year. Receives 300 submissions/year. 33% of books from first-time authors; 95% from unagented writers.** "Contract is arranged through Associated University Presses of Cranbury, New Jersey. We are a *selection* committee only." Nonauthor subsidy publishes 2% of books. Publishes book 1 year after acceptance of ms. Reports in 2 weeks on queries. *Writer's Market* recommends allowing 2 months for reply.

O-- Fairleigh Dickinson publishes books for the academic market.

**Nonfiction:** Reference, scholarly books. Subjects include art, business/economics, Civil War, film, history, Jewish studies, literary criticism, music, philosophy, politics, psychology, sociology, women's studies. Looking for scholarly books in all fields; no nonscholarly books. Query with outline and sample chapters. Reviews artwork/photos as part of ms package.
**Recent Title(s):** *Between Old Worlds and New: Occasional Writings on Music*, by Wilfrid Mellers.

---

**FOR INFORMATION** on book publishers' areas of interest, see the nonfiction and fiction sections in the Book Publishers Subject Index.

**Tips:** "Research must be up to date. Poor reviews result when authors' bibliographies and notes don't reflect current research. We follow *Chicago Manual of Style* (14th edition) style in scholarly citations. We will consider collections of unpublished conference papers or essay collections, if they relate to a strong central theme and have scholarly merit."

**FAIRVIEW PRESS**, 2450 Riverside Ave. S., Minneapolis MN 55454. (800)544-8207. Fax: (612)672-4980. Website: http://www.press.fairview.org. **Acquisitions:** Lane Stiles, managing editor; Stephanie Billecke, editor. Estab. 1988. Publishes hardcover and trade paperback originals and reprints. **Publishes 20-30 titles/year. Receives 3,000 queries and 500 mss/year. 40% of books from first-time authors; 65% from unagented writers. Pays 8-12% royalty on wholesale price. Offers $500-2,500 advance.** Publishes book 1 year after acceptance of ms. Accepts simultaneous submissions. Reports in 3 months on proposals. Book catalog and ms guidelines free.

O⌐ Fairview Press publishes books and related materials that educate families and individuals about their physical and emotional health, and motivate them to seek positive changes in themselves and their communities. Currently emphasizing health, medicine, seniors/aging, grief. De-emphasizing parenting/childcare, psychology, sociology.

**Nonfiction:** Reference, self-help. Subjects include child guidance/parenting, health, psychology, sociology, social and family issues. "We publish books on issues that impact families and the communities in which they live. Manuscripts that are essentially one person's story are rarely saleable." Submit proposal package, including outline, 2 sample chapters, author information, marketing ideas and SASE. Reviews artwork/photos as part of ms package. Send photocopies.

**Recent Title(s):** *A Family Caregiver's Guide to Planning and Decision Making for the Elderly*, by Janis A. Wilkinson.

**Tips:** Audience is general reader, especially families. "Tell us what void your book fills in the market; give us an angle. Tell us who will buy your book. We have moved away from recovery books and have focused on health and medical issues."

**FALCON PUBLISHING, INC.**, Landmark Communications, Box 1718, Helena MT 59624. (406)442-6597. Fax: (406)442-0384. E-mail: falcon@falconguide.com. Website: http://www.FalconOutdoors.com. **Acquisitions:** Glenn Law, editorial director; Charlene Patterson, editorial assistant (Two Dot Books: regional and western history, western Americana). Estab. 1978. Publishes hardcover and trade paperback originals. **Publishes 80 titles/year. Receives 350 queries and 30 mss/year. 20% of books from first-time authors; 95% from unagented writers. Pays royalty on net sales.** Publishes book 1-2 years after acceptance of ms. Accepts simultaneous submissions. Reports in 2 months on queries. Book catalog for $2.50.

O⌐ Falcon Press is primarily interested in ideas for recreational guidebooks and books on regional outdoor subjects. "Falcon is committed to the concept of 'green publishing': promoting the responsible and safe use of the natural environment, as well as its preservation. We consider ideas for recreational guidebooks and books on regional outdoor subjects." Currently emphasizing outdoor recreation, regional themes, regional history.

**Imprint(s):** Chockstone, Falcon Guide, Insiders', Sky House, ThreeForks (cookbooks), **Two Dot**.

**Nonfiction:** Illustrated book, guide books. Subjects include nature/environment, recreation, travel. Query with SASE. "We can only respond to queries submitted on the topics listed above. No fiction, no poetry." Reviews artwork/photos as part of the ms package. Send transparencies.

**Recent Title(s):** *Allen and Mike's Really Cool Telemark Tips*, by Allen O'Bannon and Mike Clellan.

**Tips:** "Authors of guidebooks must hike the hikes and ride the trails."

**FANFARE**, Bantam Dell Publishing Group, Random House, Inc., 1540 Broadway, New York NY 10036. (212)354-6500. Fax: (212)782-9523. Website: http://www.bdd.com. **Acquisition:** Beth de Guzman, senior editor; Wendy McCurdy, senior editor; Stephanie Kip, editor. **Published 30 titles/year. 10-15% of books from first-time authors; less than 5% from unagented writers. Royalty and advance negotiable.** Publishes book 18 months after acceptance of ms. Accepts simultaneous submissions. Reports in 3 months on queries; 4 months on requested proposals and mss.

O⌐ Fanfare "publishes a range of the best voices in women's fiction from brand new to established authors."

**Fiction:** Publishes romance and women's contemporary fiction only. Adventure/romance, historical/romance, suspense/romance, western/romance. Length: 90,000-120,000 words. Query with SASE. *No unsolicited mss.*

**Recent Title(s):** *Lady Reckless*, by Leslie LaFoy (historical romance).

**Tips:** "We advise that writers review the titles we have published in the past several years to get an idea of what we are looking for. Be aware of our needs in terms of length and content of manuscripts."

**FARRAR STRAUS & GIROUX BOOKS FOR YOUNG READERS**, Farrar Straus Giroux, Inc., 19 Union Square West, New York NY 10003. (212)741-6900. Fax: (212)633-2427. **Acquisitions:** Margaret Ferguson, editor-in-chief. Estab. 1946. Publishes hardcover and trade paperback originals. **Publishes 50 titles/year. Receives 6,000 queries and mss/year. 10% of books from first-time authors; 50% from unagented writers. Pays 6% royalty on retail price for paperbacks, up to 10% for hardcovers. Offers $3,000-15,000 advance.** Publishes book 18 months after acceptance of ms. Accepts simultaneous submissions, if informed. Reports in 2 months on queries, 3 months on mss. Book catalog for 9×12 SAE with $1.87 postage. Manuscript guidelines for #10 SAE.

O⌐ "We publish original and well-written material for all ages."

**Imprint(s):** Aerial Fiction, Francis Foster Books, Mirasol/Libros Juveniles, R&S Books, Sunburst Paperbacks.

**Fiction:** Juvenile, picture books, young adult. Query with SASE; considers complete ms. "We still look at unsolicited manuscripts, but for novels we prefer synopsis and sample chapters. Always enclose SASE for any materials author wishes returned. Query status of submissions in writing—no calls, please."

**Recent Title(s):** *Belle Prater's Boy*, by Ruth White (Newbery Honor novel, ages 9-12).
**Tips:** Audience is full age range, preschool to young adult. Specializes in literary fiction.

**FARRAR, STRAUS & GIROUX, INC.**, 19 Union Square West, New York NY 10003.  Fax: (212)633-2427. Estab. 1946. **Publishes 120 titles/year. Receives 5,000 submissions/year. Pays variable royalty. Offers advance.** Publishes book 18 months after acceptance.
   ○→ Farrar, Straus & Giroux is one of the most respected publishers of top-notch commercial-literary fiction and specialized nonfiction, as well as cutting-edge poetry. Publishes hardcover originals.
**Imprint(s):** Faber & Faber Inc. (U.K.-originated books), **Farrar Straus & Giroux Books for Young Readers, Hill & Wang, Noonday Press, North Point Press**, Sunburst Books.
**Nonfiction and Fiction:** Query.
**Recent Title(s):** *Slaves in the Family*, by Edward Ball (nonfiction); *Gain*, by Richard Powers (fiction); *Birthday Letters*, by Ted Hughes (poetry).

**FAWCETT JUNIPER**, Ballantine Books, 201 E. 50th St., New York NY 10022. (212)751-2600. **Acquisitions:** Leona Nevler, editor. **Publishes 24 titles/year. Pays royalty. Offers advance.** Publishes book 1 year after acceptance of ms. Accepts simultaneous submissions. Reports in 6 months on queries.
**Nonfiction:** Adult books.
**Fiction:** Mainstream/contemporary, young adult (12-18). No children's books. Query.
**Recent Title(s):** *The Moral Compass of the American Lawyer; The First Horseman.*

**THE FEMINIST PRESS AT THE CITY UNIVERSITY OF NEW YORK**, Wingate Hall, City College/CUNY, Convent Ave. at 138th St., New York NY 10031. (212)650-8890. Fax: (212)650-8893. **Acquisitions:** Jean Casella, editorial director. Estab. 1970. Publishes hardcover and trade paperback originals and reprints. **Publishes 22 titles/year. Receives 1,000 submissions/year. 20% of books from first-time authors; 80% from unagented writers. Pays royalty on net price. Offers $250 average advance.** Accepts simultaneous submissions. Reports in 4 months on proposals. Book catalog for 8½×11 SASE. Ms guidelines for #10 SASE.
   ○→ "Our primary mission is to publish works of fiction by women which preserve and extend women's literary traditions. We emphasize work by multicultural/international women writers."
**Nonfiction:** "We look for nonfiction work which challenges gender-role stereotypes and documents women's historical and cultural contributions. No monographs. Note that we generally publish for the college classroom as well as the trade." Children's (ages 8 and up)/juvenile, primary materials for the humanities and social science classroom and general readers, with a special emphasis on multicultural and international characters and settings. Subjects include ethnic, gay/lesbian, government/politics, health/medicine, history, language/literature, music, sociology, translation, women's issues/studies and peace, memoirs, international. Send proposal package, including materials requested in guidelines. Reviews artwork/photos as part of ms package. Send photocopies and SASE.
**Fiction:** "The Feminist Press publishes fiction reprints only. No original fiction is considered."
**Recent Title(s):** *A Cross and a Star*, by Marjorie Agosin (memoirs of a Jewish girl in Chile).

**FERGUSON PUBLISHING COMPANY**, 200 W. Jackson, 7th Floor, Chicago IL 60606. Website: http://www.fergpu bco.com. **Acquisitions:** Holli Cosgrove, editorial director. Estab. 1940. Publishes hardcover originals. **Publishes 15 titles/year. Reports in 3 months on queries. Pays by project.**
   ○→ "We are primarily a career education publisher that publishes for schools and libraries."
**Nonfiction:** Reference. "We publish work specifically for the junior high/high school/college library reference market. Works are generally encyclopedic in nature. Our current focus is career encyclopedias. We consider manuscripts that cross over into the trade market. No mass market, poetry, scholarly, or juvenile books, please." Query or submit outline and 1 sample chapter.
**Recent Title(s):** *What Can I Do Now?*, edited by Holli Cosgrove.
**Tips:** "We like writers who know the market—former or current librarians or teachers or guidance counselors."

**FILTER PRESS**, P.O. Box 95, Palmer Lake CO 80133-0095. (719)481-2420. Fax: (719)481-2420. E-mail: filter.press@ cwix.com. **Acquisitions:** Doris Baker, president. Estab. 1956. Publishes trade paperback originals and reprints. **Publishes 4-6 titles/year. Pays 10-12% royalty on wholesale price.** Publishes ms an average of 8 months after acceptance.
   ○→ Filter Press specializes in nonfiction of the West.
**Nonfiction:** Subjects include Americana, anthropology/archaeology, cooking/foods/nutrition, crafts and crafts people of the Southwest, memoirs, women writers of the West. "We're interested in the history and natural history of the West." Query with outline and SASE. Reviews artwork/photos as part of ms package.
**Recent Title(s):** *Rivers of Wind*, by Gary N. Penley (memoir).

**░N░ FIRE ENGINEERING BOOKS & VIDEOS**, PennWell Publishing Co., Park 80 W., Plaza 2, Saddle Brook NJ 07663. (201)845-0800. Fax: (201)845-6275. E-mail: 74677.1505@compuserve.com. Website: http://www.fireengineerin g.com. **Acquisitions:** William Manning, editor; Diane Feldman, managing editor; James Bacon, book editor. Publishes hardcover and softcover originals. **Publishes 10 titles/year. Receives 24 queries/year. 75% of books from first-time authors; 100% from unagented writers. Pays 15% royalty on net sales.** Publishes book 1 year after acceptance of ms. No simultaneous submissions. Reports in 3 months on proposals. Book catalog free.

☞ Fire Engineering publishes textbooks relevant to firefighting and training. Training firefighters and other emergency responders. Currently emphasizing reserve training, preparedness for terrorist threats, natural disasters, first response to fires and emergencies.

**Nonfiction:** Reference, technical, textbook. Subjects include firefighter training, public safety. Submit outline and 2 sample chapters, and biographical sketch.

**Recent Title(s):** *Truck Company Operations*, by John W. Mittendorf.

**Tips:** "No human interest stories, technical training only."

**FIREBRAND BOOKS**, 141 The Commons, Ithaca NY 14850. (607)272-0000. **Acquisitions:** Nancy K. Bereano, publisher. Estab. 1985. Publishes hardcover and trade paperback originals. **Publishes 6-8 titles/year. Receives 400-500 submissions/year. 50% of books from first-time authors; 90% from unagented writers. Pays 7-9% royalty on retail price, or makes outright purchase.** Publishes book 18 months after acceptance. Accepts simultaneous submissions, if so noted. Reports in 1 month on queries. *Writer's Market* recommends allowing 2 months for reply. Book catalog free.

☞ "Our diverse audience includes feminists, lesbians, ethnic audiences, and other progressive people."

**Nonfiction:** Personal narratives, essays. Subjects include feminism, lesbianism. Submit complete ms.

**Fiction:** Considers all types of feminist and lesbian fiction.

**Recent Title(s):** *Don't Explain*, by Jewelle Gomez.

**FISHER BOOKS**, 5335 W. Massingale Rd., Tucson AZ 85743. (520)744-6110. Fax: (520)744-0944. Website: http://www.fisherbooks.com. **Acquisitions:** Sarah Trotta, managing editor. Estab. 1987. Publishes trade paperback originals and reprints. **Publishes 16 titles/year. 25% of books from first-time authors; 75% from unagented writers. Pays 10-15% royalty on wholesale price.** Accepts simultaneous submissions. Book catalog for 8½×11 SAE with 3 first-class stamps.

☞ Fisher Books publishes how-to and self-help titles focusing on pregnancy and childcare. Currently emphasizing pregnancy, childcare, parenting. De-emphasizing business.

**Nonfiction:** Subjects include automotive, business, cooking/foods/nutrition, pregnancy/childcare, regional gardening, family health, self-help. Submit outline and sample chapter with SASE. *No unsolicited mss.*

**Recent Title(s):** *Baby Tips™ Series* (childcare).

**FLORICANTO PRESS**, Inter American Corp., 650 Castro St., Suite 120-331, Mountain View CA 94041. (415)552-1879. Fax: (415)793-2662. E-mail: floricanto@msn. Website: http://www.floricantopress.com. Publishes hardcover and trade paperback originals and reprints. **Publishes 6 titles/year. Receives 200 queries/year. 60% of books from first-time authors; 5% from unagented writers. Pays 5% royalty on wholesale price. Offers $500-1,500 advance.** Rejected mss destroyed. Reports in 3 months on queries, 7 months on mss. Book catalog for #10 SASE.

☞ Floricanto Press is "dedicated to promoting Latino thought and culture."

**Nonfiction:** Biography, cookbook, reference. Subjects include anthropology/archaeology, ethnic (Hispanic), health/medicine, history, language/literature, psychology, women's issues/studies. "We are looking primarily for nonfiction popular (but serious) titles that appeal the general public on Hispanic subjects." Submit outline and sample chapter(s).

**Fiction:** Adventure, erotica, ethnic (Hispanic), literary, occult, romance, short story collections. "On fiction we prefer contemporary works and themes." Submit synopsis and 1 sample chapter.

**Recent Title(s):** *Far from My Mother's Home*, by Barbara Jujica (short stories); *Cinco de Mayo: A Symbol of Mexican Resistance* (nonfiction).

**Tips:** Audience is general public interested in Hispanic culture. "Submit material as described, on DOS disk, graphic art for cover. We need authors that are willing to promote their work heavily."

**FOCAL PRESS**, Butterworth Heinemann, Reed Elsevier (USA) Inc., 225 Wildwood Ave., Woburn MA 01801-2041. Fax: (781)904-2640. E-mail: marie.lee@bhusa.com. Website: http://www.bh.com/fp/. **Acquisitions:** Marie Lee, publisher; Lauren Lavery, associate editor (photography, theater). Estab. US, 1981; UK, 1938. Publishes hardcover and paperback originals and reprints. **Publishes 40-45 UK-US titles/year; entire firm publishes 200 titles/year. Receives 500-700 submissions/year. 25% of books from first-time authors; 90% from unagented writers. Pays 10-12% royalty on net receipts. Offers modest advance.** Publishes book 9 months after acceptance. Accepts simultaneous submissions. Reports in 2 months. Book catalog and ms guidelines for SASE.

☞ Focal Press publishes reference material in all areas of the media, from audio, broadcasting, and cinematography, through to journalism, radio, television, video, and writing. Currently emphasizing graphics, animation and multimedia.

**Nonfiction:** How-to, reference, technical and textbooks in media arts: photography, film and cinematography, broadcasting, theater and performing arts and audio, sound and media technology. High-level scientific/technical monographs are also considered. "We do not publish collections of photographs or books composed primarily of photographs. Our books are text-oriented, with artwork serving to illustrate and expand on points in the text." Query preferred, or submit outline and sample chapters. Reviews artwork/photos as part of ms package.

**Recent Title(s):** *The Film Developing Cookbook*, by Steve Anchell and Bill Troop.

**Tips:** "Our advances and royalties are more carefully determined with an eye toward greater profitability for all our publications."

**FODOR'S TRAVEL PUBLICATIONS, INC.**, Random House, Inc. 201 E. 50th, New York NY 10022. **Acquisitions**: Karen Cure, editorial director. Estab. 1936. Publishes trade paperback originals. **Publishes 150 titles/year. Receives 100 queries and 4 mss/year. Most titles are collective works, with contributions as works for hire. Most contributions are updates of previously published volumes.** Publishes book 1 year after acceptance of ms. Accepts simultaneous submissions. Reports in 2 months on queries. Book catalog free.

O—¬ Fodor's publishes travel books on many regions and countries.

**Nonfiction:** Travel guides, some illustrated. "We're not interested in travel literature or in proposals for general travel guidebooks. We are interested in unique approaches to favorite destinations. Writers seldom review our catalog or our list and often query about books on topics that we're already covering. Beyond that, it's important to review competition and to say what the proposed book will add." Query or submit outline, sample chapter(s) and proposal package, including competition review and review of market with SASE. "Do not send originals without first querying as to our interest in the project."

**Recent Title(s):** *France '99*, by Fodor's (travel guide).

**Tips:** "In preparing your query or proposal, remember that it's the only argument Fodor's will hear about why your book will be a good one and why you think it will sell; and it's also best evidence of your ability to create the book you propose. Craft your proposal well and carefully so that it puts your best foot forward."

**FOGHORN PRESS**, Avalon Travel Publishing, Avalon Publishing Group, 5855 Beaudry St., Emeryville CA 94608. (510)595-3664. Website: http://www.foghorn.com. **Acquisitions:** Dave Morgan, publisher; Kyle Morgan, editor-in-chief. Estab. 1985. Publishes trade paperback originals and reprints. **Publishes 30 titles/year. Receives 500 queries and 200 mss/year. 10% of books from first-time authors; 98% from unagented writers. Pays 12% royalty on wholesale price; occasional work-for-hire.** Publishes book 18 months after acceptance of ms. Accepts simultaneous submissions. Reports in 1 month on queries, 2 months on proposals and mss. Book catalog free.

O—¬ Foghorn publishes outdoor recreation guidebooks.

**Nonfiction:** Outdoor recreation guidebooks. Subjects include nature/environment, recreation (camping, hiking, fishing), sports, outdoors, leisure. Submit proposal package, including outline or chapter headings, résumé, 2 or more sample chapters, marketing plan, author information.

• At press time Foghorn was purchased by Avalon Publishing Group and will join Moon Publications to form Avalon Travel Publishing

**Tips:** "We are expanding our list nationally in the formats we already publish (camping, hiking, fishing, dogs) as well as developing new formats to test California."

**FORGE**, Tom Doherty Associates, LLC, 175 Fifth Ave., 14th Floor, New York NY 10010. (212)388-0100. Fax: (212)388-0191. Website: http://www.tor.com. **Acquisitions:** Melissa Ann Singer, senior editor (western/historical, medical or biotechnological thriller, mysteries, contemporary women's fiction, historical, women's or health issues, horror/occult); Natalia Aponte, editor (western/historical, Women of the West, contemporary mystery, women's fiction, suspense/thriller, historical); Claire Eddy, editor (science fiction and fantasy, contemporary and historical mystery, historical suspense). Publishes hardcover, trade paperback and mass market paperback originals, trade and mass market paperback reprints. **Receives 5,000 mss/year. 2% of books from first-time authors; a few from unagented writers. Royalties: paperback, 6-8% first-time authors, 8-10% established authors; hardcover, 10% first 5,000, 12½% second 5,000, 15% thereafter.** Offers advance. Reports in 4 months on proposals. Book catalog for 9×12 SASE with 2 first-class stamps.

O—¬ "TDA publishes the best of past, present, and future—meaning that we cover all ground in fiction from historicals set in prehistory to the sharpest contemporary fiction to the acknowledged best in science fiction and fantasy."

**Nonfiction:** Subjects include health/medicine, women's issues/studies. Query with outline and 3 sample chapters.

**Fiction:** Historical, horror, mainstream/contemporary, mystery, suspense, thriller; general fiction of all sorts. "We handle a wide range of books; if you're not sure if a project is right for us, phone us and ask." Query with synopsis and 3 sample chapters.

**Recent Title(s):** *Paris Never Leaves You*, by Adréana Robbins; *Honor Thy Wife* by Norman Bogrer.

**FORTRESS PRESS**, Augsburg Fortress Publishers. Box 1209, Minneapolis MN 55440. (612)330-3300. Fax: (612)330-3455. Website: http://www.augsburgfortress.org. **Acquisitions**: Dr. Henry F. French, editorial director; Dr. K.C. Hanson, acquisitions editor; J. Michael West, senior editor. Estab. 1855. Publishes hardcover and trade paperback originals. **Publishes 45 titles/year. Receives 500-700 queries/year. 5-10% of books from first-time authors. Pays royalty on retail price. No advance.** Publishes book 1 year after acceptance of ms. Accepts simultaneous submissions. Reports in 3 months on proposals. Book catalog free (call 1-800-328-4648). Manuscript guidelines available online.

O—¬ Fortress Press publishes academic books in Biblical studies, theology, Christian ethics, church history, and professional books in pastoral care and counseling.

**Nonfiction:** Subjects include church history, religion, women's issues/studies, African-American studies. Query with annotated toc, brief cv, sample chapter (introduction) and SASE. Please study guidelines before submitting.

**Recent Title(s):** *Theology of the Old Testament*, by Walter Bruggeman.

**FORUM**, Prima Publishing, 3875 Atherton Rd., Rocklin CA 95765. (916)632-4400. Fax: (916)632-4403. **Acquisitions:** Steven Martin, editorial director. Publishes hardcover and trade paperback originals and reprints. **Publishes 10-15 titles/ year. 25% of books from first-time authors; 5% from unagented writers. Pays variable advance and royalty.**

Publishes book 1 year after acceptance of ms. Accepts simultaneous submissions. Reports in 1 month on queries and proposals, 2 months on mss.

○→ "Forum publishes business books that contribute to the marketplace of ideas."

**Nonfiction:** Subjects include libertarian/conservative thought, business/economics, government/politics, history, religion, current affairs, individual empowerment. Query with outline, 1 sample chapter and SASE.

**Recent Title(s):** *Reagan on Leadership*, by James Strock (business).

■ **FORWARD MOVEMENT PUBLICATIONS**, 412 Sycamore St., Cincinnati OH 45202. Fax: (513)721-0729. E-mail: forward.movement@ecunet.org. Website: http://www.dfms.org/forward-movement. **Acquisitions:** Reverend Edward S. Gleason, editor and director. Estab. 1934. Publishes trade paperback originals. **Publishes 12 titles/year. 50% of books from first-time authors; 100% from unagented writers. Pays one-time honorarium.** Reports in 1 month on queries and proposals, 2 months on mss. Book catalog for 9×12 SAE with $1.43 postage.

○→ "Forward Movement was established in 1934 'to help reinvigorate the life of the church.' Many titles focus on the life of prayer, where our relationship with God is centered, death, marriage, baptism, recovery, joy, the Episcopal Church and more."

**Nonfiction:** Essays. Religious subjects. "We publish a variety of types of books, but they all relate to the lives of Christians. We are an agency of the Episcopal Church." Query with SASE.

**Fiction:** Episcopal for middle school (ages 8-12) readers. Query with SASE.

• The editor notes that this publisher is just beginning to seek middle school (ages 8-12) fiction in their subject area.

**Recent Title(s):** *Letting Go*, by Reverend Dr. Edmund D. Campbell, Jr.

**Tips:** Audience is primarily members of mainline Protestant churches.

**WALTER FOSTER PUBLISHING, INC.**, A Quarto Group Company, 23062 La Cadena Dr., Laguna Hills CA 92653. (949)380-7510. Fax: (949)380-7575. **Acquisitions:** Mark McIntosh, creative director. Publishes trade paperback originals. **Publishes 40-100 titles/year. Receives 10-20 queries/year. 50% of books from first-time authors; 100% from unagented writers. Makes outright purchase. No advance.** Publishes book 1-2 years after acceptance of ms. Accepts simultaneous submissions. Reports in 2 months on queries, 6 months on proposals and mss. "Don't call us, we'll call you." Book catalog free.

○→ Walter Foster publishes instructional how-to art/craft instruction as well as licensed products.

**Nonfiction:** How-to. Arts and crafts subjects. Submit proposal package, including query letter, color photos/examples of artwork. Reviews artwork/photos as part of ms package. Send color photocopies or color photos. "Send enough samples of your artwork to prove your qualifications."

**Recent Title(s):** *Papier-Mâché* (art instruction).

Ⓐ **FOUL PLAY**, W.W. Norton, 500 Fifth Ave., New York NY 10110. (212)354-5500. Fax: (212)869.0856. Website: http://www.wwnorton.com. **Acquisitions:** Candace Watt, editor. Estab. 1996. Publishes hardcover originals and reprints. **0% from unagented writers. Pays royalty on retail price. Advance varies.** Publishes book 1 year after acceptance of ms. Reporting time varies. Book catalog free from W.W. Norton (same address).

○→ "We publish a broad range of mysteries, from cozies to hard-boiled to traditional."

**Fiction:** Mystery, suspense. *Agented submissions only.*

**FOUR WALLS EIGHT WINDOWS**, 39 W. 14th St., Room 503, New York NY 10011. Fax: (212)206-8799. E-mail: edit@fourwallseightwindows.com. Website: http://www.fourwallseightwindows.com. Estab. 1987. Publisher: John Oakes. **Acquisitions:** Acquisitions Editor. Estab. 1987. Publishes hardcover originals, trade paperback originals and reprints. **Publishes 20 titles/year. Receives 3,000 submissions/year. 15% of books from first-time authors; 50% from unagented writers. Pays royalty on retail price. Advance varies widely.** Publishes book 1-2 years after acceptance. Reports in 2 months on queries. Book catalog for 6×9 SAE with 3 first-class stamps.

○→ Emphasizing fine literature and quality nonfiction, Four Walls Eight Windows has a reputation for carefully edited and distinctive books.

**Imprint(s):** No Exit.

**Nonfiction:** Political, investigative. Subjects include art/architecture, government/politics, history, language/literature, nature/environment, science. No New Age. Query with outline and SASE. All mss without SASE discarded.

**Fiction:** Feminist, literary, science fiction. "No romance, popular." Query first with outline/synopsis and SASE.

**Recent Title(s):** *Genesis: The Story of Apollo 8*, by Robert Zimmerman (science); *Arcade*, by Gordon Lish (fiction).

**FOX CHAPEL PUBLISHING**, 1970 Broad St., East Petersburg PA 17520. **Acquisitions:** John Alan. Publishes hardcover and trade paperback originals and trade paperback reprints. **Publishes 12-20 titles/year. 80% of books from first-time authors; 100% from unagented writers. Pays royalty or makes outright purchase. Advance varies.** Publishes book 6-18 months after acceptance of ms. Accepts simultaneous submissions. Reports in 2 months on queries.

○→ Fox Chapel publishes woodworking and woodcarving titles for professionals and hobbyists.

**Nonfiction:** Woodworking, woodcarving and related titles. Query. Reviews artwork/photos as part of ms package. Send photocopies.

**Recent Title(s):** *Fireplace and Mantel Ideas—100 Classic Designs.*

**Tips:** "We're looking for knowledgeable artists, woodworkers first, writers second to write for us. Our market is for avid woodworking hobbyists and professionals."

**FRANCISCAN UNIVERSITY PRESS**, University Blvd., Steubenville OH 43952. Fax: (614)283-6427. Website: http://esoptron.umd.edu/fusfolder/press.html. **Acquisitions:** James Fox, executive director. Publishes trade paperback originals and reprints. **Publishes 4 titles/year. 5% of books from first-time authors; 100% from unagented writers. Pays 5-15% royalty on retail price.** Publishes book 1 year after acceptance of ms. Reports in 3 months on proposals. Book catalog and ms guidelines free.

   **O-π** "We seek to further the Catholic and Franciscan mission of Franciscan University of Steubenville by publishing quality popular-level Catholic apologetics and biblical studies. In this manner we hope to serve Pope John Paul II's call for a new evangelization of today's Catholics."

**Nonfiction:** Popular level Catholic theology. Subjects include catechetics, scripture, Catholic apologetics. Query with cv and SASE.

**Recent Title(s):** *Let the Fire Fall*, by Fr. Michael Scanlan.

**Tips:** "95% of our publications are solicited from authors who have already been published."

**THE FREE PRESS**, Simon & Schuster, 1230 Avenue of the Americas, New York NY 10020. (212)698-7000. Fax: (212)632-4989. Website: http://www.simonsays.com. **Acquisitions:** Liz Maguire, editorial director; Paul Golob, associate editor; Chad Conway, associate editor; Robert Wallace, senior editor (business); Bruce Nichols, senior editor (history); Paul Golob (current events/politics); Philip Rapapport, editor (psychology/social work/self-help); Steven Morrow, editor (science, math, literature, art). Estab. 1947. **Publishes 120 titles/year. Receives 3,000 submissions/year. 15% of books from first-time authors; 50% of books from unagented writers. Pays variable royalty.** Publishes book 1 year after acceptance of ms. Reports in 2 months.

   **O-π** The Free Press publishes serious adult nonfiction.

**Nonfiction:** professional books and college texts in the social sciences, humanities and business. Reviews artwork/photos as part of ms package. "We look for an identifiable target audience, evidence of writing ability." Accepts nonfiction translations. Query with 1-3 sample chapters, outline before submitting mss.

**Recent Title(s):** *The Death of Outrage*, by William Bennett.

**FREE SPIRIT PUBLISHING INC.**, 400 First Ave. N., Suite 616, Minneapolis MN 55401-1730. (612)338-2068. Fax: (612)337-5050. E-mail: help4kids@freespirit.com. Publisher: Judy Galbraith. **Acquisitions:** Caryn Pernu, acquisitions editor. Estab. 1983. Publishes trade paperback originals and reprints. **Publishes 30 titles/year. 25% of books from first-time authors; 75% from unagented writers. Offers advance.** Book catalog and ms guidelines free.

   **O-π** "We believe passionately in empowering kids to learn to think for themselves and make their own good choices."

**Imprint(s):** Self-Help for Kids®, Free Spirited Classroom® Series, Self-Help for Teens®.

**Nonfiction:** Self-Help for Kids ®. Subjects include child guidance/parenting, education (pre-K-12, but not textbooks or basic skills books like reading, counting, etc.), health (mental/emotional health—*not* physical health—for/about children), psychology (for/about children), sociology (for/about children). No fiction, poetry or autobiographies. Query with outline, 2 sample chapters and SASE. Send photocopies. "Many of our authors are teachers, counselors or others involved in helping kids."

**Recent Title(s):** *What On Earth Do You Do When Someone Dies*, by Trevor Romain.

**Tips:** "Our audience is children, teens, teachers, parents and youth counselors. We are concerned with kids' mental/emotional well-being and are especially looking for books written directly to kids in a language they can understand. We are not looking for academic or religious materials, nor books that analyze problems with the nation's school systems. Instead we want books that offer practical, positive advice so kids can help themselves."

**FRIENDS UNITED PRESS**, 101 Quaker Hill, Richmond IN 47374. (765)962-7573. Fax: (765)966-1293. Website: http://www.fum.org. **Acquisitions:** Barbara Bennett Mays, editor/manager. Estab. 1968. **Publishes 5 titles/year. Receives 100 queries and 80 mss/year. 50% of books from first-time authors; 99% from unagented writers. Pays 7½% royalty.** Publishes ms 1 year after acceptance of ms. Accepts simultaneous submissions. Reports in 3 months. Book catalog and ms guidelines free.

   **O-π** "Friends United Press publishes books that reflect Quaker religious practices and testimonies, and energize and equip Friends and others through the power of the Holy Spirit to gather people into fellowships where Jesus Christ is loved, known and obeyed 'as Teacher and Lord.' "

**Nonfiction:** Biography, humor, children's/juvenile, reference, textbook. Religious subjects. "Authors should be Quaker and should be familiar with Quaker history, spirituality and doctrine." Submit proposal package. Reviews artwork/photos as part of ms package. Send photocopies.

**Fiction:** Historical, juvenile, religious. "Must be Quaker-related." Query.

**Recent Title(s):** *The Fairest Isle*, by Mary Langford (history of Friends in Jamaica).

**Tips:** "Spirituality manuscripts must be in agreement with Quaker spirituality."

**GATFPRESS**, Graphic Arts Technical Foundation, 200 Deer Run Rd., Sewickley PA 15143-2600. (412)741-6860. Fax: (412)741-2311. E-mail: poresick@gatf.com. Website: http://www.gatf.org. **Acquisitions:** Peter Oresick, director of publications; Tom Destree, editor in chief; Amy Woodall, managing editor (graphic arts, communication, book publishing, printing). Estab. 1924. Publishes trade paperback originals and hardcover reference texts. **Publishes 15 titles/year. Receives 25 submissions/year. 50% of books from first-time authors; 100% from unagented writers. Pays 5-15% royalty on retail price.** Publishes book 6 months after acceptance. Reports in 1 month on queries. *Writer's*

*Market* recommends allowing 2 months for reply. Book catalog for 9×12 SAE with 2 first-class stamps. Manuscript guidelines for #10 SASE.

> "GATF's mission is to serve the graphic communications community as the major resource for technical information and services through research and education." Currrently emphasizing career guides for graphic communications.

**Nonfiction:** How-to, reference, technical, textbook. Subjects include printing/graphic communications and electronic publishing. "We primarily want textbook/reference books about printing and related technologies. However, we are expanding our reach into general computing and electronic communications." Query with SASE or submit outline, sample chapters and SASE. Reviews artwork/photos as part of ms package.

**Recent Title(s):** *Understanding Digital Imposition,* by Hal Hinderliter.

**Tips:** "We are publishing titles that are updated more frequently, such as *On-Demand Publishing.* Our scope now includes reference titles geared toward general audiences interested in computers, imaging, and Internet as well as print publishing."

**GAY SUNSHINE PRESS and LEYLAND PUBLICATIONS,** P.O. Box 410690, San Francisco CA 94141-0690. Website: http://www.gaysunshine.com. **Acquisitions:** Winston Leyland, editor. Estab. 1970. Publishes hardcover originals, trade paperback originals and reprints. **Publishes 6-8 titles/year. Pays royalty or makes outright purchase.** Reports in 6 weeks on queries. Book catalog for $1.

> Gay history, sex, politics, and culture are the focus of the quality books published by Gay Sunshine Press. Leyland Publications publishes books on popular aspects of gay sexuality and culture. "We seek innovative literary nonfiction and fiction depicting gay themes and lifestyles."

**Nonfiction:** How-to and gay lifestyle topics. "We're interested in innovative literary nonfiction which deals with gay lifestyles." No long personal accounts, academic or overly formal titles. Query. "After we respond positively to your query, submit outline and sample chapters with SASE." *All unsolicited mss are returned unopened.*

**Fiction:** Erotica, ethnic, experimental, historical, mystery, science fiction, translation. "Interested in well-written novels on gay themes; also short story collections. We have a high literary standard for fiction." Query. "After we respond positively to your query, submit outline/synopsis and sample chapters with SASE." *All unsolicited mss returned unopened.*

**Recent Title(s):** *Partings at Dawn: An Anthology of Japanese Gay Literature.*

**GEM GUIDES BOOK COMPANY,** 315 Cloverleaf Dr., Suite F, Baldwin Park CA 91706-6510. (626)855-1611. Fax: (626)855-1610. **Acquisitions:** Kathy Mayerski, editor. Estab. 1965. **Publishes 6-8 titles/year. Receives 40 submissions/year. 30% of books from first-time authors; 100% from unagented writers. Pays 6-10% royalty on retail price. Estab. 1965.** Publishes book 1 year after acceptance. Accepts simultaneous submissions. Reports in 3 months.

> "Gem Guides prefers nonfiction books for the hobbyist in rocks and minerals; lapidary and jewelry-making; travel and recreation guide books for the West and Southwest; and other regional local interest."

**Imprint(s):** Gembooks.

**Nonfiction:** Gem Guides specializes in books on earth sciences, lapidary and jewelry-making, nature books, also travel/local interest titles for the Western US. Subjects include hobbies, Western history, nature/environment, recreation, travel. Query with outline/synopsis and sample chapters with SASE. Reviews artwork/photos as part of ms package.

**Recent Title(s):** *Gold Mining for Fun and Profit,* by Gail Butler.

**Tips:** "We have a general audience of people interested in recreational activities. Publishers plan and have specific book lines in which they specialize. Learn about the publisher and submit materials compatible with that publisher's product line."

**GENERAL PUBLISHING GROUP,** 2701 Ocean Park Blvd., Suite 140, Santa Monica CA 90405. (310)314-4000. Fax: (310)314-8080. E-mail: editorial@gpgbooks.com. **Acquisitions:** Editorial Director. Estab. 1991. Publishes hardcover and trade paperback originals. **Publishes 50 titles/year. Pays royalty.** Publishes ms 8 months after acceptance. Accepts simultaneous submissions. Reports in 4 months on queries.

> General Publishing Group specializes in popular culture, entertainment, politics and humor titles.

**Nonfiction:** Biography, coffee table book, gift book, humor, illustrated book. Subjects include Americana, art/architecture, music/dance, photography, entertainment/media, politics. Query with proposal package, including sample chapters, toc and SASE. Reviews artwork as part of ms package. Send photocopies.

**Recent Title(s):** *Pepsi: 100 Years,* by Bob Stoddard; *Inside the Playboy Mansion,* by Gretchen Edgren.

**LAURA GERINGER BOOKS,** HarperCollins Children's Books, 10 E. 53rd St., New York NY 10022. (212)207-7000. Website: http://www.harpercollins.com. **Acquisitions:** Laura Geringer, senior vice president/publisher; Susan Kassirer, senior editor. Publishes hardcover originals. **Publishes 15-20 titles/year. 5% of books from first-time authors; 25% from unagented writers. Pays 10-12½% on retail price.** Advance varies. Publishes ms 6-12 months after acceptance of ms for novels, 1-2 years after acceptance of ms for picture books. Reports in 2 weeks on queries, 1 month on proposals, 4 months on mss. Book catalog for 8×10 SAE with 3 first-class stamps. Manuscript guidelines for #10 SASE.

> "We look for books that are out of the ordinary, authors who have their own definite take, and artists that add a sense of humor to the text."

**Fiction:** Children's, adventure, fantasy, historical, humor, literary, picture books, young adult. "A mistake writers often make is failing to research the type of books an imprint publishes, therefore sending inappropriate material." Query with SASE for picture books; submit complete ms with SASE for novels.

**Recent Title(s):** *If You Give a Pig a Pancake*, by Laura Nurmeroff; illustrated by Felicia Bend.

**GESSLER PUBLISHING CO., INC.**, 10 E. Church Ave., Roanoke VA 24011. (540)345-1429. Fax: (540)342-7172. E-mail: gesslerco@aol.com. Website: http://www.gessler.com. **Acquisitions:** Richard Kurshan, CEO. Estab. 1932. Publishes trade paperback originals and reprints. **Publishes 75 titles/year. Receives 50 queries and 25 mss/year. 5% of books from first-time authors; 90% from unagented writers, "very few, if any, are agented." Pays 10-20% royalty on retail price. Offers $250-500 advance.** Publishes book 9 months after acceptance of ms. Accepts simultaneous submissions. Reports in 3 days on queries, 3 weeks on mss. *Writer's Market* recommends allowing 2 months for reply. Book catalog free.

○☞ Gessler publishes high-quality language-learning materials for the education market.

**Nonfiction:** Textbook. Subjects include education, language/literature, multicultural. "We publish supplementary language learning materials. Our products assist teachers with foreign languages, ESL, and multicultural activities." Query first, then submit outline/synopsis with 2-3 sample chapters or complete ms with cover letter and SASE. Reviews artwork/photos as part of ms package. Send photocopies.

**Recent Title(s):** *Buenviaje*, by Maria Koonce (Spanish workbook).

**Tips:** Elementary/middle school/high school audience. "Writers need to be more open-minded when it comes to understanding not everyone learns the same way. They may have to be flexible when it comes to revising their work to accommodate broader teaching/learning methods."

**GIFTED EDUCATION PRESS**, 10201 Yuma Court, P.O. Box 1586, Manassas VA 20109. (703)369-5017. **Acquisitions**: Maurice Fisher, publisher. Estab. 1981. Publishes mass market paperback originals. **Publishes 10 titles/year. Receives 75 queries and 25 mss/year. 90% of books from first-time authors; 100% from unagented writers. Pays 10-12% royalty on retail price.** Publishes book 3 months after acceptance of ms. Accepts simultaneous submissions. Reports in 1 month. Book catalog free. Manuscript guidelines for #10 SASE.

○☞ Gifted Education Press publishes books on multiple intelligences, humanities education for gifted children and how to parent gifted children. Currently emphasizing multiple intelligences. De-emphasizing humanities.

**Nonfiction:** Reference, textbook, teacher's guides. Subjects include child guidance/parenting, computers/electronics, education, language/literature, philosophy, psychology, science. "Writers must indicate their expertise in the subject and propose challenging topics for teachers and gifted students." Query or submit outline with SASE. *All unsolicited mss returned.* Reviews artwork/photos as part of ms package.

**Recent Title(s):** *Applying Multiple Intelligences to Gifted Education: I'm Not Just an IQ Score!*, by Colleen Willard-Holt and Dan Holt.

**Tips:** Audience is parents and teachers of gifted students, university professors and graduate students. "We are looking for clear, straight forward and well-organized writing. Expertise in the topical areas is required."

**N GIFTED PSYCHOLOGY PRESS, INC.**, Anodyne, Inc., P.O. Box 5057, Scottsdale AZ 85261. (602)954-4200. Fax: (602)954-0185. E-mail: giftedbook@earthlink.net. Website: http://www.GiftedPsychologyPress.com. **Acquisitions:** James T. Webb, president. Estab. 1986. Publishes trade paperback originals. **Publishes 4-5 titles/year. Receives 10 queries and 10 mss/year. 25% of books from first-time authors; 100% from unagented writers. Pays 9-15% royalty on retail price. Offers $0-750 advance.** Publishes book 6 months after acceptance of ms. Accepts simultaneous submissions. Reports in 2 months on queries, 3 months on proposals, 4 months on mss. Book catalog and ms guidelines free or on website.

○☞ Gifted Psychology Press publishes books on the social/emotional/interpersonal needs of gifted and talented children and adults for parents and teachers of gifted and talented youngsters.

**Nonfiction:** Biography, humor, reference, self-help, textbook, educational, assessment scales. Subjects include child guidance/parenting, education, women's issues/studies, gifted/talented children and adults. Submit proposal package, including outline, 3 sample chapters and an explanation of how work differs from similar published books.

**Recent Titles:** *Iowa Acceleration Scale*, by Assouline and Colangelo (assessment scale).

**Tips:** "Manuscripts should be clear, cogent, and well-written and should pertain to gifted, talented, and creative persons and/or issues."

**GLENBRIDGE PUBLISHING LTD.**, 6010 W. Jewell Ave., Denver CO 80232-7106. Fax: (303)987-9037. **Acquisitions:** James A. Keene, editor. Estab. 1986. Publishes hardcover originals and reprints, trade paperback originals. **Publishes 6-8 titles/year. Pays 10% royalty.** Publishes book 1 year after acceptance of ms. Accepts simultaneous submissions. Reports in 2 months on queries. Book catalog for 6×9 SASE. Manuscript guidelines for #10 SASE.

○☞ "Glenbridge has an eclectic approach to publishing. We look for titles that have long-term capabilities."

**Nonfiction:** Subjects include Americana, business/economics, history, music, philosophy, politics, psychology, sociology, cookbooks. Query with outline/synopsis, sample chapters and SASE.

**Recent Title(s):** *Train Your Dog in One Hour*, by Sandy Butler.

**THE GLENLAKE PUBLISHING COMPANY, LTD.**, 1261 W. Glenlake, Chicago IL 60660. (773)262-9765. Fax: (773)262-9436. E-mail: glenlake@ix.netcom.com. Website: http://www.glenlake.com. **Acquisitions:** Barbara Craig, editor. Estab. 1995. Publishes hardcover originals. **Publishes 20 titles/year. Receives 50 queries and 5 mss/year. 25%**

of books from first-time authors; 100% from unagented writers. **Pays 10-15% royalty on wholesale price. Offers $1,500 average advance.** Publishes book 2 months after acceptance of ms. Accepts simultaneous submissions. Reports in 1 month on queries. Book catalog free.

○➡ "Glenlake is an independent book publisher whose primary objective is to promote the advancement of current thinking in the areas of business, finance, economics, applied statistics, computer applications to business and statistics, and environmental science and engineering."

**Nonfiction:** Subjects include business/economics, computers/electronics, money/finance. Submit proposal package, including author's bio, outline, 1 sample chapter and SASE.

**Recent Title(s):** *International Handbook of Corporate Finance*, by Brian Terry.

**THE GLOBE PEQUOT PRESS, INC.**, P.O. Box 833, Old Saybrook CT 06475-0833. (860)395-0440. Fax: (203)395-1418. President/Publisher: Linda Kennedy. **Acquisitions:** Shelly Wolf, submissions editor. Estab. 1947.Publishes hardcover originals, paperback originals and reprints. **Publishes 150 titles/year. Receives 1,500 submissions/year. 30% of books from first-time authors; 70% from unagented writers. Average print order for a first book is 4,000-7,500. Makes outright purchase or pays 10% royalty on net price. Offers advance.** Publishes book 1 year after acceptance of ms. Accepts simultaneous submissions. Reports in 3 months. Book catalog for 9 × 12 SASE.

○➡ Globe Pequot is among the top sources for travel books in the United States and offers the broadest selection of travel titles of any vendor in this market.

**Nonfiction:** Travel guidebooks (regional OK) and outdoor recreation. No doctoral theses, fiction, genealogies, memoirs, poetry or textbooks. Submit outline, table of contents, sample chapter and résumé/vita. Reviews artwork/photos.

**Recent Title(s):** *Legendary Light Houses*, by John Grant.

**DAVID R. GODINE, PUBLISHER, INC.**, 9 Hamilton Place, Boston MA 02108. Website: http://www.godine.com. **Acquisitions:** Mark Polizzotti, editorial director. Estab. 1970. Publishes hardcover and trade paperback originals and reprints. **Publishes 25 titles/year. Pays royalty on retail price.** Publishes book 3 years after acceptance of ms. Book catalog for 5 × 8 SAE with 3 first-class stamps.

○➡ "Our particular strengths are books about the history and design of the written word, literary essays, and the best of world fiction in translation. We also have an unusually strong list of children's books, all of them printed in their entirety with no cuts, deletions, or side-stepping to keep the political watchdogs happy."

**Nonfiction:** Biography, coffee table book, cookbook, illustrated book, children's/juvenile. Subjects include Americana, art/architecture, gardening, nature/environment, photography, literary criticism, current affairs. *No unsolicited mss.*

**Fiction:** Literary, novel, short story collection, children's/juvenile. *No unsolicited manuscripts.*

**Recent Title(s):** *The Corner in the Marais: Memoir of a Paris Neighborhood*, by Alex Karmel (nonfiction); *The Disobedience of Water*, by Sena Jeter Naslund (fiction); *Beyond*, by Albert Goldbarth (poetry).

■ **GOLDEN WEST PUBLISHERS**, 4113 N. Longview, Phoenix AZ 85014. (602)265-4392. Fax: (602)279-6901. **Acquisitions:** Hal Mitchell, editor. Estab. 1973. Publishes trade paperback originals. **Publishes 15-20 titles/year. Receives 200 submissions/year. 50% of books from first-time authors; 100% from unagented writers. Prefers mss on work-for-hire basis. No advance.** Publishes book an average of 6 months after acceptance. Accepts simultaneous submissions. Reports in 1 month on queries, 2 months on mss.

○➡ "We seek to provide quality, affordable cookbooks and books about the Southwest to the marketplace. We are currently featuring Cooking Across America Cook Book Series™ plus state and regional cookbooks." Currently emphasizing cooking across America. De-emphasizing southwest history.

**Nonfiction:** Cookbooks, books on the Southwest and West. Subjects include cooking/foods, Southwest history and outdoors, travel. Query. Reviews artwork/photos as part of ms package.

**Recent Title(s):** *Wisconsin Cook Book*, by Wade.

**Tips:** "We are interested in Arizona and Southwest material, and regional and state cookbooks for the entire country, and welcome material in these areas."

**GOVERNMENT INSTITUTES/ABS.**, 4 Research Place, Suite 200, Rockville MD 20850-3226. (301)921-2355. Fax: (301)921-0373. E-mail: giinfo@govinst.com. Website: http://www.govinst.com. **Acquisitions:** Russ Bahorsky, acquisitions editor (occupational safety and health, quality, ISO 9000, the Internet); Charlene Ikonomou (environmental compliance and sciences, marine industry), editors. Estab. 1973. Publishes hardcover and softcover originals and CD-ROM/disk products. **Publishes 45 titles/year. Receives 100 submissions/year. 50% of books from first-time authors; 100% from unagented writers. Pays royalty or makes outright purchase.** Publishes book 5 months after acceptance. Accepts simultaneous submissions, if so noted. Reports in 2 months. Book catalog free.

○➡ "Our mission is to be the leading global company providing practical, accurate, timely and authoritative information desired by people concerned with environment, health and safety, telecommunications, and other regulatory and technical topics." Currently emphasizing practical information for the business community. De-emphasizing books on issues and theories.

**Nonfiction:** Reference, technical. Subjects include environmental law, occupational safety and health, environmental engineering, telecommunications, employment law, FDA matters, industrial hygiene and safety, real estate with an environmental slant, management systems, Quality, ISO 9000, Internet business. Needs professional-level titles in those areas. Also looking for international environmental topics. Submit outline and at least 1 sample chapter.

**Recent Title(s):** *Environmental Guide to the Internet*, by Murphy/Briggs-Erickson.

**Tips:** "We also conduct courses. Authors are frequently invited to serve as instructors."

**THE GRADUATE GROUP**, P.O. Box 370351, West Hartford CT 06137-0351. **Acquisitions:** Mara Whitman, president; Robert Whitman, vice president. Estab. 1964. Publishes trade paperback originals. **Publishes 50 titles/year. Receives 100 queries and 70 mss/year. 60% of books from first-time authors; 85% from unagented writers. Pays 20% royalty on retail price.** Publishes book 3 months after acceptance of ms. Accepts simultaneous submissions. Reports in 1 month. Book catalog and ms guidelines free.

> O→ "The Graduate Group helps college and graduate students better prepare themselves for rewarding careers and helps people advance in the workplace." Currently emphasizing test preparation, career advancement and materials for prisoners.

**Nonfiction:** Reference. Subjects include test taking, directories, dictionaries, career/internships, law, medicine, law enforcement, corrections, how to succeed, self-motivation, education, professional development, building self-esteem, learning networking skills, working with the disabled and gifted, summer/year round opportunities for students, assisting the elderly, financial planning, business, international. Send complete ms and SASE with sufficient postage.

**Recent Title(s):** *Interviewing for Results, Careers in Law Enforcement.*

**Tips:** Audience is career planning offices; college, graduate school and public libraries. "We are open to all submissions, especially those involving career planning, internships and other nonfiction titles. Looking for books on law enforcement, books for prisoners and reference books on subjects/fields students would be interested in. We want books on helping students and others to interview, pass tests, gain opportunity, understand the world of work, networking, building experience, preparing for advancement, preparing to enter business, improving personality and building relationships."

**GRAYWOLF PRESS**, 2402 University Ave., Suite 203, St. Paul MN 55114. (651)641-0077. Fax: (651)641-0036. Website: http://www.graywolfpress.org. Editor/publisher: Fiona McCrae. Executive Editor: Anne Czarniecki. **Acquisitions:** Jeffrey Shotts (poetry, nonfiction); Katie Dublinski, editorial assistant (fiction, nonfiction). Estab. 1974. Publishes trade cloth and paperback originals and reprints. **Publishes 16 titles/year. Receives 2,500 queries/year. 20% of books from first-time authors; 50% from unagented writers. Pays royalty on retail price. Offers $1,000-6,000 advance on average.** Publishes book 18 months after acceptance of ms. Reports in 3 months on queries. Book catalog free. Manuscript guidelines for #10 SASE.

> O→ Graywolf Press is an independent, nonprofit publisher dedicated to the creation and promotion of thoughtful and imaginative contemporary literature essential to a vital and diverse culture.

**Nonfiction:** Language/literature/culture. Query with SASE.

**Fiction:** Literary. "Familiarize yourself with our list first." Query with SASE.

**Poetry:** "We are interested in linguistically challenging work." Query sample with SASE.

**Recent Title(s):** *Readings*, by Sven Birkerts (nonfiction); *Salvation & Other Disasters*, by Josip Novakovich (fiction); *The Way It Is*, by William Stafford (poetry).

**▚ GREAT QUOTATIONS PUBLISHING**, 1967 Quincy Ct., Glendale Heights IL 60139. (630)582-2800. Fax: (630)582-2813. **Acquisitions:** Diane Voreis, acquisitions editor. Estab. 1991. **Publishes 30 titles/year. Receives 1,500 queries and 1,200 mss/year. 50% of books from first-time authors; 80% from unagented writers. Pays 3-10% royalty on net sales or makes outright purchase of $300-3,000. Offers $200-1,200 advance.** Publishes book 6 months after acceptance of ms. "We publish new books twice a year, in July and in January." Accepts simultaneous submissions. Reports in 6 months with SASE. Book catalog for $2. Manuscript guidelines for #10 SASE.

> O→ Great Quotations seeks original material for the following general categories: children, humor, inspiration, motivation, success, romance, tributes to mom/dad/grandma/grandpa, etc.

**Nonfiction:** Humor, illustrated book, self-help, quotes. Subjects include business/economics, child guidance/parenting, nature/environment, religion, sports, women's issues/studies. "We look for subjects with identifiable markets, appealing to the general public. We do not publish children's books or others requiring multicolor illustration on the inside. Nor do we publish highly controversial subject matter." Submit outline and 2 sample chapters. Reviews artwork/photos as part of ms package. Send photocopies, transparencies.

**Poetry:** "We would be most interested in upbeat and juvenile poetry."

**Recent Title(s):** *Secret Language of Men*, by Sherry Weaver (gift book).

**Tips:** "Our books are physically small and generally a very quick read. They are available at gift shops and book shops throughout the country. We are aware that most of our books are bought on impulse and given as gifts. We need strong, clever, descriptive titles; beautiful cover art and brief, positive, upbeat text. Be prepared to submit final manuscript on computer disk, according to our specifications. (It is not necessary to try to format the typesetting of your manuscript to look like a finished book.)"

**▚ GREENE BARK PRESS**, P.O. Box 1108, Bridgeport CT 06601. (203)372-4861. Fax: (203)371-5856. Website: http://www.bookworld.com/greenebark. **Acquisitions:** Thomas J. Greene, publisher; Michele Hofbauer, associate publisher. Estab. 1991. Publishes hardcover originals. **Publishes 5 titles/year. Receives 100 queries and 6,000 mss/year. 60% of books from first-time authors; 100% from unagented writers. Pays 10-15% royalty on wholesale price.** Publishes book 1 year after acceptance of ms. Accepts simultaneous submissions. Reports in 3 months on mss. Book catalog for $2; ms guidelines with SASE.

> O→ Greene Bark Press only publishes books for children and young adults, mainly picture and read-to books. "All of our titles appeal to the imagination and encourage children to read and explore the world through books.

We only publish children's fiction—all subjects—but in reading picture book format appealing to ages 3-9 or all ages."

**Fiction:** Juvenile. Submit entire ms with SASE. No queries or ms by e-mail.

**Recent Title(s):** *Excuse Me, Are You A Dragon*, by Rhett Bransom Pennell.

**Tips:** Audience is "children who read to themselves and others. Mothers, fathers, grandparents, godparents who read to their respective children, grandchildren. Include SASE, be prepared to wait, do not inquire by telephone."

**GREENHAVEN PRESS, INC.**, P.O. Box 289009, San Diego CA 92198-9009. (619)485-7424. Fax: (619)485-9549. **Acquisitions:** David M. Hangen, managing editor. Estab. 1970. **Publishes approximately 100 anthologies/year; all anthologies are works for hire. Makes outright purchase of $1,000-3,000.** Publishes ms 1 year after acceptance of ms. Book catalog for 9×12 SAE with 3 first-class stamps.

O→ Greenhaven Press publishes hard and softcover educational supplementary materials and (nontrade) nonfiction anthologies on contemporary issues, literary criticism and history for high school and college readers. These anthologies serve as supplementary educational material for high school and college libraries and classrooms. Currently emphasizing literary and historical topics, and social-issue anthologies.

**Nonfiction:** "We produce tightly formatted anthologies on contemporary issues, literary criticism, and history for high school- and college-level readers. We are looking for freelance book editors to research and compile these anthologies; we are not interested in submissions of single-author manuscripts. Each series has specific requirements. Potential book editors should familiarize themselves with our catalog and anthologies." Query. No unsolicited mss.

**Recent Title(s):** *Biomedical Ethics* (Opposing Viewpoints Series).

**GREENWILLOW BOOKS**, William Morrow & Co., 1350 Avenue of the Americas, New York NY 10019. (212)261-6500. Website: http://www.williammorrow.com. Senior Editor: Elizabeth Shub. **Acquisitions:** Editorial Department, Greenwillow Books. Estab. 1974. Publishes hardcover originals and reprints. **Publishes 60-70 titles/year. 1% of books from first-time authors; 30% from unagented writers. Pays 10% royalty on wholesale price for first-time authors. Advance varies.** Publishes ms 2 years after acceptance of ms. Accepts simultaneous submissions, if so noted. Reports in 3 months on mss. Book catalog for 9×12 SAE with $2 postage. Manuscript guidelines for #10 SASE.

O→ Greenwillow Books publishes quality picture books and fiction for young readers of all ages, and nonfiction primarily for children under seven years of age.

**Fiction:** Juvenile, picture books: fantasy, historical, humor, literary, mystery. Send complete ms with SASE. Reviews artwork with submissions. Send photocopies.

**Recent Title(s):** *Lilly's Purple Plastic Purse*, by Kevin Henkes.

**GREENWOOD PRESS**, Greenwood Publishing Group, 88 Post Rd. W., Westport CT 06881. (203)226-3571. Fax: (203)222-1502. Website: http://www.greenwood.com. **Acquisitions:** Peter Kracht, executive editor. Establ 1967. Publishes hardcover originals. **Publishes 200 titles/year. Receives 1,000 queries/year. 25% of books from first-time authors. Pays variable royalty on net price. Offers advance rarely.** Publishes book 1 year after acceptance of ms. Accepts simultaneous submissions. Reports in 6 months on queries. Book catalog and ms guidelines online.

O→ Greenwood Press publishes reference materials for the entire spectrum of libraries, as well as scholarly monographs in the humanities and the social and behavioral sciences.

**Nonfiction:** Reference. Query with proposal package, including scope, organization, length of project, whether a complete ms is available or when it will be, cv or résumé and SASE. *No unsolicited mss.*

**Recent Title(s):** *John Grisham: A Critical Companion*, by Mary Beth Pringle.

**N GREENWOOD PUBLISHING GROUP**, Reed-Elsevier (USA) Inc., 88 Post Rd. W, Westport CT 06881. (203)226-3571. Fax: (203)222-1502. Website: http://www.greenwood.com. Executive Vice President: Jim Sabin. **Acquisitions:** Reference Publishing: Academic Reference—Cynthia Harris (history and economics, ext. 460, charris@greenwood.com); George Butler (anthropology, education, literature, drama and sociology, ext. 461, gbutler@greenwood.com); Alicia Merritt (art and architecture, music and dance, philosophy and religion, popular culture, ext. 443, amerritt@greenwood.com); Nita Romer (multicultural and women's studies, gerontology, media, political science and law, psychology, ext. 445, nromer@greenwood.com); Interdisciplinary studies, such as African-American studies are handled by all editors; contact js@greenwood.com. Secondary School Reference—Barbara Rader (literature, history, women's studies, school librarianship, ext. 442, brader@greenwood.com); Emily Birch (sociology, psychology, arts, religion, sports and recreation, ext. 448, ebirch@greenwood.com). Academic and Trade: Alan Sturmer (economics, business, law, ext. 475, asturmer@greenwood.com); Dan Eades (history and military studies, ext. 479, deades@greenwood.com); Jane Garry (library science, pregnancy, parenting, alternative medicine, education, and anthropology, ext. 480, jgarry@greenwood.com). Professional Publishing: Eric Valentine (Quorum Books, ext. 471, evalentine@greenwood.com). Publishes hardcover and trade paperback originals. **Publishes 700 titles/year. Pays royalty on net price. Offers advance rarely.** Publishes book 1 year after acceptance of ms. Accepts simultaneous submissions. Book catalog and ms guidelines online.

O→ The Greenwood Publishing Group consists of five distinguished imprints with one unifying purpose: to provide the best possible reference, professional, text, and scholarly resources in the humanities and the social and behavioral sciences.

**Imprint(s):** Auburn House, Bergin & Garvey, **Greenwood Press**, **Praeger Publishers**, Quorum Books.

**Nonfiction:** Reference, textbook. Subjects include anthropology/archaeology, business/economics, child guidance/

parenting, education, government/politics, history, language/literature, military/war, music/dance, philosophy, psychology, religion, sociology, sports, women's issues/studies. Query with proposal package, including scope, organization, length of project, whether a complete ms is available or when it will be, cv or résumé and SASE. *No unsolicited mss.*
**Recent Title(s):** *From the Unthinkable to the Unavoidable*, edited by Carol Rittner and John Roth (religion/Holocaust studies); *The Feminist Encyclopedia of German Literature*, edited by Friederike Eigler and Susanne Kord; *The Fighting Pattons*, by Brian Sobel (military).
**Tips:** "No interest in fiction, drama, poetry—looking for serious, scholarly, analytical studies of historical problems." Greenwood Publishing maintains an excellent website, providing complete catalog, ms guidelines and editorial contacts.

**GROLIER PUBLISHING**, Grolier Inc., 90 Sherman Turnpike, Danbury CT 06816. (203)797-3500. Fax: (203)797-3197. Executive Editor: Mark Friedman. Estab. 1895. Publishes hardcover and trade paperback originals.
    O-- "Grolier Publishing is a leading publisher of reference, educational and children's books. We provide parents, teachers and librarians with the tools they need to enlighten children to the pleasure of learning and prepare them for the road ahead."
**Imprint(s): Children's Press**, Grolier Educational, **Orchard Books, Franklin Watts.**

**A GROSSET & DUNLAP PUBLISHERS**, Penguin Putnam Inc., 345 Hudson St., New York NY 10014. Associate Publisher: Ronnie Ann Herman. **Acquisitions:** Jane O'Connor, president. Estab. 1898. Publishes hardcover (few) and paperback originals. **Publishes 175 titles/year.** Publishes book 18 months after acceptance. Reports in 2 months.
    O-- Grosset & Dunlap publishes children's books that examine new ways of looking at the world of a child.
**Imprint(s):** Planet Dexter, **Price Stern Sloan.**
**Nonfiction:** Juveniles. Subjects include nature, science. *Agented submissions only.*
**Fiction:** Juveniles. *Agented submissions only.*
**Recent Title(s):** *Dragon Slayers' Academy* series, *Zack Files* series.
**Tips:** "Nonfiction that is particularly topical or of wide interest in the mass market; new concepts for novelty format for preschoolers; and very well-written easy readers on topics that appeal to primary graders have the best chance of selling to our firm."

**GROUP PUBLISHING, INC.**, 1515 Cascade Ave., Loveland CO 80538. Fax: (970)669-1994. E-mail: kloesche@aol.com. Website: http://www.grouppublishing.com. **Acquisitions:** Kerri Loesche, editorial assistant; Paul Woods (curriculum); Dennis McLaughlin (adult acquisitions); Jim Kochenburger (children's acquisitions); Amy Simpson (youth books). Estab. 1974. Publishes trade paperback originals. **Publishes 20-30 titles/year. Receives 200-400 queries and 300-500 mss/year. 30% of books from first-time authors; 95% from unagented writers. Pays up to 10% royalty on wholesale price or makes outright purchase. Offers up to $1,000 advance.** Publishes book 18 months after acceptance of ms. Accepts simultaneous submissions. Reports in 2 months on queries, 6 months on proposals. Book catalog for 9 × 12 SAE with 2 first-class stamps. Manuscript guidelines for #10 SASE.
    O-- "Our mission is to encourage Christian growth in children, youth and adults."
**Imprint(s):** Group (contact Amy Simpson), Vital Ministry (contact Dennis McLaughlin).
**Nonfiction:** How-to, adult, youth and children's ministry resources. Subjects include education, religion and any subjects pertinent to adult, youth or children's ministry in a church setting. "We're an interdenominational publisher of resource materials for people who work with adults, youth or children in a Christian church setting. We also publish materials for use directly by youth or children (such as devotional books, workbooks or Bibles stories). Everything we do is based on concepts of active and interactive learning as described in *Why Nobody Learns Much of Anything at Church: And How to Fix It*, by Thom and Joani Schultz. We need new, practical, hands-on, innovative, out-of-the-box ideas—things that no one's doing . . . yet." Submit proposal package, including outline, 2 sample chapters, introduction to the book (written as if the reader will read it), and sample activities if appropriate.
**Recent Title(s):** *The Dirt on Learning*, by Thom and Joani Schultz.
**Tips:** "We're seeking proposals for CD-ROM projects. Submit same as proposal package above."

**GROVE/ATLANTIC, INC.**, 841 Broadway, New York NY 10003. (212)614-7850. Fax: (212)614-7886. Publisher: Morgan Entrekin. **Acquisitions:** Joan Bingham, executive editor. Elizabeth Schmitz, senior editor/director of subsidiary rights. Estab. 1952. Publishes hardcover originals, trade paperback originals and reprints. **Publishes 60-70 titles/year. Receives 1000s queries/year. 10-15% of books from first-time authors; "very few" from unagented writers. Pays 7½-15% royalty on retail price. Advance varies considerably.** Publishes book 1 year after acceptance of ms. Accepts simultaneous submissions. "Because of volume of queries, Grove/Atlantic can only respond when interested—though SASE might generate a response." Book catalog free.
    O-- Grove/Atlantic publishes serious nonfiction and literary fiction.
**Imprint(s):** Grove Press (estab. 1952), Atlantic Monthly Press (estab. 1917).
**Nonfiction:** Biography. Subjects include government/politics, history, travel. Query with SASE. *No unsolicited mss.*
**Fiction:** Experimental, literary, translation. Query with SASE. *No unsolicited mss.*
**Poetry:** "We try to publish at least one volume of poetry every list." Query. *No unsolicited mss.*
**Recent Title(s):** *Black Hawk Dawn: A Story of Modern War*, by Mark Bowden.

**ALDINE DE GRUYTER**, Walter de Gruyter, Inc., 200 Saw Mill River Rd., Hawthorne NY 10532. Website: http://www.degruyter.de. **Acquisitions:** Dr. Richard Koffler, executive editor. Publishes hardcover and academic paperback originals. **Publishes 15-25 titles/year. Receives several hundred queries and 100 mss/year. 15% of books from first-time authors; 99% from unagented writers. Pays 7½-10% royalty on net sales.** Publishes book 9 months after acceptance of ms. Accepts simultaneous submissions. Reports in 2 months on proposals. Book catalog free. Ms guidelines only after contract.

○━ Aldine de Gruyter is an academic nonfiction publisher.

**Nonfiction:** Textbook (rare), course-related monographs and edited volumes. Subjects include anthropology (biological); sociology, human services, evolutionary psychology. "Aldine's authors are academics with Ph.D's and strong publication records. No poetry or fiction." Submit 1-2 sample chapters, proposal package, including c.v., market, competing texts, etc., reviews of earlier work.

**Recent Title(s):** *Thinking About Social Problems*, by Donileen R. Loseke.

**Tips:** Audience is professors and upper level and graduate students.

**GRYPHON HOUSE, INC.**, P.O. Box 207, Beltsville MD 20704. (301)595-9500. Fax: (301)595-0051. Website: http://www.ghbooks.com. **Acquisitions:** Kathy Charner, editor-in-chief. Estab. 1971. Publishes trade paperback originals. **Publishes 6 titles/year. Pays royalty on wholesale price.** Reports in 3 months.

○━ Gryphon House publishes books of creative educational activities for parents and teachers to do with young children ages 0-8.

**Nonfiction:** How-to, education. Submit outline, 2-3 sample chapters and SASE.

**Recent Title(s):** *Global Art*, by Maryann Kohl and Jean Potter; *The I Can't Sing Book*, by Jackie Silberg.

**GRYPHON PUBLICATIONS**, P.O. Box 209, Brooklyn NY 11228. **Acquisitions:** Gary Lovisi, owner/publisher. Publishes trade paperback originals and reprints. **Publishes 10 titles/year. Receives 500 queries and 1,000 mss/year. 60% of books from first-time authors; 90% from unagented writers. No advance.** Makes outright purchase by contract, price varies. Publishes book 2 years after acceptance of ms. Reports in 1 month on queries. *Writer's Market* recommends allowing 2 months for reply. Book catalog and ms guidelines for #10 SASE.

**Imprint(s):** Paperback Parade Magazine, Hardboiled Magazine, Other Worlds Magazine, Gryphon Books, Gryphon Doubles.

**Nonfiction:** Reference, bibliography. Subjects include hobbies, literature and book collecting. "We need well-written, well-researched articles, but query first on topic and length. Writers submit material that is not fully developed/researched." Query with SASE. Reviews artwork/photos as part of ms package. Send photocopies (slides, transparencies may be necessary later).

**Fiction:** Mystery, science fiction, suspense, urban horror, hardboiled fiction. "We want cutting-edge fiction, under 3,000 words with impact!" For short stories, query or submit complete ms. For novels, send 1-page query letter with SASE.

**Tips:** "We are very particular about novels and book-length work. A first-timer has a better chance with a short story or article. On anything over 6,000 words *do not* send manuscript, send *only* query letter with SASE."

**N GUILFORD PUBLICATIONS, INC.**, 72 Spring St., New York NY 10012. (212)431-9800. Fax: (212)966-6708. E-mail: info@guilford.com. Website: http://www.guilford.com. **Acquisitions:** Seymour Weingarten, editor-in-chief; Rochelle Serwator, editor (neuropsychology, social work); Kitty Moore, senior editor (psychology/psychiatry. family, child clinical, culture); Christopher Jennison, senior editor (education, school psychology); Peter Wissoker, editor (geography, communication, social theory). Estab. 1978. Publishes hardcover and trade paperback originals and trade paperback reprints. **Publishes 75 titles/year. Receives 200 queries and 50 mss/year. 30% of books from first-time authors; 90% from unagented writers. Pays 0-15% royalty on wholesale price. Offers $500-5,000 advance.** Publishes book 7 months after acceptance of ms. Accepts simultaneous submissions. Reports in 1 month on queries and proposals, 2 months on mss. Book catalog and ms guidelines free or on website.

○━ Guilford Publications publishes quality trade and professional titles in psychology, psychiatry and the behavioral sciences, including addictions, gender issues and child abuse; as well as cultural studies, philosophy, politics, geography, communication and education. Products include books, journals and videos.

**Nonfiction:** Self-help, technical, textbook. Subjects include child guidance/parenting, education, gay/lesbian, government/politics, health/medicine, philosophy, psychology, sociology, women's issues/studies. Query with SASE. Submit proposal package, including outline, 2 sample chapters and curriculum vitae.

**Recent Titles:** *Your Defiant Child*, by Russell A. Barkley (parenting).

**Tips:** "Projects must be solidly research-based."

**GULF PUBLISHING COMPANY**, P.O. Box 2608, Houston TX 77252-2608. (713)520-4465. Fax: (713)520-4438. Website: http://www.gulfpub.com. **Acquisitions:** Phil Carmical, acquisitions editor (science/technical, self-help, business, children's); Kim Kilmer, acquisitions editor (field guides, cookbooks, Texana). Estab. 1916. Publishes hardcover and trade paperback originals and reprints. **Publishes 60-65 titles/year. Receives 1,000 queries and 400 mss/year. 50% of books from first-time authors; 90% from unagented writers. Pays royalty.** Publishes book 18 months after acceptance of ms. Accepts simultaneous submissions. Reports in 1 month on queries, 3 months on proposals and mss. Book catalog and ms guidelines free.

○━ Gulf publishes technical and Texana titles. "We are expanding to publish books for a more general nonfiction audience. The titles include, but are not necessarily limited to, outdoor field guides, general cookbooks, business books, self-help books, and books on human resources and training."

**Imprint(s):** Maverick (Hank the Cowdog Audiobooks); Lonestar (Texana); Cashman Dudley (business).
**Nonfiction:** Cookbook, how-to, reference, self-help, technical, Texana. Subjects include business/economics, cooking/foods/nutrition, money/finance, nature/environment, regional. Submit proposal package, including cover letter, outline, résumé, sample chapters and SASE. Reviews artwork/photos as part of ms package. Send color copies, slides or actual photos.
**Fiction:** Juvenile, picture books. "Primarily, we are interested in picture books for young readers (ages 8-13)." Submit synopsis, sample chapter and SASE.
**Recent Title(s):** *HRD Trends Worldwide*, by Jack Phillips (business/human resource).
**Tips:** "We are always looking for general business books and children's fiction of very high quality. We will also be launching a new line of dog-training books."

**HACHAI PUBLISHING**, 156 Chester Ave., Brooklyn NY 11218. (718)633-0100. Website: http://www.hachai.com. **Acquisitions**: Dina Rosenfeld, editor. Estab. 1988. Publishes hardcover originals. **Publishes 6 titles/year. Makes $1,000 outright purchase.** Accepts simultaneous submissions. Reports in 2 months on mss. Book catalog free. Manuscript guidelines for #10 SASE.
  ○━ "Hachai is dedicated to producing high quality Jewish children's literature, ages 2 through 10. Story should promote universal values such as sharing, kindness, etc."
**Nonfiction:** Children's/juvenile. Jewish religious subjects. Submit complete ms with SASE. Reviews artwork/photos as part of ms package. Send photocopies.
**Recent Title(s):** *Nine Spoons*, by Marci Stillerman (nonfiction); *On the Ball*, by Dina Rosenfeld (fiction).
**Tips:** "We are looking for books that convey the traditional Jewish experience in modern times or long ago; traditional Jewish observance such as Sabbath and Holidays and mitzvos such as mezuzah, blessings etc.; positive character traits (middos) such as honesty, charity, respect, sharing, etc. We are also interested in biographies of spiritually great men and women in Jewish history; problem novels, historical fiction and tales of adventure for young readers (8-11) written with a traditional Jewish perspective; and highlighting the relevance of Torah in making important choices. Please, no animal stories, romance, violence, preachy sermonizing."

**HALF HALT PRESS, INC.**, P.O. Box 67, Boonsboro MD 21713. (301)733-7119. Fax: (301)733-7408. **Acquisitions:** Elizabeth Carnes, publisher. Estab. 1986. Publishes 90% hardcover and trade paperback originals and 10% reprints. **Publishes 15 titles/year. Receives 150 submissions/year. 25% of books from first-time authors; 50% from unagented authors. Pays 10-12½% royalty on retail price. Offers advance by agreement.** Publishes book 1 year after acceptance of ms. Reports in 1 month on queries. *Writer's Market* recommends allowing 2 months for reply. Book catalog for 6×9 SAE with 2 first-class stamps.
  ○━ "We publish high-quality nonfiction on equestrian topics, books that help riders and trainers do something better."
**Nonfiction:** Instructional: horse and equestrian-related subjects only. "We need serious instructional works by authorities in the field on horse-related topics, broadly defined." Query with SASE. Reviews artwork/photos as part of ms package.
**Recent Title(s):** *Practical Eventing*, by Sally O'Connor.
**Tips:** "Writers have the best chance selling us well-written, unique works that teach serious horse people how to do something better. If I were a writer trying to market a book today, I would offer a straightforward presentation, letting the work speak for itself, without hype or hard sell. Allow publisher to contact writer, without frequent calling to check status. They haven't forgotten the writer but may have many different proposals at hand; frequent calls to 'touch base,' multiplied by the number of submissions, become an annoyance. As the publisher/author relationship becomes close and is based on working well together, early impressions may be important, even to the point of being a consideration in acceptance for publication."

**ALEXANDER HAMILTON INSTITUTE**, 70 Hilltop Rd., Ramsey NJ 07446-1119. (201)825-3377. Fax: (201)825-8696. Website: http://www.ahipubs.com. **Acquisitions:** Brian L.P. Zevnik, editor-in-chief; Gloria Ju, editor; Amy Knierim, editor. Estab. 1909. Publishes 3-ring binder and paperback originals. **Publishes 5-10 titles/year. Receives 50 queries and 10 mss/year. 25% of books from first-time authors; 95% from unagented writers. Pays 5-8% royalty on retail price or makes outright purchase ($3,500-7,000). Offers $3,500-7,000 advance.** Publishes book 10 months after acceptance. Accepts simultaneous submissions. Reports in 1 month on queries, 2 months on mss.
  ○━ Alexander Hamilton Institute publishes "non-traditional" management books for upper-level managers and executives. Currently emphasizing legal issues for HR/personnel. De-emphasizing how-to business management.
**Nonfiction:** Executive/management books. The first audience is overseas, upper-level managers. "We need how-to and skills building books. *No* traditional management texts or academic treatises." The second audience is US personnel executives and high-level management. Subject is legal personnel matters. "These books combine court case research and practical application of defensible programs." Submit outline, 3 paragraphs on each chapter, examples of lists, graphics, cases.
**Recent Title(s):** *Employer's Guide to Record-Keeping Requirements*.
**Tips:** "We sell exclusively by direct mail to managers and executives around the world. A writer must know his/her field and be able to communicate practical systems and programs."

**HAMPTON ROADS PUBLISHING COMPANY, INC.**, 134 Burgess Lane, Charlottesville VA 22902. (804)296-2772. Fax: (804)296-5096. E-mail: hrpc@hrpub.com. Website: http://hrpub.com. **Acquisitions:** Frank DeMarco, chief editor (metaphysical/visionary fiction); Robert S. Friedman, president (metaphysical/alternative medicine); Ken Eagle Feather, marketing director (spiritual paths/Toltec). Estab. 1989. Publishes hardcover and trade paperback originals. **Publishes 25-30 titles/year. Receives 1,000 queries and 1,500 mss/year. 50% of books from first-time authors; 70% from unagented writers. Pays royalty. Offers $1,000-100,000 advance.** Publishes book 1 year after acceptance of ms. Accepts simultaneous submissions. Reports in 1 month on queries and proposals, 5 months on mss. Book catalog free. Manuscript guidelines free.

Oᴙ "Our reason for being is to impact, uplift and contribute to positive change in the world. We publish books that will enrich and empower the evolving consciousness of mankind."

**Nonfiction:** How-to, illustrated book, self-help. Spirituality subjects. Submit full ms. Reviews artwork/photos as part of the ms package. Send photocopies and SASE.

**Fiction:** Spiritual, visionary fiction. "Fiction should have one or more of the following themes: spiritual, inspirational, metaphysical, i.e., past life recall, out of body experiences, near death experience, paranormal." Query or submit synopsis with full ms and SASE.

**Recent Title(s):** *Cosmic Journeys*, by Rosalind McKnight (nonfiction); *Getting There*, by Michael Roads (fiction).

■ **HANCOCK HOUSE PUBLISHERS**, 1431 Harrison Ave., Blaine WA 98230-5005. (604)538-1114. Fax: (604)538-2262. E-mail: hancock@uniserve.com. **Acquisitions:** David Hancock, publisher; Nancy Miller, editor. Estab. 1971. Publishes hardcover and trade paperback originals and reprints. **Publishes 14 titles/year. Receives 300 submissions/year. 50% of books from first-time authors; 90% from unagented writers. Pays 10% royalty.** Accepts simultaneous submissions. Publishes book up to 1 year after acceptance. Book catalog free. Manuscript guidelines for #10 SASE.

Oᴙ Hancock House Publishers, seeks agriculture, natural history, animal husbandry, conservation and popular science titles with a regional (Pacific Northwest), national or international focus.

**Nonfiction:** Biography, how-to, reference, technical. Pacific Northwest history and biography, nature guides, native culture, and international natural history. "Centered around Pacific Northwest, local history, nature guide books, international ornithology and Native Americans." Submit outline, 3 sample chapters and proposal package, including selling points with SASE. Reviews artwork/photos as part of ms package. Send photocopies.

**Recent Title(s):** *Bushplanes of the North*, by Robert Grant (aviation/history).

**HANSER GARDNER PUBLICATIONS**, 6915 Valley Ave., Cincinnati OH 45244. (513)527-8977. Fax: (513)527-8950. Website: http://www.gardnerweb.com. **Acquisitions:** Woody Chapman. Estab. 1993. Publishes hardcover and paperback originals and reprints. **Publishes 5-10 titles/year. Receives 40-50 queries and 5-10 mss/year. 75% of books from first-time authors; 100% from unagented writers. Pays 10-15% royalty on net receipts. No advance.** Publishes book 10 months after acceptance of ms. Accepts simultaneous submissions. Reports in 2 weeks on queries, 1 month on proposals and mss. Book catalog and ms guidelines free.

Oᴙ Hanser Gardner publishes training and practical application titles for metalworking, machining and finishing shops/plants.

**Nonfiction:** How-to, technical, textbook. Subjects include metalworking and finishing processes, and related management topics. "Our books are primarily basic introductory-level training books and books that emphasize practical applications. Strictly deal with subjects above." Query with résumé, preface, outline, sample chapter, comparison to competing or similar titles. Reviews artwork/photos as part of ms package. Send photocopies.

**Recent Title(s):** *Industrial Painting*, by Norman R. Roobol (industrial reference).

**Tips:** "Our readers and authors occupy various positions within small and large metalworking, machining and finishing shops/plants. We prefer that interested individuals write, call, or fax us with their queries first, so we can send them our proposal guideline form."

⧉ **HARBOR PRESS**, 5713 Wollochet Dr. NW, Gig Harbor WA 98335. Fax: (253)851-5191. President/Publisher: Harry R. Lynn. **Acquisitions:** Deborah Young, senior editor. Estab. 1985. Publishes hardcover and trade paperback originals and reprints. **Publishes 8-10 titles/year. Negotiates competitive royalties on wholesale price or makes outright purchase.**

Oᴙ Harbor Press publishes consumer-oriented health and self-improvement titles for both trade and mail-order markets.

**Nonfiction:** Health, self-improvement. Subjects include health/medicine, nutrition. Query with proposal package, including outline, 3 sample chapters, synopsis and SASE. Reviews artwork/photos as part of ms package. Send photocopies.

**Recent Title(s):** *Healing Back Pain Naturally: The Mind-Body Program Proven to Work.*

**HARCOURT INC.**, (formerly Harcourt Brace & Company), Children's Books Division, 525 B St., Suite 1900, San Diego CA 92101. (619)261-6616. Fax: (619)699-6777. Website: http://www.harcourtbooks.com/Childrens/childrn.html. Publisher: Louise Pelan. Estab. 1919. Publishes hardcover originals and trade paperback reprints.

Oᴙ Harcourt Inc. owns some of the world's most prestigious publishing imprints—imprints which distinguish quality products for the juvenile, educational, scientific, technical, medical, professional and trade markets worldwide.

**Imprint(s):** Browndeer Press, Gulliver Books, Gulliver Green, Magic Carpet, Red Wagon, Silver Whistle, Voyager Paperbacks.
**Nonfiction and Fiction:** Agented submissions or query letters only with SASE. *No unsolicited mss.* No phone calls.
**Recent Title(s):** *Home Run*, by Robert Burleigh; *My Name is Georgia*, by Jeanette Winter.

**HARCOURT INC.**, (formerly Harcourt Brace & Company), Trade Division, 525 B St., Suite 1900, San Diego, CA 92101. (619)699-6560. Fax: (619)699-5555. Website: http://www.harcourtbooks.com. **Acquisitions**: David Hough, managing editor; Jane Isay, editor-in-chief (science, math, history, language); Drenka Willen, senior editor (poetry, fiction in translation, history); Walter Bode, editor (history, geography, American fiction). Publishes hardcover and trade paperback originals and trade paperback reprints. **Publishes 120 titles/year. 5% of books from first-time authors; 5% from unagented writers. Pays 6-15% royalty on retail price. Offers $2,000 minimum advance.** Accepts simultaneous mss.
>  O― Harcourt Inc. owns some of the world's most prestigious publishing imprints—imprints which distinguish quality products for the juvenile, educational, scientific, technical, medical, professional and trade markets worldwide. Currently emphasizing science and math.

**Imprint(s):** Harvest (contact Andre Bernard).
**Nonfiction:** Publishes all categories *except* business/finance (university texts), cookbooks, self-help, sex. Agented submissions or query letters only with SASE. *No unsolicited mss.*
**Recent Title(s):** *Africans in America*, by Charles Johnson and Patricia Smith (nonfiction); *East of the Mountains*, by David Guterson (fiction); *Jackstraws*, by Charles Simic (poetry).

**HARPERBUSINESS**, HarperCollins Publishers, 10 E. 53rd St., New York NY 10036. (212)207-7006. Website: http://www.harpercollins.com. **Acquisitions:** Adrian Zackheim, senior vice president/publisher; David Conti, executive editor; Laureen Rowland, senior editor. Estab. 1991. Publishes hardcover, trade paperback and mass market paperback originals, hardcover and trade paperback reprints. **Publishes 50-55 titles/year. Receives 500 queries and mss/year. 1% of books from first-time authors; 10% from unagented writers. Pays royalty on retail price; varies. Offers advance.** Accepts simultaneous submissions. Reports in 2 months on proposals and mss. Book catalog free.
>  O― HarperBusiness publishes "the inside story on ideas that will shape business practices and thinking well into the next millennium, with cutting-edge information and visionary concepts." Currently emphasizing finance, motivation, technology.

**Nonfiction:** Biography (economics); business/economics, marketing subjects. "We don't publish how-to, textbooks or things for academic market; no reference (tax or mortgage guides), our reference department does that. Proposals need to be top notch, especially for unagented writers. We tend not to publish people who have no business standing. Must have business credentials." Submit proposal package with SASE.
**Recent Title(s):** *Direct From Dell*, by Michael Dell.
**Tips:** Business audience: managers, CEOs, consultants, some academics. "We accept more unagented proposals, but they tend to come from authors who are already well established in their fields."

**HARPERCOLLINS CHILDREN'S BOOKS**, HarperCollins Publishers, 10 E. 53rd St., New York NY 10022. (212)207-7000. Website: http://www.harpercollins.com. Editor-in-Chief: Kate Morgan Jackson. **Acquisitions:** Alix Reid, executive editor; Robert Warren, editorial director; Phoebe Yeh, executive editor. Publishes hardcover originals. **Publishes 350 titles/year. Receives 200 queries and 5,000 mss/year. 5% of books from first-time authors; 25% from unagented writers. Pays 10-12½% royalty on retail price.** Advance varies. Publishes novel 1 year, picture books 2 years after acceptance of ms. Accepts simultaneous submissions. Reports in 1 month on queries and proposals, 4 months on mss. Book catalog for 8×10 SASE with 3 first-class stamps. Ms guidelines for #10 SASE.
>  O― "We have no rules for subject matter, length or vocabulary, but look instead for ideas that are fresh and imaginative, good writing that involves the reader is essential."

**Imprint(s):** Joanna Cotler Books (Joanna Cotler, editorial director); Michael DiCapua Books (Michael DiCapua, editorial director); **Laura Geringer Books** (Laura Geringer, editorial director); HarperFestival (Mary Alice Moore, editorial director); HarperTrophy (Ginee Seo, editorial director).
**Fiction:** Adventure, fantasy, historical, humor, juvenile, literary, picture books, young adult. Query *only* with SASE. no unsolicited mss.
**Recent Title(s):** *Today I Feel Silly*, by Jamie Lee Curtis (picture book); *Ella Enchanted*, by Gail Carson Levine (novel).

🅐 **HARPERCOLLINS PUBLISHERS**, 10 E. 53rd St., New York NY 10022. (212)207-7000. Website: http://www.harpercollins.com. Publishes hardcover fiction and nonfiction. **Publishes 120-150 titles a year.** Reports on solicited queries in 6 weeks. *Agented submissions only.*
>  O― "HarperCollins, one of the largest English language publishers in the world, is a broad-based publisher with strengths in serious nonfiction and quality fiction, commercial fiction, business and professional, children's, educational, general interest, and religious and spiritual books, self-help books as well as multimedia titles."

**Imprint(s):** Cliff Street Books (contact Diane Reverand), **Ecco Press**, Harper Adult Trade; HarperAudio, **HarperBusiness**, **HarperCollins**, **HarperCollins Children's Books**, HarperEdge, **HarperEntertainment**, HarperFlamingo (contact Susan Weinberg), HarperHorizon, **HarperLibros**, HarperPaperbacks, **HarperPerennial**, HarperPrism, HarperResource, **HarperSanFrancisco**, HarperTrophy, HarperVoyager, **Regan Books**, **Zondervan Publishing House**.
**Nonfiction:** Americana, animals, art, biography, business/economics, current affairs, cookbooks, health, history, how-

to, humor, music, nature, philosophy, politics, psychology, reference, religion, science, self-help, sociology, sports, travel. *Agented submissions only. No unsolicited queries or mss.*

**Fiction:** Adventure, fantasy, gothic, historical, mystery, science fiction, suspense, western, literary. "We look for a strong story line and exceptional literary talent." *Agented submissions only. No unsolicited queries or mss.*

**Recent Title(s):** *The Poisonwood Bible*, by Barbara Kingsolver; *The Professor and the Mad Man*, by Simon Winchester.

**HARPERENTERTAINMENT,** (formerly HarperActive), HarperCollins Publishers, 10 E. 53rd St., New York NY 10022. (212)207-7000. Editorial Director/Vice President: Hope Innelli. **Acquisitions:** Lara Comstock, editor. Estab. 1997. **20% of books from first-time authors. Writer-for-hire arrangements mostly. Fees vary.** Reports in 3-12 months on mss. Book catalog and mss guidelines not available.

   O➡ "A newly formed imprint, HarperEntertainment is dedicated to publishing sports, movie and TV tie-ins, celebrity bios and books reflecting trends in popular culture."

**Nonfiction:** Children's/juvenile, biographies, movie and TV-tie ins. "The bulk of our work is done by experienced writers for hire, but we are open to original ideas." Query with outline and SASE.

**Fiction:** Humor, juvenile, movie and TV tie-ins. Query with synopsis and SASE.

**Recent Title(s):** *Mary-Kate & Ashley's New Adventures.*

**HARPERLIBROS,** HarperCollins Publishers, 10 E. 53rd St., New York NY 10022. (212)207-7000. Fax: (212)207-7145. Website: http://www.harpercollins.com. **Acquisitions:** Terry Karten, editorial director. Estab. 1994. Publishes hardcover and trade paperback originals. **Publishes 10 titles/year. Receives 250 queries/year. 30% of books from first-time authors. Pays variable royalty on net price. Advance varies.** Publishes book 1 year after acceptance of ms.

   O➡ "Harper Libros offers Spanish language editions of selected HarperCollins titles, sometimes reprints, sometimes new books that are published simultaneously in English and Spanish. The list mirrors the English-language list of HarperCollins in that we publish both literary and commercial fiction and nonfiction titles including all the different HarperCollins categories, such as self-help, spirituality, etc."

**Imprint(s):** Harper Arco Iris (children's).

**Nonfiction:** How-to, self-help. Subjects include business/economics, ethnic, spirituality, women's health. Query. *No unsolicited mss.*

**Fiction:** Literary. Query. *No unsolicited mss.*

**Recent Title(s):** *Salud: A Latina's Guide to Total Health*, by Jane Delgado, MD (women's health).

Ⓐ **HARPERPERENNIAL,** HarperCollins Publishers, 10 E. 53rd St., New York NY 10036. (212)207-7000. Website: http://www.harpercollins.com. **Acquisitions:** Acquisitions Editor. Estab. 1963. Publishes trade paperback originals and reprints. **Publishes 100 titles/year. Receives 500 queries/year. 5% of books from first-time authors; 2% from unagented writers. Pays 5-7½% royalty. Advance varies.** Publishes book 6 months after acceptance of ms. Reports in 2 weeks on queries, 1 month on mss. Book catalog free.

   O➡ Harper Perennial publishes a broad range of adult literary fiction and nonfiction paperbacks.

**Nonfiction:** Biography, cookbook, how-to, humor, illustrated book, reference, self-help. Subjects include Americana, animals, business/economics, child guidance/parenting, education, ethnic, gay/lesbian,history, language/literature, mental health, military/war, money/finance, music/dance, nature/environment, philosophy, psychology/self-help psychotherapy, recreation, regional, religion/spirituality, science, sociology, sports, translation, travel, women's issues/studies. "Our focus is ever-changing, adjusting to the marketplace. Mistakes writers often make are not giving their background and credentials—why they are qualified to write the book. A proposal should explain why the author wants to write this book; why it will sell; and why it is better or different from others of its kind." *Agented submissions only.*

**Fiction:** Ethnic, feminist, literary. "Don't send us novels—go through hardcover." *Agented submissions only.*

**Poetry:** "Don't send poetry unless you have been published in several established literary magazines already." *Agented submissions only.* Query with 10 sample poems.

**Recent Title(s):** *God of Small Things*, by Arundhati Roy.

**HARPERSANFRANCISCO,** HarperCollins Publishers, 353 Sacramento St., Suite 500, San Francisco CA 94111-3653. (415)477-4400. Fax: (415)477-4444. E-mail: hcsanfrancisco@harpercollins.com. Senior Vice President: Diane Gedymin. **Acquisitions:** Liz Perle, editor-at-large (women's studies, psychology, personal growth, inspiration); Douglas Adams, senior editor (Hebrew Bible, Judaism, religion, health, sexuality); John Loudon, executive editor (religious studies, biblical studies, psychology/personal growth, Eastern religions). Estab. 1977. Publishes hardcover originals, trade paperback originals and reprints. **Publishes 75 titles/year. Receives about 10,000 submissions/year. 5% of books from first-time authors. Pays royalty.** Publishes book within 18 months after acceptance.

   O➡ HarperSanFrancisco publishes books that "nurture the mind, body and spirit; support readers in their ongoing self-discovery and personal growth; explore the essential religious and philosophical issues of our time; and present the rich and diverse array of the wisdom traditions of the world to a contemporary audience."

**Nonfiction:** Biography, how-to, reference, self-help. Subjects include psychology, religion, self-help, spirituality. Query. *No unsolicited mss.*

**Recent Title(s):** *Journey to the Heart*, by Melody Beattie (nonfiction); *The Alchemist*, by Paulo Cuelho (fiction).

**HARVARD BUSINESS SCHOOL PRESS**, Harvard Business School Publishing Corp., 60 Harvard Way, Boston MA 02163. (617)495-6700. Fax: (617)496-8066. Website: http://www.hbsp.harvard.edu. Director: Carol Franco. **Acquisitions:** Marjorie Williams, executive editor; Kirsten Sandberg, senior editor; Hollis Heimbouch, senior editor; Nikki Sabin, acquisitions editor. Estab. 1984. Publishes hardcover originals. **Publishes 35-45 titles/year. Receives 500 queries and 300 mss/year. 20% of books from first-time authors; 10% from unagented writers. Pays escalating royalty on retail price. Advances vary widely depending on author and market for the book.** Publishes book 9 months after acceptance of ms. Accepts simultaneous submissions. Reports in 1 month on proposals and mss. Book catalog and ms guidelines free.

    ○┅ The Harvard Business School Press publishes books for an audience of senior and general managers and business scholars. HBS Press is the source of the most influential ideas and conversation that shape business worldwide.

**Nonfiction:** Business/economics subjects. Submit proposal package, including outline with sample chapters.

**Recent Title(s):** *Net Worth*, by John Hagel and Mark Singer.

**Tips:** "Take care to really look into the type of business books we publish. They are generally not handbooks, how-to manuals, policy-oriented, dissertations, edited collections, or personal business narratives."

**THE HARVARD COMMON PRESS**, 535 Albany St., Boston MA 02118-2500. (617)423-5803. Fax: (617)423-0679 or (617)695-9794. **Acquisitions:** Bruce P. Shaw, president/publisher. Associate Publisher: Dan Rosenberg. Estab. 1976. Publishes hardcover and trade paperback originals and reprints. **Publishes 12 titles/year. Receives 1,000 submissions/year. 20% of books from first-time authors; 40% of books from unagented writers. Pays royalty. Offers average $4,000 advance.** Publishes book 1 year after acceptance of ms. Accepts simultaneous submissions. Reports in 2 months. Book catalog for 9×12 SAE with 3 first-class stamps. Manuscript guidelines for SASE.

    ○┅ "We want strong, practical books that help people gain control over a particular area of their lives." Currently emphasizing cooking, childcare/parenting, health. De-emphasizing general instructional books, travel.

**Imprint(s):** Gambit Books.

**Nonfiction:** Subjects include cooking, childcare/parenting, health, travel. "A large percentage of our list is made up of books about cooking, child care and parenting; in these areas we are looking for authors who are knowledgeable, if not experts, and who can offer a different approach to the subject. We are open to good nonfiction proposals that show evidence of strong organization and writing, and clearly demonstrate a need in the marketplace. First-time authors are welcome." Accepts nonfiction translations. Submit outline and 1-3 sample chapters. Reviews artwork/photos.

**Recent Title(s):** *The Basque Table*, by Teresa Barrenchea.

**Tips:** "We are demanding about the quality of proposals; in addition to strong writing skills and thorough knowledge of the subject matter, we require a detailed analysis of the competition."

**HARVARD UNIVERSITY PRESS**, 79 Garden St., Cambridge MA 02138. (617)495-2600. Fax: (617)495-5898. Website: http://www.hup.harvard.edu. **Acquisitions:** Aïda D. Donald, assistant director/editor-in-chief (history, contemporary affairs, sociology with historical emphasis, women's studies with historical emphasis); Lindsay Waters, executive editor for the humanities (literary criticism, philosophy, multicultural studies); Michael G. Fisher, executive editor for science and medicine (medicine, neuroscience, science, astronomy); Joyce Seltzer, senior executive editor (history, contemporary affairs); Michael Aronson, senior acquisitions editor for social sciences (sociology, economics, law, political science); Margaretta Fulton, general editor for the humanities (classics, religion, music, art, Jewish studies, women's studies); Elizabeth Knoll, senior editor for the behavioral sciences (behavioral sciences, neuroscience, education). Estab. 1913. **Publishes 130 titles/year.**

    ○┅ Harvard University Press publishes scholarly books and works of general interest in the humanities, the social and behavioral sciences, the natural sciences, and medicine. Does not normally publish poetry, fiction, festschriften, memoirs, symposia, or unrevised doctoral dissertations.

**Imprint(s):** The Belknap Press.

**Nonfiction:** Reference. Subjects include art/architecture, business/economics, ethnic, government/politics, history, language/literature, music, philosophy, psychology, religion, science, sociology, women's issues/studies. Query with SASE.

**Recent Title(s):** *Florence: A Portrait*, by Michael Levey (history).

**HASTINGS HOUSE**, Eagle Publishing Corp., 9 Mott Ave., Suite 203, Norwalk CT 06850. (203)838-4083. Fax: (203)838-4084. E-mail: info@upub.com. Website: http://www.upub.com. Publisher: Peter Leers. **Acquisitions:** Rachel Borst. Publishes hardcover and trade paperback originals and reprints. **Publishes 20 titles/year. Receives 600 queries and 900 mss/year. 10% of books from first-time authors; 40% from unagented writers. Pays 8-10% royalty on retail price on trade paperbacks. Offers $1,000-10,000 advance.** Publishes book 6-10 months after acceptance of ms. Reports in 2 months.

    ○┅ "We are looking for books that address consumer needs. We are primarily focused on expanding our Daytrips Travel Series nationally and internationally along with related travel books and select nonfiction." Currently de-emphasizing humor and cookbooks.

**Nonfiction:** Biography, cookbook, how-to, reference, self-help, consumer. Subjects include business/economics, cooking/foods/nutrition, health/medicine, psychology, travel, writing. Query or submit outline.

**Recent Title(s):** *Great American Mansions*, by Merril Folsom.

**HATHERLEIGH PRESS**, 1114 First Ave., New York NY 10021. (212)832-1584. Fax: (212)308-7930. E-mail: info@h atherleigh.com. Website: http://www.hatherleigh.com. Editor-In-Chief: Frederic Flach, M.D. **Acquisitions:** Adam Cohen, managing editor. Estab. 1995. Publishes hardcover originals, trade paperback originals and reprints. **Publishes 10-12 titles/year. Receives 20 queries and 20 mss/year. Pays 5-15% royalty on retail price or makes outright purchase. Offers $500-5,000 advance.** Publishes book 6 months after acceptance of ms. Reports in 2 months on queries. Book catalog free.

○┬ Hatherleigh Press publishes general self-help titles and reference books for mental health professionals.

**Imprint(s):** Red Brick Books—new fiction imprint (Kevin J. Moran, acquisitions editor); Five Star Fitness Publishing.
**Nonfiction:** Reference, self-help, technical. Subjects include health/medicine, psychology. Submit outline and 1 sample chapter with SASE. Reviews artwork/photos as part of ms package. Send photocopies.
**Recent Title(s):** *Women and Anxiety*, by Helen DeRosis, M.D.
**Tips:** Audience is mental health professionals. Submit a clear outline, including market and audience for your book.

**THE HAWORTH PRESS, INC.**, 10 Alice St., Binghamton NY 13904. Website: http://www.haworthpressinc.com. **Acquisitions:** Bill Palmer, managing editor. Estab. 1973. Publishes hardcover and trade paperback originals. **Publishes 100 titles/year. Receives 500 queries and 250 mss/year. 60% of books from first-time authors; 98% from unagented writers. Pays 7½-15% royalty on wholesale price. Offers $500-1,000 advance.** Publishes book 1 year after acceptance of ms. Reports in 2 months on proposals. Manuscript guidelines free.

○┬ The Haworth Press is primarily a scholarly press.

**Imprint(s):** The Harrington Park Press, Haworth Pastoral Press, Haworth Food Products Press.
**Nonfiction:** Reference, textbook. Subjects include agriculture/horticulture, business/economics, child guidance/parenting, cooking/foods/nutrition, gay/lesbian, health/medicine, money/finance, psychology, sociology, women's issues/studies. "No 'pop' books." Submit proposal package, including outline and 1-3 sample chapters and author bio. Reviews artwork/photos as part of ms package. Send photocopies.
**Recent Title(s):** *Reviving the Tribe*, by Eric Rofes (gay & lesbian).

**HAY HOUSE, INC.**, P.O. Box 5100, Carlsbad CA 92018-5100. (760)431-7695. Fax: (760)431-6948. Website: http://www.hayhouse.com. **Acquisitions:** Jill Kramer, editorial director. Estab. 1985. Publishes hardcover and trade paperback originals. **Publishes 40 titles/year. Receives 1,200 submissions/year. 10% of books are from first-time authors; 25% from unagented writers. Pays standard royalty.** Publishes book 10-15 months after acceptance of ms. Accepts simultaneous submissions. Reports in 3 weeks. *Writer's Market* recommends allowing 2 months for reply. Book catalog free. Does not respond or return mss without SASE.

○┬ "We publish books, audios and videos that help heal the planet."

**Imprint(s):** Astro Room.
**Nonfiction:** Primarily self-help. Subjects include relationships, mind/body health, nutrition, education, astrology, environment, health/medicine, money/finance, nature, philosophy/New Age, psychology, spiritual, sociology, women's and men's issues/studies. "Hay House is interested in a variety of subjects as long as they have a positive self-help slant to them. No poetry, children's books or negative concepts that are not conducive to helping/healing ourselves or our planet." Query or submit outline, sample chapters and SASE.
**Recent Title(s):** *Passage to Power: Natural Menopause Revolution*, by Leslie Keaton.
**Tips:** "Our audience is concerned with our planet, the healing properties of love, and general self-help principles. If I were a writer trying to market a book today, I would research the market thoroughly to make sure there weren't already too many books on the subject I was interested in writing about. Then I would make sure I had a unique slant on my idea. SASE a must!"

**N.** **HAZELDEN PUBLISHING**, P.O. Box 176, Center City MN 55012. Website: http://www.hazelden.org. **Acquisitions:** Rebecca Post, executive editor. Estab. 1954. Publishes hardcover and trade paperback originals and trade paperback reprints. **Publishes 80 titles/year. Receives 2,500 queries and 1,000 mss/year. 30% of books from first-time authors; 50% from unagented writers. Pays 8% royalty on retail price. Offers advance based on first year sales projections.** Publishes book 1 year after acceptance of ms. Accepts simultaneous submissions. Reports in 6 months. Book catalog or ms guidelines free.

○┬ Hazelden is a trade, educational and professional publisher specializing in psychology, self-help, and spiritual books that help enhance the quality of people's lives. Products include gift books, curriculum, workbooks, audio and video, computer-based products and wellness products. "We specialize in books on addiction/recovery, spirituality/personal growth, chronic illness and prevention topics related to chemical and mental health."

**Nonfiction:** Gift book, how-to, self-help. Subjects include child guidance/parenting, gay/lesbian, health/medicine, memoirs, psychology, spirituality. Query with SASE. Submit proposal package, including outline, 2 sample chapters, market analysis and author qualifications.
**Recent Title(s):** *Stop Being Mean to Yourself*, by Melody Beattie (self-help).
**Tips:** Audience includes "consumers and professionals interested in the range of topics related to chemical and emotional health, including spirituality, self-help and addiction recovery."

**HEALTH COMMUNICATIONS, INC.**, 3201 SW 15th St., Deerfield Beach FL 33442. (954)360-0909. Website: http://www.hci-online.com. **Acquisitions:** Christine Belleris, editorial co-director; Matthew Diener, editorial co-director; Allison Janse, associate editor; Lisa Drucker, associate editor. Publishes hardcover and trade paperback originals. Estab.

1976. **Publishes 40 titles/year. 20% of books from first-time authors; 90% from unagented writers. Pays 15% royalty on net price.** Publishes book 9 months after acceptance of ms. Accepts simultaneous submissions. Reports in 1 month on queries, 3 months on proposals and mss. Book catalog for 8½×11 SASE. Manuscript guidelines for #10 SASE.

> O→ "We are the Life Issues Publisher. Health Communications, Inc., strives to help people grow and improve their lives from physical and emotional health to finances and interpersonal relationships." Currently emphasizing visionary fiction—fiction with a message."

**Nonfiction:** Gift book, self-help. Subjects include child guidance/parenting, inspiration, psychology, spirituality, women's issues/studies, recovery. Submit proposal package, including outline, 2 sample chapters, vitae, marketing study and SASE. No phone calls. Reviews artwork/photos as part of ms package. Send photocopies.

**Recent Title(s):** *Chicken Soup for the Couple's Soul* by Canfield, Hansen, DeAngelis and Donnelly (nonfiction); *Wings of Destiny*, by Catherine Lanigan (fiction).

**Tips:** Audience is composed primarily of women, aged 25-60, interested in personal growth and self-improvement. "Please do your research in your subject area. We publish general self-help books and are expanding to include new subjects such as business self-help and possibly alternative healing. We need to know why there is a need for your book, how it might differ from other books on the market and what you have to offer to promote your work."

**HEALTH INFORMATION PRESS (HIP)**, PMIC (Practice Management Information Corp.), 4727 Wilshire Blvd., Los Angeles CA 90010. (213)954-0224. Fax: (213)954-0253. E-mail: pmiceditor@aol.com. Website: http://medicalbookstore.com. **Acquisitions:** Kathryn Swanson, managing editor. Publishes hardcover originals, trade paperback originals and reprints. **Publishes 8-10 titles/year. Receives 100 queries and 50 mss/year. 10% of books from first-time authors; 90% from unagented writers. Pays 10-15% royalty on net receipts. Offers $1,500-5,000 average advance.** Publishes books 18 months after acceptance of ms. Reports in 6 months. Book catalog and ms guidelines for #10 SASE.

> O→ Health Information Press publishes books for consumers who are interested in taking an active role in their health care.

**Nonfiction:** How-to, illustrated book, reference, self-help. Subjects include health/medicine, psychology, science. "We seek to simplify health and medicine for consumers." Submit proposal package, including outline, 3-5 sample chapters, curriculum vitae or résumé and letter detailing who would buy the book and the market/need for the book. Reviews artwork/photos as part of the ms package.

**Recent Title(s):** *Questions & Answers on AIDS*, by Lyn Frumkin, M.D.

**HEALTH PRESS**, P.O. Box 1388, Santa Fe NM 87504. (505)982-9373. Fax: (505)983-1733. E-mail: hthprs@trail.com. Website: http://www.healthpress.com. **Acquisitions:** Corie Conwell, editor. Estab. 1988. Publishes hardcover and trade paperback originals. **Publishes 4 titles/year. 90% of books from first-time authors; 90% from unagented writers. Pays standard royalty on wholesale price.** Publishes book 1 year after acceptance of ms. Accepts simultaneous submissions. Reports in 2 months on proposals. Book catalog free.

> O→ Health Press publishes books by health care professionals on cutting-edge patient education topics.

**Nonfiction:** Subjects include health/medicine, patient education. Submit proposal package, including résumé, outline and 3 complete chapters. Reviews artwork/photos as part of ms package. Send photocopies.

**Recent Title(s):** *Blueberry Eyes*, by Monica Dorscoll Beatty, illustration by Peg Michel (children's book concerning eye treatment).

**HEALTHWISE PUBLICATIONS**, Piccadilly Books, P.O. Box 25203, Colorado Springs CO 80936-5203. (719)550-9887. Publisher: Bruce Fife. **Acquisitions**: Submissions Department. Publishes hardcover and trade paperback originals and trade paperback reprints. **Pays 15-10% royalty on retail price.** Publishes book 1 year after acceptance of ms. Accepts simultaneous submissions.

> O→ Healthwise specializes in the publication of books on health and fitness written with a holistic or natural health viewpoint.

**Nonfiction:** Diet, nutrition, exercise, alternative medicine and related topics. Query with sample chapters. Reports only if interested.

**Recent Title(s):** *Panic Free: Eliminate Anxiety/Panic Attacks Without Drugs*, by Lynne Freeman, Ph.D. (health/psychology).

**WILLIAM S. HEIN & CO., INC.**, (formerly Fred B. Rothman & Co.), 1285 Main St., Buffalo NY 14209-1987. (716)882-2600. Fax: (716)883-8100. E-mail: wsheinco@class.org. **Acquisitions:** Attn: Editorial Manager. Estab. 1961. **Publishes 20 titles/year. Receives 60 queries and 20 mss/year. 20% of books from first-time authors; 100% from unagented writers. Pays 10-25% royalty on net price.** Publishes book 9 months after acceptance of ms. Accepts simultaneous submissions. Does not return submissions. Reports in 3 months. Book catalog free.

> O→ William S. Hein & Co. publishes reference books for law librarians, legal researchers and those interested in legal writing.

**Nonfiction:** Reference. Subjects include law and librarianship. Submit proposal package, including outline, 3 sample chapters and intended audience.

**Recent Title(s):** *Courts Counselors & Correspondents: A Media Relations Analysis of the Legal System*, by Richard Stack (public relations/law).

**HEINEMANN**, Reed Elsevier (USA) Inc., 361 Hanover St., Portsmouth NH 03801. Fax: (603)431-7840. Website: http://www.heinemann.com. **Acquisitions:** Leigh Peake, executive editor (education); Lisa Barnett, senior editor (performing arts); William Varner, acquisitions editor (literacy); Lisa Luedeke, acquisitions editor (Boynton/Cook). Estab. 1977. Publishes hardcover and trade paperback originals. **Publishes 80-100 titles/year. 50% of books from first-time authors; 75% from unagented writers. Pays royalty on wholesale price. Advance varies widely.** Publishes book 9 months after acceptance of ms. Accepts simultaneous submissions. Reports in 3 months on proposals. Book catalog free. Manuscript guidelines for #10 SASE.

O→ Heinemann specializes in theater and education titles. "Our goal is to offer a wide selecton of books that satisfy the needs and interests of educators from kindergarten to college." Currently emphasizing literacy education, K-12 education through technology.

**Imprint(s):** Boynton/Cook Publishers, Beeline Books.

**Nonfiction:** How-to, reference. Subjects include parenting as it relates to school education, education, gay/lesbian issues, language arts, women's issues/studies, drama. "Our goal is to provide books that represent leading ideas within our niche markets. We publish very strictly within our categories. We do not publish classroom textbooks." Query. Submit proposal package, including table of contents, outline, 1-2 sample chapters.

**Recent Title(s):** *Word Matters*, by Irene Fountas and Gay-sa Pirrell.

**Tips:** "Keep your queries (and manuscripts!) short, study the market, be realistic and prepared to promote your book!"

**HELIX BOOKS**, Perseus Books Group, One Jacob Way, Reading MA 01867 (781)944-3700, ext. 2853. Fax: (781)944-8243. Website: http://www.aw.com. **Acquisitions**: Jeffrey Robbins, executive editor (physics, astronomy, complexity); Amanda Cook, editor (biology, evolution, complexity). Estab. 1992. Publishes hardcover and trade paperback originals and reprints. **Publishes 30 titles/year. Receives 160 queries/year. 50% of books from first-time authors; 60% from unagented writers. Pays 7½-15% royalty on retail price "sliding scale based on number of copies sold." Offers $5,000 and up advance.** Publishes book 6 months after acceptance of ms. Accepts simultaneous submissions but prefers exclusive. Reports in 1 month on queries. Book catalog free.

O→ "Helix Books presents the world's top scientists and science writers sharing with the general public the latest discoveries and their human implications, across the full range of scientific disciplines." Currently emphasizing physics/astronomy, biology, evolution, complexity. De-emphasizing earth sciences, philosophy of science, neuroscience.

**Nonfiction:** Science. Query or submit outline, 2 sample chapters and proposal package, including market analysis, competition analysis, audience description, chapter outlines/table of contents, why topic is hot, why author is the one to write this book, 25-word synopsis that explains why the proposed book will be the best ever written about this topic.

**Recent Title(s):** *The Memory of It All*, by Richard P. Kynmen.

**HELLGATE PRESS**, PSI Research, 300 N. Valley Dr., Grants Pass OR 97526. (503)479-9464. Fax: (503)476-1479. Website: http://www.psi-research.com/hellgate.htm. **Acquisitions:** Emmett Ramey, president. Estab. 1996. **Publishes 20-25 titles/year. Pays royalty.** Publishes books 6 months after acceptance of ms. Accepts simultaneous submissions. Reports in 2 months on queries. Book catalog and ms guidelines for #10 SASE.

O→ Hellgate Press specializes in military history, other military topics and travel.

**Nonfiction:** Subjects include history, military/war, travel. Query with outline, sample chapter and SASE. Reviews artwork/photos as part of the ms package. Send photocopies.

**Recent Title(s):** *Pilots, Man Your Planes!*, by Wilbur Morrison.

**HENDRICK-LONG PUBLISHING CO., INC.**, P.O. Box 25123, Dallas TX 75225-1123. (214)358-4677. Fax: (214)352-4768. E-mail: hendrick-long@worldnet.att.net. **Acquisitions:** Joann Long. Estab. 1969. Publishes hardcover and trade paperback originals and hardcover reprints. **Publishes 8 titles/year. Receives 500 submissions/year. 90% of books from unagented writers. Pays royalty on selling price.** Publishes book 18 months after acceptance. Reports in 1 month on queries, 2 months if more than query sent. Book catalog for 8½×11 or 9×12 SAE with 4 first-class stamps. Manuscript guidelines for #10 SASE.

O→ Hendrick-Long publishes historical fiction and nonfiction primarily about Texas and the Southwest for children and young adults.

**Nonfiction:** Biography, history. Texas and Southwest-focused material for children and young adults. Query or submit outline and 2 sample chapters. Reviews artwork/photos as part of ms package; send photocopies, no original art.

**Fiction:** Texas and the Southwest-focused material for kindergarten through young adult. Query or submit outline/synopsis and 2 sample chapters.

**Recent Title(s):** *Lone Star Justice: Supreme Court Justice Tom C. Clark*, by Evan Young (young adult); *Terror from the Gulf: A Hurricane in Galveston*, by Martha T. Jones.

**HENDRICKSON PUBLISHERS, INC.**, 140 Summit St., P.O. Box 3473, Peabody MA 01961-3473. Fax: (978)531-8146. E-mail: DPenwell@hendrickson.com or PAlexander@hendrickson.com. **Acquisitions:** Dan Penwell, manager of trade products; Patrick Alexander, editorial director (academic). Estab. 1983. Publishes hardcover and trade paperback originals and reprints. **Publishes 35 titles/year. Receives 200 submissions/year. 10% of books from first-time authors; 100% from unagented writers.** Publishes book an average of 1 year after acceptance of ms. Accepts simultaneous submissions (if so notified). Reports in 2 months. Book catalog and ms guidelines for SASE.

O→ Hendrickson publishes "books that give insight into Bible understanding (academically) and encourage spiritual

growth (popular trade)." Currently emphasizing Bible reference. De-emphasizing fiction.
**Nonfiction:** Religious subjects. "We will consider any quality manuscript specifically related to biblical studies and related fields. Also, nonfiction books in a more popular vein that give a hunger to studying, understanding and applying Scripture; books that encourage spiritual growth, such as personal devotionals." Submit outline and sample chapters.
**Recent Title(s):** *Dictionary of Early Christian Beliefs*, edited by David Bercot.

**HENSLEY PUBLISHING**, (formerly Virgil Hensley), 6116 E. 32nd St., Tulsa OK 74135-5494. (918)664-8520. Website: http://www.hensleypublishing.com. **Acquisitions:** Terri Kalfas, editor. Estab. 1965. Publishes hardcover and paperback originals. **Publishes 5-10 titles/year. Receives 800 submissions/year. 50% of books from first-time authors; 50% from unagented writers. Pays 5% minimum royalty on gross sales or makes outright purchase of $250 minimum for study aids.** Publishes ms 18 months after acceptance of ms. Reports in 2 months on queries. Manuscript guidelines for #10 SASE.
    O━ Hendrickson publishes Bible-centered books, devotionals and curriculum that offer the reader a wide range of topics. Currently emphasizing shorter studies.
**Nonfiction:** Bible study curriculum. Subjects include child guidance/parenting, money/finance, men's and women's Christian education, prayer, prophecy, Christian living, large and small group studies, discipleship, adult development, parenting, personal growth, pastoral aids, church growth, family. "We do not want to see anything non-Christian." No New Age, poetry, plays, sermon collections. Query with synopsis and sample chapters.
**Recent Title(s):** *Men in the Bible: Examples to Live By*, by Don Charles (Bible study).
**Tips:** "Submit something that crosses denominational lines directed toward the large Christian market, not small specialized groups. We serve an interdenominational market—all Christian persuasions. Our goal is to get readers back into studying their Bible instead of studying about the Bible."

**HERITAGE BOOKS, INC.**, 1540-E Pointer Ridge Place, Bowie MD 20716-1859. (301)390-7708. Fax: (301)390-7193. **Acquisitions:** Karen Ackerman, editorial supervisor. Estab. 1978. Publishes hardcover and paperback originals and reprints. **Publishes 100 titles/year. Receives 300 submissions/year. 25% of books from first-time authors; 100% from unagented writers. Pays 10% royalty on list price.** Accepts simultaneous submissions. Reports in 1 month. *Writer's Market* recommends allowing 2 months for reply. Book catalog for SAE.
    O━ "We particularly desire to publish nonfiction titles dealing with history and genealogy."
**Nonfiction:** History and genealogy including how-to and reference works, as well as conventional histories and genealogies. "Ancestries of contemporary people are not of interest. The titles should be either of general interest or restricted to Eastern U.S. and Midwest, United Kingdom, Germany. Material dealing with the present century is usually not of interest." Query or submit outline with SASE. Reviews artwork/photos.
**Tips:** "The quality of the book is of prime importance; next is its relevance to our fields of interest."

**HEYDAY BOOKS**, Box 9145, Berkeley CA 94709-9145. Fax: (510)549-1889. E-mail: heyday@heydaybooks.com. **Acquisitions:** Malcolm Margolin, publisher. Estab. 1974. Publishes hardcover originals, trade paperback originals and reprints. **Publishes 8-10 titles/year. Receives 200 submissions/year. 50% of books from first-time authors; 90% of books from unagented writers. Pays 8-10% royalty on net price.** Publishes book 8 months after acceptance of ms. Reports in 1 week on queries, 5 weeks on mss. *Writer's Market* recommends allowing 2 months for reply. Book catalog for 7×9 SAE with 3 first-class stamps.
    O━ Heyday Books publishes nonfiction books with a strong California focus. "We publish books about native Americans, natural history, history, and recreation, with a strong California focus."
**Nonfiction:** Books about California only. Subjects include Americana, history, nature, travel. Query with outline and synopsis. Reviews artwork/photos.
**Recent Title(s):** *Gold Rush: A Literary Exploration*, edited by Michael Kowalewski (anthology).
**Tips:** "Give good value, and avoid gimmicks."

**[N] HI WILLOW RESEARCH & PUBLISHING**, P.O. Box 720400, San Jose CA 95172-0400. (831)660-0589. Fax: (831)634-1456. E-mail: david@lmcsource.com. Website: http://www.LMC.source.com. Estab. 1978. Publishes trade paperback originals. **Publishes 5 titles/year. Receives 10 queries and 10 mss/year. 50% of books from first-time authors; 100% from unagented writers. Pays 10-15% royalty on net. No advance.** Publishes book 3 months after acceptance of ms. Accepts simultaneous submissions. Reports in 1 month on queries. Book catalog and ms guidelines free.
**Nonfiction:** Library, information science. Submit outline and 1 sample chapter. Reviews artwork/photos as part of ms package. Send photocopies.
**Recent Title(s):** *Reinvent Your School's Library in the Age of Technology*.

**HIGH PLAINS PRESS**, P.O. Box 123, 539 Cassa Rd., Glendo WY 82213. Fax: (307)735-4590. **Acquisitions:** Nancy Curtis, publisher. Estab. 1986. Publishes hardcover and trade paperback originals. **Publishes 4 titles/year. Receives 300 queries and 200 mss/year. 80% of books from first-time authors; 95% from unagented writers. Pays 10% royalty on wholesale price. Offers $100-600 advance.** Publishes book 2 years after acceptance of ms. Accepts simultaneous submissions. Reports in 1 month on queries and proposals, 3 months on mss. Book catalog and ms guidelines for 8½×10 SASE.

○─ "What we sell best is history of the Old West, particularly things relating to Wyoming. We also publish one book of poetry a year in our Poetry of the American West series."

**Nonfiction:** Biography, Western Americana, Americana, art/architecture, history, nature/environment, regional. "We focus on books of the American West, mainly history." Submit outline. Reviews artwork/photos as part of ms package. Send photocopies.

**Poetry:** "We only seek poetry closely tied to the Rockies. Do not submit single poems." Query with complete ms.

**Recent Title(s):** *Wind River Adventure*, by Edward J. Farlow (nonfiction); *Close at Hand*, by Mary Lou Sanelli (poetry).

**HIGHSMITH PRESS**, P.O. Box 800, Fort Atkinson WI 53538-0800. (920)563-9571. Fax: (920)563-4801. E-mail: hpress@highsmith.com. Website: http://www.hpress.highsmith.com. **Acquisitions:** Donald J. Sager, publisher. Estab. 1990. Publishes hardcover and paperback originals. **Publishes 20 titles/year. Receives 500-600 queries and 400-500 mss/year. 30% of books from first-time authors; 100% from unagented writers. Pays 10-12% royalty on net sales price. Offers $250-1,000 advance.** Publishes book 6 months after acceptance of ms. Accepts simultaneous submissions. Reports in 1 month on queries, 2 months on proposals, 3 months on mss. Book catalog and ms guidelines free.

○─ Highsmith Press publishes educational, professional, and informational resources to meet the practical needs of librarians, educators, readers, library users, colleges, media specialists, schools and related institutions, and to help them fulfill their valuable functions.

**Imprint(s):** Alleyside Press, Upstart Books (creative supplemental reading, library and critical thinking skills materials designed to expand the learning environment).

**Nonfiction:** Reference, professional. Subjects include education, language/literature, multicultural, professional (library science), teacher activity. "We are primarily interested in reference and library professional books, library and study skills, curricular and activity books for teachers and others who work with preschool through high school youth." Query with outline and 1-2 sample chapters. Reviews artwork/photos as part of ms package. Send transparencies.

**Fiction:** No longer accepting children's picture book mss. "Our current emphasis is on storytelling collections for preschool-grade 6. We prefer stories that can be easily used by teachers and children's librarians, multicultural topics, and manuscripts that feature fold and cut, flannelboard, tangram, or similar simple patterns that can be reproduced."

**Recent Title(s):** *How to Get a Job If You're a Teenager*, by Cindy Pervola and Debby Hobgood; *Great Asian Stories*, by Cathy Spagnoli (fiction).

**HILL AND WANG**, Farrar Straus & Giroux, Inc., 19 Union Square W., New York NY 10003. (212)741-6900. Fax: (212)633-9385. **Acquisitions:** Elisabeth Sifton, publisher; Lauren Osborne, senior editor. Estab. 1956. Publishes hardcover and trade paperback originals. **Publishes 12 titles/year. Receives 1,500 queries/year. 5% of books from first-time authors; 50% from unagented writers. Pays 7½% royalty on retail price. Advances "vary widely from a few hundred to several thousand dollars."** Publishes book 1 year after acceptance of ms. Accepts simultaneous submissions. Reports in 2 months. Book catalog free.

○─ Hill and Wang publishes serious nonfiction books, primarily in history and the social sciences.

**Nonfiction:** Cross-over academic and trade books. Subjects include government/politics, history (primarily American, some European and African history), public policy, sociology, women's issues, some drama. Submit outline, sample chapters, letter explaining rationale for book and SASE. Reviews artwork/photos as part of ms package. Send samples.

**Fiction:** *Not* considering new fiction.

**Recent Title(s):** *Modern Media: A Family Story of Slavery and Child-Murder from the Old South*, by Steven Weisenburger.

**HIPPOCRENE BOOKS INC.**, 171 Madison Ave., New York NY 10016. (212)685-4371. Fax: (212)779-9338. E-mail: hippocre@ix.netcom.com. Website: http://www.hippocrenebooks.com. President/Publisher: George Blagowidow. **Acquisitions:** Carol Chitnis, managing editor (cooking, classic poetry, travel, Polish interest); Nadia Hassani, associate editor (foreign language dictionaries, leaning guides); Kara Migliorelli, associate editor (illustrated histories, weddings, proverbs). Estab. 1971. Publishes hardcover and trade paperback originals. **Publishes 100 titles/year. Receives 250 submissions/year. 10% of books from first-time authors; 95% from unagented writers. Pays 6-10% royalty on retail price. Offers $2,000 advance.** Publishes book 16 months after acceptance of ms. Accepts simultaneous submissions. Reports in 2 months. Book catalog for 9 × 12 SAE with 5 first-class stamps. Manuscript guidelines for #10 SASE.

○─ Hippocrene publishes reference books of international interest, often bilingual, in the fields of cookery, travel, language and literature. It specializes in foreign language dictionaries and learning guides and also publishes ethnic cuisine cookbooks, travel and history titles. Currently emphasizing cookery, history and foreign language. De-emphasizing military history and travel.

**Nonfiction:** Reference. Subjects include foreign language, Judaic reference, ethnic and special interest travel, military history, bilingual love poetry, bilingual proverbs, international cookbooks, Polish interest, foreign language, dictionaries and instruction. Submit proposal including outline, 2 sample chapters, toc.

---

**ALWAYS ENCLOSE** a self-addressed, stamped envelope (SASE) with all your queries and correspondence.

**Recent Title(s):** *Wedded Strangers: The Challenges of Russian-American Marriages*, by Lynn Visson (nonfiction); *Classic American Love Poems* (poetry).
**Tips:** "Our recent successes in publishing general books considered midlist by larger publishers is making us more of a general trade publisher. We continue to do well with reference books like dictionaries, atlases and language studies. We ask for proposal, sample chapter, and table of contents. We then ask for material if we are interested."

**HI-TIME PUBLISHING**, N90 W16890 Roosevelt Dr., Menomonee Falls WI 53051-7933. (414)502-4222. Fax: (414)502-4224. Senior Editor: Lorraine M. Kukulski. **Publishes 6 titles/year. Receives 20 queries, 10 mss/year. Payment method may be outright purchase, royalty or down payment plus royalty.** Book catalog and ms guidelines free.
**Nonfiction:** Textbook, religion. "We publish religious education material for Catholic junior high through adult programs. Most of our material is contracted in advance and written by persons with theology or religious education backgrounds." Query with SASE.
**Recent Title(s):** *The Way of the Cross for Teenagers.*

**HOHM PRESS**, P.O. Box 2501, Prescott AZ 86302. Fax: (520)717-1779. E-mail: pinedr@goodnet.com. **Acquisitions:** Regina Sara Ryan, managing editor. Estab. 1975. Publishes hardcover and trade paperback originals. **Publishes 6-8 titles/year. 50% of books from first-time authors. Pays 10-15% royalty on net sales. No advance.** Publishes book 18 months after acceptance of ms. Accepts simultaneous submissions. Reports in 3 months on queries. Book catalog for $1.50.
  O-π Hohm Press publishes a range of titles in the areas of psychology and spirituality, herbistry, alternative health methods and nutrition. Currently emphasizing health alternatives.
**Nonfiction:** Self-help. Subjects include alternative health/medicine, philosophy, religious (Hindu, Buddhist, Sufi or translations of classic texts in major religious traditions). "We look for writers who have an established record in their field of expertise. The best buy of recent years came from two women who fully substantiated how they could market their book. We believed they could do it. We were right." Query with SASE.
**Poetry:** "We are not accepting poetry at this time except for translations of recognized religious/spiritual classics." Query.
**Recent Title(s):** *The Yoga Tradition*, by Georg Feuerstein (nonfiction); *For Love of the Dark One: Songs of Mirabai*, by Andrew Schelling (poems).

**ℕ. HOLIDAY HOUSE INC.**, 425 Madison Ave., New York NY 10017. (212)688-0085. Fax: (212)421-6134. Editor-in-Chief: Regina Griffin. **Acquisitions:** Lisa Hopp, associate editor. Estab. 1935. Publishes hardcover originals. **Publishes 50 titles/year. Receives 3,000 submissions/year. 2-5% of books from first-time authors; 50% from unagented writers. Pays royalty on list price, range varies. Offers $2,000-10,000 advance.** Publishes book 1-2 years after acceptance of ms. Query. Manuscripts not returned without SASE. Manuscript guidelines for #10 SASE.
  O-π Holiday House publishes children's and young adult books for the school and library markets. "We have a commitment to publishing first-time authors and illustrators. We specialize in quality hardcovers from picture books to young adult, both fiction and nonfiction, primarily for the school and library market." Currently emphasizing literary middle-grade novels.
**Nonfiction:** American history, biography, natural history, science. Submit query only with SASE. Reviews artwork/photos as part of ms package. Send photocopies only—no originals—to Claire Counihan, art director.
**Fiction:** Adventure, ethnic, historical, humor, juvenile, picture books, easy readers. Query first with SASE.
**Recent Title(s):** *Young Black & Determined: A Biography of Lornide Hershey*, by Pat and Fred McKissack (nonfiction); *I Was a Third Grade Science Project*, by M.J. Auch (fiction).
**Tips:** "We are not geared toward the mass market, but toward school and library markets. We need picturebook texts with strong stories and writing. We do not publish board books or novelties."

**HOLLIS PUBLISHING COMPANY**, Puritan Press, Inc., 95 Runnells Bridge Rd., Hollis NH 03049. (603)889-4500. Fax: (603)889-6551. E-mail: books@hollispublishing.com. Website: http://www.hollispublishing.com. **Acquisitions:** Rebecca Shannon, editor. Publishes hardcover and trade paperback originals. **Publishes 5 titles/year. Receives 25 queries and 15 mss/year. 50% of books from first-time authors; 100% from unagented writers. Pays 5-10% royalty on retail price.** Publishes book within 6 months of acceptance of ms. Reports in 1 month on queries and proposals, 2 months on mss. Book catalog free. Manuscript guidelines for #10 SASE.
  O-π Hollis publishes books on social policy, US government and politics, current events and recent events, intended for use by professors and their students, college and university libraries and the general reader. Currently emphasizing works about education, the Internet, government, history-in-the-making, social values and politics.
**Nonfiction:** Biography, scholarly. Subjects include Americana, anthropology/archaeology, education, ethnic, government/politics, history, memoirs, nature/environment, regional, sociology, travel. Query with outline and 2 sample chapters with SASE.
**Recent Title(s):** *democracy.com? Visions of Governance in a Networked World*, edited by Elaine Ciulla Kamarck and Joseph S. Nye, Jr.

**HOLMES PUBLISHING GROUP**, P.O. Box 623, Edmonds WA 98020. E-mail: jdh@jdholmes.com. CEO: J.D. Holmes. **Acquisitions:** L.Y. Fitzgerald. Estab. 1983. Publishes hardcover and trade paperback originals and reprints.

Publishes 40 titles/year. Receives 120 queries and 80 mss/year. 20% of books from first-time authors; 20% from unagented writers. Pays 10% royalty on net revenue. Publishes book 4 months after acceptance of ms. Reports in 2 months.

   0—¬ Holmes publishes informative spiritual titles on philosophy, metaphysical and religious subjects, and alternative medicine and health.

**Imprint(s):** Alchemical Press, Alexandrian Press, Contra/Thought, Sure Fire Press.

**Nonfiction:** Self-help. Subjects include health/medicine, occult, philosophy, religion, metaphysical. "We do not publish titles that are more inspirational than informative." Query only with SASE.

   ● Holmes Publishing Group no longer publishes fiction.

**Recent Title(s):** *Soul of Your Pet*, by Scott S. Smith.

**HENRY HOLT & COMPANY BOOKS FOR YOUNG READERS**, Henry Holt & Co., Inc., 115 W. 18th St., New York NY 10011. (212)886-9200. Associate Publisher: Laura Godwin (picture books, chapter books and middle grade). Senior Editor: Marc Aronson (young adult). Senior Editor: Christy Ottaviano (picture books, chapter books and middle grade). Associate Editor: Margaret Garrou. **Acquisitions:** BYR Submissions. Estab. 1866 (Holt). Publishes hardcover originals. **Publishes 70-80 titles/year. 5% of books from first-time authors; 50% from unagented writers. Pays royalty on retail price. Offers $3,000 and up advance.** Publishes book 18 months after acceptance of ms. Reports in 5 months on queries and mss. Book catalog and ms guidelines free with SASE.

   0—¬ "Henry Holt Books for Young Readers publishes highly original and cutting-edge fiction and nonfiction for all ages, from the very young to the young adult."

**Imprint(s):** Books by Michael Hague; Books by Bill Martin Jr. and John Archimbault; Edge Books (cutting-edge young adult books); Owlet Paperbacks; Redfeather Books (chapter books for ages 7-10), W-5 Reference.

**Nonfiction:** Children's/juvenile, illustrated book. Query with SASE.

**Fiction:** Juvenile: adventure, animal, contemporary, fantasy, history, humor, multicultural, religion, sports, suspense/mystery. Picture books: animal, concept, history, humor, multicultural, religion, sports. Young adult: contemporary, fantasy, history, multicultural, nature/environment, problem novels, sports. Query with SASE.

**Recent Title(s):** *Robber and Me*, by Josef Holub (juvenile fiction).

**HENRY HOLT & COMPANY, INC.**, 115 W. 18th St., New York NY 10011. (212)886-9200. President: John Sterling. **Acquisitions:** Sara Bershtel, editorial director of Metropolitan Books (literary fiction, politics, history); Elizabeth Stein, adult trade editor; Elizabeth Crossman, editor (cooking); David Sobel, senior editor (science, culture, history, health); (Mr.) Tracy Brown, executive editor (adult literary fiction, culture, popular music, biography); Amelia Sheldon, editor, Owl Books (lifestyle, health, self help, women's studies). Query before submitting.

   0—¬ Holt is a general interest publisher of quality fiction and nonfiction.

**Imprint(s):** John Macrae Books, Metropolitan Books, **Owl Books, Henry Holt & Company Books for Young Readers** (Books by Michael Hague, Books by Bill Martin Jr. and John Archambault, Owlet Paperbacks, Redfeather Books, W5 Reference).

**Recent Title(s):** *When Things Start to Think*, by Neil Gershenfeld; *The Giant, O'Brien*, by Hilary Mankel.

**HOLY CROSS ORTHODOX PRESS**, Hellenic College, 50 Goddard Ave., Brookline MA 02445. Fax: (617)850-1460. **Acquisitions:** Anton C. Vrame, Ph.D., managing editor. Estab. 1974. Publishes trade paperback originals. **Publishes 8 titles/year. Imprint publishes 2 titles/year.** Receives 10-15 queries and 10-15 mss/year. 85% of books from first-time authors; 100% from unagented writers. Pays 8-12% royalty on retail price. Publishes book 18 months after acceptance of ms. Accepts simultaneous submissions. Reports in 6 months on mss. Book catalog free.

   0—¬ Holy Cross publishes titles that are rooted in the tradition of the Eastern Orthodox Church.

**Imprint(s):** Hellenic College Press.

**Nonfiction:** Academic. Subjects include ethnic, religion (Greek Orthodox). "Holy Cross Orthodox Press publishes scholarly and popular literature in the areas of Orthodox Christian theology and Greek letters. Submissions are often far too technical usually with a very limited audiences." Submit outline and complete ms. Reviews artwork/photos as part of the manuscript package. Send photocopies.

**Recent Title(s):** *Christianity: Lineaments of a Sacred Tradition*, by Philip Sherrard.

**N** **HOME PLANNERS, LLC**, 3275 West Ina Rd., #110, Tucson AZ 85741. (520)297-8200. Fax: (520)297-6219. E-mail: paulette@torchlake.com. Website: http://www.homeplanners.com. **Acquisitions:** Paulette Mulvin, special projects and acquisitions editor. Estab. 1946. Publishes hardcover and trade paperback originals. **Publishes 12-15 titles/year. Receives 8-10 queries and 2-3 mss/year. 80% of books from first-time authors; 100% from unagented writers. Pays outright purchase of $5,000-18,000. No advance.** Publishes book 6 months after acceptance of ms. Accepts simultaneous submissions. Reports in 2 months on queries, 4 months on proposals, 6 months on mss. Book catalog free.

   0—¬ Home Planners publishes home plan, landscape, interior design books and magazines and construction plans. "We are primarily interested in how-to or reference titles. We may consider personal experience or technical stories but only if unusual and exceptionally well done."

**Nonfiction:** How-to, reference. Subjects include art/architecture, gardening, homebuilding/home improvement/remodeling. Query with SASE. Submit proposal package, including outline and 1 sample chapter. Reviews artwork/photos as part of ms package. Send photocopies.

**Recent Titles:** *Beds & Borders,* by Susan A. Roth (how-to/reference).

**Tips:** "Have some experience in architecture, building or remodeling. Previous publishing or magazine writing in the field preferred."

**HONOR BOOKS,** P.O. Box 55388, Tulsa OK 74155. (918)496-9007. **Acquisitions:** Catherine Dodd, acquisitions secretary. Publishes hardcover and trade paperback originals. **Publishes 60 titles/year. Receives 1,000 queries and 500 mss/year. 2% of books from first-time authors. 70% of books from unagented writers. Pays royalty on wholesale price, makes outright purchase or assigns work for hire. Advance negotiable.** Publishes book 2 years after acceptance of ms. Accepts simultaneous submissions. Reports in 1 month on queries, 3 months on proposals. Ms guidelines for #10 SASE.

○━ "We are a Christian publishing house with a mission to inspire and encourage people to draw near to God and to enjoy His love and grace."

**Nonfiction:** Devotionals, motivation, seasonal/holiday gift books, "portable" inspiration. Subjects are geared toward the "felt needs" of people. No autobiographies or teaching books. Query with outline, writing sample and proposal package, including table of contents, synopsis and author bio, SASE. Reviews artwork/photos as part of the ms package. Send photocopies.

**Recent Title(s):** *Breakfast for the Soul.*

**Tips:** "Our books are for busy, achievement-oriented people who are looking for a balance between reaching their goals and knowing that God loves them unconditionally. Our books should challenge spiritual growth, victorious living and an intimate knowledge of God. Write about what you are for and not what you are against. We look for scripts that are biblically correct and which edify the reader."

**HOUGHTON MIFFLIN BOOKS FOR CHILDREN,** Houghton Mifflin Company, 222 Berkeley St., Boston MA 02116. (617)351-5959. Fax: (617)351-1111. Website: http://www.hmco.com. **Acquisitions:** Amanda Sullivan, submissions coordinator. Publishes hardcover and trade paperback originals and reprints. **Firm publishes 100 titles/year. Receives 5,000 queries and 12,000 mss/year. 10% of books from first-time authors; 70% from unagented writers. Pays 5-10% royalty on retail price. Advance dependent on many factors.** Publishes book 18 months after acceptance of ms. Accepts simultaneous submissions. Reports in 4 months. Book catalog for 9×12 SASE with 3 first-class stamps. Manuscript guidelines for #10 SASE.

○━ "Houghton Mifflin gives shape to ideas that educate, inform, and above all, delight."

**Imprint(s):** Sandpiper Paperback Books (Eden Edwards, editor).

**Nonfiction:** Biography, children's/juvenile, humor, illustrated book. Subjects include agriculture/horticulture, Americana, animals, anthropology, art/architecture, ethnic, gardening, history, language/literature, music/dance, nature/environment, recreation, regional, science, sports, travel. Interested in "innovative science books, especially about scientists 'in the field' and what they do." Submit outline and 2 sample chapters with SASE. Mss not returned without appropriate-sized SASE. Reviews artwork/photos as part of ms package. Send photocopies.

**Fiction:** Adventure, ethnic, historical, humor, juvenile (early readers), literary, mystery, picture books, suspense, young adult, board books. Submit full ms with appropriate-sized SASE.

**Recent Title(s):** *Hamburger Heaven,* by Yei; *Snake Scientist,* by Montgomery.

**Tips:** "Faxed or e-mailed manuscripts and proposals are not considered."

**HOUGHTON MIFFLIN COMPANY,** 222 Berkeley St., Boston MA 02116. (617)351-5000. Fax: (617)351-1202. Website: http://www.hmco.com. Vice President: Arthur S. Battle Jr. Senior Editor: Anton Mueller. Executive Editor: Janet Silver. **Acquisitions:** Submissions Editor. Estab. 1832. Publishes hardcover and trade paperback originals and reprints. **Publishes 60 hardcovers, 30-40 paperbacks/year. 10% of books from first-time authors; 20% from unagented writers. Hardcover: pays 10-15% royalty on retail price, sliding scale or flat rate based on sales; paperback: 7½% flat fee, but negotiable. Advance varies.** Publishes book 1-2 years after acceptance of ms. Accepts simultaneous submissions. Reports in 3 months. Book catalog and ms guidelines free.

○━ "Houghton Mifflin gives shape to ideas that educate, inform and delight. In a new era of publishing, our legacy of quality thrives as we combine imagination with technology, bringing you new ways to know."

**Imprint(s):** Chapters Publishing Ltd., Clarion Books, Peter Davison Books, Walter Lorraine Books, **Houghton Mifflin Books for Children**, Mariner Paperbacks, Sandpiper Paperbacks, Frances Tenenbaum Books.

**Nonfiction** Biography, childrens/juvenile, language/literature, military/war, money/finance, music/dance, nature/environment, philosophy, photography, psychology, recreation, regional, religion, science, sociology, sports, travel, women's issues/studies. "We are not a mass market publisher. Our main focus is serious nonfiction. We do practical self-help but not pop psychology self-help." Query with outline, 1 sample chapter and SASE. Reviews artwork/photos as part of ms package. Send photocopies.

**Fiction:** Adventure, confession, ethnic, fantasy, feminist, gay/lesbian, historical, humor, literary, mainstream/contemporary, mystery, short story collections, suspense. "We are not a mass market publisher. Study the current list." Query with 3 sample chapters or complete mss and SASE.

**Poetry:** "At this point we have an established roster of poets we use. It is hard for first-time poets to get published by Houghton Mifflin."

**Recent Title(s):** *Bogart: A Life in Hollywood,* by Jeffrey Meyers; *American Pastoral,* by Philip Roth.

**HOUSE OF COLLECTIBLES**, Ballantine Publishing Group, Random House, Inc., 201 E. 50th St., New York NY 10022. Website: http://www.randomhouse.com. **Acquisitions:** Laura Paczosa, editor. Publishes trade and mass market paperback originals. **Publishes 25-28 titles/year. Receives 200 queries/year. 1% of books from first-time authors; 85% from unagented writers. Pays royalty on retail price, varies. Offers advance against royalties, varies.** Publishes book 6 months after acceptance of ms. Accepts simultaneous submissions, if so noted. Reports in 3 months on queries. Book catalog free from Ballantine.

O→ "One of the premier publishing companies devoted to books on a wide range of antiques and collectibles, House of Collectibles publishes books for the seasoned expert and the beginning collector alike."
**Imprint(s):** Official Price Guide series.
**Nonfiction:** How-to (related to collecting antiques and coins), reference books. Subjects include hobbies, recreation. "We are happy to hear from collectors with a particular expertise. Something may strike us, or be timely. We are expanding beyond price guides." Query or submit outline, 3 sample chapters with SASE.
**Recent Title(s):** *Official Price Guide to Records*, by Jerry Osborne.
**Tips:** " We have been publishing price guides and other books on antiques and collectibles for over 35 years and plan to meet the needs of collectors, dealers and appraisers well into the 21st century."

**HOWELL BOOK HOUSE**, Macmillan General Reference, 1633 Broadway, New York NY 10019. (212)654-8500. **Acquisitions:** Dominique DeVito, editor-in-chief; Don Stevens, associate publisher; Seymour Weiss, executive editor (dogs, birds); Beth Adelman, editor (dogs, cats, birds); Amanda Pisani, editor (dogs, cats, fish, reptiles). Publishes hardcover originals, trade paperback originals and reprints. **Publishes 60-100 titles/year. Receives 3,000 queries/year. 15% of books from first-time authors; 40% from unagented writers. Pays royalty on retail price or net sales, or makes outright purchase or work-for-hire assignments. Offers variable advance.** Publishes book 1 year after acceptance of ms. Accepts simultaneous submissions. Reports in 2 months on queries and mss, 1 month on proposals.

O→ Howell Book House is a publisher of reference books for owners of companion animals: horses, dogs, cats, fish, birds, reptiles, small mammals and exotics. "Our mission is to publish the highest quality and most useful information and reference books on pet and animal subjects." Currently emphasizing dogs.
**Nonfiction:** How-to, reference. Subjects include animals, recreation. Submit outline with 1 sample chapter and proposal package, including table of contents, author's credentials, target audience and market analysis. Reviews artwork/photos as part of ms package. Send photocopies. SASE for returns.
**Recent Title(s):** *The Rottweiler: Centuries of Service*, by Linda Michels and Catherine Thompson.

**HOWELL PRESS, INC.**, 1713-2D Allied Lane, Charlottesville VA 22903. (804)977-4006. Fax: (804)971-7204. E-mail: howellpres@aol.com. Website: http://www.howellpress.com. **Acquisitions:** Ross A. Howell, president. Estab. 1985. **Publishes 10-13 titles/year. Receives 500 submissions/year. 10% of books from first-time authors; 80% from unagented writers. Pays 5-7% royalty on net retail price. "We generally offer an advance, but amount differs with each project and is generally negotiated with authors on a case-by-case basis."** Publishes book 18 months after acceptance of ms. Reports in 2 months. Book catalog for 9×12 SAE with 4 first-class stamps. Manuscript guidelines for #10 SASE.

O→ Howell Press publishes and distributes books in the categories of history, transportation, gardening, cooking and regional (Mid-Atlantic and Southeastern U.S.) interest. Currently emphasizing regional subjects, quilting, Civil War history. De-emphasizing memoirs (military).
**Nonfiction:** Illustrated books, historical texts. Subjects include aviation, military history, cooking, maritime history, motor sports, gardening, transportation, quilting, travel and regional (Mid-Atlantic and Southeastern U.S.). "Generally open to most ideas, as long as writing is accessible to average adult reader. Our line is targeted, so it would be advisable to look over our catalog before querying to better understand what Howell Press does." Query with outline and sample chapters with SASE. Reviews artwork/photos as part of ms package. Does not return mss without SASE.
**Recent Title(s):** *The Burning: Sheridan in the Shenandoah Valley*, by John Heatwole.
**Tips:** "Focus of our program has been illustrated books, but we will also consider nonfiction manuscripts that would not be illustrated."

**HOWELLS HOUSE**, P.O. Box 9546, Washington DC 20016-9546. (202)333-2182. **Acquisitions:** W.D. Howells, publisher. Estab. 1988. Publishes hardcover and trade paperback originals and reprints. **Publishes 4 titles/year; each imprint publishes 2-3 titles/year. Receives 2,000 queries and 300 mss/year. 50% of books from first-time authors; 60% from unagented writers. Pays 15% net royalty or makes outright purchase. May offer advance.** Publishes book 8 months after ms development completed. Reports in 2 months on proposals.

O→ "Our interests are institutions and institutional change."
**Imprint(s):** The Compass Press, Whalesback Books.
**Nonfiction:** Biography, illustrated book, textbook. Subjects include Americana, anthropology/archaeology, art/architecture, business/economics, education, government/politics, history, military/war, photography, science, sociology, translation. Query.
**Fiction:** Historical, literary, mainstream/contemporary. Query.

**N: HUDSON HILLS PRESS, INC.**, 122 E. 25th St., 5th Floor, New York NY 10010-2936. (212)674-6005. Fax: (212)674-6045. **Acquisitions:** Paul Anbinder, president/publisher. Estab. 1978. Publishes hardcover and paperback originals. **Publishes 15 titles/year. Receives 50-100 submissions/year. 15% of books from first-time authors; 90%**

**from unagented writers. Pays 4-6% royalty on retail price. Offers $3,500 average advance.** Publishes book 1 year after acceptance of ms. Accepts simultaneous submissions. Reports in 2 months. Book catalog for 6×9 SAE with 2 first-class stamps.

O→ Hudson Hills Press publishes books about art and photography, including monographs.

**Nonfiction:** Art, photography. Query first, then submit outline and sample chapters. Reviews artwork/photos as part of ms package.

**N: HUMAN KINETICS PUBLISHERS, INC.**, P.O. Box 5076, Champaign IL 61825-5076. (217)351-5076. Fax: (217)351-2674. **Acquisitions:** Ted Miller, director (trade); Loarn Robertson, director (academic); Martin Barnard, trade senior acquisitions editor (fitness, running, golf, tennis, cycling, fishing); Scott Wikgren, academic director (physical education, youth fitness and physical activity, recreation); Mike Bahrke, academic acquisitions editor (exercise physiology, strength and conditioning, health-fitness leadership, personal training, nutrition, supplements); Loarn Robertson, academic acquisitions editor (biomechanics, anatomy, athletic training, cardiac rehab, test/measurement); Judy Wright, academic acquisitions editor (dance, motor, learning/behavior/performance/development, gymnastics, adapted physical education, older adults); Steve Pope, academic acquisitions editor (sport psychology, sport history, sport sociology, sport management, women and sport, recreation and leisure); Dale Lloyd, American fitness alliance director (youth fitness, fitness testing). Publisher: Rainer Martens. Estab. 1974. Publishes hardcover and paperback text and reference books, trade paperback originals, software and audiovisual. **Publishes 120 titles/year. Receives 300 submissions/year. 30% of books from first-time authors; 90% of books from unagented writers. Pays 10-15% royalty on net income.** Publishes book an average of 18 months after acceptance. Accepts simultaneous submissions. Reports in 2 months. Book catalog free.

O→ Human Kinetics publishes books which accurately interpret sport and fitness training and techniques, physical education, sports sciences and sports medicine for coaches, athletes and fitness enthusiasts and professionals in the physical action field.

**Imprint(s):** HK Trade, HK Academic.

**Nonfiction:** How-to, reference, self-help, technical and textbook. Subjects include health, recreation, sports, sport sciences and sports medicine, and physical education. Especially interested in books on fitness; books on all aspects of sports technique or how-to books and coaching books; books which interpret the sport sciences and sports medicine, including sport physiology, sport psychology, sport pedagogy and sport biomechanics. No sport biographies, sport record or statistics books or regional books. Submit outline and sample chapters. Reviews artwork/photos as part of ms package.

**Recent Title(s):** *Running Within*, by Jerry Lynch and Warren Scott.

**HUMANICS PUBLISHING GROUP**, P.O. Box 7400, Atlanta GA 30357. (404)874-2176. Fax: (404)874-1976. E-mail: humanics@mindspring.com. **Acquisitions:** Gary Wilson, editor. Estab. 1976. Publishes trade paperback originals. **Publishes 10 titles/year; imprints: Humanics Trade, 2; Humanics Learning, 10. Receives 5,000 queries/year. 70% of books from first-time authors. Pays 10% royalty on wholesale price. Offers $500-3,000 advance.** Publishes book 1-12 months after acceptance of ms. Accepts simultaneous submissions, if so noted. Responds only if interested. Book catalog free. Manuscript guidelines for #10 SASE.

O→ Humanics Trade publishes "books for the mind, body and spirit." Currently emphasizing management, leadership, self-development.

**Imprint(s):** Humanics Trade, Humanics Learning.

**Nonfiction:** Children's/juvenile, illustrated book, self-help. Subjects include child guidance/parenting, philosophy, spirituality (e.g., taoism), New Age. Query with outline, 1 sample chapter and SASE.

**Recent Title(s):** *The Tao of Design*, by Carl Garant.

**Tips:** "For our activity books, audience is parents and educators looking for books which will enrich their children's lives. For our trade books, audience is anyone interested in positive, healthy self-development. We are looking for quality and creativity. As a small publisher, we don't waste our time or an author's time on books that are not of lasting importance or value. Taoism and Zen high interest."

**HUNGRY MIND PRESS**, 1648 Grand Ave., St. Paul MN 55105. Fax: (651)699-7190. E-mail: hmindpress@aol.com. **Acquisitions:** Pearl Kilbride. Publishes hardcover originals, trade paperback originals and reprints. **Publishes 8-10 titles/year. Receives 200 queries and 300 mss/year. 25% of books from unagented writers. Royalties and advances vary.** Publishes book 10 months after acceptance of ms. Accepts simultaneous submissions. Reports in 2 months on proposals. Book catalog for 6×9 SAE and 2 first-class stamps. Manuscript guidelines for #10 SASE.

O→ Hungry Mind Press publishes adult-level, literary fiction and nonfiction.

**Nonfiction and Fiction:** Literary, adult fiction and nonfiction. No how-to or self-help/instructional mss. Submit proposal package, including letter, outline and at least one sample chapter with SASE.

**Recent Title(s):** *Siberian Dawn*, by Jeffrey Taylor (travel) and *The River Warren*, by Kent Meyers (fiction).

**HUNTER HOUSE**, P.O. Box 2914, Alameda CA 94501. (510)865-5282. Fax: (510)865-4295. Website: http://www.hunterhouse.com. Publisher: Kiran S. Rana. **Acquisitions:** Jeanne Brondino, acquisitions coordinator. Estab. 1978. Publishes hardcover and trade paperback originals and reprints. **Publishes 12 titles/year. Receives 200-300 queries and 100 mss/year. 50% of books from first-time authors; 80% from unagented writers. Pays 12-15% royalty on net receipts, defined as selling price. Offers $250-2,500 advance.** Publishes book 1-2 years after acceptance of final ms. Accepts simultaneous submissions. Reports in 2 months on queries, 3 months on proposals, 6 months on mss. Book catalog and ms guidelines for 8½×11 SAE with 3 first-class stamps.

O→ Hunter House publishes health books (especially women's health), self-help health, sexuality and couple relationships, violence prevention and intervention. Currently de-emphasizing human rights.

**Nonfiction:** Reference, (only health reference); self-help, social issues. "Health books (especially women's health) should focus on emerging health issues or current issues that are inadequately covered and be written for the general population. Family books: Our current focus is sexuality and couple relationships, and alternative lifestyles to high stress. Community topics include violence prevention, violence intervention and human rights. We also publish specialized curricula for counselors and educators in the areas of violence prevention and trauma in children." Query with proposal package, including synopsis, table of contents and chapter outline, sample chapter, target audience information, competition and what distinguishes the book. Send photocopies, proposals generally not returned, requested mss returned with SASE. Reviews artwork/photos as part of ms package.

**Recent Title(s):** *Free Yourself From an Abusive Relationship*, by Andrea Lissette and Richard Kraus.

**Tips:** Audience is concerned people who are looking to educate themselves and their community about real-life issues that affect them. "Please send as much information as possible about *who* your audience is, *how* your book addresses their needs, and *how* you reach that audience in your ongoing work."

**HUNTER PUBLISHING, INC.**, 130 Campus Dr., Edison NJ 08818. Fax: (561)546-8040. E-mail: hunterp@bellsouth.net. Website: http://www.hunterpublishing.com. **Acquisitions:** Kim André, editor; Lissa Dailey. President: Michael Hunter. Estab. 1985. **Publishes 100 titles/year. Receives 300 submissions/year. 10% of books from first-time authors; 75% from unagented writers. Pays royalty. Offers negotiable advance.** Publishes book 5 months after acceptance of ms. Accepts simultaneous submissions. Reports in 3 weeks on queries, 1 month on ms. *Writer's Market* recommends allowing 2 months for reply. Book catalog for #10 SAE with 4 first-class stamps.

O→ Hunter Publishing publishes practical guides for travelers going to the Caribbean, U.S., Europe, South America, and the far reaches of the globe.

**Imprint(s):** Adventure Guides, Romantic Weekends Guides, Alive Guides.

**Nonfiction:** Reference, travel guides. "We need travel guides to areas covered by few competitors: Caribbean Islands, South and Central America, regional U.S. from an active 'adventure' perspective." No personal travel stories or books not directed to travelers. Query or submit outline/synopsis and sample chapters. Reviews artwork/photos as part of ms package.

**Recent Title(s):** *Adventure Guide to Canada's Atlantic Provinces*, by Barbara Radcliffe-Rogers.

**Tips:** "Guides should be destination-specific, rather than theme-based alone. Thus, 'travel with kids' is too broad; 'Florida with Kids' is OK. Make sure the guide doesn't duplicate what other guide publishers do. We need active adventure-oriented guides and more specialized guides for travelers in search of the unusual."

**ICC PUBLISHING, INC.**, International Chamber of Commerce, 156 Fifth Ave., Suite 308, New York NY 10010. (212)206-1150. Fax: (212)633-6025. E-mail: iccpub@interport.net. Website: http://www.iccwbo.org. **Acquisitons:** Rachelle Bijou, director. Estab. 1980. Publishes paperback originals. **Publishes 10 titles/year. Pays royalty or makes outright purchase.** Publishes book 1 year after acceptance of ms. Accepts simultaneous submissions. Reports in 1 month. Book catalog and ms guidelines free.

O→ ICC publishes essential books and reference materials on all facets of international trade and business.

**Nonfiction:** Reference, technical. Subjects include international trade and business. Query or submit proposal package, including outline, table of contents and 3 sample chapters with SASE.

**Recent Title(s):** *Inc. Terms Q&A*; *Import-Export Basics*, by Charles del Busto.

**Tips:** "Our specific audience includes those in the fields of international trade, law, banking, as well as the general public."

**ICON EDITIONS**, Westview Press, Perseus Books Group, 10 E. 53rd St., New York NY 10036. (212)207-7282. **Acquisitions:** Cass Canfield, Jr., editor. Estab. 1973. Publishes hardcover and trade paperback originals and reprints. **Publishes 6 titles/year. Receives hundreds of queries/year. 25% of books from first-time authors; 80% from unagented writers. Royalty and advance vary.** Publishes book 18 months after acceptance of ms. Accepts simultaneous submissions, if so noted. Returns submissions with SASE if author requests. Book catalog free.

O→ Icon Editions focuses on books in architecture, art history and art criticism for the academic and semi-academic market, college and university market.

**Nonfiction:** Books for academic and semi-academic market. Subjects include art/architecture, art history, art criticism. Query with SASE. Reviews artwork/photos as part of ms package "if we're interested." Send photocopies.

**Recent Title(s):** *The Methodologies of Art*, by Laurie Schneider Adams.

**N ICONOGRAFIX, INC.**, 1830A Hanley Rd., P.O. Box 446, Hudson WI 54020. (715)381-9755. Fax: (715)381-9756. **Acquisitions:** Richard Seymour, president. Estab. 1992. Publishes trade paperback originals. **Publishes 20 titles/year. Receives 50 queries and 20 mss/year. 25% of books from first-time authors; 100% from unagented writers. Pays 10% royalty on wholesale price or makes outright purchase of $1,000-2,000. Offers $1,000-2,000 advance.** Publishes book 1 year after acceptance of ms. Accepts simultaneous submissions. Reports in 1 month on queries, 3 months on proposals and mss. Book catalog and ms guidelines free.

O→ Iconografix publishes special historical interest photographic books for transportation equipment enthusiasts.

**Nonfiction:** Photo albums. Subjects include transportation. Query with SASE. Reviews artwork/photos as part of ms package. Send prints (8×10 preferred).

**ICS PUBLICATIONS**, Institute of Carmelite Studies, 2131 Lincoln Rd. NE, Washington DC 20002. (202)832-8489. Fax: (202)832-8967. Website: http://www.ocd.or.at/ics. **Acquisitions:** Steven Payne, O.C.D., editorial director. Publishes hardcover and trade paperback originals and reprints. **Publishes 8 titles/year. Receives 10-20 queries and 10 mss/ year. 10% of books from first-time authors; 90-100% from unagented writers. Pays 2-6% royalty on retail price or makes outright purchase. Offers $500 advance.** Publishes book 2 years after acceptance of ms. Accepts simultaneous submissions, if so noted. Reports in 2 months on proposals. Book catalog for 7×10 SAE with 2 first-class stamps. Writer's guidelines for #10 SASE.
    O➔ "Our audience consists of those interested in the Carmelite tradition or in developing their life of prayer and spirituality."
**Nonfiction:** Religious (should relate to Carmelite spirituality and prayer). "We are looking for significant works on Carmelite history, spirituality, and main figures (Saints Teresa, John of the Cross, Therese of Lisieux, etc.). Too often we receive proposals for works that merely repeat what has already been done, are too technical for a general audience, or have little to do with the Carmelite tradition and spirit." Query or submit outline and 1 sample chapter.
**Recent Title(s):** *Carmelite Spirituality in the Teresian Tradition*, by Paul-Marie of the Cross.

**IDE HOUSE PUBLISHERS**, 122 N. Fairlawn Dr., Round Lake Park IL 60073-3186. (847)546-7753. Website: http:// www.publishers-associates.com. Please note: Ide House is a member of Publishers Associates. All mss and other commu- nications must be addressed to Publishers Associates—a consortium of independent publishers. **Acquistions:** Ryan Idol, senior editor (gay/lesbian studies); Jane Seymour, liberal studies coordinator; Nalinda Downs, senior editor (women's studies); David Ashford, associate editor (US politics); Mary Meeks, associate editor (Third World politics); James Davidson, associate editor (European politics). Estab. 1979. Publishes hardcover and trade paperback originals. **Pub- lishes 10 titles/year. Receives 300 queries and 500 mss/year. 70% of books from first-time authors; 100% from unagented writers. Pays 4-7% royalty on retail price.** Publishes book 1 year after acceptance of ms. Reports in 1 month on queries and proposals, 4 months on mss. Book catalog for 6×9 SAE with 5 first-class stamps. Manuscript guidelines for #10 SASE.
    ● At press time we received a number of complaints about Ide House and Publishers Associates that we were unable to resolve for this edition.
**Imprint(s):** Hercules Press (Bryan Estevez, executive senior vice president/editor).
**Nonfiction:** Women's history. Subjects include gay/lesbian, government/politics (liberal only), history, women's issues/ studies. "We accept only nonsexist/nonhomophobic scholarly works." Query with outline and 2 sample chapters. All unsolicited mss returned unopened.
**Recent Title(s):** *What America Wants, America Gets*, by Joe Sharpnack (politics/humor); *Darvik*, by Tim Oates (3rd world poetry/epic).
**Tips:** "Inaugurating poetry branch. We are emphasizing a quest for liberal politics and budgeted for 100 titles in 1996- 1998."

**IDEALS CHILDREN'S BOOKS**, Hambleton-Hill Publishing, Inc., 1501 County Hospital Rd., Nashville TN 37218. **Acquisitions:** Bethany Snyder, editor. Publishes children's hardcover and trade paperback originals. **Publishes 25 titles/ year. Receives 300 queries and 2,000-2,500 mss/year. 10% of books from first-time authors; 10% from unagented writers. Pay determined by individual contract.** Publishes book up to 2 years after acceptance of ms. Reports in 6 months on queries, proposals and mss. Manuscript guidelines for #10 SASE.
    O➔ Ideals Children's Books publishes fiction and some nonfiction for toddlers to 8-year-olds. This publisher accepts only unsolicited manuscripts from agents, members of the Society of Children's Book Writers & Illustrators, and previously published book authors who may submit with a list of writing credits.
**Nonfiction:** Children's. Subjects include Americana, nature/environment, science, sports. Submit proposal package.
**Fiction:** Submit complete ms with SASE. No middle grade or young adult novels.
**Recent Title(s):** *The Littlest Uninvited One*, by Charles Tazewell, illustrated by Gail Tribble (picture book); *Discovery Readers* (science/nature).
**Tips:** "We are not interested in anthropomorphism or alphabet books. We are seeking original, child-centered fiction for the picture book format."

**IDEALS PUBLICATIONS INC.**, 535 Metroplex Dr., Suite 250, Nashville TN 37211. (615)333-0478. Publisher: Patricia Pingry. **Acquisitions:** Copy Editor. Estab. 1944. Uses short prose and poetry. Also publishes *Ideals* magazine. **Publishes 8-10 hardbound books, 12-14 childrens titles. Advance varies. Most material from unagented submis- sions.** Accepts simultaneous submissions. Accepts previously published material. Send information about when and where the piece previously appeared. Publishes book 18 months after acceptance of ms. Reports in 2 months only with SASE. Manuscript guidelines free with SASE.
    O➔ Ideals publishes highly illustrated seasonal, nostalgic, inspirational and patriotic coffee table books, including a travel book series, and children's picture and board books.
**Nonfiction:** Biography, coffee table books. Subjects include travel, inspirational, nostalgic, patriotic, historical, how- to, self-help.
**Recent Title(s):** *Barefoot Days* (children's poetry).

**IDYLL ARBOR, INC.**, P.O. Box 720, Ravensdale WA 98051. (425)432-3231. Fax: (425)432-3726. E-mail: editors@idyllarbor.com. **Acquisitions:** Tom Blaschko. Publishes hardcover and trade paperback originals and trade paperback reprints. **Publishes 6 titles/year. 50% of books from first-time authors; 100% from unagented writers. Pays 8-15% royalty on wholesale price or retail price.** Publishes book 1 year after acceptance of ms. Accepts simultaneous submissions. Reports in 1 month on queries, 2 months on proposals, 4 months on mss. Book catalog and ms guidelines free.

O— Idyll Arbor publishes practical information on the current state and art of health care practice. Currently emphasizing therapies (recreational, occupational, music, horticultural), activity directors in long term care facilities, and social service professionals.

**Nonfiction:** Technical, textbook. Subjects include agriculture/horticulture (used in long term care activities or health care—therapy), health/medicine (for therapists, social service providers and activity directors), recreation (as therapy). "Idyll Arbor is currently developing a line of *Personal Health* books where each one explains a condition or a closely related set of medical or psychological conditions. The target audience is the person or the family of the person with the condition. We want to publish a book that explains a condition at the level of detail expected of the average primary care physician so that our readers can address the situation intelligently with specialists. We look for manuscripts from authors with recent clinical experience. Good grounding in theory is required, but practical experience is more important." Query preferred with outline and 1 sample chapter. Reviews artwork as part of ms package. Send photocopies.
**Recent Title(s):** *Idyll Arbor's Glossary for Therapists*, by Joan Burlingame and Thomas K. Skalko (health care reference).
**Tips:** "The books must be useful for the health practitioner who meets face to face with patients *or* the books must be useful for teaching undergraduate and graduate level classes. We are especially looking for therapists with a solid clinical background to write on their area of expertise."

**ILR PRESS**, Cornell University Press, Sage House, 512 E. State St., Ithaca NY 14850. (607)277-2338 ext. 232. Fax: (607)277-2374. **Acquisitions:** F. Benson, editor. Estab. 1945. Publishes hardcover and trade paperback originals and reprints. **Publishes 12-15 titles/year. Pays royalty.** Reports in 2 months on queries. Book catalog free.

O— "We are interested in manuscripts with innovative perspectives on current workplace issues that concern both academics and the general public."

**Nonfiction:** All titles relate to industrial relations and/or workplace issues including relevant work in the fields of history, sociology, political science, economics, human resources, and organizational behavior. Needs for the next year include mss on workplace problems, employment policy, immigration, current history, and dispute resolution for academics and practitioners. Query or submit outline and sample chapters.
**Recent Title(s):** *Capital Moves: RCA's 70-Year Quest for Cheap Labor*, by Jefferson Cowie.
**Tips:** "Manuscripts must be well documented to pass our editorial evaluation, which includes review by academics in related fields."

**IMAGE BOOKS**, Doubleday Broadway Publishing Group, Random House, Inc., 1540 Broadway, New York NY 10036. (212)354-6500. Fax: (212)782-8911. Website: http://www.bdd.com. **Acquisitions:** Trace Murphy, senior editor. Estab. 1956. Publishes hardcover originals and reprints, trade paperback originals and reprints, mass market paperback originals and reprints. **Publishes 12 titles/year. Receives 500 queries/year; receives 300 mss/year. 10% of books from first-time writers; no unagented writers. Pays royalty on net price. Advance varies.** Publishes book 18 months after acceptance of ms. Accepts simultaneous submissions. Reports in 3 months on proposals.

O— Image Books has grown from a classic Catholic list to include a variety of current and future classics, maintaining a high standard of quality as the finest in religious paperbacks.

**Nonfiction:** Biography, cookbook, gift book, how-to, humor, illustrated book, reference, self-help. Subjects include philosophy, psychology, religious/inspirational, world wisdom traditions, women's issues/studies. Query. Prefers agented submissions. Reviews artwork as part of ms package. Send photocopies.
**Recent Title(s):** *The Inner Voice of Love*, by Henri J.M. Nouwen (inspirational).

**IMPACT PUBLISHERS, INC.**, P.O. Box 910, San Luis Obispo CA 93406-0910. (805)543-5911. Fax: (805)543-4093. **Acquisitions:** Freeman Porter, acquisitions editor. Estab. 1970. Publishes trade paperback originals. **Publishes 6 titles/year. Receives 250 queries and 250 mss/year. 40% of books from first-time authors; 60% from unagented writers. Pays 10% royalty on net receipts.** Publishes book 12-18 months after acceptance of ms. Accepts simultaneous submissions. Reports in 5 months on proposals. Book catalog and ms guidelines free.

O— "Our purpose is to make the best human services expertise available to the widest possible audience: children, teens, parents, couples, individuals seeking self-help and personal growth, and human service professionals." Currently emphasizing professional resources for "The Practical Therapist Series." De-emphasizing children's books.

**Imprint(s):** American Source Books, Little Imp Books.
**Nonfiction:** Children's/juvenile, self-help. Subjects include child guidance/parenting, health/medicine, psychology (professional), caregiving/eldercare. "All our books are written by qualified human service professionals and are in the fields of mental health, personal growth, relationships, aging, families, children and professional psychology. We are currently seeking to expand our professional list." Submit proposal package, including short résumé or vita, book description, audience description, outline, 1-3 sample chapters and SASE.
**Recent Title(s):** *Is That All There Is?* (nonfiction).

**Tips:** "Don't call to see if we have received your submission. Include a self-addressed, stamped postcard if you want to know if manuscript arrived safely. We prefer a non-academic, readable style. We publish only popular psychology and self-help materials written in 'everyday language' by professionals with advanced degrees and significant experience in the human services."

**INCENTIVE PUBLICATIONS, INC.**, 3835 Cleghorn Ave., Nashville TN 37215-2532. (615)385-2934. Fax: (615)385-2967. E-mail: incentiv@nashville.net. Website: http://www.nashville.net./~incentiv. **Acquisitions:** Jennifer Janke, editor. Estab. 1970. Publishes paperback originals. **Publishes 25-30 titles/year. Receives 350 submissions/year. 25% of books from first-time authors; 100% from unagented writers. Pays royalty or makes outright purchase.** Publishes book an average of 1 year after acceptance. Reports in 1 month on queries.
- Incentive publishes developmentally appropriate teacher/parent resource materials and educational workbooks for children in grades K-12.

**Nonfiction:** Teacher resource books in pre-K through 12th grade. Query with synopsis and detailed outline.
**Recent Title(s):** *Character Education Grades K-6 and 6-12 Years 1 & 2*, by Heidel and Mersereau.

**INDIANA UNIVERSITY PRESS**, 601 N. Morton St., Bloomington IN 47404-3797. (812)855-4203. Fax: (812)855-8507. E-mail: iupress@indiana.edu. Website: http://www.indiana.edu/~iupress/. Estab. 1950. Managing Editor: Jane Lyle. **Acquisitions:** Robert J. Sloan (civil war, classical studies, drama/performance, paleontology, history, medical/ethics, philanthropy, science and religion), Janet Rabinowitch (art, African studies, Jewish studies, philosoophy, Middle East studies, Russian and East European studies), John Gallman (Asian studies, politics), Joan Catapano (dance, film studies, gay/lesbian/gender studies, Black studies, film, women's studies), Jeffrey Ankrom (music). Estab. 1951. Publishes hardcover originals, paperback originals and reprints. **Publishes 175 titles/year. 30% of books from first-time authors; 98% from unagented writers. Nonauthor subsidy publishes 9% of books. Pays maximum 10% royalty on retail price. Offers occasional advance.** Publishes book 1 year after acceptance of ms. Reports in 2 months. Book catalog and ms guidelines free.
- Indiana University Press's mandate is "to serve the world of scholarship and culture as a professional publisher and also to represent and reflect the major strengths of Indiana University." Indiana's list is especially strong in the humanities, the social sciences and regional studies.

**Nonfiction:** Scholarly books on humanities, history, philosophy, religion, Jewish studies, Black studies, criminal justice, translations, semiotics, public policy, film, music, philanthropy, social sciences, regional materials, African studies, Russian Studies, women's studies, and serious nonfiction for the general reader. Also interested in textbooks and works with course appeal in designated subject areas. Query with prospectus, sample chapter, CV, book length and discussion of the market. "Queries should include as much descriptive material as is necessary to convey scope and market appeal to us." Reviews artwork/photos.
**Recent Title(s):** *The Complete Dinosaur*, edited by James O. Forlow and Michael Brett-Surman.

**INFO NET PUBLISHING**, 34188 Coast Highway, Suite C, Dana Point CA 92629. (949)489-9292. Fax: (949)489-95495. E-mail: infonetpub@aol.com Website: http://www.infonetpublishing.com. **Acquisitions:** Herb Wetenkamp, president. Estab. 1987. Publishes hardcover and trade paperback originals. **Publishes 6 titles/year. Receives 50 queries and 20 mss/year. 80% of books from first-time authors; 85% from unagented writers. Pays 7-10% royalty on wholesale price or makes outright purchase of $1,000-10,000. Offers $1,000-2,000 advance in some cases.** Publishes book 10 months after acceptance of ms. Accepts simultaneous submissions. Reports in 2 months. Book catalog for 10×12 SAE and 2 first-class stamps. Manuscript guidelines for #10 SASE.
- Info Net publishes for easily identified niche markets; specific markets with some sort of special interest, hobby, avocation, profession, sport or lifestyle.

**Nonfiction:** Biography, children's/juvenile, gift book, how-to, reference, self-help, technical. Subjects include Americana and collectibles, aviation/aircraft archaeology, business/economics (retailing), history, hobbies, military/war, nature/environment, recreation, regional, science, sports, travel, women's issues/studies. "We are looking for specific niche market books, not general titles, other than self-help. Do not repeat same formula as other books. Offer something new, in other words." Submit outline, 3 sample chapters, proposal package, including demographics, marketing plans/data with SASE. Reviews artwork/photos as part of the ms package. Send photocopies.
**Recent Title(s):** *The Survival Guide for Today's Career Woman*, by Rayner (women's issues/self help).
**Tips:** "Please check to be sure similar titles are not already published covering the exact same subject matter. Research the book you are proposing."

**INNER TRADITIONS INTERNATIONAL**, P.O. Box 388, 1 Park St., Rochester VT 05767. (802)767-3174. Fax: (802)767-3726. E-mail: info@gotoit.com. Website: http://www.gotoit.com. Managing Editor: Rowan Jacobsen. **Acquisitions:** Jon Graham, editor. Estab. 1975. Publishes hardcover and trade paperback originals and reprints. **Publishes 60 titles/year. Receives 3,000 submissions/year. 10% of books from first-time authors; 20% from unagented writers. Pays 8-10% royalty on net receipts. Offers $1,000 average advance.** Publishes book 1 year after acceptance of ms. Reports in 3 months on queries, 6 months on mss. Book catalog and ms guidelines free.
- Inner Traditions publishes works representing the spiritual, cultural and mythic traditions of the world and works on alternative medicine and holistic health that combine contemporary thought with the knowledge of the world's great healing traditions. Currently emphasizing alternative health.

**Imprint(s):** Destiny Audio Editions, Destiny Books, Destiny Recordings, Healing Arts Press, Inner Traditions, Inner

Traditions En Español, Inner Traditions India, Park Street Press.
**Nonfiction:** Subjects include anthropology/archaeology, natural foods, cooking, nutrition, health/alternative medicine, history and mythology, indigenous cultures, music/dance, nature/environment, ethnobotony business, esoteric philosophy, psychology, world religions, women's issues/studies, New Age. "We are interested in the relationship of the spiritual and transformative aspects of world cultures." Query or submit outline and sample chapters with SASE. Does not return mss without SASE. Reviews artwork/photos as part of ms package.
**Recent Title(s):** *The Temple of Man*, by Schwaller de Lubicz.
**Tips:** "We are not interested in autobiographical stories of self-transformation. We do not accept any electronic submissions (via e-mail). We are not currently looking at fiction."

**INNISFREE PRESS**, 136 Roumfort Rd., Philadelphia PA 19119. (215)247-4085. Fax: (215)247-2343. E-mail: InnisfreeP@aol.com. Website: http://www.innisfreepress.com. **Acquisitions:** Marcia Broucek, publisher. Estab. 1996. Publishes trade paperback originals. **Publishes 6-8 titles/year. Receives 500 queries and 300 mss/year. 50% of books from first-time authors; 90% from unagented writers. Pays 10-15% royalty on wholesale price.** Publishes book 1 year after acceptance of ms. Accepts simultaneous submissions. Reports in 1 month on queries; 2 months on proposals; 3 months on mss. Book catalog and ms guidelines free.
  ○ "Innisfree's mission is to publish books that nourish individuals both emotionally and spiritually; to offer books that 'call to the deep heart's core' " Currently emphasizing women's issues, spirituality. De-emphasizing child guidance/parenting.
**Nonfiction:** Spiritually focused self-help and personal growth. Subjects include child guidance/parenting, health/medicine, holistic body/mind/spirit, nature/environment, psychology, religion, women's issues/studies. No poetry or children's material or "survival" manuscripts, please. Query with proposal package, including outline, 2 sample chapters, potential audience, and what makes the book unique, with SASE. Reviews artwork as part of ms package. Send photocopies.
**Recent Title(s):** *The Tao of Eating: Feed Your Soul through Everyday Experiences with Food*, by Linda Harper.
**Tips:** "Our books respond to the needs of today's seekers—people who are looking for deeper meaning and purpose in their lives, for ways to integrate spiritual depth into hectic, stressful days."

**INTERCULTURAL PRESS, INC.**, P.O. Box 700, Yarmouth ME 04096. (207)846-5168. Fax: (207)846-5181. E-mail: books@interculturalpress.com. Website: http://www.interculturalpress.com. **Acquisitions:** Judy Carl-Hendrick, managing editor. Estab. 1980. Publishes hardcover and trade paperback originals. **Publishes 8-12 titles/year. Receives 50-80 submissions/year. 50% of books from first-time authors; 95% of books from unagented writers. Pays royalty. Offers small advance occasionally.** Publishes book within 2 years after acceptance. Accepts simultaneous submissions. Reports in 2 months. Book catalog and ms guidelines free.
  ○ Intercultural Press publishes materials related to intercultural relations, including the practical concerns of living and working in foreign countries, the impact of cultural differences on personal and professional relationships and the challenges of interacting with people from unfamiliar cultures, whether at home or abroad.
**Nonfiction:** Reference, textbook and theory. "We want books with an international or domestic intercultural or multicultural focus, especially those on business operations (how to be effective in intercultural business activities), education (textbooks for teaching intercultural subjects, for instance) and training (for Americans abroad or foreign nationals coming to the United States). Our books are published for educators in the intercultural field, business people engaged in international business, managers concerned with cultural diversity in the workplace, and anyone who works in an occupation where cross-cultural communication and adaptation are important skills. No manuscripts that don't have an intercultural focus." Accepts nonfiction translations. Query with outline or proposal. *No unsolicited mss.*
**Recent Title(s):** *Figuring Foreigners Out: A Practical Guide*, by Craig Storti.

**INTERLINK PUBLISHING GROUP, INC.**, 46 Crosby St., Northampton MA 01060. (413)582-7054. Fax: (413)582-7057. E-mail: interpg@aol.com. Website: http://www.interlinkbooks.com. **Acquisitions:** Michel Moushabeck, publisher. Estab. 1987. Publishes hardcover and trade paperback originals. **Publishes 50 titles/year. Receives 600 submissions/year. 30% of books from first-time authors; 50% from unagented writers. Pays 6-8% royalty on retail price.** Publishes book 18 months after acceptance. Accepts simultaneous submissions. Reports in 1 month on queries. *Writer's Market* recommends allowing 2 months for reply. Book catalog and ms guidelines free.
  ○ Interlink publishes a general trade list of adult fiction and nonfiction with an emphasis on books that have a wide appeal while also meeting high intellectual and literary standards.
**Imprint(s):** Crocodile Books, USA; Interlink Books; Olive Branch Press.
**Nonfiction:** World travel, world history and politics, ethnic cooking, world music. Submit outline and sample chapters.
**Fiction:** Ethnic, international feminist. "Adult fiction—We are looking for translated works relating to the Middle East, Africa or Latin America. Juvenile/Picture Books—Our list is full for the next two years. No science fiction, romance, plays, erotica, fantasy, horror." Submit outline/synopsis and sample chapters.
**Recent Title(s):** *House of the Winds*, by Mia Yun.
**Tips:** "Any submissions that fit well in our publishing program will receive careful attention. A visit to your local bookstore or library to look at some of our books before you send in your submission is recommended."

**INTERNATIONAL FOUNDATION OF EMPLOYEE BENEFIT PLANS**, P.O. Box 69, Brookfield WI 53008-0069. (414)786-6700. Fax: (414)786-8780. E-mail: books@ifebp.org. Website: http://www.ifebp.org. **Acquisitions:** Dee Birschel, senior director of publications. Estab. 1954. Publishes hardcover and trade paperback originals. **Publishes 10**

titles/year. **Receives 20 submissions/year. 15% of books from first-time authors; 80% from unagented writers. Pays 5-15% royalty on wholesale and retail price.** Publishes book 1 year after acceptance. Reports in 3 months on queries. Book catalog free. Manuscript guidelines for SASE.

    O→ IFEBP publishes general and technical monographs on all aspects of employee benefits—pension plans, health insurance, etc.

**Nonfiction:** Reference, technical, consumer information, textbook. Subjects limited to health care, pensions, retirement planning, and employee benefits. Query with outline.

**Recent Title(s):** *Health Care Cost Management—A Basic Guide, Third Edition*, by Madelon Lubin.

**Tips:** "Be aware of interests of employers and the marketplace in benefits topics, for example, how AIDS affects employers, health care cost containment."

**N INTERNATIONAL MARINE**, The McGraw-Hill Companies, P.O. Box 220, Camden ME 04843-0220. Fax: (207)236-6314. **Acquisitions:** Jonathan Eaton, editorial director (boating, marine nonfiction). Estab. 1969. Publishes hardcover and paperback originals. **Publishes 40 titles/year. receives 500-700 mss/year. 30% of books from first-time authors; 80% from unagented writers. Pays standard royalties based on net price. Offers advance.** Publishes book 1 year after acceptance. Reports in 2 months. Book catalog and ms guidelines for SASE.

    O→ International Marine publishes "good books about boats."

**Imprint(s): Ragged Mountain Press** (sports and outdoor books that take you off the beaten path).

**Nonfiction:** "Marine and outdoor nonfiction. A wide range of subjects include: boat design, seamanship, boat mainte-nance, etc." All books are illustrated. "Material in all stages welcome." Query first with outline and 2-3 sample chapters. Reviews artwork/photos as part of ms package.

**Recent Nonfiction Title(s):** *Electrics Simplified*, by Don Casey (how-to); *Mountaineering: A Woman's Guide*, by Andrea Gabbard.

**Tips:** "Writers should be aware of the need for clarity, accuracy and interest. Many progress too far in the actual writing.

**INTERNATIONAL MEDICAL PUBLISHING**, P.O. Box 479, McLean VA 22101-0479. (703)519-0807. Fax: (703)519-0806. E-mail: masterso@patriot.net. Website: http://www.medicalpublishing.com. **Acquisitions:** Thomas Masterson, MD, editor. Estab. 1991. Publishes mass market paperback originals. **Publishes 11 titles/year. Receives 20 queries and 2 mss/year. 5% of books from first-time authors; 100% from unagented writers. Pays royalty on gross receipts.** Publishes book 8 months after acceptance of ms. Reports in 2 months on queries. Book catalog free.

    O→ IMP publishes books to make life easier for doctors in training. "We're branching out to also make life easier for people with chronic medical problems."

**Nonfiction:** Reference, textbook. Health/medicine subjects. "We distribute only through medical and scientific book-stores. Think about practical material for doctors-in-training. We are interested in handbooks. Online projects are of interest." Query with outline.

**Recent Title(s):** *Day-by-Day Diabetes Calendar*, by Resa Levetan, M.D.

**N INTERNATIONAL PUBLISHERS CO., INC.**, P.O. Box 3042, New York NY 10116-3042. (212)366-9816. Fax: (212)366-9820. E-mail: service@intpubnyc.com. **Acquisitions:** Betty Smith, president. Estab. 1924. Publishes hardcover originals, trade paperback originals and reprints. **Publishes 5-6 titles/year. Receives 50-100 mss/year. 10% of books from first-time authors. Pays 5-7½% royalty on paperbacks; 10% royalty on cloth. No advance.** Publishes book 6 months after acceptance of ms. Accepts simultaneous submissions. Reports in 1 month on queries with SASE, 6 months on mss. Book catalog and ms guidelines for SAE with 55¢ postage.

    O→ International Publishers Co., Inc. emphasizes books based on Marxist science.

**Nonfiction:** Biography, reference, textbook. Subjects include Americana, economics, history, philosophy, politics, art, social sciences, Marxist-Leninist classics. "Books on labor, black studies and women's studies based on Marxist science have high priority." Query or submit outline, sample chapters and SASE. Reviews artwork/photos as part of ms package.

**Recent Title(s):** *Vladimir and Nadya—The Lenin Story*, by Mary Hamilton-Dann.

**Tips:** No fiction or poetry.

**INTERNATIONAL SCHOLARS PUBLICATIONS, INC.**, 7831 Woodmont Ave., #345, Bethesda MD 20814. (301)654-7335. E-mail: austinisp1@aol.com. Website: http://www.interscholars.com. **Acquisitions**: Dr. Robert West. Estab. 1993. Publishes hardcover and trade paperback originals, hardcover reprints. **Publishes 120 titles/year. Receives 1,720 queries and 800 mss/year. 80% of books from first-time authors; 100% from unagented writers. Pays 8-12% royalty on wholesale price.** Publishes book 8 months after acceptance of ms. Accepts simultaneous submissions. Reports in 2 months on queries and mss, 1 month on proposals. Book catalog and ms guidelines for #10 SASE.

    O→ International Scholars Publications is an independent publishing house founded by scholars from a variety of traditions united by the goal of affirming the richness and diversity of contemporary scholarship.

**Imprint(s):** Catholic Scholars Publications, Christian Universities Press, University Press for West Africa.

**Nonfiction:** Biography, reference, scholarly, textbook. Subjects include art/architecture, education, ethnic, government/politics, history, language/literature, military/war, money/finance, philosophy, psychology, religion, science, sociology, women's issues/studies, Africa. "Research monographs and revised dissertations welcome. Some submissions do not contain enough information or have work condition problems." Query with outline, 2 sample chapters, cv and SASE.

**Recent Title(s):** *Youth Street Gangs*, by Vernon Harlan (criminal justice).

**Tips:** "Audience are upscale readers who enjoy an intellectual challenge. Focus on concept, contents, size of work and why it should be released."

**INTERNATIONAL WEALTH SUCCESS**, P.O. Box 186, Merrick NY 11570-0186. (516)766-5850. Fax: (516)766-5919. **Acquisitions:** Tyler G. Hicks, editor; Steven D. Hicks, associate editor. Estab. 1967. **Publishes 10 titles/year. Receives 100 submissions/year. 100% of books from first-time authors; 100% from unagented writers. Pays 10% royalty on wholesale or retail price. Buys all rights. Offers usual advance of $1,000, but this varies depending on author's reputation and nature of book.** Publishes book 4 months after acceptance. Reports in 1 month. Book catalog and ms guidelines for 9×12 SAE with 3 first-class stamps.

   O⊸ "We publish nonfiction books and periodicals to help Beginning Wealth Builders choose, start, finance, and succeed in their own home-based or externally-quartered small business. Currently looking for books on e-commerce—doing business on the Internet.

**Nonfiction:** Self-help, how-to. "Techniques, methods, sources for building wealth. Highly personal, how-to-do-it with plenty of case histories. Books are aimed at wealth builders and are highly sympathetic to their problems. These publications present a wide range of business opportunities while providing practical, hands-on, step-by-step instructions aimed at helping readers achieve their personal goals in as short a time as possible while adhering to ethical and professional business standards." Financing, business success, venture capital, etc. Length: 60,000-70,000 words. Query. Reviews artwork/photos.

**Recent Title(s):** *Real Estate Finance Secrets Revealed*, by Huey Walsh.

**Tips:** "With the mass layoffs in large and medium-size companies there is an increasing interest in owning your own business. So we will focus on more how-to hands-on material on owning—and becoming successful in—one's own business of any kind. Our market is the BWB—Beginning Wealth Builder. This person has so little money that financial planning is something they never think of. Instead, they want to know what kind of a business they can get into to make some money without a large investment. Write for this market and you have millions of potential readers. Remember—there are a lot more people *without* money than *with* money."

**INTERSTATE PUBLISHERS, INC.**, 510 N. Vermilion St., P.O. Box 50, Danville IL 61834-0050. (217)446-0500. Fax: (217)446-9706. E-mail: info-ipp@ippinc.com. Website: http://www.ippinc.com. **Acquisitions:** Ronald L. McDaniel, vice president, editorial. Estab. 1914. Publishes hardcover originals. **Publishes 20 titles/year. Receives 100 queries and 25 mss/year. 50% of books from first-time authors; 100% from unagented writers. Pays 10% royalty on actual money received from sales.** Publishes book 6 months after acceptance of ms. Accepts simultaneous submissions, if so noted. Reports in 2 months on proposals. Book catalog (specify high school or college) for 9×12 SAE with 4 first-class stamps.

   O⊸ Interstate Publishers publishes textbooks and related materials that infuse science concepts into agricultural education.

**Nonfiction:** Textbook, ancillary materials for each textbook. Subjects include agriculture/horticulture, education (middle school, high school, college). Submit proposal package, including prospectus, outline, 2 sample chapters and SASE. Reviews artwork/photos as part of ms package. Send photocopies.

**Recent Title(s):** *Wildlife Management: Science & Technology*, by Charles A. Stutzenbaker, et al.

**Tips:** "Our audience is students who are interested in agriculture. They may simply want to become literate on the subject, or they may be preparing for a career in the new science-oriented agriculture. The career may well be off the farm and in areas such as landscaping, food technology, biotechnology, plant and soil science, etc. Educational texts must demonstrate fair and balanced treatment of the sexes, minorities, and persons with disabilities."

**INTERVARSITY PRESS**, P.O. Box 1400, Downers Grove IL 60515. (630)887-2500. Fax: (630)887-2520. E-mail: mail@iupress.com. Website: http://www.iupress.com. **Acquisitions:** David Zimmerman, assistant editor; Linda Doll, editor (general, Christian living); Andy Le Pean, editorial director (academic); Jim Hoover, assistant editorial director (academic, reference); Cindy Bunch-Hotaling, editor (Bible study, Christian living). Estab. 1947. Publishes hardcover originals, trade paperback and mass market paperback originals. **Publishes 70-80 titles/year. Receives 1,500 queries and 1,000 mss/year. 15% of books from first-time authors; 85% from unagented writers. Pays negotiable flat fee or royalty on retail price. Offers negotiable advance.** Publishes book 2 years after acceptance of ms. Accepts simultaneous submissions. Reports in 2 months on proposals. Book catalog for 9×12 SAE and 5 first-class stamps. Manuscript guidelines for #10 SASE.

   O⊸ InterVarsity Press publishes a full line of books from an evangelical Christian perspective targeted to an open-minded audience. "We serve those in the university, the church and the world, by publishing books from a Christian evangelical perspective."

**Imprint(s):** Academic (contact: Andy LePean); Bible Study; General; Popular; Reference (contact Dan Reid).

**Nonfiction:** Religious subjects. Writers need cv/résumé and detailed table of contents with query and SASE.

**Recent Title(s):** *Knowing with the Heart*, by Ray Clouser.

**INTERWEAVE PRESS**, 201 E. Fourth St., Loveland CO 80537. (970)669-7672. Fax: (970)667-8317. **Acquisitions:** Judith Durant, craft book editor; Doree Pitkin, herb book editor. Estab. 1975. Publishes hardcover and trade paperback originals. **Publishes 10-15 titles/year. Receives 50 submissions/year. 60% of books from first-time authors; 98% from unagented writers. Pays 10% royalty on net receipts.** Publishes book 1 year after acceptance of ms. Accepts simultaneous submissions, if so noted. Reports in 2 months. Book catalog and ms guidelines free.

   O⊸ Interweave Press publishes instructive and inspirational titles relating to the fiber arts and herbal topics.

**Nonfiction:** How-to, technical. Subjects limited to fiber arts—basketry, spinning, knitting, dyeing and weaving—and herbal topics—gardening, cooking, medical herbs and lore. Submit outline/synopsis and sample chapters. Reviews artwork/photos as part of ms package.

**Recent Title(s):** *What the Ladies Won't Tell You*, by Logan Chamberlain.

**Tips:** "We are looking for very clear, informally written, technically correct manuscripts, generally of a how-to nature, in our specific fiber and herb fields only. Our audience includes a variety of creative self-starters who appreciate inspiration and clear instruction. They are often well educated and skillful in many areas."

**ITALICA PRESS**, 595 Main St., Suite 605, New York NY 10044-0047. (212)935-4230. Fax: (212)838-7812. E-mail: inquiries@italicapress.com. Website: http://www.italicapress.com. **Acquisitions:** Ronald G. Musto and Eileen Gardiner, publishers. Estab. 1985. Publishes trade paperback originals. **Publishes 6 titles/year. Receives 75 queries and 20 mss/year. 50% of books from first-time authors; 100% from unagented writers. Pays 7-15% royalty on wholesale price.** Publishes book 1 year after acceptance of ms. Accepts simultaneous submissions. Reports in 1 month on queries. Book catalog free. Guidelines on website.

○→ Italica Press publishes English translations of modern Italian fiction and medieval and Renaissance nonfiction.

**Nonfiction:** "We publish *only* English translations of medieval and Renaissance source materials and English translations of modern Italian fiction." Query. Reviews artwork/photos as part of ms package. Send photocopies.

**Tips:** "We are interested in considering a wide variety of medieval and Renaissance topics (not historical fiction), and for modern works we are only interested in translations from Italian fiction."

**JAIN PUBLISHING CO.**, P.O. Box 3523, Fremont CA 94539. (510)659-8272. Fax: (510)659-0501. E-mail: mail@jainpub.com. Website: http://www.jainpub.com. **Acquisitions:** M.K. Jain, editor-in-chief. Estab. 1989. Publishes hardcover and trade paperback originals and reprints. **Publishes 6 titles/year. Receives 300 queries/year. 100% from unagented writers. Pays up to 15% royalty on net sales. Offers occasional advance.** Publishes book 1-2 years after acceptance of ms. Reports in 3 months on mss, if interested. Book catalog and ms guidelines available on website.

○→ Jain Publishing Company is a general trade and college textbook publisher with a diversified list in subjects such as business/management, computers/internet, health/healing and religions/philosophies. "We also publish fine pocket-size motivational/inspirational giftbooks and vegetarian cookbooks. Our goal is to provide quality reading material at reasonable prices." Currently emphasizing health/healing.

**Imprint(s): Asian Humanities Press.**

**Nonfiction:** Computers/Internet, foods/nutrition (vegetarian), health/healing (alternative), philosophies/religions (Eastern), business/management, reference, textbooks. "Manuscripts should be thoroughly researched and written in an 'easy to read' format. Preferably between 60,000-100,000 words." Submit proposal package, including cv and list of prior publications. Reviews artwork/photos as part of ms package. Send photocopies. Does not return submissions.

**Recent Title(s):** *Menopause: A Basic Guide for Women*, by Alan J. Silverstein, M.D. (health/healing).

**Tips:** Continued emphasis on undergraduate textbooks. "We're interested more in user-oriented books than general treatises."

**JAMESON BOOKS INC.**, 722 Columbus St., P.O. Box 738, Ottawa IL 61350. (815)434-7905. Fax: (815)434-7907. **Acquisitions:** Jameson G. Campaigne, publisher/editor. Estab. 1986. **Publishes hardcover originals. Publishes 12 titles/year. Receives 500 queries/year; 300 mss/year. 33% of books from first-time authors; 33% from unagented writers. Pays 6-15% royalty on retail price. Offers $1,000-25,000 advance.** Publishes book 1 year after acceptance of ms. Accepts simultaneous submissions. Reports in 6 months on queries. Book catalog for 8 × 10 SASE.

○→ Jameson Books publishes conservative politics and economics; Chicago area history; and biographies.

**Nonfiction:** Biography. Subjects include business/economics, history, politics, regional (Chicago area). Query with sample chapter and SASE (essential). *Submissions not returned without SASE.*

**Fiction:** Interested in pre-cowboy frontier fiction. Query with 1 sample chapter and SASE.

**Recent Title(s):** *Politics as a Noble Calling*, by F. Clifton White (memoirs); *Yellowstone Kelly: Gentleman and Scout*, by Peter Bowen (fiction).

**⟦N⟧ THOMAS JEFFERSON UNIVERSITY PRESS**, 100 E. Normal St., Kirksville MO 63501-4221. (816)785-4525. Fax: (816)785-4181. E-mail: tjup@truman.edu. Website: http://www.truman.edu/tjup. **Acquisitions:** Paula Presley, director/editor-in-chief (reference works/bibliography/history); Nancy Reschly, poetry editor (contemporary narrative poetry); Raymond Mentzer, general editor (early modern history, literature, biography). **Publishes 4-6 titles/year. Pays 25% maximum royalty on net sales.**

○→ Thomas Jefferson University Press publishes books in the humanities and social sciences with high standards of production quality. Currently emphasizing humanities, social sciences, early modern history, literature, church history. De-emphasizing theology.

**Nonfiction:** Biography, illustrated book, textbook and monographs on Americana, anthropology/archaeology, art/architecture, government/politics, history, language/literature, philosophy, religion and sociology.

**Poetry:** Original poetry and translations.

**Recent Title(s):** *Bethsaida*, by Aran/Freund (archaeology); *Naked Heart*, by Pagliaro (biography/history); *Marriage and Divorce in the Thought of Martin Bucer*, by H.J. Selderhuis (nonfiction); *The Rose Inside*, by David Keplinger.

**JEWISH PUBLICATION SOCIETY**, 1930 Chestnut St., Philadelphia PA 19103. (215)564-5925. Fax: (215)564-6640. E-mail: jewishbook@aol.com. Website: http://www.jewishpub.org. **Acquisitions**: Dr. Ellen Frankel, editor-in-chief; Bruce Black, children's editor. Estab. 1888. Publishes hardcover and trade paperback originals, trade paperback reprints. **Publishes 12 titles/year. 20% of books from first-time authors; 75% from unagented writers. Pays 10% royalty on wholesale price. Offers $1,000-4,000 advance.** Publishes book 18 months after acceptance. Accepts simultaneous submissions, if noted. Reports in 3 months on proposals. Book catalog free.

    O→ The Jewish Publication Society is a nonprofit educational association formed for the purpose of promoting Jewish culture by disseminating a wide variety of religious and secular works in the U.S. and abroad.

**Nonfiction:** Children's/juvenile, reference, trade books. Subjects include history, language/literature, religion, women's issues/studies. "No monographs or textbooks. We do not accept memoirs, biographies, art books, coffee-table books, fiction or poetry." Children's books include picture books, biography, history, religion, young middle readers; young adult include biography, history, religion, sports. Query with proposal package including outline, description and proposed table of contents, cv and SASE.

**Recent Title(s):** *Engendering Judaism*, by Rachel Adler; *The Shema*, by Norman Lamm.

**Tips:** "Our audience is college-educated Jewish readers interested in Bible, Jewish history or Jewish practice, as well as young readers."

**JIST WORKS, INC.**, 720 N. Park Ave., Indianapolis IN 46202-3431. (317)264-3720. Fax: (317)264-3763. E-mail: jistworks@aol.com. Website: http://www.jistworks.com. **Acquisitions**: Michael Cunningham, managing editor. Estab. 1981. Publishes trade paperback originals and reprints. **Publishes 40 titles/year. Receives 300 submissions/year. 60% of books from first time authors; majority from unagented writers. Pays 5-12% royalty on wholesale price or makes outright purchase (negotiable).** Publishes book 1 year after acceptance. Accepts simultaneous submissions. Reports in 3 months on queries. Book catalog and ms guidelines for 9×12 SAE with 6 first-class stamps.

    O→ "Our purpose is to provide quality career, job search, and other living skills information, products, and services that help people manage and improve their lives—and the lives of others."

**Imprint(s):** Park Avenue Publications (business and self-help that falls outside of the JIST topical parameters).

**Nonfiction:** How-to, career, reference, self-help, software, video, textbook. Specializes in job search, self-help and career related topics. "We want text/workbook formats that would be useful in a school or other institutional setting. We also publish trade titles, all reading levels. Will consider books for professional staff and educators, appropriate software and videos." Query with SASE. Reviews artwork/photos as part of ms package.

**Recent Title(s):** *Résumé Magic*, by Susan Britton Whitcomb.

**Tips:** "Institutions and staff who work with people of all reading and academic skill levels, making career and life decisions or people who are looking for jobs are our primary audience, but we're focusing more on business and trade topics for consumers."

**JOSSEY-BASS/PFEIFFER**, 350 Sansome St., San Francisco CA 94104. (415)433-1740.Fax: (415)433-1711. E-mail: mholt@jbp.com. Website: http://www.pfeiffer.com. **Acquisitions**: Matthew Holt, editor. **Publishes 25-50 titles/year. 25% of books from first-time authors; 95% of books from unagented writers. Pays 10% average royalty.** Publishes book 1 year after acceptance of ms. Accepts simultaneous submissions. Reports in 2 months on queries.

    O→ Jossey-Bass/Pfeiffer specializes in human resource development titles in the fields of business, management and training.

**Nonfiction:** Subjects include management, human resource development, training, both books and instruments. Query with SASE; proposal guidelines on website.

**Recent Title(s):** *Web-Based Training*, by Margaret Driscoll.

    ● Jossey-Bass was recently purchased by John Wiley & Sons, but will remain located in San Francisco.

**JOURNEY BOOKS**, Bob Jones University Press, 1700 Wade Hampton Blvd., Greenville SC 29614-0001. **Acquisitions:** Gloria Repp, acquisitions editor. Estab. 1974. Publishes trade paperback originals and reprints. **Publishes 11 titles/year. Receives 180 queries and 570 mss/year. 10% of books from first-time authors; 100% from unagented writers. Makes outright purchase of $500-1,250; royalties to established authors.** Publishes book 18 months after acceptance. Accepts simultaneous submissions. Reports in 2 months on mss. Book catalog and ms guidelines free.

    O→ Journey Books publishes nonfiction and fiction "reflecting a Christian perspective. Journey rarely publishes biblical fiction and doesn't publish romance, poetry or drama."

**Nonfiction:** Biography (for teens), children's/juvenile. Subjects include animals, gardening, history, sports. "We're looking for concept books on almost any subject suitable for children. We also like biographies." Submit outline and 3 sample chapters.

**Fiction:** Juvenile, young adult. "We're looking for well-rounded characters and plots with plenty of action suitable for a Christian audience. Avoid being preachy." Submit synopsis and 5 sample chapters or complete ms.

**Recent Title(s):** *Danger Follows*; *Escape*.

**Tips:** "Our readers are children ages two and up, teens and young adults. We're looking for high-quality writing that reflects a Christian standard of thought and features well-developed characters capable of dynamic changes, in a convincing plot. Most open to: first chapter books, adventure, biography."

**JUDSON PRESS**, P.O. Box 851, Valley Forge PA 19482-0851. (610)768-2128. Fax: (610)768-2441. E-mail: judsonpress@juno.com. Website: http://www.judsonpress.com. Publisher: Kristy Arnesen Pullen. **Acquisitions:** Randy Frame;

Mary Nicol, senior editor. Estab. 1824. Publishes hardcover and paperback originals. **Publishes 20-30 titles/year. Receives 750 queries/year. Pays royalty or makes outright purchase.** Publishes book 10 months after acceptance of ms. Accepts simultaneous submissions. Reports in 3 months. Enclose return postage. Book catalog for 9×12 SAE with 4 first-class stamps. Manuscript guidelines for #10 SASE.

O→ "Our audience is mostly church members and leaders who seek to have a more fulfilling personal spiritual life and want to serve Christ in their churches and other relationships. We have a large African American readership."

**Nonfiction:** Adult religious nonfiction of 30,000-80,000 words. Query with outline and sample chapter.

• Judson Press also publishes a quarterly journal, *The African American Pulpit*; call for submission guidelines.

**Recent Title(s):** *Breathing New Life Into Lent*, by Robert Stowe, Donna Schaper, Anne McKinstry and Janet Powers.

**Tips:** "Writers have the best chance selling us practical books assisting clergy or laypersons in their ministry and personal lives. Our audience consists of Protestant church leaders and members. Be sensitive to our workload and adapt to the market's needs. Books on multicultural issues are very welcome."

**KALMBACH PUBLISHING CO.**, 21027 Crossroads Circle, P.O. Box 1612, Waukesha WI 53187-1612. Fax: (414)798-6468. E-mail: tspohn@kalmbach.com. Website: http://books.kalmbach.com. Editor-in-Chief: Dick Christianson (model railroading, toy trains, railfanning). **Acquisitions:** Terry Spohn, senior acquisitions editor (railroading, scale modeling, miniatures); Kent Johnson, acquisitions editor (model railroading, toy trains). Estab. 1934. Publishes hardcover and paperback originals, paperback reprints. **Publishes 15-20 titles/year. Receives 100 submissions/year. 85% of books from first-time writers; 100% from unagented writers. Pays 10% royalty on net. Offers $1,500 average advance.** Publishes book 18 months after acceptance. Reports in 2 months.

O→ Kalmbach publishes reference materials and how-to publications for serious hobbyists in the railfan, model railroading, plastic modeling and toy train collecting/operating hobbies.

**Nonfiction:** Hobbies, how-to, amateur astronomy, railroading. "Our book publishing effort is in railroading and hobby how-to-do-it titles *only*." Query first. "I welcome telephone inquiries. They save me a lot of time, and they can save an author a lot of misconceptions and wasted work." In written query, wants detailed outline of 2-3 pages and a complete sample chapter with photos, drawings, and how-to text. Reviews artwork/photos as part of ms package.

**Recent Title(s):** *Building the Messerschmidt BF-109*, by Hjermstad and Phillips.

**Tips:** "Our books are about half text and half illustrations. Any author who wants to publish with us must be able to furnish good photographs and rough drawings before we'll consider contracting for his book."

**KAR-BEN COPIES, INC.**, 6800 Tildenwood Ln., Rockville MD 20852. (800)452-7236. Fax: (301)881-9195. E-mail: karben@aol.com. Website: http://www.karben.com. **Acquisitions:** Madeline Wikler, editor (juvenile Judaica). Estab. 1976. Publishes hardcover and trade paperback originals. **Publishes 8-10 titles/year. Receives 50-100 queries and 300-400 mss/year. 5% of books from first-time authors; 100% from unagented writers. Pays 5-8% royalty of net sales. Offers $500-2,500 advance.** Publishes book 10 months after acceptance of ms. Accepts simultaneous submissions. Reports in 1 month. Book catalog free or on website. Manuscript guidelines for 9×12 SAE with 2 first-class stamps.

O→ Kar-Ben Copies publishes Jewish books, calendars and cassettes, fiction and nonfiction, for preschool and primary children interested in Jewish holidays and traditions.

**Nonfiction:** Children's/juvenile (Judaica only). Religious subjects. "Jewish themes only!" Submit complete ms.

**Fiction:** Juvenile, religious. "Jewish themes and young kids only!"

**Recent Title(s):** *Kids Love Israel*, by Barbara Sofer (travel guide for families); *Once Upon a Shabbos*, by Jacqueline Jules (folktale for Shabbot).

**Tips:** "Do a literature search to make sure similar title doesn't already exist."

**KENSINGTON**, 850 Third Ave., 16th Floor, New York NY 10022. (212)407-1500. Fax: (212)935-0699. Website: http://www.kensingtonbooks.com. **Acquisitions:** Ann LaFarge, executive editor (romance, fiction); Tracy Bernstein, editorial director (pop culture, spiritual, New Age, parenting, health); Paul Dinas, editor-in-chief (nonfiction, true crime thrillers); Kate Duffy, editorial director (historical, regency, romance); John Scognamiglio, editorial director (romance, mystery thrillers, gay fiction); Hillary Sares, editor (Precious Gem romances); Karen Thomas, senior editor (Arabesque multicultural romances); Diane Stockwell, editor (Encanto, Hispanic romances). Estab. 1975. Publishes hardcover originals, trade paperback originals and reprints. **Kensington publishes 300 titles/year; Pinnacle 60; Zebra 140-170; Arabesque 48. Receives 6,000 queries/year. 3-5% of books from first-time authors. Pays royalty on retail price, varies by author and type of book.** Advance varies by author and type of book. Publishes book 18 months after acceptance of ms. Accepts simultaneous submissions. Reports in 1 month on queries; 3 months on mss. Book catalog for #10 SASE. Manuscript guidelines for SASE or on website.

O→ Kensington focuses on profitable niches and uses aggressive marketing techniques to support its books.

**Imprint(s):** Arabesque, Bouquet, Encanto, **Kensington**, Pinnacle, Precious Gems, **Zebra**.

**Nonfiction:** Self-help. Subjects include alternative health/medicine, pop culture, true crime, biography, humor, current events. Query with outline and SASE. *No unsolicited mss. Agented submissions only.* Reviews artwork/photos as part of the ms package, if integral to project. Send photocopies.

**Fiction:** Mystery, romance, suspense, women's, thriller, gay fiction, epic westerns. Query with synopsis and SASE. *No unsolicited mss. No unagented writers.*

**Tips:** Agented submissions only, except for submissions to Arabesque, Bouquet, Encanto and Precious Gems.

**KENT STATE UNIVERSITY PRESS**, P.O. Box 5190, Kent OH 44242-0001. (330)672-7913. Fax: (330)672-3104. **Acquisitions:** John T. Hubbell, director (history, regional); Julia Morton, editor-in-chief (literary criticism). Estab. 1965. Publishes hardcover and paperback originals and some reprints. **Publishes 30-35 titles/year. Nonauthor subsidy publishes 20% of books. Standard minimum book contract on net sales. Offers advance rarely.** Reports in 3 months. Book catalog free.

> O–¬ Kent State publishes primarily scholarly works and titles of regional interest. Currently emphasizing U.S. history, literary criticism. De-emphasizing European history.

**Nonfiction:** Especially interested in "scholarly works in history and literary studies of high quality, any titles of regional interest for Ohio, scholarly biographies, archaeological research, the arts, and general nonfiction. Always write a letter of inquiry before submitting manuscripts. We can publish only a limited number of titles each year and can frequently tell in advance whether or not we would be interested in a particular manuscript. This practice saves both our time and that of the author, not to mention postage costs. If interested we will ask for complete manuscript. Decisions based on inhouse readings and two by outside scholars in the field of study." Enclose return postage.
**Recent Title(s):** *George B. McClellan and Civil War History*, by Thomas J. Rowland; *Outlaws of the Purple Cow*, by Lester Goran (short stories).
**Tips:** "We are cautious about publishing heavily-illustrated manuscripts."

**KINSEEKER PUBLICATIONS**, P.O. Box 184, Grawn MI 49637-0184. (616)276-7653. E-mail: kinseeker6@aol.com. Website: http://www.angelfire.com/biz/Kinseeker/index.html. **Acquisitions:** Victoria Wilson, editor. Estab. 1986. Publishes trade paperback originals. **Publishes 6 titles/year. 95% of books from unagented writers. Pays 10-25% royalty on retail price. No advance.** Publishes book 8 months after acceptance. Reports in 3 months. Book catalog and ms guidelines for #10 SASE.

> O–¬ Kinseeker publishes books to help people researching their family histories.

**Imprint(s):** Roundsky Press.
**Nonfiction:** How-to, reference books. Subjects are local history and genealogy. Query or submit outline and sample chapters. Reviews artwork/photos as part of ms package.
**Recent Title(s):** *Tickling Your Ancestral Funnybone*, by Janet Elaine Smith (genealogy).

**B. KLEIN PUBLICATIONS**, P.O. Box 6578, Delray Beach FL 33482. (561)496-3316. Fax: (561)496-5546. **Acquisitions:** Bernard Klein, editor-in-chief. Estab. 1946. Publishes hardcover and paperback originals. **Publishes 5 titles/year. Pays 10% royalty on wholesale price, "but we're negotiable. Advance depends on many factors."** Markets books by direct mail and mail order. Accepts simultaneous submissions. Reports in 2 months. Book catalog for #10 SASE.

> O–¬ B. Klein Publications specializes in directories, annuals, who's who books, bibliography, business opportunity, reference books.

**Nonfiction:** Business, hobbies, how-to, reference, self-help, directories and bibliographies. Query or submit outline and sample chapters.
**Recent Title(s):** *Guide to American Directories*, by Bernard Klein.

**KLUWER ACADEMIC/PLENUM PUBLISHING**, Perseus Books Group, 233 Spring St., 7th Floor, New York NY 10013-1578. (212)620-8000. Fax: (212)463-0742. E-mail: frankd@plenum.com. Website: http://www.plenum.com. **Acquisitions:** Frank K. Darmstadt, editor. Plenum estab. 1946. Publishes scholarly hardcover originals. **Pays variable royalty. Advance varies.**

> O–¬ Kluwer Academic publishes scholarly books for professionals interested in the latest of scientific information or research. Currently emphasizing professional books.

**Nonfiction:** Scholarly texts. Subjects include social sciences, medical sciences, psychology, psychiatry, gender studies, health. Submit outline, sample chapters, résumé, vita and review sources. "Please don't e-mail proposals!"
**Recent Title(s):** *Truth, Proof, and Infinity*, by Peter Fletcher.
**Tips:** "Kluwer caters to the needs and interests of the professional reader. We encourage authors who are passionate about their work! Writers have the best chance selling authoritative, well-written, serious information in areas of health, mental health, social sciences and contemporary issues. Our audience consists of informed researchers and professionals and students in human, life and social sciences. If I were a writer trying to market a book today, I would say something interesting, important and useful, and say it well. Authors/editors must have an academic background; should be familiar with preparing manuscript in camera-ready form."

**ALFRED A. KNOPF AND CROWN BOOKS FOR YOUNG READERS**, Random House, Inc., 201 E. 50th St., New York NY 10022. (212)782-5623. Website: http://www.randomhouse.com/kids. Vice President/Publishing Director: Simon Boughton. Associate Publishing Director: Andrea Cascardi. Executive Editor: Nancy Siscoe. **Acquisitions:** Send mss to Crown/Knopf Editorial Department. Publishes hardcover originals, trade paperback reprints. **Publishes 60 titles/year. 10% of books from first-time authors; 40% from unagented writers. Pays 4-10% royalty on retail price. Offers advance of $3,000 and up.** Publishes book 1-2 years after acceptance of ms. Accepts simultaneous submissions. Reports in 3 months on mss. Book catalog for 9×12 SASE. Manuscript guidelines free.

> O–¬ Knopf is known for high quality literary fiction, and is willing to take risks with writing styles. It publishes for children ages 4 and up. Crown is known for books young children immediately use and relate to. It focuses on children ages 2-6. Crown also publishes nonfiction for all ages.

**Imprint(s): Alfred A. Knopf Books for Young Readers, Crown Books for Young Readers**, Knopf Paperbacks,

Dragonfly.
**Nonfiction:** Children's/juvenile, biography. Subjects include ethnic, history, nature/environment, science. Query with entire ms and SASE.
**Fiction:** Juvenile, literary, picture books, young adult. Query with entire ms and SASE.
**Recent Title(s):** *Sammy Keyes and the Hotel Thief*, by Wendelin van Draanen (fiction); *Emeline at the Circus*, by Marjorie Priceman (picture book).

**ALFRED A. KNOPF, INC.**, Knopf Publishing Group, Random House, Inc., 201 E. 50th St., New York NY 10022. (212)751-2600. **Acquisitions:** Senior Editor. Estab. 1915. Publishes hardcover and paperback originals. **Publishes 200 titles/yearly. 15% of books from first-time authors; 30% from unagented writers. Royalty and advance vary.** Publishes book 1 year after acceptance of ms. Accepts simultaneous submissions, if so noted. Reports in 3 months. Book catalog for 7½×10½ SAE with 5 first-class stamps.
   **O⇥** Knopf is a general publisher of quality nonfiction and fiction.
**Nonfiction:** Book-length nonfiction, including books of scholarly merit. Preferred length: 50,000-150,000 words. "A good nonfiction writer should be able to follow the latest scholarship in any field of human knowledge, and fill in the abstractions of scholarship for the benefit of the general reader by means of good, concrete, sensory reporting." Query. Reviews artwork/photos as part of ms package.
**Fiction:** Publishes book-length fiction of literary merit by known or unknown writers. Length: 40,000-150,000 words. Query with sample chapters.
**Recent Title(s):** *Consilience*, by Edward O. Wilson (nonfiction); *The Wind-Up Bird Chronicle*, by Haruki Murakami (fiction); *Ten Commandments*, by J.D. McClatchy (poetry).

**Ⓝ KNOWLEDGE, IDEAS & TRENDS, INC. (KIT)**, 1131-0 Tolland Turnpike, Suite 175, Manchester CT 06040. (860)646-0745. **Acquisitions:** Ruth Kimball-Bailey, editor. Publishes hardcover and trade paperback originals. **Publishes 4-5 titles/year. 80% of books from first-time authors; 100% from unagented writers. Pays royalty on wholesale price or advance against royalty. Advance varies.** Publishes book 18 months after acceptance of ms. Accepts simultaneous submissions. Reports in 3 months on mss. Book catalog and ms guidelines free.
**Nonfiction:** Biography, humor, reference, self-help. Subjects include anthropology/archaeology, history, psychology, sociology, women's issues/studies. Send outline and 3 sample chapters. Reviews artwork/photos as part of ms package. Send photocopies.
**Recent Title(s):** *The Other Side of Ethel Mertz: The Life Story of Vivian Vance*, by Frank Castelluccio and Alvin Walker (biography); *Button, Button, Who Has the Button*, by Ruth Harriet Jacobs, Ph.D. (drama).
**Tips:** "Audience is general readers, academics, older women, sociologists."

**Ⓝ KODANSHA AMERICA, INC.**, 575 Lexington Ave., 23rd Floor, New York NY 10022. (917)322-6200. Fax: (212)935-6929. **Acquisitions:** Editorial Department. Estab. 1989 (in US). Publishes 70% hardcover and trade paperback originals; 30% trade paperback reprints in Kodansha Globe series. **Publishes 25-30 titles/year. Receives 3,000 submissions/year. 20% of books from first-time authors; 10% from unagented writers. Pays 6-15% royalty on retail price. Offers $2,000 (reprints), $10,000 (original) average advances.** Publishes book 9 months after acceptance of ms. Accepts simultaneous submissions. Reports in up to 3 months.
**Nonfiction:** Anthropology/archaeology, cooking, history, inspirational, self-help, spirituality, memoir, nature/environment, philosophy, psychology, religion, science, sociology, translation, East/West and Asian subjects. No fiction. Query.
**Recent Title(s):** *In the Garden of Our Dreams*.
**Tips:** "Our focus is on nonfiction titles of a cross-cultural nature, well-researched, written with authority, bringing something of a world view and a fresh eye to the general reading public. We are especially interested in titles with staying power, which will sell as well in five years' time as now. Potential authors should be aware of what comparable titles are on the market, and from whom."

**Ⓝ KOGAN PAGE U.S.**, Kogan Page Ltd., 163 Central Ave., #2, Dover NH 03820. (603)749-9171. Fax: (603)749-6155. E-mail: bizbks@aol.com. Website: http://www.kogan-page.co.uk. **Acquisitions:** Spencer Smith (business). Publishes hardcover and trade paperback originals. **Publishes 100 titles/year. Pays royalty. Advances vary.** Publishes book 1 year after acceptance of ms. Accepts simultaneous submissions. Reports in 1 month on queries, 2 months on proposals. Book catalog on request or on website.
   **O⇥** Kogan Page U.S. publishes books in business, management, finance, international business and education for business people and educators.
**Nonfiction:** How-to, reference, self-help, textbook. Subjects business/economics. Query with SASE. Submit outline, 2 sample chapters, competition and market analysis. Reviews artwork/photos as part of ms package. Send photocopies.
**Recent Title(s):** *Millennium Countdown*, by Kusmirak (business/computer).

**KREGEL PUBLICATIONS**, Kregel, Inc., P.O. Box 2607, Grand Rapids MI 49501. E-mail: dennis@kregel.com. Website: http://www.gospelcom.net/kregel. **Acquisitions:** Dennis R. Hillman, publisher. Estab. 1949. Publishes hardcover and trade paperback originals and reprints. **Publishes 80 titles/year. Receives 150 queries and 100 mss/year. 5% of books from first-time authors; 100% from unagented writers. Pays 8-14% royalty on wholesale price or makes outright purchase of $500-1,000. Offers negotiated advance.** Publishes book 1 year after acceptance of ms.

Accepts simultaneous submissions. Reports in 2 months on queries and proposals. Book catalog for 9 × 12 SAE with 3 first-class stamps. Manuscript guidelines for #10 SASE.

O━ "Our mission as an evangelical Christian publisher is to provide—with integrity and excellence—trusted, biblically-based resources that challenge and encourage individuals in their Christian lives."

**Imprint(s):** Kregel Classics.

**Nonfiction:** Biography (Christian), reference, textbook. Religious subjects. "We serve evangelical Christian readers and those in career Christian service." Query with outline, 2 sample chapters, bio and market comparison.

**Recent Title(s):** *Suicide: A Christian Response,* by Gary Stewart and Timothy Demy.

**Tips:** "Looking for titles with broad appeal in the area of biblical studies and spiritual living. Projects are first evaluated on the basis of a proposal. Do not send complete manuscripts."

**KRIEGER PUBLISHING CO.**, P.O. Box 9542, Melbourne FL 32902-9542. (407)724-9542. Fax: (407)951-3671. E-mail: info@krieger-pub.com. Website: http://www.web4u.com/krieger-publishing/. **Acquisitions:** Elaine Harland, manager/editor (natural history/sciences and veterinary medicine); Michael W. Galbraith, series editor (adult education); Gordon Patterson, series editor (essays compiled to explore issues and concerns of scholars); Donald M. Waltz, series editor (space sciences). Estab. 1969. Publishes hardcover and paperback originals and reprints. **Publishes 60 titles/year. Receives 50-60 submissions/year. 30% of books from first-time authors; 100% from unagented writers. Pays royalty on net price.** Publishes book 1 year after acceptance of ms. Reports in 3 months. Book catalog free.

O━ "We provide accurate and well-documented scientific and technical titles for text and reference use, college level and higher."

**Imprint(s):** Anvil Series, Orbit Series, Public History.

**Nonfiction:** College reference, technical, textbook. Subjects include history, space science, herpetology, chemistry, physics, engineering, adult education, veterinary medicine, natural history, math. Query. Reviews artwork/photos as part of ms package.

**Recent Title(s):** *Taking the Stars: Celestial Navigation From Argonauts to Astronauts,* by Peter Ifland.

**KROSHKA BOOKS**, 6080 Jericho Turnpike, Suite 207, Commack NY 11725-2808. (516)499-3103. Fax: (516)499-3146. E-mail: novascience@earthlink.net. **Acquisitions:** Frank Columbus, editor-in-chief; Nadya Columbus, editor. Publishes hardcover and paperback originals. **Publishes 150 titles/year. Receives 1,000 queries/year. Pays royalty.** Publishes book 6-12 months year after acceptance. Accepts simultaneous submissions. Reports in 1 month.

O━ "Virtually all areas of human endeavor fall within our scope of interest."

**Imprint:** Troitsa Books.

**Nonfiction:** Biography, technical. Subjects include anthropology, business/economics, computers/electronics, nutrition, education, government/politics, health/medicine, history, money/finance, nature/environment, philosophy, psychology, recreation, religion, science, sociology, software, sports, childhood development. Query. Reviews artwork/photos as part of ms package. Send photocopies.

**Recent Title(s):** *Firemania,* by Carl Chiarelli.

**KUMARIAN PRESS, INC.**, 14 Oakwood Ave., West Hartford CT 06119-2127. (860)233-5895. Fax: (860)233-6072. E-mail: kpbooks@aol.com. Website: http://www.kpbooks.com. **Acquisitions:** Linda Beyus, acquisitions editor. Estab. 1977. Publishes hardcover and trade paperback originals. **Publishes 8-12 titles/year. Pays royalty of 7-10% of net.** Accepts simultaneous submissions, if so noted. Reports in 1 month on queries and proposals. Book catalog and ms guidelines free.

O━ Kumarian Press publishes books and other media that will have a positive social and economic impact on the lives of people living in "Third World" conditions, no matter where they live. "We publish books for professionals, academics, students interested in global affairs which includes international development, peace and conflict resolution, environmental sustainability, globalization, NGOs, women and gender."

**Nonfiction:** Professional, academic. Subjects include economics, government/politics, nature/environment, sociology, women's issues/studies, microenterprise, globalization, international development, sustainability. "Kumarian Press looks for mss that address world issues and promote change. Areas of interest include, but are not limited to: international development, peace and conflict resolution, gender, NGOs, Third World studies, environment and works that link the shared problems faced by both the North and the South." Submit proposal package including outline, 1-2 sample chapters, cv or résumé, intended readership, detailed table of contents and projected word count with SASE.

**Recent Title(s):** *Aiding Violence: the Development Enterprise in Rwanda,* by Peter Urin.

Ⓝ **LAKE VIEW PRESS**, P.O. Box 578279, Chicago IL 60657. **Acquisitions:** Paul Elitzik, director. Publishes hardcover and trade paperback originals. **Publishes 5 titles/year. Receives 100 queries and 10 mss/year. 100% of books from unagented writers. Pays 6-10% royalty on wholesale price.** Publishes book 1 year after acceptance of ms. Reports in 1 month on queries. *Writer's Market* recommends allowing 2 months for reply. Query with toc, c.v. and SASE. No sample chapters. Book catalog for 5½ × 8½ SASE.

O━ Lake View Press publishes scholarly nonfiction in sociology, criminology and film written in a manner accessible to a nonprofessional reader.

**Nonfiction:** Biography, reference, technical. Subjects include government/politics, history, language/literature, sociology, women's issues/studies. Query.

**Recent Title(s):** *Forsaking our Children: Bureaucracy & Reform in the Child Welfare System,* by John M. Hagedorn.

**LANDMARK SPECIALTY BOOKS**, (formerly Antique Trader Books), Landmark Specialty Publications, 150 W. Brambleton Ave., Norfolk VA 23510-2075. Website: http://www.collect.com. **Acquisitions**: Allan Miller, managing editor (toys and other popular collectibles); Tony Lillis, acquisitions editor (antiques, music memorabilia, military collectibles). Kyle Husfloen, consulting editor (antiques, glass, furniture, porcelain, metalware). Publishes hardcover and trade paperback originals. **Publishes 30 titles/year. Receives 58 queries and 20 mss/year. 60% of books from first-time authors; 100% from unagented writers. Pays 10-15% royalty on wholesale price. Offers $2,000-8,000 advance.** Publishes book 10 months after acceptance of ms. Accepts simultaneous submissions. Reports in 3 months on proposals. Book catalog and ms guidelines free.
  Oπ Antique Trader Books publishes annuals, reference books, collector's guides and price guides for all areas of collecting. "We provide high-quality, informative, comprehensive, accurate and entertaining price guides and reference books on the subject of antiques and collectibles." Currently emphasizing traditional antiques—glass, furniture, metalware, military collectibles.
**Imprint(s)**: Antique Trader Books, Tuff Stuff Books.
**Nonfiction**: Price guides. Subjects include hobbies (antiques and collectibles). Query or submit outline and 2 sample chapters and SASE. Reviews artwork/photos as part of ms package. Send duplicate prints or transparencies only.
**Recent Title(s)**: *The Bean Family Pocket Guide*, by Shawn Brecka.
**Tips**: "Audience includes collectors of just about everything and anything."

**PETER LANG PUBLISHING**, 275 Seventh Ave., New York NY 10001. (212)647-7700. Fax: (212)647-7707. Website: http://www.peterlang.com. Managing Director: Christopher S. Myers. Senior Editor: Heidi Burns, Ph.D. **Acquisitions**: Owen Lancer, editor. Estab. 1952. Publishes mostly hardcover originals. **Publishes 300 titles/year. 75% of books from first-time authors; 98% from unagented writers. Pays 10-20% royalty on net price. No advance.** Publishes book 1 year after acceptance. Reports in 3 months. Book catalog free.
  Oπ Peter Lang publishes scholarly monographs in the humanities and social sciences.
**Nonfiction**: Reference works, scholarly monographs. Subjects include education, literary criticism, Germanic and Romance languages, art history, business/economics, American and European political science, history, music, philosophy, psychology, religion, sociology, biography, mass media, theology, women's studies, cultural studies. All books are scholarly monographs, textbooks, reference books, reprints of historic texts, critical editions or translations. "We do not publish original fiction or poetry. We seek scholarly and critical editions only." No mss shorter than 200 pages. Query with cv and synopsis or sample chapter. Fully refereed review process.
**Recent Title(s)**: *Moral Outrage in Education*, by David Purple.
**Tips**: "Besides our commitment to specialist academic monographs, we are one of the few US publishers who publish books in most of the modern languages. A major advantage for Lang authors is international marketing and distribution of all titles. Translation rights sold for many titles."

**LANGENSCHEIDT PUBLISHING GROUP**, 46-35 54th Rd., Maspeth NY 11378. (800)432-MAPS. Fax: (718)784-0640. E-mail: spohja@langenscheidt.com. **Acquisitions**: Sue Pohja, acquisitions; Christine Cardone, editor. Estab. 1983. Publishes hardcover and trade paperback originals. **Publishes over 100 titles/year; imprint publishes 20 titles/year. Receives 25 queries and 15 mss/year. 100% of books from unagented writers. Pays royalty or makes outright purchase.** Publishes book 6 months after acceptance of ms. Accepts simultaneous submissions. Reports in 2 months on proposals. Book catalog free.
  Oπ Langenscheidt Publishing Group publishes maps, travel guides, foreign language dictionary products and educational materials.
**Imprint(s)**: ADC Map, American Map, Arrow Map, Creative Sales, Hagstrom Map, Hammond Map, Insight Guides, Trakker Map.
**Nonfiction**: Reference. Foreign language subjects. "Any foreign language that fills a gap in our line is welcome." Submit outline and 2 sample chapters (complete ms preferred.)
**Recent Title(s)**: *Diccionario Universal* (foreign language).
**Tips**: "Any item related to our map, foreign language dictionary and travel products could have potential for us."

**■ LARK BOOKS**, Altamont Press, 50 College St., Asheville NC 28801. E-mail: carol.taylor@larkbooks.com. Website: http://www.larkbooks.com. **Acquisitons**: Carol Taylor, publisher. Estab. 1976. Publishes hardcover and trade paperback originals and reprints. **Publishes over 50 titles/year. Receives 300 queries and 100 mss/year. 80% of books from first-time authors; 90% from unagented writers. Offers up to $2,500 advance.** Publishes book 1 year after acceptance of ms. Accepts simultaneous submissions. Reports in 2 months.
  Oπ Lark Books publishes high quality, highly illustrated books, primarily in the crafts/leisure markets celebrating the creative spirit. "We work closely with book clubs. Our books are either how-to, 'gallery' or combination books."
**Nonfiction**: Coffee table book, cookbook, how-to, illustrated book, children's/juvenile. Subjects include gardening, hobbies, nature/environment, crafts. Query first. If asked, submit outline and 1 sample chapter, sample projects, table of contents. Reviews artwork/photos as part of ms package. Send transparencies if possible.
**Recent Title(s)**: *Complete Book of Floorcloths*, by Cathy Cooper.
**Tips**: "We publish both first-time and seasoned authors. In either case, we need to know that you have substantial expertise on the topic of the proposed book—that we can trust you to know what you're talking about. If you're great at your craft but not so great as a writer, you might want to work with us as a coauthor or as a creative consultant."

**Ⓐ LAUREL BOOKS**, Bantam Dell Publishing Group, Random House, Inc., 1540 Broadway, New York NY 10036. (212)354-6500. **Acquisitions:** Maggie Crawford, editorial director. Publishes trade paperback and mass market originals. **Publishes 4 titles/year.**
**Fiction:** Literary anthologies. *Agented submissions only.*

**MERLOYD LAWRENCE BOOKS**, Perseus Book Group, 102 Chestnut St., Boston MA 02108. **Acquisitions:** Merloyd Lawrence, president. Estab. 1982. Publishes hardcover and trade paperback originals. **Publishes 7-8 titles/year. Receives 400 submissions/year. 25% of books from first-time authors; 20% from unagented writers. Pays royalty on retail price.** Publishes book 1 year after acceptance of ms. Accepts simultaneous submissions.
**Nonfiction:** Child development, health/medicine, nature/environment, psychology, social science. Query with SASE only. *All queries with SASE read and answered.* No unsolicited mss read.
**Recent Title(s):** *Respect: An Exploration*, by Sara Lawrence-Lightfoot; *Growth of the Mind*, by Stanley Greenspan.

**Ⓝ LEADERSHIP PUBLISHERS, INC.**, Talented and Gifted Education, P.O. Box 8358, Des Moines IA 50301-8358. (515)278-4765. Fax: (515)270-8303. **Acquisitions:** Lois F. Roets, editorial director. Estab. 1982. **Publishes 5 titles/year. Receives 20 queries and 25 mss/year. Pays 10% royalty of sales** or makes outright purchse of smaller mss. Publishes book 1 year after acceptance of ms. Reports in 3 months. Book catalog and ms guidelines for 9 × 12 SAE with 2 first-class stamps.
   Oₙ Leadership Publishers publishes enrichment programs and teacher reference books for education of the talented and gifted.
**Nonfiction:** Textbook. Education subjects. Submit outline and 2 sample chapters with SASE. "Queries and manuscripts with SASE will be returned, others will not be acknowledged nor returned."

**Ⓝ LEARNING PUBLICATIONS, INC.**, 5351 Gulf Dr., Holmes Beach FL 34217. (941)778-6651. Fax: (941)778-6818. E-mail: lpi@bhip.infi.net. Website: http://www.bhip.infi.net/~lpi. **Acquisitions:** Ruth Erickson, editor. Estab. 1975. Publishes trade paperback originals and reprints. **Publishes 10-15 titles/year. Receives 150 queries and 50 mss/year. 50% of books from first-time authors; 100% from unagented writers. Pays 5-10% royalty.** Publishes book 1 year after acceptance of ms. Accepts simultaneous submissions. Reports in 1 month on queries and proposals, 4 months on mss. Book catalog free. Manuscript guidelines for #10 SASE.
   Oₙ "We specifically market by direct mail to education and human service professionals materials to use with students and clients."
**Nonfiction:** Reference, textbook, curricula and manuals for education and human service professionals. Subjects include education, psychology, sociology, women's issues/studies. "Writers interested in submitting manuscripts should request our guidelines first." Query and submit outline and/or table of contents, 1 sample chapter, proposal package, including one-page synopsis and résumé with SASE. Reviews artwork/photos as part of ms package. Send photocopies.
**Recent Title(s):** *Process-Oriented Group Therapy for Men and Women Sexually Abused as Children*, by Carolyn Knight, Ph.D. (psychology/therapy).
**Tips:** "Learning Publications has a limited, specific market. Writers should be familiar with who buys our books."

**Ⓝ LEBHAR-FRIEDMAN BOOKS**, Lebhar-Friedman, Inc., 425 Park Ave., New York NY 10022-3556. (212)756-5204. Fax: (212)756-5128. E-mail: fscatoni@lf.com. Website: http://www.lfbooks.com. **Acquisitions:** Frank R. Scatoni, associate editor; Paul Frumkin, senior editor; Geoff Colson, publisher. Publishes hardcover originals and reprints, trade paperback originals and reprints. **Publishes 10-15 titles/year. Receives over 100 queries and over 100 mss/year. 50% of books from first-time authors; 40% from unagented writers. Pays 7½-15% royalty on retail price. Offers competitive advances.** Publishes book 1 year after acceptance of ms. Accepts simultaneous submissions. Reports in 1 month on queries, 2 months on proposals, 3 months on mss. Book catalog and ms guidelines on website.
**Nonfiction:** Biography, coffee table book, cookbook, gift book, how-to, humor, illustrated book, multimedia, reference, self-help, technical, textbook. Subjects include agriculture/horticulture, Americana, animals, anthropology/archaeology, art/architecture, business/economics, child guidance/parenting, computers/electronics, cooking/foods/nutrition, creative nonfiction, education, ethnic, gardening, government/politics, health/medicine, history, hobbies, language/literature, memoirs, money/finance, nature/environment, philosophy, photography, psychology, recreation, regional, religion, science, sociology, software, spirituality, travel, women's issues/women's studies. Query with SASE or submit proposal package, including outline and 2 sample chapters. Reviews artwork as part of ms package. Reviews photocopies, not originals.
**Recent Title(s):** *A Taste of Hollywood: The Story of Ma Maison*, by Patrick Terrail (entertainment/memoir); *Last Suppers*, by James Dickerson (pop culture/cooking).

**LEE & LOW BOOKS**, 95 Madison Ave., New York NY 10016. (212)779-4400. Fax: (212)683-1894. Website: http://www.leeandlow.com. **Acquisitions:** Louise May, senior editor. Estab. 1991. **Publishes 12 titles/year.** Send complete ms with SASE. Reports in 5 months. Encourages new writers. Manuscript guidelines on website.
   Oₙ "Our goals are to meet a growing need for books that address children of color, and to present literature that all children can identify with. We only consider multicultural children's picture books." Currently emphasizing material for 2-5 year olds.
**Recent Title(s):** *Elizabeth's Doll*, by Stephanie Stuve-Bodeen, illustrated by Christy Hale.
**Tips:** "Of special interest are stories set in contemporary America. We are interested in fiction as well as nonfiction.

We do not consider folktales, fairy tales or animal stories."

**J & L LEE CO.**, P.O. Box 5575, Lincoln NE 68505. **Acquisitions:** James L. McKee, publisher. Publishes trade paperback originals and reprints. **Publishes 5 titles/year. Receives 25 queries and 5-10 mss/year. 20% of books from first-time authors; 60% from unagented writers. Pays 10% royalty on retail price or makes outright purchase of $100 minimum. Rarely offers advance.** Publishes book 10 months after acceptance of ms. Accepts simultaneous submissions. Reports in 6 months on queries and mss, 1 month on proposals. Book catalog free.

   O⌐ "Virtually everything we publish is of a Great Plains nature."

**Imprint(s):** Salt Creek Press, Young Hearts.

**Nonfiction:** Biography, reference. Subjects include Americana, history, regional. Query.

**Recent Title(s):** *Lay of the Land*, by Brent Olson.

**LEHIGH UNIVERSITY PRESS**, Linderman Library, 30 Library Dr., Lehigh University, Bethlehem PA 18015-3067. (610)758-3933. Fax: (610)974-2823. E-mail: inlup@lehigh.edu. **Acquisitions:** Philip A. Metzger, director. Estab. 1985. Publishes hardcover originals. **Publishes 10 titles/year. Receives 90-100 queries and 50-60 mss/year. 70% of books from first-time authors; 100% from unagented writers. Pays royalty.** Publishes book 18 months after acceptance of ms. Accepts simultaneous submissions. Reports in 3 months. Book catalog and ms guidelines free.

   O⌐ Lehigh University Press is an academic press publishing scholarly monographs. "We are especially interested in works on 18th century studies and the history of technology, but consider works of quality on a variety of subjects."

**Nonfiction:** Biography, reference, academic. Subjects include Americana, art/architecture, history, language/literature, science. Submit 1 sample chapter and proposal package.

**Recent Title(s):** *Machiavelli Redeemed: Retrieving His Humanist Perspectives on Equality, Power and Glory*, by Robert A. Kocis.

**LEISURE BOOKS**, 276 Fifth Ave., Suite 1008, New York NY 10001-0112. (212)725-8811. Fax: (212)532-1054. E-mail: dorchedit@dorchesterpub.com. **Acquisitions:** Jennifer Bonnell, editorial assistant; Kate Seaver, editorial assistant; Alicia Condon, editorial director; Don D'Auria, senior editor (Westerns, technothrillers, horror); Christopher Keeslar, editor. Estab. 1970. Publishes mass market paperback originals and reprints. **Publishes 160 titles/year. Receives thousands of mss/year. 20% of books from first-time authors; 20% from unagented writers. Pays royalty on retail price. Advance negotiable.** Publishes book 18 months after acceptance of ms. Reports in 6 months on queries. Book catalog free (800)481-9191. Manuscript guidelines for #10 SASE.

   O⌐ Leisure Books is seeking historical romances, westerns, horror and technothrillers.

**Imprint(s): Love Spell** (romance), **Leisure** (romance, western, techno, horror).

**Fiction:** Historical romance (90,000-100,000 words); time-travel romance (90,000 words); futuristic romance (90,000 words); westerns (75,000-115,000 words); horror (90,000 words); technothrillers (90,000 words). "We are strongly backing historical romance. All historical romance should be set pre-1900. Horrors and westerns are growing as well. No sweet romance, gothic, science fiction, erotica, contemporary women's fiction, mainstream or action/adventure." Query or submit outline/synopsis and first 3 sample chapters only. "No material returned without SASE."

**Recent Title(s):** *Mine to Take*, by Dara Joy (romance).

**LERNER PUBLISHING GROUP**, 241 First Ave. N., Minneapolis MN 55401. (612)332-3344. Website: http://www.lernerbooks.com. **Editor-in-Chief:** Mary Rodgers. **Acquisitions:** Jennifer Martin, editor. Estab. 1959. Publishes hardcover originals, trade paperback originals and reprints. **Publishes 150-175 titles/year; First Avenue Edition, 30; Carolrhoda, 50-60; Runestone Press, 3. Receives 1,000 queries and 300 mss/year. 20% of books from first-time authors; 95% from unagented writers. Pays 3-8% royalty on net price (approximately 60% of books) or makes outright purchase of $1,000-3,000 (for series and work-for-hire). Offers $1,000-3,000 advance.** Publishes book 2 years after acceptance of ms. Submissions accepted March 1 to March 31 and October 1 to October 31, only. Accepts simultaneous submissions. Reports in 4 months on proposals. Catalog for 9×12 SAE with 6 first-class stamps. Manuscript guidelines for #10 SASE. "Requests for catalogs and submissions guidelines must be clearly addressed as such on envelope."

   O⌐ "Our goal is to publish books that educate, stimulate and stretch the imagination, foster global awareness, encourage critical thinking and inform, inspire and entertain." Currently emphasizing biographies. De-emphasizing fiction.

**Imprint(s): Carolrhoda Books**; First Avenue Editions (paperback reprints for hard/soft deals only); Lerner Publica-

**FOR EXPLANATIONS OF THESE SYMBOLS,**
**SEE THE INSIDE FRONT AND BACK COVERS OF THIS BOOK.**

tions; Runestone Press.

**Nonfiction:** Children's/juvenile (grades 3-10). Subjects include art/architecture, biography, ethnic, history, nature/environment, science, sports, aviation, geography. Query with outline, 1-2 sample chapters, SASE.

**Fiction:** Juvenile (middle grade). "We are not actively pursuing fiction titles." Query with synopsis, 1-2 sample chapters and SASE.

**Recent Title(s):** *Emily Dickinson: Singular Poet*, by Carol Dommermuth-Costa (biography).

**LIFETIME BOOKS, INC.**, 2131 Hollywood Blvd., Suite 305, Hollywood FL 33073. (954)925-5242. Fax: (954)925-5244. E-mail: lifetime@shadow.net. Website: http://www.lifetimebooks.com. **Acquisitions:** Callie Rucker, senior editor. Estab. 1943. Publishes hardcover and trade paperback originals. **Publishes 20-25 titles/year. Receives 1,500-2,00 queries and 1,000 mss/year. 95% of books from first-time authors; 95% from unagented writers. Pays negotiable royalty on retail price. Offers advance of $0-10,000.** Publishes book 4 months after acceptance. Accepts simultaneous submissions. Reports in 1 month on queries and proposals, 2 months on mss. Book catalog and ms guidelines for #10 SASE.

○┓ "Lifetime Books is committed to inspiring readers to improve all aspects of their lives by providing how-to and self-help information which can help them obtain such a goal."

**Imprint(s):** Compact Books (contact Donald Lessne); Fell Publishers; Lifetime Periodicals.

**Nonfiction:** Children's/juvenile, cookbooks, giftbooks, reference, how-to, self-help. Subjects include animals, business and sales, child guidance/parenting, cooking/food/nutrition, education, ethnic, health/medicine, hobbies, bio/exposé, money/finance, philosophy, psychology, religion, sports. "We are interested in material on business, health and fitness, self-improvement and reference. We will not consider topics that only appeal to a small, select audience." Submit outline, author bio, publicity ideas, proposals and 3 sample chapters. Reviews artwork as part of ms package. Send photocopies. No poetry, no fiction, no short stories, no children's.

**Recent Title(s):** *The Leader Within You* (business/inspiration).

**Tips:** "We are most interested in well-written, timely nonfiction with strong sales potential. Our audience is very general. Learn markets and be prepared to help with sales and promotion. Show us how your book is unique, different or better than the competition."

**LIGUORI PUBLICATIONS**, One Liguori Dr., Liguori MO 63057. (314)464-2500. Fax: (314)464-8449. E-mail: 104626.1563@compuserve.com. Website: http://www.liguori.org. Publisher: Thomas M. Santa, C.SS.R. **Acquisitions:** Judith A. Bauer, managing editor (Trade Group); Patricia Kossman, executive editor (Trade Group, New York office 718/229-8001, ext. 231 or 232, Fax: 718/631-5339.); Kass Dotterweich and Elsie McGrath, managing editors (Catechetical and Pastoral Resources Group); Scott Guillot, software engineer (Electronic Publishing). Estab. 1943. The Trade Group publishes hardcover and trade paperback originals and reprints under the Liguori and Liguori/Triumph imprints; publishes 30 titles/year. The Catechetical and Pastoral Resources Group publishes paperback originals and reprints under the Liguori and Libros Liguori imprints: **Publishes 50 titles/year, including Spanish-language titles. The Electronic Publishing Division publishes 4 titles/year under the Faithware® imprint. Royalty varies or purchases outright. Advance varies.** Publishes 2 years after acceptance of ms. Prefers no simultaneous submissions. Reports in 2 months on queries and proposals, 3 months on mss. Author guidelines on request.

○┓ Liguori Publications, faithful to the charism of Saint Alphonsus, is an apostolate within the mission of the Denver Province. Its mission, a collaborative effort of Redemptorists and laity, is to spread the gospel of Jesus Christ primarily through the print and electronic media. It shares in the Redemptorist priority of giving special attention to the poor and the most abandoned. Currently emphasizing practical spirituality, spiritual slant on secular topics.

**Imprint(s):** Faithware®, Libros Liguori, Liguori Books, Liguori/Triumph.

**Nonfiction:** Inspirational, devotional, prayer, Christian-living, self-help books. Religious subjects. Mostly adult audience; limited children/juvenile. Query with annotated outline, 1 sample chapter, SASE. Query for CD-ROM and Internet publishing. Publishes very few electronic products received unsolicited.

**Recent Title(s):** *Simple Truths* by Fulton J. Sheen (spirituality).

**LIMELIGHT EDITIONS**, Proscenium Publishers, Inc., 118 E. 30th St., New York NY 10016. Fax: (212)532-5526. E-mail: jjlmlt@idt.net. Website: http://www.limelighteditions.com. **Acquisitions:** Melvyn B. Zerman, president; Roxanna Font, assistant publisher. Estab. 1983. Publishes hardcover and trade paperback originals, trade paperback reprints. **Publishes 14 titles/year. Receives 150 queries and 40 mss/year. 15% of books from first-time authors; 20% from unagented writers. Pays 7½ (paperback)-10% (hardcover) royalty on retail price. Offers $500-2,000 advance.** Publishes book 10 months after acceptance of ms. Reports in 1 month on queries and proposals, 3 months on mss. Book catalog and ms guidelines free.

○┓ Limelight Editions publishes books on film, theater, music and dance. "Our books make a strong contribution to their fields and deserve to remain in print for many years."

**Nonfiction:** Biography, historical, humor, instructional—most illustrated—on music/dance or theater/film. "All books are on the performing arts *exclusively*." Query with proposal package, including 2-3 sample chapters, outline with SASE. Reviews artwork/photos as part of ms package. Send photocopies.

**Recent Title(s):** *Zero Dances: A Biography of Zero Mostel*, by Arthur Sainer.

**LION PUBLISHING**, Chariot Victor Publishing, 4050 Lee Vance View, Colorado Springs CO 80918-7102. (719)536-3271. Fax: (719)536-3269. **Acquisitions:** Karen Artl, product manager. Publishes hardcover and trade paperback originals. **Published 10 titles/year. Pays variable royalty on wholesale price. Advance varies.** Publishes book 18 months after acceptance of ms. Accepts simultaneous submissions, if so noted. Reports in 3 months on queries.

> ○➞ "Lion Publishing's books are more 'seeker-sensitive' than Chariot; more accessible to the 'unchurched.' Lion seeks to lead the way with Spiritual Growth products."

**Nonfiction:** Biography, gift book, devotional. Subjects include child guidance/parenting, religion, marriage/family, inspirational, Christian living. Query or submit outline, 1 sample chapter with SASE.

**Fiction:** Religious. Query with complete ms. *Writer's Market* recommends query with SASE first.

**Recent Title(s):** *What a Wonderful World!*, by Pat Alexander (stories and poems); *The Lord's Prayer for Children*, by Lois Rock.

> ● Lion Publishing originates and distributes books in the United Kingdom and the United States. The numbers listed above do not include titles originating in and distributed solely in the UK.

**Tips:** "All Lion books are written from a Christian perspective. However, they must speak primarily to a general audience. Half of our titles are children's books, yet we receive few manuscripts of publishable quality and almost no nonfiction of *any* kind. In short, we need high-quality nonfiction of all types that fit our guidelines."

**LIPPINCOTT WILLIAMS & WILKENS**, (formerly Lippincott-Raven), 227 E. Washington Sq., Philadelphia PA 19106. (215)238-4200. Fax: (215)238-4227. Website: http://www.LWW.com. **Acquisitions:** Janice Ryan, vice president/publisher; Anne S. Patterson, vice president/publisher (medical); Timothy Butterfield, executive vice president Education/Reference; Donna Hilton, vice president/editor-in-chief, nursing. Estab. 1792. Publishes hardcover originals. **Publishes 325 titles/year. Pay rates vary depending on type of book, whether the author is the principal or contributing author and amount of production necessary.** Accepts simultaneous submissions, if so noted. Reports in 3 months on proposals.

> ○➞ The mission of Lippincott Williams & Wilkens is to disseminate healthcare information, including basic science, for medical and nursing students and ongoing education for practicing nursing and clinicians.

**Imprint(s):** Lippincott.

**Nonfiction:** Reference, textbook, manuals, atlases on health/medicine subjects. "We do not publish for the layperson." Query with proposal package including outline, table of contents, cv, proposed market and how your ms differs, estimate number of trim size pages and number and type of illustrations (line drawing, half-tone, 4-color).

**Recent Title(s):** *Washington Manual of Medical Therapeutics*, 29th ed.

**Tips:** Audience is medical and nursing students, medical students and practicing nurses and clinicians.

**LITTLE, BROWN AND CO., INC.**, Time Warner Inc., 1271 Avenue of the Americas, New York NY 10020. (212)522-8700. Editor-in-Chief: Michael Pietsch. **Acquisitions:** Editorial Department, Trade Division. Estab. 1837. Publishes hardcover originals and paperback originals and reprints. **Publishes 100 titles/year. "Royalty and advance agreements vary from book to book and are discussed with the author at the time an offer is made."**

> ○➞ "The general editorial philosophy for all divisions continues to be broad and flexible, with high quality and the promise of commercial success as always the first considerations."

**Imprint(s):** Back Bay Books; **Bulfinch Press**; **Little, Brown and Co. Children's Books**.

**Nonfiction:** "Issue books, autobiography, biographies, culture, cookbooks, history, popular science, nature and sports." Query *only. No unsolicited mss or proposals.*

**Fiction:** Contemporary popular fiction as well as fiction of literary distinction. Query *only. No unsolicited mss.*

**Recent Title(s):** *Naked*, by David Sedaris (nonfiction); *Blood Work*, by Michael Connelly (fiction).

Ⓐ **LITTLE, BROWN AND CO., CHILDREN'S BOOKS**, 3 Center Plaza, Boston MA 02108. (617)227-0730. Website: http://www.littlebrown.com. Editorial Director/Associate Publisher: Maria Modugno. Executive Editor: Megan Tingley. **Acquisitions:** Leila Little. Estab. 1837. Publishes hardcover originals, trade paperback originals and reprints. **Firm publishes 60-70 titles/year. Pays royalty on retail price. Offers advance to be negotiated individually.** Publishes book 2 years after acceptance of ms. Accepts simultaneous submissions, if so noted. Reports in 1 month on queries, 2 months on proposals and mss.

> ○➞ Little, Brown and Co. publishes books on a wide variety of nonfiction topics which may be of interest to children and are looking for strong writing and presentation, but no predetermined topics.

**Nonfiction:** Children's/juvenile, middle grade and young adult. Subjects include animals, art/architecture, ethnic, gay/lesbian, history, hobbies, nature/environment, recreation, science, sports. Writers should avoid "looking for the 'issue' they think publishers want to see, choosing instead topics they know best and are most enthusiastic about/inspired by." *Agented submissions only.*

**Fiction:** All juvenile/young adult; picture books. Categories include adventure, ethnic, fantasy, feminist, gay/lesbian, historical, humor, mystery, science fiction and suspense. "We are looking for strong fiction for children of all ages in any area, including multicultural. We always prefer full manuscripts for fiction." *Agented submissions only.*

**Recent Title(s):** *The Tale I Told Sasha*, by Nancy Willard, illustrated by David Christiana.

**Tips:** "Our audience is children of all ages, from preschool through young adult. We are looking for quality material that will work in hardcover—send us your best."

**LITTLE SIMON**, Simon & Schuster Children's Publishing Division, Simon & Schuster, 1230 Avenue of the Americas, New York NY 10020. (212)698-7200. Website: http://www.simonandschuster.com. Vice President/Publisher: Robin Corey. **Acquisitions:** Alison Weir, editorial director; Laura Hunt, senior editor. Publishes novelty books only. **Publishes 75 titles/year. 5% of books from first-time authors; 5% from unagented writers. Pays 2-5% royalty on retail price for original, non-licensed mss.** Publishes book 6 months after acceptance of ms. Reports on queries in 8 months.

⊶ "Our goal is to provide fresh material in an innovative format for pre-school to age eight. Our books are often, if not exclusively, illustrator driven."

**Nonfiction:** Children's/juvenile novelty books. "Novelty books include many things that do not fit in the traditional hardcover or paperback format, such as pop-up, board book, scratch and sniff, glow in the dark, open the flap, etc." Query only with SASE. *All unsolicited mss returned unopened.*

**Recent Title(s):** *Giggle Bugs*, by David A. Carter (flap book with sound chip).

**LITTLE TIGER PRESS**, % Futech, N16 W23390 Stoneridge Dr., Waukesha WI 53188. (414)544-2001. Fax: (414)544-2022. **Acquisitions:** Jody A. Linn. Estab. 1995. Publishes hardcover originals. **Publishes 20-25 titles/year. Receives 300 queries and 1,800 mss/year. 75% of books from first-time authors; 85% from unagented writers. Pays 7½-10% royalty on retail price or for first-time authors makes outright purchase of $800-2,500. Offers $2,000 minimum advance.** Publishes book 1 year after acceptance of ms. Accepts simultaneous submissions. Reports in 2 months on queries and proposals, 3 months on mss. Book catalog for 9×11 SASE with 3 first-class stamps. Manuscript guidelines for #10 SASE.

⊶ "We focus on bringing new talent into the field of children's books and publishing appealing, funny, and memorable titles. Our goal is to provide books that will win the hearts of adults as well as children."

**Imprint:** Futech.

**Fiction:** Humor, juvenile, picture books. "Humorous stories, stories about animals, children's imagination, or realistic fiction are especially sought." Send ms with SASE.

**Recent Title(s):** *Smudge*, by Julian Sykes (picture hard core).

**Tips:** "Audience is children 3-8 years old. We are looking for simple, basic picture books, preferably humorous, that children will enjoy again and again. We do not have a multicultural or social agenda."

**LIVINGSTON PRESS**, Station 22, University of West Alabama, Livingston AL 35470. **Acquisitions:** Joe Taylor, director. Estab. 1984. Publishes hardcover and trade paperback originals. **Publishes 4-6 titles/year; imprint publishes 1 title/year. 20% of books from first-time authors; 90% from unagented writers. Pays 12½% of book run.** Publishes book 18 months after acceptance of ms. Accepts simultaneous submissions. Reports in 1 month on queries; 1 year on mss.

⊶ Livingston Press publishes topics such as southern literature and quirky fiction. Currently emphasizing short stories. De-emphasizing poetry.

**Imprint(s):** Swallow's Tale Press.

**Nonfiction:** Local history, folklore only. Query. *All unsolicited mss returned.*

**Fiction:** Experimental, literary, short story collections. Query with SASE.

**Recent Title(s):** *Longrider*, by Mark Edmonds (nonfiction); *Detecting Metal*, by Fred Bonnie (fiction); *Hard Facts*, by Peter Huggins.

**Poetry:** "We publish very little poetry, mostly books we have asked to see." Query with SASE.

**Recent Poetry Title(s):** *Flight From Valhalla*, by Michael Bugeja (poetry); *Hunter-Gatherer*, by R.T. Smith; *Lizard Fever*, by Eugene Walter.

**Tips:** "Our readers are interested in literature, often quirky literature."

**LLEWELLYN PUBLICATIONS**, Llewellyn Worldwide, Ltd., P.O. Box 64383, St. Paul MN 55164-0383. (612)291-1970. Fax: (612)291-1908. E-mail: lwlpc@llewellyn.com. Website: http://www.llewellyn.com. **Acquisitions:** Nancy J. Mostad, acquisitions manager (New Age, metaphysical, occult, self-help, how-to books); Barbara Wright, acquisitions editor (kits and decks). Estab. 1901. Publishes trade and mass market paperback originals. **Publishes 100 titles/year. Receives 2,000 submissions/year. 30% of books from first-time authors; 90% from unagented writers. Pays 10% royalty on moneys received both wholesale and retail.** Accepts simultaneous submissions. Reports in 3 months. Book catalog for 9×12 SAE with 4 first-class stamps. Manuscript guidelines for SASE.

⊶ Llewellyn publishes New Age fiction and nonfiction exploring "new worlds of mind and spirit." Currently emphasizing astrology, wicca, alternative health and healing, tarot. De-emphasizing fiction, channeling.

**Nonfiction:** How-to, self-help. Subjects include nature/environment, health and nutrition, metaphysical/magic, astrology, tarot, women's issues/studies. Submit outline and sample chapters. Reviews artwork/photos as part of ms package.

---

**MARKET CONDITIONS** are constantly changing! If this is 2001 or later, buy the newest edition of *Writer's Market* at your favorite bookstore or order directly from Writer's Digest Books.

**Fiction:** Metaphysical/occult, which is authentic and educational, yet entertaining.
**Recent Title(s):** *Teen Witch*, by Silver RavenWolf (nonfiction).

**LOCUST HILL PRESS**, P.O. Box 260, West Cornwall CT 06796-0260. (860)672-0060. Fax: (860)672-4968. **Acquisitions:** Thomas C. Bechtle, publisher. Estab. 1985. Publishes hardcover originals. **Publishes 12 titles/year. Receives 150 queries and 20 mss/year. 100% of books from unagented writers. Pays 12-18% royalty on retail price.** Publishes book 6 months after acceptance of ms. Accepts simultaneous submissions. Reports in 1 month. *Writer's Market* recommends allowing 2 months for reply. Book catalog free.
  O— Locust Hill Press specializes in scholarly reference and bibliography works for college and university libraries worldwide, as well as monographs and essay collections on literary subjects.
**Nonfiction:** Reference. Subjects include ethnic, language/literature, women's issues/studies. "Since our audience is exclusively college and university libraries (and the occasional specialist), we are less inclined to accept manuscripts in 'popular' (i.e., public library) fields. While bibliography has been and will continue to be a specialty, our Locust Hill Literary Studies is gaining popularity as a series of essay collections and monographs in a wide variety of literary topics." Query.
**Recent Title(s):** *Thornton Wilder: New Essays*, by Martin Blank, Dalma Brunaver and David Izzo.
**Tips:** "Remember that this is a small, very specialized academic publisher with no distribution network other than mail contact with most academic libraries worldwide. Please shape your expectations accordingly. If your aim is to reach the world's scholarly community by way of its libraries, we are the correct firm to contact. But *please*: no fiction, poetry, popular religion, or personal memoirs."

**LONE EAGLE PUBLISHING CO.**, 2337 Roscomare Rd., Suite 9, Los Angeles CA 90077-1851. (310)471-8066 or 1-800-FILMBKS. Fax: (310)471-4969. E-mail: info@loneeagle.com. Website: http://www.loneeagle.com. **Acquisitions:** Jeff Black, editor. Estab. 1982. Publishes perfectbound and trade paperback originals. **Publishes 15 titles/year. Receives 100 submissions/year. 80% of books from unagented writers. Pays 10% royalty minimum on net income wholesale. Offers $500-1,000 average advance.** Publishes book 1 year after acceptance of ms. Accepts simultaneous submissions. Reports quarterly on queries. Book catalog free.
  O— Lone Eagle Publishing Company publishes reference directories that contain comprehensive and accurate credits, personal data and contact information for every major entertainment industry craft. Lone Eagle also publishes many 'how-to' books for the film production business, including books on screenwriting, directing, budgeting and producing, acting, editing, etc.
**Nonfiction:** Technical, how-to, reference. Film and television subjects. "We are looking for books in film and television, related topics or biographies." Submit outline, toc and sample chapters. Reviews artwork/photos as part of ms package.
**Recent Title(s):** *Elements of Style for Screenwriters*, by Paul Argentina.
**Tips:** "A well-written, well-thought-out book on some technical aspect of the motion picture (or video) industry has the best chance. Pick a subject that has not been done to death, make sure you know what you're talking about, get someone well-known in that area to endorse the book and prepare to spend a lot of time publicizing the book. Completed manuscripts have the best chance for acceptance."

**LONELY PLANET PUBLICATIONS**, 150 Linden St., Oakland CA 94607-2538. (510)893-8555. Fax: (510)893-8563. E-mail: info@lonelyplanet.com. Website: http://www.lonelyplanet.com. **Acquisitions:** Mariah Bear, publishing manager (travel guide books); Roslyn Bullas, publishing manager (Picses). Estab. 1973. Publishes trade paperback originals. **Publishes 60 titles/year. Receives 500 queries and 100 mss/year. 5% of books from first-time authors; 50% from unagented writers. Makes outright purchase or negotiated fee—⅓ on contract, ⅓ on submission, ⅓ on approval.** Publishes book 2 years after acceptance of ms. Accepts simultaneous submissions. Reports in 3 months on queries. Manuscript guidelines for #10 SASE.
  O— Lonely Planet publishes travel guides, atlases, travel literature, diving and snorkeling guides.
**Nonfiction:** Travel guides, phrasebooks atlases and travel literature exclusively. "Request our catalog first to make sure we don't already have a similar book or call and see if a similar book is on our production schedule." Submit outline or proposal package. Reviews artwork/photos as part of ms package. Send photocopies.
**Recent Title(s):** *Diving and Snorkeling in Baja*.

🅐 **LONGSTREET PRESS, INC.**, 2140 Newmarket Parkway, Suite 122, Marietta GA 30067. (770)980-1488. Fax: (770)859-9894. President/Editor: Chuck Perry. **Acquisitions:** Editorial Department. Estab. 1988. Publishes hardcover and trade paperback originals. **Publishes 45 titles/year. Receives 2,500 submissions/year. 10% of books from first-time authors; none from unagented writers. Pays royalty.** Publishes book 1 year after acceptance of ms. Accepts simultaneous submissions. Reports in 3 months. Book catalog for 9×12 SAE with 4 first-class stamps. Manuscript guidelines for #10 SASE.
  O— Although Longstreet Press publishes a number of genres, their strengths have been humor, business, guidebooks, cookbooks, and fiction. "As Southern publishers, we look for regional material."
**Nonfiction:** Biography, coffee table book, cookbook, humor, illustrated book, reference. Subjects include Americana, cooking/foods/nutrition, gardening, history, language/literature, nature/environment, photography, regional, sports, women's issues/studies. "No poetry, scientific or highly technical, textbooks of any kind, erotica." *Agented submissions only.*
**Fiction:** Literary, mainstream/contemporary. *Agented fiction only.*

**Recent Title(s):** *Hill Country*, by Janice Woods Windle.

**LOOMPANICS UNLIMITED**, P.O. Box 1197, Port Townsend WA 98368-0997. Fax: (360)385-7785. E-mail: loompse ditor@olympus.net. Website: http://www.loompanics.com. President: Michael Hoy. **Acquisitions:** Vanessa McGrady, chief editor. Estab. 1975. Publishes trade paperback originals. **Publishes 15 titles/year. Receives 500 submissions/year. 40% of books from first-time authors; 100% from unagented writers. Pays 10-15% royalty on wholesale or retail price or makes outright purchase of $100-1,200. Offers $500 average advance.** Publishes book 1 year after acceptance of ms. Accepts simultaneous submissions. Reports in 2 months. Author guidelines free. Book catalog for $5, postpaid.

    O⟶ The mission statement offered by Loompanics is "no more secrets—no more excuses—no more limits! We publish how-to books with an edge. We are always looking for beat-the-system books on crime, tax avoidance, survival, drug manufacture, revenge and self-sufficiency."

**Nonfiction:** How-to, reference, self-help. "In general, works about outrageous topics or obscure-but-useful technology written authoritatively in a matter-of-fact way." Subjects include the underground economy, crime, drugs, privacy, self-sufficiency, anarchism and "beat the system" books. "We are looking for how-to books in the fields of espionage, investigation, the underground economy, police methods, how to beat the system, crime and criminal techniques. We are also looking for similarly-written articles for our catalog and its supplements. No cookbooks, inspirational, travel, management or cutesy-wutesy stuff." Query or submit outline/synopsis and sample chapters. Reviews artwork/photos.

**Recent Title(s):** *Drink as Much as You Want and Live Longer*, by Fred Beyerlein.

**Tips:** "Our audience is young males looking for hard-to-find information on alternatives to 'The System.' Your chances for success are greatly improved if you can show us how your proposal fits in with our catalog."

**LOTHROP, LEE & SHEPARD BOOKS**, William Morrow & Co., 1350 Avenue of the Americas, New York NY 10019-6641. (212)261-6640. Fax: (212)261-6648. **Acquisitions:** Susan Pearson, editor-in-chief; Melanie Donovan, senior editor. Estab. 1859. Publishes hardcover originals only. **Publishes 30 titles/year. Fewer than 2% of books from first-time authors; 25% of books from unagented writers. Royalty and advance vary according to type of book.** Publishes book within 2 years of acceptance of artwork. Reports in 3 months.

    O⟶ Lothrop, Lee & Shepard publishes children's books only, including fiction, nonfiction and poetry for children from preschool through YA.

**Fiction and Nonfiction:** Publishes picture books, general nonfiction, poetry and novels. Looks for "organization, clarity, creativity, literary style." Query with samples. *No unsolicited mss.*

**Recent Title(s):** *Bound for America*, by James Haskins and Kathleen Benson, illustrated by Floyd Cooper (nonfiction).

**LOUISIANA STATE UNIVERSITY PRESS**, P.O. Box 25053, Baton Rouge LA 70894-5053. (504)388-6294. Fax: (504)388-6461. **Acquisitions:** L.E. Phillabaum, director; Maureen G. Hewitt, assistant director and editor-in-chief; John Easterly, executive editor; Sylvia Frank, acquisitions editor. Estab. 1935. Publishes hardcover originals, hardcover and trade paperback reprints. **Publishes 70-80 titles/year. Receives 800 submissions/year. 33% of books from first-time authors. 95% from unagented writers. Pays royalty on list and net price.** Publishes book 1 years after acceptance of ms. Reports in 1 month on queries. *Writer's Market* recommends allowing 2 months for reply. Book catalog and ms guidelines free.

**Nonfiction:** Biography and literary poetry collections. Subjects include anthropology/archaeology, art/architecture, ethnic, government/politics, history, language/literature, military/war, music/dance, philosophy, photography, regional, sociology, women's issues/studies. Query or submit outline and sample chapters.

**Recent Title(s):** *The Collected Poems of Robert Penn Warren* (poetry); *Lee and His Generals in War and Memory*, by Gary W. Gallagher (history).

**Tips:** "Our audience includes scholars, intelligent laymen, general audience."

**THE LOVE AND LOGIC PRESS, INC.**, Cline/Fay Institute, Inc., 2207 Jackson St., Golden CO 80401. Fax: (303)278-3894. Website: http://www.loveandlogic.com. **Acquisitions:** Nancy Lucero, president/publisher (multiculturalism, social change, community organizing, progressive social work practice); Jeannie Jacobson, product development specialist (education, design). Publishes hardcover and trade paperback originals. **Publishes 5-12 titles/year. 10% of books from first-time authors; 100% from unagented writers. Pays 7½-12% royalty on wholesale price. Offers $500-5,000 advance.** Publishes book 18 months after acceptance of ms. Accepts simultaneous submissions. Reports in 1 month on queries and proposals; 3 months on mss. Book catalog free.

    O⟶ "We publish titles which help empower parents, teachers and others who help young people, and which help these individuals become more skilled and happier in their interactions with children. Our titles stress building personal responsibility in children and helping them become prepared to function well in the world." Currently emphasizing parenting, classroom management. De-emphasizing psychology, self-help.

**Nonfiction:** Self-help. Subjects include child guidance/parenting, education, health/medicine, psychology, sociology, current social issue trends. "We consider any queries/proposals falling into the above categories (with the exception of parenting) but especially psychology/sociology and current social issues and trends." No mss or proposals in New Age category, personal recovery stories, i.e., experiences with attempted suicide, drug/alcohol abuse, institutionalization or medical experiences. Query with SASE. Reviews artwork/photos as part of ms package. Send photocopies.

**Recent Title(s):** *Humor, Play and Laughter: Stress-proofing Life With Your Kids*, by Joseph Michelli, Ph.D.

**LOVE SPELL**, Leisure Books, Dorchester Publishing Co., Inc., 276 Fifth Ave., Suite 1008, New York NY 10001-0112. (212)725-8811. **Acquisitions**: Jennifer Bonnell, editorial assistant; Kate Seaver, editorial assistant; Christopher Keeslar, editor. Publishes mass market paperback originals. **Publishes 48 titles/year. Receives 1,500-2,000 queries and 150-500 mss/year. 30% of books from first-time authors; 25-30% from unagented writers. Pays 4% royalty on retail price for new authors. Offers $2,000 average advance for new authors.** Publishes book 1 year after acceptance of ms. Reports in 6 months on mss. Book catalog free (800)481-9191. Manuscript guidelines for #10 SASE.

    O→ Love Spell publishes the quirky sub-genres of romance: time-travel, paranormal, futuristic. "Despite the exotic settings, we are still interested in character-driven plots." Love Spell is developing a new humor line including both contemporary and historical romances.

**Fiction:** Romance: historical, time travel, paranormal, futuristic, legendary lover. Query or submit synopsis and first 3 sample chapters only. "No material will be returned without a SASE. "Books industry-wide are getting shorter; we're interested in 90,000 words."

**Recent Title(s):** *Love Me Tender*, by Sandra Hill.

**LOWELL HOUSE**, NTC/Contemporary, 2020 Avenue of the Stars, Suite 300, Los Angeles CA 90067. **Acquisitions**: Bud Sperry, senior editor (trade health, nonfiction, mental health, cookbooks); Peter Hoffman, senior editor (natural and alternative trade titles); Michael Artenstein, editor-in-chief (fiction, nonfiction); Brenda Pope-Ostron, editorial director (juvenile, educational titles). Publishes hardcover originals, trade paperback originals and reprints. **Publishes 120 titles/ year. 60% of books from first-time authors; 75% from unagented writers. Pays royalty on retail price.** Publishes book 20 months after acceptance of ms. Accepts simultaneous submissions. Reports in 3 months on proposals. Book catalog for 9×12 SAE with $3 postage.

    O→ Lowell House publishes reference titles in health, parenting and adult education that emphasizes alternative, natural health. Currently emphasizing health.

**Imprint(s):** Anodyne, Draw Science, Extension Press, 50 Nifty, Classics, Gifted & Talented, Legacy Press, Woman to Woman.

**Nonfiction:** Reference. Subjects include child guidance/parenting, cooking/foods/nutrition, education, health/medicine, money/finance, psychology, recreation, sports, women's issues/studies. "Juvenile division does not accept outside submissions." Query or submit outline, 1 sample chapter and SASE.

**Recent Title(s):** *Nixon's Enemies*, by Kenneth Karz.

**Tips:** "Submit a well-constructed proposal that clearly delineates the work's audience, its advantages over previously published books in the area, a detailed outline, and synopsis and the writer's cv or background.

**LOYOLA PRESS**, 3441 N. Ashland Ave., Chicago IL 60657-1397. (773)281-1818 ext. 300. Fax: (773)281-0152. E-mail: schroeder@loyolapress.com. **Acquisitions**: Jim Manney, acquisitions editor. Estab. 1912. Publishes hardcover and trade paperback originals and reprints. **Publishes 20 titles/year. Receives 500 submissions/year. 10% of books from first-time authors; 60% from unagented writers. Pays variable royalty as percentage of net sales. Small advance.** Publishes book 1-2 years after acceptance of ms. Accepts simultaneous submissions. Reports in 2 months. Book catalog for 8½×11 SASE.

**Imprint(s):** Jesuit Way, Seeker's Guides, Wild Onion.

**Nonfiction:** Practical spirituality with Catholic Christian flavor. Subjects include prayer and meditation, personal relationships, spiritual wisdom for everyday life, scripture study for nonspecialists, the Catholic tradition. *Jesuit Way* books focus on Jesuit history, biography, and spirituality. *Seeker's Guides* are short introductions to various aspects of Christian living. *Wild Onion* books highlight religion in Chicago. Query before submitting ms.

**Recent Title(s):** *Bumping into God*.

**Tips:** "We need authors who are experts in their field, yet who can communicate their knowledge to beginners without talking down; authors who love the Catholic spiritual tradition and can open up its riches to others; authors who write simply and clearly—and with style. The winning combination is expertise + spirituality + style."

**LUCENT BOOKS**, P.O. Box 289011, San Diego CA 92198-9011. (619)485-7424. Fax: (619)485-8019. **Acquisitions**: Lori Shein, managing editor. Estab. 1988. Publishes hardcover educational supplementary materials and (nontrade) juvenile nonfiction. **Publishes 125 books/year. 5% of books from first-time authors; 95% from unagented writers. Makes outright purchase of $2,500-3,000.** Query for book catalog and ms guidelines; send 9×12 SAE with 3 first-class stamps.

    O→ Lucent publishes nonfiction for a middle school audience providing students with resource material for academic studies and for independent learning.

**Nonfiction:** Juvenile. "We produce tightly formatted books for middle grade readers. Each series has specific requirements. Potential writers should familiarize themselves with our material." Series deal with history, current events, social issues. All are works for hire, by assignment only. No unsolicited mss. "Once title is assigned, authors submit outline and first chapter."

**Recent Title(s):** *Teen Smoking*, by Eleanor H. Ayer (teen issues).

**Tips:** "We expect writers to do thorough research using books, magazines and newspapers. Biased writing—whether liberal or conservative—has no place in our books. We prefer to work with writers who have experience writing nonfiction for middle grade students. We are looking for experienced writers, especially those who have written nonfiction books at young adult level."

**THE LYONS PRESS**, 31 W. 21st St., New York NY 10010. (212)620-9580. Fax: (212)929-1836. **Acquisitions:** Bryan Oettel, editor-in-chief (outdoor activity, adventure, sports); Lilly Golden, senior editor (sports, cooking); Bryan Oettel, senior editor, (all subjects); Becky Koh, editor (sports, health); Christopher Pavone, managing editor. Estab. 1984 (Lyons & Burford), 1997 (The Lyons Press). Publishes hardcover and trade paperback originals and reprints. **Publishes 110-120 titles/year. 30% of books from first-time authors; 60% from unagented writers. Pays varied royalty on retail price.** Publishes book 1 year after acceptance of ms. Accepts simultaneous submissions. Reports in 3 weeks on queries. *Writer's Market* recommends allowing 2 months for reply. Book catalog free.

　○┅ The Lyons Press publishes practical and literary books, chiefly centered on outdoor subjects—natural history, all sports, gardening, horses, fishing. Currently emphasizing adventure, sports. De-emphasizing hobbies, travel.

**Nonfiction:** Subjects include Americana, animals, cooking/foods/nutrition, gardening, health, hobbies, nature/environment, science, sports, travel. Query.

**Recent Title(s):** *The Search for the Giant Squid*, by Richard Ellis (nature).

**Tips:** The Lyons Press has teamed up to develop books with L.L. Bean, *Field & Stream*, The Nature Conservancy and *Golf Magazine*.

**MACMILLAN BRANDS**, Macmillan General Reference, 1633 Broadway, New York NY 10019. (212)654-8500. Fax: (212)654-4822. Website: http://www.mgr.com. **Acquisitions:** Susan Clarey, publisher; Anne Ficklen, executive editor (Weight Watchers, Betty Crocker); Jim Willhite, editor (Burpee gardening); Emily Nolan, editor (Weight Watchers, Betty Crocker). Publishes hardcover originals, trade paperback originals and reprints. **Publishes 60-100 titles/year. Receives 3,000 queries/year. 15% of books from first-time authors; 5% from unagented writers. Pays royalty on retail price or net sales, or makes outright purchase or work-for-hire assignments. Offers variable advance.** Publishes book 1 year after acceptance of ms. Accepts simultaneous submissions. Reports in 2 months on queries and mss, 1 month on proposals.

　○┅ Macmillan Brands publishes cooking and gardening reference titles.

**Nonfiction:** Cookbook, how-to, reference. Subjects include cooking/foods/nutrition, gardening. Submit outline, 1 sample chapter and proposal package, including table of contents, author credentials, target audience and market analysis. Reviews artwork/photos as part of ms package. Send photocopies.

　● At press time, Macmillan General Reference was for sale.

**MACMILLAN COMPUTER PUBLISHING USA**, 201 W. 103rd St., Indianapolis IN 46290. (317)581-3500. Website: http://www.mcp.com.

**Imprint(s):** Brady Games, Macmillan Online, Macmillan Software, **Que, Sams.**

**MACMILLAN CONSUMER REFERENCE**, 1633 Broadway, New York NY 10019. (212)654-8500.

**Imprints:** Macmillan Computer Publishing, Macmillan General Reference, Macmillan Library Reference.

　● At press time Macmillan General Reference and Macmillan Library Reference were for sale. The children's Library Reference imprints, Crestwood House, Dillon Press, Julian Messner, New Discovery, Silver Burdett Press and Silver Press, were closed prior to the sale.

**MACMILLAN GENERAL REFERENCE**, 1633 Broadway, New York NY 10019. (212)654-8500. Fax: (212)654-4822. Website: http://www.mgr.com. **Acquisitions**: Gary Krebs, managing editor. Publishes hardcover originals, trade paperback originals and reprints. **Publishes 400-500 titles/year. Receives 10,000 queries/year. 15% of books from first-time authors; 5% from unagented writers. Pays royalty on retail price or net sales or makes outright purchase or work-for-hire assignments. Offers $1,000-1,000,000 advance depending on imprint.** Publishes book 1 year after acceptance of ms. Accepts simultaneous submissions. Reports in 2 months on queries and mss, 1 month on proposals.

　○┅ Macmillan General Reference publishes popular reference in travel, pet books, consumer information, careers, test preparation, tax guides, cooking, gardening, sports, health, history, psychology, parenting, writing guides, atlases, dictionaries, music, the arts, business, parenting, science, religion.

**Imprint(s):** Arco (contact Marie Butler, publisher); **Howell Book House** (contact Kathy Nebenhaus, publisher); **Macmillan Brands and Cookbooks** (contact Susan Clarey, publisher), Macmillan Lifestyle Guides (contact Kathy Nebenhaus, publisher); **Macmillan Travel** (contact Mike Spring, publisher).

**Nonfiction:** Biography, cookbook, gift book, how-to, illustrated book, multimedia (disk/CD-ROM/cassette with book), reference, self-help. Subjects include Americana, animals, anthropology/archaeology, art/architecture, business/economics, child guidance/parenting, computers/electronics, cooking/foods/nutrition, education, ethnic, gardening, gay/lesbian, government/politics, health/medicine, history, hobbies, language/literature, military/war, money/finance, music/dance, nature/environment, psychology, recreation, religion, science, sociology, software, sports, travel, women's issues/studies, pets, consumer affairs. Submissions must have an original and interesting idea, good credentials and writing skills and an understanding of the market, and audience. Submit outline, 1 sample chapter and proposal package, including table of contents, author credentials, market competition and audience assessment. Reviews artwork/photos as part of ms package. Send photocopies.

　● At press time, Macmillan General Reference was for sale.

Ⓐ **MACMILLAN TRAVEL**, Macmillan General Reference, 1633 Broadway, New York NY 10019. (212)654-8500. Fax: (212)654-4822. Website: http://www.frommers.com **Acquisitions**: Michael Spring, publisher. Publishes trade paperback originals and reprints. **Publishes 60-100 titles/year. Receives 3,000 queries/year. 15% of books from first-time authors. Pays royalty on retail price or net sales, or makes outright purchase or work-for-hire assignments. Offers variable advance.** Publishes book 1 year after acceptance of ms. Accepts simultaneous submissions. Reports in 2 months on queries and mss, 1 month on proposals.

**O─** Macmillan Travel publishes regional travel guides that fit destination-specific formats or series.

**Nonfiction:** Subjects include regional, travel. *Agented submissions only.*

**Recent Title(s):** *The Complete Idiots Guide to Paris*, by Suzanne Kellener.

● At press time, Macmillan General Reference was for sale.

**MACMURRAY & BECK**, 1649 Downing St., Denver CO 80218. Fax: (303)832-2158. E-mail: ramey@macmurraybeck .com. Website: http://www.macmurraybeck.com. **Acquisitions:** Frederick Ramey, executive editor; Leslie Koffler, associate editor; Greg Michelson, fiction. Estab. 1989. Publishes hardcover and trade paperback originals. **Publishes 5-8 titles/year. 90% of books from first-time authors; 20% from unagented writers. Pays 8-12% royalty on retail price. Offers $2,000-5,000 advance.** Publishes book 18 months after acceptance of ms. Accepts simultaneous submissions. Reports in 3 months on queries and proposals, 4 months on mss. Book catalog $2. Manuscript guidelines free.

**O─** "We are interested in reflective personal narrative of high literary quality both fiction and nonfiction."

**Imprint(s):** Divina (speculative, spiritual and metaphysical, contact Leslie Koffler).

**Nonfiction:** "We are looking for personal narratives and extraordinary perspectives." Submit outline and 2 sample chapters with SASE. Reviews artwork/photos as part of ms package. Send photocopies.

**Fiction:** Literary. "We are most interested in debut novels of life in the contemporary West, but we select for voice and literary merit far more than for subject or narrative." Writers often make the mistake of "submitting genre fiction when we are in search of strong literary fiction." Submit synopsis and 3 sample chapters with SASE.

**Recent Title(s):** *Swimming in Trees*, by Maria Stokes Katzenbach; *Hummingbird House*, by Patricia Henley.

**MADISON BOOKS**, Rowman and Littlefield Publishing Group, 4720 Boston Way, Lanham MD 20706. (301)459-3366. Fax: (301)459-2118. **Acquisitions:** Alyssa Theodore, acquisitions editor; Julie Kirsch, vice president of production. Estab. 1984. Publishes hardcover originals, trade paperback originals and reprints. **Publishes 40 titles/year. Receives 1,200 submissions/year. 15% of books from first-time authors; 65% from unagented writers. Pays 10-15% royalty on net price.** Publishes ms 1 year after acceptance. Reports in 2 months. Book catalog and ms guidelines for 9×12 SAE with 4 first-class stamps.

**Nonfiction:** History, biography, contemporary affairs, trade reference. Query or submit outline and sample chapter. *No unsolicited mss.*

**MAGE PUBLISHERS INC.**, 1032 29th St. NW, Washington DC 20007. (202)342-1642. Fax: (202)342-9269. E-mail: info@mage.com. Website: http://www.mage.com. **Acquisitions:** Amin Sepehri, assistant to publisher. Estab. 1985. Publishes hardcover originals and reprints, trade paperback originals. **Publishes 4 titles/year. Receives 40 queries and 20 mss/year. 10% of books from first-time authors; 95% from unagented writers. Pays variable royalty. Offers $250-1,500 advance.** Publishes book 8-16 months after acceptance of ms. Accepts simultaneous submissions. Reports in 1 month on queries and proposals, 3 months on mss. Book catalog free.

**O─** Mage publishes books relating to Persian/Iranian culture.

**Nonfiction:** Biography, children's/juvenile, coffee table book, cookbook, gift book, illustrated book. Subjects include anthropology/archaeology, art/architecture, cooking/foods/nutrition, ethnic, history, language/literature, music/dance, sociology, translation. Query. Reviews artwork/photos as part of ms package. Send photocopies.

**Fiction:** Ethnic, feminist, historical, literary, mainstream/contemporary, short story collections. Must relate to Persian/Iranian culture. Query.

**Poetry:** Must relate to Persian/Iranian culture. Query.

**Recent Title(s):** *A Taste of Persia*, by N. Batmanglis (cooking); *The Lion and the Throne*, by Ferdowsi (mythology).

**Tips:** Audience is the Iranian-American community in America and Americans interested in Persian culture.

**MAIN STREET BOOKS**, Doubleday Broadway Publishing Group, Random House, Inc., 1540 Broadway, New York NY 10036. (212)354-6500. **Acquisitions:** Gerald Howard, editor-in-chief; Jennifer Griffen, senior editor. Estab. 1992. Publishes hardcover originals, trade paperback originals and reprints. **Publishes 20-30 titles/year. Receives 600 queries, 200 mss/year. 25% of books from first-time authors. Offers advance and royalties.** Publishes book 18 months after acceptance of ms. Accepts simultaneous submissions, if so noted. Reports in 1 month on queries, 6 months on mss. Doubleday book catalog and ms guidelines free.

**O─** "Main Street Books continues the tradition of publishing backlists, but we are focusing more on 'up front' books and big sellers in the areas of self-help, fitness and popular culture."

**Nonfiction:** Cookbook, gift book, how-to, humor, self-help. Subjects include Americana, animals, business/economics, child guidance/parenting, cooking/foods/nutrition, education, ethnic, gay/lesbian, health/fitness, money/finance, music/dance, nature/environment, pop psychology, pop culture. Query with SASE, but agented submissions only of manuscripts. Reviews artwork/photos as part of ms package, "but never send unless requested."

**Recent Title(s):** *Checklist for Your First Baby*, by Susan Kagen Podell, M.S., R.D. (parenting/childcare); *Quit Your Job and Get Big Raises*, by Gordon Miller (business).

**N MANATEE PUBLISHING**, P.O. Box 6467, Titusville FL 32782. (407)267-9800. Fax: (407)267-8076. **Acquisitions:** Crystal Holton, editor (children's stories). Publishes trade paperback originals and reprints. **Publishes 6 titles/ year. Receives 200 queries and 100 mss/year. 90% of books from first-time authors; 100% from unagented writers. Pays 10-15% royalty on wholesale price.** Publishes book 1 year after acceptance of ms. Accepts simultaneous submissions. Reports in 1 month. Book catalog and ms guidelines for #10 SASE.
**Nonfiction:** Children's/juvenile, illustrated book. Subjects include child guidance/parenting, education. Submit complete ms. *Writer's Market* recommends query with SASE. Reviews artwork/photos as part of ms package. Send photocopies.
**Fiction:** Juvenile, picture books, children's books. Submit complete ms. *Writer's Market* recommends query with SASE.
**Recent Title(s):** *All About Frogs*, by Larry Block (children's fiction).

**N MARCH STREET PRESS**, 3413 Wilshire, Greensboro NC 27408. Phone/fax: (336)282-9754. E-mail: rbixby@-aol.com. Website: http://users.aol.com/marchst. **Acquisitions:** Robert Bixby, editor/publisher. Publishes literary chapbooks. **Publishes 6-10 titles/year. Receives 12 queries and 30 mss/year. 50% of books from first-time authors; 100% from unagented writers. Pays 15% royalty. Offers advance of 10 copies.** Estab. 1988. Publishes book 6 months after acceptance of ms. Accepts simultaneous submissions. Reports in 3 months on mss. Book catalog and ms guidelines for #10 SASE.
    O→ March Street publishes poetry chapbooks.
**Poetry:** "My plans are based on the submissions I receive, not vice versa." Submit complete ms.
**Recent Title(s):** *Everything I Need*, by Keith Taylor.
**Tips:** "Audience is extremely sophisticated, widely read graduates of M.A., M.F.A. and Ph.D. programs in English and fine arts. Also lovers of significant, vibrant and enriching verse regardless of field of study or endeavor. Most beginning poets, I have found, think it beneath them to read other poets. This is the most glaring flaw in their work. My advice is to read ceaselessly. Otherwise, you may be published, but you will never be accomplished."

**MARINER BOOKS**, Houghton Mifflin, 222 Berkeley St., Boston MA 02116. (617)351-5000. Fax: (617)351-1202. Website: http://www.hmco.com. **Acquisitions:** John Radziewicz. Estab. 1997. Publishes trade paperback originals and reprints. **Advance and royalty vary.** Reports in 2 months on mss.
    O→ Houghton Mifflin books give shape to ideas that educate, inform and delight. Mariner is an eclectic list that notably embraces fiction.
**Nonfiction:** Subjects include biography, education, government/politics, history, philosophy, political thought, sociology. Query with SASE.
**Fiction:** Literary, contemporary. Submit synopsis with SASE.
**Recent Title(s):** *The Road to Ubar*, by Nicholas Clapp (history); *The Coast of Good Intentions*, by Michael Byers (fiction); *Rules for Dance*, by Mary Oliver (poetry).

**MARLOR PRESS, INC.**, 4304 Brigadoon Dr., St. Paul MN 55126. (651)484-4600. Fax: (651)490-1182. **Acquisitions:** Marlin Bree, publisher. Estab. 1981. Publishes trade paperback originals. **Publishes 6 titles/year. Receives 100 queries and 25 mss/year. Pays 8-10% royalty on wholesale price.** Publishes book 8 months after final acceptance. Reports in 3 months. Book catalog for 6×9 SAE with 2 first-class stamps. Manuscript guidelines for #10 SASE.
    O→ Currently emphasizing general interest boating and how-to travel books.
**Nonfiction:** Travel, boating, children's books. "Primarily how-to stuff. No anecdotal reminiscences or biographical materials. No fiction or poetry." Query first; submit outline with sample chapters only when requested. *No unsolicited mss.* Do not send full ms. Reviews artwork/photos as part of ms package.
**Recent Title(s):** *Going Abroad: the Bathroom Survival Guide*, by Eva Newman.

**MARLOWE & COMPANY**, Avalon Publishing Group, 841 Broadway, 4th Floor, New York NY 10003. (212)614-7880. Publisher: Neil Ortenberg. **Acquisitions:** Gayle Watkins, acquisitions editor. Estab. 1993. Publishes hardcover and trade paperback originals and reprints. **Publishes 60 titles/year. Receives 800 queries/year. 5% of books from first-time authors; 5% from unagented writers. Pays 10% royalty on retail price for hardcover, 6% for paperback. Offers advance of 50% of anticipated first printing.** Publishes book 1 year after acceptance of ms. Book catalog free.
    O→ Currently emphasizing spirituality, health, religion.
**Nonfiction:** Health/medicine, New Age, history. Query with SASE. *No unsolicited submissions.*
**Fiction:** Literary. "We are looking for literary, rather than genre fiction." *No unsolicited submissions.*
    • Marlowe & Company is closed to submissions at this time.
**Recent Title(s):** *Dog Soldiers: Societies of the Plains*, by Thomas Mails (history); *Amistad*, by David Pesci (fiction).

**MASQUERADE BOOKS**, Crescent Publishing, 801 Second Ave., New York NY 10017. (212)661-7878. Fax: (212)983-2548. E-mail: masqbks@aol.com. **Acquisitions:** Marti Hohmann, editor-in-chief (upscale erotica). Estab. 1989. Publishes trade paperback and mass market paperback originals and reprints. **Publishes 40 titles/year. Receives 500 queries and 1,000 mss/year. 10% of books from first-time authors; 95% from unagented writers. Pays 5% royalty on retail price. Offers $1,200 advance.** Publishes book 1 year after acceptance of ms. Reports in 1 month on queries and proposals, 3 months on mss. Manuscript guidelines free.
    O→ Masquerade publishes upscale, literary erotica.

**Nonfiction:** Subjects include gay/lesbian, self-help, sex, women's issues/studies. Submit proposal package, including cover letter with bio, outline, 3 sample chapters and SASE.
**Fiction:** Erotica, gay/lesbian, literary, short story collections, translation. Writing in all categories must be erotic or thematically concerned with sex and/or sexuality. Query or submit synopsis, 3 sample chapters, author bio and SASE.
**Recent Title(s):** *Neptune & Surf*, by Marilyn Jaye Lewis.
**Tips:** "Please do not send poorly written material that is better placed in skin mags. We are always interested in well-done contemporary S&M and writing by women."

**MASTERS PRESS**, NTC/Contemporary Group, 1214 W. Boston Post Rd., #302, Mamaroneck NY 10543. (914)834-8284. Website: http://www.masterspress.com. Editorial Director: John T. Nolan. **Acquisitions:** Ken Samelson, acquisitions editor. Estab. 1986. Publishes hardcover and trade paperback originals. **Publishes 45-50 titles/year; imprint publishes 20 titles/year. Receives 60 queries and 50 mss/year. 25% of books from first-time authors; 75% from unagented writers. Pays 10-15% royalty. Offers $1,000-5,000 advance.** Publishes book 1 year after acceptance of ms. Accepts simultaneous submissions. Reports in 2 months on proposals. Book catalog free.
   O➥ "Our audience is sports enthusiasts and participants, people interested in fitness."
**Nonfiction:** Biography, how-to, reference, self-help. Subjects include recreation, sports, fitness. Submit outline, 2 sample chapters, author bio and marketing ideas.
**Recent Title(s):** *Our House: A Tribute to Fenway Park*, by Kurt Smith.

**[N] MAUPIN HOUSE PUBLISHING INC.**, P.O. Box 90148, Gainesville FL 32607-0148. Fax: (352)373-5588. E-mail: jgraddy@maupinhouse.com. **Acquisitions**: Julia Graddy, co-publisher. Publishes trade paperback originals and reprints. **Publishes 7 titles/year. Pays 5-10% royalty on retail price. Reports in 2 months on queries.**
   O➥ Maupin House publishes teacher resource books for language arts teachers K-12.
**Nonfiction:** Publishes nonfiction books on language art education. "We are looking for practical, in-classroom resource materials. Classroom teachers are our top choice as authors." Query with SASE.
**Fiction:** Juvenile for grades 3-5. "We are interested in fiction that features a child set in historical Florida."
   ● Maupin House has increased its number of titles published from 3 to 7 in the past year.
**Recent Title(s):** *Teaching Writing Skills with Children's Literature*, by Dierking and McElveen.

**MAYFIELD PUBLISHING COMPANY**, 1280 Villa St., Mountain View CA 94041. Fax: (650)960-0826. Website: http://www.mayfieldpub.com. **Acquisitions:** Ken King, (philosophy, religion); Holly Allen, (communications); Frank Graham, (psychology, parenting); Jan Beatty, (anthropology, theater, art); Renee Deljon, (English); Michele Sordi, (health, physical eduction); Serina Beauparlant (sociology, women's studies). Estab. 1947. **Publishes 70-80 titles/year.** Accepts simultaneous submissions. Manuscript guidelines free.
   O➥ Mayfield publishes textbooks for college level courses in the humanities and social sciences.
**Nonfiction:** Textbook (*college only*). Subjects include anthropology/archaeology, art, child guidance/parenting, communications/theater, health/physical education, English composition, music/dance, philosophy, psychology, religion, sociology, women's studies. Submit proposal package including outline, table of contents, sample chapter, description of proposed market.

**MBI PUBLISHING**, Chronicle Publishing, 729 Prospect Ave., P.O. Box 1, Osceola WI 54020-0001. (715)294-3345. Fax: (715)294-4448. E-mail: mbibks@motorbooks.com. Website: http://www.motorbooks.com. Publishing Director: Zack Miller. **Acquisitions:** Lee Klancher, senior acquisitions editor (tractors, stock car racing, motorcycles); Mike Haenggi, acquisitions editor (aviation, military history); Keith Mathiowetz, acquisitions editor (American cars, Americana, railroading collectibles); Paul Johnson, acquisitions editor (automotive how-to, boating); Christopher Batio, acquisitions editor (Americana, collectibles); John Adams-Graf, acquisitions editor (foreign cars, vintage racing). Estab. 1973. Publishes hardcover and paperback originals. **Publishes 125 titles/year. Receives 200 queries and 50 mss/year. 95% of books from unagented writers. Pays 12% royalty on net receipts. Offers $5,000 average advance.** Publishes book 1 year after acceptance. Accepts simultaneous submissions. Reports in 3 months. Free book catalog. Manuscript guidelines for #10 SASE.
   O➥ MBI is a transportation-related publisher: cars, motorcycles, racing, trucks, tractors, boats, bicycles—also Americana, aviation and military history.
**Imprint(s):** Bay View, Bicycle Books, Crestline, Zenith Books.
**Nonfiction:** Coffeetable book, gift book, how-to, illustrated book. Subjects include Americana, history, hobbies, how-to, military/war, photography (as they relate to cars, trucks, motorcycles, motor sports, aviation—domestic, foreign and military). Accepts nonfiction translations. Query with SASE. "State qualifications for doing book." Reviews artwork/photos as part of ms package. Send photocopies.
**Recent Title(s):** *America's Special Forces*, by David Bohrer (modern military).

**[N] [★] McDONALD & WOODWARD PUBLISHING CO.**, 325 Dorrence Rd., Granville OH 43023. (740)321-1140. Fax: (740)321-1141. Website: http://www.mwpubco.com. **Acquisitions:** Jerry N. McDonald, managing partner/publisher. Estab. 1986. Publishes hardcover and trade paperback originals. **Publishes 8 titles/year. Receives 100 queries and 20 mss/year. 50% of books from first-time authors; 100% from unagented writers. Pays 10% royalty on net receipts.** Publishes book 1 year after acceptance of ms. Accepts simultaneous submissions. Reports in 2 weeks. Book catalog free.

○─ "McDonald & Woodward publishes books in natural and cultural history." Currently emphasizing travel, natural history. De-emphasizing self-help.

**Nonfiction:** Biography, coffee table book, how-to, illustrated book, self-help. Subjects include Americana, animals, anthropology, ethnic, history, nature/environment, science, travel. Query or submit outline and sample chapters. Reviews artwork/photos as part of ms package. Send photocopies.

**Recent Title(s):** *The Snowflake Man*, by Duncan C. Blanchard.

**Tips:** "We are especially interested in additional titles in our 'Guides to the American Landscape' series. Should consult titles in print for guidance. We want well-organized, clearly written, substantive material."

**MARGARET K. McELDERRY BOOKS**, Simon & Schuster Children's Publishing Division, Simon & Schuster, 1230 Sixth Ave., New York NY 10020. (212)698-7200. Fax: (212)698-2796. Website: http://www.simonsayskids.com. Vice President/Publisher: Brenda Bowen. Editor-at-Large: Margaret K. McElderry. **Acquisitions:** Emma D. Dryden, senior editor (books for preschoolers to 16-year-olds); Karen Riskin, assistant editor (middle grade fiction, quality picture books). Estab. 1971. Publishes quality material for preschoolers to 16-year-olds, but publishes only a few YAs. Publishes hardcover originals. **Publishes 25 titles/year. Receives 5,000 queries/year. 10% of books from first-time authors; 50% from unagented writers. Average print order is 4,000-6,000 for a first teen book; 7,500-10,000 for a first picture book. Pays royalty on retail price: 10% fiction; picture book, 5% author, 5% illustrator. Offers $5,000-6,000 advance for new authors.** Publishes book up to 2 years after contract signing. Manuscript guidelines for #10 SASE.

○─ "We are more interested in superior writing and illustration than in a particular 'type' of book." Currently emphasizing young picture books. De-emphasizing picture books with a lot of text.

**Nonfiction:** Children's/juvenile, adventure, biography, history. "Read. The field is competitive. See what's been done and what's out there before submitting. Looks for originality of ideas, clarity and felicity of expression, well-organized plot and strong characterization (fiction) or clear exposition (nonfiction); quality. We will accept one-page query letters for picture books or novels." *No unsolicited mss.*

**Fiction:** Juvenile only. Adventure, fantasy, historical, mainstream/contemporary, mystery, science fiction. Query with SASE. *No unsolicited mss.*

**Poetry:** Query with 3 sample poems.

**Recent Title(s):** *The Planet Hunters*, by Dennis B. Fradin (nonfiction); *Hurry, Hurry, Mary Dear!*, by N.M. Bodecker, illustrated by Erik Blevgad (fiction); *The Rainbow Hand*, by Janet Wong (poetry).

**Tips:** "Freelance writers should be aware of the swing away from teen-age novels to books for younger readers and of the growing need for beginning chapter books for children just learning to read on their own."

**McFARLAND & COMPANY, INC., PUBLISHERS**, Box 611, Jefferson NC 28640. (336)246-4460. Fax: (336)246-5018. E-mail: mcfarland@skybest.com. Website: http://www.mcfarlandpub.com. **Acquisitions:** Robert Franklin, president/editor-in-chief; Steve Wilson, senior editor; Virginia Tobiassen, editor; Marty McGees, assistant editor. Estab. 1979. Publishes reference books and scholarly, technical and professional monographs. Publishes mostly hardcover and a few "quality" paperback originals; a non-"trade" publisher. **Publishes 165 titles/year. Receives 1,200 submissions/year. 70% of books from first-time authors; 95% from unagented writers. Pays 10-12½% royalty on net receipts. No advance.** Publishes book 10 months after acceptance. Reports in 2 weeks.

○─ McFarland publishes serious nonfiction in a variety of fields, including general reference, performing arts, sports (particularly baseball); women's studies, librarianship, literature, Civil War, history and international studies. Currently emphasizing radio history, medieval studies, automotive history.

**Nonfiction:** Reference books and scholarly, technical and professional monographs. Subjects include African American studies (very strong), art, business, chess, Civil War, drama/theater, cinema/radio/TV (very strong), health, history, librarianship (very strong), music, pop culture, sociology, sports/recreation (very strong), women's studies (very strong), world affairs (very strong). Reference books are particularly wanted—fresh material (i.e., not in head-to-head competition with an established title). "We prefer manuscripts of 250 or more double-spaced pages." No fiction, New Age, exposés, poetry, children's books, devotional/inspirational works, Bible studies or personal essays. Query with outline and sample chapters. Reviews artwork/photos as part of ms package.

**Recent Title(s):** *United States Congressional Elections, 1788-1997*, by Michael J. Dubin; *The Cultural Encyclopedia of Baseball*, by Jonathan Fraser Light.

**Tips:** "We want well-organized knowledge of an area in which there is not information coverage at present, plus reliability so we don't feel we have to check absolutely everything. Our market is worldwide and libraries are an important part." McFarland also publishes two journals, *American Literary Realism* and *Journal of Information Ethics*.

**McGRAW-HILL COMPANIES**, 1221 Avenue of the Americas, New York NY 10020. Website: http://www.mcgraw-hill.com. Divisions include **Business McGraw Hill; Computing McGraw Hill;** Glencoe/McGraw Hill; McGraw-Hill Higher Education; McGraw Hill Inc./TAB Books; McGraw-Hill Ryerson (Canada), **Osborne/McGraw-Hill**, McGraw-Hill Professional Book Group. General interest publisher of nonfiction.

**McGREGOR PUBLISHING**, 4532 W. Kennedy Blvd., Suite 233, Tampa FL 33609. (813)805-2665 or (888)405-2665. Fax: (813)832-6177. E-mail: mcgregpub@aol.com. **Acquisitions:** Dave Rosenbaum, acquisitions editor. Publishes hardcover and trade paperback originals. **Publishes 4-6 titles/year. Receives 100 queries and 20 mss/year. 75% of books from first-time authors; 80% from unagented writers. Pays 10-12% on retail price; 13-16% on wholesale**

**price. Advances vary.** Publishes book 1 year after acceptance of ms. Accepts simultaneous submissions. Reports in 2 months on queries and proposals, 3 months on mss. Book catalog and ms guidelines free.

○➟ "We publish nonfiction books that tell the story behind the story."

**Nonfiction:** Biography, how-to, self-help. Subjects include business/economics, ethnic, history, money/finance, regional, sports. "We're always looking for regional nonfiction titles, and especially for sports, biographies, true crime, self-help and how-to books." Query or submit outline with 2 sample chapters.

● McGregor no longer publishes fiction.

**Recent Title(s):** *If They Don't Win It's a Shame: The Year the Marlins Bought the World Series*, by Rosenbaum.

**Tips:** "We pride ourselves on working closely with an author and producing a quality product with strong promotional campaigns."

**MEADOWBROOK PRESS**, 5451 Smetana Dr., Minnetonka MN 55343. (612)930-1100. Fax: (612)930-1940. **Acquisitions:** Joseph Gredler, submissions editor (general submissions, poetry); Jason Sanford, editor (fiction). Estab. 1975. Publishes trade paperback originals and reprints. **Publishes 20 titles/year. Receives 1,500 queries/year. 15% of books from first-time authors. Pays 10% royalty.** Publishes book 1 year after acceptance. Accepts simultaneous submissions. Reports in 3 months on queries. Book catalog and ms guidelines for #10 SASE.

○➟ Meadowbrook is a family-oriented press which specializes in parenting books, party books, humorous quote books, humorous children's poetry books, children's activity books and juvenile fiction. Currently emphasizing party planning. De-emphasizing parenting.

**Nonfiction:** How-to, humor, reference. Subjects include baby/childcare, cooking/foods/nutrition, senior citizens, children's activities, relationships. No academic or autobiography. Query with outline and sample chapters. "We prefer a query first; then we will request an outline and/or sample material." Send for guidelines.

**Fiction:** Children's fiction ages 7-12. Query with SASE.

**Poetry:** Children's humorous poetry and light verse for adults. Query with SASE.

**Recent Title(s):** *Baby Play and Learn*, by Penny Warner (nonfiction); *Girls to the Rescue Book #6*, Bruce Lansky (fiction); *Lighten Up!*, by Bruce Lansky (poetry).

**Tips:** "Always send for fiction and poetry guidelines before submitting material. We do not accept unsolicited picture book submissions." Meadowbrook has several series, including Girls to the Rescue, Newfangled Fairy Tales and Kids Pick the Funniest Poems.

**[N] MEDICAL PHYSICS PUBLISHING**, 4513 Vernon Blvd., Madison WI 53705. (608)262-4021. Fax: (608)265-2121. E-mail: mpp@medicalphysics.org. Website: http://www.medicalphysics.org. **Acquisitions:** John Cameron, vice president; Betsey Phelps, managing editor. Estab. 1985. Publishes hardcover and trade paperback originals and reprints. **Publishes 8-10 titles/year; imprint publishes 3-5 titles/year. Receives 10-20 queries/year. 100% of books from unagented writers. Pays 10% royalty on wholesale price.** Publishes book 6 months after acceptance of ms. Accepts simultaneous submissions. Reports in 6 months on mss. Book catalog free.

○➟ "We are a nonprofit, membership organization publishing affordable books in medical physics and related fields." Currently emphasizing biomedical engineering. De-emphasizing books for the general public.

**Imprint(s):** Cogito Books.

**Nonfiction:** Reference books, textbooks, and symposium proceedings in the fields of medical physics and radiology. Also distribute Ph.D. theses in these fields. Submit entire ms. Reviews artwork/photos as part of ms package. Send disposable copies.

**Recent Nonfiction Title(s):** *Radiation Protection Dosimetry*, by Jack Simmons and David Watt.

**MERCURY HOUSE**, 736 Clementina St., Suite 300, San Francisco CA 94103. (415)626-7874. Fax: (415)626-7875. Website: http://www.wenet.net/~mercury/. **Acquisitions:** (Ms.) K. Janene-Nelson, managing editor. Estab. 1984. Publishes hardcover originals and trade paperbacks originals and reprints. **Publishes 8 titles/year. Pays 10-15% royalty on retail price. Offers $3,000-5,000 advance.** Publishes book 1 year after acceptance of ms. Reports in 3 months. Catalog for 55¢ postage.

○➟ "Mercury House is a nonprofit corporation guided by a dedication to literary values. It exists to promote professional publishing services to writers largely abandoned by market-driven commercial presses. Our purpose is to promote the free exchange of ideas, including minority viewpoints, by providing our writers with both an enduring format and the widest possible audience for their work."

**Nonfiction:** Biography, essays, memoirs. Subjects include anthropology, ethnic, gay/lesbian, politics/current affairs, language/literature, literary current affairs, nature/environment, philosophy, translation, literary travel, women's issues/studies, human rights/indigenous peoples. "Within the subjects we publish, we are above all a literary publisher looking for high quality writing and innovative book structure, research, etc." Query with 1 sample chapter.

**Fiction:** Ethnic, experimental, feminist, gay/lesbian, historical, literary, short story collections, literature in translation. "Very limited spots. We prefer sample chapters to determine writing style. It's very important to submit only if the subject is appropriate (as listed), though we do enjoy mutations/blending of genres (high quality, thoughtful work!)." No mainstream, thrillers, sexy books." Query first.

**Recent Title(s):** *Face of the Deep*, by Thomas Farber (Pacific Ocean travel and exploration biography); *House by the Sea*, by Rebecca Fromer (biography, Jewish Holocaust in Greece).

**Tips:** "Our reader is a person who is discriminating about his/her reading material, someone who appreciates the extra care we devote to design, paper, cover, and exterior excellence to go along with the high quality of the writing itself.

Be patient with us concerning responses: it's easier to reject the manuscript of a nagging author than it is to decide upon it. The manner in which an author deals with us (via letter or phone) gives us a sense of how it would be to work with this person for a whole project; good books with troublesome authors are to be avoided."

**MERIWETHER PUBLISHING LTD.**, 885 Elkton Dr., Colorado Springs CO 80907-3557. (719)594-4422. **Acquisitions:** Arthur Zapel, Theodore Zapel, Rhonda Wray, editors. Estab. 1969. Publishes paperback originals and reprints. **Publishes 10-12 books/year; 50-60 plays/year. Receives 1,200 submissions/year. 50% of books from first-time authors; 90% from unagented writers. Pays 10% royalty on retail price or makes outright purchase.** Publishes book 6 months after acceptance. Accepts simultaneous submissions. Reports in 2 months. Book catalog and ms guidelines for $2.

   O⤝ Meriwether publishes theater books, games and videos; speech resources; plays, skits and musicals; and resources for gifted students. "We specialize in books on the theatre arts and religious plays for Christmas, Easter and youth activities. We also publish musicals for high school performers and churches." Currently emphasizing musicals.

**Nonfiction:** How-to, reference, educational, humor. Also textbooks. Subjects include art/theater/drama, music/dance, recreation, religion. "We publish unusual textbooks or trade books related to the communication or performing arts and how-to books on staging, costuming, lighting, etc. We are not interested in religious titles with fundamentalist themes or approaches—we prefer mainstream religion titles." Query or submit outline/synopsis and sample chapters.

**Recent Title(s):** *Theatre Games and Beyond*, by Amiel Schotz.

**Fiction:** Plays and musicals—humorous, mainstream, mystery, religious, suspense.

**Tips:** "Our educational books are sold to teachers and students at college and high school levels. Our religious books are sold to youth activity directors, pastors and choir directors. Our trade books are directed at the public with a sense of humor. Another group of buyers is the professional theatre, radio and TV category. We focus more on books of plays and short scenes and textbooks on directing, staging, make-up, lighting, etc."

**N⃞ MESORAH PUBLICATIONS, LTD.**, 4401 Second Ave., Brooklyn NY 11232. (718)921-9000. Fax: (718)680-1875. E-mail: artscroll@mesorah.com. Website: http://www.artscroll.com. **Acquisitions:** (Mrs.) D. Schechter, literary editor. Estab. 1976. Publishes hardcover and trade paperback originals. **Publishes 50 titles/year. Receives 50 queries and 200 mss/year. 30% of books from first-time authors; 100% from unagented writers. Pays 3-10% royalty on retail price. No advance.** Publishes book 1 year after acceptance of ms. Accepts simultaneous submissions. Reports in 2 months.

   O⤝ Mesorah publishes Judaica, Bible study, Talmud, liturgical materials, history, books on the Holocaust for an Orthodox Jewish audience.

**Imprints:** Shaar Press, Tamar Books.

**Nonfiction:** Biography, children's/juvenile, coffee table book, cookbook, gift book, reference, self-help, textbook. Subjects include business/economics, child guidance/parenting, creative nonfiction, education, ethnic, history, memoirs, philosophy, religion, spirituality, translation. Query with SASE, or submit proposal package, including outline and 2 sample chapters or completed ms. Reviews artwork/photos as part of ms package. Send photocopies.

**Fiction:** Adventure, historical, juvenile, mainstream/contemporary, mystery, religious. Query with SASE, or submit proposal package, including synopsis and 2 sample chapters, or completed ms.

**Recent Title(s):** *Twerski on Spirituality*, by Dr. A.J. Twerski (spirituality); *The Runaway*, by Chaim Eliav (suspense).

**THE MESSAGE COMPANY**, 4 Camino Azul, Sante Fe NM 87505. (505)474-0998. **Acquisitions:** James Berry, president. Publishes trade paperback originals and reprints. **Publishes 6-8 titles/year. Receives 20 queries and 12 mss/year. 80% of books from first-time authors; 100% from unagented writers. Pays 6-8% royalty on retail price or makes outright purchase of $500-2,000. No advance.** Publishes book 3 months after acceptance of ms. Accepts simultaneous submissions. Book catalog for 6×9 SAE with 2 first-class stamps.

   O⤝ The Message Company packages alternative topics for the mainstream market.

**Nonfiction:** How-to. Subjects include business/economics (spirituality in business-related only), government/politics (freedom/privacy issues only), science (new energy/new science only). Submit proposal package, including outline and sample chapters. Reviews artwork/photos as part of ms package. Send photocopies.

**Recent Title(s):** *Physics of Love*, by Dale Pond.

**N⃞ METAL POWDER INDUSTRIES FEDERATION**, 105 College Rd. E., Princeton NJ 08540. (609)452-7700. Fax: (609)987-8523. E-mail: info@mpif.org. **Acquisitions:** Cindy Jablonowski, publications manager; Peggy Lebedz, assistant publications manager. Estab. 1946. Publishes hardcover originals. **Publishes 10 titles/year. Pays 3-12½% royalty on wholesale or retail price. Offers $3,000-5,000 advance.** Reports in 1 month.

   O⤝ Metal Powder Industries publishes monographs, textbooks, handbooks, design guides, conference proceedings, standards, and general titles in the field of powder metullary or particulate materials.

**Nonfiction:** Work must relate to powder metallurgy or particulate materials.

**Recent Title(s):** *Advances in Powder Metallurgy and Particulate Materials* (conference proceeding).

**N⃞ METAMORPHOUS PRESS**, P.O. Box 10616, Portland OR 97296-0616. (503)228-4972. Fax: (503)223-9117. E-mail: metabooks@metamodels.com. Website: http://www.metamodels.com/meta/mann.html. Publisher: David Balding. Editorial Director: Lori Vannorsdel. **Acquisitions:** Nancy Wyatt-Kelsey, acquisitions editor. Estab. 1982. Publishes trade paperback originals and reprints. **Publishes 4-5 titles/year. Receives 2,500 submissions/year. 90% of books from first-time authors; 90% from unagented writers. Pays minimum 10% profit split on wholesale prices. No advance.** Publishes book 1 year after acceptance. Accepts simultaneous submissions. Reports in 3 months. Book catalog and ms guidelines for 9×12 SAE with 3 first-class stamps or on website.

> **O—** "Our primary editorial screen is 'will this (behavioral science) book further define, explain or support the concept that we are responsible for our reality or assist people in gaining control of their lives?' " Currently emphasizing NLPE, enneagram, Ericksonian Hypnosis. De-emphasizing New Age.

**Imprint(s):** Grinder & Associates (Lori Vannorsdel, editorial director).

**Nonfiction:** How-to, reference, self-help, technical, textbook—all related to behavioral science and personal growth. Subjects include business and sales, health, psychology, sociology, education, science and new ideas in behavioral science. "We are interested in any well-proven new idea or philosophy in the behavioral science areas." Submit idea, outline, and table of contents only. Reviews artwork/photos as part of ms package.

**Recent Title(s):** *Enneagram Spectrum of Personality Styles*, by Wagner; *Framework of Excellence*, by C. Miliner; *Patterns of Therapeutic Technology of Milton Erickson, vols 1-2*, by Bandler & Grinder (hypnotherapy).

**MEYERBOOKS, PUBLISHER**, P.O. Box 427, Glenwood IL 60425-0427. (708)757-4950. **Acquisitions:** David Meyer, publisher. Estab. 1976. Publishes hardcover and trade paperback originals and reprints. **Publishes 5 titles/year. Pays 10-15% royalty on wholesale or retail price. No advance.** Reports in 3 months on queries.

**Imprint(s):** David Meyer Magic Books.

**Nonfiction:** History, reference. Subjects include Americana, herbal studies, history of stage magic. Query with SASE.

**Recent Title(s):** *The Hanlon Brothers: Their Amazing Acrobatics, Pantomimes and Stage Specials*, by McKinven (theatrical history).

**MICHIGAN STATE UNIVERSITY PRESS**, 1405 S. Harrison Rd., Manly Miles Bldg., Suite 25, East Lansing MI 48823-5202. (517)355-9543. Fax: (800)678-2120; local/international (517)432-2611. E-mail: msupress@pilot.msu.edu. Website: http://www.pilot.msu.edu/unit/msupress. **Acquisitions:** Martha Bates, acquisitions editor. Estab. 1947. Publishes hardcover and softcover originals. **Publishes 35 titles/year. Receives 1,000 submissions/year. 75% of books from first-time authors; 100% from unagented writers. Royalties vary.** Publishes ms 18 months after acceptance of ms. Book catalog and ms guidelines for 9×12 SASE.

> **O—** Michigan State University publishes scholarly books that further scholarship in their particular field. In addition they publish nonfiction that addresses, in a more contemporary way, social concerns, such as diversity, civil rights, the environment.

**Imprint(s):** Colleagues, Lotus.

**Nonfiction:** Scholarly, trade. Subjects include Afro-American studies, American regional history, American literature and criticism, American studies, business, Canadian studies, contemporary African studies, contemporary civil rights history, creative nonfiction, Great Lakes regional, labor studies, legal studies, Native American studies, women's studies. Series: Canadian Series, Schoolcraft Series, Rhetoric and Public Affairs Series, Native American Series, Colleagues Books. Query with outline and sample chapters. Reviews artwork/photos.

**Recent Title(s):** *High-Tech Betrayal*, by Victor Devinatz.

**MIDDLE ATLANTIC PRESS**, 10 Twosome Dr., Box 600, Moorestown NJ 08057. Website: http://www.koen.com/midatintro.html. **Acquisitions:** Terence Doherty, acquisitions editor. Publishes trade paperback originals and mass market paperback originals. **Publishes 4-6 titles/year. Receives 50 queries and 12 mss/year. 5% of books from first-time authors; 50% from unagented writers. Offers $3,000-5,000 advance.** Publishes book 3 months after acceptance of ms. Accepts simultaneous submissions. Reports in 1 week on queries, 1 month on proposals.

> **O—** Middle Atlantic Press is a regional publisher focusing on New York, New Jersey, Pennsylvania and Delaware.

**Imprint(s):** MAP.

**Nonfiction:** Mid-Atlantic states focus, cookbooks. Subjects include history, recreation, regional, sports. Submit proposal package, outline with 3 sample chapters and SASE. Sometimes reviews artwork/photos as part of ms package. Send photocopies.

> ● Middle Atlantic no longer publishes fiction.

**Recent Title(s):** *Filling in the Seams*, by Chris Edwards (sports); *Julie and the Marigold Boy*, by Larona Homer (fiction); and *Phantom of the Pine*, by James F. McCloy and Ray Miller Jr. (history/folklore).

**MID-LIST PRESS**, Jackson, Hart & Leslie, 4324 12th Ave S., Minneapolis MN 55407-3218. Website: http://www.midlist.org. Publisher: Marianne Nora. **Acquisitions:** Lane Stiles, senior editor. Estab. 1989. Publishes hardcover and trade paperback originals. **Publishes minimum 4 titles/year. Pays 40-50% royalty of profits. Offers $500-1,000 advance.** Send SASE for First Series guidelines and/or general submission guidelines; also available online.

> **O—** Mid-List Press publishes books of high literary merit and fresh artistic vision by new and emerging writers.

**Recent Title(s):** *Prairie Son*, by Donald Clausen (creative nonfiction); *The Hand Before the Eye*, by Donald Friedman (fiction); *White*, by Jennifer O'Grady (poetry).

**Tips:** Mid-List Press is an independent press. In addition to publishing the annual winners of the Mid-List Press First Series Awards, Mid-List Press publishes fiction and creative nonfiction by first-time and established writers.

**MIDMARCH ARTS PRESS**, 300 Riverside Dr., New York NY 10025-5239. (212)666-6990. **Acquisitions**: S. Moore, editor (art/literature). Estab. 1975. Publishes hardcover and trade paperback originals. **Publishes 4-6 titles/year. Receives 60-100 queries and 15 mss/year. 1% of books from first-time authors; 100% from unagented writers. Pays 10% minimum royalty on retail price.** Publishes book 3 months after acceptance of ms. Reports in 3 months. Book catalog and ms guidelines for #10 SASE.

O─┐ Midmarch Arts Press publishes books on the arts, art history, criticism and poetry.

**Nonfiction:** Subjects include art/architecture, photography. Query. Reviews artwork/photos as part of ms package. Send photocopies.

**Poetry:** Query.

**Recent Title(s):** *Art and Politics in the 1930s: Americanism, Marxism, Modernism* (art history).

**MILKWEED EDITIONS**, 430 First Ave. N., Suite 400, Minneapolis MN 55401-1743. (612)332-3192. Website: http://www.milkweed.org. **Acquisitions:** Emilie Buchwald, publisher; Elisabeth Fitz, manuscript coordinator (fiction, children's fiction, poetry); City as Home editor (literary writing about cities); World as Home editor (literary writing about the natural world). Estab. 1980. Publishes hardcover originals and paperback originals and reprints. **Publishes 20 titles/year. Receives 2,000 submissions/year. 30% of books from first-time authors; 70% from unagented writers. Pays 7½% royalty on list price. Advance varies.** Publishes work 1-2 years after acceptance. Accepts simultaneous submissions. Reports in 6 months. Book catalog for $1.50. Manuscript guidelines for SASE.

O─┐ Milkweed Editions publishes literary fiction for adults and middle grade readers, nonfiction, memoir and poetry. "Our vision is focused on giving voice to writers whose work is of the highest literary quality and whose ideas engender personal reflection and cultural action." Currently emphasizing nonfiction about the natural world.

**Nonfiction:** Literary. Subjects include language/literature, nature/environment. Send ms with SASE for our response.

**Fiction:** Literary. Novels for adults and for readers aged 8-14. High literary quality. Send ms with SASE.

**Recent Title(s):** *Thirst*, by Ken Kalfur (fiction); *Shedding Life*, by Miroslav Hulub (nonfiction); *Eating Bread & Honey*, by Pattiana Rogers (poetry).

**Tips:** "We are looking for excellent writing in fiction, nonfiction, poetry, and children's novels, with the intent of making a humane impact on society. Send for guidelines. Acquaint yourself with our books in terms of style and quality before submitting. Many factors influence our selection process, so don't get discouraged. Nonfiction is focused on literary writing about the natural world, including living well in urban environments. We no longer publish children's biographies. We read poetry in January and June only."

**MILKWEEDS FOR YOUNG READERS**, Imprint of Milkweed Editions, 430 First Ave. N., Suite 400, Minneapolis MN 55401-1743. (612)332-3192. Fax: (612)332-6248. Website: http://www.milkweed.org. Children's Reader: Elisabeth Fitz. Estab. 1984. Publishes hardcover and trade paperback originals. **Publishes 1-2 titles/year. 25% of books from first-time authors; 70% from unagented writers. Pays 7½% royalty on retail price. Advance varies.** Publishes book 1 year after acceptance of ms. Accepts simultaneous submissions. Reports in 2 months on queries, 6 months on mss. Book catalog for $1.50. Manuscript guidelines for #10 SASE.

O─┐ "Milkweeds for Young Readers are works that embody humane values and contribute to cultural understanding." Currently emphasizing natural world, urban environments. De-emphasizing fantasy.

**Fiction:** For ages 8-12: adventure, animal, fantasy, historical, humor, environmental, mainstream/contemporary. Query with 2-3 sample chapters and SASE.

**Recent Title(s):** *Treasure of Panther Peak*, by Aileen Kilgore Henderson.

**THE MILLBROOK PRESS INC.**, 2 Old New Milford Rd., Brookfield CT 06804. Fax: (203)775-5643. Website: http://www.millbrookpress.com. Senior Vice President/Publisher: Jean Reynolds. Amy Shields and Laura Walsh, senior editors. **Acquisitions:** Meghann Hall, manuscript coordinator. Estab. 1989. Publishes hardcover and paperback originals. **Publishes 150 titles/year. Pays varying royalty on wholesale price or makes outright purchase. Advance varies.** Publishes book 1 year after acceptance of ms. Reports in 1 month on queries and proposals. Book catalog for 9 × 12 SAE with 4 first-class stamps. Manuscript guidelines for #10 SASE.

O─┐ Millbrook Press publishes quality children's books of curriculum-related nonfiction for the school/library market.

**Imprint(s): Twenty-First Century Books** (Pat Culleton, publisher).

**Nonfiction:** Children's/juvenile. Subjects include animals, anthropology/archaeology, ethnic, government/politics, health/medicine, history, hobbies, nature/environment, science, sports. Specializes in general reference, social studies, science, arts and crafts, multicultural and picture books. "Mistakes writers most often make when submitting nonfiction are failure to research competing titles and failure to research school curriculum." Query or submit outline and 1 sample chapter.

**Recent Title(s):** *Fabulous Frogs*, by Linda Glaser.

**N: MILLENNIUM PRESS**, Skeptics Society, P.O. Box 338, Altadena CA 91001. (818)794-3119. **Acquisitions:** Michael Shermer, editor. "Millennium Press strives to publish skeptical/scientific books supporting and embodying the scientific method and critical thinking." Estab. 1988. Publishes hardcover and trade paperback originals. **Publishes 4 titles/year. Receives 100 queries and 10 mss/year. 30% of books from first-time authors; 100% from unagented writers. Pays 10% or negotiable royalty on retail price. Offers negotiable advance.** Publishes book 8 months after acceptance of ms. Accepts simultaneous submissions. Reports in 1 month on queries, 2 months on proposals, 3 months on mss. Book catalog and ms guidelines free.

**Imprint(s): Skeptic Magazine**.

**Nonfiction:** Reference, technical. Subjects include history, religion, science. Submit outline, 1 sample chapter, proposal package, including table of contents and author biography. Reviews artwork/photos as part of the ms package. Send photocopies.

**Recent Nonfiction Title(s):** *Bible Prophecy: Failure or Fulfillment?*, by Tim Callahan; *Who Wrote the Gospels?*, by Randel Helms; *Creationism*, by Tom McIver.

**MINNESOTA HISTORICAL SOCIETY PRESS**, Minnesota Historical Society, 345 Kellogg Blvd. W., St. Paul MN 55102-1906. (651)296-2264. Fax: (651)297-1345. Website: http://www.mnhs.org. **Acquisitions:** Ann Regan, managing editor. Estab. 1849. Publishes hardcover and trade paperback originals, trade paperback reprints. **Publishes 10 titles/ year; each imprint publishes 5 titles/year. Receives 100 queries and 25 mss/year. 50% of books from first-time authors; 100% from unagented writers. Royalties are negotiated.** Publishes book 14 months after acceptance. Reports in 1 month on queries. *Writer's Market* recommends allowing 2 months for reply. Book catalog free.

    O➞ Minnesota Historical Society Press publishes both scholarly and general interest books that contribute to the understanding of Minnesota and Midwestern history.

**Imprint(s):** Borealis Books (reprints only); Midwest Reflections (memoir and personal history).

**Nonfiction:** Regional works only: biography, coffee table book, cookbook, illustrated book, reference. Subjects include anthropology/archaeology, art/architecture, history, memoir, photography, regional, women's issues/studies, Native American studies. Query with proposal package including letter, outline, vita, sample chapter. Reviews artwork/photos as part of ms package. Send photocopies.

**Recent Title(s):** *Shaping My Feminist Life: A Memoir*, by Kathleen C. Ridder.

**Tips:** Minnesota Historical Society Press is getting many inappropriate submissions from their listing. *A regional connection is required.*

**MINSTREL BOOKS**, Pocket Books for Young Readers, Simon & Schuster, 1230 Avenue of the Americas, New York NY 10020. (212)698-7669. Website: http://www.simonsayskids.com. Editorial Director: Patricia MacDonald. **Acquisitions:** Attn: Manuscript proposals. Estab. 1986. Publishes hardcover originals and reprints, trade paperback originals. **Publishes 125 titles/year. Receives 1,200 queries/year. Less than 25% from first-time authors; less than 25% from unagented writers. Pays 6-8% royalty on retail price. Advance varies.** Publishes book 2 years after acceptance of ms. Accepts simultaneous submissions. Reports in 3 months on queries. Book catalog and ms guidelines free.

    O➞ "Minstrel publishes fun, kid-oriented books, the kinds kids pick for themselves, for middle grade readers, ages 8-12."

**Nonfiction:** Children's/juvenile—middle grades, ages 8-12. Subjects include celebrity biographies and books about TV shows. Query with outline, sample chapters and SASE.

**Fiction:** Middle grade fiction for ages 8-12: animal stories, fantasy, humor, juvenile, mystery, science fiction, suspense. No picture books. "Thrillers are very popular, and 'humor at school' books." Query with synopsis/outline, sample chapters and SASE.

**Recent Title(s):** *Aliens Stole My Body*, by Bruce Coville.

**Tips:** "Hang out with kids to make sure your dialogue and subject matter are accurate."

**MITCHELL LANE PUBLISHERS**, P.O. Box 200, Childs MD 21916-0200. Fax: (410)392-4781. **Acquisitions:** Barbara Mitchell, publisher. Estab. 1993. Publishes hardcover and trade paperback originals. **Publishes 8-15 titles/year. 10% of books from first-time authors; 100% from unagented writers. Makes outright purchase on work-for-hire basis. No advance.** Publishes book 1 year after acceptance of ms. Reports only if interested. Book catalog free.

    O➞ Mitchell Lane publishes multicultural biographies for children and young adults.

**Nonfiction:** Multicultural, biography. Ethnic subjects. Query with SASE.

**Recent Title(s):** *Rafael Palmeiro: Living the American Dream*, by E. Brandt (biography); *Rain Forest Girl*, by Chalise Miner (nonfiction).

**MODERN LANGUAGE ASSOCIATION OF AMERICA**, Dept. WM, 10 Astor Pl., New York NY 10003. (212)475-9500. Fax: (212)477-9863. **Acquisitions:** Joseph Gibaldi, director of book acquisitions and development. Director of MLA Book Publications: Martha Evans. Estab. 1883. Publishes hardcover and paperback originals. **Publishes 15 titles/year. Receives 125 submissions/year. 100% of books from unagented writers. Pays 5-10% royalty on net proceeds.** Publishes book 1 year after acceptance. Reports in 2 months on mss. Book catalog free.

    O➞ The MLA publishes on current issues in literary and linguistic research and teaching of language and literature at postsecondary level.

**Nonfiction:** Scholarly, professional. Language and literature subjects. No critical monographs. Query with outline.

**🅽 ⬛** **MOMENTUM BOOKS, LTD.**, 6964 Crooks Rd., #1, Troy MI 48098. (248)828-3666. Fax: (248)828-0142. E-mail: momentumbooks@glis.net. **Acquisitions:** Franklin Foxx, editor. Estab. 1987. **Publishes 6 titles/year. Receives 100 queries and 30 mss/year. 95% of books from first-time authors; 100% from unagented writers. Pays 10-15% royalty. No advance.**

    O➞ Momentum Books publishes regional books and general interest nonfiction.

**Nonfiction:** Biography, cookbook, guides. Subjects include cooking/foods/nutrition, government/politics, history, memoirs, military/war, sports, travel. Submit proposal package, including outline, 3 sample chapters and marketing outline.
**Recent Title(s):** *To Strike at a King*, by Mike Ranville (history).

**MONACELLI PRESS**, 10 E. 92nd St., New York NY 10128. (212)831-0248. **Acquisitions:** Andrea Monfried, editor. Estab. 1994. Publishes hardcover and trade paperback originals. **Publishes 25-30 titles/year. Receives over 100 queries and mss/year. 10% of books from first-time authors; 90% from unagented writers. Pays royalty on retail price. Offers occasional advance, amount negotiable.** Publishes book 18 months after acceptance of ms. Accepts simultaneous submissions. Reports in 3 months on queries. Book catalog free.
  O→ Monacelli Press produces high-quality illustrated books in architecture, fine arts, decorative arts, landscape and photography.
**Nonfiction:** Coffee table book. Subjects include art/architecture. Query with outline, 1 sample chapter and SASE. Reviews artwork/photos as part of ms package. Send transparencies, duplicate slides best. (Monacelli does not assume responsibility for unsolicited artwork; call if you are uncertain about what to send.)
**Recent Title(s):** *Jim Dine: The Alchemy of Images*, text by Marco Livingstone with commentary by Jim Dine.

**MOODY PRESS**, Moody Bible Institute, 215 W. Locust St., Chicago IL 60610. (800)678-8001. Fax: (800)678-0003. Vice President/Executive Editor: Greg Thorton. **Acquisitions:** Acquisitions Coordinator. Estab. 1894. Publishes hardcover, trade and mass market paperback originals and hardcover and mass market paperback reprints. **Publishes 60 titles/year; imprint publishes 5-10 titles/year. Receives 1,500 queries and 2,000 mss/year. Less than 1% of books from first-time authors; 99% from unagented writers. Royalty varies. Offers $500-5,000 advance.** Publishes book 6 months after acceptance of ms. Accepts simultaneous submissions but prefers not to. Reports in 2 months. Book catalog for 9×12 SAE with 4 first-class stamps. Guidelines for #10 SASE.
  O→ "The mission of Moody Press is to educate and edify the Christian and to evangelize the non-Christian by ethically publishing conservative, evangelical Christian literature and other media for all ages around the world; and to help provide resources for Moody Bible Institute in its training of future Christian leaders."
**Imprint(s):** Northfield Publishing, Moody Children & Youth (contact Ella Linvall).
**Nonfiction:** Children's/juvenile, gift book, general Christian living. Subjects include child guidance/parenting, money/finance, religion, women's issues/studies. "Look at our recent publications, and convince us of what sets your book apart from all the rest on bookstore shelves and why it's consistent with our publications. Many writers don't do enough research of the market or of our needs." Query with outline, 3 sample chapters, table of contents, author's own market study showing why book will be successful and SASE.
**Recent Nonfiction Title(s):** *Management by Proverbs*, by Michael Zigarelli.
**Fiction:** Religious. "We are not currently accepting fiction submissions."
**Tips:** "Our audience consists of general, average Christian readers, not scholars. Know the market and publishers. Spend time in bookstores researching."

**N: MOON PUBLICATIONS, INC.**, Avalon Travel Publishing, Avalon Publishing Group, 5855 Beaudry St., Emeryville CA 94608. (510)595-3664. Website: http://www.moon.com. **Publisher:** Bill Newlin. **Editorial Director:** Pauli Galin. Estab. 1973. Publishes trade paperback originals. **Publishes 15 titles/year. Receives 100-200 submissions/year. 50% from first-time authors; 95% from unagented writers. Pays royalty on net price. Offers advance of up to $10,000.** Publishes book an average of 9 months after acceptance. Accepts simultaneous submissions. Reports in 2 months. Book catalog and proposal guidelines for 7½×10½ SAE with 2 first-class stamps.
  O→ "Moon Publications publishes comprehensive, articulate travel information to North and South America, Asia and the Pacific."
**Nonfiction:** "We specialize in travel guides to Asia and the Pacific Basin, the United States, Canada, the Caribbean, Latin America and South America, but are open to new ideas. Our guides include in-depth cultural and historical background, as well as recreational and practical travel information. We prefer comprehensive guides to entire countries, states, and regions over more narrowly defined areas such as cities, museums, etc. Writers should write first for a copy of our guidelines. Proposal required with outline, table of contents, and writing sample. Author should also be prepared to provide photos, artwork and base maps. No fictional or strictly narrative travel writing; no how-to guides." Reviews artwork/photos as part of ms package.
**Recent Nonfiction Title(s):** *New York Handbook*, by Christiane Bird (travel); *Tennessee Handbook*, by Jeff Bradley (travel); *Dominican Republic Handbook*, by Gaylord Dold (travel).
  ● At press time Avalon Publishing acquired Foghorn Press and will combine Moon and Foghorn to form Avalon Travel Publishing.
**Tips:** "Moon Travel Handbooks are designed by and for independent travelers seeking the most rewarding travel

---

**VISIT THE WRITER'S DIGEST WEBSITE** at http://www.writersdigest.com for hot new markets, daily market updates, writers' guidelines and much more.

experience possible. Our Handbooks appeal to all travelers because they are the most comprehensive and honest guides available. Check our website."

**MOREHOUSE PUBLISHING CO.**, 4475 Linglestown Rd., Harrisburg PA 17112. (717)541-8130. Fax: (717)541-8136. E-mail: morehouse@morehouse.com. Website: http://www.morehousegroup.com. **Acquisitions:** Debra K. Farrington, editorial director. Estab. 1884. Publishes hardcover and paperback originals. **Publishes 35 titles/year. 50% from first-time authors. Pays 10% net royalties. Offers small advance.** Publishes books within 18 months of acceptance. Accepts simultaneous submissions. Reports in 2 months. Guidelines available upon request.

○┅ Morehouse Publishing has traditionally published for the Episcopal Church and the Anglican Communion.

**Nonfiction:** "In addition to its line of books for the Episcopal church, it also publishes books of practical value from within the Christian tradition for clergy, laity, academics, professionals, and seekers." Subjects include spirituality, biblical studies, liturgics, congregational resorces, women's issues, devotions and meditations, and issues around Christian life. Submit outline, 1-2 sample chapters, résumé or cv, and market analaysis.

**Fiction:** Christian children's picture books for ages 3-8. Submit entire ms (no more than 1,500 words) and résumé/cv.

**Recent Title(s):** *Living with Contradiction: An Introduction to Benedictine Spirituality*, by Esther de Waal; *Jenny's Prayer*, by Annette Griessman, illustrated by Mary Ann Lard.

**△ WILLIAM MORROW AND CO.**, 1350 Avenue of the Americas, New York NY 10019. (212)261-6500. Fax: (212)261-6595. Website: http://www.williammorrow.com. Editorial Director: Lisa Queen. Managing Editor: Kim Lewis. **Acquisitions:** Pam Hoenig, associate publisher (Hearst Books, Hearst Marine Books); David Reuther, editor-in-chief (Beech Tree Books, Morrow Junior Books, Mulberry Books); Susan Pearson, editor-in-chief (Lothrop, Lee & Shepard Books); Toni Sciarra, editor (Quill Trade Paperbacks); Susan Hirschman (Greenwillow Books); Betty Nichols Kelly, editor-at-large. Estab. 1926. **Publishes 200 titles/year. Receives 10,000 submissions/year. 30% of books from first-time authors; 5% from unagented writers. Pays standard royalty on retail price. Advance varies.** Publishes book 2 years after acceptance of ms. Reports in 3 months.

○┅ William Morrow publishes a wide range of titles that receive much recognition and prestige. A most selective house.

**Imprint(s):** Beech Tree Books (juvenile); **Greenwillow Books** (juvenile); Hearst Books; Hearst Marine Books; **Lothrop, Lee & Shepard Books** (juvenile); **Morrow Junior Books** (juvenile); Mulberry Books (juvenile); Quill Trade Paperbacks; Tupelo Books; Rob Weisbach Books.

**Nonfiction and Fiction:** Publishes adult fiction, nonfiction, history, biography, arts, religion, poetry, how-to books, cookbooks. Length: 50,000-100,000 words. *Agented submissions only. No unsolicited mss or proposals.*

**Recent Title(s):** *The Last Party: The Life and Times of Studio 54*, by Anthony Haden-Guest (social history); *Van Gogh's Bad Cafe*, by Frederic Tuten.

**MORROW JUNIOR BOOKS**, William Morrow and Co., 1350 Avenue of the Americas, New York NY 10019. (212)261-6691. Publisher: Barbara Lalicki. **Acquisitions:** Meredith Carpenter, executive editor; Rosemary Brosnan, executive editor; Andrea Curley, senior editor; Marisa Miller, assistant editor. Publishes hardcover originals. **Publishes 50 titles/year. All contracts negotiated individually. Offers variable advance.**

○┅ Morrow Junior Books is one of the nation's leading publishers of books for children, including bestselling fiction and nonfiction.

**Nonfiction:** Juveniles (trade books). No textbooks. Query. *No unsolicited mss.*

**Fiction:** Juveniles (trade books). Query. *No unsolicited mss.*

**Recent Title(s):** *Ramona's World*, by Beverly Cleary; *Joan of Arc*, by Diane Stanley.

**⊞ ⊠ MOUNTAIN N'AIR BOOKS**, P.O. Box 12540, La Crescenta CA 91224. (818)951-4150. **Acquisitions:** Gilberto d'Urso, owner. Publishes trade paperback originals. **Publishes 6 titles/year. Receives 50 queries and 35 mss/year. 75% of books from first-time authors; 100% from unagented writers. Pays 5-10% royalty on retail price or makes outright purchase. No advance.** Publishes book 6 months after acceptance with ms. Reports in 2 weeks on queries and 2 months on mss. Manuscript guidelines for #10 SASE.

○┅ Mountain N'Air publishes books for those generally interested in the outdoors and travel.

**Imprint(s):** Bearly Cooking.

**Nonfiction:** Biography, cookbook, how-to. Subjects include cooking/foods/nutrition, nature/environment, recreation, travel/adventure. Submit outline with 2 sample chapters. Reviews artwork/photos as part of the ms package. Send photocopies.

**Recent Title(s):** *The Nose Knows*, by Battista (restaurant guide).

**⊠ MOUNTAIN PRESS PUBLISHING COMPANY**, P.O. Box 2399, Missoula MT 59806-2399. (406)728-1900. Fax: (406)728-1635. E-mail: mtnpress@montana.com. Website: http://www.mtnpress.com. **Acquisitions:** Kathleen Ort, editor-in-chief (natural history/science/outdoors); Gwen McKenna, editor (history); Jennifer Carey, assistant editor (Roadside Geology and Tumblweed Series). Estab. 1948. Publishes hardcover and trade paperback originals. **Publishes 15 titles/year. Receives 250 submissions/year. 50% of books from first-time authors; 90% from unagented writers. Pays 7-12% on wholesale price.** Publishes book 2 years after acceptance. Reports in 3 months. Book catalog free.

○┅ "We are expanding our Roadside Geology and Roadside History series (done on a state by state basis). We are interested in well-written regional field guides—plants, flowers and birds—and readable history and natural history."

**Nonfiction:** Western history, nature/environment, regional, earth science, creative nonfiction. "No personal histories or journals." Query or submit outline and sample chapters. Reviews artwork/photos as part of ms package.

**Recent Title(s):** *From Earth to Herbalist: An Earth Conscious Guide to Medicinal Plants*, by Gregory Tilford; *William Henry Jackson: Framing the Frontier*, by Douglas Waitley.

**Tips:** "Find out what kind of books a publisher is interested in and tailor your writing to them; research markets and target your audience. Research other books on the same subjects. Make yours different. Don't present your manuscript to a publisher—*sell* it to him. Give him the information he needs to make a decision on a title. Please learn what we publish before sending your proposal. We are a 'niche' publisher."

**THE MOUNTAINEERS BOOKS**, 1001 SW Klickitat Way, Suite 201, Seattle WA 98134-1162. (206)223-6303. Fax: (206)223-6306. E-mail: mbooks@mountaineers.org. Executive Director: Art Freeman. Managing Editor: Cindy Bohn. **Acquisitions:** Margaret Foster, editor-in-chief. Estab. 1961. Publishes 95% hardcover and trade paperback originals and 5% reprints. **Publishes 40 titles/year. Receives 150-250 submissions/year. 25% of books from first-time authors; 98% from unagented writers. Pays royalty on net sales. Offers advance.** Publishes book 1 year after acceptance. Reports in 3 months. Book catalog and ms guidelines for 9×12 SAE with $1.33 postage.

> Mountaineers Books specializes in expert, authoritative books dealing with mountaineering, hiking, backpacking, skiing, snowshoeing, canoeing, bicycling, etc. These can be either how-to-do-it or where-to-do-it (guidebooks). Currently emphasizing regional conservation and natural history.

**Nonfiction:** Guidebooks for national and international adventure travel, recreation, natural history, conservation/environment, non-competitive self-propelled sports, outdoor how-to. Does *not* want to see "anything dealing with hunting, fishing or motorized travel." Submit author bio, outline and minimum of 2 sample chapters. Accepts nonfiction translations. Looks for "expert knowledge, good organization." Also interested in nonfiction adventure narratives.

**Recent Title(s):** *Himalaya Alpine-Style: The Most Challenging Routes on the Highest Peaks*, by Andy Fashawe and Stephen Venables.

• See the Contests and Awards section for information on the Barbara Savage/"Miles From Nowhere" Memorial Award for outstanding adventure narratives offered by Mountain Books.

**Tips:** "The type of book the writer has the best chance of selling our firm is an authoritative guidebook (*in our field*) to a specific area not otherwise covered; or a how-to that is better than existing competition (again, *in our field*)."

**JOHN MUIR PUBLICATIONS**, Agora Inc., P.O. Box 613, Santa Fe NM 87504. (505)982-4078. Fax: (505)988-1680. **Acquisitions:** Cassandra Conyers, acquisitions manager. Estab. 1969. Publishes trade paperback originals. **Publishes 60-70 titles/year. Receives 1,000 queries and 50 mss/year. 60% of books from first-time authors; 90% from unagented writers. Pays 10% average royalty on wholesale price or makes outright purchase occasionally. Offers $3,500 average advance.** Publishes book 1 year after acceptance of ms. Accepts simultaneous submissions if noted in cover letter. Reports in 6 weeks on queries, 4 months on proposals. Book catalog for 9×12 SAE and 3 first-class stamps. Manuscript guidelines for #10 SASE.

> "We make the complex simple in the areas of independent travel and alternative health. We live in a busy time so our expert authors sort through time-sapping and money-wasting alternatives to offer our readers the best information for decision-making." Currently emphasizing natural health and special-interest travel.

**Nonfiction:** Adult travel and natural health. "We are continuing our commitment to adult travel titles and are seeking unique travel-related manuscripts. We are refining our list, and we're particularly interested in natural health. Do your homework to see what kinds of books we publish." Query or submit outline, 1-2 sample chapters and proposal package, including competition, résumé, marketing ideas with SASE. Reviews artwork/photos as part of ms package. Send photocopies or transparencies.

**Recent Title(s):** *Healing Centers and Retreats*, by Jennifer Miller.

**Tips:** "Audience is culturally minded, adults interested in independent travel and wanting to share enthusiasm with their children. They are somewhat adventurous and interested in multicultural themes. John Muir publishes nonfiction, so don't send us your great fiction idea. Check the competition. We don't want to see your idea if it's already on the store shelves. We are particularly interested in seeing special-interest travel proposals for the U.S. (domestic) traveler."

**MULTNOMAH PUBLISHERS, INC.**, P.O. Box 1720, Sisters OR 97759. (541)549-1144. E-mail: lstillwell@multnomahpubl.com. **Acquisitions:** Don Goodman; Rod Morris (general fiction); Karen Ball (romance and women's fiction). Estab. 1987. Publishes hardcover and trade paperback originals. **Publishes 120 titles/year. Receives 2,400 queries and 1,200 mss/year. 2% of books from first-time authors; 50% from unagented writers. Pays royalty on wholesale price.** Publishes book 1-2 years after acceptance of ms. Accepts simultaneous submissions. Reports in 3 months on queries. Manuscript guidelines for #10 SASE.

> Multnomah publishes books on Christian living and family enrichment, devotional and gift books and fiction.

**Imprint(s):** Alabaster, Multnomah Books, Palisades.

• Gold'n'Honey children's books was sold to Zondervan for the Zonderkidz imprint.

**Nonfiction:** Children, coffee table book, gift book, humor, illustrated book. Subjects include child guidance/parenting, religion. Submit proposal package, including outline/synopsis, 3 sample chapters and market study with SASE. Reviews artwork/photos as part of ms package. Send photocopies.

**Fiction:** Adventure, historical, humor, mystery, religious, romance, suspense, western. Submit synopsis, 3 sample

chapters with SASE.
**Recent Title(s):** *Stories for the Families*, by Alice Gray (nonfiction); *Publish & Perish*, by Sally Wright (mystery).

**MUSTANG PUBLISHING CO.**, P.O. Box 770426, Memphis TN 38177-0426. **Acquisitions:** Rollin Riggs, editor. Estab. 1983. Publishes hardcover and trade paperback originals. **Publishes 10 titles/year. Receives 1,000 submissions/ year. 50% of books from first-time authors; 90% of books from unagented writers. Pays 6-8% royalty on retail price.** Publishes book 1 year after acceptance. Accepts simultaneous submissions. Reports in 1 month. *Writer's Market* recommends allowing 2 months for reply. Book catalog for $2 and #10 SASE. No phone calls, please.

O━ Mustang publishes general interest nonfiction for an adult audience.

**Nonfiction:** How-to, humor, self-help. Subjects include Americana, hobbies, recreation, sports. "Our needs are very general—humor, travel, how-to, etc.—for the 18-to 60-year-old market." Query or submit outline and sample chapters with SASE. Reviews artwork as part of ms package. Send photocopies.

**Recent Title(s):** *How to Be a Way Cool Grandfather*, by Steen (how-to); *The Complete Book of Golf Games* by Johnston (sports).

**Tips:** "From the proposals we receive, it seems that many writers never go to bookstores and have no idea what sells. Before you waste a lot of time on a nonfiction book idea, ask yourself, 'How often have my friends and I actually *bought* a book like this?' We are not interested in first-person travel accounts or memoirs."

**🅐 THE MYSTERIOUS PRESS**, Warner Books, 1271 Avenue of the Americas, New York NY 10020. (212)522-5144. Fax: (212)522-7990. Website: http://www.warnerbooks.com. **Acquisitions:** William Malloy, editor-in-chief; Sara Ann Freed, executive editor; Susanna Einstein, associate editor. Estab. 1976. Publishes hardcover and mass market editions. **Publishes 36 titles/year. No agented writers. Pays standard, but negotiable, royalty on retail price. Amount of advance varies widely.** Publishes book an average of 1 year after acceptance of ms. Reports in 2 months.

O━ The Mysterious Press publishes well-written crime/mystery/suspense fiction.

**Fiction:** Mystery, suspense, crime/detective novels. No short stories. Query. *Agented submissions only.*

**Recent Title(s):** *Home Fires*, by Margaret Maron.

**🅝 MYSTIC SEAPORT MUSEUM**, 75 Greenmanville Ave., Mystic CT 06355-0990. (203)572-0711. Fax: (203)572-5326. **Acquisitions:** Joseph Gribbins, publications director. Estab. 1970. Publishes hardcover and trade paperback originals and reprints. **Publishes 4-6 titles/year. Pays 15% royalty on wholesale price.** Reports in 3 months.

O━ "We strive to publish significant new work in the areas of American maritime, yachting and small-craft history and biography." Mystic Seaport Museum has enlarged its focus from New England to North America.

**Imprint(s):** American Maritime Library.

**Nonfiction:** "We need serious, well-documented biographies, studies of economic, social, artistic, or musical elements of American maritime (not naval) history; books on traditional boat and ship types and construction (how-to). We are now interested in all North American maritime history—not, as in the past, principally New England. We like to see anything and everything, from queries to finished work." Query with outline and 3 sample chapters and SASE.

**Recent Nonfiction Title(s):** *America and the Sea: A Maritime History*, by Benjamin W. Labarce, et. al.

**THE NAIAD PRESS, INC.**, P.O. Box 10543, Tallahassee FL 32302. (850)539-5965. Fax: (850)539-9731. Website: http://www.naiadpress.com. **Acquisitions:** Barbara Grier, editorial director. Estab. 1973. Publishes paperback originals. **Publishes 31 titles/year. Receives over 1,500 submissions/year. 20% of books from first-time authors; 99% from unagented writers. Pays 15% royalty on wholesale or retail price. No advance.** Publishes book 2 years after acceptance. Reports in 4 months. Book catalog and ms guidelines for 6×9 SAE and $1.50 postage and handling.

O━ The Naid Press publishes lesbian fiction, preferably lesbian/feminist fiction.

**Fiction:** "We are not impressed with the 'oh woe' school and prefer realistic (i.e., happy) novels. We emphasize fiction and are now heavily reading manuscripts in that area. We are working in a lot of genre fiction—mysteries, short stories, fantasy—all with lesbian themes, of course. We have instituted an inhouse anthology series, featuring short stories only by our own authors (authors who have published full length fiction with us or those signed to do so)." Query.

**Recent Title(s):** *Past Due*, by Claire McNab (mystery).

**Tips:** "There is tremendous world-wide demand for lesbian mysteries from lesbian authors published by lesbian presses, and we are doing several such series. We are no longer seeking science fiction. Manuscripts under 50,000 words have twice as good a chance as over 50,000."

**NARWHAL PRESS, INC.**, 1629 Meeting St., Charleston SC 29405-9408. (803)853-0510. Fax: (803)853-2528. E-mail: shipwrex@aol.com. Website: http://www.shipwrecks.com. **Acquisitions:** Dr. E. Lee Spence, chief editor (marine archaeology, shipwrecks); Dr. Terry Frazier, managing editor (novels, marine histories, military); Roni L. Smith, associate editor (novels, children's books). Estab. 1994. Publishes hardcover and trade paperback originals. **Publishes 10 titles/ year. Receives 100 queries and 50 mss/year. 75% of books from first-time authors; 100% from unagented writers. Pays 10-15% royalty on wholesale price. Offers $1,000-2,000 advance.** Publishes book 3 months after acceptance of ms. Accepts simultaneous submissions. Reports in 2 weeks on queries, 1 month on mss.

O━ Narwhal Press specializes in books about shipwrecks and marine archaeology and history.

**Nonfiction:** Biography, children's/juvenile, how-to, reference. Subjects include anthropology/archaeology, history, memoirs, military/war. "We are constantly searching for titles of interest to shipwreck divers, marine archaeologists, Civil War buffs, etc., but we are expanding our titles to include novels, children's books, modern naval history and personal memoirs." Query or submit outline and 3 sample chapters and SASE. Reviews artwork/photos as part of ms package. Send photocopies.

**Fiction:** Historical, juvenile, mainstream/contemporary, military/war, young adult, dive-related. "We prefer novels with a strong historical context. We invite writers to submit fiction about undersea adventures. Best to call or write first." Query, then submit synopsis and 3 sample chapters and SASE.

**Recent Title(s):** *The Hunley: Submarines, Sacriface & Success in the Civil War*, by Mark Ragan (history); *Budapest Betrayal*, by Mimi Hallman (historical novel).

**Tips:** "Become an expert in your subject area. Polish and proofread your writing."

**NATIONAL TEXTBOOK CO.**, NTC/Contemporary Publishing Group, 4255 W. Touhy Ave., Lincolnwood IL 60646. (847)679-5500. Fax: (847)679-2494. President/CEO: Mark R. Pattis. Vice President/Publisher: Steve Van Thournout. Editorial Director: Cindy Krejcsi. **Acquisitions:** N. Keith Fry, director of foreign language publishing (world languages and ESL); Bill Kelleher, executive editor (high school language arts); Kathleen Manatt, executive editor (high school social studies); Marisa L'Heureux, executive editor (NTC College language arts); Betsy Lancefield (VGM Career Horizons); Lynn Mooney (NTC Business Books). Estab. 1962. Publishes original textbooks for education and trade market, and software. **Publishes 100-150 titles/year. Receives 1,000 submissions/year. 10% of books from first-time authors. 75% from unagented writers. Manuscripts purchased on either royalty or fee basis.** Publishes book 1 year after acceptance. Reports in 3 months. Book catalog and ms guidelines for 6×9 SAE and 2 first-class stamps.

○━ "We are a niche-oriented educational publisher of supplementary and core curricular materials."

**Nonfiction:** Textbooks. Major emphasis being given to world language and languages arts classroom texts, especially secondary level material, and business and career subjects (marketing, advertising, sales, etc.). Send sample chapter and outline or table of contents.

**Recent Title(s):** *Hammer's German Grammar and Usage*; *Theatre—Art in Action*; *Advertising Principles*.

**NATUREGRAPH PUBLISHERS, INC.**, P.O. Box 1047, Happy Camp CA 96039. (530)493-5353. Fax: (530)493-5240. E-mail: nature@sisgtel.net or naturgraph@aol.com. Website: http://members.aol.com/naturegraph/homepage.htm. **Acquisitions:** Barbara Brown, editor-in-chief; Keven Brown, editor. Estab. 1946. Publishes trade paperback originals. **Publishes 5 titles/year. Pays 8-10% royalty on wholesale price. No advance.** Reports in 1 month on queries, 2 months on proposals and mss.

○━ Naturegraph publishes "books for a better world. Within our niches of nature and Indian subjects, we hope the titles we choose to publish will benefit the world in some way."

**Nonfiction:** Primarily publishes nonfiction for the layman in natural history (biology, geology, ecology, astronomy); American Indian (historical and contemporary); outdoor living (backpacking, wild edibles, etc.); crafts and how-to. "Our primary niches are nature and Native American subjects with adult level, non-technical language and scientific accuracy. First, send for our free catalog. Study what kind of books we have already published." Submit outline and 2 sample chapters with SASE.

**Recent Title(s):** *Animals of the Western Rangelands*, by Ernest H. Elms.

**Tips:** "Please—always send a stamped reply envelope. Publishers get hundreds of manuscripts yearly; not just yours."

**THE NAUTICAL & AVIATION PUBLISHING CO.**, 1250 Saivmont Ave., Mt. Pleasant SC 29464. (843)856-0561. Fax: (843)856-3164. President/Publisher: Jan Snouck-Hurgronje. **Acquisitions:** Amanda McCall, editor. Estab. 1979. Publishes hardcover originals and reprints. **Publishes 10-12 titles/year. Receives 500 submissions/year. Pays 10-14% royalty on net selling price. Rarely offers advance.** Accepts simultaneous submissions. Book catalog free.

○━ The Nautical & Aviation Publishing Co. publishes military history—fiction and reference.

**Nonfiction:** Reference. Subjects include history, American wars. Query with synopsis and 3 sample chapters. Reviews artwork/photo as part of package.

**Fiction:** Historical. Submit outline/synopsis and sample chapters.

**Recent Title(s):** *Fort Macon: A History*, by Paul Branch.

**Tips:** "We are primarily a nonfiction publisher, but will review historical fiction of military interest of literary merit."

**NAVAL INSTITUTE PRESS**, US Naval Institute, 291 Wood Ave., Annapolis MD 21402-5035. Fax: (410)269-7940. E-mail: esecunda@usni.org. Website: http://www.usni.org. Press Director: Ronald Chambers. **Acquisitions:** Paul Wilderson, executive editor; Mark Gatlin, senior acquisitions editor; Eric Mills, acquisitions editor. Estab. 1873. **Publishes 80 titles/year. Receives 700-800 submissions/year. 50% of books from first-time authors; 85% from unagented writers. Pays 5-10% royalty on net sales.** Publishes book 1 year after acceptance. Book catalog free with 9×12 SASE. Manuscript guidelines for #10 SASE.

○━ The U.S. Naval Institute Press publishes general and scholarly books of professional, scientific, historical and literary interest to the naval and maritime community.

**Imprint(s):** Bluejacket Books (paperback reprints).

**Nonfiction:** "We are interested in naval and maritime subjects and in broad military topics, including government policy and funding. Specific subjects include: tactics, strategy, navigation, history, biographies, aviation, technology and others." Query letter strongly recommended.

**Fiction:** Limited fiction on military and naval themes.

**Recent Title(s):** *Wolf: U-Boat Commanders in World War II*, by Jordan Vause (nonfiction); *Rising Wind*, by Dick Couch (modern military thriller).

■ **NEAL-SCHUMAN PUBLISHERS, INC.**, 100 Varick St., New York NY 10013. (212)925-8650. Fax: (212)219-8916. E-mail: charles@neal-schuman.com. Website: http://www.neal-schuman.com. **Acquisitions:** Charles Harmon, director of publishing. Estab. 1976. Publishes hardcover and trade paperback originals. **Publishes 30 titles/year. Receives 500 submissions/year. 75% of books from first-time authors; 90% from unagented writers. Pays 10% royalty on net sales. Offers advances infrequently.** Publishes book 1 year after acceptance. Reports in 1 month on proposals. *Writer's Market* recommends allowing 2 months for reply. Book catalog and ms guidelines free.
- ☞ "Neal-Schuman publishes books about libraries, information science and the use of information technology, especially in education and libraries."

**Nonfiction:** Reference, Internet guides, textbook, texts and professional books in library and information science. "We are looking for many books about the Internet." Submit proposal package, including vita, outline, preface and sample chapters.

**Recent Title(s):** *Internet Power Searching*, by Phil Bradley.

**THOMAS NELSON PUBLISHERS**, NelsonWord Publishing Group, Box 141000, Nashville TN 37214-1000. Corporate address does not accept unsolicited mss; no phone queries. **Acquisitions:** Janet Thoma (Janet Thoma Books, 1157 Molokai, Tega Cay SC 29715, fax: 803/548-2684); Victor Oliver (Oliver-Nelson Books, 1360 Center Dr., Suite 102-B, Atlanta GA 30338, fax: 770/391-9784); Mark Roberts (religious, reference, academic or professional only), P.O. Box 141000, Nashville TN 37214, fax: 615/391-5225). Estab. 1984. **Publishes 150-200 titles/year. Pays royalty on net sales with rates negotiated for each project.** Publishes books 1-2 years after acceptance. Reports in 3 months. Accepts simultaneous submissions, if so noted.
- ☞ Thomas Nelson publishes Christian lifestyle nonfiction and fiction.

**Imprint(s):** Janet Thoma Books, Oliver-Nelson Books, **Tommy Nelson**.

**Nonfiction:** Adult inspirational, motivational, devotional, self-help, Christian living, prayer and evangelism, reference/Bible study. Query with SASE, then send brief, prosaic résumé, 1-page synopsis and 1 sample chapter to one of the acquisitions editors at the above locations with SASE.

**Fiction:** Seeking successfully published commercial fiction authors who write for adults from a Christian perspective. Send brief, prosaic résumé, 1-page synopsis and 1 sample chapter to one of the acquisitions editors at the above locations with SASE.

**Recent Title(s):** *Exploring the New Testament World*, by Albert A. Bell, Jr.; *Spine Chillers*, by Fred E. Katz.

**TOMMY NELSON**, Thomas Nelson, Inc., 404 BNA Dr., Bldg. 200, Suite 508, Nashville TN 37217. Fax: (615)902-2415. Website: http://www.tommynelson.com. Publishes hardcover and trade paperback originals. **Publishes 50-75 titles/year. Receives 1,000 mss/year. 5% of books from first-time authors; 50% from unagented writers. Pays royalty on wholesale price or makes outright purchase. Pays $1,000 minimum advance.** Publishes book 18 months after acceptance of ms. No simultaneous submissions.
- ☞ Tommy Nelson publishes children's Christian nonfiction and fiction for boys and girls up to age 14. "We honor God and serve people through books, videos, software and Bibles for children that improve the lives of our customers."

**Imprint(s):** Word Kids.

**Nonfiction:** Children's/juvenile. Religious subjects (Christian evangelical). *No unsolicited submissions.*

**Fiction:** Adventure, juvenile, mystery, picture books, religious. "No stereotypical characters without depth." *No unsolicited submissions.*

**Recent Title(s):** *50 Money Making Ideas for Kids*, by Allen & Lauree Burkett (money making projects); *Butterfly Kisses*, by Bob Carlisle (father's reflections on daughter).

**Tips:** "Know the CBA market. Check out the Christian bookstores to see what sells and what is needed."

**NELSON-HALL PUBLISHERS**, 111 N. Canal St., Chicago IL 60606. (312)930-9446. Senior Editor: Richard O. Meade. **Acquisitions:** Editorial Director. Estab. 1909. Publishes hardcover and paperback originals. **Publishes 30 titles/year. Receives 200 queries and 20 mss/year. 90% of books submitted by unagented writers. Pays 5-15% royalty on wholesale price.** Publishes book 1 year after acceptance. Accepts simultaneous submissions. Reports in 1 month on queries.
- ☞ Nelson-Hall publishes college textbooks and, more rarely, general scholarly books in the social sciences.

**Nonfiction:** Subjects include anthropology/archaeology, government/politics, criminology, psychology, sociology. Query with outline, 2 sample chapters, cv.

**Recent Title(s):** *Risky Business: America's Fascination with Gambling*, by Ron Pavalko.

Ⓐ **NEW AMERICAN LIBRARY**, Penguin Putnam Inc., 375 Hudson St., New York NY 10014. (212)366-2000. Website: http://www.penguin.com. Executive Editor: Carolyn Nichols. **Acquisitions:** Ellen Edwards, executive editor (commercial women's fiction—mainstream novels and contemporary romances; mysteries in a series and single title suspense; nonfiction of all types for a general audience); Laura Anne Gilman, executive editor (science fiction/fantasy/horror, mystery series, New Age); Audrey LaFehr, executive editor (contemporary and historical romance, women's suspense, multicultural fiction); Hilary Ross, associate executive editor (romances, Regencies); Doug Grad, senior editor (thrillers, suspense novels, international intrigue, technothrillers, military fiction and nonfiction, adventure nonfiction); Joe Pittman, senior editor (mysteries, suspense, thrillers, horror, commerical fiction); Dan Slater, editor (historical fiction, adult westerns, thrillers, military fiction and nonfiction, true crime, media tie-ins); Don Hymans, associate editor (classics, adventure/exploration); Cecilia Oh, associate editor (romance, Regency, commercial women's fiction, inspirational nonfiction); Genny Ostertag, associate editor (suspense, multicultural commercial fiction, women's fiction). Publishes mass market paperback originals and reprints. **Publishes 500 titles/year. Receives 20,000 queries and 10,000 mss/year. 30-40% of books from first-time authors; 5% from unagented writers. Advance and royalty negotiable.** Publishes book 2 years after acceptance of ms. Reports in 6 months.

○━ NAL publishes commercial fiction and nonfiction for the popular audience.
**Imprint(s):** Mentor, Onyx, **ROC**, Signet, Signet Classic, Signet Reference, Topaz.
**Nonfiction:** Biography, how-to, reference, self-help. Subjects include animals, child guidance/parenting, cooking/foods/nutrition, ethnic, health/medicine, language/literature, military/war, money/finance, psychology, sports. "Looking for reference and annual books." *Agented submission only.*
**Fiction:** Erotica, ethnic, fantasy, historical, horror, literary, mainstream/contemporary, mystery, occult, romance, science fiction, suspense, western. "Looking for writers who can deliver a book a year (or faster) of consistent quality." *Agented submissions only.*
**Recent Title(s):** *Down at the End of Lonely Street*, by Peter Harry Brown and Pat H. Broeske (biography of Elvis Presley); *Mortal Fear*, by Greg Iles (thriller).

**THE NEW ENGLAND PRESS, INC.**, P.O. Box 575, Shelburne VT 05482. (802)863-2520. Fax: (802)863-1510. E-mail: nep@together.net. Website: http://www.nepress.com. **Acquisitions:** Mark Wanner, managing editor. Publishes hardcover and trade paperback originals. **Publishes 6-8 titles/year. Receives 500 queries and 200 mss/year. 50% of books from first-time authors; 90% from unagented writers. Pays royalty on wholesale price. No advance.** Estab. 1978. Publishes book 15 months after acceptance of ms. Accepts simultaneous submissions. Reports in 3 months. Book catalog free.

○━ The New England Press publishes high-quality trade books of regional northern New England interest. Currently emphasizing young adult historical, Vermont history.
**Nonfiction:** Biography, young adult, illustrated book. Subjects include nature, history, regional, Vermontiana. "Nonfiction submissions must be based in Vermont and have northern New England topics. No memoirs or family histories. Identify potential markets and ways to reach them in cover letter." Submit outline and 2 sample chapters with SASE. Reviews artwork/photos as part of the ms package. Send photocopies.
**Fiction:** "We look for very specific subject matters based on Vermont history and heritage. We are also interested in historical novels for young adults based in New Hampshire and Maine. We do not publish contemporary adult fiction of any kind." Submit synopsis and 2 sample chapters with SASE.
**Recent Title(s):** *Alexander Twilight: Vermont's African-American Pioneer*, by Michael Hahn (nonfiction); *Father By Blood*, by Louella Bryant (fiction).
**Tips:** "Our readers are interested in all aspects of Vermont and northern New England, including hobbyists (railroad books) and students (young adult fiction and biography). No agent is needed, but our market is extremely specific and our volume is low, so send a query or outline and writing samples first. Sending the whole manuscript is discouraged. We will not accept projects that are still under development or give advances."

**NEW HARBINGER PUBLICATIONS**, 5674 Shattuck Ave., Oakland CA 94609. Fax: (510)652-5472. E-mail: nhelp@newharbinger.com. Website: http://www.newharbinger.com. **Acquisitions:** Kristin Beck, acquisitions manager; Catharine Sutker, acquisitions editor. Estab. 1979. **Publishes 36 titles/year. Receives 750 queries and 200 mss/year. 60% of books from first-time authors; 95% from unagented writers. Pays 12% royalty on wholesale price. Offers $0-3,000 advance.** Publishes book 1 year after acceptance of ms. Accepts simultaneous submissions. Reports in 1 month on queries and proposals, 2 months on mss. Book catalog and ms guidelines free.

○━ "We look for psychology and health self-help books that teach the average reader how to master essential skills. Our books are also read by mental health professionals who want simple, clear explanations of important psychological techniques and health issues."
**Nonfiction:** Self-help (psychology/health), textbooks. Subjects include anger management, anxiety, coping, health/medicine, psychology. "Authors need to be a qualified psychotherapist or health practitioner to publish with us." Submit proposal package, including outline, 3 sample chapters, competing titles and why this one is special.
**Recent Title(s):** *Healing Fear*, by Ed Bourne.
**Tips:** Audience includes psychotherapists and lay readers wanting step-by-step strategies to solve specific problems. "Our definition of a self-help psychology or health book is one that teaches essential life skills. The primary goal is to train the reader so that, after reading the book, he or she can deal more effectively with problems."

**NEW HOPE PUBLISHERS**, Division of Woman's Missionary Union, P.O. Box 12065, Birmingham AL 35202-2065. (205)991-8100. Fax: (205)991-4015. Website: http://www.newhopepubl.com. **Acquisitions:** Jennifer Law, editor; Leslie Caldwell, editorial specialist. **Publishes 15 titles/year. Receives 100 queries and 60 mss/year. 25% of books**

from first-time authors; **98% from unagented writers. Pays 7-10% royalty on retail price or makes outright purchase.** Publishes book 2 years after acceptance of ms. Reports in 6 months on mss. Book catalog for 9×12 SAE with 3 first-class stamps. Manuscript guidelines for #10 SASE.

O→ "Our goal is to provide resources to motivate and equip women to share the hope of Christ."

**Imprint(s): New Hope**, Woman's Missionary Union.

**Nonfiction:** How-to, children's/juvenile (religion), personal spiritual growth. Subjects include child guidance/parenting (from Christian perspective), education (Christian church), religion (Christian faith—must relate to missions work, culture and multicultural issues, Christian concerns, Christian ethical issues, spiritual growth, etc.), women's issues/studies from Christian perspective. "We publish Christian education materials that focus on missions work or educational work in some way. Teaching helps, spiritual growth material, ideas for working with different audiences in a church, etc.—missions work overseas or church work in the U.S., women's spiritual issues, guiding children in Christian faith." Submit outline and 3 sample chapters for review. Submit complete ms for acceptance decision.

**Recent Title(s):** *Glimpses of Christian Everyday Life*, by Karla Worley.

**NEW HORIZON PRESS**, P.O. Box 669, Far Hills NJ 07931. (908)604-6311. Fax: (908)604-6330. **Acquisitions:** Dr. Joan S. Dunphy, publisher (nonfiction, social cause, true crime). Estab. 1983. Publishes hardcover and trade paperback originals. **Publishes 12 titles/year. 90% of books from first-time authors; 50% from unagented writers. Pays standard royalty on net price. Pays advance.** Publishes book 2 years after acceptance of ms. Accepts simultaneous submissions. Book catalog and ms guidelines free.

O→ New Horizon publishes adult nonfiction featuring true stories of uncommon heroes, true crime, social issues and self help. Introducing a new line of children's self-help.

**Imprints:** Small Horizons.

**Nonfiction:** Biography, children's/juvenile, how-to, self-help. Subjects include child guidance/parenting, creative nonfiction, government/politics, health/medicine, nature/environment, psychology, women's issues/studies, true crime. Submit proposal package, including outline, 3 sample chapters, author bio with photo, résumé and marketing information.

**Recent Title(s):** *Titanic Adventure*, by Jennifer Carter and Joel Hirschhorn (biography/women's issues).

**Tips:** "We are a small publisher, thus it is important that the author/publisher have a good working relationship. The author must be willing to sell his book."

**NEW WORLD LIBRARY**, Whatever Publishing, Inc., 14 Pamaron Way, Novato CA 94949. (415)884-2100. Fax: (415)884-2199. E-mail: escort@nwlib.com. Website: http://www.nwlib.com. Publisher: Marc Allen. **Acquisitions:** Becky Benenate, editorial director. Estab. 1979. Publishes hardcover and trade paperback originals and reprints. **Publishes 35 titles/year. 10% of books from first-time authors; 50% from unagented writers. Pays 12-16% royalty on wholesale price for paperback; 12-20% royalty on wholesale price for hardcover. Offers $0-200,000 advance.** Publishes book 18 months after acceptance of ms. Accepts simultaneous submissions. Reports in 2 months. Book catalog and ms guidelines free.

O→ NWL is dedicated to publishing books and cassettes that inspire and challenge us to improve the quality of our lives and our world.

**Imprint(s):** Nataraj.

**Nonfiction:** Gift book, self-help. Subjects include business/prosperity, cooking/foods/nutrition, ethnic (African-American, Native American), money/finance, nature/environment, personal growth, psychology, religion, women's issues/studies. Query or submit outline, 1 sample chapter and author bio with SASE. Reviews artwork/photos as part of ms package. Send photocopies.

**Recent Title(s):** *The Art of Becoming Yourself*, by Sabrina Ward Harrison.

**NEW YORK UNIVERSITY PRESS**, 70 Washington Square S., New York NY 10012. (212)998-2575. Fax: (212)995-3833. Website: http://www.nyupress.nyu.edu. **Acquisitions:** Eric Zinner (cultural studies, literature, media, anthropology); Jennifer Hammer (Jewish studies, psychology, religion, women's studies); Niko Pfund (business, history, law); Stephen Magro (social sciences). Estab. 1916. Hardcover and trade paperback originals. **Publishes 150 titles/year. Receives 800-1,000 queries/year. 30% of books from first-time authors; 90% from unagented writers. Advance and royalty on net receipts varies by project.** Publishes book 8 months after acceptance of ms. Accepts simultaneous submissions. Reports in 1 month on proposals (peer reviewed).

O→ New York University Press embraces ideological diversity. "We often publish books on the same issue from different poles to generate dialogue, engender and resist pat categorizations."

**Nonfiction:** Subjects include anthropology/archaeology, art/architecture, business/economics, computers/electronics, education, ethnic, gay/lesbian, government/politics, health/medicine, history, language/literature, military/war, money/finance, music/dance, nature/environment, philosophy, photography, psychology, regional, religion, sociology, sports, travel, women's issues/studies. Submit proposal package, including outline, 1 sample chapter and with SASE. Reviews artwork/photos as part of the ms package. Send photocopies.

**Fiction and Poetry:** Publishes *only* contest winners for the NYU Press Prizes.

**Recent Title(s):** *Kosovo: A Short History*, by Noel Malcolm.

**NEWCASTLE PUBLISHING CO., INC.**, 13419 Saticoy, N. Hollywood CA 91605. (818)787-4378. Fax: (213)780-2007. Editor-in-Chief: Daryl Saunders. **Acquisitions:** Erik Bradford, editor; Jodi Grossblatt, editor. Estab. 1970. Publishes trade paperback originals and reprints. **Publishes 10 titles/year. Receives 300 submissions/year. 70% of books**

from first-time authors; **95% of books from unagented writers. Pays 5-10% royalty on retail price. No advance.**
Publishes book an average of 8 months after acceptance of ms. Accepts simultaneous submissions. Reports in 1 month.
*Writer's Market* recommends allowing 2 months for reply. Free book catalog. Manuscript guidelines for SASE.

    **O─π** Newcastle publishes quality paperbacks for the discerning reader.

**Nonfiction:** How-to, self-help, metaphysical, New Age and practical advice for older adults. Subjects include health
(physical fitness, diet and nutrition), psychology. No biography, travel, children's books, poetry, cookbooks or fiction.
Query or submit outline and sample chapters. Looks for "something to grab the reader so that he/she will readily
remember that passage."

**Recent Title(s):** *Celtic Mythology.*

**Tips:** "Check the shelves in the larger bookstores on the subject of the manuscript being submitted. A book on life
extension, holistic health, or stress management has the best chance of selling to our firm along with books geared for
older adults on personal health issues, etc."

**NEWJOY PRESS**, P.O. Box 3437, Ventura CA 93006. (800)876-1373. Fax: (805)984-0503. E-mail: njpublish@aol.c
om. **Acquisitions**: Joy Nyquist, publisher. Publishes trade paperback originals. **Publishes 7-10 titles/year. Pays 10-
15% royalty on retail price.** Reports in 4 months.

    **O─π** "Our plan is to publish quality books in an easy-to-read style. We publish traveler's help books, recovery books
    (focus on relapse prevention) and self-help books (focus on women's issues)." Currently emphasizing traveler's
    help books. De-emphasizing self-help books.

**Nonfiction:** Publishes chemical dependency relapse prevention books; self-help books with focus on women's issues;
traveler's help books. Submit (by mail only) a proposal with outline, sample chapter and author's qualifications. Previous
marketing experience and a strong marketing plan along with a commitment to marketing is very important.

**Recent Title(s):** *Relapse Traps: How to Escape or Avoid Them,* by Robert Ramsey, Ed.D.

**Tips:** "Newjoy Press is looking for books written by qualified persons who offer relevant information based on research
and expertise on their subject. In addition, the authors must have a strong marketing plan and marketing skills such as
public speaking."

**A** **NEWSTAR PRESS**, NewStar Press, Dove Entertainment, 8955 Beverly Blvd., Los Angeles CA 90048. Website:
http://www.newstarmedia.com. **Acquisitions**: Beth Lieberman, editorial director. Estab. 1994. Publishes hardcover originals, trade paperback originals and reprints. **Publishes 25 titles/year. Receives 1,000 queries and 250 mss/year. 5%
of books from first-time authors; 1% from unagented writers. Pays royalty on retail price. Advance varies.**
Publishes book 1 year after acceptance of ms. Accepts simultaneous submissions. Reports in 2 months.

    **O─π** NewStar Press publishes a diverse list of nonfiction titles.

**Nonfiction:** Biography, how-to, reference, self-help. Subjects include Americana, business and economics, child guid-
ance/parenting, cooking/foods/nutrition, government/politics, health/medicine, money/finance, psychology, regional, science. *Agented submissions only. All unsolicited mss returned unopened.*

**Fiction:** *Agented submissions only.*

**Recent Title(s):** *The Complete Guide to Nutritional Supplements,* by Brenda Adderly, M.H.A.

**NIGHTSHADE PRESS**, P.O. Box 76, Troy ME 04987. (207)948-3427. Fax: (207)948-5088. E-mail: potatoeyes@unin
ets.net. Website: http://www.maineguide.com/giftshop/potatoeyes. Estab. 1989. Publishes hardcover and trade paperback
originals. **Publishes 4-5 titles/year. Pays royalty on retail price. No advance.** Reports in 2 months on queries and
proposals, 3 months on mss.

    ● Nightshade Press also publishes the literary magazine *Potato Eyes.*

**Fiction:** Contemporary, feminist, humor/satire, literary, mainstream, regional. No religious, romance, preschool, juvenile, young adult, psychic/occult. Query with SASE.

**Poetry:** Submit 3-5 poems with SASE.

**Recent Title(s):** *Every Day A Visitor,* by Richard Abrons (short story collection); *Bone Music,* by Howard Nelson.

**N** **NO STARCH PRESS**, 555 Dettaro St., Suite 250, San Francisco CA 94107. (415)863-9900. Fax: (415)863-9950.
**Acquisitions:** William Pollock, publisher. Estab. 1994. Publishes trade paperback originals. **Publishes 6-10 titles/year.
Receives 100 queries and 5 mss/year. 80% of books from first-time authors; 90% from unagented writers. Pays
10-15% royalty on wholesale price. Offers negotiable advance.** Publishes book 4 months after acceptance of ms.
Accepts simultaneous submissions. Book catalog free.

    **O─π** No Starch Press publishes informative, easy to read computer books for non-computer people to help them get
    the most from their hardware and software. Currently de-emphasizing trade nonfiction related to the technology
    business and/or cyberculture.

**Imprint(s):** No Starch Comix.

**Nonfiction:** How-to, reference, technical. Subjects include computers/electronics, hobbies, software. Only considers
computer-related books or underground comics. Submit outline, 1 sample chapter, bio, market rationale. Reviews art-
work/photos as part of ms package. Send photocopies.

**Recent Title(s):** *Steal This Computer Book,* by Wally Wang; *The Color Printer Idea Book,* by Kay Hall.

**Tips:** "No fluff—content, content, content or just plain fun. Understand how your book fits into the market. Tell us
why someone, anyone, will buy your book. Be enthusiastic."

**NODIN PRESS**, Micawber's Inc., 525 N. Third St., Minneapolis MN 55401. (612)333-6300. Fax: (612)359-5737. **Acquisitions:** Norton Stillman, publisher. Publishes hardcover and trade paperback originals. **Publishes 4 titles/ year. Receives 20 queries and 20 mss/year. 75% of books from first-time authors; 100% from unagented writers. Pays 10% royalty. Offers $250-1,000 advance.** Publishes book 20 months after acceptance of ms. Accepts simultaneous submissions. Reports in 6 months on queries. Book catalog or ms guidelines free.

O── Nodin Press publishes Minnesota guidebooks.

**Nonfiction:** Biography, regional guide book. Subjects include ethnic history, sports, travel. Query.

**Recent Title(s):** *Minnesota Free, The State's Best No-Charge Attractions*, by Jim Morse (nonfiction); *Lessons on the Journey*, by David Nimmer.

**NOONDAY PRESS**, Farrar Straus & Giroux, Inc., 19 Union Square W., New York NY 10003. (212)741-6900. Fax: (212)633-9385. **Acquisitions:** Elisabeth Dyssegaard, executive editor. Publishes trade paperback originals and reprints. **Publishes 70 titles/year. Receives 1,500-2,000 queries/mss per year. Pays 6% royalty on retail price. Advance varies.** Publishes book 1 year after acceptance of ms. Accepts simultaneous submissions. Reports in 2 months on queries and proposals. Book catalog and ms guidelines free.

O── Noonday emphasizes literary nonfiction and fiction, as well as fiction and poetry reprints.

**Nonfiction:** Biography. Subjects include child guidance/parenting, education, language/literature. Query with outline, 2-3 sample chapters, cv, cover letter discribing project and SASE. *No unsolicited mss.*

**Fiction:** Literary. Mostly reprints of classic authors.

**Recent Title(s):** *Message from My Father*, by Calvin Trillin (memoir); *Enemies: A Love Story*, by Isaac Bashevis Singer (fiction).

**NORTH LIGHT BOOKS**, F&W Publications, 1507 Dana Ave., Cincinnati OH 45207. Editorial Director: Greg Albert. **Acquisitions:** Acquisitions Coordinator. Publishes hardcover and trade paperback how-to books. **Publishes 40-45 titles/ year. Pays 10-20% royalty on net receipts. Offers $4,000 advance.** Accepts simultaneous submissions. Reports in 1 month. Book catalog for 9×12 SAE with 6 first-class stamps.

O── North Light Books publishes art, craft and design books, including watercolor, drawing, colored pencil and decorative painting titles that emphasize illustrated how-to art instruction.

**Nonfiction:** Watercolor, drawing, colored pencil, decorative painting, craft and graphic design instruction books. Interested in books on watercolor painting, basic drawing, pen and ink, colored pencil, decorative painting, table-top crafts, basic design, computer graphics, layout and typography. Do not submit coffee table art books without how-to art instruction. Query or submit outline and examples of artwork (transparencies and photographs).

**Recent Title(s):** *Painting Fresh Florals in Watercolor*, by Arleta Peck.

**NORTH POINT PRESS**, Farrar Straus & Giroux, Inc., 19 Union Square W., New York NY 10003. (212)741-6900. Fax: (212)633-9385. Editorial Director: Rebecca Saletan. Editor: Ethan Nosowsky. **Acquisitions:** Katrin Wilde. Estab. 1980. Hardcover and trade paperback originals. **Publishes 25 titles/year. Receives hundreds of queries and hundreds of mss/year. 20% of books from first-time authors. Pays standard royalty rates. Advance varies.** Publishes book 18 months after acceptance of ms. Accepts simultaneous submissions. Reports in 2 months on queries and proposals, 3 months on mss. Manuscript guidelines for #10 SASE.

O── "We are a broad-based literary trade publisher—high quality writing only."

**Nonfiction:** Subjects include nature/environment, food/gardening, history, religion (no New Age), music, memoir/ biography, sports, travel. "Be familiar with our list. No genres." Query with outline, 1-2 sample chapters and SASE.

**Recent Title(s):** *Out of Sheer Rage*, by Geoff Dyer.

**NORTHEASTERN UNIVERSITY PRESS**, 360 Huntington Ave., 416CP, Boston MA 02115. (617)373-5480. Fax: (617)373-5483. Website: http://www.neu.edu/nupress. **Acquisitions:** William Frohlich, director (music, criminal justice); John Weingartner, senior editor (history, law and society); Terri Teleen, editor (women's studies). Estab. 1977. Publishes hardcover originals and trade paperback originals and reprints. **Publishes 40 titles/year. Receives 500 queries and 100 mss/year. 50% of books from first-time authors; 90% from unagented writers. Pays 5-15% royalty on wholesale price. Offers $500-5,000 advance.** Publishes book 1 year after acceptance of ms. Accepts simultaneous submissions. Reports in 1 month. Book catalog and ms guidelines free.

O── Northeastern University Press publishes scholarly and general interest titles in the areas of American history, criminal justice, law and society, women's studies, African-American literature, ethnic studies and music. Currently emphasizing American studies. De-emphasizing literary studies.

**Nonfiction:** Biography, adult trade scholarly monographs. Subjects include Americana, criminal justice, ethnic, law/ society, history, memoirs, music/dance, regional, women's issues/studies. Query or submit proposal package, including outline, 1-2 sample chapters and SASE. Reviews artwork/photos as part of ms package. Send photocopies.

**Fiction:** Literary. Majority of fiction titles are reissues. Query.

**Recent Title(s):** *No State Haven: Stories of Women in Prison*, by Lori B. Girshick (nonfiction); *Peyton Place*, by Grace Metalious (fiction).

**NORTHERN ILLINOIS UNIVERSITY PRESS**, DeKalb IL 60115-2854. (815)753-1826/753-1075. Fax: (815)753-1845. **Acquisitions:** Mary L. Lincoln, director/editor-in-chief; Martin Johnson, acquisitions editor (history, politics). Estab. 1965. **Publishes 18-20 titles/year. Pays 10-15% royalty on wholesale price.** Book catalog free.

O→ NIU Press publishes both specialized scholarly work and books of general interest to the informed public. "We publish mainly history, politics, anthropology, and other social sciences. We are interested also in studies on the Chicago area and midwest and on literature in translation." Currently emphasizing literature in translation. De-emphasizing literary criticism.

**Nonfiction:** "Publishes mainly history, political science, social sciences, philosophy, literary criticism and regional studies. No collections of previously published essays, no unsolicited poetry." Accepts nonfiction translations. Query with outline and 1-3 sample chapters.

**Recent Title(s):** *Cleaning Up the Great Lakes*, by Terry Kehoe.

**NORTHFIELD PUBLISHING**, Moody Press, 215 W. Locust St., Chicago IL 60610. (800)678-8001. Fax: (800)678-0003. **Acquisitions:** Acquisitions Coordinator. **Publishes 5-10 titles/year. Less than 1% of books from first-time authors; 95% from unagented writers. Pays royalty on net receipts. Offers $500-50,000 advance.** Publishes books 8 months after acceptance of ms. Accepts simultaneous submissions, but prefers not to. Reports in 2 months on queries. Book catalog for 9 × 12 SAE with 2 first-class stamps. Manuscript guidelines for #10 SASE.

O→ "Northfield publishes a line of books for non-Christians or those exploring the Christian faith. While staying true to Biblical principles, we eliminate some of the Christian wording and scriptual references to avoid confusion."

**Nonfiction:** Biographies (classic). Subjects include business/economics, child guidance/parenting, finance. Query with outline, 2-3 sample chapters, table of contents, author's market study of why this book will be successful and SASE.

**Recent Title(s):** *Loving Solutions*, by Gary Chapman (marriage helps).

**NORTHLAND PUBLISHING CO., INC.**, P.O. Box 1389, Flagstaff AZ 86002-1389. (520)774-5251. Fax: (520)774-0592. E-mail: editorial@northlandpub.com. Website: http://www.northlandpub.com. **Acquisitions:** Stephanie Bucholz, adult editor (western and southwestern art and cookery); Aimee Jackson, kids editor (picture books, especially humor). Estab. 1958. Publishes hardcover and trade paperback originals. **Publishes 25 titles/year. Imprint publishes 10 titles/year. Receives 4,000 submissions/year. 25% of books from first-time authors; 50% from unagented writers. Pays royalty on net receipts. Offers advance.** Publishes book 2 years after acceptance. Accepts simultaneous submissions. Reports in 3 months. Call for book catalog and ms guidelines.

O→ "Northland is well regarded in the publishing industry as a publisher of quality nonfiction books on the material culture and indigenous peoples of the American West, including fine art, history, natural history and cookbooks. Under our new imprint, Rising Moon, we publish picture books for children with universal themes."

**Imprint(s):** Rising Moon (books for young readers).

**Nonfiction:** Biography, children's/juvenile, coffee table book, cookbook, gift book, illustrated book (picture books). Subjects include animals (children's and adult natural history), anthropology/archaeology (Native America), art/architecture (multi-author/artist only), cooking/foods/nutrition (cookbooks, Southwest), ethnic (Native Americans, Hispanic), history (natural and Native America), hobbies (collecting/arts), nature/environment (picture books), regional (Southwestern and Western US). Submit outline and 2-3 sample chapters with SASE. No fax or e-mail submissions. Reviews artwork/photos as part of the ms package. "Artwork should be sent to the Art Director unless it is critical to understanding the proposal."

**Fiction:** Picture books. Submit synopsis and 3 sample chapters with SASE. "No dummy books! For picture books, send complete manuscript with SASE."

**Recent Title(s):** *Art of the Hopi*, by Jerry & Lois Jacka (adult); *California A-Z*, by Dorothy H. Weaver (children's).

**Tips:** "Our audience is composed of general interest readers."

**NORTHWORD PRESS**, Creative Publishing International, Inc., 5900 Green Oak Dr., Minnetonka MN 55343. (612)936-4700. Fax: (612)933-1456. **Acquisitions:** Barbara K. Harold, editorial director. Estab. 1984. Publishes hardcover and trade paperback originals. **Publishes 15-20 titles/year. Receives 600 submissions/year. 50% of books are from first-time authors; 90% are from unagented writers. Pays 10-15% royalty on wholesale price. Offers $2,000-20,000 advance.** Publishes book 1 year after acceptance. Accepts simultaneous submissions. Reports in 3 months on queries. Book catalog for 9 × 12 SASE with 7 first-class stamps. Manuscript guidelines for SASE.

O→ NorthWord Press publishes exclusively nature and wildlife titles for adults, teens, and children.

**Nonfiction:** Coffee table books, introductions to wildlife and natural history, guidebooks, children's illustrated books; nature and wildlife subjects exclusively. Query with outline, sample chapters and SASE.

**Recent Title(s):** *Chased By the Light*, by Jim Brandenburg.

**Tips:** "No poetry, fiction or memoirs. We have expanded to include exotic and non-North American topics."

**W.W. NORTON CO., INC.**, 500 Fifth Ave., New York NY 10110. Fax: (212)869-0856. Website: http://www.wwnorton.com. **Acquisitions:** Robert Weil, executive editor. Edwin Barber; Jill Bialosky (literary fiction, biography, memoirs); Amy Cherry (history, biography, women's issues, African-American, health); Carol Houck-Smith (literary fiction, travel memoirs, behavioral sciences, nature); Starling Lawrence, editor-in-chief; Angela von der Leppe (trade nonfiction, behavioral sciences, earth sciences, astronomy, neuro-science, education); Jim Mairs (history, biography, illustrated books); Alane Mason (serious nonfiction cultural and intellectual history, illustrated books, literary fiction and memoir); W. Drake McFeely, president (nonfiction, particularly science and social science). Estab. 1923. Publishes hardcover and paperback originals and reprints. **Publishes 300 titles/year. Pays royalty.** Reports in 2 months.

O→ General trade publisher of fiction, poetry and nonfiction, educational and professional books. "W.W. Norton

Co. strives to carry out the imperative of its founder to 'publish books not for a single season, but for the years' in the areas of fiction, nonfiction and poetry."

**Imprint(s): Backcountry Publications, Countryman Press, Foul Play Press, Outside Books, W.W. Norton**.

**Nonfiction and Fiction:** Subjects include antiques and collectibles, architecture, art/design, autobiography/memoir, biography, business, child care, cooking, current affairs, family, fiction, games, health, history, law, literature, music, mystery, nature, nautical topics, photography, poetry, politics/political science, reference, religion, sailing, science, self-help, transportation, travel. *College Department:* Subjects include biological sciences, economics, psychology, political science, and computer science. *Professional Books* specializes in psychotherapy. "We are not interested in considering books from the following categories: juvenile or young adult, religious, occult or paranormal, genre fiction (formula romances, sci-fi or westerns), and arts and crafts. Please give a brief description of your submission, your writing credentials, and any experience, professional or otherwise, which is relevant to your submission. Submit 2 or 3 sample chapters, one of which should be the first chapter, with SASE. No phone calls. Address envelope and letter to The Editors."

**Recent Title(s):** *Hitler*, by Ian Kershaw (nonfiction); *Voyage of the Narwhal*, by Andrea Barrett (fiction).

**NOVA PRESS**, 11659 Mayfield Ave., Suite 1, Los Angeles CA 90049. (310)207-4078. Fax: (310)571-0908. E-mail: novapress@aol.com. Website: http://www.testprepcenter.com. **Acquisitions:** Jeff Kolby, president. Estab. 1993. Publishes trade paperback originals. **Publishes 10 titles/year. Pays 10-22½% royalty on net price.** Publishes book 6 months after acceptance of ms. Book catalog free.

    O⊶ Nova Press publishes only test prep books for college entrance exams, and closely related reference books, such as college guides and vocabulary books.

**Nonfiction:** Test prep books for college entrance exams. How-to, self-help, technical. Education, software subjects.

**Recent Title(s):** *The Art of Academic Finesse*, by Eric Evans.

**NTC/CONTEMPORARY PUBLISHING GROUP**, 4255 W. Touhy Ave., Lincolnwood IL 60646-1975. (847)679-5500. Fax: (847)679-2494. E-mail: ntcpub2@aol.com. Editorial Director: John T. Nolan. **Acquisitions:** Danielle Egan-Miller, business editor; Rob Taylor, associate editor; Denise Betts, assistant editor; Betsy Lancefield, senior editor; Anne Knudsen, executive editor. Estab. 1947. Publishes hardcover originals and trade paperback originals and reprints. **Publishes 850 titles/year. Receives 9,000 submissions/year. 10% of books from first-time authors; 25% of books from unagented writers. Pays 6-15% royalty on retail price.** Publishes book 1 year after acceptance. Accepts simultaneous submissions. Reports in 2 months. Manuscript guidelines for SASE.

    O⊶ "We are a midsize, niche-oriented, backlist-oriented publisher. We publish exclusively nonfiction in general interest trade categories plus travel, reference and quilting books."

**Imprint(s):** Contemporary Books, Country Roads Press, Keats Publishing, **Lowell House, Masters Press,** NTC Business Books, **NTC Publishing Group, National Textbook Company,** Passport Books, Peter Bedrick Books, **The Quilt Digest Press, VGM Career Horizons**.

**Nonfiction:** Cookbooks, how-to, humor, reference, self-help. Subjects include business, careers, child guidance/parenting, crafts (especially quilting), marketing, cooking, health/fitness, nutrition, pet care, popular culture, psychology, real estate, sports, travel, women's studies. Submit outline, sample chapters and SASE. Reviews artwork/photos as part of ms package.

**Recent Title(s):** *How Men Have Babies*, by Alan Thicke.

**⌈N⌉ OAK KNOLL PRESS**, 310 Delaware St., New Castle DE 19720. (302)328-7232. Fax: (302)328-7274. E-mail: oakknoll@oakknoll.com. Website: http://www.oakknoll.com. **Acquisitions:** Editor. Estab. 1976. Publishes hardcover and trade paperback originals and reprints. **Publishes 35 titles/year. Receives 100 queries and 100 mss/year. 50% of books from first-time authors; 100% from unagented writers. Pays 10% royalty on income.** Publishes book 18 months after acceptance of ms. Accepts simultaneous submissions. Reports in 1 month on queries. *Writer's Market* recommends allowing 2 months for reply. Book catalog free.

    O⊶ Oak Knoll specializes in books about books—preserving the art and lore of the printed word.

**Nonfiction:** Book arts. Subjects include printing, papermaking, bookbinding, book collecting, etc. Query. Reviews artwork/photos as part of ms package. Send photocopies.

**Recent Title(s):** *Historical Scripts*, by Stan Knight; *Printing on the Iron Handpress*, by Richard-Gabriel Rummonds.

**OASIS PRESS**, PSI Research, 300 N. Valley Dr. Grants Pass OR 97526, Grants Pass OR 97526. (503)479-9464. Fax: (503)476-1479. **Acquisitions:** Emmett Ramey, president. Estab. 1975. Publishes hardcover, trade paperback and binder originals. **Publishes 20-30 books/year. Receives 90 submissions/year. 60% of books from first-time authors; 90% from unagented writers. Pays 10% royalty on the net received, except wholesale sales. No advance.** Publishes book 6 months after acceptance. Accepts simultaneous submissions. Reports in 2 months (initial feedback) on queries. Book catalog and ms guidelines for SASE.

    O⊶ Oasis Press publishes books for small business or individuals who are entrepreneurs or owners or managers of small businesses (1-300 employees).

**Imprint(s): Hellgate Press**.

**Nonfiction:** How-to, reference, textbook. Subjects include business/economics, computers, education, money/finance, retirement, exporting, franchise, finance, marketing/public relations, relocations, environment, taxes, business start up and operation. Needs information-heavy, readable mss written by professionals in their subject fields. Interactive where appropriate. Authorship credentials less important than hands-on experience qualifications. Query for unwritten material or to check current interest in topic and orientation. Submit outline/synopsis and sample chapters. Reviews artwork/photos as part of ms package.

**Recent Title(s):** *Before You Go Into Business, Read This*, by Ira Nottonson.

**Tips:** "Best chance is with practical, step-by-step manuals for operating a business, with worksheets, checklists. The audience is made up of entrepreneurs of all types: small business owners and those who would like to be; attorneys, accountants and consultants who work with small businesses; college students; dreamers. Make sure your information is valid and timely for its audience, also that by virtue of either its content quality or viewpoint, it distinguishes itself from other books on the market."

**OHIO STATE UNIVERSITY PRESS**, 1070 Carmack Rd., Columbus OH 43210. (614)292-6930. Fax: (614)292-2065. E-mail: ohiostatepress@osu.edu. Website: http://www.sbs.ohio-sate.edu/osu-press. **Acquisitions:** Charlotte Dihoff, assistant director/editor-in-chief; Barbara Hanrahan, director. Estab. 1957. **Publishes 30 titles/year. Pays royalty.** Reports in 3 months; ms held longer with author's permission.

&#x2022;&#x2500; Ohio State University Press publishes scholarly nonfiction, and offers short fiction and short poetry prizes. Currently emphasizing criminal justice and American history. De-emphasizing political science and European studies.

**Imprint(s):** Sandstone Books.

**Nonfiction:** Scholarly studies with special interests in African American studies, business and economic history, criminology, literary criticism, political science regional studies, teaching and higher education, Victorian studies, women's and gender studies, women's health. Query with outline and sample chapters and SASE.

**Recent Title(s):** *Seasoning: A Poet's Year*, by David Young (memoir); *Women Drinking Benedictine*, by Sharon Dilworth.

**Tips:** "Publishes some poetry and fiction in addition to the prizes. Query first."

**OHIO UNIVERSITY PRESS**, Scott Quadrangle, Athens OH 45701. (740)593-1155. Fax: (740)593-4536. Website: http://www.ohiou.edu/oupress/. **Acquisitions:** Gillian Berchowitz, senior editor (contemporary history, African studies, Appalachian studies); David Sanders, director (literature, literary criticism, midwest and frontier studies, Ohioana); James Webb, series editor (environmental history). Estab. 1964. Publishes hardcover and trade paperback originals and reprints. **Publishes 40-45 titles/year. Receives 500 queries and 50 mss/year. 20% of books from first-time authors; 95% from unagented writers. Pays 7-10% royalty on net sales. No advance.** Publishes book 1 year after acceptance of ms. Reports in 1 month on queries and proposals, 2 months on mss. Book catalog free. Manuscript guidelines for #10 SASE.

&#x2022;&#x2500; Ohio University Press publishes and disseminates the fruits of research and creative endeavor, specifically in the areas of literary studies, regional works, philosophy, contemporary history, African studies and frontier Americana. Its charge to produce books of value in service to the academic community and for the enrichment of the broader culture is in keeping with the university's mission of teaching, research and service to its constituents.

**Imprint(s):** Ohio University Monographs in International Studies (Gillian Berchowitz); Swallow Press (David Sanders, director).

**Nonfiction:** Biography, reference, scholarly. Subjects include African studies, agriculture/horticulture, Americana, animals, anthropology/archaeology, art/architecture, ethnic, gardening, government/politics, history, language/literature, military/war, nature/environment, philosophy, regional, sociology, travel, women's issues/studies. Query with proposal package, including outline, sample chapter and SASE. "We prefer queries or detailed proposals, rather than manuscripts, pertaining to scholarly projects that might have a general interest. Proposals should explain the thesis and details of the subject matter, not just sell a title." Reviews artwork/photos as part of ms package. Send photocopies.

**Recent Title(s):** *A Paris Year: Dorothy & James T. Farrell, 1931-1932*, by Edgar Brandh (nonfiction); *Your Madness, Not Mine*, by Makuchi (fiction); *Selected Poems of Yvor Winters*, by R.L. Barth, ed. (poetry).

**Tips:** "Rather than trying to hook the editor on your work, let the material be compelling enough and well-presented enough to do it for you."

**THE OLIVER PRESS, INC.**, 5707 W. 36th St., Minneapolis MN 55416-2510. (612)926-8981. Fax: (612)926-8965. E-mail: theoliverpress@mindspring.com. Website: http://www.oliverpress.com. **Acquisitions:** Denise Sterling, editor. Estab. 1991. Publishes hardcover originals. **Publishes 10 titles/year. Receives 100 queries and 20 mss/year. 10% of books from first-time authors; 100% from unagented writers. Makes outright purchase of $800-2,000.** Publishes book 1 year after acceptance of ms. Accepts simultaneous submissions. Reports in 2 months on queries. Book catalog for 6×9 SAE with 3 first-class stamps. Manuscript guidelines for #10 SASE.

&#x2022;&#x2500; "We publish collective biographies for ages 10 and up. Although we cover a wide array of subjects, all are published in this format." Currently emphasizing science, business, government.

**Nonfiction:** Children's/juvenile collective biographies only. Subjects include business/economics, ethnic, government/politics, health/medicine, military/war, nature/environment, science. Query with SASE.

**Recent Title(s):** *Construction: Building the Impossible*, by Nathan Aaseng.

**Tips:** "Audience is primarily junior and senior high school students writing reports."

**N ONE ON ONE COMPUTER TRAINING**, Mosaic Media, 2055 Army Trail Rd., Suite 100, Addison IL 60101. (630)628-0500. Fax: (630)628-0550. **Acquisitions:** Natalie Young, manager product development. Estab. 1976. **Publishes 10-20 titles/year. 100% of books from unagented writers. Pays 5-10% royalty (rarely) or makes outright purchase of $3,500-10,000. Advance depends on purchase contract.** Publishes book 3 months after acceptance of ms. Reports in 2 months on queries, 3 months on proposals. Book catalog free.

○➤ One on One Computer Training publishes computer hardware and software self-help and technical titles for users to learn or become more advanced. Currently emphasizing computer softwae, IT, Internet, programming. De-emphasizing computer security, certification programs.

**Imprint(s):** FlipTrack Learning Systems.

**Nonfiction:** How-to, self-help, technical. Subjects include computers, software, IT, Internet programming, software certification and computer security. Query. All unsolicited mss returned unopened.

**Recent Title(s):** *Working Smarter With the Internet.*

**ONE WORLD**, Ballantine Publishing Group, Random House, Inc., 201 E. 50th St., New York NY 10022. (212)572-2620. Fax: (212)940-7539. Website: http://www.randomhouse.com. **Acquisitions:** Cheryl Woodruff, publisher (multicultural fiction and nonfiction, spirituality and health); Gary Brozek, editor (multicultural and general fiction and nonfiction). Estab. 1991. Publishes hardcover, trade paperback and mass market, originals, trade and mass market paperback reprints. **Publishes 8-10 titles/year. Receives 1,200 queries and mss/year. 25% of books from first-time authors; 5% from unagented writers. Pays 8-12% royalty on retail price, varies from hardcover to mass market. Advance varies.** Publishes book 18 months after acceptance of ms. Accepts simultaneous submissions, if so noted. Reports in 6 months. Book catalog and ms guidelines for #10 SASE.

○➤ "One World's list includes books written by and focused on African Americans, Native Americans, Asian Americans and Latino Americans. We concentrate on *American* multicultural experiences." Currently looking for high-quality commercial fiction. No romance.

**Nonfiction:** Biography, health, inspirational, memoir, narrative nonfiction, self-help, spirituality. "We are dealing with American people of color." Query or submit proposal package including 200 pages with SASE. Reviews artwork/photos as part of ms package, where germane. Send photocopies.

**Fiction:** "We are looking for outstanding contemporary fiction. In the past, topics have mostly been 'pre-Civil rights era and before.'" Query with synopsis, 3 sample chapters (100 pages) and SASE.

**Recent Title(s):** *Willow Weep for Me*, by Meri-Ana Nana Danquah (nonfiction); *Gingersnaps*, by Delorys Welch-Tyson (fiction).

**Tips:** "For first-time authors, have a completed manuscript. You won't be asked to write on speculation."

**N ONJINJINKTA PUBLISHING**, The Betty Eadie Press, P.O. Box 25490, Seattle WA 98125. (206)433-8978. Fax: (206)246-4088. E-mail: peter@embracedbythelight.com. Website: http://www.Embracedbythelight.com. **Acquisitions:** Peter Orullian, senior editor. Publishes hardcover, trade paperback and mass market paperback originals and reprints. **Publishes 8-12 titles/year; imprint publishes 4-6 titles/year. Receives 500 queries and 100 mss/year. 50% of books from first-time authors; 80% from unagented writers. Pays 5-15% royalty on retail price. Offers $1,000-10,000 advance.** Publishes book 18 months after acceptance of ms. Accepts simultaneous submissions. Reports in 2 months on queries and proposals, 3 months on mss. Book catalog for 9×12 SAE with 4 first-class stamps. Manuscript guidelines for #10 SASE.

○➤ Onjinjinkta publishes the future work of Betty Eadie (*Embraced by the Light*) and inspirational works by other writers.

**Imprint(s):** Wambly Publishing (contact Peter Orullian, editor)

**Nonfiction:** Children's/juvenile, humor, self-help. Subjects include Americana, creative nonfiction, military/war, music/dance, nature/environment, regional, religion, spirituality. Submit proposal package, including outline, 1 sample chapter, author bio and SASE.

**Fiction:** Adventure, fantasy, horror, humor, mainstream/contemporary, military/war, mystery, regional, religious, science fiction, spiritual, suspense. Submit proposal package including synopsis, 1 sample chapter and author bio.

**Poetry:** Query.

**Recent Title(s):** *Embraced by the Light*, by Betty J. Eadie (spiritual nonfiction); *The Adventure of Caterpillar Jones*, by Jim and Jon Hixon (juvenile fiction).

**Tips:** "Nonfiction audience is thoughtful, hopeful individuals who seek self-awareness. Fiction audience is readers who desire to be engaged in the high art of escapism. We can only publish a short list each year; your book must target its market forcefully, and its story must express and invoke fresh ideas on the ancient themes."

**N ORANGE FRAZER PRESS, INC.**, 37½ W. Main St., P.O. Box 214, Wilmington OH 45177. (937)382-3196. Fax: (937)383-3159. Website: http://www.orangefrazer.com. **Acquisitions:** John Baskin, editor (Ohio sports, Ohio history); Marcy Hawley, editor (Ohio reference, Ohio travel). Publishes hardcover and trade paperback originals and reprints. **Publishes 10 titles/year. Receives 50 queries and 40 mss/year. 50% of books from first-time authors; 99% from unagented writers. Pays 10-12% royalty on wholesale price.** Publishes book 18 months after acceptance of ms. Accepts simultaneous submissions. Reports in 2 months on queries, 1 month on proposals and mss. Book catalog free.

**Nonfiction:** Biography, coffee table book, cookbook, gift book, humor, illustrated book, reference, textbook. Subjects include art/architecture, cooking/foods/nutrition, education, history, memoirs, nature/environment, photography, recre-

ation, regional (Ohio), sports, travel, women's issues/women's studies. Submit proposal package, including outline, 1 sample chapter and SASE. Reviews artwork/photos as part of ms package. Send photocopies or transparencies.
**Recent Title(s):** *I Beg to Differ: Politically Correct, Proudly Midwest, Potentially Funny*, by Laura Pulfer (humorous commentary); *The 1997/1998 Ohio Almanac*, edited by Mike O'Bryant.

**N: ORBIS BOOKS**, P.O. Box 308, Maryknoll NY 10545-0308. (914)941-7590. Executive Director: Michael Leach. **Acquisitions:** Robert Ellsberg, editor-in-chief. Estab. 1970. Publishes hardcover and trade paperback originals. **Publishes 50-55 titles/year. Receives 1,500 queries and 700 mss/year. 2% of books from first-time authors; 99% from unagented writers. Pays 10-15% royalty on wholesale price net. Offers $500-3,000 advance.** Publishes book 15 months after acceptance of ms. Reports in 2 months on proposals. Book catalog and ms guidelines free.
    O— "We seek books illuminating religious and social situations of Third World Christians, the lessons of the Third World for the North, global dimensions of Christian faith and the challenge of the world church."
**Nonfiction:** Reference. Subjects include spirituality, theology, religion. Submit proposal package, including outline, summary, 10-20 page chapter of intro."
**Recent Title(s):** *Praying with Icons*, by Jim Forest.

**ORCHARD BOOKS**, Grolier Publishing, 95 Madison Ave., New York NY 10016. (212)951-2650. President/Publisher: Judy V. Wilson. **Acquisitions:** Sarah Caguiat, editor; Ana Cerro, editor. Estab. 1987. Publishes hardcover and trade paperback originals. **Publishes 60-70 titles/year. Receives 1,600 queries/year. 25% of books from first-time authors; 50% from unagented writers. Pays 6-10% royalty on retail price. Advance varies.** Publishes book 1 year after acceptance of ms. Reports in 3 months on queries.
    O— Orchard specializes in children's picture books.
**Nonfiction:** Children's/juvenile, illustrated book. Subjects include animals, history, nature/environment. Query with SASE. *"No unsolicited mss at this time. Queries only! Be as specific and enlightening as possible about your book."* Reviews artwork/photos as part of the ms package. Send photocopies.
**Fiction:** Picture books, young adult, middle reader, board book, novelty. Query with SASE. *No unsolicited mss, please.*
**Recent Title(s):** *An Extraordinary Life*, by Pringle and Marstall (nonfiction); *The Pig Who Ran a Red Light*, by Paul Brett Johnson (fiction).
**Tips:** "Go to a bookstore and read several Orchard Books to get an idea of what we publish. Write what you feel and query us if you think it's 'right.' It's worth finding the right publishing match."

**ORCHISES PRESS**. P.O. Box 20602, Alexandria VA 22320-1602. (703)683-1243. E-mail: rlathbur@osfl.gmu.edu. Website: http://mason.gmu.edu/~rlathbur. **Acquisitions:** Roger Lathbury, editor-in-chief. Estab. 1983. Publishes hardcover and trade paperback originals and reprints. **Publishes 4-5 titles/year. Receives 600 queries and 200 mss/year. 1% of books from first-time authors; 95% from unagented writers. Pays 36% of receipts after Orchises has recouped its costs.** Publishes book 1 year after acceptance. Accepts simultaneous submissions. Reports in 3 months. Book catalog for #10 SASE.
    O— Orchises Press is a general literary publisher specializing in poetry (but not new fiction) with selected reprints and textbooks.
**Nonfiction:** Biography, how-to, humor, reference, technical, textbook. No real restrictions on subject matter. Query. Reviews artwork/photos as part of the ms package. Send photocopies.
**Poetry:** Poetry must have been published in respected literary journals. Publishes free verse, but has strong formalist preferences. Query or submit 5 sample poems.
**Recent Title(s):** *Is This the End of Little Rico?*, by Daniel Ort (nonfiction); *The Potato Eaters*, by Leonard Nathan (poetry).
**Tips:** "Show some evidence of appealing to a wider audience than simply people you know."

**N: OREGON STATE UNIVERSITY PRESS**, 101 Waldo Hall, Corvallis OR 97331-6407. (541)737-3166. Fax: (541)737-3170. **Acquisitions:** Warren Slesinger, acquiring editor. Estab. 1965. Publishes hardcover and paperback originals. **Publishes 15-20 titles/year. Receives 100 submissions/year. 75% of books from first-time authors; 100% of books from unagented writers. Pays royalty on net receipts. No advance.** Publishes book 1 year after acceptance. Reports in 3 months. Book catalog for 6×9 SAE with 2 first-class stamps. Writer's guidelines for SASE.
    O— Oregon State University Press publishes several scholarly and specialized books and books of particular importance to the Pacific Northwest. "OSU Press plays an essential role by publishing books that may not have a large audience, but are important to scholars, students and librarians in the region."
**Nonfiction:** Publishes scholarly books in history, biography, geography, literature, natural resource management, with strong emphasis on Pacific or Northwestern topics. Submit outline and sample chapters.
**Recent Title(s):** *Planning a New West*, by Carl Abbott, Sy Adler and Margorie Post Abbott..
**Tips:** Send for an authors' guidelines pamphlet.

**ORYX PRESS**, 4041 N. Central Ave., Suite 700, Phoenix AZ 85012. (602)265-2651. Fax: (602)265-6250. E-mail: info@oryxpress.com. Website: http://www.oryxpress.com/. President: Phyllis B. Steckler. **Acquisitions:** Donna Sanzone, Henry Rasof, acquisitions editors; Martha Wilke (submission). Estab. 1975. **Publishes 50 titles/year. Receives 500 submissions/year. 40% of books from first-time authors; 80% from unagented writers. Pays 10% royalty on**

**net receipts. Offers moderate advances.** Publishes book 9 months after acceptance of manuscript. Proposals via Internet welcomed. Reports in 1 month. Book catalog and author guidelines free.

○╼ Oryx Press publishes print and/or electronic reference resources for public, college and university, K-12 school, business and medical libraries, and professionals.

**Nonfiction:** Directories, dictionaries, encyclopedias, in print and electronic formats (online and CD-ROM), and other general reference works; special subjects: business, education, consumer health care, government information, gerontology, social sciences. Query or submit outline/rationale and samples. Queries/mss may be routed to other editors in the publishing group.

**Recent Title(s):** *Storytelling Encyclopedia: Historical, Cultural and Multiethnic Approaches to Oral Traditions Around the World*, edited by David Leeming (reference).

**Tips:** "We are accepting and promoting more titles over the Internet. We are also looking for up-to-date, relevant ideas to add to our established line of print and electronic works."

**OSBORNE/MCGRAW-HILL**, The McGraw-Hill Companies, 2600 10th St., Berkeley CA 94710. (510)548-2805. **Acquisitions:** Scott Rogers, editor-in-chief. Estab. 1979. Publishes computer trade paperback originals. **Publishes 100 titles/year. Receives 120 submissions/year. 30% of books from first-time authors. Pays 8-12% royalty on wholesale price. Offers $5,000 average advance.** Publishes book an average of 6 months after acceptance. Accepts simultaneous submissions. Reports in 2 months. Book catalog free.

○╼ Osborne publishes technical computer books and software.

**Nonfiction:** Software, technical. Computer subjects. Query with outline and sample chapters. Reviews artwork/photos as part of ms package.

**Recent Title(s):** *Microsoft Office 2000: The Complete Reference*, by Stephen L. Nelson and Peter Weverka.

**[N̄] OSPREY PUBLISHING LIMITED**, SBM Inc., 443 Park Ave. S., #801, New York NY 10016. (212)685-5560. Fax: (212)685-5836. E-mail: ospreyusa@aol.com. Website: http://www.osprey-publishing.co.uk. **Acquisitions:** Lee Johnson, managing editor (military, uniforms, battles); Shaun Barrington, managing editor (aviation, automotive). Publishes hardcover and trade paperback originals. **Publishes 78 titles/year. Receives "hundreds" queries/year. 25% of books from first-time authors; 100% from unagented writers. Makes outright purchases of $1,000-5,000. Offers advance.** Publishes book 6 months after acceptance of ms. Reports in 2 months. Book catalog free or on website.

○╼ Osprey Publishing produces high-quality nonfiction series in the areas of military and aviation history and automotive titles. Lines include Air Combat, Aircraft of the Aces, Campaign, Elite, Men at Arms, New Vanguard, Warrior.

**Nonfiction:** Biography, illustrated book, military history, aviation, automotive. Subjects include history, hobbies, military/war. Query with SASE. Reviews artwork/photos as part of ms package. Send photocopies.

**Recent Title(s):** *Retreat Hell*, by Martin Marix-Evans (WWI history).

**Tips:** "Osprey history books appeal to everyone with an interest in history: Teachers, students, history buffs, re-enactors, model makers, researchers, writers, movie production companies, etc. Known for meticulous research and attention to detail, our books are considered accurate and informative. Please do not send manuscript. We publish mainly in series in specific monographic format. Please provide academic credentials and subject matter of work. Artist references must be provided by author."

**OUR SUNDAY VISITOR, INC.**, 200 Noll Plaza, Huntington IN 46750-4303. (219)356-8400. Fax: (219)359-9117. E-mail: oursunvis@osv.com. President/Publisher: Robert Lockwood. Editor-in-Chief: Greg Erlandson. **Acquistions:** Jackie Lindsey, acquisitions editor. Estab. 1912. Publishes paperback and hardbound originals. **Publishes 20-30/year. Receives over 100 submissions/year. 10% of books from first-time authors; 90% from unagented writers. Pays variable royalty on net receipts. Offers $1,000 average advance.** Publishes book 1 year after acceptance. Reports in 3 months. Author's guide and catalog for SASE.

○╼ "We are a Catholic publishing company seeking to educate and deepen our readers in their faith." Currently emphasizing reference, apologetics and catechetics. De-emphasizing inspirational.

**Nonfiction:** Catholic viewpoints on current issues, reference and guidance, family, prayer and devotional books, and Catholic heritage books. Prefers to see well-developed proposals as first submission with annotated outline and definition of intended market. Reviews artwork/photos as part of ms package.

**Recent Title(s):** *Encyclopedia of Saints*, by Bunson.

**Tips:** "Solid devotional books that are not first-person, well-researched church histories or lives of the saints and catechetical books have the best chance of selling to our firm. Make it solidly Catholic, unique, without pious platitudes."

**[A] THE OVERLOOK PRESS**, Distributed by Penguin Putnam, 386 W. Broadway, New York NY 10012. (212)965-8400. Fax: (212)965-9839. Publisher: Peter Mayer. **Acquisitions:** (Ms.) Tracy Karns, editor. Estab. 1971. Publishes hardcover and trade paperback originals and hardcover reprints. **Publishes 40 titles/year. Receives 300 submissions/year. Pays 3-15% royalty on wholesale or retail price.** Reports in 5 months. Book catalog free.

○╼ Overlook Press publishes fiction, children's books and nonfiction.

**Imprint(s):** Elephant's Eye, Tusk Books.

**Nonfiction:** Art, architecture, biography, current events, design, film, health/fitness, history, how-to, lifestyle, martial arts, music, popular culture, New York State regional. No pornography. *Agented submissions only.*

**Fiction:** Literary fiction, fantasy, foreign literature in translation. *Agented submissions only.*

**N ★ THE OVERMOUNTAIN PRESS**, P.O. Box 1261, Johnson City TN 37605. (423)926-2691. Fax: (423)929-2464. **Acquisitions:** Elizabeth L. Wright, editor. Estab. 1970. Publishes hardcover and trade paperback originals and hardcover and trade paperback reprints. **Publishes 15-20 titles/year. Receives 500 queries and 100 mss/year. 50% of books from first-time authors; 100% from unagented writers. Pays 7½-15% royalty on wholesale price. No advance.** Publishes book 1 year after acceptance of ms. Accepts simultaneous submissions. Reports in 1 month on queries, 6 months on proposals and mss. Book catalog and ms guidelines free.

O—π The Overmountain Press publishes primarily Appalachian history. Audience is people interested in history of Tennessee, Virginia, North Carolina, Kentucky, and all aspects of this region—Revolutionary War, Civil War, county histories, historical biographies, etc. Currently emphasizing county history, Civil War history, revised war history. De-emphasizing fiction.

**Nonfiction:** Biography, children's/juvenile, cookbook. Subjects include Americana, cooking/foods/nutrition, history, military/war, nature/environment, photography, regional, Native American. Submit proposal package, including outline, 3 sample chapters and marketing suggestions. Reviews artwork/photos as part of ms package. Send photocopies.
**Fiction:** Picture books.
**Recent Title(s):** *Between the States: Bristol TN/VA During the Civil War*, by V.N. "Bud" Phillips (nonfiction); *Appalachian ABCs*, by Francie Hall (children's ABC book).
**Tips:** "Please submit a proposal. Please no phone calls."

**RICHARD C. OWEN PUBLISHERS INC.**, P.O. Box 585, Katonah NY 10536. Fax: (914)232-3977. Website: http://www.rcowen.com. **Acquisitions:** Janice Boland, director of children's books; Amy Haggblom, project editor (professional development, teacher-oriented books). Estab. 1982. Publishes hardcover and paperback originals. **Publishes 23 titles/year. Receives 150 queries and 1,000 mss/year. 99% of books from first-time authors; 100% from unagented writers. Pays 5% royalty on wholesale price.** Publishes book 3 years after acceptance of ms. Accepts simultaneous submissions, if so noted. Reports in 1 month on queries and proposals, 2 months on mss. Manuscript guidelines for SASE with 52¢ postage.

O—π "Our focus is literacy education with a meaning-centered perspective. We are also seeking manuscripts for our new collection of short, snappy stories for children in third grade. Subjects include humor, careers, mysteries, science fiction, folktales, women, fashion trends, sports, music, myths, journalism, history, inventions, planets, architecture, plays, adventure, technology, vehicles."

**Nonfiction:** Children's/juvenile humor, illustrated book. Subjects include animals, nature/environment, gardening, music/dance, recreation, science, sports. "Our books are for 5-7-year-olds. The stories are very brief—under 100 words—yet well structured and crafted with memorable characters, language and plots." Send for ms guidelines, then submit complete ms with SASE.
**Fiction:** Picture books. "Brief, strong story line, believable characters, natural language, exciting—child-appealing stories with a twist. No lists, alphabet or counting books." Send for ms guidelines, then submit full ms with SASE.
**Poetry:** Poems that excite children, fun, humorous, fresh. No jingles. Must rhyme without force or contrivance. Send for ms guidelines, then submit complete ms with SASE.
**Recent Title(s):** *Saguaro*, by Anne Massey Ecton (nonfiction); *Dogs at School*, by Suzanne Hardin (fiction); *There Was a Mouse*, by Pat Blanchard and Joanne Suhr (poetry).
**Tips:** "We don't respond to queries. Please do not e-mail us. Because our books are so brief it is better to send entire ms. We publish books with intrinsic value for young readers—books they can read with success, books with supports and challenges to take them to the next learning point. We believe students become enthusiastic, independent, life-long learners when supported and guided by skillful teachers. The professional development work we do and the books we publish support these beliefs."

**OWL BOOKS**, Henry Holt & Co., Inc., 115 W. 18th St., New York NY 10011. (212)886-9200. Website: http://www.hholt.com. **Acquisitions:** David Sobel, senior editor. Estab. 1996. Publishes trade paperback originals. **Firm publishes 135-140 titles/year; imprint publishes 50-60 titles/year. 30% of books from first-time authors; 5% from unagented writers. Pays 6-7½% royalty on retail price. Advance varies.** Publishes book 1 year after acceptance of ms. Accepts simultaneous submissions. Reports in 3 months on proposals.

O—π "We are looking for original, great ideas that have commercial appeal, but that you can respect."
**Nonfiction:** "Broad range." Subjects include art/architecture, biography, cooking/foods/nutrition, gardening, health/medicine, history, language/literature, nature/environment, regional, sociology, sports, travel. Query with outline, 1 sample chapter and SASE.
**Fiction:** Literary fiction. Query with synopsis, 1 sample chapter and SASE.
**Recent Title(s):** *White Boy Shuffle*, by Paul Beatty; *The Debt to Pleasure*, by John Lanchester.

**OXFORD UNIVERSITY PRESS**, 198 Madison Ave., New York NY 10016. (212)726-6000. Website: http://www.oup-usa.org/. **Acquisitions:** Joan Bossert, vice president/editorial director. Laura Brown, director (trade publishing). Estab. 1896. Publishes hardcover and trade paperback originals and reprints. **Publishes 1,500 titles/year. 40% of books from first-time authors; 80% from unagented writers. Pays 0-15% royalty on wholesale price or retail price. Offers $0-40,000 advance.** Publishes book 10 months after acceptance of ms. Accepts simultaneous submissions. Reports in 3 months on proposals. Book catalog free.

O—π "We publish books that make a significant contribution to the literature and research in a number of disciplines, which reflect the departments at the University of Oxford."

**Nonfiction:** Biography, children's/juvenile, reference, technical, textbook. Subjects include archaeology, art/architecture, business/economics, computers/electronics, gay/lesbian, government/politics, health/medicine, history, language/literature, law, military/war, music/dance, nature/environment, philosophy, psychology and psychiatry, religion, science, sociology, women's issues/studies. Oxford is an academic, scholarly press. Submit outline, sample chapters and cv. Reviews artwork/photos as part of ms package (but not necessary).

**PACIFIC BOOKS, PUBLISHERS**, P.O. Box 558, Palo Alto CA 94302-0558. (650)965-1980. **Acquisitions:** Henry Ponleithner, editor. Estab. 1945. **Publishes 6-12 titles/year. Pays 7½-15% royalty. No advance.** Reports in 1 month. *Writer's Market* recommends allowing 2 months for reply. Book catalog and guidelines for 9×12 SASE.
- Pacific Books publishes general interest and scholarly nonfiction including professional and technical books, and college textbooks.

**Nonfiction:** General interest, professional, technical and scholarly nonfiction trade books. Specialties include western Americana and Hawaiiana. Looks for "well-written, documented material of interest to a significant audience." Also considers text and reference books for high school and college. Accepts artwork/photos and translations. Query with outline and SASE.
**Recent Title(s):** *The Magnificient Rogues of San Francisco*, by Charles F. Adams (regional history).

**PACIFIC PRESS PUBLISHING ASSOCIATION**, Book Division, P.O. Box 5353, Nampa ID 83653-5353. (208)465-2511. Fax: (208)465-2531. E-mail: editor.book@pacificpress.com. Website: http://www.pacificpress.com. **Acquisitions:** Jerry Thomas (children's stories, devotional, biblical). Estab. 1874. Publishes hardcover and trade paperback originals and reprints. **Publishes 35 titles/year.** Receives 600 submissions and proposals/year. **Up to 35% of books from first-time authors; 100% from unagented writers. Pays 8-16% royalty on wholesale price. Offers $300-1,500 average advance depending on length.** Publishes book 10 months after acceptance. Reports in 3 months. Manuscript guidelines available at website or send #10 SASE.
- Pacific Press is an exclusively religious publisher of the Seventh-day Adventist denomination. "We are looking for practical, how-to oriented manuscripts on religion, health, and family life that speak to human needs, interests and problems from a Biblical perspective. We publish books that promote a stronger relationship with God, deeper Bible study, and a healthy, helping lifestyle."

**Nonfiction:** Biography, cookbook (vegetarian), how-to, juvenile, self-help. Subjects include cooking/foods (vegetarian only), health, nature, religion, family living. "We can't use anything totally secular or written from other than a Christian perspective." Query or request information on how to submit a proposal. Reviews artwork/photos.
**Recent Title(s):** *Stand at the Cross*, by Lonnie Melashenko and John McClarty; *Prayer Warriors*, by Celeste Perrino Walker.
**Tips:** "Our primary audience is members of the Seventh-day Adventist denomination. Almost all are written by Seventh-day Adventists. Books that are doing well for us are those that relate the Biblical message to practical human concerns and those that focus more on the experiential rather than theoretical aspects of Christianity. We are assigning more titles, using less unsolicited material—although we still publish manuscripts from freelance submissions and proposals."

**PACIFIC VIEW PRESS**, P.O. Box 2657, Berkeley CA 94702. **Acquisitions:** Pam Zumwalt, acquisitions editor. Estab. 1992. Publishes hardcover and trade paperback originals. **Publishes 4-6 titles/year. 50% of books from first-time authors; 100% from unagented writers. Pays 10% maximum royalty on net. Offers $1,000-5,000 advance.** Publishes book 1 year after acceptance. Accepts simultaneous submissions. Reports in 2 months on queries and proposals. Book catalog free. Writer's guidelines for #10 SASE.
- Pacific View Press publishes books for persons professionally/personally aware of the growing importance of the Pacific Rim and/or the modern culture of these countries, especially China.

**Nonfiction:** Children's/juvenile (Asia/multicultural only), reference, textbook (Chinese medicine only), contemporary Pacific Rim affairs. Subjects include business/economics (Asia and Pacific Rim only), health/medicine (Chinese medicine), history (Asia), regional (Pacific Rim), travel (related to Pacific Rim). Query with proposal package including outline, 1-2 chapters, target audience and SASE.
**Recent Title(s):** *Made in China: Ideas and Inventions from Ancient China*, by Suzanne Williams (illustrated Chinese history for kids).
**Tips:** "Audience is business people, academics, travelers, etc."

**PAGEMILL PRESS**, Circulus Publishing Group, Inc., 2716 Ninth St., Berkeley CA 94710. (510)848-3600. Fax: (510)848-1326. E-mail: circulus@aol.com. **Acquisitions:** Tamara Traeder, publisher (psychology/women's issues); Roy M. Carlisle, editorial director (psychology/dreamwork). Publishes trade paperback originals. **Publishes 2 titles/year.** Receives 200 queries and 100 mss/year. **Pays 10-16% royalty on wholesale price. Offers $1,000-3,000 average advance.** Publishes book 9 months after acceptance of ms. Accepts simultaneous submissions. Reports in 3 months. Book catalog and ms guidelines free.
- PageMill Press publishes books in the fields of psychology and personal growth.

**Nonfiction:** Self-help. Subjects include psychology, women's issues/women's studies, dreamwork. Query with proposal package, including outline and SASE. Reviews artwork as part of ms package. Send photocopies.
**Recent Title(s):** *Slow Dance*, by Bonnie Sher Klein (stroke victim memoir).
**Tips:** "Our authors explore the intellectual, psychological, and spiritual dimensions of our daily lives, such as the mind/body connection, the power of myth and dreams in everyday circumstances, the role of the unconscious in human

interactions, and the integration of a fuller experience of the body in life's activities."

**PALADIN PRESS**, P.O. Box 1307, Boulder CO 80306-1307. (303)443-7250. Fax: (303)442-8741. E-mail: editoria l@paladin-press.com. Website: http://www.paladin-press.com. President/Publisher: Peder C. Lund. **Acquisitions:** Jon Ford, editorial director. Estab. 1970. Publishes hardcover and paperback originals and paperback reprints. **Publishes 50 titles/year. 50% of books from first-time authors; 100% from unagented writers. Pays 10-12-15% royalty on net sales.** Publishes book 1 year after acceptance. Accepts simultaneous submissions. Reports in 2 months. Book catalog free.

**O—** Paladin Press publishes the "action library" of nonfiction in military science, police science, weapons, combat, personal freedom, self-defense, survival, "revenge humor." Currently emphasizing personal freedom, financial freedom.

**Imprint(s):** Sycamore Island Books.

**Nonfiction:** "Paladin Press primarily publishes original manuscripts on military science, weaponry, self-defense, personal privacy, financial freedom, espionage, police science, action careers, guerrilla warfare, fieldcraft and 'creative revenge' humor. If applicable, send sample photographs and line drawings with complete outline and sample chapters." Query with outline and sample chapters.

**Recent Title(s):** *The Modern Identity Changer*, by Sheldon Charrett.

**Tips:** "We need lucid, instructive material aimed at our market and accompanied by sharp, relevant illustrations and photos. As we are primarily a publisher of 'how-to' books, a manuscript that has step-by-step instructions, written in a clear and concise manner (but not strictly outline form) is desirable. No fiction, first-person accounts, children's, religious or joke books. We are also interested in serious, professional videos and video ideas (contact Michael Janich)."

**PANTHEON BOOKS**, Knopf Publishing Group, Random House, Inc., 201 E. 50th St., 25th Floor, New York NY 10022. (212)751-2600. Fax: (212)572-6030. Editorial Director: Dan Frank. Senior Editor: Shelley Wagner. Executive Editor: Erroll McDonald. **Acquisitions:** Adult Editorial Department. Estab. 1942. **Pays royalty. Offers advance.**

**O—** Pantheon Books publishes both Western and non-Western authors of literary fiction and important nonfiction.

**Nonfiction:** History, politics, autobiography, biography, interior design. Query.

**Recent Title(s):** *Confederates in The Attic*, by Tony Horwitz; *All Over But the Shoutin'*, by Ric Bragg.

**PAPIER-MACHE PRESS**, 627 Walker St., Watsonville CA 95076. (408)763-1420. Fax: (408)763-1422. Website: http://www.ReadersNdex.com/papiermache. **Acquisitions:** Shirley Coe, acquisitions editor. Estab. 1984. **Publishes 4-6 titles/year. Pays royalty.** Accepts simultaneous submissions. Book catalog and ms guidelines free.

**O—** "Our goal is to produce attractive, accessible books that deal with contemporary personal, social and political issues. We focus primarily on midlife women and aging and have a national reputation for 'gentle consciousness raising.' "

**Fiction:** "We publish theme anthologies that include fiction and poetry." Write for submission guidelines.

**Recent Title(s):** *One Small Step: Moving Beyond Trauma and Therapy to a Life of Joy*, by Yvonne Dolan, MA (self-help); *Grow Old Along with Me—The Best Is Yet to Be*, edited by Sandra Haldeman Martz (fiction).

**Tips:** Audience is women, 35-55 years old. Always request submission guidelines before submitting.

**PARACLETE PRESS**, P.O. Box 1568, Orleans MA 02653. (508)255-4685. **Acquisitions:** Lillian Miao, CEO. Estab. 1981. Publishes hardcover and trade paperback originals. **Publishes 14 titles/year. Receives 156 queries and 60 mss/ year. 80% of books from unagented writers. Pays 10-12% royalty. Offers advance.** Publishes book 18 months after acceptance of ms. Accepts simultaneous submissions. Reports in 2 months on queries, proposals and mss. Book catalog and ms guidelines for 8½×11 SASE and 4 first-class stamps.

**Nonfiction:** Prayer, spirituality. religious subjects. No poetry or children books. Submit outline with sample chapters.

● Paraclete no longer publishes fiction.

**Recent Title(s):** *Awake My Heart-Psalms for Life*, edited by Frederick Bassett (Psalms paperback); *Creative Prayer*, by Brigid Herman (paperback); *Things in Heaven and Earth*, by various authors (hardcover).

**PARAGON HOUSE PUBLISHERS**, 2700 University Ave. W., Suite 200, St. Paul MN 55114-1016. (651)644-3087. Fax: (651)644-0997. E-mail: paragon@paragonhouse.com. Website: http://www.paragonhouse.com. **Acquisitions:** Laureen Enright, acquisitions editor (general). Estab. 1982. Publishes hardcover and trade paperback originals and trade paperback reprints. **Publishes 12-15 titles/year; each imprint publishes 2-5 titles/year. Receives 400 queries and 75 mss/year. 7% of books from first-time authors; 90% from unagented writers. Pays 7-15% royalty on net sales. Offers $500-1,500 advance.** Publishes book 1 year after acceptance of ms. Accepts simultaneous submissions. Reports in 3 months. Book catalog on website. Manuscript guidelines for #10 SASE.

**Imprints:** PWPA Books (Dr. Gordon L. Anderson); Althena Books (Laureen Enright); New Era Books (Dr. Thomas Walsh); ICUS Books (Laureen Enright).

**Nonfiction:** Textbook. Subjects include government/politics, multicultural, nature/environment, philosophy, religion, sociology, spirituality, women's issues/studies. Submit proposal package, including outline, 2 sample chapters and summary, market breakdown and SASE for return of material.

**Recent Titles:** *Beyond the Human Species*, by Georges Van Vrekhem (nonfiction).

**PARKWAY PUBLISHERS, INC.**, Box 3678, Boone NC 28607. Phone/fax: (704)265-3993. E-mail: aluri@netins.net. Website: http://www.netins.net/showcase/alurir. **Acquisitions:** Rao Aluri, president. Publishes hardcover and trade paperback originals. **Publishes 4-6 titles/year. Receives 15-20 queries and 10 mss/year. 75% of books from first-time authors; 100% from unagented writers. Pays 10-15% royalty on net price. No advance.** Publishes book 8 months after acceptance. Reports in 1 month on queries, 2 months on mss. Book catalog on website.

    O─┓ Parkway publishes books on the local history and culture of Western North Carolina. "We prefer manuscripts suitable for tourism industry/market. We are located on Blue Ridge Parkway and our primary industry is tourism. We are interested in books which present the history and culture of western North Carolina to the tourist market."

**Nonfiction:** Reference, technical. Subjects include history, culture and tourism of western North Carolina. Prefers complete ms with SASE. *Writer's Market* recommends sending a query with SASE first.

**Recent Title(s):** *Parkway Byways*, by James Hinkel (travel); *Fire and Rain*, by Michael R. Revere (poetry).

**PASSEGGIATA PRESS**, P.O. Box 636, Pueblo CO 81002. (719)544-7889. **Acquisitions:** Donald E. Herdeck, publisher/editor-in-chief; Harold Ames, Jr., general editor. Estab. 1973. Publishes hardcover and paperback originals. **Publishes 10-20 titles/year. Receives 200 submissions/year. 15% of books from first-time authors; 99% from unagented writers. Nonauthor-subsidy publishes 5% of books. Pays 10% royalty. Offers advance "only on delivery of complete manuscript which is found acceptable; usually $300."** Accepts simultaneous submissions. Reports in 1 month.

    O─┓ "We search for books that will make clear the complexity and value of non-Western literature and culture."

**Nonfiction:** Specializes in African, Caribbean, Middle Eastern (Arabic and Persian) and Asian-Pacific literature, criticism and translation, Third World literature and history, fiction, poetry, criticism, history and translations of creative writing, including bilingual texts (Arabic language/English translations). Query with outline, table of contents. Reviews artwork/photos as part of ms package. State availability of photos/illustrations.

**Fiction:** Query with synopsis, plot summary (1-3 pages).

**Poetry:** Submit 5-10 sample poems.

**Recent Title(s):** *Appreciating the Difference: The Biography of Three Continents Press*, by D. Herdeck; *The House on Arnus Square*, by Samad Attar (novel travel from Arabic); *Not Yet Africa*, by Kevin Gordon (travel log).

**Tips:** "We are always interested in genuine contributions to understanding non-Western culture. We need a *polished* translation, or original prose or poetry by non-Western authors *only*. Critical and cross-cultural studies are accepted from any scholar from anywhere."

**PASSPORT PRESS**, P.O. Box 1346, Champlain NY 12919-1346. **Acquisitions:** Jack Levesque, publisher. Estab. 1975. Publishes trade paperback originals. **Publishes 4 titles/year. 25% of books from first-time authors; 100% from unagented writers. Pays 6% royalty on retail price.** Publishes book 9 months after acceptance.

    O─┓ Passport Press publishes practical travel guides on specific countries. Currently emphasizing offbeat countries.

**Imprint(s):** Travel Line Press.

**Nonfiction:** Travel books only, not travelogues. Especially looking for mss on practical travel subjects and travel guides on specific countries. Send 1-page query only. Reviews artwork/photos as part of ms package.

**Recent Title(s):** *Honduras and the Bay Islands*, by Panet & Glassman.

**PAULINE BOOKS & MEDIA**, Daughters of St. Paul, 50 St. Paul's Ave., Jamaica Plain MA 02130-3491. (617)522-8911. Fax: (617)541-9805. Website: http://www.pauline.org. **Acquisitions:** Sister Mary Mark Wickenheiser, FSP, acquisitions (adult); Sister Patricia Edward Jablonski, acquisitions (children); Sister Madonna Ratliff, FSP, acquisitions editor (adult). Estab. 1948. Publishes trade paperback originals and reprints. **Publishes 25-35 titles/year. Receives approximately 1,300 proposals/year. Pays authors 8-12% royalty on net sales.** Publishes ms 2-3 years after acceptance. Reports in 3 months. Book catalog for 9×12 SAE with 4 first-class stamps.

    O─┓ "As a Catholic publishing house, we serve the Church by responding to the hopes and needs of all people with the Word of God, in the spirit of St. Paul. Pauline Books and Media publishes in the areas of faith and moral values, family formation, spiritual growth and development, children's faith formation, instruction in the Catholic faith for young adults and adults. Works consonant with Catholic theology are sought." Currently emphasizing saints/biographies, popular presentation of Catholic faith, biblical prayer. De-emphasizing pastoral ministry, teen fiction.

**Nonfiction:** Saints' biographies, juvenile, spiritual growth and faith development. Subjects include child guidance/ parenting, religion teacher resources, Scripture. No strictly secular mss. Query with SASE. *No unsolicited mss.*

**Fiction:** Juvenile. Query only with SASE. *No unsolicited mss.*

**Recent Title(s):** *Images for Prayer: Matthew, Mark, Luke, John*, by Robert J. Knopp (nonfiction); *Poetry as Prayer: The Hound of Heaven* (poetry).

**PAULIST PRESS**, 997 Macarthur Blvd., Mahwah NJ 07430. (201)825-7300. Fax: (201)825-8345. **Acquisitions:** Lawrence E. Boadt, president/editorial director. Managing Editor: Donald Brophy. Estab. 1865. Publishes hardcover and paperback originals and paperback reprints. **Publishes 90-100 titles/year. Receives 500 submissions/year. 5-8% of books from first-time authors; 95% from unagented writers. Nonauthor subsidy publishes 1-2% of books. Usually pays royalty on retail price. Usually offers advance.** Publishes book 10 months after acceptance. Reports in 2 months.

**O—** Paulist Press publishes Christian and Catholic theology, spirituality and religion titles.
**Imprint(s):** HiddenSpring (spirituality, self-help, well-being, religion; contact Jan-Erik Guerth, 335 E. 90th St., New York NY 10128, (212)534-7646, fax: (212)534-7035).
**Nonfiction:** Philosophy, religion, self-help, textbooks (religious). Accepts nonfiction translations from German, French and Spanish. "We would like to see theology (Catholic and ecumenical Christian), popular spirituality, liturgy, and religious education texts." Submit outline and 2 sample chapters. Reviews artwork/photos as part of ms package.

**PBC INTERNATIONAL INC.**, 1 School St., Glen Cove NY 11542. (516)676-2727. Fax: (516)676-2738. Website: http://www.dir-dd.com/pbc.html. Publisher: Mark Serchuck. **Acquisitions:** Lisa Maruca, managing director. Estab. 1980. Publishes hardcover and paperback originals. **Publishes 18 titles/year. Receives 100-200 submissions/year. Most of books from first-time authors and unagented writers done on assignment. Pays royalty and/or flat fees.** Accepts simultaneous submissions. Reports in 2 months. Book catalog for 9×12 SASE.
**O—** PBC International is the publisher of full-color visual idea books for the design, marketing and graphic arts professional. "Edited for trend-making design professionals and style-conscious consumers, our books bring the reader a fresh contemporary point of view—one that presents spaces that are inviting and employ a mix of elements, a depth of composition and, above all, are current and modern."
**Nonfiction:** Subjects include design, graphic art, architecture/interior design, packaging design, marketing design, product design. No submissions not covered in the above listed topics. Query with outline and sample chapters with SASE. Reviews artwork/photos as part of ms package.

**PEACHTREE CHILDREN'S BOOKS**, Imprint of Peachtree Publishers, Ltd. 494 Armour Circle NE, Atlanta GA 30324. (404)876-8761. Fax: (404)875-2578. E-mail: peachtree@mindspring.com. Website: http://peachtreebooks.com. President/Publisher: Margaret Quinlin. **Acquisitions:** Helen Harriss, submissions editor. Publishes hardcover and trade paperback originals. **Publishes 18-20 titles/year. 25% of books from first-time authors; 25% from unagented writers. Pays royalty on retail price. Advance varies.** Publishes book 18 months after acceptance of ms. Accepts simultaneous submissions. Reports in 3 months on queries, 4 months on manuscripts. Book catalog for $1.35 first-class postage. Manuscript guidelines for #10 SASE.
**O—** "We publish a broad range of subjects and perspectives, with emphasis on innovative plots and strong writing."
**Imprint(s):** Free Stone, Peachtree Jr.
**Nonfiction:** Children's/juvenile. Subjects include health, history, regional. Submit complete ms with SASE. *Writer's Market* recommends a query with SASE first.
**Fiction:** Juvenile, picture books, young adult. Submit ms with SASE.
**Recent Title(s):** *About Mammals*, by Sills & Sills (children's picture book); *Polar Star*, by Sally Gundley.

**PEACHTREE PUBLISHERS, LTD.**, 494 Armour Circle NE, Atlanta GA 30324-4888. (404)876-8761. Fax: (404)875-2578. **Acquisitions:** Sarah Helyar Smith (children's, juvenile, young adult, adult), Amy Sproull (regional/outdoors). Estab. 1978. Publishes hardcover and trade paperback originals. **Publishes 20-25 titles/year.** Approximately 65% of Peachtree's list consists of children's books. **Receives up to 18,000 submissions/year. 25% of books from first-time authors; 75% from unagented writers. Prefers to work with previously published authors. Pays 7½-15% royalty.** Publishes book 2 years after acceptance. Reports in 6 months on queries. Book catalog for 9×12 SAE with 3 first-class stamps.
**O—** Peachtree Publishers specializes in children's books, juvenile chapter books, young adult, regional guidebooks, parenting and self-help. Currently emphasizing adult nonfiction, self help, regional guides, children's, juvenile, young adult. De-emphasizing adult cooking, gardening.
**Imprint(s): Peachtree Children's Books** (Peachtree Jr., Free Stone).
**Nonfiction:** General. Subjects include children's titles and juvenile chapter books, history, health, humor, biography, general gift, recreation, self-help. No technical or reference. Submit outline and sample chapters. Reviews artwork/photos as part of ms package. Send photocopies.
**Fiction:** Literary, juvenile, young adult, mainstream. No fantasy, science fiction or romance. Submit sample chapters.
**Recent Title(s):** *Arthritis of the Hip and Knee*, by Allen Brander Stulberg (adult); *Rough Waters*, by S.L. Rottman (young adult); *Thirteen Monsters*, by Kevin Shortsleeve (children's).

**PELICAN PUBLISHING COMPANY**, 1000 Burmaster, P.O. Box 3110, Gretna LA 70053. (504)368-1175. Website: http://www.pelicanpub.com. President/Publisher: Milburn Calhoun. **Acquisitions:** Nina Kooij, editor-in-chief. Estab. 1926. Publishes hardcover, trade paperback and mass market paperback originals and reprints. **Publishes 80 titles/year. Receives 5,000 submissions/year. 15% of books from first-time authors; 90% from unagented writers. Pays royalty on actual receipts.** Publishes book 9-18 months after acceptance. Reports in 1 month on queries. Writer's guidelines for SASE.
**O—** "We believe ideas have consequences. One of the consequences is that they lead to a bestselling book. We publish books to improve and uplift the reader." Currently emphasizing Irish titles.
**Nonfiction:** Biography, coffee table book (limited), popular history, sports, architecture, illustrated book, juvenile, motivational, inspirational, Scottish, Irish, editorial cartoon. Subjects include Americana (especially Southern regional, Ozarks, Texas, Florida and Southwest); business (popular motivational, if author is a speaker); history; music (American artforms: jazz, blues, Cajun, R&B); politics (special interest in conservative viewpoint); religion (for popular audience mostly, but will consider others). *Travel:* Regional and international. *Motivational:* with business slant. *Inspirational:*

author must be someone with potential for large audience. *Cookbooks*: "We look for authors with strong connection to restaurant industry or cooking circles, i.e., someone who can promote successfully." Query with SASE. "We require that a query be made first. This greatly expedites the review process and can save the writer additional postage expenses." No multiple queries or submissions. Reviews artwork/photos as part of ms package. Send photocopies only.

**Fiction:** Historical, Southern, juvenile. "We publish maybe one novel a year, usually by an author we already have. Almost all proposals are returned. We are most interested in historical Southern novels." No young adult, romance, science fiction, fantasy, gothic, mystery, erotica, confession, horror, sex or violence. Submit outline/synopsis and 2 sample chapters with SASE.

**Recent Title(s):** *Was Jefferson Davis Right?*, by James Ronald Kennedy and Walter Donald Kennedy (history); *Lucky O'Leprechaun*, by Jana Dillon.

**Tips:** "We do extremely well with cookbooks, travel and popular histories. We will continue to build in these areas. The writer must have a clear sense of the market and knowledge of the competition. A query letter should describe the project briefly, give the author's writing and professional credentials, and promotional ideas."

**PENCIL POINT PRESS, INC.**, 277 Fairfield Rd., Fairfield NJ 07004. **Acquisitions:** Gene Garone, publisher (all areas); Patricia Cominsky (math, science). **Publishes 12 titles/year. Receives 12 queries and 12 mss/year. 100% of books from first-time authors. Pays 5-16% royalty or makes outright purchase of $25-50/page. No advance.** Publishes book 1 year after acceptance. Accepts simultaneous submissions. Reports in 2 months on proposals. Book catalog free.

⊶ Pencil Point publishes educational supplemental materials for teachers of all levels. Currently emphasizing professional reference. De-emphasizing language arts.

**Nonfiction:** Reference, technical, textbook. Education subjects, including professional reference, music, science, mathematics, language arts, ESL and special needs. Prefers supplemental resource materials for teachers grades K-12 and college (especially mathematics). Submit proposal package, including outline, 2 sample chapters and memo stating rationale and markets.

**Recent Title(s):** *Earthscope: Exploring Relationships Affecting Our Global Environment*, by Wright H. Gwyn.

**Tips:** Audience is K-8 teachers, 9-12 teachers and college-level supplements. No children's trade books or poetry.

**PENGUIN PUTNAM INC.**, 375 Hudson St., New York NY 10014. Website: http://www.penguinputnam.com. President: Phyllis Grann. General interest publisher of both fiction and nonfiction.

**Imprint(s): The Penguin Group:** *Hardcover:* Allen Lane, **DAW, Dutton,** Penguin Press, Viking; **Viking Studio,** *Paperback:* Arkana, **DAW,** Mentor, Meridian, Onyx, Penguin, Penguin Classics, Plume, **Roc, Signet,** Signet Classics, Topaz; *Children's:* **Dial Books for Young Readers, Dutton Children's Books,** Puffin, **Viking Children's Books,** Frederick Warne. **The Putnam Berkley Publishing Group:** *Hardcover:* Ace/Putnam, **Boulevard, Price Stern Sloan,** Putnam, **G.P. Putnam's Sons,** Riverhead, **Jeremy P. Tarcher;** *Paperback:* Ace, **Berkley Books,** HP Books, Jove, **Perigee, Price Stern Sloan,** Prime Crime, Riverhead Books; *Children's:* **Grosset & Dunlap,** PaperStar, **Philomel Books, Price Stern Sloan, G.P. Putnam's Sons,** Wee Sing.

**PENNSYLVANIA HISTORICAL AND MUSEUM COMMISSION,** Imprint of the Commonwealth of Pennsylvania, P.O. Box 1026, Harrisburg PA 17108-1026. (717)787-8099. Fax: (717)787-8312. Website: http://www.state.pa.us. **Acquisitions:** Diane B. Reed, chief, publications and sales division. Estab. 1913. Publishes hardcover and paperback originals and reprints. **Publishes 6-8 titles/year. Receives 25 submissions/year. Pays 5-10% royalty on retail price. Makes outright purchase or sometimes makes special assignments.** Publishes book 18 months after acceptance. Accepts simultaneous submissions. Reports in 4 months. Prepare mss according to the *Chicago Manual of Style*.

⊶ "We have a tradition of publishing scholarly and reference works, as well as more popularly styled books that reach an even broader audience interested in some aspect of Pennsylvania."

**Nonfiction:** All books must be related to Pennsylvania, its history or culture: biography, illustrated books, reference, technical and historic travel. No fiction. "The Commission seeks manuscripts on Pennsylvania, specifically on archaeology, history, art (decorative and fine), politics and biography." Query or submit outline and sample chapters. Guidelines and proposal forms available.

**Recent Title(s):** *Prehistoric Cultures of Eastern Pennsylvania*, by Jay Custer (archaeology).

**Tips:** "Our audience is diverse—students, specialists and generalists—all of them interested in one or more aspects of Pennsylvania's history and culture. Manuscripts must be well researched and documented (footnotes not necessarily required depending on the nature of the manuscript) and interestingly written. Manuscripts must be factually accurate, but in being so, writers must not sacrifice style."

**[N] [✉] PENNYWHISTLE PRESS**, P.O. Box 734, Tesuque NM 87574. (505)982-0000. Fax: (505)982-0066. E-mail: pnywhistle@aol.com. **Acquisitions:** Victor di Suvero, publisher. **Publishes 6 titles/year. Receives 400 queries and 500 mss/year. 50% of books from first-time authors; 100% from unagented writers. Pays $100, chapbook plus 50 copies of book to author.** Publishes book 1 year after acceptance. Accepts simultaneous submissions. Reports in 1 month on queries, 2 months on proposals, 3 months on mss. Book catalog for 4×12 SAE with 1 first-class stamp. Manuscript guidelines free.

⊶ Pennywhistle publishes only poetry chapbooks.

**Poetry:** Submit 30 sample poems.

**Recent Title(s):** *¡ Saludos! Poems of New Mexico.*

**PERFECTION LEARNING CORPORATION**, 10520 New York Ave., Des Moines IA 50322-3775. (515)278-0133. Fax: (515)278-2980. Website: http://www.plconline.com. **Acquisitions:** Sue Thies, senior editor (books division); Terry Ofner, senior editor (curriculum division). Estab. 1926. Publishes hardcover and trade paperback originals. **Publishes 50-60 fiction and informational; 150 teacher's resources titles/year. Pays 5-8% royalty on retail price. Offers $300-500 advance.** Reports in 5 months on proposals.

　　O—¬ "Perfection Learning is dedicated to publishing literature-based materials that enhance teaching and learning in Pre K-12 classrooms and libraries."

**Imprint(s):** Cover-to-Cover.

**Nonfiction:** Publishes nonfiction and curriculum books, including workbooks, literature anthologies, teacher guides, literature tests, and niche textbooks for grades 3-12. "We are publishing hi-lo informational books for students in grades 2-8, reading levels 1-4." Query or submit outline with SASE; for curriculum books, submit proposal and writing sample with SASE.

**Fiction:** "We are publishing hi-lo fiction in a variety of genres for students in grades 2-8, reading levels 1-4." Submit 2-3 sample chapters with SASE.

**Recent Title(s):** *The Rattlesnake Necklace*, by Linda Baxter (hi-lo historical fiction); *The Iditarod*, by Monica Devine (hi-lo informational book in a narrative style).

**PERIGEE BOOKS**, Penguin Putnam Inc., 375 Hudson St., New York NY 10014. (212)366-2000. **Acquisitions:** John Duff, editor. Publishes trade paperback originals and reprints. **Publishes 12-15 titles/year. Receives hundreds of queries/year; 30 proposals/year. 30% first-time authors; 10% unagented writers. Pays 7½-15% royalty. Offers $5,000-150,000 advance.** Publishes book 18 months after acceptance of ms. Reports in 2 months. Catalog free. Manuscript guidelines given on acceptance of ms.

**Nonfiction:** Prescriptive books. Subjects include health/fitness, child care, spirituality. Query with outline. Prefers agented mss, but accepts unsolicited queries.

**THE PERMANENT PRESS/SECOND CHANCE PRESS**, 4170 Noyac Rd., Sag Harbor NY 11963. (516)725-1101. Website: http://www.thepermanentpress.com. **Acquisitions:** Judith Shepard, editor. Estab. 1978. Publishes hardcover originals. **Publishes 12 titles/year. Receives 7,000 submissions/year. 60% of books from first-time authors; 60% from unagented writers. Pays 10-15% royalty on wholesale price. Offers $1,000 advance for Permanent Press books; royalty only on Second Chance Press titles.** Publishes book 18 months after acceptance. Accepts simultaneous submissions. Reports in 6 months on queries. Book catalog for 8×10 SAE with 7 first-class stamps. Manuscript guidelines for #10 SASE.

　　O—¬ Permanent Press publishes literary fiction. Second Chance Press devotes itself exclusively to re-publishing fine books that are out of print and deserve continued recognition. "We endeavor to publish quality writing—primarily fiction—without regard to authors' reputations or track records." Currently emphasizing literary fiction. De-emphasizing poetry, short story collections.

**Nonfiction:** Biography, autobiography, historical. No scientific and technical material, academic studies. Query.

**Fiction:** Literary, mainstream, mystery. Especially looking for high line literary fiction, "artful, original and arresting." No genre fiction, poetry or short stories. Query with first 20 pages.

**Recent Title(s):** *A Soldier's Book*, by Joanna Higgins (fiction).

**Tips:** "Audience is the silent minority—people with good taste. We are interested in the writing more than anything and long outlines are a turn-off. The SASE is vital to keep track of things, as we are receiving ever more submissions. No fax queries will be answered. We aren't looking for genre fiction but a compelling, well-written story." Permanent Press does not employ readers and the number of submissions it receives has grown. If the writer sends a query or manuscript that the press is not interested in, a reply may take six weeks. If there is interest, it may take 3 to 6 months.

**PERSPECTIVES PRESS**, P.O. Box 90318, Indianapolis IN 46290-0318. (317)872-3055. E-mail: ppress@iquest.net. Website: http://www.perspectivespress.com. **Acquisitions:** Pat Johnston, publisher. Estab. 1982. Publishes hardcover and trade paperback originals. **Publishes 4 titles/year. Receives 200 queries/year. 95% of books from first-time authors; 95% from unagented writers. Pays 5-15% royalty on net sales.** Publishes book 1 year after acceptance. Reports in 1 month on queries to schedule a full reading. *Writer's Market* recommends allowing 2 months for reply. Book catalog and writer's guidelines for #10 SAE with 2 first-class stamps or on website.

　　O—¬ "Our purpose is to promote understanding of infertility issues and alternatives, adoption and closely-related child welfare issues, and to educate and sensitize those personally experiencing these life situations, professionals who work with such clients, and the public at large."

**Nonfiction:** How-to, juvenile and self-help books on health, psychology and sociology. Must be related to infertility, adoption, alternative routes to family building. "No adult fiction!" Query with SASE.

**Recent Title(s):** *Choosing Assisted Reproduction*, by Susan Cooper and Ellen Glazer.

**Tips:** "For adults, we are seeking infertility and adoption decision-making materials, books dealing with adoptive or foster parenting issues, books to use with children, books to share with others to help explain infertility, adoption, foster care, third party reproductive assistance, special programming or training manuals, etc. For children, we will consider adoption or foster care-related fiction manuscripts that are appropriate for preschoolers and early elementary school children. We do not consider YA. Nonfiction manuscripts are considered for all ages. No autobiography, memoir or adult fiction. While we would consider a manuscript from a writer who was not personally or professionally involved in these issues, we would be more inclined to accept a manuscript submitted by an infertile person, an adoptee, a birthparent, an adoptive parent or a professional working with any of these."

**PETER PAUPER PRESS, INC.**, 202 Mamaroneck Ave., White Plains NY 10601-5376. **Acquisitions:** Solomon M. Skolnick, creative director. Estab. 1928. Publishes hardcover originals. **Publishes 40-50 titles/year. Receives 700 queries and 300 mss/year. 40% of books from first-time authors; 100% from unagented writers. Makes outright purchase only.** Publishes ms 1 year after acceptance. Reports in 1 month. *Writer's Market* recommends allowing 2 months for reply. Manuscript guidelines for #10 SASE.

    O– PPP publishes small format, illustrated gifts for occasions and in celebration of specific relationships such as Mom, sister, friend, teacher, grandmother, granddaughter.

**Nonfiction:** Subjects include specific relationships or special occasions (graduation, Mother's Day, Christmas, etc.). "We do not publish narrative works. We publish brief, original quotes, aphorisms, and wise sayings. *Please do not send us other people's quotes.*" Submit outline with SASE.

**Recent Title(s):** *A Friend for All Seasons*, compiled by Helen H. Moore.

**Tips:** "Our readers are primarily female, age 20 and over, who are likely to buy a 'gift' book in a stationery, gift, book or boutique store. Writers should become familiar with our previously published work. We publish only small-format illustrated hardcover gift books of between 750-4,000 words. We have no interest in work aimed at men."

**A.K. PETERS, LTD.**, 63 South Ave., Natick MA 01760. (781)235-2210. Fax: (781)235-2404. E-mail: editorial@akpeters.com. Website: http://www.akpeters.com. **Acquisitions:** Alice and Klaus Peters, publishers. Publishes hardcover originals and reprints. **Publishes 20 titles/year. Receives 50 queries and 30 mss/year. 75% of books from first-time authors; 100% from unagented writers. Pays 15-20% royalty on net price.** Publishes book 4 months after acceptance of ms. Accepts simultaneous submissions. Reports in 3 months. Book catalog and ms guidelines free.

    O– "A.K. Peters, Ltd. publishes scientific/technical/medical books and popular nonfiction titles related to science and technology."

**Nonfiction:** Biography, multimedia (format: CD-ROM), technical, textbook. Subjects include computers/electronics, health/medicine, science, software, mathematics. "We are predominantly a publisher of mathematics and computer science, but we are very interested in expanding our list in robotics and health/medicine as well. Stories of people behind the science are also of interest. Proposals for nonfiction should be well organized and well written, clearly noting audience and purpose." Submit proposal package, including outline or table of contents with sample chapters or full ms. Description of target audience also helpful. Reviews artwork/photos as part of the ms package. Send photocopies.

**Recent Title(s):** *Drawbridge Up: Mathematics—A Cultural Anathema*, by Hans Magnus Enzensberger.

**PHI DELTA KAPPA EDUCATIONAL FOUNDATION**, P.O. Box 789, Bloomington IN 47402. (812)339-1156. Fax: (812)339-0018. E-mail: special.pubs@pdkintl.org. Website: http://www.pdkintl.org. **Acquisitions:** Donovan R. Walling, editor of special publications. Estab. 1906. Publishes hardcover and trade paperback originals. **Publishes 24-30 titles/year. Receives 100 queries and 50-60 mss/year. 50% of books from first-time authors; 100% from unagented writers. Pays honorarium of $500-5,000.** Publishes book 9 months after acceptance of ms. Reports in 3 months on proposals. Book catalog and ms guidelines free.

    O– "We publish books for educators—K-12 and higher education. Our professional books are often used in college courses but are never specifically designed as textbooks."

**Nonfiction:** How-to, reference, essay collections. Subjects include child guidance/parenting, education, legal issues. Query with outline and 1 sample chapter. Reviews artwork/photos as part of ms package.

**Recent Title(s):** *The Truth about America's Schools: The Bracey Reports, 1991-97*, by Gerald W. Bracey (school performance, evaluation and reform).

**PHILOMEL BOOKS**, Penguin Putnam Inc., 345 Hudson St., New York NY 10014. (212)414-3610. **Acquisitions:** Patricia Lee Gauch, editorial director; Michael Green, senior editor. Estab. 1980. Publishes hardcover originals. **Publishes 20-25 titles/year. Receives 2,600 submissions/year. 15% of books from first-time authors; 30% from unagented writers. Pays standard (7½-15%) royalty. Advance negotiable.** Publishes book 1-2 years after acceptance. Reports in 3 months on queries. Book catalog for 9×12 SAE with 4 first-class stamps. Request book catalog from marketing department of Putnam Publishing Group.

    O– "We look for beautifully written, engaging manuscripts for children and young adults."

**Fiction:** Children's picture books (ages 3-8); middle-grade fiction and illustrated chapter books (ages 7-10); young adult novels (ages 10-15). Particularly interested in picture book mss with original stories and regional fiction with a distinct voice. Historical fiction OK. Unsolicited mss accepted for picture books only; query first for long fiction. Always include SASE. No series or activity books.

**Recent Title(s):** *Shake Rag*, by Amy Littlesugar.

**Tips:** "We prefer a very brief synopsis that states the basic premise of the story. This will help us determine whether or not the manuscript is suited to our list. If applicable, we'd be interested in knowing the author's writing experience or background knowledge. We try to be less influenced by the swings of the market than in the power, value, essence of the manuscript itself."

**PICADOR USA**, St. Martin's Press, 175 Fifth Ave., New York NY 10010. **Acquisitions:** George Witte. Estab. 1994. Publishes hardcover originals and trade paperback originals and reprints. **Publishes 70-80 titles/year. 30% of books**

from first-time authors. Publishes "few" unagented writers. **Pays 7½-12½% royalty on retail price. Advance varies.** Publishes book 18 months after acceptance of ms. Accepts simultaneous submissions. Reports in 2 months on queries. Book catalog for 9×12 SASE and $2.60 postage. Manuscript guidelines for #10 SASE.

    **O-π** Picador publishes high-quality literary fiction and nonfiction. "We are open to a broad range of subjects, well written by authoritative authors."

**Nonfiction:** Subjects include language/literature, philosophy, biography/memoir, cultural history, narrative books with a point of view on a particular subject. "When submitting queries, be aware of things outside the book, including credentials, that may affect our decision." Query only with SASE. No phone queries.

**Fiction:** Literary. Query only with SASE.

**Recent Title(s):** *Fashionable Nonsense*, by Alan Sokal and Jean Bricmont (science/philosophy); *The Hiawatha*, by David Treuer (fiction).

**⊠ PICCADILLY BOOKS**, P.O. Box 25203, Colorado Springs CO 80936-5203. (719)550-9887. Publisher: Bruce Fife. **Acquisitions:** Submissions Department. Estab. 1985. Publishes hardcover and trade paperback originals and trade paperback reprints. **Publishes 5-8 titles/year. Receives 200 submissions/year. 70% of books from first-time authors; 95% from unagented writers. Pays 10% royalty on retail price.** Publishes book 1 year after acceptance. Accepts simultaneous submissions. Responds only if interested.

    **O-π** Picadilly publishes books on humor, entertainment, performing arts, skits and sketches, and writing.

**Nonfiction:** How-to books on entertainment, humor, performing arts, writing and small business. "We have a strong interest in subjects on clowning, magic, puppetry and related arts, including comedy skits and dialogs." Query with sample chapters.

**Recent Title(s):** *The World's Funniest Clown Skits*, by Barry DeChant.

**Tips:** "Experience has shown that those who order our books are either kooky or highly intelligent or both. If you like to laugh, have fun, enjoy games, or have a desire to act like a jolly buffoon, we've got the books for you."

**⊠ PICTON PRESS**, Picton Corp., P.O. Box 250, Rockport ME 04856-0250. (207)236-6565. Fax: (207)236-6713. E-mail: sales@pictonpress.com. Website: http://www.pictonpress.com. **Acquisitions:** Candy McMahan Perry, office manager. Publishes hardcover and mass market paperback originals and reprints. **Publishes 30 titles/year. Receives 30 queries and 15 mss/year. 50% of books from first-time authors; 100% from unagented writers. Pays 0-10% royalty on wholesale price or makes outright purchase.** Publishes book 6 months after acceptance of ms. Reports in 2 months on queries and proposals, 3 months on mss. Book catalog free.

    **O-π** "Picton Press is one of America's oldest, largest and most respected publishers of genealogical and historical books specializing in research tools for the 17th, 18th and 19th centuries."

**Imprint(s):** Cricketfield Press, New England History Press, Penobscot Press, **Picton Press**.

**Nonfiction:** Reference, textbook. Subjects include Americana, genealogy, history, vital records. Query with outline.

**Recent Title(s):** *Nemesis At Potsdam*, by Alfred de Zayas.

**THE PILGRIM PRESS**, United Church Board for Homeland Ministries, 700 Prospect Ave. E., Cleveland OH 44115-1100. (216)736-3715. Fax: (216)736-3703. E-mail: stavet@ucc.org. **Acquisitions:** Timothy G. Staveteig, editorial director. Estab. 1985. Publishes hardcover and trade paperback originals. **Publishes 55 titles/year. 30% of books from first-time authors; 80% from unagented writers. Pays standard royalties and advances where appropriate.** Publishes book an average of 18 months after acceptance. Reports in 3 months on queries. Book catalog and ms guidelines free.

**Nonfiction:** Ethics, social issues with a strong commitment to justice—addressing such topics as public policy, sexuality and gender, economics, medicine, gay and lesbian concerns, human rights, minority liberation and the environment—primarily in a Christian context, but not exclusively.

**Recent Title(s):** *Seeds of Racism in the Soul of America*, by Paul Griffin.

**Tips:** "We are concentrating more on academic and trade submissions. Writers should send books about contemporary social issues. Our audience is liberal, open-minded, socially aware, feminist, church members and clergy, teachers and seminary professors."

**PILOT BOOKS**, 127 Sterling Ave., P.O. Box 2102, Greenport NY 11944. (516)477-1094. Fax: (516)477-0978. E-mail: feedback@pilotbooks@aol.com. Website: http://www.pilotbooks.com. **Acquisitions:** Robert Ungerleider, publisher; Ruth Gruen, editor. Estab. 1959. Publishes paperback originals. **Publishes 10-15 titles/year. Receives 200-300 submissions/year. 30% of books from first-time authors; 90% from unagented writers. Offers standard royalty contract based on retail price. Offers $250 usual advance, but this varies.** Publishes book an average of 8 months after acceptance. Reports in 2 months. Book catalog and guidelines for #10 SASE.

    **O-π** "Pilot Books offers readers well-organized, well-written 'how' and 'where'-to books on a variety of timely topics."

**Nonfiction:** Publishes "personal, business and career guides, senior and budget travel information and books on new ideas and trends for today's older adult. We prefer authors with credentials in the field they're writing about." Length: 25,000-50,000 words. Send outline with SASE. Reviews artwork/photos as part of ms package.

**Recent Title(s):** *How to Buy a Franchise*, by James A. Meaney.

**PIÑATA BOOKS**, Arte Publico Press, University of Houston, Houston TX 77204-2174. (713)743-2841. Fax: (713)743-2847. **Acquisitions:** Nicolas Kanellos, president. Estab. 1994. Publishes hardcover and trade paperback originals. **Publishes 10-15 titles/year. 60% of books from first-time authors. Pays 10% royalty on wholesale price. Offers $1,000-3,000 advance.** Publishes book 2 years after acceptance of ms. Accepts simultaneous submissions. Reports in 1 month on queries, 6 months on mss. Book catalog free. Manuscript guidelines for #10 SASE.

   ○━ Piñata Books is dedicated to the publication of children's and young adult literature focusing on U.S. Hispanic culture.

**Nonfiction:** Children's/juvenile. Ethnic subjects. "Pinata Books specializes in publication of children's and young adult literature that authentically portrays themes, characters and customs unique to U.S. Hispanic culture." Query with outline/synopsis, 2 sample chapters and SASE.

**Fiction:** Adventure, juvenile, picture books, young adult. Query with synopsis, 2 sample chapters and SASE.

**Poetry:** Appropriate to Hispanic theme. Submit 10 sample poems.

**Recent Title(s):** *Silent Dancing: A Partial Remembrance of a Puerto Rican Childhood*, by Judith Ortiz-Cofer (memoir, ages 11-adult); *Tun-ta-ca-tun*, edited by Sylvia Pena (children's poetry, preschool to young adult).

**Tips:** "Include cover letter with submission explaining why your manuscript is unique and important, why we should publish it, who will buy it, etc."

**PINEAPPLE PRESS, INC.**, P.O. Box 3899, Sarasota FL 34230. (941)359-0886. **Acquisitions:** June Cussen, editor. Estab. 1982. Publishes hardcover and trade paperback originals. **Publishes 20 titles/year. Receives 1,500 submissions/year. 20% of books from first-time authors; 80% from unagented writers. Pays 6½-15% royalty on retail price. Seldom offers advance.** Publishes book 18 months after acceptance. Accepts simultaneous submissions. Reports in 3 months. Book catalog for 9×12 SAE with $1.24 postage.

   ○━ "We are seeking quality nonfiction on diverse topics for the library and book trade markets."

**Nonfiction:** Biography, how-to, reference, regional (Florida), nature. Subjects include animals, history, gardening, nature. "We will consider most nonfiction topics. Most, though not all, of our fiction and nonfiction deals with Florida." No pop psychology or autobiographies. Query or submit outline/brief synopsis, sample chapters and SASE.

**Fiction:** Literary, historical, mainstream, regional (Florida). No romance, science fiction, children's. Submit outline/brief synopsis and sample chapters.

**Recent Title(s):** *Art Lover's Guide to Florida*, by Anne Jeffrey and Aletta Dreller; *Myra Sims*, by Janis Owens (literature).

**Tips:** "Learn everything you can about book publishing and publicity and agree to actively participate in promoting your book. A query on a novel without a brief sample seems useless."

**PIPPIN PRESS**, 229 E. 85th St., P.O. Box 1347, Gracie Station, New York NY 10028. (212)288-4920. Fax: (732)225-1562. **Acquisitions:** Barbara Francis, president and editor-in-chief; Joyce Segal, senior editor. Estab. 1987. Publishes hardcover originals. **Publishes 4-6 titles/year. Receives 1,500 queries/year. 80% of queries from unagented writers. Pays royalty.** Publishes book 2 years after acceptance. Reports in 3 weeks on queries. *Writer's Market* recommends allowing 2 months for reply. Book catalog for 6×9 SASE. Manuscript guidelines for #10 SASE.

   ○━ Pippin publishes general nonfiction and fiction for children ages 4-12.

**Nonfiction:** Children's books: autobiography, biography, humor. Subjects include animals, history, language/literature, nature, science. General nonfiction for children ages 4-10. Query with SASE only. *No unsolicited mss.* Reviews artwork/photos as part of ms package. Send photocopies.

**Fiction:** Historical fiction, humor, mystery, picture books. "We're especially looking for small chapter books for 7- to 11-year olds, especially by people of many cultures." Also interested in humorous fiction for ages 7-11. Query with SASE only.

**Recent Title(s):** *A Visit From the Leopard*, by Catherine Mudiko-Piwang and Edward Frascino; *Abigail's Drum*, by John A. Minahan, illustrated by Robert Quackenbush (historical fiction).

**Tips:** "Read as many of the best children's books published in the last five years as you can. We are looking for multi-ethnic fiction and nonfiction for ages 7-10, as well as general fiction for this age group. I would pay particular attention to children's books favorably reviewed in *School Library Journal*, *The Booklist*, *The New York Times Book Review*, and *Publishers Weekly*."

**PLANNERS PRESS**, American Planning Association, 122 S. Michigan Ave., Chicago IL 60603. Fax: (312)431-9985. E-mail: slewis@planning.org. Website: http://www.planning.org. **Acquisitions:** Sylvia Lewis, director of publications. Estab. 1928. Publishes hardcover and trade paperback originals. **Publishes 4-6 titles/year. Receives 20 queries and 6-8 mss/year. 50% of books from first-time authors; 100% from unagented writers. Pays 7½-12% royalty on retail price.** Publishes book 1 year after acceptance. Reports in 1 month on queries, 2 months on proposals and mss. Book catalog and ms guidelines free.

   ○━ "Our books have a narrow audience of city planners and often focus on the tools of city planning."

**Nonfiction:** Technical (specialty-public policy and city planning). Government/political subjects. Submit 2 sample chapters and table of contents. Reviews artwork/photos as part of ms package. Send photocopies.

**Recent Title(s):** *Citistate Seattle; Transportation and Land Use Innovations.*

**PLANNING/COMMUNICATIONS**, 7215 Oak Ave., River Forest IL 60305. (708)366-5200. E-mail: dl@jobfinders online.com. Website: http://jobfindersonline.com. **Acquisitions:** Daniel Lauber, president. Estab. 1979. Publishes hardcover, trade and mass market paperback originals, trade paperback reprints. **Publishes 3-6 titles/year. Receives 30 queries and 3 mss/year. 50% of books from first-time authors; 100% from unagented writers. Pays 15-20%**

**royalty on net sales.** Publishes book 1 year after acceptance of ms. Accepts simultaneous submissions. Reports in 2 months on queries, 3 months on proposals and mss. Book catalog for $2. Manuscript guidelines for #10 SASE.

O→ Planning Communications publishes books on career, self-help financial books, sociology, urban planning and politics.

**Nonfiction:** Careers, self-help, résumés, cover letters, interviewing. Subjects include business/economics (careers), education, government/politics, money/finance, sociology. Submit outline and 3 sample chapters with SASE. Reviews artwork/photos as part of ms package. Send photocopies.

**Recent Title(s):** *Flight Attendant Job Finder & Career Guide*, by Tim Kirkwood; *From Making Profit to Making a Difference: Careers in Nonprofits for Business Professionals*, by Richard King.

**PLATINUM PRESS INC.**, 311 Crossways Park Dr., Woodbury NY 11797. (516)364-1800. Fax: (516)364-1899. **Acquisitions:** Herbert Cohen (mysteries, detective, hunting, fishing, outdoor, woodworking). Estab. 1990. Publishes hardcover originals and reprints. **Publishes 100 titles/year; each imprint publishes 30 titles/year. 25% of books from first-time authors; 25% from unagented writers. Pays 5-10% royalty on retail price. Offers $500-750 advance.** Accepts simultaneous submissions.

O→ Platinum Press publishes nonfiction gardening, history, religion and military and mystery fiction.

**Imprint(s):** Detective Book Club, Home Craftsman Book Club, Outdoor Sportsman Library, Platinum Press.
**Nonfiction:** Gardening, history, military/war, religion subjects. Query with SASE.
**Fiction:** Mystery, suspense. Query with SASE.
**Recent Title(s):** *U.S. Army Survival Manual.*

**PLAYERS PRESS, INC.**, P.O. Box 1132, Studio City CA 91614-0132. (818)789-4980. **Acquisitions:** Robert W. Gordon, vice president, editorial. Estab. 1965. Publishes hardcover and trade paperback originals, and trade paperback reprints. **Publishes 35-70 titles/year. Receives 200-1,000 submissions/year. 15% of books from first-time authors; 80% from unagented writers. Pays royalty on wholesale price.** Publishes book within 2 years of acceptance. Reports on queries in 1 month, up to 1 year on mss. Book catalog and guidelines for 9×12 SAE with 5 first-class stamps.

O→ Players Press publishes support books for the entertainment industries: theater, film, television, dance and technical. Currently emphasizing how-to books. De-emphasizing children's.

**Nonfiction:** Juvenile and theatrical drama/entertainment industry. Subjects include the performing arts, costume, theater and film crafts. Needs quality plays and musicals, adult or juvenile. Query. Reviews artwork/photos as part of package.
**Plays:** Subject matter includes adventure, confession, ethnic, experimental, fantasy, historical, horror, humor, mainstream, mystery, religious, romance, science fiction, suspense, western. Submit complete ms for theatrical plays only. Plays must be previously produced. "No novels or story books are accepted."
**Recent Title(s):** *Theatre Management*, by Kevin Marshall and Sue Celentano.
**Tips:** "Plays, entertainment industry texts, theater, film and TV books have the only chances of selling to our firm."

**PLEASANT COMPANY PUBLICATIONS**, 8400 Fairway Pl., Middleton WI 53562. Fax: (608)836-1999. Website: http://www.americangirl.com. **Acquistions:** Jennifer Hirsch, submissions editor. Estab. 1986. Publishes hardcover and trade paperback originals. **Publishes 25-30 title/year. Receives 400 queries and 400 mss/year. 90% of books from unagented writers. "Payment varies extremely depending on the nature of the work." Advance varies.** Accepts simultaneous submissions. Reports in 2 months. Book catalog for SASE.

O→ "Pleasant Company publishes fiction and nonfiction for girls 7-12 under its two imprints, The American Girls Collection® and American Girl Library®. The company relies primarily on its own team of writers, editors, and designers to produce its books and print products."

**Imprint(s):** The American Girls Collection, American Girl Library.
**Nonfiction:** Children's/juvenile for girls, ages 7-12. Subjects include contemporary lifestyle, activities, how-to. Query.
**Fiction:** Juvenile for girls, ages 7-12. Subjects include contemporary and historical fiction, mysteries. "We are seeking high-quality contemporary fiction about girls ages 9-12 for new, non-series imprint. No romance, fantasy, picture books, rhyme or stories about talking animals." Query.
**Recent Title(s):** *Oops! The Manners Guide for Girls*, by Nancy Holyoke (nonfiction); *Meet Josefina, An American Girl*, by Valerie Tripp (fiction).

**PLEXUS PUBLISHING, INC.**, 143 Old Marlton Pike, Medford NJ 08055-8750. (609)654-6500. Fax: (609)654-4309. **Acquisitions:** Thomas Hogan, editorial director. Estab. 1977. Publishes hardcover and paperback originals. **Publishes 4-5 titles/year. Receives 10-20 submissions/year. 70% of books from first-time authors; 90% from unagented writers. Pays 10-20% royalty on wholesale price; buys some booklets outright for $250-1,000. Offers $500-1,000 advance.** Accepts simultaneous submissions/year. Reports in 3 months. Book catalog and guidelines for 10×13 SAE with 4 first-class stamps.

**Nonfiction:** Biography (of naturalists), reference. Subjects include plants, animals, nature, life sciences. "We will consider any book on a nature/biology subject, particularly those of a reference (permanent) nature that would be of lasting value to high school and college audiences, and/or the general reading public (ages 14 and up). Authors should have authentic qualifications in their subject area, but qualifications may be by experience as well as academic training." No gardening, philosophy or psychology; generally not interested in travel but will consider travel that gives sound ecological information. Also interested in mss of about 20-40 pages in length for feature articles in *Biology Digest* (guidelines available with SASE). Query. Reviews artwork as part of ms package. Send photocopies.

**Tips:** "We will give serious consideration to well-written manuscripts that deal even indirectly with biology/nature subjects. For example, *Exploring Underwater Photography* (a how-to for divers) and *The Literature of Nature* (an anthology of nature writings for college curriculum) were accepted for publication."

**POPULAR CULTURE INK**, P.O. Box 1839, Ann Arbor MI 48106. (734)677-6351. **Acquisitions:** Tom Schultheiss, publisher. Estab. 1989. Publishes hardcover originals and reprints. **Publishes 4-6 titles/year. Receives 50 queries and 20 mss/year. 100% of books from first-time authors; 100% from unagented writers. Pays variable royalty on wholesale price. Offers variable advance.** Publishes book 2 years after acceptance. Accepts simultaneous submissions. Reports in 1 month. *Writer's Market* recommends allowing 2 months for reply. Book catalog and ms guidelines free.

○━ Popular Culture Ink publishes directories and reference books for radio, TV, music and other entertainment subjects.

**Nonfiction:** Reference. Subjects include music, popular entertainment. Query with SASE.

**Recent Title(s):** *Surfin' Guitars*, by Robert Dalley (1960s surf music).

**Tips:** Audience is libraries, avid collectors. "Know your subject backwards. Make sure your book is unique."

**POPULAR WOODWORKING BOOKS**, F&W Publications, 1507 Dana Ave., Cincinnati OH 45207. (513)531-2690. **Acquisitions:** Mark Thompson, acquisitions editor. Publishes hardcover and trade paperback originals and reprints. **Publishes 10-12 titles/year. Receives 30 queries and 10 mss/year. 50% of books from first-time authors; 95% from unagented writers. Pays 10-20% royalty on net receipts. Offers $3,000-5,000 advance.** Publishes book 1 year after acceptance of ms. Accepts simultaneous submissions. Reports in 1 month. Book catalog and ms guidelines for 9 × 12 SAE with 6 first-class stamps.

**Nonfiction:** How-to, illustrated book, woodworking/wood crafts. "We publish heavily illustrated how-to woodworking books that show, rather than tell, our readers how to accomplish their woodworking goals." Query with proposal package, including outline, transparencies and SASE. Reviews artwork/photos as part of ms package. Send transparencies. "Always submit copies of transparencies. We will not be responsible for lost or stolen transparencies!"

**Recent Title(s):** *How to Build Classic Garden Furniture*, by Danny Proulx.

**Tips:** "Our books are for 'advanced beginner' woodworking enthusiasts."

**POSSIBILITY PRESS**, (formerly Success Publishers), One Oakglade Circle, Hummelstown PA 17036-9525. (717)566-0468. Fax: (717)566-6423. E-mail: posspress@aol.com. **Acquisitions:** Mike Markowski, publisher; Marjorie L. Markowski, editor-in-chief. Estab. 1981. Publishes trade paperback originals. **Publishes 10 titles/year. Receives 1,000 submissions/year. 90% of books from first-time authors; 100% from unagented writers. Royalties vary.** Publishes book 1 year or less after acceptance. Reports in 2 months. Manuscript guidelines for #10 SAE and 2 first-class stamps.

○━ "Our mission is to help the people of the world grow and become the best they can be, through the written and spoken word."

**Imprint(s): Aviation Publishers, Health Publishers, Possibility Press**.

**Nonfiction:** How-to, self-help. Subjects include business, current significant events, pop-psychology, success/motivation, inspiration, entrepreneurship, sales marketing, network marketing and homebased business topics, and human interest success stories.

**Recent Title(s):** *Focus On The Dream*, by Jeff Smith.

**Tips:** "Our focus is on creating and publishing bestsellers written by authors who speak and consult. We're looking for authors who are serious about making a difference in the world."

**PPI PUBLISHING**, P.O. Box 292239, Kettering OH 45429. (937)294-5057. **Acquisitions:** Shary Price, managing editor. Publishes age-specific paperback originals. **Publishes 10-15 titles/year. Receives 200 queries and 50 mss/year. 90% of books from first-time authors; 100% from unagented writers. Pays 10% royalty on retail price.** Publishes book 10 months after acceptance of ms. Accepts simultaneous submissions. Reports in 2 months on queries, 3 months on proposals, 2 months on mss. Catalog and guidelines for 9 × 12 SASE and 2 first-class stamps. Manuscript guidelines for #10 SASE.

○━ "PPI Publishing seeks to provide top-quality, well researched, up-to-the-minute information on the 'hot' issues for teens with distribution mostly to schools and public libraries."

**Nonfiction:** Children/young adult, how-to, self-help. Subjects include motivational; social issues such as AIDS, abortion, teenage drinking; environmental issues such as the Rainforest and the ozone layer; teen sexuality, "hot youth topics," career guidance. Publishes books in the Fall. Query or submit outline with 3 sample chapters with SASE. Reviews artwork/photos as part of the ms package. Send photocopies.

---

**MARKET CONDITIONS** are constantly changing! If this is 2001 or later, buy the newest edition of *Writer's Market* at your favorite bookstore or order directly from Writer's Digest Books.

**Recent Title(s):** *AIDS: Facts, Issues, Choices,* by Faith H. Brynie, Ph.D.

**Tips:** Readers are students in grades 7-12 and their teachers. "We're looking for quality material on 'hot' topics that will appeal to middle school/high school students. Submit fresh topics with logical thought and writing."

**PRACTICE MANAGEMENT INFORMATION CORP. (PMIC),** 4727 Wilshire Blvd., Los Angeles CA 90010. (213)954-0224. Fax: (213)954-0253. E-mail: pmiceditor@aol.com. Website: http://www.medicalbookstore.com. **Acquisitions:** Kathryn Swanson, managing editor. Estab. 1986. Publishes hardcover originals. **Publishes 21 titles/year. Receives 100 queries and 50 mss/year. 10% of books from first-time authors; 90% from unagented writers. Pays 12½% royalty on net receipts. Offers $1,000-5,000 advance.** Publishes book 18 months after acceptance of ms. Reports in 6 months on queries. Book catalog and ms guidelines for #10 SASE.

    O-¬ PMIC helps doctors with the business of medicine with books for doctors, medical office and hospital staff, medical managers, insurance coding/billing personnel.

**Imprint(s): PMIC, Health Information Press.**

**Nonfiction:** Reference, technical, textbook, medical practice management, clinical, nonfiction. Subjects include business/economics, health/medicine, science. Submit proposal package, including outline and letter stating who is the intended audience, the need/market for such a book, as well as outline, 3-5 sample chapters and curriculum vitae/résumé.

**Recent Title(s):** *Hematology,* by Richert E. Goyette, M.D.

**N̈ PRAEGER PUBLISHERS,** The Greenwood Publishing Group, Inc., 88 Post Road W., Westport CT 06881. (203)226-3571. Fax: (203)226-6009. Publisher: Peter Kracht. **Acquisitions:** Heather Stainer (history, military); Nita Romer (psychology); Elizabeth Clinton (sociology); Cynthia Harris (economics); Pamela St. Clair (cultural studies, media); James Sabin (politics). Estab. 1949. Publishes paperback originals. **Publishes 250 titles/year. Receives 1,200 submissions/year. 5% of books from first-time authors; 90% from unagented writers. Pays 6½-12% royalty on net sales. Rarely offers advance.** Publishes book an average of 1 year after acceptance. Accepts simultaneous submissions. Reports in 1 month. *Writer's Market* recommends allowing 2 months for reply. Book catalog and manuscript guidelines available on website.

    O-¬ Praeger publishes scholarly trade and advanced texts in the social and behavioral sciences and communications, international relations and military studies.

**Nonfiction:** "We are looking for scholarly works in women's studies, sociology, psychology, contemporary history, military studies, political science, economics, international relations. No language and literature." Query with proposal package, including: scope, organization, length of project; whether a complete ms is available, or when it will be; cv or résumé with SASE. No unsolicited ms.

**Recent Title(s):** *An American Paradox: Censorship in a Nation of Free Speech,* by Patrick Garry; *Black and Right: The Bold New Voice of Black Conservatives in America,* edited by Stan Faryna, Brad Stetson and Joseph G. Conti; *Assault on the Left: The FBI and the Sixties Antiwar Movement,* by James Kirkpatrick Davis.

**PRAIRIE OAK PRESS,** 821 Prospect Place, Madison WI 53703. (608)255-2288. **Acquisitions:** Jerry Minnich, president. Estab. 1991. Publishes hardcover originals, trade paperback originals and reprints. **Publishes 6-8 titles/year. Pays royalty or makes outright purchase. Offers $500-1,000 advance.** Reports in 3 months on proposals.

    O-¬ Prairie Oak publishes exclusively Upper Great Lakes regional nonfiction.

**Imprint(s):** Prairie Classics, Acorn Guides.

**Nonfiction:** History, folklore, gardening, sports, travel, architecture, other general trade subjects. "Any work considered must have a strong tie to Wisconsin and/or the Upper Great Lakes region." Query or submit outline and 1 sample chapter with SASE.

**Recent Title(s):** *Wisconsin with Kids,* by Visser (family travel guide).

**Tips:** "When we say we publish regional works only, we mean Wisconsin, Minnesota, Michigan, Illinois. Please do not submit books of national interest. We cannot consider them."

**PRECEPT PRESS,** Bonus Books, 160 E. Illinois St., Chicago IL 60611. (312)467-0580. Fax: (312)467-9271. E-mail: bb@bonus-books.com. Website: http://www.bonus-books.com. **Acquisitions:** Jean Kang, assistant editor. Estab. 1970. Publishes hardcover and trade paperback originals. **Publishes 20 titles/year. Receives 300 queries and 100 mss/year. 25% of books from first-time authors; 90% from unagented writers. Pays royalty.** Publishes book 8 months after acceptance. Accepts simultaneous submissions if so noted. Reports in 3 months on proposals. Manuscript guidelines for #10 SASE.

    O-¬ Precept Press features a wide variety of books for the technical community. Currently emphasizing cultural and film theory.

**Nonfiction:** Reference, technical, clinical, textbook. Subjects include business, CD-ROM, medical and oncology texts. Query with SASE.

**Recent Title(s):** *Handbook of Chemotherapy Regimens for Gynecologic Cancers,* by Maurie Markman.

**PRESIDIO PRESS,** 505B San Marin Dr., Suite 300, Novato CA 94945-1340. (415)898-1081, ext. 125. Fax: (415)898-0383. **Acquisitions:** E.J. McCarthy, executive editor. Estab. 1974. Publishes hardcover originals and reprints. **Publishes 24 titles/year. Receives 1,600 submissions/year. 35% of books from first-time authors; 65% from unagented writers. Pays 15-20% royalty on net receipts. Advance varies.** Publishes book 18 months after acceptance. Reports within 1 month on queries. Book catalog and ms guidelines for 7½×10½ SAE with 4 first-class stamps.

☞ "We publish the finest and most accurate military history and military affairs nonfiction, plus entertaining and provocative fiction related to military affairs."

**Imprint(s):** Lyford Books.

**Nonfiction:** Subjects include military history and military affairs. Query with SASE. Reviews artwork/photos as part of ms package. Send photocopies.

**Fiction:** Men's action-adventure, thriller, mystery, military, historical. Query with SASE.

**Recent Title(s):** *The Biographical History of World War II*, by Mark M. Boatner III; *Proud Legions*, by John Antal (military fiction).

**Tips:** "Study the market. Find out what publishers are publishing, what they say they want and so forth. Then write what the market seems to be asking for, but with some unique angle that differentiates the work from others on the same subject. We feel that readers of hardcover fiction are looking for works of no less than 80,000 words."

**PRICE STERN SLOAN, INC.**, Penguin Putnam Inc., 345 Hudson, New York NY 10014. (212)951-8700. Fax: (212)951-8694. Editorial Director: Jon Anderson. **Acquisitions:** Submissions Editor (juvenile submissions); Calendars Editor (calendar submissions). Estab. 1963. **Publishes 80 titles/year (95% children's). Makes outright purchase. Offers advance.** Reports in 3 months. Catalog for 9×12 SAE with 5 first-class stamps. Manuscript guidelines for SASE. Address to "Catalog Request" or "Manuscript Guidelines."

☞ Price Stern Sloan publishes quirky mass market novelty series for children and adult page-a-day calendars.

**Imprint(s):** Doodle Art®, I Can Read Comics, Mad Libs®, Mad Mysteries®, Mr. Men & Little Miss™, Plugged In®, Serendipity®, Travel Games to Go, Troubador Press, Wee Sing®.

**Nonfiction and Fiction:** Mass market juvenile series and adult page-a-day calendars only. Do not send *original* artwork or ms. *No unsolicited mss.* "Most of our titles are unique in concept as well as execution."

**Recent Title(s):** The *Plugged In™ When Your Parents Split Up* . . Alys Swan Jackson (nonfiction); *Kermit's ABC*, illustrated by Stef de Renver (fiction).

**Tips:** "Price Stern Sloan has a unique, humorous, off-the-wall feel."

■ **PRIDE & IMPRINTS**, 7419 Ebbert Dr. SE, Port Orchard WA 98367. E-mail: mail@pride-imprints.com. Website: www.pride-imprints.com. **Acquisitions:** (Ms.) Cris Newport, senior editor. Estab. 1989. Publishes trade paperback originals and reprints. **Publishes 10 titles/year. Receives 5,200 queries and 15,000 mss/year. 50% of books from first-time authors; 50% from unagented writers. Pays 10-15% royalty on wholesale price.** Publishes book 1-2 years after acceptance of ms. Accepts simultaneous submissions. Reports in 6 months on mss. Book catalog and ms guidelines for $2. Guidelines also available at website.

☞ "We publish work that is revolutionary in content, sheds light on misconceptions and challenges stereotypes." De-emphasizing poetry, contemporary fiction.

**Imprint(s):** Little Blue Works, RAMPANT Gaming.

**Nonfiction:** Biography, children's/juvenile, cookbook, how-to, humor, illustrated book, reference, self-help. Subjects include business/economics, cooking/foods/nutrition, education, gay/lesbian, history, language/literature, money/finance, philosophy, psychology. Submit synopsis and first 50 pages with SASE. Reviews artwork/photos as part of the ms package. Send photocopies.

**Fiction:** Adventure, cyberfiction, erotica, ethnic, experimental, fantasy, feminist, future fiction, gay/lesbian, gothic, historical, humor, juvenile, literary, mystery, occult, plays, science fiction, suspense, young adult. "We look for work that challenges the way we see the world." Submit general synopsis, chapter-by-chapter synopsis and first 50 pages with SASE.

**Poetry:** "We look for poetry that others might consider 'too wild, too risky, too truthful.' A collection must have at least 100 poems for us to consider it." Submit complete ms.

**Recent Title(s):** *Write Your Autobiography*, by Bette Lou Tobin (nonfiction); *Bones Become Flowers*, by Jess Mowry (fiction); *Cape Cod Light*, by Michael Hattersley (poetry).

**Tips:** "We publish for almost every audience. Read several of our books before sending anything."

**PRIMA PUBLISHING**, P.O. Box 1260, Rocklin CA 95677-1260. (916)632-4400. Website: http://www.primapublishing.com. President/Founder: Ben Dominitz. **Acquisitions:** *Lifestyles Division:* Steven Martin, editorial director; Susan Silva, acquisitions editor; Jamie Miller, acquisitions editor; Denise Sternad, acquisitions; Lorna Dolley, acquisitions; Julie McDonald, acquisitions. *Prima Games Division:* Debra Kempker, publisher; Stacy DeFoe, product manager; Amy Raynor, product manager. *PrimaTech Division:* Matthew Carleson, publisher; Dan J. Foster, managing editor; Deborah F. Abshier, acquisitions editor; Jenny Watson, acquisitions editor. Estab. 1984. Publishes hardcover originals and trade paperback originals and reprints. **Publishes 300 titles/year. Receives 750 queries/year. 10% of books from first-time authors; 30% from unagented writers. Pays 15-20% royalty on wholesale price. Advance varies.** Publishes book 18 months after acceptance. Accepts simultaneous submissions. Reports in 3 months. Catalog for 9×12 SAE with 8 first-class stamps. Writer's guidelines for #10 SASE.

☞ "Books for the way we live, work and play."

**Nonfiction:** Business, parenting, education, alternative and traditional health, entertainment, writing, biography, self-help. Subjects include cooking/foods, crafts, history, pets, politics, psychology, relationships, sports, current affairs, network marketing. "We want books with originality, written by highly qualified individuals. No fiction at this time." Query with SASE.

**Tips:** "Prima strives to reach the primary and secondary markets for each of its books. We are known for promoting our books aggressively. Books that genuinely solve problems for people will always do well if properly promoted. Try to picture the intended audience while writing the book. Too many books are written to an audience that doesn't exist."

**[N] PRO/AM MUSIC RESOURCES, INC.**, 63 Prospect St., White Plains NY 10606. (914)448-9327. **Acquisitions:** Thomas P. Lewis, publisher. Publishes hardcover and trade paperback originals. **Publishes 5 titles/year. Receives 20 mss/year. 50% of books from first-time authors. Pays 10% royalty on retail price. No advance.** Publishes book 1 year after acceptance of ms. Accepts simultaneous submissions. Book catalog for #10 SASE.
- Pro/Am publishes only nonfiction music titles.

**Nonfiction:** Music only. Query with SASE.
**Recent Title(s):** *History Through the Opera Glass*, by George Jelliner; *Performing Bach's Keyboard Music*, by George Kochevitsky; *The Music of My Time*, by Joan Peyser.

**[N] PROFESSIONAL PUBLICATIONS, INC.**, 1250 Fifth Ave., Belmont CA 94002-3863. (415)593-9119. Fax: (415)592-4519. E-mail: ppi@ppi2pass.com. **Acquisitions:** Aline Magee, acquisitions editor. Estab. 1975. Publishes hardcover and paperback originals and video and audio cassettes, and CD-ROMs. **Publishes over 30 titles/year. Receives 100-200 submissions/year.** Publishes book 18 months after acceptance of ms. Accepts simultaneous submissions. Reports in 2 weeks on queries. *Writer's Market* recommends allowing 2 months for reply. Book catalog and ms guidelines free.
- PPI publishes for engineering architecture, land surveying and interior design professionals preparing to take examinations for national licensing. Professional Publications wants only professionals practicing in the field to submit material. Currently emphasizing engineering exam review. De-emphasizing architecture exam review.

**Nonfiction:** Reference, technical, textbook. Subjects include engineering mathematics, engineering, land surveying, architecture, interior design. Especially needs "review books for all professional licensing examinations." Query or submit outline and sample chapters. Reviews artwork/photos as part of ms package.
**Recent Title(s):** *Civil Surveying Practice Exam*, by James Monroe Jr., PE.
**Tips:** "We specialize in books for working professionals: engineers, architects, land surveyors, interior designers, etc. The more technically complex the manuscript is the happier we are. We love equations, tables of data, complex illustrations, mathematics, etc. In technical/professional book publishing, it isn't always obvious to us if a market exists. We can judge the quality of a manuscript, but the author should make some effort to convince us that a market exists. Facts, figures, and estimates about the market—and marketing ideas from the author—will help sell us on the work."

**PROMPT PUBLICATIONS**, Howard W. Sams & Co., 2647 Waterfront Parkway E. Dr., Indianapolis IN 46214-2041. (317)298-5400. Fax: (317)298-5604. E-mail: cdrake@in.net. Website: http://www.hwsams.com. **Acquisitions:** Loretta L. Yates, managing editor. Publishes trade paperback originals and reprints. **Publishes 30 titles/year. Receives 50-75 queries and 30 mss/year. 40% of books from first-time authors; 90% from unagented writers. Pays royalty on retail price based on author's experience. Advance varies.** Publishes book 1 year after acceptance of ms. Reports in 2 months on queries, 4 months on proposals, 6 months or more on mss. Book catalog free.
- "Our mission is to produce quality and reliable electronics technology publications in either book or CD-ROM form, to meet the needs of the engineer, technician, hobbyist and average consumer." Currently emphasizing cutting-edge electronics technology. De-emphasizing electronics project books.

**Nonfiction:** How-to, reference, technical, textbook. Subjects include audio/visual, computers/electronics, electronics repair, energy, science (electricity). "Books should be written for beginners *and* experts, hobbyists *and* professionals. We do not publish books about software. We like manuscripts about cutting-edge technology, household electronics, professional electronics, troubleshooting and repair, component cross-references and how to create or assemble various electronic devices." Established authors query; new authors send complete ms or proposal with SASE. Reviews artwork/photos as part of ms package. Send photocopies or sketches ("we have technicians to produce illustrations if necessary").
**Recent Title(s):** *Semiconductor Cross Reference on CD-ROM*, by Howard W. Sams.
**Tips:** Audience is trade consumers, electronics/technical hobbyists, professionals needing reference books, and technical schools. "Please keep in mind that most technical books have a short shelf life, and write accordingly. Remember, also, that it takes a while for a book to be published, so keep notes on updating your material when the book is ready to print. When submitting, above all, *be patient*. It can take up to a year for a publisher to decide whether or not to publish your book."

**[N] [★] PROSTAR PUBLICATIONS INC.**, 3 Church Circle, #109, Annapolis MD 21401. (310)577-1975. Fax: (310)577-9272. Website: http://www.nauticalbooks.com. **Acquisitions:** Peter Griffes, president (marine-related/how-to/business); Cathryn Pisarski, editor (history/memoirs). Estab. 1965. Publishes trade paperback originals. **Publishes 35 titles/year; imprint publishes 10-15. Receives 60 queries and 25 mss/year. 50% of books from first-time authors; 100% from unagented writers. Pays 15% royalty on wholesale price. Rarely offers advance.** Publishes book 1 year after acceptance of ms. Accepts simultaneous submissions. Reports in 1 month on queries, 3 months on proposals. Book catalog on website.
- "Originally, ProStar published only nautical books. At present, however, we are expanding. Any quality nonfiction book would be of interest."

**Imprints:** Lighthouse Press (Peter Griffes).
**Nonfiction:** Coffee table book, how-to, illustrated book, reference, technical. Subjects include art/architecture, business/

economics, history, memoirs, nature/environment, nautical, travel. Query. Reviews artwork/photos as part of ms package. Send photocopies.

**Recent Titles:** *A Practical Guide to Coastal Navigation*, by Jeff Markell (nautical book)

**Tips:** "We prefer to work directly with the author; we seldom work with agents. Send in a well-written query letter, and we will give your book serious consideration."

**PRUETT PUBLISHING**, 7464 Arapahoe Rd., Suite A-9, Boulder CO 80303. (303)449-4919. Fax: (303)443-9019. E-mail: pruettbks@aol.com. Publisher: Jim Pruett. **Acquisitions:** Robert Sheldon, editor. Estab. 1959. Publishes hardcover paperback and trade paperback originals and reprints. **Publishes 10-15 titles/year. 60% of books are from first-time authors; 100% from unagented writers. Pays 10-12% royalty on net income.** Publishes book 18 months after acceptance of ms. Accepts simultaneous submissions. Reports in 2 months on queries. Book catalog and ms guidelines free.

    ○┐ Pruett Publishing strives to convey to our customers and readers a respect of the American West, in particular the spirit, traditions, and attitude of the region. "We publish books in the following subject areas: outdoor recreation, regional history, environment and nature travel and culture."

**Nonfiction:** Regional history, guidebooks, nature, biography. Subjects include Western Americana, archaeology (Native American), Western history, nature/environment, recreation (outdoor), regional/ethnic cooking/foods (Native American, Mexican, Spanish), regional travel, regional sports (cycling, hiking, fishing). "We are looking for nonfiction manuscripts and guides that focus on the Rocky Mountain West." Submit proposal package. Reviews artwork/photos and formal proposal as part of ms package.

**Recent Title(s):** *Colorado Nature Almanac: A Month-by-Month Guide to the State's Wildlife and Wild Places*, by Stephen R. Jones and Ruth Carol Cusman.

**Tips:** "There has been a movement away from large publisher's mass market books and towards small publisher's regional interest books, and in turn distributors and retail outlets are more interested in small publishers. Authors don't need to have a big name to have a good publisher. Look for similar books that you feel are well produced—consider design, editing, overall quality and contact those publishers. Get to know several publishers, and find the one that feels right—trust your instincts."

**PUFFIN BOOKS**, Penguin Putnam Inc., 345 Hudson St., New York NY 10014-3657. (212)366-2000. Website: http://www.penguin.com/childrens. President/Publisher: Tracy Tang. **Acquisitions:** Sharyn November, senior editor; Kristin Gilson, executive editor; Joy Peskin, assistant editor. Publishes trade paperback originals and reprints. **Publishes 175-200 titles/year. Receives 300 queries and mss/year. 1% of books by first-time authors; 5% from unagented writers. Royalty and advance vary.** Publishes book 1 year after acceptance of ms. Accepts simultaneous submissions, if so noted. Reports in 1 month on mss. Book catalog for 9×12 SASE with 7 first-class stamps; send request to Marketing Department.

    ○┐ Puffin Books publishes high-end trade paperbacks and paperback reprints for preschool children, beginning and middle readers, and young adults.

**Imprint(s):** PaperStar.

**Nonfiction:** Biography, children's/juvenile, illustrated book, young children's concept books (counting, shapes, colors). Subjects include education (for teaching concepts and colors, not academic), women in history. " 'Women in history' books interest us." Query. *No unsolicited mss.*

**Fiction:** Picture books, young adult novels, middle grade and easy-to-read grades 1-3. "We publish mostly paperback reprints. We do few original titles." Query. *No unsolicited mss.*

**Tips:** "Our audience ranges from little children 'first books' to young adult (ages 14-16). An original idea has the best luck."

**PURDUE UNIVERSITY PRESS**, 1207 South Campus Courts, Bldg. E, West Lafayette IN 47907-1207. (765)494-2038. **Acquisitions:** Thomas Bacher, director (technology, business, veterinary medicine, philosophy); Margaret Hunt, managing editor (Central European studies, regional, literature). Estab. 1960. Publishes hardcover and trade paperback originals and trade paperback reprints. **Publishes 14-20 titles/year. Receives 600 submissions/year. Pays 7½-15% royalty.** Publishes book 9 months after acceptance. Reports in 2 months. Book catalog and ms guidelines for 9×12 SASE.

    ○┐ "We look for books that look at the world as a whole and offer new thoughts and insights into the standard debate." Currently emphasizing technology, human-animal issues, business. De-emphasizing literary studies.

**Nonfiction:** "We publish work of quality scholarship and titles with regional (Midwest) flair. Especially interested in innovative contributions to the social sciences and humanities that break new barriers and provide unique views on

**FOR EXPLANATIONS OF THESE SYMBOLS,**
**SEE THE INSIDE FRONT AND BACK COVERS OF THIS BOOK.**

current topics. Expanding into veterinary medicine, engineering and business topics. Always looking for new authors who show creativity and thoroughness of research." Print and electronic projects accepted. Query before submitting.
**Poetry:** One book selected each year by competition. Send SASE for guidelines.
**Recent Title(s):** *Seeds of Hope: An Engineer's WWII Leters*, by William Sabel (nonfiction); *Murderer's Row*, by Edwin Schorb (poetry).

**G.P. PUTNAM'S SONS**, (Adult Trade), Penguin Putnam, Inc., 375 Hudson, New York NY 10014. (212)366-2000. Fax: (212)366-2666. Website: http://www.putnam.com. **Acquisitions:** Acquisitions Editor. Publishes hardcover and trade paperback originals. **5% of books from first-time authors; none from unagented writers. Pays variable advance on retail price.** Accepts simultaneous submissions. Reports in 6 months on queries. Request book catalog through mail order department. Manuscript guidelines free.
**Imprint(s): Perigee, Price Stern Sloan, Putnam** (children's), **Jeremy P. Tarcher**.
**Nonfiction:** Biography, celebrity-related topics, contemporary affairs, cookbook, self-help. Subjects include animals, business/economics, child guidance/parenting, cooking/foods/nutrition, health/medicine, military/war, nature/environment, religion/inspirational, science, sports, travel, women's issues/studies. Query with SASE. *No unsolicited mss.*
**Fiction:** Adventure, literary, mainstream/contemporary, mystery, suspense, women's. Query with synopsis, *brief* writing sample (the shorter the better) and SASE. Prefers agented submissions.
**Recent Title(s):** *Lindbergh*, by A. Scott Berg (nonfiction); *Rainbow Six*, by Tom Clancy (adventure).

**G.P. PUTNAM'S SONS BOOKS FOR YOUNG READERS**, Penguin Putnam Books for Young Readers, Penguin Putnam Inc., 345 Hudson St., New York NY 10014. (212)414-3610. **Acquisitions:** Manuscript editor. Publishes hardcover originals. **Publishes 40 titles/year. Receives 2,500 submissions/year. 20% of books from first-time authors; 30% from unagented writers. Pays standard royalty. Advance negotiable.** Publishes book 2 years after acceptance of ms. Reports in 2 months on queries and unsolicited mss.
**Fiction:** Children's picture books (ages 3-8); middle-grade fiction and illustrated chapter books (ages 7-10); older middle-grade fiction (ages 10-14) some young adult (ages 14-18). Particularly interested in middle-grade fiction with strong voice, literary quality, high interest for audience, poignancy, humor, unusual settings or plots. Historical fiction OK. Unsolicited mss accepted for picture books only; query first for fiction. Always include SASE or no response. No science fiction, no series or activity books, no board books.
**Recent Title(s):** *Cowboy Bunnies*, by Christine Loomis, illustrated by Ora Eitan (picture book); *Rules of the Road*, by Joan Bauer (middle-grade novel).

**QUE**, Macmillan Computer Publishing USA, 201 W. 103rd St., Indianapolis IN 46290. (317)581-3500. Website: http://www.mcp.com/que/. Vice President/Publisher: James Price. **Acquisitions:** Holly Allender, acquisitions editor (Linut/Unity networking, programming, ERP); Gretchen Ganser, acquisitions editor (Linut/Unity networking, programming, ERP); Karen Whitehouse, acquisitions editor (applications, web, graphics, MacIntosh); Jamie Milazzo, acquisitions editor (applications, web, graphics, MacIntosh); Stephanie McComb, acquisitions editor (Idiot's Guides, Easy Series, Quick Reference Series); Jiri Byus, acquisitions editor (Windows 2000, hardware, certification); Tracy Williams, acquisitions editor (Windows 2000, hardware, certification). Publishes hardcover, trade paperback and mass market paperback originals and reprints. **Publishes 200 titles/year. 85% of books from unagented writers. Pays variable royalty on wholesale price or makes work-for-hire arrangements. Advance varies.** Accepts simultaneous submissions. Reports in 1 month on proposals. Catalog and ms guidelines free.
**Nonfiction:** Computer books.
**Recent Title(s):** *Easy Windows '98*.

**QUEST BOOKS**, Theosophical Publishing House, P.O. Box 270, Wheaton IL 60189. (630)665-0130. Fax: (630)665-8791. E-mail: questbooks@aol.com. Website: htpp://www.theosophica.org. **Acquisitions:** Brenda Rosen, executive editor. Publishes hardcover originals and trade paperback originals and reprints. **Publishes 12-15 titles/year. Receives 500 queries and 100 mss/year. 50% of books from first-time authors; 75% from unagented writers. Pays 10-13% on wholesale price. Offers $3,000-10,000 advance.** Publishes book 20 months after acceptance of ms. Accepts simultaneous submissions. Reports in 1 month on queries, 2 months on proposals, 3 months on mss. Book catalog and ms guidelines free.
    **O—π** "TPH is dedicated to the promotion of the unity of humanity and the encouragement of the study of religion, philosophy and science, to the end that we may better understand ourselves and our place in the universe."
**Nonfiction:** Biography, illustrated book, self-help. Subjects include anthropology/archaeology, art/architecture, health/medicine, music/dance, nature/environment, travel, self-development, self-help, philosophy (holistic), psychology (transpersonal), Eastern and Western religions, theosophy, comparative religion, men's and women's spirituality, Native American spirituality, holistic implications in science, health and healing, yoga, meditation, astrology. "Our speciality is high-quality spiritual nonfiction with a self-help aspect. Great writing is a must. We seldom publish 'personal spiritual awakening' stories. No submissions accepted that do not fit the needs outlined above." Accepts nonfiction translations. Query or submit proposal package, including author bio, contents, sample chapter and SASE. Reviews artwork/photos as part of ms package. Send photocopies.
**Recent Title(s):** *The Forsaken Garden*, by Nancy Ryley (health/spirituality).
**Tips:** "Our audience includes the 'New Age' community, seekers in all religions, general public, professors, and health professionals. Read a few recent Quest titles. Know our books and our company goals. Explain how your book or proposal

relates to other Quest titles. Quest gives preference to writers with established reputations/successful publications."

**QUILL DRIVER BOOKS/WORD DANCER PRESS**, 8386 N. Madsen Ave., Clovis CA 93611. (559)322-5917. Fax: (559)322-5967. E-mail: sbm12@csufresno.edu. **Acquisitions:** Stephen Blake Mettee, publisher. Publishes hardcover and trade paperback originals and reprints. **Publishes 10-12 titles/year. (Quill Driver Books: 4/year, Word Dancer Press: 6-8/year). 50% of books from first-time authors; 95% from unagented writers. Pays 4-10% royalty on retail price. Offers $500-5,000 advance.** Publishes book 9 months after acceptance. Accepts simultaneous submissions. Reports in 1 month on queries and proposals, 3 months on mss. Book catalog and ms guidelines for #10 SASE.

    **O—** "We publish a modest number of books per year, each of which, we hope, makes a worthwhile contribution to the human community, and we have a little fun along the way." Currently emphasizing books to enhance the lifestyles of those over 50.

**Nonfiction:** Biography, how-to, reference, general nonfiction. Subjects include Californiana, regional, fund-raising, writing. Query with proposal package. Reviews artwork/photos as part of ms package. Send photocopies.

**Recent Title(s):** *The Memory Manual: Ten Simple Things You Can Do To Improve Your Memory after 50.*

**THE QUILT DIGEST PRESS**, NTC/Contemporary Publishing Group, 4255 W. Touhy, Lincolnwood IL 60646. (847)679-5500. Fax: (847)679-2494. **Acquisitions:** Anne Knudsen, executive editor. Publishes hardcover and trade paperback originals. **Publishes 10-12 titles/year. Receives 100 queries and 30 mss/year. 20% of books from first-time authors; 80% from unagented writers. Pays royalty on wholesale price.** Publishes book 1 year after acceptance of ms. Accepts simultaneous submissions. Reports in 2 months. Book catalog and ms guidelines free.

    **O—** Quilt Digest Press publishes quilting and sewing craft books.

**Nonfiction:** How-to. Subjects include hobbies, crafts/quilting. Submit outline, bio, sample, photos and SASE. Reviews artwork/photos as part of ms package. Send color photocopies.

**Recent Title(s):** *Circles of the East*, by Kumik Sudo.

**QUITE SPECIFIC MEDIA GROUP LTD.**, 260 Fifth Ave., Suite 703, New York NY 10001. (212)725-5377. Fax: (212)725-8506. E-mail: info@quitespecificmedia.com. Website: http://www.quitespecificmedia.com. **Acquisitions:** Ralph Pine, editor-in-chief. Estab. 1967. Publishes hardcover originals, trade paperback originals and reprints. **Publishes 12 titles/year. Receives 300 queries/year and 100 mss/year. 75% of books from first-time authors; 85% from unagented writers. Pays royalty on wholesale price.** Advance varies. Publishes book 18 months after acceptance. Accepts simultaneous submissions. Reports "as quickly as possible." Book catalog and ms guidelines free.

    **O—** Quite Specific Media Group is an umbrella company of five imprints specializing in costume and fashion, theater and design.

**Imprint(s):** Costume & Fashion Press, Drama Publishers, By Design Press, Entertainment Pro, Jade Rabbit

**Nonfiction:** Texts, guides, manuals, directories, reference and multimedia—for and about performing arts theory and practice: acting, directing; voice, speech, movement; makeup, masks, wigs; costumes, sets, lighting, sound; design and execution; technical theater, stagecraft, equipment; stage management; producing; arts management, all varieties; business and legal aspects; film, radio, television, cable, video; theory, criticism, reference; playwriting; theater and performance history; costume and fashion. Accepts nonfiction and technical works in translations also. Query with 1-3 sample chapters and SASE; no complete mss. Reviews artwork/photos as part of ms package.

**Recent Title(s):** Recently co-published books with the Victoria and Albert Museum, London.

**RACE POINT PRESS**, P.O. Box 770, Provincetown MA 02657. Vice President: Roselyn Callahan. Publishes trade paperback originals. **Publishes 5 titles/year. Pays 7-12% royalty on wholesale price or makes outright purchase.** Reports in 2 months on proposals.

**Nonfiction:** How-to, reference, self-help, technical. Subjects include art/architecture, health/medicine, aging. "Our focus is on books for the senior market which highlight available programs or practical advice on accessing needed services." Query or submit outline or proposal package, including 2 sample chapters and probable completion date; author biography. *All unsolicited mss returned unopened.*

**Recent title(s):** *The Medicare Answer Book*, 3rd ed., by Connacht Cash (technical).

**RAGGED MOUNTAIN PRESS**, International Marine/The McGraw-Hill Companies, P.O. Box 220, Camden ME 04843-0220. (207)236-4837. Fax: (207)236-6314. **Acquisitions:** Thomas McCarthy, acquisitions editor; Jonathan Eaton, editorial director. Estab. 1969. Publishes hardcover and trade paperback originals and reprints. **Publishes 40 titles/year; imprint publishes 15, remainder are International Marine. Receives 200 queries and 100 mss/year. 30% of books from first-time authors; 90% from unagented writers. Pays 10-15% royalty on net price. Offers advance.** Publishes book 1 year after acceptance of ms. Accepts simultaneous submissions. Reports in 1 month on queries. *Writer's Market*

---

**TO RECEIVE REGULAR TIPS AND UPDATES** about writing and Writer's Digest publications via e-mail, send an e-mail with "SUBSCRIBE NEWSLETTER" in the body of the message to "newsletter-request@writersdigest.com."

recommends allowing 2 months for reply. Book catalog for $9 \times 12$ SAE with 10 first-class stamps. Manuscript guidelines for #10 SASE.

O→ Ragged Mountain Press publishes "books that take you off the beaten path."
**Nonfiction:** Outdoor-related how-to, guidebooks, essays. Subjects include camping, fly fishing, snowshoeing, backpacking, canoeing, outdoor cookery, skiing, snowboarding, survival skills and wilderness know-how, birdwatching, natural history, climbing and kayaking. "Ragged Mountain publishes nonconsumptive outdoor and environmental issues books of literary merit or unique appeal. Be familiar with the existing literature. Find a subject that hasn't been done or has been done poorly, then explore it in detail and from all angles." Query with outline and 1 sample chapter. Reviews artwork/photos as part of ms package. Send photocopies.
**Recent Title(s):** *The Ragged Mountain Press Pocket Guide to Wilderness Medicine and First Aid*, by Paul G. Gill, Jr., M.D.

**⊠ RAINBOW BOOKS, INC.**, P.O. Box 430, Highland City FL 33846. (941)648-4420. Fax: (941)648-4420. E-mail: rbibooks@aol.com. **Acquisitons:** Betsy A. Lampe, editorial director. Estab. 1979. Publishes hardcover and trade paperback originals. **Publishes 12-15 titles/year. Receives 300 queries and 100 mss/year. 90% of books from first-time authors; 80% from unagented writers. Pays 6-12% royalty on retail price. Offers advance.** Publishes book 1 year after acceptance of ms. Accepts simultaneous submissions. Reports in 1 month on queries and proposals, 2 months on mss. Manuscript guidelines for #10 SASE.

O→ Rainbow Books publishes self-help/how-to books for the layman, and is also interested in seeing the same type of nonfiction books for ages 8 to 14 years. "We have begun a limited line of mystery fiction, up to approximately 80,000 words. We publish no other fiction."
**Nonfiction:** Biography, children's/juvenile, how-to, self-help. Subjects include animals, business/economics, child guidance/parenting, education, gardening, hobbies, money/finance, nature/environment, philosophy, psychology, recreation, science, sociology, sports, women's issues/studies. "We want books that provide authoritative answers to questions in layman language. We have also begun a list of 3rd-to-8th grade titles for young people along the same lines as our adult general nonfiction. Writers must include background credentials for having written the book they propose." Query with SASE. Reviews artwork/photos as part of ms package. Send photocopies.
**Fiction:** "We will publish 2 mystery fiction titles in 1999. Mainly, we're looking for well-written mystery books that deserve to be published." Submit synopsis and complete ms and SASE with sufficient postage.
**Recent Title(s):** *Learning Disabilities 101: A Primer for Parents*, by Mary Cathryn Haller (nonfiction); *Revenge of the Gypsy Queen*, by Kris Neri (mystery fiction).
**Tips:** "We are addressing an adult population interested in answers to questions, and also 8- to 14-year-olds of the same mindset. Be professional in presentation of queries and manuscripts, and always provide a return mailer with proper postage attached in the event the materials do not fit our list."

**RAINBOW PUBLISHERS**, P.O. Box 261129, San Diego CA 92196. (619)271-7600. **Acquisitions:** Christy Allen, editor. Estab. 1951. **Publishes 20 titles/year. Receives 250 queries and 100 mss/year. 50% of books from first-time authors. Pays flat fee or royalty based on wholesale price.** Publishes book 3 years after acceptance of ms. Accepts simultaneous submissions. Reports in 3 months on queries, proposals and mss. Book catalog for $9 \times 12$ SAE with 2 first-class stamps. Manuscript guidelines for #10 SASE.

O→ "Rainbow Publishers strives to publish Bible-based materials that contribute to, inspire spiritual growth and development in children and adults and meet the needs of readers in the Christian realm, preferably evangelical." Currently emphasizing women's interests, 5th- and 6th-grade interests. De-emphasizing men's issues, skits and plays.
**Imprint(s):** Rainbow (reproducible activity books); Legacy (nonfiction Bible-teaching books for kids and adults).
**Nonfiction:** How-to, textbook. "We publish reproducible activity books for Christian teachers to use in teaching the Bible to children ages 2-12 and Bible-teaching books for children and adults." Query with outline, sample pages, age level, introduction. "We use freelance artists. Send a query and photocopies of art samples."
**Recent Title(s):** *Home & Back*, by Linda Washington (reproducible series).
**Tips:** "We are seeking manuscripts for *both* the children's and adult Christian book market, focusing on Christian education."

**Ⓐ RANDOM HOUSE CHILDREN'S PUBLISHING**, Random House, Inc., 201 E. 50th St., New York NY 10022. (212)751-2600. Fax: (212)940-7685. Website: http://www.randomhouse/com/kids. Vice President/Publishing Director: Kate Klimo. **Acquisitions:** Ruth Koeppel, senior editor/licensing director (Stepping Stones); Heidi Kilgras, editor (Step into Reading); Stephanie St. Pierre, senior editor (Picturebacks). Estab. 1935. Publishes hardcover, trade paperback, and mass market paperback originals and reprints. **Publishes 200 titles/year. Receives 1,000 queries/year. Pays 1-6% royalty or makes outright purchase. Advance varies.** Publishes book 1 year after acceptance of ms. Accepts simultaneous submissions. Reports in 3 weeks-6 months. Book catalog free.

O→ "Random House Books aim to create books that nurture the hearts and minds of children, providing and promoting quality books and a rich variety of media that entertain and educate readers from 6 months to 12 years."
**Imprint(s):** Random House Books for Young Readers, **Alfred A. Knopf and Crown Children's Books**, Dragonfly.
**Nonfiction:** Children's/juvenile. Subjects include animal, history, nature/environment, popular culture, science, sports. *Agented submissions only. No unsolicited mss.*

**Fiction:** Humor, juvenile, mystery, picture books, young adult. "Familiarize yourself with our list. We look for original, unique stories. Do something that hasn't been done." *Agented submissions only. No unsolicited mss.*
**Recent Title(s):** *Shooting Stars: The Women of Pro Basketball*, by Bill Gutman; *The Mermaids' Lullaby*, by Kate Spohn, (glitter book about mermaids).

**RANDOM HOUSE, INC.**, 201 E. 50th St., New York NY 10022. (212)751-2600. Website: http://www.randomhouse. com.
**Imprint(s):** *Ballantine Publishing Group:* **Ballantine**, Columbine, **Del Rey, Fawcett** (Crest, Gold Medal, Juniper), **House of Collectibles**, Ivy Books, Library of Contemporary Thought, One World. *Bantam:* **Bantam Books, Crime Line, Fanfare, Spectra, Broadway Books.** *Crown Publishing Group:* Bell Tower, **Clarkson Potter,** Crown Publishers, Harmony Books, Living Language, Park Lane Press, Three Rivers Press. *Dell:* **Delacorte Press, Delta, Dell Publishing Island, Dell Trade Paperbacks, Dial Press, Delta Trade Paperbacks.** *Doubleday:* **Anchor Books, Currency, Doubleday Religious Division, Image Books, Main Street Books, Nan A. Talese.** *Knopf Publishing Group:* Everyman's Library, **Alfred A. Knopf, Pantheon, Schocken, Vintage Books.** *Random House Audio Publishing Group:* BDD Audio Publishing, Random House Audio Publishing. *Random House Children's Publishing:* **Bantam Books for Young Readers, Crown Books for Young Readers,** CTW Publishing, **Delacorte Press Books for Young Readers, Doubleday Books for Young Readers,** Dragonfly, First Choice Chapter Books, **Knopf Books for Young Readers,** Laurel-Leaf, Picture Yearling, **Random House Children's Publishing,** Skylark, Starfire, Yearling. *Random House Information Group:* Princeton Review, Random House Reference and Information Publishing, **Times Books.** *Random House Trade Publishing Group:* Random House Adult Trade Books, Villard Books, Modern Library. *Random House Diversified Publishing Group:* Children's Classics, Crescent Books, Derrydale, Gramercy Books, Jelly Bean Press, Random House Large Print Publishing, Wings Books. *Fodor's Travel Publications:* **Fodor's.** *Random House New Media. Random House Direct Marketing. Random House International.*

**RAWSON ASSOCIATES**, Simon & Schuster, 1230 Avenue of the Americas, New York NY 10020. (212)632-4941. **Acquisitions:** Eleanor Rawson, publisher. Publishes hardcover originals. **Publishes 5 titles/year. Receives "hundreds" of queries/year. Less than 10% of books from first-time authors. Pays royalty. Offers advance.** *Writer's Market* recommends allowing 2 months for a reply.
  O➡ Rawson Associates publishes nonfiction. "We are interested in original concepts that deal with issues of concern to many people."
**Nonfiction:** Subjects include business, contemporary lifestyle concerns, health/medicine, psychology. "We are looking for author's with strong credentials and ability to assist in marketing work." Query or submit outline with 1 sample chapter and credentials with SASE. Reviews artwork/photos as part of the ms package. Send photocopies.
**Recent Title(s):** *Buffettology*, by Mary Buffett and David Clark.

**RED HEN PRESS**, Valentine Publishing Group, P.O. Box 902582, Palmdale CA 93590-2582. Phone/fax: (818)831-0649. E-mail: redhen@vpg.net. Website: http://www.vpg.net. **Acquisitions:** Mark E. Cull, publisher/editor (fiction); Katherine Gale, poetry editor (poetry, literary fiction). Estab. 1993. Publishes trade paperback originals. **Publishes 6 titles/year. Receives 2,000 queries and 500 mss/year. 10% of books from first-time authors; 90% from unagented writers. Pays 10% royalty on retail price.** Publishes book 1 year after acceptance of ms. Accepts simultaneous submissions. Reports in 1 month on queries, 2 months on proposals, 3 months on mss. Book catalog and ms guidelines free.
  O➡ Red Hen Press specializes in literary fiction and poetry.
**Nonfiction:** Biography, children's/juvenile, cookbooks. Subjects include anthropology/archaeology, ethnic, gay/lesbian, language/literature, travel, women's issues/studies. Query with SASE. Reviews artwork/photos as part of ms package. Send photocopies.
**Fiction:** Ethnic, experimental, feminist, gay/lesbian, historical, literary, mainstream/contemporary, poetry, poetry in translation, short story collections. "We prefer high-quality literary fiction." Query with SASE.
**Poetry:** Query with 5 sample poems.
**Recent Titles:** *Highway Trade*, by John Domini (short story collection); *The Sun Takes Us Away*, by Benjamin Sultam (lyric poetry).
**Tips:** "Audience reads poetry, literary fiction, intelligent nonfiction. If you have an agent, we may be too small since we don't pay advances. Write well. Send queries first. Be willing to help promote your own book."

**REFERENCE PRESS INTERNATIONAL**, P.O. Box 4126, Greenwich CT 06831. (203)622-6860. Fax: (203)622-5983. E-mail: ml2626@aol.com. **Acquisitions:** Cheryl Lacoff, senior editor. Publishes hardcover and trade paperback originals. **Publishes 6 titles/year. Receives 50 queries and 20 mss/year. 75% of books from first-time authors; 90% from unagented writers. Pays royalty or makes outright purchase. Advance determined by project.** Publishes book 6 months after acceptance. Accepts simultaneous submissions. Reports in 3 months. Book catalog for #10 SASE.
  O➡ Reference Press specializes in instructional, reference and how-to titles.
**Nonfiction:** How-to, illustrated book, multimedia (audio, video, CD-ROM), reference, technical, educational, instructional. Subjects include Americana, art/architecture, business/economics, hobbies, money/finance, gardening, photography, anything related to the arts or crafts field. "Follow the guidelines as stated concerning subjects and types of books we're looking for." Query with outline, 1-3 sample chapters and SASE. Reviews artwork/photos as part of ms package. Send photocopies.

**Recent Title(s):** *Who's Who in the Peace Corps*, (alumni directory).

**REFERENCE SERVICE PRESS**, 5000 Windplay Dr., Suite 4, El Dorado Hills CA 95762. (916)939-9620. Fax: (916)939-9626. E-mail: findaid@aol.com. Website: http://www.rspfunding.com. **Acquisitions:** Stuart Hauser, acquisitions editor. Estab. 1977. Publishes hardcover originals. **Publishes 10-20 titles/year. 100% of books from unagented writers. Pays 10% or higher royalty.** Publishes book 6 months after acceptance. Accepts simultaneous submissions. Reports in 2 months. Book catalog for #10 SASE.

O→ "We are interested only in directories and monographs dealing with financial aid."

**Nonfiction:** Reference for financial aid seekers. Subjects include education, ethnic, military/war, women's issues/studies, disabled. Submit outline and sample chapters.

**Recent Title(s):** *College Student's Guide to Merit and Other No-Need Funding, 1998-2000.*

**Tips:** "Our audience consists of librarians, counselors, researchers, students, re-entry women, scholars and other fund-seekers."

**A** **REGAN BOOKS**, HarperCollins, 10 E. 53rd St., New York NY 10022. (212)207-7400. Fax: (212)207-6951. Website: http://www.harpercollins.com. **Acquisitions:** Judith Regan, president/publisher. Estab. 1994. Publishes hardcover and trade paperback originals. **Publishes 30 titles/year. Receives 7,500 queries and 5,000 mss/year. Pays royalty on retail price. Advance varies.** Publishes book 1 year after acceptance of ms. Accepts simultaneous submissions. Reports in 3 months on proposals.

O→ Regan Books publishes general fiction and nonfiction: biography, self-help, style and gardening books, and is known for contemporary topics and controversial authors and titles.

**Nonfiction:** Biography, coffee table book, cookbook, gift book, illustrated book, reference, self-help. All subjects. *Agented submissions only. No unsolicited mss.* Reviews artwork as part of ms package. Send photocopies.

**Fiction:** All categories. *Agented submissions only. No unsolicited mss.*

**Recent Title(s):** *I Know This Much Is True*, by Wally Lamb.

**A** **REGNERY PUBLISHING, INC.**, Eagle Publishing, One Massachusetts Ave., NW, Washington DC 20003. Fax: (202)546-8759. Publisher: Alfred S. Regnery. Executive Editor: Harry Crocker. Managing Editor: David Dortman. **Acquisitions:** Submissions Editor. Estab. 1947. Publishes hardcover and paperback originals and reprints. **Publishes 30 titles/year. 0% of books from unagented writers. Pays 8-15% royalty on retail price. Offers $0-50,000 advance.** Publishes book 1 year after acceptance. No fax submissions. Reports in 6 months on proposals.

O→ Regnery publishes conservative, well-written, well-produced, sometimes controversial books. Currently emphasizing health books.

**Imprint(s):** Gateway Editions, LifeLine Press.

**Nonfiction:** Biography, business/economics, current affairs, health/medicine, history. *Agented submissions only. No unsolicited mss.*

**Recent Title(s):** *Gore: A Political Biography*, by Rob Zelnick (nonfiction); *The Adventures of Inspector Lestrade*, by M.J. Trow (fiction).

**Tips:** "We seek high-impact, headline-making, bestseller treatments of pressing current issues by established experts in the field."

**RENAISSANCE BOOKS**, Renaissance Media, 5858 Wilshire Blvd., Suite 200, Los Angeles CA 90036. (323)939-1840. **Acquisitions:** Kimbria Hays, production coordinator; Arthur Morey, managing editor; James Robert Parish, editor (show business); Richard F.X. O'Connor, editor (general nonfiction); Joe McNeely, editor (New Age/psychology). Publishes hardcover and trade paperback originals. **Publishes 30 titles/year. Receives 300 queries/year. 10% of books from first-time authors; 30% from unagented writers. Pays royalty on retail price. Advance varies widely.** Publishes book 6 months after acceptance of ms. Accepts simultaneous submissions. Reports in 2 months on proposals. Book catalog free.

O→ Renaissance publishes a wide range of nonfiction trade books.

**Nonfiction:** Biography, cookbook, how-to, reference, self-help. Subjects include Americana, animals, business and economics, child guidance/parenting, cooking/foods/nutrition, government/politics, health/medicine, history, hobbies, money/finance, psychology, recreation, sociology, sports, entertainment, show business. Submit outline and 2 sample chapter with SASE.

**Recent Title(s):** *Powerful Prayers*, by Larry King (religious).

**Tips:** "Include as much marketing information as possible in your proposal. Why will your book sell in today's marketplace?"

**REPUBLIC OF TEXAS PRESS**, Wordware Publishing, Inc., 2320 Los Rios Blvd., Suite 200, Plano TX 75074. (972)423-0090. Fax: (972)881-9147. E-mail: gbivona@wordware.com. Website: http://www.wordware.com. **Acquisitions:** Ginnie Bivona, Diane Stultz, James S. Hill. Publishes trade and mass market paperback originals. **Publishes 25-30 titles/year. Receives 400 queries and 300 mss/year. 80% of books from unagented writers. Pays 8-12% royalty on wholesale price.** Publishes book 9 months after acceptance of ms. Reports in 2 months. Book catalog and ms guidelines for SASE.

O→ Republic of Texas Press specializes in Texas and Southwestern humor, history, trivia, cookbooks and ghost stories. Also interested in specialized travel books.

**Nonfiction:** History, Texana material, general interest. Subjects include Old West, Southwest, cookbooks, military, women of the West, ghost stories, humor, biography. Submit TOC, 2 sample chapters, target audience and author bio.
**Recent Title(s):** *Fixxin' to Be Texan*, by Helen Bryant; *Exploring Texas with Children*, by Sharry Bruckner.

**RESOURCE PUBLICATIONS, INC.**, 160 E. Virginia St., Suite #290, San Jose CA 95112-5876. (408)286-8505. Fax: (408)287-8748. E-mail: orders@rpinet.com. Website: http://www.rpinet.com/ml/ml.html. **Acquisitions:** Nick Wagner, editorial director (religious books). Estab. 1973. Publishes trade paperback originals. **Produces 20 titles/year. 30% of books from first-time authors; 95% from unagented writers. Pays 8% royalty (for a first project). Rarely offers advance.** Reports in 10 weeks. Catalog for 9 × 12 SAE with postage for 10 ozs. Manuscript guidelines for #10 SASE.
    **O—** Resource Publications publishes books to help liturgists and ministers make the imaginative connection between liturgy and life.
**Nonfiction:** How-to, self-help. Subjects include child guidance/parenting, education, music/dance, religion, professional ministry resources for worship, education, clergy and other leaders, for use in Roman Catholic and mainline Protestant churches. Submit proposal. Reviews artwork as part of freelance ms package.
**Fiction:** Fables, anecdotes, faith sharing stories, any stories useful in preaching or teaching. Query.
**Recent Title(s):** *Nun Better* (short stories); *Dreams That Help You Mourn*, by Lois Hendricks (dreams in grieving).
**Tips:** "We are publishers and secondarily we are book packagers. Pitch your project to us for publication first. If we can't take it on on that basis, we may be able to take it on as a packaging and production project."

**RESURRECTION PRESS, LTD.**, P.O. Box 248, Williston Park NY 11596. (516)742-5686. Fax: (516)746-6872. **Acquisitions:** Emilie Mackney, publisher. Publishes trade paperback originals and reprints. **Publishes 6-8 titles/year; imprint publishes 4 titles/year. Receives 100 queries and 100 mss/year. 25% of books from first-time authors; 100% from unagented writers. Pays 5-10% royalty on retail price. Offers $250-2,000 advance.** Publishes book 1 year after acceptance of ms. Accepts simultaneous submissions. Reports in 1 month on queries and proposals, 2 months on mss. Book catalog and ms guidelines free.
    **O—** Resurrection Press publishes religious, devotional and inspirational titles.
**Imprint(s):** Spirit Life Series.
**Nonfiction:** Self-help. Religious subjects. Wants mss of no more than 200 double-spaced typewritten pages. Query with outline and 2 sample chapters. Reviews artwork/photos as part of ms package. Send photocopies.
**Recent Title(s):** *The Joy of Being a Eucharistic Minister*, by Mitch Finely.

**FLEMING H. REVELL PUBLISHING**, Baker Book House, P.O. Box 6287, Grand Rapids MI 49516. Fax: (616)676-2315. Website: http://www.bakerbooks.com. **Acquisitions:** Linda Holland, editorial director; Bill Petersen, senior acquisitions editor; Jane Campbell, senior editor (Chosen Books). Estab. 1870. Publishes hardcover, trade paperback and mass market paperback originals and reprints. **Publishes 50 titles/year; imprint publishes 10 titles/year. Receives 750 queries and 1,000 mss/year. 1% of books from first-time authors; 75% from unagented writers. Pays 14-18% royalty on wholesale price.** Publishes book 1 year after acceptance of ms. Accepts simultaneous submissions. Reports in 3 months. Manuscript guidelines for #10 SASE.
    **O—** Revell publishes to the heart (rather than to the head). For 125 years, Revell has been publishing evangelical books for the personal enrichment and spiritual growth of general Christian readers.
**Imprint(s):** Chosen Books, Spire Books.
**Nonfiction:** Biography, coffee table book, how-to, self-help. Subjects include child guidance/parenting, Christian Living. Query with outline and 2 sample chapters.
**Fiction:** Religious. Submit synopsis and 2 sample chapters.
**Recent Title(s):** *God's Guidance*, by Elisabeth Elliot (nonfiction); *A Time of War*, by Gilbert Morris (fiction).

**REVIEW AND HERALD PUBLISHING ASSOCIATION**, 55 W. Oak Ridge Dr., Hagerstown MD 21740. (301)791-7000. **Acquisitions:** Jeannette R. Johnson, acquisitions editor. Estab. 1861. Publishes hardcover, trade paperback and mass market paperback originals and reprints. **Publishes 40-50 titles/year. Receives 200 queries and 350 mss/year. 50% of books from first-time authors; 95% from unagented writers. Pays 7-15% royalty. Offers $500-1,000 advance.** Publishes book 18 months after acceptance of ms. Accepts simultaneous submissions. Reports in 1 month on queries and proposals, 2 months on mss. Book catalog for 10 × 13 SASE. Manuscript guidelines for #10 SASE.
    **O—** "Through print and electronic media, the Review and Herald Publishing Association nurtures a growing relationship with God by providing products that teach and enrich people spiritually, mentally, physically and socially as we near Christ's soon second coming. We belong to the Seventh Day Adventist denomination."
**Nonfiction:** Biography, children's/juvenile, cookbook, gift book, humor, multimedia, reference, self-help, textbook, Christian lifestyle, inspirational. Subjects include animals, anthropology/archaeology, child guidance/parenting, cooking/foods/nutrition, education, health/medicine, history, nature/environment, philosophy, religion, women's issues/studies. Submit proposal package, including 3 sample chapters and cover letter with SASE.
**Fiction:** Adventure, historical, humor, juvenile, mainstream/contemporary, religious, all Christian-living related. Submit synopsis and or 3 sample chapters.
**Recent Title(s):** *The Appearing*, by Penny Estes Wheeler; *Incredible Answers to Prayer*, by Roger Morneau.

◼ **MORGAN REYNOLDS PUBLISHING**, 620 S. Elm St., Suite 384, Greensboro NC 27406. Fax: (336)275-1152. E-mail: morganreynolds@www.morganreynolds.com. Website: http://www.morganreynolds.com. **Acquisitions**: John Riley, editor. Publishes hardcover originals. **Publishes 10-12 titles/year. Receives 200-250 queries and 75-100 mss/year. 50% of books from first-time authors; 100% from unagented writers. Pays 8-12% royalty on wholesale price. Offers $500-1,000 advance.** Publishes book 8 months after acceptance of ms. Accepts simultaneous submissions. Reports in 2 months.

    ○➤ Morgan Reynolds publishes books on young adult biographies, well-known historical and contemporary figures and people and events too often left out of the textbooks. "Our goal is to continue to publish lively, informative and original works of non-fiction." Currently emphasizing biographies of successful business people.

**Nonfiction:** Biography. Subjects include Americana, business/economics, government/politics, history, language/literature, military/war, money/finance, women's issues/studies, all young adult/juvenile oriented. No children's books. "We publish nonfiction for juvenile and young adult readers. We publish titles in our five series: Notable Americans, World Writers, Great Events, Champions of Freedom, Great Athletes—as well as high-quality non-series works. We plan to expand our biography lines. We are interested in well-written books on prominent women from ancient and medieval times." Submit outline, 3 sample chapters with SASE. Reviews artwork/photos as part of ms package. Send photocopies.

**Recent Title(s):** *Bram Stoker: Author of Dracula*, by Nancy Whitelaw.

**Tips:** "Research the markets before submitting. We spend too much time dealing with manuscripts that shouldn't have been submitted."

**RISING TIDE PRESS**, 3831 N. Oracle Rd., Tucson AZ 85705-3254. (520)888-1140. E-mail: rtpress@aol.com. **Acquisitions:** Alice Frier, senior editor (nonfiction, romance); Lee Boojamra, editor/publisher (mystery, science fiction). Estab. 1991. Publishes trade paperback originals. **Publishes 10-15 titles/year. Receives 1,000 queries and 600 mss/year. 75% of books from first-time authors; 100% from unagented writers. Pays 10-15% royalty on wholesale price.** Publishes book 15 months after acceptance. *No* simultaneous submissions. Reports in 1 week on queries, 1 months on proposals, 3 months on mss. Book catalog for $1. Writer's guidelines for #10 SASE.

    ○➤ "Our books are for, by and about lesbian lives. They change lives and help create a better society. We seek to promote social justice and equal rights for lesbians and gay men."

**Nonfiction:** Lesbian nonfiction. Query with outline, entire ms and *large* SASE. *Writer's Market* recommends a query with SASE first. Reviews artwork/photos as part of ms package. Send photocopies.

**Fiction:** Lesbian fiction only. Adventure, erotica, fantasy, historical, horror, humor, literary, mainstream/contemporary, mystery, occult, romance, science fiction, suspense, mixed genres. "Major characters must be lesbian. Primary plot must have lesbian focus and sensibility." Query with synopsis or entire ms and SASE. *Writer's Market* recommends a query with SASE first.

**Recent Title(s):** *No Escape*, by Nancy Sanra.

**Tips:** "We welcome unpublished authors. We do *not* consider agented authors. Any material submitted should be proofed. No multiple submissions."

**ROC BOOKS**, Penguin Putnam Inc., 375 Hudson St., New York NY 10014. (212)366-2000. Website: http://www.penguinputnam.com. **Acquisitions:** Laura Anne Gilman, executive editor; Jennifer Heddle, assistant editor. Publishes mass market, trade and hardcover originals. **Publishes 36 titles/year. Receives 500 queries/year. Pays royalty. Advance negotiable.** Accepts simultaneous submissions. Report in 2-3 months on queries.

    ○➤ "We're looking for books that are a good read, that people will want to pick up time and time again."

**Fiction:** Fantasy, horror, science fiction. "ROC tries to strike a balance between fantasy and science fiction." Query with synopsis and 1-2 sample chapters. *"We discourage unsolicited submissions."*

**Recent Title(s):** *Heir to the Shadows*, by Anne Bishop.

**ROCKBRIDGE PUBLISHING CO.**, Howell Press, P.O. Box 351, Berryville VA 22611-0351. (540)955-3980. Fax: (540)955-4126. E-mail: cwpub@visuallink.com. Website: http://rockbpubl.com. **Acquisitions:** Katherine Tennery, publisher. Estab. 1989. Publishes hardcover original and reprints, trade paperback originals. **Publishes 4-6 titles/year. Pays royalty on wholesale price. No advance.** Reports in 3 months on proposals. Writer's guidelines available on website.

    ○➤ Rockbridge publishes nonfiction books about the Civil War, Virginia tour guides, Virginia/Southern folklore and ghost stories.

**Nonfiction:** "We are developing a series of travel guides to the country roads in various Virginia counties. The self-guided tours include local history, identify geographic features, etc. We are also looking for material about the Civil War, especially biographies, and expanding interests from Virginia to other southern states, notably Georgia." Query with outline, 3 sample chapters, author credentials and SASE.

**Recent Title(s):** *The Burning: Sheridan in the Shenandoah Valley*, by John Heatwole.

**RODALE BOOKS**, Rodale, 400 S. Tenth St., Emmaus PA 18098. Website: http://www.rodalepress.com. Vice President, Active Living Books: Neil Wertheimer. Editorial Director for Health and Fitness Books: Deborah Yost. **Acquisitions:** Sally Reith, acquisitions editor. Estab. 1932. Publishes hardcover originals, trade paperback originals and reprints. **Publishes 75-100 titles/year; imprints publish 10-15 titles/year. Pays 6-15% royalty on retail price.** Publishes book 18 months after acceptance of ms. Accepts simultaneous submissions. Reports in 1 month on queries, 2 months on proposals and mss. Book catalog and ms guidelines free.

○━ "Our mission is to show people how they can use the power of their bodies and minds to make their lives better."

**Imprint(s): Daybreak Books** (Neil Wertheimer, vice president/publisher); Rodale Reach (Susan Clarey, executive editor).

**Nonfiction:** Cookbook, how-to, self-help. Subjects include cooking/foods/nutrition, gardening, health/medicine (men's, women's, alternative, seniors), quilting and pets. "Our publications focus on the individual and what you can do to make life more natural, more self-reliant and more healthful." Query or submit proposal package including 1-2 sample chapters, author's resume and SASE.

**Recent Title(s):** *Prayer, Faith & Healing*, by Kenneth W. Caine and Brian Kaufman; *1001 Ingenious Gardening Ideas*, edited by Deborah Martin.

**Tips:** "We're looking for authors who can dig deeply for facts and details, report accurately and write with flair."

**THE ROSEN PUBLISHING GROUP**, 29 E. 21st St., New York NY 10010. (212)777-3017. Fax: (212)253-6915. E-mail: rosened@erols.com. **Acquisitions:** Erin M. Hovanec, young adult editorial division leader. Estab. 1950. Publishes hardcover and trade paperback originals. **Publishes 300 titles/year. Receives 150 queries and 75 mss/year. 50% of books from first-time authors; 95% from unagented writers. Pays 6-10% royalty on retail price or makes outright purchase of $175-1,000. May offer $500-1,000 advance.** Publishes books about 9 months after acceptance of ms. Reports in 2 months on proposals. Book catalog and ms guidelines free.

○━ The Rosen Publishing Group publishes young adult titles for sale to school and public libraries. Each book is aimed at teenage readers and addresses them directly.

**Imprint(s):** Power Kids Press (nonfiction for grades K-4 that are supplementary to the curriculum. Topics include conflict resolution, character-building, health, safety, drug abuse prevention, history, self-help, religion, science and multicultural titles. **Contact:** Kristen Ward, Power Kids Press editorial division leader). Rosen Central (nonfiction for grades 5-9 on a wide range of topics, mostly related to the curriculum. Topics include social issues, health, sports, self-esteem, history and science. **Contact:** Amy Haugers, editor).

**Nonfiction:** Juvenile, self-help, young adult, reference. Submit outline and 1 sample chapter. Books should be written at K-4 or 8th grade reading level. Areas of particular interest include multicultural ethnographic studies; careers; coping with social, medical and personal problems; values and ethical behavior; drug abuse prevention; self-esteem; social activism; religion.

**Recent Title(s):** *Teen Witnesses to the Holocaust* series; *African-American Arts and Culture* series.

**Tips:** "The writer has the best chance of selling our firm a book on vocational guidance or personal social adjustment, or high-interest, low reading-level material for teens."

**ROWMAN & LITTLEFIELD PUBLISHERS, INC.**, 4720 Boston Way, Lanham MD 20706. (301)459-3366. **Acquisitions:** Jon Sisk, associate publisher. Estab. 1969. Publishes hardcover and trade paperback originals and reprints. **Publishes 250 titles/year. Receives 2,000 queries and 1,000 mss/year. 95% from unagented writers. Pays 5-15% royalty on wholesale price. Advance varies.** Publishes book 6 months after acceptance of ms. Accepts simultaneous submissions.

○━ Rowman & Littlefield publishes scholarly books on a variety of nonfiction subjects in the humanities and social sciences.

**Nonfiction:** Biography, reference, textbook, scholarly. Subjects include anthropology/archaeology, business/economics, education, ethnic, gay/lesbian, government/politics, history, language/literature, military/war, money/finance, philosophy, psychology, religion, sociology, translations, women's issues/studies. Query with proposal, including outline, proposed toc, cv and SASE.

**ROWMAN & LITTLEFIELD PUBLISHING GROUP**, 4720 Boston Way, Lanham MD 20706. (301)459-3366. Publishes hardcover and trade paperback originals and reprints. **Publishes 600 titles/year.**

**Imprint(s): Ivan R. Dee,** Derrydale Press, Lexington Books, New Amsterdam Books, **Rowman & Littlefield Publishers, Madison Books, Scarecrow Press,** University Press of America, Vestal Press.

**ROXBURY PUBLISHING CO.**, P.O. Box 491044, Los Angeles CA 90049. (310)473-3312. **Acquisitions:** Claude Teweles, executive editor. Estab. 1981. Publishes hardcover and paperback originals and reprints. **Publishes 15-25 titles/year. Pays royalty.** Accepts simultaneous submissions. Reports in 2 months.

○━ Roxbury publishes college textbooks in the humanities and social sciences only.

**Nonfiction:** College-level textbooks *only*. Subjects include humanities, speech, developmental studies, social sciences, sociology, criminology, criminal justice. Query, submit outline/synopsis and sample chapters, or submit complete ms. *Writer's Market* recommends a query with SASE first.

**N: RUDI PUBLISHING**, 12 Geary St., Suite 508, San Francisco CA 94108. (415)392-6940. Fax: (415)392-6942. E-mail: rudi3@ix.netcom.com. Website: http://www.rudipublishing.com. **Acquisitions:** Terri Boekhoff, publisher; Carolyn West, acquisitions editor. Publishes hardcover and trade paperback originals. **Publishes 5 titles/year. Receives 200 queries and 70 mss/year. 50% of books from first-time authors; 100% from unagented writers. Pays 7-12% royalty on wholesale price. No advance.** Publishes book 18 months after acceptance of ms. Accepts simultaneous submissions. Reports in 3 months on queries and proposals, 6 months on mss. Book catalog and ms guidelines free.

O—¬ Rudi Publishing publishes nonfiction titles that provide important information or promote awareness and understanding.

**Nonfiction:** How-to, self-help. Subjects include career and personal development, cultural studies, ethnic, history, sports. Submit proposal package, including outline, 3 sample chapters, detailed toc, market analysis, author cv and SASE. Reviews artwork/photos as part of ms package. Send transparencies. "But we rarely publish art-heavy books.

**Recent Title(s):** *Love at Mid-Life*, by Richard A. Osing (relationships/self-help).

**Tips:** "Clearly know and understand the audience for your book and be able to communicate that audience to us. Understand that the author is the most important spokesperson for the work."

**RUNNING PRESS BOOK PUBLISHERS**, 125 S. 22nd St., Philadelphia PA 19103. (215)567-5080. Fax: (215)568-2919. President/Publisher: Stuart Teacher. **Acquisitions:** Maryellen Lewis, assistant to the editorial director; Nancy Steele, director of acquisitions; Brian Perrin, associate publisher; Jennifer Worick; Mary McGuire Ruggiero, acquiring editor (cookbooks); Patty Smith, acquiring editor (children's projects); Greg Jones, acquiring editor (photography and general nonfiction); Jason Rekulak, acquiring editor (novelty and general nonfiction). Estab. 1972. Publishes hardcover originals, trade paperback originals and reprints. **Publishes 150 titles/year. Receives 600 queries/year. 50% of books from first-time authors; 30% from unagented writers. Payment varies. Advances varies.** Publishes book 6-18 months after acceptance of ms. Accepts simultaneous submissions. Reports in 6 weeks on queries. Book catalog free. Manuscript guidelines for #10 SASE.

O—¬ "Running Press and Courage Books publish nonfiction trade and promotional titles, including pop culture books, cookbooks, quote books, children's learning kits, photo-essay books."

**Imprint(s):** Courage Books.

**Nonfiction:** Children's/juvenile, how-to, self-help. Subjects include art/architecture, cooking/foods/nutrition, recreation, science, craft, how-to. Query with outline, contents, synopsis and SASE. Reviews artwork/photos as part of the ms package. Send photocopies; "no originals."

**Recent Title(s):** *Twins*, by Ruth and Rachel Sandweiss.

**RUTGERS UNIVERSITY PRESS**, 100 Joyce Kilmer Ave., Piscataway NJ 08854-8099. (732)445-7762. Fax: (732)445-7039. E-mail: marlie@rci.rutgers.edu. Website: http://rutgerspress.rutgers.edu. **Acquisitions:** Leslie Mitchner, editor-in-chief/associate director (humanities);  David Myers, acquiring editor (social sciences); Helen Hsu, senior editor (science, regional books). Estab. 1936. Publishes hardcover originals and trade paperback originals and reprints. **Publishes 70 titles/year. Receives up to 1,500 queries and up to 300 books/year. Up to 30% of books from first-time authors; 70% from unagented writers. Pays 7½-15% royalty on retail or net price. Offers $1,000-10,000 advance.** Publishes book 1 year after acceptance of ms. Accepts simultaneous submissions, if so noted. Reports in 1 month on proposals. Book catalog free.

O—¬ "Our press aims to reach audiences beyond the academic community with accessible scholarly and regional books."

**Nonfiction:** Books for use in undergraduate courses. Subjects include anthropology, African-American studies, Asian-American studies, education, gay/lesbian, government/politics, gender studies, health/medicine, history of science, literature, literary criticism, multicultural studies, nature/environment, regional, religion, human evolution, sociology, translation, women's studies, ecology, media studies. Submit outline and 2-3 sample chapters. Reviews artwork/photos as part of the ms package. Send photocopies.

**Recent Title(s):** *Pretty in Punk: Girls' Gender Resistance in a Boys' Subculture*, by Lauraine Leblanc.

**Tips:** Both academic and general audiences. "Many of our books have potential for undergraduate course use. We are more trade-oriented than most university presses. We are looking for intelligent, well-written and accessible books. Avoid overly narrow topics."

**RUTLEDGE HILL PRESS**, 211 Seventh Ave. N.,  Nashville TN 37219-1823. (615)244-2700. Fax: (615)244-2978. **Acquisitions:** Mike Towle, executive editor. Estab. 1982. Publishes hardcover and trade paperback originals and reprints. **Publishes 60 titles/year. Receives 1,500 submissions/year. 25% of books from first-time authors; 60% from unagented writers. Pays 10-20% royalty on net price.** Publishes book 1 year after acceptance. Reports in 2 months. Book catalog for 9×12 SAE with 4 first-class stamps.

O—¬ "We are a publisher of market-specific books, focusing on particular genres or regions."

**Nonfiction:** Biography, cookbook, humor, regional travel, Civil War history, quilt books, sports. "The book should have a unique marketing hook other than the subject matter itself. Books built on new ideas and targeted to a specific U.S. region are welcome. Please, no fiction, children's, academic, poetry or religious works, and we won't even look at *Life's Little Instruction Book* spinoffs or copycats." Submit cover letter that includes brief marketing strategy and author bio, outline and sample chapters. Reviews artwork/photos as part of ms package.

**Recent Title(s):** *No Ordinary Joe*, by Michael O'Brien.

**SAE INTERNATIONAL**, Society of Automotive Engineers, 400 Commonwealth Dr., Warrendale PA 15096. (724)776-4841. **Acquisitions:** Jeff Worsinger, product manager; Edward Manns, product manager. Estab. 1905. Publishes hardcover and trade paperback originals. **Publishes 25-30 titles/year. Receives 250 queries and 75 mss/year. 30-40% of books from first-time authors; 100% from unagented writers. Pays royalty with possible advance.** Publishes book within 1 year after acceptance of ms. Accepts simultaneous submissions. Reports in 2 months. Book catalog and ms guidelines free.

**O—** "Automotive means anything self-propelled. We are a professional society serving this area, which includes aircraft, spacecraft, marine, rail, automobiles, trucks and off-highway vehicles." Currently emphasizing automotive safety engineering.

**Imprint(s): SAE International**, STS Press.

**Nonfiction:** Biography, multimedia (CD-ROM), reference, technical, textbook. Automotive and aerospace subjects. "Request submission guidelines. Clearly define your book's market or angle." Query with SASE. Reviews artwork/photos as part of ms package. Send photocopies.

**Recent Title(s):** *Automotive Technology, Engine Testing: Theory and Practice*.

**Tips:** "Audience is automotive engineers, technicians, car buffs, aerospace engineers, technicians and historians."

**SAFARI PRESS INC.**, 15621 Chemical Lane, Building B, Huntington Beach CA 92649-1506. (714)894-9080. Fax: (714)894-4949. E-mail: info@safaripress.com. Website: http://www.safaripress.com. **Acquisitions:** Jacqueline Neufeld, editor. Estab. 1984. Publishes hardcover originals and reprints and trade paperback reprints. **Publishes 6-15 titles/year. 50% of books from first-time authors; 99% from unagented writers. Pays 8-15% royalty on wholesale price.** No simultaneous submissions. Book catalog for $1. "Request our 'Notice to Prospective Authors.' "

**O—** Safari Press publishes books only on big-game hunting, firearms and wingshooting; this includes African, North American, European, Asian, and South American hunting and wingshooting.

**Nonfiction:** Biography, how-to, adventure stories. Subjects include hunting, firearms, wingshooting—"nothing else. We discourage autobiographies, unless the life of the hunter or firearms maker has been exceptional. We routinely reject manuscripts along the lines of 'Me and my buddies went hunting for . . . and a good time was had by all!' No fishing." Query with outline and SASE.

**Recent Title(s):** *American Man-Killers*, by Don Zaidle; *Jim Corbett, Master of the Jungle*, by Tim Werling.

**N SAGAMORE PUBLISHING**, 804 N. Neil St., Suite 100, Champaign IL 61820. (217)359-5940. Fax: (217)359-5975. E-mail: books@sagamorepub.com. Website: http://www.sagamorepub.com. **Acquisitions:** Joseph Bannon, CEO (parks, recreation, leisure); Tom Bast, director of acquistions (outdoor recreation). Estab. 1974. Publishes hardcover and trade paperback originals. **Publishes 10-12 titles/year. Receives 30-40 queries and 25-30 mss/year. 40% of books from first-time authors; 100% from unagented writers. Pays 7-15% royalty. No advance.** Publishes book 6 months after acceptance of ms. Accepts simultaneous submissions. Reports in 1 month. Book catalog and ms guidelines free or on website.

**O—** "Sagamore Publishing has been a leader in the parks and recreation field for over 20 years. We are now expanding into the areas of tourism and recreation for special populations such as people with autism or ADD/ADHD, and outdoor adventure and wildlife."

**Nonfiction:** Reference, textbook. Subjects include education, health/medicine, nature/environment, recreation, outdoor adventure, tourism. Submit proposal package, including outline, 1 sample chapter and market projections. Reviews artwork/photos as part of ms package. Send photocopies.

**Recent Titles:** *Outdoor Recreation in American Life*, by Ken Cordell (textbook/reference).

**Tips:** "We strongly encourage potential authors to submit a marketing prospective with any manuscript they submit."

**ST. ANTHONY MESSENGER PRESS**, 1615 Republic St., Cincinnati OH 45210-1298. (513)241-5615. Fax: (513)241-0399. E-mail: stanthony@americancatholic.org. Website: http://www.americancatholic.org. Publisher: The Rev. Jeremy Harrington, O.F.M. **Acquisitions:** Kathleen Carroll, editor (children's books); Lisa Biedenbach, managing editor. Estab. 1970. Publishes trade paperback originals. **Publishes 15-20 titles/year. Receives 200 queries and 50 mss/year. 5% of books from first-time authors; 100% from unagented writers. Pays 10-12% royalty on net receipts of sales. Offers $1,000 average advance.** Publishes book 18 months after acceptance. Reports in 1 month on queries, 2 months on proposals and mss. Book catalog for 9×12 SAE with 4 first-class stamps. Manuscript guidelines free.

**O—** "St. Anthony Messenger Press/Franciscan Communications seeks to communicate the word that is Jesus Christ in the styles of Saints Francis and Anthony. Through print and electronic media marketed in North America and worldwide, we endeavor to evangelize, inspire and inform those who search for God and seek a richer Catholic, Christian, human life. Our efforts help support the life, ministry and charities of the Franciscan Friars of St. John the Baptist Province, who sponsor our work."

**Nonfiction:** History, religion, Catholic identity and teaching, prayer and spirituality resources, scripture study. Children's books with Catholic slant, family-based religious education programs. Query with outline and SASE. Reviews artwork/photos as part of ms package.

**Recent Title(s):** *Practicing Catholic*, by Archbishop Daniel Pilarczyk; *Can You Find Bible Heroes? Introducing Your Child to the Old Testament*, by Phillip Gallery and illustrated by Janet Harlow.

**Tips:** "Our readers are ordinary 'folks in the pews' and those who minister to and educate these folks. Writers need to know the audience and the kind of books we publish. Manuscripts should reflect best and current Catholic theology and doctrine." St. Anthony Messenger Press especially seeks books which will sell in bulk quantities to parishes, teachers, pastoral ministers, etc. They expect to sell at least 5,000 to 7,000 copies of a book.

**ST. BEDE'S PUBLICATIONS**, St. Scholastica Priory, P.O. Box 545, Petersham MA 01366-0545. (978)724-3407. Fax: (978)724-3574. **Acquisitions:** Acquisitions Editor. Estab. 1977. Publishes hardcover originals, trade paperback originals and reprints. **Publishes 8-12 titles/year. Receives 100 submissions/year. 30-40% of books from first-time**

authors; **98% from unagented writers. Nonauthor subsidy publishes 10% of books. Pays 5-10% royalty on wholesale price or retail price. No advance.** Publishes book 2 years after acceptance of ms. Accepts simultaneous submissions. Reports in 2 months. Book catalog and ms guidelines for 9×12 SAE and 2 first-class stamps.

    O↝ St. Bede's Publications is owned and operated by the Roman Catholic nuns of St. Scholastica Priory. The publications are seen as as apostolic outreach. Their mission is to make available to everyone quality books on spiritual subjects such as prayer, scripture, theology and the lives of holy people.

**Nonfiction:** Textbook (theology), religion, prayer, spirituality, hagiography, theology, philosophy, church history, related lives of saints. "We are always looking for excellent books on prayer, spirituality, liturgy, church or monastic history. Theology and philosophy are important also. We publish English translations of foreign works in these fields if we think they are excellent and worth translating." No submissions unrelated to religion, theology, spirituality, etc., and no poetry, fiction or children's books. Query or submit outline and sample chapters with SASE. Does not return submissions without adequate postage.

**Recent Title(s):** *Truthful Living*, by Michael Casky; *The Invisible Father*, by Louise Bouyer (translated from French).

**Tips:** "There seems to be a growing interest in monasticism among lay people, and we will be publishing more books in this area. For our theology/philosophy titles our audience is scholars, colleges and universities, seminaries, etc. For our other titles (i.e. prayer, spirituality, lives of saints, etc.) the audience is above-average readers interested in furthering their knowledge in these areas."

**ⓃⒾ ST. JEROME'S PRESS**, P.O. Box 33192, Baltimore MD 21218-0401. (410)235-5089. Fax: (410)235-5089. E-mail: stjeromespress@hotmail.com. **Acquisitions:** John W. Sweeley, D.D., editor (religion, theology, adoption, spirituality). Publishes hardcover and trade paperback originals. **Publishes 10-12 titles/year. 95% of books from first-time authors; 95% from unagented writers. Pays 8-10% royalty. No advance.** Publishes book 9 months after acceptance of ms. Accepts simultaneous submissions. Reports in 3 months on mss. Manuscript guidelines for #10 SASE.

    O↝ "We publish scholarly works, monographs, dissertations. First person inspirational accepted but must be good writing."

**Nonfiction:** Reference, technical, scholarly. Subjects include anthropology/archaeology, philosophy, religion, spirituality, adoption, theology. Submit proposal package or complete ms. *Writer's Market* recommends a query first.

**Fiction:** Religious, spiritual. "Must reflect mainstream Christian values, a good story, and well written."

**Recent Titles:** *Adoption: The Case for Open Records*, by John W. Sweeley, D.D.

**Tips:** "Present your best writing and tell the story so the reader doesn't want to put the book down."

**ST. MARTIN'S PRESS, SCHOLARLY & REFERENCE DIVISION**, St. Martin's Press, 175 Fifth Ave., New York NY 10010. (212)982-3900. Fax: (212)777-6359. Website: http://www.stmartins.com. **Acquisitions:** Michael Flamini, senior editor (history, politics, education, religion); Karen Wolny, editor (politics); Kirsti Long, editor (literature, cultural studies, anthropology). Publishes hardcover and trade paperback originals. **Firm publishes 700 titles/year. Receives 500 queries and 600 mss/year. 25% of books from first-time authors; 75% from unagented writers. Pays royalty: trade, 7-10% list; other, 7-10% net. Advance varies.** Publishes book 7 months after acceptance of ms. Accepts simultaneous submissions. Reports in 1 month on proposals. Book catalog and ms guidelines free.

    O↝ "We remain true to our origin as a scholarly press . . . with the backing of St. Martin's Press we are able to make books more accessible."

**Nonfiction:** Reference, scholarly. Subjects include business/economics, government/politics, history, language/literature, philosophy, religion, sociology, women's issues/studies, humanities, social studies. "We are looking for good solid scholarship." Query with proposal package including outline, 3-4 sample chapters, prospectus, cv and SASE. "We like to see as much completed material as possible." Reviews artwork/photos as part of ms package.

**Recent Title(s):** *Property and Prosperity Through the Ages*, by Tom Bethell.

**ⓃⒾ ★ SAINT MARY'S PRESS**, 702 Terrace Heights, Winona MN 55987-1320. (800)533-8095. Fax: (800)344-9225. Website: http://www.smp.org. **Acquisitions:** Carl Koch, series editor (spirituality); Steve Nagel, editor (young adult fiction). Estab. 1943. Publishes trade paperback originals. **Imprint publishes 20-30 titles/year. Receives 300 queries and 150 mss/year. 70% of books from first-time authors; 100% from unagented writers. Pays 8-12% royalty on wholesale price. No advance.** Publishes book 14 months after acceptance of ms. Accepts simultaneous submissions. Book catalog free or on website. Manuscript guidelines free.

**Nonfiction:** Subjects include memoirs, regional, spirituality. Query with SASE or submit proposal package, including outline, 1 sample chapter and brief author biography.

**Fiction:** Religious, young adult. "We are looking for young adult novels of 40,000 words that are character-driven: They need to portray the struggle toward adulthood, whatever the genre or historical circumstances. We want unforgetable characters."

**Poetry:** "The poetry should have connections to the spiritual journey." Query. Submit 10 sample poems.

**Recent Titles:** *Painting with C.S. Lewis*, by Charles Taliaferro (spirituality); *Serafin*, by Sophie Masson (young adult fiction); *Woman Un-bent*, by Irene Zimmerman (poetry).

**Tips:** "Do research of Saint Mary Press book lives before submitting proposal."

**SAMS**, Macmillan Computer Publishing USA, 201 W. 103rd St., Indianapolis IN 46290. (317)581-3500. Website: http://www.mcp.com/sams/. Publisher/Vice President: James Price. **Acquisitions:** Angela Kozlowski, acquisitions editor (unleashed series, Pine North Guides); Steve Anglin, acquisitions editor (operating systems, certification, professional programming); Randi Roger, acquisitions editor (applications, web); Chris Webb, acquisitions editor (programming); Sharon Cox, acquisitions editor (programming). Estab. 1951. Publishes trade paperback originals. **Publishes 160 titles/ year. 30% of books from first-time authors; 95% from unagented writers. Pays royalty on wholesale price, negotiable. Advance negotiable.** Publishes book 1 year after acceptance of ms. Accepts simultaneous submissions if noted; "however, once contract is signed, Sams Publishing retains first option rights on future works on same subject." Reports in 6 weeks on queries. Manuscript guidelines free.

　　O━ Sams has made a major commitment to publishing books that meet the needs of computer users, programmers, administrative and support personnel, and managers.

**Nonfiction:** Computer subjects. Query with SASE.

**Recent Title(s):** *Pure JFC Swing.*

**SANTA MONICA PRESS LLC**, P.O. Box 1076, Santa Monica CA 90406. **Acquisitions:** Minju Pak, editorial director. Estab. 1991. Publishes trade paperback originals. **Publishes 6-10 titles/year. Receives 200-300 queries and mss/year. 75% of books from first-time authors; 75% from unagented writers. Pays 4-10% royalty on wholesale price. Offers $500-2,500 advance.** Publishes book 1 year after acceptance of ms. Accepts simultaneous submissions. Reports in 2 months on proposals. Book catalog and ms guidelines for #10 SASE.

　　O━ Santa Monica Press Publishes two lines of books: general how-to books written in simple, easy-to-understand terms; and books which explore popular culture from an offbeat perspective.

**Nonfiction:** Gift book, how-to, illustrated book reference. Subjects include Americana, pop culture, health/medicine, music/dance, sports, theater, film, general how-to. Submit proposal package, including outline, 2-3 sample chapters, biography, marketing potential of book with SASE. All unsolicited mss returned unopened. Reviews artwork/photos as part of the ms package. Send photocopies.

**Recent Title(s):** *Offbeat Marijuana: The Life and Times of the World's Grooviest Plant*, by Saul Rubin (popular culture/current affairs); *Collecting Sins*, by Steven Sobel (fiction).

**Tips:** "Our how-to books provide readers with practical guidance in a wide variety of subjects, from letter writing to health care. These handy guides are written in simple, easy-to-understand terms. Our offbeat books explore popular culture from an offbeat perspective. These large format books feature hundreds of graphics and photos and are written for the naturally curious reader who possesses a healthy sense of humor."

**SARABANDE BOOKS, INC.**, 2234 Dundee Rd., Suite 200, Louisville KY 40205. (502)458-4028. Fax: (502)458-4065. E-mail: sarabandeb@aol.com. Website: http://www.sarabandebooks.org. **Acquisitions**: Sarah Gorham, editor-in-chief. Publishes hardcover and trade paperback originals. **Publishes 8 titles/year. Receives 500 queries and 2,000 mss/ year. 35% of books from first-time authors; 75% from unagented writers. Pays 10% royalty on actual income received. Offers $500-2,000 advance.** Publishes book 18 months after acceptance of ms. Accepts simultaneous submissions. Reports in 3 months on queries, 6 months on mss. Book catalog free. Manuscript guidelines for #10 SASE.

　　O━ Sarabande publishes works of lasting literary value.

**Fiction:** Literary, novellas, short story collections. "We do not publish novels." Query with 1 sample story, 1 page bio, listing of publishing credits and SASE. *Submissions in September only.*

**Poetry:** "Poetry of superior artistic quality. Otherwise no restraints or specifications." Query and submit 10 sample poems. *Submissions in September only.*

**Recent Title(s):** *Stealing Glimpses: On Poetry, Poets and Things in Between*, by Molly McQuade (nonfiction); *A Gram of Mars*, by Becky Hagenston (fiction); *Bad Judgment*, by Cathleen Calbert (poetry).

**Tips:** Sarabande publishes for a general literary audience. "Know your market. Read—and buy—books of literature."

**SAS INSTITUTE INC.**, SAS Campus Dr., Cary NC 27513-2414. (919)677-8000. Fax: (919)677-4444. E-mail: sasbbu @unx.sas.com. Website: http://www.sas.com. **Acquisitions:** David D. Baggett, editor-in-chief. Estab. 1976. Publishes hardcover and trade paperback originals. **Publishes 40 titles/year. Receives 10 submissions/year. 50% of books from first-time authors; 100% from unagented writers. Payment negotiable. Offers negotiable advance.** Reports in 2 weeks on queries. Book catalog and ms guidelines free.

　　O━ SAS Institute publishes books for SAS software users, "both new and experienced."

**Nonfiction:** Software, technical, textbook, statistics. "SAS Institute's Publications Division publishes books developed and written inhouse. Through the Books by Users program, we also publish books by SAS users on a variety of topics relating to SAS software. We want to provide our users with additional titles to supplement our primary documentation and to enhance the users' ability to use the SAS System effectively. We're interested in publishing manuscripts that describe or illustrate using any of SAS Institute's software products. Books must be aimed at SAS software users, either new or experienced. Tutorials are particularly attractive, as are descriptions of user-written applications for solving real-life business, industry or academic problems. Books on programming techniques using the SAS language are also desirable. Manuscripts must reflect current or upcoming software releases, and the author's writing should indicate an understanding of the SAS System and the technical aspects covered in the manuscript." Query. Submit outline/synopsis and sample chapters. Reviews artwork/photos as part of ms package.

**Recent Title(s):** *The Little SAS Book: A Primer*, by Lora D. Delunch and Susan J. Slaughter.

**Tips:** "If I were a writer trying to market a book today, I would concentrate on developing a manuscript that teaches or illustrates a specific concept or application that SAS software users will find beneficial in their own environments or can adapt to their own needs."

**SASQUATCH BOOKS**, 615 Second Ave., Suite 260, Seattle WA 98104. (206)467-4300. Fax: (206)467-4301. E-mail: books@sasquatchbooks.com. Website: http://www.sasquatchbooks.com. President: Chad Haight. **Acquisitions:** Gary Luke, editorial director; Kate Rogers, editor (travel). Estab. 1986. Publishes regional hardcover and trade paperback originals. **Publishes 30 titles/year. 20% of books from first-time authors; 75% from unagented writers. Pays royalty on cover price. Offers wide range of advances.** Publishes ms 6 months after acceptance. Reports in 3 months. Book catalog for 9 × 12 SAE with 2 first-class stamps.

O—¬ Sasquatch Books publishes adult nonfiction from the Northwest, specializing in travel, cooking, gardening, history and nature.

**Nonfiction:** Subjects include regional art/architecture, cooking, foods, gardening, history, nature/environment, recreation, sports, travel and outdoors. "We are seeking quality nonfiction works about the Pacific Northwest and West Coast regions (including Alaska to California). In this sense we are a regional publisher, but we do distribute our books nationally." Query first, then submit outline and sample chapters with SASE.

**Recent Title(s):** *Naturalistic Gardening*, by Ann Lovejoy.

**Tips:** "We sell books through a range of channels in addition to the book trade. Our primary audience consists of active, literate residents of the West Coast."

**SCARECROW PRESS, INC.**, Rowman & Littlefield Publishing Group, 4720 Boston Way, Lanham MD 20706. (301)459-3366. Fax: (301)459-2118. Website: http://www.scarecrowpress.com. **Acquisitions:** Shirley Lambert, editorial director; Katie Regen, assistant editor. Estab. 1950. Publishes hardcover originals. **Publishes 165 titles/year. Receives 600-700 submissions/year. 70% of books from first-time authors; 99% from unagented writers. Pays 8% royalty on net of first 1,000 copies; 10% of net price thereafter. No advance.** Publishes book 18 months after receipt of ms. Reports in 2 months. Book catalog for 9 × 12 SAE and 4 first-class stamps.

O—¬ Scarecrow Press publishes several series: The Historical Dictionary series, which includes countries, religious, international organizations; and Composers of North America. "We consider any scholarly title likely to appeal to libraries. Emphasis is on reference material."

**Nonfiction:** Reference books and meticulously prepared annotated bibliographies, indices and books on women's studies, ethnic studies, music, movies, stage. library and information science, parapsychology, fine arts and handicrafts, social sciences, religion, sports, literature and language. Query.

**Recent Title(s):** *The Holocaust in Literature for Youth: A Guide and Resource Book*, by Edward T. Sullivan.

**SCHIRMER BOOKS**, Macmillan Reference, 1633 Broadway, New York NY 10019-6785. (212)654-8414. Fax: (212)654-4745. **Acquisitions:** Richard Carlin, executive editor. Publishes hardcover and paperback originals, related CDs, CD-ROMs, audiocassettes. **Publishes 50 books/year. Receives 250 submissions/year. 25% of books from first-time authors; 75% of books from unagented writers.** Publishes book 1 year after acceptance of ms. Reports in 4 months. Book catalog and ms guidelines for SASE.

O—¬ Schirmer publishes scholarly and reference books on the performing arts. Currently emphasizing popular music, including rock and jazz.

**Nonfiction:** Publishes college texts, biographies, scholarly, reference, and trade on the performing arts specializing in music, film and theatre. Submit outline/synopsis, sample chapters and current vita. Reviews artwork/photos as part of ms package. "Submit only if central to the book, not if decorative or tangential."

**Recent Title(s):** *Billboard's American Rock and Roll in Review*, by Jay Warner.

**Tips:** "The writer has the best chance of selling our firm a music book with a clearly defined, reachable audience, either scholarly or trade. Must be an exceptionally well-written work of original scholarship prepared by an expert who has a thorough understanding of correct manuscript style and attention to detail (see the *Chicago Manual of Style*)."

**SCHOCKEN BOOKS**, Knopf Publishing Group, Random House, Inc., 201 E. 50th St., New York NY 10022. (212)572-2559. Fax: (212)572-6030. Website: http://www.randomhouse.com/schocken. **Acquisitions:** Arthur Samuelson, editorial director; Cecelia Cancellaro, editor. Estab. 1933. Publishes hardcover originals and reprints, trade paperback originals and reprints. **Publishes 24 titles/year. A small percentage of books are from first-time writers; small percentage from unagented writers. Pays royalty on net price. Advance varies.** Accepts simultaneous submissions. Book catalog free.

O—¬ "Schocken publishes a broad nonfiction list of serious, solid books with commercial appeal, as well as reprints of classics." Schocken has a commitment to publishing Judaica, and also specializes in the areas of religious, cultural and women's studies.

**Nonfiction:** Subjects include education, ethnic, government/politics, health/medicine, history, Judaica, nature/environment, philosophy, cultural studies, religion, women's issues/studies. Submit proposal package, including "whatever is necessary to make the case for your book."

**Fiction:** Reprints classics.

**Recent Title(s):** *The Monk and The Philosopher: A Father and Son Discuss Life's Eternal Questions*.

**SCHOLASTIC INC.**, Book Group, 555 Broadway, New York NY 10012. (212)343-6100. Estab. 1920. Website: http://www.scholastic.com. Publishes trade paperback originals for children ages 4-young adult. Publishes juvenile hardcover picture books, novels and nonfiction. **All divisions: Pays advance and royalty on retail price.** Reports in 6 months. Manuscript guidelines for #10 SASE.

O—¬ "We are proud of the many fine, innovative materials we have created—such as classroom magazines, book clubs, book fairs, and our new literacy and technology programs. But we are most proud of our reputation as 'The Most Trusted Name in Learning.' "

**Imprint(s): Blue Sky Press** (contact Bernette Ford), **Cartwheel Books** (contact Bernette Ford), Arthur Levine Books (contact Arthur Levine), Mariposa (contact Susanna Pasternac), **Scholastic Press** (contact Elizabeth Szabla), Scholastic Reference & Gallimard (contact Wendy Barish), Scholastic Trade Paperback (contact Craig Walker).

**Nonfiction:** Publishes nonfiction for children ages 4 to teen. Query.

**Fiction:** Hardcover—open to all subjects suitable for children. Paperback—family stories, mysteries, school, friendships for ages 8-12, 35,000 words. YA fiction, romance, family and mystery for ages 12-15, 40,000-45,000 words for average to good readers. Queries welcome. Unsolicited manuscripts discouraged.

**Recent Title(s):** *The Great Fire*, by Jim Murphy; *Out of the Dust*, by Karen Hesse.

**Tips:** New writers for children should study the children's book field before submitting.

**SCHOLASTIC PRESS**, Scholastic Inc., 555 Broadway, New York NY 10012. (212)343-6100. Website: http://www.scholastic.com. **Acquisitions:** Elizabeth Szabla, editorial director. Publishes hardcover originals. **Publishes 50 titles/year. Receives 2,500 queries/year. 5% of books from first-time authors. Pays royalty on retail price. Royalty and advance vary.** Publishes book 18-24 months after acceptance of ms. Reports in 6 months on queries.

O—¬ Scholastic Press publishes a range of picture books, middle grade and young adult novels.

**Nonfiction:** Children's/juvenile, general interest. *Agented submissions only.*

**Fiction:** Juvenile, picture books. *Agented submissions only.*

**Recent Title(s):** *Out of the Dust*, by Karen Hesse (fiction).

**SCHOLASTIC PROFESSIONAL PUBLISHING**, Scholastic, Inc., 555 Broadway, New York NY 10012. Website: http://www.scholastic.com. Vice President/Editor-in-Chief: Terry Cooper. **Acquisitions:** Adriane Rozier, editorial production coordinator. Estab. 1989. **Publishes 80-100 books/year. Offers standard contract.** Reports in 2 months. Book catalog for 9 × 12 SAE.

**Nonfiction:** Elementary and middle-school level enrichment—all subject areas, including math and science and theme units, integrated materials, writing process, management techniques, teaching strategies based on personal/professional experience in the classroom and technology ideas. Production is limited to printed matter: resource and activity books, professional development materials, reference titles. Length: 6,000-12,000 words. Query with table of contents, outline and sample chapter.

**Recent Titles(s):** *Perfect Poems for Teaching Phonics*; *12 Write-and-Read Math Storybooks*.

**Tips:** "Writer should have background working in the classroom with elementary or middle school children, teaching pre-service students, and/or solid background in developing supplementary educational materials for these markets."

**D&F SCOTT PUBLISHING, INC.**, P.O. Box 821653, North Richland Hills TX 76182. (817)788-2280. Fax: (817)788-9232. E-mail: bibal@cmpu.net. Website: http://www.dfscott.com. **Acquisitions:** Dr. William R. Scott, president. Publishes hardcover and trade paperback originals. **Publishes 20 titles/year. Receives 50 queries/year and 15 mss/year. 10% of books from first-time authors; 100% from unagented writers. Pays 10-20% royalty on wholesale price. No advance.** Publishes book 6 months after acceptance of ms. Accepts simultaneous submissions. Reports in 3 months. Book catalog and ms guidelines free.

O—¬ "BIBAL Press was established as the publishing agency of BIBAL Corporation, a nonprofit institute founded for the purpose of encouraging the study of biblical archaeology and literature."

**Imprints:** BIBAL Press, Smithfield Press, WestWind Press.

**Nonfiction:** How-to, reference, textbook. Subjects include anthropology/archaeology, religion. Submit proposal package, including table of contents, 2 sample chapters and SASE. Reviews artwork/photos as part of the ms package. Send photocopies.

**Recent Title(s):** *Witness: Images of Auschwitz*, by Alexandre Oler.

**SCRIBNER**, Simon & Schuster, 1230 Avenue of the Americas, New York NY 10020. (212)698-7000. **Acquisitions:** Jillian Blake, editor. Publishes hardcover originals. **Publishes 70-75 titles/year. Receives thousands of queries/year. 20% of books from first-time authors; none from unagented writers. Pays 7½-12½% royalty on wholesale price. Advance varies.** Publishes book 9 months after acceptance of ms. Accepts simultaneous submissions. Reports in 3 months on queries.

**Imprint(s): Rawson Associates; Lisa Drew Books;** Scribner Classics (reprints only); Scribner Poetry (by invitation only).

**Nonfiction:** Subjects include education, ethnic, gay/lesbian, health/medicine, history, language/literature, nature/environment, philosophy, psychology, religion, science, biography, criticism. *Agented submissions only.*

**Fiction:** Literary, mystery, suspense. *Agented submissions only.*

**Poetry:** Publishes few titles; by invitation only.

**Recent Title(s):** *Angela's Ashes*, by Frank McCourt (memoir, National Book Award and Pulitzer Prize winner); *Underworld*, by Don DeLillo.

**SEAL PRESS**, 3131 Western Ave., Suite 410, Seattle WA 98121. Fax: (206)285-9410. E-mail: sealprss@scn.org. Website: http://www.sealpress.com. **Acquisitions:** Faith Conlon, editor/publisher. Jennie Goode, managing editor. Publishes hardcover and trade paperback originals. **Publishes 14 titles/year. Receives 500 queries and 500 mss/year. 25%**

of books from first-time authors; **80% from unagented writers. Pays 6-10% royalty on retail price. Offers $500-1,000 advance.** Publishes book 18 months after acceptance of ms. Accepts simultaneous submissions. Reports in 2 months on queries. Book catalog and ms guidelines for SASE.

**O—** "Seal Press is an independent feminist book publisher interested in original, lively, radical, empowering and culturally diverse nonfiction by women addressing contemporary issues from a feminist perspective or speak positively to the experience of being female." Currently emphasizing women outdoor adventurists, young feminists. De-emphasizing fiction unless lesbian.

**Imprint(s):** Adventura Books, Djuna Books, Live Girls.

**Nonfiction:** Self-help, literary nonfiction essays. Subjects include child guidance/parenting, ethnic, gay/lesbian, health/medicine, nature/outdoor writing, travel, women's issues/studies, popular culture. Query with SASE. Reviews artwork/photos as part of ms package. Send photocopies.

**Fiction:** Ethnic, feminist, gay/lesbian, literary. "We are interested in alternative voices that aren't often heard from." Query with synopsis and SASE. *No unsolicited mss.*

**Recent Title(s):** *Adios, Barbie*, edited by Ophira Edut (nonfiction); *Behind the Limbo Silence*, by Elizabeth Nunez (fiction).

● Seal Press is not publishing poetry or mysteries at this time.

**Tips:** "Our audience is generally composed of women interested in reading about contemporary issues addressed from a feminist perspective."

**[N] SEASTONE**, Ulysses Press, P.O. Box 3440, Berkeley CA 94703. (510)601-8301. Fax: (510)601-8307. E-mail: ulypress@aol.com. **Acquisitions:** Ray Riegert, editorial director. Publishes trade paperback originals. **Publishes 10 titles/year. Receives 100 queries and 10 mss/year. 10% of books from first-time authors; 75% from unagented writers. Pays 12-16% royalty on wholesale price. Offers $2,000-8,000 advance.** Publishes book 6 months after acceptance of ms. Accepts simultaneous submissions. Reports in 2 months on proposals. Book catalog free.

**Nonfiction:** Religion, spirituality. Submit proposal package, including outline, 2 sample chapters and market analysis with SASE. Reviews artwork/photos as part of ms package. Send photocopies.

**SEAWORTHY PUBLICATIONS, INC.**, 507 Sunrise Dr., Port Washington WI 53074. (414)268-9250. Fax: (414)268-9208. E-mail: publisher@seaworthy.com. Website: http://www.seaworthy.com. **Acquisitions:** Joseph F. Janson, publisher. Publishes trade paperback originals, hardcover originals and reprints. **Publishes 8 titles/year. Receives 60 queries and 20 mss/year. 60% of books from first-time authors; 100% from unagented writers. Pays 15% royalty on wholesale price. Offers $1,000 advance.** Publishes book 6 months after acceptance of ms. Reports in 1 month. Book catalog and ms guidelines for #10 SASE.

**O—** Seaworthy Publications is a nautical book publisher that primarily publishes books of interest to recreational boaters and serious bluewater cruisers, including cruising guides, how-to and first-person adventure. Currently emphasizing guidebooks, how-to. De-emphasizing first-person adventure.

**Nonfiction:** Regional guide books, first-person adventure, illustrated book, reference, technical—all dealing with boating. Subjects include cooking/foods/nutrition, nautical history, hobbies of sailing and boating, regional boating guide books, sport sail racing, world travel. Query with 3 sample chapters and SASE. Reviews artwork/photos as part of ms package. Send photocopies or color prints.

● Seaworthy Publications is not accepting fiction or poetry at this time.

**Recent Title(s):** *We Followed Odysseus*, by Hal Roth (historical nonfiction adventure).

**Tips:** "Our audience consists of sailors, boaters, and those interested in the sea, sailing or long distance cruising and racing."

**[N] [★] SELF-COUNSEL PRESS**, 1704 N. State St., Bellingham WA 92225. (360)676-4530. **Acquisitions:** Lori Ledingham, managing editor (business/legal). Estab. 1977. Publishes trade paperback originals and reprints. **Publishes 12 titles/year. Receives 1,000 queries/year. 30% of books from first-time authors; 90% from unagented writers. Pays 10% royalty on net price. Rarely pays advance.** Publishes book 8 months after acceptance of ms. Accepts simultaneous submissions. Reports in 4 months. Book catalog and ms guidelines free.

**O—** Self-Counsel Press publishes a range of quality self-help publication books written in practical, non-technical style by recognized experts in the fields of business, financial, personal or legal guidance for people who want to help themselves. "We also publish a writing series."

**Nonfiction:** How-to, reference, self-help. Subjects include business/economics, computers/electronics, money/finance, legal issues for laypeople. Submit proposal package, including outline, 2 sample chapters and résumé.

**Recent Title(s):** *Start and Run an Exporting Business*, by Laurel Delaney (business).

● This publisher also has offices in Canada.

**SERENDIPITY SYSTEMS**, P.O. Box 140, San Simeon CA 93452. (805)927-5259. E-mail: bookware@thegrid.net. Website: http://www.thegrid.net/bookware/bookware.htm. **Acquisitions:** John Galuszka, publisher. **Publishes 6-12 titles/year; each imprint publishes 0-6 titles/year. Receives 600 queries and 150 mss/year. 95% of books from unagented writers. Pays 25-33% royalty on wholesale price or on retail price, "depending on how the book goes out."** Publishes book 2 months after acceptance of ms. Accepts simultaneous submissions. Electronic submissions required. Reports in 1 month on mss. *Writer's Market* recommends allowing 2 months for reply. Book catalog available online. Manuscript guidelines for #10 SASE, or on the Internet.

O— "Since 1986 Serendipity Systems has promoted and supported electronic publishing with electronic books for IBM-PC compatible computers."

**Imprint(s):** Books-on-Disks™, Bookware™.

**Nonfiction:** "We only publish reference books on literature, writing and electronic publishing." Query first with SASE. Submit entire ms on disk in ASCII or HTML files. Queries by e-mail; mss, summaries with sample chapters and long documents should be sent by postal mail.

**Fiction:** "We want to see *only* works which use (or have a high potential to use) hypertext, multimedia, interactivity or other computer-enhanced features. No romance, religious, occult, New Age, fantasy, or children's mss. Submit entire ms on disk in ASCII or HTML files. Query first.

**Recent Title(s):** *The Electronic Publishing Forum* (nonfiction); *Sideshow*, by Marian Allen.

**Tips:** "Check our guidelines on the Internet for the latest information."

**SERGEANT KIRKLAND'S PRESS**, 912 Lafayette Blvd., Fredericksburg VA 22401-5617. (540)899-5565. Fax: (540)899-7643. E-mail: sgt_kirklands_press@bigfoot.com. Website: http://www.Kirklands.org. **Acquisitions:** Pia S. Seagrave, Phd.D., editor-in-chief. Publishes hardcover and trade paperback originals, hardcover reprints. **Publishes 22-24 titles/year. Receives 300 queries and 120 mss/year. 70% of books from first-time authors; 90% from unagented writers. Pays 8-10% royalty on wholesale price. No advance.** Publishes book 6 months after acceptance of ms. Accepts simultaneous submissions. Reports in 2 months on queries and proposals; 4 months on mss. Book catalog free. Manuscript guidelines for #10 SASE.

O— Currently emphasizing American history of academic and regional interest—colonial, Civil War, WWII and Vietnam periods.

**Nonfiction:** Biography, reference. Subjects include Americana, anthropology/archaeology, ethnic, government/politics, history, military/war, regional. Submit complete ms. *Writer's Market* recommends a query first. Reviews artwork/photos as part of ms package. Send photocopies.

**Recent Titles:** *Platoon: Bravo Company*, by Robert Hemphill (Vietnam)

**Tips:** "Have your work professionally edited and be sure it meets the general standards of The Chicago Manual of Style."

**SEVEN STORIES PRESS**, 140 Watts St., New York NY 10013. (212)226-8760. Website: http://www.sevenstories.com. **Acquisitions:** Daniel Simon, Greg Ruggiero, Paul Abruzzo, Michael Maurkin. Estab. 1995. Publishes hardcover and trade paperback originals. **Publishes 20-25 titles/year. 15% of books from first-time authors; 15% from unagented writers. Pays 7-15% royalty on retail price.** Publishes book 1-3 years after acceptance. Accepts simultaneous submissions. Reports in 3 months. Book catalog and manuscript guidelines free.

O— Seven Stories Press publishes literary/activist fiction and nonfiction "on the premise that both are works of the imagination and that there is no contradiction in publishing the two side by side."

**Nonfiction:** Biography. Subjects include general nonfiction. Query only. No unsolicited ms. Responds only if interested.

**Fiction:** Contemporary. Query only. SASE required. *No unsolicited mss.*

**Recent Title(s):** *Dark Alliance*, by Gary Webb (investigative reporting); *Grand Central Winter*, by Lee Stringer (literary memoir); *Parable of the Talents*, by Octavia E. Butler.

**HAROLD SHAW PUBLISHERS**, 388 Gundersen Dr., P.O. Box 567, Wheaton IL 60189. (630)665-6700. **Acquisitions:** Lori McCullough, editorial assistant. Estab. 1967. Publishes mostly trade paperback originals and reprints. **Publishes 40 titles/year. Receives 1,000 submissions/year. 10-20% of books from first-time authors; 90% from unagented writers. Offers 5-10% royalty on retail price. Offers $500-1,000 advance.** Sometimes makes outright purchase of $375-2,500 for Bible studies and compilations. Publishes book 18 months after acceptance of ms. Reports in 3-6 months. Guidelines for #10 SASE. Catalog for 9×12 SAE with 5 first-class stamps.

O— "We publish a wide range (full circle) of books from a Christian perspective for use by a broad range of readers."

**Nonfiction:** Subjects include marriage, family and parenting, self-help, mental health, spiritual growth, Bible study and literary topics. "We are looking for adult general nonfiction with different twists—self-help manuscripts with fresh insight and colorful, vibrant writing style. No autobiographies or biographies accepted. Must have a Christian perspective for us even to review the manuscript." Query with SASE.

**Recent Title(s):** *Bright Evening Star*, by Madeleine L'Engle.

**Tips:** "Get an editor who is not a friend or a spouse who will tell you honestly whether your book is marketable. It will save a lot of your time and money and effort. Then do an honest evaluation. Who would read the book other than yourself? If it won't sell 5,000 copies, it's not very marketable and most publishers wouldn't be interested."

**THE SIDRAN PRESS**, The Sidran Foundation, 2328 W. Joppa Rd., Suite 15, Lutherville MD 21093. (410)825-8888. Fax: (410)337-0747. E-mail: sidran@sidran.org. Website: http://www.sidran.org. **Acquisitions:** Esther Giller, director. Estab. 1991. Publishes hardcover originals and trade paperback originals and reprints. **Publishes 5-6 titles/year. Receives 75 queries and 40 mss/year. 20% of books from first-time authors; 95% from unagented writers. Pays 8-10% royalty on wholesale price.** Publishes book 1 year after acceptance of ms. No simultaneous submissions. Reports in 1 month on queries, 3 months on proposals, 6 months on mss. Book catalog and ms guidelines free.

O— "Sidran Press is the publishing component of a nonprofit organization devoted to advocacy, education and research in support of people with psychiatric disabilities related to extremely traumatic life experiences."

Exclusively publishes books about traumatic stress and dissociative conditions, nonfiction, practical tools for recovery, education and training materials for professionals, self-help workbooks. Currently emphasizing practical recovery tools, professional training, application of research. De-emphasizing biography, autobiography or first-person recovery narratives.

**Nonfiction:** Reference, self-help, textbook, professional. Subjects include psychiatry, expressive therapies, psychology. Specializes in trauma/abuse/domestic violence and mental health issues. Query with proposal package including outline, 2-3 sample chapters, introduction, competing titles, market information.

**Recent Nonfiction Title(s):** *Unspeakable Truths and Happy Endings: Human Cruelty and the New Trauma Therapy*, by Rebecca Coffey.

**SIERRA CLUB BOOKS**, Dept. WM, 85 Second, San Francisco CA 94105. (415)977-5500. Fax: (415)977-5793. **Acquisitions:** James Cohee, senior editor. Estab. 1962. Publishes hardcover and paperback originals and reprints. **Publishes 30 titles/year. Receives 1,000 submissions/year. 50% of books from unagented writers. Royalties vary by project. Offers $3,000-15,000 average advance.** Publishes book 18 months after acceptance. Reports in 2 months.

O➞ The Sierra Club was founded to help people to explore, enjoy and preserve the nation's forests, waters, wildlife and wilderness. The books program publishes quality trade books about the outdoors and the protection of natural resources.

**Imprint(s):** Sierra Club Books for Children.

**Nonfiction:** A broad range of environmental subjects: outdoor adventure, descriptive and how-to, women in the outdoors; landscape and wildlife pictorials; literature, including travel and works on the spiritual aspects of the natural world; travel and trail; natural history and current environmental issues, including public health and uses of appropriate technology; gardening; general interest; and children's books. "Specifically, we are interested in literary natural history, environmental issues such as nuclear power, self-sufficiency, politics and travel, and juvenile books with an ecological theme." Does *not* want "proposals for large color photographic books without substantial text; how-to books on building things outdoors; books on motorized travel; or any but the most professional studies of animals." Query first, then submit outline and sample chapters. Reviews artwork/photos as part of ms package. Send photocopies.

**Recent Title(s):** *Seven Wonders: Timeless Travels for a Healthier Planet.*

**SILHOUETTE BOOKS**, 300 E. 42nd St., New York NY 10017. (212)682-6080. Fax: (212)682-4539. Website: http://www.romance.net. Editorial Director, Silhouette Books, Harlequin Historicals: Tara Gavin. **Acquisitions:** Mary Theresa Hussey, senior editor (Silhouette Romance); Karen Taylor Richman, senior editor (Silhouette Special Editions); Joan Marlow Golan, senior editor (Silhouette Desires); Leslie Wainger, executive senior editor/editorial coordinator (Silhouette Intimate Moments); Tracy Farrell, senior editor/editorial coordinator (Harlequin Historicals). Estab. 1979. Publishes mass market paperback originals. **Publishes 350 titles/year. Receives 4,000 submissions/year. 10% of books from first-time authors; 50% from unagented writers. Pays royalty.** Publishes book 1-3 years after acceptance. Manuscript guidelines for #10 SASE.

O➞ Silhouette publishes contemporary adult romances.

**Imprint(s):** *Silhouette Romances* (contemporary adult romances, 53,000-58,000 words); *Silhouette Desires* (contemporary adult romances, 55,000-60,000 words); *Silhouette Intimate Moments* (contemporary adult romances, 80,000-85,000 words); *Silhouette Yours Truly* (contemporary adult romances, 53,000-58,000 words); *Harlequin Historicals* (adult historical romances, 95,000-105,000 words).

**Fiction:** Romance (contemporary and historical romance for adults). "We are interested in seeing submissions for all our lines. No manuscripts other than the types outlined. Manuscript should follow our general format, yet have an individuality and life of its own that will make it stand out in the readers' minds." Send query letter, 2 page synopsis and SASE to head of imprint. *No unsolicited mss.*

**Recent Title(s):** *The MacGregor Grooms*, by Nora Roberts.

**Tips:** "The romance market is constantly changing, so when you read for research, read the latest books and those that have been recommended to you by people knowledgeable in the genre. We are actively seeking new authors for all our lines, contemporary and historical."

**SIMON & SCHUSTER**, 1230 Avenue of the Americas, New York NY 10020. Website: http://www.simonsays.com. *Adult Trade:* Simon & Schuster Trade (Fireside, **The Free Press**, Kaplan, **Scribner [Lisa Drew, Rawson Associates**, Scribner], Simon & Schuster, Touchstone); *Simon & Schuster Children's Publishing:* (Aladdin Paperbacks, **Atheneum Books for Young Readers, Margaret K. McElderry Books**), Nickelodeon, Simon Spotlight **[Little Simon]**, **Simon & Schuster Books for Young Readers**, Simon & Schuster New Media; *Mass Market:* Pocket Books (Pocket Books for Young Adults **[Archway Paperbacks, Minstrel Books**, Pocket Books for Young Adults, Pocket Pulse], MTV Books, Nickelodeon, *Star Trek*, Washington Square Press).

**SIMON & SCHUSTER BOOKS FOR YOUNG READERS**, Simon & Schuster Children's Publishing Division, 1230 Avenue of the Americas, New York NY 10020. (212)698-2851. Website: http://www.simonandschuster.com. or http://www.simonsayskids.com. **Acquisitions:** Stephanie Owens Lurie, editorial director, vice president/associate publisher (humorous picture books, fiction, nonfiction); Kevin Lewis, editor (African-American/multicultural picture books, humorous picture books, middle-grade); David Gale, senior editor (young adult/middle grade novels); Michele Coppola, editor (toddler books, middle-grade fiction); Rebecca Davis, editor (character-centered picture books and poetry). Publishes hardcover originals. **Publishes 80-90 titles/year. Receives 2,500 queries and 10,000 mss/year. 5-10% of books**

**from first-time authors; 40% from unagented writers. Pays 4-12% royalty on retail price. Advance varies.** Publishes book 1-3 years after acceptance of ms. Accepts simultaneous submissions. Reports in 2 months on queries. Manuscript guidelines for #10 SASE.

○━ "The three adjectives we use to describe our imprint are fresh, family-oriented and accessible. We're looking for writing-edge fiction, family-oriented picture books that are character-oriented." Currently emphasizing middle grade humor/adventure stories. De-emphasizing nonfiction.

**Nonfiction:** Children's/juvenile. Subjects include animals, ethnic, history, nature/environment. "We're looking for innovative, appealing nonfiction especially for younger readers. Please don't submit education or textbooks." Query with SASE only. *All unsolicited mss returned unread.*

**Fiction:** Fantasy, historical, humor, juvenile, mystery, picture books, science fiction, young adult. "Fiction needs to be fresh, unusual and compelling to stand out from the competition. We're not looking for problem novels, stories with a moral, or rhymed picture book texts." Query with SASE only. *All unsolicited mss returned unread.*

**Poetry:** "Most of our poetry titles are anthologies; we publish very few stand-alone poets." No picture book ms in rhymed verse. Query.

**Recent Title(s):** *Ghosts of the White House*, by Charyl Harness (nonfiction); *Heaven*, by Angela Johnson (fiction); *Climb Into My Lap*, selected by Lee Bennett Hopkins (poetry).

**Tips:** "We're looking for fresh, original voices and unexplored topics. Don't do something because everyone else is doing it. Try to find what they're *not* doing. We publish mainly for the bookstore market, and are looking for books that will appeal directly to kids."

**SKIDMORE-ROTH PUBLISHING, INC.**, 400 Inverness Dr., S. #260, Englewood CO 80112. (303)662-8793. Fax: (303)662-8079. E-mail: info@skidmore-roth.com. Website: http://www.skidmore-roth.com. **Acquisitions:** Lynn Kendall, editor. Estab. 1987. Publishes trade paperback originals. **Publishes 24 titles/year. Receives 10 queries and 24 mss/year. 50% of books from first-time authors; 100% from unagented writers. Pays 4-8% royalty on wholesale price or makes outright purchase of $2,500-10,000.** Publishes book 9 months after acceptance of ms. Accepts simultaneous submissions. Reports in 2 weeks on proposals.

○━ Skidmore-Roth publishes medical books and material for medical professionals worldwide.

**Nonfiction:** Reference, textbook. Health/medicine subjects. "We are looking for proposals in areas where there is currently a lack of publication."

**Recent Title(s):** *EMS Field Protocol Manual*, by Jon Apfelbaum.

**Tips:** "Audience is licensed nurses working in hospitals, long term care facilities, subacute centers, home health, HMO's and medical clinics, nurse assistants and nurse aides, nursing students and other allied health professions."

**SKY PUBLISHING CORP.**, 49 Bay State Rd., Cambridge MA 02138. (617)864-7360. Fax: (617)864-6117. E-mail: postmaster@skypub.com. Website: http://www.skypub.com. President/Publisher: Richard Tresch Fienberg. **Acquisitions:** J. Kelly Beatty, senior editor; Carolyn Collins Petersen, editor, books and products; Sally MacGillivray, publications manager. Estab. 1941. **Publishes 4 titles/year.** Publishes hardcover and trade paperback originals on topics of interest to serious amateur astronomers as well as *Sky & Telescope: The Essential Magazine of Astronomy* and *Skywatch: Your Guide to Stargazing and Space Exploration.* Nonfiction only. Magazine articles: pays 20¢/word. **Books: pays 10% royalty on net sales.** Magazine author and book proposal guidelines available. Catalog free.

○━ Sky Publishing Corporation will be an advocate of astronomy and space science through its products and services and will aggressively promote greater understanding of these disciplines among laypeople.

**Recent Title(s):** *The Deep Sky: An Introduction*, by Philip S. Harrington.

**SLACK INC.**, 6900 Grove Rd., Thorofare NJ 08086. (609)848-1000. Fax: (609)853-5991. E-mail: adrummond@slackinc.com. Website: http://www.slackinc.com. **Acquisitions:** Amy E. Drummond, editorial director. Estab. 1960. Publishes hardcover and softcover originals. **Publishes 32 titles/year. Receives 80 queries and 23 mss/year. 75% of books from first-time authors; 100% from unagented writers. Pays 10% royalty.** Publishes book 8 months after acceptance. Accepts simultaneous submissions. Reports in 4 months on queries, 1 month on proposals, 3 months on mss. Book catalog and ms guidelines free.

○━ Slack publishes academic textbooks and professional reference books on various medical topics.

**Nonfiction:** Textbook (medical). Subjects include ophthalmology, athletic training, physical therapy, occupational therapy. Submit proposal package, including outline, 2 sample chapters, market profile and cv. Reviews artwork/photos as part of ms package. Send photocopies.

**Recent Title(s):** *Occupational Therapy: Enabling Function and Well Being*, by Christiansen and Baum.

**THE SMITH**, The Generalist Association, Inc., 69 Joralemon St., Brooklyn NY 11201-4003. (718)834-1212. Website: http://members.aol.com/thesmith1. **Acquisitions:** Harry Smith, publisher/editor; Michael McGrinder, associate editor. Estab. 1964. Publishes hardcover and trade paperback originals. **Publishes 3-5 titles/year. Receives 2,500 queries/year. 50% of books from first-time authors; more than 90% from unagented writers. Pays royalty. Offers $500-1,000 advance.** Publishes book 9 months after acceptance. Accepts simultaneous submissions. Reports in 3 months. Guidelines for #10 SASE.

○━ The Smith publishes literature of "outstanding artistic quality."

**Nonfiction:** Literary essays, language and literature. "The 'how' is as important as the 'what' to us. Don't bother to send anything if the prose itself is not outstanding. We don't publish anything about how to fix your car or your soul."

Query with proposal package including outline and sample chapter. Reviews artwork/photos as part of ms package. Send photocopies. No registered mail.
**Fiction:** Experimental, literary. "Emphasis is always on artistic quality. A synopsis of almost any novel sounds stupid." Query with 1 sample chapter. *No complete mss. No registered mail.*
**Poetry:** "No greeting card sentiments, no casual jottings." Submit 7-10 sample poems. No complete ms. Do not send registered mail.
**Recent Title(s):** *The Cleveland Indian*, by Luke Salisbury (novel); *Your Heart Will Fly Away*, by David Rigsbee (poetry).

**SMITH AND KRAUS PUBLISHERS, INC.**, One Main St., P.O. Box 127, Lyme NH 03768. (603)643-6431. **Acquisitions:** Marisa Smith, president/publisher. Estab. 1990. Publishes hardcover and trade paperback originals. **Publishes 35-40 books/year. 10% of books from first-time authors; 10-20% from unagented writers. Pays 10% royalty of net on retail price. Offers $500-2,000 advance.** Publishes book 1 year after acceptance. Reports in 1 month on queries, 2 months on proposals, 4 months on mss. Book catalog free.
**Nonfiction and Fiction:** Drama, theater. Query with SASE. Does not return submissions.
**Recent Title(s):** *Horton Foote: Collected Plays Volume III*; *Plays of Fairy Tales (Grades K-3)*, by L.E. McCullough.

**GIBBS SMITH, PUBLISHER**, P.O. Box 667, Layton UT 84041. (801)544-9800. Fax: (801)544-5582. Website: http://www.gibbs~smith.com. **Acquisitions:** Madge Baird, editorial director (humor, western); Gail Yngve, editor (gift books, architecture, interior decorating, poetry); Suzanne Taylor, editor (children's, rustic living, outdoor activities and picture); Linda Nimori, editor. Estab. 1969. Publishes hardcover and trade paperback originals. **Publishes 50 titles/year. Receives 1,500-2,000 submissions/year. 8-10% of books from first-time authors; 50% from unagented writers. Pays 6-15% royalty on gross receipts. Offers $2,000-3,000 advance.** Publishes book 1-2 years after acceptance of ms. Accepts simultaneous submissions, if so noted. Reports in 1 month on queries, 10 weeks on proposals and mss. Book catalog for 9×12 SAE and $2.13 in postage. Manuscript guidelines free.
  O─╖ "We publish books that enrich and inspire humankind." Currently emphasizing interior design and home reference. De-emphasizing novels and short stories.
**Imprint(s):** Peregrine Smith Books, Gibbs Smith Junior.
**Nonfiction:** Children's/juvenile, illustrated book, textbook. Subjects include architecture, humor, interior design, nature, regional. Query or submit outline, several completed sample chapters and author's cv. Reviews artwork/photos as part of the ms package. Send sample illustrations if applicable.
**Fiction:** Only short works oriented to gift market. Submit synopsis with sample illustration if applicable.
**Poetry:** "Our annual poetry contest accepts entries only in April. Charges $15 fee. Prize: $500." Submit complete ms.
**Recent Title(s):** *Mexican Country Style*, by Witynski and Carr (nonfiction); *The Lesson*, by Carol Lynn Pearson (fiction).

**SOCIAL SCIENCE EDUCATION CONSORTIUM**, P.O. Box 21270, Boulder CO 80308-4270. (303)492-8154. Fax: (303)449-3925. E-mail: singletl@stripe.colorado.edu. **Acquisitions:** Laurel R. Singleton, managing editor. Estab. 1963. Publishes trade paperback originals. **Publishes 8 titles/year. 25% of books from first-time authors; 100% from unagented writers. Pays 8-12% royalty on net sales (retail price minus average discount).** Publishes book 6 months after acceptance. Accepts simultaneous submissions. Reports in 1 month on proposals.
  O─╖ "We publish materials to help K-12 social studies teachers enrich their curriculum—through lessons on new topics, that take students deeper than a traditional text would, or involve innovative teaching strategies." Currently emphasizing history, geography and civics education.
**Nonfiction:** Teacher resources. Subjects include education, government/politics, history; must include teaching applications. "We publish titles of interest to social studies teachers particularly; we do not generally publish on such broad educational topics as discipline, unless there is a specific relationship to the social studies/social sciences." Submit outline and 1-2 sample chapters.
**Recent Title(s):** *Service Learning in the Middle School Curriculum: Staff Development Handbook*, by Ron Schukar and Laurel Singelton.
**Tips:** "The mission of the SSEC is threefold: (1) to provide leadership for social science education, (2) to promote a larger role for the social sciences in the curriculum, and (3) to close the gap between frontier thinking in the social sciences and the curriculum."

**SOHO PRESS, INC.**, 853 Broadway, New York NY 10003. (212)260-1900. Website: http://www.sohopress.com. **Acquisitions:** Juris Jurjevics, publisher/editor-in-chief; Laura Hruska, associate publisher; Melanie Fleishman, editor/director of marketing. Estab. 1986. Publishes hardcover and trade paperback originals. **Publishes 35 titles/year. Receives 5,000 submissions/year. 75% of books from first-time authors; 50% from unagented writers. Pays 7½-15% royalty on retail price. Offers advance.** Publishes book within 1 year after acceptance. Accepts simultaneous submissions. Reports in 2 months. Book catalog for 6×9 SAE with 2 first-class stamps.
  O─╖ Soho Press publishes literary fiction, mysteries set overseas, and in the U.S., multicultural fiction and nonfiction.
**Nonfiction:** Literary nonfiction: travel, autobiography, biography, etc. No self-help. Submit outline and sample chapters.
**Fiction:** Adventure, ethnic, feminist, historical, literary, mainstream/contemporary, mystery, suspense. Submit complete ms with SASE. *Writer's Market* recommends query with SASE first.
**Recent Title(s):** *Hokkaido Highway Blues: Hitchhiking Japan*, by Will Ferguson (nonfiction); *The Farming of Bones*,

by Edwidge Danticat (fiction).

**Tips:** "Soho Press publishes discerning authors for discriminating readers, finding the strongest possible writers and publishing them." Soho Press also publishes two book series: Hera (historical fiction reprints with accurate and strong female lead characters) and Soho Crime (mysteries set overseas, noir, procedurals).

**SOUNDPRINTS**, The Trudy Corp., 353 Main Ave., Norwalk CT 06851. (203)846-2274. Fax: (203)846-1776. E-mail: sndprnts@ix.netcom.com. Website: http://www.soundprints.com. **Acquisitions:** Stephanie Smith, editorial assistant. Estab. 1988. Publishes hardcover originals. **Publishes 12-14 titles/year. Receives 200 queries/year. 20% of books from first-time authors; 90% of books from unagented writers. Makes outright purchase. No advance.** Publishes book 2 years after acceptance of ms. Accepts simultaneous submissions. Reports on queries in 3 months. Book catalog for $9 \times 12$ SASE with $1.21 postage. Manuscript guidelines for #10 SASE.

    O—π Soundprints publishes picture books that portray a particular animal and its habitat. All books are reviewed for accuracy by curators from the Smithsonian Institution and other wildlife experts.

**Nonfiction:** Children's/juvenile, animals. "We focus on worldwide wildlife and habitats. Subject animals must be portrayed realistically and must not be anthropomorphic. Meticulous research is required." Query with SASE. Does not review photos. (All books are illustrated in full color.)

**Fiction:** Juvenile. "Most of our books are under license from the Smithsonian Institution or The Nature Conservancy, and are closely curated fictional stories based on fact. We never do stories of anthropomorphic animals. When we publish juvenile fiction, it will be about wildlife or history and all information in the book *must* be accurate." Query.

**Recent Title(s):** *Bluestem Horizon: A Story of a Tallgrass Prairie*, by Evelyn Lee; illustrated by Krista Brauckmann-Towns.

**Tips:** "Our books are written for children from ages four through eight. Our most successful authors can craft a wonderful story which is derived from authentic wildlife or historic facts. First inquiry to us should ask about our interest in publishing a book about a specific animal or habitat."

**SOURCEBOOKS, INC.,** P.O. Box 372, Naperville IL 60566. (630)961-3900. Fax: (630)961-2168. Publisher: Dominique Raccah. **Acquisitions:** Todd Stocke, managing editor (nonfiction trade); Mark Warda (Legal Survival Guides self-help/law series); Deborah Werksman (Hysteria Publications). Estab. 1987. Publishes hardcover and trade paperback originals. **Publishes 70 titles/year. 50% of books from first-time authors; 75% from unagented writers. Pays 6-15% royalty on wholesale price.** Publishes book 1 year after acceptance. Accepts simultaneous submissions. Reports in 3 months on queries. Book catalog and ms guidelines for $9 \times 12$ SASE.

    O—π Sourcebooks publishes many forms of nonfiction titles, generally in the how-to and reference areas, including books on parenting, self-help/psychology, business and health. Focus is on practical, useful information and skills. It also continues to publish in the reference, New Age, history, current affairs and travel categories. Currently emphasizing humor, gift, women's interest, New Age.

**Imprint(s):** Casablanca Press, Legal Survival Guides, Sphinx Publishing (self-help legal), Hysteria Publications (women's humor/gift book).

**Nonfiction:** *Small Business Sourcebooks:* books for small business owners, entrepreneurs and students. "A key to submitting books to us is to explain how your book helps the reader, why it is different from the books already out there (please do your homework) and the author's credentials for writing this book." *Sourcebooks:* gift books, self-help, general business, and how to. "Books likely to succeed with us are self-help, art books, parenting and childcare, psychology, women's issues, how-to, house and home, humor, gift books or books with strong artwork." Query or submit outline and 2-3 sample chapters (not the first). *No complete mss.* Reviews artwork/photos as part of ms package.

**Recent Title(s):** *We Interrupt This Broadcast*, by Joe Garner (history).

**Tips:** "Our market is a decidedly trade-oriented bookstore audience. We also have very strong penetration into the gift store market. Books which cross over between these two very different markets do extremely well with us. Our list is a solid mix of unique and general audience titles and series-oriented projects. In other words, we are looking for products that break new ground either in their own areas or within the framework of our series of imprints. We love to develop books in new areas or develop strong titles in areas that are already well developed."

**SOUTH END PRESS**, 7 Brookline St., Cambridge MA 02139. (617)547-4002. Fax: (617)547-1333. **Acquisitions:** Acquisitions Department. Estab. 1977. Publishes hardcover and trade paperback originals and reprints. **Publishes 15 titles/year. Receives 400 queries and 100 mss/year. 50% of books from first-time authors; 95% from unagented writers. Pays 11% royalty on wholesale price. Occasionally offers $500-2,500 advance.** Publishes book 9 months after acceptance. Accepts simultaneous submissions. Reports in up to 3 months on queries and proposals. Book catalog and ms guidelines free.

    O—π South End Press publishes nonfiction political books with a new left/feminist/multicultural perspective.

**Nonfiction:** Subjects include economics, education, ethnic, gay/lesbian, government/politics, health/medicine, history, nature/environment, philosophy, science, sociology, women's issues/studies, political. Query or submit 2 sample chapters including intro or conclusion and annotated toc. Reviews artwork as part of ms package. Send photocopies.

**Recent Title(s):** *Zapata's Disciple: Essays*, by Martin Espada.

**SOUTHERN ILLINOIS UNIVERSITY PRESS**, P.O. Box 3697, Carbondale IL 62902-3697. (618)453-2680. Fax: (618)453-1221. **Acquisitions:** Jim Simmons, editorial director (film, theater, aviation, American history); Karl Kageff, sponsoring editor (composition, rhetoric, criminology); Rick Stetter, director (military history, criminology, trade nonfiction). Estab. 1956. Publishes hardcover and trade paperback originals and reprints. **Publishes 50-60 titles/year; imprint publishes 4-6 titles/year. Receives 800 queries and 300 mss/year. 45% of books from first-time authors; 100% from unagented writers. Pays 5-10% royalty on wholesale price. Rarely offers advance.** Publishes book 1 year after receipt of a final ms. Reports in 3 months. Book catalog and ms guidelines free.

O— "To serve the academy and serious readers of the Mississippi Valley." Currently emphasizing theater, film, baseball. De-emphasizing literary criticism, philosophy.

**Imprint(s):** Shawnee Books (contact Lisa Bayer, director of marketing).

**Nonfiction:** Biography, reference, textbook. Subjects include Americana, history, regional, sports, women's issues/studies. Query with proposal package, including synopsis, table of contents, author's vita with SASE.

**Recent Title(s):** *The World Wars Through the Female Gaze*, by Jean Gallagher (literature/history).

**SOUTHERN METHODIST UNIVERSITY PRESS**, P.O. Box 415, Dallas TX 75275. Fax: (214)768-1432. Website: http://www.smu.edu/~press. **Acquisitions:** Kathryn Lang, senior editor. Estab. 1937. Publishes hardcover and trade paperback originals and reprints. **Publishes 10-15 titles/year. Receives 500 queries and 500 mss/year. 75% of books from first-time authors; 95% from unagented writers. Pays up to 10% royalty on wholesale price. Offers $500 advance.** Publishes book 1 year after acceptance. Reports in 1 month on queries and proposals, 1 year on mss.

O— Southern Methodist University publishes in the fields of literary fiction, ethics and human values, film and theater, regional studies and theological studies. Currently emphasizing literary fiction. De-emphasizing scholarly, narrowly focused studies.

**Nonfiction:** Subjects include medical ethics/human values, film/theater, regional history, theology. Query with outline, 3 sample chapters, table of contents and author bio. Reviews artwork/photos as part of the ms package. Send photocopies.

**Fiction:** Literary novels and short story collections. Query.

**Recent Title(s):** *A Complicated Situation*, by Jane Mullen (short story collection); *Between Two Silences: Talking with Peter Brook*, edited by Dale Moffitt (conversations with the world-renowned stage director).

**SOUTHFARM PRESS**, Haan Graphic Publishing Services, Ltd., P.O. Box 1296, Middletown CT 06457. (860)346-8798. Fax: (860)347-9931. E-mail: haan/southfarm@usa.net. Publisher: Walter J. Haan. **Acquisitions:** Wanda P. Haan, editor-in-chief. Estab. 1983. Publishes trade hardcover and paperback originals. **Publishes 5 titles/year. 90% from first-time authors; 100% from unagented writers. Pays 5-10% royalty on retail price. No advance.** Publishes book 1 year after acceptance of ms. Accepts simultaneous submissions. Reports in 1 month. *Writer's Market* recommends allowing 2 months for reply.

O— Southfarm publishes primarily history and military/war nonfiction. Currently emphasizing air wars, poetry. No longer publishing on dog breeds.

**Nonfiction:** Subjects include history, military/war. Submit outline/synopsis and sample chapters.

**Recent Title(s):** *The Emperor's Angry Guest*, by Ralph Knox (nonfiction); *Life Is A Poem*, by Evelyn Brill Stark (poetry).

**SPECTRA**, Bantam Dell Publishing Group, Random House, Inc., 1540 Broadway, New York NY 10036. (212)782-9418. Fax: (212)782-9523. Website: http://www.bdd.com. **Acquisitions:** Anne Lesley Groell, editor. Estab. 1984. Publishes hardcover, trade and mass market paperback originals and reprints. **Receives hundreds of queries and 500 mss/year. 20% of books from first-time authors. Pays 8-10% royalty on wholesale price. Pays $5,000 and up advance.** Publishes book 1 year after acceptance of ms. Accepts simultaneous submissions, if so noted. Reports in 8 months. Manuscript guidelines for #10 SASE.

O— "Spectra has a high-quality list of fantasy and science fiction, but we buy across the board."

**Fiction:** Fantasy, science fiction, humorous fantasy and science fiction. "We try to have a high-quality list. If we love and are passionate about what we're reading, we'll do what we can to work with it." Submit synopsis, 3 sample chapters with SASE.

**Recent Title(s):** *Antarctica*, by Kim Stanley Robinson (science fiction); *A Clash of Kings*, by George R.R. Martin (fantasy).

**Tips:** "We publish books for an adult audience. We like to bring new authors in, but be aware we already have a crowded list and cannot buy as freely as we'd like."

**THE SPEECH BIN, INC.**, 1965 25th Ave., Vero Beach FL 32960-3062. (561)770-0007. **Acquisitions:** Jan J. Binney, senior editor. Estab. 1984. Publishes trade paperback originals. **Publishes 10-20 titles/year. Receives 500 mss/year. 50% of books from first-time authors; 90% from unagented writers. Pays negotiable royalty on wholesale price.** Publishes ms 1 year after acceptance. Reports within 3 months if SASE included. Book catalog for 9×12 SASE and $1.48 postage.

O— Publishes professional materials for specialists in rehabilitation, particularly speech-language pathologists and audiologists, special educators, occupational and physical therapists, and parents and caregivers of children and adults with developmental and post-trauma disabilities."

**Nonfiction:** How-to, illustrated book, juvenile (preschool-teen), reference, textbook, educational material and games for both children and adults. Subjects include health, communication disorders and education for handicapped persons. Query or submit outline and sample chapters with SASE. Reviews artwork as part of ms package. Send photocopies.

**Fiction:** "Booklets or books for children and adults about handicapped persons, especially with communication disorders." Query or submit outline/synopsis and sample chapters. "This is a potentially new market for The Speech Bin."

**Recent Title(s):** *Living Skills for the Head-Injured Child*, by Julie Buxton and Kelly Godfree (nonfiction); *Artic-Pic*, by Denise Grigas.

**Tips:** "Books and materials must be clearly presented, well written and competently illustrated. We have added books and materials for use by other allied health professionals. We are also looking for more materials for use in treating adults and very young children with communication disorders. Please do not fax manuscripts to us." The Speech Bin is increasing their number of books published per year and is especially interested in reviewing treatment materials for adults and adolescents.

**[N] SPENCE PUBLISHING COMPANY**, 501 Elm St., Suite 450, Dallas TX 75202. (214)939-1700. Fax: (214)939-1800. Website: http://www.spencepublishing.com. **Acquisitions:** Mitchell Muncy, editor-in-chief. Estab. 1995. Publishes hardcover and trade paperback originals. **Publishes 10-12 titles/year. Pays 10-15% royalty on net receipts. No advance.** Accepts simultaneous submissions. Reports in 1 month on queries, 2 months on proposals. Book catalog free or on website. Manuscript guidelines for #10 SASE.
   O— Spence publishes nonfiction books of commentary on social and cultural issues related to education, ethics, religion and public life, politics, law, marriage and the family, and the arts.
**Nonfiction:** Subjects include education, government/politics, philosophy, religion, sociology, women's issues/studies. Query with SASE or submit proposal package, including outline, 1 sample chapter and SASE.

**SPINSTERS INK**, 32 E. First St., #330, Duluth, MN 55802. (218)727-3222. Fax: (218)727-3119. E-mail: spinsters@spinsters-ink.com. Website: http://www.spinsters-ink.com. **Acquisitions:** Nancy Walker. Estab. 1978. Publishes trade paperback originals and reprints. **Publishes 6 titles/year. Receives 400 submissions/year. 50% of books from first-time authors; 95% from unagented writers. Pays 7-11% royalty on retail price.** Publishes book 18 months after acceptance. Reports in 4 months. Book catalog free. Manuscript guidelines for SASE.
   O— "Spinsters Ink publishes novels and nonfiction works that deal with significant issues in women's lives from a feminist perspective: books that not only name these crucial issues, but—more important—encourage change and growth. We are committed to publishing works by women writing from the periphery, fat women, Jewish women, lesbians, old women, poor women, rural women, women examining classism, women of color, women with disabilities, women who are writing books that help make the best in our lives more possible."
**Nonfiction:** Feminist analysis for positive change. Subjects include women's issues. "We do not want to see work by men or anything that is not specific to women's lives (humor, children's books, etc.)." Query. Reviews artwork/photos as part of ms package.
**Fiction:** Ethnic, women's, lesbian. "We do not publish poetry or short fiction. We are interested in fiction that challenges, women's language that is feminist, stories that treat lifestyles with the diversity and complexity they deserve. We are also interested in genre fiction, especially mysteries." Submit outline/synopsis and sample chapters.
**Recent Title(s):** *Turnip Blues*, by Helen Campbell (fiction).

**STACKPOLE BOOKS**, 5067 Ritter Rd., Mechanicsburg PA 17055. Fax: (717)796-0412. E-mail: stackpoleedit@paonline.com. Website: http://www.stackpolebooks.com. **Acquisitions:** Judith Schnell, editorial director (fly fishing, sports); William C. Davis, editor (history); Mark Allison, editor (nature, photography); Ed Skender, editor (military guides); Kyle Weaver (Pennsylvania). Estab. 1935. Publishes hardcover and paperback originals and reprints. **Publishes 75 titles/year. Pays industry standard royalty.** Publishes book 1 year after acceptance. Reports in 1 month. *Writer's Market* recommends allowing 2 months for reply.
   O— "Stackpole maintains a growing and vital publishing program by featuring authors who are experts in their fields, from outdoor activities to Civil War history."
**Nonfiction:** Outdoor-related subject areas—nature, wildlife, outdoor skills, outdoor sports, fly fishing, paddling, climbing, crafts and hobbies, photography, history especially Civil War and military guides. Query. Does not return unsolicited mss. Reviews artwork/photos as part of ms package.
**Recent Title(s):** *Exploring the Appalachian Trail Guides* (5-book hiking series).
**Tips:** "Stackpole seeks well-written, authoritative manuscripts for specialized and general trade markets. Proposals should include chapter outline, sample chapter and illustrations and author's credentials."

**STA-KRIS, INC.**, P.O. Box 1131, Marshalltown IA 50158. (515)753-4139. President: Kathy Wagoner. Publishes hardcover and trade paperback originals. **Publishes 4 titles/year. Pays negotiated royalty on wholesale price or makes outright purchase. Advance negotiable.** Publishes book 1 year after acceptance. Accepts simultaneous submissions. Reports in 2 months on queries and proposals, 4 months on mss. Book catalog free.
**Nonfiction:** Coffee table book, gift book, illustrated book, self-help. "We publish nonfiction gift books that portray universal feelings, truths and values or have a special occasion theme, plus small format compilations of statements about professions, issues, attitudes, etc." Query with proposal package including synopsis, bio, published credits.
**Recent Title(s):** *The Grandparents' Memory Book*, by Teri Harrison.
**Tips:** "Our audience tends to be women ages 20 and older. We are an independent publisher who supports the marketing of their books with great energy and knowledge. We are currently looking for projects that would fit nicely in the gift store market."

**STANDARD PUBLISHING**, Standex International Corp., 8121 Hamilton Ave., Cincinnati OH 45231. (513)931-4050. Publisher/Vice President: Eugene H. Wigginton. **Acquisitions:** Lisa Caldwell (children's books); Ruth Frederick (children's ministry resources); Dale Reeves (empowered youth products); Jim Eichenberger (solid foundation resources of ministry to adults). Estab. 1866. Publishes hardcover and paperback originals and reprints. **Pays royalty.** Publishes book 18 months after acceptance. Reports in 3 months. Manuscript guidelines for #10 SASE; send request to Jolene Barnes.

○— Standard specializes in religious books for children and religious education.

**Nonfiction:** Children's picture books, Christian education (teacher training, working with volunteers), quiz, puzzle, crafts (to be used in Christian education). Query with SASE.

**Recent Title(s):** *The Young Reader's Bible* (nonfiction); *Be Brave Anna!* (fiction).

**STANFORD UNIVERSITY PRESS**, Stanford CA 94305-2235. (650)723-9434. Fax: (605)725-3457. Website: http://www.sup.org. Editorial Director: Pamela Holway. Senior Editor: Muriel Bell. Humanities Editor: Helen Tartar. **Acquisitions:** Norris Pope, director. Estab. 1925. **Publishes 120 titles/year. Receives 1,500 submissions/year. 40% of books from first-time authors; 95% from unagented writers. Pays up to 15% royalty ("typically 10%, often none"). Sometimes offers advance.** Publishes book 14 months after receipt of final ms. Reports in 6 weeks.

○— Stanford University Press publishes scholarly books in the humanities, social sciences and natural history, high-level textbooks and some books for a more general audience.

**Nonfiction:** History and culture of China, Japan and Latin America; literature, criticism, and literary theory; political science and sociology; European history; anthropology, linguistics and psychology; archaeology and geology; medieval and classical studies. Query with prospectus and an outline. Reviews artwork/photos as part of ms package.

**Recent Title(s):** *The Leisure Ethic*, by William A. Gleason and Charles W. Chesnutt.

**Tips:** "The writer's best chance is a work of original scholarship with an argument of some importance."

**STARBURST PUBLISHERS**, P.O. Box 4123, Lancaster PA 17604. (717)293-0939. Fax: (717)293-1945. E-mail: starburst@starburstpublishers.com. Website: http://www.starburstpublishers.com. **Acquisitions:** David A. Robie, editor-in-chief. Estab. 1982. Publishes hardcover and trade paperback originals. **Publishes 15-20 titles/year. Receives 1,000 queries and mss/year. 50% of books from first-time authors, 75% from unagented writers. Pays 6-16% royalty on wholesale price. Advance varies.** Publishes book 1 year after acceptance of ms. Accepts simultaneous submissions. Reports in 1 month on queries. *Writer's Market* recommends allowing 2 months for reply. Book catalog for 9 × 12 SASE with 4 first-class stamps. Manuscript guidelines for #10 SASE.

○— Starburst publishes quality self-help, health and inspirational titles for the trade and religious markets. Currently emphasizing inspirational gift books. De-emphasizing fiction.

**Nonfiction:** General nonfiction, cookbook, gift book, how-to, self-help, Christian. Subjects include business/economics, child guidance/parenting, cooking/foods/nutrition, counseling/career guidance, education, gardening, health/medicine, money/finance, nature/environment, psychology, real estate, recreation, religion. "We are looking for contemporary issues facing Christians and today's average American." Submit proposal package including outline, 3 sample chapters, author's biography and SASE. Reviews artwork/photos as part of ms package. Send photocopies.

**Fiction:** Inspirational. "We are only looking for good wholesome fiction that inspires or fiction that teaches self-help principles." Submit outline/synopsis, 3 sample chapters, author's biography and SASE.

**Recent Title(s):** *Revelation/Daniel*. by Daymond Duck (nonfiction); *The Fragile Thread*, by Aliske Webb (fiction).

**Tips:** "Fifty percent of our line goes into the Christian marketplace, fifty percent into the general marketplace. We have direct sales representatives in both the Christian and general (bookstore, library, health and gift) marketplace. Write on an issue that slots you on talk shows and thus establishes your name as an expert and writer."

**STEEPLE HILL**, Harlequin Enterprises, 300 E. 42nd St., New York NY 10017. Website: http://www.romance.net. **Acquisitions:** Tara Gavin, editorial director; Tracy Farrell, senior editor. Acquisitions Editors: Melissa Jeglinski, Ann Leslie Tuttle, Patience Smith, Karen Kosztolnyik and all Silhouette/Harlequin Historicals editors. Estab. 1997. Publishes mass market paperback originals. **Pays royalty.** Manuscript guidelines for #10 SASE.

○— "This series of contemporary, inspirational love stories portrays Christian characters facing the many challenges of life, faith and love in today's world."

**Imprint(s):** Love Inspired.

**Fiction:** Christian romance (70,000 words). Query or submit synopsis and 3 sample chapters with SASE.

**Recent Title(s):** *With Baby in Mind*, by Arlene James.

**Tips:** "Drama, humor and even a touch of mystery all have a place in this series. Subplots are welcome and should further the story's main focus or intertwine in a meaningful way. Secondary characters (children, family, friends, neighbors, fellow church members, etc.) may all contribute to a substantial and satisfying story. These wholesome tales of romance include strong family values and high moral standards. While there is no premarital sex between characters, a vivid, exciting romance that is presented with a mature perspective, is essential. Although the element of faith must clearly be present, it should be well integrated into the characterizations and plot. The conflict between the main characters should be an emotional one, arising naturally from the well-developed personalities you've created. Suitable stories should also impart an important lesson about the powers of trust and faith."

**N STEMMER HOUSE PUBLISHERS**, 2627 Caves Rd., Owings Mills MD 21117. (410)363-3690. E-mail: stemmer house@home.com. Website: http://www.stemmer.com. **Acquisitions:** Barbara Holdridge, president (design, natural history, children's books, gardening, cookbooks). Estab. 1975. Publishes hardcover and trade paperback originals. **Publishes 3-5 titles/year; imprint publishes 2 titles/year. Receives 2,000 queries and 1,500 mss/year. 50% of books from**

**first-time authors; 90% from unagented writers. Pays 5-10% royalty on wholesale price. Offers $300 advance.** Publishes book 1-2 years after acceptance of ms. Accepts simultaneous submissions. Reports in 2 weeks. Book catalog for 9×12 SAE and 2 first-class stamps. Manuscript guidelines for #10 SASE.

○━ Stemmer House publishes nonfiction illustrated books for adults and children in the arts and humanities, cookbooks, gardening, children's books and audio cassettes. Currently emphasizing natural history. De-emphasizing adult and children's fiction.

**Imprints:** The International Design Library, The NatureEncyclopedia Series.

**Nonfiction:** Biography, children's/juvenile, cookbook, illustrated book. Subjects include animals, art/architecture, gardening, multicultural, nature/environment. Query with SASE or submit proposal package, including outline, 3 sample chapters and cover letter. Reviews artwork/photos as part of ms package. Send photocopies and transparencies.

**Recent Titles:** *Floral Designs from Traditional Printed Handkerchiefs*, by Phoebe Erb.

**STENHOUSE PUBLISHERS**, P.O. Box 360, York ME 03909. (207)363-9198. Fax: (207)363-9730. E-mail: philippa @stenhouse.com. Website: http://www.stenhouse.com. **Acquisitions:** Philippa Stratton, editorial director. Estab. 1993. Publishes paperback originals. **Publishes 15 titles/year. Receives 300 queries/year. 30% of books from first-time authors; 99% from unagented writers. Pays royalty on wholesale price. Offers "very modest" advance.** Publishes book 6 months after delivery of final ms. Reports in 1 month on queries, 2 months on proposals, 3 months on mss. Book catalog and ms guidelines free or on website.

○━ Stenhouse publishes books that support teachers' professional growth by connecting theory and practice, and specializes in literacy education.

**Nonfiction:** Exclusively education, specializing in literacy. "All our books are a combination of theory and practice." Query with outline. Reviews artwork/photos as part of ms package. Send photocopies.

**Recent Title(s):** *Methods that Matter: Six Structures for Best Practice Classrooms*, by Harvey Danielle and Marilyn Bizar; *Craft Lessons: Teaching Writing K-8*, by Ralph Fletcher.

**STERLING PUBLISHING**, 387 Park Ave. S., New York NY 10016. (212)532-7160. Fax: (212)213-2495. **Acquisitions:** Sheila Anne Barry, acquisitions manager. Estab. 1949. Publishes hardcover and paperback originals and reprints. **Publishes 350 titles/year. Pays royalty. Offers advance.** Publishes book 1 year after acceptance. Reports in 4 months. Guidelines for SASE.

○━ Sterling publishes highly illustrated, accessible, hands-on, practical books for adults and children.

**Imprint(s):** Sterling/Chapelle; Sterling/Tamos; Sterling/Silver; Sterling/Godsfield; Sterling/SIR.

**Nonfiction:** Alternative lifestyle, fiber arts, games and puzzles, health, how-to, hobbies, children's humor, children's science, nature and activities, pets, recreation, reference, sports, wine, gardening, art, home decorating, dolls and puppets, ghosts, UFOs, woodworking, crafts, medieval, Celtic subjects, alternative health and healing, new consciousness. Query or submit detailed outline and 2 sample chapters with photos if applicable.

**Recent Title(s):** *The Great Rubber Stamp Book*, by Dee Gruenig.

**STIPES PUBLISHING CO.**, P.O. Box 526, Champaign IL 61824-9933. (217)356-8391. Fax: (217)356-5753. E-mail: stipes@soltec.com. **Acquisitions:** Benjamin H. Watts, (engineering, science, business); Robert Watts (agriculture, music and physical education). Estab. 1925. **Publishes hardcover and paperback originals. Publishes 15-30 titles/year. Receives 150 submissions/year. 50% of books from first-time authors; 95% from unagented writers. Pays 15% maximum royalty on retail price.** Publishes book 4 months after acceptance. Reports in 2 months.

○━ Stipes Publishing is "oriented towards the education market and educational books with some emphasis in the trade market."

**Nonfiction:** Technical (some areas), textbooks on business/economics, music, chemistry, CADD, AUTO-CADD, agriculture/horticulture, environmental education, and recreation and physical education. "All of our books in the trade area are books that also have a college text market. No books unrelated to educational fields taught at the college level." Submit outline and 1 sample chapter.

**Recent Title(s):** *Keyboard Musicianship, Book One*, by James Lykeetal (music).

**STOEGER PUBLISHING COMPANY**, 5 Mansard Court, Wayne NJ 07470. (973)872-9500. Fax: (973)872-2230. **Acquisitions:** David Perkins, vice president. Estab. 1925. Publishes trade paperback originals. **Publishes 12-15 titles/ year. Royalty varies, depending on ms.** Accepts simultaneous submissions. Reports in 1 month. Book catalog for #10 SAE with 2 first-class stamps.

○━ Stoeger publishes books on hunting, shooting sports, fishing, cooking, nature and wildlife.

**FOR EXPLANATIONS OF THESE SYMBOLS,**
**SEE THE INSIDE FRONT AND BACK COVERS OF THIS BOOK.**

**Nonfiction:** Specializing in reference and how-to books that pertain to hunting, fishing and appeal to gun enthusiasts. Submit outline and sample chapters.
**Recent Title(s):** *Gun Trader's Guide*, by Toby Bridges.

**STONE BRIDGE PRESS**, P.O. Box 8208, Berkeley CA 94707. (510)524-8732. Fax: (510)524-8711. E-mail: sbp@ston ebridge.com. Website: http://www.stonebridge.com/. **Acquisitions:** Peter Goodman, publisher. Estab. 1989. Publishes hardcover and trade paperback originals. **Publishes 6 titles/year; imprint publishes 2 titles/year. Receives 100 queries and 75 mss/year. 15-20% of books from first-time authors; 90% from unagented writers. Pays royalty on wholesale price. Advance varies.** Publishes book 2 years after acceptance. Accepts simultaneous submissions. Reports in 1 month on queries and proposals, 4 months on mss. Book catalog free.
    ○┬ Stone Bridge Press strives "to publish and distribute high-quality informational tools about Japan."
**Imprint(s):** The Rock Spring Collection of Japanese Literature.
**Nonfiction:** How-to, reference. Subjects include art/architecture, business/economics, government/politics, language/ literature, philosophy, translation, travel, women's issues/studies. "We publish Japan- (and some Asia-) related books only." Query with SASE. Reviews artwork/photos as part of ms package. Send photocopies.
**Recent Title(s):** *365 Views of Mt. Fuji*, *The Animé Companion*, *Saké Pure & Simple*.
**Tips:** Audience is "intelligent, worldly readers with an interest in Japan based on personal need or experience. No children's books or commercial fiction. Realize that interest in Japan is a moving target. Please don't submit yesterday's trends or rely on a view of Japan that is outmoded. Stay current!"

**STONEWALL INN**, St. Martin's Press, 175 Fifth Ave., New York NY 10010. (212)674-5151. Website: http://www.sto newallinn.com. **Acquisitions:** Keith Kahla, general editor. Publishes trade paperback originals and reprints. **Publishes 20-23 titles/year. Receives 3,000 queries/year. 40% of books from first-time authors; 25% from unagented writers. Pays standard royalty on retail price. Advance varies.** Publishes book 1 year after acceptance of ms. Accepts simultaneous submissions. Reports in 6 months on queries. Book catalog free.
    ○┬ Stonewall Inn is an imprint for gay and lesbian themed fiction, nonfiction and mysteries. Currently emphasizing literary fiction. De-emphasizing mysteries.
**Nonfiction:** Subjects include nearly every aspect of gay/lesbian studies. "We are looking for well-researched sociological works; author's credentials count for a great deal." Query with SASE.
**Fiction:** Gay/lesbian, literary, mystery. "Anybody who has any question about what a gay novel is should go out and read half a dozen. For example, there are hundreds of 'coming out' novels in print." Query with SASE.
**Recent Title(s):** *The Pleasure Principle*, by Michael Bronski (nonfiction); *An Arrow's Flight*, by Mark Merlis (fiction).

**STONEYDALE PRESS**, 523 Main St., Stevensville MT 59870. (406)777-2729. Fax: (406)777-2521. **Acquisitions:** Dale A. Burk, publisher. Estab. 1976. Publishes hardcover and trade paperback originals. **Publishes 4-6 titles/year. Receives 40-50 queries and 6-8 mss/year. 90% of books from unagented writers. Pays 12-15% royalty.** Publishes book 18 months after acceptance of ms. Reports in 2 months. Book catalog available.
    ○┬ "We seek to publish the best available source books on big game hunting, historical reminiscence and outdoor recreation in the Northern Rocky Mountain region."
**Nonfiction:** How-to hunting books, historical reminiscences. Query.
**Recent Title(s):** *Lewis & Clark in the Bitterroot*; *Self-Defense for Nature Lovers*.

**STOREY PUBLISHING**, Schoolhouse Rd., Pownal VT 05261. (802)823-5200. Fax: (802)823-5819. Website: http:// www.storey.com. **Acquisitions:** Margaret J. Lydic, editorial director; Deborah Balmuth (natural beauty and healing/ health, crafts, herbs); Deborah Burns (animals, horses, birds, farming); Gwen Steege (gardening, crafts); Dan Callahan (building). Estab. 1983. Publishes hardcover and trade paperback originals and reprints. **Publishes 45 titles/year. Receives 350 queries and 150 mss/year. 25% of books from first-time authors; 80% from unagented writers. Pays royalty or makes outright purchase.** Publishes book within 2 years of acceptance. Accepts simultaneous submissions. Reports in 1 month on queries, 3 months on proposals and mss. Book catalog and ms guidelines free.
    ○┬ "We publish practical information that encourages personal independence in harmony with the environment."
**Nonfiction:** Subjects include garden and home, herbs, natural health and beauty, birds and nature, animals, beer and wine, cooking and crafts, building, home-based business. Occasionally reviews artwork/photos as part of the ms package.
**Recent Title(s):** *Herbal Tea Gardens*, by Marietta Marshall Marcin.

**STORY LINE PRESS**, P.O. Box 1240, Ashland OR 97520. (541)512-8792. Fax: (541)512-8793. **Acquisitions:** Robert McDowell, publisher/editor. Estab. 1985. Publishes hardcover and trade paperback originals. **Publishes 12-16 titles/ year. Receives 500 queries and 1,000 mss/year. 10% of books from first-time authors; most from unagented writers. Pays 10-15% royalty on retail price or makes outright purchase of $250-1,500. Offers $0-3,000 advance.** Publishes book 1-2 years after acceptance of ms. Accepts simultaneous submissions. Reports in 1 month on queries, 3 months on mss. Book catalog free. Manuscript guidelines for #10 SASE.
    ○┬ "Story Line Press exists to publish the best stories of our time in poetry, fiction and nonfiction. Seventy-five percent of our list includes a wide range of poetry and books about poetry. Our books are intended for the general and academic reader. We are working to expand the audience for serious literature."
**Nonfiction:** Literary. Subjects include authors/literature. Query with SASE.
**Fiction:** Literary, no popular genres. "We currently have a backlist through the year 2000. Please send query letter

first." Query with SASE.

**Poetry:** Backlist for publication is through the year 2000.

**Recent Title(s):** *Oh Jackie*, by Mandy Benz (fiction); *The Muse Strikes Back* (poetry anthology).

**Tips:** "We strongly recommend that first-time poetry authors submit their book-length manuscript in the Nicholas Roerich Poetry Contest." See the Contests & Awards section for details.

**STYLUS PUBLISHING, LLC**, 22883 Quicksilver Dr., Sterling VA 20166. **Acquisitions**: John von Knorring, publisher. Estab. 1996. Publishes hardcover and trade paperback originals. **Publishes 6-10 titles/year. Receives 50 queries and 6 mss/year. 50% of books from first-time authors; 100% from unagented writers. Pays 5-10% royalty on wholesale price.** Publishes book 6 months after acceptance of ms. Reports in 1 month. Book catalog and ms guidelines free.

○➔ Stylus specializes in books on higher education and business training.

**Nonfiction:** Subjects include business and training, education. Query or submit outline, 1 sample chapter with SASE. Reviews artwork/photos as part of ms package. Send photocopies.

**Recent Title(s):** *Internet Based Learning*, edited by Deanie French, et al.

**SUCCESS PUBLISHING**, 3419 Dunham Rd., Warsaw NY 14569-9735. (716)786-5663. **Acquisitions:** Allan H. Smith, president (home-based business); Ginger Smith (business), Dana Herbison (home/craft), Robin Garretson (fiction). Estab. 1982. Publishes mass market paperback originals. **Publishes 6 titles/year. Receives 175 submissions/year, 10 mss/year. 90% of books from first-time authors; 100% from unagented writers. Pays 7-12% royalty.** Offers $500-1,000 advance. Publishes book 10 months after acceptance. Accepts simultaneous submissions. Reports in 2 months. Book catalog and ms guidelines for #10 SAE with 2 first-class stamps.

○➔ Success publishes guides that focus on the needs of the home entrepeneur to succeed as a viable business. Currently emphasizing starting a new business. De-emphasizing self-help/motivation books.

**Nonfiction:** Children's/juvenile, how-to, self-help. Subjects include child guidence/parenting, business/economics, hobbies, money/finance, craft/home-based business. "We are looking for books on how-to subjects such as home business and sewing." Query.

**Recent Title(s):** *How to Find a Date/Mate*, by Dana Herbison.

● Success Publishing notes that it is looking for ghostwriters.

**Tips:** "Our audience is made up of housewives, hobbyists and owners of home-based businesses."

**SUDBURY PRESS**, Profitable Technology, Inc., 40 Maclean Dr., Sudbury MA 01776. Fax: (978)443-0734. E-mail: press@intertain.com. Website: http://www.sudburypress.com. **Acquisitions:** Susan Gray, publisher. Publishes hardcover and mass market paperback originals. **Publishes 4 titles/year. Receives 100 queries and 100 mss/year. 100% of books from first-time authors; 100% from unagented writers. Pays 10% royalty on wholesale price. Offers $3,000 advance.** Publishes book 6 months after acceptance. Reports in 3 months. Book catalog on Internet.

○➔ Sudbury Press publishes only cozy mysteries and autobiographies and biographies of women.

**Nonfiction:** "We want biographies and autobiographies of ordinary women in extraordinary circumstances."

**Recent Title(s):** *To Auschwitz and Back: My Personal Journey*, by Ruth Bindefeld Neray.

**SUMMERS PRESS, INC.**, also known as Business Publishing, 950 Westbank Dr., Suite 204, Austin TX 78746. **Acquisitions:** Mark Summers, editor. Estab. 1989. Publishes hardcover originals. **Publishes 5 titles/year. Some books from first-time authors. Pays royalty on retail price or makes outright purchase. Offers advance. Also makes outright purchase.** Accepts simultaneous submissions.

○➔ Summers Press publishes reference books for businesses.

**Nonfiction:** Reference, technical, legal references for businesses. Subjects include employment, health, and safety law. Includes software. "Manuscript should be easily accessible, use short sentences, and attempt to convey complex information on a 10-12th grade reading level." Query with outline, 1 chapter and SASE.

**Recent Nonfiction Title(s):** *OSHA Compliance Guide*, (reference book for businesses).

**THE SUMMIT PUBLISHING GROUP**, 2000 E. Lamar Blvd., Suite 600, Arlington TX 76006. (817)588-3013. **Acquisitions:** Jill Bertolet, publisher; Veronica Palmer, acquisitions editor; DeNell Russell, submissions editor; Katherine Bear, submissions editor. Estab. 1990. Publishes hardcover originals, trade paperback originals and reprints. **Publishes 35 titles/year. 40% of books from first-time authors; 80% from unagented writers. Pays 5-20% royalty on wholesale price. Offers $2,000 and up advance.** Publishes book 6 months after acceptance of ms. Accepts simultaneous submissions. Reports in 1 month on queries and proposals, 3 months on mss.

○➔ Summit Publishing Group publishes contemporary books with a nationwide appeal. "We target the adult market with biography, self-help, how-to, gift and coffee table books." Currently emphasizing self-help, biography, cookbooks. De-emphasizing children's/juvenile.

**Imprints:** Legacy Books (corporate private label organizational publications).

**Nonfiction:** Biography, children's/juvenile, coffee table book, cookbook, gift book, how-to, humor, self-help. Subjects include art/architecture, business/economics, cooking, ethnic, gardening, government/politics, health/medicine, history, hobbies, military/war, money/finance, nature/environment, recreation, regional, religion, science, sociology, sports, women's issues/studies. Submit proposal package including outline, 2 sample chapters, table of contents, proposal marketing letter and résumé with SASE. Reviews artwork/photos as part of ms package. Send photocopies.

**Recent Title(s):** *On the Brink*, by Norman Brinker.

**Tips:** "Books should have obvious national-distribution appeal, be of a contemporary nature and be marketing-driven: author's media experience and contacts a strong plus."

**★ SUNSTONE PRESS**, P.O. Box 2321, Santa Fe NM 87504-2321. (505)988-4418. **Acquisitions:** James C. Smith, Jr., president. Estab. 1971. Publishes paperback and hardcover originals. **Publishes 25 titles/year. Receives 400 submissions/year. 70% of books from first-time authors; 100% from unagented writers. Pays 7½-15% royalty on wholesale price.** Publishes book 18 months after acceptance. Reports in 1 month.

    **O→** "Sunstone Press has traditionally focused on Southwestern themes, especially for nonfiction. However, in the past 18 months, general fiction titles have become very successful nationwide."

**Imprint(s):** Sundial Publications.

**Nonfiction:** How-to series craft books. Books on the history, culture and architecture of the Southwest. "Looks for strong regional appeal (Southwestern)." Query with SASE. Reviews artwork/photos as part of ms package.

**Fiction:** Publishes material with Southwestern theme. Query with SASE.

**Recent Title(s):** *Cowboy in the Roundhouse: A Political Life*, by Bruce King as told to Charles Poling (nonfiction); *Assignment Homicide*, by Jeanne Toomey (fiction).

**Tips:** This publisher's focus is the Southwestern US but it receives many, many submissions outside this subject.

**N. SWAN-RAVEN & CO.**, Blue Water Publishing, Inc., P.O. Box 190, Mill Spring NC 28756. (828)894-8444. Fax: (828)894-8454. E-mail: bluewaterp@aol.com. Website: http://www.5thworld.com/bluewater. **Acquisitions:** Pamela Meyer, publisher. Publishes trade paperback originals. **Publishes 6 titles/year. Receives 40 queries and 25 mss/month. 80% of books from first-time authors; 90% from unagented writers. Pays 5-12% royalty on wholesale price.** Publishes book 16 months after acceptance of ms. Accepts simultaneous submissions. Reports in 2 months on mss. Book catalog and ms guidelines for SASE with 55¢ postage.

    **O→** "Swan-Raven strives to preserve the Earth by publishing books that draw on the ancient wisdom of indigenous cultures to bring information from the otherworlds to our world."

**Nonfiction:** Subjects include health, philosophy, women's issues/studies, spiritual, future speculation. Query with outline. Reviews artwork/photos as part of ms package. Send photocopies.

**Recent Title(s):** *The Voice: of the Infinite in the Small*, by Joanne Lauck (ecology).

**SWEDENBORG FOUNDATION**, P.O. Box 549, West Chester PA 19381-0549. (610)430-3222. Fax: (610)430-7982. E-mail: acquisition@swedenborg.com. Executive Director/Publisher: Deborah Forman. **Acquisitions:** Susan Poole, acquisitions editor. Estab. 1849. Publishes hardcover and trade paperback originals and reprints. **Publishes 6-10 titles/year; imprints publish 4 titles/year. Pays 5-10% royalty on net receipts or makes outright purchase. Offers $500 minimum advance.** Reports in 3 months on queries, 6 months on proposals, 9 months on mss. Book catalog and ms guidelines free.

    **O→** "The Swedenborg Foundation publishes books by and about Emanuel Swedenborg (1688-1772), his ideas, how his ideas have influenced others, and related topics. A Chrysalis book is an adventurous, spiritually focused book presented with a nonsectarian perspective that appeals to open-minded, well-educated seekers of all traditions. Appropriate topics include—but are not limited to—science, mysticism, spiritual growth and development, wisdom traditions, healing and spirituality, as well as subjects that explore Swedenborgian concepts, such as: near-death experience, angels, biblical interpretation, mysteries of good and evil, etc. These books will foster a searching approach to the spiritual basis of reality."

**Imprint(s):** Chrysalis Books, Swedenborg Foundation Press.

**Nonfiction:** Spiritual growth and development, science and spirituality. Subjects include philosophy, psychology, religion. Query with proposal package, including synopsis, outline, sample chapter and SASE. Reviews artwork/photos as part of ms package. Send photocopies.

**Recent Nonfiction Title(s):** *Hidden Millennium: The Doomsday Fallacy*, by Stephen Koke.

    • The Swedenborg Foundation also publishes *Chrysalis Reader*, listed in Consumer Magazines/Religious.

**Tips:** "Most readers of our books are thoughtful, well-read individuals seeking resources for their philosophical, spiritual or religious growth. Especially sought are nonfiction works that bridge contemporary issues to spiritual insights."

**SYRACUSE UNIVERSITY PRESS**, 1600 Jamesville Ave., Syracuse NY 13244-5160. (315)443-5534. Fax: (315)443-5545. **Acquisitions:** Robert A. Mandel, director. Estab. 1943. **Averages 80 titles/year. Receives 600-700 submissions/year. 25% of books from first-time authors; 75% from unagented writers. Nonauthor subsidy publishes 20% of books. Pays royalty on net sales.** Publishes book an average of 15 months after acceptance of ms. Simultaneous submissions discouraged. Book catalog for 9×12 SAE with 3 first-class stamps.

    **O→** Currently emphasizing television, Jewish studies, Middle East topics. De-emphasizing peace studies.

**Nonfiction:** "Special opportunity in our nonfiction program for freelance writers of books on New York state, sports history, Jewish studies, the Middle East, religious studies, television and popular culture. We have published regional books by people with limited formal education, but authors were thoroughly acquainted with their subjects, and they wrote simply and directly about them. Provide precise descriptions of subjects, along with background description of project. The author must make a case for the importance of his or her subject." Query with outline and at least 2 sample chapters. Reviews artwork/photos as part of ms package.

**SYSTEMS CO., INC.**, P.O. Box 339, Carlsborg WA 98324. (360)683-6860. **Acquisitions:** Richard H. Peetz, Ph.D., president. Estab. 1981. Publishes hardcover and trade paperback originals. **Publishes 3-5 titles/year. 50% of books from first-time authors; 100% from unagented writers. Pays 20% royalty on wholesale price after costs.** Publishes book 6 months after acceptance of ms. Accepts simultaneous submissions. Reports in 2 months. Book catalog free. Manuscript guidelines for $1.

O—¬ "We publish succinct and well-organized technical and how-to-do-it books with minimum filler." De-emphasizing business/economics, health/medicine.

**Nonfiction:** How-to, self-help, technical, textbook. Subjects include business/economics, automotive, health/medicine, money/finance, nature/environment, science/engineering. Submit outline, 2 sample chapters and SASE. Reviews artwork/photos as part of ms package. Send photocopies.

**Recent Title(s):** *Existentialism & Folklore*, by J.S. Hescher, M.D.

**Tips:** "Our audience consists of people in technical occupations, people interested in doing things themselves. In submitting nonfiction, writers often make the mistake of picking a common topic with lots of published books in print."

[A] **NAN A. TALESE**, Doubleday Broadway Publishing Group, Random House, Inc., 1540 Broadway, New York NY 10036. (212)782-8918. Fax: (212)782-9261. Website: http://www.nantalese.com. **Acquisitions:** Nan A. Talese, editorial director. Publishes hardcover originals. **Publishes 15 titles/year. Receives 400 queries and mss/year. Pays variable royalty on retail price. Advance varies.** Publishes book 8 months after acceptance of ms. Accepts simultaneous submissions. Reports in 1 week on queries, 2 months on proposals and mss.

O—¬ Nan A. Talese publishes nonfiction with a powerful guiding narrative and relevance to larger cultural trends and interests, and literary fiction of the highest quality.

**Nonfiction:** Biography, gift book, select. Subjects include art/architecture, history, philosophy, current trends. *Agented submissions only.*

**Fiction:** Literary. "We're interested in everything literary. No genre fiction or low-market stuff." *Agented submissions only.*

**Recent Title(s):** *Amsterdam*, by Ian McEwan.

**Tips:** "Audience is highly literate people interested in literary books. We want well-written material."

**JEREMY P. TARCHER, INC.**, Penguin Putnam, Inc., 375 Hudson St., New York NY 10014. (212)366-2000. Website: http://www.penguinputnam.com. Publisher: Joel Fotinos. **Acquisitions:** Mitch Horowitz, senior editor; Wendy Hubbert, senior editor; David Groff, editor; Joel Fotinos, publisher (nonfiction). Estab. 1965. Publishes hardcover and trade paperback originals and reprints. **Publishes 30-40 titles/year. Receives 500 queries and 500 mss/year. 10% of books from first-time authors; 5% from unagented writers. Pays 5-8% royalty on retail price. Offers advance.** Accepts simultaneous submissions. Book catalog free.

O—¬ Although Tarcher is not a religion imprint per se, Jeremy Tarcher's vision was to publish ideas and works about human consciousness that were large enough to include matters of spirit and religion.

**Nonfiction:** How-to, self-help. Subjects include business/economics, child guidance/parenting, gay/lesbian, health/medicine, nature/environment, philosophy, psychology, religion, women's issues/studies. Query with SASE.

**Recent Title(s):** *Sweat Your Prayers*, by Gabrielle Roth (spirituality, psychology).

**Tips:** "Audience seeks personal growth through books. Understand the imprint's focus and categories. We stick with the tried and true."

**TAYLOR PUBLISHING COMPANY**, 1550 W. Mockingbird Lane, Dallas TX 75235. (214)819-8560. Fax: (214)819-8580. Website: http://www.taylorpub.com. President: Craig Von Pelt. Publisher/Editorial Director: Lynn Brooks. **Acquisitions:** Michael Emmerich, senior editor (sports, history, pop culture, gardening, health); Camille N. Cline, editor (pop culture, history, health, gardening). Estab. 1981. Publishes hardcover and softcover originals. **Publishes 35 titles/year. Receives 1,500 submissions/year. 25% of books from first-time authors; 25% from unagented writers.** Publishes book 1-2 years after acceptance. Accepts simultaneous submissions. Reports in 3 months. Book catalog and ms guidelines for 10×13 SASE.

O—¬ "We publish solid, practical books that should backlist well. We look for authors who are expert authors in their field and already have some recognition through magazine articles, radio appearances or their own TV or radio show. We also look for speakers or educators."

**Nonfiction:** Gardening, sports, popular culture, parenting, health, home improvement, how-to, popular history, biography, miscellaneous nonfiction. Submit outline, sample chapter, an overview of the market and competition and an author bio as it pertains to proposed subject matter. Reviews artwork as part of ms package.

**Recent Title(s):** *Midwest Landscape Design*, by Susan McClure.

**TCU PRESS**, (formerly Texas Christian University Press), P.O. Box 298300, TCU, Fort Worth TX 76129. (817)257-7822. Fax: (817)257-5075. **Acquisitions:** Judy Alter, director; James Ward Lee, acquisitions consultant. Estab. 1966. Publishes hardcover originals, some reprints. **Publishes 12 titles/year. Receives 100 submissions/year. 10% of books from first-time authors; 75% from unagented writers. Nonauthor-subsidy publishes 10% of books. Pays 10% royalty on net price.** Publishes book 16 months after acceptance. Reports in 3 months on queries.

O—¬ TCU publishes "scholarly works and regional titles of significance focusing on the history and literature of the American West."

**Nonfiction:** American studies, literature and criticism. Query. Reviews artwork/photos as part of ms package.

**Fiction:** Regional fiction, by invitation only. *Please do not query.*
**Recent Title(s):** *Giant Country: Essays on Texas*, by Don Graham.
**Tips:** "Regional and/or Texana nonfiction has best chance of breaking into our firm."

**TEACHERS COLLEGE PRESS**, 1234 Amsterdam Ave., New York NY 10027. (212)678-3929. Fax: (212)678-4149. Website: http://www.tc.columbia.edu/tcpress. Director: Carole P. Saltz. **Acquisitions:** Brian Ellerbeck, executive acquisitions editor. Estab. 1904. Publishes hardcover and paperback originals and reprints. **Publishes 60 titles/year. Pays industry standard royalty.** Publishes book 1 year after acceptance. Reports in 2 months. Catalog free.
> Teachers College Press publishes a wide range of educational titles for all levels of students: early childhood to higher education. "Publishing books that respond to, examine and confront issues pertaining to education, teacher training and school reform."

**Nonfiction:** "This university press concentrates on books in the field of education in the broadest sense, from early childhood to higher education: good classroom practices, teacher training, special education, innovative trends and issues, administration and supervision, film, continuing and adult education, all areas of the curriculum, computers, guidance and counseling and the politics, economics, philosophy, sociology and history of education. We have recently added women's studies to our list. The Press also issues classroom materials for students at all levels, with a strong emphasis on reading and writing and social studies." Submit outline and sample chapters.
**Recent Title(s):** *How Schools Might Be Governed and Why*, by Seymour Sarason.

**TEACHING & LEARNING COMPANY**, 1204 Buchanan St., P.O. Box 10, Carthage IL 62321-0010. (217)357-2591. Fax: (217)357-6789. E-mail: tandlcom@adams.net. Website: http://www.teachinglearning.com. **Acquisitions:** Jill Eckhardt, managing editor. Estab. 1994. **Publishes 60 titles/year. Receives 25 queries and 200 mss/year. 25% of books from first-time authors; 98% from unagented writers. Pays royalty.** Accepts simultaneous submissions. Reports in 3 months on queries, 9 months on proposals and mss. Book catalog and ms guidelines free.
> Teaching & Learning Company publishes teacher resources (supplementary activity/idea books) for grades pre K-8.

**Nonfiction:** Subjects include teacher resources: language arts, reading, math, science, social studies, arts and crafts, responsibility education. No picture books or storybooks. Submit table of contents, introduction, 3 sample chapters with SASE. Reviews artwork/photos as part of ms package. Send photocopies.
**Recent Title(s):** *Mind Over Manners*, by Greta Barclay Lipson.
**Tips:** "Our books are for teachers and parents of pre K-8th grade children."

**TEMPLE UNIVERSITY PRESS**, USB, 1601 N. Broad St., Philadelphia PA 19122-6099. (215)204-8787. Fax: (215)204-4719. E-mail: tempress@astro.ocis.temple.edu. Website: http://www.temple.edu. **Acquisitions:** Michael Ames, consulting editor; Janet Francendese, editor-in-chief; Doris Braendel, senior acquisitions editor. Estab. 1969. **Publishes 60 titles/year. Pays up to 10% royalty on wholesale price.** Publishes book 10 months after acceptance. Reports in 2 months. Book catalog free.
> "Temple University Press has been publishing useful books on Asian-Americans, law, gender issues, film, women's studies and other interesting areas for nearly 30 years for the goal of social change."

**Nonfiction:** American history, sociology, women's studies, health care, ethics, labor studies, photography, urban studies, law, Latin American studies, African-American studies, Asian-American studies, public policy and regional (Philadelphia area). "No memoirs, fiction or poetry." Uses *Chicago Manual of Style*. Reviews artwork/photos. Query.
**Recent Title(s):** *Heroes in Hard Times: Cop Action Movies in the U.S.*, by Neal King (cinema/gender studies).

**TEN SPEED PRESS**, P.O. Box 7123, Berkeley CA 94707. (510)559-1600. Fax: (510)524-1052. E-mail: info@tenspeed.com. Publisher: Kirsty Melville. Publisher/Editorial Director: Phillip Wood. **Acquisitions:** Address submissions to "Acquisitions Department." Estab. 1971. Publishes trade paperback originals and reprints. **Firm publishes 100 titles/year; imprints average 70 titles/year. 25% of books from first-time authors; 50% from unagented writers. Pays 8-12% royalty on retail price. Offers $2,500 average advance.** Publishes book 1 year after acceptance. Accepts simultaneous submissions. Reports in 3 months on queries. Book catalog for 9×12 SAE with 6 first-class stamps. Manuscript guidelines for #10 SASE.
> Ten Speed Press publishes authoritative books for an audience interested in innovative, proven ideas.

**Imprint(s): Celestial Arts, Tricycle Press**.
**Nonfiction:** Cookbook, how-to, reference, self-help. Subjects include business and career, child guidance/parenting, cooking/foods/nutrition, gardening, health/medicine, money/finance, nature/environment, recreation, science. "We mainly publish innovative how-to books. We are always looking for cookbooks from proven, tested sources—successful restaurants, etc. *Not* 'Grandma's favorite recipes.' Books about the 'new science' interest us. No biographies or autobiographies, first-person travel narratives, fiction or humorous treatments of just about anything." Query or submit outline and sample chapters.
**Recent Title(s):** *The Joy of Not Working*, by Ernie Zelinski.
**Tips:** "We like books from people who really know their subject, rather than people who think they've spotted a trend to capitalize on. We like books that will sell for a long time, rather than nine-day wonders. Our audience consists of a well-educated, slightly weird group of people who like food, the outdoors and take a light but serious approach to business and careers. Study the backlist of each publisher you're submitting to and tailor your proposal to what you perceive as their needs. Nothing gets a publisher's attention like someone who knows what he or she is talking about,

and nothing falls flat like someone who obviously has no idea who he or she is submitting to."

**TEXAS A&M UNIVERSITY PRESS**, College Station TX 77843-4354. (409)845-1436. Fax: (409)847-8752. E-mail: fdl@tampress.tamu.edu. Website: http://www.tamu.edu/upress. **Acquisitions:** Noel Parsons, editor-in-chief (military, eastern Europe, natural history, agriculture, nautical archaeology); Mary Lenn Dixon, managing editor (political science, presidential studies, anthropology, borderlands, western history). Estab. 1974. **Publishes 50 titles/year. Nonauthorsubsidy publishes 25% of books. Pays in royalties.** Publishes book 1 year after acceptance. Reports in 1 month. *Writer's Market* recommends allowing 2 months for reply. Book catalog free.

    O—¬ Texas A&M University Press publishes a wide range of nonfiction, scholarly trade and crossover books of regional and national interest, "reflecting the interests of the university, the broader scholarly community, and the people of our state and region."

**Nonfiction:** Books on Texas and the Southwest, military studies, American and western history, Texas and western literature, Mexican-US borderlands studies, nautical archaeology, women's studies, ethnic studies, natural history, the environment, presidential studies, economics, business history, architecture, Texas and western art and photography, agriculture and veterinary medicine. Query.

**Recent Title(s):** *Land of the Desert Sun: Texas' Big Bend Country*, by D. Gentry Steele.

**Tips:** Proposal requirements are posted on the website.

**TEXAS STATE HISTORICAL ASSOCIATION**, 2.306 Richardson Hall, University Station, Austin TX 78712. (512)471-1525. **Acquisitions:** George B. Ward, assistant director. Estab. 1897. Publishes hardcover and trade paperback originals and reprints. **Publishes 8 titles/year. Receives 50 queries and 50 mss/year. 10% of books from first-time authors; 95% from unagented writers. Pays 10% royalty on net cash proceeds.** Publishes book 1 year after acceptance. Reports in 2 months on mss. Catalog and ms guidelines free.

    O—¬ "We are interested in scholarly historical articles and books on any aspect of Texas history."

**Nonfiction:** Biography, coffee table book, illustrated book, reference. Historical subjects. Query. Reviews artwork/photos as part of ms package. Send photocopies.

**Recent Title(s):** *El Llano Estacado: Exploration and Imagination on the High Plains of Texas and New Mexico, 1536-1860*, by John Miller Morris (history).

**N: TEXAS WESTERN PRESS**, The University of Texas at El Paso, El Paso TX 79968-0633. (915)747-5688. Fax: (915)747-7515. Director: John Bristol. **Acquisitions:** Bobbi McConnaughey Gonzales. Estab. 1952. Publishes hardcover and paperback originals. **Publishes 7-8 titles/year. Pays standard 10% royalty.** Reports in 2 months. Catalog and ms guidelines free.

    O—¬ Texas Western Press publishes books on the history and cultures of the American Southwest, especially historical and biographical works about West Texas, New Mexico, northern Mexico and the US-Mexico borderlands. Currently emphasizing developing border issues, economic issues of the border. De-emphasizing coffee table books.

**Imprint(s):** Southwestern Studies.

**Nonfiction:** Scholarly books. Historic and cultural accounts of the Southwest (West Texas, New Mexico, northern Mexico and Arizona). Also art, photographic books, Native American and limited regional fiction reprints. Occasional technical titles. "Our *Southwestern Studies* use manuscripts of up to 30,000 words. Our hardback books range from 30,000 words up. The writer should use good exposition in his work. Most of our work requires documentation. We favor a scholarly, but not overly pedantic, style. We specialize in superior book design." Query with outline. Follow *Chicago Manual of Style*.

**Recent Title(s):** *Frontier Cavalryman*, by Marcos Kinevan.

**Tips:** Texas Western Press is interested in books relating to the history of Hispanics in the US, will experiment with photo-documentary books, and is interested in seeing more 'popular' history and books on Southwestern culture/life. "We try to treat our authors professionally, produce handsome, long-lived books and aim for quality, rather than quantity of titles carrying our imprint."

**THUNDER'S MOUTH PRESS**, Avalon Publishing Group, 841 Broadway, 4th Floor, New York NY 10003. (212)614-7880. Publisher: Neil Ortenberg. **Acquisitions:** Gayle Watkins, acquisitions editor. Estab. 1982. Publishes hardcover and trade paperback originals and reprints, almost exclusively nonfiction. **Publishes 70-80 titles/year. Receives 1,000 submissions/year. 15% of books from unagented writers. Pays 7-10% royalty on retail price. Offers $15,000 average advance.** Publishes book 8 months after acceptance. Reports in 2 months on queries.

**Nonfiction:** Biography, politics, popular culture. *No unsolicited mss.* "No queries, please."

**Recent Title(s):** *Hindsight*, by Boris Vallejo.

**TIDE-MARK PRESS**, P.O. Box 280311, East Hartford CT 06128-0311. (860)289-0363. Fax: (860)289-3654. **Book Acquisitions:** Carol Berto, editor. Publishes hardcover originals. **Publishes 2-3 titles/year and over 50 calendars. Receives 50-100 queries/year. 50% of books from first-time authors; most from unagented writers. Pays 10% on net sales. Advances vary with projects.** Publishes book 18 months after acceptance of ms. Reports in 1 month.

    O—¬ Tide-Mark focuses on illustrations and text about journeys of discovery into the natural world.

**Nonfiction:** Coffee table book, gift book, calendars. "The explorer/illustrator can be a scientist with a camera, a perceptive traveler, or someone thoroughly grounded in a particular landscape or region." Reviews artwork/photos as part of the ms package. Call for proposal guidelines.

**Recent Title(s):** *Tall Ships, An International Guide*, by Thad Koza.

**TIDEWATER PUBLISHERS**, Cornell Maritime Press, Inc., P.O. Box 456, Centreville MD 21617-0456. (410)758-1075. Fax: (410)758-6849. **Acquisitions:** Charlotte Kurst, managing editor. Estab. 1938. Publishes hardcover and paperback originals. **Publishes 7-9 titles/year. Receives 150 submissions/year. 41% of books from first-time authors; 99% from unagented writers. Pays 7½-15% royalty on retail price.** Publishes book 1 year after acceptance. Reports in 2 months. Book catalog for 10×13 SAE with 5 first-class stamps.

O→ Tidewater Publishers issues adult nonfiction works related to the Chesapeake Bay area, Delmarva or Maryland in general. "The only fiction we handle is juvenile and must have a regional focus."

**Nonfiction:** Cookbook, history, illustrated book, juvenile, reference. Regional subjects only. Query or submit outline and sample chapters. Reviews artwork/photos as part of ms package.

**Fiction:** Regional juvenile fiction only. Query or submit outline/synopsis and sample chapters.

**Recent Title(s):** *Twilight on the Bay: The Excursion Boat Empire of B.B. Wills*, by Brian J. Cudahy.

**Tips:** "Our audience is made up of readers interested in works that are specific to the Chesapeake Bay and Delmarva Peninsula area. We do not publish personal narratives, adult fiction or poetry."

**TIMES BOOKS**, Random House, Inc., 201 E. 50th St., New York NY 10022. (212)751-2600. Website: www.randomhouse.com. Vice President/Publisher: Carle Frelmuth. **Acquisitions:** Elizabeth Rapoport (health, family, education); John Mahaney (business); Philip Turner (consumer affairs, history, biography, current events); Stanley Newman (crossword puzzles). Estab. 1959. Publishes hardcover and paperback originals and reprints. **Publishes 50-60 titles/year. Pays royalty. Offers average advance.** Publishes book 1 year after acceptance. Reports in 2 months for reply.

O→ "Times Books is noted for its books on business, current affairs and political commentary, as well as a popular line of puzzles and games."

**Nonfiction:** Business/economics, science and medicine, history, biography, women's issues, family, cookbooks, current affairs. Query. *No Unsolicited mss.* Reviews artwork/photos as part of ms package.

**Recent Title(s):** *East and West*, by Christopher Patten (current affairs/politics).

**TIMES BUSINESS**, Random House, Inc., 201 E. 50th St., New York NY 10022. (212)572-2275. Fax: (212)572-4949. Website: http://www.randomhouse.com. **Acquisitions:** John Mahaney, executive editor. Estab. 1995. Publishes hardcover and trade paperback originals. **Publishes 20-25 titles/year. 50% of books from first-time authors; 15% from unagented writers. Pays negotiable royalty on list price; hardcover on invoice price. Advance negotiable.** Publishes book 9 months after acceptance of ms. Accepts simultaneous submissions. Reports in 1 month on proposals. Book catalog free from Random House (same address). Manuscript guidelines for #10 SASE.

**Nonfiction:** Subjects include business/economic, money/finance, management, technology and business. Query with proposal package including outline, 1-2 sample chapters, market analysis and SASE.

**Recent Title(s):** *Profit Zone*, by Adrian Zlywotzky and David Morrison.

**TODD PUBLICATIONS**, P.O. Box 635, Nyack NY 10960. (914)358-6213. E-mail: toddpub@aol.com. **Acquisitions:** Barry Klein, president. Estab. 1962. Publishes hardcover and trade paperback originals. **Publishes 5 titles/year. 1% of books from first-time authors. Pays 5-15% royalty on wholesale price. Publishes book 6 months after acceptance.** Accepts simultaneous submissions. Reports in 2 months on proposals. Book catalog free. Manuscript guidelines for #10 SASE.

O→ Todd publishes and distributes reference books and directories of all types.

**Nonfiction:** How-to, reference, directories, self-help. Subjects include business/economics, ethnic, health/medicine, money/finance, travel. Submit 2 sample chapters.

**Recent Title(s):** *Directory Of Mastercard & Visa Credit Card Sources*; *Insider's Guide To Bank Cards With No Credit Check*; *Indian Country Address Book*.

**TOR BOOKS**, Tom Doherty Associates, LLC, 175 Fifth Ave., New York NY 10010. **Acquisitions:** Patrick Nielsen Hayden, senior editor. Estab. 1980. Publishes hardcover originals and trade and mass market paperback originals and reprints. **Publishes 150-200 books/year. 2-3% of books from first-time authors; 3-5% from unagented writers. Pays royalty on retail price.** Publishes book 1-2 years after acceptance. No simultaneous submissions. "No queries please." Reports in 2-6 months on proposals and mss. Book catalog for 9×12 SAE with 2 first-class stamps; ms guidelines for SASE.

O→ "Tor Books publishes what is arguably the largest and most diverse line of science fiction and fantasy ever produced by a single English-language publisher."

**Fiction:** Adventure, fantasy, historical, horror, science fiction. Submit synopsis and 3 sample chapters.

**Recent Title(s):** *Path of Daggers*, by Robert Jordan (fantasy).

**Tips:** "We're never short of good sf or fantasy, but we're always open to solid, technologically knowledgeable hard science fiction or thrillers by writers with solid expertise."

**TORAH AURA PRODUCTIONS**, 4423 Fruitland Ave., Los Angeles CA 90058. (213)585-7312. Website: http://www.torahaura.com. **Acquisitions:** Jane Golub. Estab. 1982. Publishes hardcover and trade paperback originals. **Pub-**

lishes 25 titles/year; imprint publishes 10 titles/year. **Receives 5 queries and 10 mss/year. 2% of books from first-time authors; 100% from unagented writers. Pays 10% royalty on wholesale price.** Publishes book 3 years after acceptance of ms. Accepts simultaneous submissions. Reports in 6 months on mss. Book catalog free.

O—¬ Torah Aura publishes mostly educational materials for Jewish classrooms.

**Imprint(s): Alef Design Group.**

**Nonfiction:** Children's/juvenile, textbook. Subjects include language/literature (Hebrew), religion (Jewish). No picture books. Query with SASE. Reviews artwork/photos as part of ms package. Send photocopies.

**Fiction:** Juvenile, picture books, religious, young adult. All fiction must have Jewish interest. Query with SASE.

**Recent Title(s):** *The Bible from Alef to Tau,* by Penina V. Adelman.

**TOTEM BOOKS**, Icon Books PLC, P.O. Box 223, Canal St., Station, New York NY 10013. (212)431-9368. Fax: (212)966-5768. E-mail: totem@theliteraryagency.com. **Acquisitions:** Richard Appignanesi, editorial director (nonfiction, psychology, philosophy); Duncan Heath, executive editor (science, music, language). Estab. 1994. Publishes trade paperback originals. **Publishes 12 titles/year. Receives 10 queries and 2 mss/year. 30% of books from first-time authors; 75% from unagented writers. Pays 4% royalty on retail price.** Publishes book 15 months after acceptance of ms. Reports in 2 months on queries.

O—¬ Totem Books publishes graphic study guides for high school, college and junior college students. Currently emphasizing philosophy/psychology—extracts or works in progress.

**Imprint(s):** The Encounter Series, The Introducing Series.

**Nonfiction:** Biography, reference, graphic study guides. Subjects include anthropology, language/literature, music, philosophy, psychology, religion, science, sociology, women's issues/studies. Query with SASE.

**Recent Title(s):** *Introducing Heidegger,* by Jeff Collins.

**Tips:** "Study our books and recognize that we only publish collaborations of author and illustrator. We publish accessible graphic study guides that combine text and fully integrated black & white illustrations to communicate complex and esoteric subjects—without over simplification."

**TOTLINE PUBLICATIONS**, Frank Schaffer Publications, Inc., P.O. Box 2250, Everett WA 98203-0250. (206)353-3100. E-mail: totline@gte.net. **Acquisitions:** Mina McMullin, managing editor (book mss); Submissions Editor (single activity ideas). Estab. 1975. Publishes educational activity books and parenting books for teachers and parents of 2-6-year-olds. **Publishes 50-60 titles/year. 100% from unagented writers. Makes outright purchase plus copies of book/newsletter author's material appears in.** Book catalog and ms guidelines free on written request.

O—¬ Totline publishes educationally and developmentally appropriate books for 2-, 3-5-, and 6-year-olds.

**Nonfiction:** Illustrated activity books for parents and teachers of 2-6-year-olds. Subjects include animals, art, child guidance/parenting, cooking with kids, foods and nutrition, education, ethnic, gardening, hobbies, language/literature, music, nature/environment, science. Considers activity book and single activity submissions from early childhood education professionals. Considers parenting activity mss from parenting experts. Query with SASE. No children's storybooks, fiction or poetry.

**Recent Title(s):** *Multisensory Theme-A-Saurus,* edited by Gayle Bittinger.

**Tips:** "Our audience is teachers and parents who work with children ages 2-6. Write for submission requirements. We are especially interested in parent-child activities for 0- to 3-year-olds and teacher-child activities for toddler groups."

**TOWER PUBLISHING**, 588 Saco Rd., Standish ME 04084. (207)642-5400. Fax: (207)642-5463. E-mail: tower@ime .net. Website: www.ime.net/tower. **Acquisitions:** Michael Lyons, president. Estab. 1772. Publishes hardcover originals and reprints, trade paperback originals. **Publishes 15 titles/year. Receives 60 queries and 30 mss/year. 10% of books from first-time authors; 90% from unagented writers. Pays royalty on net receipts. No advance.** Publishes book 6 months after acceptance of ms. Accepts simultaneous submissions. Reports in 1 month on queries, 2 months on proposals and mss. Book catalog and guidelines free.

O—¬ Tower Publishing specializes in business and professional directories and legal books.

**Nonfiction:** Reference. Business/economics subjects. Looking for legal books of a national stature. Query with outline.

**TRAFALGAR SQUARE PUBLISHING**, P.O. Box 257, N. Pomfret VT 05053-0257. (802)457-1911. Fax: (802)457-1913. E-mail: tsquare@sover.net. Website: http://www.horseandriderbooks.com. Publisher: Caroline Robbins. **Acquisitions:** Martha Cook, managing editor. Estab. 1987. Publishes hardcover and trade paperback originals and reprints. **Publishes 10 titles/year. Pays royalty.** Reports in 2 months.

O—¬ "We publish high quality instructional books for horsemen and horsewomen, always with the horse's welfare in mind."

**Nonfiction:** Books about horses. "We publish books for intermediate to advanced riders and horsemen. No stories, children's books or horse biographies." Query with proposal package, including outline, 1-2 sample chapters, letter of writer's qualifications and audience for book's subject.

**Recent Title(s):** *Cross-Train Your Horse,* by Jane Savoie.

**TRANS-ATLANTIC PUBLICATIONS, INC.**, 311 Bainbridge St., Philadelphia PA 19147. Fax: (215)925-7412. E-mail: rsmolin@lx.netcom. com. Website: http://www.transatlanticpub.com. **Acquisitions:** Ron Smolin. Estab. 1984. Publishes hardcover, trade paperback and mass market paperback originals. **Publishes 100 titles/year. Imprint publishes 20 titles/year. Receives 500 queries and 500 mss/year. 15% of books from first-time authors; 20% from unagented**

writers. **Pays 7½-12% royalty on retail price. Offers $2,000-10,000 advance.** Publishes book 11 months after acceptance of ms. Accepts simultaneous submissions.

○→ Trans-Atlantic publishes a wide variety of nonfiction and fiction and distributes a wide variety of business books published in England.

**Imprint(s):** Bainbridge Books.
**Nonfiction:** Biography, coffee table book, illustrated book, reference. Subjects include animals, art/architecture, nutrition, creative nonfiction, gay/lesbian, government/politics, health/medicine, history, nature/environment, philosophy, photography, science, sex, sociology, sports. Query. Reviews artwork/photos as part of ms package. Send photocopies.
**Fiction:** Adventure, experimental, humor, literary, mainstream/contemporary, mystery, plays, science fiction, suspense, young adult. Query with 2 sample chapters and SASE.
**Recent Title(s):** *Japan's Hidden Face*, by T. Abe (nonfiction); *God Does Play Dice*, by Klara Samuels (holocaust autobiography).

**TRANSNATIONAL PUBLISHERS, INC.,** 411 Saw Mill River Rd., Ardsley NY 10502. (914)693-5100. Fax: (914)693-4430. E-mail: transbooks@aol.com. Website: http://www.transnationalpubs.com. Editor: Maria Angelini. **Acquisitions:** Adriana Maida, acquisitions editor. Estab. 1980. **Publishes 15-20 titles/year. Receives 40-50 queries and 30 mss/year. 60% of books from first-time authors; 95% from unagented writers. Pays 10% royalty of net revenue. Offers no advance.** Publishes book 9 months after acceptance of ms. Accepts simultaneous submissions. Reports in 1 month. Book catalog and ms guidelines free.

○→ "We provide specialized publications for the teaching of law and law-related subjects in law school classroom, clinic and continuing legal education settings."

**Nonfiction:** Reference, technical, textbook. Subjects include business/economics, government/politics, women's issues/studies. Query or submit proposal package, including table of contents, introduction, sample chapter with SASE.
**Recent Title(s):** *Women and International Human Rights*, by Kelly Askin and Doreen Koerig.

**TREASURE LEARNING SYSTEMS,** Treasure Publishing, 1133 Riverside Ave., Fort Collins CO 80524. (970)484-8483. Fax: (970)495-6700. E-mail: mark@treasurelearning.com. Website: http://www.treasurelearning.com. **Acquisitions:** Mark A. Steiner, senior editor. Publishes hardcover originals. **Publishes 4 titles/year. Receives 150 queries and 150 mss/year. 50% of books from first-time authors; 80% from unagented writers. Pays royalty on retail price or makes outright purchase. Offers $5,000 advance.** Publishes book 6 months after acceptance of ms. Accepts simultaneous submissions. Reports in 1 month on queries and mss, 2 months on proposals. Book catalog and ms guidelines free.

○→ "Treasure Learning Systems exists to help the Church fulfill the Great Commission. We create and distribute Christian education resources which feature excellence in biblical content, educational methodology and product presentation. Our primary responsibility is to serve the local and international Church."

**Nonfiction:** Children's/juvenile, illustrated book. Subjects include education, Bible stories. All books are Christian oriented. "No novels or shallow content." Query with SASE. Reviews artwork/photos. Send photocopies.
**Poetry:** Must be Christian oriented.
**Recent Title(s):** *Discipleland* (elementary Bible study).

**TRICYCLE PRESS,** Ten Speed Press, P.O. Box 7123, Berkeley CA 94707. (510)559-1600. Fax: (510)524-1052. Website: www.tenspeed.com. **Acquisitions:** Nicole Geiger, publisher. Publishes hardcover and trade paperback originals. **Publishes 12-14 titles/year. 20% of books from first-time authors; 60% from unagented authors. Pays 15-20% royalty on wholesale price (lower if book is illustrated). Offers $0-9,000 advance.** Publishes book 1 year after acceptance of ms. Accepts simultaneous submissions. Reports in 3 months on submissions (no query letters!) Book catalog for 9 × 12 SAE and 3 first-class stamps in postage; ms guidelines for #10 SASE; or one large envelope for both.

○→ "Tricycle Press looks for something outside the mainstream; books that encourage children to look at the world from a possibly alternative angle."

**Nonfiction:** Children's/juvenile, how-to, self-help, picture books, activity books. Subjects include art/architecture, gardening, health/medicine, nature/environment, science, geography. Submit complete ms for activity books; 2-3 chapters or 20 pages for others. Reviews artwork/photos as part of ms package. Send photocopies.
**Fiction:** Picture books. Submit complete ms for picture books. Query with synopsis and SASE for all others.
**Recent Title(s):** *G is for Googol: A Math Alphabet Book*, by David Schwartz, illustrated by Marissa Moss (math); *Hey, Little Ant*, by Phillip and Hannah Hoose, illustrated by Debbie Tilley (picture book).

**TRILOGY BOOKS,** 3579 E. Foothill Blvd., #236, Pasadena CA 91105. (626)797-0390. Fax: (626)797-7036. E-mail: 72274,44@compuserve.com. **Acquisitions:** Marge Wood, publisher. Publishes trade paperback originals. **Publishes 4 titles/year. Pays 10% royalty on net revenues. Advance varies.** Publishes book 1 year after acceptance of ms. Accepts simultaneous submissions. Reports in 1 month on queries. Book catalog and ms guidelines free.

○→ Trilogy publishes women's studies, self-help and psychology that have both mainstream and scholarly appeal.

**Nonfiction:** Subjects include women's history, women's issues/studies, self-help, psychology. Query.
**Recent Title(s):** *Beauty Bites Beast: Awakening the Warrior in Women and Girls*, by Ellen Snortland.

**TRINITY PRESS INTERNATIONAL,** The Morehouse Group, P.O. Box 1321, Harrisburg PA 17105. **Acquisitions:** Harold Rast, publisher. Estab. 1989. Publishes trade paperback originals and reprints. **Publishes 40 titles/year. Pays**

**10% royalty on wholesale price.** Publishes book 9 months after acceptance of ms. Accepts simultaneous submissions. Book catalog free.

O–π Trinity Press International is an ecumenical publisher of serious books on theology and the Bible for the religious academic community, religious professionals, and serious book readers.

**Nonfiction:** Textbook, Christian/theological studies. Subjects include history (as relates to the Bible), translation (biblical/Christian texts). Submit outline and 1 sample chapter.

**Recent Title(s):** *Christology Revisited*, by John Macquarrie.

**TROITSA BOOKS**, Kroshka Books, 6080 Jericho Turnpike, Suite 207, Commack NY 11725-2808. (516)499-3103. Fax: (516)499-3146. E-mail: novascience@earthlink.net. **Acquisitions:** Frank Columbus, editor-in-chief; Nadya Columbus, editor. Publishes hardcover and paperback originals. Publishes book up to 1 year after acceptance of ms. Accepts simultaneous submissions. Reports in 1 month.

O–π This imprint is devoted to Christianity.

**Nonfiction:** Christianity. Subjects include biography, history, inspirational, sermons, prayer books, memoirs. Query with SASE. Reviews artwork/photos as part of ms package. Send photocopies.

**Recent Title(s):** *In His Own Words: The Beliefs and Teachings of Jesus*, by Albert Kirby Griffin.

**TSR, INC.**, Wizards of the Coast, P.O. Box 707, Renton WA 98057-0707. (425)226-6500. Executive Editor: Mary Kirchoff. **Acquisitions:** Novel Submissions Editor. Estab. 1975. Publishes hardcover and trade paperback originals and trade paperback reprints. **Publishes 40-50 titles/year. Receives 600 queries and 300 mss/year. 25% of books from first-time authors; 35% from unagented authors. Pays 4-8% royalty on retail price. Offers $4,000-6,000 average advance.** Publishes book 1 year after acceptance of ms. Accepts simultaneous submissions. Reports in 2 months on queries. Guidelines for #10 SASE.

O–π TSR publishes science fiction and fantasy titles.

**Imprint(s):** Dragonlance® Books; Forgotten Realms® Books; Grayhawk Novels; Legend of the Fire Rings Novels; Magic: The Gathering® Books; Star*Drive Books.

**Nonfiction:** "All of our nonfiction books are generated inhouse."

**Fiction:** Fantasy, gothic, humor, science fiction short story collections. "We currently publish only work-for-hire novels set in our trademarked worlds. No violent or gory fantasy or science fiction." Request guidelines, then query with outline/synopsis and 3 sample chapters.

**Recent Title(s):** *The Silent Blade*, by R.A. Salvatore, in *The Forgotten Realms* series.

**Tips:** "Our audience largely is comprised of highly imaginative 12-30 year-old males."

**TURTLE PRESS**, S.K. Productions Inc., P.O. Box 290206, Wethersfield CT 06129-0206. (860)529-7770. Fax: (860)529-7775. E-mail: editorial@turtlepress.com. Website: http://www.turtlepress.com. **Acquisitions:** Cynthia Kim, editor. Publishes hardcover originals, trade paperback originals and reprints. **Publishes 4-6 titles/year. Pays 8-10% royalty. Offers $500-1,000 advance.** Reports in 1 month on queries. *Writer's Market* recommends allowing 2 months for reply.

O–π Turtle Press publishes sports and martial arts nonfiction and juvenile fiction for a specialty niche audience.

**Nonfiction:** How-to, martial arts, philosophy, self-help, sports. "We prefer tightly targeted topics on which there is little or no information available in the market, particularly for our sports and martial arts titles." Query with SASE

**Fiction:** "We have just begun a line of children's martial arts adventure stories and are very much interested in submissions to expand this line." Query with SASE.

**Recent Title(s):** *Weight Training for Martial Artists*, by Jennifer Lawler (martial arts).

**CHARLES E. TUTTLE CO.**, 153 Milk St., 5th Floor, Boston MA 02109. **Acquisitions:** Michael Lewis, acquisitions editor. Estab. 1832. Publishes hardcover and trade paperback originals and reprints. **Publishes 60 titles/year. Receives over 1,000 queries/year. 20% of books from first-time authors; 60% from unagented writers. Pays 5-10% royalty on net or retail price, depending on format and kind of book.** Publishes book 18 months after acceptance of ms. Accepts simultaneous submissions. Reports in 3 months on proposals.

O–π "Tuttle is America's leading publisher of books on Japan and Asia."

**Nonfiction:** Self-help, Eastern philosophy, alternative health. Subjects include cooking/foods/nutrition (Asian related), philosophy, Buddhist, Taoist, religion (Eastern). Submit query, outline and SASE. Cannot guarantee return of ms.

**Recent Title(s):** *Martial Artist's Way*, by Sifu Glen Doyle.

**TWENTY-FIRST CENTURY BOOKS**, Millbrook Press, 2 Old New Milford Rd., Brookfield CT 06804. (203)740-2220. Publisher: Pat Culleton. Editor: Dominic Barth. **Acquisitions:** Editorial Department. Publishes hardcover originals. **Publishes 40 titles/year. Receives 200 queries and 50 mss/year. 20% of books from first-time writers; 75% from unagented writers. Pays 5-8% royalty on net price.** Publishes book 18 months after acceptance of ms. Accepts simultaneous submissions. Reports in 3 months on proposals.

O–π Twenty-First Century Books publishes nonfiction science, technology and social issues titles for children and young adults.

**Nonfiction:** Children's and young adult nonfiction. Subjects include government/politics, health/medicine, history, military/war, nature/environment, science, current events and social issues. "We publish primarily in series of four or more titles, for ages 10 and up, grades 5-8 (middle grade), and single titles for grades 7 and up. No picture books,

fiction or adult books." Submit proposal package including outline, sample chapter and SASE. Does not review artwork.
**Recent Title(s):** *Science Concepts* series (grades 5-8).
**Tips:** "We are now accepting single titles for both middle grade and young adult readers."

**29TH STREET PRESS**, (formerly Duke Press), Duke Communications International, 221 E. 29th St., Loveland CO 80538. (970)663-4700. Fax: (970)203-2756. E-mail: mcconnta@duke.com. Website: http://www.dukepress.com. **Acquisitions:** Tricia McConnell, acquisitions editor, (AS/400); Mick Gusinde-Duffy, acquisitions editor (Windows NT). Estab. 1982. Publishes trade paperback originals. **Publishes 20-25 titles/year. Receives 20 queries and 5 mss/year. 75% of books from first-time authors; 90% from unagented writers. Pays 10-15% royalty on wholesale price. Offers no advance.** Publishes book 4 months after acceptance of complete ms. Accepts simultaneous submissions. Reports in 1 month on proposals. Book catalog and ms guidelines free.
   O─╖ 29th Street Press publishes books for MIS managers, students, programmers, and system operators working on an IBM AS/400 midrange computer or a Windows NT platform and financial controllers.
**Nonfiction:** Technical, textbook, multimedia (CD-ROM). Subjects include IBM AS/400 midrange computer, accounting software and Windows NT operating system. Submit proposal package including overview, table of contents, sample chapter, schedule, target audience, competing products, marketing plan, personal information, résumé, list of previous publications.
**Recent Title(s):** *TCP/IP and the AS/400*, by Michael Ryan.
**Tips:** "Authors must have technical knowledge and experience on an IBM AS/400 or Windows NT."

**TWO DOT**, Falcon Publishing Co. Inc., Box 1718, Helena MT 59624. (406)442-6597. Fax: (406)442-0384. E-mail: falcon@falconguide.com. Website: http://www.falconguide.com. **Acquisitions:** Megan Hiller, editor. Publishes hardcover and trade paperback originals. **Publishes 10 titles/year. 30% of books from first-time authors; 100% from unagented writers. Pays 8-12½% on net. Offers minimal advance.** Publishes book 1 year after acceptance of ms. Accepts simultaneous submissions. Reports in 3 months. Book catalog for 9×12 SASE with 3 first-class stamps. Manuscript guidelines for SASE.
   O─╖ "Two Dot looks for lively writing for a popular audience, well-researched, on western themes." Currently emphasizing popular history, western history, regional history, western Americana, cooking/foods. De-emphasizing scholarly writings, children's books, fiction, poetry.
**Nonfiction:** Subjects include Americana (western), cooking/foods/nutrition, history, regional. Two state by state series of interest: *More Than Petticoats*, on notable women; and *It Happened In . . .* state histories. Submit outline, 1 sample chapter and SASE. Reviews artwork/photos as part of the ms package. Send photocopies.
**Recent Title(s):** *Charles M. Russell Legacy*, by Larry Peterson.

**TYNDALE HOUSE PUBLISHERS, INC.**, 351 Executive Dr., P.O. Box 80, Wheaton IL 60189-0080. (630)668-8300. Website: http://www.tyndale.com. **Acquisitions:** Manuscript Review Committee. Estab. 1962. Publishes hardcover and trade paperback originals and mass paperback reprints. **Publishes 100 titles/year. 5-10% of books from first-time authors. Average first print order for a first book is 5,000-10,000. Royalty and advance negotiable.** Publishes book 18 months after acceptance. Reports in up to 2 months. Book catalog and ms guidelines for 9×12 SAE with 9 first-class stamps.
**Nonfiction:** Christian growth/self-help, devotional/inspirational, theology/Bible doctrine, children's nonfiction, contemporary/critical issues." Send query or synopsis with SASE. *No unsolicited mss.*
   O─╖ Tyndale House publishes "practical, user-friendly Christian books for the home and family."
**Fiction:** "Biblical, historical and other Christian themes. No short story collections. Youth books: character building stories with Christian perspective. Especially interested in ages 10-14." Send query or synopsis with SASE. *No unsolicited mss.*
**Recent Title(s):** *Left Behind*, by Jerry Jenkins and Tim LaHaye; *The Last Sin Eater*, by Francine Rivers.

**ULYSSES PRESS**, P.O. Box 3440, Berkeley CA 94703. (510)601-8301. Fax: (510)601-8307. E-mail: ulysses@ulyssespress.com. **Acquisitions:** Ray Riegert, editorial director. Estab. 1982. Publishes trade paperback originals. **Publishes 10-15 titles/year. 25% of books from first-time authors; 75% from unagented writers. Pays 12-16% royalty on wholesale price. Offers $2,000-4,000 advance.** Publishes book 6 months after acceptance. Accepts simultaneous submissions. Reports in 2 months on proposals. Book catalog free.
   O─╖ Ulysses publishes travel, spirituality and health books.
**Imprint(s):** Seastone (hidden travel series).
**Nonfiction:** Health, spirituality, travel. Submit proposal package including outline, 2 sample chapters and market analysis with SASE. Reviews artwork/photos as part of ms package. Send photocopies. "Only proposals accompanied by a SASE will be returned."
**Recent Title(s):** *The Music of Silence*.

**UNITY BOOKS**, Unity School of Christianity, 1901 NW Blue Parkway, Unity Village MO 64065-0001. (816)524-3550 ext. 3190. Fax: (816)251-3552. E-mail: sprice@unityworldhq.org. Website: http://www.unityworldhq.org. **Acquisitions:** Michael Maday, editor; Raymond Teague, associate editor. Estab. 1889. Publishes hardcover and trade paperback originals and reprints. **Publishes 16 titles/year. Receives 100 queries and 500 mss/year. 30% of books from first-time authors; 95% from unagented writers. Pays 10-15% royalty on net receipts.** Publishes book 13 months after acceptance of final ms. Reports in 1 month on queries and proposals, 2 months on mss. Book catalog and ms guidelines free.

   o━ "Unity Books publishes metaphysical Christian books based on Unity principles, as well as inspirational books on metaphysics and practical spirituality. All manuscripts must reflect a spiritual foundation and express the Unity philosophy, practical Christianity, universal principles, and/or metaphysics."

**Nonfiction:** Inspirational, self-help, reference (spiritual/metaphysical). Subjects include health (holistic), philosophy (perennial/New Thought), psychology (transpersonal), religion (spiritual/metaphysical Bible interpretation/modern Biblical studies). "Writers should be familiar with principles of metaphysical Christianity but not feel bound by them. We are interested in works in the related fields of holistic health, spiritual psychology and the philosophy of other world religions." Query with book proposal, including cover letter, summarizing unique features and suggested sales and marketing strategies, toc or project outline and 1-3 sample chapters with SASE. Reviews artwork/photos as part of ms package. Send photocopies.

**Recent Title(s):** *Prayer Works*, by Rosemary Ellen Guiley.

**UNIVELT, INC.**, P.O. Box 28130, San Diego CA 92198. (760)746-4005. Fax: (760)746-3139. Website: http://univelt.st aigerland.com. **Acquisitions:** Robert H. Jacobs, publisher. Estab. 1970. Publishes hardcover originals. **Publishes 8 titles/ year. Receives 20 submissions/year. 5% of books from first-time authors; 5% from unagented writers. Nonauthor-subsidy publishes 10% of books. Pays 10% royalty on actual sales. No advance.** Publishes book 4 months after acceptance. Reports in 1 month. Book catalog and ms guidelines for SASE.

   o━ Univelt publishes astronautics, spaceflight, aerospace technology and history titles.

**Imprint(s):** American Astronautical Society, National Space Society.

**Nonfiction:** Publishes in the field of aerospace, especially astronautics, including application of aerospace technology to Earth's problems. Call, and then submit outline and 1-2 chapters. Reviews artwork/photos as part of ms package.

**Recent Title(s):** *Strategies for Mars: A Guide to Human Exploration, Volume 86*, edited by Carol Stoker and Carter Emmart.

**Tips:** "Writers have the best chance of selling manuscripts on the history of astronautics (we have a history series) and astronautics/spaceflight subjects. We publish for the American Astronautical Society."

**N: THE UNIVERSITY OF AKRON PRESS**, 374B Bierce Library, Akron OH 44325-1703. (330)972-5342. Fax: (330)972-5152. E-mail: press@uakron.edu. Website: http://www.uakron.edu/uapress. **Acquisitions:** Elton Glaser, director. Estab. 1988. Publishes hardcover and trade paperback originals. **Publishes 4-5 titles/year. Receives 40-60 queries and over 500 mss/year** (because of poetry contest). **20% of books from first-time authors; 100% from unagented writers. Pays 4-10% royalty on wholesale price.** Publishes book 14 months after acceptance of ms. Accepts simultaneous submissions (only for poetry contest.) Reports in 1 month on queries, 2 months on proposals, 5 months on mss. Book catalog free. Manuscript guidelines for #10 SASE.

   o━ "The University of Akron Press strives to be the University's ambassador for scholarship and creative writing at the national and international levels." Currently emphasizing technology and the environment, Ohio history and culture, poetry. De-emphasizing fiction.

**Nonfiction:** Scholarly, Ohio history. Subjects include regional, technology and environment. "We publish mostly in our two nonfiction series: Technology and the Environment; Ohio history and culture. Writers often do not submit material suitable to our series books." Query. Reviews artwork/photos as part of ms package. Send photocopies.

**Poetry:** Follow the guidelines and submit manuscripts only for the contest.

**Recent Title(s):** *Wheels of Fortune: The Story of Rubber in Akron*, by Steve Love and David Giffels (regional nonfiction); *Winter Morning with Crow*, by Clare Rossini (poetry).

**Tips:** "We have mostly an audience of general educated readers, with a more specialized audience of public historians, sociologists and political scientists for the scholarly series."

**UNIVERSITY OF ALABAMA PRESS**, P.O. Box 870380, Tuscaloosa AL 35487-0380. Fax: (205)348-9201. Website: http://www.uapress.ua.edu. **Acquisitions:** Nicole Mitchell, director (history, political science, regional interest); Curtis Clark, assistant director/editor-in-chief (American literature, communications, Jewish studies, public administration); Judith Knight, acquisition editor (archaeology). Estab. 1945. Publishes nonfiction hardcover and paperbound originals and fiction paperback reprints. **Publishes 45-50 titles/year. Receives 300 submissions/year. 70% of books from first-time authors; 95% from unagented writers.** Publishes book 1 year after acceptance. Book catalog free. Manuscript guidelines for SASE.

**Nonfiction:** Considers upon merit almost any subject of scholarly interest, but specializes in communications, political science and public administration, literary criticism and biography, history, Jewish studies and archaeology of the Southeastern United States. Accepts nonfiction translations. Reviews artwork/photos as part of ms package.

**Fiction:** Reprints of works by contemporary Southern writers.

**Tips:** University of Alabama Press responds to an author within 2 weeks upon receiving the manuscript. If they think it is unsuitable for Alabama's program, they tell the author at once. If the manuscript warrants it, they begin the peer-review process, which may take two to four months to complete. During that process, they keep the author fully informed.

**UNIVERSITY OF ALASKA PRESS**, P.O. Box 756240, 1st Floor Gruening Bldg., UAF, Fairbanks AK 99775-6240. (907)474-5831. Fax: (907)474-5502. E-mail: fypress@uaf.edu. Website: http://www.uaf.edu/uapress. Manager: Debbie Gonzalez. **Acquisitions:** Pam Odom. Estab. 1967. Publishes hardcover originals, trade paperback originals and reprints.

**Publishes 5-10 titles/year. Receives 100 submissions/year. Pays 7½-10% royalty on net sales.** Publishes book within 2 years after acceptance. Reports in 2 months. Book catalog free.

O→ "The mission of the University of Alaska Press is to encourage, publish and disseminate works of scholarship that will enhance the store of knowledge about Alaska and the North Pacific Rim, with a special emphasis on the circumpolar regions."

**Imprint(s):** Classic Reprints, LanternLight Library, Oral Biographies, Rasmuson Library Historical Translation Series.

**Nonfiction:** Biography, reference, technical, textbook, scholarly nonfiction relating to Alaska-circumpolar regions. Subjects include agriculture/horticulture, Americana (Alaskana), animals, anthropology/archaeology, art/architecture, education, ethnic, government/politics, health/medicine, history, language, military/war, nature/environment, regional, science, translation. Nothing that isn't northern or circumpolar. Query or submit outline. Reviews copies of artwork/ photos as part of ms package.

**Recent Title(s):** *The Iñupiaq Eskimo Nations of Northwest Alaska*, by Ernest S. Burch, Jr.

**Tips:** "Writers have the best chance with scholarly nonfiction relating to Alaska, the circumpolar regions and North Pacific Rim. Our audience is made up of scholars, historians, students, libraries, universities, individuals."

**THE UNIVERSITY OF ARKANSAS PRESS**, 201 Ozark Ave., Fayetteville AR 72701-1201. (501)575-3246. Fax: (501)575-6044. E-mail: uaprinfo@cavern.uark.edu. Website: http://www.uark.edu/~uaprinfo. Director: John Coghland, acting director. **Acquisitions:** Kevin Brock, acquisitions editor. Estab. 1980. Publishes hardcover and trade paperback originals and reprints. **Publishes 30 titles/year. Receives 1,000 submissions/year.** 30% of books from first-time authors; 95% from unagented writers. Pays 10% royalty on net receipts from hardcover; 6% on paper. Publishes book 1 year after acceptance of ms. Accepted mss must be submitted on disk. Reports in up to 3 months. Book catalog for 9×12 SAE with 5 first-class stamps. Manuscript guidelines for #10 SASE.

O→ The University of Arkansas Press publishes books on Orzark studies, Civil War in the West, black community studies, American music forms, literary studies and poetics.

**Nonfiction:** Arkansas and regional studies, African-American studies, Southern history and literature, Modernist studies (literature). "Our current needs include literary criticism and history. We won't consider manuscripts for general textbooks, juvenile or religious studies, fiction, or anything requiring a specialized or exotic vocabulary." Query or submit outline, sample chapters, and current résumé or cv.

**Recent Title(s):** *The Wilderness Within: American Women Writers on Spiritual Quest*, by Kristina K. Groover.

**UNIVERSITY OF CHICAGO PRESS**, 5801 Ellis Ave., Chicago IL 60637. (773)702-7700. Fax: (773)702-9756. **Acquisitions**: Susan Abrams, editor (biological science, history of science); T. David Brent, editor (anthropology, philosophy, psychology); Penelope Kaiserlian, editor (geography); Douglas Mitchell, editor (sociology, history); Alan Thomas, editor (literary criticism and theory, religious studies); John Tryneski, editor (political science, law, education); Susan Bielstein, editor (art, architecture, classics, women's studies). Estab. 1891. Publishes hardcover originals, trade paperback originals and reprints. **Publishes 260 titles/year.** 10% of books from first-time authors; 95% from unagented writers. Pays 5-10% royalty on hardcover, 7½% for paperback on net receipts for first-time authors. Advance varies. Publishes book 1 year after acceptance of ms. No simultaneous submissions. Reports in 3 weeks on proposals. Catalog free, call marketing department.

O→ University of Chicago is a scholarly and academic press that also publishes books for a wider audience.

**Nonfiction:** Subjects include anthropology/archaeology, art/architecture, biological sciences, business/economics, education, ethnic, gay/lesbian, government/politics, history, history of science, language/literature, money/finance, music/ dance, philosophy, psychology, religion, sociology, translation, women's issues/studies, law, physical sciences, linguistics. Prefers authors with established credentials. Query or submit proposal package, including prospectus, table of contents, 2-3 sample chapters and author's cv with SASE. Reviews artwork/photos as part of ms package. Send photocopies. No e-mail submissions.

**Poetry:** Publishes 4 titles/year by invitation. *No unsolicited submissions.*

**Recent Title(s):** *The Last Dinosaur Book*, by W.J.T. Mitchell; *A Poet's Guide to Poetry*, by Mary Kinzie.

**UNIVERSITY OF GEORGIA PRESS**, 330 Research Dr., Athens GA 30602-4901. (706)369-6130. Fax: (706)369-6131. E-mail: ugapress@uga.edu. Executive Editor/Director: Karen Orchard. **Acquisitions:** David Des Jardines, acquisition editor. Estab. 1938. Publishes hardcover originals, trade paperback originals and reprints. **Publishes 85 titles/year; imprint publishes 10-15 titles/year. Receives 600 queries/year.** 33% of books from first-time authors; 66% from unagented writers. Pays 7-10% royalty on net price. Rarely offers advance; amount varies. Publishes book 1 year after acceptance of ms. Reports in 2 months on queries. Book catalog free. Manuscript guidelines for #10 SASE.

**Imprint(s):** Brown Thrasher Books, David Des Jardines, acquisition editor (paperback originals and reprints, Southern history, literature and culture).

**Nonfiction:** Subjects include Americana, anthropology/archaeology, art/architecture, government/politics, history, language/literature, nature/environment, regional. Query or submit outline with 1 sample chapter, author's bio with SASE. Reviews artwork/photos as part of ms package if essential to book.

**Fiction:** Literary. "Most successful novels to date have been literary and have dealt with Southwestern themes and characters in a southern setting."

**Poetry:** Published only through contemporary poetry series competition. Query first for guidelines and submission periods; $15 submission fee required.

**Recent Title(s):** *From Selma to Sorrow: The Life and Death of Viola Liuzzo*, by Mary Stanton (biography); *Daughter of My People*, by James Kilgo (novel); *After I was Dead*, by Laura Mullen (poetry).

**UNIVERSITY OF ILLINOIS PRESS**, 1325 S. Oak St., Champaign IL 61820-6903. (217)333-0950. Fax: (217)244-8082. E-mail: uipress@uiuc.edu. Website: http://www.press.uillinois.edu. **Acquisitions:** Willis Regier, director/editor-in-chief. Estab. 1918. Publishes hardcover and trade paperback originals and reprints. **Publishes 100-110 titles/year. 50% of books from first-time authors; 95% from unagented writers. Nonauthor-subsidy publishes 10% of books. Pays 0-10% royalty on net sales. Offers $1,000-1,500 advance (rarely).** Publishes book 1 year after acceptance. Reports in 1 month. Book catalog for 9×12 SAE with 2 first-class stamps.
  O➤ University of Illinois Press publishes "scholarly books and serious nonfiction" with a wide range of study interests.
**Nonfiction:** Biography, reference, scholarly books. Subjects include Americana, history (especially American history), music (especially American music), politics, sociology, philosophy, sports, literature. Always looking for "solid, scholarly books in American history, especially social history; books on American popular music, and books in the broad area of American studies." Query with outline.
**Recent Title(s):** *Atomic Spaces: Living on the Manhattan Project*, by Peter Bacon Hales.
**Tips:** "Serious scholarly books that are broad enough and well-written enough to appeal to nonspecialists are doing well for us in today's market."

**UNIVERSITY OF IOWA PRESS**, 119 W. Park Rd., Iowa City IA 52242-1000. (319)335-2000. Fax: (319)335-2055. Website: http://www.uiowa.edu/~uipress. **Acquisitions:** Holly Carver, director. Estab. 1969. Publishes hardcover and paperback originals. **Publishes 35 titles/year. Receives 300-400 submissions/year. 30% of books from first-time authors; 95% from unagented writers. Pays 7-10% royalty on net price.** Publishes book 1 year after acceptance. Reports within 6 months. Book catalog and ms guidelines free.
  O➤ "We publish authoritative, original nonfiction that we market mostly by direct mail to groups with special interests in our titles and by advertising in trade and scholarly publications."
**Nonfiction:** Publishes anthropology, archaeology, British and American literary studies, history (Victorian, U.S., regional Latin American), jazz studies, history of photography and natural history. Looks for evidence of original research; reliable sources; clarity of organization; complete development of theme with documentation, supportive footnotes and/or bibliography; and a substantive contribution to knowledge in the field treated. Query or submit outline. Use *Chicago Manual of Style*. Reviews artwork/photos as part of ms package.
**Fiction and Poetry:** Currently publishes the Iowa Short Fiction Award selections and winners of the Iowa Poetry Prize Competition. Query regarding poetry or fiction before sending ms.
**Recent Title(s):** *A Whitman Chronology*, by Joann Krieg.
**Tips:** "Developing a series in creative nonfiction."

**N UNIVERSITY OF MAINE PRESS**, 5717 Corbett Hall, Orono ME 04469-5717. (207)581-1408. **Acquisitons:** Director. Publishes hardcover and trade paperback originals and reprints. **Publishes 4 titles/year. Receives 50 queries and 25 mss/year. 10% of mss from first-time authors; 90% from unagented writers.** Publishes book 1 year after acceptance of ms. Accepts simultaneous submissions. *Writer's Market* recommends allowing 2 months for reply.
**Nonfiction:** "We are an academic book publisher, interested in scholarly works on regional history, regional life sciences, Franco-American studies. Authors should be able to articulate their ideas on the potential market for their work." Query.
**Recent Title(s):** *Maine: The Pine Tree State*, by Judd, et.al. (history of Maine).
**Fiction:** Rarely. "The University of Maine Press publishes primarily regional fiction: Maine, New England, Canadian Maritimes." Query.

**UNIVERSITY OF MISSOURI PRESS**, 2910 LeMone Blvd., Columbia MO 65201. (573)882-7641. Fax: (573)884-4498. Website: http://www.system.missouri.edu/upress. Director: Beverly Jarrett. **Acquisitions:** (Mr.) Clair Willcox, acquisitions editor. Estab. 1958. Publishes hardcover and paperback originals and paperback reprints. **Publishes 55 titles/year. Receives 500 submissions/year. 25-30% of books from first-time authors; 90% from unagented writers. Pays up to 10% royalty on net receipts. No advance.** Publishes book 1 year after acceptance of ms. Reports in 6 months. Book catalog free.
  O➤ University of Missouri Press publishes primarily scholarly nonfiction in the social sciences and also some short fiction collections.
**Nonfiction:** Scholarly publisher interested in history, literary criticism, political science, journalism, social science, some art history. Also regional books about Missouri and the Midwest. No mathematics or hard sciences. Query or submit outline and sample chapters. Consult *Chicago Manual of Style*.
**Fiction:** "Collections of short fiction are considered throughout the year; the press does not publish novels. Queries should include sample story, a table of contents and a brief description of the manuscript that notes its length."
**Recent Title(s):** *Praying for Base Hits*, by Bruce Clayton (nonfiction); *Veneer*, by Steve Yarbrough.

**UNIVERSITY OF NEVADA PRESS**, MS 166, Reno NV 89557. (775)784-6573. Fax: (775)784-6200. E-mail: dalrympl@scs.unr.edu. Director: Ronald E. Latimer. Editor-in-Chief: Margaret F. Dalrymple. **Acquisitions:** Trudy McMurrin, acquisitions editor. Estab. 1961. Publishes hardcover and paperback originals and reprints. **Publishes 35 titles/year.**

**20% of books from first-time authors; 99% from unagented writers. Pays average of 10% royalty on net price.** Publishes book 1 year after acceptance of ms. Preliminary report in 2 months. Book catalog and ms guidelines free.

O─╖ "We are the first university press to sustain a sound series on Basque studies—New World and Old World."

**Nonfiction:** Specifically needs regional history and natural history, literature, current affairs, ethnonationalism, gambling and gaming, anthropology, biographies, Basque studies. No juvenile books. Submit complete ms. *Writer's Market* recommends a query with SASE first. Reviews photocopies of artwork/photos as part of ms package.

**Recent Title(s):** *Small Craft Warnings: Stories*, by Kate Braverman.

**UNIVERSITY OF NEW MEXICO PRESS**, 1720 Lomas Blvd. NE, Albuquerque NM 87131-1591. (505)277-2346. E-mail: unmpress@unm.edu. Director: Elizabeth Hadas. **Acquisitions:** Barbara Guth, managing editor (women's studies, chicano/a studies); Dana Asbury, editor (art, photography); Larry Durwood Ball, editor (western Americana, anthropology); David V. Holby, editor (Latin American studies, history). Estab. 1929. Publishes hardcover originals and trade paperback originals and reprints. **Publishes 70 titles/year. Receives 600 submissions/year. 12% of books from first-time authors; 90% from unagented writers. Royalty varies.** *Writer's Market* recommends allowing 2 months for reply. Book catalog free.

O─╖ "The Press is well known as a publisher in the fields of anthropology, archaeology, Latin American studies, photography, architecture and the history and culture of the American West, fiction, some poetry, Chicano/a studies and works by and about American Indians."

**Nonfiction:** Biography, illustrated book, scholarly books. Subjects include anthropology/archaeology, art/architecture, ethnic, history, photography. "No how-to, humor, juvenile, self-help, software, technical or textbooks." Query. Reviews artwork/photos as part of ms package. Send photocopies.

**Recent Title(s):** *Bone Voyage: A Journey in Forensic Anthropology*, by Stanley Rhine (nonfiction); *El Camino del Rio*, Jim Sanderson (fiction).

**UNIVERSITY OF NORTH TEXAS PRESS**, P.O. Box 311336, Denton TX 76203-1336. Fax: (940)565-4590. E-mail: vick@acad.admin.unt.edu or wright@acad.admin.unt.edu. Website: http://www.unt.edu/untpress or http://www.tamu.edu/upress. **Acquisitions**: Frances B. Vick, director. Charlotte Wright, associate director. Estab. 1987. Publishes hardcover and trade paperback originals and reprints. **Publishes 15-20 titles/year. Receives 500 queries and mss/year. 95% of books from unagented writers. Pays 7½-10% royalty of net.** Publishes book 2 years after acceptance of ms. Reports in 3 months on queries. Book catalog for 8½×11 SASE.

O─╖ UNT Press believes that university presses should be on the cutting edge and is not averse to the different or unusual. We are dedicated to producing the highest quality scholarly, academic and general interest books. We are committed to serving all peoples by publishing stories of their cultures and experiences that have been overlooked. Currently emphasizing folklore, multicultural topics, women's issues, history, Texana and western Americana.

**Nonfiction:** Biography, reference. Subjects include agriculture/horticulture, Americana, ethnic, government/politics, history, language/literature, military/war, regional. Query with SASE. Reviews artwork/photos as part of ms package. Send photocopies.

**Poetry:** Offers the Vassar Miller Prize in Poetry, an annual, national competition with a $1,000 prize and publication of the winning manuscript each fall. Query first with SASE.

**Recent Title(s):** *Stories from an Animal Sanctuary*, by Lynn Curry (natural science/natural history); *Panhandle Cowboy*, by John Erickson (fiction).

**Tips:** "We have series called War and the Southwest; Practical Guide Series; Texas Folklore Society Publications series; the Western Life Series; Literary Biographies of Texas Writers series."

**UNIVERSITY OF OKLAHOMA PRESS**, 1005 Asp Ave., Norman OK 73019-0445. (405)325-5111. Fax: (405)325-4000. Website: http://www.ou.edu/oupress. **Acquisitions:** Jean Hurtado, acquisitions editor (American Indian studies, western history, classics); Ron Chrisman, acquisitions editor (paperbacks, military history); Kimberly Wiar, senior acquisitions editor (American Indian literature, political science, natural history, literary criticism). Estab. 1928. Publishes hardcover and paperback originals and reprints. **Publishes 100 titles/year. Pays standard royalty for comparable books.** Publishes book 18 months after acceptance. Reports in 3 months. Book catalog for $1 and 9×12 SAE with 6 first-class stamps.

O─╖ University of Oklahoma Press publishes books for both a scholarly and general audience.

**Imprint(s):** Oklahoma Paperbacks.

**Nonfiction:** Publishes American Indian studies, Western US history, political science, literary theory, natural history, women's studies, classical studies, Mesoamerican studies, military history. No unsolicited poetry or fiction. Query with outline, 1-2 sample chapters and author résumé. Use *Chicago Manual of Style* for ms guidelines. Reviews artwork/photos as part of ms package.

**Recent Title(s):** *Preparing America's Foreign Policy for the 21st Century*, by David L. Boren and Edward J. Perkins (political science); *Dark River: A Novel*, by Louis Owens (American Indian literature).

**UNIVERSITY OF PENNSYLVANIA PRESS**, 4200 Pine St., Philadelphia PA 19104-4011. (215)898-6261. Fax: (215)898-0404. Website: http://www.upenn.edu/pennpress. Director: Eric Halpern. **Acquisitions:** Jerome Singerman, humanities editor; Patricia Smith, social sciences editor; Jo Joslyn, art and architecture editor; Robert Hockhart, history editor. Estab. 1890. Publishes hardcover and paperback originals and reprints. **Publishes 75 titles/year. Receives 650**

submissions/year. **10-20% of books from first-time authors; 95% from unagented writers. Royalty determined on book-by-book basis.** Publishes book 10 months after delivery of final ms. Reports in 3 months or less. Book catalog for 9×12 SAE with 6 first-class stamps.
**Nonfiction:** Publishes American history, literary criticism, women's studies, cultural studies, ancient studies, medieval studies, business, anthropology, folklore, art history, architecture. "Serious books that serve the scholar and the professional, student and general reader." Follow the *Chicago Manual of Style*. Query with outline, résumé or vita. *No unsolicited mss.* Reviews artwork as part of ms package. Send photocopies.
**Recent Title(s):** *ABC of Architecture*, by James F. O'Gorman.

**UNIVERSITY OF SCRANTON PRESS**, University of Scranton, Scranton PA 18510-4660. (717)941-4228. Fax: (717)941-4309. E-mail: rousseaur1@uofs.edu. Website: http://www.viamall.com (catalog). **Acquisitions:** Richard Rousseau, director. Estab. 1981. Publishes hardcover and paperback originals. **Publishes 5 titles/year. Receives 200 queries and 45 mss/year. 60% of books from first-time authors; 100% from unagented writers. Pays 10% royalty.** Publishes book 1 year after acceptance. Reports in 1 month on queries. Book catalog and ms guidelines free.
　　O╼ The University of Scranton Press, a member of the Association of Jesuit University Presses, publishes primarily scholarly monographs in theology, philosophy and the culture of northeast Pennsylvania.
**Imprint(s):** Ridge Row Press.
**Nonfiction:** Scholarly monographs. Subjects include art/architecture, language/literature, philosophy, religion, sociology. Looking for clear editorial focus: theology/religious studies; philosophy/philosophy of religion; scholarly treatments; the culture of northeast Pennsylvania. Query or submit outline and 2 sample chapters.
**Poetry:** Only poetry related to northeast Pennsylvania.
**Recent Title(s):** *Living in Two Cities: Augustinian Projectures in Political Thought*, by Eugene TeSelle.

**UNIVERSITY OF SOUTH CAROLINA PRESS**, 937 Assembly St., 8th Floor, Columbia SC 29208. **Acquisitions:** Barry Blose, acquisitions editor (literature, religious studies, rhetoric, social work); Alexander Moore, acquisitions editor (history, regional studies, culinary history). Estab. 1944. Publishes hardcover originals, trade paperback originals and reprints. **Publishes 50 titles/year. Receives 1,200 queries/year and 250 mss/year. 30% of books from first-time authors; 95% from unagented writers. Pays 7½-20% royalty on wholesale price. Offers $1,000-5,000 advance.** Publishes book 13 months after acceptance of ms. Accepts simultaneous submissions. Reports in 3 months on mss. Book catalog and ms guidelines free on request.
　　O╼ "We focus on scholarly monographs and regional trade books of lasting merit."
**Nonfiction:** Biography, illustrated book, reference, monograph. Subjects include art/architecture, culinary history, language/literature, military/war, regional, rhetoric, religion, communication, international relations. "Do not submit entire unsolicited manuscripts or projects with limited scholarly value." Submit proposal package, including outline, 2 sample chapters, cv and résumé with SASE. Reviews artwork/photos as part of the ms package. Send photocopies.
**Poetry:** "All poetry is published as part of the James Dickey Contemporary Poetry Series and is selected by the series editor, Richard Howard." Submit "some" sample poems.
**Recent Title(s):** *South Carolina: A History*, by Walter Edgar; *"Ulysses"—En-Gendered Perspectives*, edited by Devlin and Marilyn Reizbaum.

**THE UNIVERSITY OF TENNESSEE PRESS**, 293 Communications Bldg., Knoxville TN 37996-0325. Fax: (423)974-3724. E-mail: utpress2@utk.edu. Website: http://www.sunsite.utk.edu/utpress/. **Acquisitions:** Joyce Harrison, acquisitions editor (scholarly books); Jennifer Siler, director (Civil War, regional trades, fiction). Estab. 1940. **Publishes 30 titles/year. Receives 450 submissions/year. 35% of books from first-time authors; 99% from unagented writers. Nonauthor-subsidy publishes 10% of books. Pays negotiable royalty on net receipts.** Book catalog for 12×16 SASE with 2 first-class stamps. Manuscript guidelines for SASE.
　　O╼ "Our mission is to stimulate scientific and scholarly research in all fields; to channel such studies, either in scholarly or popular form, to a larger number of people; and to extend the regional leadership of the University of Tennessee by stimulating research projects within the South and by non-university authors."
**Nonfiction:** American studies *only*, in the following areas: African-American studies; Appalachian studies, religion (history, sociology, anthropology, biography only), folklore/folklife, history, literary studies, vernacular architecture, historical archaeology, and material culture. Submissions in other fields, and submissions of poetry, textbooks, plays and translations, are not invited. Prefers "scholarly treatment and a readable style. Authors usually have Ph.D.s." Submit outline, author vita and 2 sample chapters. Reviews artwork/photos as part of ms package.
**Fiction:** Regional. Query with synopsis and author biographical information.
**Recent Title(s):** *Wildflowers of the Southern Mountains*, by Richard Smith.
**Tips:** "Our market is in several groups: scholars; educated readers with special interests in given scholarly subjects; and the general educated public interested in Tennessee, Appalachia and the South. Not all our books appeal to all these groups, of course, but any given book must appeal to at least one of them."

**UNIVERSITY OF TEXAS PRESS**, P.O. Box 7819, Austin TX 78713-7819. Fax: (512)320-0668. E-mail: castiron@mail.utexas.edu. Website: http://www.utexas.edu/utpress/. **Acquisitions:** Theresa May, assistant director/executive editor (social sciences, Latin American studies); James Burr, acquisition editor (humanities, classics); Sheri Englund, acquisitions editor (science). Estab. 1952. **Publishes 80 titles/year. Receives 1,000 submissions/year. 50% of books from first-time authors; 99% from unagented writers. Pays royalty usually based on net income. Offers advance**

**occasionally.** Publishes book 18 months after acceptance of ms. Reports in up to 3 months. Book catalog and ms guidelines free.

○━ "In addition to publishing the results of advanced research for scholars worldwide, UT Press has a special obligation to the people of its state to publish authoritative books on Texas."

**Nonfiction:** General scholarly subjects: natural history, American, Latin American, Native American, Chicano and Middle Eastern studies, classics and the ancient world, film, contemporary regional architecture, archaeology, anthropology, geography, ornithology, environmental studies, biology, linguistics, women's literature, literary biography (Modernist period). Also uses specialty titles related to Texas and the Southwest, national trade titles and regional trade titles. Accepts nonfiction translations related to above areas. Query or submit outline and 2 sample chapters. Reviews artwork/photos as part of ms package.

**Fiction:** Latin American and Middle Eastern fiction only in translation.

**Recent Title(s):** *Chicano Politics and Society in the Late Twentieth Century*, edited by David Montejano.

**Tips:** "It's difficult to make a manuscript over 400 double-spaced pages into a feasible book. Authors should take special care to edit out extraneous material. We look for sharply focused, in-depth treatments of important topics."

**UNIVERSITY PRESS OF COLORADO**, 4699 Nautilus Court, Suite 403, Boulder CO 80301. (303)530-5337. Fax: (303)530-5306. Director: Luther Wilson. **Acquisitions:** Yashka Hallein, acquisitions editor. Estab. 1965. Publishes hardcover and paperback originals. **Publishes 40 titles/year. Receives 1,000 submissions/year. 50% of books from first-time authors; 95% from unagented writers. Pays 7½-15% royalty contract on net price.** Publishes book 2 years after acceptance of ms. Reports in 6 months. Book catalog free.

○━ "We are a university press. Books should be solidly researched and from a reputable scholar."

**Nonfiction:** Scholarly, regional and environmental subjects. Length: 250-500 pages. Query first with table of contents, preface or opening chapter and SASE. Reviews artwork/photos as part of ms package.

**Fiction:** Limited fiction series; works of fiction on the trans-Mississippi West, by authors residing in the region. Query with SASE.

**Recent Title(s):** *Innocents on the Ice: A Memoir of Antarctic Exploration 1957*, by John C. Bohrendt (nonfiction); *October Revolution*, by Tom LaMarr (fiction); *Palma Cathedral*, by Michael White (poetry).

**Tips:** "We have series on the Women's West and on Mesoamerican worlds."

**UNIVERSITY PRESS OF KANSAS**, 2501 W. 15th St., Lawrence KS 66049-3905. (785)864-4154. Fax: (785)864-4586. E-mail: mail@newpress.upress.ukans.edu. **Acquisitions:** Michael J. Briggs, editor-in-chief (military history, political science, law); Nancy Scott Jackson, acquisitions editor (western history, American studies, environmental studies, women's studies, philosophy); Fred M. Woodward, director, (political science, presidency, regional). Estab. 1946. Publishes hardcover originals, trade paperback originals and reprints. **Publishes 50 titles/year. Receives 600 queries/year. 20% of books from first-time authors; 98% from unagented writers. Pays 5-15% royalty on net price.** Publishes book 10 months after acceptance of ms. Reports in 1 month on proposals. Book catalog and ms guidelines free.

○━ The University Press of Kansas publishes scholarly books that advance knowledge and regional books that contribute to the understanding of Kansas, the Great Plains and the Midwest.

**Nonfiction:** Biography. Subjects include Americana, anthropology/archaeology, government/politics, history, military/war, nature/environment, philosophy, regional, sociology, women's issues/studies. "We are looking for books on topics of wide interest based on solid scholarship and written for both specialists and informed general readers. Do not send unsolicited complete manuscripts." Submit cover letter, cv, and prospectus, outline or sample chapter. Reviews artwork/photos as part of the ms package. Send photocopies.

**Recent Title(s):** *Nixon's Vietnam War*, by Jeffrey Kimbal.

**UNIVERSITY PRESS OF KENTUCKY**, 663 S. Limestone, Lexington KY 40508-4008. (606)257-2951. Fax: (606)257-2984. Website: http://www.uky.edu/UniversityPress/. **Acquisitions:** Nancy L. Grayson, editor-in-chief. Estab. 1951. Publishes hardcover and paperback originals and reprints. **Publishes 60 titles/year. Royalty varies. No advance.** Publishes ms 1 year after acceptance. Reports in 2 months on queries. Book catalog free.

○━ "We are a scholarly publisher, publishing chiefly for an academic and professional audience."

**Nonfiction:** Biography, reference, monographs. "Strong areas are American history, literature, women's studies, film studies, American and African-American studies, folklore, Kentuckiana and regional books, Appalachian studies, Irish studies and military history. No textbooks, genealogical material, lightweight popular treatments, how-to books or books unrelated to our major areas of interest." The Press does not consider original works of fiction or poetry. Query.

**Recent Title(s):** *Baseball's Pivotal Era, 1945-1951*, by William Marshall.

**UNIVERSITY PRESS OF MISSISSIPPI**, 3825 Ridgewood Rd., Jackson MS 39211-6492. (601)982-6205. Fax: (601)982-6217. E-mail: press@ihl.state.ms.us. Director/Editor-in-Chief: Seetha Srinivasan. **Acquisitions:** Craig Gill, senior editor (regional studies, anthropology, military history); Anne Stascavage, editor (performance art, literature). Acquisitions Editor. Estab. 1970. Publishes hardcover and paperback originals and reprints. **Publishes 55 titles/year. Receives 750 submissions/year. 20% of books from first-time authors; 90% from unagented writers. "Competitive royalties and terms."** Publishes book 1 year after acceptance. Reports in 3 months. Catalog for 9×12 SAE with 3 first-class stamps.

○━ "University Press of Mississippi publishes scholarly and trade titles, as well as special series, including: American Made Music; Author and Artist; Comparative Diaspora Studies; Faulkner and Yoknapatawpha; Fiction

Series; Folk Art and Artists; Folklife in the South; Literary Conversations; Natural History; Performance Studies in Culture; Studies in Popular Culture; Understanding Health and Sickness; Writers and Their Work."

**Imprint(s):** Muscadine Books (regional trade), Banner Books (literary reprints).

**Nonfiction:** Americana, biography, history, politics, folklife, literary criticism, ethnic/minority studies, art, photography, music, health, popular culture with scholarly emphasis. Interested in southern regional studies and literary studies. Submit outline, sample chapters and cv. "We prefer a proposal that describes the significance of the work and a chapter outline." Reviews artwork/photos as part of ms package.

**Fiction:** Commissioned trade editions by prominent writers.

**Recent Title(s):** *Light of the Spirit; Portraits of Southern Outsider Artists*, by Karekin Goekjian and Robert Peacock.

**UNIVERSITY PRESS OF NEW ENGLAND**, (includes Wesleyan University Press), 23 S. Main St., Hanover NH 03755-2048. (603)643-7100. Fax: (603)643-1540. E-mail: university.press@dartmouth.edu. Website: http://www.dartmouth.edu/acad-inst/upne/. Director: Richard Abel. **Acquisitions:** Phil Pochoda, editorial director (American/northeastern studies, fiction, biography, cultural studies); Phyllis Deutsch, editor (Jewish studies, art, biography, American studies, French studies); April Ossmann, assistant editor (poetry, nature, performance studies, American/regional studies); Suzanna Tamminen, editor-in-chief (poetry [for Wesleyan], music, performance studies). Estab. 1970. Publishes hardcover and trade paperback originals, trade paperback reprints. **Publishes 75-80 titles/year. Pays standard royalty. Offers advance occasionally.** Reports in 2 months. Book catalog and guidelines for 9×12 SAE with 5 first-class stamps.

    O─ "University Press of New England is a consortium of university presses. Some books—those published for one of the consortium members—carry the joint imprint of New England and the member: Wesleyan, Dartmouth, Brandeis, Tufts, University of New Hampshire and Middlebury College. We publish academic studies for an academic audience (mostly American studies and Jewish studies) as well as nonfiction aimed at the educated reader/intellectual. We also encourage regional (New England) work (academic, fiction, poetry or otherwise)." Currently emphasizing American studies, cultural studies. De-emphasizing fiction.

**Nonfiction:** Americana (New England), art, biography, music, nature, American studies, Jewish studies, performance studies, regional (New England). No festschriften, unrevised doctoral dissertations, or symposium collections. Submit outline, 1-2 sample chapters with SASE. *No electronic submissions.*

**Fiction:** *Only* New England novels and reprints.

**Recent Title(s):** *Acts of Memory & Cultural Recall in the Present*, by Miehe Bal, Jonathan Crewe, Leo Spitzer, editors (cultural studies); *Lost Daughters*, by Laurie Alberts (novel).

**THE URBAN LAND INSTITUTE**, (formerly ULI), 1025 Thomas Jefferson St. N.W., Washington DC 20007-5201. (202)624-7000. Fax: (202)624-7140. **Acquisitions:** Rachelle Levitt, vice president/publisher. Estab. 1936. Publishes hardcover and trade paperback originals. **Publishes 15-20 titles/year. Receives 20 submissions/year. 2% of books from first-time authors; 100% of books from unagented writers. Pays 10% royalty on gross sales. Offers $1,500-2,000 advance.** Publishes book 6 months after acceptance. Book catalog and ms guidelines for 9×12 SAE.

    O─ The Urban Land Institute publishes technical books on real estate development and land planning.

**Nonfiction:** "The majority of manuscripts are created inhouse by research staff. We acquire two or three outside authors to fill schedule and subject areas where our list has gaps. We are not interested in real estate sales, brokerages, appraisal, making money in real estate, opinion, personal point of view, or manuscripts negative toward growth and development." Query. Reviews artwork/photos as part of ms package.

**Recent Title(s):** *Urban Parks and Open Space.*

**UTAH STATE UNIVERSITY PRESS**, 7800 Old Main Hill, Logan UT 84322-7800. (435)797-1362. Fax: (435)797-0313. Website: http://www.usu.edu/~usupress. **Acquisitions:** Michael Spooner, director (composition, poetry); John Alley, editor (history, folklore, fiction). Estab. 1972. Publishes hardcover and trade paperback originals and reprints. **Publishes 15 titles/year. Receives 170 submissions/year. 8% of books from first-time authors. Pays royalty on net price. No advance.** Publishes book 18 months after acceptance. Reports in 1 month on queries. Book catalog free. Manuscript guidelines for SASE.

    O─ Utah State University Press publishes scholarly works in the academic areas noted below. Currently interested in book-length scholarly manuscripts dealing with folklore studies or composition studies.

**Nonfiction:** Biography, reference and textbooks on folklore, Americana and the West. Query with SASE. Reviews artwork/photos as part of ms package. Send photocopies.

**Recent Title(s):** *Wiring the Writing Center*, edited by Eric H. Hobson; *People of the West Desert*, by Craig Denton; *The Hammered Dulcimer*, by Lisa Williams (poetry).

**Tips:** Utah State University Press also sponsors the annual May Swenson Poetry Award.

**VAN DER PLAS PUBLICATIONS**, 1282 Seventh Ave., San Francisco CA 94122-2526. (415)665-8214. Fax: (415)753-8572. Publisher/Editor: Rob van der Plas. Estab. 1997. Publishes hardcover and trade paperback originals. **Publishes 6 titles/year. Receives 15 submissions/year. 10% of books from first-time authors. 100% from unagented writers. Pays 12% of net royalty. No advance.** Publishes book an average of 1 year after acceptance. Accepts simultaneous submissions. Reports in 3 months. Book catalog and ms guidelines for #10 SASE.

**Nonfiction:** How-to, technical. Subjects include recreation, sports. Submit complete ms. Artwork/photos essential as part of the ms package.

**Recent Titles:** *100 Years of Bicycle Components and Accessory Design.*

**Tips:** "Writers have a good chance selling us books with better and more illustrations and a systematic treatment of the subject. First check what is on the market and ask yourself whether you are writing something that is not yet available and wanted."

**N VANDAMERE PRESS**, AB Associates International, Inc., P.O. Box 5243, Arlington VA 22205. **Acquisitions:** Jerry Frank, editor. Estab. 1984. Publishes hardcover and trade paperback originals and reprints. **Publishes 8-15 titles/ year. Receives 750 queries and 2,000 mss/year. 25% of books from first-time authors; 90% from unagented writers. Pays royalty on revenues generated.** Publishes book 1-3 years after acceptance of ms. Accepts simultaneous submissions. Reports in 6 months.

○➤ Vandamere publishes general fiction as well as nonfiction of historical, biographical or regional interest. Currently emphasizing history and biography.

**Nonfiction:** Subjects include Americana, biography, disability/healthcare issues, education, history, military/war, regional (Washington D.C./Mid-Atlantic). Submit outline and 2-3 sample chapters. Reviews artwork/photos as part of ms package. Send photocopies.

**Fiction:** General fiction including adventure, erotica, humor, mystery, suspense. Submit synopsis and 5-10 sample chapters. *Writer's Market* recommends sending a query with SASE first.

**Recent Title(s):** *Blackbird Fly Away*, by Hugh Gregory Gallagher (nonfiction); *Holy War*, by Alexander M. Grace.

**Tips:** "Authors who can provide endorsements from significant published writers, celebrities, etc., will *always* be given serious consideration. Clean, easy-to-read, *dark* copy is essential. Patience in waiting for replies is essential. All unsolicited work is looked at, but at certain times of the year our review schedule will stop." No response without SASE.

**VANDERBILT UNIVERSITY PRESS**, Box 1813, Station B, Nashville TN 37235. (615)322-3585. Fax: (615)343-8823. E-mail: vupress@vanderbilt.edu. Website: http://www.vanderbilt.edu/VUPress. **Acquisitions:** Charles Backus, director. Among other titles, publishes Vanderbilt Library of American Philosophy (Herman J. Saatkamp, editor); Vanderbilt Issues in Higher Education (John Braxton, editor) and Innovations in Applied Mathematics (Larry Schumacher, editor). Also distributes for and co-publishes with the Country Music Foundation. Estab. 1940. Publishes hardcover originals and trade paperback originals and reprints. **Publishes 15-20 titles/year. Receives 350-400 queries/year. 25% of books from first-time authors; 90% from unagented writers. Pays 15% maximum royalty on net income. Sometimes offers advance.** Publishes book 10 months after acceptance of ms. No simultaneous submissions. Reports in 3 months on proposals. Book catalog and ms guidelines free.

○➤ "Vanderbilt University Press, the publishing arm of the nation's leading research university, has maintained a strong reputation as a publisher of distinguished titles in the humanities, social sciences, education, medicine and regional studies, for both academic and general audiences, responding to rapid technological and cultural changes, while upholding high standards of scholarly publishing excellence."

**Nonfiction:** Biography, textbook, scholarly. Subjects include Americana, anthropology/archaeology, education, government/politics, health/medicine, history, language/literature, music and popular culture, nature/environment, philosophy, regional, religion, translation, women's issues/studies. Submit outline, 1 sample chapter and cv. Reviews artwork/photos as part of ms package. Send photocopies.

**Recent Title(s):** *In Love with Life: Reflections on the Joy of Living and Why We Hate to Die*, by John Lacks.

**Tips:** "Our audience consists of scholars and educated general readers."

**N VENTURE PUBLISHING, INC.**, 1999 Cato Ave., State College PA 16801. Fax: (814)234-1651. E-mail: vpublish@venturepublish.com. Website: http://www.venturepublish.com. **Acquisitions:** Geof Godbey, editor. Estab. 1979. Publishes hardcover originals and reprints. **Publishes 6-8 titles/year. Receives 50 queries and 20 mss/year. 40% of books from first-time authors; 100% from unagented writers. Pays royalty on wholesale price. Offers advance.** Publishes book 9 months after acceptance of ms. Reports in 1 month on queries; 2 months on proposals and mss. Book catalog and ms guidelines free.

○➤ Venture Publishing produces quality educational publications, also workbooks for professionals, educators, and students in the fields of recreation, parks, leisure studies, therapeutic recreation and long term care.

**Nonfiction:** Textbook, college academic, professional. Subjects include nature/environment (outdoor recreation management and leadership texts), recreation, sociology (leisure studies), long-term care nursing homes, therapeutic recreation. "Textbooks and books for recreation activity leaders high priority." Submit outline and 1 sample chapter.

**Recent Title(s):** *Programming for Parks, Recreation, and Leisure Services: A Servant Approach*, by Don DeGraaf, Debra Jordan, Kathy DeGraaf.

**VERSO**, 180 Varick St., 10th Fl., New York NY 10014. (212)807-9680. Fax: (212)807-9152. E-mail: versoinc@aol.com. Website: http://www.verso-nlr.com. **Acquisitions:** Colin Robinson, managing director. Estab. 1970. Publishes hardcover

---

**ALWAYS SUBMIT** unsolicited manuscripts or queries with a self-addressed, stamped envelope (SASE) within your country or a self-addressed envelope with International Reply Coupons (IRC) purchased from the post office for other countries.

and trade paperback originals. **Publishes 40-60 titles/year. Receives 300 queries and 150 mss/year. 10% of mss from first-time authors, 95% from unagented writers. Pays royalty.** Publishes book 1 year after acceptance of ms. Accepts simultaneous submissions. Reports in 5 months. Book catalog free.

○⊶ "Our books cover politics, culture, and history (among other topics), but all come from a critical, Leftist viewpoint, on the border between trade and academic."

**Nonfiction:** Illustrated book. Subjects include economics, government/politics, history, philosophy, sociology and women's issues/studies. "We are loosely affiliated with *New Left Review* (London). We are not interested in academic monographs." Submit proposal package, including at least 1 sample chapter.

**Recent Title(s):** *Wall Street*, by Doug Henwood (politics/economics).

**VGM CAREER HORIZONS**, NTC/Contemporary Publishing Group, 4255 W. Touhy Ave., Lincolnwood IL 60646-1975. (847)679-5500. Fax: (847)679-2494. Editorial Group Director: John Nolan. **Acquisitions:** Betsy Lancefield, editor. Estab. 1963. Publishes hardcover and paperback originals. **Publishes 100 titles/year. Receives 250-300 submissions/year. 15% of books from first-time authors; 95% from unagented writers. Pays royalty or makes outright purchase. Advance varies.** Publishes book 1 year after acceptance of ms. Accepts simultaneous submissions. Reports in 3 months. Book catalog and ms guidelines for 9×12 SAE with 5 first-class stamps.

○⊶ VGM publishes career-focused titles for job seekers, career planners, job changers, students and adults in education and trade markets.

**Nonfiction:** Textbook and general trade on careers in medicine, business, environment, etc. Query or submit outline and sample chapters.

**Recent Title(s):** *Career Change*, by Dr. David P. Hellard.

**Tips:** VGM also hires revision authors to handle rewrites and new editions of existing titles.

**Ⓐ VIKING**, Penguin Putnam Inc., 375 Hudson St., New York NY 10014. (212)366-2000. **Acquisitions:** Barbara Grossman, publisher. Publishes hardcover and trade paperback originals. **Pays 10-15% royalty on retail price. Advance negotiable.** Publishes book 1 year after acceptance of ms. Accepts simultaneous submissions. Report in 6 months on queries.

○⊶ Viking publishes a mix of academic and popular fiction and nonfiction.

**Nonfiction:** Subjects include biography, business/economics, child guidance/parenting, cooking/foods/nutrition, health/medicine, history, language/literature, music/dance, philosophy, women's issues/studies. *Agented submissions only.*

**Fiction:** Literary, mainstream/contemporary, mystery, suspense. *Agented submissions only.*

**Recent Title(s):** *Without a Doubt*, by Marcia Clark (popular culture); *Out to Canaan*, by Jan Karon (novel).

**VIKING CHILDREN'S BOOKS**, Penguin Putnam Inc., 375 Hudson St., New York NY 10014. (212)366-2000. Editor-in-Chief: Elizabeth Law. **Acquisitions:** Submissions Editors. Publishes hardcover originals. **Publishes 80 books/year. Receives 7500 queries/year. 25% of books from first-time authors; 33% from unagented writers. Pays 10% royalty on retail price.** Advance negotiable. Publishes book 1 year after acceptance of ms. Report in 4 months on queries.

○⊶ Viking Children's Books publishes high-quality trade books for children including fiction, nonfiction, and novelty books for pre-schoolers through young adults.

**Nonfiction:** Children's books. Query with outline, 3 sample chapters and SASE.

**Fiction:** Juvenile, young adult. Submit complete ms for novels, picture books and chapter books with SASE.

**Recent Title(s):** *See Through History*, series by various authors (history); *The Awful Aardvarks Go to School*, by Reeve Lindbergh (picture book).

**VIKING STUDIO**, (formerly Penguin Studio), Penguin Putnam, Inc., 375 Hudson St., New York NY 10014. (212)366-2191. Website: http://www.penguinputnam.com. **Acquisitions:** Christopher Sweet, executive editor (art, music, history, photography, fashion, religion); Cyril Nelson, senior editor (arts & crafts, decorative arts); Marie Timell, senior editor (nonfiction general interest, astrology, New Age); Rachel Tsutsumi, associate editor, (art, architecture, photography, fashion, design, travel). Publishes hardcover originals. **Publishes 35-40 titles/year. Receives 300 submissions/year. Less than 10% of books are from first-time authors; less than 5% from unagented writers.** Publishes book 1 year after acceptance. Accepts simultaneous submissions. Reports in 2 months.

○⊶ Viking Studio publishes high-quality nonfiction, illustrated hardcover/trade books.

**Nonfiction:** Subjects include Americana, architecture, photography, New Age/metaphysics, art, photography, popular culture, astrology, architecture, fashion. Reviews artwork as part of ms package. Send photocopies.

**Recent Title(s):** *The Rolling Stones: A Life on the Road*, by The Rolling Stones.

**Ⓐ VILLARD BOOKS**, Random House Inc., 201 E. 50th St., New York NY 10022. (212)572-2878. Publisher: Ann Godoff. Estab. 1983. Publishes hardcover and trade paperback originals. **Publishes 55-60 titles/year. 95% of books are agented submissions. Advances and royalties; negotiated separately.** Accepts simultaneous submissions.

○⊶ "Villard Books is the publisher of savvy and sometimes quirky bestseller hardcovers and trade paperbacks."

**Nonfiction and Fiction:** Commercial nonfiction and fiction. *Agented submissions only.* Submit outline/synopsis and up to 50 pages in sample chapters. *No unsolicited submissions.*

**Recent Title(s):** *Marriage Shock: The Emotional Transformation of Women Into Wives*, by Dalma Heyn (relationships).

**VINTAGE**, Knopf Publishing Group, Random House Inc., 201 E. 50th St., New York NY 10020. Vice President: LuAnn Walther. Editor-in-Chief: Martin Asher. **Acquisitions:** Submissions Dept. Publishes trade paperback originals and reprints. **Publishes 200 titles/year. Receives 600-700 mss/year. 5% of books from first time-authors; less than 1% from unagented writers. Pays 4-8% on retail price. Offers $2,500 and up advance.** Publishes book 1 year after acceptance of ms. Accepts simultaneous submissions. Reports in 6 months.
**Nonfiction:** Subjects include anthropology/archaeology, biography, business/economics, child guidance/parenting, education, ethnic, gay/lesbian, government/politics, health/medicine, history, language/literature, military/war, nature/environment, philosophy, psychology, regional, science, sociology, translation, travel, women's issues/studies. Submit outline and 2-3 sample chapters. Reviews artwork as part of ms package. Send photocopies.
**Fiction:** Literary, mainstream/contemporary, short story collections. Submit synopsis with 2-3 sample chapters.
**Recent Title(s):** *A Civil Action*, by Harr (current affairs); *Snow Falling on Cedars*, by Guterson (contemporary).

**N** **VINTAGE IMAGES**, P.O. Box 4699, Silver Spring MD 20914. (301)879-6522. Fax: (301)879-6524. E-mail: vimages@erols.com. Website: http://www.vintageimages.com. **Acquisitions:** Brian Smolens, president. Publishes trade paperback originals. **Publishes 8 titles/year. Pays 4-8% royalty on wholesale price or makes outright purchase of $500-2,500. No advance.** Publishes book 5 months after acceptance of ms. No simultaneous submissions. Manuscript guidelines for #10 SASE.
**Nonfiction:** Poster books. Photography subjects. Send for guidelines. Query with SASE. *All unsolicited mss returned unopened.*
**Tips:** "We are interested in creative writers who can weave a humorous/dramatic theme around 36 vintage photos (early 1900s)."

**VISTA PUBLISHING, INC.**, 422 Morris Ave., Suite #1, Long Branch NJ 07740. (732)229-6500. Fax: (732)229-9647. E-mail: czagury@vistapubl.com. Website: http://www.vistapubl.com. **Acquisitions:** Carolyn Zagury, president. Estab. 1991. Publishes trade paperback originals. **Publishes 12 titles/year. Receives 200 queries and 125 mss/year. 75% of books from first-time authors; 100% from unagented writers. Pays 50% royalty on wholesale or retail price.** Publishes book 2-3 years after acceptance of ms. Accepts simultaneous submissions. Reports in 3 months on mss. Book catalog and ms guidelines free.
  **O—** Vista publishes books by nurses and allied health professionals. Currently emphasizing clinical nursing issues and topics. De-emphasizing fiction and mysteries.
**Nonfiction:** Nursing and career related. Subjects include business, child guidance/parenting, creative nonfiction, health/medicine, women's issues/studies, specific to nursing and allied health professionals. Submit full ms and SASE. *Writer's Market* recommends query with SASE first. Reviews artwork/photos as part of ms package. Send photocopies.
**Fiction:** Horror, multicultural, mystery, poetry, short story collections, nursing medical. "We specialize in nurse and allied health professional authors." Submit full ms and SASE.
**Poetry:** Nursing-related. Submit complete ms.
**Recent Title(s):** *Child Abuse: A Quick Reference*, by Cynthia Feinan and Winfred Coleman (nonfiction); *Things Hidden*, by Helen Osterman (fiction); *Not So Perfect, Perfect Parent*, by Leah Johnston Rowbotham (poetry).
**Tips:** "It's always worth the effort to submit your manuscript."

**VOYAGEUR PRESS**, 123 N. Second St., Stillwater MN 55082. (651)430-2210. Fax: (651)430-2211. E-mail: mdregni @voyageurpress.com or tberger@voyageurpress.com. **Acquisitions:** Todd R. Berger (regional travel and photography. Michael Dregni, editorial director. Estab. 1972. Publishes hardcover and trade paperback originals. **Publishes 30 titles/year. Receives 1,200 queries and 500 mss/year. 10% of books from first-time authors; 90% from unagented writers. Pays royalty.** Publishes book 1 year after acceptance of ms. Accepts simultaneous submissions. Reports in 3 months. Book catalog and ms guidelines free.
  **O—** "Voyageur Press is internationally known as a leading publisher of quality natural history, wildlife and regional books."
**Nonfiction:** Coffee table book (and smaller format photographic essay books), cookbook. Subjects include natural history, nature/environment, Americana, collectibles, history, outdoor recreation, regional. Query or submit outline. Reviews artwork/photos. Send transparencies—duplicates and tearsheets only.
**Recent Title(s):** *This Old Tractor* (stories and photos about farm tractors); *Last Standing Woman* (Native American novel).
**Tips:** "We publish books for a sophisticated audience interested in natural history and cultural history of a variety of subjects. Please present as focused an idea as possible in a brief submission (one page cover letter; two page outline or proposal). Note your credentials for writing the book. Tell all you know about the market niche and marketing possibilities for proposed book."

**WADSWORTH PUBLISHING COMPANY**, International Thomson Publishing, Inc., 10 Davis Dr., Belmont CA 94002. (650)595-2350. Fax: (650)637-7544. Website: http://www.thomson.com/wadsworth.html. **Acquisitions:** Sean Wakely, editorial director; Peter Adams, editor (philosophy/religion); Karen Austin, editor (communications, radio/TV/film); Clark Baxter, publisher (history/political science/music); Deirdre Cavanaugh, executive editor (communications, speech and theater); Halee Dinsey, editor (sociology/anthropology [upper level]); Lisa Gebo, senior editor (psychology and helping professions); Sabra Horne, senior editor (criminal justice); Eve Howard, publisher (sociology [intro level]); Dianne Lindsay, editor (education/special education); Vicki Knight, executive editor (psychology); Peter Marshall, publisher (health/nutrition); Eileen Murphy, editor (counseling and social work); Stacey Purviance, editor (psychology); Marianne Tafliner, senior editor (psychology). Estab. 1956. Publishes hardcover and paperback originals and software. **Publishes 240 titles/year. 35% of books from first-time authors; 99% of books from unagented writers. Pays 5-15% royalty on net price. Advances not automatic policy.** Publishes ms 1 year after acceptance. Accepts simultaneous submissions. Book catalog (by subject area) and ms guidelines available.

  ○━ Wadsworth publishes college-level textbooks in social sciences, humanities, education and college success.

**Nonfiction:** Textbooks and multimedia products: higher education only. Subjects include anthropology, counseling, criminal justice, education, health, music, nutrition, philosophy, psychology, religious studies, sociology, speech and mass communications, broadcasting, TV and film productions, college success. Query or submit outline/synopsis and sample chapters.

**Recent Title(s):** *Production and Operations Management*, 7th edition, by Norman Gaither.

**J. WESTON WALCH, PUBLISHER**, P.O. Box 658, Portland ME 04104-0658. (207)772-2846. Fax: (207)774-7167. Website: http://www.walch.com. **Acquisitions:** Lisa French, editor-in-chief. Estab. 1927. **Publishes 100 titles/year. Receives 300 submissions/year. 10% of books from first-time authors; 95% from unagented writers. Offers 8-12% royalty on gross receipts. Advances negotiable.** Publishes book 18 months after acceptance of ms. Reports in 4 months. Book catalog for 9 × 12 SAE with 5 first-class stamps. Manuscript guidelines for #10 SASE.

  ○━ Publishes educational softcover originals for grades 6-adult in the US and Canada.

**Nonfiction:** Subjects include art, business, technology, economics, English, geography, government, history, literacy, mathematics, middle school, science, social studies, special education. "We publish only supplementary educational material for grades six to adult in the U.S. and Canada. Formats include books, reproducibles, posters and mixed packages. Most titles are assigned by us, though we occasionally accept an author's unsolicited submission. We have a great need for author/artist teams and for authors who can write at third- to seventh-grade levels. We do *not* want basic texts or anthologies. All authors should have educational experience at the secondary level. *Query first. No unsolicited mss.* Looks for sense of organization, writing ability, knowledge of subject, skill of communicating with intended audience." Reviews artwork/photos as part of ms package.

**Recent Title(s):** *Graphic Organizers for Social Studies Classes*, by Daniel J. Barnekow.

**WALKER AND CO.**, Walker Publishing Co., 435 Hudson St., New York NY 10014. Fax: (212)727-0984. Publisher: George Gibson. Editors: Jacqueline Johnson, Michael Seidman. Juvenile Publisher: Emily Easton. Juvenile Editor: Soyung Pak. **Acquisitions:** Submissions Editor or Submissions Editor-Juvenile. Estab. 1959. Publishes hardcover and trade paperback originals. **Publishes 70 titles/year. Receives 3,500 submissions/year. Pays royalty on retail price, 7½-12% on paperback, 10-15% on hardcover. Offers competitive advances.** Material without SASE will not be returned. Reports in 3 months. Book catalog and ms guidelines for 9 × 12 SAE with 3 first-class stamps.

  ○━ Walker publishes general nonfiction on a variety of subjects as well as mysteries, children's books and large print religious reprints. Currently emphasizing science, history, technology, math. De-emphasizing music, bio, self-help, sports.

**Nonfiction:** Biography, history, science and natural history, health, juvenile, music, nature and environment, reference, popular science, sports/baseball, and self-help books. Query with SASE. No phone calls.

**Fiction:** Adult mystery, juvenile fiction and picture books. Query with SASE.

**Recent Title(s):** *Galileo's Daughter*, by Dava Sobel (history/biography/science); *E = MC²*, by David Bodanis (history/science); *Zarafa*, by Michael Allin (history); *Captain's Command*, by Anna Myers (juvenile).

Ⓐ **WARNER ASPECT**, Warner Books, 1271 Avenue of the Americas, New York NY 10020. (212)522-7200. Editor-in-Chief: Betsy Mitchell. Publishes hardcover, trade paperback, mass market paperback originals and mass market paperback reprints. **Publishes 30 titles/year. Receives 500 queries and 350 mss/year. 5-10% of books from first-time authors; 1% from unagented writers. Pays royalty on retail price. Offers $5,000-up advance.** Publishes book 1 year after acceptance of ms. Reports in 3 months on mss.

  ○━ "We're looking for 'epic' stories in both fantasy and science fiction."

**Fiction:** Fantasy, science fiction. "Sample our existing titles—we're a fairly new list and pretty strongly focused." Mistake writers often make is "hoping against hope that being unagented won't make a difference. We simply don't have the staff to look at unagented projects."

**Recent Title(s):** *The Barbed Coil*, by J.V. Jones (fantasy).

**WARNER BOOKS**, Time & Life Building, 1271 Avenue of the Americas, New York NY 10020. (212)522-7200. President, Maureen Egen. **Acquisitions:** (Ms.) Jamie Raab, senior vice president/publisher (general nonfiction, commercial fiction); Rick Horgan, vice president/executive editor (popular culture, general nonfiction, thriller fiction); Amy Einhorn, executive editor, trade paperback (popular culture, business, fitness, self-help); Claire Zion, executive editor, mass market (women's fiction, spirituality and human potential); Rick Wolff, executive editor (business, humor, sports); Betsy Mitchell, executive editor (science fiction); Caryn Karmatz Rudy, senior editor (fiction, general nonfiction, popular culture); Rob McMahon (fiction, business, sports); Diana Baroni, editor (health, fitness, general nonfiction); Jessica Papin, associate editor (commercial fiction, general nonfiction); John Aherne, associate editor (popular culture, fiction, general nonfiction); William Malloy, editor-in-chief, Mysterious Press (mysteries, cookbooks); Sara Ann Freed, executive editor (mysteries, suspense); Susanna Einstein, associate editor (mysteries, literary fiction). Estab. 1961. Publishes hardcover, trade paperback and mass market paperback originals and reprints. **Publishes 350 titles/year. Pays variable**

**royalty. Advance varies.** Publishes book 2 years after acceptance of ms. Responds in 4 months.

   Oπ Warner publishes general interest fiction and nonfiction.

**Imprint(s): Mysterious Press** (mystery/suspense), **Warner Aspect** (science fiction and fantasy), Warner Vision.

**Nonfiction:** Biography, business, cooking, current affairs, health, history, home, humor, popular culture, psychology, reference, self-help, sports, spirituality and human potential. Query with SASE.

**Fiction:** Fantasy, horror, mainsteam, mystery, romance, science fiction, suspense, thriller. Query with SASE.

**Recent Title(s):** *Honk and Holler Opening Soon*, by Billie Letts; *Something More*, by Sarah Ban Breathnach; *Live Now, Age Later*, by Isadore Rosenfeld, M.D.

**WASHINGTON STATE UNIVERSITY PRESS**, Pullman WA 99164-5910. (800)354-7360. Fax: (509)335-8568. E-mail: pkeithc@wsu.edu. Website: http://www.publications.wsu.edu/wsupress. Director: Thomas H. Sanders. **Acquisitions:** Keith Petersen, editor; Glen Lindeman, editor. Estab. 1928. Publishes hardcover originals, trade paperback originals and reprints. **Publishes 10 titles/year. Receives 300-400 submissions/year. 50% of books from first-time writers; mostly unagented authors. Pays 5% minimum royalty, graduated according to sales.** Publishes book 18 months after acceptance of ms. Reports on queries in 2 months.

   Oπ WSU Press publishes books on the history, pre-history, culture, and politics of the West, particularly the Pacific Northwest.

**Nonfiction:** Subjects include Americana, art, biography, environment, ethnic studies, history (especially of the American West and the Pacific Northwest), politics, essays. "We seek manuscripts that focus on the Pacific Northwest as a region. No romance novels, how-to books, gardening books or books used specifically as classroom texts. We welcome innovative and thought-provoking titles in a wide diversity of genres, from essays and memoirs to history, anthropology and political science." Submit outline and sample chapters. Reviews artwork/photos as part of ms package.

**Recent Title(s):** *Not Just Trees: The Legacy of a Douglas-Fir Forest*, by Jane Claire Dirks-Edmunds.

**Tips:** "We have developed our marketing in the direction of regional and local history and have attempted to use this as the base upon which to expand our publishing program. In regional history, the secret is to write a good narrative—a good story—that is substantiated factually. It should be told in an imaginative, clever way. Have visuals (photos, maps, etc.) available to help the reader envision what has happened. Tell the regional history story in a way that ties it to larger, national, and even international events. Weave it into the large pattern of history. We have published our first book of essays and a regional cookbook and will do more in these and other fields if we get the right manuscript."

**FRANKLIN WATTS**, Grolier Publishing, 90 Sherman Turnpike, Danbury CT 06816. (203)797-6802. Website: http://publishing.grolier.com/publishing.html. Publisher: John Selfridge. **Acquisitions:** Mark Friedman, executive editor; Melissa Stewart, senior editor (science); Douglas Hill, senior editor (reference). Estab. 1942. Publishes hardcover and softcover originals. **Publishes 150 titles/year. 5% of books from first-time authors; 95% from unagented writers. Advance varies.** Publishes book 18 months after acceptance of ms. Accepts simultaneous submissions. Reports in 4 months on queries. Book catalog for $3.

   Oπ Franklin Watts publishes nonfiction books for the library market (K-12) to supplement textbooks.

**Nonfiction:** History, science, social issues, biography. Subjects include education, language/literature, American and world history, politics, natural and physical sciences, sociology. Multicultural, curriculum-based nonfiction lists published twice a year. Strong also in the area of contemporary problems and issues facing young people. No humor, coffee table books, fiction, picture books, poetry, cookbooks or gardening books. Query with outline and SASE. *No unsolicited mss.* No phone calls. Prefers to work with unagented authors.

**Recent Title(s):** *The Asante Kingdom*, by Carol Thompson.

**Tips:** Most of this publisher's books are developed inhouse; less than 5% come from unsolicited submissions. However, they publish several series for which they always need new books. Study catalogs to discover possible needs.

**WEATHERHILL, INC.**, 41 Monroe Turnpike, Trumbull CT 06611. (203)459-5090. Fax: (203)459-5095. E-mail: weatherhill@weatherhill.com. Website: http://www.weatherhill.com. **Acquisitions:** Raymond Furse, editorial director. Estab. 1962. Publishes hardcover and trade paperback originals and reprints. **Publishes 36 titles/year. Receives 250 queries and 100 mss/year. 20% of books from first-time authors; 95% from unagented writers. Pays 12-18% royalty on wholesale price. Offers advances up to $10,000. Publishes books 8 months after acceptance of ms.** Accepts simultaneous submissions. Reports in 1 month on proposals. Book catalog and ms guidelines free.

   Oπ Weatherhill publishes exclusively Asia-related nonfiction and Asian fiction and poetry in translation.

**Imprint(s):** Weatherhill, Tengu Books.

**Nonfiction:** Asia-related topics only. Biography, coffee table book, cookbook, gift book, how-to, humor, illustrated book, reference, self-help. Subjects include anthropology/archaeology, art/architecture, cooking/foods/nutrition, gardening, history, language/literature, music/dance, nature/environment, photography, regional, religion, sociology, translation, travel. Submit outline, 2 sample chapters and sample illustrations (if applicable). Reviews artwork/photos as part of ms package. Send photocopies.

**Fiction:** "We publish only important Asian writers in translation. Asian fiction is a hard sell. Authors should check funding possibilities from appropriate sources: Japan Foundation, Korea Foundation, etc." Query with synopsis.

**Poetry:** Only Asian poetry in translation. Query.

**Recent Title(s):** *The Jewelry of Nepal; Vegetarian Sushi Made Easy.*

**WEIDNER & SONS PUBLISHING**, P.O. Box 2178, Riverton NJ 08077. (609)486-1755. Fax: (609)486-7583. E-mail: weidner@waterw.com. Website: http://www.waterw.com/~weidner. **Acquisitions:** James H. Weidner, president. Estab. 1967. Publishes hardcover and trade paperback originals and reprints. **Publishes 10-20 titles/year; imprint publishes 10 titles/year. Receives hundreds of queries and 50 mss/year. 100% of books from first-time authors; 90% from unagented writers. Pays 10% maximum royalty on wholesale price.** Accepts simultaneous submissions. Reports in 1 month on queries.

○⇥ Weidner & Sons publishes primarily science, text and reference books for scholars, college students and researchers.

**Imprint(s):** Bird Sci Books, Delaware Estuary Press, Hazlaw Books, Medlaw Books, Pulse Publications, Tycooly Publishing USA.

**Nonfiction:** Reference, technical, textbook. Subjects include agriculture/horticulture, animals, business/economics, child guidance/parenting, computers/electronics, education, gardening, health/medicine, hobbies (electronic), language/literature, nature/environment, psychology, science and ecology/environment. "We do not publish fiction; never poetry. No topics in the 'pseudosciences': occult, astrology, New Age and metaphysics, etc." Query or submit outline and sample chapters with return postage and SASE required. Include e-mail address for faster response. Reviews artwork/photos as part of ms package. Send photocopies. "Suggest 2 copies of ms, double spaced, along with PC disk in Word, Word Perfect, Write or Pagemaker."

**Recent Title(s):** *The Huntington Sexual Behavior Scale.*

**SAMUEL WEISER, INC.**, P.O. Box 612, York Beach ME 03910-0612. (207)363-4393. Fax: (207)363-5799. E-mail: email@weiserbooks.com. **Acquisitions:** Eliot Stearns, editor. Estab. 1956. Publishes hardcover originals and trade paperback originals and reprints. **Publishes 18-20 titles/year. Receives 200 submissions/year. 50% of books from first-time authors; 98% from unagented writers. Pays 10% royalty on wholesale and retail price. Offers $500 average advance.** Publishes book 18 months after acceptance of ms. Reports in 3 months. Book catalog free.

○⇥ Samuel Weiser looks for strong books in Eastern philosophy, metaphysics, esoterica of all kinds (tarot, astrology, qabalah, magic, etc.) written by teachers and people who know the subject.

**Nonfiction:** How-to, self-help. Subjects include health, music, philosophy, psychology, religion. "We don't want a writer's rehash of all the astrology books in the library, only texts written by people with strong backgrounds in the field. No poetry or novels." Submit complete ms. *Writer's Market* recommends query with SASE first. Reviews artwork/photos as part of ms package.

**Recent Title(s):** *Ayurvedic Healing for Women: A Modern Interpretation of Ayurvedic Gynecology*, by Atreya.

**Tips:** "Most new authors do not check permissions, nor do they provide proper footnotes. If they did, it would help. We look at all manuscripts submitted to us. We are interested in seeing freelance art for book covers."

**WESCOTT COVE PUBLISHING CO.**, P.O. Box 130, Stamford CT 06904. (203)322-0998. **Acquisitions:** Julius M. Wilensky, president. Estab. 1968. Publishes trade paperback originals and reprints. **Publishes 4 titles/year. Receives 15 queries and 10 mss/year. 25% of books from first-time authors; 95% from unagented writers. Pays 5-10% royalty on retail price. Offers $1,000-1,500 advance.** Publishes book 1 year after acceptance of ms. Accepts simultaneous submissions. Reports in 1 month on queries. Book catalog free.

○⇥ "We publish the most complete cruising guides, each one an authentic reference for the area covered."

**Nonfiction:** How-to, humor, illustrated book, reference, nautical books. Subjects include history, hobbies, regional, travel. "All titles are nautical books; half of them are cruising guides. Mostly we seek out authors knowledgeable in sailing, navigation, cartography and the area we want covered. Then we commission them to write the book." Query with outline, 1-2 sample chapters, author's credentials and SASE.

**Recent Title(s):** *First Time Around*, by Jamie Bryson; *Chesapeake Bay Cruising Guide*—Volume I, Upper Bay, by Tom Heale.

**WESLEYAN UNIVERSITY PRESS**, 110 Mount Vernon St., Middletown CT 06459. (860)685-2420. **Acquisitions:** Suzanna Tamminen, editor-in-chief. Estab. 1957. Publishes hardcover originals and paperbacks. **Publishes 25-30 titles/year. Receives 1,500 queries and 1,000 mss/year. 10% of books from first-time authors; 80% from unagented writers. Pays 0-10% royalty. Offers up to $3,000 advance.** Publishes book 1 year after acceptance of ms. Accepts simultaneous submissions. Reports in 1 month on queries, 2 months on proposals, 3 months on mss. Book catalog free. Manuscript guidelines for #10 SASE.

○⇥ Wesleyan University Press is a scholarly press with a focus on cultural studies.

**Nonfiction:** Biography, textbook, scholarly. Subjects include art/architecture, ethnic, gay/lesbian, history, language/literature, music/dance, philosophy, sociology, theater, film. Submit outline, proposal package, including: introductory letter, curriculum vitae, table of contents. Reviews artwork/photos as part of ms package. Send photocopies.

**Fiction:** Science fiction. "We publish very little fiction, less than 3% of our entire list."

**Poetry:** "Writers should request a catalog and guidelines." Submit 5-10 sample poems.

**Recent Title(s):** *Thieves of Paradise*, by Yusef Kommunyakaa (poetry).

■ **WESTCLIFFE PUBLISHERS**, P.O. Box 1261, Englewood CO 80150. (303)935-0900. Fax: (303)935-0903. E-mail: westclif@westcliffepublishers.com. **Acquisitions:** Linda Doyle, associate publisher; Kristin Iverson, managing editor. Estab. 1981. Publishes hardcover originals, trade paperback originals and reprints. **Publishes 23 titles/year. Receives 100 queries and 60 mss/year. 75% of books from first-time authors; 100% from unagented writers. Pays**

**3-15% royalty on retail price. Offers advance of up to 50% of the first year's royalties.** Publishes book 18 months after acceptance of ms. Accepts simultaneous submissions. Reports in 1 month. Book catalog free.

O→ "Westcliffe Publishers produces the highest quality in regional photography and essays for our coffee table-style books and calendars. As an eco-publisher our mission is to foster environmental awareness by showing the beauty of the natural world." Currently emphasizing children's regional books.

**Nonfiction:** Coffee table book, gift book, illustrated book, reference. Subjects include Americana, animals, gardening, nature/environment, photography, regional, travel. "Writers need to do their market research to justify a need in the marketplace." Submit outline with proposal package. Westcliffe will contact you for photos, writing samples.

**Recent Title(s):** *Margaret's Magnificent Colorado Adventure*, by Julie Dannenberg.

**Tips:** Audience are nature and outdoors enthusiasts and photographers. "Just call us!"

**N** **WESTERN PSYCHOLOGICAL SERVICES**, Manson Western Corp., 12031 Wilshire Blvd., Los Angeles CA 90025. Phone/fax: (310)478-2061. E-mail: smanson@wpspublish.com. **Acquisitions:** Susan Madden, director of marketing. Estab. 1948. Publishes trade paperback originals. **Publishes 6 titles/year. Receives 6 queries and 12 mss/year. 75% of books from first-time authors; 80% from unagented writers. Pays 5-10% royalty on retail price. No advance.** Publishes book 1 year after acceptance of ms. Accepts simultaneous submissions. Reports in 1 month. Book catalog free.

O→ Western Psychological Services publishes books used by therapists, counselors, social workers and others in the helping field working with children 5-12 years old.

**Nonfiction:** Self-help. Child guidance/parenting subjects. Submit complete ms. *Writer's Market* recommends a query first. Reviews artwork/photos as part of ms package. Send photocopies.

**Fiction:** Expressing feelings, understanding and dealing with emotional problems. Submit complete ms. *Writer's Market* recommends a query first.

**Recent Title(s):** *Attention Disorders in Children*, by Richard Morriss, Ph.D. (assessment and treatment of school-related behaviors); *Bart Speaks Out: Breaking the Silence on Suicide*, by Linda Golman (expressing feelings).

**WESTVIEW PRESS**, Perseus Books Group, 5500 Central Ave., Boulder CO 80301-2877. (303)444-3541. Fax: (303)449-3356. Website: http://www.westviewpress.com. Executive Editor: Leo Wiegman. **Acquisitions:** Marcus Boggs, publisher. Karl Yambert, Katherine Murphy, senior acquisitions editors. Rob Williams, Sarah Warner, Andrew Day, editors. Estab. 1975. Publishes hardcover and trade paperback originals and reprints. **Publishes 300 titles/year. Receives 1,000 queries and 500 mss/year. 25% of books from first-time authors; 90% from unagented writers. Pays 8-15% royalty on net receipts. Advance varies, $0-20,000 and up.** Publishes book 1 year after acceptance of ms. Accepts simultaneous submissions, if so noted. Reports in 1 week on queries, 6 weeks on proposals and mss. Book catalog available on Website. Manuscript guidelines free.

O→ Westview Press publishes a wide range of general interest and scholarly nonfiction (including undergraduate and graduate-level textbooks) in the social sciences and humanities.

**Imprint(s):** Icon Editions (Cass Canfield).

**Nonfiction:** Biography, reference, textbook, trade, monograph. Subjects include anthropology, art/architecture (criticism and history), education, ethnic (cultural studies), government/politics, history, military/war (history), psychology, religious studies, sociology, women's issues/studies. "Know our focus. We publish books of original scholarship. To gain our interest, write a book that is both original and interesting." Query or submit proposal package including outline, 3 sample chapters, table of contents with SASE. Reviews artwork/photos as part of ms package, if germane. Send photocopies.

**Recent Title(s):** *International Encyclopedia of Public Administration*, by Shafritz.

**WHISPERING COYOTE PRESS, L.P.**, 300 Crescent Court, Suite 860, Dallas TX 75201. Fax: (214)871-5577 or (214)319-7298. **Acquisitions:** Mrs. Lou Alpert, editor. Estab. 1990. **Publishes 6 titles/year. 20% of books from first-time authors; 90% from unagented writers. Pays 8% royalty on retail price of first 10,000 copies, 10% after (combined author and illustrator). Offers $2,000-8,000 advance (combined author, illustrator).** Publishes book 2 years after acceptance of ms. Accepts simultaneous submissions. Reports in 3 months. Book catalog and ms guidelines for #10 SAE with 55¢ postage.

O→ "Our focus is on children's picture books ages 4-11. We try to publish a product that is child-friendly and will encourage children to love reading."

**Fiction:** Juvenile picture books, adventure, fantasy. "We only do picture books." Submit complete ms to 7130 Alexander Dr., Dallas TX 75214. All material must include an SASE. If author is illustrator also, submit sample art. Send photocopies, no original art. No holiday-specific books.

**Poetry:** "We like poetry—if it works in a picture book format. We are not looking for poetry collections."

**Recent Title(s):** *The First Starry Night*, by Jann Shaddox Isom (fiction); *Hey Diddle Diddle*, by Kin Eagle (extended rhyme).

**N** **WHITE CLIFFS MEDIA, INC.**, Editorial Department: 400 Del Verde, Circle #2, Sacramento CA 95833. **Acquisitions:** Lawrence Aynesmith. Estab. 1985. White Cliffs publishes music titles for an academic and general audience. Publishes hardcover and trade paperback originals. **Publishes 5-10 titles/year. 50% of books from first-time authors; 50% from unagented writers. Pays 5-12% royalty or makes outright purchase.** Publishes book 1 year after acceptance. No simultaneous submissions. Reports in 2 months on queries, 4 months on proposals, 6 months on mss. Book catalog for #10 SASE.

**Nonfiction:** Biography, textbook. Subjects include anthropology, ethnic, music/dance. Query. Reviews artwork/photos as part of ms package. Send photocopies.

**Recent Title(s):** *Drum Circle Spirit*, by Arthur Hull.

**Tips:** "Distribution is more difficult due to the large number of publishers. Writers should send proposals that have potential for mass markets as well as college texts, and that will be submitted and completed on schedule. Our audience reads college texts, general interest trade publications. If I were a writer trying to market a book today, I would send a book on music comparable in quality and mass appeal to a book like Stephen Hawking's *A Brief History of Time*."

**WHITE MANE BOOKS**, White Mane Publishing Company Inc., 63 W. Burd St., P.O. Box 152, Shippensburg PA 17257. (717)532-2237. Fax: (717)532-7704. **Acquisitions:** Martin K. Gordon, president (White Mane Books); Harold Collier, vice president (other imprints). Estab. 1987. Publishes hardcover, and trade paperback originals and reprints. **Publishes 60 titles/year; each imprint publishes 12-18 titles/year. Receives 300 queries and 50 mss/year. 50% of books from first-time authors; 75% from unagented writers. Pays royalty on monies received.** Publishes book 18 months after acceptance of ms. Accepts simultaneous submissions. Reports in 1 month on queries and proposals, 3 months on mss. Book catalog and ms guidelines free.

   ☞ "White Mane Books both publish military history with the emphasis on the American Civil War." Currently emphasizing World War II.

**Imprints:** Back Street Books (military history, emphasis on American Civil War); Ragged Edge Press (religious); WMkids (historically based children's fiction).

**Nonfiction:** Adult/reference, children's/juvenile. Subjects include history, military/war. Query with SASE. Reviews artwork/photos as part of ms package. Send photocopies.

**Fiction:** Historical, juvenile. Query with SASE.

**ALBERT WHITMAN AND CO.**, 6340 Oakton St., Morton Grove IL 60053-2723. (847)581-0033. **Acquisitions:** Kathleen Tucker, editor-in-chief. Estab. 1919. Publishes hardcover originals and paperback reprints. **Publishes 30 titles/year. Receives 5,000 submissions/year. 20% of books from first-time authors; 70% from unagented writers. Pays 10% royalty for novels; 5% for picture books.** Publishes book an average of 18 months after acceptance of ms. Accepts simultaneous submissions. Reports in 5 months. Book catalog for 8×10 SAE and 2 first-class stamps. Manuscript guidelines for #10 SASE.

   ☞ Albert Whitman publishes "good books for children ages 2-12."

**Nonfiction:** "All books are for ages 2-12." Concept books about special problems children have, easy science, social studies, math. Query.

**Fiction:** "All books are for ages 2-12." Adventure, ethnic, fantasy, historical, humor, mystery, picture books and concept books (to help children deal with problems). "We need easy historical fiction and picture books. No young adult and adult books." Submit outline/synopsis and sample chapters (novels) and complete ms (picture books).

**Recent Title(s):** *Sugar Was My Best Food: Diabetes and Me*, by Carol Peacock, Adair Gregory and Kyle Gregory (autobiography); *Missing: One Stuffed Rabbit*, by Maryann Cocca-Leffler.

**Tips:** "There is a trend toward highly visual books. The writer can most easily sell us strong picture book text that has good illustration possibilities. We sell mostly to libraries, but our bookstore sales are growing."

**THE WHITSTON PUBLISHING CO.**, P.O. Box 958, Troy NY 12181-0958. Phone/fax: (518)283-4363. E-mail: whitson@capital.net. Website: http://www.whitston.com. **Acquisitions:** Jean Goode, editorial director. Estab. 1969. Publishes hardcover originals. **Averages 20 titles/year. Receives 100 submissions/year. 50% of books from first-time authors; 100% from unagented writers. Pays 10% royalty on price of book (wholesale or retail) after sale of 500 copies.** Publishes book 1 year after acceptance. Reports in 6 months. Book catalog for $1.

   ☞ Whitston focuses on Modern American and English literature and bibliographies.

**Nonfiction:** "We publish scholarly and critical books in the arts, humanities and some of the social sciences. We also publish bibliographies. We are interested in scholarly monographs and collections of essays." Query. Reviews artwork/photos as part of ms package.

**Recent Title(s):** *Harlem Renaissance Re-examined: A Revised and Expanded Edition*, edited by Victor A. Kramer and Robert A. Russ.

**MARKUS WIENER PUBLISHERS INC.**, 231 Nassau St., Princeton NJ 08542. (609)971-1141. **Acquisitions:** Shelley Frisch, editor-in-chief. Estab. 1981. Publishes hardcover originals and trade paperback originals and reprints. **Publishes 20-25 titles/year; imprint publishes 5 titles/year. Receives 50-150 queries and 50 mss/year. Pays 10% royalty on net sales.** Publishes book 1 year after acceptance. Reports in 2 months on queries and proposals. Book catalog free.

   ☞ Markus Wiener publishes textbooks in history subjects and regional world history.

**Imprint(s):** Princeton Series on the Middle East, Topics in World History.

**Nonfiction:** Textbook. History subjects, Caribbean studies, Middle East, Africa.

**Recent Title(s):** *Challenges to Democracy* (Middle East studies).

**MICHAEL WIESE PRODUCTIONS**, 11288 Ventura Blvd., Suite 821, Studio City CA 91604. (818)379-8799. Website: http://www.mwp.com. **Acquisitions:** Ken Lee, vice president. Estab. 1981. Publishes trade paperback originals.

**Publishes 4-6 titles/year. Receives 10-15 queries/year. 90% of books from first-time authors. Pays 7-10% royalty on retail price. Offers $500-1,000 advance.** Publishes book 10 months after acceptance of ms. Accepts simultaneous submissions. Reports in 1 month on queries and proposals, 2 months on mss. Book catalog free.

O– Michael Wiese publishes how-to books for professional film or video makers, film schools and bookstores.

**Nonfiction:** How-to. Subjects include professional film and videomaking. Call before submitting nonfiction; submit outline with 3 sample chapters.

**Recent Title(s):** *The Writer's Journey*, by Christopher Vogler.

**Tips:** Audience is professional filmmakers, writers, producers, directors, actors and university film students.

**WILD FLOWER PRESS**, Blue Water Publishing, P.O. Box 190, Mill Spring NC 28756. (828)894-8444. Fax: (828)894-8454. E-mail: bluewaterp@aol.com. Website: http://www.5thworld.com or http://bluewater.com. President: Pam Meyer. **Acquisitions:** Brian Crissey; Julie Sherar, editor. Publishes hardcover originals and trade paperback originals and reprints. **Publishes 6 titles/year. Receives 50 queries and 25 mss/month. 80% of books from first-time authors; 90% from unagented writers. Pays 7½-15% royalty.** Publishes book 16 months after acceptance of ms. Accepts simultaneous submissions. Reports in 2 months on mss. Book catalog and ms guidelines for SASE with 55¢ postage.

O– "Wild Flower Press strives to preserve the Earth by publishing books that develop new wisdom about our emerging planetary citizenship, bringing information from the outerworlds to our world."

**Nonfiction:** Books about extraterrestrial research and experiences. Submit outline. Reviews artwork/photos as part of ms package. Send photocopies.

**Recent Title(s):** *The Psychic Sasquatch*, by Jack Lapseritis.

**N WILDCAT CANYON PRESS**, Circulus Publishing Group, Inc., 2716 Ninth St., Berkeley CA 94710. (510)848-3600. Fax: (510)848-1326. E-mail: circulus@aol.com. **Acquisitions:** Julienne Bennett, publisher (relationships/gift books); Roy M. Carlisle, editorial director (psychology/relationships). Publishes trade paperback originals. **Publishes 8 titles/year. Receives 500 queries and 300 mss/year. Pays 10-16% royalty on wholesale price. Offers $1,000-3,000 advance.** Publishes book 9 months after acceptance of ms. Accepts simultaneous submissions. Reports in 3 months. Book catalog and ms guidelines free.

O– Wildcat Canyon Press publishes books primarily for women that embrace and enhance such relationship subjects as friendship, spirituality, women's issues, and home and family, all with a focus on self-help and personal growth.

**Nonfiction:** Gift book, self-help. Subjects include psychology, women's issues/women's studies, relationships. Query with proposal package, including outline and SASE. Reviews artwork/photos as part of ms package. Send photocopies.

**Recent Title(s):** *Independent Women*, by Debra Sands Miller (psychology/women's issues).

**Tips:** "As a proactive publishing house we commission most of our titles and we are primarily interested in solicited queries and proposals. We do not publish fiction or poetry."

**WILDER PUBLISHING CENTER**, 919 Lafond Ave., St. Paul MN 55104. (612)659-6013. Fax: (612)642-2061. E-mail: vlh@wilder.org. Website: http://www.wilder.org. **Acquisitions:** Vincent Hyman, editorial director. Publishes trade paperback originals. **Publishes 4-6 titles/year. Receives 30 queries and 15 mss/year. 75% of books from first-time authors; 100% from unagented writers. Pays 10% royalty on net.** Books are sold through direct mail; average discount is 15%. **Offers $1,000-3,000 advance.** Publishes book 1 year after acceptance of ms. Accepts simultaneous submissions, if so noted. Reports in 1 month on queries and proposals, 3 months on mss. Book catalog and ms guidelines free or on website.

O– Wilder Publishing Center emphasizes community and nonprofit organization management and development.

**Nonfiction:** Nonprofit management, organizational development, community organizing. Subjects include government/politics, sociology. "We are in a growth mode and welcome proposals in these areas. We are seeking manuscripts that report 'best practice' methods using handbook or workbook formats." Phone query OK before submitting proposal with detailed chapter ouline, 1 sample chapter and SASE.

**Recent Title(s):** *Consulting with Nonprofits: A Practitioner's Guide*.

**Tips:** "Writers must be practitioners with a passion for their work and experience presenting their techniques at conferences. Freelance writers with an interest in our niches could do well searching out and teaming up with such practitioners as our books sell very well to a tightly-targeted market."

**WILDERNESS PRESS**, 2440 Bancroft Way, Berkeley CA 94704-1676. (510)843-8080. Fax: (510)548-1355. E-mail: mail@wildernesspress.com. Website: http://www.wildernesspress.com. **Acquisitions:** Caroline Winnett, publisher. Mike Jones, associate publisher. Estab. 1967. Publishes paperback originals. **Publishes 10 titles/year. Receives 150 submissions/year. 20% of books from first-time authors; 95% from unagented writers. Pays 8-10% royalty on retail price. Offers $1,000 average advance.** Publishes book 8 months after acceptance of ms. Reports in 1 month. Book catalog free. Manuscript guidelines for SASE.

O– "We seek to publish the most accurate, reliable and useful outdoor books and maps for self-propelled outdoor activities for hikers, kayakers, skiers, snowshoers, backpackers."

**Nonfiction:** "We publish books about the outdoors. Most are trail guides for hikers and backpackers, but we also publish how-to books about the outdoors. The manuscript must be accurate. The author must research an area in person. If writing a trail guide, you must walk all the trails in the area your book is about. Outlook must be strongly conservationist. Style must be appropriate for a highly literate audience." Request proposal guidelines.

**Recent Title(s):** *Showshoe Trails of Tahoe*, by Michael C. Write.

**JOHN WILEY & SONS, INC.**, 605 Third Ave., New York NY 10158. Website: http://www.wiley.com. Editor-in-Chief/Senior Editor of African-American Books: Carole Hall. **Acquisitions**: Editorial Department. Estab. 1807. Publishes hardcover originals, trade paperback originals and reprints. **Pays "competitive royalty rates."** Accepts simultaneous submissions. Book catalog and ms guidelines free with #10 SASE.

   O⟳ "The General Interest group publishes books for the consumer market."

**Nonfiction:** Biography, how-to, children's/juvenile, reference, self-help. Subjects include child guidance/parenting, current affairs, health/medicine, history, hospitality, military/war, psychology, science, women's issues/studies, African American interest. Query.

**Recent Title(s):** *The New York Public Library Business Desk Reference.*

**WILLIAMSON PUBLISHING CO.**, P.O. Box 185, Church Hill Rd., Charlotte VT 05445. Website: http://www.williamsonbooks.com. **Acquisitions**: Susan Williamson, editorial director. Estab. 1983. Publishes trade paperback originals. **Publishes 15 titles/year. Receives 1,000 queries/year. 75% of books from first-time authors; 90% from unagented writers. Pays royalty or flat fee on retail price. Offers standard advance.** Publishes book 18 months after acceptance. Accepts simultaneous submissions, but prefers 6 months exclusivity. Reports in 4 months with SASE. Book catalog for 8½×11 SAE with 4 first-class stamps. Manuscript guidelines on website.

   O⟳ "Our mission is to help every child fulfill his/her potential and experience personal growth through active learning. We want 'our kids' to be able to work toward a culturally rich, ethnically diverse, peaceful nation and global community." Currently emphasizing creative approaches to specific areas of science, history, cultural experiences, diversity.

**Nonfiction:** Children's/juvenile, children's creative learning books on subjects ranging from science, art, to early learning skills. Adult books include parenting, psychology, cookbook, how-to, self-help. "Williamson has four very successful children's book series: *Little Hands*® (ages 2-6), *Kids Can!*® (ages 6-12), *Tales Alive*® (folktales plus activities, age 4-10) and *Kaleidoscope Kids*® (96-page, single subject, ages 7-12). They must incorporate learning through doing. *No picture books, story books, or fiction please!* Please don't call concerning your submission. It never helps your review, and it takes too much of our time. With an SASE, you'll hear from us." Submit outline, 2-3 sample chapters and SASE.

   ● Williamson's big success is its *Kids Can!*® and *Kaleidoscope Kids*™. *Pyramids* and *Knights and Castles* both won American Bookseller Pick of the Lists and Children's Book Council Notable Book Award series.

**Recent Title(s):** *Monarch Magic*, by Lynn Rosenblatt.

**Tips:** "Our children's books are used by kids, their parents, and educators. They encourage self-discovery, creativity and personal growth. Our books are based on the philosophy that children learn best by doing, by being involved. Our authors need to be excited about their subject area and equally important, excited about kids."

**WILLOW CREEK PRESS**, P.O. Box 147, 9931 Highway 70 W., Minocqua WI 54548. (715)358-7010. Fax: (715)358-2807. E-mail: ljevert@newnorth.net. Website: http://www.willowcreekpress.com. **Acquisitions**: Laura Evert, managing editor. Estab. 1986. Publishes hardcover and trade paperback originals and reprints. **Publishes 25 titles/year. Receives 400 queries and 150 mss/year. 15% of books from first-time authors; 50% from unagented writers. Pays 6-15% royalty on wholesale price. Offers $2,000-5,000 advance.** Publishes book 10 months after acceptance of ms. Accepts simultaneous submissions. Reports in 2 months.

   O⟳ Willow Creek specializes in nature, outdoor and animal books, cookbooks, calendars and videos with high-quality photography.

**Nonfiction:** Coffee table book, cookbook, how-to, humor, illustrated book. Subjects include wildlife, pets, cooking/foods/nutrition, gardening, hobbies, nature/environment, photography, recreation, sports. Submit outline and 1 sample chapter with SASE for return of materials. Reviews artwork/photos as part of ms package. Send photocopies.

**Fiction:** Adventure, humor, picture books, short story collections. Submit synopsis and 2 sample chapters.

**Recent Title(s):** *Birdwatching for Cats*, by George H. Harrison.

**WILSHIRE BOOK CO.**, 12015 Sherman Rd., North Hollywood CA 91605-3781. (818)765-8579. Website: http://www.mpowers.com. Publisher: Melvin Powers. **Acquisitions**: Marcia Grad, senior editor. Estab. 1947. Publishes trade paperback originals and reprints. **Publishes 25 titles/year. Receives 3,000 submissions/year. 80% of books from first-time authors; 75% from unagented writers. Pays standard royalty.** Publishes book 6 months after acceptance of ms. Reports in 2 months. Welcomes telephone calls to discuss mss or book concepts.

   O⟳ "You are not only what you are today, but also what you choose to become tomorrow."

**Nonfiction:** Self-help, motivation/inspiration/spiritual, psychology, recovery, how-to. Subjects include personal success, entrepreneurship, marketing on the Internet, mail order, horsemanship. Min. 60,000 words. Requires detailed chapter outline, 3 sample chapters and SASE. Accepts queries and complete mss. Reviews artwork/photos as part of ms package. Send photocopies.

**Fiction:** Allegories that teach principles of psychological/spiritual growth or offer guidance in living. Minimum 30,000 words. Requires synopsis, 3 sample chapters and SASE. Accepts complete mss.

**Recent Title(s):** *Guide to Rational Living*, by Albert Ellis, Ph.D. and Robert Harper, Ph.D.; *The Princess Who Believed in Fairy Tales*, by Marcia Grad.

**Tips:** "We are vitally interested in all new material we receive. Just as you hopefully submit your manuscript for publication, we hopefully read every one submitted, searching for those that we believe will be successful in the marketplace. Writing and publishing must be a team effort. We need you to write what we can sell. We suggest that you read the successful books mentioned above or others that are similar to the manuscript you want to write. Analyze them to discover what elements make them winners. Duplicate those elements in your own style, using a creative new approach and fresh material, and you will have written a book we can catapult onto the bestseller list."

**WINDSOR BOOKS**, Windsor Marketing Corp., P.O. Box 280, Brightwaters NY 11718-0280. (516)321-7830. Website: http://www.windsorpublishing.com. **Acquisitions:** Jeff Schmidt, managing editor. Estab. 1968. Publishes hardcover and trade paperback originals, reprints, and very specific software. **Publishes 8 titles/year. Receives approximately 40 submissions/year. 60% of books from first-time authors; 90% from unagented writers. Pays 10% royalty on retail price; 5% on wholesale price (50% of total cost). Offers variable advance.** Publishes book an average of 6 months after acceptance of ms. Accepts simultaneous submissions. Reports in 2 weeks on queries. *Writer's Market* recommends allowing 2 months for reply. Book catalog and ms guidelines free.

○┅ "Our books are for serious investors."

**Nonfiction:** How-to, technical. Subjects include business/economics (investing in stocks and commodities). Interested in books on strategies, methods for investing in the stock market, options market and commodity markets. Query or submit outline and sample chapters. Reviews artwork/photos as part of ms package.

**Tips:** "We sell through direct mail to our mailing list and other financial lists. Writers must keep their work original; this market tends to have a great deal of information overlap among publications."

**Ⓝ WINSLOW PRESS**, 770 E. Atlantic Ave., Suite 201, Delray Beach FL 33483. (561)274-8084. Fax: (561)274-8533. Website: http://www.winslowpress.com. Publishes hardcover originals. **Publishes 3-5 titles/year. Receives 150 queries and 2,000 mss/year. 80% of books from first-time authors; 80% from unagented writers. Pays royalty. Sometimes offers advance.** Accepts simultaneous submissions. Reports in 1 month on queries and proposals, 3 months on mss. Book catalog for 8×10 SAE with 75¢ first-class stamps.

**Nonfiction:** Children's/juvenile. History subjects. Query with SASE. Reviews artwork/photos as part of ms package. Send photocopies.

**Fiction:** Adventure, ethnic, fantasy, historical, humor, juvenile, multicultural, mystery, picture books, poetry, science fiction, sports, suspense, young adult. Submit complete ms.

**Poetry:** Submit several sample poems.

**WISDOM PUBLICATIONS**, 199 Elm St., Somerville MA 02144. (617)776-7416, ext. 25. Fax: (617)776-7844. E-mail: editorial@wisdompubs.org. Website: http://www.widsompubs.org. Publisher: Timothy McNeill. **Acquisitions:** E. Gene Smith, acquisitions editor. Estab. 1976. Publishes hardcover originals, trade paperback originals and reprints. **Publishes 12-15 titles/year. Receives 240 queries/year. 50% of books from first-time authors; 95% from unagented writers. Pays 4-8% royalty on wholesale price (net).** Publishes book within 2 years after acceptance of ms. Book catalog and ms guidelines free on website.

○┅ Wisdom Publications is dedicated to making available authentic Buddhist works for the benefit of all. "We publish translations, commentaries and teachings of past and contemporary Buddhist masters and original works by leading Buddhist scholars."

**Nonfiction:** Subjects include philosophy (Buddhist or comparative Buddhist/Western), Buddhism, Buddhist texts and Tibet. Query with SASE. Reviews artwork/photos as part of ms package. Send photocopies.

**Poetry:** Buddhist. Query with SASE.

**Recent Title(s):** *Imagine All the People*, by the Dalai Lama (nonfiction); *Vast as the Heavens, Deep as the Sea*, by Khunu Rinpoche (poetry).

**Tips:** "We are basically a publisher of Buddhist books—all schools and traditions of Buddhism. Please see our catalog or our website *before* you send anything to us to get a sense of what we publish."

**WOODBINE HOUSE**, 6510 Bells Mill Rd., Bethesda MD 20817. (301)897-3570. Fax: (301)897-5838. E-mail: info@woodbinehouse.com. **Acquisitions:** Susan Stokes, editor. Estab. 1985. Publishes hardcover and trade paperback originals and reprints. **Publishes 8 titles/year. 90% of books from unagented writers. Pays 10-12% royalty.** Publishes book 18 months after acceptance of ms. Accepts simultaneous submissions. Reports in 2 months. Book catalog and ms guidelines for 6×9 SAE with 3 first-class stamps.

○┅ Woodbine House publishes books for or about individuals with disabilities to help those individuals and their families live fulfilling and satisfying lives in their communities.

**Nonfiction:** Publishes books for and about children and adults with disabilities. No personal accounts or general parenting guides. Submit outline and 3 sample chapters with SASE. Reviews artwork/photos as part of ms package.

**Fiction:** Children's picture books. Submit entire ms with SASE.

**Recent Title(s):** *Fine Motor Skills in Children with Down Syndrome*, by Maryanne Bruni.

**Tips:** "Do not send us a proposal on the basis of this description. Examine our catalog and a couple of our books to make sure you are on the right track. Put some thought into how your book could be marketed (aside from in bookstores). Keep cover letters concise and to the point; if it's a subject that interests us, we'll ask to see more."

**WOODHOLME HOUSE PUBLISHERS**, 1829 Reisterstown Rd., #130, Baltimore MD 21208. (410)653-7903. Fax: (410)653-7904. **Acquisitions:** Gregg A. Wilhelm, director. Estab. 1996. Publishes hardcover and trade paperback originals. **Publishes 5 titles/year. Receives 100 queries and 50 mss/year. 50% of books from first-time authors; 80% from unagented writers. Pays 5-15% royalty on retail price.** Publishes book 9 months after acceptance of ms. Accepts simultaneous submissions. Reports in 1 month on queries; 3 months on mss. Manuscript guidelines for #10 SASE.

    ◯┱ Woodholme is a regional-interest publisher (mid-Atlantic/Chesapeake Bay area) covering a variety of genres.
**Nonfiction:** Biography, guidebooks, history, memoir. Regional subjects. Submit proposal package, including cover letter, outline/synopsis, author bio and SASE. Reviews artwork/photos as part of ms package. Send photocopies.
**Fiction:** Short story collections, regional interest. "Setting/people/place should have regional flavor. We are impressed with work that possesses a strong sense of place." Query or submit synopsis with 1 sample chapter and SASE.
**Recent Title(s):** *Wish You Were Here!: A Guide to Baltimore City for Natives and Newcomers*, by Carolyn Males.
**Tips:** "Audience is interested in the Chesapeake Bay and Mid-Atlantic area, radiating out from Baltimore, Maryland."

**WORDWARE PUBLISHING, INC.**, 2320 Los Rios Blvd., Plano TX 75074. (972)423-0090. Fax: (972)881-9147. E-mail: jhill@wordware.com. Website: http://www.wordware.com. President: Russell A. Stultz. **Acquisitions:** J. Hill Parkleyter. Estab. 1983. Publishes trade paperback and mass market paperback originals. **Publishes 50-60 titles/year. Receives 100-150 queries and 50-75 mss/year. 40% of books from first-time authors; 95% from unagented writers. Pays 8% royalty on wholesale price. Offers advance.** Publishes book 6 months after acceptance of ms. Accepts simultaneous submissions. Reports in 2 months. Book catalog and ms guidelines free.

    ◯┱ Wordware publishes computer/electronics books covering a broad range of technologies for professional programmers and developers.
**Imprint(s): Republic of Texas Press.**
**Nonfiction:** Reference, technical, textbook. Subjects include computers, electronics. "Wordware publishes advanced titles for developers and professional programmers." Submit proposal package, including table of contents, 2 sample chapters, target audience summation, competing books.
**Recent Title(s):** *Developers Guide to Delphi Troubleshooting*, by Clay Shannon.

■ **WORKMAN PUBLISHING CO.**, 708 Broadway, New York NY 10003. (212)254-5900. Fax: (212)254-8098. Website: http://www.workman.com. **Acquisitions:** Sally Kovalchik, editor-in-chief (gardening, popular reference, humor); Suzanne Rafer, executive editor (cookbook, child care, parenting, teen interest); Ruth Sullivan, senior editor (humor, fashion, health); Liz Carey, senior editor (crafts, children, humor); Michaela Muntean, senior editor (children's). Estab. 1967. Publishes hardcover and trade paperback originals. **Publishes 40 titles/year. Receives thousands of queries/year. Open to first-time authors. Pays variable royalty on retail price. Advance varies.** Publishes book 1 year after acceptance of ms. Accepts simultaneous submissions. Reports in 5 months. Book catalog free.

    ◯┱ "We are a trade paperback house specializing in a wide range of popular nonfiction. We publish no adult fiction and very little children's fiction. We also publish a full range of full color wall and Page-A-Day® calendars."
**Imprint(s): Algonquin Books of Chapel Hill**, Artisan.
**Nonfiction:** Cookbooks, gift books, how-to, humor. Subjects include child guidance/parenting, gardening, health/medicine, sports, travel. Query with sample chapters and SASE. Reviews artwork/photos as part of ms package "if relevant to project. Don't send anything you can't afford to lose."
**Recent Title(s):** *The Yogi Book*, by Yogi Berra; *Brain Quest*, by Chris Welles Feder (best-selling educational game).

**WORLD LEISURE**, P.O. Box 160, Hampstead NH 03841. (617)569-1966. Fax: (617)561-7654. E-mail: wleisure@aol.com. **Acquisitions:** Charles Leocha, president. Estab. 1977. Publishes trade paperback originals. **Publishes 3-5 titles/year. Pays royalty or makes outright purchase. No advance.** Reports in 2 months on proposals.

    ◯┱ World Leisure specializes in travel books, activity guidebooks and self-help titles.
**Nonfiction:** "We will be publishing annual updates to *Ski Europe* and *Skiing America*. Writers planning any ski stories should contact us for possible add-on assignments at areas not covered by our staff. We also will publish general travel titles such as Travelers' Rights, Family travel guides, guidebooks about myths and legends, the *Cheap Dates* (affordable activity guidebooks) series and self/help books such as *Getting To Know You*, and *A Woman's ABCs of Life*." Submit outline, intro chapter and annotated table of contents with SASE.
**Recent Title(s):** *Seababies and Their Friends*, by Cathleen Arone.

**WRITE WAY PUBLISHING**, 10555 E. Dartmouth, Suite 210, Aurora CO 80014 Website: http://www.writewaypub.com. **Acquisitions:** Dorrie O'Brien, owner/editor. Estab. 1993. Publishes hardcover and trade paperback originals. **Publishes 10-15 titles/year. Receives 1,000 queries and 350 mss/year. 50% of books from first-time authors; 95% from unagented writers. Pays 8-10% royalty on wholesale price. No advance.** Publishes book within 3 years after acceptance of ms. Accepts simultaneous submissions. Reports in 1 month on queries; 9 months on mss. Book brochure and ms guidelines for SASE.

    ◯┱ Write Way is a fiction-only small press concentrating on mysteries, soft science fiction, fairy tale/fantasy and horror/thrillers.
**Fiction:** Fantasy, horror, mystery, science fiction. Query with short synopsis, first 1-2 chapters and postage with proper-sized box or envelope. "We only consider completed works."
**Recent Title(s):** *For the Time Being*, by M. DesJardin.
**Tips:** "We find that lengthy outlines and/or synopsis are unnecessary and much too time-consuming for our editors to read. We prefer a very short plot review and one to two chapters to get a feel for the writer's style. If we like what we read, then we'll ask for the whole manuscript."

**WRITER'S DIGEST BOOKS**, F&W Publications, 1507 Dana Ave., Cincinnati OH 45207. (513)531-2690. Fax: (513)531-7107. Website: http://www.writersdigest.com. Editor: Jack Heffron. **Acquisitions:** Acquisitions Coordinator. Estab. 1920. Publishes hardcover and paperback originals. **Publishes 28 titles/year. Receives 500 queries and 50 mss/ year. No books from first-time authors; 40% unagented writers. Pays 10-20% royalty on net receipts. Offers average advance of $5,000 and up.** Accepts simultaneous submissions, if so noted. Publishes book 18 months after acceptance of ms. Reports in 2 months. Book catalog for 9×12 SAE with 6 first-class stamps.

    ○┅ Writer's Digest Books is the premiere source for books about writing, publishing instructional and reference books for writers that concentrate on the creative technique and craft of writing rather than the marketing of writing.

**Nonfiction:** Instructional and reference books for writers. "Our instruction books stress results and how specifically to achieve them. Should be well-researched, yet lively and readable. Our books concentrate on writing techniques over marketing techniques. We do *not* want to see books telling readers how to crack specific nonfiction markets: *Writing for the Computer Market* or *Writing for Trade Publications*, for instance. Concentrate on broader writing topics. In the offices here we refer to a manuscript's 4T value—manuscripts must have information writers can Take To The Typewriter. We are continuing to grow our line of reference books for writers with our Howdunit series, and *A Writer's Guide to Everyday Life* series. References must be usable, accessible, and, of course, accurate." Query or submit outline and sample chapters with SASE. "Be prepared to explain how the proposed book differs from existing books on the subject." *No fiction or poetry.*

**Recent Title(s):** *The Marshall Plan for Novel Writing*, by Evan Marshall.

**Tips:** "Writer's Digest Books also publishes instructional books for photographers and songwriters, but the main thrust is on writing books. The same philosophy applies to songwriting and photography books: they must instruct about the creative craft, as opposed to instructing about marketing."

**ℕ WYNDHAM HALL PRESS**, 52857 C.R. 21, Bristol IN 46507. (219)848-4834. Website: http://www.wyndhamhall.com. **Acquisitions:** Milton L. Clayton, publisher. Estab. 1981. Publishes hardcover and trade paperback originals and reprints. **Publishes 20 titles/year. Receives 100 queries and 50 mss/year. 90% of books from first-time authors; 100% from unagented writers. Pays 10-15% on wholesale price.** Publishes book 4 months after acceptance of ms. Accepts simultaneous submissions. Reports in 1 month. Book catalog and ms guidelines free.

    ○┅ Wyndham Hall was begun by a college professor, and the focus is on scholarly texts. Ninety percent of authors are affiliated with universities and education.

**Nonfiction:** Reference, textbook. Subjects include education, ethnic, government/politics, health/medicine, philosophy, psychology, religion, science, sociology. "We publish serious scholarly work. Writers must include their credentials or qualifications for writing the book." Submit proposal package, including completed ms and qualifications. Reviews artwork/photos as part of ms package. Send photocopies.

**Recent Title(s):** *The Bosnia Files; China's Transition Toward a Market Economy; Civil Society and Democracy.*

**YALE UNIVERSITY PRESS**, 302 Temple St., New Haven CT 06520. (203)432-0960. Fax: (203)432-0948. Website: http://www.yale.edu/yup. **Acquisitions:** Jonathan Brent, editorial director (humanities, Cold War studies, annuals of communism, philosophy); Charles Grench, editor-in-chief (anthropology, history, Judaic studies, religion, women's studies); Jean E. Thomson Black, editor (science, medicine); John S. Covell, senior editor (economics, law, political science); Harry Haskell, editor (music, classics, archaeology, performing arts); Richard Miller, assistant editor, (poetry); Judy Metro, senior editor (art, art history, architecture, geography); Susan Arellano, senior editor (education, psychiatry, psychology, sociology). Estab. 1908. Publishes hardcover and trade paperback originals. **Publishes 225 titles/year. Receives 8,000 queries and 400 mss/year. 15% of books from first-time authors; 85% from unagented writers. Pays 0-15% royalty on net price. Offers $500-50,000 advance (based on expected sales).** Publishes book 1 year after acceptance of ms. Accepts simultaneous submissions, if so noted. Reports in 1 month on queries, 2 months on proposals, 3 months on mss. Book catalog and ms guidelines for #10 SASE.

    ○┅ Yale University Press publishes scholarly and general interest books.

**Nonfiction:** Biography, illustrated book, reference, textbook, scholarly works. Subjects include Americana, anthropology/archaeology, art/architecture, economics, education, history, language/literature, medicine, military/war, music/dance, philosophy, psychology, religion, science, sociology, women's issues/studies. "Our nonfiction has to be at a very high level. Most of our books are written by professors or journalists, with a high level of expertise." Query by letter with SASE. "We'll ask if we want to see more. No unsolicited manuscripts. We won't return them." Reviews artwork/photos as part of ms package. Send photocopies, not originals.

**Poetry:** Publishes 1 book each year. Submit complete ms to Yale Series of Younger Poets Competition. Open to poets under 40 who have not had a book previously published. Submit ms of 48-64 pages in February. Entry fee: $15. Send SASE for rules and guidelines.

**Recent Title(s):** *Bill Evans: How My Heart Sings*, by Peter Pettinger.

**Tips:** "Audience is scholars, students and general readers."

**YMAA PUBLICATION CENTER**, 4354 Washington St., Roslindale MA 02131. (800)669-8892. Fax: (617)323-7417. Website: http://www.ymaa.com. **Acquisitions:** David Ripianzi, editor. Estab. 1982. Publishes hardcover and trade paperback originals and reprints. **Publishes 6 titles/year. Pays royalty on retail price. No advance.** Reports in 2 months on proposals.

    ○┅ "YMAA publishes books on Chinese Chi Kung (Qigong), Taijiquan and Chinese martial arts. We are expanding our focus to include books on healing, wellness, meditation and subjects related to Chinese culture and Chinese medicine."

**Nonfiction:** "We are most interested in Chinese martial arts, Chinese medicine and Chinese Qigong. We publish Eastern thought, health, meditation, massage and East/West synthesis. We no longer publish or solicit books for children. We also produce instructional videos to accompany our books on traditional Chinese martial arts, meditation, massage and Chi Kung." Send proposal with outline, 1 sample chapter and SASE.

**Recent Title(s):** *Tai Chi Secrets of the Ancient Masters*, by Dr. Yang Jwing Ming.

**Tips:** "If you are submitting health-related material (Qigong/Chinese medicine etc.) please list *specific benefits* readers can expect."

**ZEBRA BOOKS**, Kensington, 850 Third Ave., 16th Floor, New York NY 10022. (212)407-1500. Website: http://www.kensingtonbooks.com. **Acquisitions**: Ann Lafarge, editor; Kate Duffy, senior editor (historical, regency, romance); John Scognamiglio, senior editor (romance, mystery, thrillers, pop culture); Hillary Sares (Precious Gem romances). Publishes hardcover originals, trade paperback and mass market paperback originals and reprints. **Publishes 140-170 titles/year. 5% of books from first-time authors; 30% from unagented writers. Pays variable royalty and advance.** Publishes book 18 months after acceptance of ms. Accepts simultaneous submissions. Reports in 1 month on queries, in 3 months on mss. Book catalog for #10 SASE.

O— Zebra Books is dedicated to women's fiction, which includes, but is not limited to romance.

**Fiction:** Romance, women's fiction. Query with synopsis and SASE. *No unsolicited submissions.*

**ZOLAND BOOKS, INC.**, 384 Huron Ave., Cambridge MA 02138. (617)864-6252. Fax: (617)661-4998. **Acquisitions:** Roland Pease, Jr., publisher/editor. Estab. 1987. Publishes hardcover and trade paperback originals. **Publishes 14 titles/year. Receives 700 submissions/year. 15% of books from first-time authors; 40% from unagented writers. Pays 7½% royalty on retail price.** Publishes book 18 months after acceptance of ms. Reports in 3 months. Book catalog for 6½ × 9½ SAE with 2 first-class stamps.

O— Zoland Books is an independent publishing company producing fiction, poetry and art books of literary interest.

**Nonfiction:** Biography, art book. Subjects include art/architecture, language/literature, nature/environment, photography, regional, translation, travel, women's issues/studies. Query. Reviews artwork/photos as part of ms package.

**Fiction:** Literary, short story collections. Submit complete ms. *Writer's Market* recommends querying with SASE first.

**Recent Title(s):** *Glorie*, by Caryn James; *In the Pond*, by Ha Jin; *Camelot*, by Caryl Rivers.

**Tips:** "We are most likely to publish books which provide original, thought-provoking ideas, books which will captivate the reader and are evocative."

**ZONDERVAN PUBLISHING HOUSE**, HarperCollins Publishers, 5300 Patterson Ave. SE, Grand Rapids MI 49530-0002. (616)698-6900. E-mail: zpub@zph.com. Website: http://www.zondervan.com. Publisher: Scott Bolinder. Editors: David Lambert, Sandy Vander Zicht. **Acquisitions:** Manuscript Review Editor. Estab. 1931. Publishes hardcover and trade paperback originals and reprints. **Publishes 120 titles/year. Receives 3,000 submissions/year. 20% of books from first-time authors; 80% from unagented writers. Pays 14% royalty on net amount received on sales of cloth and softcover trade editions; 12% royalty on net amount received on sales of mass market paperbacks. Offers variable advance.** Reports in 3 months on proposals. SASE required. Guidelines for #10 SASE. To receive a recording about submissions call (616)698-6900 ext. 3447.

O— "Our mission is to be the leading Christian communications company meeting the needs of people with resources that glorify Jesus Christ and promote biblical principles."

**Imprint(s):** Zonderkidz.

**Nonfiction and Fiction:** Biography, autobiography, self-help, devotional, contemporary issues, Christian living, Bible study resources, references for lay audience; some adult fiction; youth and children's ministry, teens and children. Academic and Professional Books: college and seminary textbooks (biblical studies, theology, church history); preaching, counseling, discipleship, worship, and church renewal for pastors, professionals and lay leaders in ministry; theological and biblical reference books. All from religious perspective (evangelical). Submit outline/synopsis, 1 sample chapter, and SASE for return of materials.

**Recent Title(s):** *Perennial: Meditations for the Seasons of Life*, by Twila Paris; *Every Hidden Thing*, by Athol Dickson (mystery).

---

**MARKETS THAT WERE** listed in the 1999 edition of *Writer's Market* but do not appear this year are listed in the General Index with a notation explaining why they were omitted.

# Canadian Book Publishers

Canadian book publishers share the same mission as their U.S. counterparts—publishing timely books on subjects of concern and interest to a targetable audience. Most of the publishers listed in this section, however, differ from U.S. publishers in that their needs tend toward subjects that are specifically Canadian or intended for a Canadian audience. Some are interested in submissions from Canadian writers only. There are many regional Canadian publishers that concentrate on region-specific subjects, and many Quebec publishers will consider only works in French.

U.S. writers hoping to do business with Canadian publishers should take pains to find out as much about their intended markets as possible. The listings will inform you about what kinds of books the companies publish and tell you whether they are open to receiving submissions from nonCanadians. To further target your markets and see very specific examples of the books they are publishing, send for catalogs from publishers or check their websites.

There has always been more government subsidy of publishing in Canada than in the U.S. However, with continued cuts in such subsidies, government support is on the decline. There are a few author-subsidy publishers in Canada and writers should proceed with caution when they are made this offer.

Publishers offering author-subsidy arrangements (sometimes referred to as "joint venture," "co-publishing" or "cooperative publishing") are not listed in *Writer's Market*. If one of the publishers in this section offers you an author-subsidy arrangement or asks you to pay for all or part of the cost of any aspect of publishing (printing, marketing, etc.) or asks you to guarantee the purchase of a number of books yourself, please let us know about that company immediately.

Despite a healthy book publishing industry, Canada is still dominated by publishers from the U.S. Two out of every three books found in Canadian bookstores are published in the U.S. These odds have made some Canadian publishers even more determined to concentrate on Canadian authors and subjects. Canadian publishers that accept manuscripts only from Canadian authors are indicated by the ⌧ symbol. Writers interested in additional Canadian book publishing markets should consult *Literary Market Place* (R.R. Bowker & Co.), *The Canadian Writer's Guide* (Fitzhenry & Whiteside) and *The Canadian Writer's Market* (McClelland & Stewart).

## INTERNATIONAL MAIL

U.S. postage stamps are useless on mailings originating outside of the U.S. When enclosing a self-addressed envelope for return of your query or manuscript from a publisher outside the U.S., you must include International Reply Coupons (IRCs) or postage stamps from that country. Canadian stamps are sold online at http://www.canadapost.ca. IRCs are available at your local post office and can be redeemed for stamps of any country. You can cut a substantial portion of your international mailing expenses by sending disposable proposals and manuscripts (i.e., photocopies or computer printouts which the recipient can recycle if she is not interested), instead of paying postage for the return of rejected material. Please note that the cost for items such as catalogs is expressed in the currency of the country in which the publisher is located.

**For a list of publishers according to their subjects of interest, see the nonfiction and fiction sections of the Book Publishers Subject Index. Information on book publishers and producers listed in the previous edition of *Writer's Market* but not included in this edition can be found in the General Index.**

**N** ◼ **ADVENTURE BOOK PUBLISHERS**, Durksen Enterprises Ltd., #712-3545-32 Ave. NE, Calgary, Alberta T1Y 3M1 Canada. (403)285-6844. E-mail: adventure@puzzlesbyshar.com. Website: http://www.puzzlesbyshar.com/adventurebooks. Publishes digital books. **Publishes 12-20 titles/year. Receives 60-80 queries and 40 mss/year. 100% of books from first-time authors; 100% from unagented writers. Pays 20-50% royalty on retail price. No advance.** Publishes book 7 months after acceptance of ms. Accepts simultaneous submissions. Reports in 1 month on queries and proposals, 3 months on mss. Book catalog on website. Manuscript guidelines on website or provided by e-mail to invited authors.

**Nonfiction:** Biography, children's/juvenile, cookbook, how-to, humor, self-help. Subjects include Americana, animals, cooking/foods/nutrition, creative nonfiction, history, military/war, nature/environment. Query with synopsis via e-mail. Reviews artwork/photos as part of ms package. Send GIF images via e-mail.

**Fiction:** Adventure, historical, horror, humor, juvenile, mainstream/contemporary, military/war, mystery, occult, romance, science fiction, short story collections, suspense, western, young adult. "Graphic sex/violence in excess is not necessary to tell a good or compelling story." Query with synopsis via e-mail.

**Recent Title(s):** *Who! Me?*, by Sharon Kuntz (humor); *Star Ranger*, by Robert Blacketer (science fiction).

**Tips:** "We specialize in unpublished writers since they are the ones who need the most help and encouragement. As such, we do not encourage agency submissions."

**THE ALTHOUSE PRESS**, U.W.O., Faculty of Education, 1137 Western Rd., London, Ontario N6G 1G7 Canada. (519)661-2096. Fax: (519)661-3833. E-mail: press@julian.uwo.ca. Website: http://www.uwo.ca./edu/press. Director: Dr. David Radcliffe. **Acquisitions:** Katherine Butson, editorial assistant. Publishes trade paperback originals and reprints. **Publishes 1-5 titles/year. Receives 30 queries and 19 mss/year. 100% of books from unagented writers. Pays 10% royalty on net price. Offers $300 advance.** Accepts simultaneous submissions. Reports in 2 weeks on queries, 4 months on mss. Book catalog and manuscript guidelines free.

> **O—** "The Althouse Press publishes both scholarly research monographs in education, and professional books and materials for educators in elementary schools, secondary schools and faculties of education." De-emphasizing curricular or instructional materials intended for use by elementary or secondary school students.

**Nonfiction:** Education subjects. Query. Reviews artwork/photos as part of ms package. Send photocopies.

**Recent Title(s):** *For the Love of Teaching*, by Brent Kilbourn.

**Tips:** Audience is practicing teachers and graduate education students.

**N** **ANVIL PRESS**, 204-A E. Broadway, Vancouver, British Columbia V5T 1W2 Canada. (604)876-8710. Fax: (604)879-2667. E.-mail: subter@pinc.com. Website: http://www.anvilpress.com. **Acquisitions:** Brian Kaufman. "Anvil Press publishes contemporary adult fiction, poetry and drama, giving voice to up-and-coming Canadian writers, exploring all literary genres, discovering, nurturing and promoting new Canadian literary talent." Publishes trade paperback originals. **Publishes 6 titles/year. Receives 300 queries/year. 80% of books from first-time authors; 70% from unagented writers. Pays 10-15% on wholesale price. Offers $200-400 advance.** Publishes ms 8 months after acceptance of ms. Reports in 2 months on queries and proposals, 6 months on mss. Book catalog for 9×12 SAE with 2 first-class stamps. Manuscript guidelines for #10 SASE.

> ● Anvil Press also publishes the literary magazine *sub-Terrain* and sponsors several contests, including the 3-Day Novel Writing Contest, the *sub-Terrain* Short Story Contest, the Last Poems Contest and the Creative Nonfiction Contest.

**Fiction:** Literary, plays, short story collections. Contemporary, modern literature—no formulaic or genre. Query with 2 sample chapters and SASE.

**Poetry:** "Get our catalog, look at our poetry, read *sub-Terrain* magazine (our quarterly literary magazine). We do very little poetry in book form—maybe 1-2 titles per year." Query with 12 sample poems.

**Recent Title(s):** *Where Words Like Manarchs Fly, A Cross Generational Anthology of Mexican Poets in Translation*, edited by George McWhirter; *Dry Shore (a comic strip)*, by Rod Filbrandt; and *Gas Tank & Other Stories*, by Dennis E. Bolen.

**Tips:** Audience is young, informed, educated, aware, with an opinion, culturally active (films, books, the performing arts). "No U.S. authors, unless selected as the winner of our 3-Day Novel Contest. Research the appropriate publisher for your work."

**N** **BETWEEN THE LINES**, 720 Bathurst St., Suite #404, Toronto, Ontario M5S 2R4 Canada. (416)535-9914. Fax: (416)535-1484. E-mail: btlbooks@web.net. Website: http://www.btlbooks.com. **Acquisitions:** Ruth Bradley-St-Cyr, acquisitions and managing editor. Publishes trade paperback originals. **Publishes 10 titles/year. Receives 150 queries and 25 mss/year. 80% of books from first-time authors; 95% from unagented writers. Pays 10% royalty on retail price. No advance.** Publishes book 1 year after acceptance of ms. Accepts simultaneous submissions. Reports in 2 months on queries and proposals, 4 months on mss. Book catalog and ms guidelines for 8½×11 SAE and IRCs.

> **O—** "We are a left-wing house concentrating on politics and public policy issues, social issues, gender issues, development, education and the environment. We only publish Canadian authors."

**Nonfiction:** Biography, reference, textbook. Subjects include education, gay/lesbian, government/politics, health, history, memoirs, sociology, women's issues/studies. Submit proposal package, including outline, 2-3 sample chapters and table of contents. Reviews artwork/photos as part of ms package.

**[N]** **[symbol] BLIZZARD PUBLISHING**, 73 Furby St., Winnipeg, Manitoba R3C 2A2 Canada. (204)775-2923. Fax: (204)775-2947. E-mail: info@blizzard.mb.ca. **Acquisitions:** Managing Editor (drama, theory and plays, nonfiction); Clarise Foster, assistant managing editor; David Fuller, co-ordinator (plays). Publishes trade paperback originals. **Publishes 9-10 titles/year. Receives 150 queries and 25 mss/year. 80% of books from first-time authors; 97% from unagented authors. Pays 18% royalty on retail price. Offers $200 advance.** Publishes book 1 year after acceptance of ms. Accepts simultaneous submissions. Reports in 6 months. Book catalog for 10×12 SAE with $2 IRC. Manuscript guidelines for #10 IRC.
**Imprint(s):** Bain & Cox (nonfiction).
**Nonfiction:** Drama, plays, dramatic theory, essays criticism. Subjects include art/architecture, cooking/foods/nutrition. "Nonfiction tends to focus on the arts and deals with primarily Canadian issues although not exclusive. We publish some historical books—but they must have a unique angle and the focus is usually Canadian." Query with sASE.
**Recent Titles:** *Cupboard Love: Dictionary of Culinary Curiosities*, by Mark Morton (cooking/etimology/reference).

**[symbol] BOREALIS PRESS, LTD.**, 9 Ashburn Dr., Nepean, Ontario K2E 6N4 Canada. Fax: (613)829-7783. Editorial Director: Frank Tierney. E-mail: borealis@istar.ca. **Acquisitions:** Glenn Clever, senior editor. Estab. 1972. Publishes hardcover and paperback originals. **Publishes 10-12 titles/year. Receives 400-500 submissions/year. 80% of books from first-time authors; 95% from unagented writers. Pays 10% royalty on net price. No advance.** Publishes book 18 months after acceptance. No multiple submissions. Reports in 2 months. Book catalog for $3 and SASE.
**Imprint(s):** Tecumseh Press.
**Nonfiction:** "Only material Canadian in content." Biography, children's/juvenile, reference. Subjects include government/politics, history, language/literature. Query with outline, 2 sample chapters and SASE. *No unsolicited mss.* Reviews artwork/photos as part of ms package. Looks for "style in tone and language, reader interest and maturity of outlook."
**Fiction:** "Only material Canadian in content and dealing with significant aspects of the human situation." Adventure, ethnic, historical, juvenile, literary, romance, short story collections, young adult. Query with synopsis, 1-2 sample chapters and SASE. *No unsolicited mss.*
**Recent Title(s):** *How Parliament Works, 5th edition*, by John Beiermi; *A Critical Edition*, edited by Elizabeth Thompson (fiction).

**THE BOSTON MILLS PRESS**, Stoddart Publishing, 132 Main St., Erin, Ontario N0B 1T0 Canada. (519)833-2407. Fax: (519)833-2195. E-mail: books@boston-mills.on.ca. Website: http://www.boston-mills.on.ca. President: John Denison. **Acquisitions:** Noel Hudson, managing editor. Estab. 1974. Publishes hardcover and trade paperback originals. **Publishes 20 titles/year. Receives 100 submissions/year. 40% of books from first-time authors; 95% from unagented writers. Pays 8-15% royalty on retail price. No advance.** Publishes book 18 months after acceptance. Accepts simultaneous submissions. Reports in 2 months. Book catalog free.
   **O—π** Boston Mills Press publishes specific market titles of Canadian and American interest including history, transportation and regional guidebooks.
**Nonfiction:** Coffee table book, gift book, illustrated books. Subjects include art/architecture, cooking/foods/nutrition, creative nonfiction, gardening, guidebooks, history, nature, recreation, regional. "We're interested in anything to do with Canadian or American history—especially transportation." No autobiographies. Query. Reviews artwork/photos as part of ms package. Send photocopies.
**Recent Title(s):** *Rosedale*, by William M. Gray.
**Tips:** "We can't compete with the big boys so we stay with short-run specific market books that bigger firms can't handle. We've done well this way so we'll continue in the same vein."

**[N]** **BPS BOOKS**, The British Psychological Society, St. Andrews House, 48 Princess Rd. E, Leicester LE1 7DR United Kingdom. Phone: (+44)116 254 9568. Fax: (+44)116 247 0787. E-mail: books@bps.org.uk. Website: http://www.bps.org.uk. **Acquisitions:** Joyce Collins, publisher; Jon Reed, senior editor. Publishes trade paperback originals. **Publishes 12 titles/year. Receives 30 queries and 15-20 mss/year. 25% of books from first-time authors; 95% from unagented writers. Pays 7-12% royalty on retail price. No advance.** Publishes book 1 year after acceptance of ms. Reports in 2 months. Book catalog free or on website. Manuscript guidelines free.
**Nonfiction:** Multimedia (CD-ROM), reference, textbook, professional and educational. Subjects include education, psychology. Submit proposal package, including outline and 1 sample chapter and CV.
**Recent Title(s):** *Altruism and Aggression*, by Anne Campbell.
**Tips:** "We publish psychology for managers, teachers, medical and healthcare professionals, students and practicing psychologists. We do not publish self-help or popular psychology or fiction. Please give us an indication of your qualifications for writing this particular book. We are a professional and learned society, and all submissions will go to an editorial board of practicing psychologists."

**[N]** **[symbol] CANADIAN LIBRARY ASSOCIATION**, 200 Elgin St., Suite 602, Ottawa, Ontario K2P 1L5 Canada. (613)232-9625. Fax: (613)563-9895. E-mail: emorton@cla.ca. Website: http://www.cla.amlibs.ca. **Acquisitions:** Elizabeth Morton, editor, (Feliciter/Monographs). Publishes trade paperback originals. **Publishes 4 titles/year. Receives 10 queries and 5 mss/year. 50% of books from first-time authors; 100% from unagented writers. Pays 10% minimum royalty on wholesale price. No advance.** Publishes book 6 months after acceptance of ms. Reports in 1 month on queries, 3 months on proposals and mss. Book catalog and manuscript guidelines free.
   **O—π** "CLA publishes practical/professional/academic materials with a Canadian focus or direct Canadian application

as a service to CLA members and to contribute to the professional development of library staff."
**Nonfiction:** Reference, professional, academic. Subjects include history, library science. Query with outline. Reviews artwork/photos as part of ms package. Send photocopies.
**Recent Title(s):** *Understanding Telecommunications and Public Policy: A Guide for Libraries.*
**Tips:** Audience is library and information scientists.

**CANADIAN PLAINS RESEARCH CENTER**, University of Regina, Regina, Saskatchewan S4S 0A2 Canada. (306)585-4795. Fax: (306)585-4699. **Acquisitions**: Brian Mlazgar, coordinator. Estab. 1973. Publishes scholarly paperback originals and some casebound originals. **Publishes 5-6 titles/year. Receives 10-15 submissions/year. 35% of books from first-time authors. Nonauthor-subsidy publishes 80% of books.** Publishes book 2 years after acceptance. Reports in 6 months. Book catalog and ms guidelines free. Also publishes *Prairie Forum*, a scholarly journal. Publishes scholarly research on the Canadian plains.
**Nonfiction:** Biography, illustrated book, technical, textbook, scholarly. Subjects include business and economics, history, nature, politics, sociology. "The Canadian Plains Research Center publishes the results of research on topics relating to the Canadian Plains region, although manuscripts relating to the Great Plains region will be considered. Material *must* be scholarly. Do not submit health, self-help, hobbies, music, sports, psychology, recreation or cookbooks unless they have a scholarly approach. For example, we would be interested in acquiring a pioneer manuscript cookbook, with modern ingredient equivalents, if the material relates to the Canadian Plains/Great Plains region." Submit complete ms. *Writer's Market* recommends query with SASE first. Reviews artwork/photos as part of ms package.
**Recent Title(s):** *Discover Saskatchewan*, by Nilson (guide to historic sites and markers).
**Tips:** "Pay attention to manuscript preparation and accurate footnoting, according to *Chicago Manual of Style.*"

**CARSWELL THOMSON PROFESSIONAL PUBLISHING**, The Thomson Corp., One Corporate Plaza, 2075 Kennedy Rd., Scarborough, Ontario M1T 3V4 Canada. (416)298-5024. Fax: (416)298-5094. E-mail: rfreeman@carswell .com. Website: http://www.carswell.com. **Acquisitions**: Robert Freeman, vice president, legal group. Publishes hardcover originals. **Publishes 150-200 titles/year. 30-50% of books from first-time authors. Pays 5-15% royalty on wholesale price. Offers $1,000-5,000 advance.** Publishes book 6 months after acceptance of ms. Accepts simultaneous submissions. Reports in 3 months. Book catalog and ms guidelines free.
    O─┐ Carswell Thomson is Canada's national resource of information and legal interpretations for law, accounting, tax and business professionals.
**Nonfiction:** Legal, tax and business reference. "Canadian information of a regulatory nature is our mandate." Submit proposal package, including résumé and outline.
**Recent Title(s):** *The Internet Handbook for Canadian Lawyers*, by M. Drew Jackson and Timothy L. Taylor.
**Tips:** Audience is Canada and persons interested in Canadian information; professionals in law, tax, accounting fields; business people interested in regulatory material.

**CHA PRESS**, Canadian Healthcare Association, 17 York St., Ottawa, Ontario K1N 9J6 Canada. (613)241-8005, ext. 264. E-mail: chapress@canadian-healthcare.org. **Acquisitions**: Eleanor Sawyer, director of publishing. Publishes softcover specialty textbooks. **Publishes 8-10 titles/year. Receives 7 queries and 3 mss/year. 60% from first-time authors, 90% from unagented writers. Pays 10-17% royalty on retail price or makes outright purchase of $250-1,000. Offers $500-1,500 advance.** Publishes book 8 months after acceptance of ms. Accepts simultaneous submissions. Reports in 3 months. Book catalog and ms guidelines free.
    O─┐ CHA Press strives to be Canada's health administration textbook publisher. We serve readers in our broad continuum of care in regional health authorities, hospitals and health care facilities and agencies, which are governed by trustees.
**Nonfiction:** How-to, textbook. Subjects include health/medicine, history, management, healthcare policy, healthcare administration. Query with outline and with SASE.
**Tips:** "Audience is healthcare facility managers (senior/middle); policy analysts/researchers; nurse practitioners and other healthcare professionals; trustees. "CHA Press is looking to expand its frontlist for 1999-2000 on issues specific to Canadian healthcare system reform; continuum of care issues; integrated health delivery. Don't underestimate amount of time it will take to write or mistake generic 'how-to' health for mass media as appropriate for CHA's specialty press."

**N⃞ CHARLTON PRESS**, 2040 Yonge St., Suite 208, Toronto, Ontario M4S 1Z9 Canada. Fax: (416)488-4656. **Acquisitions**: Jean Dale, managing editor. Publishes trade paperback originals and reprints. **Publishes 15 titles/year. Receives 30 queries and 5 mss/year. 10% of books from first-time authors; 100% from unagented writers. Pays 10% minimum royalty on wholesale price or makes variable outright purchase. Offers $1,000 advance.** Publishes book 6 months after acceptance of ms. Accepts simultaneous submissions. Reports in 1 month on queries and proposals, 2 months on mss. Book catalog free on request.
**Nonfiction:** Reference (price guides on collectibles). Subjects include numismatics, toys, military badges, ceramic collectibles, sport cards. Submit outline. Reviews artwork/photos as part of ms package. Send photocopies.
**Recent Title(s):** *Royal Doulton Figurines*, by J. Dale (reference guide).

**CHEMTEC PUBLISHING**, 38 Earswick Dr., Toronto-Scarborough, Ontario M1E 1C6 Canada. (416)265-2603. Fax: (416)265-1399. E-mail: chemtec@interlog.com. Website: http://chemtec.org/. **Acquisitions**: Anna Wypych, president. Publishes hardcover originals. **Publishes 5 titles/year. Receives 10 queries and 7 mss/year. 20% of books from first-**

time authors. **Pays 5-15% royalty on retail price.** Publishes book 6 months after acceptance of ms. Accepts simultaneous submissions. Reports in 2 months on queries, 4 months on mss. Book catalog and ms guidelines free.

○━ Publishes books on polymer chemistry, physics and technology. "Special emphasis is given to process additives and book which treat subject in comprehensive manner."

**Nonfiction:** Technical, textbook. Subjects include environment, science, chemistry, polymers. Submit outline or sample chapter(s).

**Recent Title(s):** *Handbook of Fillers*, by George Wypych.

**Tips:** Audience is industrial research and universities.

**CREATIVE BOUND INC.**, Box 424, 151 Tansley Dr., Carp, Ontario K0A 1L0 Canada. (613)831-3641. Fax: (613)831-3643. E-mail: cbound@igs.net. Website: http://www.wellnet.ca/creativebound. **Acquisitions:** Gail Baird, president. Publishes trade paperback originals. **Publishes 6-8 titles/year. Receives 250 queries and 80 mss/year. 30% of books from first-time authors; 100% from unagented writers. Pays 11-15% royalty on wholesale price. No advance.** Publishes book 5 months after acceptance of ms. Accepts simultaneous submissions. Reports in 1 month on queries, 3 months on proposals and mss. Book catalog free.

○━ "We publish books that "inspire, help and heal" in four categories: mind/body/spirit, personal growth, healing/recovery, parenting."

**Nonfiction:** Child guidance/parenting, psychology, spirituality, women's issues/studies. Submit proposal package, including outline and sample chapters. Reviews artwork/photos as part of ms package "only if absolutely central to work." Send photocopies.

**Recent Title(s):** *Laughter, Love and Limits: Parenting for Life*, by Dr. Maggie Mamen (nonfiction).

**ECRITS DES FORGES**, C.P. 335, 1497 Laviolette, Trois-Rivières, Quebec G9A 5G4 Canada. (819)379-9813. Fax: (819)376-0774. E-mail: ecrits.desforges@aiqnet.com. **Acquisitions:** Gaston Bellemare, president. Publishes hardcover originals. **Publishes 40 titles/year. Receives 30 queries and 1,000 mss/year. 10% of books from first-time authors; 90% from unagented writers. Pays 10-30% royalty. Offers 50% advance.** Publishes book 9 months after acceptance of ms. Accepts simultaneous submissions. Reports in 9 months. Book catalog free.

**Poetry:** Poetry only and written in *French*. Submit 20 sample poems.

**Recent Title(s):** *Écrits profanes*, by Sor Juana Ines de la Cruz.

**ECW PRESS**, 2120 Queen St. E., Suite 200, Toronto, Ontario M4E 1E2 Canada. (416)694-3348. Fax: (416)698-9906. E-mail: ecw@sympatico.ca. President: Jack David (nonfiction); Michael Holmes, literary editor (fiction, poetry). Estab. 1979. Publishes hardcover and trade paperback originals. **Publishes 20 titles/year. Receives 400 submissions/year. 50% of books from first-time authors; 80% from unagented writers. Nonauthor-subsidy publishes up to 5% of books. Pays 10% royalty on retail price.** Accepts simultaneous submissions. Reports in 2 months. Book catalog free.

**Nonfiction:** Particularly interested in popular biography, sports books and general trade books. Query. Reviews artwork/photos as part of ms package.

**Recent Title(s):** *Bite Me! Sarah Michelle Gellar and Buffy the Vampire Slayer*, by Nikki Stafford (nonfiction); *Pontypool Changes Everything*, by Tony Burgess (fiction); *Digressions of a Naked Party Girl*, by Sky Gilbert (poetry).

**Tips:** No unsolicited fiction or poetry mss. "We're looking for sports books and music biographies; please query first."

**EDGE SCIENCE FICTION AND FANTASY PUBLISHING**, Box 75064 Cambrian PO, Calgary, Alberta T2K 6J8 Canada. (403)282-5206. Fax: (403)254-0456. E-mail: editor@cadivision.com. Website: http://www.edgewebsite.com. **Acquisitions:** Jessie Tambay, Martha Nagel, Mike Bonde, Grant Lital, acquisitions editors. Editorial Manager: Lynn Jennyc. Publishes hardcover and trade paperback originals. **Publishes 3-12 titles/year. Receives 40 queries and 400 mss/year. 50% of books from first-time authors; 75% from unagented writers. Pays 10% royalty on wholesale price. Offers $500-1,000 advance.** Publishes book 1 year after acceptance of ms. Accepts simultaneous submissions. Reports in 3 months on queries and proposals; 2-6 months on mss. Book catalog not available. Ms guidelines for #10 SASE. (If from US, use IRCs, not US stamps.)

○━ "Our goal is to publish quality science fiction and fantasy novels that attract a strong readership and generate interest within the industry."

**Fiction:** Fantasy, science fiction. "We are looking for all types of fantasy and science fiction, except juvenile/young adult." Submit synopsis and 3 sample chapters with SASE.

**Recent Titles:** *The Black Chalice*, by Marie Jakober (historical fantasy); *Keeper's Child*, by Leslie Davis (science fiction).

**Tips:** "Audience is anyone who enjoys a well written science fiction or fantasy novels. Polish your manuscript before you submit it. Get your manuscript critiqued by others before you submit it."

**ÉDITIONS LOGIQUES/LOGICAL PUBLISHING**, P.O. Box 10, Station D, Montreal, Quebec H3K 3B9 Canada. (514)933-2225. Fax: (514)933-8823. E-mail: logique@cam.org. Website: http://www.logique.com. **Acquisitions:** Louis-Philippe Hebert, president and general manager. "Les Éditions Logiques will only publish books translated or written in French." Publishes hardcover, trade and mass market paperback originals and reprints. **Publishes 75 titles/year. Receives 200 queries and 100 mss/year. 40% of books from first-time authors; 100% from unagented writers. Pays 6-10% royalty on retail price. Offers advance up to $1,000.** Publishes book 6 months after acceptance of ms. Reports in 2 months. Book catalog free.

**Nonfiction:** Biography, coffee table book, cookbook, how-to, humor, illustrated book, children's/juvenile, reference, self-help, technical, textbook and computer books. "We aim to the contemporary adult: technology, environment, learning, trying to cope and live a happy life. Writers should offer some insight on the reality of today." Submit outline, 2-3 sample chapters and pictures if required. Reviews artwork as part of the ms package. Send photocopies.

**Fiction:** Erotica, experimental, fantasy, literary, mainstream/contemporary and science fiction. "Be modern." Submit complete ms only. *Writer's Market* recommends query with SASE first.

**Recent Title(s):** *Relaxer*, (self-help, health); *L'ermite* (romance).

**Tips:** "Our audience consists of contemporary men and women. French manuscripts only, please, or a copy of English book if already published and French rights are available."

**EMPYREAL PRESS**, P.O. Box 1746, Place Du Parc, Montreal, Quebec HZW 2R7 Canada. Publishes trade paperback originals. **Publishes 1-4 titles/year. 50% of books from first-time authors; 90% from unagented writers. Pays 10% royalty on wholesale price. Offers $300 (Canadian) advance.** Book catalog for #10 SASE.

➤ "Our mission is the publishing of Canadian and other literature which doesn't fit into any standard 'mold'— writing which is experimental yet grounded in discipline, imagination."

**Fiction:** Experimental, feminist, gay/lesbian, literary, short story collections. Query. *No unsolicited mss.*

**Recent Title(s):** *Reality Games*, by Louis Dudek.

**FERNWOOD PUBLISHING LTD.**, P.O. Box 9409, Station A, Halifax, Nova Scotia B3K 5S3 Canada. (902)422-3302. **Acquisitions**: Errol Sharpe, publisher (social science); Wayne Antony, editor (social science). Publishes trade paperback originals. **Publishes 12-15 titles/year. Receives 80 queries and 30 mss/year. 40% of books from first-time authors; 100% from unagented writers. Pays 7-10% royalty on wholesale price.** Publishes book 1 year after acceptance of ms. Accepts simultaneous submissions. Reports in 6 weeks on proposals. Book catalog and ms guidelines free.

➤ "Fernwood's objective is to publish critical works which challenge existing scholarship."

**Nonfiction:** Biography, reference, textbook. Subjects include anthropology/archaeology, education, ethnic, gay/lesbian, government/politics, health/medicine, history, language/literature, nature/environment, philosophy, sociology, sports, translation, women's issues/studies, Canadaiana. "Our main focus is in the social sciences and humanities, emphasizing labor studies, women's studies, gender studies, critical theory and research, political economy, cultural studies and social work—for use in college and university courses." Submit proposal package, including outline, table of contents, sample chapters. Reviews artwork/photos as part of ms package. Send photocopies.

**Recent Title(s):** *Yesterday's News: How Canada's Newspapers are Failing Us*, by John Miller.

**FITZHENRY & WHITESIDE, LTD.**, 195 Allstate Parkway, Markham, Ontario L3R 4T8 Canada. (905)477-9700. Fax: (905)477-9179. **Acquisitions**: Richard Dionne, editor. Estab. 1966. Publishes hardcover and paperback originals and reprints. **Publishes 20 titles/year, text and trade. Royalty contract varies. Advance negotiable.** Enclose return postage.

**Nonfiction:** Topics of interest to Canadians: history, nature, Native studies, language, reference, children's, young adult. Submit outline and 1 sample chapter with IRCs.

**Fiction:** Children's, young adult only. Query with SASE.

**Recent Title(s):** *The Lucy Maud Montgomery Album*, edited by McCabe and Heilbrom.

**GOOSE LANE EDITIONS**, 469 King St., Fredericton, New Brunswick E3B 1E5 Canada. (506)450-4251. **Acquisitions**: Laurel Boone, editorial director. Estab. 1956. **Publishes 12-14 titles/year. Receives 500 submissions/year. 20% of books from first-time authors; 75-100% from unagented writers. Pays royalty on retail price.** Reports in 6 months. Manuscript guidelines for SASE (Canadian stamps or IRCs).

➤ Goose Lane publishes fiction and nonfiction from well-read authors with finely crafted literary writing skills.

**Nonfiction:** Biography, illustrated book, literary history (Canadian). Subjects include art/architecture, history, language/literature, nature/environment, translation, women's issues/studies. No crime, confessional, how-to, self-help, medical, legal or cookbooks. Query first.

**Fiction:** Experimental, feminist, historical, literary, short story collections. "Our needs in fiction never change: substantial, character-centred literary fiction. No children's, YA, mainstream, mass market, genre, mystery, thriller, confessional or sci-fi fiction." Query with SASE first.

**Recent Title(s):** *The Brennen Siding Trilogy*, by Herb Curtis (novel); *Reservation X: The Power of Place in Aboriginal Contemporary Art*, edited by Gerald McMaster (nonfiction).

**Tips:** "Writers should send us outlines and samples of books that show a very well-read author who has thought long and deeply about the art of writing and, in either fiction or nonfiction, has something of Canadian relevance to offer. We almost never publish books by non-Canadian authors, and we seldom consider submissions from outside the country. Our audience is literate, thoughtful and well-read. If I were a writer trying to market a book today, I would contact the targeted publisher with a query letter and synopsis, and request manuscript guidelines. Purchase a recent book from the publisher in a relevant area, if possible. Never send a complete manuscript blindly to a publisher. *Never* send a manuscript or sample without an SASE with IRC's or sufficient return postage in Canadian stamps."

**GUERNICA EDITIONS**, 27 Humewood Dr., Toronto, Ontario M6C 2W3 Canada. (416)658-9888. Fax: (416)657-8885. **Acquisitions**: Antonio D'Alfonso, editor/publisher (poetry, nonfiction, novels); Pasquale Verdicchio, editor (Canadian reprints); Joseph Pivato, editor (essays); Ken Scambray, editor (U.S. reprints). Estab. 1978. Publishes trade paperback originals, reprints and software. **Publishes 20 titles/year. Receives 1,000 submissions/year. 5% of books from first-time authors. Pays 8-10% royalty on retail price or makes outright purchase of $200-5,000. Offers 10¢/word advance for translators.** IRCs required: "American stamps are of no use to us in Canada." Reports in 1 month on queries, 6 months on proposals, 1 year on mss. Book catalog for SASE/IRC.

  **O—π** Guernica Editions is an independent press dedicated to the bridging of cultures. "We do original and translations of fine works. We are seeking less poetry, more prose, essays, novels, and translations into English."

**Nonfiction:** Biography, art, film, history, music, philosophy, politics, psychology, religion, literary criticism, ethnic history, multicultural comparative literature, creative nonfiction, gay/lesbian, government/politics, sex, women's issues/studies. Query with SASE.

**Fiction:** Original works and translations. Subjects include ethnic, feminist, gay/lesbian, literary, multicultural, poetry, poetry in translation. "We wish to open up into the fiction world and focus less on poetry. Also specialize in European, especially Italian, translations." Query with SASE (IRCs).

**Poetry:** "We wish to have writers in translation. Any writer who has translated Italian poetry is welcomed. Full books only. Not single poems by different authors, unless modern, and used as an anthology. First books will have no place in the next couple of years." Submit samples.

**Recent Title(s):** *Wop*, by Salvatore LaGumina (nonfiction); *The Embrace*, by Irene Guilford (fiction); *Labor Songs*, by Diane Raptosh (poetry).

**[N]** **HARLEQUIN ENTERPRISES, LTD.**, Subsidiary of Torstar Corporation, Corporate Office: 225 Duncan Mill Rd., Don Mills, Ontario M3B 3K9 Canada. (416)445-5860. Chairman and Chief Executive Officer: Brian E. Hickey. Editorial divisions: Harlequin Books (Randall Toye, editorial director); Silhouette Books (Isabel Swift, vice president editorial; for editorial requirements, see separate listing, under Silhouette Books); and Worldwide Library/Gold Eagle Books (Randall Toye, editorial director; see separate listing under Worldwide Library). Estab. 1949. Submissions for Harlequin Intrigue, Harlequin American Romance and Harlequin Historicals should be directed to the designated editor and sent to Harlequin Books, 300 E. 42nd St., New York NY 10017. (212)682-6080. Romance and Presents submissions should be sent to Harlequin Mills and Boon, Eton House, 18-24 Paradise Rd., Richmond Surey TW9 1SR United Kingdom. All other submissions should be directed to the Canadian address. Publishes mass market paperback originals. **Publishes 780 titles/year; receives 10,000 submissions annually. 10% of books from first-time authors; 20% from unagented writers. Pays royalty. Offers advance.** Publishes book 1 year after acceptance. Reports in 6 weeks on queries. *Writer's Market* recommends allowing 2 months for reply. Writer's guidelines free.

**Imprint(s):** Harlequin Romance and Harlequin Presents (Karin Stoecker, director UK); Harlequin Superromance (Paula Eykelhof, senior editor); Harlequin Temptation (Birgit Davis-Todd, senior editor); Harlequin Intrigue and Harlequin American Romance (Debra Matteucci, senior editor and editorial coordinator); Harlequin Historicals (Tracy Farrell, senior editor).

**Fiction:** Adult contemporary and historical romance, including novels of romantic suspense (Intrigue), short contemporary romance (Presents and Romance), long contemporary romance (Superromance), short contemporary sensuals (Temptation) and adult historical romance (Historicals). "We welcome submissions to all of our lines. Know our guidelines and be familiar with the style and format of the line you are submitting to. Stories should possess a life and vitality that makes them memorable for the reader." *Writer's Market* recommends sending a query with SASE first.

**Tips:** "Harlequin's readership comprises a wide variety of ages, backgrounds, income and education levels. The audience is predominantly female. Because of the high competition in women's fiction, readers are becoming very discriminating. They look for a quality read. Read as many recent romance books as possible in all series to get a feel for the scope, new trends, acceptable levels of sensuality, etc."

**HARPERCOLLINS PUBLISHERS LTD.**, 55 Avenue Rd., Suite 2900, Toronto, Ontario M5R 3L2 Canada. (416) 975-9334. **Acquisitions:** Iris Tupholme, vice president/publisher/editor-in-chief. Publishes hardcover and trade paperback originals and reprints, mass market paperback reprints. **Publishes 45 titles/year. Pays 8-15% royalty on retail price. Offers from $1,500 to over six figures advance.** Publishes book 18 months after acceptance.

**Nonfiction:** Biography, children's/juvenile, self-help. Subjects include business and economics, gardening, gay/lesbian, government/politics, health/medicine, history, language/literature, money/finance, nature/environment, religion, travel, women's issues/studies. *No unsolicited mss.* Query first with SASE and appropriate Canadian postage or IRCs.

**Fiction:** Ethnic, experimental, feminist, juvenile, literary, mainstream/contemporary, picture books, religious, short story collections, young adult. *No unsolicited mss.* Query first with SASE and appropriate Canadian postage or IRCs.

**Recent Title(s):** *The Red Shoes—Margaret Atwood Starting Out*, by Rosemary Sullivan (nonfiction); *The White Bone*, by Barbara Goudy (fiction).

**F.P. HENDRIKS PUBLISHING**, 4806-53 St., Stettler, Alberta T0C 2L2 Canada. (403)742-6483. **Acquisitions:** Faye Boer, managing editor. **Publishes 2-5 titles/year. Receives 30 queries and 20 mss/year. 80% of books from first-time authors; 100% from unagented writers. Pays 10% royalty. Offers $250-1,000 advance depending on author.** Publishes book 18 months after acceptance of ms. Accepts simultaneous submissions. Reports in 2 months on queries, 3 months on proposals, 6 months on mss. Book catalog free.

  **O—π** "Primary focus is teacher's resources in English/language arts and sciences including lessons and activities with solid theoretical background." Currently emphasizing sports/health books with solid educational perspective.

**Nonfiction:** Teacher's resources, self-help, textbook. Subjects include child guidance/parenting, education, health/

medicine, language/literature, science, sports. Submit outline with SASE. Reviews artwork/photos as part of ms package. Send photocopies.

**Fiction:** Adventure, fantasy, humor, juvenile, mystery, science fiction, young adult. "We plan to begin publishing young adult fiction in the above categories to commence 2000-2001. Must include accompanying teacher resources or outline for same. Beware of lack of attention to intended audience; lack of attention to elements of plot." Submit synopsis with SASE. "Full length novels only."

**Recent Title(s):** *From Your Child's Teacher*, by David Platt, Robin Bright, Lisa McMullin.

**Tips:** "Primary audience is teachers of elementary, middle school, junior high in English/language arts and science."

**HORSDAL & SCHUBART PUBLISHERS LTD.**, 623-425 Simcoe St., Victoria, British Columbia V8V 4T3 Canada. Fax: (250)360-0829. **Acquisitions**: Marlyn Horsdal, editor. Publishes hardcover originals and trade paperback originals and reprints. **Publishes 8-10 titles/year. 50% of books from first-time authors; 100% from unagented writers. Pays 15% royalty on wholesale price. Negotiates advance.** Publishes books 6 months after acceptance of ms. Accepts simultaneous submissions. Reports in 1 month on queries. Book catalog free.

O—π "We concentrate on Western and Northern Canada and nautical subjects and offer useful information, to give readers pause for thought, to encourage action to help heal the Earth." Currently emphasizing environment, wider areas. De-emphasizing regional histories.

**Nonfiction:** Subjects include anthropology/archaeology, art/architecture, biography, government/politics, history, nature/environment, recreation, regional. Query with outline, 2-3 sample chapters and SASE or SAE with IRCs. Reviews artwork/photos as part of ms package. Send photocopies.

**Recent Title(s):** *Heart of the Raincoast*, by Alexandra Morton (nonfiction); *Spring Rain*, by Bet Oliver (fiction).

**◼◤◥ HOUSE OF ANANSI PRESS**, 34 Lesmill Rd., Toronto, Ontario M3B 2T6 Canada. (416)445-3333. Fax: (416)445-5967. E-mail: info@anansi.ca. Website: http://www.anansi.ca. **Acquisitions:** Martha Sharpe, publisher. Publishes hardcover and trade paperback originals. **Publishes 10-15 titles/year. Receives 750 queries/year. 5% of books from first-time authors; 99% from unagented writers. Pays 8-15% royalty on retail price. Offers $500-2,000 advance.** Publishes book 9 months after acceptance of ms. Accepts simultaneous submissions. Reports in 2 months on queries, 3 months on proposals, 4 months on mss.

O—π "Our mission is to publish the best new literary writers in Canada and to continue to grow and adapt along with the Canadian literary community, while maintaining Anansi's rich history."

**Nonfiction:** Biography, critical thought, literary criticism. Subjects include anthropology, gay/lesbian, government/politics, history, language/literature, philosophy, science, sociology, women's issues/studies, only Canadian writers. "Our nonfiction list is literary, but not overly academic. Some writers submit academic work better suited for university presses or pop-psychology books, which we do not publish." Submit outline with 2 sample chapters and SASE. Send photocopies of artwork/photos.

**Fiction:** "We publish literary fiction by Canadian authors." Experimental, feminist, gay/lesbian, literary, short story collections. "Authors must have been published in established literary magazines and/or journals. We only want to consider sample chapters." Submit synopsis, 2 sample chapters with SASE.

**Poetry:** "We only publish book-length works by Canadian authors. Poets must have a substantial résumé of published poems in literary magazines or journals. We only want samples from a ms." Submit 10-15 sample poems or 15 pages.

**Recent Title(s):** *The Expanding Prison: The Crisis in Crime and Punishment and the Search for Alternatives*, by David Cayley (nonfiction); *The Plight of Happy People in an Ordinary World*, by Natalee Caple (fiction); *A Frame of the Book*, by Erin Mouré (poetry).

**Tips:** "Submit often to magazines and journals. Read and buy other writers' work. Know and be a part of your writing community."

**INSTITUTE OF PSYCHOLOGICAL RESEARCH, INC./INSTITUT DE RECHERCHES PSYCHOLOGIQUES, INC.**, 34 Fleury St. W., Montréal, Québec H3L 1S9 Canada. (514)382-3000. Fax: (514)382-3007. **Acquisitions:** Marie-Paule Chevrier, general director. Estab. 1958. Publishes hardcover and trade paperback originals and reprints. **Publishes 12 titles/year. Receives 15 submissions/year. 10% of books from first-time authors, 100% from unagented writers. Pays 10-12% royalty.** Publishes book 6 months after acceptance of ms. Reports in 2 months.

O—π Institute of Psychological Research publishes psychological tests and science textbooks for a varied professional audience.

**Nonfiction:** Textbooks, psychological tests. Subjects include philosophy, psychology, science, translation. "We are looking for psychological tests in French or English." Submit complete ms. *Writer's Market* recommends a query with SASE first.

**Recent Title(s):** *Épreuve individuelle d'habileté mentale*, by Jean-Marc Chevrier (intelligence test).

**Tips:** "Psychologists, guidance counselors, professionals, schools, school boards, hospitals, teachers, government agen-

---

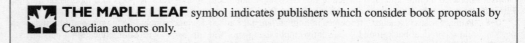 **◼◤◥ THE MAPLE LEAF** symbol indicates publishers which consider book proposals by Canadian authors only.

cies and industries comprise our audience."

**ISER BOOKS**, Institute of Social and Economic Research, Memorial University of Newfoundland, A 1044, St. John's A1K 1A9 Newfoundland. (709)737-8343. Fax: (709) 737-7560. E-mail: iser-books@morgan.ucs.mun.ca. Website: http://www.mun.ca/iser/. **Acquisitions:** Al Potter, manager. Publishes trade paperback originals. **Publishes 3-4 titles/year. Receives 10-20 queries and 10 mss/year. 45% of books published are from first-time authors; 85% from unagented writers. Pays 6-10% royalty on wholesale price. No advance.** Publishes book 4 months after acceptance of ms. Reports in 1 month on queries, 2 months on proposals; 3-4 months on mss. Book catalogue, ms guidelines free.

    ○┅ Iser Books publishes research within such disciplines and in such parts of the world as are deemed of relevance to Newfoundland and Labrador.

**Nonfiction:** Biography, reference. Subjects include agriculture/horticulture, anthropology/archaeology, ethic, government/politics, history, multicultural, recreation, regional, sociology, translation, women's issues/studies. Query with SASE. Submit proposal package, including outline and 2-3 sample chapters.

**Recent Title(s):** *Literacy for Living*, by William Fagan (ethnography/literacy).

**JESPERSON PUBLISHING, LTD.**, Jesperson Press, 39 James Lane, St. John's, New Foundland A1E 3H3 Canada. (709)753-0633. Fax: (709)753-5507. E-mail: jpress@public.nfld.com. Website: http://www.bcity.com/jesperson. **Acquisitions:** JoAnne Soper-Cook, editor. Publishes trade paperback originals. **Publishes 10-12 titles/year. Receives 100 queries and 75 mss/year. 10% of books from first-time authors; 100% from unagented writers. Pays 10% royalty on retail price. No advance.** Publishes book 18 months after acceptance of ms. Accepts simultaneous submissions. Reports in 1 month on queries, 3 months on proposals and mss. Book catalog and ms guidelines free or on website.

    ○┅ "We are interested in solid writing, a good grasp of the English language, and a New Foundland angle." Currently emphasizing solid fiction, creative nonfiction. De-emphasizing poetry, children's books.

**Nonfiction:** Humor, historical/cultural. Subjects include creative nonfiction, education, history, military/war, women's issues/studies. Query with SASE. Reviews artwork/photos as part of ms package. Send photocopies.

**Fiction:** Experimental, feminist, historical, humor, literary, military/war, multicultural, poetry, regional, short story collections. Query with SASE.

**Poetry:** Query.

**Recent Titles:** *Beside Myself*, by Peggy Smith Krachun (nonfiction); *Tales From the Frozen Ocean*, by Dwain Campbell (fiction); *Shadows of the Heart*, by Nellie Strowbridge (poetry).

**Tips:** "Do not send SASE with U.S. postage!!!"

**LONE PINE PUBLISHING**, 10426 81st Ave., #206, Edmonton, Alberta T6E 1X5 Canada. (403)433-9333. Fax: (403)433-9646. Website: http://www.lonepinepublishing.com. **Acquisitions:** Nancy Foulds, editorial director. Estab. 1980. Publishes trade paperback originals and reprints. **Publishes 12-20 titles/year. Receives 800 submissions/year. 75% of books from first-time authors; 95% from unagented writers. Pays royalty.** Reports in 2 months on queries. Book catalog free.

    ○┅ "We publish recreational and natural history titles, and some popular history as well as excellent quality native guide books (e.g., bird identification guides, plant guide)." De-emphasizing popular history, travel.

**Imprint(s):** Lone Pine, Home World, Pine Candle and Pine Cone.

**Nonfiction:** Nature/recreation guide books. Subjects include animals, anthropology/archaeology, botany/ethnobotany, gardening, nature/environment ("this is where most of our books fall"). The list is set for the next year and a half, but we are interested in seeing new material. Submit outline and sample chapters. Reviews artwork/photos as part of ms package. Do not send originals. Send SASE with sufficient international postage if you want your ms returned.

**Recent Title(s):** *Plants of the Rocky Mountains*, by Linda Kershaw, Andy MacKinnon and Jim Pojar.

**Tips:** "Writers have their best chance with recreational or nature guidebooks. Most of our books are strongly regional in nature."

**JAMES LORIMER & CO., PUBLISHERS**, 35 Britain St., Toronto, Ontario M5A 1R7 Canada. (416)362-4762. Fax: (416)362-3939. **Acquisitions:** Diane Young, senior editor. Publishes trade paperback originals. **Publishes 20 titles/year. Receives 150 queries and 50 mss/year. 10% of books from first-time authors; 100% from unagented writers. Pays 5-10% royalty on retail price. Offers negotiable advance.** Publishes book 6 months after acceptance of ms. Reports in 4 months on proposals. Book catalog for #10 SASE.

    ○┅ "James Lorimer & Co. publishes Canadian authors only, on Canadian issues/topics. For juvenile list, realistic themes only, especially mysteries and sports."

**Nonfiction:** Children's/juvenile. Subjects include business and economics, government/politics, history, sociology, women's issues/studies. "We publish Canadian authors only and Canadian issues/topics only." Submit outline, 2 sample chapters and résumé.

**Fiction:** Juvenile, young adult. "No fantasy, science fiction, talking animals; realistic themes only. Currently seeking chapter books for ages 7-11 and sports novels for ages 9-13 (Canadian writers only)." Submit synopsis and 2 sample chapters.

**Recent Title(s):** *The Winning Edge*, by Michele Bossley (skating).

**LYNX IMAGES, INC.**, 104 Scollard St., Toronto, Ontario M5R 1G2 Canada. (416)925-8422. Fax: (925)952-8352. E-mail: info@lynximages.com. Website: http://www.lynximages.com. **Acquisitions:** Russell Floren, president; Andrea Gutsche, director; Barbara Chesholm, producer. Publishes hardcover and trade paperback originals. **Publishes 6 titles/ year. Receives 100 queries and 50 mss/year. 80% of books from first-time authors; 80% from unagented writers. Makes outright purchase of $6,000-15,000. Offers 40% advance.** Publishes book 6 months-1 year after acceptance of ms. Accepts simultaneous submissions. Reports in 6 months on mss. Book catalog free.
**Profile:** "Lynx Images specializes in high-quality projects on Great Lakes and Canadian history. Our approach is to actively search out and document vanishing pieces of our heritage, bringing history alive with gripping and engaging stories." Currently emphasizing Canadian history, Great Lakes, general history, travel.
**Nonfiction:** Coffee table book, gift book, multimedia (video). Subjects include history, nature/environment, travel. Submit proposal package, including sample chapter. Reviews artwork/photos as part of ms package. Send photocopies or other formats.
**Recent Title(s):** *Superior: Under the Shadow of the Gods*, by Barbara Chisholm.

**MARCUS BOOKS**, P.O. Box 327, Queensville, Ontario L0G 1R0 Canada. (905)478-2201. Fax: (905)478-8338. **Acquisitions:** Tom Rieder, president. Publishes trade paperback originals and reprints. **Publishes 1 title/year. Receives 12 queries and 6 mss/year. 90% of books from first-time authors; 100% from unagented writers. Pays 10% royalty on retail price.** Publishes book 6 months after acceptance of ms. Reports in 4 months on mss. Book catalog for $1.
**Nonfiction:** "Interested in alternative health and esoteric topics." Submit outline and 3 sample chapters.

**MARITIMES ARTS PROJECTS PRODUCTIONS**, Box 596, Station A, Fredericton, New Brunswick E3B 5A6 Canada. (506)454-5127. Fax: (506)454-5127. E-mail: jblades@nbnet.nb.ca. **Acquisitions:** Joe Blades, publisher. Publishes Canadian-authored trade paperback originals and reprints. **Publishes 8-12 titles/year. 50% of books from first-time authors; 100% from unagented writers. Pays 10% royalty on retail price or 10% of print run. Offers $0-100 advance.** Publishes book 1-1½ years after acceptance of ms. Reports in 6-12 months on mss. Book catalog for 9×12 SAE with 2 first-class Canadian stamps in Canada. Manuscript guidelines for #10 SASE (Canadian postage or IRC).
○→ "We are a small literary and regional Canadian publishing house."
**Imprint(s):** Broken Jaw Press, Book Rat, SpareTime Editions, Dead Sea Physh Products.
**Nonfiction:** Illustrated book. Subjects include history, language/literature, nature/environment, regional, women's issues/studies, criticism, culture. Query with SASE (Canadian postage or IRC). Reviews artwork/photos as part of ms package. Send photocopies, transparencies.
**Fiction:** Literary.
**Recent Title(s):** *Best in Life*, by Ted Mouradian (nonfiction); *Like Minds*, by Shannon Friesion (fiction); *Tunnel of the Green Prow*, by Nela Rio (poetry).
**Tips:** "We don't want unsolicited manuscripts or queries."

**Ⓝ McCLELLAND & STEWART INC.**, 481 University Ave., Suite 900, Toronto, Ontario M5G 2E9 Canada. (416)598-1114. Imprints are McClelland & Stewart, New Canadian Library. Publishes hardcover, trade paperback and mass market paperback originals and reprints. **Publishes 80 titles/year. Receives thousands of queries/year. 10% of books from first-time authors; 30% from unagented writers. Pays 10-15% royalty on retail price (hardcover rates). Offers advance.** Publishes book 1 year after acceptance of ms. Reports in 3 months on proposals.
**Nonfiction:** Biography, coffee table book, how-to, humor, illustrated book, children's/juvenile, reference, self-help, textbook. Subjects include agriculture/horticulture, animals, art/architecture, business and economics, Canadiana, child guidance/parenting, cooking/foods/nutrition, education, gardening, gay/lesbian, government/politics, health/medicine, history, hobbies, language/literature, military/war, money/finance, music/dance, nature/environment, philosophy, photography, psychology, recreation, religion, science, sociology, sports, translation, travel, women's issues/studies. "We publish books by Canadian authors or on Canadian subjects." Submit outline; all unsolicited mss returned unopened.
**Fiction:** Experimental, historical, humor, literary, mainstream/contemporary, mystery, short story collections. "We publish quality fiction by prize-winning authors." Query. *No unsolicited mss. All unsolicited mss returned unopened.*
**Poetry:** "Only Canadian poets should apply. We publish only four titles each year." Query. *No unsolicited mss.*
**Recent Title(s):** *Memoirs*, by Pierre Trudeau (political memoir nonfiction); *The Love of a Good Woman*, by Alice Munro (fiction); *Handwriting*, by Michael Ondaatje (poetry).

**McGRAW-HILL RYERSON LIMITED**, The McGraw-Hill Companies, 300 Water St., Whitby, Ontario L1N 9B6 Canada. Fax: (416)430-5020. Website: http://www.mcgrawhill.ca. **Acquisitions:** Joan Homewood, publisher. McGraw-Hill Ryerson, Ltd., publishes books on Canadian business and personal finance for the Canadian market. Publishes hardcover and trade paperback originals and revisions. **Publishes 20 new titles/year. 75% of books are revisions. 15% of books from first-time authors; 85% from unagented writers. Pays 7½-10% royalty on retail price. Offers $4,000 average advance.** Publishes book 1 year after acceptance. Accepts simultaneous submissions. Reports in 6 months on queries.
**Nonfiction:** How-to, reference, professional. Subjects include small business, management, personal finance, Canadian military history, training for business skills. "No books and proposals that are American in focus. We publish primarily

for the Canadian market, but work with McGraw-Hill U.S. on business, management and training titles." Query. Submit outline and sample chapters.
**Recent Title(s):** *Guarantee Your Child's Financial Future*, by Ben McLean.
**Tips:** "Writers have the best chance of selling us nonfiction business and personal finance books with a distinctly Canadian focus. Proposal guidelines are available. Thorough market research on competitive titles increases chances of your proposal getting serious consideration, as does endorsement by or references from relevant professionals."

**MEKLER & DEAHL, PUBLISHERS**, 237 Prospect St. S., Hamilton, Ontario L8M 2Z6 Canada. (905)312-1779. Fax: (905)312-8285. E-mail: meklerdeahl@globalserve.net. **Acquisitions:** James Deahl, editor (poetry). "Books must be very well written, and have a market for us to be interested." Publishes trade paperback originals and reprints. **Publishes 4-6 titles/year. No books from first-time authors; 100% from unagented writers. Pays 10-12% royalty on retail price.** Publishes book 10 months after acceptance. Accepts simultaneous submissions. Reports in 6 months.
**Imprint(s):** Unfinished Monument Press (literature); Hamilton Haiku Press.
**Poetry:** "We have a special interest in people's poetry." Query with SASE. "No unsolicited manuscripts, please."
**Recent Title(s):** *Sing for the Inner Ear*, edited by Al Purdy (poetry).

■ **NEWEST PUBLISHERS LTD.**, 201, 8540- 109 St., Edmonton, Alberta T6G 1E6 Canada. (403)432-9427. Fax: (403)433-3179. E-mail: newest@planet.eon.net. **Acquisitions:** Liz Grieve, managing editor. Estab. 1977. Publishes trade paperback originals. **Publishes 8 titles/year. Receives 200 submissions/year. 40% of books from first-time authors; 90% from unagented writers. Pays 10% royalty.** Publishes book 2 years after acceptance. Accepts simultaneous submissions. Reports in 6 months on queries. Book catalog for 9 × 12 SAE with 4 first-class Canadian stamps or IRCs.
○── "We only publish Western Canadian authors. Our audience consists of people interested in the west and north of Canada; teachers, professors."
**Nonfiction:** Literary/essays (Western Canadian authors). Subjects include ethnic, government/politics (Western Canada), history (Western Canada), Canadiana. Query.
**Fiction:** Literary. Submit outline/synopsis and sample chapters.
**Recent Title(s):** *Crybaby!*, by Janice Williamson (nonfiction); *The Blood Girls*, by Meira Cook (fiction); *Martin Yesterday*, by Brad Fraser (drama).
**Tips:** "Trend is towards more nonfiction submissions. Would like to see more full-length literary fiction."

■ **NORBRY PUBLISHING**, 15838 Shaws Creek Rd., Terra Cotta, Ontario L0P 1N0 Canada. (905)838-2800. Fax: (905)838-0214. E-mail: norbry@norbry.com. Website: http://www.norbry.com. **Acquisitions:** Rebecca Pembry, president (accounting). Publishes mass market paperback originals. **Publishes 9 titles/year. Receives 12 queries and no mss/year. No books from first-time writers; 100% from unagented writers. Pays 2-20% royalty on retail price. No advance.** Publishes book 6 months after acceptance of ms. Accepts simultaneous submissions. Book catalog and ms guidelines free.
**Nonfiction:** Multimedia (CD-ROM), textbook. Subjects include business/economics, computers/electronics, education, software. Query with SASE. Reviews artwork as part of ms package. Send photocopies.
**Recent Title(s):** *Learning Simple Accounting 6.0 for Windows*, by Harvey Freedman and James McLachlin.

■ **ORIGIN OF BOOKS**®, Citi Services Limited, 12 York Place, Leeds LS1 2DS United Kingdom. E-mail: leeds@or iginofbooks.com. Website: http://www.originofbook.com. **Acquisitions:** Katerina Theohari-Smith, director; Greg Lloyd Smith, publisher. Publishes hardcover, trade paperback and mass market paperback originals and hardcover, trade paperback and mass market paperback reprints. **Publishes 18-25 titles/year; imprint publishes 18-25/year. Receives 1,500 queries and 185 mss/year. 80% of books from first-time authors; 20% from unagented writers. Pays 10-18% royalty on wholesale price. Offers negotiable advance.** Publishes book 9 months after acceptance of ms. Accepts simultaneous submissions. Reports in 3 months on queries and proposals, 6 months on mss. Book catalog for #10 SASE. Manuscript guidelines free.
**Imprints:** The Origin of Books®.
**Nonfiction:** Biography, children's/juvenile, coffee table book, cookbook, gift book, how-to, humor, illustrated book, self-help. Subjects include art/architecture, business/economics, child guidance/parenting, computers/electronics, cooking/foods/nutrition, creative nonfiction, gardening, gay/lesbian, government/politics, hobbies, language/literature, memoirs, money/finance, multicultural, nature/environment, philosophy, photography, psychology, recreation, regional, sex, software, translation, travel, women's issues/studies. Query with IRCs. Reviews artwork/photos as part of ms package. Send photocopies.
**Fiction:** Erotica, gay/lesbian, humor, picture books, poetry, poetry in translation, romance, suspense. Query with IRCs.
**Poetry:** Query with IRCs.
**Recent Title(s):** *Footnotes To a Scoundrel*, by Brian Richards (nonfiction biography).
**Tips:** "We prefer electronic submissions at submissions@originofbooks.com."

■ **OWL BOOKS**, 179 John St., Suite 500, Toronto, Ontario M5T 3G5 Canada. Fax: (416)340-9769. E-mail: owlbook s@owl.on.ca. Website: http://www.owl.on.ca. **Acquisitions:** Sheba Meland, publishing director. Estab. 1976. Publishes hardcover and trade paperback originals. **Publishes 10 titles/year. Receives 100 queries and 500 mss/year. 15% of books from first-time authors; 80% from unagented writers. Pays royalty on retail price.** Publishes book 18 months after acceptance of ms. Accepts simultaneous submissions. Reports in 3 months. Catalog and ms guidelines for #10 SAE with IRC. (No US stamps).

○┅ "We publish books for children that educate and inform them about their world in a way that is fun." Currently emphasizing science, nature, activity. De-emphasizing storybooks.

**Nonfiction:** Children's/juvenile. Subjects include animals, hobbies, nature/environment, science and science activities. "We are closely affiliated with the discovery-oriented children's magazines *Owl* and *Chickadee*, and concentrate on fresh, innovative nonfiction and picture books with nature/science themes, and quality children's craft/how-to titles." Submit proposal package, including outline, vita and 3 sample chapters. Reviews artwork/photos as part of ms package. Send photocopies or transparencies (not originals).

**Fiction:** Picture books. Submit complete ms. *Writer's Market* recommends a query with SASE first.

**Recent Title(s):** *The Inuksuk Book*, by Mary Wallace (nonfiction); *Quennu and the Cave Bear*, by Marie Day (fiction).

**Tips:** "To get a feeling for our style of children's publishing, take a look at some of our recent books and at *Owl* and *Chickadee* magazines. We publish Canadian authors in the main but will occasionally publish a work from outside Canada if it strikingly fits our list."

**PACIFIC EDUCATIONAL PRESS**, Faculty of Education, University of British Columbia, Vancouver, British Columbia V6T 1Z4 Canada. Fax: (604)822-6603. E-mail: cedwards@interchange.ubc.ca. **Acquisitions:** Catherine Edwards, director. Publishes trade paperback originals. **Publishes 6-8 titles/year. Receives 200 submissions/year. 15% of books from first-time authors; 100% from unagented writers.** Accepts simultaneous submissions, if so noted. Reports in 6 months on mss. Book catalog and ms guidelines for 9×12 SAE with IRCs.

○┅ Pacific Educational Press "publishes books on the subject of education for an adult audience of teachers, scholars, librarians and parents." Currently emphasizing literature, education, social studies education, and international issues and experiences in education.

**Recent Title(s):** *Teaching to Wonder: Responding to Poetry in the Secondary Classroom*, by Carl Leggs.

**[N] PEDLAR PRESS**, P.O. Box 26, Station P, Toronto, Ontario M5S 2S6 Canada. (416)926-8110. Fax: (416)513-1805. E-mail: feralgrl@interlog.com. **Acquisitions:** Beth Follett, editor (fiction, poetry). Publishes hardcover and trade paperback originals. **Publishes 3-5 titles/year. Receives 50-60 mss/year. 50% of books from first-time authors; 100% from unagented writers. Pays 10-15% royalty on retail price. Offers $400-800 advance.** Publishes book 1 year after acceptance of ms. Accepts simultaneous submissions. Reports in 1 month on queries, 6 months on mss. Book catalog and ms guidelines for #10 SASE.

**Nonfiction:** Gift book, humor, illustrated book. Subjects include creative nonfiction, gay/lesbian, language/literature, sex, women's issues/studies. Query with SASE or submit proposal package, including outline and 5 sample chapters. Reviews artwork/photos as part of ms package. Send photocopies.

**Fiction:** Erotica, experimental, feminist, gay/lesbian, humor, literary, picture books, poetry, short story collections, translation. Query with SASE or submit proposal package, including synopsis and 5 sample chapters.

**Recent Titles:** *Fishing Up The Moon*, by Anne Hines (novel); *Sex Libris*, by Antonella Brion (poetry).

**Tips:** "We select manuscripts according to our taste. Be familiar with some if not most of our recent titles."

**[■] PENGUIN BOOKS CANADA LTD.**, The Penguin Group, 10 Alcorn Ave., Suite 300, Toronto, Ontario M4V 3B2 Canada. (416)925-0068. **Acquisitions:** Jackie Kaiser, senior editor (cooking, biography, social issues); Meg Masters, executive editor (sports, biography, business); Cynthia Good, president/publisher.

**Nonfiction:** Any Canadian subject by Canadian authors. Query. *No unsolicited mss.*

**Recent Title(s):** *Titans*, by Peter C. Newuer (business); *Home From the Vinyl Cafe*, by Stuart McLear (fiction).

**[■] PLAYWRIGHTS CANADA PRESS**, Playwrights Union of Canada, 54 Wolseley St., 2nd Floor, Toronto, Ontario M5T 1A5 Canada. (416)703-0201. Fax: (416)703-0059. E-mail: cdplays@interlog.com. Website: http://www.puc.ca. **Acquisitions:** Angela Rebeiro, publisher. Estab. 1972. Publishes paperback originals and reprints of plays by Canadian citizens or landed immigrants. **Receives 40 submissions/year. 50% of plays from first-time authors; 50% from unagented authors. Pays 10% royalty on list price.** Publishes 1 year after acceptance. Reports in up to 1 year. Play catalog for $5. Accepts children's plays.

○┅ "Playwrights Canada Press publishes only drama which has received professional production."

**Recent Title(s):** *Patience*, by Jason Sherman.

**[N] [■] POLESTAR BOOK PUBLISHERS**, P.O. Box 5238, Station B, Victoria, British Columbia V8R 6N4 Canada. (250)361-9718. Fax: (250)361-9738. E-mail: pstarvic@direct-ca. Website: http://mypage.direct.ca/p/polestar. **Acquisitions:** Lynn Henry, managing editor (fiction, teen fiction, poetry, general nonfiction). Publishes trade paperback originals. **Publishes 12 titles/year. Receives 150-200 queries and 200 mss/year. 40% of books from first-time authors; 60% from unagented writers. Pays 8-12% royalty on retail price. Offers $200-2,000 advance.** Publishes book 18 months after acceptance of ms. Accepts simultaneous submissions. Reports in 6 months. Book catalog for 9×12 SAE with IRCs or on website. Manuscript guidelines for #10 SAE with IRCs or on website.

**Nonfiction:** Children's/juvenile. Subjects include cooking/foods/nutrition, creative nonfiction, gardening, gay/lesbian, language/literature, multicultural, nature/environment, recreation, sports, women's issues/studies. Query with SASE.

**Fiction:** Ethnic, feminist, gay/lesbian, literary, multicultural, poetry, young adult. Query with SASE.

**Poetry:** Submit 15 sample poems.

**Recent Title(s):** *Too Many Men on the Ice*, by J. Stevens/J. Avery (women's hockey, nonfiction); *Pool-Hopping*, by Ann Fleming (short stories, fiction); *Inward to the Bones*, by K. Braid (poetry).
**Tips:** "We only publish Canadian authors."

**N PORTHOLE PRESS LTD.**, 2832 Heath Dr., Victoria, British Columbia V9A 2J5 Canada. Phone/fax: (250)386-7458. **Acquisitions:** Diana Gault. Publishes trade paperback originals. **Publishes 2 titles/year. Receives 6-10 queries and 10-12 mss/year. 30% of books from first-time authors; 100% from unagented writers. Pays royalty on retail price. Offers negotiable advance.** Publishes book 6 months after acceptance of ms. Accepts simultaneous submissions. Book catalog and ms guidelines for #10 SAE with IRCs.
**Nonfiction:** Illustrated book, reference. Subjects include history (west coast only), child survival (emergency preparedness for children). Submit proposal package, including outline. Reviews artwork/photos as part of ms package. Send photocopies.
**Recent Title(s):** *The Story of Sidney*, by Peter Grant (west coast history).
**Tips:** "Submit within advertised publishing, program scope. Send SASE that will fit submission. Obtain a book (from the library) in each publishing category before deciding to submit your own work."

**N PRESS GANG PUBLISHERS**, 1723 Grant St., Vancouver, British Columbia V5L 2Y6 Canada. (604)251-3315. Fax: (604)251-3329. E-mail: pgangpub@portal.ca. Website: http://www.pressgang.bc.ca. **Acquisitions:** Barbara Kuhne. Publishes trade paperback originals. **Publishes 6-8 titles/year. Receives 750-1,000 mss/year. Pays royalty on retail price. No advance.** Reports in 3 months. Book catalog free. Manuscript guidelines free or on website.
**Nonfiction:** Subjects include creative nonfiction, gay/lesbian, psychology, women's issues/studies. Query with SASE.
**Fiction:** Feminist, gay/lesbian, literary, short story collections. Query with SASE.

**PRODUCTIVE PUBLICATIONS**, P.O. Box 7200 Station A, Toronto, Ontario M5W 1X8 Canada. (416)483-0634. Fax: (416)322-7434. **Acquisitions:** Iain Williamson, owner. Estab. 1985. Publishes trade paperback originals. **Publishes 24 titles/year. Receives 160 queries and 40 mss/year. 80% of books from first-time authors; 100% from unagented writers. Pays 10-15% royalty on wholesale price.** Publishes book 3 months after acceptance of ms. Reports in 1 month on queries and proposals, 3 months on mss. Accepts simultaneous submissions. Book catalog free.
O— "Productive publishes books to help readers succeed and to help readers meet the challenges of the new information age and global marketplace." Interested in books on business computer software, the Internet for business purposes, investment, stock market and mutual funds, etc. Currently emphasizing computers, software, personal finance. De-emphasizing jobs, how to get employment.
**Nonfiction:** How-to, reference, self-help, technical. Subjects include business and economics, computers and electronics, health/medicine, hobbies, money/finance, software (business). "We are interested in small business/entrepreneurship/employment/self-help (business)/how-to/health and wellness—100 to 300 pages." Submit outline. Reviews artwork as part of ms package. Send photocopies.
**Recent Title(s):** *Stock Market Panic*, by Dave Skariea.
**Tips:** "We are looking for books written by *knowledgeable, experienced experts* who can express their ideas *clearly* and *simply.*"

**N RAINCOAST BOOK DISTRIBUTION LIMITED**, 8680 Cambie St., Vancouver, British Columbia V6P 6M9 Canada. **Acquisitions:** Brian Scrivener, editorial director. Publishes hardcover and trade paperback originals and reprints. **Publishes 20-25 titles/year. Receives 800 queries and 500 mss/year. 1% of books from first-time authors; 80% from unagented writers. Pays 8-12% royalty on retail price. Offers $1,000-6,000 advance.** Publishes book within 2 years after acceptance of ms. Reports in 2 months on queries and proposals, 3 months on mss. Book catalog and ms guidelines for #10 IRCs
**Imprint(s):** Raincoast Books.
**Nonfiction:** Children's, coffee table book, cookbook, gift book, illustrated book. Subjects include animals, art/architecture, cooking/foods/nutrition, history, nature/environment, photography, recreation, regional, sports, travel, business, Canadian subjects and native studies/issues. "We are expanding rapidly and plan on publishing a great deal more over the next two or three years, particularly nonfiction. Proposals should be focused and include background information on the author. Include a market study or examination of competition. We like to see proposals that cover all the bases and offer a new approach to the subjects we're interested in." Query first with SASE. *No unsolicited mss.*
**Fiction:** Children's picture books. "Our interest is high-quality children's picture books with Canadian themes." Query first with SASE. *No unsolicited mss.*
**Recent Title(s):** *Shocking Beauty*, by Thomas Hobbs (gardening); *The Dragon New Year*, by David Bouchard (children's picture book).
**Tips:** "We have very high standards. Our books are extremely well designed and the texts reflect that quality. Be focused in your submission. Know what you are trying to do and be able to communicate it. Make sure the submission is well organized, thorough, and original. We like to see that the author has done some homework on markets and competition, particularly for nonfiction."

**RED DEER PRESS**, (formerly Red Deer College Press), Box 5005, 56th Ave. and 32nd St., Red Deer, Alberta T4N 5H5 Canada. (403)342-3321. Fax: (403)357-3639. E-mail: vmix@admin.rdc.ab.ca. **Acquisitions:** Dennis Johnson, managing editor (nonfiction); Aritha van Herk, fiction editor; Nicole Markotic, poetry editor; Joyce Doolittle, drama

editor; Peter Carver, childrens' acquisitions editor. Publishes trade paperback originals and occasionally reprints. **Publishes 14-17 titles/year. Receives 1,700 queries and 2,000 mss/year. 20% of books from first-time authors; 90% from unagented writers. Pays 8-10% royalty on retail price.** Publishes book 1 year after acceptance of ms. Accepts simultaneous submissions. Reports in 6 months.
**Imprint(s):** Northern Lights Books for Children, Northern Lights Young Novels, Discovery Books, Roundup Books, Writing West, Prairie Garden Books, History Along the Highway.
**Nonfiction:** Children's/juvenile, humor, illustrated books. Subjects include anthropology/archaeology/paleontology, cooking/foods/nutrition, gardening, history (local/regional), nature/environment (local/regional), regional, travel. Nonfiction list focuses on regional history, paleontology, and some true crime, travel, gardening—much with a regional (Canadian) emphasis. "Writers should assess their competition in the marketplace and have a clear understanding of their potential readership." Query with SASE. Reviews artwork/photos as part of ms package. Send photocopies.
**Fiction:** Adventure, ethnic, experimental, historical, humor, juvenile, literary, mainstream/contemporary, picture books, plays (occasionally), short story collections (occasionally), western, young adult. Adult fiction list includes well-established Canadian writers writing literary fiction, though the press is open to accepting other forms if tastefully and skillfully done. Query.
**Poetry:** Send cover letter, SASE and 8-10 sample poems (not exceeding 20 pages).
**Recent Title(s):** *Reaching North: A Celebration of the Subarctic*, by Jamie Bastedo (nonfiction); *Restlessness*, by Aritha van Herk (fiction); *Flat Side*, by Monty Reid (poetry).
**Tips:** Audience varies from imprint to imprint. "Know as much as you can about the potential market/readership for your book and indicate clearly how your book is different from or better than others in the same genre." Accepts very few unsolicited manuscripts each year. Prefers Canadian authors with proven track record.

**REIDMORE BOOKS INC.**, 18228-102 Ave., Edmonton, Alberta T5S 1S7 Canada. (780)444-0912. Fax: (780)444-0933. E-mail: reidmore@compusmart.ab.ca. Website: http://www.reidmore.com. **Acquisitions:** Leah-Ann Lymer, senior editor. Estab. 1979. Publishes hardcover originals. **Publishes 10-12 titles/year. Receives 50 submissions/year. 60% of books from first-time authors; 100% from unagented writers. Subsidy publishes 5% of books. Pays royalty.** Publishes book 1 year after acceptance. Reports in 8 months on queries. Book catalog free.
○⚓ Reidmore publishes social studies for kindergarten to grade 12.
**Nonfiction:** Textbook. Subjects include ethnic, government/politics, history, geography and social studies. Query. Most manuscripts are solicited by publisher from specific authors.
**Recent Title(s):** *Century of Change: Europe from 1789 to 1918*, by Mitchner and Tuffs (grades 10-12).

**ROCKY MOUNTAIN BOOKS**, #4 Spruce Centre SW, Calgary, Alberta T3C 3B3 Canada. (403)249-9490. Fax: (403)249-2968. E-mail: tonyd@rmbooks.com. Website: http://www.rmbooks.com. **Acquisitions:** Tony Daffern, publisher. **Publishes trade paperback originals. Publishes 5 titles/year. Receives 30 queries/year. 75% of books from first-time authors; 100% from unagented writers. Pays 10% royalty. Offers $1,000-2,000 advance.** Publishes book 1 year after acceptance. Reports in 1 month on queries. *Writer's Market* recommends allowing 2 months for reply. Book catalog and ms guidelines free.
○⚓ "We are focused on Western Canada and also mountaineering."
**Nonfiction:** How-to. Subjects include nature/environment, recreation, travel. "Our main area of publishing is outdoor recreation guides to Western and Northern Canada." Query.
**Recent Title(s):** *GPS Made Easy*, 2nd edition, by Lawrence Letham (how-to).

◤◢ **RONSDALE PRESS**, 3350 W. 21st Ave., Vancouver, British Columbia V6S 1G7 Canada. Website: http://www.ronsdalepress.com. **Acquisitions:** Ronald B. Hatch, director (fiction, poetry, social commentary); Veronica Hatch, managing director (children's literature). Publishes trade paperback originals. **Publishes 8 titles/year. Receives 100 queries and 200 mss/year. 60% of books from first-time authors; 95% from unagented writers. Pays 10% royalty on retail price.** Publishes book 1 year after acceptance of ms. Accepts simultaneous submissions. Reports in 1 week on queries, 1 month on proposals, 3 months on mss. Book catalog for #10 SASE. Writers *must* be Canadian citizens or landed immigrants.
○⚓ Ronsdale publishes fiction, poetry, regional history, biography and autobiography, books of ideas about Canada, as well as children's books.
**Nonfiction:** Biography, children's/juvenile. No picture books. Subjects include history, language/literature, nature/environment, regional.
**Fiction:** Novels, short story collections, children's literature. Query with at least 80 pages.
**Poetry:** "Poets should have published some poems in magazines/journals and should be well-read in contemporary masters." Submit complete ms.
**Recent Poetry Title(s):** *Does Canada Matter? Liberalism and the Illusion of Sovereignty*, by Clarence Bolt (nonfiction); *Daruma Days*, by Terry Watada (fiction); *Taking the Breath Away*, by Harold Rhenisch (poetry).
**Tips:** "We aim to publish the best Canadian writers. We are particularly interested in books that help Canadians know one another better. Ronsdale Press is a literary publishing house, based in Vancouver, and dedicated to publishing books from across Canada, books that give Canadians new insights into themselves and their country."

**SELF-COUNSEL PRESS**, 1481 Charlotte Rd., North Vancouver, British Columbia V7J 1H1 Canada. (604)986-3366. Also 1704 N. State Street, Bellingham, WA 98225. (360)676-4530. **Acquisitions:** Lori Ledingham, managing editor.

Estab. 1970. Publishes trade paperback originals. **Publishes 15-20 titles/year. Receives 1,000 submissions/year. 80% of books from first-time authors; 95% from unagented writers. Pays 10% royalty on net receipts.** Publishes book 9 months after acceptance. Accepts simultaneous submissions. Reports in 2 months. Book catalog and ms guidelines for 9×12 SAE.

   **O→** "We are looking for business and legal titles written for the layperson that allow readers to take the solution to their needs or problems into their own hands and succeed. We do not publish personal self-help account or fiction." Currently emphasizing business and legal—financial. De-emphasizing family, lifestyle, psychology.

**Nonfiction:** How-to, self-help. Subjects include business, law, reference. Query or submit outline and sample chapters.

**Recent Title(s):** *Computer Crisis 2000*, by W. Michael Fletcher.

**Tips:** "The Self-Counsel author is an expert in his or her field of business or law and capable of conveying practical, specific information to the layperson."

**SHORELINE,** 23 Ste.-Anne, Ste.-Anne-de-Bellevue, Quebec H9X 1L1 Canada. Phone/fax: (514)457-5733. E-mail: bookline@total.net. Website: http://www.total.net/~bookline. **Acquisitions:** Judy Isherwood, editor. "Our mission is to support new authors by publishing literary works of considerable merit." Publishes trade paperback originals. **Publishes 3 titles/year. Pays 10% royalty on retail price.** Publishes book 1 year after acceptance. Reports in 1 month on queries, 4 months on ms. Book catalog for 50¢ postage.

**Nonfiction:** Biography, essays, humour, illustrated book, reference. Subjects include: America, art, Canada, education, ethnic, health/mental health, history, mediation, regional, religion, Mexico, Spain, the Arctic, travel, women's studies.

**Recent Title(s):** *Alaska Burning*, by Jerry Nelson.

**Tips:** Audience is "adults and young adults who like their nonfiction personal, different and special. Beginning writers welcome, agents unnecessary. Send your best draft (not the first!), make sure your heart is in it."

**N** **SIMON & PIERRE PUBLISHING CO. LTD.,** A Subsidiary of Dundurn Press, Suite 301, 2181 Queen St. E., Toronto, Ontario M4E 1E5 Canada. (416)463-0313. **Acquisitions:** Carl Brand, director of operations. Estab. 1972. Publishes hardcover and trade paperback originals and reprints. **Publishes 6-8 titles/year. Receives 300 submissions/year. 50% of books are from first-time authors; 85% from unagented writers. Trade book royalty 10-15% on retail price. Education royalty 8% of net. Offers $500 average advance.** Publishes book an average of 1 year after acceptance. Accepts simultaneous submissions. Reports in 3 months on queries. Ms guidelines free.

   **O→** Simon & Pierre publishes "Canadian themes by Canadian authors," both fiction and nonfiction literary and contemporary subjects such as Sherlockian literature and drama.

**Nonfiction:** Reference, drama, language/literature, music/dance (drama), Sherlockian literature and criticism. "We are looking for Canadian drama and drama related books." Query or submit outline and sample chapters. Sometimes reviews artwork/photos as part of ms package.

**Fiction:** Adventure, literary, mainstream/contemporary, mystery, plays (Canadian, must have had professional production). "No romance, sci-fi or experimental." Query or submit outline/synopsis and sample chapters.

**Recent Fiction Title(s):** *Found: A Body*, by Betsy Struthers (novel).

**Tips:** "We are looking for Canadian themes by Canadian authors. Special interest in drama and drama related topics; also Sherlockian. If I were a writer trying to market a book today, I would check carefully the types of books published by a publisher before submitting manuscript; books can be examined in bookstores, libraries, etc.; should look for a publisher publishing the type of book being marketed. Clean manuscripts essential; if work is on computer disk, give the publisher that information. Send information on markets for the book, and writer's résumé, or at least why the writer is an expert in the field. Covering letter is important first impression."

**N** **SKYFOOT TECHNICAL,** 283 McAlpine Ave. S., Welland, Ontario L3B 1T8 Canada. (905)708-1784. E-mail: pboucher@skyfoot-technical.nu. Website: http://www.skyfoot-technical.nu. Publishes trade paperback originals. **Publishes 2-5 titles/year. Pays 10% royalty on wholesale price.** Publishes book 1 year after acceptance of ms. Accepts simultaneous submissions. Reports within 1 month on queries, 2 months on proposals, 3 months on mss.

**Nonfiction:** How-to, reference, technical. Subjects include computers/electronics, hobbies, science, Native, New Age. "We are a new, small technical publisher looking for quality manuscripts for niche book publication. We stress content quality, low price and interesting subject matter, rather than esthetics. All publications are 8½×11, side-stapled or loose-leaf format, depending on subject matter." Submit *very* short query about manuscript or proposal via e-mail or voice mail.

**Tips:** "Leave a voice mail or e-mail regarding your book or idea. We will get back to you and if interested, will tell you how to send the work to us. Please visit our website to get an understanding of what we are looking for. Our books are not mass-market, so nobody is going to make a lot of money. However, we do offer the chance of publication and some income from the product. As such, new or unpublished writers are most welcome."

---

**ALWAYS SUBMIT** unsolicited manuscripts or queries with a self-addressed, stamped envelope (SASE) within your country or a self-addressed envelope with International Reply Coupons (IRC) purchased from the post office for other countries.

**SNOWAPPLE PRESS**, Box 66024, Heritage Postal Outlet, Edmonton, Alberta T6J 6T4 Canada. **Acquisitions**: Vanna Tessier, editor. Publishes hardcover originals, trade paperback originals and reprints, mass market paperback originals and reprints. **Publishes 5-6 titles/year. Receives 300 queries/year. 50% of books from first-time authors; 100% from unagented writers. Pays 10-50% royalty on retail price or makes outright purchase of $100 or pays in copies. Offers $100-200 advance.** Publishes book 2 years after acceptance. Accepts simultaneous submissions. Reports in 1 month on queries, 3 months on proposals and mss.

　○━ "We focus on topics that are interesting, unusual and controversial."

**Fiction:** Adventure, ethnic, experimental, fantasy, feminist, historical, literary, mainstream/contemporary, mystery, picture books, short story collections, young adult. Query with SASE.

**Poetry:** Query with SASE or SAE and IRC.

**Recent Title(s):** *The Last Waltz of Chopin* (translation), by Gilberto Finzi (fiction); *Moodseeds*, by Vanna Tessier (poetry).

**Tips:** "We are a small press that will publish original, interesting and entertaining fiction and poetry."

**SOUND AND VISION PUBLISHING LIMITED**, 359 Riverdale Ave., Toronto, Ontario M4J 1A4 Canada. (416)465-2828. Fax: (416)465-0755. E-mail: musicbooks@soundandvision.com. Website: http://www.soundandvision.com. **Acquisitions:** Geoff Savage. Publishes hardcover trade paperback originals. **Publishes 2-4 titles/year. Receives 25 queries/year. 85% of books from first-time authors; 100% from unagented writers. Pays royalty on wholesale price. Offers $500-2,000 advance.** Reports in 1 month.

　○━ Sound And Vision specializes in books on music with a humorous slant.

**Nonfiction:** Music/humor subjects. Query with SASE.

**Recent Title(s):** *The Composers, A Hystery of Music*, by Kevin Reeves (music, humor).

**N** **STODDART KIDS**, 34 Lesmill Rd., Toronto, Ontario M3B 2T6 Canada. (416)445-3333. Fax: (416)445-5967. E-mail: kelly.jones@ccmailgw.genpub.com. **Acquisitions:** Kathryn Cole, publisher/COO; Kelly Jones, assistant editor. Publishes hardcover and trade paperback and mass market paperback originals. **Publishes 30 titles/year. Receives 450 queries/year. 20% of books from first-time authors; 70% from unagented writers. Pays 6-10% royalty.** Publishes book 18 months after acceptance of ms. Reports in 1 month on queries. Book catalog for 9×12 SAE with 2 IRCs.

　○━ "Stoddart Kids publishes books for preschoolers to young adult. It offers the finest literature and illustrations from across North America and reflects the experiences, values and personalities of its multicultural population. Stoddart Kids books offer quality, cultural diversity, rich language and subject matter with award-winning art."

**Nonfiction:** Children's/juvenile. Subjects include creative nonfiction, history, multicultural, nature/environment, science. Query with SASE only. Reviews artwork/photos as part of ms package. Send photocopies.

**Fiction:** Historical, juvenile, literary, multicultural, mystery, picture books, suspense, young adult. "No science fiction or fantasy." Query with SASE.

**Recent Titles:** *Ahmek*, by Patrick Watson (historical fiction).

**STODDART PUBLISHING CO., LTD.**, General Publishing Co., Ltd., 34 Lesmill Rd., Toronto, Ontario M3B 2T6 Canada. **Acquisitions:** Donald G. Bastian, managing editor. Publishes hardcover, trade paperback and mass market paperback originals and trade paperback reprints. **Publishes 100 titles/year. Receives 1,200 queries and mss/year. 10% of books from first-time authors; 50% from unagented writers. Pays 8-10% royalty on retail price.** Publishes book 1 year after acceptance of ms. Accepts simultaneous submissions. Reports in 2 months. Book catalog and ms guidelines for #10 SASE.

　○━ Stoddart publishes "important Canadian books" for a general interest audience. Currently emphasizing money/finance, sports, business. De-emphasizing coffee table book, cookbook, gardening.

**Imprint(s):** Stoddart Kids (Kathryn Cole, publisher).

**Nonfiction:** Biography, coffee table book, cookbook, gift book, how-to, humor, illustrated book, self-help. Subjects include art/architecture, business and economics, child guidance/parenting, computers and electronics, cooking/foods/nutrition, gardening, government/politics, health/medicine, history, language/literature, military/war, money/finance, nature/environment, psychology, science, sociology, sports. Submit outline, 2 sample chapters, résumé, with SASE.

**Recent Title(s):** *The Eatons*, by Rod McQueen (nonfiction); *Save Me, Joe Louis*, by M.T. Kelly (fiction).

**THOMPSON EDUCATIONAL PUBLISHING INC.**, 14 Ripley Ave., Suite 104, Toronto, Ontario M6S 3N9 Canada. (416)766-2763. Fax: (416)766-0398. E-mail: publisher@thompsonbooks.com. Website: www.thompsonbooks.com. **Acquisitions:** Keith Thompson, president. **Publishes 10 titles/year. Receives 15 queries and 10 mss/year. 80% of books from first-time authors; 100% from unagented writers. Pays 10% royalty on net price.** Publishes book 1 year after acceptance. Reports in 1 month. Book catalog free.

　○━ Thompson Educational specializes in high-quality educational texts in the social sciences and humanities.

**Nonfiction:** Textbook. Subjects include business and economics, education, government/politics, sociology, women's issues/studies. Submit outline and 1 sample chapter and résumé.

**Recent Title(s):** *Biomedical Ethics: Cases and Concepts for Health Care Professionals*, by Saul Ross and David Malloy.

**TRILOBYTE PRESS**, 1486 Willowdown Rd., Oakville, Ontario L6L 1X3 Canada. (905)847-7366. Fax: (905)847-3258. E-mail: admin@successatschool.com. Website: http://www.successatschool.com. Publisher: Danton H. O'Day,

Ph.D. Publishes trade paperback originals. **Publishes 3-4 titles/year. Receives 50 queries and 20 mss/year. 50% of books from first-time authors; 100% from unagented writers. Pays 10% royalty on wholesale price. No advance.** Publishes book 8 months after acceptance of ms. Accepts simultaneous submissions. Reports in 1 month on queries, 2 months on proposals, 3 months on mss. Book catalog and ms guidelines are available on website.

**Nonfiction:** How-to, reference, self-help, textbook. Subjects include education, health/medicine, science. "We are continually looking for guides to help students succeed in school and in their careers." Query with proposal package, including outline, 2 sample chapters, qualifications of author and SASE. Reviews artwork/photos as part of ms package. Send photocopies.

**Recent Title(s):** *Write on Track—The Teaching Kit*, by Philip Dimitroff.

**Tips:** Audience is "people from high school through college age who want to do their best in school. Think about your submission—why us and why is your book worth publishing? Who will read it and why?"

**TURNSTONE PRESS**, 607-100 Arthur St., Winnipeg, Manitoba R3B 1H3 Canada. (204)947-1555. Fax: (204)942-1555. E-mail: editor@turnstonepress.mb.ca. Website: http://www.turnstonepress.com. **Acquisitions:** Manuela Dias, managing editor. Estab. 1971. Publishes trade paperback originals. **Publishes 10-12 titles/year. Receives 1,000 mss/year. 25% of books from first-time authors; 75% from unagented writers. Pays 10% royalty on retail price. Offers $100-500 advance.** Publishes book 1 year after acceptance of ms. Reports in 4 months. Book catalog free with SASE. Publishes Canadians and permanent residents only.

O— "Turnstone Press is a literary press that publishes Canadian writers with an emphasis on writers from, and writing on, the Canadian west. We are interested in publishing experimental/literary works that mainstream publishers may not be willing to work with." Currently emphasizing nonfiction-travel, memoir, eclectic novels. De-emphasizing formula or mainstream work.

**Imprint(s):** Ravenstone (literary genre fiction).

**Nonfiction:** Turnstone Press would like to see more nonfiction books, particularly travel, nature, memoir, women's writing. Query with SASE.

**Fiction:** Adventure, ethnic, experimental, feminist, gothic, humor, literary, mainstream/contemporary, mystery, short story collections, women's. Would like to see more novels. Query with SASE (Canadian postage) first.

**Poetry:** Submit complete ms.

**Recent Title(s):** *Island of the Human Heart: A Women's Travel Odyssey*, by Laurie Gough (nonfiction); *The Drum King*, by Richelle Kosar (fiction); *Elizabeth Went West*, by Jan Horner (poetry).

**Tips:** "Writers are encouraged to view our list and check if submissions are appropriate. Would like to see more women's writing, travel, memoir, life-writing as well as eclectic novels. Would like to see 'non-formula' genre writing, especially *literary* mystery, gothic and noir for our new imprint."

**THE UNITED CHURCH PUBLISHING HOUSE (UCPH)**, 3250 Bloor St. W., 4th Floor, Etobicoke, Ontario M8X 2Y4 Canada. (416)231-5931. Fax: (416)232-6004. E-mail: aturner@uccan.org. Website: http://www.uccan.org/ucph. **Acquisitions:** Ann Turner. Publishes trade paperback originals from Canadian authors only. **Publishes 13 titles/year. Receives 500 queries and 200 mss/year. 90% of books from first-time authors; 99% from unagented writers. Pays 10% royalty on retail price. Offers $500-2,000 advance.** Publishes book 1 year after acceptance. Reports in 1 month on queries, 6 months on proposals, 1 year on mss. Proposal guidelines free with SASE.

O— "We are committed to publishing books and resources that help people to engage in Christian ministry. We are further committed to engaging readers, regardless of denomination or faith, in consideration of the spiritual aspects of their lives."

**Nonfiction:** Subjects relate to United Church of Canada interests only, in the following areas: ethnic, gay/lesbian, history, multicultural, music/dance, philosophy, psychology, religion, sociology, women's issues/studies, theology and biblical studies. Query first. *No unsolicited mss.* Reviews artwork/photos as part of the ms package. Send photocopies.

**Recent Title(s):** *Circle of Grace: Worship and Prayer in the Everyday*, by Keri K. Wehlander.

**Tips:** "Along with reflections or new insights, present ideas of how this might be applied in church or community life."

**THE UNIVERSITY OF ALBERTA PRESS**, 141 Athabasca Hall, Edmonton, Alberta T6G 2E8 Canada. (780)492-3662. Fax: (780)492-0719. E-mail: uap@gpu.srv.ualberta.ca. Website: http://www.ualberta.ca/~uap. **Acquisitions:** Glenn Rollans, director. Estab. 1969. Publishes hardcover and trade paperback originals and trade paperback reprints. **Publishes 18-25 titles/year. Receives 400 submissions/year. 60% of books from first-time authors; majority from unagented writers. Pays 10% royalty on net price.** Publishes book within 1 year after acceptance. Reports in 3 months. Book catalog and ms guidelines free.

O— The University of Alberta publishes books on the Canadian West, the North, multicultural studies, health sciences, the environment, earth sciences, native studies, Canadian history, natural science and Canadian prairie literature." Currently emphasizing Canadian prairie literature.

**Nonfiction:** "Our interests include the Canadian West, the North, multicultural studies, health science and native studies." Submit table of contents, 1-2 chapters, sample illustrations and cv.

**Recent Title(s):** *Shredding the Public Interest*, by Kevin Taft (nonfiction); *What the Crow Said*, by Robert Kroetsch (fiction); *Apostrophes II: Through You I*, by E.D. Blodgett (poetry).

**Tips:** "Since 1969, the University of Alberta Press has earned recognition and awards from the Association of American University Presses, the Alcuin Society, the Book Publishers Association of Alberta and the Bibliographical Society of

Canada, among others. Now we're growing—in the audiences we reach, the numbers of titles we publish, and our energy for new challenges. But we're still small enough to listen carefully, to work closely with our authors, to explore possibilities. Our list is strong in Canadian, western and northern topics, but it ranges widely."

**UNIVERSITY OF OTTAWA PRESS**, 542 King Edward, Ottawa, Ontario K1N 6N5 Canada. (613)562-5246. Fax: (613)562-5247. E-mail: press@uottawa.ca. Website: http://www.uopress.uottawa.ca. **Acquisitions:** Vicki Bennett, editor-in-chief; Professor Jean Delisle, director translation collection (translation, history of translation, teaching translation); Chad Gaffield, Guy Lecklaire, directors Institute Canadian Studies (Canadian studies); Gilles Paquet, director collection (governance). Estab. 1936. **Publishes 22 titles/year; 10 titles/year in English. Receives 250 submissions/year. 20% of books from first-time authors; 95% from unagented writers. Determines nonauthor subsidy by preliminary budget. Pays 5-10% royalty on net price.** Publishes book 6 months after acceptance. Reports in 1 month on queries, 6 months on mss. Book catalog and author's guide free.

    O— The University Press publishes books for the scholarly and educated general audiences. They were "the first *officially* bilingual publishing house in Canada. Our goal is to help the publication of cutting edge research—books written to be useful to active researchers but accessible to an interested public." Currently emphasizing French in North America, language rights, social justice, translation, Canadian studies. De-emphasizing medieval studies, criminology.

**Nonfiction:** Reference, textbook, scholarly. Subjects include criminology, education, Canadian government/politics, Canadian history, language/literature, nature/environment, philosophy, religion, sociology, translation, women's issues/studies. Submit outline/synopsis, sample chapters and cv.

**Recent Title(s):** *The Fallacy of Race & the Shoah*, by Naomi Kramer.

**Tips:** *No unrevised theses!* "Envision audience of academic specialists and (for some books) educated public."

**UPNEY EDITIONS**, 19 Appalachian Crescent, Kitchener, Ontario N2E 1A3 Canada. **Acquisitions**: Gary Brannon, publisher. Publishes trade paperback originals. **Publishes 2-4 titles/year. Receives 200 queries and 100 mss/year. 33% of books from first-time authors; 100% from unagented writers. Pays 10% royalty on wholesale price.** Publishes book 9 months after acceptance. Reports in 1 month. Book catalog for #10 SASE (Canadian).

    O— Currently emphasizing foreign travel and lifestyle, also retirement topics. De-emphasizing nature/environment.

**Nonfiction:** Biography, reference. Subjects include Americana, art/architecture, history (with Canada/USA connections or Canadian history), language/literature, military/war, retirement, travel. "Remember that we are a Canadian small press, and our readers are mostly Canadians! We are specifically interested in popular history with cross-border U.S. Canada connection; also, popular travel literature (particularly Europe), but it must be witty and critically honest. No travel guides, cycling, hiking or driving tours! We prefer words to paint pictures rather than photographs, but line art will be considered. Queries or submissions that dictate publishing terms turn us right off. So do submissions with no SASE or submissions with return U.S.postage stamps. Enclose sufficient IRCs or we cannot return material." Length: 50,000 words maximum. Query with outline, 2 sample chapters and SASE for Canada. "We prefer to see manuscripts well thought out chapter by chapter, not just a first chapter and a vague idea of the rest." Reviews artwork/photos as part of ms package. Send photocopies.

**Recent Title(s):** *Villages of the Grand*, by Robert Higgins.

**Tips:** "We will consider any nonfiction topic with the exception of religion, politics and finance. City/regional/destination specific travel material expertly illustrated with pen and ink sketches will catch our attention. Although our titles are directed to a general audience, our sales and marketing are focused on libraries (public, high school, college) 70% and 30% on bookstores. We are dismayed by the 'pushy' attitude of some submissions. We will not even look at 'finished package, ready-to-print' submissions, which seem to be growing in number. The authors of these instant books clearly need a printer and/or investor and not a publisher. Electronic, preformatted submissions on disk are welcome—we are a Mac, QuarkXPress environment."

**VANWELL PUBLISHING LIMITED**, 1 Northrup Crescent, P.O. Box 2131, St. Catharines, Ontario L2M 6P5 Canada. (905)937-3100. Fax: (905)937-1760. **Acquisitions:** Angela Dobler, general editor; Simon Kooter, editor (military). Estab. 1983. Publishes trade originals and reprints. **Publishes 5-7 titles/year. Receives 100 submissions/year. Publishes Canadian authors only. 85% of books from first-time authors; 100% from unagented writers. Pays 8-15% royalty on wholesale price. Offers $200 average advance.** Publishes book 1 year after acceptance of ms. Reports in 3 months on queries. Book catalog free.

    O— "Vanwell is considered Canada's leading naval heritage publisher. We also publish military aviation, biography, WWII and WWI histories. Recently publishing children's fiction and nonfiction, but not picture books. We are seeing an increased demand for biographical nonfiction for ages 10-14."

**Nonfiction:** All military/history nature. Query with SASE. Reviews artwork/photos as part of ms package.

**Recent Title(s):** *A Crown of Life: the World of John McCrae*, by Dianne Graves (biography); *C-Growl: The Daring Little Airplane* (fiction).

**Tips:** "The writer has the best chance of selling a manuscript to our firm which is in keeping with our publishing program, well written and organized. Our audience: older male, history buff, war veteran; regional tourist; students. *Canadian* only military/aviation, naval, military/history and children's nonfiction have the best chance with us."

**WALL & EMERSON, INC.**, 6 O'Connor Dr., Toronto, Ontario M4K 2K1 Canada. (416)467-8685. Fax: (416)696-2460. E-mail: wall@wallbooks.com. Website: http://www.wallbooks.com. **Acquisitions:** Byron E. Wall, president (history of science, mathematics); Martha Wall, vice president. Estab. 1987. Publishes hardcover and trade paperback originals and reprints. **Publishes 3 titles/year. 50% of books from first-time authors; 100% from unagented writers. Pays royalty of 8-15% on wholesale price.** Publishes book 2 years after acceptance. Accepts simultaneous submissions. Reports in 3 months.

**O→** "We are most interested in textbooks for college courses that meet well-defined needs and are targeted to their audiences." Currently emphasizing adult education, engineering. De-emphasizing social work.

**Nonfiction:** Reference, textbook. Subjects include adult education, health/medicine, philosophy, science, mathematics. "We are looking for any undergraduate college text that meets the needs of a well-defined course in colleges in the U.S. and Canada." Submit outline and sample chapters.

**Recent Title(s):** *Introduction to Industrial Ergonomics,* by T.M. Fraser.

**Tips:** "Our audience consists of college undergraduate students and college libraries. Our ideal writer is a college professor writing a text for a course he or she teaches regularly. If I were a writer trying to market a book today, I would identify the audience for the book and write directly to the audience throughout the book. I would then approach a publisher that publishes books specifically for that audience."

**WHITECAP BOOKS LTD.,** 351 Lynn Ave., North Vancouver, British Columbia V7J 2C4 Canada. (604)980-9852. Fax: (604)980-8197. E-mail: bkwiz@pinc.com. Website: http://www.whitecap.ca. **Acquisitions:** Robin Rivers, editorial director. Whitecap Books publishes a wide range of nonfiction with a Canadian and international focus. Publishes hardcover and trade paperback originals. **Publishes 24 titles/year. Receives 150 queries and 300 mss/year. 20% of books from first-time authors; 90% from unagented writers. Royalty and advance negotiated for each project.** Publishes book 18 months after acceptance. Accepts simultaneous submissions. Reports in 2 months on proposals.

**Nonfiction:** Coffee table book, cookbook, children's/juvenile. Subjects include animals, gardening, history, nature/environment, recreation, regional, travel. "We require an annotated outline. Writers should take the time to research our list. This is especially important for children's writers." Submit outline, 1 sample chapter, table of contents and SASE with international postal voucher for submission from the U.S. Send photocopies, not original material.

**Recent Title(s):** *100 Best Plants,* by Steve Whysall.

**Tips:** "We want well-written, well-researched material that presents a fresh approach to a particular topic."

**[N] WUERZ PUBLISHING, LTD.,** 895 McMillan Ave., Winnipeg, Manitoba R3M 0T2 Canada. (204)453-7429. **Acquisitions:** Steve Wuerz. Publishes trade paperback originals and reprints. **Publishes 12 titles/year. Receives 25 queries and 12 mss/year. 90% of books from first-time authors; 100% from unagented writers. Pays 10-15% royalty on wholesale price.** Publishes book 1-2 years after acceptance of ms. Reports in 1 month on queries and proposals, 2 months on mss.

**O→** Publishes books on science and native languages.

**Nonfiction:** Multimedia, textbook. Subjects include language/literatuare, nature/environment, science. "Do not ask for our marketing plans before we've seen your manuscript." Query or submit outline with 3 sample chapters and proposal package. Reviews artwork/photos as part of ms package. Send photocopies.

**Recent Nonfiction Title(s):** *Environmental Chemistry,* by Ondrus (college textbook); *General Relativity & Cosmology,* by Chow (college text); *Cree-English, English-Cree* (bilingual dictionary).

**[N] YORK PRESS LTD.,** 152 Boardwalk Dr., Toronto, Ontario M4L 3X4 Canada. E-mail: yorkpress@sympatico.ca. Website: http://www3.sympatico.ca/yorkpress. **Acquisitions:** Dr. S. Elkhadem, general manager/editor. Estab. 1975. Publishes trade paperback originals. **Publishes 10 titles/year. Receives 50 submissions/year. 10% of books from first-time authors; 100% from unagented writers. Pays 10-20% royalty on wholesale price.** Publishes book 6 months after acceptance. Reports in 2 weeks. *Writer's Market* recommends allowing 2 months for reply.

**O→** "We publish scholarly books and creative writing of an experimental nature."

**Nonfiction and Fiction:** Reference, textbook, scholarly. Especially needs literary criticism, comparative literature and linguistics and fiction of an experimental nature by well-established writers. Query.

**Recent Title(s):** *Herman Melville: Romantic & Prophet,* by C.S. Durer (scholarly literary criticism); *The Moonhare,* by Kirk Hampton (experimental novel).

**Tips:** "If I were a writer trying to market a book today, I would spend a considerable amount of time examining the needs of a publisher *before* sending my manuscript to him. The writer must adhere to our style manual and follow our guidelines exactly."

---

**MARKETS THAT WERE** listed in the 1999 edition of *Writer's Market* but do not appear this year are listed in the General Index with a notation explaining why they were omitted.

# Small Presses

"Small press" is a relative term. Compared to the dozen or so conglomerates, the rest of the book publishing world may seem to be comprised of small presses. A number of the publishers listed in the Book Publishers section consider themselves small presses and cultivate the image. For our classification, small presses are those that publish three or fewer books per year.

The publishing opportunities are slightly more limited with the companies listed here than with those in the Book Publishers section. Not only are they publishing fewer books, but small presses are usually not able to market their books as effectively as larger publishers. Their print runs and royalty arrangements are usually smaller. It boils down to money, what a publisher can afford, and in that area, small presses simply can't compete with conglomerates.

However, realistic small press publishers don't try to compete with Penguin Putnam or Random House. They realize everything about their efforts operates on a smaller scale. Most small press publishers get into book publishing for the love of it, not solely for the profit. Of course, every publisher, small or large, wants successful books. But small press publishers often measure success in different ways.

Many writers actually prefer to work with small presses. Since small publishing houses are usually based on the publisher's commitment to the subject matter, and since they necessarily work with far fewer authors than the conglomerates, small press authors and their books usually receive more personal attention than the larger publishers can afford to give them. Promotional dollars at the big houses tend to be siphoned toward a few books each season that they have decided are likely to succeed, leaving hundreds of "midlist" books underpromoted, and, more likely than not, destined for failure. Since small presses only commit to a very small number of books every year, they are vitally interested in the promotion and distribution of each one.

Just because they publish three or fewer titles per year does not mean small press editors have the time to look at complete manuscripts on spec. In fact, the editors with smaller staffs often have even less time for submissions. The procedure for contacting a small press with your book idea is exactly the same as it is for a larger publisher. Send a one-page query with SASE first. If the press is interested in your proposal, be ready to send an outline or synopsis, and/or a sample chapter or two. Be patient with their reporting times; small presses can be slower to respond than larger companies. You might consider simultaneous queries, as long as you note this, to compensate for the waiting game.

For more information on small presses, see *Novel & Short Story Writer's Market* and *Poet's Market* (Writer's Digest Books), and *Small Press Review* and *The International Directory of Little Magazines and Small Presses* (Dustbooks).

**For a list of publishers according to their subjects of interest, see the nonfiction and fiction sections of the Book Publishers Subject Index. Information on book publishers and producers listed in the previous edition of *Writer's Market* but not included in this edition can be found in the General Index.**

**ACADA BOOKS**, 1850 Union St., Suite 1236, San Francisco CA 94123. President: Brian Romer. Publishes college textbooks. **Publishes 3 titles/year. Receives 50 queries/year; 20 mss/year. 33% of books from first-time authors; 100% from unagented writers. Royalty varies.** Publishes book 4 months after acceptance of ms. Accepts simultaneous submissions. Reports in 2 months on proposals. Manuscript guidelines free.
**Nonfiction:** Textbook. Subjects include business, criminal justice, communications, politics, history, nature/environment, psychology, sociology.

**ACCENT BOOKS,** (formerly Accent on Living), Cheever Publishing, Inc., P.O. Box 700, Bloomington IL 61702. (309)378-2961. Fax: (309)378-4420. **Acquisitions:** Betty Garee, editor. **Publishes 2 titles/year. Receives 50 queries and 150 mss/year. 90% of books from first-time authors; 90% from unagented writers. Makes outright purchase.** Publishes book 3 months after acceptance of ms. Accepts simultaneous submissions. Reports on queries in 1 month. Book catalog for 8×10 SAE with 2 first-class stamps. Manuscript guidelines for #10 SASE.

☞ Accent Books publishes books pertaining to the physically disabled who are trying to live an independent life.
**Nonfiction:** How-to, humor, self-help. Subjects include business/economics, child guidance/parenting, cooking/foods/ nutrition, education, gardening, money/finance, recreation, religion, travel. All pertaining to physically disabled. Query. Reviews artwork/photos as part of ms package. Send snapshots or slides. Recent title: *Good Grief,* by Dee Bissell/ Michael Cruerer.

**ACME PRESS,** P.O. Box 1702, Westminster MD 21158-1702. (410)848-7577. Managing Editor: Ms. E.G. Johnston. Estab. 1991. Publishes hardcover and trade paperback originals. **Publishes 1-2 titles/year. Pays 50% of profits. Offers small advance.** Reports in 2 months on mss.
**Fiction:** Humor. "We accept submissions on any subject as long as the material is humorous; prefer full-length novels. No cartoons or art (text only). No pornography, poetry, short stories or children's material." Submit outline, first 50-75 pages and SASE. Recent title: *Hearts of Gold,* by James Magorian (comic mystery).
**Tips:** "We are always looking for the great comic novel."

**AFRIMAX, Inc.,** 703 Shannon Lane, Kirksville MO 63501. (660)665-0757. President: Emmanuel Nnadozie. Publishes trade paperback originals. **Publishes 4 titles/year. Pays 8% royalty. No advance.** Reports in 5 months on queries, 1 month on proposals, 3 months on mss. Manuscript guidelines free on request.
**Nonfiction:** How-to and textbook. Subjects include business and economics, ethnic, money/finance, regional, travel. "International business & African business related interests. They do not carefully consider the audience and present the materials in the most appropriate way." Query. Recent title: *African Culture & American Business in Africa,* by Emmanuel Nnadozie (business/how-to).
**Tips:** Audience includes business managers, business educators, students.

**[N] AHSAHTA PRESS,** Boise State University, Dept. of English, 1910 University Dr., Boise ID 83725-1525. (208)426-1999. Fax: (208)426-4373. E-mail: ttrusky@boisestate.edu. Co-Editor: Tom Trusky. Estab. 1974. Publishes Western American poetry in trade paperback. Reads SASE samplers annually, January-March. Not reading until 2000.

**ALETHEIA PUBLICATIONS,** 46 Bell Hollow Rd., Putnam Valley NY 10579. Publisher: Carolyn Smith. Imprint: Social Change Press. Publishes trade paperback originals and reprints. **Publishes 3 titles/year. Imprint publishes 2 titles/year. Receives 10 queries and 3 mss/year. 90% of books from first-time authors; 100% from unagented writers. Pays 10% royalty on retail price. No advance.** Publishes book 8 months after acceptance of ms. Accepts simultaneous submissions. Reports in 1 month on queries, 2 months on proposals, 3 months on mss.

☞ "We specialize in books for and about Americans who have lived or are living overseas in the Foreign Service, the military and other contexts. We also publish books about freelance editing and writing."
**Nonfiction:** Subjects include sociology, editing. Submit proposal package, including rationale, sample chapters, table of contents and SASE. Recent title: *The Accidental Diplomat: Dilemmas of the Trailing Spouse,* by Katherine L. Hughes.
**Tips:** Audience is Americans who have lived overseas and freelance editors and writers. Audience for Social Change Press is sociologists interested in urban problems and culture.

**AMERICAN CATHOLIC PRESS,** 16565 S. State St., South Holland IL 60473. (312)331-5845. Editorial Director: Rev. Michael Gilligan, Ph.D. Estab. 1967. Publishes hardcover originals and hardcover and paperback reprints. "Most of our sales are by direct mail, although we do work through retail outlets." **Publishes 4 titles/year. Makes outright purchase of $25-100. No advance.**
**Nonfiction:** "We publish books on the Roman Catholic liturgy—for the most part, books on religious music and educational books and pamphlets. We also publish religious songs for church use, including Psalms, as well as choral and instrumental arrangements. We are interested in new music, meant for use in church services. Books, or even pamphlets, on the Roman Catholic Mass are especially welcome. We have no interest in secular topics and are not interested in religious poetry of any kind."

**AMIGADGET PUBLISHING COMPANY,** P.O. Box 1696, Lexington SC 29071. (803)957-1106. Fax: (803)957-7495. E-mail: jaygross@calweb.com. Website: http://www.calweb.com/~jaygross. Editor-in-Chief: Jay Gross. Publishes hardcover and trade paperback originals. **Publishes 2 titles/year. Pays royalty or makes outright purchase. Advance negotiable.** Reports in 6 months.
**Nonfiction:** "Niche markets are our specialty. No books on Windows." Query only with SASE. No mss. Recent title: *How to Start Your Own Underground Newspaper,* by J. Gross (how-to).

**[N] ANHINGA PRESS,** P.O. Box 10595, Tallahassee FL 32302. (850)521-9920. Fax: (850)442-6323. E-mail: info@a nhinga.org. Website: http://www.anhinga.org. Acquisitions Editors: Rick Campbell, Joann Gardner, Van Brock. Publishes hardcover and trade paperback originals. **Publishes 3-4 titles/year. Pays 10% royalty on retail price and offers Anhinga prize of $2,000. No advance.** Reports in 2 months.

**Poetry:** We like good poetry. Query or submit 10 sample poems. Recent title: *The Secret History of Water*, by Silvia Curbelo.

**ARIADNE PRESS**, 4817 Tallahassee Ave., Rockville MD 20853-3144. (301)949-2514. President: Carol Hoover. Estab. 1976. "Our purpose is to promote the publication of emerging fiction writers." Publishes hardcover and trade paperback originals. **Publishes 1 book/year. Pays 10% royalty on retail price. No advance.** Reports in 1 month on queries, 3 months on mss.
- This publisher is currently interested in novels by emerging writers and offers an annual novel-writing contest.
**Fiction:** Adventure, feminist, historical, humor, literary, mainstream/contemporary. "We look for exciting and believable plots, strong themes, and non-stereotypical characters who develop in fascinating and often unpredictable directions." Query with 1-2 page plot summary, bio and SASE. "Send brief plot summary. Please do not send sample chapters unless requested." Recent title: *Family Blood*, by Mary Hazzard.

**AUTO BOOK PRESS**, P.O. Bin 711, San Marcos CA 92079-0711. (760)744-3582. Editorial Director: William Carroll. Estab. 1955. Publishes hardcover and paperback originals. **Publishes 2-4 titles/year. Pays negotiated royalty on wholesale price. Advance varies.** Reports in 1 month on queries.
**Nonfiction:** Automotive material only: technical or definitive how-to. Query with SASE. Recent title: *Two Wheels to Panama*.

**BALCONY PRESS**, 512 E. Wilson, Suite 306, Glendale CA 91206. (818)956-5313. E-mail: ann@balconypress.com. Publisher: Ann Gray. Publishes hardcover and trade paperback originals. **Publishes 4-5 titles/year. Pays 10% royalty on wholesale price. No advance.** Reports in 1 month on queries and proposals; 3 months on mss. Book catalog free.
**Nonfiction:** Biography, coffee table books and illustrated books. Subjects include art/architecture, ethnic, gardening, history (relative to design, art and architecture) and regional. "We are interested in the human side of design as opposed to technical or how-to. We like to think our books will be interesting to the general public who might not otherwise select an architecture or design book." Query by telephone or letter. Submit outline and 2 sample chapters with introduction if applicable. Recent title: *Artful Players: Artistic Life in Early San Francisco*, by Birgitta Hjalmavson.
**Tips:** Audience consists of architects, designers and the general public who enjoy those fields. "Our books typically cover California subjects but that is not a restriction. It's always nice when an author has strong ideas about how the book can be effectively marketed. We are not afraid of small niches if a good sales plan can be devised."

**BANDANNA BOOKS**, 319-B Anacapa St., Santa Barbara CA 93101. (805)564-3559. Fax: (805)564-3278. E-mail: bandana@bandanabooks.com.25. Website: http://www.bandannabooks.com. Publisher: Sasha Newborn. Editor: Joan Blake. Publishes trade paperback originals and reprints. **Publishes 3 titles/year. Receives 300 queries and 100 mss/year. 25% of books from first-time authors; 100% from unagented writers. Pays negotiable royalty on net receipts. Offers up to $1,000 advance.** Accepts simultaneous submissions. Reports in 4 months on proposals.
**Nonfiction:** Textbooks for college students, some illustrated. Subjects include education, history, literature, language, translations. "Bandanna Books seeks to humanize the classics, history, language in non-sexist, modernized translations, using direct and plain language." Submit query letter, table of contents and first chapter. Reviews artwork/photos as part of ms package. Send photocopies. Recent title: *Don't Panic: The Procrastinator's Guide to Writing an Effective Term Paper*, by Steven Posusta.
**Tips:** "Our readers have a liberal arts orientation. Inventive, professional, well-thought-out presentations, please. Always include a SASE for reply."

**BLACK HERON PRESS**, P.O. Box 95676, Seattle WA 98145. Publisher: Jerry Gold. Publishes hardcover and trade paperback originals. **Publishes 4 titles/year. Pays 8-9% royalty on retail price.** Reports in 3 months on queries, 6 months on proposals and mss.
**Profile:** "Black Heron Press publishes literary fiction—lately we've tended toward surrealism/science fiction (not fantasy) and social fiction; writers should look at some of our titles."
**Fiction:** High quality, innovative fiction. Query with cover letter, 3 sample chapters and SASE. Recent title: *Story Story Story*, by Jim Schumock.
**Tips:** "Readers should look at some of our books before submitting—they are easily available. Most submissions we see are competently done but have been sent to the wrong press. We do not publish self-help books or romances."

**BLISS PUBLISHING CO.**, P.O. Box 920, Marlborough MA 01752. (508)779-2827. Publisher: Stephen H. Clouter. Publishes hardcover and trade paperback originals. **Publishes 2-4 titles/year. Pays 10-15% royalty on wholesale price. No advance.** Reports in 2 months.
**Nonfiction:** Biography, illustrated book, reference, textbook. Subjects include government/politics, history, music/dance, nature/environment, recreation, regional. Submit proposal package, including outline, table of contents, 3 sample chapters, brief author biography, table of contents, SASE. Recent title: *Ninnuock, The Algonkian People of New England*, by Steven F. Johnson.

**BLUE SKY MARKETING, INC.**, P.O. Box 21583, St. Paul MN 55121. (612)456-5602. President: Vic Spadaccini. Publishes hardcover and trade paperback originals. **Publishes 3 titles/year. Pays royalty on wholesale price.** Reports in 3 months. Manuscript guidelines for 6×9 SAE with 4 first-class stamps.

**Nonfiction:** Gift book, how-to. Subjects include humor, regional, self-help, house and home. "Ideas must be unique. If it's been done, we're not interested!" Submit proposal package, including outline, 1 sample chapter, author bio, intended market, analysis comparison to competing books with SASE. Recent title: *31 Days to Ruin Your Relationship*, by Tricia Seymour and Rusty Barrier.

**Tips:** "Our books are primarily 'giftbooks,' sold to women in specialty stores, gift shops and bookstores."

**[N] BOOKHAVEN PRESS, LLC**, P.O. Box 1243, 401 Amherst Ave., Moon Township PA 15108. (412)262-5578. Orders: (800)782-7424. Fax: (412)262-5147. Website: http://www.members@aol.com/bookhaven. Publisher: Dennis Damp. **Acquisitions:** Victor Richards, editorial manager. Publishes trade paperback originals. **Publishes 2 titles/year. 100% of books from first-time authors; 100% from unagented writers. Pays 7-12% royalty on wholesale price. No advance.** Does not return submissions; sends form letter for rejection, destroys originals. Reports in 3 months on queries, 1 month on proposals, 2 months on mss. Book catalog free.

**Nonfiction:** How-to, reference. Subjects include business/economics, education, money/finance and careers. "We look for well-developed manuscripts from computer literate writers. All manuscripts must be available in IBM computer format (Word Perfect preferred)." Submit outline and 2 sample chapters. Recent title: *Health Care Job Explosion! High Growth Health Care Careers & Job Locator*, by Dennis Damp.

**BRIGHT RING PUBLISHING, INC.**, P.O. Box 31338, Bellingham WA 98228-3338. (360)734-1601. Fax: (360)676-1271. E-mail: maryann@brightring.com. Website: http://www.brightring.com/books. Owner: Mary Ann Kohl. Publishes trade paperback originals on creative ideas for children. **Publishes 1 title/year. Pays 3-5% royalty on net price. Offers $500 advance.** Reports in 2 months. Ms guidelines for SASE.

○➡ "We want to bring creative art ideas to children, encouraging process, not product."

**Nonfiction:** "Only books which specifically fit our format will be considered: art or creative activities with 1) materials 2) procedure 3) variations/extensions. One idea per page, about 150 ideas total. No crafts, fiction, picture books, poetry." Query with 1-2 sample chapters or submit proposal package, including complete book, with SASE. *Writer's Market* recommends sending a query with SASE first. Recent title: *Great Artists: Hands-On Art for Children in the Styles of the Great Masters.*

**Tips:** "Send for guidelines first. Check out books at the library or bookstore to see what style the publisher likes. Submit only ideas that specifically relate to the company's list."

**[N] BULL PUBLISHING CO.**, 110 Gilbert, Menlo Park CA 94025-2833. (650)332-2855. Fax: (650)327-3300. **Acquisitions:** James Bull, publisher (self-care, nutrition, women's health, weight control); Lansing Hayes, publisher (mental health). Estab. 1974. Publishes hardcover and trade paperback originals. **Publishes 2-4 titles/year. Pays 10-16% royalty on wholesale price (net to publisher).** Publishes ms an average of 6 months after acceptance. Book catalog free.

○➡ Bull Publishing publishes health and nutrition books for the public with an emphasis on self-care, women's health, weight control and mental health.

**Nonfiction:** How-to, self-help. Subjects include self-care, nutrition, fitness, child health and nutrition, health education, mental health. "We look for books that fit our area of strength: responsible books on health that fill a substantial public need, and that we can market primarily through professionals." Submit outline and sample chapters. Reviews artwork/photos as part of ms package. Recent title: *Exercise Beats Arthritis*, by Sayce and Fraser.

**CADMUS EDITIONS**, P.O. Box 126, Tiburon CA 94920. Director: Jeffrey Miller. Publishes hardcover and trade paperback originals. **Publishes 3-4 titles/year. Pays negotiated royalty. No advance.** Reports in 1 month.

**Fiction:** Literary fiction. "We seek only truly distinguished work." Query with SASE. Recent title: *The Tangier Diaries, 1962-1978*, by John Hopkins (nonfiction).

**Poetry:** Query with SASE. Recent title: *Wandering into the Wind*, by Sāntoka, translated by Cid Corman (Haiku poetry of last wandering itinerant monk in Japan).

**CALYX BOOKS**, P.O. Box B, Corvallis OR 97339-0539. (541)753-9384. Also publishes *Calyx, A Journal of Art & Literature by Women*. Director: Margarita Donnelly. Managing Editor: Micki Reaman. Estab. 1986 for Calyx Books; 1976 for Calyx, Inc. Publishes fine literature by women, fiction, nonfiction and poetry. **Publishes 3 titles/year. Pays 10-15% royalty on net receipts; amount of advance depends on grant support.** Reports in 1 year.

● Calyx is open to submissions from January 1-March 15, 2000.

**Nonfiction:** Outline, 3 sample chapters and SASE. Recent title: *The Violet Shyness of Their Eyes*, by Barbara Scot.

**Fiction:** Literary fiction by women. "Please do not query." Send 3 sample chapters, bio, outline, synopsis and SASE during open book ms period only. Recent title: *Switch*, by Carol Guess.

**Poetry:** "We only publish 1 poetry book a year." Submit 10 poems, table of contents, bio and SASE. Recent title: *Indian Singing*, by Gail Tremblay.

**Tips:** "Please be familiar with our publications."

**CAROUSEL PRESS**, P.O. Box 6038, Berkeley CA 94706-0038. (510)527-5849. Editor and Publisher: Carole T. Meyers. Estab. 1976. Publishes trade paperback originals and reprints. **Publishes 1-2 titles/year. Pays 10-15% royalty on wholesale price. Offers $1,000 advance.** Reports in 1 month on queries.

**Nonfiction:** Family-oriented travel and other travel books. Query with outline, 2 sample chapters and SASE. Recent title: *Dream Sleeps: Castle & Palace Hotels of Europe*, by Pamela L. Barrus (guide).

**CASSANDRA PRESS**, P.O. Box 868, San Rafael CA 94915. (415)382-8507. President: Gurudas. Estab. 1985. Publishes trade paperback originals. **Publishes 3 titles/year. Receives 200 submissions/year. 50% of books from first-time authors; 50% from unagented writers. Pays 6-8% maximum royalty on retail price. Advance rarely offered.** Publishes book 1 year after acceptance. Accepts simultaneous submissions. Reports in 3 weeks on queries, 3 months on mss. Book catalog and ms guidelines free.
**Nonfiction:** New Age, how-to, self-help. Subjects include cooking/foods/nutrition, health/medicine (holistic health), philosophy, psychology, religion (New Age), metaphysical, political tyranny. "We like to do around 3 titles a year in the general New Age, metaphysical and holistic health fields. No children's books or novels." Submit outline and sample chapters. Recent title: *Treason the New World Order*, by Gurudas (political).

**☒ CENTER FOR AFRICAN-AMERICAN STUDIES PUBLICATIONS**, University of California at Los Angeles, 160 Haines Hall, 405 Hilgard Ave., Los Angeles CA 90095-1545. (310)206-6340. Publishes hardcover and trade paperback originals. "All manuscripts should be scholarly works about the African-American experience. Authors should be able to demonstrate a thorough knowledge of the subject matter. Not interested in autobiographies, poetry or fiction." Recent title: *The Woman, the Writer and Caribbean Society*, edited by Helen Pyne-Timothy.
**Nonfiction:** Textbooks. Subjects include anthropology, art/architecture, business/economics, ethnic, government/politics, history, music/dance, psychology, scholarly, sociology, women's issues.

**CLARITY PRESS INC.**, 3277 Roswell Rd. NE, #469, Atlanta GA 30305. (404)231-0649. Fax: (404)231-3899. E-mail: clarity@islandnet.com. Website: http://www.bookmasters.com/clarity. Contact: Annette Gordon. Estab. 1984. Publishes mss on minorities, human rights in U.S., Middle East and Africa. Publishes hardcover and trade paperback originals. **Publishes 4 titles/year.** Reports in 3 months on queries only if interested.
**Nonfiction:** Human rights/minority issues. No fiction. Query with author's bio, synopsis and endorsements. Responds *only* if interested, so do *not* enclose SASE. Recent title: *The Legacy of IBO Landing: Gullah Roots of African American Culture*, by M.L. Goodwine (anthology).
**Tips:** "Check our titles on website."

**CROSSQUARTER BREEZE**, P.O. Box 8756, Santa Fe NM 87504. (505)438-9846. Owner: Therese Francis. Publishes trade paperback originals and reprints. **Publishes 3-5 titles/year. Receives 8 queries/year. 90% of books from first-time authors. Pays 8-10% royalty on wholesale or retail price.** Publishes book 6 months after acceptance of ms. Accepts simultaneous submissions. Reports in 2 months on queries. Book catalog for $1.75.
  **O─** "We emphasize personal sovereignty, self responsibility and growth with pagan or pagan-friendly emphasis for young adults and adults." Currently emphasizing new thought medicine, especially herbs. De-emphasizing preachy children's.
**Nonfiction:** Children's/juvenile, how-to, self-help. Subjects include health/medicine, nature/environment, philosophy, religion (pagan only). Query with SASE. Reviews artwork/photos as part of the ms package. Send photocopies. Recent title: *20 Herbs to Take Outdoors*, by Therese Francis.
**Tips:** "Audience is earth-conscious people looking to grow into balance of body, mind, emotion and spirit."

**☒ DOWN THERE PRESS**, Open Enterprises Cooperative, Inc., 938 Howard St., #101, San Francisco CA 94103-4114. (415)974-8985 ext. 205. Fax: (415)974-8989. E-mail: goodvibe@well.com. Website: http://www.goodvibes.com/dtp/dtp.html. Publishes trade paperback originals. **Publishes 2 titles/year. Pays 12-15% royalty on wholesale price. Offers $1,000-2,000 advance.** Publishes book 18 months after acceptance of ms. Accepts simultaneous submissions. Reports in 2 months on queries, 3 months on proposals and mss. Book catalog for #10 SASE or on website. Manuscript guidelines for #10 SASE or on website.
  **O─** Publishes books for "adults interested in learning more about their own and others' sexuality in a playful and literate way."
**Nonfiction:** Illustrated, self-help. Subjects include gay/lesbian, photography, psychology, sex, women's issues/studies. Query with SASE or submit proposal package, including 1-2 sample chapters and synopsized toc and SASE. Recent title: *The Good Vibrations Guide: Adult Videos* (reference).
**Fiction:** Erotica, short story collections (erotic). Submit proposal package including synopsis, 1-2 sample chapters and SASE or completed ms for short stories. Recent title: *Sex Toy Tales*, edited by Cathy Winks and Anne Semans (erotic short stories).
**Tips:** "Our publication program is small and focused. Read our catalog and some of our books. We are looking for a pan-sexual, sex-positive view of sex."

**DRY BONES PRESS**, P.O. Box 640345, San Francisco CA 94164. (415)252-7341. Website: http://www.drybones.com. Editor/Publisher: J. Rankin. Publishes hardcover and trade paperback originals and reprints and mass market paperback originals. **Publishes 2-4 titles/year. Pays 6-10% royalty on retail price.** Publishes book 2 years after acceptance of ms. Accepts simultaneous submissions, if so noted. Reports in 2 months.
**Nonfiction:** California Gold Rush, reference, technical. Subjects include health/medicine, history, philosophy, regional, religion, translation, nursing patient writing. Submit outline, 1-2 sample chapters and proposal package, including marketing ideas with SASE. Recent title: *Coming Home*, by Grace Elizabeth Skye (sex abuse survivor account).

**Fiction:** Historical, humor/satire, mainstream/contemporary, mystery, plays, religious, science fiction. "Looking for unique items, with solid quality. No maudlin sentimentality or failure to develop insight or characters." Submit synopsis, 1-2 sample chapters with SASE. Recent title: *Aquarius*, by Richard Epstein (satire/social commentary).

**EARTH-LOVE PUBLISHING HOUSE LTD.**, 3440 Youngfield St., Suite 353, Wheat Ridge CO 80033. (303)233-9660. Fax: (303)233-9354. Director: Laodeciae Augustine. Publishes trade paperback originals. **Publishes 1-2 books/year. Pays 6-10% royalty on wholesale price.** Reports in 1 month on queries and proposals, 3 months on mss.
**Nonfiction:** Metaphysics and minerals. Query with SASE. Recent title: *Love Is In The Earth—Kaleidoscope Pictorial Supplement*, by Melody (metaphysical reference).

**[N] EASTERN PRESS**, P.O. Box 881, Bloomington IN 47402-0881. Publisher: Don Y. Lee. Estab. 1981. Publishes hardcover originals and reprints. **Publishes 3 titles/year. Pays by arrangement with author. No advance.** Reports in 3 months.
O— "Our publications are involved with English and Asian language(s) for higher academic works." Currently emphasizing humanities and social science in East Asia.
**Nonfiction:** Academic books on Asian subjects and pedagogy on languages. Query with outline and SASE. Recent title: *Autohaiku*, by Don Y. Lee (6×9 hardcover).

**ECOPRESS**, 1029 NE Kirsten Place, Corvallis OR 97330. (541)758-7545. E-mail: ecopress@peak.org. Editor-in-Chief: Christopher Beatty. Publishes hardcover originals, trade paperback originals and reprints. **Publishes 2-4 titles/year. Pays 6-15% royalty on publisher's receipts. Offers $0-5,000 advance.** Reports in 1 month on queries and proposals, 3 months on mss. Manuscript guidelines for #10 SASE or submit electronically.
**Nonfiction:** How-to. Subjects include nature/environment, recreation (outdoor, hiking), science, sports (outdoor, fishing). "The work must have some aspect that enhances environmental awareness. Do a competitive analysis and create a marketing plan for your book or proposal." Query with SASE by electronic or regular mail. Recent title: *The Trinity Alps Companion*, by Wayne Moss.
**Tips:** "A major focus of Ecopress is outdoor guides, especially river and hiking guides. Other nonfiction will be considered. All Ecopress books must have an environmental perspective."

**[N] EDUCATIONAL SYSTEMS ASSOCIATES, INC.**, P.O. Box 96, Kearney NE 68848-0096. (308)234-6261.
**Acquisitions:** Melanie Gregory, administrative assistant (educational materials). Publishes trade paperback originals. **Publishes 4 titles/year. Receives 40 queries and 20 mss/year. 100% of books from unagented writers. Pays 10% royalty on wholesale. No advance.** Publishes book 1 year after acceptance of ms. Accepts simultaneous submissions. Reports in 1 month on queries, 3 months on mss. Book catalog and ms guidelines free.
**Nonfiction:** Textbook. Subjects include education, science. Query with SASE or submit completed ms. Recent title: *A Classroom Teacher's Practical Guide to Multicultural Education*, by Tom Continé.

**EMERALD WAVE**, Box 969, Fayetteville AR 72702. Contact: Maya Harrington. Publishes trade paperback originals. **Publishes 1-3 titles/year. Pays 7-10% royalty. No advance.** Reports in 1 month on queries, 3 months on mss.
O— "We publish thoughtful New Age books which relate to everyday life and/or the environment on this planet with enlightened attitudes. Nothing poorly written, tedious to read or too 'out there.' It's got to have style too."
**Nonfiction:** Spiritual/metaphysical New Age. Subjects include health, environment, philosophy, psychology. Submit outline and 3 sample chapters with SASE. Recent title: *Spirit at Work*, by Lois Grant (angels/healing).

**THE FAMILY ALBUM**, Rt. 1, Box 42, Glen Rock PA 17327. (717)235-2134. Fax: (717)235-8765. E-mail: ronbiblio@delphi.com. Contact: Ron Lieberman. Estab. 1969. Publishes hardcover originals and reprints and software. **Publishes 2 titles/year. Pays royalty on wholesale price.**
**Nonfiction:** "Significant works in the field of (nonfiction) bibliography. Worthy submissions in the field of Pennsylvania history, folk art and lore. We are also seeking materials relating to books, literacy, and national development. Special emphasis on Third World countries, and the role of printing in international development." No religious material or personal memoirs. Submit outline and sample chapters.

**FIESTA CITY PUBLISHERS, ASCAP**, P.O. Box 5861, Santa Barbara CA 93150. (805)681-9199. President: Frank E. Cooke. Associate Editor: John Harris (musical material). Publishes hardcover and mass market paperback originals. **Publishes 2-3 titles/year. Pays 5-20% royalty on retail price. No advance.** Reports in 1 month on queries, 2 months on proposals. Book catalog and ms guidelines for #10 SASE.
**Nonfiction:** "Seeking originality." Children's/juvenile, cookbook, how-to, humor and musical plays. "Prefers material appealing to young readers, especially related to music: composing, performing, etc." Query with outline and SASE. Recent title: *The Piano*, by Philip Gurlik, R.T.T. (technician's guide for piano owners).
**Plays:** Musical plays only. "Must be original, commercially viable, preferably short, with eye-catching titles. Must be professionaly done and believable. Avoid too much detail." Query with 1 or 2 sample chapters and SASE. Recent title: *Break Point*, by Frank Cooke a.k.a. Eddie Franck (young people's musical).
**Tips:** "Looking for material which would appeal to young adolescents in the modern society. Prefer little or no violence with positive messages. Carefully-constructed musical plays always welcome for consideration."

**FRONT ROW EXPERIENCE**, 540 Discovery Bay Blvd., Byron CA 94514-9454. Phone/fax: (510)634-5710. Contact: Frank Alexander, editor. Estab. 1974. Imprint is Kokono. Publishes trade paperback originals and reprints. **Publishes 1-2 titles/year. Pays 10% royalty on income received. No advance.** Reports in 1 month.

   **O—** Publishes books on movement education and coordination activities for pre-K to 6th grade.

**Nonfiction:** Teacher/educator edition paperback originals. "We're always focused on movement education advitities and lesson plans for pre-k to the 6th grade. Recent title: *Perceptual-Motor Lesson Plans, Level 2.*

**Tips:** "Be on target—find out what we want and only submit queries."

**GAMBLING TIMES, INC.**, 16140 Valerio St., Suite B, Van Nuys CA 91406-2916. (818)781-9355. Fax: (818)781-3125. Publisher: Stanley R. Sludikoff. Publishes hardcover and trade paperback originals. **Publishes 2-4 titles/year. Pays 4-11% royalty on retail price.** Reports in 2 months on queries, 3 months on proposals, 6 months on mss.

**Nonfiction:** How-to and reference books on gambling. Submit proposal package, including ms and SASE. *Writer's Market* recommends sending a query with SASE first. Recent title: *Book of Tells*, by Caro (poker).

**Tips:** "All of our books serve to educate the public about some aspect of gambling."

**GOOD BOOK PUBLISHING COMPANY**, P.O. Box 837, Kihei HI 96753-0837. Phone/fax: (808)874-4876. E-mail: dickb@dickb.com. Publisher: Richard G. Burns. Publishes trade paperback originals and reprints. **Publishes 4 titles/year. Pay 10% royalty. No advance.** Reports in 2 months.

**Nonfiction:** Spiritual roots of Alcoholics Anonymous. Query with SASE. Recent title: *The Golden Text of A.A.: God, A.A. & Real Spirituality.*

**[N] HardPressed PUBLISHING**, P.O. Box 27094, Jacksonville FL 32205-0094. (904)384-2856. Fax: (904)388-9185. E-mail: Hpressed@aol.com. Website: http://www.HPressed.com. **Acquisitions:** Ellyn Pearson, acquisitions editor. Publishes trade paperback originals. **Publishes 3 titles/year. Pays 20-50% royalty on wholesale price. No advance.** No simultaneous submissions. Reports back in 1 month on queries and proposals, 2 months on mss. Book catalog and ms guidelines on website.

**Nonfiction:** Gift book, humor, self-help. Child guidance/parenting (accessible, funny, user-friendly), creative nonfiction, money/finance (light-hearted, accessible, user-friendly), spirituality. Query with SASE or submit proposal package, including outline, 1 sample chapter and brief bio. Recent title: *Life's Little Recipe Book*, by Karen Wynn (cookbook parody).

**Tips:** Audience is intelligent readers who take on new projects and challenges to improve their lives. "We like humor—but not for its own sake. We're interested in books that provide genuinely helpful information—but in a light and humorous way."

**HEMINGWAY WESTERN STUDIES SERIES**, Boise State University, 1910 University Dr., Boise ID 83725. (208)426-1999. Fax: (208)426-4373. E-mail: ttrusky@boisestate.edu. Editor: Tom Trusky. Publishes multiple edition artists' books which deal with Rocky Mountain political, social and environmental issues. Write for author's guidelines and catalog.

**HERBAL STUDIES LIBRARY**, 219 Carl St., San Francisco CA 94117. (415)564-6785. Fax: (415)564-6799. Owner: J. Rose. Publishes trade paperback originals. **Publishes 3 titles/year. Pays 5-10% royalty on retail price. Offers $500 advance.** Reports in 1 month on mss with SASE. *Writer's Market* recommends allowing 2 months for reply.

**Nonfiction:** How-to, reference, self-help. Subjects include gardening, health/medicine, herbs and aromatherapy. No New Age. Query with sample chapter and SASE. Recent title: *The Aromatherapy Book: Applications and Inhalations*, by Jeanne Rose.

**ILLUMINATION ARTS**, P.O. Box 1865, Bellevue WA 98009. (425)644-7185. Editorial Director: Ruth Thompson. Publishes hardcover originals. **Publishes 1-3 titles/year. Receives 200-250 queries and 100 mss/year. 50% of books from first-time authors; 90% from unagented writers. Pays royalty.** Publishes book 1-2 years after acceptance of ms. Reports in 2 weeks on queries and proposals, 1 month on mss.

   **O—** Illumination Arts publishes inspirational/spiritual children's nonfiction and fiction. Currently emphasizing adventure, humorous stories with inspirational and spiritual values. De-emphasizing Bible based stories.

**Nonfiction:** Children's/juvenile. Child guidance/parenting subjects. "Our books are all high quality, inspirational/spiritual. Send for our guidelines. Stories need to be exciting and inspirational for children." Query with complete ms and SASE. Recent title: *The Right Touch*, by Sandy Kleven (book to help children avoid sexual abuse).

**Fiction:** Juvenile, picture books. "All are inspirational/spiritual. No full-length novels. Send for guidelines. Some writers do not include sufficient postage to return manuscripts. A few writers just do not have a grasp of correct grammar. Some are dull or uninteresting." Query with complete ms and SASE. Recent title: *Sky Castle*, by Sandra Hanken.

**Tips:** "Audience is looking for a spiritual message and children who enjoy stories that make them feel self assured."

**IN PRINT PUBLISHING**, P.O. Box 20765, Sedona AZ 86336-9758. (520)284-5298. Fax: (520)284-6283. Publisher/Editor: Tomi Keitlen. Estab. 1991. Publishes trade paperback originals. **Publishes 3-5 titles/year. Pays 6-10% royalty on retail price. Offers $250-500 advance.** Reports in 2 months on queries and proposals, 3 months on mss.

   • Because of a large number of submissions, In Print Publishing has suspended review of new ms until March, 2000.

**Nonfiction:** "We are an eclectic publisher interested in books that have current impact: political, spiritual, financial, medical, environmental problems. We are interested in books that will leave a reader with hope. We are also interested in books that are metaphysical, books that give ideas and help for small business management and books that have impact in all general subjects. No violence, sex or poetry." Query with SASE. Recent title: *The Chicken Came First*, by Chandler Everett.

**Tips:** "We are interested in books about Angels. We are also interested in short books that will be part of a Living Wisdom Series™. These books must be no more than 18,000-20,000 words. We are not interested in any books that are over 300 pages—and are more likely interested in 75,000 words or less. Find areas that are not overdone and offer new insight to help others."

**INDIANA HISTORICAL SOCIETY**, 315 W. Ohio St., Indianapolis IN 46202-3299. (317)232-1882. Fax: (317)233-3109. Director of Publications: Thomas A. Mason. Estab. 1830. Publishes hardcover originals. **Publishes 3 titles/year. Pays 6% royalty on retail price.** Reports in 1 month.
**Nonfiction:** "We seek book-length manuscripts that are solidly researched and engagingly written on topics related to the history of Indiana." Query with SASE. Recent title: *Sherman Minton: New Deal Senator, Cold War Justice*, by Linda C. Gugin and James E. St. Clair.

**INTERTEXT**, 2633 E. 17th Ave., Anchorage AK 99508-3207. **Acquisitions:** Sharon Ann Jaeger, editor (20th Century poetry, literary theory). Estab. 1982. Publishes trade paperback originals. **Publishes 1-2 titles/year. Pays 10% royalty after costs are met. No advance.** Reports in 6 months on queries.
**Nonfiction:** "Only *solicited* nonfiction will be published, usually translations of essays by noted international authors or literary criticism or theory. (No immediate plans as we have a backlog of other titles.)" Query with SASE. "No response without it in most cases."
**Poetry:** "We look for poetry that is rich in imagery, is skillfully crafted, is powerful and compelling and that avails itself of the varied resonance and melody of the language. Cannot use religious verse. We expect book manuscripts to run 48-96 pages. (Please do *not* send an entire manuscript unless we specifically ask to see it.)" Submit 3-5 sample poems by first-class mail with SASE. Recent title: *Pelted with Petals: The Burmese Poems*, by Kyi May Kaung (poetry).
**Tips:** "Intertext is extremely selective; thus beginners should submit elsewhere. We regret that we cannot offer critiques of rejected work. Queries and samples lacking SASE cannot be returned. Poets we admire include William Stafford, Gary Snyder, W.S. Merwin, Sarah Kirsch, António Ramos Rosa, Rainer Maria Rilke, Louis Hammer, Tomas Tranströmer and Bob Perelman. We are moving toward electronic (and inventory-free) publishing."

**IVY LEAGUE PRESS, INC.**, P.O. Box 3326, San Ramon CA 94583-8326. 1-(888)IVY-PRESS or (925)736-0601. Fax: (925)736-0602. E-mail: ivyleaguepress@worldnet.att.net. Editor: Maria Thomas. Publishes hardcover, trade paperback and mass market paperback originals. Reports in 3 months.
• Ivy League is focusing more on medical thrillers with black physician protagonists, although it still welcomes Judaica and other submissions.
**Nonfiction:** Subjects include health/medicine, Judaica and self-help nonfiction. Query with SASE. Recent title: *Jewish Divorce Ethics*, by Bulka.
**Fiction:** Medical suspense. Query with SASE. Recent title: *Allergy Shots*, by Litman.

**JELMAR PUBLISHING CO., INC.**, P.O. Box 488, Plainview NY 11803. (516)822-6861. President: Joel J. Shulman. Publishes hardcover and trade paperback originals. **Publishes 2-5 titles/year. Pays 25% royalty after initial production and promotion expenses of first and successive printings.** Reports in 1 week. *Writer's Market* recommends allowing 2 months for reply.
**Nonfiction:** How-to and technical subjects on the packaging, package printing and printing fields. "The writer must be a specialist and recognized expert in the field." Query with SASE. Recent title: *Graphic Design for Corrugated Packaging*, by Donald G. McCaughey Jr. (graphic design).

**JOHNSTON ASSOCIATES, INTERNATIONAL (JASI)**, P.O. Box 313, Medina WA 98039. (425)454-3490. Fax: (425)462-1355. E-mail: jasibooks@aol.com. Publisher: Ann Schuessler. Contact: Rosanne Cohn, marketing director. Publishes trade paperback originals. **Publishes 3-5 titles/year. Receives 150 queries and 8 ms/year. Pays 10-15% royalty on wholesale price. Advance varies.** Publishes book 1-3 years after acceptance of ms. Accepts simultaneous submissions. Reports in 3 months. Book catalog and ms guidelines for #10 SASE.
**Nonfiction:** Recreation, regional (any region), travel and other nonfiction. "We are interested in books that hit unique niches or look at topics in new, unique ways." Query with proposal package, including outline, sample chapter, target market, competition, reason why the book is different and SASE. Recent title: *Discover Washington with Kids* by Suzanne Monson.
**Tips:** "We are interested in books that fit unique niches or look at a topic in a unique way."

**KALI PRESS**, P.O. Box 2169, Pagosa Springs CO 81147. (970)264-5200. E-mail: info@kalipress.com. Contact: Cynthia Olsen. Publishes trade paperback originals. **Publishes 3 titles/year. Pays 8-10% royalty on net price. No advance.** Reports in 1 month on queries, 6 weeks on proposals, 2 months on mss.
☞ "We specialize in complementary health which encompasses body, mind and spiritual topics." Currently emphasizing new alternative healing modalities.

**Nonfiction:** Natural health and spiritual nonfiction. Subjects include education on natural health issues. Query with 2 sample chapters and SASE. Reviews artwork/photos as part of ms package. Send photocopies. Recent title: *Australian Tea Tree First Aid for Animals*, by Cheyanne West.

**LAHONTAN IMAGES**, 210 S. Pine St., Susanville CA 96130. (530)257-6747. Fax: (530)251-4801. Owner: Tim I. Purdy. Estab. 1986. Publishes hardcover and trade paperback originals. **Publishes 2 titles/year. Pays 10-15% royalty on wholesale or retail price. No advance.** Reports in 2 months.
**Nonfiction:** Publishes nonfiction books pertaining to northeastern California and western Nevada. Query with outline and SASE. Recent title: *Maggie Greeno*, by George McDow Jr. (biography).

**LAUREATE PRESS**, 2710 Ohio St., Bangor ME 04401. Editor: Robyn Beck. Publishes trade paperback originals. **Publishes 3 titles/year.**
**Nonfiction:** Fencing subjects only—how-to, technical. Query letter only. Recent title: *The Science of Fencing*, by William Gaugler (fencing-technical); *On Fencing*, by Aldo Nadi.
**Tips:** Audience is recreational and competitive fencers worldwide, not martial arts or reenactment.

**LINTEL**, 24 Blake Lane, Middletown NY 10940. (212)674-4901. Editorial Director: Walter James Miller. Estab. 1978. Publishes hardcover originals and reprints and trade paperback originals. **Publishes 2 titles/year. Authors get 100 copies originally, plus royalties after all expenses are cleared.** Reports in 2 months on queries, 4 months on proposals, 6 months on ms.
**Nonfiction:** "So far all our nonfiction titles have been textbooks. Query with SASE. Recent title: *Writing a Television Play, Second Edition*, by Michelle Cousin (textbook).
**Fiction:** Publishes experimental fiction, art poetry and selected nonfiction. Query with SASE.
**Poetry:** Submit 5 sample poems. Recent title: *Mud River*, by Judy Aygildiz (hardcover with art work).

**MAGNUS PRESS**, P.O. Box 41157, San Jose CA 95160. (408)226-8638. Editorial Director: Warren Angel. Publishes trade paperback originals and reprints. **Publishes 2 titles/year. Pays royalty on retail price. No advance.** Reports in 1 month on queries and proposals, 2 months on mss.
**Nonfiction:** Subjects include religious Biblical study. "We publish popularly written biblical studies; little outside that." Query with SASE. Recent title: *Yes We Can Love One Another*, by Warren Angel (Biblical study).

**MARLTON PUBLISHERS, INC.**, P.O. Box 223, Severn MD 21144. (800)859-1073. President: Bruce Rory. Marlton publishes Christian suspense novels for adults. Publishes hardcover, trade paperback originals and mass market pocketbook originals. **Publishes 3 titles/year. Makes outright purchase, price negotiable.**
**Fiction:** Ethnic, religious, romance, suspense. "Company plans to publish 3-10 Christian suspense novels per year; paperbacks less than 25,000 words. We publish real-life, mature stories for adults. It should deal with contemporary issues which today's Christian adults are trying to harmonize with their faith." *Agented submissions only.* Recent title: *Extreme Flashbacks*, by Ralph Thomas (suspense).

**McGAVICK FIELD PUBLISHING**, P.O. Box 854, Allyn WA 98524-0854. (360)275-4081. Fax: (360)705-8006. E-mail: nannies@abc.nanny.com. Website: http://www.abcnanny.com. **Acquisitions:** Phyllis McGavick, co-owner (children's issues), Frances Hernan, co-owner (human resource issues regarding all forms of child care). **Publishes 2 titles/1999; 6 planned for 2000. 75% of books from first-time authors; 75% from unagented writers. Pays 15-25% royalty on sliding scale on retail price. Advance varies.** Publishes book 9 months after acceptance of ms. Accepts simultaneous submissions. Book catalog and ms guidelines free.
**Nonfiction:** How-to, humor, self-help handbooks for hiring child care, household employees and for securing all forms of child care. Subjects include employment issues, child care issues and second careers. Submit proposal package, including outline, 2 sample chapters, market research and competition or submit complete ms. "We are looking for short projects of 100 printed pages or under." Reviews artwork/photos as part of ms package. Send photocopies. Recent title: *The ABCs of Hiring a Nanny*, by Frances Anne Hernan (handbook for hiring child care).
**Tips:** "We are looking for writers with professional backgrounds in all forms of hiring and employing child care that is desperately needed in a very troubled industry. Large profits are made at the expense of the children, parent employers and society in general."

**MEGA MEDIA PRESS**, 3838 Raymert Dr., #203, Las Vegas NV 89121. (702)433-5388. President: Lillian S. Payn. Publishes trade paperback originals. **Publishes 3 titles/year. Pay varies.** Reports in 1 month.
**Nonfiction:** Subjects include business and economics, software. Query. Recent title: *Consultant's Little Instruction Book*, Ray Payn (business).

**MENUS AND MUSIC**, 1462 66th St., Emeryville CA 94608. (510)658-9100. Fax: (510)658-1605. **Acquisitions:** Sharon O'Connor, president (music, food, love). Publishes trade paperback originals and reprints. **Publishes 2 titles/year. Receives 5 queries/year. Pays 7-10% royalty. No advance.** Accepts simultaneous submissions. Reports in 1 month on queries and proposals, 3 months on mss. Book catalog and ms guidelines free.
**Nonfiction:** Coffee table book, cookbook, gift book. Subjects include Americana, art/architecture, cooking/foods/nutrition, gardening, hobbies, music/dance, photography, recreation, travel. Submit proposal package, including outline

and 1 sample chapter. Reviews artwork/photos as part of ms package. Send photocopies.

**Fiction:** Humor (women), multimedia, poetry, poetry in translation. "We are especially interested in proposals that will appeal to women, gift buyers, or books that can be paired with music." Submit proposal package, including synopsis and 1 sample chapter.

**Poetry:** Submit 3 sample poems.

**Tips:** "Our books are primarily bought by women who are interested in cooking, music and travel. We have excellent distribution in the gift industry and good distribution in the book trade. We are interested in high-quality work—we have completed books with New York's Metropolitan Opera and the San Francisco Ballet. Our books are beautiful and sell well for years."

**MOSAIC PRESS MINIATURE BOOKS**, 358 Oliver Rd., Cincinnati OH 45215-2615. (513)761-5977. Publisher: Miriam Irwin. Estab. 1977. **Publishes 1 nonfiction book/year.** "Subjects range widely. Please query."

**NEW ENGLAND CARTOGRAPHICS, INC.**, P.O. Box 9369, North Amherst MA 01059. (413)549-4124. Fax: (413)549-3621. E-mail: gcolopes@crocker.com. President: Christopher Ryan. Editor: Valerie Vaughan. Publishes trade paperback originals and reprints. **Publishes 3 titles/year. Pays 5-10% royalty on retail price. No advance.** Reports in 2 months.

**Nonfiction:** Outdoor recreation nonfiction subjects include nature/environment, recreation, regional. "We are interested in specific 'where to' in the area of outdoor recreation guidebooks of the northeast U.S." Topics of interest are hiking/backpacking, skiing, canoeing etc. Query with outline, sample chapters and SASE. Reviews artwork/photos as part of ms package. Send photocopies. Recent title: *24 Great Rail Trails of New Jersey*, by Della Penner.

**NEWSAGE PRESS**, P.O. Box 607, Troutdale OR 97060-0607. (503)695-2211. Fax: (503)695-5406. E-mail: newsage @teleport.com. Website: http://www.teleport.com/~newsage. Publisher: Maureen R. Michelson. Marketing Communications: Ericka Stork. "NewSage Press book address a myriad of social concerns, from environmental issues to women's issues to health issues." Estab. 1985. Publishes hardcover and trade paperback originals. Recent title: *Eating with Conscience: The Bioethics of Food*, by Dr. Michael W. Fox and *Conversations with Animals*, by Lydia Hiby with Bonnie Weintraub.

**[N] NEXT DECADE, INC.**, 39 Old Farmstead Rd., Chester NJ 07930. (908)879-6625. Fax: (908)879-6625. Website: http://www.nextdecade.com. **Acquisitions:** Barbara Kimmel, president (reference, self-help, how-to). Publishes trade paperback originals. **Publishes 2-4 titles/year. Receives 50 queries and 10 mss/year. 50% of books from first-time authors; 10% from unagented writers. Pays 10-15% royalty on wholesale price. Advances vary. Publishes book 1 year after acceptance of ms.** Accepts simultaneous submissions. Reports in 1 month. Catalog on website.

**Nonfiction:** How-to, reference, self-help. Subjects include business/economics, child guidance/parenting, cooking/foods/nutrition, health/medicine, hobbies, money/finance, multicultural, recreation. "We don't publish in all areas listed above, but would consider submissions." Query with SASE. Recent title: *Citizenship Made Simple*, by Barbara Kimmel and Alan Lubner (reference).

**Tips:** "We are interested in reference/how-to that would have broad mass market appeal. We are a small, award-winning press that successfully publishes a handful of books each year. Do not submit if you are looking for a large advance."

**NICOLAS-HAYS**, Box 612, York Beach ME 03910. (207)363-4393. Publisher: B. Lundsted. Publishes hardcover originals and trade paperback originals and reprints. **Publishes 2-4 titles/year. Pays 15% royalty on wholesale price. Offers $200-500 advance.** Reports in 2 months.

**Nonfiction:** Publishes self-help; nonfiction. Subjects include philosophy (Eastern), psychology (Jungian), religion (alternative), women's issues/studies. Query with outline, 3 sample chapters and SASE. Recent title: *Ring of Power*, by Jean Shinoda Bolen.

**Tips:** "We only publish books that are the lifework of authors—our editorial plans change based on what the author writes."

**OBERLIN COLLEGE PRESS**, Rice Hall, Oberlin College, Oberlin OH 44074. (440)775-8408. Business Manager: Heather Smith. Editors: David Young, Alberta Turner, David Walker. Imprints are *Field Magazine: Contemporary Poetry & Poetics*, Field Translation Series, Field Poetry Series. Publishes hardcover and trade paperback originals. **Publishes 2-3 titles/year. Pays 7½-10% royalty on retail price. Offers $500 advance.** Reports in 1 month on queries and proposals, 2 months on mss.

**Poetry:** *Field Magazine*—submit up to 5 poems with SASE for response; *Field* Translation Series—Query with SASE and sample poems; *Field* Poetry Series—no unsolicited mss, enter mss in *Field* Poetry Prize held annually in May. Send SASE for guidelines after October 1st. Recent title: *Ill Lit*, by Franz Wright.

**OCEAN VIEW BOOKS**, P.O. Box 102650, Denver CO 80250. Editor: Lee Ballentine. Publishes hardcover originals and trade paperback originals. **Publishes 2 titles/year. 100% from unagented writers. Pays negotiable royalty.** Reports in 2 months on queries, "if there is interest."

**Fiction:** Literary, science fiction, fiction about the 1960s. "Ocean View Books is an award-winning publisher of new speculative and slipstream fiction, poetry, criticism, surrealism and science fiction." Recent title: *All the Visions*, by Rudy Rucker.

**C. OLSON & CO.**, P.O. Box 100-WM, Santa Cruz CA 95063-0100. (408)459-9700. E-mail: bittersweet@jps.net. Owner: Clay Olson. Estab. 1981. Publishes trade paperback originals. **Publishes 1-2 titles/year. Royalty negotiable.** Reports in 2 months on queries.
**Nonfiction:** "We are looking for nonfiction manuscripts or books that can be sold at natural food stores and small independent bookstores on health and on how to live a life which improves the earth's environment. Also interested in a photo book for young children about the horrors and tragedy of wars." Query first with SASE. Recent title: *World Health, Carbon Dioxide & The Weather*, by J. Recklaw (ecology).

**N OZARK MOUNTAIN PUBLISHING, INC.**, P.O. Box 754, Huntsville AR 72740. Phone/fax: (501)738-2348. Website: http://www.ozarkmt.com. **Acquisitions:** Nancy Garrison. Publishes hardcover and trade paperback originals and mass market paperback reprints. **Publishes 3-4 titles/year. Receives 100 queries and 100 mss/year. 25% of books from first-time authors; 90% from unagented writers. Pays 10% royalty on wholesale price. Offers $500 advance.** Publishes book 18 months after acceptance of ms. Accepts simultaneous submissions. Reports in 3 months. Book catalog free or on website.
**Nonfiction:** Biography. Subjects include spirituality, New Age/metaphysical. Query with SASE or submit proposal package, including outline and 2 sample chapters. "No phone calls, please." Recent nonfiction title: *The Forgotten Woman*, by Arun and Sunanda GAndhi (biography).

**PACIFIC VIEW PRESS**, P.O. Box 2657, Berkeley CA 94702. (510)849-4213. President: Pam Zumwalt. Publishes hardcover and trade paperback originals. **Publishes 3 titles/year. Pays 5-10% royalty on wholesale price. Offers $500-2,000 advance.** Reports in 2 months. Book catalog free.
**Nonfiction:** Subjects include Asia-related business and economics, Asian current affairs, Chinese medicine, nonfiction Asian-American multicultural children's books. "We are only interested in Pacific Rim related issues. Do not send proposals outside our area of interest." Query with proposal package, including outline, 1 sample chapter, author background, audience info and SASE. No unsolicited mss. Recent title: *The Great Taiwan Bubble: The Rise and Fall of an Emerging Stock Market*, by Steven R. Champion.

**N PARROT PRESS**, 42307 Osgood Rd., Unit N, Fremont CA 94539. (510)659-1030. Editor: Jennifer Hubbard. **Publishes 3 titles/year. Pays 10-15% royalty on gross sales (wholesale, retail price).**
**Nonfiction:** How-to, reference, self-help. Pet birds only. "We publish nonfiction books written for pet bird owners. We are most interested in well-researched books on pet bird husbandry, health care, diet and species profiles. Good, clear, accessible writing is a requirement." Submit outline and 1-3 sample chapters with SASE.

**PARTNERS IN PUBLISHING**, P.O. Box 50347, Tulsa OK 74150. Phone/fax: (918)835-8258. Editor: P.M. Fielding. Estab. 1976. Publishes trade paperback originals. **Publishes 1-2 titles/year. Pays royalty on wholesale price. No advance.** Reports in 2 months on queries.
• This press reports being deluged with submissions having nothing to do with learning disabilities.
**Nonfiction:** "Understand that we are only interested in older teen and young adults with learning disabilities." Biography, how-to, reference, self-help, technical and textbooks on learning disabilities, special education for youth and young adults. Query with SASE. Recent title: *Enhancing Self-Esteem for Exceptional Learners*, by John R. Moss and Elizabeth Ragsdale (for parents and teachers who deal with exceptional youth and young adults).

**POGO PRESS, INCORPORATED**, 4 Cardinal Lane, St. Paul MN 55127-6406. E-mail: pogopres@minn.net. Website: http://www.pogopress.com. Vice President: Leo J. Harris. Publishes trade paperback originals. **Publishes 3 titles/year. Pays royalty on wholesale price.** Publishes book 6 months after acceptance. Reports in 2 months. Book catalog free.
**Nonfiction:** "We limit our publishing to Breweriana, history, art, popular culture and travel odysseys. Our books are heavily illustrated." Query. Reviews artwork/photos as part of ms package. Send photocopies. Recent title: *The Far Islands and Other Cold Places—Travel Essays of a Victorian Lady*, by Elizabeth Taylor.

**N THE POST-APOLLO PRESS**, 35 Marie St., Sausalito CA 94965. Publisher: Simone Fattal. Publishes trade paperback originals and reprints. **Publishes 2-3 titles/year. Pays 5-7% royalty on wholesale price. No advance.** Reports in 3 months. Book catalog and ms guidelines for #10 SASE.
**Nonfiction:** Essay, letters. Subjects include art/architecture, language/literature, translation, women's issues/studies. Query. Recent title: *Rumi & Sufism*, Eva de Vitray-Meyerovitch (religion/philosophy).
**Fiction:** Ethnic, experimental, feminist, gay/lesbian, humor, literary, plays. Submit 1 sample chapter and SASE. Recent title: *A Beggar At Damascus Gate*, by Yasmine Zahran (novel).
**Poetry:** Experimental/translations. Submit 1-5 sample poems and SASE. Recent title: *There*, by Etel Adnan.
**Tips:** "We are interested in writers with a fresh and original vision. We often publish women who are well-known in their country, but new to the American reader."

**N POT SHARD PRESS**, P.O. Box 215, Comptche CA 95427. (707)937-1443. **Acquisitions:** M.L. Harrison Mackie, publisher. Publishes paperback originals and reprints. **Publishes 2 titles/year. Pays negotiable royalty. No advance.** Publishes book 6 months after acceptance of ms.
**Poetry:** Mss by request only. Recent title: *Say Yes Quickly*, by Mary Brodish O'Connor.

**ᴺ POTENTIALS DEVELOPMENT, INC.**, 779 Cayuga St., Unit 1, Lewiston NY 14092. (716)754-9476. Fax: (800)372-1236. President: C.B. Seide. Estab. 1978. Publishes paperback originals. **Averages 1 title/year. Pays at least 5% royalty on sales of first 3,000 copies; 8% thereafter. No advance.** Reports in 2 months. Book catalog and ms guidelines for 9×12 SASE.
**Nonfiction:** Submit outline and/or 1-3 sample chapters with SASE. Recent title: *Sense-sational Activities for the Senses*, by Kathy Hughes.

**PRAKKEN PUBLICATIONS, INC.**, P.O. Box 8623, Ann Arbor MI 48107-8623. (313)975-2800. Fax: (313)975-2787. Publisher: George Kennedy. Book Editor: Susanne Peckham. Estab. 1934. Publishes educational hardcover and paperback originals as well as educational magazines. **Publishes 3 book titles/year. Pays 10% royalty on net sales (negotiable with production costs).** Reports in 2 months if reply requested and SASE furnished. Book catalog for #10 SASE.
**Nonfiction:** Industrial, vocational and technology education and related areas; general educational reference. "We are currently interested in manuscripts with broad appeal in any of the specific subject areas of industrial arts, technology education, vocational-technical education, and reference for the general education field." Submit outline and sample chapters. Recent title: *Outdoor Power Equipment Electrical Systems*, by Bill Schuster.
**Tips:** "We have a continuing interest in magazine and book manuscripts which reflect emerging issues and trends in education, especially vocational, industrial and technological education."

**PUCKERBRUSH PRESS**, 76 Main St., Orono ME 04473-1430. (207)581-3832 or 866-4808. Publisher/Editor: Constance Hunting. Estab. 1971. Publishes trade paperback originals and reprints of literary fiction and poetry. **Publishes 3-4 titles/year. Pays 10-15% royalty on wholesale price.** Reports in 1 month on queries; 2 months on proposals; 3 months on ms.
**Nonfiction:** Belles lettres, translations. Query with SASE. Recent title: *Art Notes*, by Farnham Blair.
**Fiction:** Literary and short story collections. Recent title: *Young*, by Miriam Colwell (novel).
**Poetry:** Highest literary quality. Submit complete ms with SASE. Recent title: *Translations of Celan*, by Muska Nagel.
**Tips:** "We are looking for serious literary work by unknown or known authors."

**PUPPY HOUSE PUBLISHING COMPANY, LLC**, P.O. Box 1539, New York NY 10021. Publishes hardcover and trade paperback originals. **Publishes 3 titles/year.** Royalty varies. Reports in 1 month.
    ⚬━ Puppy House seeks to publish exceptional children's books.
**Nonfiction:** Children's/juvenile, coffee table book. Subjects include animals, art/architecture. Query with SASE.
**Fiction:** Juvenile, picture books, young adult. Query with SASE.
**Tips:** "We are looking for innovative and well-written children's books for all ages, especially picture books. Our foremost requirement is excellence of concept and writing."

**RED EYE PRESS, INC.**, P.O. Box 65751, Los Angeles CA 90065. President: James Goodwin. Publishes trade paperback originals. **Publishes 2 titles/year. Pays 8-12% royalty on retail price. Offers $1-2,000 advance.** Reports in 1 month on queries, 3 months on mss.
**Nonfiction:** How-to, gardening, reference books. Query with outline, 2 sample chapters and SASE. Recent title: *Hashish!*, by Robert Connell Clarke.

**RED WHEELBARROW PRESS, INC.**, P.O. Box 33143, Austin TX 78764. President: L.C. Sajbel. Publishes hardcover and trade paperback originals and reprints. **Publishes 1-5 titles/year. 90% of books from first-time authors; 90% for unagented writers. Pays 10% royalty on retail price.** Publishes book 1 year after acceptance of ms. Reports in 4 months on mss. Manuscript guidelines for #10 SASE.
    • Red Wheelbarrow accepts submissions January through April only.
**Nonfiction:** Children's/juvenile, humor. Americana subjects. "We hope to find manuscripts that deal with original nonfiction topics in which children ages 6-12 would be interested and from which they would learn, including (for example) local geography or biographies or obscure archeological finds that children could connect with their studies. Poor grammar or punctuation make it difficult to trust that the author has thoroughly checked other details in text." Submit 3-5 sample chapters and outline with SASE January to April.
**Fiction:** Adventure, humor, juvenile, literary, short story collections. "We will be focusing on children's literature. Make me care about your characters! No one is interested in a story if they are not engaged by the protagonist. We also accept poetry for children *only*." Submit synopsis and 3-5 sample chapters with SASE. Recent title: *The Ambitious Baker's Batter*, by Wendy Seese (juvenile).
**Tips:** "We are looking for fresh, new writers and thought-provoking literature. For children and adults, we feel that literature should be fun and challenging."

**ᴺ REFERENCE PUBLICATIONS, INC.**, P.O. Box 344, Algonac MI 48001-0344. (810)794-5722. Fax: (810)794-7463. Estab. 1975. Publishes hardcover originals. **Pays 10% royalty on wholesale price. No advance.** Reports in 1 month. *Writer's Market* recommends allowing 2 months for reply.
**Nonfiction:** Publishes Africana, Americana, and botany reference books. Query. Recent title: *Medical Plants of China*, by James A. Duke and Edward S. Ayensu.

**THE RIEHLE FOUNDATION**, P.O. Box 7, Milford OH 45150. Fax: (513)576-0022. **Acquisitions:** Mrs. B. Lewis, general manager. Estab. 1976. Publishes trade paperback originals and reprints. **Publishes 2-4 titles/year. Receives 100 queries and 30 mss/year. 50% of books from first-time authors; 100% from unagented writers. Pays royalty.** Publishes book 6 months after acceptance of ms. Accepts simultaneous submissions. Reports in 3 months on mss. Book catalog and ms guidelines for #10 SASE.

    **O⇥** "We are only interested in materials which are written to draw the reader to a deeper love for God." Currently emphasizing prayer/meditational/inspirational books.

**Nonfiction:** Biography, reference, devotional. Subjects include religion (Roman Catholic). Submit entire ms, curriculum vitae, a statement of your purpose and intentions for writing the book and your intended audience with SASE. Reviews artwork/photos as part of ms package. Send photocopies.

**Fiction:** Religious, short story collections; all with Roman Catholic subjects. Submit entire ms with SASE. Recent title: *Exodus: The Road to Freedom*, by Michael Brown.

**RISING STAR PRESS**, P.O. Box BB, Los Altos CA 94023. (650)966-8920. Fax: (650)968-2658. E-mail: editor@rising starpress.com. Website: http://www.risingstarpress.com. **Acquisitions:** Editorial Director. Publishes hardcover originals and reprints, trade paperback originals and reprints. Rising Star publishes quality books that inform and inspire. **Publishes 2-4 titles/year. Pays 10-15% royalty on wholesale price. Offers $1,000-8,000 advance.** Publishes book 6 months after acceptance of ms. Accepts simultaneous submissions. Reports in 2 months on proposals.

    **O⇥** "Rising Star selects manuscripts based on benefit to the reader. We are interested in a wide variety of nonfiction topics." Currently emphasizing social issues. De-emphasizing metaphysical, personal finance.

**Nonfiction:** Biography, humor, self-help. Subjects include education, health/medicine, language/literature, philosophy, regional, religion, social issues, sociology, spirituality. "Authors need to be able to answer these questions: Who will benefit from reading this? Why? Mistakes writers often make are not identifying their target market early and shaping the work to address it." Query with proposal package including outline, 2 sample chapters, target market, author's connection to market, and author's credentials, with SASE. "We do *not* publish fiction, children's books, or poetry." Recent title: *Linus Pauling on Peace*, edited by Barbara Marinaui and Ramesh Krishnamurthy.

**[N] JAMES RUSSELL**, P.O. Box 10121, Suite 2098, Eugene OR 97440. Phone/fax: (775)348-8711. E-mail: scrnplay@ powernet.net. Website: http://www.powernet.net/~scrnplay. **Acquisitions:** James Russell, publisher. Publishes trade paperback originals. **Publishes 2 titles/year. Receives 10 queries and 2 mss/year. 90% of books from first-time authors; 90% from unagented writers. Pays 5-7% royalty on wholesale price.** Publishes book 1 year after acceptance of ms. Accepts simultaneous submissions. Reports in 1 month. Book catalog and ms guidelines on website.

**Nonfiction:** How-to, technical. Subjects include sports (including gambling, shooting), screenwriting, theatrical, movies, TV. Query with SASE. *All unsolicited mss returned unopened.* Reviews artwork/photos as part of ms package. Send simple line art illustrations. Wants less photos, more illustrations, at least 40/ms.

**Fiction:** Historical (Nevada), humor, plays (script format), regional (Nevada), religious (Christian), sports (competitive), western (Nevada). Books are 150-200 pages long. Query with SASE. *All unsolicited mss returned unopened.* Recent title: *Trap Shooting Secrets*, by James Russell (sports how-to).

**Tips:** Audience is tourists, professionals. "Never send a manuscript unless we request in writing to do so. Do not call. Always send #10 SASE with query. Keep query to one page. New unagented writers may submit, but follow the rules above. Visit our website for more information. We are a new publishing firm."

**RUSSIAN INFORMATION SERVICES**, 89 Main St., Suite 2, Montpelier VT 05602. (802)223-4955. Website: http://solar.ini.utk.edu/rispubs/ **Acquisitions:** Stephanie Ratmeyer, vice president. Publishes trade paperback originals and reprints. **Publishes 2-3 titles/year. Receives 20-30 queries and 10 mss/year. 50% of books from first-time authors; 100% from unagented writers. Pays 8-12% royalty on retail price.** Publishes book 8 months after acceptance of ms. Accepts simultaneous submissions. Reports in 2 months on mss. Book catalog free.

    **O⇥** "Audience is business people and independent travelers to Russia and the former Soviet Union."

**Nonfiction:** Reference, travel, business. Subjects include business/economics, language/literature, travel. "Our editorial focus is on Russia and the former Soviet Union." Submit proposal package, including ms, summary and cv. Reviews artwork/photos as part of ms package. Send photocopies. Recent title: *Survival Russian*, by Ivanov (language).

**Tips:** RIS also publishes *Russian Life*, a monthly magazine on Russian history, travel, culture and life. See the Ethnic/ Minority section of Consumer Magazines.

**[N] SALVO PRESS**, P.O. Box 9095, Bend OR 97702. Phone/fax: (541)330-8746. E-mail: sschmidt@bendnet.com. Website: http://www.salvopress.com. **Acquisitions:** Scott Schmidt, publisher. Publishes trade paperback originals. **Publishes 3 titles/year. Receives 100 queries and 50 mss/year. 50% of books from first-time authors; 50% from unagented writers. Pays 8-15% royalty on retail price. No advance.** Publishes book 9 months after acceptance of ms. Reports in 1 month on queries, 2 months on mss. Book catalog and ms guidelines on website.

**Fiction:** Mystery, suspense, espionage, thriller. Query with SASE. "Our needs change. Check our website." Recent title: *Extreme Faction*, by Trevor Scott (thriller).

**Tips:** "Salvo Press also sponsors the annual Mystery Novel Award. Send SASE for guidelines or check the website for them."

**SOUND VIEW PRESS**, 170 Boston Post Rd., Madison CT 06443. President: Peter Hastings Falk. Estab. 1985. Publishes hardcover and trade paperback originals, dictionaries, exhibition records, and price guides exclusive to fine art. All titles are related.

**SPECTACLE LANE PRESS INC.**, P.O. Box 1237, Mt. Pleasant SC 29465-1237. Phone/fax: (843)971-9165. Editor: James A. Skardon. Publishes nonfiction hardcover and trade paperback originals. **Publishes 2-3 titles/year. Pays 6-10% royalty on wholesale price. Offers $500-1,000 advance.** Reports in 1 month on queries, 2 months on mss. **Nonfiction:** "More celebrity and TV-oriented humor and sports and family-oriented life-style subjects holding closely to current trends. "Query first. Then send outline and 3 chapters with SASE if we are interested." Recent title: *The Difference Between Cats & Dogs*, by Bob Zahn (cartoons).

**STEEL BALLS PRESS**, P.O. Box 807, Whittier CA 90608. Owner: R. Don Steele. Website: http://steelballs.com. "We publish only controversial nonfiction." Publishes hardcover and trade paperback originals. **Publishes 2-3 titles/year. Pays 10% royalty on retail price after break-even. No advance.** Guidelines available on website. **Nonfiction:** How-to, self-help. Subjects include business and economics, money/finance, psychology, sociology, women's issues/studies. No humor, homeless, incest/molestation, save-the-world. Query (1 page) *only* with SASE. Any more than one page query will not be replied to nor returned. Recent title: *Sex, Truth and Audiotape*, by Joanna B. Lopez (self-help for divorced men).
**Tips:** "Write a persuasive one-page query letter. Explain who will buy and why."

**THE SUGAR HILL PRESS**, 216 Stoddard Rd., Hancock NH 03449-5102. Publisher: L. Bickford. Estab. 1990. Publishes trade paperback originals. **Publishes 1 title/year. Pays 15-20% royalty on publisher's revenues. No advance.** Reports in 2 months on proposals.
○━ "Our books focus on helping school personnel—secretaries, guidance counselors, administrators—make the most of their school's investment in school administration software."
**Nonfiction:** "We publish technical manuals for users of school administrative software *only*. (These are supplemental materials, not the manuals which come in the box.) A successful writer will combine technical expertise with crystal-clear prose." Query with outline and 1 sample chapter. Recent title: *A Report Cards Handbook*, by Geoffrey D. Hirsch.

**⦂Ｎ⦂ THE SYSTEMSWARE CORPORATION**, 973C Russell Ave., Gaithersburg MD 20879. (301)948-4890. Fax: (301)926-4243. Editor: Pat White. Estab. 1987.
**Nonfiction:** "We specialize in innovative books and periodicals on Knowledge Engineering or Applied Artificial Intelligence and Knowledge Based Systems. We also develop intelligent procurement-related software packages for large procurement systems." Query with SASE first.

**TAMARACK BOOKS, INC.**, P.O. Box 190313, Boise ID 83719-0313. (800)962-6657. (208)387-2656. Fax: (208)387-2650. President/Owner: Kathy Gaudry. General Editor: Maggie Chenore. Publishes trade paperback originals and reprints. **Publishes 3-5 titles/year. Pays 5-15% royalty.** Reports in 4 months on queries, 6 months on mss.
○━ "We publish nonfiction history of the American West and are avidly seeking women's books. Time period preference is for pre-1900s." Currently emphasizing "pioneer women who have made a difference, whether they have name recognition or not."
**Nonfiction:** History and illustrated books on West for people living in or interested in the American West. "We are looking for manuscripts for a popular audience, but based on solid research. We specialize in mountain man, women's issues and outlaw history prior to 1940 in the West, but will look at any good manuscript on Western history prior to 1940." Query with outline and SASE. Recent title: *Competitive Struggle, America's Western Fur Trading Posts, 1764-1865*, by R.G. Robertson.
**Tips:** "We look for authors who want to actively participate in the marketing of their books."

**TAMBRA PUBLISHING**, P.O. Box 3044, Montclair CA 91763. E-mail: tambra_publishing@juno.com. Editor: Tambra Campbell. Publisher: Kathy Gulley. Publishes hardcover and trade paperback originals. Estab. 1985. Publishes how-to books on character interpretation, a handwriting analysis; also accepts well-written screenplays and manuscripts with good storylines that can be adapted into screenplays. **Pays royalty on retail price.** Reports in 2 months on queries, 4 months on mss.
**Nonfiction:** Psychology—personality analysis for parenting, self-help, matchmaking, compatibility, employee screening. Query with SASE first, or send table of contents, author bio and statement on how your book differs from those already published, outline, 3-4 sample chapters and SASE. Recent title: *Celebrity Handwriting*, by K.G. Stevens.

**⦂Ｎ⦂ TECHNICAL BOOKS FOR THE LAYPERSON, INC.**, P.O. Box 391, Lake Grove NY 11755. (540)877-1477. Contact: Mary Lewis. Publishes trade paperback originals. **Publishes 3 titles/year. Pays 10-40% royalty on actual earnings. No advance.** Reports in 2 months on mss. Book catalog and ms guidelines free. *Absolutely no phone calls.*
**Nonfiction:** How-to, reference, self-help, technical, textbook. "Our primary goal is consumer-friendliness ('Books by consumers for consumers'). All topics are considered. There is a preference for completed work which equips an ordinary consumer to deal with a specialized or technical area." Submit 1 sample chapter. Recent title: *Common Blood Tests*, by Gifford (medical reference).

**Tips:** "Our audience is the consumer who needs very explicit information to aid in making good purchasing decisions." Format chapter for camera-ready copy, with text enclosed in 4½×7 area (including headers and footers).

**TIA CHUCHA PRESS**, A Project of The Guild Complex, P.O. Box 476969, Chicago IL 60647. (773)377-2496. Fax: (773)252-5388. Director: Luis Rodriguez. Publishes trade paperback originals. **Publishes 2-4 titles/year. Receives 25-30 queries and 150 mss/year. Pays 10% royalty on wholesale price. Offers $500-1,000 advance.** Reports in 9 months on mss. Publishes book 1 year after acceptance. Book catalog and ms guidelines free.
**Poetry:** "No restrictions as to style or content. We do cross-cultural and performance-oriented poetry. It has to work on the page, however." Submit complete ms with SASE. Recent title: *Talisman*, by Afaa M. Weave.
**Tips:** Audience is "those interested in strong, multicultural, urban poetry—the best of bar-cafe poetry. Annual manuscript deadline is June 30. Send your best work. No fillers. We read in the summer; we decide in the fall what books to publish for the following year."

**VALIANT PRESS, INC.**, P.O. Box 330568, Miami FL 33233. (305)665-1889. President: Charity Johnson. Estab. 1991. Publishes hardcover and trade paperback originals. **Publishes 1-3 titles/year. Pays royalty on net receipts. Offers minimal advance.** Reports in 2 months.
**Nonfiction:** "We are interested in nonfiction books on Florida subjects." Submit proposal package, including outline, 2-3 sample chapters, author's background, marketing info with SASE. Recent title: *The Biltmore, Beacon for Miami, Revised and Expanded*, by Helen Muir.

**VITESSE PRESS**, 45 State St., Suite 367, Montpelier VT 05602. (802)229-4243. Fax: (802)229-6939. E-mail: dickmfield@aol.com. Website: http://www.Acornpub.com. Editor: Richard H. Mansfield. Estab. 1985. Publishes trade paperback originals. **Publishes 3 titles/year. Pays 7-10% royalty. No advance.** Reports in 1 month on queries.
**Nonfiction:** Regional mountain biking guides (Eastern), outdoor recreation books. Especially interested in cycling-related books. Recent title: *Cycling Along the Canals of New York*, by Louis Rossi.

**WAYFINDER PRESS**, P.O. Box 217, Ridgway CO 81432-0217. (970)626-5452. Owner: Marcus E. Wilson. Estab. 1980. Publishes trade paperback originals. **Publishes 2 titles/year. Pays 8-10% royalty on retail price.** Reports in 1 month.
**Nonfiction:** Illustrated book, reference. Subjects include Americana, government/politics, history, nature/environment, photography, recreation, regional, travel. "We are looking for books on western Colorado: history, nature, recreation, photo, and travel. No books on subjects outside our geographical area of specialization." Query or submit outline/synopsis, sample chapters and SASE. Reviews artwork/photos as part of ms package. Recent title: *Ouray—Chief of the Utes*, by P. David Smith.
**Tips:** "Writers have the best chance selling us tourist-oriented books. Our audience is the local population and tourists."

**N WESTERN NEW YORK WARES INC.**, P.O. Box 733, Ellicott Station, Buffalo NY 14205. (716)832-6088. Website: http://www.wnybooks.com. **Acquisitions:** Brian S. Meyer, publisher (regional history); Matthew Pitts, marketing manager (sports, regional travel). Publishes trade paperback originals. **Publishes 3 titles/year. Pays 50% of net profits on all runs. No advance.** Publishes book 1 year after acceptance on ms. Accepts simultaneous submissions. Reports in 1 month. Book catalog free or on website. Manuscript guidelines for #10 SASE.
**Nonfiction:** Regional history focusing on upstate Western New York (Buffalo, Niagara Falls, Chautauqua, Allegheny). Subjects include art/architecture, history, photography, travel. Query with SASE. Recent title: *Daring Niagara: 50 Death-Defying Stunts at Niagra Falls*, by Paul Gromosiak.

**N WOODBRIDGE PRESS**, P.O. Box 209, Santa Barbara CA 93102. (805)965-7039. Fax: (805)963-0540. E-mail: woodpress@aol.com. Website: http://www.woodbridgepress.com. Editor: Howard Weeks. Estab. 1971. Publishes hardcover and trade paperback originals. **Publishes 2-3 titles/year. Pays 10-15% on wholesale price.** Accepts simultaneous submissions. Reports in 2 months with SASE. Book catalog free.
   O— "We publish books by expert authors on special forms of gardening, vegetarian cooking, very limited self-help psychology and humor."
**Nonfiction:** Cookbook (vegetarian), self-help. Subjects include agriculture/horticulture, cooking/foods/nutrition, gardening, health, psychology (popular). Query. Reviews artwork/photos as part of ms package. Recent title: *Love Yourself So Hate the Weight*, by Brother Craig (weight loss).

---

**MARKETS THAT WERE** listed in the 1999 edition of *Writer's Market* but do not appear this year are listed in the General Index with a notation explaining why they were omitted.

# Book Producers

Book producers provide services for book publishers, ranging from hiring writers to editing and delivering finished books. Most book producers possess expertise in certain areas and will specialize in producing books related to those subjects. They provide books to publishers who don't have the time or expertise to produce the books themselves (many produced books are highly illustrated and require intensive design and color-separation work). Some work with on-staff writers, but most contract writers on a per-project basis.

Most often a book producer starts with a proposal; contacts writers, editors and illustrators; assembles the book; and sends it back to the publisher. The level of involvement and the amount of work to be done on a book by the producer is negotiated in individual cases. A book publisher may simply require the specialized skill of a particular writer or editor, or a producer could put together the entire book, depending on the terms of the agreement.

Writers have a similar working relationship with book producers. Their involvement depends on how much writing the producer has been asked to provide. Writers are typically paid by the hour, by the word, or in some manner other than on a royalty basis. Writers working for book producers usually earn flat fees. Writers may not receive credit (a byline in the book, for example) for their work, either. Most of the contracts require work for hire, and writers must realize they do not own the rights to writing published under this arrangement.

The opportunities are good, though, especially for writing-related work, such as fact checking, research and editing. Writers don't have to worry about good sales. Their pay is secured under contract. Finally, writing for a book producer is a good way to broaden experience in publishing. Every book to be produced is different, and the chance to work on a range of books in a number of capacities may be the most interesting aspect of all.

Book producers most often want to see a query detailing writing experience. They keep this information on file and occasionally even share it with other producers. When they are contracted to develop a book that requires a particular writer's experience, they contact the writer. There are well over 100 book producers, but most prefer to seek writers on their own. The book producers listed in this section have expressed interest in being contacted by writers. For a list of more producers, contact the American Book Producers Association, 160 Fifth Ave., Suite 625, New York NY 10010, or look in *Literary Market Place* (R.R. Bowker).

**For a list of publishers according to their subjects of interest, see the nonfiction and fiction sections of the Book Publishers Subject Index. Information on book publishers and producers listed in the previous edition of *Writer's Market* but not included in this edition can be found in the General Index.**

**A.G.S. INCORPORATED,** P.O. Box 460313, San Francisco CA 94146. Contact: Mr. Yenne. Averages 10-12 titles/year. 15% of books from first-time authors; 100% from unagented writers. Makes outright purchase. Reports in 2 months if interested.
  • A.G.S. Incorporated does not work with out-of-area writers.
**Nonfiction:** Coffee table book, illustrated book, reference. Subjects include Americana, animals, history, military/war, photography, transportation. Query with SASE.

**B&B PUBLISHING, INC.,** P.O. Box 96, Walworth WI 53184-0096. (414)275-9474. Fax: (414)275-9530. President: William Turner. Submissions Editor: Naomi Kirchschlager. Produces supplementary educational materials for grades K-12. 10% of books from first-time authors, 90% from unagented writers. Payment varies, mostly "work-for-hire" contracts. Reports in 3 months. Book catalog and ms guidelines for SASE.
  • B&B Publishing also publishes a regional southeastern Wisconsin quarterly magazine, *At the Lake*.

**Nonfiction:** Especially interested in curriculum based material in social studies, reading, writing, math and regional southeastern Wisconsin human interest feature ideas. Query. Reviews artwork/photos as part of ms package.
**Recent Title(s):** *Geotrax* (geography).

**N: BOOKWRIGHTS PRESS**, 2255 Westover Dr., Charlottesville VA 22901. Phone/fax: (804)823-8223. Publisher: Mayapriya Long. Produces hardcover and trade paperback originals. Averages 4 titles/year. 40% of books from first-time authors; 100% from unagented writers. Pays royalty. Reports in 2 months.
**Nonfiction:** How-to, self-help, technical, textbook. Subjects include cooking, foods & nutrition, gardening, military/war, regional, religion, Eastern religion. Query with résumé via e-mail or mail. "Do not send manuscript."
**Recent Title(s):** *Sentimental Journeys* (regional); *Pagan Resurrection Myths and the Resurrection of Christ* (religious/scholarly).
**Fiction:** Historical, mainstream, Asian, Indian fiction. Query or submit proposal.
**Recent Title(s):** *Mandalay's Child* (fiction).
**Tips:** "No unsolicited manuscripts. Query first. When requested, send manuscript on disk with accompanying hard copy."

**ALISON BROWN CERIER BOOK DEVELOPMENT, INC.**, 815 Brockton Lane N., Plymouth MN 55410. (612)449-9668. Fax: (612)449-9674. "The vast majority of books start with our ideas or those of a publisher, not with proposals from writers. We do not act as authors' agents." Produces hardcover and trade paperback originals. Produces 4 titles/year. 50% of books from first-time authors; 90% from unagented writers. Payment varies with the project. Reports in 3 weeks. *Writer's Market* recommends allowing 2 months for reply.
   **O—** Currently emphasizing health, business self-help. De-emphasizing cookbooks.
**Nonfiction:** How-to, popular reference, self-help. Subjects include child guidance/parenting, cooking/foods/nutrition, health, sports, business self-help, women's interest. Query with SASE.
**Recent Title(s):** *When the Man You Love Won't Take Care of His Health*, by Ken Goldberg, M.D. (Golden Books).
**Tips:** "I often pair experts with writers and like to know about writers and journalists with co-writing experience."

**COMPASS PRODUCTIONS**, 211 E. Ocean Blvd., #360, Long Beach CA 90802. (562)432-7613. Fax: (562)495-0445. Vice President: Dick Dudley. Produces hardcover originals. **Pays 2-8% royalty on wholesale price for total amount of books sold to publisher. Offers $2,000 advance for idea/text.** Reports in 6 weeks. *Writer's Market* recommends allowing 2 months for reply.
   **O—** Compass Productions is interested in pop-up and novelty (attachments) only. Subjects include early learning, nature, fiction and nonfiction
**Nonfiction:** Humor, juvenile, ("all our books are pop-up and novelty books"). Subjects include Americana, animals, education, recreation, regional, religion, sports (concept-early age books). Query with SASE.
**Fiction:** Adventure, fantasy, horror, humor, juvenile, mystery, religious. Query with SASE.
**Recent Title(s):** *Safety City* (nonfiction); *Eeirie Feary Feeling* (fiction).
**Tips:** "Keep in mind our books are *pop-up*, *dimensional*, or novelty *only*! Short verse, couplets or short nonfiction text for 6-7 spreads per book."

**COURSE CRAFTERS, INC.**, 33 Low St., 2nd Floor, Newburyport MA 01950. (978)465-2040. Fax: (978)465-5027. E-mail: lise@coursecrafters.com. Website: http://www.coursecrafters.com. President: Lise B. Ragan. Produces textbooks, language materials (Spanish/ESL) and publishes packages for early childhood/family learning that feature storytelling and music. Makes outright purchase. Manuscript guidelines vary based upon project-specific requirements.
**Nonfiction:** Textbook. "We package materials that teach language. We are particularly looking for innovative approaches and visually appealing presentations." Subjects include language, education (preschool-adult), and early childhood. Submit résumé, publishing history and clips. Reviews artwork/photos as part of ms package.
**Tips:** "Mail (or fax) résumé with list of projects related to specific experience with ESL, bilingual and/or foreign language textbook development. Also interested in storytellers and musicians for our new audio/game packages."

**GLEASON GROUP, INC.**, 6 Old Kings Hwy., Norwalk CT 06850. (203)847-6658. President: Gerald Gleason. Produces 4-8 titles/year. Work-for-hire.
**Nonfiction:** Textbooks about software with CD-ROMs. Submitt résumé. *No unsolicited mss.*
**Recent Title(s):** *Word 2000: A Professional Approach.*
**Tips:** "If writer is well versed in the most recent Microsoft Office software, and has written technical or software-related material before, he/she can send us their résumé."

**LOUISE B. KETZ AGENCY**, 1485 First Ave., Suite 4B, New York NY 10021. (212)535-9259. President: Louise B. Ketz. Produces and agents hardcover and paperback originals. Averages 3-5 titles/year. 90% of books from unagented writers. Pays flat fees and honoraria to writers. Reports in 6-8 weeks.
**Nonfiction:** Biography, reference. Subjects include Americana, business and economics, history, military/war, science, sports. Submit proposal.
**Recent Title(s):** *British Writers: Dictionary of American History, Supplement.*
**Tips:** "It is important for authors to list their credentials relevant to the book they are proposing (i.e., why they are qualified to write that nonfiction work). Also helps if author defines the market (who will buy the book and why)."

**GEORGE KURIAN REFERENCE BOOKS**, Box 519, Baldwin Place NY 10505. Phone/fax: (914)962-3287. President: George Kurian. Editors: Jeff Schultz (general); Henry Sapinda (religion, education, business). "We seek to provide accurate information on issues of global interest." Produces hardcover originals. Produces 6 titles/year. 10% of books from first-time authors; 50% from unagented writers. Pays 10-15% royalty on net receipts. Reports in 3 months. Book catalog for 8½×11 SAE with 2 first-class stamps. Manuscript guidelines for #10 SASE.

○━ "Our goal is to publish innovative reference books for the library and trade market." Currently emphasizing international affairs, religion, education, children's

**Imprints:** International Encyclopedia Society; UN Studies Forum.

**Nonfiction:** Biography, illustrated book, reference. Subjects include Americana, business and economics, education, ethnic, government/politics, history, military/war, philosophy, photography, science, religion, travel. Query or submit proposal.

**Recent Title(s):** *Compendium of the 21st Century.*

**LAMPPOST PRESS INC.**, 1172 Park Ave., New York NY 10128-1213. (212)876-9511. President: Roseann Hirsch. Estab. 1987. Produces hardcover, trade paperback and mass market paperback originals. Averages 25 titles/year. 50% of books from first-time authors; 85% from unagented writers. Pays 50% royalty or makes outright purchase.

**Nonfiction:** Biography, cookbook, how-to, humor, illustrated book, juvenile, self-help. Subjects include child guidance/parenting, cooking/foods/nutrition, gardening, health, money/finance, women's issues. Query or submit proposal. Reviews artwork/photos as part of ms package.

**McCLANAHAN BOOK COMPANY INC.**, 23 W. 26th St., New York NY 10010. (212)725-1515. Vice President, Managing Director: Jeanne Firestone. Produces 50-60 titles/year. 5% of books from first-time authors; 90% from unagented writers. Makes outright purchase. Reports within 3 months to submissions with SASE.

○━ "Our goal is to provide entertaining books with an underlying educational value to the mass market—for children ages 2-10 years old." Currently emphasizing science topics. De-emphasizing story book topics.

**Nonfiction:** Juvenile. Submit proposal only. Reviews artwork/photos as part of ms package.

**Recent Title(s):** *Know-It-Alls.*

**NEW ENGLAND PUBLISHING ASSOCIATES, INC.**, P.O. Box 5, Chester CT 06412. (860)345-READ. Fax: (860)345-3660. E-mail: nepa@nepa.com. President: Elizabeth Frost-Knappman; Vice President/Treasurer: Edward W. Knappman. Staff: Victoria Harlow, Ron Formica, Christopher Ceplenski and Kristine Schiavi. Estab. 1983. "Our mission is to provide personalized service to a select list of mainly nonfiction clients." NEPA develops adult and young adult reference and information titles and series for the domestic and international markets. Produces hardcover and trade paperback originals. 20% of books from first-time authors. Reports in 2 months.

● Elizabeth Frost-Knappman's *Women's Progress in America* was selected by *Choice* as Outstanding Reference Book of the Year.

**Tips:** "Revise, revise, revise."

**NEWMARKET PRESS**, 18 E. 48th St., Suite 1501, New York NY 10017. (212)832-3575. Fax: (212)832-3629. Assistant Editor: Rachel Reiss. Managing Editor: Elissa Altman. Produces hardcover and trade paperback originals. Produces 25-30 titles/year. Pays royalty. Catalog for SAE 9×12 and $1.01 postage. Manuscript guidelines for #10 SASE.

○━ Currently emphasizing movie tie-in/companion books, self-help. De-emphasizing fiction.

**Nonfiction:** General nonfiction, self-help. Subjects include child guidance/parenting, cooking/foods/nutrition, film, health, money/finance, psychology. Query with SASE or submit proposal.

**Recent Title(s):** *Whose Body Is It Anyway? Smart Alternative & Traditional Health Choices for Your Total Well-Being,* by Joan Kenley, Ph.D.

**Tips:** "Check out other Newmarket titles before submitting to get a sense of the kind of books we publish. Be patient!"

**N: PUBLICOM, INC.**, 411 Massachusetts Ave., Acton MA 01720-3739. (978)263-5773. Fax: (978)263-7553. Vice President (Publicom Textbook Services): Patricia White. Vice President (tradebooks): Patricia Moore. "We create and support superior publishing teams in service to educational (textbook) publishers, and we publish exemplary tradebooks that promote learning, compassion and self-reliance." Produces hardcover and trade paperback originals under the imprint VanderWyk & Burnham. Produces or publishes 5-20 titles/year. 50% of books from first-time authors; 50% from unagented writers. "Work for hire" for textbooks; pays 3-10% royalty or makes variable outright purchase. Offers up to $3,000 advance for trade publishing. Reports in 6 months.

**Nonfiction:** Biography, self-help, textbook. Subjects include school disciplines K-college, tradebook topics in social sciences, business, child guidance/parenting, education, aging. Submit proposal, résumé, publishing history and clips.

**Recent Title(s):** *How to Enjoy Your Retirement—Activities from A-Z,* by Wagner & Day (aging).

**SACHEM PUBLISHING ASSOCIATES, INC.**, P.O. Box 412, Guilford CT 06437-0412. (203)453-4328. Fax: (203)453-4320. E-mail: sachempublishing@guilfordct.com. President: Stephen P. Elliott. Estab. 1974. Produces hardcover originals for publishers. Produces 3 titles/year. 5% of books from first-time authors; 100% from unagented writers. Pays royalty or works for hire. Reports in 1 month. *Writer's Market* recommends allowing 2 months for reply.

**Nonfiction:** Reference. Subjects include Americana, government/politics, history, military/war. Submit résumé and

publishing history.
**Recent Title(s):** *American Heritage Encyclopedia of American History*, by John Mack Faragher, general editor.

**SILVER MOON PRESS**, 160 Fifth Ave., New York NY 10010. (212)242-6499. Fax: (212)242-6799. E-mail: silvermp @aol.com. Website: http://www.silvermoonpress.com. Editorial Assistant: Karin Lillebo. Publisher: David Katz. "We publish mainly American historical fiction for age group 8-12." Produces hardcover originals. Produces 2-4 books/year. 10% of books from first-time authors; 90% from unagented writers. Pays 7-12% royalty. Book catalog free.
**Nonfiction:** Juvenile. Subjects include education, history, Revolutionary War, science, sports. Submit proposal. Reviews artwork/photos as part of ms package.
**Fiction:** Historical, juvenile, multicultural, mystery. Submit 3 sample chapters or synopsis along with SASE.
**Recent Title(s):** *A Secret Party in Boston Harbor*, Kris Hemphill (nonfiction).

**2M COMMUNICATIONS LTD.**, 121 W. 27th St., New York NY 10001. (212)741-1509. Fax: (212)691-4460. Editorial Director: Madeleine Morel. Produces hardcover, trade paperback and mass market paperback originals. Produces 15 titles/year. 50% of books from first-time authors. Reports in 2 weeks. *Writer's Market* recommends allowing 2 months for reply.
**Nonfiction:** Biography, cookbook, how-to, humor. Subjects include child guidance/parenting, cooking/foods/nutrition, ethnic, gay/lesbian, health, psychology, women's studies. Query or submit proposal with résumé and publishing history.

**N VERNON PRESS, INC.**, 398 Columbus Ave., #355, Boston MA 02116-6008. (617)437-0388. Fax: (617)437-0894. E-mail: vernpres@tiac.net. Contact: Brian Hotchkiss, co-creative director, editorial; Peter Blaiwas, co-creative director (art & art history, popular culture, music/dance, design. Produces hardcover and trade paperback originals. **Produces 8-12 titles/year. 30% of books from first-time authors. 60% from unagented writers. Pays 60-70% royalty on net receipts or pays work-for-hire fee based on individual project.** Reports in 6 weeks.
**Nonfiction:** Children's/juvenile, coffee table book, gift book, illustrated book. Subjects include Americana, art/architecture, gardening, history, hobbies, language/literature, music/dance, photography, recreation, regional, religion, translation, travel, women's issues/studies. Submit proposal. Reviews artwork/photos as part of ms package. Send photocopies or duplicate transparencies.
**Fiction:** Picture books, poetry, poetry in translation, translation. Query.
**Recent Title(s):** *Golf at the Water's Edge*, by Brenda and John McGuire (gift, Abbeville); *The Story of Digby and Marie*, by Robert Shure (literary fiction, St. Martin's).

**N DANIEL WEISS ASSOCIATES, INC.**, 33 W. 17th St., 11th Floor, New York NY 10011. Editorial Assistant: Jennifer Klein. Estab. 1987. Produces mass market paperback originals. Produces 135 titles/year. 10% of books from first-time authors; 40% from unagented writers. Pays 1-4% royalty on retail price or makes outright purchase of $1,500-6,500 "depending on author's experience." Offers $1,500-6,500 advance. Reports in 2 months. Guidelines for #10 SASE.
**Fiction:** Adventure, historical, horror, juvenile, science-fiction, young adult. "Middle grade, young adult and early reader. Mostly series fiction. Ask for guidelines prior to submission. We no longer accept unsolicited manuscripts."
**Recent Title(s):** Series: Roswell High, Countdown, Spy Girls.
**Tips:** "We need writers for Love Stories, Sweet Valley High and Sweet Valley University."

**THE WONDERLAND PRESS**, 160 Fifth Ave., Suite 723, New York NY 10010. (212)989-2550. President: John Campbell. Produces hardcover and trade paperback originals and mass market paperback originals. Produces 50 titles/year. 80% of books from first-time authors, 90% from unagented writers. Payment depends on the book: sometimes royalty with advance, sometimes work-for-hire. Reports in 3 weeks.
**Nonfiction:** Biography, coffee table book, how-to, humor, illustrated book, reference, self-help. Subjects include business and economics, education, gardening, gay/lesbian, history, money/finance, photography, psychology, art. Submit proposal with sample chapter(s). Reviews artwork/photos as part of ms package.
**Recent Title(s):** *The Essential Jackson Pollock* (Abrams).
**Tips:** "Always submit in writing, never by telephone. Know your market intimately. Study the competition and decide whether there is a genuine need for your book, with a market base that will justify publication. Send us an enthused, authoritative, passionately written proposal that shows your mastery of the subject and that makes us say, 'Wow, we want that!' "

---

**MARKETS THAT WERE** listed in the 1999 edition of *Writer's Market* but do not appear this year are listed in the General Index with a notation explaining why they were omitted.

# Consumer Magazines

Selling your writing to consumer magazines is as much an exercise of your marketing skills as it is of your writing abilities. Editors of consumer magazines are looking not simply for good writing, but for good writing which communicates pertinent information to a specific audience— their readers. Why are editors so particular about the readers they appeal to? Because it is only by establishing a core of faithful readers with identifiable and quantifiable traits that magazines attract advertisers. And with many magazines earning up to half their income from advertising, it is in their own best interests to know their readers' tastes and provide them with articles and features that will keep their readers coming back.

## APPROACHING THE CONSUMER MAGAZINE MARKET

Marketing skills will help you successfully discern a magazine's editorial slant and write queries and articles that prove your knowledge of the magazine's readership to the editor. The one complaint we hear from magazine editors more than any other is that many writers don't take the time to become familiar with their magazine before sending a query or manuscript. Thus, editors' desks become cluttered with inappropriate submissions—ideas or articles that simply will not be of much interest to the magazine's readers.

You can gather clues about a magazine's readership—and thus establish your credibility with the magazine's editor—in a number of ways:

• Start with a careful reading of the magazine's listing in this section of *Writer's Market*. Most listings offer very straightforward information about their magazine's slant and audience.
• Send for a magazine's writer's guidelines, if available. These are written by each particular magazine's editors and are usually quite specific about their needs and their readership.
• If possible, talk to an editor by phone. Many will not take phone queries, particularly those at the higher-profile magazines. But many editors of smaller publications will spend the time to help a writer over the phone.
• Perhaps most important, read several current issues of the target magazine. Only in this way will you see firsthand the kind of stories the magazine actually buys.
• Check a magazine's website. Often writer's guidelines and a selection of articles are included in a publication's online version. A quick check of archived articles lets you know if ideas you want to propose have already been covered.

Writers who can correctly and consistently discern a publication's audience and deliver stories that speak to that target readership will win out every time over writers who simply write what they write and send it where they will.

## AREAS OF CURRENT INTEREST

Today's consumer magazines reflect societal trends and interests. As baby boomers age and the so-called "Generation X" comes along behind, magazines arise to address their concerns, covering topics of interest to various subsets of both of those wide-ranging demographic groups. Some areas of special interest now popular among consumer magazines include gardening, health & fitness, family leisure, computers, travel, fashion and cooking.

As in the book publishing business, magazine publishers are experimenting with a variety of approaches to marketing their publications electronically, whether on the Internet, the World Wide Web or via CD-ROM. For tips on how to write for online magazines, see the article on page 78 by Michael Ray Taylor, followed by the details on a number of high-profile online magazines, by Anthony Tedesco on page 83.

## WHAT EDITORS WANT

In nonfiction, editors continue to look for short feature articles covering specialized topics. They want crisp writing and expertise. If you are not an expert in the area about which you are writing, make yourself one through research.

Always query before sending your manuscript. Don't e-mail or fax a query unless an editor specifically mentions an openness to this in the listing. Publishing, despite all the electronic advancements, is still a very paper-oriented industry. Once a piece has been accepted, however, many publishers now prefer to receive your submission via disk or modem so they can avoid re-keying the manuscript. Some magazines will even pay an additional amount for disk submission.

Fiction editors prefer to receive complete short story manuscripts. Writers must keep in mind that marketing fiction is competitive and editors receive far more material than they can publish. For this reason, they often do not respond to submissions unless they are interested in using the story. Before submitting material, check the market's listing for fiction requirements to ensure your story is appropriate for that market. More comprehensive information on fiction markets can be found in *Novel & Short Story Writer's Market* (Writer's Digest Books).

Many writers make their articles do double duty, selling first or one-time rights to one publisher and second serial or reprint rights to another noncompeting market. The heading, **Reprints**, offers details when a market indicates they accept previously published submissions, with submission form and payment information if available.

When considering magazine markets, be sure not to overlook opportunities with Canadian and international publications. Many such periodicals welcome submissions from U.S. writers and can offer writers an entirely new level of exposure for their work.

Regardless of the type of writing you do, keep current on trends and changes in the industry. Trade magazines such as *Writer's Digest*, *Folio:* and *Advertising Age* and will keep you abreast of start-ups and shutdowns and other writing/business trends.

## PAYMENT

Writers make their living by developing a good eye for detail. When it comes to marketing material, the one detail of interest to almost every writer is the question of payment. Most magazines listed here have indicated pay rates; some give very specific payment-per-word rates while others state a range. Any agreement you come to with a magazine, whether verbal or written, should specify the payment you are to receive and when you are to receive it. Some magazines pay writers only after the piece in question has been published. Others pay as soon as they have accepted a piece and are sure they are going to use it.

In *Writer's Market*, those magazines that pay on acceptance have been highlighted with the phrase **pays on acceptance** set in bold type. Payment from these markets should reach you faster than from markets who pay on publication. There is, however, some variance in the industry as to what constitutes payment "on acceptance"—some writers have told us of two- and three-month waits for checks from markets that supposedly pay on acceptance. It is never out of line to ask an editor when you might expect to receive payment for an accepted article.

So what is a good pay rate? There are no standards; the principle of supply and demand operates at full throttle in the business of writing and publishing. As long as there are more writers than opportunities for publication, wages for freelancers will never skyrocket. Rates vary widely from one market to the next, however, and the news is not entirely bleak. One magazine industry source puts the average pay rate for consumer magazine feature writing at $1.25 a word, with "stories that require extensive reporting . . . more likely to be priced at $2.50 a word." In our opinion, those estimates are on the high side of current pay standards. Smaller circulation magazines and some departments of the larger magazines will pay a lower rate.

Editors know that the listings in *Writer's Market* are read and used by writers with a wide range of experience, from those as-yet unpublished writers just starting out, to those with a successful, profitable freelance career. As a result, many magazines publicly report pay rates in the lower end of their actual pay ranges. Experienced writers will be able to successfully negotiate higher pay rates for their material. Newer writers should be encouraged that as your reputation grows (along with your clip file), you will be able to command higher rates. The article How Much Should I Charge? gives you an idea of pay ranges for different freelance jobs.

## WHAT'S NEW THIS YEAR?

We've added several features to make *Writer's Market* even more helpful in your search for the right magazine markets, features you won't find in any other writer's guide.

Many magazines are taking advantage of electronic media—and you should too. This year we've added information on whether a magazine accepts queries by e-mail or fax in addition to regular mail, and whether writers' guidelines are available online or by e-mail. We use a small computer icon to indicate that a magazine's website carries original online-only content and the online editor to address your query to.

Some areas of a magazine are more open to newer writers than others. Often writers unknown to the editor can break in with shorter features, columns or departments. This year we've added a key symbol ( ⚷ ) to identify the best ways to break in to *that* particular magazine.

### Information at-a-glance

Last year we made some changes to help you access the information you need as efficiently as possible. Most immediately noticeable, we added a number of symbols at the beginning of each listing to quickly convey certain important information. In the Consumer Magazine section, symbols identify comparative payment rates ( **$—$ $ $ $** ); new listings ( **N** ); "opportunity" markets ( **✖** ) that are at least 75% freelance written, appear quarterly or more frequently, and buy a high number of manuscripts; and magazines that do not accept freelance submissions ( **⊘** ). Different sections of *Writer's Market* include other symbols; check the front and back inside covers for an explanation of all the symbols used throughout the book.

We also highlighted important information in boldface, the "quick facts" you won't find in any other market book, but should know before you submit your work. To clearly identify the editorial "point person" at each magazine, the word "**Contact:**" identifies the appropriate person to query at each magazine. We also highlight what percentage of the magazine is freelance written, how many manuscripts a magazine buys per year of nonfiction, fiction, poetry and fillers and respective pay rates in each category.

**Information on publications listed in the previous edition of *Writer's Market* but not included in this edition may be found in the General Index.**

## ANIMAL

The publications in this section deal with pets, racing and show horses, and other domestic animals and wildlife. Magazines about animals bred and raised for the market are classified in the Farm category of Trade, Technical & Professional Journals. Publications about horse racing can be found in the Sports section.

**$ $** **AKC GAZETTE**, American Kennel Club, 260 Madison Ave., New York NY 10016. Fax: (212)696-8272. Website: http://www.akc.org/gazet.htm. Editor-in-Chief: Diane Vasey. **Contact:** Josh Adams, features editor. **85% freelance written.** Monthly association publication "slanted to interests of fanciers of purebred dogs as opposed to commercial interests or pet owners. We require solid expertise from our contributors—we are *not* a pet magazine." Estab. 1889. Circ. 60,000. Pays on publication. Publishes ms an average of 6 months after acceptance. Byline given. Offers 10% kill fee. Buys first North American serial rights, international and electronic rights. Submit seasonal material 6 months in advance. Reports in up to 2 months. Writer's guidelines for #10 SASE.

**Nonfiction:** General interest, historical, how-to, humor, photo feature, profiles, dog art, travel, training and canine performance sports. No poetry, tributes to individual dogs, or fiction. **Buys 30-40 mss/year.** Query with or without published clips. Length: 1,000-3,000 words. **Pays $200-400.** Pays expenses of writers on assignment.

**Photos:** State availability of photos with submission. Reviews color transparencies and prints only. Offers $25-150/ photo. Captions, model releases and identification of subjects required. Buys one-time rights. Photo contest guidelines for #10 SASE.

**Fiction:** Annual short fiction contest only. Guidelines for #10 SASE.

⬛ The online magazine carries original content not found in the print edition. Contact: Sori Tietjen.

**Tips:** "Contributors should be involved in the dog fancy or expert in area they write about (veterinary, showing, field trialing, obedience, training, dogs in legislation, dog art or history or literature). All submissions are welcome but author must be a credible expert or be able to interview and quote the experts. Veterinary articles must be written by or with veterinarians. Humorous features are personal experiences relative to purebred dogs that have broader applications. For features generally, know the subject thoroughly and be conversant with jargon peculiar to the sport of dogs."

**$ AMERICA'S CUTTER**, Published by GoGo Communications, Inc., 201 W. Moore, Suite 200, Terrell TX 75160. (972)563-7001. Fax: (972)563-7004. E-mail: acutterl@airmail.net. Website: http://www.americascutter.com. **Contact:** Carroll Brown Arnold, publisher/editor. **25% freelance written.** Works with a small number of new/unpublished writers each year. Bi-monthly magazine covering cutting horses, their owners, trainers and riders. Estab. 1995. Circ. 5,000. Pays on publication. Publishes ms 3 months after acceptance. Byline given. Buys one-time, North American serial rights. Query by mail, e-mail, fax. Reports in 1 month. Sample copy $4.25 or on website.

**Nonfiction:** Informational and historical articles on cutting horse competition and equipment; new products; interviews/ profiles. Length: 250-1,500 words. **Pays $10-150.**

**Photos:** Send photo with submission. Reviews 35mm slide transparencies, 5×7 and 8×10 photos, color and b&w. Pays $5-15/photo.

**Poetry:** Accepts some poetry geared toward cutters and cutting horse owners and trainers. **Pays $5-25.**

**Tips:** "We are interested only in cutting horse-related subjects. Writing style should show a deep interest in horses coupled with knowledge of the world of cutting. We are looking for the 'hidden' success stories in our industry."

**⬛ ⬛ ANIMALS**, Massachusetts Society for the Prevention of Cruelty to Animals, 350 S. Huntington Ave., Boston MA 02130. (617)522-7400. Fax: (617)522-4885. Editor: Joni Praded. Managing Editor: Paula Abend. **90% freelance written.** Bimonthly magazine publishing "articles on wildlife (American and international), domestic animals, balanced treatments of controversies involving animals, conservation, animal welfare issues, pet health and pet care." Estab. 1868. Circ. 100,000. **Pays on acceptance.** Publishes ms an average of 5 months after acceptance. Byline given. Offers negotiable kill fee. Buys one-time rights or makes work-for-hire assignments. Submit seasonal material 6 months in advance. Reports in 6 weeks. Sample copy for $2.95 and 9×12 SAE with 4 first-class stamps. Writer's guidelines for #10 SASE.

**Nonfiction:** Exposé, general interest, how-to, opinion and photo feature on animal and environmental issues and controversies, plus practical pet-care topics. "*Animals* does not publish breed-specific domestic pet articles or 'favorite pet' stories. Poetry and fiction are also not used." **Buys 50 mss/year.** Query with published clips. Length: 2,200 words maximum. Sometimes pays the expenses of writers on assignment.

**Photos:** State availability of photos with submission, if applicable. Reviews contact sheets, 35mm transparencies and 5×7 or 8×10 prints. Payment depends on usage size and quality. Captions, model releases and identification of subjects required. Buys one-time rights.

**Columns/Departments:** Books (book reviews of books on animals and animal-related subjects). **Buys 18 mss/year.** Query with published clips. Length: 300 words maximum. Profile (women and men who've gone to extraordinary lengths to aid animals). Length: 800 words maximum. **Buys 6 mss/year.** Query with clips.

**Tips:** "Present a well-researched proposal. Be sure to include clips that demonstrate the quality of your writing. Stick to categories mentioned in *Animals'* editorial description. Combine well-researched facts with a lively, informative writing style. Feature stories are written almost exclusively by freelancers. We continue to seek proposals and articles that take a humane approach. Articles should concentrate on how issues affect animals, rather than humans."

**$ $ APPALOOSA JOURNAL**, Appaloosa Horse Club, 5070 Hwy. 8 West, P.O. Box 8403, Moscow ID 83843-0903. (208)882-5578. Fax: (208)882-8150. E-mail: journal@appaloosa.com. **Contact:** Robin Hirzel, editor. **20-40% freelance written.** Monthly magazine covering Appaloosa horses. Estab. 1946. Circ. 25,000. Pays on publication. Publishes ms an average of 3 months after acceptance. Byline given. Buys first North American serial rights. Reports in 1 month on queries; 2 months on mss. Sample copy and writer's guidelines free.

● *Appaloosa Journal* no longer accepts material for columns.

**Nonfiction:** Historical, interview/profile, photo feature. **Buys 15-20 mss/year.** Query with or without published clips, or send complete ms. Length: 1,000-3,000 words. **Pays $100-400.** Sometimes pays expenses of writers on assignment.

**Photos:** Send photos with submission. Payment varies. Captions and identification of subjects required.

**Tips:** "Articles by writers with horse knowledge, news sense and photography skills are in great demand. If it's a solid article about an Appaloosa, the writer has a pretty good chance of publication. A good understanding of the breed and the industry is helpful. Make sure there's some substance and a unique twist."

**[N] $ $ ASPCA ANIMAL WATCH,** The American Society for the Prevention of Cruelty to Animals, 424 E. 92nd St., New York NY 10128-6804. (212)876-7700. Fax: (212)410-0087. E-mail: publications@aspca.org. Website: http://www.aspca.org. Editor: Cindy A. Adams. **Contact:** Marion Lane, senior editor. **20-30% freelance written.** Quarterly magazine covering animal welfare. "The ASPCA's mission is to alleviate pain, fear and suffering in all animals. ASPCA *Animal Watch* is the voice of the ASCPA, it is our primary means of communicating with and educating our membership. In addition to in-depth, timely coverage and original reporting on important issues, *Animal Watch* provides practical advice on companion animal care. The ASCPA promotes the adoption and responsible care of pets, and through the magazine we encourage excellent stewardship in areas such as diet, exercise and veterinary care." Estab. 1992. Circ. 214,000. Pays on publication. Publishes ms an average of 4 months after acceptance. Byline given. Offers 50% kill fee. Buys first North American serial rights. Editorial lead time 6 months. Submit seasonal material 6 months in advance. Accepts queries by mail, fax. Accepts simultaneous submissions. Reports in 2 months on queries; 3 months on mss. Sample copy for #10 SAE with 4 first-class stamps or on website. Writer's guidelines for #10 SASE.
**Nonfiction:** Exposé, general interest, historical/nostalgic, how-to, interview/profile, photo feature, travel. No stories told from animals' point of view, religious stories, fiction or poetry, articles with strident animal rights messages or articles with gory details. **Buys 25-30 mss/year.** Query with published clips. Length: 650-2,500 words. **Pays $75-600.** Sometimes pays expenses of writers on assignment.
**Photos:** State availability of photos with submission. Reviews transparencies and prints. Offers $75-300/photo or negotiates payment individually. Captions, model releases and identification of subjects required. Buys one-time rights.
**Columns/Departments:** Humane Living (profiles, short news stories), 400-700 words; Animals Abroad (first person by someone abroad), 650-700 words; Animals & the Law (balanced report on a legal or legislative subject), 650-700 words. **Buys 10 mss/year.** Query with or without published clips or send complete ms. **Pays $75-175.**
**Tips:** "The most important assets for an *Animal Watch* contributor are familiarity with the animal welfare movement in the U.S., the ability to write lively, well-researched articles. We are always looking for positive stories about people and groups and businesses who are helping to protect animals in some way and may inspire others to do the same. We know the problems—share with us some solutions, some approaches that are working. Everything we publish should include 'How you can help. . . .' We are as likely to assign a feature as a short piece for one of the departments."

**$ $ CAT FANCY,** Fancy Publications, Inc., P.O. Box 6050, Mission Viejo CA 92690. (949)855-8822. Fax: 949-855-0654. E-mail: aluke@fancypubs.com Website: http://www.animalnetwork.com. **Contact:** Amanda Luke, editor. **80-90% freelance written.** Monthly magazine mainly for women ages 25-54 interested in all phases of cat ownership. Estab. 1965. Circ. 303,000. Pays on publication. Publishes ms an average of 6 months after acceptance. Buys first North American serial rights. Byline given. Absolutely no simultaneous submissions. Submit seasonal material 4 months in advance. Reports in 3 months. Sample copy for $5.50. Writer's guidelines for SASE.
**Nonfiction:** Historical, medical, how-to, humor, informational, personal experience, photo feature, technical; must be cat oriented. **Buys 5-7 mss/issue.** Query by mail first with published clips. Length: 500-3,000 words. **Pays $35-400; special rates for photo/story packages.**
**Photos:** Photos purchased with or without accompanying ms. Pays $50 minimum for color prints; $50-200 for 35mm or 2¼ × 2¼ color transparencies; occasionally pays more for particularly outstanding or unusual work. Photo guidelines for SASE; then send prints and transparencies. Model release required.
**Columns/Departments:** Cat Newsline (news of national interest to cat lovers), 1,000 words maximum; Kids for Cats (short stories, how-to, crafts, puzzles for 10-16 year olds); Feline Friends (once or twice/year, readers' special cats).
**Poetry:** Short, cat-related poems. Submit any number but always with SASE.
**Fiction:** Not reviewing fiction at this time.
**Fillers:** Newsworthy or unusual; items with photos. Query first. Buys 5/year. Length: 500-1,000 words. Pays $35-100.
**Tips:** "Most of the articles we receive are profiles of the writers' own cats or profiles of cats that have recently died. We reject almost all of these stories. What we need are well-researched articles that will give our readers the information they need to better care for their cats or to help them fully enjoy cats. Please review past issues and notice the informative nature of articles before querying us with an idea. *Please query first.*"

**$ $ CATS MAGAZINE,** Primedia Special Interests, 260 Madison Ave., 8th Floor, New York NY 10016. E-mail: info@catsmag.com. Website: http://www.catsmag.com. **Contact:** Jane W. Reilly, editor-in-chief. **80% freelance written.** Monthly magazine for owners and lovers of cats. Estab. 1945. Circ. 127,000. **Pays on acceptance.** Byline given. Buys all rights. Editorial works 6 months in advance. Accepts queries by mail, fax.
**Nonfiction:** General interest (concerning cats); how-to (care, etc. for cats); health-related; personal experience; travel. Query. Length 1,500-2,500 words. **Pays $50-500.**
**Photos:** State availability of photos with submissions. Reviews color slides, 2¼ × 2¼ transparencies. Identification of subjects required. Buys all rights.
**Columns/Departments:** Cat Tales (true cat-theme short stories), 250-1,000 words. Buys Cat Tales on spec only. Do not query. **Pays $25.**
**Tips:** "Writer must show an affinity for cats. Extremely well-written, thoroughly researched, carefully thought-out articles have the best chance of being accepted. Innovative topics or a new twist on an old subject are always welcomed."

**$ CATSUMER REPORT, Consumer Magazine for Cat Owners**, Good Communications, P.O. Box 10069, Austin TX 78766-1069. (512)454-6090. Fax: (512)454-3420. E-mail: gooddogmag@aol.com. Website: http://www.prod ogs.com/dmn/gooddog. Publisher: Ross Becker. **Contact:** Judi Becker, editor/managing editor. **90% freelance written.** Bimonthly magazine for consumers/laypeople. "*CATsumer Report* is fun, easy, conversational read, but the reader should also learn while enjoying the publication." Estab. 1994. Pays on publication. Byline given. Kill fee varies. Buys first North American serial rights. Editorial lead time 4 months. Submit seasonal material 4 months in advance. Accepts simultaneous submissions. Sample copy and writer's guidelines for SAE.
**Nonfiction:** General interest, humor, interview/profile, new product, opinion, personal experience. No fiction or poetry. **Buys 30 mss/year.** Send complete ms. Length: 700-1,200 words. Rates negotiable.
**Tips:** "E-mail me a cover letter and include the manuscript (as an e-mail message, not an attached file). It's faster."

**$ $ THE CHRONICLE OF THE HORSE**, P.O. Box 46, Middleburg VA 20118-0046. (540)687-6341. Fax: (540)687-3937. Website: http://www.chronofhorse.com. Editor: John Strassburger. Managing Editor: Nancy Comer. **Contact:** Beth Rasin, assistant editor. **80% freelance written.** Weekly magazine about horses. "We cover English riding sports, including horse showing, grand prix jumping competitions, steeplechase racing, foxhunting, dressage, endurance riding, handicapped riding and combined training. We are the official publication for the national governing bodies of many of the above sports. We feature news, how-to articles on equitation and horse care and interviews with leaders in the various fields." Estab. 1937. Circ. 22,000. **Pays for features on acceptance**; news and other items on publication. Publishes ms an average of 4 months after acceptance. Byline given. Buys first North American rights and makes work-for-hire assignments. Submit seasonal material 3 months in advance. Query by mail. Reports in 10 weeks. Sample copy for $2 and 9×12 SAE. Writer's guidelines for #10 SASE or on website.
**Nonfiction:** General interest; historical/nostalgic (history of breeds, use of horses in other countries and times, art, etc.); how-to (trailer, train, design a course, save money, etc.); humor (centered on living with horses or horse people); interview/profile (of nationally known horsemen or the very unusual); technical (horse care, articles on feeding, injuries, care of foals, shoeing, etc.). Length: 6-7 pages. **Pays $125-200.** News of major competitions, "clear assignment with us first." Length: 1,500 words. **Pays $150.** Small local competitions, 800 words. **Pays $50-75.** Special issues: Steeplechase Racing (January); American Horse in Sport and Grand Prix Jumping (February); Horse Show (March); Intercollegiate (April); Kentucky 4-Star Preview (April); Junior and Pony (April); Combined Training (May); Dressage (June); Hunt Roster (September); Vaulting and Handicapped (November); Stallion (December). No Q&A interviews, clinic reports, Western riding articles, personal experience or wild horses. **Buys 300 mss/year.** Query or send complete ms. Length: 300-1,225 words. **Pays $25-200.**
**Photos:** State availability of photos. Accepts prints or color slides. Accepts color for b&w reproduction. Pays $25-30. Identification of subjects required. Buys one-time rights.
**Columns/Departments:** Dressage, Combined Training, Horse Show, Horse Care, Racing over Fences, Young Entry (about young riders, geared for youth), Horses and Humanities, Hunting. Query or send complete ms. Length: 300-1,225 words. **Pays $25-200.**
**Poetry:** Light verse, traditional. No free verse. **Buys 30/year.** Length: 5-25 lines. **Pays $15.**
**Fillers:** Anecdotes, short humor, newsbreaks, cartoons. **Buys 300/year.** Length: 50-175 lines. **Pays $10-20.**
> The online magazine carries original content not found in the print edition and includes writer's guidelines. Contact: Erin Harty, online editor.
**Tips:** "Get our guidelines. Our readers are sophisticated, competitive horsemen. Articles need to go beyond common knowledge. Freelancers often attempt too broad or too basic a subject. We welcome well-written news stories on major events, but clear the assignment with us."

**$ $ DOG FANCY**, Fancy Publications, Inc., P.O. Box 6050, Mission Viejo CA 92690-6050. Fax: (949)855-3045. E-mail: Sbiller@fancypubs.com. Website: http://www.dogfancy.com. Editor: Betty Liddick. **Contact:** Steven Biller, managing editor. **95% freelance written.** Monthly magazine for men and women of all ages interested in all phases of dog ownership. Estab. 1970. Circ. 286,000. Pays on publication. Publishes ms an average of 6 months after acceptance. Byline given. Offers $100 kill fee. Buys first North American serial and non-exclusive electronic and other rights. Submit seasonal material 6 months in advance. Accepts simultaneous submissions. Reports in 2 months. Sample copy for $5.50. Writer's guidelines for #10 SASE.
**Nonfiction:** Book excerpts, general interest, how-to, humor, inspirational, interview/profile, new product, personal experience, photo feature, travel. "No stories written from a dog's point of view, poetry, anything that advocates irresponsible dog care, tributes to dogs that have died or beloved family pets." **Buys 100 mss/year.** Query by mail. Length: 850-1,500 words. **Pays $200-500.**
**Photos:** State availability of photos with submission. Reviews contact sheets, transparencies and prints. Offers no additional payment for photos accepted with ms. Model release, identification of subjects required. Buys one-time and electronic rights.
**Columns/Departments:** Dogs on the Go (travel with dogs), 600-700 words; Dogs That Make a Difference (heroic dogs), 800 words. **Buys 24 mss/year.** Query. **Pays $300-400.**
**Fiction:** Occasionally publishes novel excerpts.
> The online magazine carries original content not found in the print edition. Contact: John Fultz, online editor.
**Tips:** "We're looking for the unique experience that enhances the dog/owner relationship—with the dog as the focus of the story, not the owner. Medical articles are assigned to veterinarians. Note that we write for a lay audience (non-

technical), but we do assume a certain level of intelligence. Read the magazine before making a pitch. Make sure your query is clear, concise and relevant."

**N** **$** **DOG SPORTS MAGAZINE**, 231 Orin Way, Douglas WY 82633. (307)358-3487. Fax: (307)358-4752. E-mail: dsm@coffey.com. Website: http://www.dogsports.com. Editor: Cheryl Carlson. **Contact:** Laurel Johnson, producer. **5% freelance written.** Monthly tabloid covering working dogs. Estab. 1979. Circ. 2,000. Pays on publication. Publishes ms an average of 1 month after acceptance. Byline given. Buys first North American serial and reprint rights. Editorial lead time 1 month. Submit seasonal material 1 month in advance. Accepts queries by mail, e-mail. Accepts simultaneous submissions. Sample copy free or on website.
**Nonfiction:** Essays, general interest, how-to (working dogs), humor, interview/profile, technical. **Buys 5 mss/year.** Send complete ms. **Pays $50.**
**Reprints:** Accepts previously published submissions.
**Photos:** State availability of photos with submission. Reviews prints. Offers no additional payment for photos accepted with ms. Captions and identification of subjects required. Buys all rights.

**☆** **$ $** **DOG WORLD, The Authority on Dog Care**, Primedia Special Interest Publications, 500 N. Dearborn. Suite 1100, Chicago IL 60610. (312)396-0600. Fax: (312)467-7118. E-mail: dogworld3@aol.com. Website: http://www.dogworldmag.com. **Contact:** Donna Marcel, editor. **95% freelance written.** Monthly magazine covering dogs. "We write for the serious dog enthusiasts, breeders, veterinarians, groomers, etc., as well as a general audience interested in in-depth information about dogs." Estab. 1915. Circ. 61,000. **Pays on acceptance.** Byline given. Buys first North American serial rights. Editorial lead time 10 weeks. Submit seasonal material 4 months in advance. Reports in 6 months. Writer's guidelines free.
**Nonfiction:** General interest on dogs including health care, veterinary medicine, grooming, legislation, responsible ownership, show awards, obedience training, show schedules, Junior Showmanship, kennel operations, dog sports, breed spotlights and histories, how-to, interview/profile, new products, personal experience, travel. No fluffy poems or pieces about dogs. Special issues: July (breed standards); February (puppy). **Buys approximately 80 mss/year.** Query with SASE. Length: 3,000-3,500 words. Payment negotiated. Sometimes pays the expenses of writers on assignment.
**Reprints:** Rarely publishes reprints. Send tearsheet of article, typed ms with rights for sale noted, and information about when and where the article previously appeared. Payment negotiated on individual basis.
**Photos:** State availability of photos with submission. Offers no additional payment for photos accepted with ms; occasionally negotiates payment individually for professional photos. Current rate for a cover photo is $300; inside color photo $50-175; b&w $25-50, depending on size used. Payment on publication. Buys one-time rights.
**Tips:** "Get a copy of editorial calendar, stay away from 'fluffy' pieces—we run very few. Be able to translate technical/medical articles into what average readers can understand. Mention accompanying art—very important."

**$** **DOGGONE, The Newsletter About Fun Places to Go And Cool Stuff to Do With Your Dog**, P.O. Box 651155, Vero Beach FL 32965-1155. Fax: (561)569-8434. E-mail: doggonenl@aol.com. Website: http://www.doggonefun.com. **Contact:** Wendy Ballard, publisher. "*DogGone* is a bimonthly travel and activity newsletter for dog owners. All destination pieces are written with a dog slant, including lodgings that accept pets, dog-allowed tourist attractions, parks, hiking trails, walking tours, even restaurants with outdoor seating that don't mind a pooch on the porch." Estab. 1993. Circ. 3,000. Pays on publication. Publishes ms an average of 4 months after acceptance. Buys first rights and electronic rights. Editorial lead time 4 months. Submit seasonal material 4 months in advance. Query by mail, e-mail. Reports in 1 month. Sample copy for 9×12 SASE and 3 first-class stamps. Writer's guidelines for #10 SASE.
**Nonfiction:** Travel, exposé, historical, how-to, personal experience. "No poetry or 'My dog is the best because . . .' articles." Query with published clips or send complete ms. Length: 300-1,000 words. **Pays $34-100.** Writers may opt to accept subscription to *DogGone* as partial payment.
**Reprints:** Send photocopy of article and information about when and where it previously appeared. **Pays $34-100.**
**Photos:** Send photos with submission. Reviews prints or slides. Offers no additional payment for photos accepted with ms. Captions required. Buys rights with ms.
**Columns/Departments:** Beyond Fetch (creative activities to enjoy with dogs), 300-900 words; Parks Department (dogs-allowed national, state, regional parks), 300 words; Visiting Vet (travel-related), 300 words; Touring (walking or driving tours with pets-allowed stops), 600-900 words; Worth a Paws (pet-friendly stops near highways/interstates). Query with published clips or send complete ms. **Pays $34-100.**
**Fillers:** Facts, dogs-allowed events. Length: 50-200 words. **Pays $15.**
**Tip:** "Submit an entertaining yet informative manuscript about a personal travel experience with your dog. Make me want to recreate your vacation for myself."

**☆** **$** **DRESSAGE TODAY**, Fleet Street Publishing, 656 Quince Orchard Rd., Suite 600, Gaithersburg MD 20878. (301)977-3900. Fax: (301)990-9015. E-mail: dtletters@aol.com. Editorial Director: Mary Kay Kinnish. **Contact:** Stacey Wigmore, assistant editor. **70% freelance written.** Monthly. "*Dressage Today* presents national and international news and developments associated with the art and sport of dressage. Expands reader's knowledge of this classical, universal equestrian discipline. Serves as a conscience for good of sport, horses and riders; provides a forum for discussion and debate with respect to the sport. Enhances self-awareness and self-improvement through articles that address mental, physical and emotional aspects of the sport." Estab. 1994. Circ. 36,000. **Pays on acceptance.** Publishes ms an average of 6 months after acceptance. Byline given. Offers 25% kill fee. Buys first North American serial rights and makes work-for-hire assignments. Editorial lead time 3 months. Submit seasonal material 6 months in advance. Query by mail, e-mail, fax, phone. Reports in 2 months. Writer's guidelines for #10 SASE.

**Nonfiction:** Book excerpts, general interest, historical/nostalgic, how-to (dressage training for horse and/or rider, equine management), humor, interview/profile, opinion, personal experience, product reviews, technical. **Buys 36 mss/year.** Query with or without published clips. Length: 500-3,000 words. **Pays $150-300 for assigned articles, $100 maximum for unsolicited articles.** Sometimes pays expenses of writers on assignment.

**Reprints:** Sometimes accepts previously published submissions. Send photocopy of article or typed ms with rights for sale noted and information about when and where the article previously appeared. Negotiates payment individually.

**Photos:** State availability of photos with submission or send photos with submission. Reviews transparencies and 4×6 or 3×5 prints). Negotiates payment individually. Captions and identification of subjects required. Buys one-time rights.

**Columns/Departments:** The Arena (short, newsworthy items), 200-400 words; Book/video reviews, 500 words. **Buys 12-24 mss/year.** Query. **Pays $25-50.**

**Fiction:** Humorous, slice-of-life vignettes. For example, "800-word articles that epitomize the relationship with dressage horses." No articles about horses dying. Query. Length: 650-1,000 words.

**Tips:** "Send résumé with relevant clips. Call on phone. Be willing to start out with a smaller piece."

**$ $THE GAITED HORSE, The One Magazine for all Gaited Horses,** 4 Cadence L.L.C., 8008 Elk-to-Hwy Rd., P.O. Box 259, Elk WA 99009. Fax: (509)292-8330. E-mail: editor@thegaitedhorse.com. Website: http://www.thegaitedhorse.com. **Contact:** Rhonda Hart, editor. Quarterly magazine. "Subject matter must relate in some way to gaited horses." Estab. 1998. Circ. 5,000. Pays on publication. Publishes ms an average of 2 months after acceptance. Byline given. Buys first North American serial rights or makes work-for-hire assignments. Editorial lead time 4 months. Submit seasonal material 4 months in advance. Accepts simultaneous submissions. Reports in 6 weeks on queries; 1 month on mss. Sample copy for $3; writer's guidelines free or on website.

**Nonfiction:** Book excerpts, essays, exposé, general interest (gaited horses), historical/nostalgic, how-to, humor, interview/profile, new product, personal experience, photo experience, photo features, travel, anything related to gaited horses, lifestyles, art, etc. "No 'My first horse' stories." **Buys 25 mss/year.** Query and/or send complete ms. Length: 1,000-2,500 words. **Pays $50-300.**

**Photos:** State availability of photos with submission or send photos with submission. Reviews prints (3×5 or larger). Negotiates payment individually. Captions, model releases and identification of subjects required. Buys one-time rights.

**Columns/Departments:** Through the Legal Paces (equine owners rights & responsibilities; Horse Cents (financial advice for horse owners); Health Check (vet advice); Smoother Trails (trail riding); all 500-1,000 words. **Buys 24 mss/year.** Query. **Pays $100.**

**Fillers:** Anecdotes, newsbreaks, short humor. **Buys 20/year.** Length: 5-300 words. **Pays $10-50.**

**Tips:** "We are actively seeking to develop writers from within the various gaited breeds and equine disciplines. If you have a unique perspective on these horses, we would love to hear from you."

**$ GOOD DOG!, Consumer Magazine for Dog Owners,** P.O. Box 10069, Austin TX 78766-1069. (512)454-6090. Fax: (512)454-3420. E-mail: gooddogmag@aol.com. Website: http://www.prodogs.com/dmn/gooddog. Publisher: Ross Becker. **Contact:** Judi Becker, editor. **90% freelance written.** Bimonthly magazine for consumers/laypeople. "*Good Dog!* is a fun, easy, conversational read but the reader should also learn while enjoying the publication." Estab. 1988. Pays on publication. Byline given. Buys first North American serial rights. Editorial lead time 4 months. Submit seasonal material 4 months in advance. Query by mail, e-mail, phone. Accepts simultaneous submissions. Sample copy and writer's guidelines for SAE.

**Nonfiction:** General interest, humor, interview/profile, new product, opinion, personal experience. No fiction or poetry. **Buys 30 mss/year.** Send complete ms. Length: 700-1,200 words. Rates negotiable.

**Photos:** Send photos with submission. Reviews 4×6 or larger prints. Negotiates payment individually. Identification of subjects required with label of photo owner/address.

**Tips:** "E-mail a cover letter and manuscript (as an e-mail message not an attached file). It's faster this way."

**$ THE GREYHOUND REVIEW,** P.O. Box 543, Abilene KS 67410-0543. (785)263-4660. Fax: (785)263-4689. E-mail: nga@jc.net. Website: http://www.nga.jc.net. Editor: Gary Guccione. **Contact:** Tim Horan, managing editor. **20% freelance written.** Monthly magazine covering greyhound breeding, training and racing. Estab. 1911. Circ. 4,000. **Pays on acceptance.** Byline given. Buys first rights. Submit seasonal material 2 months in advance. Reports in 2 weeks on queries; 1 month on mss. Sample copy for $3. Writer's guidelines free.

**Nonfiction:** How-to, interview/profile, personal experience. "Articles must be targeted at the greyhound industry: from hard news, special events at racetracks to the latest medical discoveries. Do not submit gambling systems." **Buys 24 mss/year.** Query. Length: 1,000-10,000 words. **Pays $85-150.** Sometimes pays the expenses of writers on assignment.

**Reprints:** Send photocopy of article. Pays 100% of the amount paid for an original article.

**Photos:** State availability of photos with submission. Reviews 35mm transparencies and 8×10 prints. Offers $10-50/photo. Identification of subjects required. Buys one-time rights.

**$ $HORSE ILLUSTRATED, The Magazine for Responsible Horse Owners,** Fancy Publications, Inc., P.O. Box 6050, Mission Viejo CA 92690-6050. (949)855-8822. Fax: (949)855-3045. E-mail: joltmann@fancypubs.com. Website: http://www.horseillustrated.com. Contact: Mora Harris, associate editor, ext 422. **90% freelance written.** Prefers to work with published/established writers but will work with new/unpublished writers. Monthly magazine covering all aspects of horse ownership. "Our readers are adults, mostly women, between the ages of 18 and 40; stories should be geared to that age group and reflect responsible horse care." Estab. 1976. Circ. 190,000. Pays on publication. Publishes ms an average of 8 months after acceptance. Byline given. Buys one-time rights; requires first North American rights among equine publications. Submit seasonal material 6 months in advance. Reports in 3 months. Sample copy for $3.50. Writer's guidelines for #10 SASE.

**Nonfiction:** How-to (horse care, training, veterinary care), photo feature. No "little girl" horse stories, "cowboy and Indian" stories or anything not *directly* relating to horses. "We are looking for longer, more authoritative, in-depth features on trends and issues in the horse industry. Such articles must be queried first with a detailed outline of the article and clips. We rarely have a need for fiction." **Buys 20 mss/year.** Query or send complete ms. Length: 1,000-2,000 words. **Pays $100-300 for assigned articles; $50-300 for unsolicited articles.**

**Photos:** Send photos with submission. Reviews 35mm transparencies, medium format transparencies and 5×7 prints.

**Tips:** "Freelancers can break in at this publication with feature articles on Western and English training methods; veterinary and general care how-to articles; and horse sports articles. We rarely use personal experience articles. Submit photos with training and how-to articles whenever possible. We have a very good record of developing new freelancers into regular contributors/columnists. We are always looking for fresh talent, but certainly enjoy working with established writers who 'know the ropes' as well. We are accepting less freelance work—much is now assigned and contracted."

**$ $ THE HORSE, Your Guide to Equine Health Care,** P.O. Box 4680, Lexington KY 40544-4680. (606)276-6771. Fax: (606)276-4450. E-mail: kherbert@thehorse.com. Website: http://www.thehorse.com. **Contact:** Kimberly S. Herbert, editor. **75% freelance written.** Monthly magazine covering equine health and care. *The Horse* is "an educational/news magazine geared toward the professional, hands-on horse owner." Estab. 1983. Circ. 36,000. Pays on publication. Publishes ms an average of 2 months after acceptance. Byline given. Buys first world and electronic rights, "depending on the writer." Query by mail, e-mail, fax, phone. Reports in 2 months on queries. Sample copy for $2.95 or on website. Writer's guidelines free.

**Nonfiction:** How-to, technical, topical interviews. "No first-person experiences not from professionals; this is a technical magazine to inform horse owners." **Buys 90 mss/year.** Query with published clips. Length: 500-5,000 words. **Pays $75-650.**

**Photos:** Send photos with submission. Reviews transparencies. Offers $10-150/photo. Captions and identification of subjects required.

**Columns/Departments:** Up Front (news on horse health), 100-500 words; Equinomics (economics of horse ownership), 2,500 words. **Buys 40 mss/year.** Query with published clips. **Pays $50-350.**

The online magazine carries original content not found in the print edition.

**Tips:** "We publish reliable horse health information from top industry professionals from around the world. Manuscript must be submitted electronically or on disk."

**N $ HORSES ALL,** North Hill Publications, 278-19 St. NE, Calgary, Alberta T2E 8P7 Canada. (403)248-9993. Fax: (403)248-8838. E-mail: nhpubs@cadvision.com **Contact:** Vanessa Peterelli, editor. **40% freelance written.** Eager to work with new/unpublished writers. Monthly tabloid for horse owners and the horse industry. Estab. 1977. Circ. 7,000. Pays on publication. Publishes ms an average of 3 months after acceptance. Byline given. Offers 30% kill fee. Buys first North American serial rights. Submit seasonal material 3 months in advance. Accepts queries by mail, e-mail, fax. Accepts simultaneous submissions. Sample copy and writer's guidelines for SAE.

**Nonfiction:** Book excerpts, essays, general interest, historical/nostalgic, how-to (training, horse care and maintenance), inspirational, interview/profile, personal experience, photo feature. "We would prefer more general stories, no specific local events or shows." **Buys 3 mss/year.** Query. Length: 800-1,400 words. **Pays $50-75 (Canadian) for solicited articles only.**

**Reprints:** Accepts previously published submissions.

**Photos:** Send photos with submission. Reviews prints 3×4 or larger. Negotiates payment individually. Captions, model releases, identification of subjects required. Buys one-time rights.

**Tips:** "Our writers must be knowledgeable about horses and the horse industry, and be able to write features in a readable, conversational manner, but in third person only, please. While we do include coverage of major events in our publication, we generally require that these events take place in Canada. Any exceptions to this general rule are evaluated on a case-by-case basis."

**$ I LOVE CATS,** I Love Cats Publishing, 450 Seventh Ave., Suite 1701, New York NY 10123. (212)244-2351. Fax: (212)244-2367. E-mail: yankee@dancom.com. Website: http://www.iluvcats.com. **Contact:** Lisa Allmendinger, editor. **100% freelance written.** Bimonthly magazine covering cats. "*I Love Cats* is a general interest cat magazine for the entire family. It caters to cat lovers of all ages. The stories in the magazine include fiction, nonfiction, how-to, humorous and columns for the cat lover." Estab. 1989. Circ. 100,000. Pays on publication. Publishes ms an average of 1 year after acceptance. Byline given. No kill fee. Buys all rights. Must sign copyright consent form. Editorial lead time 6 months. Submit seasonal material 9 months in advance. Accepts queries by mail, e-mail. Reports in 2 months. Sample copy for $4. Writer's guidelines for #10 SASE, website or by e-mail.

**Nonfiction:** Essays, general interest, how-to, humor, inspirational, interview/profile, new product, opinion, personal experience, photo feature. No poetry. **Buys 100 mss/year.** Send complete ms. Length: 500-1,500 words. **Pays $50-150, contributor copies or other premiums "if requested."** Sometimes pays expenses of writers on assignment.

**Photos:** Send photos with submission. Offers no additional payment for photos accepted with ms. Identification of subjects required. Buys all rights.

**Fiction:** Adventure, fantasy, historical, humorous, mainstream, mystery, novel excerpts, slice-of-life vignettes, suspense. "This is a family magazine. No graphic violence, pornography or other inappropriate material. *I Love Cats* is strictly 'G-rated.' " **Buys 100 mss/year.** Send complete ms. Length: 500-1,500 words. **Pays $50-150.**

**Fillers:** Anecdotes, facts, short humor. **Buys 25/year. Pays $25.**

**Tips:** "Please keep stories short and concise. Send complete ms with photos, if possible. I buy lots of first-time authors. Nonfiction pieces with color photos are always in short supply. With the exception of the standing columns, the rest of the magazine is open to freelancers. Be witty, humorous or take a different approach to writing."

**$ $ MUSHING**, Stellar Communications, Inc., P.O. Box 149, Ester AK 99725-0149. (907)479-0454. Fax: (907)479-3137. E-mail: editor@mushing.com. Website: http://www.mushing.com. Publisher: Todd Hoener. **Contact:** Enrico Sassi, managing editor. Bimonthly magazine on "all aspects of the growing sports of dogsledding, skijoring, carting, dog packing and weight pulling. *Mushing* promotes responsible dog care through feature articles and updates on working animal health care, safety, nutrition and training." Estab. 1987. Circ. 6,000. Pays on publication. Publishes ms an average of 4 months after acceptance. Byline given. Buys first serial and second serial (reprint) rights. Submit seasonal material 4 months in advance. Accepts queries by mail, e-mail, fax, phone. Reports in 8 months. Sample copy for $5, $6 US to Canada. Writer's guidelines free; call or e-mail for information.

**Nonfiction:** Historical, how-to, humor, interview/profile, new product, personal experience, photo feature, technical, innovations, travel. "We consider articles on canine health and nutrition, sled dog behavior and training, musher profiles and interviews, equipment how-to's, trail tips, expedition and race accounts, innovations, sled dog history, current issues, personal experiences and humor." Themes: Iditarod and long-distance racing (January/February); Expeditions/Peak of Race Season (March/April); health and nutrition (May/June); musher and dog profiles, summer activities (July/August); equipment, fall training (September/October); races and places (November/December). Prefers query with or without published clips and SASE, considers complete ms and SASE. Length: 1,000-2,500 words. **Pays $50-250 for articles.** Payment depends on length and quality. Pays expenses of writers on assignment, if prearranged.

**Photos:** Send photos with submission. Reviews contact sheets, transparencies, prints. Prefers 8×10 glossy prints or negatives for b&w. Offers $20-165/photo. Captions, model releases, identification of subjects required. Buys one-time and second reprint rights. We look for good b&w and quality color for covers and specials.

**Columns/Departments:** Query with or without published clips and SASE or send complete ms with SASE. Length: 500-1,000 words.

**Fiction:** Considers short, well-written and relevant or timely fiction. Query or send complete ms with SASE. Pay varies.

**Fillers:** Anecdotes, facts, cartoons, newsbreaks, short humor, puzzles. Length: 100-250 words. **Pays $20-35.**

**Tips:** "Read our magazine. Know something about dog-driven, dog-powered sports."

**$ $ PAINT HORSE JOURNAL**, American Paint Horse Association, P.O. Box 961023, Fort Worth TX 76161-0023. (817)834-2742. Fax: (817)838-7368. E-mail: ddodds@apha.com. Website: http://www.apha.com. **Contact:** Dan Streeter, senior copy editor. **10% freelance written.** Works with a small number of new/unpublished writers each year. Monthly magazine for people who raise, breed and show Paint horses. Estab. 1966. Circ. 30,000. **Pays on acceptance.** Publishes ms an average of 3 months after acceptance. Buys first North American serial rights plus reprint rights occasionally. Pays negotiable kill fee. Byline given. Phone queries OK, but prefers written query. Submit seasonal material 3 months in advance. Query by mail, e-mail, fax. Reports in 1 month. Writers guidelines available upon request. Sample copy $4.

**Nonfiction:** General interest (personality pieces on well-known owners of Paints); historical (Paint horses in the past—particular horses and the breed in general); how-to (train and show horses); photo feature (Paint horses). Now seeking informative well-written articles on recreational riding. **Buys 4-5 mss/issue.** Send complete ms. Length: 1,000-2,000 words. **Pays $35-450.**

**Reprints:** Accepts previously published articles. Send typed ms with rights for sale noted and information about when and where the article previously appeared. For reprints, pays 30-50% of the amount paid for an original article.

**Photos:** Send photos with ms. Offers no additional payment for photos accepted with accompanying ms. Uses 3×5 or larger b&w or color glossy prints; 35mm or larger color transparencies. Captions required. Photos must illustrate article and must include Paint Horses.

**Tips:** "*PHJ* needs breeder-trainer articles, Paint horse marketing and timely articles from areas throughout the US and Canada. We are looking for more recreational and how-to articles. We are beginning to cover equine activity such as trail riding, orienteering and other outdoor events. Photos with copy are almost always essential. Well-written first person articles are welcomed. Submit items that show a definite understanding of the horse business. Be sure you understand precisely what a Paint horse is as defined by the American Paint Horse Association. Use proper equine terminology."

**$ $ PETS MAGAZINE**, Moorshead Magazines, Ltd., 505 Consumers Rd., Suite 500, Toronto, Ontario M2J 4V8 Canada. (416)491-3699. Fax: (416)491-3996. E-mail: pets@moorshead.com. Website: http://www.moorshead.com/pets. **Contact:** Edward Zapletal, editor. **40% freelance written.** Bimonthly magazine for "pet owners, primarily cat and dog owners, but we also cover rabbits, guinea pigs, hamsters, gerbils, birds and fish. Issues covered include: pet health care, nutrition, general interest, grooming, training humor, human-animal bond stories. No fiction! No poetry!" Estab. 1983. Circ. 51,000. Pays within 30 days of publication. Publishes ms an average of 2 months after acceptance. Byline given.

Offers 50% kill fee. Buys first North American serial rights or other negotiable rights. Editorial lead time 3 months. Submit seasonal material 2 months in advance. Sample copy for #10 SAE with IRCs. Writer's guidelines for 9½×4 SAE with IRCs. "Please no U.S. postage on return envelope."
**Nonfiction:** General interest, humor, new product, personal experience, veterinary medicine, human interest (i.e., working animal), training and obedience. No fiction. **Buys 10 mss/year.** Query. Length: 500-1,500 words. **Pays 12-18¢/word (Canadian funds).**
**Reprints:** Considers reprints of previously published submissions. **Pays 6-9¢/word.**
**Photos:** Prefers good color pictures or slides. Reviews photocopies. Identification of subjects required. Buys one-time rights.
**Columns/Departments:** Grooming Your Pet (mostly dogs and cats), 300-400 words. **Buys 6-12 mss/year.** Query.
**Fillers:** Facts. **Buys 5/year.** Length: 20-100 words. **Pays $10-20.**
**Tips:** "Always approach with a query letter first. E-mail is good if you've got it. We'll contact you if we like what we see. I like writing to be friendly, informative, well-balanced with pros and cons. Remember, we're catering to pet owners, and they are a discriminating audience."

**$ $ THE QUARTER HORSE JOURNAL**, P.O. Box 32470, Amarillo TX 79120. (806)376-4811. Fax: (806)349-6400. E-mail: aqhajrnl@arnet. Website: http://www.aqha.com. Editor-in-Chief: Jim Jennings. **Contact:** Jim Bret Campbell, editor. **20% freelance written.** Prefers to work with published/established writers. Monthly official publication of the American Quarter Horse Association. Estab. 1948. Circ. 78,000. **Pays on acceptance.** Publishes ms an average of 6 months after acceptance. Buys first North American serial rights. Submit seasonal material 6 months in advance. Accepts queries by mail, e-mail, fax. Reports in 2 months. Sample copy and writer's guidelines for SAE.
**Nonfiction:** How-to (fitting, grooming, showing, or anything that relates to owning, showing, or breeding); informational (educational clinics, current news); interview (feature-type stories—must be about established horses or people who have made a contribution to the business); personal opinion; and technical (equine updates, new surgery procedures, etc.). **Buys 20 mss/year.** Length: 800-1,800 words. **Pays $150-300.**
**Photos:** Purchased with accompanying ms. Captions required. Send prints or transparencies. Uses 4×6 color glossy prints, 2¼×2¼, 4×5 or 35mm color transparencies. No additional pay for photos accepted with accompanying ms.
**Tips:** "Writers must have a knowledge of the horse business."

**★ $ $ REPTILE & AMPHIBIAN HOBBYIST**, T.F.H. Publications, One TFH Plaza, Neptune NJ 07753. (732)988-8400, ext. 235. Fax: (732)988-9635. E-mail: rephob@aol.com. Website: http://www-tfh.com. **Contact:** Tom Mazorlig, editor. Editor-in-chief: Marilee Talman. **100% freelance written.** "Colorful, varied monthly covering reptiles and amphibians as pets aimed at beginning to intermediate hobbyists. Pet shop distribution. Writers must know their material, including scientific names, identification, general terrarium maintenance." Estab. 1995. Circ. 30,000. Pays 60 days after acceptance. Publishes ms 6 months after acceptance. Byline given. Buys all rights, multiple rights or non-exclusive rights. Editorial lead time 2 months. Reports in 1 month on queries; 2 months on mss. Sample copy for $4.50. Writer's guidelines free.
**Nonfiction:** General interest, interview/profile, personal experience, photo feature, technical, travel. **Buys 120 mss/year.** Query. Length: 1,500-2,000 words. **Pays $100-120.**
**Photos:** Send photos with submission. Reviews transparencies and prints. Offers $20/photo. Captions, model releases and identification of subjects required. Buys all rights.
**Columns/Departments:** Herp People (profiles herp-related personalities); In Review (book reviews); Invertebrate Corner (terrarium invertebrates), all 1,500 words. **Buys 45 mss/year.** Query. **Pays $75-100.**
**Tips:** "Talk to the editor before sending anything. A short telephone conversation tells more about knowledge of subject matter than a simple query. I'll read anything, but it is very easy to detect an uninformed author. Very willing to polish articles from new writers."

**$ $ THE RETRIEVER JOURNAL**, Wildwood Press, P.O. Box 968, Traverse City MI 49685. (616)946-3712. Fax: (616)946-9588. E-mail: editor@villagepress.com. Website: http://www.villagepress.com/wildwood. Managing Editor: Bob Butz. **Contact:** Steve Smith, editor. **65% freelance written.** Bimonthly magazine covering retriever training and hunting with retrievers. *"The Retriever Journal* is geared to the retriever owner who hunts all game—upland and waterfowl—with a retriever. We cover major field trials and tests. We use some well-written 'how-to' and 'where-to' in each issue." Estab. 1995. Circ. 18,000. Pays on publication. Publishes ms an average of 8 months after acceptance. Byline given. Offers 40% kill fee. Buys first North American serial rights. Editorial lead time 8 months. Submit seasonal material 8 months in advance. Accepts queries by mail, e-mail, fax. Reports in 1 month on queries; 2 months on mss. Sample copy for $6.50. Writer's guidelines for #10 SASE.
**Nonfiction:** Essays, how-to, humor, nostalgia, personal experience, photo feature. Feature stories should focus on the use of retrieving breeds in hunting, training techniques, trialing, canine medicine, and the traditions of hunting with retrievers. Features on shotguns and shotgunning, wildlife species, and conservation topics are also in demand. "No 'dead dog' stories or stories from the animal's point of view." **Buys 15-30 mss/year.** Query or send complete ms. Length: 1,500-2,200 words. **Pays $300-500 for assigned articles; $250-400 for unsolicited articles.**
**Photos:** State availability of photos with submission. Reviews transparencies. Offers no additional payment for photos accepted with ms. Buys one-time rights.
**Fiction:** Humorous, slice-of-life vignettes. "Fiction is acceptable, but it must have the dog at the forefront of the story." **Buys 4-6 mss/year.** Send complete ms.

**Fillers:** Anecdotes, short humor. "There is an ongoing need for shorter featurettes and short filler pieces, such as training tips, vet tips, humor, dog-related news, product reviews, quotable quotes, and book reviews. These should be 150-1,000 words." **Buys 6-8/year.** Length: 700-1,500 words. **Pays $150-300.**

**Tips:** "Be familiar with past issues of *The Retriever Journal.* Since we only publish 6 times a year, submitting 'new' and 'fresh' material is important—don't send us a story similar to something we ran a year ago."

**$ $** THE WESTERN HORSEMAN, World's Leading Horse Magazine Since 1936, Western Horseman, Inc., P.O. Box 7980, Colorado Springs CO 80933-7980. (719)633-5524. Fax: (719)633-1392. E-mail: pclose@westernho rseman.com. Website: http://www.westernhorseman.com. **Contact:** Pat Close, editor. **50% freelance written.** Works with a small number of new/unpublished writers each year. Monthly magazine for horse owners covering horse care and training. Estab. 1936. Circ. 225,000. **Pays on acceptance.** Publishes ms an average of 5 months after acceptance. Buys one-time and North American serial rights. Byline given. Submit seasonal material 6 months in advance. Accepts queries by mail, e-mail, fax, phone. Reports in 3 weeks. Sample copy for $5. Writer's guidelines for #10 SASE.

**Nonfiction:** How-to (horse training, care of horses, tips, ranch/farm management, etc.), informational (on rodeos, ranch life, historical articles of the West emphasizing horses). **Buys 250 mss/year.** Query; no fax material. Length: 500-2,500 words. **Pays $100-600, "sometimes higher by special arrangement."**

**Photos:** Send photos with ms. Offers no additional payment for photos. Uses 5×7 or 8×10 b&w glossy prints and 35mm transparencies. Captions required.

**Tips:** "Submit clean copy, double spaced, with professional quality photos. Stay away from generalities. Writing style should show a deep interest in horses coupled with a wide knowledge of the subject. Almost all of the freelance articles we buy are accompanied by photographs or illustrations. In fact, the quality of the photos or illustrations sometimes makes the difference as to whether we buy an article."

# ART & ARCHITECTURE

Listed here are publications about art, art history, specific art forms and architecture written for art patrons, architects, artists and art enthusiasts. Publications addressing the business and management side of the art industry are listed in the Art, Design & Collectibles category of the Trade section. Trade publications for architecture can be found in Building Interiors, and Construction & Contracting sections.

**$ $** THE AMERICAN ART JOURNAL, Kennedy Galleries, Inc., 730 Fifth Ave., New York NY 10019. (212)541-9600. Fax: (212)977-3833. **Contact:** Jayne A. Kuchna, editor-in-chief. Prefers to work with published/established writers; works with a small number of new/unpublished writers each year. "Annual scholarly magazine of American art history of the 17th, 18th, 19th and 20th centuries, including painting, sculpture, architecture, photography, cultural history, etc., for people with a serious interest in American art, and who are already knowledgeable about the subject. Readers are scholars, curators, collectors, students of American art, or persons with a strong interest in Americana." Circ. 2,000. **Pays on acceptance.** Publishes ms an average of 6 months after acceptance. Byline given. Buys all rights, but will reassign rights to writer. Reports in 2 months. Sample copy for $18.

**Nonfiction:** "All articles are about some phase or aspect of American art history. No how-to articles or reviews of exhibitions. No book reviews or opinion pieces. No human interest approaches to artists' lives. No articles written in a casual or 'folksy' style. *Writing style must be formal and serious.*" **Buys 10-15 mss/year.** Submit complete ms "with good cover letter." No queries. Length: 2,500-8,000 words. **Pays $400-600.**

**Photos:** Purchased with accompanying ms. Captions required. Uses b&w only. Offers no additional payment for photos accepted with accompanying ms.

**Tips:** "Articles *must be* scholarly, thoroughly documented, well-researched, well-written and illustrated. Whenever possible, all manuscripts must be accompanied by b&w photographs, which have been integrated into the text by the use of numbers."

**$ $** AMERICAN INDIAN ART MAGAZINE, American Indian Art, Inc., 7314 E. Osborn Dr., Scottsdale AZ 85251-6401. (602)994-5445. Fax: (602)945-9533. **Contact:** Roanne P. Goldfein, editor. **97% freelance written.** Works with many new/unpublished writers each year. Quarterly magazine covering Native American art, historic and contemporary, including new research on any aspect of Native American art north of the US/Mexico border. Estab. 1975. Circ. 30,000. Pays on publication. Publishes ms an average of 3 months after acceptance. Byline given. Buys one-time and first rights. Reports in 3 weeks on queries; 3 months on mss. Writer's guidelines for #10 SASE.

**Nonfiction:** New research on any aspect of Native American art. No previously published work or personal interviews with artists. **Buys 12-18 mss/year.** Query. Length: 1,000-2,500 words. **Pays $75-300.**

**Photos:** An article usually requires between eight and fifteen photographs. (Photos should be glossy 8×10 prints; color photos should be transparencies; 35mm slides are acceptable.) Buys one-time publication rights to photos. Fee schedules and reimbursable expenses are decided upon by the magazine and the author.

**Tips:** "The magazine is devoted to all aspects of Native American art. Some of our readers are knowledgeable about the field and some know very little. We seek articles that offer something to both groups. Articles reflecting original research are preferred to those summarizing previously published information."

**$ $ $AMERICAN STYLE, The Art of Living Creatively**, The Rosen Group, 3000 Chestnut Ave., Suite 304, Baltimore MD 21211. (410)889-3093. Fax: (410)243-7089. E-mail: hoped@rosengrp.com. Website: http://www.america nstyle.com. **Contact:** Hope Daniels, editor. **50% freelance written.** Quarterly magazine covering handmade American Crafts. Estab. 1994. Circ. 50,000. Pays on publication. Publishes ms an average of 6 months after acceptance. Byline given. Buys first North American serial rights. Editorial lead time 6-9 months. Submit seasonal material 1 year in advance. Query by mail, e-mail, fax. Sample copy for $3. Writer's guidelines for #10 SASE.
   • *American Style* is especially interested in travel articles on arts/resort destinations, profiles of contemporary craft collectors and studio artists.
**Nonfiction:** Specialized arts/crafts interests. Query with published clips. Length: 300-2,500 words. **Pays $500-800.** Sometimes pays expenses of writers on assignment.
**Photos:** Send color photos with submission. Reviews oversized transparencies and 35mm slides. Negotiates payment individually. Captions required.
**Columns/Departments:** Artist Profiles, Artful Dining, 700-1,000 words. Query with published clips. **Pays $300-500.**
**Tips:** "Contact editor about upcoming issues, article ideas. Concentrate on contemporary American craft art, such as ceramics, wood, fiber, glass, etc. No hobby crafts."

**[N] $ $ $ $ART & ANTIQUES**, Trans World Publishing, Inc., 2100 Powers Ferry Rd., Atlanta GA 30339. (770)955-5656. Fax: (770)952-0669. Editor: Barbara S. Tapp. **Contact:** Patti Verbanas, managing editor. **90% freelance written.** Magazine published 11 times/year covering fine art and antique collectibles and the people who collect them and/or create them. "*Art & Antiques* is the authoritative source for elegant, sophisticated coverage of the treasures collectors love, the places to discover them and the unique ways collectors use them to enrich their environments." Circ. 196,000. **Pays on acceptance.** Publishes ms an average of 6 months after acceptance. Byline given. Offers 25% kill fee or $250. Buys first North American serial rights. Editorial lead time 8 months. Submit seasonal material 6 months in advance. Reports in 6 weeks on queries, 2 months on mss. Sample copy and writer's guidelines free.
**Nonfiction:** Essays, how-to, interview/profile, photo feature, travel. Features are expanded, more in-depth articles that fit into any of the departments listed below. "We publish one 'interior design with art and antiques' focus feature a month. Special issues: Designing with art & antiques (September); Asian art & antiques (October); Contemporary art (December). No academic articles on artists, especially deceased ones. **Buys 200 mss/year.** Query with or without published clips. Length: 200-2,000 words. **Pays $200-2,000.** Pays expenses of writers on assignment.
**Photos:** Send photos with submission. Reviews contact sheets, transparencies, prints. Captions, identification of subjects required. Buys one-time rights.
**Columns/Departments:** *Art & Antiques* Update (trend coverage and timely news of issues and personalities), 100-350 words; Review (thoughts and criticisms on a variety of worldwide art exhibitions throughout the year), 600-800 words; Value Judgments (experts highlight popular to undiscovered areas of collecting), 600-800 words; Emerging Artists (an artist on the cusp of discovery), 600-800 words; Collecting (profiles fascinating collectors, their collecting passions and the way they live with their treasures), 800-900 words; Discoveries (collections in lesser-known museums and homes open to the public), 800-900 words; Studio Session (peek into the studio of an artist who is currently hot or is a revered veteran allowing the reader to watch the artist in action), 800-900 words; Then & Now (the best reproductions being created today and the craftspeople behind the work), 800-900 words; World View (major art and antiques news worldwide; visuals preferred but not necessary), 600-800 words; Travelling Collector (hottest art and antiques destinations, dictated by those on editorial calendar; visuals preferred but not necessary), 800-900 words; Essay (first-person piece tackling a topic in a non-academic way; visuals preferred, but not necessary); Books (reviews of important books), 100-400 words; Profile (profiles those who are noteworthy and describes their interests and passions; very character-driven and should reveal their personalities), 600-800 words. **Buys 200 mss/year.** Query with or without published clips. **Pays $200-800.**
**Fillers:** Facts, newsbreaks. **Buys 22 mss/year.** Length: 150-350 words. **Pays $200.**
**Tips:** "Send scouting shots with your queries. We are a very visual magazine and no idea will be considered without visuals. We are good about responding to writers in a timely fashion—excessive phone calls are not appreciated, but do check in if you haven't heard from us in a month. We like colorful, lively and creative writing. Have fun with your query. Multiple queries in a submission are allowed."

**[N] $ $ART REVUE MAGAZINE**, Innovative Artists, 302 W. 13th St., Loveland CO 80537. Phone/fax: (970)669-0625. E-mail: artrevue@aol.com. **Contact:** Jan McNutt, editor. **85% freelance written.** Quarterly magazine covering fine art of sculpture and painting. "Articles are focused on fine art: how to, business of art, profiles of artists, museums, galleries, art businesses, art shows and exhibitions. Light and breezy articles on artists, their personalities and their work. We are not particularly interested in an artist's philosophy or their 'art statements.' " Estab. 1990. Circ. 8,000. Pays on publication. Publishes ms an average of 3 months after acceptance. Byline given. Buys first rights. Editorial lead time 3 months. Submit seasonal material 6 months in advance. Reports in 1 month on queries, 3 months on mss. Sample copy for $3. Writer's guidelines for #10 SASE.
**Nonfiction:** Essays, how-to, humor, interview/profile, new product, opinion, personal experience, photo feature, technical, travel. No crafts, pottery, doll-making, inspirational, religious, tie-dying. Special issues: Galleries and Gallery Owners (February); Artists in the West, North, South, East (May). **Buys 4-6 mss/year.** Query or preferably send complete ms. Length: 500-2,000 words. **Pays $100 and up.**
**Photos:** State availability of photos with submission. Reviews prints. Offers no additional payment for photos accepted

with ms. Identification of subjects required. Acquires one-time rights.

**Columns/Departments:** Art Matters (interesting art happenings), 100-200 words; Meet . . . (short q&a with artist), 100-300 words; Frivolous Art (interesting, eclectic, fun), 50-100 words. **Buys 6 mss/year.** Query. **Pays $25-50.**

**Tips:** "Write about unusual, fun, interesting artists or art happenings, galleries or museums. Don't try to be too serious. Put in your personality as well as what you're writing about. We're more interested in style than formula."

**N $ ART TIMES, A Literary Journal and Resource for All the Arts**, P.O. Box 730, Mount Marion NY 12456-0730. Phone/fax: (914)246-6944. E-mail: arttimes@ulster.net. Website: http://www.ulster.net/~arttimes. **Contact:** Raymond J. Steiner, editor. **10% freelance written.** Prefers to work with published/established writers; works with a small number of new/unpublished writers each year. Monthly tabloid covering the arts (visual, theater, dance, etc.). "*Art Times* covers the art fields and is distributed in locations most frequented by those enjoying the arts. Our copies are sold at newsstands and are distributed throughout upstate New York counties as well as in most of the galleries in Soho, 57th Street and Madison Avenue in the metropolitan area; locations include theaters, galleries, museums, cultural centers and the like. Our readers are mostly over 40, affluent, art-conscious and sophisticated. Subscribers are located across U.S. and abroad (Italy, France, Germany, Greece, Russia, etc.)." Estab. 1984. Circ. 19,000. Pays on publication. Publishes ms an average of 4 years after acceptance. Byline given. Buys first serial rights. Submit seasonal material 8 months in advance. Accepts simultaneous submissions. Reports in 3 months on queries; 6 months on mss. Sample copy for 9 × 12 SAE with 6 first-class stamps. Writer's guidelines for #10 SASE or on website.

**Fiction:** Raymond J. Steiner, fiction editor. "We're looking for short fiction that aspires to be *literary*. No excessive violence, sexist, off-beat, erotic, sports, or juvenile fiction." **Buys 8-10 mss/year.** Send complete ms. Length: 1,500 words maximum. **Pays $25 maximum (honorarium) and 1 year's free subscription.**

**Poetry:** Raymond J. Steiner, poetry editor. Poet's Niche. Avant-garde, free verse, haiku, light verse, traditional. "We prefer well-crafted 'literary' poems. No excessively sentimental poetry." **Buys 30-35 poems/year.** Submit maximum 6 poems. Length: 20 lines maximum. Offers contributor copies and 1 year's free subscription.

**Tips:** "Be advised that we are presently on an approximate four-year lead for short stories, two-year lead for poetry. We are now receiving 300-400 poems and 40-50 short stories per month. We only publish two to three poems and one story each issue. Be familiar with *Art Times* and its special audience. *Art Times* has literary leanings with articles written by a staff of scholars knowledgeable in their respective fields. Although an 'arts' publication, we observe no restrictions (other than noted) in accepting fiction/poetry other than a concern for quality writing—subjects can cover anything and not specifically arts."

**$ $ $ THE ARTIST'S MAGAZINE**, F&W Publications, Inc., 1507 Dana Ave., Cincinnati OH 45207-1005. (513)531-2690, ext. 467. Fax: (513)531-2902. E-mail: tamedit@aol.com. Website: http://www.artistsmagazine.com. Editor: Sandra Carpenter. **Contact:** Senior Editor. **80% freelance written.** Works with a large number of new/unpublished writers each year. Monthly magazine covering primarily two-dimensional art instruction for working artists. "Ours is a highly visual approach to teaching the serious amateur artist techniques that will help him improve his skills and market his work. The style should be crisp and immediately engaging." Circ. 250,000. Pays on publication. Publishes ms an average of 6 months after acceptance. Bionote given for feature material. Offers 25% kill fee. Buys first North American serial and second serial (reprint) rights. Reports in 3 months. Sample copy for $3 and 9 × 12 SAE with 3 first-class stamps. Writer's guidelines for #10 SASE.

• Writers must have working knowledge of art techniques. This magazine's most consistent need is for instructional feature articles written in the artist's voice.

**Nonfiction:** Instructional only—how an artist uses a particular technique, how he handles a particular subject or medium, or how he markets his work. "The emphasis must be on how the reader can learn some method of improving his artwork, or the marketing of it." No unillustrated articles; no seasonal material; no travel articles; no profiles. **Buys 60 mss/year.** Query first; all queries must be accompanied by slides, transparencies, prints or tearsheets of the artist's work as well as the artist's bio, and the writer's bio and clips. Length: 1,200-1,800 words. **Pays $200-350 and up.** Sometimes pays the expenses of writers on assignment.

**Photos:** "Transparencies—in 4 × 5 or 35mm slide format—are required with every accepted article since these are essential for our instructional format. Full captions must accompany these." Buys one-time rights.

**Columns/Departments:** "Two departments are open to freelance writers." Swipe File is a collection of tips and suggestions, including photos and illustrations. No query required. Length: up to 100 words. **Pays $10 and up.** Drawing Board is a monthly column that covers basic art or drawing skills. Query first with illustrations. Length: 1,200 words. **Pays $250 and up.**

**Tips:** "Look at several current issues and read the author's guidelines carefully. Submissions must include artwork. Remember that our readers are fine artists and illustrators."

**$ $ $ ART-TALK**, Box 8508, Scottsdale AZ 85252. (602)948-1799. Fax: (602)994-9284. Editor: Bill Macomber. **Contact:** Thom Romeo. **30% freelance written.** Newspaper published 9 times/year covering fine art. "*Art-Talk* deals strictly with fine art, the emphasis being on the Southwest. National and international news is also covered. All editorial is of current interest/activities and written for the art collector." Estab. 1981. Circ. 42,000. **Pays on acceptance.** Publishes ms an average of 2 months after acceptance. Byline given. Buys first North American serial rights and makes work-for-hire assignments. Editorial lead time 3 months. Submit seasonal material 4 months in advance. Accepts simultaneous submissions. Reports in 2 weeks on queries; 1 month on mss. Sample copy free.

**Nonfiction:** Exposé, general interest, humor, interview/profile, opinion, personal experience, photo feature. No articles on non-professional artists (e.g., Sunday Painters) or about a single commercial art gallery. **Buys 12-15 mss/year.** Query with published clips. Length: 500-4,000 words. **Pays $75-800 for assigned articles; $50-750 for unsolicited articles.** Sometimes pays expenses of writers on assignment.

**Photos:** State availability of photos with submission. Reviews transparencies, prints. Offers no additional payment for photos accepted with ms. Captions, identification of subjects required. Buys one-time rights.

**Columns/Departments:** Maintains 9 freelance columnists in different cities. **Buys 38 mss/year.** Query with published clips. **Pays $100-175.**

**Tips:** "Good working knowledge of the art gallery/auction/artist interconnections. Should be a part of the 'art scene' in an area known for art."

**⚡ $ $C, international contemporary art,** C Arts Publishing and Production, Inc., P.O. Box 5, Station B, Toronto, Ontario M5T 2T2. (416)539-9495. Fax: (416)539-9903. E-mail: cmag@istar.ca. Website: http://www.CMagazine.com. **Contact:** Joyce Mason, editor/publisher. **80% freelance written.** Quarterly magazine covering international contemporary art. "*C* provides a vital and vibrant forum for the presentation of contemporary art and the discussion of issues surrounding art in our culture, including feature articles, dialogue, reviews and reports, as well as original artists' projects." Estab. 1983. Circ. 7,000. Pays on publication. Publishes ms an average of 4 months after acceptance. Byline given. Offers kill fee. Editorial lead time 3 months. Accepts simultaneous submissions, if so noted. Reports in 6 weeks on queries; 4 months on mss. Sample copy for $10 (US). Writer's guidelines for #10 SASE.

**Nonfiction:** Essays, general interest, opinion, personal experience. **Buys 50 mss/year.** Query. Length: 1,000-3,000 words. **Pays $150-500 (Canadian), ($105-350 US).**

**Photos:** State availability of photos with submission or send photos with submission. Reviews 4×5 transparencies or 8×10 prints. Offers no additional payment for photos accepted with ms. Captions required. Buys one-time rights.

**Columns/Departments:** Reviews (review of art exhibitions), 500 words. **Buys 30 mss/year.** Query. **Pays $100 (Canadian) ($170 US).**

**$ $FUSE MAGAZINE, A magazine about issues of art & culture,** ARTONS Publishing, 401 Richmond St. W., #454, Toronto, Ontario M5V 3A8 Canada. (416)340-8026. Fax: (416)340-0494. E-mail: fuse@interlog.com. Website: http://www.fusemagazine.org. **Contact:** Petra Chevrier, managing editor. **100% freelance written.** Quarterly magazine covering art and art criticism; analysis of cultural and political events as they impact on art production and exhibition. Estab. 1976. Circ. 2,500. Pays on publication. Publishes ms an average of 4 months after acceptance. Byline given. Offers 50% kill fee for commissioned pieces only. Buys first North American serial rights all languages. Editorial lead time 4 months. Submit seasonal material 2 months in advance. Accepts simultaneous submissions. Accepts queries by mail only. Sample copy for $5 (US funds if outside Canada). Writer's guidelines for #10 SAE with IRCs.

**Nonfiction:** Essays, interview/profile, opinion, art reviews. **Buys 50 mss/year.** Query with published clips and detailed proposal or send complete ms. Length: 800-6,000 words. **Pays 10¢/word or $100 for reviews (Canadian funds).**

**Photos:** State availability of photos with submission. Reviews 5×7 prints. Offers no additional payment for photos accepted with ms. Captions required.

**Columns/Departments:** **Buys 10 mss/year. Pays 10¢/word.**

**Tips:** Send detailed, but not lengthy, proposals or completed manuscripts for review by the editorial board.

**Ⓝ $ $INDIAN ARTIST, Magazine of Contemporary Native American Arts,** Indian Artist, Inc., 1807 2nd St., #61, Santa FE NM 87505. (505)982-1600. Fax: (505)983-0790. E-mail: 104472.3914@compuserve.com. Website: http://www.indianartistmag@compuserve.com. **Contact:** Michael Hice, editor. **70% freelance written.** Magazine published 5 times a year covering Native American arts. "Focus on the people who make Indian art—pottery to music—and those who make it possible." Estab. 1995. Circ. 45,000. **Pays on acceptance.** Publishes ms an average of 2 months after acceptance. Byline given. Offers 50% kill fee. Buys first North American serial, one-time and electronic rights. Editorial lead time 3 months. Submit seasonal material 3 months in advance. Accepts queries by mail, e-mail, fax, phone. Reports in 2 weeks. Sample copy for $3. Writer's guidelines for #10 SASE.

**Nonfiction:** Essays, humor, inspirational, interview/profile, opinion. **Buys 40 mss/year.** Query with published clips. No unsolicited mss. Length: 250-1,500 words. **Pays $75-500.** Pays expenses of writers on assignment.

**Photos:** State availability of photos with submission. Reviews 4×5 transparencies and prints. Negotiates payment individually. Captions and identification of subjects required. Buys one-time rights.

**Columns/Departments:** Profiles (interviews with artists), 250-1,500 words; Features (areas of Indian art), 2,000 words; Reviews (books, exhibits, critical look), 300 words. **Buys 10 mss/year.** Query. **Pays $100-500.**

**Tips:** "Call or write for guidelines to discuss ideas. Writers who have a great idea or person(s) they want to write about, are to send a one-page query letter on (1) Why you want to write about this person or subject; (2) Why, in context, you feel this person or subject is important; (3) What qualifies you as the writer. Include two samples of your writing. If you are Native (not necessary), please indicate your tribe."

**$ $THE MAGAZINE ANTIQUES,** Brant Publications, 575 Broadway, New York NY 10012. (212)941-2800. Fax: (212)941-2819. E-mail: brantpubs@aol.com. **Contact:** Allison Ledes, editor. **75% freelance written.** Monthly. "Articles should present new information in a scholarly format (with footnotes) on the fine and decorative arts, architecture, historic preservation and landscape architecture." Estab. 1922. Circ. 65,835. Pays on publication. Publishes ms an average of 6 months after acceptance. Byline given. Buys all rights. Editorial lead time 6 months. Submit seasonal material 6 months in advance. Reports in 3 weeks on queries; 6 months on mss. Sample copy for $10.50.

**Nonfiction:** Historical/nostalgic, scholarly. **Buys 50 mss/year**. Query with cv. Length: 2,850-3,000 words. **Pays $250-500**. Sometimes pays expenses of writers on assignment.

**Photos:** State availability of photos with submission. Reviews contact sheets, negatives, transparencies and prints. Captions and identification of subjects required. Buys one-time rights.

**$ $ $ METROPOLIS, The Magazine of Architecture and Design**, Bellerophon Publications, 61 W. 23rd St., New York NY 10010. (212)722-5050. Fax: (212)627-9988. E-mail: edit@metropolismag.com. Website: http://www.metropolismag.com. Editor-in-Chief: Marissa Bartolucci. **Contact:** Jared Hohlt, managing editor. **80% freelance written.** Monthly magazine (combined issues February/March and August/September) for consumers interested in architecture and design. Estab. 1981. Circ. 48,000. **Pays on acceptance.** Publishes ms an average of 3 months after acceptance. Byline given. Makes work-for-hire assignments. Submit calendar material 6 weeks in advance. Reports in 8 months. Sample copy for $4.95.

**Nonfiction:** Contact: Susan Szenasy, editor-in-chief. Essays (design, architecture, urban planning issues and ideas), profiles (of multi-disciplinary designers/architects). No profiles on individual architectural practices, information from public relations firms, or fine arts. **Buys 30 mss/year.** Length: 500-2,000 words. **Pays $100-1,000.**

**Photos:** State availability of or send photos with submission. Reviews contact sheets, 35mm or 4×5 transparencies, or 8×10 b&w prints. Payment offered for certain photos. Captions required. Buys one-time rights.

**Columns/Departments:** Insites (short takes on design and architecture), 100-600 words; **pays $50-150.** In Print (book review essays: focus on issues covered in a group of 2-4 books), 2,500-3,000 words; The Metropolis Observed (architecture and city planning news features and opinion), 750-1,500 words; **pays $200-500.** Visible City (historical aspects of cities), 1,500-2,500 words; **pays $600-800;** direct queries to Kira Gould, managing editor. By Design (the process of design), 1,000-2,000 words; **pays $600-800;** direct queries to Janet Rumble, senior editor. **Buys approximately 40 mss/year.** Query with published clips.

**Tips:** "We're looking for ideas, what's new, the obscure or the wonderful. Keep in mind that we are interested *only* in the consumer end of architecture and design. Send query with examples of photos explaining how you see illustrations working with article. Also, be patient and don't expect an immediate answer after submission of query."

**$ $ MIX, The Magazine of Independent Art and Culture**, Parallélogramme Artist-Run Culture and Publishing, Inc., 401 Richmond St. #446, Toronto, Ontario M5V 3A8 Canada. (416)506-1012. Fax: (416)340-8458. E-mail: mix@web.net. Website: http://www.mix.web.net/mix/. **Contact:** Karen Augustine, editor. Managing Editor: Danyèle Fortin. **90% freelance written.** Quarterly magazine covering artist-run gallery activities. "*Mix* represents and investigates contemporary artistic practices and issues, especially in the progressive Canadian artist-run scene." Estab. 1973. Circ. 3,500. Pays on publication. Publishes an average of 6 months after acceptance. Byline given. Offers 25-50% kill fee. Buys first North American serial rights. Editorial lead time 6 months. Submit seasonal material 4 months in advance. Reports in 2 months on queries; 3 months on mss. Sample copy for $6.50, 8½×9¾ SASE and 6 first-class stamps. Writer's guidelines free.

**Nonfiction:** Essays, interview/profile. **Buys 12-20 mss/year.** Query with published clips. Length: 750-3,500 words. **Pays $100-400.** Sometimes pays expenses of writers on assignment.

**Reprints:** Send photocopy of article and information about when and where the article previously appeared.

**Photos:** State availability of photos with submission. Captions and identification of subjects required. Buys one-time rights.

**Columns/Departments:** Extracts, 1,000-2,500 words; Heiroglyphs, 2,000-3,000 words; Interviews, 2,000-3,000 words. Query with published clips. **Pays $50-200.**

**Tips:** "Read the magazine and other contemporary art magazines. Understand the idea 'artist-run.' "

**$ $ U.S. ART: All the News That Fits Prints**, MSP Communications, 220 S. Sixth St., Suite 500, Minneapolis MN 55402. (612)339-7571. Fax: (612)339-5806. E-mail: sgilbert@mspcommunications.com. Publisher: Frank Sisser. **Contact:** Tracy McCormick, managing editor. **40% freelance written.** Monthly magazine that reflects current events in the limited-edition-print market and educates collectors and the trade about the market's practices and trends. Circ. 55,000. Distributed primarily through a network of 900 galleries as a free service to their customers. Pays on acceptance. Publishes ms 3-4 months after acceptance. Byline given. Offers 25% kill fee. Buys all rights "for a period of 60 days following publication of article." Editorial lead time 2-4 months. Departments/columns are staff-written. Query by mail, e-mail, fax. Reports in 2-3 months. Sample copy and writer's guidelines for SASE.

**Nonfiction:** Two artist profiles per issue; an average of 6 features per issue including roundups of painters whose shared background of geographical region, heritage, or currently popular style illustrates a point; current events and exhibitions; educational topics on buying/selling practices and services available to help collectors purchase various print media. **Buys 4 mss/year.** Length: 1,000-2,000 words. **Pays $300-500 for features.**

**Photos:** Color transparencies are preferred. B&w photos considered for the staff-written columns. Returns materials after 2 months.

**Tips:** "We are open to writers whose backgrounds are not arts-specific. We generally do not look for art critics but prefer general-assignment reporters who can present factual material with flair in a magazine format. We also are open to opinion pieces from experts (gallery owners, publishers, consultants, show promoters) within the industry."

**N $ WESTART**, P.O. Box 6868, Auburn CA 95604. (530)885-0969. **Contact:** Martha Garcia, editor-in-chief. Semimonthly 12-page tabloid emphasizing art for practicing artists and artists/craftsmen; students of art and art patrons.

Estab. 1961. Circ. 4,000. Pays on publication. Byline given. Buys all rights. Query or submit complete ms with SASE for reply or return. Phone queries OK. Sample copy and writer's guidelines free.
**Nonfiction:** Informational, photo feature, profile. No hobbies. **Buys 6-8 mss/year.**Length: 700-800 words. **Pays 50¢/column inch.**
**Photos:** Purchased with or without accompanying ms. Send b&w prints. Pays 50¢/column inch.
**Tips:** "We publish information which is current—that is, we will use a review of an exhibition only if exhibition is still open on the date of publication. Therefore, reviewer must be familiar with our printing and news deadlines."

**$ $ $ WILDLIFE ART, The Art Journal of the Natural World**, Pothole Publications, Inc. 52230 W. 73rd St., Suite A, Edina MN 55439 or P.O. Box 390026, Edina MN 55439. E-mail: pbarry@mail.winternet.com. Website: http://www.wildlifeartmag.com. Editor-in-Chief: Robert Koenke. **Contact:** Rebecca Hakala Rowland, editor. **80% freelance written.** Bimonthly magazine. "*Wildlife Art* is the world's largest wildlife art magazine. Features cover interviews on living artists as well as wildlife art masters, illustrators and conservation organizations. Audience is publishers, collectors, galleries, museums, show promoters worldwide." Estab. 1982. Circ. 50,000. **Pays on acceptance.** Publishes ms an average of 6 months after acceptance. Byline given. Negotiable kill fee. Buys second serial (reprint) rights. Accepts queries by mail, fax, phone. Reports in 6 months. Sample copy for 9×12 SAE with 10 first-class stamps. Writer's guidelines for #10 SASE.
**Nonfiction: Buys 40 mss/year.** Query with published clips; include samples of artwork. Length: 800-5,000 words. **Pays $150-900.**
**Columns/Departments: Buys up to 6 mss/year. Pays $100-300.**
**Tips:** Best way to break in is to offer concrete story ideas; new talent; a new unique twist of artistic excellence.

# ASSOCIATIONS

Association publications allow writers to write for national audiences while covering local stories. If your town has a Kiwanis, Lions or Rotary Club chapter, one of its projects might merit a story in the club's magazine. If you are a member of the organization, find out before you write an article if the publication pays members for stories; some associations do not. In addition, some association publications gather their own club information and rely on freelancers solely for outside features. Be sure to find out what these policies are before you submit a manuscript. Club-financed magazines that carry material not directly related to the group's activities are classified by their subject matter in the Consumer and Trade sections.

**$ COMEDY WRITERS ASSOCIATION NEWSLETTER**, P.O. Box 23304, Brooklyn NY 11202-0066. (718)855-5057. **Contact:** Robert Makinson, editor. **10% freelance written.** Semiannual newsletter on comedy writing for association members. Estab. 1989. **Pays on acceptance.** Publishes ms 3 months after acceptance. Byline given. Buys all rights. Reports in 2 weeks on queries; 1 month on mss. Sample copy for $5. Guidelines for #10 SASE.
**Nonfiction:** How-to, articles about marketing, directories, Internet, new trends. Query. Length: 250-500 words. "You may submit articles and byline will be given if used, but at present payment is only made for jokes. Emphasis should be on marketing, not general humor articles."
**Tips:** "The easiest way to be mentioned in the publication is to submit short jokes. (Payment is $1-3 per joke.) Jokes for professional speakers preferred. Include SASE when submitting jokes."

**[N] $ $ DAC NEWS, Official Publication of the Detroit Athletic Club**, Detroit Athletic Club, 241 Madison Ave., Detroit MI 48226. Managing Editor: Jesse Wick. **Contact:** John Bluth, editor/publisher. **10% freelance written.** Magazine published 9 times/year. "*DAC News* is the magazine for Detroit Athletic Club members. It covers club news and events, plus general interest features." Estab. 1916. Circ. 3,600. Pays on publication. Publishes ms an average of 3 months after acceptance. Byline given. Buys one-time rights or makes work-for-hire assignments. Editorial lead time 3 months. Submit seasonal material 3 months in advance. Reports in 1 month. Sample copy free.
**Nonfiction:** General interest, historical/nostalgic, photo feature. "No fiction or poetry. No politics or social issues—this is an entertainment magazine. We do not accept unsolicited mss or queries for travel articles." **Buys 2-3 mss/year.** Query. Length: 1,000-5,000 words. **Pays $100-600.** Sometimes pays the expenses of writers on assignment.
**Reprints:** Accepts previously published submissions.
**Photos:** State availability of photos with submission. Reviews transparencies and 4×6 prints. Negotiates payment individually. Captions, model releases and identification of subjects required. Buys one-time rights.
**Tips:** "Review our editorial calendar. It tends to repeat from year to year, so a freelancer with a fresh approach to one of these topics will get our attention quickly. It helps if articles have some connection with the D.A.C., but this is not absolutely necessary. We also welcome articles on Detroit history, Michigan history, or automotive history."

**$ $ THE ELKS MAGAZINE**, 425 W. Diversey, Chicago IL 60614-6196. (773)755-4740. Fax: (773)755-4792. E-mail: elksmag@elks.org. Website: http://www.elksmag.com. **Contact:** Anna L. Idol, managing editor. Editor: Fred D. Oakes. **25% freelance written.** Will work with published or unpublished writers. Magazine published 10 times/year with basic mission of being the "voice of the Elks." All material concerning the news of the Elks is written in-house. Freelance, general interest articles are to be upbeat, wholesome, informative, with family appeal. Estab. 1922. Circ. 1,200,000. **Pays on acceptance.** Buys first North American serial rights, print only. Reports within 1 month. Sample copy and writer's guidelines for 9×12 SAE with 4 first-class stamps or on website.

**Nonfiction:** "We're really interested in seeing manuscripts on business, technology, history, or just intriguing topics, ranging from science to sports." No fiction, politics, religion, controversial issues, travel, first person, fillers or verse. **Buys 2-3 mss/issue.** Send complete ms. "No queries." Length: 1,500-3,000 words. **Pays 20¢ per word.**

**Tips:** "Check our website. Freelance articles are noted on the Table of Contents, but are not reproduced online, as we purchase only one-time print rights. If possible, please advise where photographs may be found. Photographs taken and submitted by the writer are paid for separately at $25 each. Please try us first. We'll get back to you soon."

**$ $ $ KIWANIS**, 3636 Woodview Trace, Indianapolis IN 46268-3196. (317)875-8755. Fax: (317)879-0204. E-mail: cjonak@kiwanis.org. Website: http://www.kiwanis.org. Managing Editor: Chuck Jonak. **60-75% freelance written.** Magazine published 10 times/year for business and professional persons and their families. Estab. 1917. Circ. 260,000. **Pays on acceptance.** Buys first serial rights. Offers 40% kill fee. Publishes ms an average of 3 months after acceptance. Byline given. Accepts queries by mail, e-mail, fax. Reports within 1 month. Sample copy and writer's guidelines for 9×12 SAE with 5 first-class stamps; writer's guidelines also on website.

**Nonfiction:** Articles about social and civic betterment, small-business concerns, children, science, education, religion, family, health, recreation, etc. Emphasis on objectivity, intelligent analysis and thorough research of contemporary issues. Positive tone preferred. Concise, lively writing, absence of clichés, and impartial presentation of controversy required. When applicable, include information and quotations from international sources. Avoid writing strictly to a US audience. "We have a continuing need for articles of international interest. In addition, we are very interested in proposals that concern helping youth, particularly prenatal through age five: day care, developmentally appropriate education, early intervention for at-risk children, parent education, safety and health." **Buys 40 mss/year.** Length: 1,500-2,500 words. **Pays $400-1,000.** "No fiction, personal essays, profiles, travel pieces, fillers or verse of any kind. A light or humorous approach is welcomed where the subject is appropriate and all other requirements are observed." Usually pays the expenses of writers on assignment. Query first. Must include SASE for response.

● Ranked as one of the best markets for freelance writers in *Writer's Yearbook* magazine's annual "Top 100 Markets," January 1999.

**Photos:** "We accept photos submitted with manuscripts. Our rate for a manuscript with good photos is higher than for one without." Model release and identification of subjects required. Buys one-time rights.

**Tips:** "We will work with any writer who presents a strong feature article idea applicable to our magazine's audience and who will prove he or she knows the craft of writing. First, obtain writer's guidelines and a sample copy. Study for general style and content. When querying, present detailed outline of proposed manuscript's focus and editorial intent. Indicate expert sources to be used, as well as article's tone and length. Present a well-researched, smoothly written manuscript that contains a 'human quality' with the use of anecdotes, practical examples, quotations, etc."

**$ $ THE LION**, 300 22nd St., Oak Brook IL 60523-8815. (630)571-5466. Fax: (630)571-8890. E-mail: lions@lions clubs.org. Website: http://www.lionsclubs.org. **Contact:** Robert Kleinfelder, senior editor. **35% freelance written.** Works with a small number of new/unpublished writers each year. Monthly magazine covering service club organization for Lions Club members and their families. Estab. 1918. Circ. 600,000. **Pays on acceptance.** Publishes ms an average of 5 months after acceptance. Buys all rights. Byline given. Accepts queries by mail, fax, phone. Reports in 6 weeks. Sample copy and writer's guidelines free.

**Nonfiction:** Informational (issues of interest to civic-minded individuals) and photo feature (must be of a Lions Club service project). No travel, biography or personal experiences. Welcomes humor, if sophisticated but clean; no sensationalism. Prefers anecdotes in articles. **Buys 4 mss/issue.** Query. Phone queries OK. Length: 500-2,200. **Pays $100-750.** Sometimes pays the expenses of writers on assignment.

**Photos:** Purchased with or without accompanying ms or on assignment. Captions required. Query for photos. B&w and color glossies at least 5×7 or 35mm color slides. Total purchase price for ms includes payment for photos accepted with ms. "Be sure photos are clear and as candid as possible."

**Tips:** "Send detailed description of proposed article. Query first and request writer's guidelines and sample copy. Incomplete details on how the Lions involved actually carried out a project and poor quality photos are the most frequent mistakes made by writers in completing an article assignment for us. We are geared increasingly to an international audience. Writers who travel internationally could query for possible assignments, although only locally related expenses could be paid."

**$ THE OPTIMIST**, Optimist International, 4494 Lindell Blvd., St. Louis MO 63108. (314)371-6000. Fax: (314)371-6006. E-mail: magazine@optimist.org. Website: http://www.optimist.org. **Contact:** Dena Hull, managing editor. **5% freelance written.** Bimonthly magazine about the work of Optimist clubs and members for members of the Optimist clubs in the United States and Canada. Circ. 130,000. **Pays on acceptance.** Publishes ms an average of 4 months after acceptance. Buys first North American serial rights. Submit seasonal material 3 months in advance. Accepts queries by mail, e-mail, fax. Reports in 1 month. Sample copy and writer's guidelines for 9×12 SAE with 4 first-class stamps.

**Nonfiction:** Human interest, profiles, humor. "We want articles about the activities of local Optimist clubs. These volunteer community-service clubs are constantly involved in projects, aimed primarily at helping young people. With over 4,000 Optimist clubs in the US and Canada, writers should have ample resources. Some large metropolitan areas boast several dozen clubs. We are also interested in feature articles on individual club members who have in some way distinguished themselves, either in their club work or their personal lives. Good photos for all articles are a plus and can mean a bigger check." Will also consider short (200-400 word) articles that deal with self-improvement or a philosophy of optimism. **Buys 1-2 mss/issue.** Query. "Submit a letter that conveys your ability to turn out a well-written article and tells exactly what the scope of the article will be." Length: 800-1,200 words. **Pays $100 and up.**

**Reprints:** Send photocopy of article and information about when and where the article previously appeared. Pays 50% of amount paid for an original article.

**Photos:** State availability of photos. Payment negotiated. Captions preferred. Buys all rights. "No mug shots or people lined up against the wall shaking hands."

**Tips:** "Find out what the Optimist clubs in your area are doing, then find out if we'd be interested in an article on a specific club project. All of our clubs are eager to talk about what they're doing. Just ask them and you'll probably have an article idea. We would like to see short pieces on the positive effect an optimistic outlook on life can have on an individual. Examples of famous people who overcame adversity because of their positive attitude are welcome."

**[N] $ PERSPECTIVE**, Pioneer Clubs, P.O. Box 788, Wheaton IL 60189-0788. (630)293-1600. Fax: (630)293-3053. E-mail: bparat@yahoo.com. Website: http://www.pioneerclubs.org. **Contact:** Rebecca Powell Parat, editor. **15% freelance written.** Works with a number of new/unpublished writers each year. Triannual magazine for "volunteer leaders of clubs for girls and boys age 2-grade 12. Clubs are sponsored by local churches throughout North America." Estab. 1967. Circ. 24,000. **Pays on acceptance.** Publishes ms an average of 6 months after acceptance. Byline given. Buys full rights for assigned articles, first North American serial rights for unsolicited mss, and second serial (reprint) rights. Submit seasonal material 9 months in advance. Query by mail, e-mail, fax, phone. Reports in 2 months. Writer's guidelines and sample copy for $1.75 and 9×12 SAE with 6 first-class stamps.

**Nonfiction:** Informational (relationship skills, leadership skills); inspirational (stories of leaders and children in Pioneer Clubs); interview (Christian education leaders, club leaders); personal experience (of club leaders). **Buys 2-3 mss/year.** Length: 1,000-1,500 words. **Pays $60-130.**

**Reprints:** Send photocopy of article or typed ms with rights for sale noted and information about when and where the article previously appeared.

**Columns/Departments:** Storehouse (game, activity, outdoor activity, service project suggestions—all related to club projects for age 2 through grade 12). **Buys 2-3 mss/year.** Submit complete ms. Length: 150-250 words. **Pays $8-15.**

**Tips:** "Submit articles directly related to club work, practical in nature, i.e., ideas for leader training in communication, discipline, teaching skills. However, most of our articles are assigned. Writers who have contact with a Pioneer Clubs program in their area and who are interested in working on assignment are welcome to contact us."

**[logo] $ $ RECREATION NEWS**, Official Publication of the Washington DC Chapter of the National Employee Services and Recreation Association, P.O. Box 32335, Calvert Station, Washington DC 20007-0635. (202)965-6960. Fax: (202)965-6964. E-mail: recreation_news@mcimail.com. **Contact:** Henry T. Dunbar, editor. **85% freelance written.** Monthly guide to leisure-time activities for federal and private industry workers covering outdoor recreation, travel, fitness and indoor pastimes. Estab. 1979. Circ. 104,000. Pays on publication. Publishes ms an average of 8 months after acceptance. Byline given. Buys first rights and second serial (reprint) rights. Submit seasonal material 10 months in advance. Accepts queries by mail, e-mail. Accepts simultaneous submissions. Reports in 2 months. Sample copy and writer's guidelines for 9×12 SAE with $1.05 in postage.

**Nonfiction: Contact:** Articles Editor. Leisure travel (mid-Atlantic travel only); sports; hobbies; historical/nostalgic (Washington-related); personal experience (with recreation, life in Washington). Special issues: Skiing (December). **Buys 45 mss/year.** Query with published clips. Length: 800-2,000 words. **Pays from $50-300.**

**Reprints:** Send photocopy of article or typed ms with rights for sale noted, and information about where and when article previously appeared. **Pays $50.**

**Photos: Contact:** Photo Editor. State availability of photos with query letter or ms. Uses b&w prints. Pays $25. Uses color transparency on cover only. Pays $50-125 for transparency. Captions and identification of subjects required.

**Tips:** "Our writers generally have a few years of professional writing experience and their work runs to the lively and conversational. We like more manuscripts in a wide range of recreational topics, including the off-beat. The areas of our publication most open to freelancers are general articles on travel and sports, both participational and spectator, also historic in the DC area. In general, stories on sites visited need to include info on nearby places of interest and places to stop for lunch, to shop, etc."

**$ $ $ THE ROTARIAN**, Rotary International, 1560 Sherman Ave., Evanston IL 60201-4818. (847)866-3000. Fax: (847)866-9732. E-mail: prattc@riorc.mhs.compuserve.com. Website: http://www.rotary.org. Editor-in-chief: Willmon L. White. **Contact:** Charles W. Pratt, editor; Cary Silver, managing editor. **40% freelance written.** Monthly magazine for Rotarian business and professional men and women and their families, schools, libraries, hospitals, etc. "Articles should appeal to an international audience and in some way help Rotarians help other people. The organization's rationale is one of hope, encouragement and belief in the power of individuals talking and working together." Estab. 1911. Circ. 514,565. **Pays on acceptance.** Byline usually given. Kill fee negotiable. Buys one-time or all rights. Reports in 3 weeks. Sample copy for 9×12 SAE with 6 first-class stamps. Writer's guidelines for #10 SASE.

**Nonfiction:** General interest, humor, sports, inspirational, photo feature, travel, business, environment. No fiction, religious or political articles. Query with published clips. Length: 1,500 words maximum. Negotiates payment.

**Reprints:** Send tearsheet or photocopy of article or typed ms with rights for sale noted and information about when and where the article previously appeared. Negotiates payment.

**Photos:** State availability of photos. Reviews contact sheets and transparencies. Usually buys one-time rights.

**Columns/Departments:** Manager's Memo (business), Executive Health, Personal Computing, Executive Lifestyle, Earth Diary, Travel Tips, Trends. Length: 800 words. Query.

**Tips:** "The chief aim of *The Rotarian* is to report Rotary International news. Most of this information comes through Rotary channels and is staff written or edited. The best field for freelance articles is in the general interest category. These run the gamut from humor pieces and 'how-to' stories to articles about such significant concerns as business management, world health and the environment."

**$ $ SCOUTING**, Boy Scouts of America, 1325 W. Walnut Hill Lane, P.O. Box 152079, Irving TX 75015-2079. (972)580-2367. Fax: (972)580-2079. E-mail: 103064.3363@compuserve.com. Website: http://www.bsa.scouting.org. **Contact:** Jon C. Halter, editor. Executive Editor: Scott Daniels. **80% freelance written.** Magazine published 6 times/year on Scouting activities for adult leaders of the Boy Scouts, Cub Scouts, Venture and BSA Learning for Life programs. Estab. 1913. Circ. 1,000,000. **Pays on acceptance.** Offers 25% kill fee. Publishes ms an average of 9-18 months after acceptance. Byline given. Buys first North American serial rights. Editorial lead time 6-12 months. Submit seasonal material 1 year in advance. Submit by mail or fax. Accepts simultaneous submissions. Accepts queries by mail, fax. Reports in 1 month on queries; 2 months on mss. Sample copy for $1 and 9×12 SAE with 4 first-class stamps. Writer's guidelines for #10 SASE or on website.

**Nonfiction:** Program activities; leadership techniques and styles; profiles; inspirational; occasional general interest for adults (humor, historical, nature, social issues, trends). **Buys 30-40 mss/year.** Query with published clips and SASE. Length: 600-1,200 words. **Pays $750-1,000 for assigned articles; $300-750 for unsolicited articles.** Pays expenses of writers on assignment.

● Ranked as one of the best markets for freelance writers in *Writer's Yearbook* magazine's annual "Top 100 Markets," January 1999.

**Reprints:** Send photocopy of article and information about where and when the article previously appeared. "First-person accounts on Scouting experiences (previously published in local newspapers, etc.) are a popular subject."

**Photos:** State availability of photos with submission. Reviews transparencies and prints. Identification of subjects required. Buys one-time rights.

**Columns/Departments:** Way it Was (Scouting history), 1,000 words; Family Talk (family—raising kids, etc.), 600-750 words. **Buys 8-12 mss/year.** Query. **Pays $300-500.**

**Fillers:** Anecdotes, short humor. **Buys 25-30/year.** Length: 50-150 words. **Pays $25 on publication.** "Limited to personal accounts of humorous or inspirational scouting experiences."

**$ $ THE TOASTMASTER**, Toastmasters International, 23182 Arroyo Vista, Rancho Santa Margarita CA 92688 or P.O. Box 9052, Mission Viejo, CA 92690-7052. (714)858-8255. Fax: (714)858-1207. E-mail: sfrey@toastmasters.org. Website: http://www.toastmasters.org. Associate Editor: Mary Frances Conley. **Contact:** Suzanne Frey, editor. **50% freelance written.** Monthly magazine on public speaking, leadership and club concerns. "This magazine is sent to members of Toastmasters International, a nonprofit educational association of men and women throughout the world who are interested in developing their communication and leadership skills. Members range from novice speakers to professional orators and come from a wide variety of backgrounds." Estab. 1932. Circ. 170,000. **Pays on acceptance.** Publishes ms an average of 10 months after acceptance. Byline given. Buys second serial (reprint), first-time or all rights. Submit seasonal material 3 months in advance. Accepts simultaneous submissions. Reports in 6 weeks on queries; 1 month on mss. Sample copy for 9×12 SAE with 4 first-class stamps. Writer's guidelines for #10 SASE.

**Nonfiction:** Book excerpts, how-to (communications related), humor (only if informative; humor cannot be off-color or derogatory), interview/profile (only if of a very prominent member or former member of Toastmasters International or someone who has a valuable perspective on communication and leadership). **Buys 50 mss/year.** Query. Length: 1,000-2,500 words. **Pays $100-250.** Sometimes pays expenses of writers on assignment. "Toastmasters members are requested to view their submissions as contributions to the organization. Sometimes asks for book excerpts and reprints without payment, but original contribution from individuals outside Toastmasters will be paid for at stated rates."

**Reprints:** Send typed ms with rights for sale noted and information about when and where the article previously appeared. Pays 50-70% of amount paid for an original article.

**Photos:** Reviews b&w prints. No additional payment for photos accepted with ms. Captions required. Buys all rights.

**Tips:** "We are looking primarily for 'how-to' articles on subjects from the broad fields of communications and leadership which can be directly applied by our readers in their self-improvement and club programming efforts. Concrete examples are useful. Avoid sexist or nationalist language."

**$ $ VFW MAGAZINE**, Veterans of Foreign Wars of the United States, 406 W. 34th St., Kansas City MO 64111. (816)756-3390. Fax: (816)968-1169. Website: http://www.vfw.org. **Contact:** Rich Kolb, editor-in-chief. **40% freelance written.** Monthly magazine on veterans' affairs, military history, patriotism, defense and current events. "*VFW Magazine* goes to its members worldwide, all having served honorably in the armed forces overseas from World War II through Bosnia." Circ. 2,000,000. **Pays on acceptance.** Offers 50% kill fee on commissioned articles. Buys first rights. Submit seasonal material 6 months in advance. Considers simultaneous queries. Reports in 2 months. Sample copy for 9×12 SAE with 5 first-class stamps.

○→ Break in with "fresh and innovative angles on veterans' rights; stories on little-known exploits in U.S. Military history. Will be particularly in the market for Korean War battle accounts during 2000-2003. Upbeat articles about severely disabled veterans who have made good; feel-good patriotism pieces; current events as they relate to defense policy; health and retirement updates are always useful."

**Nonfiction:** Veterans' and defense affairs; recognition of veterans and military service; current foreign policy; American armed forces abroad and international events affecting U.S. national security are in demand. Resolutions passed each August at VFW national convention; recent legislation and veteran concerns. **Buys 25-30 mss/year.** Query with 1-page outline, résumé and published clips. Length: 1,000 words. **Pays up to $500 maximum unless otherwise negotiated.**

• Ranked as one of the best markets for freelance writers in *Writer's Yearbook* magazine's annual "Top 100 Markets," January 1999.

**Reprints:** Considers previously published submissions.

**Photos:** Send photos with submission. Color transparencies (2¼ × 2¼) preferred; b&w prints (5 × 7, 8 × 10). Reviews contact sheets, negatives, transparencies and prints. Captions, model releases and identification of subjects required. Buys first North American rights.

**Tips:** "Absolute accuracy and quotes from relevant individuals are a must. Bibliographies useful if subject required extensive research and/or is open to dispute. Consult *The Associated Press Stylebook* for correct grammar and punctuation. Please enclose 3-sentence biography describing your military service in the field in which you are writing." Welcomes member and freelance submissions. No phone queries.

# ASTROLOGY, METAPHYSICAL & NEW AGE

Magazines in this section carry articles ranging from shamanism to extraterrestrial phenomena. With the coming millennium, there is increased interest in spirituality, angels, near death experiences, mind/body healing and other New Age concepts and figures. The following publications regard astrology, psychic phenomena, metaphysical experiences and related subjects as sciences or as objects of serious study. Each has an individual personality and approach to these phenomena. If you want to write for these publications, be sure to read them carefully before submitting.

★ $ **ASTROLOGY YOUR DAILY HOROSCOPE,** Popular Magazine Group, Inc.,7002 W. Butler Pike, Ambler PA 19002. **Contact:** Arthur Ofner, editor-in-chief. **90% freelance written.** Monthly magazine covering astrology and horoscopes. *"Astrology Your Daily Horoscope* is a monthly astrology magazine that covers all facets of astrology, including weekly and daily predictions, advice from astrologers, prophetic numerology, lunar forecasts, birthday horoscopes, and forecasts about love, money and health issues. Feature articles relate to planetary transits, how astrology is used in individual lives, and how-to articles. Publishes ms an average of 6 months after acceptance. Byline given. Buys all rights. Editorial lead time 4 to 6 months. Submit seasonal material 6 months in advance. Reports in 2 months. Sample copy for $4.95. Writer's guidelines for #10 SASE.

**Nonfiction:** Book excerpts, how-to (e.g., interpret a natal chart), chart analysis of celebrities. Special issue: Astrology Annual (Fall). **Buys 48 mss/year.** Send complete ms. Length: 1,300-3,250 words. **Pays $52-130.**

**Tips:** "With query include complete description of concept, working title, estimated word length, and whether or not any charts will be used. If proposed article is time-sensitive, include date it needs to be published by. For manuscript— must be well written, astrologically accurate and of likely interest to our target audience. If text areas are lengthy, put in subheads. For all—please include name, address, phone number and social security number. On first page of ms include total word count."

$ $ **FATE,** Llewellyn Worldwide, Ltd., P.O. Box 64383, St. Paul MN 55164-0383. Fax: (651)291-1908. E-mail: fate@LLewellyn.com. Website: http://www.fatemag.com. **Contact:** Editor. **70% freelance written.** Estab. 1948. Circ. 65,000. Pays after publication. Byline given. Buys all rights. Query by mail, e-mail. Reports in 3 months or more. Sample copy and writer's guidelines for $3 and 9 × 12 SAE with 5 first-class stamps or on website.

**Nonfiction:** Personal psychic and mystical experiences, 350-500 words. **Pays $25.** Articles on parapsychology, Fortean phenomena, cryptozoology, spiritual healing, flying saucers, new frontiers of science, and mystical aspects of ancient civilizations, 500-3,000 words. Must include complete authenticating details. Prefers interesting accounts of single events rather than roundups. "We very frequently accept manuscripts from new writers; the majority are individual's first-person accounts of their own psychic/mystical/spiritual experiences. We do need to have all details, where, when, why, who and what, included for complete documentation. We ask for a notarized statement attesting to truth of the article." Query first. **Pays 10¢/word.**

**Fillers:** Fillers are especially welcomed and must be be fully authenticated also, and on similar topics. Length: 50-300 words.

**Photos:** Buys slides. prints, or digital photos/illustrations with mss. Pays $10.

▣ The online magazine carries original content not found in the print edition and includes writer's guidelines. Contact online editor.

**Tips:** "We would like more stories about *current* paranormal or unusual events."

★ $ $ **GNOSIS, A Journal of the Western Inner Traditions,** Lumen Foundation, P.O. Box 14217, San Francisco CA 94114. (415)974-0600. Fax: (415)974-0366. E-mail: smoley@well.com (queries). Website: http://www.lu

men.org. **Contact:** Richard Smoley, editor. **75% freelance written.** Quarterly magazine covering esoteric spirituality. "*Gnosis* is a journal covering the esoteric, mystical, and occult traditions of Western civilization, including Judaism, Christianity, Islam, and Paganism." Estab. 1985. Circ. 15,000. Pays on publication. Publishes ms an average of 3 months after acceptance. Byline given. Buys first North American serial rights. Editorial lead time 5 months. Submit seasonal material 5 months in advance. Reports in 1 month on queries; 4 months on mss. Sample copy for $9 or on website. Writer's guidelines for #10 SASE or on website.

● At press time it was learned that *Gnosis* has ceased publication.

**Nonfiction:** Book excerpts, essays, religious. Theme issue articles (esoteric traditions and practices, past and present); interviews with spiritual teachers, authors, and scholars. Special issues: Egypt, Summer 1999 (deadline: February 1, 1999); Archetypal Psychology, Fall 1999 (deadline: May 1, 1999); The Rosicrucians, Winter 2000 (deadline: August 1, 1999). **Buys 32 mss/year.** Query by mail with published clips. Length: 1,000-5,000 words. **Pays $100-300 for assigned articles; $50-200 for unsolicited articles.** All contributors also receive 4 copies plus a year's subscription.

**Photos:** State availability of photos with submissions. Reviews contact sheets, prints. Offers $50-125/photo. Captions, identification of subjects required. Buys one-time rights.

**Columns/Departments:** News & Notes (items of current interest in esoteric spirituality), 1,000 words. **Pays $100-250 per article.** Book Reviews (reviews of new books in the field), 250-1,000 words. **Pays $50 per book reviewed. Buys 45 mss/year.** Query with published clips.

**Tips:** "We give strong preference to articles related to our issue themes (available with writer's guidelines). "If you have a topic you would like to pursue, we encourage you to send us a short query letter—well ahead of the deadline date—before you begin writing. If possible, include a clipping or Xerox of writing you've done, if you think we may not be already familiar with your style. Please note: we cannot pay 'kill fees.' All submissions are 'on spec.' We reserve the right to copy-edit material for style, grammar and conciseness. If major rewriting or editing is called for, we will try to contact the author before publishing. We generally try to avoid cuteness, recycling of material available elsewhere, or story ideas more appropriate to other focused publications such as *Yoga Journal* or *Shaman's Drum*. No faxed or e-mail submissions or queries, please."

**$ $ LAPIS, The inner meaning of contemporary life**, New York Open Center, 83 Spring St., New York NY 10012. (212)334-0210. Fax: (212)219-1347. E-mail: nyoc@aol.com. Website: http://www.opencenter.org. Editor: Ralph White. Managing Editor: Susan Meckler. **Contact:** Cathy Mars, associate editor. **95% freelance written.** Magazine published 3 times/year. "*Lapis* contains the finest in holistic writing today. Articles by world leaders, scholars, philosophers, artists and adventurers provide in-depth exploration of new trends in consciousness and current affairs. Addressing both the inner world of soul and spirit and the outer world of politics, society, and ecology, *Lapis* occupies a unique niche in contemporary publications." Estab. 1995. Circ. 20,000. Pays on publication. Publishes ms an average of 2 months after acceptance. Byline given. Buys first rights or second serial (reprint) rights. Editorial lead time 3 months. Query by mail, e-mail, fax, phone. Reports in 2 weeks on queries; 2 months on mss. Sample copy $5 or on website; writer's guidelines free.

**Nonfiction:** Book excerpts, essays, general interest, humor, inspirational, interview/profile, opinion, personal experience, photo feature, religious, travel. **Buys 50-60 mss/year.** Send complete ms. Length: 1,000-5,000 words. **Pays $100-500.**

**Reprints:** Send photocopy of article or short story or typed ms with rights for sale noted and information about when and where the article or story previously appeared. Negotiable payment.

**Photos:** State availability of photos with submission. Reviews contact sheets, transparencies, 8×10 prints. Negotiates payment individually. Identification of subjects required. Buys one-time rights.

**Columns/Departments:** The World, Traditions, Lovers of Wisdom, Society, Freedom and Poetry.

**Fiction:** Ethnic, historical, humorous, mystery, slice-of-life vignettes. Publishes novel excerpts. **Buys 5 mss/year.** Send complete ms. Length: 1,000-5,000 words. **Pays $100-500.**

**Poetry:** Avant-garde, free verse, haiku, spiritual. **Buys 3-5 poems/year.** Submit maximum 3 poems. **Pays $50-200.**

**Tips:** "Submissions should always be crisp, meaningful and enlightening. *Lapis* is a channel for deeper and more spiritual understanding of issues and experiences. We're looking for wise voices."

**$ $ MAGICAL BLEND MAGAZINE, A Primer for the 21st Century**, P.O. Box 600, Chico CA 95927. (916)893-9037. Fax: (916)893-9076. E-mail: magical@crl.com. Website: http://www.magicalblend.com. **Contact:** Michael Peter Langerin, editor. **50% freelance written.** Bimonthly magazine covering social and mystical transformation. "*Magical Blend* endorses no one pathway to spiritual growth, but attempts to explore many alternative possibilities to help transform the planet." Estab. 1980. Circ. 65,000. Pays on publication. Publishes ms an average of 2 months after acceptance. Byline given. Reports in 2 months. Sample copy free. Writer's guidelines for #10 SASE.

**Nonfiction:** Book excerpts, essays, general interest, inspirational, interview/profile, religious. "Articles must reflect our standards: see our magazine. No poetry or fiction." **Buys 24 mss/year.** Send complete ms. Length: 1,000-5,000 words. Pay varies. Contributor copies.

**Photos:** State availability of photos with submission. Reviews transparencies. Negotiates payment individually. Model releases, identification of subjects required. Buys all rights.

**Fillers:** Newsbreaks. **Buys 12-20/year.** Length: 300-450 words. Pay varies.

**$ $ $ NEW AGE: The Journal for Holistic Living**, 42 Pleasant St., Watertown MA 02472. (617)926-0200. Fax: (617)924-2967. E-mail: forum@newage.com. Website: http://www.newage.com Executive Editor: Luise Light. Editor: Jennifer Cook. **Contact:** Patricia Lang, editorial assistant. **35% freelance written.** Works with a small number of new/unpublished writers each year. Bimonthly magazine emphasizing "personal fulfillment and social change. The audience we reach is college-educated, social-service/hi-tech oriented, 25-55 years of age, concerned about social values, humanitarianism and balance in personal life." Estab. 1974. Cir. 275,000. Publishes ms 5 months after acceptance. Byline given. Offers 25% kill fee. Buys first North American serial and reprint rights. Submit seasonal material 6 months in advance. Accepts simultaneous submissions. Reports in 3 months on queries. Sample copy for $5 and 9 × 12 SAE. Guidelines for #10 SASE.

**Nonfiction:** Book excerpts, exposé, general interest, how-to (travel on business, select a computer, reclaim land, plant a garden), behavior, trend pieces, humor, inspirational, interview/profile, new product, food, sci-tech, music, media, nutrition, holistic health, education, personal experience. **Buys 60-80 mss/year.** Query with published clips. No phone calls. The process of decision making takes time and involves more than one editor. An answer cannot be given over the phone." Length: 200-4,000 words. **Pays $50-2,500.** Pays the expenses of writers on assignment.

**Reprints:** Send tearsheet or photocopy of article.

**Photos:** State availability of photos. Model releases, identification of subjects required. Buys one-time rights.

**Columns/Departments:** Body/Mind; Reflections; Upfront. **Buys 60-80 mss/year.** Query with published clips. Length: 250-1,500 words. **Pays $50-850.**

**Tips:** "Submit short, specific news items to the Upfront department. Query first with clips. A query is one to two paragraphs—if you need more space than that to *present* the idea, then you don't have a clear grip on it. The next open area is columns: Reflections often takes first-time contributors. Read the magazine and get a sense of type of writing run in column. In particular we are interested in seeing inspirational, first-person pieces that highlight an engaging idea, experience or issue. We are also looking for new cutting-edge thinking."

**N $ PANGAIA, Exploring the Pagan World**, Blessed Bee, Inc., Box 641, Point Arena CA 95468. (707)882-2052. Fax: (707)882-2793. E-mail: dcdarling@saber.net. Editor: D.C. Darling. **95% freelance written.** Quarterly spiritual magazine covering the neo-pagan movement worldwide. "*PanGaia* is for all people who share a deep love and commitment to the earth. *PanGaia* is dedicated to helping explore our spiritual, emotional and mundane lives in a way which respects all persons, creatures, and the Earth, and which has immediate application to our everyday lives. We encourage folks of all paths to send their work, but our focus is on material which expresses an Earth-centered spirituality." Estab. 1997. Pays on publication. Publishes ms an average of 1 year after acceptance. Byline given. Buys first North American serial, one-time, second serial (reprint) or electronic rights. Editorial lead time 4 months. Submit seasonal material 6 months in advance. Accepts queries by mail, e-mail. Reports in 6 weeks on queries; 6 months on mss. Sample copy for $5. Writer's guidelines for #10 SASE.

**Nonfiction:** Book excerpts, essays, historical/nostalgic, inspirational, interview/profile, personal experience, photo feature, religious, travel. No material on correlated topics, commercial promotion or personal diatribes. **Buys 20 mss/year.** Send complete ms. Length: 500-3,000 words. **Pays $10-100.**

**Reprints:** Accepts previously published submissions.

**Photos:** State availability of photos with submission. Reviews prints. Negotiates payment individually. Captions and identification of subjects required. Buys one-time rights.

**Columns/Departments:** Sacred Place; Sacred Path; Scientific Mysticism and Worldwide Paganism. **Buys 16 mss/year.** Send complete ms.

**Fiction:** Adventure, ethnic, fantasy, historical, humorous, religious, science fiction. No grim or abstract stories. **Buys 4 mss/year.** Send complete ms. Length: 1,000-3,000 words. **Pays $10-50.**

**Poetry:** Buys 2 poems/year. Submit maximum 4 poems.

**$ $ PARABOLA, The Magazine of Myth and Tradition**, The Society for the Study of Myth and Tradition, 656 Broadway, New York NY 10012-2317. (212)505-9037. Fax: (212)979-7325. E-mail: parabola@panix.com. Website: http://www.parabola.org. **Contact:** Natalie Baan, managing editor. Quarterly magazine "devoted to the exploration of the quest for meaning as expressed in the myths, symbols, and tales of the religious traditions. Particular emphasis is on the relationship between this wisdom and contemporary life." Estab. 1976. Circ. 40,000. Pays on publication. Publishes ms 3 months after acceptance. Byline given. Offers kill fee for assigned articles only (usually $100). Buys first North American serial, first, one-time or second serial (reprint) rights. Editorial lead time 4 months. Accepts queries by mail, e-mail, fax. Accepts simultaneous submissions. Reports in 3 weeks on queries; on mss "variable—for articles directed to a particular theme, we usually respond the month after the deadline (so for an April 8 deadline, we are likely to respond in May). Articles not directed to themes may wait four months or more!" Sample copy for $6.95 current issue; $8.95 back issue. Writers guidelines and list of themes for SASE, via e-mail or on website.

**Nonfiction:** Book excerpts, essays, photo feature. Send for current list of themes. No articles not related to specific themes. Special issues: Threshold: where change takes place (deadline: October 8,1999), The Riddle: questions, enigmas, mysteries (deadline: January 8, 2000.) **Buys 15-40 mss/year.** Query. Length: 1,500-3,000 words. **Pays $100 minimum.** Sometimes pays expenses of writers on assignment.

**Reprints:** Send photocopy of article or short story (must include copy of copyright page) and information about when and where the article or short story previously appeared.

**Photos:** State availability of photos with submission. Reviews contact sheets, any transparencies and prints. Identification of subjects required. Buys one-time rights.

**Columns/Departments:** Tangents (reviews of film, exhibits, dance, theater, video, music relating to theme of issue), 1,500-2,000 words; Book Reviews (reviews of current books in religion, spirituality, mythology and tradition), 500 words; Epicycles (retellings of myths and folk tales of all cultures—no fiction or made-up mythology!), under 2,000 words. **Buys 20-40 unsolicited mss/year.** Query. **Pays $75.**

**Fiction:** "We *very* rarely publish fiction; must relate to upcoming theme." Query. Publishes novel excerpts.

**Tips:** "Each issue of *Parabola* is organized around a theme. Examples of themes we have explored in the past include Rite of Passage, Sacred Space, The Child, Ceremonies, Addiction, The Sense of Humor, Hospitalilty, The Hunter and The Stranger."

**N $ SHAMAN'S DRUM, A Journal of Experiential Shamanism**, Cross-Cultural Shamanism Network, P.O. Box 97, Ashland OR 97520. (541)552-0839. **Contact:** Timothy White, editor. **75% freelance written.** Quarterly educational magazine of cross-cultural shamanism. "*Shaman's Drum* seeks contributions directed toward a general but well-informed audience. Our intent is to expand, challenge, and refine our readers' and our understanding of shamanism in practice. Topics include indigenous medicineway practices, contemporary shamanic healing practices, ecstatic spiritual practices, and contemporary shamanic psychotherapies. Our overall focus is cross-cultural, but our editorial approach is culture-specific—we prefer that authors focus on specific ethnic traditions or personal practices about which they have significant firsthand experience. We are looking for examples of not only how shamanism has transformed individual lives but also practical ways it can help ensure survival of life on the planet. We want material that captures the heart and feeling of shamanism and that can inspire people to direct action and participation, and to explore shamanism in greater depth." Estab. 1985. Circ. 14,000. Publishes ms 6 months after acceptance. Buys first North American serial and first rights. Editorial lead time 1 year. Reports in 3 months. Sample copy for $5. Writer's guidelines for #10 SASE.

**Nonfiction:** Book excerpts, essays, interview/profile (please query), opinion, personal experience, photo feature. *No fiction, poetry or fillers.* **Buys 16 mss/year.** Send complete ms. Length: 5,000-8,000 words. "**We pay 5-8¢/word,** depending on how much we have to edit. We also send two copies and tearsheets in addition to cash payment."

**Reprints:** Accepts rarely. Send typed ms with rights for sale noted and information about when and where the article previously appeared. Pays 50% of amount paid for an original article.

**Photos:** Send photos with submission. Reviews contact sheets, transparencies and all size prints. Offers $40-50/photo. Identification of subjects required. Buys one-time rights.

**Columns/Departments:** Judy Wells, Earth Circles editor. Earth Circles (news format, concerned with issues, events, organizations related to shamanism, indigenous peoples and caretaking Earth. Relevant clippings also sought. Clippings paid with copies and credit line), 500-1,500 words. **Buys 8 mss/year.** Send complete ms. **Pays 5-8¢/word.** Reviews: Timothy White, editor (in-depth reviews of books about shamanism or closely related subjects such as indigenous lifestyles, ethnobotany, transpersonal healing and ecstatic spirituality), 500-1,500 words. "Please query us first and we will send *Reviewer's Guidelines.*" **Pays 5-8¢/word.**

**Tips:** "All articles must have a clear relationship to shamanism, but may be on topics which have not traditionally been defined as shamanic. We prefer original material that is based on, or illustrated with, first-hand knowledge and personal experience. Articles should be well documented with descriptive examples and pertinent background information. Photographs and illustrations of high quality are always welcome and can help sell articles."

**$ UFO UNIVERSE**, Goodman Media, 1700 Broadway, New York NY 10019-5905. Phone/fax: (212)685-4080. **Contact:** T.G. Beckley, editor. Quarterly magazines covering UFOs, conspiracy and occult subjects. Pays on publication. Byline given. Buys first North American serial rights, second serial (reprint) rights or all rights or makes work-for-hire assignments. Editorial lead time 6 months. Query by mail, fax. Reports in 6 weeks on queries. Sample copy for $5 plus $2 postage. Writer's guidelines for #10 SASE.

**Nonfiction:** Book excerpts, exposé, how-to, inspirational, personal experience, travel. **Buys 70-80 mss/year.** Query. Length: 2,500-3,500 words. **Pays $100.**

**Reprints:** Accepts previously published submissions.

**Photos:** State availability or send photos with submission. Reviews prints. Captions required.

**Fillers:** Length: 300-1,000 words. **Pays $25.**

**Tips:** "Know the subject and have something new to offer!"

**$ WHOLE LIFE TIMES**, P.O. Box 1187, Malibu CA 90265. (310)317-4200. Fax: (310)317-4206. E-mail: wholelifex @aol.com. Website: http://www.wholelifetimes.com. **Contact:** Abigail Lewis, editor. Monthly tabloid covering the holistic lifestyle. Estab. 1979. Circ. 55,000. Pays within 30 days after publication for feature stories only. Buys first North American serial rights. Accepts queries by mail, e-mail, fax. Sample copy for $3. Writer's guidelines for #10 SASE.

**Nonfiction:** Exposé, how-to, health, healing, inspirational, interview/profile, spiritual, food, travel, leading-edge information, revelant celebrity profiles. Special issues: Healing Arts (October), Food & Nutrition (November), Spirituality (December), New Beginnings (January), Relationships (February); Longevity (March), Travel (April), Arts and Cultures (May), Vitamins and Supplements (June), Women's (July), Men's (August). **Buys 45 mss/year.** Query with published clips or send complete ms. Length: 800-1,500 words. **Pays 5-10¢/word for feature stories only.**

**Reprints:** E-mail, fax or mail typed ms or send Macintosh, Microsoft Word diskette of ms with rights for sale noted and information about when and where the article previously appeared. Pays 50% of amount paid for an original article.

**Columns/Departments:** Healing, Parenting, Finance, Food, Personal Growth, Relationships, Humor, Travel, Sexuality, Spirituality and Psychology. Length: 750-1,200 words.

**Tips:** "Queries should show an awareness of current topics of interest in our subject area. We welcome investigative reporting and are happy to see queries that address topics in a political context. We are especially looking for articles on health and nutrition."

# AUTOMOTIVE & MOTORCYCLE

Publications in this section detail the maintenance, operation, performance, racing and judging of automobiles and recreational vehicles. Publications that treat vehicles as means of shelter instead of as a hobby or sport are classified in the Travel, Camping & Trailer category. Journals for service station operators and auto and motorcycle dealers are located in the Trade Auto & Truck section.

**N ✶ $ $ AMERICAN IRON MAGAZINE,** TAM Communications Inc., 1010 Summer St., Stamford CT 06905. (203)425-8777. Fax: (203)425-8775. **Contact:** Chris Maida, editor. **80% freelance written.** Monthly family-oriented magazine covering Harley-Davidson and other US brands with a definite emphasis on Harleys. Circ. 80,000. Pays on publication. Publishes ms an average of 6 months after acceptance. Byline given. Reports in 1 month on queries with SASE. Sample copy for $3.
**Nonfiction:** "Clean and non-offensive. Stories include bike features, touring stories, how-to tech stories with step-by-step photos, historical pieces, profiles, events, opinion and various topics of interest to the people who ride Harley-Davidsons." No fiction. **Buys 60 mss/year. Pays $250 for touring articles with slides to first-time writers.** Payment for other articles varies.
**Photos:** Submit color slides or large transparencies. No prints. Send SASE for return of photos.
**Tips:** "We're not looking for stories about the top ten biker bars or do-it-yourself tattoos. We're looking for articles about motorcycling, the people and the lifestyle. If you understand the Harley mystique and can write well, you've got a good chance of being published."

**✶ $ AMERICAN WOMAN MOTORSCENE,** American Woman Motorscene, 2424 Coolidge Rd., Suite 203, Troy, MI 48084. (248)614-0017. Fax: (248)614-8929. E-mail: courtney@americanwomanmag.com. Website: http://www.americanwomanmag.com. **Contact:** Jenny Bonk, associate editor. **80% freelance written.** Bimonthly automotive/adventure lifestyle and service-oriented magazine for women. Estab. 1988. Circ. 100,000. Pays on publication 2 months after acceptance. Byline always given. Buys first rights and second serial (reprint) rights or makes work-for-hire assignments. Submit seasonal material 4 months in advance. Reports in 2 months. For a sample copy send $1.50 and SASE.
**Nonfiction:** Humor, inspirational, interview/profile, new product, photo feature, travel, lifestyle. No articles depicting women in motorsports or professions that are degrading, negative or not upscale. **Buys 30 mss/year.** Send complete ms. Length 250-1,500 words. **Pay depends on quantity, quality and content. Byline—$100.**
**Reprints:** Send photocopy of article and information about when and where the article previously appeared.
**Photos:** Send photos with submission. Reviews contact sheets. Black and white or Kodachrome 64 preferred. Captions, model releases and identification of subjects required. Buys all rights.
**Columns/Departments:** Automall, Idle Chatter, 100-750 words. "Humor is best."
**Fillers:** Anecdotes, facts, gags to be illustrated by cartoonist, newsbreaks, short humor. **Buys 12/year.** Length: 25-100 words. Negotiable.

▣ The online magazine contains material not found in the print edition and includes writer's guidelines.

**Tips:** "The *AWM* reader is typically career and/or family oriented, independent, and adventurous. She demands literate, entertaining and useful information from a magazine enabling her to make educated buying decisions. It helps if the writer is into cars and trucks. We are a lifestyle type of publication more than a technical magazine. Positive attitudes wanted."

**$ ASPHALT ANGELS MAGAZINE,** (formerly *Harley Women/Asphalt Angels Magazine*), Thunder Press, Inc., Publications, P.O. Box 608, Marion IL 62959. (618)964-9411. Fax: (618)964-9711. E-mail: asphltmag@aol.com. Website: http://www.asphaltangels.com. **Contact:** Genevieve Smith, editor. **50% freelance written.** Bimonthly magazine for motorcycle and Harley female enthusiasts. Estab. 1985. Circ. 60,000. Pays on publication. Publishes ms an average of 2 months after acceptance. Byline given. Buys first rights. Editorial lead time 2 months. Submit seasonal material 2 months in advance. Accepts queries by mail, e-mail, fax. Accepts simultaneous submissions. Sample copy and writer's guidelines free.
**Nonfiction:** General interest, historical/nostalgic, how-to (technical motorcycle), humor, interview/profile, new product, personal experience, photo feature, technical. **Buys 35 mss/year.** Query with published clips. Length: 200-2,000 words. **Pays $5/100 words, up to 600 words.** Sometimes pays expenses of writers on assignment.
**Reprints:** Send photocopy of article or typed ms with rights for sale noted and information about when and where the article previously appeared. Pays 100% of amount paid for an original article.
**Photos:** Send photos. Captions, model releases, identification of subjects required. Buys one-time rights.
**Poetry:** Avant-garde, free verse, haiku, light verse, traditional. **Buys 6 poems/year. Pays 5¢/word,** 600 words max.
**Fillers:** Anecdotes, facts, gags to be illustrated by cartoonist, newsbreaks, short humor. No pay.

**$ $ AUTO RESTORER**, (formerly *Classic Auto Restorer*), Fancy Publications, Inc., P.O. Box 6050, Mission Viejo CA 92690-6050. (949)855-8822. Fax: (949)855-3045. **Contact:** Ted Kade, editor. **85% freelance written.** Monthly magazine on auto restoration. "Our readers own old cars and they work on them. We help our readers by providing as much practical, how-to information as we can about restoration and old cars." Estab. 1989. Pays on publication. Publishes ms an average of 3 months after acceptance. Buys first North American serial or one-time rights. Submit seasonal material 4 months in advance. Reports in 2 months. Sample copy for $5.50. Writer's guidelines free.
**Nonfiction:** How-to (auto restoration), new product, photo feature, technical, product evaluation. **Buys 60 mss/year.** Query with or without published clips. Length: 200-2,500 words. **Pays $150/published page, including photos and illustrations.**
**Photos:** Send photos with submission. Reviews contact sheets, transparencies and 5×7 prints. Technical drawings that illustrate articles in black ink are welcome. Offers no additional payment for photos accepted with ms.
**Tips:** "Query first. Interview the owner of a restored car. Present advice to others on how to do a similar restoration. Seek advice from experts. Go light on history and non-specific details. Make it something that the magazine regularly uses. Do automotive how-tos."

**⭐ $ $ AUTOMOBILE QUARTERLY, The Connoisseur's Magazine of Motoring Today, Yesterday, and Tomorrow**, Kutztown Publishing Co., P.O. Box 348, 15076 Kutztown Rd., Kutztown PA 19530-0348. (610)683-3169. Fax: (610)683-3287. Publishing Director: Jonathan Stein. **Contact:** Karla Rosenbusch, senior editor. Assistant Editor: Stuart Wells. **85% freelance written.** Quarterly hardcover magazine covering "automotive history, with excellent photography." Estab. 1962. Circ. 13,000. **Pays on acceptance.** Publishes ms an average of 1 year after acceptance. Byline given. Buys first international serial rights. Editorial lead time 9 months. Reports in 2 weeks on queries; 2 months on mss. Sample copy for $19.95.
**Nonfiction:** Essays, historical/nostalgic, photo feature, technical. **Buys 25 mss/year.** Query by mail or fax. Length: 3,500-8,000 words. **Pays approximately 30¢/word.** Sometimes pays expenses of writers on assignment.
**Photos:** State availability of photos with submission. Reviews 4×5, 35mm and 120 transparencies and historical prints. Buys one-time rights.
**Tips:** "Study the publication, and stress original research."

**$ $ $ $ AUTOWEEK**, Crain Communications, 1400 Woodbridge, Detroit MI 48207. (313)446-6000. Fax: (313)446-0347. E-mail: letters@autoweek.com. Website: http://www.autoweek.com. Editor: Matt DeLorenzo. Managing Editor: Larry Edsall. **Contact:** Todd Lasga, features editor. **33% freelance written.** "*AutoWeek* is the country's only weekly magazine for the auto enthusiast." Estab. 1958. Circ. 300,000. Pays on publication. Publishes ms an average of 1 month after acceptance. Byline given. Buys first North American serial rights. Accepts queries by mail, e-mail, phone, fax.
**Nonfiction:** Historical/nostalgic, interview/profile, new product, travel. **Buys 100 mss/year.** Query. Length: 700-3,000 words. **Pays $1/word.** Sometimes pays expenses of writers on assignment.

**$ $ BRITISH CAR MAGAZINE**, 343 Second St., Suite H, Los Altos CA 94022-3634. (650)949-9680. Fax: (650)949-9685. E-mail: britcarmag@aol.com. Website: http://www.britishcar.com. **Contact:** Gary G. Anderson, editor and publisher. **50% freelance written.** Bimonthly magazine covering British cars. "We focus upon the cars built in Britain, the people who buy them, drive them, collect them, love them. Writers must be among the aforementioned. Written by enthusiasts for enthusiasts." Estab. 1985. Circ. 30,000. Pays on publication. Publishes ms an average of 3 months after acceptance. Byline given. Buys all rights, unless other arrangements made. Submit seasonal material 4 months in advance. Reports in 1 month. Sample copy for $5. Writer's guidelines for #10 SASE.
● The editor is looking for more technical and restoration articles by knowledgeable enthusiasts and professionals.
**Nonfiction:** Historical/nostalgic; how-to (repair or restoration of a specific model or range of models, new technique or process); humor (based upon a realistic nonfiction situation); interview/profile (famous racer, designer, engineer, etc.); photo feature; technical. **Buys 30 mss/year.** Send complete ms. "Include SASE if submission is to be returned." Length: 750-4,500 words. **Pays $2-5/column inch for assigned articles; $2-3/column inch for unsolicited articles.**
**Photos:** Send photos with submission. Reviews transparencies and prints. Offers $15-75/photo. Captions and identification of subjects required. Buys all rights, unless otherwise arranged.
**Columns/Departments:** Update (newsworthy briefs of interest, not too timely for bimonthly publication), approximately 50-175 words. **Buys 20 mss/year.** Send complete ms.
**Tips:** "Thorough familiarity of subject is essential. *British Car* is read by experts and enthusiasts who can see right through superficial research. Facts are important, and must be accurate. Writers should ask themselves 'I know I'm interested in this story, but will most of *British Car* readers appreciate it?' "

**$ $ $ $ CAR AND DRIVER**, Hachette Filipacchi Magazines, Inc., 2002 Hogback Rd., Ann Arbor MI 48105-9795. (734)971-3600. Fax: (734)971-9188. E-mail: spence1cd@aol.com. Website: http://www.caranddriver.com. **Contact:** Steve Spence, managing editor. Monthly magazine for auto enthusiasts; college-educated, professional, median 24-35 years of age. Estab. 1956. Circ. 1,200,000. **Pays on acceptance.** Byline given. Offers 25% kill fee. Buys first North American serial rights. Query by mail, e-mail, fax. Reports in 2 months.
**Nonfiction:** Articles about automobiles, new and old. Informational articles on cars and equipment, some satire and humor and personalities, past and present, auto-related. Informational, humor, historical, think articles and nostalgia. All road tests are staff-written. "Unsolicited manuscripts are not accepted. Query letters must be addressed to the

Managing Editor. *Rates are generous, but few manuscripts are purchased from outside."* **Buys 1 freelance ms/year. Pays maximum $3,000/feature; $750-1,500/short piece.** Pays expenses of writers on assignment.

**Photos:** Color slides and b&w photos sometimes purchased with accompanying mss.

■ The online magazine carries original content not found in the print edition. Contact: Brad Nevin, online editor.

**Tips:** "It is best to start off with an interesting query and to stay away from nuts-and-bolts ideas because that will be handled in-house or by an acknowledged expert. Our goal is to be absolutely without flaw in our presentation of automotive facts, but we strive to be every bit as entertaining as we are informative. We do not print this sort of story: 'My Dad's Wacky, Lovable Beetle.' "

**⬥ $ $ CC MOTORCYCLE MAGAZINE**, Motomag Corp., P.O. Box 808, Nyack NY 10960. (914)353-MOTO. Fax: (914)353-5240. E-mail: motomag@aol.com. Website: http://www.moto-mag.com. **Contact:** Mark Kalan, publisher/ editor. **90% freelance written.** Monthly magazine featuring "positive coverage of motorcycling in America—riding, travel, racing and tech." Estab. 1989. Circ. 30,000. Pays on publication. Publishes ms 2 months after acceptance. Byline given. Buys one-time rights. Editorial lead time 3 months. Submit seasonal material 3 months in advance. Accepts simultaneous submissions. Reports in 1 month. Sample copy for $3. Writer's guidelines for #10 SASE.

**Nonfiction:** Essays, general interest, historical/nostalgic, how-to, humor, inspirational, interview/profile, new product, personal experience, photo feature, technical, travel. Special issues: Annual Edition; Laconia's 75th Anniversary (racing at NIHS) Speedway; Daytona Beach Biketoberfest; Summer touring stories—travel. **Buys 12 mss/year.** Query with published clips. Length: 1,000-2,000 words. **Pays $50-250 for assigned articles; $25-125 for unsolicited articles.** Sometimes pays expenses of writers on assignment.

**Reprints:** Send tearsheet or photocopy of article or short story. No payment. Publishes novel excerpts.

**Photos:** State availability of photos with submission. Reviews contact sheets, transparencies. Negotiates payment individually. Captions, model releases, identification of subjects required. Buys one-time rights.

**Fiction:** Adventure, fantasy, historical, romance, slice-of-life vignettes. All fiction must be motorcycle related. **Buys 6 mss/year.** Query with published clips. Length: 1,500-2,500 words. **Pays $50-250.**

**Poetry:** Avant-garde, free verse, haiku, light verse, traditional. Must be motorcycle related. **Buys 6 poems/year.** Submit 12 maximum poems. Length: open. **Pays $10-50.**

**Fillers:** Anecdotes, cartoons. **Buys 12/year.** Length: 100-200 words. **Pays $10-50.**

**Tips:** "Ride a motorcycle and be able to construct a readable sentence!"

**$ $ MUSTANG & FORDS MAGAZINE**, Petersen Publishing Company, 6420 Wilshire Blvd., Los Angeles CA 90048. Fax: (323)782-2000. E-mail: smartj@petersenpub.com. **Contact:** Jim Smart, senior editor. **30% freelance written.** Monthly magazine covering vintage post-war Fords, Mercurys, Lincolns. "Anyone who writes to this audience better know Fords. Our audience is primarily early Ford performance buffs. Our typical reader is an aging baby boomer who loves old Fords. Most of them drive new Fords." Estab. 1980. Circ. 100,000 subscribers, plus 75,000 newsstand. Pays on publication. Byline given. Offers $100 kill fee. Buys all rights. Editorial lead time 4 months. Reports in 3 weeks on queries. Sample copy and writer's guidelines free.

**Nonfiction:** New product, photo feature, technical. Query. Length: 300-1,500 words. **Pays $100-250/page.** Sometimes pays expenses of writers on assignment.

**Photos:** Send photos with submission. Reviews contact sheets, negatives, transparencies. Offers no additional payment for photos accepted with ms. Captions, model releases, identification of subjects required. Buys one-time rights.

**Columns/Departments: Buys 48 mss/year.** Query with published clips. Pay varies.

**$ RIDER**, TL Enterprises, Inc., 2575 Vista Del Mar Dr., Ventura CA 93001. (805)667-4100. Fax: (805)667-4378. E-mail: editor@ridermagazine.com. Managing Editor: Donya Carlson. **Contact:** Mark Tuttle, Jr., editor. **50% freelance written.** Monthly magazine on motorcycling. "*Rider* serves owners and enthusiasts of road and street motorcycling, focusing on touring, commuting, camping and general sport street riding." Estab. 1974. Circ. 140,000. Pays on publication. Publishes ms an average of 6-12 months after acceptance. Byline given. Offers 25% kill fee. Buys first North American serial rights. Editorial lead time 4 months. Submit seasonal material 6 months in advance. Reports in 2 months. Sample copy for $2.95. Writer's guidelines for #10 SASE.

○┅ "The articles we do buy often share the following characteristics: 1. The writer queried us in advance by regular mail (not by telephone or e-mail) to see if we needed or wanted the story. 2. The story was well written and of proper length. 3. The story had sharp, uncluttered photos taken with the proper film—*Rider* does not buy stories without photos."

**Nonfiction:** General interest, historical/nostalgic, how-to (re: motorcycling), humor, interview/profile, personal experience. Does not want to see "fiction or articles on 'How I Began Motorcycling.' " **Buys 30 mss/year.** Query. Length: 500-1,500 words. **Pays $100 minimum for unsolicited articles.**

**Photos:** Send photos with submission. Reviews contact sheets, transparencies and 5×7 prints (b&w only). Offers no additional payment for photos accepted with ms. Captions required. Buys one-time rights.

**Columns/Departments:** Rides, Rallies & Clubs (favorite ride or rally), 800-1,000 words. **Buys 15 mss/year.** Query. **Pays $150.**

**Tips:** "We rarely accept manuscripts without photos (slides or b&w prints). Query first. Follow guidelines available on request. We are most open to feature stories (must include excellent photography) and material for 'Rides, Rallies and Clubs.' Include information on routes, local attractions, restaurants and scenery in favorite ride submissions."

**$ $ $ ROAD & TRACK**, Hachette Filipacchi Magazines Inc., P.O. Box 1757, 1499 Monrovia Ave., Newport Beach CA 92663. (949)720-5300. Fax: (949)631-2757. Editor: Thomas L. Bryant. **Contact:** Ellida Maki, managing editor. **25% freelance written.** Monthly automotive magazine. Estab. 1947. Circ. 740,000. Pays on publication. Publishes ms an average of 6 months after acceptance. Kill fee varies. Buys first rights. Editorial lead time 3 months. Reports in 1 month on queries; 2 months on mss.

**Nonfiction:** Automotive interest. No how-to. Query. Length: 2,000 words. Pay varies. Pays expenses of writers on assignment.

**Photos:** State availability of photos with submissions. Reviews transparencies, prints. Negotiates payment individually. Model releases required. Buys one-time rights.

**Columns/Department:** Reviews (automotive), 500 words. Query. Pay varies.

**Fiction:** Automotive. Query. Length: 2,000 words. Pay varies.

**Tips:** "Because mostly written by staff or assignment, we rarely purchase unsolicited manuscripts—but it can and does happen! Writers must be knowledgeable about enthusiast cars."

**$ $ TRUCKIN', World's Leading Sport Truck Publication**, McMullen Argus Publishing, 774 S. Placentia Ave., Placentia CA 92870. (714)939-2400. Fax: (714)572-1864. **Contact:** Kevin Wilson, editor. Vice President Editorial: Steve Stillwell. **15% freelance written.** Monthly magazine covering customized sport trucks. "We purchase events coverage, technical articles and truck features, all having to be associated with customized ½ ton pickups and mini-trucks." Estab. 1975. Circ. 200,000. Pays on publication. Buys all rights unless previously agreed upon. Editorial lead time 3 months. Submit seasonal material 6 months in advance. Reports in 2 weeks on queries; 1 month on mss. Sample copy for $4.50. Writer's guidelines free.

**Nonfiction:** How-to, new product, photo feature, technical, events coverage. **Buys 50 mss/year.** Query. Length: 1,000 words minimum. Pay negotiable. Sometimes pays expenses of writers on assignment.

**Photos:** Send photos with submission. Reviews contact sheets and transparencies. Captions, model releases, identification of subjects required. Buys all rights unless previously agreed upon.

**Columns/Departments:** Bill Blankenship. Insider (latest automotive/truck news), 2,000 words. **Buys 70 mss/year.** Send complete ms. **Pays $25 minimum.**

**Fillers:** Bill Blankenship. Anecdotes, facts, newsbreaks. **Buys 50/year.** Length: 600-1,000 words. Pay negotiable.

**Tips:** "Send all queries and submissions in envelopes larger than letter size to avoid being detained with a mass of reader mail. Send complete packages with transparencies and contact sheets (with negatives). Submit hard copy and a computer disc when possible. Editors purchase the materials that are the least complicated to turn into magazine pages! All materials have to be fresh/new and primarily outside of California."

**$ $ VETTE MAGAZINE**, McMullen Argus Publishing, 774 S. Placentia Ave., Placentia CA 92870. (714)939-2400. Fax: (714)572-1864. E-mail: bobw@mcmullenargus.com. Website: http://www.vetteweb.com. **Contact:** Bob Wallace, editor-in-chief. Monthly magazine covering all subjects related to the Corvette automobile. "Our readership is extremely knowledgeable about the subject of Corvettes. Therefore, writers must know the subject thoroughly and be good at fact checking." Estab. 1976. Circ. 40,000. Buys first North American serial rights. Submit seasonal material 4 months in advance. Query for electronic submissions. Sample copy for 9×12 SAE with 6 first-class stamps.

**Nonfiction:** General interest, historical/nostalgic, how-to, interview/profile, new product, personal experience, photo feature, technical, travel. **Buys 120 mss/year.** Query by mail with published clips. Length: 400-2,700 words. **Pay varies.**

**Photos:** State availability of photos with submission. Reviews contact sheets. Offers no additional payment for photos accepted with ms. Captions and model releases required. Buys one-time rights.

**Columns/Departments:** Reviews, Q&A. 400-500 words. **Buys 12-20 mss/year.** Query. **Pay varies.**

**$ $ $ $ VIPER MAGAZINE, The Magazine for Dodge Viper Enthusiasts**, J.R. Thompson Co., 31690 W. 12 Mile Rd., Farmington Hills MI 48334-4459. (248)553-4566. Fax: (248)553-2138. E-mail: jrt@jrthompson.com. **Contact:** Mark Giannatta, editor-in-chief. Editorial Director: John Thompson. **40% freelance written.** Quarterly magazine covering "all Vipers—all the time." Also the official magazine of the Viper Club of America. "Speak to *VM* readers from a basis of Viper knowledge and enthusiasm. We take an honest, journalistic approach to all stories, but we're demonstrably and understandably proud of the Dodge Viper sports car, its manufacturer and employees." Estab. 1995. Circ. 15,000. **Pays on acceptance.** Publishes ms an average of 4 months after acceptance. Byline given. Buys first rights or second serial (reprint) rights. Editorial lead time 5 months. Submit seasonal material 6 months in advance. Query by mail, e-mail, fax, phone. Reports in 1 week. Writer's guidelines for #10 SASE or by e-mail.

**Nonfiction:** Query. Length: 400-1,500 words. **Pays $1/word.** Sometimes pays expenses of writers on assignment.

**Reprints:** Send information about when and where the article previously appeared. Payment varies.

**Photos:** State availability or send photos with submission. Negotiates payment individually. Captions, model releases and identification of subjects required. Buys all rights.

**Columns/Departments:** SnakeBites (coverage of Viper Club of America events such as local chapter activities, fundraising, track days, etc.), under 200 words; Competition (competitive Viper events such as road-racing, drag-racing, etc.), under 200 words. **Pays $1/word.**

**Fillers:** Anecdotes, facts, gags to be illustrated by cartoonist, newsbreaks, short humor. Length: 25-100 words. **Pays $1/word.**

**Tips:** "Being a Viper owner is a good start, since you have been exposed to our 'culture' and probably receive the magazine. This is an even more specialized magazine than traditional auto-buff books, so knowing Vipers is essential."

**N** **$** **WOMEN WITH WHEELS, Quarterly Publication on Automobiles,** Women With Wheels, 1718 North-field Square, Suite A, Northfield IL 60093. (847)501-3519. Fax: (847)501-3519 or (847)392-1582. E-mail: womwwheels @aol.com. **Contact**: Susan Frissell, Ph.D., publisher/editorial director. **2% freelance written** (looking to increase). Quarterly newsletter covering auto-related, women-oriented subjects. "*WWW* is a quarterly publication on automobiles, written for women. Caters to women who not only own their own vehicles, but are responsible for purchasing and maintaining them. *WWW* is written to educate and inform women, in a jargon-free way. Audience is 18-75 years old, average income $31,000, employed in all professions." Estab. 1989. Circ. 1,000. Pays on publication. Publishes ms an average of 6 months after acceptance. Byline given. Buys first North American and one-time rights. Editorial lead time 4 months. Submit seasonal material 3 months in advance. Query by mail, e-mail, fax, phone. Accepts simultaneous submissions. Reports in 6 weeks on queries; 3 months on mss. Sample copy and writer's guidelines for #10 SASE with 2 first-class stamps.

**Nonfiction:** Book excerpts, historical/nostalgic, how-to, humor, interview/profile, new product, opinion, personal experience, technical, travel. Special issue: National Car Care Month (Fall). No articles loaded with automotive jargon. **Buys 2-5 mss/year.** Send complete ms. Length: 100-2,000 words. **Pays $5 for assigned articles; $3.50 for unsolicited articles.**

**Reprints:** Accepts previously published submissions.

**Photos:** State availability of photos with submission. Reviews 3½×5 prints. Offers no additional payment for photos accepted with ms. Captions and identification of subjects required. Buys one-time rights.

**Columns/Departments:** New Products (auto-related), 50 words; Autosmarts (up-and-coming auto trends), 100 words; Features (personal stories), 500-1,500 words; Auto How-to (do-it-yourself hints), 300-1,000 words. **Buys 2-5 mss/year.** Query. **Pays $3.50-10.**

**Fillers:** Anecdotes, facts, gags to be illustrated by cartoonist, newsbreaks, short humor. **Buys 5/year.** Length: 25-100 words. **Pays $1-5.**

**Tips:** "Request a sample copy and writer's guidelines. All departments open to freelancers. Looking to increase number of freelancers. Especially interested in those wanting to build a portfolio and students with passion for automobiles. Will also consider personal stories related to purchasing, maintaining automobiles. Just about anything automotive."

# AVIATION

Professional and private pilots and aviation enthusiasts read the publications in this section. Editors want material for audiences knowledgeable about commercial aviation. Magazines for passengers of commercial airlines are grouped in the Inflight category. Technical aviation and space journals and publications for airport operators, aircraft dealers and others in aviation businesses are listed under Aviation & Space in the Trade section.

**$ $ $ $** **AIR & SPACE/SMITHSONIAN MAGAZINE**, 370 L'Enfant Promenade SW, 10th Floor, Washington DC 20024-2518. (202)287-3733. Fax: (202)287-3163. E-mail: airspacedt@aol.com. Website: http://www.airspacemag.c om. Editor: George Larson. **Contact:** Linda Shiner, executive editor. **80% freelance written.** Prefers to work with published/established writers. Bimonthly magazine covering aviation and aerospace for a non-technical audience. "The emphasis is on the human rather than the technological, on the ideas behind the events. Features are slanted to a technically curious, but not necessarily technically knowledgeable audience. We are looking for unique angles to aviation/ aerospace stories, history, events, personalities, current and future technologies, that emphasize the human-interest aspect." Estab. 1985. Circ. 284,000. **Pays on acceptance.** Byline given. Offers kill fee. Buys first North American serial rights. Adapts from soon to be published books. Accepts queries by mail, e-mail, fax. Reports in 3 months. Sample copy for $5. Guidelines for #10 SASE or on website.

    **○┅** "We're looking for 'reader service' articles—a collection of helpful hints and interviews with experts that would help our readers enjoy their interest in aviation. An example: An article telling readers how they could learn more about the space shuttle, where to visit, how to invite an astronaut to speak to their schools, what books are most informative, etc."

**Nonfiction:** Book excerpts, essays, general interest (on aviation/aerospace), historical/nostalgic, humor, photo feature, technical. **Buys 50 mss/year.** Query with published clips. Length: 1,500-3,000 words. **Pays $1,500-3,000 average.** Pays expenses of writers on assignment.

    ● The editors are actively seeking stories covering space and general or business aviation.

**Photos:** State availability of illustrations with submission. Reviews 35mm transparencies. Refuses unsolicited material.

**Columns/Departments:** Above and Beyond (first person), 1,500-2,000 words; Flights and Fancy (whimsy), approximately 800 words; From the Field (science or engineering in the trenches), 1,200 words; Collections (profiles of unique museums), 1,200 words. **Buys 25 mss/year.** Query with published clips. **Pays $1,000 maximum.** Soundings (brief items, timely but not breaking news), 500-700 words. **Pays $150-300.**

**Tips:** "Soundings is most open to freelancers. We continue to be interested in stories about space exploration."

**✪** **$** **BALLOON LIFE**, Balloon Life Magazine, Inc., 2336 47th Ave. SW, Seattle WA 98116-2331. (206)935-3649. Fax: (206)935-3326. E-mail: tom@balloonlife.com. Website: http://www.balloonlife.com. **Contact:** Tom Hamilton, editor-in-chief. **75% freelance written.** Monthly magazine for sport of hot air ballooning. Estab. 1986. Circ. 4,000.

Pays on publication. Byline given. Offers 50-100% kill fee. Buys non-exclusive all rights. Submit seasonal material 4 months in advance. Reports in 3 weeks on queries; 1 month on mss. Sample copy for $9 \times 12$ SAE with $2 postage. Writer's guidelines for #10 SASE.

**Nonfiction:** Book excerpts, general interest, events/rallies, safety seminars, balloon clubs/organizations, how-to (flying hot air balloons, equipment techniques), interview/profile, new product, letters to the editor, technical. **Buys 150 mss/ year.** Query with or without published clips, or send complete ms. Length: 1,000-1,500 words. **Pays $50-75 for assigned articles; $25-50 for unsolicited articles.** Sometimes pays expenses of writers on assignment.

**Reprints:** Send photocopy of article or short story or typed ms with rights for sale noted and information about when and where the article or story previously appeared. Pays 100% of amount paid for an original article or story.

**Photos:** Send photos with submission. Reviews transparencies, prints. Offers $15/inside photo, $50/cover. Identification of subjects required. Buys non-exclusive all rights.

**Columns/Departments:** Hangar Flying (real life flying experience that others can learn from), 800-1,500 words; Crew Quarters (devoted to some aspect of crewing), 900 words; Preflight (a news and information column), 100-500 words; **pays $50.** Logbook (recent balloon events—events that have taken place in last 3-4 months), 300-500 words; **pays $20. Buys 60 mss/year.** Send complete ms.

**Fiction:** Humorous. **Buys 3-5 mss/year.** Send complete ms. Length: 800-1,500 words. **Pays $50.**

**Tips:** "This magazine slants toward the technical side of ballooning. We are interested in articles that help to educate and provide safety information. Also stories with manufacturers, important individuals and/or of historic events and technological advances important to ballooning. The magazine attempts to present articles that show 'how-to' (fly, business opportunities, weather, equipment). Both our Feature Stories section and Logbook section are where most manuscripts are purchased."

**$ CESSNA OWNER MAGAZINE**, Jones Publishing, Inc., N7450 Aanstad Rd., P.O. Box 5000, Iola WI 54945. (715)445-5000. Fax: (715)445-4053. E-mail: aircraft@aircraftownergroup.com. Website: http://www.aircraftowner-group.com. **Contact:** Bruce Loppnow, publisher and editor. **50% freelance written.** Monthly magazine covering Cessna single and twin engine aircraft. "*Cessna Owner Magazine* is the official publication of the Cessna Owner Organization (C.O.O.). Therefore, our readers are Cessna aircraft owners, renters, pilots, and enthusiasts. Articles should deal with buying/selling, flying, maintaining, or modifying Cessnas. The purpose of our magazine is to promote safe, fun, and affordable flying." Estab. 1975. Circ. 6,000. Pays on publication. Publishes ms an average of 3 months after acceptance. Byline given. Buys first, one-time or second serial (reprint) rights or makes work-for-hire assignment on occasion. Editorial lead time 1 month. Submit seasonal material 3 months in advance. Reports in 2 weeks on queries; 1 month on mss. Sample copy and writer's guidelines free.

**Nonfiction:** Historical/nostalgic (of specific Cessna models), how-to (aircraft repairs and maintenance), new product, personal experience, photo feature, technical (aircraft engines and airframes). "We are always looking for articles about Cessna aircraft modifications. We also need articles on Cessna twin-engine aircraft. April, July, and October are always big issues for us, because we attend various airshows during these months and distribute free magazines. Feature articles on unusual, highly-modified, or vintage Cessnas are especially welcome during these months. Good photos are also a must." Special issues: Engines (maintenance, upgrades); Avionics (purchasing, new products). **Buys 24 mss/year.** Query. Length: 1,500-3,500 words. **Pays 7-11¢/word.**

**Reprints:** Send typed ms with rights for sale noted and information about when and where the article previously appeared.

**Photos:** Send photos with submission. Reviews $3 \times 5$ and larger prints. Captions and identification of subjects required.

**Tips:** "Always submit a hard copy or ASCII formatted computer disk. Color photos mean a lot to us, and manuscripts stand a much better chance of being published when accompanied by photos. Freelancers can best get published by submitting articles on aircraft modifications, vintage planes, restorations, flight reports, twin-engine Cessnas, etc."

**$ FLYER**, N.W. Flyer, Inc., P.O. Box 39099, Lakewood WA 98439-0099. (253)471-9888. Fax: (253)471-9911. E-mail: kirk.gormley@flyer-online.com. Website: http://www.flyer-online.com. **Contact:** Kirk Gormley, editor. **30% freelance written.** Prefers to work with published/established writers. Biweekly tabloid covering general, regional, national and international aviation stories of interest to pilots, aircraft owners and aviation enthusiasts. Estab. 1949. Circ. 35,000. Pays 1 month after publication. Publishes ms an average of 3 months after acceptance. Byline given. Buys one-time and first North American serial rights; on occasion second serial (reprint) rights. Submit seasonal material 2 months in advance. Reports in 2 months. Sample copy for $3.50. Writer's and style guidelines for #10 SASE.

**Nonfiction:** "We stress news. A controversy over an airport, a first flight of a new design, storm or flood damage to an airport, a new business opening at your local airport—those are the sort of projects that may get a new writer onto our pages, if they arrive here soon after they happen. We are especially interested in reviews of aircraft." Personality pieces involving someone who is using his or her airplane in an unusual way, and stories about aviation safety are of interest. Query first on historical, nostalgic features and profiles/interviews. Many special sections throughout the year; send SASE for list. **Buys 100 mss/year.** Query or send complete ms. Length: 500-2,000 words. **Pays up to $10/printed column inch maximum.** Rarely pays the expenses of writers on assignment.

**Reprints:** Accepts previously published submissions from noncompetitive publications, if so noted. Payment varies.

**Photos:** Shoot clear, up-close photos, preferably color prints or slides. Send photos with ms. Captions and photographer's ID required. Pays $10/b&w photo and $50/cover photo 1 month after publication.

**Tips:** "The longer the story, the less likely it is to be accepted. A 1,000-word story with good photos is the best way to see your name in print. If you are covering controversy, send us both sides of the story. Most of our features and news stories are assigned in response to a query."

**$ MOUNTAIN PILOT MAGAZINE**, Wiesner Publishing Co. LLC, 7009 S. Potomac St., Englewood CO 80112. (303)662-5284. Fax: (303)397-7619. E-mail: ehuber@mountainpilot.com. Website: http://www.mountainpilot.com. **Contact:** Edward Huber, editor. **50% freelance written.** Quarterly. *"Mountain Pilot* is the only magazine that serves pilots operating or planning to operate in the mountainous states. Editorial material focuses on mountain performance— flying, safety and education." Considers anything on mountain flying or destination, also camping at mountain airstrips. Estab. 1985. Circ. 15,000. Pays on publication. Publishes ms an average of 6 months after acceptance. Byline given. Buys first rights. Editorial lead time 3 months. Submit seasonal material 6 months in advance. Offers $25 kill fee. Accepts queries by mail, e-mail, fax. Reports in 3 weeks. Writer's guidelines for #10 SASE.
**Nonfiction:** Regular features include: aviation experiences, technology, high-altitude maintenanace and flying, cold-weather tips and pilot techniques. **Buys 18-35 manuscripts/year.** Send cover letter with copy of manuscript, Mac or DOS file saved as text only, unformed ASCII, or in QuarkXPress (Mac) on 3½-inch floppy diskette, author's bio and photo. Length: 1,000 max words. **Pays $100/published page** (includes text and photos).
**Reprints:** Send tearsheet or photocopy of article or short story and information about when and where the article previously appeared.
**Photos:** Send photos with submission (copies acceptable for evaluation). Credit line given.
**Columns/Departments:** Mountain airports, lodging, survival, mountain flying, travel, product news and reviews, industry news. *Mountain Pilot* purchases first serial rights. May consider second serial reprinting rights; query with ms. Captions, model releases and identification of subjects required. **Buys 6 mss/year.** Query. **Pays $50.**

**$ $ PIPERS MAGAZINE**, Jones Publishing, Inc., N7450 Aanstad Rd., P.O. Box 5000, Iola WI 54945. (715)445-5000. Fax: (715)445-4053. E-mail: aircraft@aircraftownergroup.com. Website: http://www.aircraftownergroup.com. **Contact:** Bruce Loppnow, publisher/editor. **50% freelance written.** Monthly magazine covering Piper single and twin engine aircraft. *"Pipers Magazine* is the official publication of the Piper Owner Society (P.O.S). Therefore, our readers are Piper aircraft owners, renters, pilots, mechanics and enthusiasts. Articles should deal with buying/selling, flying, maintaining or modifying Pipers. The purpose of our magazine is to promote safe, fun and affordable flying." Estab. 1988. Circ. 5,000. Pays on publication. Publishes ms an average of 3 months after acceptance. Buys first, one-time or second serial (reprint) rights or makes work-for-hire assignment on occasion. Editorial lead time 1 month. Submit seasonal material 3 months in advance. Reports in 2 weeks on queries; 1 month on mss. Sample copy and writer's guidelines free.
**Nonfiction:** Historical/nostalgic (of specific models of Pipers), how-to (aircraft repairs & maintenance), new product, personal experience, photo feature, technical (aircraft engines and airframes). "We are always looking for articles about Piper aircraft modifications. We also are in need of articles on Piper twin engine aircraft, and late-model Pipers. April, July, and October are always big issues for us, because we attend airshows during these months and distribute free magazines." Feature articles on unusual, highly-modified, vintage, late-model, or ski/float equipped Pipers are especially welcome. Good photos are a must. **Buys 24 mss/year.** Query. Length: 1,500-3,500 words. **Pays 7-11¢/word.**
**Reprints:** Send typed ms with rights for sale noted and information about when and where the article previously appeared.
**Photos:** Send photos with submissions. Reviews transparencies, 3×5 and larger prints. Offers no additional payment for photos accepted. Captions, identification of subjects required.
**Tips:** "Always submit a hard copy or ASCII formatted computer disk. Color photos mean a lot to us, and manuscripts stand a much greater chance of being published when accompanied by photos. Freelancers can best get published by submitting articles on aircraft modifications, vintage planes, late-model planes, restorations, twin-engine Pipers, etc."

**$ $ PLANE AND PILOT**, Werner Publishing Corp., 12121 Wilshire Blvd., Suite 1200, Los Angeles CA 90025. (310)820-1500. Fax: (310)826-5008. E-mail: editors@planeandpilot.com. Website: http://www.planeandpilotmag.com. Editor: Lyn Freeman. **Contact:** Jenny Shearer, managing editor. **100% freelance written.** Monthly magazine that covers general aviation. "We think a spirited, conversational writing style is most entertaining for our readers. We are read by private and corporate pilots, instructors, students, mechanics and technicians—everyone involved or interested in general aviation." Estab. 1964. Circ. 130,000. Pays on publication. Publishes ms an average of 3 months after acceptance. Byline given. Kill fee negotiable. Buys all rights. Submit seasonal material 4 months in advance. Reports in 2 months. Sample copy for $5.50. Writer's guidelines free or on website.
**Nonfiction:** How-to, new product, personal experience, technical, travel, pilot proficiency and pilot reports on aircraft. **Buys 75 mss/year.** Submit query with idea, length and the type of photography you expect to provide. Length: 1,000-1,800 words. **Pays $200-500.** Rates vary depending on the value of the material as judged by the editors. Pays expenses of writers on assignment.
**Reprints:** Send photocopy of article or typed ms with rights for sale noted with information about when and where the article previously appeared. Pays 50% of amount paid for original article.
**Photos:** Submit suggested heads, decks and captions for all photos with each story. Submit b&w photos in proof sheet form with negatives or 8×10 prints with glossy finish. Submit color photos in the form of 2¼×2¼ or 4×5 or 35mm transparencies in plastic sleeves. Offers $50-300/photo. Buys all rights.
**Columns/Departments:** Readback (any newsworthy items on aircraft and/or people in aviation), 100-300 words; Jobs & Schools (a feature or an interesting school or program in aviation), 1,000-1,500 words; and Travel (any traveling

done in piston-engine aircraft), 1,000-2,500 words. **Buys 30 mss/year.** Send complete ms. **Pays $200-500.** Rates vary depending on the value of the material as judged by the editors.
**Tips:** "Pilot proficiency articles are our bread and butter. Manuscripts should be kept under 1,800 words."

**⌘ $ $ $ PRIVATE PILOT,** Y-Visionary, Inc., 265 S. Anita Dr., #120, Orange CA 92868. (714)939-9991, ext. 234. Fax: (714)939-9909. E-mail: aircrftdr@aol.com. Website: http://www.privatepilotmag.com. **Contact:** Bill Fedorko, editorial director or Amy Maclean, managing editor. **85% freelance written.** Monthly magazine covering general aviation. Estab. 1965. Circ. 85,000. Pays on publication. Publishes ms an average of 4 months after acceptance. Byline given. Buys first North American serial rights. Editorial lead time 3 months. Submit seasonal material 6 months in advance. Accepts queries by mail, e-mail, fax. Reports in 6 weeks on queries; 2 months on mss. Writer's guidelines for #10 SASE.
**Nonfiction:** General interest, how-to, personal experience, travel, aircraft types. **Buys 100 mss/year.** Query. Length: 1,000-2,500 words. **Pays $400-850. Sometimes pays expenses of writers on assignment.**
**Photos:** State availability of photos with submission. Reviews 35mm transparencies. Negotiates payment individually. Model releases and identification of subjects required. Buys one-time rights.
**Tips:** "Send good queries. Readers are pilots who want to read about aircraft, places to go and ways to save money."

**$ WOMAN PILOT,** Aviatrix Publishing, Inc., P.O. Box 485, Arlington Heights IL 60006-0485. (847)797-0170. Fax: (847)797-0161. E-mail: womanpilot@womanpilot.com Website: http://www.womanpilot.com. **Contact:** Danielle Clarneaux, editor. **80% freelance written.** Bimonthly magazine covering women who fly all types of aircraft and careers in all areas of aviation. Personal profiles, historical articles and current aviation events. Estab. 1993. Circ. 5,000. Pays on publication. Publishes ms an average of 5 months after acceptance. Byline given. Buys first North American serial rights. Editorial lead time 4 months. Sample copy for $3. Writer's guidelines for #10 SASE.
**Nonfiction:** Book excerpts, historical/nostalgic, humor, interview/profile, new product, personal experience, photo feature. **Buys 35 mss/year.** Query with published clips or send complete ms. Length: 500-3,000 words. **Pays $20-55 for assigned articles; $20-40 for unsolicited articles; and contributor copies.**
**Reprints:** Send tearsheet or photocopy of article or short story or typed ms with rights for sale noted and information about when and where the article or short story previously appeared.
**Photos:** State availability or send photos/photocopies with submission. Negotiates payment individually. Captions, model releases, identification of subjects required. Buys one-time rights.
**Fiction:** Adventure, historical, humorous, slice-of-life vignettes. **Buys 4 mss/year.** Query with or without published clips. Length: 500-2,000 words. **Pays $20-35.**
**Fillers:** Cartoons. **Buys 6/year. Pays $10-20.**
**Tips:** "If a writer is interested in writing articles from our leads, she/he should send writing samples and explanation of any aviation background. Include any writing background."

## BUSINESS & FINANCE

Business publications give executives and consumers a range of information from local business news and trends to national overviews and laws that affect them. National and regional publications are listed below in separate categories. Magazines that have a technical slant are in the Trade section under Business Management, Finance or Management & Supervision categories.

## National

**Ⓝ $ $ $ BUSINESS ASSET, BUSINESS SENSE, YOUR BUSINESS,** Baumer Financial Publishing, 820 W. Jackson Blvd., #450, Chicago IL 60607. (312)627-1020. Fax: (312)627-1105. E-mail: baumerfpub@aol.com. **Contact:** Soo Ji Min, editor. **50% freelance written.** Quarterly magazine covering small business and entrepreneurs. Estab. 1998. Circ. *Business Asset* 25,000; *Business Sense* 85,000; *Your Business* 15,000. Pays on publication. Publishes ms an average of 4 months after acceptance. Byline given. Offers 33% kill fee. Buys first North American serial rights. Editorial lead time 6 months. Submit seasonal material 6 months in advance.
**Nonfiction:** How-to (finance, legal, technology, marketing, management, HR, insurance), small business profiles. No humor, personal experience, religious, opinion, book excerpts, travel. **Buys 40 mss/year.** Query with published clips. Length: 800-2,000 words. **Pays 75¢/word.**
**Photos:** State availability of photos with submission. Offers no additional payment for photos accepted with ms. Identification of subjects required. Buys one-time rights.
**Columns/Departments:** Technology, Legal, Insurance, Marketing (for small business owners), 800-900 words. **Buys 20 mss/year.** Query with published clips. **Pays 50¢/word.**

**Ⓝ $ $ DOLLARS AND SENSE, What's Left in Economics,** Economic Affairs Bureau, 1 Summer St., Somerville MA 02143. (617)628-8411. Fax: (617)628-2025. E-mail: dollars@igc.org. Website: http://www.dollarsandsense.org. **Contact:** Abby Scher and Marc Breslow, co-editors. **10% freelance written.** Bimonthly magazine covering economics, environmental and social justice. "We explain the workings of the U.S. and international economics, and provide leftist perspectives on current economic affairs. Our audience is a mix of activists, organizers, academics, liberals, unionists and other socially concerned people." Estab. 1974. Circ. 8,000. Pays on publication. Publishes ms an average of 4 months after acceptance. Byline given. Offers 30% kill fee. Buys all rights. Editorial lead time 3 months. Submit seasonal material 2 months in advance. Reports in 1 month. Sample copy for $4.50 or on website; writer's guidelines also on website.

**Nonfiction:** Exposé, political economics. **Buys 6 mss/year.** Query by mail with published clips. Length: 700-2,500 words. **Pays $0-200.** Sometimes pays expenses of writers on assignment.

**Photos:** State availability of photos with submission. Negotiates payment individually. Captions and identification of subjects required. Buys one-time rights.

**Tips:** "Be familiar with our magazine and the types of communities interested in reading us. *Dollars and Sense* is a progressive economics magazine that explains in a popular way both the workings of the economy and struggles to change it. Articles may be on the environment, the World Bank, community organizing, urban conflict, inflation, unemployment, union reform, welfare, changes in government regulation . . . a broad range of topics that have an economic theme. Find samples of our latest issue on our homepage."

**$ $ENTREPRENEUR MAGAZINE**, 2392 Morse Ave., Irvine CA 92614-6234. (714)261-2325. Fax: (714)755-4211. E-mail: entmag@entrepreneurmag.com. Website: http://www.entrepreneurmag.com. **Contact:** Rieva Lesonsky, editor, or Peggy Reeves Bennett, articles editor. **40% freelance written.** "Readers are small business owners seeking information on running a better business. *Entrepreneur* readers already run their own businesses. They have been in business for several years and are seeking innovative methods and strategies to improve their business operations. They are also interested in new business ideas and opportunities, as well as current issues that affect their companies." **Pays on acceptance.** Publishes ms an average of 5 months after acceptance. Byline given. Buys first international rights. Submit seasonal material 6 months in advance of issue date. Accepts queries by mail, fax. Reports in 3 months. Sample copy for $7 from Order Deaprtment. Writer's guidelines for #10 SASE (please write "Attn: Writer's Guidelines" on envelope) or on website.

• *Entrepreneur* publishes the bimonthly *Entrepreneur International* which covers the latest in U.S. trends and franchising for an international audience. (This is not written for a U.S. audience.) They encourage writers with expertise in this area to please query with ideas. Sample copy $6.50 from Order Department.

**Nonfiction:** How-to (information on running a business, dealing with the psychological aspects of running a business, profiles of unique entrepreneurs), current news/trends and their effect on small business. **Buys 10-20 mss/year.** Query with clips of published work and SASE or query by fax. Length: 2,000 words. Payment varies. Columns not open to freelancers.

• Ranked as one of the best markets for freelance writers in *Writer's Yearbook* magazine's annual "Top 100 Markets," January 1999.

**Photos:** "We use color transparencies to illustrate articles. Please state availability with query." Uses standard color transparencies. Buys first rights.

**Tips:** "Read several issues of the magazine! Study the feature articles versus the columns. Probably 75 percent of our freelance rejections are for article ideas covered in one of our regular columns. It's so exciting when a writer goes beyond the typical, flat 'business magazine query'—how to write a press release, how to negotiate with vendors, etc.— and instead investigates a current trend and then develops a story on how that trend affects small business. In your query, mention companies you'd like to use to illustrate examples and sources who will provide expertise on the topic."

**$ $ENTREPRENEUR'S BUSINESS START-UPS**, (formerly *Business Start-Ups*), Entrepreneur Media, Inc., 2392 Morse Ave., Irvine CA 92614. (949)261-2083. Fax: (949)755-4211. E-mail: bsumag@entrepreneurmag.com. Website: http://www.bizstartups.com. **Contact:** Karen Axelton, managing editor. **65% freelance written.** Monthly magazine for young entrepreneurs (age 23 to 35). "We target tech-savvy, upscale and educated readers who are preparing to start a business within the next year or have started a business within the past 2 years. Articles cover ideas for hot businesses to start; how-to advice to help new entrepreneurs run and grow their businesses; cutting-edge technology, management and marketing trends; motivational topics and more." Estab. 1989. Circ. 200,000. **Pays on acceptance.** Byline given. Offers 20% kill fee. Buys first time international rights. Submit seasonal material 6 months in advance. Accepts queries by mail, e-mail. Reports in 3 months on queries. Sample copy for $3 and $3 shipping. Writer's guidelines for SASE (please write: "Attn: Writer's Guidelines" on envelope).

**Nonfiction:** "Our readers don't necessarily have tons of money, but they make up for it in attitude, energy and determination. They're seeking ideas for hot businesses to start; how-to advice to help them run and grow their businesses; cutting-edge articles to keep them on top of the latest business trends; and motivational articles to get (and keep) them psyched up. No matter what your topic, articles should be packed with real-life examples of exciting young entrepreneurs doing things in new and different ways, plus plenty of pull-outs, sidebars and tips that can be presented in an eye-catching style. Types of features we are seeking include: Psychological (staying motivated, sparking creativity, handling stress, overcoming fear, etc.); Profiles of successful young entrepreneurs with original, creative, outrageous ideas and strategies others can learn from; Operating articles (how-to advice for running a business, such as finding financing, choosing a partner, marketing on a shoestring, etc.); Issues (examination of how a current issue affects young entrepreneurs); Industry round-ups (articles covering a particular industry and highlighting several young entrepreneurs in that industry, for example, gourmet food entrepreneurs, cigar entrepreneurs, specialty travel entrepreneurs); Tech. We are always seeking people who can write interestingly and knowledgeably about technology. Feature length: 1,200-1,800 words. **Pays $400 and up for features, $100 for briefs.**

● Ranked as one of the best markets for freelance writers in *Writer's Yearbook* magazine's annual "Top 100 Markets," January 1999.

**Reprints:** Send tearsheet of article and info about when and where the article previously appeared. Pay varies.

**Photos:** Daryl Hoopes, art director. State availability of photos with submission. Identification of subjects required.

**Columns/Departments:** Biz 101 (management/operations topics such as management trends, legal issues, insuring your business and other things new entrepreneurs must know to run a successful business), 300-500 words; Hot Biz (spotlights a hot business to start. Examples include niche greeting cards, catering and personal coaching. The column explains why this industry is hot and its growth prospects, and spotlights several successful entrepreneurs who share their start-up secrets), 1,000 words.

**Tips:** "We are looking for irreverent, creative writers who can approach topics in new ways in terms of style, format and outlook. You must write in a way our audience can relate to. They want a lot of info, fast, with specifics on where to get more info and follow up. They're skeptical and don't believe everything they read. Tone should sound like a friend giving another friend the 'inside scoop'—not like a professor lecturing from an ivory tower. Humor helps a lot. How *not* to break in: Send a résumé without a query (I hate this!) or writing samples that are full of vague generalities."

■ **$ $ INCOME OPPORTUNITIES**, NewsLine, 5300 City Plex Tower, 2448 E. 81st St., Tulsa OK 74137-4207. (918)491-6100, ext. 108. Fax: (918)491-9410. E-mail: editor@incomeops.com. Website: http://www.incomeops.com. Managing Editor: Steven M. Brown. **Contact:** André Hinds, executive editor. **70% freelance written.** Bimonthly magazine covering small business and franchise opportunities. "*Income Opportunities* targets an audience that includes the entrepreneur in all of us, the person with a dream of casting off the corporate shackles and becoming his or her own boss, and the individual who simply wants to supplement his or her regular income with money-making, work-from-home opportunities." Estab. 1956. Circ. 185,000. **Pays on acceptance.** Publishes ms an average of 3 months after acceptance. Byline given. Offers 50% kill fee. Buys first North American serial rights. Editorial lead time 3 months. Submit seasonal material 3 months in advance. Accepts queries and mss by mail, e-mail, fax. Reports in 6 weeks on queries; 6 weeks on mss. Writer's guidelines for #10 SASE.

**Nonfiction:** How-to (money-making, small business or entrepreneurial concepts), interview/profile (individuals who are successful small business owners). Does not want autobiographies, historical small-business start-ups (such as Sears). **Buys 60 mss/year.** Send complete ms. Length: 1,200-1,600 words. **Pays $300-500.**

● Ranked as one of the best markets for freelance writers in *Writer's Yearbook* magazine's annual "Top 100 Markets," January 1999.

**Photos:** State availability of photos with submission. Reviews 35mm transparencies and 3×5 prints. Offers no additional payment for photos accepted with ms. Identification of subjects required. Buys one-time rights.

**Fillers:** Steven M. Brown, managing editor. Money-making, small business or entrepreneurial tips. **Buys 42/year.** Length: 150-300 words. **Pays $50.**

**Tips:** "We need tips to help start-up businesses become profitable quickly. The stories that catch our eye are concise, informative and have a good hook, such as '12 Ways to Slash Your Taxes' or 'How to Double Your Income Next Year.' "

**$ $ $ INDEPENDENT BUSINESS: America's Small Business Magazine**, Group IV Communications, Inc., 860 Via de la Paz, #D-4, Pacific Palisades CA 90272. (805)496-6156, ext. 18. Fax: (805)496-5469. E-mail: gosmallbiz@aol.com. Website: http://www.yoursource.com. **Contact:** Daniel Kehrer, editor. **75% freelance written.** Bimonthly magazine for small and independent business. "We publish only practical 'how-to' articles of interest to small business owners all across America." Estab. 1989. Circ. 630,000. **Pays on acceptance.** Publishes ms an average of 4 months after acceptance. Byline given. Offers 25% kill fee. Buys first rights. Reports in 6 months. Sample copy for $4. Writer's guidelines for #10 SASE.

**Nonfiction:** How-to articles for operating a small business. No "generic" business articles, articles on big business, how to start a business or general economic theory. **Buys 80-100 mss/year.** Query with résumé and published clips; do not send mss. Length: 1,000-2,000 words. **Pays $500-1,500.** Pays expenses of writers on assignment.

**Columns/Departments:** Tax Tactics, Money Matters, Small Business Computing, Marketing Moves, Ad-visor, Your Employees, Managing Smart, Selling Smart, Business Cost-Savers, all 1,000-2,000 words. **Buys 40-50 mss/year.** Query with résumé and published clips. **Pays $500-1,500.**

**Tips:** "Talk to small business owners anywhere in America about what they want to read, what concerns or interests them in running a business. All areas open, but we use primarily professional business writers with top credentials in the field. Please read magazine before submitting query!"

■ **$ $ $ $ INDIVIDUAL INVESTOR**, Individual Investor Group, 125 Broad St., 14th Floor, New York NY 10004. (212)742-2277. Fax: (212)742-0747. Website: http://www.iionline.com. **Contact:** Paul Libassi, editor. **40% freelance written.** Monthly magazine covering stocks, mutual funds and personal finance. "Our readers range from novice to experienced investors. Our articles aim to be lively, informative, interesting, and to uncover 'undiscovered' investing opportunities." Circ. 500,000. **Pays on acceptance.** Publishes ms an average of 3 months after acceptance. Byline given. Buys all rights. Editorial lead time 2 months. Submit seasonal material 4 months in advance. Sample copy free.

**Columns/Departments:** Paul Libassi, editor. Educated Investor (investing basics and special topics), 1,500 words.

**Buys 12 mss/year.** Query with published clips. **Pays up to $1/word.**

**Tips:** "Most ideas are generated inhouse and assigned to a stable of freelancers."

■✖ $**THE NETWORK JOURNAL, Black Professional and Small Business News**, The Network Journal Communication, 139 Fulton St., Suite 407, New York, NY 10038. (212)962-3791. Fax: (212)962-3537. E-mail: tnj@obe 1.com. Website: http://www.tnj.com. Editor: Tania Padgett. **Contact:** Cameron Brown, managing editor. **25% freelance written.** Monthly tabloid covering business and career articles. *The Network Journal* caters to Black professionals and small-business owners, providing quality coverage on business, financial, technology and career news germane to the Black community. Estab. 1993. Circ. 11,000. Pays on publication. Byline given. Buys all rights. Editorial lead time 2 months. Submit seasonal material 3 months in advance. Accepts queries by mail, e-mail, fax, phone. Accepts simultaneous submissions. Sample copy for $1 or on website. Writer's guidelines for SASE or on website.

**Nonfiction:** How-to, interview/profile. Send complete ms. Length: 1,200-1,500 words. **Pays $40.** Sometimes pays expenses of writers on assignment.

**Reprints:** Accepts previously published submissions.

**Photos:** Send photos with submission. Offers $20/photo. Identification of subjects required. Buys one-time rights.

**Columns/Departments:** Book reviews, 700-800 words; career management and small business development, 800 words. **Pays $25.**

◼ The online magazine carries original content not found in the print version and includes writer's guidelines. Contact: Michael Prince, online editor.

**Tips:** "We are looking for vigorous writing and reporting for our cover stories and feature articles. Pieces should have gripping leads, quotes that actually say something and that come from several sources. Unless it is a column, please do not submit a one-source story. Always remember that your article must contain a nutgraph—that's usually the third paragraph telling the reader what the story is about and why you are telling it now. Editorializing should be kept to a minimum. If you're writing a column, make sure your opinions are well-supported."

▨ ✖ $ $ $ $**PROFIT, The Magazine for Canadian Entrepreneurs**, CB Media Limited, 777 Bay St., 5th Floor, Toronto, Ontario Canada M5W 1A7. (416)596-5999. Fax: (416)596-5111. E-mail: profit@cbmedia.ca. Website: http://www.profitguide.com. **Contact:** Ian Portsmouth, senior editor. **80% freelance written.** Published 8 times/ year magazine covering small and medium business. "We specialize in specific, useful information that helps our readers manage their businesses better. We want Canadian stories only." Estab. 1982. Circ. 110,000. **Pays on acceptance.** Publishes ms an average of 2 months after acceptance. Byline given. Kill fee varies. Buys first North American serial rights and non-exclusive electronic rights. Submit seasonal material 6 months in advance. Query by mail, e-mail, fax, phone. Reports in 1 month on queries; 6 weeks on mss. Sample copy for 9×12 SAE with 84¢ postage (Canadian). Writer's guidelines free.

**Nonfiction:** How-to (business management tips), strategies and Canadian business profiles. **Buys 50 mss/year.** Query with published clips. Length: 800-2,000 words. **Pays $500-2,000 (Canadian).** Pays expenses of writers on assignment. State availability of photos with submission.

**Columns/Departments:** Finance (info on raising capital in Canada), 700 words; Marketing (marketing strategies for independent business), 700 words. **Buys 80 mss/year.** Query with published clips. Length: 200-800 words. **Pays $150-600 (Canadian).**

◼ The online magazine carries original material not found in the print edition. Contact: Rick Spence.

**Tips:** "We're wide open to freelancers with good ideas and some knowledge of business. Read the magazine and understand it before submitting your ideas—which should have a Canadian focus."

$ $ $ $**REPORT ON BUSINESS MAGAZINE**, Globe and Mail, 444 Front St. W., Toronto Ontario M5V 2S9 Canada. (416)585-5499. E-mail: robmag@globeandmail.ca. Website: http://www.robmagnet.com/. Editor: Patricia Best. **Contact:** Trish Wilson, senior editor. **50% freelance written.** Monthly "business magazine like *Forbes* or *Fortune* which tries to capture major trends and personalities." Circ. 300,000. **Pays on acceptance.** Publishes ms an average of 4 months after acceptance. Byline given. Offers 50% kill fee. Buys first North American serial rights. Query for electronic submissions. Reports in 3 weeks. Free sample copy.

**Nonfiction:** Book excerpts, exposé, interview/profile, new product, photo feature. Special issue: quarately technology report. **Buys 30 mss/year.** Query with published clips. Length: 2,000-4,000 words. **Pays $200-3,000.** Pays expenses of writers on assignment.

**Tips:** "For features send a one-page story proposal. We prefer to write about personalities involved in corporate events."

★ $ $**TECHNICAL ANALYSIS OF STOCKS & COMMODITIES, The Trader's Magazine**, Technical Analysis, Inc., 4757 California Ave. SW, Seattle WA 98116-4499. (206)938-0570. Fax: (206)938-1307. E-mail: editor@tr aders.com. Website: http://www.traders.com. Publisher: Jack K. Hutson. **Contact:** Thomas R. Hartle, editor. **75% freelance written.** Eager to work with new/unpublished writers. Magazine covers methods of investing and trading stocks, bonds and commodities (futures), options, mutual funds and precious metals. Estab. 1982. Circ. 56,000. Pays on publication. Publishes ms an average of 3 months after acceptance. Byline given. Buys all rights; however, second serial (reprint) rights revert to the author, provided copyright credit is given. Reports in 3 weeks on queries; 1 month on mss. Sample copy for $5. Writer's guidelines for #10 SASE or on website.

**Nonfiction:** Reviews (new software or hardware that can make a trader's life easier, comparative reviews of software books, services, etc.); how-to (trade); technical (trading and software aids to trading); utilities (charting or computer programs, surveys, statistics or information to help the trader study or interpret market movements); humor (unusual incidents of market occurrences, cartoons). "No newsletter-type, buy-sell recommendations. The article subject must relate to trading psychology, technical analysis, charting or a numerical technique used to trade securities or futures. Virtually requires graphics with every article." **Buys 150 mss/year.** Query with published clips if available or send complete ms. Length: 1,000-4,000 words. **Pays $100-500.** (Applies per inch base rate and premium rate—write for information). Sometimes pays expenses of writers on assignment.

**Reprints:** Send tearsheet or photocopy of article or typed ms with rights for sale noted and information about when and where the article appeared.

**Photos:** Christine M. Morrison, art director. State availability of art or photos. Pays $60-350 for b&w or color negatives with prints or positive slides. Captions, model releases and identification of subjects required. Buys one-time and reprint rights.

**Columns/Departments: Buys 100 mss/year.** Query. Length: 800-1,600 words. **Pays $50-300.**

**Fillers:** Karen Wasserman, fillers editor. Jokes and cartoons on investment humor. Must relate to trading stocks, bonds, options, mutual funds, commodities or precious metals. **Buys 20/year.** Length: 500 words. **Pays $20-50.**

**Tips:** "Describe how to use technical analysis, charting or computer work in day-to-day trading of stocks, bonds, commodities, options, mutual funds or precious metals. A blow-by-blow account of how a trade was made, including the trader's thought processes, is the very best received story by our subscribers. One of our primary considerations is to instruct in a manner that the layperson can comprehend. We are not hypercritical of writing style."

**N $ WORDS FOR SALE**, 1149 Granada Ave., Salinas CA 93906. **Contact:** Lorna Gilbert, submission editor.

**Nonfiction:** "Since 1968, we have sold almost every kind of written material to a wide variety of individual and corporate clients. We deal in both the written as well as the spoken word. From humorous one liners and nightclub acts, to informative medical brochures, political speeches, and almost everything in between. We are not agents. We are a company that provides original written material created especially for the specific needs of our current clients. Therefore, do not send us a sample of your work. As good as it may be, it is almost certainly unrelated to our current needs. Instead begin by finding out what our clients want and write it for them. What could be simpler? It gets even better: *We buy sentences!* That's right. Forget conceiving, composing, editing and polishing endless drafts of magazine articles or book manuscripts. Simply create the type of sentence or sentences we're looking for and we'll buy one or more of them. We respond promptly. We pay promptly." **Pays $1 and up/sentence. Pays on acceptance."** All submissions must include SASE or they will not be returned.

**Tips:** "The key to your selling something to us, is to *first* find out *exactly* what we are currently buying. To do this simply mail us a #10 SASE and we will promptly send you a list of what we are anxious to buy at this time."

**$ $ $ YOUR MONEY**, Consumers Digest Inc., 8001 Lincoln Ave., 6th Floor, Skokie IL 60077-2403. (847)763-9200. Fax: (847)763-0200. E-mail: bhessel@consumersdigest.com. Website: http://www.consumersdigest.com. **Contact:** Brooke Hessel, assistant editor. **75% freelance written.** Bimonthly magazine on personal finance. "We cover the broad range of topics associated with personal finance—spending, saving, investing earning, etc." Estab. 1979. Circ. 500,000. **Pays on acceptance.** Publishes ms an average of 2 months after acceptance. Byline given. Offers 50% kill fee. Buys first rights and second serial (reprint) rights. Query by mail, e-mail, fax. Reports in 3 months (or longer) on queries. Do not send computer disks. Sample copy and writer's guidelines for 9×12 SAE with 4 first-class stamps. Writer's guidelines for #10 SASE.

● *Your Money* has been receiving more submissions and has less time to deal with them. Accordingly, they often need more than three months reporting time.

**Nonfiction:** How-to. "No first-person success stories or profiles of one company." Financial planning: debt management, retirement, funding education; investment: stocks and bonds, mutual funds, collectibles, treasuries, CDs; consumer-oriented topics: travel, car bargains, etc. **Buys 25 mss/year.** Send complete ms or query and clips. Include stamped, self-addressed postcard for more prompt response. Length: 1,500-2,500 words. **Pays 60¢/word.** Pays expenses of writers on assignment.

**Tips:** "Know the subject matter. Develop real sources in the investment community. Demonstrate a reader-friendly style that will help make the sometimes complicated subject of investing more accessible to the average person. Fill manuscripts with real-life examples of people who actually have done the kinds of things discussed—people we can later photograph. Although many of our readers are sophisticated investors, we provide jargon-free advice for people who may not be sophisticated. Articles must be thoroughly researched and professionally written. We ask writers to supply documentation: phone numbers of people interviewed, original sources of facts and figures, annual reports of recommended companies, etc. Sidebars, charts, tables, and graphs are frequently used, and these are expected from writers. Authors must be well-acquainted with the areas they discuss and should be prepared to render subjective and objective opinions about profit potential and risk."

# Regional

**$ $ ALASKA BUSINESS MONTHLY**, Alaska Business Publishing, 501 W. Northern Lights Blvd., Suite 100, Anchorage AK 99503-2577. (907)276-4373. Fax: (907)279-2900. E-mail: editor@akbizmag.com. Website: http://www.a

kbizmag.com. **Contact:** Debbie Cutler, editor. **80% freelance written.** Monthly magazine covering Alaska-oriented business and industry. "Our audience is Alaska business men and women who rely on us for timely features and up-to-date information about doing business in Alaska." Estab. 1985. Circ. 10,000. Pays on publication. Publishes ms an average of 2 months after acceptance. Byline given. Offers $50 kill fee. Buys first North American serial rights, first rights, one-time rights or makes work-for-hire assignments. Editorial lead time 2 months. Submit seasonal material 3 months in advance. Query by mail, e-mail, fax, phone. Reports in 2 weeks on queries; 1 month on mss. Sample copy for 9×12 SAE and 6 first-class stamps. Writer's guidelines free.
**Nonfiction:** Humor, interview/profile, new product, opinion, technical, business. No fiction, poetry or anything not pertinent to Alaska. **Buys approx. 150 mss/year.** Send complete ms. Length: 500-2,500 words. **Pays $100-300.** Sometimes pays expenses of writers on assignment.
**Photos:** Send photos with submission. Reviews 35mm or larger transparencies and 5×7 or larger prints. Offers $25-400/photo. Captions, model releases and identification of subjects required. Buys one-time rights.
**Columns/Departments:** Required Reading (business book reviews); Small Business Profile, 500 words. **Buys 12 mss/year.** Send complete ms. **Pays $100-150.**
**Tips:** "Send a well-written manuscript on a subject of importance to Alaska businesses. Include photos."

**Ⓝ $ $ ATLANTIC BUSINESS MAGAZINE,** Communications Ten Limited, 197 Water St., St. John's, Newfoundland A1C 6E7 Canada. (709)726-9300. Fax: (709)726-3013. E-mail: dchafe@abmaginf.ca. Website: http://www.webazine.nf.ca. Managing Editor: Edwina Hutton. **Contact:** Dawn Chafe, editor. **60% freelance written.** Published bimonthly covering business in Atlantic Canada. "We discuss positive business developments, emphasizing that the four Atlantic provinces are a great place to do business." Estab. 1989. Circ. 30,000. Pays on publication. Publishes ms an average of 1 month after acceptance. Byline given. Buys one-time rights. Editorial lead time 2 months. Accepts queries by mail, e-mail, fax, phone. Sample copy and writer's guidelines for free.
**Nonfiction:** Exposé, general interest, interview/profile, new product. "We don't want religious, technical or scholarly material. We are not an academic magazine." **Buys 36 mss/year.** Query with published clips. Length: 1,500-2,400 words. **Pays $300-750.** Sometimes pays expenses of writers on assignment.
**Photos:** Send photos with submission. Reviews contact sheets, transparencies and prints. Negotiates payment individually. Captions and identification of subjects required. Buys one-time rights.
**Columns/Departments:** Query with published clips.
**Tips:** "Writers should submit their areas of interest as well as samples of their work and if possible, suggested story ideas."

**⧗ $ $ $ BC BUSINESS,** Canada Wide Magazines & Communications Ltd., 4180 Lougheed Highway, 4th Floor, Burnaby, British Columbia V5C 6A7 Canada. (604)299-7311. Fax: (604)299-9188. **Contact:** Bonnie Irving, editor. **80% freelance written.** Monthly magazine "reports on significant issues and trends shaping the province's business environment. Stories are lively, topical and extensively researched." Circ. 26,000. Pays 2 weeks prior to publication. Publishes ms an average of 2 months after acceptance. Byline given. Kill fee varies. Buys first Canadian rights. Editorial lead time 4 months. Submit seasonal material 4 months in advance. Query by mail, fax, phone. Accepts simultaneous submissions. Reports in 6 weeks. Writer's guidelines free.
**Nonfiction:** Query with published clips. Length: 800-3,000 words. **Pays 40-60¢/word,** depending on length of story (and complexity). Sometimes pays expenses of writers on assignment.
**Photos:** State availability of photos with submission.

**$ $ BOULDER COUNTY BUSINESS REPORT,** 3180 Sterling Circle, Suite 201, Boulder CO 80301-2338. (303)440-4950. Fax: (303)440-8954. E-mail: jwlewis@bcbr.com. Website: http://www.bcbr.com. **Contact:** Jerry W. Lewis, editor. **75% freelance written.** Prefers to work with local published/established writers; works with a small number of new/unpublished writers each year. Monthly newspaper covering Boulder County business issues. Offers "news tailored to a monthly theme and read primarily by Colorado businesspeople and by some investors nationwide. Philosophy: Descriptive, well-written articles that reach behind the scene to examine area's business activity." Estab. 1982. Circ. 18,000. Pays on publication. Publishes ms an average of 1 month after acceptance. Byline given. Buys one-time rights and second serial (reprint) rights. Reports in 1 month on queries; 2 weeks on mss. Sample copy for $1.44.
**Nonfiction:** Interview/profile, new product, examination of competition in a particular line of business. "All our issues are written around three or four monthly themes. No articles are accepted in which the subject has not been pursued in depth and both sides of an issue presented in a writing style with flair." **Buys 120 mss/year.** Query with published clips. Length: 250-2,000 words. **Pays $50-200.**
**Photos:** State availability of photos with query letter. Reviews b&w contact sheets. Pays $10 maximum for b&w contact sheet. Identification of subjects required. Buys one-time rights and reprint rights.
**Tips:** "Must be able to localize a subject. In-depth articles are written by assignment. The freelancer located in the Colorado area has an excellent chance here."

**$ $ BUSINESS LIFE MAGAZINE,** Business Life Magazine, Inc., 4101-A Piedmont Pkwy., Greensboro NC 27410-8110. (336)812-8801. Fax: (336)812-8832. E-mail: lbouchey@bizlife.com. Website: http://www.bizlife.com. **Contact:** Lisa M. Bouchey, editor-in-chief. **30% freelance written.** "*Business Life* is a monthly, full-color magazine profiling businesses and business people that have ties to the Piedmont Triad, are headquartered here, or have an impact on the lives of local business people." Estab. 1989. Circ. 14,000. Pays on the 15th of the month of publication. Publishes ms 3 months after acceptance. Byline given. Offers ⅓ kill fee. Buys first rights and second serial (reprint) rights. Editorial lead time 2 months. Submit seasonal material 5 months in advance. Accepts queries by mail, e-mail, fax. Accepts simultaneous submissions. Reports in 3 weeks on queries. Sample copy for 9×12 SASE and $3 postage. Guidelines for SASE.

**Nonfiction:** Book excerpts, general interest, interview/profile, travel. No articles without ties to NC or the Piedmont Triad region (except travel). **Buys 45 mss/year**. Query with published clips. Length: 1,800-2,500 words. **Pays $200-250.**

**Photos:** State availability of photos with submission. Reviews transparencies (2×3). Negotiates payment individually. Captions and identification of subjects required. Buys one-time rights.

The online magazine carries original content not found in the print edition. Contact: Lisa M. Bouchey, online editor.

**Tips:** "Story should be of interest to readers in our area, either with a national angle that impacts people here or a more 'local' approach (a profile in the Piedmont Triad). We are primarily a regional publication."

**$ $ BUSINESS NH MAGAZINE**, 404 Chestnut St., Suite 201, Manchester NH 03101-1831. (603)626-6354. Fax: (603)626-6359. E-mail: bnhmag@aol.com. **Contact:** Janet Phelps, editor. **50% freelance written.** Monthly magazine with focus on business, politics and people of New Hampshire. "Our audience consists of the owners and top managers of New Hampshire businesses." Estab. 1983. Circ. 13,000. Pays on publication. Publishes ms an average of 2 months after acceptance. Byline given. Query by e-mail, fax.

**Nonfiction:** Features—how-to, interview/profile. **Buys 24 mss/year.** Query with published clips and résumé. "No unsolicited manuscripts; interested in New Hampshire writers only." Length: 750-2,500 words. **Pays $75-350.**

**Photos:** Both b&w and color photos used. Pays $40-80. Buys one-time rights.

**Tips:** "I *always* want clips and résumé with queries. Freelance stories are almost always assigned. Stories *must* be local to New Hampshire."

**$ $ $ BUSINESS NORTH CAROLINA**, Red Hand Media, 5435 77 Center Dr., Suite 50, Charlotte NC 28217-0711. (704)523-6987. Fax: (704)523-4211. E-mail: bnc@businessnc.com. Editor: David Kinney. **Contact:** Terry Noland, managing editor. **60% freelance written**. Monthly magazine covering business in North Carolina. "We seek to show not only trends and events but the human face of commerce." Estab. 1981. Circ. 30,000. **Pays on acceptance**. Publishes ms an average of 2 months after acceptance. Byline sometimes given. Offers 25% kill fee. Makes work-for-hire assignments. Editorial lead time 2 months. Accepts queries by mail, phone. Reports in 2 weeks. Sample copy for $3.50.

**Nonfiction:** Book excerpts, exposé, general interest, interview/profile, photo feature. No how-to, general trend stories or new product reviews. **Buys 25 mss/year**. Query with published clips. Length: 2,000-4,000 words. **Pays $400-800**. Pays expenses of writers on assignment.

**Columns/Departments:** People (profiles of business people), and Tattlers (gossipy, insider news items) 500 words; Professions (issues dealing with a particular profession or unusual occupation), 1,300 words; Money (highlighting a particular stock's performance), 1,000 words. **Buys 65 mss/year**. Query with published clips. **Pays $100-350.**

**Tips:** "The People department—short personality profiles—is the most common place for new freelancers to break in. If they can pitch us on an idea, that helps. Knowledge of North Carolina is a plus. Do not pitch how-to/service pieces. Corporate or personality profiles welcome. Issue stories must have strong North Carolina tie. In general, we like stories with an edge to them."

**$ $ CHARLESTON REGIONAL BUSINESS JOURNAL**, Setcom, Inc., P.O. Box 446, Charleston SC 29402. (843)723-7702. Fax: (843)723-7060. E-mail: info@crbj.com. Website: http://www.crbj.com. Editor: William Settlemyer. Managing Editor: Renee Johnson. **Contact:** Catherine Fahey, associate editor. **60% freelance written.** Bimonthly newspaper covering local business. "We publish articles of interest to small business owners in the Charleston area, preferably with a local slant." Estab. 1994. Circ. 7,000. Pays on publication. Publishes ms an average of 1 month after acceptance. Byline given. Offers $40 kill fee. Buys all rights. Editorial lead time 1 month. Submit seasonal material 2 months in advance. Accepts queries by mail, e-mail, fax. Accepts simultaneous submissions. Reports in 2 weeks on queries. Sample copy online at website.

**Nonfiction:** Interview/profile (business people), technical, other of interest to small business owners, women business owners. No how-to's. **Buys 100 mss/year.** Query with published clips. Length: 400-900 words. **Pays $40-200.** Sometimes pays expenses of writers on assignment.

**Photos:** State availability of photos with submission. Reviews e-mail photos (jpeg, 170 resolution minimum). Offers $30/photo. Identification of subjects required. Buys one-time rights.

**$ COAST BUSINESS**, Ship Island Holding Co., P.O. Box 1209, Gulfport MS 39502. Fax: (228)594-0074. E-mail: coastbusiness@nse.com. **Contact:** Lauren Thompson, editor. **10% freelance written.** Biweekly tabloid covering business. "*Coast Business* covers local and national business news and issues. Our readers represent the business community of the Mississippi Gulf Coast." Estab. 1989. Circ. 8,000. Pays on publication. Publishes ms an average of 1 month after acceptance. Byline given. Buys first North American serial rights. Editorial lead time 3 months. Submit seasonal material 3 months in advance. Reports in 2 weeks on queries; 1 month on mss. Sample copy for $1.

**Nonfiction:** How-to, interview/profile, new product, opinion. All articles must be business related. **Buys 26 mss/year.** Query with published clips. Length: 700-1,500 words. **Pays $50-150.** Sometimes pays expenses of writers on assignment.

**Photos:** Send photos with submission. Reviews prints. Negotiates payment individually. Captions, identification of subjects required. Buys one-time rights.

**Columns/Departments:** Computers (product reviews, tips); Finance (personal or business); Law (business); Small Business Q&A; Tax; Travel (business); all 700-750 words. Query with published clips. **Pays $50-75.**

**Tips:** "Our audience is the business community of the Mississippi Gulf Coast. We cover local news as well as national issues that affect the way the Coast does business."

**$ $ CRAIN'S DETROIT BUSINESS**, Crain Communications Inc., 1400 Woodbridge Ave., Detroit MI 48207-3110. (313)446-6000. Fax: (313)446-1687. E-mail: jmelton@crain.com. Website: http://crainsdetroit.com. Editor: Mary Kramer. Executive Editor: Cindy Goodaker. **Contact:** James Melton, special sections editor. **15% freelance written.** Weekly tabloid covering business in the Detroit metropolitan area—specifically Wayne, Oakland, Macomb, Washtenaw and Livingston counties. Estab. 1985. Circ. 150,000 readership. Pays on publication. Publishes ms an average of 1 month after acceptance. Byline given. Buys all rights and all electronic rights. Accepts queries by mail, e-mail. Sample copy for $1.

• *Crain's Detroit Business* uses only area writers and local topics.

**Nonfiction:** New product, technical, business. **Buys 100 mss/year.** Query with published clips. Length: 30-40 words/column inch. **Pays $10/column inch.** Pays expenses of writers on assignment.

**Photos:** State availability of photos with submissions.

**Tips:** "Contact special sections editor in writing with background and, if possible, specific story ideas relating to our type of coverage and coverage area. We only use *local* writers."

**N $ IN BUSINESS WINDSOR**, Cornerstone Publications Inc., 1614 Lesperance Rd., Tecumseh, Ontario N8N 1Y3 Canada. (519)735-2080. Fax: (519)735-2082. E-mail: inbiz@mnsi.net. Website: http://www.inbizwin.com. Associate Editor: Mark Malone. **Contact:** Gordon Hillman, publisher. **20% freelance written.** Monthly magazine covering business. "We focus on issues/ideas which are of interest to businesses in and around Windsor and Essex County (Ontario). Most stories deal with business and finance but we occasionally write about, for example, health and sports." Estab. 1988. Circ. 10,000. Pays on publication. Publishes ms an average of 2 months after acceptance. Byline given. Buys first rights. Editorial lead time 3 months. Submit seasonal material 3 months in advance. Accepts queries by mail, e-mail, fax and phone. Reports in 2 weeks on queries; 1 month on mss. Sample copy for $3.50.

**Nonfiction:** General interest, how-to, interview/profile. **Buys 25 mss/year.** Query with published clips. Length: 1,000-2,500 words. **Pays $50-150.** Sometimes pays expenses of writers on assignment.

**$ $ $ INGRAM'S**, Show-Me Publishing, Inc., 306 E. 12th St., Suite 1014, Kansas City MO 64106. (816)842-9994. Fax: (816)474-1111. **Contact:** Patrick Lowry, editor. **50% freelance written.** Monthly magazine covering Kansas City business/executive lifestyle for "upscale, affluent business executives and professionals. Looking for sophisticated writing with style and humor when appropriate." Estab. 1975. Circ. 26,000. **Pays on acceptance.** Publishes ms an average of 2 months after acceptance. Byline given. Buys first rights and Internet rights. Editorial lead time 2 months. Submit seasonal material 3 months in advance. Reports in 6 weeks on queries. Sample copy for $3 current, $5 back.

**Nonfiction:** How-to (businesses and personal finance related), interview/profile (KC execs and politicians, celebrities), opinion. **Buys 30 mss/year.** Query with published clips. "All articles must have a Kansas City angle. We don't accept unsolicited manuscripts except for opinion column." Length: 500-3,000 words. **Pays $175-500 maximum.** Sometimes pays expenses of writers on assignment.

**Columns/Departments:** Say-So (opinion), 1,500 words. **Buys 12 mss/year. Pays $175 maximum.**

**Tips:** "Writers must understand the publication and the audience—knowing what appeals to a business executive, entrepreneur, or professional in Kansas City."

**N ★ $ INLAND EMPIRE BUSINESS JOURNAL**, Daily Planet Publishing, Inc., 8560 Vineyard Ave., Suite 306, Rancho Cucamonga CA 91730-4352. (909)484-9765. Fax: (909)391-3160. E-mail: busjournal@.com. Managing Editor: Ingrid Anthony. **Contact:** Robert Perry, assistant editor. **80% freelance written.** Monthly magazine covering business related news and features occuring in or pertinent to the "Inland Empire" of Southern California—Riverside and San Bernardino counties. "Audience: decision makers in the two-county area, including CEOs, CFOs, COOs, regional and branch managers, entrepreneurs, politicians and bureaucrats. Philosophy: politically conservative, caters to employer-entrepreneur-professional." Estab. 1988. Circ. 30,000. Pays 30 days after publication. Publishes ms an average of 1 month after acceptance. Byline sometimes given. Buys first North American serial rights or makes work-for-hire assignments. Editorial lead time 2 weeks. Submit seasonal material 1 month in advance. Query by mail, e-mail, fax, phone. Reports in 3 weeks on queries. Sample copy for $2 plus $1.70 postage. AP guidelines.

**Nonfiction:** Opinion. **Buys 60 mss/year.** Query with published clips. Length: 300-1,500 words. **Pays 5¢/word.** Sometimes pays expenses of writers on assignment.

**Photos:** State availability of photos with query or send photos with submission. Reviews negatives, transparencies or 4×6 prints. Offers $7.50-15/photo. Captions and identification of subjects required. Buys one-time rights.

**Columns/Departments:** Exporting (how-to); The Employers Group (employer issues); Corner on the Market (marketing info); Manager's Bookshelf (business book reviews); Mead on Wine (wine reviews); Executive Time Out (travel and photos); all 850 words. Query with published clips.

**$ $ JOHNSON COUNTY BUSINESS TIMES**, Sun Publications Inc., 7373 W. 107th St., Overland Park KS 66212-2547. (913)649-8778. Fax: (913)381-9889. E-mail: jcbt@sunpublications.com. **Contact:** Christine Perez, editor.

**5% freelance written.** Weekly magazine covering Johnson County business news. "Our magazine is written for local CEOs." Estab. 1994. Circ. 15,000. **Pays on acceptance.** Publishes ms an average of 1 month after acceptance. Byline given. Offers 25% kill fee. Buys first rights. Editorial lead time 1 month. Submit seasonal material 3 months in advance. Reports in 2 weeks on queries. Sample copy for $1.50 plus postage. Writer's guidelines for $1.50 plus postage.

**Nonfiction:** How-to (business stories), interview/profile, business trend stories. **Buys 10 mss/year.** Query with published clips. Length: 600-3,000 words. **Pays $75-500.** Sometimes pays expenses of writers on assignment.

**Photos:** State availability of photos with submission. Reviews negatives. Negotiates payment individually. Identification of subjects required. Buys all rights.

**Columns/Departments:** Query with published clips. **Pays $75-200.**

**Tips:** "Propose specific, well-thought-out ideas that are a good fit for our audience. Stories must have a local angle."

**$ $ THE LANE REPORT**, Lane Communications Group, 201 E. Main St., 14th Floor, Lexington KY 40507. (606)244-3522. Fax: (606)244-3555. E-mail: lanereport@aol.com. Website: http://www.lanereport.com. **Contact:** John Gaver, editorial director. **50% freelance written.** Monthly magazine covering statewide business. Estab. 1986. Circ. 13,000. **Pays on acceptance.** Byline given. Offers 50% kill fee. Buys one-time rights. Editorial lead time 6 weeks. Submit seasonal material 3 months in advance. Accepts queries by mail, e-mail, fax. Accepts simultaneous submissions. Reports in 1 month. Sample copy and guidelines free.

**Nonfiction:** Essays, exposé, interview/profile, new product, photo feature. No fiction. **Buys 30-40 mss/year.** Query with published clips. Length: 500-2,000 words. **Pays $100-375.** Sometimes pays expenses of writers on assignment.

**Reprints:** Accepts previously published submissions.

**Photos:** State availability of photos with submission. Reviews contact sheets, negatives, transparencies, prints. Negotiates payment individually. Identification of subjects required. Buys one-time rights.

**Columns/Departments:** Copy Klatsch, Small Business Advisor, Financial Advisor, Exploring Kentucky, Perspective. All less than 1,000 words.

▣ The online magazine carries original content not found in the print edition. Contact: John Gaver or Chris Taylor, online editors.

**Ⓝ $ $ METRO JOURNAL, Oklahoma City's Business Magazine**, Arlan Brown Publishing Co., 3923 N. Pennsylvania, Oklahoma City OK 73112. (405)525-0100. Fax: (405)525-0112. E-mail: metro@telepath.com. Managing Editor: Hugh Jones. **Contact:** Dayna Avery, associate editor. **10-20% freelance written.** Monthly business magazine covering all business topics and real estate. "*Metro Journal* covers business related issues from small business to personal finance. We also cover the real estate market in Oklahoma City." Estab. 1993. Circ. 5,000. Pays on publication. Byline given. Offers 50% kill fee. Editorial lead time 1 month. Submit seasonal material 3 months in advance. Accepts queries by mail, e-mail, fax, phone. Accepts simultaneous submissions. Sample copy free. Writer's guidelines by e-mail.

**Nonfiction:** Exposé, how-to (business related), humor, interview/profile, new product, personal experience, photo feature, travel. Special issues: small business survival guide, special environmental issue, OKC properties (leasing guide), special construction and development. **Buys 10 mss/year.** Query with published clips. Length: 500-1,000 words. **Pays 10-20¢/word for assigned articles; 5-10¢/word for unsolicited articles.** Sometimes pays writers with contributor copies or other premiums. Sometimes pays expenses of writers on assignment.

**Reprints:** Accepts previously published submissions.

**Photos:** Send photos with submission. Negotiates payment individually. Captions, model releases and identification of subjects required. Buys all rights.

**Columns/Departments:** Small Business Advisor (how-to articles), Money Matters (financial advisor), Stock Watch (OKC-based companies), all 750 words. Query with published clips. **Pays 10-20¢/word.**

**$ $ PACIFIC BUSINESS NEWS**, 863 Halekauwila St., Honolulu HI 96813. (808)596-2021. Fax: (808)591-2321. E-mail: pbn@lava.net. Website: http://www.amcity.com/pacific/. **Contact:** Bernie Silver, editor. **5% freelance written.** Weekly business newspaper. Estab. 1963. Circ. 14,500. Pays on publication. Byline given. Offers 50% kill fee. Buys all rights. Editorial lead time 1 month. Query by mail, e-mail, fax, phone. Reports in 2 weeks on queries. Sample copy free.

**Nonfiction:** Feature articles, opinion. Query with published clips. Length: 750-1,000 words. **Pays $200.**

**Photos:** State availability of photos with submission. Reviews negatives. Offers no additional payment for photos accepted with ms. Captions required. Buys all rights.

**✠ $ $ PHILADELPHIA ENTERPRISER**, Business Pursuits, Inc., 3000 Valley Forge Circle, Suite G10, King of Prussia PA 19406. (610)783-7202. Fax: (610)783-7206. E-mail: publisher@enterpriser.com. Website: http://www.enterpriser.com. **Contact:** Bob Calandra, editor. **90% freelance written.** "Bimonthly conversational style magazine targeting practical advice for owners of emerging growth companies." Estab. 1994. Circ. 20,351. **Pays on acceptance.** Publishes ms an average of 1 month after acceptance. Byline given. Offers 50% kill fee. Buys first North American serial rights. Editorial lead time 1 month. Submit seasonal material 2 months in advance. Accepts queries by mail, e-mail, fax. Sample copy for $3.95.

**Nonfiction:** How-to, humor, inspirational, interview/profile, new product, travel. **Buys 56 mss/year.** Query with published clips. Length: 800-2,000 words. **Pays $265-660 for assigned articles; $160-400 for unsolicited articles.**

**Photos:** Send photos with submission. Reviews negatives. Offers no additional payment for photos accepted with ms.

Captions and identification of subjects required. Buys all rights.
**Columns/Departments: Buys 56 mss/year.** Query with published clips. **Pays $800-2,000.**
**Tips:** "Send us article ideas with first right of refusal on new topics of interest to business owners."

**$ $PITTSBURGH BUSINESS TIMES**, American City Business Journals, Inc., 2313 E. Carson St., Suite 200, Pittsburgh PA 15203-2158. (412)481-6397. Fax: (412)481-9956. E-mail: bittimes@aol.com. Website: http://www.amcity .com/pittsburgh/. Managing Editor: Betsy Benson. **Contact:** Paul Furiga, editor. **10% freelance written.** Weekly business journal. "*The Business Times* is the first and foremost source of business information for business executives in the Pittsburgh region and focuses on excellent reporting, fine writing and breaking news." Estab. 1981. Circ. 13,500. Pays on publication. Publishes ms an average of 1 month after acceptance. Byline given. Offers negotiable kill fee. Buys all rights. Editorial lead time 2 months. Reports in 1 week on queries; 2 weeks on mss. Sample copy and writer's guidelines free.
**Nonfiction:** Exposé, general interest, how-to, interview. "No first-person pieces; stories promoting any specific person/ entity or company." **Buys 20-40 mss/year.** Query with published clips. Length: 200-2,000 words. **Pays $50-200.** Sometimes pays expenses of writers on assignment.
**Photos:** State availability of photos with submission. Reviews contact sheets. Negotiates payment individually. Identification of subjects required. Buys all rights.
**Columns/Departments:** Michael Miller, special reports editor. Strategies (how-to stories on business issues), 800 words. **Buys 10-15 mss/year.** Query with published clips. **Pays $50-200.**
**Tips:** "Understand the focus and audience of weekly business journals, which are written for a highly literate, information-hungry, sophisticated group of readers. Always query first. One-page letters with a focused, one-paragraph story description are best."

**$ $SACRAMENTO BUSINESS JOURNAL**, American City Business Journals Inc., 1401 21st St., Suite 200, Sacramento CA 95814-5221. (916)447-7661. Fax: (916)447-2243. E-mail: bbuchanan@amcity.com. Website: http:// www.amcity.com/sacramento. Editor: Lee Wessman.**Contact:** Bill Buchanan, associate editor. **5% freelance written.** Weekly newspaper covering the Sacramento area's economy. "Our readers are decision makers. They own or manage companies, or are community leaders who want to know what's happening. They expect sophisticated, well-researched news. And they don't read fluff." Estab. 1984. Circ. 14,000. Pays on publication. Publishes ms an average of 1 month after acceptance. Byline sometimes given. Offers 50% kill fee. Buys all rights or makes work-for-hire assignments. Editorial lead time 2 months. Submit seasonal material 2 months in advance. Accepts queries by mail, e-mail, fax, phone. Reports in 3 weeks on queries. Sample copy for $2 and SAE with 2 first-class stamps.
**Nonfiction:** Humor, interview/profile, new product, opinion, local business news and trends. "No public relations stories on behalf of specific companies or industries. No thinly sourced stories." **Buys 60 mss/year.** Query with published clips. Length: 500-1,500 words. **Pays $125-200.** Sometimes pays expenses of writers on assignment.
**Photos:** State availability of photos with submission. Reviews contact sheets, prints. Offers $25-50 maximum/photo. Captions and identification of subjects required. Buys one-time rights.
**Columns/Departments:** Gary Chazen, associate editor. Small Biz (meaningful successes or failures), 750 words; Focus (industry trends), 1,200 words. **Buys 20 mss/year.** Query. **Pays $100-175.**
The online magazine carries original content not included in the print edition. Contact: Lee Wessman, online editor.
**Tips:** "Most of our freelance work is done on assignment with a three-week turnaround. We look for a regular stable of writers who can get an assignment, do the research and produce a well-focused story that reflects the drama of business and doesn't avoid controversy."

**$ $UTAH BUSINESS**, Olympus Publishers, 85 E. Fort Union Blvd., Midvale UT 84047-1531. Fax: (801)568-0812. E-mail: editor@utahbusiness.com. Website: http://www.utahbusiness.com. **Contact:** Matt Wright, associate editor. Editor: Brian Pittman. **80% freelance written.** "*Utah Business* is a monthly magazine focusing on the people, practices, and principles that drive Utah's economy. Audience is business owners and executives." Estab. 1983. Circ. 35,000. Pays on publication. Publishes ms an average of 2-3 months after acceptance. Byline given. Buys first rights and makes work-for-hire assignments. Editorial lead time 3 months. Submit seasonal material 2-3 months in advance. Accepts simultaneous submissions. Reports in 6 weeks on queries; 2 months on mss. Sample copy for 8½ × 11 SAE with 4 first-class stamps. Writer's guidelines for #10 SASE.
**Nonfiction:** How-to (business), interview/profile (business), new product, technical (business/technical), policy and politics. "No cake recipes. Nothing in first person. There is no self-only information." **Buys 200 mss/year.** Send complete ms. Length: 700-3,000 words. **Pays 25¢/word.** Sometimes pays expenses of writers on assignment.
**Reprints:** Accepts previously published submissions.
**Photos:** State availability of photos with submission. Reviews negatives. Offers no additional payment for photos accepted with ms. Identification of subjects required. Buys one-time rights.
**Columns/Departments:** Books/Travel/Money (direct, informative, advice, how-to), 650-700 words; In The News (business, Utah relevant news), 1,200 words; Features (Utah relevant conceptual stories), 2,000-3,000 words. **Buys 80 mss/year.** Send complete ms. **Pays 25¢/word.**
**Fillers:** Facts, newsbreaks. **Buys 20/year.** Length: 120-500 words. **Pays 25¢/word.**
**Tips:** "Use common sense; tailor your queries and stories to this market. Use AP style and colorful leads. Read the magazine first!"

**$ $VERMONT BUSINESS MAGAZINE**, 2 Church St., Burlington VT 05401-4445. (802)863-8038. Fax: (802)863-8069. E-mail: vtbizmag@together.net. Website: http://www.vtbusinessmagazine.com. **Contact:** Timothy McQuiston, editor. **80% freelance written.** Monthly tabloid covering business in Vermont. Circ. 8,000. Pays on publication. Publishes ms an average of 1 month after acceptance. Byline given. Buys one-time rights. Reports in 2 months. Sample copy for 11×14 SAE with 7 first-class stamps.

**Nonfiction:** Business trends and issues. **Buys 200 mss/year.** Query with published clips. Length: 800-1,800 words. **Pays $100-200.**

**Reprints:** Send tearsheet of article and information about when and where the article previously appeared.

**Photos:** Send photos with submission. Reviews contact sheets. Offers $10-35/photo. Identification of subjects required.

**Tips:** "Read daily papers and look for business angles for a follow-up article. We look for issue and trend articles rather than company or businessman profiles. Note: magazine accepts Vermont-specific material *only*. The articles *must* be about Vermont."

# CAREER, COLLEGE & ALUMNI

Three types of magazines are listed in this section: university publications written for students, alumni and friends of a specific institution; publications about college life for students; and publications on career and job opportunities. Literary magazines published by colleges and universities are listed in the Literary & "Little" section.

**N AMERICAN CAREERS**, Career Communications, Inc., 6701 W. 64th St., Overland Park KS 66202. Fax: (913)362-4864. **Contact:** Mary Pitchford, editor. **50% freelance written.** High school and vocational/technical school student publication published 3 times during school year covering careers, career statistics, skills needed to get jobs. Many stories are provided at no charge by authors in business, education and government. Estab. 1990. Circ. 500,000. **Pays on acceptance.** Byline sometimes given. Buys all rights and makes work-for-hire assignments. Query by mail. Reports in 1 month. Sample copy for $2. Writer's guidelines for SASE.

**Nonfiction:** Career and education features related to 6 basic career paths: arts and communication; business, management and related technology; health services; human services; industrial and engineering technology; and natural resources and agriculture. **Buys 10 mss/year.** Query with published clips. Deadlines: June 1 (Fall); September 1 (Winter); December 1 (Spring). Length: 300-750 words. **Pay varies.** Pays expenses of writers on assignment.

**Reprints:** Send photocopy of article or typed ms with rights for sale noted and information about when and where the article previously appeared. Pays 25% of amount paid for an original article.

**Photos:** State availability of photos with submission. Negotiates payment individually. Captions, model releases and identification of subjects required.

**Columns/Departments:** Reality Check (brief career-related facts), 25-100 words; Career Profile, 250-300 words. Some reviewing of current related books. **Buys 6 mss/year.** Negotiates payment.

**Tips:** "Letters of introduction or query letters with samples and resumes are ways we get to know writers. Samples should include how-to articles and career-related articles. Articles written for teenagers also would make good samples. Short feature articles on careers, career-related how-to articles and self-assessment tools (10-20 point quizzes with scoring information) are primarily what we publish."

**$ $THE BLACK COLLEGIAN, The Career & Self Development Magazine for African American Students**, Black Collegiate Services, Inc., 140 Carondelet St., New Orleans LA 70130. (504)523-0154. Fax: (504)523-0271. E-mail: robert@black-collegian.com. Website: http://www.black-collegian.com. Contact: Robert Miller, editor. **25% freelance written.** Magazine biannually published (October and February) during school year for African-American college students and recent graduates with an interest in career and job information, African-American cultural awareness, personalities, history, trends and current events. Estab. 1970. Circ. 109,000. Buys one-time rights. Pays on publication. Byline given. Submit seasonal and special interest material 2 months in advance of issue date. Accepts queries by mail, e-mail, fax. Reports in 6 months. Sample copy for $4 and 9×12 SAE. Writer's guidelines for #10 SASE.

**Nonfiction:** Material on careers, sports, black history, news analysis. Articles on problems and opportunities confronting African-American college students and recent graduates. Book excerpts, exposé, general interest, historical/nostalgic, how-to (develop employability), opinion, personal experience, profile, inspirational. **Buys 40 mss/year** (6 unsolicited). Query with published clips and send complete ms. Length: 500-1,500 words. **Pays $100-500.**

**Photos:** State availability of or send photos with query or ms. Black and white photos or color transparencies purchased with or without ms. 8×10 prints preferred. Captions, model releases and identification of subjects required. Pays $35/b&w; $50/color.

The online magazine carries original content not included in the print edition. Contact: Kathy De Joie, online editor.

**$ $CAREER FOCUS, For Today's Rising Professional**, Communications Publishing Group, Inc., 3100 Broadway, Suite 660, Kansas City MO 64111-2413. (816)960-1988. Fax: (816)960-1989. **Contact:** Neoshia Michelle Paige, executive editor. **80% freelance written.** Bimonthly magazine "devoted to providing positive insight, information, guidance and motivation to assist Blacks and Hispanics (ages 21-40) in their career development and attainment of goals." Estab. 1988. Circ. 250,000. Pays on publication. Byline often given. Buys second serial (reprint) rights and makes work-for-hire assignments. Submit seasonal material 6 months in advance. Accepts simultaneous submissions. Reports in 2 months. Sample copy for 9×12 SAE with 4 first-class stamps. Writer's guidelines for #10 SASE.

• The editor notes that if the writer can provide the manuscript on 3.25 disk, saved in generic ASCII, pay is $10 higher and chance of acceptance is greater.

**Nonfiction:** Book excerpts, general interest, historical, how-to, humor, inspirational, interview/profile, personal experience, photo feature, technical, travel. Length: 750-2,000 words. **Pays $150-400 for assigned articles; 12¢/word for unsolicited articles.** Sometimes pays expenses of writers on assignment.

**Reprints:** Send tearsheet of article or short story and information about when and where the article previously appeared. Pays 6¢/word.

**Photos:** State availability of photos with submission. Reviews transparencies. Pays $20-25/photo. Captions, model releases and identification of subjects required. Buys all rights.

**Columns/Departments:** Profiles (striving and successful Black and Hispanic young adult, ages 21-40). **Buys 15 mss/year.** Send complete ms. Length: 500-1,000 words. **Pays $50-250.**

**Fiction:** Adventure, ethnic, historical, humorous, mainstream, slice-of-life vignettes. **Buys 3 mss/year.** Send complete ms. Length: 500-2,000 words. Pay varies.

**Fillers:** Anecdotes, facts, gags to be illustrated by cartoonist, newsbreaks, short humor. **Buys 10/year.** Length: 25-250 words. **Pays $25-100.**

**Tips:** For new writers: Submit full ms that is double-spaced; clean copy only. If available, send clips of previously published works and résumé. Should state when available to write. Most open to freelancers are profiles of successful and striving persons including photos. Profile must be of a Black or Hispanic adult living in the US. Include on first page of ms name, address, phone number, Social Security number and number of words in article.

**$ $ CARNEGIE MELLON MAGAZINE,** Carnegie Mellon University, Bramer House, Pittsburgh PA 15213-3890. (412)268-2132. Fax: (412)268-6929. Editor: Ann Curran. Estab. 1914. Quarterly alumni publication covering university activities, alumni profiles, etc. Circ. 67,000. **Pays on acceptance.** Byline given. Reports in 1 month. Sample copy for $2 and 9×12 SAE.

**Nonfiction:** Book reviews (faculty alumni), general interest, humor, interview/profile, photo feature. "We use general interest stories linked to Carnegie Mellon activities and research." No unsolicited mss. **Buys 10-15 features and 5-10 alumni profiles/year.** Query with published clips. Length: 800-2,000 words. **Pays $250-750 or negotiable rate.**

**Poetry:** Avant-garde, traditional. Poet or topic must be related to Carnegie Mellon University. No previously published poetry. **Pays $25.**

**$ $ $ CAROLINA ALUMNI REVIEW,** UNC General Alumni Association, P.O. Box 660, Chapel Hill NC 27514-0660. (919)962-1208. Fax: (919)962-0010. E-mail: alumni@unc.edu. Website: http://alumni.unc.edu **Contact:** Regina Oliver, editor. Bimonthly University of North Carolina alumni magazine seeking understanding of issues and trends in higher education. Estab. 1912. Circ. 55,000. **Pays on acceptance.** Publishes ms an average of 6 months after acceptance. Byline given. Buys first North American serial rights and second serial (reprint) rights (for electronic republishing). Editorial lead time 1 year. Query by mail, e-mail, fax.

**Nonfiction:** Interview/profile, photo feature. Nothing unrelated to UNC or higher education. **Buys 15 mss/year.** Query with published clips. Length: 750-2,500 words. **Pays $200-1,000.** "We take very few unsolicited pieces." Pays the expenses of writers on assignment with limit agreed upon in advance.

**Photos:** State availability of photos with submission. Reviews contact sheets, negatives, transparencies or prints. Offers $25-700/photo. Identification of subjects required. Buys one-time and electronic republishing rights.

**Tips:** "Be familiar with *Chronicle of Higher Education* and other journals covering higher education, including other alumni magazines."

**N $ $ THE CHRISTIAN COLLEGE HANDBOOK,** Kipland Publishing House, P.O. Box 1357, Oak Park IL 60304. (708)524-5070. Fax: (708)524-5174. E-mail: kipland7@aol.com. Website: http://www.collegefocus.com. **Contact:** Tonya Eichelberger. **85% freelance written.** Annual magazine covering college planning. "*The Christian College Handbook* is a college planning guide for high school juniors and seniors and expresses the value of a Christian college or university education." Estab. 1994. Circ. 265,000. **Pays on acceptance.** Publishes ms 4 months after acceptance. Byline given. Buys all rights. Editorial lead time 4 months. Accepts queries by mail, e-mail, fax. Sample copy for $3. Writer's guidelines for free.

**Nonfiction:** How-to, interview/profile, personal experience. First person and how-to features focus on all topics of interest to high schoolers planning for college. No fiction or poetry. **Buys 18-25 mss/year.** Query with published clips. Length: 800-1,200 words. **Pays 8-15¢/word.** Sometimes pays expenses of writers on assignment.

**Photos:** State availability of photos with submission. Negotiates payment individually. Captions, model releases, identification of subjects required.

**Tips:** "We are open to working with new, unpublished authors, especially college graduates, current college students, college professors, admissions personnel, career counselors, and financial aid officers. Visit our website to view articles previously published in *The Christian College Handbook.*"

**$ $ CIRCLE K MAGAZINE**, 3636 Woodview Trace, Indianapolis IN 46268-3196. Fax: (317)879-0204. E-mail: ckimagazine@kiwanis.org. Website: http://www.circlek.org. **Contact:** Amy L. Wiser, executive editor. **60% freelance written.** "Our readership consists almost entirely of above-average college students interested in voluntary community service and leadership development. They are politically and socially aware and have a wide range of interests." Published 5 times/year. Circ. 15,000. **Pays on acceptance.** Buys first North American serial rights. Byline given. Query by mail, e-mail. Reports in 2 months. Sample copy and writer's guidelines for large SAE with 3 first-class stamps.
**Nonfiction:** Articles published in *Circle K* are of 2 types—serious and light nonfiction. "We are interested in general interest articles on topics concerning college students and their lifestyles, as well as articles dealing with careers, community concerns and leadership development. No first person confessions, family histories or travel pieces." Query. Length: 1,500-2,000 words. **Pays $150-400.**
**Photos:** Purchased with accompanying ms. Captions required. Total purchase price for ms includes payment for photos.
**Tips:** "Query should indicate author's familiarity with the field and sources. Subject treatment must be objective and in-depth, and articles should include illustrative examples and quotes from persons involved in the subject or qualified to speak on it. We are open to working with new writers who present a good article idea and demonstrate that they've done their homework concerning the article subject itself, as well as concerning our magazine's style. We're interested in college-oriented trends, for example: entrepreneur schooling, high-tech classrooms, music, leisure and health issues."

**$ COLLEGE BOUND, The Magazine for High School Students By College Students**, Ramholtz Publishing Inc., 2071 Clove Rd., Suite 206, Staten Island NY 10304-1643. (718)273-5700. Fax: (718)273-2539. E-mail: editorial@collegebound.net. Website: http://www.collegebound.net. **Contact:** Gina LaGuardia, editor-in-chief. **85% freelance written.** Bimonthly magazine "written by college students for high school students and is designed to provide an inside view of college life." Estab. 1987. Circ. 95,000. Pays on publication. Publishes ms an average of 4 months after acceptance. Byline given. Buys first and second rights. Editorial lead time 4 months. Submit seasonal material 4 months in advance. Accepts simultaneous submissions. Reports in 5 weeks. Sample copy and writer's guidelines for 9×12 SASE.
**Nonfiction:** How-to (apply for college, prepare for the interview, etc.), personal experience (college experiences). **Buys 30 mss/year.** Query with published clips. Length: 800-1,000 words. **Pays $50-75.**
**Reprints:** Send photocopy of article.
**Photos:** Send photos with submission. Reviews prints. Offers no additional payment for photos accepted with ms. Buys one time rights.
**Columns/Departments:** Campus Cool (unique traditions from different colleges), 100-150 words; Clip Notes (admissions facts and advice, as well as interesting tidbits on "happenings" related to junior and senior students' lifestyles, 75-200 words); Focus (in-depth profile of a community organization, student-founded group or other group of interest); Applause! (schools that have won awards, super student profiles, big scholarship winners, etc.); Soul Story (first person account of the college application process); That's Life (issues outside the academic realm, i.e., money tips, current events, social commentary); all 500-1,000 words. **Buys 30 mss/year.** Query with published clips. **Pays $15-75.**
**Fillers:** Anecdotes, facts, newsbreaks, short humor. **Buys 10/year.** Length: 50-200 words. **Pays $15-25.**
**Tips:** "College students from around the country are welcome to serve as correspondents to provide our teen readership with personal accounts on all aspects of college. Give us your expertise on everything from living with a roommate, choosing a major, and joining a fraternity or sorority, to college dating, interesting course offerings on your campus, how to beat the financial headache and other college application nightmares."

**$ COLLEGE BOUND.NET, A Student's Interactive Guide to College Life**, Ramholtz Publishing, Inc., 2071 Clove Rd., Staten Island NY 10304. (718)273-5700. Fax: (718)273-2539. E-mail: editorial@collegebound.net. Website: http://www.collegebound.net. **Contact:** Gina LaGuardia, editor-in-chief. **60% freelance written.** "Online magazine for students making the transition from high school to college." Estab. 1996. Pays on publication. Publishes ms an average of 4 months after acceptance. Byline given. Buys first rights and second serial (reprint) rights. Editorial lead time 4 months. Submit seasonal material 4 months in advance. Reports in 2 months on queries. Writer's guidelines for #10 SASE.
**Nonfiction:** Essays, general interest, how-to, inspirational, interview/profile, new product, personal experience, student travel. Query. Length: 300-700 words. **Pays $15-65.** Sometimes pays the expenses of writers on assignment.
**Reprints:** Send photocopy of article.
**Photos:** State availability of photos with submission. Reviews transparencies and prints. Offers no additional payment for photos accepted with ms. Captions and identification of subjects required.
**Columns/Departments:** Digital Details (technology), Money, Food, Sports, Music, Shout!, Go Girl. Length: 300-500 words. **Buys 30 mss/year.** Query with published clips. **Pays $15-40.**
**Fillers:** Anecdotes, facts, newsbreaks, short humor. **Buys 10/year.** Length: 50 words.

**$ $ COLLEGE PREVIEW, A Guide for College-Bound Students**, Communications Publishing Group, 3100 Broadway, Suite 660, Kansas City MO 64110. (816)960-1988. Fax: (816)960-1989. **Contact:** Neoshia Michelle Paige, editor. **80% freelance written.** Quarterly educational and career source guide. "Contemporary guide designed to inform and motivate Black and Hispanic young adults, ages 16-21 years old about college preparation, career planning and life survival skills." Estab. 1985. Circ. 600,000. Pays on publication. Byline often given. Buys first serial and second serial (reprint) rights or makes work-for-hire assignments. Submit seasonal material 6 months in advance.

Accepts simultaneous submissions. Reports in 2 months. Sample copy for 9 × 12 SAE with 4 first-class stamps. Writer's guidelines for #10 SASE.

● The editor notes that if the writer can provide the manuscript on 3.25 disk, saved in generic ASCII, pay is $10 higher and chance of acceptance is greater.

**Nonfiction:** Book excerpts or reviews, general interest, how-to (dealing with careers or education), humor, inspirational, interview/profile (celebrity or "up and coming" young adult), new product (as it relates to young adult market), personal experience, photo feature, technical, travel. Send complete ms. Length: 750-2,000 words. **Pays $150-400 for assigned articles; 12¢/word for unsolicited articles.** Sometimes pays expenses of writers on assignment.

**Reprints:** Send photocopy of article or short story or typed ms with rights for sale noted and information about when and where the article previously appeared. **Pays 6¢/word.**

**Photos:** State availability of photos with submission. Reviews transparencies. Offers $20-$25/photo. Captions, model releases and identification of subjects required. Will return photos—send SASE.

**Columns/Departments:** Profiles of Achievement (striving and successful minority young adults ages 16-35 in various careers). **Buys 30 mss/year.** Send complete ms. Length: 500-1,500. **Pays 10¢/word.**

**Fiction:** Adventure, ethnic, historical, humorous, mainstream, slice-of-life vignettes. **Buys 3 mss/year.** Send complete ms. Length: 500-2,000 words. Pay varies.

**Fillers:** Anecdotes, facts, gags to be illustrated by cartoonist, newsbreaks, short humor. **Buys 10/year.** Length: 25-250 words. **Pays $25-100.**

**Tips:** For new writers—send complete ms that is double spaced; clean copy only. If available, send clips of previously published works and résumé. Should state when available to write. Include on first page of ms name, address, phone, Social Security number, word count and SASE.

**★ $ $ DIRECT AIM, For Today's Career Strategies**, Communications Publishing Group, 3100 Broadway, Pen Tower, Suite 660, Kansas City MO 64110. (816)960-1988. Fax: (816)960-1989. **Contact:** Neoshia Michelle Paige, editor. **80% freelance written.** Quarterly educational and career source guide for Black and Hispanic college students at traditional, non-traditional, vocational and technical institutions. "This magazine informs students about college survival skills and planning for a future in the professional world." Buys second serial (reprint) rights or makes work-for-hire assignments. Submit seasonal material 6 months in advance. Accepts simultaneous submissions. Reports in 2 months. Sample copy for 9 × 12 SAE with 4 first-class stamps. Writer's guidelines for #10 SASE.

● The editor notes that if the writer can provide the manuscript on 3.25 disk, saved in generic ASCII, pay is $10 higher and chance of acceptance is greater.

**Nonfiction:** Book excerpts or reviews, general interest, how-to (dealing with careers or education), humor, inspirational, interview/profile (celebrity or "up and coming" young adult), new product (as it relates to young adult market), personal experience, photo feature, technical, travel. Query or send complete ms. Length: 750-2,000 words. **Pays $150-400 for assigned articles; 12¢/word for unsolicited articles.** Sometimes pays expenses of writers on assignment.

**Reprints:** Send photocopy of article or typed ms with rights for sale noted and information about when and where the article previously appeared. **Pays 6¢/word.**

**Photos:** State availability of photos with submission. Reviews transparencies. Offers $20-25/photo. Captions, model releases and identification of subjects required. Will return photos.

**Columns/Departments:** Profiles of Achievement (striving and successful minority young adult age 18-35 in various technical careers). **Buys 25 mss/year.** Send complete ms. Length: 500-1,500. **Pays $50-250.**

**Fiction:** Publishes novel excerpts. Adventure, ethnic, historical, humorous, mainstream, slice-of-life vignettes. **Buys 3 mss/year.** Send complete ms. Length: 500-2,000 words. Pay varies.

**Fillers:** Anecdotes, facts, gags to be illustrated by cartoonist, newsbreaks, short humor. **Buys 30/year.** Length: 25-250 words. **Pays $25-100.**

**Tips:** For new writers—send complete ms that is double spaced; clean copy only. If available, send clips of previously published works and résumé. Should state when available to write. Include on first page of ms name, address, phone, Social Security number and word count. Photo availability is important."

**★ $ $ DIVERSITY MONTHLY: CAREER OPPORTUNITIES & INSIGHTS,** (formerly *EEO Bimonthly*), CASS Recruitment Media/CASS Communications, Inc., 1800 Sherman Ave., Evanston IL 60201-3769. (847)733-3100. Fax: (847)475-8807. E-mail: casspubs@casscom.com. Website: http://www.casscom.com. Senior Editor: Liz Harmon. **Contact:** Robert Shannon, executive editor. **85% freelance written.** Monthly magazine covering "career management for minorities, women and people with disabilities, either new to the workforce or entering the workforce. Readers are (or will be) white-collar professionals, usually in technical fields." Estab. 1967. Circ. 13,000. **Pays on acceptance.** Publishes ms an average of 3 months after acceptance. Byline given. Buys first North American serial rights. Editorial lead time 3 months. Accepts queries by mail, e-mail, fax. Accepts simultaneous submissions. Reports in 3 weeks on queries; 2 months on mss. Sample copy for 10 × 12 SAE with 6 first-class stamps. Writer's guidelines for #10 SASE or by e-mail.

**Nonfiction:** How-to (career management fundamentals), interview/profile, new product (career/workplace-related), job/career/salary trends specific to minorities and women. **Buys 30-40 mss/year.** Query with published clips. Length: 1,800-2,400 words. **Pays $350-600 for assigned articles; $300-500 for unsolicited articles.** Sometimes pays expenses of writers on assignment.

**Reprints:** Accepts previously published submissions.

**Photos:** State availability of photos with submission. Reviews transparencies and prints. Offers no additional payment for photos accepted with ms. Identification of subjects required. Buys one-time rights.

**Columns/Departments:** Coach's Corner (advice column for specific minority/professional group), 1,500 words. **Buys 10 mss/year.** Query with published clips. **Pays $350-450.**

**Tips:** "Remember our audience—minorities, women and persons with disabilities. Where possible, address at least a portion of your article to at least a white-collar segment of our audience."

**$ $ EQUAL OPPORTUNITY, The Nation's Only Multi-Ethnic Recruitment Magazine for Black, Hispanic, Native American & Asian American College Grads**, Equal Opportunity Publications, Inc., 1160 E. Jericho Turnpike, Suite 200, Huntington NY 11743-5405. (516)421-9469. Fax: (516)421-0359. E-mail: info@aol.com. Website: http://www.eop.com. **Contact:** James Schneider, editor. **70% freelance written.** Prefers to work with published/established writers. Triannual magazine covering career guidance for minorities. "Our audience is 90% college juniors and seniors; 10% working graduates. An understanding of educational and career problems of minorities is essential." Estab. 1967. Circ. 15,000, distributed through college guidance and placement offices. Pays on publication. Publishes ms an average of 6 months after acceptance. Byline given. Buys first rights. Editorial lead time 6 months. Submit seasonal material 6 months in advance. Accepts queries by mail, e-mail, fax, phone. Reports in 2 weeks on queries, 1 month on mss. Sample copy and writer's guidelines for 9 × 12 SAE with 5 first-class stamps.

**Nonfiction:** Book excerpts and articles (job search techniques, role models); general interest (specific minority concerns); how-to (job-hunting skills, personal finance, better living, coping with discrimination); humor (student or career related); interview/profile (minority role models); opinion (problems of minorities); personal experience (professional and student study and career experiences); technical (on career fields offering opportunities for minorities); travel (on overseas job opportunities); and coverage of Black, Hispanic, Native American and Asian American interests. **Buys 10 mss/year.** Query or send complete ms. Deadline dates: fall (June 10); winter (September 15); spring (January 1). Length: 1,000-2,000 words. **Pays 10¢/word.** Sometimes pays expenses of writers on assignment.

**Reprints:** Send information about when and where the article previously appeared. **Pays 10¢/word.**

**Photos:** Prefers 35mm color slides and b&w. Captions and identification of subjects required. Buys all rights. Pays $15/photo use.

**Tips:** "Articles must be geared toward questions and answers faced by minority and women students."

**⚡ $ $ FIRST OPPORTUNITY, Today's Career Options**, Communications Publishing Group, 3100 Broadway, Suite 660, Kansas City MO 64111. (816)960-1988. Fax: (816)960-1989. **Contact:** Neoshia Michelle Paige, editor. **80% freelance written.** Resource publication focusing on advanced vocational/technical educational opportunities and career preparation for Black and Hispanic young adults, ages 16-21. Circ. 500,000. Pays on publication. Byline sometimes given. Buys second serial (reprint) rights or makes work-for-hire assignments. Submit seasonal material 6 months in advance. Accepts simultaneous submissions. Reports in 2 months. Sample copy for 9 × 12 SAE with 4 first-class stamps. Writer's guidelines for #10 SASE.

• The editor notes that if the writer can provide the manuscript on 3.25 disk, saved in generic ASCII, pay is $10 higher and chance of acceptance is greater.

**Nonfiction:** Book excerpts or reviews, general interest, how-to (dealing with careers or education), humor, inspirational, interview/profile (celebrity or "up and coming" young adult), new product (as it relates to young adult market), personal experience, photo feature, technical, travel. Length: 750-2,000 words. **Pays $150-400 for assigned articles; 12¢/word for unsolicited articles.** Sometimes pays expenses of writers on assignment.

**Reprints:** Send photocopy of article or typed ms with rights for sale noted and information about when and where the article previously appeared. **Pays 6¢/word.**

**Photos:** State availability of photos with submission. Prefers transparencies. Offers $20-25/photo. Captions, model releases, identification of subjects required. Buys all rights.

**Columns/Departments:** Profiles of Achievement (striving and successful minority young adult, age 16-35 in various vocational or technical careers). **Buys 15 mss/year.** Send complete ms. Length: 500-1,500. **Pays $50-250.**

**Fiction:** Adventure, ethnic, historical, humorous, mainstream, slice-of-life vignettes. **Buys 3 mss/year.** Send complete ms. Length: 500-5,000 words. Pay varies.

**Fillers:** Anecdotes, facts, gags to be illustrated by cartoonist, newsbreaks, short humor. **Buys 10/year.** Length: 25-250 words. **Pays $25-100.**

**Tips:** For new writers—send complete ms that is double spaced; clean copy only. If available, send clips of previously published works and résumé. Should state when available to write. Include on first page of ms name, address, phone, Social Security number and word count. Photo availability is important.

**$ FLORIDA LEADER (for college students)**, P.O. Box 14081, Gainesville FL 32604-2081. (352)373-6907. Fax: (352)373-8120. E-mail: oxendine@compuserve.com. Website: http://www.floridaleader.com. Publisher: W.H. "Butch" Oxendine, Jr. Managing Editor: Kay Quinn. **Contact:** Teresa Beard, assistant editor. **10% freelance written.** Triannual "college magazine, feature-oriented, especially activities, events, interests and issues pertaining to college students." Estab. 1981. Circ. 27,000. Publishes ms an average of 2 months after acceptance. Byline given. Submit seasonal material 6 months in advance. Query by mail, e-mail, fax. Reports in 2 months on queries. Sample copy and writer's guidelines for $3.50, 9 × 12 SAE and 5 first-class stamps.

**Nonfiction:** How-to, humor, interview/profile, feature—all multi-sourced and Florida college related. "What Florida Students Think" is the third issue (published in September) and is the only one for which outside help is necessary.

Query with SASE by July to be considered for this issue. Length: 900 words. **Pays $35-75.** Sometimes pays expenses of writers on assignment.

**Photos:** State availability of photos with submission. Reviews negatives and transparencies. Captions, model releases, identification of subjects required.

■ The online magazine carries original content not found in the print edition. Contact: Teresa Beard and Butch Oxendine, online editors.

**⊠ $ $ $NOTRE DAME MAGAZINE**, University of Notre Dame, 538 Grace Hall, Notre Dame IN 46556-5612. (219)631-5335. Fax: (219)631-6767. E-mail: ndmag.1@nd.edu. Website: http://www.nd.edu. Managing Editor: Carol Schaal.**Contact:** Kerry Temple, editor. **75% freelance written.** Quarterly magazine covering news of Notre Dame and education and issues affecting contemporary society. "We are a university magazine with a scope as broad as that found at a university, but we place our discussion in a moral, ethical, spiritual context reflecting our Catholic heritage." Estab. 1972. Circ. 142,000. **Pays on acceptance.** Publishes ms an average of 1 year after acceptance. Byline given. Kill fee negotiable. Buys first serial and electronic rights. Reports in 1 month. Sample copy free on website. Writer's guidelines on website.

**Nonfiction:** Opinion, personal experience, religion. **Buys 35 mss/year.** Query with clips of published work. Length: 600-3,000 words. **Pays $250-1,500.** Sometimes pays expenses of writers on assignment.

**Photos:** State availability of photos. Reviews b&w contact sheets, transparencies and 8×10 prints. Model releases and identification of subjects required. Buys one-time rights.

**Columns/Departments:** Perspectives (essays, often written in first-person, deal with a wide array of issues—some topical, some personal, some serious, some light). Query with published clips or submit ms.

**Tips:** "The editors are always looking for new writers and fresh ideas. However, the caliber of the magazine and frequency of its publication dictate that the writing meet very high standards. The editors value articles strong in storytelling quality, journalistic technique, and substance. They do not encourage promotional or nostalgia pieces, stories on sports, or essays which are sentimentally religious."

**$ $OREGON QUARTERLY, The Magazine of the University of Oregon**, 5228 University of Oregon, Chapman Hall, Eugene OR 97403-5228. (541)346-5048. Fax: (541)346-5571. E-mail: quarterly@oregon.uoregon.edu. Website: http://www.uoregon.edu/~oq. **Contact:** Guy Maynard. Assistant Editor: Kathleen Holt. **50% freelance written.** Quarterly university magazine of people and ideas at the University of Oregon and the Northwest. Estab. 1919. Circ. 100,000. Pays on publication. Publishes ms an average of 3 months after acceptance. Byline given. Offers 20% kill fee. Buys first North American serial rights. Query by mail, e-mail. Reports in 2 months. Sample copy for 9×12 SAE with 4 first-class stamps or on website.

○┅ Break in to the magazine with a profile (400 or 800 words) of a University of Oregon alumnus. Best to query first.

**Nonfiction:** Northwest issues and culture from the perspective of UO alumni and faculty. **Buys 30 mss/year.** Query with published clips. Length: 250-2,500 words. **Pays $50-500.** Sometimes pays expenses of writers on assignment.

**Reprints:** Send photocopy of article and information about when and where the article previously appeared. Pays 50% of the amount paid for an original article.

**Photos:** State availability of photos with submission. Reviews 8×10 prints. Offers $10-25/photo. Identification of subjects required. Buys one-time rights.

**Fiction:** Publishes novel excerpts.

**Tips:** "Query with strong, colorful lead; clips."

**⊠ $ $ THE PENN STATER**, Penn State Alumni Association, 11 Old Main, University Park PA 16802. (814)865-2709. Fax: (814)863-5690. E-mail: pennstater@psu.edu. Website: http://www.alumni.psu.edu. **Contact:** Tina Hay, editor. **75% freelance written.** Bimonthly magazine covering Penn State and Penn Staters. Estab. 1910. Circ. 120,000. **Pays on acceptance.** Publishes ms an average of 4 months after acceptance. Byline given. Offers 50% kill fee. Buys first North American serial rights or second serial (reprint) rights. Web rights negotiable. Editorial lead time 3 months. Submit seasonal material 6-8 months in advance. Accepts simultaneous submissions. Accepts queries by mail, e-mail, fax. Reports in 2 months on queries. Sample copy and writer's guidelines free.

**Nonfiction:** Book excerpts (by Penn Staters), general interest, historical/nostalgic, humor (sometimes), interview/profile, personal experience (sometimes), book reviews, photo feature, science/research. Stories must have Penn State connection. **Buys 20 mss/year.** Query with published clips and SASE. *No unsolicited mss.* Length: 400-2,500 words. Pays competitive rates. Pays expenses of writers on assignment.

**Reprints:** Send photocopy of article and information about when and where it previously appeared. Payment varies.

**Photos:** Send photos with submission. Reviews transparencies and prints. Negotiates payment individually. Captions required. Buys one-time rights.

**Tips:** "We are especially interested in attracting writers who are savvy in creative nonfiction/literary journalism. All stories must have a Penn State tie-in."

**$ $THE PURDUE ALUMNUS**, Purdue Alumni Association, Purdue Memorial Union 160, 101 N. Grant St., West Lafayette IN 47906-6212. (765)494-5184. Fax: (765)494-9179. **Contact:** Tim Newton, editor. **50% freelance written.** Prefers to work with published/established writers; works with small number of new/unpublished writers each year. Bimonthly magazine covering subjects of interest to Purdue University alumni. Estab. 1912. Circ. 65,000. Pays on publication. Publishes ms an average of 2 months after acceptance. Byline given. Buys first rights and makes work-for-hire assignments. Submit seasonal material 6 months in advance. Accepts simultaneous submissions. Reports in 2 weeks on queries; 1 month on mss. Sample copy for 9×12 SAE with 2 first-class stamps.

**Nonfiction:** Book excerpts, general interest, historical/nostalgic, humor, interview/profile, personal experience. Focus is on alumni, campus news, issues and opinions of interest to 65,000 members of the Alumni Association. Feature style, primarily university-oriented. Issues relevant to education. **Buys 12-20 mss/year.** Length: 1,500-2,500 words. **Pays $250-500.** Pays expenses of writers on assignment.

**Reprints:** Accepts previously published submissions.

**Photos:** State availability of photos. Reviews b&w contact sheet or 5×7 prints.

**Tips:** "We have 300,000 living, breathing Purdue alumni. If you can find a good story about one of them, we're interested. We use local freelancers to do campus pieces."

**$ $ RIPON COLLEGE MAGAZINE**, P.O. Box 248, Ripon WI 54971-0248. (920)748-8364. Fax: (920)748-9262. E-mail: booneL@mac.ripon.edu. Website: http://www.ripon.edu. **Contact:** Loren J. Boone, editor. **15% freelance written.** Quarterly magazine that "contains information relating to Ripon College and is mailed to alumni and friends of the college." Estab. 1851. Circ. 14,000. Pays on publication. Publishes ms an average of 3 months after acceptance. Byline given. Not copyrighted. Makes work-for-hire assignments. Query by mail, e-mail, fax, phone. Reports in 2 weeks.

**Nonfiction:** Historical/nostalgic, interview/profile. **Buys 4 mss/year.** Query with or without published clips, or send complete ms. Length: 250-1,000 words. **Pays $25-350.**

**Photos:** State availability of photos with submission. Reviews contact sheets. Offers additional payment for photos accepted with ms. Captions and model releases are required. Buys one-time rights.

**Tips:** "Story ideas must have a direct connection to Ripon College."

**[N] $ $ $ $ RUTGERS MAGAZINE**, Rutgers University, Alexander Johnston Hall, New Brunswick NJ 08903. (732)932-7315, ext. 618. Fax: (732)932-8412. E-mail: lchambe@ur.rutgers.edu. **Contact:** Lori Chambers, editor. **50% freelance written.** Quarterly university magazine of "general interest, but articles must have a Rutgers University or alumni tie-in." Circ. 110,000. **Pays on acceptance.** Publishes ms an average of 4 months after acceptance. Byline given. Pays 30-35% kill fee. Buys first North American serial rights. Submit seasonal material 8 months in advance. Query by mail, e-mail, fax. Reports in 1 month. Sample copy for $3 and 9×12 SAE with 5 first-class stamps.

**Nonfiction:** Essays, general interest, historical/nostalgic, science/research, interview/profile, arts/humanities, and photo feature. No articles without a Rutgers connection. **Buys 15-20 mss/year.** Query with published clips. Length: 2,000-4,000 words. **Pays $1,800-2,200.** Pays expenses of writers on assignment.

**Fiction:** Novel excerpts.

**Photos:** State availability of photos with submission. Payment varies. Identification of subjects required. Buys one-time rights.

**Columns/Departments:** Business, Opinion, Sports, Alumni Profiles (related to Rutgers), 1,200-1,800 words. **Buys 6-8 mss/year.** Query with published clips. Pays competitively.

**Tips:** "Send an intriguing query backed by solid clips. We'll evaluate clips and topic for most appropriate use."

**[N] $ STUDENT LEADER (for college students)**, Oxendine Publishing Inc., P.O. Box 14081, Gainesville FL 32604-2081. (352)373-6907. Fax: (352)373-8120. E-mail: oxendine@compuserve.com. Website: http://www.studentleader.com. Editor: W.H. "Butch" Oxendine Jr. **Contact:** Kay Quinn, managing editor. **30% freelance written.** Published 3 times/year. Magazine covering student government, leadership. Estab. 1993. Circ. 200,000. Pays on publication. Byline given. Buys all rights. Submit seasonal material 4 months in advance. Query by mail, e-mail, fax. Reports in 1 month on queries. Sample copy for #10 SAE with 3 first-class stamps or on website. Writer's guidelines for #10 SASE.

**Nonfiction:** How-to, humor, new product, opinion, leadership development news/tips for college students. Readers include student government officers, resident assistants, honor society leaders, volunteer coordinators, fraternity/sorority members. "No lengthy individual profiles or articles without primary or secondary sources of attribution." **Buys 2 mss/year.** Query. Length: 900 words. Pay varies. Pays contributor copies to students or first-time writers.

**Photos:** State availability of or send photos with submission. Reviews contact sheets, negatives, transparencies. Offers $50/photo maximum. Captions, model releases, identification of subjects required. Buys all rights.

**Columns/Departments: Buys 2 mss/year.** Query with SASE. Length: 250-1,000 words. **Pays $100 maximum.**

**Fillers:** Facts, newsbreaks, tips. **Buys 2/year.** Length: 100 words minimum. No payment for fillers.

■ The online magazine carries original content not found in the print edition. Contact: Kay Quinn and Butch Oxendine, online editors.

**Tips:** "Read other high school and college publications for current ideas, interests. Send outlines or manuscripts for review. All sections open to freelance work. Always looking for lighter, humorous articles, as well as features on colleges and universities, careers, jobs. Multi-sourced (5-10) articles are best."

**★ $ SUCCEED, The Magazine for Continuing Education**, Ramholtz Publishing Inc., 2071 Clove Rd., Suite 206, Staten Island NY 10304-1643. (718)273-5700. Fax: (718)273-2539. E-mail: editorial@collegebound.net **Contact:** Gina LaGuardia, editor-in-chief. **85% freelance written.** Quarterly magazine. "*SUCCEED*'s readers are interested in continuing education, whether it be for changing careers or enhancing their current career." Estab. 1994. Circ. 155,000. Pays on publication. Publishes ms an average of 4 months after acceptance. Byline given. Buys first and second rights.

Editorial lead time 4 months. Submit seasonal material 4 months in advance. Accepts simultaneous submissions. Reports in 5 weeks. Sample copy for $1.50. Writer's guidelines for 9×12 SASE.

**Nonfiction:** Essays, exposé, general interest, how-to (change careers), interview/profile (interesting careers); new product, opinion, personal experience. **Buys 25 mss/year.** Query with published clips. Length: 1,000-1,500 words. **Pays $75-125.** Sometimes pays expenses of writers on assignment.

**Reprints:** Send photocopy of article.

**Photos:** Send photos with submission. Reviews negatives, prints. Offers no additional payment for photos accepted with ms. Captions and identification of subjects required. Buys one-time rights.

**Columns/Departments:** Tech Zone (new media/technology), 300-700 words; To Be... (personality/career profile), 600-800 words; Financial Fitness (finance, money management), 100-300 words. Solo Success (how readers can "do it on their own," with recommended resources, books, and software. **Buys 10 mss/year.** Query with published clips. **Pays $15-70.**

**Fillers:** Facts, newsbreaks. **Buys 5/year.** Length: 50-200 words.

**Tips:** "Here are some topics we're interested in covering for future issues: Finding a Career That Fits, Retirement Strategies, Ethics in the Business World, Returning to School: Portfolio Assessment."

**[N] TOMORROW'S CHRISTIAN GRADUATE,** Kipland Publishing House, P.O. Box 1357, Oak Park IL 60304. (708)524-5070. Fax: (708)524-5174. E-mail: kipland7@aol.com. Website: http://www.christiangraduate.com. **Contact**: Tonya Eichelberger, editor. **85% freelance written.** Annual magazine covering seminary and graduate school planning. *"Tomorrow's Christian Graduate* is a planning guide for adults pursuing a seminary or Christian graduate education and expresses the value of a seminary or Christian graduate education." Estab. 1998. Circ. 150,000. **Pays on acceptance.** Publishes ms 4 months after acceptance. Byline given. Buys all rights. Editorial lead time 4 months. Accepts queries by mail, e-mail, fax. Sample copy for $3. Writer's guidelines free.

**Nonfiction:** How-to, interview/profile, personal experience. First-person and how-to features focus on all topics of interest to adults pursuing graduate studies. No fiction or poetry. **Buys 18-25 mss/year.** Query with published clips. Length: 800-1,600 words. **Pays 8-15¢/word for assigned articles, 6-15¢/word for unsolicited articles.** Sometimes pays expenses of writers on assignment.

**Photos:** State availability of photos with submission. Negotiates payment individually. Captions, model releases, identification of subjects required.

**Tips:** "We are open to working with new/unpublished authors, especially current graduate students, graduate professors, admissions personnel, career counselors, and financial aid officers. Visit our website to view previously published articles."

**$ U, The National College Magazine,** American Collegiate Network Inc., 1800 Century Park E., #820, Los Angeles CA 90067-1511. (310)551-1381. Fax: (310)551-1659. E-mail: editor@umagazine.com. Website: http://www.umagazine.com. **Contact:** Frances Huffman, editor. **50% freelance written.** Magazine published 6 times/year "for college students by college students covering news, lifestyle and entertainment that relates to college students and college life." Estab. 1987. Circ. 1,500,000. **Pays on acceptance.** Publishes ms an average of 3 months after acceptance. Byline given. Buys all rights. Editorial lead time 3 months. Submit seasonal material 3 months in advance. Reports in 2 months. Accepts queries by mail, e-mail, fax. Sample copy and writer's guidelines free.

**O–** Best bet to break in is to have clips that show that your writing style is "u." Material: humorous, irreverent, edgy, conversational.

**Nonfiction:** Exposé, general interest, historical/nostalgic, humor, interview/profile, opinion, photo feature, travel. No articles that do not relate to college students or college life. **Buys 150-200 mss/year.** Query with published clips. Length: 250-1,000 words. **Pays $25-100.** Sometimes pays expenses of writers on assignment.

**Photos:** Reviews transparencies, prints. Negotiates payment individually. Buys all rights.

**Columns/Departments:** U. Life (college news, lifestyle, trends), 200-300 words; 15 Minutes (profile of outstanding student), 200 words; Byte Me (technology), 200 words; R&R (entertainment, reviews). **Buys 100 mss/year.** Query with published clips. **Pays $25-35.**

**Tips:** Contributors must be enrolled as a college student. *"U* is written in 'college speak.' The tone is conversational, lively, engaging, smart, hip, and a little irreverent. Write articles as if you were talking to your friends at school. *U* is a magazine, not a newspaper—no inverted pyramid stories please! Magazine style requires a punchy lead that grabs the reader, a compelling main body and a witty walk-off."

**$ $ US BLACK ENGINEER/HISPANIC ENGINEER, And Information Technology,** Career Communications Group, Inc., 729 E. Pratt St., Suite 504, Baltimore MD 21202-3101. (410)244-7101. Fax: (410)752-1837. Website: http://www.blackfamily.net.net **Contact:** Garland L. Thompson, managing editor. **80% freelance written.** Quarterly magazine. "Both of our magazines are designed to bring technology issues home to people of color. We look at careers in technology and what affects career possibilities, including education. But we also look at how technology affects Black Americans and Latinos." Estab. 1976. Circ. 20,000. Pays on publication. Publishes ms an average of 1 month after acceptance. Byline given. Offers 50% kill fee. Makes work-for-hire assignments. Editorial lead time 2 months. Accepts quries by mail, e-mail, phone, fax. Reports in 2 weeks. Sample copy and ms guidelines for #10 SASE.

**Nonfiction:** How-to (plan a career, get a first job, get a good job), interview/profile, new product, technical (new technologies and people of color involved with them (Capitol Hill/federal reportage on technology and EEO issues). No opinion pieces, first-person articles, routine profiles with no news peg or grounding in science/technology issues.

**Length:** 650-1,800 words. **Pays $250-600**. Sometimes pays expenses of writers on assignment.
**Photos:** State availability of photos with submission. Negotiates payment individually. Captions, model releases, identification of subjects required. Buys all rights.
**Columns/Departments:** Color of Technology (did you know that . . .?), 800 words; Pros on the Move (Black/Hispanic career moves), 500 words; Greatest Challenge (up from the roots), 650 words; Surfing the Net (websites of interest), 650 words; New in Print (books), 350 words; Community News (relating to science and tech people), 650 words. **Buys 30 mss/year.** Query with published clips. **Pays $250-300.**

▣ The online magazine carries original content not found in the print edtion. Contact: Garland Thompson, online editor.

**Tips:** "Call or come see me. Also contact us about covering our conferences, Black Engineer of the Year Awards and Women of Color Technology Awards."

[N] **$ WHAT MAKES PEOPLE SUCCESSFUL,** The National Research Bureau, Inc., 320 Valley St., Burlington IA 52601. (319)752-5415. Fax: (319)752-3421. **Contact:** Nancy Heinzel, editor. **75% freelance written.** Quarterly magazine. Estab. 1948. Circ. 1,500. Pays on publication. Publishes ms an average of 1 year after acceptance. Buys all rights. Submit seasonal material 8 months in advance of issue date. Accepts queries by mail, phone, fax. Sample copy and writer's guidelines for #10 SAE with 2 first-class stamps. Eager to work with new/unpublished writers; works with a small number each year.
**Nonfiction:** How-to (be successful); general interest (personality, employee morale, guides to successful living, biographies of successful persons, etc.); experience; opinion. No material on health. **Buys 3-4 mss/issue.** Query with outline. Length: 500-700 words. **Pays 4¢/word.**
**Tips:** Short articles (rather than major features) have a better chance of acceptance because all articles are short.

[N] **$ $ $ $ WORKING AT HOME,** Success Holdings, LLC, 733 Third Ave., New York NY 10017. Fax: (212)949-7002. **Contact:** Jodie Green, editor. **80% freelance written.** Quarterly publication covering home-based businesses. "We are a service publication, bringing the reader actionable strategies for working at home in a way that's better, smarter and more successful." Estab. 1997. Circ. 300,000. Pays after mss clears fact checking. Publishes ms an average of 6 months after acceptance. Byline given. Offers 20% kill fee. Buys one-time or all rights. Editorial lead time 6 months. Submit seasonal material 6 months in advance.
**Nonfiction:** Book excerpts, how-to. **Buys more than 50 mss/year.** Query by mail with published clips. Length: 600-2,000 words. **Pays up to $1/word.** Sometimes pays expenses of writers on assignment.
**Columns/Departments:** Query with published clips. **Pays up to $1/word.**

**$ $ WPI JOURNAL,** Worcester Polytechnic Institute, 100 Institute Rd., Worcester MA 01609-2280. Fax: (508)831-5820. E-mail: wpi-journal@wpi.edu. Website: http://www.wpi.edu/+journal. **Contact:** Michael Dorsey, editor. **50% freelance written.** Quarterly alumni magazine covering science and engineering/education/business personalities for 25,000 alumni, primarily engineers, scientists, managers, national media. Estab. 1897. Circ. 28,000. Pays on publication. Publishes ms an average of 6 months after acceptance. Byline given. Buys one-time rights. Accepts queries by mail, e-mail, fax. Accepts simultaneous submissions. Query for electronic submissions. Requires hard copy also. Reports in 1 month on queries. Sample copy on website.
**Nonfiction:** Interview/profile (alumni in engineering, science, etc.); photo feature; features on people and programs at WPI. Query with published clips. Length: 1,000-4,000 words. Pays negotiable rate. Sometimes pays expenses of writers on assignment.
**Reprints:** Accepts previously published submissions.
**Photos:** State availability of photos with query or ms. Reviews b&w contact sheets. Pays negotiable rate. Captions required.

▣ The online magazine carries original content not included in the print edition.

**Tips:** "Submit outline of story and/or ms of story idea or published work. Features are most open to freelancers. Keep in mind that this is an alumni magazine, so most articles focus on the college and its graduates."

# CHILD CARE & PARENTAL GUIDANCE

Magazines in this section address the needs and interests of families with children. Some publications are national in scope, others are geographically specific. Some offer general advice for parents, while magazines such as *Catholic Parent* answer the concerns of smaller groups. Other markets that buy articles about child care and the family are included in the Religious and Women's sections and in the Trade Education & Counseling section. Publications for children can be found in the Juvenile and Teen & Young Adult sections.

[N] **$ ALASKA PARENTING,** Wick Communications, 5751 E. Mayflower Ct., Wasilla AK 99654. (907)376-3289. Fax: (907)352-2277. E-mail: editor@alaska.net. Managing Editor: Bill Hitchcock. **Contact:** Victoria Naegele, editor (AKParenting@knix.net); (907)895-5471). **30-60% freelance written.** Monthly magazine covering family, children, parenting. "This magazine focuses on Alaska's families. Articles should have a connection to Alaska either via an Alaska writer or Alaska subject matter. No boilerplate stories. Issues are thematic. Request guidelines and theme calendar." Estab. 1992. Circ. 18,200. Pays 30 days after publication. Byline given. Offers 50% kill fee. Buys first North American serial or one-time rights. Editorial lead time 3 months. Submit seasonal material 4 months in advance. Accepts queries by mail, e-mail, fax. No phone. Accepts simultaneous submissions. Reports in 6 weeks on queries; 2 months on mss. Sample copy for 9×12 SASE with 5 ounces of postage. Guidelines and theme calendar for #10 SASE.

**Nonfiction:** Essays, general interest, historical/nostalgia, how-to, humor, inspirational, interview/profile, personal experience, photo feature, travel. *Note:* all must related to Alaska or Alaskans. Special issues: Creative kids (March); Back to School (August). No generic first-person articles; no "I visited Alaska once and . . ." Writers must understand the uniqueness of Alaska. **Buys 20-35 mss/year.** Query with clips, but complete mss OK. Length: 750-2,000 words. **Pays $20-50.**

**Photos:** State availability of photos with submission. Reviews 35mm negatives, 35mm transparencies and any size prints, color preferred, b&w OK. Negotiates payment individually. Also considers cover shots. Captions, photo releases and identification of subjects required. Buys one-time rights.

**Columns/Departments:** The Laugh Frontier (first-person humor regarding life in Alaska), 400-600 words; Parenting Pipeline (first-person sharing experiences that will inspire, uplift, enlighten, inform or otherwise aid other Alaska families, need not relate to theme), 400-600 words; Make It Together (theme- or holiday-related craft and cooking projects for families—requires illustration), 250-500 words. **Buys 20-25 mss/year.** Query or send complete ms. **Pays $20 for Laugh Frontier or Parenting Pipeline; $15 (total) for Make It Together; $15-25 for other columns as assigned.**

**$ $ $AMERICAN BABY MAGAZINE, For Expectant and New Parents**, Primedia Communications, 249 W. 17th St., New York NY 10011-5300. (212)462-3500. Fax: (212)367-8332. Website: http://www.americanbaby.com. **Contact:** Eilzabeth Haas, editorial assistant. Editor-in-Chief: Judith Nolte. **70% freelance written.** Prefers to work with published/established writers; works with a small number of new/unpublished writers each year. Monthly magazine addressing health, medical and childcare concerns for expectant and new parents, particularly those having their first child or those whose child is between the ages of birth and 2 years old. Mothers are the primary readers, but fathers' issues are equally important. "A simple, straightforward, clear approach is mandatory." Estab. 1938. Circ. 1,650,000. **Pays on acceptance.** Publishes ms an average of 6 months after acceptance. Byline given. Offers 25% kill fee. Buys first North American serial rights. Editorial lead time 5 months. Submit seasonal material 6 months in advance. Accepts simultaneous submissions. Accepts queries by mail. Reports in 1 month on queries; 2 months on mss. Sample copy for 9×12 SAE with 6 first-class stamps. Writer's guidelines for #10 SASE.

● Ranked as one of the best markets for freelance writers in *Writer's Yearbook* magazine's annual "Top 100 Markets," January 1999.

**Nonfiction:** Book excerpts, essays, general interest, how-to (some aspect of pregnancy or baby care), humor, new product and personal experience. "No 'hearts and flowers' or fantasy pieces." Full-length articles should offer helpful expert information on some aspect of pregnancy or child care; should cover a common problem of child-raising, along with solutions; or should give expert advice on a psychological or practical subject. Articles about products, such as toys and nursery furniture, are not accepted, as these are covered by staff members. **Buys 60 mss/year.** Query with published clips or send complete ms. Length: 1,000-2,000 words. **Pays $750-1,200 for assigned articles; $600-800 for unsolicited articles.** Pays the expenses of writers on assignment.

**Reprints:** Send photocopy of article and information about when and where the article previously appeared. Pays 50% of amount paid for an original article.

**Photos:** State availability of photos with submission. Reviews transparencies and prints. Model release and identification of subjects required. Buys one-time rights.

**Columns/Departments:** Personal Experience, 900-1,200 words, **pays $500**; Short Items, Crib Notes (news and feature items) and Medical Update, 50-250 words, **pays $100.**

**Tips:** "Get to know our style by thoroughly reading the magazine. Don't send something we recently published. Our readers want to feel connected to other parents, both to share experiences and to learn from one another. They want reassurance that the problems they are facing are solvable and not uncommon. They want to keep up with the latest issues affecting their new family, particularly health and medical news, but they don't have a lot of spare time to read. We forgo the theoretical approach to offer quick-to-read, hands-on information that can be put to use immediately."

**$AT-HOME MOTHER**, At-Home Mothers' Resource Center, 406 E. Buchanan Ave., Fairfield IA 52556-3810. E-mail: ahmrc@lisco.com. Website: http://www.at-home-mothers.com. **Contact:** Jeanette Lisefski, editor. **100% freelance written.** Quarterly magazine. "*At-Home Mother* provides support for at-home mothers and features up-beat articles that reinforce their choice to stay at home with their children, helping them to find maximum fulfillment in this most cherished profession. Through education and inspiration, we also help those mothers who want to stay at home find ways to make this goal a reality." Pays on publication. Publishes ms an average of 3-12 months after acceptance. Byline given. Buys first North American serial rights or second serial (reprint) rights. Editorial lead time 3 months. Accepts queries by mail, e-mail. Accepts simultaneous submissions. Reports in 1 month on queries; 3 months on mss. Sample copy for $4. Writer's guidelines for #10 SASE.

○▬ Break in with upbeat, positive articles containing experiences by other mothers in answers to mother's concerns relating to all aspects of at-home mothering.

**Nonfiction:** Essays, how-to, humor, inspirational, interview/profile, personal experience, photo feature. Features and departments focus on: Choosing Home, Earning at Home, Earning by Saving at Home, Mothers' Self-Esteem and Happiness at Home, Managing at Home, Celebrating Motherhood, Heart-to-Heart Parenting, Flexible Work Options, Teaching at Home, Learning at Home. **Buys 100 mss/year.** Query with or without published clips. Length: 500-2,500 words. **Pays $25-150.**

**Reprints:** Send photocopy of article or typed ms with rights for sale noted and information about when and where the article previously appeared. Pays 50% of amount paid for an original article.

**Photos:** Send photos with submission. Reviews prints or slides. Offers $10-150. Model releases required. Buys one-time rights.

**Columns/Departments:** Book reviews, 300-400 words. Query with or without published clips. **Pays $10-50.**

**Poetry:** Free verse, light verse, traditional. **Buys 8 poems/year.** Length: 4-50 lines. **Pays $10-50.**

**Fillers:** Anecdotes, facts, short humor. **Buys 12/year.** Length: 20-500 words. **Pays $10-50.**

**Tips:** "Follow our writer's guidelines. Write specifically to at-home mothers."

**$ ATLANTA PARENT/ATLANTA BABY,** 2346 Perimeter Park Dr., Suite 101, Atlanta GA 30346. (770)454-7599. Fax: (770)454-7699. E-mail: atlparent@family.com. Website: http://www.atlantaparent.com. Editor: Liz White. **Contact:** Peggy Middendorf, managing editor. **50% freelance written.** *Atlanta Parent* is a monthly tabloid covering parenting of children from birth-16 years old. Offers "down-to-earth help for parents." Estab. 1983. Circ. 80,000. *Atlanta Baby* magazine is published 4 times/year for expectant and new parents. Circ. 30,000. Pays on publication. Publishes ms 3 months after acceptance. Byline given. Buys one-time rights. Submit seasonal material 6 months in advance. Accepts queries by mail, e-mail. Reports in 4 months. Sample copy for $3.

**Nonfiction:** General interest, how-to, humor, interview/profile, travel. Special issues: Private school (January); Camp (February); Health and Fitness (March); Birthday Parties (April); Maternity and Mothering (May); Childcare (July); Back-to-school (August); Teens (October); Holidays (November/December). No first-person accounts or philosophical discussions. **Buys 60 mss/year.** Query with or without published clips, or send complete ms. Length: 800-2,100 words. **Pays $15-30.** Sometimes pays expenses of writers on assignment.

**Reprints:** Send tearsheet or photocopy of article or typed ms with rights for sale noted and information about when and where the article previously appeared. Pays $15-30.

**Photos:** State availability of photos with submission and send photocopies. Reviews 3×5 photos "b&w preferably." Offers $10/photo. Buys one-time rights.

**Tips:** "Articles should be geared to problems or situations of families and parents. Should include down-to-earth tips and be clearly written. No philosophical discussions or first-person narratives."

**$ $ $ $ BABY TALK,** The Parenting Group, 1325 Avenue of the Americas, 27th Floor, New York NY 10019-6026. (212)522-8989. Fax: (212)522-8750. **Contact:** Susan Kane, editor-in-chief. **Mostly freelance written.** Magazine published 10 times/year. "*Baby Talk* is written primarily for women who are considering pregnancy or who are expecting a child, and parents of children from birth through 18 months, with the emphasis on pregnancy through first six months of life." Estab. 1935. Circ. 1,725,000. Reports in 2 months.

**Nonfiction:** Features cover pregnancy, the basics of baby care, infant/toddler health, growth and development, juvenile equipment and toys, work and day care, marriage and sex, "approached from a how-to, service perspective. The message—Here's what you need to know and why—is delivered with smart, crisp style. The tone is confident and reassuring (and, when appropriate, humorous and playful), with the backing of experts. In essence, *Baby Talk* is a training manual of parents facing the day-to-day dilemmas of new parenthood." Query in writing with SASE. No phone calls, please. Length: 1,000-2,000 words. **Pays $500-2,000,** depending on length, degree of difficulty, and the writer's previous experience.

**Columns/Departments:** Several departments are written by regular contributors. Length: 100-1,250 words. **Pays $100-$1,000.** Query in writing with SASE.

**Tips:** "Please familiarize yourself with the magazine before submitting a query. Take the time to focus your story idea; scattershot queries are a waste of everyone's time."

**$ BAY AREA BABY,** United Advertising Publications, 401 Alberto Way, Suite A, Los Gatos CA 95032-5404. (408)358-1414. Fax: (408)356-4903. E-mail: writers@bayareaparent.com. Senior editor: Mary Brence Martin. Magazine published 3 times a year covering pregnancy and new parenthood (usually first-time). "*Bay Area Baby* targets pregnant couples and new (usually first-time) parents. We provide local, up-to-the-minute information on pregnancy and babies." Estab. 1986. Circ. 60,000. Pays on publication. Publishes ms an average of 6 months after acceptance. Byline given. Buys first rights. Editorial lead time 4 months. Submit seasonal material 6 months in advance. Accepts simultaneous submissions. Reports in 2 months. Sample copy for 8½×11½ SAE with 5 first-class stamps. Writer's guidelines for #10 SASE.

**Nonfiction:** Book excerpts, essays, interview/profile, personal experience (must be related to pregnancy or new parenthood). **Buys 9 mss/year.** Send complete ms. Length: 600-1,400 words. **Pays 6¢/word.** Sometimes pays expenses of writers on assignment.

**Reprints:** Accepts previously published submissions.

**Photos:** State availability of photos with submission. Reviews contact sheets, transparencies, prints. Offers $10-15/photo. Buys one-time rights.

**N $ BAY AREA PARENT MAGAZINE**, United Advertising Publications, 401 Alberto Way, Suite A, Los Gatos CA 95032-5404. Fax: (408)356-4903. Regional Manager: Lynn Berardo. **Contact:** Mary Brence Martin, managing editor. **80% freelance written.** Works with locally-based published/established writers and some non-local writers. Monthly tabloid of resource information for parents and teachers. Circ 77,000. Pays on publication. Publishes ms an average of 6 months after acceptance. Byline given. Buys one-time rights. Submit seasonal material 4 months in advance. Accepts simultaneous submissions. Sample copy for 9×12 SAE with 10 first-class stamps. Writer's guidelines for #10 SASE.

**Nonfiction:** Book excerpts (related to our interest group); exposé (health, psychology); how-to (related to kids/parenting); humor; interview/profile; photo feature; travel (with kids, family). Special issues: Music (March); Art and Kid's Birthdays (April); Summer Camps and Vacations (May); Family Fun (May); Health and Medicine (October); Working Parents (July); Fashion and Sports (August); Back-to-School (September). No poetry or fiction. **Buys 45-60 mss/year.** Query or send complete ms. Length: 150-1,500 words. **Pays 6-9¢/word.** Sometimes pays expenses of writers on assignment.

**Reprints:** Send typed ms with rights for sale noted and information about when and where the article previously appeared.

**Photos:** State availability of photos. Prefers b&w contact sheets and/or 3×5 b&w prints. Pays $10-15. Model release required. Buys one-time rights.

**Columns/Departments:** Child Care, Family Travel, Birthday Party Ideas, Baby Page, Toddler Page, Adolescent Kids. **Buys 36 mss/year.** Send complete ms. Length: 400-1,200 words. **Pays 6-9¢/word.**

**Tips:** "Submit new, fresh information concisely written and accurately researched. We also produce *Bay Area Baby Magazine*, published three times a year; *Valley Parent* Magazine, which focuses on central Contra Costa County and southern Alameda County; and *Bay Area Parent of Teens*, a subscription-only publication for parents of adolescents."

**$ BIG APPLE PARENT/QUEENS PARENT**, Family Communications, Inc., 9 E. 38th St., 4th Floor, New York NY 10016. (212)889-6400. Fax: (212)689-4958. E-mail: parentspaper@mindspring.com. Website: http://www.bigapple parents.com. **Contact:** Helen Freedman, managing editor. **95% freelance written.** Monthly tabloids covering New York City family life. "*BAP* readers live in high-rise Manhattan apartments; it is an educated, upscale audience. Often both parents are working full time in professional occupations. Child-care help tends to be one-on-one, in the home. Kids attend private schools for the most part. While not quite a suburban approach, some of our *QP* readers do have backyards (though most live in high-rise apartments). It is a more middle-class audience in Queens. More kids are in day care centers; majority of kids are in public schools." Estab. 1985. *Big Apple* circ. 67,000, *Queens* circ. 52,000. Pays end of month following publication. Byline given. Offers 50% kill fee. Buys first New York City rights. Reserves the right to publish an article in either or both the Manhattan and Queens editions and online. Submit seasonal material 3 months in advance. Accepts simultaneous submissions. Reports immediately; however, request no submissions during the summer months. Sample copy and writer's guidelines free.

**Nonfiction:** Essays, exposé, general interest, how-to, inspirational, interview/profile, opinion, photo feature, family health, education. **Buys 60-70 mss/year.** Query by mail, fax or e-mail or send complete ms. Length: 600-1,000 words. **Pays $35-50.** Sometimes pays expenses of writers on assignment. "We are not buying any more humor or personal parenting essays through end of 1999, but we're *always* looking for news and coverage of controversial issues."

**Reprints:** Send tearsheet or photocopy of article or typed ms with rights for sale noted and information about when and where the article previously appeared. Pays same as article rate.

**Photos:** State availability of or send photos with submission. Reviews contact sheets, prints. Offers $20/photo. Captions required. Buys one-time rights.

**Columns/Departments:** Dads; Education; Family Finance. **Buys 50-60 mss/year.** Send complete ms.

**Tips:** "We have a very local focus; our aim is to present articles our readers cannot find in national publications. To that end, news stories and human interest pieces must focus on New York and New Yorkers. Child-raising articles must include quotes from New York and Queens' experts and sources. We are always looking for news and newsy pieces; we keep on top of current events, frequently giving issues that may relate to parenting a local focus so that the idea will work for us as well."

**N $ $ CATHOLIC FAITH & FAMILY**, Circle Media, 33 Rossotto Dr., Hamden CT 06514. (203)288-5600. Fax: (203)288-5157. E-mail: editor@twincircle.com. **Contact:** Loretta Seyer, editor. **95% freelance written.** Weekly magazine. "We publish inspirational articles that focus on living/raising your children as Catholics. We look for articles on Catholic traditions, some travel pieces (usually to religious or educational family life), features on people living the Catholic life in a unique way." Estab. 1966. Circ. 8,000. Pays on publication. Byline given. Buys first rights. Accepts queries by mail, e-mail, fax.

**Nonfiction:** Inspirational, interview/profile, opinion, religious, travel. Send complete ms. Length: 1,000-2,000 words. **Pays $75-400.**

**Photos:** State availability of photos with submission or send photos with submission. Reviews prints. Identification of subjects required.

**Columns/Departments:** Hearth & Home (recipes, crafts, games, parties, traditions that celebrate/teach Catholic traditions/faith), 1,000 words. **Pays $75-175.**

**N $ CATHOLIC PARENT**, Our Sunday Visitor, 200 Noll Plaza, Huntington IN 46750-4310. (219)356-8400. Fax: (219)356-8472. E-mail: cp@osv.com. Website: http://www.osv.com. **Contact:** Woodeene Koenig-Bricker, editor.

**95% freelance written.** Bimonthly magazine. "We look for practical, realistic parenting articles written for a primarily Roman Catholic audience. The key is practical, not pious." Estab. 1993. Circ. 36,000. **Pays on acceptance.** Publishes ms an average of 6 months after acceptance. Byline given. Kill fee varies. Buys first North American serial rights. Editorial lead time 6 months. Submit seasonal material 6 months in advance. Accepts simultaneous submissions. Reports in 2 months. Sample copy for $3.

> • *Catholic Parent* is extremely receptive to first-person accounts of personal experiences dealing with parenting issues that are moving, emotionally engaging and uplifting for the reader. Bear in mind the magazine's mission to provide practical information for parents.

**Nonfiction:** Essays, how-to, humor, inspirational, personal experience, religious. **Buys 50 mss/year.** Send complete ms. Length: 850-1,200 words. Pay varies. Sometimes pays expenses of writers on assignment.
**Photos:** State availability of photos with submissions.
**Columns/Departments:** This Works (parenting tips), 200 words. **Buys 50 mss/year.** Send ms. **Pays $15-25.**
**Tips:** No poetry, fiction.

**$ $ CHICAGO PARENT, Connecting with Families,** Wednesday Journal, Inc., 141 S. Oak Park Ave., Oak Park IL 60302-2972. (708)386-5555. Fax: (708)524-8360. E-mail: chiparent@aol.com. Website: http://chicagoparent.com. **Contact:** Sharon Bloyd-Peshkin, editor. **50% freelance written.** Monthly. "We are a highly local parenting publication with a strong preference for local writers, although we are open to others. We cover a gamut of issues, doing everything from investigative features and in-depth reporting to service pieces on child health and daycare issues." Estab. 1988. Circ. 125,000 in four zones. Pays on publication. Publishes ms 1-2 months after acceptance. Byline given. Offers 10% kill fee. Buys first rights; reprint rights at 20%, online at 10% of original ms payment. Editorial lead time 3-4 months. Submit seasonal material 4-5 months in advance. Query by mail, e-mail, fax. Reports in 1 month. Sample copy for $3 and SASE with $1.65 postage. Writer's guidelines for #10 SASE.
**Nonfiction:** Book excerpts, profiles, general parenting interest, how-to (parent-related), humor, investigative features. Few essays. Special issues include Healthy Woman, Chicago Baby, Healthy Child. **Buys 120 mss/year.** Query with published clips. Length: 800-3,000 words. **Pays $100-350 for assigned articles, $35-200 for unsolicited articles.** Sometimes pays expenses of writers on assignment.
**Photos:** State availability of photos with submission or send photos with submission. Reviews contact sheets, negatives, any transparencies, any prints. Offers $0-40/photo. Negotiates payment individually. Buys one-time rights.
**Columns/Departments:** Healthy Kids (kids' health issues); Single Parent (legal or other issues for single parents); Parent on the Payroll (issues of reconciling work and home life), all 850 words. **Buys 30 mss/year.** Query with published clips or send complete ms. **Pays $100.**

**★ $ $ $ $ CHILD,** Gruner + Jahr, 375 Lexington Ave., New York NY 10017-5514. (212)499-2000. Fax: (212)499-2038. E-mail: childmag@aol.com. Editor-in-Chief: Pamela Abrams. Managing Editor: Elizabeth Roberta. **Contact:** Julie Savacool, editorial assistant. **95% freelance written.** Monthly magazine for parenting. Estab. 1986. Circ. 930,000. **Pays on acceptance.** Byline given. Offers 25% kill fee. Buys first North American serial, first, one-time and second serial (reprint) rights. Editorial lead time 3 months. Submit seasonal material 6 months in advance. Reports in 2 months. Sample copy for $3.95. Writer's guidelines free.

> • Ranked as one of the best markets for freelance writers in *Writer's Yearbook* magazine's annual "Top 100 Markets," January 1999.

**Nonfiction:** Book excerpts, general interest, interview/profile, new product, photo feature, travel. No poetry. **Buys 50 feature mss/year, 25-30 short pieces/year.** Query with published clips. Length: 650-2,500 words. **Pays $1/word.** Sometimes pays expenses of writers on assignment.
**Photos:** State availability of photos with submission. Reviews transparencies. Negotiates payment individually. Buys one-time rights.
**Columns/Departments:** First Person (mother's or father's perspective); Lesson Learned (experience mother or father learned from). Query with published clips. **Buys 100 mss/year.** Length: 1,500 words. **Pays $1/word.**

> • *Child* receives too many inappropriate submissions. Please consider your work carefully before submitting.

**Tips:** "Stories should include opinions from experts as well as anecdotes from parents to illustrate the points being made. Service is key."

**★ $ $ CHRISTIAN PARENTING TODAY,** Christianity Today, Inc., 465 Gundersen Dr., Carol Stream IL 60188-2489. (630)260-6200. Fax: (630)260-0114. E-mail: cptmag@aol.com. Editor: Carala Barnhill. Associate Editor: Lisa Jack. **Contact:** Lori McCullough. **90% freelance written.** Bimonthly magazine "strives to be a positive, practical magazine that targets real needs of today's family with authoritative articles based on real experience, fresh research and the timeless truths of the Bible. *CPT* provides parents information that spans birth to 14 years of age in the following areas of growth: spiritual, social, emotional, physical, academic." Estab. 1988. Circ. 90,000. **Pays on acceptance.** Byline given. Buys first North American serial or second serial (reprint) rights. Submit seasonal material 8 months in advance. Reports in 2 months. Sample copy for 9×12 SAE with $3 postage. Writer's guidelines for #10 SASE.
**Nonfiction:** Book excerpts, how-to, humor, inspirational, religious. Feature topics of greatest interest: practical guidance in spiritual/moral development and values transfer; practical solutions to everyday parenting issues; tips on how to enrich readers' marriages; ideas for nurturing healthy family ties; family activities that focus on parent/child interaction; humorous pieces about everyday family life. **Buys 50 mss/year.** Query only. Length: 750-2,000 words. **Pays 12-20¢/ word.**

**Reprints:** Send photocopy of article and typed ms with rights for sale noted and information about when and where the article previously appeared.

**Photos:** State availability of photos with submission. Do not submit photos without permission. Reviews transparencies. Model release required. Buys one-time rights.

**Columns/Departments:** Ideas That Work (family-tested parenting ideas from our readers), 25-100 words **(pays $25)**; Life In Our House (entertaining, true, humorous stories about your family), 25-100 words **(pays $25)**; Your Child Today (spiritual development topics from a Christian perspective), 420-520 words **(pays $150)**. Submissions become property of *CPT*. Submissions to *Life In Our House* and *Ideas That Work* are not acknowledged or returned.

**Tips:** "Tell it like it is. Readers have a 'get real' attitude that demands a down-to-earth, pragmatic take on topics. Don't sugar-coat things. Give direction without waffling. If you've 'been there,' tell us. The first-person, used appropriately, is OK. Don't distance yourself from readers. They trust people who have walked in their shoes. Get reader friendly. Fill your article with nuts and bolts: developmental information, age-specific angles, multiple resources, sound-bite sidebars, real-life people and anecdotes and realistic, vividly explained suggestions."

**🔲 $ $ DALLAS FAMILY MAGAZINE, The Magazine for Today's Parents**, Family Publications, Inc., 2501 Oak Lawn Ave., Suite 600, Dallas TX 75219. (214)521-2021. Fax: (214)522-9270. E-mail: dallasfam@aol.com. **Contact:** Ann S. Sentilles, editor. **50% freelance written.** Monthly tabloid covering parenting/families. "It is our mission to provide information, resources, perspective and support to parents—to strengthen families and their communities." Estab. 1993. Circ. 80,000. Pays 30 days after publication. Byline given. Offers 25% kill fee. Buys first North American serial or all rights. Editorial lead time 2 months. Submit seasonal material 3 months in advance. Accepts queries by mail, e-mail, fax. Reports in 1 month. Sample copy and writer's guidelines free.

**Nonfiction:** Essays, how-to (parenting families), humor, interview/profile, new product, personal experience (only occasionally), photo feature, travel. **Buys 12-20 mss/year.** Query with published clips. Length: 750-2,500 words. **Pays $125-400 for assigned articles; $50-300 for unsolicited articles.**

**Photos:** State availability of photos with submission. Identification of subjects required. Buys one-time rights.

**Tips:** "Send a fully developed story idea that demonstrates reporting and writing skills and understanding of the parenting niche market."

**⭐ $ $ FAMILY DIGEST, The Black Mom's Best Friend!,** Family Digest Association, 696 San Ramon Valley Blvd., #349, Danville CA 94526. Fax: (925)838-4948. **Contact:** Darryl Mobley, associate editor. **90% freelance written.** Quarterly magazine covering women's services. "Our mission: Help black moms/female heads-of-household get more out of their roles as wife, mother, homemaker. Editorial coverage includes parenting, health, love and marriage, travel, family finances, and beauty and style . . . All designed to appeal to black moms." Estab. 1997. Circ. 2,100,000. Pays on publication. Publishes ms an average of 6 months after acceptance. Byline sometimes given. Buys first North American serial rights, second serial (reprint) rights, or makes work-for-hire assignments. Editorial lead time 2 months. Submit seasonal material 3 months in advance. Accepts simultaneous submissions. Reports in 1 month. Writer's guidelines free by e-mail or for SASE and 2 first-class stamps.

**Nonfiction:** Book excerpts, general interest (dealing with relationships), historical/nostalgic, how-to, humor, inspirational, interview/profile, personal experience. "We are not political. We do not want articles that blame others. We do want articles that improve the lives of our readers." Query with published clips. Length: 1,000-3,000 words. **Pays $100-500.** Sometimes pays expenses of writers on assignment.

**Reprints:** Accepts previously published submissions.

**Photos:** State availability of or send photos with submission. Reviews negatives, transparencies, prints. Offers no additional payment for photos accepted with ms. Captions, model releases, identification of subjects required.

**Columns/Departments:** Parenting, love and marriage, health, family finances, beauty and style, A Better You! (personal development). **Buys 100 mss/year.** Query with published clips. **Pays $100-500.**

**Fiction:** Erotica, ethnic, historical, humorous, novel excerpts, romance. Query with published clips.

**Fillers:** Anecdotes, facts, gags to be illustrated by cartoonist, short humor. **Buys 100 mss/year.** Length: 50-250 words.

**⭐ $ THE FAMILY DIGEST,** P.O. Box 40137, Fort Wayne IN 46804. **Contact:** Corine B. Erlandson, editor. **95% freelance written.** Bimonthly digest-sized magazine. "*The Family Digest* is dedicated to the joy and fulfillment of the Catholic family and its relationship to the Catholic parish." Estab. 1945. Circ. 150,000. Pays within 1-2 months of acceptance. Publishes ms usually within 1 year after acceptance. Byline given. Buys first North American rights. Submit seasonal material 7 months in advance. Reports in 2 months. Sample copy and writer's guidelines for 6×9 SAE with 2 first-class stamps.

**Nonfiction:** Family life, parish life, how-to, seasonal, inspirational, prayer life, Catholic traditions. Send ms with SASE. No poetry or fiction. **Buys 60 unsolicited mss/year.** Length: 750-1,200 words. **Pays $40-60/article.**

**Reprints:** Prefers previously unpublished articles. Send typed ms with rights for sale noted and information about when and where the article previously appeared. Pays 5¢/word.

**Fillers:** Anecdotes, tasteful humor based on personal experience. **Buys 3/issue.** Length: 25-100 words maximum. **Pays $20 on acceptance.** Cartoons: Publishes 5 cartoons/issue, related to family and Catholic parish life. **Pays $35/cartoon on acceptance.**

**Tips:** "Prospective freelance contributors should be familiar with the publication and the types of articles we accept and publish. We are especially looking for upbeat articles which affirm the simple ways in which the Catholic faith is expressed in daily life. Articles on family and parish life, including seasonal articles, how-to pieces, inspirational, prayer, spiritual life and Church traditions, will be gladly reviewed for possible acceptance and publication."

**$ $ $ $ FAMILY LIFE**, Hachette-Filipacchi Magazines, Inc., 1633 Broadway, 41st Floor, New York NY 10019-6708. (212)767-4918. Fax: (212)489-4561. E-mail: familylife@aol.com. **Contact:** Peter Herbst, editor-in-chief. **60% freelance written.** Magazine published 10 times/year for parents of children ages 3-12. Estab. 1993. Circ. 500,000. **Pays on acceptance.** Publishes ms an average of 4 months after acceptance. Byline given. Offers 25% kill fee. Buys first worldwide rights. Editorial lead time 6 months. Submit seasonal material 8 months in advance. Accepts simultaneous submissions. Accepts queries by mail, e-mail, fax. Reports in 6 weeks on queries. Sample copy for $3, call (201)451-9420. Writer's guidelines for #10 SASE. "No calls please."

**Nonfiction:** Parenting book excerpts, essays and articles on family topics, general interest, new product, photo feature, travel health. Does not want to see articles about children under 3 or childbirth. Feature length: 2,000-3,500 words. Query with published clips. **Pays $1/word.** Pays expenses of writers on assignment.

• Ranked as one of the best markets for freelance writers in *Writer's Yearbook* magazine's annual "Top 100 Markets," January 1999.

**Photos:** State availability of photos with submission. Reviews transparencies. Negotiates payment individually. Buys one-time rights.

**Columns/Departments:** Family Matters section in the front of the book (newsy shorts on parenting topics, interesting travel destinations and the latest health issues), 150-250 words. Individual columns: Parent to Parent (story by a parent about life with his or her child that epitomizes one issue in child-rearing); Motherhood (changes and challenges that being a mother brings to a woman's life); Family Affairs (personal issues parents face as their children grow up); School Smart (today's educational issues); House Calls (health); Chip Chat (the latest in family computing). Length: 1,000-1,500 words. Query with published clips.

▣ The online magazine carries original content not found in the print edition. Contact: Tess Ghilaga, online editor.

**Tips:** "Our readers are parents of children ages 3-12 who are interested in getting the most out of family life. Most are college educated and work hard at a full-time job. We want fresh articles dealing with the day-to-day issues that these families face, with personal insight and professional opinion on how to handle them."

**$ FAMILY TIMES**, Family Times, Inc., 10 Main St., #3C, Christiana DE 19702. (302)224-3020. Fax: (302)224-3024. E-mail: ftimes@family.com. Website: http://www.delawarefamily.com. **Contact:** Denise Yearian, editor. **50% freelance written.** Monthly tabloid for parenting. "Our targeted distribution is to parents via a controlled network of area schools, daycares, pediatricians and places where families congregate. We only want articles related to parenting, children's issues and enhancing family life." Estab. 1990. Circ. 35,000. Pays on publication. Publishes ms an average of 2 months after acceptance. Byline given. Buys one-time or second serial (reprint) rights. Editorial lead time 2 months. Submit seasonal material 2 months in advance. Accepts simultaneous submissions. Reports in 3 months on mss. Sample copy for 3 first-class stamps.

**Nonfiction:** Book excerpts, how-to parenting, inspirational, interview/profile, new product, opinion, personal experience, photo feature, travel, children, parenting. Special issues: Technology/Education (January); Fitness (February); Summer Camps (March); Environment (April); Birthdays (May); Summer Fun (June); Pregnancy & Birth (July); After-School Activities (August); Back-To-School (September); Childcare Options (October); Health & Safety (November); Holiday Celebrations (December). **Buys 60 mss/year.** Send complete ms. Length: 750-1,000 words. **Pays $30 minimum for assigned articles; $25 for unsolicited articles.**

**Reprints:** Send tearsheet or photocopy of article or typed ms with rights for sale noted.

**Photos:** State availability of photos with submission. Negotiates payment individually. Identification of subjects required. Buys one-time rights.

**Columns/Departments: Pays $25-50.**

**Tips:** "Work with other members of PPA (Parenting Publications of America) since we all share our writers and watch others' work. We pay little but you can sell the same story to 30 other publications in different markets. Online use offers additional author credit and payment based on accesses. We are most open to general features."

**$ $ GREAT EXPECTATIONS, Today's Parent Group**, 269 Richmond St. W, Toronto, Ontario M5V 1X1 Canada. (416)569-8680. Fax: (416)496-1991. Website: http://www.todaysparent.com. **Contact:** Susan Spicer, assistant editor. Editor: Holly Bennett. **100% freelance written.** Consumer magazine published 3 times a year. "*GE* helps, supports and encourages expectant and new parents with news and features related to pregnancy, birth, human sexuality and parenting." Estab. 1973. Circ. 200,000. **Pays on acceptance.** Publishes ms an average of 8 months after acceptance. Bylines given. Buys first North American serial rights. Editorial lead time 6 months. Reports in 6 weeks on queries. Sample copy and writer's guidelines for #10 SASE.

**Nonfiction:** Features about pregnancy, labor and delivery, post-partum issues. **Buys 12 mss/year.** Query with published clips. Length: 700-2,000 words. **Pays $400-1,200.** Sometimes pays expenses of writers on assignment.

**Photos:** State availability of photos with submission. Negotiates payment individually. Rights negotiated individually.

**Tips:** "Our writers are professional freelance writers with specific knowledge in the childbirth field. *GE* is written for a Canadian audience using Canadian research and sources."

**$ $ GROWING PARENT**, Dunn & Hargitt, Inc., P.O. Box 620, Lafayette IN 47902-0620. (765)423-2624. Fax: (765)742-8514. **Contact:** Nancy Kleckner, editor. **40-50% freelance written.** Works with a small number of new/

unpublished writers each year. "We do receive a lot of unsolicited submissions but have had excellent results in working with some unpublished writers. So, we're always happy to look at material and hope to find one or two jewels each year." Monthly newsletter which focuses on parents—the issues, problems, and choices they face as their children grow. "We want to look at the parent as an adult and help encourage his or her growth not only as a parent but as an individual." Estab. 1973. Pays on publication. Publishes ms an average of 6 months after acceptance. Byline given. Buys first North American serial rights; maintains exclusive rights for three months. Submit seasonal material 6 months in advance. Reports in 2 weeks. Sample copy and writer's guidelines for 5×8 SAE with 2 first-class stamps.

**Nonfiction:** "We are looking for informational articles written in an easy-to-read, concise style. We would like to see articles that help parents deal with the stresses they face in everyday life—positive, upbeat, how-to-cope suggestions. We rarely use humorous pieces, fiction or personal experience articles. Writers should keep in mind that most of our readers have children under two years of age." **Buys 15-20 mss/year.** Query. Length: 1,000-1,500 words; will look at shorter pieces. **Pays 10-15¢/word.**

**Reprints:** Send tearsheet of article and information about when and where it previously appeared.

**Tips:** "Submit a very specific query letter with samples."

**⚑ $ $ $ $ HEALTHY KIDS**, Primedia, 249 W. 17th St., New York NY 10011-5300. (212)462-3300. Fax: (212)367-8332. Website: http://www.healthykids.com. Editor: Laura Broadwell. **Contact:** Jeanette Bogren, editorial assistant. **90% freelance written.** Bimonthly magazine that addresses all elements that go into the raising of a healthy, happy child, from basic health-care information to an analysis of a child's growing mind and behavior patterns. Extends the wisdom of the pediatrician into the home, and informs parents of young children (ages birth to 10 years) about proper health care. The only magazine produced for parents in association with the American Academy of Pediatrics, the nonprofit organization of more than 55,000 pediatricians dedicated to the betterment of children's health. To ensure accuracy, all articles are reviewed by an Editorial Advisory Board comprised of distinguished pediatricians. Estab. 1989. Circ. 1,550,000. **Pays on acceptance.** Byline given. Offers 33% kill fee. Buys first North American rights. Submit seasonal material at least 6 months in advance. Reports in 2 months. Writer's guidelines for #10 SASE.

**Nonfiction:** How to help your child develop as a person, keep safe, keep healthy. No poetry, fiction, travel or product endorsement. Special issues: Good Eating!—A complete guide to feeding your family (February/March). Query by mail. No unsolicited mss. Length: 2,000-2,500 words. **Pays $1,500-2,500.** Pays expenses of writers on assignment.

**Columns/Departments:** Focus On . . . (an informal conversation with a pediatrician, in a question-and-answer format, about a timely health issue); Let's Eat (advice on how to keep mealtimes fun and nutritious, along with some child-friendly recipes); Behavior Basics (a helpful article on how to deal with some aspect of a child's behavior—from first friendships to temper tantrums). **Buys 20 mss/year.** Query. Length: 1,500-1,800 words. **Pays $1,200-1,500.**

⬛ The online magazine carries original content not found in the print edition. Contact: Jill Laurinaitis, online editor.

**Tips:** "A simple, clear approach is mandatory. Articles should speak with the voice of medical authority in children's health issues, while being helpful and encouraging, cautionary but not critical, and responsible but not preachy. All articles should include interviews with appropriate Academy-member pediatricians and other health care professionals."

**$ $ KIDS: ACTIVITIES FOR FAMILIES, Woman's Day Special Interest Publications**, Hachette-Filipacchi Magazines, 1633 Broadway, New York NY 10019. Fax: (212)767-5612. Editor: Carolyn Gatto. **Contact:** Janice Wright, managing editor. "This semiannual magazine is a resource guide for parents who want to stimulate their child's creativity by exploring crafts, cooking, and other home-based leisure time activities, including holiday ideas. Complete how-to for crafts, games and activities are provided. Ideas should be of interest to children ages 3 to 13, but need not span the entire range. 95% of the readers are female, with a median age of 41." **Pays on acceptance.** Publishes ms an average of 3 months after acceptance. Offers up to 25% kill fee. Buys first worldwide serial or second serial (printing) rights. Editorial lead time 6 months. Submit seasonal material 10 months in advance. Reports in 3 months. Writer's guidelines for #10 SASE.

**Nonfiction:** How-to (crafts & activities for families), new products, reviews of children's books, videos, software, music & other media. **Buys 30 mss/year.** Query with published clips. Length: 250-1,000 words. Payment varies based on length, writer, importance. Sometimes pays expenses of writers on assignment.

**Reprints:** Accepts previously published submissions.

**Photos:** State availability of photos with submissions. Model releases required. Buys one-time rights.

**Columns/Departments:** Query with published clips. Payment varies based on length, writer, and level of amount of research required.

**Tips:** "Send a brief, clear query letter with relevant clips, and be patient. Potential reviewers must query, stating qualifications: Do not send unsolicited reviews."

**⚑ $ $ L.A. PARENT, The Magazine for Parents in Southern California**, 443 E. Irving Dr., Suite D, Burbank CA 91504-2447. (818)846-0400. Fax: (818)841-4380. E-mail: laparent@family.com. Website: http://www.laparent.com. **Contact:** Christina Elston, editor. **80% freelance written.** Prefers to work with published/established writers, but works with a small number of new/unpublished writers each year. Monthly tabloid covering parenting. Estab. 1980. Circ. 200,000. **Pays on acceptance.** Publishes ms an average of 4 months after acceptance. Byline given. Buys first and reprint rights. Submit seasonal material 4 months in advance. Accepts queries by mail, e-mail, fax. Accepts simultaneous queries. Reports in 3 months. Sample copy and writer's guidelines for $2 and 11×14 SAE with 5 first-class stamps.

• *L.A. Parent* is looking for more articles pertaining to infants and early childhood.

**Nonfiction:** General interest, how-to. Special issues: High Potential Parenting and Nutrition of the Young Child. "We focus on generic parenting for ages 0-12 and Southern California activities for families, and do round-up pieces, i.e., a guide to private schools, art opportunities." **Buys 60-75 mss/year.** Query with clips of published work. Length: 1,000 words. **Pays $250-350 plus expenses.**

**Reprints:** Send photocopy of article or typed ms with rights for sale noted and information about when and where the article previously appeared. Pays $50 on average for reprints.

**Tips:** "We will be using more contemporary articles on parenting's challenges. If you can write for a 'city magazine' in tone and accuracy, you may write for us. We look for a sophisticated tone in covering the joys and demands of being a mom or dad in the 90s."

**$ LONG ISLAND PARENTING NEWS**, RDM Publishing, P.O. Box 214, Island Park NY 11558. (516)889-5510. Fax: (516)889-5513. E-mail: liparent@family.com. Website: http://www.LIPN.com. **Contact:** Heather Hart, editor. Director: Andrew Elias. **70% freelance written.** Free community newspaper published monthly "for concerned parents with active families and young children. Our slogan is: 'For parents who care to know.' " Estab. 1989. Circ. 57,000. Pays on publication. Publishes ms an average of 3 months after acceptance. Byline given (also 1-3 line bio, if appropriate). Buys one-time rights. Editorial lead time 2 months. Submit seasonal material 3 months in advance. Accepts simultaneous submissions. Reports in 3 months. Sample copy for $3 and 9×12 SAE with 5 first-class stamps. Guidelines free.

**Nonfiction:** Book excerpts, essays, general interest, how-to, humor, interview/profile, new product, opinion, personal experience, travel. Needs articles covering childcare, childbirth/maternity, schools, camps and back-to-school. **Buys 30-50 mss/year.** Query with or without published clips, or send complete ms. Length: 500-2,000 words. **Pays $40-200.** "Sometimes trade article for advertising space." Sometimes pays expenses of writers on assignment.

**Reprints:** Send photocopy of article or typed ms with rights for sale noted and information about when and where the article previously appeared. Negotiates fee.

**Photos:** Send photos, preferably b&w, with submission. Negotiates payment individually. Reviews 4×5 prints. Offers $5-50/photo. Captions, model releases required. Buys one-time rights.

**Columns/Departments:** On the Island (local, national and international news of interest to parents); Off The Shelf (book reviews); Fun & Games (toy and game reviews); KidVid (reviews of kids' video); The Beat (reviews of kids' music); Monitor (reviews of computer hardware and software for kids); The Big Picture (reviews of kids' films); Soon Come (for expectant parents); Educaring (parenting info and advice); Something Special (for parents of kids with special needs); Growing Up (family health issues); On the Ball (sports for kids); Family Matters (essays on family life); Words Worth (storytelling); Getaway (family travel); Teen Time (for parents of teenagers). **Buys 20-30 mss/year.** Send complete ms. Length: 300-2,000 words. **Pays $40-200.**

**Tips:** "*Long Island Parenting News* is dedicated to educate, inform and inspire parents (from pregnancy to teens) in the development of their understanding, appreciation, and celebration of their families."

**$ MAMA'S LITTLE HELPER**, Turquoise Butterfly Press, P.O. Box 1127, Athens OH 45701-1127. (740)664-3030. E-mail: turqbutfly@bright.net. Website: http://www.angelfire.com/biz2/turquoisebutterfly. **Contact**: Terri Andrews, editor. "We are the only parenting support group via the mail for ADHD parents. We focus on all aspects of raising spirited children." Buys one-time rights. Sample copy for $3.50. Writer's guidelines for #10 SASE.

**Nonfiction:** "Our primary goal is to support and assist parents of hyperactive, ADHD, spirited and energetic children with guidance, information, tried and tested tips and medical information. Topics include: Ritalin, diet, positive discipline, stress-busting, car trips, restaurants, dealing with schools and siblings, recipes, ADHD history. Length: 900-1,500 words for features, 100-900 words for personal stories, interviews, humor, etc. Send complete ms with word count and SASE. Include researched citations. **Pays 1¢/word or contributor copies.**

**⊠ $ METRO PARENT MAGAZINE**, All Kids Considered, Ltd., 24567 Northwestern Hwy., Suite 150, Southfield MI 48075-2412. (248)352-0990. Fax: (248)352-5066. E-mail: metropar@family.com. Website: http://family.com. **Contact:** Susan DeMaggio, editor. **100% freelance written.** Monthly tabloid covering parenting/family issues. "*Metro Parent* is a local parenting publication geared toward parents with children under the age of 12. We look for sound, pertinent information for our readers, preferably using local experts as sources." Estab. 1986. Distributed throughout Oakland, Macomb and Wayne Counties and the city of Ann Arbor. Circ. 70,000. Pays on publication. Publishes ms an average of 2 months after acceptance. Byline given. Buys one-time rights. Editorial lead time 3 months. Submit seasonal material 4 months in advance. Accepts simultaneous submissions. Accepts queries by mail, e-mail, fax. Sample copy and writer's guidelines free or on website.

**Nonfiction:** Book excerpts, general interest, how-to, humor, inspirational, interview/profile, new product, travel. Special issues: Metro Baby Magazine (geared for expectant parents, August, March); Camps (January-May); Birthdays (May); Back to School (August/September); and Holiday issues (October, November, December, February). **Buys 25 mss/year.** Query with published clips. Length: 500-3,000 words. **Pays $75-150 for assigned articles.**

**Reprints:** Send photocopy and information about when and where the article previously appeared. **Pays $35.**

**Photos:** State availability of photos with submission. Reviews 4×6 prints. Negotiates payment individually. Captions, model releases, identification of subjects required. Buys one-time rights.

**Columns/Departments:** Short Stuff (new products), 100 words; Mixed Media (video, movie, books, audio, software), 700 (total) words; Boredom Busters (craft ideas, games & activities), 700 words; Let's Party! (fun, unique ideas for parties and other celebrations), 700 words. **Buys 35 mss/year.** Query with published clips. **Pays $30-50.**

**$ METROKIDS MAGAZINE, The Resource for Delaware Valley Families**, Kidstuff Publications, Inc., 1080 N. Delaware Ave., #702, Philadelphia PA 19125-4330. (215)291-5560. Fax: (215)291-5563. E-mail: metrokids@family.com. Website: http://www.metrokids.com. **Contact:** Amanda Hathaway, executive editor. **80% freelance written.** Monthly tabloid providing information for parents and kids in Philadelphia, South Jersey and surrounding counties. Estab. 1990. Circ. 90,000. Pays on publication. Byline given. Buys one-time rights. Submit seasonal material 4 months in advance. Accepts queries by mail, e-mail, fax. Reports in up to 8 months on queries. Guidelines for #10 SASE.

**Nonfiction:** General interest, how-to, new product, travel, parenting, health. Special issues: Baby First (April; pregnancy, childbirth, first baby); Camps (December-June); Special Kids (October; children with special needs); Vacations and Theme Parks (May, June); What's Happening (January; guide to events and activities); Healthy Times (July; family and especially children's health). **Buys 40 mss/year.** Query with published clips. Prefers mss to queries. Length: 800-1,500 words maximum. **Pays $1-50.** Sometimes pays expenses of writers on assignment.

**Reprints:** Send photocopy of article and information about when and where it previously appeared. Pays $20-40.

**Photos:** State availability of photos with submission. Captions required. Buys one-time rights.

**Columns/Departments:** Book Beat (book reviews); Bytesize; Body Wise (health); Dollar Sense (finances); all 500-700 words. **Buys 25 mss/year.** Query. **Pays $1-50.**

**Tips:** "Send a query letter several months before a scheduled topical issue; then follow-up with a telephone call. We are interested in feature articles (on specified topics) or material for our regular columns (with a regional/seasonal base). Articles should cite expert sources and the most up-to-date theories and facts. We are looking for a journalistic-style of writing. Editorial calendar available on request. We are also interested in finding local writers for assignments."

**N $ $ NEW ENGLAND BOOMING**, P.O. Box 1200, Boston MA 02130. (617)522-1515. Fax: (617)522-1694. E-mail: kaleel@nebooming.com. Travel Editor: Kaleel Sakakeeny. **Contact:** Bill Lindsay, editor-in-chief. **70% freelance written.** Monthly magazine covering baby boomers. Estab. 1997. Circ. 50,000. Pays on publication. Byline given. Offers 33% kill fee. Buys first North American serial rights and electronic rights. Editorial lead time 1 month. Accepts queries by e-mail, fax. Accepts simultaneous submissions. Reports in 3 weeks on queries. Sample copy for 20¢ and SASE. Writer's guidelines free with #10 SASE.

**Nonfiction: Pays $400 for features.**

**Photos:** State availability of photos with submission. Reviews transparencies. Offers $35/photo. Captions required. Buys one-time rights.

**Columns/Departments: Buys 120 mss/year. Pays $200 departments; $400 features.**

**$ NEW MOON NETWORK: FOR ADULTS WHO CARE ABOUT GIRLS**, New Moon Publishing, Inc., P.O. Box 3620, Duluth MN 55803. (218)728-5507. Fax: (218)728-0314. E-mail: newmoon@cp.duluth.mn.us. Website: http://www.newmoon.org. **Contact:** Joe Kelly, editor. **10% freelance written.** Bimonthly magazine covering adults (parents, teachers, others) who work with girls age 8-14. "*New Moon Network* is the companion publication to *New Moon: The Magazine For Girls and Their Dreams*. It is written by and for adults—parents, teachers, counselors and others—who are working to raise healthy, confident girls. Its goal is to celebrate girls and support their efforts to hang onto their voices, strengths and dreams as they move from being girls to becoming women." Estab. 1992. Circ. 3,000. Pays on publication. Publishes ms an average of 2 months after acceptance. Byline given. Buys first rights and second serial (reprint) rights. Editorial lead time 3 months. Submit seasonal material 4 months in advance. Accepts simultaneous submissions. Reports in 1 month on queries; 2 months on mss. Sample copy for $6.50. Writer's guidelines free.

**Nonfiction:** Essays, general interest, historical/nostalgic, humor, inspirational, interview/profile, opinion, personal experience, photo feature, religious, technical, book reviews. Editorial calendar available. **Buys 6 mss/year.** Query. Length: 750-1,500 words. **Pays 4-8¢/word.**

**Reprints:** Send photocopy of article or short story and information about when and where it previously appeared.

**Photos:** State availability of photos with submissions (prefers b&w). Reviews 4×5 prints. Negotiates payment individually. Captions, model releases, identification of subjects required. Buys one-time rights.

**Columns/Departments:** Mothering (personal experience), 900 words; Fathering (personal experience), 900 words; Current Research (girl-related), 900-1,800 words; Book Reviews, 900 words. **Buys 3 mss/year.** Query. **Pays 4-8¢/word.**

**Fiction:** Humorous, slice-of-life vignettes, multicultural/girl centered. **Buys 1 mss/year.** Query. Length: 900-1,800 words. **Pays 4-8¢/word.**

**Tips:** "Writers and artists who comprehend our goals have the best chance of publication. Refer to our guidelines and upcoming themes. We are not looking for advice columns or 'twelve tips for being a successful parent' formula articles. Write for clarity and ease of understanding, rather than in an 'academic' style."

**$ $ NEW YORK FAMILY, CONNECTICUT FAMILY, WESTCHESTER FAMILY**, United Advertising Publications, 141 Halstead Ave., Mamaroneck NY 10543-2652. (914)381-7474. Fax: (914)381-7672. E-mail: fpg@family.com. Website: http://www.nyfamily.com; ctfamily.com; westchesterfam.com. **Contact:** Betsy F. Woolf, editor. **90% freelance written.** Monthly magazine "that serves as a local parenting resource." Estab. 1986. Circ. 175,000. Pays on publication. Publishes ms an average of 6 months after acceptance. Byline given. Offers $25 kill fee. Buys first or second serial (reprint) rights; prefers first rights. Editorial lead time 4 months. Submit seasonal material 4 months in advance. Writer's guidelines available online.

**Nonfiction:** How-to (home, raising kids), humor, personal experience, travel (for parenting market). Special issue: Baby Guide (2/year). No articles unrelated to parenting and the home. **Buys 100 mss/year.** Query with published clips. Length: 800-1,200 words. **Pays $50-200 for assigned articles; $50-125 for unsolicited articles.**

**Reprints:** Accepts previously published materials.

**Photos:** Send photos with submission. Reviews prints (5 × 7). Negotiates payment individually. Model releases required. Buys one-time rights.

**N $ $ NORTHWEST FAMILY MAGAZINE**, MMB Publications, Inc., 1155 N. State St., #414, Bellingham WA 98225. (360)734-3025. Fax: (360)734-1550. E-mail: nwfamily@family.com. Website: http://www.nwfamily.com. Managing Editor: Katey Roemmele. **Contact:** Lisa Laskey, editor. **50% freelance written.** Monthly parenting magazine. "We are a parenting resource publication whose goal is to help families with everyday issues they face. We are especially concerned with issues particular to the Northwest and western Washington State." Estab. 1995. Circ. 55,000. Pays on publication. Publishes ms an average of 6 months after acceptance. Byline sometimes given. Buys one-time rights. Editorial lead time 3 months. Submit seasonal material 6 months in advance. Accepts queries by mail, e-mail. Accepts simultaneous submissions. Reports in 3 weeks on queries; 3 months on mss. Sample copy for $1.25. Writer's guidelines for #10 SASE.

**Nonfiction:** Katey Roemmele, managing editor. Essays, general interest, how-to relating to children and parenting, humor, inspirational, interview/profile, new product, personal experience, photo feature, travel with kids. **Buys 40-50 mss/year.** Send complete ms. Length: 300-1,600 words. **Pays 10¢/word for assigned articles; $25-45 for unsolicited articles** (depending on length). Sometimes pays expenses of writers on assignment.

**Reprints:** Accepts previously published submissions.

**Photos:** State availability of photos with submission. Reviews negatives and any size prints. Negotiates payment individually. Model releases required. Buys one-time rights.

**Columns/Departments:** Katey Roemmele, managing editor. School News (information about schools, especially local), 100-300 words; Bulletin Board (quick information for families), 100-300 words; Reviews (videos/books/products for families), 100-300 words. **Buys 8-10 mss/year.** Send complete ms. **Pays $10-20.**

**Poetry:** Lisa Laskey, editor. Avant garde, free verse, haiku, light verse, traditional. "No heavy or negative content." **Buys 6 poems/year.** Submit maximum 5 poems. Length: 6-25 lines. **Pays $5-20.**

**Tips:** "Send entire article with word count. Topic should apply to parents (regional focus increases our need for your article) and be addressed in a positive manner—'How to' not 'How not to.'"

**N $ PARENTING BAY AREA TEENS**, United Advertising Publications, 401 Alberto Way, Suite A, Los Gatos CA 95032. Editor: Lora White. **Contact:** Mary Brence Martin. Estab. 1996. Circ. 80,000. Monthly magazine covering issues of interest to parents of adolescents. Publishes ms 6 months after acceptance of ms. Pays on publication. Byline given. Buys first rights. Editorial lead time 6 months. Submit seasonal material 6 months in advance. Accepts simultaneous submissions. Reports in 2 months. Sample copy for 8½ × 11 SASE with 4 first-class stamps. Writer's guidelines for #10 SASE.

**Nonfiction: Pays 6¢/word.**

**Photos:** State availability of photos with submission. Pays $10-15/photo.

**$ $ $ $ PARENTING MAGAZINE**, 1325 Avenue of the Americas, 27th Floor, New York NY 10019-6026. (212)522-8989. Fax: (212)522-8699. Editor-in-Chief: Janet Chan. Executive Editor: Lisa Bain. **Contact:** Articles Editor. Magazine published 10 times/year "for parents of children from birth to twelve years old, with the most emphasis put on the under-sixes, and covering both the psychological and practical aspects of parenting." Estab. 1987. **Pays on acceptance.** Byline given. Offers 25% kill fee. Buys first rights. Sample copy for $2.95 and 9 × 12 SAE with 5 first-class stamps. Writer's guidelines for #10 SASE.

● Ranked as one of the best markets for freelance writers in *Writer's Yearbook* magazine's annual "Top 100 Markets," January 1999.

**Nonfiction:** Articles editor. Book excerpts, humor, investigative reports, personal experience, photo feature. **Buys 20-30 features/year.** Query with or without published clips. No phone queries, please. Length: 1,000-3,000 words. **Pays $500-2,000.** Sometimes pays expenses of writers on assignment.

**Columns/Departments:** Family Reporter (news items relating to children/family), 100-400 words; Ages and Stages (health, nutrition, new products and service stories), 100-500 words; Children's Health, 100-500 words. **Buys 50-60 mss/year.** Query to the specific departmental editor. **Pays $50-500.**

**Tips:** "The best guide for writers is the magazine itself. Please familiarize yourself with it before submitting a query."

**$ $ PARENTS' PRESS, The Monthly Newspaper for Bay Area Parents**, 1454 Sixth St., Berkeley CA 94710-1431. (510)524-1602. Fax: (510)524-0912. E-mail: parentsprs@aol.com. Website: http://members.aol.com/parentsprs/index.html. **Contact:** Dixie M. Jordan, editor. **50% freelance written.** Monthly tabloid for parents. Estab. 1980. Circ. 75,000. Pays within 45 days of publication. Publishes ms an average of 4 months after acceptance. Kill fee varies (individually negotiated). Buys all rights, second serial (reprint) and almost always Northern California Exclusive rights. Submit seasonal material 6 months in advance. Accepts queries by mail, e-mail. Reports in 3 months. Sample copy for $3. Writer's guidelines and editorial calendar for #10 SASE. Rarely considers simultaneous submissions.

○⊸ Break in with short articles focusing on one or more interesting places to go/activities to do with children in the San Francisco Bay Area.

**Nonfiction:** Book excerpts, well-researched articles on children's health, development, education, family activities and travel. "We require a strong Bay Area focus in almost all articles. Use quotes from experts and Bay Area parents. Please, no child-rearing tips or advice based on personal experience." Special annual issues include Pregnancy, Birth

& Baby, Family Travel, Back to School. **Buys 30-50 mss/year.** Query with or without published clips, or send complete ms. Length: 300-3,000 words; 1,500-2,000 average. **Pays $50-500 for assigned articles; $25-250 for unsolicited articles.** Will pay more if photos accompany article. Negotiable. Will negotiate fees for special projects written by Bay Area journalists.

**Reprints:** Send photocopy of article with rights for sale noted and information about when and where the article previously appeared and where else it is being submitted. Pays up to $50.

**Photos:** State availability of photos with submission. Reviews prints, any size, b&w only. Offers $10-15/photo. Model release and identification of subject required. Buys one-time rights.

**$ $PARENT.TEEN, The Magazine for Bay Area Families with Teens**, Parents' Press, 1454 Sixth St., Berkeley CA 94710. (510)524-1602. Fax: (510)524-0912. E-mail: parentsprs@aol.com. Website: http://members.aol. com/parentsprs/index.html. **Contact:** Dixie M. Jordan, editor. **75% freelance written.** Monthly magazine for parents of teens. Estab. 1997. Circ. 80,000. Pays within 60 days of publication. Publishes ms an average of 3 months after acceptance. Kill fee varies (individually negotiated). Buys all rights, second serial (reprint) and almost always Northern California Exclusive rights. Submit seasonal material 6 months in advance. Accepts queries by mail, e-mail. Reports in 2 months. Sample copy for $3. Writer's guidelines and editorial calendar for #10 SASE or on website.

> ○→ Break in with profiles of offbeat colleges or programs, especially California/West Coast and articles on innovative programs operated by teens in the Bay Area. Examples have been teenage members of Search & Rescue, a teen-run wildlife museum, teen-produced programs for National Public Radio.

**Nonfiction:** Regular features, open to all, cover adolescent medicine, teen psychology, youth culture and trends, education, college preparation, work, sports, sex, gender roles, family relationships, legal topics, financial issues and profiles of interesting teens, colleges and programs. "We require a strong Bay Area focus in most articles. Use quotes from experts and Bay Area teens." **Buys 40 mss/year.** Query with clips or send complete ms on spec. "We pay for lively, information-packed content, not length." Length: 500-1,200 words. **Pays $150-500.**

**Reprints:** Send a photocopy of article with rights for sale noted and information about when and where the article previously appeared. Pays up to $50.

**Photos:** State availability of photos with submission. Payment rates higher for mss with photos. Photos only: $15-50 for one-time rights (b&w). Reviews color slides for cover; contact art director Renee Benoit before sending. Photos returned only if accompanied by SASE. Model releases and subject identification required.

**Columns/Departments: Pays $5-10** for "grab bag" items, ranging from one sentence to one paragraph on "weird facts about teens" or teen-related Bay Area news item. Submissions must cite sources of information.

**Tips:** "We do not commission stories by writers who are unknown to us, so your best bet is to send us original articles on spec or already published articles offered for reprint rights. We are looking for writers who can pack a lot of information in as few words as possible in lively prose. No first-person 'How I Got My Kid Through Teenhood.' "

**$SAN DIEGO FAMILY MAGAZINE, San Diego County's Leading Resource for Parents & Educators Who Care!**, P.O. Box 23960, San Diego CA 92193-3960. (619)685-6970. Fax: (619)685-6978. E-mail: sandiegofamily. com. Website: http://sandiegofamily.com. **Contact:** Sharon Bay, editor-in-chief. **75% freelance written.** Monthly magazine for parenting and family issues. "*SDFM* strives to provide informative, educational articles emphasizing positive parenting for our typical readership of educated mothers, ages 25-45, with an upper-level income. Most articles are factual and practical, a few are humor and personal experience. Editorial emphasis is uplifting and positive." Estab. 1982. Circ. 120,000. Pays on publication. Byline given. Buys first, one-time or second serial (reprint) rights. Editorial lead time 2 months. Submit seasonal material 3 months in advance. Reports in 2 months on queries; 3 months on mss. Sample copy and writer's guidelines for $3.50 with 9×12 SAE.

**Nonfiction:** How-to, parenting, new baby help, enhancing education, family activities, interview/profile (influential or noted persons or experts included in parenting or the welfare of children) and articles of specific interest to or regarding San Diego (for California) families/children/parents/educators. "No rambling, personal experience pieces." **Buys 75 mss/year.** Send complete ms. Length: 800 words maximum. **Pays $1.25/column inch.** "Byline and contributor copies if writer prefers."

**Reprints:** Send typed ms with rights for sale noted and information about when and where the article previously appeared.

**Photos:** State availability of photos with submission. Reviews contact sheets and 3½×5 or 5×7 prints. Negotiates payment individually. Identification of subjects preferred. Buys one-time rights.

**Columns/Departments:** Kids' Books (topical book reviews), 800 words. **Buys 12 mss/year.** Query with published clips. **Pays $1.25/column inch minimum.**

**Fillers:** Facts and newsbreaks (specific to the family market). **Buys 10/year.** Length: 50-200 words. **Pays $1.25/column inch minimum.**

**$ $SAN FRANCISCO PENINSULA PARENT**, United Advertising Publications, 1480 Rollins Rd., Burlingame CA 94010-2307. (650)342-9203. Fax: (650)342-9276. E-mail: sfpp@aol.com. Website: http://family.com/homepage.ht ml. **Contact:** Lisa Rosenthal, editor. **25% freelance written.** Monthly magazine geared to parents of children from birth to teens. "We provide articles that empower parents with the essential parenting skills they need and offer local resource information." Estab. 1984. Circ. 70,000. Pays on publication. Publishes ms 3-6 months after acceptance. Byline given. Offers 50% kill fee. Buys first and second serial (reprint) rights. Editorial lead time 5 months. Submit seasonal material 4 months in advance. Accepts queries by mail, e-mail, fax. Reports in 3 months on queries; 4 months on mss. Sample copy and writer's guidelines free.

**Nonfiction:** Humor, interview/profile, travel (family-related). No articles that preach to parents, no first-person memories. **Buys 8 mss/year.** Query with or without published clips. Length: 800-1,200 words. **Pays $100-200 for assigned articles; $25-100 for unsolicited articles.** Sometimes pays expenses of writers on assignment.

**Reprints:** Send tearsheet or photocopy of article or typed ms with rights for sale noted and information about when and where the article previously appeared. **Pays $25-50.**

**Photos:** State availability of photos with submission. Offers $25-$50/photo; negotiates payment individually. Captions and model releases required. Buys one-time rights.

**Columns/Departments:** Healthbeat (health news for families), 1,000 words; Parents of Teens Column, 1,000 words. **Buys 2 mss/year.** Query with or without published clips. **Pays $25-100.**

**⊠ $ $ $ $ SESAME STREET PARENTS**, Children's Television Workshop, 1 Lincoln Plaza, 3rd Floor, New York NY 10023-7129. (212)875-6470. Fax: (212)875-6105. Editor-in-Chief: Susan Lapinski. **Contact:** Patti Jones, assistant editor. **80% freelance written.** Magazine published 10 times/year for parents of preschoolers that accompanies every issue of Sesame Street Magazine. Circ. 1,000,000. **Pays on acceptance.** Byline given. Offers 33% kill fee. Buys varying rights. Submit seasonal material 7 months in advance. Reports in 2 months on queries. Sample copy for 9 × 12 SAE with 6 first-class stamps. Writer's guidelines for #10 SASE.

**Nonfiction:** Child development/parenting, how-to (practical tips for parents of preschoolers), interview/profile, personal experience, book excerpts, essays, photo feature, travel (with children). **Buys 100 mss/year.** Query with published clips or send complete ms. Length: 500-2,000 words. **Pays $300-2,000 for articles.**

**Reprints:** Send typed ms with rights for sale noted and information about when and where the article previously appeared. Negotiates payment.

**Photos:** State availability of photos with submission. Model releases, identification of subjects required. Buys one-time or all rights.

**$ $ $ SUCCESSFUL STUDENT**, Imagination Publishing, 820 W. Jackson Blvd., Suite 450, Chicago IL 60607. (312)627-1020. Fax: (312)627-1105. **Contact:** Eva Dienel, editor. **30% freelance written.** Semiannual magazine published for customers of Sylvan Learning Centers covering education. "We focus on education-related issues and study habits and tips. We frequently use expert writers and/or sources." Circ. 550,000. Pays on publication. Publishes ms an average of 5 months after acceptance. Byline given. Offers 33% kill fee. Buys first North American serial rights. Editorial lead time 6 months. Accepts simultaneous submissions.

**Nonfiction:** Book excerpts, essays, how-to (tips on studying, etc.), inspirational, interview/profile, new product. No parenting stories. Query by mail only with published clips and SASE. **Buys 2-4 mss/year.** Length: 300-1,700 words. **Pays 50¢/word.** Pays expenses of writers on assignment.

**Reprints:** Accepts previously published submissions.

**Photos:** State availability of photos with submission. Negotiates payment individually. Buys one-time rights.

**Tips:** "We're looking for writers with strong voices and an understanding of our editorial categories, who have the ability to write clearly and concisely. Because many of our stories include expert sources, our writers have enough of an education background to recognize these people. We frequently ask writers to pull short facts or tips into sidebars to complement the main stories. Stories are carefully reviewed for accuracy and appropriateness by the editorial staff and an advisory board from Sylvan Learning Systems."

**$ $ TOLEDO AREA PARENT NEWS**, Toledo Area Parent News, Inc., 1120 Adams St., Toledo OH 43624-1509. (419)244-9859. Fax: (419)244-9871. E-mail: erin@toledocitypaper.com. Website: http://family.go.com/Local/tole. **Contact:** Erin Kramer, editor. **20% freelance written.** Monthly tabloid for Northwest Ohio/Southeast Michigan parents. Estab. 1992. Circ. 50,000. Pays on publication. Publishes ms an average of 1 month after acceptance. Byline given. Makes work-for-hire assignments. Editorial lead time 3 months. Accepts queries by mail, e-mail, fax. Reports in 1 month. Sample copy for $1.50.

**Nonfiction:** "We use only local writers, by assignment only." General interest, interview/profile, opinion. "We accept queries and opinion pieces only. Send cover letter and clips to be considered for assignments." **Buys 10 mss/year.** Length: 1,000-2,500 words. **Pays $75-125.**

**Photos:** State availability of photos with submission. Negotiates payment individually. Identification of subjects required. Buys all rights.

**Tips:** "We love humorous stories that deal with common parenting issues or features on cutting-edge issues."

**$ $ TUESDAY'S CHILD MAGAZINE, Parenting Kids of All Abilities**, Lynn Martens-Publisher, P.O. Box 270046, Fort Collins CO 80527. (970)416-7416. Fax: (970)686-0780. E-mail: tueskid@frii.com. Website: http://www.tuesdayschild.com. **Contact:** Sarah Asmus McCarthy, editor. **60% freelance written.** Bimonthly consumer magazine covering parenting children with disabilities. Circ. 10,000. Pays on publication. Byline given. Offers 50% kill fee. Buys first North American serial rights. Editorial lead time 2 months. Submit seasonal material 3 months in advance. Accepts queries by mail, e-mail. Sample copy and writer's guidelines free.

**Nonfiction:** General interest, how-to, humor, inspirational, interview/profile, new product, personal experience, photo feature, technical, travel, disability related issues. **Buys 20 mss/year.** Query or query with published clips. Length: 800-5,000 words. **Pays $100/magazine page.**

**Reprints:** Accepts previously published submissions.

**Photos:** State availability of photos with submissions. Offers no additional payment for photos accepted with ms. Buys one-time rights.

**Columns/Departments:** Parent's Place, Kid Ability, Feature, Rec & Fun, Alternatives. **Buys 20 mss/year.** Query. **Pays $100/magazine page.**

**Poetry:** Free verse, light verse, traditional. **Buys 1 poem/year.** Submit maximum 2 poems. Length: 5-25 words.

**⊠ $ $ TWINS, The Magazine for Parents of Multiples,** The Business Word, Inc., 5350 S. Roslyn St., Suite 400, Englewood CO 80111-2125. (303)290-8500 or (888)55TWINS. Fax: (303)290-9025. E-mail: twins.editor@business word.com. Website: http://www.twinsmagazine.com. Editor-in-Chief: Susan J. Alt. Managing Editor: Marge D. Hansen. **Contact:** Betsy McLinda, assistant editor. **80% freelance written.** Bimonthly magazine covering parenting multiples. "*TWINS* is an international publication that provides informational and educational articles regarding the parenting of twins, triplets and more. All articles must be multiple specific and have an upbeat, hopeful and/or positive ending." Estab. 1984. Circ. 55,000. Pays on publication. Byline given. Buys first North American serial rights. Editorial lead time 3 months. Submit seasonal material 5 months in advance. Accepts queries by mail, e-mail, fax, phone. Accepts simultaneous submissions. Reporting time varies. Sample copy for $5 or on website. Writer's guidelines for #10 SASE.

**Nonfiction:** Personal experience (first-person parenting experience) and professional experience as it relates to multiples. Nothing on cloning, pregnancy reduction or fertility issues. **Buys 12 mss/year.** Query with or without published clips or send complete ms. Length: 1,300 words. **Pays $25-250 for assigned articles; $25-75 for unsolicited articles.**

**Photos:** State availability of photos with submission. Offers no additional payment for photos accepted with ms. Identification of subjects required.

**Columns/Departments:** On Being Parents (parenting multiples/personal essay), 800-850 words; Special Miracles (miraculous stories about multiples with a happy ending), 800-850 words. **Buys 12-20 mss/year.** Query with or without published clips or send complete ms. **Pays $25-75.** "All department articles must have a happy ending, as well as teach a lesson that parents of multiples can learn from."

**$ VALLEY PARENT MAGAZINE,** United Advertising Publications, 401 Alberto Way, Suite A, Los Gatos CA 95032-5405. (408)358-1414. Fax: (408)356-4903. E-mail: writers@bayareaparent.com. Regional Manager: Lynn Berardo. **Contact:** Mary Brence Martin, managing editor. **43% freelance written.** Monthly magazine covering parenting children ages birth through early teens. "The information we are most likely to use is local, well-researched and geared to our readers." Estab. 1992. Circ. 55,000. Pays on publication. Publishes ms an average of 6 months after acceptance. Byline given. Buys first rights. Editorial lead time 6 months. Submit seasonal material 6 months in advance. Accepts simultaneous submissions. Reports in 2 months. Sample copy for 8½×12 SAE with 5 first-class stamps. Writer's guidelines for #10 SASE.

**Nonfiction:** Book excerpts, interview/profile, opinion, personal experience (all parenting-related). Send complete ms with SASE. **Buys 22 mss/year.** Length: 900-2,000 words. **Pays 6-9¢/word.**

**Reprints:** Send tearsheet or photocopy of article or typed ms with rights for sale noted and information about when and where the article previously appeared. Pays 100% of amount paid for an original article.

**Photos:** State availability of photos with submission. Reviews contact sheets, negatives, transparencies, prints. Offers $10-15/photo. Buys one-time rights.

**Columns/Departments:** First Year, 950-1,000 words. Query with published clips or send complete ms with SASE. **Pays 6-9¢/word.**

**$ VALLEYKIDS PARENT NEWS,** 3403 Shoemaker Dr., Columbia MO 65202-0935. (573)815-0831. Fax: (573)815-0832. E-mail vjnimmo@juno.com. **Contact:** Vivian J. Nimmo, editor. **50% freelance written.** Monthly tabloid featuring "suggestions for busy parents who care about their children." Estab. 1992. Circ. 61,000. Pays on publication. Publishes ms an average of 2 months after acceptance. Byline given. Buys one-time rights and makes work-for-hire assignments. Editorial lead time 3 months. Submit seasonal material 3 months in advance. Accepts simultaneous submissions. Accepts queries by e-mail. Reports in 2 months on queries; 3 months on mss. Sample copy for $1. Writer's guidelines free.

**Nonfiction:** General interest, how-to, inspirational. No self-promotional pieces. **Buys 60-70 mss/year.** Send complete ms. Length: 600-1,200 words. **Pays $25-50.**

**Reprints:** Accepts previously published submissions.

**Photos:** State availability of photos with submission. Buys one-time rights.

**Tips:** "Query by e-mail with the title of article, length, fee expected and brief summary of content. If asked, submit article by e-mail."

**Ⓝ ⊠ $ WESTERN NEW YORK FAMILY,** Western New York Family Inc., P.O. Box 265, 287 Parkside Ave., Buffalo NY 14215-0265. (716)836-3486. Fax: (716)836-3680. E-mail: wny_fam@family.com. Website: http://www.wes ternnewyork.com. **Contact:** Michele Miller, editor/publisher. **90% freelance written.** Monthly magazine covering parenting in Western NY. "Readership is largely composed of families with children ages newborn to 12 years. Although most subscriptions are in the name of the mother, 91% of fathers also read the publication. Strong emphasis is placed on how and where to find family-oriented events, as well as goods and services for children, in Western New York." Estab. 1984. Circ. 22,500. Pays on publication. Publishes ms up to 18 months after acceptance. Byline given. Buys one-time, second serial (reprint) or simultaneous (non-local) rights. Editorial lead time 3 months. Submit seasonal material

3 months in advance. Accepts queries by mail, e-mail, fax. Accepts simultaneous submissions (non-local). Reports only if interested. Sample copy for $2.50 and $9 \times 12$ SAE with 3 first-class stamps. Guidelines for #10 SASE or by e-mail.

**O—** Break in is with either a "cutting edge" topic that is new and different in it's relevance to parenting in the 90s or a "timeless" topic which is "evergreen" and can be kept on file to fill last minute holes.

**Nonfiction:** How-to (craft projects for kids, holiday, costume, etc.), humor (as related to parenting), personal experience (parenting related), travel (family destinations). Special issues: Birthday Celebrations (January); Cabin Fever (February); Having A Baby (March); Education & Enrichment (April); Mother's Day (May); Father's Day (June); Summer Fun (July and August); Back to School (September); Halloween Happenings (October); Family Issues (November); and Holiday Happenings (December). **Buys 50 mss/year.** Send complete ms. Length: 750-3,000 words. **Pays $50-100 for assigned articles; $20-40 for unsolicited articles.** Sometimes pays expenses of writers on assignment.

**Reprints:** Accepts previously published submissions.

**Photos:** State availability of photos with submission. Reviews $3 \times 5$ prints. Offers no additional payment for photos accepted with ms. Captions, model releases and identification of subjects required. Buys one-time rights.

**Columns/Departments:** Family Travel: Destination Fun!, 1,000 words; It's Dad's Turn (father's viewpoint), 750 words. **Buys 24 mss/year.** Send complete ms. **Pays $20-40.**

**Fillers:** Facts. **Buys 10/year.** Length: 450 words. **Pays $20.**

**Tips:** "We are interested in well-researched, nonfiction articles on surviving the newborn, preschool, school age and adolescent years. Our readers want practical information on places to go and things to do in the Buffalo area and nearby Canada. They enjoy humorous articles about the trials and tribulations of parenthood as well as 'how-to' articles (i.e., tips for finding a sitter, keeping your sanity while shopping with preschoolers, ideas for holidays and birthdays, etc.). Articles on making a working parent's life easier are of great interest as are articles written by fathers. We prefer a warm, conversational style of writing."

**$ $ $ $ WORKING MOTHER MAGAZINE,** MacDonald Communications, 135 W. 50th St., 16th Floor, New York NY 10020-1201. (212)445-6100. Fax: (212)445-6174. E-mail: wmedit@womweb.com. **Contact:** Kathryn Cartwright, senior editor. **90% freelance written.** Prefers to work with published/established writers; works with a small number of new/unpublished writers each year. Monthly magazine for women who balance a career with the concerns of parenting. Circ. 925,000. Publishes ms an average of 4 months after acceptance. Byline given. Buys all rights. Pays 20% kill fee. Submit seasonal material 6 months in advance. Accepts queries by mail. Sample copy for $4. Writer's guidelines for SASE.

**Nonfiction:** Service, humor, child development, material pertinent to the working mother's predicament. Query to *Working Mother Magazine*. **Buys 9-10 mss/issue.** Length: 1,500-2,000 words. Pays expenses of writers on assignment.

**Tips:** "We are looking for pieces that help the reader. In other words, we don't simply report on a trend without discussing how it specifically affects our readers' lives and how they can handle the effects. Where can they look for help if necessary?"

**$ $ $ YOUR BABY,** Today's Parent Group, 269 Richmond St. W., Toronto, Ontario M5V 1X1 Canada. Fax: (416)496-1991. Website: http://www.todaysparent.com. **Contact:** Susan Spicer, assistant editor. Editor: Holly Bennett. **100% freelance written.** Magazine published 3 times a year covering parenting from birth to age 2. "Articles of interest to parents of young children about child development, care, health and parenting issues." **Pays on acceptance.** Publishes ms an average of 8 months after acceptance. Byline given. Buys first North American serial rights. Editorial lead time 6 months. Reports in 6 weeks on queries. Sample copy and writer's guidelines for #10 SASE.

**Nonfiction:** Features about parenting young children. **Buys 12 mss/year.** Query with published clips. Length: 500-1,500 words. **Pays $400-1,000.** Sometimes pays expenses of writers on assignment.

**Tips:** "Our writers are professional freelance writers. *YB* is written for a Canadian audience and we insist on Canadian research, anecdotes, sources and relevance."

# COMIC BOOKS

**$ CARTOON WORLD,** P.O. Box 1164, Kent WA 98035. E-mail: cartoonworld@usa.net. **Contact:** Vic Stredicke, editor. (253)854-6649. Monthly newsletter for professional and serious amateur cartoonists who want to find new places to sell their cartoons. Circ. 300. **Pays on acceptance.** Byline given. Offers counsel to new writers. Submit seasonal material 3 months in advance. Accepts queries by mail, e-mail, phone, fax. Reports in 1 month. Sample copy free.

**Nonfiction:** "Want articles about the business of cartooning. Most features should be first-person accounts of cartoon editing, creating ideas, work habits." All cartoons run must have been published elsewhere. Length: 1,000 words. **Pays $5/page/feature.**

**Reprints:** Note where previously appeared. **Pays $5/page.**

**$ MIXXZINE, Entertainment for the New Millenium,** Mixx Entertainment, Inc., 746 W. Adams Blvd., Los Angeles CA 90089-7725. (213)743-2519. Fax: (213)749-7199. E-mail: info@mixxonline.com. **Contact:** Stu Levy, CEO. **50% freelance written.** Bimonthly magazine covering Japanese comics and animation (manga, anime). "*MixxZine* readers are the most up-to-date on Japanese comics and animation and are interested in learning more about Japanese culture." Estab. 1997. Circ. 50,000. Pays on publication. No byline. Makes work-for-hire assignments. Editorial lead time 3 months. Submit seasonal material 3 months in advance. Accepts queries by e-mail, fax. Accepts simultaneous submissions. Sample copy for $2.50.

**Nonfiction:** New product. **Buys 3 mss/year.** Query with published clips. Length: 500-4,000 words. **Pays $100/feature articles.**

**Photos:** State availability of photos with submission. Reviews 8½ × 11 prints. Offers no additional payment for photos accepted with ms. Buys all rights.

**$ $WIZARD: THE COMICS MAGAZINE,** Wizard Entertainment, 151 Wells Ave., Congers NY 10920-2036. (914)268-2000. Fax: (914)268-0053. E-mail: aekardon@aol.com. Website: http://www.wizardworld.com. Editor: Brian Cunningham. Senior Editor: Joe Yanarella. **Contact:** Andrew Kardon, managing editor. **70% freelance written.** Monthly magazine covering comics and action figures. Estab. 1991. Circ. 300,000. Pays on publication. Publishes ms an average of 3 months after acceptance. Byline given. Offers 50% kill fee. Buys all rights. Editorial lead time 4 months. Accepts queries by mail, e-mail, fax. Reports in 6 weeks. Sample copy and writer's guidelines free.

**Nonfiction:** Historical/nostalgic, how-to, humor, interview/profile, new product, personal experience, photo feature, first person diary. No columns or opinion pieces. **Buys 100 mss/year.** Query with or without published clips. Length: 250-4,000 words. **Pays 15-20¢/word.** Sometimes pays expenses of writers on assignment.

**Photos:** State availability of photos with submission. Negotiates payment individually. Identification of subjects required. Buys all rights.

**Columns/Departments:** Time Travel (classic moment in comic history), 500 words; Coming Attractions (comic book-related movies and TV shows), 150-500 words. Query with published clips. **Pays $75-500.**

**Tips:** "Send plenty of samples showing the range of your writing styles. Have a good knowledge of comic books. Read a few issues to get the feel of the conversational 'Wizard Style.' "

# CONSUMER SERVICE & BUSINESS OPPORTUNITY

Some of these magazines are geared to investing earnings or starting a new business; others show how to make economical purchases. Publications for business executives and consumers interested in business topics are listed under Business & Finance. Those on how to run specific businesses are classified by category in the Trade section.

**$ $AMERICAN VENTURE, For Entrepreneurs & Accredited Investors,** Fusion International, Inc., 621 SW Alder, Suite 630, Portland OR 97205. (503)221-9981. Fax: (503)221-9987. E-mail: avce@aol.com. Website: http://www.avce.com. **Contact:** Douglas Clements, editor-in-chief. **75% freelance written.** "Quarterly magazine contains articles written for individuals and companies that invest in new ventures and people that manage new ventures. Articles should *not* favor tax-funded programs or laws that restrict economic freedom. Articles should be consistent with free-market economics." Estab. 1997. Circ. 25,000. Pays on publication. Publishes ms an average of 2 months after acceptance. Byline given. Buys all rights. Editorial lead time 2 months. Submit seasonal material 2 months in advance. Accepts simultaneous submissions. Accepts queries by mail, e-mail. Sample copy and writer's guidelines on website.

O─ Break in with an interesting story of how a start-up venture battled many problems, overcame them with creative solutions and ultimately succeeded.

**Nonfiction:** Essays, exposé, general interest, historical/nostalgic, how-to, inspirational, interview/profile, new product, opinion, personal experience. **Buys 15 mss/year.** Query with published clips. Length: 500-1,250 words. **Pays $50-300.**

**Reprints:** Accepts previously published submissions.

**Photos:** State availability of photos with submission. Reviews contact sheets. Negotiates payment individually. Buys one-time rights.

**Columns/Departments:** Investor's Perspective (investor talks about his philosophy, deals), 750 words; Success Against the Odds (entrepreneur who succeeded despite much adversity), 1,000 words; Secret of Their Success (story of the early days of a famous company), 1,000 words; Innovators (a company with a revolutionary new product/service), 750 words. **Buys 10 mss/year.** Query with or without published clips. **Pays $50-300.**

**Fillers:** Anecdotes, facts, newsbreaks, short humor. **Buys 5/year.** Length: 100-300 words. **Pays $30-150.**

**Tips:** "Articles should contain interesting new information that venture capitalists and entrepreneurs can use. No boring, obvious tracts. We like 'war stories' from investors and entrepreneurs that are inspirational. Articles that illustrate the beauty of free-market capitalism are favored."

**$ $JERRY BUCHANAN'S INFO MARKETING REPORT,** TOWERS Club Press, Inc., P.O. Box 2038, Vancouver WA 98668-2038. (360)574-3084. Fax: (360)576-8969. **Contact:** Jerry Buchanan, editor. **5-10% freelance written.** Works with a small number of unpublished writers each year. Monthly of 10 or more pages on entrepreneurial enterprises, reporting especially on self-publishing of how-to reports, books, audio and video tapes, seminars, etc. "Bypassing big trade publishers and marketing your own work directly to consumer (mail order predominantly)." Estab. 1974. Circ. 10,000. Pays on publication. Publishes ms an average of 2 months after acceptance. Byline given. Buys one-time rights. Reports in 2 weeks. Sample copy for $15 and 6 × 9 SASE.

**Nonfiction:** Exposé (of mail order fraud); how-to (personal experience in self-publishing and marketing); book reviews of new self-published nonfiction how-to-do-it books (must include name and address of author). "Welcomes well-written articles of successful self-publishing/marketing ventures. Must be current, and preferably written by the person who actually did the work and reaped the rewards. There's very little we will not consider, *if* it pertains to unique money-making enterprises that can be operated from the home." **Buys 10 mss/year.** Send complete ms. Fax submissions accepted of no more than 3 pages. Length: 500-1,500 words. **Pays $150-250.** Pays extra for b&w photo and bonus for excellence in longer ms.

**Reprints:** Send tearsheet or photocopy of article or typed ms with rights for sale noted and information about when and where the article previously appeared. Pays 10% of the amount paid for an original article.

**Tips:** "The most frequent mistake made by writers in completing an article for us is that they think they can simply rewrite a newspaper article and be accepted. That is only the start. We want them to find the article about a successful self-publishing enterprise, and then go out and interview the principal for a more detailed how-to article, including names and addresses. We prefer that writer actually interview a successful self-publisher. Articles should include how idea first came to subject; how they implemented and financed and promoted the project; how long it took to show a profit and some of the stumbling blocks they overcame; how many persons participated in the production and promotion; and how much money was invested (approximately) and other pertinent how-to elements of the story. Glossy photos (b&w) of principals at work in their offices will help sell article."

**N** **★** **$ ECONOMIC FACTS,** The National Research Bureau, Inc., 320 Valley St., Burlington IA 52601. (319)752-5415. Fax: (319)752-3421. **Contact:** Nancy Heinzel, editor. **75% freelance written.** Quarterly magazine. Estab. 1948. Pays on publication. Publishes ms an average of 1 year after acceptance. Byline given. Buys all rights. Sample copy and writer's guidelines for #10 SAE with 2 first-class stamps.

• Eager to work with new/unpublished writers; works with a small number of new/unpublished writers each year.

**Nonfiction:** General interest (private enterprise, government data, graphs, taxes and health care). **Buys 10 mss/year.** Query with outline of article. Length: 500-700 words. **Pays 4¢/word.**

**★** **$ $ HOME BUSINESS MAGAZINE,** United Marketing & Research Company, Inc., 9582 Hamilton Ave. #368, Huntington Beach CA 92646. Fax: (714)962-7722. E-mail: henderso@ix.netcom.com. Website: http://www.home businessmag.com. **Contact:** Stacy Ann Henderson, editor-in-chief. **75% freelance written.** "*Home Business Magazine* covers every angle of the home-based business market including: cutting edge editorial by well-known authorities on sales and marketing, business operations, the home office, franchising, business opportunities, network marketing, mail order and other subjects to help readers choose, manage and prosper in a home-based business; display advertising, classified ads and a directory of home-based businesses; technology, the Internet, computers and the future of home-based business; home-office editorial including management advice, office set-up, and product descriptions; business opportunities, franchising and work-from-home success stories." Estab. 1993. Circ. 80,000. Pays on publication. Publishes ms an average of 4 months after acceptance. Byline given. Buys first, one-time, second serial (reprint) rights or makes work-for-hire assignments. Editorial lead time 2 months. Submit seasonal material 3 months in advance. Accepts queries by mail, e-mail, fax, phone. Accepts simultaneous submissions. Sample copy for 9 × 12 SASE with 8 first-class stamps or on website. Writer's guidelines for #10 SASE.

**Nonfiction:** Book excerpts, general interest, how-to (home business), inspirational, interview/profile, new product, personal experience, photo feature, technical, mail order, franchise, business management, Internet, finance network marketing. No non-home business related topics. **Buys 40 mss/year.** Send complete ms with 9 × 12 SASE with 8 first-class stamps. Length: 265-3,200 words. **Pays $67-500 for assigned articles; $0-200 for unsolicited articles.** Pays with contributor copies or other premiums on request or per pre-discussed arrangement with magazine.

**Reprints:** Accepts previously published submissions.

**Photos:** Send photos with submission. Offers no additional payment for photos accepted with ms. Identification of subjects required. Buys one-time rights.

**Columns/Departments:** Marketing & Sales; Money Corner; Home Office; Management; Technology; Working Smarter; Franchising; Network Marketing, all 265-1,200 words. Send complete ms. **Pays $0-200.**

▣ The online magazine carries original content not found in the print edition. Contact: Ted Wooley, online editor.

**Tips:** "Send complete information by mail as per our writer's guidelines and e-mail if possible. We encourage writers to submit Feature Articles (2-4 page) and Departmental Articles (⅓-1½ page). Please submit polished, well-written, organized material. It helps to provide subheadings within the article. Boxes, lists and bullets are encouraged because they make your article easier to read, use and reference by the reader. A primary problem in the past is that articles do not stick to the subject of the title. Please pay attention to the focus of your article and to your title."

**$ $ $ $ KIPLINGER'S PERSONAL FINANCE,** 1729 H St. NW, Washington DC 20006. (202)887-6400. Fax: (202)331-1206. Website: http://www.kiplinger.com. Editor: Ted Miller. **Contact:** Christine Pulfrey, senior editorial assistant. **Less than 10% freelance written.** Prefers to work with published/established writers. Monthly magazine for general, adult audience interested in personal finance and consumer information. "*Kiplinger's* is a highly trustworthy source of information on saving and investing, taxes, credit, home ownership, paying for college, retirement planning, automobile buying and many other personal finance topics." Estab. 1947. Circ. 1,300,000. **Pays on acceptance.** Publishes ms an average of 2 months after acceptance. Buys all rights. Reports in 1 month.

**Nonfiction:** "Most material is staff-written, but we accept some freelance. Thorough documentation is required for fact-checking." Query with clips of published work. Pays expenses of writers on assignment.

**Tips:** "We are looking for a heavy emphasis on personal finance topics."

**⯀ $MONEY SAVING IDEAS**, The National Research Bureau, 320 Valley St., Burlington IA 52601. (319)752-5415. Fax: (319)752-3421. **Contact:** Nancy Heinzel, editor. **75% freelance written.** Quarterly magazine that features money saving strategies. "We are interested in money saving tips on various subjects (insurance, travel, heating/cooling, buying a house, ways to cut costs and balance checkbooks). Our audience is mainly industrial and office workers." Estab. 1948. Circ. 1,000. Pays on publication. Publishes ms an average of 1 year after acceptance. Byline given. Buys all rights. Sample copy and writers guidelines for #10 SAE with 2 first-class stamps. Writer's guidelines for #10 SASE.
**Nonfiction:** How-to (save on grocery bills, heating/cooling bills, car expenses, insurance, travel). Query with or without published clips, or send complete ms. Length: 500-700 words. **Pays 4¢/word.**
**Tips:** "Follow our guidelines. Keep articles to stated length, double-spaced, neatly typed. If writer wishes rejected manuscript returned include SASE. Name, address and word length should appear on first page."

**⯀ $ $SPARE TIME MAGAZINE, The Magazine of Money Making Opportunities**, Kipen Publishing Corp., 5810 W. Oklahoma Ave., Milwaukee WI 53219. (414)543-8110. Fax: (414)543-9767. Email: editor@spare-time.com. Website: http://www.spare-time.com. **Contact:** Peter Abbott, editor. **75% freelance written.** Magazine published monthly except July covering affordable money-making opportunities. "We publish information the average person can use to begin and operate a spare-time business or extra income venture, with the possible goal of making it fulltime." Estab. 1955. Circ. 300,000. Pays on publication. Publishes ms an average of 3 months after acceptance. Byline given. Buys first North American serial rights. Editorial lead time 2 months. Submit seasonal material 3 months in advance. Accepts simultaneous submissions, query first. Reports in 1 month on queries; 2 months on mss. Sample copy for $2.50. Writer's guidelines and editorial calendar for #10 SASE.
**Nonfiction:** Book excerpts and reviews (small business related), how-to (market, keep records, stay motivated, choose opportunity), interview/profile and personal experience (small business related). Special issues: Starting a new business (January); Hobby businesses (February); Taxes (March); Low cost franchising (April); Sales and marketing (May/June); Education and training (August). **Buys 24-54 mss/year.** Query with SASE. Length: up to 1,100 words (cover story: 1,500-2,000 words; installment series, three parts up to 1,100 words each). **Pays 15¢/word upon publication.** Sometimes pays expenses of writers on assignment.
**Reprints:** Send photocopy of article or typed ms with information about when and where the article previously appeared. Pays 50% of amount paid for an original article.
**Photos:** State availability of photos with submission. Reviews contact sheets, 3×5 or larger prints. Pays $15/published photo. Captions, identification of subjects required. Buys one-time rights.
**Tips:** "It is always best to query. At all times keep in mind that the audience is the average person, not over-educated in terms of business techniques. The best pieces are written in lay language and relate to that type of person."

**⯀ $THE UNDERGROUND SHOPPER**, Talk Productions, 1508 E. Belt Line Rd., Carrollton TX 75006. (972)245-1144. E-mail: queries@undergroundshopper.com. **Contact:** Rebecca Taverner, senior editor. Eager to work with new/unpublished writers. Monthly magazine for consumers who are interested in getting more but paying less. **Pays on acceptance.** Byline given. Buys first rights, some second rights. Submit seasonal/holiday material 4 months in advance. Query by mail, e-mail. Reports in 1 month. Sample copy and writer's guidelines for $1.50 postage and SASE.
**Nonfiction:** How-to, new product, personal experience, consumer tips. Query. Length 400-2,000 words. **Pays $50-150 for first-time freelancers.**
**Photos:** State availability of photos with query. Offers $5-25 per photo to freelance photographers. Buys first rights and reprint rights.
**Fillers:** Anecdotes, facts and consumer information. Length: 50 words maximum. **Pays $10-20.**
**Tips:** "Interested only in articles focused on "Living the good life . . . at half the price. Submissions should give consumers information on how to save money in every aspect of their lives."

# CONTEMPORARY CULTURE

These magazines often combine politics, current events and cultural elements such as art, literature, film and music, to examine contemporary society. Their approach to institutions is typically irreverent and investigative. Some, like *Madison*, report on alternative culture and appeal to a young adult "Generation X" audience. Others treat mainstream culture for a baby boomer generation audience.

**⯀ $ $ $ $A&U AMERICA'S AIDS MAGAZINE**, Art & Understanding, Inc., 25 Monroe St., Albany NY 12210. (518)426-9010. Fax: (518)436-5354. E-mail: mailbox@aumag.org. Website: http://www.aumag.org. **Contact:** David Waggoner, editor. **50% freelance written.** Monthly magazine covering cultural responses to AIDS/HIV. Estab. 1991. Circ. 175,000. Pays on publication. Publishes ms an average of 3 months after acceptance. Byline given. Offers 20% kill fee. Buys first North American serial rights. Editorial lead time 6 months. Accepts queries by mail, e-mail, fax, phone. Accepts simultaneous submissions. Reports in 1 month on queries; 2 months on mss. Sample copy for $5. Writer's guidelines for #10 SASE.
**Nonfiction:** Book excerpts, essays, general interest, how-to, humor, interview/profile, new product, opinion, personal

experience, photo feature, reviews (film, theater, art exhibits, video, music, other media), travel, medical news. **Buys 120 mss/year.** Query with published clips. Length: 800-4,800 words. **Pays $250-2,500 for feature articles and cover stories; $50-150 for reviews.** Sometimes pays expenses of writers on assignment.

**Photos:** State availability of photos with submission. Reviews contact sheets, transparencies (up to 4×5), prints (5×7 to 8×10) Offers $50-500/photo. Captions, model releases, identification of subjects required. Buys one-time rights.

**Columns/Departments:** The Culture of AIDS (reviews of books, music, film), 800 words; Viewpoint (personal opinion), 900-1,500 words; MediaWatch (mass media opinion), 800-1,200 words. **Buys 100 mss/year.** Send complete ms. **Pays $100-250.**

**Fiction:** Unpublished work only. Send complete ms. Length: 5,000 words maximum (2,500-4,000 words preferred). **Pays $150-500.**

**Poetry:** Any length/style (shorter works preferred). **Pays $75-150.**

**N $ $ BORDERLINES**, Borderlines Magazine Soc., 400 Dovercourt Rd., Toronto M6J 3E7 Canada. Fax: (416)534-2301. E-mail: borderln@idirect.com. Managing Editor: J. Jenkinson. **Contact:** S. Fogel. **70% freelance written.** Quarterly magazine. "We are a leading edge arts/culture publication, especially interested in voices underrepresented in mainstream media." Estab. 1984. Circ. 3,000. Pays on publication. Publishes ms an average of 4 months after acceptance. Buys simultaneous rights. Editorial lead time 2 months. Accepts queries by mail, e-mail, fax. Reports in 4 months. Sample copy for $5.

**Nonfiction:** Essays, reviews. **Buys 10 mss/year.** Query or send ms. Length: 1,000-2,500 words. **Pays $100-300.**

**Photos:** Send photos with submission.

**Columns/Departments: Pays $100-300.**

**Fiction:** Experimental, novel excerpts. **Buys 5 mss/year.** Length: 1,000-2,500 words. **Pays $100-300.**

**N BOSTON REVIEW**, E53-407, M.I.T., Cambridge MA 02139. (617)253-3642. E-mail: bostonreview@mit.edu. Website: http://www.bostonreview.mit.edu. Editor: Josh Cohen. **Contact:** Jefferson Decker, managing editor. **90% freelance written.** Bimonthly magazine of cultural and political analysis, reviews, fiction and poetry. "The editors are committed to a society and culture that foster human diversity and a democracy in which we seek common grounds of principle amidst our many differences. In the hope of advancing these ideals, the *Review* acts as a forum that seeks to enrich the language of public debate." Estab. 1975. Circ. 20,000. Publishes ms an average of 3 months after acceptance. Byline given. Buys first American serial rights. Reports in 6 months. Sample copy $5 or on website. Writer's guidelines for #10 SASE or on website.

● The Boston Review also offers a poetry contest. See Contests & Awards/Poetry section.

**Nonfiction:** Critical essays and reviews. Query with clips. "We do not accept unsolicited book reviews: if you would like to be considered for review assignments, please send your résumé along with several published clips." **Buys 125 mss/year.**

**Fiction:** Jodi Daynard, fiction editor. "I'm looking for stories that are emotionally and intellectually substantive and also interesting on the level of language. Things that are shocking, dark, lewd, comic, or even insane are fine so long as the fiction is *controlled* and purposeful in a masterly way. Subtlety, delicacy and lyricism are attractive too." **Buys 8 mss/year.** Length: 1,200-5,000 words.

**Poetry:** Mary Jo Bang and Timothy Donnelly, poetry editors.

**N $ $ BRUTARIAN, The Magazine That Dares To Be**, Box 25222, Arlington VA 22202. E-mail: brutarian1@juno.com. **Contact:** Dominick Salemi, editor. **100% freelance written.** Quarterly magazine covering popular and unpopular culture. "A healthy knowledge of the great works of antiquity and an equally healthy contempt for most of what passes today as culture." Estab. 1991. Circ. 3,000. Pays on publication. Publishes ms an average of 3 months after acceptance. Byline given. Buys first or one-time rights. Editorial lead time 2 months. Submit seasonal material 6 months in advance. Reports in 1 week on queries; 2 months on mss. Sample copy for $6.

○ Break in with an interview with an up-and-coming rock band, film actor/actress or director or popular writer.

**Nonfiction:** Book excerpts, essays, exposé, general interest, humor, interview/profile, reviews of books, film and music. **Buys 10-20 feature articles/year.** Send complete ms. Length: 1,000-10,000 words. **Pays $100-400.** Sometimes pays expenses of writers on assignment.

**Reprints:** Send typed ms with rights for sale noted and information about when and where the article previously appeared. Pays 50% of amount paid for an original article.

**Photos:** State availability of photos with submission. Reviews contact sheets. Offers no additional payment for photos accepted with ms. Caption, model releases, identification of subjects required. Buys one-time rights.

**Columns/Departments:** Celluloid Void (critiques of cult and obscure films), 500-1,000 words; Brut Library (critiques of books), 500-1,000 words; Audio Depravation (short critiques of odd, R&B, jazz and R&R music), 50-100 words. **Buys "hundreds" of mss/year.** Send complete ms. **Pays $5-100.**

**Fiction:** Adventure, confession, erotica, experimental, fantasy, horror, humorous, mystery, novel excerpts, suspense. **Buys 8-10 mss/year.** Send complete ms. Length: 1,000-10,000 words. **Pays $100-500**, 10¢/word for established writers. Publishes novel excerpts.

**Poetry:** Avant-garde, free verse, traditional. **Buys 10-15 poems/year.** Submit maximum 3 poems. Length: 25-1,000 lines. **Pays $20-200.**

**Tips:** "Send résumé with completed manuscript. Avoid dry tone and excessive scholasticism. Do not cover topics or issues which have been done to death unless you have a fresh approach or new insights on the subject."

◪ $**CAFE EIGHTIES MAGAZINE, The Perfect Blend of Yesterday's Grinds and What's Brewing in Your Mind Today**, 1562 First Ave., Suite 180, New York NY 10028. (212)570-5599. Fax: (212)861-0588. E-mail: kim@cafe80s.com. Website: http://www.cafe80s.com. **Contact:** Kimberly Brittingham, publisher/editor-in-chief. **90% freelance written.** Quarterly magazine. *"Cafe Eighties* is created by and for the mini-generation that 'came of age' in the early-to-mid 1980s. We want our stories to be told. We want *Cafe Eighties* to serve as a forum, a scrapbook, a storybook, a historical reference and an all-encompassing diary of who we are and the events and trends that lead us into today." Estab. 1993. Circ. 2,500. Pays on publication. Publishes ms 1 year after acceptance. Byline given. Buys one-time and second serial (reprint) rights and makes work-for-hire assignments. Submit seasonal material 9 months in advance. Accepts queries by mail, e-mail. Accepts simultaneous submissions. Reports in 1 week on queries; 2 months on mss. Sample copy for $5. Writer's guidelines for #10 SASE or on website.

◳ The magazine carries original online content and includes writer's guidelines. Contact: Kimberly Brittingham.

**Nonfiction:** Essays, general interest, humor, interview/profile, new product, opinion, personal experience, photo feature, travel. "No subject matter that does not pertain to a 25-35 readership." **Buys 40 mss/year.** Query. Length: 300-4,000 words. **Pays 3¢/published word plus $20.** Sometimes pays expenses of writers on assignment.
**Reprints:** Accepts previously published submissions.
**Photos:** State availability of photos with submission. Reviews contact sheets. Negotiates payment individually. Identification of subjects required. Buys one-time rights.
**Columns/Departments:** Books; Retro Reviews. **Buys 20 mss/year.** Query. **Pays 3¢/published word plus $20.**
**Fillers:** Facts, gags to be illustrated by cartoonist, short humor. **Buys 20/year. Pays $5-20.**
**Tips:** "Approach us with specific ideas in mind. If you've already put some thought into a potential feature for *Cafe Eighties*, even if you're only bringing us a skeleton of an idea, you're more likely to gain an assignment in the near future. We'll brainstorm with you to develop a project that suits your interests as well as our editorial needs."

$**CANADIAN DIMENSION**, Dimension Publications Inc., 91 Albert St., Room 2-B, Winnipeg, Manitoba, R3B 1G5 Canada. Fax: (204)957-1519. E-mail: info@canadiandimension.mb.ca. Website: http://www.canadiandimension.mb.ca/cd/index.htm. **80% freelance written. Contact:** George Harris. Bimonthly magazine "that makes sense of the world. We bring a socialist perspective to bear on events across Canada and around the world. Our contributors provide in-depth coverage on popular movements, peace, labour, women, aboriginal justice, environment, third world and eastern Europe." Estab. 1963. Circ. 4,000. Pays on publication. Publishes ms an average of 6 months after acceptance. Copyrighted by *CD* after publication. Accepts simultaneous submissions. Reports in 6 weeks on queries. Sample copy for $2. Writer's guidelines for #10 SAE with IRC.
**Nonfiction:** Interview/profile, opinion, reviews, political commentary and analysis, journalistic style. **Buys 8 mss/year.** Length: 500-2,000 words. **Pays $25-100.**
**Reprints:** Sometimes accepts previously published submissions. Send typed ms with rights for sale noted (electronic copies when possible) and information about when and where the article previously appeared.

Ⓝ $**CANNABIS CULTURE**, P.O. Box 15, 199 W. Hastings St.,Vancouver, British Columbia V6B 1H4 Canada. (604)669-9069. Fax: (604)669-9038. E-mail: muggles@cannabisculture.com. Website: http://www.cannabisculture.com. **Contact:** Dana Larsen, editor. **25% freelance written.** Bimonthly magazine covering marijuana and hemp. "Marijuana is good—prohibition is wrong." Estab. 1994. Circ. 35,000. Pays on publication. Publishes ms an average of 4 months after acceptance. Byline given. Offers 50% kill fee. Not copyrighted. Buys first rights or one-time rights and rights for website use. Editorial lead time 2 months. Submit seasonal material 6 months in advance. Accepts queries by mail, e-mail, fax, phone. Accepts simultaneous submissions. Reports in 1 month. Sample copy for $6.
**Nonfiction:** Current events, historical/nostalgic, how-to (grow marijuana), interview/profile, legal and cultural issues, new product, personal experience, travel. "No articles on why pot is good/illegal. We know." **Buys 3-6 mss/year.** Send complete ms. Length: 1,000-4,000 words. **Pays 4¢/word minimum.** Sometimes pays expenses of writers on assignment.
**Reprints:** Send tearsheet of article and information about when and where the article previously appeared. Pays 100% of amount paid for an original article.
**Photos:** Send photos with submission. Reviews prints. Offers $30 minimum, negotiates payment individually. Caption, identification of subjects required. Buys one-time rights.
**Fillers:** Newsbreaks. Length: 50-1,000 words. **Pays 4¢/word.**
**Tips:** "Be obsessed with all things marijuana and hemp. We need timely information and breaking news on cannabis."

◪ $ $**CURIO**, Curio Magazine, Inc., 81 Pondfield Rd., Suite 264, Bronxville NY 10708. (914)961-8649. Fax: (914)779-4033. E-mail: genm20b@prodigy.com. **Contact:** Mickey Z., editor. **80% freelance written.** Quarterly magazine covering politics, art, culture and photography. "Our readers are socially aware and independent with strong opinions and a definite sense of humor." Estab. 1996. Circ. 50,000. Pays on publication. Publishes ms an average of 3 months after acceptance. Byline given. Offers $25 kill fee. Buys first North American serial rights. Editorial lead time 3 months. Submit seasonal material 3 months in advance. Accepts simultaneous submissions. Sample copy for $6. Writer's guidelines for #10 SASE.
**Nonfiction:** Book excerpts, general interest, how-to (i.e., throw a movie punch), humor, interview/profile, new product, opinion, personal experience, travel. **Buys 20 mss/year.** Send complete ms. Length: 300-3,000 words. **Pays $140/page.** Pays writers with contributor copies or other premium for poetry or if specifically negotiated with writer.
**Photos:** "*Curio* offers photographers 6 pages to layout their own work for $300. Photo essay may be approved by art

director." Captions, model releases and identification of subjects required. Buys one-time rights, plus use in future "best of" issues and for publicity, if needed.

**Reprints:** Send photocopy of article. Pays contributors copy only.

**Columns/Departments:** Interrogation (Q&A interviews); Reviews (film, art, music, television, video, photography, radio, food, restaurants, etc.), 300 words. **Buys 100 mss/year.** Send complete ms. **Pays $105-140/page.**

**Fillers:** Anecdotes, facts, gags to be illustrated by cartoonist, short humor. **Pays $0-25.**

**Tips:** "Send complete manuscript. Don't call us, we will call you. But, if you move, please give us your new address."

**⊠ $ $FIRST THINGS,** Institute on Religion & Public Life, 156 Fifth Ave., Suite 400, New York NY 10010. (212)627-1985. Fax: (212)627-2184. E-mail: ft@firstthings.com. Website: http://www.firstthings.com. **Contact:** James Nuechterlein, editor. Editor-in-Chief: Richard John Neuhaus. Managing Editor: Matthew Berke. Associate Editor: Daniel Moloney. **70% freelance written.** "Intellectual journal published 10 times/year containing social and ethical commentary in broad sense, religious and ethical perspectives on society, culture, law, medicine, church and state, morality and mores." Estab. 1990. Circ. 32,000. Pays on publication. Publishes ms an average of 4 months after acceptance. Byline given. Kill fee varies. Buys all rights. Editorial lead time 2 months. Submit seasonal material 5 months in advance. Reports in 3 months on mss. Sample copy and writer's guidelines for SAE.

**Nonfiction:** Essays, opinion. **Buys 60 mss/year.** Send complete double-spaced ms. Length: 1,500 words for Opinion; 4,000-6,000 words for long articles. **Pays $300-800.** Sometimes pays expenses of writers on assignment.

**Poetry:** Traditional. **Buys 25-30 poems/year.** Length: 4-40 lines. **Pays $50.**

**Tips:** "We prefer complete manuscripts (hard copy, double-spaced) to queries, but will reply if unsure."

**$ $FRANCE TODAY,** FrancePress Inc., 1051 Divisadero St., San Francisco CA 94115. (415)921-5100. Fax: (415)921-0213. E-mail: fpress@francepress.com. Website: http://www.francepress.com. **Contact:** Cara Ballard, editor. **90% freelance written.** Bimonthly tabloid covering contemporary France. "*France Today* is a feature publication on contemporary France including sociocultural analysis, business, trends, current events and travel." Estab. 1989. Circ. 25,000. Pays on publication. Publishes ms an average of 5 months after acceptance. Byline given. Buys first North American and second serial (reprint) rights. Submit seasonal material 4 months in advance. Accepts queries by mail, e-mail, fax. Reports in 3 months. Sample copy for 10×13 SAE with 5 first-class stamps.

**Nonfiction:** Essays, exposé, general interest, historical, humor, interview/profile, personal experience, travel. "No travel pieces about well-known tourist attractions." Special issues: Paris, France on the Move, France On a Budget, Summer Travel, The French Palate, French Around the World, France Adventure. **Buys 50 mss/year.** Query with or without published clips, or send complete ms. Length: 500-2,000 words. **Pays $150-300.**

**Reprints:** Send typed ms with rights for sale noted and information about when and where the article previously appeared. Pay varies.

**Photos:** Offers $25/photo. Identification of subjects required. Buys one-time rights.

**$ $ $HIGH TIMES,** Trans High Corp., 235 Park Ave. S., 5th Floor, New York NY 10003-1405. (212)387-0500. Fax: (212)475-7684. E-mail: hteditor@hightimes.com. Website: http://www.hightimes.com. Publisher: Mike Edison. News Editor: Dean Latimer. **Contact:** Steven Hager, editorial director. **30% freelance written.** Monthly magazine covering marijuana and the counterculture. Estab. 1974. Circ. 250,000. Pays on publication. Byline given. Offers 20% kill fee. Buys one-time or all rights or makes work-for-hire assignments. Submit seasonal material 6 months in advance. Accepts queries by mail, e-mail, fax. Reports in 1 month on queries; 4 months on mss. Sample copy for $5 and #10 SASE. Writer's guidelines for SASE or on website.

**Nonfiction:** Book excerpts, exposé, humor, interview/profile, new product, personal experience, photo feature, travel. **Buys 30 mss/year.** Send complete ms. Length: 2,000-7,000 words. **Pays $300-1,000.** Sometimes pays expenses of writers on assignment.

**Reprints:** Send tearsheet of article or typed ms with rights for sale noted. Pays in ad trade.

**Photos:** Shirley Halperin, photo editor. Send photos with submission. Pays $25-400, $400 for cover photos, $350 for centerfold. Captions, model release, identification of subjects required. Buys all rights or one-time use.

**Columns/Departments:** Steve Bloom, music editor; Chris Simunek, cultivation editor; Steve Wishnia, views editor. Drug related books, news. **Buys 10 mss/year.** Query with published clips. Length: 100-2,000 words. **Pays $25-300.**

**Fillers:** Frank Max, cartoon editor. Gags to be illustrated by cartoonist, newsbreaks, short humor. **Buys 10 mss/year.** Length: 100-500 words. **Pays $10-50.**

**Tips:** "Although promoting the legalization and cultivation of medicinal plants, primarily cannabis, is central to our mission, *High Times* does not promote the indiscriminate use of such plants. We are most interested in articles on cannabis cultivation, the history of hemp, the rise of the modern hemp industry, the history of the counterculture and countercultural trends and events. The best way for new writers to break in is through our news section. We are always looking for regional stories involving the Drug War that have national significance. This includes coverage of local legal battles, political controversies, drug testing updates and legalization rally reports. All sections are open to good, professional writers."

**⊠ $IMPLOSION, A Journal of the Bizarre and Eccentric,** Implosion Publishing, 1921 E. Colonial Dr., Orlando FL 32803. (407)898-5573. E-mail: info@implosion-mag.com. Website: http://www.implosion-mag.com. **Contact:** Cynthia Conlin, editor. **75% freelance written.** Quarterly magazine. "As the title implies, *Implosion* is a publication devoted to the bizarre. Everything we publish falls into this realm." Estab. 1995. Circ. 22,000. Pays within 30 days of publication. Publishes ms an average of 6 months after acceptance. Byline given. Buys first North American serial rights or one-time rights. Editorial lead time 6 months. Accepts queries by mail, e-mail. Accepts simultaneous submissions. Reports in 1 month on queries; 4 months on mss. Sample copy for $5 or on website. Writer's guidelines for #10 SASE or on website.

**Nonfiction:** Exposé, interview/profile, photo feature, travel, strange. **Buys 30 mss/year.** Send complete ms. Length: 1,000-5,000 words. **Pays $20-100 for assigned articles; $15-50 for unsolicited articles.** Sometimes pays expenses of writers on assignment.

**Photos:** Send photos with submission. Reviews contact sheets, 4×5 transparencies, 4×6 prints. Negotiates payment individually. Captions, model releases and identification of subjects required. Buys one-time rights.

**Columns/Departments:** Book reviews (must be unusual and bizarre), 250-500 words; CD reviews (must be unusual and bizarre), 250-500 words. **Buys 50 mss/year.** Send complete ms. **Pays $10.**

**Fiction:** Experimental, horror, science fiction. "The volume of unsolicited fiction is astronomical. Read the magazine to understand the format." **Buys 15 mss/year.** Send complete ms. Length: 200-5,000 words. **Pays $10-25.**

**Tips:** "We are especially interested in reviewing interviews with odd and eccentric musicians, filmmakers, artists, etc. Also, we have an on-going need for book reviews. We've got more fiction manuscripts than we know what to do with."

**N $ $ $ $ MADISON**, Attic Communications, LLC, 140 W. 57th St., 9th Floor, New York NY 10019. (212)957-0017. Fax: (212)957-0380. E-mail: scohen@madison-magazine.com. Editor: Fred Moore. **Contact:** Scott Lyle Cohen, associate editor. **60% freelance written.** Lifestyle magazine published 8 times/year covering entertainment, art, architecture, fashion, food, design, etc. Estab. 1998. Circ. 275,000. Pays on publication. Publishes ms an average of 3 months after acceptance. Byline given. Not copyrighted. Buys first North American serial rights. Editorial lead time 3 months. Submit seasonal material 4 months in advance. Accepts simultaneous submissions. Reports in 3 weeks on queries; 1 month on mss. Sample copy for $4.95 and SASE with 9 first-class stamps.

**Nonfiction:** Book excerpts and reviews, essays, exposé, general interest, humor, interview/profile, personal experience, photo feature, travel, design, architecture, food. No how-to, self-help, service. Query with published clips. Length: 1,000-4,000 words. **Pays $500-1,750, open to negotiation.**

**Photos:** State availability of photos with submission. Reviews contact sheets. Negotiates payment individually. Buys one-time rights.

**Fiction:** Adventure, condensed novels, humorous, novel excerpts, serialized novels. Query with published clips. Length: 500-1,750. **Pays $500-1,750.**

**Tips:** "Understand fully our voice. We publish intelligent, encompassing works that speak to a reader of a like mindset. Be creative. Break the rules."

**$ NEW HAVEN ADVOCATE, News & Arts Weekly**, New Mass Media Inc., 1 Long Wharf Dr., New Haven CT 06511-5991. (203)789-0010. Fax: (203)787-1418. E-mail: editor@newhavenadvocate.com. Website: http://www.ne whavenadvocate.com. **Contact:** Joshua Mamis, editor. **10% freelance written.** Weekly tabloid. "Alternative, investigative, cultural reporting with a strong voice. We like to shake things up." Estab. 1975. Circ. 55,000. Pays on publication. Byline given. Buys on speculation. Buys one-time rights. Editorial lead time 1 month. Submit seasonal material 2 months in advance. Accepts simultaneous submissions. Reports in 1 month.

**Nonfiction:** Book excerpts, essays, exposé, general interest, humor, interview/profile. **Buys 15-20 mss/year.** Query with published clips. Length: 750-2,000 words. **Pays $50-150.** Sometimes pays expenses of writers on assignment.

**Photos:** State availability of photos with submission. Captions, model releases, identification of subjects required. Buys one-time rights.

**Tips:** "Strong local focus; strong literary voice, controversial, easy-reading, contemporary, etc."

**N $ $ $ NOTORIOUS, People Breaking the Rules**, Notorious Entertainment LLC, 37 E. 28th St., Suite 906, New York NY 10016. Fax: (212)685-7831. E-mail: feedback@notorious.com. Executive Editor: Scott Baldinger. **Contact:** Scott or Alex. **30% freelance written.** Bimonthly magazine covering "people breaking the rules and changing the world," a lifestyle/profile magazine, young and hip, multicultural upstarts. *Notorious* magazine has been editorially redefined—presenting innovative people who are changing the world with their unique brand of individuality. Its mission is to inform and inspire, to educate and elevate the infinite range of individual possibility. *Notorious'* new direction will include interviews with celebrities who reveal their fears in creating their identity, profiles of unknown upstarts, and lavish travel and fashion layouts. Investigative features will explore cautionary tales of individuals who take their dreams to the breaking point. *Notorious* is for everyone who wants to live a sexy, daring life, a life that makes a difference." Estab. 1997; relaunched 1999. Circ. 200,000. Pays on publication. Publishes ms an average of 2 months after acceptance. Byline given. Offers 25% kill fee. Buys all rights. Editorial lead time 3-4 months. Submit seasonal material 3 months in advance. Accepts queries by mail, fax. Reports in 1 month on queries; 2 months on mss.

**Nonfiction:** Essays, exposé, general interest, humor, interview/profile, opinion, photo feature, travel. Query. Length: 500-5,000 words. **Pays $250-2,000 for assigned articles; $100-1,000 for unsolicited articles.** Sometimes pays expenses of writers on assignment.

**Photos:** State availability of photos with submission.

**Columns/Departments:** Contact: Scott Baldinger, executive editor. Notorious People, 200-400 words. The Good Life, (500 words). Query with or without published clips. **Pays $100-500.**

**$ $ $ $** **ROLLING STONE**, Wenner Media Inc., 1290 Avenue of the Americas, New York NY 10104. (212)484-1616. This magazine did not respond to our request for information. Query before submitting.

**UTNE READER**, 1624 Harmon Place, Suite 330, Minneapolis MN 55403. (612)338-5040. Fax: (612)338-6043. E-mail: editor@utne.com. Website: http://www.utne.com. **Contact:** Craig Cox, managing editor. Accepts queries by mail, e-mail, phone, fax.
   ● The *Utne Reader* has been a finalist three times for the National Magazine Award for general excellence.
**Reprints:** Accepts previously published submissions. Send tearsheet or photocopy of article or typed ms with rights for sale noted and information about when and where the article previously appeared.
   O→ Break in with submissions for 'New Planet.'
**Tips:** "State the theme(s) clearly, let the narrative flow, and build the story around strong characters and a vivid sense of place. Give us rounded episodes, logically arranged."

**$** **YES! A Journal of Positive Futures**, Positive Futures Network, P.O. Box 10818, Bainbridge Island WA 98110. (206)842-0216. Fax: (206)842-5208. E-mail: editors@futurenet.org. Website: http://www.futurenet.org. Editor: Sarah van Gelder. **Contact:** Tracy Rysavy, associate editor. Quarterly magazine emphasizing sustainability and community. "Interested in stories on building a positive future: sustainability, overcoming divisiveness, ethical business practices, etc." Estab. 1996. Circ. 14,000. Pays on publication. Byline given. Buys various rights. Editorial lead time 4 months. Accepts queries by mail, e-mail, fax. Accepts simultaneous submissions. Reports in 6 months on mss; 1 month on queries. Free sample copy or on website. Writer's guidelines for #10 SASE or on website.
**Nonfiction:** Book excerpts, essays, how-to, humor, interview/profile, personal experience, photo feature, technical, environmental. "No negativity or blanket prescriptions for changing the world." Query with published clips. "Please contact us for a detailed call for submission before each issue." Length: 200-3,500 words. Pays writers with 1-year subscription and 2 contributor copies. **Pays $20-50 (negotiable).** Sometimes pays expenses of writers on assignment.
**Reprints:** Send photocopy of article or typed ms with rights for sale noted and information about when and where the article previously appeared. Pays 100% of amount paid for an original article.
**Photos:** State availability of photos with submission. Reviews contact sheets, negatives, transparencies and prints. Offers $20-75/photo. Identification of subjects required. Buys one-time rights.
**Columns/Departments:** Query with published clips. **Pays $20-60.**
**Poetry:** Avant-garde, free verse, haiku, light verse, traditional. **Buys 2-3 poems/year.** Submit maximum 10 poems.
**Tips:** "Read and become familiar with the publication's purpose, tone and quality. We are about facilitating the creation of a better world. We are looking for writers who want to participate in that process. *Yes!* is less interested in bemoaning the state of our problems and more interested in highlighting promising solutions. We are highly unlikely to accept submissions that simply state the author's opinion on what needs to be fixed and why. Our readers know *why* we need to move towards sustainability; they are interested in *how* to do so."

# DETECTIVE & CRIME

Fans of detective stories want to read accounts of actual criminal cases, detective work and espionage. Markets specializing in crime fiction are listed under Mystery publications.

**$ $** **DETECTIVE CASES**, Detective Files Group, Globe Communications Corp., 1350 Sherbrooke St. West, Suite 600, Montreal, Quebec H3G 2T4 Canada. (514)849-7733. **Contact:** Dominick A. Merle, editor-in-chief. Bimonthly magazine. See *Detective Files*.

**$ $** **DETECTIVE DRAGNET**, Detective Files Group, Globe Communications Corp., 1350 Sherbrooke St. West, Suite 600, Montreal, Quebec H3G 2T4 Canada. (514)849-7733. **Contact:** Dominick A. Merle, editor-in-chief. Bimonthly 72-page magazine. See *Detective Files*.

**$ $** **DETECTIVE FILES**, Detective Files Group, Globe Communications Corp., 1350 Sherbrooke St. West, Suite 600, Montreal, Quebec H3G 2T4 Canada. (514)849-7733. **Contact:** Dominick A. Merle, editor-in-chief. **100% freelance written.** Bimonthly magazine featuring "narrative accounts of true murder mysteries leading to arrests and convictions." **Pays on acceptance.** Publishes ms an average of 6 months after acceptance. Byline given. Buys all rights. Reports in 2 weeks on queries; 2 months on mss. Sample copy and writer's guidelines for SASE.
**Nonfiction:** True crime cases only; no fiction. Query. Length: 3,000-6,000 words. **Pays $250-350.**
**Photos:** Send photos with submission. Offers no additional payment for photos accepted with ms. Captions, identification of subjects required. Buys all rights.
**Tips:** "Build suspense and police investigation leading to arrest. No smoking gun or open and shut cases. Neatness, clarity and pace will help you make the sale."

**$ $** **HEADQUARTERS DETECTIVE**, Detective Files Group, Globe Communications Corp., 1350 Sherbrooke St. West, Suite 600, Montreal, Quebec H3G 2T4 Canada. (514)849-7733. **Contact:** Dominick A. Merle, editor-in-chief. Bimonthly magazine; 72 pages. See *Detective Files*.

**$ P. I. MAGAZINE, America's Private Investigation Journal**, 755 Bronx, Toledo OH 43609. (419)382-0967. Fax: (419)382-0967. E-mail: pimag1@aol.com. Website: http://www.PIMALL.com. **Contact:** Bob Mackowiak, editor/publisher. **75% freelance written.** "Audience includes professional investigators and mystery/private eye fans." Estab. 1988. Circ. 5,200. Pays on publication. Publishes ms an average of 3 months after acceptance. Buys one-time rights. Submit seasonal material 3 months in advance. Accepts simultaneous submissions. Reports in 3 months on queries; 4 months on mss. Sample copy for $6.75.

**Nonfiction:** Interview/profile, personal experience and accounts of real cases. **Buys 4-10 mss/year.** Send complete ms. Length: 1,000 words and up. **Pays $75 minimum for unsolicited articles.**

**Photos:** Send photos with submission. May offer additional payment for photos accepted with ms. Model releases, identification of subjects required. Buys one-time rights.

**Tips:** "The best way to get published in *P.I.* is to write a detailed story about a professional P.I.'s true-life case. No fiction, please. Unsolicited fiction manuscripts will not be returned."

**$ $ STARTLING DETECTIVE**, Detective Files Group, Globe Communications Corp., 1350 Sherbrooke St. West, Suite 600, Montreal, Quebec H3G 2T4 Canada. (514)849-7733. **Contact:** Dominick A. Merle, editor-in-chief. Bimonthly 72-page magazine. See *Detective Files.*

**$ $ TRUE POLICE CASES**, Detective Files Group, Globe Communications Corp., 1350 Sherbrooke St. West, Suite 600, Montreal, Quebec H3G 2T4 Canada. (514)849-7733. **Contact:** Dominick A. Merle, editor-in-chief. Bimonthly 72-page magazine. Buys all rights. See *Detective Files.*

# DISABILITIES

These magazines are geared toward disabled persons and those who care for or teach them. A knowledge of disabilities and lifestyles is important for writers trying to break in to this field; editors regularly discard material that does not have a realistic focus. Some of these magazines will accept manuscripts only from disabled persons or those with a background in caring for disabled persons.

**N $ $ ABILITIES, Canada's Lifestyle Magazine for People with Disabilities**, Canadian Abilities Foundation, #501-489 College St., Toronto, Ontario M6G 1A5, Canada. (416)923-1885. Fax: (416)923-9829. E-mail: able@inte rlog.com. Website: http://indie.ca/abilities/. Editor: Raymond Cohen. **Contact:** Lisa Bendall, managing editor. **50% freelance written.** Quarterly magazine covering disability issues. "*Abilities* provides information, inspiration and opportunity to its readers with articles and resources covering health, travel, sports, products, technology, profiles, employment, recreation and more." Estab. 1987. Circ. 50,000. Pays on publication. Publishes ms an average of 3 months after acceptance. Byline given. Offers 50% kill fee. Buys first rights. Editorial lead time 3 months. Submit seasonal material 4 months in advance. Accepts queries by mail, e-mail, fax. Reports in 3 months. Sample copy free. Writer's guidelines for #10 SASE, on website or by e-mail.

**Nonfiction:** Book excerpts, general interest, how-to, humor, inspirational, interview/profile, new product, opinion, personal experience, photo feature, travel. Does not want "articles that 'preach to the converted'—contain info that people with disabilities likely already know, such as what it's like to have a disability." **Buys 30-40 mss/year.** Query or send complete ms. Length: 500-2,500 words. **Pays $50-400 (Canadian) for assigned articles; $50-300 (Canadian) for unsolicited articles.**

**Reprints:** Sometimes accepts previously published submissions (if stated as such).

**Photos:** State availability of photos with submission.

**Columns/Departments:** The Lighter Side (humor), 600 words. Profile, 1,200 words.

**Tips:** "Do not contact by phone—send something in writing. Send a great idea that we haven't done before and make a case for why you'd be able to do a good job with it. Be sure to include a relevant writing sample."

**$ $ ACCENT ON LIVING**, P.O. Box 700, Bloomington IL 61702-0700. (309)378-2961. Fax: (309)378-4420. E-mail: acntlvng@aol.com. Website: http://www.blvd.com/accent. **Contact:** Betty Garee, editor. **75% freelance written.** Eager to work with new/unpublished writers. Quarterly magazine for physically disabled persons and rehabilitation professionals. Estab. 1956. Circ. 20,000. Buys first and second (reprint) rights. Byline usually given. Pays on publication. Publishes ms an average of 6 months after acceptance. Accepts queries by mail, e-mail, fax, phone. Reports in 1 month. Sample copy and writer's guidelines for $3.50 and #10 SAE with 7 first-class stamps. Writer's guidelines for #10 SASE.

**Nonfiction:** Articles about new devices that would make a disabled person with limited physical mobility more independent; should include description, availability and photos. Medical breakthroughs for disabled people. Intelligent discussion articles on acceptance of physically disabled persons in normal living situations; topics may be architectural barriers, housing, transportation, educational or job opportunities, organizations, or other areas. How-to articles concerning everyday living, giving specific, helpful information so the reader can carry out the idea himself/herself. News articles about active disabled persons or groups. Good strong interviews. Vacations, accessible places to go, sports, organizations, humorous incidents, self-improvement and sexual or personal adjustment—all related to physically handicapped persons. "We are looking for upbeat material." **Buys 50-60 unsolicited mss/year.** Query with SASE. Length: 250-1,000 words. **Pays 10¢/word for published articles** (after editing and/or condensing by staff).

**Reprints:** Send tearsheet and information about when and where the article previously appeared. Pays 10¢/word.

**Photos:** Pays $10 minimum for b&w photos purchased with accompanying captions. Amount will depend on quality of photos and subject matter. Pays $50 and up for four-color cover photos. "We need good-quality color or b&w photos (or slides and transparencies)."

**Tips:** "Ask a friend who is disabled to read your article before sending it to *Accent*. Make sure that he/she understands your major points and the sequence or procedure."

**$ $ ACTIVE LIVING**, Disability Today Publishing Group, Inc., 132 Main St. E., Suite 1, Grimsby, Ontario L3M 1P1 Canada. (905)309-1639. Fax: (905)309-1640. E-mail: activliv@aol.com. **Contact:** Theresa MacInnis, managing editor. **70% freelance written.** Bimonthly magazine. "*Active Living* is about how to improve health, fitness and mobility, where to enjoy accessible leisure and travel, and what to look for in new therapeutic, recreational and/or sporting activities for people with a disability." Estab. 1990. Circ. 75,000. Pays on publication. Publishes ms an average of 3 months after acceptance. Byline given. Buys one-time or second serial (reprint) rights. Editorial lead time 3 months. Submit seasonal material 6 months in advance. Accepts queries by mail, e-mail, fax. Sample copy $5.50. Writer's guidelines for #10 SAE and IRC.

**Nonfiction:** Health and fitness, inspirational, interview/profile, new product, personal experience, photo feature, recreation, travel. Annual features: O&P feature section (February); Kids (December). **Buys 12 mss/year.** Query with SAE and IRC. Length: 1,000-1,500 words. **Pays 18¢/word.**

**Reprints:** Send tearsheet, photocopy or typed ms on disk with rights for sale noted and information about when and where the article previously appeared. Pay negotible.

**Photos:** Send photos with submission. Reviews 4×6 prints. Offers no additional payment for photos accepted with ms. Model releases and identification of subjects required. Buys one-time rights.

**Columns/Departments:** Sports (disabled sports), 800 words; Alternative Therapies, 600 words; Destinations (travel), 600 words; Nutrition, 600 words; Take Note (news), include 5-6 items of 200-300 words. Health; Fitness; Getting Started; O&P (orthotics & prosthetics); Ask the Experts; 750 words. **Buys 24 mss/year.** Query. **Pays 18¢/word.**

**Fiction:** Occasionally publishes novel excerpts.

**Tips:** "Write on how to improve health, fitness or how to play/adapt a sport. Provide outline for a series of contributions; identify experience in field of disability. Unsolicited manuscripts and photos will not be returned. No phone queries. Please avoid labeling or use of disparaging language like 'the disabled,' confined, crippled."

**$ $ $ $ ARTHRITIS TODAY**, Arthritis Foundation. 1330 W. Peachtree St., Atlanta GA 30309. (404)872-7100. Fax: (404)872-9559. E-mail: atmail@arthritis.org. Website: http://www.arthritis.org. Editor: Cindy T. McDaniel. Managing Editor: Shannon Wilder. Executive Editor: Marcy O'Koon. **Contact:** Michele Taylor, editorial coordinator. **50% freelance written.** Bimonthly magazine about living with arthritis; latest in research/treatment. "*Arthritis Today* is written for the more than 43 million Americans who have arthritis and for the millions of others whose lives are touched by an arthritis-related disease. The editorial content is designed to help the person with arthritis live a more productive, independent and painfree life. The articles are upbeat and provide practical advice, information and inspiration." Estab. 1987. Circ. 600,000. **Pays on acceptance.** Offers 25% kill fee. Buys first North American serial rights but requires unlimited reprint rights in any Arthritis Foundation-affiliated endeavor. Editorial lead time 6 months. Submit seasonal material 6 months in advance. Accepts queries by mail, e-mail, fax. Considers simultaneous submissions. Reports in 2 months. Sample copy for 9×11 SAE with 4 first-class stamps. Writer's guidelines for #10 SASE.

● Ranked as one of the best markets for freelance writers in *Writer's Yearbook* magazine's annual "Top 100 Markets," January 1999.

**Nonfiction:** General interest, how-to (tips on any aspect of living with arthritis), service, inspirational, opinion, personal experience, photo feature, technical, nutrition, general health and lifestyle. **Buys 60-70 unsolicited mss/year.** Query with published clips or send complete ms. Length: 150-2,000 words. **Pays $150-2,000.** Pays expenses of writers on assignment.

**Photos:** Send photos with submission. Reviews prints. Negotiates payment individually. Identification of subjects required. Buys one-time rights.

**Columns/Departments:** Research Spotlight (research news about arthritis); LifeStyle (travel, leisure), 100-300 words; Well Being (arthritis-specific medical news), 100-300 words; Hero (personal profile of people with arthritis), 100-300 words. **Buys 10 mss/year.** Query with published clips. **Pays $150-300.**

**Fillers:** Facts, gags to be illustrated by cartoonist, short humor. **Buys 10/year.** Length: 40-100 words. **Pays $80-150.**

**Tips:** "Our readers are already well-informed. We need ideas and writers that give in-depth, fresh, interesting information that truly adds to their understanding of their condition and their quality of life. Quality writers are more important than good ideas. The staff generates many of our ideas but needs experienced, talented writers who are good reporters to execute them. Please provide published clips. In addition to articles specifically about living with arthritis, we look for articles to appeal to an older audience on subjects such as hobbies, general health, lifestyle, etc."

**$ $ ASTHMA MAGAZINE, Strategies For Taking Control**, Lifelong Publications, 3 Bridge St., Newton MA 02158. (617)964-4910. Fax: (617)964-8095. E-mail: asthmamag@aol.com. **Contact:** Rachel Butler, editor-in-chief. **50% freelance written.** Bimonthly. "*Asthma Magazine* offers unbiased education for people with asthma. We are an independent publication (not sponsored by any drug company) and we provide indepth education to help the asthmatic manage his/her disease and live an active and healthy life." Estab. 1995. Circ. 100,000. Pays on publication. Publishes ms an average of 1 month after acceptance. Byline given. Offers 25% kill fee. Buys all rights. Editorial lead time 6 weeks. Submit seasonal material 3 months in advance. Accepts queries by mail, e-mail, fax, phone. Sample copy and writer's guidelines free.

**Nonfiction: Buys 4 features/issue.** How-to, inspirational, interview/profile, new product (usually a news blurb, not a full article), personal experience, technical, travel—all related to the subject matter. **Buys 12-15 mss/year.** Query with published clips. Length: 800-1,200 words. **Pays $200-500.**

**Photos:** State availability of photos with submission. Reviews prints. Offers no additional payment for photos accepted with ms. Buys all rights.

**Columns/Departments:** Hear My Story (personal experience of a person with asthma or article about someone who has accomplished something significant despite their asthma, or someone in the asthma/medical field); 900 words. Query with published clips. **Pays $250.**

**Tips:** "We look for writers who have had experience writing for the medical community for either clinicians or patients. Writing must be clear, concise and easy to understand (7th-9th grade reading level), as well as thoroughly researched and medically accurate."

**$ $ CAREERS & the disABLED**, Equal Opportunity Publications, 1160 E. Jericho Turnpike, Suite 200, Huntington NY 11743. (516)421-9421. Fax: (516)421-0359. E-mail: info@aol.com. Website: http://www.eop.com. **Contact:** James Schneider, editor. **60% freelance written.** Quarterly magazine "offers role-model profiles and career guidance articles geared toward disabled college students and professionals and promotes personal and professional growth." Pays on publication. Publishes ms an average of 6 months after acceptance. Estab. 1967. Circ. 10,000. Byline given. Buys first North American serial rights. Editorial lead time 6 months. Submit seasonal material 6 months in advance. Accepts simultaneous submissions. Reports in 3 weeks. Sample copy and writer's guidelines for 9×12 SAE with 5 first-class stamps.

**Nonfiction:** Essays, general interest, how-to, interview/profile, new product, opinion, personal experience. **Buys 30 mss/year.** Query. Length: 1,000-2,500 words. **Pays 10¢/word, $350 maximum.** Sometimes pays the expenses of writers on assignment.

**Reprints:** Send information about when and where the article previously appeared.

**Photos:** State availability of or send photos with submission. Reviews transparencies, prints. Offers $15-50/photo. Captions, identification of subjects required. Buys one-time rights.

**Tips:** "Be as targeted as possible. Role model profiles and specific career guidance strategies that offer advice to disabled college students are most needed."

**N $ DIABETES INTERVIEW**, Kings Publishing, 3715 Balboa St., San Francisco CA 94121. (415)387-4002. Fax: (415)387-3604. E-mail: daniel@diabetesworld.com or sharon@diabetesworld.com. Website: http://www.diabetesworld.com. **Contact:** Sharon Kellaher or Daniel Trecroci, editors. Managing Editor: Melissa Settlay. **40% freelance written.** Monthly tabloid covering diabetes care. "*Diabetes Interview* covers the latest in diabetes care, medications and patient advocacy. Personal accounts are welcome as well as medical-oriented articles by MDs, RNs and CDEs (certified diabetes educators)." Estab. 1991. Circ. 40,000. Pays on publication. Publishes ms 2 months after acceptance. Byline given. Buys all rights. Editorial lead time 2 months. Submit seasonal material 2 months in advance. Accepts queries by mail, e-mail, fax, phone. Sample copy on website and writer's guidelines free.

**Nonfiction:** Essays, how-to, inspirational, interview/profile, new product, opinion, personal experience. **Buys 25 mss/year. Pays $50 for smaller articles, $150 for features.**

**Reprints:** Accepts previously published submissions.

**Photos:** State availability or send photos with submission. Negotiates payment individually.

**Tips:** "Be actively involved in the diabetes community or have diabetes. However, writers need not have diabetes to write an article, but it must be diabetes-related."

**$ $ DIABETES SELF-MANAGEMENT**, R.A. Rapaport Publishing, Inc., 150 W. 22nd St., Suite 800, New York NY 10011-2421. (212)989-0200. Fax: (212)989-4786. E-mail: editor@diabetes-self-mgmt.com. Website: http://www.diabetes-self-mgmt.com. **Contact:** James Hazlett, editor-in-chief. **20% freelance written.** Bimonthly. "We publish how-to health care articles for motivated, intelligent readers who have diabetes and who are actively involved in their own health care management. All articles must have immediate application to their daily living." Estab. 1983. Circ. 415,000. Pays on publication. Publishes ms an average of 3 months after acceptance. Byline given. Offers 20% kill fee. Buys all rights. Submit seasonal material 6 months in advance. Accepts queries by mail, e-mail, fax, phone. Reports in 6 weeks. Sample copy for $3.50 and 9×12 SAE with 6 first-class stamps or on website. Writer's guidelines for #10 SASE.

**Nonfiction:** How-to (exercise, nutrition, diabetes self-care, product surveys), technical (reviews of products available, foods sold by brand name, pharmacology), travel (considerations and prep for people with diabetes). **Buys 10-12 mss/year.** Query with published clips. Length: 1,500-2,500 words. **Pays $400-700 for assigned articles; $200-700 for unsolicited articles.**

**Tips:** "The rule of thumb for any article we publish is that it must be clear, concise, useful, and instructive, and it must have immediate application to the lives of our readers. If your query is accepted, expect heavy editorial supervision."

**$ DIALOGUE**, Blindskills, Inc., P.O. Box 5181, Salem OR 97301-0181. (800)860-4224; (503)581-4224. Fax: (503)581-0178. E-mail: blindskl@teleport.com. Website: http://www.teleport.com/blindskl. **Contact:** Carol M. McCarl, editor. **85% freelance written.** Quarterly journal covering the visually impaired. Estab. 1961. Circ. 1,100. Pays on publication. Publishes ms an average of 8 months after acceptance. Byline given. Buys first rights. Editorial lead time 3 months. Submit seasonal material 3 months in advance. Sample copy $6. Writer's guidelines for #10 SASE.

**Nonfiction:** Essays, general interest, historical/nostalgic, how-to, humor, interview/profile, new product, personal experience. Prefer material by visually impaired writers. No controversial, explicit sex or religious or political topics. **Buys 20 mss/year.** Send complete ms. Length: 500-1,200 words. **Pays $10-35 for assigned articles; $10-25 for unsolicited articles.**

**Reprints:** Send tearsheet or photocopy of article or short story or typed ms with rights for sale noted and information about when and where the article or story previously appeared.

**Columns/Departments:** All material should be relative to blind and visually impaired readers. Careers, 1,000 words; What's New & Where to Get It (resources, new product), 2,500 words; What Do You Do When . . . ? (dealing with sight loss), 1,000 words. **Buys 40 mss/year.** Send complete ms. **Pays $10-25.**

**Fiction:** Adventure, humorous, science fiction, slice-of-life vignettes, first person experiences. Prefer material by visually impaired writers. No controversial, explicit sex. No religious or political. **Buys 6-8 mss/year.** Query with complete ms. Length: 800-1,200 words. **Pays $15-25.**

**Poetry:** Free verse, light verse, traditional. Prefer material by visually impaired writers. No controversial, explicit sex or religious or political topics. **Buys 15-20 poems/year.** Submit maximum 5 poems. Length: 20 lines maximum. **Pays $10-15.**

**Fillers:** Anecdotes, facts, newsbreaks, short humor. Length: 50-150 words. No payment.

**Tips:** Send SASE for free writers guidelines, $6 for sample in Braille, cassette or large print.

**$ $ HEARING HEALTH**, Voice International Publications, Inc., P.O. Drawer V, Ingleside TX 78362-0500. Fax: (512)776-3278. E-mail: ears2u@hearinghealthmag.com. Website: http://www.hearinghealthmag.com. **Contact:** Paula Bonillas, editor. **20% freelance written.** Bimonthly magazine covering issues and concerns pertaining to hearing and hearing loss. Estab. 1984. Circ. 20,000. Pays on publication. Byline given. Buys one-time rights. Editorial lead time 2 months. Submit seasonal material 4 months in advance. Accepts queries by mail, fax. Accepts simultaneous submissions. Reports in 6 weeks on queries; 2 months on mss. Sample copy for $2 or on website. Writer's guidelines for #10 SASE.

**Nonfiction:** Books excerpts, essays, exposé, general interest, historical/nostalgic, humor, inspirational, interview/profile, new product, opinion, personal experience, photo feature, technical, travel. No self-pitying over loss of hearing. Query with published clips. Length: 500-2,000 words. **Pays $75-200.** Sometimes pays expenses of writers on assignment.

**Reprints:** Accepts previously published submissions, if so noted.

**Photos:** State availability of photos with submission. Reviews contact sheets. Negotiates payment individually. Captions, model releases, identification of subjects required. Buys one-time rights.

**Columns/Departments:** Kidink (written by kids with hearing loss), 300 words; People (shares stories of successful, everyday people who have loss of hearing), 300-400 words. **Buys 2 mss/year.** Query with published clips.

**Fiction:** Fantasy, historical, humorous, novel excerpts, science fiction. **Buys 2 mss/year.** Query with published clips. Length: 400-1,500 words.

**Poetry:** Avant-garde, free verse, light verse, traditional. **Buys 2/year.** Submit 2 poems max. Length: 4-50 lines.

**Fillers:** Anecdotes, facts, gags to be illustrated, newsbreaks, short humor. **Buys 6/year.** Length: 25-1,500 words.

**Tips:** "We look for fresh stories, usually factual but occasionally fictitious, about coping with hearing loss. A positive attitude is a must for *Hearing Health.* Unless one has some experience with deafness or hearing loss—whether their own or a loved one's—it's very difficult to 'break in' to our publication. Experience brings about the empathy and understanding—the sensitivity—and the freedom to write humorously about any handicap or disability."

**$ KALEIDOSCOPE: International Magazine of Literature, Fine Arts, and Disability**, Kaleidoscope Press, 701 S. Main St., Akron OH 44311-1019. (330)762-9755. Fax: (330)762-0912. **Contact:** Gail Willmott, senior editor. Subscribers include individuals, agencies and organizations that assist people with disabilities and many university and public libraries. Estab. 1979. Circ. 1,500. **75% freelance written.** Semiannual. Byline given. Rights return to author upon publication. Eager to work with new/unpublished writers; appreciates work by established writers as well. Especially interested in work by writers with a disability, but features writers both with and without disabilities. "Writers without a disability must limit themselves to our focus, while those with a disability may explore any topic (although we prefer original perspectives about experiences with disability)." Accepts queries by mail, fax. Reports in 3 weeks, acceptance or rejection may take 6 months. Sample copy for $4 prepaid. Guidelines free for SASE.

**Nonfiction:** Personal experience essays, book reviews and articles related to disability. Special issues: The Created Environment (January, deadline August); Disability and Memoir/Biography (July, deadline March). Submit photocopies with SASE for return of work. Please type submissions. All submissions should be accompanied by an autobiographical sketch. May include art or photos that enhance works, prefer b&w with high contrast. **Publishes 8-14 mss/year.** Maximum 5,000 words. **Pays $10-125 plus 2 copies.**

**Reprints:** Send typed ms with rights for sale noted and information about when and where the article previously appeared. Publishes novel excerpts.

**Fiction:** Short stories, novel excerpts. Traditional and experimental styles. Works should explore experiences with disability. Use people-first language. Maximum 5,000 words.

**Poetry:** Limit 5 poems/submission. **Publishes 12-20 poems/year.** Do not get caught up in rhyme scheme. High quality with strong imagery and evocative language. Reviews any style.

**Tips:** "Inquire about future themes of upcoming issues. Sample copy very helpful. Works should not use stereotyping, patronizing or offending language about disability. We seek fresh imagery and thought-provoking language."

**N** **$ $ $ MIRACLES**, McMurry Publishing, 1010 E. Missouri, Phoenix AZ 85014. Fax: (602)395-5853. **Contact:** Stephanie Thurrott, editor. **80% freelance written.** Triannual magazine covering the Children's Miracle Network. *"Miracles* is a magazine custom published for the Children's Miracle Network, a nonprofit organization that raises money to help sick and injured children." Estab. 1997. Circ. 75,000. **Pays on acceptance.** Byline sometimes given. Offers 20% kill fee. Buys all rights. Editorial lead time 6 months. Sample copy for 11×13 SAE with 10 first-class stamps.
**Nonfiction:** General interest, how-to, inspirational, interview/profile. **Buys 20 mss/year.** Query with published clips. Length: 100-1,800 words. **Pays 50¢/word.** Sometimes pays expenses of writers on assignment.
**Photos:** State availability of photos with submission. Negotiates payment individually. Captions, model releases and identification of subjects required.

# ENTERTAINMENT

This category's publications cover live, filmed or videotaped entertainment, including home video, TV, dance, theater and adult entertainment. In addition to celebrity interviews, most publications want solid reporting on trends and upcoming productions. Magazines in the Contemporary Culture and General Interest sections also use articles on entertainment. For those publications with an emphasis on music and musicians, see the Music section.

**$ $ ANGLOFILE, British Entertainment & Pop Culture**, The Goody Press, P.O. Box 33515, Decatur GA 30033. (404)633-5587. Fax: (404)321-3109. **Contact:** William P. King, editor. Managing Editor: Leslie T. King. **15% freelance written.** Monthly newsletter. "News and interviews on British entertainment, past and present, from an American point of view." Circ. 3,000. Pays on publication. Publishes ms an average of 6 months after acceptance. Byline given. Buys all rights. Reports in 2 months. Free sample copy.
**Nonfiction:** Justin Stonehouse, articles editor. Book excerpts, essays, historical/nostalgic, interview/profile, opinion, personal experience, photo feature, and travel. "No articles written for general audience." **Buys 5 mss/year.** Send complete ms. Length: 1,500 words. **Pays $25-250.**
**Reprints:** Send tearsheet or photocopy of story with information about when and where the article previously appeared. Payment negotiable.
**Photos:** Send photos with submission. Reviews prints. Offers $10-25/photo. Identification of subjects required. Buys all rights.

**$ CINEASTE, America's Leading Magazine on the Art and Politics of the Cinema**, Cineaste Publishers, Inc., 200 Park Ave. S., #1601, New York NY 10003. Phone/fax: (212)982-1241. E-mail: cineaste@cineaste.com. **Contact:** Gary Crowdus, editor-in-chief. **30% freelance written.** Quarterly magazine covering motion pictures with an emphasis on social and political perspective on cinema. Estab. 1967. Circ. 10,000. Pays on publication. Publishes ms an average of 4 months after acceptance. Byline given. Offers 50% kill fee. Buys first North American serial rights. Editorial lead time 3 months. Submit seasonal material 4 months in advance. Accepts queries by mail, e-mail, fax. Reports in 1 month. Sample copy $5. Writer's guidelines for #10 SASE.
**Nonfiction:** Essays, historical/nostalgic, humor, interview/profile, opinion. **Buys 20-30 mss/year.** Query with published clips. Length: 2,000-5,000 words. **Pays $30-100.** Pays in contributor copies at author's request.
**Photos:** State availability of photos with submission. Reviews transparencies, 8×10 prints. Offers no additional payment for photos accepted with ms. Identification of subjects required. Buys one-time rights.
**Columns/Departments:** Homevideo (topics of general interest or a related group of films); A Second Look (new interpretation of a film classic or a reevaluation of an unjustly neglected release of more recent vintage); Lost and Found (film that may or may not be released or otherwise seen in the US but which is important enough to be brought to the attention of our readers); Festivals (film festivals of particular political importance); all 1,000-1,500 words. Query with published clips. **Pays $50 minimum.**
**Tips:** "We dislike academic jargon, obtuse Marxist teminology, film buff trivia, trendy 'buzz' phrases, and show biz references. We do not want our writers to speak of how they have 'read' or 'decoded' a film, but to view, analyze and interpret same. The author's processes and quirks should be secondary to the interests of the reader. Warning the reader of problems with specific films is more important to us than artificially 'puffing' a film because its producers or politics are agreeable. One article format we encourage is an omnibus review of several current films, preferably those not reviewed in a previous issue. Such an article would focus on films that perhaps share a certain political perspective, subject matter or generic concerns (e.g., films on suburban life, or urban violence, or revisionist Westerns). Like individual Film Reviews, these articles should incorporate a very brief synopsis of plots for those who haven't seen the films. The main focus, however, should be on the social issues manifested in each film and how it may reflect something about the current political/social/esthetic climate."

**★ CINEFANTASTIQUE MAGAZINE, The Review of Horror, Fantasy and Science Fiction Films**, P.O. Box 270, Oak Park IL 60303. (708)366-5566. Fax: (708)366-1441. **Contact:** Frederick S. Clarke, editor. **100% freelance**

**written.** Willing to work with new/unpublished writers. Monthly magazine covering horror, fantasy and science fiction films. Estab. 1970. Circ. 30,000. Pays on publication. Publishes ms an average of 6 months after acceptance. Byline given. Buys all magazine rights. Reports in 2 months or longer. Sample copy for $7 and 9×12 SAE.

**Nonfiction:** Historical/nostalgic (retrospects of film classics); interview/profile (film personalities); new product (new film projects); opinion (film reviews, critical essays); technical (how films are made). **Buys 100-125 mss/year.** Query with published clips and SASE for return of ms. Length: 1,000-10,000 words.

**Photos:** State availability of photos with query letter or ms.

**Tips:** "Study the magazine to see the kinds of stories we publish. Develop original story suggestions; develop access to film industry personnel; submit reviews that show a perceptive point of view."

**$ DANCE INTERNATIONAL**, Vancouver Ballet Society, 1415 Barclay St., Vancouver, British Columbia V6G 1J6 Canada. (604)681-1525. Fax: (604)681-7732. E-mail: danceint@direct.ca. Editor: Maureen Riches. **Contact:** Tamar Satov, contributing editor. **100% freelance written.** Quarterly magazine covering dance arts. "Articles and reviews on current activities in world dance, with occasional historical essays; reviews of dance films, video and books." Estab. 1973. Circ. 3,500. Pays on publication. Publishes ms an average of 3 months after acceptance. Byline given. Offers 50% kill fee. Buys one-time rights. Editorial lead time 3 months. Submit seasonal material 6 weeks in advance. Accepts queries by mail, e-mail, fax. Reports in 2 weeks on queries; 1 month on mss. Sample copy and guidelines for SAE.

**Nonfiction:** Book excerpts, essays, historical/nostalgic, interview/profile, personal experience, photo feature. **Buys 100 mss/year.** Query. Length: 1,200-2,200 words. **Pays $40-150.**

**Reprints:** Accepts previously published submissions.

**Photos:** Send photos with submission. Reviews prints. Offers no additional payment for photos accepted with ms. Identification of subjects required.

**Columns/Departments:** Kaija Pepper, copy editor. Dance Bookshelf (recent books reviewed), 1,200 words; Regional Reports (events in each region), 1,200-2,000 words. **Buys 100 mss/year.** Query. **Pays $60-70.**

**Tips:** "Send résumé and samples of recent writings."

**$ $ DRAMATICS MAGAZINE**, Educational Theatre Association, 2343 Auburn Ave., Cincinnati OH 45219. (513)421-3900. Fax: (513)421-7077. E-mail: pcorathers@etassoc.org. Website: http://www.etassoc.org. **Contact:** Donald Corathers, editor-in-chief. **70% freelance written.** Works with small number of new/unpublished writers. For theater arts students, teachers and others interested in theater arts education. Magazine published monthly, September-May. Estab. 1929. Circ. 40,000. **Pays on acceptance.** Publishes ms an average of 3 months after acceptance. Buys first North American serial rights. Byline given. Submit seasonal material 3 months in advance. Accepts queries by mail, e-mail, fax. Accepts simultaneous submissions. Reports in 3 months; longer on unsolicited mss. Sample copy for 9×12 SAE with 5 first-class stamps. Guidelines free or on website.

**Nonfiction:** How-to (technical theater, directing, acting, etc.), informational, interview, photo feature, humorous, profile, technical. **Buys 30 mss/year.** Submit complete ms. Length: 750-3,000 words. **Pays $50-400.** Rarely pays expenses of writers on assignment.

**Reprints:** Send tearsheet or photocopy of article or play, or typed ms with rights for sale noted and information about when and where it previously appeared. Pays up to 75% of amount paid for an original article.

**Photos:** Purchased with accompanying ms. Uses b&w photos and transparencies. Query. Total purchase price for ms usually includes payment for photos.

**Fiction:** Drama (one-act and full-length plays). "No plays for children, Christmas plays or plays written with no attention paid to the conventions of theater." Prefers unpublished scripts that have been produced at least once. **Buys 5-9 mss/year.** Send complete ms. **Pays $100-400.**

**Tips:** "The best way to break in is to know our audience—drama students, teachers and others interested in theater—and to write for them. Writers who have some practical experience in theater, especially in technical areas, have a leg-up here, but we'll work with anybody who has a good idea. Some freelancers have become regular contributors. Others ignore style suggestions included in our writer's guidelines."

**N ⌧ $ $ EAST END LIGHTS, The Quarterly Magazine for Elton John Fans**, Voice Communications Corp., P.O. Box 760, New Baltimore MI 48047. (810)949-7900. Fax: (810)949-2217. E-mail: eastendlts@aol.com. **Contact:** Tom Stanton, editor. **90% freelance written.** Quarterly magazine covering Elton John. "In one way or another, a story must relate to Elton John, his activities or associates (past and present). We appeal to discriminating Elton fans. No gushing fanzine material. No current concert reviews." Estab. 1990. Circ. 1,700. Pays 3 weeks after publication. Publishes ms an average of 3 months after acceptance. Byline given. Offers 100% kill fee. Buys first rights and second serial (reprint) rights. Submit seasonal material 3 months in advance. Accepts queries by mail, e-mail, fax. Reports in 2 months. Sample copy $2.

**Nonfiction:** Book excerpts, essays, exposé, general interest, historical/nostalgic, humor and interview/profile. **Buys 20 mss/year.** Query with or without published clips or send complete ms. Length: 400-1,000 words. **Pays $75-250 for assigned articles; $75-150 for unsolicited articles.** Pays with contributor copies only if the writer requests.

**Reprints:** Send tearsheet or photocopy of article or typed ms with rights for sale noted and information about when and where the article previously appeared. Pays 50% of amount paid for an original article.

**Photos:** State availability of photos with submission. Reviews negatives and 5×7 prints. Offers $40-75/photo. Buys one-time rights and all rights.

**Columns/Departments:** Clippings (non-wire references to Elton John in other publications), maximum 200 words.

**Buys 12 mss/year.** Send complete ms. Length: 50-200 words. **Pays $20-50.**
**Tips:** "Approach with a well-thought-out story idea. We prefer interviews with Elton-related personalities—past or present; try to land an interview we haven't done. We are particularly interested in music/memorabilia collecting of Elton material."

**$ $FANGORIA: Horror in Entertainment**, Starlog Communications, Inc., 475 Park Ave. S., 8th Floor, New York NY 10016. (212)689-2830. Fax: (212)889-7933. **Contact:** Anthony Timpone, editor. **95% freelance written.** Works with a small number of new/unpublished writers each year. Magazine published 10 times/year covering horror films, TV projects, comics, videos and literature and those who create them. "We emphasize the personalities and behind-the-scenes angles of horror filmmaking." Estab. 1979. Pays on publication. Publishes ms an average of 3 months after acceptance. Byline given. Buys all rights. Submit seasonal material 4 months in advance. Reports in 6 weeks. "We provide an assignment sheet (deadlines, info) to writers, thus authorizing queried stories that we're buying." Sample copy for $6 and 10×13 SAE with 4 first-class stamps. Writer's guidelines for #10 SASE.
  • *Fangoria* is looking for more articles on independent filmmakers and better-known horror novelists.
**Nonfiction:** Book excerpts; interview/profile of movie directors, makeup FX artists, screenwriters, producers, actors, noted horror/thriller novelists and others—with genre credits; special FX and special makeup FX how-it-was-dones (on filmmaking only). Occasional "think" pieces, opinion pieces, reviews, or sub-theme overviews by industry professionals. **Buys 100 mss/year.** Query by letter (never by phone) with ideas and published clips. Length: 1,000-3,500 words. **Pays $100-250.** Rarely pays expenses of writers on assignment. Avoids most articles on science fiction films—see listing for sister magazine *Starlog* in *Writer's Market* Science Fiction consumer magazine section.
**Photos:** State availability of photos. Reviews b&w and color prints and transparencies. "No separate payment for photos provided by film studios." Captions, identification of subjects required. Photo credit given.
**Columns/Departments:** Monster Invasion (exclusive, early information about new film productions; also mini-interviews with filmmakers and novelists). Query with published clips. Length: 300-500 words. **Pays $45-75.**
  • *Fangoria* emphasizes that it does not publish fiction or poetry.
**Tips:** "Other than recommending that you study one or several copies of *Fangoria*, we can only describe it as a horror film magazine consisting primarily of interviews with technicians and filmmakers in the field. Be sure to stress the interview subjects' words—not your own opinions as much. We're very interested in small, independent filmmakers working outside of Hollywood. These people are usually more accessible to writers, and more cooperative. *Fangoria* is also sort of a *de facto* bible for youngsters interested in movie makeup careers and for young filmmakers. We are devoted only to *reel* horrors—the fakery of films, the imagery of the horror fiction of a Stephen King or a Clive Barker— *we do not* want nor would we *ever* publish articles on real-life horrors, murders, etc. A writer must *like* and *enjoy* horror films and horror fiction to work for us. If the photos in *Fangoria* disgust you, if the sight of *(stage)* blood repels you, if you feel 'superior' to horror (and its fans), you aren't a writer for us and we certainly aren't the market for you. We love giving new writers their *first* chance to break into print in a national magazine. We are currently looking for Vancouver-, Arizona- and Las Vegas-based correspondents."

**⊠ $ $FILM COMMENT**, Film Society of Lincoln Center, 70 Lincoln Center Plaza, New York NY 10023. (212)875-5610. Fax: (212)875-5636. E-mail: rtjfc@aol.com. Website: http://www.filmlinc.com. **Contact:** Richard T. Jameson, editor. **100% freelance written.** Bimonthly magazine covering film criticism and film history, "authoritative, personal writing (not journalism) reflecting experience of and involvement with film as an art form." Estab. 1962. Circ. 30,000. Pays on publication. Publishes ms an average of 2 months after acceptance. Byline given. Offers 50% kill fee (assigned articles only). Editorial lead time 6 weeks. Accepts queries by mail, e-mail, fax, phone. Accepts simultaneous submissions. Reports in 2 weeks. Guidelines free.
**Nonfiction:** Essays, historical, interview, opinion. **Buys 100 mss/year.** Send complete ms. "We respond to queries, but rarely *assign* a writer we don't know." Length: 800-8,000 words. "We don't use a separate pay scale for solicited or unsolicited. **There is no fixed rate, but roughly based on 3 words/$1.**"
**Photos:** State availability of photos. No additional payment for photos accepted with ms. Buys one-time rights.
**Tips:** "We are more or less impervious to 'hooks,' don't worry a whole lot about 'who's hot who's not,' or tying in with next fall's surefire big hit (we think people should write about films they've seen, not films that haven't even been finished). We appreciate good writing (writing, not journalism) on subjects in which the writer has some personal investment and about which he or she has something noteworthy to say. Demonstrate ability and inclination to write *FC*-worthy articles. We read and consider everything we get, and we do print unknowns and first-timers. Probably the writer with a shorter submission (1,000-2,000 words) has a better chance than with an epic article that would fill half the issue."

**$ $KPBS ON AIR MAGAZINE**, **San Diego's Guide to Public Broadcasting**, KPBS Radio/TV, 5200 Campanile Dr., San Diego CA 92182-5400. (619)594-3766. Fax: (619)265-6417. Website: http://www.kpbs.org. **Contact:** Michael Good, editor. **15% freelance written.** Monthly magazine on public broadcasting programming and San Diego arts. "Our readers are very intelligent, sophisticated and rather mature. Your writing should be, too." Estab. 1970. Circ. 63,000. Pays on publication. Publishes ms an average of 1 month after acceptance. Byline given. Offers 50% kill fee. Not copyrighted. Buys first North American serial rights. Submit seasonal material 3 months in advance. Accepts queries by mail, fax, phone. Reports in 3 months. Sample copy for 9×12 SAE with 4 first-class stamps.
**Nonfiction:** Interview/profile of PBS personalities and/or artists performing in San Diego, opinion, profiles of public TV and radio personalities, backgrounds on upcoming programs. Nothing over 1,500 words. **Buys 60 mss/year.** Query

with published clips. Length: 300-1,500 words. **Pays 20¢/word, 28¢/word if the article is received via modem or computer disk.** Sometimes pays expenses of writers on assignment.

**Reprints:** Rarely accepts reprints of previously published submissions. Send tearsheet or typed ms with rights for sale noted and information about when and where the article previously appeared. **Pays 25¢/word.**

**Photos:** State availability of photos with submission. Reviews transparencies, 5×7 prints. Offers $30-300/photo. Identification of subjects required. Buys one-time rights.

**Columns/Departments:** On the Town (upcoming arts events in San Diego), 800 words; Short Takes (backgrounds on public TV shows), 500 words; Radio Notes (backgrounders on public radio shows), 500 words. **Buys 35 mss/year.** Query with or without published clips. **Pays 20¢/word; 28¢/word if the article is received via modem or disk.**

**Tips:** "Feature stories for national writers are most open to freelancers. Arts stories for San Diego writers are most open. Read the magazine, then talk to me."

**N $ $ NATIONAL EXAMINER, America's Favorite Family Weekly**, Globe Communications Corp., 5401 Broken Sound Blvd., Boca Raton FL 33487. (561)997-7733. Fax: (561)997-5595. E-mail: examtab@aol.com or examtab @gate.net. Editor-in-Chief: Brian Williams. **Contact:** Roger Capettini (ext. 1106) or Chris Benquhe (ext. 1036). Weekly magazine covering entertainment, general interest, crime, health, celebrity reporting. *"The National Examiner* is a general interest magazine that specializes in celebrity reporting, Hollywood gossip, human interest stories and cutting edge health reporting." Estab. 1972. Circ. 500,000. Pays on publication. Byline given. Buys all rights. Editorial lead time 5 days. Submit seasonal material 2 months in advance. Accepts queries by mail, e-mail, fax, phone. Reports in 2 weeks. Sample copy and writer's guidelines for SAE.

**Nonfiction:** How-to, humor, inspirational, crime, celebrity. **Pays $200** for leads for page 1 **plus $200** if writing story. **Pays $40** for shorts **plus $20** if writing story.

**Photos:** State availability of photos with submission or send photos with submission. Captions, model releases and identification of subjects required. Buys one-time and all rights.

**N $ THE NEWFOUNDLAND HERALD**, Sunday Herald Ltd., Box 2015, St. John's, Newfoundland A1C 5R7 Canada. (709)726-7060. Fax: (709)726-8227/6971. E-mail: newfoundland.herald@nf.sympatico.ca. **Contact:** Karen Dawe, managing editor. **25% freelance written.** Weekly entertainment magazine. "We prefer Newfoundland and Labrador-related items." Estab. 1946. Circ. 30,000. Pays on publication. Publishes ms an average of 2 months after acceptance. Byline given. Buys first North American serial, one-time or all rights. Editorial lead time 4 months. Submit seasonal material 3 months in advance. Accepts queries by mail, e-mail, fax. Sample copy for $5. Guidelines free via fax ($1 by mail).

**Nonfiction:** General interest, investigative news, how-to, interview/profile, travel. No opinion, humor, poetry, fiction, satire. **Buys 500 mss/year.** Query with published clips. Length: 700-2,500 words. **Pays $30 minimum.** Sometimes pays expenses of writers on assignment.

**Reprints:** Send typed ms with rights for sale noted (Mac disk or e-mail attachment of text preferred).

**Photos:** Send photos with submission. Offers $7.50-25/photo. Captions required. Buys one-time rights.

**Columns/Departments:** Music (current artists), Video/Movies (recent releases/themes), TV shows (Top 20); all 1,500-2,500 words. **Buys 500 mss/year.** Query with published clips.

**Tips:** "Know something about Newfoundlanders and Labradorians—for example, travel writers should know where we like to travel. Query first. No opinion pieces, satire, humor or poetry is purchased; fiction is not accepted. Original cartoons which focus on local politics will be considered. Photos should be submitted with all articles. Please use color 35mm print or slide film. No b&w photos unless otherwise requested. Please read several issues of the magazine before submitting any material to the *Herald*."

**$ $ $ $ PEOPLE**, Time Inc. Magazine Co., Time & Life Bldg., Rockefeller Center, New York NY 10020. (212)522-1212. Fax: (212)522-0536. Website: http://www.people.com. This magazine did not respond to our request for information. Query before submitting.

**★ $ $ THE READERS SHOWCASE**, Suggitt Group Ltd., 950 Canada Trust Tower, 10104-103 Ave., Edmonton, Alberta T5J 0H8 Canada. (780)413-6163. Fax: (780)413-6185. E-mail: readers@suggitt.com. Website: http://www.s uggitt.com. **Contact:** Maureen Hutchison, senior editor. **80-100% freelance written.** Bimonthly magazine covering books available at the Canadian SmithBooks and Coles bookstores. *"The Readers Showcase* consists of author interviews, book reviews, lifestyle pieces, industry news, contests, book-related editorials, etc." Estab. 1993. Circ. 400,000 (1,000,000 in December). Pays within 30 days of publication. Publishes ms an average of 1 month after acceptance. Byline given. Offers 50% kill fee. Editorial lead time 2 months. Submit seasonal material 2 months in advance. Accepts queries by mail, e-mail, fax. Accepts simultaneous submissions. Sample copy and writer's guidelines free.

**Nonfiction:** Book excerpts, lifestyle issues, interview/profile, book reviews. **Buys 300 mss/year.** Query with published clips. Length: 300-2,000 words. **Pay rates vary, starting at 25¢/word.**

**Reprints:** Accepts previously published submissions.

**Tips:** Writer's best bet to break in is to "provide writer samples, along with a résumé and covering letter, indicating what you could offer to the magazine. Indicate your areas of interest. Writers should be prepared to be flexible regarding deadlines and assignment choices. Most importantly, writers' articles must be informative, yet inviting to the reader."

**$ $ RIGHT ON!**, Sterling's Magazines, 233 Park Ave. S., New York NY 10003. (212)780-3519. **Contact**: Cynthia Horner, editorial director. **10% freelance written.** Monthly black entertainment magazine for teenagers and young adults. Circ. 250,000. Pays on publication. Publishes ms an average of 3 months after acceptance. Byline given. Buys all rights. Submit seasonal material 4 months in advance. Reports in 1 month on queries.
**Nonfiction:** Interview/profile. "We only publish entertainment-oriented stories or celebrity interviews." **Buys 15-20 mss/year.** Query with or without published clips, or send ms. Length: 500-4,000 words. **Pays $50-200.**
**Photos:** State availability of photos with submission. Reviews transparencies, 8 × 10 b&w prints. Offers no additional payment for photos accepted with ms. Identification of subjects required. Buys one-time or all rights.

**$ $ $ SATELLITE ORBIT**, Commtek Communications Corp., Suite 600, 8330 Boone Blvd., Vienna VA 22003. (703)827-0511. Fax: (703)827-0159. E-mail: satorbit@aol.com. Website: http://www.orbitmagazine.com. **Contact:** Laura Fries, senior editor. **25% freelance written.** Monthly magazine on television available to owners of large satellite dishes. Estab. 1979. **Pays on acceptance.** Publishes an average of 2 months after acceptance. Offers 10% kill fee. Buys first or second rights. Reports in 1 month.
**Nonfiction:** "Wants to see articles on satellite programming, equipment, television trends, sports and celebrity interviews." Query with published clips and SASE. *No unsolicited mss.* **Buys 24 mss/year.** Length: 700 words. **Pays 50¢/word.**
**Reprints:** Pays 20% of amount paid for an original article.

**✪ $ $ SCI-FI ENTERTAINMENT**, Sovereign Media, 11305 Sunset Hills Rd., Reston VA 20190. (703)471-1556. E-mail: scottedelman@erols.com. **Contact:** Scott Edelman, editor. **100% freelance written.** Published 9 times/year. Magazine covering science fiction movies and television—old, new, upcoming fantasy. Estab. 1994. Circ. 70,000. Pays 30 days after acceptance. Publishes ms an average of 1 month after acceptance. Byline given. Offers 10% kill fee. Buys first world rights. Editorial lead time 1 month. Submit seasonal material 3 months in advance. Accepts simultaneous submissions. Reports in 2 weeks on queries; 1 month on mss. Sample copy for $4.95. Guidelines for #10 SASE.
**Nonfiction:** General interest, historical/nostalgic, interview/profile, new product (games), opinion, personal experience, photo feature. **Buys 100 mss/year.** Query. Length: 2,000-3,000 words. **Pays $200-500.** Sometimes pays expenses of writers on assignment.
**Photos:** State availability of photos with submissions. Offers no additional payment for photos accepted with ms. Identification of subjects required. Buys one-time rights.
**Columns/Departments:** Infinite Channels (games), 2,300 words; Video (video reviews), 2,400 words; Books (books on movies), 2,500 words. **Buys 6 mss/year.** Query with published clips.

**$ $ SOAP OPERA UPDATE**, Bauer Publishing, 270 Sylvan Ave., Englewood Cliffs NJ 07632. (201)569-6699. Fax: (201)569-2510. **Contact:** Richard Spencer, editor-in-chief. **25% freelance written.** Biweekly. "We cover daytime and prime time soap operas with preview information, in-depth interviews and exclusive photos, history, character sketches, events where soap stars are seen and participate." Estab. 1988. Circ. 288,000. Pays on publication. Byline given. Buys first North American serial rights. Submit seasonal material 3 months in advance. Accepts queries by mail, fax. Reports in 1 month.
**Nonfiction:** Humor, interview/profile. "Only articles directly about actors, shows or history of a show." **Buys 100 mss/year.** Query with published clips. Length: 750-2,200 words. **Pays $400.** Sometimes pays expenses of writers on assignment.
**Photos:** State availability of photos with submission. Reviews transparencies. Offers $25. Captions and identification of subjects required. Buys all rights.
**Tips:** "Come up with fresh, new approaches to stories about soap operas and their people. Submit ideas and clips. Take a serious approach; don't talk down to the reader. All articles must be well written and the writer must be knowledgeable about his subject matter."

**$ $ STEPPIN' OUT MAGAZINE**, Collins Communications, Inc., 381 Broadway, Westwood NJ 07675. (201)358-2929. Fax: (201)358-2824. E-mail: stepoutmag@aol.com. Website: http://www.steppinoutmagazine.com. **Contact:** Chauncé Hayden, editor. **20% freelance written.** Weekly regional entertainment magazine. "*Steppin' Out* targets younger readers. Submissions should be hip and timely." Estab. 1988. Circ. 70,000. Pays on publication. Publishes ms an average of 1 month after acceptance. Byline given. Offers 20% kill fee. Buys one-time and second serial (reprint) rights. Editorial lead time 2 months. Submit seasonal material 2 months in advance. Accepts simultaneous submissions. Reports in 2 weeks on queries; 1 month on mss. Sample copy for $5.
**Nonfiction:** Exposé, general interest, humor, interview/profile, opinion, personal experience, photo feature, travel. **Buys 20 mss/year.** Query with published clips. Length: 500-2,000 words. **Pays $20-500 for assigned articles; $20-100 for unsolicited articles.** Sometimes pays expenses of writers on assignment.
**Reprints:** Accepts previously published submissions.
**Photos:** State availability of photos with submission. Reviews any size prints. Offers no additional payment for photos accepted with ms. Captions, model releases and identification of subjects required. Buys one-time rights.
**Columns/Departments:** More Music (music-national); 24-7 (opinion); Bar Fly (young adult), all 200 words. **Buys 10 mss/year.** Query with published clips. **Pays $20-100.**
**Fiction:** Humorous, slice-of-life vignettes.
**Fillers:** Anecdotes, facts, gags to be illustrated by cartoonist, newsbreaks, short humor. **Buys 20/year.** Length: 50-500

words. **Pays $20-100.**
**Tips:** "Keep it simple, write honestly and don't be afraid to voice your opinion."

**[N]** **$** **THEATREFORUM, International Theatre Journal**, UCSD Department of Theatre, 9500 Gilman Dr., La Jolla CA 92093-0344. (619)534-6598. Fax: (619)534-1080. E-mail: theatreforum@ucsd.edu./ **Contact:** Jim Carmody, editor-in-chief. **75% freelance written.** Semiannual magazine covering performance, theatrical and otherwise. "*Theatre-Forum* is an international journal of theater, performance art, dance theater, music theater and forms yet to be devised. We publish performance texts, interviews with artists on their creative process, and articles about innovative productions and groups. Written by and for members of both the academic and artistic community, we represent a wide variety of aesthetic and cultural interests." Estab. 1992. Circ. 2,000. Pays on publication. Byline given. Buys one-time rights or anthology rights for scripts. Editorial lead time 4 months. Accepts queries by mail, e-mail, fax. Reports in 1 month on queries; 2 months on mss. Sample copy for $5. Writer's guidelines for #10 SASE.
　　**O–¬** Break in with "a sophisticated, insightful piece on a new, innovative and not widely known performance. We do not publish any articles not related to a specific performance or play."
**Nonfiction:** Essays, interview/profile, photo feature, performance criticism. Buys 10-12 mss/year. Query with published clips. Length: 1,000-5,000 words. Pays 5¢/word.
**Photos:** State availability of photos with submission. Negotiates payment individually. Identification of subjects required. Buys one-time rights.
**Scripts:** Previously published plays are not considered. Buys 4-6 mss/year. Query with published clips. Pays $200.
**Tips:** "We are interested in documenting, discussing, and disseminating innovative and provocative theaterworks. Non-traditional and inventive texts (plays) are welcome. We also publish in-depth analyses of innovative theatrical productions. We are interested in finding artists who want to write about other artists."

**$** **$** **TV GUIDE**, 1211 Avenue of the Americas, New York NY 10036. Contact: Editor (National Section). 50% freelance written. Prefers to work with published/established writers but works with a small number of new/unpublished writers each year. Weekly. Estab. 1953. Circ. 13,000,000.
**Nonfiction:** "The national editorial section looks at the shows, the stars and covers the medium's impact on news, sports, politics, literature, the arts, science and social issues through reports, profiles, features and commentaries."

**$** **$** **$** **XXL MAGAZINE**, Harris Publications, 1115 Broadway, 8th Floor, New York NY 10010. E-mail: annag@h arris-pub.com. **Contact:** Anna Gebbie, managing editor. **50% freelance written.** Bimonthly. "*XXL* is hip-hop on a higher level, an upscale urban lifestyle magazine." Estab. 1997. Circ. 175,000. Pays on publication. Byline given. Offers 25% kill fee. Buys all rights. Editorial lead time 4 months. Submit seasonal material 3 months in advance. Accepts queries by mail, e-mail.
**Nonfiction:** Interview/profile, music, entertainment, luxury materialism. Query with published clips. Length: 200-5,000 words. **Pays 50¢/word.** Pays expenses of writers on assignment.
**Photos:** State availability of photos with submission. Reviews contact sheets, transparencies, prints. Negotiates payment individually. Captions, model releases required. Buys "3 month no-see" rights.
**Tips:** "Please send clips, query and cover letter by mail or e-mail."

# ETHNIC & MINORITY

Ideas and concerns of interest to specific nationalities and religions are covered by publications in this category. General interest lifestyle magazines for these groups are also included. Many ethnic publications are locally oriented or highly specialized and do not wish to be listed in a national publication such as *Writer's Market*. Query the editor of an ethnic publication with which you're familiar before submitting a manuscript, but do not consider these markets closed because they are not listed in this section. Additional markets for writing with an ethnic orientation are located in the following sections: Career, College & Alumni; Juvenile; Literary & "Little"; Men's; Women's; and Teen & Young Adult.

**[N]** **$** **$** **AFRICAN ACCESS MAGAZINE, Mainstreaming Africa**, 812-22nd Ave. NW, Calgary, Alberta T2M 1P2 Canada. (403)210-2726. Fax: (403)210-2484. E-mail: editor@africanaccess.com. Website: http://www.africanaccess .com. **Contact:** Chris Roberts, editor. **50% freelance written.** A consumer/trade hybrid magazine published quarterly covering business, investment and travel in Africa. "*AfriCan Access Magazine* is Canada's guide to the African Renaissance. Our audience is internationally oriented: business, investment and travel interest in Africa. Articles should have a North American-African connection." Estab. 1998. Circ. 5,000. Pays on publication. Publishes ms an average of 1-2 months after acceptance. Byline given. Offers 20% kill fee. Buys first North American serial, one-time or electronic rights. Editorial lead time 1-2 months. Accepts queries by mail, e-mail, fax, phone. Accepts simultaneous submissions. Reports in 2 weeks on queries; 1 month on mss. Sample copy for $5. Writer's guidelines on website.
**Nonfiction:** Book excerpts/reviews, essays, exposé, general interest, how-to (do business, case studies, travel, invest), interview/profile, opinion, personal experience, photo feature, travel, investment/political analysis. "If Africa isn't part

of the story, we aren't interested." **Buys 20 mss/year.** Query with published clips. Length: 600-2,000 words. **Pays $100-400 for assigned articles; $50-300 for unsolicited articles (Canadian).** Pays sometimes in copies and/or advertising.
**Reprints:** Accepts previously published submissions.
**Photos:** State availability of photos with submission. Negotiates payment individually. Captions and identification of subjects required. Buys one-time rights.
**Columns/Departments:** Recommended Reading: Reviews (book, film, TV, video, art reviews), 100-300 words; NGO Profile (work of an NGO active in Africa), 500-750 words; Travel Stories (humorous/adventure first person), 200-400 words; Business Profiles (detailed how-to look at SMEs active overseas), 400-750 words; Cyber Africa (Africa on the Internet, best sites), 200-350 words. **Buys 8-12 mss/year.** Query with published clips or send complete ms. **Pays $100.**
🖥 The online magazine carries original content not found in the print edition.
**Tips:** "If a writer has first hand experience in Africa, has studied Africa, or is African, that helps! We want practical stories our readers can use."

⭐ **$ AIM MAGAZINE**, AIM Publishing Company, 7308 S. Eberhart Ave., Chicago IL 60619-0554. (773)874-6184. Fax: (206)543-2746. Managing Editor: Dr. Myron Apilado. **Contact:** Ruth Apilado, associate editor. **75% freelance written.** Works with a small number of new/unpublished writers each year. Quarterly magazine on social betterment that promotes racial harmony and peace for high school, college and general audience. Estab. 1975. Circ. 10,000. Pays on publication. Publishes ms an average of 3 months after acceptance. Offers 60% kill fee. Not copyrighted. Buys one-time rights. Submit seasonal material 6 months in advance. Accepts queries by mail, phone. Accepts simultaneous submissions. Reports in 2 months on queries. Sample copy and guidelines for $4 and 9×12 SAE with $1.70 postage.
**Nonfiction:** Exposé (education); general interest (social significance); historical/nostalgic (Black or Indian); how-to (create a more equitable society); profile (one who is making social contributions to community); book reviews and reviews of plays "that reflect our ethnic/minority orientation." No religious material. **Buys 16 mss/year.** Send complete ms. Length: 500-800 words. **Pays $25-35.**
**Photos:** Reviews b&w prints. Captions, identification of subjects required.
**Fiction:** Ethnic, historical, mainstream, suspense. "Fiction that teaches the brotherhood of man." **Buys 20 mss/year.** Send complete ms. Length: 1,000-1,500 words. **Pays $25-35.**
**Poetry:** Avant-garde, free verse, light verse. No "preachy" poetry. **Buys 20 poems/year.** Submit maximum 5 poems. Length: 15-30 lines. **Pays $3-5.**
**Fillers:** Jokes, anecdotes, newsbreaks. **Buys 30/year.** Length: 50-100 words. **Pays $5.**
**Tips:** "Interview anyone of any age who unselfishly is making an unusual contribution to the lives of less fortunate individuals. Include photo and background of person. We look at the nations of the world as part of one family. Short stories and historical pieces about Blacks and Indians are the areas most open to freelancers. Subject matter of submission is of paramount concern for us rather than writing style. Articles and stories showing the similarity in the lives of people with different racial backgrounds are desired."

**$ ALBERTA SWEETGRASS**, Aboriginal Multi-Media Society of Alberta, 15001 112th Ave., Edmonton, Alberta T5M 2V6 Canada. (800)661-5469. Fax: (403)455-7639. E-mail: wind@ammsa.com. Website: http://www.ammsa.com. **Contact:** Debora Lockyer Steel, managing editor. Monthly tabloid newspaper. **50% freelance written.** "Alberta Sweetgrass is a community paper which focuses on people from within Alberta's first nations, métis and non-status aboriginal communities." Estab. 1993. Circ. 7,500. Pays 10th of month following publication. Accepts queries by mail, e-mail, fax, phone. Sample copy free. Writer's guidelines available on website and production schedule available upon request.
**Nonfiction:** Features, general interest, interview/profile, opinion, photo feature, travel, community-based stories, all with an Alberta angle (no exceptions). **Usually runs 2-3 focus sections/month.** Query. Length: 400-1,200 words. **Pays $3/published inch for one-source stories; $3.60 for multiple sources** (less for excess editorial work).
**Reprints:** Pays 50% of amount paid for an original article.
**Photos:** State availability of photos with submission. Offers $15/b&w photo; $50/color cover; $15/inside color.
**Columns/Departments:** Book/Film/Art Reviews (Alberta Aboriginal), 450-500 words; Briefs (community news shorts), 150-200 words.
**Tips:** "Aboriginal knowledge is definitely an asset in order to send us usable stories, but even if you aren't familiar with Aboriginal culture, but are still a good writer, bounce a story idea off the editor and do the interview. That way, you will begin to learn more about Aboriginal culture."

**$ $ ARMENIAN INTERNATIONAL MAGAZINE**, 207 S. Brand Blvd., Suite 205, Glendale CA 91204. (818)246-7979. Fax: (818)246-0088. E-mail: aim4m@well.com. **Contact:** Salpi H. Ghazarian, editor/publisher. **50% freelance written.** Monthly magazine about the Caucasus and the global Armenian diaspora. "Special reports and features about politics, business, education, culture, interviews and profiles. Each month, *AIM* is filled with essential news, situation analysis, and indepth articles with local and international coverage of events that affect Armenian life." Estab. 1989. Circ. 10,000. Pays on publication. Publishes ms an average of 3 months after acceptance. Byline given. Buys all rights. Accepts queries by mail, e-mail, fax. Reports in 2 weeks on queries; 6 weeks on mss.
**Nonfiction:** General interest, historical, interview/profile, photo feature and travel. Special issue: Armenian restaurants around the world. **Buys 60 mss/year.** Query by mail, fax or e-mail with published clips. Length: 600-1,200 words. **Pays $50-400 for assigned articles; $50-200 for unsolicited articles.** Sometimes pays expenses of writers on assignment.
**Reprints:** Send photocopy of article.

**Photos:** State availability of photos with submission. Reviews negatives, transparencies and prints. Offers $10-50/photo. Captions and identification of subjects required.
**Fiction:** Publishes novel excerpts upon approval.
**Tips:** "Have an interesting take on Armenian issues and their global significance or global issues and their significance for Armenia or Armenians."

**$ $ THE B'NAI B'RITH INTERNATIONAL JEWISH MONTHLY,** 1640 Rhode Island Ave. NW, Washington DC 20036. (202)857-2708. Fax: (202)296-1092. E-mail: sfreed@bnaibrith.org. Website: http://bnaibrith.org/ijm. Editor: Eric Rozenman. **Contact:** Stacey Freed, managing editor. **50% freelance written.** Bimonthly magazine covering Jewish affairs. Estab. 1886. Circ. 200,000. **Pays on acceptance.** Publishes ms an average of 3 months after acceptance. Byline given. Offers 25% kill fee. Buys first North American serial rights. Editorial lead time 3 months. Submit seasonal material 6 months in advance. Accepts queries by mail, e-mail, fax. Accepts simultaneous submissions. Reports in 1 month. Sample copy for $2 and 9×13 SAE with 2 first-class stamps. Writer's guidelines free.
**Nonfiction:** General interest pieces of relevance to the Jewish community of US and abroad; interview/profile, photo feature. Buys 15-25 mss/year. Query by mail, fax or e-mail with published clips. Length: 750-2,500 words. **Pays $400-750 for assigned articles; $300-600 for unsolicited articles.** Sometimes pays expenses of writers on assignment.
**Photos:** State availability of photos with submission. Reviews contact sheets, 2×3 transparencies and prints. Pays $150/page for color, $100/page for b&w. Identification of subjects required. Buys one-time rights.
**Tips:** "Know what's going on in the Jewish world. Look at other Jewish publications also. Writers should submit clips with their queries. The best way to break into the *Jewish Monthly* is to submit a range of good story ideas accompanied by clips. We aim to establish relationships with writers and we tend to be loyal. We generally do not publish first-person essays, commentaries, and we do not do book reviews."

**$ CONGRESS MONTHLY,** American Jewish Congress, 15 E. 84th St., New York NY 10028. (212)879-4500. **Contact:** Rochelle Mancini, managing editor. **90% freelance written.** Bimonthly magazine. "*Congress Monthly*'s readership is popular, but well-informed; the magazine covers political, social, economic and cultural issues of concern to the Jewish community in general and to the American Jewish Congress in particular." Estab. 1933. Circ. 35,000. Pays on publication. Publishes ms an average of 3 months after acceptance. Byline given. Buys one-time rights. Submit seasonal material 2 months in advance. No simultaneous submissions. Reports in 2 months.
**Nonfiction:** General interest ("current topical issues geared toward our audience"). No technical material. Query only. *No unsolicited mss.* Length: 2,000-2,500 words. Book reviews, 1,000-1,500 words; author profiles, film and theater reviews, travel. Payment amount determined by author experience and article length.
**Photos:** State availability of photos. Reviews b&w prints. "Photos are paid for with payment for ms."

**$ $ DIMENSIONS, the Magazine of Jewish Lifestyle in South Florida,** Skarco Press Inc., One Prospect Park Business Center, 5251 N.W. 33rd Ave., Fort Lauderdale FL 33309. (954)252-9393. Fax: (954)252-9391. E-mail: ljanasz@gate.net. **Contact:** Linda Janasz, editor-in-chief. **Quarterly magazine covering Jewish lifestyle in Southern Florida, geared toward 35-55-year-olds. Estab. 1995. Circ. 40,000. Pays on publication. Byline given. Buys first North American and second serial rights. Editorial lead time 4 months. Submit seasonal material 4 months in advance. Accepts queries by mail, e-mail. Accepts simultaneous submissions. Reports in 2 months. Sample copy for $3 plus $1.24 postage.
**Nonfiction:** Book excerpts, general interest, interview/profile (with celebrity or well-known person), religious (Jewish), family matters, health and well-being, fashion, travel. **Buys 10 mss/year.** Query with published clips. Length: 600-2,000 words. **Pays $100-300.**
**Photos:** State availability of photos with submission. Negotiates payment individually. Captions, model releases, identification of subjects required.
**Tips:** "Writers should understand our market and readers' lifestyle: Jewish professionals, families and singles aged 30s-50s, affluent, upscale, living in South Florida. Very cosmopolitan."

**⊘ EBONY MAGAZINE** does not accept freelance writing.

**$ $ $ EMERGE, Black America's Newsmagazine,** BET Holdings, Inc., 1 BET Plaza, 1900 W Place NE, Washington DC 20018. (202)608-2093. Fax: (202)608-2598. E-mail: emergemag@msbet.com. Website: http://www.emergemag.com. Managing Editor: Florestine Purnell. **Contact:** George E. Curry, editor. **80% freelance written.** African-American news monthly. "*Emerge* is a general interest publication reporting on a wide variety of issues from health to sports to politics, almost anything that affects Black Americans. Our audience is comprised primarily of African-Americans 25-49, individual income of $55,000, professional and college educated." Estab. 1989. Circ. 200,000. **Pays on acceptance.** Publishes ms an average of three months after acceptance. Byline given. Offers 25% kill fee. Buys first North American serial rights. Submit seasonal material 6 months in advance. Accepts queries by mail, e-mail, fax. Reports in 8 weeks. Sample copy for $3 and 9×12 SAE or on website. Writer's guidelines for #10 SAE with 2 first-class stamps or on website.
● Ranked as one of the best markets for freelance writers in *Writer's Yearbook* magazine's annual "Top 100 Markets," January 1999.
**Nonfiction:** Essays, exposé, general interest, historical/nostalgic, humor, interview/profile, technical, travel. "We are not interested in standard celebrity pieces that lack indepth reporting, as well as analysis, or pieces dealing with interpersonal relationships." Query with published clips. Length: 600-2,000 words. **Pays 60-75¢/word.**

**Photos:** State availability of photos with submission. Reviews contact sheets. Negotiated payment. Captions, model releases, indentification of subjects required. Buys one-time rights.

**Columns/Departments:** Cover to Cover (review and news on new books or magazines), 650-750 words; Destinations (experiences, culture and adventure in far-off places or unique approaches to familiar destinations), 650-750 words; Dialogue (short-formed Q&A with African-American newsmakers and scholars), 2,000 words; Education (news and trends), 650-750 words; Etcetera (stories or insights—often humorous), 750 words; Film (what's new and of interest to African-American moviegoers and home videos), 750-1,800 words; Gallery (critical perspective and news about visual arts and artists), 650-750 words; International (covers all corners of the globe from an Afrocentric perspective), 650-1,200 words; Media (behind the scenes insight on television and radio shows, their stars and creators), 650-750 words; Perspective (personal thought and experience) 1,200-2,000 words; Religion, 650-750 words; Speaking Volumes (interview with new authors or publishers), 650-750 words; Theatre (spotlight on the world of theatre and dance), 650-750 words; Take Note (musical artists, new releases and trends), 650-750 words; and The Last Word (full-page opinion piece), 650-750 words. Query.

**Tips:** "If a writer doesn't have a completed manuscript, then he should mail a query letter with clips. No phone calls. First-time authors should be extremely sensitive to the *Emerge* style and fit within these guidelines as closely as possible. We do re-write and re-edit pieces. We are a news monthly so articles must be written with a 3-month lead time in mind. Writers must assist our research department during fact checking process and closing. Read at least six issues of the publication before submitting ideas."

**✠ $ $ESTYLO MAGAZINE,** Latina Lifestyle, Mandalay Publishing, 3660 Wilshire Blvd., Suite 530, Los Angeles CA 90010. (213)383-6300. Fax: (213)383-6499. E-mail: Estylo@aol.com. Editor: Juana I. Gallegos. **Contact:** Denise M. Castañon, managing editor. **75% freelance written.** "Bimonthly fashion, beauty and entertainment magazine for the affluent and mobile Latina. It contains a variety of features and departments devoted to cuisine, health, fitness, beauty, fashion and entertainment topics." Estab. 1997. Circ. 50,000. Pays on publication. Publishes ms an average of 2 months after acceptance. Byline given. Buys first rights. Editorial lead time 3 months. Submit seasonal material 3 months in advance. Query by mail, e-mail. Accepts simultaneous submissions. Reports in 2 weeks. Writer's guidelines for #10 SASE.

**Nonfiction:** Exposé, general interest, how-to (career, fitness, health), interview/profile, new product, photo feature, religious. **Buys 15-20 mss/year.** Query with published clips. Length: 1,200 words. **Pays $100 minimum.** Sometimes pays expenses of writers on assignment.

**Reprints:** Send photocopy of article.

**Photos:** State availability of photos with submission. Reviews contact sheets. Negotiates payment individually. Captions, model releases, identificiation of subjects required. Buys all rights.

**Columns/Departments: Buys 15-20 mss/year.** Query with published clips. Length: 800-1,200 words. **Pays $100 minimum.**

**$ $GERMAN LIFE,** Zeitgeist Publishing Inc., 226 N. Adams St., Rockville MD 20850-1829. (301)294-9081. Fax: (301)294-7821. E-mail: editor@GermanLife.com. Website: http://www.GermanLife.com. **Contact:** Heidi L. Whitesell, editor. **50% freelance written.** Bimonthly magazine covering German-speaking Europe. "*German Life* is for all interested in the diversity of German-speaking culture, past and present, and in the various ways that the United States (and North America in general) has been shaped by its German immigrants. The magazine is dedicated to solid reporting on cultural, historical, social and political events." Estab. 1994. Circ. 40,000. Pays on publication. Publishes ms an average of 6 months after acceptance. Byline given. Buys first North American serial rights. Editorial lead time 4 months. Submit seasonal material 6 months in advance. Accepts queries by mail, e-mail. Reports in 2 months on queries; 3 months on mss. Sample copy for $4.95 and SAE with 4 first-class stamps. Writer's guidelines free.

**Nonfiction:** Exposé, general interest, historical/nostalgic, how-to (German crafts, recipes, gardening), interview/profile, opinion (only for final column), photo feature, travel. Special issues: Oktoberfest-related (October); seasonal relative to Germany, Switzerland or Austria (December); travel to German-speaking Europe (April); education or politics in German-speaking Europe (August). **Buys 50 mss/year.** Query with published clips. Length: 1,000-2,000 words. **Pays $200-500 for assigned articles; $200-350 for unsolicited articles.** Sometimes pays expenses of writers on assignment.

**Photos:** State availability of photos with submission. Reviews color transparencies, 5×7 color or b&w prints. Offers no additional payment for photos accepted with ms. Identification of subjects required. Buys one-time rights.

**Columns/Departments:** German-Americana (regards specific German-American communities, organizations and/or events past or present), 1,500 words; Profile (portrays prominent Germans, Americans, or German-Americans), 1,000 words; At Home (cuisine, home design, gardening, crafts, etc. relating to German-speaking Europe), 800 words; Library (reviews of books, videos, CDs, etc.), 300 words. **Buys 30 mss/year.** Query with published clips. **Pays $130-300.**

**Fillers:** Anecdotes, facts, newsbreaks, short humor. Length: 100-300 words. **Pays $50-150.**

**Tips:** "The best queries include several informative proposals. Ideally, clips show a background in a German-related topic, but more importantly, a flair for 'telling stories.' Majority of articles present a human interest angle. Even though *German Life* is a special interest magazine, writers should avoid overemphasizing autobiographical experiences/stories."

**$ $HADASSAH MAGAZINE,** 50 W. 58th St., New York NY 10019. (212)688-0937. Fax: (212)446-9521. **Contact:** Joan Michel, associate editor. **90% freelance written.** Works with small number of new/unpublished writers each year. Monthly (except combined issues June/July and August/September). "*Hadassah* is a general interest, Jewish feature and literary magazine. We speak to our readers on a vast array of subjects ranging from politics to parenting, to midlife crisis to Mideast crisis. Our readers want coverage on social and economic issues, the arts, travel and health." Circ. 334,000. Buys first rights (with travel and family articles, buys all rights). Sample copy and writer's guidelines for 9×13 SASE.

**Nonfiction:** Primarily concerned with Israel, Jewish communities around the world and American civic affairs as relates to the Jewish community. "We are also open to art stories that explore trends in Jewish art, literature, theater, etc. Will not assign/commission a story to a first-time writer for Hadassah." **Buys 10 unsolicited mss/year.** Send query and writing samples by mail. No phone queries. Length: 1,500-2,000 words. **Pays $350 minimum, $75 for reviews.** Sometimes pays expenses of writers on assignment.

**Photos:** "We buy photos only to illustrate articles, with the exception of outstanding color photos from Israel which we use on our covers. We pay $175 and up for a suitable cover photo." Offers $50 for first photo; $35 for each additional. "Always interested in striking cover (color) photos, especially of Israel and Jerusalem."

**Columns/Departments:** "We have a Family column and a Travel column, but a query for topic or destination should be submitted first to make sure the area is of interest and the story follows our format."

**Fiction:** Short stories with strong plots and positive Jewish values. No personal memoirs, "schmaltzy" or shelter magazine fiction. "We continue to buy very little fiction because of a backlog." Length: 1,500 words maximum. **Pays $300 minimum.** "Require proper size SASE."

**Tips:** "We are interested in reading articles that offer an American perspective on Jewish affairs (1,500 words). For example, a look at the presidential candidates from a Jewish perspective. Send query of topic first."

**$ HERITAGE FLORIDA JEWISH NEWS**, P.O. Box 300742, Fern Park FL 32730-0742. (407)834-8787. Fax: (407)831-0507. E-mail: heritagefl@aol.com. Publisher/Editor: Jeffrey Gaeser. **Contact:** Christine L. Allen, managing editor. **20% freelance written.** Weekly tabloid on Jewish subjects of local, national and international scope, except for special issues. "Covers news of local, national and international scope of interest to Jewish readers and not likely to be found in other publications." Estab. 1976. Circ. 3,500. Pays on publication. Publishes ms an average of 2 months after acceptance. Byline given. Buys first North American serial, first, one-time, second serial (reprint) or simultaneous rights. Submit seasonal material 3 months in advance. Accepts queries by mail, e-mail, fax. Reports in 1 month. Sample copy for $1 and 9×12 SASE.

**Nonfiction:** General interest, interview/profile, opinion, photo feature, religious, travel. "Especially needs articles for these annual issues: Rosh Hashanah, Financial, Chanukah, Celebration (wedding and bar mitzvah), Passover, Health and Fitness, Education, Travel. No fiction, poems, first-person experiences." **Buys 50 mss/year.** Send complete ms. Length: 500-1,000 words. **Pays 50¢/column inch.**

**Reprints:** Send typed ms with rights for sale noted.

**Photos:** State availability of photos with submission. Reviews b&w prints up to 8×10. Offers $5/photo. Captions, identification of subjects required. Buys one-time rights.

**$ THE HIGHLANDER**, Angus J. Ray Associates, Inc., 560 Green Bay Rd., Suite 204, Winnetka IL 60093. **Contact:** Sharon Kennedy Ray, editor. **50% freelance written.** Works with a number of new/unpublished writers each year. Bimonthly magazine covering Scottish history, clans, genealogy, travel/history, and Scottish/American activities. Estab. 1961. Circ. 35,000. **Pays on acceptance.** Publishes ms an average of 6 months after acceptance. Byline given. Buys first North American serial and second serial (reprint) rights. Submit seasonal material 6 months in advance. Reports in 1 month. Sample copy for $5. Writer's guidelines free.

**Nonfiction:** Historical/nostalgic. "No fiction; no articles unrelated to Scotland." **Buys 100 mss/year.** Query. Length: 750-2,000 words. **Pays $75-150.**

**Reprints:** Send tearsheet or photocopy of article or typed ms with information about when and where the article previously appeared. Pays 50% of amount paid for an original article.

**Photos:** State availability. Prefers color photos, but include transparencies, maps, and/or line or historical drawings to illustrate your work. Identification of subjects required. Writer must provide one-time rights. Artwork returned after publication.

**Tips:** "Articles should be related to Scotland in a time span of roughly 1300 to 1900, although there is some flexibility in the time. We are not concerned with modern Scotland or with current problems or issues in Scotland."

**⊠ $ $ HISPANIC**, 99 Ponce de Leon, Suite 600, Coral Gables, FL 33134. (305)442-2462. Fax: (305)443-7650. E-mail: editor@hisp.com. Website: http://www.hisp.com. Publisher: Alfredo J. Estrada. **Contact:** Katherine A. Diaz, managing editor. **80% freelance written.** Monthly English-language magazine for the US Hispanic community. "*Hispanic* is a general interest publication emphasizing political issues, business news, and cultural affairs." Estab. 1987. Circ. 250,000. Pays on publication. Publishes ms an average of 4 months after acceptance. Byline given. Offers 25% kill fee. Buys all rights, puts some features on the Internet (*Hispanic Online*). Editorial lead time 3 months. Accepts queries by mail, e-mail, fax.

**Nonfiction:** General interest, business news, career strategies, politics, investigative pieces, culture features, opinion, personal essays. **Buys 200 mss/year.** Query in writing or submit ms on spec. Length: 1,400-3,500 words. **Pays $200-450.** Pays phone expenses, "but these must be cleared with editors first."

**Photos:** State availability of photos with submission. Reviews transparencies. Offers $25-500/photo. Captions, model releases, identification of subjects required.

**Columns/Departments:** Forum (op-ed), portfolio (product coverage, travel destinations, book, film and music reviews, money tips, cars). **Pays $75.**

The online magazine carries original material not found in the print edition. Contact: Enrique Gonzalez, online editor.

**Tips:** "We prefer a tone that doesn't overexplain the Hispanic perspective (such as not explaining Hispanic symbolism or translating Spanish words to English). Generally, the point of view should be inclusive: 'we' rather than 'they.' "

**$ $ $ ITALIAN AMERICA, Official Publication of the Order Sons of Italy in America**, Order Sons of Italy in America, 219 E St. NE, Washington DC 20002. (202)547-2900. E-mail: bkdedit@.com. **Contact:** Brenda Dalessandro, editor. **50% freelance written.** Quarterly magazine. "*Italian America* strives to provide timely information about OSIA, while reporting on individuals, institutions, issues and events of current or historical significance in the Italian-American community." Estab. 1996. Circ. 65,000. Pays on publication. Publishes ms an average of 3 months after acceptance. Byline given. Offers 50% kill fee. Buys first North American serial rights. Editorial lead time 3 months. Accepts simultaneous submissions. Sample copy and writer's guidelines free.

**Nonfiction:** Essays, exposé, historical, current events, nostalgic, interview/profile, opinion, personal experience, travel. **Buys 10 mss/year.** Query with published clips. Length: 500-2,500 words. **Pays $150-1,000.** Sometimes pays expenses of writers on assignment.

**Photos:** State availability of photos with submission. Reviews contact sheets. Negotiates payment individually. Identification of subjects required. Buys one-time rights.

**Columns/Departments:** Community Notebook (Italian American life), 500 words; Postcard from Italy (life in Italy today), 750 words; Reviews (books, films by or about Italian Americans), 500 words. **Buys 5 mss/year.** Send complete ms. **Pays $100-500.**

**⊠ $ $ JEWISH ACTION**, Union of Orthodox Jewish Congregations of America, 11 Broadway, 14th Floor, New York NY 10004-1302. (212)613-8146. Fax: (212)564-9058. E-mail: charlott@ou.org. Website: http://www.ou.org. Editor: Charlotte Friedland. **Contact:** Tova Ovits, assistant editor. **80% freelance written.** "Quarterly magazine offering a vibrant approach to Jewish issues, Orthodox lifestyle and values." Circ. 30,000. Pays 8 weeks after publication. Byline given. Submit seasonal material 4 months in advance. Reports in 3 months. Sample copy and guidelines for 9 × 12 SAE with 5 stamps.

    **०–** Break in with a query for "Just Between Us" column.

**Nonfiction:** Current Jewish issues, history, biography, art, inspirational, humor, music and book reviews. Query with published clips. **Buys 30-40 mss/year.** Length: 1,000-3,000 words, including footnotes. **Pays $100-300 for assigned articles; $75-150 for unsolicited articles.**

**Photos:** Send photos with submission. Identification of subjects required.

**Fiction:** Must have relevance to Orthodox reader. Length: 1,000-2,000 words.

**Poetry:** Limited number accepted. **Pays $25-75.**

**Columns/Departments:** Just Between Us (personal opinion on current Jewish life and issues), 1,000 words. **Buys 4 mss/year.** Jewish Living (section pertaining to holidays, contemporary Jewish practices), 1,000-1,500 words. **Buys 10 mss/year.**

**Tips:** "Remember that your reader is well educated and has a strong commitment to Orthodox Judaism. Articles on the Holocaust, holidays, Israel and other common topics should offer a fresh insight. Because the magazine is a quarterly, we do not generally publish articles which concern specific timely events."

**⊠ ⊠ $ MIDSTREAM, A Monthly Jewish Review**, 110 E. 59 St., New York NY 10022-1373. **Contact:** Joel Carmichael, editor. **90% freelance written.** Works with a small number of new/unpublished writers each year. Bimonthly magazine. "*Midstream* magazine is the Zionist periodical of record; in fact, there is no other journal of its kind which publishes Zionist historiography on a monthly basis in the world." Estab. 1954. Circ. 10,000. Pays after publication. Publishes ms an average of 6 months after acceptance. Byline given. Buys first North American serial rights. Accepts queries by mail, fax, phone. Reports in 3 months. Fiction guidelines for #10 SASE.

**Nonfiction:** "Articles offering a critical interpretation of the past, searching examination of the present, and affording a medium for independent opinion and creative cultural expression. Articles on the political and social scene in Israel, on Jews in Russia, the US and elsewhere. **Pays 5¢/word.**

**Fiction:** Primarily of Jewish and related content. **Pays 5¢/word.**

**Poetry:** Primarily of Jewish and related content. **Pays 5¢/word.**

**Tips:** "A book review is a good way to start. Send us a sample review or a clip, let us know your area of interest, suggest books you would like to review. For longer articles, give a brief account of your background or credentials in this field. Send query describing article or ms with cover letter. Since we are a bimonthly, we look for critical analysis rather than a 'journalistic' approach."

**$ $ MINORITY ADVANCEMENT PROFILE (MAP)**, 30 N. Raymond, Suite 211, Pasadena CA 91103. (626)577-1984. Fax: (626)577-1490. E-mail: info@mapnews.com. Website: http://www.mapnews.com. Publisher: Darrell R. Dansby. Senior Editor: Jeanetta M. Standefor. **Contact:** Editorial Staff. **40% freelance written.** Bimonthly business newsletter written for minority entrepreneurs and career professionals covering all aspects of business and careers. "We provide how-to information for starting and growing small businesses, profiles of successful entrepreneurs, career advancement advice and profiles of successful career professionals." Estab. 1996. Circ. 28,000. Pays on publication. Publishes ms an average of 2 months after acceptance. Byline given. Buys first rights and second serial (reprint) rights. Submit seasonal material 2 months in advance. Accepts queries by mail, e-mail, fax. Accepts simultaneous submissions. Reports in 2 months. Sample copy for $3. Writer's guidelines for #10 SASE with "Attn: Writer's Guidelines" on envelope.

**Nonfiction:** Book excerpts, how-to (business/career issues), humor, inspirational, interview/profile, new product, technical. No entertainment, travel, general interest. "We seek 'how-to-do-it-better' articles for starting and growing a small business or various aspects of career advancement. Please read the newsletter and writer's guidelines before querying. Articles covering up-to-date practical business and career information and interviews or profiles of successful entrepreneurs and career professionals are welcome." Query with published clips. Length: 300-1,000 words. **Pays $100-500.**

**Reprints:** Accepts previously published submissions.

**Photos:** State availability of photos with submission. Captions, model releases, identification of subjects required. Pays $5-20/photo. Buys one-time rights.

**Columns/Departments:** Entrepreneur/Career Profiles, 900-950 words; MAP Hall of Shame (humorous personal, business or work experiences), 100 words; Entrepreneur Report (timely, professional, practical information for entrepreneurs), 500-600 words; Career Management (how-to advice and opportunities for career advancement), 500-600 words; Keeping You in the Know (personal, career, business advice and information), 200-300 words; Product Review and Recommendation (books, product and service reviews), 100-150 words; Just Ask Us . . . Q&A (business and career advice), 250-300 words. Query with published clips. **Pays $100-500.**

**Fillers:** Anecdotes, facts, gags to be illustrated, newsbreaks, short humor. Length: 100-500 words. **Pays $50-200.**

The online magazine carries original content not found in the print edition and includes writer's guidelines. Contact: Jeanetta M. Standefor, online editor.

**Tips:** "MAP addresses the specific needs of minority entrepreneurs and career professionals. Each issue combines dual information, issues and events about and from the minority perspective. Profiles, departments and columns are most open to freelancers."

**$ $ $ MOMENT, The Magazine of Jewish Culture & Opinion**, 4710 41st St. NW, Washington DC 20016. (202)364-3300. Fax: (202)364-2636. E-mail: editor@momentmag.com. Publisher/Editor: Hershel Shanks. Managing Editor: David Holzel. **Contact:** Joshua Rolnick, assistant editor. **90% freelance written.** "*Moment* is an independent Jewish bimonthly general interest magazine that specializes in cultural, political, historical, religious and 'lifestyle' articles relating chiefly to the North American Jewish community and Israel." Estab. 1975. Circ. 65,000. Pays on publication. Publishes ms an average of 6 months after acceptance. Byline given. Buys first North American serial rights. Editorial lead time 3 months. Submit seasonal material 6 months in advance. Accepts queries by mail, e-mail, fax. Accepts simultaneous submissions. Reports within 1 month on queries; 3 months on mss. Sample copy for $4.50 and SAE. Writer's guidelines free.

**Nonfiction:** "We look for meaty, colorful, thought-provoking features and essays on Jewish trends and Israel. We occasionally publish book excerpts, memoirs and profiles." **Buys 25-30 mss/year.** Query with published clips. Length: 2,500-4,000 words. **Pays $200-1,200 for assigned articles; $40-500 for unsolicited articles.**

**Photos:** State availability of photos with submission. Negotiates payment individually. Identification of subjects required. Buys one-time rights.

**Columns/Departments:** Notes and News/5759—snappy pieces of not more than 250 words about quirky events in Jewish communities, news and ideas to improve Jewish living; Olam (The Jewish World)—first-person pieces, humor and colorful reportage of 800-1,500 words; Book reviews (fiction and nonfiction) are accepted but generally assigned, 400-800 words. **Buys 30 mss/year.** Query with published clips. **Pays $50-250.**

**Tips:** "Stories for *Moment* are usually assigned, but unsolicited manuscripts are often selected for publication. Successful features offer readers an in-depth journalistic treatment of an issue, phenomenon, institution, or individual. The more the writer can follow the principle of 'show, don't tell,' the better. The majority of the submissions we receive are about The Holocaust and Israel. A writer has a better chance of having an idea accepted if it is not on these subjects."

**N $ $ NA'AMAT WOMAN, Magazine of NA'AMAT USA, the Women's Labor Zionist Organization of America**, NA'AMAT USA, 200 Madison Ave., New York NY 10016. (212)725-8010. Fax: (212)447-5187. Website: http://www.naamatusa@naamat.org. **Contact:** Judith A. Sokoloff, editor. **80% freelance written.** Magazine published 4 times/year covering Jewish themes and issues; Israel; women's issues; and social and political issues. Estab. 1926. Circ. 25,000. Pays on publication. Byline given. Not copyrighted. Buys first North American serial, one-time, first serial and second serial (reprint) rights to book excerpts and makes work-for-hire assignments. Accepts queries by mail, fax. Reports in 3 months. Writer's guidelines for SASE.

**Nonfiction:** Exposé, general interest (Jewish), historical/nostalgic, interview/profile, opinion, personal experience, photo feature, travel, art and music. "All articles must be of particular interest to the Jewish community." **Buys 20 mss/year.** Query with clips of published work or send complete ms. **Pays 10¢/word.**

**Photos:** State availability of photos. Pays $25-45 for 4×5 or 5×7 prints. Captions, identification of subjects required. Buys one-time rights.

**Columns/Departments:** Film and book reviews with Jewish themes. **Buys 20 mss/year.** Query with clips of published work or send complete ms. **Pays 10¢/word.**

**Fiction:** Historical/nostalgic, humorous, women-oriented and novel excerpts. "Intelligent fiction with Jewish slant. No maudlin nostalgia or trite humor." **Buys 3 mss/year.** Send complete ms. Length: 1,200-3,000 words. **Pays 10¢/word.**

**$ $ NATIVE PEOPLES MAGAZINE, The Arts and Lifeways**, 5333 N. Seventh St., Suite C-224, Phoenix AZ 85014-2804. (602)252-2236. Fax: (602)265-3113. E-mail: editorial@nativepeoples.com. Website: http://www.nativepeo

ples.com. **Contact**: Priscilla Thomas, editorial coordinator or Ben Winton, editor. Quarterly full-color magazine on Native Americans. "The primary purpose of this magazine is to offer a sensitive portrayal of the arts and lifeways of native peoples of the Americas." Estab. 1987. Circ. 95,000. Pays on publication. Byline given. Buys one-time rights. Accepts queries by mail, e-mail, fax. Reports in 1 month on queries; 2 months on mss. Writer's guidelines sent or online. "Extremely high-quality reproduction with full color throughout."

**Nonfiction:** Book excerpts (pre-publication only), historical/nostalgic, interview/profile, personal experience, photo feature. **Buys 35 mss/year.** Query with published clips. Length: 1,500-3,000 words. **Pays 25¢/word.**

**Photos:** State availability of photos with submission. Reviews transparencies (all formats) but prefers 35mm slides. Offers $45-150/page rates. Pays $250 for cover photos. Identification of subjects required. Buys one-time rights.

**Columns/Departments:** In the News (profiles of tribal members who achieved success in area of difficulty). Length: 300 words accompanied by b&w photo of individual. Byline given.

**Tips:** "We are extremely focused upon authenticity and a positive portrayal of present-day traditional and cultural practices. Our readership has been expanded to include Native American students in schools throughout the country. This is being done for the purpose of giving young people a sense of pride in their heritage and culture, to offer role models and potential career considerations. Therefore, it is extremely important that the Native American point of view be incorporated in each story."

**N** **$ $ RUSSIAN LIFE, RIS Publications**, 89 Main St., #2, Montpelier VT 05602. Phone/fax: (802)223-4955. E-mail: ruslifeispubs.com. Website: http://www.rispubs.com. Editor: Mikhail Ivanov. **Contact:** Paul Richardson, publisher. **40% freelance written.** Bimonthly magazine covering Russian culture, history, travel and business. "Our readers are informed Russophiles with an avid interest in all things Russian. But we do not publish personal travel journals or the like." Estab. 1956. Circ. 15,000. Pays on publication. Publishes ms 2 months after acceptance. Byline given. Offers $25 kill fee. Buys first rights. Editorial lead time 2 months. Submit seasonal material 3 months in advance. Reports in 1 month: Sample copy for 9×12 SAE with 6 first-class stamps. Writer's guidelines for #10 SASE.

**Reprints:** Accepts previously published submissions.

**Nonfiction:** General interest, photo feature, travel. No personal stories, i.e., "How I came to love Russia." **Buys 15-20 mss/year.** Query. Length: 1,000-6,000 words. **Pays $100-300.**

**Photos:** Send photos with submission. Reviews contact sheets. Negotiates payment individually. Captions required. Buys one-time rights.

**Tips:** "A straightforward query letter with writing sample or manuscript (not returnable) enclosed."

**$ $ SCANDINAVIAN REVIEW**, The American-Scandinavian Foundation, 15 E. 65th St., New York NY 10021. (212)879-9779. Fax: (212)249-3444. Website: http://www.amscan.org. **Contact:** Adrienne Gyongy, editor. **75% freelance written.** Triannual magazine for contemporary Scandinavia. Audience: members, embassies, consulates, libraries. Slant: popular coverage of contemporary affairs in Scandinavia. Estab. 1913. Circ. 4,000. Pays on publication. Publishes ms 2 months after acceptance. Byline given. Buys first North American serial and second serial (reprint) rights. Editorial lead time 3 months. Submit seasonal material 3 months in advance. Reports in 6 weeks on queries. Sample copy on website and writer's guidelines free.

**Nonfiction:** General interest, interview/profile, photo feature, travel (must have Scandinavia as topic focus). Special issue: Scandinavian travel. *No pornography.* **Buys 30 mss/year.** Query with published clips. Length: 1,500-2,000 words. **Pays $300 maximum.**

**Reprints:** Accepts previously published submissions, though unpublished mss are preferred.

**Photos:** State availability or send photos with submission. Reviews 3×5 transparencies or prints. Pays $25-50/photo; negotiates payment individually. Captions required. Buys one-time rights.

**N** **$ TAKE PRIDE! COMMUNITY**, Topaz Realty, Inc., 1014 Franklin St. SE, Grand Rapids MI 49507-1327. (616)243-1919. Fax: (616)243-6844. E-mail: wmathis@triton.net. Website: http://www.takepride.com. President/CEO: Walter L. Mathis, Sr. **Contact:** Joy Milano, editor. **50% freelance written.** Bimonthly magazine and weekly tabloid covering education and economic empowerment for all people especially African-Americans. Estab. 1991. Circ. 5,000. Pays on publication. Publishes ms an average of 1 month after acceptance. Byline given. Buys one-time rights and makes work-for-hire assignments. Editorial lead time 1 month. Submit seasonal material 1 month in advance. Accepts queries by mail, e-mail. Accepts simultaneous submissions. Reports in 2 weeks on queries; 1 month on mss. Sample copy and writer's guidelines on website.

**Nonfiction:** Exposé, general interest, historical/nostalgic, how-to, humor, inspirational, interview/profile, opinion, religious, technical. Special issue: MLK Day (January). **Buys 4 mss/year.** Query with or without published clips or send complete ms. Length: 200-1,500 words. **Pays $25.**

**Photos:** State availability of photos or send photos with submission. Reviews 3×5 prints. Negotiates payment individually. Model releases and identification of subjects required. Buys one-time rights.

**Columns/Departments:** Inspirational (religious, advice); Education; Economics, all 350 words. Query with or without published clips or send complete ms. **Pays $25.**

**Fillers:** Shawn Commons, graphic designer. Facts, gags to be illustrated by cartoonist, newsbreaks, short humor. Length: 50 words. **Pays $10.**

**Tips:** "Get in touch with our target audience and write about what is important to them. A writer's best bet to break in to this magazine is to present issues and facts relevant to all aspects of the African-American community. Dare to say what needs to be said and to tell it like it is whether it is 'popular' or not."

**N** **$** THE UKRAINIAN WEEKLY, Ukrainian National Association, 2200 Route 10, P.O. Box 280, Parsippany NJ 07054. (973)292-9800. Fax: (973)644-9510. E-mail: staff@ukrweekly.com. Website: http://www.ukrweekly.com. **Contact:** Roma Hadzewycz, editor-in-chief. **30% freelance written** (mostly by a corps of regular contributors). Weekly tabloid covering news and issues of concern to Ukrainian community, primarily in North America but also around the world, and events in Ukraine. "We have news bureaus in Kyiv, capital of Ukraine, and in Toronto." Estab. 1933. Circ. 10,000. Pays on publication. Publishes ms an average of 1 month after acceptance. Byline given. Buys first North American serial and second serial (reprint) rights or makes work-for-hire assignments. Submit seasonal material 1 month in advance. Reports in 1 month. Sample copy for 9×12 SAE with 3 first-class stamps.

**Nonfiction:** Book excerpts, essays, exposé, general interest, historical/nostalgic, interview/profile, opinion, personal experience, photo feature, news events. Special issues: Easter, Christmas, anniversary of Ukraine's independence proclamation (August 24, 1991), student scholarships, anniversary of Chornobyl nuclear accident and year-end review of news. **Buys 80 mss/year.** Query with published clips. Length: 500-2,000 words. **Pays $45-100 for assigned articles; $25-100 for unsolicited articles.** Sometimes pays expenses of writers on assignment.

**Reprints:** Send typed ms with rights for sale noted and information about when and where the article previously appeared. Pays 25-50% of amount paid for an original article.

**Photos:** Send photos with submission. Reviews contact sheets, negatives and 3×5, 5×7 or 8×10 prints. Offers no additional payment for photos accepted with ms.

**Columns/Departments:** News & Views (commentary on news events), 500-1,000 words. **Buys 10 mss/year.** Query. **Pays $25-50.**

**Tips:** "Become acquainted with the Ukrainian community in the US and Canada. The area of our publication most open to freelancers is community news—coverage of local events. We put more emphasis on events in Ukraine now that it has re-established its independence."

**$ $** UPSCALE MAGAZINE, Exposure to the World's Finest, Upscale Communications, Inc., 600 Bronner Brothers Way SW, Atlanta, GA 30310. (404)758-7467. Fax: (404)755-9892. E-mail: upscale8@mindspring.com. Website: http://www.upscale8@mindspring.com. Editor-in-Chief: Sheila Bronner. **Contact:** Sylviette McGill, managing editor. **75-80% freelance written.** Monthly magazine covering topics that inspire, inform or entertain African-Americans. "*Upscale* is a general interest publication featuring a variety of topics—beauty, health and fitness, business news, travel, arts, relationships, entertainment and other issues that affect day-to-day lives of African-Americans." Estab. 1989. Circ. 242,000. Byline given. Offers 25% kill fee. Buys all rights in published form. Editorial lead time 4 months. Submit seasonal material 6 months in advance. Sample copy for $2. Writer's guidelines for #10 SASE

**Nonfiction:** Book excerpts/reviews, general interest, historical/nostalgic, inspirational, interview/profile, personal experience, religious, travel. **Buys 135 mss/year.** Query by mail or fax. Length varies. **Pays $100 minimum.**

**Photos:** State availability of photos with submission. Reviews contact sheets, transparencies, prints. Negotiates payment individually. Captions, model releases, identification of subjects required. Buys one-time or reprint rights.

**Columns/Departments:** Kim Hamilton, Body & Soul/Living editor. Positively You, Viewpoint (personal inspiration/perspective). **Buys 25 mss/year.** Query by mail or fax.

**Fiction:** Publishes novel excerpts.

**Tips:** "No unsolicited fiction, poetry or essays. Unsolicited nonfiction is accepted for our Positively You and Viewpoint sections. Queries for exciting and informative nonfiction story ideas are welcomed."

**$ $** VISTA MAGAZINE, The Magazine for all Hispanics, Horizon, a U.S. Communications Company, 999 Ponce de Leon Blvd., Suite 600, Coral Gables FL 33134. (305)442-2462. Fax: (305)443-7650. E-mail: jlobaco@aol.com. Website: http://www.vistamagazine.com. **Contact:** Julia Bencomo Lobaco, editor. **50% freelance written.** Monthly "Sunday supplement style magazine targeting Hispanic audience. Dual-language, Spanish/English, 50/50%. Stories appear in one language or another, not both. Topics of general interest, but with a Hispanic angle." Estab. 1985. Circ. 1,100,000. Pays on publication. Publishes ms an average of 2 months after acceptance. Byline given. Offers 25% kill fee. Buys first North American serial rights. Editorial lead time 2 months. Submit seasonal material 4 months in advance. Accepts queries by mail, e-mail, fax, phone. Sample copy free or on website.

**Nonfiction:** Exposé, general interest, historical/nostalgic, how-to (home improvement), inspirational, interview/profile, new product, opinion, personal experience, photo feature, travel. "No creative writing, poems, etc." **Buys 40-50 mss/year.** Query with published clips. Length: 500-1,600 words. **Pays $250-450.** Sometimes pays expenses of writers on assignment.

**Photos:** State availability of photos with submission.

**Columns/Departments:** Voices (personal opinion re: Hispanic-related theme), 500 words. **Pays $100.**

**Tips:** "Query by phone is usually best."

# FOOD & DRINK

Magazines appealing to gourmets, health-conscious consumers and vegetarians are classified here. Some publications emphasize "the art and craft" of cooking for food enthusiasts who enjoy developing these skills as a leisure activity. Another popular trend stresses healthy eating and food choices. Many magazines in the Health & Fitness category present a holistic approach to well-being through nutrition and fitness for healthful living. Magazines in General Interest and Women's categories also buy articles on food topics. Journals aimed at food processing, manufacturing and retailing are in the Trade section.

**$ $ $ $BON APPETIT, America's Food and Entertaining Magazine**, Condé Nast Publications, Inc., 6300 Wilshire Blvd., Los Angeles CA 90048. (323)965-3600. Fax: (323)937-1206. **Contact:** Barbara Fairchild, executive editor. Editor-in-Chief: William J. Garry. **10% freelance written.** Monthly magazine that covers fine food, restaurants and home entertaining. "*Bon Appetit* readers are upscale food enthusiasts and sophisticated travelers. They eat out often and entertain four to six times a month." Estab. 1975. Circ. 1,331,853. **Pays on acceptance.** Byline given. Negotiates rights. Submit seasonal material 1 year in advance. Reports in 6 weeks. Guidelines for #10 SASE.
• Ranked as one of the best markets for freelance writers in *Writer's Yearbook* magazine's annual "Top 100 Markets," January 1999.
**Nonfiction:** Travel (restaurant or food-related), food feature, dessert feature. "No cartoons, quizzes, poetry, historic food features or obscure food subjects." **Buys 45 mss/year.** Query with published clips. Length: 750-2,000 words. **Pays $500-1,800.** Pays expenses of writers on assignment.
**Photos:** Never send photos.
**Tips:** "We are most interested in receiving travel stories from freelancers. They must have a good knowledge of food (as shown in accompanying clips) and a light, lively style with humor. Nothing long and pedantic please."

**$ $ $COOKING & ENTERTAINING, Woman's Day Special Interest Publications**, Hachette-Filipacchi Magazines, 1633 Broadway, New York NY 10019. Fax: (212)767-5612. E-mail: wdspecials@aol.com. Editor: Carolyn Gatto. **Contact:** Janice Wright, managing editor. Triannual magazine covering food, cooking, entertaining. "This magazine is full of ideas for seasonal get-togethers for spring, summer and the holidays, from festive food (a major focus) to fanciful decorating to table settings. Helpful articles, from the best equipment to prepare-ahead strategies to highlights of seasonal foods are also included. The average reader is female and 43 years old." **Pays on acceptance.** Publishes ms an average of 3 months after acceptance. Byline given. Offers up to 25% kill fee. Buys first worldwide serial or second serial (printing) rights. Editorial lead time 6 months. Submit seasonal material 10 months in advance. Reports in 3 months. Sample copy not available; writer's guidelines for #10 SASE.
**Nonfiction:** How-to (party planning, cooking, cleanup, grocery shopping), new product, photo features (tabletop settings). **Buys 15 mss/year.** Query with published clips. Length: 250-1,000 words. Payment varies based on length, writer, importance. Sometimes pays expenses of writers on assignment.
**Reprints:** Accepts previously published submissions.
**Photos:** State availability of photos with submission. Model releases required. Buys one-time rights.
**Columns/Departments:** Query with published clips. Payment varies based on length, writer, and level/amount of research required.

**⬟ $ $ $ $COOKING LIGHT, The Magazine of Food and Fitness**, P.O. Box 1748, Birmingham AL 35201-1681. (205)877-6000. Fax: (205)877-6600. Website: http://cookinglight.com. Editor: Douglas Crichton. Executive Editors: Nathalie Dearing, Rod Davis. **Contact:** Rod Davis (food and fitness). **75% freelance written.** Magazine published 10 times/year on healthy recipes and fitness information. "*Cooking Light* is a positive approach to a healthier lifestyle. It's written for healthy people on regular diets who are counting calories or trying to make calories count toward better nutrition. Moderation, balance and variety are emphasized. The writing style is fresh, upbeat and encouraging, emphasizing that eating a balanced, varied, lower-calorie diet and exercising regularly do not have to be boring." Estab. 1987. Circ. 1,350,000. **Pays on acceptance.** Publishes ms an average of 1 year after acceptance. Byline sometimes given. Offers 33% kill fee. Submit seasonal material 1 year in advance. Reports in 1 year.
**Nonfiction:** Personal experience on nutrition, healthy recipes, fitness/exercise. Back up material a must. **Buys 150 mss/year.** Must query with résumé and published clips; no unsolicited mss. Response guaranteed with SASE. Length: 400-2,000 words. **Pays $250-2,000.** Pays expenses of writers on assignment.
▣ The online magazine contains original content not found in the print edition. Contact: Tim Jackson, online editor.
**Tips:** "Emphasis should be on achieving a healthier lifestyle through food, nutrition, fitness, exercise information. In submitting queries, include information on professional background. Food writers should include examples of healthy recipes which meet the guidelines of *Cooking Light.*"

**$ $ $ $FOOD & WINE**, American Express Publishing Corp., 1120 Avenue of the Americas, New York NY 10036. (212)382-5618. Editor-in-Chief: Dana Cowin. Managing Editor: Mary Ellen Ward. Executive Editor: Pamela Kaufman. Food Editor: Tina Ujlaki. Monthly magazine for "active people for whom eating, drinking, entertaining, dining out and travel are central to their lifestyle." Estab. 1978. Circ. 855,286. **Pays on acceptance.** Byline given. Offers 25% kill fee. Buys first world rights. Submit seasonal material 9 months in advance. Reports in 3 weeks on queries; 2 weeks on mss. Sample copy for $5.
• *Food & Wine* notes that they are very selective in choosing outside freelance writers.
**Nonfiction:** Food trends and news, how-to, kitchen and dining room design, travel. Query with published clips. **Buys 125 mss/year.** Length: 1,000-3,000 words. **Pays $800-2,000.** Pays expenses of writers on assignment.
**Photos:** State availability of photos with submission. No unsolicited photos or art. Offers $100-450/photo. Model

releases and identification of subjects required. Buys one-time rights.

**Columns/Departments:** Restaurants, Travel, Style, Food, Health, Cooking Openers/Well-being, Cooking Fast, Cooking Master. **Buys 120 mss/year.** Query with published clips. Length: 800-3,000 words. **Pays $800-2,000.**

🖥 The online magazine carries original content not found in the print edition. Contact: Ann Shields, online editor.

**Tips:** "Good service, good writing, up-to-date information, interesting article approach and appropriate point of view for *F&W*'s audience are important elements to keep in mind. Look over several recent issues before writing query."

**$ $ $ $ GOURMET**, Condé Nast Publications, Inc., 560 Lexington Ave., New York NY 10022. (212)880-2712. Website: http://www.gourmet.com. Publisher: Ruth Reichl. **Contact:** Gina Sanders, editor. Affluent monthly magazine emphasizing fine dining. "*Gourmet, The Magazine of Good Taste*, encompasses fine dining and entertaining, world travel, cooking, including elegant table settings, wines and spirits, shopping, culture and history, art and antiques." This magazine did not respond to our request for information. Query before submitting.

**$ $ HOME COOKING**, House of White Birches, Publishers, 306 E. Parr Rd., Berne IN 46711. (219)589-4000, ext. 396. Fax: (219)589-8093. E-mail: home_cooking@whitebirches.com. Website: http://www.whitebirches.com. **Contact:** Shelly Vaughan, editor. Managing Editor: Barb Sprunger. **60% freelance written.** "*Home Cooking* delivers dozens of kitchen-tested recipes from home cooks every month. Special monthly features offer recipes, tips for today's busy cooks, techniques for food preparation, nutritional hints and more. Departments cover topics to round out the cooking experience." Circ. 75,000. **Pays within 45 days after acceptance.** Publishes ms an average of 8 months after acceptance. Byline given. Buys all or first rights, occasionally one-time rights. Editorial lead time 6 months. Submit seasonal material 8 months in advance. Accepts queries by mail, e-mail. Accepts simultaneous submissions. Reports in 1 month on queries; 2 months on mss. Sample copy for 6×9 SAE and 2 first-class stamps. Editorial calendar for #10 SASE.

**Nonfiction:** How-to, humor, interview/profile, new product, personal experience, recipes, book reviews, all in food/cooking area. No health/fitness or travel articles. **Buys 85 mss/year.** Query or send complete ms. Length: 250-750 words plus 6-8 recipes. **Pays $20-300 for assigned articles; $20-175 for unsolicited articles.** Sometimes pays expenses of writers on assignment.

**Reprints:** Accepts previously published submissions.

**Photos:** State availability of photos with submission. Reviews prints. Negotiates payment individually. Model releases and identification of subjects required. Buys one-time rights.

**Columns/Departments:** Dinner Tonight (complete 30-minute meal with preparation guide), 500 words; Your Invitation to Dinner (complete meal to serve 6-12 guests), 600 words; Stirring Comments (book and product reviews), 100 words; Pinch of Sage (hints for the home cook), 200-500 words. **Buys 48 mss/year.** Query or send complete ms. **Pays $20-100.**

**Fillers:** Anecdotes, facts, newsbreaks, short humor. **Buys 10/year.** Length: 10-150 words. **Pays $15-25.**

**Tips:** "Departments are most open to new writers. All submissions should be written specifically for our publication. Be sure to check spelling, grammar and punctuation before mailing. If that means setting aside your manuscript for two weeks to regain your objectivity, do it. A sale two weeks later beats a rejection earlier. If you follow our style in your manuscript, we know you've read our magazine."

**$ $ KASHRUS MAGAZINE, The Bimonthly for the Kosher Consumer and the Trade**, Yeshiva Birkas Reuven, P.O. Box 204, Parkville Station, Brooklyn NY 11204. (718)336-8544. **Contact:** Rabbi Yosef Wikler, editor. **25% freelance written.** Prefers to work with published/established writers, but will work with new/unpublished writers. Bimonthly magazine covering kosher food industry and food production. Estab. 1980. Circ. 10,000. Pays on publication. Publishes ms an average of 2 months after acceptance. Byline given. Offers 50% kill fee. Buys first or second serial (reprint) rights. Submit seasonal material 2 months in advance. Accepts queries by mail, phone. Accepts simultaneous submissions. Reports in 1 week on queries, 2 weeks on mss. Sample copy for $3.

**Nonfiction:** General interest, interview/profile, new product, personal experience, photo feature, religious, technical and travel. Special issues feature: International Kosher Travel (October); Passover (March). **Buys 8-12 mss/year.** Query with published clips. Length: 1,000-1,500 words. **Pays $100-250 for assigned articles; up to $100 for unsolicited articles.** Sometimes pays expenses of writers on assignment.

**Reprints:** Send tearsheet or photocopy of article and information about when and where the article previously appeared. Pays 25-50% of amount paid for an original article.

**Photos:** State availability of photos with submission. Offers no additional payment for photos accepted with ms. Acquires one-time rights.

**Columns/Departments:** Book Review (cook books, food technology, kosher food), 250-500 words; People in the News (interviews with kosher personalities), 1,000-1,500 words; Regional Kosher Supervision (report on kosher supervision in a city or community), 1,000-1,500 words; Food Technology (new technology or current technology with accompanying pictures), 1,000-1,500 words; Travel (international, national), must include Kosher information and Jewish communities, 1,000-1,500 words; Regional Kosher Cooking, 1,000-1,500 words. **Buys 8-12 mss/year.** Query with published clips. **Pays $50-250.**

**Tips:** "*Kashrus Magazine* will do more writing on general food technology, production, and merchandising as well as human interest travelogs and regional writing in 2000 than we have done in the past. Areas most open to freelancers are interviews, food technology, cooking and food preparation, dining, regional reporting and travel. We welcome stories on the availability and quality of Kosher foods and services in communities across the U.S. and throughout the world."

Some of our best stories have been by non-Jewish writers about kosher observance in their region. We also enjoy humorous articles. Just send a query with clips and we'll try to find a storyline that's right for you, or better yet, call us to discuss a storyline."

**✪ $ $** **RISTORANTE**, Foley Publishing, P.O. Box 73, Liberty Corner NJ 07938. (908)766-6006. Fax: (908)766-6607. E-mail: barmag@aol.com. Website: http://www.bartender.com. **Contact:** Raymond Foley, publisher or Jaclyn Foley, editor. **75% freelance written.** Bimonthly magazine covering "Italian anything! *Ristorante—The magazine for the Italian Connoisseur.* For Italian restaurants and those who love Italian food, travel, wine and all things Italian!" Estab. 1994. Circ. 40,000. Pays on publication. Publishes ms an average of 3 months after acceptance. Byline sometimes given. Buys first North American and one-time rights. Editorial lead time 3 months. Submit seasonal material 3 months in advance. Reports in 1 month on queries; 2 months on mss. Sample copy and writer's guidelines for 9 × 12 SAE and 4 first-class stamps.
**Nonfiction:** Book excerpts, general interest, historical/nostalgic, how-to (prepare Italian foods), humor, new product, opinion, personal experience, travel. **Buys 25 mss/year.** Send complete ms. Length: 100-1,000 words. **Pays $100-350 for assigned articles; $75-300 for unsolicited articles.** Sometimes pays expenses of writers on assignment.
**Reprints:** Send tearsheet or photocopy of article and information about when and where the article previously appeared. Pays 25% of amount paid for an original article.
**Photos:** Send photos with submission. Reviews 3 × 5 prints. Negotiates payment individually. Captions, model releases required. Buys one-time rights.
**Columns/Departments:** Send complete ms. **Pays $50-200.**
**Fillers:** Anecdotes, facts, short humor. **Buys 10/year. Pays $10-50.**

**$ $ $ $** **SAVEUR**, Meigher Communications, 100 Avenue of the Americas, New York NY 10013. (212)334-1212. Fax: (212)334-1260. Editor-in-Chief: Dorothy Kalins. Editor: Colman Andrews. Bimonthly. "*Saveur* covers the world of food to make cooking, eating, and reading about food more satisfying." This magazine did not respond to our request for information. Query before submitting.

**$ $ $** **VEGETARIAN TIMES**, 4 High Ridge Park, Stamford CT 06905. (203)321-1758. Fax: (203)322-1966. **Contact:** Donna Sapolin, editorial director. **50% freelance written.** Prefers to work with published/established writers; works with small number of new/unpublished writers each year. Monthly magazine. Circ. 320,000. Buys first serial or all rights. Byline given unless extensive revisions are required or material is incorporated into a larger article. **Pays on acceptance.** Publishes ms an average of 4 months after acceptance. Submit seasonal material 6 months in advance. Accepts queries by mail or fax. No phone queries. Reports in 3 months. Writer's guidelines for #10 SASE.
**Nonfiction:** Features articles that inform readers about how vegetarianism relates to diet, cooking, lifestyle, natural health, consumer choices, natural foods, environmental concerns and animal welfare. "All material should be well-documented and researched, and written in a sophisticated and lively style." Informational, how-to, personal experience, interview, investigative. Query with published clips. Length: average 2,000 words. **Pays $100-1,000,** sometimes higher, depending on length and difficulty of piece. Also uses 200-500-word items for news department. Sometimes pays expenses of writers on assignment.
**Photos:** Payment negotiated/photo.
**Tips:** "You don't have to be a vegetarian to write for *Vegetarian Times,* but it is vital that your article have a vegetarian perspective. The best way to pick up that slant is to read several issues of the magazine (no doubt a tip you've heard over and over). We are looking for stories that go beyond the obvious 'Why I Became a Vegetarian.' A well-written provocative query plus samples of your best writing will increase your chances of publication."

**$ $** **WINE SPECTATOR**, M. Shanken Communications, Inc., 387 Park Ave. S., New York NY 10016. (212)684-4224. Fax: (212)684-5424. E-mail: winespec@mshanken.com. Website: http://www.winespectator.com. **Contact:** Jim Gordon, managing editor. **20% freelance written.** Prefers to work with published/established writers. Biweekly newsmagazine. Estab. 1976. Circ. 250,000. Pays within 30 days of publication. Publishes ms an average of 2 months after acceptance. Byline given. Buys all rights and makes work-for-hire assignments. Submit seasonal material 4 months in advance. Accepts queries by mail, fax. Reports in 3 months. Sample copy for $5. Writer's guidelines for #10 SASE.
**Nonfiction:** General interest (news about wine or wine events); interview/profile (of wine, vintners, wineries); opinion; travel, dining and other lifestyle pieces; photo feature. No "winery promotional pieces or articles by writers who lack sufficient knowledge to write below just surface data." Query. Length: 100-2,000 words average. **Pays $50-500.**
**Photos:** Send photos with ms. Pays $75 minimum for color transparencies. Captions, model releases, identification of subjects required. Buys all rights.
■ The online magazine carries original content not found in the print edition. Contact: Jane Shufer, online editor.
**Tips:** "A solid knowledge of wine is a must. Query letters essential, detailing the story idea. New, refreshing ideas which have not been covered before stand a good chance of acceptance. *Wine Spectator* is a consumer-oriented *news magazine,* but we are interested in some trade stories; brevity is essential."

**N** **$ $** **WINE X MAGAZINE, Wine, Food and an Intelligent Slice of Vice**, X Publishing, Inc., 4184 Sonoma Mountain Rd., Santa Rosa CA 95404-9503. (707)545-0992. Fax: (707)542-7062. E-mail: winex@wco.com. Website: http://www.winexwired.com. **Contact:** Darryl Roberts, editor/publisher. **100% freelance written.** Biweekly magazine covering wine and other beverages. "*Wine X* is a lifestyle magazine for young adults featuring wine, beer, spirits, music, movies, fashion, food, coffee, celebrity interviews, health/fitness." Estab. 1997. Circ. 35,000. Pays on publication. Published ms 3 months after acceptance. Byline given. Not copyrighted. Buys first North American serial and electronic rights. Editorial lead time 3 months. Submit seasonal material 4 months in advance. Accepts queries by mail, e-mail, fax. Reports in 3 weeks on queries; 3 months on mss. Sample copy for $5. Guidelines online at website.

**Nonfiction:** Essays, personal experience, photo feature. No restaurant reviews, wine collector profiles. **Buys 6 mss/ year.** Query. Length: 500-1,500 words. **Pays $50-250 for assigned articles; $50-150 for unsolicited articles.** Sometimes pays expenses of writers on assignment.

**Photos:** Reviews transparencies. Offers no additional payment for photos accepted with ms. Model releases and identification of subjects required. Buys one-time rights.

**Columns/Departments:** Wine, Other Beverages, Lifestyle, all 1,000 words. **Buys 72 mss/year.** Query.

**Fiction: Buys 6 mss/year.** Query. Length: 1,000-1,500 words. **No pay for fiction.**

**Poetry:** Avant garde, free verse, haiku, light verse, traditional. **Buys 2 poems/year.** Submit maximum 3 poems. Length: 10-1,500 lines.

**Fillers:** Short humor. **Buys 6/year.** Length: 100-500 words. **Pays $0-50.**

**Tips:** "See our website."

# GAMES & PUZZLES

These publications are written by and for game enthusiasts interested in both traditional games and word puzzles and newer role-playing adventure, computer and video games. Other puzzle markets may be found in the Juvenile section.

**$ $ CHESS LIFE**, United States Chess Federation, 3054 NYS Route 9W, New Windsor NY 12553-7698. (914)562-8350. Fax: (914)561-2437 or (914)236-4852. E-mail: chesslife-uscf@juno.com. Website: http://www.uschess.org. **Contact:** Glenn Petersen, editor. **15% freelance written.** Works with a small number of new/unpublished writers each year. Monthly. "*Chess Life* is the official publication of the United States Chess Federation, covering news of most major chess events, both here and abroad, with special emphasis on the triumphs and exploits of American players." Estab. 1939. Circ. 70,000. Publishes ms an average of 8 months after acceptance. Byline given. Offers 50% kill fee. Buys first or negotiable rights. Submit seasonal material 8 months in advance. Accepts simultaneous submissions. Reports in 3 months. Sample copy and writer's guidelines for $9 × 11$ SAE with 5 first-class stamps.

**Nonfiction:** General interest, historical, interview/profile, technical—all must have some relation to chess. No "stories about personal experiences with chess." **Buys 30-40 mss/year.** Query with samples "if new to publication." Length: 3,000 words maximum. **Pays $100/page (per 800-1,000 words).** Sometimes pays expenses of writers on assignment.

**Reprints:** Send tearsheet or photocopy of article or short story or typed ms with rights for sale noted and information about when and where the article or story previously appeared.

**Photos:** Reviews b&w contact sheets and prints, and color prints and slides. Captions, model releases and identification of subjects required. Buys all or negotiable rights. **Pays $25-35 inside; $100-300 for covers.**

**Columns/Departments:** Chess Review (brief articles on unknown chess personalities and "Chess in Everyday Life."

**Fiction:** Short stories and novel excerpts. "Chess-related, high quality." **Buys 2-3 mss/year.** Pays variable fee.

**Fillers:** Cartoons, poems, puzzles. Submit with samples and clips. Buys first or negotiable rights. **Pays $25 upon acceptance.**

**Tips:** "Articles must be written from an informed point of view—not from view of the curious amateur. Most of our writers are specialized in that they have sound credentials as chessplayers. Freelancers in major population areas (except New York and Los Angeles, which we already have covered) who are interested in short personality profiles and perhaps news reporting have the best opportunities. We're looking for more personality pieces on chessplayers around the country; not just the stars, but local masters, talented youths, and dedicated volunteers. Freelancers interested in such pieces might let us know of their interest and their range. Could be we know of an interesting story in their territory that needs covering. Examples of published articles include a locally produced chess television program, a meeting of chess set collectors from around the world, chess in our prisons, and chess in the works of several famous writers."

**$ $ GAMEPRO**, IDG Games Media Group, 501 Second St., Suite 500, San Francisco CA 94107. (415)979-9845. Fax (415) 546-5225. Website: http://www.gamepro.com. Publisher: John Rousseau. **Contact:** Kathy Skaggs, managing editor. Monthly magazine. "*GamePro* is a multi-platform interactive gaming magazine covering the electronic game market. It is edited for the avid online, video and PC game enthusiast. The editorial includes a mix of news, reviews, strategy and specific topical sections such as Fighter's Edge, Role Player's Realm and the Sports Pages." Estab. 1988. Circ. 500,000. Query before submitting. Accepts queries by mail, e-mail, phone, fax.

    The online magazine carries original content not found in the print edition. Contact: George Chronis, online editor.

**$ $ $ $ GAMES MAGAZINE**, Games Publications, Inc., 7002 W. Butler Pike, Suite 210, Ambler PA 19002. (215)643-6385. Fax: (215)628-3571. E-mail: gamespub@itw.com. **Contact:** R. Wayne Schmittberger, editor-in-chief. **50% freelance written.** Magazine published 9 times/year covering puzzles and games. "*Games* is a magazine of puzzles, contests, and features pertaining to games and ingenuity. It is aimed primarily at adults and has an emphasis on pop culture." Estab. 1977. Circ. 175,000. Pays on publication. Publishes ms an average of 4 months after acceptance. Byline given. Offers 25% kill fee. Buys first North American serial rights, first rights, one-time rights, second serial (reprint) rights, all rights or makes work-for-hire assignments. Editorial lead time 3 months. Submit seasonal material 6 months in advance. Accepts simultaneous submissions. Reports in 6 weeks on queries; 3 months on mss. Sample copy for $5. Writer's guidelines for #10 SASE.

**Nonfiction:** Photo features, puzzles, games. **Buys 3 mss/year; 100 puzzles/year.** Query. Length: 1,500-2,500 words. **Pays $1,000-1,750.** Sometimes pays expenses of writers on assignment.

**Reprints:** Accepts previously published submissions.

**Photos:** State availability of photos with submission. Reviews contact sheets, negatives, transparencies, prints. Negotiates payment individually. Captions, model releases, identification of subjects required. Buys one-time rights.

**Columns/Departments:** Gamebits (game/puzzle news), 250 words; Games & Books (product reviews), 350 words; Wild Cards (short text puzzles), 100 words. **Buys 50 mss/year.** Query. **Pays $25-250.**

**Fiction:** Interactive adventure and mystery stories. **Buys 1-2 mss/year.** Query. Length: 1,500-2,500 words. **Pays $1,000-1,750.**

**Tips:** "Look for real-life people, places, or things that might in some way be the basis for a puzzle."

**$ SCHOOL MATES**, United States Chess Federation, 186 Route 9W, New Windsor NY 12553-5794. (914)562-8350 ext. 152. Fax: (914)561-CHES (2437). E-mail: scholastic_uscf@juno.com. Website: http://www.uschess.org. Publication Director: Jay Hastings. **Contact:** Beatriz Marinello, editor. **10% freelance written.** Bimonthly magazine of chess for the beginning (some intermediate) player. Includes instruction, player profiles, chess tournament coverage, listings. Estab. 1987. Circ. 30,000. Pays on publication. Publishes ms an average of 6 months after acceptance. Byline given. Publication copyrighted "but not filed with Library of Congress." Buys first rights. Editorial lead time 2 months. Submit seasonal material 3 months in advance. Accepts queries by e-mail. Accepts simultaneous submissions. Reports in 6 months. Sample copy and writer's guidelines free.

**Nonfiction:** How-to, humor, personal experience (chess, but not "my first tournament"), photo feature, technical, travel and any other chess related item. **Buys 10-20 mss/year.** Query. Length: 250-1,000 words. **Pays $50/1,000 words, $20 minimum.** "We are not-for-profit; we try to make up for low $ rate with complimentary copies." Sometimes pays expenses of writers on assignment.

**Reprints:** Send tearsheet, photocopy of article or typed ms with rights for sale noted and information about when and where the article previously appeared. Pays 100% of amount paid for an original article.

**Photos:** Send photos with submission. Reviews prints. Offers $25/photo for first time rights. Captions, identification of subjects required. Buys one-time rights, pays $15 for subsequent use.

**Columns/Departments:** Test Your Tactics/Winning Chess Tactics (explanation, with diagrams, of chess tactics; 8 diagrammed chess problems, e.g., "white to play and win in 2 moves"); Basic Chess (chess instruction for beginners). Query with published clips. **Pays $50/1,000 words ($20 minimum).**

**Tips:** "Know your subject; chess is a technical subject, and you can't fake it. Human interest stories on famous chess players or young chess players can be 'softer,' but always remember you are writing for children, and make it lively. We use the Frye readability scale (3rd-6th grade reading level), and items written on the appropriate reading level do stand out immediately! We are most open to human interest stories, puzzles, cartoons, photos. We are always looking for an unusual angle, e.g., (wild example) a kid who plays chess while surfing, or (more likely) a blind kid and how she plays chess with her specially-made chess pieces and board, etc."

# GAY & LESBIAN INTEREST

The magazines listed here cover a wide range of politics, culture, news, art, literature and issues of general interest to gay and lesbian communities. Magazines of a strictly sexual content are listed in the Sex section.

**$ $ THE ADVOCATE**, Liberation Publications, Inc., 6922 Hollywood Blvd., 10th Floor, Suite 1000, Los Angeles CA 90028-6148. (213)871-1225. Fax: (213)467-6805. E-mail: newsroom@advocate.com. **Contact**: Judy Wieder, editor-in-chief. Biweekly magazine covering national news events with a gay and lesbian perspective on the issues. Estab. 1967. Circ. 80,000. Pays on publication. Byline given. Buys first North American serial rights. Responds in 1 month. Sample copy for $3.95. Writer's guidelines for #10 SASE.

**Nonfiction:** Exposé, interview/profile, news reporting and investigating. "Here are elements we look for in all articles: *Angling*: An angle is the one editorial tool we have to attract a reader's attention. An *Advocate* editor won't make an assignment unless he or she has worked out a very specific angle with you. Once you've worked out the angle with an editor, don't deviate from it without letting the editor know. Some of the elements we look for in angles are: a news hook; an open question or controversy; a 'why' or 'how' element or novel twist; national appeal; and tight focus. *Content*: Lesbian and gay news stories in all areas of life: arts, sciences, financial, medical, cyberspace, etc. *Tone*: Tone is the element that makes an emotional connection. Some characteristics we look for: toughness; edginess; fairness and evenhandedness; multiple perspectives." Special issues: gays on campus, coming out interviews with celebrities, HIV and health. Query. Length: 1,200 words. **Pays $550.**

**Columns/Departments:** Arts & Media (news and profiles of well-known gay or lesbians in entertainment) is most open to freelancers. Query. Length: 750 words. **Pays $100-500.**

**Fiction:** Publishes novel excerpts.

**Tips:** *"The Advocate* is a unique newsmagazine. While we report on gay and lesbian issues and are published by one of the country's oldest and most established gay-owned companies, we also play by the rules of mainstream-not gay-community-journalism."

**N ⊠ $ $ ALTERNATIVE FAMILY MAGAZINE,** AFM Publishing, P.O. Box 7179, Van Nuys CA 91409. (818)909-0314. Fax: (818)909-3792. E-mail: altfammag@aol.com. Website: http://www.altfammag.com. Managing Editor: John Quinlan. **Contact:** Kelly Taylor, editor-in-chief. **90% freelance written.** Bimonthly magazine covering general parenting and topics more specific to gay and lesbian parenting. "Editorial content must be diverse to reflect gay and lesbian parenting. Topics might also include product information, nutrition, safety, medicine, general health, financial information and children's interest. Also publishes articles of interest to parents-to-be." Estab. 1998. Circ. 8,000. Pays on publication. Publishes ms an average of 3 months after acceptance. Byline given. Offers 25% kill fee. Buys first North American serial rights. Editorial lead time 2 months. Submit seasonal material 3 months in advance. Accepts simultaneous submissions. Reports in 6 weeks on queries; 2 months on mss. Sample copy for $3.95 and 9 × 12 SAE with 6 first-class stamps. Writer's guidelines for #10 SASE.

**Nonfiction:** Book excerpts, essays, general interest, how-to, humor, inspirational, interview/profile, new product, opinion, personal experience, photo feature, travel. "No articles that focus on heterosexual parents or interests." **Buys 20 mss/year.** Send complete ms. Length: 200-3,000 words. **Pays $25-300 for assigned articles; $25-300 for unsolicited articles.**

**Reprints:** Accepts previously published submissions.

**Photos:** Send photos with submission. Reviews contact sheets, transparencies and prints. Negotiates payment individually. Captions, model releases and identification of subjects required. Buys one-time rights.

**Columns/Departments:** Gadgets (product information), 150 words; Your Health (health topics for entire family), 200 words; Baby Tips, 25 words and up. **Buys 15 mss/year.** Send complete ms. **Pays $10-200.**

**Fillers:** Facts, gags to be illustrated by cartoonist, newsbreaks, short humor. **Buys 5-10/year.** Length: 75-300 words. **Pays $5-30.**

**Tips:** "We're looking for general parenting articles, tips and topics for our audience of gay, lesbian, bisexual, transgendered audience of parents and expectant parents—keeping in mind that our reader audience also includes single GLBT parents."

**$ BAY WINDOWS, New England's Largest Gay and Lesbian Newspaper,** Bay Windows, Inc., 631 Tremont St., Boston MA 02118-2034. (617)266-6670. Fax: (617)266-5973. E-mail: news@baywindows.com. Website: http://www.baywindows.com. Editor: Jeff Epperly. Arts Editor: Rudy Kikel. **Contact:** Loren King, assistant editor. **30-40% freelance written.** Weekly newspaper of gay news and concerns. *"Bay Windows* covers predominantly news of New England, but will print non-local news and features depending on the newsworthiness of the story. We feature hard news, opinion, news analysis, arts reviews and interviews." Estab. 1983. Publishes ms within 2 months of acceptance, pays within 2 months of publication. Byline given. Offers 50% kill fee. Rights obtained vary, usually first serial rights. Simultaneous submissions accepted if other submissions are outside of New England. Submit seasonal material 3 months in advance. Accepts queries by mail, e-mail, fax, phone. Reports in 3 months. Sample copy for $5. Writer's guidelines for #10 SASE.

**Nonfiction:** Hard news, general interest with a gay slant, interview/profile, opinion, photo features. **Publishes 200 mss/year.** Query with published clips or send complete ms. Length: 500-1,500 words. **Pay varies: $25-100 news, arts.**

**Reprints:** Send tearsheet or photocopy of article and information about when and where the article previously appeared. Pays 75% of amount paid for an original article.

**Photos:** Pays $25/published photo. Model releases and identification of subjects required.

**Columns/Departments:** Film, music, dance, books, art. Length: 500-1,500 words. **Buys 200 mss/year. Pays $25-100.** Letters, opinion to Jeff Epperly, editor; news, features to Loren King, assistant editor; arts, reviews to Rudy Kikel, arts editor.

**Poetry:** All varieties. **Publishes 50 poems/year.** Length: 10-30 lines. No payment. **Contact:** Rudy Kikel.

**Tips:** "Too much gay-oriented writing is laden with the clichés and catch phrases of the movement. Writers must have intimate knowledge of gay community; however, this doesn't mean that standard English usage isn't required. We look for writers with new, even controversial perspectives on the lives of gay men and lesbians. While we assume gay is good, we'll print stories which examine problems within the community and movement. No pornography or erotica."

**$ $ CURVE MAGAZINE,** Outspoken Enterprises, Inc., 1 Haight St., #B, San Francisco CA 94102. Fax: (415)863-1609. E-mail: curvemag@aol.com. Editor-in-chief: Frances Stevens. **Contact:** Gretchen Lee, managing editor. **40% freelance written.** Bimonthly magazine covering lesbian general interest categories. "We want dynamic and provocative articles written by, about and for lesbians." Estab. 1991. Circ. 68,000. Pays on publication. Byline given. Offers 25% kill fee. Buys first North American serial rights. Editorial lead time 3 months. Submit seasonal material 3 months in advance. Accepts queries by mail, e-mail, fax. Sample copy for $3.95 with $2 postage. Writer's guidelines free.

**Nonfiction:** Book excerpts, essays, exposé, general interest, how-to, humor, interview/profile, opinion, photo feature, travel. Special issues: Pride issue (June/July); Music issue (August/September). No fiction or poetry. **Buys 25 mss/year.** Query. Length: 200-2,500 words. **Pays $40-300.** Sometimes pays expenses of writers on assignment.

**Photos:** Send photos with submission. Offers $50-100/photo; negotiates payment individually. Captions, model releases, identification of subjects required. Buys one-time rights.

**Columns/Departments: Buys 72 mss/year.** Query. **Pays $75-300.**

**Tips:** Feature articles generally fit into one of the following categories: Celebrity profiles (lesbian, bisexual or straight women who are icons for the lesbian community or actively involved in coalition-building with the lesbian community). Community segment profiles—e.g., lesbian firefighters, drag kings, sports teams (multiple interviews with a variety of women in different parts of the country representing a diversity of backgrounds). Non-celebrity profiles (activities of "unknown" or low-profile lesbian and bisexual activists/political leaders, athletes, filmmakers, dancers, writers, musicians, etc.). Controversial issues (spark a dialogue about issues that divide us as a community, and the ways in which lesbians of different backgrounds fail to understand and support one another. We are not interested in inflammatory articles that incite or enrage readers without offering a channel for action). Trends (community trends in a variety of areas, including sports, fashion, image, health, music, spirituality and identity). Visual essays (most of our fashion and travel pieces are developed and produced in-house. However, we welcome input from freelancers and from time to time publish outside work).

**$ $ GIRLFRIENDS MAGAZINE, Lesbian culture, politics and entertainment**, 3415 Cesar Chavez, Suite 101, San Francisco CA 94110. (415)648-9464. Fax: (415)648-4705. E-mail: staff@gfriends.com. Website: http://www.gfriends.com. Editorial Director: Heather Findlay. **Contact:** Kathleen Hildenbrand, managing editor. Monthly lesbian magazine. *"Girlfriends* provides its readers with intelligent, entertaining and visually-pleasing coverage of culture, politics and entertainment—all from an informed and critical lesbian perspective." Estab. 1994. Circ. 75,000. Pays on publication. Publishes ms an average of 6 months after acceptance. Byline given. Offers 25% kill fee. Buys first rights, use for advertising/promoting *Girlfriends.* Editorial lead time 3 months. Submit seasonal material 6 months in advance. Accepts simultaneous submissions. Reports in 3 weeks on queries; 2 months on mss. Sample copy for $4.95 plus $1.50 s/h. Writer's guidelines for #10 SASE.

**Nonfiction:** Investigative features, celebrity profiles, exposé, humor, interviews, photo feature, travel. Special features: best lesbian restaurants in the US; best places to live. Special issues: sex issue, gay pride issue, breast cancer issue. **Buys 20-25 mss/year.** Query with published clips. Length: 1,000-3,500 words. **Pays 10¢/word.**

**Reprints:** Send photocopy of article or typed ms with rights for sale noted and information about when and where the article previously appeared. Negotiable payment.

**Photos:** Send photos with submissions. Reviews contact sheets, 4×5 or 2¼×2¼ transparencies, prints. Offers $30-250/photo. Captions, model releases, identification of subjects required. Buys one-time rights, use for advertising/promoting *GF.*

**Columns/Departments:** Book reviews, 900 words; Music reviews, 600 words; Travel, 600 words. Query with published clips. **Pays 10¢/word.**

• *Girlfriends* is not accepting fiction, poetry or fillers.

**Tips:** "Be unafraid of controversy—articles should focus on problems and debates raised around lesbian culture, politics, and sexuality. Avoid being 'politically correct.' Photographers should aim for the suggestive, not the explicit. We don't want just to know what's happening in the lesbian world, we want to know how what's happening in the world affects lesbians."

**$ $ THE GUIDE, To Gay Travel, Entertainment, Politics and Sex**, Fidelity Publishing, P.O. Box 990593, Boston MA 02199-0593. (617)266-8557. Fax: (617)266-1125. E-mail: theguide@guidemag.com. Website: http://www.guidemag.com. **Contact:** French Wall, editor. **25% freelance written.** Monthly magazine on the gay and lesbian community. Estab. 1981. Circ. 30,000. **Pays on acceptance.** Publishes ms an average of 2 months after acceptance. Kill fee negotiable. Buys first-time rights. Submit seasonal material 2 months in advance. Accepts queries by mail, e-mail. Accepts simultaneous submissions. Reports in 3 months. Sample copy for 9×12 SAE with 8 first-class stamps. Writer's guidelines for #10 SASE.

**Nonfiction:** Book excerpts (if yet unpublished), essays, exposé, general interest, historical/nostalgic, humor, interview/profile, opinion, personal experience, photo feature, religious. **Buys 24 mss/year.** Query with or without published clips or send complete ms. Length: 500-5,000 words. **Pays $75-220.**

**Reprints:** Occasionally buys previously published submissions. Pays 100% of amount paid for an original article.

**Photos:** Send photos with submission. Reviews contact sheets. Offers no additional payment for photos accepted with ms (although sometimes negotiable). Captions, model releases, identification of subjects preferred; releases required sometimes. Buys one-time rights.

**Tips:** "Brevity, humor and militancy appreciated. Writing on sex, political analysis and humor are particularly appreciated. We purchase very few freelance travel pieces; those that we do buy are usually on less commercial destinations."

**$ $ HERO MAGAZINE**, (formerly *Arrow Magazine*), HERO Publishing, LLC, 8581 Santa Monica Blvd., #430, West Hollywood CA 90069. (310)360-8022. E-mail: editor@heromag.com. Website: http://www.heromag.com. **Contact:** Paul Horne, editorial director. **90% freelance written.** Bimonthly magazine for pro-commitment gay men with emphasis on relationships, romance and family, in addition to entertainment, pop culture and technology. Estab. 1996. Circ. 100,000. Pays on publication. Publishes ms an average of 2 months after acceptance. Byline given. Buys one-time rights. Editorial lead time 2 months. Submit seasonal material 4 months in advance. Reports in 1 month on queries. Sample copy for $4.95. Writer's guidelines on website.

**Nonfiction:** Book excerpts, essays, general interest, how-to, humor, inspirational, interview/profile, opinion, personal experience, photo feature, technology, travel. "*HERO* selects articles which challenge and broaden the current depiction of gay men in the media. Therefore, erotic material and overtly sexual submissions will likely be overlooked." Query with published clips. No queries by fax or e-mail. **Buys 30 mss/year**. Length: 300-4,000 words. **Pays 10-50¢/word for print publication only**, not for online publication.

**Reprints:** Accepts previously published submissions.

**Photos:** Send photos with submission. Reviews contact sheets. Offers no additional payment for photos accepted with ms. Model releases required. Buys one time rights.

**Columns/Departments:** Book (book features and reviews), 300-1,000 words. Family (profiles of gay fathers, children of gay parents), Youth (out gay kids making a difference); Boy Toys (technology, high-tech gadgets); Music and Theatre (interviews and reviews); Spirituality, all 500-1,000 words. **Buys 20 mss/year**. Query with published clips. **Pays 10-50¢/word.**

**Tips:** "*HERO* is not the typical gay lifestyle magazine. We are the first and only national magazine for gay men that features commitment, romance, family and a balanced approach to life and our features are all practical, positive and inspirational. Successful freelances will read the magazine and get a feel for our audience and vision before querying. Please keep query letters brief and concise. HERO readers should be moved and/or inspired by what they read in the magazine."

**$ LAMBDA BOOK REPORT, A Review of Contemporary Gay and Lesbian Bisexual & Transgender Literature,** Lambda Literary Foundation, P.O. Box 73910, Washington DC 20056-3910. (202)462-7924. Fax: (202)462-5264. E-mail: lbreditor@aol.com. **Contact:** Jim Marks, managing editor. **90% freelance written.** Monthly magazine that covers gay/lesbian literature. "*Lambda Book Report* devotes its entire contents to the discussion of gay, lesbian, bisexual and transgender books and authors. Any other submissions would be inappropriate." Estab. 1987. Circ. 11,000. Pays 90 days after publication. Byline given. Buys first rights. Reports in 2 months. Sample copy for $4.95. Guidelines free.

● This editor sees an increasing need for writers familiar with economic and science/medical-related topics.

**Nonfiction:** Book excerpts, essays (on gay literature), interview/profile (of authors), book reviews. "No historical essays, fiction or poetry." Query with published clips. Length: 200-2,000 words. **Pays $15-125 for assigned articles; $5-25 for unsolicited articles.**

**Photos:** Send photos with submission. Reviews contact sheets. Offers $10-25/photo. Model releases required. Buys one-time rights.

**Tips:** "Assignments go to writers who query with 2-3 published book reviews and/or interviews. It is helpful if the writer is familiar with gay and lesbian literature and can write intelligently and objectively on the field. Review section is most open. Clips should demonstrate writers' knowledge, ability and interest in reviewing gay books."

**[N] $ $ METRO SOURCE,** MetroSource Publishing Inc., 180 Varick St., 5th Floor, New York NY 10014. (212)691-5127. Fax: (212)741-2978. E-mail: metrosource@aol.com. **Contact:** Eva Leonard, editor. **70% freelance written.** Quarterly magazine. "*MetroSource* is a celebration and exploration of urban gay and lesbian life. *MetroSource* is an upscale, glossy, four-color lifestyle magazine targeted to an urban, professional gay and lesbian readership." Estab. 1990. Circ. 55,000. Pays on publication. Publishes ms an average of 6 months after acceptance. Byline given. Buys all rights. Editorial lead time 6 months. Submit seasonal material 4 months in advance. Accepts queries by mail, e-mail, fax, phone. Accepts simultaneous submissions. Sample copy for $5.

**Nonfiction:** Exposé, interview/profile, photo feature, travel. No opinion pieces. **Buys 20 mss/year.** Query with published clips. Length: 1,000-2,500 words. **Pays $100-500.**

**Photos:** State availability of photos with submission. Negotiates payment individually. Captions and model releases required.

**Columns/Departments:** Book reviews and health columns (both of interest to gay and lesbian audience), word lengths vary. Query with published clips. **Pays $100-700.**

**$ MOM GUESS WHAT NEWSPAPER,** 1725 L St., Sacramento CA 95814. (916)441-6397. Fax: (916)441-6422. E-mail: info@mgwnew.com. Website: http://www.mgwnews.com. **Contact:** Linda Birner, editor. **80% freelance written.** Works with small number of new/unpublished writers each year. Biweekly tabloid covering gay rights and gay lifestyles. A newspaper for gay men, lesbians and their straight friends in the State Capitol and the Sacramento Valley area. First and oldest gay newspaper in Sacramento. Estab. 1977. Circ. 21,000. Publishes ms an average of 3 months after acceptance. Byline given. Buys all rights. Submit seasonal material 3 months in advance. Reports in 2 months. Sample copy for $1. Writer's guidelines for 10×13 SAE with 4 first-class stamps or on website.

**Nonfiction:** Interview/profile and photo feature of international, national or local scope. **Buys 8 mss/year.** Query. Length: 200-1,500 words. Payment depends on article. Pays expenses of writers on special assignment.

**Reprints:** Send tearsheet or photocopy and information about when and where previously appeared. Pay varies.

**Photos:** Send photos with submission. Reviews 5×7 prints. Offers no additional payment for photos accepted with ms. Captions and identification of subjects required. Buys one-time rights.

**Columns/Departments:** News, Restaurants, Political, Health, Film, Video, Book Reviews. **Buys 12 mss/year.** Query. Payment depends on article.

**Tips:** "*MGW* is published primarily from volunteers. With some freelancers payment is made. Put requirements in your cover letter. Byline appears with each published article; photos credited. Editors reserve right to edit, crop, touch up, revise, or otherwise alter manuscripts, and photos, but not to change theme or intent of the work. Enclose SASE postcard for acceptance or rejection. We will not assume responsibility for returning unsolicited material lacking sufficient return postage or lost in the mail."

**$ OUTSMART**, Up & Out Communications, 3406 Audubon Place, Houston TX 77006. (713)520-7237. Fax: (713)522-3275. E-mail: outsmartmagazine.com. Website: http://www.outsmartmagazine.com. **Contact:** Greg Jeu, publisher. **70% freelance written.** Monthly magazine covering gay and lesbian issues. "*OutSmart* provides positive information to gay men, lesbians and their associates to enhance and improve the quality of our lives." Estab. 1994. Circ. 15,000. Pays on publication. Publishes ms an average of 2 months after acceptance. Byline given. Buys one-time rights and simultaneous rights. Editorial lead time 2 months. Submit seasonal material 2 months in advance. Accepts queries by mail, e-mail. Accepts simultaneous submissions. Reports in 6 weeks on queries; 2 months on mss. Sample copy and writer's guidelines for SASE.

**Nonfiction:** Historical/nostalgic, interview/profile, opinion, personal experience, photo feature, travel, health/wellness, local/national news. **Buys 10 mss/year.** Send complete ms. Length: 700-2,000 words. **Pays $20-60.**

**Reprints:** Send photocopy of article.

**Photos:** State availability of photos with submission. Reviews 4×6 prints. Negotiates payment individually. Identification of subjects required. Buys one-time rights.

■ The online magazine carries original content not found in the print edition.

**Tips:** "Outsmart is a mainstream publication that covers culture, politics, personalities, entertainment and health/wellness as well as local and national news and events. It is our goal to address the diversity of the lesbian and gay community, fostering understanding among all Houston's citizens."

**[N] $ THE WASHINGTON BLADE**, Washington Blade, Inc., 1408 U St., NW, Washington DC 20009-3916. (202)797-7000. Fax: (202)797-7040. E-mail: news@washblade.com or arts@washblade.com or forum@washblade.com. Website: http://www.washblade.com. **Contact:** Greg Varner, arts editor or Lyn Stoesen, opinion editor. **20% freelance written.** Nation's oldest and largest weekly news tabloid covering the gay/lesbian community. "Articles (subjects) should be written from or directed to a gay perspective." Estab. 1969. Circ. 50,000. Pays in 1 month. Publishes ms an average of 1 month after acceptance. Byline given. Offers kill fee. Buys first North American serial rights. Submit seasonal material 1 month in advance. Accepts queries by mail, e-mail, fax. Reports in 2 months.

○┱ The greatest opportunities for freelancers are in the arts section. "We look for features, reviews and profiles with a Washington, DC, area angle. Story ideas on books, travel, lifestyles, exhibitions are all considered. Send query to Greg Varner, arts editor (arts@washblade.com)."

**Nonfiction:** Most news stories are staff-generated; writers with news or news feature ideas should query first.

**Reprints:** Send typed ms with rights for sale noted and information about when and where the article previously appeared.

**Photos:** "A photo or graphic with feature/lifestyle articles is particularly important. Photos with news stories are appreciated." Send photos by mail or e-mail. Pays $25 minimum. Captions preferred. On assignment, photographer paid mutually agreed upon fee, with expenses reimbursed. Publication retains all rights.

**Columns/Departments:** Arts (books, travel and profiles of gay figures in the arts). **Pays 10-12¢/word.** Send submissions to Greg Varner, arts editor. Opinion columns 1-2 times/week (reactions to political developments, cultural observations, and moving or funny personal stories), 900 words. **Pays $25.** Send submissions to Lyn Stoesen, opinion editor. No sexually explicit material.

**Tips:** "We have a highly competent and professional staff of news reporters, and it is difficult to break in here as a freelancer covering news. Include a résumé, good examples of your writing, and know the paper before you send a manuscript for publication. We look for writers who are credible and professional, and for copy that is accurate, fair, timely, and objective in tone. We do not work with writers who play fast and loose with the facts. Before you send anything, become familiar with our publicationn. We get a lot of material that is completely inapprorpiate. Do not send sexually explicit material."

**[N] $ THE JAMES WHITE REVIEW, A Gay Men's Literary Quarterly**, P.O. Box 73910, Washington DC 20056-3910. (202)462-7924. E-mail: jwrmerla@aol.com. Publisher: Jim Marks. **Contact:** Patrick Merla, editor. **100% freelance written.** Quarterly tabloid covering gay men. Estab. 1983. Circ. 6,000. Byline given. Buys first North American serial rights. Editorial lead time 3 months. Submit seasonal material 3 months in advance. Reports in 3 months on queries. Sample copy for $4.95. Writer's guidelines for #10 SASE.

**Nonfiction:** Book excerpts and essays. **Buys 4 mss/year.** Send complete ms. Length: 2,000 words maximum. **Pays $20-50 minimum.**

**Photos:** Send photos with submission. Reviews prints. Negotiates payment individually. Buys one-time rights.

**Fiction:** Confession, erotica, experimental, fantasy, historical, novel excerpts and serialized novels. **Buys 20 mss/year.** Send complete ms. Length: 2,000 words maximum. **Pays $50 maximum.**

**Poetry:** Avant-garde, free verse and traditional. **Buys 80 poems/year.** Submit no more than 8 poems, or no more than 250 lines of verse (whichever is less). **Pays $20.**

# GENERAL INTEREST

General interest magazines need writers who can appeal to a broad audience—teens and senior citizens, wealthy readers and the unemployed. Each magazine still has a personality that suits its audience—one that a writer should study before sending material to an editor. Other markets for general interest material are in these Consumer categories: Contemporary Culture, Ethnic/Minority, Inflight, Men's, Regional and Women's.

**$ $ THE AMERICAN LEGION MAGAZINE**, P.O. Box 1055, Indianapolis IN 46206-1055. (317)630-1200. Fax: (317)630-1280. E-mail: tal@legion.org. Website: http://www.legion.org. Editorial Administrator: Patricia Marschand. **Contact**: John Raughter, executive editor. **70% freelance written.** Monthly magazine. "Working through 15,000 community-level posts, the honorably discharged wartime veterans of The American Legion dedicate themselves to God, country and traditional American values. They believe in a strong defense; adequate and compassionate care for veterans and their families; community service; and the wholesome development of our nation's youth. We publish articles that reflect these values. We inform our readers and their families of significant trends and issues affecting our nation, the world and the way we live. Our major features focus on the American flag, national security, foreign affairs, business trends, social issues, health, education, ethics and the arts. We also publish selected general feature articles, articles of special interest to veterans, and question-and-answer interviews with prominent national and world figures." Prefers to work with published/established writers, but works with a small number of new/unpublished writers each year. Estab. 1919. Circ. 2,800,000. Buys first North American serial rights. Reports in 6 weeks on submissions. **Pays on acceptance.** Publishes ms an average of 6 months after acceptance. Byline given. Accepts queries by mail, e-mail, fax. Reports in 2 months. Sample copy for $3.50 and 9×12 SAE with 6 first-class stamps. Writer's guidelines for #10 SASE.
**Nonfiction:** Query with SASE first, will only consider unsolicited mss that are of interest to military veterans. Query should explain the subject or issue, article's angle and organization, writer's qualifications and experts to be interviewed. Well-reported articles or expert commentaries cover issues/trends in world/national affairs, contemporary problems, general interest, sharply-focused feature subjects. Monthly Q&A with national figures/experts. Few personality profiles. No regional topics or promotion of partisan political agendas. **Buys 50-60 mss/year.** Length: 500-2,000 words. **Pays 40¢/word and up.** Pays phone expenses of writers on assignment.
**Photos:** On assignment.
**Tips:** "Queries by new writers should include clips/background/expertise; no longer than 1½ pages. Submit suitable material showing you have read several issues. *The American Legion Magazine* considers itself '*the* magazine for a strong America.' Reflect this theme (which includes economy, educational system, moral fiber, social issues, infrastructure, technology and national defense/security). We are a general interest, national magazine, not a strictly military magazine. We are widely read by members of the Washington establishment and other policy makers. No unsolicited jokes. No phone queries."

**■ $ $ THE AMERICAN SCHOLAR**, The Phi Beta Kappa Society, 1785 Massachusetts Ave., NW, 4th Floor, Washington DC 20036. (202)265-3808. Fax: (202)265-0083. E-mail: scholar@pbk.org. Editor: Anne Fadiman. **Contact:** Jean Stipicevic, managing editor. **100% freelance written.** Quarterly magazine. "Our articles are written by scholars and experts but written in nontechnical language for an intelligent audience. Material covers a wide range in the arts, sciences, current affairs, history and literature." Estab. 1932. Circ. 25,000. Pays on publication. Byline given. Offers 50% kill fee. Buys first rights. Editorial lead time 6 months. Submit seasonal material 6 months in advance. Accepts queries by mail, e-mail, fax. Reports in 2 weeks on queries; 2 months on ms. Sample copy for $6.95. Writer's guidelines for #10 SASE.
**Nonfiction:** Book excerpts (prior to publication only), essays, historical/nostalgic, humor. **Buys 40 mss/year.** Query. Length: 3,000-5,000 words. **Pays $500.**
**Columns/Departments: Buys 16 mss/year.** Query. Length: 3,000-5,000 words. **Pays $500.**
**Poetry:** Rob Farnsworth, poetry editor. **Buys 20/year.** Submit maximum 3 poems. Length: 34-75 lines. **Pays $50.** "Write for guidelines."
**Tips:** "The section most open to freelancers is the book review section. Query and send samples of reviews written. No phone queries."

**$ $ $ $ THE ATLANTIC MONTHLY**, 77 N. Washington St., Boston MA 02114. Editor: William Whitworth. Managing Editor: Cullen Murphy. **Contact**: Michael Curtis, senior editor. Monthly magazine of arts and public affairs. "Seeks fiction that is clear, tightly written with strong sense of 'story' and well-defined characters." Circ. 500,000. **Pays on acceptance.** Byline given. Buys first North American serial rights. Accepts queries by mail, fax. Simultaneous submissions discouraged. Reporting time varies.
**Nonfiction:** Book excerpts, essays, general interest, humor, personal experience, religious, travel. Query with or without published clips or send complete ms with SASE. All unsolicited mss must be accompanied by SASE. Length: 1,000-6,000 words. Payment varies. Sometimes pays expenses of writers on assignment.
**Fiction:** Literary and contemporary fiction. **Buys 12-15 mss/year.** Send complete ms. Length: 2,000-6,000 words preferred. **Pays $3,000.**
**Poetry:** Peter Davison, poetry editor. **Buys 40-60 poems/year.**
 ■ The online magazine carries original content not found in the print edition. Contact: Wen Stephenson, online editor.
**Tips:** Writers should be aware that this is not a market for beginner's work (nonfiction and fiction), nor is it truly for intermediate work. Study this magazine before sending only your best, most professional work. When making first

contact, "cover letters are sometimes helpful, particularly if they cite prior publications or involvement in writing programs. Common mistakes: melodrama, inconclusiveness, lack of development, unpersuasive characters and/or dialogue."

**$ $ CAPPER'S**, Ogden Publications, Inc., 1503 SW 42nd St., Topeka KS 66609-1265. (913)274-4346. Fax: (913)274-4305. E-mail: npeavler@kspress.com. Website: http://www.cappers.com. **Contact:** Ann Crahan, editor. Associate Editors: Cheryl Ptacek, Heather Reynolds, Melanie Kitchner. **25% freelance written.** Works with a small number of new/unpublished writers each year. Biweekly tabloid emphasizing home and family for readers who live in small towns and on farms. Estab. 1879. Circ. 240,000. **Pays for poetry and fiction on acceptance;** articles on publication. Publishes ms an average of 3-6 months after acceptance. Buys one-time serial rights only. Submit seasonal material at least 3 months in advance. Reports in 4 months; 10 months for serialized novels. Sample copy for $1.95. Writer's guidelines for #10 SASE.
**Nonfiction:** Historical (local museums, etc.), inspirational, nostalgia, budget travel (Midwest slants), people stories (accomplishments, collections, etc.). **Buys 50 mss/year.** Submit complete ms. Length: 700 words maximum. **Pays $2.50/ inch. Pays additional $5 if used on website.**
**Reprints:** Send typed ms with rights for sale noted and information about when and where the article previously appeared.
**Photos:** Purchased with accompanying ms. Submit prints. Pays $5-15 for b&w glossy prints. Purchase price for ms includes payment for photos. Limited market for color photos (35mm color slides); pays $10-30 for color photos, $40 for covers. Additional payment of $5 if used on website.
**Columns/Departments:** Heart of the Home (homemakers' letters, recipes, hints); Community Heartbeat (volunteerism). Submit complete ms. Length: 300 words maximum. **Pays approximately $2 per printed inch.**
**Fiction:** "We buy very few fiction pieces—longer than short stories, shorter than novels." Adventure and romance mss. No explicit sex, violence or profanity. **Buys 4-5 mss/year.** Query. Length: 7,500-45,000 words. **Pays $75-300.**
**Poetry:** Free verse, haiku, light verse, traditional, nature, inspiration. "The poems that appear in *Capper's* are not too difficult to read. They're easy to grasp. We're looking for everyday events and down-to-earth themes." **Buys 5-6/issue.** Limit submissions to batches of 5-6. Length: 4-16 lines. **Pays $10-15.**
**Tips:** "Study a few issues of our publication. Most rejections are for material that is too long, unsuitable or out of character for our magazine (too sexy, too much profanity, wrong kind of topic, etc.). On occasion, we must cut material to fit column space."

**$ $ THE CHRISTIAN SCIENCE MONITOR**, 1 Norway St., Boston MA 02115. (617)450-2000. Website: http:// www.csmonitor.com. **Contact:** Scott Armstrong (National); Clayton Jones (International), Amelia Newcomb (Learning); Jim Bencivenga (Ideas); Gregory Lamb (Arts & Leisure); David Scott (Home Front); Lynde McCormick (Work & Money). International newspaper issued daily except Saturdays, Sundays and holidays in North America; weekly international edition. Estab. 1908. Circ. 95,000. Buys all newspaper rights worldwide for 3 months following publication. Buys limited number of mss, "top quality only." Publishes original (exclusive) material only. Pays on publication. Reports in 1 month. Writer's guidelines for #10 SASE.
**Nonfiction:** In-depth features and essays. The newspaper includes 5 sections: Learning (education and life-long learning); Arts & Leisure; Ideas (religion, ethics, science and technology, environment, book reviews); Home Front (home and community issues); and Work & Money. Query to the appropriate section editor. **Pays $200 average.** Home Forum page buys essays of 400-900 words. **Pays $150 average.**
**Poetry:** Traditional, blank and free verse. Seeks non-religious poetry of high quality and of all lengths up to 75 lines. **Pays $35-75 average.**
**Tips:** "Style should be bright but not cute, concise but thoroughly researched. Try to humanize news or feature writing so reader identifies with it. Avoid sensationalism. Accent constructive, solution-oriented treatment of subjects."

**$ $ $ $ CIVILIZATION**, Capital Publications, 575 Lexington Ave., New York NY 10022. (212)223-3100. Fax: (212)832-4883. **Contact:** Regan Solmo, managing editor. Bimonthly magazine. "*Civilization* is the membership magazine of the Library of Congress covering contemporary culture. Well-known writers contribute articles on the arts, travel, government, history, education, biography and social issues." Estab. 1994. Circ. 200,000. Pays ⅓ on acceptance, ⅔ on publication, for exclusive 90-day rights to features.
**Nonfiction:** *Civilization*'s departments and columns are staff written, but virtually all features come from freelancers. **Pays up to $5,000.** (Pay depends on subject matter, quality and the amount of time a writer has put into a piece.)
**Tips:** "*Civilization* is not a history magazine. We are a magazine of American culture. The key thing for us is that when we do look into the past, we connect it to the present." The magazine is now giving more emphasis to contemporary subjects. We take relatively few over-the-transom pieces. But we do look at everything that comes in, and sometimes we pick up something that looks really impressive. We put an enormous stress on good writing. Subject is important, but unless a writer can show us a sheaf of clips, we won't get started with them. There is a *Civilization* sensibility that we try to maintain. If you don't know the magazine well, you won't really understand what we're trying to do." To break in, look to contemporary subjects and the arts—including fine arts, the lively arts and book reviews.

**$ $ $ DIVERSION**, 1790 Broadway, New York NY 10019. (212)969-7500. Fax: (212)969-7557. Contact: Tom Passavant, editor-in-chief. Monthly magazine covering travel and lifestyle, edited for physicians. "*Diversion* offers an eclectic mix of interests beyond medicine. Regular features include stories on domestic and foreign travel destinations, discussions of food and wine, sports columns, guidance on gardening and photography, and information on investments and finance. The editorial reflects its readers' affluent lifestyles and diverse personal interests. Although *Diversion* doesn't cover health subjects, it does feature profiles of doctors who excel at nonmedical pursuits." Estab. 1973. Circ. 176,000. Pays 3 months after acceptance. Offers 25% kill fee. Editorial lead time 4 months. Sample copy $4.50. Guidelines available. Responds in 1 month.

● Ranked as one of the best markets for freelance writers in *Writer's Yearbook* magazine's annual "Top 100 Markets," January 1999.

**Nonfiction:** "We have more than enough travel articles. More interested in culture, the arts, sports, etc." **Buys 70 ms/ year.** Length: 1,800-2,000 words. **Pays $50-1,200.** Query with proposal, published clips and author's credentials.
**Columns/Departments:** Travel, food & wine, photography, gardening, finance. Length: 1,200 words. Pays $500-750. Query with proposal, published clips and author's credentials.

**$ $ $ $ EQUINOX: Canada's Magazine of Discovery**, Malcolm Publishing, 11450 Albert-Hudon Blvd., Montreal North, Quebec H1G 3J9 Canada. (514)327-4464. Fax: (514)327-0514. E-mail: eqxmag@globetrotter.net. **Contact**: Kendra Tobey, departments editor. Bimonthly magazine "encompassing the worlds of human cultures and communities, the natural world and science and technology. *Equinox* is Canada's world-class magazine of discovery. It serves a large readership of intelligent Canadians who share a desire to learn more about themselves, their country, and the world around them. Its editorial range is eclectic, with a special emphasis on biology, ecology, wildlife, the earth sciences, astronomy, medicine, geography, natural history, the arts, travel and adventure. Throughout the theme is that of discovery and, in many cases, rediscovery. While exploring the unfamiliar, *Equinox* also provides fresh insights into the familiar." Estab. 1982. Circ. 120,000. **Pays on acceptance.** Byline given. Offers 50% kill fee. Buys first North American serial rights only. Submit seasonal queries 1 year in advance. Accepts queries by mail, e-mail, fax. Reports in 2 months. Sample copy for $5 and SAE with Canadian postage or IRCs. Writer's guidelines for #10 SASE (U.S. writers must send IRCs, not American stamps).

● Ranked as one of the best markets for freelance writers in *Writer's Yearbook* magazine's annual "Top 100 Markets," January 1999.

**Nonfiction:** Book excerpts (occasionally). No travel articles. Should have Canadian focus. Query with SAE including Canadian postage or IRCs. Length: 1,500-5,000 words. **Pays $1,500-3,500 (Canadian) negotiated.**
**Reprints:** Accepts previously published submissions. Send tearsheet of article and information about when and where the article previously appeared. Pays 30% of amount paid for an original article.
**Photos:** Send photos with ms. Reviews color transparencies—must be of professional quality; no prints or negatives. Captions and identification of subjects required. Pays $110-350. Pays $500 for covers. Sometimes pays package fees.
**Columns/Departments:** Nexus (current science that isn't covered by daily media) 250-350 words. **Pays $250 (Canadian).** Pursuits (service section for active living) 200-1,000 words. **Pays $250-900 (Canadian).** Query with published clips.
**Tips:** "Submit ideas for short photo essays as well as longer features. We welcome queries by mail and e-mail."

**✪ $ $ GRIT: American Life and Traditions**, Ogden Publications, 1503 SW 42nd St., Topeka KS 66609-1265. (785)274-4300. Fax: (785)274-4305. E-mail: grit@cjnetworks.com. Website: http://www.grit.com. **Contact:** Donna Doyle, editor-in-chief. **80% freelance written.** Open to new writers. "*Grit* is Good News. As a wholesome, family-oriented magazine published for more than a century and distributed nationally, *Grit* features articles about family lifestyles, traditions, values and pastimes. *Grit* accents the best of American life and traditions—past and present. Our readers cherish family values and appreciate practical and innovative ideas. Many of them live in small towns and rural areas across the country; others live in cities but share many of the values typical of small-town America." Estab. 1882. Circ. 200,000. Pays on publication. Byline given. Buys all and first rights. Submit seasonal material 3 months in advance. Sample copy and writer's guidelines for $4 and 11 × 14 SASE with 4 first-class stamps.

○� How to break in: Departments such as Readers True Stories, Pet Tales, Looking Back, Profile, Seasonal Readers Memories (Easter, Christmas, Mother's Day), Poetry.

**Nonfiction:** Need features (timely, newsworthy, touching but with a *Grit* angle), profiles, humor, readers' true stories, outdoor hobbies, collectibles. Also articles on gardening, crafts, hobbies, leisure pastimes. The best way to sell work is by reading each issue cover to cover. Special issues: Gardening (January-October); Health (twice a year). **Features pay 15-22¢/word plus $25-200 each for photos depending on quality and placement.** Main features run 1,200 to 1,500 words. Department features average 800-1,000 words. Department pay varies on placement and length. Flat rate for photo and article.
**Fiction:** Short stories, 1,500-2,000 words; may also purchase accompanying art if of high quality and appropriate. Need serials (romance, westerns, mysteries) of at least 3,500 words. Send ms with SASE to Fiction Dept.
**Photos:** Professional quality photos (b&w prints or color slides) increase acceptability of articles. Photos: $25-200 each in features according to quality, placement and color/b&w.
**Tips:** "Articles should be directed to a national audience. Sources identified fully. Our readers are warm and loving. They want to read about others with heart. Send us something that will make us cry with joy."

**$ $ $ $ HARPER'S MAGAZINE**, 666 Broadway, 11th Floor, New York NY 10012. (212)614-6500. Fax: (212)228-5889. Editor: Lewis H. Lapham. **Contact:** Ann Gollin, editor's assistant. **90% freelance written.** Monthly magazine for well-educated, socially concerned, widely read men and women who value ideas and good writing. "*Harper's Magazine* encourages national discussion on current and significant issues in a format that offers arresting facts and intelligent opinions. By means of its several shorter journalistic forms—Harper's Index, Readings, Forum, and Annotation—as well as with its acclaimed essays, fiction, and reporting, *Harper's* continues the tradition begun with its first issue in 1850: to inform readers across the whole spectrum of political, literary, cultural, and scientific affairs." Estab. 1850. Circ. 216,000. Rights purchased vary with author and material. Pays negotiable kill fee. **Pays on acceptance.** Reports in 2 weeks. Publishes ms an average of 3 months after acceptance. Sample copy for $3.95.

• *Harper's Magazine* won the 1998 National Magazine Award for Feature Writing.

**Nonfiction:** "For writers working with agents or who will query first only, our requirements are: public affairs, literary, international and local reporting and humor." No interviews; no profiles. Complete ms and query must include SASE. No unsolicited poems will be accepted. Publishes one major report per issue. Length: 4,000-6,000 words. Publishes one major essay/issue. Length: 4,000-6,000 words. "These should be construed as topical essays on all manner of subjects (politics, the arts, crime, business, etc.) to which the author can bring the force of passionate and informed statement."

**Reprints:** Accepts previously published material for its "Readings" section. Send typed ms with rights for sale noted and information about when and where the article previously appeared.

**Fiction: Publishes 1 short story/month. Generally pays 50¢-$1/word.**

**Photos:** Contact: Angela Riechers, art director. Occasionally purchased with mss; others by assignment. Pays $50-500.

**Tips:** "Some readers expect their magazines to clothe them with opinions in the way that Bloomingdale's dresses them for the opera. The readers of *Harper's Magazine* belong to a different crowd. They strike me as the kind of people who would rather think in their own voices and come to their own conclusions."

⬛★ **$ $ $ $** HOPE MAGAZINE, How to be Part of the Solution, Hope Publishing, Inc., P.O. Box 160, Brooklin ME 04616. (207)359-4651. Fax: (207)359-8920. E-mail: info@hopemag.com. Website: http://www.hopemag.c om. Editor-in-Chief/Publisher: Jon Wilson. Editor: Kimberly Ridley. Assistant Editor: Amy Rawe. **Contact:** Adrienne Bassler, editorial assistant. **90% freelance written.** Quarterly magazine covering humanity at its best and worst. "We strive to evoke empathy among readers." Estab. 1996. Circ. 22,000. Pays on publication. Publishes ms an average of 6 months after acceptance. Byline given. Offers 20% kill fee. Buys first, one-time or second serial (reprint) rights. Editorial lead time 4 months. Submit seasonal material 6 months in advance. Accepts queries by mail, e-mail, fax. Accepts simultaneous submissions. Reports in 6 months. Sample copy for $5. Writer's guidelines for #10 SASE.

**Nonfiction:** Book excerpts, essays, general interest, interview/profile, personal experience, photo feature. Nothing explicitly religious, political or New Age. **Buys 50-75 mss/year.** Query with published clips or writing samples and SASE. Length: 250-4,000 words. **Pays $50-2,000.** Sometimes pays expenses of writers on assignment.

**Photos:** State availability of or send photos with submission. Reviews contact sheets and 5×7 prints. Negotiates payment individually. Captions and identification of subjects required. Buys one-time rights.

**Columns/Departments:** Contact Departments Editor. Signs of Hope (inspiring dispatches/news) 250-500 words. **Buys 50-60 mss/year.** Query with published clips or send complete ms and SASE. **Pays $50-150.**

**Tips:** "Write very personally, and very deeply. We're not looking for shallow 'feel-good' pieces. Approach uncommon subjects. Cover the ordinary in extraordinary ways. Go to the heart. Surprise us. Many stories we receive are too 'soft.' Absolutely no phone queries."

**$ $ $ $** LIFE, Time & Life Bldg., Rockefeller Center, New York NY 10020. (212)522-1212. **Contact:** Isolde Motley, managing editor. **10% freelance written.** Prefers to work with published/established writers; rarely works with new/unpublished writers. Monthly general interest picture magazine for people of all ages, backgrounds and interests. "*Life* shows the world through the power of pictures. It explores domestic and international news, business, the arts, lifestyle and human interest stories." Estab. 1936. Circ. 1,500,000. **Pays on acceptance.** Publishes ms an average of 3 months after acceptance. Byline given. Buys first North American serial rights. Submit seasonal material 4 months in advance. Accepts simultaneous submissions. Reports in 2 months.

**Nonfiction:** "We've done articles on anything in the world of interest to the general reader and on people of importance. It's extremely difficult to break in since we buy so few articles. Most of the magazine is pictures. We're looking for very high quality writing. We select writers whom we think match the subject they are writing about." Query with clips of previously published work. Length: 1,000-4,000 words.

**$ $ $ $** NATIONAL GEOGRAPHIC MAGAZINE, 1145 17th St. NW, Washington DC 20036. (202)857-7000. Fax: (202)828-6667. Website: http://www.nationalgeographic.com. Editor: William Allen. **Contact:** Oliver Payne, senior assistant editor, manuscripts. **60% freelance written.** Prefers to work with published/established writers. Monthly magazine for members of the National Geographic Society. "Timely articles written in a compelling, 'eyewitness' style. Arresting photographs that speak to us of the beauty, mystery, and harsh realities of life on earth. Maps of unprecedented detail and accuracy. These are the hallmarks of *National Geographic* magazine. Since 1888, the *Geographic* has been educating readers about the world." Circ. 9,200,000.

**Nonfiction:** *National Geographic* publishes general interest, illustrated articles on science, natural history, exploration, cultures and geographical regions. Of the freelance writers assigned, a few are experts in their fields; the remainder are established professionals. Fewer than 1% of unsolicited queries result in assignments. Query (500 words with clips of published magazine articles by mail to Senior Assistant Editor Oliver Payne. Do not send mss. Before querying, study recent issues and check a *Geographic Index* at a library since the magazine seldom returns to regions or subjects covered within the past 10 years. Length: 2,000-8,000 words. Pays expenses of writers on assignment.

**Photos:** Photographers should query in care of the Photographic Division.

■ The online magazine carries original content not included in the print edition. Contact: Mark Holmes, online editor.

**Tips:** "State the theme(s) clearly, let the narrative flow, and build the story around strong characters and a vivid sense of place. Give us rounded episodes, logically arranged."

**$ $ $ THE NEW YORK TIMES**, 229 W. 43rd St., New York NY 10036. (212)556-1234. Fax: (212)556-3830. *The New York Times Magazine* appears in *The New York Times* on Sunday. The *Arts and Leisure* section appears during the week. The *Op Ed* page appears daily.

**Nonfiction:** *Lives:* "Most articles are assigned but some unsolicited material is published, especially in the "Lives" column, a weekly personal-essay feature. Views should be fresh, lively and provocative on national and international news developments, science, education, family life, social trends and problems, arts and entertainment, personalties, sports and the changing American scene." Length: 900 words. **Pays $1,000.** Address unsolicited essays with SASE to the "Lives" Editor. *Arts and Leisure:* Wants "to encourage imaginativeness in terms of form and approach—stressing ideas, issues, trends, investigations, symbolic reporting and stories delving deeply into the creative achievements and processes of artists and entertainers—and seeks to break away from old-fashioned gushy, fan magazine stuff." Length: 1,500-2,000 words. **Pays $100-350,** depending on length. Address unsolicited articles with SASE to the Arts and Leisure Articles Editor. *Op Ed page:* "The Op Ed page is always looking for new material and publishes many people who have never been published before. We want material of universal relevance which people can talk about in a personal way. Wehn writing for the Op Ed page, there is no formula, but the writing itself should have some polish. Don't make the mistake of pontificating on the news. We're not looking for more political columnists." Length: 750 words. **Pays $150.**

**$ $ $ $ THE NEW YORKER**, 20 W. 43rd St., New York NY 10036-7441. (212)536-5400. Fax: (212)536-5735. Editor: David Remnick. Weekly. Estab. 1925. Circ. 750,000. *"The New Yorker* is a national magazine edited to address current issues, ideas and events. The magazine blends domestic and international news analysis with in-depth features, critiques and humorous observations on politics and business, culture and the arts, education, style, science, sports and literature." *The New Yorker* is one of today's premier markets for nonfiction, fiction and poetry. To submit material, please direct your ms to the appropriate editor, (i.e., nonficton, fiction or poetry) and enclose SASE. The editors deal with a tremendous number of submissions every week; writers should be prepared to wait at least 2 or 3 months for a reply. **Pays on acceptance.**

**Tips:** "We are always happy to welcome new contributors to our pages. We have no guidelines as such. If you feel that your work might be right for us, please send your submission (prose typed double-spaced; poetry single-spaced, and no more than six poems at a time) to the appropriate editors—Fact, Fiction, Talk of the Town, or Poetry. If you plan to submit a long nonfiction piece, however, you should send a query letter, with a detailed proposal, to the Fact Editors. Please include SASE with any submission."

**$ $ $ NEWSWEEK**, 251 W. 57th St., New York NY 10019. (212)445-4000. Circ. 3,180,000. Contact: Pam Hamer. *"Newsweek* is edited to report the week's developments on the newsfront of the world and the nation through news, commentary and analysis." Accepts unsolicited mss for My Turn, a column of personal opinion. The 850-900 word essays for the column must be original, not published elsewhere and contain verifiable facts. **Payment is $1,000, on publication.** Buys non-exclusive world-wide rights. Reports in 2 months only on submissions with SASE.

**THE OXFORD AMERICAN, The Southern Magazine of Good Writing**, The Oxford American, Inc., P.O. Drawer 1156, Oxford MS 38655. (601)236-1836. Fax: (601)236-3141. E-mail: oxam@watervalley.net. Editor: Marc Smirnoff. **Contact:** Kelly Caudle, managing editor. **30-50% freelance written.** Bimonthly magazine covering the South. *"The Oxford American* is a general-interest literary magazine about the South." Estab. 1992. Circ. 30,000. Pays 30 days after publication. Publishes ms an average of 6 months after acceptance. Byline given. Offers 25% kill fee. Buys first North American serial rights and one-time rights. Editorial lead time 2 months. Submit seasonal material 4 months in advance. Accepts queries by mail, e-mail. Reports in 3 weeks on queries; 3 months on mss. Sample copy for $6.50. Writer's guidelines for #10 SASE.

**Nonfiction:** Essays, general interest, humor, personal experience, reporting, profiles, memoirs concerning the South. **Buys 6 mss/year.** Query with published clips or send complete ms. Pay varies. Sometimes pays expenses of writers on assignment.

**Reprints:** Send tearsheet, photocopy or typed ms with info about when and where the article previously appeared.

**Photos:** Negotiates payment individually. Captions required. Buys one-time rights.

**Columns/Departments:** Send complete ms. Pay varies.

**Fiction:** Publishes novel excerpts. **Buys 10 mss/year.** Send complete ms. Pay varies.

**Tips:** "Like other editors, I stress the importance of being familiar with the magazine. Those submitters who know the magazine always send in better work because they know what we're looking for. To those who don't bother to at least flip through the magazine, let me point out we only publish articles with some sort of Southern connection."

**$ $ $ $ PARADE**, Parade Publications, Inc., 711 Third Ave., New York NY 10017. (212)450-7000. Fax: (212)450-7284. **Contact:** Dakila D. Divina, articles editor. Weekly magazine for a general interest audience. **90% freelance written.** Circ. 37,000,000. **Pays on acceptance.** Publishes ms an average of 3 months after acceptance. Kill fee varies in amount. Buys first North American serial rights. Reports in 6 weeks on queries. Writer's guidelines for #10 SASE.

**Nonfiction:** General interest (on health, trends, social issues or anything of interest to a broad general audience); interview/profile (of news figures, celebrities and people of national significance); and "provocative topical pieces of news value." Spot news events are not accepted, as *Parade* has a 6-week lead time. No fiction, fashion, travel, poetry, cartoons, nostalgia, regular columns, quizzes or fillers. Unsolicited queries concerning celebrities, politicians, sports figures, or technical are rarely assigned. Address single-page queries to Articles Editor; include SASE. Length of published articles: 800-1,500 words. **Pays $2,500 minimum.** Pays expenses of writers on assignment.

**Tips:** "Send a well-researched, well-written paragraph query targeted to our national market. No phone or fax queries. Keep subject tightly focused—you should be able to state the point or theme in three or four sentences."

**$ $ $ $ READER'S DIGEST**, Reader's Digest Rd., Pleasantville NY 10570-7000. E-mail: readersdigest@notes .compuserve.com. Website: http://www.readersdigest.com. **Contact:** Editorial Correspondence. Monthly general interest magazine. "We are looking for contemporary stories of lasting interest that give the magazine variety, freshness and originality." Estab. 1922. Circ. 15,000,000. **Pays on acceptance.** Byline given. Buys exclusive world periodical rights, electronic rights, among others. Editorial lead time 3 months. Submit seasonal material 6 months in advance. Accepts queries by mail, e-mail, fax. Address article queries and tearsheets of published articles to the editors.

● Ranked as one of the best markets for freelance writers in *Writer's Yearbook* magazine's annual "Top 100 Markets," January 1999.

**Nonfiction:** Book excerpts, essays, exposé, general interest, historical/nostalgic, humor, inspirational, interview/profile, opinion, personal experience. **Buys 100 mss/year.** Query with published clips. Does not read or return unsolicited mss. Length: 2,500-4,000 words. **Original article rates generally begin at $5,000.**

**Reprints:** Send tearsheet or photocopy with rights for sale noted and information about where and when the article appeared. Pays $1,200/*Reader's Digest* page for World Digest rights (usually split 50/50 between original publisher and writer).

**Columns/Departments:** "Original contributions become the property of *Reader's Digest* upon acceptance and payment. Life-in-These-United States contributions must be true, unpublished stories from one's own experience, revealing adult human nature, and providing appealing or humorous sidelights on the American scene." Length: 300 words maximum. **Pays $400 on publication.** True, unpublished stories are also solicited for Humor in Uniform, Campus Comedy, Tales Out of School and All in a Day's Work. Length: 300 words maximum. **Pays $400 on publication.** Towards More Picturesque Speech—the first contributor of each item used in this department is paid $50 for original material, $35 for reprints. For items used in Laughter, the Best Medicine, Personal Glimpses, Quotable Quotes, Notes From All Over, Points to Ponder and elsewhere in the magazine payment is as follows; to the *first* contributor of each from a published source, $35. For original material, $30/*Reader's Digest* two-column line. Previously published material must have source's name, date and page number. Contributions cannot be acknowledged or returned. Send complete anecdotes to *Reader's Digest*, Box LL, Pleasantville NY 10570, or fax to (914)238-6390. CompuServe address is notes:readersdigest or use readersdigest@notes.compuserve.com from other online services and the Internet."

**Tips:** "Roughly half the 30-odd articles we publish every month are reprinted from magazines, newspapers, books and other sources. The remaining 15 or so articles are original—most of them assigned, some submitted on speculation. While many of these are written by regular contributors—on salary or on contract—we're always looking for new talent and for offbeat subjects that help give our magazine variety, freshness and originality. Above all, in the writing we publish, *The Digest* demands accuracy—down to the smallest detail. Our worldwide team of 60 researchers scrutinizes every line of type, checking every fact and examining every opinion. For an average issue, they will check some 3500 facts with 1300 sources. So watch your accuracy. There's nothing worse than having an article fall apart in our research checking because an author was a little careless with his reporting. We make this commitment routinely, as it guarantees that the millions of readers who believe something simply because they saw it in *Reader's Digest* have not misplaced their trust."

**$ READERS REVIEW**, The National Research Bureau, Inc., 320 Valley St., Burlington IA 52601. (319)752-5415. Fax: (319)752-3421. **Contact:** Nancy Heinzel, editor. **75% freelance written.** Quarterly magazine. Estab. 1948. Pays on publication. Publishes ms an average of 1 year after acceptance. Buys all rights. Submit seasonal material 7 months in advance of issue date. Sample copy and writers guidelines for #10 SAE with 2 first-class stamps.

● The *Readers Review* works with a small number of new/unpublished writers each year, and is eager to work with new/unpublished writers.

**Nonfiction:** General interest (steps to better health, attitudes on the job); how-to (perform better on the job, do home repairs, car maintenance); travel. **Buys 10-12 mss/year.** Query with outline or submit complete ms. Length: 500-700 words. **Pays 4¢/word.**

**Tips:** "Writers have a better chance of breaking in our publication with short articles."

**$ $ REAL PEOPLE, The Magazine of Celebrities and Interesting People**, Main Street Publishing Co., Inc., 450 Seventh Ave., Suite 1701, New York NY 10123. (212)244-2351. Fax: (212)244-2367. E-mail: mrs-2@idt.net. **Contact:** Alex Polner, editor. **75% freelance written.** Bimonthly magazine for ages 30 and up focusing on celebs and show business, but also interesting people who might appeal to a national audience. Estab. 1988. Circ. 100,000. Pays on publication. Byline given. Pays 33% kill fee. Buys all rights. Submit seasonal material 6 months in advance. Reports on queries in 6 weeks. Sample copy for $4 and 8×11 SAE with 3 first-class stamps. Guidelines for #10 SASE.

**Nonfiction:** Interview/profile. Q&A formats are not encouraged. "We do a fall preview of TV and film in September. Material must be in by June. Other seasonal stories are 3-6 months in advance." **Buys 80 mss/year.** Query with published clips and SASE. Length: 200-1,500 words. **Pays $200-500 for assigned articles; $100-250 for unsolicited articles.**
**Columns/Departments:** Contact: Brad Hamilton. Newsworthy shorts—up to 200 words. "We are doing more shorter (75-250 word) pieces for our 'Real Shorts' column." Psst (gossip), 100 words; Follow-up (humor), 100 words. **Pays $25-50.**
**Photos:** State availability of photos with submissions. Reviews 5×7 prints and/or slides or hi-res photos on disk. Offers no additional payment for photos accepted with ms. Captions, model releases and identification of subjects required. Buys one-time rights.
**Tips:** "We are mainly interested in articles/interviews with celebrities of national prominence (Hollywood, music, authors, politicians, businesspeople in the media). Profiles must be based on personal interviews. As a rule, profiles should be tough, revealing, exciting and entertaining."

**$ REUNIONS MAGAZINE,** P.O. Box 11727, Milwaukee WI 53211-0727. (414)263-4567. Fax: (414)263-6331. E-mail: reunions@execpc.com. Website: http://www.reunionsmag.com. **Contact:** Edith Wagner, editor. **75% freelance written.** Quarterly magazine covering reunions—all aspects, all types. "*Reunions Magazine* is primarily for people actively involved with family, class, military and other reunions. We want easy, practical ideas about organizing, planning, researching/searching, attending or promoting reunions." Estab. 1990. Circ. 18,000. Pays on publication. Publishes ms an average of 1 year after acceptance. Byline given. Buys one-time rights. Editorial lead time minimum 6 months. Submit seasonal material 1 year in advance. Accepts queries by mail, e-mail, fax; appreciates e-mail submissions. Reports in 1 year. Sample copy free or on website. Writer's guidelines for #10 SASE or on website.
**Nonfiction:** Historical/nostalgic, how-to, humor, interview/profile, new product, personal experience, reunion recipes with reunion anecdote, photo feature, travel—all must be reunion-related. Needs reviewers for books, videos, software (include your requirements). Special issues: Ethnic/African-American family reunions (Winter); Food and Kids features (Summer); Golf and Travel features (Autumn); reunions in various sections of the US. **Buys 25 mss/year.** Query with published clips. Length: 500-2,500 words. **Pays $25.** Often rewards with generous copies.
**Reprints:** Send tearsheet or photocopy of article or typed ms with rights for sale noted and information about when and where the article previously appeared. Usually pays $10.
**Photos:** State availability of photos with submission. Reviews contact sheets, negatives, 35mm transparencies and prints. Offers no additional payment for photos accepted with ms. Captions, model releases and identification of individuals or small groups required. Buys one-time rights. Always looking for vertical cover photos that scream: "Reunion!"
**Fillers:** Anecdotes, facts, news, short humor—must be reunion-related. **Buys 20/year.** Length: 50-250 words. **Pays $5.**
The online magazine carries original content and includes writer's guidelines. Contact: Edith Wagner, online editor.
**Tips:** "Write a lively account of an interesting or unusual reunion, either upcoming or soon afterward while it's hot. Tell readers why reunion is special, what went into planning it and how attendees reacted. Our *Masterplan* section is a great place for a freelancer to start. Send us how-tos or tips on any aspect of reunion organizing. Open your minds to different types of reunions—they're all around!"

**$ $ $ ROBB REPORT, The Magazine for the Luxury Lifestyle**, 1 Acton Place, Acton MA 01720. (978)263-7749. Fax: (978)929-9679. E-mail: robb@robbreport.com. Website: http://www.robbreport.com. **Contact:** Steven Castle, editor. **60% freelance written.** Monthly magazine. "We are a lifestyle magazine geared toward active, affluent readers. Addresses upscale autos, luxury travel, boating, technology, lifestyles, watches, fashion, sports, investments, collectibles." Estab. 1976. Circ. 100,000. Pays on publication. Byline given. Offers 50% kill fee. Buys all rights or first North American serial rights. Submit seasonal material 5 months in advance. Accepts queries by mail, fax. Reports in 2 months on queries; 1 month on mss. Sample copy for $10.95 plus shipping and handling. Writer's guidelines for #10 SASE.
**Nonfiction:** General interest (autos, lifestyle, etc.), interview/profile (business owners/entrepreneurs), new product (autos, boats, consumer electronics), travel (international and domestic). No essays, bargain travel. Special issues: Home issue (September); Watch issue (November). **Buys 60 mss/year.** Query with published clips if available. Length: 500-3,500 words. **Pays $150-2,000.** Sometimes pays expenses of writers on assignment.
**Photos:** State availability of photos with submission. Payment depends on article. Buys one-time rights.
The online magazine carries original material not found in the print edition. Contact: Steven Castle.
**Tips:** "Show zest in your writing, immaculate research and strong thematic structure, and you can handle most any assignment. We want to put the reader there, whether the article is about test driving a car, fishing for marlin, touring a luxury home or profiling a celebrity. The best articles will be those that tell stories, with all the details about products or whatever else you may be writing about placed in that context. Anecdotes should be used liberally, especially for leads, and the fun should show in your writing."

**$ $ THE SATURDAY EVENING POST,** The Saturday Evening Post Society, 1100 Waterway Blvd., Indianapolis IN 46202. (317)636-8881. Fax: (317)637-0126. E-mail: satevepst@aol.com. Website: http://www.satevepost.org. **Contact:** Patricia Perry, managing editor. Travel Editor: Holly Miller. **30% freelance written.** Bimonthly general interest, family-oriented magazine focusing on physical fitness, preventive medicine. "Ask almost any American if he or she has heard of *The Saturday Evening Post*, and you will find that many have fond recollections of the magazine from their childhood days. Many readers recall sitting with their families on Saturdays awaiting delivery of their *Post* subscription in the mail. *The Saturday Evening Post* has forged a tradition of 'forefront journalism.' *The Saturday Evening Post* continues to stand at the journalistic forefront with its coverage of health, nutrition, and preventive medicine." Estab. 1728. Circ. 500,000. Pays on publication. Publishes ms an average of 3 months after acceptance. Byline given. Buys second serial (reprint) and all rights. Submit seasonal material 4 months in advance. Accepts queries by mail, fax. Accepts simultaneous submissions. Reports in 1 month on queries; 6 weeks on mss. Writer's guidelines for #10 SASE or on website.

**Nonfiction:** Book excerpts, general interest, how-to (gardening, home improvement), humor, interview/profile, travel. "No political articles or articles containing sexual innuendo or hypersophistication." **Buys 25 mss/year.** Query with or without published clips, or send complete ms. Length: 750-2,500 words. **Pays $200 minimum**, negotiable maximum for assigned articles. Sometimes pays expenses of writers on assignment.

**Photos:** State availability of photos with submission. Reviews negatives and transparencies. Offers $50 minimum, negotiable maxmium per photo. Model release, identification required. Buys one-time or all rights.

**Columns/Departments:** Travel (destinations); Post Scripts (well-known humorists); Post People (activities of celebrities). **Buys 16 mss/year.** Query with published clips or send complete ms. Length: 750-1,500 words. **Pays $150 minimum**, negotiable maximum.

**Poetry:** Light verse.

**Fillers:** Post Scripts Editor: Steve Pettinga. Anecdotes, short humor. **Buys 200/year.** Length: 300 words. **Pays $15.**

**Tips:** "Areas most open to freelancers are Health, Post Scripts and Travel. For travel we like text-photo packages, pragmatic tips, side bars and safe rather than exotic destinations. Query by mail, not phone. Send clips."

⭐ **$ $ $ $ SATURDAY NIGHT**, Saturday Night Magazine Ltd., 184 Front St. E, Suite 400, Toronto, Ontario M5A 4N3 Canada. Phone: (416)368-7237. Fax: (416)368-5112. E-mail: editorial@saturdaynight.ca. Website: http://www.saturdaynight.ca/. Editor: Paul Tough. **Contact:** Tara Ariano, assistant to the editor. **95% freelance written.** Monthly magazine. Readership is urban concentrated. Well-educated, with a high disposable income. Average age is 43. Estab. 1887. Circ. 410,000. Pays on receipt of a publishable ms. Byline given. Offer 50% kill fee. Buys first North American serial rights. Editorial lead time 4 months. Submit seasonal material 4 months in advance. Accepts queries by mail, e-mail, phone, fax. Accepts simultaneous submissions. Sample copy for $3.50. Writer's guidelines free.

**Nonfiction:** Book excerpts, essays, general interest, interview/profile, opinion, personal experience, photo feature. **Buys 100 mss/year.** Query. Length: 200-5,000 words. **Pays $1/word.**

**Photos:** State availability of photos with submission. Negotiates payment individually. Model releases and identification of subjects required. Buys one-time rights.

**Columns/Departments:** Surveyor (short, interesting stories) 200-1,200 words; Canadian Letters, 500-1,200 words; The Passing Show (humor), 570-1,000 words; One Moment (history) 750-1,000 words. Query. **Pays $1/word.**

**Fiction:** Publishes novel excerpts.

🖥 The online magazine carries original content not found in the print edition. Contact: Tara Ariano, online editor.

**$ $ $ $ SMITHSONIAN MAGAZINE**, 900 Jefferson Dr., Washington DC 20560-0406. (202)786-2900. E-mail: siarticles@aol.com. Website: http://www.smithsonianmag.si.edu. **Contact:** Marlane A. Liddell, articles editor. **90% freelance written.** Prefers to work with published/established writers. Monthly magazine for associate members of the Smithsonian Institution; 85% with college education. "*Smithsonian Magazine*'s mission is to inspire fascination with all the world has to offer by featuring unexpected and entertaining editorial that explores different lifestyles, cultures and peoples, the arts, the wonders of nature and technology, and much more. The highly educated, innovative readers of *Smithsonian* share a unique desire to celebrate life, seeking out the timely as well as the timeless, the artistic as well as the academic and the thought-provoking as well as the humorous." Circ. 2,300,000. Buys first North American serial rights. "Payment for each article to be negotiated depending on our needs and the article's length and excellence." **Pays on acceptance.** Publishes ms an average of 6 months after acceptance. Editorial leadtime 2 months. Submit seasonal material 3 months in advance. Reports in 2 months. Sample copy for $5, % Judy Smith. Writer's guidelines for #10 SASE or on website.

● Ranked as one of the best markets for freelance writers in *Writer's Yearbook* magazine's annual "Top 100 Markets," January 1999.

○━ "We consider focused subjects that fall within the general range of Smithsonian Institution interests, such as: cultural history, physical science, art and natural history. We are always looking for offbeat subjects and profiles. We do not consider fiction, poetry, travel features, political and news events, or previously published articles. We publish only twelve issues a year, so it is difficult to place an article in *Smithsonian*, but please be assured that all proposals are considered."

**Nonfiction:** "Our mandate from the Smithsonian Institution says we are to be interested in the same things which now interest or should interest the Institution: cultural and fine arts, history, natural sciences, hard sciences, etc." Query with clips. Buys 120-130 feature articles (up to 5,000 words) and 12 short pieces (750 words)/year. Pays various rates per feature, $1,500 per short piece. Pays expenses of writers on assignment.

**Photos:** Purchased with or without ms and on assignment. Captions required. Pays $400/full color page. "Illustrations are not the responsibility of authors, but if you do have photographs or illustration materials, please include a selection of them with your submission. In general, 35mm color transparencies or black-and-white prints are perfectly acceptable. Photographs published in the magazine are usually obtained through assignments, stock agencies or specialized sources.

No photo library is maintained and photographs should be submitted only to accompany a specific article proposal."

**Columns/Departments: Buys 12-15 department articles/year.** Length: 1,000-2,000 words. Back Page humor, 1,000 words. **Pays $1,000 per department article.**

**Tips:** "We prefer a written proposal of one or two pages as a preliminary query. The proposal should convince us that we should cover the subject, offer descriptive information on how you, the writer, would treat the subject and offer us an opportunity to judge your writing ability. Background information and writing credentials and samples are helpful. All unsolicited proposals are sent to us on speculation and you should receive a reply within eight weeks. Please include a self-addressed stamped envelope. We also accept proposals via electronic mail at siarticles@aol.com. If we decide to commission an article, the writer receives full payment on acceptance of the manuscript. If the article is found unsuitable, one-third of the payment serves as a kill fee."

**N ☒ $ $ $ $ SOLIMAR, Living in the New Millennium**, Solimar, Inc., 3717 Mt. Diablo Blvd., #109, Lafayette CA 94549. Fax: (925)284-9473. E-mail: lesliebranscum@earthlink.net. Website: http://www.solimarmagazine. com. Editor: Sunni Taliaferro. Managing Editor: Sarah Lenz. **Contact:** Leslie Branscum, editorial assistant. **80% freelance written.** Quarterly magazine covering lifestyle. "*Solimar* gives practical examples of how to bring dreams to life through telling real life stories or personal expressions that are *not* preachy." Estab. 1999. Circ. 50,000. **Pays on acceptance** or on publication. Publishes ms an average of 3 months after acceptance. Byline given. Offers 50% kill fee. Buys first North American serial and electronic rights. Editorial lead time 1 year. Submit seasonal material 1 year in advance. Accepts queries by mail, e-mail, fax. Reports in 2 weeks on queries; 3 months on mss. Sample copy for $3 and mailing label. Writer's guidelines for #10 SASE or by e-mail.

**Nonfiction:** Book excerpts, inspirational, interview/profile, new product, personal experience, photo feature, travel. No dissertations; no gossip; no "pollyanna," criticism; no sarcasm. **Buys 60 mss/year.** Query with or without published clips. Length: 300-3,000 words. **Pays $225-2,250.** Sometimes pays expenses of writers on assignment.

**Reprints:** Accepts previously published submissions.

**Photos:** State availability of photos with submission. Reviews 2¼×2¼ transparencies and 5×7 prints. Negotiates payment individually. Captions, model releases and identification of subjects required. Buys one-time rights and electronic rights.

**Columns/Departments:** Self, Family, Community, World, Features, Celebrity, Travel, Arts, all 300-750 words. **Buys 16 mss/year.** Query with published clips. **Pays $225-560.**

**Fiction:** Experimental, novel excerpts, serialized novels, slice-of-life vignettes. **Buys 20 mss/year.** Query with published clips. Length: 300-2,000 words. **Pays $225-1,500.**

**Poetry:** Avant-garde, free verse, haiku, light verse, traditional. No erotica; no "bashing." **Buys up to 20 poems/year.** Submit maximum 5 poems. Length: up to 750 lines. **Pays $50.**

**Fillers:** Anecdotes, gags to be illustrated by cartoonist, short humor. **Buys 60/year.** Length: up to 150 words. **Pays $25.**

**Tips:** "The focus of our magazine is to give practical examples of how to bring dreams to life. We do this by telling stories from real life, not through preaching. All submissions, whether fiction, nonfiction, poetry, photography or art need to leave our readers with a good feeling. Stories about people who are having a positive impact on their community; celebrities who live their lives in inspirational ways, and uplifting stories about any kind of relationship are especially wanted. Query letters need to be concise and explain exactly how the piece relates to our editorial mission."

**☒ $ $ $ THE SUN, A Magazine of Ideas**, The Sun Publishing Company, 107 N. Roberson St., Chapel Hill NC 27516. (919)942-5282. Website: http://www.thesunmagazine.org. **Contact:** Sy Safransky, editor. **90% freelance written.** Monthly general interest magazine. "We are open to all kinds of writing, though we favor work of a personal nature." Estab. 1974. Circ. 40,000. Pays on publication. Publishes ms an average of 6 months after acceptance. Byline given. Buys first or one-time rights. Reports in 1 month on queries; 3 months on mss. Sample copy for $5. Send SASE for writer's guidelines or see website.

**Nonfiction:** Book excerpts, essays, general interest, interview, opinion, personal experience, spiritual. **Buys 36 mss/year.** Send complete ms. Length: 7,000 words maximum. **Pays $300-1,500.** "Complimentary subscription is given in addition to payment (applies to payment for *all* works, not just nonfiction)."

**Reprints:** Send photocopy of article or short story and information about when and where the article or story previously appeared. Pays 50% of amount paid for an original article or story.

**Photos:** Send b&w photos with submission. Offers $50-200/photo. Model releases preferred. Buys one-time rights.

**Fiction:** Experimental, literary. "We avoid stereotypical genre pieces like sci-fi, romance, western and horror. Read an issue before submitting." **Buys 30 mss/year.** Send complete ms. Length: 7,000 words maximum. **Pays $300-1,000 for original fiction.**

    ● Ranked as one of the best markets for fiction writers in *Writer's Digest* magazine's last "Fiction 50."

**Poetry:** Free verse, prose poems, short and long poems. **Buys 24 poems/year.** Submit maximum 6 poems. **Pays $50-200.**

**TIME**, Time Inc. Magazine, Time & Life Bldg., 1271 Avenue of the Americas, New York NY 10020. (212)522-1212. Fax: (212)522-0323 **Contact:** Walter Isaacson, managing editor. Weekly magazine. "*Time* covers the full range of information that is important to people today—breaking news, national and world afairs, business news, societal and lifestyle issues, culture and entertainment news and reviews." Estab. 1923. Circ. 4,150,000. This magazine did not respond to our request for information. Query before submitting.

**$ $ $ $ TOWN & COUNTRY**, The Hearst Corp., 1700 Broadway, New York NY 10019. (212)903-5000. Fax: (212)765-8308. **Contact**: John Cantrell, deputy editor. **40% freelance written.** Monthly lifestyle magazine. *"Town & Country* is a lifestyle magazine for the affluent market. Features focus on fashion, beauty, travel, interior design, and the arts as well as individuals' accomplishments and contributions to society." Estab. 1846. Circ. 488,000. **Pays on acceptance.** Offers 25% kill fee. Buys first North American serial and electronic rights. Reports in 1 month on queries.

● Ranked as one of the best markets for freelance writers in *Writer's Yearbook* magazine's annual "Top 100 Markets," January 1999.

**Nonfiction:** "We're looking for engaging service articles for a high income, well-educated audience, in numerous categories: travel, personalities, interior design, fashion, beauty, jewelry, health, city news, country life news, the arts, philanthropy." **Buys 25 mss/year.** Length: column items, 100-300 words; feature stories, 800-2,000 words. Special issues: Annual home issue (October 1998); Annual weddings issue (February 1999); Annual travel issue (April 1999). **Pays $2/word.** Query with clips before submitting.

**Tips:** "We have served the affluent market for over 150 years, and our writers need to be expert in the needs and interests of that market."

**★ $ $ $ TROIKA; Wit, Wisdom & Wherewithal**, Lone Tout Publications, Inc., P.O. Box 1006, Weston CT 06883. (203)227-5377. Fax: (203)222-9332. E-mail: etroika@aol.com. Website: http://www.troikamagazine.com. **Contact**: Celia Meadow, editor. **80% freelance written.** Quarterly magazine covering general interest, lifestyle. "A magazine for men and women seeking a balanced, three-dimensional lifestyle: personal achievement, family commitment, community involvement. Readers are upscale, educated, 30-50 age bracket. The *Troika* generation is a mix of what is called the X generation and the baby boomers. We are that generation. We grew up with sex, drugs and rock 'n roll, but now it really is our turn to make a difference, if we so choose." Estab. 1993. Circ. 120,000. Pays on publication. Publishes ms an average of 6 months after acceptance. Byline given. Buys first North American and Internet serial rights. Editorial lead time 3 months. Submit seasonal material 6 months in advance. Accepts queries by mail, e-mail. Accepts simultaneous submissions. Reports in 2 months. Sample copy for $5 or on website. Guidelines for #10 SASE or on website.

**Nonfiction:** Essays, exposé, general interest, historical/nostalgic, how-to (leisure activities, pro bono, finance), humor, inspirational, interview/profile (non-celebrity), opinion, personal experience. No celebrity profiles. **Buys 60-80 mss/year.** Query or send complete ms. Length:1,800-3,000 words. **Pays $250-1,000 for assigned articles; $250-400 for first appearance of unsolicited articles.**

**Reprints:** Send photocopy with information about when and where the article or story previously appeared.

**Photos:** State availability of photos with submission. Reviews negatives, transparencies. Offers no additional payment for photos accepted with ms. Captions, model releases, identification of subjects required.

**Columns/Departments:** Literati; Pub Performances (literary, theater, arts, culture); Blueprints (architecture, interior design, fashion); Body of Facts (science); Hippocratic Horizons (health); Home Technology; Capital Commitments (personal finance); all 750-1,200 words. **Buys 40-60 mss/year.** Query or send complete ms. **Pays $250 maximum.**

**Fiction:** Adventure, confession, experimental, fantasy, historical, mainstream, mystery, novel excerpts, slice-of-life vignettes, suspense. **Buys 4-8 mss/year.** Send complete ms. Length: 3,000 words maximum. **Pays $250 maximum.**

**VANITY FAIR**, Condé Nast Publications, Inc., 350 Madison Ave., New York NY 10017. (212)880-8800. Publisher: Chris Garrett. Monthly. *"Vanity Fair* presents the issues, events and people that define our times. This chronicle of contemporary culture features art, entertainment, politics, business, and the media." This magazine did not respond to our request for information. Query before submitting.

**★ $ $ THE WORLD & I, The Magazine for Lifelong Learners**, News World Communications, Inc., 3600 New York Ave. NE, Washington DC 20002. (202)635-4000. Fax: (202)269-9353. E-mail: theworldandi@mcimail.com. Website: http://www.worldandi.com. Editor: Morton A. Kaplan. Executive Editor: Michael Marshall. **Contact**: Gary Rowe, editorial office coordinator. **90% freelance written.** Monthly magazine. "A broad interest magazine for the thinking, educated person." Estab. 1986. Circ. 30,000. Pays on publication. Publishes ms an average of 6 months after acceptance. Byline given. Offers 20% kill fee. Buys all rights. Submit seasonal material 5 months in advance. Reports in 6 weeks on queries; 10 weeks on mss. Sample copy for $5 and 9×12 SASE. Guidelines for #10 SASE.

**Nonfiction:** "Description of Sections: Current Issues: Politics, economics and strategic trends covered in a variety of approaches, including special report, analysis, commentary and photo essay. The Arts: International coverage of music, dance, theater, film, television, craft, design, architecture, photography, poetry, painting and sculpture—through reviews, features, essays, opinion pieces and a 6-page Gallery of full-color reproductions. Life: Surveys all aspects of life in 22 rotating subsections which include: Travel and Adventure (first person reflections, preference given to authors who provide photographic images), Profile (people or organizations that are "making a difference"), Food and Garden (must be accompanied by photos), Education, Humor, Hobby, Family, Consumer, Trends, and Health. Send SASE for complete list of subsections. Natural Science: Covers the latest in science and technology, relating it to the social and historical context, under these headings: At the Edge, Impacts, Nature Walk, Science and Spirit, Science and Values, Scientists: Past and Present, Crucibles of Science and Science Essay. Book World: Excerpts from important, timely books (followed by commentaries) and 10-12 scholarly reviews of significant new books each month, including untranslated works from abroad. Covers current affairs, intellectual issues, contemporary fiction, history, moral/religious issues and the social sciences. Currents in Modern Thought: Examines scholarly research and theoretical debate across the wide range of disciplines in the humanities and social sciences. Featured themes are explored by several contributors. Investigates theoretical issues raised by certain current events, and offers contemporary reflection on issues drawn from the whole history of human thought. Culture: Surveys the world's people in these subsections: Peoples (their unique characteristics and cultural symbols), Crossroads (changes brought by the meeting of cultures), Patterns (photo essay depicting the daily life of a distinct culture), Folk Wisdom (folklore and practical wisdom and their present forms), and Heritage (multicultural backgrounds of the American people and how they are bound to the world). Photo Essay: Patterns, a 6- or 8-page photo essay, appears monthly in the Culture section. Emphasis is placed on comprehensive photographic coverage of a people or group, their private or public lifestyle, in a given situation or context. Accompanying word count: 300-500 words. Photos must be from existing stock, no travel subsidy. Life & Ideals, a 6- or 8-page photo essay, occasionally appears in the Life section. First priority is given to those focused on individuals or organizations that are "making a difference." Accompanying word count: 700-1,000 words. 'No *National Enquirer*-type articles.' " **Buys 1,200 mss/year.** Query with published clips and SASE. Length: 1,000-5,000 words. Pays on a per-article basis that varies according to the length of the article, the complexity of special research required, and the experience of the author. Seldom pays expenses of writers on assignment.

**Reprints:** Send typed ms with rights for sale noted and information about when and where the article previously appeared.

**Fiction:** Publishes novel excerpts.

**Poetry:** Contact: Arts Editor. Avant-garde, free verse, haiku, light verse, traditional. **Buys 4-6 poems/year.** Query with maximum 5 poems. **Pays $30-75.**

**Photos:** State availability of photos with submission. Reviews contact sheets, transparencies and prints. Payment negotiable. Model releases and identification of subjects required. Buys one-time rights.

**Tips:** "We accept articles from journalists, but also place special emphasis on scholarly contributions. It is our hope that the magazine will enable the best of contemporary thought, presented in accessible language, to reach a wider audience than would normally be possible through the academic journals appropriate to any given discipline."

# HEALTH & FITNESS

The magazines listed here specialize in covering health and fitness topics for a general audience. Health and fitness magazines have experienced a real boom lately. Most emphasize developing healthy lifestyle choices in exercise, nutrition and general fitness. Many magazines offer alternative healing and therapies that are becoming more mainstream, such as medicinal herbs, health foods and a holistic mind/body approach to well-being. As wellness is a concern to all demographic groups, publishers have developed editorial geared to specific audiences: African-American women, older readers, men, women. Also see the Sports/Miscellaneous section where publications dealing with health and particular sports may be listed. For magazines that cover healthy eating, refer to the Food & Drink section. Many general interest publications are also potential markets for health or fitness articles. Magazines covering health topics from a medical perspective are listed in the Medical category of Trade.

**$ $ AMERICAN FITNESS,** 15250 Ventura Blvd., Suite 200, Sherman Oaks CA 91403. (818)905-0040. Fax: (818)990-5468. Website: http://www.afaa.com. Publisher: Roscoe Fawcett. **Contact:** Peg Jordan, R.N., editor-at-large. **75% freelance written.** Eager to work with new/unpublished writers. Bimonthly magazine covering exercise and fitness, health and nutrition. "We need timely, in-depth, informative articles on health, fitness, aerobic exercise, sports nutrition, age-specific fitness and outdoor activity." Circ. 36,000. Pays 6 weeks after publication. Publishes ms an average of 6 months after acceptance. Byline given. Buys all rights. Submit seasonal material 4 months in advance. Accepts queries by mail, fax. Accepts simultaneous submissions. Reports in 6 weeks. Sample copy for $3 and SAE with 6 first-class stamps. Writer's guidelines for SAE.

**Nonfiction:** Health and fitness, including women's issues (pregnancy, family, pre- and post-natal, menopause and eating disorders); new research findings on exercise techniques and equipment; aerobic exercise; sports nutrition; sports medicine; innovations and trends in aerobic sports; tips on teaching exercise and humorous accounts of fitness motivation; physiology; exposé (on nutritional gimmickry); historical/nostalgic (history of various athletic events); inspirational (sports leader's motivational pieces); interview/profile (fitness figures); new product (plus equipment review); personal experience (successful fitness story); photo feature (on exercise, fitness, new sport); youth and senior fitness; travel (activity adventures). No articles on unsound nutritional practices, popular trends or unsafe exercise gimmicks. **Buys 18-25 mss/year.** Query with published clips or send complete ms. Length: 800-1,200 words. **Pays $200 for features, $80 for news.** Sometimes pays expenses of writers on assignment.

**Reprints:** Accepts previously published submissions.

**Photos:** Sports, action, fitness, aquatic aerobics, aerobics competitions and exercise classes. "We are especially interested in photos of high-adrenalin sports like rock climbing and mountain biking." Pays $0 for b&w prints; $35 for transparencies. Captions, model release and identification of subjects required. Usually buys all rights; other rights purchased depend on use of photo.

**Columns/Departments:** Research (latest exercise and fitness findings); Alternative paths (non-mainstream approaches to health, wellness and fitness); Strength (latest breakthroughs in weight training); Clubscene (profiles and highlights of fitness club industry); Adventure (treks, trails and global challenges); Food (low-fat/non-fat, high-flavor dishes); Homescene (home workout alternatives); Clip 'n' Post (concise exercise research to post in health clubs, offices or on refrigerators). Query with published clips or send complete ms. Length: 800-1,000 words. **Pays $100-140.**

**Tips:** "Make sure to quote scientific literature or good research studies and several experts with good credentials to validate exercise trend, technique, or issue. Cover a unique aerobics or fitness angle, provide accurate and interesting findings, and write in a lively, intelligent manner. Please, no first person accouts of 'how I lost weight or discovered running.' *AF* is a good place for first-time authors or regularly published authors who want to sell spin-offs or reprints."

**$ $AMERICAN HEALTH**, Reader's Digest Rd., Pleasantville NY 10570. (914)238-1000. Fax: (914)244-5656. Website: http://www.americanhealth.com. Editor: Miriam Arond. **Contact:** Editorial. **70% freelance written.** Women's health magazine published 10 times/year covering both scientific and "lifestyle" aspects of women's health, including medicine, fitness, nutrition and psychology. Estab. 1982. Circ. 1,000,000. **Pays on acceptance.** Publishes ms an average of 6 months after acceptance. Byline or tagline given. Offers 25% kill fee. Buys first North American serial rights. Accepts queries by mail, fax. Sample copy for $3. Writer's guidelines for #10 SASE.

**Features:** News-based articles usually with a service angle; well-written pieces with an investigative or unusual slant; profiles (health, fitness or celebrity related). No mechanical research reports, unproven treatments. "Stories should be written clearly, without jargon. Information should be new, authoritative and helpful to readers." **Buys 60-70 mss/year.** Query with 2 published clips. Length: 800-2,000 words. Payment varies. Pays expenses of writers on assignment.

**Reprints:** Send information about when and where the article previously appeared.

**Columns/Departments:** Medicine, Alternative Medicine, Fitness, Diet/Nutrition, Medical Mystery, Lifestyle, Mental Health, Healthscope, Family, Dental. Other news sections from time to time. **Buys 100 mss/year.** Query with published clips.

**Tips:** "*American Health* relies on outside contributors for most of our articles. The magazine needs good ideas and good articles from experienced journalists and writers. Feature queries should be short (no longer than a page) and to the point. Give us a good angle and a paragraph of background. Queries only. We are not responsible for material not accompanied by a SASE."

**$ $BETTER HEALTH**, Better Health Magazine, 1450 Chapel St., New Haven CT 06511-4440. (203)789-3972. Fax: (203)789-4053. **Contact:** Cynthia Wolfe Boynton, editor/publishing director. **90% freelance written.** Prefers to work with published/established writers; will consider new/unpublished writers. Bimonthly magazine devoted to health, wellness and medical issues. Estab. 1979. Circ. 500,000. **Pays on acceptance.** Byline given. Offers 20% kill fee. Buys first rights. Query first; do not send article. Sample copy for $2.50. Writer's guidelines for #10 SASE.

**Nonfiction:** Wellness/prevention issues are of prime interest. New medical techniques or nonmainstream practices are not considered. No fillers, poems, quizzes, seasonal, heavy humor, inspirational or personal experience. Length: 1,500-3,000 words. **Pays $300-700.**

**$ $BETTER NUTRITION**, Intertec/Primedia, 5 Penn Plaza, 13th Floor, New York NY 10001. (212)613-9757. Fax: (212)563-3028. E-mail: jamesg@cowles.com. **Contact:** James J. Gormley, editor. **57% freelance written.** Monthly magazine covering nutritional news and approaches to optimal health. "Since 1938, *Better Nutrition*'s mission has been to inform our readers about the latest breakthroughs in nutritional (and lifestyle) approaches to optimal health and ongoing research into supplementation with vitamins, botanicals, minerals and other natural products." Estab. 1938. Circ. 480,000. Pays on publication. Publishes ms an average of 2 months after acceptance. Byline given. Offers 50% kill fee. Rights purchased vary. Editorial lead time 3 months. Accepts queries by mail, e-mail, fax. Sample copy free.

**Nonfiction:** Clinical research crystallized into accessible articles on nutrition, health, alternative medicine, disease prevention, FDA exposés. Each issue has a featured article (e.g., February, Healthy Heart; April, Organic). **Buys 120-180 mss/year.** Query. Length: 630-1,500 words. **Pays $200-400.** Sometimes pays expenses of writers on assignment.

**Photos:** State availability of photos with query. Reviews $4 \times 5$ transparencies and $3 \times 5$ prints. Negotiates payment individually. Captions, model releases, identification of subjects required if applicable. Buys one-time rights or non-exclusive reprint rights.

**Columns/Departments:** Health Watch; Nutrition News; Women's Health; Earth Medicine; Healing Herbs; Better Hair, Skin & Nails; Herb Update; Health in Balance; Book Zone; Supplement Update; Natural Energy; Children's Health; Sports Nutrition; Earth Watch; Homeopathy; Botanical Medicine; Meatless Meals; Trim Time; Healthier Pets; Ayurvedic Medicine; Longevity; Healing Herbs; Frontiers of Science.

**Fillers:** Nutrition-related crossword puzzles, sidebars, charts and lists.

**Tips:** "Be on top of what's newsbreaking in nutrition and supplementation. Interview experts. Be available for one-week-assignment/in-our-hands turnarounds. Fact-check, fact-check, fact-check. Find out what distinguishes us from other consumer-directed industry publications. Send in a résumé (including Social Security/IRS number), a couple of clips and a list of article possibilities."

**$ $DELICIOUS!, Your Magazine of Natural Living**, New Hope Communications, 1301 Spruce St., Boulder CO 80304. E-mail: delicious@newhope.com. Editor: Kathryn Arnold. **Contact:** Heather Prouty, senior editor. **85% freelance written.** Monthly magazine covering natural products, nutrition, alternative medicines, herbal medicines. "*Delicious!* magazine empowers natural foods store shoppers to make health-conscious choices in their lives. Our goal is to improve consumers' perception of the value of natural methods in achieving health. To do this, we educate consumers on nutrition, disease prevention, botanical medicines and natural personal care products." Estab. 1985. Circ. 420,000. **Pays on acceptance**. Publishes ms an average of 6 months after acceptance. Byline given. Offers 20% kill fee. Editorial lead time 4 months. Submit seasonal material 6-8 months in advance. Accepts simultaneous submissions. Reports in 3 months. Sample copy and writer's guidelines free.

● Ranked as one of the best markets for freelance writers in *Writer's Yearbook* magazine's annual "Top 100 Markets," January 1999.

**Nonfiction:** Book excerpts, how-to, personal experience (regarding natural or alternative health), health nutrition, herbal medicines, alternative medicine. **Buys 150 mss/year.** Query with published clips. Length: 500-2,000 words. **Pays $100-700 for assigned articles; $50-300 for unsolicited articles.**

**Photos:** State availability of photos with submission. Reviews 3×5 prints. Offers no additional payment for photos accepted with ms. Identification of subjects required. Buys one-time rights.

**Columns/Departments:** Herbal Kingdom (scientific evidence supporting herbal medicines) 1,500 words; Nutrition (new research on diet for good health) 1,200 words; Dietary Supplements (new research on vitamins/minerals, etc.) 1,200 words. Query with published clips. **Pays $100-500.**

● New Hope Communications and *Delicious!* were sold to Penton Media.

**Tips:** "Highlight any previous health/nutrition/medical writing experience. Demonstrate a knowledge of natural medicine, nutrition, or natural products. Health practitioners who demonstrate writing ability are ideal freelancers."

**$ $ $ FDA CONSUMER**, 5600 Fishers Lane, Rockville MD 20857. (301)827-7130. Fax: (301)443-9057. Website: http://www.fda.gov. **Contact:** FDA Consumer Editor. **10% freelance written.** Prefers to work with experienced health and medical writers. Bimonthly magazine for general public interested in health issues. A federal government publication (Food and Drug Administration). Circ. 25,000. Pays after acceptance. Publishes ms an average of 3 months after acceptance. Byline given. Not copyrighted. Pays 50% kill fee. "All rights must be assigned to the USA so that the articles may be reprinted without permission. This includes electronic rights. We cannot be responsible for any work by writer not agreed upon by prior contract."

**Nonfiction:** "Upbeat feature articles of an educational nature about FDA regulated products and specific FDA programs and actions to protect the consumer's health and pocketbook. Articles based on health topics connected to food, drugs, medical devices, and other products regulated by FDA. All articles subject to clearance by the appropriate FDA experts as well as acceptance by the editor. All articles based on prior arrangement by contract." Query with résumé and clips only. **Buys 5-10 freelance mss/year.** Length: 2,000-2,500 words. **Pays $800-950** for "first-timers"; **$1,200** for those who have previously published in *FDA Consumer*. Pays phone and mailing expenses.

**Photos:** Black and white photos are purchased on assignment only.

**Tips:** "Besides reading the feature articles in *FDA Consumer*, a writer can best determine whether his/her style and expertise suit our needs by submitting a résumé and clips; story suggestions are generated inhouse."

**$ $ $ $ FITNESS MAGAZINE**, 375 Lexington Ave., New York NY 10017-5514. (212)499-2000. Fax: (212)499-1568. **Contact:** Jennifer Cook, executive editor. Published 10 times/year for women in their twenties and thirties who are interested in fitness and living a healthy life. **Pays on acceptance**. Byline given. Offers 20% kill fee. Buys first North American serial rights. Reports in 2 months on queries. Writer's guidelines for #10 SASE.

● Ranked as one of the best markets for freelance writers in *Writer's Yearbook* magazine's annual "Top 100 Markets," January 1999.

**Nonfiction:** "We need timely, well-written nonfiction articles on exercise and fitness, beauty, health, diet/nutrition, and psychology. We always include boxes and sidebars in our stories." **Buys 80-100 mss/year.** Query. Length: 1,500-2,500 words. **Pays $1,500-2,500.** Pays expenses of writers on assignment.

**Reprints:** Accepts previously published submissions. Send photocopy of article. Negotiates fee.

**Columns/Departments: Buys 60 mss/year.** Query. Length: 600-1,200 words. **Pays $800-1,500.**

**Tips:** "Our pieces must get inside the mind of the reader and address her needs, hopes, fears and desires. *Fitness* acknowledges that getting and staying fit is difficult in an era when we are all time-pressured."

**$ $ $ $ HEALTH**, Time, Inc., Two Embarcadero Center, Suite 600, San Francisco CA 94111. (415)248-2700. Editor-in-Chief: Barbara Paulsen. **Contact:** Kristin Kloberdanz, editorial assistant. Magazine published 8 times/year on health, fitness and nutrition. "Our readers are predominantly college-educated women in their 30s and 40s. Edited to focus not on illness, but on events, ideas and people." Estab. 1987. Circ. 1,050,000. **Pays on acceptance**. Byline given. Offers 25% kill fee. Buys first North American serial rights. Accepts simultaneous submissions. Reports in 2 months on queries. Sample copy for $5 to "Back Issues." Writer's guidelines for #10 SASE. "No phone calls, please."

● *Health* stresses that writers must send for guidelines before sending a query, and that only queries that closely follow the guidelines get passed on to editors.

**Nonfiction: Buys 25 mss/year.** No unsolicited mss. Query with published clips and SASE. Length: 1,200 words. **Pays $1,800.** Pays the expenses of writers on assignment.

**Columns/Departments:** Food, Mind, Healthy Looks, Fitness.

**Tips:** "We look for well-articulated ideas with a narrow focus and broad appeal. A query that starts with an unusual local event and hooks it legitimately to some national trend or concern is bound to get our attention. Use quotes, examples and statistics to show why the topic is important and why the approach is workable. We need to see clear evidence of credible research findings pointing to meaningful options for our readers. Stories should offer practical advice and give clear explanations."

**$ $ HEALTH FOR WOMEN, Woman's Day Special Interest Publications**, Hachette-Filipacchi Magazines, 1633 Broadway, New York NY 10019. Fax: (212)767-5612. Editor: Carolyn Gatto. **Contact:** Janice Wright, managing editor. Semiannual consumer magazine covering women, health, fitness. "This magazine aims at helping the reader take care of herself and live a healthy lifestyle. Topics include weight control and reduction, exercise, food, emotions, and broader health issues. Exercise must be from a qualified professional in the field. The largest group of readers is in the 18 to 34 age group. Research guidelines will be supplied upon assignment." **Pays on acceptance**. Publishes ms an average of 3 months after acceptance. Byline given. Offers up to 25% kill fee. Buys first worldwide serial or second serial (printing) rights. Editorial lead time 6 months. Submit seasonal material 10 months in advance. Reports in 3 months. Sample copy not available; writer's guidelines for #10 SASE.

**Nonfiction:** How-to (diet, fitness), new product, service for women's health issues. **Buys 40 mss/year**. Query with published clips. Length: 250-1,000 words. Payment varies based on length, writer, importance. Sometimes pays expenses of writers on assignment.

**Reprints:** Accepts previously published submissions.

**Photos:** State availability of photos with submission. Model releases required. Buys one-time rights.

**Columns/Departments: Buys 6 mss/year**. Query with published clips. Payment varies based on length, writer, and level/amount of research required.

**Tips:** "Send a brief, clear query letter with relevant clips, and be patient."

**N $ HOLISTIC LIVING MAGAZINE A Celebration of Life**, HHAPA, 366 Nassau St., Princeton NJ 08540. (609)924-8711. Fax: (609)924-3836. E-mail: mchollow@pipeline.com. Website: http://www.holisticliving.org. **Contact:** Michele Hollow, editor. **70% freelance written**. Bimonthly magazine covering holistic health. Estab. 1981. Circ. 150,000. Pays on publication. Byline given. Buys all rights. Editorial lead time 4 months. Submit seasonal material 6 months in advance. Accepts queries by mail, e-mail, fax. Accepts simultaneous submissions. Reports in 10 weeks. Sample copy for $3. Writer's guidelines for #10 SASE.

**Nonfiction:** Alternative medicine, interview/profile, personal experience, nutrition, holistic health, spiritual. Query. Length: 250-1,500 words. **Pays up to $100 maximum for cover articles.** All writers get bios at the end of their articles.

**Reprints:** Accepts previously published submissions.

**Photos:** State availability of photos with submission or send photos with submission. Offers no additional payment for photos accepted with ms. Model releases and identification of subjects required.

**Columns/Departments:** The Holistic House, The Holistic Child, The Holistic Pet, Astrology, Book Reviews and First Person. Query.

**Tips:** "Opportunity exists for unpublished and published writers. We need first-person articles on uplifting issues— example: Patch Adams, MD, wrote about his Gesundheit Institute. Articles on herbs, nutrition, alternative therapies must be backed up with scientific research. Query editor with writing sample."

**$ $ $ LET'S LIVE MAGAZINE**, Franklin Publications, Inc., 320 N. Larchmont Blvd., P.O. Box 74908, Los Angeles CA 90004-3030. (323)469-3901. Fax: (323)469-9597. E-mail: letslive@earthlink.net. Editor-in-Chief: Beth Salmon. **Contact:** Nicole Brechka, assistant editor or Elizabeth Coombs, senior editor. Monthly magazine emphasizing health and preventive medicine. "Our editorial mission at *Let's Live* is to encourage readers to manage and promote their own health and well-being by providing well-researched, authoritative and practical information on preventive and complementary medicine, natural health products and the importance of an active lifestyle." **95% freelance written.** Works with a small number of new/unpublished writers each year; expertise in health field helpful. Estab. 1933. Circ. 1,700,000. Pays within 30 days of submission. Publishes ms an average of 4 months after acceptance. Buys all rights. Byline given. Submit seasonal material 6 months in advance. Accepts queries by mail, e-mail. Reports in 2 months on queries; 3 months on mss. Sample copy for $5 and 10×13 SAE with 6 first-class stamps. Writer's guidelines for #10 SASE.

● The editors are looking for more cutting-edge, well-researched natural health information that is substantiated by experts and well-respected scientific research literature.

**Nonfiction:** General interest (effects of vitamins, minerals, herbs and nutrients in improvement of health or afflictions); historical (documentation of experiments or treatment establishing value of nutrients as boon to health); how-to (enhance natural beauty, exercise/bodybuilding, acquire strength and vitality, improve health of adults and/or children and prepare tasty, healthy meals); interview (benefits of research in establishing prevention as key to good health); personal opinion (views of orthomolecular doctors or their patients on value of health foods toward maintaining good health); profile (background and/or medical history of preventive medicine, M.D.s or Ph.D.s, in advancement of nutrition). Manuscripts must be well-researched, reliably documented and written in a clear, readable style. **Buys 2-4 mss/issue.** Query with published clips and SASE. Length: 1,200-1,400 words. **Pays $850-1,000 for features.**

**Columns/Departments:** Sports Nutrition (Expert Column, Your Personal Trainer), Natural Medicine Chest, Herbs for Health, Millennium Medicine. Query with published clips and SASE. Length: 1,200-1,400 words. **Pays $500.**

**Photos:** Send photos. Pays $50 for 8×10 color prints, 35mm transparencies. Captions, model releases required.

**Tips:** "We want writers with experience in researching nonsurgical medical subjects and interviewing experts with the ability to simplify technical and clinical information for the layman. A captivating lead and structural flow are essential. The most frequent mistakes made by writers are in writing articles that are too technical; in poor style; written for the wrong audience (publication not thoroughly studied), or have unreliable documentation or overzealous faith in the topic reflected by flimsy research and inappropriate tone."

**$ $ MASSAGE MAGAZINE, Keeping Those Who Touch—In Touch**, 200 Seventh Ave. #240, Santa Cruz CA 95062. (408)477-1176. Fax: (408)477-2918. E-mail: edit@massagemag.com. Website: http://www.massagemag.com. **Contact:** Karen Menehan, editor. **60% freelance written.** Prefers to work with published/established writers, but works with a number of new/unpublished writers each year. Bimonthly magazine on massage-bodywork and related healing arts. Estab. 1985. Circ. 35,000. Pays on publication. Publishes ms an average of 1 year after acceptance. Byline given. Buys first North American rights. Accepts queries by mail, e-mail. Reports in 1 month on queries; 2 months on mss. Sample copy and writer's guidelines free.

**Nonfiction:** General interest, historical/nostalgic, how-to, experiential, inspirational, interview/profile, photo feature, technical, travel. Length: 600-2,000 words. **Pays $25-250 for articles.**

**Reprints:** Send tearsheet of article and typed ms with rights for sale noted and information about when and where the article previously appeared. Pays 50-75% of amount paid for an original article.

**Photos:** Send photos with submission. Offers $10-25/photo. Identification of subjects and photographer required. Buys one-time rights.

**Columns/Departments:** Touching Tales (experiential); Profiles; Table Talk (news briefs); Practice Building (business); Technique; Body/mind. Length: 800-1,200 words. **Pays $60-150** for most of these columns.

**Fillers:** Facts, news briefs. Length: 100-800 words. **Pays $125 maximum.**

**Tips:** "In-depth feature articles that detail the benefits of massage are a high priority."

**$ $ $ MEN'S FITNESS**, Men's Fitness, Inc., 21100 Erwin St., Woodland Hills CA 91367-3712. (818)884-6800. Fax: (818)704-5734. Website: http://www.mensfitness.com. **Contact:** Dean Brierly, managing editor. **80% freelance written.** Works with small number of new/unpublished writers each year. Monthly magazine for health-conscious men (core readership ages 18-35). Provides reliable, entertaining guidance for the active male in all areas of lifestyle. Estab. 1984. Circ. 430,000. Pays 1 month after acceptance. Publishes ms an average of 4 months after acceptance. Offers 33% kill fee. Buys all rights. Submit seasonal material 8 months in advance. Reports in 2 months. Writer's guidelines for 9×12 SAE. Query before sending ms.

**Nonfiction:** Service, informative, inspirational and scientific feature articles written for men. Few interviews or regional news unless extraordinary. Query with published clips. Length: 800-1,200 words. **Pays $1/word.**

**Columns/Departments:** Nutrition, Mind, Appearance, Sexuality, Health. Length: 1,200-1,500 words. **Pays $1/word.**

**Tips:** "We look for writing that is informative *and* accessible, crafted in an entertaining, conversational style. A proven track record of previously published, similarly-themed material will enhance your chances of acceptance."

**$ $ $ MEN'S HEALTH**, Rodale, 33 E. Minor St., Emmaus PA 18098. (610)967-5171. Fax: (610)967-7725. E-mail: tmcgrat1@rodalepress.com. Website: http://www.menshealth.com. Editor: Michael Lafavore. Executive Editor: Peter Moore. **Contact:** Tom McGrath, senior editor. **50% freelance written.** Prefers to work with established/published writers. Magazine published 10 times/year covering men's health and fitness. "*Men's Health* is a lifestyle magazine showing men the practical and positive actions that make their lives better, with articles covering fitness, nutrition, relationships, travel, careers, grooming and health issues." Estab. 1986. Circ. 1,511,000. **Pays on acceptance.** Offers 25% kill fee. Buys all rights. Accepts queries by mail, fax. Responds in 3 weeks. Writer's guidelines for SASE.

o➤ Freelancers have the best chance with the front-of-the-book piece, Malegrams.

**Nonfiction:** "Authoritative information on all aspects of men's physical and emotional health. We rely on writers to seek out the right experts and to either tell a story from a first-person vantage or get good anecdotes." **Buys 30 features/year, 360 short pieces/year.** Query with published clips and SASE. Length: 1,200-4,000 words for features, 100-300 words for short pieces. **Pays $1,000-5,000 for features, $100-500 for short pieces.**

• Ranked as one of the best markets for freelance writers in *Writer's Yearbook* magazine's annual "Top 100 Markets," January 1999.

**Columns/Departments: Buys 80 mss/year.** Length: 750-1,500 words. **Pays $750-2,000.**

▣ The online magazine carries original content not included in the print edition. Contact: Amy Donohue, online editor.

**Tips:** "We have a wide definition of health. We believe that being successful in every area of your life is being healthy. The magazine focuses on all aspects of health, from stress issues to nutrition to exercise to sex. It is 50% staff written, 50% from freelancers. The best way to break in is not by covering a particular subject, but by covering it within the magazine's style. There is a very particular tone and voice to the magazine. A writer has to be a good humor writer as well as a good service writer. Prefers mail queries. No phone calls, please."

**$ $ $ MUSCLE & FITNESS**, The Science of Living Super-Fit, Weider Health & Fitness, 21100 Erwin St., Woodland Hills, CA 91367. (818)884-6800. Fax: (818)595-0463. Website: http://www.muscle-fitness.com. Editor: Bill Geiger. **Contact:** Vincent Scalisi, editorial director; Bill Geiger, editor (training and other articles); Jo Ellen Krumm, managing editor (nutrition and food articles). **50% freelance written.** Monthly magazine covering bodybuilding and fitness for healthy, active men and women. It contains a wide range of features and monthly departments devoted to all areas of bodybuilding, health, fitness, injury prevention and treatment, and nutrition. Editorial fulfills two functions: information and entertainment. Special attention is devoted to how-to advice and accuracy. Estab. 1950. Circ. 500,000. **Pays on acceptance.** Publishes ms an average of 2 months after acceptance. Offers 25-40% kill fee. Buys all rights and second serial (reprint) rights. Editorial lead time 5 months. Submit seasonal material 5 months in advance. Accepts simultaneous submissions. Reports in 2 weeks on queries.

• Ranked as one of the best markets for freelance writers in *Writer's Yearbook* magazine's annual "Top 100 Markets," January 1999.

**Nonfiction:** Bill Geiger. Book excerpts, how-to (training), humor, interview/profile, photo feature. **Buys 120 mss/year.** "All features and departments are written on assignment." Query with published clips. Length: 800-1,800 words. **Pays $250-800.** Pays expenses of writers on assignment.

**Reprints:** Send photocopy of article or typed ms with rights for sale noted and information about when and where the article previously appeared. Payment varies.

**Photos:** State availability of photos with submission.

**Tips:** "Know bodybuilders and bodybuilding. Read our magazine regularly (or at least several issues), come up with new information or a new angle on our subject matter (bodybuilding training, psychology, nutrition, diets, fitness, etc.), then pitch us in terms of providing useful, unique, how-to information for our readers. Send a one-page query letter (as described in *Writer's Market*) to sell us on your idea and on you as the best writer for that article. Send a sample of your published work. If we like your idea and assign the article, be sure to research and fact-check it thoroughly, write and edit it carefully and turn it in on time. Act like a professional even if you're just beginning your freelance career."

**N ☆ $ $MUSCLE MAG INTERNATIONAL**, 6465 Airport Rd., Mississauga, Ontario L4V 1E4 Canada. Fax: (905)678-9236. Editor: Johnny Fitness. **80% freelance written.** "We do not care if a writer is known or unknown; published or unpublished. We simply want good instructional articles on bodybuilding." Monthly magazine for 16- to 60-year-old men and women interested in physical fitness and overall body improvement. Estab. 1972. Circ. 300,000. Buys all rights. **Pays on acceptance.** Publishes ms an average of 4 months after acceptance. Byline given. Sample copy for $5 and 9×12 SAE. Reports in 2 months. Submit complete ms with IRCs.

**Nonfiction:** Articles on ideal physical proportions and importance of supplements in the diet, training for muscle size. Should be helpful and instructional and appeal to young men and women who want to live life in a vigorous and healthy style. "We would like to see articles for the physical culturist on new muscle building techniques or an article on fitness testing." Informational, how-to, personal experience, interview, profile, inspirational, humor, historical, expose, nostalgia, personal opinion, photo, spot news, new product, merchandising technique. "Also now actively looking for good instructional articles on Hardcore Fitness." **Buys 200 mss/year.** Length: 1,200-1,600 words. **Pays 20¢/word.** Sometimes pays the expenses of writers on assignment.

**Columns/Departments:** Nutrition Talk (eating for top results), Shaping Up (improving fitness and stamina). Length: 1,300 words. **Pays 20¢/word.**

**Photos:** Color and b&w photos are purchased with or without ms. Pays $50 for 8×10 glossy exercise photos; $50 for 8×10 b&w posing shots. Pays $200-1,000 for color cover and $50 for color used inside magazine (transparencies). More for "special" or "outstanding" work.

**Fillers:** Newsbreaks, puzzles, quotes of the champs. Length: open. **Pays $10 minimum.**

**Tips:** "The best way to break in is to seek out the muscle-building 'stars' and do in-depth interviews with biography in mind. Color training picture support essential. Writers have to make their articles informative in that readers can apply them to help gain bodybuilding success. Specific fitness articles should quote experts and/or use scientific studies to strengthen their theories. Write strong articles full of 'how-to' information. We want to genuinely help our readers build better, fitter, stronger bodies."

**$ $ $ $NATURAL HEALTH**, Weider Publications, Inc., 70 Lincoln St., 5th Floor, Boston MA 02111. (617)753-8900. Fax: (617)457-0966. E-mail: naturalhealth@weiderpub.com. Website: http://www.naturalhealthmag.com. Editor: Bill Thomson. **Contact:** Clare Horn, research editor. **50% freelance written.** Magazine published 9 times/year covering alternative health and natural living. "We are an authoritative guide to the best in mind, body and spirit self-care." Estab. 1971. Circ. 425,000. **Pays on acceptance.** Publishes ms an average of 3 months after acceptance. Byline given. Offers 33% kill fee. Buys first rights and reprint rights. Editorial lead time 6 months. Submit seasonal material 6 months in advance. Accepts simultaneous submissions. Reports in 3 months on queries. Sample articles on website.

O— Break in with a well-researched health brief or News & Notes piece.

**Nonfiction:** Book excerpts, exposé, how-to, inspirational, personal experience. No fiction, reprints from other publications or event coverage. **Buys 20 mss/year.** Query by mail with published clips. Length: 150-3,000 words. **Pays $75-2,000.** Sometimes pays the expenses of writers on assignment.

**Photos:** State availability of photos with submission. Buys one-time rights.

**Columns/Departments:** My Story (personal account of illness or condition treated naturally), 1,500 words. **Buys 9 mss/year. Pays $250.** Health Brief (information-dense piece on a widely-used natural food, rememdy or supplement—"strictly the facts"), 750 words. **Buy 20 mss/year. Pays $400-$500.** New & Notes (health, fitness, body care news briefs), 125 words. **Buys 20 mss/year. Pays $75.** Readers On (personal reflections on selected topics; see latest issue for topic), 100-500 words. **Pays $100.** Query.

**Tips:** "Read the magazine. The recipes are always vegan. The products are non-chemical. Read books written by the advisory board members. Andrew Weil, James Gordon, Joseph Pizzorno, Jennifer Jacobs, etc."

**$ $ $ $ NEW CHOICES, Living Even Better After 50**, Reader's Digest Publications, Inc., Reader's Digest Rd., Plesantville NY 10510. Fax: (914)244-5888. E-mail: newchoices@readersdigest.com. **Contact:** Elaine Rubino, editorial administrative assistant. Magazine published 10 times/year covering retirement lifestyle. "*New Choices* is a lifestyle and service magazine for adults 50 and over. Editorial focuses on travel, health, fitness, investments, food and home." Estab. 1960. Circ. 604,000.

**Nonfiction:** Planning for retirement, personal health and fitness, financial strategies, housing options, travel, profiles/interviews (celebrities and newsmakers), relationships, leisure pursuits, various lifestyle/service subjects. **Buys 60 mss/year.** Length: 750-2,000 words. **Pays $1/word,** negotiable. Query with 2-3 published clips and SASE. No phone calls.

**Columns/Departments:** Personal essays, online bargains, taxes, cooking, travel, style. **Buys 84 mss/year.** Pay varies. Query with 2-3 published clips. No phone calls.

**$ $ $ OXYGEN!, Serious Fitness for Serious Women,** Muscle Mag International, 6465 Airport Rd., Mississauga, Ontario L4V 1E4 Canada. (905)678-7311. Fax: (905)678-9236. **Contact:** Pamela Cottrell, editor. **70% freelance written.** Bimonthly magazine covering women's health and fitness. "*Oxygen* encourages various exercise, good nutrition to shape and condition the body." Estab. 1997. Circ. 180,000. **Pays on acceptance.** Publishes ms an average of 4 months after acceptance. Byline given. Offers 25% kill fee. Buys all rights. Editorial lead time 3 months. Submit seasonal material 6 months in advance. Accepts queries by mail, fax. Reports in 5 weeks on queries; 2 months on mss. Sample copy for $5.

**Nonfiction:** Exposé, how-to (training and nutrition), humor, inspirational, interview/profile, new product, personal experience, photo feature. No "poorly researched articles that do not genuinely help the readers towards physical fitness, health and physique." **Buys 100 mss/year.** Send complete ms. Length: 1,400-1,800 words. **Pays $250-1,000.** Sometimes pays expenses of writers on assignment.

**Reprints:** Send tearsheet, photocopy or typed manuscript with rights for sale noted and information about when and where the article previously appeared. Pay varies.

**Photos:** State availability of or send photos with submission. Reviews contact sheets, 35mm transparencies, prints. Offers $35-500. Identification of subjects required. Buys all rights.

**Columns/Departments:** Nutrition (low fat recipes), 1,700 words; Weight Training (routines and techniques), 1,800 words; Aerobics (how-tos), 1,700 words. **Buys 50 mss/year.** Send complete ms. **Pays $150-500.**

**Tips:** "Every editor of every magazine is looking, waiting, hoping and praying for the magic article. The beauty of the writing has to spring from the page; the edge imparted has to excite the reader because of its unbelievable information."

**PREVENTION,** Rodale, 33 E. Minor St., Emmaus, PA 18098. (610)967-5171. Fax: (610)967-7654. Editor: Anne Alexander. **Contact:** Denise Foley, senior staff editor, features. Monthly magazine covering health and fitness. "*Prevention* is for readers who take an active role in achieving and maintaining good health and fitness for themselves and their families. Stressing health promotion and disease prevention, *Prevention* features practical guidance on nutrition, diet and food preparation, medical care, alternative medicine, fitness, weight control, skin care and personal psychology with a mind-body component." Estab. 1950. Circ. 3,519,000. Accepts queries by mail, fax. "No phone queries, please."

• *Prevention* reports that it is buying more freelance pieces than in the past.

**Tips:** *Prevention,* "America's Leading Health Magazine," is a market only for the most experienced freelancers. "We are not a good market for somebody who's interested in breaking into the health market. The monthly aims to inform readers about current developments in health. Because this information is medically and scientifically specialized, expertise and research are primary requirements. Only experienced health writers should query the magazine. Query us with a well-written, block buster new idea or a new spin on an old idea. Demonstrate you're well-versed on health and medicine and can bring a sophisticated perspective to a piece."

**$ $ RHYTHM OF THE DRUM, Our Wholistic Magazine,** P.O. Box 470379, Los Angeles CA 90047-0379. (800)324-DRUM. Fax: (323)756-3656. **Contact:** Jacquetta Y. Parhams, publisher. **20% freelance written.** Semiannual magazine covering wholistic health (health and fitness). "*Rhythm of the Drum* deals with all aspects of our health—the physical, mental, emotional, spiritual, financial, political, etc., health. *The Drum* covers issues and solutions facing Africans all over the globe with respect to the whole health of individuals, the family and the community." Estab. 1994. Circ. 10,000. Pays on publication. Publishes ms an average of 6 months after acceptance. Byline given. Offers 15% kill fee. Buys one-time and second serial (reprint) rights. Editorial lead time 4 months. Submit seasonal material 6 months in advance. Accepts simultaneous submissions. Reports in 6 weeks on queries. Please request guidelines before querying. Sample copy for $2.50 and 9×12 SASE with 4 first-class stamps. Writer's guidelines for #10 SASE.

**Nonfiction:** Book excerpts, essays, exposé, historical/nostalgic, how-to, inspirational, interview/profile, new product, opinion, personal experience, photo feature, religious, technical, travel, cartoons, puzzles, political. Special issue: Black History Month/Anniversary Issue (February). Query with published clips if available. Length: 25-2,000 words. **Pays $10-500 for assigned articles; $3-240 for unsolicited articles.**

**Reprints:** Send tearsheet or photocopy of article with rights for sale noted and information about when and where it previously appeared.

**Photos:** Send photos. Reviews 8½×11 transparencies and 3×5 or larger prints. Offers no additional payment for photos accepted with ms. Negotiates payment individually. Model releases and identification of subjects required.

**Columns/Departments:** The Political Skinny (political); Tree of Life (physical health); Ourstory (our history); Safety First (being careful in- and outdoors); The Dollars & $ense of It (economics and finance); Spiritually Speaking (spiritual health and growth); Sci-Non-Fi (the sciences).

**Poetry:** Avant-garde, free verse, haiku, light verse, traditional. **Buys 10 poems/year.** Submit maximum 2 poems. Length: 1-50 lines. **Pays $5-100.**

**Fillers:** Anecdotes, facts, newsbreaks. **Buys 8/year.** Length: 5-50 words. **Pays 50¢-$5.**

**Tips:** "*Rhythm of the Drum* is an uplifting magazine of enlightenment. Articles that denigrate other peoples will be rejected. We do not need to tear down others to build ourselves up. Photos, charts, maps, graphs and other photo-ready artwork are encouraged but not required; many articles are published without artwork."

**$ $ $ $ SHAPE MAGAZINE,** Weider Health & Fitness, 21100 Erwin St., Woodland Hills CA 91367. (818)595-0593. Fax: (818)992-6895. Website: http://www.shapemag.com. Editor-in-Chief: Barbara Harris. **Contact:** Peg Moline, editorial director. **70% freelance written.** Prefers to work with published/established writers. Monthly magazine covering women's health and fitness. "*Shape* reaches women who are committed to the healthful, active lifestyles. Our readers are participating in a variety of sports and fitness related activities, in the gym, at home and outdoors, and they are also proactive about their health and are nutrition conscious." Estab. 1981. Circ. 900,000. **Pays on acceptance.** Offers 33% kill fee. Buys all rights and reprint rights. Submit seasonal material 8 months in advance. Reports in 2 months. Sample copy for 9×12 SAE and 4 first-class stamps.
- Weider also publishes *Fit Pregnancy* (for pregnant and postpartum women); and *Jump* (for teenage girls).

**Nonfiction:** Book excerpts; exposé (health, fitness, nutrition related); how-to (get fit); interview/profile (of fit women); health/fitness, recipes. "We use some health and fitness articles written by professionals in their specific fields. No articles that haven't been queried first." Special issues: every September is an anniversary issue. **Buys 27 features/year, 36-54 short pieces/year.** Query with clips of published work. Length: 3,000 words for features, 1,000 words for short pieces. **Pays $1/word.**
- Ranked as one of the best markets for freelance writers in *Writer's Yearbook* magazine's annual "Top 100 Markets," January 1999.

**Photos:** Submit slides or photos with photographer's name or institution to be credited. Provide necessary captions and all model releases.

**Tips:** "Review a recent issue of the magazine. Provide source verification materials and sources for items readers may buy, including 800 numbers. Not responsible for unsolicited material. We reserve the right to edit any article."

**★ $ $ VIBRANT LIFE, A Magazine for Healthful Living,** Review and Herald Publishing Assn., 55 W. Oak Ridge Dr., Hagerstown MD 21740-7390. (301)393-4019. Fax: (301)393-4055. E-mail: vleditor@rhpa.org. Website: http://www.vibrantlife.com. **Contact:** Larry Becker, editor. **80% freelance written.** Enjoys working with published/established writers; works with a small number of new/unpublished writers each year. Bimonthly magazine covering health articles (especially from a prevention angle and with a Christian slant). Estab. 1845. Circ. 50,000. **Pays on acceptance.** "The average length of time between acceptance of a freelance-written manuscript and publication of the material depends upon the topics: some immediately used; others up to 2 years." Byline always given. Offers 50% kill fee. Buys first serial, first world serial, or sometimes second serial (reprint) rights. Submit seasonal material 9 months in advance. Accepts queries by mail, e-mail, fax. Reports in 2 months. Sample copy for $1. Guidelines for #10 SASE.
- Ranked as one of the best markets for freelance writers in *Writer's Yearbook* magazine's annual "Top 100 Markets," January 1999.

**Nonfiction:** Interview/profile (with personalities on health). "We seek practical articles promoting better health and a more fulfilled life. We especially like features on breakthroughs in medicine, and most aspects of health. We need articles on how to integrate a person's spiritual life with their health. We'd like more in the areas of exercise, nutrition, water, avoiding addictions of all types and rest—all done from a wellness perspective." **Buys 50-60 feature articles/year, 6-12 short pieces/year.** Send complete ms. Length: 500-1,500 words for features, 25-250 words for short pieces. **Pays $75-300 for features, $25-40 for short pieces.**

**Reprints:** Send tearsheet of article and information about when and where the article previously appeared. Pays 50% of amount paid for an original article.

**Photos:** Send photos with ms. Needs 35mm transparencies. Not interested in b&w photos.

**Columns/Departments: Buys 12-18 department artices/year.** Length: 500-650 words. **Pays $75-175.**

**Tips:** "*Vibrant Life* is published for baby boomers, particularly young professionals, age 35-50. Articles must be written in an interesting, easy-to-read style. Information must be reliable; no faddism. We are more conservative than other magazines in our field. Request a sample copy, and study the magazine and writer's guidelines."

**$ $ VIM & VIGOR, America's Family Health Magazine,** 1010 E. Missouri Ave., Phoenix AZ 85014-2601. (602)395-5850. Fax: (602)395-5853. E-mail: jennw@mcpub.com. Website: http://www.vigormagazine.com **Contact:** Jennifer Daack Woolson, associate publisher/editor. **75% freelance written.** Quarterly magazine covering health and healthcare. Estab. 1985. Circ. 1,100,000. **Pays on acceptance.** Publishes ms an average of 3 months after acceptance. Byline given. Buys all rights. Sample copy for 9×12 SAE with 8 first-class stamps or on website. Writer's guidelines for #10 SASE.

**Nonfiction:** Health, diseases, medical breakthroughs, exercise/fitness trends, wellness, and healthcare. "Absolutely no complete manuscripts will be accepted. All articles are assigned. Send samples of your style. Any queries regarding story ideas will be placed on the following year's conference agenda and will be addressed on a topic-by-topic basis." **Buys 12 mss/year.** Send published clips by mail or e-mail. Length: 1,000-1,500 words. **Pays $500.** Pays expenses of writers on assignment.

The online magazine carries original content not included in the print edition.

**$ $ VITALITY MAGAZINE, Toronto's Monthly Wellness Journal**, 356 Dupont St., Toronto, Ontario M5R 1V9 Canada. (416)964-0528. **Contact:** Julia Woodford, editor. **50% freelance written.** Monthly magazine covering holistic health, nutritional medicine. "We give top priority to well-researched articles on nutritional medicine, healing properties of foods and herbs, environmental health issues, natural lifestyles, alternative healing for cancer, arthritis, heart disease, etc. Organic foods and issues. Estab. 1989. Circ. 41,000. Pays on publication. Publishes ms 3 months after acceptance. Byline given. Buys first rights, one-time rights or second serial (reprint) rights. Editorial lead time 3 months. Submit seasonal material 3 months in advance. Accepts simultaneous submissions. Reports "when we have time." Sample copy for $2 (cash only).

**Nonfiction:** Book excerpts, exposé, how-to (on self-health care), inspirational, personal experience. "Nothing endorsing drugs, surgery, pharmaceuticals. No submissions from public relations firms." **Buys 8-12 mss/year.** Send complete ms. Length 1,000-1,800 words. **Pays 10¢/word (Canadian).**

**Reprints:** Send photocopy of article or typed ms with rights for sale noted and information about when and where the article previously appeared. Pays 10¢/word (Canadian) for reprints.

**Photos:** Send photos with submission. Offers $25-30 (Canadian)/photo. Identification of subjects required. Buys one-time rights.

**Fillers:** Facts, newsbreaks.

**Tips:** "Must have a good working knowledge of subject area and be patient if not responded to immediately. Features are most open to freelancers. Write well, give me the facts, but do it in layman's terms. A sense of humor doesn't hurt. All material must be relevant to our *Canadian* readership audience. If you're doing a critical piece on products in the marketplace, give me brand names."

**$ $ $ $ THE WALKING MAGAZINE**, Walking Inc., 45 Bromfield St., Boston MA 02108. (617)574-0076. Fax: (617)338-7433. **Contact:** Lori Lundberg. **60% freelance written.** Bimonthly magazine covering health and fitness. *"The Walking Magazine* is written for healthy, active adults who are committed to fitness walking as an integral part of their lifestyle. Each issue offers advice on exercise techniques, diet, nutrition, personal care and contemporary health issues. It also covers information on gear and equipment, competition and travel, including foreign and domestic destinations for walkers." Estab. 1986. Circ. 650,000. **Pays on acceptance.** Offers 25% kill fee. Editorial lead time 3 months. Accepts simultaneous submissions. Responds in 2 months. Sample copy for $3.95. Guidelines for SASE.

**Nonfiction:** Walks for travel and adventure, fitness, health, nutrition, fashion, equipment, famous walkers, and other walking-related topics. **Buys 35-42 mss/year.** Query with published clips (no more than 3). Length: 1,500-2,500 words. **Pays $750-2,500.**

**Columns/Departments:** Walking Shorts, Your Self, Health, Nutrition, Active Beauty, Walk It Off, Events, Walking Gear (gear and equipment), Ramblings (back page essay), 300-1,200 words. Query with clips. **Pays $150-600.**

**$ $ $ WEIGHT WATCHERS MAGAZINE**, Healthy Living, Inc., P.O. Box 12847, Birmingham AL 35202-2847. (205)877-6000. Fax: (205)877-5790. E-mail: wwmag@mindspring.com. Editor-in-Chief: Kate Greer. Editorial Coordinator: Chris O'Connell. Executive Editor: Melissa Chessher Aspell. Food Editor: Alyson Haynes. Fitness and Health Editor: Kate Neale Cooper. Beauty and Fashion Editor: Melissa Bigner. **Contact:** Matthew Solan, articles editor. **Approximately 80% freelance written.** Magazine published 9 times/year mostly for women interested in healthy lifestyle/behavior information/advice, including news on health, nutrition, fitness, beauty, fashion, psychology and food/recipes. Success and before-and-after stories also welcome. Estab. 1968. Circ. 1,000,000. **Pays on acceptance.** Offers 33% kill fee. Buys first North American rights. Editorial lead time 3-12 months. Accepts queries by mail, e-mail, fax. Sample copy and writer's guidelines for $1.95 and 9×12 SASE.

● Ranked as one of the best markets for freelance writers in *Writer's Yearbook* magazine's annual "Top 100 Markets," January 1999.

**Nonfiction:** Covers fitness, nutrition, psychology, health clubs, spas, beauty, fashion, style, travel and products for both the kitchen and an active lifestyle. "We are interested in general health, nutrition and behavorial/psychological articles (stories with a strong weight loss angle always a plus). Some fitness—everything from beginner to advanced ideas—freelanced out. Personal triumph/success stories of individuals who lost weight also of interest. Back page a humorous look at some aspect of getting/staying in shape or achieving better health. Our articles have an authoritative yet friendly tone. How-to and service information crucial for all stories. To expedite fact-checking, we require a second, annotated manuscript including names, phone numbers, journal/newsletter citations of sources." Buys 18-25 mss/year. Send detailed queries with published clips and SASE. Average article length: 700-1,500 words. **Pays $1/word, "depending on the writer."**

**Reprints:** Pays 33% of amount paid for an original article.

**Columns/Departments:** Accepts editorial in health, fitness, beauty, fashion, inspiration, nutrition. **Buys 20-25 mss/year.** Length: 500-1,200 words. **Pays $1/word.**

**Tips:** "Well developed, tightly written queries always a plus, as are ideas that have a strong news peg. Trend pieces welcome and we're always on the lookout for a fresh angle on an old topic. Sources must be reputable; we prefer subjects to be medical professionals with university affiliations who are published in their field of expertise. Lead times require stories to be seasonal, long-range and forward-looking. Keep in mind that a trend today may be old news in six months. We're looking for fresh, innovative stories that yield worthwhile information for our readers—the latest exercise alternatives, a suggestion of how they can reduce stress, nutritional information that may not be common knowledge, suggestions from experts on skin care, reassurance about their lifestyle or health concerns, etc."

✫ $ $ $ **YOGA JOURNAL**, 2054 University Ave., Berkeley CA 94704. (510)841-9200. Website: http://www.yogajournal.com. **Contact:** Kathryn Arnold, editor-in-chief; Jeanne Ricci, managing editor. **75% freelance written.** Bimonthly magazine covering yoga, holistic health, conscious living, spiritual practices, ecology and nutrition. Estab. 1975. Circ. 108,000. Publishes mss an average of 10 months after acceptance. Byline given. Offers kill fee on assigned articles. Buys first North American serial rights. Submit seasonal material minimum 4 months in advance. Reports in approx. 3 months. Sample copy $3.50. Writer's guidelines free.

**Nonfiction:** Book excerpts; how-to (yoga, exercise, etc.); inspirational (yoga or related); profile/interview; opinion; photo feature; yoga-related travel. "Yoga is a main concern, but we also highlight other conscious living/New Age personalities and endeavors (nothing too 'woo-woo')." **Buys 50-60 mss/year.** Query with SASE. Length: 2,500-6,000 words. **Pays $1,000-3,000.**

**Reprints:** Submit tearsheet or photocopy of article with information about when and where the article previously appeared and rights for sale noted.

**Columns/Departments:** Health (self-care; well-being); Body-Mind (hatha Yoga; other body-mind modalities; meditation; yoga philosophy; Western mysticism); Community (service; profiles; organizations; events). Length: 1,500-2,000 words. **Pays $600-800.** Living (books; video; arts; music), 800 words. **Pays $250-300.** World of Yoga, Spectrum (brief yoga and healthy living news/events/fillers), 150-600 words. **Pays $50-150.**

**Tips:** "Please read our writer's guidelines before submission. Do not e-mail or fax unsolicited manuscripts."

✫ $ $ **YOUR HEALTH**, Globe Communications Corp., 5401 NW Broken Sound Blvd., Boca Raton FL 33487. (561)997-7733. E-mail: yhealth@aol.com. Website: http://www.yourhealthmag.com. Associate Editor: Lisa Rappa. **Contact:** Susan Gregg, editor. **80% freelance written.** Magazine published 8 times/year on health and fitness. "*Your Health* is dedicated to presenting timely health and medical information to consumers. Our audience is healthy, middle-class + concerned about improving and maintaining highest levels of physical, emotional and spiritual health. Emphasis on self-care and prevention (through sound nutrition, exercise, and behavioral and spiritual health) as opposed to treatment of disease. We give readers information that will help them take charge of their health and become a health partner with—rather than patient of—their doctors." Estab. 1962. Circ. 50,000. Pays on publication. Byline given. Buys first North American serial and second serial (reprint) rights. Submit seasonal material 3 months in advance. Reports in 1 month on queries; 6 weeks on mss. Sample copy and writer's guidelines free.

**Nonfiction:** Book excerpts, general interest, how-to (on general health and fitness topics), inspirational, interview/profile, medical breakthroughs, natural healing and alternative medicine, new products, celebrities. "Give us something new and different." **Buys 75-100 mss/year.** Query with published clips or send complete ms. Length: 800-1,500 words. **Pays 20¢/word for original ms.**

**Reprints:** Send tearsheet and information about when and where the article previously appeared. **Pays $75-200.**

**Photos:** Send photos with submission. Reviews contact sheets, negatives, transparencies, prints. Offers $50-200/photo. Captions, model releases, identification of subjects required. Buys one-time rights.

**Columns/Departments:** Nutrition (general nutrition and healthful eating, supplements). Weight Loss (sensible advice from experts on how to achieve permanent weight loss without "dieting"; evaluation of new diet fads, books or trends). Cooking (recipes and low-fat cooking tips). Fitness (cardiovascular conditioning, strength training, stretching, exercise for weight loss, sports activities, movement therapies such as yoga, tai chi, Pilates). Behavior (mind/body emotional and spiritual health, stress management, relationships). Successful Aging (health and fitness after 50; profiles of successful agers). Alternative Medicine (our approach: alternative and natural remedies or therapies should be used as an adjunct to, not replacement for, traditional treatments and prevention strategies. Sources and experts for these stories should be reputable, responsible advocates). Women (preventive health issues; skin care and beauty). Men (preventive health issues). Sexual Health. Parenting. Remedies (sensible advice for common ailments such as headaches, back pain, allergies, colds, everyday aches and pains, etc.). Healthy Getaways (fitness/adventure travel; wellness vacations). Length: 600-800 words. **Pays 20¢/word.**

**Tips:** "Freelancers can best break in by offering us stories of national interest that we won't find through other channels, such as wire services. Well-written self-help articles, especially ones that focus on natural prevention and cures, are always welcome. We're looking for more natural health and alternative therapy stories."

# HISTORY

Listed here are magazines and other periodicals written for historical collectors, genealogy enthusiasts, historic preservationists and researchers. Editors of history magazines look for fresh accounts of past events in a readable style. Some publications cover an era, while others may cover a region or subject area, such as aviation history.

✫ **AMERICAN HERITAGE**, 60 Fifth Ave., New York NY 10011. (212)206-5500. Fax: (212)620-2332. E-mail: mail@americanheritage.com. Website: http://www.americanheritage.com. **Contact:** Richard Snow, editor. **70% freelance written.** Magazine published 8 times/year. "*American Heritage* writes from a historical point of view on politics, business, art, current and international affairs, and our changing lifestyles. The articles are written with the intent to enrich the reader's appreciation of the sometimes nostalgic, sometimes funny, always stirring panorama of the American experience." Circ. 300,000. Usually buys first North American rights or all rights. Byline given. **Pays on acceptance.**

Publishes ms an average of 6-12 months after acceptance. Before submitting material, "check our index to see whether we have already treated the subject." Submit seasonal material 1 year in advance. Reports in 2 months. Writer's guidelines for #10 SASE.

**Nonfiction:** Wants "historical articles by scholars or journalists intended for intelligent lay readers rather than for professional historians." Emphasis is on authenticity, accuracy and verve. "Interesting documents, photographs and drawings are always welcome. Query. Style should stress readability and accuracy." **Buys 30 unsolicited mss/year.** Length: 1,500-6,000 words. Pay varies. Sometimes pays the expenses of writers on assignment.

**Tips:** "We have over the years published quite a few 'firsts' from young writers whose historical knowledge, research methods and writing skills met our standards. The scope and ambition of a new writer tell us a lot about his or her future usefulness to us. A major article gives us a better idea of the writer's value. Everything depends on the quality of the material. We don't really care whether the author is 20 and unknown, or 80 and famous, or vice versa. No phone calls, please."

**$ $ $ AMERICAN HISTORY**, 6405 Flank Dr., Harrisburg PA 17112-2750. (717)657-9555. Website: http://www.thehistorynet.com. **Contact:** Tom Huntington, editor. **60% freelance written.** Bimonthly magazine of cultural, social, military and political history published for a general audience. Estab. 1966. Circ. 120,000. **Pays on acceptance.** Byline given. Buys first rights. Reports in 10 weeks on queries. Writer's guidelines for #10 SASE or online. Sample copy and guidelines for $5 (includes 3rd class postage) or $4 and 9 × 12 SAE with 4 first-class stamps.

**Nonfiction:** Features biographies of noteworthy historical figures and accounts of important events in American history. Also includes pictorial features on artists, photographers and graphic subjects. "Material is presented on a popular rather than a scholarly level." Query by mail only with published clips and SASE. "Query letters should be limited to a concise 1 page proposal defining your article with an emphasis on its unique qualities." **Buys 20 mss/year.** Length: 2,000-4,000 words depending on type of article. **Pays $500-800.**

**Photos:** Welcomes suggestions for illustrations.

■ The online magazine contains content not included in the print edition. Contact: Christine Teehky, managing editor.

**Tips:** "Key prerequisites for publication are thorough research and accurate presentation, precise English usage and sound organization, a lively style, and a high level of human interest. Submissions received without return postage will not be considered or returned. Inappropriate materials include: fiction, book reviews, travelogues, personal/family narratives not of national significance, articles about collectibles/antiques, living artists, local/individual historic buildings/landmarks and articles of a current editorial nature. Currently seeking articles on significant Civil War subjects. No phone, fax or e-mail queries, please."

**★ $ $ AMERICA'S CIVIL WAR**, Primedia History Group, 741 Miller Dr., SE, Suite D-2, Leesburg VA 20175-8920. (703)771-9400. Fax: (703)779-8345. E-mail: cheryls@cowles.com. Website: http://www.thehistorynet.com. **Contact:** Roy Morris, Jr., editor. Managing Editor: Carl Von Wodtke. **95% freelance written.** Bimonthly magazine of "popular history and straight historical narrative for both the general reader and the Civil War buff covering strategy, tactics, personalities, arms and equipment." Estab. 1988. Circ. 125,000. Pays on publication. Publishes ms up to 2 years after acceptance. Byline given. Buys all rights. Accepts queries by mail, e-mail, fax. Reports in 3 months on queries; 6 months on mss. Sample copy for $5. Writer's guidelines for #10 SASE or online.

**Nonfiction:** Book excerpts, historical, travel. No fiction or poetry. **Buys 24 mss/year.** Query. Length: 3,500-4,000 words and should include a 500-word sidebar. **Pays $300 maximum.**

**Photos:** Send photos with submission or cite sources. "We'll order." Captions and identification of subjects required.

**Columns/Departments:** Personality (probes); Ordnance (about weapons used); Commands (about units); Eyewitness to War (about appropriate historical sites). **Buys 24 mss/year.** Query. Length: 2,000 words. **Pays up to $150.**

■ The online magazine carries original content not found in the print edition. Contact: Roger Vance. Includes writer's guidelines.

**Tips:** "All stories must be true. We do not publish fiction or poetry. Write an entertaining, informative and unusual story that grabs the reader's attention and holds it. Include suggested readings in a standard format at the end of your piece. Manuscript must be typed, double-spaced on one side of standard white 8½ × 11, 16 to 30 pound paper—no onion skin paper or dot matrix printouts. All submissions are on speculation. Prefer subjects to be on disk (IBM- or Macintosh-compatible floppy disk) as well as a hard copy. Choose stories with strong art possibilities."

**N $ THE ARTILLERYMAN**, Historical Publications, Inc., 234 Monarch Hill Rd., Tunbridge VT 05077. (802)889-3500. Fax: (802)889-5627. E-mail: mail@civilwarnews.com. ("attention: the Artilleryman"). **Contact:** Kathryn Jorgenson, editor. **60% freelance written.** Quarterly magazine covering antique artillery, fortifications and crew-served weapons 1750-1900 for competition shooters, collectors and living history reenactors using artillery. "Emphasis on Revolutionary War and Civil War but includes everyone interested in pre-1900 artillery and fortifications, preservation, construction of replicas, etc." Estab. 1979. Circ. 2,200. Pays on publication. Publishes ms an average of 6 months after acceptance. Byline given. Not copyrighted. Buys one-time rights. Accepts queries by mail, e-mail, fax, phone. Accepts simultaneous submissions. Reports in 3 weeks. Sample copy and writer's guidelines for 9 × 12 SAE with 4 first-class stamps.

**Nonfiction:** Historical; how-to (reproduce ordnance equipment/sights/implements/tools/accessories, etc.); interview/profile; new product; opinion (must be accompanied by detailed background of writer and include references); personal experience; photo feature; technical (must have footnotes); travel (where to find interesting antique cannon). Interested in "artillery *only*, for sophisticated readers. Not interested in other weapons, battles in general." **Buys 24-30 mss/year.** Send complete ms. Length: 300 words minimum. **Pays $20-60.** Sometimes pays the expenses of writers on assignment.

**Reprints:** Send tearsheet or photocopy of article and information about when and where the article previously appeared. Pays 100% of amount paid for an original article.

**Photos:** Send photos with ms. Pays $5 for $5 \times 7$ and larger b&w prints. Captions, identification of subjects required.

**Tips:** "We regularly use freelance contributions for Places-to-Visit, Cannon Safety, The Workshop and Unit Profiles departments. Also need pieces on unusual cannon or cannon with a known and unique history. To judge whether writing style and/or expertise will suit our needs, writers should ask themselves if they could knowledgeably talk *artillery* with an expert. Subject matter is of more concern than writer's background."

**$ $AVIATION HISTORY,** Primedia History Group, 741 Miller Dr., SE, Suite D-2, Leesburg VA 20175-8920. (703)771-9400. Fax: (703)779-8345. E-mail: cheryls@cowles.com. Website: http://www.thehistorynet.com. **Contact:** Arthur Sanfelici, editor. Managing Editor: Carl von Wodtke. **95% freelance written.** Bimonthly magazine covering military and civilian aviation from first flight to the jet age. It aims to make aeronautical history not only factually accurate and complete, but also enjoyable to varied subscriber and newsstand audience. Estab. 1990. Circ. 80,000. Pays on publication. Publishes ms up to 2 years after acceptance. Byline given. Buys all rights. Editorial lead time 6 months. Submit seasonal material 1 year in advance. Accepts queries by mail, e-mail, fax. Accepts simultaneous submissions. Reports in 3 months on queries; 6 months on mss. Sample copy for $5. Writers guidelines for #10 SASE or online.

**Nonfiction:** Book excerpts, historical/nostalgic, interview/profile, personal experience, travel. **Buys 24 mss/year.** Query. Length: Feature articles should be 3,500-4,000 words, each with a 500-word sidebar, author's biography and book suggestions for further reading. **Pays $300.**

**Photos:** State availability of art and photos with submission, cite sources. "We'll order." Reviews contact sheets, negatives, transparencies. Identification of subjects required. Buys one-time rights.

**Columns/Departments:** People and Planes, Enduring Heritage, Aerial Oddities, Art of Flight; all 2,000 words. **Pays $150.** Book reviews, 300-750 words; **Pays minimum $30.**

The online magazine carries original content not found in the print edition and includes writer's guidelines. Contact: Roger Vance.

**Tips:** "Choose stories with strong art possibilities. Include a hard copy as well as an IBM- or Macintosh-compatible floppy disk. Write an entertaining, informative and unusual story that grabs the reader's attention and holds it. All stories must be true. We do not publish fiction or poetry."

**$ $CHICAGO HISTORY, The Magazine of the Chicago Historical Society**, Chicago Historical Society, Clark St. at North Ave., Chicago IL 60614-6099. (312)642-4600. Fax: (312)277-2066. E-mail: adams@chicagohistory.org. Website: http://www.chicagohistory.org. **Contact:** Rosemary Adams, editor-in-chief. **100% freelance written.** Works with a small number of new/unpublished writers each year. Quarterly magazine covering Chicago history: cultural, political, economic, social and architectural. Estab. 1945. Circ. 9,500. Pays on publication. Publishes ms an average of 1 year after acceptance. Byline given. Buys all rights. Submit seasonal material 9 months in advance. Reports in 4 months. Sample copy for $3.50 and $9 \times 12$ SAE with 3 first-class stamps or on website. Writer's guidelines free or on website.

**Nonfiction:** Book excerpts, essays, historical, photo feature. Articles should be "analytical, informative, and directed at a popular audience with a special interest in history." No "cute" articles, no biographies. **Buys 8-12 mss/year.** Query or send complete ms. Length: approximately 4,500 words. **Pays $150-250.**

**Photos:** Send photocopies with submission; no originals. Offers no additional payment for photos accepted with ms. Identification of subjects required.

**Tips:** "A freelancer can best break in by 1) calling to discuss an article idea with editor; and 2) submitting a detailed outline of proposed article. All sections of *Chicago History* are open to freelancers, but we suggest that authors do not undertake to write articles for the magazine unless they have considerable knowledge of the subject and are willing to research it in some detail. We require a footnoted manuscript, although we do not publish the notes."

**$ $CIVIL WAR TIMES ILLUSTRATED**, 6405 Flank Dr., Harrisburg PA 17112. (717)657-9555. Fax: (717)657-9552. E-mail: cwt@cowles.com. Website: http://www.thehistorynet.com. Editor: Jim Kushlan. 90% freelance written. Works with a small number of new/unpublished writers each year. Magazine published 7 times/year. Estab. 1962. Circ. 50,000. **Pays on acceptance.** Publishes an average of 18 months after acceptance. Buys all rights. Submit seasonal material 1 year in advance. Reports in 8 months on mss. Sample copy for $5.50. Writer's guidelines for SASE.

**Nonfiction:** Profile, photo feature, Civil War historical material. "Positively no fiction or poetry." **Buys 20 freelance mss/year.** Length: 2,500-5,000 words. **Pays $75-600.**

**Photos:** Renée Myers, art director.

**Tips:** "We're very open to new submissions. Send submissions after examining writer's guidelines and several recent issues. Include photocopies of photos that could feasibly accompany the article. Confederate soldiers' diaries and letters are welcome."

**$ $COLUMBIAD, A Quarterly Review of the War Between the States**, Primedia Enthusiast Publications, 741 Miller Dr. SE, Suite D-2, Leesburg VA 20175. (703)771-9400. Fax: (703)779-8345. E-mail: columbiad@thehistorynet.com. Website: http://www.thehistorynet.com. Managing Editor: Carl Von Wedtke. **Contact:** Christopher Anderson, editor. **95% freelance written.** Quarterly journal covering American Civil War history. Estab. 1997. Circ. 3,500.

**Pays on acceptance**. Publishes ms an average of 6 months after acceptance. Byline given. Buys first, second serial (reprint), electronic and exclusive worldwide publication rights to the 120th day after the end of the mail date of the issue in which the article appears. Editorial lead time 6 months. Submit seasonal material 1 year in advance. Accepts queries by mail, e-mail, fax. Accepts simultaneous submissions. Reports in 3 months on queries; 6 months on mss. Sample copy for $12 (some articles website). Writer's guidelines for #10 SASE or online.

**Nonfiction:** Historical/nostalgic. No reenactment stories. **Buys 30 mss/year.** Query preferred; also accepts complete mss. Length: 5,000-10,000 words. **Pays $400-650 for assigned articles; $100-650 for unsolicited articles.**

**Photos:** State availability of or send photos with submission. Reviews transparencies and prints. Negotiates payment individually. Identification of subjects required. Buys all rights.

**Columns/Departments:** Notes from the Field (news of events, discoveries, research pertaining to Civil War), 2,500 words; Book reviews (analytical and in-depth review of recently released CW books). **Buys 8 mss/year.** Query or send complete ms. **Pays $100-300.**

▣ The online magazine carries original content not found in the print edition and includes writer's guidelines. Contact: Roger Vance.

**Tips:** "The entire American Civil War and anything related to it form the legitimate subject matter of *Columbiad*. Articles should not have been published elsewhere; if an article has been published previously, the author must note this in the query or cover letter. Talks and papers delivered verbally may, however, be submitted as articles, but the author should note when and where the speech was given. Articles should represent substantial research in primary and appropriate secondary source materials, and should embody a well-reasoned, documented inner logic. Graceful, clear writing is crucial. Examine a copy of two of *Columbiad* for examples of what the editors are looking for. All articles should be annotated. Footnotes or margin notes in the manuscript are preferred. Notes should contain complete information about sources; in the case of books, they should include the author's entire name, the exact title, place of publication, publisher, year of publication, and pages cited. In the case of reprinted books, the original year of publication should be noted, followed by the publication information relating to the reprint. Informational notes are acceptable and may be used to include parenthetical material of interest. Articles should be submitted both as hard copy and with an IBM- or Macintosh-compatible 3½" or 5¼" floppy disk. Articles submitted only as hard copy will be considered nonetheless. Hard copy should be clearly legible."

**$ $ GATEWAY HERITAGE**, Missouri Historical Society, P.O. Box 11940, St. Louis MO 63112-0040. (314)746-4557. Fax: (314)746-4548. **Contact:** Matt Heidenry, editor. **75% freelance written.** Quarterly magazine covering Missouri history. "*Gateway Heritage* is a popular history magazine which is sent to members of the Missouri Historical Society. Thus, we have a general audience with an interest in history." Estab. 1980. Circ. 6,200. Pays on publication. Publishes ms an average of 6 months after acceptance. Byline given. Offers $75 kill fee. Buys first North American serial rights. Editorial lead time 6 months. Submit seasonal material 1 year in advance. Reports in 2 weeks on queries; 2 months on mss. Sample copy for 9×12 SAE with 7 first-class stamps. Writer's guidelines for #10 SASE.

**Nonfiction:** Book excerpts, historical/nostalgic, interview/profile, personal experience, photo feature. No genealogies. **Buys 12-15 mss/year.** Query with published clips. Length: 3,500-5,000 words. **Pays $200.**

**Photos:** State availability of photos with submission.

**Columns/Departments:** Literary Landmarks (biographical sketches and interviews of famous Missouri literary figures) 1,500-2,500 words; Missouri Biographies (biographical sketches of famous and interesting Missourians) 1,500-2,500 words; Gateway Album (excerpts from diaries and journals) 1,500-2,500 words. **Buys 6-8 mss/year.** Query with published clips. **Pays $100.**

**Tips:** "Ideas for our departments are a good way to break into *Gateway Heritage*."

**N $ $ $ $ MHQ, The Quarterly Journal of Military History**, Primedia Enthusiast Publications, 741 Miller Dr. SE, Suite D-2, Leesburg VA 20175-8920. (703)771-9400. Fax: (703)779-8345. E-mail: mhq@thehistory.net.com. Website: http://www.thehistorynet.com. Editor: Rod Paschell. Managing Editor: Carl Von Wodtke. **Contact:** Christopher Anderson, senior editor. **100% freelance written.** Quarterly magazine covering military history. "*MHQ* offers readers in-depth articles on the history of warfare from ancient times into the 20th century. Authoritative features and departments cover military strategies, philosophies, campaigns, battles, personalities, weaponry, espionage and perspectives, all written in a lively and readable style. Articles are accompanied by classical works of art, contemporary illustrations, photographs and maps. Readers include serious students of military tactics, strategy, leaders and campaigns, as well as general world history enthusiasts. Many readers are currently in the military or retired officers." Estab. 1988. Circ. 30,000. Pays on publication. Byline given. Buys first, second serial (reprint), electronic and exclusive worldwide publication rights to the 120th day after the end of the on-sale period for the issue in which the article appears. Editorial lead time 10 months. Submit seasonal material 1 year in advance. Accepts queries by mail, e-mail, fax. Accepts simultaneous submissions. Reports in 3 months on queries; 6 months on mss. Sample copy for $23 (hardcover), $13 (softcover); some articles on website. Writer's guidelines for #10 SASE or online.

**Nonfiction:** Historical, personal experience, photo feature. No stories pertaining to collectibles or reenactments. **Buys 50 mss/year.** Query preferred; also accepts complete ms. Length: 1,000-5,000 words. **Pays $800-2,000 for assigned articles; $400-2,000 for unsolicited articles.**

**Photos:** Send photos (preferred) or state availability of photos with submission. Reviews transparencies and prints. Negotiates payment individually. Identification of subjects required. Buys all rights.

**Columns/Departments:** Artist on War (description of artwork of a military nature); Experience of War (first-person accounts of military incidents); Strategic View (discussion of military theory, strategy); Arms & Men (description of military hardware or unit), all up to 3,000 words. **Buys 20 mss/year.** Send complete ms. **Pays $400-800.**

■ The online magazine carries original content not included in the print edition and includes writer's guidelines. Contact: Roger Vance.

**Tips:** "All stories must be true—we publish no fiction. Although we are always looking for variety, some subjects—World War II, the American Civil War, and military biography, for instance—are the focus of so many proposals that we are forced to judge them by relatively rigid criteria. We are always glad to consider articles on these subjects. However, less common ones—medieval, Asian, or South American military history, for example—are more likely to attract our attention. The likelihood that articles can be effectively illustrated often determines the ultimate fate of manuscripts. Many otherwise excellent articles have been rejected due to a lack of suitable art or photographs. Regular departments—columns on strategy, tactics, and weaponry, as well as book, film and video reviews—average 1,500 words. Our contributing editors provide most departments, but we often consider unsolicited proposals, especially for 'Experience of War,' which is personal reminiscence. These stories need not be combat experiences per se, but must be true, first-person narratives. While the information we publish is scholarly and substantive, we prefer writing that is light, anecdotal, and above all, engaging, rather than didactic."

■ **$ $ MILITARY HISTORY,** Primedia History Group, 741 Miller Dr., SE, Suite D-2, Leesburg VA 20175-8920. (703)771-9400. Fax: (703)779-8345. E-mail: cheryls@cowles.com. Website: http://www.thehistorynet.com. **Contact:** Jon Guttman, editor. Managing Editor: Carl Von Wodtke. **95% freelance written.** Circ. 150,000. "We'll work with anyone, established or not, who can provide the goods and convince us as to its accuracy." Bimonthly magazine covering all military history of the world. "We strive to give the general reader accurate, highly readable, often narrative popular history, richly accompanied by period art." Pays on publication. Publishes ms 2 years after acceptance. Byline given. Buys all rights. Submit anniversary material at least 1 year in advance. Accepts queries by mail, e-mail, fax. Reports in 3 months on queries; 6 months on mss. Sample copy for $5. Writer's guidelines for #10 SASE or online.

**Nonfiction:** Historical; interview (military figures of commanding interest); personal experience (only occasionally). **Buys 18 mss, plus 6 interviews/year.** Query with published clips. "Submit a short, self-explanatory query summarizing the story proposed, its highlights and/or significance. State also your own expertise, access to sources or proposed means of developing the pertinent information." Length: 4,000 words with a 500-word sidebar. **Pays $400.**

**Columns/Departments:** Intrigue, Weaponry, Perspectives, Personality and review of books, video, CD-ROMs, software—all relating to military history. **Buys 24 mss/year.** Query with published clips. Length: 2,000 words. **Pays $200.**

■ The online magazine carries content not found in the print edition and includes writer's guidelines. Contact: Roger Vance.

**Tips:** "We would like journalistically 'pure' submissions that adhere to basics, such as full name at first reference, same with rank, and definition of prior or related events, issues cited as context or obscure military 'hardware.' Read the magazine, discover our style, and avoid subjects already covered. Pick stories with strong art possibilities (*real* art and photos), send photocopies, tell us where to order the art. Avoid historical overview; focus upon an event with appropriate and accurate context. Provide bibliography. Tell the story in popular but elegant style. Include a hard copy as well as an IBM- or Macintosh-compatible floppy disk."

**$ $ PERSIMMON HILL,** National Cowboy Hall of Fame and Western Heritage Center, 1700 NE 63rd St., Oklahoma City OK 73111. (405)478-6404. Fax: (405)478-4714. E-mail: nchf@aol.com. Website: http://www.cowboyhalloffame.org. **Contact:** M.J. Van Deventer, editor. **70% freelance written.** Prefers to work with published/established writers; works with a small number of new/unpublished writers each year. Quarterly magazine for an audience interested in Western art, Western history, ranching and rodeo, including historians, artists, ranchers, art galleries, schools, and libraries. Estab. 1970. Circ. 15,000. Pays on publication. Publishes ms up to 2 years after acceptance. Buys first rights. Byline given. Reports in 3 months. Sample copy for $9 and 12 first-class stamps or on website. Writer's guidelines for #10 SASE or on website.

**Nonfiction:** Historical and contemporary articles on famous Western figures connected with pioneering the American West, Western art, rodeo, cowboys, etc. (or biographies of such people), stories of Western flora and animal life and environmental subjects. "We want thoroughly researched and historically authentic material written in a popular style. May have a humorous approach to subject. No broad, sweeping, superficial pieces; i.e., the California Gold Rush or rehashed pieces on Billy the Kid, etc." Length: 1,500 words. **Buys 35-50 mss/year.** Query with clips. **Pays $150-250.**

**Photos:** Glossy b&w prints or color transparencies purchased with ms, or on assignment. Pays according to quality and importance for b&w and color photos. Suggested captions required.

**Tips:** "Send us a story that captures the spirit of adventure and individualism that typifies the Old West or reveals a facet of the Western lifestyle in contemporary society. Excellent illustrations for articles are essential! We lean toward scholarly, historical, well-researched articles. We're less focused on western celebrities than some of the other contemporary magazines."

**$ $ $ $ PRESERVATION MAGAZINE,** National Trust for Historic Preservation, 1785 Massachusetts Ave. NW, Washington DC 20036. (202)588-6388. **Contact:** Robert Wilson, editor. **75% freelance written.** Prefers to work with published/established writers. Bimonthly covering preservation of historic buildings in the US. "We cover subjects related in some way to place. Most entries are features, department or opinion pieces." Circ. 250,000. Pays on publication. Publishes ms an average of 1 month after acceptance. Byline given. Offers variable kill fee. Buys one-time rights. Reports in 2 months on queries. No writer's guidelines.

**Nonfiction:** Features, news, profiles, opinion, photo feature, travel. **Buys 30 mss/year.** Query with published clips.

Length: 500-3,500 words. Sometimes pays expenses of writers on assignment, but not long-distance travel.
**Tips:** "Do not send or propose histories of buildings, descriptive accounts of cities or towns or long-winded treatises."

**$ $ $ TIMELINE**, Ohio Historical Society, 1982 Velma Ave., Columbus OH 43211-2497. (614)297-2360. Fax: (614)297-2367. E-mail: cduckworth@ohiohistory.org. **Contact:** Christopher S. Duckworth, editor. **90% freelance written.** Works with a small number of new/unpublished writers each year. Bimonthly magazine covering history, prehistory and the natural sciences, directed toward readers in the Midwest. Estab. 1885. Circ. 19,000. **Pays on acceptance.** Publishes ms an average of 1 year after acceptance. Byline given. Offers $75 minimum kill fee. Buys first North American serial or all rights. Submit seasonal material 6 months in advance. Reports in 3 weeks on queries; 6 weeks on mss. Sample copy for $6 and 9×12 SAE. Writer's guidelines for #10 SASE.
**Nonfiction:** Book excerpts, essays, historical, profile (of individuals), photo feature. Topics include the traditional fields of political, economic, military, and social history; biography; the history of science and technology; archaeology and anthropology; architecture; the fine and decorative arts; and the natural sciences including botany, geology, zoology, ecology, and paleontology. **Buys 22 mss/year.** Query. Length: 1,500-6,000 words. Also vignettes of 500-1,000 words. **Pays $100-900.**
**Photos:** Send photos with submission. Submissions must include ideas for illustration. Reviews contact sheets, transparencies, 8×10 prints. Captions, model releases, identification of subjects required. Buys one-time rights.
**Tips:** "We want crisply written, authoritative narratives for the intelligent lay reader. An Ohio slant may strengthen a submission, but it is not indispensable. Contributors must know enough about their subject to explain it clearly and in an interesting fashion. We use high-quality illustration with all features. If appropriate illustration is unavailable, we can't use the feature. The writer who sends illustration ideas with a manuscript has an advantage, but an often-published illustration won't attract us."

**$ $ TRACES OF INDIANA AND MIDWESTERN HISTORY**, Indiana Historical Society, 315 W. Ohio St., Indianapolis IN 46202-3299. (317)232-1877. Fax: (317)233-3109. E-mail: rboomhower@statelib.lib.in.us. Website: http://www.indianahistory.org/traces.htm. Executive Editor: Thomas A. Mason. **Contact:** Ray E. Boomhower, managing editor. **80% freelance written.** Quarterly magazine on Indiana and Midwestern history. "Conceived as a vehicle to bring to the public good narrative and analytical history about Indiana in its broader contexts of region and nation, *Traces* explores the lives of artists, writers, performers, soldiers, politicians, entrepreneurs, homemakers, reformers, and naturalists. It has traced the impact of Hoosiers on the nation and the world. In this vein, the editors seek nonfiction articles that are solidly researched, attractively written, and amenable to illustration, and they encourage scholars, journalists, and freelance writers to contribute to the magazine." Estab. 1989. Circ. 11,000. **Pays on acceptance.** Publishes ms an average of 6 months after acceptance. Byline given. Buys one-time rights. Submit seasonal material 1 year in advance. Reports in 3 months on mss. Sample copy and writer's guidelines for $5.25 (make checks payable to Indiana Historical Society) and 9×12 SAE with 7 first-class stamps or on website. Writer's guidelines only for #10 SASE.
**Nonfiction:** Book excerpts, historical essays, historical photographic features on topics of biography, literature, folklore, music, visual arts, politics, economics, industry, transportation and sports. **Buys 20 mss/year.** Send complete ms. Length: 2,000-4,000 words. **Pays $100-500.**
**Photos:** Send photos with submission. Reviews contact sheets, photocopies, transparencies and prints. Pays "reasonable photographic expenses." Captions, permissions and identification of subjects required. Buys one-time rights.
**Tips:** "Freelancers should be aware of prerequisites for writing history for a broad audience. Should have some awareness of this magazine and other magazines of this type published by midwestern and western historical societies. Preference is given to subjects with an Indiana connection and authors who are familiar with *Traces*. Quality of potential illustration is also important."

**⚑ $ TRUE WEST and OLD WEST**, Western Periodicals, Inc., P.O. Box 2107, Stillwater OK 74076-2107. (405)743-3370. Fax: (405)743-3374. E-mail: western@cowboy.net. Website: http://www.cowboy.net/western. **Contact:** Marcus Huff, editor. **100% freelance written.** Works with a small number of new/unpublished writers each year. *True West* (monthly), and *Old West* (quarterly) are magazines on Western American history from prehistory to 1930. "We want reliable research on significant historical topics written in lively prose for an informed general audience. More recent topics may be used if they have a historical angle or retain the Old West flavor of trail dust and saddle leather." Estab. 1953. Circ. 40,000. **Pays on acceptance.** Sends galleys. Publishes ms an average of 4 months after acceptance. Byline given. Buys first North American serial rights. Editorial lead time 3 months. Submit seasonal material 6 months in advance. Accepts simultaneous submissions. Reports in 1 month on queries; 2 months on mss. Sample copy for $2 and 9×12 SAE. Writer's guidelines for #10 SASE.
**Nonfiction:** Historical/nostalgic, how-to, humor, photo feature, travel, Native Americans, trappers, miners, cowboys, ranchers, pioneers, military ghost towns, lost mines, women and minorities. "We do not want rehashes of worn-out stories, historical fiction or history written in a fictional style." Special issue: ghost stories published every October (deadline June 5.) **Buys 150 mss/year.** Query. Ideal length: 2,000 words, maximum length 4,000 words; shorter pieces, especially humor, 300-1,500 words. **Pays 3-6¢/word.**
**Photos:** "We usually need from four to eight photos for each story, and we rely on writers to provide them." Send photos with accompanying query or ms. "Appropriate maps enhance our articles, and we appreciate receiving sketches for our artists to work from." Pays $10 for b&w prints. Identification of subjects required. Buys one-time rights.
**Columns/Departments:** Western Roundup—200-300-word short articles on historically oriented places to go and

things to do in the West. Should include one b&w print. **Buys 24 mss/year.** Send complete ms. **Pays $25-75.**
**Fillers:** Short humor. **Buys 12/year.** Length: 500-1,000 words. **Pays 3-6¢/word.**
**Tips:** "Do original research on fresh topics. Stay away from controversial subjects unless you are truly knowledgable in the field. Read our magazines and follow our guidelines. A freelancer is most likely to break in with us by submitting thoroughly researched, lively prose on relatively obscure topics. First-person accounts rarely fill our needs. Historical accuracy and strict adherence to the facts are essential. We much prefer material based on primary sources (archives, court records, documents, contemporary newspapers and first-person accounts) to those that rely mainly on secondary sources (published books, magazines, and journals). Note: We are currently trying to take *True West* and *Old West* back to their 'roots' by publishing shorter pieces. Ideal length is between 1,500-3,000 words."

**$ $VIETNAM**, Primedia History Group, 741 Miller Dr. SE, #D-2, Leesburg VA 20175-8920. (703)771-9400. Fax: (703)779-8345. E-mail: cheryls@cowles.com. Website: http://www.thehistorynet.com. **Contact:** Colonel Harry G. Summers, Jr., editor. Managing Editor: Carl Von Wodtke. **90% freelance written.** Bimonthly magazine that "provides in-depth and authoritative accounts of the many complexities that made the war in Vietnam unique, including the people, battles, strategies, perspectives, analysis and weaponry." Estab. 1988. Circ. 115,000. Pays on publication. Publishes ms up to 2 years after acceptance. Byline given. Buys all rights. Accepts queries by mail, e-mail, fax. Reports in 3 months on queries; 6 months on mss. Sample copy for $5. Writer's guidelines for #10 SASE.
**Nonfiction:** Book excerpts (if original), historical, interview, personal/experience, military history. "Absolutely no fiction or poetry; we want straight history, as much personal narrative as possible, but not the gung-ho, shoot-em-up variety, either." **Buys 24 mss/year.** Query. Length: 4,000 words maximum. **Pays $300 for features, sidebar 500 words.**
**Photos:** Send photos with submission or state availability and cite sources. Identification of subjects required.
**Columns/Departments:** Arsenal (about weapons used, all sides); Personality (profiles of the players, all sides); Fighting Forces (various units or types of units: air, sea, rescue); Perspectives. Query. Length: 2,000 words. **Pays $150.**
  The online magazine carries original content not found in the print edition and includes writer's guidelines. Contact: Roger Vance.
**Tips:** "Choose stories with strong art possibilities. Send hard copy plus an IBM- or Macintosh-compatible floppy disk. All stories must be true. We do not publish fiction or poetry. All stories should be carefully researched, third-person articles or firsthand accounts that give the reader a sense of experiencing historical events."

**$ $WILD WEST**, Primedia History Group, 741 Miller Dr., SE, Suite D-2, Leesburg VA 20175-8920. (703)771-9400. Fax: (703)779-8345. E-mail: cheryls@cowles.com. Website: http://www.thehistorynet.com. **Contact:** Gregory Lalire, editor. Managing Editor: Carl Von Wodtke. **95% freelance written.** Bimonthly magazine on history of the American frontier, from its eastern beginnings to its western terminus. "*Wild West* covers the popular (narrative) history of the American West—events, trends, personalities, anything of general interest." Estab. 1988. Circ. 200,000. Pays on publication. Publishes ms an average of 2 years after acceptance. Byline given. Buys all rights. Editorial lead time 6 months. Submit seasonal material 1 year in advance. Accepts queries by mail, e-mail, fax. Accepts simultaneous submissions. Reports in 3 months on queries; 6 months on mss. Sample copy for $5. Writer's guidelines for #10 SASE or online.
**Nonfiction:** Book excerpts, historical/nostalgic, humor, personal experience, travel. No fiction or poetry—nothing current. **Buys 36 mss/year.** Query. Length: 4,000 words with a 500-word sidebar. **Pays $300.**
**Photos:** State availability of photos with submission; cite sources. Reviews negatives, transparencies. Offers no additional payment for photos accepted with ms. Captions, identification of subjects required. Buys one-time rights.
**Columns/Departments:** Travel; Gun Fighters & Lawmen, 2,000 words; Personalities; Warriors & Chiefs, 2,000 words; Artist West, 2,000 words; Books Reviews, 500 words. **Buys 36 mss/year.** Query. **Pays $150 for departments, book reviews by the word, minimum $30.**
  The online magazine carries original content not found in the print edition and includes writer's guidelines. Contact: Roger Vance.
**Tips:** "Always query the editor with your story idea. Successful queries include a description of sources of information and suggestions for color and black-and-white photography or artwork. The best way to break into our magazine is to write an entertaining, informative and unusual story that grabs the reader's attention and holds it. We favor carefully researched, third-person articles or firsthand accounts that give the reader a sense of experiencing historical events. Include a hard copy as well as an IBM- or Macintosh-compatible floppy disk."

**$ $WORLD WAR II**, Primedia History Group, 741 Miller Dr., SE, Suite D-2, Leesburg VA 20175-8920. (703)771-9400. Fax: (703)779-8345. E-mail: cheryls@cowles.com. Website: http://www.thehistorynet.com. **Contact:** Michael Haskew, editor. Managing Editor: Carl Von Wodtke. **95% freelance written.** Prefers to work with published/established writers. Bimonthly magazine covering "military operations in World War II—events, personalities, strategy, national policy, etc." Estab. 1986. Circ. 200,000. Pays on publication. Publishes ms an average of 2 years after acceptance. Byline given. Buys all rights. Submit anniversary-related material 1 year in advance. Accepts queries by mail, e-mail, fax. Reports in 3 months on queries; 6 months or more on mss. Sample copy for $5. Writer's guidelines for #10 SASE or online.
**Nonfiction:** World War II military history. No fiction. **Buys 24 mss/year.** Query. Length: 4,000 words with a 500-word sidebar. **Pays $200.**
**Photos:** State availability of art and photos with submission. For photos and other art, send photocopies and cite sources. "We'll order." Captions and identification of subjects required.

**Columns/Departments:** Undercover (espionage, resistance, sabotage, intelligence gathering, behind the lines, etc.); Personalities (WW II personalities of interest); Armaments (weapons, their use and development), all 2,000 words. **Pays $100.** Book reviews, 300-750 words. **Buys 18 mss/year (plus book reviews).** Query with SASE.

■ The online magazine contains content not found in the print edition and includes writer's guidelines. Contact: Roger Vance. Includes writer's guidelines.

**Tips:** "List your sources and suggest further readings in standard format at the end of your piece—as a bibliography for our files in case of factual challenge or dispute. All submissions are on speculation. Include a hard copy as well as an IBM- or Macintosh-compatible floppy disk. All stories must be true. We do not publish fiction or poetry. Stories should be carefully researched."

**N** ✕ **$ YESTERDAY'S MAGAZETTE, The Magazine of Memories**, Independent Publishing Co., P.O. Box 18566, Sarasota FL 34276. Editor: Ned Burke. **95% freelance written.** Bimonthly magazine of nostalgia. Estab. 1973. Circ. 2,500. Pays on publication. Publishes ms an average of 6 months after acceptance. Byline given. Buys first rights. Submit seasonal/holiday material 4 months in advance. Reports in 2 months. Sample copy for $3 and 9 × 12 SAE with 4 first-class stamps. Writer's guidelines free.

**Nonfiction:** General interest, historical/nostalgic, humor, inspirational, interview/profile ('yesterday' celebrities), opinion, personal experience, photo feature and photo. Special "Christmas" issue, deadline November 15, featuring "My Favorite Christmas Memory." **Buys 100 mss/year.** Send complete ms. Length: 100-1,500 words. **Pays $5-25 for unsolicited articles.** Pays for most short articles, poems, etc.

**Photos:** Send photos with submission. Reviews 5 × 7 prints. Offers $5-10 for photos accepted with ms. Identification of subjects required. Buys one-time rights.

**Columns/Departments:** The Way We Were (a look at certain period of time—40s, 50s, etc.); When I Was a Kid (childhood memories); In A Word (objects from the past—'ice box,' etc.); Yesterday Trivia (quiz on old movie stars, TV shows, etc.), all 300-750 words. **Buys 12 mss/year.** Send complete ms. Length: 500-750 words. **Pays $5-10.**

**Fiction:** Historical, humorous, slice-of-life vignettes. "No modern settings." **Buys 12 mss/year.** Send complete ms. Length: 750-2,500 words. **Pays $5-25.**

**Poetry:** Traditional. Nothing other than traditional. **Buys 50 poems/year.** Submit maximum 5 poems. Length: 4-32 lines. **Pays $5 and/or contributor copies.**

**Fillers:** Anecdotes, short humor. **Buys 5/year.** Length: 50-250 words. **Pays $5 and/or contributor copies.**

**Tips:** "We would like to see more 40s, 50s and 60s pieces, especially with photos. It's hard to reject any story with a good photo. All areas are open, especially 'Plain Folks Page' which uses letters, comments and opinions of readers."

# HOBBY & CRAFT

Magazines in this category range from home video to cross-stitch. Craftspeople and hobbyists who read these magazines want new ideas while collectors need to know what is most valuable and why. Collectors, do-it-yourselfers and craftspeople look to these magazines for inspiration and information. Publications covering antiques and miniatures are also listed here. Publications covering the business side of antiques and collectibles are listed in the Trade Art, Design & Collectibles section.

**$ $ ANTIQUE REVIEW**, P.O. Box 538, Worthington OH 43085-0538. (614)885-9757. Fax: (614)885-9762. E-mail: editor@antiquereviewohio.com. Website: http://www.antiquereviewohio.com. **Contact:** Charles Muller, editor. **60% freelance written.** Eager to work with new/unpublished writers. Monthly tabloid for an antique-oriented readership, "generally well-educated, interested in Early American furniture and decorative arts, as well as folk art." Estab. 1975. Circ. 10,000. Pays on publication date assigned at time of purchase. Publishes ms an average of 2 months after acceptance. Byline given. Buys first North American serial and second (reprint) rights. Accepts queries by mail, phone. Reports in 3 months. Free sample copy and writer's guidelines for #10 SASE.

● *Antique Review* has added a new section focusing on trends and collectibles.

**Nonfiction:** "The articles we desire concern history and production of furniture, pottery, china, and other quality Americana. In some cases, contemporary folk art items are acceptable. We are also interested in reporting on antiques shows and auctions with statements on conditions and prices." **Buys 5-8 mss/issue.** Query with clips of published work. Query should show "author's familiarity with antiques, an interest in the historical development of artifacts relating to early America and an awareness of antiques market." Length: 200-2,000 words. **Pays $100-200.** Sometimes pays expenses of writers on assignment.

**Reprints:** Accepts previously published submissions if not first printed in competitive publications. Send tearsheet or photocopy of article or typed ms with rights for sale noted and information about when and where the article previously appeared. Pays 100% of amount paid for an original article.

**Photos:** Send photos with query. Payment included in ms price. Uses 3 × 5 or larger glossy b&w or color prints. Captions required. Articles with photographs receive preference.

**Tips:** "Give us a call and let us know of specific interests. We are more concerned with the background in antiques than in writing abilities. The writing can be edited, but the knowledge imparted is of primary interest. A frequent mistake is being too general, not becoming deeply involved in the topic and its research. We are interested in primary research into America's historic material culture."

**$ $ THE ANTIQUE TRADER WEEKLY**, P.O. Box 1050, Dubuque IA 52004-1050. (319)588-2073, ext. 121. Fax: (800)531-0880. E-mail: traderpubs@aol.com. **Contact:** Kyle Husfloen, editor. **50% freelance written.** Works with a small number of new/unpublished writers each year. Weekly newspaper for collectors and dealers in antiques and collectibles. Estab. 1957. Circ. 60,000. Publishes ms an average of 1 year after acceptance. Buys all rights. Payment at beginning of month following publication. Submit seasonal material 4 months in advance. Sample copy for $1 and #10 SASE. Writer's guidelines free.

**Nonfiction:** "We invite authoritative and well-researched articles on all types of antiques and collectors' items and in-depth stories on specific types of antiques and collectibles. No human interest stories. We do not pay for brief information on new shops opening or other material printed as a service to the antiques hobby." **Buys 60 mss/year.** Query or submit complete ms. Length: 1,000-2,000 words. **Pays $50-150 for features; $150-250 for feature cover stories.**

**Photos:** Submit a liberal number of good color photos to accompany article. Uses 35mm slides for cover. Offers no additional payment for photos accompanying mss.

**Tips:** "Send concise, polite letter stating the topic to be covered in the story and the writer's qualifications. No 'cute' letters rambling on about some 'imaginative' story idea. Writers who have a concise yet readable style and know their topic are always appreciated. I am most interested in those who have personal collecting experience or can put together a knowledgeable and informative feature after interviewing a serious collector/authority."

**$ AUTOGRAPH COLLECTOR**, Odyssey Publications, 510-A South Corona Mall, Corona CA 91719. (909)734-9636. Fax: (909)371-7139. E-mail: DBTOGI@aol.com. Website: http://www.AutographCollector.com. **Contact:** Ev Phillips, editor. **80% freelance written.** Monthly magazine covering the autograph collecting hobby. "The focus of *Autograph Collector* is on documents, photographs or any collectible item that has been signed by a famous person, whether a current celebrity or historical figure. Articles stress how and where to locate celebrities and autograph material, authenticity of signatures and what they are worth." Byline given. Negotiable kill fee. Buys all rights. Editorial lead time 2 months. Submit seasonal material 3 months in advance. Accepts queries by mail, e-mail, fax, phone. Reports in 2 weeks on queries; 1 month on mss. Sample copy and writer's guidelines free.

**Nonfiction:** Historical/nostalgic, how-to, interview/profile, personal experience. "Articles must address subjects that appeal to autograph collectors and should answer six basic questions: Who is this celebrity/famous person? How do I go about collecting this person's autograph? Where can I find it? How scarce or available is it? How can I tell if it's real? What is it worth?" **Buys 25-35 mss/year.** Query. Length: 1,750-2,250 words. **Pays 5¢/word.** Sometimes pays expenses of writers on assignment.

**Photos:** State availability of photos with submission. Reviews transparencies, prints. Offers $3/photo. Captions, identification of subjects required. Buys one-time rights.

**Columns/Departments:** "*Autograph Collector* buys 8-10 columns per month written by regular contributors. Send query for more information." **Buys 90-100 mss/year.** Query. **Pays $50 or as determined on a per case basis.**

**Fillers:** Anecdotes, facts. **Buys 20-25/year.** Length: 200-300 words. **Pays $15.**

**Tips:** "Ideally writers should be autograph collectors themselves and know their topics thoroughly. Articles must be well-researched and clearly written. Writers should remember that *Autograph Collector* is a celebrity-driven magazine and name recognition of the subject is important."

**$ $ BECKETT BASEBALL CARD MONTHLY**, Statabase, Inc., 15850 Dallas Pkwy., Dallas TX 75248. (972)991-6657. Fax: (972)233-6488. Website: http://www.beckett.com. Editorial Director: Rudy Klancnik. **Contact:** Tracy Hackler, senior editor. **60% freelance written.** Monthly magazine on baseball card and sports memorabilia collecting. "Our readers expect our publication to be entertaining and informative. Our slant is that hobbies are fun and rewarding. Especially wanted are how-to-collect articles." Estab. 1984. **Pays on acceptance.** Publishes ms an average of 4 months after acceptance. Byline given. Pays $50 kill fee. Buys all rights. Submit seasonal material 6 months in advance. Reports in 1 month. Sample copy for $3.95. Writer's guidelines free.

**Nonfiction:** How-to, humor, interview/profile, new product, opinion, personal experience, photo feature, technical. Special issues: Spring training (February); season preview (April); All-Star game (July); Hobby Awards (August); World Series (October). No articles that emphasize speculative prices and investments. **Buys 50 mss/year.** Send complete ms. Length: 300-1,500 words. **Pays $100-400 for assigned articles; $50-200 for unsolicited articles.** Sometimes pays expenses of writers on assignment.

**Photos:** Send photos with submission. Reviews 35mm transparencies, 5×7 or larger prints. Offers $10-300/photo. Captions, model releases and identification of subjects required. Buys one-time rights.

**Fiction:** Humorous only.

**Tips:** "A writer for *Beckett Baseball Card Monthly* should be an avid baseball fan and card collector with passion for the hobby and an enthusiasm for sharing his/her interests with others. Articles must be factual, but not overly statistic-laden. First person (not research) articles presenting the writer's personal experiences told with wit and humor, and emphasizing the stars of the game, are *always* wanted. Acceptable articles must be of interest to our two basic reader segments: teenaged boys and their middle-aged fathers who are re-experiencing an interest in baseball card collecting. Prospective writers should not write down to either group!"

**$ $** BECKETT BASKETBALL CARD MONTHLY, Statabase, Inc., 15850 Dallas Pkwy., Dallas TX 75248. (972)991-6657. Fax: (972)991-8930. Website: http://www.beckett.com. Publisher: Dr. James Beckett. Editorial Director: Rudy Klancnik. **Contact:** Joel Brown, associate editor. **30% freelance written.** Monthly magazine on basketball card and sports memorabilia collecting. "Our readers expect our publication to be entertaining and informative. Our slant is that hobbies are fun and rewarding. Especially wanted are articles dealing directly with the hobby of basketball card and memorabilia collecting." Estab. 1990. Circ. 200,000. **Pays on acceptance.** Publishes ms an average of 4 months after acceptance. Byline given. Pays $50 kill fee. Buys first North American serial rights. Submit seasonal material 6 months in advance. Accepts queries by mail, e-mail, fax. Reports in 1 month. Sample copy for $3.99.
**Nonfiction:** How-to, humor, interview/profile, new product, opinion, photo feature, technical. No articles that emphasize speculative prices and investments. **Buys 145 mss/year.** Send complete ms. Length: 300-1,500 words. **Pays $100-400 for assigned articles; $100-200 for unsolicited articles.** Sometimes pays expenses of writers on assignment.
**Photos:** Send photos with submission. Reviews 35mm transparencies, 5×7 or larger prints. Offers $10-300/photo. Captions, model releases and identification of subjects required. Buys one-time rights.
**Tips:** "A writer for *Beckett Basketball Monthly* should be an avid sports fan and basketball card collector with an enthusiasm for sharing his/her hobby interests with others. Articles must be factual and entertaining, but not overly statistic-laden."

**$ $** BECKETT FOOTBALL CARD MONTHLY, Statabase, Inc., 15850 Dallas Pkwy., Dallas TX 75248. (214)991-6657. Fax: (972)233-6488. Website: http://www.beckett.com. Editorial Director: Rudy Klancnik. **Contact:** Mike Pagel, associate editor. **85% freelance written.** Monthly magazine on football card and sports memorabilia collecting. "Our readers expect our publication to be entertaining and informative. Our slant is that hobbies are fun and rewarding. Especially wanted are well-written articles on great football card sets, past and present." Estab. 1989. **Pays on acceptance.** Publishes ms an average of 4 months after acceptance. Byline given. Pays $50 kill fee. Buys all rights. Submit seasonal material 6 months in advance. Reports in 1 month. Sample copy for $3.95. Writer's guidelines free.
**Nonfiction:** Historical/nostalgic, how-to, humor, interview/profile, new product, opinion, personal experience, photo feature, technical. Special issues: Super Bowl (January); NFL draft (April); Hobby Awards (August). No articles that emphasize speculative prices and investments. Buys 145 mss/year. Send complete ms. Length: 300-1,500 words. Pays $100-400 for assigned articles; $50-200 for unsolicited articles. Sometimes pays expenses of writers on assignment.
**Photos:** Send photos with submission. Reviews 35mm transparencies, 5×7 or larger prints. Offers $10-300/photo. Captions, model releases, identification of subjects required. Buys one-time rights.
**Fiction:** Humorous only.
**Tips:** "A writer for *Beckett Football Card Monthly* should be an avid sports fan and/or a collector with an enthusiasm for sharing his/her interests with others. Articles must be factual, but not overly statistic-laden. Acceptable articles must be of interest to our two basic reader segments: teenaged boys and their middle-aged fathers who are re-experiencing a nostalgic renaissance of their own childhoods. Prospective writers should write down to neither group!"

**$ $** BECKETT HOCKEY COLLECTOR, Statabase, Inc., 15850 Dallas Pkwy., Dallas TX 75248. (972)991-6657. Fax: (972)233-6488. Website: http://www.beckett.com. **Contact:** Al Muin, associate editor. **75% freelance written.** Monthly magazine on hockey, hockey card and memorabilia collecting. "Our readers expect our publication to be entertaining and informative, with intense coverage of the hockey collectibles market." Our slant is that hobbies are fun and rewarding. Especially wanted are how-to-collect articles." Estab. 1990. **Pays on acceptance.** Publishes ms an average of 3 months after acceptance. Byline given. Pays $50 kill fee. Buys all rights. Submit seasonal material 6 months in advance. Reports in 1 month. Sample copy for $3.95. Writer's guidelines free.
**Nonfiction:** New collecting ideas, great collections in North America, interview/profile, new product, opinion, personal experience, photo feature, technical. Special issues: All-Star game (February); Hobby Awards (August); draft (June); season preview (October). No articles that emphasize speculative prices and investments. Buys 145 mss/year. Send complete ms. Length: 300-1,500 words. Pays $100-400 for assigned articles; $50-200 for unsolicited articles. Sometimes pays expenses of writers on assignment.
**Photos:** Send photos with submission. Reviews 35mm transparencies, 5×7 or larger prints. Offers $10-300/photo. Captions, model releases and identification of subjects required. Buys one-time rights.
**Fiction:** Humorous only.
**Tips:** "A writer for *Beckett Hockey Monthly* should be an avid sports fan and/or a collector with an enthusiasm for sharing his/her interests with others. Articles must be factual, but not overly statistic-laden. Acceptable articles must be of interest to our two basic reader segments: teenaged boys and their middle-aged fathers who are re-experiencing a nostalgic renaissance of their own childhoods. Prospective writers should write down to neither group!" .

**$ $** BECKETT RACING MONTHLY, Statabase, Inc., 15850 Dallas Pkwy., Dallas TX 75248. (972)991-6657. Fax: (972)991-8930. E-mail: markzeske@beckett.com. Website: http://www.beckett.com. Editor: Dr. James Beckett. Editorial Director: Rudy J. Klancnik. **Contact:** Mark Zeske, senior editor. **85% freelance written.** Monthly magazine on racing card, die-cast and sports memorabilia collecting. "Our readers expect our publication to be entertaining and informative. Our slant is that racing collectibles are fun and rewarding. Especially wanted are articles dealing directly with the hobby of card collecting." Estab. 1994. Circ. 100,000 **Pays on acceptance.** Publishes ms an average of 4 months after acceptance. Byline given. Pays $50 kill fee. Buys all rights. Submit seasonal material 6 months in advance. Reports in 1 month. Sample copy for $3.95. Writer's guidelines free.
**Nonfiction:** Historical/nostalgic, how-to, interview/profile, new product, opinion, personal experience, photo feature,

technical. No articles that emphasize speculative prices and investments. Send complete ms. Length: 300-1,500 words. **Pays $100-400 for assigned articles; $100-200 for unsolicited articles.** Sometimes pays expenses of writer on assignment.

**Photos:** Send photos with submission. Reviews 35mm transparencies, 5×7 or larger prints. Offers $10-300/photo. Captions, model releases and identification of subjects required. Buys one-time rights.

**Fiction:** Humorous only.

**Tips:** "A writer for *Beckett Racing Monthly* should be an avid racing fan in touch with the growing racing collectibles field. Articles must be factual, but not overly statistic-laden. First person (not research) articles presenting the writer's personal experiences told with wit and humor, and emphasizing the stars of the sport, are always wanted."

**$ $** BECKETT SPORTS COLLECTIBLES AND AUTOGRAPHS, Statbase, Inc., 15850 Dallas Pkwy., Dallas TX 75248. (972)991-6657. Fax: (972)991-8930. E-mail: mpagel@beckett.com. Website: http://www.beckett.com. Editor: Dr. James Beckett. Editorial Director: Rudy J. Klancnik. **Contact:** Mike Payne, managing editor. **85% freelance written.** Monthly magazine offering coverage of sports, collectibles and autographs from stars of all sports. "Our readers expect our publication to be entertaining and informative. Our slant is that sports collectibles are fun and rewarding." Estab. 1991. Circ. 73,128. **Pays on acceptance.** Publishes ms an average of 4 months after acceptance. Byline given. Pays $50 kill fee. Buys all rights. Submit seasonal material 8 months in advance. Reports in 1 month. Sample copy for $2.95. Writer's guidelines free.

**Nonfiction:** Historical/nostalgic (for collectibles only), how-to, humor, interview/profile, new product, opinion, personal experience, photo feature, technical. Special issues: card sets in review (January); baseball draft special (June). No articles that emphasize speculative prices and investments on cards. **Buys 50 mss/year.** Send complete ms. Length: 300-1,500 words. **Pays $100-400 for assigned articles; $50-200 for unsolicited articles.** Sometimes pays expenses of writers on assignment.

**Photos:** Send photos with submission. Reviews 35mm transparencies, 5×7 or larger prints. Offers $25-300/photo. Captions, model releases and identification of subjects required. Buys one-time rights.

**Tips:** "A writer for *Beckett Sports Collectibles and Autographs* should be an avid sports fan and/or a collector with an enthusiasm for sharing his/her interests with others. Acceptable articles must be of interest to both experienced collectors, and newer hobbyists entering the field"

**★ $** BREW YOUR OWN, The How-to Homebrew Beer Magazine, 216 F St., Suite 160, Davis CA 95616. (530)758-4596. Fax: (530)758-7477. E-mail: edit@byo.com. Website: http://www.byo.com. Managing Editor: Gailen Jacobs. **Contact:** Craig Bystrynski, editor. **85% freelance written.** Monthly magazine covering home brewing. "Our mission is to provide practical information in an entertaining format. We try to capture the spirit and challenge of brewing while helping our readers brew the best beer they can." Estab. 1995. Circ. 42,000. Pays on publication. Publishes ms 4 months after acceptance. Byline given. Offers 25% kill fee. Buys all rights. Editorial lead time 3 months. Submit seasonal material 3 months in advance. Reports in 2 months. Writer's guidelines for #10 SASE.

**Nonfiction:** How-to (home brewing), informational pieces on equipment, ingredients and brewing methods. Length: 1,500-3,000 words. Humor (related to home brewing), interview/profile, personal experience, historical, trends. Length: 800-2,000 words. **Buys 75 mss/year.** Query with published clips and SASE. **Pays $50-150** depending on length, complexity of article and experience of writer. Sometimes pays expenses of writers on assignment.

**Photos:** State availability of photos with submission. Reviews contact sheets, transparencies, 5×7 prints. Negotiates payment individually. Captions required. Buys all rights.

**Columns/Departments:** News (humorous, unusual news about homebrewing), 50-250 words; Last Call (humorous stories about homebrewing), 700 words. **Buys 12 mss/year.** Query with or without published clips. **Pays $50.**

**Tips:** "*Brew Your Own* is for anyone who is interested in brewing beer, from beginners to advanced all-grain brewers. We seek articles that are straightforward and factual, not full of esoteric theories or complex calculations. Our readers tend to be intelligent, upscale, and literate."

**N ★ $** BREWING TECHNIQUES, The Art and Science of Small-Scale Brewing, New Wine Press, P.O. Box 3222, Eugene OR 97403-0222. (541)687-2993. Fax: (541)687-8534. E-mail: editor@brewtech.com. Website: http://www.brewingtechniques.com. Editor-in-Chief: Stephen Mallery. **Contact:** Deb Jolda, managing editor. **90% freelance written.** Bimonthly peer-reviewed magazine covering brewing: advanced home brewing and professional (small-scale) brewing. "*BT* is the only magazine in the industry that focuses on brewers themselves across both home and professional markets. Our readers are passionate about beer and always strive for improvements to their own brews. They are typically well-educated, often with scientific or technical backgrounds. They expect accurate, cutting-edge information that is presented without condescension. We expect the same high standards of our authors." Estab. 1993. Circ. 10,000. Pays on publication. Publishes ms an average of 3 months after acceptance. Byline given. Offers 100% kill fee for solicited mss. Buys first North American serial, electronic and second serial (reprint) rights (for material as published; author retains rights to original submissions). Editorial lead time 2-4 months. Submit seasonal material 4 months in advance. Accepts queries by mail, e-mail (preferred), fax, phone. Reports in 1 week on queries; 1 month on mss. Sample copy free or sample articles on website. Writer's guidelines by e-mail or website.

**Nonfiction:** Book reviews, essays, general interest, historical/nostalgic, how-to (practical articles about brewing tips and tricks, innovations, equipment), humor, interview/profile, personal experience, technical, travel. **Buys 30-40 mss/year.** Query. Length: 250-3,000 words. **Pays $25 minimum** (if the author is willing, subscription in lieu of payment).

**Photos:** State availability of photos with submission. Reviews 3×5 prints (preferred, not essential). Offers $10-25/

photo. Captions and identification of subjects required.

**Columns/Departments:** Home Brewers Corner and Craft Brewers Corner (tips, tricks, anecdotes, profiles, news), 250 words maximum; Book Reviews (books about brewing as opposed to beer), 500 words. **Buys 12-24 mss/year.** Query. **Pays $25 minimum.**

**Tips:** "Optimally, you'll be a brewer yourself, or at least have a fair knowledge of beer and brewing. Be flexible in your subject matter and approach, and be willing to work with us to produce an excellent article (read: your work does not end with the submission). Do your homework! It's easiest for all of us if you do your research before submitting and ensure that the content is accurate. Dot your 'i's' and cross your 't's' and we'll be impressed."

**N: BULLETIN, Magazine of the Ontario Handweavers and Spinners,** 450 Westheights Dr., P.O. Box 44009, Kitchener, Ontario N2N 3G7 Canada. E-mail: dburns@golden.net. Website: http://www3.sympatico.ca/ontario.handweavers.spinners. Editor: Ron Abbott. **Contact:** Dianne Burns, content editor. **80-90% freelance written.** Quarterly magazine covering handweaving, spinning, fibre arts. "Our readers are weavers and spinners. All articles deal with some aspect of these crafts." Estab. 1957. Circ. 1,000. Pays within 30 days after publication. Buys one-time rights. Editorial lead time 4 months. Submit seasonal material 4 months in advance. Accepts simultaneous submissions. Reports in 2 months on mss. Sample copy for $3 (Canadian) or on website. Writer's guidelines for #10 SASE or by e-mail.

**Nonfiction:** How-to, interview/profile, new production, opinion, personal experiences, technical. No articles from writers not involved in weaving, spinning, dying, knitting, basketry, felt making, paper making, sheep raising, craft supplies, etc. **Buys 40-50 mss/year.** Send complete ms. Length: 750-1,000 words. **Pays $75-150 (Canadian).**

**Reprints:** Accepts previously published submissions.

**Photos:** Send photos with submission. Reviews 4×6 prints. Offers no additional payment for photos accepted with ms. Captions, identification of subjects required. Buys one-time rights.

**Columns/Departments:** Variations on a Wheel (specific type of spinning wheel), 750-1,000 words; Profile (about a handweaver or spinner, well-known or professional), 750-1,000 words. **Buys 4-12 mss/year.** Send complete ms. **Pays $75-150 Canadian).**

**Fiction:** Humorous, slice-of-life vignettes, if they deal with weaving, spinning or other related crafts. **Buys 0-3 mss/year.** Send complete ms. Length: 500-750 words. **Pays $10-50 Canadian.**

**Tips:** "Contributors must have an understanding of our craft. This magazine is FOR and BY numbers of the Ontario Handweavers and Spinners. Members range from beginners to masters. We welcome articles from knowledgeable men and women who love the fibre arts as much as we do and who can offer something new, interesting, and informative to these age old crafts. And please, spell my name correctly."

**$ $ CAR MODELER,** Kalmbach Publishing Co., 21027 Crossroads Circle, P.O. Box 1612, Waukesha WI 53187-1612. (414)796-8776. Fax: (414)796-1383. E-mail: editor@carmodeler.com. Website: http://www.Kalmbach.com/carmodeler/carmodeler.html. **Contact:** Kirk Bell, senior editor.
  ● *Car Modeler* has changed to an annual, published in April. Their freelance needs have decreased significantly.

**$ CERAMICS MONTHLY,** American Ceramic Society, P.O. Box 6102, Westerville OH 43086. (614)523-1660. Fax: (614)891-8960. E-mail: editorial@ceramicmonthly.org. **Contact:** Ruth C. Butler, editor. **50% freelance written.** Monthly magazine, except July and August, covering the ceramic art and craft field. "Technical and business information for potters and ceramic artists." Estab. 1953. Circ. 39,000. Pays on publication. Byline given. Editorial lead time 3 months. Submit seasonal material 6 months in advance. Accepts queries by mail, e-mail, fax, phone. Reports in 6 weeks on queries; 2 months on mss. Sample copy for cost plus $2 s&h. Writer's guidelines for #10 SASE or on website.

**Nonfiction:** Essays, how-to, interview/profile, opinion, personal experience, technical. **Buys 100 mss/year.** Send complete ms. Length: 500-3,000 words. **Pays 7¢/word.**

**Photos:** Send photos with submission. Reviews transparencies (2 ¼×2¼ or 4×5). Offers $15 for black and white; $25 for color photos. Captions required.

**Columns/Departments:** Up Front (workshop/exhibition review), 500-1,000 words. **Buys 20 mss/year.** Send complete ms. **Pays 7¢/word.**

**$ $ CLASSIC TOY TRAINS,** Kalmbach Publishing Co., 21027 Crossroads Circle, Waukesha WI 53187. (414)796-8776. Fax: (414)796-1142. E-mail: editor@classtrain.com. Website: http://www.kalmbach.com/ctt/toytrains.html. **Contact:** Neil Besougloff, editor. **75-80% freelance written.** Magazine published 9 times/year covering collectible toy trains (O, S, Standard, G scale, etc.) like Lionel, American Flyer, Marx, Dorfan, etc. "For the collector and operator of toy trains, *CTT* offers full-color photos of layouts and collections of toy trains, restoration tips, operating information, new product reviews and information, and insights into the history of toy trains." Estab. 1987. Circ. 72,000. **Pays on acceptance.** Publishes ms an average of 1 year after acceptance. Byline given. Buys all rights. Editorial lead time 3 months. Submit seasonal material 6 months in advance. Accepts queries by mail, e-mail, fax, phone. Reports in 3 weeks on queries; 1 month on mss. Sample copy for $4.95 plus s&h. Writer's guidelines for #10 SASE or on website.

**Nonfiction:** General interest, historical/nostalgic, how-to (restore toy trains; design a layout; build accessories; fix broken toy trains), interview/profile, personal experience, photo feature, technical. **Buys 90 mss/year.** Query. Length: 500-5,000 words. **Pays $75-500.** Sometimes pays expenses of writers on assignment.

**Photos:** Send photos with submission. Reviews 4×5 transparencies; 5×7 prints preferred. Offers no additional payment for photos accepted with ms or $15-75/photo. Captions required. Buys all rights.

**Fillers:** Uses cartoons. **Buys 6 fillers/year. Pays $30.**

**Tips:** "It's important to have a thorough understanding of the toy train hobby; most of our freelancers are hobbyists themselves. One-half to two-thirds of *CTT*'s editorial space is devoted to photographs; superior photography is critical."

**$ $ COLLECTOR EDITIONS**, Collector Communications Corp., 170 Fifth Ave., New York NY 10010-5911. (212)989-8700. Fax: (212)645-8976. **Contact:** Joan M. Pursley, editor. **40% freelance written.** Works with a small number of new/unpublished writers each year. Published 7 times/year, it covers porcelain and glass collectibles and limited-edition prints. "We specialize in contemporary (post-war ceramic and glass) collectibles, including reproductions, but also publish articles about antiques, if they are being reproduced today and are generally available." Estab. 1973. Circ. 96,000. Pays within 30 days of acceptance. Publishes ms an average of 6 months after acceptance. Buys first North American serial rights. "First assignments are always done on a speculative basis." Reports in 2 months. Sample copy for $2. Writer's guidelines for #10 SASE.
**Nonfiction:** "Short features about collecting, written in tight, newsy style. We specialize in contemporary (postwar) collectibles. Values for pieces being written about should be included." Informational, interview, profile, exposé, nostalgia. Special issues: Christmas Collectibles (December). **Buys 15-20 mss/year.** Query with sample photos. Length: 800-1,500 words. **Pays $250-400.** Sometimes pays expenses of writers on assignment.
**Photos:** B&w and color photos purchased with accompanying ms with no additional payment. Captions are required. "We want clear, distinct, full-frame images that say something."
**Columns/Departments:** Staff written; not interested in freelance columns.
**Tips:** "Unfamiliarity with the field is the most frequent mistake made by writers in completing an article for us."

**$ $ COLLECTOR'S MART, Contemporary Collectibles**, Limited Edition Art & Gifts, Krause Publications, 700 E. State St., Iola WI 54990. (715)445-2214. Fax: (715)445-4087. E-mail: sieberm@krause.com. Website: http://www.krause.com. **Contact:** Mary L. Sieber, editor. **50% freelance written.** Bimonthly magazine covering contemporary collectibles, for collectors of all types. Estab. 1976. Circ. 170,000. Pays on publication. Publishes ms an average of 6 months after acceptance. Byline given. Buys perpetual but non-exclusive rights. Editorial lead time 2 months. Submit seasonal material 4 months in advance. Accepts queries by mail, e-mail, fax, phone. Reports in 1 month on mss. Writer's guidelines not available.
**Nonfiction:** Buys 35-50 mss/year. Send complete ms. Length: 1,000-2,000 words. **Pays $50-300.**
**Photos:** Send only color photos with submission. Reviews transparencies, prints. Offers no additional payment for photos accepted with ms. Captions required. Buys one-time rights.

**N $ $ COLLECTORS NEWS & THE ANTIQUE REPORTER**, P.O. Box 156, Grundy Center IA 50638-0156. (319)824-6981. Fax: (319)824-3414. E-mail: collect@collectors-news.com. Website: http://collectors-news.com. **Contact:** Linda Kruger, managing editor. **20% freelance written.** Estab. 1959. Works with a small number of new/unpublished writers each year. Monthly magazine-size publication on newsprint covering antiques, collectibles and nostalgic memorabilia. Circ. 13,000. Byline given. Pays on publication. Publishes ms an average of 1 year after acceptance. Buys first rights and makes work-for-hire assignments. Submit seasonal material 3 months in advance. Accepts queries by mail, e-mail, fax, phone. Reports in 2 weeks on queries; 6 weeks on mss. Sample copy for $4 and 9×12 SAE. Writer's guidelines free.
**O—** Break in with articles on internet/computers and collecting; celebrity collectors; collectors with unique and/or extensive collections; music collectibles; transportation collectibles; advertising collectibles; bottles; glass, china and silver; primitives; furniture; jewelry; lamps; western; textiles; toys; black memorabilia; political collectibles; movie memorabilia and any 20th century and timely subjects.
**Nonfiction:** General interest (any subject re: collectibles, antique to modern); historical/nostalgic (relating to collections or collectors); how-to (display your collection, care for, restore, appraise, locate, add to, etc.); interview/profile (covering individual collectors and their hobbies, unique or extensive; celebrity collectors, and limited edition artists); technical (in-depth analysis of a particular antique, collectible or collecting field); and travel (coverage of special interest or regional shows, seminars, conventions—or major antique shows, flea markets; places collectors can visit, tours they can take, museums, etc.). Special issues: 12-month listing of antique and collectible shows, flea markets and conventions, (January includes events January-December; June includes events June-May); international contemporary collectibles expo (September); holidays (October-December). **Buys 70 mss/year.** Query with sample of writing. Length: 800-1,000 words. **Pays $1/column inch.**
**Photos:** "Articles accompanied by photographs are given first consideration." A selection of 2-8 prints is suggested. "Articles are eligible for full-color front page consideration when accompanied by quality color prints, color slides, and/or color transparencies. Only one article is highlighted on the cover per month. Any article providing a color photo selected for front page use receives an additional $25." Reviews color or b&w prints. Payment for photos included in payment for ms. Captions required. Buys first rights.
**Tips:** "Present a professionally written article with quality illustrations—well researched and documented information."

**$ $ CQ VHF, Ham Radio Above 50 MHz**, CQ Communications, Inc., 25 Newbridge Rd., Hicksville NY 11801. (516)681-2922. Fax: (516)681-2926. E-mail: cq-vhf@cq-vhf.com. Website: http://www.cq-vhf.com. **Contact:** Richard Moseson, editor. Managing Editor: Edith Lennon. **90% freelance written.** Monthly magazine covering amateur (ham) radio. "All of our articles must be related to amateur (ham) radio and its usage on frequencies above 50 MHz. Since many of our readers are either new to ham radio or new to specific aspects of the hobby, we require that all technical terminology and on-air abbreviations be explained, either within the main text or in a sidebar. Don't assume prior knowledge of your topic, but assume that the reader is an intelligent person who will understand a well-written and clearly-explained article. Writing style is friendly and informal, but not 'cute.' " Estab. 1996. Circ. 30,000. Pays 1-2 months after publication. Publishes ms an average of 6 months after acceptance. Byline given. Buys first North American serial rights and second serial (reprint) rights. Editorial lead time 3 months. Submit seasonal material 4 months in advance. Reports in 3 weeks on queries; 2 months on mss. Sample copy and writer's guidelines free via e-mail, on website or for #10 SASE.

**Nonfiction:** How-to, interview/profile, new product (reviews), opinion (Op-Ed pays in 1-year subscription only), personal experience, photo feature, technical. "All articles must be related to VHF ham radio. No 'How My 5-Year-Old Got Her Ham License' or any article that is not related to VHF ham radio." **Buys 60-70 mss/year.** Query. Length: 2,000-3,500 words. **Pays $40/page.**

**Reprints:** Accepts previously published submissions, if so noted.

**Photos:** Send photos with submissions. Reviews 3½×5 or 4×6 prints. Offers no additional payment for photos accepted with ms. Captions, identification of subjects required. Buys one-time rights.

**Tips:** "You must be familiar with ham radio and/or ham radio operators. If you are writing about a related topic, you must be able to show how it ties in with ham radio above 50 MHz. If you're not a ham, try to find a ham radio club in your area. Find out what they're up to that might be interesting to write about, and be a reporter—ask if you can tag along; take notes, conduct interviews, take pictures. And don't be afraid to ask the hams to translate 'hamspeak' into English for you. You can't explain what you don't understand. E-mail queries get the quickest reply."

**$ $ CRAFTS MAGAZINE**, 2 News Plaza, Peoria IL 61656. Fax: (309)679-5454. E-mail: crafts@primedrasi.com. **Contact:** Miriam Olson, editor. Magazine published 10 times/year covering crafts and needlecrafts, mostly how-to projects using products found in a craft, needlework or fabric store. Estab. 1977. Circ. 330,000. **Pays on acceptance.** Byline given. Buys all rights. Editorial lead time 5 months. Accepts queries by mail, e-mail, fax. Reports in 1 month on queries. Writer's guidelines for #10 SASE.

**Nonfiction:** All how-to articles. "We also publish a quarterly scrapbooking (memory-album-making) issue called *Snapshot Memories.*" **Buys 400 mss/year.** Query with photo or sketch of how-to project. **Pays $150-400.**

**Tips:** "Project should use readily-available supplies. Project needs to be easily duplicated by reader. Most projects are made for gifts, home decorating accents, wearables and holidays, especially Christmas. Include a photo of the project; second best is a clear, labeled sketch. Must know likes, dislikes and needs of today's crafter and have in-depth knowledge of craft products. *Crafts* is a mix of traditional techniques plus all the latest trends and fads."

**$ $ CRAFTS 'N' THINGS**, Clapper Communications Companies, 2400 Deven, Suite 375, Des Plaines IL 60018-4618. (847)635-5800. Fax: (847)635-6311. E-mail: npiorkowski@clapper.com. Website: http://www.clapper.com. **Contact:** Nona Piorkowski, associate editor. **90% freelance written.** How-to and craft project magazine published 10 times/year. "We publish craft project instructions for beginner to intermediate level hobbyists." Estab. 1975. Circ. 311,000. Publishes ms an average of 4 months after acceptance. Byline given. Buys all rights. Submit seasonal material 6 months in advance. Accepts queries by mail, fax.

**Nonfiction:** How-to craft projects: include time it takes to complete, cost of supplies used, and skill level; new product (for product review column). Send SASE for list of issue themes and writer's guidelines. **Buys 240 mss/year.** Send complete ms with photos, instructions and SASE. **Pays $50-400.** Offers listing exchange as a product source instead of payment in some cases.

**Reprints:** Send photocopy of article and information about when and where the article previously appeared.

The online magazine carries original content not found in the print edition. Contact: Elaine Petersen, online editor.

**Tips:** "Query for guidelines and list of themes and deadlines. How-to articles are the best bet for freelancers. A how-to project will have a good chance for acceptance if it is quick, easy, and has broad appeal; supplies are limited and easy to find; cost is $10 or less; takes less than 5 hours to complete."

**$ $ CROCHET WORLD**, House of White Birches, P.O. Box 776, Henniker NH 03242. Fax: (219)589-8093. E-mail: www.whitebirches.com. Website: http://www.whitebirches.com. **Contact:** Susan Hankins, editor. **100% freelance written.** Bimonthly magazine covering crochet patterns. "*Crochet World* is a pattern magazine devoted to the art of crochet. We also feature a Q&A column, letters (swap shop) column and occasionally non-pattern manuscripts, but it must be devoted to crochet." Estab. 1978. Circ. 75,000. Pays on publication. Byline given. Buys all rights. Editorial lead time 4 months. Submit seasonal material 6 months in advance. Reports in 1 month. Sample copy for $2. Writer's guidelines free.

**Nonfiction:** How-to (crochet). **Buys 0-2 mss/year.** Send complete ms. Length: 500-1,500 words. **Pays $50.**

**Columns/Departments:** Touch of Style (crocheted clothing); It's a Snap! (quick one-night simple patterns); Pattern of the Month, first and second prize each issue. **Buys dozens of patterns/year.** Send complete pattern. **Pays $40-300.**

**Poetry:** Strictly crochet-related. **Buys 0-5 poems/year.** Submit maximum 2 poems. Length: 6-20 lines. **Pays $10-20.**

**Fillers:** Anecdotes, facts, short humor. **Buys 0-10/year.** Length: 25-200 words. **Pays $5-30.**

**Tips:** "Be aware that this is a pattern generated magazine for crochet designs. I prefer the actual item sent along with complete directions/graphs etc., over queries. In some cases a photo submission or good sketch will do. Crocheted designs must be well-made and original and directions must be complete. Write for Designer's Guidelines which detail how to submit designs. Non-crochet items, such as fillers, poetry *must* be crochet-related, not knit, not sewing, etc."

**[N] $ DANCING USA, For the Romance of Ballroom Dance**, DOT Publications Inc., 10600 University Ave. NW, Minneapolis MN 55448-6166. (612)757-4414. Fax: (612)757-6605. E-mail: ballroom@dancingusa.com. Website: http://www.dancingusa.com. **Contact:** Patti Johnson, editor. **60% freelance written.** Bimonthly magazine covering ballroom, swing and Latin dance. "Techniques to broaden your dance styles. Inspiring stories spark romance, enliven relationships. Learn communication on the dance floor. Expert source: videos, CDs, shoes, where to go. Music reviews: big band, swing, Latin. Reminisce: ballrooms, big bands, step history." Estab. 1983. Circ. 20,000. Pays on publication. Publishes ms an average of 6 months after acceptance. Byline given. Buys first North American serial rights. Editorial lead time 3 months. Submit seasonal material 4 months in advance. Accepts queries by mail, e-mail, fax. Reports in 2 months on queries; 3 months on mss. Sample copy for $4.50.

**Nonfiction:** Book excerpts, exposé, historical/nostalgic, how-to (dance), humor, inspirational, interview/profile, new product, opinion, personal experience, photo feature, technical, travel (all related to partner dance and music). **Buys 30-40 mss/year.** Send complete ms. Length: 100-1,500 words. **Pays $25-35 for assigned articles; $10-35 for unsolicited articles.**

**Photos:** Send photos with submission. Reviews 3×5 or other sized prints. Offers no additional payment for photos accepted with ms.

**Fiction:** Adventure, confession, fantasy, historical, humorous, mystery, romance, slice-of-life vignettes (all related to partner dance). **Buys 2-4 mss/year.** Send complete ms. Length: 100-1,200 words. **Pays $10-35.**

**Poetry:** Avant-garde, free verse, haiku, light verse, traditional. **Buys 6 poems/year.** Submit maximum 3 poems. **Pays $10-20.**

**Tips:** The 3 to 9 feature articles per issue from freelancers include: humor, dancer profiles, history of dance or music, teacher/expert guidance, how to promote dance, Latin music and dance, tango music and dance. Regular departments generally submitted by freelancers or developed by staff: Speaking Of (8-10 short pieces on news, trends, facts, issues, people and quotes); Twinkles (4-6 short pieces on how the world revolves around dance; includes poetry, inspirational, history); Ballroom Gallery (focus on 1-2 places to dance that have regular weekly dancing, usually large floor, historical or new); Where to go dancing (different state covered each issue by staff writer); Hotstuff (good reading, viewing, partaking of films, products review).

**$ $ DECORATIVE ARTIST'S WORKBOOK**, F&W Publications, Inc., 1507 Dana Ave., Cincinnati OH 45207-1005. (513)531-2690, ext. 461. Fax: (513)531-2902. E-mail: dawedit@aol.com. **Contact:** Anne Hevener, editor. Estab. 1987. **75% freelance written.** Bimonthly magazine covering decorative painting projects and products of all sorts. Offers "straightforward, personal instruction in the techniques of decorative painting." Circ. 90,000. **Pays on acceptance.** Byline given. Offers 25% kill fee. Buys first North American serial rights. Submit seasonal material 8 months in advance. Reports in 1 month. Sample copy for $4.65 and 9×12 SAE with 5 first-class stamps.

**Nonfiction:** How-to (related to decorative painting projects), new products, techniques, artist profiles. **Buys 30 mss/year.** Query with slides or photos. Length: 1,200-1,800 words. **Pays 15-25¢/word.**

**Photos:** Send photos with submission. Reviews 35mm, 4×5 transparencies and quality photos. Offers no additional payment for photos accepted with ms. Captions required. Buys one-time rights.

**Tips:** "Find a design, surface or technique that is fresh and new to decorative painting. The more you know—and can prove you know—about decorative painting the better your chances. I'm looking for experts in the field who, through their own experience, can artfully describe the techniques involved. How-to articles are most open to freelancers. Be sure to query with photo/slides, and show that you understand the extensive graphic requirements for these pieces and can provide painted progressives—slides or illustrations that show works in progress."

**[▲] $ DOLL WORLD The Magazine for Doll Lovers**, House of White Birches, 306 E. Parr Rd., Berne IN 46711. (219)589-8741. Fax: (219)589-8093. E-mail: doll_world@whitebirches.com. Website: http://www.whitebirches.com. **Contact:** Vicki Steensma, editor. **90% freelance written.** Bimonthly magazine covering doll collecting, restoration. "Interested in informative articles about doll history and costumes, interviews with doll artists and collectors, and how-to articles." Estab. 1978. Circ. 54,000. Pays pre-publication. Byline given. Buys all rights. Submit seasonal material 9 months in advance. Accepts queries by mail, fax. Reports in 2 months. Writer's guidelines for SASE.

**Nonfiction:** How-to, interview/profile. Special issues: Play dolls of the '50s (April 2000; deadline: September 1, 1999); Grandma's attic: Dolls through the generations (June 2000; deadline: November 1, 1999); Fashion dolls forever (August 2000; deadline: December 1, 1999); Fantasy, Fairies and Friends (October 2000; deadline: February 1, 2000); Christmas past making Christmas present (December 2000; deadline: April 1, 2000). **Buys 100 mss/year.** Send complete ms. **Pays $50 and up.**

**Photos:** Send top-quality photos. Captions and identification of subjects required.

**Tips:** "Choose a specific manufacturer and talk about his dolls or a specific doll—modern or antique—and explore its history and styles made. Be descriptive, but do not overuse adjectives. Use personal conversational tone."

**$ $ DOLLHOUSE MINIATURES**, Kalmbach Publishing Co., 21027 Crossroads Circle, Waukesha WI 53187-9951. (414)798-6618. Fax: (414)796-1383. E-mail: jlange@dhminiatures.com. Website: http://www.dhminiatures.com. Editor: Jane D. Lange. **Contact:** Christine Paul, managing editor. **50% freelance written.** Monthly magazine covering dollhouse scale miniatures. "*Dollhouse Miniatures* is aimed at passionate miniatures hobbyists. Our readers take their miniatures seriously and do not regard them as toys. We avoid 'cutesiness' and treat our subject as a serious art form and/or an engaging leisure interest." Estab. 1971. Circ. 47,000. **Pays on acceptance.** Byline given. Buys all rights but will revert rights by agreement. Submit seasonal material 1 year in advance. Reports in 3 weeks on queries; 2 months on mss. Sample copy for $3.95. Writer's guidelines for #10 SASE.

**Nonfiction:** How-to miniature projects in 1″, ½″, ¼″ scales, interview/profile (artisans or collectors), photo feature (dollhouses, collections, museums). No articles on miniature shops or essays. **Buys 120 mss/year.** Query with few sample photos. Length: 1,000-1,500 words for features, how-to's may be longer. **"Payment varies, but averages $150."**

**Photos:** Send photos with submission. Requires 35mm slides and larger, 3×5 prints. "Photos are paid for with manuscript. Seldom buy individual photos." Captions preferred; identification of subjects required. Buys all rights.

**Tips:** "It is essential that writers for *Dollhouse Miniatures* be active miniaturists, or at least very knowledgeable about the hobby. Our readership is intensely interested in miniatures and will discern lack of knowledge or enthusiasm on the part of an author. A writer can best break in to magazine by sending photos of work, credentials and a story outline. Photographs must be sharp and properly exposed to reveal details. Photos showing scale are especially appreciated. For articles about subjects in the Chicago/Milwaukee area, we can usually send our staff photographer."

**N $ DOLLMAKING, Your Resource for Creating & Costuming Modern Porcelain Dolls**, Jones Publishing, N7450 Aanstad Rd., P.O. Box 5000, Iola WI 54945. (715)445-5000. Fax: (715)445-4053. E-mail: dollmaking@doll makingartisan.com. Website: http://www.dollmakingartisan.com. **Contact:** Stacy D. Carlson, editor. **50% freelance written.** Bimonthly magazine covering porcelain dollmaking. "*Dollmaking*'s intent is to entertain and inform porcelain and sculpted modern doll artists and costumers with the newest projects and techniques. It is meant to be a resource for hobby enthusiasts." Estab. 1985. Circ. 15,000. Pays on publication. Byline sometimes given. Buys all rights. Editorial lead time 4 months. Submit seasonal material 4 months in advance. Accepts queries by mail, e-mail, fax, phone. Sample copy online at website. Writer's guidelines free.

**Nonfiction:** Inspirational, interview/profile, personal experience. **Buys 12 mss/year.** Query. Length: 800 words. **Pays $75-150.**

**Photos:** State availability of photos with submission. Reviews 2½×2½ transparencies. Negotiates payment individually. Buys all rights.

**Columns/Departments:** Dressmaker's Forum (dressmaking and sewing tips for dolls), 1,000 words; Sewing Q&A (readers write in with sewing questions), 1,600 words. **Buys 2-3 mss/year.** Query. **Pays $75.**

**Fillers:** Anecdotes. **Buys 6/year.** Length: 500-800 words. **Pays $55-75.**

**Tips:** "The best way to break in is to send a manuscript of something the author has written concerning porcelain dollmaking and costuming. The article may be a personal story, a special technique used when making a doll, a successful doll fundraiser, sewing tips for dolls, or anything that would be of interest to a serious doll artisan. If no manuscript is available, at least send a letter of interest."

**⊠ $ $ $ ELECTRONICS NOW**, Gernsback Publications, Inc., 500 Bi-County Blvd., Farmingdale NY 11735. (516)293-3000. Fax: (516)293-3115. E-mail claron@gernsback.com Website: http://www.gernsback.com. **Contact:** Carl Laron, editor. **75% freelance written.** Monthly magazine on electronics technology and electronics construction, such as communications, computers, test equipment, components, video and audio. Estab. 1929. Circ. 104,000. **Pays on acceptance.** Publishes ms an average of 6 months after acceptance. Byline given. Buys all rights. Submit seasonal material 6 months in advance. Accepts queries by mail, e-mail. Reports in 2 months on queries; 4 months on mss. Sample copy and writer's guidelines free or on website.

**Nonfiction:** How-to (electronic project construction), humor (cartoons), new product. **Buys 150-200 mss/year.** Send complete ms. Length: 1,000-10,000 words. **Pays $200-800 for assigned articles; $100-800 for unsolicited articles.**

**Photos:** Send photos with submission. Offers no additional payment for photos accepted with ms. Captions, model releases and identification of subjects required. Buys all rights.

**N $ $ $ FAMILY TREE MAGAZINE, Discover, Preserve & Celebrate Your Family's History**, F&W Publications, 1507 Dana Ave., Cincinnati OH 45207. (513)531-2690. Fax: (513)531-2902. E-mail: ftmedit@fwpubs. com. Website: http://www.familytreemagazine.com. **Contact:** David A. Fryxell, editorial director. **75% freelance written.** Bimonthly magazine covering family history, heritage and genealogy. "*Family Tree Magazine* is a general-interest consumer magazine that helps readers discover, preserve and celebrate their family's history. We cover genealogy, ethnic heritage, personal history, genealogy Web sites and software, scrapbooking, photography and photo preservation, and other ways that families connect with their past." Estab. 1999. Circ. 250,000. **Pays on acceptance.** Publishes ms an average of 6 months after acceptance. Byline given. Offers 25% kill fee. Buys first rights and electronic rights. Editorial lead time 8 months. Submit seasonal material 8 months in advance. Accepts queries by mail, e-mail. Accepts simultaneous submissions. Reports in 1 month on queries. Sample copy for $5. Writer's guidelines for #10 SASE or online at website.

**Nonfiction:** Book excerpts, historical/nostalgic, how-to (genealogy), new product (photography, computer), technical (genealogy software, photography equipment), travel (with ethnic heritage slant). **Buys 50 mss/year.** Query with published clips. Length: 1,000-3,500 words. **Pays $250-800.** Sometimes pays expenses of writers on assignment.

**Reprints:** Accepts previously published submissions.

**Photos:** State availability of photos with submission. Reviews transparencies and 8×10 prints. Negotiates payment individually. Captions required. Buys one-time rights.

**$ $ FIBERARTS, The Magazine of Textiles**, Altamont Press, 50 College St., Asheville NC 28801. (828)253-0467. Fax: (828)253-7952. E-mail: fiberarts@larkbooks.com. Website: http://www.larkbooks.com/fiberarts. **Contact:**

Ann Batchelder, editor. **100% freelance written.** Eager to work with new writers. Magazine published 5 times/year covering textiles as art and craft (contemporary trends in fiber sculpture, weaving, quilting, surface design, stitchery, papermaking, basketry, felting, wearable art, knitting, fashion, crochet, mixed textile techniques, ethnic dying, fashion, eccentric tidbits, etc.) for textile artists, craftspeople, hobbyists, teachers, museum and gallery staffs, collectors and enthusiasts. Estab. 1975. Circ. 25,250. Pays 30 days after publication. Publishes ms an average of 4 months after acceptance. Byline given. Buys first rights. Editorial guidelines and style sheet available. Sample copy for $5 and 10×12 SAE with 2 first-class stamps. Writer's guidelines for #10 SAE with 2 first-class stamps.

**Nonfiction:** Historical, artist interview/profile, opinion, photo feature, technical, education, trends, exhibition reviews, textile news. Query with brief outline prose synopsis and SASE. Include a few visuals that might accompany the article. No phone queries. "Please be very specific about your proposal. Also an important consideration in accepting an article is the kind of photos—35mm slides and/or b&w glossies—that you can provide as illustration. We like to see photos in advance." Length: 250-2,000 words plus 4-5 photos. **Pays $100-400,** depending on article. Rarely pays the expenses of writers on assignment or for photos.

**Photos:** B&w photos or color slides must accompany every article. The more photos to choose from, the better. Full photo captions are essential. Please include a separate, number-keyed caption sheet. The names and addresses of those mentioned in the article or to whom the visuals are to be returned are necessary.

**Columns/Departments:** Swatches (new ideas for fiber, unusual or offbeat subjects, work spaces, resources and marketing, techniques, materials, equipment, design and trends), 400 words. **Pays $100.** Profile (focuses on one artist), 400 words and one photo. **Pays $100.** Reviews (exhibits and shows; summarize quality, significance, focus and atmosphere, then evaluate selected pieces for aesthetic quality, content and technique—because we have an international readership, brief biographical notes or quotes might be pertinent for locally or regionally known artists), 400 words and 3-5 photos. **Pays $100.** (Do not cite works for which visuals are unavailable; you are not eligible to review a show in which you have participated as an artist, organizer, curator or juror.)

**Tips:** "Our writers are very familiar with the textile field, and this is what we look for in a new writer. Familiarity with textile techniques, history or events determines clarity of an article more than a particular style of writing. The writer should also be familiar with *Fiberarts*, the magazine. While the professional is essential to the editorial depth of *Fiberarts*, and must find timely information in the pages of the magazine, this is not our greatest audience. Our editorial philosophy is that the magazine must provide the non-professional textile enthusiast with the inspiration, support, useful information, and direction to keep him or her excited, interested, and committed. No phone queries."

**$ $FINE TOOL JOURNAL,** Antique & Collectible Tools, Inc., 27 Fickett Rd., Pownal ME 04069. (207)688-4962. Fax: (207)688-4831. E-mail: ceb@finetoolj.com. Website: http://www.finetoolj.com. **Contact:** Clarence Blanchard, editor. **90% freelance written.** "The *Fine Tool Journal* is a quarterly magazine specializing in older or antique hand tools from all traditional trades. Readers are primarily interested in woodworking tools, but some subscribers have interests in such areas as leatherworking, wrenches, kitchen and machinist tools. Readers range from beginners just getting into the hobby to advanced collectors and organizations." Estab. 1970. Circ. 2,500. Pays on publication. Publishes ms an average of 6 months after acceptance. Byline given. Offers $50 kill fee. Buys first and second serial (reprint) rights. Editorial lead time 3-9 months. Submit seasonal material 6 months in advance. Accepts queries by mail, e-mail, fax. Reports in 2 months on queries; 3 months on mss. Sample copy for $5. Guidelines for SASE.

**Nonfiction:** General interest, historical/nostalgic, how-to (make, use, fix and tune tools), interview/profile, personal experience, photo feature, technical. "We're looking for articles about tools from all trades. Interests include collecting, preservation, history, values and price trends, traditional methods and uses, interviews with collectors/users/makers, etc. Most articles published will deal with vintage, pre-1950, hand tools. Also seeking articles on how to use specific tools or how a specific trade was carried out. However, how-to articles must be detailed and not just of general interest. We do on occasion run articles on modern toolmakers who produce traditional hand tools." **Buys 24 mss/year.** Send complete ms. Length: 400-2,000 words. **Pays $50-200.** Sometimes pays expenses of writers on assignment.

**Reprints:** Accepts previously published submissions.

**Photos:** Send photos with submission. Reviews 4×5 prints. Negotiates payment individually. Model releases, identification of subjects required. Buys all rights.

**Columns/Departments:** Stanley Tools (new finds and odd types), 300-400 words; Tips of the Trade (how to use tools), 100-200 words. **Buys 12 mss/year.** Send complete ms. **Pays $30-60.**

**Tips:** "The easiest way to get published in the *Journal* is to have personal experience or know someone who can supply the detailed information. We are seeking articles that go deeper than general interest and that knowledge requires experience and/or research. Short of personal experience find a subject that fits our needs and that interests you. Spend some time learning the ins and outs of the subject and with hard work and a little luck you will earn the right to write about it."

**$ $FINE WOODWORKING,** The Taunton Press, P.O. Box 5506, Newtown CT 06470-5506. (203)426-8171. Fax: (203)270-6751. E-mail: jkolle@taunton.com. Website: http://www.taunton.com. Editor: Tim Schreiner. **Contact:** Jeff Kolle, managing editor. Bimonthly magazine on woodworking in the small shop. "All writers are also skilled woodworkers. It's more important that a contributor be a woodworker than a writer. Our editors (also woodworkers) will fix the words." Estab. 1975. Circ. 270,000. **Pays on acceptance.** Byline given. Kill fee varies; "editorial discretion." Buys first rights and rights to republish in anthologies and use in promo pieces. Submit seasonal material 6 months in advance. Accepts simultaneous submissions. Reports in 2 months. Writer's guidelines free.

    ○━ "We're looking for good articles on almost all aspects of woodworking from the basics of tool use, stock preparation and joinery to specialized techniques and finishing. We're especially keen on articles about shop-built tools, jigs and fixtures or any stage of design, construction, finishing and installation of cabinetry and furniture. Whether the subject involves fundamental methods or advanced techniques, we look for high-quality workmanship, thoughtful designs, safe and proper procedures."

**Nonfiction:** How-to (woodworking). **Buys 120 mss/year.** Query with proposal letter. "No specs—our editors would rather see more than less." **Pays $150/magazine page.** Sometimes pays expenses of writers on assignment.

**Photos:** Send photos with submission. Reviews contact sheets, negatives, transparencies, prints. Captions, model releases, identification of subjects required. Buys one-time rights.

**Columns/Departments:** Notes & Comment (topics of interest to woodworkers); Question & Answer (woodworking Q & A); Methods of Work (shop tips); Tools & Materials (short reviews of new tools). **Buys 400 items/year.** Length varies. **Pays $10-150/published page.**

    The online magazine carries original content not found in the print edition. Contact: Ruth Dobsevage, online editor.

**Tips:** "Send for authors guidelines and follow them. Stories about woodworking reported by non-woodworkers are *not* used. Our magazine is essentially reader-written by woodworkers."

**$ $FINESCALE MODELER**, Kalmbach Publishing Co., 21027 Crossroads Circle, P.O. Box 1612, Waukesha WI 53187. (414)796-8776. Fax: (414)796-1383. E-mail: tthompson@finescale.com. Website: http://www.finescale.com. Editor: Terry Thompson. **80% freelance written.** Eager to work with new/unpublished writers. Magazine published 10 times/year "devoted to how-to-do-it modeling information for scale model builders who build non-operating aircraft, tanks, boats, automobiles, figures, dioramas, and science fiction and fantasy models." Circ. 80,000. **Pays on acceptance.** Publishes ms an average of 14 months after acceptance. Byline given. Buys all rights. Reports in 6 weeks on queries; 3 months on mss. Sample copy for $9 × 12$ SAE with 3 first-class stamps. Writer's guidelines free.

**Nonfiction:** How-to (build scale models); technical (research information for building models). Query or send complete ms. Length: 750-3,000 words. **Pays $55/published page minimum.**

    • *Finescale Modeler* is especially looking for how-to articles for car modelers.

**Photos:** Send color photos with ms. Pays $7.50 minimum for transparencies and $5 minimum for color prints. Captions and identification of subjects required. Buys one-time rights.

**Columns/Departments:** *FSM* Showcase (photos plus description of model); *FSM* Tips and Techniques (model building hints and tips). **Buys 25-50 Tips and Techniques/year.** Query or send complete ms. Length: 100-1,000 words. **Pays $25-50.**

**Tips:** "A freelancer can best break in first through hints and tips, then through feature articles. Most people who write for *FSM* are modelers first, writers second. This is a specialty magazine for a special, quite expert audience. Essentially, 99% of our writers will come from that audience."

**$ $FONS AND PORTER'S SEW MANY QUILTS**, Oxmoor House, 2100 Lakeshore Dr., Birmingham AL 35209. Fax: (205)877-6078. Website: http://www.fonsandporter.com. Editor: Susan Cleveland. Managing Editor: Rhonda Richards. **Contact:** Pat Wilens, features editor. **10% freelance written.** Bimonthly magazine covering quilting. "*Sew Many Quilts* is published for beginning to intermediate quilters. We feature 8-10 projects per issue and one large feature related to quilting." Estab. 1996. Circ. 139,000. **Pays on acceptance.** Publishes ms an average of 8-12 months after acceptance. Byline given. Buys first, second serial (reprint) and all rights. Editorial lead time 8-12 months. Submit seasonal material 1 year in advance. Accepts simultaneous submissions. Reports in 2 weeks on queries; 2 months on mss. Writer's guidelines for #10 SASE.

**Nonfiction:** Historical/nostalgic, how-to quilting, humor, interview/profile, photo feature. "No articles that cannot be supported with visuals." **Buys 12 mss/year.** Send complete ms. Length: 1,000-3,000 words. **Pays $100-300.**

**Photos:** State availability of photos with submission or send photos with submission. Reviews $4 × 5$ transparencies and $4 × 6$ prints. Offers no additional payment for photos accepted with ms. Identification of subjects required. Buys all rights.

**Tips:** "Send us a draft in the mail. We will contact you within two months to let you know if the work is accepted or rejected."

**$ $GENEALOGICAL COMPUTING**, Ancestry Inc., 266 W. Center St., Orem UT 84057. (801)426-3500. Fax: (801)426-3501. E-mail: gceditor@ancestry.com. Website: http://www.ancestry.com. **Contact:** Matthew Helm, editor. **85% freelance written.** Quarterly magazine covering genealogy and computers. Estab. 1980. Circ. 8,000. Pays on publication. Publishes ms an average of 4 months after acceptance. Byline given. Buys all rights. Editorial lead time 4 months. Submit seasonal material 4 months in advance.

**Nonfiction:** How-to, interview/profile, new product, technical. **Buys 40 mss/year.** Query by mail. Length: 1,500-2,500 words. **Pays $40-200.**

**Reprints:** Accepts previously published submissions. Pays 75% of amount paid for an original article.

**$ $GREAT AMERICAN CRAFTS**, Krause Publications, 700 E. State St., Iola WI 54990-0001. (715)445-2214. Fax: (715)445-4087. Website: http://www.krause.com. Editor: Julie Stephani. Managing Editor: Bill Stephani. **Contact:** Sandra Sparks, associate editor. **75% freelance written.** Bimonthly magazine covering general crafts. "*Great American Crafts* contains projects using needlework, knitting, crocheting, sewing, quilting, clay, painting and general projects for beginning and intermediate crafters. Subscribers get book discounts and other special benefits." Estab. 1998. Pays on publication. Publishes ms an average of 6 months after acceptance. Byline given. Buys all rights and occasional second serial (reprint) or makes work-for-hire assignments. Editorial lead time 4 months. Submit seasonal material 6 months in advance. Accepts queries by mail, fax. Writer's guidelines free.

**Nonfiction:** How-to (craft project directions), new product, photo feature. **Buys 300 mss/year for craft projects.** Query. **Pays $50-250.**

**Photos:** Send photos with submission. Offers no additional payment for photos accepted with ms. Model releases and identification of subjects required. Buys all rights.

**Columns/Departments:** Bill Stephani, managing editor. **Pays $50-250.**

**Tips:** "To submit an original design to *Great American Crafts* magazine, please include the following: designer's name, address, daytime phone number, clear photo or detailed sketch, brief paragraph describing the project. If your design is accepted for publication, we will call you to discuss the contract, fee, and deadlines. You will be asked to send us the project and instructions at this time. Instructions must be typed. We prefer to receive them on disk along with a hard copy. Include the following: complete materials list, detailed step-by-step instructions, full-size patterns if needed, illustrations and charts if needed."

**$ $ THE HOME SHOP MACHINIST**, 2779 Aero Park Dr., P.O. Box 1810, Traverse City MI 49685. (616)946-3712. Fax: (616)946-3289. E-mail: jrice@villagepress.com. Website: http://www.villagepress.com. **Contact:** Joe D. Rice, editor. **95% freelance written.** Bimonthly magazine covering machining and metalworking for the hobbyist. Circ. 34,000. Pays on publication. Publishes ms an average of 2 years after acceptance. Byline given. Buys first North American serial rights only. Reports in 2 months. Free sample copy and writer's guidelines for 9 × 12 SASE.

**Nonfiction:** How-to (projects designed to upgrade present shop equipment or hobby model projects that require machining), technical (should pertain to metalworking, machining, drafting, layout, welding or foundry work for the hobbyist). No fiction or "people" features. **Buys 40 mss/year.** Query or send complete ms. Length: open—"whatever it takes to do a thorough job." **Pays $40/published page, plus $9/published photo.**

**Photos:** Send photos with ms. Pays $9-40 for 5 × 7 b&w prints; $70/page for camera-ready art; $40 for b&w cover photo. Captions and identification of subjects required.

**Columns/Departments:** Book Reviews; New Product Reviews; Micro-Machining; Foundry. "Become familiar with our magazine before submitting." Query first. **Buys 25-30 mss/year.** Length: 600-1,500 words. **Pays $40-70/page.**

**Fillers:** Machining tips/shortcuts. No news clippings. **Buys 12-15/year.** Length: 100-300 words. **Pays $30-48.**

**Tips:** "The writer should be experienced in the area of metalworking and machining; should be extremely thorough in explanations of methods, processes—always with an eye to safety; and should provide good quality b&w photos and/ or clear dimensioned drawings to aid in description. Visuals are of increasing importance to our readers. Carefully planned photos, drawings and charts will carry a submission to our magazine much farther along the path to publication."

**$ $ HOT TOYS**, Beckett Publications, 15850 Dallas Pkwy., Dallas TX 75248. (972)991-6657. Fax: (972)387-2248. E-mail: dkale@beckett.com. Website: http://www.beckett.com. **Contact:** Doug Kale, editor. Managing Editor: Mike Payne. **80% freelance written.** Monthly magazine covering toys ranging from action figures to yo-yo's. "We're reaching the consumer of toys, toy enthusiasts, as well as collectors." Estab. 1998. Circ. 120,000. **Pays on acceptance.** Byline given. Buys all rights. Editorial lead time 3 months. Submit seasonal material 3 months in advance. Accepts simultaneous submissions. Sample copy for $4.95, writer's guidelines for #10 SASE.

**Nonfiction:** General interest, historical/nostalgic, how-to, humor, interview/profile, new product, personal experience, photo feature. "We're also looking for authors for book publishing." **Pays $100-250.**

**Photos:** State availability of photos with submission. Reviews contact sheets, negatives, transparencies and prints. Negotiates payment individually. Buys all rights.

**N $ IN THE FLESH**, Art & Ink Enterprises, 5 Marine View Plaza, Suite 207, Hoboken NJ 07030. (201)653-2700. Fax: (201)653-7892. E-mail: inkeditor@hotmail.com. Website: http://www.InTheFlesh.com. Managing editor: Scot Rienecker. **Contact:** Jean-Chris Miller, editorial director. **33% freelance written.** Quarterly magazine covering all aspects of body modification. "Our subjects and audience are extremely diverse. Subjects include tatooing, piercing, branding, corsetry, scarification, implants, as well as historical accounts of these practices." Estab. 1995. Circ. 50,000. Pays on publication. Publishes ms an average of 3 months after acceptance. Byline sometimes given. Buys first rights. Editorial lead time 3 months. Submit seasonal material 4 months in advance. Accepts queries by mail, e-mail, fax. Accepts simultaneous submissions. Sample copy $7. Writer's guidelines for #10 SASE.

**Nonfiction:** Essays, historical/nostalgic, humor, inspirational, interview/profile, new product, opinion, personal experience, photo feature, religious (pertaining to body modification rituals). **Buys 4 mss/year.** Query. Length: 500-4,000 words. **Pays $50-150.**

**Photos:** Send photos with submission. Reviews transparencies, prints. Negotiates payment individually. Model releases, identification of subjects required. Buys one-time rights.

**Fiction:** "We accept all types of fiction pertaining to body modification, as long as it isn't too long." **Buys 4 mss/ year.** Query with published clips. Length: 500-3,000 words. **Pays up to $50.**

**Fillers:** Anecdotes, facts, gags to be illustrated by cartoonist, newsbreaks, short humor. **Buys 20/year.** Length: 500 words maximum. **Pays up to $50.**

**Tips:** "We encourage people to send in a duplicate rather than their only copy of a manuscript. If they'd like materials returned, make sure to enclose SASE with adequate postage."

**N** **JOY OF COLLECTING**, Publications International, 7373 N. Cicero, Lincolnwood IL 60646. Fax: (847)676-3671. Editor: Sarah Hauber. **Contact:** Jeff Mintz, vice president, acquisitions editor. **100% freelance written.** Bimonthly magazine covering contemporary limited edition and open edition collectibles. We cover only "new" collectibles—no secondary market or antiques. Estab. 1997. Circ. 175,000. **Pays on acceptance.** Publishes ms an average of 4 months after acceptance. Byline given. Buys all rights. Editorial lead time 6 months. Submit seasonal material 6 months in advance. Reports in 1 month on queries; 2 months on mss. Sample copy and writer's guidelines for SAE.

**Nonfiction:** How-to, interview/profile, new product, personal experience, photo feature. No antiques, memorabilia or secondary market coverage. **Buys 50 mss/year.** Query with published clips. Length varies per assignment.

**Reprints:** Accepts previously published material.

**Photos:** Send photos with submission. Reviews transparencies and prints. Negotiates payment individually. Captions, model releases and identification of subjects required. Buys one-time rights.

**Tips:** "Our target audience is mostly middle-aged women in a lower to middle income bracket. Prices should only occasionally be mentioned; they should never be the focus of an article. When covering a general theme, skew the coverage toward the more affordable prices. It's not necessary to avoid the more expensive manufacturers entirely, but reserve more space for the lower end of the price range. Our goal is to portray collecting as accessible and fun for everyone. Send a query with clips and a solid cover letter that allows us to evaluate your background. Do not send manuscript."

**$ $ KITPLANES, For designers, builders and pilots of experimental aircraft**, A Primedia Publication, 8745 Arrow Dr., Suite 105, San Diego CA 92123. (619)694-0491. Fax: (619)694-8147. E-mail: dave@kitplanes.com. Website: http://www.kitplanes.com. Managing Editor: Keith Beveridge. **Contact:** Dave Martin, editor. **70% freelance written.** Eager to work with new/unpublished writers. Monthly magazine covering self-construction of private aircraft for pilots and builders. Estab. 1984. Circ. 83,000. Pays on publication. Publishes ms an average of 3 months after acceptance. Byline given. Buys exclusive complete serial rights. Submit seasonal material 6 months in advance. Accepts queries by mail, e-mail. Reports in 2 weeks on queries; 6 weeks on mss. Sample copy for $5. Writer's guidelines free.

**Nonfiction:** How-to, interview/profile, new product, personal experience, photo feature, technical, general interest. "We are looking for articles on specific construction techniques, the use of tools, both hand and power, in aircraft building, the relative merits of various materials, conversions of engines from automobiles for aviation use, installation of instruments and electronics." No general-interest aviation articles, or "My First Solo" type of articles. **Buys 80 mss/year.** Query. Length: 500-3,000 words. **Pays $70-600,** including story photos.

**Photos:** State availability of or send photos with query or ms. Pays $300 for cover photos. Captions and identification of subjects required. Buys one-time rights.

**Tips:** "*Kitplanes* contains very specific information—a writer must be extremely knowledgeable in the field. Major features are entrusted only to known writers. I cannot emphasize enough that articles must be directed at the individual aircraft builder. We need more 'how-to' photo features in all areas of homebuilt aircraft."

**N $ KNITTING DIGEST**, House of White Birches, 306 E. Parr Rd., Berne IN 46711. (219)589-4000. Fax: (219)589-8093. E-mail: knitting_digest@whitebirches.com. Website: http://www.whitebirches.com. **Contact:** Jeanne Stauffer, editor. **100% freelance written.** Bimonthly magazine covering knitting designs and patterns. "We print only occasional articles, but are always open to knitting designs and proposals." Estab. 1993. Circ. 50,000. Pays within 2 months. Publishes ms 6 months after acceptance. Byline given. Offers 100% kill fee. Buys all rights. Accepts queries by mail, e-mail. Accepts simultaneous submissions. Reports in 2 months on queries; 6 months on mss. Guidelines for SASE.

**Nonfiction:** How-to (knitting skills); technical (knitting field). **Buys 4-6 mss/year.** Send complete ms. Length: 500 words maximum. Pay varies. Also pays in contributor copies.

**Tips:** "Clear concise writing. Humor is appreciated in this field, as much as technical tips. The magazine is a digest, so space is limited. All submissions must be typed and double-spaced."

**$ $ KNIVES ILLUSTRATED, The Premier Cutlery Magazine**, 265 S. Anita Dr., Suite 120, Orange CA 92868-3310. (714)939-9991, ext. 201. Fax: (714)939-9909. E-mail: budlang@pacbell.net. Website: http://www.KnivesIllustrated.com. **Contact:** Bud Lang, editor. **40-50% freelance written.** Bimonthly magazine covering high-quality factory and custom knives. "We publish articles on different types of factory and custom knives, how-to-make knives, technical articles, shop tours, articles on knife makers and artists. Must have knowledge about knives and the people who use and make them. We feature the full range of custom and high tech production knives, from miniatures to swords, leaving nothing untouched. We're also known for our outstanding how-to articles and technical features on equipment, materials and knife making supplies. We do not feature knife maker profiles as such, although we do spotlight some makers by featuring a variety of their knives and insight into their background and philosophy." Estab. 1987. Circ. 35,000. Pays on publication. Byline given. Editorial lead time 3 months. Accepts queries by mail, e-mail, fax, phone. Reports in 2 weeks on queries. Sample copy available. Writer's guidelines for #10 SASE.

**Nonfiction:** How-to, interview/profile, photo features, technical. **Buys 35-40 mss/year.** Query first. Length: 400-2,000 words. **Pays $100-500 minimum.**

**Photos:** Send photos with submission. Reviews 35mm, 2¼×2¼, 4×5 transparencies, 5×7 prints. Negotiates payment individually. Captions, model releases, identification of subjects required.

**Tips:** "Most of our contributors are involved with knives, either as collectors, makers, engravers, etc. To write about this subject requires knowledge. A 'good' writer can do OK if they study some recent issues. If you are interested in submitting work to *Knives Illustrated* magazine, it is suggested you analyze at least two or three different editions to get a feel for the magazine. It is also recommended that you call or mail in your query to determine if we are interested in the topic you have in mind. While verbal or written approval may be given, all articles are still received on a speculation basis. We cannot approve any article until we have it in hand, whereupon we will make a final decision as to its suitability for our use. Bear in mind we do not suggest you go to the trouble to write an article if there is doubt we can use it promptly."

**LAPIDARY JOURNAL**, 60 Chestnut Ave., Suite 201, Devon PA 19333-1312. (610)293-1112. Fax: (610)293-1717. E-mail: editorialj@aol.com. Website: http://www.lapidaryjournal.com. Editor: Merle White. **Contact:** Hazel Wheaton, managing editor. **70% freelance written.** Monthly magazine covering gem, bead and jewelry arts. "Our audience is hobbyists who usually have some knowledge of and proficiency in the subject before they start reading. Our style is conversational and informative. There are how-to projects and profiles of artists and materials." Estab. 1947. Circ. 53,000. **Pays on acceptance.** Publishes ms an average of 4 months after acceptance. Byline given. Buys one-time and worldwide rights. Editorial lead time 3 months. Accepts queries by mail, e-mail. Sample copy on website.
**Nonfiction:** How-to jewelry/craft, interview/profile, new product, personal experience, technical, travel. Special issues: Bead Annual, Gemstone Annual, Jewelry Design issue. **Buys 100 mss/year.** Query. Sometimes pays some expenses of writers on assignment.
**Reprints:** Send photocopy of article.

**$ $ THE LEATHER CRAFTERS & SADDLERS JOURNAL**, 331 Annette Court, Rhinelander WI 54501-2902. (715)362-5393. Fax: (715)362-5391. Managing Editor: Dorothea Reis. **Contact:** William R. Reis, publisher. **100% freelance written.** Bimonthly magazine. "A leather-working publication with how-to, step-by-step instructional articles using full-size patterns for leathercraft, leather art, custom saddle, boot and harness making, etc. A complete resource for leather, tools, machinery and allied materials plus leather industry news." Estab. 1990. Circ. 9,000. Pays on publication. Publishes ms an average of 2 months after acceptance. Byline given. Buys first North American serial and second serial (reprint) rights. Submit seasonal material 6 months in advance. Accepts queries by mail, fax, phone. Accepts simultaneous submissions. Reports in 1 month. Sample copy for $5. Writer's guidelines for #10 SASE.
  O— Break in with a how-to, step-by-step leather item article from beginner through masters and saddlemaking.
**Nonfiction:** How-to (crafts and arts and any other projects using leather). "I want only articles that include hands-on, step-by-step, how-to information." **Buys 75 mss/year.** Send complete ms. Length: 500-2,500 words. **Pays $20-250 for assigned articles; $20-150 for unsolicited articles.**
**Reprints:** Send tearsheet or photocopy of article. Pays 50% of amount paid for an original article.
**Columns/Departments:** Beginners, Intermediate, Artists, Western Design, Saddlemakers, International Design and Letters (the open exchange of information between all peoples). Length: 500-2,500 words on all. **Buys 75 mss/year.** Send complete ms. **Pays 5¢/word.**
**Photos:** Send good contrast color print photos and full-size patterns and/or full-size photo-carve patterns with submission. Lack of these reduces payment amount. Captions required.
**Fillers:** Anecdotes, facts, gags illustrated by cartoonist, newsbreaks. Length: 25-200 words. **Pays $5-20.**
**Tips:** "We want to work with people who understand and know leathercraft and are interested in passing on their knowledge to others. We would prefer to interview people who have achieved a high level in leathercraft skill."

**$ LINN'S STAMP NEWS**, Amos Press, 911 Vandemark Rd., P.O. Box 29, Sidney OH 45365. (937)498-0801. Fax: (800)340-9501. E-mail: linns@linns.com. Website: http://www.linns.com. Editor: Michael Laurence. **Contact:** Michael Schrieber, managing editor. **50% freelance written.** Weekly tabloid on the stamp collecting hobby. "All articles must be about philatelic collectibles. Our goal at *Linn's* is to create a weekly publication that is indispensable to stamp collectors." Estab. 1928. Circ. 70,000. Pays within one month of publication. Publishes ms an average of 1 month after acceptance. Byline given. Buys first North American serial rights. Submit seasonal material 2 months in advance. Reports in 2 weeks on mss. Free sample copy. Writer's guidelines for #10 SAE with 2 first-class stamps.
**Nonfiction:** General interest, historical/nostalgic, how-to, interview/profile, technical, club and show news, current issues, auction realization and recent discoveries. "No articles merely giving information on background of stamp subject. Must have philatelic information included." **Buys 300 mss/year.** Send complete ms. Length: 500 words maximum. **Pays $20-50.** Rarely pays expenses of writers on assignment.
**Photos:** Good illustrations a must. Send photos with submission. Provide captions on separate sheet of paper. Prefers crisp, sharp focus, high-contrast glossy b&w prints. Offers no additional payment for photos accepted with ms. Captions required. Buys all rights.
**Tips:** "Check and double check all facts. Footnotes and bibliographies are not appropriate to our newspaper style. Work citation into the text. Even though your subject might be specialized, write understandably. Explain terms. *Linn's* features are aimed at a broad audience of relatively novice collectors. Keep this audience in mind. Do not write down to the reader but provide information in such a way to make stamp collecting more interesting to more people. Embrace readers without condescending to them."

**N ✪ $ LOST TREASURE, INC.**, P.O. Box 451589, Grove OK 74345. Fax: (918)786-2192. E-mail: managingeditor@losttreasure.com. Website: http://www.losttreasure.com. **Contact:** Patsy Beyerl, managing editor. **75% freelance written.** Monthly and annual magazines covering lost treasure. Estab. 1966. Circ. 55,000. Pays on publication. Byline given. Buys all rights. Accepts queries by mail, e-mail, fax. Reports in 1 month on queries, 2 months on ms. Writers guidelines for #10 SASE. Sample copy and guidelines for $10 \times 13$ SAE with $1.47 postage or on website. Editorial calendar for *Lost Treasure* for SASE.

**Nonfiction:** *Lost Treasure*, a monthly, is composed of lost treasure stories, legends, folklore, how-to articles, treasure hunting club news, who's who in treasure hunting, tips. Length: 500-1,500 words. *Treasure Cache*, an annual, contains stories about documented treasure caches with a sidebar from the author telling the reader how to search for the cache highlighted in the story. **Buys 225 mss/year.** Length: 1,000-2,000 words. Query on *Treasure Cache* only. Fax OK. **Pays 4¢/word.**

**Photos:** Black & white or color prints, hand-drawn or copied maps, art with source credit with mss will help sell your story. Pays $5/published photo. We are always looking for cover photos with or without accompanying ms. Pays $100/published photo. Must be 35mm color slides, vertical. Captions required.

**Tips:** "We are only interested in treasures that can be found with metal detectors. Queries welcome but not required. If you write about famous treasures and lost mines, be sure we haven't used your selected topic recently and story must have a new slant or new information. Source documentation required. How-tos should cover some aspect of treasure hunting and how-to steps should be clearly defined. If you have a *Treasure Cache* story we will, if necessary, help the author with the sidebar telling how to search for the cache in the story. *Lost Treasure* articles should coordinate with theme issues when possible."

**[N] $ $ MEMORY MAKERS**, The First Source for Scrapbooking Ideas, Satellite Press, 465 W. 115th Ave., #6, Denver CO 80234. (303)452-1968. Fax: (303)452-3582. E-mail: editorial@memorymakersmagazine.com. Editor: Michele Gerbrandt. **Contact:** Deborah Mock, managing editor. **25% freelance written.** Bimonthly magazine covering scrapbooking, hobbies and crafts. "*Memory Makers* is an international magazine that showcases ideas and stories of scrapbookers. It includes articles with information, instructions, and products that apply to men and women who make creative scrapbooks." Estab. 1996. Circ. 170,000. Pays on project completion. Publishes ms 4 months after acceptance. Byline given. Buys all rights. Editorial lead time 6 months after acceptance. Submit seasonal material 6 months in advance. Accepts queries by mail, e-mail, fax. Accepts simultaneous submissions. Reports in 1 month on queries. Guidelines for #10 SASE.

**Nonfiction:** Historical/nostalgic, how-to (scrapbooking techniques), inspirational, interview/profile, new product, personal experience, travel (all related to scrapbooking). No "all-encompassing how-to scrapbook" articles. **Buys 6-10 mss/year.** Query with published clips. Length: 1,000-1,500 words. Pays **$100-750.**

**Columns/Departments:** Keeping It Safe (issues surrounding the safe preservation of scrapbooks), Scrapbooking 101 (how-to scrapbooking techniques for beginners), Photojournaling (new and useful ideas for improving scrapbook journaling), Sure Shots (photography and camera usage tips), all 600-800 words. Query with published clips. **Pays $150-300.**

**$ $ MONITORING TIMES**, Grove Enterprises Inc., P.O. Box 98, Brasstown NC 28902-0098. (704)837-9200. Fax: (828)837-2216. E-mail: mteditor@grove-ent.com. Website: http://www.grove-ent.com. **Contact:** Rachel Baughn, managing editor. Publisher: Robert Grove. **20% freelance written.** Monthly magazine for radio hobbyists. Estab. 1982. Circ. 30,000. Pays on publication. Publishes ms an average of 4 months after acceptance. Byline given. Buys first North American serial rights and limited reprint rights. Submit seasonal material 4 months in advance. Reports in 1 month. Sample copy and writer's guidelines for $9 \times 12$ SAE and 9 first-class stamps.

**Nonfiction:** General interest, how-to, humor, interview/profile, personal experience, photo feature, technical. **Buys 72 mss/year.** Query. Length: 1,000-2,500 words. **Pays $50/published page average.**

**Reprints:** Send photocopy of article and information about when and where the article previously appeared. Pays 25% of amount paid for an original article.

**Photos:** Send photos with submission. Captions required. Buys one-time rights.

**Columns/Departments:** "Query managing editor."

**Tips:** "Need articles on radio communications systems and shortwave broadcasters. We are accepting more technical projects."

**[X] PACK-O-FUN, Projects For Kids & Families**, Clapper Communications, 2400 Devon Ave., Des Plaines IL 60018-4618. (847)635-5800. Fax: (847)635-6311. E-mail: 72567.1066@compuserve.com. Website: http://www.clapper.com. Editor: Billie Ciancio. **Contact:** Georgianne Detzner, managing editor. **85% freelance written.** Bimonthly magazine covering crafts and activities for kids and those working with kids. Estab. 1951. Circ. 102,000. Pays 45 days after signed contract. Byline given. Buys all rights. Editorial lead time 8 months. Submit seasonal material 8 months in advance. Accepts simultaneous submissions. Accepts queries by mail, e-mail, fax. Reports in 2 months. Sample copy for $3.50 or on website.

**Nonfiction:** "We request quick and easy, inexpensive crafts and activities. Projects must be original, and complete instructions are required upon acceptance." Pay is negotiable.

**Reprints:** Send tearsheet of article and information about when and where the article previously appeared.

**Photos:** Photos of project may be submitted in place of project at query stage.

**Tips:** "*Pack-O-Fun* is looking for original how-to projects for kids and those working with kids. Write simple instructions for crafts to be done by children ages 5-13 years. We're looking for recyclable ideas for throwaways. We seldom accept fiction unless accompanied by a craft. It would be helpful to check out our magazine before submitting."

**$ POP CULTURE COLLECTING**, Odyssey Publications, Inc., 510-A South Corona Mall, Corona CA 91719. (909)734-9636. Fax: (909)371-7139. E-mail: DBTOGI@aol.com. **Contact:** Ev Phillips, editor. **80% freelance written.** Monthly magazine for people interested in collecting celebrity or pop culture-related memorabilia. "Focus is on movie and TV props, costumes, movie posters, rock 'n' roll memorabilia, animation art, space or sports memorabilia, even vintage comic books, newspapers and magazines. Any collectible item that has a celebrity or pop culture connection and evokes memories. *Pop Culture Collecting* likes to profile people or institutions with interesting and unusual collections and tell why they are meaningful or memorable. Articles stress how to find and collect memorabilia, how to preserve and display it, and determine what it is worth." Estab. 1995. Circ. 15,000. Pays on publication. Publishes ms 3 months after acceptance. Byline given. Offers negotiable kill fee. Buys all rights. Editorial lead time 2 months. Submit seasonal material 3 months in advance. Accepts queries by mail, e-mail, fax, phone. Reports in 2 weeks on queries; 1 month on mss. Sample copy and writer's guidelines free.

**Nonfiction:** Historical/nostalgic, how-to, interview/profile, personal experience, description of celebrity memorabilia collections. "No material not related to celebrity memorabilia, such as antiques. Articles must address subjects that appeal to collectors of celebrity or pop culture memorabilia and answer the following: What are these items? How do I go about collecting them? Where can I find them? How scarce or available are they? How can I tell if they're real? What are they worth?" **Buys 25-35 mss/year.** Query. Length: 1,400-1,600 words. **Pays 5¢/word.** Sometimes pays expenses of writers on assignment.

**Photos:** State availability of photos with submission. Reviews transparencies and prints. Offers $3/photo. Captions and identification of subjects required. Buys one-time rights.

**Columns/Departments:** "We print 8-10 columns a month written by regular contributors." Send query for more information. **Buys 90-100 mss/year. Pays $50 or as determined on a per case basis.**

**Tips:** "Writers ideally should be collectors of celebrity or pop culture memorabilia and know their topics thoroughly. Feature articles must be well-researched and clearly written. Writers should remember that *Pop Culture Collecting* is a celebrity/pop culture/nostalgia magazine. For this reason topics dealing with antiques or other non-related items are not suitable for publication."

**$ POPULAR COMMUNICATIONS**, CQ Communications, Inc., 25 Newbridge Rd., Hicksville NY 11801. (516)681-2922. Fax: (516)681-2926. E-mail: popularcom.@aol.com. Website: http://www.popular-communications.com. **Contact:** Harold Ort, editor. **25% freelance written.** Monthly magazine covering the radio communications hobby. Estab. 1982. Circ. 50,000. Pays on publication. Publishes ms an average of 6 months after acceptance. Buys first North American serial rights. Editorial lead time 3 months. Submit seasonal material 6 months in advance. Accepts queries by mail, e-mail, fax. Reports in 1 month on queries; 2 months on mss. Sample copy free. Writer's guidelines for #10 SASE.

**Nonfiction:** General interest, how-to, new product, photo feature, technical. **Buys 6-10 mss/year.** Query. Length: 1,800-3,000 words. **Pays $35/printed page.**

**Photos:** State availability of photos with submission. Negotiates payment individually. Captions, model releases, identification of subjects required.

**Tips:** "Be a radio enthusiast with a keen interest in ham, shortwave, amateur, scanning or CB radio."

**$ $ POPULAR ELECTRONICS**, Gernsback Publications, Inc., 500 Bi-County Blvd., Farmingdale NY 11735-3931. (516)293-3000. Fax: (516)293-3115. E-mail: peeditor@gernsback.com. Website: http://www.gernsback.com. **Contact:** Konstantinos Karagiannis, managing editor. **80% freelance written.** Monthly magazine covering hobby electronics—"features, projects, ideas related to audio, radio, experimenting, test equipment, computers, antique radio, communications, amateur radio, consumer electronics, state-of-the-art, etc." Circ. 78,000. **Pays on acceptance.** Byline given. Buys all rights. Submit seasonal material 9 months in advance. Accepts queries by mail, e-mail. Reports in 1 month. Free sample copy, "include mailing label." Writer's guidelines for #10 SASE or on website.

**Nonfiction:** General interest, how-to, photo feature, technical. **Buys 200 mss/year.** Query or send complete ms. Length: 1,000-3,500 words. **Pays $150-600.**

**Photos:** Send photos with submission. Wants b&w glossy photos. Offers no additional payment for photos accepted with ms. Captions required. Buys all rights.

**Tips:** "All areas are open to freelancers. Project-type articles and other 'how-to' articles have best success. Devices that inferface with PCs or have practical applications around the home especially appeal to our readers."

**$ $ $ $ POPULAR MECHANICS**, Hearst Corp., 224 W. 57th St., 3rd Floor, New York NY 10019. (212)649-2000. Fax: (212)586-5562. E-mail: popularmechanics@hearst.com. Website: http://www.popularmechanics.com. **Contact:** Joe Oldham, editor-in-chief. Managing Editor: Sarah Deem. **Up to 50% freelance written.** Monthly magazine on automotive, home improvement, science, boating, outdoors, electronics. "We are a men's service magazine that tries to address the diverse interests of today's male, providing him with information to improve the way he lives. We cover stories from do-it-yourself projects to technological advances in aerospace, military, automotive and so on." Estab. 1902. Circ. 1,400,000. **Pays on acceptance.** Publishes ms an average of 6 months after acceptance. Byline given. Offers 25% kill fee. Buys all rights. Submit seasonal material 6 months in advance. Reports in 3 weeks on queries; 1 month on mss. Writer's guidelines for SASE.

**Nonfiction:** General interest, how-to (shop projects, car fix-its), new product, technical. Special issues: Boating Guide (February); Home Improvement Guide (April); Consumer Electronics Guide (May); New Cars Guide (October); Woodworking Guide (November). No historical, editorial or critique pieces. **Buys 2 mss/year.** Query with or without published clips or send complete ms. Length: 500-1,500 words. **Pays $500-1,500 for assigned articles; $300-1,000 for unsolicited articles.** Sometimes pays expenses of writers on assignment.

**Photos:** Usually assigns a photographer. "If you have photos, send with submission." Reviews slides and prints. Offers no additional payment for photos accepted with ms. Captions, model releases and identification of subjects required. Buys all rights.

**Columns/Departments:** New Cars (latest and hottest cars out of Detroit and Europe), Car Care (Maintenance basics, How It Works, Fix-Its and New products: send to Don Chaikin. Electronics, Audio, Home Video, Computers, Photography: send to Toby Grumet. Boating (new equipment, how-tos, fishing tips), Outdoors (gear, vehicles, outdoor adventures): send to Cliff Gromer. Home & Shop Journal: send to Steve Willson. Science (latest developments), Tech Update (breakthroughs) and Aviation (sport aviation, homebuilt aircraft, new commercial aircraft, civil aeronautics): send to Jim Wilson. All columns are about 800 words.

■ The online magazine contains material not found in the print edition. Contact: Bill Rhodes, online editor.

**$ $ POPULAR WOODWORKING**, F&W Publications, 1507 Dana Ave., Cincinnati OH 45207. (513)531-2690, ext 407. Fax: (513)531-7107. E-mail: popwood@fwpubs.com. Editor: Steve Shanesy. **Contact:** Christopher Schwarz, managing editor. **35% freelance written.** "*Popular Woodworking* is a bimonthly magazine that invites woodworkers of all levels into a community of professionals who share their hard-won shop experience through in-depth projects and technique articles, which help the readers hone their existing skills and develop new ones. Related stories increase the readers' understanding and enjoyment of their craft. Any project submitted must be aesthetically pleasing, of sound construction and offer a challenge to readers. On the average, we use four features per issue. Our primary needs are 'how-to' articles on woodworking projects. Our secondary need is for articles that will inspire discussion concerning woodworking. Tone of articles should be conversational and informal, as if the writer is speaking directly to the reader. Our readers are the woodworking hobbyist and small woodshop owner. Writers should have an extensive knowledge of woodworking, or be able to communicate information gained from woodworkers." Estab. 1981. Circ. 284,000. **Pays on acceptance.** Publishes ms an average of 10 months after acceptance. Byline given. Buys first world rights. Submit seasonal material 6 months in advance. Reports in 2 months. Sample copy and writer's guidelines for $4.50 and 9 × 12 SAE with 6 first-class stamps.

**Nonfiction:** How-to (on woodworking projects, with plans); humor (woodworking anecdotes); technical (woodworking techniques). Special issues: Shop issue, Outdoor Projects issue, Tool issue, Holiday Projects issue. **Buys 20 mss/year.** Query with or without published clips or send complete ms. **Pay starts at $150/published page.** "The project must be well designed, well constructed, well built and well finished. Technique pieces must have practical application."

**Reprints:** Send photocopy of article or typed ms with rights for sale noted and information about when and where the article previously appeared. Pays 25% of amount paid for an original article.

**Photos:** Send photos with submission. Reviews color only, slides and transparencies, 3 × 5 glossies acceptable. Offers no additional payment for photos accepted with ms. Photographic quality may affect acceptance. Need sharp close-up color photos of step-by-step construction process. Captions and identification of subjects required.

**Columns/Departments:** Tricks of the Trade (helpful techniques), Out of the Woodwork (thoughts on woodworking as a profession or hobby, can be humorous or serious), 500-1,500 words. **Buys 6 mss/year.** Query.

**Tips:** "Write an 'Out of the Woodwork' column for us and then follow up with photos of your projects. Submissions should include materials list, complete diagrams (blueprints not necessary), and discussion of the step-by-step process. We have become more selective on accepting only practical, attractive projects with quality construction. We are also looking for more original topics for our other articles."

**$ QUILT WORLD**, House of White Birches, 306 E. Parr Rd., Berne IN 46711. (219)589-4000. Fax: (207)794-3290. E-mail: hatch@agate.net. **Contact:** Sandra L. Hatch, editor. **100% freelance written.** Works with a small number of new/unpublished writers each year. Bimonthly magazine covering quilting. "*Quilt World* is a general quilting publication. We accept articles about special quilters, techniques, coverage of unusual quilts at quilt shows, special interest quilts, human interest articles and patterns. We include 5-8 patterns in every issue. Reader is 30-70 years old, midwestern." Circ. 130,000. Pays 45 days after acceptance. Byline given. Buys all, first and one-time rights. Submit seasonal material 10 months in advance. Accepts queries by mail, e-mail. Reports in 3 months. Writer's guidelines for #10 SASE.

**Nonfiction:** How-to, interview/profile (quilters), technical, new product (quilt products), photo feature. **Buys 18-24 mss/year.** Query or send complete ms. Length: open. **Pays $50-100.**

**Reprints:** Send photocopy of article and information about when and where it previously appeared.

**Photos:** Send photos with submission. Reviews transparencies and prints. Offers $15/photo (except covers). Identification of subjects required. Buys all or one-time rights.

**Tips:** "Read several recent issues for style and content."

**N $ $ QUILTER'S NEWSLETTER MAGAZINE**, 741 Corporate Circle, Suite A, Golden CO 80401-5622. (303)278-1010. Fax: (303)277-0370. E-mail: maustin@primediasi.com. Senior Features Editor: Jeannie Spears. **Contact:** Mary Leman Austin, executive director. Magazine published 10 times/year. Estab. 1969. Circ. 200,000. Pays on publication, sometimes on acceptance. Buys first North American serial rights or second rights. Accepts queries by mail, e-mail, fax, phone. Reports in 2 months. Free sample copy.

**Nonfiction:** "We are interested in articles on the subject of quilts and quiltmakers *only*. We are not interested in anything relating to 'Grandma's Scrap Quilts' but could use fresh material." **Buys 25 mss/year.** Submit complete ms. **Pays 10¢/word minimum, usually more.**

**Reprints:** Send tearsheet of article or typed ms with rights for sale noted and information about when and where the article previously appeared.

**Photos:** Additional payment for photos depends on quality.

**Fillers:** Related to quilts and quiltmakers only.

**Tips:** "Be specific, brief, and professional in tone. Study our magazine to learn the kind of thing we like. Send us material which fits into our format but which is different enough to be interesting. Realize that we're the top-selling quilt magazine on the market and that we're aspiring to be even better, then send us the cream off the top of your quilt material."

**⭐ $ $ QUILTING TODAY MAGAZINE**, Chitra Publications, 2 Public Ave., Montrose PA 18801. (570)278-1984. Fax: (570)278-2223. E-mail: chitra@epix.net. Website: http://www.quilttownusa.com. **Contact:** Editorial Team. **80% freelance written.** Bimonthly magazine on quilting, traditional and contemporary. "We seek articles that will cover one or two full pages (800 words each); informative to the general quilting public, present new ideas, interviews, instructional, etc." Estab. 1986. Circ. 70,000. Pays on publication. Publishes ms an average of 6 months after acceptance. Byline given. Buys second serial (reprint) rights. Submit seasonal material 8 months in advance. Reports in 1 month on queries; 2 months on mss. Writer's guidelines for SASE.
  • *Quilting Today Magazine* has a department appearing occasionally—"History Lessons," featuring a particular historical style or period in quiltmaking history.

**Nonfiction:** Book excerpts, essays, how-to (for various quilting techniques), humor, interview/profile, new product, opinion, personal experience, photo feature. "No articles about family history related to a quilt or quilts unless the quilt is a masterpiece of color and design, impeccable workmanship." **Buys 20-30 mss/year.** Query with or without published clips, or send complete ms. Length: 800-1,600 words. **Pays $75/full page of published text.**

**Reprints:** Occasionally accepts previously published submissions. Send photocopy of article or typed ms with rights for sale noted and information about when and where the article previously appeared. Pays $75/published page.

**Photos:** Send photos with submission. Reviews 35mm slides and larger transparencies. Offers $20/photo. Captions, identification of subjects required. Buys all rights unless rented from a museum.

**Columns/Departments:** Quilters Lesson Book (instructional), 800-1,600 words. **Buys 10-12 mss/year.** Send complete ms. **Pays up to $75/column.**

**Tips:** "Query with ideas; send samples of prior work so that we can assess and suggest assignment. Our publications appeal to traditional quilters (generally middle-aged) who use the patterns in each issue. Must have excellent photos."

**$ $ $ RAILMODEL JOURNAL**, Golden Bell Press, 2403 Champa St., Denver CO 80205. **Contact:** Robert Schleicher, editor. **80% freelance written.** "Monthly magazine for advanced model railroaders. 100% photo journalism. We use step-by-step how-to articles with photos of realistic and authentic models." Estab. 1989. Circ. 16,000. Pays on publication. Byline given. Offers 100% kill fee. Buys first and second serial (reprint) rights. Editorial lead time 6 months. Submit seasonal material 6 months in advance. Reports in 4 months on queries; 8 months on mss. Sample copy for $4.50. Writer's guidelines free.

**Nonfiction:** Historical/nostalgic, how-to, photo feature, technical. "No beginner articles or anything that could even be mistaken for a toy train." **Buys 70-100 mss/year.** Query. Length: 200-5,000 words. **Pays $60-800.** Sometimes pays expenses of writers on assignment.

**Photos:** Send photos with submission. Reviews contact sheets, 35mm transparencies and 5×7 prints. Captions, model releases and identification of subjects required. Buys one-time and reprint rights.

**Tips:** "Writers must understand dedicated model railroaders who recreate 100% of their model cars, locomotives, buildings and scenes from specific real-life prototypes. Close-up photos a must."

**$ RENAISSANCE MAGAZINE**, Phantom Press, 13 Appleton Rd., Nantucket MA 02554. Fax: (508)325-5992. E-mail: renzine@compuserve.com. **Contact:** Kim Guarnaccia, managing editor. **90% freelance written.** Quarterly magazine covering the history of the Middle Ages and the Renaissance. "Our readers include historians, reenactors, roleplayers, medievalists and Renaissance Faire enthusiasts." Estab. 1996. Circ. 25,000. Pays on publication. Publishes ms an average of 1 year after acceptance. Byline given. Buys North American serial rights. Editorial lead time 6 months. Submit seasonal material 4 months in advance. Reports in 3 weeks on queries; 2 months on mss. Sample copy for $6. Writer's guidelines for #10 SASE.

**Nonfiction:** Essays, exposé, historical/nostalgic, how-to, interview/profile, new product, opinion, photo feature, religious, travel. No fiction. **Buys 25 mss/year.** Query or send ms with SASE. Length: 1,000-5,000 words. **Pays 5¢/word.** Pays writers with 2 contributor copies or other premiums upon request.

**Reprints:** Accepts previously published submissions.

**Photos:** State availability of photos with submission. Reviews contact sheets, any size negatives, transparencies and prints. Offers no additional payment for photos accepted with ms or negotiates payment individually. Captions, model releases and identification of subjects required. Buys all rights.

**Columns/Departments:** Book reviews, 500 words. Include original or good copy of book cover. **Pays 5¢/word.**

**Tips:** "Send in all articles in the standard manuscript format with photos/slides or illustrations for suggested use. Writers *must* be open to critique and all historical articles should also include a recommended reading list. An SASE must be included to receive a response to any submission."

**$ $ RUG HOOKING MAGAZINE**, Stackpole Magazines, 500 Vaughn St., Harrisburg PA 17110-2220. (717)234-5091. Fax: (717)234-1359. E-mail: rughook@paonline.com. Website: http://www.rughookingonline.com. Editor: Patrice Crowley. **Contact:** Brenda Wilt, assistant editor. **75% freelance written.** Magazine published 5 times/year covering the craft of rug hooking. "This is the only magazine in the world devoted exclusively to rug hooking. Our readers are both novices and experts. They seek how-to pieces, features on fellow artisans and stories on beautiful rugs new and old." Estab. 1989. Circ. 10,000. **Pays on acceptance.** Publishes ms an average of 1 year after acceptance. Byline given. Buys all rights. Editorial lead time 6 months. Submit seasonal material 6 months in advance. Accepts queries by mail, e-mail, fax. Reports in 2 months. Sample copy for $5.

**Nonfiction:** How-to (hook a rug or a specific aspect of hooking), personal experience. **Buys 30 mss/year.** Query with published clips. Length: 825-2,475 words. **Pays $74.25-222.75.** Sometimes pays expenses of writers on assignment.

**Reprints:** Send photocopy of article and information about when and where the article previously appeared.

**Photos:** Send photos with submission. Reviews 2×2 transparencies, 3×5 prints. Negotiates payment individually. Identification of subjects required. Buys all rights.

**☆ $ $ SCALE AUTO ENTHUSIAST**, Kalmbach Publishing Co., 21027 Crossroads Circle, P.O. Box 1612, Waukesha WI 53187-1612. (414)796-8776. Fax: (414)796-1383. E-mail: editor@scaleautomag.com. Website: http://www.kalmbach.com/scaleauto/scaleauto.html. **Contact:** Kirk Bell, senior editor. **70% freelance written.** Bimonthly magazine covering model car building. "We are looking for model builders, collectors and enthusiasts who feel their models and/or modeling techniques and experiences would be of interest and benefit to our readership." Estab. 1979. Circ. 75,000. Pays on publication. Publishes ms an average of 6 months after acceptance. Byline given. Buys all rights. Editorial lead time 4 months. Submit seasonal material 3 months in advance. Accepts queries by mail, e-mail, fax, phone. Reports in 1 month on queries; 3 months on mss. Sample copy and writer's guidelines free or on website.

**Nonfiction:** Book excerpts, historical/nostalgic, how-to (build models, do different techniques), interview/profile, personal experience, photo feature, technical. Query or send complete ms. Length: 750-3,000 words. **Pays $75-100/published page.**

**Photos:** Send photos and negatives with submission. Prefers b&w glossy prints and 35mm color transparencies. When writing how-to articles be sure to take photos *during* project. Negotiates payment individually. Captions, model releases, identification of subjects required. Buys all rights.

**Columns/Departments: Buys 50 mss/year.** Query. **Pays $75-100/published page.**

**Tips:** "First and foremost, our readers like how-to material: how-to paint, how-to scratchbuild, how-to chop a roof, etc. Basically, our readers want to know how to make their own models better. Therefore, any help or advice you can offer is what modelers want to read. Also, the more photos you send, taken from a variety of views, the better choice we have in putting together an outstanding article layout. Send us more photos than you would ever possibly imagine we could use. This permits us to pick and choose the best of the bunch."

**☆ $ $ SEW NEWS, The Fashion Magazine for People Who Sew**, Primedia Special Interest Publications, 741 Corporate Circle, Suite A, Golden CO 80401. (303)278-1010. Fax: (303)277-0370. E-mail: sewnews@aol.com. Website: http://www.sewnews.com. **Contact:** Linda Turner Griepentrog, editor. **90% freelance written.** Works with a small number of new/unpublished writers each year. 12 issues/year covering fashion-sewing. "Our magazine is for the beginning home sewer to the professional dressmaker. It expresses the fun, creativity and excitement of sewing." Estab. 1980. Circ. 261,000. **Pays on acceptance.** Publishes ms an average of 6 months after acceptance. Byline given. Buys all rights. Submit seasonal material 6 months in advance. Accepts queries by mail, e-mail, fax. Reports in 2 months. Sample copy for $4.95. Writer's guidelines for #10 SAE with 2 first-class stamps or on website.

● All stories submitted to *Sew News* must be on disk.

**Nonfiction:** How-to (sewing techniques), interview/profile (interesting personalities in home-sewing field). **Buys 200-240 ms/year.** Query with published clips if available. Length: 500-2,000 words. **Pays $25-500.**

**Photos:** Send photos. Prefers color photographs or slides. Payment included in ms price. Identification of subjects required. Buys all rights.

▣ The online magazine carries original content not found in the print edition and includes writer's guidelines.

**Tips:** "Query first with writing sample and outline of proposed story. Areas most open to freelancers are how-to and sewing techniques; give explicit, step-by-step instructions plus rough art. We're using more home decorating content."

**$ SHUTTLE SPINDLE & DYEPOT**, Handweavers Guild of America, Inc., 3327 Duluth Highway, Two Executive Concourse, Suite 201, Duluth GA 30096. (770)495-7702. Fax: (770)495-7703. E-mail: 73744.202@compuserve.com. Website: http://www.weavespindye.org. Publications Manager: Pat King. **Contact:** Sandra Bowles, editor-in-chief. **60% freelance written.** "Quarterly membership publication of the Handweavers Guild of America, Inc., *Shuttle Spindle & Dyepot* magazine seeks to encourage excellence in contemporary fiber arts and to support the preservation of techniques and traditions in fiber arts. It also provides inspiration for fiber artists of all levels and develops public awareness and appreciation of the fiber arts. *Shuttle Spindle & Dyepot* appeals to a highly educated, creative and very knowledgeable audience of fiber artists and craftsmen—weavers, spinners, dyers and basket makers." Estab. 1969. Circ. 30,000. Pays on publication. Publishes ms 6 months after acceptance. Byline given. Buys first North American serial, reprint and electronic rights. Editorial lead time 8 months. Submit seasonal material 8 months in advance. Accepts queries by mail, e-mail, fax, phone. Sample copy for $7.50 plus shipping. Writer's guidelines on website.

○➡ Articles featuring up-and-coming artists, new techniques, cutting-edge ideas and designs, fascinating children's activities, and comprehensive fiber collections are a few examples of "best bet" topics.

**Nonfiction:** Inspirational, interview/profile, new product, personal experience, photo feature, technical, travel. "No self-promotional and no articles from those without knowledge of area/art/artists." **Buys 40 mss/year.** Query with published clips. Length: 1,000-2,000 words. **Pays $75-150.**

**Photos:** State availability of photos with query. Offers no additional payment for photos accepted with ms. Captions, model releases and identification of subjects required.

**Columns/Departments:** Books and Videos, News and Information, Calendar and Conference, Travel and Workshop, Guildview (all fiber/art related). **Buys 8 mss/year.** Query with published clips. **Pays $50-75.**

**Tips:** "Become knowledgeable about the fiber arts and artists. The writer should provide an article of importance to the weaving, spinning, dyeing and basket making community. Query by telephone (once familiar with publication) by appointment helps editor and writer."

**$ SPORTS COLLECTORS DIGEST**, Krause Publications, 700 E. State St., Iola WI 54990. (715)445-2214. Fax: (715)445-4087. E-mail: kpsports@aol.com. **Contact:** Tom Mortenson, editor. Estab. 1952. **50% freelance written.** Works with a small number of new/unpublished writers each year. Weekly sports memorabilia magazine. "We serve collectors of sports memorabilia—baseball cards, yearbooks, programs, autographs, jerseys, bats, balls, books, magazines, ticket stubs, etc." Circ. 52,000. Pays after publication. Publishes ms an average of 3 months after acceptance. Byline given. Buys first North American serial rights only. Submit seasonal material 3 months in advance. Reports in 5 weeks on queries; 2 months on mss. Free sample copy. Writer's guidelines for #10 SASE.

**Nonfiction:** General interest (new card issues, research on older sets); historical/nostalgic (old stadiums, old collectibles, etc.); how-to (buy cards, sell cards and other collectibles, display collectibles, ways to get autographs, jerseys and other memorabilia); interview/profile (well-known collectors, ball players—but must focus on collectibles); new product (new card sets); personal experience ("what I collect and why"-type stories). No sports stories. "We are not competing with *The Sporting News*, *Sports Illustrated* or your daily paper. Sports collectibles only." **Buys 100-200 mss/year.** Query. Length: 300-3,000 words; prefers 1,000 words. **Pays $50-125.**

**Reprints:** Send tearsheet of article. Pays 100% of amount paid for an original article.

**Photos:** Unusual collectibles. Send photos. Pays $5-15 for b&w prints. Identification of subjects required. Buys all rights.

**Columns/Departments:** "We have all the columnists we need but welcome ideas for new columns." **Buys 100-150 mss/year.** Query. Length: 600-3,000 words. **Pays $90-125.**

**Tips:** "If you are a collector, you know what collectors are interested in. Write about it. No shallow, puff pieces; our readers are too smart for that. Only well-researched articles about sports memorabilia and collecting. Some sports nostalgia pieces are OK. Write only about the areas you know about."

**$ SUNSHINE ARTIST, America's Premier Show & Festival Publication**, Palm House Publishing Inc., 2600 Temple Dr., Winter Park FL 32789. (407)539-1399. Fax: (407)539-1499. E-mail: sunart@sunshineartists.com. Website: http://www.sunshineartist.com. Publisher: David Cook. **Contact:** Amy Detwiler, editor. Monthly magazine covering art shows in the United States. "We are the premier-marketing/reference magazine for artists and crafts professionals who earn their living through art shows nationwide. We list more than 2,000 shows monthly, critique many of them and publish articles on marketing, selling and other issues of concern to professional show circuit artists." Estab. 1972. Circ. 12,000. Pays on publication. Publishes ms an average of 3 months after acceptance. Byline given. Buys first North American serial rights. Reports within 2 months. Sample copy for $5.

**Nonfiction:** "We publish articles of interest to artists and crafts professionals who travel the art show circuit. Current topics include marketing, computers and RV living." No how-to. **Buys 5-10 freelance mss/year.** Query or ms. Length: 1,000-2,000 words. **Pays $50-150 for accepted articles.**

**Reprints:** Send photocopy of article and information about when and where the article previously appeared.

**Photos:** Send photos with submission. Offers no additional payment for photos accepted with ms. Captions, model releases and identification of subjects required.

**★ $ $ TEDDY BEAR REVIEW**, Collector Communications Corp., 170 Fifth Ave., New York NY 10010. (212)989-8700. **Contact:** Stephen L. Cronk, editor. **75% freelance written.** Works with a small number of new/unpublished writers each year. Bimonthly magazine on teddy bears for collectors, enthusiasts and bearmakers. Estab. 1985. Pays 30 days after acceptance. Byline given. Buys first North American serial rights. Submit seasonal material 6 months in advance. Sample copy and writer's guidelines for $2 and 9×12 SAE.

**Nonfiction:** Book excerpts, historical, how-to, interview/profile. No nostalgia on childhood teddy bears. **Buys 30-40 mss/year.** Query with photos and published clips. Length: 900-1,800 words. **Pays $100-350.** Sometimes pays the expenses of writers on assignment "if approved ahead of time."

**Photos:** Send photos with submission. Reviews transparencies and b&w prints. Offers no additional payment for photos accepted with ms. Captions required. Buys one-time rights.

**Tips:** "We are interested in good, professional writers around the country with a strong knowledge of teddy bears. Historical profile of bear companies, profiles of contemporary artists and knowledgeable reports on museum collections are of interest."

**$ $ THREADS**, Taunton Press, 63 S. Main St., P.O. Box 5506, Newtown CT 06470. (203)426-8171. **Contact:** Chris Timmons, editor. Bimonthly magazine covering sewing, garment construction, and related fabric crafts (quilting and embroidery). "We're seeking proposals from hands-on authors who first and foremost have a skill. Being an experienced writer is of secondary consideration." Estab. 1985. Circ. 176,000. Pays $150/page. Byline given. Offers $150 kill fee. Buys one-time rights or reprint rights in article collections. Editorial lead time 4 months minimum. Query for electronic submissions. Reports in 1-2 months. Writer's guidelines free.

**Nonfiction:** "We prefer first-person experience."

**Columns/Departments:** Notes (current events, new products, opinions); Book reviews; Tips; Closures (stories of a humorous nature). Query. **Pays $150/page.**

**Tips:** "Send us a proposal (outline) with photos of your own work (garments, samplers, etc.)."

**$ $ TODAY'S COLLECTOR**, The Nation's Antiques and Collectibles Marketplace, Krause Publications, 700 E. State St., Iola WI 54990. (715)445-2214. Fax: (715)445-4087. E-mail: ellingboes@krause.com. Website: http://www.krause.com. **Contact:** Steve Ellingboe, editor. **50% freelance written.** Monthly magazine covering antiques and collectibles. "*Today's Collector* is for serious collectors of all types of antiques and collectibles." Estab. 1993. Circ. 85,000. Pays on publication. Publishes ms an average of 6 months after acceptance. Byline given. Offers $25-50 kill fee. Buys perpetual but non-exclusive rights. Editorial lead time 2 months. Submit seasonal material 4 months in advance. Accepts simultaneous submissions. Reports in 1 month on mss. Sample copy free.

**Nonfiction:** How-to (antiques and collectibles). No articles that are too general—specific collecting areas only. **Buys 60-75 mss/year.** Send complete ms. Length: 500-3,000 words. **Pays $50-200.**

**Reprints:** Send typed ms with rights for sale noted and information about when and where the article previously appeared. Pays 50% of amount paid for an original article.

**Photos:** Send photos with submission. Reviews transparencies, prints. Offers no additional payment for photos accepted with ms. Captions required. Buys one-time rights.

**Tips:** "I want detailed articles about specific collecting areas—nothing too broad or general. I need lots of information about pricing and values, along with brief history and background."

**[N] [★] $ TOY CARS & VEHICLES**, Krause Publications, 700 E. State St., Iola WI 54990-0001. (715)445-2214. Fax: (715)445-4087. E-mail: korbecks@krause.com. Website: http://www.collectit.net. **Contact:** Sharon Korbeck, editor. **85-90% freelance written.** Monthly tabloid covering collectible toy vehicles/models. "We cover the hobby market for collectors of die-cast models, model kit builders and fans of all types of vehicle toys." Estab. 1998. Circ. 17,000. Pays on publication. Publishes ms an average of 6-12 months after acceptance. Byline given. Buys perpetual, non-exclusive rights. Editorial lead time 2-4 months. Submit seasonal material 6 months in advance. Accepts simultaneous submissions. Reports in 2 weeks on queries; 2 months on mss. Sample copy for $2.99. Writer's guidelines for SASE.

**Nonfiction:** How-to, interview/profile, new product. **Buys 25 mss/year.** Query by mail with published clips. Length: 800-1,500 words. **Pays $30-100.** Sometimes pays expenses of writers on assignment.

**Photos:** Send photos with submission. Reviews negatives, 3×5 transparencies and 3×5 prints. Offers no additional payment for photos accepted with ms. Captions, model releases and identification of subjects required. Buys one-time rights.

**Columns/Departments:** The Checkered Flag (nostalgic essays about favorite toys), 500-800 words; Helpful Hints (tips about model kit buildings, etc.), 25-35 words; model reviews (reviews of new die-cast and model kits), 100-350 words. **Buys 25 mss/year.** Query with published clips. **Pays $30-100.**

**Tips:** "Our magazine is for serious hobbyists looking for info about kit building, model quality, new product info and collectible value."

**$ TOY FARMER**, Toy Farmer Publications, 7496-106 Ave. SE, LaMoune ND 58458-9404. (701)883-5206. Fax: (701)883-5209. President: Claire D. Scheibe. Publisher: Cathy Scheibe. **Contact:** Delanee Fox, editorial assistant. **65% freelance written.** Monthly magazine covering farm toys. Youth involvement is strongly encouraged. Estab. 1978. Circ. 27,000. Pays on publication. Publishes ms an average of 1 month after acceptance. Byline given. Buys first North American serial rights. Editorial lead time 3 months. Submit seasonal material 3 months in advance. Accepts queries by mail, fax. Accepts previously published submissions. Reports in 1 month on queries; 2 months on mss. Sample copy for $4. Writer's guidelines for #10 SASE.

**Nonfiction:** General interest, historical/nostalgic, humor, new product, technical. **Buys 100 mss/year.** Query with published clips. 800-1,500 words. **Pays 10¢/word.** Sometimes pays expenses of writers on assignment.

**Photos:** State availability of photos with submission. Reviews transparencies. No additional payment for photos accepted with ms. Buys one-time rights.

**Columns/Departments: Buys 36 mss/year.** Query with published clips. **Pays 10¢/word.**

**$ $ [★] TOY SHOP**, Krause Publications, 700 E. State St., Iola WI 54990. (715)445-2214. Fax: (715)445-4087. E-mail: korbecks@krause.com. Website: http://www.krause.com. **Contact:** Sharon Korbeck, editor. **85-90% freelance written.** Biweekly tabloid covering toy collecting. "We cover primarily vintage collectible toys from the 1930s-present. Stories focus on historical toy companies, the collectibility of toys and features on prominent collections." Estab. 1988. Circ. 40,000. Pays on publication. Publishes ms an average of 8-30 months after acceptance. Byline given. Buys "perpetual, nonexclusive rights." Editorial lead time 2-4 months. Submit seasonal material 6 months in advance. Accepts queries by mail, e-mail. Accepts simultaneous submissions. Reports in 2 months. Sample copy for $3.98. Writer's guidelines on website.

**Nonfiction:** Historical/nostalgic (toys, toy companies), interview/profile (toy collectors), new product (toys), photo feature (toys), features on old toys. No opinion, broad topics or poorly researched pieces. **Buys 100 mss/year.** Query. Length: 500-1,500 words. **Pays $50-200.** Contributor's copies included with payment. Sometimes pays expenses of writers on assignment.

**Reprints:** Send photocopy of article and information about when and where the article previously appeared.

**Photos:** State availability of or send photos with submission. Reviews negatives, transparencies, 3×5 prints. Negotiates payment individually. Captions, model releases, identification of subjects required. Rights purchased with ms rights.

**Columns/Departments:** Collector Profile (profile of toy collectors), 700-1,000 words; Toy I Loved (essay on favorite toys), 500-750 words. **Buys 25 mss/year.** Query. **Pays $50-150.**

**Tips:** "Articles must be specific. Include historical info, quotes, photos with story. Talk with toy dealers and get to know how big the market is."

**$ $ TOY TRUCKER & CONTRACTOR,** Toy Farmer Limited, 7496 106th Ave. SE, LaMoure ND 58458-9404. (701)883-5206. Fax: (701)883-5209. E-mail: zekesez@aol.com. President: Claire Scheibe. Publisher: Cathy Scheibe.
**Contact:** Delanee Fox, editorial assistant. **75% freelance written.** Monthly consumer magazine covering collectible toys. "We are a magazine on hobby and collectible toy trucks and construction pieces." Estab. 1990. Circ. 6,500. Pays on publication. Publishes ms an average of 3 months after acceptance. Byline given. Buys first North American serial rights. Editorial lead time 3 months. Submit seasonal material 3 months in advance. Reports in 1 month on queries; 2 months on mss. Sample copy for $4. Writer's guidelines free on request.
**Nonfiction:** Historical/nostalgic, interview/profile, new product, technical. **Buys 35 mss/year.** Query. Length: 800-2,400. **Pays 10¢/word. Sometimes pays expenses of writers on assignment.**
**Reprints:** Accepts previously published submissions.
**Photos:** Send photos with submission. Offers no additional payment for photos accepted with ms. Captions, model releases and identification of subjects required.

**✴ $ $ TOYFARE, The Toy Magazine,** Wizard Entertainment Group, 151 Wells Ave., Congers NY 10920. (914)268-2000. Fax: (914)268-0053. E-mail: toyfarettm@aol.com. Website: http://www.toyfare.com. Managing Editor: Joe Yanarella. **Contact:** Matthew Senreich, editor. **70% freelance written.** Monthly magazine covering action figures and collectible toys. Estab. 1997. Pays on publication. Byline given. Offers 50% kill fee. Buys all rights. Editorial lead time 4 months. Submit seasonal material 4 months in advance. Accepts queries by mail, e-mail, fax. Sample copy and writer's guidelines for SAE.
**Nonfiction:** Historical/nostalgic, how-to, humor, interview/profile, new product, personal experience, photo feature, technical. No column or opinion pieces. **Buys 75-100 mss/year.** Query with published clips. Length: 250-4,000 words. **Pays 15¢/word.**
**Photos:** State availability of photos with submission. Negotiates payment individually. Identification of subjects required. Buys all rights.
**Columns/Departments:** Toy Story (profile of past toy line), Sneak Peek (profile of new action figure); both 750-900 words. Query with published clips. **Pays $75-100.**

**$ $ TRADITIONAL QUILTER, The Leading Teaching Magazine for Creative Quilters,** All American Crafts, Inc., 243 Newton-Sparta Rd., Newton NJ 07860. (973)383-8080. Fax: (973)383-8133. E-mail: craftpub@aol.com.
**Contact:** Laurette Koserowski, editor. **45% freelance written.** Bimonthly magazine on quilting. Estab. 1988. Pays on publication. Byline given. Buys first or all rights. Submit seasonal material 6 months in advance. Reports in 2 months. Sample copy for 9×12 SAE with 4 first-class stamps. Writer's guidelines for #10 SASE.
**Nonfiction:** Quilts and quilt patterns with instructions, quilt-related projects, guild news, interview/profile, photo feature—all quilt related. Query with published clips. Length: 350-1,000 words. **Pays 10-12¢/word.**
**Photos:** Send photos with submission. Reviews all size transparencies and prints. Offers $10-15/photo. Captions and identification of subjects required. Buys one-time or all rights.
**Columns/Departments:** Feature Teacher (qualified quilt teachers with teaching involved—with slides); Profile (award-winning and interesting quilters); The Guilded Newsletter (reports on quilting guild activities, shows, workshops, and retreats). Length: 1,000 words maximum. **Pays 10¢/word, $15/photo.**

**$ $ TRADITIONAL QUILTWORKS, The Pattern Magazine for Traditional Quilters,** Chitra Publications, 2 Public Ave., Montrose PA 18801. (570)278-1984. Fax: (570)278-2223. E-mail: chitra@epix.net. Website: http://www.quilttownusa.com. **Contact:** Editorial Team. **50% freelance written.** Bimonthly magazine on quilting. "We seek articles of an instructional nature, profiles of talented teachers, articles on the history of specific areas of quiltmaking (patterns, fiber, regional, etc.)." Estab. 1988. Circ. 70,000. Pays on publication. Publishes ms an average of 6 months after acceptance. Byline given. Buys second serial (reprint) rights. Submit seasonal material 8 months in advance. Reports in 2 months. Writer's guidelines for SASE.
**Nonfiction:** Historical, instructional, quilting education. "No light-hearted entertainment." **Buys 12-18 mss/year.** Query with photos, with or without published clips, or send complete ms. "Publication hinges on photo quality." Length: 1,500 words maximum. **Pays $75/published page of text.**
**Reprints:** Send photcopy of article and information about when and where the article previously appeared. Payment varies depending on amount of material used.
**Photos:** Send photos with submission. Reviews 35mm slides and larger transparencies (color). Offers $20/photo. Captions, model releases and identification of subjects required. Buys all rights.

**Tips:** "Our publications appeal to traditional quilters, generally middle-aged and mostly who use the patterns in the magazine. Publication hinges on good photo quality."

**$ $ VIDEOMAKER, Camcorders, Computers, Tools & Techniques for Creating Video**, York Publishing, P.O. Box 4591, Chico CA 95927. (530)891-8410. Fax: (530)891-8443. E-mail: editor@videomaker.com. Website: http://www.videomaker.com. Editor: Matt York. **Contact:** Chuck Peters, managing editor. **75% freelance written.** Monthly magazine on video production. "Our audience encompasses video camera users ranging from broadcast and cable TV producers to special-event videographers to video hobbyists . . . labeled professional, industrial, 'prosumer' and consumer. Editorial emphasis is on video*making* (production and exposure), *not* reviews of commercial videos. Personal video phenomenon is a young 'movement'; readership is encouraged to participate—get in on the act, join the fun." Estab. 1986. Circ. 90,000. Pays on publication. Publishes ms an average of 6 months after acceptance. Byline given. Buys all rights. Submit seasonal material 6 months in advance. Accepts queries by mail, e-mail. Accepts simultaneous submissions. Reports in 3 months. Sample copy for 9 × 12 SAE with 9 first-class stamps. Writer's guidelines free.
**Nonfiction:** How-to (tools, tips, techniques for better videomaking); interview/profile (notable videomakers); product probe (review of latest and greatest or innovative); personal experience (lessons to benefit other videomakers); technical (state-of-the-art audio/video). Articles with comprehensive coverage of product line or aspect of videomaking preferred. **Buys 70 mss/year.** Query with or without published clips, or send complete ms. Length: open. **Pays 10¢/word.**
**Reprints:** Send tearsheet and information about when and where the article previously appeared. Payment negotiable.
**Photos:** Send photos and/or other artwork with submissions. Reviews contact sheets, transparencies and prints. Captions required. Payment for photos accepted with ms included as package compensation. Buys one-time rights.
**Columns/Departments:** Sound Track (audio information); Getting Started (beginner's column); Quick Focus (brief reviews of current works pertaining to video production); Profitmaker (money-making opportunities); Edit Points (tools and techniques for successful video editions). **Buys 40 mss/year. Pays 10¢/word.**
**Tips:** "Comprehensiveness a must. Article on shooting tips covers *all* angles. Buyer's guide to special-effect generators cites *all* models available. Magazine strives for an 'all-or-none' approach. Most topics covered once (twice tops) per year, so we must be thorough. Manuscript/photo package submissions helpful. *Videomaker* wants videomaking to be fulfilling and fun."

**$ $ VOGUE KNITTING**, Butterick Company, 161 Sixth Ave., New York NY 10013-1205. (212)620-2577. Fax: (212)620-2731. Editor: Trisha Malcolm. Managing Editor: Daryl Brower. **50% freelance written.** Quarterly magazine that covers knitting. "High fashion magazine with projects for knitters of all levels. In-depth features on techniques, knitting around the world, interviews, bios and other articles of interest to well-informed readers." Estab. 1982. Circ. 500,000. Pays on publication. Byline given. Publishes ms an average of 4 months after acceptance. Buys first North American serial rights. Editorial lead time 6 months. Submit seasonal material 3 months in advance. Query by mail or fax. Accepts simultaneous submissions. Reports in 3 months. Writer's guidelines free.
**Nonfiction:** How-to, humor, inspirational, interview/profile, personal experience, photo feature, travel. **Buys 3-6 mss/year.** Query. Length: 300-900 words. **Pays $250 minimum.**
**Photos:** Send photos with submission. Reviews contact sheets, negatives. Offers no additional payment. Captions, model releases and identification of subjects required. Buys all rights.

**$ $ WEEKEND WOODCRAFTS**, EGW Publishing Inc., 1041 Shary Circle, Concord CA 94518. (925)671-9852. Fax: (925)671-0692. E-mail: rjoseph@egw.com. Website: http://www.weekendwoodcrafts.com. **Contact:** Robert Joseph, editor. Bimonthly magazine covering woodworking/crafts. "Projects that can be completed in one weekend." Estab. 1992. Circ. 91,000. **Pays half on acceptance and half on publication.** Publishes ms an average of 3 months after acceptance. Byline given. Buys first rights. Editorial lead time 2 months. Submit seasonal material 2 months in advance. Accepts queries by mail, e-mail. Accepts simultaneous submissions. Reports in 2 months. Sample copy on website and writer's guidelines free.
**Nonfiction:** How-to (tips and tech), woodworking projects. **Buys 10 mss/year.** Send complete ms. Length: 400-1,500 words. **Pays $100-500.**
**Photos:** Send photos with submission. Reviews contact sheets and print (4×6). Offers no additional payment for photos accepted with ms. Buys all rights.
**Tips:** "Build simple and easy weekend projects, build one- to two-hour projects."

**$ $ WOODSHOP NEWS**, Soundings Publications Inc., 35 Pratt St., Essex CT 06426-1185. (860)767-8227. Fax: (860)767-1048. E-mail: woodshopnews@worldnet.att.net. Website: http://www.woodshopnews.com. Editor: Thomas K. Clark. **Contact:** A.J. Hamler, associate editor. **20% freelance written.** Monthly tabloid "covering woodworking for professionals and hobbyists. Solid business news and features about woodworking companies. Feature stories about interesting amateur woodworkers. Some how-to articles." Estab. 1986. Circ. 100,000. Pays on publication. Publishes ms an average of 6 months after acceptance. Byline given. Offers 25% kill fee. Buys first North American serial rights. Submit seasonal material 4 months in advance. Reports in 1 month. Sample copy on website and writer's guidelines free.
   • *Woodshop News* needs writers in major cities in all regions except the Northeast. Also looking for more editorial opinion pieces.
**Nonfiction:** How-to (query first), interview/profile, new product, opinion, personal experience, photo feature. Key word is "newsworthy." No general interest profiles of "folksy" woodworkers. **Buys 12-15 mss/year.** Query with

published clips or submit ms. Length: 100-1,200 words. **Pays $50-400 for assigned articles; $40-250 for unsolicited articles; $40-100 for workshop tips.** Pays expenses of writers on assignment.

**Photos:** Send photos with submission. Reviews contact sheets and prints. Offers $20-35/b&w photo; $250/4-color cover, usually with story. Captions and identification of subjects required. Buys one-time rights.

**Columns/Departments:** Pro Shop (business advice, marketing, employee relations, taxes etc. for the professional written by an established professional in the field), 1,200-1,500 words. **Buys 12 mss/year.** Query. **Pays $200-250.**

**Fillers:** Small filler items, briefs, or news tips that are followed up by staff reporters. **Pays $10.**

**Tips:** "The best way to start is a profile of a business or hobbyist woodworker in your area. Find a unique angle about the person or business and stress this as the theme of your article. Avoid a broad, general-interest theme that would be more appropriate to a daily newspaper. Our readers are woodworkers who want more depth and more specifics than would a general readership. If you are profiling a business, we need standard business information such as gross annual earnings/sales, customer base, product line and prices, marketing strategy, etc. Black and white 35 mm photos are a must. We need more freelance writers from the Mid-Atlantic, Midwest and West Coast."

**$ $ WOODWORK, A Magazine For All Woodworkers**, Ross Periodicals, P.O. Box 1529, Ross CA 94957-1529. (415)382-0580. Fax: (415)382-0587. E-mail: woodwrkmag@aol.com. **Contact:** John Lavine, editor. Publisher: Tom Toldrian. **90% freelance written.** Bimonthly magazine covering woodworking. "We are aiming at a broad audience of woodworkers, from the hobbyist to professional. Articles run the range from the simple to the complex. We cover such subjects as carving, turning, furniture, tools old and new, design, techniques, projects and more. We also feature profiles of woodworkers, with the emphasis being always on communicating woodworking methods, practices, theories and techniques. Suggestions for articles are always welcome." Estab. 1986. Circ. 80,000. Pays on publication. Byline given. Buys first North American serial and second serial (reprint) rights. Sample copy for $5 and 9 × 12 SAE with 6 first-class stamps. Writer's guidelines for #10 SASE.

**Nonfiction:** How-to (simple or complex, making attractive furniture), interview/profile (of established woodworkers that make attractive furniture), photo feature (of interest to woodworkers), technical (tools, techniques). "Do not send a how-to unless you are a woodworker." Query first. Length: 1,500-2,000 words. **Pays $150/published page.**

**Photos:** Send photos with submission. Reviews 35mm slides. Pays higher page rate for photos accepted with ms. Captions and identification of subjects required. Buys one-time rights. Photo guidelines available on request.

**Columns/Departments:** Tips and Techniques column **pays $35-75.** Interview/profiles of established woodworkers. Bring out woodworker's philosophy about the craft, opinions about what is happening currently. Good photos of attractive furniture a must. Section on how-to desirable. Query with published clips. **Pays $150/published page.**

**Tips:** "Our main requirement is that each article must directly concern woodworking. If you are not a woodworker, the interview/profile is your best, really only chance. Good writing is essential as are good photos. The interview must be entertaining, but informative and pertinent to woodworkers' interests. Include sidebar written by the profile subject."

# HOME & GARDEN

The baby boomers' turn inward, or "cocooning," has caused an explosion of publications in this category. Gardening magazines in particular have blossomed, as more people are developing leisure interests at home. Some magazines here concentrate on gardens; others on the how-to of interior design. Still others focus on homes and gardens in specific regions of the country. Be sure to read the publication to determine its focus before submitting a manuscript or query.

**$ $ $ ADDITIONS & DECKS, Woman's Day Special Interest Publications**, Hachette-Filipacchi Magazines, 1633 Broadway, New York NY 10019. Fax: (212)767-5612. Editor: Carolyn Gatto. **Contact:** Julie Sinclair, managing editor. Semiannual magazine covering information and ideas for homeowners about adding space, indoors or out. "This magazine is for anyone who's thinking of or is engaged in the process of adding on to their home, indoors or out. It showcases design ideas and includes planning strategies for increasing living space. Legal and financial issues and tips on working with professionals are included." **Pays on acceptance.** Publishes ms an average of 3 months after acceptance. Byline given. Offers up to 25% kill fee. Buys first worldwide serial or second serial (printing) rights. Editorial lead time 6 months. Submit seasonal material 10 months in advance. Reports in 2 months. Sample copy not available; writer's guidelines for #10 SASE.

**Nonfiction:** How-to (do-it-yourself information, hire and work with professionals), new products, photo feature (homes with dramatic expansions or beautiful decks), technical (info about materials, procedures that a homeowner should know). **Buys 20 mss/year.** Query with published clips. Length: 250-1,000 words. Payment varies based on length, writer, importance. Sometimes pays expenses of writers on assignment.

**Reprints:** Accepts previously published submissions.

**Photos:** Send before & after photos with query. Model releases required. Buys one-time rights.

**Columns/Departments:** Step by Step (how-to instructions for 1 or 2 relevant projects that can be completed in a day or two), 400-800 words; Legal Issues (relevant legal issues: awareness and what to do), 400-800 words; Money Matters (relevant financial issues: awareness and what to do). Up Close and Personal (formatted Q&A with artist or outstanding professional in relevant area), 300 words. **Buys 6 mss/year.** Query with published clips. Payment varies based on length, writer, and level/amount of research required.

**Tips:** "Send a brief, clear query letter with relevant clips, and be patient. Before and after photos are very helpful, as are floor plans. Photo(s) of weekend project ideas are also helpful."

**\$ \$ THE AMERICAN GARDENER, A Publication of the American Horticultural Society**, 7931 E. Boulevard. Dr., Alexandria VA 22308-1300. (703)768-5700. Fax: (703)768-7533. E-mail: editor@ahs.org. Website: http://www.ahs.org. **Contact:** David J. Ellis, editor. Managing Editor: Mary Yee. **90% freelance written.** Bimonthly magazine covering gardening and horticulture. "*The American Gardener* is the official publication of the American Horticultural Society (AHS), a national, nonprofit, membership organization for gardeners, founded in 1922. AHS is dedicated to educating and inspiring people of all ages to become successful, environmentally responsible gardeners by advancing the art and science of horticulture. Readers of *The American Gardener* are avid amateur gardeners; about 22% are professionals. Most prefer not to use synthetic pesticides." Estab. 1922. Circ. 26,000. Pays on publication. Publishes ms an average of 6 months after acceptance. Byline given. Offers 25% kill fee. Buys first North American serial rights; negotiates electronic rights separately. Editorial lead time 14 weeks. Submit seasonal material 1 year in advance. Reports in 3 months on queries if SASE included. Sample copy for \$4. Writer's guidelines for #10 SASE.
**Nonfiction:** Book excerpts, essays, historical, how-to (landscaping, environmental gardening), inspirational, interview/profile, personal experience, technical (explain science of horticulture to lay audience), children and nature, plants and health, city gardening, humor. **Buys 30 mss/year.** Query with published clips. Length: 750-2,000 words. **Pays \$100-500** depending on article's length, complexity, author's horticultural background, and publishing experience. Pays with contributor copies or other premiums when other horticultural organizations contribute articles.
**Reprints:** Send photocopy of article with information about when and where the article previously appeared. Pay varies.
**Photos:** State availability of photos with submission. Reviews transparencies, prints; these must be accompanied by postage-paid return mailer. Pays \$50-200/photo. Identification of subjects required. Buys one-time rights. Sometimes pays expenses of writers on assignment.
**Columns/Departments:** Offshoots (humorous, sentimental or expresses an unusual viewpoint), 1,200 words; Conservationist's Notebook (articles about individuals or organizations attempting to save endangered species or protect natural areas), 750 words; Natural Connections (explains a natural phenomenon—plant and pollinator relationships, plant and fungus relationships, parasites—that may be observed in nature or in the garden), 750 words; Urban Gardener (looks at a successful small space garden—indoor, patio, less than a quarter-acre; a program that successfully brings plants to city streets or public spaces; or a problem of particular concern to city dwellers), 750-1,500 words; Planting the Future (children and youth gardening programs), 750 words; Plants and Your Health (all aspects of gardening and health, from sunburn, poison ivy and strained backs to herbal medicines), 750 words; Regional Happenings (events that directly affect gardeners only in 1 area, but are of interest to others: an expansion of a botanical garden, a serious new garden pest, the launching of a regional flower show, a hot new gardening trend), 250-500 words. **Buys 20 mss/year.** Query with published clips. **Pays \$50-200.**
**Tips:** "We run very few how-to articles. Our readers are advanced, passionate amateur gardeners; about 20 percent are horticultural professionals. Our articles are intended to bring this knowledgeable group new information, ranging from the latest scientific findings that affect plants, to the history of gardening and gardens in America."

**\$ \$ \$ \$ AMERICAN HOMESTYLE & GARDENING MAGAZINE**, Gruner & Jahr USA Publishing, 375 Lexington Ave., New York NY 10017. (212)499-2000. Fax: (212)499-1536. Editor-in-Chief: Douglas Turshen. **Contact:** Leah Rosch. Magazine published 10 times/year. "*American Homestyle & Gardening* is a guide to complete home design. It is edited for homeowners interested in decorating, building and remodeling products. It focuses on a blend of style, substance and service." Estab. 1986. Circ. 1,000,000. **Pays on acceptance.** Byline given. Offers 25% kill fee. Buys first North American serial rights. Writer's guidelines for #10 SASE.
**Nonfiction:** Writers with expertise in design, decorating, building or gardening. "Because stories begin with visual elements, queries without scouting photos rarely lead to assignments." Length: 750-2,000 words. **Pays \$750-2,500.** Pays expenses of writers on assignment.
**Tips:** "Writers must have knowledge of interior design, remodeling or gardening."

**\$ \$ ATLANTA HOMES AND LIFESTYLES**, 1100 Johnson Ferry Rd., Suite 595, Atlanta GA 30342. (404)252-6670. Fax: (404)252-6673. E-mail: obloise@atlantahomsmag.com. Website: http://www.atlantahandl.com. **Contact:** Oma Bloise, editor. **65% freelance written.** Magazine published 10 times/year. "*Atlanta Homes and Lifestyles* is designed for the action-oriented, well-educated reader who enjoys his/her shelter, its design and construction, its environment, and living and entertaining in it." Estab. 1983. Circ. 33,091. Pays on publication. Byline given. Publishes ms an average of 6 months after acceptance. Pays 25% kill fee. Buys all rights. Reports in 3 months. Sample copy for \$3.95.
**Nonfiction:** Historical, interview/profile, new products, well-designed homes, antiques (Q&A), photo features, gardens, local art, remodeling, food, preservation, entertaining. "We do not want articles outside respective market area, not written for magazine format, or that are excessively controversial, investigative or that cannot be appropriately illustrated with attractive photography." **Buys 35 mss/year.** Query with published clips. Length: 500-750 words. **Pays \$350 for features.** Sometimes pays expenses of writers on assignment "if agreed upon in advance of assignment."
**Reprints:** Send tearsheet or photocopy of article and information about where and when it previously appeared. Pays 50% of amount paid for an original article.
**Photos:** Send photos with submission; most photography is assigned. Reviews transparencies. Offers \$40-50/photo. Captions, model releases and identification of subjects required. Buys one-time rights.
**Columns/Departments:** Short Takes (newsy items on home and garden topics); Quick Fix (simple remodeling ideas);

Cheap Chic (stylish decorating that is easy on the wallet); Digging In (outdoor solutions from Atlanta's gardeners); Big Fix (more extensive remodeling projects); Real Estate News; Interior Elements (hot new furnishings on the market); Weekender (long or short weekend getaway subjects). Query with published clips. **Buys 25-30 mss/year.** Length: 350-500 words. **Pays $50-200.**

**[N] [★] $ BACKHOME: Your Hands-On Guide to Sustainable Living**, Wordsworth Communications, Inc., P.O. Box 70, Hendersonville NC 28793. (828)696-3838. Fax: (828)696-0700. E-mail: backhome@ioa.com. Website: http://www.BackHomemagazine.com. **Contact:** Lorna K. Loveless, editor. **80% freelance written.** Bimonthly magazine. *"BackHome* encourages readers to take more control over their lives by doing more for themselves: productive organic gardening; building and repairing their homes; utilizing alternative energy systems; raising crops and livestock; building furniture; toys and games and other projects; creative cooking. *BackHome* promotes respect for family activities, community programs and the environment." Estab. 1990. Circ. 24,000. Pays on publication. Publishes ms 3-12 months after acceptance. Byline given. Offers $25 kill fee at publisher's discretion. Buys first North American serial rights. Editorial lead time 3 months. Submit seasonal material 3-6 months in advance. Accepts queries by mail, e-mail, fax. Reports in 6 weeks on queries; 2 months on mss. Sample copy for $5 or on website. Writer's guidelines for SASE.
**Nonfiction:** How-to (gardening, construction, energy, home business), interview/profile, personal experience, technical, self-sufficiency. **Buys 80 mss/year.** Query. Length: 750-5,000 words. **Pays $25** (approximately)/printed page.
**Reprints:** Send photocopy of article and information about when and where the article previously appeared. **Pays $25/printed page.**
**Photos:** Send photos with submission: 35mm slides and color prints. Offers additional payment for photos published. Identification of subjects required. Buys one-time rights.
**Tips:** "Very specific in relating personal experiences in the areas of gardening, energy, and homebuilding how-to. Third-person approaches to others' experiences are also acceptable but somewhat less desirable. Clear color photo prints, especially those in which people are prominent, help immensely when deciding upon what is accepted."

**$ $ $ BEST IDEAS FOR CHRISTMAS, Woman's Day Special Interest Publications**, Hachette-Filipacchi Magazines, 1633 Broadway, New York NY 10019. Fax: (212)767-5612. E-mail: wdspecials@aol.com. Editor: Carolyn Gatto. **Contact:** Janice Wright, managing editor. Annual magazine covering crafts, holiday, lifestyle. "This magazine offers ideas and how-to information for all the fun aspects of the holidays—cooking, entertaining, decorating the home and making, wrapping and giving gifts." **Pays on acceptance.** Publishes ms an average of 3 months after acceptance. Byline given. Offers up to 25% kill fee. Buys first worldwide serial or second serial (printing) rights. Editorial lead time 6 months. Submit seasonal material 10 months in advance. Reports in 3 months. Sample copy not available; writer's guidelines for #10 SASE.
**Nonfiction:** Historical/nostalgic (where various traditions come from); how-to (crafts); interview/profile (notable people with holiday connections); new product; photo feature (homes decorated for the holidays); designs for ornaments and other Christmas decorations. **Buys 5 mss/year.** Query with published clips. Length: 250-1,000 words. Payment varies based on length, writer, importance. Sometimes pays expenses of writers on assignment.
**Reprints:** Accepts previously published submissions.
**Photos:** Send photos of craft with query. Model releases required. Buys one-time rights.
**Columns/Departments:** Query with published clips. Payment varies based on length, writer, and level/amount of research required.
**Tips:** "Send a brief, clear query letter with relevant clips, and be patient."

**$ $ $ $ BETTER HOMES AND GARDENS**, 1716 Locust St., Des Moines IA 50309-3023. (515)284-3044. Fax: (515)284-3763. Website: http://www.bhglive.com. Editor-in-Chief: Jean LemMon. Editor (Building): Joan McCloskey. Editor (Food & Nutrition): Nancy Byal. Editor (Garden/Outdoor Living): Mark Kane. Editor (Health): Martha Miller. Editor (Education & Parenting): Richard Sowienski. Editor (Money Management, Automotive, Electronics): Lamont Olson. Editor (Features & Travel): Nina Elder. Editor (Interior Design): Sandy Soria. **10-15% freelance written.** *"Better Homes and Gardens* provides home service information for people who have a serious interest in their homes." Estab. 1922. Circ. 7,605,000. **Pays on acceptance.** Buys all rights. "We read all freelance articles, but much prefer to see a letter of query rather than a finished manuscript."
**Nonfiction:** Travel, education, gardening, health, cars, money management, home entertainment. "We do not deal with political subjects or with areas not connected with the home, community, and family." Pays rates "based on estimate of length, quality and importance." No poetry.
● Most stories published by this magazine go through a lengthy process of development involving both editor and writer. Some editors will consider *only* query letters, not unsolicited manuscripts.
**Tips:** Direct queries to the department that best suits your story line.

**$ $ BIRDS & BLOOMS**, Reiman Publications, 5925 Country Lane, Greendale WI 53129. Editor: Tom Curl. **Contact:** Ken Wysocky, managing editor. **15% freelance written.** Bimonthly magazine focusing on the "beauty in your own backyard. *Birds & Blooms* is a sharing magazine that lets backyard enthusiasts chat with each other by exchanging personal experiences. This makes *Birds & Blooms* more like a conversation than a magazine, as readers share tips and tricks on producing beautiful blooms and attracting feathered friends to their backyards." Estab. 1995. Circ. 1,500,000. Pays on publication. Publishes ms an average of 7 months after acceptance. Byline given. Buys all rights. Editorial lead time 2 months. Submit seasonal material 4 months in advance. Accepts simultaneous submissions.

Reports in 1 month on queries; 2 months on mss. Sample copy for $2, 9 × 12 SAE and $1.95 postage. Writer's guidelines for SASE.

**Nonfiction:** Essays, how-to, humor, inspirational, personal experience, photo feature, natural crafting and "plan" items for building backyard accents. No bird rescue or captive bird pieces. **Buys 12-20 mss/year.** Send complete ms. Length: 250-1,000 words. **Pays $100-400.**

**Photos:** Trudi Bellin, photo coordinator. Send photos with submission. Reviews transparencies and prints. Identification of subjects required. Buys one-time rights.

**Columns/Departments:** Backyard Banter (odds, ends and unique things); Bird Tales (backyard bird stories); Local Lookouts (community backyard happenings); all 200 words. **Buys 12-20 mss/year.** Send complete ms. **Pays $50-75.**

**Fillers:** Anecdotes, facts, gags to be illustrated by cartoonist. **Buys 25/year.** Length: 10-250 words. **Pays $10-75.**

**Tips:** "Focus on conversational writing—like you're chatting with a neighbor over your fence. Manuscripts full of tips and ideas that people can use in backyards across the country have the best chance of being used. Photos that illustrate these points also increase chances of being used."

**$ $ $ COASTAL LIVING**, Southern Progress Corp., 2100 Lakeshore Dr., Birmingham AL 35209. (205)877-6000. Fax: (205)877-6990. E-mail: lynn_carter@spc.com. Website: http://www.coastallivingmag.com. **Contact:** Lynn Carter, managing editor. Bimonthly magazine "for those who live or vacation along our nation's coasts. The magazine emphasizes home design and travel, but also covers a wide variety of other lifestyle topics and coastal concerns." Estab. 1997. Circ. 375,000. Reports in 2 months.

**Nonfiction:** The magazine is roughly divided into 5 areas, with regular features, columns and departments for each area. **Currents** offers short, newsy features of 30-75 words on *New Products and Ideas* (fun accessories to upscale furnishings), *Happenings* (interesting events), and *Coastal Curiosities* (facts and statistics about the shore). **Travel** includes Getaways, Nature Travel and Sporting Life. **Homes** places the accent on casual living, with "warm, welcoming houses and rooms designed for living. Sections include *Building and Remodeling*, *Good Decisions* (featuring a particular construction component of building or remodeling, with installation or maintenance techniques), *New Communities* (profiles of environmentally sensitive coastal developments); and *Decorating*. **Food** is divided into *Entertaining* (recipes and tips) and *Seafood Primer* (basics of buying and preparing seafood). The **Lifestyle Service** section is a catch all of subjects to help readers live better and more comfortably: *The Good Life* (profiles of people who have moved to the coast), *Coastal Home* (original plans for the perfect coastal home), *So You Want to Live In...* (profiles of coastal communities), etc. Query with SASE.

**Photos:** State availability of photos with submission.

The online magazine carries original content not found in the print edition. Contact: Susan Haynes, online editor.

**Tips:** "Query us with ideas that are very specifically targeted to the columns that are currently in the magazine."

**$ $ COLORADO HOMES & LIFESTYLES**, Wiesner Publishing, LLC, 7009 S. Potomac St., Englewood CO 80112-4029. (303)662-5204. Fax: (303)397-7619. E-mail: emcgraw@winc.usa.com. Website: http://www.coloradohandl.com. Associate Editor: Jenna Samelson. **Contact:** Evalyn McGraw, editor. **70% freelance written.** "Bimonthly upscale shelter magazine—glossy, 4-color—containing beautiful homes, gardens, travel articles, art and artists, food and wine, architecture, calendar, antiques, etc. All of Colorado is included. Geared toward home-related and lifestyle areas, personality profiles, etc." Estab. 1981. Circ. 35,000. **Pays on acceptance.** Publishes ms an average of 6 months after acceptance. Byline given. Offers 15% kill fee. Buys first North American serial rights. Editorial lead time 3 months. Submit seasonal material 1 year in advance. Accepts queries by mail, e-mail, fax. Sometimes accepts simultaneous submissions. Reports in 1 month. Sample copy and writer's guidelines for SASE.

● The editor reports that *Colorado Homes & Lifestyles* is doing many more lifestyle articles and needs more unusual and interesting worldwide travel stories.

**Nonfiction:** Fine homes and furnishings, regional interior design trends, interesting personalities and lifestyles, gardening and plants—all with a Colorado slant. Book excerpts, general interest, historical/nostalgic, new product, photo feature, travel. No personal essays, religious, humor, technical. Special issues: Mountain Homes and Lifestyles (people, etc.) (January/February); Great Bathrooms (March/April); Home of the Year Contest (July/August); Great Kitchens (September/October). **Buys 40-50 mss/year.** Query with published clips. Length: 1,000-1,500 words. **Pays $125-300 for assigned articles; $125-200 for unsolicited articles.** Sometimes pays the expenses of writers on assignment. Provide sources with phone numbers.

**Columns/Departments:** Gardening (informative); Artisans (profile of Colorado artisans/craftspeople and work); Travel (worldwide, personal experience preferred); Architecture (Colorado), all 1,100-1,300 words. **Buys 60-75 mss/year.** Query with published clips. **Pays $125-200.**

**Reprints:** Send photocopy of article or typed ms with rights for sale noted and information about when and where the article previously appeared. Pays 35-50% of amount paid for an original article.

**Photos:** Send photos with ms. Reviews 35mm, 4 × 5 and 2¼ color transparencies and b&w glossy prints. Identification of subjects required. Title and caption suggestions appreciated. Please include photographic credits.

**Fiction:** Occasionally publishes novel excerpts.

**Tips:** "Send query, lead paragraph, clips (published and unpublished, if possible). Send ideas for story or stories. Include some photos, if applicable. The more interesting and unique the subject the better. A frequent mistake made by writers is failure to provide material with a style and slant appropriate for the magazine, due to poor understanding of the focus of the magazine."

✖ **$ $ $ COTTAGE LIFE**, Quarto Communications, 54 St. Patrick St., Toronto, Ontario M5T 1V1 Canada. (416)599-2000. Fax: (416)599-0708. E-mail: dzimmer@cottagelife.com. Managing Editor: Penny Caldwell. **Contact:** David Zimmer, editor. **80% freelance written.** Bimonthly magazine. "*Cottage Life* is written and designed for the people who own and spend time at waterfront cottages throughout Canada and bordering U.S. states. The magazine has a strong service slant, combining useful "how-to" journalism with coverage of the people, trends, and issues in cottage country. Regular columns are devoted to boating, fishing, watersports, projects, real estate, cooking, nature, personal cottage experience, and environmental, political, and financial issues of concern to cottagers." Estab. 1988. Circ. 70,000. **Pays on acceptance.** Publishes ms an average of 2 months after acceptance. Byline given. Offers 50-100% kill fee. Buys first North American serial rights.

**Nonfiction:** Book excerpts, exposé, historical/nostalgic, how-to, humor, interview/profile, personal experience, photo feature, technical. **Buys 90 mss/year.** Query with published clips and SAE with Canadian postage or IRCs. Length: 1,500-3,500 words. **Pays $100-2,200 for assigned articles; $50-1,000 for unsolicited articles.** Sometimes pays expenses of writers on assignment. Query first.

**Columns/Departments:** On the Waterfront (front department featuring short news, humor, human interest, and service items). Length: 400 words. **Pays $100.** Cooking, Real Estate, Fishing, Nature, Watersports, Personal Experience and Issues. Length: 150-1,200 words. Query with published clips and SAE with Canadian postage or IRCs. **Pays $100-750.**

**Tips:** "If you have not previously written for the magazine, the 'On the Waterfront' section is an excellent place to break in."

**$ $ $ COUNTRY JOURNAL**, Cowles Enthusiast Media, 4 High Ridge Park, Stamford CT 06905. (203) 321-1778. Fax: (203) 322-1966. E-mail: cntryjrnl@cowles.com. **Contact:** Josh Garskof, editor. Bimonthly magazine. "*Country Journal* covers homes, tools, and projects, emphasizing craftsmanship, quality, value and usefuness." Estab. 1974. Circ. 154,344. Pays on publication. Buys all rights. Editorial lead time 6 months. Reports in 3 months.

**Nonfiction:** Features cover gardening, food, health, the natural world, small-scale farming, land conservation, the environment, energy and other issues affecting country life. **Buys 50 mss/year.** Length: 2,500 words. **Pay varies.** Query by mail with published clips, a list of sources and details as to why you are an authority on the subject, as well as your qualifications for writing the piece.

**Reprints:** Send photocopy of article with information about when it previously appeared.

**Photos:** Photographs and/or drawings are critical for the acceptance of any article. Original color transparencies, 35mm or larger—no dupes; also accepts b&w prints 5×7 or larger with white borders; no negatives.

**Columns/Departments:** Sentinel (brief ideas, information and resources for country life. This department is a good way for new writers to break into the magazine), 300-600 words. Housesmith (projects, procedures, tools and other subjects dealing with home and grounds maintenance and improvement), 1,000-1,500 words. Making Do (simple, inexpensive ways of fixing, building and improvising, up to 1,000 words.

**Tips:** "We are looking for short (1,000 words or less), first-person accounts of living in or moving to the country. We look for experts in gardening, home repair, etc. We also look for writers who live in country locales across North America and can write about people, trends and issues that are concerns in their area but have a nationwide relevancy."

**$ $ $ COUNTRY LIVING**, The Hearst Corp., 224 W. 57th St., New York NY 10019. (212)649-3509. **Contact:** Marjorie Gage, senior editor. Monthly magazine covering home design and interior decorating with an emphasis on "country" style. "A lifestyle magazine for readers who appreciate the warmth and traditions associated with American home and family life. Each monthly issue embraces American country decorating and includes features on furniture, antiques, gardening, home building, real estate, cooking, entertaining and travel." Estab. 1978. Circ. 1,816,000.

**Nonfiction:** Most open to freelancers: antiques articles from authorities, personal essay. **Buys 20-30 mss/year.** Pay varies. Send complete ms and SASE.

**Columns/Departments:** Most open to freelancers: Readers Corner. Pay varies. Send complete ms and SASE.

**Tips:** "Know the magazine, know the market and know how to write a good story that will interest *our* readers."

Ⓝ **$ $ COUNTRY SAMPLER**, Country Sampler, Inc., 707 Kautz Rd., St. Charles IL 60174. (630)377-8000. Fax: (630) 377-8194. Website: http://www.sampler.com. Publisher: Margaret B. Kernan. **Contact:** Susan Wagner, features editor. Bimonthly magazine. "*Country Sampler* is a country decorating magazine and a country product catalog." Estab. 1984. Circ. 525,160. Accepts queries by mail, fax.

**Nonfiction:** "Furniture, accessories and decorative accents created by artisans throughout the country are displayed and offered for purchase directly from the maker. Fully decorated room settings show the readers how to use the items in their homes to achieve the warmth and charm of the country look."

**Tips:** "Send photos and story idea for a country style house tour. Story should be regarding decorating tips and techniques."

**$ $ $ DECORATING IDEAS, Woman's Day Special Interest Publications**, Hachette-Filipacchi Magazines, 1633 Broadway, New York NY 10019. Fax: (212)767-5612. Editor: Carolyn Gatto. **Contact:** Julie Sinclair, managing editor. Consumer magazine published 3 times a year covering home decorating. "This magazine aims to inspire and teach readers how to create a beautiful home." **Pays on acceptance.** Publishes ms an average of 3 months after acceptance. Byline given. Offers up to 25% kill fee. Buys first worldwide serial or second serial (printing) rights. Editorial lead time 6 months. Submit seasonal material 10 months in advance. Reports in 2 months. Sample copy not available; writer's guidelines for #10 SASE.

**Nonfiction:** How-to (home decor projects for beginner/intermediate skill levels—sewing, woodworking, painting, etc.), new product, photo feature, technical, collectibles, hard to find services, unique stores. **Buys 30 mss/year.** Query with published clips. Length: 250-1,000 words. Payment varies based on length, writer, importance. Sometimes pays expenses of writers on assignment.

**Reprints:** Accepts previously published submissions.

**Photos:** Send representative photos with query. Model releases required. Buys one-time rights.

**Columns/Departments:** Step by Step (how-to instructions for 1 or 2 relevant projects that can be completed in a day or two), 400-800 words. **Buys 3 mss/year.** Query with published clips. Payment varies based on length, writer, and level/amount of research required.

**Tips:** "Send a brief, clear query letter with relevant clips, and be patient. Before and after photos are very helpful, as are photos of ideas for Step by Step column. In addition to specific ideas and projects (for which how-to information is provided), we look at decorating trends, provide advice on how to get the most design for your money (with and without help from a professional), and highlight noteworthy new products and services."

**N $ $ DESIGN TIMES, The Art of Interiors**, Regis Publishing Co., Inc., 1 Design Center Place, Suite 249, Boston MA 02210. (617)443-0636. Fax: (617)443-0637. E-mail: dtimes@aol.com. Website: http://www.designtimes.net. **Contact:** Norma Mushkat, managing editor. **75% freelance written.** Bimonthly magazine covering high-end residential interior design nationwide. "Show, don't tell. Readers want to look over the shoulders of professional interior designers. Avoid cliché. Love design." Estab. 1988. Circ. 20,000. Pays on publication. Publishes ms an average of 4 months after acceptance. Byline given. Offers 10% kill fee. Buys all rights. Editorial lead time 3 months. Submit seasonal material 6 months in advance. Accepts queries by mail, e-mail, fax. Accepts simultaneous submissions. Reports in 1 month. Sample copy for 10×13 SAE with 10 first-class stamps or on website.

**Nonfiction:** Residential interiors. **Buys 25 mss/year.** Query with published clips. Length: 1,200-3,000 words. Pay varies. Sometimes pays the expenses of writers on assignment.

**Photos:** State availability of photos with submission. Reviews 4×5 transparencies, 9×10 prints. Negotiates payment individually. Caption, model releases, identification of subject required. Buys one-time rights.

**Columns/Departments: Pays $100-150.**

**Tips:** "A home owned by a well-known personality or designer would be a good feature query. Since the magazine is so visual, great photographs are a big help. Also, recognition of the topic in the design industry."

**$ $ EARLY AMERICAN HOMES**, Primedia, 6405 Flank Dr., Harrisburg PA 17112. Fax: (717)657-9552. Website: http://www.thehistorynet.com. **Contact:** Mimi Handler, editor. **20% freelance written.** Bimonthly magazine for "people who are interested in capturing the warmth and beauty of the 1600 to 1840 period and using it in their homes and lives today. They are interested in antiques, traditional crafts, architecture, restoration and collecting." Estab. 1970. Circ. 130,000. **Pays on acceptance.** Publishes ms an average of 1 year after acceptance. Buys worldwide rights. Accepts queries by mail, fax. Reports in 3 months. Sample copy and writer's guidelines for 9×12 SAE with 4 first-class stamps.

• Ranked as one of the best markets for freelance writers in *Writer's Yearbook* magazine's annual "Top 100 Markets," January 1999.

**Nonfiction:** "Social history (the story of the people, not epic heroes and battles), travel to historic sites, antiques and reproductions, restoration, architecture and decorating. We try to entertain as we inform. We're always on the lookout for good pieces on any of our subjects. Would like to see more on how real people did something great to their homes." **Buys 40 mss/year.** Query or submit complete ms. Length: 750-3,000 words. **Pays $100-600.** Pays expenses of writers on assignment.

The online magazine carries original content not included in the print edition. Contact: Jeanmarie Andrews, online editor.

**Tips:** "Our readers are eager for ideas on how to bring early America into their lives. Conceive a new approach to satisfy their related interests in arts, crafts, travel to historic sites, and especially in houses decorated in the early American style. Write to entertain and inform at the same time. Be prepared to help us with sources for illustrations."

**$ $ FINE HOMEBUILDING**, The Taunton Press, 63 S. Main St., P.O. Box 5506, Newtown CT 06470-5506. (800) 283-7252. Fax: (203) 270-6751. E-mail: fh@taunton.com. Website: http://www.taunton.com. **Contact:** Kevin Ireton, editor. "*Fine Homebuilding* is a bimonthly magazine for builders, architects, contractors, owner/builders and others who are seriously involved in building new houses or reviving old ones." Estab. 1981. Circ. 247,712. Pays half on acceptance, half on publication. Publishes ms 1 year after acceptance. Byline given. Offers on acceptance payment as kill fee. Buys first and reprint rights. Reports in 1 month. Writer's guidelines for SASE.

**Nonfiction:** "We're interested in almost all aspects of home building, from laying out foundations to capping cupolas." Query with outline, description, photographs, sketches and SASE. **Pays $150/published page** with "a possible bonus on publication for an unusually good manuscript."

**Photos:** "Take lots of work-in-progress photos. Color print film, ASA 400, from either Kodak or Fuji works best. If you prefer to use slide film, use ASA 100. Keep track of the negatives; we will need them for publication. If you're not sure what to use or how to go about it, feel free to call for advice."

**Columns/Departments:** Tools & Materials, Reviews, Questions & Answers, Tips & Techniques, Cross Section, What's the Difference?, Finishing Touches, Great Moments. Query with outline, description, photographs, sketches and SASE. **Pays $150/published page.**

**Tips:** "Our chief contributors are home builders, architects and other professionals. We're more interested in your point of view and technical expertise than your prose style. Adopt an easy, conversational style and define any obscure terms for non-specialists. We try to visit all our contributors and rarely publish building projects we haven't seen, or authors we haven't met."

**$ $ FLOWER AND GARDEN MAGAZINE**, 4645 Belleview, Kansas City MO 64112. (816)531-5730. Fax: (816)531-3873. E-mail: kcpublishing@earthlink.net. **Contact:** Angela M. Hughes, senior editor. **80% freelance written.** Works with a small number of new/unpublished writers each year. Bimonthly picture magazine. *"Flower & Garden* focuses on ideas that can be applied to the home garden and outdoor environs, primarily how-to, but also historical and background articles are considered if a specific adaptation can be obviously related to home gardening." Estab. 1957. Circ. 300,000. **Pays on acceptance.** Publishes ms an average of 1 year after acceptance. Buys first-time nonexclusive reprint rights. Byline given. Accepts queries by mail, e-mail, fax. Reports in 2 months. Sample copy for $3. Writer's guidelines for #10 SASE.

● The editor tells us good quality photos accompanying articles are more important than ever.

**Nonfiction:** Interested in illustrated articles on how to do certain types of gardening and descriptive articles about individual plants. Flower arranging, landscape design, house plants and patio gardening are other aspects covered. "The approach we stress is practical (how-to-do-it, what-to-do-it-with). We emphasize plain talk, clarity and economy of words. An article should be tailored for a national audience." **Buys 20-30 mss/year.** Query. Length: 500-1,000 words. Rates vary depending on quality and kind of material and author's credentials, **$200-500.**

**Reprints:** Sometimes accepts previously published articles. Send typed ms with rights for sale noted, including information about when and where the article previously appeared.

**Photos:** Color slides and transparencies preferred, 35mm and larger but 35mm slides or prints not suitable for cover. Submit cover photos as 2¼ × 2¼ or larger transparencies. An accurate packing list with appropriately labeled photographs and numbered slides with description sheet (including Latin botanical and common names) must accompany submissions. In plant or flower shots, indicate which end is up on each photo. Photos are paid for on publication, $60-175 inside, $300 for covers.

**Tips:** "The prospective author needs good grounding in gardening practice and literature. Offer well-researched and well-written material appropriate to the experience level of our audience. Photographs help sell the story. Describe special qualifications for writing the particular proposed subject."

**$ $ $ GARDEN DESIGN**, 100 Avenue of the Americas, New York NY 10013. (212)334-1212. Fax: (212)334-1260. E-mail: gardendesign@meigher.com. Editor: Douglas Brenner. **Contact:** Jennifer Matlack, assistant editor. Magazine published 8 times/year devoted to the fine art of garden design. Circ. 325,000. Pays 2 months after acceptance. Byline given. Buys first North American rights. Submit seasonal material 6 months in advance. Sample copy for $5. Writer's guidelines for #10 SASE.

**Nonfiction:** "We look for literate writing on a wide variety of garden-related topics—history, architecture, the environment, furniture, decorating, travel, personalities." Query by mail with outline, published clips and SASE. Length: 200-1,200 words. Sometimes pays expenses of writer or photographer on assignment.

**Photos:** Submit scouting photos when proposing article on a specific garden.

**Tips:** "Our greatest need is for extraordinary private gardens. Scouting locations is a valuable service freelancers can perform, by contacting designers and garden clubs in the area, visiting gardens and taking snapshots for our review. All departments of the magazine are open to freelancers. Familiarize yourself with our departments and pitch stories accordingly. Writing should be as stylish as the gardens we feature."

**$ $ $ GARDENING & OUTDOOR LIVING, Woman's Day Special Interest Publications**, Hachette-Filipacchi Magazines, 1633 Broadway, New York NY 10019. Fax: (212)767-5612. Editor: Carolyn Gatto. **Contact:** Janice Wright, managing editor. Annual magazine covering gardening, home outdoor space (decks, lawn, patios). "This magazine, which appears in the spring, aims to give readers inspiration, practical advice, and how-to's." **Pays on acceptance.** Publishes ms an average of 3 months after acceptance. Byline given. Offers up to 25% kill fee. Buys first worldwide serial or second serial (printing) rights. Editorial lead time 6 months. Submit seasonal material 10 months in advance. Reports in 3 months. Sample copy not available; writer's guidelines for #10 SASE.

**Nonfiction:** How-to, new product (gardens or outdoor home spaces), photo features (beautiful gardens; inviting outdoor home settings), technical (care for), travel (gardens around US). **Buys 50 mss/year.** Query with published clips. Length: 250-1,000 words. Payment varies. Sometimes pays expenses of writers on assignment.

**Reprints:** Accepts previously published submissions.

**Photos:** State availability of or send representative photos with query. Model releases required. Buys one-time rights.

**Columns/Departments:** Step by Step (how-to instructions for 1 or 2 relevant projects that can be completed in a day or two), 400-800 words. **Buys 2 mss/year.** Query with published clips. Payment varies based on length, writer, and level/amount of research required.

**Tips:** "Send a brief, clear query letter with relevant clips, and be patient."

**$ $ THE HERB COMPANION**, Interweave Press, 201 E. Fourth St., Loveland CO 80537-5655. (970)669-7672. Fax: (970)669-6117. E-mail: HerbCompanion@HCPress.com. Website: http://www.Interweave.com. **Contact:** Robyn Griggs Lawrence, editor. **80% freelance written.** Bimonthly magazine about herbs: culture, history, culinary, crafts and some medicinal use for both experienced and novice herb enthusiasts. Circ. 110,000. Pays on publication. Byline given.

Buys first North American serial rights. Editorial lead time 4 months. Query in writing. Reports in 2 months. Sample copy for $4. Guidelines for #10 SASE.

**Nonfiction:** Practical horticultural, original recipes, historical, how-to, herbal crafts, profiles, helpful hints and book reviews. Submit detailed query or ms. Length: 4 pages or 1,000 words. **Pays $175/published page.**

**Photos:** Send photos with submission. Transparencies preferred. Returns photos and artwork.

**Tips:** "New approaches to familiar topics are especially welcome. If you aren't already familiar with the content, style and tone of the magazine, we suggest you read a few issues. Technical accuracy is essential. Please use scientific as well as popular names for plants and cover the subject in depth while avoiding overly academic presentation. Information should be made accessible to the reader, and we find this is best accomplished by writing from direct personal experience where possible and always in an informal style."

**$ HOME DIGEST, The Homeowner's Family Resource Guide**, Home Digest International Inc., 268 Lakeshore Rd. E, Unit 604, Oakville, Ontario L6J 7S4 Canada. (905)844-3361. Fax: (905)849-4618. E-mail: homedigest@canada.c om. **Contact:** William Roebuck, editor. **40% freelance written.** Magazine published 5 times/year covering house, home and life management for families in stand-alone houses in the greater Toronto region. "*Home Digest* has a strong service slant, combining useful how-to journalism with coverage of the trends and issues of home ownership and family life. In essence, our focus is on the concerns of families living in their own homes." Estab. 1995. Circ. 522,000. Pays on publication. Publishes ms an average of 3 months after acceptance. Byline given. Buys first North American serial rights. Editorial lead time 3 months. Submit seasonal material 3 months in advance. Accepts queries by mail, e-mail, fax. Accepts simultaneous submissions. Reports in 1 month. Sample copy for 9×6 SASE and 2 Canadian stamps. Writer's guidelines for #10 SASE.

**Nonfiction:** General interest, how-to (household hints, basic home renovation, decorating), humor (living in Toronto), inspirational. No travel, opinion, puff pieces. **Buys 10 mss/year.** Query. Length: 350-7500 words. **Pays $50-125** (Canadian).

**Reprints:** Accepts previously published submission.

**Photos:** Send photos with submission. Reviews transparencies and prints. Offers $10-20 per photo. Captions, model releases, and identification of subjects required. Buys one-time rights.

**Columns/Departments:** Household Hints (tested tips that work); Healthy Living (significant health/body/fitness news); all 300-350 words. **Buys 10 mss/year.** Query. **Pays $40-75** (Canadian).

**Fillers:** Anecdotes, facts. **Buys 25/year.** Length: 10-30 words. **Pays $2.50-5** (Canadian).

**Tips:** "Base your ideas on practical experiences. We're looking for 'uncommon' advice that works."

**$ $ $ HOME REMODELING, Woman's Day Special Interest Publications**, Hachette-Filipacchi Magazines, 1633 Broadway, New York NY 10019. Fax: (212)767-5612. E-mail: wdspecials@aol.com. Editor: Carolyn Gatto. **Contact:** Julie Sinclair, managing editor. Quarterly magazine covering home improvement, upgrades, repairs. "This guide is for anyone who is thinking about remodeling all or part of their home and features design ideas, new products and materials, along with detailed service information about how to save time, money and energy on large and small projects." **Pays on acceptance.** Publishes ms an average of 3 months after acceptance. Byline given. Offers up to 25% kill fee. Buys first worldwide serial or second serial (printing) rights. Editorial lead time 6 months. Submit seasonal material 10 months in advance. Reports in 2 months. Sample copy not available; writer's guidelines for #10 SASE.

**Nonfiction:** How-to (planning & construction), new product, photo features (dramatic successfully remodeled homes), technical (information about materials procedures that a homeowner should know), healthy home issues. **Buys 60 mss/ year.** Query with published clips. Length: 250-1,000 words. Payment varies based on length, writer, importance. Sometimes pays expenses of writers on assignment.

**Reprints:** Accepts previously published submissions.

**Photos:** Send representative photos with query. Model releases required. Buys one-time rights.

**Columns/Departments:** Step by Step (how-to instructions for one or two relevant projects that can be completed in a day or two), 400-800 words; Legal Issues (relevant legal issues: awareness and what-to-do), 400-800 words; Money Matters (relevant financial issues: awareness and what-to-do); Up Close and Personal (formatted Q&A with outstanding professional in relevant area), 300 words. **Buys 12 mss/year.** Query with published clips. Payment varies based on length, writer, and level/amount of research required.

**Tips:** "Send a brief, clear query letter with relevant clips, and be patient. Before and after photos are very helpful, as are floor plans. Photos for Step by Step department also helpful."

**$ $ HOMES & COTTAGES**, The In-Home Show Ltd., 6557 Mississauga Rd., Suite D, Mississauga, Ontario L5N 1A6 Canada. (905)567-1440. Fax: (905)567-1442. E-mail: jimhc@pathcom.com. Website: http://www.homesandcottage s.com. Editor: Janice Naisby. **Contact:** Jim Adair, editor-in-chief. **50% freelance written.** Magazine published 8 times/ year covering building and renovating; "technically comprehensive articles." Estab. 1987. Circ. 64,000. Pays on publication. Publishes mss average of 2 months after acceptance. Byline given. Offers 10% kill fee. Buys first North American serial rights. Editorial lead time 3 months. Submit seasonal material 3 months in advance. Sample copy for SAE. Writer's guidelines for SASE.

**Nonfiction:** Humor (building and renovation related), new product, technical. **Buys 32 mss/year.** Query. Length: 1,000-2,000 words. **Pays $300-750.** Sometimes pays expenses of writers on assignment.

**Photos:** Send photos with submission. Reviews transparencies and prints. Negotiates payment individually. Captions and identification of subjects required. Buys one-time rights.

**Tips:** "Read our magazine before sending in a query. Remember that you are writing to a Canadian audience."

**$ $ $**HORTICULTURE, American Gardening at Its Best, 98 N. Washington St., Boston MA 02114. (617) 742-5600. Fax: (617) 367-6364. E-mail: tfischer@primediasi.com. Website: http://www.hortmag.com. **Contact:** Thomas Fischer, executive editor. Magazine published 8 times/year. "*Horticulture*, the country's oldest gardening magazine, is designed for active amateur gardeners. Our goal is to offer a blend of text, photographs and illustrations that will both instruct and inspire readers." Circ. 300,000. Byline given. Offers kill fee. Buys one-time or first North American serial rights. Submit seasonal material 10 months in advance. Accepts queries by mail, e-mail, fax. Reports in 3 months. Writer's guidelines for SASE.

   • Ranked as one of the best markets for freelance writers in *Writer's Yearbook* magazine's annual "Top 100 Markets," January 1999.

**Nonfiction:** "We look for an encouraging personal experience, anecdote and opinion. At the same time, a thorough article should to some degree place its subject in the broader context of horticulture." **Buys 15 mss/year.** Query with published clips, subject background material and SASE. Include disk where possible. Length: 1,000-2,000 words. **Pays $600-1,500.** Pays expenses of writers on assignment if previously arranged with editor.

**Columns/Departments:** Query with published clips, subject background material and SASE. Include disk where possible. Length: 100-1,500 words. **Pays $50-750.**

**Tips:** "We believe every article must offer ideas or illustrate principles that our readers might apply on their own gardens. No matter what the subject, we want our readers to become better, more creative gardeners."

**$ $ $**HOUSE BEAUTIFUL, The Hearst Corp., 1700 Broadway, New York NY 10019-5905. (212)903-5100. Fax: (212)586-3439. Website: http://www.housebeautiful.com. Publisher: Cindy Sperling Spengler. Editor: Margaret Kennedy. Monthly magazine covering home design and interior decorating. This magazine did not respond to our request for information. Query with SASE before submitting.

**$ $ $**KITCHENS & BATHS, Woman's Day Special Interest Publications, Hachette-Filipacchi Magazines, 1633 Broadway, New York NY 10019. Fax: (212)767-5612. Editor: Carolyn Gatto. **Contact:** Julie Sinclair, managing editor. Quarterly magazine. **Pays on acceptance.** Publishes ms an average of 3 months after acceptance. Byline given. Offers up to 25% kill fee. Buys first worldwide serial or second serial (printing) rights. Editorial lead time 6 months. Submit seasonal material 10 months in advance. Reports in 2 months. Sample copy not available; writer's guidelines for #10 SASE.

**Nonfiction:** How-to (design tips, problem solving), new product, photo features (homes with beautiful kitchens & baths), technical (information about plumbing, hardware, materials relevant to a consumer). **Buys 50 mss/year.** Query with published clips. Length: 250-1,000 words. Payment varies based on length, writer, importance. Sometimes pays expenses of writers on assignment.

**Reprints:** Accepts previously published submissions.

**Photos:** Send photos with query. Model releases required. Buys one-time rights.

**Columns/Departments:** Step by Step (how-to instructions for one or two relevant projects that can be completed in a day or two), 400-800 words; Legal Issues (relevant legal issues: awareness and what-to-do), 400-800 words; Lessons Learned (personal experiences gained by homeowner while remodeling), 400-800 words; Up Close and Personal (formatted Q&A with relevant, outstanding artist or professional), 300 words; Money Matters (relevant financial issues: awareness and what-to-do). **Buys 12 mss/year.** Query with published clips. Payment varies based on length, writer, and level/amount of research required.

**Tips:** "Send a brief, clear query letter with relevant clips, and be patient. Before and after photos are very helpful, as are floor plans. Whether readers are planning a new home, remodeling or even just redecorating, here they'll find designs and products that are innovative, efficient, and environmentally sound. Advice about trends and storage and safety information, ideas for home kitchen and bathrooms. This magazine showcases hundreds of the newest, brightest, and boldest ideas for these two important rooms in the home."

**N $ $**LOG HOME DESIGN IDEAS, H+S Media, 1620 S. Lawe St., Suite 2, Appleton WI 54915. (920)830-1701. Fax: (920)830-1710. E-mail: editor@athenet.net. Website: http://www.lhdi.com. **Contact:** Teresa Hilgenberg, editor. **Less than 20% freelance written.** Bimonthly magazine covering log homes. "We are a full-color, slick publication devoted to log homes, their design, decoration and the delight log home owners have for their lifestyle. Our readers are couples 30-35 years of age who either own a log home or dream of owning a modern manufactured or handcrafted log home." Estab. 1994. Circ. 200,000. Pays on publication. Publishes ms an average of 6-12 months after acceptance. Byline given. Buys first rights. Editorial lead time 9 months. Submit seasonal material year in advance. Accepts queries by mail, e-mail, fax, phone. Reports in 6 months. Sample copy not available.

**Nonfiction:** Essays, how-to, interview/profile, personal experience, photo feature, technical. Limited historical and nostalgic. **Buys 2-6 mss/year.** Send complete ms. Length: 500-1,200 words. **Pays $100-500.** Sometimes pays expenses of writers on assignment.

**Photos:** Send photos with submission. Reviews contact sheets, negatives, 2½×2½ and 4×5 transparencies—only color. Negotiates payment individually. Captions, model releases, identification of subjects required. Buys one-time rights.

**Columns/Departments:** "We will consider well-written columns on interior decor, how-to/technical, 'folksy' essays.

Show us what you can do, it may become a regular feature." Length: 250-600 words. **Buys 6 mss/year.** Send complete ms. **Pays $50-300.**

**Tips:** "Concentrate on satisfied log home owners and their experiences while planning, building and decorating their homes. We're also looking for new columns with a laid-back, folksy bent that will appeal to log home owners who have discovered the good life. The right columns could become regular features."

**$ $LOG HOME LIVING,** Home Buyer Publications Inc., 4200-T Lafayette Center Dr., Chantilly VA 20151. (703)222-9411. Fax: (703)222-3209. E-mail: jbrewster@homebuyerpubs.com. Website: http://www.loghomeliving.com. **Contact:** Janice Brewster, editor. **50% freelance written.** Monthly magazine for enthusiasts who are dreaming of, planning for, or actively building a log home. Estab. 1989. Circ. 132,000. **Pays on acceptance.** Publishes ms an average of 6 months after acceptance. Byline given. Offers $100 kill fee. Buys first or second serial (reprint) rights. Editorial lead time 6 months. Submit seasonal material 6 months in advance. Reports in 6 weeks. Sample copy for $4. Writer's guidelines for #10 SASE.

     • Ranked as one of the best markets for freelance writers in *Writer's Yearbook* magazine's annual "Top 100 Markets," January 1999.

**Nonfiction:** Book excerpts, how-to (build or maintain log home), interview/profile (log home owners), personal experience, photo feature (log homes), technical (design/decor topics), travel. "We do not want historical/nostalgic material." **Buys 6 mss/year.** Query. Length: 1,000-2,000 words. **Pays $250-500.** Pays expenses of writers on assignment.

**Reprints:** Send tearsheet or photocopy of article and information about when and where the article previously appeared. Pays 50% of amount paid for an original article.

**Photos:** State availability of photos with submission. Reviews contact sheets, 4×5 transparencies and 4×6 prints. Negotiates payment individually. Buys one-time rights.

**$ $LOG HOMES ILLUSTRATED,** Goodman Media Group, Inc., 1700 Broadway, New York NY 10019. (212)541-7100. Fax: (212)245-1241. Website: http://www.goodmanmediagroup.com. Editor: Roland Sweet. **Contact:** Stacy Durr Albert, managing editor. **30-40% freelance written.** Bimonthly magazine. "*Log Homes Illustrated* presents full-color photo features and inspirational stories of people who have fulfilled their dream of living in a log home. We show readers how they can make it happen too." Estab. 1994. Circ. 126,000. Pays on publication. Publishes ms 6 months after acceptance. Byline given. Buys first rights or second serial (reprint) rights. Editorial lead time 4 months. Submit seasonal material 6 months in advance. Accepts simultaneous submissions. Sample copy for $3.99.

**Nonfiction:** Book excerpts, how-to (gardening, building), profile (architects), new product, personal experience, photo feature, technical, travel. Special issues: Annual Buyer's Guide; PLANS issue. "We tend to stay away from articles that focus on just one craftsman, promotional pieces." **Buys 20-25 mss/year.** Query by mail with published clips or send complete ms. Length: 1,200-3,000 words. **Pays $300-600.** Pays expenses of writers on assignment with limit agreed upon in advance.

**Reprints:** Accepts previously published submissions.

**Photos:** Send photos with submission. Reviews 4×5 transparencies, slides or prints. Negotiates payment individually. Captions required. Buys one-time rights.

**Columns/Departments:** Diary (personal glimpses of log experience), 1,200-2,000 words; Going Places (visiting a log B&B, lodge, etc.), 1,200-2,000 words; Worth a Look (log churches, landmarks, etc.), 1,200-2,000 words; Gardening (rock gardens, water gardens, etc.), 2,000-3,000 words. **Buys 15 mss/year.** Query with published clips or send complete ms. **Pays $300-600.**

**Tips:** "Professional photos frequently make the difference between articles we accept and those we don't. Look for unique log structures in your travels, something we may not have seen before. We also consider carefully researched articles pertaining to insuring a log home, financing, contracting, etc."

**$ $MOUNTAIN LIVING,** Wiesner Publishing, 7009 S. Potomac St., Englewood CO 80112. (303)397-7600. Fax: (303)397-7619. E-mail: rawlings@winc.usa.com. Website: http://www.mtnliving.com. **Contact:** Irene Rawlings, editor. **90% freelance written.** Bimonthly magazine covering "shelter and lifestyle issues for people who live in, visit or hope to live in the mountains." Estab. 1994. Circ. 35,000. **Pays on acceptance.** Publishes ms an average of 4 months after acceptance. Byline given. Offers 15% kill fee. Buys first North American serial rights. Editorial lead time 6 months. Submit seasonal material 6 months in advance. Accepts queries by mail, e-mail. Accepts simultaneous submissions. Reports in 6 weeks on queries; 2 months on mss. Sample copy for $5 or on website. Writer's guidelines for #10 SASE.

**Nonfiction:** Book excerpts, essays, historical/nostalgic, interview/profile, personal experience, photo feature, travel, home features. **Buys 30 mss/year.** Query with published clips. Length: 1,200-2,000 words. **Pays $50-400.** Sometimes pays expenses of writers on assignment.

     • Ranked as one of the best markets for freelance writers in *Writer's Yearbook* magazine's annual "Top 100 Markets," January 1999.

**Reprints:** Send photocopy of article or typed ms with rights for sale noted. Payment varies.

**Photos:** State availability of photos with submission. Negotiates payment individually. Buys one-time rights.

**Columns/Departments:** Architecture, Art, Gardening, Sporting Life, Travel (often international), Off the Beaten Path (out-of-the-way mountain areas in U.S.), History, Health, Cuisine, Environment, Destinations (an art-driven department featuring a beautiful mountain destination in U.S.—must be accompanied by quality photograph), Trail's End (mountain-related essays). **Buys 35 mss/year.** Query with published clips. Length: 300-1,500 words. **Pays $50-300.**

**Tips:** "A deep understanding of and respect for the mountain environment is essential. Think out of the box. We love to be surprised. Write a brilliant, short query and always send clips."

**$ $ $ OLD-HOUSE INTERIORS**, Gloucester Publishers, 2 Main St., Gloucester MA 01930. (978)283-3200. Fax: (978)283-4629. **Contact:** Regina Cole, senior editor. **55% freelance written.** Bimonthly magazine for "furnishing residential period houses with a knowledge of historic house styles." Estab. 1994. Circ. 160,000. **Pays on acceptance.** Publishes ms 6 months after acceptance. Byline given. Offers 25% kill fee. Buys first North American serial rights. Editorial lead time 9 months. Submit seasonal material 1 year in advance. Reports in 1 month on queries; 2 months on mss. Sample copy and writer's guidelines for SASE.

O→ Break in with departments, such as Before and After, showing a dramatic change.

**Nonfiction:** Historical, decorator's how-to, interview/profile, opinion, photo feature, technical, travel, historic house tours. No nostalgia. **Buys 25 mss/year.** Query by mail. Length: 300-1,500 words. **Pays $25-1,500.** Sometimes pays expenses of writers on assignment.

**Photos:** State availability of photos with submission or send photos with submission. Negotiates payment individually. Captions and identification of subjects required. Buys one-time rights.

**Columns/Departments:** History of Furniture (academic), 1,200 words; Open House (friendly, informational), 400 words; Period Accents (informative), 750 words. Query. **Pays $25-1,500.**

**Tips:** "Writers should know that we are not a decorating magazine, but rather a beautifully photographed, intelligently written guide on finishing and furnishing period homes of every era."

**$ $ $ $ ORGANIC GARDENING**, Rodale, 33 E. Minor, Emmaus PA 18098. (610)967-8363. Fax: (6610)967-7846. E-mail: sweidal@rodalepress.com. Website: http://www.organicgardening.com. **Contact:** Sandra Weida, office coordinator. **75% freelance written.** Magazine published 6 times/year. "*Organic Gardening* is for gardeners who garden, who enjoy gardening as an integral part of a healthy lifestyle. Editorial shows readers how to grow anything they choose without chemicals. Editorial details how to grow flowers, edibles and herbs, as well as information on ecological landscaping. Also organic topics including soil building and pest control." Circ. 700,000. Pays between acceptance and publication. Buys all rights. Reports in 2 months on queries and mss.

● Ranked as one of the best markets for freelance writers in *Writer's Yearbook* magazine's annual "Top 100 Markets," January 1999.

**Nonfiction:** "The natural approach to the whole home landscape." Query with published clips and outline. **Pay varies, up to $1/word for experienced writers.**

▣ The online magazine carries original content not found in the print edition. Contact: Scott Meyer, online editor.

**Ⓝ $ $ POPULAR HOME AUTOMATION, The How-to Guide to Home Technology**, EH Publishing, 526 Boston Post Rd., Suite 150, Wayland MA 01778. (508)358-3400. Fax: (508)358-5195. E-mail: kparon@ehpub.com. Website: http://www.pophome.com. Editor: Leo Soderman. **Contact:** Katina Paron, associate editor. **70% freelance written.** Bimonthly magazine covering home technology and automation. "*Popular Home Automation* is geared for hands-on do-it-yourselfers who are technologically savvy." Estab. 1996. Circ. 7,500. Pays 30 days after publication. Publishes ms an average of 3 months after acceptance. Byline given. Offers 25% kill fee. Buys first North American serial rights. Editorial lead time 2 months. Submit seasonal material 4 months in advance. Accepts queries by mail, e-mail, fax. Accepts simultaneous submissions. Reports in 1 month on queries; 3 months on mss. Sample copy for $5 or on website.

**Nonfiction:** How-to, interview/profile, new product, opinion, personal experience, technical. **Buys 20-35 mss/year.** Query with published clips. Length: 700-3,000 words. **Pays 10-45¢/word.** "Pays in contributor copies or other premiums on writer's request." Pays expenses of writers on assignment.

**Photos:** Send photos with submission. Offers no additional payment for photos accepted with ms. Identification of subjects required. Buys one-time rights.

**Columns/Departments:** The Last Word (humor/opinion on home technology), 750 words. **Buys 6 mss/year.** Query with published clips. **Pays 10-25¢/word.**

▣ The online magazine carries original content not found in the print edition. Contact: Leo Soderman, online editor.

**Ⓝ $ $ ROMANTIC HOMES**, Y-Visionary Publishing, 265 S. Anita Dr., Orange CA 92868. (714)939-9991. Fax: (714)939-9909. Website: http://www.romantichomesmag.com. Editor: Eileen Paulin. **Contact:** Cathy Yarnovich, executive managing editor. **40% freelance written.** Bimonthly magazine covering home decor. "*Romantic Homes* is the magazine for women who want to create a warm, intimate, and casually elegant home—a haven that is both a gathering place for family and friends and a private refuge from the pressures of the outside world. The *Romantic Homes* reader is personally involved in the decor of her home. Features offer unique ideas and how-to advice on decorating, home furnishings, and gardening. Departments focus on floor and wall coverings, paint, textiles, refinishing, architectural elements, artwork, travel and entertaining. Every article responds to the reader's need to create a beautiful, attainable environment, providing her with the style ideas and resources to achieve her own romantic home." Estab. 1994. Circ. 140,000. **Pays on acceptance.** Publishes ms an average of 2 months after acceptance. Byline given. Buys all rights. Editorial lead time 4 months. Submit seasonal material 6 months in advance. Accepts queries by mail, fax. Accepts simultaneous submissions. Reports in 2 weeks on queries; 2 months on mss. Writer's guidelines for SASE.

**Nonfiction:** How-to. "Not just for dreaming, *Romantic Homes* combines unique ideas and inspirations with practical how-to advice on decorating, home furnishings, remodeling and gardening for readers who are actively involved in improving their homes. Every article responds to the reader's need to know how to do it and where to find it." **Buys 150 mss/year.** Query with published clips. Length: 1,000-1,200 words. **Pays $500.**

**Photos:** State availability of photos or send photos with submission. Reviews transparencies. Captions, model releases and identification of subjects required. Buys all rights.

**Columns/Departments:** Departments cover antiques, collectibles, artwork, shopping, travel, refinishing, architectural elements, flower arranging, entertaining and decorating, 400-500 words. **Pays $350.**

**$ $ SAN DIEGO HOME/GARDEN LIFESTYLES**, Mckinnon Enterprises, Box 719001, San Diego CA 92171-9001. (619)571-1818. Fax: (619)571-1889. E-mail: sdhg@sen.rr.com. Senior Editor: Phyllis Van Doren. **Contact:** Wayne Carlson, editor. **50% freelance written.** Monthly magazine covering homes, gardens, food, intriguing people, real estate, art, culture, and local travel for residents of San Diego city and county. Estab. 1979. Circ. 50,000. Pays on publication. Publishes ms an average of 3 months after acceptance. Byline given. Buys first North American serial rights only. Submit seasonal material 3 months in advance. Reports in 3 months. Sample copy for $4.

**Nonfiction:** Residential architecture and interior design (San Diego-area homes only); remodeling (must be well-designed—little do-it-yourself); residential landscape design; furniture; other features oriented towards upscale readers interested in living the cultured good life in San Diego. Articles must have local angle. Query with published clips. Length: 700-2,000 words. **Pays $50-350.**

**Tips:** "No out-of-town, out-of-state subject material. Most freelance work is accepted from local writers. Gear stories to the unique quality of San Diego. We try to offer only information unique to San Diego—people, places, shops, resources, etc. We plan more food and entertaining-at-home articles and more articles on garden products. We also need more in-depth reports on major architecture, environmental, and social aspects of life in San Diego and the border area."

**$ $ $ SOUTHERN ACCENTS**, Southern Progress Corp., 2100 Lakeshore Dr., Birmingham AL 35209. (205)877-6000. Fax: (205)877-6990. E-mail: lynn_carter@spc.com. Website: http://www.southernaccents.com. **Contact:** Lynn Carter, managing editor. "*Southern Accents* celebrates the best of the South." Estab. 1977. Circ. 370,000. Reports in 2 months.

**Nonfiction:** "Each issue features the finest homes and gardens along with a balance of features that reflect the affluent lifestyles of its readers, including architecture, antiques, entertaining, collecting and travel." Query by mail with SASE, clips and photos.

▣ The online magazine carries original content not found in the print edition. Contact: Diane Shirah, online editor.

**Tips:** "Query us only with specific ideas targeted to our current columns."

**$ $ $ STYLE AT HOME**, Telemedia Communications, Inc., 25 Sheppard Ave. W., Suite 100, Toronto, Ontario M2N 6S7 Canada. (416)733-7600. Fax: (416)218-3632. E-mail: letters@styleathome.com. **Contact:** Gail Johnston Habs, editor. Managing Editor: Laurie Grassi. **90% freelance written.** Home decor magazine published 8 times/year. "The number one magazine choice of Canadian women aged 25 to 54 who own a home and have a serious interest in decorating. Provides an authoritative, stylish collection of inspiring and accessible interiors, decor projects; reports on style design trends." Estab. 1997. Circ. 204,000. **Pays on acceptance.** Byline given. Offers 50% kill fee. Buys first rights. Editorial lead time 3 months. Submit seasonal material 4 months in advance. Accepts queries by mail, e-mail, fax. Reports in 1 months on queries, 1 week on mss. Sample copy for $1.75 plus tax. Writer's guidelines free.

🔦 Break in by "familiarizing yourself with the type of interiors we show. Be very up-to-date with the design and home decor market in Canada. Provide a lead to a fabulous home or garden."

**Nonfiction:** Interview/new product. "No how-to; these are planned in-house." **Buys 100 mss/year.** Query with published clips; include scouting shots with interior story queries. Length: 100-800 words. **Pays $100-1,000.** Sometimes pays expenses of writers on assignment.

**Photos:** State availability of photos with submission. Reviews transparencies. Negotiates payment individually. Captions required. Buys one-time rights.

**Columns/Departments:** Query with published clips. **Pays $100-500.**

**$ $ TEXAS GARDENER, The Magazine for Texas Gardeners, by Texas Gardeners**, Suntex Communications, Inc., P.O. Box 9005, Waco TX 76714-9005. (254)848-9393. Fax: (254)848-9779. E-mail: suntex@calpha.com. Editor: Chris S. Corby. **Contact:** Tammy Mathis, managing editor. **80% freelance written.** Works with a small number of new/unpublished writers each year. Bimonthly magazine covering vegetable and fruit production, ornamentals and home landscape information for home gardeners in Texas. Estab. 1981. Circ. 30,000. Pays on publication. Publishes ms an average of 4 months after acceptance. Byline given. Buys first North American serial and all rights. Submit seasonal material 6 months in advance. Accepts queries by mail, e-mail, fax. Reports in 2 months. Sample copy for $2.75 and SAE with 5 first-class stamps. Writer's guidelines for #10 SASE.

**Nonfiction:** How-to, humor, interview/profile, photo feature. "We use feature articles that relate to Texas gardeners. We also like personality profiles on hobby gardeners and professional horticulturists who are doing something unique." **Buys 50-60 mss/year.** Query with clips of published work. Length: 800-2,400 words. **Pays $50-200.**

**Photos:** "We prefer superb color and b&w photos; 90% of photos used are color." Send photos. Pays negotiable rates for 2¼ or 35mm color transparencies and 8×10 b&w prints and contact sheets. Model release and identification of subjects required.

**Columns/Departments:** Between Neighbors. **Pays $25.**

**Tips:** "First, be a Texan. Then come up with a good idea of interest to home gardeners in this state. Be specific. Stick to feature topics like 'How Alley Gardening Became a Texas Tradition.' Leave topics like 'How to Control Fire Blight' to the experts. High quality photos could make the difference. We would like to add several writers to our group of regular contributors and would make assignments on a regular basis. Fillers are easy to come up with in-house. We want good writers who can produce accurate and interesting copy. Frequent mistakes made by writers in completing an article assignment for us are that articles are not slanted toward Texas gardening, show inaccurate or too little gardening information or lack good writing style."

**$ $ TIMBER HOMES ILLUSTRATED**, Goodman Media Group, Inc., 1700 Broadway, New York NY 10019. (212)541-7100. Fax: (212)245-1241. Website: http://www.goodmanmediagroup.com. Editor: Roland Sweet. **Contact:** Stacy Durr Albert, managing editor. **30% freelance written.** Quarterly. "*Timber Homes Illustrated* presents full-color photo features and stories about timber-frame, log, post-and-beam and other classic wood homes. We feature stories of homeowners who've achieved their dream and encouragement for those who dream of owning a timber home." Estab. 1996. Circ. 75,000. Pays on publication. Byline given. Buys first North American serial rights or second serial (reprint) rights. Editorial lead time 4 months. Submit seasonal material 6 months in advance. Accepts simultaneous submissions. Sample copy for $3.99.

**Nonfiction:** Book excerpts, historical/nostalgic, how-to (building), interview/profile (architects), personal experience, photo feature, travel. Special issue: Annual Buyer's Directory. No self-promotion pieces about furniture designers, etc. **Buys 15 mss/year.** Query with published clips or send complete ms. Length: 1,200-3,000 words. **Pays $300-600.** Pays expenses of writers on assignment with limit agreed upon in advance.

**Reprints:** Accepts previously published submissions.

**Photos:** Send photos with submission. Reviews 4×5 transparencies, slides or prints. Negotiates payment individually. Captions required. Buys one-time rights.

**Columns/Departments:** Traditions (history of timber-framing), 1,200-3,000 words; Interior Motives (decorating timber homes), 1,200-2,200 words; Space & Place (decor ideas, timber-frame components), 1,200-2,000 words. **Buys 10 mss/year.** Query with published clips or send complete ms. **Pays $300-600.**

**Tips:** "We suggest including photos with your submission. Present a clear idea of where and how your story will fit into our magazine. We are always interested in seeing timber structures other than homes, such as wine vineyards or barns. Look for something unique—including unique homes."

**$ $ $ TODAY'S HOMEOWNER**, 2 Park Ave., New York NY 10016. (212)779-5000. Fax: (212)725-3281. Website: http://www.todayshomeowner.com. Editor: Paul Spring. Managing Editor: Steven Saltzman. **Contact:** Fran Donegan, executve editor. **10% freelance written.** Prefers to work with published/established writers. "If it's good, and it fits the type of material we're currently publishing, we're interested, whether writer is new or experienced." Magazine published 10 times/year for the active home and car owner. "Articles emphasize an active, home-oriented lifestyle. Includes information useful for maintenance, repair and renovation to the home and family car. Information on how to buy, how to select products useful to homeowners/car owners. Emphasis in home-oriented articles is on good design, inventive solutions to styling and space problems, useful home-workshop projects." Estab. 1928. Circ. 950,000. **Pays on acceptance.** Publishes ms an average of 4 months after acceptance. Byline given. Buys first North American serial rights. Reports in 3 months. Query.

O⟶ Break in with a submissions to the Homeowner's Digest department.

**Nonfiction:** Feature articles relating to homeowner, 1,500-2,500 words. "This may include personal home-renovation projects, professional advice on interior design, reports on different or unusual construction methods, energy-related subjects, outdoor/backyard projects, etc. No high-tech subjects such as aerospace, electronics, photography or military hardware. Most of our automotive features are written by experts in the field, but fillers, tips, how-to repair, or modification articles on the family car are welcome. Articles on construction, tool use, refinishing techniques, etc., are also sought. **Pays $300 minimum for features;** fees based on number of printed pages, photos accompanying mss., etc." Query only; *no unsolicited mss.* Pays expenses of writers on assignment.

**Photos:** Photos should accompany mss. Pays $600 and up for transparencies for cover. Inside color: $300/1 page, $500/2, $700/3, etc. Captions and model releases required.

▪ The online magazine carries original content not found in the print edition. Contact: Peter Noah, online editor.

**Tips:** "The most frequent mistake made by writers in completing an article assignment for *Today's Homeowner* is not taking the time to understand its editorial focus and special needs."

**N $ $ VICTORIAN HOMES**, Y-Visionary Publishing L.P., 265 S. Anita Dr., Suite 120, Orange CA 92868-3310. (714)939-9991, ext. 332. Fax: (714)939-9909. E-mail: ekotite@pacbell.net. Managing Editor: Cathy Yarnovich. **Contact:** Erika Kotite, editor. **90% freelance written.** Bimonthly magazine covering Victorian home restoration and decoration. "*Victorian Homes* is read by Victorian home owners, restorers, house museum management and others interested in the Victorian revival. Feature articles cover home architecture, interior design, furnishings and the home's history. Photography is *very* important to the feature." Estab. 1981. Circ. 100,000. **Pays on acceptance.** Publishes ms an average of 6-12 months after acceptance. Byline given. Offers $50 kill fee. Buys first North American serial and one-time rights. Editorial lead time 4 months. Submit seasonal material 1 year in advance. Accepts queries by mail, e-mail, fax. Accepts simultaneous submissions. Reports in 6 weeks on queries; 2 months on mss. Sample copy and writer's guidelines for SAE.

**Nonfiction:** How-to (create period style curtains, wall treatments, bathrooms, kitchens, etc.), photo feature. "Article must deal with structures—no historical articles on Victorian people or lifestyles." **Buys 30-35 mss/year.** Query. Length: 800-1,800 words. **Pays $300-500.** Sometimes pays expenses of writers on assignment.

**Photos:** State availability of photos with submission. Reviews 2¼×2¼ transparencies. Negotiates payment individually. Captions required. Buys one-time rights.

**$ $ $ WALLS, WINDOWS & FLOORS, Woman's Day Special Interest Publications**, Hachette-Filipacchi Magazines, 1633 Broadway, New York NY 10019. Fax: (212)767-5612. Editor: Carolyn Gatto. **Contact:** Julie Sinclair, managing editor. Magazine published 3 times a year covering home decorating ideas focused on walls, windows, and floors. **Pays on acceptance.** Publishes ms an average of 3 months after acceptance. Byline given. Offers up to 25% kill fee. Buys first worldwide serial or second serial (printing) rights. Editorial lead time 6 months. Submit seasonal material 10 months in advance. Reports in 2 months. Sample copy not available; writer's guidelines for #10 SASE.

**Nonfiction:** How-to (floor, walls and window treatments), interview/profile (designers), new product, photo features, technical (information about paint, wallpaper, floor coverings). **Buys 40 mss/year.** Query with published clips. Length: 250-1,000 words. Payment varies. Sometimes pays expenses of writers on assignment.

**Reprints:** Accepts previously published submissions.

**Photos:** Send photos with query. Model releases required. Buys one-time rights.

**Columns/Departments:** Query with published clips. Payment varies based on length, writer, and level/amount of research required.

**Tips:** "Tips from professionals, how-to's and timesaving techniques make this a hands-on magazine that deals with all sorts of ways to color, cover, and decorate these surfaces of the home. Many ideas are presented in a problem/solving format so readers can easily achieve the looks that express their own personal style. Product and trend information keep readers current. Send a brief, clear query letter with relevant clips, and be patient. Before and after photos are very helpful."

# HUMOR

Publications listed here specialize in gaglines or prose humor, some for readers and others for performers or speakers. Other publications that use humor can be found in nearly every category in this book. Some have special needs for major humor pieces; some use humor as fillers; many others are interested in material that meets their ordinary fiction or nonfiction requirements but also has a humorous slant. The majority of humor articles must be submitted as complete manuscripts on speculation because editors usually can't know from a query whether or not the piece will be right for them.

**$ FUNNY TIMES, A Monthly Humor Review**, Funny Times, Inc., P.O. Box 18530, Cleveland Heights OH 44118. (216)371-8600. Fax: (216)371-8696. E-mail: ft@funnytimes.com. Website: http://www.funnytimes.com. **Contact:** Raymond Lesser, Susan Wolpert, editors. **10% freelance written.** Monthly tabloid for humor. "*Funny Times* is a monthly review of America's funniest cartoonists and writers. We are the *Reader's Digest* of modern American humor with a progressive/peace-oriented/environmental/politically activist slant." Estab. 1985. Circ. 50,000. Pays on publication. Publishes ms an average of 3 months after acceptance. Byline given. Buys one-time or second serial (reprint) rights. Editorial lead time 2 months. Accepts simultaneous submissions. Reports in 3 months on mss. Sample copy for $3 or 9×12 SAE with 4 first-class stamps. Writer's guidelines for #10 SASE.

**Nonfiction:** Essays (funny), humor, interview/profile, opinion (humorous), personal experience (absolutely funny). "We only publish humor or interviews with funny people (comedians, comic actors, cartoonists, etc.). Everything we publish is very funny. If your piece isn't extremely funny then don't bother to send it. Don't send us anything that's not outrageously funny. Don't send anything that other people haven't already read and told you they laughed so hard they peed their pants." **Buys 36 mss/year.** Send complete ms. Length: 1,000 words. **Pays $50 minimum for unsolicited articles.**

**Reprints:** Accepts previously published submissions.

**Fiction:** Humorous. **Buys 6 mss/year.** Query with published clips. Length: 500 words. **Pays $50-150.**

**Fillers:** Short humor. **Buys 6/year. Pays $20.**

**Tips:** "Send us a small packet (1-3 items) of only your very funniest stuff. If this makes us laugh we'll be glad to ask for more. We particularly welcome previously published material that has been well-received elsewhere."

**$ LATEST JOKES**, P.O. Box 23304, Brooklyn NY 11202-0066. (718)855-5057. **Contact:** Robert Makinson, editor. **20% freelance written.** Bimonthly newsletter of humor for TV and radio personalities, comedians and professional speakers. Estab. 1974. **Pays on acceptance.** Byline given. Buys all rights. Reports in 2 months. Sample copy for $3 and SASE.

● The editor says jokes for public speakers are most needed.

**Nonfiction:** Humor (short jokes). "No way-out, vulgar humor. Jokes about human tragedy also unwelcome." Send up to 20 jokes with SASE. **Pays $1-3/joke.**

**Tips:** "No famous personality jokes. Clever statements are not enough. Be original and surprising. Our emphasis is on jokes for professional speakers."

**N ☒ $ $ MAD MAGAZINE**, 1700 Broadway, New York NY 10019. (212)506-4850. Website: http://www.mad mag.com. **Contact:** Editorial Dept. **100% freelance written.** Monthly magazine "always on the lookout for new ways to spoof and to poke fun at hot trends." Estab. 1952. **Pays on acceptance.** Publishes ms an average of 6 months after acceptance. Byline given. Buys all rights. Submit seasonal material 6 months in advance. Reports in 10 weeks. Sample articles on website. Writer's guidelines for #10 SASE.

**Nonfiction:** Satire, parody. "We're *not* interested in formats we're already doing or have done to death like 'what they say and what they really mean.' " **Buys 400 mss/year.** "Submit a premise with three or four examples of how you intend to carry it through, describing the action and visual content. Rough sketches desired but not necessary. One-page gags: two to eight panel cartoon continuities at minimum very funny, maximum hilarious!" **Pays minimum of $400/** *MAD* page. "*Don't* send previously published submissions, riddles, advice columns, TV or movie satires, book manuscripts, top ten lists, articles about Alfred E. Neuman, poetry, essays, short stories or other text pieces."

**Tips:** "Have fun! Remember to think visually! Surprise us! Freelancers can best break in with satirical nontopical material. Include SASE with each submission. Originality is prized. We like outrageous, silly and/or satirical humor."

**☒ $ NEW HUMOR MAGAZINE**, New Communications, Inc. Publishers, P.O. Box 216, Lafayette Hill PA 19444. Fax: (215)487-2670. E-mail: Newhumor@aol.com. Website: http://www.gohumor.com. Managing Editor: Suzanne Savaria. **Contact:** Edward Savaria Jr., editor-in-chief. **90% freelance written.** Bimonthly magazine covering humor. "Tasteful, intelligent and funny. Looking for clean humor in a sense that funny stories, jokes and poems do not have to sink to sexist, bathroom or ethnic subjects to be humorous." Estab. 1994. Circ. 9,500. Pays on publication. Publishes ms an average of 4 months after acceptance. Byline given. Buys first North American serial, second serial (reprint) or simultaneous rights. Editorial lead time 4 months. Submit seasonal material 4 months in advance. Accepts simultaneous submissions. Reports in 1 month on queries. Sample copy for $3. Writer's guidelines for #10 SASE.

**Nonfiction:** Book excerpts, essays, humor, interview/profile, new product (humorous), travel. **Buys 12 mss/year.** Send complete ms. Length: 250-1,000 words. **Pays $25-50.**

**Reprints:** Send photocopy of article or short story or typed ms with rights for sale noted. Pays same amount paid for an original article or story.

**Columns/Departments:** Open to Column Ideas, 250-750 words. **Pays $25-50.**

**Fiction:** Humorous, novel excerpts. **Buys 40 mss/year.** Send complete ms. Length: 25-1,500 words. **Pays $25-50.**

**Poetry:** Avant-garde, free verse, haiku, light verse. **Buys 30 poems/year.** Submit maximum 10 poems. Length: 1-50 lines. **Pays $5-15.**

**Fillers:** Anecdotes, short humor. **Buys 20/year.** Length: 25-300 words. **Pays $10-25.**

**Tips:** "If you think it's funny—it might be. Test stories on friends, see if they laugh. Don't be afraid to send odd humor—something completely different."

**N $ WORDS FOR SALE**, 1149 Granada Ave., Salinas CA 93906. **Contact:** Lorna Gilbert, submission editor.

**Nonfiction:** "Since 1968, we have sold almost every kind of written material to a wide variety of individual and corporate clients. We deal in both the written as well as the spoken word. From humorous one liners and nightclub acts, to informative medical brochures, political speeches, and almost everything in between. We are not agents. We are a company that provides original written material created especially for the specific needs of our current clients. Therefore, do not send us a sample of your work. As good as it may be, it is almost certainly unrelated to our current needs. Instead begin by finding out what our clients want and write it for them. What could be simpler? It gets even better: *We buy sentences!* That's right. Forget conceiving, composing, editing and polishing endless drafts of magazine articles or book manuscripts. Simply create the type of sentence or sentences we're looking for and we'll buy one or more of them. We respond promptly. We pay promptly." **Pays $1 and up/sentence. Pays on acceptance."** All submissions must include SASE or they will not be returned.

**Tips:** "The key to your selling something to us, is to *first* find out *exactly* what we are currently buying. To do this simply mail us a #10 SASE and we will promptly send you a list of what we are anxious to buy at this time."

# INFLIGHT

Most major inflight magazines cater to business travelers and vacationers who will be reading, during the flight, about the airline's destinations and other items of general interest.

**$ ABOARD MAGAZINE**, 100 Almeria Ave., Suite 220, Coral Gables FL 33134. Fax: (305)441-9739. E-mail: aboard@worldnet.att.net. Website: http://www.aboardmagazines.com. Managing Editor: Lyng-Hou Ramirez. **Contact:** Michael Mut, editorial assistant. **40% freelance written.** Bimonthly bilingual inflight magazine designed to reach travelers to and from Latin America, carried on 15 major Latin-American airlines. Estab. 1976. Circ. 180,000. Pays on publication. Byline given. Buys one-time or simultaneous rights. Accepts queries by mail, e-mail, fax. Accepts simultaneous submissions. Reports in 2 months.

**Nonfiction:** General interest, new product, business, science, art, fashion, photo feature, technical, travel. "No controversial or political material." Query with SASE. **Buys 50 mss/year.** Length: 1,200-1,500 words. **Pays $100-150.**

**Reprints:** Send photocopy of article or typed ms with rights for sale noted and information about when and where the article previously appeared. Pays 0-50% of amount paid for an original article.

**Photos:** Send photos with submission. Reviews 35mm slides or transparencies only. Offers no additional payment for photos accepted with ms. Offers $20/photo minimum. Identification of subjects required. Buys one-time rights.

**Fillers:** Facts. **Buys 6/year.** Length: 800-1,200 words. **Pays $100.**

**Tips:** "Send article with photos. We need lots of travel material on Chile, Ecuador, Bolivia, El Salvador, Honduras, Guatemala, Uruguay, Nicaragua, Paraguay, Venezuela, Dominican Republic."

**$ $ ABOVE & BEYOND, The Magazine of the North**, Above & Beyond Ltd., P.O. Box 13142, Kanata, Ontario K2K 1X3 Canada. (613)599-4190. Fax: (613)599-4191. E-mail: editor@above-n-beyond.com. Website: http://www.above-n-beyond.com. **Contact:** Season Osborne, editor. **100% freelance written.** Quarterly inflight magazine for First Air, Canada's 3rd largest airline serving Northern Canada. Estab. 1988. Circ. 30,000. Pays on publication. Publishes ms an average of 4 months after acceptance. Byline given. Offers 50% kill fee. Buys first North American serial rights. Editorial lead time 8 months. Submit seasonal material 1 year in advance. Accepts queries by mail, e-mail, fax, phone. Sample copy and writer's guidelines for $6 (Canadian) and SASE.

**Nonfiction:** "We are interested in feature articles pertaining to: political, social and economic activities from a northern perspective; outdoor and recreational activities; profile pieces on northern individuals, communities and destinations; wildlife, fishing and hunting; travel features. We don't want articles about new products being used in the North or any articles that don't concern the North." **Buys 20 mss/year.** Send complete ms via mail (include SASE) or e-mail. Length: 1,000-1,500 words. **Pays 25¢/word.** Sometimes pays expenses of writers on assignment.

**Reprints:** Send tearsheet of article with information about when and where the article previously appeared. Pay varies.

**Photos:** Send photos with submission. Reviews color transparencies and prints. No b&w. Pays $25/photo. Captions, identification of subjects required. Buys one-time rights.

**Tips:** "Submit clean, insightful articles about life in the North that are within our length requirements. A large part of our readership is in Northern Canada so we don't want any 'Gee, whiz, aren't things different in the North' type of articles. We're looking for stories that paint a picture. Excellent photographs are essential, yes, but don't rely on these to provide your visual images. Your words should do this so that the photos and text work harmonize."

**N $ $ $ AMERICA WEST AIRLINES MAGAZINE**, Skyword Marketing Inc., 4636 E. Elwood St., Suite 5, Phoenix AZ 85040-1963. (602)997-7200. Fax: (602)997-9875. **Contact:** Michael Derr, editor. **80% freelance written.** Monthly magazine covering business and travel/destinations. "We look for thoughtful writing, full of detail, and a writer's ability to create a sense of place." Estab. 1986. Circ. 135,000. Pays on publication. Publishes ms an average of 6 months after acceptance. Byline given. Offers 15% kill fee. Buys first North American serial rights. Editorial lead time 6 months. Submit seasonal material 6 months in advance. Accepts queries by mail, fax. Accepts simultaneous submissions. Reports in 1 month. Sample copy for $3. Writer's guidelines for #10 SASE.

**Nonfiction:** Book excerpts, essays, general interest, historical/nostalgic, humor, interview/profile, new product, personal experience, photo feature, travel. "Ours is not a traditional feature well, but a mix of short, medium and long articles, specialty subjects and special-format features, but all still with the graphic appeal of a traditional feature." No how-to, poetry or flying articles. Query with published clips. Length: 500-2,000 words. **Pays $150-1,000.** Sometimes pays expenses of writers on assignment.

**Photos:** State availability of photos with submission. Reviews transparencies. Offers $25-100/photo. Identification of subjects required. Buys one-time rights.

**Columns/Departments:** Quick Fixes (narrowly focused short articles "featuring refreshing escapes that last a weekend, an afternoon, an hour. The more offbeat, the better. In a nutshell: self-contained cleverly written pieces. Must be in the route system"), 150-400 words; Best Of (a list of some of the best things to do, see or experience in a single destination). Query with published clips.

**Fiction:** Adventure, historical, humorous, mainstream, mystery, slice-of-life vignettes. Nothing of a sexual or potentially controversial or offensive nature. **Buys 12 mss/year.** Send completed ms. Length: 200-2,000 words. **Pays $200-500.**

**Fillers:** Short humor.

**Tips:** "In general, we prefer an informal yet polished style with personal, intimate storytelling. We especially appreciate visual, robust and passionate writing—a literary flair is never out of place. Be creative and capture a sense of the people and places you write about. Present tense preferred, if appropriate. Be thorough yet concise: good reporting is crucial. We require detailed, accurate writing and look for anecdotes and lively quotes. Don't pad. Be thoughtful and fair: justify your observations. Establish a point of view: refine your theme. We don't accept material from first-time writers, and we rarely publish material from writers who send unsolicited manuscripts. We have a network of writers who send new writers our way."

**$ $ $ $ AMERICAN WAY**, P.O. Box 619640, Mail Drop 5598, Dallas/Fort Worth Airport TX 75261-9640. (817)967-1804. Fax: (817)967-1571. E-mail: americanway@compuserve.com. Website: http://www.AA.com/away. Editor-in-Chief: John H. Ostdick. Managing Editor: Elaine Srnka. **Contact:** Tiffany Franke, associate editor. **98% freelance written.** Works exclusively with published/established writers. Biweekly inflight magazine for passengers flying with

American Airlines and American Eagle. Estab. 1966. **Pays on acceptance.** Publishes ms an average of 4 months after acceptance. Buys first serial rights. Accepts queries by mail, e-mail, fax. Reports in 5 months. Request sample copy by e-mail to 74763.2710@compuserve.com.

**Nonfiction:** Travel, business, arts/culture, sports, law, fashion and computer/technology. The magazine strives to be accessible, relevant, and, most of all, entertaining." Feature articles. Query with résumé, pertinent clips and SASE. Length: 2,000-2,500 words. **Pays $2,000.**

**Fiction:** Nancy Stevens, associate editor. Length: 2,500 words maximum. **Pays $1,100.**

**Columns/Departments:** Sojourners, 200 words; 1-page departments, 400 words; departments, 800-1,000 words. **Pays $1/word.**

**Tips:** "We have few needs for new writers at this time, so the likelihood of your query being accepted is slight. We do not respond to queries sent without an SASE unless we plan to pursue them. All stories are by assignment only. If your suggestion is accepted, you will be contacted by an editor who will assign the story and negotiate the deadline and your payment."

**$ THE AUSTRALIAN WAY, Qantas Inflight Magazine**, BRW Media, G.P.O. Box 55A, Melbourne, Victoria 3001 Australia. Phone: (03)96033888. Fax: (03)96420852. E-mail: tbrentnall@brw.fairfax.com.au. **Contact:** Tom Brentnall, editor. **80% freelance written.** Monthly magazine catering to Qantas Airways passengers travelling on both internal Australian routes and overseas. It provides articles on international events, travel, the arts, science and technology, sport, natural history and humor. The focus is on elegant writing and high-quality photography. There is a heavy emphasis on Australian personalities, culture and lifestyle." Estab. 1993. Circ. 1,600,000. Pays on publication. Publishes ms an average of 2 months after acceptance. Byline given. Buys first rights. Editorial lead time 2 months. Submit seasonal material 3 months in advance. Accepts queries by mail, fax.

**Nonfiction:** General interest, historical/nostalgic, interview/profile, photo feature, travel. Query with published clips. **Buys 50 mss/year.** Length: 800-1,500 words. **Pays $500 (Australian)/1,000 words.**

**Fiction:** Publishes novel excerpts (Australian authors only).

**Photos:** State availability of photos with submission. Reviews transparencies and prints. Negotiates payment individually. Captions, identification of subjects required. Buys all rights if commissioned; one-time rights if unsolicited.

**Tips:** "Guidelines for writers available on request. Writers should entertain as well as inform both an Australian and international readership. Features can be of general interest, about personalities, or on cultural, business or sporting interests. The magazine tends to avoid travel 'destination' pieces *per se*, though it carries appropriate stories that use these locations as backdrops."

**$ $ $ $ CONTINENTAL, The Magazine of Continental Airlines**, Pohly and Partners, 101 Huntington Ave., 13th Floor, Boston MA 02199. (617)424-7700. Fax: (617)437-7714. E-mail: beaulieuk@pohlypartners.com. Website: http://www.pohlypartners.com. Managing Editor: Timothy Lyster. **Contact:** Ken Beaulieu, executive editor. **80% freelance written.** Monthly inflight magazine "for a business traveler audience. We look for the person behind the company." Estab. 1986. Circ. 400,000. Pays 30 days from invoice. Publishes ms 3 months after acceptance. Byline given. Offers 25% kill fee. Buys first international rights. Editorial lead time 4-6 months. Submit seasonal material 6 months in advance. Reports in 1 month. Sample copy and writer's guidelines for SAE.

● Ranked as one of the best markets for freelance writers in *Writer's Yearbook* magazine's annual "Top 100 Markets," January 1999.

**Nonfiction:** Business executives, destinations, entertainers and athletes, luxuries, social and political leaders. **Buys 45 mss/year.** Query with published clips and SASE. Length: 100-1,500 words. **Pays $1/word,** but occasionally varies. Pays expenses of writers on assignment.

**Reprints:** Send photocopy of article and information about when and where the article previously appeared. Pays 25% of amount paid for an original article.

**Photos:** State availability of photos with submission. Reviews transparencies. Negotiates payment individually.

**Columns/Departments:** Time Out (outdoor sports); Executive Edge (products and services for the frequent traveler); City Focus (development issues in Continental destinations); Personal Finance; Mind of the Manager (issues); Reviews in Brief (books); Fun (crosswords). **Buys 60 mss/year.** Length: 100-1,500 words. Query with SASE.

**Tips:** "Consult a recent issue of the magazine for content and style. We look for timely hooks."

**$ $ $ HEMISPHERES, Pace Communications for United Airlines**, 1301 Carolina St., Greensboro NC 27401. (336)378-6065. **Contact:** Randy Johnson, editor. **95% freelance written.** Monthly magazine for the educated, sophisticated business and recreational frequent traveler on an airline that spans the globe. Estab. 1992. Circ. 500,000. **Pays on acceptance.** Publishes ms 3 months after acceptance. Byline given. Offers 20% kill fee. Usually buys first, worldwide rights. Editorial lead time 8 months. Submit seasonal material 8 months in advance. Reports in 10 weeks on queries; 4 months on mss. Sample copy for $5. Writer's guidelines for #10 SASE.

● Ranked as one of the best markets for freelance writers in *Writer's Yearbook* magazine's annual "Top 100 Markets," January 1999.

**Nonfiction:** General interest, humor, personal experience. "Keeping 'global' in mind, we look for topics that reflect a modern appreciation of the world's cultures and environment. No 'What I did (or am going to do) on a trip to. . . .' " Query with published clips. Length: 500-3,000 words. **Pays 50¢/word and up.**

**Photo:** State availability of photos with submission. Reviews transparencies "only when we request them." Negotiates payment individually. Captions, model releases, identification of subjects required. Buys one-time rights.

**Columns/Departments:** Making a Difference (Q&A format interview with world leaders, movers, and shakers. A 500-600 word introduction anchors the interview. We want to profile an international mix of men and women representing a variety of topics or issues, but all must truly be making a difference. No puffy celebrity profiles.); On Location (A snappy selection of one or two sentences, "25 Fascinating Facts" that are obscure, intriguing, or travel-service-oriented items that the reader never knew about a city, state, country or destination.); Executive Secrets (Things that top executives know); Case Study (Business strategies of international companies or organizations. No lionizations of CEOs. Strategies should be the emphasis. "We want international candidates."); Weekend Breakway (Takes us just outside a major city after a week of business for a physically active, action-packed weekend. This isn't a sedentary "getaway" at a "property."); Roving Gourmet (Insider's guide to interesting eating in major city, resort area, or region. The slant can be anything from ethnic to expensive; not just "best." The four featured eateries span a spectrum from "hole in the wall," to "expense account lunch" and on to "big deal dining."); Collecting (Photo with lengthy caption or occasional 800-word story on collections and collecting that can emphasize travel); Eye on Sports (Global look at anything of interest in sports); Vintage Traveler (Options for mature, experienced travelers); Savvy Shopper (Insider's tour of best places in the world to shop. *Savvy Shopper* steps beyond all those stories that just mention the great shopping at a particular destination. A shop-by-shop, gallery-by-gallery tour of the best places in the world."); Science and Technology alternates with Computers (Substantive, insightful story. Not just another column on audio components or software. No gift guides!"); Aviation Journal (For those fascinated with aviation. *Aviation Journal* is an opportunity to enthrall all of those fliers who are fascinated with aviation. Topics range widely. A fall 1998 redesign of the magazine ushered in a reader-service-oriented "Great Airports" guide series, the classic DC-3, airport identifiers, Of Grape And Grain (Wine and spirits with emphasis on education, not one-upmanship); Show Business (Films, music and entertainment); Musings (Humor or just curious musings); Quick Quiz (Tests to amuse and educate); Travel News (Brief, practical, invaluable, trend-oriented tips); Book Beat (Tackles topics like the Wodehouse Society, the birth of a book, the competition between local bookshops and national chains. Please, no review proposals. Slant—what the world's reading—residents explore how current best sellers tell us what their country is thinking.). Length: 1,400 words. Query with published clips. **Pays 50¢/word and up.**

**Fiction:** Adventure, humorous, mainstream, slice-of-life vignettes. **Buys 4 mss/year.** Query. Length: 500-2,000 words. **Pays 50¢/word and up.**

**Tips:** "We increasingly require writers of 'destination' pieces or departments to 'live whereof they write.' Increasingly want to hear from U.S., U.K. or other English speaking/writing journalists (business & travel) who reside outside the U.S. in Europe, South America, Central America and the Pacific Rim—all areas that United flies. We're not looking for writers who aim at the inflight market. *Hemispheres* broke the fluffy mold of that tired domestic genre. Our monthly readers are a global mix on the cutting edge of the global economy and culture. They don't need to have the world filtered by US writers. We want a Hong Kong restaurant writer to speak for that city's eateries, so we need English speaking writers around the globe. That's the 'insider' story our reader's respect. We use resident writers for departments such as Roving Gourmet, Savvy Shopper, On Location, 3 Perfect Days (which became a cable TV program in September 1998) and Weekend Breakaway, but authoritative writers can roam in features. Sure we cover the US, but with a global view: No 'in this country' phraseology. 'Too American' is a frequent complaint for queries. We use UK English spellings in articles that speak from that tradition and we specify costs in local currency first before US dollars. Basically, all of above serves the realization that today, 'global' begins with respect for 'local.' That approach permits a wealth of ways to present culture, travel and business for a wide readership. We anchor that with a reader service mission that grounds everything in 'how to do it.' "

**N** **$ $ $** KWIHI, **The In-Flight Magazine of Air Aruba**, ABARTA Metro Publishing, 11900 Biscayne Blvd., Suite 300, Miami FL 33181-2726. (305)892-6644. Fax: (305)892-1005. **Contact:** Jenny Bronson, editor. **50-75% free-lance written.** Quarterly magazine covering Aruba. "*Kwihi* is written for vacationing passengers of Air Aruba. Articles focus on activities, sports, entertainment, dining and other subjects of interest to visitors of the island of Aruba." Estab. 1995. Circ. 10,000. **Pays on acceptance.** Publishes ms an average of 2 months after acceptance. Byline given. Buys all rights. Editorial lead time 3 months. Submit seasonal material 3 months in advance. Accepts queries by mail, e-mail, fax.

**Nonfiction:** Interview/profile (locals), travel (Aruba only). **Buys 12 mss/year.** Query with published clips. Length: 500-3,000 words. **Pays $250-1,500.**

**Photos:** State availability of photos with submission. Negotiates payment individually. Identification of subjects required.

**Columns/Departments:** On the Island & Off the Cuff (island news, travel tidbits, book reviews), 150-200 words each, total column is around 2,500; Personality Profile (profile of interesting Arubans—artists, business owners, etc.), 1,000 words. Query with published clips. **Pays $100-500.**

**N** **$ $** RENO AIR APPROACH, Adventure Media Inc., 650 S. Orcas St., Suite 103, Seattle WA 98108. (206)762-1922. Fax: (206)762-1886. Senior Editor: Andrew Tarica. **Contact:** Heidi Schuessler, editor. **80% freelance written.** Monthly inflight magazine for Reno Air. "First and foremost, all queries must have a connection to the cities where Reno Air flies (mostly West Coast destinations). We're especially interested in things to see and do that are not on every tourism brochure: think 'off-the-beaten path.' Also, we want to meet the people behind the story, whether it's a business short or a feature." Estab. 1997. Circ. 500,000. Pays on publication. Publishes ms an average of 3 months after acceptance. Byline given. Offers 25% kill fee. Buys first North American serial rights. Editorial lead time 3 months.

Submit seasonal material 6 months in advance. Reports in 2 months. Sample copy for $2. Writer's guidelines free by e-mail.

**Nonfiction:** Essays, general interest, interview/profile, new product, photo feature (relevant to our route system), travel, business (success stories, interesting niche market, business profiles). Special issues: Ski Guide to the West (December) and Golf Guide (June). No how-to/service pieces (basically anything second person) or religious. **Buys 120 mss/year.** Query by mail with published clips. Length: 250-2,500 words. **Pays 25-35¢/word for assigned articles; 20-25¢/word for unsolicited articles.**

**Photos:** State availability of photos with submission. Negotiates payment individually. Captions, model releases and identification of subjects required. Buys one-time rights.

**Columns/Departments:** Andrew Tarica, senior editor. Face to Face (ordinary people doing extraordinary things), 1,200 words; On the Map (an interesting aspect of one city we fly to), 1,600 words; Leisure Time (where to maximize your free time), 1,600 words. Query with published clips. **Pays 20-30¢/word.**

**Tips:** "Start with front-of-the-book departments (business profiles, hotel reviews, restaurant profiles). If you can do a good job with a 600-word story, we'll feel more comfortable assigning longer pieces. Query by mail with one or two well-thought out ideas, and why they'd work for our magazine."

**$ $ $ $SKY**, Pace Communications for Delta Air Lines, 1301 Carolina St., Greensboro NC 27401. E-mail: skymag@aol.com. Website: http://www.delta-sky.com. **Contact:** Mickey McLean, managing editor. Published monthly for business and leisure travelers aboard Delta Air Lines. **Pays on acceptance.** Byline given. Offers 25% kill fee. Buys first worldwide serial rights. Accepts queries by mail, e-mail. Reports in 4 months. Sample copy for $7.50.

 • Ranked as one of the best markets for freelance writers in *Writer's Yearbook* magazine's annual "Top 100 Markets," January 1999.

**Nonfiction:** "Needs timely, interesting and informative articles on business, technology, travel, sports and humor." **Buys 48 mss/year.** Query with published clips. Length: 1,500-3,000 words. **Pays $1,500-3,000.** Pays the expenses of writers on assignment.

**Columns/Departments: Buys 180 mss/year.** Query with published clips. **Pays $1,000-1,500.** Length: 1,000-1,500 words.

**Fillers:** Length: 100-400 words. **Pays $75-300.**

**Tips:** "*USA Today* said *Sky* is 'redefining inflight magazines.' We don't want run-of-the-mill inflight articles; we want fresh—sometimes humorous—takes on business, technology, travel and sports."

**$ $ $ $SOUTHWEST AIRLINES SPIRIT**, 4333 Amon Carter Blvd., Fort Worth TX 76155-9616. (817)967-1804. Fax: (817)967-1571. E-mail: 102615.376@compuserve.com. Website: http://www.spiritmag.com. **Contact:** John Clark, editor. Monthly magazine for passengers on Southwest Airlines. Estab. 1992. Circ. 280,000. **Pays on acceptance.** Byline given. Buys first North American serial and electronic rights. Reports in 1 month on queries.

 • Ranked as one of the best markets for freelance writers in *Writer's Yearbook* magazine's annual "Top 100 Markets," January 1999.

**Nonfiction:** "Seeking accessible, entertaining, relevant and timely glimpses of people, places, products and trends in the regions Southwest Airlines serves. Newsworthy/noteworthy topics; well-researched and multiple source only. Experienced magazine professionals only. Business, travel, technology, sports and lifestyle (food, fitness and culture) are some of the topics covered in *Spirit*." Special issues: Destination: Little Rock, Restaurants: Steakhouses, Estate Planning, Nutrition: Weight Food (September 1998); Destination: Undertermined, Restaurants: French, Financial Advisers, Fitness: Quickies (October 1998); Destination: San Diego, Hotel Dining, Housing Affordability, Nutrition: Organic (November 1998); *Spirit's* Annual Holiday Feature, Destination: Las Vegas, Restaurants: Middle Eastern, College Loans, Fitness: Sick Workouts (December 1998). **Buys 48 mss/year.** Query with published clips. Length: 2,500 words. **Pays $2,000.** Pays expenses of writers on assignment.

**Columns/Departments: Buys 21 mss/year.** Query with published clips. Length: 1,200-2,200 words. Pay varies.

**Fillers: Buys 12/year.** Length: 250 words. Pay varies.

**$ $ $ $TWA AMBASSADOR**, 4636 E. Elwood St., Suite 5, Phoenix AZ 85040-1963. **Contact:** Ellen Alperstein, consulting editor. Monthly magazine for foreign and domestic TWA passengers. Estab. 1968. Circ. 223,000. **Pays on acceptance.** Byline given. Offers 25% kill fee. Buys first rights. Reports in 6 weeks on queries. Sample copy for 9×12 SASE plus $2.17 postage (no checks or postal coupons—US postage only). Writer's guidelines for #10 SASE, attn. Rich.

 • Ranked as one of the best markets for freelance writers in *Writer's Yearbook* magazine's annual "Top 100 Markets," January 1999.

**Nonfiction:** "We need solid journalism stylishly rendered. We look for first-rate reporting by professionals with a track record. Also, essays and commentaries, the first one usually on spec. Stories cover a range of general interest topics—business, sports, entertainment, food, media, money, family and more. No traditional travel stories or service pieces." **Buys 40-45 mss/year.** Query with published clips. Length: 700-2,500 words. **Pays 75¢-$1/word.** Pays expenses of writers on assignment.

**Columns/Departments: Buys 45-50 mss/year.** Query with published clips. Length: 500-1,200 words. **Pays 75¢-$1/word.**

**Fiction:** "We accept fiction but buy very little."

**Tips:** "We have a small staff and a huge volume of mail—please query with SASE."

☆ **$ $ $ $** U.S. AIRWAYS ATTACHÉ, Pace Communications, 1301 Carolina St., Greensboro NC 27401. Fax: (336)378-8278. E-mail: AttacheAir@aol.com. Editor: Jay Heinrichs. Editorial Assistant: Kendra Gemma. **Contact:** Lance Elko, managing editor. **75% freelance written.** Monthly magazine for travelers on U.S. Airways. Estab. 1997. Circ. 441,000. **Pays on acceptance.** Publishes ms an average of 4 months after acceptance. Byline given. Offers 25% kill fee. Buys first global serial rights for most articles. Editorial lead time 3 months. Accepts queries by mail, e-mail, fax. Reports in 1 month on queries. Sample copy for $7.50 or on website. Writer's guidelines for #10 SASE.

**Nonfiction:** Essays, food, general interest, lifestyle, sports, travel. Features are highly visual, focusing on some unusual or unique angle of travel, food, business, or other topic approved by an *Attaché* editor." **Buys 60 mss/year.** Query with published clips. Length: 350-2,500 words. Pay varies with freelancers' degree of experience and expertise. Sometimes pays expenses of writers on assignment.

**Photos:** State availability of photos with submission. Reviews contact sheets, negatives, transparencies. Negotiates payment individually. Model releases, identification of subjects required. Buys one-time rights.

**Columns/Departments:** *Passions* includes several topics such as "Vices," "Food," "Golf," "Sporting," "Shelf Life," and "Things That Go"; *Paragons* features short lists of the best in a particular field or category, as well as 400-word pieces describing the best of something—for example, the best home tool, the best ice cream in Paris, and the best reading library. Each piece should lend itself to highly visual art; *Informed Sources* are departments of expertise and first-person accounts. They include "How It Works," "Home Front," "Improvement," and "Genius at Work." **Buys 50-75 mss/year.** Query with published clips. Pay varies with freelancers' degree of experience and expertise.

**Tips:** "We look for cleverly written, entertaining articles with a unique angle, particularly pieces that focus on 'the best of' something. Study the magazine for content, style and tone. Queries for story ideas should be to the point and presented clearly. Any correspondence should include SASE."

☆ **$ $ $** WASHINGTON FLYER MAGAZINE, #111, 1707 L St., NW, Washington DC 20036. Fax: (202)331-2043. **Contact:** Stefanie Berry, associate editor. **75% freelance written.** Bimonthly inflight magazine for business and pleasure travelers at Washington National and Washington Dulles International airports INSI. "Primarily affluent, well-educated audience that flies frequently in and out of Washington, DC." Estab. 1989. Circ. 180,000. **Pays on acceptance.** Byline given. Offers 25% kill fee. Buys first North American rights. Submit seasonal material 4 months in advance. Reports in approximately 10 weeks. Sample copy and writer's guidelines for 9×12 SAE with $2 postage.

• Ranked as one of the best markets for freelance writers in *Writer's Yearbook* magazine's annual "Top 100 Markets," January 1999.

**Nonfiction:** General interest, interview/profile, travel, business. One international destination feature per issue, determined 6 months in advance. One feature per issue on aspect of life in Washington. **Buys 20-30 mss/year.** Query with published clips and SASE. Length: 800-1,200 words. **Pays $500-900.**

**Photos:** State availability of photos. Reviews negatives and transparencies (almost always color). Considers additional payment for top-quality photos accepted with ms. Identification of subjects required. Buys one-time rights.

**Columns/Departments:** Washington Insider, Travel, Hospitality, Airports and Airlines, Restaurants, Shopping. Query with SASE. Length: 800-1,200 words. **Pays $500-900.**

**Tips:** "Know the Washington market and issues relating to frequent business/pleasure travelers as we move toward a global economy. With a bimonthly publication schedule it's important that stories remain viable as possible during the magazine's two-month 'shelf life.' No telephone calls, please and understand that most assignments are made in August for the coming year."

Ⓝ **$ $** WINGTIPS, The Official Magazine of COMAIR, Graf/X Publishing, 3000 N. 2nd St., Minneapolis MN 55411. (612)588-7571. Fax: (610)588-2265. E-mail: http://www.graf-x.net. **Contact:** Inflight Editor. Bimonthly inflight magazine for COMAIR airlines. "Wingtips covers travel, business, sports and profiles. Locations mentioned in articles must match with Comair flight routes." Estab. 1995. Circ. 32,000. Pays 60 days after publication. Byline given. Offers 50% kill fee. Buys first North American serial rights, second serial rights and makes work-for-hire assignments. Editorial lead time 4 months. Submit seasonal material 4 months in advance. Accepts simultaneous submissions. Reports in 6 weeks on queries, 2 months on mss. Sample copy for 8×11 SAE with 3 first-class stamps. Writer's guidelines for #10 SASE.

**Nonfiction:** Book excerpts, general interest, how-to, humor, interview/profile, personal experience, travel. **Buys 20-30 mss/year.** Query with published clips. Length: 750-2,500 words. **Pays $50-500 for assigned articles; $10-250 for unsolicited articles.** Sometimes pays expenses of writers on assignment.

**Reprints:** State availability of photos with submission. Negotiates payment individually.

**Tips:** "Since this publication doubles as an airline marketing tool, the writers with the best chance are the ones who can write a piece with a positive slant, that is still informative and stylistic. Work published here needs to be ultimately positive but not sterile. Also, we need more health-related submissions."

# JUVENILE

Just as children change and grow, so do juvenile magazines. Children's magazine editors stress that writers must read recent issues. A wide variety of issues are addressed in the numerous magazines for the baby boom echo. Respecting nature, developing girls' self-esteem and establishing good healthy habits all find an editorial niche. This section lists publications for children up to age 12. Magazines for young people 13-19 appear in the Teen and Young Adult category. Many of the following publications are produced by religious groups and, where possible, the specific denomination is given. A directory for juvenile markets, *Children's Writer's & Illustrator's Market*, is available from Writer's Digest Books.

**$ $AMERICAN GIRL**, Pleasant Company Publications, 8400 Fairway Place, Middleton WI 53562. (608)836-4848. Fax: (608)831-7089. E-mail: readermail@ag.pleasantco.com. Website: http://www.americangirl.com. Editor: Sarah Jane Brian. Managing Editor: Barbara Stretchberry. **Contact:** Magazine Department Assistant. **5% freelance written.** Bimonthly 4-color magazine covering hobbies, crafts, profiles and history of interest to girls ages 8-12. Estab. 1992. Circ. 750,000. **Pays on acceptance.** Byline given for larger features, not departments. Offers 50% kill fee. Buys all rights, occasionally first North American serial rights. Editorial lead time 6 months. Submit seasonal material 6 months in advance. Accepts simultaneous submissions. Reports in 3 months on queries. Sample copy for 9 × 12 SAE with $1.93 postage. Writer's guidelines for #10 SASE.

- Best opportunity for freelancers is the Girls Express section. "We're looking for short profiles of girls who are into sports, the arts, interesting hobbies, cultural activities, and other areas. A key: The girl must be the 'star' and the story must be from her point of view. Be sure to include the age of the girls you're pitching to us. If you have any photo leads, please send those, too. We also welcome how-to stories—how to send away for free things, hot ideas for a cool day, how to write the President and get a response. In addition, we're looking for easy crafts that can be explained in five simple steps. Stories in Girls Express have to be told in no more than 175 words. We prefer to receive ideas in query form rather than finished manuscripts."

**Nonfiction:** General contemporary interest, how-to. No historical profiles about obvious female heroines—Annie Oakley, Amelia Earhart; no romance or dating. **Buys 3-10 mss/year.** Query by mail with published clips. Length: 100-800 words, depending on whether it's a feature or for a specific department. **Pays $300 minimum for feature articles.** Pays expenses of writers on assignment.

**Reprints:** Accepts reprints of previously published fiction.

**Photos:** State availability of photos with submission. "We prefer to shoot." Buys all rights.

**Fiction:** Adventure, condensed novels, ethnic, historical, humorous, slice-of-life vignettes. No romance, science fiction, fantasy. **Buys 6 mss/year.** Query with published clips. Length: 2,300 words maximum. **Pays $500 minimum.**

**Columns/Departments:** Girls Express (short profiles of girls with unusual and interesting hobbies that other girls want to read about), 175 words, query; Giggle Gang (puzzles, games, etc—especially looking for seasonal).

▣ The online magazine carries original content not found in the print edition.

**$BABYBUG**, Carus Corporation, P.O. Box 300, Peru IL 61354. (815)224-6656. Editor-in-Chief: Marianne Carus. **Contact:** Paula Morrow, editor. **50% freelance written.** Board-book magazine published every 6 weeks. "*Babybug* is 'the listening and looking magazine for infants and toddlers,' intended to be read aloud by a loving adult to foster a love of books and reading in young children ages 6 months-2 years." Estab. 1994. Circ. 45,000. Pays on publication. Publishes ms an average of 18 months after acceptance. Byline given. Buys first, second serial (reprint) or all rights. Editorial lead time 8-10 months. Submit seasonal material 1 year in advance. Accepts simultaneous submissions, if so noted. Sample copy for $5. Writer's guidelines for #10 SASE.

**Nonfiction:** General interest and "World Around You" for infants and toddlers. **Buys 5-10 mss/year.** Send complete ms. Length: 1-10 words. **Pays $25.**

**Fiction:** Adventure, humorous and anything for infants and toddlers. **Buys 5-10 mss/year.** Send complete ms. Length: 2-8 short sentences. **Pays $25.**

**Poetry: Buys 8-10 poems/year.** Submit maximum 5 poems. Length: 2-8 lines. **Pays $25.**

**Tips:** "Imagine having to read your story or poem—out loud—fifty times or more! That's what parents will have to do. Babies and toddlers demand, 'Read it again!' Your material must hold up under repetition."

⬥ **$ $BOYS' LIFE**, Boy Scouts of America, P.O. Box 152079, Irving TX 75015-2079. **Contact:** W.E. Butterworth IV, managing editor. **75% freelance written.** Prefers to work with published/established writers; works with small number of new/unpublished writers each year. Monthly magazine covering activities of interest to all boys ages 8-18. Most readers are Scouts or Cub Scouts. Estab. 1911. Circ. 1,300,000. **Pays on acceptance.** Publishes ms an average of 1 year after acceptance. Buys one-time rights. Reports in 2 months. Sample copy for $3 and 9 × 12 SAE. Writer's guidelines for #10 SASE.

● Ranked as one of the best markets for freelance writers in *Writer's Yearbook* magazine's annual "Top 100 Markets," January 1999.

**Nonfiction:** Mike Goldman, articles editor. Subject matter is broad, everything from professional sports to American history to how to pack a canoe. Look at a current list of the BSAs more than 100 merit badge pamphlets for an idea of the wide range of subjects possible. Major articles run 500-1,500 words; preferred length is about 1,000 words including sidebars and boxes. **Pays $400-1,500.** Uses strong photo features with about 500 words of text. Separate payment or assignment for photos. **Buys 60 major articles/year.** Also needs how-to features and hobby and crafts ideas. Query in writing with SASE. No phone queries. Pays expenses of writers on assignment.

**Columns:** Contact: special features editor. "Science, nature, earth, health, sports, space and aviation, cars, computers, entertainment, pets, history, music are some of the columns for which we use 300-750 words of text. This is a good place to show us what you can do." **Buys 75-80 columns/year. Pays $250-300.** Query first in writing.

**Fiction:** Shannon Lowry, associate editor. Humor, mystery, science fiction and adventure. Short stories 1,000-1,500 words; rarely longer. **Buys 12-15 short stories/year.** Send complete ms with SASE. **Pays $750 minimum.**

● Ranked as one of the best markets for fiction writers by *Writer's Digest* magazine's "Fiction 50," June 1999.

**Fillers:** Also buys freelance comics pages and scripts.

**Tips:** "We strongly recommend reading at least 12 issues of the magazine before you submit queries. We are a good market for any writer willing to do the necessary homework."

**N ✪ $ BOYS QUEST**, Bluffton News Publishing, 103 N. Main, P.O. Box 227, Bluffton OH 45817. (419)358-4610. Editor: Marilyn Edwards. **Contact:** Virginia Edwards, assistant editor. **70% freelance written.** Bimonthly magazine covering boys ages 6-12, with a mission to inspire boys to read, maintain traditional family values, and emphasize wholesome, innocent childhood interests. Estab. 1995. Circ. 4,000. Pays on publication. Byline given. Buys first North American serial rights. Editorial lead time 1 year. Submit seasonal material 1 year in advance. Accepts simultaneous submissions. Reports in 1 month on queries; 2 months on mss. Sample copy for $3.95. Guidelines for #10 SASE.

**Nonfiction:** General interest, historical/nostalgic, how-to (building), humor, interview/profile, personal experience. Send complete ms. Length: 300-700 words with photos. **Pays 5¢/word.**

**Reprints:** Send photocopy of article or short story or typed ms with rights for sale noted. **Pays 5¢/word.**

**Photos:** State availability of photos or send with submission. Offers $10/photo. Model releases required. Buys one-time rights.

**Columns/Departments:** Send complete ms. **Pays 5¢/word.**

**Fiction:** Adventure, historical, humorous. Send complete ms. Length: 300-700 words. **Pays 5¢/word.**

**Poetry:** Traditional. **Buys 25-30 poems/year.** Length: 10-30 lines. **Pays $10-15.**

**Tips:** "We are looking for lively writing, most of it from a young boy's point of view—with the boy or boys directly involved in an activity that is both wholesome and unusual. We need nonfiction with photos and fiction stories—around 500 words—puzzle, poems, cooking, carpentry projects, jokes and riddles. Nonfiction pieces that are accompanied by black and white photos are far more likely to be accepted than those that need illustrations."

**$ BREAD FOR GOD'S CHILDREN**, Bread Ministries, Inc., P.O. Box 1017, Arcadia FL 34265. (941)494-6214. Fax: (941)993-0154. E-mail: bread@desoto.net. **Contact:** Judith M. Gibbs, editor. **10% freelance written.** "An interdenominational Christian teaching publication published 8 times/year written to aid children and youth in leading a Christian life." Estab. 1972. Circ. 10,000. Pays on publication. Publishes ms an average of 6 months after acceptance. Byline given. Buys first rights. Accepts simultaneous submissions. Reports in 6 months on mss. Three sample copies for 9×12 SAE and 5 first-class stamps. Writer's guidelines for #10 SASE.

○→ Break in with a good story about a 6-10 year old gaining insight into a spiritual principle—without an adult preaching the message to him.

**Nonfiction:** Christian values. "We are looking for writers who have a solid knowledge of Biblical principles and are concerned for the youth of today keeping the principles. Our stories must be well-written, with the story itself getting the message across—no preaching, moralizing or tag endings." **Buys 5 mss/year.** Send complete ms. Length: 500-800 words. **Pays $15-25.**

**Reprints:** Send tearsheet of article or short story and information about when and where the article or story previously appeared.

**Columns/Departments:** Let's Chat (children's Christian values), 500-700 words; Teen Page (youth Christian values), 600-800 words; Idea Page (games, crafts, Bible drills). **Buys 3-5 mss/year.** Send complete ms. **Pays $25.**

**Fiction:** No fantasy, science fiction, or non-Christian themes. **Buys 15-20 mss/year.** Send complete ms. Length: 600-800 words (young children), 900-1,500 words (older children). **Pays $30-50.**

**Tips:** "Follow usual guidelines for careful writing, editing, and proofreading. We get many manuscripts with misspellings, poor grammar, careless typing. Know your subject—writer should know the Lord to write about the Christian life. Study the publication and our guidelines."

**$ $ CALLIOPE: The World History Magazine for Young People**, Cobblestone Publishing, Inc., 30 Grove St., Peterborough NH 03458-1454. (603)924-7209. Fax: (603)924-7380. E-mail: editorial@cobblestone.mv.com. Website: http://www.cobblestonepub.com. Editors: Rosalie and Charles Baker. **Contact:** Rosalie F. Baker. **50% freelance written.** Prefers to work with published/established writers. Magazine published 9 times/year covering world history (East and West) through 1800 AD for 8- to 14-year-olds. Articles must relate to the issue's theme. Circ. 13,000. Pays on publication. Byline given. Buys all rights. Prefers not to accept simultaneous submissions. Sample copy for $4.50 and 7½×10½ SASE with 4 first-class stamps or on website. Writer's guidelines for SASE or on website.

**Nonfiction:** Essays, general interest, historical/nostalgic, how-to (activities), recipes, humor, interview/profile, personal experience, photo feature, technical, travel. Articles must relate to the theme. No religious, pornographic, biased or sophisticated submissions. **Buys 30-40 mss/year.** Query with published clips. Length: feature articles 700-800 words. Supplemental nonfiction 300-600 words. **Pays 20-25¢/printed word.**

**Photos:** State availability of photos with submission. Reviews contact sheets, color slides and b&w prints. Buys one-time rights. Pays $15-100 (color cover negotiated).

**Fiction:** All fiction must be theme-related. **Buys 10 mss/year.** Query with published clips. Length: up to 800 words. **Pays 20-25¢/printed word.**

**Columns/Departments:** Activities (crafts, recipes, projects); up to 700 words. Pays on an individual basis.

**Fillers:** Puzzles and Games (no word finds). Crossword and other word puzzles using the vocabulary of the issue's theme. Mazes and picture puzzles that relate to the theme. Pays on an individual basis.

**Tips:** "A query must consist of all of the following to be considered (please use non-erasable paper): a brief cover letter stating the subject and word length of the proposed article; a detailed one-page outline explaining the information to be presented in the article; an extensive bibliography of materials the author intends to use in preparing the article; a self-addressed stamped envelope. (Authors are urged to use primary resources and up-to-date scholarly resources in their bibliography.) Writers new to *Calliope* should send a writing sample with the query. If you would like to know if your query has been received, please also include a stamped postcard that requests acknowledgement of receipt. In all correspondence, please include your complete address as well as a telephone number where you can be reached."

**$ $ CHICKADEE MAGAZINE, Discover a World of Fun**, The Owl Group, Bayard Press Canada, 179 John St., Suite 500, Toronto, Ontario M5T 3G5 Canada. (416)340-2700. Fax: (416)340-9769. E-mail: chickadeenet@owl.on.ca. Website: http://www.owl.on.ca. **Contact:** Angela Keenlyside, editorial assistant. **25% freelance written.** Magazine published 9 times/year for 6- to 9-year-olds. "We aim to interest children in the world around them in an entertaining and lively way." Estab. 1979. Circ. 110,000 Canada and US. Pays on publication. Byline given. Buys all rights. Accepts queries by mail, e-mail. Reports in 3 months. Sample copy for $4 and SAE ($2 money order or IRCs). Writer's guidelines for SAE ($2 money order or IRCs).

**Nonfiction:** How-to (easy and unusual arts and crafts); personal experience (real children in real situations). No articles for older children; no religious or moralistic features.

**Photos:** Send photos with ms. Reviews 35mm transparencies. Identification of subjects required.

**Fiction:** Adventure (relating to the 6-9-year-old), humor. No talking animal stories or religious articles. Send complete ms with $2 money order or IRCs for handling and return postage. **Pays $200** (US).

**Tips:** "A frequent mistake made by writers is trying to teach too much—not enough entertainment and fun."

**⊠ $ $ CHILDREN'S DIGEST**, Children's Better Health Institute, P.O. Box 567, Indianapolis IN 46206-0567. (317)636-8881. Fax: (317)684-8094. **Contact:** Daniel Lee, editor. **85% freelance written.** Works with a small number of new/unpublished writers each year. Magazine published 8 times/year covering children's health for preteen children. Estab. 1950. Pays on publication. Publishes ms an average of 1 year after acceptance. Byline given. Buys all rights. Submit seasonal material 8 months in advance. Submit *only* complete mss. "No queries, please." Reports in 2 months. Sample copy for $1.25. Writer's guidelines for #10 SASE.

• *Children's Digest* would like to see more photo stories about current events and topical matters and more nonfiction in general.

**Nonfiction:** Historical, craft ideas, health, nutrition, fitness and sports. "We're especially interested in factual features that teach readers about fitness and sports or encourage them to develop better health habits. We are *not* interested in material that is simply rewritten from encyclopedias. We try to present our health material in a way that instructs *and* entertains the reader." **Buys 15-20 mss/year.** Send complete ms. Length: 500-1,000 words. **Pays up to 12¢/word.**

**Photos:** State availability of full color or b&w photos. Payment varies. Model releases and identification of subjects required. Buys one-time rights.

**Fiction:** Adventure, humorous, mainstream, mystery. Stories should appeal to both boys and girls. "We need some stories that incorporate a health theme. However, we don't want stories that preach, preferring instead stories with implied morals. We like a light or humorous approach." **Buys 15-20 mss/year.** Length: 500-1,500 words. **Pays up to 12¢/word.**

**Poetry: Pays $20 minimum.**

**⊠ $ $ CHILDREN'S PLAYMATE**, Children's Better Health Institute, P.O. Box 567, Indianapolis IN 46206-0567. (317)636-8881, ext. 267. Fax: (317)684-8094. Website: www.satevepost.org/kidsonline. **Contact:** (Ms.) Terry Harshman, editor. **75% freelance written.** Eager to work with new/unpublished writers. Magazine published 8 times/year for children ages 6-8. "We are looking for articles, stories, poems, and activities with a health, sports, fitness or nutritionally oriented theme. We also publish general interest fiction and nonfiction. We try to present our material in a positive light, and we try to incorporate humor and a light approach wherever possible without minimizing the seriousness of what we are saying." Estab. 1929. Buys all rights. Byline given. Pays on publication. Submit seasonal material 8 months in advance. Reports in 3 months; sometimes may hold mss for up to 1 year, with author's permission. Sample copy for $1.25. Writer's guidelines for #10 SASE.

**Nonfiction:** "A feature may be an interesting presentation on good health, exercise, proper nutrition and safety." **Buys 40 mss/year.** Include word count. Length: 500 words maximum. Submit complete ms; no queries. Material will not be returned unless accompanied by a SASE." **Pays up to 17¢/word.**

**Fiction:** Short stories for beginning readers, not over 600 words. Seasonal stories with holiday themes. Humorous stories, unusual plots. Vocabulary suitable for ages 6-8. Submit complete ms. Include word count with stories. **Pays up to 17¢/word.**

**Fillers:** Recipes, crafts, puzzles, dot-to-dots, color-ins, hidden pictures, mazes. **Buys 30 fillers/year.** Payment varies. Prefers camera-ready activities. Activity guidelines for #10 SASE.

**Tips:** "We're especially interested in features, stories, poems and articles about health, nutrition, fitness, and fun."

**$ $ CLUBHOUSE MAGAZINE**, Focus on the Family, 8605 Explorer Dr., Colorado Springs CO 80920. Fax: (719)531-3499. Website: http://www.family.org. Editor: Jesse Florea. **Contact:** Annette Bourland, associate editor. **25% freelance written.** Monthly magazine geared for Christian kids ages 8-12. Estab. 1987. Circ. 105,000. **Pays on acceptance.** Byline given. Buys one-time rights. Editorial lead time 5 months. Submit seasonal material 7 months in advance. Sample copy for $1.50. Writer's guidelines for #10 SASE.
**Nonfiction:** Essays, general interest, historical/nostalgic, how-to, humor, inspirational, interview/profile, personal experience, photo feature, religious experience. **Buys 3 mss/year.** Send complete ms. Length: 800-1,200 words. **Pays $25-450 for assigned articles; 10-25¢/word for unsolicited articles.** Sometimes pays expenses of writers on assignment.
**Photos:** Send photos with submission. Reviews contact sheets, transparencies. Negotiates payment individually. Captions, model releases, identification of subjects required. Buys negotiable rights.
**Columns/Departments:** Lookout (news/kids in community), 50 words. **Buys 2 mss/year.** Send complete ms. **Pays $25-150.**
**Fiction:** Adventure, fantasy, holiday, humor, historical, religious (Christian), mystery, western, children's literature (Christian), novel excerpts. **Buys 10 mss/year.** Send complete ms. Length: 400-2,000 words. **Pays $200-450.**
**Fillers:** Buys 2 facts, newsbreaks/year. Length: 40-100 words. **Pays $25-150.**

**✖ $ $ COBBLESTONE: Discover American History**, Cobblestone Publishing, 30 Grove St., Suite C, Peterborough NH 03458-1457. (603)924-7209. Fax: (603)924-7380. Website: http://www.cobblestonepub.com. **Contact:** Meg Chorlian, editor. **100% freelance written** (except letters and departments); approximately 1 issue/year is by assignment only. Prefers to work with published/established writers. Monthly magazine (September-May) covering American history for children ages 8-14. "Each issue presents a particular theme, making it exciting as well as informative. Half of all subscriptions are for schools." Circ. 35,000. Pays on publication. Publishes ms an average of 4 months after acceptance. Byline given. Offers 50% kill fee if assigned. Buys all rights. All material must relate to monthly theme. Editorial lead time 8 months. Accepts simultaneous submissions. Reports in 4 months. Sample copy for $4.95 and 7½×10½ SAE with 4 first-class stamps. Writer's guidelines and query deadlines with SASE.
**Nonfiction:** Historical, interview, plays, biography, recipes, activities, personal experience. "Request a copy of the writer's guidelines to find out specific issue themes in upcoming months." No material that editorializes rather than reports. **Buys 80 mss/year.** Query by mail with published clips, outline and bibliography. Length: Feature articles 600-800 words. Supplemental nonfiction 300-500 words. **Pays 20-25¢/printed word.**
**Photos:** State availability of photos with submission. Reviews contact sheets, transparencies, prints. Offers $15-50 for non-professional quality, up to $100 for professional quality. Captions, identification of subjects required. Buys one-time rights. Photos must relate to theme.
**Fiction:** Adventure, ethnic, historical, biographical fiction, relating to theme. "Has to be very strong and accurate." **Buys 5 mss/year.** Length: 500-800 words. Query with published clips. **Pays 20-25¢/printed word.**
**Poetry:** Free verse, light verse, traditional. **Buys 5 poems/year.** Length: up to 50 lines. Pays on an individual basis. Must relate to theme.
**Columns/Departments:** Puzzles and Games (no word finds); crossword and other word puzzles using the vocabulary of the issue's theme.
**Tips:** "All material is considered on the basis of merit and appropriateness to theme. Query should state idea for material simply, with rationale for why material is applicable to theme. Request writer's guidelines (includes themes and query deadlines) before submitting a query. Include SASE. In general, please keep in mind that we are a magazine for children ages 8-14. We want the subject to be interesting and historically accurate, but not condescending to our readers. Queries should include a detailed outline and a bibliography."

**$ $ COUNSELOR**, Scripture Press Publications, 4050 Lee Vance View, Colorado Springs CO 80918. (719)536-0100. Fax: (719)536-3045. **Contact:** Janice K. Burton, editor. **60% freelance written.** Quarterly Sunday School take-home paper with 13 weekly parts. "Our readers are 8-10 years old. All materials attempt to show God's working in the lives of children. Must have a true Christian slant, not just a moral implication." **Pays on acceptance.** Publishes ms an average of 1-2 years after acceptance. Byline given. Buys all or one-time rights with permission to reprint. Editorial lead time 1 year. Submit seasonal material 1 year in advance. Reports in 1-2 months on mss. Sample copy and writer's guidelines for #10 SASE.
**Nonfiction:** Inspirational (stories), interview/profile, personal experience, religious. All stories must have a spiritual perspective. Show God at work in a child's life. **Buys 10-20 mss/year.** Send complete ms with SASE. Length: 800-850 words. **Pays 10¢/word.**
**Reprints:** Send typed ms with rights for sale noted and information about when and where the article previously appeared.
**Columns/Departments:** God's Wonders (seeing God through creation and the wonders of science), Kids in Action (kids doing unusual activities to benefit others), Around the World (missions stories from child's perspective), all 300-350 words. Send complete ms. **Pays 10¢/word.**
**Fiction:** Adventure, ethnic, religious. **Buys 10-15 mss/year.** Send complete ms. Length: 800-850 words. **Pays 10¢/word.**
**Fillers:** Buys 8-12 puzzles, games, fun activities/year. Length: 150 words maximum. **Pays 10¢/word.**
**Tips:** "Show a real feel for the age level. Know your readers and what is age appropriate in terms of concepts and

vocabulary. Submit only best quality manuscripts. We're looking for lively, interesting, true stories that show children how biblical principles can be applied to their everyday lives; stories that are Christ centered, not merely moral and true-to-life fiction with lots of action and dialogue that shows the Holy Spirit at work in the lives of children. Stories that reveal inner attitudes, spiritual conflicts, good decision-making, effects of prayer, issues of Christian character, salvation. If submitting nonfiction, you must include permission from story's subject."

**$ CRAYOLA KIDS MAGAZINE**, Co-published by Meredith Corporation and Binney & Smith Properties, Inc., 1716 Locust St., Des Moines IA 50309-3023. (515)284-2390. Fax: (515)284-3412. E-mail: bpalar@mdp.com. **Contact:** Barbara Hall Palar, editor. **25% freelance written.** Bimonthly magazine covering children (ages 3-8). "Our mission is to excite families with young children about the magic of reading and the wonder of creativity. We do that by reprinting a children's trade book (in its entirety) and by presenting open-ended crafts and fun puzzles and activities related to a particular theme." Estab. 1994. Circ. 550,000 subscribers plus newsstand. **Pays on acceptance.** Publishes ms an average of 4 months after acceptance. Byline sometimes given. Buys second serial (reprint) and all rights, makes work-for-hire assignments. Editorial lead time 8 months. Submit seasonal material anytime. Accepts simultaneous submissions, if so noted. Reports in 3 weeks on queries; 4 months on mss. Sample copy for $2.95 and writer's guidelines for #10 SASE.
**Nonfiction:** How-to/kids' crafts—seasonal and theme-related, puzzles. **Buys 30-40 mss/year.** Themes: "Ancient Culture," "On the Farm," "Space," "Back to School," "Rain Forest," "Halloween," "Tall Tales & Legends," "Holidays" and "Far North." Query. Length: 250 words maximum. **Pays $50-300 for assigned articles; $30-150 for unsolicited articles.**
**Fillers:** "For fillers we want ideas for visual puzzles that are fresh and fun. Do not send art except as a rough indicator of how the puzzle works."
**Tips:** "We're looking for crafts and family activities involving children ages 4 to 11. Send a sample with crafts—they should be made from easy-to-find materials, be fun to make and then play with and should be kid-tested. Send for list of themes before submitting crafts or puzzles or activities that are not seasonal."

**$ $ CRICKET**, Carus Publishing Co., P.O. Box 300, Peru IL 61354-0300. (815)224-6656. **Contact:** Marianne Carus, editor-in-chief. Monthly general interest literary magazine for children ages 9-14. Estab. 1973. Circ. 74,000. Pays on publication. Byline given. Buys first publication rights in the English language. Submit seasonal material 1 year in advance. Reports in 3 months. Sample copy and writer's guidelines for $5 and 9×12 SAE. Writer's guidelines only for #10 SASE.
• *Cricket* is looking for more fiction and nonfiction for the older end of its 9-14 age range. It also seeks humorous stories and mysteries (*not* detective spoofs).
**Nonfiction:** Adventure, biography, foreign culture, geography, history, natural science, science, social science, sports, technology, travel. (A short bibliography is required for *all* nonfiction articles.) Send complete ms. Length: 200-1,500 words. **Pays up to 25¢/word.**
**Reprints:** Send typed ms with rights for sale noted and information about when and where the article previously appeared. Pays 50% of amount paid for an original article.
**Fiction:** Adventure, ethnic, fairy tales, fantasy, historical, humorous, mystery, novel excerpts, science fiction, suspense, western. No didactic, sex, religious or horror stories. **Buys 75-100 mss/year.** Send complete ms. Length: 200-2,000 words. **Pays up to 25¢/word.**
**Poetry: Buys 20-30 poems/year.** Length: 50 lines maximum. **Pays up to $3/line.**

**$ CRUSADER MAGAZINE**, P.O. Box 7259, Grand Rapids MI 49510-7259. (616)241-5616. Fax: (616)241-5558. E-mail: cadets@aol.com. Website: http://www.gospelcom.net/cadets/. **Contact:** G. Richard Broene, editor. **40% freelance written.** Works with a small number of new/unpublished writers each year. Magazine published 7 times/year. "*Crusader Magazine* shows boys 9-14 how God is at work in their lives and in the world around them." Estab. 1958. Circ. 13,000. **Pays on acceptance.** Byline given. Publishes ms an average of 8 months after acceptance. Rights purchased vary with author and material; buys first serial, one-time, second serial (reprint) and simultaneous rights. Accepts simultaneous submissions. Reports in 2 months. Sample copy and writer's guidelines for 9×12 SAE with $1.01 in postage.
**Nonfiction:** Articles about young boys' interests: sports, outdoor activities, bike riding, science, crafts, etc., and problems. Emphasis is on a Christian multi-racial perspective, but no simplistic moralisms. Informational, how-to, personal experience, interview, profile, inspirational, humor. Special issues: Created for Service (September/October); Justice and Mercy (November); Loneliness (December); Honesty (January); Smoking and Drugs (February); Contentment (March); and The Great Outdoors (April/May). **Buys 20-25 mss/year.** Submit complete ms. Length: 500-1,500 words. **Pays 2-5¢/word.**
**Reprints:** Send typed ms with rights for sale noted. Pay varies.
**Photos:** Pays $4-25 for b&w photos purchased with mss.
**Columns/Departments:** Project Page—uses simple projects boys 9-14 can do on their own.
**Fiction:** "Considerable fiction is used. Fast-moving stories that appeal to a boy's sense of adventure or sense of humor are welcome. Avoid preachiness. Avoid simplistic answers to complicated problems. Avoid long dialogue and little action." Length: 900-1,500 words. **Pays 2¢/word minimum.**
**Fillers:** Uses short humor and any type of puzzles as fillers.
**Tips:** "Best time to submit stories/articles is early in calendar year—in March or April. Also remember readers are boys ages 9-14. Stories must reflect or add to the theme of the issue."

**$ $ CURIOCITY FOR KIDS**, Thomson Newspapers, 730 N. Franklin, Suite 706, Chicago IL 60610. Fax: (312)573-3810. E-mail: dscott@ttmedia.com. Website: http://www.freezone.com. **Contact:** Andrew Scott, editor. **10% freelance written.** Monthly magazine. "*Curiocity* is a kid-driven magazine that uses humor and a light-hearted, inquisitive approach to inform and entertain kids 7-12 about people, places and things around the country and around the town." Estab. 1994. Circ. 250,000. Pays on publication. Publishes ms an average of 2 months after acceptance. Offers 50% kill fee. Buys all rights. Editorial lead time 2 months. Submit seasonal material 5 months in advance. Reports in 1 month. Sample copy $5.

**Nonfiction:** Interested mostly in profiles of outstanding and unusual kids; new angles and how-tos for sports stories; and fun takes on educational topics. Length: 300-600 words. **Pays: $100-200.**

**Photos:** State availability of photos with submission. Offers no additional payment for photos accepted with ms. Identification of subjects required.

**Tips:** "We publish only a small percentage of freelance stories, so we prefer queries to be right on target for our needs. No fiction, please. Just query us in our range of needs; please include clips of other published works."

**⚑ $ $ CURRENT HEALTH 1, The Beginning Guide to Health Education**, General Learning Communications, 900 Skokie Blvd., Suite 200, Northbrook IL 60062-4028. (847)205-3000. Fax: (847)564-8197. E-mail: ruben@glc omm.com. **Contact:** Carole Rubenstein, senior editor. **95% freelance written.** An educational health periodical published monthly, September-April/May. "Our audience is 4th-7th grade health education students. Articles should be written at a 5th grade reading level. As a curriculum supplementary publication, info should be accurate, timely, accessible and highly readable." Estab. 1976. Circ. 152,000. Pays on publication. Publishes ms an average of 6 months after acceptance. Buys all rights.

**Nonfiction:** Health curriculum. **Buys 70 mss/year.** Query with introductory letter, résumé and clips. *No unsolicited mss. Articles are on assignment only.* Length: 950-2,000 words. **Pays $150-450.**

**Tips:** "We are looking for good writers with preferably an education and/or health background, who can write for the age group in a scientifically accurate way. Ideally, the writer should be an expert in the area in which he or she is writing. All topics are open to freelancers: disease, drugs, fitness and exercise, psychology, nutrition, first aid and safety, environment, and personal health."

**⚑ $ DISCOVERIES**, Word Action Publishing Co., 6401 The Paseo, Kansas City MO 64131. Fax: (816)333-4439. Editor: Virginia Folsom. **Contact:** Kathleen M. Johnson, assistant editor. **75% freelance written.** Weekly Sunday school take-home paper. "Our audience is third and fourth graders. We require that the stories relate to the Sunday school lesson for that week." Circ. 5,000. Pays on publication. Publishes ms an average of 1 year after acceptance. Byline given. Buys second serial (reprint) rights or multi-use rights. Accepts simultaneous submissions. Reports in 6 weeks on queries; 2 months on mss. Sample copy and writer's guidelines for #10 SASE.

**Reprints:** Send typed ms with rights for sale noted and information about when and where the article previously appeared.

**Fiction:** Religious. Must relate to our theme list. **Buys 45 mss/year.** Send complete ms. Length: 400-500 words. **Pays $20-25.**

**Fillers:** Gags to be illustrated by cartoonist, puzzles, Bible trivia (need bibliography documentation). **Buys 100/year.** Length: 50-200 words. **Pays $15.**

**Tips:** "Follow our theme list, read the Bible verses that relate to the theme. September 1999 begins our new curriculum."

**⚑ $ DISCOVERY TRAILS**, (formerly *Junior Trails*), Gospel Publishing House, 1445 Boonville Ave., Springfield MO 65802-1894. (417)862-2781. **Contact:** Sinda S. Zinn, editor. **98% freelance written.** Weekly 4-page Sunday school take-home paper. *Discovery Trails* is written for boys and girls 10-12 (slanted toward older group). Fiction, adventure and mystery stories showing children applying Christian principles in everyday living are used in the paper. **Pays on acceptance.** Publishes ms an average of 12-18 months after acceptance. Byline given. Buys one-time, second serial (reprint) and simultaneous rights. Editorial lead time 12-18 months. Submit seasonal material 18 months in advance. Accepts simultaneous submissions. Reports in 2 months. Sample copy and writer's guidelines for #10 SASE.

**Nonfiction:** Humor, religious. Wants articles with reader appeal, emphasizing some phase of Christian living and historical, scientific or natural material with a spiritual lesson. **Buys 15-20 mss/quarter.** Send complete ms. Length: 500 words maximum. **Pays 7-10¢/word.**

**Reprints:** Send typed ms with rights for sale noted and information about when and where the article previously appeared. Pays 7¢/word for second rights.

**Fiction:** Adventure, historical, humorous, mystery. No Bible fiction, "Halloween" or "Santa Claus" stories. Wants fiction that presents realistic characters working out their problems according to Bible principles, presenting Christianity in action without being preachy. Serial stories acceptable. **Buys 80-90 mss/year.** Send complete ms. Length: 1,000 words (except for serial stories). **Pays 7-10¢/word.**

**Poetry:** Light verse, traditional. **Buys 10 poems/year.** Submit maximum 2-3 poems. **Pays $5-15.**

**Tips:** "Follow the guidelines, remember the story should be interesting—carried by dialogue and action rather than narration—and appropriate for a Sunday school take-home paper. Don't send groups of stories in one submission."

**Ⓝ $ $ DOLPHIN LOG**, The Cousteau Society, 61 E. 8th St., New York NY 10003. (212)673-9097. Fax: (212)673-9183. Editor: Risa Rao. **30-40% freelance written.** Bimonthly nonfiction magazine covering marine biology, ecology, natural history and the environment. "*Dolphin Log* is an educational publication for children ages 7-13 offered by The Cousteau Society. Subject matter encompasses all areas related to our global water system. The philosophy of the magazine is to delight, instruct and instill an environmental ethic and understanding of the interconnectedness of living organisms, including people." Estab. 1981. Circ. 80,000. Pays on publication. Publishes ms an average of 1 year after acceptance. Byline given. Buys one-time, reprint and translation rights. Reports in 3 months. Sample copy for $2 (make checks payable to The Cousteau Society) and 9×12 SAE with 3 first-class stamps. Writer's guidelines for SASE.

**Nonfiction:** General interest (per guidelines); how-to (water-related crafts or science); photo feature (marine subject). "Of special interest are articles on specific marine creatures, and games involving an ocean/water-related theme which develop math, reading and comprehension skills. Experiments that can be conducted at home and demonstrate a phenomenon or principle of science are wanted, as are clever crafts or art projects which also can be tied to an ocean theme. No 'talking' animals. First-person accounts are discouraged, as are fictional narratives and articles that address the reader." **Buys 8-12 mss/year.** Query or send complete ms. Length: 400-600 words. **Pays $75-250.**

**Photos:** Send photos with query or ms (duplicates only). Prefers underwater animals, water photos with children, photos that explain text. Pays $75-200/photo. Identification of subjects required. Buys one-time and translation rights.

**Columns/Departments:** Discovery (science experiments or crafts a young person can easily do at home), 50-250 words; Creature Feature (lively article on one specific marine animal), 200-300 words. Buys 1 mss/year. Send complete ms. **Pays $25-100.**

**Poetry:** No "talking" animals or dark or religious themes. **Buys 1-2 poems/year. Pays $10-100.**

**Tips:** "Find a lively way to relate scientific facts to children without anthropomorphizing. We need to know material is accurate and current. Articles should feature an interesting marine creature and contain factual material that's fun to read. We are especially interested in material that draws information from current scientific research."

⊠ **$ $ FACES, People, Places and Cultures**, Cobblestone Publishing, 30 Grove St., Peterborough NH 03458. (603)924-7209. Fax: (603)924-7380. E-mail: faces@cobblestonepub.com. Website: http://www.cobblestonepub.com. **Contact:** Elizabeth Crooker, editor. **90-100% freelance written.** Monthly magazine published during school year. "*Faces* stands apart from other children's magazines by offering a solid look at one subject and stressing strong editorial content, color photographs throughout and original illustrations. *Faces* offers an equal balance of feature articles and activities, as well as folktales and legends." Estab. 1984. Circ. 15,000. Pays on publication. Publishes ms an average of 4 months after acceptance. Byline given. Offers 50% kill fee. Buys all rights. Editorial lead time 1 year. Accepts queries by mail, e-mail, fax. Accepts simultaneous submissions. Sample copy for $4.95 and 7½×10½ SAE with 4 first-class stamps or on website. Writer's guidelines for #10 SASE.

**Nonfiction:** Historical/nostalgic, humor, interview/profile, personal experience, photo feature, travel, recipes, activities (puzzles, mazes). All must relate to theme. **Buys 45-50 mss/year.** Query with published clips. Length: 300-1,000. **Pays 20-25¢/word.**

**Reprints:** Send tearsheet of article or short story. Pay is negotiable.

**Photos:** State availability of photos with submission or send copies of related images for photo researcher. Reviews contact sheets, transparencies, prints. Offers $15-100 (for professional). Negotiates payment individually (for non-professional). Captions, model releases, identification of subjects required. Buys one-time rights.

**Fiction:** Ethnic, historical, retold legends or folktales. Depends on theme. Query with published clips. Length: 500-1,000 words. **Pays 20-25¢/word.**

**Poetry:** Avant-garde, free verse, haiku, light verse, traditional. Length: 100 words maximum. Pays on individual basis.

**Tips:** "Freelancers should send for a sample copy of magazine and a list of upcoming themes and writer's guidelines. The magazine is based on a monthly theme (upcoming themes include the Koreas, The Dominican Republic, Bosnia). We appreciate professional queries that follow our detailed writer's guidelines."

⊠ **$ $ THE FRIEND**, 50 E. North Temple, Salt Lake City UT 84150-3226. Fax: (801)240-5997. **Contact:** Vivian Paulsen, managing editor. **50% freelance written.** Eager to work with new/unpublished writers as well as established writers. Monthly publication of The Church of Jesus Christ of Latter-Day Saints for children ages 3-11. Circ. 350,000. **Pays on acceptance.** Buys all rights. Submit seasonal material 8 months in advance. Reports in 2 months. Sample copy and writer's guidelines for $1.50 and 9×12 SAE with 4 first-class stamps.

**Nonfiction:** Subjects of current interest, science, nature, pets, sports, foreign countries, things to make and do. Special issues: Christmas, Easter. "Submit only complete manuscript with SASE—no queries, please." Length: 1,000 words maximum. **Pays 10¢/word minimum.**

**Fiction:** Seasonal and holiday stories, stories about other countries and their children. Wholesome and optimistic; high motive, plot and action. Character-building stories preferred. Length: 1,200 words maximum. Stories for younger children should not exceed 250 words. Submit complete ms. **Pays 10¢/word minimum.**

**Poetry:** Serious, humorous, holiday. Any form with child appeal. **Pays $25 minimum.**

**Tips:** "Do you remember how it feels to be a child? Can you write stories that appeal to children ages 3-11 in today's world? We're interested in stories with an international flavor and those that focus on present-day problems. Send material of high literary quality slanted to our editorial requirements. Let the child solve the problem—not some helpful, all-wise adult. No overt moralizing. Nonfiction should be creatively presented—not an array of facts strung together. Beware of being cutesy."

**$ $ $ GIRL'S LIFE**, Monarch Publishing, 4517 Harford Rd., Baltimore MD 21214. Fax: (410)254-0991. Website: http://www.girlslife.com. Editor: Karen Bokram. **Contact:** Kelly A. White, senior editor. Bimonthly magazine covering girls ages 8-15. Estab. 1994. Circ. 980,000. Pays on publication. Publishes ms an average of 3 months after acceptance.

Byline given. Buys first exclusive North American serial rights. Editorial lead time 5 months. Submit seasonal material 6 months in advance. Reports in 3 months. Sample copy for $5 or on website. Writer's guidelines for #10 SASE.

**Nonfiction:** Beauty, book excerpts, essays, general interest, how-to, humor, inspirational, interview/profile, new product, relationship, sports, travel. Special issues: Back to School (August/September); Fall, Halloween (October/November); Holidays, Winter (December/January); Valentine's Day, Crushes (February/March); Spring, Mother's Day (April/May); and Summer, Father's Day (June/July). **Buys 20 mss/year.** Query by mail with published clips. Submit complete mss on spec only. Length: 700-2,000 words. **Pays $150-800.**

**Photos:** State availability of photos with submission. Reviews contact sheets, negatives, transparencies. Negotiates payment individually. Captions, model releases, identification of subjects required.

**Columns/Departments:** Outta Here! (travel information); Sports (interesting); Huh? (explain something like Watergate or Woodstock, at anniversary of an event); Try It! (new stuff to try); all 1,200 words. **Buys 12 mss/year.** Query with published clips. **Pays $150-450.**

**Fiction:** Publishes novel excerpts.

   ■ The online magazine carries original content not found in the print edition. Contact: Miki Hicks, online editor.

**Tips:** Send queries with published writing samples and detailed résumé. "Have new ideas, a voice that speaks to our audience—not *down* to our audience, and supply artwork (i.e. color slides)."

**$ $ GUIDEPOSTS FOR KIDS**, P.O. Box 638, Chesterton IN 46304. Fax: (219)926-3839. Website: http://www.gp 4k.org. **Contact:** Betsy Kohn, managing editor. **30% freelance written.** Bimonthly magazine for kids. "*Guideposts for Kids* is a value-centered, fun-to-read kids magazine for 7-12-year-olds (with an emphasis on the upper end of this age bracket). Issue-oriented, thought-provoking. No preachy stories." *Guideposts For Kids* is very interested in seasonal stories, especially Thanksgiving and Christmas. Estab. 1990. Circ. 200,000. **Pays on acceptance.** Byline given. Offers 25% kill fee. Buys all rights. Editorial lead time 6 months. Submit seasonal material 6 months in advance. Accepts queries by mail, fax. Reports in 6 weeks. Sample copy for $3.25. Writer's guidelines for #10 SASE.

   ○→ Break in with short nonfiction on topics of general interest, under 500 words, and "Featuring Kids," profiles of interesting kids 7-12, 250 words.

**Nonfiction:** Issue-oriented, thought-provoking features, general interest, humor, interview/profile, photo essays, technical (technology). No articles with adult voice/frame of reference or Sunday-School-type articles. **Buys 20 mss/year.** Query with SASE. Length: 150-1,500 words. **Pays $125-400.** Sometimes pays expenses of writers on assignment.

**Photos:** State availability of or send photos with submission. Negotiates payment individually. Identification of subjects required. Buys one-time rights.

**Columns/Departments:** Tips from the Top (Christian athletes and celebrities), 650 words; Featuring Kids (profiles of interesting kids), 200-300 words. **Buys 15 mss/year.** Query or send complete ms with SASE. **Pays $100-350.**

**Fiction:** Adventure, fantasy, historical, humorous, mystery, suspense. **Buys 8 mss/year.** Send complete ms and SASE. Length: 500-1,300 words. **Pays $175-350.**

**Fillers:** Facts, short humor, puzzles, mazes, jokes. **Buys 8-10/year.** Length: 300 words maximum. **Pays $25-175.** Finders fee ($20-25) for news clippings used.

**Tips:** "Before you submit to one of our departments, study the magazine. In most of our pieces, we look for a strong kid voice/viewpoint. We do not want preachy or overtly religious material. Looking for value-driven stories and profiles. In the fiction arena, we are very interested in historical and mysteries. In nonfiction, we welcome tough themes and current issues. This is not a beginner's market."

**⊠ $ HIGHLIGHTS FOR CHILDREN**, 803 Church St., Honesdale PA 18431-1824. (570)253-1080. Managing Editor: Christine French Clark. **Contact:** Beth Troop, manuscript coordinator. **80% freelance written.** Monthly magazine for children ages 2-12. Estab. 1946. Circ. 3,000,000. **Pays on acceptance.** Buys all rights. Reports in about 2 months. Sample copy free. Writer's guidelines for #10 SASE.

**Nonfiction:** "We need articles on science, technology and nature written by persons with strong backgrounds in those fields. Contributions always welcomed from new writers, especially engineers, scientists, historians, teachers, etc., who can make useful, interesting facts accessible to children. Also writers who have lived abroad and can interpret the ways of life, especially of children, in other countries in ways that will foster world brotherhood. Sports material, biographies and articles of general interest to children. Direct, original approach, simple style, interesting content, not rewritten from encyclopedias. State background and qualifications for writing factual articles submitted. Include references or sources of information." Length: 900 words maximum. **Pays $100 minimum.** Articles geared toward our younger readers (3-7) especially welcome, up to 400 words. Also buys original party plans for children ages 4-12, clearly described in 300-600 words, including drawings or samples of items to be illustrated. Also, novel but tested ideas in crafts, with clear directions and made-up models. Projects must require only free or inexpensive, easy-to-obtain materials. Especially desirable if easy enough for early primary grades. Also, fingerplays with lots of action, easy for very young children to grasp and to dramatize. Avoid wordiness. We need creative-thinking puzzles that can be illustrated, optical illusions, brain teasers, games of physical agility and other 'fun' activities." **Pays minimum $50 for party plans; $25 for crafts ideas; $25 for fingerplays.**

   ● Ranked as one of the best markets for freelance writers in *Writer's Yearbook* magazine's annual "Top 100 Markets," January 1999.

**Photos:** Color 35mm slides, photos or art reference materials are helpful and sometimes crucial in evaluating mss.

**Fiction:** Unusual, meaningful stories appealing to both girls and boys, ages 2-12. "Vivid, full of action. Engaging plot, strong characterization, lively language." Prefers stories in which a child protagonist solves a dilemma through his or her own resources. Seeks stories that the child ages 8-12 will eagerly read, and the child ages 2-7 will begin to read and/or will like to hear when read aloud (400-900 words ). "We publish stories in the suspense/adventure/mystery, fantasy and humor category, all requiring interesting plot and a number of illustration possiblities. Also need rebuses (picture stories 125 words or under), stories with urban settings, stories for beginning readers (100-400 words), sports and horse stories and retold folk tales. We also would like to see more material of 1-page length (300-500 words), both fiction and factual. War, crime and violence are taboo." **Pays $100 minimum.**

• Ranked as one of the best markets for fiction writers in *Writer's Digest* magazine's "Fiction 50," June 1999.

**Tips:** "We are pleased that many authors of children's literature report that their first published work was in the pages of *Highlights*. It is not our policy to consider fiction on the strength of the reputation of the author. We judge each submission on its own merits. With factual material, however, we do prefer that writers be authorities in their field or people with first-hand experience. In this manner we can avoid the encyclopedic article that merely restates information readily available elsewhere. We don't make assignments. Query with simple letter to establish whether the nonfiction subject is likely to be of interest. A beginning writer should first become familiar with the type of material that *Highlights* publishes. Include special qualifications, if any, of author. Write for the child, not the editor. Write in a voice that children understand and relate to. Speak to today's kids, avoiding didactic, overt messages. Even though our general principles haven't changed over the years, we are contemporary in our approach to issues. Avoid worn themes."

**✪ $ HOPSCOTCH, The Magazine for Girls**, Bluffton News Publishing & Printing Co., P.O. Box 164, Bluffton OH 45817-0164. (419)358-4610. Editor: Marilyn B. Edwards. **Contact:** Becky Jackman, editorial assistant. **90% freelance written.** Bimonthly magazine on basic subjects of interest to young girls. "*Hopscotch* is a digest-size magazine with a four-color cover and two-color format inside. It is designed for girls ages 6-12, with youngsters 8, 9 and 10 the specific target age; it features pets, crafts, hobbies, games, science, fiction, history, puzzles, careers, etc." Estab. 1989. Pays on publication. Byline given. Buys first or second rights. Submit seasonal material 8 months in advance. Accepts simultaneous submissions. Reports in 3 weeks on queries; 2 months on mss. Sample copy for $3.95. Writer's guidelines, current theme list and needs for #10 SASE.

• *Hopscotch* has a sibling magazine, *Boys' Quest*, for ages 6-13, with the same old-fashioned values as *Hopscotch*.

**Nonfiction:** General interest, historical/nostalgic, how-to (crafts), humor, inspirational, interview/profile, personal experience, pets, games, fiction, careers, sports, cooking. "No fashion, hairstyles, sex or dating articles." **Buys 60 mss/ year.** Send complete ms. Length: 400-1,000 words. **Pays 5¢/word.**

**Reprints:** Send tearsheet or photocopy of article or typed ms with rights for sale noted. **Pays 5¢/word.**

**Photos:** Send photos with submission. Prefers b&w photos, but color photos accepted. Offers $5-10/photo. Captions, model releases and identification of subjects required. Buys one-time rights.

**Columns/Departments:** Science—nature, crafts, pets, cooking (basic), 400-700 words. Send complete ms. **Pays $10-35/column.**

**Fiction:** Adventure, historical, humorous, mainstream, mystery, suspense. **Buys 15 mss/year.** Send complete ms. Length: 600-900 words. **Pays 5¢/word.**

**Poetry:** Free and light verse, traditional. "No experimental or obscure poetry." Send 6 poems max. **Pays $10-30.**

**Tips:** "Almost all sections are open to freelancers. Freelancers should remember that *Hopscotch* is a bit old-fashioned, appealing to *young* girls (6-12). We cherish nonfiction pieces that have a young girl or young girls directly involved in unusual and/or worthwhile activities. Any piece accompanied by decent photos stands an even better chance of being accepted."

**$ $ HUMPTY DUMPTY'S MAGAZINE**, Children's Better Health Institute, P.O. Box 567, Indianapolis IN 46206-0567. (317)636-8881. **Contact:** Nancy S. Axelrad, editor. **75% freelance written.** Magazine published 8 times/ year covering health, nutrition, hygiene, fitness and safety for children ages 4-6. "Our publication is designed to entertain and to educate young readers in healthy lifestyle habits. Fiction, poetry, pencil activities should have an element of good nutrition or fitness." Estab. 1948. Circ. 350,000. Pays on publication. Publishes ms 8 months after acceptance. Byline given. Buys all rights. Editorial lead time 8 months. Submit seasonal material 10 months in advance. Accepts simultaneous submissions. Reports in 3 months. Sample copy for $1.25. Writer's guidelines for #10 SASE.

**Nonfiction:** "We are open to nonfiction on almost any age-appropriate subject, but we especially need material with a health theme—nutrition, safety, exercise, hygiene. We're looking for articles that encourage readers to develop better health habits without preaching. Very simple factual articles that creatively teach readers about their bodies. We use several puzzles and activities in each issue—dot-to-dot, hidden pictures and other activities that promote following instructions, developing finger dexterity and working with numbers and letters." **Buys 3-4 mss/year.** Submit complete ms with word count. Length: 500 words maximum. **Pays 22¢/word.**

**Photos:** Send photos with submission. Offers no additional payment for photos accepted with ms. Buys all rights.

**Columns/Departments:** Mix & Fix (no-cook recipes), 100 words. **Buys 8 mss/year.** Send complete ms. Pay varies.

**Fiction:** Humorous, mainstream, folktales retold. "We use some stories in rhyme and a few easy-to-read stories for the beginning reader. All stories should work well as read-alouds. Currently we need sports/fitness stories. We try to present our health material in a positive light, incorporating humor and a light approach wherever possible. Avoid stereotyping. Characters in contemporary stories should be realistic and reflect good, wholesome values." **Buys 4-6 mss/year.** Submit complete ms with word count. Length: 350 words maximum. **Pays 22¢/word.**

**Poetry:** Free verse, light verse, traditional. Short, simple poems. **Buys 6-8 poems/year.** Submit 2-3 poems at one time. **Pays $20 minimum.**

**Tips:** "Get to know the magazine before submitting material."

**$ $** JACK AND JILL, Children's Better Health Institute, P.O. Box 567, Indianapolis IN 46206-0567. (317)636-8881. Fax: (317)684-8094. **Contact:** Daniel Lee, editor. **50% freelance written.** Magazine published 8 times/year for children ages 7-10. Estab. 1938. Circ. 200,000. Pays on publication. Publishes ms an average of 8 months after acceptance. Buys all rights. Byline given. Submit seasonal material 8 months in advance. No queries. Reports in 10 weeks. May hold material being seriously considered for up to 1 year. "Material will not be returned unless accompanied by SASE with sufficient postage." Sample copy for $1.25. Writer's guidelines for #10 SASE.

    ○→ Break in to with nonfiction about ordinary kids with a news hook—something that ties in with current events, matters the kids are seeing or television and in mainstream news—i.e., space exploration, scientific advances, sports, etc.

**Nonfiction:** "Because we want to encourage youngsters to read for pleasure and for information, we are interested in material that will challenge a young child's intelligence *and* be enjoyable reading. Our emphasis is on good health, and we are in particular need of articles, stories, and activities with health, safety, exercise and nutrition themes. We try to present our health material in a positive light—incorporating humor and a light approach wherever possible without minimizing the seriousness of what we are saying." Straight factual articles are OK if they are short and interestingly written. "We would rather see, however, more creative alternatives to the straight factual article. Items with a news hook will get extra attention. We'd like to see articles about interesting kids involved in out-of-the-ordinary activities. We're also interested in articles about people with unusual hobbies for our Hobby Shop department." **Buys 10-15 nonfiction mss/year.** Length: 500-800 words. **Pays 17¢/word minimum.**

**Photos:** When appropriate, photos should accompany ms. Reviews sharp, contrasting b&w glossy prints. Sometimes uses color slides, transparencies or good color prints. Pays $15 for photos. Buys one-time rights.

**Fiction:** May include, but is not limited to, realistic stories, fantasy adventure—set in past, present or future. "All stories need a well-developed plot, action and incident. Humor is highly desirable. Stories that deal with a health theme need not have health as the primary subject." **Buys 20-25 mss/year.** Length: 500-800 words (short stories). **Pays 15¢/word minimum.**

**Fillers:** Puzzles (including various kinds of word and crossword puzzles), poems, games, science projects, and creative craft projects. We get a lot of these. To be selected, an item needs a little extra spark and originality. Instructions for activities should be clearly and simply written and accompanied by models or diagram sketches. "We also have a need for recipes. Ingredients should be healthful; avoid sugar, salt, chocolate, red meat and fats as much as possible. In all material, avoid references to eating sugary foods, such as candy, cakes, cookies and soft drinks."

**Tips:** "We are constantly looking for new writers who can tell good stories with interesting slants—stories that are not full of out-dated and time-worn expressions. We like to see stories about kids who are smart and capable, but not sarcastic or smug. Problem-solving skills, personal responsibility and integrity are good topics for us. Obtain *current* issues of the magazine and *study* them to determine our present needs and editorial style."

**KIDZ CHAT**, (formerly *R-A-D-A-R*), 8121 Hamilton Ave., Cincinnati OH 45231. (513)931-4050. Fax: (513)931-0950. **Contact:** Gary Thacker, editor. **75% freelance written.** Weekly for children in grades 3 and 4 in Christian Sunday schools. Estab. 1866 (publishing house). Rights purchased vary with material; prefers buying first serial rights, but will buy second (reprint) rights. Occasionally overstocked. **Pays on acceptance.** Reports in 3 months. Sample copy and writer's guidelines and theme list for #10 SASE.

**$ LADYBUG, the Magazine for Young Children**, Carus Publishing Co., P.O. Box 300, Peru IL 61354-0300. (815)224-6656. Editor-in-Chief: Marianne Carus. **Contact:** Paula Morrow, editor. Monthly general interest magazine for children ages 2-6. "We look for quality writing—quality literature, no matter the subject." Estab. 1990. Circ. 134,000. Pays on publication. Byline given. Buys first publication rights in the English language. Submit seasonal material 1 year in advance. Reports in 3 months. Sample copy and guidelines for $4 and 9×12 SAE. Guidelines only for #10 SASE.

    ● *Ladybug* needs even more activities based on concepts (size, color, sequence, comparison, etc.) and interesting, appropriate nonfiction. Also needs articles and parent-child activities for its parents' section. See sample issues.

**Nonfiction:** Can You Do This?, 1-2 pages; The World Around You, 2-4 pages; activities based on concepts (size, color, sequence, comparison, etc.), 1-2 pages. **Buys 35 mss/year.** Send complete ms; no queries. "Most *Ladybug* nonfiction is in the form of illustration. We'd like more simple science, how-things-work and behind-the-scenes on a preschool level." Length: 250-300 words maximum. **Pays up to 25¢/word.**

**Fiction:** Adventure, ethnic, fantasy, folklore, humorous, mainstream, mystery. **Buys 30 mss/year.** Send complete ms. Length: 850 words maximum. **Pays up to 25¢/word.**

**Poetry:** Light verse, traditional, humorous. **Buys 20 poems/year.** Submit *maximum* 5 poems. Length: 20 lines maximum. **Pays up to $3/line.**

**Fillers:** Anecdotes, facts, short humor. **Buys 10/year.** Length: 250 words maximum. **Pays up to 25¢/word.** "We welcome interactive activities: rebuses, up to 100 words; *original* fingerplays and action rhymes (up to 8 lines)."

**Tips:** "Reread manuscript *before* sending in. Keep within specified word limits. Study back issues before submitting to learn about the types of material we're looking for. Writing style is paramount. We look for rich, evocative language and a sense of joy or wonder. Remember that you're writing for preschoolers—be age-appropriate but not condescending. A story must hold enjoyment for both parent and child through repeated read-aloud sessions. Remember that we live in a multicultural world. People come in all colors, sizes, physical conditions and have special needs. Be inclusive!"

■ **$ LIVE, A Weekly Journal of Practical Christian Living**, Gospel Publishing House, 1445 Boonville Ave., Springfield MO 65802-1894. (417)862-2781. Fax: (417)862-6059. E-mail: l-live@gph.org. Website: http://www.home.a g.org/sscl/. **Contact:** Paul W. Smith, adult curriculum editor. **100% freelance written.** Quarterly magazine for weekly distribution covering practical Christian living. "*LIVE* is a take-home paper distributed weekly in young adult and adult Sunday school classes. We seek to encourage Christians in living for God through fiction and true stories which apply biblical principles to everyday problems." Estab. 1928. Circ. 125,000. **Pays on acceptance.** Publishes ms an average of 18 months after acceptance. Byline given. Buys first rights or second serial (reprint) rights. Editorial lead time 8-12 months. Submit seasonal material 12-18 months in advance. Accepts queries by mail, e-mail, fax, phone. Accepts simultaneous submissions. Reports in 2 weeks on queries; 2 months on mss. Sample copy and writer's guidelines for #10 SASE or writer's guidelines *only* on website.

**Nonfiction:** Inspirational, religious. No preachy articles or stories that refer to religious myths (e.g. Santa Claus, Easter bunny, etc.) **Buys 50-100 mss/year.** Send complete ms. Length: 400-1,500 words. **Pays 7-10¢/word.**

**Reprints:** Send tearsheet, photocopy or typed ms with rights for sale noted and information about when and where the article previously appeared. Pays 70% of amount paid for an original article.

**Photos:** Send photos with submission. Reviews 35mm transparencies and 3×4 prints or larger. Offers $35-60/photo. Identification of subjects required. Buys one-time rights.

**Fiction:** Religious, inspirational. No preachy fiction, fiction about Bible characters or stories that refer to religious myths (e.g. Santa Claus, Easter bunny, etc.). No science or Bible fiction. **Buys 50-100 mss/year.** Send complete ms. Length: 800-1,600 words. **Pays 7-10¢/word.**

**Poetry:** Free verse, haiku, light verse, traditional. **Buys 36-48 poems/year.** Submit maximum 3 poems. Length: 12-25 lines. **Pays $35-60.**

**Fillers:** Anecdotes, short humor. **Buys 12-36/year.** Length: 300-600 words. **Pays 7-10¢/word.**

**Tips:** "Don't moralize or be preachy. Provide human interest articles with Biblical life application. Stories should consist of action, not just thought-life; interaction, not just insight. Heroes and heroines should rise above failures, take risks for God, prove that scriptural principles meet their needs. Conflict and suspense should increase to a climax! Avoid pious conclusions. Characters should be interesting, believable and realistic. Avoid stereotypes. Characters should be active, not just pawns to move the plot along. They should confront conflict and change in believable ways. Describe the character's looks and reveal his personality through his actions to such an extent that the reader feels he has met that person. Readers should care about the character enough to finish the story. Feature racial, ethnic and regional characters in rural and urban settings."

**$ $ $ MUSE**, Carus Publishing, 332 S. Michigan, #2000, Chicago IL 60604. (312)939-1500. Fax: (312)939-8150. E-mail: muse@caruspub.com. Website: http://www.musemag.com. Editor: Diane Lutz. **Contact:** Submissions Editor, the Cricket Magazine Group. **100% freelance written.** Nonfiction magazine for children published 10 times/year. Estab. 1996. Pays 60 days after acceptance or upon acceptance. Offers 50% kill fee. Buys all rights. Accepts queries by mail, e-mail, fax. Reports in 3 months. Sample copy for $5 or on website. Guidelines for #10 SASE.

**Nonfiction:** Children's. "The goal of *Muse* is to give as many children as possible access to the most important ideas and concepts underlying the principle areas of human knowledge. It will take children seriously as developing intellects by assuming that, if explained clearly, the ideas and concepts of an article will be of interest to them. Articles should meet the highest possible standard of clarity and transparency aided, wherever possible, by a tone of skepticism, humor and irreverence." Please send SASE for writer's guidelines first. Query with published clips, résumé and possible topics. Length: 1,000-2,500 words. **Pays 50¢/word for assigned articles; 25¢/word for unsolicited articles;** plus 3 free copies of issue in which article appears.

**Tips:** "Unsolicited manuscripts should be sent to Submissions Editor, The Cricket Magazine Group."

**$ MY FRIEND, The Catholic Magazine for Kids**, Pauline Books & Media/Daughters of St. Paul, 50 St. Paul's Ave., Jamaica Plain, Boston MA 02130-3495. (617)522-8911. Fax: (617)541-9805. E-mail: myfriend@pauline.org. Website: http://www.pauline.org. (click on Kidstuff). Editor-in-Chief: Sister Rose Pacatte, fsp. **Contact:** Sister Kathryn James Hermes, fsp, editor. **40% freelance written.** Magazine published 10 times/year for children ages 6-12. "*My Friend* is a 32-page monthly Catholic magazine for boys and girls. Its goal is to celebrate the Catholic Faith—as it is lived by today's children and as it has been lived for centuries." Circ. 12,000. Pays on editorial completion of the issue (five months ahead of publication date). Buys serial rights. Accepts queries by mail, e-mail. Reports in 2 months. Sample copy for $2.95. Writer's guidelines for #10 SASE. No theme lists.

**Nonfiction:** How-to, religious, technical, media-related articles, real-life features. "This year we are emphasizing cultural and ecumenical themes. We prefer authors who have a rich background and mastery in these areas. We are looking for fresh perspectives into a child's world that are imaginative, unique, challenging, informative, current and fun. We prefer articles that are visual, not necessarily text-based—articles written in 'windows' style with multiple points of entry." Send complete ms. Length: 150-800 words. **Pays $35-100.** Pays in contributor copies by prior agreement with an author "who wishes to write as a form of sharing our ministry."

**Photos:** Send photos with submission.

**Fiction:** "We are looking for stories that immediately grab the imagination of the reader. Good dialogue, realistic character development, current lingo are necessary. A child protagonist must resolve a dilemma through his or her own resources. We prefer seeing a sample or submission of a story. Often we may not be able to use a particular story but the author will be asked to write another for a specific issue based on his or her experience, writing ability, etc. At this time we are especially analyzing submissions for the following: intercultural relations, periodic appearance of a child living with a disability or a sibling of a child or adult with a disability, realistic and current issues kids face today and computer literacy."

• *My Friend* needs "fun fiction with a message relevant to a child's life."

**Fillers:** Puzzles and jokes. "We need new creative ideas, small-size puzzles, picture puzzles, clean jokes." **Jokes pay $7. Puzzles pay $10-15.**

**Tips:** "We have a strong commitment to working with our authors to produce material that is factual, contemporary and inspiring. We prefer those authors who write well and are able to work as a team with us. We need stories that are relevant, have substance, include detail, and are original. Try science fiction for moral issues, etc."

**N ✕ $ NATURE FRIEND**, Carlisle Press, 2727 TR 421, Sugarcreek OH 44681. (330)852-1900. Fax: (330)852-3285. Managing Editor: Elaine Troyer. **Contact:** Marvin Wenyerd, owner/editor. **80% freelance written.** Monthly Christian nature magazine. "*Nature Friend* includes stories, puzzles, science experiments, nature experiments—all submissions need to honor God as creator." Estab. 1983. Circ. 8,000. Pays on publication. Publishes ms an average of 6-10 months after acceptance. Byline given. Buys first or one-time rights. Editorial lead time 4 months. Submit seasonal material 2 months in advance. Accepts queries by mail, fax. Accepts simultaneous submissions. Reports in 4 weeks on queries; 4 months on mss. Sample copy for $2.50 postage paid. Writer's guidelines for 40¢ postage paid.

**Nonfiction:** How-to (nature, science experiments), photo feature, religious, articles about interesting/unusual animals. No poetry, evolution, animals depicted in captivity. **Buys 50 mss/year.** Send complete ms. Length: 250-1,200 words. **Pays 5¢/word.**

**Photos:** Send photos with submission. Reviews any transparencies and prints. Offers $35-50/photo. Captions and identification of subjects required. Buys one-time rights.

**Columns/Departments:** Learning By Doing, Hands on! Hands on! Hands on (anything about nature), 500-1,000 words. **Buys 20 mss/year.** Send complete ms.

**Fillers:** Facts, puzzles, and short essays on something current in nature. **Buys 35/year.** Length: 150-250 words. **Pays 5¢/word.**

**Tips:** "We want to bring joy to children by opening the world of God's creation to them. We endeavor to educate with science experiments, stories, etc. We endeavor to create a sense of awe about nature's creator and a respect for His creation."

**$ NEW MOON: THE MAGAZINE FOR GIRLS & THEIR DREAMS**, New Moon Publishing, Inc., P.O. Box 3620, Duluth MN 55803-3620. (218)728-5507. Fax: (218)728-0314. E-mail: girl@newmoon.org. Website: http://www.newmoon.org. **Contact:** Bridget Grosser or Deb Mylin, managing editors. **25% freelance written.** Bimonthly magazine covering girls ages 8-14, edited by girls aged 8-14. "In general, all material should be pro-girl and feature girls and women as the primary focus. *New Moon* is for every girl who wants her voice heard and her dreams taken seriously. *New Moon* celebrates girls, explores the passage from girl to woman and builds healthy resistance to gender inequities. The New Moon girl is true to herself and *New Moon* helps her as she pursues her unique path in life, moving confidently into the world." Estab. 1992. Circ. 35,000. Pays on publication. Publishes ms 6-12 months after acceptance. Byline given. Offers 50% kill fee. Buys one-time or all rights. Editorial lead time 5 months. Submit seasonal material 8 months in advance. Accepts queries by mail, e-mail, fax. Accepts simultaneous submissions. Reports in 8 months. Sample copy for $6.50 or on website. Guidelines for SASE or on website.

**Nonfiction:** Essays, general interest, humor, inspirational, interview/profile, opinion, personal experience, photo feature, religious, technical, travel, multicultural/girls from other countries. Special issues: The Moon Issue (Jan/Feb 2000, deadline July 1, 1999); Medieval Times (March/April 2000, deadline September 1, 1999); 25 Beautiful Girls (picked by readers. May/June 2000, deadline November 1, 1999); Dreams & Nightmare (July/August 2000, deadline January 1, 2000); Education & Learning (September/October 2000, deadline March 1, 2000); Clothes & Fashion Throughout History (November/December 2000, deadline May 1, 2000). No fashion, beauty or dating. **Buys 20 mss/year.** Query or send complete ms. Length: 300-1,000 words. **Pays 8-10¢/word for assigned articles; 5-10¢/word for unsolicited articles.**

**Reprints:** Send typed ms with rights for sale noted and information about when and where the article previously appeared. Negotiates fee.

**Photos:** State availability of photos with submission. Reviews contact sheets, transparencies, 4×5 prints. Negotiates payment individually. Captions and identification of subjects required. Buys one-time rights.

**Columns/Departments:** Global Village (girl's life in a non-North American country, usually but not always written by a girl), 900 words; Women's Work (profile of a woman and her job(s)), 600-1,200 words; She Did It (real girls doing real things), 300-600 words; Herstory (historical woman relating to theme), 600-1,200 words. **Buys 10 mss/year.** Query. **Pays 8-10¢/word.**

**Fiction:** Adventure, fantasy, historical, humorous, slice-of-life vignettes, all girl-centered. **Buys 6 mss/year.** Query or send complete ms. Length: 300-1,200 words. **Pays 8-12¢/word.**

**Poetry:** No poetry by adults.

**Tips:** "Please read *New Moon* before submitting to get a sense of our style. Writers and artists who comprehend our goals have the best chance of publication. We love creative articles—both nonfiction and fiction—that are not condescending to our readers. Keep articles to suggested word lengths; avoid stereotypes. Refer to our guidelines and upcoming themes."

**$ $ OWL MAGAZINE, The Discovery Magazine for Children**, Owl Group (owned by Bayard Press), 179 John St., Suite 500, Toronto, Ontario M5T 3G5 Canada. (416)340-2700. Fax: (416)340-9769. E-mail: owl@owlkids.com.

Website: http://www.owl.on.ca. **Contact:** Elizabeth Siegel, editor. **25% freelance written.** Works with small number of new writers each year. Magazine published 9 times/year covering science and nature. Aims to interest children in their environment through accurate, factual information about the world presented in an easy, lively style. Estab. 1976. Circ. 75,000. Pays on publication. Publishes ms an average of 3 months after acceptance. Byline given. Buys all rights. Submit seasonal material 1 year in advance. Accepts queries by mail, e-mail, fax. Reports in 3 months. Sample copy for $4.28. Writer's guidelines for SAE (large envelope if requesting sample copy) and money order for $1 postage (no stamps please).

**Nonfiction:** Personal experience (real life children in real situations); photo feature (natural science, international wildlife, and outdoor features); science, nature and environmental features. No problem stories with drugs, sex or moralistic views, or talking animal stories. **Buys 6 mss/year.** Query with clips of published work. Length: 500-1,500 words. **Pays $200-500** (Canadian).

**Photos:** State availability of photos. Reviews 35mm transparencies. Identification of subjects required. Send for photo package before submitting material.

**Tips:** "Write for editorial guidelines first. Review back issues of the magazine for content and style. Know your topic and approach it from an unusual perspective. Our magazine never talks down to children. Our articles have a very light conversational tone and this must be reflected in any writing that we accept. We would like to see more articles about science and technology that aren't too academic."

**$ $ POCKETS,** The Upper Room, 1908 Grand Ave., P.O. Box 189, Nashville TN 37202-0189. (615)340-7333. Fax: (615)340-7267. E-mail: pockets@upperroom.org. Website: http://www.upperroom.org. Editor: Janet R. Knight. **Contact:** Lynn Gilliam, associate editor. **60% freelance written.** Eager to work with new/unpublished writers. Monthly magazine (except February) covering children's and families' spiritual formation. "We are a Christian, inter-denominational publication for children 6-11 years of age. Each issue reflects a specific theme." Estab. 1981. Circ. 94,000. **Pays on acceptance.** Byline given. Buys first North American serial rights. Submit seasonal material (both secular and liturgical) 1 year in advance. Reports in 10 weeks on mss. Sample copy for 7½×10½ or larger SASE with 4 first-class stamps. Writer's guidelines and themes for #10 SASE or on website.

• *Pockets* publishes fiction and poetry, as well as short, short stories (500-800 words) for children 4-7. They publish one of these stories per issue.

**Nonfiction:** Interview/profile, religious (retold scripture stories), personal experience. Each issue reflects a specific theme; themes available with #10 SASE. No violence or romance. **Buys 5 mss/year.** Length: 400-1,000 words. **Pays 14¢/word.**

**Reprints:** Accepts one-time previously published submissions. Send typed ms with rights for sale noted and information about when and where the article previously appeared. Pays 100% of amount paid for an original article.

**Photos:** Send photos with submission. No photos unless they accompany an article. Reviews contact sheets, transparencies or prints. $25/photo. Buys one-time rights.

**Columns/Departments:** Refrigerator Door (poetry and prayer related to themes), maximum of 24 lines; Pocketsful of Love (family communications activities), 300 words; Peacemakers at Work (profiles of children working for peace, justice and ecological concerns), 300-800 words. **Buys 20 mss/year. Pays 14¢/word.** Activities/Games (related to themes). **Pays $25 and up.** Kids Cook (simple recipes children can make alone or with minimal help from an adult). **Pays $25.**

**Fiction:** Adventure, ethnic, slice-of-life. "Submissions do not need to be overtly religious. They should reflect daily living, lifestyle and problem-solving based on living as faithful disciples. They should help children experience the Christian life that is not always a neatly wrapped moral package but is open to the continuing revelation of God's will for their lives." **Buys 44 mss/year.** Length: 600-1,500 words. **Pays 14¢/word.**

• Ranked as one of the best markets for fiction writers in *Writer's Digest* magazine's "Fiction 50," June 1999.

**Poetry: Buys 22 poems/year.** Length: 4-24 lines. **Pays $2/line. Pays $25 minimum.**

▣ The online magazine carries original content not found in the print edition and includes writer's guidelines, themes and fiction-writing contest guidelines. Contact: Lynn Gilliam, associate editor.

**Tips:** "Theme stories, role models and retold scripture stories are most open to freelancers. We are also looking for nonfiction stories about children involved in peace/justic/ecology efforts. Poetry is also open. It is very helpful if writers send for themes. These are *not* the same as writer's guidelines. We have an annual Fiction Writing Contest. Contest guidelines available with #10 SASE or on our website. Writer's guidelines, themes, and contest guidelines, are all available on our website at http://www.upperroom.org."

**$ POWER AND LIGHT,** 6401 The Paseo, Kansas City MO 64131. (816)333-7000. Fax: (816)333-4439. E-mail: mprice@nazarene.org. Associate Editor: Matt Price. **Contact:** Beula Postlewait, editor. **Mostly freelance written.** Weekly magazine for boys and girls ages 11-12 using WordAction Sunday School curriculum. Estab. 1992. Publishes ms an average of 1 year after acceptance. Buys multiple use rights. Accepts queries by mail, e-mail, fax, phone. Reports in 3 months. "Minimal comments on pre-printed form are made on rejected material." Sample copy and guidelines for SASE.

**Fiction:** Stories with Christian emphasis on high ideals, wholesome social relationships and activities and right choices. Informal style. Submit complete ms. Length: 500-700 words. **Pays 5¢/word.**

**Tips:** "All themes and outcomes should conform to the theology and practices of the Church of the Nazarene."

⊘ **$ $ RANGER RICK**, National Wildlife Federation, 8925 Leesburg Pike, Vienna VA 22184. (703)790-4274. Gerald Bishop, editor. **40% freelance written.** Monthly magazine for children from ages 7-12, with the greatest concentration in the 7-10 age bracket.
- Because of a backup in submissions, the editorial staff at *Ranger Rick* is not accepting queries or unsolicited manuscripts until further notice.

✪ **$ $ SPIDER, The Magazine for Children**, The Cricket Magazine Group, P.O. Box 300, Peru IL 61354. (815)224-6656. Fax: (815)224-6615. Editor-in-Chief: Marianne Carus. Editor: Laura Tillotson. **Contact:** Submissions Editor. **80% freelance written.** Monthly magazine covering literary, general interest. "*Spider* introduces 6- to 9-year-old children to the highest quality stories, poems, illustrations, articles and activities. It was created to foster in beginning readers a love of reading and discovery that will last a lifetime. We're looking for writers who respect children's intelligence." Estab. 1994. Circ. 87,000. Pays on publication. Publishes ms an average of 4 years after acceptance. Byline given. Buys first North American serial rights (for stories, poems, articles), second serial (reprint) rights or all rights (for crafts, recipes, puzzles). Editorial lead time 9 months. Accepts simultaneous submissions. Reports in 4 months on mss. Sample copy for $5. Writer's guidelines for #10 SASE.
**Nonfiction:** Adventure, biography, geography, history, science, social science, sports, technology, travel. A bibliography is required with all nonfiction submissions. **Buys 6-8 mss/year.** Send complete ms. Length: 300-800 words. **Pays 25¢/word.**
**Reprints:** Note rights for sale and information about when and where article previously appeared.
**Photos:** Send photos with submission (prints or slide dupes OK). Reviews contact sheets, 35mm to 4×4 transparencies, 8×10 maximum prints. Offers $35-50/photo. Captions, model releases, identification of subjects required. Buys one-time rights.
**Fiction:** Adventure, ethnic, fantasy, historical, humorous, mystery, science fiction, suspense, realistic fiction, folk tales, fairy tales. No romance, horror, religious. **Buys 15-20 mss/year.** Send complete ms. Length: 300-1,000 words. **Pays 25¢/word.**
- Ranked as one of the best magazines for fiction writers in *Writer's Digest* magazine's "Fiction 50," June 1998.
**Poetry:** Free verse, traditional, nonsense, humorous, serious. No forced rhymes, didactic. **Buys 10-20 poems/year.** Submit maximum 5 poems. Length: 20 lines maximum. **Pays $3/line maximum.**
**Fillers:** Puzzles, mazes, games, brainteasers, math and word activities. **Buys 15-20/year.** Payment depends on type of filler.
**Tips:** "We'd like to see more of the following: nonfiction, particularly photoessays, that focuses on an angle rather than providing an overview; puzzles and 'takeout page' activity ideas; folktales and humorous stories. Most importantly, do not write down to children."

**$ $ $ SPORTS ILLUSTRATED FOR KIDS**, Time-Warner, Time & Life Building, 1271 Sixth Ave., New York NY 10020. (212)522-5437. Fax: (212)522-0120. Managing Editor: Neil Cohen. **Contact:** Kirsten Rosanen. **20% freelance written.** Monthly magazine on sports for children 8 years old and up. Content is divided 20/80 between sports as played by kids, and sports as played by professionals. Estab. 1989. **Pays on acceptance.** Publishes ms an average of 3 months after acceptance. Byline given. Offers 25% kill fee. Buys all rights. For sample copy call (800)992-0196. Writer's guidelines for #10 SASE.
**Nonfiction:** Games, general interest, how-to, humor, inspirational, interview/profile, photo feature, puzzles. **Buys 15 mss/year.** Query with published clips. Length: 100-1,500 words. **Pays $75-1,000 for assigned articles; $75-800 for unsolicited articles.** Pays expenses of writers on assignment.
**Photos:** State availability of photos with submission. Buys one-time rights.
**Columns/Departments:** The Worst Day I Ever Had (tells about day in pro athlete's life when all seemed hopeless), 150 words.

**$ STONE SOUP, The Magazine by Young Writers and Artists**, Children's Art Foundation, P.O. Box 83, Santa Cruz CA 95063-0083. (831)426-5557. Fax: (831)426-1161. E-mail: editor@stonesoup.com. Website: http://www.stonesoup.com. **Contact:** Ms. Gerry Mandel, editor. **100% freelance written.** Bimonthly magazine of writing and art by children, including fiction, poetry, book reviews, and art by children through age 13. Estab. 1973. Audience is children, teachers, parents, writers, artists. "We have a preference for writing and art based on real-life experiences; no formula stories or poems." Pays on publication. Publishes ms an average of 3 months after acceptance. Buys all rights. Submit seasonal material 6 months in advance. Reports in 1 month. Sample copy for $4 or on website. Writer's guidelines for SASE or on website.
**Nonfiction:** Book reviews. **Buys 12 mss/year.** Query with SASE. **Pays $25.**
**Reprints:** Send photocopy of article or story and information about when and where the article or story previously appeared. Pays 100% of amount paid for an original article or story.
**Fiction:** Adventure, ethnic, experimental, fantasy, historical, humorous, mystery, science fiction, slice-of-life vignettes, suspense. "We do not like assignments or formula stories of any kind." **Accepts 60 mss/year.** Send complete ms with SASE. **Pays $25 for stories.** Authors also receive 2 copies and discounts on additional copies and on subscriptions.
**Poetry:** Avant-garde, free verse. **Accepts 20 poems/year.** Pays $25/poem. (Same discounts apply.)
**Tips:** "All writing we publish is by young people ages 13 and under. We do not publish any writing by adults. We can't emphasize enough how important it is to read a couple of issues of the magazine. We have a strong preference

for writing on subjects that mean a lot to the author. If you feel strongly about something that happened to you or something you observed, use that feeling as the basis for your story or poem. Stories should have good descriptions, realistic dialogue and a point to make. In a poem, each word must be chosen carefully. Your poem should present a view of your subject and a way of using words that are special and all your own."

**N $ TOGETHER TIME**, WordAction Publishing Company, 6401 The Paseo, Kansas City MO 64131. Website: http://www.nazarene.org. Editor: Melissa Hammer. **Contact:** Kathleen Johnson, assistant editor. Weekly children's story paper published weekly featuring a children's Sunday school theme. "*Together Time* is a full-color weekly story paper for three and four year olds which correlates directly with the WordAction Sunday school curriculum. It is designed to connect Sunday school learning with the daily living experiences and growth of the child." Circ. 5,000. Pays on publication. Publishes ms an average of 6-12 months after acceptance. Byline given. Buys multi-use rights. Editorial lead time 1 year. Submit seasonal material 1 year in advance. Accepts simultaneous submissions. Reports in 2 weeks on queries; 1 month on mss. Sample copy and writer's guidelines for #10 SASE.
**Nonfiction:** Religious. "Does not want to see anything that does not match our theme-list." **Buys 30 mss/year.** Send complete ms. Length: 200-350 words. **Pays $10-25.**
**Reprints:** Accepts previously published submissions.
**Columns/Departments:** Crafts/activities and finger plays (both simple, 3-4 year old level of understanding). **Buys 30 mss/year.** Send complete ms. **Pays 25¢/per line-$15.**
**Fiction:** Religious. "Does not want to see anything that does not match our theme-list." **Buys 30 mss/year.** Send complete ms. Length: 200-350 words. **Pays $10-25.**
**Poetry:** Free verse. "Avoid portrayals of extremely precocious, abnormally mature children." **Buys 20 poems/year.** Submit maximum 5 poems. Length: 4-12 lines. **Pays 25¢/line.**

**N $ TOUCH, Touching Girls' Hearts with God's Love**, GEMS Girls' Clubs, P.O. Box 7259, Grand Rapids MI 49510. (616)241-5616. Fax: (616)241-5558. Editor: Jan Boone. **Contact:** Carol Smith, managing editor. **80% freelance written.** Works with new and published/established writers. Monthly magazine "to show girls ages 9-14 how God is at work in their lives and in the world around them. Our readers are mainly girls from Christian homes who belong to GEMS Girls' Clubs, a relationship-building club program available through churches. The May/June issue annually features material written by our readers." Estab. 1971. Circ. 13,000. Pays on publication. Publishes ms an average of 1 year after acceptance. Byline given. Buys second serial (reprint) and first North American serial rights. Submit seasonal material 1 year in advance. Accepts simultaneous submissions. Reports in 2 months. Sample copy for 9×12 SAE with 3 first-class stamps and $1. Writer's guidelines for #10 SASE.
**Nonfiction:** Biographies and autobiographies of "heroes of the faith." Informational (write for issue themes); humor (need much more); inspirational (seasonal and holiday); interview; multicultural materials; travel; personal experience (avoid the testimony approach); photo feature (query first); religious. "Because our magazine is published around a monthly theme, requesting the letter we send out twice a year to our established freelancers would be most helpful. We do not want easy solutions or quick character changes from bad to good. No pietistic characters. No "new girl at school starting over after parents' divorce" stories. Constant mention of God is not necessary if the moral tone of the story is positive. We do not want stories that always have a happy ending." Special issues: School Surprises (September); Stand Tall, Fall On Your Knees (October); Thankfulness (November); Modeling Christmas (December); Get Out Of Your Rut! (January); Love Is . . . (February); True Adventure (March); Getting In Shape (April); Annual Get-in-Touch issue written by *Touch* readers, the girl's themselves (May/June). **Buys 10 unsolicited mss/year.** Submit complete ms. Length: 200-800 words. **Pays $10-20** plus 2 copies.
**Reprints:** Send typed ms with rights for sale noted and information about when and where the article previously appeared.
**Photos:** Purchased with or without ms. Reviews 5×7 or 8×10 clear color glossy prints. Appreciate multicultural subjects. Pays $25-50 on publication.
**Columns/Departments:** How-to (crafts); puzzles and jokes; quizzes. Length: 200-400 words. Submit complete ms. Pay varies.
**Fiction:** Adventure (that girls could experience in their hometowns or places they might realistically visit); historical; humorous; mystery (believable only); romance (stories that deal with awakening awareness of boys are appreciated); slice-of-life vignettes; suspense (can be serialized); religious (nothing preachy). **Buys 20 mss/year.** Submit complete ms. Length: 400-1,000 words. **Pays $20-50.**
**Poetry:** Free verse, haiku, light verse, traditional. **Buys 5/year.** Length: 15 lines maximum. **Pays $5-15 minimum.**
**Tips:** "Prefers not to see anything on the adult level, secular material or violence. Writers frequently over-simplify the articles and often write with a Pollyanna attitude. An author should be able to see his/her writing style as exciting and appealing to girls ages 9-14. The style can be fun, but also teach a truth. Subjects should be current and important to *Touch* readers. Use our theme update as a guide. We would like to receive material with a multicultural slant."

**$ $ TURTLE MAGAZINE FOR PRESCHOOL KIDS**, Children's Better Health Institute, P.O. Box 567, Indianapolis IN 46206-0567. (317)636-8881. Fax: (317)684-8094. **Contact:** Terry Harshman, editor. **90% freelance written.** Bimonthly magazine (monthly March, June, September, December). General interest, interactive magazine with the purpose of helping preschoolers develop healthy minds and bodies. Circ. 300,000. Pays on publication. May hold mss for up to 1 year before acceptance/publication. Byline given. Buys all rights. Submit seasonal material 8 months in advance. Reports in 3 months. Sample copy for $1.25. Writer's guidelines for #10 SASE.

**Nonfiction:** "Uses very simple science experiments. These should be pretested. Also publish simple, healthful recipes." **Buys 24 mss/year.** Length: 150-300 words. **Pays up to 22¢/word.**

**Fiction:** All should have single-focus story lines and work well as read-alouds. "Most of the stories we use have a character-building bent, but are not preachy or overly moralistic. We are in constant need of stories to help a preschooler appreciate his/her body and what it can do; stories encouraging active, vigorous play; stories about good health. We are also in need of short (50-150 words) rebus stories. We no longer buy stories about 'generic' turtles because we now have PokeyToes, our own trade-marked turtle character. All should 'move along' and lend themselves well to illustration. Writing should be energetic, enthusiastic and creative—like preschoolers themselves. No queries, please." **Buys 50 mss/year.** Length: 150-300 words. **Pays up to 22¢/word.**

**Poetry:** "We're especially looking for action rhymes to foster creative movement in preschoolers. We also use short verse on our back cover."

**Tips:** "We are trying to include more material for our youngest readers. Stories must be age-appropriate for two- to five-year-olds, entertaining and written from a healthy lifestyle perspective."

**$ $ U.S. KIDS, A Weekly Reader Magazine**, Children's Better Health Institute, P.O. Box 567, Indianapolis IN 46206-0567. (317)636-8881. Webstie: http://www.satevepost.org/kidsonline. **Contact:** Nancy S. Axelrad, editor. **50% freelance written.** Published 8 times/year featuring "kids doing extraordinary things, especially activities related to heatlh, sports, the arts, interesting hobbies, the environment, computers, etc." Reading level appropriate for 1st to 3rd grade readers. Estab. 1987. Circ. 230,000. Pays on publication. Publishes ms an average of 4 months after acceptance. Byline given. Buys all rights. Editorial lead time 6 months. Submit seasonal material 6 months in advance. Reports in 4 months on mss. Sample copy for $2.95 or on website. Writer's guidelines for #10 SASE.

• *U.S. Kids* is being re-targeted for a younger audience.

**Nonfiction:** Especially interested in articles with a health/fitness angle. Also general interest, how-to, interview/profile, science, kids using computers, multicultural. **Buys 16-24 mss/year.** Send complete ms. Length: 400 words maximum. **Pays up to 25¢/word.**

**Photos:** State availability of photos with submission. Reviews contact sheets or color photocopies, negatives, transparencies, prints. Negotiates payment individually. Captions, model releases, identification of subjects required. Buys one-time rights.

**Columns/Departments:** Real Kids (kids doing interesting things); Fit Kids (sports, healthy activities); Computer Zone. Length: 300-400 words. Send complete ms. **Pays up to 25¢/word.**

**Fiction:** Adventure, rebus, historical, humorous, mainstream, suspense. No anthropomorphized animals or objects. **Buys 8 mss/year.** Send complete ms. Length: 400-800 words. **Pays up to 25¢/word.**

**Poetry:** Light verse, traditional, kid's humorous, health/fitness angle. **Buys 6-8 poems/year.** Submit maximum 6 poems. Length: 8-24 lines. **Pays $25-50.**

**Fillers:** Facts, newsbreaks (related to kids, especially kids' health), short humor, puzzles, games, activities. Length: 200-500 words. **Pays 25¢/word.**

**Tips:** "We are re-targeting magazine for first-, second-, and third-graders and looking for fun and informative articles on activities and hobbies of interest to younger kids. Special emphasis on fitness, sports and health. Availability of good photos a plus."

**N ☆ $ $ WILD OUTDOOR WORLD (W.O.W.)**®, Rocky Mountain Elk Foundation, P.O. Box 1329, Helena MT 59624. (406)449-1335. Fax: (406)449-9197. E-mail: carolync@MT.net. **Contact:** Carolyn Zieg Cunningham, editorial director. **75% freelance written.** Magazine published 5 times/year covering North American wildlife for children ages 8-12. "W.O.W. emphasizes the conservation of North American wildlife and habitat. Articles reflect sound principles of ecology and environmental education. It stresses the 'web of life,' nature's balance and the importance of habitat." Estab. 1993. Circ. 150,000. **Pays on acceptance.** Publishes ms an average of 18 months after acceptance. Byline given. Buys first North American and electronic rights. Editorial lead time 4 months. Submit seasonal material 8 months in advance. Accepts queries by mail, e-mail, fax. Accepts simultaneous submissions. Reports in 2 months. Sample copy for 9×12 SAE with 3 first-class stamps. Writer's guidelines for #10 SASE.

O—₪ Break in with scientific accuracy, strong *habitat* focus; both educational and fun to read.

**Nonfiction:** Life histories and habitat needs of wild animals. How-to (children's outdoor-related projects, camping, hiking, other healthy outdoor pursuits), interview/profile, personal experience. No anthropomorphism, no domestic animal stories. **Buys 24-30 mss/year.** Query. Length: 600-850 words. **Pays $100-300 maximum.**

**Photos:** State availability of photos with submission. Reviews 35mm transparencies. Offers $50-250/photo. Captions, model releases, identification of subjects required. Buys one-time rights. *No unsolicited photos.*

**Columns/Departments:** Making a Difference (kids' projects that improve their environment and surrounding habitat), 500 words; Short Stuff (short items, puzzles, games, interesting facts about nature), 300 words. **Buys 25-30 mss/year.** Query. **Pays $50-100.**

**Fiction:** Adventure (outdoor, nature and exploring, ethical, "hunting" stories that reflect good sportsmanship and behavior). "We haven't used fiction, but are willing to consider stories that reflect outdoors and environmental ethics, caring for the land and animals." Query. Length: 600-850 words. **Pays $100-300.**

• *W.O.W.* is overstocked and not accepting poetry.

**Fillers:** Facts. **Buys 15-20/year.** Length: 300 words maximum. **Pays $50-100.**

**Tips:** "Because our publisher is a nonprofit whose mission is to conserve habitat for wildlife, we look for a gentle conservation/habitat/environmental ethics message. Stories should be scientifically accurate because the magazine is used in many classrooms. We also look for a hopeful, light-hearted, fun style."

**⊠ $ WONDER TIME**, 6401 The Paseo Blvd., Kansas City MO 64131-1213. (816)333-7000. Fax: (816)333-4439. E-mail: dfillmore@nazarene.org. or pcraft@nazarene.org. **Contact:** Donna Fillmore, editor. **75% freelance written.** "Willing to read and consider appropriate freelance submissions." Published weekly by WordAction for children ages 6-8. Correlates to the Bible Truth in the weekly Sunday School lesson. Pays on publication. Publishes ms an average of 1 year after acceptance. Byline given. Buys rights to reuse and all rights for curriculum assignments. Accepts queries by mail, e-mail. Reports in 2 months. Sample copy and writer's guidelines for 9×12 SAE with 2 first-class stamps.
**Fiction:** Buys stories portraying Christian attitudes without being preachy. Uses true-to-life stories teaching honesty, truthfulness, kindness, helpfulness or other important spiritual truths, and avoiding symbolism. Also, stories about real life problems children face today. "God should be spoken of as our Father who loves and cares for us; Jesus, as our Lord and Savior." **Buys 40 mss/year.** Length: 250-350 words. **Pays $25 on publication.**
**Tips:** "Any stories that allude to church doctrine must be in keeping with Wesleyan beliefs. Avoid fantasy, precocious children or personification of animals. Write on a first to second grade readability level."

# LITERARY & "LITTLE"

Fiction, poetry, essays, book reviews and scholarly criticism comprise the content of the magazines listed in this section. Some are published by colleges and universities, and many are regional in focus.

Everything about "little" literary magazines is different than other consumer magazines. Most carry few or no ads, and many do not seek them. Circulations under 1,000 are common. And sales often come more from the purchase of sample copies than from the newsstand.

The magazines listed in this section cannot compete with the pay rates and exposure of the high-circulation general interest magazines also publishing fiction and poetry. But most "little" literary magazines don't try. They are more apt to specialize in publishing certain kinds of fiction or poetry: traditional, experimental, works with a regional sensibility, or the fiction and poetry of new and younger writers. For that reason, and because fiction and poetry vary so widely in style, writers should *always* invest in the most recent copies of the magazines they aspire to publish in.

Many "little" literary magazines pay contributors only in copies of the issues in which their works appear. *Writer's Market* lists only those that pay their contributors in cash. However, *Novel & Short Story Writer's Market* includes nonpaying fiction markets, and has in-depth information about fiction techniques and markets. The same is true of *Poet's Market* for nonpaying poetry markets (both books are published by Writer's Digest Books). Many literary agents and book editors regularly read these magazines in search of literary voices not found in mainstream writing. There are also more literary opportunities listed in the Contests and Awards section.

**N $ ACM (Another Chicago Magazine)**, Left Field Press, 3709 N. Kenmore, Chicago IL 60613. (773)248-7665. **Contact:** Sara Skolnik, managing editor. **98% freelance written.** Open to new/unpublished writers. Biannual literary journal. Estab. 1977. Circ. 2,500. Pays on publication. Publishes ms an average of 6 months after acceptance. Byline given. Buys first serial rights. Accepts queries by mail, fax. Accepts simultaneous queries and submissions. Reports in 3 months. Sample copy for $8. Writer's guidelines for #10 SASE.
**Nonfiction:** S.L. Wisenberg, nonfiction editor. Interview (contemporary poets and fiction writers), essays (contemporary literature), reviews of small press publications. **Buys 5-6 mss/year.** Query. Length: 1,000-20,000 words. **Pays $5-25.**
**Fiction:** Sharon Solwitz, fiction editor. Serious ethnic and experimental fiction, novel excerpts. **Buys 10-20 mss/year.** Send complete ms. Length: 50-10,000 words. **Pays $5-25.**
**Poetry:** Serious poetry. No light verse or inspirational. **Buys 50 poems/year.** Length: 1-1,000 lines. **Pays $5-25.**

**N $ AFRICAN AMERICAN REVIEW**, Indiana State University, Department of English, ISU, Terre Haute IN 47809. (812)237-2968. Fax: (812)237-4382. E-mail: wsmalloy@amber.indstate.edu. Website: http://web.indstate.edu:80/Artsci/AAR. Managing Editor: Connie LeComte. **Contact:** Joe Weixlmann, editor. **65% freelance written.** Quarterly magazine covering African-American literature and culture. "Essays on African-American literature, theater, film, art and culture generally; interviews; poetry and fiction by African-American authors; book reviews." Estab. 1967. Circ. 4,500. Pays on publication. Publishes ms an average of 1 year after acceptance. Byline given. Buys first North

American serial rights. Editorial lead time 1 year. Reports in 1 month on queries; 3 months on mss. Sample copy for $5. Writer's guidelines for #10 SASE.

**Nonfiction:** Essays, interview/profile. **Buys 30 mss/year.** Query. Length: 3,500-6,000 words. **Pays $50-150.** Pays in contributor copies upon request.

**Photos:** State availability of photos with submission. Offers no additional payment for photos accepted with ms. Captions required.

**Fiction:** Ethnic. **Buys 4 mss/year.** Send complete ms. Length: 2,500-5,000 words. **Pays $50-150.**

**$ AGNI**, Dept. WM, Boston University, 236 Bay State Rd., Boston, MA 02215. (617)353-7135. Fax: (617)353-7136. E-mail: agni@bu.edu. Website: http://www.webdelsol.com/AGNI. **Contact:** Askold Melnyczuk, editor; Colette Kelso, managing editor. Biannual literary magazine. "*AGNI* publishes poetry, fiction and essays. Also regularly publishes translations and is committed to featuring the work of emerging writers. We have published Derek Walcott, Joyce Carol Oates, Sharon Olds, John Updike, and many others. Estab. 1972. Circ. 2,000. Pays on publication. Publishes ms an average of 6 months after acceptance. Byline given. Buys first North American serial rights and rights to reprint in *AGNI* anthology (with author's consent). Editorial lead time 6 months. Accepts simultaneous submissions. Reports in 2 weeks on queries; 6 months on mss. Sample copy for $9 or on website. Writer's guidelines for #10 SASE.

**Fiction:** Short stories. **Buys 6-12 mss/year.** Send complete ms with SASE. **Pays $20-150.**

**Poetry: Buys more than 140/year.** Submit maximum 5 poems with SASE. **Pays $20-150.**

**Tips:** "It is important to look at a copy of *AGNI* before submitting, to see if your work might be compatible. Please write for guidelines or a sample."

**$ $ ALASKA QUARTERLY REVIEW**, ESB 208, University of Alaska-Anchorage, 3211 Providence Dr., Anchorage AK 99508. (907)786-6916. E-mail: ayaqr@uaa.alaska.edu. Website: http://www.uaa.alaska.edu/aqr. **Contact:** Ronald Spatz, executive editor. **95% freelance written.** Prefers to work with published/established writers; eager to work with new/unpublished writers. Semiannual magazine publishing fiction, poetry, literary nonfiction and short plays in traditional and experimental styles. Estab. 1982. Circ. 2,200. Pays honorariums on publication when funding permits. Publishes ms an average of 6 months after acceptance. Byline given. Buys first North American serial rights. Upon request, rights will be transferred back to author after publication. Reports in 4 months. Sample copy for $5. Writer's guidelines for SASE or on website.

• *Alaska Quarterly* reports they are always looking for freelance material and new writers.

**Nonfiction:** Literary nonfiction: essays and memoirs. **Buys 0-5 mss/year.** Query. Length: 1,000-20,000 words. **Pays $50-200** subject to funding; pays in contributor's copies and subscriptions when funding is limited.

**Reprints:** Accepts previously published submissions under special circumstances (special anthologies or translations). Send photocopy of article or short story or typed ms with rights for sale noted and information about when and where the article previously appeared.

**Fiction:** Experimental and traditional literary forms. No romance, children's or inspirational/religious. Publishes novel excerpts. **Buys 20-30 mss/year.** Send complete ms. Length: Up to 20,000 words. **Pays $50-200** subject to funding; pays in contributor's copies and subscriptions when funding is limited.

**Drama:** Experimental and traditional one-act plays. **Buys 0-2 mss/year.** Query. Length: Up to 20,000 words but prefers short plays. **Pays $50-200** subject to funding; contributor's copies and subscriptions when funding is limited.

**Poetry:** Avant-garde, free verse, traditional. No light verse. **Buys 20-65 poems/year.** Submit maximum 10 poems. **Pays $10-50** subject to availability of funds; pays in contributor's copies and subscriptions when funding is limited.

The online magazine carries original content not found in the print edition and includes writer's guidelines.

**Tips:** "All sections are open to freelancers. We rely almost exclusively on unsolicited manuscripts. *AQR* is a nonprofit literary magazine and does not always have funds to pay authors."

**$ AMELIA MAGAZINE**, Amelia Press, 329 E St., Bakersfield CA 93304. (661)323-4064. E-mail: amelia@light speed.net. **Contact:** Frederick A. Raborg, Jr., editor. **100% freelance written.** Eager to work with new/unpublished writers. "*Amelia* is a quarterly international magazine publishing the finest poetry and fiction available, along with expert criticism and reviews intended for all interested in contemporary literature. *Amelia* also publishes two separate magazines each year: *Cicada* and *SPSM&H*." Estab. 1983. Circ. 1,750. **Pays on acceptance.** Publishes ms an average of 6 months after acceptance. Byline given. Offers 50% kill fee. Buys first North American serial rights. Submit seasonal material 2 months in advance. Reports in 3 months on mss. Sample copy for $9.95 (includes postage). Writer's guidelines for #10 SASE.

• An eclectic magazine, open to greater variety of styles—especially genre and mainstream stories unsuitable for other literary magazines. Receptive to new writers.

**Nonfiction:** Historical/nostalgic (in the form of belles lettres); humor (in fiction or belles lettres); interview/profile (poets and fiction writers); opinion (on poetry and fiction only); personal experience (as it pertains to poetry or fiction in the form of belles lettres); travel (in the form of belles lettres only); criticism and book reviews of poetry and small press fiction titles. "Nothing overtly slick in approach. Criticism pieces must have depth; belles lettres must offer important insights into the human scene." **Buys 8 mss/year.** Send complete ms and SASE. Length: 1,000-2,000 words. **Pays $25** or by arrangement. Sometimes pays the expenses of writers on assignment.

**Fiction:** Adventure, book excerpts (original novel excerpts only), erotica (of a quality seen in Anais Nin or Henry Miller only), ethnic, experimental, fantasy, historical, horror, humorous, mainstream, mystery, novel excerpts, science fiction, suspense, western. "We would consider slick fiction of the quality seen in *Esquire* or *Vanity Fair* and more excellent submissions in the genres—science fiction, wit, Gothic horror, traditional romance, stories with complex *raisons d'être*; avant-garde ought to be truly avant-garde." No pornography ("good erotica is not the same thing"). **Buys 24-36 mss/year.** Send complete ms. Length: 1,000-5,000 words, sometimes longer. "Longer stories really have to sparkle." **Pays $35** or by arrangement for exceptional work.

● Ranked as one of the best markets for fiction writers in *Writer's Digest* magazine's "Fiction 50," June 1999.

**Poetry:** Avant-garde, free verse, haiku, light verse, traditional. "No patently religious or stereotypical newspaper poetry." **Buys 100-240 poems**/year depending on lengths. Prefers submission of at least 3 poems. Length: 3-100 lines. "Shorter poems stand the best chance." **Pays $2-25.**

**Tips:** "*Have something to say* and say it well. If you insist on waving flags or pushing your religion, then do it with subtlety and class. We enjoy a good cry from time to time, too, but sentimentality does not mean we want to see mush. Read our fiction carefully for depth of plot and characterization, then try very hard to improve on it. With the growth of quality in short fiction, we expect to find stories of lasting merit. I also hope to begin seeing more critical essays which, without sacrificing research, demonstrate a more entertaining obliqueness to the style sheets, more 'new journalism' than MLA. In poetry, we also often look for a good 'storyline' so to speak. Above all we want to feel a sense of honesty and value in every piece. No e-mail manuscript submissions."

**N** **$ ANTIETAM REVIEW**, 41 S. Potomac, Hagerstown MD 21740-5512. Phone/fax: (301)791-3132. **Contact:** Susanne Kass, editor. **100% freelance written.** Annual magazine of fiction (short stories), poetry and b&w photography. Estab. 1982. Circ. 1,500. Pays on publication. Byline given. Accepts queries by mail, phone. Reports in 2 months. Sample copy for $3.15 (back issue), $5.25 (current issue). Writer's guidelines for SASE.

**Fiction:** Novel excerpts (if work as independent pieces), short stories of a literary quality. No religious, romance, erotica, confession, horror or condensed novels. **Buys 9 mss/year.** Query or send complete ms. Length: 5,000 words. **Pays $50-100.**

**Poetry:** Crystal Brown. Avant-garde, free verse, traditional. Does not want to see haiku, religious and most rhyme. **Buys 20-25 poems/year.** Submit 5 poems maximum. **Pays $20.**

**Tips:** "Spring 2000 annual issue will need fiction, poetry and b&w photography not previously published. Still seeking high quality work from both published and emerging writers. Writers must live in or be native of, Maryland, Pennsylvania, Delaware, Virginia, West Virginia or District of Columbia. Also we now have a summer Literary Contest. We consider materials from September 1 through February 1. Offers cash prize and publication in *Antietam Review*."

**$ THE ANTIGONISH REVIEW**, St. Francis Xavier University, P.O. Box 5000, Antigonish, Nova Scotia B2G 2W5 Canada. (902)867-3962. Fax: (902)867-5563. E-mail: tar@stfx.ca. Website: http://www.antigonish.com/review/. Managing Editor: Gertrude Sanderson. **Contact:** George Sanderson, editor. **100% freelance written.** Quarterly literary magazine. Estab. 1970. Circ. 850. Pays on publication. Publishes ms an average of 2-4 months after acceptance. Byline given. Offers variable kill fee. Rights retained by author. Editorial lead time 4 months. Submit seasonal material 4 months in advance. Accepts queries by mail, e-mail, fax, phone. Reports in 4 months on mss; 1 month on queries. Sample copy for $4 or on website. Writer's guidelines for #10 SASE or on website.

**Nonfiction:** Essays, interview/profile, book reviews/articles. No academic pieces. **Buys 15-20 mss/year.** Query. Length: 1,500-5,000 words. **Pays $50-150.**

**Fiction:** Literary. No erotica. **Buys 35-40 mss/year.** Send complete ms. Length: 500-5,000 words. **Pays in copies.**

**Poetry: Buys 100-125 poems/year.** Submit maximum 5 poems. **Pays in copies.**

**Tips:** "Send for guidelines and/or sample copy. Send ms with cover letter and SASE with submission."

**$ ANTIOCH REVIEW**, P.O. Box 148, Yellow Springs OH 45387-0148. **Contact:** Robert S. Fogarty, editor. Quarterly magazine for general, literary and academic audience. Estab. 1941. Circ. 5,100. Byline given. Pays on publication. Publishes ms an average of 10 months after acceptance. Rights revert to author upon publication. Reports in 2 months. Sample copy for $6. Writer's guidelines for #10 SASE.

**Nonfiction:** "Contemporary articles in the humanities and social sciences, politics, economics, literature and all areas of broad intellectual concern. Somewhat scholarly, but never pedantic in style, eschewing all professional jargon. Lively, distinctive prose insisted upon." Length: 2,000-8,000 words. **Pays $10/published page.**

**Fiction:** "Quality fiction only, distinctive in style with fresh insights into the human condition." No science fiction, fantasy or confessions. **Pays $10/published page.**

**Poetry:** No light or inspirational verse. "We do not read poetry May 1-September 1."

**N** **$ BANGTALE PRESS**, P.O. Box 83984, Phoenix AZ 85071-3984. (602)993-4989. E-mail: bangtale@primenet. com. **Contact:** William Edward Dudley, editor. **75% freelance written.** Semiannual magazine. "We actively seek

---

**ALWAYS SUBMIT** unsolicited manuscripts or queries with a self-addressed, stamped envelope (SASE) within your country or a self-addressed envelope with International Reply Coupons (IRC) purchased from the post office for other countries.

poetry that is telling and doesn't complicate itself through evasive word salad but seeks understanding and gives emotion. We want short stories and essays that in their own way have a poetic underpinning. We lean toward works that explore how different cultures enrich our lives and increase our sense of the world's people. Above all we encourage writing as an instrument that disentangles your thought process. (We would rather see your ideas than set up restrictions.) We encourage humor and irony." Publishes ms 10 months after acceptance. Byline given. Buys one-time rights. Editorial lead time 4 months. Accepts queries by mail, e-mail. Reports in 1 month. Sample copy for $5.

**Nonfiction:** Cultural interest, book excerpts, essays, humor, interview/profile, personal experience. **Buys 5 mss/year.** Send complete ms hard copy and if available disk with indication of the program in which it was written. Length: 300-1,000 words. **Pays $25-50.**

**Photos:** Reviews artistic 3×5 prints (b&w). Negotiates payment individually.

**Fiction:** Experimental, character studies, humor, novel excerpts, slice-of-life vignettes. Publishes novel excerpts. Send complete ms hard copy and if available disk with indication of the program in which it was written. Length: 300-3,000 words. **Pays $25-50.**

**Poetry:** Anything poetic, free verse, light verse. Submit maximum 15 poems. Pays contributor's copy.

**Tips:** "Use quality in language that is humane, humorous, passionate, delightfully understandable, culturally forward, and unexpected."

**$ BLACK WARRIOR REVIEW**, P.O. Box 862936, Tuscaloosa AL 35486-0027. (205)348-4518. Website: http://www.sa.ua.edu/osm/bwr. **90% freelance written.** Semiannual magazine of fiction, poetry, essays and reviews. Estab. 1974. Circ. 2,000. Pays on publication. Publishes ms an average of 6 months after acceptance. Byline given. Buys first rights. Reports in 2 weeks on queries; 3 months on mss. Sample copy for $8. Writer's guidelines for #10 SASE.

● Consistently excellent magazine. Placed stories and poems in recent *Best American Short Stories*, *Best American Poetry* and *Pushcart Prize* anthologies.

**Nonfiction:** Interview/profile, book reviews and literary/personal essays. **Buys 5 mss/year.** No queries; send complete ms. **Pays up to $100** and 2 contributor's copies.

**Fiction:** Christopher Manlove, fiction editor. **Buys 10 mss/year.** Publishes novel excerpts if under contract to be published. One story/chapter per envelope, please. **Pays up to $150** and 2 contributor's copies.

**Poetry:** Susan Goslee, poetry editor. Submit 3-6 poems. **Buys 50 poems/year. Pays up to $75** and 2 copies.

**Tips:** "Read the *BWR* before submitting; editors change each year. Send us your best work. Submissions of photos and/or artwork is encouraged. We sometimes choose unsolicited photos/artwork for the cover. Address all submissions to the appropriate genre editor."

**$ BOMB MAGAZINE**, 594 Broadway, #905, New York NY 10012. (212)431-3943. Fax: (212)431-5880. E-mail: bomb@echonyc.com. Website: http://www.bombsite.com. **Contact:** Betsy Sussler, editor-in-chief. Quarterly magazine covering art, literature, film, theater and music. Estab. 1981. Circ. 25,000. Pays on publication. Publishes ms an average of 6 months after acceptance. Byline given. Buys one-time rights. Reports in 4 months. Sample copy for $4.50 and 10 first-class stamps or on website.

**Nonfiction:** Book excerpts. "Literature only." Query by mail only. Length: 250-5,000 words. **Pays $100 minimum.**

**Fiction:** Short stories. "No commercial fiction." **Buys 20 mss/year.** Send complete ms. Length: 250-5,000 words. **Pays $100 minimum.**

**Poetry:** Avant-garde. **Buys 10/year.** Submit maximum 5 poems. **Pays $50.**

**■ $ $ BOULEVARD**, Opojaz, Inc., 4579 Laclede Ave., #332, St. Louis MO 63108-2103. **Contact:** Richard Burgin, editor. **100% freelance written.** Triannual literary magazine covering fiction, poetry and essays. "*Boulevard* is a diverse literary magazine presenting original creative work by well-known authors, as well as by writers of exciting promise." Estab. 1985. Circ. 3,500. Pays on publication. Publishes ms an average of 9 months after acceptance. Byline given. No kill fee. Buys first North American serial rights. Accepts simultaneous submissions. Reports in 2 weeks on queries; 2 months on mss. Sample copy for $7. Writer's guidelines for #10 SASE.

**Nonfiction:** Book excerpts, essays, interview/profile. "No pornography, science fiction, children's stories or westerns." **Buys 8 mss/year.** Send complete ms. Length: 8,000 words maximum. **Pays $50-250** (sometimes higher).

**Fiction:** Confession, experimental, mainstream, novel excerpts. "We do not want erotica, science fiction, romance, western or children's stories." **Buys 20 mss/year.** Send complete ms. Length: 8,000 words maximum. **Pays $50-250** (sometimes higher). Publishes novel excerpts.

**Poetry:** Avant-garde, free verse, haiku, traditional. "Do not send us light verse." **Buys 80 poems/year.** Submit maximum 5 poems. Length: up to 200 lines. **Pays $25-250** (sometimes higher).

**Tips:** "Read the magazine first. The work *Boulevard* publishes is generally recognized as among the finest in the country. We continue to seek more good literary or cultural essays. Send only your best work."

**$ $ THE CAPILANO REVIEW**, The Capilano Press Society, 2055 Purcell Way, North Vancouver, British Columbia V7J 3H5 Canada. Fax: (604)983-7520. E-mail: bsherrin@capcollege.bc.ca. Website: http://www.capcollege.bc.ca/dept/TCR/tcr. **Contact:** Robert Sherrin, editor. **100% freelance written.** "Triannual visual and literary arts magazine that publishes only what the editors consider to be the very best fiction, poetry, or visual art being produced. *TCR* editors are interested in fresh, original work that stimulates and challenges readers. Over the years, the magazine has developed a reputation for pushing beyond the boundaries of traditional art and writing. We are interested in work that is new in concept and in execution." Estab. 1972. Circ. 1,000. Pays on publication. Byline given. Buys first North American serial rights. No simultaneous submissions please. Reports in 1 month on queries; 5 months on mss. Sample copy for $9 or on website. Writer's guidelines for #10 SASE with IRC or Canadian stamps or on website.

**Fiction:** Literary. **Buys 10-15 mss/year.** Length: 6,000 words maximum. Send complete ms with SASE and Canadian postage or IRCs. **Pays $50-200.** Publishes previously unpublished novel excerpts.

**Poetry:** Avant-garde, free verse. **Buys 40 poems/year.** Submit 5-10 unpublished poems with SASE. **Pays $50-200.**

**$THE CHARITON REVIEW**, Truman State University, Kirksville MO 63501-9915. (660)785-4499. Fax: (660)785-7486. **Contact:** Jim Barnes, editor. **100% freelance written.** Semiannual (fall and spring) magazine covering contemporary fiction, poetry, translation and book reviews. Circ. 600. Pays on publication. Publishes ms an average of 3-6 months after acceptance. Byline given. Buys first North American serial rights. Reports in 1 week on queries; 1 month on mss. Sample copy for $5 and 7×10 SAE with 4 first-class stamps.

**Nonfiction:** Essays, essay reviews of books. **Buys 2-5 mss/year.** Send complete ms. Length: 1,000-5,000. **Pays $15.**

**Fiction:** Ethnic, experimental, mainstream, novel excerpts, traditional. Publishes novel excerpts if they can stand alone. "We are not interested in slick or sick material." **Buys 6-10 mss/year.** Send complete ms. Length: 1,000-6,000 words. **Pays $5/page (up to $50).**

**Poetry:** Avant-garde, traditional. **Buys 50-55 poems/year.** Submit maximum 5 poems. Length: open. **Pays $5/page.**

**Tips:** "Read *Chariton*. Know the difference between good literature and bad. Know what magazine might be interested in your work. We are not a trendy magazine. We publish only the best. All sections are open to freelancers. Know your market or you are wasting your time—and mine. Do *not* write for guidelines; the only guideline is excellence."

**$CICADA**, *Amelia Magazine*, 329 E St., Bakersfield CA 93304. (661)323-4064. **Contact:** Frederick A. Raborg, Jr., editor. **100% freelance written.** Quarterly magazine covering Oriental fiction and poetry (haiku, etc.). "Our readers expect the best haiku and related poetry forms we can find. Our readers circle the globe and know their subjects. We include fiction, book reviews and articles related to the forms or to the Orient." Estab. 1984. Circ. 600. Pays on publication. Publishes ms an average of 6 months after acceptance. Byline given. Offers 50% kill fee. Buys first North American serial rights. Editorial lead time 2 months. Submit seasonal material 3 months in advance. Accepts simultaneous submissions. Reports in 2 weeks on queries, 3 months on mss. Sample copy for $4.95. Guidelines for #10 SASE.

**Nonfiction:** Essays, general interest, historical/nostalgic, humor, interview/profile, opinion, personal experience, travel. **Buys 1-3 mss/year.** Send complete ms. Length: 500-2,500 words. **Pays $10.**

**Photos:** Send photos with submission. Reviews 5×7 or 8×10 b/w prints. Offers $10-25/photo. Model releases required. Buys one-time rights.

**Fiction:** Adventure, erotica, ethnic, experimental, fantasy, historical, horror, humorous, mainstream, mystery, romance, science fiction, slice-of-life vignettes, suspense. **Buys 4 mss/year.** Send complete ms. Length: 500-2,500 words. **Pays $10-20.**

**Poetry: Buys 400 poems/year.** Submit maximum 12 poems. Length: 1-50 lines. **Pays 3 "best of issue" poets $10.**

**Fillers:** Anecdotes, short humor. Buys 1-4/year. Length: 25-500 words. No payment for fillers.

**Tips:** "Writers should understand the limitations of contemporary Japanese forms particularly. We also use poetry based on other Asian ethnicities and on the South Seas ethnicities. Don't be afraid to experiment within the forms. Be professional in approach and presentation."

**$ $CONFRONTATION, A Literary Journal**, Long Island University, Brookville NY 11548. (516)299-2720. Fax: (516)299-2735. Assistant to Editor: Michael Hartnett.**Contact:** Martin Tucker, editor-in-chief. **75% freelance written.** Semiannual literary magazine. "We are eclectic in our taste. Excellence of style is our dominant concern." Estab. 1968. Circ. 2,000. Pays on publication. Publishes ms an average of 1 year after acceptance. Byline given. "Rarely offers kill fee." Buys first North American serial, first, one-time or all rights. Accepts simultaneous submissions. Reports in 3 weeks on queries; 2 months on mss. Sample copy for $3.

**Nonfiction:** Essays, personal experience. **Buys 15 mss/year.** Send complete ms. Length: 1,500-5,000 words. **Pays $100-300 for assigned articles; $15-300 for unsolicited articles.**

**Photos:** State availability of photos with submission. Offers no additional payment for photos accepted with ms. Buys one-time rights.

**Fiction:** Jonna Semeiks. Experimental, mainstream, slice-of-life vignettes, novel excerpts (if they are self-contained stories). "We judge on quality, so genre is open." **Buys 60-75 mss/year.** Send complete ms. Length 6,000 words maximum. **Pays $25-250.**

**Poetry:** Katherine Hill-Miller. Avant-garde, free verse, haiku, light verse, traditional. **Buys 60-75 poems/year.** Submit maximum 6 poems. Length open. **Pays $10-100.**

**Tips:** "Most open to fiction and poetry."

**$DESCANT, Descant Arts & Letters Foundation**, P.O. Box 314, Station P, Toronto, Ontario M5S 2S8. (416)593-2557. E-mail: descant@web.net. Editor: Karen Mulhallen. **Contact:** Tara Ferris, managing editor. Quarterly literary journal. Estab. 1970. Circ. 1,200. Pays on publication. Publishes ms 16 months after acceptance. Editorial lead time 4 months. Submit seasonal material 4 months in advance. Accepts queries by mail, e-mail. Sample copy for $8. Writer's guidelines for SASE.

**Nonfiction:** Book excerpts, essays, historical/nostalgic, interview/profile, personal experience, photo feature, travel. Query or send complete ms. **Pays $100** honorarium plus 1 year's subscription.

**Photos:** State availability of photos with submission. Reviews contact sheets and prints. Offers no additional payment

for photos accepted with ms. Buys one-time rights.
**Fiction:** Send complete ms. **Pays $100.**
**Poetry:** Free verse, light verse, traditional. Submit maximum 10 poems. **Pays $100.**
**Tips:** "Familiarize yourself with our magazine before submitting."

**$ $ $ DOUBLETAKE**, 1317 W. Pettigrew St., Durham NC 27705. (919)660-3669. Fax: (919)660-3668. Website: http://www.doubletakemagazine.org. **Contact:** Fiction Editor. **Pays on acceptance.** Byline given. Buys first North American serial rights. Accepts simultaneous submissions. Reports in 3 months on mss. Sample copy for $12. Writer's guidelines for #10 SASE or on website.
**Fiction:** "We accept realistic fiction in all of its variety. We look for stories with a strong, narrative voice and an urgency in the writing." **Buys 12 mss/year.** Send complete ms with cover letter. No preferred length. **Pays competitively.**
  ● *DoubleTake* received the 1998 National Magazine Award for General Excellence for magazines with circulation under 100,000.
  ▣ The online magazine carries original content not found in the print edition and includes writer's guidelines.
**Tips:** "Be careful of stories that are too leisurely paced. Also, the essential conflict of the story should be discernible to the reader. We're interested in how a character is changed in some way be the end of the story."

**$ DREAMS OF DECADENCE**, P.O. Box 2988, Radford VA 24143-2988. (540)633-2220. Fax: (540)633-2220. E-mail: dnapublications@iname.com. Website: sfsite.com/dnaweb/home.htm. **Contact:** Angela Kessler, editor. Quarterly literary magazine featuring vampire fiction and poetry. Pays on publication. Publishes ms an average of 6 months after acceptance. Buys first North American serial rights. Accepts queries by mail, e-mail. Accepts simultaneous submissions. Reports in 1 month. Sample copy for $5. Writer's guidelines for #10 SASE or on website.
**Fiction:** "I like elegant prose with a Gothic feel. The emphasis is on dark fantasy rather than horror. No vampire feeds, vampire has sex, someone becomes a vampire pieces." **Buys 30-40 mss/year.** Send complete ms. Length: 1,000-15,000 words. **Pays 1-5¢/word.**
**Poetry:** "Looking for all forms; however, the less horrific and the more explicitly vampiric a poem is, the more likely it is to be accepted." Pays in copies.
**Tips:** "We look for atmospheric, well-written stories with original ideas, not rehashes."

**$ $ EVENT**, Douglas College, P.O. Box 2503, New Westminster, British Columbia V3L 5B2 Canada. (604)527-5293. Fax: (604)527-5095. E-mail: event@douglas.bc.ca. **Contact:** Calvin Wharton, assistant editor. **100% freelance written.** Triannual magazine containing fiction, poetry and reviews. "We are eclectic and always open to content that invites involvement. Generally, we like strong narrative." Estab. 1971. Circ. 1,000. Pays on publication. Publishes ms an average of 8 months after acceptance. Byline given. Buys first North American serial rights. Accepts queries by mail, fax, phone. Accepts simultaneous submissions. Reports in 1 month on queries; 4 months on mss. Sample copy for $5. Guidelines for #10 SASE.
  ● *Event* does not read manuscripts in July.
**Fiction:** Christine Dewar, fiction editor. "We look for readability, style and writing that invites involvement." **Buys 12-15 mss/year.** Send complete ms. Length: 5,000 words. Submit maximum 2 stories. **Pays $22/page to $500.**
**Poetry:** Gillian Garding-Russell, poetry editor. Free verse and prose poems. No light verse. "In poetry, we tend to appreciate the narrative and sometimes the confessional modes." **Buys 30-40 poems/year.** Submit maximum 10 poems. **Pays $25-500.**

**⊞ ✪ $ THE FIDDLEHEAD**, Campus House, University of New Brunswick, P.O. Box 4400, Fredericton, New Brunswick E3B 5A3 Canada. (506)453-3501. Fax: (506)453-4599. E-mail: fid@nbnet.nb.ca. Editor: Ross Leckie. **Contact:** S. Campbell, managing editor. **90% freelance written.** Eager to work with new/unpublished writers. Quarterly magazine covering poetry, short fiction and book reviews. Estab. 1945. Circ. 1,000. Pays on publication. Publishes ms an average of 1 year after acceptance. Not copyrighted. Buys first North American serial rights. Submit seasonal material 6 months in advance. Reports in 6 months. Sample copy $9.
**Fiction:** Norm Rauvin. "Stories may be on any subject—acceptance is based on quality alone." **Buys 30 mss/year.** Send complete ms. Length: 50-3,000 words. **Pays $10/page.**
**Poetry:** Julie Dennison and Eric Hill, poetry editors. Avant-garde, free verse, light verse. "Poetry may be on any subject—acceptance is based on quality alone." **Buys 100 poems/year.** Submit maximum 10 poems. **Pays $12/page; $100 maximum.** Offers annual poetry and  short fiction contest with different themes. Deadline is always December 15th.
**Tips:** "Quality alone is the criterion for publication. *Canadian return postage or IRCs* should accompany all manuscripts."

**⊞ ✪ $ FIREWEED, A Feminist Quarterly of Writing, Politics, Art and Culture**, Fireweed Inc., P.O. Box 279, Station B, Toronto, Ontario M5T 2W2 Canada. (416)504-1339. E-mail: fireweed@web.net. **Contact:** Suzanne Methot, managing editor. **100% freelance written.** Quarterly perfect-bound book covering feminist/women's. "*Fireweed* is a forum for the writings of women; diverse cultural, sexual and regional communities; tackles dominant power relations of sex, race, class and sexuality; challenging space for dialogue and inquiry into women's cultural resistance and expression." Estab. 1978. Circ. 1,500. Pays on publication. Publishes ms an average of 1 year after acceptance.

Byline and bio given. Offers 50% kill fee. Buys first North American serial rights. Editorial lead time 3 months. Accepts simultaneous submissions. Reports in 6 months on queries; 1 year on mss. Sample copy for $5. Writer's guidelines for #10 SAE; include IRC.

**Nonfiction:** Book excerpts, essays, general interest, historical/nostalgic, humor, interview/profile, opinion, personal experience, photo feature, visual art, comics. Special issues: Sex-Trade Workers (spring '99); Heavy Girls (summer '99). Does not want to see travel, science, literary criticism, children's. **Buys 75-100 mss/year.** Send complete ms. Length: 5,000 words. **Pays $30/first page, $10 each additional page.**

**Reprints:** Accepts previously published submissions.

**Photos:** Send photos with submission (not originals). Negotiates payment individually.

**Fiction:** Confession, erotica, ethnic, experimental, historical, humorous, novel excerpts. No children's, full mss (we publish excerpts only). **Buys 30-50 mss/year.** Send partial ms. Length: 5,000 words. **Pays $30/first page, $10 each additional page.**

**Poetry:** Avant garde, free verse, haiku, light verse, traditional, prose poetry. **Buys 20-40 poems/year.** Submit maximum 5 poems. Length: open. **Pays $30.**

**Tips:** "Fireweed maintains a commitment to publishing new and established writers. Writers should submit work that challenges feminist/women's literary and aesthetic genres—we are committed to publishing a diversity of voices (that is, there is no one formula). Note: We hate people who send us SASEs with US postage (don't do this)."

**★ $ FIRST WORD BULLETIN,** Amick Associates Magazines, 2046 Lothbury Dr., Fayetteville NC 28304-5666. E-mail: gw83@correo.interlink.es. Website: http://www.interlink.es/peraso/first. Editor: G.W. Amick. **Contact:** Mary Margaret Swain, editorial assistant. **60-80% freelance written.** Quarterly magazine printed in Madrid, Spain, with worldwide distribution to the English-speaking community. "Our audience is the general public, but the magazine is specifically aimed at writers who wish to get published for credits. We welcome unpublished writers; since our audience is mainly writers we expect high-quality work. We like writers who have enough self-confidence to be willing to pay the postage to get to us. They should write for guidelines first and then follow them to the letter." Estab. 1995. Pays on publication. Publishes ms an average of 6 months after acceptance. Byline given. Offers 10% kill fee or $5. Buys first world or second serial (reprint) rights. Editorial lead time 3 months. Submit seasonal material 5 months in advance. Accepts simultaneous submissions. Reports in 3 weeks on queries; 2 months on mss. Sample copy for $3.50 and SAE with $3.50 postage or 4 IRCs. Writer's guidelines for SAE with $2 postage or 2 IRCs.

• First Word is based in Spain at Calle Domingo Fernandez 5, Box 500, 28036 Madrid Spain.

**Nonfiction:** General interest, how-to, humor, personal experience, environment, self-help, preventive medicine, literary, experimental. **Buys 40 mss/year.** Send complete ms. Length: 500-4,000 words. **Pays 2½¢/word up to $50.** Pays in contributor copies for fillers, bullets, pieces less than 50 words.

**Reprints:** Send tearsheet or photocopy of article or short story and information about when and where the article previously appeared. **Pays 2½¢/word up to $50.**

**Fiction:** Adventure, environment, experiment, humorous, mainstream, self-help. No smut, pornography, science fiction, romance/love stories or horror. **Buys 10-30 mss/year.** Send complete ms. Length: 500-4,000 words. **Pays 2½¢/word up to $50.**

**Poetry:** Free verse, light verse. "We are not interested in poetry per se, but will accept poetry as a sidebar or filler." **Buys 4-8 poems/year.** Submit maximum 1 poem. Length: 14 lines for filler; 24 lines for sidebar. **Pays 2½¢/word up to $50.**

**Fillers:** Anecdotes, facts, gags to be illustrated by cartoonist, short humor. **Buys 32/year.** Length: 10-80 words. **Pays 2½¢/word up to $50.**

**Tips:** "Write for guidelines. Pay close attention to the market study. Follow directions to the letter. Get the editor's name correct. Don't request return of manuscript, ask for the first page only to save postage. If you submit a self-help article, don't let God do all the work. For an environmental article, study the subject carefully and get your facts correct. Use positive thinking at all times. I still feel strong about ecology, but I would like to see something on alternative medicine, homeopathy, perhaps some exotic stories on medicines from herbs in Brazil and Venezuela. I need crossword puzzles also."

**$ FRANK, An International Journal of Contemporary Writing & Art,** Association Frank, 32 rue Edouard Vaillant, Montreuil France. Phone: (33)(1)48596658. Fax: (31)(1)48596668. E-mail: poetry@frankonline.org or fiction@frankonline.org. Website: http://www.paris-anglo.com/frank. **Contact:** David Applefield, editor. **80% freelance written.** Bilingual magazine covering contemporary writing of all genres. "Writing that takes risks and isn't ethnocentric is looked upon favorably." Estab. 1983. Circ. 4,000. Pays on publication. Publishes ms an average of 1 year after acceptance. Byline given. Buys one-time rights. Editorial lead time 6 months. Reports in 1 month on queries; 2 months on mss. Sample copy for $10. Writer's guidelines for #10 SASE or on website.

• As of Fall '99, *Frank* is offering $2,000 in prize money plus publication with its poetry and fiction contests.

**Nonfiction:** Interview/profile, travel. **Buys 2 mss/year.** Query. **Pays $100.** Pays in contributor copies by agreement.

**Photos:** State availability of photos with submission. Negotiates payment individually. Buys one-time rights.

**Fiction:** Experimental, international, novel excerpts. **Buys 8 mss/year.** Send complete ms. Length: 1-3,000 words. **Pays $10/printed page.**

**Poetry:** Avant-garde, translations. **Buys 20 poems/year.** Submit maximum 10 poems. **Pays $20.**

**Tips:** "Suggest what you do or know best. Avoid query form letters—we won't read the ms. Looking for excellent literary/cultural interviews with leading American writers or cultural figures."

**$ THE GETTYSBURG REVIEW**, Gettysburg College, Gettysburg PA 17325. (717)337-6770. Managing Editor: Emily Ruark Clarke. **Contact:** Peter Stitt, editor. Quarterly literary magazine. "Our concern is quality. Manuscripts submitted here should be extremely well-written." Estab. 1988. Circ. 4,000. Pays on publication. Byline given. Buys first North American serial rights. Editorial lead time 1 year. Submit seasonal material 9 months in advance. Accepts queries by mail, fax. Reports in 1 month on queries; 3 months on mss. Sample copy for $7. Writer's guidelines for #10 SASE. Reading period September-May. No simultaneous submissions.
**Nonfiction:** Essays. **Buys 20/year.** Send complete ms. Length: 3,000-7,000. **Pays $25/page.**
**Fiction:** High quality, literary. Publishes novel excerpts. **Buys 20 ms/year.** Send complete ms. Length: 2,000-7,000. **Pays $25/page.**
**Poetry:** **Buys 50 poems/year.** Submit maximum 3 poems. **Pays $2/line.**

**$ $ GLIMMER TRAIN STORIES**, Glimmer Train Press, Inc., 710 SW Madison St., #504, Portland OR 97205. (503)221-0836. Fax: (503)221-0837. Website: http://www.GlimmerTrain.com. Co-editor: Susan Burmeister-Brown. **Contact:** Linda Burmeister Davies, co-editor. **90% freelance written.** Quarterly magazine covering short fiction. "We are interested in well-written, emotionally-moving short stories published by unknown, as well as known, writers." Estab. 1991. Circ. 16,000. **Pays on acceptance.** Byline given. Buys first rights. Accepts simultaneous submissions. Reports in 3 months on mss. Sample copy for $9.95 or on website. Writer's guidelines for #10 SASE or on website.
**Fiction:** "We are not restricted to any types." **Buys 32 mss/year.** Send complete ms. Length: 1,200-8,000 words. **Pays $500.**
● Ranked as one of the best markets for fiction writers in *Writer's Digest* magazine's "Fiction 50," June 1999.
**Tips:** "Manuscripts should be sent to us in the months of January, April, July and October. Be sure to include a sufficiently-stamped SASE. We are particularly interested in receiving work from new writers." See *Glimmer Train*'s contest listings in Contest and Awards section.

**$ GRAIN LITERARY MAGAZINE**, Saskatchewan Writers Guild, P.O. Box 1154, Regina, Saskatchewan S4P 3B4 Canada. (306)244-2828. Fax: (306)244-0255. E-mail: grain.mag@sk.sympatico.ca. Website: http://www.skwriter.com. Business Administrator: Jennifer Still. **Contact:** Elizabeth Philips, editor. **100% freelance written.** Quarterly literary magazine covering poetry, fiction, creative nonfiction, drama. "*Grain* publishes writing of the highest quality, both traditional and nontraditional in nature. The *Grain* editors' aim: To publish work that challenges readers; to encourage promising new writers; and to produce a well-designed, visually interesting magazine." Estab. 1973. Circ. 1,500. Pays on publication. Publishes ms an average of 11 months after acceptance. Byline given. Buys first, Canadian, serial rights. Editorial lead time 6 months. Accepts queries by mail, e-mail, fax, phone. Reports in 1 month on queries; 4 months on mss. Sample copy for $7 or on website. Writer's guidelines for #10 SASE or on website.
**Nonfiction:** Interested in creative nonfiction.
**Photos:** Review transparencies and prints. Submit 12-20 slides and b&w prints, short statement (200 words) and brief resume. Pays $100 for front cover art, $30/photo.
**Fiction:** Literary fiction of all types. "No romance, confession, science fiction, vignettes, mystery." **Buys 40 mss/year.** Query or send 2 stories maximum or 30 pages of novel-in-progress and SAE with postage or IRCs. Does not accept e-mail submissions, but will respond by e-mail—save on stamps. **Pays $30-100.**
● Ranked as one of the best markets for fiction writers in *Writer's Digest* magazine's "Fiction 50," June 1999.
**Poetry:** Avant-garde, free verse, haiku, traditional. "High quality, imaginative, well-crafted poetry. No sentimental, end-line rhyme, mundane." **Buys 78 poems/year.** Submit maximum 10 poems and SASE with postage or IRCs. **Pays $30-100.**

**$ $ GRANTA, The Magazine of New Writing**, 2-3 Hanover Yard, Noel Rd., London NI 8BE England. Phone: 0701 704 9776. Fax: 0701 704 0474. E-mail: editorial@grantamag.co.uk. **Contact:** Ian Jack, editor. Quarterly magazine. "*Granta* magazine publishes fiction, reportage, biography and authobiography, history, travel and documentary photography. It rarely publishes 'writing about writing.' The realistic narrative—the story—is its primary form." *Granta* has been called "the most impressive literary magazine of its time" by the *London Daily Telegraph*, and has published Salman Rushdie, Martin Amis, Saul Bellow and Paul Theroux, among others. Estab. 1979. Circ. 90,000. Pays on publication. Rights purchased vary. Reports in 1 month on queries; up to 3 months on mss.
**Nonfiction:** Reportage, biography, autobiography, history, travel.
**Fiction:** Literary. No fantasy, science fiction, romance, historical, occult or other genre fiction. **Buys 1-2 mss/year.**

Query by mail. Length: varies. **Pays £75-5,000** (British pounds).

**Tips:** "We're looking for the best in realistic narrative or stories—originality of voice or subject, without jargon, contrivance or self-conscious 'performance.' Either the story or your treatment of it should be, in some way, unique. If it's a nonfiction piece, it should have a story and yet not neglect facts entirely. If it's fiction, originality and personality certainly count." No poetry and no e-mail submissions.

**$ HAPPY**, 240 E. 35th St., Suite 11A, New York NY 10016. E-mail: bayardx@aol.com. **Contact:** Bayard, editor. Pays on publication. Byline given. Buys one-time rights. Accepts queries by mail, e-mail. Accepts simultaneous and previously published submissions. Reports in 1 month on mss. Sample copy for $9. Writer's guidelines for #10 SASE.
**Fiction:** Novel excerpts, short stories. "We accept anything that's beautifully written. Genre isn't important. It just has to be incredible writing." **Buys 100-130 mss/year.** Send complete ms with cover letter. Length: 250-5,000 words. **Pays $5/1,000 words.**
**Tips:** "If you imagine yourself Ernest Hemingway, you and your work have been dead for 30 years and are of no interest to us."

**$ HIGH PLAINS LITERARY REVIEW**, 180 Adams St., Suite 250, Denver CO 80206. (303)320-6828. Fax: (303)320-0463. Managing Editor: Phyllis A. Harwell. **Contact:** Robert O. Greer, Jr., editor-in-chief. **80% freelance written.** Triannual literary magazine. "The *High Plains Literary Review* publishes short stories, essays, poetry, reviews and interviews, bridging the gap between commercial quarterlies and academic reviews." Estab. 1986. Circ. 1,200. Pays on publication. Byline given. Buys first North American serial rights. Accepts simultaneous submissions. Reports in 3 months. Sample copy for $4. Writer's guidelines for #10 SASE.
  ● Its unique editorial format—between commercial and academic—makes for lively reading. Could be good market for that "in between" story.
**Nonfiction:** Essays, reviews. **Buys 20 mss/year.** Send complete ms. Length: 10,000 words maximum. **Pays $5/page.**
**Fiction:** Ethnic, historical, humorous, mainstream. **Buys 12 mss/year.** Send complete ms. Length: 10,000 words maximum. **Pays $5/page.**
**Poetry:** **Buys 45 poems/year. Pays $10/page.**

**$ INDIANA REVIEW**, Indiana University, 1020 E. Kirkwood, Bloomington IN 47405-7103. (812)855-3439. Website: http://www.indiana.edu/~inreview/. **Contact:** Brian Leung, editor. **100% freelance written.** Semiannual magazine. "*Indiana Review*, a non-profit organization run by IU graduate students, is a journal of previously unpublished poetry and fiction. Literary interviews and essays also considered. We publish innovative fiction and poetry. We're interested in energy, originality and careful attention to craft. While we publish many well-known writers, we also welcome new and emerging poets and fiction writers." Estab. 1982. Pays on publication. Byline given. Buys first North American serial rights. Reports within 4 months. Sample copy for $8. Writer's guidelines for SASE or on website.
**Nonfiction:** Essays. No strictly academic articles dealing with the traditional canon. Query with author bio, previous publications and SASE. Length: 7,500 maximum. **Pays $5/page.**
**Fiction:** Experimental, mainstream, novel excerpts. "We look for daring stories which integrate theme, language, character and form. We like polished writing, humor and fiction which has consequence beyond the world of its narrator." **Buys 12 mss/year.** Send complete ms. Length: 250-15,000. **Pays $5/page.**
  ● Ranked as one of the best markets for fiction writers in *Writer's Digest* magazine's "Fiction 50," June 1999.
**Poetry:** Avant-garde, free verse. Looks for inventive and skillful writing. **Buys 80 mss/year.** Submit up to 5 poems at one time only. Length: 5 lines minimum. **Pays $5/page.**
**Tips:** "Read us before you submit. Often reading is slower in summer and holiday months. Only submit work to journals you would proudly subscribe to, then subscribe to a few. Take care to read the latest two issues and specifically mention work you identify with and why. Submit work that 'stacks up' with the work we've published."

**$ INDIGENOUS FICTION**, I.F. Publishing, P.O. Box 2078, Redmond WA 98073-2078. E-mail: deckr@earthlink.n et. **Contact:** Sherry Decker, editor. **98% freelance written.** Semiannual magazine covering short fiction, poetry and art. "We want literary—fantasy, dark fantasy, science fiction, horror, mystery and mainstream. We enjoy elements of the supernatural or the unexplained, odd, intriguing characters and beautiful writing. Most accepted stories will be between 2,500-4,500 words in length." Estab. 1998. Circ. 250. Pays on publication. Publishes ms an average of 6 months after acceptance. Byline given. Buys first North American serial and second serial (reprint) rights. Editorial lead time 6 months. Submit seasonal material 6 months in advance. Accepts simultaneous submissions. Reports in 2 weeks on queries; 1 month on mss. Sample copy for $6. Writer's guidelines for SASE.
**Fiction:** Adventure, experimental, fantasy, dark fantasy, horror, humorous, mainstream, mystery, science fiction, suspense, odd, bizarre, supernatural and the unexplained. "No porn, abuse of children, gore; no it was all a dream, evil cat, unicorn or sweet nostalgic tales. No vignettes or slice-of-life (without beginning, middle and end)." **Buys 30 mss/year.** Send complete ms, cover letter and credits. Length: 500-8,000 words, usually 2,000-4,500 words. **Pays $5-20.**
**Poetry:** Free verse, haiku, light verse, traditional. No poetry that neither tells a story nor evokes an image. **Buys 20 poems/year.** Submit maximum 5 poems. Length: 3-30 lines. **Pays $5.**
**Fillers:** Short humor. **Buys 6/year.** Length: 100-500 words. **Pays $5.**
**Tips:** "Proper manuscript format; no e-mail or fax submissions. No disks unless asked. We like beautiful, literary writing where something happens in the story. By literary we don't mean a long, rambling piece of beautiful writing for the sake of beauty—we mean characters and situations, fully developed, beautifully. Ghosts, time travel, parallel

words, 'the bizarre'—fine! Vampires? Well, okay, but no clichés or media tie-ins. Vampire tales should be bone-chillingly dark, beautiful, erotic or humorous. Everything else has been done. Writers we admire: Joyce Carol Oates, Ray Bradbury, Pat Conroy, Dale Bailey, Tanith Lee."

**N** **$ $** **INKLINGS: Threads of Truth From Art & Story**, Paradox Publishing, 1650 Washington St., Denver CO 80203. (303)861-8517. Fax: (303)861-0659. E-mail: inklings@paradoxpub.com. Website: http://www.paradoxpub.c om. Publisher: Brad Hicks. Managing Editor: Kristy Johnson. **Contact:** Jo Kadlecek, editor. **50-75% freelance written.** Quarterly magazine covering literature and the arts. "*Inklings* is a quarterly literary magazine and arts discussion bridging classic literature and art with popular culture in the spirit of the 'Inklings' of Oxford: C.S. Lewis, J.R.R. Tolkien, Charles Williams and friends." Estab. 1994. Circ. 10,000. Pays on publication. Publishes ms an average of 3 months after acceptance. Byline given. Buys first North American serial rights. Accepts queries by mail, e-mail, fax. Sample copy for $5 US/$7 foreign. Writer's guidelines and theme list for #10 SASE.
**Nonfiction:** Essays, interview/profile, personal experience, reviews of books, theatre, film and music. "No inspirational pieces." **Buys 40 mss/year.** Send complete ms. Length: 250-3,000 words. **Pays $25-100.**
**Photos:** State availability of photos with submission.
**Fiction:** Laura Wright/Nancy Hicks, fiction editors. Adventure, condensed novels, confession, erotica, ethnic, experimental, fantasy, historical, horror, humorous, mainstream, mystery, novel excerpts, religious, romance, science fiction, serialized novels, slice-of-life vignettes, suspense, western. "Do not submit fiction over 3,500 words." **Buys 8 mss/ year.** Query or send complete ms. Length: up to 3,500 words. **Pays $100.**
**Poetry:** Susan Kauffman and Kristy Johnson, poetry editors. Avant garde, free verse, haiku, light verse, traditional. **Buys 24-32 poems/year.** Submit maximum 10 poems. Length: 2-100 lines. **Pays $25.**
**Tips:** "*Inklings* exists as a vital catalyst to encourage honest dialogue and affecting stories relating from the common human experience—by writers who approach their craft truthfully irrespective of their religion, nationality, race, or political worldview. *Inklings* publishes poetry, essays, reviews, interviews, and fiction of lasting merit, honestly written with depth of plot, characterization and meaning, with thoughtful insight into the human condition. *Inklings* will never publish a submission which refuses to acknowledge the legitimate human needs of all individuals and cultures. A wide variety of arts-related literary content is reflected in *Inklings*—preferably material that adheres to a redemptive vision of life (as opposed to an abysmal, hopeless view). Though not exclusively, preference will be given to submissions written to correspond with our themes."

**N** **$** **THE IOWA REVIEW**, 369 EPB, The University of Iowa, Iowa City IA 52242. (319)335-0462. Fax: (319)335-2535. E-mail: iareview@blue.weeg.uiowa.edu. Website: http://www.uiowa.edu/~iareview/. Editor: David Hamilton. **Contact:** Mary Hussmann, editor. Triannual magazine. Estab. 1970. Buys first North American and non-exclusive anthology, classroom and online serial rights. Reports in 3 months. Sample copy and writer's guidelines for $6 or on website.
**Nonfiction, Fiction and Poetry:** "We publish essays, reviews, novel excerpts, stories and poems and would like for our essays not always to be works of academic criticism. We have no set guidelines as to content or length." **Buys 65-85 unsolicited mss/year.** Submit complete ms with SASE. **Pays $1/line for verse; $10/page for prose.**
  • This magazine uses the help of colleagues and graduate assistants. Its reading period is September-January 31.

**$** **JAPANOPHILE PRESS**, P.O. Box 7977, 415 N. Main St., Ann Arbor MI 48107. E-mail: susanlapp@aol.com. Website: http://www.japanophile.com. **Contact:** Susan Lapp, editor or Ashby Kinch, associate editor. **80% freelance written.** Works with a small number of new/unpublished writers each year. Quarterly magazine for literate people interested in Japanese culture anywhere in the world. Estab. 1974. Pays on publication. Publishes ms an average of 3 months after acceptance. Buys first North American serial rights. Accepts queries by mail, e-mail, fax. Reports in 3 months. Sample copy for $4, postpaid or on website. Writer's guidelines for #10 SASE.
**Nonfiction:** "We want material on Japanese culture in *North America or anywhere in the world*, even Japan. We want articles, preferably with pictures, about persons engaged in arts of Japanese origin: a Virginia naturalist who is a haiku poet, a potter who learned raku in Japan, a vivid 'I was there' account of a Go tournament in California. We would like to hear more about what it's like to be a Japanese in the U.S. Our particular slant is a certain kind of culture wherever it is in the world: Canada, the U.S., Europe, Japan. The culture includes flower arranging, haiku, sports, religion, travel, art, photography, fiction, etc. It is important to study the magazine." **Buys 8 mss/issue.** Query preferred but not required. Length: 1,800 words maximum. **Pays $8-20.**
**Reprints:** Send information about when and where the article was previously published. Pays up to 100% of amount paid for original article.
**Photos:** Pays $10-20 for glossy prints. "We prefer b&w people pictures."
**Columns/Departments:** Regular columns and features are Tokyo Topics and Japan in North America. "We also need columns about Japanese culture in various American cities." Query. Length: 1,000 words. **Pays $1-20.**
**Fiction:** Experimental, mainstream, mystery, adventure, humorous, romance, historical. Themes should relate to Japan or Japanese culture. Length: 1,000-4,000 words. Annual contest pays $100 to best short story (contest reading fee $5). Should include 1 or more Japanese and non-Japanese characters in each story.
**Poetry:** Traditional, avant-garde and light verse related to Japanese culture or any subject in a Japanese form such as haiku. Length: 3-50 lines. **Pays $1-20.**
**Fillers:** Newsbreaks, clippings and short humor of up to 200 words. **Pays $1-5.**
**Tips:** "We want to see more articles about Japanese culture worldwide, including unexpected places, but especially

U.S., Canada and Europe. Lack of convincing fact and detail is a frequent mistake."

**$ THE JOURNAL**, Ohio State University, 421 Denney Hall, 164 W. 17th Ave., Columbus OH 43210. (614)292-4076. Fax: (614)292-7816. E-mail: thejournal05@postbox.acs.ohio-state.edu. Website: http://www.cohums.ohio-state.edu/english/journals/the_journal/homepage.htm. **Contact:** Kathy Fagan, Michelle Herman, editors. **100% freelance written.** Semiannual literary magazine. "We're open to all forms; we tend to favor work that gives evidence of a mature and sophisticated sense of the language." Estab. 1972. Circ. 1,500. Pays on publication. Byline given. Buys first North American serial rights. Reports in 2 weeks on queries; 2 months on mss. Sample copy for $7 or on website. Writer's guidelines for #10 SASE or on website.
**Nonfiction:** Essays, interview/profile. **Buys 2 mss/year.** Query. Length: 2,000-4,000 words. **Pays $25 maximum.**
**Columns/Departments:** Reviews of contemporary poetry, 2,000-4,000 words. **Buys 2 mss/year.** Query. **Pays $25.**
**Fiction:** Novel excerpts, literary short stories. **Pays $25 minimum.**
**Poetry:** Avant-garde, free verse, traditional. **Buys 100 poems/year.** Submit maximum 5 poems/year. **Pays $25.**

**$ KALLIOPE, a journal of women's literature & art**, Florida Community College at Jacksonville, 3939 Roosevelt Blvd., Jacksonville FL 32205. (904)381-3511. Website: http://www.fccj.org/kalliope/kalliope.htm. **Contact:** Mary Sue Koeppel, editor. **100% freelance written.** Triannual magazine. "*Kalliope* publishes poetry, short fiction, reviews, and b&w art, usually by women artists. We look for artistic excellence." Estab. 1978. Circ. 1,600. Pays on publication. Publishes ms an average of 3 months after acceptance. Buys first rights. Reports in 1 week on queries. Sample copy for $7 (recent issue) or $4 (back copy). Writer's guidelines for #10 SASE or on website.
**Nonfiction:** Interview/profile, reviews of new works of poetry and fiction. **Buys 6 mss/year.** Send complete ms. Length: 500-2,000 words. **Pays $10 honorarium.**
• *Kalliope's* reading period is September through May.
**Fiction:** Ethnic, experimental, fantasy, humorous, literary, slice-of-life vignettes, novel excerpts. **Buys 12 mss/year.** Send complete ms. Length: 100-2,000 words. **Pays $10.**
**Poetry:** Avant-garde, free verse, haiku, light verse, traditional. **Buys 75 poems/year.** Submit 3-5 poems. Length: 2-120 lines. **Pays $10 if finances permit.**
**Tips:** "We publish the best of the material submitted to us each issue. (We don't build a huge backlog and then publish from that backlog for years.) Although we look for new writers and usually publish several with each issue alongside already established writers, we love it when established writers send us their work. We've recently published Tess Gallagher, Enid Shomer and one of the last poems by Denise Levertov. Send a bio with all submissions."

**$ THE KENYON REVIEW**, Kenyon College, Gambier OH 43022. (740)427-5208. Fax: (740)427-5417. E-mail: kenyonreview@kenyon.edu. Website: http://www.kenyonreview.com. **Contact:** Doris Jean Dilts, operations coordinator; David H. Lynn, editor. **100% freelance written.** Triannual magazine covering contemporary literature and criticism. "An international journal of literature, culture and the arts dedicated to an inclusive representation of the best in new writing, interviews and criticism from established and emerging writers." Estab. 1939. Circ. 4,500. Pays on publication. Publishes ms 1 year after acceptance. Byline given. Buys first, one-time rights. Editorial lead time 1 year. Submit seasonal material 1 year in advance. Sample copy for $8. Writer's guidelines for 4×9 SASE.
• *The Kenyon Review* will not be accepting unsolicited mss from April 1999 to September 2000 because of a backlog of accepted mss. The editors apologize for any disappointment or inconvenience.

**[N] $ THE KIT-CAT REVIEW**, 244 Halstead Ave., Harrison NY 10528. (914)835-4833. **Contact:** Claudia Fletcher, editor. **100% freelance written.** Quarterly literary magazine. "*The Kit-Cat Review* is named after the 18th Century Kit-Cat Club, whose members included Addison, Steele, Congreeve, Vanbrugh and Garth. Its purpose is to promote/discover excellence and originality. Some issues are part anthology." Estab. 1998. Circ. 100. **Pays on acceptance.** Byline given. Buys one-time rights. Accepts queries by mail, phone. Reports in 1 week on queries, 1 month on mss. Sample copy $2.
**Nonfiction:** Book excerpts, essays, general interest, historical/nostalgic, humor, interview/profile, personal experience, travel. **Buys 2 mss/year.** Send complete ms. Length: up to 6,000 words. **Pays $25-100.**
**Fiction:** Experimental, novel excerpts, slice-of-life vignettes. No stories with "O. Henry-type formula endings." **Buys 20 mss/year.** Send complete ms. Length: up to 6,000 words. **Pays $25-100.**
**Poetry:** Free verse, traditional. No excessively obscure poetry. **Buys 100 poems/year.** Two issues (spring, autumn) include a poetry award of $1000. **Pays $10-100.**
**Tips:** "Obtaining a sample copy is strongly suggested."

**[★] $ LEGIONS OF LIGHT**, Box 874, Margaretville, NY 12455. Phone/fax: (914)586-2759. E-mail: beth@stepahead.net. Website: http://www.stepahead.net/~lol/legions.htm. **Contact:** Elizabeth Mami, editor. **100% freelance written.** Bimonthly magazine. "*Legions of Light* accepts all material except graphic violence or sex. All ages read the magazine, all subjects welcomed." Estab. 1990. Circ. 2,000. Pays on publication. Publishes ms an average of 1 year after acceptance. Byline sometimes given. Buys one-time rights. Editorial lead time 4 months. Submit seasonal material 6 months in advance. Accepts queries by mail, e-mail. Accepts simultaneous submissions. Reports in 6 weeks on queries. Sample copy for $3. Guidelines for #10 SASE or on website.
**Nonfiction:** Historical/nostalgic, humor, inspirational, humor/profile, personal experience, religious. No graphic violence or adult material. **Buys 10-20 mss/year.** Send complete ms. Length: 500-1,500 words. **Pays $5-10.**
**Reprints:** Accepts previously published submissions. Send photocopy of article or short story. Publishes novel excerpts.

**Photos:** State availability of photos with submission. Reviews 3×5 prints. Offers no additional payment for photos accepted with ms. Identification of subjects required. Buys one-time rights.

**Fiction:** Adventure, ethnic, experimental, fantasy, historical, horror, humorous, mainstream, mystery, religious, romance, science fiction, slice-of-life vignettes, suspense, western. No adult or graphic violence. **Buys 20-30 mss/year.** Query or send complete ms. Length: 1,500 words maximum. **Pays $5-10.**

**Poetry:** Avant-garde, free verse, haiku, light verse, traditional. No erotica. **Buys 15-20 poems/year. Pays $5-10.**

■ The online magazine carries original content not found in the print edition and includes writer's guidelines.

**Fillers:** Anecdotes, facts, newsbreaks, short humor. Buys 5-15/year. **Pays $5-10.**

**Tips:** "*Legions of Light* caters to unpublished talent, especially children. Subscribers are used first, but subscribing is *not* a requirement to be accepted for publication. All are accepted, but due to overload, it does take time to actually get published. All will though. Calls and reminders are encouraged. I eventually get every one in."

**$ LIBIDO, The Journal of Sex & Sensibility**, Libido, Inc., 5318 N. Paulina St., Chicago IL 60640. (773)275-0842. Fax: (773)275-0752. E-mail: rune@mcs.com. Co-editors: Marianna Beck and Jack Hafferkamp. **Contact**: J.L. Beck, submissions editor. **50% freelance written.** Quarterly magazine covering literate erotica. "*Libido* is about sexuality. Orientation is not an issue, writing ability is. The aim is to enlighten as often as it is to arouse. Humor—sharp and smart—is important, so are safer sex contexts." Estab. 1988. Circ. 10,000. Pays on publication. Byline given. Kill fee "rare, but negotiable." Buys one-time or second serial (reprint) rights. Editorial lead time 3 months. Submit seasonal material 4 months in advance. Payment negotiable. Reports in 6 months. Sample copy for $8. Writer's guidelines for #10 SASE.

**Nonfiction:** Book excerpts, essays, historical/nostalgic, humor, photo feature, travel. "No violence, sexism or misty memoirs." **Buys 10-20 mss/year.** Send complete ms. Length: 300-2,500 words. **Pays $50 minimum for assigned articles; $15 minimum for unsolicited articles.** Pays contributor copies "when money isn't an issue and copies or other considerations have equal or higher value." Sometimes pays expenses of writers on assignment.

**Reprints:** Send photocopy of article or short story or typed ms with rights for sale noted and information about when and where the material previously appeared. Pays 100% of amount paid for an original article.

**Photos:** Reviews contact sheets and 5×7 and 8×10 prints. Negotiates payment individually. Model releases required. Buys one-time rights.

**Fiction:** Erotica, short novel excerpts. **Buys 20 mss/year.** Send complete ms. Length: 800-2,500 words. **Pays $20-50.**

**Poetry:** Uses humorous short erotic poetry. No limericks. **Buys 10 poems/year.** Submit maximum 3 poems. **Pays $15.**

**Tips:** "*Libido*'s guidelines are purposely simple and loose. All sexual orientations are appreciated. The only taboos are exploitative and violent sex. Send us a manuscript—make it short, sharp and with a lead that makes us want to read. If we're not hooked by paragraph three, we reject the manuscript."

**$ $ THE MALAHAT REVIEW**, The University of Victoria, P.O. Box 1700, STN CSC, Victoria, British Columbia V8W 2Y2 Canada. (250)721-8524. E-mail: malahat@uvic.ca (for queries only). Website: http://web.uvic.ca/malahat. **Contact:** Marlene Cookshaw, acting editor. **100% freelance written.** Eager to work with new/unpublished writers. Quarterly covering poetry, fiction, drama and reviews. Estab. 1967. Circ. 1,000. **Pays on acceptance.** Publishes ms up to 6 months after acceptance. Byline given. Offers 100% kill fee. Buys first world rights. Accepts queries by mail, e-mail, phone. Reports in 2 weeks on queries; 3 months on mss. Sample copy for $8. Sample articles and guidelines on website.

**Nonfiction:** "Query first about review articles, critical essays, interviews and visual art which we generally solicit." Include SASE with Canadian postage or IRCs. **Pays $30/magazine page.**

**Photos:** Pays $25 for b&w prints. Captions required. Pays $100 for color print used as cover.

**Fiction: Buys 20 mss/year.** Send complete ms up to 20 pages. **Pays $30/magazine page.**

**Poetry:** Avant-garde, free verse, traditional. Length: 5-10 pages. **Buys 100/year. Pays $30/magazine page.**

**Tips:** "Please do not send more than one manuscript (the one you consider your best) at a time. See the *Malahat Review's* long poem and novella contests in Contest & Awards section."

**$ $ MANOA, A Pacific Journal of International Writing**, University of Hawaii Press, 1733 Donaghho Rd., Honolulu HI 96822. (808)956-3070. Fax: (808)956-7808. E-mail: fstewart@hawaii.edu. Website: http://www2.hawaii.edu/mjournal. Managing Editor: Patricia Matsueda. **Contact:** Frank Stewart, editor. Semiannual literary magazine. "High quality literary fiction, poetry, essays, personal narrative, reviews. About half of each issue devoted to U.S. writing, and half new work from Pacific and Asian nations. Our audience is primarily in the U.S., although expanding in Pacific countries. U.S. writing need not be confined to Pacific settings or subjects." Estab. 1989. Circ. 2,500. Pays on publication. Byline given. Buys first North American serial or non-exclusive, one-time reprint rights. Editorial lead time 6 months. Submit seasonal material 8 months in advance. Reports in 3 weeks on queries; 2 months on poetry mss, 4 months on fiction. Sample copy for $10. Writer's guidelines free with SASE.

**Nonfiction:** Frank Stewart, editor. Book excerpts, essays, interview/profile, creative nonfiction or personal narrative related to literature or nature. Lisa Ottiger, reviews editor. Book reviews on recent books in arts, humanities and natural sciences, usually related to Asia, the Pacific or Hawaii or published in these places. No Pacific exotica. **Buys 3-4 mss/year,** excluding reviews. Query or send complete ms. Length: 1,000-5,000 words. **Pays $25/printed page.**

**Fiction:** Ian MacMillan, fiction editor. "We're potentially open to anything of literary quality, though usually not genre fiction as such." Publishes novel excerpts. No Pacific exotica. **Buys 12-18 mss/year** in the US (excluding translation).

Send complete ms. Length: 1,000-7,500. **Pays $100-500** normally ($25/printed page).

**Poetry:** Frank Stewart, editor. No light verse. **Buys 40-50 poems/year.** Send 5-6 poems minimum. **Pays $25.**

**Tips:** "Although we are a Pacific journal, we are a general interest U.S. literary journal, not limited to Pacific settings or subjects."

**$ THE MASSACHUSETTS REVIEW**, South College, University of Massachusetts, Amherst MA 01003-9934. (413)545-2689. Fax: (413)577-0740. E-mail: massrev@external.umass.edu. Website: http://www.litline.org/html/massre view.html. Editors: Mary Heath, Jules Chametzky, Paul Jenkins. Quarterly magazine. Estab. 1959. Pays on publication. Publishes ms 6-18 months after acceptance. Buys first North American serial rights. Accepts queries by mail, e-mail, fax. Reports in 3 months. Does not return mss without SASE. Sample copy for $7 with 3 first-class stamps. Sample articles and writer's guidelines on website.

**Nonfiction:** Articles on literary criticism, women, public affairs, art, philosophy, music and dance. No reviews of single books. Send complete ms or query with SASE. Length: 6,500 words average. **Pays $50.**

**Fiction:** Publishes one short story per issue. Length: 25-30 pages maximum. **Pays $50.**

**Poetry:** Submit 6 poems maximum. **Pays 35¢/line to $10 minimum.**

**Tips:** "No manuscripts are considered June-October. No fax or e-mail submissions."

**[N] $ $ MERLYN'S PEN, Fiction, Essays and Poems by America's Teens**, Merlyn's Pen Inc., 4 King St., East Greenwich RI 02818. (401)885-5175. Fax: (401)885-5222. E-mail: merlynspen@aol.com. Website: http://www.mer lynspen.com. Editor: R. James Stahl. **Contact:** Zachary Davis, manuscript coordinator. **100% freelance written.** Annual. "We publish fiction, essays and poems by America's teen writers, age 11-19 exclusively." Estab. 1985. Circ. 5,000. Pays on publication. Publishes ms an average of 6 months after acceptance. Byline given. Buys all rights. Editorial lead time up to 10 months. Reports in 3 months. Sample articles and writer's guidelines on website.

**Nonfiction:** Essays, exposé, general interest, historical/nostalgic, how-to, humor, opinion, personal experience, travel. **Buys 10 mss/year.** Send complete ms. Length: 100-5,000 words. **Pays $25-200.**

**Fiction:** Adventure, experimental, fantasy, historical, horror, humorous, mainstream, mystery, romance, science fiction, slice-of-life vignettes, suspense. **Buys 40 mss/year.** Send complete ms. Length: 100-5,000 words. **Pays $20-250.**

**Poetry:** Avant garde, free verse, haiku, light verse, traditional. **Buys 25 poems/year.** Submit 3 poems maximum. Length: 3-250 lines. **Pays $20-250.**

**Tips:** "**Contributors must be between ages 11-19.** We select about 50 pieces out of 10,000 received and we do respond. Writers *must* use *our* cover sheet, which is on website or free by calling (800)247-2027."

**$ MICHIGAN QUARTERLY REVIEW**, 3032 Rackham Bldg., University of Michigan, Ann Arbor MI 48109-1070. E-mail: dorisk@umich.edu. Website: http://www.umich.edu/~mqr. **Contact:** Laurence Goldstein, editor. **75% freelance written.** Prefers to work with published/established writers. Quarterly. Estab. 1962. Circ. 1,500. Publishes ms an average of 1 year after acceptance. Pays on publication. Buys first serial rights. Reports in 2 months. Sample copy for $2.50 with 2 first-class stamps.

● The Lawrence Foundation Prize is a $1,000 annual award to the best short story published in the *Michigan Quarterly Review* during the previous year.

**Nonfiction:** "*MQR* is open to general articles directed at an intellectual audience. Essays ought to have a personal voice and engage a significant subject. Scholarship must be present as a foundation, but we are not interested in specialized essays directed only at professionals in the field. We prefer ruminative essays, written in a fresh style and which reach interesting conclusions. We also like memoirs and interviews with significant historical or cultural resonance." **Buys 35 mss/year.** Query by mail. Length: 2,000-5,000 words. **Pays $100-150.**

**Fiction and Poetry:** No restrictions on subject matter or language. **Buys 10 mss/year.** "We are very selective. We like stories which are unusual in tone and structure, and innovative in language." Send complete ms. **Pays $10/published page.**

**Tips:** "Read the journal and assess the range of contents and the level of writing. We have no guidelines to offer or set expectations; every manuscript is judged on its unique qualities. On essays—query with a very thorough description of the argument and a copy of the first page. Watch for announcements of special issues which are usually expanded issues and draw upon a lot of freelance writing. Be aware that this is a university quarterly that publishes a limited amount of fiction and poetry; that it is directed at an educated audience, one that has done a great deal of reading in all types of literature."

**$ $ THE MISSOURI REVIEW**, 1507 Hillcrest Hall, University of Missouri, Columbia MO 65211. (573)882-4474. Fax: (573)884-4671. E-mail: moreview@showme.missouri.edu. Website: http://www.missourireview.org. **Contacts:** Speer Morgan, editor; Greg Michalson, poetry editor; Evelyn Somers, nonfiction editor. **100% freelance written.** Triannual literary magazine. "We publish contemporary fiction, poetry, interviews, personal essays, cartoons, special features—such as 'History as Literature' series and 'Found Text' series—for the literary and the general reader interested in a wide range of subjects." Estab. 1978. Circ. 6,500. Pays on signed contract. Byline given. Buys first rights. Editorial lead time 4-6 months. Accepts queries by mail, phone. Reports in 2 weeks on queries; 3 months on mss. Sample copy for $7 or on website. Writer's guidelines for #10 SASE or on website.

**Nonfiction:** Evelyn Somers, nonfiction editor. Book excerpts, essays. No literary criticism. **Buys 10 mss/year.** Send complete ms. **Pays $15-20/printed page up to $750.**

**Fiction:** Mainstream, literary, novel excerpts. No genre fiction. **Buys 25 mss/year.** Send complete ms. **Pays $15-20/**

printed page up to $750.

&bull; Ranked as one of the best markets for fiction writers in *Writer's Digest* magazine's "Fiction 50," June 1999.

**Poetry:** Greg Michalson, poetry editor. Publishes 3-5 poetry features of 6-12 pages each per issue. "Please familiarize yourself with the magazine before submitting poetry." **Buys 50 poems/year. Pays $125-250.**

The online magazine carries original content not found in the print edition and includes writer's guidelines. Contact: Speer Morgan, online editor.

**Tips:** "Send your best work. We'd especially like to see more personal essays."

---

**$ NEW ENGLAND REVIEW**, Middlebury College, Middlebury VT 05753. (802)443-5075. E-mail: nereview@middlebury.edu. Website: http://www.middlebury.edu/~nereview/. Editor: Stephen Donadio. Managing Editor: Jodee Stanley Rubins. **Contact** on envelope: Poetry, Fiction, or Nonfiction Editor; on letter: Stephen Donadio. Quarterly magazine. Serious literary only. Estab. 1978. Circ. 2,000. Pays on publication. Publishes ms an average of 6 months after acceptance. Byline given. Buys first North American serial rights. Accepts simultaneous submissions. Reads September 31 to May 31 (postmark dates). Reports in 2 weeks on queries; 3 months on mss. Sample copy for $7. Writer's guidelines for #10 SASE.

**Nonfiction:** Serious literary only. **Buys 20-25 mss/year.** Send complete ms. Length: 7,500 words maximum, though exceptions may be made. **Pays $10/page, $20 minimum** plus 2 copies.

**Reprints:** Rarely accepts previously published submissions, (if out of print or previously published abroad only.)

**Fiction:** Serious literary only, novel excerpts. **Buys 25 mss/year.** Send complete ms. Send 1 story at a time. **Pays $10/page, minimum $20** plus 2 copies.

**Poetry:** Serious literary only. **Buys 75-90 poems/year.** Submit 6 poems max. **Pays $10/page or $20** and 2 copies.

**Tips:** "We consider short fiction, including shorts, short-shorts, novellas, and self-contained extracts from novels. We consider a variety of general and literary, but not narrowly scholarly, nonfiction: long and short poems; speculative, interpretive, and personal essays; book reviews; screenplays; graphics; translations; critical reassessments; statements by artists working in various media; interviews; testimonies; and letters from abroad. We are committed to exploration of all forms of contemporary cultural expression in the United States and abroad. With few exceptions, we print only work not published previously elsewhere."

---

**$ NEW LETTERS**, University of Missouri-Kansas City, University House, 5101 Rockhill Rd., Kansas City MO 64110-2499. (816)235-1168. Fax: (816)235-2611. Managing Editor: Robert Stewart. **Contact:** James McKinley, editor. **100% freelance written.** Quarterly magazine. "*New Letters* is intended for the general literate reader. We publish literary fiction, nonfiction, essays, poetry. We also publish art." Estab. 1934. Circ. 1,800. Pays on publication. Publishes ms an average of 5 months after acceptance. Byline given. Buys first North American serial rights. Editorial lead time 6 months. Submit seasonal material 6 months in advance. Accepts simultaneous submissions. Reports in 1 month on queries; 3 months on mss. Sample copy for $5.50 (current issue). Writer's guidelines for #10 SASE.

&bull; Submissions are not read between May 15 and October 15.

**Nonfiction:** Essays. No self-help, how-to or non-literary work. **Buys 6-8 mss/year.** Send complete ms. Length: 5,000 words maximum. **Pays $40-100.**

**Photos:** Send photos with submission. Reviews contact sheets, $2 \times 4$ transparencies, prints. Offers $10-40/photo. Buys one-time rights.

**Fiction:** No genre fiction. **Buys 12 mss/year.** Send complete ms. Length: 5,000 words maximum. **Pays $30-75.**

**Poetry:** Avant-garde, free verse, haiku, traditional. No light verse. **Buys 40 poems/year.** Submit maximum 3 poems. Length: open. **Pays $10-25.**

---

**$ $ NORTH CAROLINA LITERARY REVIEW: A Magazine of Literature, Culture, and History**, English Dept., East Carolina University, Greenville NC 27858-4353. (252)328-1537. Fax: (252)328-4889. E-mail: bauerm@mail.ecu.edu. **Contact:** Margaret Bauer, editor. Annual literary magazine published in spring covering North Carolina writers, literature, culture, history. "Articles should have a North Carolina slant. First consideration is always for quality of work. Although we treat academic and scholarly subjects, we do not wish to see jargon-laden prose; our readers, we hope, are found as often in bookstores and libraries as in academia. We seek to combine best elements of magazine for serious readers with best of scholarly journal." Estab. 1992. Circ. 750. Pays on publication. Publishes ms within 1 year after acceptance. Byline given. Buys first North American serial rights. Rights returned to writer on request. Editorial lead time 6 months. Accepts queries by mail, e-mail. Reports in 1 month on queries, 3 months on mss, 6 months on unsolicited mss. Sample copy for $10. Writer's guidelines for SASE or via e-mail.

**Nonfiction:** Book excerpts, essays, exposé, general interest, historical/nostalgic, humor, interview/profile, opinion, personal experience, photo feature, travel, reviews, short narratives; surveys of archives. "No jargon-laden academic articles." **Buys 25-35 mss/year.** Query with published clips. Length: 500-5,000 words. **Pays $50 minimum.**

**Photos:** State availability of photos with query. Reviews $5 \times 7$ or $8 \times 10$ prints; snapshot size or photocopy OK. Negotiates payment individually. Captions and identification of subjects required, releases when appropriate. Buys one-time rights.

**Columns/Departments:** Archives (survey of North Carolina-writer archives), 500-1,500 words; Thomas Wolfe (Wolfe-related articles/essays), 1,000-2,000 words; Readers/Writers Places (bookstores or libraries, or other places readers and writers gather), 500-1,500; Black Mountain College, 1,000-2,000 words; Reviews (essay reviews of North Carolina-related literature (fiction, creative nonfiction, poetry). **Buys 10 mss/year.** Send complete ms. **Pays $50-150.**

**Fiction:** Must be North Carolina related—either by a NC-connected writer or set in NC. Adventure, ethnic, experimental,

fantasy, historical, horror, humorous, mainstream, mystery, novel excerpts, romance, science fiction, slice-of-life vignettes, suspense, western. **Buys 3-4 mss/year.** Query. Length: 5,000 words maximum. **Pays $50-300.**
**Poetry: Buys 8-10 poems/year.** Length: 30-150 lines. **Pays $25-50.** NC poets only.
**Fillers: Buys 2-10/year.** Length: 50-300 words. **Pays $10-25.**
**Tips:** "By far the easiest way to break in is with special issue sections. We are especially interested in reports on conferences, readings, meetings that involve North Carolina writers, and personal essays or short narratives with strong sense of place. We are more interested in essays that use creative nonfiction approaches than in straight articles of informational nature. See back issues for other departments. These are the only areas in which we encourage unsolicited manuscripts; but we welcome queries and proposals for all others. Interviews are probably the other easiest place to break in; no discussions of poetics/theory, etc., except in reader-friendly (accessible) language; interviews should be personal, more like conversations, that explore connections between a writer's life and his/her work."

**$ NOSTALGIA, A Sentimental State of Mind,** Nostalgia Publications, P.O. Box 2224, Orangeburg SC 29116. **Contact:** Connie L. Martin, editor. **100% freelance written.** Semiannual magazine for "true, personal experiences that relate faith, struggle, hope, success, failure and rising above problems common to all." Estab. 1986. Circ. 1,000. Pays on publication. Publishes ms an average of 1 year after acceptance. Byline given. Buys one-time rights. Submit seasonal material 6 months in advance. Reports in 6 weeks on queries. Sample copy for $5. Writer's guidelines for #10 SASE.
**Nonfiction:** General interest, historical/nostalgic, humor, inspirational, opinion, personal experience, photo feature, religious and travel. Does not want to see anything with profanity or sexual references. **Buys 20 mss/year.** Send complete ms. Length: 1,500 words. **Pays $25 minimum.** Pays contributor copies if preferred. Short Story Awards $600 annually.
**Reprints:** Send tearsheet, typed ms or photocopy of article or short story and information about when and where the article previously appeared. Payment varies.
**Photos:** State availability of photos with submission. Offers no additional payment for photos with ms.
**Poetry:** Free verse, haiku, light verse, traditional and modern prose. "No ballads; no profanity; no sexual references." Submit 3 poems maximum. Length: no longer than 45-50 lines preferably. Poetry Awards $600 annually.
**Tips:** Write for guidelines before entering contests. Short Story Award (deadlines March 31 and August 31); Poetry Award (deadlines June 30 and December 31). Entry fees reserve future edition.

**$ $ THE PARIS REVIEW,** 45-39 171st Place, Flushing NY 11358. Submit mss to 541 E. 72nd St., New York NY 10021. (212)861-0016. Fax: (212)861-4504. Website: http://www.parisreview.com. **Contact:** George A. Plimpton, editor. Quarterly magazine. Buys all rights. Pays on publication. Accepts queries by mail. Reporting time varies. Address submissions to proper department. Sample copy for $11. Writer's guidelines for #10 SASE (from Flushing Office). Reporting time often 6 months or longer.
**Fiction:** Study the publication. Query. No length limit. **Pays up to $600.** Annual Aga Khan Fiction Contest award of $1,000.
**Poetry:** Richard Howard, poetry editor. Study the publication. **Pays $35 minimum** varies according to length. Awards $1,000 in Bernard F. Conners Poetry Prize contest.

**$ $ PARNASSUS, Poetry in Review,** Poetry in Review Foundation, 205 W. 89th St., #8-F, New York NY 10024. (212)362-3492. Fax: (212)875-0148. E-mail: parnew@aol.com. Managing Editor: Ben Downing. **Contact:** Herbert Leibowitz, editor. Semiannual trade paperback-size magazine covering poetry and criticism. Estab. 1972. Circ. 1,500. Pays on publication. Publishes ms an average of 5 months after acceptance. Byline given. Buys one-time rights. Sample copy for $15.
**Nonfiction:** Essays. **Buys 30 mss/year.** Query with published clips. Length: 1,500-7,500 words. **Pays $50-300.** Sometimes pays writers in contributor copies or other premiums rather than a cash payment upon request.
**Poetry:** Accepts most types of poetry including avant-garde, free verse, traditional. **Buys 3-4 unsolicited poems/year.**

**[N] $ PIG IRON SERIES,** Pig Iron Press, P.O. Box 237, Youngstown OH 44501-0237. (330)747-6932. Fax: (330)747-0599. **Contact:** Jim Villani, publisher. **95% freelance written.** Annual thematic serial emphasizing literature/ art for writers, artists and intelligent lay audience interested in popular culture. Circ. 1,000. Buys one-time rights. Pays on publication. Publishes ms an average of 18 months after acceptance. Byline given. Reports in 4 months. Sample copy $5. Writer's guidelines and current theme list for #10 SASE.
**Nonfiction:** General interest, personal opinion, criticism, new journalism and lifestyle. **Buys 6-12 mss/year.** Query. Length: 6,000 words max. **Pays $5/page min.**
**Reprints:** Send information about when and where the article previously appeared.
**Photos:** Send photos with query. Pays $5 minimum for 5×7 or 8×10 b&w glossy prints. Buys one-time rights.
**Fiction:** Narrative fiction, living history, novel excerpts, psychological fiction, environment, avant-garde, experimental, metafiction, satire, parody. **Buys 4-12 mss/issue.** Submit complete ms. Length: 6,000 words max. **Pays $5 min.**
**Poetry:** Avant-garde and free verse. **Buys 25-50/issue.** Submit in batches of 5 or less. Length: open. **Pays $5 minimum.**
**Tips:** "Looking for fiction and poetry that is sophisticated, elegant, mature and polished. Interested in literary works that are consistent with the fundamental characteristics of modern and contemporary literature, including magical realism, metafiction, new journalism, living history and populist."

**$ $ $ $ PLAY THE ODDS,** The Big Dog Press, P.O. Box 55498, Little Rock AR 72215-5498. Phone/fax: (501)224-9452. **Contact:** Tom Raley, editor. Monthly consumer magazine covering gambling. "We cover gambling activities all across the country. We offer tips, reviews, instructions and advice. We also cover cruise lines since most have casinos on board." Estab. 1997. **Pays on acceptance**. Publishes ms an average of 4 months after acceptance. Buys one-time rights. Accepts simultaneous submissions. Accepts queries by mail. Reports in 3 weeks on queries; 2 months on mss. Sample copy for $2. Writer's guidelines for #10 SASE.

● Ranked as one of the best markets for freelance writers in *Writer's Yearbook* magazine's annual "Top 100 Markets," January 1999.

**Nonfiction:** Primarily dealing with casino gaming, *Play the Odds* also covers horse racing, dog racing, sports wagering and online casinos. Also features service articles on entertainment, lodging, and dining facilities located in or near gaming resorts. **Buys 85-145 mss/year.** Length: 800 words. **Pays $500-1,750.**

**Fiction:** Adventure, fantasy (science fantasy), horror, mystery/suspense (cozy, private eye/hardboiled, romantic suspense), science fiction (soft sociological), senior citizen/retirement, sports, westerns (traditional). **Buys 12-20 mss/year.** Length: 600-800 words. **Pays $1,500-3,000.**

● *Play the Odds* was ranked among the best markets for fiction writers in *Writer's Digest's* "Fiction 50," June 1999.

**Columns/Departments:** Reviews (shows, games, hotels, casinos, books), up to 300 words; humorous fillers, up to 80 words. **Buys 24-36 reviews/year; 36-60 fillers/year. Pays $50-350.**

▣ The online magazine carries original content not found in the print edition. Contact: Lisa Nimitz, online editor.

**Tips:** In nonfiction, the editor advises that a writer present an aspect or area of gaming which is out of the mainstream. In fiction, "we look for fast-paced stories with real characters. The stories should be fun, enjoyable and the main character doesn't need to be trying to save the world. Few, if any of us, do that. We do, however, get in bad situations. You must write what you enjoy writing about. If you don't want to write a story about gambling or a gambler, it will show in your work. If it is something you want, that will also show in your work and we will notice."

**$ PLEIADES**, Pleiades Press, Dept. of English & Philosophy, Central Missouri State University, Warrensburg MO 64093. (660)543-4425. Fax: (660)543-8544. E-mail: kdp8106@cmsu2.cmsu.edu. **Contact:** R.M. Kinder and Kevin Prufer, editors. **100% freelance written.** Semiannual journal (5½×8½ perfect bound). "We publish contemporary fiction, poetry, interviews, literary essays, special-interest personal essays, reviews. We're especially interested in cross genre pieces and ethnic explorations. General and literary audience." Estab. 1991. Circ. 1,300. Pays on publication. Publishes ms an average of 9 months after acceptance. Byline given. Buys first North American and second serial (reprint) rights (occasionally requests rights for WordBeat, TV, radio reading, website). Editorial lead time 9 months. Submit seasonal material 9 months in advance. Accepts queries by mail, e-mail, phone. Accepts simultaneous submissions. Reports in 2 months. Sample copy for $5 (back issue), $6 (current issue). Writer's guidelines for #10 SASE.

**Nonfiction:** Book excerpts, essays, interview/profile, reviews. "Nothing pedantic, slick or shallow." **Buys 4-6 mss/year.** Send complete ms. Length: 2,000-4,000 words. **Pays $10.**

**Fiction:** R.M. Kinder, editor. Ethnic, experimental, humorous, mainstream, novel excerpts, magic realism. No science fiction, fantasy, confession, erotica. **Buys 16-20 mss/year.** Send complete ms. Length: 2,000-6,000 words. **Pays $10.**

**Poetry:** Kevin Prufer, editor. Avant-garde, free verse, haiku, light verse, traditional. "Nothing didactic, pretentious, or overly sentimental." **Buys 40-50 poems/year.** Submit maximum 6 poems. **Pays $3/poem "or one year subscription, poets choice."**

**Tips:** "We're always looking for book reviews. We're most interested in insightful, articulate reviews of small-press books of poetry and fiction. Show care for your material and your readers—submit quality work in a professional format. Include cover letter with brief bio and list of publications. Include SASE."

**$ $ PLOUGHSHARES**, Emerson College, Dept. M, 100 Beacon St., Boston MA 02116. Website: http://www.emerson.edu/ploughshares/. **Contact:** Don Lee, editor. Triquarterly magazine for "readers of serious contemporary literature." Circ. 6,000. Pays on publication. Publishes ms an average of 6 months after acceptance. Buys first North American serial rights. Accepts simultaneous submissions, if so noted. Reports in 5 months. Sample copy for $8 (back issue). Writer's guidelines for SASE.

● A competitive and highly prestigious market. Rotating and guest editors make cracking the line-up even tougher, since it's difficult to know what is appropriate to send. The reading period is August 1 through March 31.

**Nonfiction:** Personal and literary essays (accepted only occasionally). Length: 5,000 words maximum. **Pays $25/printed page, $50-$250.** Reviews (assigned). Length: 500 words maximum. **Pays $30.**

**Fiction:** Literary, mainstream. **Buys 25-35 mss/year.** Length: 300-6,000 words. **Pays $25/printed page, $50-250.**

● Ranked as one of the best markets for fiction writers in *Writer's Digest* magazine's "Fiction 50," June 1999.

**Poetry:** Traditional forms, blank verse, free verse and avant-garde. Length: open. **Pays $25/printed page, $50-$250.**

**Tips:** "We no longer structure issues around preconceived themes. If you believe your work is in keeping with our general standards of literary quality and value, submit at any time during our reading period."

**[N] $ POTTERSFIELD PORTFOLIO**, Stork and Press, P.O. Box 40, Station A, Sydney, Nova Scotia B1P 6G9 Canada. Fax: (902)567-6609. E-mail: lars@atcon.com. Managing Editor: Douglas Arthur Brown. Literary magazine published 3 times a year. "*Pottersfield Portfolio* is always looking for poetry and fiction that provides fresh insights and delivers the unexpected. The stories and poems that capture our attention will be the ones that most effectively blend an intriguing voice with imaginative language. Our readers expect to be challenged, enlightened and entertained." Estab. 1979. Circ. 500. Pays on publication. Publishes ms an average of 3-6 months after acceptance. Byline given. Buys first North American serial rights. Editorial lead time 3-6 months. Submit seasonal material 9 months in advance.

Reports in 3 weeks on queries; 6 months on mss. Writer's guidelines for #10 SASE.

**Nonfiction:** Book excerpts, essays, interview/profile, photo feature. **Buys 6 mss/year.** Query by mail. Length: 500-5,000 words. **Pays $5-25 (Canadian).**

**Fiction:** Contact fiction editor. Experimental, novel excerpts, short fiction. No fantasy, horror, mystery, religious, romance, science fiction, western. **Buys 12-15 mss/year.** Send complete ms. Length: 500-5,000 words. **Pays $5-25.**

**Poetry:** Contact poetry editor. Avant garde, free verse, traditional. **Buys 15-20 poems/year.** Submit maximum 10 poems. **Pays $5-25.**

**$ THE PRAIRIE JOURNAL of Canadian Literature**, P.O. Box 61203, Brentwood Postal Services, 217K-3630 Brentwood Rd. NW, Calgary, Alberta T2L 2K6 Canada. Website: http://www.ampa.ab.ca **Contact:** A. Burke, editor. **100% freelance written.** Semiannual magazine of Canadian literature. Estab. 1983. Circ. 600. Pays on publication; "honorarium depends on grant." Byline given. Buys first North American serial rights. Reports 6 months. Sample copy for $6 and IRC (Canadian stamps) or 50¢ payment for postage. Writer's guidelines on website.

**Nonfiction:** Interview/profile, scholarly, literary. **Buys 5 mss/year.** Query first. Include IRCs. **Pays $25-100.**

**Photos:** Send photocopies of photos with submission. Offers additional payment for photos accepted with ms. Identification of subjects required. Buys first North American rights.

**Fiction:** Literary. **Buys 10 mss/year.** Send complete ms. Pays contributor copies or honoraria for literary work.

**Poetry:** Avant-garde, free verse. **Buys 10 poems/year.** Submit maximum 6-10 poems.

**Tips:** "Commercial writers are advised to submit elsewhere. Art needed, black and white pen and ink drawings or good-quality photocopy. Do not send originals. We are strictly small press editors interested in highly talented, serious artists. We are oversupplied with fiction but seek more high-quality poetry, especially the contemporary long poem or sequences from longer works. We welcome freelancers."

**$ PRESS**, Daniel Roberts, Inc., 125 W. 72nd St., Suite 3-M, New York NY 10023. E-mail: pressltd@aol.com. Editor: Daniel Roberts. **Contact:** Sean Anthony, managing editor. **100% freelance written.** Quarterly literary magazine containing poetry and fiction with "clarity, memorable lines, captivating plots and excellence." Estab. 1995. Circ. 15,000. **Pays on acceptance.** Publishes ms an average of 3 months after acceptance. Byline given. Buys first rights. Editorial lead time 3 months. Reports in 2 months on queries; 1 year on mss. Sample copy for $9.24. Guidelines for #10 SASE.

**Fiction:** "While almost all forms are acceptable, prose poems and more experimental writing (stories that don't actually tell a story) are discouraged." **Buys 40 mss/year.** Send complete ms. Length: up to 25 typed pages. **Pays $100.**

**Poetry:** Avant-garde, free verse, haiku, light verse, traditional. "All poems must make sense. That is all complicated rhythms and fanciful word choices, all emotional and psychological gestures must have a public value as well as a personal value." No careless, seasonal, immature poetry. **Buys 120 poems/year.** Submit maximum 3 poems. **Pays $50.**

**$ PRISM INTERNATIONAL**, Department of Creative Writing, Buch E462-1866 Main Mall, University of British Columbia, Vancouver, British Columbia V6T 1Z1 Canada. (604)822-2514. Fax: (604)822-3616. E-mail: prism@unixg.ubc.ca. Website: http://www.arts.ubc.ca/prism. Executive Editor: Laisha Rosnau. **Contact:** Jennica Harper, Kiera Miller, editors. **100% freelance written.** Eager to work with new/unpublished writers. Quarterly magazine emphasizing contemporary literature, including translations, for university and public libraries, and private subscribers. Estab. 1959. Circ. 1,200. Pays on publication. Publishes ms an average of 4 months after acceptance. Buys first North American serial rights. Accepts queries by mail, e-mail, fax. Reports in 6 months. Sample copy for $5 or on website. Writer's guidelines for #10 SAE with 1 first-class Canadian stamp (Canadian entries) or 1 IRC (US entries) or on website.

**Nonfiction:** "*Creative* nonfiction that reads like fiction." No reviews, tracts or scholarly essays.

**Fiction:** Experimental, traditional, novel excerpts. **Buys 3-5 mss/issue.** Send complete ms. Length: 5,000 words maximum. **Pays $20/printed page** and 1-year subscription. Publishes novel excerpts up to 25 double-spaced pages.

**Poetry:** Avant-garde, traditional. **Buys 20 poems/issue.** Submit maximum 6 poems. **Pays $20/printed page** and 1-year subscription.

**Drama:** One-acts preferred. **Pays $20/printed page** and 1-year subscription.

**Tips:** "We are looking for new and exciting fiction. Excellence is still our number one criterion. As well as poetry, imaginative nonfiction and fiction, we are especially open to translations of all kinds, very short fiction pieces and drama which work well on the page. Translations must come with a copy of the original language work. Work may be submitted through e-mail or our website. We pay an additional $10/printed page to selected authors whose work we place on our on-line version of *Prism*."

**$ $ QUARTERLY WEST**, University of Utah, 200 S. Central Campus Dr., Rm. 317, Salt Lake City UT 84112-9109. (801)581-3938. Website: http://chronicle.utah.edu/QW/QW.html. **Contact:** Margot Schilpp, editor. Semiannual magazine. "We publish fiction, poetry, and nonfiction in long and short formats, and will consider experimental as well as traditional works." Estab. 1976. Circ. 1,900. Pays on publication. Publishes ms an average of 6 months after acceptance. Buys first North American serial and all rights. Accepts simultaneous submissions, if so noted. Reports in 6 months on mss. Sample copy for $7.50 or on website. Writer's guidelines for #10 SASE or on website.

**Nonfiction:** Essays, interview/profile, book reviews. **Buys 4-5 mss/year.** Send complete ms with SASE. Length: 10,000 words maximum. **Pays $25.**

**Fiction:** Contact: Gerry Hart and Rebekah Lindberg. Ethnic, experimental, humorous, mainstream, novel excerpts, short shorts, slice-of-life vignettes, translations. **Buys 20-30 mss/year.** Send complete ms with SASE. Pays $25-500.

No preferred lengths; interested in longer, fuller short stories and short shorts. Length: 50-125 pages. **Pays $25-500.**
**Poetry:** Contact: Heidi Blitch and Melanie Figg. Avant-garde, free verse, traditional. **Buys 30-50 poems/year.** Submit 5 poems maximum. **Pays $15-100.**
**Tips:** "We publish a special section or short shorts every issue, and we also sponsor a biennial novella contest. We are open to experimental work—potential contributors should read the magazine! We solicit quite frequently, but tend more toward the surprises—unsolicited. Don't send more than one story per submission, but submit as often as you like. Biennial novella competition guidelines available upon request with SASE."

**$ $ QUEEN'S QUARTERLY, A Canadian Review**, Queen's University, Kingston, Ontario K7L 3N6 Canada. (613)533-2667. Fax: (613)533-6822. E-mail: qquarter@post.queensu.ca. Website: http://info.queensu.ca/quarterly. **Contact:** Joan Harcourt, literary editor. Quarterly magazine covering a wide variety of subjects, including science, humanities, arts and letters, politics and history for the educated reader. **15% freelance written.** Estab. 1893. Circ. 3,000. Pays on publication. Publishes ms an average of 3 months after acceptance. Byline given. Buys first North American serial rights. Accepts queries by mail, e-mail, fax. Requires 1 double-spaced hard copy and 1 copy on disk in WordPerfect. Reports in 1 month on mss. *Writer's Market* recommends allowing 2 months for reply. Sample copy $6.50 or on website. Writer's guidelines on website.
**Fiction:** Historical, humorous, mainstream and science fiction. No fantasy. Publishes novel excerpts. **Buys 8-12 mss/year.** Send complete ms. Length: 4,000 words maximum. **Pays $150-250.**
**Poetry:** Avant-garde, free verse, haiku, light verse, traditional. No "sentimental, religious, or first efforts by unpublished writers." **Buys 25/year.** Submit maximum 6 poems. Length: open. **Pays $100-200.**
**Tips:** "Poetry and fiction are most open to freelancers. Don't send less than the best. No multiple submissions. No more than six poems or two stories per submission. We buy very few freelance submissions."

**$ RARITAN A Quarterly Review**, 31 Mine St., New Brunswick NJ 08903. (732)932-7887. Fax: (732)932-7855. Editor: Richard Poirier. **Contact:** Stephanie Volmer, managing editor. Quarterly magazine covering literature, general culture. Estab. 1981. Circ. 3,500. Pays on publication. Publishes ms 1 year after acceptance. Byline given. Buys first North American serial rights. Editorial lead time 5 months. Accepts simultaneous submissions.
**Nonfiction:** Book excerpts, essays. **Buys 50 mss/year.** Send complete ms. Length 15-30 pages. **Pays $100.**
 ● Raritan no longer accepts previously published submissions.

**[N] $ RIVER STYX, Big River Association**, 634 N. Grand Blvd., 12th Floor, St. Louis MO 63103. (314)533-4541. Fax: (314)533-3345. Website: http://www.riverstyx.org. Senior Editors: Quincy Troupe and Michael Castro. **Contact:** Richard Newman, editor. Triannual literary magazine. "*River Styx* publishes the highest quality fiction, poetry, interviews, essays and visual art. We are an internationally distributed multicultural literary magazine." Estab. 1975. Pays on publication. Publishes ms an average of 12 months after acceptance. Byline given. Buys one-time rights. Manuscripts read May-November. Accepts simultaneous submissions, if so noted. Reports in 4 months on mss. Sample copy for $7. Writer's guidelines for #10 SASE or on website.
**Nonfiction:** Essays, interviews. **Buys 2-5 mss/year.** Send complete ms. Pays 2 contributor copies, plus one-year subscription; **$8/page** if funds are available.
 ● The River Styx has won several prizes, including Best American Poetry 1994, 1996, 1998; Pushcart Prize; and Stanley Hanks Prizes.
**Photos/Art:** Send with submission. Reviews 5×7 or 8×10 b&w prints or color. Also slides. Pays 2 contributor copies, plus one-year subscription; $8/page if funds are available. Buys one-time rights.
**Fiction:** Literary, novel excerpts. **Buys 6-9 mss/year.** Send complete ms. Pays 2 contributor copies, plus one-year subscription; **$8/page** if funds are available.
**Poetry:** Traditional, free verse, avant-garde. No religious. **Buys 40-50 poems/year.** Submit 3-5 poems. Pays 2 contributor copies, plus one-year subscription. **$8/page** if funds are available.

**[N] $ ROOM OF ONE'S OWN, A Canadian Feminist Quarterly of Literary Criticism**, West Coast Feminist Literary Magazine Society, P.O. Box 46160, Station D, Vancouver, British Columbia V6J 5G5 Canada. Website: http://www.islandnet.com/room/enter. **Contact:** Growing Room Collective. **100% freelance written.** Quarterly literary journal of feminist literature. Estab. 1975. Circ. 1,000. Pays on publication. Publishes ms an average of 8 months after acceptance. Byline given. Buys first North American serial rights. Editorial lead time 9 months. Reports in 3 months on queries; 6 months on mss. Sample copy for $7 or on website. Writer's guidelines for #10 SAE with 2 IRCs (US postage not valid in Canada) or on website.
**Nonfiction:** Essays, interview/profile, reviews. **Buys 1-2 mss/year.** Send complete ms. Length: 1,000-2,500 words. **Pays $25 (Canadian)** and 1-year subscription.
**Photos:** Send photos with submission. Reviews prints. Offers no additional payment for photos accepted with ms. Buys one-time rights.
**Fiction:** Adventure, ethnic, experimental, fantasy, humorous, mainstream, slice-of-life vignettes, science fiction, feminist literature. **Buys 80 mss/year.** Length: 2,000-5,000 words. **Pays $25 (Canadian).**
**Poetry:** Avant-garde, free verse. "Nothing light, undeveloped." **Buys 20 poems/year.** Submit maximum 8 poems. Length: 3-80 lines. **Pays $25 (Canadian).**

⭐ **$ $ ROSEBUD, The Magazine For People Who Enjoy Good Writing**, Rosebud, Inc., P.O. Box 459, Cambridge WI 53523. (608)423-9609. (800)786-5669. Website: http://www.hyperionstudio.com/rosebud. **Contact:** Rod Clark, editor. **100% freelance written.** Quarterly magazine "for people who love to read and write. Our readers like good storytelling, real emotion, a sense of place and authentic voice." Estab. 1993. Circ. 9,000. Pays on publication. Publishes ms an average of 2 months after acceptance. Byline given. Buys one-time or second serial (reprint) rights. Editorial lead time 3 months. Submit seasonal material 3 months in advance. Accepts simultaneous submissions. Sends acknowledgment postcard upon receipt of submission and reports in 1-5 months. Sample copy for $5.95 or sample articles on website. Writer's guidelines for SASE or on website.

**Nonfiction:** Book excerpt, essays, general interest, historical/nostalgic, humor, interview/profile, personal experience, travel. "No editorializing." **Buys 6 mss/year.** Send complete ms and SASE. Length: 1,200-1,800 words. **Pays $45-195** plus 3 copies.

**Reprints:** Send tearsheet, photocopy or typed ms with rights for sale noted. Pays 100% of amount paid for an original article.

**Photos:** State availability of photos with submission. Offers no additional payment for photos accepted with ms. Captions, model releases and identification of subjects required. Buys one-time rights.

**Fiction:** Ethnic, experimental, historical, humorous, mainstream, novel excerpts, slice-of-life vignettes, suspense. "No formula pieces." **Buys 80 mss/year.** Send complete ms and SASE. Length: 1,200-1,800 words. **Pays $45-195** plus 3 copies.

 • Ranked as one of the best markets for fiction writers in *Writer's Digest* magazine's "Fiction 50," June 1999.

**Poetry:** Avant-garde, free verse, traditional. No inspirational poetry. **Buys 36 poems/year.** Submit maximum 5 poems. Length: open. **Pays $45-195** and 3 contributor's copies.

 The online magazine carries original content not found in the print edition.

**Tips:** "Something has to 'happen' in the pieces we choose, but what happens inside characters is much more interesting to us than plot manipulation. We prefer to respond with an individualized letter (send SASE for this) and recycle submitted manuscripts. We will return your manuscript only if you send sufficient postage. We can only give detailed editorial feedback on pieces we are going to buy."

**$ SHORT STUFF, for Grown-ups**, Bowman Publications, P.O. Box 7057, Loveland CO 80537. (970)669-9139. **Contact:** Donna Bowman, editor. **98% freelance written.** Bimonthly magazine. "We are perhaps an enigma in that we publish only clean stories in any genre. We'll tackle any subject, but don't allow obscene language or pornographic description. Our magazine is for grown-ups, *not* X-rated 'adult' fare." Estab. 1989. Circ. 10,400. Payment and contract on publication. Byline given. Buys first North American serial rights. Editorial lead time 3 months. Submit seasonal material 3 months in advance. Reports in 6 months on mss. Sample copy for $1.50 and 9×12 SAE with 5 first-class stamps. Writer's guidelines for #10 SASE.

**Nonfiction:** Humor. Special issues: "We are holiday oriented and each issue reflects the appropriate holidays." **Buys 20 mss/year.** Most nonfiction is staff written. Send complete ms. Length: 500-1,500 words. **Pays $10-50.**

**Photos:** Send photos with submission. Offers no additional payment for photos accepted with ms. Identification of subjects required. Buys one-time rights.

**Fiction:** Adventure, historical, humorous, mainstream, mystery, romance, science fiction (seldom), suspense, western. **Buys 144 mss/year.** Send complete ms. Length: 500-1,500 words. **Pays $10-50.**

**Fillers:** Anecdotes, short humor. **Buys 200/year.** Length: 20-500 words. **Pays $1-5.**

**Tips:** "Don't send floppy disks or cartridges. Do include cover letter about the author, not a synopsis of the story. We are holiday oriented; mark on *outside* of envelope if story is for Easter, Mother's Day, etc. We receive 500 manuscripts each month. This is up about 200%. Because of this, I implore writers to send one manuscript at a time. I would not use stories from the same author more than once an issue and this means I might keep the others too long."

**N $ SING HEAVENLY MUSE!, Women's Poetry and Prose**, Sing Heavenly Muse! Inc., Box 13320, Minneapolis MN 55414. **Contact:** Editorial Circle. **100% freelance written.** Annual journal of women's literature. Circ. 500. Pays on publication. Publishes ms an average of 1 year after acceptance. Byline given. Buys first North American serial rights. Reports in 6 months. Sample copy for $4. Writer's guidelines for #10 SASE.

**Fiction:** Women's literature, journal pieces, memoir and novel excerpts. **Buys 15-20 mss/year.** Length: 10,000 words maximum. **Pays $15-25;** contributors receive 2 free copies.

**Poetry:** Avant-garde, free verse, haiku, light verse, traditional. **Buys 75-100/year.** No length limit. **Pays $15-25.**

**Tips:** "To meet our needs, writing must be feminist and women-centered. Reading periods vary. Issues are often related to a specific theme; always query for guidelines, upcoming themes and reading periods before submitting."

**$ THE SOUTHERN REVIEW**, 43 Allen Hall, Louisiana State University, Baton Rouge LA 70803-5001. (225)388-5108. Fax: (225)388-5098. E-mail: bmacon@unix1.sncc.lsu.edu. **Contact:** Michael Griffith, associate editor. **100% freelance written.** Works with a moderate number of new/unpublished writers each year. Quarterly magazine "with emphasis on contemporary literature in the United States and abroad, and with special interest in Southern culture and history." Estab. 1935. Circ. 3,100. Pays on publication. Publishes ms an average of 6 months after acceptance. Byline given. Buys first serial rights only. No queries. Reports in 2 months. Sample copy for $6. Writer's guidelines for #10 SASE. Reading period: September through May.

**Nonfiction:** Essays with careful attention to craftsmanship, technique and seriousness of subject matter. "Willing to publish experimental writing if it has a valid artistic purpose. Avoid extremism and sensationalism. Essays should exhibit thoughtful and sometimes severe awareness of the necessity of literary standards in our time." Emphasis on contemporary literature, especially southern culture and history. No footnotes. **Buys 25 mss/year.** Length: 4,000-10,000 words. **Pays $12/page.**

**Fiction and Poetry:** Short stories of lasting literary merit, with emphasis on style and technique, also novel excerpts. Length: 4,000-8,000 words. **Pays $12/page.**

**Poetry:** Length: 1-4 pages. **Pays $20/page.**

**$ SPORT LITERATE, Honest Reflections on Life's Leisurely Diversions**, Pint Size Publications, P.O. Box 577166, Chicago IL 60657-7166. Fax: (773)929-0818. E-mail: sportlit@aol.com. Website: http://www.avalon.net/~librar ian/sportliterate/. **Contact:** William Meiners and Jotham Burrello editor. **95% freelance written.** Quarterly literary journal covering leisure/sport . . . life outside the daily grind of making a living. "*Sport Literate* publishes the highest quality nonfiction and poets on themes of leisure and sport. Our writers use a leisure activity to explore a larger theme. The writing is allegoric. We serve a broad audience." Estab. 1995. Circ. 1,500. Pays on publication. Publishes ms an average of 3 months after acceptance. Byline given. Buys first North American serial rights. Editorial lead time 3 months. Submit seasonal material 4 months in advance. Accepts queries by mail, e-mail. Reports in 3 weeks on queries; 2 months on mss. Sample copy for $5.75 or on website. Writer's guidelines for #10 SASE or on website.

**Nonfiction:** Essays, historical/nostalgic, humor, interview/profile, personal experience, travel, creative nonfiction. No book reviews, straight reporting on sports. **Buys 28 mss/year.** Send complete ms. Length: 250-5,000 words. **Pays up to $20.**

**Poetry: Contact:** Jennifer Richter, poetry editor. Avant-garde, free verse, haiku, light verse, traditional. **Buys 25 poems/ year.** Submit maximum 5 poems. Length: 10 lines. **Pays up to $20.**

**Tips:** "We like to explore all the avenues of the creative nonfiction form—personal essays, literary journalism, travel pieces, historical, humor and interviews—as they relate to our broad definition of sport. We only publish fiction from the famous or the dead. Read any publication that you're submitting to. It can be a great time saver."

**$ SPSM&H**, *Amelia Magazine*, 329 E St., Bakersfield CA 93304. (661)323-4064. **Contact:** Frederick A. Raborg, Jr., editor. **100% freelance written.** Quarterly magazine featuring fiction and poetry with Romantic or Gothic theme. "*SPSM&H* (Shakespeare, Petrarch, Sidney, Milton and Hopkins) uses one short story in each issue and 20-36 sonnets, plus reviews of books and anthologies containing the sonnet form and occasional articles about the sonnet form or about some romantic or Gothic figure or movement. We look for contemporary aspects of the sonnet form." Estab. 1984. Circ. 600. Pays on publication. Publishes ms an average of 6 months after acceptance. Byline given. Offers 50% kill fee. Buys first North American serial rights. Editorial lead time 2 months. Submit seasonal material 3 months in advance. Accepts simultaneous submissions. Reports in 2 weeks on queries; 3 months on mss. Sample copy for $4.95. Writer's guidelines for #10 SASE.

**Nonfiction:** Essays, general interest, historical/nostalgic, humor, interview/profile, opinion and anything related to sonnets or to romance. **Buys 1-4 mss/year.** Send complete ms. Length: 500-2,000 words. **Pays $10.**

**Photos:** Send photos with submission. Reviews 8×10 or 5×7 b&w prints. Offers $10-25/photo. Model releases required. Buys one-time rights.

**Fiction:** Confession, erotica, experimental, fantasy, historical, humor, humorous, mainstream, mystery, romance, slice-of-life vignettes. **Buys 4 mss/year.** Send complete ms. Length: 500-2,500 words. **Pays $10-20.**

**Poetry:** Sonnets, sonnet sequences. **Buys 140 poems/year.** Submit maximum 10 poems. Length: 14 lines. Two "best of issue" poets each receive $14.

**Fillers:** Anecdotes, short humor. **Buys 2-4/year.** Length: 25-500 words. No payment for fillers.

**Tips:** "Read a copy certainly. Understand the limitations of the sonnet form and, in the case of fiction, the requirements of the romantic or Gothic genres. Be professional in presentation, and realize that neatness does count. Be contemporary and avoid Victorian verse forms and techniques. Avoid convolution and forced rhyme. Idiomatics ought to be contemporary. Don't be afraid to experiment. We consider John Updike's 'Love Sonnet' to be the extreme to which poets may experiment."

**N $ THE STRAIN, Interactive Arts Magazine**, 1307 Diablo, Houston TX 77532-3004. **Contact:** Norman Clark Stewart Jr., editor. **80% freelance written.** Monthly literary magazine. Estab. 1987. Circ. 200. Pays on publication. Publishes ms up to 3 years after acceptance. Byline given. Buys first, one-time or second serial rights. Makes work-for-hire assignments. Reports in up to 2 years.

**Nonfiction:** Alicia Alder, articles editor. Essays, exposé, how-to, humor, photo feature, technical. **Buys 2-20 mss/year.** Send complete ms. **Pays $5 minimum.**

**Reprints:** Send typed ms with rights for sale noted and information about when and where article previously appeared.

**Photos:** Send photos with submissions. Reviews transparencies and prints. Model releases and identification of subjects required. Buys one-time rights.

**Columns/Departments:** Charlie Mainze, editor. Multi-media performance art. Send complete ms. **Pays $5 minimum.**

**Fiction:** Michael Bond, editor. **Buys 1-35 mss/year.** Send complete ms. **Pays $5 minimum.**

**Poetry:** Annas Kinder, editor. Avant-garde, free verse, light verse, traditional. **Buys 100/year.** Submit maximum 5 poems. **Pays $5 minimum.**

**$ THE STRAND MAGAZINE**, P.O. Box 1418, Birmingham MI 48012-1418. (800)300-6652. Fax: (248)874-1046. E-mail: strandmag@worldnet.att.net. **Contact:** A.F. Gulli, managing editor. Quarterly magazine covering mysteries, short stories, essays, book reviews. "Mysteries and short stories written in the classic tradition of this century's great authors." Estab. 1998. Pays on publication. Publishes ms an average of 4 months after acceptance. Byline given. Buys first North American serial rights. Reports in 1 month on queries; 4 months on mss. Guidelines for #10 SASE.
**Fiction:** Horror, humorous, mystery, suspense. Send complete ms. Length: 2,000-6,000 words. **Pays $25-150.**

**[N] $ TAMPA REVIEW**, University of Tampa Press, 401 W. Kennedy Blvd., Tampa FL 33606. (813)253-6266. Editor: Richard B. Mathews. Semiannual literary magazine. An international literary journal publishing art and literature from Florida and Tampa Bay as well as new work and translations from throughout the world. Estab. 1988. Circ. 500. Pays on publication. Publishes ms an average of 10 months after acceptance. Byline given. Buys first North American serial rights. Editorial lead time 6-18 months. Reports in 5 months on mss. Sample copy for $5. Guidelines for SASE.
**Nonfiction:** Paul Linnehan, nonfiction editor. Essays, general interest, interview/profile, personal experience. No "how-to" articles; fads; journalistic reprise etc. **Buys 6 mss/year.** Send complete ms. Length: 250-7,500 words. **Pays $10/ printed page.**
**Photos:** State availability of photos with submission. Reviews contact sheets, negatives, transparencies, prints. Offers $10/photo. Caption identification of subjects required. Buys one-time rights.
**Fiction:** Lisa Birnbaum and Kathleen Ochshorn, fiction editors. Literary. **Buys 6 mss/year.** Send complete ms. Length: 200-5,000 words. **Pays $10/printed page.**
**Poetry:** Don Morrill and Kathryn Van Spanckeren, poetry editors. Avant-garde, free verse, haiku, light verse, traditional, visual/experimental. No greeting card verse; hackneyed, sing-song, rhyme-for-the-sake-of-rhyme. **Buys 45 poems/year.** Submit up to 10 poems at one time. Length: 2-225 lines.
**Tips:** "Send a clear cover letter stating previous experience or background. Our editorial staff considers submissions between September and December for publication in the following year."

**$ THEMA**, Box 8747, Metairie LA 70011-8747. (504)887-1263. E-mail: bothomos@juno.com. Website: http://www.l itline.org/html/THEMA.html. **Contact:** Virginia Howard, editor. **100% freelance written.** Triannual literary magazine covering a different theme for each issue. "*Thema* is designed to stimulate creative thinking by challenging writers with unusual themes, such as 'laughter on the steps' and 'jogging on ice.' Appeals to writers, teachers of creative writing and general reading audience." Estab. 1988. Circ. 350. **Pays on acceptance.** Byline given. Buys one-time rights. Accepts queries by mail, e-mail. Reports in 5 months on mss (after deadline for particular issue). Sample copy for $8. Writer's guidelines for #10 SASE or on website. Upcoming themes for SASE.
**Fiction:** Adventure, ethnic, experimental, fantasy, historical, humorous, mainstream, mystery, religious, science fiction, slice-of-life vignettes, suspense, western, novel excerpts. "No erotica." Special issues: Toby came today (November 1, 1999); Addie hasn't been the same . . . (March 1, 2000); Scraps (July 1, 2000). **Buys 30 mss/year.** Send complete ms and *specify theme* for which it is intended. **Pays $10-25.**
  ● Ranked as one of the best markets for fiction writers in *Writer's Digest* magazine's "Fiction 50," June 1999.
**Reprints:** Send typed ms with rights for sale noted and information about when and where the article previously appeared. Pays same amount paid for original story or poem.
**Poetry:** Avant-garde, free verse, haiku, light verse, traditional. No erotica. **Buys 27 poems/year.** Submit maximum 3 poems. Length: 4-50 lines. **Pays $10.**
**Tips:** "Be familiar with the themes. *Don't submit* unless you have an upcoming theme in mind. Specify the target theme on the first page of your manuscript or in a cover letter. Put your name on *first* page of manuscript only. (All submissions are judged in blind review after the deadline for a specified issue.) Most open to fiction and poetry. Don't be hasty when you consider a theme—mull it over and let it ferment in your mind. We appreciate interpretations that are carefully constructed, clever, subtle, well thought out."

**⊠ $ $ THE THREEPENNY REVIEW**, P.O. Box 9131, Berkeley CA 94709. (510)849-4545. **Contact:** Wendy Lesser, editor. **100% freelance written.** Works with small number of new/unpublished writers each year. Quarterly literary tabloid. "We are a general interest, national literary magazine with coverage of politics, the visual arts and the performing arts as well." Estab. 1980. Circ. 9,000. **Pays on acceptance.** Publishes ms an average of 1 year after acceptance. Byline given. Buys first North American serial rights. Reports in 1 month on queries; 2 months on mss. Does *not* read mss in summer months. Sample copy for $7 and 10×13 SAE with 5 first-class stamps. Writer's guidelines for SASE.
**Nonfiction:** Essays, exposé, historical, personal experience, book, film, theater, dance, music and art reviews. **Buys 40 mss/year.** Query with or without published clips, or send complete ms. Length: 1,500-4,000 words. **Pays $200.**
**Fiction:** No fragmentary, sentimental fiction. **Buys 10 mss/year.** Send complete ms. Length: 800-4,000 words. **Pays $200.**
  ● Ranked as one of the best markets for fiction writers in *Writer's Digest* magazine's last "Fiction 50."
**Poetry:** Free verse, traditional. No poems "without capital letters or poems without a discernible subject." **Buys 30 poems/year.** Submit 5 poems maximum. **Pays $100.**
**Tips:** "Nonfiction (political articles, memoirs, reviews) is most open to freelancers."

**[N] $ TICKLED BY THUNDER, Helping Writers Get Published**, Tickled by Thunder, 7385 129 St., Surrey, British Columbia V3W 7B8 Canada. (604)591-6095. E-mail: thunder@istar.ca. Website: http://www.home.ca/~thunder.

**Contact:** L. Lindner, publisher/editor. **100% freelance written.** Quarterly literary magazine on writing. "Our readers are generally writers hoping to improve their craft and gain writing experience/credits." Estab. 1990. Circ. 1,000. Pays on publication. Publishes ms an average of 4 months after acceptance. Byline given. Buys one-time rights. Editorial lead time 4 months. Submit seasonal material 6 months in advance. Accepts queries by mail, e-mail. Accepts simultaneous submissions. Reports in 6 weeks on queries; 4 months on mss. Sample copy for $2.50 or sample articles on website. Writer's guidelines for #10 SASE or on website.

**Nonfiction:** Interview/profile, opinion, personal experience (must relate to writing). Does not want to see articles not slanted to writing. **Buys 4 mss/year.** Send complete ms. Length: 300-2,000 words. **Pays 5¢-$5/line.**

**Photos:** State availability of photos with submission. Model releases and identification of subjects required. Buys one-time rights.

**Fiction:** Experimental, fantasy, humorous, mainstream, mystery, religious, science fiction, slice-of-life vignettes, suspense, western. No bad language—not even "damn" or "hell." **Buys 8-12 mss/year.** Send complete ms. Length: 300-2,000 words. **Pays 10¢-$5/line.**

**Poetry:** Avant garde, free verse, haiku, light verse, traditional. "No stuff that requires a manual to understand." **Buys 12-20 poems/year.** Submit maximum 7 poems. Length: 50 lines. **Pays 2¢-$2/line.**

**N $ $ $ TIN HOUSE**, McCormack Communications. 2601 NW Thurman St., Portland OR 97210. (503)274-4393. Fax: (503)222-1154. E-mail: tinhouse@europa.com. Editor-in-Chief: Win McCormack. Managing Editor: Holly Macarthur. **Contact:** Rob Spillman, Elissa Chapell, editors. **75% freelance written**. Quarterly literary magazine. "We are a general interest literary quarterly. Our watchword is quality. Our audience is people interested in literature in all its aspects, from the mundane to the exalted." Estab. 1998. Circ. 5,000. Pays on publication. Publishes ms up to 1 year after acceptance. Byline given. Offers 25-50% kill fee. Buys first North American serial rights and anthology rights. Editorial lead time 6 months. Submit seasonal material 6 months in advance. Accepts simultaneous submissions. Reports in 6 weeks on queries, 3 months on mss. Sample copy $15.

**Nonfiction:** Book excerpts, essays, general interest, interview/profile, personal experience. Query or send complete ms. Length: up to 2,000 words. **Pays $50-800 for assigned articles; $50-500 for unsolicited articles.** Sometimes pays expenses of writers on assignment.

**Photos:** State availability of photos with submission. Reviews prints. Offers no additional payment for photos accepted with ms. Buys one-time rights.

**Columns/Departments:** Lost and Found (mini-reviews of forgotten or under appreciated books), to 5,000 words; Readable Feasts (fiction or nonfiction literature with recipes), 2,000-3,000 words; Pilgrimmage (journey to a personally significant place, especially literary), 2,000-3,000 words. **Buys 15-20 mss/year.** Query or send complete ms. **Pays $50-500.**

**Fiction:** Experimental, mainstream, novel excerpts. **Buys 15-20 mss/year.** Send complete ms. Length: up to 3,000 words. **Pays $200-800.**

**Poetry:** Amy Bartlett, poetry editor. Avant-garde, free verse, traditional. No prose masquerading as poetry. **Buys 40-800 poems/year.** Submit 5 poems/batch. **Pays $50-150.**

**Fillers:** Tucker Malarkey, senior editor. Interesting literary facts or anecdotes *with*citations. Length: up to 100 lines. **Pays $0-10.**

**Tips:** "We seek: boldness of concept, intense level of energy and emotion, precision of observation, deployment of imagination, grace of style. We require both an investment of strong feeling and great professional care from the writer."

**$ TRIQUARTERLY**, 2020 Ridge Ave., Northwestern University, Evanston IL 60208-4302. (847)491-3490. Fax: (847)467-2096. Website: http://triquarterly.nwu.edu. **Contact:** Susan Firestone Hahn, editor. **70% freelance written.** Eager to work with new/unpublished writers. Triannual magazine of fiction, poetry and essays, as well as artwork. Estab. 1964. Pays on publication. Publishes ms an average of 1 year after acceptance. Buys first serial and nonexclusive reprint rights. Reports in 3 months. Study magazine before submitting. Sample copy for $5. Writer's guidelines for #10 SASE.

● *TriQuarterly* has had several stories published in the *O. Henry Prize* anthology and *Best American Short Stories* as well as poetry in *Best American Poetry.*

**Nonfiction:** Query before sending essays (no scholarly or critical essays except in special issues).

**Fiction and Poetry:** No prejudice against style or length of work; only seriousness and excellence are required. Publishes novel excerpts. **Buys 20-50 unsolicited mss/year.** Payment varies depending on grant support. Does not accept or read mss between April 1 and September 30.

**$ VIRGINIA QUARTERLY REVIEW**, University of Virginia, One West Range, Charlottesville VA 22903. (804)924-3124. Fax: (804)924-1397. E-mail: jco7e@virginia.edu. **Contact:** Staige D. Blackford, editor. Quarterly magazine. "A national journal of literature and thought." Estab. 1925. Circ. 4,000. Pays on publication. Publishes ms an average of 1 year after acceptance. Byline given. Buys first rights. Editorial lead time 6 months. Submit seasonal material 6 months in advance. Reports in 2 weeks on queries; 2 months on mss. Sample copy $5. Guidelines for #10 SASE or on website.

**Nonfiction:** Book excerpts, essays, general interest, historical/nostalgic, humor, inspirational, personal experience, travel. Send complete ms. Length: 2,000-4,000 words. **Pays $10/page maximum.**

**Fiction:** Adventure, ethnic, historical, humorous, mainstream, mystery, novel excerpts, romance. Send complete ms. Length: 2,000-4,000 words. **Pays $10/page maximum.**

**Poetry:** Gregory Orr, poetry editor. All types. Submit maximum 5 poems. Pays $1/line.

**WASCANA REVIEW OF CONTEMPORARY POETRY AND SHORT FICTION,** University of Regina, Department of English, Regina, Saskatchewan S45 0A2 Canada. Fax: (306)585-4827. E-mail: Kathleen.wall@uregina.ca **Contact:** Kathleen Wall, editor. **100% freelance written.** Semiannual magazine covering contemporary poetry and short fiction. "We seek poetry and short fiction that combines craft with risks, pressure with grace. Critical articles should articulate a theoretical approach and also explore either poetry or short fiction. While we frequently publish established writers, we also welcome—and seek to foster—new voices." Estab. 1966. Circ. 300. Pays on publication. Publishes ms an average of 4 months after acceptance. Buys first North American rights. Editorial lead time 4 months. Accepts queries mail, e-mail, fax, phone. Reports in 1 week on queries; 2 months on mss. Guidelines for #10 SASE.
**Columns/Departments:** Reviews of contemporary poetry and short fiction (ask for guidelines), 1,000-1,500 words. **Buys 8 mss/year.** Query. **Pays $3/printed page.**
**Fiction:** No genre-bound fiction, or stories with sentimental or predictable endings. **Buys 8-10 mss/year.** Send complete ms. **Pays $3/printed page** plus 2 contributor's copies.
**Poetry:** Troni Grande. Avant-garde, free verse. No sentimental, feel-good verse, no predictable rhyme and meter. **Buys 40 poems/year.** Submit maximum 5 poems. **Pays $10/printed page** plus contributor's copies.
**Tips:** "The best advice I can give is to read back issues to ensure that what you write and what we publish are in sync. We publish a wide variety of poetry and short fiction and seek to include more traditional voices and cutting edge experimenters."

**$ WESTERN HUMANITIES REVIEW,** University of Utah, English Dept., LNCO 3500, Salt Lake City UT 84112-1107. (801)581-6070. Fax: (801)585-5167. E-mail: whr.lists@m.cc.utah.edu. **Contact:** Jenny Mueller, managing editor. Quarterly magazine for educated readers. Estab. 1947. Circ. 1,200. Pays on publication. Publishes ms up to 1 year after acceptance. Buys all rights. Accepts queries by mail, phone. Accepts simultaneous submissions. Reports in 5 months.
**Nonfiction:** Barry Weller, editor-in-chief. Authoritative, readable articles on literature, art, philosophy, current events, history, religion and anything in the humanities. Interdisciplinary articles encouraged. Departments on film and books. **Buys 4-5 unsolicited mss/year. Pays $50-100.**
**Fiction:** Karen Brennan, fiction editor. Any type, including experimental. **Buys 8-12 mss/year.** Send complete ms. **Pays $100** on average.
**Poetry:** Richard Howard, poetry editor.
**Tips:** "Because of changes in our editorial staff, we urge familiarity with *recent* issues of the magazine. Inappropriate material will be returned without comment. We do not publish writer's guidelines because we think that the magazine itself conveys an accurate picture of our requirements."

**[N] WHETSTONE,** Barrington Area Arts Council, Box 1266, Barrington IL 60011. (847)382-5626. Co-Editors: S. Berris, M. Portnoy. **Contact:** J. Tolle, co-editor. **100% freelance written.** Annual literary magazine featuring fiction, creative nonfiction and poetry. "We publish work by emerging and established authors for readers hungry for poetry and prose of substance." Estab. 1982. Circ. 700. Pays on publication. Publishes ms up to 14 months after acceptance. Byline given. Not copyrighted. Buys first North American serial rights. Accepts simultaneous submissions. Reports in 5 months on mss. Sample copy and writer's guidelines for $5.
**Nonfiction:** Creative essay. "No articles." **Buys 0-3 mss/year.** Send complete ms. Length: 500-5,000 words. Pays with 2 copies and variable cash payment.
**Fiction:** Novel excerpts (literary) and short stories. **Buys 10-12 mss/year.** Send complete ms. Length: 500-5,000 words. Pays with 2 copies and variable cash payment.
**Poetry:** Free verse, traditional. "No light verse, for children, political poems." **Buys 10-20 poems/year.** Submit maximum 7 poems. Pays with 2 copies and variable cash payment.
**Tips:** "We look for fresh approaches to material. We appreciate careful work. Send us your best. We welcome unpublished authors. Though we pay in copies and small monetary amounts that depend on the generosity of our patrons and subscribers, we offer prizes for work published in *Whetstone*. For the last 4 years these prizes have totaled $750, and were given to two or three writers. The editors make their decisions at the time of publication. This is not a contest. In addition, we nominate authors for *Pushcart*; *Best American Short Stories*; *Poetry and Essays*; *O. Henry Awards*; *Best of the South*; Illinois Arts Council Awards; and other prizes and anthologies as they come to our attention. Though our press run is moderate, we work for our authors and offer a prestigious vehicle for their work."

**[N] $ WILLOW SPRINGS,** 705 W. First Ave., Eastern Washington University, Spokane WA 99201. (509)623-4349. **Contact:** Christopher Howell, editor. **100% freelance written.** Semiannual literary magazine. "We publish quality contemporary poetry, fiction, nonfiction and works in translation." Estab. 1977. Circ. 1,500. Publishes ms an average of 10 months after acceptance. Byline given. Acquires first publication rights. Editorial lead time 2 months. Reports in 2 months. Sample copy for $5. Writer's guidelines for #10 SASE.
• A magazine of growing reputation. Takes part in the AWP Intro Award program.
**Nonfiction:** Essays. **Accepts 4 mss/year.** Send complete ms. **Pays $20-50** plus 2 contributor copies.
**Fiction:** Literary fiction only. "No genre fiction, please." **Accepts 5-8 mss/year.** Send complete ms.
**Poetry:** Avant-garde, free verse. "No haiku, light verse or religious." **Accepts 50-80 poems/year.** Submit maximum 6 poems. Length: 12 pages maximum.
**Tips:** "We do not read manuscripts in June, July and August."

**N** **$ WRITER'S BLOCK MAGAZINE, Canada's Leading Literary Digest**, Box 32, 9944-33 Ave., Edmonton, Alberta T6N 1E8 Canada. (780)464-6623. Fax: (780)464-5524. **Contact:** Shaun Donnelly, publisher/editor. **100% freelance written.** Semiannual magazine covering genre fiction. "We look for outstanding genre fiction and poetry (i.e., horror, mystery, romance, science fiction and western). Estab. 1994. Circ. 5,000. Pays on publication. Publishes ms an average of 6 months after acceptance. Byline given. Offers 50% kill fee. Buys first North American serial rights. Editorial lead time 6 months. Submit seasonal material 6 months in advance. Accepts simultaneous submissions. Reports in 2 weeks on queries; 3 months on mss. Sample copy for $5. Writer's guidelines for #10 SASE.

　　**O⌐** "New writers have a better chance via the contest rather than regular submission because they aren't competing with writers like Koontz!"

**Nonfiction:** Humor, photo feature, book reviews. **Buys 4-8 mss/year.** Send complete ms. Length: 250-5,000 words. **Pays 2-5¢/word.**

**Reprints:** Accepts previously published submissions.

**Photos:** Send photos with submission. Reviews prints. Negotiates payment individually. Buys one-time rights.

**Columns/Departments:** Book reviews (genre fiction), 250-1,000 words. **Buys 2-4 mss/year.** Send complete ms. **Pays 2-5¢/word.**

**Fiction:** Adventure, fantasy, horror, humorous, mainstream, mystery, romance, science fiction, suspense, western. "No sex or profanity." **Buys 8-12 mss/year.** Send complete ms. Length: 500-5,000 words. **Pays 2-5¢/word.**

**Poetry:** Krista Fisher, associate editor. Avant garde, free verse, haiku, light verse, traditional. **Buys 8-12 poems/year.** Submit maximum 5 poems. **Pays $5-25.**

**N** **$ THE WRITER'S PUBLISHING**, The Writer's Publisher, Box 55, Tofino, British Columbia V0R 2Z0. (800)655-0506. Fax: (250)725-2513. E-mail: writerspubl@bc.sympatico.ca. Editor: Rebecca Tuck. **100% freelance written.** Quarterly literary magazine. Estab. 1996. Circ. 200. Pays on publication. Publishes ms an average of 3-4 months after acceptance. Byline sometimes given. Not copyrighted. Buys one-time rights. Editorial lead time 3 months. Accepts queries by mail, e-mail, fax, phone. Accepts simultaneous submissions. Reports in 1 month. Sample copy for $5. Writer's guidelines for SAE.

**Nonfiction:** Essays, general interest, humor, inspirational, opinion, personal experience, travel. Send complete ms. Length: 5,000 words maximum. **Pays $25.**

**Reprints:** Accepts previously published submissions.

**Fiction:** Adventure, condensed novels, confession, erotica, ethnic, experimental, fantasy, historical, horror, humorous, mainstream, mystery, novel excerpts, religious, romance, science fiction, serialized novels, slice-of-life vignettes, suspense, western. **Buys 200 mss/year.** Send complete ms. Length: 5,000 words maximum. **Pays $25.**

**Poetry:** **Buys 80 poems/year.** Length: 1,000 lines maximum. **Pays $25.**

**$ YELLOW SILK: Journal of Erotic Arts**, verygraphics, Box 6374, Albany CA 94706. (510)644-4188. **Contact:** Lily Pond, editor. **90% freelance written.** Prefers to work with published/established writers. Annual international journal of erotic literature and visual arts. "Editorial policy: Nature. Spirit. Eros. Our publication is literary, not pornographic. The quality of the literature is as important as the erotic content." Pays on publication. Byline given. Buys all publication rights for 1 year following publication, at which time they revert to author, non-active and reprint electronic and anthology rights for duration of copyright.

**Nonfiction:** Book excerpts, essays, humor, reviews. "We often have theme issues, but non-regularly and usually not announced in advance. No pornography. No romance-novel type writing, sex fantasies. No first-person accounts or blow-by-blow descriptions. No articles. No novels." **Buys 30 mss/year.** Send complete ms. All submissions should be typed, double-spaced, with name, address and phone number on each page; always enclose SASE. No specified length requirements.

**Reprints:** Send short story and information about when and where the article previously appeared.

**Fiction:** Erotic literature, including ethnic, experimental, fantasy, humorous, mainstream, novel excerpts, science fiction. See "Nonfiction." **Buys 12-16 mss/year.** Send complete ms.

**Poetry:** Avant-garde, free verse, haiku, light verse, traditional. "No greeting-card poetry." **Buys 12-16 poems/year.** No limit on number of poems submitted, "but don't send book-length manuscripts."

**Tips:** "The best way to get into *Yellow Silk* is produce excellent, well-crafted work that includes eros freshly, with strength of voice, beauty of language, and insight into character. I'll tell you what I'm sick of and have, unfortunately, been seeing more of lately: the products of 'How to Write Erotica' classes. This is not brilliant fiction; it is poorly written fantasy and not what I'm looking for."

**$ $ $ ZOETROPE: ALL STORY**, AZX Publications, 260 Fifth Ave. #1200, New York NY 10001-6408. (212)696-5720. Fax: (212)696-5845. Website: http://www.zoetrope-stories.com. **Contact:** Adrienne Brodeur, editor-in-chief. Quarterly literary magazine specializing in high caliber short fiction. "*Zoetrope: All Story* bridges the worlds of fiction and film by publishing stories alongside essays and reprints of classic stories that were adapted for the screen." Open to outstanding work by beginning and established writers. Estab. 1997. Circ. 40,000. Publishes ms 6 months after acceptance. Byline given. Buys first serial rights and 2 year film option. Accepts simultaneous submissions. Reports in 5 months. Sample copy on website. Guidelines for SASE or on website.

　　● Ranked as one of the best markets for fiction writers in *Writer's Digest* magazine's "Fiction 50," June 1999. *Zoetrope* does not accept submissions from June 1 through August 31.

**Fiction:** Literary, mainstream/contemporary, one act plays. 7,000 words maximum. No short shorts or reprints. Receives

6,000 submissions/year. **Buys 32-40 ms/year.** Query with SASE and complete ms (1 story maximum). **Pays $1,200.**
    ■ The online magazine carries original content not found in the print edition and includes writer's guidelines.

**Tips:** "*Zoetrope* considers unsolicited submissions of short stories no longer than 7,000 words. Excerpts from larger works, screenplays, treatments and poetry will be returned unread. We are unable to respond to submissions without SASE."

**$ ZYZZYVA, The Last Word: West Coast Writers & Artists**, 41 Sutter St., Suite 1400, San Francisco CA 94104-4987. (415)752-4393. Fax: (415)752-4391. E-mail: editor@zyzzyva.org. Website: http://www.zyzzyva.org. **Contact:** Howard Junker, editor. **100% freelance written.** Works with a small number of new/unpublished writers each year. "We feature work by West Coast writers only. We are essentially a literary magazine, but of wide-ranging interests and a strong commitment to nonfiction." Estab. 1985. Circ. 3,500. **Pays on acceptance.** Publishes ms an average of 3 months after acceptance. Byline given. Buys first North American serial rights and one-time anthology rights. Accepts queries by mail, e-mail, fax. Reports in 1 week on queries; 1 month on mss. Sample copy and writer's guidelines for $5 or on website.
**Nonfiction:** Book excerpts, general interest, historical/nostalgic, humor, personal experience. **Buys 15 mss/year.** Query by mail or e-mail. Length: open. **Pays $50.**
**Photos:** Copies or slides only.
**Fiction:** Ethnic, experimental, humorous, mainstream. **Buys 20 mss/year.** Send complete ms. Length: open. **Pays $50.**
    ● Ranked as one of the best markets for fiction writers in *Writer's Digest* magazine's "Fiction 50," June 1999.
**Poetry: Buys 20 poems/year.** Submit maximum 5 poems. Length: 3-200 lines. **Pays $50.**
**Tips:** "West Coast writers means those currently living in California, Alaska, Washington, Oregon or Hawaii."

# MEN'S

Magazines in this section offer features on topics of general interest primarily to men. Magazines that also use material slanted toward men can be found in Business & Finance, Child Care & Parental Guidance, Ethnic/Minority, Gay & Lesbian Interest, General Interest, Health & Fitness, Military, Relationships and Sports sections. Magazines featuring pictorial layouts accompanied by stories and articles of a sexual nature, both gay and straight, appear in the Sex section.

**$ $ $ CIGAR AFICIONADO**, M. Shanken Community, Inc., 387 Park Ave. S., New York NY 10016. (212)684-4224. Fax: (212)684-5424. Website: http://www.cigaraficionado.com. Editor: Marvin Shanken. **Contact**: Gordon Mott, managing editor. **75% freelance written.** Bimonthly magazine covering cigars. Estab. 1992. Circ. 400,000. **Pays on acceptance.** Publishes ms an average of 9 months after acceptance. Byline given. Offers 25% kill fee. Buys all rights. Editorial lead time 3 months. Submit seasonal material 3 months in advance. Reports in 2 months. Sample copy and writer's guidelines for SASE.
    ● Ranked as one of the best markets for freelance writers in *Writer's Yearbook* magazine's annual "Top 100 Markets," January 1999.
**Nonfiction: Buys 80-100 features/year.** Query. Length: 2,000 words. Pay varies. Sometimes pays expenses of writers on assignment.
**Columns/Departments: Buys 20 short pieces year.** Length: 1,000 words. Pay varies.

**$ CIGAR LIFESTYLES MAGAZINE**, Made Ya Look! Inc., 1845 Oak St., #12, Northfield IL 60093. (847)446-1735. Fax: (847)446-1699. E-mail: yalook@aol.com. **Contact**: Editorial Department. Editor: Patrick Grady. Managing Editor: Roger Blackshaw. **90% freelance written.** Quarterly magazine covering cigars and male lifestyles. "*Cigar Lifestyles Magazine* offers a look at the good life and easy living." Estab. 1995. Circ. 300,000. Pays on publication. Byline sometimes given. Offers 25% kill fee. Buys all rights. Editorial lead time 1 month. Submit seasonal material 3 months in advance. Accepts simultaneous submissions. Reports in 1 month on queries; 2 months on mss. Sample copy and writer's guidelines for $3.50.
**Nonfiction:** Book excerpts, essays, exposé, humor, inspirational, interview/profile, new product, photo feature, travel. **Buys 50 mss/year.** Query with published clips. Length: 750-1,500 words. Sometimes pays expenses of writers on assignment. Pay varies.
**Reprints:** Accepts previously published submissions.
**Photos:** Send photos with submission. Reviews 5 × 10 prints. Offers no additional payment for photos accepted with ms. Model releases and identification of subjects required. Buys all rights.
**Fillers:** Anecdotes, facts, gags to be illustrated by cartoonist, newsbreaks, short humor. **Buys 75-100/year.** Length: 500-750 words. Pay varies.
**Tips:** "Call us and fax us information. Stories with photos are your best chance. Good photos help."

**$ $ $ $ GENTLEMEN'S QUARTERLY**, 4 Times Square, New York NY 10036. (212)880-8800. Editor-in-Chief: Arthur Cooper. **Contact:** Martin Beiser, managing editor. Mark Adams, senior editor (health-related articles).

Prefers to work with established/published writers. **60% freelance written.** Circ. 650,000. Monthly magazine emphasizing fashion, general interest and service features for men ages 25-45 with a large discretionary income. **Pays on acceptance.** Byline given. Pays 25% kill fee. Submit seasonal material 6 months in advance. Accepts queries by mail and fax. Reports in 1 month.

O➡ Break in through the columns, especially Contraria, Enthusiasms or First Person.

**Nonfiction:** Politics, personality profiles, lifestyles, trends, grooming, nutrition, health/fitness, sports, travel, money, investment and business matters. **Buys 4-6 mss/issue.** Query with published clips. Length: 1,500-4,000 words. Pay varies.

**Columns/Departments:** Query with published clips. Length: 1,000-2,500 words. Pay varies.

**Fiction:** Ilena Silverman, assistant managing editor.

**Tips:** "Major features are usually assigned to well-established, known writers. Pieces are almost always solicited."

**$ $ $ HEARTLAND USA**, UST Publishing, 1 Sound Shore Dr., Greenwich CT 06830-7251. (203)622-3456. Fax: (203)863-5393. E-mail: husaedit@aol.com. **Contact:** Brad Pearson, editor. **95% freelance written.** Bimonthly magazine for working men. "*HUSA* is a general interest lifestyle magazine for adult males—active outdoorsmen. The editorial mix includes hunting, fishing, sports, automotive, how-to, country music, human interest and wildlife." Estab. 1991. Circ. 901,000. **Pays on acceptance.** Byline given. Offers 20% kill fee. Buys first North American serial and second serial (reprint) rights. Submit seasonal material 1 year in advance. Accepts queries by mail, e-mail, fax. Accepts simultaneous submissions. Reports in 1 month on queries. Sample copy on request. Writer's guidelines for #10 SASE.

**Nonfiction:** Book excerpts, general interest, historical/nostalgic, how-to, humor, inspirational, interview/profile, new product, personal experience, photo feature, technical, travel. "No fiction or dry expository pieces." **Buys 30 mss/year.** Query with or without published clips or send complete ms. Length: 350-1,200 words. **Pays 50-80¢/word** for assigned articles; 25-80¢/word for unsolicited articles. Sometimes pays expenses of writers on assignment.

● Ranked as one of the best markets for freelance writers in *Writer's Yearbook* magazine's annual "Top 100 Markets," January 1999.

**Reprints:** Send photocopy of article and information about when and where the article previously appeared. Pays 25% of amount paid for an original article.

**Photos:** Send photos with submission. Reviews transparencies. Identification of subjects required. Buys one-time rights.

**Tips:** "Features with the possibility of strong photographic support are open to freelancers, as are our departments. We look for a relaxed, jocular, easy-to-read style, and look favorably on the liberal use of anecdote or interesting quotations. Our average reader sees himself as hardworking, traditional, rugged, confident, uncompromising and daring."

**$ $ $ $ THE INTERNATIONAL, The Magazine of Adventure and Pleasure for Men**, Tomorrow Enterprises, 2228 E. 20th St., Oakland CA 94606. (510)532-6501. Fax: (510)536-5886. E-mail: tonyattomr@aol.com. **Contact:** Mr. Anthony L. Williams, managing editor. **70% freelance written.** Monthly magazine covering "bush and seaplane flying, seafaring, pleasure touring, etc. with adventure stories from all men who travel on sexual tours to Asia, Latin America, The Caribbean and the Pacific." Estab. 1997. Circ. 5,000. Pays on publication. Publishes ms 2 months after acceptance. Buys first rights. Editorial lead time 2 months. Submit seasonal material 3 months in advance. Accepts queries by mail, e-mail. Accepts simultaneous submissions. Reports in 2 weeks on queries; 2 months on mss. Writer's guidelines free.

**Nonfiction:** Exposé, general interest, historical/nostalgic, humor, interview/profile, opinion, personal experience, photo feature, travel. Seafaring stories of all types published with photos. Military and veteran stories also sought, as well as ex-pats living abroad. Especially interested in airplane flying stories with photos. No pornography, no family or "honeymoon" type travel. **Buys 40-50 mss/year.** Query or send complete ms. Length: 700 words max. **Pays $100-2,000 for assigned articles, $25-1,000 for unsolicited articles.** Sometimes pays expenses of writers on assignment.

**Photos:** Send photos with submission. Reviews negatives and 5×6 prints. Offers no additional payment for photos accepted with ms. Identification of subjects required. Buys one-time rights or all rights.

**Columns/Departments:** Asia/Pacific Beat; Latin America/Caribbean Beat (Nightlife, Adventure, Air & Sea), 450 words; Lifestyles Abroad (Expatriate Men's Doings Overseas), 600-1,000 words. **Buys 25 mss/year.** Query or send complete ms. **Pays $25-1,000.**

**Fillers:** Anecdotes, facts, gags to be illustrated by cartoonist, newsbreaks, short humor. **Buys 25/year.** Length: 200-600 words. **Pays $25-100.**

**Tips:** "If a single male lives in those parts of the world covered, and is either a pleasure tourist, pilot or seafarer, we are interested in his submissions. He can visit our upcoming website or contact us directly. Stories from female escorts or party girls are also welcomed."

**$ $ $ $ MAXIM, The Best Thing to Happen to Men Since Women**, 1040 Sixth Ave, 23rd Floor, New York City NY 10018. Fax: (212)302-2635. E-mail: editors@maximmag.com. **Contact:** Steve Perrine, co-editor. **50% freelance written.** Monthly magazine. "*Maxim* covers every aspect of real men's real lives, from sports and sex to health and fitness to fashion and beer with irreverence, edge and humor." Estab. 1996. Circ. 1,250,000. **Pays on acceptance.** Publishes ms an average of 1 month after acceptance. Byline sometimes given. Offers 20% kill fee. Buys all rights. Editorial lead time 3 months. Submit seasonal material 6 months in advance. Accepts simultaneous submissions. Reports in 6 weeks on queries; 2 months on mss. Writer's guidelines for #10 SASE.

**Nonfiction:** Book excerpts, humorous essays, expose, general interest, how-to, humor, new product, personal experience, photo features. **Buys hundreds of mss/year.** Query by mail or e-mail. Length: 200-3,000 words. **Pays $1/word**

minimum for assigned articles; 50¢/word minimum for unsolicited articles. Pays expenses of writers on assignment.
**Reprints:** Accepts previously published submissions.
**Photos:** State availability of photos with submission. Negotiates payment individually. Identification of subjects required. Buys all rights.
**Columns/Departments:** Circus Maxims (service with irreverence and weird news items), 200-500 words. Query. **Pays $1/word**.

**$ $ $ P.O.V.** , BYOB Ventures/Freedom Communications, 56 W. 22nd St., 3rd Floor, New York NY 10010. (212)367-7600. Website: http://www.povmag.com. Editor: Randall Lane. **Contact:** Ty Wenger, features editor. **60% freelance written.** Published monthly. "*P.O.V.* is geared toward driven, successful, ambitious young men who are looking for advice on how to get the most out of their careers, investments and leisure time. Our stories reflect that mission." Estab. 1995. Circ. 360,000. Pays on publication. Publishes ms an average of 3 months after acceptance. Byline given. Offers 20% kill fee. Buys first North American serial and electronic rights. Editorial lead time 3-6 months. Submit seasonal material 5 months in advance. Reports in 6 months. Sample copy for $3 plus postage or on website. Writer's guidelines for #10 SASE or on website.
**Nonfiction:** Exposé, general interest, how-to (business), interview, travel, personal finance, stories. "No 'memory' essays or personal experience (unless it relates specifically to our audience)." **Buys 200 mss/year.** Query by mail with published clips. Length: 250-3,500 words. **Pays 50¢/word.** Sometimes pays expenses of writers on assignment.
**Photos:** State availability of photos with submission. Negotiates payment individually. Captions, identification of subjects required. Buys one-time rights.
**Columns/Departments:** Bargains & Scams (consumer advice), 1,100 words; Five Tips (quick tips for life/careers/money), 600 words; Sweat (health, nutrition, fitness), 1,000 words; Profiles (successful up-and-comers in their 20s/early 30s), 600 words. Query by mail with published clips.

    The online magazine carries original content not found in the print edition and includes writer's guidelines. Contact: Larry Smith, editor-at-large.
**Tips:** "Numerous story ideas that show a strong familiarity with the editorial content of the magazine are critical. Solid writing experience for national magazines is preferred. Pitch to specific departments; it's easier to break in with shorter pieces, particularly those with career/business angles. We are also always seeking comprehensively reported stories about issues, people and trends affecting our demographic."

**$ $ $ $ SMOKE MAGAZINE, Life's Burning Desires**, Lockwood Publications, 130 W. 42nd St., New York NY 10036. (212)391-2060. Fax: (212)827-0945. E-mail: cigarbar@aol.com. Website: http://www.smokemag.com. Editor: Alyson Boxman. Managing Editor: Andy Marinkovich. **Contact:** Michael Malone, associate editor. **75% freelance written.** Quarterly magazine covering cigars and men's lifestyle issues. "A large majority of *Smoke's* readers are affluent men, ages 28-40; active, educated and adventurous." Estab. 1995. Circ. 175,000. Pays 2 months after publication. Publishes ms an average of 3 months after acceptance. Byline given. Offers 25% kill fee. Buys first rights. Editorial lead time 2 months. Submit seasonal material 6 months in advance. Accepts queries by mail, e-mail, fax. Accepts simultaneous submissions. Reports in 6 weeks on queries; 3 months on mss. Sample copy for $4.95; writer's guidelines for #10 SASE.
**Nonfiction:** Essays, exposé, general interest, historical/nostalgic, how-to, humor, interview/profile, opinion, personal experience, photo feature, travel. **Buys 25 mss/year.** Query with published clips. Length: 1,500-3,000 words. **Pays $500-2,500.** Sometimes pays expenses of writers on assignment.
**Photos:** State availability of photos with submission. Reviews transparencies (2¼ × 2¼). Negotiates payment individually. Identification of subjects required.
**Columns/Departments:** Romeo (men's humor); y Julieta (men's humor written by women); What Lew Says (cigar industry news); all 1,500 words. **Buys 20 mss/year.** Query with published clips. **Pays $500-2,000.**
**Fiction:** Adventure, condensed novels, confession, experimental, fantasy, historical, humorous, mainstream, mystery, novel excerpts, serialized novels, slice-of-life vignettes, suspense, western. **Buys 4 mss/year.** Query with published clips. Length: 3,000-5,000 words. **Pays $500-1,000.**
**Fillers:** Anecdotes, facts, gags to be illustrated by cartoonist, newsbreaks, short humor. **Buys 12/year.** Length: 200-500 words. **Pays $200-500.**

    The online magazine carries original content not found in the print edition. Contact: Chris O'Hara, online editor.
**Tips:** "Send a short, clear query with clips. Go with your field of expertise: cigars, sports, music, true crime, etc. . . . ."

**N □ $ UNGROOM'D, The Men's Perspective on Marriage**©, Marrying Man Group, Inc., 11901 Santa Monica Blvd., Suite 504, West Los Angeles CA 90025. (310)840-2393. Fax: (818)623-0255. E-mail: mbl@ungroomd.c om. Website: http://www.ungroomd.com. Managing Editor: Ramin Ramhormozi. **Contact:** Michael B. Lehrman, editor-in-chief. **95% freelance written.** Weekly online magazine covering marriage from the man's perspective. "*unGROOM'd* will strive to incorporate a balance between journalistic, personal experience and resource content that focuses on preparing the groom for marriage. Through insightful, informative and entertaining content, presented in a mature and intelligent forum, unGROOM'd sets a new standard in marriage and wedding journalism that will shift the way society views the topic of marriage. The publication does not imitate or take cues from the mainstream, instead challenging the traditional views of men and the marriage process." Estab. 1997. Circ. 75,000. **Pays on acceptance.** Byline given. Buys electronic rights. Editorial lead time 2 months. Accepts queries by e-mail, website. Sample copy and writer's guidelines on website.

**Nonfiction:** Book excerpts, general interest, historical/nostalgic, how-to (pick the best tux, groomsmen's gifts, photographer, location, plan a bachelor party), humor, interview/profile, personal experience, religious, travel. Special issues: Sex (February); Money (April); Fatherhood (June); Weddings (October). **Buys 4 mss/year.** Query. Length: 500-800 words. **Pays 5¢/word.** Sometimes pays writers with premiums under special circumstances.

**Photos:** Send photos with submission. Reviews transparencies. No additional payment for photos accepted with ms.

**Columns/Departments:** Now Featuring (cover stories on marriage), 800-1,200 words; Tying the Knot (walking down the aisle in style—the "big day"), 500-800 words; Mind Over Marriage (the psychology of men, women & marriage), 500-800 words; Incomes Outcome (information on investing, financial planning, home buying and the marriage tax), 500-800 words; His Castle (life at home and the balance between your space and your spouse), 500-800 words. **Buys 24-36 mss/year for each department.** Query. **Pays 5¢/word.**

**Fiction:** Erotica, humorous, mainstream, slice-of-life vignettes. **Buys 24-36 mss/year.** Query. Length: 500-800 words. **Pays 5¢/word.**

**Fillers:** Anecdotes, facts, newsbreaks, short humor. **Buys 20-30/year.** Does not pay for fillers.

**Tips:** "Writers can visit www.ungroomd.com and click into 'Be a Writer" for more information on submitting material to unGROOM'd."

# MILITARY

These publications emphasize military or paramilitary subjects or other aspects of military life. Technical and semitechnical publications for military commanders, personnel and planners, as well as those for military families and civilians interested in Armed Forces activities are listed here. Publications covering military history can be found in the History section.

**$ $ AMERICAN SURVIVAL GUIDE**, Y-Visionary Publishing, 265 S. Anita Dr., Suite 120, Orange CA 92868-3310. Fax: (714)939-9909. E-mail: jim4asg@aol.com. **Contact:** Jim Benson, editor. Scott Stoddard, managing editor. **50% freelance written.** Monthly magazine covering "self-reliance, defense, meeting day-to-day and possible future threats—survivalism for survivalists." Circ. 60,000. Pays on publication. Publishes ms up to 1 year after acceptance. Byline given. Submit seasonal material 5 months in advance. Sample copy for $6. Writer's guidelines for SASE.
- *American Survival Guide* is always looking for more good material with quality artwork (photos). They want articles on recent events and new techniques, etc. giving the latest available information to their readers.

**Nonfiction:** Exposé (political); how-to; interview/profile; personal experience (how I survived); photo feature (equipment and techniques related to survival in all possible situations); emergency medical; health and fitness; communications; transportation; food preservation; water purification; self-defense; terrorism; nuclear dangers; nutrition; tools; shelter; etc. "No general articles about how to survive. We want specifics and single subjects." **Buys 60-100 mss/year.** Query or send complete ms. Length: 1,500-2,000 words. **Pays $160-400.** Sometimes pays some expenses of writers on assignment.

**Photos:** Send photos with ms. "One of the most frequent mistakes made by writers in completing an article assignment for us is sending photo submissions that are inadequate." Captions, model releases and identification of subjects mandatory. Buys exclusive one-time rights.

**Tips:** "We need hard copy with computer disk and photos or other artwork. Prepare material of value to individuals who wish to sustain human life no matter what the circumstance. This magazine is a text and reference."

**$ $ ARMY MAGAZINE**, Box 1560, Arlington VA 22210. (703)841-4300. Fax: (703)841-3505. E-mail: armymag@ausa.org. Website: http://www.ausa.org/armyzine/. **Contact:** Mary Blake French, editor. **70% freelance written.** Prefers to work with published/established writers. Monthly magazine emphasizing military interests. Estab. 1904. Circ. 90,000. Pays on publication. Publishes ms an average of 5 months after acceptance. Byline given except for back-up research. Buys all rights. Submit seasonal material 3 months in advance. Accepts queries by mail, fax. Sample copy and writer's guidelines for 9×12 SAE with $1 postage or on website.
- *Army Magazine* looks for shorter articles.

**Nonfiction:** Historical (military and original); humor (military feature-length articles and anecdotes); interview; new product; nostalgia; personal experience dealing especially with the most recent conflicts in which the US Army has been involved (Desert Storm, Panama, Grenada); photo feature; profile; technical. No rehashed history. "We would like to see more pieces about little-known episodes involving interesting military personalities. We especially want material lending itself to heavy, contributor-supplied photographic treatment. The first thing a contributor should recognize is that our readership is very savvy militarily. 'Gee-whiz' personal reminiscences get short shrift, unless they hold their own in a company in which long military service, heroism and unusual experiences are commonplace. At the same time, Army readers like a well-written story with a fresh slant, whether it is about an experience in a foxhole or the fortunes of a corps in battle." **Buys 8 mss/issue.** Submit complete ms (hard copy and disk). Length: 1,500 words, but shorter items, especially in 1,000 to 1,500 range, often have better chance of getting published. **Pays 12-18¢/word.** No unsolicited book reviews.

**Photos:** Submit photo material with accompanying ms. Pays $25-50 for 8×10 b&w glossy prints; $50-350 for 8×10 color glossy prints or 2¼×2¼ transparencies; will also accept 35mm. Captions preferred. Buys all rights. Pays $35-50 for cartoon with strong military slant.

**Columns/Departments:** Military news, books, comment (*New Yorker*-type "Talk of the Town" items). **Buys 8/issue.** Submit complete ms. Length: 1,000 words. **Pays $40-150.**

**N** **$ $ ARMY/NAVY/AIR FORCE/MARINE CORPS TIMES**, Army Times Publishing Co., 6883 Commercial Dr., Springfield VA 22159. (703)750-9000. Fax: (703)750-8622. Websites: http://www.armytimes.com; http://www.navy times.com; http://www.airforcetimes.com; http://www.marinecorpstimes.com. **Contact:** Chris Lawson, managing editor, *Army Times*; Alex Neill, managing editor, *Navy Times*; Julie Bird, managing editor, *Air Force Times*; Phillip Thompson, managing editor, *Marine Corps Times*. Weeklies edited separately for Army, Navy, Marine Corps, and Air Force military personnel and their families. They contain career information such as pay raises, promotions, news of legislation affecting the military, housing, base activities and features of interest to military people. Estab. 1940. Circ. 230,000. **Pays on acceptance.** Byline given. Offers kill fee. Buys first rights. Accepts queries by mail, e-mail, phone. Accepts simultaneous submissions. Reports in 1 month on queries. Sample copy and writer's guidelines for SASE.

**Nonfiction:** Features of interest to career military personnel and their families. No advice pieces. Query. **Buys 150-175 mss/year.** Length: 750-2,000 words. **Pays $100-500.**

**Columns/Departments: Buys 75 mss/year.** Length: 500-900 words. **Pays $75-125.**

The online magazine carries original content not found in the print editions. Contact: Neff Hudson, online editor.

**Tips:** Looking for "stories on active duty, reserve and retired military personnel; stories on military matters and localized military issues; stories on successful civilian careers after military service."

**★ $ $ NAVAL HISTORY**, US Naval Institute, 291 Wood Rd., Annapolis MD 21402-5035. (410)295-1079. Fax: (410)269-7940. E-mail: fschultz@usni.org. Website: http://www.usni.org. **Contact:** Fred L. Schultz, editor-in-chief. Kimberly Couranz and Colin Babb, associate editors. **90% freelance written.** Bimonthly magazine covering naval and maritime history, worldwide. "We are committed, as a publication of the 126-year-old US Naval Institute, to presenting the best and most accurate short works in international naval and maritime history. We do find a place for academicians, but they should be advised that a good story generally wins against a dull topic, no matter how well researched." Estab. 1988. Circ. 40,000. **Pays on acceptance.** Publishes ms an average of 2 years after acceptance. Byline given. Buys first North American serial rights; occasionally allows rights to revert to authors. Editorial lead time 6 months. Submit seasonal material 6 months in advance. Accepts queries by mail, e-mail, fax, phone. Reports in 1 month on queries; 2 months on mss. Sample copy for $3.50 and SASE or on website. Writer's guidelines for #10 SASE or on website.

**Nonfiction:** Book excerpts, essays, historical/nostalgic, humor, inspirational, interview/profile, personal experience, photo feature, technical. **Buys 50 mss/year.** Query. Length: 1,000-3,000 words. **Pays $300-500 for assigned articles; $75-400 for unsolicited articles.**

**Photos:** State availability of photos with submission. Reviews contact sheets, transparencies, 4×6 or larger prints and digital submissions or CD-ROM. Offers $10 minimum. Captions, model releases, identification of subjects required. Buys one-time rights.

**Fillers:** Anecdotes, news breaks (naval-related), short humor. **Buys 40-50/year.** Length: 50-1,000 words. **Pays $10-50.**

**Tips:** "A good way to break in is to write a good, concise, exciting story supported by primary sources and substantial illustrations. Naval history-related news items (ship decommissionings, underwater archaeology, etc.) are also welcome. Because our story bank is substantial, competition is severe. Tying a topic to an anniversary many times is an advantage. We still are in need of Korean and Vietnam War-era material."

**N ★ $ $ NORTH & SOUTH, The Magazine of Civil War Conflict**, North & South Magazine Inc., 33756 Black Mountain Rd., Tollhouse CA 93667. (559)855-8637. Fax: (559)855-8639. E-mail: kpoulter@aol.com. Website: http://www.northandsouthmagazine.com. **Contact:** Keith Poulter, publisher/editor. **100% freelance written.** Magazine published seven times a year covering the era of the American Civil War. "*North & South* specializes in fresh and accurate history. Most contributors are academics engaged in ongoing research. End notes (citations) are required. Audience is Civil War buffs." Estab. 1997. Circ. 16,000. Pays on publication. Publishes ms up to 15 months after acceptance. Byline given. Buys first North American serial rights. Editorial lead time 3 months. Submit seasonal material 6 months in advance. Accepts queries by mail, e-mail, fax, phone. Reports in 2 weeks on queries; 2 months on mss. Sample copy for $4.95. Writer's guidelines for SAE with 1 first-class stamp.

**Nonfiction:** Historical. "No emotional diatribes, material already published, or poorly researched work. **Buys 35 mss/ year.** Query. Length: 1,000-10,000 words. **Pays 10-15¢/word.**

**Photos:** State availability of photos with submission. Reviews negatives, 5×4 transparencies and prints. Negotiates payment individually. Identification of subjects required. Buys one-time rights.

**Columns/Departments:** Briefings (200 word reviews of new and upcoming books) and Knapsack (snippets of Civil War interest). **Buys 40 mss/year.** Query. **Pays 10¢/word.**

**Fillers:** Anecdotes, facts. **Buys 5/year.** Length: 50-200 words. **Pays 10¢/word.**

**Tips:** "Do not submit your manuscript unless based on original research using primary sources. *North & South* is looking for fresh material, or new slants on standard material. All contributions should be well-researched history, not unauthenticated anecdotes. Articles will vary from the biography of a single individual, to accounts and analyses of battles and campaigns, to pieces on broad subjects such as tactics, strategy, logistics, etc. Though the content should be more substantial than the often shallow pieces printed in other magazines, the style should not be too dry or academic.

*North & South* is intended to be a popular magazine as well as a reliable source for historical information! *Do not submit unsolicited manuscripts."*

**$ $ OFF DUTY MAGAZINE**, 3505 Cadillac Ave., Suite O-105, Costa Mesa CA 92626-1500. (714)549-7172. Fax: (714)549-4222. E-mail: odutyedit@aol.com. Website: http://www.offduty.com. **Contact:** Tom Graves, managing editor. **30% freelance written.** Magazine published 8 times/year covering the leisure-time activities and interests of the military community. "Our audience is solely military members and their families; many of our articles could appear in other consumer magazines, but we always slant them toward the military; i.e. where to get a military discount when traveling." Estab. 1970. Circ. 514,000. **Pays on acceptance.** Publishes ms an average of 3 months after acceptance. Byline given. Buys one-time rights. Submit seasonal material at least 4 months in advance. Accepts queries by mail, e-mail, fax, phone. Accepts simultaneous submissions. Reports in 2 months on queries. Sample copy for 9 × 12 SAE with 6 first class stamps or sample articles on website. Writer's guidelines for SASE.
**Nonfiction:** Travel, finance, lifestyle (with a military angle), interview/profile (music and entertainment). "Must be familiar with *Off Duty* and its needs." **Buys 30-40 mss/year.** Query. Length: 800-1,800 words. **Pays $150-500.**
● Editor is not interested in seeing war reminiscences. Insightful "how to" articles on military lifestyles and benefits desired.
**Reprints:** Send tearsheet or photocopy of article and information about when and where the article previously appeared. Pays 50% of amount paid for an original article.
**Photos:** State availability of photos with submission. Reviews contact sheets, websites or sample prints/slides. Offers $50-300/photo; more for cover. Captions and identification of subjects required. Buys one-time rights. Unsolicited photos not returned without SASE.
**Columns/Departments:** Dialogue—A Forum for Women (active-duty, spouse or dependent, subjects related to both off-duty and on-duty life). Length: 1,200 words. Address them to "Dialogue." **Pays $150.**
**Tips:** "Get to know the military community and its interests beyond the stereotypes. Query with the idea of getting on our next year's editorial calendar. We choose our primary topics at least six months in advance. Send queries with lists of story ideas, not just one."

**PARAMETERS: U.S. Army War College Quarterly**, US Army War College, Carlisle Barracks PA 17013-5050. (717)245-4943. E-mail: awca-parameters@carlisle-emh2.army.mil. Website: http://carlisle-www.army.mil/usawc/Param eters/. **Contact:** Editor, *Parameters.* **100% freelance written.** Prefers to work with published/established writers or experts in the field. Readership consists of senior leadership of US defense establishment, both uniformed and civilian, plus members of the media, government, industry and academia interested in national and international security affairs, military strategy, military leadership and management, art and science of warfare, and military history (provided it has contemporary relevance). Estab. 1971. Circ. 13,500. Pays on publication. Publishes ms an average of 6 months after acceptance. Byline given. Not copyrighted; unless copyrighted by author, articles may be reprinted with appropriate credits. Buys first serial rights. Accepts queries by mail, e-mail, fax, phone. Accepts queries by mail, e-mail, fax, phone. Reports in 6 weeks. Sample copy and writer's guidelines for SASE or on website.
**Nonfiction:** Articles are preferred that deal with current security issues, employ critical analysis and provide solutions or recommendations. Liveliness and verve, consistent with scholarly integrity, appreciated. Theses, studies and academic course papers should be adapted to article form prior to submission. Documentation in complete endnotes. Submit complete ms. Length: 4,500 words average, preferably less. **Pays $150** average (including visuals).
**Tips:** "Make it short; keep it interesting; get criticism and revise accordingly. Write on a contemporary topic. Tackle a subject only if you are an authority. No fax submissions."

**$ $ PROCEEDINGS**, U.S. Naval Institute, 291 Wood Rd., Annapolis MD 21402-5035. (410)268-6110. Fax: (410)295-1049. Website: http://www.usni.org. Editor: Fred H. Rainbow. **Contact:** John G. Miller, managing editor. **80% freelance written**. Monthly magazine covering Navy, Marine Corps, Coast Guard. Estab. 1873. Circ. 100,000. **Pays on acceptance.** Publishes ms an average of 3-9 months after acceptance. Byline given. Buys all rights. Editorial lead time 3 months. Reports in 2 months on submissions. Sample copy for $3.95. Writer's guidelines free.
**Nonfiction:** Essays, historical/nostalgic, interview/profile, photo feature, technical. **Buys 100-125 mss/year**. Query or send complete ms. Length: 3,000 words. **Pays $60-150/printed page** for unsolicited articles.
**Photos:** State availability of or send photos with submission. Reviews transparencies and prints. Offers $25/photo maximum. Buys one-time rights.
**Columns/Departments:** Comment & Discussion (letters to editor), 7,500 words; Commentary (opinion), 1,000 words; Nobody Asked Me, But . . . (opinion), less than 1,000 words. **Buys 150-200 mss/year**. Query or send complete ms. **Pays $32-150.**
**Fillers:** Anecdotes. **Buys 20/year**. Length: 100 words. **Pays $25.**

**$ $ $ THE RETIRED OFFICER MAGAZINE**, 201 N. Washington St., Alexandria VA 22314-2539. (800)245-8762. Fax: (703)838-8179. E-mail: editor@troa.org. Website: http://www.troa.org. Editor: Col. Warren S. Lacy, USA-Ret. Managing Editor: Joanne Hodges. **Contact:** Heather Lyons, senior editor. **60% freelance written.** Prefers to work with published/established writers. Monthly magazine for officers of the 7 uniformed services and their families. "*The Retired Officer Magazine* covers topics such as current military/political affairs; recent military history, especially Vietnam and Korea; travel; finance; hobbies; health and fitness; and military family and retirement lifestyles." Estab. 1945. Circ. 395,000. **Pays on acceptance.** Publishes ms an average of 1 year after acceptance. Byline given. Buys first

North American serial rights. Accepts queries by mail, e-mail, fax. Reports on material accepted for publication within 3 months. Sample copy and writer's guidelines for 9×12 SASE with 6 first-class stamps or on website.

**Nonfiction:** Current military/political affairs, health and wellness, recent military history, travel, military family lifestyle. Emphasis now on current military and defense issues. "We rarely accept unsolicited manuscripts. We look for detailed query letters with résumé, sample clips and SASE attached. We do not publish poetry or fillers." **Buys 48 mss/ year.** Length: 800-2,500 words. **Pays up to $1,350.**

**Photos:** Query with list of stock photo subjects. Pays $20 for each 8×10 b&w photo (normal halftone) used. Original slides or transparencies must be suitable for color separation. Pays $75-200 for inside color; $300 for cover.

■ The online magazine carries original content not found in the print edition and includes writer's guidelines. Contact: Ronda Reid, online editor.

# MUSIC

Music fans follow the latest industry news in these publications that range from opera to hip hop. Types of music and musicians or specific instruments are the sole focus of some magazines. Publications geared to the music industry and professionals can be found in the Trade Music section. Additional music and dance markets are found in the Contemporary Culture and Entertainment sections.

**$ AMERICAN SONGWRITER**, 1009 17th Ave. S., Nashville TN 37212-2201. (615)321-6096. Fax: (615)321-6097. E-mail: asongmag@aol.com. Website: http://www.songnet.com/asongmag/. **Contact:** Vernell Hackett, editor. **30% freelance written.** Bimonthly magazine about songwriters and the craft of songwriting for many types of music, including pop, country, rock, metal, jazz, gospel, and r&b. Estab. 1984. Circ. 5,000. Pays on publication. Publishes ms an average of 2 months after acceptance. Offers 25% kill fee. Buys first North American serial rights. Reports in 2 months. Sample copy for $4. Writer's guidelines for SASE.

**Nonfiction:** General interest, interview/profile, new product, technical, home demo studios, movie and TV scores, performance rights organizations. No fiction. **Buys 20 mss/year.** Query with published clips. Length: 300-1,200 words. **Pays $25-60.**

**Reprints:** Send tearsheet or photocopy of article and information about when and where the article previously appeared. Pays same amount as paid for an original article.

**Photos:** Send photos with submission. Reviews 3×5 prints. Offers no additional payment for photos accepted with ms. Identification of subjects required. Buys one-time rights.

**Tips:** "*American Songwriter* strives to present articles which can be read a year or two after they were written and still be pertinent to the songwriter reading them."

**$ $ $ $ AUDIO, The Equipment Authority**, Hachette Filipacchi Magazines, Inc., 1633 Broadway, New York NY 10019. Fax: (212)767-5633. E-mail: alofft@hfmmag.com or coreygreenberg@csi.com. Managing Editor: Kay Blummenthal. **Contact:** Alan Lofft, senior editor; Corey Greenberg, editor. **90% freelance written.** Monthly magazine covering high-performance audio and audio/video equipment. Estab. 1947. Circ. 110,000. Pays on publication. Publishes ms an average of 2 months after acceptance. Byline given. Buys first North American serial rights and electronic rights. Editorial lead time 3 months. Accepts simultaneous submissions. Sample copy for $6.95.

**Nonfiction:** Essays, how-to, interview/profile, new product, technical. **Buys 20 mss/year.** Query. Length: 1,500-5,000 words. **Pays $100-2,500.** Sometimes pays the expenses of writers on assignment.

**Photos:** State availability of photos with submission. Negotiates payment individually. Buys one-time and electronic rights.

**Columns/Departments:** Ivan Berger, technical editor. Playback (short equipment reviews), 250 words; Spectrum (news), 600 words; Music reviews, 250 words. **Buys 130 mss/year.** Query. **Pays $100-500.**

**★ $ $ BLUEGRASS UNLIMITED**, Bluegrass Unlimited, Inc., P.O. Box 111, Broad Run VA 20137-0111. (540)349-8181 or (800)BLU-GRAS. Fax: (540)341-0011. E-mail: editor@blugrassmusic.com. Editor: Peter V. Kuykendall. **Contact:** Sharon Watts, managing editor. **80% freelance written.** Prefers to work with published/established writers. Monthly magazine on bluegrass and old-time country music. Estab. 1966. Circ. 27,000. Pays on publication. Publishes ms an average of 4 months after acceptance. Byline given. Kill fee negotiated. Buys first North American serial, one-time, all rights and second serial (reprint) rights. Submit seasonal material 4 months in advance. Reports in 2 weeks on queries; 2 months on mss. Sample copy free. Writer's guidelines for #10 SASE.

**Nonfiction:** General interest, historical/nostalgic, how-to, interview/profile, personal experience, photo feature, travel. No "fan"-style articles. **Buys 75-80 mss/year.** Query with or without published clips. Length: open. **Pays 8-10¢/word.**

**Reprints:** Send photocopy or typed ms with rights for sale noted and information about when and where the article previously appeared. Payment is negotiable.

**Photos:** State availability of or send photos with query. Reviews 35mm transparencies and 3×5, 5×7 and 8×10 b&w and color prints. Pays $50-150 for transparencies; $25-50 for b&w prints; $50-250 for color prints. Identification of subjects required. Buys one-time and all rights.

**Fiction:** Ethnic, humorous. **Buys 3-5 mss/year.** Query. Length: negotiable. **Pays 8-10¢/word.**
**Tips:** "We would prefer that articles be informational, based on personal experience or an interview with lots of quotes from subject, profile, humor, etc."

**$ $ CHAMBER MUSIC**, Chamber Music America, 305 Seventh Ave., New York NY 10001-6008. (212)242-2022. Website: http://www.chamber-music.org. **Contact:** Johanna B. Keller, editor or Karissa Krenz, assistant editor. Bimonthly magazine covering chamber music. Estab. 1977. Circ. 13,000. Pays on publication. Publishes ms an average of 5 months after acceptance. Byline given. Offers kill fee. Buys first publication rights. Editorial lead time 8 months.
**Nonfiction:** Issue-oriented stories of relevance to the chamber music field written by top music journalists and critics, or music practitioners. **Buys 50 mss/year.** Query with clips by mail only. Length: 2,500-3,500 words. **Pays $500 minimum.** Sometimes pays expenses of writers on assignment.
**Photos:** State availability of photos with submission. Offers no additional payment for photos accepted with ms.

**N ⚏ $ $ $ $ GUITAR MAGAZINE**, Cherry Lane Music, 6 E. 32nd St., New York NY 10016. Fax: (212)251-0840. E-mail: editors@guitarmag.com. Website: http://www.guitarmag.com. **Contact:** Jon Chappell, editor-in-chief or Jon Wiederhorn, managing editor. **75% freelance written.** Monthly magazine covering guitars, music, technology. Estab. 1983. Circ. 175,000. Pays on publication. Publishes ms an average of 1 month after acceptance. Byline given. Offers 50% kill fee. Buys one-time rights. Editorial lead time 3 months. Accepts queries by mail, e-mail, fax. Accepts simultaneous submissions. Sample copy on website.
**Nonfiction:** Book excerpts, essays, exposé, general interest, historical/nostalgic, how-to, humor, interview/profile, new product, opinion, personal experience, photo feature, technical. **Buys 48 mss/year.** Send complete ms. Length: 700-4,000 words. **Pays $75-2,000.** Sometimes pays expenses of writers on assignment.
**Reprints:** Accepts previously published submissions.
**Photos:** State availability of photos with submission. Offers $25-500/photo. Captions and identification of subjects required. Buys one-time rights.
**Columns/Departments:** Groundwire (newsy items on guitars and music), 250 words; Encore (humor on guitar and music experience), 800 words. **Buys 12 mss/year.** Send complete ms. **Pays $75-2,000.**
▪ The online magazine carries original content not found in the print edition. Contact: Jon Chappell, online editor.
**Tips:** "E-mail pitches with sample heads and subheads, a brief synopsis and mock lead."

**N $ $ $ GUITAR ONE, The Magazine You Can Play**, Cherry Lane Magazines, 6 E. 32nd St., 11th Floor, New York NY 10016. Fax: (212)251-0840. E-mail: guitarone@cherrylane.com. Website: http://www.guitar-one.com. Managing Editor: Jeff Bauer. **Contact:** Jeff Schroedl (jschroedl@halleonard.com), editor-in-chief. **50% freelance written.** Magazine published 9 times/year covering music and guitar. Estab. 1995. Circ. 100,000. **Pays on acceptance.** Byline given. Offers 100% kill fee. Makes work-for-hire assignments. Editorial lead time up to 6 months. Submit seasonal material 5 months in advance. Accepts queries by e-mail. Accepts simultaneous submissions. Reports in 2 months on mss. Sample copy by e-mail.
**Nonfiction:** Interview/profile (with guitarists). **Buys 15 mss/year.** Query with published clips. Length: 2,000-5,000 words. **Pays $300-1,200 for assigned articles; $150-800 for unsolicited articles.** Sometimes pays expenses of writers on assignment.
**Photos:** State availability of photos with submission. Reviews negatives, transparencies and prints. Negotiates payment individually. Buys one-time rights.
**Tips:** "Find an interesting feature with a nice angle that pertains to guitar enthusiasts. Submit a well-written draft or samples of work."

**$ $ GUITAR PLAYER MAGAZINE**, Miller Freeman, Inc., 411 Borel Ave., Suite 100, San Mateo CA 94402. (650)358-9500. Fax: (650)358-9216. E-mail: guitplyr@mfi.com. Website: http://www.guitarplayer.com. Editor-in-chief: Michael Molenda. **Contact:** Kyle Swenson, features editor. **15% freelance written.** Monthly magazine for persons "interested in guitars, guitarists, manufacturers, guitar builders, equipment, careers, etc." Circ. 135,000. Buys first serial and all reprint rights. **Pays on acceptance.** Publishes ms an average of 3 months after acceptance. Byline given. Accepts queries by mail, e-mail, fax. Reports in 6 weeks. Writer's guidelines for #10 SASE.
**Nonfiction:** Publishes "wide variety of articles pertaining to guitars and guitarists: interviews, guitar craftsmen profiles, how-to features—anything amateur and professional guitarists would find fascinating and/or helpful. In interviews with 'name' performers, be as technical as possible regarding strings, guitars, techniques, etc. We're not a pop culture magazine, but a magazine for musicians. The essential question: What can the reader take away from a story to become a better player?" **Buys 30-40 mss/year.** Query. Length: open. **Pays $250-450.** Sometimes pays expenses of writers on assignment.
**Photos:** Reviews b&w glossy prints. Buys 35mm color transparencies. Payment varies. Buys one time rights.
▪ The online magazine carries original content not found in the print edition. Contact: Lonnii Gause, online editor.

**$ $ MODERN DRUMMER**, 12 Old Bridge Rd., Cedar Grove NJ 07009. (201)239-4140. Fax: (201)239-7139. Features Editor: William F. Miller. Managing Editor: Rick Van Horn. **Contact:** Ronald Spagnardi, editor-in-chief. Monthly magazine for "student, semi-pro and professional drummers at all ages and levels of playing ability, with varied specialized interests within the field." **60% freelance written.** Circ. 102,000. Pays on publication. Publishes ms an average of 3 months after acceptance. Buys all rights. Reports in 2 weeks. Sample copy for $4.95. Guidelines for #10 SASE.

**Nonfiction:** How-to, informational, interview, new product, personal experience, technical. "All submissions must appeal to the specialized interests of drummers." **Buys 40-50 mss/year.** Query or submit complete ms. Length: 5,000-8,000 words. **Pays $200-500.**

**Reprints:** Accepts previously published submissions.

**Photos:** Purchased with accompanying ms. Reviews 8×10 b&w prints and color transparencies.

**Columns/Departments:** Music columns: Jazz Drummers Workshop, Rock Perspectives, Rock 'N' Jazz Clinic, Driver's Seat (Big Band), In The Studio, Show Drummers Seminar, Teachers Forum, Drum Soloist, The Jobbing Drummer, Strictly Technique, Shop Talk, Latin Symposium. Profile columns: Portraits, Up & Coming, From the Past. Book Reviews, Record Reviews, Video Reviews. "Technical knowledge of area required for most columns." **Buys 40-50 mss/year.** Query or submit complete ms. Length: 500-1,000 words. **Pays $50-150.**

**Tips:** "*MD* is looking for music journalists rather than music critics. Our aim is to provide information, not to make value judgments. Therefore, keep all articles as objective as possible. We are interested in how and why a drummer plays a certain way; the readers can make their own decisions about whether or not they like it."

**N ⭐ $ ON THE DOWNLOW, Underground Hip-Hop Zine,** Myriad Publication, 1201 Jordan St., Longview TX 75602. Phone/fax: (903)238-9381 or (888)522-6826. E-mail: pureanoint@aol.com. **Contact:** LaTosha Stanfield-Addison, editor-in-chief/creator. **90% freelance written.** Monthly magazine covering underground hip-hop music news. "The writers must live and breathe hip-hop music. It is for the purist, the outspoken, and the romantic lovers of the art of hip-hop and rap." Estab. 1993. Pays on publication. Publishes ms an average of 3 months after acceptance. Byline given. Buys all rights. Editorial lead time 2 months. Submit seasonal material 2 months in advance. Accepts queries by mail, e-mail, fax, phone. Accepts simultaneous submissions. Sample copy and writer's guidelines for SAE or on website.

**Nonfiction:** Book excerpts, exposé, historical/nostalgic, humor, inspirational, interview/profile, opinion, photo feature, religious. **Buys 200 mss/year.** Send complete ms. Length: 800-2,000 words. **Pays $75-100 for assigned articles; $25-50 for unsolicited articles.** Also pays in concert tickets, backstage passes, new unreleased music from new and professional artists. Sometimes pays expenses of writers on assignment.

**Photos:** Send photos with submission. Reviews 8×10 maximum prints. Offers no additional payment for photos accepted with ms. Captions, model releases, identification of subjects required. Buys all rights.

**Columns/Departments:** Record Album Review (open minded objectivity), 50 words; Honies (beautiful women with a hip-hop edge), 25 words; For the Love of (a passionate review of a pioneering hip-hop artist), 800 words. **Buys 175 mss/year.** Send complete ms. **Pays $30-75.**

**Fiction:** Erotica, ethnic, experimental, humorous, slice-of-life vignettes, futuristic, psychedelic, inner city superheroes. "It has to be an overwhelming 'live and die hip-hop' attitude in every sentence." **Buys 15 mss/year.** Send complete ms. Length: 800-2,000 words. **Pays $60-80.**

**Poetry:** Avant-garde, free verse, traditional, deep psychedelic thoughts on paper. "Go light on the traditional." **Buys 175 poems/year.** Submit maximum 2 poems. Length: 20-80 lines. **Pays $35-50.**

**Fillers:** Facts, newsbreaks. **Buys 350/year.** Length: 25-150 words. **Pays $10-25.**

**Tips:** "You must express a genuine love for hip-hop in everything you write. No one-hit wonder stories or flash in the pan artists. We need writers who cover artists who have an agenda of long standing career goals of becoming part of this institution we call hip-hop. If you submitted queries or mss between 1993-1999, *please resubmit!*"

**$ $ $ OPERA NEWS,** Metropolitan Opera Guild, Inc., 70 Lincoln Center Plaza, New York NY 10023-6593. (212)769-7080. Fax: (212)769-7007. Website: http://www.operanews.com. Editor/Publisher: Rudolph S. Rauch. Executive Editor: Brian Kellow. **Contact:** Kitty March. **75% freelance written.** Monthly magazine for people interested in opera; the opera professional as well as the opera audience. Estab. 1936. Circ. 120,000. Pays on publication. Publishes ms an average of 4 months after acceptance. Byline given. Buys first serial rights only. Sample copy for $4.

**⊶** Break in by "showing incisive knowledge of opera and the opera scene. We look for knowledgeable and informed writers who are capable of discussing opera in detailed musical terms—but in an engaging way."

**Nonfiction:** Most articles are commissioned in advance. Monthly issues feature articles on various aspects of opera worldwide; biweekly issues contain articles related to the broadcasts from the Metropolitan Opera. Emphasis is on high quality writing and an intellectual interest to the opera-oriented public. Informational, personal experience, interview, profile, historical, think pieces, personal opinion, opera reviews. "Also willing to consider quality fiction and poetry on opera-related themes though acceptance is rare." Query by mail. Length: 1,500-2,800 words. **Pays $450-1,200.** Sometimes pays expenses of writers on assignment.

**Photos:** State availability of photos with submission. Buys one-time rights.

**Columns/Departments:** Buys 24 mss/year.

**$ $ PROFILE,** (formerly *Release Ink Magazine*), Vox Publishing, 2525-C Lebanon Pike, Box 6, Nashville TN 37214. (615)872-8080, ext. 3320. Fax: (615)872-9786. E-mail: cameron@voxcorp.com. Website: http://www.profilemag azine.com. Editor: Chris Well. **Contact:** Suzie Waltner, editorial coordinator. **70% freelance written.** Bimonthly magazine covering Christian books, music, art and more. "*Profile* is the only magazine of its kind, covering the spectrum of Christian products from books and music to children's resources and gifts. It reaches the core Christian retail customer—

females between the ages of 21 and 50." Estab. 1998. Circ. 95,000. Pays within 30 days after publication. Publishes ms an average of 2 months after acceptance. Byline sometimes given. Buys first North American serial rights and electronic rights. Editorial lead time 6 months. Submit seasonal material 4 months in advance. Accepts queries by mail, e-mail, fax. Sample copy for $5.

**Nonfiction:** Artist interview/profile. No essays, inspirational pieces. **Buys 20-30 mss/year.** Query with published clips. Length: 500-2,500 words. **Pays 6-10¢/word.** Sometimes pays expenses of writers on assignment.

**Photos:** State availability of photos with submission. Offers no additional payment for photos accepted with ms. Identification of subjects required. Buys one-time rights.

■ The online magazine carries content not found in the print edition. Contact: Cameron Strang, online editor.

**Columns/Departments:** Noteworthy (brief profiles of Christian music artists), 400-600 words; Between the Lines (brief profiles of people writing/making books), 400-600 words; Showcase (reviews of Christian books and music), 250 words. **Buys 30 mss/year.** Query with published clips. **Pays 6-10¢/word.**

**Tips:** "We're looking for people who can exhibit working knowledge of the authors, books and artists we cover. We also want to be convinced that they've read our magazine."

**$ $ RAP SHEET**, James Communications, Inc., 2270 Centinela Ave., Box B-40, Los Angeles CA 90064. (310)670-7200. Fax: (310)670-6236. E-mail: editor@rapsheet.com. Website: http://www.rapsheet.com. Editor: Darryl James. **Contact:** Darnell Jenkins, features editor. Monthly newspaper covering hip hop artists, music and culture. Estab. 1992. Circ. 100,000. Pays on publication. Byline given. Editorial lead time 2 months. Accepts queries by mail, e-mail, fax, phone.

**Nonfiction:** Exposé, general interest, historical/nostalgic, interview/profile, photo feature, technical. Query with published clips. Length: 500-3,500. **Pays $50-300.** Sometimes pays expenses of writers on assignment.

**Photos:** Send photos with submission. Negotiates payment individually.

**Columns/Departments:** Check the Wax, Trax (album and single reviews), albums (200-300 words) singles (100 words); Back in the Day (profile on old school hip hop artist) 500-800 words; On the set (hip hop related film news) 1,000 words. **Buys 50 mss/year.** Query with published clips. **Pays $50-300.**

■ The online magazine carries original content not found in the print edition. Contact: Humphrey Riley, online editor.

**Tips:** "Submit writing samples consistent with our style and format. Explain specifically how you would like to contribute and offer ideas. Articles must be well organized, containing a powerful lead, thesis statement, body and conclusion. Writing the traditional, biography-styled profile is discouraged. The biography only works with extremely interesting life stories, which are rare. Instead, we prefer the writer to familiarize his/herself with the artist's background through research, finding the most intriguing things about the artist. Then, the story should be shaped around that information. Again, the articles must be tightly focused, avoiding rambling, and drifting off to unrelated subjects."

**$ RELEASE MAGAZINE, Christian Music Covered in Style**, Vox Publishing, 2525-C Lebanon Pike, Box 6, Nashville TN 37214. (615)872-8080. Fax: (615)872-9786. E-mail: editorial@voxcorp.com. Website: http://www.release magazine.com. Editor: Chris Well. **Contact:** Suzie Waltner, editorial coordinator. **50% freelance written.** Bimonthly magazine covering Christian pop music/artists. "*Release* is the most widely-circulated magazine in the Christian music industry, reaching its fans through retail stores and individual subscriptions. Its core audience is the 12- to 30-year-old pop or mainstream music fan." Estab. 1991. Circ. 110,000. Pays within 30 days after publication. Publishes ms an average of 2 months after acceptance. Byline given. Buys first North American serial rights and electronic rights. Editorial lead time 6 months. Submit seasonal material 4 months in advance. Sample copy for $5.

**Nonfiction:** Artist interview/profile, new product reviews. "We have an annual 'year in review' issue that features the newsmakers of the year and the winners of the Readers' Choice poll." No essays, non-Christian music-related articles. **Buys 45 mss/year.** Query with published clips. Length: 500-2,500 words. **Pays 6-10¢/word.**

**Columns/Departments:** Word on the Street (Christian artist news), 500-700 words; Views On the New (new music/product reviews), 200-300 words; Faces (brief artist profiles), 600-800 words. **Buys 10-15 mss/year.** Query with published clips. **Pays 6-10¢/word.**

■ The online magazine carries original content not found in the print edition. Contact: Chris Well, online editor.

**Tips:** "We're looking for people who can exhibit working knowledge of the music and artists we cover, and can convince us that they've read our magazine."

**$ RELIX MAGAZINE, Music for the Mind**, P.O. Box 94, Brooklyn NY 11229. (718)258-0009. E-mail: relixedit@aol.com. Website: http://www.relix.com. **Contact:** Toni A. Brown, editor. **60% freelance written.** Eager to work with new/unpublished writers. Bimonthly magazine covering classic rock 'n' roll music and specializing in Grateful Dead and other San Francisco and 60s-related groups, but also offering new music alternatives, such as "Roots Rock" and "Jam Bands." Estab. 1974. Circ. 70,000. Pays on publication. Publishes ms an average of 6 months after acceptance. Byline given. Buys all rights. Reports in 1 year. Sample copy for $5.

**Nonfiction:** Historical/nostalgic, interview/profile, new product, personal experience, photo feature, technical. Feature topics include blues, bluegrass, rock, jazz and world music; also deals with environmental and cultural issues. Special issue: year-end special. Query by mail with published clips if available or send complete ms. Length: 1,200-3,000 words. **Pays $1.75/column inch.**

**Reprints:** Send photocopy of article and information about when and where the article previously appeared.

**Photos:** "Whenever possible, submit promotional photos with articles."
**Fiction:** Publishes novel excerpts.
**Columns/Departments:** Query with published clips, if available, or send complete ms. Pays variable rates.
**Tips:** "The most rewarding aspects of working with freelance writers are fresh writing and new outlooks."

★ $ **7BALL MAGAZINE, Modern Rock on Cue**, Vox Publishing, 2525-C Lebanon Pike, Box 6, Nashville TN 37214. (615)872-8080. Fax: (615)872-9786. E-mail: 7ball@7ball.com. Website: http://www.7ball.com. Editor: Chris Well. **Contact:** Cameron Strang, managing editor. **70% freelance written.** Bimonthly magazine covering Christian modern rock/alternative music. "*7ball*—the fastest growing magazine in Christian music—captivates the teenage and young adult music lover whose tastes include modern rock, alternative, hip-hop and other styles of music with an edge." Estab. 1995. Circ. 52,000. Pays within 30 days after publication. Publishes ms an average of 2 months after acceptance. Byline given. Buys first North American serial rights and electronic rights. Editorial lead time 6 months. Submit seasonal material 4 months in advance. Accepts queries by mail, e-mail. Sample copy for $5 or on website.
**Nonfiction:** Artist interview/profile, media that is of interest to rock fans (extreme sports, video, etc.). **Buys 20 mss/year.** Query with published clips. Length: 500-2,500 words. **Pays 6-10¢/word.** Sometimes pays expenses of writers on assignment.
**Photos:** State availability of photos with submission. Offers no additional payment for photos accepted with ms. Identification of subjects required. Buys one-time rights.
**Columns/Departments:** Bankshots (brief artist profiles), 400-800 words; Reviews (new music/product reviews), 200-300 words. **Buys 80 mss/year.** Query with published clips. **Pays 6-10¢/word.**
▣ The online magazine carries original content not found in the print edition. Contact: Cameron Strang, online editor.
**Tips:** "We're looking for people who can exhibit working knowledge of the music and artists we cover and can convince us that they've read our magazine."

Ⓝ $ $ **SYMPHONY**, American Symphony Orchestra League, 1156 15th St. NW, Suite 800, Washington DC 20005. (202)776-0212. Fax: (202)776-0224. E-mail: editor@symphony.org. **Contact:** Melinda Whiting, editor. **50% freelance written.** Bimonthly magazine for the orchestra industry and classical music enthusiasts covering classical music, orchestra industry, musicians. "Writers should be knowledgeable about classical music and have critical or journalistic/repertorial approach." Circ. 20,000. **Pays on acceptance.** Publishes ms an average of 2 months after acceptance. Byline given. Buys first and one-time rights. Editorial lead time 6 months. Submit seasonal material 8 months in advance. Accepts simultaneous submissions "but we must be first to publish." Sample copy and guidelines for SAE.
**Nonfiction:** Book excerpts, essays/commentary, profile, opinion, personal experience (rare), photo feature (rare), issue features, trend pieces (by assignment only; pitches welcome). Does not want to see reviews, interviews. **Buys 30 mss/year.** Query with published clips. Length: 900-3,500 words. **Pays $150-600 for assigned articles; $0-400 for unsolicited articles.** Sometimes pays expenses of writers on assignment.
**Photos:** State availability of photos or send photos with submission. Reviews contact sheets, negatives, transparencies and prints. Offers no additional payment for photos accepted with ms. Captions and identification of subjects required. Buys one-time rights.
**Columns/Departments:** Repertoire (orchestral music—essays), 1,000 words; Recordings (noteworthy recordings by American orchestras—essays, not reviews), 1,000 words. **Buys 4 mss/year.** Query with published clips.
**Tips:** "We need writing samples before assigning pieces. We prefer to craft the angle with the writer, rather than adapt an existing piece. Pitches and queries should demonstrate a clear relevance to the American orchestra industry and should be timely."

Ⓝ $ **TRADITION**, Nat. Trad. C.M.A., P.O. Box 492, Anita IA 50020. Phone/fax: (712)762-4363. Editor: Bob Everhart. **20% freelance written.** Bimonthly magazine covering pioneer and old-time music. "Our 2,500 members are devoted fans of old-time, traditional mountain, country, bluegrass and folk music. Everything we print must be directed toward that audience." Estab. 1976. Circ. 2,500. Pays on publication. Publishes ms an average of 3 months after acceptance. Byline sometimes given. Buys one-time rights. Editorial lead time 3 months. Submit seasonal material 3 months in advance. Accepts simultaneous submissions. Reports in 3 months. Sample copy for $4 and SASE. Writer's guidelines for $4.
**Nonfiction:** Book excerpts, essays, general interest, historical/nostalgic, personal experience, travel. **Buys 6-8 mss/year.** Query by mail. **Pays $5-25.** "Sometimes pays in contributor copies."
**Reprints:** Accepts previously published submissions.
**Photos:** State availability of photos with submission. Offers no additional payment for photos accepted with ms. Identification of subjects required. Buys one-time rights.
**Poetry:** Traditional.
**Fillers:** Anecdotes, facts, short humor.

Ⓝ $ $ **ULTIMATE AUDIO**, En Garde Enterprises, Inc., 1 New York Plaza, Suite 214, New York NY 10004. Fax: (718)796-2825. E-mail: edultimate@aol.com. Website: http://www.ultimateaudio.com. Editor: Tom O'Neil. Managing Editor: Kelli Shriver. **Contact:** Myles Astor, publisher. **100% freelance written.** Quarterly magazine. "Our magazine covers the finest in high-end audio equipment and music. Our writers use highly resolving audio systems to review and evaluate electronics, digital playback equipment, speakers and accessories. We cover all genres of music—on LP and

CD—with an emphasis on the sound and performance." Estab. 1997. Circ. 10,000. Pays on publication (when subsequent issue is published). Publishes ms an average of 1-4 months after acceptance. Byline given. Buys first, second serial (reprint) or electronic rights. Editorial lead time 4 months. Submit seasonal material 4 months in advance. Accepts queries by mail, e-mail, fax, phone. Reports in 2 weeks on queries; 1 month on mss. Sample copy for $3.

**Nonfiction:** General interest, how-to, interview/profile, new product, opinion, technical. **Buys 4 mss/year.** Query. Length: 300-2,500 words. **Pays $100-500.** Sometimes pays expenses of writers on assignment.

**Columns/Departments:** Conversations With (interviews with women in audio), 2,500 words; Ultimate Vinyl Archivist (collectible records), 3,000 words. **Buys 1 ms/year.** Query. **Pays $150-500.**

# MYSTERY

These magazines buy fictional accounts of crime, detective work, mystery and suspense. Skim through other sections to identify markets for fiction; some will consider mysteries. Markets for true crime accounts are listed under Detective & Crime.

**$ HARDBOILED**, Gryphon Publications, P.O. Box 209, Brooklyn NY 11228. **Contact:** Gary Lovisi, editor. **100% freelance written.** Quarterly magazine covering crime/mystery fiction and nonfiction. "Hard-hitting crime fiction and columns/articles and reviews on hardboiled crime writing and private-eye stories—the newest and most cutting-edge work and classic reprints." Estab. 1988. Circ. 1,000. Pays on publication. Publishes ms an average of 6-18 months after acceptance. Byline given. Offers 100% kill fee. Buys one-time rights. Editorial lead time 6 months. Submit seasonal material 6 months in advance. Reports in 2 weeks on queries; 1 month on mss. Sample copy for $7. Writer's guidelines for #10 SASE.

**Nonfiction:** Book excerpts, essays, exposé. Query first. **Buys 4-6 mss/year.** Length: 500-3,000 words. **Pays 1 copy. Reprints:** Query first.

**Photos:** State availability of photos with submission.

**Columns/Departments:** Various review columns/articles on hardboiled writers. Query first. **Buys 2-4 mss/year.**

**Fiction:** Mystery, hardboiled crime and private-eye stories *all* on the cutting-edge. **Buys 40 mss/year.** Send complete ms. Length: 500-3,000 words. **Pays $5-50,** depending on length and quality.

**◩ $ ALFRED HITCHCOCK'S MYSTERY MAGAZINE**, Dell Magazines, 475 Park Ave. S, New York NY 10016. Editor: Cathleen Jordan. **100% freelance written.** Monthly magazine featuring new mystery short stories. Circ. 215,000 paid; 615,000 readers. **Pays on acceptance.** Byline given. Buys first and foreign rights. Submit seasonal material 7 months in advance. Reports in 2 months. Sample issue for $4. Writer's guidelines for SASE.

**Fiction:** Original and well-written mystery and crime fiction. "Because this is a mystery magazine, the stories we buy must fall into that genre in some sense or another. We are interested in nearly every kind of mystery, however: stories of detection of the classic kind, police procedurals, private eye tales, suspense, courtroom dramas, stories of espionage, and so on. We ask only that the story be about crime (or the threat or fear of one). We sometimes accept ghost stories or supernatural tales, but those also should involve a crime." Length: up to 14,000 words. Send complete ms with SASE. **Pays 8¢/word.**

**Tips:** "No simultaneous submissions, please. Submissions sent to *Alfred Hitchcock's Mystery Magazine* are not considered for or read by *Ellery Queen's Mystery Magazine*, and vice versa."

**$ MURDEROUS INTENT, Mystery Magazine**, Madison Publishing Co., P.O. Box 5947, Vancouver WA 98668-5947. (360)695-9004. Fax: (360)693-3354. E-mail: madison@teleport.com. Website: http://www.teleport.com/~madison. **Contact:** Margo Power, editor. **90% freelance written.** Quarterly magazine covering mystery. "Everything in *Murderous Intent* is mystery/suspense related. We bring you quality nonfiction articles, columns, interviews and 10-12 (or more) pieces of short mystery fiction per issue. You'll find stories and interviews by Carolyn Hart, Ed Gorman, Barbara Paul, Jerimiah Healy and many more excellent authors." Estab. 1994. Circ. 5,000. **Pays on acceptance.** Publishes ms an average of 12-18 months after acceptance. Byline given. Offers 100% kill fee or $10. Buys first North American serial rights. Submit seasonal material 6 months in advance. Accepts queries by e-mail only with brief synopsis and word count. "No hard copy submissions." Reports in 1 week. Sample copy for $5.95, 9×12 SAE and 4 first-class stamps or on website. Writer's guidelines for #10 SASE or on website.

**O→** Break in with very short, 500-700 nonfiction mystery related fillers and 4-8 line mystery verse.

**Nonfiction:** Humor (mystery); interview/profile (mystery authors), 500-700 words. **Buys 4-8 per issues.** Mystery-related nonfiction, 2,000-4,000 words. **Pays $10.** Sometimes pays expenses of writers on assignment. **Buys 8-12 mss/ year.** Query by e-mail with published clips.

**Photos:** State availability of photos and artwork with submission. Offers no additional payment for photos accepted with ms or negotiates payment individually. Captions, model releases, identification of subjects required. Buys one-time rights.

**Fiction:** Humorous (mystery), mystery. "Please don't send anything that is not mystery/suspense-related in some way." **Buys 48-52 mss/year.** Query by e-mail. Preferred length: 2,000-4,000 words. **Pays $10.**

● Ranked as one of the best markets for fiction writers in *Writer's Digest* magazine's "Fiction 50," June 1999.

**Poetry:** Free verse, haiku, light verse, limerick, traditional. Nothing that is not mystery/suspense-related. **Buys 12-36**

**poems/year.** Length: 4-16 lines. **Pays $2-5.**
**Fillers:** Anecdotes, facts, cartoons, jokes. All fillers must be mystery related. Length: 25-200 words. **Pays $2-5.**

▣ The online magazine carries original content not found in the print edition and includes writer's guidelines. Contact: Margo Power, online editor.

**Tips:** "Send us mysteries like the ones you love to read—as long as they fit within our guidelines. We love humorous mysteries, mysteries and suspense with exotic settings (kitchens, bathrooms, islands, etc.) good puzzles, all around good stories with characters we can't forget. We also seek permission to include select stories and articles on the website. There is no additional payment at this time."

**$ THE MYSTERY REVIEW, A Quarterly Publication for Mystery Readers,** C. von Hessert & Associates, P.O. Box 233, Colborne, Ontario K0K 1S0 Canada. US: P.O. Box 488, Wellesley Island NY 13640-0488. (613)475-4440. Fax: (613)475-3400. E-mail: 71554.551@compuserve.com. Website: http://www.inline-online.com/mystery/. **Contact:** Barbara Davey, editor. **80% freelance written.** Quarterly magazine covering mystery and suspense. "Our readers are interested in mystery and suspense books, films. All topics related to mystery—including real life unsolved mysteries." Estab. 1992. Circ. 5,000 (80% of distribution is in US). Pays on publication. Publishes ms an average of 6 months after acceptance. Byline given. Buys first North American serial rights. Editorial lead time 6 months. Submit seasonal material 6 months in advance. Reports in 6 weeks on queries; 1 month on mss. Does not assume responsibility for unsolicited manuscripts. Sample copy for $5. Writer's guidelines for #10 SASE.
**Nonfiction:** Interview/profile. Query by mail. Length: 2,000-5,000 words. **Pays $30 maximum.**
**Photos:** Send photos with submission. Reviews 5×7 b&w prints. Offers no additional payment for photos accepted with ms. Model releases, identification of subjects required. Buys all rights.
**Columns/Departments:** Book reviews (mystery/suspense titles only), 500 words; Truly Mysterious ("unsolved," less-generally-known, historical or contemporary cases; photos/illustrations required), 2,000-5,000 words; Book Shop Beat (bookstore profiles; questionnaire covering required information available from editor), 500 words. **Buys 50 mss/ year.** Query with published clips. **Pays $10-30.**
**Fillers:** Puzzles, trivia, shorts (items related to mystery/suspense). **Buys 4/year.** Length: 100-500 words. **Pays $10-20.**

**★ $ $ NEW MYSTERY, The World's Best Mystery,** Crime and Suspense Stories, 175 Fifth Ave., 2001 The Flatiron Bldg., New York NY 10010. E-mail: newmyste@erols.com. Website: http://www.NewMystery.com. Editor: Charles Raisch III. **Contact:** Editorial Committee. **100% freelance written.** Quarterly magazine featuring mystery short stories and book reviews. Estab. 1989. Circ. 120,000. **Pays on acceptance.** Publishes ms an average of 6 months after acceptance. Byline given. Does not return mss. Buys first North American serial or all rights. Editorial lead time 6 months. Submit seasonal material 1 year in advance. Reports in 2 months on mss. Not responsible for unsolicited mss. Sample copy for $7 and 9×12 SAE with 4 first-class stamps.
  ● *Find Miriam,* a short story by Stuart M. Kaminsky appearing on *NewMystery.com,* has been nominated for the Edgar Allen Poe Award for '98 Best Mystery Short Story.
**Nonfiction:** New product, short book reviews. **Buys 40 mss/year.** Send complete ms. Length: 250-2,000 words. **Pays $20-50.**
**Fiction:** Mystery, crime, noire, police procedural, child-in-jeopardy, suspense. **Buys 50 mss/year.** Send complete ms. Length: 2,000-6,000 words. **Pays $50-500.**
**Fillers:** Acrostic or crossword puzzles. **Pays $25-50.**

**★ $ ELLERY QUEEN'S MYSTERY MAGAZINE,** Dell Magazine Fiction Group, 475 Park Ave. S., 11th Floor, New York NY 10016. (212)686-7188. Fax: (212)686-7414. **Contact:** Janet Hutchings, editor. **100% freelance written.** Magazine published 11 times/year featuring mystery fiction. Estab. 1941. Circ. 500,000 readers. **Pays on acceptance.** Publishes ms an average of 6 months after acceptance. Byline given. Buys first serial or second serial (reprint) rights. Accepts simultaneous submissions. Reports in 3 months. Writer's guidelines for #10 SASE.
**Fiction:** Special consideration given to "anything timely and original. We publish every type of mystery: the suspense story, the psychological study, the private-eye story, the deductive puzzle—the gamut of crime and detection from the realistic (including stories of police procedure) to the more imaginative (including 'locked rooms' and impossible crimes). We always need detective stories. No sex, sadism or sensationalism-for-the-sake-of-sensationalism, no gore or horror. Seldom publishes parodies or pastiches. **Buys up to 13 mss/issue.** Length: 10,000 words maximum; occasionally higher but not often. Also buys 2-3 short novels/year of up to 20,000 words, by established authors and minute mysteries of 250 words. Short shorts of 1,500 words welcome. **Pays 3-8¢/word,** occasionally higher for established authors. Send complete ms with SASE.
**Poetry:** Short mystery verses, limericks. Length: 1 page, double-spaced maximum.
**Tips:** "We have a Department of First Stories to encourage writers whose fiction has never before been in print. We publish an average of 11 first stories every year."

# NATURE, CONSERVATION & ECOLOGY

These publications promote reader awareness of the natural environment, wildlife, nature preserves and ecosystems. Many of these "green magazines" also concentrate on recycling and related issues, and a few focus on environmentally-conscious sustainable living. They do not publish recreation or travel articles except as they relate to conservation or nature. Other markets for this kind of material can be found in the Regional; Sports (Hiking & Backpacking in particular); and Travel, Camping & Trailer categories, although magazines listed there require that nature or conservation articles be slanted to their specialized subject matter and audience. Some publications listed in Juvenile and Teen, such as *Wild Outdoor World* or *Owl*, focus on nature-related material for young audiences, while others occasionally purchase such material.

**$ $ $ AMERICAN FORESTS**, American Forests, P.O. Box 2000, Washington DC 20013. (202)955-4500. Fax: (202)887-1075. E-mail: mrobbins@amfor.org. Website: http://www.amfor.org. **Contact:** Michelle Robbins, editor. **75% freelance written** (mostly assigned). Quarterly magazine "of trees and forests, published by a nonprofit citizens' organization for the advancement of intelligent management and use of our forests, soil, water, wildlife and all other natural resources necessary for an environment of high quality." Estab. 1895. Circ. 21,000. **Pays on acceptance.** Publishes ms an average of 8 months after acceptance. Byline given. Buys one-time rights. Submit seasonal material 5 months in advance. Reports in 2 months. Sample copy for $2. Writer's guidelines for SASE.
● This magazine is looking for more urban and suburban-oriented pieces.
**Nonfiction:** General interest, historical, how-to, humor, inspirational. All articles should emphasize trees, forests, forestry and related issues. **Buys 2-3 mss/issue.** Query by mail or send résumé and clips to be considered for assignment. Length: 1,200-2,000 words. **Pays $250-800.**
**Reprints:** Send tearsheet of article or typed ms with rights for sale noted and information about when and where the article previously appeared. Pays 50% of amount paid for an original article.
**Photos:** Send photos. Offers no additional payment for photos accompanying ms. Uses 8×10 b&w glossy prints; 35mm or larger transparencies, originals only. Captions required. Buys one-time rights.
**Tips:** "Query should have honesty and information on photo support. We *do not* accept fiction or poetry at this time."

**★ $ $ $ THE AMICUS JOURNAL**, 40 W. 20th St., New York NY 10011. (212)727-2700. Fax: (212)727-1773. E-mail: amicus@nrdc.org. Website: http:///www.nrdc.org/eamicus/index.html. **Contact:** Kathrin Day Lassila, editor. **80% freelance written.** Quarterly magazine covering national and international environmental issues. "*The Amicus Journal* is intended to provide the general public with a journal of thought and opinion on environmental affairs, particularly those relating to policies of national and international significance." Estab. 1979. Circ. 250,000. Pays on publication. Publishes ms an average of 6 months after acceptance. Offers 25% kill fee. Buys first North American serial rights (and print/electronic reprint rights). Submit seasonal material 6 months in advance. Reports in 3 months on queries. Sample copy for $4 with 9×12 SAE or on website. Writer's guidelines for SASE.
● Submissions must be of the highest writing quality only and must be grounded in thorough knowledge of subject.
**Nonfiction:** Exposé, interview/profile, essays, reviews. Query by mail with published clips. **Buys 35 mss/year.** Length: 200-3,500 words. Pay negotiable. Sometimes pays expenses of writers on assignment.
**Photos:** State availability of photos with submission. Reviews contact sheets, color transparencies, 8×10 b&w prints. Negotiates payment individually. Captions, model releases, identification of subjects required. Buys one-time rights.
**Columns/Departments:** News & Comment (summary reporting of environmental issues, tied to topical items), 700-2,000 words; International Notebook (new or unusual international environmental stories), 700-2,000 words; People, 2,000 words; Reviews (in-depth reporting on issues and personalities, well-informed essays on books of general interest to environmentalists interested in policy and history), 500-1,000 words. Query with published clips. Pay negotiable.
**Poetry:** Brian Swann. Avant-garde, free verse, haiku, others. All poetry should be rooted in nature. Must submit with SASE. **Buys 16 poems/year.** Length: 1 ms page. **Pays $50** plus a year's subscription.
**Tips:** "Please stay up to date on environmental issues, and review *The Amicus Journal* before submitting queries. Except for editorials all departments are open to freelance writers. Queries should precede manuscripts, and manuscripts should conform to the Chicago Manual of Style. *Amicus* needs interesting environmental stories—of local, regional or national import—from writers who can offer an on-the-ground perspective. Accuracy, high-quality writing, and thorough knowledge of the environmental subject are vital."

**$ $ $ $ AUDUBON, The Magazine of the National Audubon Society**, National Audubon Society, 700 Broadway, New York NY 10003-9501. Fax: (212)477-9069. Website: http://magazine.audubon.org. Lisa Gosselin, editor in chief. **Contact:** Editorial Office. **85% freelance written.** Bimonthly magazine "reflecting nature with joy and reverence and reporting the issues that affect and endanger the delicate balance and life on this planet." Estab. 1887. Circ. 460,000. **Pays on acceptance.** Byline given. Buys first North American serial rights, second serial (reprint) rights on occasion. Reports in 3 months. Sample copy for $5 for magazine and postage or on website. Writer's guidelines for #10 SASE.
● Ranked as one of the best markets for freelance writers in *Writer's Yearbook* magazine's annual "Top 100 Markets," January 1999.
**Nonfiction:** Essays, investigative, historical, humor, interview/profile, opinion, photo feature, book excerpts (well in advance of publication). Query by mail before submission. "No fax or e-mail queries, please." Length: 150-3,000 words. **Pays $1,100-4,000.** Pays expenses of writers on assignment.
**Photos:** Query with photographic idea before submitting slides. Reviews 35mm transparencies. Offers page rates per

photo on publication. Captions and identification of subjects required. Write for photo guidelines.

**Tips:** "*Audubon* articles deal with the natural and human environment. They cover the remote as well as the familiar. What they all have in common, however, is that they have a story to tell, one that will not only interest *Audubon* readers, but that will interest everyone with a concern for the affairs of humans and nature. We want good solid journalism. We want stories of people and places, good news and bad: humans and nature in conflict, humans and nature working together, humans attempting to comprehend, restore and renew the natural world. We are looking for new voices and fresh ideas. Among the types of stories we seek: profiles of individuals whose life and work illuminate some issues relating to natural history, the environment, conservation, etc.; balanced reporting on environmental issues and events here in North America and abroad; analyses of events, policies, and issues from fresh points of view. We do not publish fiction or poetry. We're not seeking first person meditations on 'nature,' accounts of wild animals rescue or taming, or birdwatching articles."

**$ THE BEAR DELUXE MAGAZINE**, (formerly *The Bear Essential Magazine*) Orlo, P.O. Box 10342, Portland OR 97296. (503)242-1047. Fax: (503)243-2645. E-mail: bear@orlo.org. Website: http://www.orlo.org. Managing Editor: Matt Buckingham. **Contact:** Thomas L. Webb, editor. **80% freelance written.** Quarterly magazine. "*The Bear Deluxe Magazine* provides a fresh voice amid often strident and polarized environmental discourse. Street level, solution-oriented and non-dogmatic, *The Bear Deluxe* presents lively creative discussion to a diverse readership." Estab. 1993. Circ. 17,000. Pays on publication. Publishes ms 2 months after acceptance. Byline given. Offers 25% kill fee. Buys first rights. Editorial lead time 3 months. Submit seasonal material 4 months in advance. Query by mail, e-mail, fax. Accepts simultaneous and previously published submissions. Reports in 1 month on queries; 2 months on mss. Sample copy for $3. Writer's guidelines for #10 SASE or on website.

**Nonfiction:** Book excerpts, essays, exposé, general interest, humor, interview/profile, new product, opinion, personal experience, photo feature, travel, artist profiles. Publishes 1 theme/year. Send #10 SASE for theme. **Buys 40 mss/year.** Query with published clips. Length: 250-4,500 words. **Pays 5¢/word.** Sometimes pays expenses of writers on assignment.

**Photos:** State availability of photos with submission. Reviews contact sheets, transparencies and 8×10 prints. Offers $15-30/photo. Model releases and identification of subjects required. Buys one-time rights.

**Columns/Departments:** Reviews (almost anything), 300 words; Hands-On (individuals or groups working on eco-issues, getting their hands dirty), 1,200 words; Talking Heads (creative first person), 500 words; News Bites (quirk of eco-news), 300 words; Portrait of an Artist (artist profiles), 1,200 words. **Buys 16 mss/year.** Query with published clips. **Pays 5¢/word, subscription and copies.**

**Fiction:** Adventure, condensed novels, historical, horror, humorous, mystery, novel excerpts, science fiction, western. "Stories must have some environmental context." **Buys 8 mss/year.** Send complete ms. Length: 750-4,500 words. **Pays 5¢/word.**

**Poetry:** Avant-garde, free verse, Haiku, light verse, traditional. **Buys 16-20 poems/year.** Submit 5 poems maximum. Length: 50 lines maximum. **Pays $10, subscription and copies.**

**Fillers:** Facts, newsbreaks, short humor and "found writing." **Buys 10/year.** Length: 100-750 words. **Pays 5¢/word, subscription and copies.**

**Tips:** "Offer to be stringer for future ideas. Get a copy of the magazine and guidelines, and query us with specific nonfiction ideas and clips. We're looking for original, magazine-style stories, not fluff or PR. Fiction, essay and poetry writers should know we have an open and blind review policy and should keep sending their best work even if rejected once. Be as specific as possible in queries."

**$ $ BIRD WATCHER'S DIGEST**, Pardson Corp., P.O. Box 110, Marietta OH 45750. (740)373-5285. E-mail: editor@birdwatchersdigest.com. Website: http://www.birdwatchersdigest.com. **Contact:** William H. Thompson III, editor. **60% freelance written.** Works with a small number of new/unpublished writers each year. Bimonthly magazine covering natural history—birds and bird watching. "*BWD* is a nontechnical magazine interpreting ornithological material for amateur observers, including the knowledgeable birder, the serious novice and the backyard bird watcher; we strive to provide good reading and good ornithology." Estab. 1978. Circ. 90,000. Pays on publication. Publishes ms 1-2 years-after acceptance. Byline given. Buys one-time, first serial and second serial (reprint) rights. Submit seasonal material 6 months in advance. Reports in 2 months. Sample copy for $3.99. Writer's guidelines for #10 SASE or on website.

**Nonfiction:** Book excerpts, how-to (relating to birds, feeding and attracting, etc.), humor, personal experience, travel (limited—we get many). "We are especially interested in fresh, lively accounts of closely observed bird behavior and displays and of bird-watching experiences and expeditions. We often need material on less common species or on unusual or previously unreported behavior of common species." No articles on pet or caged birds; none on raising a baby bird. **Buys 75-90 mss/year.** Send complete ms. All submissions must be accompanied by SASE. Length: 600-3,500 words. **Pays from $50.**

**Reprints:** Accepts previously published submissions.

**Photos:** Send photos with ms. Pays $10 min for b&w prints; $50 min for transparencies. Buys one-time rights.

The online magazine carries content not found in the print edition and includes writer's guidelines.

**Tips:** "We are aimed at an audience ranging from the backyard bird watcher to the very knowledgeable birder; we include in each issue material that will appeal at various levels. We always strive for a good geographical spread, with material from every section of the country. We leave very technical matters to others, but we want facts and accuracy, depth and quality, directed at the veteran bird watcher and at the enthusiastic novice. We stress the joys and pleasures of bird watching, its environmental contribution, and its value for the individual and society."

**$ $ $ CALIFORNIA WILD, Natural Science for Thinking Animals**, California Academy of Sciences, Golden Gate Park, San Francisco CA 94118. (415)750-7116. Fax: (415)221-4853. Website: http://www.calacademy.org/calwild. **Contact**: Keith Howell, editor. **75% freelance written.** Quarterly magazine covering natural sciences and the environment. "Our readers' interests range widely from ecology to geology, from endangered species to anthropology, from field identification of plants and birds to armchair understanding of complex scientific issues." Estab. 1948. Circ. 32,000. Pays prior to publication. Publishes ms an average of 3 months after acceptance. Byline given. Offers 50% kill fee (maximum $200). Buys first North American serial or one-time rights. Editorial lead time 3 months. Submit seasonal material 6 months in advance. Query by mail, fax. Reports in 6 weeks on queries; 6 months on mss. Sample copy for 9×12 SASE or on website. Writer's guidelines for #10 SASE or on website.

**Nonfiction:** Personal experience, photo feature, biological and earth sciences. No travel pieces. Mostly California stories, but also from Pacific Ocean countries. **Buys 20 mss/year.** Query with published clips. Length: 1,000-3,000 words. **Pays $250-1,000 for assigned articles; $200-800 for unsolicited articles.** Sometimes pays expenses of writers on assignment.

**Photos:** State availability of photos with submission. Reviews transparencies. Offers $75-150/photo. Model releases and identification of subjects required. Buys one-time rights.

**Columns/Departments:** Trail Less Traveled (unusual places); Wild Lives (description of unusual plant or animal); Science Track (innovative student, teacher, young scientist), all 1,000-1,500 words; Skywatcher (research in astronomy), 2,000-3,000 words. **Buys 12 mss/year.** Query with published clips. **Pays $200-400.**

**Fillers:** Facts. **Pays $25-50.**

**Tips:** "We are looking for unusual and/or timely stories about California environment or biodiversity."

**⊠ $ $ E THE ENVIRONMENTAL MAGAZINE**, Earth Action Network, P.O. Box 5098, Westport CT 06881-5098. (203)854-5559. Fax: (203)866-0602. E-mail: info@emagazine.com. Website: http://www.emagazine.com. **Contact:** Jim Motavalli, editor. **60% freelance written.** Bimonthly magazine. "*E Magazine* was formed for the purpose of acting as a clearinghouse of information, news and commentary on environmental issues." Estab. 1990. Circ. 50,000. Pays on publication. Byline given. Buys first North American serial rights. Editorial lead time 3 months. Submit seasonal material 6 months in advance. Query by mail, e-mail, fax. Accepts simultaneous submissions. Sample copy for $5 or on website. Writer's guidelines for #10 SASE or on website.

**Nonfiction:** Exposé (environmental), how-to (the "Green Living" section), interview/profile, new products and book reviews. No fiction or poetry. **Buys 100 mss/year.** Query with published clips. Length: 100-4,200 words. **Pays 20¢/word.** On spec or free contributions welcome.

**Photos:** State availability of photos. Reviews printed samples, e.g., magazine tearsheets, postcards, etc. to be kept on file. Negotiates payment individually. Identification of subjects required. Buys one-time rights.

**Columns/Departments:** In Brief/Currents (environmental news stories/trends), 400-1,000 words; Interviews (environmental leaders), 2,200 words; Green Living; Your Health; Going Green (travel); Eco-home; Green Business; Consumer News; New & Different Products (each 700-1,200 words). Query with published clips. **Pays 20¢/word.** On spec or free contributions welcome.

**Tips:** "Contact us to obtain writer's guidelines and back issues of our magazine. Tailor your query according to the department/section you feel it would be best suited for. Articles must be lively, well-researched, fair-sided and relevant to a mainstream, national readership."

**$ $ ENVIRONMENT**, Heldref Publications, 1319 18th St. NW, Washington DC 20036-1802. (202)296-6267. Fax: (202)296-5149. E-mail: env@heldref.org. Website: http://www.heldref.org. **Contact:** Barbara T. Richman, managing editor. **2% freelance written.** Magazine published 10 times/year for high school and college students and teachers, scientists, business and government executives, citizens interested in environment or effects of technology and science in public affairs. Estab. 1958. Circ. 8,000. Buys all rights. Byline given. Pays on publication to professional writers. Accepts queries by mail, fax. Publishes ms an average of 4 months after acceptance. Reports in 3 months. Sample copy $8. Guidelines on website.

**Nonfiction:** Scientific and environmental material, effects of science on policymaking and vice versa. Query or submit 3 double-spaced copies of complete ms. Preferred length: 2,500-4,000 words for full-length article. **Pays $100-300.** "All full-length articles must offer readers authoritative analyses of key environmental problems. Articles must be annotated (referenced), and all conclusions must follow logically from the facts and arguments presented." Prefers articles centering around policy-oriented, public decision-making, scientific and technological issues.

**Photos:** Send photos with submission. Include captions and credits.

**Columns/Departments:** Focus: (education, energy, economics, public opinion, elucidating small portion of a larger problem), 1,000-1,700/words; Report on Reports (reviews of institutions and government reports), 1,500-2,000 words; Commentary, 750 words; Books of Note, 100-150.

**Tips:** "Address a large, global problem by looking at specific examples. Avoid overgeneralizations, one-sided arguments, and jargon."

**⊠ $ $ HIGH COUNTRY NEWS**, High Country Foundation, P.O. Box 1090, Paonia CO 81428-1090. (303)527-4898. E-mail: betsym@HCN.org. Website: http://www.hcn.org. **Contact:** Betsy Marston, editor. **80% freelance written.** Works with a small number of new/unpublished writers each year. Biweekly tabloid covering Rocky Mountain West, the Great Basin and Pacific Northwest environment, rural communities and natural resource issues in 10 western states for environmentalists, politicians, companies, college classes, government agencies, grass roots activists, public land managers, etc. Estab. 1970. Circ. 19,000. Pays on publication. Publishes ms an average of 2 months after acceptance. Byline given. Buys one-time rights. Query by mail, e-mail. Reports in 1 month. Sample copy and writer's guidelines for SAE or on website.

**Nonfiction:** Reporting (local issues with regional importance); exposé (government, corporate); interview/profile; personal experience; centerspread photo feature. **Buys 100 mss/year.** Query. Length: up to 3,000 words. **Pays 20¢/word minimum.** Sometimes pays expenses of writers on assignment for lead stories.

**Reprints:** Send tearsheet of article and info about when and where the article previously appeared. Pays 15¢/word.

**Photos:** Send photos with ms. Prefers b&w prints. Captions and identification of subjects required.

**Columns/Departments:** Roundups (topical stories), 800 words; opinion pieces, 1,000 words.

**Tips:** "We use a lot of freelance material, though very little from outside the Rockies. Familiarity with the newspaper is a must. Start by writing a query letter. We define 'resources' broadly to include people, culture and aesthetic values, not just coal, oil and timber."

**$ $ $ $ INTERNATIONAL WILDLIFE,** National Wildlife Federation, 8925 Leesburg Pike, Vienna VA 22184-0001. (703)790-4510. Fax: (703)790-4544. E-mail: pubs@nwf.org. Website: http://www.nwf.org/nwf. **Contact:** Jonathan Fisher, editor. **85% freelance written.** Prefers to work with published/established writers. Bimonthly magazine for persons interested in natural history and the environment in countries outside the US. Estab. 1971. Circ. 300,000. **Pays on acceptance.** Publishes ms an average of 4 months after acceptance. Buys exclusive first time worldwide rights and nonexclusive worldwide rights after publication. "We are now assigning most articles but will consider detailed proposals for quality feature material of interest to a broad audience." Accepts queries by mail, e-mail, fax. Reports in 6 weeks. Writer's guidelines for #10 SASE.

● Ranked as one of the best markets for freelance writers in *Writer's Yearbook* magazine's annual "Top 100 Markets," January 1999.

**Nonfiction:** Focuses on world wildlife, environmental problems and peoples' relationship to the natural world as reflected in such issues as population growth, pollution, resource utilization, food production, etc. Stories deal with non-US subjects. Especially interested in articles on animal behavior and other natural history, first-person experiences by scientists in the field, well-reported coverage of wildlife-status case studies which also raise broader themes about international conservation and timely issues. Query. Length: 2,000 words. Examine past issues for style and subject matter. **Pays $2,000** minimum for long features. Sometimes pays expenses of writers on assignment.

**Photos:** Purchases top-quality color photos; prefers packages of related photos and text, but single shots of exceptional interest and sequences also considered. Prefers Kodachrome or Fujichrome transparencies. Buys one-time rights.

**Tips:** "*International Wildlife* readers include conservationists, biologists, wildlife managers and other wildlife professionals, but the majority are not wildlife professionals. In fact, *International Wildlife* caters to the unconverted—those people who may have only a passing interest in wildlife. Consequently, our writers should avoid a common pitfall: talking only to an 'in group.' *International Wildlife* is in competition with television and hundreds of other periodicals for the limited time and attention of busy people. So our functions include attracting readers with engaging subjects, pictures and layouts; then holding them with interesting and entertaining, as well as instructional, text."

**N ☆ $ $ MOUNTAINFREAK, for freaks like us,** Lungta, LLC, P.O. Box 4149, 122½ N. Oak St., Telluride CO 81435. (970)728-9731. Fax: (970)728-9821. E-mail: freaks@mountainfreak.com. Website: http://www.mountainfreak.com. **Contact:** Suzanne Cheavens, senior editor. **90% freelance written.** Quarterly magazine. "Our magazine is one that aims for entertainment, enlightenment, pulse-pounding adventure, conscientious living, spiritual awakening and healing of both the soul and the body. Ambitious, yes. Possible, most definitely. *Mountainfreak* is the magazine for those who cannot accept the status quo and who believe that life is how you script it for yourself." Estab. 1996. Circ. 25,000. Pays on publication. Publishes ms an average of 1 year after acceptance. Byline given. Offers 33% kill fee. Buys first rights or makes work-for-hire assignments. Editorial lead time 1 year. Submit seasonal material 1 year in advance. Accepts simultaneous submissions. Sample copy for $5 or on website. Writer's guidelines for SASE or on website.

**Nonfiction:** Book excerpts, essays, exposé, general interest, how-to, humor, inspirational, interview/profile, new product, personal experience, technical, travel. "Our readers are interested in the how-tos of alternative living. Some topics that have appeared in our pages include cob building, permaculture and solar energy. Organic gardening, soapmaking and herbal remedies for the common cold have also been featured in *Mountainfreak*. Think about preserving a healthy, sustainable environment for our children's children and submit accordingly. Nothing preachy and don't be afraid to interview the naysayers of your topics." **Buys 100 mss/year.** Query by mail with published clips. Length: 250-3,000 words. **Pays 10-25¢/word for assigned articles; 10-20¢/word for unsolicited articles.**

**Photos:** Send photos with submission. Reviews original transparencies. Offers $25-400/photo or negotiates payment individually. Captions required. Buys one-time rights.

**Columns/Departments:** Smoke Signals (mostly environmental but political can work, too), 500-750 words; Grooves n Such (new, mainstream music), 500-700 words; Getting High (alternative health, i.e., yoga, acupuncture, etc.), 750-1,500 words; Art Beat (interesting art news and features. Think beyond mainstream. Send queries to Karen Metzger, Art Beat editor, same address); Playground (fun adventure and treading lightly); Good Biz (a profile of companies creating quality products while maintaining conscientious business ethnics); Yummy Grub (good healthy food and recipes); Touch the Earth (living sustainably); Cosmic Raze (messages from alternative realities). We've published pieces on astrology, firewalking and Indian temple dances; Profile (interesting, dynamic people who have made a difference in mountain cultures). Query with published clips. **Pays 10-20¢/word.**

**Fiction:** No religious, serialized novels, romance (love is OK). Query with published clips. Length: 500-3,500 words. **Pays 10-25¢/word.** "Outdoor-oriented fiction is good but writers should not be limited to the genre. I react to good writing and captivating storytelling, not any particular style. This is probably our most subjectively-chosen section. My tastes are varied and in *Mountainfreak* the fiction writer will find lots of room to move. I'm not looking for established writers necessarily but writing that exudes self-confidence and imagination is attractive."

**Poetry:** Avant garde, free verse, haiku, light verse, traditional. Does not want to see religious, though spiritual is fine. Avoid Grateful Dead references. **Buys 12-15 poems/year.** Submit maximum 5 poems. **Pays $25.**

■   The online magazine carries content not found in the print edition. Contact: Susan Cheavens or Mark Steele.

**Tips:** "Writers should compose pieces with an awareness of the intelligence of our readers and their decidedly different take on life. Never be afraid to get too 'out there.' Our readers have fantastic imaginations. Never insult them. If a writer is talking about an outdoor adventure, remember that many readers have done that, too. Write from a spiritual perspective. We're not about peak bagging or first ascents, we're about worshipping the outdoors, the mountains, the air, the water. We'd like to hear from gentle travelers that are not out to conquer, but to understand. Excellent, thoughtful, original queries are a good start. Though *Mountainfreak* is slicker and more professional than our seminal, black and white publications, we are still 'freaky' compared to the mainstream media. Be true to your self. Don't try to sell me anything, just offer your best work. Know our magazine well. We have a lot of departments so finding a fit may not be as difficult as one might think. Our mission statement and writer's guidelines will either make sense to you or not. If they make sense, give it a try. We are small, growing and want people as hungry as we are to help us put out the word. Spell my name right, demonstrate an outstanding grasp of grammar and spelling (one must know the rules before one can break them,) and go out on a limb. Writers that supply captioned, excellent photos have a huge leg-up on those who do not. An exception to this would be fiction submissions. And, I must see writing samples. If you are a yet-to-be-published writer, send your favorite work. This is a unique magazine and I cannot get a sense of 'you' unless I see how you express yourself.'"

**N   $ $ $ NATIONAL PARKS**, 1776 Massachusetts Ave. NW, Washington DC 20036. (202)223-6722. Fax: (202)659-0650. E-mail: npmag@npca.org. Website: http://www.npca.org/. Editor-in-Chief: Linda Rancourt. **Contact:** Elizabeth Daerr, editorial assistant. **85% freelance written.** Prefers to work with published/established writers. Bimonthly magazine for a largely unscientific but highly educated audience interested in preservation of National Park System units, natural areas and protection of wildlife habitat. Estab. 1919. Circ. 400,000. **Pays on acceptance.** Publishes ms an average of 2 months after acceptance. Offers 33% kill fee. Buys first North American serial and second serial (reprint) rights. Reports in 5 months. Sample copy for $3 and 9×12 SAE or on website. Guidelines for #10 SASE.

**Nonfiction:** Exposé (on threats, wildlife problems in national parks); descriptive articles about new or proposed national parks and wilderness parks; natural history pieces describing park geology, wildlife or plants; new trends in park use; legislative issues. All material must relate to national parks. No poetry, philosophical essays or first person narratives. No unsolicited mss. Length: 2,000-2,500 words. **Pays $1,000 for full-length features; $500 for service articles.**

**Photos:** Send photos with submission. No color prints or negatives. Prefers color slides and transparencies. Pays $25-325 inside; $500 for covers. Captions required. Buys first North American serial rights. Send for guidelines first. Not responsible for unsolicited photos.

**Tips:** "Articles should have an original slant or news hook and cover a limited subject, rather than attempt to treat a broad subject superficially. Specific examples, descriptive details and quotes are always preferable to generalized information. The writer must be able to document factual claims, and statements should be clearly substantiated with evidence within the article. *National Parks* does not publish fiction, poetry, personal essays or 'My trip to . . .' stories."

**N   $ $ $ $ NATIONAL WILDLIFE**, National Wildlife Federation, 8925 Leesburg Pike, Vienna VA 22184-0001. (703)790-4524. Fax: (703)827-2585. **Contact:** Bob Strohm, editor-in-chief; Mark Wexler, editor. **75% freelance written,** "but assigns almost all material based on staff ideas. Assigns few unsolicited queries." Bimonthly magazine. "Our purpose is to promote wise use of the nation's natural resources and to conserve and protect wildlife and its habitat. We reach a broad audience that is largely interested in wildlife conservation and nature photography." Estab. 1963. Circ. 660,000. **Pays on acceptance.** Publishes ms an average of 1 year after acceptance. Offers 25% kill fee. Buys all rights. Submit seasonal material 8 months in advance. Reports in 6 weeks. Writer's guidelines for #10 SASE.

● Ranked as one of the best markets for freelance writers in *Writer's Yearbook* magazine's annual "Top 100 Markets," January 1999.

**Nonfiction:** General interest (2,500-word features on wildlife, new discoveries, behavior, or the environment); how-to (an outdoor or nature related activity); personal experience (outdoor adventure); photo feature (wildlife); short 700-word features on an unusual individual or new scientific discovery relating to nature. "Avoid too much scientific detail. We prefer anecdotal, natural history material." **Buys 50 mss/year.** Query with or without published clips. Length: 750-2,500 words. **Pays $500-2,000.** Sometimes pays expenses of writers on assignment.

**Photos:** John Nuhn, photo editor. Send photos or send photos with query. Prefers Kodachrome or Fujichrome transparencies. Buys one-time rights.

**Tips:** "Writers can break in with us more readily by proposing subjects (initially) that will take only one or two pages in the magazine (short features)."

**$ $ $ $ NATURAL HISTORY**, Natural History Magazine, Central Park W. at 79th St., New York NY 10024. (212)769-5500. Fax: (212)769-5511. E-mail: nhmag@amnh.org. **Contact:** Bruce Stutz, editor-in-chief. **15% freelance**

**written.** Monthly magazine for well-educated, ecologically aware audience: professional people, scientists and scholars. Circ. 400,000. **Pays on acceptance.** Publishes ms an average of 3 months after acceptance. Byline given. Buys first serial rights and becomes agent for second serial (reprint) rights. Submit seasonal material at least 6 months in advance.

● Ranked as one of the best markets for freelance writers in *Writer's Yearbook* magazine's annual "Top 100 Markets," January 1999.

**Nonfiction:** Uses all types of scientific articles except chemistry and physics—emphasis is on the biological sciences and anthropology. "We always want to see new research findings in almost all branches of the natural sciences—anthropology, archeology, zoology and ornithology. We find it is particularly difficult to get something new in herpetology (amphibians and reptiles) or entomology (insects), and would like to see material in those fields." **Buys 60 mss/year.** Query by mail or submit complete ms. Length: 1,500-3,000 words. **Pays $500-2,500,** additional payment for photos used.

**Photos:** Rarely uses 8×10 b&w glossy prints; pays $125/page maximum. Much color is used; pays $300 for inside and up to $600 for cover. Buys one-time rights.

**Columns/Departments:** Journal (reporting from the field); Findings (summary of new or ongoing research); Naturalist At Large; The Living Museum (relates to the American Museum of Natural History); Discovery (natural or cultural history of a specific place).

**Tips:** "We expect high standards of writing and research. We favor an ecological slant in most of our pieces, but do not generally lobby for causes, environmental or other. The writer should have a deep knowledge of his subject, then submit original ideas either in query or by manuscript. Acceptance is more likely if article is accompanied by high-quality photographs."

**$ NATURE CANADA**, Canadian Nature Federation, 1 Nicholas St., Suite 606, Ottawa, Ontario KIN 7B7 Canada. Fax: (613)562-3371. E-mail: cnf@cnf.ca. Website: www.cnf.ca. **Contact:** Barbara Stevenson, editor. Quarterly membership magazine covering conservation, natural history and environmental/naturalist community. "*Nature Canada* is written for an audience interested in nature. Its content supports the Canadian Nature Federation's philosophy that all species have a right to exist regardless of their usefulness to humans. We promote the awareness, understanding and enjoyment of nature." Estab. 1971. Circ. 16,000. Pays on publication. Publishes ms an average of 3 months after acceptance. Byline given. Offers $100 kill fee. Buys one-time rights. Editorial lead time 3 months. Submit seasonal material 6 months in advance. Reports in 3 months on mss. Sample copy for $5. Writer's guidelines for SASE.

**Nonfiction:** Canadian environmental issues and natural history. **Buys 20 mss/year.** Query by mail with published clips. Length: 2,000-4,000 words. **Pays 25¢/word (Canadian).**

**Photos:** State availability of photos with submission. Offers $40-100/photo (Canadian). Identification of subjects required. Buys one-time rights.

**Columns/Departments:** The Green Gardener (naturalizing your backyard), 1,200 words; Small Wonder (on less well-known species such as invertebrates, nonvascular plants, etc.), 800-1,500 words; Connections (Canadians making a difference for the environment), 1,000-1,500 words; Pathways (about natural places to visit). **Buys 16 mss/year.** Query with published clips. **Pays 25¢/word** (Canadian).

**Tips:** "Our readers are knowledgeable about nature and the environment so contributors should have a good understanding of the subject. We also deal exclusively with Canadian issues and species."

**$ $ $ SEASONS, Ontario's Nature and Environment Magazine**, Federation of Ontario Naturalists, 355 Lesmill Rd., Don Mills, Ontario M3B 2W8 Canada. (416)444-8419. E-mail: seasons@ontarionature.org. Website: http://www.ontarionature.org. **Contact:** Nancy Clark, editor. **75% freelance written.** Quarterly magazine. "*Seasons* focuses on Ontario natural history, parks and environmental issues, with appeal for general readers as well as naturalists." Estab. 1963 (published as *Ontario Naturalist* 1963-1980). Circ. 16,000. Pays on publication. Publishes ms an average of 6 months after acceptance. Byline given. Offers 50% kill fee. Buys first Canadian serial rights. Editorial lead time 6 months. Submit seasonal material 1 year in advance. Accepts queries by mail, e-mail, fax, phone. Reports in 2-3 months. Sample copy for $7.20. Writer's guidelines for #10 SASE.

**Nonfiction:** Essays, general interest, how-to (identify species, be a better birder, etc.), opinion, personal experience, photo feature, travel. No cute articles about cute animals or biology articles cribbed from reference books. **Buys 16-20 mss/year.** Query with published clips. Length: 1,500-3,000 words. **Pays $350-1,000.** Sometimes pays expenses of writers on assignment.

**Photos:** State availability of photos with submission. Reviews 35mm transparencies. Negotiates payment individually. Model releases, identification of subjects required. Buys one-time rights.

**Columns/Departments:** Naturalist's Notebook (tips on birding, improving naturalist's skills), 700 words. **Buys 4 mss/year.** Query with published clips. **Pays $200-400.**

**$ $ $ $ SIERRA**, 85 Second St., 2nd Floor, San Francisco CA 94105-3441. (415)977-5656. Fax: (415)977-5794. E-mail: sierra.letters@sierraclub.org. Website: http://www.sierraclub.org. Editor-in-Chief: Joan Hamilton. Senior Editors: Reed McManus, Paul Rauber. **Contact:** Robert Schildgen, managing editor. Works with a small number of new/unpublished writers each year. Bimonthly magazine emphasizing conservation and environmental politics for people who are well educated, activist, outdoor-oriented and politically well informed with a dedication to conservation. Estab. 1893. Circ. 550,000. **Pays on acceptance.** Publishes ms an average of 4 months after acceptance. Byline given. Kill fees negotiable when a story is assigned. Buys first North American serial rights. Query by mail, e-mail, fax. Reports in 2 months. Sample copy for $3 and SASE. Writer's guidlines on website.

● Ranked as one of the best markets for freelance writers in *Writer's Yearbook* magazine's annual "Top 100 Markets," January 1999.

**Nonfiction:** Exposé (well-documented articles on environmental issues of national importance such as energy, wilderness, forests, etc.); general interest (well-researched nontechnical pieces on areas of particular environmental concern); photo feature (photo essays on threatened or scenic areas); journalistic treatments of semi-technical topics (energy sources, wildlife management, land use, waste management, etc.). No "My trip to . . ." or "why we must save wildlife/nature" articles; no poetry or general superficial essays on environmentalism; no reporting on purely local environmental issues. Special issues: Travel (March/April 2000). **Buys 5-6 mss/issue.** Query with published clips. Length: 800-3,000 words. **Pays $450-2,000.** Pays limited expenses of writers on assignment.

**Reprints:** Send photocopy or typed ms with rights for sale noted and information about when and where the article previously appeared. Pay negotiable.

**Photos:** Larissa Zimberoff, art and production manager. Send photos. Pays $300 maximum for transparencies; more for cover photos. Buys one-time rights.

**Columns/Departments:** Food for Thought (food's connection to environment—include a recipe); Good Going (adventure journey); Hearth & Home (advice for environmentally sound living); Body Politics (health and the environment); Way to Go (wilderness trips), 750 words. **Pays $500.** Lay of the Land (national/international concerns), 500-700 words. Pay varies. Natural Resources (book reviews), 200-300 words. **Pays $50.**

**Tips:** "Queries should include an outline of how the topic would be covered and a mention of the political appropriateness and timeliness of the article. Statements of the writer's qualifications should be included."

**$WHOLE EARTH,** Point Foundation, 1408 Mission Ave., San Rafael CA 94901. (415)256-2800. Fax: (415)256-2808. E-mail: editor@wholeearthmag.com. Website: http://www.wholeearthmag.com. Editor: Peter Warshall. Managing Editor: Michael Stone. Assistant Editor: Nicole Parizeau. **Contact:** Attn. Submissions. **80% freelance written.** "Quarterly periodical supplement, descendent of the Whole Earth catalog. Evaluates tools, ideas and practices to sow the seeds for a long-term, viable planet." Estab. 1971. Circ. 30,000. Pays on publication. Publishes ms an average of 6 months after acceptance. Byline given. Buys one-time rights to articles; all rights to reviews. Editorial lead time 3 months. Accepts queries by mail, e-mail, fax. Accepts simultaneous submissions. Reports in 1 month on queries (no promises). Writer's guidelines for SASE or on website.

**Nonfiction:** Book reviews, essays, exposé, general interest, historical/nostalgic, how-to, humor, interview/profile, new product, personal experience, photo feature, religious, travel. "No dull repeats of old ideas or material; no 'goddess' material." Query or send complete ms. Length: 500-3,000 words. Pay negotiable. Pays writers with contributor copies or other premiums by agreement, usually for reviews.

**Reprints:** Accepts previously published submissions.

**Photos:** State availability of photos with submission. Negotiates payment individually. Buys one-time rights.

**Fiction:** Adventure, erotica, ethnic, experimental, humorous, novel excerpts, science fiction, slice-of-life vignettes. **Buys 2-4 mss/year.** Query or send complete ms. Length: 500-3,000 words. Pay negotiable.

**Poetry:** Peter Warshall, editor. Avant-garde, free verse, haiku, light verse, traditional. No long works. **Buys 1-4 poems/year.** Length: 100 lines maximum. Pay negotiable.

The online magazine carries original content not found in the print edition.

**Tips:** "We like your personal voice: intimate, a lively conversation with an attentive friend. We like ideas, thoughts and events to appear to stand independent and clear of the narrator. Don't send a variation on an idea. Show us you did your homework."

# PERSONAL COMPUTERS

Personal computer magazines continue to evolve. The most successful have a strong focus on a particular family of computers or widely-used applications and carefully target a specific type of computer use, although as technology evolves, some computers and applications fall by the wayside. Be sure you see the most recent issue of a magazine before submitting material.

**$ $ $COMPUTER BUYER'S GUIDE & HANDBOOK,** Bedford Communications, 150 Fifth Ave., Suite 714, New York NY 10011. Fax: (212)807-0589. E-mail: editleigh@aol.com. Website: http://www.bedfordmags.com. Editor: David A. Finck. **Contact:** Leigh Friedman, managing editor. **60% freelance written.** Monthly magazine covering computer hardware, software and peripherals; industry trends. "Publication is geared toward the computer buyer, with an emphasis on the small office." Estab. 1982. Pays on publication. Publishes ms an average of 3 months after acceptance. Byline given. Offers 25% kill fee. Buys all rights. Editorial lead time 4 months. Accepts queries by mail, e-mail. Reports in 4 weeks. Sample copy on website; writer's guidelines not available.

**Nonfiction:** How-to (e.g., how to install a CD-ROM drive), technical, hands-on reviews. **Buys 80-100 mss/year.** Query with published clips. "Will not accept unsolicited articles or manuscripts." Length: 600-5,500 words. **Pays $150-1,250 for assigned articles.** Sometimes pays expenses of writers on assignment.

**Tips:** "Send résumé with feature-length (technology-related, if possible) clips to editorial offices. Unsolicited manuscripts are not accepted or returned."

✦ **$ $ $ COMPUTER CURRENTS, Real World Solutions for Business Computing**, Computer Currents Publishing, 1250 Ninth St., Berkeley CA 94710. (510)527-0333. Fax: (510)527-4106. E-mail: editorial@compcurr.com. Website: http://www.currents.net. **Contact:** Robert Luhn, editor-in-chief. **90% freelance written.** Biweekly magazine "for fairly experienced PC and Mac business users. We provide where to buy, how to buy and how to use information. That includes buyers guides, reviews, tutorials and more." Estab. 1983. Circ. 700,000. **Pays on acceptance.** Byline given. Offers 20% kill fee. Buys all rights. Editorial lead time 2 months. Submit seasonal material 2 months in advance. Accepts queries by mail, e-mail, fax. Reports in 2 weeks on queries; 2 months on mss. Sample copy for 10 × 12 SAE with $5 postage or on website. Writer's guidelines for #10 SASE or via e-mail or on website.

**Nonfiction:** Book excerpts, exposé, how-to (using PC or Mac products), new product, opinion, technical. Special issues: Holiday Gift Guide (November). "No fiction, poetry or 'I just discovered PCs' essays." **Buys 40 mss/year.** Query with published clips and SASE. Length: 1,000-2,500 words. **Pays $700-2,000.** Sometimes pays expenses of writers on assignment.

**Reprints:** Send tearsheet or typed ms with rights for sale noted and information about when and where the article previously appeared. Pays 10-40% of amount paid for an original article.

**Photos:** State availability of photos with submission. Reviews 35mm transparencies, 8 × 10 prints. Offers no additional payment for photos accepted with ms. Buys first North American and nonexclusive reprint rights.

**Columns/Departments:** Robert Luhn. "Previews & Reviews" of new and beta hardware, software and services, 300-600 words; Features (PC, Mac, hardware, software, investigative pieces), 1,000-2,500 words. **Buys 60 mss/year.** Query with published clips and SASE. **Pays $50-500.**

▨ The online magazine carries original content not found in the print edition. Contact Robert Luhn, online editor.

**Tips:** "Writers must know PC or Mac technology and major software and peripherals. Know how to write, evaluate products critically, and make a case for or against a product under review. *Computer Currents* is the magazine for the rest of us. We don't torture test 500 printers or devote space to industry chit-chat. Instead, we provide PC and Mac users with real-world editorial they can use every day when determining what to buy, where to buy it, and how to use it. Along with supplying this kind of nitty-gritty advice to both small and large business users alike, we also demystify the latest technologies and act as a consumer advocate. We're also not afraid to poke fun at the industry, as our annual 'Year in Review' issue and biweekly 'Gigglebytes' column demonstrate."

**$ COMPUTERCREDIBLE MAGAZINE**, Assimilations, Inc., 1249 W. Jordan River Dr., South Jordan UT 84095-8250. (801)254-5432. Fax: (801)253-1040. E-mail: computer@credible.com. Website: http://www.credible.com. Editor: Rick Simi. **Contact:** Kerry Simi, managing editor. **100% freelance written.** Monthly magazine covering computers. Estab. 1995. Circ. 35,000. **Pays on acceptance.** Publishes ms an average of 1 month after acceptance. Byline given. Buys first North American serial rights, electronic rights, and second serial (reprint) rights. Accepts queries by mail, e-mail. Sample copy for $1. Writer's guidelines for #10 SASE or on website.

**Nonfiction:** General interest, how-to, humor, interview/profile, new product, opinion, technical. **Buys 40 mss/year.** Length: 650-1,500 words. **Pays 5-10¢/word.**

**Reprints:** Accepts previously published submissions.

**Photos:** State availability of photos with submission.

**Columns/Departments:** **Buys 40 mss/year.** Send complete ms. **Pays 5-10¢/word.**

**Fiction:** Humorous. **Buys 6 mss/year.** Send complete ms. Length: 650-1,000 words. **Pays 5-10¢/word.**

**Fillers:** Facts, short humor. Length: 250-650 words. **Pays 5-10¢/word.**

**Tips:** "Our diverse readership allows us to print articles in varying styles (technical, light-hearted, instructional). We are looking for fiction and non-fiction writers who can explain technical information to our experienced readers without confusing the novice reader. We look for writers who can provide interesting points of view, solutions, and humorous anecdotes on issues facing the computer user."

⋈ **$ $ $ LAPTOP BUYER'S GUIDE AND HANDBOOK**, Bedford Communications, Inc., 150 Fifth Ave., Suite 714, New York NY 10011. (212)807-8720. Fax: (212)807-0589. E-mail: Editleigh@aol.com. Website: http://www.bedfordmags.com. Editor: David A. Finck. **Contact:** Leigh Friedman, managing editor. **60% freelance written.** Monthly magazine covering mobile computing and communication. "*LBG&H* is a buyer's guide for first and second time notebook computer buyers. Editorial content is written in plain English that explains technical specifications and industry trends in a way that can be understood by a novice, without condescension." Estab. 1990. Circ. 60,000. Pays on publication. Publishes ms an average of 3 months after acceptance. Byline given. Offers 25% kill fee. Buys all rights. Editorial lead time 4 months. Accepts queries by mail, e-mail. Sample articles on website

**Nonfiction:** How-to (hardware installations), new product, technical. **Buys 80 mss/year.** Query. Length: 2,500-5,000 words. **Pays $750-1,250.** Sometimes pays expenses of writers on assignment.

**Columns/Departments:** Eye on Technology (new products), 600 words; Tech View (explain an aspect of computer technology), 3,500 words; Spotlight on Software (review a number of products within a class), 3,500 words. **Pays $150-750.**

**Tips:** "Writers' résumés with feature-length (technology-related if possible) clips are accepted. No unsolicited stories are purchased or manuscripts accepted. All freelance work is by assignment."

**$ $ $ $ MACADDICT**, Imagine Media, 150 North Hill Dr., Suite 40, Brisbane CA 94005. (415)468-4684. Fax: (415)468-4686. E-mail: dreynolds@macaddict.com. Managing Editor: Jeff T. Herton. **Contact:** David Reynolds, editor.

**25% freelance written.** Monthly magazine covering Macintosh computers. "*MacAddict* is a magazine for Macintosh computer enthusiasts of all levels. Writers must know, love and own Macintosh computers." Estab. 1996. Circ. 160,000. Pays on publication. Publishes ms an average of 3 months after acceptance. Byline given. Buys all rights. Editorial lead time 3 months. Submit seasonal material 5 months in advance. Accepts queries by mail, e-mail. Accepts simultaneous submissions. Reports in 1 month.

**Nonfiction:** General interest, how-to, new product, photo feature, technical. No humor, case studies, personal experiences, essays. **Buys 30 mss/year.** Query with or without published clips and SASE. Length: 750-5,000 words. **Pays $50-2,500.** Sometimes pays expenses of writers on asssignment.

**Photos:** State availability of photos with submission. Negotiates payment individually. Captions, model releases, identification of subjects required. Buys one-time rights.

**Columns/Departments:** Reviews (always assigned), 300-750 words; How-to's (detailed, step-by-step), 500-4,000 words; features, 1,000-4,000 words. **Buys 30 mss/year.** Query with or without published clips. **Pays $50-2,500.**

**Fillers:** Mark Simmons, senior editor. Get Info. **Buys 20/year.** Length: 50-500 words. **Pays $25-200.**

■ The online magazine carries original content not found in the print edition. Contact: David Reynolds, online editor.

**Tips:** "Send us an idea for a short one to two page how-to and/or send us a letter outlining your publishing experience and areas of Mac expertise so we can assign a review to you (reviews editor is Jennifer Ho). Your submission should have great practical hands-on benefit to a reader, be fun to read in the author's natural voice, and include lots of screenshot graphics. We require electronic submissions. Impress our reviews editor with well-written reviews of Mac products and then move up to bigger articles from there."

**$ $ $ SMART COMPUTING**, Sandhills Publishing, 131 W. Grand Dr., Lincoln NE 68521. (800)544-1264. Fax: (402)479-2104. E-mail: editor@smartcomputing.com. Website: http://www.smartcomputing.com. Managing Editor: Trevor Meers. **Contact:** Ron Kobler, editor-in-chief. **45% freelance written.** Monthly. "We focus on plain-English computing articles with an emphasis on tutorials that improve productivity without the purchase of new hardware." Estab. 1990. Circ. 300,000. **Pays on acceptance.** Publishes ms 2 months after acceptance. Byline given. Offers 25% kill fee. Buys all rights. Editorial lead time 4 months. Submit seasonal material 4 months in advance. Accepts queries by mail, e-mail. Accepts simultaneous submissions. Reports in 1 month. Sample copy for $7.99. Writer's guidelines for SASE.

○━ Break in with "any article containing little-known tips for improving software and hardware performance and Web use. We're also seeking clear reporting on key trends changing personal technology."

**Nonfiction:** How-to, new product, technical. No humor, opinion, personal experience. **Buys 250 mss/year.** Query with published clips. Length: 800-3,200 words. **Pays $240-960.** Pays the expenses of writers on assignment up to $75.

**Photos:** Send photos with submission. Offers no additional payment for photos accepted with ms. Captions required. Buys all rights.

■ The online magazine carries original content not found in the print edition. Contact: Meredith Witulski, online editor.

**Tips:** "Focus on practical, how-to computing articles. Our readers are intensely productivity-driven. Carefully review recent issues. We receive many ideas for stories printed in the last six months."

**$ $ $ $ WINDOWS MAGAZINE**, CMP Media Inc., 1 Jericho Plaza, Jericho NY 11753. (516)733-8300. Fax: (516)733-8390. Website: http://www.winmag.com. Senior Managing Editor: Donna Tapellini. Monthly magazine for business users of Windows hardware and software. "*Windows* contains information on how to evaluate, select, acquire, implement, use, and master Windows-related software and hardware." Estab. 1990. Circ. 800,000. **Pays on acceptance.** Byline given. Offers 25% kill fee. Accepts queries by mail, e-mail, phone, fax. Reports in 1-2 months on queries. Sample copy and writer's guidelines available.

**Nonfiction:** How-to, technical. **Buys 30 mss/year.** Query with published clips. Length: 1,500-4,000 words. **Pays $1,200-3,000.**

■ The online magazine carries original material not found in the print edition. Contact: Nancy Wanoff, online editor.

**Tips:** Needs "clear, entertaining, technical features on Windows hardware and software." Wants to see "how-to and how-to-buy articles, and insider's look at new products." Should be well-written, entertaining and technically accurate. "We concentrate on hands-on tips and how-to information."

**◆ $ $ $ WIRED MAGAZINE**, Condé Nast Magazines, 520 Third St., 4th Floor, San Francisco CA 94107-1815. (415)276-5000. Fax: (415)276-5150. E-mail: submit@wired.com. Website: http://www.wired.com. Editor/Publisher: Dana Lyon. Editor-in-Chief: Katrina Heron. **Contact:** Christina Gangei, editorial assistant. **95% freelance written.** Monthly magazine covering technology and digital culture. "We cover the digital revolution and related advances in computers, communications and lifestyles." Estab. 1993. Circ. 350,000. **Pays on acceptance.** Publishes ms an average of 3 months after acceptance. Byline given. Offers 25% kill fee. Buys all rights for items less than 1,000 words, first North American serial rights for pieces over 1,000 words. Editorial lead time 3 months. Reports in 3 weeks. Sample copy for $4.95. Guidelines for #10 SASE or e-mail to guidelines@wired.com.

**Nonfiction:** Essays, interview/profile, opinion. "No poetry or trade articles." **Buys 85 features, 130 short pieces, 200 reviews, 36 essays and 50 other mss/year.** Query. Pays expenses of writers on assignment.

# PHOTOGRAPHY

Readers of these magazines use their cameras as a hobby and for weekend assignments. To write for these publications, you should have expertise in photography. Magazines geared to the professional photographer can be found in the Professional Photography section.

**[N] $ $ BALIAN'S OUTDOOR & NATURE PHOTOGRAPHY**, (formerly Shutterbug's Outdoor & Nature Photography), 1042 N. Camino Real, Suite B-123, Encinitas CA 92024. E-mail: qstat_esb@compuserve.com Website: http://www.outdoorandnature.com. **Contact:** Edward Balian, editorial director. Quarterly. "Primarily a how-to magazine for outdoor photo enthusiasts. We buy only illustrated articles." Estab. 1995. Circ. 40,000. Pays on publication. Publishes ms an average of 6 months after acceptance. Byline given. Buys first North American serial rights. Editorial lead time 6 months. Submit seasonal material 12 months in advance. Accepts simultaneous submissions. Reports in 6 weeks on queries; 1 month on mss. Sample copy for 11×14 SAE and 3 first-class stamps. Writer's guidelines for #10 SASE or by e-mail (required before any submission).

**Nonfiction:** How-to, technical. "No vacation photography; destination-oriented travel stories." **Buys 40 mss/year.** Query by mail with published clips. Length: 1,500-2,500 words. **Pay varies.**

**Photos:** State availability of photos with submission. Reviews contact sheets and any prints. Offers no additional payment for photos accepted with ms. Captions required. Buys one-time rights.

**Columns/Departments:** Pro Tips (pro photographer's tips on some topic) and So What's New? (survey of photo equipment), both 1,800 words. **Buys 16 mss/year.** Query with published clips. **Pay varies.**

**Tips:** "Above all, *ONP* is a 'how-to' magazine. Hence, we seek a strong educational component, in a conversational style, i.e., 'Here's how I do it . . . here's how you can too.' Specifics as to technique and equipment (including brands, models, distributors) will be expected by our readers. Submit query with non-returnable samples of photos and previously published articles. Preference is given to pro and semi-pro photographers with proven expertise on any one topic."

**$ NATURE PHOTOGRAPHER**, Nature Photographer Publishing Co., Inc., P.O. Box 690518, Quincy MA 02269. (617)847-0095. Fax: (617)847-0952. E-mail: mjsquincy@pipeline.com and helen_marty@yahoo.com. **Contact:** Helen Longest-Slaughter Saccone and Evamarie Mathaey, co-editors-in-chief/photo editors. **65% freelance written.** Bimonthly magazine "emphasizing nature photography that uses low-impact and local less-known locations, techniques and ethics. Articles include how-to, travel to world-wide wilderness locations, and how nature photography can be used to benefit the environment and environmental education of the public." Estab. 1990. Circ. 25,000. Pays on publication. Buys one-time rights. Submit seasonal material 8 months in advance. Query by mail, e-mail. Accepts simultaneous submissions. Reports in 2 months. Sample copy for 9×12 SAE with 6 first-class stamps. Guidelines for #10 SASE.

**Nonfiction:** How-to (underwater, exposure, creative techniques, techniques to make photography easier, low-impact techniques, macro photography, large-format, wildlife), photo feature, technical, travel. No articles about photographing in zoos or on game farms. **Buys 12-18 mss/year.** Query with published clips or writing samples. Length: 750-2,500 words. **Pays $75-150.**

**Reprints:** Send photocopy of article and information about when and where the article previously appeared. Pays 75% of amount *Nature Photographer* pays for an original article.

**Photos:** Send photos upon request. Do not send with submission. Reviews 35mm, 2¼×2¼ and 4×5 transparencies. Offers no additional payment for photos accepted with ms. Identification of subjects required. Buys one-time rights.

**Tips:** "Query with original, well-thought-out ideas and good writing samples. Make sure you send SASE. Areas most open to freelancers are travel, how-to and conservation articles with dramatic slides to illustrate the articles. Must have good, solid research and knowledge of subject. Be sure to obtain guidelines by sending SASE with request before submitting query. If you have not requested guidelines within the last year, request an updated version of guidelines."

**$ $ $ PHOTO TECHNIQUES**, Preston Publications, Inc., 6600 W. Touhy Ave., Niles IL 60714. (847)647-2900. Fax: (847)647-1155. E-mail: michaeljohnston@ameritech.net. Publisher: S. Tinsley Preston III. Managing Editor: Bert Stern. **Contact:** Mike Johnston, editor. **50% freelance written.** Bimonthly publication covering photochemistry, lighting, optics, processing and printing, Zone System, special effects, sensitometry, etc. Aimed at advanced workers. Prefers to work with experienced photographer-writers; happy to work with excellent photographers whose writing skills are lacking. "Article conclusions often require experimental support." Estab. 1979. Circ. 35,000. Pays within 2 weeks of publication. Publishes ms an average of 8 months after acceptance. Byline given. Buys one-time rights. Sample copy for $5. Writer's guidelines with #10 SASE.

**Nonfiction:** Special interest articles within above listed topics; how-to, technical product reviews, photo features. Query or send complete ms. Length open, but most features run approximately 2,500 words or 3-4 magazine pages. **Pays $200-1,000** for well-researched technical articles.

**Photos:** Photographers have a much better chance of having their photos published if the photos accompany a written article. Manuscript payment includes payment for photos. Prefers 8×10 b&w and color prints. Captions, technical information required. Buys one-time rights.

**Tips:** "Study the magazine! Virtually all writers we publish are readers of the magazine. We are now more receptive than ever to articles about photographers, history, aesthetics and informative backgrounders about specific areas of the photo industry or specific techniques. Successful writers for our magazine are doing what they write about."

⊘ **POPULAR PHOTOGRAPHY** does not accept freelance submissions.

# POLITICS & WORLD AFFAIRS

These publications cover politics for the reader interested in current events. Other publications that will consider articles about politics and world affairs are listed under Business & Finance, Contemporary Culture, Regional and General Interest. For listings of publications geared toward the professional, see Government & Public Service in the Trade section.

**$ $ CHURCH & STATE, Americans United for Separation of Church and State**, 1816 Jefferson Place, NW, Washington DC 20036. (202)466-3234. Fax: (202)466-2587. Website: http://www.au.org. **Contact:** Joseph Conn, editor. **10% freelance written.** Prefers to work with published/established writers. Monthly magazine emphasizing religious liberty and church/state relations matters. Strongly advocates separation of church and state. Readership is well-educated. Estab. 1947. Circ. 33,000. **Pays on acceptance.** Publishes ms an average of 2 months after acceptance. Buys all rights. Accepts simultaneous submissions. Accepts queries by mail. Reports in 2 months. Sample copy and writer's guidelines for 9×12 SAE with 3 first-class stamps.
**Nonfiction:** Exposé, general interest, historical, interview. **Buys 11 mss/year.** Query. Length: 800-1,600 words. **Pays $150-300.** Sometimes pays expenses of writers on assignment.
**Reprints:** Send tearsheet of article, photocopy of article or typed ms with rights for sale noted and information about when and where the article previously appeared.
**Photos:** Send photos with query. Pays negotiable fee for b&w prints. Captions preferred. Buys one-time rights.
**Tips:** "We're looking for feature articles on underreported local church-state controversies. We also consider 'viewpoint' essays that offer a unique or personal take on church-state issues."

**$ $ EMPIRE STATE REPORT, The Magazine of Politics and Public Policy in New York State**, 33 Century Hill Dr., Latham NY 12210. (518)738-0001. Fax: (518)783-0005. E-mail: mcpowers@empirestatereport.com. Website: http://www.empirestatereport.com. **Contact:** Mary Caroline Powers, editor. **75% freelance written.** Monthly magazine providing "timely political and public policy articles and analysis of the business of government for local and state public officials in New York State. Anything that would be of interest to them is of interest to us." Estab. 1983. Circ. 16,000. Pays 2 months after publication. Byline given. Buys first North American serial rights. Accepts queries by mail, e-mail, fax, phone. Reports in 1 month on queries; 2 months on mss. Sample copy for $4.50 with 9×12 SASE or on website.
**Nonfiction:** Essays, exposé, interview/profile and opinion. "Writers should send for our editorial calendar." **Buys 48 mss/year.** Query with published clips. Length: 500-4,500 words. **Pays $100-700.** Sometimes pays expenses of writers on assignment.
**Photos:** Send photos with submission. Reviews any size prints. Offers $100-2,000/photo. Identification of subjects required. Buys one-time rights.
**Columns/Departments:** ESR Notebook (short news stories about state politics), 300-900 words; Perspective (opinion pieces), 900-950 words. Perspectives do not carry remuneration.
**Tips:** "Send us a query. If we are not already working on the idea, and if the query is well written, we might work something out with the writer."

**Ⓝ $ $ EUROPE**, Delegation of the European Commission, 2300 M St. NW, 3rd Floor, Washington DC 20037. (202)862-9555. Fax: (202)429-1766. Website: http://www.eurunion.org. Managing Editor: Peter Gwin. **Contact:** Robert Guttman, editor-in-chief. **50% freelance written.** Monthly magazine for anyone with a professional or personal interest in Europe and European/US relations. Estab. 1963. Circ. 75,000. Pays on publication. Publishes ms an average of 3 months after acceptance. Byline given. Offers 50% kill fee. Buys first serial and all rights. Editorial lead time 2 months. Submit seasonal material 4 months in advance. Query by mail, e-mail, fax, phone. Reports in 6 months. Sample articles on website.
**Nonfiction:** General interest, historical/nostalgic, interview/profile. Interested in current affairs (with emphasis on economics, business and politics), the Single Market and Europe's relations with the rest of the world. Publishes monthly cultural travel pieces, with European angle. "High quality writing a must. We publish articles that might be useful to people (primarily American readers) with a professional interest in Europe." Query or submit complete ms or article outline. Include résumé of author's background and qualifications. **Buys 20 mss/year.** Length: 600-1,500 words. **Pays $50-500 for assigned articles; $50-400 for unsolicited articles.**
**Columns/Departments:** Arts & Leisure (book, art, movie reviews, etc.), 200-800 words. **Pays $50-250.**
**Photos:** Photos purchased with or without accompanying mss. Buys b&w and color. Pays $25-35 for b&w print, any size; $100 for inside use of transparencies; $450 for color used on cover; per job negotiable.
**Tips:** "We are always interested in stories that connect Europe to the U.S.—especially business stories. Company profiles, a U.S. company having success or vice versa, are a good bet."

**$ $ THE NATION**, 33 Irving Place, 8th Floor, New York NY 10003. (212)209-5400. Fax: (212)982-9000. Editor: Katrina Vanden Heuvel. **Contact:** Peggy Suttle, assistant to editor. **75% freelance written.** Estab. 1865. Works with a

small number of new/unpublished writers each year. Weekly magazine "firmly committed to reporting on the issues of labor, national politics, business, consumer affairs, environmental politics, civil liberties, foreign affairs and the role and future of the Democratic Party." Buys first serial rights. Free sample copy and writer's guidelines for 6×9 SASE.
**Nonfiction:** "We welcome all articles dealing with the social scene, from an independent perspective." Queries encouraged. **Buys 100 mss/year.** Length: 2,000 words maximum. **Pays $225-300.** Sometimes pays expenses of writers on assignment.
**Columns/Departments:** Editorial, 500-700 words. **Pays $75.**
**Poetry:** Contact: Grace Schulman, poetry editor. Send poems with SASE. *The Nation* publishes poetry of outstanding aesthetic quality. **Pays $1/poem.**

**$ $ $ NATIONAL REVIEW**, 215 Lexington Ave., New York NY 10016. E-mail: articles@nationalreview.com. Website: http://www.nationalreview.com. Articles Editor: Naomi Schaefer. Biweekly magazine featuring political commentary from a conservative viewpoint. Pays on publication. Byline given. Kill fee varies. Buys all rights. Accepts queries by mail, e-mail, phone, fax. Reports in 2 months.
**Nonfiction:** Send complete ms. Length: 800-2,000 words. **Pays $250/printed page.** Sometimes pays expenses of writers on assignment.
**Columns/Departments:** Length: 900 words. **Pays $250/printed page.**
**Fillers:** Length: 1,000 words. **Pays $250/printed page.**

**N $ $ NEW JERSEY REPORTER, A Journal of Public Issues**, The Center for Analysis of Public Issues, 64 Nassau St., Princeton NJ 08542. (609)924-9750. Fax: (609)924-0363. E-mail: njreporter@rcn.com. Website: http://njreporter.org. **Contact:** Mark Magyar, editor. **90% freelance written.** Prefers to work with published/established writers but will consider proposals from others. Bimonthly magazine covering New Jersey politics, public affairs and public issues. "*New Jersey Reporter* is a hard-hitting and highly respected magazine published for people who take an active interest in New Jersey politics and public affairs, and who want to know more about what's going on than what newspapers and television newscasts are able to tell them. We publish a great variety of stories ranging from analysis to exposé." Estab. 1970. Circ. 3,200. Pays on publication. Byline given. Buys all rights. Accepts queries by mail, e-mail, fax, phone. Reports in 1 month. Sample copy available on request or on website.
**Nonfiction:** Book excerpts, exposé, interview/profile, opinion. "We like articles from specialists (in planning, politics, economics, corruption, etc.)—particularly if written by professional journalists—but we reject stories that do not read well because of jargon or too little attention to the actual writing of the piece. Our magazine is interesting as well as informative." **Buys 18-25 mss/year.** Query with published clips. Length: 1,000-4,000 words. **Pays $100-600.**
**Tips:** "Queries should be specific about how the prospective story is an issue that affects or will affect the people of New Jersey and its government. The writer's résumé should be included. Stories—unless they are specifically meant to be opinion—should come to a conclusion but avoid a 'holier than thou' or preachy tone. Allegations should be scrupulously substantiated. Our magazine represents a good opportunity for freelancers to acquire great clips. Our publication specializes in longer, more detailed, analytical features. The most frequent mistake made by writers in completing an article for us is too much personal opinion versus reasoned advocacy. We are less interested in opinion than in analysis based on sound reasoning and fact. *New Jersey Reporter* is a well-respected publication, and many of our writers go on to nationally respected newspapers and magazines."

**N $ $ POLICY REVIEW: The Journal of American Citizenship**, The Heritage Foundation, 214 Massachusetts Ave. NE, Washington DC 20002. (202)546-4400. Editor: Adam Meyerson. **Contact:** D.W. Miller, managing editor; Joe Loconte, deputy editor. Bimonthly magazine. "We have been described as 'the most thoughtful, the most influential and the most provocative publication of the intellectual right.' *Policy Review* illuminates the families, communities, voluntary associations, churches and other religious organizations, business enterprises, public and private schools, and local governments that are solving problems more effectively than large, centralized, bureaucratic government." Estab. 1977. Circ. 30,000. Pays on publication. Byline given.
**Nonfiction:** "We are looking especially for articles on private and local institutions that are putting the family back together, cutting crime, improving education and repairing the bankruptcy of government." **Buys 4 mss/year.** Send complete ms. Length: 2,000-6,000 words. **Pays average $500.**

**$ $ THE PROGRESSIVE**, 409 E. Main St., Madison WI 53703-2899. (608)257-4626. Fax: (608)257-3373. E-mail: progressive@peacenet.org. Website: http://www.progressive.org. **Contact:** Matthew Rothschild, editor. **75% freelance written.** Monthly. Estab. 1909. Pays on publication. Publishes ms an average of 6 weeks after acceptance. Byline given. Buys all rights. Reports in 1 month. Sample copy for 9×12 SAE with 4 first-class stamps or sample articles on website. Guidelines for #10 SASE.
    ○➔ Break in through the "On the Line" section.
**Nonfiction:** Primarily interested in articles which interpret, from a progressive point of view, domestic and world affairs. Occasional lighter features. "*The Progressive* is a *political* publication. General-interest material is inappropriate." Query by mail. Length: 500-4,000 words maximum. **Pays $100-500.**
**Tips:** "*The Progressive* is always looking for writers who can describe and explain political, social and economic developments in a way that will interest non-specialists. We like articles that recount specific experiences of real people to illustrate larger points. We're looking for writing that is thoughtful, clear and graceful, conversational and non-academic. Display some familiarity with our magazine, its interests and concerns, its format and style. We want query

letters that fully describe the proposed article without attempting to sell it—and that give an indication of the writer's competence to deal with the subject."

**$ $ $ REASON, Free Minds and Free Markets**, Reason Foundation, 3415 S. Sepulveda Blvd., Suite 400, Los Angeles CA 90034. (310)391-2245. Fax: (310)391-4395. E-mail: editor@reason.com. Editor: Virginia Postrel. **Contact**: Mariel Garza, assistant managing editor. **50% freelance written.** Monthly magazine covering politics, current events, culture, ideas. "*Reason* covers politics, culture and ideas from a dynamic libertarian perspective. It features reported works, opinion pieces, and book reviews." Estab. 1968. Circ. 55,000. **Pays on acceptance.** Byline given. Offers 33% kill fee. Buys first North American serial rights, first rights or all rights. Editorial lead time 2 months. Submit seasonal material 3 months in advance. Reports in 6 weeks on queries; 2 months on mss. Sample copy for $4. Writer's guidelines for #10 SASE.
**Nonfiction:** Book excerpts, essays, exposé, general interest, humor, interview/profile, opinion. No products, personal experience, how-to, travel. **Buys 50-60 mss/year.** Query with published clips. Length: 1,000-5,000 words. **Pays $250-1,000.** Sometimes pays expenses of writers on assignment.
**Tips:** "We prefer queries of no more than one or two pages with specifically developed ideas about a given topic rather than more general areas of interest. Enclosing a few published clips also helps."

**$ $ TOWARD FREEDOM, A progressive perspective on world events**, Toward Freedom Inc., P.O. Box 468, Burlington VT 05422-0468. (802)658-2523. Fax: (802)658-3738. E-mail: tfmag@aol.com. Website: http://www.to wardfreedom.com. **Contact:** Greg Guma, editor. **75% freelance written.** Political magazine published 8 times/year covering politics/culture, focus on Third World, Europe and global trends. "*Toward Freedom* is an internationalist journal with a progressive perspective on political, cultural, human rights and environmental issues around the world. Also covers the United Nations, the post-nationalist movements and U.S. foreign policy." Estab. 1952. Circ. 3,500. Pays on publication. Byline given. Kill fee "rare–negotiable." Buys first North American serial and one-time rights. Editorial lead time 1 month. Accepts queries by mail, e-mail. Reports in 3 months. Sample copy for $3. Writer's guidelines for #10 SASE or on website.
**Nonfiction:** Features, essays, book reviews, interview/profile, opinion, personal experience, travel, foreign, political analysis. Special issues: Women's Visions (March); Global Media (December/January). No how-to, fiction. **Buys 80-100 mss/year.** Query. Length: 700-2,500 words. **Pays up to 10¢/word.**
**Photos:** Send photos with submission, if available. Reviews any prints. Offers $35 maximum/photo. Identification of subjects required. Buys one-time rights.
**Columns/Departments:** *TF* Reports (from foreign correspondents), UN, Beyond Nationalism, Art and Book Reviews, 800-1,200 words. **Buys 20-30 mss/year.** Query. **Pays up to 10¢/word.** Last Word (creative commentary), 900 words. **Buys 8/year.** Query. **Pays $100.**
  The online magazine carries original content not found in the print edition and includes guidelines.
**Tips:** "Except for book or other reviews, writers should have first-hand knowledge of country, political situation, foreign policy, etc., on which they are writing. Occasional cultural 'travelogues' accepted, especially those that would enlighten our readers about a different way of life. Writing must be professional."

**N $ $ $ WORLD POLICY JOURNAL**, World Policy Institute, Suite 413, 65 Fifth Ave., New York NY 10003. (212)229-5808. Fax: (212)229-5579. Fax: (206)815-3445. Website: http://www.worldpolicy.org. Editor: James Chace. **Contact:** Linda Wrigley, managing editor. Estab. 1983. **10% freelance written.** "We are eager to work with new or unpublished writers as well as more established writers." A quarterly journal covering international politics, economics, and security issues, as well as historical and cultural essays, book reviews, profiles, and first-person reporting from regions not covered in the general media. "We hope to bring principle and proportion, as well as a sense of reality and direction to America's discussion of its role in the world." Circ. 5,000. Pays on publication. Publishes ms an average of 3 months after acceptance. Byline given. Buys all rights. Accepts queries by mail, fax. Reports in 3 months. Sample copy for $7.50 and 9×12 SAE with 10 first-class stamps.
**Nonfiction:** Articles that "define policies that reflect the shared needs and interests of all nations of the world." Query. Length: 2,500-4,500 words. Pays variable commission rate.

# PSYCHOLOGY & SELF-IMPROVEMENT

These publications focus on psychological topics, how and why readers can improve their own outlooks, and how to understand people in general. Many General Interest, Men's and Women's publications also publish articles in these areas. Magazines treating spiritual development appear in the Astrology, Metaphysical & New Age section, as well as in Religion, while markets for holistic mind/body healing strategies are listed in Health & Fitness.

**$ $ $ $ PSYCHOLOGY TODAY**, Sussex Publishers, Inc., 49 E. 21st St., 11th Floor, New York NY 10010. (212)260-7210, ext. 134. Fax: (212)260-7445. E-mail: psychtoday@aol.com. **Contact:** Camille Chatterjee, news editor. Bimonthly magazine. "*Psychology Today* explores every aspect of human behavior, from the cultural trends that shape the way we think and feel to the intricacies of modern neuroscience. We're sort of a hybrid of a science magazine, a health magazine and a self-help magazine. While we're read by many psychologists, therapists and social workers, most of our readers are simply intelligent and curious people interested in the psyche and the self." Estab. 1967. Circ. 331,400. Pays on publication. Publishes ms an average of 3 months after acceptance. Byline given. Buys first North American serial rights. Editorial lead time 5 months. Accepts queries by mail. Reports in 1 month. Sample copy for $3.50. Writer's guidelines for #10 SASE.

**Nonfiction:** "Nearly any subject related to psychology is fair game. We value originality, insight and good reporting; we're not intereted in stories or topics that have already been covered *ad nauseum* by other magazines unless you can provide a fresh new twist and much more depth. We're not interested in simple-minded 'pop psychology.' " No fiction, poetry or first-person essays on "How I Conquered Mental Disorder X." **Buys 20-25 mss/year.** Query with published clips. Length: 1,500-4,000 words. **Pays $1,000-2,500.**

**Columns/Departments:** Contact: News Editor. News & Trends (short pieces, mostly written by staff, occasionally by freelancers), 150-300 words; Query with published clips to news editor. **Pays $150-300.**

**N** **$ROSICRUCIAN DIGEST**, Rosicrucian Order, AMORC, 1342 Naglee Ave., San Jose CA 95191-0001. (408)947-3600. Website: http://www.rosicrucian.org. **Contact:** Robin M. Thompson, editor-in-chief. **50% freelance written.** Works with a small number of new/unpublished writers each year. Quarterly magazine (international) emphasizing mysticism, science, philosophy and the arts for educated men and women of all ages seeking alternative answers to life's questions. **Pays on acceptance.** Publishes ms an average of 6 months after acceptance. Buys first serial and second serial (reprint) rights. Byline given. Submit seasonal material 5 months in advance. Reports in 2 months. Free sample copy. Writer's guidelines for #10 SASE.

**Nonfiction:** How to deal with life—and all it brings us—in a positive and constructive way. Informational articles—new ideas and developments in science, the arts, philosophy and thought. Historical sketches, biographies, human interest, psychology, philosophical and inspirational articles. "We are always looking for good articles on the contributions of ancient civilizations to today's civilizations, the environment, ecology, inspirational (non-religious) subjects." No religious, astrological or political material or articles promoting a particular group or system of thought. Buys variable amount of mss/year. Query by mail. Length: 1,000-1,500 words. **Pays 6¢/word.**

**Reprints:** Prefers typed ms with rights for sale noted and information about when and where the article previously appeared, but tearsheet or photocopy acceptable. Pays 50% of amount paid for an original article; 100% "if article is really good and author has rights."

**Photos:** Purchased with accompanying ms. Send prints. Pays $10/8 × 10 b&w glossy print.

**Fillers:** Short inspirational or uplifting (not religious) anecdotes or experiences. **Buys 6/year.** Query. Length: 22-250 words. **Pays 2¢/word.**

**Tips:** "We are looking for well-written articles with a positive, constructive approach to life in these trying times. This seems to be a time of indecision and apathy in many areas, and we are encouraged when we find an article that lets the reader know that he/she can get involved, take positive action, make a change in his/her life. We are also looking for articles about how other cultures outside our own deal with the big questions, problems and changes in life, i.e., the questions of 'Who am I?', 'Where do I fit in?', 'How can I direct my own life and learn how to experience inner peace?', the role of elders in passing on culture to new generations, philosophical aspects of other cultures that can help us grow today."

**$SCIENCE OF MIND MAGAZINE**, 3251 W. Sixth St., P.O. Box 75127, Los Angeles CA 90075-0127. (213)388-2181. Fax: (213)388-1926. E-mail: sdelgado@scienceofmind.com. Website: http://www.scienceofmind.com. Editor: Elaine Sonne. **Contact:** Sylvia Delgado, editorial associate. **30% freelance written.** Monthly magazine that features articles on spirituality, self-help and inspiration. "Our publication centers on oneness of all life and spiritual empowerment through the application of Science of Mind principles." Pays on publication. Publishes ms an average of 5 months after acceptance. Byline given. Buys first North American serial rights. Submit seasonal material 6 months in advance. Accepts queries by mail, e-mail, phone, fax. Reports in 3 months. Writer's guidelines for SASE.

**Nonfiction:** Book excerpts, inspirational, personal experience of Science of Mind, spiritual. **Buys 35-45 mss/year.** Query by mail only with SASE. Length: 750-2,000 words. **Pays $25/printed page.** Pays copies for some features written by readers.

**Photos:** Reviews 35mm transparencies and 5×7 or 8 × 10 b&w prints. Buys one-time rights.

**Poetry:** Inspirational and Science of Mind oriented. "We are not interested in poetry not related to Science of Mind principles." **Buys 10-15 poems/year.** Length: 7-25 lines. Send 3 poems maximum. **Pays $25.**

**Tips:** "We are interested in first person experiences of a spiritual nature having to do with the Science of Mind."

# REGIONAL

Many regional publications rely on staff-written material, but others accept work from freelance writers who live in or know the region. The best regional publication to target with your submissions is usually the one in your hometown, whether it's a city or state magazine or a Sunday supplement in a newspaper. Since you are familiar with the region, it is easier to propose suitable story ideas.

Listed first are general interest magazines slanted toward residents of and visitors to a particular region. Next, regional publications are categorized alphabetically by state, followed by Canada. Publications that report on the business climate of a region are grouped in the regional division of the Business & Finance category. Recreation and travel publications specific to a geographical area are listed in the Travel, Camping & Trailer section. Keep in mind also that many regional publications specialize in specific areas, and are listed according to those sections. Regional publications are not listed if they only accept material from a select group of freelancers in their area or if they did not want to receive the number of queries and manuscripts a national listing would attract. If you know of a regional magazine that is not listed, approach it by asking for writer's guidelines before you send unsolicited material.

## General

**$ $ BLUE RIDGE COUNTRY**, Leisure Publishing, P.O. Box 21535, Roanoke VA 24018-9900. (703)989-6138. Fax: (703)989-7603. E-mail: leisure@roanoke.infi.net. Website: http://www.blueridgecountry.com. **Contact**: Kurt Rheinheimer, editor-in-chief. **75% freelance written.** Bimonthly magazine. "The magazine is designed to celebrate the history, heritage and beauty of the Blue Ridge region. It is aimed at the adult, upscale readers who enjoy living or traveling in the mountain regions of Virginia, North Carolina, West Virginia, Maryland, Kentucky, Tennessee, South Carolina and Georgia." Estab. 1988. Circ. 75,000. Pays on publication. Publishes ms an average of 8 months after acceptance. Byline given. Offers $50 kill fee for commissioned pieces only. Buys first and second serial (reprint) rights. Submit seasonal material 6 months in advance. Query by mail, e-mail, fax. Reports in 2 months. Sample copy for 9×12 SAE with 6 first-class stamps or on website. Writer's guidelines for #10 SASE.
**Nonfiction:** General interest, historical/nostalgic, personal experience, photo feature, travel, history. "Looking for more backroads travel, history and legend/lore pieces." **Buys 25-30 mss/year.** Query with or without published clips or send complete ms. Length: 500-1,800 words. **Pays $50-250 for assigned articles; $25-250 for unsolicited articles.**
**Photos:** Send photos with submission. Prefers transparencies. Offers $10-25/photo and $100 for cover photo. Identification of subjects required. Buys one-time rights.
**Columns/Departments:** Country Roads (shorts on people, events, travel, ecology, history, antiques, books). **Buys 12-24 mss/year.** Query. **Pays $10-40.**
**Tips:** "Freelancers needed for regional departmental shorts and 'macro' issues affecting whole region. Need field reporters from all areas of Blue Ridge region. Also, we need updates on the Blue Ridge Parkway, Appalachian Trail, national forests, ecological issues, preservation movements."

**$ $ GUESTLIFE, Monterey Bay/New Mexico/Houston/Clearwater**, Desert Publications, Inc., 303 N. Indian Canyon Dr., Palm Springs CA 92262. (760)325-2333. Fax: (760)325-7008. E-mail: edit@desert-resorts.com. Website: http://www.guestlife.com. **Contact**: Jaime Cannon, managing editor. **75% freelance written.** Annual prestige hotel room magazine covering history, highlights and activities of the area named (ex. *Monterey Bay GuestLife*). "*GuestLife* focuses on its respective area and is placed in hotel rooms in that area for the affluent vacationer." Estab. 1978. Pays 30 days after publication. Publishes ms an average of 3-9 months after acceptance. Byline given. Offers 25% kill fee. Buys electronic and all rights. Editorial lead time 6 months. Accepts queries by mail, e-mail. Reports in 6 weeks on queries; 6 months on mss. Sample copy for 10×12 SAE and 5 first-class stamps.
**Nonfiction:** Historical/nostalgic, photo feature, travel. **Buys 3 mss/year.** Query with published clips. Length: 300-800 words. **Pays $150-300.**
**Photos:** State availability of photos with submission. Reviews duplicate transparencies. Negotiates payment individually. Captions required. Buys all rights.

**$ $ NORTHWEST TRAVEL**, Northwest Regional Magazines, 1525 12th St., P.O. Box 18000, Florence OR 97439. (541)997-8401. (800)348-8401. Fax: (541)997-1124. E-mail: judy@ohwy.com. Co-editors: Jim Forst, Jason F. Jensen **Contact**: Judy Fleagle, co-editor. **60% freelance written.** Bimonthly magazine. "We like energetic writing about popular activities and destinations in the Pacific Northwest. *Northwest Travel* aims to give readers practical ideas on where to go in the region. Magazine covers Oregon, Washington, Idaho and British Columbia; occasionally Alaska and Western Montana." Estab. 1991. Circ. 50,000. Pays after publication. Publishes ms an average of 8 months after acceptance. Buys first North American serial rights. Submit seasonal material 6 months in advance. Accepts queries by mail, e-mail. Reports in 1 month on queries; 3 months on mss. Sample copy for $4.50. Writer's guidelines for #10 SASE.
• *Northwest Travel* needs more North Idaho stories.
**Nonfiction:** Book excerpts, general interest, historical/nostalgic, interview/profile (rarely), photo feature, travel (only in Northwest region). "No cliché-ridden pieces on places that everyone covers." **Buys 40 mss/year.** Query with or without published clips. Length: 1,250-2,000 words. **Pays $100-350** for feature articles and 2-5 contributor copies.
**Reprints:** Rarely accepts reprints of previously published submissions. Send photocopy of article or short story and information about when and where the article appeared. Pays 60% of amount paid for an original article.
**Photos:** State availability of photos with submission. Uses transparencies (prefers dupes). Captions, model releases

(cover photos), credits and identification of subjects required. Buys one-time rights.

**Columns/Departments:** Restaurant Features, 1,000 words. Pays $125. Worth a Stop (brief items describing places "worth a stop"), 300-350 words. **Buys 25-30 mss/year.** Send complete ms. **Pays $50.** Back Page (photo and text package on a specific activity, season or festival with some technical photo info), 80 words and 1 slide. **Pays $75.**

**Tips:** "Write fresh, lively copy (avoid clichés) and cover exciting travel topics in the region that haven't been covered in other magazines. A story with stunning photos will get serious consideration. The department most open to freelancers is the Worth a Stop department. Take us to fascinating and interesting places we might not otherwise discover."

**$ $ NOW AND THEN, The Appalachian Magazine**, Center for Appalachian Studies and Services, P.O. Box 70556-ETSU, Johnson City TN 37614-0556. (423)439-6173. Fax: (423)439-6340. E-mail: woodsidj@etsu.edu. Website: http://cass.etsu.edu/n&t/guidelin.html. Managing Editor: Nancy Fischman. **Contact:** Jane Harris Woodside, editor-in-chief. **80% freelance written.** Magazine published 3 times/year covering Appalachian region from Southern New York to Northern Mississippi. "*Now & Then* accepts a variety of writing genres: fiction, poetry, nonfiction, essays, interviews, memoirs and book reviews. All submissions must relate to Appalachia and to the issue's specific theme. Our readership is educated and interested in the region." Estab. 1984. Circ. 1,000. Pays on publication. Publishes ms an average of 4 months after acceptance. Byline given. Buys all rights. Editorial lead time 6 months. Query by mail, e-mail, fax, phone. Accepts simultaneous submissions. Reports in 5 months. Sample copy for $5. Writer's guidelines for #10 SASE or on website.

**Nonfiction:** Book excerpts, essays, general interest, historical/nostalgic, humor, interview/profile, opinion, personal experience, photo feature, book reviews of books from and about Appalachia. "We don't consider articles which have nothing to do with Appalachia; articles which blindly accept and employ regional stereotypes (dumb hillbillies, poor and downtrodden hillfolk and miners)." Special issues: Appalachian Museums and Archives (November 1 deadline); Appalachian Accents (language; March 1 deadline); Appalachian Rivers and Valleys (July 1 deadline). Query with published clips. Length: 1,000-2,500 words. **Pays $15-250 for assigned articles; $15-100 for unsolicited articles.** Sometimes pays expenses of writers on assignment.

**Reprints:** Send typed ms with rights for sale noted and information about when and where the article previously appeared. Pays 100% of amount paid for an original article. Typically $15-60.

**Photos:** State availability of photos with submission. Offers no additional payment for photos accepted with ms. Captions and identification of subjects required. Buys one-time rights.

**Fiction:** Adventure, ethnic, experimental, fantasy, historical, humorous, mainstream, slice-of-life vignettes. "Fiction has to relate to Appalachia and to the issue's theme in some way." **Buys 3-4 mss/year.** Send complete ms. Length: 750-2,500 words. **Pays $15-100.**

**Poetry:** Free verse, haiku, light verse, traditional. "No stereotypical work about the region. I want to be surprised and embraced by the language, the ideas, even the form." **Buys 25-30 poems/year.** Submit 5 poems maximum. **Pays $10.**

**Tips:** "Get the Writers' Guidelines and read them carefully. Show in your cover letter that you know what the theme of the upcoming issue is and how your submission fits the theme."

**N ✕ $ ROCKY MOUNTAIN RIDER, The Magazine About Horses, People & the West**, Rocky Mountain Rider Magazine, P.O. Box 1011, Hamilton MT 59840. (406)363-4085. Fax: (406)363-1056. **Contact:** Natalie Riehl, editor. **90% freelance written.** Monthly magazine "aiming to satisfy the interests of a wide range of readers involved in a horse and Western lifestyle. Our readers are authentic Westerners, not dudes. They appreciate the values of honesty, generosity and hard work. We carry informative articles, personality profiles, book excerpts, cowboy poetry and humor." Estab. 1993. Circ. 14,000. Pays on publication. Publishes ms an average of 6 months after acceptance. Byline given. Buys one-time rights. Submit seasonal material 6 months in advance. Accepts simultaneous submissions. Reports in 1 month on queries; 2 months on mss. Sample copy free. Writer's guidelines for #10 SASE.

**Nonfiction:** Book excerpts, essays, general interest, historical/nostalgic, humor, interview/profile, new product, personal experience, photo feature, travel, cowboy poetry. **Buys 100 mss/year.** Send complete ms. Length: 500-2,000 words. **Pays $15-90.**

**Photos:** Send photos with submission. Reviews 3×5 prints. Offers no additional payment for photos accepted with ms or $5/photo. Captions, identification of subjects required. Buys one-time rights.

**Poetry:** Light verse, traditional. **Buys 25 poems/year.** Submit maximum 10 poems. Length: 6-36 lines. **Pays $10.**

**Fillers:** Anecdotes, facts, gags to be illustrated by cartoonist, short humor. Length: 200-750 words. **Pays $15.**

**Tips:** "*RMR* is looking for positive, human interest stories that appeal to an audience of horsepeople, ranchers and folks who love living in the West. Pieces may include profiles of unusual people or animals, history, humor, anecdotes, coverage of regional events and new products. We aren't looking for many 'how to' or training articles, and are not currently looking at any fiction."

**$ $ $ $ SUNSET MAGAZINE**, Sunset Publishing Corp., 80 Willow Rd., Menlo Park CA 94025-3691. (650)321-3600. Fax: (650)327-7537. Website: http://www.sunsetmagazine.com. Editor-in-Chief: Rosalie Muller Wright. **Contact:** P. Fish, senior travel editor; K. Brenzel, senior garden editor. Monthly magazine covering the lifestyle of the Western states. "*Sunset* is a Western lifestyle publication for educated, active consumers. Editorial provides localized information on gardening and travel, food and entertainment, home building and remodeling." Freelance articles should be timely and only about the 13 Western states. Pays on acceptance. Byline given. Accepts queries by mail. Guidelines for freelance travel items for #10 SASE addressed to Editorial Services.

**Nonfiction:** "Travel items account for the vast majority of *Sunset*'s freelance assignments, although we also contract out some short garden items. However, *Sunset* is largely staff-written." Travel in the West. **Buys 50-75 mss/year.** Length: 550-750 words. **Pays $1/word.** Query before submitting.

**Columns/Departments:** Departments open to freelancers are: Building & Crafts, Food, Garden, Travel. *Travel Guide* length: 300-350 words. Direct queries to the specific editorial department.

**Tips:** "Here are some subjects regularly treated in *Sunset*'s stories and Travel Guide items: outdoor recreation (i.e., bike tours, bird-watching spots, walking or driving tours of historic districts); indoor adventures (i.e., new museums and displays, hands-on science programs at aquariums or planetariums, specialty shopping); special events (i.e., festivals that celebrate a region's unique social, cultural, or agricultural heritage). Also looking for great weekend getaways, backroad drives, urban adventures and culinary discoveries such as ethnic dining enclaves. Planning and assigning begins a year before publication date."

**[N] $ $ SYMBOL, Peachtree's Symbol of Southern Lifestyle**, Pasco Publishers, Inc., 120 Interstate N. Pkwy. E., #445, Atlanta GA 30339. (770)956-1207. Fax: (770)988-8976. E-mail: symbolmag@aol.com. Website: http://www.symbolmagazine.com. **Contact:** Jane G. Gaston, managing editor. **20-25% freelance written.** Monthly magazine covering lifestyle in the Southern states. "We embrace the Southern lifestyle and cater to high-end consumers who travel frequently and far, buy second homes, quality furnishings, artwork, jewelry and contribute to their community regularly. Primary readership is women, aged 35 and above, with household incomes of $100,000 and up. Writing should be positive and slanted to the above consumer primarily." Estab. 1998. Circ. 110,000. Pays on publication. Publishes ms an average of 4-6 months after acceptance. Byline given. Buys one-time and electronic rights. Editorial lead time 3 months. Submit seasonal material 4 months in advance. Accepts queries by mail, e-mail, fax. Accepts simultaneous submissions. Reports in 3-4 weeks on queries; 3-4 months on mss. Sample copy for an 8×10 SAE with $3 in stamps or sample articles on website. Writer's guidelines for #10 SASE (will e-mail at no charge).

**Nonfiction:** Essays, general interest, historical/nostalgic, how-to (remodeling, crafts, etc.), interview/profile, personal experience, photo feature, travel, city profile. Publishes a remodeling supplement each March "which may consist of features on specific remodeled homes, blueprints for consideration, new cabinets, countertops, fixtures, etc., plus people in the industry." Does not want to see "anything we can do inhouse (i.e. Atlanta-based pieces)." **Buys 5-10 mss/year.** Query with published clips. Length: 1,000-2,500 words. **Pays $100-350 for assigned articles; $100-250 for unsolicited articles.** Pays contributor copies and other premiums on travel assignments.

**Photos:** State availability of photos with submission. Reviews 4×4 transparencies, 5×7 prints, and slides; all must be color. Offers no additional payment for photos accepted with ms. Identification of subjects required. Buys one-time rights.

**Columns/Departments:** Food/Wine (profiles; no restaurant reviews), 1,200 words; Folks (personality profiles), 1,200 words; Well Being (health and fitness), 1,500 words. **Buys 2-5 mss/year.** Query with published clips. **Pays $85-200.**

**Tips:** "Really know the format and subject matter, follow guidelines, submit manuscripts of real interest."

**[N] [★] VILLAGE PROFILE**, Progressive Publishing, Inc., 936 W. Lake St., Roselle IL 60172. (630)582-8888. Fax: (630)582-8895 or 582-1233. E-mail: profiles@mindspring.com. Website: http://www.villageprofile.com. Managing Editor: Dan Janezick. **Contact:** Juli Bridgers, editor. **90% freelance written.** Annual local community guides covering over 30 states. "We publish community guides and maps for (primarily) chambers of commerce across the U.S. Editorial takes on a factual, yet upbeat, positive view of communities. Writers need to be able to make facts and figures 'friendly,' to present information to be used by residents as well as businesses as guides are used for economic development." Estab. 1988. Publishes 350 projects/year. **Pays on acceptance.** Publishes ms 3 months after acceptance. Byline given. Offers 100% kill fee on completed projects. Buys all rights, electronic rights, and makes work-for-hire assignments. Editorial lead time 2 months. Accepts queries by mail, fax. Sample copy for 9×12 SAE. Writer's guidelines free.

**Nonfiction:** **Buys 200 mss/year** Query with published clips. Length: 1,000-4,000 words. **Pays $200-500.** Sometimes pays expenses of writers on assignment.

**Photos:** State availability of photos. Negotiates payment individually. Identification of subjects required.

**Tips:** "Writers must meet deadlines, know how to present a positive image of a community without going overboard with adjectives and adverbs! Know how to find the info you need if our contact (typically a busy chamber executive) needs your help doing so. Availability to 'cover' a region/area is a plus."

**$ $ $ YANKEE**, Yankee Publishing Inc., P.O. Box 520, Dublin NH 03444-0520. (603)563-8111. Fax: (603)563-8252. E-mail: queries@yankeepub.com. Website: http://www.newengland.com. Editor: Judson D. Hale, Sr. Managing Editor: Tim Clark. **Contact:** Jeanne Wheaton, editorial assistant. **50% freelance written.** Monthly magazine that features articles on New England. "Our mission is to express and perhaps, indirectly, preserve the New England culture—and to do so in an entertaining way. Our audience is national and has one thing in common—they love New England." Estab. 1935. Circ. 700,000. Pays within 30 days of acceptance. Byline given. Offers 33% kill fee. Buys first rights. Submit seasonal material 6 months in advance. Accepts simultaneous submissions. Reports in 2 months on queries. Writer's guidelines for #10 SASE.

**Nonfiction:** Essays, general interest, historical/nostalgic, humor, interview/profile, personal experience. "No 'good old days' pieces, no dialect humor and nothing outside New England!" **Buys 30 mss/year.** Query with published clips and SASE. Length: 250-2,500 words. **Pays $100-1,500.** Pays expenses of writers on assignment.

• Ranked as one of the best market for freelance writers in *Writers Yearbook* magazine's annual "Top 100 Markets," January 1999.

**Photos:** Send photos with submission. Reviews contact sheets and transparencies. Offers $50-150/photo. Identification

of subjects required. Buys one-time rights.
**Columns/Departments:** New England Sampler (short bits on interesting people, anecdotes, historical oddities), 100-400 words, **pays $50-200.** Great New England Cooks (profile recipes), 500 words, **pays $800.** Recipe with a History (family favorites that have a story behind them), 100-200 words plus recipe, **pays $50.** I Remember (nostalgia focused on specific incidents), 400-500 words, **pays $200.** Travel, 25-200 words, query first, **pays $25-250. Buys 80 mss/year.** Query with published clips and SASE.
**Fiction:** Edie Clark, fiction editor. "We publish high-quality literary fiction that explores human issues and concerns in a specific place—New England." Publishes novel excerpts. **Buys 6 mss/year.** Send complete ms. Length: 500-2,500 words. **Pays $1,000.**
  • Ranked as one of the best markets for fiction writers in *Writer's Digest* magazine's "Fiction 50," June 1999.
**Poetry:** Jean Burden, poetry editor. "We don't choose poetry by type. We look for the best. No inspirational, holiday-oriented, epic, limericks, etc." **Buys 40 poems/year.** Submit maximum 3 poems. Length: 2-20 lines. **Pays $50.**
**Tips:** "Submit lots of ideas. Don't censor yourself—let *us* decide whether an idea is good or bad. We might surprise you. Remember we've been publishing for 60 years, so chances are we've already done every 'classic' New England subject. Try to surprise us—it isn't easy. These departments are most open to freelancers: New England Sampler; I Remember; Recipe with a History. Study the ones we publish—the format should be apparent. It is to your advantage to read several issues of the magazine before sending us a query or a manuscript."

# Alabama

**$ $ ALABAMA HERITAGE**, University of Alabama, Box 870342, Tuscaloosa AL 35487-0342. (205)348-7467. Fax: (205)348-7434. **Contact:** Suzanne Wolfe, editor. **50% freelance written.** "*Alabama Heritage* is a nonprofit historical quarterly published by the University of Alabama and the University of Alabama at Birmingham for the intelligent lay reader. We are interested in lively, well-written and thoroughly researched articles on Alabama/Southern history and culture. Readability and accuracy are essential." Estab. 1986. Pays on publication. Byline given. Buys first rights and second serial (reprint) rights. Reports in 1 month. Sample copy for $6. Writer's guidelines for #10 SASE.
**Nonfiction:** Historical. "We do not want fiction, poetry, book reviews, articles on current events or living artists and personal/family reminiscences." **Buys 10 mss/year.** Query. Length: 1,500-5,000 words. **Pays $100 minimum.** Also sends 10 copies to each author plus 1-year subscription.
**Photos:** Reviews contact sheets. Identification of subjects required. Buys one-time rights.
**Tips:** "Authors need to remember that we regard history as a fascinating subject, not as a dry recounting of dates and facts. Articles that are lively and engaging, in addition to being well researched, will find interested readers among our editors. No term papers, please. All areas are open to freelance writers. Best approach is a written query."

**$ ALABAMA LIVING**, Alabama Rural Electric Assn., P.O. Box 244014, Montgomery AL 36124. (334)215-2732. Fax: (334)215-2733. E-mail: area@mindspring.com. Website: http://www.areapower.com. **Contact:** Darryl Gates, editor. **10% freelance written.** Monthly magazine covering rural electric consumers. "Our magazine is an editorially balanced, informational and educational service to members of rural electric cooperatives. Our mix regularly includes Alabama history, nostalgia, gardening, outdoor and consumer pieces." Estab. 1948. Circ. 330,000. Pays on publication. Publishes ms an average of 3 months after acceptance. Byline given. Publication is not copyrighted. Buys second serial (reprint) rights. Editorial lead time 3 months. Submit seasonal material 4 months in advance. Accepts simultaneous submissions. Reports in 1 month on queries. Sample copy free or on website.
  O⚡ "The best way to break into *Alabama Living* is to give us a bit of history or nostalgia about Alabama or the Southeast."
**Nonfiction:** Historical/nostalgic, rural-oriented. Special issues: Gardening (March); Holiday Recipes (December). **Buys 6 mss/year.** Send complete ms (copy). Length: 300-750 words. **Pays $100 minimum for assigned articles; $50 minimum for unsolicited articles.**
**Reprints:** Send typed ms with rights for sale noted. **Pays $50.**

**$ $ BIRMINGHAM WEEKLY**, Birmingham Weekly Publishing Co., Inc., 2101 Magnolia Ave. S., Birmingham AL 35205. (205)322-2426. E-mail: thulen@bhamweekly.com. **Contact:** Tara Hulen, editor. **40% freelance written.** "We are an alternative newsweekly; alternative in the sense that we're an alternative to daily papers and TV news. We are edgy, hip, well written but based in solid journalism. Our audience is 18-54, educated with disposable income and an irreverant but intelligent point of view." Estab. 1997. Circ. 22,000. Pays on publication. Publishes ms an average of 2 weeks after acceptance. Byline given. Editorial lead time 3 weeks. Submit seasonal material 2 months in advance. Accepts queries by mail, e-mail. Accepts simultaneous submissions. Reports in 2 weeks on queries. Sample copy free.
**Nonfiction:** Essays, exposé, general interest, historical/nostalgic, humor, interview/profile. "No opinion columns, i.e., op-ed stuff. We are strictly interested in stories that have a Birmingham connection, except in reviews, where the requirement is for readers to be able to buy the CD or book or see the film in Birmingham." Query with or without published clips. Length: 100-1,000 words. **Pays 10¢/word.** Sometimes pays expenses of writers on assignment.
**Columns/Departments:** Sound Advice (CD reviews), 100 words; Between the Covers (book reviews), 300 words. Query with or without published clips. **Pays 10¢/word.**

**N** **$ $** **BLACK & WHITE, Birmingham's City Paper**, Black & White, Inc., 1312 20th St. S, Birmingham AL 35205. (205)933-0460. E-mail: blkwhite@aol.com. Managing Editor: Kerry Echols. **Contact:** Alison Nichols, editor. **25% freelance written.** Free biweekly city paper covering arts, entertainment news, film, music in Birmingham and anything that strikes our fancy. Audience covers the spectrum. Estab. 1992. Circ. 29,000. Pays 21 days after publication. Publishes ms an average of 1 month after acceptance. Byline given. Offers $50-100 kill fee. Buys one-time rights and local rights in market area. Editorial lead time 3 weeks. Submit seasonal material 1 month in advance. Accepts simultaneous submissions. Reports in 2 weeks on queries; 2 months on mss. Sample copy for $10×12$ with 4 first-class stamps. Writer's guidelines for #10 SASE.

**Nonfiction:** Alison Nichols, editor. Essays, general interest, interview/profile, opinion, photo feature, travel. Special issues: Music; restaurants. No fiction, poetry. **Buys 10 mss/year.** Query. Length: 200-8,000 words. **Pays $50-600.** Sometimes pays expenses of writers on assignment.

**Reprints:** Accepts previously published submissions.

**Photos:** State availability of photos with submission. Reviews contact sheets. Negotiates payment individually. Identification of subjects required. Buys one-time rights.

**Columns/Departments:** Kerry Echols, managing editor. Record/CD reviews (music), 200 words; In Print (book reviews), 600-800 words; Cinema (film revision), 400-1,000 words. **Buys 100 mss/year.** Query with published clips. **Pays $50-125.**

**Fillers:** Kerry Echols, managing editor. Cartoons. **Buys 90/year. Pays $10-20.**

**Tips:** "Send a simple, short e-mail pitch/query and/or sample of your work."

## Alaska

**★** **$ $ $** **ALASKA, The Magazine of Life on the Last Frontier**, 619 E. Ship Creek Ave., Suite 329, Anchorage AK 99501. (907)272-6070. Fax: (907)258-5360. E-mail: alaskaed@pobox.alas/ca.net. General Manager: David C. Foster. **Contact:** Donna Rae Thompson, editorial assistant. **70% freelance written.** Eager to work with new/unpublished writers. Monthly magazine covering topics "uniquely Alaskan." Estab. 1935. Circ. 205,000. Pays on publication. Publishes ms an average of 6 months after acceptance. Byline given. Buys first or one-time rights. Submit seasonal material 1 year in advance. Reports in 2 months. Sample copy for $3 and $9×12$ SAE with 7 first-class stamps. Writer's guidelines for #10 SASE.

**Nonfiction:** Historical/nostalgic, adventure, how-to (on anything Alaskan), outdoor recreation (including hunting, fishing), humor, interview/profile, personal experience, photo feature. Also travel articles and Alaska destination stories. No fiction or poetry. **Buys 40 mss/year.** Query by mail. Length: 100-2,500 words. **Pays $100-1,250.**

**Photos:** Send photos. Reviews 35mm or larger transparencies. Captions and identification of subjects required.

**Tips:** "We're looking for top-notch writing—original, well-researched, lively. Subjects must be distinctly Alaskan. A story on a mall in Alaska, for example, won't work for us; every state has malls. If you've got a story about a Juneau mall run by someone who is also a bush pilot and part-time trapper, maybe we'd be interested. The point is *Alaska* stories need to be vivid, focused and unique. Alaska is like nowhere else—we need our stories to be the same way."

## Arizona

**N** **$ $** **ARIZONA FOOTHILLS MAGAZINE**, Media That Deelivers, Inc. P.O. Box 93014, Phoenix AZ 85070-3014. (602)460-5203. Fax: (602)460-5776. E-mail: reneedee@azfoothillsmag.com. Website: http://www.azfoothillsmagazine.com. Editor: Renee Dee. **Contact:** Jeffrey James, departments editor. **50% freelance written.** Monthly magazine covering lifestyle. Estab. 1996. Circ. 40,000. Pays on publication. Publishes ms an average of 2-6 months after acceptance. Byline given. Buys first North American serial rights. Editorial lead time 2-6 months. Submit seasonal material 3-4 months in advance. Reports in 1 month. Sample copy and writer's guidelines for #10 SASE.

**Nonfiction:** Renee Dee, publisher. General interest, how-to (decorate, plant, outdoor recreation), humor, inspirational, interview/profile, new product, personal experience, photo feature, travel, fashion, decor, arts. **Buys 30 mss/year.** Query with published clips. Length: 900-2,000 words. **Pays 15¢/word for assigned articles; 10¢/word for unsolicited articles.** Sometimes pays in ads, contributor copies. Sometimes pays expenses of writers on assignment (limit agreed upon in advance).

**Reprints:** Accepts previously published material.

**Photos:** Send photos with submission. Reviews contact sheets and transparencies. Negotiates payment individually. Captions, model releases and identification of subjects required. Buys one-time rights.

**Columns/Departments:** Road-Tested Travel (in-state AZ travel); Great Escapes (outside AZ); Live Well (health and fitness); Your Money (finance). **Buys 21 mss/year.** Query with published clips. **Pays 10¢/word.**

**Tips:** "We prefer stories that appeal to my audience written with an upbeat, contemporary approach and reader service in mind."

**$ $** **ARIZONA HIGHWAYS**, 2039 W. Lewis Ave., Phoenix AZ 85009-9988. (602)271-5900. Fax: (602)254-4505. Website: http://www.arizonahighways.com. **Contact:** Rebecca Mong, senior editor. **100% freelance written.**

State-owned magazine designed to help attract tourists into and through Arizona. Estab. 1925. Circ. 425,000. **Pays on acceptance.** Buys first serial rights. Reports in up to 1 month. Writer's guidelines for SASE.

**O–** Break in with "a concise query written with flair, backed by impressive clips that relate to the kind of writing that appears in *Arizona Highways.*"

**Nonfiction:** Feature subjects include narratives and exposition dealing with history, anthropology, nature, wildlife, armchair travel, out of the way places, small towns, Old West history, Indian arts and crafts, travel, etc. Travel articles are experience-based. All must be oriented toward Arizona. **Buys 6 mss/issue.** Query with a lead paragraph and brief outline of story. "We deal with professionals only, so include list of current credits." Length: 600-2,000 words. **Pays 35-55¢/word.** Pays expenses of writers on assignment.

**Photos:** "We use transparencies of medium format, 4×5, and 35mm when appropriate to the subject matter, or they display exceptional quality or content. We prefer 35mm at 100 ISO or slower. Each transparency *must* be accompanied by information attached to each photograph: where, when, what. No photography will be reviewed by the editors unless the photographer's name appears on *each* and *every* transparency." Pays $100-600 for "selected" transparencies. Buys one-time rights.

**Columns/Departments:** Departments include Focus on Nature, Along the Way, Back Road Adventure, Great Weekends, Hike of the Month and Arizona Humor. "Back Road and Hikes also must be experience-based."

**Tips:** "Writing must be of professional quality, warm, sincere, in-depth, well-peopled and accurate. Avoid themes that describe first trips to Arizona, the Grand Canyon, the desert, Colorado River running, etc. Emphasis is to be on Arizona adventure and romance as well as flora and fauna, when appropriate, and themes that can be photographed. Double check your manuscript for accuracy. Our typical reader is a 50-something person with the time, the inclination and the means to travel."

**N $ CAREFREE ENTERPRISE MAGAZINE, Arizona's Second-Oldest Magazine**, Carefree Enterprise Magazine, Inc., P.O. Box 1145, Carefree AZ 85377. (602)488-3098. E-mail: cfmagazine@aol.com. Website: http://www.carefreeenterprise.com. Editor: Fran Barbano. **Contact:** Susan Smyth, assistant editor. **50% freelance written.** Magazine published 11 times year. "CEM is a good news publication. We dwell on the positive, uplifting, and inspiring influences of life. We promote our areas and people. (We have readers across the country and overseas.)" Estab. 1963. Circ. 3,200. Pays within 3 months after publication. Publishes ms up to 1 year after acceptance. Byline given. Buys first North American serial, first, one-time and second serial rights. Editorial lead time 3 months. Submit seasonal material 6 months in advance. Accepts queries by mail, e-mail. Reports in 4 months. Sample copy for $2 with 12×15 SAE with $1.93 postage or $4, includes postage. Writer's guidelines for #10 SASE.

**Nonfiction:** Book excerpts, general interest, historical/nostalgic, humor, inspirational, interview/profile, personal experience, photo feature, travel, health, alternative medicine. "Nothing negative or controversial." **Buys 50 mss/year.** Query with published clips or send complete ms. Length: 800-3,000 words. **Pays $50 for assigned articles; $5-50 for unsolicited articles.**

**Reprints:** Accepts previously published submissions.

**Photos:** State availability of photos with submission or send photos with submission. Reviews transparencies and prints (up to 8×10). Offers $5/photo. Captions, model releases and identification of subjects required. Buys one-time rights.

**Columns/Departments:** Stephanie Bradley, assistant editor. Health, new column (no hot topics—general interest), 300-600 words; golf (profile a course or pro), 300-500 words. **Buys 18 mss/year.** Query with published clips or send complete ms. **Pays $20-35.**

**Fiction:** General interest, historical, inspirational, humorous. **Pays up to $50 for feature.** Serial pays up to $50 for each part.

**Poetry:** Avant garde, free verse, haiku, light verse, traditional. "Nothing negative, controversial or unacceptable to families." **Buys 4-12 poems/year.** Submit maximum 3 poems. **Pays $5-25.**

**Fillers:** Anecdotes, facts, short humor. **Buys 12-50/year.** Length: 100-500 words. **Pays $15-35.**

**Tips:** "We are particularly easy to work with. New and established writers should be familiar with our publication and audience (upscale, affluent, world-travelers, multiple home-owners). Our youngest columnist is a 14-year-old blind girl who writes from a teen's point of view and often touches on blindness, and how others interact with handicapped individuals. Our oldest regular columnist is 90 years old and writes on desert flora & fauna. We are open and receptive to any/all good news, upbeat, family-oriented material. We could use more humor, inspiration, travel (regional and worldwide) and positive solutions to everyday challenges. We like to feature profiles of outstanding people (no politics) who are role model material."

**N $ $ $ PHOENIX**, Cities West Publishing, Inc., 5555 N. Seventh Ave., #B-200, Phoenix AZ 85013-1755. (602)207-3750. Fax: (602)207-3777. **Contact:** Robert Stieve, managing editor. **70% freelance written.** Monthly magazine covering regional issues, personalities, events, customs and history of the Southwest, state of Arizona and metro Phoenix. Estab. 1966. Circ. 50,000. Pays on publication. Publishes ms an average of 5 months after acceptance. Byline given. Offers 10% kill fee. Buys first North American serial rights and one-time rights. Submit seasonal material 6 months in advance. Accepts simultaneous submissions. Reports in 2 months. Sample copy for $3 and 9×12 SAE with 5 first-class stamps. Writer's guidelines for #10 SASE.

**Nonfiction:** Book excerpts, essays, investigative, general interest, historical/nostalgic, how-to, humor, inspirational, interview/profile, opinion, personal experience, photo feature, religious, technical, travel. "No material dealing with travel outside the region or other subjects that don't have an effect on the area." **Buys 50 mss/year.** Query with published clips. Length: 5,000 words. **Pays $750-1,500.** Sometimes pays expenses of writers on assignment.

**Reprints:** Send tearsheet or photocopy of article and/or typed ms with rights for sale noted and information about when and where the article previously appeared. Pays 50% of their fee for an original article.
**Photos:** Send photos with submissions. Reviews contact sheets, negatives, transparencies, prints. Offers $25-100/photo. Captions, model releases and identification of subjects required. Buys one-time rights.
**Fiction:** Query with published clips.
**Fillers: Buys 6/year.** Length: 1,000 words. **Pays $400.**
**Tips:** "Our audience is well-educated, upper middle-class Phoenicians. Articles should be of local or regional interest with vivid descriptions that put the reader in the story and present new information or a new way of looking at things. We are not afraid of opinion."

**[N] SCOTTSDALE LIFE**, The City Magazine, CitiesWest, 4041 N. Central, #A-100, Phoenix AZ 85012. (602)234-0840. Fax: (602)277-7857. E-mail: sdalelife@aol.com. **Contact:** Karlin McCarthy, editor. **50% freelance written.** Bimonthly magazine covering city and lifestyle, fashion, entertaining, people, business, society, dining. Estab. 1998. Circ. 40,000. Pays on publication. Byline given. Offers 10% kill fee. Buys all rights and electronic rights. Editorial lead time 2 months. Submit seasonal material 4 months in advance. Accepts queries by mail, e-mail. Reports in 1 month on queries. Sample copy free.
**Nonfiction:** Essays, expose, general interest, historical/nostalgic, how-to, humor, inspirational, interview/profile, new product, personal experience, photo feature, travel—all relating to the Arizona reader. Special issues: Real Estate, Beauty & Health, Art, Golf, Lifestyle. **Buys 20 mss/year** Query with or without published clips. Length: 1,000-2,000 words. **Pay varies.**
**Photos:** State availability of photos with submission. Reviews transparencies, prints. Negotiates payment individually. Captions, model releases, identification of subjects required. Buys all rights.
**Columns/Departments:** City (briefs, mini-profiles); Artful Diversions (gallery reviews), both 300-500 words; Good Taste (dining reviews), 700 words. **Buys 50 mss/year.** Query with published clips. **Pay varies.**
**Fiction:** Adventure, historical, humorous, novel excerpts, lsice-of-life vignettes, Western. **Buys 2 mss/year.** Query with published clips. Length: 500-1,000 words. **Pay varies.**
**Poetry:** Cowboy poetry. **Buys 2-5 poems/year.**
**Tips:** "No idea is a bad idea. Do not fax or phone unless you have written first. Look for the local angle or a way to make the idea relevant to the Phoenix/Scottsdale reader. Suggest photo possibilities."

**$ $ TUCSON LIFESTYLE**, Citizen Publishing Company of Wisconsin, Inc., dba Old Pueblo Press, Suite 12, 7000 E. Tanque Verde Rd., Tucson AZ 85715-5318. (520)721-2929. Fax: (520)721-8665. E-mail: tucsonlife@aol.com. **Contact:** Scott Barker, executive editor. **90% freelance written.** Prefers to work with published/established writers. Monthly magazine covering Tucson-related events and topics. Estab. 1982. Circ. 27,000. **Pays on acceptance.** Publishes ms an average of 6 months after acceptance. Byline given. Buys first Arizona rights. Submit seasonal material 1 year in advance. Accepts queries by mail, e-mail, fax. Reports in 2 months on queries; 3 months on mss. Sample copy for $2.95 plus $3 postage. Writer's guidelines free.
**Nonfiction:** All stories need a Tucson angle. Historical/nostalgic, humor, interview/profile, personal experience, travel, local stories. "We do not accept *anything* that does not pertain to Tucson or Arizona." **Buys 20 mss/year. Pays $50-500.** Sometimes pays expenses of writers on assignment.
**Photos:** Reviews contact sheets, 2¼ × 2¼ transparencies and 5 × 7 prints. Query about electronic formats. Offers $25-100/photo. Identification of subjects required. Buys one-time rights.
**Columns/Departments:** In Business (articles on Tucson businesses and business people); Lifestylers (profiles of interesting Tucsonans); Travel (Southwest, Baja and Mexico). Query. **Pays $100-200.**
**Tips:** Features are most open to freelancers. "Style is not of paramount importance; good, clean copy with interesting lead is a must."

# California

**[N] $ ANGELENO, The Toast of Los Angeles**, 5670 Wilshire Blvd., Suite 700, Los Angeles CA 90036. (312)787-4600. Fax: (312)787-4628. **50% freelance written.** Bimonthly luxury lifestyle magazine. "We cover the good things in life—fashion, fine dining, home design, the arts—from a sophisticated, cosmopolitan, well-to-do perspective." Estab. 1999. Circ. 50,000. Pays 2 months after receipt of invoice. Byline given. Offers 50% kill fee. Buys first and all rights in this market. Editorial lead time 6 months. Submit seasonal material 6 months in advance. Reports in 1 month. Sample copy $7.15 for current issue; $8.20 for back issue. Writer's guidelines for #10 SASE.
**Nonfiction:** General interest, how-to (culinary, home design), interview/profile, photo feature (occasional), travel. No fiction; *no unsolicited mss.* Query with published clips only. Length: 500-4,500 words. Pays expenses of writers on assignment.
**Photos:** State availability of photos with submission. Reviews transparencies and prints. Buys one-time first rights.

**$ $ BRNTWD MAGAZINE**, PTL Productions, 2118 Wilshire Blvd., #1060, Santa Monica CA 90403. (310)390-0251. Fax: (310)390-0261. E-mail: brntwdmag@aol.com. **Contact:** Dylan Nugent, editor. **100% freelance written.** Quarterly magazine covering entertainment, business, lifestyles, reviews. "Wanting in-depth interviews with top entertainers, politicians and similar individuals. Also travel, sports, adventure." Estab. 1995. Circ. 63,000. Pays on publication. Byline given. Editorial lead time 2-3 months. Submit seasonal material 3 months in advance. Accepts simultaneous submissions. Sample copy for $2. Writer's guidelines not available.

**Nonfiction:** Book excerpts, exposé, general interest, historical/nostalgic, humor, interview/profile, new product, opinion, personal experience, photo feature, travel. **Buys 80 mss/year.** Query with published clips. Length: 1,000-2,500 words. **Pays 10-15¢/word.**

**Photos:** State availability of photos with submission. Reviews contact sheets, negatives, transparencies, prints. Offers no additional payment for photos accepted with ms. Captions and identification of subjects required.

**Columns/Departments:** Reviews (film/books/theater/museum), 100-500 words; Sports (Southern California angle), 200-600 words. **Buys 20 mss/year.** Query with published clips or send complete ms. **Pays 10-15¢/word.**

**Tips:** "Los Angeles-based writers preferred for most articles."

**N** **$ $ L.A. WEEKLY**, Stern Publishing, 6715 Sunset Blvd., Los Angeles CA 90020. (323)465-9909. Fax: (323)465-3220. Website: http://www.laweekly.com. Editor: Sue Horton. Managing Editor: Kateri Butler. **Contact:** Janet Duckworth, features editor; Tom Christie, arts editor; Charles Rappleye, news editor. **40% freelance written.** Weekly newspaper. "*L.A. Weekly* provides a fresh, alternative look at Los Angeles. We have arts coverage, news analysis and investigative reporting and a comprehensive calendar section." Estab. 1978. Circ. 220,000. Pays on publication. Byline given. Offers 33% kill fee. Buys first North American serial and electronic rights. Accepts queries by mail, e-mail, fax. Reports in 1 month on queries; 4 months on mss. Sample copy on website.

**Nonfiction:** Essays, exposé, interview/profile, personal experience. "No fashion, health, religion, food, fiction or poetry. We buy hundreds of assigned articles from freelancers but very few unsolicited manuscripts." Query with published clips. **Pays 34¢/word.**

**Photos:** State availability of photos with submission.

**Columns/Departments:** First Person (essays drawn from personal experiences), 1,400 words; Real Gone (travel column), 800 words. Query with published clips. **Pays 34¢/word basic rate.**

**$ $ $ ORANGE COAST MAGAZINE, The Magazine of Orange County**, Orange Coast Kommunications Inc., 3701 Birch St., Suite 100, Newport Beach CA 92660-2618. (949)862-1133. Fax: (949)862-0133. E-mail: ocmag@aol.com. Website: http://www.orangecoast.com. **Contact:** Patrick Mott, editor. **95% freelance written.** Monthly magazine "designed to inform and enlighten the educated, upscale residents of Orange County, California; highly graphic and well researched." Estab. 1974. Circ. 40,000. **Pays on acceptance.** Publishes ms an average of 4 months after acceptance. Byline given. Offers 20% kill fee. Buys one-time rights. Submit seasonal material at least 6 months in advance. Accepts queries by mail, e-mail, fax. Accepts simultaneous submissions. Reports in 2 months. Sample copy for $2.95 and 10×12 SAE with 8 first-class stamps. Writer's guidelines for SASE.

   **O—** Break in with Short Cuts (topical briefs of about 200 words), pays $50; Close Up (short 600 word profiles of Orange County people), pays $200.

**Nonfiction:** Exposé (Orange County government, politics, business, crime), general interest (with Orange County focus); historical/nostalgic, guides to activities and services, interview/profile (prominent Orange County citizens), local sports, travel. Special issues: Health and Fitness (January); Dining and Entertainment (March); Home and Garden (June); Resort Guide (November); Holiday (December). **Buys 100 mss/year.** Query or send complete ms. Absolutely no phone queries. Length: 2,000-3,000 words. **Pays $400-800.**

   ● Ranked as one of the best markets for freelance writers in *Writer's Yearbook* magazine's annual "Top 100 Markets," January 1999.

**Reprints:** Send tearsheet or photocopy of article or typed ms with rights for sale noted and information about when and where the article previously appeared.

**Columns/Departments:** Most departments are not open to freelancers. **Buys 200 mss/year.** Query or send complete ms. Length: 1,000-2,000 words. **Pays $200 maximum.**

**Fiction:** Buys only under rare circumstances. Send complete ms. Length: 1,000-5,000 words. **Pays $250.**

**Tips:** "Most features are assigned to writers we've worked with before. Don't try to sell us 'generic' journalism. *Orange Coast* prefers articles with specific and unusual angles focused on Orange County. A lot of freelance writers ignore our Orange County focus. We get far too many generalized manuscripts."

**$ $ ORANGE COUNTY WOMAN**, Orange Coast Publishing, 3701 Birch, Suite 100, Newport Beach CA 92660. (949)862-1133. Fax: (949)862-0133. E-mail: ocmag@aol.com. Website: http://www.orangecoast.com. **Contact:** Janine Robinson, editor. **90% freelance written.** "*Orange County Woman* is published monthly for the educated and affluent woman of Orange County, California." Estab. 1997. Circ. 65,000. **Pays on acceptance.** Publishes ms an average of 2 months after acceptance. Byline given. Offers 20% kill fee. Buys first North American serial and electronic rights. Editorial lead time 2 months. Submit seasonal material 4 months in advance. Accepts queries by mail, e-mail, fax. Accepts simultaneous submissions. Sample copy and writer's guidelines for SASE.

**Nonfiction:** Essays, exposé, general interest, historical/nostalgic, how-to, humor, inspirational, interview/profile, new product, personal experience, photo feature, travel. Query with published clips or send complete ms and SASE. Length: 100-1,500 words. **Pays $50-300.**

**Reprints:** Send information about when and where the article previously appeared.

**Photos:** State availability of photos with submission or send photos with submission. Reviews contact sheets, negatives, transparencies, prints. Negotiates payment individually. Captions, model releases and identification of subjects required. Buys one-time rights.

**Tips:** "We are looking for profiles or trends related to women in Orange County—both for mothers and professionals. Read previous issues to gauge the range of story ideas and how they were handled. Write about real women in real situations; let their stories crystallize the broader issues. Remember that you are writing for an audience that generally is literate, affluent and sophisticated, but avoid dry intellectual discourse. Our readers are busy women."

**N $ PALO ALTO WEEKLY**, Embarcadero Publishing Co., 703 High St., P.O. Box 1610, Palo Alto CA 94302. (415)326-8210. Fax: (415)326-3928. Website: http://www.paweekly.com/paw/home.html. Editor: Brian Aronstam. **Contact:** Kate Manning, assistant to the editor. **5% freelance written.** Semiweekly tabloid focusing on local issues and local sources. Estab. 1979. Circ. 48,000. Pays on publication. Publishes ms an average of 1 month after acceptance. Byline given. Offers 50% kill fee. Buys first rights. Submit seasonal material 2 months in advance. Reports in 2 weeks. Sample copy for 9×12 SAE with 2 first-class stamps.

• *Palo Alto Weekly* covers sports and has expanded its arts and entertainment coverage. It is still looking for stories in Palo Alto/Stanford area or features on people from the area.

**Nonfiction:** General interest, historical/nostalgic, interview/profile, photo feature. Special issues: Together (weddings—mid February); Interiors (May, October). Nothing that is not local; no travel. **Buys 25 mss/year.** Query by mail with published clips. Length: 700-1,000 words. **Pays $35-60.**

**Reprints:** Accepts previously published submissions. Payment is negotiable.

**Photos:** Send photos with submission. Reviews contact sheets and 5×7 prints. Offers $10 minimum/photo. Captions, model releases and identification of subjects required. Buys one-time rights.

**Tips:** "Writers have the best chance if they live within circulation area and know publication and area well. DON'T send generic, broad-based pieces. The most open sections are food, interiors and sports. Longer 'cover story' submissions may be accepted. Keep it LOCAL."

**$ $ SACRAMENTO MAGAZINE**, 4471 D St., Sacramento CA 95819. Fax: (916)452-6061. Managing Editor: Darlena Belushin McKay. **Contact:** Krista Minard, editor. **100% freelance written.** Works with a small number of new/unpublished writers each year. Monthly magazine with a strong local angle on politics, local issues, human interest and consumer items for readers in the middle to high income brackets. Estab. 1975. Circ. 19,610. Pays on publication. Publishes ms 3 months after acceptance. Rights vary; generally buys first North American serial rights and electronic rights, rarely second serial (reprint) rights. Reports in 2 months. Sample copy for $4.50. Writer's guidelines for #10 SASE.

O➔ Break in with submissions to City Lights.

**Nonfiction:** Local issues vital to Sacramento quality of life. **Buys 5 unsolicited feature mss/year.** Query first in writing ("no e-mail, fax or phone queries will be answered"). Length: 1,500-3,000 words, depending on author, subject matter and treatment. **Pays minimum $250.** Sometimes pays expenses of writers on assignment.

**Photos:** Send photos. Payment varies depending on photographer, subject matter and treatment. Captions (including IDs, location and date) required. Buys one-time rights.

**Columns/Departments:** Business, home and garden, media, parenting, first person essays, regional travel, gourmet, profile, sports, city arts (1,000-1,800 words); City Lights (250-300 words). **Pays $50-400.**

**N $ $ SACRAMENTO NEWS & REVIEW**, Chico Community Publishing, 1015 20th St., Sacramento CA 95814. (916)498-1234. Fax: (916)498-7920. E-mail: melindaw@newsreview.com. Website: http://www.newsreview.com. **Contact:** Melinda Welsh, executive editor. **25% freelance written.** News and entertainment published weekly. "We are an alternative news and entertainment weekly. We maintain a high literary standard for submissions; unique or alternative slant. Publication aimed at a young, intellectual audience; submissions should have an edge and strong voice." Estab. 1989. Circ. 90,000. Pays on publication. Publishes ms an average of 1-2 months after acceptance. Byline given. Offers 10% kill fee. Buys first rights. Editorial lead time 1-2 months. Submit seasonal material 2 months in advance. Accepts queries by mail, e-mail, fax. Accepts simultaneous submissions. Reports in 1 month on queries; 2 months on mss. Sample copy for 50¢. Writer's guidelines for #10 SASE.

**Nonfiction:** Essays, exposé, general interest, humor, interview/profile, personal experience. Publishes holiday gift guides (November/December). Does not want to see travel, product stories, business profile. **Buys 6-10 mss/year.** Query with published clips. Length: 750-2,800 words. **Pays $40-300.** Sometimes pays expenses of writers on assignment.

**Photos:** State availability of photos with submission. Reviews 8×10 prints. Negotiates payment individually. Identification of subjects required. Buys one-time rights.

**Columns/Departments:** In the Mix (CD/TV/book reviews), 150-750 words. **Buys 10-15 mss/year.** Query with published clips. **Pays $10-300.**

**$ $ $ $ SAN FRANCISCO, Focus on the Bay Area**, 243 Vallejo St., San Francisco CA 94111. (415)398-2800. Fax: (415)398-6777. E-mail: melanie@sanfran.com. Website: http://www.sanfran.com. **Contact:** Melanie Haiken, managing editor. **80% freelance written.** Prefers to work with published/established writers. Monthly city/regional magazine. Estab. 1968. Circ. 180,000. Pays on publication. Publishes ms an average of 2 months after acceptance. Byline given. Offers 25% kill fee. Submit seasonal material 5 months in advance. Reports in 2 months. Sample copy for $2.95. Writer's guidelines for SASE.

• Ranked as one of the best markets for freelance writers in *Writer's Yearbook* magazine's annual "Top 100 Markets," January 1999.

**Nonfiction:** Exposé, interview/profile, the arts, politics, public issues, sports, consumer affairs and travel. All stories should relate in some way to the San Francisco Bay Area (travel excepted). Query with published clips. Length: 400-4,000 words. **Pays $100-2,000** plus some expenses.

**N ☆ $ $ $ SAN JOSE, The Magazine for Silicon Valley**, Renaissance Publications, Inc., 4 N. Second St., Suite 550, San Jose CA 95113. Fax: (408)975-9900. E-mail: dave@sanjosemagazine.com. Website: http://www.sanjosemagazine.com. Editor: Gilbert Sangari. **Contact:** Dave Clarke, managing editor. **80% freelance written.** Bimonthly magazine. "As the lifestyle magazine for those living at center of the technological revolution, we cover the people and places that make Silicon Valley the place to be for the new millenium. All stories must have a local angle, though they should be of national relevance." Estab. 1997. Circ. 60,000. Pays on publication. Publishes ms an average of 3 months after acceptance. Byline given. Offers 25% or $100 kill fee. Buys first North American serial rights. Editorial lead time 18 weeks. Submit seasonal material 6 months in advance. Accepts queries by mail, e-mail, fax. Accepts simultaneous submissions. Reports in 1 month. Sample copy for $5. Writer's guidelines for #10 SASE.

• Ranked as one of the best markets for freelance writers in *Writer's Yearbook* magazine's annual "Top 100 Markets," January 1999.

**Nonfiction:** General interest, interview/profile, photo feature, travel. "No technical, trade or articles without a tie-in to Silicon Valley". **Buys 120 mss/year.** Query with published clips. Length: 850-2,500 words. **Pays $50-850.** Sometimes pays expenses of writers on assignment.

**Photos:** State availability of photos with submission. Offers no additional payment for photos accepted with ms. Captions, model releases and identification of subjects required. Buys one-time rights.

**Columns/Departments:** Health (service, useful); Lifestyle (upscale); Getaways (travel) and Home Folio (home decor), all 850-1,200 words. **Buys 50 mss/year.** Query with published clips. **Pays $50-350.**

**Tips:** "Study our magazine for style and content. Nothing is as exciting as reading a tightly-written query and discovering a new writer."

**$ VENTURA COUNTY & COAST REPORTER**, VCR Inc., 1567 Spinnaker Dr., Suite 202, Ventura CA 93001. (805)658-2244. Fax: (805)658-7803. E-mail: vcrepedit@aol.com. **Contact:** Nancy Cloutier, editor. **12% freelance written.** Works with a small number of new/unpublished writers each year. Weekly tabloid covering local news. Circ. 35,000. Pays on publication. Publishes ms an average of 2 weeks after acceptance. Byline given. Buys first North American serial rights. Accepts queries by mail, e-mail, fax. Reports in 3 weeks.

**Nonfiction:** General interest (local slant), humor, interview/profile, travel (local—within 500 miles). Ventura County slant predominates. Length: 2,000-3,000 words. **Pay varies.**

**Photos:** Send photos with ms. Reviews b&w contact sheet.

**Columns/Departments:** Entertainment, Sports, Dining News, Real Estate, Boating Experience (Southern California). Send complete ms. **Pay varies.**

**Tips:** "As long as topics are up-beat with local slant, we'll consider them."

# Colorado

**N $ $ WELCOME HOME MAGAZINE, Denver/Las Vegas**, Welcome Home Magazine, LLC, 79 Spyglass Dr., Littleton CO 80123. (303)797-8400. Website: http://denver.digitalcity.com/welcomehome. **Contact:** Mary Sweeney, assistant publisher. Quarterly publication. "*Welcome Home* is a resource guide for newcomers and new movers. We offer useful and helpful information for two markets: Denver and Las Vegas. This is a post-move vehicle." Estab. 1990. Circ. 42,000. Pays on publication. Byline sometimes given. Buys nonexclusive rights. Editorial lead time 2 months. Submit seasonal material 4 months in advance. Accepts queries by mail, phone. Accepts simultaneous submissions. Reports in 1 month. Sample copy free or on website.

**Nonfiction:** General interest, how-to, humor, personal experience. Query with published clips. Length: 300-2,000 words. **Pays $200-300.**

**Reprints:** Accepts previously published submissions.

■ The online magazine carries original content not found in the print edition. Contact: Mary Sweeney, online editor.

# Connecticut

**$ $ $ $ NORTHEAST MAGAZINE**, *The Hartford Courant*, 285 Broad St., Hartford CT 06115-2510. (860)241-3700. Fax: (860)241-3853. E-mail: northeast@courant.com. Website: http://www.courant.com. Editor: Lary Bloom. **Contact:** Jane Bronfman, editorial assistant. **5% freelance written.** Eager to work with new/unpublished nonfiction writers. Weekly Sunday magazine for a Connecticut audience. Estab. 1982. Circ. 316,000. **Pays on accep-**

tance. Publishes ms an average of 5 months after acceptance. Byline given. Buys one-time rights. Reports in 3 months.
**Nonfiction:** "We are primarily interested in hard-hitting nonfiction articles spun off the news and compelling personal stories, as well as humor, fashion, style and home. We have a strong emphasis on Connecticut subject matter." General interest (has to have strong Connecticut tie-in); in-depth investigation of stories behind news (has to have strong Connecticut tie-in); historical/nostalgic; personal essays (humorous or anecdotal). No poetry. **Buys 10 mss/year.** Query by mail. Length: 750-2,500 words. **Pays $200-1,500.**
**Photos:** Most assigned; state availability of photos. "Do not send originals."
**Fiction:** Well-written, original short stories and (rarely) novel excerpts. Length: 750-1,500 words.
**Tips:** "Less space available for all types of writing means our standards for acceptance will be much higher. We can only print three to four short stories a year recently confined to a yearly fiction issue. It is to your advantage to read several recent issues of the magazine before submitting a manuscript or query. Virtually all our pieces are solicited and assigned by us, with about two percent of what we publish coming in 'over the transom' (four pieces of about 150 in 1998)."

## District of Columbia

**$ $ $** THE WASHINGTONIAN, 1828 L St. NW, #200, Washington DC 20036. (202)296-3600. Website: http://www.washingtonian.com. Editor: Jack Limpert. **Contact:** Pamela Danus, communications director. **20-25% freelance written.** Monthly magazine. "Writers should keep in mind that we are a general interest city-and-regional magazine. Nearly all our articles have a hard Washington connection. And, please, no political satire." Estab. 1965. Circ. 160,000. Pays on publication. Publishes ms an average of 3 months after acceptance. Byline given. Buys first North American serial rights, limited, non-exclusive electronic rights. Editorial lead time 6 weeks. Writer's guidelines for #10 SASE.
  ● Ranked as one of the best markets for freelance writers in *Writer's Yearbook* magazine's annual "Top 100 Markets," January 1999.
**Nonfiction:** Book excerpts, general interest, historical/nostalgic (with specific Washington, DC focus), interview/profile, personal experience, photo feature, travel. **Buys 15-30 mss/year.** Query by mail with published clips. **Pays 50¢/word.** Sometimes pays expenses of writers on assignment.
**Columns/Departments:** Howard Means, senior editor. First Person (personal experience that somehow illuminates life in Washington area), 650-700 words. **Buys 9-12 mss/year.** Query. **Pays $325.**
**Tips:** "The types of articles we publish include service pieces; profiles of people; investigative articles; rating pieces; institutional profiles; first-person articles; stories that cut across the grain of conventional thinking; articles that tell the reader how Washington got to be the way it is; light or satirical pieces (send the complete manuscript, not the idea, because in this case execution is everything); and fiction that tells readers how a part of Washington works or reveals something about the character or mood or people of Washington. Subjects of articles include the federal government, local government, dining out, sports, business, education, medicine, fashion, environment, how to make money, how to spend money, real estate, performing arts, visual arts, travel, health, nightlife, home and garden, self-improvement, places to go, things to do, and more. Again, we are interested in almost anything as long as it relates to the Washington area. We don't like puff pieces or what we call 'isn't-it-interesting' pieces. In general, we try to help our readers understand Washington better, to help our readers live better, and to make Washington a better place to live. Also, remember—a magazine article is different from a newspaper story. Newspaper stories start with the most important facts, are written in short paragraphs with a lot of transitions, and usually can be cut from the bottom up. A magazine article usually is divided into sections that are like 400-word chapters of a very short book. The introductory section is very important—it captures the reader's interest and sets the tone for the article. Scenes or anecdotes often are used to draw the reader into the subject matter. The next section then might foreshadow what the article is about without trying to summarize it—you want to make the reader curious. Each succeeding section develops the subject. Any evaluations or conclusions come in the closing section."

## Florida

**$ $** FLORIDA LIVING MAGAZINE, Florida Media, Inc., 3235 Duff Rd., Lakeland FL 33810. (941)858-7244. Fax: (941)859-3197. E-mail: flliving@earthlink.net. Website: http://www.flaliving.org. Publisher: E. Douglas Cifers. **Contact:** Kristen Crane, editor. Monthly lifestyle magazine covering Florida travel, food and dining, heritage, homes and gardens and all aspects of Florida lifestyle. Full calendar of events each month. Estab. 1981. Circ. 156,080. Publishes ms an average of 6 months after acceptance. Byline given. No kill fee. Buys first rights only. Submit seasonal material 1 year in advance. Accepts queries by mail, e-mail, fax. Reports in 2 months. Writer's guidelines sent on request with SASE. Not responsible for unsolicited material.
**Nonfiction:** General Florida interest, historical/nostalgic, interview/profile, travel, out-of-the-way Florida places, dining, attractions, festivals, shopping, resorts, bed & breakfast reviews, retirement, real estate, business, finance, health, recreation and sports. **Buys 50-60 mss/year.** Query or submit ms with SASE. Length: 500-1,500 words. **Pays $25-200 for assigned articles; $25-100 for unsolicited articles.**
**Photos:** Send photos with submission. Reviews 3×5 color prints and slides. Offers $6/photo. Captions required.
**Fiction:** Historical. **Buys 2-3 mss/year.** Send complete ms. Length: 1,000-3,000 words. Publishes novel excerpts. **Pays**

**$50-200.**

**$ $ ORLANDO WEEKLY**, Alternative Media Inc., 807 S. Orlando, Suite R, Winter Park FL 32789. (407)645-5888. Fax: (407)645-2547. E-mail: jtruesdell@aminc.com. Website: http://www.orlandoweekly.com. Managing Editor: Theresa Everline. **Contact:** Jeff Truesdell, editor. **50% freelance written.** Alternative weekly tabloid. "The *Orlando Weekly* covers news, entertainment, providing an alternative perspective to that provided by mainstream media. Our audience is 18-54, educated. We circulate 50,000 papers in Metropolitan Orlando." Estab. 1995. Circ. 50,000. **Pays on acceptance.** Byline given.

    ■ The online magazine carries original material not found in the print edition. Contact: Lindy Shepherd, online editor.

**Nonfiction:** Essays, exposé, general interest, interview/profile. Query. Length: 300-3,000 words. **Pays $50-250.** Sometimes pays expenses of writers on assignment.

**$ $ $ SUNSHINE: THE MAGAZINE OF SOUTH FLORIDA**, The Sun-Sentinel Co., 200 E. Las Olas Blvd., Fort Lauderdale FL 33301-2293. (305)356-4685. **60% freelance written.** Prefers to work with published/established writers, but works with a small number of new/unpublished writers each year. General interest Sunday magazine for the *Sun-Sentinel's* 800,000 readers in south Florida. Pays within 1 month of acceptance. Publishes ms an average of 2 months after acceptance. Byline given. Offers 25% kill fee for assigned material. Buys first serial rights or one-time rights in the state of Florida. Submit seasonal material 2 months in advance. Accepts simultaneous submissions. Reports in 1 month on queries; 2 months on mss. Sample copy and writer's guidelines for SAE.

**Nonfiction:** General interest, interview/profile, travel. "Articles must be relevant to the interests of adults living in south Florida." **Buys 150 mss/year.** Query with published clips. Length: 1,000-3,000 words; preferred length 2,000-2,500 words. **Pays 30-35¢/word to $1,200 maximum.**

**Reprints:** Send tearsheet or photocopy of article or typed ms with rights for sale noted and information about when and where the article previously appeared.

**Photos:** Send photos. Pays negotiable rate for 35mm and 2¼×2¼ color slides. Captions and identification of subjects required; model releases required for sensitive material. Buys one-time rights for the state of Florida.

**Tips:** "Do not phone, but do include your phone number on query letter. Keep your writing tight and concise—south Florida readers don't have the time to wade through masses of prose. We are always in the market for first-rate profiles, human-interest stories, travel stories and contributions to our regular 1,000-word features, 'First Person,' 'Weekenders' and 'Unsolved Mysteries.' "

**$ $ TALLAHASSEE MAGAZINE**, Rowland Publishing Inc., 1932 Miccosokee Rd., P.O. Box 1837, Tallahassee FL 32308. (850)878-0554. Fax: (850)656-1871. E-mail: tazzcat@yahoo.com Website: http://www.talmag.talstar.com. **Contact:** Kathleen M. Grobe, managing editor. **60-75% freelance written.** Bimonthly magazine covering Tallahassee area—North Florida and South Georgia. "*Tallahassee Magazine* is dedicated to reflecting the changing needs of a capital city challenged by growth and increasing economic, political and social diversity." Estab. 1979. Circ. 17,300. **Pays on acceptance.** Publishes ms an average of 3 months after acceptance. Byline given. Buys one-time rights. Editorial lead time 3 months. Submit seasonal material 4 months in advance. Accepts queries by mail, e-mail, fax, phone. Accepts simultaneous submissions. Accepts queries by mail, e-mail, fax, phone. Reports in 1 month. Sample copy for $2.95 and #10 SASE with 4 first-class stamps; sample articles on website. Writer's guidelines for #10 SASE.

**Nonfiction:** General interest, historical/nostalgic, how-to, humor, inspirational, interview/profile, personal experience, photo feature, travel, politics, sports lifestyles. **Buys 10 mss/year.** Query or submit ms with SASE. Length: 1,000-1,500 words. **Pays $100-250.**

**Reprints:** Send typed ms with rights for sale noted and information about when and where the article previously appeared. **Pays $100-350.**

**Photos:** State availability of photos with submission. Reviews 35mm transparencies, 3×5 prints. Offers no additional payment for photos accepted with ms. Model releases and identification of subjects required. Buys one-time rights.

**Columns/Departments:** Humor; Cooking; People and Social, all 850 words or less. **Buys 12-18 mss/year.** Query with published clips. **Pays $100.**

**Tips:** "Know the area we cover. This area is unusual in terms of the geography and the people. We are a Southern city, not a Florida city, in many ways. Know what we have published recently and don't try to sell us on an idea that we have published within three years of your query. Be lucid and concise and take enough time to get your facts straight. Make submissions on disk, either in Microsoft Word or Word Perfect."

# Georgia

**$ $ $ $ ATLANTA**, 1330 Peachtree St., Suite 450, Atlanta GA 30309. Fax: (404) 870-6219. E-mail: heather@atlantamag.emmis.com. **Contact:** Heather Moors Johnson, managing editor. Monthly magazine covering people, pleasures, useful information, regional happenings, restaurants, shopping, etc. for a general adult audience in Atlanta, including subjects in government, sports, pop culture, urban affairs, arts and entertainment. "*Atlanta* magazine articulates the special nature of Atlanta and appeals to an audience that wants to understand and celebrate the uniqueness of the region. The magazine's mission is to serve as a tastemaker by virtue of in-depth information and authoritative, provocative explorations of issues, personalities and lifestyles." Circ. 65,000. **Pays on acceptance.** Byline given. Offers 25% kill fee. Buys first North American serial rights. Accepts queries by mail, e-mail, fax. Reports in 2 months on queries. Sample copy on website.

**Nonfiction: Buys 36-40 mss/year.** Query with published clips. Length: 1,500-5,000 words. **Pays $300-2,000.** Pays expenses of writer on assignment.

● Ranked as one of the best markets for freelance writers in *Writer's Yearbook* magazine's "Top 100 Markets," January 1999.

**Columns/Departments:** Essay, travel. **Buys 30 mss/year.** Query with published clips. **Pays $500.** Length: 1,000-1,500 words.

**Fiction:** Publishes novel excerpts.

**Fillers: Buys 80/year.** Length: 75-175 words. **Pays $50-100.**

**Tips:** "Writers must know what makes their piece a story rather than just a subject."

**$ $ GEORGIA MAGAZINE**, Georgia Electric Membership Corp., P.O. Box 1707, Tucker GA 30085. (770)270-6950. Fax: (770)270-6995. E-mail: ann.orowski@georgiaemc.com. Website: http://www.Georgiamag.com. **Contact:** Ann Orowski, editor. **50% freelance written.** "We are a monthly magazine for and about Georgians, with a friendly, conversational tone and human interest topics." Estab. 1945. Circ. 260,000. Pays on publication. Publishes ms an average of 4 months after acceptance. Byline given. Buys first North American serial rights and website rights. Editorial lead time 2 months. Submit seasonal material 6 months in advance. Accepts simultaneous submissions. Reports in 1 month on subjects of interest. Sample copy for $2 each. Writer's guidelines for #10 SASE.

**Nonfiction:** Georgia-focused general interest, historical/nostalgic, how-to (in the home and garden), humor, inspirational, interview/profile, photo feature, travel. **Buys 8 mss/year.** Query with published clips. Length: 800-1,000 words; 500 words for smaller features and departments. **Pays $50-300.** Pays contributor copies upon negotiation. Sometimes pays expenses of writers on assignment.

**Photos:** State availability of photos with submission. Reviews contact sheets, transparencies, prints. Negotiates payment individually. Model releases, identification of subjects required. Buy one-time rights.

**N $ $ KNOW ATLANTA MAGAZINE**, New South Publishing, 1303 Hightower Trail, Suite 101, Atlanta GA 30350. (770)650-1102. Fax: (770)650-2848. E-mail: knowmag@aol.com. Website: http://www.knowatlanta.com. **Contact:** Cheryl Fenton, editor. **80% freelance written.** Quarterly magazine covering the Atlanta area. "Our articles offer information on Atlanta that would be useful to newcomers—homes, schools, hospitals, fun things to do, anything that makes their move more comfortable." Estab. 1986. Circ. 150,000. Pays on publication. Byline given. Offers 100% kill fee. Buys first North American serial rights. Editorial lead time 1 month. Submit seasonal material 2 months in advance. Sample copy free.

**Nonfiction:** General interest, how-to, personal experience, photo feature. No fiction. **Buys 10 mss/year.** Query by mail. Length: 1,000-2,000 words. **Pays $100-500 for assigned articles; $100-300 for unsolicited articles.** Sometimes pays expenses of writers on assignment.

**Reprints:** Accepts previously published submissions.

**Photos:** Send photos with submission. Reviews contact sheets. Negotiates payment individually. Captions and identification of subjects required. Buys one-time rights.

**$ $ NORTH GEORGIA JOURNAL**, Legacy Communications, Inc., P.O. Box 127, Roswell GA 30077. (770) 642-5569. Fax: (770)642-1415. E-mail: sumail@mindspring.com. Website: http://mindspring.com/~north.ga.travel. **Contact:** Olin Jackson, publisher. **70% freelance written.** Quarterly magazine "for readers interested in travel, history, and mountain lifestyles of north Georgia." Estab. 1984. Circ. 18,450. Pays on publication. Publishes ms an average of 5 months after acceptance. Byline given. Offers 25% kill fee. Buys first and all rights. Editorial lead time 6 months. Submit seasonal material 6 months in advance. Accepts queries by mail, e-mail, fax. Sample copy for 9×12 SAE and 8 first-class stamps or on website. Writer's guidelines for #10 SASE.

**Nonfiction:** Historical/nostalgic, how-to (survival techniques; mountain living; do-it-yourself home construction and repairs, etc.), interview/profile (celebrity), personal experience (anything unique or unusual pertaining to north Georgia mountains), photo feature (any subject of a historic nature which can be photographed in a seasonal context, i.e.—old mill with brilliant yellow jonquils in foreground), travel (subjects highlighting travel opportunities in North Georgia). Query with published clips. **Pays $75-350.**

**Photos:** Send photos with submission. Reviews contact sheets, transparencies. Negotiates payment individually. Captions, model releases, identification of subjects required. Buys all rights.

**Fiction:** Publishes novel excerpts.

**Tips:** "Good photography is crucial to acceptance of all articles. Send written queries then *wait* for a response. *No telephone calls please.* The most useful material involves a first person experience of an individual who has explored a historic site or scenic locale and *interviewed* a person or persons who were involved with or have first-hand knowledge of a historic site/event. Interviews and quotations are crucial. Articles should be told in writer's own words."

# Hawaii

**$ $ HAWAII MAGAZINE**, Fancy Publications, Inc., 1210 Auahi St., Suite 231, Honolulu HI 96814. (808)589-1515. Fax: (808)589-1616. E-mail: hawaii@fancypubs.com. **Contact:** June Kikuchi, managing editor. **60% freelance written.** Bimonthly magazine "written for residents and frequent visitors who enjoy the culture, people and places of the Hawaiian Islands." Estab. 1984. Circ. 81,000. Pays on publication. Byline given. Buys first North American serial rights. Submit seasonal material 6 months in advance. Accepts queries by mail, e-mail, fax. Reports in 1 month on queries; 6 weeks on mss. Sample copy for $3.95. Writer's guidelines for #10 SASE.
**Nonfiction:** General interest, historical/nostalgic, how-to, interview/profile, personal experience, photo feature, travel. "No articles on the following: first trip to Hawaii, how I discovered the Islands, the Hula, Poi, or Luaus." **Buys 66 mss/year.** Query with or without published clips, or send complete ms. Length: 4,000 words max. **Pays $100-500.**
**Photos:** Send photos with submission. Reviews contact sheets and transparencies. Prefers color transparencies. Offers $35/photo. Identification of subjects preferred. Buys one-time rights.
**Columns/Departments:** Backdoor Hawaii (a light or nostalgic look at culture or history), 800-1,200 words; Hopping the Islands (news, general interest items), 100-200 words. **Buys 6-12 mss/year.** Query. Length: 800-1,500 words. **Pays $100-200.** New department, WeatherWatch, focuses on Hawaii weather phenomena (450 words). **Pays $50.**
**Fiction:** Publishes novel excerpts.
**Tips:** "Freelancers must be knowledgeable about Island subjects, virtual authorities on them and must live in Hawaii. We see far too many first-person, wonderful-experience types of gushing articles. We buy articles only from people who are thoroughly grounded in the subject on which they are writing."

**$ $ HONOLULU**, Honolulu Publishing Co., Ltd., 36 Merchant St., Honolulu HI 96813. (808)524-7400. Fax: (808)531-2306. E-mail: honmag@pixi.com. **Publisher:** John Alves. **Contact:** John Heckathorn, editor. **50% freelance written.** Prefers to work with published/established writers. Monthly magazine covering general interest topics relating to Hawaii residents. Estab. 1888. Circ. 30,000. **Pays on acceptance.** Publishes ms an average of 4 months after acceptance. Byline given. Buys first-time rights. Submit seasonal material 5 months in advance. Accepts simultaneous submissions. Reports in 2 months. Sample copy for $2 and 9 × 12 SAE with 8 first-class stamps. Writer's guidelines for #10 SASE.
**Nonfiction:** Exposé, general interest, historical/nostalgic, photo feature—all Hawaii-related. "We write for Hawaii residents, so travel articles about Hawaii are not appropriate." **Buys 30 mss/year.** Query with published clips if available. Length: 2,000-3,000 words. **Pays $100-700.** Sometimes pays expenses of writers on assignment.
**Photos:** Michel Lê, art director. Send photos. Pays $75-175 for single image inside; $500 maximum for cover. Captions and identification of subjects required as well as model release. Buys one-time rights.
**Columns/Departments:** Calabash ("newsy," timely, humorous department on any Hawaii-related subject). **Buys 15 mss/year.** Query with published clips or send complete ms. Length: 50-750 words. **Pays $35-100.** First Person (personal experience or humor). **Buys 10 mss/year.** Length: 1,500 words. **Pays $200-300.**

# Idaho

**★ $ $ BOISE MAGAZINE**, Earls Communications, 800 W. Idaho St., Suite 304, Boise ID 83702. (208)338-5454. Fax: (208)338-0006. E-mail: info@boisemag.com. **Contact:** Alan Minskoff, editor. **90% freelance written.** "*Boise Magazine* is a city/regional quarterly devoted to Idaho's capital and its environs. We publish profiles, articles, reviews and features on business, sports, the arts, politics, community development and have regular departments that cover travel, design, books, food and wine as well as a calendar of events and a section entitled Valley." Estab. 1997. Circ. 10,000. Pays on publication. Byline given. Buys first rights. Editorial lead time 3 months. Submit seasonal material 6 months in advance. Reports in 6 weeks on queries; 3 months on mss. Sample copy $3.50. Guidelines for #10 SASE.
**Nonfiction:** Book excerpts, essays, general interest, humor, photo feature, travel. **Buys 12 mss/year.** Query by mail with published clip. Length: 500-3,500 words. **Pays 18-20¢/word.** Sometimes pays expenses of writers on assignment.
**Photos:** State availability of photos with submission. Negotiates payment individually. Model releases and identification of subjects required. Buys one-time rights.
**Columns/Departments:** Valley (short pieces on life around Boise), 500-1,250 words. **Buys 30 mss/year.** Query with published clips. **Pays 18-20¢/word.**
**Fiction:** Mainstream, novel excerpts, slice-of-life vignettes. No romance, science fiction, western, erotica, adventure, religious. **Buys 2-3 mss/year.** Query. Length: 1,000-2,500 words. **Pays 20¢/word.**
**Tips:** "The Valley and Book Reviews are the best entry-levels for freelance writers. Profiles and other departments are not as easy, and features are virtually all done by local writers."

# Illinois

**N ★ $ CHICAGO LIFE**, P.O. Box 11311, Chicago IL 60611-0311. (773)880-1360. E-mail: chgolife@mcs.com. **Publisher:** Pam Berns. **Contact:** Joan Black, editor. **95% freelance written.** Bimonthly magazine on Chicago life for educated, affluent professionals, 25-50 years old. Estab. 1984. Circ. 50,000. Pays on publication. Byline given. Kill fee varies. Submit seasonal material 8 months in advance. Accepts simultaneous submissions. Reports in 3 months. Sample copy for 9×12 SAE with 7 first-class stamps.

**Nonfiction:** Environment, health, interior design, exposé, how-to, photo feature, travel. **Buys 50 mss/year.** Send complete ms. Length: 400-1,200 words. **Pays $30.** Sometimes pays the expenses of writers on assignment.

**Reprints:** Send photocopy of article and information about when and where the article previously appeared.

**Photos:** Send photos with submission. Reviews contact sheets, negatives, transparencies, prints. Offers $15-30/photo. Buys one-time rights.

**Columns/Departments:** Law, Book Reviews, Travel, Health, Environment, Home Decorating. Send complete ms. Length: 500 words. **Pays $30.**

**Fillers:** Facts. **Pays $15-30.**

**Tips:** "Please send finished work with visuals (photos, if possible). Topics open include environmental concerns, health, interior design, travel, self improvement, how-to-do almost anything, entrepreneurs."

**N $ $ $ $ CHICAGO MAGAZINE**, 500 N. Dearborn, Suite 1200, Chicago IL 60610-4901. Fax: (312)222-0699. E-mail: chimagst@aol.com. Website: http://www.chicagomagazine.com. **Contact:** Shane Tritsch, managing editor. **50% freelance written.** Prefers to work with published/established writers. Monthly magazine for an audience which is "95% from Chicago area; 90% college educated; upper income, overriding interests in the arts, politics, dining, good life in the city and suburbs. Most are in 25-50 age bracket, well-read and articulate." Estab. 1968. Circ. 175,000. **Pays on acceptance.** Publishes ms an average of 3 months after acceptance. Buys first serial rights. Submit seasonal material 4 months in advance. Accepts queries by mail, e-mail. Reports in 1 month. For sample copy, send $3 to Circulation Dept. Writer's guidelines for #10 SASE.

**Nonfiction:** "On themes relating to the quality of life in Chicago: past, present, and future." Writers should have "a general awareness that the readers will be concerned, influential, longtime Chicagoans. We generally publish material too comprehensive for daily newspapers." Personal experience and think pieces, profiles, humor, spot news, historical articles, exposés. **Buys 100 mss/year.** Query; indicate "specifics, knowledge of city and market, and demonstrable access to sources." Length: 200-6,000 words. **Pays $100-$3,000 and up, depending on the story.** Pays expenses of writers on assignment.

**Photos:** Reviews b&w glossy prints, 35mm color transparencies or color prints. Usually assigned separately, not acquired from writers.

■ The online magazine carries content not found in the print edition. Contact: Tara Croft, online editor.

**Tips:** "Submit detailed queries, be business-like and avoid clichéd ideas."

**$ $ CHICAGO SOCIAL, Chicago's Monthly Social Magazine**, Prairie City Media, 727 N. Hudson Ave., #001, Chicago IL 60610. (312)787-4600. Fax: (312)787-4628. Editor: Michael Blaise Kong. Managing Editor: Royaa G. Silver. **Contact:** Katherine Cole, senior editor. **70% freelance written.** Monthly luxury lifestyle magazine. "We cover the good things in life—fashion, fine dining, the arts, etc.—from a sophisticated, cosmopolitan, well-to-do perspective." Circ. 75,000. Pays 2 months after receipt of invoice. Byline given. Offers 50% kill fee. Buys first rights and all rights in this market. Editorial lead time 6 months. Submit seasonal material 6 months in advance. Reports in 1 month. Sample copy for $7.15 for current issue; $8.20 for back issue. Writer's guidelines for #10 SASE.

**Nonfiction:** General interest, how-to (gardening, culinary, home design), interview/profile, photo feature (occasional), travel. No fiction; *no unsolicited mss.* Query with published clips only. Length: 500-4,500 words. **Pays $50-500.** Pays expenses of writers on assignment.

**Photos:** State availability of photos with submission. Reviews transparencies and prints. "We pay for film and processing only." Buys one-time rights.

**Columns/Departments:** Few Minutes With (Q&A), 800 words; City Art, Home Design, Gold List, Sporting Life (feature), 2,000 words. Query with published clips only. **Pays $0-200.**

**Tips:** "Send résumé, clips and story ideas. Mention interest and expertise in cover letter. We need writers who are knowledgeable about home design, architecture, art, culinary arts, entertainment, fashion and retail."

**★ $ $ $ NORTH SHORE, The Magazine of Chicago's North and Northwest Suburbs**, 3701 West Lake Ave., Glenview IL 60025. (847) 486-0600. Fax: (847) 486-7427. E-mail: tmcnamee@northshoremag.com. Publisher: Pioneer Press. Editor: Barry Hochfelder. **Contact:** Tom McNamee, executive editor. **75% freelance written.** Monthly magazine. "Our readers are diverse, from middle-class communities to some of the country's wealthiest zip codes. But they all have one thing in common—proximity to Chicago." Circ. 57,902. Pays on publication. Publishes ms an average of 1-3 months after acceptance. Byline given. Buys first North American serial rights. Submit seasonal material 5 months in advance. Accepts queries by mail, e-mail. Reports in 3 months.

**Nonfiction:** Book excerpts, general interest, how-to, interview/profile, photo feature, travel. Supplements: Our Health (guide to Chicago area hospitals), April; Senior Class (guide to retirement living in Chicago).

**Buys 50 mss/year.** Query with published clips. Length: 500-4,000 words. **Pays $100-1,000.** Sometimes pays expenses of writers on assignment.

**Columns/Departments:** "Prelude" (shorter items of local interest), 250 words. **Buys 12 mss/year.** Query with published clips. **Pays $50.**

**Tips:** "We're always looking for something of local interest that's fresh and hasn't been reported elsewhere. Look for local angle. Offer us a story that's exclusive in the crowded Chicago-area media marketplace. Well-written feature stories have the best chance of being published. We cover all of Chicago's north and northwest suburbs together with some Chicago material, not just the North Shore.''

**$ $WHERE CHICAGO MAGAZINE**, Miller Publishing, 1165 N. Clark St., Suite 302, Chicago IL 60610. (312)642-1896. Fax: (312)642-5467. E-mail: wherechicago@insnet.com. **Contact:** Margaret Doyle, editor. **50% freelance written** (uses freelance writers primarily for special projects). Monthly magazine covering Chicago tourism market. "Where Chicago is geared to the leisure and business traveler visiting Chicago. We are the premier source for shopping, dining, culture, nightlife and entertainment in the city and suburbs." Estab. 1985. Circ. 101,000. **Pays on acceptance.** Publishes ms an average of 2 months after acceptance. Byline given. Buys all rights. Editorial lead time 2 months. Submit seasonal material 4 months in advance. Accepts simultaneous submissions. Accepts queries by mail. Reports immediately. Sample copy free. Writer's guidelines not available.

**Nonfiction:** General interest, historical/nostalgic, interview/profile, photo feature, travel. No "personal experiences or anything not related to Chicago." Special issue: November/December (holiday supplement that focuses on shopping, dining, family entertainment and cultural events in Chicago, primarily in the magnificent mile area). **Buys 4 mss/year.** Query with published clips. Length varies. **Pay varies.**

**Photos:** State availability of photos with submission. Reviews 4×5 transparencies, 10×12 prints. Negotiates payment individually. Captions, model releases and identification of subjects required. Buys one-time rights.

**Tips:** "Don't call us—we'll call you. Best to send a query and writing samples. Pitch an idea, if you've got one."

## Indiana

**$ $INDIANAPOLIS MONTHLY**, Emmis Publishing Corp., 40 Monument Circle, Suite 100, Indianapolis IN 46204. (317)237-9288. Fax: (317)684-2080. E-mail: im-input@iquest.com. Website: http://www.indianapolismonthly.com. Editor-in-Chief: Deborah Paul. Senior Editor: Brian D. Smith. **Contact:** Sam Stall, editor. **50% freelance written.** Prefers to work with published/established writers. Monthly. "*Indianapolis Monthly* attracts and enlightens its upscale, well-educated readership with bright, lively editorial on subjects ranging from personalities to social issues, fashion to food. Its diverse content and attention to service make it the ultimate source by which the Indianapolis area lives." Estab. 1977. Circ. 45,000. Pays on publication. Publishes ms an average of 2 months after acceptance. Byline given. Offers negotiable kill fee. Buys first North American serial rights or one-time rights. Editorial lead time 3 months. Submit seasonal material 3 months in advance. Accepts queries by mail, e-mail. Accepts simultaneous submissions. Reports in 3 weeks. Sample copy for $6.10. Guidelines for #10 SASE.

• This magazine is using more first-person essays, but they must have a strong Indianapolis or Indiana tie. It will consider nonfiction book excerpts of material relevant to its readers.

**Nonfiction:** Book excerpts (by Indiana authors or with strong Indiana ties), essays, exposé, general interest, interview/profile, photo feature. Must have a strong Indianapolis or Indiana angle. No poetry, fiction or domestic humor; no "How Indy Has Changed Since I Left Town," "An Outsider's View of the 500," or generic material with no or little tie to Indianapolis/Indiana. **Buys 50 mss/year.** Query with published clips by mail or e-mail, or send complete ms. Length: 200-3,000 words. **Pays $50-600.**

**Reprints:** Accepts reprints only from non-competing markets. Send typed ms with rights for sale noted and information about when and where the article previously appeared. Pays 100% of the amount paid for an original article.

**Photos:** State availability of photos with submission. Reviews upon request. Negotiates payment individually. Captions, model releases and identification of subjects required. Buys one-time rights.

**Columns/Departments:** Sport; Health; First Person; Hoosiers at Large (essays by Indiana natives); Business; Coping; Controversy; Books, all 2,000-2,500 words. **Buys 35 mss/year. Pays $300.**

**Tips:** "Our standards are simultaneously broad and narrow: broad in that we're a general interest magazine spanning a wide spectrum of topics, narrow in that we buy only stories with a heavy emphasis on Indianapolis (and, to a lesser extent, Indiana). Simply inserting an Indy-oriented paragraph into a generic national article won't get it: all stories must pertain primarily to things Hoosier. Once you've cleared that hurdle, however, it's a wide-open field. We've done features on national celebrities—Indiana Pacers coach Larry Bird and *Mir* astronaut David Wolf of Indianapolis, to name two—and we've published two-paragraph items on such quirky topics as an Indiana gardening supply house that sells insects by mail. We also like local pieces on national celebs: one of our most popular cover stories was titled 'Oprah's Indiana Home.' Probably the easiest place to break in is our front-of-the-book section, IndyScene, a collection of short takes on trendy topics (including Homegrown, spotlighting Hoosiers making it big elsewhere). Query with clips showing lively writing and solid reporting. E-mail queries are OK, and snail mail queries should include SASE. No phone queries please."

## Kansas

**$ $KANSAS!**, Kansas Department of Commerce and Housing, 700 SW Harrison, Suite 1300, Topeka KS 66603-3957. (785)296-3479. Fax: (785)296-6988. **Contact:** Andrea Glenn, editor. **90% freelance written.** Quarterly magazine emphasizing Kansas travel attractions and events. Estab. 1945. Circ. 52,000. **Pays on acceptance.** Publishes ms an average of 1 year after acceptance. Byline given. Buys one-time rights. Submit seasonal material 8 months in advance. Reports in 2 months. Sample copy and writer's guidelines available.

**Nonfiction:** General interest, photo feature, travel. "Material must be Kansas-oriented and have good potential for color photographs. The focus is on travel with articles about places and events that can be enjoyed by the general public. In other words, events must be open to the public, places also. Query letter should clearly outline story. I'm especially interested in Kansas freelancers who can supply their own quality photos." Query by mail. Length: 750-1,250 words. **Pays $200-400.**

**Photos:** "We are a full-color photo/manuscript publication." Send photos (original transparencies only) with query. Pays $50-75 (generally included in ms rate) for 35mm or larger format transparencies. Captions required.

**Tips:** "History and nostalgia stories do not fit into our format because they can't be illustrated well with color photos. Submit a query letter describing one appropriate idea with outline for possible article and suggestions for photos."

# Kentucky

**$BACK HOME IN KENTUCKY**, Greysmith Publishing Inc., P.O. Box 681629, Franklin TN 37068-1629. (615)794-4338. Fax: (615)790-6188. **Contact:** Nanci P. Gregg, managing editor. **50% freelance written.** "Bimonthly magazine covering Kentucky heritage, people, places, events. We reach Kentuckians and 'displaced' Kentuckians living outside the state." Estab. 1977. Circ. 8,163. Pays on publication. Publishes ms an average of 6 months after acceptance. Byline given. Buys first North American serial rights. Submit seasonal material 8 months in advance. Reports in 2 months. Sample copy for $3 and 9×12 SAE with 5 first-class stamps. Writer's guidelines for #10 SASE.

● This magazine is increasing its emphasis on the "Back Home." It is interested in profiles of Kentucky gardeners, Kentucky cooks, Kentucky craftspeople.

**Nonfiction:** Historical (Kentucky-related eras or profiles), profiles (Kentucky cooks, gardeners and craftspersons), memories (Kentucky related), photo feature (Kentucky places and events), travel (unusual/little known Kentucky places). No inspirational or religion. **Buys 25 mss/year.** Query with or without published clips, or send complete ms. Length: 500-2,000 words. **Pays $50-150 for assigned articles; $15-75 for unsolicited articles.** "In addition to normal payment, writers receive 4 copies of issue containing their article." Sometimes pays expenses of writers on assignment.

**Reprints:** Occasionally accepts previously published submissions. Send tearsheet of article and information about when and where the article previously appeared. Pays 50% of amount paid for an original article.

**Photos:** Send photos with submission. Reviews transparencies and 4×6 prints. Offers no additional payment for photos accepted with ms. Model releases and identification of subjects required. Rights purchased depends on situation. Also looking for color transparencies for covers. Vertical format. Pays $50-150.

**Columns/Departments:** Kentucky travel, Kentucky crafts, Kentucky gardeners. **Buys 10-12 mss/year.** Query with published clips. Length: 500-750 words. **Pays $15-40.**

**Tips:** "We work mostly with unpublished writers who have a feel for Kentucky's people, places and events. Areas most open are little known places in Kentucky, unusual history and profiles of interesting, unusual Kentuckians."

**$ $KENTUCKY LIVING**, P.O. Box 32170, Louisville KY 40232-0170. (502)451-2430. Fax: (502)459-1611. **Contact:** Paul Wesslund, editor. **Mostly freelance written.** Prefers to work with published/established writers. Monthly feature magazine primarily for Kentucky residents. Estab. 1948. Circ. 450,000. **Pays on acceptance.** Publishes ms on average of 4-12 months after acceptance. Byline given. Buys first serial rights for Kentucky. Submit seasonal material at least 6 months in advance. Accepts simultaneous submissions (if previously published and/or submitted outside Kentucky). Reports in 1 month. Sample copy for 9×12 SAE with 4 first-class stamps.

**Nonfiction:** Kentucky-related profiles (people, places or events), recreation, travel, leisure, lifestyle articles, book excerpts. **Buys 18-24 mss/year.** Query or send complete ms. **Pays $75-125** for "short" features (600-800 words) used in section known as "Commonwealths." For major articles (800-2,000 words) **pays $150-350.** Sometimes pays the expenses of writers on assignment.

**Reprints:** Considers previously published submissions (if published outside Kentucky).

**Photos:** State availability of or send photos with submission or advise as to availability. Reviews color slides and b&w prints. Identification of subjects required. Payment for photos included in payment for ms.

**Tips:** "The quality of writing and reporting (factual, objective, thorough) is considered in setting payment price. We prefer general interest pieces filled with quotes and anecdotes. Avoid boosterism. Well-researched, well-written feature articles are preferred. All articles must have a strong Kentucky connection."

**$ $LOUISVILLE MAGAZINE**, 137 W. Muhammad Ali Blvd., Suite 101, Louisville KY 40202-1438. (502)625-0100. Fax: (502)625-0109. E-mail: loumag@loumag.com. Website: http://www.louisville.com. **Contact:** Amy Jackson Sellers, managing editor. **67% freelance written.** Monthly magazine "for and generally about people of the Louisville Metro area. Routinely covers arts, entertainment, business, sports, dining and fashion. Features range from news analysis/exposé to silly/funny commentary. We like lean, clean prose, crisp leads." Estab. 1950. Circ. 20,000. Publishes ms an average of 2-3 months after acceptance. Byline given. Offers 50% kill fee. Buys first North American serial rights. Editorial lead time 6 weeks. Submit seasonal material 6 months in advance. Accepts queries by mail, e-mail, fax. Reports in 3 months. Sample copy for $2.95 or on website.

**Nonfiction:** Book excerpts, essays, exposé, general interest, historical, interview/profile, photo feature. Special issues: City Guide (January); Kentucky Derby (April); EATS (September); Louisville Bride (December). **Buys 75 mss/year.** Query. Length: 500-3,500 words. **Pays $100-500 for assigned articles; $100-400 for unsolicited articles.**
**Photos:** State availability of photos with submissions. Reviews transparencies. Offers $25-50/photo. Identification of subjects required. Buys one-time rights.
**Columns/Departments:** End Insight (essays), 850 words. **Buys 10 mss/year.** Send complete ms. **Pays $100-150.**

# Louisiana

**$ $ SUNDAY ADVOCATE MAGAZINE,** P.O. Box 588, Baton Rouge LA 70821-0588. (225)383-1111, ext. 350. Fax: (225)388-0351. E-mail: fyarbrough@theadvocate.com. Website: http://www.TheAdvocate.com. **Contact:** Freda Yarbrough, news/features editor. **5% freelance written.** Byline given. Buys one-time rights. "Freelance features are put on our website." Estab. 1925. Pays on publication. Publishes ms up to 3 months after acceptance.
    **O—** Break in with travel articles.
**Nonfiction and Photos:** Well-illustrated, short articles; must have local, area or Louisiana angle, in that order of preference. **Buys 24 mss/year. Pays $100-200.**.
**Reprints:** Send tearsheet or typed ms with rights for sale noted and information about when and where the article previously appeared. **Pays $100-200.**
**Photos:** Photos purchased with ms. **Pays $30/published color photo.**
**Tips:** "Style and subject matter vary. Local interest is most important. No more than four to five typed, double-spaced pages."

# Maryland

**$ $ $ $ BALTIMORE MAGAZINE,** Inner Harbor East, 1000 Lancaster St., Suite 400, Baltimore MD 21202. (410)752-4200. Fax: (410)625-0280. E-mail: smarge@baltimoremag.com. Website: http://www.baltimoremag.com. **Contact:** Margaret Guroff, managing editor. **50-60% freelance written.** Monthly magazine. "Pieces must address an educated, active, affluent reader and must have a very strong Baltimore angle." Estab. 1907. Circ. 57,000. Pays within 60 days of acceptance. Byline given. Offers 30% kill fee. Buys first rights in all media. Submit seasonal material 4 months in advance. Reports in 2 months on queries; 2 weeks on assigned mss; 3 months on unsolicited mss. Sample copy for $2.95 and 9×12 SAE with 10 first-class stamps or on website. Writer's guidelines for #10 SASE.
**Nonfiction:** Book excerpt (Baltimore subject or author), essays, exposé, humor, interview/profile (w/Baltimorean), personal experience, photo feature, travel (local and regional to Maryland *only*). "Nothing that lacks a strong Baltimore focus or angle." Query by mail with published clips or send complete ms. Length: 1,000-3,000 words. **Pays $25-2,500 for assigned articles; $25-500 for unsolicited articles.** Sometimes pays expenses of writers on assignment.
**Columns/Departments:** Hot Shot, Health, Education, Sports. Length: 1,000-1,500 words. Query with published clips. "These shorter pieces are the best places to break into the magazine."
**Tips:** "Writers who live in the Baltimore area can send résumé and published clips to be considered for first assignment. Must show an understanding of writing that is suitable to an educated magazine reader and show ability to write with authority, describe scenes, help reader experience the subject. Too many writers send us newspaper-style articles. We are seeking: 1) *Human interest features*—strong, even dramatic profiles of Baltimoreans of interest to our readers. 2) *First-person accounts* of experience in Baltimore, or experiences of a Baltimore resident. 3) *Consumer*—according to our editorial needs, and with Baltimore sources. Writers new to us have most success with small humorous stories and 1,000-word personal essays that exhibit risky, original thought."

# Massachusetts

**$ $ $ $ BOSTON MAGAZINE,** Metrocorp, 300 Massachusetts Ave., Boston MA 02115. (617)262-9700. Fax: (617)267-1774. E-mail: bosmag@aol.com. Website: http://www.bostonmagazine.com. Editor: Craig Unger. **Contact:** Amy Traverso, editorial assistant. **10% freelance written.** Monthly magazine covering the city of Boston. Estab. 1972. Circ. 125,000. Pays on publication. Publishes ms an average of 3 months after acceptance. Byline given. Offers 20% kill fee. Buys first North American serial rights. Editorial lead time 2 months. Submit seasonal material 4 months in advance. Accepts queries by mail, fax. Reports in 6 weeks on queries. Writer's guidelines for SASE.
**Nonfiction:** Book excerpts, exposé, general interest, interview/profile, politics, crime, trends, fashion. **Buys 20 mss/ year.** Query. *No unsolicited mss.* Length: 1,200-12,000 words. Sometimes pays expenses of writers on assignment.
**Photos:** State availability of photos with submissions. Negotiates payment individually. Buys one-time rights.
**Columns/Departments:** Dining, Finance, City Life, Personal Style, Politics, Ivory Tower, Media, Wine, Boston Inc., Books, Theatre, Music. Query.
**Tips:** "Read *Boston*, and pay attention to the types of stories we use. Suggest which column/department your story

might best fit, and keep you focus on the city and its environs. We like a strong narrative style, with a slightly 'edgy' feel—we rarely do 'remember when' stories. Think *city* magazine."

**$ $ CAPE COD LIFE, Including Martha's Vineyard and Nantucket**, Cape Cod Life, Inc., P.O. Box 1385, Pocasset MA 02559-1385. (508)564-4466. Fax: (508)564-4470. E-mail: capelife@capecodlife.com. Website: http://www.capecodlife.com. Editor: Brian F. Shortsleeve. **Contact:** Nancy Berry, managing editor. **80% freelance written.** Bimonthly magazine focusing on "area lifestyle, history and culture, people and places, business and industry, and issues and answers for year-round and summer residents of Cape Cod, Nantucket and Martha's Vineyard as well as non-residents who spend their leisure time here." Circ. 39,500. Pays 30 days after publication. Byline given. Offers 20% kill fee. Buys first North American serial rights or makes work-for-hire assignments. Submit seasonal material 6 months in advance. Accepts queries by mail, e-mail, fax and phone. Reports in 6 months on queries and ms. Sample copy for $5. Writer's guidelines for #10 SASE.

**Nonfiction:** General interest, historical, gardening, interview/profile, photo feature, travel, marine, nautical, nature, arts, antiques. **Buys 20 mss/year.** Query with or without published clips. Length: 1,000-3,000 words. **Pays $100-400.**

**Photos:** Pays $25-225 for photos. Captions and identification of subjects required. Buys first rights with right to reprint. Photo guidelines for #10 SASE.

The online magazine carries original material not found in the print edition. Contact: Nancy Berry, online editor.

**Tips:** "Freelancers submitting *quality* spec articles with a Cape Cod and Islands angle have a good chance at publication. We like to see a wide selection of writer's clips before giving assignments. We accept more spec work written about Cape and Islands history than any other subject. We also publish *Cape Cod Home: Living and Gardening on the Cape and Islands* covering architecture, landscape design and interior design with a Cape and Islands focus."

**$ $ PROVINCETOWN ARTS**, Provincetown Arts, Inc., 650 Commercial St., Provincetown MA 02657. (508)487-3167. Fax: (508)487-8634. Website: http://www.capecodaccess.com. **Contact:** Christopher Busa, editor. **90% freelance written.** Annual magazine for contemporary art and writing. "*Provincetown Arts* focuses broadly on the artists and writers who inhabit or visit the Lower Cape, and seeks to stimulate creative activity and enhance public awareness of the cultural life of the nation's oldest continuous art colony. Drawing upon a 75-year tradition rich in visual art, literature and theater, *Provincetown Arts* offers a unique blend of interviews, fiction, visual features, reviews, reporting and poetry." Estab. 1985. Circ. 8,000. Pays on publication. Publishes ms an average of 4 months after acceptance. Offers 50% kill fee. Buys one-time and second serial (reprint) rights. Editorial lead time 6 months. Submit seasonal material 6 months in advance. Reports in 3 weeks on queries; 2 months on mss. Sample copy for $10. Writer's guidelines for #10 SASE.

**Nonfiction:** Book excerpts, essays, humor, interview/profile. **Buys 40 mss/year.** Send complete ms. Length: 1,500-4,000 words. **Pays $150 minimum for assigned articles; $125 minimum for unsolicited articles.**

**Photos:** Send photos with submission. Reviews 8 × 10 prints. Offers $20-100/photo. Identification of subjects required. Buys one-time rights.

**Fiction:** Mainstream. Also publishes novel excerpts. **Buys 7 mss/year.** Send complete ms. Length: 500-5,000 words. **Pays $75-300.**

**Poetry:** **Buys 25 poems/year.** Submit maximum 3 poems. **Pays $25-150.**

# Michigan

**$ $ $ ANN ARBOR OBSERVER**, Ann Arbor Observer Company, 201 E. Catherine, Ann Arbor MI 48104. Fax: (734)769-3375. E-mail: hilton@aaobserver.com. Website: http://www.arborweb.com. **Contact:** John Hilton, Editor. **50% freelance written.** Works with a small number of new/unpublished writers each year. Monthly magazine featuring people and events in Ann Arbor. "We depend heavily on freelancers and we're always glad to talk to new ones. We look for the intelligence and judgment to fully explore complex people and situations, and the ability to convey what makes them interesting. We've found that professional writing experience is not a good predictor of success in writing for the *Observer*. So don't let lack of experience deter you. Writing for the *Observer* is, however, a demanding job. Our readers range from U-M faculty members to hourly workers at GT Products. That means articles have to be both accurate and accessible." Estab. 1976. Circ. 61,000. Pays on publication. Publishes ms an average of 2 months after acceptance. Byline given. Accepts queries by mail, e-mail. Reports in 3 weeks on queries; several months on mss. Sample copy for 12½ × 15 SAE with $3 postage. Writer's guidelines for #10 SASE.

**Nonfiction:** Historical, investigative features, profiles, brief vignettes. Must pertain to Ann Arbor. **Buys 75 mss/year.** Length: 100-7,000 words. **Pays up to $1,000/article.** Sometimes pays expenses of writers on assignment.

**Columns/Departments:** Inside Ann Arbor (short, interesting tidbits), 200-500 words. **Pays $75.** Around Town (unusual, compelling ancedotes), 750-1,500 words. **Pays $150-200.**

**Tips:** "If you have an idea for a story, write a 100-200-word description telling us why the story is interesting. We are open most to intelligent, insightful features of up to 5,000 words about interesting aspects of life in Ann Arbor."

**$ HOUR DETROIT**, Hour Media LLC, 117 W. Third St., Royal Oak MI 48067. (248)691-1800. Fax: (248)691-4531. E-mail: rbohy@hourdetroit.com  Managing Editor: George Bulanda. Assistant Editor: Brenna Sanchez. **Contact:**

Ric Bohy, editor. **75% freelance written.** Monthly "general interest/lifestyle magazine aimed at a middle- to upper-income readership aged 17-70." Estab. 1996. Circ. 40,000. **Pays on acceptance.** Publishes ms an average of 2 months after acceptance. Byline given. Offers 30% kill fee. Buys first North American serial rights. Editorial lead time minimu 1½ months. Submit seasonal material 12 months in advance. Accepts queries by mail, e-mail, fax. Sample copy for $6.
**Nonfiction:** Book excerpts, exposé, general interest, historical/nostalgic, interview/profile, new product, photo feature, technical, travel. **Buys 150 mss/year.** Query with published clips. Length: 300-2,500 words. Sometimes pays expenses of writers on assignment.
**Photos:** State availability of photos with submission.

**$ $ LANSING CITY LIMITS**, CityLimits Magazine, Inc., 325-B N. Clippert, Lansing MI 48912. **Contact:** Marcia Cipriani, editor. **75% freelance written.** Monthly magazine covering the Lansing area. "All material must have a strong Lansing-area slant." Estab. 1994. Circ. 10,000. Pays on publication. Publishes ms an average of 3 months after acceptance. Byline given. Offers 25% kill fee. Buys first North American serial rights or one-time rights. Editorial lead time 2 months. Submit seasonal material 5 months in advance. Accepts simultaneous submissions. Reports in 1 month. Sample copy for 10×12 SASE and $5. Writer's guidelines for #10 SASE.
**Nonfiction:** Exposé, general interest, historical/nostalgic, humor, interview/profile, personal experience, travel. **Buys 30 mss/year.** Query with published clips. Length: 200-1,800 words. **Pays $50-250.** Sometimes pays expenses of writers on assignment.
**Photos:** State availability of photos with submission. Reviews transparencies. Negotiates payment individually. Model releases and identification of subjects required. Buys one-time rights.
**Columns/Departments:** Where Are They Now? (profiles of Lansing-ites), 800 words. Query with published clips. **Pays $50-150.**

# Minnesota

**$ $ LAKE SUPERIOR MAGAZINE**, Lake Superior Port Cities, Inc., P.O. Box 16417, Duluth MN 55816-0417. (218)722-5002. Fax: (218)722-4096. E-mail: edit@lakesuperior.com. Website: http://www.lakesuperior.com. Editor: Paul L. Hayden. **Contact:** Konnie LeMay, managing editor. **60% freelance written.** Works with a small number of new/unpublished writers each year. Bimonthly regional magazine covering contemporary and historic people, places and current events around Lake Superior. Estab. 1979. Circ. 20,000. Pays on publication. Publishes ms an average of 10 months after acceptance. Byline given. Offers $25 kill fee. Buys first North American serial and some second rights. Submit seasonal material 1 year in advance. Reports in 2 months. Sample copy for $3.95 and 5 first-class stamps. Writer's guidelines for #10 SASE.
**Nonfiction:** Book excerpts, general interest, historic/nostalgic, humor, interview/profile (local), personal experience, photo feature (local), travel (local), city profiles, regional business, some investigative. **Buys 45 mss/year.** Query with published clips. Length: 300-2,200 words. **Pays $80-600.** Sometimes pays the expenses of writers on assignment.
**Photos:** "Quality photography is our hallmark." Send photos with submission. Reviews contact sheets, 2×2 and larger transparencies, 4×5 prints. Offers $20 for b&w and $40 for color; $75 for covers. Captions, model releases, identification of subjects required.
**Columns/Departments:** Current events and things to do (for Events Calendar section), less than 300 words; Around The Circle (media reviews; short pieces on Lake Superior; Great Lakes environmental issues; themes, letters and short pieces on events and highlights of the Lake Superior Region); I Remember (nostalgic lake-specific pieces), up to 1,100 words; Life Lines (single personality profile with photography), up to 900 words. Other headings include Destinations, Nature, Wilderness Living, Heritage, Shipwreck, Chronicle, Lake Superior's Own, House for Sale. **Buys 20 mss/year.** Query with published clips. **Pays $90.**
**Fiction:** Ethnic, historic, humorous, mainstream, novel excerpts, slice-of-life vignettes, ghost stories. Must be targeted regionally. **Buys only 2-3 mss/year.** Query with published clips. Length: 300-2,500 words. **Pays $1-125.**
**Tips:** "Well-researched queries are attended to. We actively seek queries from writers in Lake Superior communities. We prefer manuscripts to queries. Provide enough information on why the subject is important to the region and our readers, or why and how something is unique. We want details. The writer must have a thorough knowledge of the subject and how it relates to our region. We prefer a fresh, unused approach to the subject which provides the reader with an emotional involvement. Almost all of our articles feature quality photography, color or black and white. It is a prerequisite of all nonfiction. All submissions should include a *short* biography of author/photographer; mug shot sometimes used. Blanket submissions need not apply."

**$ $ MINNESOTA MONTHLY**, 10 S. Fifth St., Suite 1000, Minneapolis MN 55402. Fax: (612)371-5801. E-mail: dmahoney@mnmo.com. Website: http://www.mnmo.com. **Contact:** David Mahoney, editor. **50% freelance written.** "*Minnesota Monthly* is a regional lifestyle publication written for a sophisticated, well-educated audience living primarily in the Twin Cities area." Estab. 1967. Circ. 80,000. **Pays on acceptance.** Accepts queries by mail, e-mail, fax. Writer's guidelines for SASE.
**Nonfiction:** Regional news and events, issues, services, places, people. "We are looking for fresh ideas and concise, compelling, well-crafted writing." Query with résumé, published clips and SASE. Length: 1,000-4,000 words. Pay negotiable.

**Columns/Departments:** In Short (Minnesota news and slice-of-life stories), fewer than 400 words; Portrait (photo-driven profile), 360 words; People (three short profiles), 250 words each; Just Asking (interview), 900 words; Showcase (arts and entertainment), 450 words; Midwest Traveler, 950-2,000 words; History; Back Page (essay), 500-600 words. Query with résumé, published clips and SASE. Pay negotiable.

**Tips:** "Our readers like to travel, eat out, attend arts events and read. With that in mind, our goal is to provide readers with the information they need to enrich their active lives."

## Mississippi

**$ COAST MAGAZINE**, Ship Island Holding Co., P.O. Box 1209, Gulfport MS 39502. (228)594-0004. Fax: (228)594-0074. **Contact:** Carla Arsaga, editor. **20% freelance written.** Bimonthly magazine. "We describe ourselves as a lifestyle magazine." Estab. 1993. Circ. 15,000. Pays on publication. Publishes ms an average of 4 months after acceptance. Byline given. Offers $25 kill fee. Buys first North American serial rights. Editorial lead time 6 months. Writer's guidelines for #10 SASE.

**Nonfiction:** General interest, historical/nostalgic, interview/profile, photo feature. All content is related to the Mississippi gulf coast. **Buys 6 mss/year.** Query by mail only with published clips. **Pays $25-150.**

**Photos:** Transparencies preferred. Negotiates payment individually. Captions, model releases, identification of subjects required. Buys all rights. Does not return unsolicited material.

**Columns/Departments:** Shelly Powers, assistant editor. Hot Shots (interesting people), 400 words; Art Scene (local artists), 750 words; Reflections (historical), 1,200 words. **Buys 6 mss/year.** Query with published clips. **Pays $25-75.**

**Tips:** "Being familiar with *Coast Magazine* and its readership is a must. Freelancers should send the editor a cover letter that is indicative of his or her writing style along with strong writing samples."

**N: $ $ MISSISSIPPI MAGAZINE**, DownHome Publications, 5 Lakeland Circle, Jackson MS 39216. Fax: (601)982-8447. **Contact:** Jane Alexander, editor. **90% freelance written.** Bimonthly magazine covering Mississippi—the state and its lifestyles. "We are interested in positive stories reflecting Mississippi's rich traditions and heritage, and focusing on the contributions the state and its natives have made to the arts, literature and culture. In each issue we showcase homes and gardens, lifestyle issues, food, business, design, art and more." Estab. 1981. Circ. 30,000. Pays on publication. Publishes ms an average of 6 months after acceptance. Byline given. Offers 50% kill fee. Buys first North American serial rights. Editorial lead time 6 months. Submit seasonal material 1 year in advance. Accepts queries by mail, fax. Accepts simultaneous submissions. Reports in 1 month on queries; 3 months on mss. Sample copy and writer's guidelines for SAE.

**Nonfiction:** General interest, historical/nostalgic, how-to (home decor), interview/profile, personal experience, travel. "No opinion, political, essay, book reviews, exposé." **Buys 15 mss/year.** Query. Length: 900-1,800 words. **Pays $150-350 for assigned articles; $75-200 for unsolicited articles.**

**Photos:** Send photos with submission. Reviews transparencies and prints. Negotiates payment individually. Captions, model releases and identification of subjects preferred. Buys one-time rights.

**Columns/Departments:** Business (positive stories about old, new or innovative people or products), 1,000 words; People (interviews and profiles of famous Mississippi natives or residents), 1,200 words. **Buys 6 mss/year.** Query. **Pays $150-300.**

## Missouri

**$ FOCUS/KANSAS CITY**, Communications Publishing Group, 3100 Broadway, #660, Kansas City MO 64111. (816)960-1988. Fax: (816)960-1989. **Contact:** Neoshia M. Paige, editor. **80% freelance written.** Quarterly magazine covering professional and business development. "Positive how-to, motivational profiles." Estab. 1994. Circ. 30,000. Pays on publication. Publishes ms an average of 6 months after acceptance. Byline given. Buys first rights. Accepts simultaneous submissions. Reports in 2 months. Sample copy for $3. Writer's guidelines for #10 SASE.

**Nonfiction:** Book excerpts, general interest, historical/nostalgic, how-to, humor, inspirational, interview/profile, personal experience, photo feature, technical, travel. **Buys 15 mss/year.** Length: 750-2,000 words. **Pays $150-400 for assigned articles; 12¢/word for unsolicited articles.** Sometimes pays expenses of writers on assignment.

**Photos:** State availability of photos with submission. Reviews transparencies. Offers $20-25 per photo. Captions, model releases and identification of subjects required. Buys all rights.

**Columns/Departments:** Profiles of Achievement (regional Kansas Citians), 500-1,500 words. **Buys 30 mss/year.** Pays 10¢/word.

**Fiction:** Adventure, ethnic, historical, humorous, mainstream, slice-of-life vignettes. **Buys 3 mss/year.** Length: 25-250 words. **Pays $25-100.**

**Fillers:** Anecdotes, facts, gags to be illustrated by cartoonist, newsbreaks, short humor. **Buys 10/year.** Length: 25-250 words. **Pays $25-100.**

**Tips:** "For new writers—send complete manuscript, double-spaced; clean copy only. If available, send clips of previously published work and résumé. Should state when available to write. Include on first page of manuscript: name, address, phone, social security number, word count and include SASE."

**$ $ $KANSAS CITY MAGAZINE**, 118 Southwest Blvd., 3rd Floor, Kansas City MO. (816)421-4111. Fax: (816)936-0509. Website: http://www.kcmag.com. **Contact:** Zim Loy, editor. **75% freelance written.** Bimonthly magazine. "Our mission is to celebrate living in Kansas City. We are a consumer lifestyle/general interest magazine focused on Kansas City, its people and places." Estab. 1994. Circ. 31,000. **Pays on acceptance.** Publishes ms an average of 3 months after acceptance. Byline given. Offers 10% kill fee. Buys first North American serial rights. Editorial lead time 4 months. Submit seasonal material 6 months in advance. Accepts queries by mail, e-mail, fax. Accepts simultaneous submissions. Sample copy for 8½×11 SAE or on website.
**Nonfiction:** Exposé, general interest, interview/profile, photo feature. **Buys 15-20 mss/year.** Query with published clips. Length: 250-3,000 words.
**Photos:** Negotiates payment individually. Buys one-time rights.
**Columns/Departments:** Entertainment (Kansas City only), 1,000 words; Food (Kansas City food and restaurants only), 1,000 words. **Buys 10 mss/year.** Query with published clips. **Pays $200-500.**

**$ $PITCHWEEKLY**, Pitch Publishing, Inc., 3535 Broadway, Suite 400, Kansas City MO 64111-2826. (816)561-6061. Fax: (816)756-0502. E-mail: brodgers@pitch.com. Website: http://www.pitch.com. **Contact:** Bruce Rodgers, editor. **75% freelance written.** Weekly alternative newspaper that covers arts, entertainment, politics and social and cultural awareness in the Kansas City metro region. Estab. 1980. Circ. 90,000. Pays 1 month from publication. Buys first or one-time rights or makes work-for-hire assignments. Editorial lead time 1 month. Submit seasonal material 2 months in advance. *Query first by mail!* Reports in 2 months.
**Nonfiction:** Exposé, humor, interview/profile, opinion, news, photo feature. Special issues: all holidays; Best of Music; Best of Film. Prefers nonfiction with local hook. **Buys 40-50 mss/year.** Query with published clips. Length: 500-5,000 words. **Pays $25-300.** Sometimes pays expenses of writers on assignment.
**Reprints:** Send tearsheet or photocopy of article or short story or typed ms with rights for sale noted and information about when and where the article previously appeared. Pays 50% of amount paid for an original article.
**Photos:** Send photos with submission. Reviews contact sheets. Pays for photos with ms: $25-75. Captions and identification of subjects required. Buys one-time rights.
**Fiction:** Holiday-theme fiction published on Christmas, Thanksgiving, Valentine's Day, Halloween, April Fool's (humor/satire). "Must be slightly off-beat and good." Length: 1,500-2,500 words. **Pays $75-200**
**Tips:** "Approach us with unusual angles on current political/social topics. Send well-written, clear, concise query with identifiable direction of proposed piece and SASE for reply or return. Previous publication in AAN paper a plus. We're looking for features and secondary features: current events in visual and performing arts (include new trends, etc.); social issues (OK to have an opinion as long as facts are well documented); liberal politics."

**$RIVER HILLS TRAVELER**, Todd Publishing, Route 4, Box 4396, Piedmont MO 63957. (314)223-7143. E-mail: btodd@semo.net. Website: http://www.deepozarks.com. **Contact:** Bob Todd, editor. **60% freelance written.** Monthly tabloid covering "outdoor sports and nature in the southeast quarter of Missouri, the east and central Ozarks. Topics like those in *Field & Stream* and *National Geographic*." Estab. 1973. Circ. 7,500. Pays on publication. Publishes ms an average of 2 months after acceptance. Byline given. Buys one-time rights. Editorial lead time 2 months. Submit seasonal material 1 year in advance. Accepts queries by mail, e-mail. Accepts simultaneous submissions. Reports in 2 months. Sample copy and writer's guidelines for SAE or on website.
**Nonfiction:** Historical/nostalgic, how-to, humor, opinion, personal experience ("Me and Joe"), photo feature, technical, travel. "No stories about other geographic areas." **Buys 80 mss/year.** Query with writing samples. Length: 1,500 maximum words. **Pays $15-50.** Sometimes pays expenses of writers on assignment.
**Reprints:** Send typed ms with rights for sale noted and information about when and where the article previously appeared.
**Photos:** Send photos with submission. Negotiates payment individually. Pays $25 for covers. Buys one-time rights.
**Tips:** "We are a 'poor man's' *Field & Stream* and *National Geographic*—about the eastern Missouri Ozarks. We prefer stories that relate an adventure that causes a reader to relive an adventure of his own or consider embarking on a similar adventure. Think of an adventure in camping or cooking, not just fishing and hunting. How-to is great, but not simple instructions. We encourage good first-person reporting."

**$ $SPRINGFIELD! MAGAZINE**, Springfield Communications Inc., P.O. Box 4749, Springfield MO 65808-4749. (417)882-4917. **Contact:** Robert C. Glazier, editor. **85% freelance written.** Eager to work with a small number of new/unpublished writers each year. "This is an extremely local and provincial monthly magazine. No *general* interest articles." Estab. 1979. Circ. 10,000. Pays on publication. Publishes ms from 3 months to 3 years after acceptance. Byline given. Buys first serial rights. Submit seasonal material 1 year in advance. Reports in 3 months on queries; 2 weeks on queries with Springfield hook; 6 months on mss. Sample copy for $5.30 and 9½×12½ SAE.
**Nonfiction:** Book excerpts (Springfield authors only), exposé (local topics only), historical/nostalgic (top priority but must be local history), how-to, humor, interview/profile (needs more on females than males), personal experience, photo feature, travel (1 page/month). Local interest *only*; no material that could appeal to other magazine elsewhere. **Buys 150 mss/year.** Query with published clips or send complete ms with SASE. Length: 500-5,000 words. **Pays $35-250.**
**Photos:** Send photos with query or ms. Reviews b&w and color contact sheets, 4×5 color transparencies, 5×7 b&w

prints. Pays $5-35 for b&w, $10-50 for color. Captions, model releases, identification of subjects required. Buys one-time rights. "Needs more photo features of a nostalgic bent."

**Columns/Departments: Buys 250 mss/year.** Query or send complete ms. Length varies, usually 500-2,500 words.

**Tips:** "We prefer writers read eight or ten copies of our magazine prior to submitting any material for our consideration. The magazine's greatest need is for features which comment on these times in Springfield. We are overstocked with nostalgic pieces right now. We also need profiles about young women and men of distinction."

## Montana

**$ $ MONTANA MAGAZINE**, Lee Enterprises, P.O. Box 5630, Helena MT 59604-5630. (406)443-2842. Fax: (406)443-5480. E-mail: editor@montanamagazine.com. Website: http://www.montanamagazine.com. **Contact:** Beverly R. Magley, editor. **90% freelance written.** Bimonthly "strictly Montana-oriented magazine that features community and personality profiles, contemporary issues, travel pieces." Estab. 1970. Circ. 40,000. Publishes ms an average of 1 year after acceptance. Byline given. Offers $50-100 kill fee on assigned stories only. Buys one-time rights. Submit seasonal material at least 12 months in advance. Query by mail, e-mail, fax. Accepts simultaneous submissions. Reports in 6 months. Sample copy for $5 or on website. Guidelines for #10 SASE or on website.

**Nonfiction:** Essays, general interest, interview/profile, photo feature, travel. Special features on summer and winter destination points. Query by September for summer material; March for winter material. No 'me and Joe' hiking and hunting tales; no blood-and-guts hunting stories; no poetry; no fiction; no sentimental essays. **Buys 30 mss/year.** Query with samples and SASE. Length: 300-3,000 words. **Pays 15¢/word for articles.** Sometimes pays the expenses of writers on assignment.

**Reprints:** Send information about when and where the article previously appeared. Pays 50% of amount paid for an original article.

**Photos:** Send photos with submission. Reviews contact sheets, 35mm or larger format transparencies, 5×7 prints. Offers additional payment for photos accepted with ms. Captions, model releases, identification of subjects required. Buys one-time rights.

**Columns/Departments:** Memories (reminisces of early-day Montana life), 800-1,000 words; Small Towns (profiles of communities), 1,500-2,000 words; Made in MT (successful cottage industries), 700-1,000 words plus b&w or color photo. Humor, 800-1,000 words. Query with samples and SASE.

**Tips:** "We avoid commonly-known topics so Montanans won't ho-hum through more of what they already know. If it's time to revisit a topic, we look for a unique slant."

## Nevada

**$ $ NEVADA MAGAZINE**, 401 N. Carson St., Carson City NV 89701-4291. (775)687-5416. Fax: (775)687-6159. E-mail: editor@nevadamagazine.com. Website: http://www.nevadamagazine.com. Editor: David Moore. **Contact:** Carolyn Graham, associate editor. **50% freelance written.** Works with a small number of new/unpublished writers each year. Bimonthly magazine published by the state of Nevada to promote tourism. Estab. 1936. Circ. 90,000. Pays on publication. Publishes ms an average of 8 months after acceptance. Byline given. Buys first North American serial rights. Submit seasonal material at least 6 months in advance. Accepts queries by mail, e-mail, fax, phone. Reports in 1 month. Sample copy for $1. Writer's guidelines for SASE.

○→ Break in with shorter departments, rather than trying to tackle a big feature. Good bets are Dining Out, Recreation, Casinoland, Side Trips, and Roadside Attractions.

**Nonfiction:** Nevada topics only. Historical, nostalgia, photo feature, people profile, recreational, travel, think pieces. "We welcome stories and photos on speculation." Publishes nonfiction book excerpts. **Buys 40 unsolicited mss/year.** Submit complete ms or query. Length: 500-1,800 words. **Pays $50-500.**

**Photos:** Denise Barr, art director. Send photo material with accompanying ms. Pays $20-100 for color transparencies and glossy prints. Name, address and caption should appear on each photo or slide. Buys one-time rights.

**Tips:** "Keep in mind the magazine's purpose is to promote Nevada tourism. Keys to higher payments are quality and editing effort (more than length). Send cover letter; no photocopies. We look for a light, enthusiastic tone of voice without being too cute; articles bolstered by facts and thorough research; and unique angles on Nevada subjects."

## New Hampshire

**$ $ NEW HAMPSHIRE EDITIONS**, Network Publications, Inc., 100 Main St., Nashua NH 03060. Fax: (603)889-5557. E-mail: editor@nheditions.com. Website: http://www.nheditions.com. **Contact:** Rick Broussard, editor. **50% freelance written.** Monthly magazine devoted to New Hampshire people, issues, business technology. "We want stories written for, by and about the people of New Hampshire with emphasis on qualities that set us apart from other states. We promote business and economic development." Estab. 1986. Circ. 24,000. Pays on publication. Byline given. Offers 25% kill fee. Buys all rights. Editorial lead time 3 months. Submit seasonal material 3 months in advance. Query

by mail, e-mail, fax. Accepts simultaneous submissions. Reports in 2 months on queries; 3 months on mss.
**Nonfiction:** Essays, general interest, historical/nostalgic, photo feature, business. **Buys 30 mss/year.** Query with published clips. Length: 800-2,000 words. **Pays $25-175.** Sometimes pays expenses of writers on assignment.
**Photos:** State availability of photos with submission. Offers no additional payment for photos accepted with ms. Captions, model releases, identification of subjects required. Rights purchased vary.

◼ The online magazine carries original content not found in the print edition. Contact: Rick Broussard, online editor.

**Tips:** Network Publications publishes 1 monthly magazine entitled *New Hampshire Editions* and "specialty" publications including *Destination New Hampshire*, *The World Trader*, *New Hampshire Legacy*, *The New Hampshire Century* and *New Hampshire Guide to the Internet & Technology*, each relating to aspects of the economic development, commerce, and diverse culture of New Hampshire. "In general, our articles deal with the people of New Hampshire—their lifestyles and interests. We also present localized stories about national and international issues, ideas and trends. We will only use stories that show our readers how these issues have an impact on their daily lives. We cover a wide range of topics, including healthcare, politics, law, real-life dramas, regional history, medical issues, business, careers, environmental issues, the arts, the outdoors, education, food, recreation, etc. Many of our readers are what we call 'The New Traditionalists'—aging Baby Boomers who have embraced solid American values and contemporary New Hampshire lifestyles."

# New Jersey

**$ $ ATLANTIC CITY MAGAZINE**, P.O. Box 2100, Pleasantville NJ 08232-1924. (609)272-7900. Fax: (609)272-7910. E-mail: epifanio@earthlink.net. **Contact:** Mike Epifanio, editor. **80% freelance written.** Works with small number of new/unpublished writers each year. Monthly regional magazine covering issues pertinent to the Jersey Shore area. Estab. 1978. Circ. 50,000. Pays on publication. Publishes ms an average of 4 months after acceptance. Byline given. Buys one-time rights. Offers variable kill fee. Submit seasonal material 6 months in advance. Reports in 6 weeks. Sample copy for $3 and 9 × 12 SAE with 6 first-class stamps. Writer's guidelines for SASE.
**Nonfiction:** Entertainment, general interest, recreation, history, lifestyle, interview/profile, photo feature, trends. "No hard news or investigative pieces. No travel pieces or any article without a south Jersey shore area/Atlantic City slant." Query. Length: 100-3,000 words. **Pays $50-500 for assigned articles; $50-350 for unsolicited articles.** Sometimes pays the expenses of writers on assignment.
**Photos:** Send photos. Reviews contact sheets, negatives, 2¼ × 2¼ transparencies, 8 × 10 prints. Pay varies. Captions, model releases, identification of subjects required. Buys one-time rights.
**Columns/Departments:** Art, Gambling, Entertainment, Sports, Dining, History, Style, Real Estate. Query with published clips. Length: 500-2,000 words. **Pays $150-400.**
**Tips:** "Our readers are a broad base of local residents and visiting tourists. We need stories that will appeal to both audiences."

**ℕ $ $ MONTAGE MAGAZINE**, The Write Approach, P.O. Box 2, Allamuchy NJ 07820. (908)979-0400. Fax: (908)813-3201. E-mail: approach@goes.com. Website: http://www.montagemag.com. Editor: Candace Botha. Executive Director: L.A. Popp. **Contact:** Lorraine McKiniry, associate editor. **60% freelance written.** Quarterly magazine covering New Jersey living. "We are a lifestyle publication covering all aspects of living in New Jersey—travel, medical, dining, antiques, photography, health, fitness, petcare, celebrity profiles, and timely topics of interest to our readers." Estab. 1995. Circ. 30,000. Pays on publication. Publishes ms an average of 2-4 months after acceptance. Byline given. Offers 25% kill fee. Buys first, electronic or all rights. Editorial lead time 6 weeks. Submit seasonal material 4 months in advance. Accepts queries by mail, e-mail, fax. Accepts simultaneous submissions. Reports in 3 weeks on queries; 2 months on mss. Sample copy for $3.50 or on website. Writer's guidelines for #10 SASE or by e-mail.
**Nonfiction:** General interest, historical/nostalgic, humor, inspirational, interview/profile, travel, medical, dining. No fiction, poetry, how to and anything morbid or sexually slanted. **Buys 40-50 mss/year.** Query with published clips. Length: 750-2,500 words. **Pays $275-450.**
**Photos:** State availability of or send photos with submission. Reviews 2 × 2 transparencies and 4 × 6 prints. Negotiates payment individually. Captions, model releases and identification of subjects required. Buys one-time or all rights (if assigned).
**Columns/Departments:** Susan Paulits, assistant editor. "We currently have writers for all our columns. However, we are always open to queries and good ideas for future columns." **Buys 40-60 mss/year.** Query with published clips. **Pays $225-350.**
**Fillers:** Susan Paulits, assistant editor. Facts, gags to be illustrated by cartoonist, short humor. **Buys 10/year.** Length: 100-250 words. **Pays $50-100.**
**Tips:** "Great grammar, proper punctuation and a sincere appreciation of the advantages for living in New Jersey will always interest the editorial staff. We are always looking for that unusual slant that spotlights a unique individual, a celebrity, an event or a topic of interest that is specific to New Jersey."

**$ $ NEW JERSEY OUTDOORS**, New Jersey Department of Environmental Protection, CN 402, Trenton NJ 08625. (609)777-4182. Fax: (609)292-3198. E-mail: njo@dep.state.nj.us. Website: http://www.state.nj.us/dep/njo. **Con-**

**tact:** Denise Damiano Mikics, editor. **75% freelance written.** Quarterly magazine highlighting New Jersey's natural and historic resources and activities related to them. Estab. 1950. Circ. 15,000. Pays on publication. Byline given. Buys one-time rights. Editorial lead time 1 year. Submit seasonal material 1 year in advance. Accepts queries by mail, e-mail, fax. Reports in 3 months. Sample copy for $4.25 or on website. Writer's guidelines for #10 SASE.

**Nonfiction:** How-to, personal experience and general interest articles and photo features about the conservation and enjoyment of natural and historic resources (e.g., fishing, hunting, hiking, camping, skiing, boating, gardening, trips to/ activities in specific New Jersey locations). "*New Jersey Outdoors* is not interested in articles showing disregard for the environment or in items demonstrating unskilled people taking extraordinary risks." **Buys 30-40 mss/year.** Query with published clips. Length: 600-2,000 words. **Pays $100-500.** Sometimes pays expenses of writers on assignment.

**Reprints:** Rarely accepts previously published submissions. Send typed ms with rights for sale noted and information about when and where the article previously appeared. Pays up to 100% of amount paid for the original article.

**Photos:** State availability of photos with submission. Reviews duplicate transparencies and prints. Offers $20-125/ photo. Buys one-time rights.

**Tips:** "*New Jersey Outdoors* generally publishes season-specific articles, planned a year in advance. Topics should be fresh, and stories should be accompanied by *great* photography. Articles and photos *must* relate to New Jersey."

**$ $THE SANDPAPER, Newsmagazine of the Jersey Shore**, The SandPaper, Inc., 1816 Long Beach Blvd., Surf City NJ 08008-5461. (609)494-5900. Fax: (609)494-1437. E-mail: lbinews@hotmail.com. **Contact:** Jay Mann, managing editor. **10% freelance written.** Weekly tabloid covering subjects of interest to Jersey shore residents and visitors. "*The SandPaper* publishes two editions covering many of the Jersey Shore's finest resort communities including Long Beach Island and Ocean City, New Jersey. Each issue includes a mix of news, human interest features, opinion columns and entertainment/calendar listings." Estab. 1976. Circ. 60,000. Pays on publication. Publishes ms an average of 1 month after acceptance. Byline given. Offers 100% kill fee. Buys first or all rights. Submit seasonal material 3 months in advance. Accepts queries by mail, e-mail, fax, phone. Accepts simultaneous submissions. Reports in 1 month. Sample copy for 9×12 SAE with 8 first-class stamps.

**Nonfiction:** Essays, general interest, historical/nostalgic, humor, opinion, environmental submissions relating to the ocean, wetlands and pinelands. Must pertain to New Jersey shore locale. Also, arts, entertainment news, reviews if they have a Jersey Shore angle. **Buys 10 mss/year.** Send complete ms. Length: 200-2,000 words. **Pays $25-200.** Sometimes pays the expenses of writers on assignment.

**Reprints:** Send photocopy of article and information about when and where the article previously appeared. Pays 25-50% of amount paid for an original article.

**Photos:** Send photos with submission. Offers $8-25/photo. Buys one-time or all rights.

**Columns/Departments:** SpeakEasy (opinion and slice-of-life, often humorous); Commentary (forum for social science perspectives); both 1,000-1,500 words, preferably with local or Jersey Shore angle. **Buys 50 mss/year.** Send complete ms. **Pays $30.**

**Tips:** "Anything of interest to sun worshippers, beach walkers, nature watchers and water sports lovers is of potential interest to us. There is an increasing coverage of environmental issues. The opinion page and columns are most open to freelancers. We are steadily increasing the amount of entertainment-related material in our publication. Articles on history of the shore area are always in demand."

# New Mexico

**⬛ $ $NEW MEXICO MAGAZINE**, Lew Wallace Bldg., 495 Old Santa Fe Trail, Santa Fe NM 87501. (505)827-7447. Editor-in-Chief: Emily Drabanski. Editor: Jon Bowman. Senior Editor: Walter K. Lopez. Associate editor: Steve Larese. **Contact any editor. 70% freelance written.** Monthly magazine emphasizing New Mexico for a college-educated readership with above average income and interest in the Southwest. Estab. 1922. Circ. 125,000. **Pays on acceptance.** Publishes ms an average of 8 months to a year after acceptance. Buys first North American serial rights. Submit seasonal material 1 year in advance. Reports in 2 months. Sample copy for $2.95. Writer's guidelines for SASE.

**Nonfiction:** New Mexico subjects of interest to travelers. Historical, cultural, informational articles. "We are looking for more short, light and bright stories for the 'Asi Es Nuevo Mexico' section. Also, we are buying 12 mss per year for our Makin' Tracks series. No columns, cartoons, poetry or non-New Mexico subjects." **Buys 7-10 mss/issue.** Query by mail. with 3 published writing samples. No phone or fax queries. Length: 250-1,500 words. **Pays $100-600.**

**Reprints:** Rarely publishes reprints but sometimes publishes excerpts from novels and nonfiction books.

**Photos:** Purchased as portfolio or on assignment. Query or send contact sheet or transparencies to Art Director John Vaughan. Pays $50-80 for 8×10 b&w glossy prints; $50-150 for 35mm—prefers Kodachrome. Photos should be in plastic-pocketed viewing sheets. Captions and model releases required. Buys one-time rights.

**Tips:** "Your best bet is to write a fun, lively short feature (200-350 words) for our Asi Es Nuevo Mexico section or send a superb short (300 words) manuscript on a little-known person, event, aspect of history or place to see in New Mexico. Faulty research will ruin a writer's chances for the future. Good style, good grammar. No generalized odes to the state or the Southwest. No sentimentalized, paternalistic views of Indians or Hispanics. No glib, gimmicky 'travel brochure' writing. No first-person vacation stories. We're always looking for well-researched pieces on unusual aspects of New Mexico and lively writing."

# New York

**$ $ ADIRONDACK LIFE**, P.O. Box 410, Jay NY 12941-0410. (518)946-2191. Fax: (518)946-7461. E-mail: aledit @westelcom.com. **Contact:** Elizabeth Folwell, editor or Galen Crane, associate editor. **70% freelance written.** Prefers to work with published/established writers. Emphasizes the Adirondack region and the North Country of New York State in articles concerning outdoor activities, history and natural history directly related to the Adirondacks. Publishes 8 issues/year, including special Annual Outdoor Guide. Estab. 1970. Circ. 50,000. Pays 45 days after acceptance. Publishes ms an average of 6 months after acceptance. Byline given. Buys first North American serial rights. Submit seasonal material 1 year in advance. Reports in 45 days. Sample copy for $3 and 9 × 12 SAE. Writer's guidelines for #10 SASE.
**Nonfiction:** "*Adirondack Life* attempts to capture the unique flavor and ethos of the Adirondack mountains and North Country region through feature articles directly pertaining to the qualities of the area ." Special issues: Outdoors (May); Single-topic Collector's issue (September). **Buys 20-25 unsolicited mss/year.** Query by mail. Length: 2,500-5,000 words. **Pays 25¢/word.** Sometimes pays expenses of writers on assignment.
**Photos:** All photos must have been taken in the Adirondacks. Each issue contains a photo feature. Purchased with or without ms or on assignment. All photos must be individually identified as to subject or locale and must bear photographer's name. Submit color transparencies or b&w prints. Pays $100 for full page, b&w or color; $300 for cover (color only, vertical in format). Credit line given.
**Columns/Departments:** Special Places (unique spots in the Adirondack Park); Watercraft; Barkeater (personal to political); Wilderness (environmental issues); Working (careers in the Adirondacks); Home; Yesteryears; Kitchen; Profile; Historic Preservation; Sporting Scene. Query by mail. Length: 1,200-2,400 words. **Pays 25¢/word.**
**Fiction:** Considers first-serial novel excerpts in its subject matter and region.
**Tips:** "Do not send a personal essay about your meaningful moment in the mountains. We need factual pieces about regional history, sports, culture and business. We are looking for clear, concise, well-organized manuscripts that are strictly Adirondack in subject. Check back issues to be sure we haven't already covered your topic. Please do not send unsolicited manuscripts via e-mail."

**$ $ $ BROOKLYN BRIDGE MAGAZINE**, 388 Atlantic Ave., Brooklyn NY 11217-1703. (719)596-7400. E-mail: bbridge@mennen.tiac.net. Website: http://www.brooklynbridgemag.com. Editor: Melissa Ennen. **Contact:** Joe Fodor, senior editor. **50% freelance written.** Monthly magazine covering Brooklyn. Estab. 1995. Circ. 40,000. Pays on publication. Byline given. Offers 25% kill fee. Buys first North American serial rights. Editorial lead time 2 months. Submit seasonal material 3 months in advance. Accepts queries by mail, e-mail, phone. Reports in 1 week on queries; 1 month on mss. Sample copy for 9 × 11 and $2.39 postage or on website.
○━ Break in with health and education stories.
**Nonfiction** Essays, exposé, general interest, historical/nostalgic, interview/profile, personal experience, photo feature, Brooklyn's health, home and education. Must be related to Brooklyn. **Buys 100 mss/year.** Query with published clips. Length: 200-3,000 words. **Pays $100-1,000.** Sometimes pays expenses of writers on assignment.
**Photos:** Offers no additional payment for photos accepted with ms. Identification of subjects required. Acquires one-time rights.
**Columns/Departments:** Family, 1,250 words; Last Exit, 850 words; Street, 1,100 words. **Buys 24 mss/year.** Query with published clips or send complete ms. **Pays $250-500.**

**$ $ $ $ NEW YORK MAGAZINE**, Primedia Magazines, 444 Madison Ave., New York NY 10022. (212)508-0700. Website: http://www.newyorkmag.com. Editor: Caroline Miller. Managing Editor: Sarah Jewler. **Contact:** John Homans, executive editor. **25% freelance written.** Weekly magazine focusing on current events in the New York metropolitan area. Circ. 433,813. **Pays on acceptance.** Offers 25% kill fee. Buys first world serial and electronic rights. Submit seasonal material 2 months in advance. Reports in 1 month. Sample copy for $3.50 or on website. Writer's guidelines for SASE.
**Nonfiction:** Exposé, general interest, profile, new product, personal experience, travel. Query by mail. **Pays $1/word.** Pays expenses of writers on assignment.
The online magazine carries original content not found in the print edition. Contact: Simon Dumenco, online editor.
**Tips:** "Submit a detailed query to John Homans, *New York*'s executive editor. If there is sufficient interest in the proposed piece, the article will be assigned."

**N ★ $ NEW YORK NIGHTLIFE**, (formerly *Long Island Update*), MM&B Publishers, 990 Motor Pkwy., Central Islip NY 11722. (516)435-8890. Fax: (516)435-8925. E-mail: nynl@aol.com. **Contact:** Susan Weiner, editor-in-chief. **75% freelance written.** Monthly magazine. "*Nightlife* features stories on topics concerning New Yorkers, from local events to new products. We also cover entertainment on both the local level and Hollywood." Estab. 1990. Circ. 56,000. Pays on publication. Publishes ms an average of 3 months after acceptance. Byline given. Buys first rights. Editorial lead time 2 months. Submit seasonal material 3 months in advance. Accepts queries by mail, e-mail, fax, phone. Reports in 2 weeks. Sample copy for 11 × 14 SAE with 8 first-class stamps. Writer's guidelines for #10 SASE.
**Nonfiction:** General interest, how-to (home remodeling, decorating, etc.), humor, interview/profile, new product, travel.

Special issues: Bridal Guide (April 1999). **Buys 100-120 mss/year.** Query with published clips. Length: 200-1,700 words. **Pays $50-125.**

**Photos:** State availability of photos with submission. Reviews 3×5 transparencies, 5×7 prints. Offers no additional payment for photos accepted with ms. Buys one-time rights. Sometimes pays $15 per photo used.

**Columns/Departments:** Business (money matters, personal finance); Gourmet (recipes, new products); Health (medical news, exercise, etc.); all 600-750 words. Query with published clips. **Pays $50.**

**Fiction:** Humorous. **Buys 8-10 mss/year.** Query with published clips. Length: 600-750 words. **Pays $50.**

**Tips:** "We're looking for a flair for creative writing and an interest in celebrities, film, food and entertainment in general. No techies! Queries are happily reviewed and responded to. Feel free to follow up with a phone call 2-3 weeks later."

**$ $NEWSDAY**, Melville NY 11747-4250. Website: http://www.newsday.com. **Contact:** Noel Rubinton, viewpoints editor. Opinion section of daily newspaper. Byline given. Estab. 1940. Circ. 555,203.

**Nonfiction:** Seeks "opinion on current events, trends, issues—whether national or local, government or lifestyle. Must be timely, pertinent, articulate and opinionated. Preference for authors within the circulation area including New York City." Length: 700-800 words. **Pays $150-200.**

**Tips:** "It helps for prospective authors to be familiar with our paper and section."

**$ $SPOTLIGHT MAGAZINE**, Meadow Publications Inc., 126 Library Lane, Mamaroneck NY 10543. (914)381-4740. Fax: (914)381-4641. E-mail: meadowpub@aol.com. **Contact:** Dana B. Asher, editor-in-chief. **30% freelance written.** Monthly lifestyle magazine for the "upscale, educated, adult audience in the New York-New Jersey-Connecticut tri-state area. We try to appeal to a broad audience throughout our publication area." Estab. 1977. Circ. 75,000. **Pays on acceptance.** Byline given. Editorial lead time 3 months. Submit seasonal material 5 months in advance. Reports in 1 month. Sample copy for $2.

● *Spotlight* is looking for human interest articles and issue-related features woven around New York, New Jersey and Connecticut.

**Nonfiction:** Book excerpts, exposé, general human interest, how-to, humor, interview/profile, new product, photo feature, illustrations. Annual special-interest guides: Wedding (February, June, September); Dining (December, July); Home Design (March, April, October); Health (July, January); Education (January, August); Holiday Gifts (November); Senior Living (May, November). No fiction or poetry. **Buys 30 mss/year.** Query. **Pays $150 minimum.**

**Photos:** State availability of or send photos with submission. Reviews transparencies and prints. Negotiates payment individually. Captions, model releases, identification of subjects required (when appropriate). Buys one-time rights.

**[N] $ $SYRACUSE NEW TIMES**, A. Zimmer, Ltd., 1415 W. Genesee St., Syracuse NY 13204. Fax: (315)422-1721. E-mail: editorial@syracusenewtimes.com. Website: http://www.newtimes.rway.com. **Contact:** Christina Schwab, managing editor. **50% freelance written.** Weekly tabloid covering news, sports, arts and entertainment. "*Syracuse New Times* is an alternative weekly that can be topical, provocative, irreverent and intensely local." Estab. 1969. Circ. 43,000. Pays on publication. Publishes ms an average of 1 month after acceptance. Byline given. Buys one-time rights. Editorial lead time 3 months. Submit seasonal material 3 months in advance. Accepts simultaneous submissions. Reports in 2 weeks on queries; 1 month on mss. Sample copy for 9×11 SAE with 2 first-class stamps. Guidelines for #10 SASE.

**Nonfiction:** Essays, general interest. **Buys 200 mss/year.** Query by mail with published clips. Length: 250-2,500 words. **Pays $25-200.**

**Reprints:** Accepts previously published submissions.

**Photos:** State availability of photos or send photos with submission. Reviews 8×10 prints and color slides. Offers $10-25/photo or negotiates payment individually. Identification of subjects required. Buys one-time rights.

**Tips:** "Move to Syracuse and query with strong idea."

**$ $TIME OUT NEW YORK**, Time Out New York Partners, LP, 627 Broadway, 7th Floor, New York NY 10012. (212)539-4444. Fax: (212)253-1174. E-mail: letters@timeoutny.com. Website: http://www.timeoutny.com. President/Editor-in-Chief: Cyndi Stivers. **Contact:** Marseart Watson, editorial assistant. **20% freelance written.** Weekly magazine covering entertainment in New York City. "Those who want to contribute to *Time Out New York* must be intimate with New York City and its environs." Estab. 1995. Circ. 55,000. **Pays on acceptance.** Publishes ms an average of 1 month after acceptance. Byline sometimes given. Offers 25% kill fee. Accepts queries by mail, e-mail, fax. Makes work-for-hire assignments. Reports in 2 months.

⊶ Pitch ideas to the editor of the section to which you would like to contribute (i.e., film, music, dance, etc.). Be sure to include clips or writing samples with your query letter.

**Nonfiction:** General interest, interview/profile, travel (primarily within NYC area), reviews of various entertainment topics. No essays, articles about trends, unpegged articles. Query with published clips. Length: 250-1,500. **Pays 20¢/ word for b&w features and $300/page for color features.**

**Columns/Departments:** Around Town (Greg Emmanuel); Art (Howard Halle); Books & Poetry (Janet Steen); Byte Me (Tom Samiljan); Cabaret (H. Scott Jolley); Check Out (Milena Damjanov); Clubs (Adam Goldstone); Comedy (Greg Emmanuel); Dance (Gia Kourlas); Eat Out (Adam Rapoport); Film (Aaron Gell); Gay & Lesbian (Les Simpson); Kids (Barbara Aria); Music: Classical & Opera (Susan Jackson); Music: Rock, Jazz, etc. (Gail O'Hara); Radio (Billie Cohen); Sports (Brett Martin); Television (John Sellers); Theater (Sam Whitehead); Video (Andrew Johnston).

**Tips:** "We're always looking for quirky, less-known news about what's going on in New York City."

# North Carolina

**[N] $ $CAROLINA COUNTRY**, North Carolina Association of Electric Cooperatives, 3400 Sumner Blvd,, Raleigh NC 27616. E-mail: carolina.country@ncemcs.com. **Contact:** Michael E.C. Gery, editor. **30% freelance written.** Monthly magazine for members of North Carolina's electric cooperatives. General interest material concerning North Carolina's culture, business, history, people. Estab. 1952. Circ. 380,000. **Pays on acceptance.** Publishes ms an average of 3 months after acceptance. Byline given. Offers 50% kill fee. Buys all rights. Editorial lead time 3 months. Submit seasonal material 3 months in advance. Accepts simultaneous and previously published submissions (if outside North Carolina). Reports in 1 month on queries; 2 months on mss. All submissions must be made via e-mail.
**Nonfiction:** General interest, historical/nostalgic, humor, photo feature. **Buys 12 mss/year.** Send complete ms electronically. Length: 600-1,500 words. **Pays $200-500.**
**Reprints:** North Carolina subjects only. Send submission via e-mail. Pay negotiable.
**Photos:** State availability of photos with submission. Reviews transparencies, prints. Negotiates payment individually. Captions, identification of subjects required. Buys one-time rights.
**Columns/Departments:** Focus (useful resource news in North Carolina), 100 words. **Buys 10 mss/year.** Send complete ms electronically. **Pays $20-100.**
**Tips:** "Interested in North Carolina information that would not likely appear in local newspapers. Our readers are rural and suburban residents."

**[★] $ $OUR STATE, Down Home in North Carolina**, Mann Media, P.O. Box 4552, Greensboro NC 27404.(336)286-0600. Fax: (336)286-0100. Website: http://www.mannmedia2@aol.com. **Contact:** Mary Ellis, editor. **95% freelance written.** Monthly magazine covering North Carolina. "*Our State* is dedicated to providing editorial about the history, destinations, out-of-the-way places and culture of North Carolina." Estab. 1933. Circ. 46,000. Pays on publication. Publishes ms 6-24 months after acceptance. Byline given. Buys first North American serial rights. Editorial lead time 4 months. Submit seasonal material 4 months in advance. Accepts queries by mail, e-mail, fax. Reports in 6 weeks on queries; 2 months on mss. Sample copy for $2.95. Guidelines for #10 SASE.
**Nonfiction:** Historical/nostalgic, humor, personal experience, photo feature, travel. **Buys 60 mss/year.** Send complete ms. Length: 1,000-1,500 words. **Pays $125-250 for assigned articles; $50-125 for unsolicited articles.** Sometimes pays expenses of writers on assignment.
**Photos:** State availability of photos with submission. Reviews 35mm or 4×5 transparencies. Negotiates payment individually. Identification of subjects required. Buys one-time rights.
**Columns/Departments:** Tar Heel Memories (remembering something specific about NC), 1,200 words; Tar Heel Profile (profile of interesting North Carolinian), 1,500 words; Tar Heel Literature (review of books by NC writers and about NC), 300 words. **Buys 40 mss/year.** Send complete ms. **Pays $50-150.**
**Tips:** "We are developing a style for travel stories that is distinctly *Our State.* That style starts with outstanding photographs, which not only depict an area, but interpret it and thus become an integral part of the presentation. Our stories need not dwell on listings of what can be seen. Concentrate instead on the experience of being there, whether the destination is a hiking trail, a bed and breakfast, a forest or an urban area. What thoughts and feelings did the experience evoke? What was happening? What were the mood and comportment of the people? What were the sounds and smells? What was the feel of the area? Did bugs get in the sleeping bag? Could you see the bottom of the lake, and if so, what was there? We want to know why you went there, what you experienced, and what impressions you came away with. With at least one travel story an issue, we run a short sidebar called *Our State* Travel Guide. It explains how to get to the destination; rates or admission costs if there are any; a schedule of when the attraction is open or list of relevant dates; and an address and phone number for readers to write or call for more information. This sidebar eliminates the need for general-service information in the story."

**[N] $ $WILMINGTON MAGAZINE**, City Publishing USA, Inc., 201 N. Front St., Wilmington NC 28401. (910)815-0600. E-mail: dbetz@wilmington.net. Managing Editor: Kristin Gibson. **Contact:** Don Betz, publisher. **100% freelance written.** Bimonthly magazine. "*Wilmington Magazine* appeals to residents, businesses and visitors alike. Our award-winning photography captures the faces and places of our community, complemented by articles that explore an indepth look at events and people." Estab. 1994. Circ. 8,000. Pays on publication. Publishes ms an average of 1 month after acceptance. Byline given. Buys first rights and one-time rights. Editorial lead time 6 weeks. Submit seasonal material 3 months in advance. Accepts simultaneous submissions. Reports in 1 month.
**Nonfiction:** Essays, general interest, historical/nostalgic, humor, interview/profile, photo feature, travel. No negative exposés or self-promotion. **Buys 4 mss/year.** Query with published clips. Length: 900-2,000 words. **Pays 10-12½¢/ word.** Sometimes pays expenses of writers on assignment.
**Photos:** Send photos with submission. Reviews transparencies. Offers $25-50/photo. Captions, model releases, identification of subjects required. Buys one-time rights.
**Columns/Departments:** Arts & Entertainment, Restaurant Spotlight, both 1,500-1,800 words. **Buys 12 mss/year.** Query with published clips. **Pays 10-12½¢/word.**
**Tips:** "Be familiar with southeastern North Carolina."

# North Dakota

**N** **$ $ NORTH DAKOTA REC/RTC MAGAZINE,** North Dakota Association of Rural Electric Cooperatives, 3201 Nygren Dr. NW, P.O. Box 727, Mandan ND 58554-0727. (701)663-6501. Fax: (701)663-3745. E-mail: kbrick@nda rec.com. Website: http://www.ndarec.com. Managing Editor: Jo Ann Winistorfer. **Contact:** Kent Brick, editor. **40% freelance written.** Consumer publication published monthly covering information of interest to memberships of electric cooperatives and telephone cooperatives. "We publish a general interest magazine for North Dakotans. We treat subjects pertaining to living and working in the northern Great Plains. We provide progress reporting on electric cooperatives and telephone cooperatives." Estab. 1954. Circ. 80,000. **Pays on acceptance.** Publishes ms an average of 6 months after acceptance. Byline given. Buys one-time rights or makes work-for-hire assignments. Editorial lead time 6 months. Submit seasonal material 6 months in advance. Accepts queries by mail, e-mail, fax. Accepts simultaneous submissions.
**Nonfiction:** General interest, historical/nostalgic, interview/profile, new product, travel. Upcoming theme issues include farm equipment sales show, home improvement and healthcare. **Buys 20 mss/year.** Query with published clips. Length: 1,500-2,000 words. **Pays $100-500 minimum for assigned articles; $300-600 for unsolicited articles.** Sometimes pays expenses of writers on assignment.
**Reprints:** Accepts previously published submissions.
**Photos:** State availability of photos with submission. Reviews contact sheets. Negotiates payment individually. Identification of subjects required. Buys one-time rights.
**Columns/Departments:** Energy use and financial planning, both 750 words. **Buys 6 mss/year.** Query with published clips. **Pays $100-300.**
**Fiction:** Historical, humorous, slice-of-life vignettes, western. **Buys 1 ms/year.** Query with published clips. Length: 1,000-2,500 words. **Pays $100-400.**
**Tips:** "Deal with what's real: real data, real people, real experiences, real history, etc."

# Ohio

**$ BEND OF THE RIVER MAGAZINE,** P.O. Box 859, Maumee OH 43537. (419)893-0022. **Contact:** R. Lee Raizk, publisher. **90% freelance written.** Monthly magazine for readers interested in northwestern Ohio history, antiques, etc. Estab. 1972. Circ. 6,500. Pays on publication. Publishes ms an average of 6 months after acceptance. Byline given. Buys one-time rights. Submit seasonal material 2 months in advance; deadline for holiday issue is November 1. Reports in up to 6 months. Sample copy for $1.25.
● This magazine reports that it is eager to work with new/unpublished writers. "We buy material that we like whether it is by an experienced writer or not."
**Nonfiction:** "We deal heavily in Northwestern Ohio history and nostalgia. We are looking for old snapshots of the Toledo area to accompany articles, personal reflection, etc." **Buys 75 unsolicited mss/year.** Submit complete ms or send query. Length: 1,500 words. **Pays $10-75.**
**Reprints:** Accepts previously published submissions. Send tearsheet of article and information about when and where the article previously appeared. Pays 100% of the amount paid for an original article.
**Photos:** Purchases b&w or color photos with accompanying mss. Pays $1 minimum. Captions required.
**Tips:** "Any Toledo area, well-researched nostalgia, local history will be put on top of the heap. If you send a picture with manuscript, it gets an A+! We pay a small amount but usually use our writers often and through the years. We're loyal."

**$ $ $ CLEVELAND MAGAZINE,** City Magazines, Inc., 1422 Euclid Ave., #730Q, Cleveland OH 44115. **Contact:** Liz Vaccariello, editor. **70% freelance written,** mostly by assignment. Monthly magazine with a strong Cleveland/ northeast Ohio angle. Estab. 1972. Circ. 50,000. Pays on publication. Publishes ms an average of 3 months after acceptance. Byline given. Offers 50% kill fee. Buys first rights and second serial (reprint) rights. Editorial lead time 6 months. Submit seasonal material 8 months in advance. Accepts simultaneous submissions. Reports in 2 months.
**Nonfiction:** Book excerpts, general interest, historical/nostalgic, humor, interview/profile. **Buys 1 ms/year.** Query with published clips. Length: 800-5,000 words. **Pays $200-800.** Sometimes pays expenses of writers on assignment.
**Columns/Departments:** City Life (Cleveland trivia/humor/info briefs), 200 words. **Buys 2 mss/year.** Query with published clips. **Pays $50.**

**$ THE LIVING MAGAZINES,** Community Publications, Inc., 179 Fairfield Ave., Bellevue KY 41073. (606)291-1412. Fax: (606)291-1417. E-mail: livingreat@aol.com. **Contact:** Linda R. Krummel, company editor-in-chief and editor of *Hyde Park Living, Indian Hill Living, Wyoming Living*; Linda Johnson, editor (*Fort Thomas Living, Fort Mitchell Living*); Paul Krummel, editor (*Blue Ash Living*); Mary Sikora, editor (*Oakwood Living*). **50% freelance written.** Group of monthly neighborhood magazines covering the people, places and events of Hyde Park, Oakwood, Wyoming, Indian Hill, and Blue Ash, Ohio; and Fort Mitchell and Fort Thomas, Kentucky. "We will not entertain submissions without a direct tie to one of our communities." Circ. 2,400 to 5,800/magazine. Pays on publication. Publishes ms 6 months after acceptance. Byline given, except for press releases. Buys one-time rights. Editorial lead time 2 months. Accepts queries by mail, fax, phone. Sample copy for $2 plus postage.
**Nonfiction:** General interest, historical/nostalgic, humor, interview/profile, photo feature. Query with published clips.

Length: 100-1,000 words. **Pays $50 maximum.** Does not pay for unsolicited articles. Sometimes pays the expenses of writers on assignment.

**Photos:** Send photos with submission. Negotiates payment individually. Identification of subjects required. Buys one-time rights. Payment negotiated.

**Fiction:** No unsolicited fiction. Query with published clips.

**Tips:** "Write feature stories specific to one of our covered community areas, and find undiscovered stories among our readers. Keep the stories positive, but can be poignant and/or investigative. Be courteous and friendly when researching the story."

**$ $ NORTHERN OHIO LIVE**, LIVE Publishing Co., 11320 Juniper Rd., Cleveland OH 44106. (216)721-1800. Fax: (216)721-2525. E-mail: tmudd@livepub.com. **Contact:** Tom Mudd, editor. Managing Editor: Kate Maloney. **70% freelance written.** Monthly magazine covering Northern Ohio news, politics, business, arts, entertainment, education and dining. "Reader demographic is mid-30s to 50s, though we're working to bring in the late 20s. Our readers are well educated, many with advanced degrees. They're interested in Northern Ohio's cultural scene and support it." Estab. 1980. Circ. 32,000. Pays 20th of publication month. Publishes ms an average of 1 month after acceptance. Byline given. Offers 50% kill fee. Buys first North American serial rights. Editorial lead time 3 months. Submit seasonal material 4 months in advance. Reports in 3 weeks on queries; 2 months on mss. Sample copy for $3.

**Nonfiction:** Essays, exposé, general interest, humor, interview/profile, photo feature, travel. All should have a Northern Ohio slant. Special issues: Gourmet Guide (restaurants) (May). "No business/corporate articles." **Buys 100 mss/year.** Query with published clips. Length: 1,000-3,500 words. **Pays $100-1,000.** Sometimes pays expenses of writers on assignment.

**Reprints:** Send photocopy of article and information about when and where the article previously appeared.

**Photos:** State availability of photos with submission. Reviews contact sheets, 4×5 transparencies and 3×5 prints. Negotiates payment individually. Identification of subjects required. Buys one-time rights.

**Columns/Departments:** News & Reviews (arts previews, personality profiles, general interest), 800-1,800 words. **Buys 60-70 mss/year.** Query with published clips. **Pays $100-150.** Place (essay), 400-450 words. **Pays $100.**

**Fiction:** Publishes novel excerpts.

**$ $ $ OHIO MAGAZINE**, Ohio Magazine, Inc., Subsidiary of Dispatch Printing Co., 62 E. Broad St., Columbus OH 43215-3522. (614)461-5083. Fax: (614)461-7648. E-mail: editorial@ohiomagazine.com. Website: http://www.ohio magazine.com. **Contact:** Shannon Jackson, editor. **70% freelance written.** Works with a small number of new/unpublished writers/year. Magazine published 10 times/year emphasizing Ohio-based travel, news and feature material that highlights what's special and unique about the state. Estab. 1978. Circ. 85,000. **Pays on acceptance.** Publishes ms an average of 6 months after acceptance. Buys all, second serial (reprint), one-time, first North American serial or first serial rights. Byline given except on short articles appearing in sections. Submit seasonal material minimum 6 months in advance. Accepts queries by mail, e-mail, fax. Reports in 3 months. Sample copy for $3 and 9×12 SAE or on website. Writer's guidelines for #10 SASE.

**Nonfiction:** Features: 1,000-3,000 words. **Pays $800-1,800.** Sometimes pays expenses of writers on assignment.

**Columns/Departments: Buys minimum 20 unsolicited mss/year.** Length: 100-1,500 words. **Pays $50-500.**

**Reprints:** Accepts previously published submissions. Send tearsheet or photocopy of article and information about when and where the article previously appeared. Pays 50% of amount paid for an original article.

**Photos:** Brooke Wenstrup, art director. Rate negotiable.

**Tips:** "Freelancers should send all queries in writing, not by telephone or fax. Successful queries demonstrate an intimate knowledge of the publication. The magazine has undergone a reformatting recently, placing an emphasis on Ohio travel, history and people that will appeal to a wide audience. We are looking to increase our circle of writers who can write about the state in an informative and upbeat style."

**$ $ OVER THE BACK FENCE, Southern and Northern Ohio's Own Magazine**, Back Fence Publishing, Inc., P.O. Box 756, Chillicothe OH 45601. (740)772-2165. Fax: (740)773-9273. E-mail: backfenc@bright.net. Website: http://www.backfence.com. **Contact:** Sarah Williamson, managing editor. Quarterly magazine. "We are a regional magazine serving 20 counties in Southern Ohio and 10 counties in Northern Ohio. *Over The Back Fence* has a wholesome, neighborly style. It appeals to readers from young adults to seniors, showcasing art and travel opportunities in the area." Estab. 1994. Circ. 15,000. Pays on publication. Publishes ms an average of 1-2 years after acceptance. Byline given. Buys one-time North American print publication rights, making some work-for-hire assignments. Editorial lead time 6-12 months. Submit seasonal material 6-12 months in advance. Accepts queries by mail, e-mail. Accepts simultaneous submissions, if so noted. Reports in 3 months. Sample copy for $4 or on website. Writer's guidelines for #10 SASE or on website.

    O⊸ Break in with personality profiles (1,000-2,000 words), short features, columns and food essays/features (100-400 words); and features (1,000-3,000 words).

**Nonfiction:** General interest, historical/nostalgic, humor, inspirational, interview/profile, personal exprience, photo feature, travel. **Buys 9-12 mss/year.** Query with or without published clips or send complete ms. Length: 750-1,000 words. **Pays 10¢/word minimum,** negotiable depending on experience.

**Reprints:** Send photocopy of article or short story and typed ms with rights for sale noted and information about when and where the article previously appeared. Pay negotiable.

**Photos:** State availability of photos or send photos with submission. Reviews color transparencies (35mm or larger),

3⅓×5 prints. Offers $25-100/photo. Captions, model releases and identification of subjects required. Buys one-time usage rights. "If photos are sent as part of a text/photo package, please request our photo guidelines and submit color transparencies."

**Columns/Departments:** The Arts, 750-1,000 words; History (relevant to a designated county), 750-1,000 words; Inspirational (poetry or short story), minimum for poetry 4 lines, short story 600-850 words; Recipes, 750-1,000 words; Profiles From Our Past, 300-600 words; Sport & Hobby, 750-1,000 words; Our Neighbors (i.e., people helping others), 750-1,000 words. All must be relevant to Southern or Northern Ohio. **Buys 24 mss/year.** Query with or without published clips or send complete ms. **Pays 10¢/word minimum,** negotiable depending on experience.

**Fiction:** Humorous. **Buys 4 mss/year.** Query with published clips. Length: 300-850 words. **Pays 10¢/word minimum**, negotiable depending on experience.

**Poetry:** Wholesome, traditional free verse, light verse and rhyming. **Buys 4 poems/year.** Submit maximum 4 poems. Length: 4-32 lines preferred. **Pays 10¢/word or $25 minimum.**

**Fillers:** Anecdotes, short humor. **Buys 0-8/year.** Length: 100 words maximum. **Pays 10¢/word or $25 minimum.**

**Tips:** "Our approach can be equated to a friendly and informative conversation with a neighbor about interesting people, places and events in Southern Ohio (counties: Adams, Athens, Clinton, Fayette, Fairfield, Gallia, Greene, Highland, Hocking, Jackson, Lawrence, Meigs, Perry, Pickaway, Pike, Ross, Scioto, Vinton, Warren and Washington) and Northern Ohio (counties: Ashland, Erie, Western Cuyahoga, Huron, Lorain, Medina, Ottawa, Richland, Sandusky and Wayne)."

## Oklahoma

**$ $ OKLAHOMA TODAY**, P.O. Box 53384, Oklahoma City OK 73152-9971. Fax: (405)522-4588. E-mail: mccune@oklahomatoday.com. Website: http://www.oklahomatoday.com. **Contact:** Louisa McCune, editor-in-chief. **80% freelance written.** Works with a small number of new/unpublished writers each year. Bimonthly magazine covering people, places and things Oklahoman. "We are interested in showing off the best Oklahoma has to offer; we're pretty serious about our travel slant but regularly run history, nature and personality profiles." Estab. 1956. Circ. 50,000. Pays on publication. Publishes ms an average of 6 months after acceptance. Byline given. Buys first serial right. Submit seasonal material 1 year in advance "depending on photographic requirements." Reports in 4 months. Sample copy for $2.50 and 9×12 SASE or on website. Writer's guidelines for #10 SASE or on website.

● *Oklahoma Today* has won Magazine of the Year, awarded by the International Regional Magazine Association, four out of the last eight years.

**Nonfiction:** Book excerpts (on Oklahoma topics); photo feature and travel (in Oklahoma). Special issues: Millenium issue (January 2000) and Art issue (Summer 2000). **Buys 40-60 mss/year.** Query by mail with published clips; no phone queries. Length: 1,000-3,000 words. **Pays $25-750.**

**Reprints:** Send photocopy of article and information about when and where the article previously appeared. Pay varies.

**Photos:** High-quality transparencies, slides, and b&w prints. "We are especially interested in developing contacts with photographers who live in Oklahoma or have shot here. Send samples and price range." Photo guidelines for SASE. Pays $50-100 for b&w and $50-750 for color; reviews 2¼ and 35mm color transparencies. Model releases, identification of subjects, other information for captions required. Buys one-time rights plus right to use photos for promotional purposes.

**Fiction:** Publishes novel excerpts.

**Tips:** "The best way to become a regular contributor to *Oklahoma Today* is to query us with one or more story ideas, each developed to give us an idea of your proposed slant. We're looking for *lively*, concise, well-researched and reported stories, stories that don't need to be heavily edited and are not newspaper style. We have a two full-time person editorial staff, and freelancers who can write and have done their homework get called again and again."

## Oregon

**$ $ CASCADES EAST**, P.O. Box 5784, Bend OR 97708-5784. (541)382-0127. Fax: (541)382-7057. E-mail: sunpub@sun-pub.com. Website: http://www.sunpub.com. Publisher: Geoff Hill. **Contact:** Jennifer Emmert, editor. **90% freelance written.** Prefers to work with published/established writers. Quarterly magazine for "all ages as long as they are interested in outdoor recreation, history, people and arts and entertainment in central Oregon: fishing, hunting, sightseeing, golf, tennis, hiking, bicycling, mountain climbing, backpacking, rockhounding, skiing, snowmobiling, etc." Estab. 1972. Circ. 10,000 (distributed throughout area resorts and motels and to subscribers). Pays on publication. Publishes ms an average of 6 months after acceptance. Byline given. Buys all rights. Submit seasonal material at least 6 months in advance. Reports in 3 months. Sample copy and writer's guidelines for $5 and 9×12 SAE.

● *Cascades East* now accepts and prefers manuscripts along with a 3.5 disk. They can translate most word processing programs. You can also send electronic submissions.

**Nonfiction:** General interest (first person experiences in outdoor central Oregon—with photos, can be dramatic, humorous or factual), historical (for feature, "Little Known Tales from Oregon History," with b&w photos), personal experience (needed on outdoor subjects: dramatic, humorous or factual). Art feature (on recognized Central Oregon artists of any medium, with color photos/transparencies and b&w photos). Homes & Living (unique custom/"dream" homes, architectural styles, alternative energy designs, interior designs, building locations, etc. in central Oregon); 1,000-2,500 words with color photos/transparencies. "No articles that are too general, sight-seeing articles that come from a travel folder, or outdoor articles without the first-person approach." **Buys 20-30 unsolicited mss/year.** Query. Length: 1,000-2,000 words. **Pays 5-15¢/word.**

**Reprints:** Send photocopy of article and information about when and where the article previously appeared.

**Photos:** "Old photos will greatly enhance chances of selling a historical feature. First-person articles need b&w photos also." Pays $10-25 for b&w; $15-100 for transparencies. Captions preferred. Buys one-time rights.

**Columns/Departments:** Short features on a successful Central Oregon businessperson making an impact on the community or excelling in the business market: local, national, or worldwide, with color/b&w photo. Query preferred. Length: 1,000-1,500 words.

**Tips:** "Submit stories a year or so in advance of publication. We are seasonal and must plan editorials for summer 2000 in the spring of '99, etc., in case seasonal photos are needed."

**$ $ OREGON COAST**, P.O. Box 18000, 1525 12st St., Florence OR 97439-0130. (541)997-8401 or (800)348-8401. Fax: (541)997-1124. Website: http://www.ohwy.com. Judy Fleagle and Jim Forst, editors. **65% freelance written.** Bimonthly regional magazine covering the Oregon Coast. Estab. 1982. Circ. 70,000. Pays after publication. Publishes ms an average of 1 year after acceptance. Byline given. Offers 33% kill fee. Buys first North American serial rights. Submit seasonal material 6 months in advance. Reports in 1 month on queries; 3 months on mss. Sample copy for $4.50. Writer's guidelines for #10 SASE.

● This company also publishes *Northwest Travel* and *Oregon Outside.*

**Nonfiction:** "A true regional with general interest, historical/nostalgic, humor, interview/profile, personal experience, photo feature, travel and nature as pertains to Oregon Coast." **Buys 55 mss/year.** Query with published clips. Length: 500-2,000 words. **Pays $75-350** plus 2-5 contributor copies.

**Reprints:** Sometimes accepts previously published submissions. Enclose clips. Send tearsheet or photocopy of article and information about when and where the article previously appeared. Pays an average of 75% of the amount paid for an original article.

**Photos:** Send photos with submission. Reviews 35mm or larger transparencies. Photo submissions with no ms or stand alone or cover photos. Captions, model releases (for covers), photo credits, identification of subjects required. Buys one-time rights.

**Fillers:** Newsbreaks (no-fee basis).

**Tips:** "Slant article for readers who do not live at the Oregon Coast. At least one historical article is used in each issue. Manuscript/photo packages are preferred over mss with no photos. List photo credits and captions for each print or slide. Check all facts, proper names and numbers carefully in photo/ms packages. Need stories with great color photos—could be photo essays. Must pertain to Oregon Coast somehow."

**$ $ OREGON OUTSIDE**, Educational Publications Foundation, P.O. Box 18000, 1525 12th St., Suite C, Florence OR 97439-0130. (800)348-8401. Fax: (541)997-1124. Website: http://www.ohwy.com. **Contact:** Judy Fleagle, managing editor. **70% freelance written.** Quarterly magazine covering "outdoor activities for experts as well as for families and older folks, from easy hikes to extreme skiing. We like first person, lively accounts with quotes, anecdotes, compelling leads and satisfying endings. Nitty-gritty info can be in sidebars. Send a rough map if needed." Estab. 1993. Circ. 20,000. Publishes ms an average of 1 year after acceptance. Byline given. Offers 33% kill fee. Buys first North American serial (stories and story/photo packages) and one-time rights (stand alone photos, covers and calendars). Editorial lead time 4 months. Submit seasonal material 6 months in advance. Reports in 2 months on queries; 3 months on mss. Sample copy for $4.50. Writer's guidelines for #10 SASE.

**Nonfiction:** Book excerpts, how-to, interview/profile, new product, personal experience, photo feature. "Nothing overdone. We like understatement." Query with published clips. Length: 800-1,750 words. **Pays $100-350.**

**Reprints:** Send photocopy of article and information about when and where the story previously appeared. Pays 60% of amount paid for an original article.

**Photos:** Send photos with submission. "We need more photos showing human involvement in the outdoors." Reviews 35mm up to 4×5 transparencies. Offers $25-75 with story, $350/cover photo, $75/stand alone, $100/calendar. Captions, model releases, identification of subjects required for cover consideration. Buys one-time rights.

**Columns/Departments:** Back Page (unusual outdoor photo with technical information), 80-100 words. Contact: Judy Fleagle. Query with photo. **Pays $75.**

**Fillers:** Newsbreaks, events. **Uses 10/year.** Length: 200-400 words. Does not pay for fillers.

**Tips:** "A short piece with a couple super photos for a 1- or 2-page article" is a freelancer's best chance for publication.

# Pennsylvania

**$ $ CENTRAL PA**, WITF, Inc., P.O. Box 2954, Harrisburg PA 17105-2954. (717)236-6000. Fax: (717)236-4628. E-mail: cenpa@witf.org. Website: http://www.cenpa.org. **Contact:** Steve Kennedy, executive editor. **90% freelance written.** Monthly magazine covering life in Central Pennsylvania. Estab. 1982. Circ. 42,000. Pays on publication. Publishes ms 4 months after acceptance. Offers 20% kill fee. Buys first North American serial rights. Editorial lead time 3 months. Submit seasonal material 6 months in advance. Accepts queries by mail, e-mail, fax. Accepts simultaneous submissions. Reports in 6 weeks. Sample copy for $3.50 and SASE. Writer's guidelines for #10 SASE.

**O—** Break in through Central Stories, Thinking Aloud, blurbs and accompanying events calendar.

**Nonfiction:** Essays, general interest, historical/nostalgic, how-to, humor, interview/profile, opinion, personal experience, photo feature, travel. Special issues: Dining/Food (January); Regional Insider's Guide (July). **Buys 50 mss/year.** Query with published clips or send complete ms. Length: 1,000-3,000 words. **Pays $200-750 for assigned articles; $50-500 for unsolicited articles.** Sometimes pays expenses of writers on assignment.

**Photos:** State availability of photos with submission. Reviews contact sheets, transparencies, prints. Negotiates payment individually. Identification of subjects required. Buys one-time rights.

**Columns/Departments:** Central Stories (quirky, newsy, regional), 300 words; Thinking Aloud (essay), 1,300 words; Cameo (interview), 800 words. **Buys 90 mss/year.** Query with published clips or send complete ms. **Pays $50-200.**

**Tips:** "Wow us with something you wrote, either a clip or a manuscript on spec. If it's off target but shows you can write well and know the region, we'll ask for more. We're looking for creative nonfiction, with an emphasis on conveying valuable information through near literary-quality narrative."

**N: $ $ PENNSYLVANIA HERITAGE,** Pennsylvania Historical and Museum Commission and the Pennsylvania Heritage Society, P.O. Box 1026, Harrisburg PA 17108-1026. (717)787-7522. Fax: (717)787-8312. E-mail: momalley@p hmc.state.pa.us. Website: http://www.paheritage.org. **Contact:** Michael J. O'Malley III, editor. **90% freelance written.** Prefers to work with published/established writers. Quarterly magazine. "*Pennsylvania Heritage* introduces readers to Pennsylvania's rich culture and historic legacy, educates and sensitizes them to the value of preserving that heritage and entertains and involves them in such a way as to ensure that Pennsylvania's past has a future. The magazine is intended for intelligent lay readers." Estab. 1974. Circ. 13,000. **Pays on acceptance.** Publishes ms an average of 1 year after acceptance. Byline given. Buys all rights. Accepts queries by mail, e-mail. Accepts simultaneous queries and submissions. Reports in 6 weeks on queries; 6 months on mss. Sample copy for $5 and 9×12 SAE or on website. Writer's guidelines for #10 SASE or on website.

● *Pennsylvania Heritage* is now considering freelance submissions that are shorter in length (2,000 to 3,000 words), pictorial/photographic essays, biographies of famous (and not-so-famous) Pennsylvanians and interviews with individuals who have helped shape, make, preserve the Keystone State's history and heritage.

**Nonfiction:** Art, science, biographies, industry, business, politics, transportation, military, historic preservation, archaeology, photography, etc. No articles which in no way relate to Pennsylvania history or culture. "Our format requires feature-length articles. Manuscripts with illustrations are especially sought for publication. We are now looking for shorter (2,000 words) manuscripts that are heavily illustrated with *publication-quality* photographs or artwork. We are eager to work with experienced travel writers for destination pieces on historical sites and museums that make 'The Pennsylvania Trail of History.' " **Buys 20-24 mss/year.** Prefers to see mss with suggested illustrations. Length: 2,000-3,500 words. **Pays $100-500.**

**Photos:** State availability of, or send photos with ms. Pays $25-100 for transparencies; $5-25 for b&w photos. Captions and identification of subjects required. Buys one-time rights.

**Tips:** "We are looking for well-written, interesting material that pertains to any aspect of Pennsylvania history or culture. Potential contributors should realize that, although our articles are popularly styled, they are not light, puffy or breezy; in fact they demand strident documentation and substantiation (sans footnotes). The most frequent mistake made by writers in completing articles for us is making them either too scholarly or too sentimental or nostalgic. We want material which educates, but also entertains. Authors should make history readable and enjoyable. Our goal is to make the Keystone State's history come to life in a meaningful, memorable way."

**$ $ $ PITTSBURGH MAGAZINE,** WQED Pittsburgh, 4802 5th Ave., Pittsburgh PA 15213. (412)622-1360. Website: http://www.pittsburghmag.com. **Contact:** Michelle Pilecki, managing editor. **60% freelance written.** "*Pittsburgh* presents issues, analyzes problems and strives to encourage a better understanding of the community. Our region is western Pennsylvania, eastern Ohio, northern West Virginia and western Maryland." Prefers to work with published/established writers. The monthly magazine is purchased on newsstands and by subscription, and is given to those who contribute $40 or more/year to public TV in western Pennsylvania. Estab. 1970. Circ. 75,000. Pays on publication. Publishes ms an average of 2 months after acceptance. Byline given. Buys first North American serial rights and second serial (reprint) rights. Offers kill fee. Submit seasonal material 6 months in advance. Reports in 2 months. Sample copy for $2 (old back issues).

● The editor reports a need for more hard news and stories targeting readers in their 30s and 40s, especially those with young families.

**Nonfiction:** "Without exception—whether the topic is business, travel, the arts or lifestyle—each story is clearly oriented to Pittsburghers and the greater Pittsburgh region of today. We have minimal interest in historical articles and do not publish fiction, poetry, advocacy or personal reminiscence pieces." Exposé, lifestyle, sports, informational, service, business, medical, profile. Must have greater Pittsburgh angle. Query in writing with outline and clips. No fax, phone or e-mail queries. *No complete mss.* Length: 3,500 words or less. **Pays $300-1,500.**

**Columns/Departments:** Upfront (short, front-of-the-book items), Weekender, Neighborhood. Length: 300 words maximum. **Pays $50-150.**

**Photos:** Query for photos. Model releases required. Pays pre-negotiated expenses of writers on assignment.

**Tips:** "Best bet to break in is through hard news with a region-wide impart or service pieces or profiles with a regional interest. The point is that we want more stories that reflect our region, not just a tiny part. And we *never* consider any story without a strong regional focus."

# Rhode Island

**N ☆ $ $ $ RHODE ISLAND MONTHLY**, The Providence Journal Company, 280 Kinsley Ave., Providence RI 02903. (401)421-2552. Fax: (401)831-5624. E-mail: rimonthly.com. Website: http://www.rimonthly.com. Editor: Paula M. Bodah. **Contact:** Sarah Francis, managing editor. **80% freelance written.** Monthly magazine. "*Rhode Island Monthly* is a general interest consumer magazine with a strict Rhode Island focus." Estab. 1988. Circ. 41,000. **Pays on acceptance.** Publishes ms an average of 3 months after acceptance. Byline given. Offers 20% kill fee. Buys all rights for 90 days from date of publication. Editorial lead time 3 months. Submit seasonal material 6 months in advance. Accepts queries by mail, e-mail, fax. Reports in 6 weeks on queries; 1 month on mss. Sample copy on website.
**Nonfiction:** Exposé, general interest, interview/profile, photo feature. **Buys 40 mss/year.** Query with published clips. Length: 1,800-3,000 words. **Pays $600-1,200.** Sometimes pays expenses of writers on assignment.

# South Carolina

**☆ $ $ CHARLESTON MAGAZINE**, P.O. Box 1794, Mt. Pleasant SC 29465-1794. (843)971-9811. Fax: (843)971-0121. E-mail: aareson@awod.com. **Contact:** Ann Holmes Areson, editor. **80% freelance written.** Quarterly magazine covering current issues, events, arts and culture, leisure pursuits, personalities as they pertain to the city of Charleston. "Each issue reflects an essential element of Charleston life and Lowcountry living." Estab. 1976. Circ. 20,000. Pays 30 days after publication. Publishes ms an average of 3 months after acceptance. Byline given. Buys one-time rights. Submit seasonal material 4 months in advance. Accepts queries by mail, fax. Reports in 1 month. Sample copies for 9×12 SAE with 5 first-class stamps. Writer's guidelines for #10 SASE.
**Nonfiction:** General interest, humor, food, architecture, sports, interview/profile, opinion, photo feature, travel, current events/issues, art. "Not interested in 'Southern nostalgia' articles or gratuitous history pieces. Must pertain to the Charleston area and its present culture." **Buys 40 mss/year.** Query with published clips with SASE. Length: 150-1,500 words. **Pays 15¢/published word.** Sometimes pays expenses of writers on assignment.
**Reprints:** Send photocopy of article and information about when and where the article previously appeared. Pay negotiable.
**Photos:** Send photos with submission if available. Reviews contact sheets, transparencies, slides. Offers $35/photo maximum. Identification of subjects required. Buys one-time rights.
**Columns/Departments:** Channel Markers (general local interest), 50-400 words; Spotlight (profile of local interest), 250-300 words; The Home Front (interiors, renovations and gardens), 1,000-1,200 words; Sporting Life (humorous, adventurous tales of life outdoors), 850-1,200 words; In Good Taste (restaurants and culinary trends in the city), 1,000-1,200 words; On the Road (travel opportunities near Charleston), 1,000-1,200 words; Southern View (personal experience about Charleston life), 750 words; The Marketplace (profiles of exceptional local businesses), 1,000-1,200 words; The Good Fight (worthwhile battles fought locally and statewide), 1,000-1,200 words; To Your Health (medicine, nutrition, exercise, healthcare), 1,000-1,200 words; The Arts (in Charleston and surrounding communities), 700 words.
**Tips:** "Charleston, although a city with a 300-year history, is a vibrant, modern community with a tremendous dedication to the arts and no shortage of newsworthy subjects. Don't bother submitting coffee-table magazine-style pieces. Areas most open to freelancers are Columns/Departments and features. Should be of local interest. We're looking for the freshest stories about Charleston—and those don't always come from insiders, but outsiders who are keenly observant. Offer a fresh perspective on issues and events. Write a story (non-fiction) that's not been told before. Profile intriguing Lowcountry residents."

**$ $ SANDLAPPER, The Magazine of South Carolina**, The Sandlapper Society, Inc., P.O. Box 1108, Lexington SC 29071-1108. (803)359-9941. Fax: (803)359-0629. E-mail: aida@sandlapper.org. Website: http://www.sandlapper.org. Executive Director: Suzanne Flowers. Editor: Robert P. Wilkins. **Contact:** Aida Rogers, associate editor. **35% freelance written.** Quarterly feature magazine focusing on the positive aspects of South Carolina. "*Sandlapper* is intended to be read at those times when people want to relax with an attractive, high-quality magazine that entertains and informs them about their state." Estab. 1989. Circ. 10,000. Pays during the dateline period. Publishes ms an average of 8-12 months after acceptance. Byline given. Buys first North American serial rights and the right to reprint. Submit seasonal material 6 months in advance. Accepts queries by mail, e-mail, fax. Sample copy on website. Writer's guidelines for SASE.
**Nonfiction:** Feature articles and photo essays about South Carolina's interesting people, places, cuisine, things to do. Occasional history articles. Query with clips and SASE. Length: 800-3,000 words. **Pays $50-500.** Sometimes pays the expenses of writers on assignment.
**Photos:** "*Sandlapper* buys black-and-white prints, color transparencies and art. Photographers should submit working cutlines for each photograph." Pays $25-75, $100 for cover or centerspread photo.
**Tips:** "We're not interested in articles about topical issues, politics, crime or commercial ventures. Avoid first-person nostalgia and remembrances of places that no longer exist. We look for top-quality literature. Humor is encouraged. Good taste is a standard. Unique angles are critical for acceptance. Dare to be bold, but not too bold."

## South Dakota

**$ DAKOTA OUTDOORS, South Dakota**, Hipple Publishing Co., P.O. Box 669, 333 W. Dakota Ave., Pierre SD 57501-0669. (605)224-7301. Fax: (605)224-9210. E-mail: dakdoor@aol.com. Website: http://www.capjournal.com\dako taoutdoors. Editor: Kevin Hipple. **Contact:** Rachel Engbrecht, managing editor. **85% freelance written.** Monthly magazine on Dakota outdoor life, focusing on hunting and fishing. Estab. 1974. Circ. 7,000. Pays on publication. Publishes ms an average of 2 months after acceptance. Byline given. Submit seasonal material 3 months in advance. Accepts simultaneous submissions. Reports in 3 months. Sample copy for 9×12 SAE with 3 first-class stamps.
**Nonfiction:** General interest, how-to, humor, interview/profile, personal experience, technical (all on outdoor topics—prefer in Dakotas). "Topics should center on fishing and hunting experiences and advice. Other topics, such as boating, camping, hiking, environmental concerns and general nature, will be considered as well." **Buys 120 mss/year.** Send complete ms. Length: 500-2,000 words. **Pays $5-50.** Sometimes pays in contributor copies or other premiums (inquire).
**Reprints:** Send typed ms with rights for sale noted and information about when and where the article previously appeared. Pays 50% of amount paid for an original article.
**Photos:** Send photos with submission. Reviews 3×5 or 5×7 prints. Offers no additional payment for photos accepted with ms or negotiates payment individually. Identification of subjects preferred. Buys one-time rights.
**Columns/Departments:** Kids Korner (outdoors column addressing kids from 12 to 16 years of age). Length: 50-500 words. **Pays $5-15.**
**Fiction:** Adventure, humorous. **Buys 15 mss/year.** Send complete ms.
**Fillers:** Anecdotes, facts, gags to be illustrated by cartoonist, newsbreaks, short humor. **Buys 10/year.** Also publishes line drawings of fish and game. Prefers 5×7 prints.
**Tips:** "Submit samples of manuscript or previous works for consideration; photos or illustrations with manuscript are helpful."

## Tennessee

**[N] $ $ MEMPHIS**, Contemporary Media, P.O. Box 256, Memphis TN 38101-0256. (901)521-9000. Fax: (901)521-0129. E-mail: memmag@mem.net. Editor: Richard Banks. **Contact:** Michael Finger, senior editor. **60% freelance written.** Works with a small number of new/unpublished writers. Estab. 1976. Circ. 21,917. Pays on publication. Publishes ms an average of 3 months after acceptance. Byline given. Offers 20% kill fee. Buys first North American serial rights. Accepts queries by mail, e-mail, fax, phone. Accepts simultaneous submissions. Reports in 2 months. Sample copy for 9×12 SAE with 8 first-class stamps. Writer's guidelines for SASE.
**Nonfiction:** Exposé, general interest, historical, how-to, humor, interview, profile. "Virtually all of our material has strong Memphis area connections." **Buys 25 freelance mss/year.** Query or submit complete ms or published clips. Length: 500-5,000 words. **Pays $50-500.** Sometimes pays expenses of writers on assignment.
**Tips:** "The kinds of manuscripts we need most have a sense of story (i.e., plot, suspense, character), an abundance of evocative images to bring that story alive and a sensitivity to issues at work in Memphis. Find something fresh and new about Memphis that we haven't discovered (and written about) before. Make us say, "I didn't know *that*." The most frequent mistakes made by writers in completing an article for us are lack of focus, lack of organization, factual gaps and failure to capture the magazine's style. Tough investigative pieces would be especially welcomed."

## Texas

**[N] $ $ AUSTIN HOME & LIVING**, Publications & Communications Inc., 505 Cypress Creek, Suite B, Cedar Park TX 78613. (512)926-4663. Fax: (512)331-3950. E-mail: homes@pcinews.com. Managing Editor: Nicole Villalpando. **75% freelance written.** Consumer publication published bimonthly. "*Austin Home & Living* showcases the homes found in Austin and provides tips on food, gardening and decorating." Estab. 1994. Circ. 20,000. Pays on publication. Publishes ms an average of 4 months after acceptance. Byline given. Offers 100% kill fee. Buys all rights. Editorial lead time 4 months. Submit seasonal material 6 months in advance. Accepts queries by mail, e-mail, fax, phone. Reports in 1 month on queries; 2 months on mss. Sample copy and writer's guidelines free.
**Nonfiction:** How-to, interview/profile, new product, travel. **Buys 18 mss/year.** Query with published clips. Length: 500-2,000 words. **Pays $200.** Pays expenses of writers on assignment.
**Photos:** State availability of photos with submission or send photos with submission. Reviews negatives, transparencies and prints. Offers no additional payment for photos accepted with ms. Captions required. Buys all rights.

**$ $ DALLAS/FORT WORTH SPECIAL OCCASIONS MAGAZINE**, (formerly *Special Occasions Sourcebook*), Abarta Metro Publishing, 4809 Cole Ave., Suite 205, Dallas TX 75205. (214)522-0050. Fax: (214)522-0504. E-mail: cchwhere@airmail.net. **Contact:** Charmaine Cooper Hussain, editor. **90% freelance written.** "Semiannual reader-service guide to planning events ranging from rehearsal dinners to debutante balls to weddings." Estab. 1997. Circ. 15,000. Pays on publication. Publishes ms 6 months after acceptance. Byline given. Buys all rights. Editorial lead time

10 months. Submit seasonal material 10 months in advance. Accepts queries by mail, e-mail. Accepts simultaneous submissions.

**Nonfiction:** How-to, photo feature. Does not want to see material not specific to the Dallas/Fort Worth area. **Buys 6 mss/year.** Query with published clips. Length: 1,000-2,500 words. **Pays $300-400 for assigned articles.** Sometimes pays expenses of writers on assignment.

**Photos:** Send photos with submission. Reviews transparencies. Negotiates payment individually. Captions, model releases and identification of subjects required. Buys one-time rights, all rights for cover photos.

**Tips:** Best way to break in is to "offer locally oriented advice about planning a party, with insider scoop about where to buy the best dresses, favors, tableware, cakes, etc."

**$ $ $ HOUSTON PRESS**, New Times, Inc., 1621 Milam, Houston TX 77002. (713)280-2400. Fax: (713)280-2496. Website: http://www.houstonpress.com. Editor: Margaret Downing. Managing Editor: Lisa Gray. Associate Editor: George Flynn. **Contact:** Kirsten Bubier, editorial administrator. **40% freelance written.** Alternative weekly tabloid covering "news and arts stories of interest to a Houston audience. If the same story could run in Seattle, then it's not for us." Estab. 1989. Pays on publication. Publishes ms an average of 2 weeks after acceptance. Byline given. Buys first North American serial and website rights. Editorial lead time 2 months. Submit seasonal material 3 months in advance. Sample copy for $3.

**Nonfiction:** Contact Lisa Gray, managing editor. Expose, general interest, interview/profile, arts reviews, music. Query with published clips. Length: 300-4,500 words. **Pays $10-1,000.** Sometimes pays expenses of writers on assignment.

**Photos:** State availability of photos with submission. Negotiates payment individually. Identification of subjects required. Buys all rights.

**$ THE 104 ZONE, KRBE's Lifestyle Magazine**, 104 KRBE (104.1 FM), 9801 Westheimer, #700, Houston TX 77057. (713)266-1000. Fax: (713)954-2344. Website: http://krbe.com. **Contact:** Charlotte Crawford, editor. **75% freelance written.** Monthly entertainment/lifestyle magazine covering music, local attractions and entertainment, consumer issues. "Our audience is 18-44. Stories should be entertaining, interesting, informative and well written." Circ. 90,000. Byline given. Makes work-for-hire assignments. Editorial lead time 6 weeks. Submit seasonal material 2 months in advance. Sample copy for SAE.

**Nonfiction:** General interest, how-to (buy/invest a home), humor, interview/profile. "We do not accept pre-written stories. We assign topics but will accept inquiries about being on writer list. We do not accept or pay for blind submissions." Length: 600-1,200 words. **Pays $75-150.** Sometimes pays expenses of writers on assignment.

**Photos:** State availability of photos with submission. Reviews 4×6 prints. Negotiates payment individually. Captions, model releases, identification of subjects required. Returns photos; gives credit to photographer.

**Tips:** "Contact the editor, provide writing samples. Prefer Houston-based writers but will consider out-of-towners."

**[N] $ $ $ PAPERCITY, Dallas Edition**, Urban Publishers, 3303 Lee Parkway, #340, Dallas TX 75219. (214)521-3439. Fax: (214)521-3178. E-mail: papercity2@aol.com. **Contact:** Rebecca Sherman, Dallas editor; Holly Moore, Houston editor. **15% freelance written.** Monthly magazine. "*Papercity* covers fashion, food, entertainment, home design and decoratives for urban Dallas and Houston. Our writing is lively, brash, sexy—it's where to read about the hottest restaurants, great chefs, where to shop, what's cool to buy, where to go and the chicest places to stay—from sexy, small hotels in New York, Los Angeles, London and Morocco, to where to buy the newest trends in Europe. We cover local parties with big photo spreads, and a hip nightlife column." Estab. 1994 (Houston); and 1998 (Dallas). Circ. 85,000 (Dallas). Pays on publication. Publishes ms an average of 1 month after acceptance. Byline given. Offers 10% kill fee. Buys first North American serial rights. Editorial lead time 2 months. Submit seasonal material 4 months in advance. Accepts queries by mail, e-mail, fax. Accepts simultaneous submissions. Reports in 3 weeks on queries; 1 month on mss. Sample copy for 9×12 SAE with $1.50 in first-class stamps. Writer's guidelines for #10 SASE or by e-mail.

**Nonfiction:** General interest, interview/profile, new product, travel, home decor, food. Special issues: Bridal (February); Travel (April); Restaurants (August). No straight profiles on anyone, especially celebrities. **Buys 10-12 mss/year.** Query with published clips. Length: 150-3,000 words. **Pays 35-50¢/word.**

**Photos:** State availability of photos with submission. Reviews contact sheets, transparencies and prints. Negotiates payment individually. Buys one-time rights.

**Tips:** "Read similar publications such as *W, Tattler, Wallpaper, Martha Stewart Living* for new trends, style of writing, hip new restaurants. We try to be very 'of the moment' so give us something in Dallas, Houston, New York, Los Angeles, London, etc. that we haven't heard yet. Chances are if other hip magazines are writing about it so will we."

**$ $ $ TEXAS HIGHWAYS, The Travel Magazine of Texas**, Box 141009, Austin TX 78714-1009. (512)483-3675. Fax: (512)483-3672. E-mail: editors@texashighways.com. Website: http://www.texashighways.com. **Contact:** Jill Lawless, managing editor. **80% freelance written.** Monthly magazine "encourages travel within the state and tells the Texas story to readers around the world." Estab. 1974. Circ. 300,000. Publishes ms 1 year after acceptance. Buys first North American serial and electronic rights. Reports in 2 months. Writer's guidelines for SASE.

**Nonfiction:** "Subjects should focus on things to do or places to see in Texas. Include historical, cultural and geographic aspects if appropriate. Text should be meticulously researched. Include anecdotes, historical references, quotations and, where relevant, geologic, botanical and zoological information." Query with description, published clips, additional background materials (charts, maps, etc.) and SASE. Include disk copy if available. Length: 1,200-2,000 words. **Pays 40-50¢/word.** Send for copy of writer's guidelines.

● Ranked as one of the best markets for freelance writers in *Writer's Yearbook* magazine's "Top 100 Markets," January 1999.

**Columns/Departments:** Contact: Ann Gallaway. Speaking of Texas (history, folklore, facts), 50-200 words. **Prints 3-5 items/month.** Send complete ms with reference sources. **Pays 40¢/word.**

**Tips:** "We like strong leads that draw in the reader immediately and clear, concise writing. Be specific and avoid superlatives. Avoid overused words. Don't forget the basics—who, what, where, why and how."

**$ $ $ TEXAS PARKS & WILDLIFE,** 3000 South I.H. 35, Suite 120, Austin TX 78704. (512)912-7000. Fax: (512)707-1913. E-mail: dick.reavis@tpwd.state.tx.us. Website: http://www.tpwmagazine.com. Managing Editor: Mary-Love Bigony. **Contact:** Dick J. Reavis, senior editor. **80% freelance written.** Monthly magazine featuring articles about Texas hunting, fishing, birding, outdoor recreation, game and nongame wildlife, state parks, environmental issues. All articles must be about Texas. Estab. 1942. Circ. 141,000. **Pays on acceptance.** Publishes ms an average of 6 months after acceptance. Byline given. Kill fee determined by contract, usually $200-250. Buys first rights. Submit seasonal material 6 months in advance. Accepts queries by mail, e-mail. Reports in 1 month on queries; 3 months on mss. Sample copy and writer's guidelines on website.

● *Texas Parks & Wildlife* needs more hunting and fishing material.

**Nonfiction:** General interest (Texas only), how-to (outdoor activities), photo feature, travel (state parks). **Buys 60 mss/year.** Query with published clips. Length: 500-2,500 words.

**Photos:** Send photos with submission. Reviews transparencies. Offers $65-350/photo. Captions and identification of subjects required. Buys one-time rights.

**Tips:** "Read outdoor pages of statewide newspapers to keep abreast of news items that can lead to story ideas. Feel free to include more than one story idea in one query letter. All areas are open to freelancers. All articles must have a Texas focus."

**$ UPTOWN HEALTH AND SPIRIT,** Up & Out Communications, 3406 Audubon Place, Houston TX 77006. (713)520-7237. Fax: (713)522-3275. Website: http://www.healthandspirit.com. **Contact:** Mari Chow, managing editor. **70% freelance written.** Bimonthly magazine covering holistic community. "In addition to a strong belief in natural and holistic based medicines and alternative therapies, *Uptown Health and Spirit* provides proven techniques in managing stress; inspiring insight for spiritual growth; news about the environment; and the latest information for individuals and juveniles who place a priority on creating healthy bodies, minds, and spirits." Estab. 1985. Circ. 32,000. Pays on publication. Publishes ms an average of 2 months after acceptance. Byline given. Buys one-time rights and simultaneous rights. Editorial lead time 2 months. Submit seasonal material 2 months in advance. Accepts simultaneous submissions. Reports in 6 weeks on queries, 2 months on mss. Sample copy and writer's guidelines for SASE.

● This company also publishes *Out Smart*, a monthly gay and lesbian magazine. Website: http://www.outsmartmagazine.com.

**Nonfiction:** Book excerpts, inspirational, interview/profile, new product. **Buys 10 mss/year.** Send complete ms. Length: 700-4,000 words. **Pays $20-200.**

**Reprints:** Send photocopy of article. Pay negotiable.

**Photos:** State availability of photos with submission. Reviews 4×6 prints. Negotiates payment individually. Identification of subjects required. Buys one-time rights.

**$ $ WHERE DALLAS MAGAZINE,** Abarta Media, 4809 Cole Ave., Suite 205, Dallas TX 75205. (214)522-0050. Fax: (214)522-0504. E-mail: cchwhere@airmail.net. **Contact:** Charmaine Cooper Hussain, editor. Website: http://www.travelfacts.com. **75% freelance written.** Monthly visitor's magazine. "*WHERE Dallas* is part of the *WHERE Magazine International* network, the world's largest publisher of travel magazines. Published in more than 40 cities around the world, travelers trust *WHERE* to guide them to the best in shopping, dining, nightlife and entertainment." Estab. 1996. Circ. 40,000. Pays on publication. Publishes ms an average of 2 months after acceptance. Byline given. Buys all rights. Editorial lead time 2 months. Submit seasonal material 2 months in advance. Accept queries by mail, e-mail. Accepts simultaneous submissions. Sample copy for $3.

**Nonfiction:** General interest, historical/nostalgic, photo feature, travel, special events. **Buys 30 mss/year.** Query with published clips, preferably by e-mail. Length: 650-1,200 words. **Pays $100-450.** Sometimes pays expenses of writers on assignment.

**Photos:** Send photos with submission. Reviews transparencies. Negotiates payment individually. Captions, model releases and identification of subjects required. Buys one-time rights, all rights on cover photos.

**Columns/Departments: Pays $100-450.**

**Tips:** Break in with "a solid idea—solid meaning the local Dallas angle is *everything*. We're looking for advice and tips that would/could only come from long-time residents."

# Utah

**$ $ SALT LAKE,** (formerly *Salt Lake City*), 240 E. Morris Ave., Suite 200, Salt Lake City UT 84115. (801)485-5100. Fax: (801)485-5133. E-mail: slmagazine@aol.com. Website: http://www.slcmag.com. Art Director: Scott Perry.

**Contact:** Barry Scholl, editor. **60% freelance written.** Bimonthly publication that caters to educated, affluent, and active citizens of the intermountain West. "Generally, our features profile people around the state, outdoor activities and attractions, and historical aspects of Utah." Estab. 1989. Circ. 18,000. Pays on publication. Publishes ms an average of 6 months after acceptance. Byline given. Offers $25 kill fee. Buys first North American serial rights. Submit seasonal material 6 months in advance. Accepts queries by mail, e-mail. Accepts simultaneous submissions. Reports in 2 months. Sample articles on website. Writer's guidelines for #10 SASE.

**Nonfiction:** Essays (health, family matters, financial), general interest, historical/nostalgic (pertaining to Utah and Intermountain West), humor, interview/profile (famous or powerful people associated with Utah business, politics, media), personal experience, photo feature, travel. "No movie reviews or current news subjects, please. Even essays need a tight local angle." **Buys 5 mss/year.** Query with 3 published clips or send complete ms and SASE. Follows Chicago style. Length: 1,000-5,000 words. **Pays $75-400 for assigned articles; $75-250 for unsolicited articles.** "Payment for a major feature is negotiable."

**Photos:** Send photos with submission. Reviews transparencies (size not important). Captions, model releases, identification of subjects required. Payment and rights negotiable. Don't send original negs/transparencies unless requested.

**Columns/Departments:** Up Close (standard personality profile), 1,200-1,500 words; Q & A of famous person, 1,200-1,500 words; Executive Signature (profile, business slant of major Utah entrepeneur); and Food (recipes must be included), 1,000-1,500 words. **Buys 5-10 mss/year.** Query with published clips or send complete ms. **Pays $75-250.**

• No longer accepting fiction and poetry. Also, more articles are being produced in-house. They are overstocked on general travel pieces and are focusing on travel pieces on the intermountain West.

**Tips:** "We are looking for well-written, well-researched, complete manuscripts. Writers are advised to refer to a sample issue before submitting work. *Salt Lake* magazine is most interested in unique, people-oriented profiles, historical pieces and stories of local interest. For instance, the magazine has covered local recreation, child abuse, education, air pollution, health care issues, wilderness, militias and local personalities. The majority of our stories are focused on Utah and the West. Please write for a free sample issue if you have never read our magazine."

# Vermont

**$ $ VERMONT LIFE MAGAZINE**, 6 Baldwin St., Montpelier VT 05602-2109. (802)828-3241. E-mail: vtlife@lif.state.vt.us. Website: http://www.vtlife.com. **Contact:** Thomas K. Slayton, editor-in-chief. **90% freelance written.** Prefers to work with published/established writers. Quarterly magazine. "*Vermont Life* is interested in any article, query, story idea, photograph or photo essay that has to do with Vermont. As the state magazine, we are most favorably impressed with pieces that present positive aspects of life within the state's borders." Estab. 1946. Circ. 85,000. Publishes ms an average of 9 months after acceptance. Byline given. Offers kill fee. Buys first serial rights. Submit seasonal material 1 year in advance. Reports in 1 month. Writer's guidelines for #10 SASE.

**Nonfiction:** Wants articles on today's Vermont, those which portray a typical or, if possible, unique aspect of the state or its people. Style should be literate, clear and concise. Subtle humor favored. No "Vermont clichés"—maple syrup, town meetings or stereotyped natives. **Buys 60 mss/year.** Query by letter essential. Length: 1,500 words average. **Pays 25¢/word.** Seldom pays expenses of writers on assignment.

**Photos:** Buys photographs with mss; buys seasonal photographs alone. Prefers b&w contact sheets to look at first on assigned material. Color submissions must be 4×5 or 35mm transparencies. Pays $75-250 inside color; $500 for cover. Gives assignments but only with experienced photographers. Query in writing. Captions, model releases, identification of subjects required. Buys one-time rights, but often negotiates for re-use rights.

**Fiction:** Publishes novel excerpts.

**Tips:** "Writers who read our magazine are given more consideration because they understand that we want authentic articles about Vermont. If a writer has a genuine working knowledge of Vermont, his or her work usually shows it. Vermont is changing and there is much concern here about what this state will be like in years ahead. It is a beautiful, environmentally sound place now and the vast majority of residents want to keep it so. Articles reflecting such concerns in an intelligent, authoritative, non-hysterical way will be given very careful consideration. The growth of tourism makes us interested in intelligent articles about specific places in Vermont, their history and attractions to the traveling public."

# Virginia

**$ $ THE ROANOKER**, Leisure Publishing Co., 3424 Brambleton Ave., P.O. Box 21535, Roanoke VA 24018-9900. (540)989-6138. Fax: (540)989-7603. E-mail: leisure@roanoke.infi.net. Website: http://www.theroanoker.com. **Contact:** Kurt Rheinheimer, editor. **75% freelance written.** Works with a small number of new/unpublished writers each year. Magazine published 6 times/year. "*The Roanoker* is a general interest city magazine for the people of Roanoke, Virginia and the surrounding area. Our readers are primarily upper-income, well-educated professionals between the ages of 35 and 60. Coverage ranges from hard news and consumer information to restaurant reviews and local history." Estab. 1974. Circ. 14,000. Pays on publication. Publishes ms an average of 4 months after acceptance. Byline given. Buys all rights; makes work-for-hire assignments. Submit seasonal material 4 months in advance. Accepts queries by mail, e-mail, fax. Reports in 2 months. Sample copy for $2 and 9×12 SAE with 5 first-class stamps or on website.

**Nonfiction:** Exposé, historical/nostalgic, how-to (live better in western Virginia), interview/profile (of well-known area personalities), photo feature, travel (Virginia and surrounding states). "We're looking for more photo feature stories based in western Virginia. We place special emphasis on investigative and exposé articles." Periodic special sections on fashion, real estate, media, banking, investing. **Buys 30 mss/year.** Query with published clips or send complete ms. Length: 1,400 words maximum. **Pays $35-200.**
**Reprints:** Occasionally accepts previously published submissions. Send tearsheet of article. Pays 50% of amount paid for an original article.
**Photos:** Send photos with ms. Reviews color transparencies. Pays $5-10 for 5×7 or 8×10 b&w prints; $10-50 for color transparencies. Captions and model releases required. Rights purchased vary.
**Tips:** "It helps if freelancer lives in the area. The most frequent mistake made by writers in completing an article for us is not having enough Roanoke-area focus: use of area experts, sources, slants, etc."

**$ $VIRGINIA DYNAMICS IN HIGHER EDUCATION**, The Reflective Publishers, Inc., P.O. Box 798, 113 E. Main St., Berryville VA 22611. (540)955-1298. Fax: (540)955-3447. E-mail: schulte@shentel.net. Editor: Garrison Ellis. **Contact:** Mark Schulte, managing editor. **80% freelance written.** Bimonthly magazine offering "reflective coverage of issues in higher education in Virginia." Estab. 1997. Pays on publication. Publishes ms an average of 4 months after acceptance. Byline given. Accepts simultaneous submissions. Writer's guidelines for #10 SASE.
**Nonfiction:** Essays, exposé, general interest, historical/nostalgic, humor, inspirational, interview/profile, new product, opinion, personal experience, religious, travel. **Buys 12 mss/year.** Query or send complete ms. "Call us." Length: 50-2,000 words. **Pays $250.** Sometimes pays expenses of writers on assignment.
**Reprints:** Accepts previously published submissions.
**Columns/Departments:** Sports, Humor, Opinion, all on Virginia higher education. **Pays $250.**
**Fillers:** Anecdotes, facts, gags to be illustrated by cartoonist, short humor.

# Washington

**N $ $SEATTLE, The Magazine for the Pacific Northwest**, Adams Publishing of the Pacific Northwest, 701 Dexter Ave. N, Suite 101, Seattle WA 98109. (206)284-1750. Fax: (206)284-2550. E-mail: lwogan@seattlemag.com. Website: http://www.seattlemag.com Editor: John Atkins. **Contact:** Lisa Wogan, managing editor. **90% freelance written.** "Monthly magazine serving the Seattle metropolitan area. Articles should be written with our readers in mind. They are interested in politics, fashion, the arts, social issues, their homes, gardens, travel and in maintaining the region's high quality of life." Estab. 1992. Circ. 55,000. Pays on publication. Publishes ms an average of 4 months after acceptance. Byline given. Offers 33% kill fee. Buys first rights or second serial (reprint) rights. Editorial lead time 6 months. Submit seasonal material 6 months in advance. Accepts queries by mail, e-mail, fax. Reports in 2 months. Sample copy and writer's guidelines for SASE.
**Nonfiction:** Book excerpts, general interest, politics and cultural criticism of issues facing the region, interview/profile, photo feature, local interest. Buys 60-75 mss/year. Query with published clips. Length: 50-2,000 words. **Pays $50 minimum for unsolicited articles.** Sometimes pays expenses of writers on assignment.
**Reprints:** Rarely accepts previously published submissions. Send photocopy of article and information about when and where the article previously appeared. Pay varies.
**Photos:** State availability of photos with submission. Negotiates payment individually. Buys one-time rights.
**Columns/Departments:** Reconnaisance, Chef's Dish, Fashion on 1st, Seattle Subconscious, Staples, Dining, Travel, Restaurants. Query with published clips. Pays $100-400.
**Tips:** "Good queries include a lead, sources and suggest how the proposed article will best fit into the magazine, and compelling reasons why the story is right for *Seattle*. In addition, they should show that the writer has read the magazine and understands its content and readership. Proposals for front and back of book contents will be assigned to new writers to the magazine more often than writers of well content. The editors do not, however, discourage feature-length queries and are especially interested in receiving trend pieces, investigative stories and cultural criticism with a local angle."

# Wisconsin

**$ $ $MILWAUKEE MAGAZINE**, 417 E. Chicago St., Milwaukee WI 53202. (414)273-1101. Fax: (414)273-0016. E-mail: jfennell@qgraph.com. **Contact:** John Fennell, editor. **40% freelance written.** Monthly magazine. "We publish stories about Milwaukee, of service to Milwaukee-area residents and exploring the area's changing lifestyle, business, arts, politics and dining." Circ. 42,000. Pays on publication. Publishes ms an average of 2 months after acceptance. Byline given. Offers 20% kill fee. Buys first rights. Submit seasonal material 6 months in advance. Accepts queries by mail, e-mail. Reports in 6 weeks. Sample copy for $4.
**Nonfiction:** Essays, exposé, general interest, historical, interview/profile, photo feature, travel, food and dining and other services. "No articles without a strong Milwaukee or Wisconsin angle." **Buys 30-50 mss/year.** Query with published clips and SASE. Full-length features: 2,500-6,000 words. **Pays $400-1,000.** Two-page "breaker" features (short on copy, long on visuals), 1,800 words. Query. **Pays $150-400.** Sometimes pays expenses of writers on assignment.

**Photos:** Send photos with submission. Reviews contact sheets, negatives, any transparencies and any prints. Offers no set rate per photo. Identification of subjects required. Buys one-time rights.

**Columns/Departments:** Steve Filmanowicz, departments editor. Insider (inside information on Milwaukee, exposé, slice-of-life, unconventional angles on current scene), up to 500 words; Mini reviews for Insider, 125 words; Endgame column (commentary), 850 words. Query with published clips. **Pays $25-125.**

**Tips:** "Pitch something for the Insider, or suggest a compelling profile we haven't already done. Submit clips that prove you can do the job. The department most open is Insider. Think short, lively, offbeat, fresh, people-oriented. We are actively seeking freelance writers who can deliver lively, readable copy that helps our readers make the most out of the Milwaukee area. Because we're only human, we'd like writers who can deliver copy on deadline that fits the specifications of our assignment. If you fit this description, we'd love to work with you."

**$ $ WISCONSIN TRAILS**, P.O. Box 5650, Madison WI 53705-1056. (608)231-2444. Fax: (608)231-1557. E-mail: klb@wistrails.com. Website: http://www.wistrails.com/guide. **Contact:** Kate Bast, managing editor. **40% freelance written.** Prefers to work with published/established writers. Bimonthly magazine for readers interested in Wisconsin and its contemporary issues, personalities, recreation, history, natural beauty and arts. Estab. 1959. Circ. 55,000. Buys first serial rights, one-time rights occasionally. Pays on publication. Submit seasonal material at least 1 year in advance. Publishes ms an average of 6 months after acceptance. Byline given. Reports in 3 months. Sample copy for 9×12 SAE with 10 first-class stamps. Writer's guidelines for #10 SASE.

O— "We're looking for active articles about people, places, events and outdoor adventures in Wisconsin. We want to publish one in-depth article of state-wide interest or concern per issue, and several short (600-1,500 words) articles about short trips, recreational opportunities, personalities, restaurants, inns and cultural activities. We're looking for more articles about out-of-the-way Wisconsin places that are exceptional in some way."

**Nonfiction:** "Our articles focus on some aspect of Wisconsin life: an interesting town or event, a person or industry, history or the arts, and especially outdoor recreation. We do not use first-person essays or biographies about people who were born in Wisconsin but made their fortunes elsewhere. No poetry. No articles that are too local for our regional audience, or articles about obvious places to visit in Wisconsin. We need more articles about the new and little-known." **Buys 3 unsolicited mss/year.** Query or send outline. "Queries accepted only in written form." Length: 1,000-3,000 words. **Pays 25¢/word.** Sometimes pays expenses of writers on assignment.

**Photos:** Purchased with or without mss or on assignment. Uses 35mm transparencies; larger format OK. Color photos usually illustrate an activity, event, region or striking scenery. Prefer photos with people in scenery. Black and white photos usually illustrate a given article. Pays $50 each for b&w on publication. Pays $50-75 for inside color; $100-200 for covers. Caption information required.

**Tips:** "When querying, submit well-thought-out ideas about stories specific to people, places, events, arts, outdoor adventures, etc. in Wisconsin. Include published clips with queries. Do some research—many queries we receive are pitching ideas for stories we recently have published. Know the tone, content and audience of the magazine. Refer to our writers' guidelines, or request them, if necessary."

# Wyoming

**$ WYOMING RURAL ELECTRIC NEWS (WREN)**, 340 West B St., Suite 101, Casper WY 82601. (307)436-5717. Fax: (307)436-8283. E-mail: wendtland@coffey.com. **Contact:** Kris Wendtland, editor. **10% freelance written.** Monthly magazine for audience of small town residents, vacation-home owners, farmers and ranchers. Estab. 1955. Circ. 32,800. Pays on publication. Publishes ms an average of 1 month after acceptance. Byline given. Buys one-time rights. Submit seasonal material 2 months in advance. Accepts queries by mail, e-mail, fax, phone. Reports in 3 months. Sample copy for SAE with 3 first-class stamps. Writer's guidelines and editorial guidelines for #10 SASE.

**Nonfiction:** We print science, ag, how-to and human interest but not fiction. Topics of interest in general include: hunting, cooking, gardening, commodities, sugar beets, wheat, oil, coal, hard rock mining, beef cattle, electric technologies such as lawn mowers, car heaters, air cleaners and assorted gadgets, surge protectors, pesticators, etc. Wants science articles with question/answer quiz at end—test your knowledge. Buys electrical appliance articles. No nostalgia. No sad stories. Articles welcome that put present and/or future in positive light. Submit complete ms. **Buys 4-10 mss/year.** Length: 500-800 words. **Pays up to $140 plus 4 copies.**

**Reprints:** Sometimes buys reprints from noncompeting markets. Send tearsheet or photocopy and information about when and where the article previously appeared. Pays 100% of amount paid for an original article.

**Photos:** Pays up to $40 for cover photos. Color only.

**Tips:** "Study an issue or two of the magazine to become familiar with our focus and the type of freelance material we're using. We're always looking for positive humor. Always looking for fresh, new writers, original perspectives. Submit entire manuscript. Don't submit a regionally set story from some other part of the country. Photos and illustrations (if appropriate) are always welcomed."

## Canada/International

**$ ATLANTIC BOOKS TODAY**, Atlantic Provinces Book Review Society, 1657 Barrington St., #502, Halifax, Nova Scotia B3J 2A1 Canada. (902)429-4454. E-mail: booksatl@istar.ca. Website: http://www.atlanticonline.nsca/index. **Contact:** Elizabeth Eve, managing editor. **50% freelance written.** Quarterly tabloid covering books and writers in Atlantic Canada. "We only accept written inquiries for stories pertaining to promoting interest in the culture of the Atlantic region." Estab. 1992. Circ. 20,000. Pays on publication. Byline given. Offers $25 kill fee. Buys one-time rights. Editorial lead time 6 months. Submit seasonal material 3 months in advance. Accepts simultaneous submissions. Reports in 1 month. Sample copy and writer's guidelines for SASE.
**Nonfiction:** Book excerpts, general interest. Query with published clips. Length: 1,000 words maximum. **Pays $120 maximum.** Sometimes pays expenses of writers on assignment.

**N $ $ $ THE BEAVER, Canada's History Magazine**, Canada's National History Society, 478-167 Lombard Ave., Winnipeg, Manitoba R3B 0T6 Canada. (204)988-9300. Fax: (204)988-9309. E-mail: cnhs@historysociety.ca. Website: http://historysociety.ca. Associate Editor: Doug Whiteway. **Contact:** Annalee Greenberg, editor. **65% freelance written.** Bimonthly history magazine covering Canadian history. Estab. 1920. Circ. 38,000. **Pays on acceptance.** Byline given. Offers $200 kill fee. Buys first North American serial rights. Editorial lead time 4 months. Submit seasonal material 8 months in advance. Accepts queries by mail, fax. Accepts simultaneous submissions. Reports in 6 weeks on queries; 2 months on mss. Sample copy for 9 × 12 SAE and 2 first-class stamps or on website. Writer's guidelines for #10 SASE or on website.
**Nonfiction:** Historical (Canadian focus), photo feature (historical). Does not want anything unrelated to Canadian history. **Buys 30 mss/year.** Query with published clips and SASE. Length: 800-4,000 words. **Pays $400-800 minimum for assigned articles; $300-600 for unsolicited articles.** Sometimes pays expenses of writers on assignment.
**Photos:** State availability of photos with submission. Offers no additional payment for photos accepted with ms. Model releases and identification of subjects required. Buys one-time rights.
**Columns/Departments:** Book and other media reviews and Canadian history subjects, 600 words ("These are assigned to freelancers with particular areas of expertise, i.e., women's history, labour history, French regime, etc.") **Buys 15 mss/year. Pays $125.**
**Tips:** "*The Beaver* is directed toward a general audience of educated readers, as well as to historians and scholars. We are in the market for lively, well-written, well-researched, and informative articles about Canadian history that focus on all parts of the country and all areas of human activity. Subject matter covers the whole range of Canadian history, with particular emphasis on social history, politics, exploration, discovery and settlement, aboriginal peoples, business and trade, war, culture and sport. Articles are obtained through direct commission and by submission. Queries should be accompanied by a stamped, self-addressed envelope. *The Beaver* publishes articles of various lengths, including long features (from 2,000 to 4,000 words) that provide an in-depth look at an event, person or era; short, more narrowly focused features (from 800 to 2,000 words); and book reviews (no longer than 600 words). Longer articles may be considered if their importance warrants publication. Articles should be written in an expository or interpretive style and present the principal themes of Canadian history in an original, interesting and informative way."

**$ BRAZZIL**, Brazzil, P.O. Box 50536, Los Angeles CA 90050. (323)255-8062. Fax: (323)257-3487. E-mail: brazzil@brazzil.com. Website: http://www.brazzil.com. **Contact:** Leda Mello, assistant editor. **60% freelance written.** Monthly magazine covering Brazilian culture. Estab. 1989. Circ. 12,000. Pays on publication. Publishes ms an average of 2 months after acceptance. Byline given. Offers 10% kill fee. Buys one-time rights. Editorial lead time 2 months. Submit seasonal material 2 months in advance. Accepts queries by mail, e-mail, fax. Accepts simultaneous submissions. Reports in 2 weeks. Sample copy free or on website.
**Nonfiction:** Book excerpts, essays, exposé, general interest, historical/nostalgic, interview/profile, personal experience, travel. "All subjects have to deal in some way with Brazil and its culture. We assume our readers know very little or nothing about Brazil, so we explain everything." **Buys 15 mss/year.** Query. Length: 800-5,000 words. **Pays $20-50.** Pays writers with contributor copies or other premiums by mutual agreement.
**Reprints:** Accepts reprints of previously published submissions. Include information about when and where the article previously appeared. Pays 50% of amount paid for an original article.
**Photos:** State availability of photos with submission. Reviews prints. Offers no additional payment for photos accepted with ms. Identification of subjects required. Buys one-time rights.
The online magazine carries original content not found in the print edition. Contact: Rodney Mello, online editor.
**Tips:** "We are interested in anything related to Brazil: politics, economy, music, behavior, profiles. Please document material with interviews and statistical data if applicable. Controversial pieces are welcome."

**$ $ BRITISH COLUMBIA REPORT**, BC Report Magazine Ltd., 305-535 Thurlow St., Vancouver, British Columbia V6E 3L2 Canada. (604)682-8202. Fax: (604)682-0963. E-mail: bcreport@axionet.com. Editor: Terry O'Neill. **Contact:** Kevin Michael Grace, managing editor. **20% freelance written.** Biweekly magazine covering British Columbia. Estab. 1989. Circ. 20,000. Pays on publication. Publishes ms 2 months after acceptance. Byline given. Offers 50% kill fee. Buys all rights. Editorial lead time 2 weeks. Accepts queries by mail, e-mail, phone, fax. Sample copy for SASE.
**Nonfiction:** News from British Columbia. **Buys 250 mss/year.** Query. Length: 250-1,250 words. **Pays $50-250 for**

**assigned articles.** Pays expenses of writers on assignment.

**Photos:** State availability of photos with submission. Negotiates payment individually. Captions required. Rights purchased negotiable.

**⚡ $ $ $ CANADIAN GEOGRAPHIC**, 39 McArthur Ave., Ottawa, Ontario K1L 8L7 Canada. (613)745-4629. Fax: (613)744-0947. E-mail: editorial@cangeo.ca. Website: http://www.cangeo.ca/. Managing Editor: Eric Harris. **Contact:** Rick Boychuk, editor. **90% freelance written.** Works with a small number of new/unpublished writers each year. Estab. 1930. Circ. 240,000. Bimonthly magazine. "*Canadian Geographic*'s colorful portraits of our ever-changing population show readers just how important the relationship between the people and the land really is." **Pays on acceptance.** Publishes ms an average of 3 months after acceptance. Buys first Canadian rights; interested only in first-time publication. Accepts queries by mail, e-mail, fax. Reports in 1 month. Sample copy for $4.25 (Canada.) and $9 \times 12$ SAE or on website.

**Nonfiction:** Buys authoritative geographical articles, in the broad geographical sense, written for the average person, not for a scientific audience. Predominantly Canadian subjects by Canadian authors. **Buys 30-45 mss/year.** *Always query first in writing and enclose SASE.* Cannot reply personally to all unsolicited proposals. Length: 1,500-3,000 words. **Pays 80¢/word minimum. Usual payment for articles ranges between $1,000-3,000.** Higher fees reserved for commissioned articles. Sometimes pays the expenses of writers on assignment.

   • *Canadian Geographic* reports a need for more articles on earth sciences.

**Photos:** Pays $75-400 for color photos, depending on published size.

**📰 $ COLLECTIBLES CANADA, Your National Guide to Limited Edition Collectible Art**, Trajan Publishing, 103 Lakeshore Rd., Suite 202, St. Catharines, Ontario L2N 2T6 Canada. (905)646-7744. Fax: (905)646-0995. E-mail: newsroom@trajan.com. Website: http://www.trajan.com/trajan. **Contact:** Joanne Keogh, editor. **60% freelance written.** Bimonthly publication covering modern day collectible art. "We provide news and profiles of limited edition collectible art from a fairly positive perspective. We attempt to be an informational tool for collectors who want to read about the products they love." Circ. 20,000. Pays 2 months after publication. Publishes ms an average of 1 month after acceptance. Byline given. Buys first North American serial rights. Editorial lead time 4 months. Submit seasonal material 5 months in advance. Accepts queries by mail, e-mail, fax, phone. Reports in 1 month. Sample copy free.

**Nonfiction:** Interview/profile, new product. "We publish both a Christmas issue and a nature issue (Jan-Feb)." No articles on antique related subjects (we are modern day collectibles). **Buys 30 mss/year.** Query with published clips. Length: 1,000-2,000 words. **Pays $100.** Sometimes pays expenses of writers on assignment.

**Photos:** State availability of photos with submission. Reviews negatives, any size transparencies and prints. Offers no additional payment for photos accepted with ms. Identification of subjects required. Buys one-time rights.

**Columns/Departments:** Book reviews (positive slant, primarily informational), 500-800 words. **Buys 2 mss/year.** Query with published clips. **Pays $50-75.**

**Tips:** "Freelancers should become familiar with the collectibles market. Always query first and send samples of your writing."

**📰 $ $ THE COTTAGE MAGAZINE, Country Living in B.C. and Alberta**, Greenheart Publications, Ltd., 322 John St., Victoria, British Columbia V8T 1T3 Canada. **Contact:** Kathy Butts, editor. **80% freelance written.** Bimonthly magazine covering recreational property in British Columbia and Alberta. Estab. 1992. Circ. 10,000. Pays on publication. Publishes ms an average of 1 month after publication. Byline given. Offers 50% kill fee. Not copyrighted. Buys first North American serial rights. Editorial lead time 2 months. Submit seasonal material 3 months in advance. Accepts simultaneous submissions. Reports in 1 month on queries; 2 months on mss. Sample copy for $2. Writer's guidelines for #10 SASE.

**Nonfiction:** General interest, historical/nostalgic, how-to, humor, interview/profile, new product, personal experience, technical. **Buys 30 mss/year.** Query. Length: 200-2,000 words. **Pays $50-300.** Sometimes pays expenses of writers on assignment (telephone expenses mostly).

**Photos:** State availability of photos with submission. Reviews contact sheets, transparencies, prints and slides. Offers no additional payment for photos accepted with ms. Buys one-time rights.

**Columns/Departments:** Utilities (solar and/or wind power), 650-700 words; Cabin Wit (humor), 650 words. **Buys 10 mss/year.** Query. **Pays $100-200.**

**Fillers:** Anecdotes, facts, gags to be illustrated by cartoonist, newsbreaks. **Buys 12/year.** Length: 50-200 words. **Pays 20¢/word.**

**📰 ⚡ $ ID MAGAZINE, The Weekly Guide to the Zeitgeist**, Macall Publishing, 123 Woolwich St., 2nd Floor, Guelph, Ontario N1H 3V1 Canada. (519)766-9853. Fax: (519)766-9891. Website: http://www.idmagazine.com. Managing Editor: Anicka Quin. **Contact:** Sherri Telenko, arts editor. **90% freelance written.** Urban weekly magazine covering pop culture, entertainment, arts, music. "*id* is a weekly guide to south-western Ontario's social happenings and current political issues." Estab. 1991. Circ. 40,000. Pays 30 days after publication. Publishes ms an average of 1 month after acceptance. Byline given. Buys one-time rights. Editorial lead time 1 months. Submit seasonal material 2 months in advance. Accepts queries by mail, e-mail, fax. Accepts simultaneous submissions. Reports in 3 weeks. Sample copy free or on website. Writer's guidelines for SAE.

**Nonfiction:** Interview/profile, research journalism. "No one source, personal experience, columns." **Buys 600 mss/**

**year.** Query with published clips. Length: 800-1,800 words. **Pays 5¢/word.** Sometimes pays expenses of writers on assignment.

**Photos:** State availability of photos with submission. Reviews contact sheets and 4×6 prints. Offers $20-70/photo. Captions, model releases and identification of subjects required. Buys one-time rights.

**Tips:** "*id* magazine's music, theater and visual arts sections focus on local events in our distribution area only (southwestern Ontario). However, we do publish one journalism-style, well researched article on a larger, national or international social issue per issue."

**▨ $ $ OUTDOOR CANADA MAGAZINE**, 340 Ferrier St., Suite 210, Markham, Ontario L3R 2Z5 Canada. (905)475-8440. Fax: (905)475-9560. E-mail: editorial@outdoorcanadamagazine.com. **Contact:** James Little, editor-in-chief. **90% freelance written.** Works with a small number of new/unpublished writers each year. Magazine published 8 times/year emphasizing noncompetitive outdoor recreation in Canada *only*. Estab. 1972. Circ. 95,000. Pays on publication. Publishes ms an average of 8 months after acceptance. Buys first rights. Submit seasonal material 1 year in advance of issue date. Byline given. *Enclose SASE or IRCs or material will not be returned.* Accepts queries by mail, e-mail, fax. Reports in 1 month. Mention *Writer's Market* in request for editorial guidelines.

**Nonfiction:** Fishing, canoeing, hunting, outdoor issues, outdoor destinations in Canada, some how-to. **Buys 35-40 mss/year, usually with photos.** Length: 2,500 words. **Pays $500 and up.**

**Reprints:** Send information about when and where the article previously appeared. Pay varies. Publishes book excerpts.

**Photos:** Emphasize people in the Canadian outdoors. Pays $100-250 for 35mm transparencies; and $400/cover. Captions and model releases required.

**Fillers:** Short news pieces. **Buys 30-40/year.** Length: 100-500 words. **Pays $50 and up.**

**N ▨ $ $ THIS MAGAZINE**, Red Maple Foundation, 401 Richmond St. W. #396, Toronto, Ontario M5V 3A8 Canada. (416)979-8400. Fax: (416)979-1143. E-mail: thismag@web.net. Website: http://www.thismag.org. Editor: Andrea Curtis. **Contact:** Sarmishta Subramanian, editor. **80% freelance written.** Bimonthly publication covering Canadian politics and culture. "*This* is Canada's leading alternative magazine. We publish stories on politics, culture and the arts that mainstream media won't touch." Estab. 1966. Circ. 6,000. Pays 8 months after publication. Publishes ms an average of 2 months after acceptance. Byline given. Buys first North American serial and electronic rights. Editorial lead time 10 weeks. Accepts queries by mail, e-mail, fax. Sample copy for $5 or on website. Writer's guidelines for #10 SASE.

**Nonfiction:** Exposé, how-to, humor, interview/profile, personal experience, photo feature. **Buys 60 mss/year.** Query with published clips. Length: 100-4,000 words. **Pays $50-500.**

**Columns/Departments: Pays $100-200.**

**$ $ UP HERE, Life at the Top of the World**, OUTCROP: The Northern Publishers, Box 1350, Yellowknife, Northwest Territories X1A 2N9 Canada. (867)920-4652. Fax: (867)873-2844. E-mail: uphere@outcrop.com. **Contact:** Cooper Langfore, editor. **70% freelance written.** Bimonthly magazine covering general interest about Canada's North. "We publish features, columns and shorts about people, wildlife, native cultures, travel and adventure in Northern Canada, with an occasional swing into Alaska. Be informative, but entertaining." Estab. 1984. Circ. 35,000. Pays on publication. Byline given. Offers 50% kill fee. Buys first North American serial rights. Editorial lead time 6 months. Submit seasonal material 1 year in advance. Reports in 4 months. Sample copy for $3.50 (Canadian) and 9×12 SASE with $1.45 Canadian postage. Writer's guidelines for legal-sized SASE and 45¢ Canadian postage.

● This publication was a finalist for Best Editorial Package, National Magazine Awards.

**Nonfiction:** Essays, general interest, historical/nostalgic, how-to, humor, interview/profile, lifestyle/culture, new product, personal experience, photo feature, technical, travel. No poetry or fiction. **Buys 30 mss/year.** Query. Length: 1,500-3,000 words. **Pays $250-750 or 15-25¢/word.** Pays with advertising space where appropriate.

**Photos:** Send photos with submission. "*Please* do not sent unsolicited original photos, slides. Photocopies are sufficient." Reviews transparencies and prints. Offers $25-350/photo (Canadian). Captions and identification of subjects required. Buys one-time rights.

**Columns/Departments:** Write for updated guidelines. **Buys 20 mss/year.** Query with published clips. **Pays $150-250 or 15-25¢/word.**

**Tips:** "We like well-researched, concrete adventure pieces, insights about Northern people and lifestyles, readable natural history. Features are most open to freelancers—travel, adventure and so on. Outer Edge (a shorter, newsy, gee-whiz section) is a good place to break in with a 50-500 word piece. We don't want a comprehensive 'How I spent my summer vacation' hour-by-hour account. We want stories with angles, articles that look at the North through a different set of glasses. Photos are important; you greatly increase your chances with top-notch images."

**$ $ WESTERN PEOPLE, Supplement to the Western Producer**, Western Producer Publications, Box 2500, Saskatoon, Saskatchewan S7K 2C4 Canada. (306)665-3500. E-mail: people@producer.com. Website: http://www.producer.com. **Contact:** Michael Gillgannon, managing editor. Weekly farm newspaper supplement "reflecting the life and people of rural Western Canada both in the present and historically." Estab. 1978. Circ. 90,000. **Pays on acceptance.** Publishes ms an average of 3 months after acceptance. Byline given. Buys first rights. Submit seasonal material 3 months in advance. Reports in 3 weeks. Sample copy for 9×12 SAE and 3 IRCs. Guidelines for #10 SAE and 2 IRCs.

**Nonfiction:** General interest, historical/nostalgic, humor, interview/profile, personal experience, photo feature. **Buys 225 mss/year.** Send complete ms. Length: 500-1,800 words. **Pays $100-275.**

**Photos:** Send photos with submission. Reviews transparencies and prints. Captions and identification of subjects required. No stand-alone photos.

**Fiction:** Adventure, historical, humorous, mainstream, mystery, romance, suspense, western stories reflecting life in rural Western Canada. **Buys 12 mss/year.** Send complete ms. Length: 1,000-2,000 words. **Pays $100-200.**

**Poetry:** Free verse, traditional, haiku, light verse. **Buys 75 poems/year.** Submit maximum 3 poems. Length: 4-50 lines. **Pays $15-50.**

**Tips:** "Western Canada is geographically very large. The approach for writing about an interesting individual is to introduce that person *neighbor-to-neighbor* to our readers."

# RELATIONSHIPS

These publications focus on lifestyles and relationships of single adults. Other markets for this type of material can be found in the Women's category. Magazines of a primarily sexual nature, gay or straight, are listed under the Sex category. Gay & Lesbian Interest contains general interest editorial targeted to that audience.

**N** **$ $ $ $ COUPLES**, Couples Magazine, LLC, 17117 W. Nine Mile Rd., Suite 1211, Southfield MI 48075. (248)559-5707. **Contact:** Ivie Jonathan Shelton, editor. **90% freelance written.** Monthly magazine designed solely to nurture, build and enhance a loving relationship between a man and a woman. **Pays on acceptance.** Byline given. Offers 10-15% kill fee. Buys all magazine rights. Reports in 1 week on queries; 3 weeks on mss. Accepts simultaneous submissions. Sample copy for $2.50 writer's guidelines for #10 SASE. Publishes ms an average of 5 months after acceptance.
- The editor reports a need for more relationship stories.

**Nonfiction:** Couples is a source of information for men and women who want to have or enhance a loving and exciting relationship with their significant other. Consequently, we need articles that address lovers etiquette, interior design ideas for creating a more seductive and romantic home environment, finding that special someone, fashion, beauty, romantic getaways, communication ideas and techniques, imaginative means and ways to spice up your sex lives, going for the gold, etc. These articles must be lively, well researched and well written and references to those experts supporting the articles. Length: 1,500-3,000 words. **Pays $1/word or more.**

**Photos:** State availability of photos with submission. Reviews contact sheets, negatives, prints. Negotiates payment individually. Model releases, identification of subjects required.

**$ $ LOVING MORE MAGAZINE**, PEP, P.O. Box 4358, Boulder CO 80306. Phone/fax: (303)543-7540. E-mail: lmm@lovemore.com. Website: http://www.lovemore.com. **Contacts:** Ryam Nearing/Brett Hill, editors. **80% freelance written.** "*Loving More* is a quarterly publication whose mission is to support, explore and enhance the many beautiful forms which families and loving relationships can take. We affirm that loving more than one can be a natural expression of health, exuberance, joy and intimacy. We view the shift from enforced monogamy and isolated families to polyamory and intentional families or tribes in the context of a larger shift toward a more balanced, peaceful and sustainable way of life." Estab. 1984. Circ. 3,000. Pays on publication. Publishes ms 6 months after acceptance. Byline given. Buys one-time rights or all rights. Editorial lead time 3 months. Submit seasonal material 6 months in advance. Accepts queries by mail, e-mail, fax. Reports in 1 month on queries. Sample copy for $6. Writer's guidelines for #10 SASE or via e-mail at writers@lovemore.com.

**Nonfiction:** Book excerpts, essays, exposé, how-to, humor, interview/profile, opinion, personal experience, photo feature. "No swinging sex, hardcore." **Buys 12-20 mss/year.** Query with published clips. Length: 750-3,000 words. **Pays $25-200.**

**Reprints:** Send information about when and where the article previously appeared. Pays 50% of amount paid for an original article.

**Photos:** Send photos with submission. Negotiates payment individually. Model releases required. Buys one-time rights.

**Poetry:** "We publish select poetry relevant to our theme."

**$ ON THE SCENE MAGAZINE**, 3507 Wyoming NE, Albuquerque NM 87111-4427. (505)299-4401. Fax: (505)299-4403. Website: http://www.onthescene-alb.com. **Contact:** Gail Skinner, editor. **60% freelance written.** Eager to work with new/unpublished writers. Monthly magazine covering lifestyles for all ages. Estab. 1979. Circ. 30,000. Pays on publication. Publishes ms within 1 year after acceptance. Byline given. Submit seasonal material 3 months in advance. Reports in 3 months. Sample copy for $3 postage or send 9×12 SAE with $1.01 postage. Writer's guidelines for #10 SASE.

**Nonfiction:** General interest, how-to, humor, inspirational, opinion, personal experience, relationships, consumer guide, travel, finance, real estate, parenting, astrology. No suggestive or pornographic material. **Buys 30 mss/year.** Send complete ms. Mss returned only if adequate SASE included. Length: 600-1,200 words. **Pays $5-35.**

**Reprints:** Send typed ms with rights for sale noted. Pays 100% of amount paid for original article.

**Photos:** Send photos with ms. Captions, model releases, identification of subjects required. Photo returned only if adequate SASE is included.

◼ The online magazine carries original content not found in the print edition.

**Tips:** "We are looking for articles that deal with every aspect of living—whether on a local or national level. Our readers are of above-average intelligence, income and education. The majority of our articles are relationships, humor and seasonal submissions. Also publishes some fiction."

**$ THE ROMANTIC, Hundreds of Creative Tips to Enrich Your Relationship**, Sterling Publications, P.O. Box 1567, Cary NC 27512-1567. (919)462-0900. Fax: (919)461-8333. E-mail: romantc@aol.com. Website: http://www.TheRomantic.com. **Contact:** Michael Webb. **20% freelance written**. Bimonthly newsletter covering the art of romance. "*The RoMANtic* aims to inspire its readers to continually improve their relationships by providing them with creative ideas, practical advice and lots of fun suggestions." Estab. 1996. Circ. 10,000. Pays on publication. Publishes ms 4 months after acceptance. Byline given. Buys first North American serial rights or second serial (reprint) rights. Editorial lead time 3 months. Submit seasonal material 4 months in advance. Accepts simultaneous submissions. Reports in 3 months on mss. Sample copy for $3.
**Nonfiction:** Inspirational, personal experience. No sex, erotica or romance novels. Send complete ms. Length: 500 words. **Pays 2¢/word**.
**Tips:** "Read one or more back issues to see the types of romantic ideas and stories that are printed."

# RELIGIOUS

Religious magazines focus on a variety of subjects, styles and beliefs. Most are sectarian, but a number approach topics such as public policy, international affairs and contemporary society from a non-denominational perspective. Fewer religious publications are considering poems and personal experience articles, but many emphasize special ministries to singles, seniors or other special interest groups. Such diversity makes reading each magazine essential for the writer hoping to break in. Educational and inspirational material of interest to church members, workers and leaders within a denomination or religion is needed by the publications in this category. Religious magazines for children and teenagers can be found in the Juvenile and Teen & Young Adult classifications. Other religious publications can be found in the Contemporary Culture and Ethnic/Minority sections as well. Spiritual topics are also addressed in Astrology, Metaphysical and New Age as well as Health & Fitness. Publications intended to assist professional religious workers in teaching and managing church affairs are classified in Church Administration & Ministry in the Trade section.

**$ AMERICA**, 106 W. 56th St., New York NY 10019. (212)581-4640. Fax: (212)399-3596. E-mail: articles@americapress.org. Website: http://wwwamericapress.org. **Contact:** Rev. Thomas J. Reese, editor. Published weekly for adult, educated, largely Roman Catholic audience. Estab. 1909. **Pays on acceptance.** Byline given. Usually buys all rights. Reports in 3 weeks. Free writer's guidelines by mail or on website.
**Nonfiction:** "We publish a wide variety of material on politics, economics, ecology and so forth. We are not a parochial publication, but almost all pieces make some moral or religious point. We are not interested in purely informational pieces or personal narratives which are self-contained and have no larger moral interest." Articles on literature, current political, social events. Length: 1,500-2,000 words. **Pays $50-200.**
**Poetry:** Contact Patrick Samway, S.J., poetry editor. Length: 15-30 lines.

**$ THE ANNALS OF SAINT ANNE DE BEAUPRÉ**, Redemptorist Fathers, P.O. Box 1000, St. Anne De Beaupré, Quebec G0A 3C0 Canada. (418)827-4538. Fax: (418)827-4530. Editor: Father Bernard Mercier, CSs.R. **Contact:** Father Roch Achard, managing editor. **80% freelance written.** Monthly religious magazine. "Our mission statement includes a dedication to Christian family values and a devotion to St. Anne." Estab. 1885. Circ. 45,000. **Pays on acceptance.** Buys first North American rights. Editorial lead time 6 months. Submit seasonal material 4 months in advance. "Please, no reprints or simultaneous submissions." Reports in 3 weeks. Sample copy and writer's guidelines for 8½ × 11 SAE and IRCs.
**Nonfiction:** Inspirational, religious. **Buys 350 mss/year.** Send complete ms. Length: 500-1,500 words. **Pays 3-4¢/word,** plus 3 copies.
**Photos:** Send photos with submission. Negotiates payment individually. Identification of subjects required. Buys one-time rights.
**Fiction:** Religious, inspirational. "No senseless, mockery." **Buys 200 mss/year.** Send complete ms. Length: 500-1,500 words. **Pays 3-4¢/word.**
**Tips:** "Write something inspirational with spiritual thrust. Reporting rather than analysis is simply not remarkable. Each article must have a spiritual theme. Please only submit first North American rights mss with the rights clearly stated. We maintain an article bank and pick from it for each month's needs which loosely follow the religious themes for each month. Right now, our needs lean towards nonfiction of approximately 1,100 words."

**$ THE ASSOCIATE REFORMED PRESBYTERIAN**, Associate Reformed Presbyterian General Synod, 1 Cleveland St., Suite 110, Greenville SC 29601-3696. (864)232-8297. Fax: (864)271-3729. E-mail: arpmaged@sprynet.com. Website: http://www.arpsynod.org. **Contact:** Ben Johnston, editor. **5% freelance written.** Works with a small number of new/unpublished writers each year. Christian magazine serving a conservative, evangelical and Reformed denomination. Estab. 1976. Circ. 6,000. **Pays on acceptance.** Publishes ms an average of 4 months after acceptance. Byline given. Not copyrighted. Buys first, one-time or second serial (reprint) rights. Submit seasonal material 4 months in advance. Accepts simultaneous submissions. Reports in 1 month. Sample copy for $1.50. Guidelines for #10 SASE.
**Nonfiction:** Book excerpts, essays, inspirational, opinion, personal experience, religious. **Buys 10-15 mss/year.** Query. Length: 400-2,000 words. **Pays $70 maximum.**
**Reprints:** Send information about when and where the article previously appeared. Pays 100% of amount paid for an original article.
**Photos:** State availability of photos with submission. Offers $25 maximum/photo. Captions and identification of subjects required. Buys one-time rights.
**Fiction:** Religious and children's. **Pays $50 maximum.**
**Tips:** "Feature articles are the area of our publication most open to freelancers. Focus on a contemporary problem and offer Bible-based solutions to it. Provide information that would help a Christian struggling in his daily walk. Writers should understand that we are denominational, conservative, evangelical, Reformed and Presbyterian. A writer who appreciates these nuances would stand a much better chance of being published here than one who does not."

**$ BIBLE ADVOCATE**, Bible Advocate Press, Church of God (Seventh Day), P.O. Box 33677, Denver CO 80233. (303)452-7973. E-mail: cofgsd@denver.net. Website: http://www.baonline.org. Editor: Calvin Burrell. **Contact:** Sherri Langton, associate editor. **25% freelance written.** Religious magazine published 10 times/year. "Our purpose is to advocate the Bible and represent the Church of God (Seventh Day) to a Christian audience." Estab. 1863. Circ. 13,500. Pays on publication. Publishes ms an average of 9 months after acceptance. Byline given. Offers 50% kill fee. Buys first and second serial (reprint) rights, plus electronic rights. Editorial lead time 3 months. Submit seasonal material 6 months in advance. Accepts queries by mail, e-mail. Accepts simultaneous submissions. Reports in 6 weeks. Sample copy for 9×12 SASE with 4 first-class stamps. Writer's guidelines for #10 SASE.
**Nonfiction:** Inspirational, interview/profile, opinion, personal experience, religious, biblical studies. No articles on Christmas or Easter. **Buys 20-25 mss/year.** Send complete ms and SASE. Length: 1,500-1,800 words long. **Pays $10-35.**
**Reprints:** Send typed ms with rights for sale noted.
**Photos:** Send photos with submission. Reviews prints. Offers payment for photos accepted with ms. Identification of subjects required.
**Columns/Departments:** Viewpoint (opinion), 500-700 words. **Buys 6 mss/year.** Send complete ms and SASE. No payment for opinion pieces.
**Poetry:** Free verse, traditional. No avant-garde. **Buys 10-12 poems/year.** Submit maximum 5 poems. Length: 5-20 lines. **Pays $10.**
**Fillers:** Anecdotes, facts. **Buys 5/year.** Length: 50-100 words. **Pays $5-10.**
> See the listing for Bible Advocate Online.
**Tips:** "Be fresh, not preachy! We're trying to reach a younger audience now, so think how you can cover contemporary and biblical topics with this audience in mind. Articles must be in keeping with the doctrinal understanding of the Church of God (Seventh Day). Therefore, the writer should become familiar with what the Church generally accepts as truth as set forth in its doctrinal beliefs. We reserve the right to edit manuscripts to fit our space requirements, doctrinal stands and church terminology. Significant changes are referred to writers for approval. No fax or handwritten submissions, please."

**$ BIBLE ADVOCATE ONLINE**, Bible Advocate Press/Church of God (Seventh Day), P.O. Box 33677, Denver CO 80233. (303)452-7973. E-mail: cofgsd@denver.net. Website: http://www.baonline.org. Editor: Calvin Burrell. **Contact:** Sherri Langton, associate editor. **75% freelance written.** "Online religious publication covering social and religious topics; more inclusive of non-Christians." Estab. 1996. Pays on publication. Publishes ms an average of 3 months after acceptance. Byline given. Offers 50% kill fee. Buys first rights and second serial (reprint) rights. Editorial lead time 3 months. Submit seasonal material 6 months in advance. Accepts queries by mail, e-mail. Accepts simultaneous submissions. Reports in 6 weeks on queries. Sample copy for 9×12 SAE and 3 first-class stamps. Writer's guidelines for #10 SASE and on website.
> "For the online magazine, write for the 'felt needs' of the reader and come up with creative ways for communicating to the unchurched."
**Nonfiction:** Inspirational, personal experience, religious. No Christmas or Easter pieces. **Buys 20-25 mss/year.** Send complete ms and SASE. Length: 1,500-1,800 words. **Pays $15-35.**
**Reprints:** Accepts previously published submissions. Send typed ms with rights for sale noted and information about when and where the article previously appeared. **Pays $15-35.**
**Photos:** Send photos with submission. Reviews prints. Offers additional payment for photos accepted with ms. Identification of subjects required. Buys one-time rights.
**Fillers:** Anecdotes, facts. **Buys 6-10/year.** Length: 50-250 words. **Pays $5-10.**
**Tips:** "Be vulnerable in your personal experiences. Show, don't tell! Delete Christian jargon and write from perspective

of a non-Christian. Articles must be in keeping with the doctrinal understanding of the Church of God (Seventh Day). Therefore, the writer should become familiar with what the Church generally accepts as truth as set forth in their doctrinal beliefs. We reserve the right to edit manuscripts to fit our space requirements, doctrinal stands and church terminology. Significant changes are referred to writers for approval. No fax or handwritten submissions, please."

**$ BRIGADE LEADER**, Christian Service Brigade, P.O. Box 150, Wheaton IL 60189. (630)665-0630. Fax: (630)665-0372. E-mail: brigadecsb@aol.com. Website: http://CSBministries.org. **Contact:** Deborah Christensen, editor. Quarterly magazine covering leadership issues for Christian Service Brigade leaders. "*Brigade Leader* is distributed to leaders with Christian Service Brigade across North America. CSB is a nonprofit, nondenominational agency dedicated to winning and training boys to serve Jesus Christ. Hundreds of churches throughout the U.S. and Canada make use of our wide range of services." Estab. 1960. Circ. 6,000. Pays on publication. Publishes ms an average of 3 months after acceptance. Byline given. Offers $35 kill fee. Buys first rights or second serial (reprint) rights. Editorial lead time 3 months. Reports in 1 week on queries. Sample copy for $1.50 and 10×13 SAE with 4 first-class stamps. Writer's guidelines for #10 SASE.
**Nonfiction:** Religious leadership. **Buys 8 mss/year.** Query only. Length: 500-1,500 words. **Pays 5-10¢/word.** Sometimes pays expenses of writers on assignment.
**Reprints:** Send typed ms with rights for sale noted. Pays 50% of amount paid for an original article.
**Photos:** State availability of photos with submission. Reviews prints. Negotiates payment. Buys one-time rights.
**Tips:** "We're looking for male writers who are familiar with Christian Service Brigade and can address leadership issues. Know *Brigade* and be able to offer practical and creative ideas for men to be better leaders."

**N $ $ CATHOLIC FORESTER**, Catholic Order of Foresters, 355 Shuman Blvd., P.O. Box 3012, Naperville IL 60566-7012. Editor: Dorothy Deer. Assistant Editor: Patricia Baron. **Contact:** Mary Ann File, associate editor. **20% freelance written.** Bimonthly magazine for members of the Catholic Order of Foresters. "*Catholic Forester* articles cover varied topics to create a balanced issue for the purpose of informing, educating and entertaining our readers." Circ. 100,000. **Pays on acceptance.** Publishes ms an average of 6-12 months after acceptance. Byline given. Offers $25 kill fee. Buys first North American serial rights. Editorial lead time 6 months. Submit seasonal material 6 months in advance. Accepts queries by mail. Reports in 2-3 months. Sample copy free for 9×12 SAE and 4 first-class stamps. Writer's guidelines free for #10 SASE.
**Nonfiction:** Humor, inspirational, religious, health, parenting, financial. **Buys 12-16 mss/year.** Send complete ms. Length: 500-1,500 words. **Pays 20-25¢/word.**
**Photos:** State availability of photos with submission. Reviews transparencies. Negotiates payment individually. Buys one-time rights.
**Fiction:** Humorous, religious. **Buys 12-16 mss/year.** Send complete ms. Length: 500-1,500 words. **Pays 20-25¢/word.**
**Poetry:** Light verse, traditional. **Buys 1 poem/year.** Submit maximum 5 poems. Length: 5-15 lines. **Pays 20-25¢/word.**
**Tips:** "Our audience covers a broad age spectrum, ranging from youth to seniors. Nonfiction topics that appeal to our members include health and wellness, money management and budgeting, parenting and family life, wildlife and environmental issues, interesting travels, historical or contemporary personalities, nostalgia and humor pieces, unusual careers or hobbies, etc. Although we are more interested in nonfiction topics, we also like to entertain our readers with humor, light fiction and short inspirational pieces. A good children's story would rate high on our list."

**$ $ CATHOLIC NEAR EAST MAGAZINE**, Catholic Near East Welfare Association, 1011 First Ave., New York NY 10022-4195. (212)826-1480. Fax: (212)826-8979. Executive Editor: Michael La Cività. **Contact:** Helen C. Packard, assistant editor. **50% freelance written.** Bimonthly magazine for a Catholic audience with interest in the Near East, particularly its current religious, cultural and political aspects. Estab. 1974. Circ. 100,000. Pays on publication. Publishes ms an average of 6 months after acceptance. Byline given. Buys all rights. Accepts queries by mail, fax. Reports in 2 months. Sample copy and writer's guidelines for 7½×10½ SAE with 2 first-class stamps.
**Nonfiction:** "Cultural, devotional, political, historical material on the Near East, with an emphasis on the Eastern Christian churches. Style should be simple, factual, concise. Articles must stem from personal acquaintance with subject matter, or thorough up-to-date research." Length: 1,200-1,800 words. **Pays 20¢/edited word.**
**Photos:** "Photographs to accompany manuscript are welcome; they should illustrate the people, places, ceremonies, etc. which are described in the article. We prefer color transparencies but occasionally use b&w. Pay varies depending on use—scale from $50-300."
**Tips:** "We are interested in current events in the regions listed above as they affect the cultural, political and religious lives of the people."

**N $ $ CELEBRATE LIFE**, American Life League, P.O. Box 1350, Stafford VA 22555. (540)659-4171. Fax: (540)659-2586. E-mail: clmag@all.org. Website: http://www.all.org/. Managing Editor: David Brandao. **Contact:** Cathy Kenyon, associate editor. **70% freelance written.** Bimonthly educational magazine covering pro-life education and human interest, pro-family issues. "We are a religious-based publication specializing in pro-life education through human-interest stories and factual presentation. Our purpose is to inspire, encourage and educate pro-life individuals and activists." Estab. 1979. Circ. 80,000. Pays on publication. Publishes ms an average of 6-8 months after acceptance. Byline given. Offers 25% kill fee. Buys first, second serial (reprint) rights or makes work-for-hire assignments. Editorial lead time 7 months. Submit seasonal material 4 months in advance. Accepts queries by mail, e-mail, fax. Accepts simultaneous submissions. Reports in 2 weeks on queries; 2-3 months on mss. Sample copy for 9 × 12 SAE and 4 first-class stamps. Writer's guidelines free by mail or e-mail.

**Nonfiction:** "No fiction, book reviews, poetry, allegory, devotionals." **Buys 40 mss/year.** Query with published clips or send complete ms. Length: 300-1,050 words. **Pays 20¢/word for assigned articles; 5-10¢/word for unsolicited articles.** Pays expenses of writers on assignment.

**Reprints:** Accepts previously published submissions.

**Photos:** State availability of photos with submission. Reviews 4 × 6 prints. Offers $10-150/photo. Identification of subjects required. Buys one-time rights.

**Fillers:** Newsbreaks. **Buys 5/year.** Length: 75-200 words. **Pays $10.**

**Tips:** "We look for inspiring, educational or motivational human-interest stories. We are religious based and pro-life. All articles must have agreement with the principles expressed in Pope John Paul II's encyclical *Humanae Vitae*. Our common themes include: abortion, post-abortion healing, sidewalk counseling, adoption and contraception."

**$ $ THE CHRISTIAN CENTURY,** Christian Century Foundation, 407 S. Dearborn St., Suite 1405, Chicago IL 60605-1150. (312)427-5380. Fax: (312)427-1302. Website: http://www.christiancentury.org. Editor/Publisher: John M. Buchanan. **Contact:** David Heim, executive editor. **90% freelance written.** Eager to work with new/unpublished writers. Weekly magazine for ecumenically-minded, progressive Protestant church people, both clergy and lay. "Authors must have a critical and analytical perspective on the church and be familiar with contemporary theological discussion." Estab. 1884. Circ. 30,000. Pays on publication. Publishes ms an average of 3 months after acceptance. Buys all rights. Editorial lead time 1 month. Submit seasonal material 4 months in advance. Accepts queries by mail, e-mail, fax. Accepts simultaneous submissions. Reports in 1 week on queries; 2 months on mss. Sample copy available for $3. Writer's guidelines on website.

**Nonfiction:** Essays, humor, interview/profile, opinion, religious. "We use articles dealing with social problems, ethical dilemmas, political issues, international affairs and the arts, as well as with theological and ecclesiastical matters. We focus on concerns that arise at the juncture between church and society, or church and culture." No inspirational. **Buys 150 mss/year.** Send complete ms; query appreciated, but not essential. All queries, mss should be accompanied by 9 × 12 SASE. Length: 1,000-3,000 words. **Pays $75-200 for assigned articles; $75-150 for unsolicited articles.**

**Photos:** State availability of photos. Reviews any size prints. Offers $25-100/photo. Buys one-time rights.

**Fiction:** Humorous, religious, slice-of-life vignettes. No moralistic, unrealistic fiction. **Buys 4 mss/year.** Send complete ms. Length: 1,000-3,000. **Pays $75-200.**

**Poetry:** Jill Peláez Baumgaertner, poetry editor. Avant-garde, free verse, haiku, traditional. No sentimental or didactic poetry. **Buys 50 poems/year.** Length: 20 lines. **Pays $50.**

The online magazine carries original content not found in the print edition and includes writer's guidelines.

**Tips:** "We seek manuscripts that articulate the public meaning of faith, bringing the resources of religious tradition to bear on such topics as poverty, human rights, economic justice, international relations, national priorities and popular culture. We are also interested in articles that examine or critique the theology and ethos of individual religious communities. We welcome articles that find fresh meaning in old traditions and which adapt or apply religious traditions to new circumstances. Authors should assume that readers are familiar with main themes in Christian history and theology; are unthreatened by the historical-critical study of the Bible; and are already engaged in relating faith to social and political issues. Many of our readers are ministers or teachers of religion at the college level."

**$ $ CHRISTIAN HOME & SCHOOL,** Christian Schools International, 3350 East Paris Ave. SE, Grand Rapids MI 49512. (616)957-1070, ext. 239. Fax: (616)957-5022. E-mail: rogers@csionline.org. Website: http://www.gospelcom .net/csi/chs. Executive Editor: Gordon L. Bordewyk. **Contact:** Roger Schmurr, senior editor. **30% freelance written.** Circ. 65,000. Works with a small number of new/unpublished writers each year. Bimonthly magazine covering family life and Christian education. "*Christian Home & School* is designed for parents in the United States and Canada who send their children to Christian schools and are concerned about the challenges facing Christian families today. These readers expect a mature, biblical perspective in the articles, not just a bible verse tacked onto the end." Estab. 1922. Pays on publication. Publishes ms an average of 4 months after acceptance. Byline given. Buys first North American serial rights. Submit seasonal material 4 months in advance. Accepts queries by mail, e-mail. Reports in 1 month. Sample copy and writer's guidelines for 9 × 12 SAE with 4 first-class stamps. Writer's guidelines only for #10 SASE or on website.

**Nonfiction:** Book excerpts, interview/profile, opinion, personal experience, articles on parenting and school life. "We publish features on issues that affect the home and school and profiles on interesting individuals, providing that the profile appeals to our readers and is not a tribute or eulogy of that person." **Buys 40 mss/year.** Send complete ms. Length: 1,000-2,000 words. **Pays $125-200.**

**Photos:** "If you have any color photos appropriate for your article, send them along."

**Tips:** "Features are the area most open to freelancers. We are publishing articles that deal with contemporary issues that affect parents. Use an informal easy-to-read style rather than a philosophical, academic tone. Try to incorporate vivid imagery and concrete, practical examples from real life. We look for manuscripts with a mature Christian perspective. Use an informal, easy-to-read style."

**[N] $ THE CHRISTIAN RESPONSE, A Newsletter for Concerned Christians,** HAPCO Industries, P.O. Box 125, Staples MN 56479-0125. (218)894-1165. E-mail: hapco@brainerd.net. Website: http://www.brainerd.net/~hapco/.

**Contact:** Hap Corbett, editor. **10% freelance written.** Consumer newsletter published bimonthly "responding to anti-Christian bias from a Christian perspective." Estab. 1993. Circ. 300. **Pays on acceptance.** Publishes ms an average of 2 months after acceptance. Byline given. Buys one-time rights. Editorial lead time 2 months. Submit seasonal material 6 months in advance. Accepts queries by mail, e-mail. Reports in 2 weeks. Sample copy for $1 (or 3 first-class stamps). Writer's guidelines for #10 SASE.
**Nonfiction:** Examples of anti-Christian bias in America. **Buys 4-6 mss/year.** Send complete ms. Length: 500 words. **Pays $5-20.**
**Fillers:** Anecdotes, facts, newsbreaks. **Buys 2-4/year.** Length: 150 words. **Pays $5-20.**
**Tips:** "We want exposés of anti-Christian bias or denial of civil rights to people because of religious beliefs."

**$ CHRISTIAN SOCIAL ACTION**, 100 Maryland Ave. NE, Washington DC 20002. (202)488-5631. Fax: (202)488-1617. E-mail: ealsguard@igc.org. **Contact:** Erik Alsgaard, editor. **2% freelance written.** Works with a small number of new/unpublished writers each year. Monthly for "United Methodist clergy and lay people interested in in-depth analysis of social issues, with emphasis on the church's role or involvement in these issues." Circ. 2,500. May buy all rights. Pays on publication. Publishes ms an average of 2 months after acceptance. Rights purchased vary with author and material. Accepts queries by mail, e-mail, fax. Returns rejected material in 5 weeks. Reports on material accepted for publication in a month. Sample copy and writer's guidelines for #10 SASE.
**Nonfiction:** "This is the social action publication of The United Methodist Church published by the denomination's General Board of Church and Society. Our publication tries to relate social issues to the church—what the church can do, is doing; why the church should be involved. We only accept articles relating to social issues, e.g., war, draft, peace, race relations, welfare, police/community relations, labor, population problems, drug and alcohol problems. No devotional, 'religious,' superficial material, highly technical articles, personal experiences or poetry." **Buys 25-30 mss/year.** "Query to show that writer has expertise on a particular social issue, give credentials, and reflect a readable writing style." Length: 2,000 words maximum. **Pays $75-125.** Sometimes pays the expenses of writers on assignment.
**Reprints:** Send tearsheet of article and information about where and when the article previously appeared. Payment negotiable.
**Tips:** "Write on social issues, but not superficially; we're more interested in finding an expert who can write (e.g., on human rights, alcohol problems, peace issues) than a writer who attempts to research a complex issue."

**⚏ $ $ CHRISTIANITY TODAY**, 465 Gundersen Dr., Carol Stream IL 60188-2498. (630)260-6200. Fax: (630)260-0114. E-mail: kdmctedit@aol.com Website: http://www.christianitytoday.net. **Contact:** Kevin D. Miller, associate editor. **80% freelance written.** Works with a small number of new/unpublished writers each year. Semimonthly magazine emphasizing orthodox, evangelical religion "covers Christian doctrine, issues, trends and current events and news from a Christian perspective. It provides a forum for the expression of evangelical conviction in theology, evangelism, church life, cultural life, and society. Special features include issues of the day, books, films, missions, schools, music and services available to the Christian market." Estab. 1956. Circ. 187,000. Publishes ms an average of 6 months after acceptance. Usually buys first serial rights. Submit seasonal material at least 8 months in advance. Accepts queries by mail, e-mail, fax, phone. Reports in 3 months. Sample copy and writer's guidelines for 9×12 SAE with 3 first-class stamps.
**Nonfiction:** Theological, ethical, historical, informational (not merely inspirational). **Buys 4 mss/issue.** *Query only.* Unsolicited mss not accepted and not returned. Length: 1,000-4,000 words. Pays negotiable rates. Sometimes pays the expenses of writers on assignment.
**Reprints:** Pays 25% of amount paid for an original article.
**Columns/Departments:** Church in Action (profiles of not-so-well-known Christians involved in significant or offbeat services). **Buys 7 mss/year.** Query only. Length: 900-1,000 words.
**Tips:** "We are developing more of our own manuscripts and requiring a much more professional quality from others. Queries without SASE will not be answered and manuscripts not containing SASE will not be returned."

**$ $ CHRYSALIS READER**, P.O. Box 549, West Chester PA 19381-0549. Fax: (804)983-1074. E-mail: lawson@aba.org. Send inquiries and mss directly to the editorial office: Route 1, Box 184, Dillwyn VA 23936-9616. **Contact:** Carol S. Lawson, editor. Managing Editor: Susanna van Rensselaer. **60% freelance written.** Biannual literary magazine on spiritually related topics. *"It is very important to send for writer's guidelines and sample copies before submitting.* Content of fiction, articles, reviews, poetry, etc., should be directly focused on that issue's theme and directed to the educated, intellectually curious reader." Estab. 1985. Circ. 3,000. Pays at page-proof stage. Publishes ms an average of 9 months after acceptance. Byline given. Buys first rights and makes work-for-hire assignments. Reports in 1 month on queries; 3 months on mss. Sample copy for $10 and 8½×11 SAE. Writer's guidelines and copy deadlines for SASE.
**Nonfiction:** Essays and interview/profile. Upcoming themes: Ages (Autumn 1999). Education (Spring 2000). **Buys 30 mss/year.** Query. Length: 2,500-3,500 words. **Pays $50-250 for assigned articles; $50-150 for unsolicited articles.**
**Photos and Illustrations:** Send suggestions for illustrations with submission. Offers no additional payment for photos accepted with ms. Captions and identification of subjects required. Buys original artwork for cover and inside copy; b&w illustrations related to theme; pays $25-150. Buys one-time rights.
**Fiction:** Robert Tucker, fiction editor. Adventure, experimental, historical, mainstream, mystery, sci-fi, related to theme of issue. **Buys 6 mss/year.** Query. Length: 2,500-3,500 words. Short fiction more likely to be published. **Pays $50-150.**
**Poetry:** Rob Lawson, senior editor. Avant-garde and traditional *but not religious.* **Buys 15 poems/year.** Submit maximum 6. **Pays $25.**

**$ $ COLUMBIA**, 1 Columbus Plaza, New Haven CT 06510. (203)772-2130. Fax: (203)777-0114. **Contact:** Richard McMunn, editor. Monthly magazine for Catholic families. Caters particularly to members of the Knights of Columbus. Estab. 1921. Circ. 1,500,000. **Pays on acceptance.** Buys first serial rights. Free sample copy and writer's guidelines.
**Nonfiction and Photos:** Fact articles directed to the Catholic layman and his family dealing with current events, social problems, Catholic apostolic activities, education, ecumenism, rearing a family, literature, science, arts, sports and leisure. Color glossy prints, transparencies or contact prints with negatives are required for illustration. Articles without ample illustrative material are not given consideration. **Pays $250-500, including photos.** Query with SASE. Length: 1,000-1,500 words. **Buys 20 mss/year.**
**Tips:** "Few unsolicited manuscripts are accepted."

**$ CONSCIENCE, A Newsjournal of Prochoice Catholic Opinion**, Catholics for a Free Choice, 1436 U St. NW, Suite 301, Washington DC 20009-3997. (202)986-6093. E-mail: cffc@igc.apc.org. **Contact:** Editor. **80% freelance written.** Sometimes works with new/unpublished writers. Quarterly newsjournal covering reproductive health and rights, including but not limited to abortion rights in the church, and church-state issues in US and worldwide. "A feminist, pro-choice perspective is a must, and knowledge of Christianity and specifically Catholicism is helpful." Estab. 1980. Circ. 12,000. Pays on publication. Publishes ms an average of 4 months after acceptance. Byline given. Buys first North American serial rights or makes work-for-hire assignments. Accepts queries by mail, e-mail. Reports in 4 months. Sample copy for 9 × 12 SAE with 4 first-class stamps. Writer's guidelines for #10 SASE.
**Nonfiction:** Book excerpts, interview/profile, opinion, issue anaylsis, a small amount of personal experience. Especially needs material that recognizes the complexity of reproductive issues and decisions, and offers original, honest insight. **Buys 8-12 mss/year.** Query with published clips or send complete ms. Length: 1,000-3,500 words. **Pays $25-150.** "Writers should be aware that we are a nonprofit organization."
**Reprints:** Sometimes accepts previously published submissions. Send typed ms with rights for sale noted and information about when and where the article previously appeared. Pays 20-30% of amount paid for an original article.
**Photos:** State availability of photos with query or ms. Prefers b&w prints. Identification of subjects required.
**Columns/Departments:** Book reviews. **Buys 6-10 mss/year.** Length: 600-1,200 words. **Pays $25-50.**
**Tips:** "Say something new on the issue of abortion, or sexuality, or the role of religion or the Catholic church, or women's status in the church. Thoughtful, well-researched and well-argued articles needed. The most frequent mistakes made by writers in submitting an article to us are lack of originality and wordiness."

**N $ THE COVENANT COMPANION**, Covenant Publications of the Evangelical Covenant Church, 5101 N. Francisco Ave., Chicago IL 60625. (773)784-3000. Fax: (773)784-4366. E-mail: covcom@compuserve.com. Website: http://www.covchurch.org. **Contact:** Jane K. Swanson-Nystrom, editor. **10-15% freelance written.** "As the official monthly periodical of the Evangelical Covenant Church, we seek to inform the denomination we serve and encourage dialogue on issues within the church and in our society." Circ. 20,000. Publishes ms an average of 2 months after acceptance. Byline given. Submit seasonal material 4 months in advance. Accepts queries by mail, e-mail. Accepts simultaneous submissions. Sample copy for $2.50 and 9 × 12 SASE. Writer's guidelines for #10 SASE.
**Nonfiction:** Humor, contemporary issues, inspirational, religious. **Buys 20-25 mss/year.** Send complete ms. Unused mss returned only if accompanied by SASE. Length: 500-2,000 words. **Pays $25-75 for assigned articles; $25-50 for unsolicited articles.**
**Reprints:** Send tearsheet, photocopy of article or typed ms with rights for sale noted and information about when and where the article previously appeared.
**Photos:** Send photos with submissions. Reviews prints. Offers no additonal payment for photos accepted with ms. Identification of subjects required. Buys one-time rights.

**$ $ DECISION**, Billy Graham Evangelistic Association, 1300 Harmon Place, Minneapolis MN 55403-1988. (612)338-0500. Fax: (612)335-1299. E-mail: submissions@bgea.org. Website: http://www.billygraham.org/decision. Interim Editor: Kersten Beckstrom. **Contact:** Bob Paulson, associate editor. **25-40% freelance written.** Works each year with small number of new/unpublished writers, as well as a solid stable of experienced writers. Monthly magazine with a mission "to set forth to every reader the Good News of salvation in Jesus Christ with such vividness and clarity that he or she will be drawn to make a commitment to Christ; to encourage, teach and strengthen Christians." Estab. 1960. Circ. 1,700,000. Pays on publication. Byline given. Buys first rights and assigns work-for-hire manuscripts, articles, projects. Include telephone number with submission. Submit seasonal material 10 months in advance; other mss published up to 18 months after acceptance. Reports in 3 months on mss. Sample copy for 9 × 12 SAE with 4 first-class stamps. Writer's guidelines for #10 SASE.
**Nonfiction:** How-to, motivational, personal experience and religious. "No personality-centered articles or articles that are issue-oriented or critical of denominations." **Buys approximately 75 mss/year.** Send complete ms. Length: 400-1,500 words. **Pays $30-260.** Pays expenses of writers on assignment.
**Photos:** State availability of photos with submission. Reviews prints. Captions, model releases and identification of subjects required. Buys one-time rights.
**Poetry:** Accepting submissions. No queries.
**Tips:** "We are seeking personal conversion testimonies and personal experience articles that show how God intervened in a person's daily life and the way in which Scripture was applied to the experience in helping to solve the problem."

The conversion testimonies describe in first person what author's life was like before he/she became a Christian, how he/she committed his/her life to Christ and what difference Christ has made in the author's life. We also are looking for vignettes on various aspects of personal evangelism. SASE required with submissions."

**$ $ DISCIPLESHIP JOURNAL**, NavPress, a division of The Navigators, P.O. Box 35004, Colorado Springs CO 80935-0004. (719)531-3571. Fax: (719)598-7128. E-mail: adam.holz@navpress.com. Website: http://www.navigato rs.org/djhome.html. **Contact:** Susan Nikaido, editor. **90% freelance written.** Works with a small number of new/ unpublished writers each year. Bimonthly magazine. "The mission of *Discipleship Journal* is to help believers develop a deeper relationship with Jesus Christ, and to provide practical help in understanding the scriptures and applying them to daily life and ministry. We prefer those who have not written for us before begin with nontheme articles about almost any aspect of Christian living. We'd like more articles that explain a Bible passage and show how to apply it to everyday life, as well as articles about developing a relationship with Jesus; reaching the world; or specific issues related to leadership and helping other believers grow." Estab. 1981. Circ. 115,000. **Pays on acceptance.** Publishes ms an average of 6 months after acceptance. Byline given. Buys first North American serial rights and second serial (reprint) rights. Submit seasonal material 6 months in advance. Reports in 6 weeks. Sample copy and writer's guidelines for $2.24 and 9×12 SAE or on website.

**Nonfiction:** Book excerpts (rarely); how-to (grow in Christian faith and disciplines; help others grow as Christians; serve people in need; understand and apply the Bible); inspirational; interview/profile (focusing on one aspect of discipleship); and interpretation/application of the Bible. No personal testimony; humor; anything not directly related to Christian life and faith; politically partisan articles. **Buys 80 mss/year.** Query with published clips and SASE only. Length: 500-2,500 words. **Pays 25¢/word for first rights.** Sometimes pays the expenses of writers on assignment.

**Reprints:** Send tearsheet of article and information about when and where the article previously appeared. Pays 25% of amount paid for an original article.

**Tips:** "Our articles are meaty, not fluffy. Study writer's guidelines and back issues and try to use similar approaches. Don't preach. Polish before submitting. About half of the articles in each issue are related to one theme. Freelancers should write to request theme list. We are looking for more practical articles on ministering to others and more articles dealing with world missions. Be vulnerable. Show the reader that you have wrestled with the subject matter in your own life. We can no longer accept unsolicited manuscripts. Query first."

**N $ $ THE DOOR**, P.O. Box 1444, Waco TX 76703-1444. E-mail: rfd3@flash.net. Contact: Robert Darden. **90% freelance written.** Works with a large number of new/unpublished writers each year. Bimonthly magazine. "*The Door* is the world's only, oldest and largest religious humor and satire magazine." Estab. 1969. Circ. 14,000. Pays on publication. Publishes ms an average of 1 year after acceptance. Buys first rights. Reports in 3 months. Sample copy for $4.50. Writer's guidelines for SASE.

**Nonfiction:** Humorous/satirical articles on church renewal, Christianity and organized religion. No book reviews. **Buys 30 mss/year.** Submit complete ms. Length: 1,500 words maximum, 750-1,000 preferred. **Pays $60-200.** Sometimes pays expenses of writers on assignment.

**Reprints:** Send typed ms with rights for sale noted and information about when and where the article previously appeared. Pays 100% of amount paid for an original article.

**Tips:** "We look for someone who is clever, on our wave length, and has some savvy about the evangelical church. We are very picky and highly selective. The writer has a better chance of breaking in with our publication with short articles since we are a bimonthly publication with numerous regular features and the magazine is only 52 pages. The most frequent mistake made by writers is that they do not understand satire. They see we are a humor magazine and conse-quently come off funny/cute (like *Reader's Digest*) rather than funny/satirical (like *National Lampoon*)." *No* poetry.

**$ DOVETAIL, A Journal By and For Jewish/Christian Families**, Dovetail Institute for Interfaith Family Re-sources, 775 Simon Greenwell Ln., Boston, KY 40107. Fax: (502)549-3543. E-mail: dif-ifr@bardstown.com. **Contact**: Mary Heléne Rosenbaum. **75% freelance written.** Bimonthly newsletter for interfaith families. "All articles must pertain to life in an interfaith (Jewish/Christian) family. We accept all kinds of opinions related to this topic." Estab. 1992. Circ. 1,500. Pays on publication. Publishes ms an average of 9 months after acceptance. Byline given. Buys first, one-time or second serial (reprint) rights. Editorial lead time 6 months. Submit seasonal material 6 months in advance. Accepts simultaneous submissions. Accepts queries by mail, e-mail, fax, phone. Electronic submissions preferred (unfo-matted text). Reports in 3 months. Sample copy for 9×12 SAE with 3 first-class stamps. Writer's guidelines free.

**Nonfiction:** Interview/profile, opinion, personal experience. No fiction. **Buys 5-8 mss/year.** Send complete ms. Length: 800-1,000 words. **Pays $20** plus 2 copies. Book reviews: 500 words. **Pays $10** plus 2 copies.

**Reprints:** Accepts previously published submissions.

**Photos:** Send photos with submission. Reviews 5×7 prints. Offers no additional payment for photos accepted with ms. Model releases and identification of subjects required. Buys one-time rights.

**Fillers:** Anecdotes, short humor. **Buys 1-2/year.** Length: 25-100 words. **Pays $10.**

**Tips:** "Write on concrete, specific topics related to Jewish/Christian intermarriage: no proselytizing, sermonizing, or general religious commentary. Successful freelancers are part of an interfaith family themselves, or have done solid research/interviews with members of interfaith families. We look for honest, reflective personal experience."

**$ EMPHASIS ON FAITH & LIVING**, Missionary Church, Inc., P.O. Box 9127, Fort Wayne IN 46899. (219)747-2027. Fax: (219)747-5331. E-mail: rlransom@aol.com. Website: http://www.mcusa.org. **Contact**: Robert Ransom, man-

aging editor. Editor: Vernon Petersen. **5% freelance written.** "Bimonthly denominational magazine targeted at the constituents of the missionary church focusing on Christian articles and news." Estab. 1969. Circ. 14,000. Pays on publication. Publishes ms an average of 4 months after acceptance. Byline given. Buys one-time rights. Editorial lead time 8 months. Submit seasonal material 6 months in advance. Accepts simultaneous submissions. Reports in 1 month on queries; 4 months on mss. Sample copy for 9×12 SAE and 2 first-class stamps. Writer's guidelines for #10 SASE.
**Nonfiction:** Inspirational, personal experience, religious. **Buys 3 mss/year.** Query. Length: 250-1,500 words. **Pays $15-50.**
**Reprints:** Send photocopy of article or short story or typed ms with rights for sale noted and information about when and where the article or story previously appeared. Negotiates payment.
**Photos:** State availability of photos with submission. Negotiates payment individually. Buys one-time rights.
**Fiction:** Religious. **Buys 1-2 mss/year.** Query. Length: 250-1,500 words. **Pays $15-50.**

**⬛⭐ $ EVANGEL**, Free Methodist Publishing House, P.O. Box 535002, Indianapolis IN 46253-5002. (317)244-3660.
**Contact:** Julie Innes, editor. **100% freelance written.** Weekly take-home paper for adults. Estab. 1897. Circ. 22,000.
Pays on publication. Publishes ms an average of 1 year after acceptance. Buys simultaneous, second serial (reprint) or one-time rights. Submit seasonal material 9 months in advance. Reports in 1 month. Sample copy and writer's guidelines for #10 SASE.
**Nonfiction:** Interview (with ordinary person who is doing something extraordinary in his community, in service to others), profile (of missionary or one from similar service profession who is contributing significantly to society), personal experience (finding a solution to a problem common to young adults; coping with handicapped child, for instance, or with a neighborhood problem. Story of how God-given strength or insight saved a situation). **Buys 100 mss/year.** Submit complete ms. Length: 300-1,000 words. **Pays 4¢/word.**
**Reprints:** Send typed ms with rights for sale noted and information about when and where the article previously appeared.
**Photos:** Purchased with accompanying ms. Captions required.
**Fiction:** Religious themes dealing with contemporary issues dealt with from a Christian frame of reference. Story must "go somewhere." **Buys 50 mss/year.** Submit complete ms.
**Poetry:** Free verse, light verse, traditional, religious. **Buys 20 poems/year.** Submit maximum 5 poems. Length: 4-24 lines. **Pays $10.**
**Tips:** "Seasonal material will get a second look. Write an attention-grabbing lead followed by an article that says something worthwhile. Relate the lead to some of the universal needs of the reader—promise in that lead to help the reader in some way. Lack of SASE brands author as a nonprofessional; I seldom even bother to read the script."

**Ⓝ $ $ EVANGELIZING TODAY'S CHILD**, Child Evangelism Fellowship Inc., Box 348, Warrenton MO 63383-0348. (314)456-4321. Fax: (314)456-2078. E-mail: etceditor@cefinc.org. **Contact:** Elsie Lippy, editor. 50% freelance written. Prefers to work with published/established writers. Bimonthly magazine. "Our purpose is to equip Christians to win the world's children to Christ and disciple them. Our readership is Sunday school teachers, Christian education leaders and children's workers in every phase of Christian ministry to children up to 12 years old." Estab. 1942. Circ. 20,000. Pays within 90 days of acceptance. Publishes ms an average of 6 months after acceptance. Byline given. Offers kill fee if assigned. Buys first serial rights. Submit seasonal material 6 months in advance. Accepts queries by mail, e-mail. Reports in 2 months. Sample copy for $2. Writer's guidelines for SASE.
**Nonfiction:** Unsolicited articles welcomed from writers with Christian education training or current experience in working with children. Buys 35 mss/year. Query. Length: 1,200. Pays 10-12¢/word.
**Reprints:** Send photocopy of article and information about when and where the article previously appeared. Pays 35% of amount paid for an original article.

**$ $ FAITH TODAY, Informing Canadian Evangelicals On Thoughts, Trends, Issues and Events**, Evangelical Fellowship of Canada, MIP Box 3745, Markham, Ontario L3R 0Y4 Canada. (905)479-5885. Fax: (905)479-4742.
E-mail: ft@efc-canada.com. Website: http://www.efc-canada.com. **Contact:** Marianne Meed Ward, managing editor. "*FT* is a bimonthly interdenominational, evangelical news/feature magazine that informs Canadian Christians on issues facing church and society, and on events within the church community. It focuses on corporate faith interacting with society rather than on personal spiritual life. Writers should have a thorough understanding of the *Canadian evangelical community*." Estab. 1983. Circ. 18,000. Pays on publication. Publishes ms an average of 6 months after acceptance. Byline given. Offers 30-50% kill fee. Buys first rights. Editorial lead time 4 months. Accepts queries by mail, e-mail, fax. Reports in 6 weeks. Sample copy and writer's guidelines free with SASE in Canadian postage.
**Nonfiction:** Religious, news feature. **Buys 75 mss/year.** Query. Length: 400-2,000 words. **Pays $100-500 Canadian,** more for cover topic material. Sometimes pays expenses of writers on assignment.
**Reprints:** Send photocopy of article. Pays 50% of amount paid for an original article.
**Photos:** State availability of photos with submission. Reviews contact sheets, prints. Identification of subjects required. Buys one-time rights.
**Tips:** "Query should include brief outline and names of the sources you plan to interview in your research. Use Canadian postage on SASE."

**Ⓝ $ FOURSQUARE WORLD ADVANCE**, International Church of the Foursquare Gospel, 1910 W. Sunset Blvd., Suite 200, P.O. Box 26902, Los Angeles CA 90026-0176. Website: http://www.foursquare.org. **Contact:** Ronald

D. Williams, editor. **5% freelance written.** Bimonthly magazine covering Devotional/Religious material, denominational news. "The official publication of the International Church of the Foursquare Gospel is distributed without charge to members and friends of the Foursquare Church." Estab. 1917. Circ. 98,000. Pays on publication. Publishes ms an average of 2 months after acceptance. Byline given. Buys first rights, one-time rights, second serial (reprint) rights and simultaneous rights. Editorial lead time 6 months. Submit seasonal material 6 months in advance. Reports in 2 weeks on queries. Sample copy and writer's guidelines free.

**Nonfiction:** Inspirational, interview/profile, personal experience, religious. **Buys 2-3 mss/year.** Send complete ms. Length: 800-1,200 words. **Pays $75.**

**Reprints:** Accepts previously published submissions.

**Photos:** State availability of photos with submission. Reviews 4×6 prints. Offers no additional payment for photos accepted with ms. Captions, model releases, identification of subjects required. Buys one-time rights.

**$ $ GROUP MAGAZINE,** Group Publishing Inc., P.O. Box 481, Loveland CO 80538. (970)669-3836. Fax: (970)669-1994. E-mail: rlawrence@grouppublishing.com. Website: http://www.grouppublishing.com. Publisher: Tim Gilmour. **Contact:** Rick Lawrence, editor. Departments Editor: Kathy Dieterich. **60% freelance written.** Bimonthly magazine covering youth ministry. "Writers must be actively involved in youth ministry. Articles we accept are practical, not theoretical, and focused for local church youth workers." Estab. 1974. Circ. 57,000. **Pays on acceptance.** Publishes ms an average of 6 months after acceptance. Byline given. Offers $20 kill fee. Buys all rights. Submit seasonal material 7 months in advance. Reports in 2 months. Sample copy for $2 and 9×12 SAE. Writer's guidelines for SASE or on website.

**Nonfiction:** How-to (youth ministry issues). No personal testimony, theological or lecture-style articles. **Buys 50-60 mss/year.** Query. Length: 250-2,200 words. **Pays $35-250.** Sometimes pays for phone calls on agreement.

**Tips:** "Submit a youth ministry idea to one of our mini-article sections—we look for tried-and-true ideas youth ministers have used with kids."

**$ $ GUIDEPOSTS MAGAZINE,** 16 E. 34th St., New York NY 10016-4397. Website: http://www.guideposts.org. **Contact:** Mary Ann O'Roark, executive editor. **30% freelance written.** Works with a small number of new/unpublished writers each year. "*Guideposts* is an inspirational monthly magazine for people of all faiths, in which men and women from all walks of life tell in true first-person narrative how they overcame obstacles, rose above failures, handled sorrow, gained new spiritual insight and became more effective people through faith in God." Estab. 1945. Publishes ms an "indefinite" number of months after acceptance. Pays 20% kill fee for assigned articles. "Many of our stories are ghosted articles, so the writer would not get a byline unless it was his/her own story." Buys all rights and second serial (reprint) rights. Reports in 2 months.

**Nonfiction and Fillers:** Articles and features should be true stories written in simple, anecdotal style with an emphasis on human interest. Short mss of approximately 250-750 words **(pays $100-250)** considered for such features as "Angels Among Us," "His Mysterious Ways" and general one-page stories. Address short items to Celeste McCauley. For full-length mss, 750-1,500 words, **pays $250-500.** All mss should be typed, double-spaced and accompanied by SASE. Annually awards scholarships to high school juniors and seniors in writing contest. **Buys 40-60 unsolicited mss/year.** Pays expenses of writers on assignment.

**Tips:** "Study the magazine before you try to write for it. Each story must make a single spiritual point that readers can apply to their own daily lives. And it may be easier to just sit down and write them than to have to go through the process of preparing a query. They should be warm, well written, intelligent and upbeat. We require personal narratives that are true and have some spiritual aspect, but the religious element can be subtle and should *not* be sermonic. A writer succeeds with us if he or she can write a true article using short-story techniques with scenes, drama, tension and a resolution of the problem presented."

**$ HOME TIMES, "A Good Little Newspaper for God & Country,"** Neighbor News, Inc., 3676 Collin Dr., #12, West Palm Beach FL 33406. (561)439-3509. E-mail: hometimes@aol.com. **Contact:** Dennis Lombard, publisher/editor. **80% freelance written.** Monthly tabloid of conservative, pro-Christian news and views. "*Home Times* is a conservative newspaper written for the general public but with a Biblical worldview and family-values slant. It is not religious or preachy. We are going on the Internet in 1999. We want to place our best writers on there too." Estab. 1988. Circ. 5,000. Pays on publication. Publishes ms an average of 3 months after acceptance. Byline given. No kill fee. Buys one-time rights. Editorial lead time 1 month. Submit seasonal material 2 months in advance. Accepts simultaneous submissions. Reports in 1 month. Sample copy for $3. Writer's guidelines for #10 SASE.

• *Home Times* is developing extended guidelines in 1999 for local stringers and freelancers, and a new editorial menu.

**Nonfiction:** Current events, essays, general interest, historical/nostalgic, how-to, humor, inspirational, interview/profile, opinion, personal experience, photo feature, religious, travel. "Nothing preachy, moralistic or with churchy slant." **Buys 35 mss/year.** Send complete ms. Length: 500-700 maximum words. **Pays $5 minimum.** Pays contributor's copies or subscriptions on mutual agreement.

**Reprints:** Send tearsheet or photocopy of article or short story and information about when and where the material previously appeared. Pays $5-10.

**Photos:** Send photos with submission. Reviews any size prints. Offers $5/photo used. Captions, model releases (when legally needed), identification of subjects required. Buys one-time rights.

**Columns/Departments: Buys 50 mss/year.** Send complete ms. **Pays $5-15.**

**Fiction:** Historical, humorous, mainstream, religious, issue-oriented contemporary. "Nothing preachy, moralistic." **Buys 5 mss/year.** Send complete ms. Length: 500-700 words. **Pays $5-25.**
**Poetry:** Free verse, light verse, traditional. **Buys 12 poems/year.** Submit 3 poems max, 2-24 lines. **Pays $5.**
**Fillers:** Anecdotes, facts, good quotes, short humor. Uses 25/year. Length: to 100 words. Pays 6 issues on acceptance.
**Tips:** "We encourage new writers. We are different from ordinary news or religious publications. We strongly suggest you read guidelines and sample issues. (Writer's subscription 12 issues for $9.) We are most open to material for new columns; journalists covering hard news in major news centers—with conservative slant. Also, lots of letters and short op-eds though we pay only in issues (6) for them."

**$ LIGHT AND LIFE MAGAZINE,** Free Methodist Church of North America, P.O. Box 535002, Indianapolis IN 46253-5002. (317)244-3660. Fax: (317)248-9055. E-mail: llmeditor@aol.com. **Contact:** Doug Newton, editor. Works with a small number of new/unpublished writers each year. Bimonthly magazine emphasizing evangelical Christianity with Wesleyan slant for a cross section of adults. Also includes discipleship guidebook and national/international and denominational religion news. Estab. 1868. Circ. 21,000. Pays on publication. Byline given. Prefers first serial rights. Accepts queries by mail. Sample copy and guidelines for $4. Writer's guidelines for SASE.
**Nonfiction:** Submit complete ms. **Pays 4¢/word, 5¢/word if submitted on disk.** Varying word lengths.
**Photos:** Purchased without accompanying ms. Send prints or slides. Pays $35 and higher for color or b&w photos.

**$ $ LIGUORIAN,** One Liguori Dr., Liguori MO 63057-9999. (314)464-2500. Fax: (314)464-8449. E-mail: aweinert@liguori.com. Website: http://www.liguori.org. Managing Editor: Cheryl Plass. **Contact:** Fr. Allen Weinert, CSSR, editor-in-chief. **25% freelance written.** Prefers to work with published/established writers. Magazine published 10 times/year for Catholics. "Our purpose is to lead our readers to a fuller Christian life by helping them better understand the teachings of the gospel and the church and by illustrating how these teachings apply to life and the problems confronting them as members of families, the church and society." Estab. 1913. Circ. 260,000. **Pays on acceptance.** Buys all rights but will reassign rights to author *after* publication upon written request. Submit seasonal material 8 months in advance. Accepts queries by mail, e-mail, fax. Reports in 6 months. Sample copy and writer's guidelines for 6×9 SAE with 3 first-class stamps or on website.
**Nonfiction:** "Pastoral, practical and personal approach to the problems and challenges of people today. No travelogue approach or unresearched ventures into controversial areas. Also, no material found in secular publications—fad subjects that already get enough press, pop psychology, negative or put-down articles." **Buys 60 unsolicited mss/year. Buys 12 fiction mss/year.** Length: 400-2,000 words. **Pays 10-12¢/word.** Sometimes pays expenses of writers on assignment.
**Photos:** Photographs on assignment only unless submitted with and specific to article.

**$ THE LIVING CHURCH,** Living Church Foundation, 816 E. Juneau Ave., P.O. Box 514036, Milwaukee WI 53203. (414)276-5420. Fax: (414)276-7483. E-mail: tlc@livingchurch.org. Managing Editor: John Schuessler. **Contact:** David Kalvelage, editor. **50% freelance written.** Weekly religious magazine on the Episcopal church. News or articles of interest to members of the Episcopal church. Estab. 1878. Circ. 9,000. Does not pay unless article is requested. Publishes ms an average of 3 months after acceptance. Byline given. Buys one-time rights. Editorial lead time 3 weeks. Submit seasonal material 1 month in advance. Accepts queries by mail, e-mail, fax. Reports in 2 weeks on queries; 1 month on mss. Sample copy free. Writer's guidelines on website.
**Nonfiction:** Opinion, personal experience, photo feature, religious. **Buys 10 mss/year.** Send complete ms. Length: 1,000 words. **Pays $25-100.** Sometimes pays expenses of writers on assignment.
**Photos:** Send photos with submission. Reviews any size prints. Offers $15-50/photo. Buys one-time rights.
**Columns/Departments:** Benediction (devotional) 250 words; Viewpoint (opinion) under 1,000 words. Send complete ms. **Pays $50 maximum.**
**Poetry:** Light verse, traditional.

**$ LIVING LIGHT NEWS,** Living Light Ministries, 5304 89 St., #200, Edmonton, Alberta T6E 5P9 Canada. (403)468-6397. Fax: (403)468-6872. E-mail: shine@livinglightnews.org. Website: http://www.livinglightnews.org. **Contact:** Jeff Caporale, editor. **75% freelance written.** Bimonthly tabloid covering Christianity. "We are an evangelical Christian newspaper slanted towards proclaiming the gospel and encouraging Christians." Estab. 1995. Circ. 20,000. Pays on publication. Publishes ms an average of 4 months after acceptance. Byline sometimes given. Offers 100% kill fee. Buys first North American serial rights, first rights, one-time rights, second serial (reprint) rights and makes work-for-hire assignments. Editorial lead time 3 months. Submit seasonal material 3 months in advance. Accepts queries by e-mail. Accepts simultaneous submissions. Sample copy for 9×12 SAE with 2 IRCs. Accepts queries by e-mail. Writer's guidelines free or on website.
**Nonfiction:** General interest, humor, inspirational, interview/profile, religious. "We have a special Christmas issue focused on the traditional meaning of Christmas." No issue-oriented, controversial stories. **Buys 5-10 mss/year.** Query. Length: 300-1,200 words. **Pays $20-125 for assigned articles; $10-70 for unsolicited articles.** Sometimes pays expenses of writers on assignment.
**Reprints:** Send photocopy of article or short story or typed ms with rights for sale noted and information about when and where it previously appeared. Pays 5¢/word.
**Photos:** State availability of photos with submission. Reviews 3×5 prints. Offers $10-50/photo. Identification of subjects required. Buys one-time rights.
**Columns/Departments:** Relationships (Christian perspective), 500 words; Finance (Christian perspective), 500

words; Book, music, video reviews (Christian perspective parenting), 250-350 words. **Buys 5-10 mss/year.** Query with published clips. **Pays $15-40.**

**Fiction:** Christmas. "We only want to see Christmas-related fiction." **Buys 2-3 mss/year.** Query with published clips. Length: 500-2,000 words. **Pays $20-100.**

**Tips:** "It is very helpful if the person is a Bible believing Christian interested in proclaiming the gospel through positive, uplifting and timely stories of interest to Christians and non-Christians."

**$ $ $ THE LUTHERAN, Magazine of the Evangelical Lutheran Church in America**, 8765 W. Higgins Rd., Chicago IL 60631-4183. (773)380-2540. Fax: (773)380-2751. E-mail: lutheran@elca.org. Website: http://www.The Lutheran.org. Editor: Edgar R. Trexler. Managing Editor: Sonia Solomonson. **Contact:** David L. Miller, senior editor. **15% freelance written.** Monthly magazine for "lay people in church. News and activities of the Evangelical Lutheran Church in America, news of the world of religion, ethical reflections on issues in society, personal Christian experience." Estab. 1988. Circ. 620,000. **Pays on acceptance.** Publishes ms an average of 6 months after acceptance. Byline given. Offers 50% kill fee. Buys first rights. Submit seasonal material 4 months in advance. Accepts queries by mail, e-mail. Reports in 6 weeks. Sample copy and writer's guidelines free.

  O═ Break in by checking out the theme list on the website and querying with ideas related to these themes.

**Nonfiction:** Inspirational, interview/profile, personal experience, photo feature, religious. "No articles unrelated to the world of religion." **Buys 40 mss/year.** Query with published clips. Length: 500-1,500 words. **Pays $400-700 for assigned articles; $100-500 for unsolicited articles.** Pays expenses of writers on assignment.

**Photos:** Send photos with submission. Reviews contact sheets, transparencies, prints. Offers $50-175/photo. Captions and identification of subjects required. Buys one-time rights.

  ▣ The online magazine carries original content not found in the print edition. Contact: Lorel Fox, online editor.

**Columns/Departments:** Lite Side (humor—church, religious), In Focus, Living the Faith, Values & Society, In Our Churches, Our Church at Work, 25-100 words. Send complete ms. **Pays $10.**

**Tips:** "Writers have the best chance selling us feature articles."

**N ⊠ $ THE LUTHERAN DIGEST**, The Lutheran Digest, Inc., P.O. Box 4250, Hopkins MN 55343. (612)933-2820. Fax: (612)933-5708. **Contact:** David L. Tank, editor. **95% freelance written.** Quarterly magazine covering Christianity from a Lutheran perspective. "Articles frequently reflect a Lutheran Christian perspective, but are not intended to be sermonettes. Popular stories show how God has intervened in a person's life to help solve a problem." Estab. 1953. Circ. 140,000. **Pays on acceptance.** Publishes ms an average of 3-6 months after acceptance. Byline given. Buys first (original articles) or second serial rights. Editorial lead time 9 months. Submit seasonal material 9 months in advance. Accepts queries by mail. Accepts simultaneous submissions. Reports in 1 month on queries; 2-4 months on mss. Sample copy for $3. Writer's guidelines free.

**Nonfiction:** Historical/nostalgic, how-to (personal or spiritual growth), humor, inspirational, personal experience, religious. Does not want to see "personal tributes to deceased relatives or friends. They are seldom used unless the subject of the article is well-known. We also avoid articles about the moment a person finds Christ as his or her personal savior." **Buys 50-60 mss/year.** Send complete ms. Length: 1,500 words. **Pays $25-50.** "For some reprint permissions and for poetry, pays writers in contributor copies or other premiums."

**Reprints:** Accepts previously published submissions. "We prefer this as we are a digest and 70-80% of our articles are reprints."

**Photos:** State availability of photos with submission. Buys one-time rights.

**Tips:** "An article that tugs on the "heart strings" just a little and closes leaving the reader with a sense of hope is a writer's best bet to breaking into *The Lutheran Digest.*"

**$ MENNONITE BRETHREN HERALD**, 3-169 Riverton Ave., Winnipeg, Manitoba R2L 2E5 Canada. (204)669-6575. Fax: (204)654-1865. E-mail: mbherald@cdnmbconf.ca. Website: http://www.cdnmbconf.ca/mb/mbherald.htm. **Contact:** Jim Coggins, editor or Susan Brandt, managing editor. **25% freelance written.** Biweekly family publication "read mainly by people of the Mennonite faith, reaching a wide cross section of professional and occupational groups, including many homemakers. Readership includes people from both urban and rural communities. It is intended to inform members of events in the church and the world, serve personal and corporate spiritual needs, serve as a vehicle of communication within the church, serve conference agencies and reflect the history and theology of the Mennonite Brethren Church." Estab. 1962. Circ. 15,500. Pays on publication. Publishes ms 6 months after acceptance. Not copyrighted. Byline given. Buys one-time rights. Accepts queries by mail, e-mail, fax. Reports in 6 months. Sample copy for $1 and 9×12 SAE with 2 IRCs.

**Nonfiction:** Articles with a Christian family orientation; youth directed, Christian faith and life, and current issues. Wants articles critiquing the values of a secular society, attempting to relate Christian living to the practical situations of daily living; showing how people have related their faith to their vocations. Send complete ms. "Articles and manuscripts not accepted for publication will be returned if a SASE (Canadian stamps or IRCs) is provided by the writer." Length: 250-1,500 words. **Pays $30-40.** Pays the expenses of writers on assignment.

**Reprints:** Send tearsheet or photocopy of article or typed ms with rights for sale noted and information about when and where the article previously appeared. Pays 70% of amount paid for an original article.

**Photos:** Photos purchased with ms.

**Columns/Departments:** Viewpoint (Christian opinion on current topics), 850 words. Crosscurrent (Christian opinion on music, books, art, TV, movies), 350 words.

**Poetry:** Length: 25 lines maximum.

**Tips:** "We like simple style, contemporary language and fresh ideas. Writers should take care to avoid religious clichés."

**$ $MESSAGE MAGAZINE**, Review and Herald Publishing, 55 West Oak Ridge Dr., Hagerstown MD 21740. (301)393-4099 ext. 2565. Fax: (301)393-4103. E-mail: message@rhpa.org. Editor: Ron Smith. Associate Editor: Dwain Esmond. **Contact:** Editorial Secretary. **10-20% freelance written.** Bimonthly magazine. "*Message* is the oldest religious journal addressing ethnic issues in the country. Our audience is predominantly black and Seventh-day Adventist; however, *Message* is an outreach magazine geared to the unchurched." Estab. 1898. Circ. 120,000. **Pays on acceptance**. Publishes ms an average of 6-12 months after acceptance. Byline given. Buys first North American serial rights; "the exception to this rule is for supplemental issues, for which we usually purchase all rights." Editorial lead time 6 months. Submit seasonal material 6 months in advance. Send complete ms. Reports in 6-9 months. Sample copy and writer's guidelines free.

**Nonfiction:** General interest to a Christian audience, how-to (overcome depression; overcome defeat; get closer to God; learn from failure, etc.), inspirational, interview/profile (profiles of famous African-Americans), personal experience (testimonies), religious. **Buys 10 mss/year.** Send complete ms. Length: 800-1,300 words. **Pays $50-300.**

**Photos:** State availability of photos with submission. Identification of subjects preferred. Buys one-time rights.

**Columns/Departments:** Voices in the Wind (community involvement/service/events/health info); Message, Jr. (stories for children with a moral, explain a biblical or moral principle); Recipes (no meat or dairy products—12-15 recipes and an intro); Healthspan (health issues); all 500 words. **Buys 12-15 mss/year.** Send complete ms for Message, Jr. and Healthspan. Query assistant editor with published clips for Voices in the Wind and Recipes. **Pays $50-300.**

**Fiction:** "We do not generally accept fiction, but when we do it's for Message, Jr. and/or has a religious theme. We buy about 3 (if that many) fictional manuscripts a year." Send complete ms. Length: 500-700 words. **Pays $50-125.**

**Fillers:** Anecdotes, facts, newsbreaks. **Buys 1-5 fillers/year.** Length: 200-500 words. **Pays $50-125.**

**Tips:** "Please look at the magazine before submitting manuscripts. *Message* publishes a variety of writing styles as long as the writing style is easy to read and flows—please avoid highly technical writing styles."

**$ THE MESSENGER OF THE SACRED HEART**, Apostleship of Prayer, 661 Greenwood Ave., Toronto, Ontario M4J 4B3 Canada. (416)466-1195. **Contact:** Rev. F.J. Power, S.J., editor. Monthly magazine for "Canadian and U.S. Catholics interested in developing a life of prayer and spirituality; stresses the great value of our ordinary actions and lives." **20% freelance written.** Estab. 1891. Circ. 15,000. Buys first rights only. Byline given. **Pays on acceptance.** Submit seasonal material 5 months in advance. Reports in 1 month. Sample copy for $1 and 7½×10½ SAE. Writer's guidelines for SASE.

**Fiction:** Religious/inspirational. Stories about people, adventure, heroism, humor, drama. **Buys 12 mss/year.** Send complete ms with SAE and IRCs. Does not return mss without SASE. Length: 750-1,500 words. **Pays 4¢/word.**

**Tips:** "Develop a story that sustains interest to the end. Do not preach, but use plot and characters to convey the message or theme. Aim to move the heart as well as the mind. Before sending, cut out unnecessary or unrelated words or sentences. If you can, add a light touch or a sense of humor to the story. Your ending should have impact, leaving a moral or faith message for the reader."

**$ THE MIRACULOUS MEDAL**, 475 E. Chelten Ave., Philadelphia PA 19144-5785. (215)848-1010. Fax: (215)848-1014. Editorial Director: Rev. William J. O'Brien, C.M. **Contact:** Mr. Charles Kelly, office manager. **40% freelance written.** Quarterly. Estab. 1915. **Pays on acceptance.** Publishes ms an average of 2 years after acceptance. Buys first North American serial rights. Buys articles only on special assignment. Accepts queries by mail. Reports in 3 months. Sample copy for 6×9 SAE with 2 first-class stamps.

**Fiction:** Should not be pious or sermon-like. Wants good general fiction—not necessarily religious, but if religion is basic to the story, the writer should be sure of his facts. Only restriction is that subject matter and treatment must not conflict with Catholic teaching and practice. Can use seasonal material, Christmas stories. Length: 2,000 words maximum. Occasionally uses short-shorts from 1,000-1,250 words. **Pays 2¢/word minimum.**

**Poetry:** Maximum of 20 lines, preferably about the Virgin Mary or at least with religious slant. **Pays 50¢/line minimum.**

**$ THE MONTANA CATHOLIC**, Diocese of Helena, P.O. Box 1729, Helena MT 59624. (406)442-5820. Fax: (406)442-5191. **Contact:** Alex Lobdell, editor. **5% freelance written.** Monthly tabloid. "We publish news and features from a Catholic perspective, particularly as they pertain to the church in western Montana." Estab. 1932. Circ. 9,200. **Pays on acceptance.** Publishes ms an average of 6 months after acceptance. Byline given. Offers 25% kill fee. Buys first, one-time, or simultaneous rights. Editorial lead time 1 month. Accepts queries by mail. Accepts simultaneous submissions. Reports in 1 month. Sample copy for $2. Writer's guidelines for #10 SASE.

**Nonfiction:** Special issues: Vocations (January); Easter; Lent; Christmas; Advent. **Buys 5 mss/year.** Send complete ms with SASE for reply and/or return of mss. Length: 400-1,200 words. **Pays 10¢/word for assigned articles; 5¢/word for unsolicited articles.**

**Photos:** Reviews contact sheets, prints. Offers $5-20/photo. Identification of subjects required. Buys one time rights.

**Tips:** "Best bets are seasonal pieces, topics related to our special supplements and features with a tie-in to western Montana—always with a Catholic angle. No poetry, please."

**$ $ MOODY MAGAZINE**, Moody Bible Institute, 820 N. LaSalle Blvd., Chicago IL 60610. (312)329-2164. Fax: (312)329-2149. E-mail: moodyedit@moody.edu. Website: http://www.moody.edu. **Contact:** Andrew Scheer, managing editor. **62% freelance written.** Bimonthly magazine for evangelical Christianity (6 issues/year). "Our readers are conservative, evangelical Christians highly active in their churches and concerned about applying their faith in daily living." Estab. 1900. Circ. 112,000. **Pays on acceptance.** Publishes ms an average of 9 months after acceptance. Byline given. Buys first North American serial rights. Submit seasonal material 9 months in advance. Query first for all submissions by mail, but not by phone. Unsolicited mss will be returned unread. Reports in 2 months. Sample copy for 9×12 SAE with $2 first-class postage. Writer's guidelines for #10 SASE.
  • Ranked as one of the best markets for freelance writers in *Writer's Yearbook* magazine's annual "Top 100 Markets," January 1999.
**Nonfiction:** Personal narratives (on living the Christian life), a few reporting articles. **Buys 55 mss/year.** "No biographies, historical articles, or studies of Bible figures." Query. Length: 1,200-2,200 words. **Pays 15¢/word for queried articles; 20¢/word for assigned articles.** Sometimes pays the expenses of writers on assignment.
**Columns/Departments:** First Person (the only article written for non-Christians; a personal conversion testimony written by the author [will accept "as told to's"]; the objective is to tell a person's testimony in such a way that the reader will understand the gospel and want to receive Christ as Savior), 800-900 words; News Focus (in-depth, researched account of current news or trend), 1,000-1,400 words. **Buys 12 mss/year.** May query by fax or e-mail for News Focus only. **Pays 15¢/word.**
**Fiction:** Will consider well-written contemporary stories that are directed toward scriptural application. Avoid clichéd salvation accounts, biblical fiction, parables, and allegories. Length: 1,200-2,000 words. **Pays 15¢/word.**
**Tips:** "We have moved to bimonthly publication, with a larger editorial well in each issue. We want articles that cover a broad range of topics, but with one common goal: to foster application by a broad readership of specific biblical principles. By publishing accounts of people's spiritual struggles, growth and discipleship, our aim is to encourage readers in their own obedience to Christ. While *Moody* continues to look for many authors to use a personal narrative style, we're also looking for some pieces that use an anecdotal reporting approach."

**N $ $ MY DAILY VISITOR**, Our Sunday Visitor, Inc., 200 Noll Plaza, Huntington IN 46750. (219)356-8400. **Contact:** Catherine and William Odell, editors. **99% freelance written.** Bimonthly magazine of Scripture meditations based on the day's Catholic mass readings. Circ. 30,000. **Pays on acceptance.** Publishes ms an average of 6 months after acceptance. Byline given. Not copyrighted. Buys one-time rights. Accepts queries by mail, e-mail. Reports in 2 months. Sample copy and writer's guidelines for #10 SAE with 2 first-class stamps. "Guest editors write on assignment basis only."
**Nonfiction:** Inspirational, personal experience, religious. **Buys 12 mss/year.** Query with published clips. Length: 150-160 words times number of days in month. **Pays $500** for 1 month (28-31) of meditations and 25 free copies.

**$ $ NEW WORLD OUTLOOK, The Mission Magazine of The United Methodist Church**, General Board of Global Ministries, 475 Riverside Dr., Room 1476, New York NY 10115. (212)870-3765. Fax: (212)870-3940. E-mail: nwo@gbgm-umc.org.nwol. Website: http://www.gbgm-umc.org/nwo/. Editor: Alma Graham. **Contact:** Christie R. House. **20% freelance written.** Bimonthly magazine covering United Methodist mission programs, projects, and personnel. "As the mission magazine of The United Methodist Church, we publish articles on or related to the mission programs, projects, institutions, and personnel of the General Board of Global Ministries, both in the United States and around the world." Estab. 1911. Circ. 30,000. Pays on publication. Publishes ms an average of 4 months after acceptance. Byline given. Offers 50% kill fee or $100. Buys all rights. Editorial lead time 4 months. Submit seasonal material 4 months in advance. Accepts queries by mail, e-mail, fax. No simultaneous or previously published submissions. Sample copy for $3.
**Nonfiction:** Photo features, mission reports, mission studies. Special issues: Urban Culture, Children of Africa (2000). **Buys 24 mss/year.** Query. Length: 500-2,000 words. **Pays $50-300.** Sometimes pays expenses of writers on assignment.
**Photos:** State availability of photos with submission. Reviews transparencies, prints. Offers $25-150/photo. Captions, identification of subjects required.
**Tips:** "Write for a list of United Methodist mission institutions, projects, or personnel in the writer's geographic area or in an area of the country or the world to which the writer plans to travel (at writer's own expense). Photojournalists have a decided advantage."

**N $ NORTHWESTERN LUTHERAN, The Word from the WELS**, WELS, 2929 N. Mayfair Rd., Milwaukee WI 53222-4398. (414)256-3888. Fax: (414)256-3899. E-mail: nl@sab.wels.net. Website: http://www.wels.net. **Contact:** Gary P. Baumler, editor. **5% freelance written.** Monthly magazine covering WELS news, topics, issues. The material usually must be written by or about WELS members. Estab. 1913. Circ. 56,000. Pays on publication. Publishes ms an average of 6 months after acceptance. Byline given. Buys one-time rights. Editorial lead time 3 months. Submit seasonal material 4 months in advance. Accepts queries by mail, e-mail, fax, phone. Reports in 2 months. Sample copy and writer's guidelines free.
**Nonfiction:** Linda Baacke, senior communications assistant. Personal experience, religious. **Buys 10 mss/year.** Query. Length: 550-1,200 words. **Pays $50/page.** Sometimes pays expenses of writers on assignment.
**Photos:** State availability of photos with submission. Reviews contact sheets. Negotiates payment individually. Captions, model releases and identification of subjects required. Buys one-time rights plus 1 month on web.
**Fillers:** Gary Baumler, editor. **Buys 1/year.**

**Tips:** "Topics should be of interest to the majority of the members of the synod—the people in the pews. Articles should have a Christian viewpoint, but we don't want sermons. We suggest you carefully read at least five or six issues with close attention to the length, content and style of the features."

**$ OBLATES**, Missionary Association of Mary Immaculate, 9480 N. De Mazenod Dr., Belleville IL 62223-1160. (618)398-4848. Fax: (618)398-8788. Managing Editor: Christine Portell. **Contact:** Mary Mohrman, manuscripts editor. **30% freelance written.** Prefers to work with published writers. Bimonthly inspirational magazine for Christians; audience mainly older Catholic adults. Circ. 500,000. **Pays on acceptance.** Usually publishes ms within 2 years after acceptance. Byline given. Buys first North American serial rights. Submit seasonal material 6 months in advance. Reports in 2 months. Sample copy and writer's guidelines for 6×9 or larger SAE with 2 first-class stamps.
**Nonfiction:** Inspirational and personal experience with positive spiritual insights. No preachy, theological or research articles. Avoid current events and controversial topics. Send complete ms; 500-600 words. "No queries." **Pays $80.**
**Poetry:** Light verse—reverent, well written, perceptive, with traditional rhythm and rhyme. "Emphasis should be on inspiration, insight and relationship with God." Submit maximum 2 poems. Length: 8-16 lines. **Pays $30.**
**Tips:** "Our readership is made up mostly of mature Americans who are looking for comfort, encouragement, and a positive sense of applicable Christian direction to their lives. Focus on sharing of personal insight to problem (i.e. death or change), but must be positive, uplifting. We have well-defined needs for an established market but are always on the lookout for exceptional work."

**[N] $ $ THE OTHER SIDE**, 300 W. Apsley St., Philadelphia PA 19144-4285. (215)849-2178. Website: http://www.theotherside.com. **Contact:** Dee Dee Risher and Doug Davidson, coeditors. **25% freelance written.** Prefers to work with published/established writers. Bimonthly magazine emphasizing "spiritual nurture, prophetic reflection, forgotten voices and artistic visions from a progressive Christian perspective." Estab. 1965. Circ. 14,000. **Pays on acceptance.** Publishes ms an average of 6 months after acceptance. Byline given. Buys all or first serial rights. Reports in 3 months. Sample copy for $4.50. Writer's guidelines for #10 SASE or on website.
**Nonfiction:** Doug Davidson, coeditor. Current social, political and economic issues in the US and around the world: personality profiles, interpretative essays, interviews, how-to's, personal experiences, spiritual reflections, biblical interpretation and investigative reporting. "Articles must be lively, vivid and down-to-earth, with a radical faith-based Christian perspective." Length: 500-3,500 words. **Pays $25-300.**
**Photos:** Cathleen Benberg, art director. Photos or photo essays illustrating current social, political, or economic reality in the US and Third World. Especially interested in creative original art offering spiritual insight and/or fresh perspectives on contemporary issues. Pays $15-75 for b&w and $50-300 for color.
**Fiction:** Robert Finegan, fiction editor. "Short stories, humor and satire conveying insights and situations that will be helpful to Christians with a radical commitment to peace and justice." Length: 300-4,000 words. **Pays $25-250.**
**Poetry:** Rod Jellema, poetry editor. "Short, creative poetry that will be thought-provoking and appealing to radical Christians who have a strong commitment to spirituality, peace and justice." Length: 3-50 lines. No more than 4 poems may be submitted at one time by any one author. **Pays $15-20.**
**Tips:** "We're looking for tightly written pieces (1,000-1,500 words) on interesting and unusual Christians (or Christian groups) who are putting their commitment to peace and social justice into action in creative and useful ways. We're also looking for provocative analytical and reflective pieces (1,000-4,000 words) dealing with contemporary social issues in the U.S. and abroad."

**$ $ OUR FAMILY**, Missionary Oblates of St. Mary's Province, P.O. Box 249, Battleford, Saskatchewan S0M 0E0 Canada. (306)937-7771. Fax: (306)937-7644. E-mail: ourfamily@marianpress.sk.ca. Website: http://www.marianpress.sk.ca/ourfamily/. **Contact:** Marie-Louise Ternier-Gommers, editor. **80% freelance written.** Prefers to work with published/established writers. Monthly magazine for Canadian Catholics. Estab. 1949. Circ. 8,000. **Pays on acceptance.** Publishes ms an average of 6 months after acceptance. Byline given. Offers 100% kill fee. Generally purchases first North American serial rights; also buys all, simultaneous, second serial (reprint) or one-time rights. Submit seasonal material 4 months in advance. Accepts queries by mail, e-mail, fax, phone. Accepts simultaneous submissions. Reports in 6 weeks. Sample copy for 9×12 SAE with $2.50 postage. Only Canadian postage or IRC useful in Canada. Writer's guidelines free on website.
**Nonfiction:** Humor (related to family life or husband/wife relations), inspirational (anything that depicts people responding to adverse conditions with courage, hope and love), personal experience (with religious dimensions), photo feature (particularly in search of photo essays on human/religious themes and on persons whose lives are an inspiration to others). Accepts phone queries. **Buys 88-100 unsolicited mss/year.** Length: 1,000-3,000 words. **Pays 7¢/word.**
**Reprints:** Send tearsheet or photocopy of article or typed ms with rights for sale noted and information about when and where the article previously appeared.
**Photos:** Photos purchased with or without accompanying ms. Pays $35 for 5×7 or larger b&w glossy prints and color photos (which are converted into b&w). Offers additional payment for photos accepted with ms (payment for these photos varies according to their quality). Free photo spec sheet for SASE.
**Poetry:** Avant-garde, free verse, haiku, light verse, traditional. **Buys 3-6 poems/issue.** Length: 3-30 lines. **Pays 75¢-$1/line.** Must have a religious dimension.
**Fillers:** Jokes, gags, anecdotes, short humor. **Buys 2-10/issue.**
**Tips:** "Writers should ask themselves whether this is the kind of an article, poem, etc. that a busy person would pick up and read in a few moments of leisure. We look for articles on the spirituality of marriage. We concentrate on recent

movements and developments in the church to help make people aware of the new church of which they are a part. We invite reflections on ecumenical experiences."

**$ PENTECOSTAL EVANGEL**, The General Council of the Assemblies of God, 1445 Boonville, Springfield MO 65802-1894. (417)862-2781. Fax: (417)862-0416. E-mail: pevangel@ag.org. Website: http://www.ag.org/evangel. Editor: Hal Donaldson. **Contact:** Ann Floyd, associate editor. **10% freelance written.** Works with a small number of new/ unpublished writers each year. Weekly magazine emphasizing news of the Assemblies of God for members of the Assemblies and other Pentecostal and charismatic Christians. Estab. 1913. Circ. 265,000. **Pays on acceptance.** Publishes ms an average of 6 months after acceptance. Byline given. Buys first serial rights, electronic rights and second serial (reprint) rights. Submit seasonal material 6 months in advance. Accepts queries by mail, e-mail, fax. Reports in 3 months. Sample copy and writer's guidelines available for $1 or on website.
**Nonfiction:** Informational (articles on homelife that convey Christian teachings), inspirational, personal experience, news, human interest, evangelical, current issues, seasonal. **Buys 3 mss/issue.** Send complete ms. Length: 500-1,200 words. **Pays $25-150.** Pays expenses of writers on assignment.
**Reprints:** Send typed ms with rights for sale noted and information about when and where the article previously appeared. Pays 30% of amount paid for original article.
**Photos:** Photos purchased without accompanying ms. Pays $30 for 8×10 b&w glossy prints; $50 for 35mm or larger color transparencies. Total purchase price for ms includes payment for photos.
**Tips:** "We publish first-person articles concerning spiritual experiences; that is, answers to prayer for help in a particular situation, of unusual conversions or healings through faith in Christ. All articles submitted to us should be related to religious life. We are Protestant, evangelical, Pentecostal, and any doctrines or practices portrayed should be in harmony with the official position of our denomination (Assemblies of God)."

**$ $ PFI WORLD REPORT**, Prison Fellowship International, P.O. Box 17434, Washington DC 20041. (703)481-0000. Fax: (703)481-0003. E-mail: cnicholson@pfi.org. **Contact:** Christopher P. Nicholson, editor. **10% freelance written.** Bimonthly newsletter covering the people and programs of Prison Fellowship in 80+ countries. Estab. 1981. Circ. 6,000. **Pays on acceptance of final draft.** Publishes ms an average of 2 months after acceptance. Byline given. Buys all rights. Editorial lead time 4 months. Submit seasonal material 4 months in advance. Accepts queries by mail, e-mail, fax. Accepts simultaneous submissions. Reports in 2 weeks on queries. Sample copy for #10 SASE or on website.
**Nonfiction:** How-to, inspirational, interview/profile, religious. No fiction or USA topics. **Buys 4 mss/year.** Query. Length: 500-750 words. **Pays $100-350.**
**Reprints:** Accepts previously published submissions.
**Photos:** State availability of photos with submission. Offers no additional payment for photos accepted with ms. Captions required. Buys one-time rights.
**Tips:** "Our audience is narrowly targetted and passionate about prison ministry. It's important to work with the affiliate P.F. ministry in whatever country you're writing about. Vague personal testimonies are not what we're looking for. Tangible examples of how God is changing lives in foreign prisons are what we're looking for."

**$ $ PIME WORLD**, P.I.M.E. Missionaries, 17330 Quincy St., Detroit MI 48221-2765. (313)342-4066. Fax: (313)342-6816. E-mail: pimemiss@flash.net. Website: http://www.rc.net/pime/. **Contact:** Paul W. Witte, managing editor. **15% freelance written.** Monthly (except July and August) magazine emphasizing foreign missionary activities of the Roman Catholic Church in Burma, India, Bangladesh, the Philippines, Hong Kong, Africa, etc., for an adult audience interested in current issues in the missions. Audience is largely high school educated, conservative in both religion and politics. Estab. 1954. Circ. 26,000. Pays on publication. Publishes ms an average of 5 months after acceptance. Byline given. Buys one-time rights. Editorial lead time 2 months. Submit seasonal material 2 months in advance. Accepts simultaneous submissions. Reports in 2 weeks on queries; 2 months on mss. Sample copy free. Writer's guidelines for #10 SASE.
**Nonfiction:** Essays, inspirational, personal experience, photo feature, religious. Informational and inspirational foreign missionary activities of the Catholic Church, Christian social commentary. **Buys 10 mss/year.** Query or send complete ms. Length: 800-1,200 words. **Pays $50-200.**
**Reprints:** Accepts previously published submissions.
**Photos:** State availability of or send photos with submission. Pays $10/color photo. Identification of subjects required. Buys one-time rights.
**Tips:** "Submit articles produced from a faith standpoint, dealing with current issues of social justice, evangelization and pastoral work in Third World countries. Interviews of missionaries accepted. Good quality color photos greatly appreciated."

**◪ $ $ THE PLAIN TRUTH, Renewing faith & values**, Plain Truth Ministries, 300 W. Green St., Pasadena CA 91129. Fax: (626)795-0107. E-mail: marlene_reed@ptm.org. Website: http://www.ptm.org. Editor: Greg Albrecht. **Contact:** Marlene Reed, assistant editor. **75-100% freelance written.** Bimonthly religious magazine. "We seek to reignite the flame of hope and faith in a world of shattered lives by illustrating the joy of a new life in Christ." Estab. 1935. Circ. 110,000. Pays on publication. Publishes ms an average of 8 months after acceptance. Byline given. Offers $50 kill fee. Buys all-language, world, one-time nonexclusive, first or reprint rights. Editorial lead time 6 months. Submit seasonal material 6 months in advance. Accepts queries by mail, e-mail. Accepts simultaneous submissions. Sample copy for 9×12 SAE with 4 first-class stamps. Guidelines for #10 SASE or on website.

**Nonfiction:** Inspirational, interview/profile, personal experience, religious. **Buys 48-50 mss/year.** Query with published clips and SASE. *No unsolicited mss.* Length: 750-2,500 words. **Pays 25¢/word.** Sometimes pays expenses of writers on assignment.

**Reprints:** Send tearsheet or photocopy of article or typed ms with rights for sale noted with information about when and where the article previously appeared with SASE for response. Pays 15¢/word.

**Photos:** State availability of photos with submission. Reviews transparencies, prints. Negotiates payment individually. Captions required. Buys one-time rights.

**Columns/Departments:** Christian People (interviews with Christian leaders), 1,500 words. **Buys 6-12 mss/year.** Send complete ms. **Pays 15-25¢/word.**

**Fillers:** Anecdotes. **Buys 0-20/year.** Length: 25-200 words. **Pays 15-25¢/word.**

 The online magazine carries original content not found in the print edition and includes writer's guidelines.

**Tips:** "Material should offer biblical solutions to real life problems. Both first person and third person illustrations are encouraged. Articles should take a unique twist on a subject. Material must be insightful and practical for the Christain reader. All articles must be well researched and biblically accurate without becoming overly scholastic. Use convincing arguments to support your Christian platform. Use vivid word pictures, simple and compelling language, and avoid stuffy academic jargon. Captivating anecdotes are vital."

**$ PRAIRIE MESSENGER, Catholic Journal**, Benedictine Monks of St. Peter's Abbey, P.O. Box 190, Muenster, Saskatchewan S0K 2Y0 Canada. (306)682-1772. Fax: (306)682-5285. E-mail: pmessenger@sk.sympatico.ca. Editor: Rev. Andrew Britz, OSB. **Contact:** Moreen Weber, associate editor. **10% freelance written.** Weekly Catholic journal with strong emphasis on social justice, Third World and ecumenism. Estab. 1904. Circ. 7,300. Pays on publication. Publishes ms an average of 4 months after acceptance. Byline given. Not copyrighted. Buys first North American serial, first, one-time, second serial (reprint) or simultaneous rights. Submit seasonal material 3 months in advance. Accepts queries by mail, e-mail, phone, fax. Reports in 2 months. Sample copy and writers guidelines for 9×12 SAE with $1 Canadian postage or IRCs.

**Nonfiction:** Interview/profile, opinion, religious. "No articles on abortion or homosexuality." **Buys 15 mss/year.** Send complete ms. Length: 250-600 words. **Pays $40-60.** Sometimes pays expenses of writers on assignment.

**Photos:** Send photos with submission. Reviews 3×5 prints. Offers $15/photo. Captions required. Buys all rights.

**$ PRESBYTERIAN RECORD**, 50 Wynford Dr., North York, Ontario M3C 1J7 Canada. (416)444-1111. Fax: (416)441-2825. E-mail: pcrecord@presbyterian.ca. Website: http://www.presbycan.ca/. **Contact:** Rev. John Congram, editor. **50% freelance written.** Eager to work with new/unpublished writers. Monthly magazine for a church-oriented, family audience. Circ. 55,000. Pays on publication. Publishes ms an average of 4 months after acceptance. Buys first serial, one-time or simultaneous rights. Submit seasonal material 3 months in advance. Accepts queries by mail, e-mail, fax, phone. Reports on accepted ms in 2 months; returns rejected material in 3 months. Sample copy and guidelines for 9×12 SAE with $1 Canadian postage or IRCs or on website.

**Nonfiction:** Material on religious themes. Check a copy of the magazine for style. Also personal experience, interview, inspirational material. No material solely or mainly American in context. No sermons, accounts of ordinations, inductions, baptisms, receptions, church anniversaries or term papers. When possible, photos should accompany manuscript; e.g., current events, historical events and biographies. Special upcoming themes: small groups in the church; conflict in the church; lay leadership. **Buys 15-20 unsolicited mss/year.** Query. Length: 600-1,500 words. **Pays $50 (Canadian).** Sometimes pays expenses of writers on assignment.

**Reprints:** Send tearsheet, photocopy of article or typed ms with rights for sale noted and information about when and where the article previously appeared.

**Photos:** Pays $15-20 for glossy photos. Uses positive transparencies for cover. Pays $50 plus. Captions required.

**Columns/Departments:** Vox Populi (items of contemporary and often controversial nature), 700 words; Mission Knocks (new ideas for congregational mission and service), 700 words.

 The online magazine carries original content not found in the print edition and includes writer's guidelines. Contact: Tom Dickey, online editor.

**Tips:** "There is a trend away from maudlin, first-person pieces redolent with tragedy and dripping with simplistic, pietistic conclusions. Writers often leave out those parts which would likely attract readers, such as anecdotes and direct quotes. Using active rather than passive verbs also helps most manuscripts."

**$ $ PRESBYTERIANS TODAY**, Presbyterian Church (U.S.A.), 100 Witherspoon St., Louisville KY 40202-1396. (502)569-5637. Fax: (502)569-8632. E-mail: today@pcusa.org. Website: http://www.pcusa.orig/pcusa/today. **Contact:** Eva Stimson, editor. Estab. 1867. **65% freelance written.** Prefers to work with published/established writers. Denominational magazine published 10 times/year covering religion, denominational activities and public issues for members of the Presbyterian Church (U.S.A.). "The magazine's puspose is to increase understanding and appreciation of what the church and its members are doing to live out their Christian faith." Estab. 1867. Circ. 82,000. **Pays on acceptance.** Publishes ms an average of 6 months after acceptance. Byline given. Offers 50% kill fee. Buys first North American serial rights. Editorial lead time 3 months. Submit seasonal material 3 months in advance. Accepts queries by mail, e-mail, fax, phone. Reports in 2 weeks on queries; 1 month on mss. Sample copy and writer's guidelines free.

**Nonfiction:** How-to (everyday Christian living), inspirational, Presbyterian programs, issues, peoples. "Most articles have some direct relevance to a Presbyterian audience; however, *Presbyterians Today* also seeks well-informed articles written for a general audience that help readers deal with the stresses of daily living from a Christian perspective." **Buys 25 mss/year.** Send complete ms. Length: 1,000-1,800 words. **Pays $300 maximum for assigned articles; $75-200 for unsolicited articles.**

**Photos:** State availability of photos. Reviews contact sheets, transparencies, b&w prints. Negotiates payment individually. Identification of subjects required. Buys one-time rights.

**$ PRESERVING CHRISTIAN HOMES**, General Youth Division, 8855 Dunn Rd., Hazelwood MO 63042. (314)837-7300. Fax: (314)837-4503. E-mail: gyouth8855@aol.com. **Contact:** Scott Graham, editor and general youth secretary. **40% freelance written.** Bimonthly magazine covering Christian home and family. "All submissions must conform to Christian perspective." Estab. 1970. Circ. 4,500. Pays on publication. Publishes ms an average of 9 months after acceptance. Byline sometimes given. Buys one-time or simultaneous rights. Editorial lead time 6 months. Submit seasonal material 6 months in advance. Accepts simultaneous submissions. Accepts queries by mail, e-mail, fax, phone. Reports in 2 weeks on queries; 2 months on mss. Sample copy for 10×13 SAE with 2 first-class stamps.

**Nonfiction:** General interest, humor, inspirational, personal experience, religious. Special issues: Mothers Day/Fathers Day. No "editorial or political." **Buys 15 mss/year.** Send complete ms. Length: 500-1,500 words. **Pays $30-40.**

**Photos:** State availability of photos with submission. Negotiates payment individually. Buys all rights.

**Fiction:** Humorous, religious, slice-of-life vignettes. **Buys 6 mss/year.** Send complete ms. Length: 500-1,500 words. **Pays $30-40.**

**Poetry:** Free verse, light verse, traditional. **Buys 3 poems/year.** Submit maximum 5 poems. Length: 10-40 lines. **Pays $20-25.**

**Fillers:** Anecdotes, facts, short humor. **Buys 2/year.** Length: 50-200 words. **Pays $10-20.**

**Tips:** "Be relevant to today's Christian families!"

**$ PURPOSE**, 616 Walnut Ave., Scottdale PA 15683-1999. (724)887-8500. Fax: (724)887-3111. E-mail: horsch@mph@org. Website: http://www.mph.org. **Contact:** James E. Horsch, editor. **95% freelance written.** Weekly magazine "for adults, young and old, general audience with varied interests. My readership is interested in seeing how Christianity works in difficult situations." Estab. 1968. Circ. 13,000. **Pays on acceptance.** Publishes an average of 8 months after acceptance. Byline given, including city, state/province. Buys one-time rights. Submit seasonal material 6 months in advance. Accepts simultaneous submissions. Reports in 3 months. Sample copy and writer's guidelines for 6×9 SAE with 2 first-class stamps.

**Nonfiction:** Inspirational stories from a Christian perspective. "I want upbeat stories that deal with issues faced by believers in family, business, politics, religion, gender and any other areas—and show how the Christian faith resolves them. *Purpose* conveys truth through quality fiction or true life stories. Our magazine accents Christian discipleship. Christianity affects all of life, and we expect our material to demonstrate this. I would like story-type articles about individuals, groups and organizations who are intelligently and effectively working at such problems as hunger, poverty, international understanding, peace, justice, etc., because of their faith." **Buys 130 mss/year.** Submit complete ms. Length: 750 words maximum. **Pays 5¢/word maximum.** Buys one-time rights only.

**Reprints:** Send tearsheet or photocopy of article or short story, or typed ms with rights for sale noted and information about when and where the material previously appeared.

**Photos:** Photos purchased with ms. Pays $5-15 for b&w (less for color), depending on quality. Must be sharp enough for reproduction; requires prints in all cases. Captions desired.

**Fiction:** Humorous, religious, historical fiction related to discipleship theme. "Produce the story with specificity so that it appears to take place somewhere and with real people. Essays and how-to-do-it pieces must include a lot of anecdotal, life exposure examples."

**Poetry:** Traditional poetry, blank verse, free verse, light verse. **Buys 130 poems/year.** Length: 12 lines maximum. **Pays $7.50-20/poem** depending on length and quality. Buys one-time rights only.

**Fillers:** Anecdotal items up to 599 words. Pays 4¢/word maximum.

**Tips:** "We are looking for articles which show the Christian faith working at issues where people hurt; stories need to be told and presented professionally. Good photographs help place material with us."

**$ QUEEN OF ALL HEARTS**, Montfort Missionaries, 26 S. Saxon Ave., Bay Shore NY 11706-8993. (516)665-0726. Fax: (516)665-4349. **Contact:** Roger Charest, S.M.M., managing editor. **50% freelance written.** Bimonthly magazine. "Subject: Mary, Mother of Jesus, as seen in the sacred scriptures, tradition, history of the church, the early Christian writers, lives of the saints, poetry, art, music, spiritual writers, apparitions, shrines, ecumenism, etc." Estab. 1950. Circ. 3,000. **Pays on acceptance.** Publishes ms an average of 6 months after acceptance. Byline given. Not copyrighted. Submit seasonal material 6 months in advance. Reports in 2 months. Sample copy for $2.50.

**Nonfiction:** Essays, inspirational, personal experience, religious. **Buys 25 ms/year.** Send complete ms. Length: 750-2,500 words. **Pays $40-60.** Sometimes pays writers in contributor copies or other premiums "by mutual agreement."

**Photos:** Send photos with submission. Reviews transparencies, prints. Pay varies. Buys one-time rights.

**Fiction:** Religious. **Buys 6 mss/year.** Send complete ms. Length: 1,500-2,500 words. **Pays $40-60.**

**Poetry:** Joseph Tusiani, poetry editor. Free verse. **Buys approximately 10 poems/year.** Submit maximum of 2 poems at one time. Pays in contributor copies.

**N $ THE QUIET HOUR**, Cook Communications Ministries, 4050 Lee Vance View, Colorado Springs CO 80918. (719)536-0100. Fax: (407)359-2850. E-mail: wilde@ao.net. Managing Editor: Doug Schmidt. **Contact:** Gary

Wilde, editor. **100% freelance written.** Devotional booklet published quarterly featuring daily devotions. *"The Quiet Hour* is the adult-level quarterly devotional booklet published by David C. Cook. The purpose of *The Quiet Hour* is to provide Bible-based devotional readings for Christians who are in the process of growing toward Christlikeness. Most often, *The Quiet Hour* is used at home, either in the morning or evening, as part of a devotional period. It may be used by individuals, couples or families. For those studying with our Bible-in-Life curriculum, it also helps them prepare for the upcoming Sunday school lesson." **Pays on acceptance**. Publishes ms an average of 14 months after acceptance. Byline given. Makes work-for-hire assignments. Editorial lead time 14 months. Accepts queries by mail. Reports in 3 months. Writer's guidelines free.

**Nonfiction:** Daily devotionals. **Buys 300 mss/year.** Query with published clips, résumé and/or list of credits. **Pays $15-35 per devotional.**

**Tips:** "Send list of credits with query—especially other devotional writing. Gear your writing to about an eighth-grade reading level, which is the same as in many newspapers and newsmagazines. You can achieve ease of understanding by using familiar words and writing mostly short sentences and paragraphs. Use no sexist language, such as the generic use of man, mankind and he. But always refer to the persons of the Trinity as masculine. Be sensitive to issues of theology and biblical interpretation. Since our customers belong to many denominations and theological traditions, confine your theological or Bible-interpretation statements (if any) to matters on which most or all evangelical Christians agree."

**$ $ REFORM JUDAISM**, Union of American Hebrew Congregations, 633 3rd Ave., New York NY 10017-6778. (212)650-4240. Website: http://www.uahc.org/rjmag/. Editor: Aron Hirt-Manheimer. **Contact:** Joy Weinberg, managing editor. **30% freelance written.** Quarterly magazine of Reform Jewish issues. *"Reform Judaism* is the official voice of the Union of American Hebrew Congregations, linking the institutions and affiliates of Reform Judaism with every Reform Jew. *RJ* covers developments within the Movement while interpreting events and Jewish tradition from a Reform perspective." Pays on publication. Publishes ms an average of 3 months after acceptance. Byline given. Offers kill fee for commissioned articles. Buys first North American serial rights. Submit seasonal material 6 months in advance. Deadlines: Spring 2000: November 1999; Summer 2000: January 2000; Fall 2000: April 2000; Winter 2000: July 2000. Reports in 2 months on queries and mss. Writer's guidelines for SASE. Sample copy for $3.50.

**Nonfiction:** Book excerpts, exposé, general interest, historical/nostalgic, inspirational, interview/profile, opinion, personal experience, photo feature, travel. **Buys 30 mss/year.** Submit complete ms with SASE. Length: cover stories: 2,500-3,500 words; major feature: 1,800-2,500 words; secondary feature: 1,200-1,500 words; department (e.g., Travel): 1,200 words; letters: 200 words maximum; opinion: 630 words maximum. **Pays 30¢/word.** Sometimes pays expenses of writers on assignment.

**Reprints:** Send tearsheet or photocopy of article or short story or typed ms with rights for sale noted and information about when and where the material previously appeared. Usually does not publish reprints.

**Photos:** Send photos with ms. Prefers 8×10/color or slides and b&w prints. Pays $25-75. Identification of subjects required. Buys one-time rights.

**Fiction:** Sophisticated, cutting-edge, superb writing. **Buys 4 mss/year.** Send complete ms. Length: 600-2,500 words. **Pays 30¢/word.** Publishes novel excerpts.

**Tips:** "We prefer a stamped postcard including the following information/checklist: _yes we are interested in publishing; _no, unfortunately the submission doesn't meet our needs; _maybe, we'd like to hold on to the article for now. Submissions sent this way will receive a faster response."

**$ $ THE REPORTER**, Women's American ORT, Inc., 315 Park Ave. S., 17th Floor, New York NY 10010. (212)505-7700. Fax: (212)674-3057. E-mail: apatz@waort.org. **Contact:** Aviva Patz, editor. **85% freelance written.** Quarterly nonprofit journal published by Jewish women's organization covering Jewish women celebrities, issues of contemporary Jewish culture, Israel, anti-semitism, women's rights, Jewish travel and the international Jewish community. Estab. 1966. Circ. 80,000. Payment time varies. Publishes ms within a year of acceptance. Byline given. Buys first North American serial rights. Submit seasonal material 6 months in advance. Reports in 3 months. Free sample copy for 9×12 SAE with 3 first-class stamps. Writer's guidelines for SASE.

**Nonfiction:** Cover feature profiles a dynamic Jewish woman making a difference in Judaism, women's issues, education, entertainment, profiles, business, journalism, sports or the arts. Send complete ms. Length varies. No more than 1,800 words. **Pays $425 and up.**

**Photos:** Send photos with submission. Identification of subjects required.

**Columns/Departments:** Education Update (trends in teaching methods, standards, censorship, etc.); Q&A (one-page interview); Last Impression (personal essay). Length: 800 words; **pays $150-300.** Up Front (short news item from Jewish world), 50-200 words; **pays $50 each.** ORT Matters, (length and pay varies). **Buys 4-6 mss/year.** Send complete ms.

**Fiction:** Publishes novel excerpts and short stories as part of "Last Impressions." **Buys 4 ms/year.** Length: 800 words. **Pays $150-300.**

**Tips:** "Simply send manuscript or query; do not call. Looking for well-written, well-researched and lively stories on relevant topics that evoke a response from the reader."

**$ REVIEW FOR RELIGIOUS**, 3601 Lindell Blvd., Room 428, St. Louis MO 63108-3393. (314)977-7363. Fax: (314)977-7362. E-mail: foppema@slu.edu. **Contact:** David L. Fleming, S.J., editor. **100% freelance written.** Bimonthly magazine for Roman Catholic priests, brothers and sisters. Estab. 1942. Pays on publication. Publishes ms an average of 9 months after acceptance. Byline given. Buys first North American serial rights; rarely buys second serial (reprint) rights. Query by mail, phone. Reports in 2 months.

**Nonfiction:** Articles on spiritual, liturgical, canonical matters only; not for general audience. Length: 1,500-5,000 words. **Pays $6/page.**

**Tips:** "The writer must know about religious life in the Catholic Church and be familiar with prayer, vows, community life and ministry."

**$ $ ST. ANTHONY MESSENGER**, 1615 Republic St., Cincinnati OH 45210-1298. Fax: (513)241-0399. E-mail: stanthony@americancatholic.org. Website: http://www.AmericanCatholic.org. **Contact:** Norman Perry, editor. **55% freelance written.** "Willing to work with new/unpublished writers if their writing is of a professional caliber." Monthly general interest magazine for a national readership of Catholic families, most of which have children or grandchildren in grade school, high school or college. Circ. 350,000. **Pays on acceptance.** Publishes ms an average of 9 months after acceptance. Byline given. Buys first worldwide serial and all electronic rights. Submit seasonal material 6 months in advance. Accepts queries by mail, e-mail, fax. Reports in 2 months. Sample copy and writer's guidelines for 9×12 SAE with 4 first-class stamps.

**Nonfiction:** How-to (on psychological and spiritual growth, problems of parenting/better parenting, marriage problems/ marriage enrichment), humor, informational, inspirational, interview, personal experience (if pertinent to our purpose), social issues, personal opinion (limited use; writer must have special qualifications for topic), profile. **Buys 35-50 mss/ year.** Length: 1,500-3,000 words. **Pays 15¢/word.** Sometimes pays the expenses of writers on assignment.

**Fiction:** Mainstream, religious. **Buys 12 mss/year.** Submit complete ms. Length: 2,500-3,000 words. **Pays 15¢/word.**

**Poetry:** *"Our poetry needs are very limited."* Submit 4-5 poems maximum. Up to 20-25 lines, "the shorter, the better." **Pays $2/line.**

The online magazine carries original content not found in the print edition. Contact: John Bookser Feister, online editor.

**Tips:** "The freelancer should ask why his or her proposed article would be appropriate for us, rather than for *Redbook* or *Saturday Review.* We treat human problems of all kinds, but from a religious perspective. Articles should reflect Catholic theology, spirituality and employ a Catholic terminology and vocabulary. We need more articles on prayer, scripture, Catholic worship. Get authoritative information (not merely library research); we want interviews with experts. Write in popular style; use lots of examples, stories and personal quotes. Word length is an important consideration."

**$ ST. JOSEPH'S MESSENGER & ADVOCATE OF THE BLIND**, Sisters of St. Joseph of Peace, St. Joseph's Home, P.O. Box 288, Jersey City NJ 07303-0288. **Contact:** Sister Mary Kuiken, CSJP, editor. **30% freelance written.** Eager to work with new/unpublished writers. Semi annual magazine. Estab. 1898. Circ. 15,500. **Pays on acceptance.** Publishes ms an average of 3 months after acceptance. Buys first serial and second serial (reprint) rights; reassigns rights back to author after publication in return for credit line in next publication. Submit seasonal material 3 months in advance (no Christmas issue). Accepts simultaneous submissions. Reports in 1 month. Sample copy and writer's guidelines for 9×12 SAE with 2 first-class stamps.

**Nonfiction:** Humor, inspirational, nostalgia, personal opinion, personal experience. **Buys 24 mss/year.** Submit complete ms. Length: 800-1,500 words. **Pays $35-50.**

**Reprints:** Send typed ms with rights for sale noted and information about when and where the article previously appeared. Pays 100% of amount paid for an original article.

**Fiction:** Romance, suspense, contemporary, mainstream, religious. **Buys 30 mss/year.** Submit complete ms. Length: 800-1,500 words. **Pays $35-50.**

**Poetry:** Light verse, traditional. **Buys 25 poems/year.** Submit 10 poems max. Length: 50-300 words. **Pays $15-25.**

**Tips:** "It's rewarding to know that someone is waiting to see freelancers' efforts rewarded by 'print'. It's annoying, however, to receive poor copy, shallow material or inane submissions. Human interest fiction, touching on current happenings, is what is most needed. We look for social issues woven into story form. We also seek non-preaching articles that carry a message that is positive."

**SCP JOURNAL and SCP NEWSLETTER**, Spiritual Counterfeits Project, P.O. Box 4308, Berkeley CA 94704-4308. (510)540-0300. Fax: (510)540-1107. E-mail: scp@dnai.com. Website: http://www.scp-inc.org/. **Contact:** Tal Brooke, editor. **5-10% freelance written.** Prefers to work with published/established writers. "The *SCP Journal* and *SCP Newsletter* are quarterly publications geared to reach demanding non-believers while giving Christians authentic insight into the very latest spiritual and cultural trends." Their targeted audience is the educated lay reader. Estab. 1975. Circ. 18,000. Pays on publication. Publishes ms an average of 6 months after acceptance. Byline given. Rights negotiable. Accepts simultaneous submissions. Reports in 3 months. Sample copy for $8.75. Writer's guidelines for SASE.

**Nonfiction:** Book excerpts, essays, exposé, interview/profile, opinion, personal experience, religious. Query by telephone. Length: 2,500-3,500 words. Pay negotiated by phone.

● Less emphasis on book reviews and more focus on specialized "single issue" topics.

**Reprints:** Call for telephone inquiry first. Send photocopy of article and ms on disk with rights for sale noted and information about when and where the article previously appeared. Payment is negotiated.

**Photos:** State available photos. Reviews contact sheets and prints or slides. Offers no additional payment for photos accepted with ms. Captions, model releases, identification of subjects required. Buys one-time rights.

**Tips:** "The area of our publication most open to freelancers is specialized topics covered by *SCP.* Do not send unsolicited samples of your work until you have checked with us by phone to see it it fits *SCP's* area of interest and publication schedule. The usual profile of contributors is that they are published within the field, have advanced degrees from top ranked universities, as well as experience that makes their work uniquely credible."

**$ SCROLL**, Deerhaven Press, 8992 Preston Rd., Suite 110-120, Frisco TX 75034-3964. (972)335-3201. E-mail: mnsurratt@aol.com. Website: http://www.deerhaven.com. **Contact:** Marshall N. Surratt, editor-in-chief. **50% freelance written.** "We offer readers help in better using computers in their ministries, churches and families. We are committed to quality reviews of faith-related software and in-depth discussion on issues relating to faith and technology." Estab. 1984. Circ. 10,000. Pays on publication. Publishes ms an average of 2 months after acceptance. Byline given. Buys first, second serial (reprint) or simultaneous rights. "Some of our articles might be published in denominational or preaching journals. These would be noncompeting. Otherwise, we ask for first rights." Editorial lead time 3 months. Submit seasonal material 3 months in advance. Accepts simultaneous submissions. Accepts queries by mail, e-mail, fax. Reports in 1 week on queries; 3 weeks on mss. Sample copy for 9×12 SAE with 5 first-class stamps. Writer's guidelines for #10 SASE.

　　⚬⇥ Break in with "articles about churches and ministries using computers and related technology. We're also interested in articles on the response of people of faith to issues brought on by technology."

**Nonfiction:** Book excerpts, essays, how-to (how to use computers in a church or ministry), interview/profile, new product, opinion, religious, technical. **Buys 15-20 mss/year.** Query with SASE. Length: 1,000-2,000 words. **Pays $50.**
**Reprints:** Accepts previously published submissions.
**Photos:** State availability of photos with submission. Reviews negatives, 35mm transparencies and 3×5 or larger prints. Offers no additional payment for photos accepted with ms. Identification of subjects required. Buys one-time rights.

**N ✪ $ THE SECRET PLACE**, Educational Ministries, ABC/USA, P.O. Box 851, Valley Forge PA 19482-0851. (610)768-2240. **Contact:** Kathleen Hayes, senior editor. **100% freelance written.** Devotional published quarterly covering Christian daily devotions. Estab. 1938. Circ. 150,000. **Pays on acceptance.** Byline given. Buys first rights. Editorial lead time 1 year. Submit seasonal material 9 months in advance. Sample copy free. Guidelines for #10 SASE.
**Nonfiction:** Inspirational. **Buys about 400 mss/year.** Send complete ms. Length: 100-200 words. **Pays $15.**
**Poetry:** Avant garde, free verse, light verse, traditional. **Buys 12-15 poems/year.** Submit maximum 6 poems. Length: 4-30 lines. **Pays $15.**

**$ SEEK**, Standard Publishing, 8121 Hamilton Ave., Cincinnati OH 45231. (513)931-4050, ext. 365. Fax: (513)931-0950. **Contact:** Eileen H. Wilmoth, editor. **98% freelance written.** Prefers to work with published/established writers. Quarterly Sunday school paper, in weekly issues for young and middle-aged adults who attend church and Bible classes. Circ. 45,000. **Pays on acceptance.** Publishes ms an average of 1 year after acceptance. Byline given. Buys first serial and second serial (reprint) rights. Submit seasonal material 1 year in advance. Accepts previously published submissions. Send tearsheet of article or typed ms with rights for sale noted. For reprints, pays 50% of amount paid for an original article. Reports in 3 months. Sample copy and writer's guidelines for 6×9 SAE with 2 first-class stamps.
**Nonfiction:** "We look for articles that are warm, inspirational, devotional, of personal or human interest; that deal with controversial matters, timely issues of religious, ethical or moral nature, or first-person testimonies, true-to-life happenings, vignettes, emotional situations or problems; communication problems and examples of answered prayers. Article must deliver its point in a convincing manner but not be patronizing or preachy. It must appeal to either men or women, must be alive, vibrant, sparkling and have a title that demands the article be read. We always need stories about families, marriages, problems on campus and life testimonies." **Buys 150-200 mss/year.** Submit complete ms. Length: 400-1,200 words. **Pays 5¢/word.**
**Reprints:** Accepts previously published submissions. Send tearsheet or photocopy of article or typed ms with rights for sale noted and information about when and where the article previously appeared. Pays 50% of amount paid for an original article.
**Photos:** B&w photos purchased with or without mss. Pays $20 minimum for good 8×10 glossy prints.
**Fiction:** Religious fiction and religiously slanted historical and humorous fiction. No poetry. Length: 400-1,200 words. **Pays 5¢/word.**

　　● Ranked as one of the best markets for fiction writers in *Writer's Digest* magazine's "Fiction 50," June 1999.
**Tips:** "Submit manuscripts which tell of faith in action or victorious Christian living as central theme. We select manuscripts as far as one year in advance of publication. Complimentary copies are sent to our published writers immediately following printing."

**$ $ SIGNS OF THE TIMES**, Pacific Press Publishing Association, P.O. Box 5353, Nampa ID 83653-5353. (208)465-2579. Fax: (208)465-2531. E-mail: mmoore@pacificpress.com. **Contact:** Marvin Moore, editor. **40% freelance written.** Works with a small number of new/unpublished writers each year. "We are a monthly Seventh-day Adventist magazine encouraging the general public to practice the principles of the Bible." Estab. 1874. Circ. 225,000. **Pays on acceptance.** Publishes ms an average of 6 months after acceptance. Byline given. Offers kill fee. Buys first North American serial rights, one-time rights, or second serial reprint rights. Editorial lead time 1 year. Submit seasonal material 1 year in advance. "Gospel articles deal with salvation and how to experience it. While most of our gospel articles are assigned or picked up from reprints, we do occasionally accept unsolicited manuscripts in this area. Gospel articles should be 1,000 to 1,200 words. Christian lifestyle articles deal with the practical problems of everyday life from a biblical and Christian perspective. These are typically 1,000 to 1,200 words. We request that authors include sidebars that give additional information on the topic wherever possible. First-person stories must illuminate a spiritual or moral truth that the individual in the story learned. We especially like stories that hold the reader in suspense or that have an unusual twist at the end. First-person stories are typically 600 to 1,000 words long." Reports in 1 month on queries; 2 months on mss. Sample copy and writer's guidelines for 9×12 SAE with 3 first-class stamps.

**Nonfiction:** General interest, how-to, humor, inspirational, interview/profile, personal experience, religious. "We want writers with a desire to share the good news of reconciliation with God. Articles should be people-oriented, well-researched and should have a sharp focus." **Buys 75 mss/year.** Query with or without published clips or send complete ms. Length: 500-1,500 words. **Pays 10-20¢/word.** Sometimes pays the expenses of writers on assignment.

**Reprints:** Send tearsheet or photocopy of article or typed ms with rights for sale noted and information about when and where the article previously appeared. Pays 50% of amount paid for an original article.

**Photos:** Merwin Stewart, photo editor. Reviews b&w contact sheets, 35mm color transparencies, 5×7 or 8×10 b&w prints. Pays $35-300 for transparencies; $20-50 for prints. Model releases and identification of subjects required (captions helpful). Buys one-time rights.

**Columns/Departments:** Send complete ms. **Pays $25-150.**

**Fillers:** "Short fillers can be inspirational/devotional, Christian lifestyle, stories, comments that illuminate a biblical text—in short, anything that might fit in a general Christian magazine. Fillers should be 500 to 600 words."

**Tips:** The audience for *Signs of the Times* includes both Christians and nonChristians of all ages. However, we recommend that our authors write with the nonChristian in mind, since most Christians can easily relate to articles that are written from a non-Christian perspective, whereas many nonChristians will have no interest in an article that is written from a Christian perspective. While *Signs* is published by Seventh-day Adventists, we mention even our own denominational name in the magazine rather infrequently. The purpose is not to hide who we are but to make the magazine as attractive to nonChristian readers as possible. We are especially interested in articles that respond to the questions of everyday life that people are asking and the problems they are facing. Since these questions and problems nearly always have a spiritual component, articles that provide a biblical and spiritual response are especially welcome. Any time you can provide us with one or more sidebars that add information to the topic of your article, you enhance your change of getting our attention. Two kinds of sidebars seem to be especially popular with readers: Those that give information in lists, with each item in the list consisting of only a few words or at the most a sentence or two; and technical information or long explanations that in the main article might get the reader too bogged down in detail. Whatever their length, sidebars need to be part of the total word count of the article. We like the articles in *Signs of the Times* to have interest-grabbing introductions. One of the best ways to do this is with anecdotes, particularly those that have a bit of suspense or conflict.

**$ SISTERS TODAY**, The Liturgical Press, St. John's Abbey, Collegeville MN 56321-2099. Fax: (320)363-7130. E-mail: mwagner@csbsju.edu. Website: http://www.csbsju/osb.sisters/public.html. **Contact:** Sister Mary Anthony Wagner, O.S.B., editor-in-chief. **80% freelance written.** Prefers to work with published/established writers. Bimonthly magazine exploring the role of women and the Church, primarily. Circ. 3,500. Pays on publication. Publishes ms several months after acceptance probably. Byline given. Buys first rights. Submit seasonal material 4 months in advance. Accepts queries by mail, fax. Sample copy for $4.50.

　　Oπ "Plug into our goal: exploring the role of women and the church."

**Nonfiction:** How-to (pray, live in a religious community, exercise faith, hope, charity etc.), informational, inspirational. Also articles concerning religious renewal, community life, worship, the role of women in the Church and in the world today. **Buys 50-60 unsolicited mss/year.** Query. Length: 500-2,500 words. **Pays $5/printed page.** Send book reviews to Sister Stephanie Weisgram, O.S.B.

**Poetry:** Sister Mary Virginia Micka, C.S.J. Free verse, haiku, light verse, traditional. **Buys 5-6 poems/issue.** Submit maximum 4 poems. **Pays $10.**

**Tips:** "Some of the freelance material evidences the lack of familiarity with *Sisters Today*. We would prefer submitted articles not to exceed eight or nine pages."

**$ SOCIAL JUSTICE REVIEW**, 3835 Westminster Place, St. Louis MO 63108-3472. (314)371-1653. **Contact:** Rev. John H. Miller, C.S.C., editor. **25% freelance written.** Works with a small number of new/unpublished writers each year. Bimonthly. Estab. 1908. Publishes ms an average of 1 year after acceptance. Not copyrighted; "however special articles within the magazine may be copyrighted, or an occasional special issue has been copyrighted due to author's request." Buys first serial rights. Sample copy for 9×12 SAE with 3 first-class stamps.

**Nonfiction:** Scholarly articles on society's economic, religious, social, intellectual, political problems with the aim of bringing Catholic social thinking to bear upon these problems. Query with SASE. Length: 2,500-3,000 words. **Pays about 2¢/word.**

**Reprints:** Send typed ms with rights for sale noted and information about when and where the article previously appeared. **Pays about 2¢/word.**

**$ SPIRITUAL LIFE**, 2131 Lincoln Rd. NE, Washington DC 20002-1199. (202)832-8489. Fax: (202)832-8967. E-mail: edodonnell@aol.com. Website: http://www.Spiritual-Life.org. **Contact:** Br. Edward O'Donnell, O.C.D., editor. **80% freelance written.** Prefers to work with published/established writers. Quarterly magazine for "largely Catholic, well-educated, serious readers. A few are non-Catholic or non-Christian." Circ. 12,000. **Pays on acceptance.** Publishes ms an average of 1 year after acceptance. Buys first North American serial rights. Reports in 2 months. Sample copy and writer's guidelines for 7×10 or larger SASE with 5 first-class stamps.

**Nonfiction:** Serious articles of contemporary spirituality and its pastoral application to everyday life. High quality articles about our encounter with God in the present day world. Language of articles should be college level. Technical terminology, if used, should be clearly explained. Material should be presented in a positive manner. Sentimental articles or those dealing with specific devotional practices not accepted. Buys inspirational and think pieces. "Brief autobiographical information (present occupation, past occupations, books and articles published, etc.) should accompany article." No fiction or poetry. **Buys 20 mss/year.** Length: 3,000-5,000 words. **Pays $50 minimum** and 2 contributor's copies. Book reviews should be sent to Br. Edward O'Donnell, O.C.D.

**$ STANDARD**, Nazarene International Headquarters, 6401 The Paseo, Kansas City MO 64131. (816)333-7000. **Contact:** Everett Leadingham, editor. **100% freelance written.** Works with a small number of new/unpublished writers each year. Weekly inspirational paper with Christian reading for adults. Estab. 1936. Circ. 160,000. **Pays on acceptance.** Publishes ms an average of 15-18 months after acceptance. Byline given. Buys one-time rights and second serial (reprint) rights. Submit seasonal material 6 months in advance. Reports in 10 weeks. Sample copy free. Writer's guidelines for SAE with 2 first-class stamps.
**Reprints:** Send tearsheet of short story.
**Fiction:** Prefers fiction-type stories *showing* Christianity in action. Send complete ms; no queries. Length: 500-1,500 words. **Pays 3½¢/word for first rights; 2¢/word for reprint rights.**
• Ranked as one of the best markets for fiction writers in *Writer's Digest* magazine's "Fiction 50," June 1999.
**Poetry:** Free verse, haiku, light verse, traditional. Buys 50 poems/year. Submit maximum 5 poems. Length: 50 lines maximum. **Pays 25¢/line.**
**Tips:** "Stories should express Christian principles without being preachy. Setting, plot and characterization must be realistic."

**$ TEACHERS INTERACTION**, Concordia Publishing House, 3558 S. Jefferson Ave., St. Louis MO 63118-3968. (314)268-1083. Fax: (314)268-1329. E-mail: NummelaTA@cphnet.org. Jean Muser, editorial associate. **Contact:** Tom Nummela, editor. **20% freelance written.** Quarterly magazine of practical, inspirational, theological articles for volunteer church school teachers. Material must be true to the doctrines of the Lutheran Church—Missouri Synod. Estab. 1960. Circ. 16,000. Pays on publication. Publishes ms an average of 1 year after acceptance. Byline given. Buys all rights. Submit seasonal material 1 year in advance. Query by mail, e-mail, fax. Reports in 3 months on mss. Sample copy for $2.75. Writer's guidelines for #10 SASE.
**Nonfiction:** How-to (practical help/ideas used successfully in own classroom), inspirational (to the church school worker—must be in accordance with LCMS doctrine), personal experience (of a Sunday school classroom nature—growth). No theological articles. **Buys 6 mss/year.** Send complete ms. Length: 1,200 words. **Pays up to $100.**
**Fillers:** "*Teachers Interaction* buys short Interchange items—activities and ideas planned and used successfully in a church school classroom." **Buys 48/year.** Length: 200 words maximum. **Pays $20.**
**Tips:** "Practical or 'it happened to me' experiences articles would have the best chance. Also short items—ideas used in classrooms; seasonal and in conjunction with our Sunday school material, Our Life in Christ. Our format includes *all* volunteer church school teachers, Sunday school teachers, Vacation Bible School, and midweek teachers, as well as teachers of adult Bible studies."

**$ THESE DAYS**, Presbyterian Publishing Corp., 100 Witherspoon St., Louisville KY 40202-1396. (502)569-0664. Fax: (502)569-5113. E-mail: kaysno@worldnet.att.net **Contact:** Kay Snodgrass, editor. **95% freelance written.** Bimonthly consumer magazine covering religious devotionals. "*These Days* is published especially for the Cumberland Presbyterian Church, The Presbyterian Church in Canada, The Presbyterian Church (U.S.A.), The United Churches of Canada, and The United Church of Christ as a personal, family and group devotional guide." Estab. 1970. Circ. 200,000. **Pays on acceptance.** Publishes ms an average of 8 months after acceptance. Byline given. Buys all rights and makes work-for-hire assignments. Editorial lead time 10 months. Submit seasonal material 12 months in advance. Reports in 1 month on queries; 6 months on mss. Sample copy for 6×9 SASE and 2 first-class stamps. Writer's guidelines for #10 SASE.
**Nonfiction:** Devotionals in our format. "Use freelance in all issues. Only devotional material will be accepted. Send for issue themes and scripture references. Enclose #10 SASE." **Buys 365 mss/year.** Query or query with published clips. Length: 200-250 words. **Pays $10.**
**Poetry:** Buys 2-6 poems/year. Submit maximum 5 poems. Length: 3-20 lines. **Pays $10.**
**Tips:** "The best way is to send a one-page query that includes your religious affiliation and your religious, writing-related experience plus a sample devotional in our format and/or published clips of similar material."

**$ $ THIS PEOPLE MAGAZINE, Exploring LDS issues and personalities**, Utah Alliance Publishing Co., P.O. Box 1629, Orem UT 84059-1629. (801)852-5200. Fax: (801)852-5202. Website: this-people.com. **Contact:** Editor. **75% freelance written.** Quarterly magazine "aimed at Mormon readers and examines Mormon issues and people in an upbeat, problem-solving way." Estab. 1979. Circ. 20,000. Pays on publication. Publishes ms an average of 6 months after acceptance. Byline given. Buys first rights. Submit seasonal material 6 months in advance. Accepts queries by mail, e-mail, fax. Reports in 2 months. Sample copy for 9×12 SAE with 8 first-class stamps. Writer's guidelines for #10 SASE.
**Nonfiction:** Essays, historical/nostalgic, humor, inspirational, interview/profile, personal experience, photo feature, travel—all Mormon oriented. No cartoons, fiction. **Buys 15-20 mss/year.** Query with or without published clips, or

send complete ms. Length: 1,000-3,500 words. **Pays $150-400 for assigned articles; $100-400 for unsolicited articles.** Sometimes pays expenses of writers on assignment.

**Reprints:** Send tearsheet or photocopy of article.

**Photos:** State availability of photos. Model releases and identification of subjects required. Buys all rights.

**Tips:** "I prefer query letters that include the first 6-8 paragraphs of an article plus an outline of the article. Clips and credits of previous publications are helpful."

**N** **X** **$** **$** **U.S. CATHOLIC**, Claretian Publications, 205 W. Monroe St., Chicago IL 60606. (312)236-7782. Fax: (312)236-8207. E-mail: uscath@claret.org. Website: http://www.uscatholic.org. Editor: Rev. Mark J. Brummel, CMF. Managing Editor: Meinrad Scherer-Emunds. **Contact:** Fran Hurst, editorial assistant. **100% freelance written.** General interest consumer magazine covering Catholic spirituality. "*U.S. Catholic* is dedicated to the belief that it makes a difference whether you're Catholic. We invite and help our readers explore the wisdom of their faith tradition and apply their faith to the challenges of the 21st century." Estab. 1963. Circ. 50,000. **Pays on acceptance.** Publishes ms an average of 6 months after acceptance. Byline given. Buys first North American serial rights. Editorial lead time 6 months. Submit seasonal material 9 months in advance. Accepts queries by mail, e-mail, fax, phone. Accepts simultaneous submissions. Reports in 2 months. Sample copy free. Writer's guidelines for #10 SASE.

**Nonfiction:** Essays, inspirational, opinion, personal experience, religious. **Buys 100 mss/year.** Send complete ms. Length: 2,500-3,500 words (depends on type of article). **Pays $250-600.** Sometimes pays expenses of writers on assignment.

**Photos:** State availability of photos with submission.

**Columns/Departments: Pays $250-600.**

**Fiction:** Maureen Abood, literary editor. Mainstream, religious, slice-of-life vignettes. **Buys 4-6 mss/year.** Send complete ms. Length: 2,500-3,000 words. **Pays $300.**

**Poetry:** Maureen Abood, literary editor. Free verse. "No light verse." **Buys 12 poems/year.** Submit maximum 5 poems. Length: 50 lines. **Pays $75.**

**THE UNITED CHURCH OBSERVER**, 478 Huron St., Toronto, Ontario M5R 2R3 Canada. (416)960-8500. Fax: (416)960-8477. E-mail: general@ucobserver.org. Website: http://www.ucobserver.org. **Contact:** Muriel Duncan, editor. **20% freelance written.** Prefers to work with published/established writers. Monthly newsmagazine for people associated with The United Church of Canada. Deals primarily with events, trends and policies having religious significance. Most coverage is Canadian, but reports on international or world concerns will be considered. Pays on publication. Publishes ms an average of 4 months after acceptance. Byline usually given. Buys first serial rights and occasionally all rights. Accepts queries by mail, e-mail, fax.

**Nonfiction:** Occasional opinion features only. Extended coverage of major issues usually assigned to known writers. No opinion pieces or poetry. Submissions should be written as news, no more than 1,200 words length, accurate and well-researched. Queries preferred. Rates depend on subject, author and work involved. Pays expenses of writers on assignment "as negotiated."

**Reprints:** Send tearsheet or photocopy of article with information about when and where the article previously appeared. Payment negotiated.

**Photos:** Buys photographs with mss. B&w should be 5×7 minimum; color 35mm or larger format. Payment varies.

**Tips:** "The writer has a better chance of breaking in at our publication with short articles; this also allows us to try more freelancers. Include samples of previous *news* writing with query. Indicate ability and willingness to do research, and to evaluate that research. The most frequent mistakes made by writers in completing an article for us are organizational problems, lack of polished style, short on research, and a lack of inclusive language."

**X** **$** **THE UPPER ROOM, Daily Devotional Guide**, P.O. Box 189, Nashville TN 37202-0189. (615)340-7252. Fax: (615)340-7006. E-mail: TheUpperRoomMagazine@upperroom.org. Website: http://www.upperroom.org. Editor and Publisher: Stephen D. Bryant. **Contact:** Office of the Managing Editor. **95% freelance written.** Eager to work with new/unpublished writers. Bimonthly magazine "offering a daily inspirational message which includes a Bible reading, text, prayer, 'Thought for the Day,' and suggestion for further prayer. Each day's meditation is written by a different person and is usually a personal witness about discovering meaning and power for Christian living through scripture study which illuminates daily life." Circ. 2.2 million (US); 385,000 outside US Pays on publication. Publishes ms an average of 1 year after acceptance. Byline given. Buys first North American serial rights and translation rights. Submit seasonal material 14 months in advance. "Manuscripts are not returned. If writers include a stamped, self addressed postcard, we will notify them that their writing has reached us. This does not imply acceptance or interest in purchase. Does not respond unless material is accepted for publication." Sample copy and writer's guidelines with a 4× SAE and 2 first-class stamps. For guidelines only send #10 envelope with stamp.

**Nonfiction:** Inspirational, personal experience, Bible-study insights. No poetry, lengthy "spiritual journey" stories. Special issues: Lent and Easter 2000; Advent 1999. **Buys 365 unsolicited mss/year.** Send complete ms. Length: 300 words maximum. **Pays $50.**

**Tips:** "The best way to break into our magazine is to send a well-written manuscript that looks at the Christian faith in a fresh way. Standard stories and sermon illustrations are immediately rejected. We very much want to find new writers and welcome good material. We are particularly interested in meditations based on Old Testament characters and stories. Good repeat meditations can lead to work on longer assignments for our other publications, which pay more. A writer who can deal concretely with everyday situations, relate them to the Bible and spiritual truths, and write clear, direct prose should be able to write for *The Upper Room*. We want material that provides for more interaction on the part of the reader—meditation suggestions, journaling suggestions, space to reflect and link personal experience with the meditation for the day. Meditations that are personal, authentic, exploratory and full of sensory detail make good devotional writing."

**$ $THE WAR CRY**, The Salvation Army, 615 Slaters Lane, Alexandria VA 22313. Fax: (703)684-5539. E-mail: warcry@usn.salvationarmy.org. Website: http://publications.salvationarmyusa.org. Managing Editor: Jeff McDonald. **Contact:** Lt. Colonel Marlene Chase, editor. **10% freelance written.** Biweekly magazine covering army news and Christian devotional writing. Estab. 1881. Circ. 500,000. **Pays on acceptance.** Publishes ms an average of 3-12 months after acceptance. Byline given. Buys one-time rights. Editorial lead time 6 weeks. Submit seasonal material 1 year in advance. Reports in 1 month. Sample copy and writer's guidelines free.
**Nonfiction:** Humor, inspirational, interview/profile, personal experience, religious. No missionary stories, confessions. **Buys 40 mss/year.** Send complete ms. **Pays up to 20¢/word for assigned articles; 10-20¢/word for unsolicited articles.** Sometimes pays expenses of writers on assignment.
**Reprints:** Send typed ms with rights for sale noted and information about when and where the article previously appeared. **Pays 15¢/word.**
**Photos:** Offers $35-200/photo. Identification of subjects required. Buys one-time rights.
**Fiction:** Religious. **Buys 2-4 mss/year.** Send complete ms. Length: 1,200-1,500 words maximum. **Pays 20¢/word.**
**Poetry:** Free verse. Inspirational only. **Buys 10-20 poems/year.** Submit maximum 5 poems. Length: 16 lines maximum. **Pays $20-50.**
**Fillers:** Anecdotes (inspirational). **Buys 10-20/year.** Length: 200-500 words. **Pays 15-20¢/word.**
**Tips:** "We are soliciting more short fiction, inspirational articles and poetry, interviews with Christian athletes, evangelical leaders and celebrities, and theme-focused articles."

**$ THE WESLEYAN ADVOCATE**, The Wesleyan Publishing House, P.O. Box 50434, Indianapolis IN 46250-0434. (317)576-8156. Fax: (317)842-1649. E-mail: communications@wesleyan.org. Executive Editor: Dr. Norman G. Wilson. **Contact:** Jerry Brecheisen, managing editor. **50% freelance written.** Monthly magazine of The Wesleyan Church. Estab. 1842. Circ. 20,000. Pays on publication. Byline given. Buys first rights or simultaneous rights (prefers first rights). Submit seasonal material 6 months in advance. Accepts simultaneous submissions. Reports in 2 weeks. Sample copy for $2. Writer's guidelines for #10 SASE.
**Nonfiction:** Humor, inspirational, religious. Send complete ms. Length: 500-700 words. **Pays $10-40 for assigned articles; $5-25 for unsolicited articles.**
**Reprints:** Send photocopy of article and typed ms with rights for sale noted and information about when and where the article previously appeared.
**Photos:** Send photos with submission. Buys one-time rights.
**Poetry:** Accepts some seasonal poetry. Length: 10-15 lines. **Pays $5-10.**
**Tips:** "Write for a guide."

**$ THE WESLEYAN WOMAN**, Wesleyan Publishing House, P.O. Box 50434, Indianapolis IN 46250. (317)570-5164. Fax: (317)570-5254. E-mail: wwi@wesleyan.org. Editor: Nancy Heer. **Contact:** Martha Blackburn, managing editor. **60-70% freelance written.** "Quarterly instruction and inspiration magazine for women 20-80. It is read by believers mainly." Estab. 1980. Circ. 4,000. Pays on publication. Byline given. Buys one-time and second serial (reprint) rights. Editorial lead time 3 months. Submit seasonal material 6 months in advance. Accepts simultaneous submissions. Sample copy and writer's guidelines free.
**Nonfiction:** General interest, how-to (ideas for service and ministry), humor, inspirational, personal experience, religious. "We look for interesting, easy-to-read articles about the Christian life that capture the readers' interest. We look for uplifting articles that grab your attention; that inspire you to reach up to God with devotion, and out to those around us with unconditional love. No 'preaching' articles that tell others what to do." **Buys 60 mss/year.** Send complete ms. Length: 200-700 words. **Pays 2-4¢/word.**
**Reprints:** Send photocopy of article or typed ms with rights for sale noted and information about when and where the article previously appeared. Pays 50-75% of amount paid for an original article.
**Photos:** Send photos with submission. Offers $30/photo. Captions and identification of subjects required. Buys one-time rights.
**Fillers:** Anecdotes, facts, newsbreaks, short humor. **Buys 20/year.** Length: 150-350 words. **Pays 2-4¢/word.**
**Tips:** "Send a complete article after seeing our guidelines. Articles that are of your personal journey are welcomed. We go for the nerve endings—touching the spots where women are hurting, perplexed or troubled. Every article must pass the text question. 'Why would today's busy, media-blitzed Christian woman want to read this article?' We seldom publish sermons and Bible studies. Our denomination has other magazines which do these."

**N** ☒ **$ $WHISPERS FROM HEAVEN**, Publications International, Ltd., 7373 N. Cicero, Lincolnwood IL 60646. (847)329-5656. Fax: (847)329-5387. E-mail: tgavin@pubint.com. Editor: Julie Greene. Managing Editor: Becky Bell. **Contact:** Theresa Gavin, associate acquisitions editor. **100% freelance written.** Bimonthly magazine covering inspirational human-interest. "We're looking for real-life experiences (personal and otherwise) that lift the human spirit and illuminate positive human traits and valves: though many stories may deal with (the overcoming of) tragedy and/or difficult times, descriptions shouldn't be too visceral and the emphasis should be on adversity overcome a positive result. *Whispers*, though inspiring, is not overtly religious." Estab. 1999. Circ. 120,000. **Pays on acceptance**. Publishes ms an average of 5 months after acceptance. Byline given. Offers 25% kill fee. Buys all rights. Editorial lead time 5 months. Submit seasonal material 5 months in advance. Accepts queries by mail, e-mail, fax, phone. Accepts simultaneous submissions. Writer's guidelines free.

**Nonfiction:** General interest, inspirational, personal experience. "Nothing overtly religious or anything that explores negative human characteristics." **Buys 150 mss/year.** Query with or without published clips. Length: 1,000-1,500 words. **Pays $100-300 for assigned articles; $100-225 for unsolicited articles.** Pays expenses of writers on assignment.

**Reprints:** Accepts previously published submissions.

**Photos:** State availability of photos with submission. Reviews negatives. Negotiates payment individually. Acquires negotiable rights.

**Tips:** "We are particularly fond of stories (when they warrant it) that have a 'twist' at the end—an extra bit of surprising information that adds meaning and provides an emotional connecting point to the story itself."

**$ WOMAN'S TOUCH**, Assemblies of God Women's Ministries Department (GPH), 1445 Boonville Ave., Springfield MO 65802-1894. (417)862-2781. Fax: (417)862-0503. E-mail: womanstouch@ag.org. **Contact:** Peggy Musgrove, editor. Managing Editor: Aleda Swartzendruber. **50% freelance written.** Willing to work with new/unpublished writers. Bimonthly inspirational magazine for women. "Articles and contents of the magazine should be compatible with Christian teachings as well as human interests. The audience is women, both homemakers and those who are career-oriented." Estab. 1977. Circ. 15,000. Pays on publication. Publishes ms an average of 8-10 months after acceptance. Byline given. Buys first, second or one-time and electronic rights. Editorial lead time 8-10 months. Submit seasonal material 10 months in advance. No queries; send ms by mail. Reports in 3 months. Sample copy for 9½ × 11 SAE with 3 first-class stamps. Writer's guidelines for #10 SASE.

**Nonfiction:** Book excerpts, general interest, inspirational, personal experience, religious, health. No fiction, poetry. **Buys 30 mss/year.** Send complete ms. Length: 200-1,000 words. **Pays $10-50 for assigned articles; $10-35 for unsolicited articles.**

**Reprints:** Send photocopy of article and information about when and where the article previously appeared. Pays 50-75% of amount paid for an original article.

**Columns/Departments:** A Final Touch (inspirational/human interest), 400 words; A Better You (health/wellness), 400 words; A Lighter Touch (true, unpublished anecdotes), 100 words. **Buys 8-10 mss/year. Pays $10-35.**

**Tips:** "Submit manuscripts on current issues of interest to women."

**$ $ THE WORLD**, Unitarian Universalist Association, 25 Beacon St., Boston MA 02108-2800. (617)742-2100. Fax: (617)742-7025. E-mail: ahoffman@uua.org. Website: http://www.uua.org. Editor-in-Chief: Tom Stites. **Contact:** Amy Hoffman. **50% freelance written.** Bimonthly magazine "to promote and inspire denominational self-reflection; to inform readers about the wide range of Unitarian Universalist values, purposes, activities, aesthetics, and spiritual attitudes, and to educate readers about the history, personalities, and congregations that comprise UUism; to enhance its dual role of leadership and service to member congregations." Estab. 1987. Circ. 115,000. **Pays on acceptance.** Publishes ms an average of 1 year after acceptance. Byline given. Buys one-time rights. Editorial lead time 3 months. Submit seasonal material 3 months in advance. Accepts queries by mail, e-mail, fax. Reports in 2 months on queries; 3 months on mss. Sample copy and writer's guidelines for 9 × 12 SASE or on website.

**Nonfiction:** All articles must have a clear UU angle. Essays, historical/nostalgic (Unitarian or Universalist focus), inspirational, interview/profile (with UU individual or congregation), commentary, photo feature (of UU congregation or project), religious. "We are planning issues on family, spirituality and welfare reform." No unsolicited poetry or fiction. **Buys 5 unsolicited mss/year.** Query with published clips. Length: 1,500-3,500 words. **Pays $400 minimum for assigned feature articles.** Sometimes pays expenses of writers on assignment.

**Photos:** State availability of photos with submission. Reviews contact sheets. Offers no additional payment for photos accepted with ms. Captions, model releases and identification of subjects required. Buys one-time rights.

**Columns/Departments:** Focus On (profiles); Community Projects (social service project profiles); Book Reviews (liberal religion, social issues, politics), 600-800 words. Query (profiles, book reviews). **Pays $75-250 for assigned articles and book reviews.**

**N: WORLD CHRISTIAN MAGAZINE**, Global Activists for the Cause of Christ, WinPress, P.O. Box 1525, Oak Park IL 60304. (708)524-5070. Fax: (708)524-5174. **Contact:** Tonya Eichelberger. Quarterly magazine covering religious missions. "*World Christian Magazine* exists to inform, encourage, provoke and mobilize this generation in obedience to the Great Commission." Estab. 1982. Circ. 30,000 (March, September, December), 150,000 (June). **Pays on acceptance.** Publishes ms 6 months after acceptance. Byline given. Buys all rights. Editorial lead time up to 6 months. Accepts queries by mail, e-mail, fax. Sample copy for $4. Writer's guidelines free.

**Nonfiction:** Book excerpts, essays, general interest, how-to, inspirational, interview/profile, opinion, personal experience, photo feature, religious, travel, some sidebars. No fiction or poetry. **Buys 50-60 mss/year.** Query with published clips. Length: 600-2,000 words. **Pays 6-15¢/word.** Sometimes pays expenses of writers on assignment.

**Photos:** State availability of photos with submission. Negotiates payment individually. Captions, model releases, identification of subjects required.

# RETIREMENT

January 1, 1996 the first baby boomer turned 50. With peak earning power and increased leisure time, this generation is able to pursue varied interests while maintaining active lives. More people are retiring in their 50s, while others are starting a business or traveling and pursuing hobbies. These publications give readers specialized information on health and fitness, medical research, finances and other topics of interest, as well as general articles on travel destinations and recreational activities.

**◩ $ $ $ ACTIVETIMES MAGAZINE**, 417 Main St., Carbondale CO 81623. **Contact**: Chris Kelly, editor. **80% freelance written.** Quarterly newspaper magazine covering over 50 market. "We target active, adults over 50. We emphasize the positive, enjoyable aspects of aging." Estab. 1992. Circ. 5,000,000. Pays on publication. Publishes ms an average of 4 months after acceptance. Byline given. Offers 50% kill fee. Buys first North American serial and electronic reprint rights. Editorial lead time 3 months. Submit seasonal material 9 months in advance. Reports in 2 months. Sample copy and guidelines for 9 × 12 SAE with 3 first-class stamps. Writer's guidelines only for #10 SASE.
**Nonfiction:** General interest, how-to, interview/profile, travel round-ups (not destination stories), outdoor, business, careers, education, housing, entertainment, books, celebrities, food, nutrition, health, products, relationships, sex, volunteerism, community service, sports/recreation. No personal essays, first person narratives or nostalgia. **Buys 30 mss/year.** Query with published clips and SASE or postcard. No SASE, no reply. Length: 400-750 words. **Pays $75-400 for assigned articles; $50-250 for unsolicited articles.**
**Photos:** State availability of photos with submission. Reviews contact sheets, 35mm transparencies, prints. Negotiates payment individually. Identification of subjects required.
**Columns/Departments:** Profile (interesting over-50), 500-600 words. **Buys 4 mss/year.** Query with published clips. **Pays $75-250.** Never-Evers (over-50 doing something never, ever did including b&w photo), 150 words. Send complete ms. **Pays $35.**
**Tips:** "Write a detailed query, with substantiating clips. Show how story will appeal to active over-50 reader. Not interested in pain, death, suffering, loss, illness and other similarly depressing subjects."

**$ ALIVE! A Magazine for Christian Senior Adults**, Christian Seniors Fellowship, P.O. Box 46464, Cincinnati OH 45246-0464. (513)825-3681. Editor: J. David Lang. **Contact**: A. June Lang, office editor. **60% freelance written.** Bimonthly magazine for senior adults ages 50 and older. "We need timely articles about Christian seniors in vital, productive lifestyles, travels or ministries." Estab. 1988. Pays on publication. Byline given. Buys first or second serial (reprint) rights. Submit seasonal material 6 months in advance. Accepts queries by mail. Reports in 2 months. Membership $15/year. Sample copy for 9 × 12 SAE with 3 first-class stamps. Writer's guidelines for #10 SASE.
**Nonfiction:** General interest, humor, inspirational, interview/profile, photo feature, religious, travel. **Buys 25-50 mss/year.** Send complete ms and SASE. Length: 600-1,200 words. **Pays $18-75.** Organization membership may be deducted from payment at writer's request.
**Reprints:** Send tearsheet, photocopy of article or typed ms with rights for sale noted and information about when and where the article previously appeared. Pays 60-75% of amount paid for an original article.
**Photos:** State availability of photos with submission. Offers $10-25. Model releases and identification of subjects required. Buys one-time rights.
**Columns/Departments:** Heart Medicine (humorous personal anecdotes; prefer grandparent/grandchild stories or anecdotes re: over-55 persons), 10-100 words; Games n' Stuff (word games, puzzles, word search), 200-500 words. **Buys 50 mss/year.** Send complete ms and SASE. **Pays $2-25.**
**Fiction:** Adventure, humorous, religious, romance (if it fits age group), slice-of-life vignettes, motivational/inspirational. **Buys 12 mss/year.** Send complete ms. Length: 600-1,500 words. **Pays $20-60.**
**Fillers:** Anecdotes, facts, gags to be illustrated, short humor. **Buys 15/year.** Length: 50-500 words. **Pays $2-15.**
**Tips:** "Include SASE and whether manuscript is to be returned or tossed."

**⟨N⟩ $ MATURE LIVING, A Magazine for Christian Senior Adults**, LifeWay Press of the Southern Baptist Convention, 127 Ninth Ave. N., Nashville TN 37234-0140. (615)251-2274. Fax: (615)251-5008. E-mail: matureliving@1 ifeway.com. Editor: Al Shackleford. **Contact**: Judy Pregel, managing editor. **70% freelance written.** Monthly leisure reading magazine for senior adults 50 and older. Estab. 1977. Circ. 350,000. **Pays on acceptance.** Byline given. Prefers to purchase all rights if writer agrees. Submit seasonal material 1 year in advance. Reports in 3 months. Sample copy for 9 × 12 SAE with 4 first-class stamps. Writer's guidelines for #10 SASE.
**Nonfiction:** General interest, historical/nostalgic, how-to, humor, inspirational, interview/profile, personal experience, photo feature, crafts, travel. No pornography, profanity, occult, liquor, dancing, drugs, gambling. **Buys 100 mss/year.** Send complete ms. Length: 600-1,200 words maximum. **Pays 5½¢/word (accepted); $75 minimum.**
**Photos:** State availability of photos with submission. Offers $10-25/photo. Pays on publication. Buys one-time rights.
**Columns/Departments:** Cracker Barrel (brief, humorous, original quips and verses), **pays $15**; Grandparents' Brag Board (something humorous or insightful said or done by your grandchild or great-grandchild), **pays $15**; Inspirational (devotional items), **pays $25**; Food (introduction and 4-6 recipes), **pays $50**; Over the Garden Fence (vegetable or flower gardening), **pays $40**; Crafts (step-by-step procedures), **pays $40**; Game Page (crossword or word-search puzzles and quizzes), **pays $40.**

**Fiction:** Humorous, mainstream, slice-of-life vignettes. No reference to liquor, dancing, drugs, gambling; no pornography, profanity or occult. **Buys 12 mss/year.** Send complete ms. Length: 900-1,200 words. **Pays 5½¢/word; $75 minimum.**

**Poetry:** Light verse, traditional, seasonal, inspirational. **Buys 30 poems/year.** Submit maximum 5 poems. Length: open. **Pays $25.**

⬧ **$ $ $ MATURE OUTLOOK**, Meredith Corp., 1716 Locust St., Des Moines IA 50309-3023. E-mail: outlook @mdp.com. **Contact:** Peggy Person, editor. **80% freelance written.** Bimonthly magazine on travel, health, nutrition, food, money and people for over-50 audience. *"Mature Outlook* is for the 50+ reader who is discovering new possibilities for a new time of life. It provides information for establishing a secure base of health and financial well-being, as well as stories of travel, hobbies, volunteerism and more. They may or may *not* be retired." Circ. 725,000. **Pays on acceptance.** Publishes ms an average 7 months after acceptance. Byline given. Offers 25% kill fee. Buys all rights or makes work-for-hire assignments. Submit all material 9 months in advance. Reports in 2 weeks. Sample copy for $3 and 9×12 SAE. Writer's guidelines for #10 SASE.

**Nonfiction:** How-to, travel, health, fitness, financial, people profiles. No poetry, celebrities or reprints. **Buys 50-60 mss/year.** Query with published clips. Length: 75-2,500 words. **Pays $50-2,000.** Pays telephone expenses of writers on assignment.

**Photos:** State availability of photos with submission. Pays for photos on publication.

**Tips:** "Please query. Please don't call. Reviews manuscripts for short articles or department briefs of 500 words or less. Travel briefs with the greatest chance of acceptance will alert readers to a little-known regional opportunity within the U.S.—a festival, museum, exhibition, scenic hiking trail, boat ride, etc."

**$ MATURE YEARS**, The United Methodist Publishing House, 201 Eighth Ave. S., Nashville TN 37202-0801. Fax: (615)749-6512. E-mail: mcropsey@umpublishing.org. **Contact:** Marvin W. Cropsey, editor. **50% freelance written.** Prefers to work with published/established writers. Quarterly magazine "designed to help persons in and nearing the retirement years understand and appropriate the resources of the Christian faith in dealing with specific problems and opportunities related to aging." Estab. 1954. Circ. 70,000. **Pays on acceptance.** Publishes ms an average of 1 year after acceptance. Buys one-time North American serial rights. Submit seasonal material 14 months in advance. Reports in 2 weeks on queries; 2 months for mss. Sample copy for $5 and 9×12 SAE. Writer's guidelines for #10 SASE.

**Nonfiction:** How-to (hobbies), inspirational, religious, travel (special guidelines), older adult health, finance issues. Especially important are opportunities for older adults to read about service, adventure, fulfillment and fun. **Buys 75-80 mss/year.** Send complete ms. Length: 900-2,000 words. **Pays $45-125.** Sometimes pays expenses of writers on assignments.

**Reprints:** Send photocopy or typed ms with rights for sale noted and information about when and where the article previously appeared. Pays 100% of amount paid for an original article.

**Photos:** Send photos with submission. Negotiates payment individually. Captions, model releases required. Buys one-time rights.

**Columns/Departments:** Health Hints (retirement, health), 900-1,500 words; Going Places (travel, pilgrimmage), 1,000-1,500 words; Fragments of Life (personal inspiration), 250-600 words; Modern Revelations (religious/inspirational), 900-1,500 words; Money Matters (personal finance), 1,200-1,800 words; Merry-Go-Round (cartoons, jokes, 4-6 line humorous verse); Puzzle Time (religious puzzles, crosswords). **Buys 4 mss/year each.** Send complete ms. **Pays $25-45.**

**Fiction:** Religious, slice-of-life vignettes, retirement years. **Buys 4 mss/year.** Send complete ms. Length: 1,000-2,000 words. **Pays $60-125.**

**Poetry:** Free verse, haiku, light verse, traditional. **Buys 24 poems/year.** Submit 6 poems maximum. Length: 3-16 lines. **Pays $5-20.**

**$ $ $ MODERN MATURITY**, American Association of Retired Persons, 601 E St., NW, Washington DC 20049. (202)434-6880. Website: http://www.aarp.org. **Contact:** Hugh Delehanty, editor. **50% freelance written.** Prefers to work with published/established writers. Bimonthly magazine. *"Modern Maturity* is devoted to the varied needs and active life interests of AARP members, age 50 and over, covering such topics as financial planning, travel, health, careers, retirement, relationships and social and cultural change. Its editorial content serves the mission of AARP seeking through education, advocacy and service to enhance the quality of life for all by promoting independence, dignity and purpose." Circ. 22,500,000. **Pays on acceptance.** Publishes ms an average of 6 months after acceptance. Byline given. Buys first North American serial rights. Submit seasonal material 6 months in advance. Accepts queries by mail. Reports in 3 months. Free sample copy and writer's guidelines.

**Nonfiction:** Careers, workplace, practical information in living, financial and legal matters, personal relationships, consumerism. Query first. *No unsolicited mss.* Length: up to 2,000 words. **Pays up to $3,000.** Sometimes pays expenses of writers on assignment.

**Photos:** Photos purchased with or without accompanying ms. Pays $250 and up for color; $150 and up for b&w.

**Fiction:** Very occasional short fiction.

**Tips:** "The most frequent mistake made by writers in completing an article for us is poor follow-through with basic research. The outline is often more interesting than the finished piece. We do not accept unsolicited manuscripts."

✦ **$ $ PRIME TIMES**, Grote Publishing, 634 W. Main St., Suite 207, Madison WI 53703-2634. **Contact:** Mary-Carel Verden, managing editor. **75% freelance written.** Bimonthly membership magazine for MEMBERS Prime Club, formerly the National Association for Retired Credit Union People (NARCUP). "*Prime Times* is a topical magazine of broad appeal to a general adult audience, emphasizing issues relevant to people over age 50. It offers timely articles on health, fitness, finance, travel, outdoor sports, consumer issues, lifestyle, home arts and family relationships. Estab. 1979. Circ. 76,000. May share a core of editorial material with sister magazine *American Times* (est. 1993), sent to financial institutions' older adult customers. Pays on publication. Publishes ms an average of 6 months after acceptance. Byline given. Buys first North American serial rights, one-time rights and second serial (reprint) rights. Editorial lead time 7 months. Submit seasonal material 8 months in advance. Query by mail. Reports in 2 months on queries; 2 months on mss. Sample copy for $3.75 and 9 × 12 SAE with 4 first-class stamps. Writer's guidelines for #10 SASE.

**Nonfiction:** Book excerpts, general interest, health/fitness, travel, historical, humor, recipes, photo features. "No nostalgia pieces, medical or financial pieces based solely on personal anecdotes, personal opinion essays, fiction or poetry." **Buys 8-12 mss/year.** Prefers to see complete ms. Length: 1,000-2,000 words. **Pays $250 minimum for full-length assigned articles; $100 minimum for unsolicited full-length articles.**

**Reprints: Buys 8-16 reprints/year.** Send photocopy or typed ms with rights for sale noted and info about when and where the article previously appeared. **Pays $50-125,** depending on length, quality and number of times published.

**Photos:** Needs professional-quality photos. State availability of or send photos with submission. Welcomes text-photo packages. Reviews contact sheets, transparencies and prints. Negotiates payment individually. Model releases and identification of subjects required. Buys one-time rights.

**Tips:** "Articles that contain useful, well-documented, up-to-date information have the best chance of publication. Don't send personal essays, or articles that repeat information readily available in mainstream media. Articles on health and medical issues *must* be founded in sound scientific method and include current data. Quotes from experts add to an article's validity. You must be able to document your research. Make it easy for us to make a decision on your submission. If the article is written, submit the entire thing—manuscript with professional-quality photos. If you query, be specific. Write part of it in the style in which you would write the article. Be sure to enclose clips. With every article we publish, something about the story must lend itself to strong graphic representation."

**$ SENIOR LIVING NEWSPAPERS**, Smith III Publications, Inc., 318 E. Pershing, Springfield MO 65806. Fax: (417)862-9079. Website: http://www.seniorlivingnewspaper.com. Editor: Robert Smith. **Contact:** Joyce O'Neal, managing editor. **10% freelance written.** Monthly newspaper covering active seniors in retirement. "For people 55 + . Positive and upbeat attitude on aging, prime of life times. Slant is directed to mid-life and retirement lifestyles. Readers are primarily well-educated and affluent retirees, homemakers and career professional. *Senior Living* informs; health, fitness-entertains; essays, nostalgia, humor, etc." Estab. 1988. Circ. 57,000. Pays 30 days after publication. Publishes ms an average of 2 months after acceptance. Byline given. Offers 25% kill fee. Buys first and second serial (reprint) rights. Editorial lead time 3 months. Submit seasonal material 3 months in advance. Reports in 2 weeks on queries; 1 month on mss. Sample copy for 9 × 12 SAE with 5 first-class stamps. Writer's guidelines for #10 SASE.

**Nonfiction:** Essays, general interest, historical/nostalgic, humor, inspirational, personal experience, photo feature, health-related. No youth oriented, preachy, sugar coated, technical articles. **Buys 30-40 mss/year.** Send complete ms. Length: 300-800 words. **Pays $35-50 for assigned articles; $5-35 for unsolicited articles.** Pays expenses of writers on assignment.

**Reprints:** Accepts previously published submissions.

**Photos:** Send photos with submission. Offers $1-5/photo. Captions, model releases and identification of subjects required. Buys one-time rights.

**Fillers:** Anecdotes, facts, short humor. **Buys 15/year.** Length: 150-250 words. **Pays $1-5.**

**Tips:** "Beginning writers who are in need of byline clips stand a good chance if they indicate that they do not require payment for article."

**$ ✦ SENIOR MAGAZINE**, 3565 S. Higuera St., San Luis Obispo CA 93401. (805)544-8711. Fax: (805)544-4450. Editor/Publisher: Gary D. Suggs. **Contact:** George Brand, managing editor. **90% freelance written.** Monthly magazine covering seniors to inform and entertain the "over-50" but young-at-heart audience. Estab. 1981. Circ. 240,000. Pays on publication. Publishes ms an average of 1 month after acceptance. Byline given. Query by mail, phone. Not copyrighted. Buys first or second rights. Accepts simultaneous submissions. Submit seasonal material 2 months in advance. Reports in 2 weeks. Sample copy for 9 × 12 SAE with $1.50 postage. Writer's guidelines for SASE.

**Nonfiction:** Health, historical/nostalgic, humor, inspirational, personal experience, unique hobbies, second careers, book reviews, personality profiles of unusual or notable people (actors, sports figures, writers, travel). Special issues: Second Careers; Going Back to School; Christmas (December); Travel (October, March). **Buys 30-75 mss/year.** Query with SASE. Length: 900-1,200 words. **Pays $1.50/inch.**

**Reprints:** Send typed ms with rights for sale noted and information about when and where the article previously appeared. Pays 100% of amount paid for an original article.

**Photos:** Send photos with submission. Reviews 8 × 10 b&w prints only. Offers $10-15/photo. Captions and identification of subjects required. Buys one-time rights. Uses mostly well known personalities.

**Columns/Departments:** Finance (investment), Taxes, Auto, Health. Length: 300-900 words. **Pays $1.50/inch.**

**[N] $ TODAY'S CHRISTIAN SENIOR**, Marketing Partners, Inc., 162 E. Main St., Elverson PA 19520. (610)286-8800. Fax: (610)286-8881. E-mail: tcpubs@mkpt.com. Editor: Jerry Thacker. **Contact:** Bryan Bice, managing editor.

**25% freelance written.** Quarterly magazine covering senior citizen issues from a conservative religious perspective. "Articles are written to help senior citizens in the areas of health, travel, finances and spirituality." Estab. 1995. Pays on publication. Publishes ms an average of 1 year after acceptance. Byline sometimes given. Buys simultaneous rights. Editorial lead time 1 year. Submit seasonal material 1 year in advance. Query by mail, fax. Accepts simultaneous submissions. Reports in 1 month on queries; 3 months on mss. Sample copy for 9×12 SAE with 4 first-class stamps. Writer's guidelines for #10 SASE.

**Nonfiction:** Historical/nostalgic, inspirational, personal experience, religious, travel. No fiction. **Buys 5 mss/year.** Send complete ms. Length: 800-1,000 words. **Pays $150.**

**Reprints:** Accepts previously published submissions.

# ROMANCE & CONFESSION

Listed here are publications that need stories of romance ranging from ethnic and adventure to romantic intrigue and confession. Each magazine has a particular slant; some are written for young adults, others to family-oriented women. Some magazines also are interested in general interest nonfiction on related subjects.

**$ BLACK SECRETS,** Sterling/McFadden Partnership, 233 Park Ave. S., 7th Floor, New York NY 10003. (212)780-3500. Fax: (212)979-7342. **Contact:** Marcia Mahan, editor. See *Intimacy/Black Romance.*

**Fiction:** "This is our most romantic magazine of the five. We use one longer story between 20-24 pages for this book, and sometimes we feature it on the cover. Save your harsh, sleazy stories for another magazine. Give us your softest, dreamiest, most imaginative, most amorous story with a male love interest we can't help but fall in love with. Make sure your story has body and not just bodies. Our readers love romance, but also require substance." **Pays $100-125.**

**Tips:** "Please request a sample and guidelines before submitting. Enclose a 9×12 SASE with 5 first-class stamps."

**$ INTIMACY/BLACK ROMANCE,** Sterling/McFadden Partnership, 233 Park Ave. S., 7th Floor, New York NY 10003. (212)780-3500. Fax: (212)979-7342. **Contact:** Marcia Mahan, editor. **100% freelance written.** Eager to work with new/unpublished writers. Bimonthly magazine of romance and love. Estab. 1982. Circ. 100,000. Pays on publication. Publishes ms an average of 2 months after acceptance. Byline given on articles only. Buys all rights. Submit seasonal material 6 months in advance. Reports in 2 months. Sample copy for 9×12 SAE with 5 first-class stamps. Writer's guidelines for #10 SASE.

**Nonfiction:** How-to (relating to romance and love) and feature articles on any aspect of relationships. **Buys 100 mss/year.** Query with published clips or send complete ms. Length: 3-5 pages. **Pays $100-125.**

**Fiction:** Confession and romance. "Stories that are too graphic in content and lack romance are unacceptable." **Buys 300 mss/year.** Accepts stories which are a bit more romantic than those written for *Jive, Black Confessions* or *Bronze Thrills.* Send complete ms (4,000-5,000 words). **Pays $100-125.**

**Tips:** "I still get excited when I read a manuscript by an unpublished writer whose use of language is magical and fresh. I'm always looking for that diamond in the fire. Send us your *best* shot. Writers who are careless, sloppy and ungrammatical are an immediate turn-off for me. Please do your homework first. Is it the type of story we buy? Is it written in ms format? Does it make one want to read it?"

**$ INTIMACY/BRONZE THRILLS,** Sterling/McFadden Partnership, 233 Park Ave. S., 5th Floor, New York NY 10003. (212)780-3500. Fax: (212)979-7342. **Contact:** Marcia Mahan, editor. Estab. 1982. See *Intimacy/Black Romance.*

**Fiction:** "Stories can be a bit more extraordinary and uninhibited than in the other magazines but still they have to be romantic. For example, we might buy a story about a woman who finds out her husband is a transsexual in *Bronze Thrills,* but not for *Jive* (our younger magazine). The stories for this magazine tend to have a harder, more adult edge of reality than the others."

**$ JIVE,** Sterling/McFadden Partnership, 233 Park Ave. S., 7th Floor, New York NY 10003. (212)780-3500. Fax: (212)979-7342. **Contact:** Marcia Mahan, editor. 100% freelance written. Eager to work with new/unpublished writers. Bimonthly magazine of romance and love. Estab. 1982. Circ. 100,000. Pays on publication. Publishes ms an average of 2 months after acceptance. Byline given on articles only. Buys all rights. Submit seasonal material 6 months in advance. Reports in 2 months on queries; 6 months on mss. Sample copy for 9×12 SASE with 5 first-class stamps. Free writer's guidelines.

**Nonfiction:** How-to (relating to romance and love) and feature articles on any aspect of relationships. "We like our articles to have a down-to-earth flavor. They should be written in the spirit of sisterhood, fun and creativity. Come up with an original idea our readers may not have thought of but will be dying to try out." **Buys 100 mss/year.** Query with published clips or send complete ms. Length: 3-5 typed pages. **Pays $100-125.**

**Fiction:** Confession and romance. "Stories that are too graphic and lack romance are unacceptable. However, all stories must contain one or two love scenes. Love scenes should allude to sex—romantic, not lewd." **Buys 300 mss/year.** Send complete ms (4,000-5,000 words). **Pays $100-125.**

**Tips:** "We are leaning toward more romantic writing styles as opposed to the more graphic stories of the past. Our audience is largely black teenagers. The stories should reinforce Black pride and should be geared toward teenage issues.

Our philosophy is to show our experiences in as positive a light as possible without promoting any of the common stereotypes that are associated with Black men, lovemaking prowess, penile size, etc. Stereotypes of any kind are totally unacceptable. The fiction section which accepts romance stories and confession stories is most open to freelancers. Also, our special features section is very open. We would also like to see stories that are set outside the US (perhaps they could be set in the Caribbean, Europe, Africa, etc.) and themes that are reflective of things happening around us in the 90s—abortion, AIDS, alienation, surrogate mothers, etc. But we also like to see stories that transcend our contemporary problems and can give us a moment of pleasure, warmth, joy and relief. The characters should be anywhere from teenage to 30s but not the typical 'country bumpkin girl who was turned out by a big city pimp' type story. Please, writers who are not Black, research your story to be sure that it depicts Black people in a positive manner. Do not make a Black character a caricature of a non-Black character. Read contemporary Black fiction to ensure that your dialogue and speech idioms are natural to the Black vernacular."

**◪ $TRUE CONFESSIONS**, Macfadden Women's Group, 233 Park Ave. S., New York NY 10003. (212)979-4800. Fax: (212)979-7342. E-mail: trueconfessionsmail@yahoo.com. **Contact**: Pat Byrdsong, editor. **100% freelance written.** Eager to work with new/unpublished writers. Monthly magazine for high-school-educated, working class women, teens through maturity. Circ. 200,000. Buys all rights. Byline given on featured columns. Pays during the last week of month of issue. Publishes ms an average of 4 months after acceptance. Submit seasonal material 8 months in advance. Reports in 15 months.

> ⚷ "If you have a strong story to tell, tell it simply and convincingly. We always have a need for 4,000-word stories with dramatic impact about dramatic events." Asian-, Latina-, Native- and African-American stories are encouraged.

**Nonfiction:** Timely, exciting, true emotional first-person stories on the problems that face today's women. The narrators should be sympathetic, and the situations they find themselves in should be intriguing, yet realistic. Many stories may have a strong romantic interest and a high moral tone; however, personal accounts or "confessions," no matter how controversial the topic, are encouraged and accepted. Careful study of a current issue is suggested. Length: 4,000-7,000 words and mini stories 1,000-1,500 words; also book lengths of 8,000-9,000 words. **Pays 5¢/word.** Submit complete ms. No simultaneous submissions. SASE required. Buys all rights.

**Columns/Departments:** Family Zoo (pet feature), 50 words or less, **pays $50 for pet photo and story.** All other features are 200-300 words: My Moment With God (a short prayer); Incredible But True (an incredible/mystical/spiritual experience); My Man (a man who has been special in your life); Woman to Woman (a point of view about a contemporary subject matter or a woman overcoming odds). Send complete ms and SASE. **Pays $65** for all features; **$75 for My Moment with God.**

**Poetry:** Poetry should rhyme. Length: 4-20 lines. **Pays $10 minimum.**

**Tips:** "Our magazine is almost 100% freelance. We purchase all stories that appear in our magazine. Read 3-4 issues before sending submissions. Do not talk down to our readers. We prefer manuscripts on disk as well as hard copy."

**N ◪ $TRUE EXPERIENCE**, The Sterling/MacFadden Partnership, 233 Park Ave. S., New York NY 10003. (212)979-4800. Fax: (212)979-7342. **Contact:** Rose Bernstein, editor. Associate Editor: Katherine Edwards. **100% freelance written.** Monthly magazine covering women's confession stories. "*True Experience* is a women's confession magazine which publishes first-person short stories on actual occurrences. Our stories cover such topics as love, romance, crime, family problems and social issues. The magazine's primary audience consists of working-class women in the South, Midwest and rural West. Our stories aim to portray the lives and problems of 'real women.' " Estab. 1928. Circ. 100,000. Pays on publication. Publishes ms an average of 4 months after acceptance. No byline. Buys all rights. Editorial lead time 4 months. Submit seasonal material 6 months in advance. Reports in 2 weeks on queries; 4 months on mss. Sample copy for $1.79. Writer's guidelines for #10 SASE.

**Nonfiction:** Confession, humorous, mystery, romance, slice-of-life vignettes. **Buys 125 mss/year.** Send complete ms. Length: 1,000-10,000 words. **Pays 3¢/word.**

**Columns/Departments:** Woman Talk (brief stories covering rites of passage in women's lives), 500-1,500 words; How We Met (anecdotes describing a couple's first meeting), 300-1,000 words. **Buys 24 mss/year.** Send complete ms. **Pays $50-75.**

**Poetry:** Light verse, traditional. **Buys 5 poems/year.** Submit maximum 10 poems. Length: 4-50 lines. **Pays $2/line.**

**Tips:** "The best way to break into our publication is to send us a well-written, interesting story with sympathetic characters. Stories focusing on topical subjects like sexual harassment, crime, AIDS, or natural disasters are most likely to receive serious considerations. No special submission methods. All stories must be written in first person."

**◪ $TRUE LIFE STORIES**, (formerly *Modern Romances*), Sterling/Macfadden Partnership, 233 Park Ave. S., New York NY 10003. (212)979-4894. Fax: (212)979-7342. **Contact:** Bridgett Gayle, editor. **100% freelance written.** Monthly magazine for family-oriented working women, ages 18-65 years old. Circ. 200,000. Pays the last week of the month of issue. Buys all rights. Submit seasonal material at least 6 months in advance. Reports in 11 months. Writer's guidelines for #10 SASE.

• This editor is especially in need of short, well-written stories (approximately 3,000-7,000 words).

**Nonfiction:** Confession stories with reader identification and a strong emotional tone; a strong emphasis on character-ization and well-defined plots. Should be realistic and compelling. No third-person material. Timely holiday stories (e.g., Christmas themes) should be submitted at least 6 months in advance (by July). **Buys 10 mss/issue.** No query letters; submit complete ms. Length: 2,500-10,000 words. **Pays 5¢/word.** Buys all rights.

**Poetry:** Light, romantic poetry and seasonal subjects. Length: 24 lines maximum. **Pays $2/line.** Look at poetry published in previous issues before submitting.

**⬛ $ TRUE ROMANCE**, Sterling/Macfadden Partnership, 233 Park Ave. S., New York NY 10003. (212)979-4800. Fax: (212)979-7342. **Contact:** Pat Vitucci, editor. **100% freelance written.** Monthly magazine for women, teens through retired, offering compelling confession stories based on true happenings, with reader identification and strong emotional tone. No third-person material. Estab. 1923. Circ. 225,000. Pays 1 month after publication. Buys all rights. Submit seasonal material at least 6 months in advance. Reports within 8 months.
**Nonfiction:** Confessions, true love stories; mini-adventures: problems and solutions; dating and marital and child-rearing difficulties. Realistic yet unique stories dealing with current problems, everyday events; strong emotional appeal. **Buys 12 stories/issue.** Submit ms. Length: 3,000-8,000 words. **Pays 3¢/word;** slightly higher rates for short-shorts.
**Columns/Departments:** That's My Child (photo and 50 words); Loving Pets (photo and 50 words), **both pay $50;** Cupid's Corner (photo and 500 words about you and spouse), **pays $100;** That Precious Moment (1,000 words about a unique experience), **pays $50.**
**Poetry:** Light romantic poetry. Length: 24 lines maximum. **Pays $10-30.**
**Tips:** "A timely, well-written story that is told by a sympathetic narrator who sees the central problem through to a satisfying resolution is *all* important to break into *True Romance*. We are always looking for interesting, emotional, identifiable stories."

**⬛ $ TRUE STORY**, Sterling/Macfadden Partnership, 233 Park Ave. S., New York NY 10003. (212)979-4800. Fax: (212)979-7342. Website: http://www.truestorymail.com. **Contact:** Tina Pappalardo, editor. **80% freelance written.** Monthly magazine for young married, blue-collar women, 20-35; high school education; increasingly broad interests; home-oriented, but looking beyond the home for personal fulfillment. Circ. 1,000,000. Buys all rights. Byline given "on articles only." Pays 1 month after publication. Submit seasonal material 1 year in advance. Reports in 1 year. Guidelines on website.
    **O—** Subject matter can range from light romances to sizzling passion, from all-out tearjerkers to happily-ever-after endings, and everything in between.
**Nonfiction:** First-person stories covering all aspects of women's interests: love, marriage, family life, careers, social problems, etc. The best direction a new writer can be given is to carefully study several issues of the magazine; then submit a fresh, exciting, well-written true story. We have no taboos. It's the handling and believability that make the difference between a rejection and an acceptance." **Buys about 125 full-length mss/year.** Submit only complete mss for stories. Length: 1,500-10,000 words. **Pays 5¢/word; $100 minimum.** Pays a flat rate for columns or departments, as announced in the magazine. Query for fact articles.
**Tips:** *"True Story* is unique because all of our stories are written from the hearts of real people, and deal with all of the issues that affect us today—parenthood, relationships, careers, family affairs, and social concerns. All of our stories are written in first person, and should be no less than 2,000 words and no more than 10,000. If you have access to a computer, we require you to send your submission on a disk, along with a clean hard copy of the story. Please keep in mind, all files must be saved as rich text format (RTF)."

# RURAL

These publications draw readers interested in rural lifestyles. Surprisingly, many readers are from urban centers who dream of or plan to build a house in the country. Magazines featuring design, construction, log homes and "country" style interior decorating appear in Home & Garden.

**$ $ THE COUNTRY CONNECTION, Ontario's Pro-Nature Magazine**, Pinecone Publishing, P.O. Box 100, Boulter, Ontario K0L 1G0 Canada. Fax: (613)332-5183. E-mail: pinecone@northcom.net. Website: web.northcom.net/pinecone. **Contact:** Gus Zylstra, editor. **75% freelance written.** Semiannual magazine covering country life and tourism. *"The Country Connection* is a magazine for true nature lovers and the rural adventurer. Building on our commitment to heritage, cultural, artistic, and outdoor themes, we continually add new topics to illuminate the country experience of people living within nature. Our goal is to chronicle rural life in its many aspects, giving 'voice' to the countryside." Estab. 1989. Circ. 10,000. Pays on publication. Publishes ms an average of 6 months after acceptance. Byline given. Buys first rights. Editorial lead time 4 months. Submit seasonal material 4 months in advance. Accepts queries by mail, e-mail. Sample copy $4.55. For writer's guidelines send #10 SAE (in Canada) or IRC (in US) or on website.
**Nonfiction:** General interest, historical/nostalgic, humor, personal experience, photo feature, lifestyle, leisure, art and culture, travel, vegetarian recipes only. No hunting, fishing, animal husbandry or pet articles. **Buys 20 mss/year.** Send complete ms. Length: 500-2,000 words. **Pays 7-10¢/word.** Sometimes pays expenses of writers on assignment.
**Photos:** Send photos with submission. Reviews transparencies and prints. Offers $10-50/photo. Captions required. Buys one-time rights.
**Columns/Departments: Pays 7-10¢/word.**
**Fiction:** Adventure, fantasy, historical, humorous, slice-of-life vignettes, country living. **Buys 4 mss/year.** Send complete ms. Length: 500-1,500 words. **Pays 7-10¢/word.**

**Tips:** "Send (original content) manuscript with appropriate support material such as photos, illustrations, maps, etc. Do not send American stamps. They have no value in Canada!"

**$ COUNTRY FOLK**, Salaki Publishing & Design, HC77, Box 608, Pittsburg MO 65724. Phone/fax: (417)993-5944. **Contact**: Susan Salaki, editor. **100% freelance written.** Bimonthly magazine. "*Country Folk* publishes true stories and history of the Ozarks." Estab. 1994. Circ. 5,000. Pays on publication. Publishes ms an average of 3 months after acceptance. Byline given. Buys first rights. Editorial lead time 2 months. Submit seasonal material 3 months in advance. Accepts queries by mail, fax, phone. Reports in 1 month on queries; 2 months on mss. Sample copy for $4. Writer's guidelines for #10 SASE.
  • *Country Folk* has increased from quarterly to bimonthly and doubled its circulation.
**Nonfiction:** Historical/nostalgic, how-to, humor, inspirational, personal experience, photo feature, true ghost stories of the Ozarks. **Buys 10 mss/year.** Send complete ms and SASE. Length: 750-1,000 words. **Pays $5-20.** Pays writers with contributor copies or other premiums if we must do considerable editing to the work.
**Photos:** Send photos with submission. Buys one-time rights.
**Fiction:** Historical, humorous, mystery, novel excerpts. **Buys 10 mss/year.** Send complete ms. Length: 750-800 words. **Pays $5-50.**
**Poetry:** Haiku, light verse, traditional. **Buys 25 poems/year.** Submit maximum 3 poems. **Pays $1-5.**
**Fillers:** Anecdotes, facts, gags to be illustrated by cartoonist, newsbreaks, short humor. **Buys 25/year. Pays $1-5.**
**Tips:** "We want material from people who are born and raised in the country, especially the Ozark region. We accept submissions in any form, handwritten or typed. Many of the writers and poets whose work we publish are first time submissions. Most of the work we publish is written by older men and women who have heard stories from their parents and grandparents about how the Ozark region was settled in the 1800s. Almost any writer who writes from the heart about a true experience from his or her youth will get published. Our staff edits for grammar and spelling errors. All the writer has to be concerned about is conveying the story."

**$ $ FARM & RANCH LIVING**, Reiman Publications, 5925 Country Lane, Greendale WI 53129. (414)423-0100. Fax: (414)423-8463. E-mail: 76150.162@compuserve.com. Website: http://www.reiman.org. **Contact**: Nick Pabst, editor. **30% freelance written.** Eager to work with new/unpublished writers. Bimonthly lifestyle magazine aimed at families that farm or ranch full time. "*F&RL* is *not* a 'how-to' magazine—it focuses on people rather than products and profits." Estab. 1978. Circ. 480,000. Pays on publication. Publishes ms an average of 6 months after acceptance. Byline given. Buys first serial rights and one-time rights. Submit seasonal material 6 months in advance. Reports in 6 weeks. Query by mail, fax. Sample copy for $2. Writer's guidelines for #10 SASE.
**Nonfiction:** Interview/profile, photo feature, nostalgia, humor, inspirational, personal experience, "Prettiest Place in the Country" (photo/text tour of ranch or farm). No how-to articles or stories about "hobby farmers" (doctors or lawyers with weekend farms); no issue-oriented stories (pollution, animal rights, etc.). **Buys 30 mss/year.** Query or send ms. Length: 600-1,200 words. **Pays $200 for text/photos package.** Payment for "Prettiest Place" negotiable.
**Reprints:** Send photocopy of article with rights for sale noted. Payment negotiable.
**Photos:** Scenic. State availability of photos with query. Pays $75-200 for 35mm color slides. Buys one-time rights.
**Fillers:** Jokes, anecdotes, short humor with farm or ranch slant. **Buys 50/year.** Length: 50-150 words. **Pays $25.**
**Tips:** "Our readers enjoy stories and features that are upbeat and positive. A freelancer must see *F&RL* to fully appreciate how different it is from other farm publications—ordering a sample is strongly advised (not available on newsstands). Photo features (about interesting farm or ranch families) and personality profiles are most open to freelancers. We can make separate arrangements for photography if writer is unable to provide photos."

**$ FARM TIMES**, 504 Sixth St., Rupert ID 83350. (208)436-1111. Fax: (208)436-9455. E-mail: farmtimes@safelink.net. Website: http://www.farmtimes.com. **Contact**: Robyn Maxfield, managing editor. **50% freelance written.** Monthly regional tabloid for agriculture-farming/ranching. "*Farm Times* is dedicated to rural living in the Intermountain and Pacific Northwest. Stories related to farming and ranching in the states of Idaho, Montana, Nevada, Oregon, Utah, Washington and Wyoming are our mainstay, but farmers and ranchers do more than just work. Human interest articles that appeal to rural readers are used on occasion." Estab. 1987. Pays on publication. Byline given. Editorial lead time 1 month. Submit seasonal material 3 months in advance. Accepts queries by mail, e-mail. Reports in 2 months on queries. Writer's guidelines for #10 SASE. Sample copy for $2.50 or on website.
**Nonfiction:** Farm or ranch issues, exposé, general interest, how-to, interview/profile, new product (few), opinion, late breaking ag news. Always runs one feature article of interest to women. No humor, essay, first person, personal experience or book excerpts. Special issues: Irrigation, Chemical/Fertilizer, Potato Production. **Buys 200 mss/year.** Query with published clips. Send complete ms. Length: 500-800 words. **Pays $1.50/column inch.**
**Reprints:** Send typed ms with rights for sale noted and information about when and where the article previously appeared. Pays 100% of amount paid for an original article.
**Photos:** Send photocopy of article and photos with submission. Reviews contact sheets with negatives, 35mm or larger transparencies and 3×5 or larger prints. Offers $7/b&w inside, $35/color front page cover. Captions, model releases, identification of subjects required. Buys one-time rights.
**Column/Departments:** Horse (horse care/technical), 500-600 words; Rural Religion (interesting churches/missions/religious activities) 600-800 words; Dairy (articles of interest to dairy farmers) 600-800 words. **Buys 12 mss/year.** Query. Send complete ms. **Pays $1.50/column inch.**
**Tips:** "Ag industry-related articles should have a Pacific Northwest and Intermountain West slant (crops, production

techniques, etc.), or how they pertain to the global market. Write tight, observe desired word counts. Feature articles can vary between agriculture and rural living. Good quality photos included with manuscript increase publication chances. Articles should have farm/ranch/rural slant on various topics: health, travel (farmers vacation, too), financial, gardening/landscape, etc."

**$ $ MOTHER EARTH NEWS**, Sussex Publishers, 49 E. 21st St., 11th Floor, New York NY 10010. (212)260-7210. Fax: (212)260-7445. E-mail: mearthnews@aol.com. Website: http://www.motherearthnews.com. Editor: Matthew Scanlon. Managing Editor: Michael Seeber. **Contact**: Marguerite Lamb, senior editor. Mostly freelance written. Bimonthly magazine emphasizing "country living and country skills, for both long-time and would-be ruralites. *Mother Earth News* is dedicated to presenting information that will help readers become more self-sufficient, financially independent, and environmentally aware." Circ. 450,000. Pays on publication. Byline given. Submit seasonal material 5 months in advance. No handwritten mss. Reports within 6 months. Publishes ms an average of 1 year after acceptance. Sample copy for $5. Writer's guidelines for #10 SASE with 1 first-class stamp.
**Nonfiction:** How-to, home business, alternative energy systems, home building, home retrofit and home maintenance, energy-efficient structures, seasonal cooking, gardening. **Buys 100-150 mss/year.** Query. "A short, to-the-point paragraph is often enough. If it's a subject we don't need at all, we can answer immediately. If it tickles our imagination, we'll ask to take a look at the whole piece. No phone queries, please." Length: 300-3,000 words. Payment negotiated. Publishes nonfiction book excerpts.
**Photos:** Purchased with accompanying ms. Send prints or transparencies. Uses 8×10 b&w glossies or any size color transparencies. Include type of film, speed and lighting used. Total purchase price for ms includes payment for photos. Captions and credits required.
**Columns/Departments:** Country Lore (down-home solutions to everyday problems); Bits & Pieces (snippets of news, events and silly happenings); Herbs & Remedies (home healing, natural medicine); Energy & Environment (ways to conserve energy while saving money; also alternative energy).
**Tips:** "Probably the best way to break in is to study our magazine, digest our writer's guidelines, and send us a concise article illustrated with color transparencies that we can't resist. When folks query and we give a go-ahead on speculation, we often offer some suggestions. Failure to follow those suggestions can lose the sale for the author. We want articles that tell what real people are doing to take charge of their own lives. Articles should be well-documented and tightly written treatments of topics we haven't already covered. The critical thing is length, and our payment is by space, not word count. *No phone queries.*"

**$ RURAL HERITAGE**, 281 Dean Ridge Lane, Gainesboro TN 38562-5039. (931)268-0655. E-mail: editor@ruralheritage.com. Website: http://www.ruralheritage.com. Publisher: Allan Damerow. **Contact**: Gail Damerow, editor. **98% freelance written.** Willing to work with a small number of new/unpublished writers. Bimonthly magazine devoted to the training and care of draft animals and other traditional country skills. Estab. 1976. Circ. 4,500. Pays on publication. Publishes ms an average of 6 months after acceptance. Byline given. Buys first English language rights. Submit seasonal material 6 months in advance. Reports in 3 months. Sample copy for $6. Writer's guidelines for #10 SASE or on website.
**Nonfiction:** How-to (crafting and farming); interview/profile (people using draft animals); photo feature. No articles on *mechanized* farming. **Buys 100 mss/year.** Query or send complete ms. Length: 1,200-1,500 words. **Pays 5¢/word.**
**Reprints:** Accepts previously published submissions, but only if previous publication had limited or regional circulation. Send tearsheet or photocopy of article, typed ms with rights for sale noted and information about when and where the article previously appeared. Pays 100% of amount paid for an original article.
**Photos:** Send photos with ms. Pays $10. Captions and identification of subjects required. Buys one-time rights. Six covers/year (color transparency or 5×7 horizontal print), animals in harness $75. Photo guidelines for #10 SASE.
**Columns/Departments:** Drafter's Features (draft animals used for farming, shows and pulls—their care); Crafting (horse-drawn implement designs and patterns), both 750-1,500 words; Humor, 750-900 words. **Pays 5¢/word.**
**Poetry:** Traditional. **Pays $5-25.**
**Tips:** "Always welcome are: 1) Detailed descriptions and photos of horse-drawn implements 2) Prices and other details of draft animal and implement auctions and sales."

**$ $ RURALITE**, P.O. Box 558, Forest Grove OR 97116-0558. (503)357-2105. Fax: (503)357-8615. E-mail: ruralite@europa.com. Website: http://www.europa.com/~ruralite/. **Contact**: Curtis Condon, editor-in-chief. **80% freelance written.** Works with new, unpublished writers "who have mastered the basics of good writing." Monthly magazine aimed at members of consumer-owned electric utilities throughout 10 western states, including Alaska. Publishes 48 regional editions. Estab. 1954. Circ. 320,000. Buys first rights, sometimes reprint rights. **Pays on acceptance.** Byline given. Accepts queries by mail, e-mail, fax. Reports in 1 month. Sample copy and writer's guidelines for 10×13 SAE with 4 first-class stamps; guidelines also on website.
**Nonfiction:** Looking for well-written nonfiction, dealing primarily with human interest topics. Must have strong Northwest perspective and be sensitive to Northwest issues and attitudes. Wide range of topics possible, from energy-related subjects to little-known travel destinations to unusual businesses located in areas served by consumer-owned electric utilities. "About half of our readers are rural and small town residents; others are urban and suburban. Topics with an obvious 'big-city' focus not accepted." Family-related issues, Northwest history (no encyclopedia rewrites), people and events, unusual tidbits that tell the Northwest experience are best chances for a sale. Special issues: Home Improvement (September 1998 and 1999); Gardening (February 1999). Query first; unsolicited manuscripts submitted without request rarely read by editors. **Buys 50-60 mss/yr.** Length 300-2,000 words. **Pays $75-400.**

**Reprints:** Send typed ms with rights for sale noted and information about when and where the article previously appeared. For reprints, pays 50% of "*our* regular freelance rates."
**Photos:** "Illustrated stories are the key to a sale. Stories without art rarely make it, with the exception of humor pieces. Black and white prints, color slides, all formats, accepted with 'razor-sharp' focus."
**Tips:** "Study recent issues. Follow directions when given an assignment. Be able to deliver a complete package (story and photos). We're looking for regular contributors to whom we can assign topics from our story list after they've proven their ability to deliver quality mss."

# SCIENCE

These publications are published for laymen interested in technical and scientific developments and discoveries, applied science and technical or scientific hobbies. Publications of interest to the personal computer owner/user are listed in the Personal Computers section. Journals for scientists and engineers are listed in Trade in various sections.

**$ $AD ASTRA, The Magazine of the National Space Society**, 600 Pennsylvania Ave. SE, Suite 201, Washington DC 20003-4316. (202)543-1900. Fax: (202)546-4189. E-mail: adastraed@aol.com. Website: http://www.nss.org/adastra. **Contact:** Frank Sietzen, Jr., editor-in-chief. **80% freelance written.** Bimonthly magazine covering the space program. "We publish non-technical, lively articles about all aspects of international space programs, from shuttle missions to planetary probes to plans for the future." Estab. 1989. Circ. 30,000. Pays on publication. Byline given. Buys first North American serial rights. Reports on queries when interested. Sample copy for 9×12 SASE. Writer's guidelines for #10 SASE.
**Nonfiction:** Book excerpts, essays, expose, general interest, interview/profile, opinion, photo feature, technical. No science fiction or UFO stories. Query with published clips. Length: 1,500-3,000 words. **Pays $150-250 for features.**
**Photos:** State availability of photos with submission. Reviews 35mm slides, 3×5 color transparencies and b&w prints. Negotiates payment. Identification of subjects required. Buys one-time rights.
**Columns/Departments:** Reviews, editorials, education. Length: 750 words. Query. **Pays $75-100.**
■ The online magazine carries original content not found in the print edition. Contact: Rob Pearlman, online editor.
**Tips:** "Require manuscripts to be accompanied by ASCII or Word or Word Perfect 7.0 floppy disk. Know the field of space technology, programs and policy. Know the players. Look for fresh angles. And, please, know how to write!"

**$ $ARCHAEOLOGY**, Archaeological Institute of America, 135 William St., New York NY 10038. (212)732-5154. Fax: (212)732-5707. E-mail: peter@archaeology.org. Website: http://www.archaeology.org. **Contact:** Peter A. Young, editor-in-chief. **5% freelance written.** "*Archaeology* combines worldwide archaeological findings with photography, specially rendered maps, drawings, and charts. Articles cover current excavations, recent discoveries, and special studies of ancient cultures. Regular features: Timelines, Newsbriefs, film and book reviews, current museum exhibits, The Forum. Two annual Travel Guides give trip planning information. We generally commission articles from professional archaeologists. The only magazine of its kind to bring worldwide archaeology to the attention of the general public." Estab. 1948. Circ. 200,000. Pays on publication. Byline given. Offers 25% kill fee. Buys first North American serial rights. Submit seasonal material 6 months in advance. Accepts simultaneous submissions. Sample copy and writer's guidelines free.
**Nonfiction:** Essays, general interest. **Buys 6 mss/year.** Query preferred. Length: 1,000-3,000 words. **Pays $750 maximum.** Sometimes pays expenses of writers on assignment.
**Photos:** Send photos with submission. Reviews 35mm color slides or 4×5 color transparencies. Identification of subjects and credits required.
**Tips:** "We reach nonspecialist readers interested in art, science, history, and culture. Our reports, regional commentaries, and feature-length articles introduce readers to recent developments in archaeology worldwide."

**★ $ $ASTRONOMY**, Kalmbach Publishing, P.O. Box 1612, Waukesha WI 53187-1612. (414)796-8776. Fax: (414)798-6468. E-mail: astro@astronomy.com. Managing Editor: David J. Eicher. **Contact:** Bonnie Gordon, editor. **75% freelance written.** Monthly magazine covering astronomy—the science and hobby of. "Half of our magazine is for hobbyists (who may have little interest in the heavens in a scientific way); the other half is directed toward armchair astronomers who may be intrigued by the science." Estab. 1973. Circ. 185,000. **Pays on acceptance.** "We are governed by what is happening in the space program and the heavens. It can be up to a year before we publish a manuscript." Byline given. Buys first North American serial, one-time and all rights. Query for electronic submissions. Reports in 1 month on queries; 2 months on mss. Writer's guidelines for SASE.
**Nonfiction:** Book excerpts, space and astronomy, how-to for astro hobbyists, humor (in the viewpoints column and about astro), new product, photo feature, technical. **Buys 100-200 mss/year.** Query. Length: 500-4,500 words. **Pays $50-500.**
**Photos:** Send photos with submission. Reviews transparencies and prints. Pays $25/photo. Captions, model releases and identification of subjects required.
**Tips:** "Submitting to *Astronomy* could be tough. (Take a look at how technical astronomy is.) But if someone is a

physics teacher (or math or astronomy), he or she might want to study the magazine for a year to see the sorts of subjects and approaches we use and then submit a proposal."

**$ $FINAL FRONTIER**, 1017 S. Mountain Ave., Monrovia CA 91016. Fax: (626)932-1036. **Contact:** Dave Cravotta, editor. Bimonthly magazine covering space exploration. "*Final Frontier* is about space technology, commerce and exploration. The missions and machines. People and politics. The adventure of space travel and discovery. Our readers are interested in all aspects of space exploration. We're looking for space-related articles with strong human interest." Estab. 1988. Circ. 75,000. **Pays on acceptance.** Byline given. Buys first North American serial rights. Offers 30% kill fee. Reports in 2 months on queries. Sample copy free for SASE with postage for 6 ounces; mark envelope "sample copy request."

**Nonfiction:** "Interview/profile, human interest, international space programs, profiles of scientists and other interesting people involved in space, fun stories about off-the-wall space subjects, new spacecraft designs and commercial space ventures." **Buys 20 mss/year.** Query with published clips and SASE. Length: 1,200-2,400 words. **Pays 40¢ a word.** Sometimes pays expenses of writers on assignment.

**Reprints:** Accepts previously published submissions from non-competing markets. **Pays 30¢/word.**

**Columns/Departments:** Buys 90 mss/year. "Notes from Earth" (news stories, mission updates, inventions, discoveries), 150-400 words; "Down to Earth" (stories about space missions, technologies and experiments with applications that directly benefit people on Earth, 450-600 words. **Pays 40¢/word.** Query with published clips and SASE.

**Fillers:** Cartoons. No UFOs or *Star Trek*, outer space subjects. Any format; appropriate for family. **Buys 6/year.** Would like to buy more. Pay negotiable.

**Tips:** Needs "strong reporting on all aspects of space. 'Notes from Earth' is the best place for new writers to break in. When querying, mention the availability of photographs or artist's conceptions. Our readers are technically savvy, but you must clearly explain the science and technology in your story, without oversimplifying. Avoid NASA jargon and acronyms. Write in a lively, engaging style—we want stories, not dry, technical reports. We do not run stories about UFOs or *Star Trek*. We no longer purchase science fiction."

**$ $SCIENCE SPECTRA, The Intl. Magazine of Contemporary Scientific Thought**, G&B Magazines Unlimited, P.O. Box 26430, Collegeville PA 19426. Website: http://www.gbhap.com/science_spectra/. Editor: Gerhart Friedlander. **Contact:** Heather Wagner, managing editor. **25% freelance written.** Quarterly magazine covering science. "Our magazine's audience is composed primarily of scientists and the 'scientifically literate.' Writers must have experience writing for a scientific audience." Estab. 1995. Circ. 10,000. Pays on publication. Byline given. Buys all rights. Editorial lead time 3 months. Reports in 1 month on queries. Accepts queries by mail. Writer's guidelines for SAE and 1 first-class stamp.

    **O→** Break in with research experience in particular scientific field about which he/she is reporting or clearly demonstrated ability to write for scientific audience.

**Nonfiction:** Interview/profile, science and technology. **Buys 10-15 mss/year.** Length: approximately 2,000 words. **Pays 25¢/word for assigned articles.**

**Photos:** Offers no additional payment for photos accepted with ms. Captions required. Buys all time rights.

**Columns/Departments:** From the Front Lines (cutting edge research/technology) 2,000 words; Portrait (profile of leading scientific figure) 2,000 words; Controversy Corner (presents both sides of current scientific debate) 2,000 words. **Buys 5-10 mss/year.** Query with published clips. **Pays 25¢/word.**

**Tips:** "Writers should include clips that demonstrate their knowledge of and/or experience in the scientific area about which they are writing. Do not send complete manuscripts; query letter with clips only."

**N $ $THE SCIENCES**, 655 Madison Ave., 16th Floor, New York NY 10021. (212)838-6727. Fax: (212)355-3795. Website: http://www.nyas.org. **Contact:** Peter Brown, editor-in-chief. **50% freelance written.** Bimonthly magazine. "*The Sciences* is the cultural magazine of science. This is the kind of magazine that scientists would come to after work, that they can talk about to a friend, a spouse, a colleague in another discipline." Pays on publication. Byline given. Query with SASE.

    **O→** Break in by offering an intimate knowledge of the scientific subject matter you want to write about. Though hard science is needed, a story must emerge from the hard science.

**Nonfiction:** Profiles, opinion, book or product reviews, features. Every piece must have "lots of science in it. It's important for writers to remember that many of our readers are members of the New York Academy of Science." Length: 3,000 words. **Pays $750.** Query with SASE.

**Columns/Departments:** Opinion, sciences news. Length: 1,000 words. Opinion pieces are always worth trying but that absolutely must include "significant scientific content." Query with SASE.

**N $ $ $SCIENTIFIC AMERICAN**, 415 Madison Ave., New York NY 10017. (212)754-0550. Fax: (212)755-1976. E-mail: editors@sciam.com. Website: http://www.sciam.com. **Contact:** Philip Yam, news editor. Monthly publication covering developments and topics of interest in the world of science. "*Scientific American* brings its readers directly to the wellspring of exploration and technological innovation. The magazine specializes in first-hand accounts by the people who actually do the work. Their personal experience provides an authoritative perspective on future growth. Over 100 of our authors have won Nobel Prizes. Complementing those articles are regular departments written by *Scientific American*'s staff of professional journalists, all specialists in their fields. . . . *Scientific American* is the authoritative source of advance information. Authors are the first to report on important breakthroughs, because they're the people who make them. . . . It all goes back to *Scientific American*'s corporate mission: to link those who use knowledge with those who create it." Estab. 1845. Circ. 666,630. Query before submitting.

**Nonfiction:** Freelance opportunities limited to news and analysis section. **Pays $1/word average.**

**$ $ $ SKY & TELESCOPE, The Essential Magazine of Astronomy**, Sky Publishing Corp., P.O. Box 9111, Belmont MA 02178. (617)864-7360. Fax: (617)576-0336. E-mail: skytel@skypub.com. Website: http://www.skypub.c om. Editor: Leif J. Robinson. **Contact:** Bud Sadler, managing editor. **15% freelance written.** Monthly magazine covering astronomy. "*Sky & Telescope* is the magazine of record for astronomy. We cover amateur activities, research news, equipment, book and software reviews. Our audience is the amateur astronomer who wants to learn more about the night sky." Estab. 1941. Circ. 120,000. Pays on publication. Publishes ms an average of 6 months after acceptance. Byline given. Buys first rights. Editorial lead time 4 months. Submit seasonal material 6-12 months in advance. Accepts queries by mail, e-mail, fax, phone. Reports in 3 weeks on queries; 1 month on mss. Sample copy for $3.99. Guidelines free by e-mail request, on website or for #10 SASE.

**Nonfiction:** Essays, historical/nostalgic, how-to, opinion, personal experience, photo feature, technical. No poetry, crosswords, new age or alternative cosmologies. **Buys 10 mss/year.** Query. Length: 1,500-4,000 words. **Pays $1,000.** Sometimes pays expenses for writers on assignment.

**Photos:** Send photos with submission. Reviews contact sheets. Negotiates payment individually. Identification of subjects required. Buys one-time rights.

**Columns/Departments:** Focal Point (opinion), 1,000 words; Books & Beyond (reviews), 800 words; Amateur Astronomers (profiles), 1,500 words. **Buys 20 mss/year.** Query. **Pays 20¢/word.**

**Tips:** "Good artwork is key. Keep the text lively and provide captions."

**★ $ $ WEATHERWISE, The Magazine About the Weather**, Heldref Publications, 1319 18th St. NW, Washington DC 20036. (202)296-6267. Fax: (202)296-5149. E-mail: ww@heldref.org. Website: http://www.weatherwis e.org. Associate Editor: Kimbra Cutlip. **Contact:** Doyle Rice, managing editor. **75% freelance written.** Bimonthly magazine covering weather and meteorology. "*Weatherwise* is America's only magazine about the weather. Our readers range from professional weathercasters and scientists to basement-bound hobbyists, but all share a common craving for information about weather as it relates to technology, history, culture, society, art, etc." Estab. 1948. Circ. 32,000. Pays on publication. Publishes ms an average of 6 months after acceptance. Byline given. Offers 25% kill fee. Buys all rights or first North American serial or second (reprint) serial rights. Editorial lead time 6 months. Submit seasonal material 6 months in advance. Accepts queries by mail, e-mail, phone, fax. Reports in 2 months on queries. Sample copy for $4 and a 9×12 SAE with 10 first-class stamps. Writer's guidelines for #10 SASE or on website.

&#8212; "First, familiarize yourself with the magazine by taking a close look at the most recent six issues. (You can also visit our website, which features the full text of many recent articles.) This will give you an idea of the style of writing we prefer in *Weatherwise*. Then, read through our writer's guidelines (available from our office or on our website) which detail the process for submitting a query letter. As for the subject matter, keep your eyes and ears open for the latest research and/or current trends in meteorology and climatology that you feel would be appropriate for the general readership of *Weatherwise*. And always keep in mind weather's awesome power and beauty—its 'fun, fury, and fascination' that so many of our readers enjoy."

**Nonfiction:** Book excerpts, essays, general interest, historical/nostalgic, how-to, humor, interview/profile, new product, opinion, personal experience, photo feature, technical, travel. Special issue: Photo Contest (September/October deadline June 1). Special issue: 1999 Weather in Review (March/April 2000). "No blow-by-blow accounts of the biggest storm to ever hit your backyard." **Buys 15-18 mss/year.** Query with published clips. Length: 1,500-2,500 words. **Pays $200-500 for assigned articles; $0-300 for unsolicited articles.** Sometimes pays expenses of writers on assignment.

**Reprints:** Send photocopy of article and information about when and where the article previously appeared. Pays 25% of amount paid for an original article. Publishes book excerpts.

**Photos:** State availability of or send photos with submission. Reviews contact sheets, negatives, transparencies, prints and electronic files. Negotiates payment individually. Captions, identification of subjects required. Buys one-time rights.

**Columns/Departments:** Front & Center (news, trends, opinion), 300-400 words; Weather Talk (folklore and humor), 1,000 words; The Lee Word (humorous first-person accounts of adventures with weather), 1,000 words. **Buys 12-15 mss/year.** Query with published clips. **Pays $0-200.**

**Tips:** "Don't query us wanting to write about broad types like the Greenhouse Effect, the Ozone Hole, El Niño, etc. If it's capitalized, you can bet you won't be able to cover it all in 2,000 words. With these topics and all others, find the story within the story. And whether you're writing about a historical storm or new technology, be sure to focus on the human element—the struggles, triumphs, and other anecdotes of individuals."

# SCIENCE FICTION, FANTASY & HORROR

These publications often publish experimental fiction and many are open to new writers. More information on these markets can be found in the Contests & Awards section under the Fiction heading.

**$ABSOLUTE MAGNITUDE, Science Fiction Adventures**, DNA Publications, P.O. Box 2988, Radford VA 24143. E-mail: dnapublications@iname.com. Website: www.sfsite/dnaweb/home.htm. **Contact:** Warren Lapine, editor-in-chief. 95% freelance written. Quarterly science fiction magazine covering science fiction short stories. "We specialize in action/adventure science fiction with an emphasis on hard science. Interested in tightly-plotted, character-driven stories." Estab. 1993. Circ. 6,000. Pays on publication. Publishes ms an average of 6 months after acceptance. Byline given. Buys first English language serial rights, first rights. Editorial lead time 6 months. Accepts simultaneous submissions. "Do not query—send completed ms." Reports in 1 month on mss. Sample copy for $5. Writer's guidelines for #10 SASE.

● This editor is still looking for tightly plotted stories that are character driven. He is now purchasing more short stories than before.

**Fiction:** Science fiction. **Buys 40 mss/year.** Send complete ms. Length: 1,000-25,000 words. **Pays 1-5¢/word.**

**Poetry:** Any form. **Buys 4 poems/issue.** Submit maximum 5 poems. Length: up to 25,000 words. **Pays 10¢/line.** Best chance with light verse.

**Tips:** "We are very interested in working with new writers but we are not interested in 'drawer-cleaning' exercises. There is no point in sending less than your best effort if you are interested in a career in writing. We do not use fantasy, horror, satire, or funny science fiction. We're looking for character-driven action/adventure based Technical Science Fiction. We want tightly plotted stories with memorable characters. Characters should be the driving force behind the action of the story; they should not be thrown in as an afterthought. We need to see both plot development and character growth. Stories which are resolved without action on the protagonist's part do not work for us; characters should not be spectators in situations completely beyond their control or immune to their influence. Some of our favorite writers are Roger Zelazny, Frank Herbert, Robert Silverberg, and Fred Saberhagen."

**$AMAZING STORIES**, Wizards of the Coast, Inc., 1801 Lind Ave. SW, Renton WA 98055. Fax: (425)204-5928. E-mail: amazing@wizards.com. Website: http://www.wizards.com. Publisher: Wendy Noritake. **Contact:** Mr. Kim Mohan, editor-in-chief. **100% freelance written.** Quarterly magazine featuring quality science fiction short stories. Estab. 1926 (bimonthly starting July 1999). Circ. 40,000. **Pays on acceptance.** Publishes ms an average of 6 months after acceptance. Byline given. Offers 33% kill fee. Buys first North American serial or all rights. Editorial lead time 6 months. Submit seasonal material 1 year in advance. Reports in 2 months on queries; 3 months on mss. Writer's guidelines free with SASE or on website.

**Nonfiction:** Opinion, reviews. **Buys 2 mss/year.** Query with published clips. Length: 1,000-2,500 words. **Pays 6-8¢/word.**

**Columns/Departments:** Query.

**Fiction:** Science fiction. **Buys 40 mss/year.** Query. Length: 1,000-8,000 words. **Pays 6-8¢/word.**

**Tips:** "Read writer's guidelines. Write a good, short query letter. Your manuscript should look professional. We are not likely to publish sword-and-sorcery fantasy; ethnic fantasy that is a rehash or an interpretation of a myth or legend; and horror that relies on gratuitous vulgarity or excessive gore to make the story work."

**$ $ANALOG SCIENCE FICTION & FACT**, Dell Magazine Fiction Group, 475 Park Avenue S., New York NY 10016. (212)698-1313. Fax: (212)698-1198. E-mail: analogsf@erols.com. Website: http://www.sfsite.com/analog. **Contact:** Dr. Stanley Schmidt, editor. **100% freelance written.** Eager to work with new/unpublished writers. For general future-minded audience. Monthly. Estab. 1930. **Pays on acceptance.** Publishes ms an average of 10 months after acceptance. Byline given. Buys first North American serial and nonexclusive foreign serial rights. Accepts queries for serials and fact articles only; query by mail. Reports in 1 month. Sample copy for $5. Writer's guidelines for #10 SASE or on website.

**Nonfiction:** Illustrated technical articles dealing with subjects of not only current but future interest, i.e., topics at the present frontiers of research whose likely future developments have implications of wide interest. **Buys about 11 mss/year.** No e-mail queries or submissions. Length: 5,000 words. **Pays 6¢/word.**

**Fiction:** "Basically, we publish science fiction stories. That is, stories in which some aspect of future science or technology is so integral to the plot that, if that aspect were removed, the story would collapse. The science can be physical, sociological or psychological. The technology can be anything from electronic engineering to biogenetic engineering. But the stories must be strong and realistic, with believable people doing believable things—no matter how fantastic the background might be." Publishes novel excerpts only if they can stand alone as independent stories. **Buys 60-100 unsolicited mss/year.** Send complete ms of short fiction; query about serials. Length: 2,000-80,000 words. **Pays 4¢/word** for novels; **5-6¢/word** for novelettes; **6-8¢/word** for shorts under 7,500 words; **$450-600** for intermediate lengths.

● Ranked as one of the best markets for fiction writers in *Writer's Digest* magazine's last "Fiction 50."

**Tips:** "In query give clear indication of central ideas and themes and general nature of story line—and what is distinctive or unusual about it. We have no hard-and-fast editorial guidelines, because science fiction is such a broad field that I don't want to inhibit a new writer's thinking by imposing 'Thou Shalt Not's.' Besides, a really good story can make an editor swallow his preconceived taboos. I want the best work I can get, regardless of who wrote it—and I need new writers. So I work closely with new writers who show definite promise, but of course it's impossible to do this with *every* new writer. No occult or fantasy."

**$ASIMOV'S SCIENCE FICTION**, Dell Magazine Fiction Group, 475 Park Avenue S., 11th Floor, New York NY 10016. (212)686-7188. Fax: (212)686-7414 (for correspondence only, no submissions). E-mail: asimovs@erols.com.

Website: http://www.asimovs.com. Executive Editor: Sheila Williams. **Contact**: Gardner Dozois, editor. **98% freelance written.** Works with a small number of new/unpublished writers each year. Published 11 times a year, including 1 double issue. Estab. 1977. Circ. 50,000. **Pays on acceptance.** Buys first North American serial and nonexclusive foreign serial rights; reprint rights occasionally. No simultaneous submissions. Accepts queries by mail. Reports in 2 months. Sample copy for $5 and 6½×9½ SAE or on website. Writer's guidelines for #10 SASE or on website.

**Reprints:** Send typed ms with rights for sale noted and information about when and where the article previously appeared.

**Fiction:** Science fiction primarily. Some fantasy and humor but no "Sword and Sorcery." No explicit sex or violence. Publishes novel excerpts; doesn't serialize novels. "It's best to read a great deal of material in the genre to avoid the use of some *very* old ideas." **Buys 10 mss/issue.** Submit complete ms and SASE with *all* submissions. Length: 750-15,000 words. **Pays 5-8¢/word.**

**Poetry:** Length should not exceed 40 lines; **pays $1/line.**

● Ranked as one of the best markets for fiction writers in *Writer's Digest* magazine's "Fiction 50," June 1999.

**Tips:** "In general, we're looking for 'character-oriented' stories, those in which the characters, rather than the science, provide the main focus for the reader's interest. Serious, thoughtful, yet accessible fiction will constitute the majority of our purchases, but there's always room for the humorous as well. Borderline fantasy is fine, but no Sword & Sorcery, please. Neither are we interested in explicit sex or violence. A good overview would be to consider that all fiction is written to examine or illuminate some aspect of human existence, but that in science fiction the backdrop you work against is the size of the Universe. Please do not send us submissions on disk. We've bought some of our best stories from people who have never sold a story before."

**N $ $ BLOODSONGS**, Implosion Publishing, 1921 E. Colonial Dr., Orlando FL 32803. (407)898-5573. Fax: (407)898-7565. E-mail: bloodsongs@implosion.com. Website: http://www.bloodsongs.com. Editor: Cynthia Conlin. **Contact:** David G. Barnett, fiction editor. **75% freelance written.** Quarterly magazine covering horror in all aspects: fiction, music, art, film and more. Estab. 1994. Circ. 14,000. Pays 30 days after publication. Publishes ms 6 months after acceptance. Byline given. Buys first North American serial rights. Sample copy for $5. Guidelines for #10 SASE.

**Fiction:** Length: up to 7,000 words. **Pays $10-20.** "Stick to horror. Dabbling in other genres, such as science fiction, mystery, is fine, as long as your story is primarily a horror tale."

**Tips:** "Your first page and opening paragraphs are the most important of the story. If your first page sucks, no one may ever get to your second. Try to grab readers with your opening. The best story openings start with some sort of action or excitement. Be careful when choosing any of the following as your subject matter: vampires, werewolves, Cthulhu monsters, serial killers, evil children, demonic possession, cannibalism, Satanism, deals with the devil, revenge from beyond the grave. These topics are cliché magnets. If you must write about them, please make sure that your approach/angle/twist really is new and unique."

**$ MARION ZIMMER BRADLEY'S FANTASY MAGAZINE**, P.O. Box 249, Berkeley CA 94701-0249. Phone/fax: (510)644-9222. E-mail: mzbfm@well.com. Website: http://www.mzbfm.com. **Contact:** Mrs. Marion Z. Bradley, editor. **100% freelance written.** Quarterly magazine of fantasy fiction. Estab. 1988. **Pays on acceptance.** Publishes ms 1 year after acceptance. Byline given. Buys first North American serial rights. Reports in 3 months. Sample copy for $4 and 9″×12″ SAE.

**Nonfiction:** "Non-fiction should be queried; it is done on commission only. *Please read a few issues before submitting so that you can see the kind of thing we do buy.*"

**Fiction:** Fantasy. No science fiction, no horror. **Buys 55-60 mss/year.** Send complete ms. Length: 300-5,500 words; short shorts, 1,000 words maximum. **Pays 3-10¢/word.** "We buy original fantasy (*not* sex fantasies) with no particular objection to modern settings, but we do want action and adventure. The primary purpose of your story should should be to entertain the reader; and although any good story has a central point behind the plot, the reader should be able to deduce it rather than having it thrust upon him. Fantasy content should start on the first page and must appear within the first three pages. We prefer strong female characters, and we will reject stories in which we find objectionable sexism. We also reject stories with bad grammar or spelling. We do not favor strong language because, although we ARE NOT a magazine aimed at children or young adults, we do have many young readers."

**Tips:** "Do not submit without first reading guidelines. Please *do not* submit: Poetry, serials, novel excerpts, children's stories, shared world stories, science fiction, hard technology, occult, horror, re-written fairy tales, radical feminism, romances (in which love, romance and marriage are the main motivations), surrealism, or avant-garde stories, stories written in the present tense, or stories about God, the Devil, or hearth-witches. Beware of: 'dime-a-dozen' subjects such as dragons, elves, unicorns, wizards, vampires, writers, sea creatures, brute warriors, ghosts, adventuring sorcerers/sorceresses, thieves/assassins, or final exams for wizards. We get dozens of these kinds of stories every week, and we reject all but the *truly* unusual and well-written ones."

**$ $ THE CRYSTAL BALL**, The Starwind Press, P.O. Box 98, Ripley OH 45167. (937)392-4549. **Contact:** Marlena Powell, editor. **90% freelance written.** Quarterly magazine covering science fiction and fantasy for young adult readers. "*We are especially targeting readers of middle school age.*" Estab. 1997. **Pays on acceptance.** Publishes ms an average of 6 months after acceptance. Byline given. Offers 100% kill fee. Buys first or second serial (reprint) rights. Editorial lead time 4 months. Accepts queries by mail, phone. Sample copy for 9×12 SAE and $3. Guidelines for #10 SASE.

**Nonfiction:** How-to (science), interview/profile, personal experience, book reviews, science information. **Buys 4-6 mss/year.** Query. Length: 900-3,000 words. **Pays ¼¢/word.**

**Reprints:** Send typed ms with rights for sale noted and information and when and where the article previously appeared. Pays 100% of amount paid for an original article.

**Photos:** Send photos with submission. Negotiates payment individually. Captions, identification of subjects required.

**Columns/Departments:** Book reviews (science fiction and fantasy), 100-200 words or less; museum reviews (science & technology, museums & centers, children's museums), 900 words. **Buys 10-15 mss/year.** Query. **Pays ¼¢/word.**

**Fiction:** Fantasy, science fiction. **Buys 10-12 mss/year.** Send complete ms. Length: 1,000-5,000 words. **Pays ¼¢/word.**

**Tips:** "Have a good feel for writing for kids. Don't 'write down' to your audience because they're kids. We look for articles of scientific and technological interest."

**N $ FLESH AND BLOOD**, 121 Joseph St., Bayville NJ 08721. E-mail: ahhh@webtv.net. Website: http://www.geo cities.com/soho/lofts/3459/fnb.html. **Contact:** Jack Fisher, editor. **90% freelance written.** Small press horror magazine published tri-annually covering horror/dark fantasy. Estab. 1997. Circ. 500. **Pays within 3 months from acceptance.** Publishes ms an average of 10 months after acceptance. Editorial lead time 1 month. Reports in 2 weeks on queries; 1 month on mss. Sample copy for $4. Writer's guidelines for #10 SASE.

**Reprints:** Accepts previously published submissions.

**Fiction:** Horror, slice-of-life vignettes, dark fantasy. "No garden-variety work. Work where the main character is a 'nut,' killer, etc." **Buys 18-24 mss/year.** Length: 500-4,000 words. **Pays ½¢/word.**

**Poetry:** Avant garde, free verse, horror/dark fantasy surreal, bizarre. "No rhyming, love pieces." **Buys 15-20 poems/ year.** Submit maximum 5 poems. Length: 3-25 lines. **Pays $5.**

**Tips:** "We like light horror over gore. Don't let the title deceive you. Surreal, bizarre, eccentric tales have a good chance. We especially like dark fantasy pieces or vignettes."

**$ $ INTERZONE, Science Fiction and Fantasy**, 217 Preston Drove, Brighton England BN1 6FL United Kingdom. 01273-504710. E-mail: interzone@cix.co.uk. Editor: David Pringle. Mostly freelance written. Monthly magazine covering science fiction and fantasy. Estab. 1982. Circ. 10,000. Pays on publication. Publishes ms an average of 3 months after acceptance. Byline given. Buys first or one-time rights. Editorial lead time 3 months. Reports in 3 months on mss. Sample copy for $6. Writer's guidelines free.

**Nonfiction:** Essays, interview/profile, opinion. Send complete ms. Length: 1,000-5,000 words. Pays by agreement.

**Photos:** State availability of photos with submissions. Offers no additional payment for photos accepted with ms.

**Fiction:** Science fiction and fantasy. **Buys 75mss/year.** Send complete ms. Length: 2,000-6,000 words. **Pays £30/1,000 words.**

**N $ THE MAGAZINE OF FANTASY & SCIENCE FICTION**, Mercury Press, P.O. Box 1806, Madison Square Station, New York NY 10159-1806. Fax: (212)982-2676. E-mail: gordonfsf@aol.com. Website: http://www.sfsite.com/ fsf/. **Contact:** Gordon Van Gelder, editor. **100% freelance written.** Monthly fantasy fiction and science fiction magazine. "*The Magazine of Fantasy and Science Fiction* publishes various types of science fiction and fantasy short stories and novellas, making up about 80% of each issue. The balance of each issue is devoted to articles about science fiction, a science column, book and film reviews, cartoons and competitions." Estab. 1949. Circ. 80,000. **Pays on acceptance.** Byline given. Buys first North American and foreign serial rights. Submit seasonal material 8 months in advance. Reports in 2 months. Sample copy for $5. Writer's guidelines for #10 SASE or on website.

**Fiction:** Fantasy, horror, science fiction. Prefers character-oriented stories. Send complete ms. No electronic submissions. Length: 2,000-20,000 words. **Pays 5-8¢/word.**

● Ranked as one of the best markets for fiction writers in *Writer's Digest* magazine's "Fiction 50," June 1999.

**Tips:** "We need more hard science fiction and humor."

**N $ ON SPEC**, The Copper Pig Writers Society, P.O. Box 4727, Edmonton, Alberta T6E 5G6 Canada. E-mail: onspec@earthling.net. Website: http://www.icomm.ca/onspec/. General Editor: Jena Snyder. Fiction Editors: Barry Hammond, Susan MacGregor, Hazel Sangster, Jena Snyder, Diane L. Walton. **95% freelance written.** Quarterly literary magazine covering Canadian science fiction, fantasy and horror. Estab. 1989. Circ. 2,000. **Pays on acceptance**. Publishes ms an average of 1 year after acceptance. Byline given. Buys first North American serial rights. Editorial lead time 6 months. Accepts queries by mail, e-mail, phone. Reports in 2 weeks on queries. Reports in 2 months after deadline on mss. Sample copy for $6. Writer's guidelines available on website.

**Nonfiction:** Commissioned only. Yearly theme issue. 2000 theme is "Future Crime." "Each year we offer $100 prize to best story by a young and upcoming author published in *On Spec* in the past year."

**Fiction:** Science fiction, fantasy, horror, magic realism. No media tie-in or shaggy-alien stories. **Buys 50 mss/year.** Send complete ms only. Length: 6,000 words maximum. **Pays $50-180 (Canadian) 3¢/word.**

**Poetry:** Barry Hammond, poetry editor. Avant-garde, free verse. "We rarely buy rhyming or religious material." **Buys 6 poems/year.** Submit maximum 10 poems. Length: 4-100 lines. **Pays $20.**

**Tips:** "We want to see stories with plausible characters, a well-constructed, consistent, and vividly described setting, a strong plot and believable emotions; characters must show us (not tell us) their emotional responses to each other and to the situation and/or challenge they face. Also: don't send us stories written for television. We don't like media tie-ins, so don't watch TV for inspiration! Read, instead! Absolutely no e-mailed or faxed submissions. Strong preference given to submissions by Canadians."

■ **$ OUTSIDE, Speculative and Dark Fiction Magazine**, C&C Clocktower Fiction, Box 260, 6549 Mission Gorge Rd., San Diego CA 92120. E-mail: outside@clocktowerfiction.com. Website: http://www.outside.clocktowerfictio n.com. **Contact:** Editorial. Editors: Brian Callahan and John Cullen. **100% freelance written.** Online magazine offering science fiction and dark imaginative and horror. "*Outside* is a paying professional magazine of science fiction and dark imaginative fiction, aimed at people who love to read well-plotted character-driven genre fiction." Estab. 1998. **Pays on acceptance.** Publishes ms an average of 3 months after acceptance. Byline given. Buys first North American serial and first North American electronic serial rights. Reports in 3 months on mss. Sample copy and guidelines on website.
**Fiction:** Horror, science fiction. "We seek well-written, character-driven fiction that is tightly plotted. Professionally executed, with attention to basics—grammar, punctuation, usage. No sword and sorcery, shared worlds, porno of any kind, excessive violence or gore beyond the legitimate needs of a story, no vulgarity unless it furthers the story (sparingly at that). No derivative works emulating TV shows or movies (e.g., Star Trek)." **Buys 12 mss/year.** Send complete ms. Length: 1,500-5,000 words. **Pays 3¢/word.**
**Tips:** "Please read the tips and guidelines on the magazine's website for further and up-to-the-moment details. *Submissions by mail only.* Traditional format, #10 SASE minimum for reply. E-mail submissions will be deleted unread."

**$ THE SILVER WEB, A Magazine of the Surreal**, Buzzcity Press, P.O. Box 38190, Tallahassee FL 32315. (850)385-8948. Fax: (850)385-4063. E-mail: annk19@mail.idt.net. **Contact:** Ann Kennedy, publisher/editor. **100% freelance written.** Semiannual literary magazine. "*The Silver Web* is a semi-annual publication featuring science fiction, dark fantasy and horror, fiction, poetry, art, and thought-provoking articles. The editor is looking for works ranging from speculative fiction to dark tales and all weirdness in between; specifically works of the surreal." Estab. 1988. Circ. 2,000. **Pays on acceptance.** Byline given. Offers 100% kill fee. Buys first North American serial, one-time or second serial (reprint) rights. Editorial lead time 2 months. Accepts simultaneous submissions. Accepts queries by mail, e-mail. Reports in 1 week on queries; 2 months on mss. Sample copy for $7.20; subscription: $12. Writer's guidelines for #10 SASE or via e-mail.
**Nonfiction:** Book excerpts, essays, interview/profile, opinion. **Buys 6 mss/year.** Query. Length: 500-8,000 words. **Pays $20-250.**
**Reprints:** Send information before submitting ms about when and where material previously appeared. Pays 100% of amount paid for an original article.
**Photos:** State availability of photos with submission. Reviews prints. Negotiates payment individually. Identification of subjects required. Buys one-time rights.
**Columns/Departments:** Book Reviews, Movie Reviews, TV Reviews, all 3,000 words. **Buys 6 mss/year.** Send complete ms. **Pays $20-250.**
**Fiction:** Experimental, horror, science fiction, dark fantasy, surreal. "We do not want to see typical storylines, endings or predictable revenge stories." **Buys 20-25 mss/year.** Send complete ms. Length: 500-8,000 words. **Pays $10-320.** Publishes novel excerpts but query first. Open to submissions January 1 to September 30.
**Poetry:** Avant-garde, free verse, haiku, light verse, traditional. **Buys 18-30/year.** Submit maximum 5 poems. **Pays $10-50.**
**Fillers:** Art fillers. **Buys 10/year. Pays $5-10.**
**Tips:** "Give us an unusual unpredictable story with strong, believable characters we care about. Surprise us with something unique. We do look for interviews with people in the field (writers, artists, filmmakers)."

**$ SPACE AND TIME**, 138 W. 70th St., 4B, New York NY 10023-4468. Website: http://www.bway.net/~cburns/ space&time.html. Editor-in-Chief: Gordon Linzner. **Contacts:** Gerard Houarner, fiction editor; Lawrence Greenberg, poetry editor. **99% freelance written.** Semiannual magazine of science fiction and fantasy. "We feature a mix of fiction and poetry in all aspects of the fantasy genre—science fiction, supernatural horror, sword & sorcery, mixed genre, unclassifiable. Its variety makes it stand out from more narrowly focused magazines. Our readers enjoy quality material that surprises and provokes." Estab. 1966. Circ. 1,500. **Pays on acceptance.** Publishes ms an average of 9 months after acceptance. Byline given. Buys first North American serial rights. Editorial lead time 1 year. Accepts queries by mail. Reports in 3 months on mss. Sample copy $6.50. Writer's guidelines for #10 SASE or on website.
**Nonfiction:** Essays on fantasy, science fiction, science, etc. "No so-called 'true' paranormal." **Buys 1-2 mss/year.** Send complete ms. Length: 1,000 words maximum. **Pays 1¢/word plus 2 contributor copies.**
**Photos/Artwork:** Art director. Artwork (could include photos). Send nonreturnable photocopies. Reviews prints. Pays $10 for interior illustration, $25 for cover, plus 2 contributor copies. Model releases required. Buys one-time rights.
**Fiction:** Gerard Houarner, fiction editor. Fantasy, horror, science fiction, mixed genre (i.e., science-fiction-mystery, western-horror, etc.) and unclassifiable; "Do not want anything that falls outside of fantasy/science fiction (but that leaves a lot). No fiction set in a franchised universe, i.e., *Star Trek*." **Buys 20-24 mss/year.** Send complete ms. Length: 10,000 words maximum. **Pays 1¢/word plus 2 contributor copies, $5 minimum.**
**Poetry:** Lawrence Greenberg, poetry editor. Avant-garde, free verse, haiku, light verse, traditional. "Do not send poetry without a solid connection to the genres we publish. Imaginative metaphors alone do not make it fantasy." **Buys 20 poems/year.** Submit maximum 5 poems. Length: no limits. **Pays 1¢/word ($5 minimum) plus 2 contributor copies.**
**Tips:** "Avoid clichés and standard plots unless you have something new to add."

**$ $ STARLOG MAGAZINE, The Science Fiction Universe**, Starlog Group, 475 Park Ave. S., 8th Floor, New York NY 10016-1689. Fax: (212)889-7933. E-mail: communications@starloggroup.com. Website: http://starlog.com. **Contact:** David McDonnell, editor. **90% freelance written.** "We are now somewhat hesitant to work with unpublished writers." Monthly magazine covering "the science fiction-fantasy genre: its films, TV, books, art and personalities." Estab. 1976. "We concentrate on interviews with actors, directors, writers, producers, special effects technicians and others. Be aware that 'sci-fi' and 'Trekkie' are seen as derogatory terms by our readers and by us." Pays on publication. Publishes ms an average of 4 months after acceptance. Byline given. Offers kill fee "only to manuscripts *written* or interviews *done for us*." Buys all rights. No simultaneous submissions. Reports in 6 weeks or less. "We provide an assignment sheet to *all* writers with deadline and other info, authorizing a queried piece. No such sheets provided for already completed stories sent in on speculation. Manuscripts *must* be submitted on computer disk or by e-mail. Printouts helpful." Sample copy for $5. Writer's guidelines for #10 SASE.

    0⇥ Break in by "doing something fresh, imaginative or innovative—or all three. Or by getting an interview we can't get. The writers who sell to us try *hard* and manage to meet one or both challenges."

**Nonfiction:** Interview/profile (actors, directors, screenwriters who've made science fiction films and science fiction novelists); coverage of science fiction fandom, etc. "We also sometimes cover science fiction/fantasy animation and comics." No personal opinion think pieces/essays. *No* first person. Avoids articles on horror films/creators. "We prefer article format as opposed to Q&A interviews." **Buys 200 mss/year.** Query first with published clips. "We accept queries by regular mail *only*, by fax if there's a critical time factor or by e-mail. No phone calls. Ever! Unsolicited phone calls *won't* be returned." Length: 500-3,000 words. **Pays $35 (500-word or less items); $50-75 (sidebars); $150-275 (1,000-4,000 word pieces).**

**Reprints:** Pays $50 for *each* reprint in each foreign edition or such.

**Photos:** State availability of photos. Pays $10-25 for color slide transparencies depending on quality. "No separate payment for photos provided by film studios." Captions, model releases, identification of subjects and credit line on photos required. Photo credit given. Buys all rights.

**Columns/Departments:** Booklog (book reviews, **$15 each,** by assignment only). **Buys 150 reviews/year.** Query with published clips. Book review, 125 words maximum. No kill fee.

    ▪ The online magazine carries original content not found in the print edition. Contact: Jeanne Provost, online editor.

**Tips:** "Absolutely *no fiction*. We do *not* publish it and we throw away fiction manuscripts from writers who *can't* be bothered to include SASE. Nonfiction only please! We are always looking for *fresh* angles on the various *Star Trek* shows, *The X-Files*, and *Star Wars*. Know your subject before you try us. Most full-length major assignments go to freelancers with whom we're already dealing. But if we like your clips and ideas, it's possible we'll give *you* a chance. No phone calls for *any* reason please—we *mean* that!"

**$ STARSHIP EARTH**, Black Moon Publishing, P.O. Box 484, Bellaire OH 43906. E-mail: shadowhorse@aol.com. Managing Editor: Kirin Lee. **Contact**: Silver Shadowhorse, fiction editor. **15% freelance nonfiction; 100% freelance fiction written.** Bimonthly magazine featuring science fiction. "*Starship Earth* is geared toward science fiction fans of all ages. We do mostly nonfiction, but do print short stories. Our nonfiction focus: profiles of actors and industry people, conventions, behind the scenes articles on films and TV shows. We do cover action/adventure films and TV as well. Heavy *Star Trek* focus. We cover classic science fiction, too." Estab. 1996. Pays on publication. Publishes ms an average of 1 year after acceptance. Byline sometimes given. Buys first or one-time rights. Editorial lead time 9-12 months. Submit seasonal material 6 months in advance. Accepts queries by mail. Reports in about 3 weeks on queries; 4 months on mss. Writer's guidelines for #10 SASE.

    ● *Starship Earth* is planning an anthology of short stories of up to 4,000 words. Stories submitted to *Starship Earth* will automatically be considered.

**Nonfiction:** General interest, how-to (relating to science fiction, writing, model building, crafts, etc.), interview/profile, new product (relating to science of science fiction), nostalgia, personal experience, photo feature, travel (relating to attending conventions), behind the scenes of film/TV science fiction, book reviews. **Buys variable number of mss/ year.** Query. Length: up to 3,000 words. Please query for longer pieces. **Pays ½-3¢/word.** Pays in copies for book or film reviews. Sometimes pays expenses of writers on assignment.

**Photos:** State availability of photos with submission. Reviews transparencies, prints. Negotiates payment individually. Captions, model releases, identification of subjects required. Buys one-time rights.

**Columns/Departments:** Jenna Dawson, assistant editor. Costumes, conventions/events, science fiction music, upcoming book, film, TV releases, film reviews, book reviews, new products; all up to 700 words. Query. **Does not pay for columns/departments pieces.**

**Fiction:** Silver Shadowhorse, editor. Fantasy, historical (with a science fiction twist), science fiction. No erotic content, horror, "Sword & Sorcery" violence, explicit language or religious material. **Buys variable number of mss/year, 12 short stories/year.** Query. Length: 500-3,000 words. **Pays ½-3¢/word.**

**Fillers:** Contact: Jenna Dawson, assistant editor. Anecdotes, facts, newsbreaks, short humor. Length: 50-250 words. **Does not pay for fillers.**

**Tips:** "Follow guidelines and present a professional package. We are willing to work with new and unpublished writers in most areas. All manuscripts must be in standard format. We are always looking for new or unusual angles on old science fiction shows/films, conventions, costumes, fx and people in the business. Articles from interviews must have sparkle and be interesting to a variety of readers. Absolutely no gossip or fluff. Anyone sending a disposable manuscript can simply include their e-mail address instead of a SASE for reply."

**$ THE URBANITE, Surreal & Lively & Bizarre**, Urban Legend Press, P.O. Box 4737, Davenport IA 52808. Website: http://members.tripod.com/theurbanite/. **Contact:** Mark McLaughlin, editor. **95% freelance written.** Triannual magazine covering surreal fiction and poetry. "We look for quality fiction with a surrealistic tone. . . . We prefer character-driven storylines. Our audience is urbane, culture-oriented, and hard to please!" Estab. 1991. Circ. 1,000. **Pays on acceptance.** Contributors to recent issues include Thomas Ligotti, Basil Copper, Caitlin Kiernan, John Pelan and Pamela Briggs. Publishes ms an average of 6 months after acceptance. Byline given. Buys first North American serial rights or second serial (reprint) rights and non-exclusive rights for public readings. "We hold readings of the magazine at various venues—like arts centers, literary conventions and libraries." Editorial leadtime 6 months. Reports in 1 month on queries; 2 months on mss. Sample copy for $5. Writer's guidelines for #10 SASE.

● Fiction from the magazine has been reprinted in *The Year's Best Fantasy and Horror* and England's *Best New Horror,* and a poem in *The Year's Best Fantastic Fiction.* The magazine has been nominated for the International Horror Guild Award.

**Nonfiction:** Essays, humor, interview/profile. Each issue has a theme. We don't publish recipes, fishing tips or music/CD reviews." **Buys up to 6 mss/year.** Query. Length: 500-3,000 words. **Pays $15-90 for assigned articles; $10-60 for unsolicited articles.**

**Reprints:** Accepts previously published submissions (but query first). Send typed ms with rights for sale noted and information about when and where the article previously appeared. Pays 100% of amount paid for an original article.

**Columns/Departments:** "We haven't run any columns, but would like to. Unfortunately, we haven't seen any queries that really thrill us." **Pays $15-90.**

**Fiction:** Experimental, fantasy (contemporary), horror, humorous, science fiction (but not "high-tech"), slipstream/cross genre, surrealism of all sorts. Upcoming theme: No. 12: The Zodiac. **Buys 54 mss/year.** Send complete ms. Length: 500-3,000 words. We do publish longer works, up to 10,000 words—but query first. **Pays $10-300 (2-3¢/word).** Publishes novel excerpts. Each issue has a Featured Writer, who receives 3¢/word, 10 contributor copies, and a lifetime subscription to the magazine.

● Ranked as one of the best markets for fiction writers in *Writer's Digest* magazine's "Fiction 50," June 1999.

**Poetry:** Avant-garde, free verse, traditional, narrative poetry. No haiku or light verse. **Buys 18 poems/year.** Submit maximum 3 poems. Length: up to 2 ms pages. **Pays $10/poem.** Each issue has a featured poet who receives 10 contributor copies.

**Tips:** "Writers should familiarize themselves with surrealism in literature: too often, we receive stories filled with genre clichés. Also: we prefer character-driven stories.We're looking to add nonfiction (at the same pay rate—2-3¢/word—as fiction). Reviews, articles, cultural commentary . . . the more unusual, the better. Don't just write because you want to see your name in print. Write because you have something to say."

**$ WICKED MYSTIC MAGAZINE,** FTWS Press, 532 La Guardia Place, #371, New York NY 10012. (718)638-1533. E-mail: wickedmyst@aol.com. Website: http://www.wickedmystic.com. **Contact:** Andre Scheluchin, editor. **90% freelance written.** Quarterly literary magazine featuring extreme, cutting-edge horror fiction and nonfiction. Estab. 1990. Circ. 10,000. Pays on publication. Publishes ms an average of 6 months after acceptance. Byline given. Buys first North American serial rights. Editorial lead time 2 months. Submit seasonal material 2 months in advance. Reports in 2 weeks on queries; 4 months on mss. Sample copy for $5.95. Writer's guidelines for #10 SASE.

**Nonfiction:** Book excerpts, essays, general interest, how-to, humor, inspirational, interview/profile, new product, opinion, personal experience, photo feature. **Buys 10 mss/year.** Send complete ms. Length: 500-4,000 words. **Pays 1¼¢/word.** Sometimes pays expenses of writers on assignment.

**Photos:** Send photos with submission. Reviews prints. Negotiates payment individually. Buys one-time rights.

**Columns/Departments:** Horror-related book, music, event reviews, all 2,000 words. **Buys 4 mss/year.** Send complete ms. **Pays 1¼¢/word.**

**Fiction:** Adventure, erotica, experimental, fantasy, horror, science fiction, suspense, novel excerpts. No mainstream fiction. **Buys 35 mss/year.** Send complete ms. Length: 500-4,000 words. **Pays 1¼¢/word.**

**Poetry:** Avant-garde, free verse, haiku, light verse, traditional. No rhyming poetry. **Buys 40 poems/year.** Submit maximum 5 poems. Length: 4-40 lines. **Pays $5-20.**

**Fillers:** Anecdotes, facts, gags to be illustrated by cartoonist, newsbreaks, short humor. **Buys 10/year.** Length: 1-75 words. **Pays $5-20.**

**Tips:** "We're not mainstream, not traditional. We need shock, twists and extremes."

# SEX

Magazines featuring pictorial layouts accompanied by stories and articles of a sexual nature, both gay and straight, are listed in this section. Dating and single lifestyle magazines appear in the Relationships section. Other markets for articles relating to sex can be found in the Men's and Women's sections.

**N ✕ $ BUMP & GRIND,** Full Deck Productions, P.O. Box 625, West Redding CT 06896. (203)744-6010. Fax: (203)794-0008. Send submissions to: Full Deck Productions, P.O. Box 893, Hudson PQ J0P 1H0 Canada. Editor: John Todds. **Contact:** Robert Lafave, publisher/managing editor. **100% freelance written.** Monthly men's magazine covering "hard-core, anything goes (not an anal title), very dirty and lusty. All Full Deck Productions titles deal with hardcore sex." Estab. 1996. Circ. 40,000. Pays on 60 day terms. Publishes ms an average of 3 months after acceptance. Byline sometimes given. Buys all rights. Editorial lead time 3 months. Accepts queries by mail, e-mail, fax, phone. Accepts simultaneous submissions. Sample copy for $5 US per issue. Writer's guidelines for #10 SASE or by e-mail.

**Fiction:** "We will not accept anything to do with violence, children, non-consenting sex or degradation." **Buys 64 mss/year.** Send complete ms. Length: 1,300-2,000 words. **Pays $15-20.**

**Tips:** See *Sticky Buns*.

**N** ✖ **$ BUTTIME STORIES**, Full Deck Productions, P.O. Box 625, West Redding CT 06896. (203)744-6010. Fax: (203)794-0008. Send submissions to: Full Deck Productions, P.O. Box 893, Hudson PQ J0P 1H0 Canada. Website: http://www.fulldeck@total.net. Editor: John Todds. **Contact:** Robert Lafave, publisher/managing editor. **100% freelance written.** Monthly men's magazine covering anal adventure. "All Full Deck Productions titles deal with hardcore sex." Estab. 1996. Circ. 40,000. Pays on 60 day terms. Publishes ms an average of 3 months after acceptance. Byline sometimes given. Buys all rights. Editorial lead time 3 months. Accepts queries by mail, e-mail, fax, phone. Accepts simultaneous submissions. Sample copy for $5 US per issue. Writer's guidelines for #10 SASE or by e-mail.

**Fiction:** "We will not accept anything to do with violence, children, non-consenting sex or degradation." **Buys 64 mss/year.** Send complete ms. Length: 1,300-2,000 words. **Pays $15-20.**

**Tips:** See *Sticky Buns*.

**N** ✖ **$ CHEATERS CLUB**, Full Deck Productions, P.O. Box 625, West Redding CT 06896. (203)744-6010. Fax: (203)794-0008. Send submissions to: Full Deck Productions, P.O. Box 893, Hudson PQ J0P 1H0 Canada. Website: http://www.fulldeck@total.net. Editor: John Todds. **Contact:** Robert Lafave, publisher/managing editor. **100% freelance written.** Monthly men's magazine covering "swingers, lesbians, couples who invite others to join them; threesomes, foursomes and moresomes." "All Full Deck Productions titles deal with hardcore sex." Estab. 1996. Circ. 40,000. Pays on 60 day terms. Publishes ms an average of 3 months after acceptance. Byline sometimes given. Buys all rights. Editorial lead time 3 months. Accepts queries by mail, e-mail, fax, phone. Accepts simultaneous submissions. Sample copy for $5 US per issue. Writer's guidelines for #10 SASE or by e-mail.

**Fiction:** "We will not accept anything to do with violence, children, non-consenting sex or degradation." **Buys 64 mss/year.** Send complete ms. Length: 1,300-2,000 words. **Pays $15-20.**

**Tips:** See *Sticky Buns*.

**N** **$ $ DRUMMER**, Desmodus, Inc., P.O. Box 410390, San Francisco CA 94141-0390. (415)252-1195. Fax: (415)252-9574. E-mail: drummhq@slip.net. **Contact:** Robert Davolt, editor/publisher. **30% freelance written.** Monthly magazine of "erotic aspects of leather and other masculine fetishes for gay men." Estab. 1975. Circ. 45,000. Byline given. Buys first North American serial rights or makes work-for-hire assignments. Written queries only. No response on unsolicited submissions. Accepts queries by mail. Sample copy for $10. Writer's guidelines for #10 SASE.

**Nonfiction:** Book excerpts, essays, historical/nostalgic, how-to, humor, interview/profile, new product, opinion, personal experience, photo feature, technical, travel. No feminine-slanted or heterosexual pieces. **Buys 15 mss/year.** Query with or without published clips, or send complete ms. Length: 1,000-15,000 words. **Pays $50-100 for assigned articles; $50-100 for unsolicited articles.**

**Photos:** Send photocopies with submission. Reviews contact sheets and transparencies. Offers $25-50/photo. Model releases, all Title 18 ID and proof of age required. Buys one-time rights on all rights.

**Fiction:** Adventure, erotica, ethnic, fantasy, historical, horror, humorous, mystery, novel excerpts, science fiction, slice-of-life vignettes, suspense, western. Must have gay "macho" erotic elements. **Buys 20-30 mss/year.** Send complete ms. Length: 1,000-7,000 words. Occasionally serializes stories. **Pays $50-100.**

🖳 The online magazine carries original content not found in the print edition.

**Tips:** "*Drummer* is a hardcore raunch magazine for gay men. Keep that in mind and you're in the ballpark."

**$ $ EXOTIC MAGAZINE**, X Publishing, 625 SW 10th Ave. #324, Portland OR 97205. Fax: (503)241-7239. E-mail: xmag@teleport.com. **Contact:** Gary Aker or 1095 Market St., Suite 409, San Francisco CA 94103. (415)252-1322. E-mail: xmagaix.netcom.com. **Contact:** Bob Armstrong. Monthly magazine covering adult entertainment, sexuality. "*Exotic* is pro-sex, informative, amusing, mature, intelligent. Our readers rent and/or buy adult videos, visit strip clubs and are interested in topics related to the adult entertainment industry and sexuality/culture. Don't talk down to them or fire too far over their heads. Many readers are computer literate and well-traveled. We're also interested in insightful fetish material. We are not a 'hard core' publication." Estab. 1993. Circ. 120,000. Pays 30 days after publication. Byline given. Buys first North American serial rights; and on-line rights; may negotiate second serial (reprint) rights. Accepts simultaneous submissions. Accepts queries by mail, e-mail, fax. Reports in 2 weeks on queries; 2 months on mss. Sample copy for 9 × 12 SASE and 5 first-class stamps. Writer's guidelines for #10 SASE.

○─ Break in by "living in Seattle, Portland or San Francisco so you can report on what's happening (with query list) in our areas of distribution. Really good cartoons, unsolicited, have an outside chance."

**Nonfiction:** Exposé, general interest, historical/nostalgic, how-to, humor, interview/profile, travel, news. No "men writing as women, articles about being a horny guy, opinion pieces pretending to be fact pieces." **Buys 36 mss/year.** Send complete ms. Length: 1,000-1,800 words. **Pays 10¢/word up to $150.**

**Reprints:** Send typed ms with rights for sale noted and information about when and where the article previously appeared. Pays 100% of amount paid for an original article.

**Photos:** Rarely buys photos. Most provided by staff. Reviews prints. Negotiates payment individually. Model releases required.

**Fiction:** We are currently overwhelmed with fiction submissions. Please only send fiction if it's really amazing. Erotica, slice-of-life vignettes. (Must present either erotic element or some "vice" of modern culture, such as gambling, music, dancing). Send complete ms. Length: 1,000-1,800 words. **Pays 10¢/word up to $150.**

**Tips:** "Read adult publications, spend time in the clubs doing more than just tipping and drinking. Look for new insights in adult topics. For the industry to continue to improve, those who cover it must also be educated consumers and affiliates. Please type, spell-check and be realistic about how much time the editor can take 'fixing' your manuscript."

**$ $ $ $ FOX MAGAZINE**, Montcalm Publishing, 401 Park Ave. S., New York NY 10016-8802. (212)779-8900. Fax: (212)725-7215. Website: http://www.gallerymagazine.com. Editorial Director: Will Romano. Managing Editor: Rich Friedman. **50% freelance written.** Prefers to work with published/established writers. Monthly magazine "focusing on features of interest to the young American man." Estab. 1982. Circ. 300,000. Pays on publication. Byline given. Offers 25% kill fee. Buys first North American serial rights or makes work-for-hire assignments. Submit seasonal material 6 months in advance. Reports in 1 month on queries; 2 months on mss. Sample copy for $8.95 (add $2 for Canadian and foreign orders). Writers' guidelines for #10 SASE.

**Nonfiction:** Investigative pieces of notable figures in adult entertainment, sex advice, porn star/stripper profiles, XXX video reviews, swinger convention news. **Buys 4-5 mss/year.** Query or send complete ms. Length: 1,500-5,000 words. **Pays $300-1,500.** "Special prices negotiated." Sometimes pays expenses of writers on assignment.

**Reprints:** Send tearsheet or photocopy of article or short story or typed ms with rights for sale noted and information about when and where the article previously appeared. Pays 25% of amount paid for an original article.

**Photos:** Send photos with accompanying ms. Pay varies. Reviews b&w or color contact sheets and negatives. Buys one-time rights. Captions preferred; model releases and photo IDs required.

**Fiction:** Erotica only (special guidelines available). **Buys 1 ms/issue.** Send complete ms. Length: 1,000-3,000 words. **Pays $350-500.**

**$ $ $ $ GALLERY MAGAZINE**, Montcalm Publishing Corp., 401 Park Ave. S., New York NY 10016-8802. (212)779-8900. Fax: (212)725-7215. Managing Editor: Rich Friedman. **Contact:** Will Romano, editorial director. **50% freelance written.** Prefers to work with published/established writers. Monthly magazine "focusing on features of interest to the young American man. *Gallery* is a magazine aimed at entertaining and educating the contemporary man. *Gallery* covers political, cultural, and social trends on a national and global level through serious and provocative investigative reports, candid interviews, human-interest features, service-oriented articles, fiction, erotica, humor and photographic portfolios of beautiful women. Each issue of *Gallery* contains our 'Heroes' feature, a first-person account of the effects of the Vietnam War, 'Toys for Men' service feature; and columns dealing with travel, entertainment news, automotives, health and fitness, and outdoor leisure activities." Estab. 1972. Circ. 500,000. Pays on publication. Byline given. Pays 25% kill fee. Buys first North American serial rights or makes work-for-hire assignments. Submit seasonal material 6 months in advance. Reports in 1 month on queries; 2 months on mss. Back issue for $8.95 (add $2 for Canadian and foreign orders). Writer's guidelines for SASE.

• *Gallery* works on Macintosh, so it accepts material on Mac or compatible disks if accompanied by hard copy.

**Nonfiction:** Investigative pieces, general interest, how-to, humor, interview, new products, profile. **Buys 4-5 mss/issue.** Query or send complete mss. Length: 1,500-3,500 words. **Pays $1,500-2,500.** "Special prices negotiated." Sometimes pays expenses of writers on assignment.

**Reprints:** Send tearsheet, photocopy or typed ms of article or story with rights for sale noted and information about when and where the article previously appeared. Pays 25% of amount paid for an original article.

**Photos:** Send photos with accompanying mss. Pay varies for b&w or color contact sheets and negatives. Buys one-time rights. Captions preferred; model release, photo ID required.

**Fiction:** Erotica only (special guidelines available). **Buys 1 ms/issue.** Send complete ms. Length: 1,000-3,000 words. **Pays $350-500.**

**$ $ GENESIS**, Magna Publications, 210 Route 4 E., Suite 401, Paramus NJ 07652. (201)843-4004. Fax: (201)843-8636. E-mail: genesismag@aol.com. Website: www.genesismagazine.com. Editor: Paul Gambino. **Contact:** Dan Davis, managing editor. **85% freelance written.** "Monthly men's sophisticate with celebrity interviews, erotic and non-erotic fiction, exposé, product and media reviews, lifestyle pieces." Estab. 1974. Circ. 450,000. Pays on publication. Publishes ms an average of 3 months after acceptance. Byline given. Offers 50% kill fee. Buys first or second serial (reprint) rights. Editorial lead time 4 months. Submit seasonal material 6 months in advance. Accepts simultaneous submissions. Reports in 1 month on queries; 2 months on mss. Sample copy for $6.99. Writer's guidelines for #10 SASE.

**Nonfiction:** Exposé, general interest, how-to, humor, interview/profile, new product, personal experience, photo feature, film, music, book, etc., reviews, lifestyle pieces. "No investigative articles not backed up by facts." **Buys 24 mss/yr.** Send complete ms. Length: 150-2,500 words. **Pays 22¢/word.** Sometimes pays expenses of writers on assignment.

**Reprints:** Send tearsheet, photocopy of article or typed ms with rights for sale noted with information about when and where the article previously appeared. Pays 50% of amount paid for an original article.

**Photos:** State availability of photos with submission. Reviews 4×5 transparencies, 8×10 prints, slides. Negotiates payment individually. Captions, model releases and identification of subjects required. Buys first/exclusive rights.

**Columns/Departments:** Film/video/B movies (interviews, sidebars), music, books, consumer products, all 150-500 words. **Buys 30 mss/year.** Query with published clips or send complete ms. Length: 2,500-3,500. **Pays 22¢/word.**

**Fiction:** Adventure, confession, erotica, fantasy, horror, humorous, mainstream, mystery, romance, science fiction, slice

of life vignettes, suspense. Publishes novel excerpts. **Buys 24 mss/year.** Query or send complete ms. Length: 2,500-3,500 words. **Pays $500.**
**Fillers:** Anecdotes, facts, newsbreaks, short humor. **Buys 24/year.** Length: 25-500 words. **Pays 22¢/word, $50 min.**
**Tips:** "Be patient, original and detail-oriented."

■ **$ $ GENT, "Home of the D-Cups,"** Firestone Publishing, Inc., 14411 Commerce Way, Suite 420, Miami Lakes FL 33016. Fax: (305)362-3120. E-mail: jack@dugent.com. Website: http://www.sexmags.com. **Contact:** Fritz Bailey, articles editor **50% freelance written.** Monthly men's sophisticate magazine with emphasis on big breasts. Estab. 1960. Circ. 150,000. Pays on publication. Byline given. Buys first North American serial and electronic rights. Editorial turnaround time 6 months. Submit seasonal material 6 months in advance. Sample copy for $7. Writer's guidelines for #10 SASE.
**Nonfiction:** How-to ("anything sexually related"), personal experience ("any and all sexually related matters"). **Buys 6-12 mss/year.** Query. Length: 1,000-2,500 words. **Pays $150.**
**Photos:** Send photos with submission. Reviews 35mm transparencies. Negotiates payment individually. Model releases and identification of subjects required. Buys first North American and second rights.
**Fiction:** Erotica, fantasy. **Buys 13 mss/year.** Send complete ms. Length: 2,500 words. **Pays $200.**
**Tips:** "An easy smooth read full of graphic sexual content involving women with big breasts. Fiction and letters!"

■ **$ $ GUYS,** First Hand Ltd., P.O. Box 1314, Teaneck NJ 07666-3441. (201)836-9177. Fax: (201)836-5055. E-mail: firsthand3@aol.com. **Contact:** William Spencer, editor. **80% freelance written.** Bimonthly magazine of erotica for gay men. "A positive, romantic approach to gay sex." Estab. 1988. Circ. 100,000. Pays on publication. Publishes ms an average of 1 year after acceptance. Byline given. Buys first North American serial or all rights. Accepts queries by mail, e-mail, fax. Reports in 6 months. Sample copy for $5.50. Writer's guidelines for #10 SASE.
**Fiction:** Erotica. **Buys 72 mss/year.** Send complete ms. Length: 1,000-10,000 words. **Pays $75-250.**
**Tips:** "We publish gay erotica—the hotter the better—if it's also well-written, it's in."

**$ $ $ $ HUSTLER,** HG Inc., 8484 Wilshire Blvd., Suite 900, Beverly Hills CA 90211. Fax: (213)651-2741. E-mail: dbuchbinder@lfp.com. Website: http://www.hustler.com. Editor: Allan MacDonell. **Contact:** David Buchbinder, features editor. **60% freelance written.** Magazine published 13 times/year. "*Hustler* is the no-nonsense men's magazine. Our audience does not need to be told whether to wear their trousers cuffed or plain. The *Hustler* reader expects honest, unflinching looks at hard topics—sexual, social, political, personality profile, true crime." Estab. 1974. Circ. 750,000. Pays as boards ship to printer. Publishes ms an average of 3 months after acceptance. Byline given. Offers 20% kill fee. Buys all rights. Editorial lead time 4 months. Submit seasonal material 6 months in advance. Query by mail, e-mail, fax. Reports in 2 weeks on queries; 1 month on mss. Writer's guidelines for #10 SASE.
● *Hustler* is most interested in profiles of dynamic ground-breaking, indomitable individuals who don't mind "flipping a bird" at the world in general.
**Nonfiction:** Book excerpts, exposé, general interest, how-to, interview/profile, personal experience, trends. **Buys 30 mss/year.** Query. Length: 3,500-4,000 words. **Pays $1,500.** Sometimes pays expenses of writers on assignment.
**Columns/Departments:** Sex Play (some aspect of sex that can be encapsulated in a limited space), 2,500 words. **Buys 13 mss/year.** Send complete ms. **Pays $750.**
**Fiction:** "Difficult fiction market. Must have two sex scenes; yet not be rote or boring." Publishes novel excerpts. **Buys 2 mss/year.** Send complete ms. Length: 3,000-3,500. **Pays $1,000.**
**Fillers: Pays $50-100.** Jokes and "Graffilthy," bathroom-wall humor.
**Tips:** "Don't try and mimic the *Hustler* style. If a writer needs to be molded into our voice, we'll do a better job of it than he or she will."

**$ HUSTLER BUSTY BEAUTIES, America's Breast Magazine,** HG Publications, Inc., 8484 Wilshire Blvd., Suite 900, Beverly Hills CA 90211. (213)651-5400. Fax: (213)651-2741. E-mail: busty@lfp.com. Website: http://www.bustybeauty.com. **Contact:** N. Morgen Hagen, associate publisher. **40% freelance written.** Men's monthly sophisticate magazine. "*Hustler Busty Beauties* is an adult title that showcases attractive large-breasted women with accompanying erotic fiction, reader letters, humor." Estab. 1974. Circ. 180,000. Pays on publication. Publishes ms an average of 6 months after acceptance. Byline given. Buys all rights. Accepts queries by mail, e-mail, fax. Reports in 1 month. Sample copy for $6 and 9×12 SAE. Free writer's guidelines.
**Columns/Departments:** LewDDD Letters (erotic experiences involving large-breasted women from first-person point-of-view), 500-1,000 words. **Buys 24-36 mss year.** Send complete ms. **Pays $50-75.**
**Fiction:** Adventure, erotica, fantasy, humorous, mystery, science fiction, suspense. "No violent stories or stories without a bosomy female character." **Buys 13 mss year.** Send complete ms. Length: 750-2,500 words. **Pays $250-500.**
**Jokes:** Appropriate for audience. **Pays $10-25.**

■ **$ IN TOUCH/INDULGE FOR MEN,** In Touch International, Inc., 13122 Saticoy St., North Hollywood CA 91605-3402. (818)764-2288. Fax: (818)764-2307. E-mail: alan@intouchformen.com. Website: http://www.intouchformen.com. **Contact:** Alan W. Mills, editor. **80% freelance written.** Works with a small number of new/unpublished writers each year. Monthly magazine covering the gay male lifestyle, gay male humor and erotica. Estab. 1973. Circ. 70,000. Pays on publication. Byline given, pseudonym OK. Buys one-time rights. Accepts simultaneous submissions. Accepts queries by mail, e-mail, fax. Reports in 2 months. Sample copy for $6.95. Writer's guidelines for #10 SASE or on website.

**Nonfiction: Rarely buys nonfiction.** Send complete ms. Length: 3,000-3,500 words. **Pays $25-75.**

**Photos:** Send photos with submission. Reviews contact sheets, transparencies, prints. Offers $25/photo. Captions, model releases, identification of subjects required. Buys one-time rights.

**Fiction:** Gay male erotica. **Buys 82 mss/year.** Send complete ms. Length: 3,000-3,500 words. **Pays $75 maximum.**

**Fillers:** Short humor. **Buys 12/year.** Length: 1,500-2,500 words. **Pays $25-50.**

The online magazine carries original content not found in the print edition and includes writer's guidelines.

**Tips:** "Our publications feature male nude photos plus three fiction pieces, several articles, cartoons, humorous comments on items from the media, photo features. We try to present positive aspects of the gay lifestyle, with an emphasis on humor. Humorous pieces may be erotic in nature. We are open to all submissions that fit our gay male format; the emphasis, however, is on humor and the upbeat. We receive many fiction manuscripts but not nearly enough unique, innovative, or even experimental material."

**N $ KEY CLUB,** Full Deck Productions, P.O. Box 625, West Redding CT 06896. (203)744-6010. Fax: (203)794-0008. Send submissions to: Full Deck Productions, P.O. Box 893, Hudson PQ J0P 1H0 Canada. Editor: John Todds. **Contact:** Robert Lafave, publisher, managing editor. **100% freelance written.** Monthly men's magazine covering "first time anal virgins, new partners, new toys, new experiences. All Full Deck Productions titles deal with hardcore sex." Estab. 1996. Circ. 40,000. Pays on 60 day terms. Publishes ms an average of 3 months after acceptance. Byline sometimes given. Buys all rights. Editorial lead time 3 months. Accepts queries by mail, e-mail, fax, phone. Accepts simultaneous submissions. Sample copy for $5 US per issue. Writer's guidelines for #10 SASE.

**Fiction:** Erotica. "We will not accept anything to do with violence, children, non-consenting sex or degradation." **Buys 64 mss/year.** Send complete ms. Length: 1,300-2,000 words. **Pays $15-20.**

**Tips:** See *Sticky Buns.*

**$ $ NUGGET,** Dugent Corp., 14411 Commerce Way, Suite 420, Miami Lakes FL 33016-1598. Fax: (305)362-3120. E-mail: editor-nugget@dugent.com. Website: http://www.dugent.com/nug/. Managing Editor: Nye Willden. **Contact:** Christopher James, editor-in-chief. **100% freelance written.** Monthly magazine covering fetish and kink. "*Nugget* is a one-of-a-kind publication which appeals to daring, open-minded adults who enjoy all forms of both kinky, alternative sex (catfighting, transvestism, fetishism, bi-sexuality, etc.) and conventional sex." Estab. 1960. Circ. 100,000. Pays on publication. Publishes ms an average of 1 year after acceptance. Byline given. Buys first North American serial rights. Editorial lead time 5 months. Submit seasonal material 1 year in advance. Accepts simultaneous submissions. Reports in 2 weeks on queries; 2 months on mss. Sample copy for $5. Writer's guidelines free.

**Nonfiction:** Interview/profile, sexual matters/trends (fetish and kink angle). **Buys 8 mss/year.** Query. Length: 2,000-3,000 words. **Pays $200 minimum.**

**Photos:** Send photos with submission. Reviews transparencies. Offers no additional payment for photos accepted with ms. Model releases required. Buys one-time second rights.

**Fiction:** Erotica, fantasy. **Buys 20 mss/year.** Send complete ms. Length: 2,000-3,000 words. **Pays $200-250.**

**Tips:** Most open to fiction submissions. (Follow guidelines for suitable topics.)

**$ OPTIONS,** AJA Publishing, P.O. Box 170, Irvington NY 10533. E-mail: dianaeditr@aol.com. Editor: Don Stone. **Contact:** Diana Sheridan, associate editor. Mostly freelance written. Sexually explicit magazine for and about bisexuals and to a lesser extent homosexuals, published 10 times/year. "Articles, stories and letters about bisexuality. Positive approach. Safe-sex encounters unless the story clearly pre-dates the AIDS situation." Estab. 1977. Circ. 100,000. Pays on publication. Publishes mss an average of 10 months after acceptance. Byline given, usually pseudonymous. Buys all rights. Buys almost no seasonal material. Accepts queries by mail, e-mail. Reports in 3 weeks. Sample copy for $2.95 and 6×9 SAE with 5 first-class stamps. Writer's guidelines for SASE.

**Nonfiction:** Essays (occasional), how-to, humor, interview/profile, opinion, personal experience (especially). All must be bisexually or gay related. Does not want "anything not bisexually/gay related, anything negative, anything opposed to safe sex, anything dry/boring/ponderous/pedantic. Write even serious topics informally if not lightly." **Buys 10 nonfiction mss/year.** Send complete ms. Length: 2,000-3,000. **Pays $100.**

**Photos:** Reviews transparencies and prints. Pays $20 for b&w photos; $200 for full color. Color or b&w sets $150. Previously published photos acceptable.

**Fiction:** "We don't usually get enough true first-person stories and need to buy some from writers. They must be bisexual, usually man/man, hot and believable. They must not read like fiction." **Buys 60 fiction mss/year.** Send complete ms. Length: 2,000-3,000. **Pays $100.**

**Tips:** "We use many more male/male pieces than female/female. Use only one serious article per issue. A serious/humorous approach is good here, but only if it's natural to you; don't make an effort for it. No longer buying 'letters'. We get enough real ones."

**N $ STICKY BUNS,** Full Deck Productions, P.O. Box 625, West Redding CT 06896. (203)744-6010. Fax: (203)794-0008. Send submissions to: Full Deck Productions, P.O. Box 893, Hudson PQ J0P 1H0 Canada. Editor: John Todds. **Contact:** Robert Lafave, publisher, managing editor. **100% freelance written.** Monthly men's magazine covering "the anal fetish as well as S&M and bondage. All Full Deck Productions titles deal with hardcore sex." Estab. 1996.

Circ. 40,000. Pays on 60 day terms. Publishes ms an average of 3 months after acceptance. Byline sometimes given. Buys all rights. Editorial lead time 3 months. Accepts queries by mail, e-mail, fax, phone. Accepts simultaneous submissions. Sample copy for $5 US per issue. Writer's guidelines for #10 SASE.

**Fiction:** Looking for "anal adventures; very sticky, lots of wet descriptions, oils, etc. We will not accept anything to do with violence, children, non-consenting sex or degradation." **Buys 64 mss/year.** Send complete ms. Length: 1,300-2,000 words. **Pays $15-20.**

**Tips:** "Story length should not exceed 2,000 words. Cut the introduction—get straight to the sex. Stories of 800-1,200 words are needed; send three of these stories to each one longer title. Open with a bang—is it interesting? Does it excite the reader? Be very descriptive and very graphic, but not violent. Be explicitly descriptive. We want to smell leather, taste the skin, and feel the action as it takes place. But the sex must be enjoyable for all participants; nobody does anything in these stories against their will."

**⃞ $ $SUCCULENT**, Swank Publications, 210 Route 4 East, Suite 401, Paramus NJ 07652-5116. Fax: (201)843-8636. E-mail: sexeditor@aol.com. **Contact:** Bob Rosen, editor. **50% freelance written.** Quarterly magazine covering beautiful women with large natural breasts. "*Succulent* is an erotic celebration of the natural breast. The writing is fun, literate, informative and sexy. Our audience is men of all ages and all types of careers who appreciate our unique perspective on sexuality." Estab. 1998. Circ. 30,000. Pays on publication. Publishes ms an average of 6 months after acceptance. Byline given. Buys all rights. Editorial lead time 4 months. Accepts queries by mail, e-mail. Accepts simultaneous submissions. Reports in 6 weeks. Sample copy for $7. Writer's guidelines for #10 SASE.

**Nonfiction:** Essays, historical/nostalgic, humor, interview/profile, opinion, personal experience, photo feature. "Read the magazine. It's obvious what we want." **Buys 4 mss/year.** Send complete ms. Length: 2,500-2,800 words. **Pays $200-250.** Sometimes pays expenses of writers on assignment.

**Photos:** Send photos with submission. Reviews contact sheets and transparencies. Negotiates payment individually. Captions, model releases and identification of subjects required. Buys 3 uses per year.

**Fiction:** Erotica. **Buys varing number of mss/year.** Send complete ms. Length: 2,500-2,800 words. **Pays $200-250.**

**◆ $ $SWANK**, Swank Publications, 210 Route 4 E., Suite 401, Paramus NJ 07652. (201)843-4004. Fax: (201)843-8636. Website: www.swank.com. Editor: Paul Gambino. **Contact:** Odette Diaz, associate editor. **75% freelance written.** Works with new/unpublished writers. Monthly magazine on "sex and sensationalism, lurid. High quality adult erotic entertainment." Audience of men ages 18-38, high school and some college education, medium income, skilled blue-collar professionals, union men, some white-collar. Estab. 1954. Circ. 400,000. Pays on publication. Publishes ms an average of 4 months after acceptance. Byline given, pseudonym if wanted. Buys first North American serial rights. Submit seasonal material 6 months in advance. Reports in 3 weeks on queries; 1 month on mss. Sample copy for $6.95. Writer's guidelines for SASE.

• *Swank* reports a need for more nonfiction, non-sex-related articles.

**Nonfiction:** Exposé (researched), adventure must be accompanied by color photographs. "We buy articles on sex-related topics, which don't need to be accompanied by photos." Interested in unusual lifestyle pieces. How-to, interviews with entertainment, sports and sex industry celebrities. Buys photo pieces on autos, action, adventure. **Buys 34 mss/year.** Query with or without published clips. **Pays $350-500.** Sometimes pays the expenses of writers on assignment. "It is strongly recommended that a sample copy is reviewed before submitting material."

**Reprints:** Send photocopy or article or short story or typed ms with rights for sale noted and information and when and where the article previously appeared. Pays 50% of amount paid for an original article.

**Photos:** Alex Suarez, art director. "Articles have a much better chance of being purchased if you have accompanying photos." Model releases required.

**Fiction:** Publishes novel excerpts. "We will consider stories that are not strictly sexual in theme (humor, adventure, detective stories, etc.) However, these types of stories are much more likely to be considered if they portray some sexual element, or scene, within their context."

**⃞ $ $WHAP! MAGAZINE, The Modern Gal's Guide to Marital Bliss**, Retro Systems, P.O. Box 69491, Los Angeles CA 90069. Phone/fax: (323)653-9427. E-mail: retrosys@wenet.net. Website: http://www.whapmag.com. Managing Editor: Mark Portier. **Contact:** Keri Pentauk, editor. **25% freelance written.** Quarterly magazine covering relationships, marriage, sex. "*Whap! Magazine* is a faux post-war women's magazine that combines feminism, fetishism and fun! We believe that gals should rule the roost and that there should be trouble, otherwise!" Estab. 1994. Circ. 27,400. Pays on publication. Publishes ms an average of 6 months after acceptance. Byline sometimes given. Offers 50% kill fee. Buys all rights. Editorial lead time 3-6 months. Accepts queries by mail, e-mail, fax. Accepts simultaneous submissions. Reports in 1 month on queries; 3 months on mss. Sample copy for $7.95 or online at website. Writer's guidelines for #10 SASE or online at website.

**Nonfiction:** Essays, exposé, general interest, historical/nostalgic, how-to (ways to make husbands more obedient and responsive to their wives), interview/profile, personal experience, photo feature. "No mistress/slave jargon; overheated mind trips; impractical ideas." **Buys 15-20 mss/year.** Query. Length: 1,000-2,000 words. **Pays $50-250.** Sometimes pays with back issues or "items from our catalog if requested."

**Photos:** State availability of photos with submission. Reviews contact sheets and 4×6 prints. Negotiates payment individually. Model releases required.

**Fiction:** Confession, erotica, historical, slice-of-life vignettes. "No vulgar or overtly violent situations." **Buys 3-6 mss/year.** Query. Length: 1,000-2,000 words. **Pays $50-250.**

**Tips:** "Go to our website, study our magazine and come up with a winning new slant guaranteed to appeal to a contemporary, mostly female readership."

**N** ✖ **$ WICKED FETISHES**, Full Deck Productions, P.O. Box 625, West Redding CT 06896. (203)744-6010. Fax: (203)794-0008. Send submissions to: Full Deck Productions, P.O. Box 893, Hudson PQ J0P 1H0 Canada. Editor: John Todds. **Contact:** Robert Lafave, publisher/managing editor. **100% freelance written.** "Monthly men's sophisticate" digest covering "fetish, domination/submission, feet, etc.—within the law. All Full Deck Productions titles deal with hardcore sex." Estab. 1996. Circ. 40,000. Pays on 60 day terms. Publishes ms an average of 3 months after acceptance. Byline sometimes given. Buys all rights. Editorial lead time 3 months. Accepts queries by mail, e-mail, fax, phone. Accepts simultaneous submissions. Sample copy for $5 US per issue. Writer's guidelines for #10 SASE.
**Fiction:** "We will not accept anything to do with violence, children, non-consenting sex or degradation." **Buys 64 mss/year.** Send complete ms. Length: 1,300-2,000 words. **Pays $15-20.**
**Tips:** See *Sticky Buns*.

# SPORTS

A variety of sports magazines, from general interest to sports medicine, are covered in this section. For the convenience of writers who specialize in one or two areas of sport and outdoor writing, the publications are subcategorized by the sport or subject matter they emphasize. Publications in related categories (for example, Hunting & Fishing; Archery & Bowhunting) often buy similar material. Writers should read through this entire section to become familiar with the subcategories. Publications on horse breeding and hunting dogs are classified in the Animal section, while horse racing is listed here. Publications dealing with automobile or motorcycle racing can be found in the Automotive & Motorcycle category. Markets interested in articles on exercise and fitness are listed in the Health & Fitness section. Outdoor publications that promote the preservation of nature, placing only secondary emphasis on nature as a setting for sport, are in the Nature, Conservation & Ecology category. Regional magazines are frequently interested in sports material with a local angle. Camping publications are classified in the Travel, Camping & Trailer category.

## Archery & Bowhunting

**$ $ BOWHUNTER, The Number One Bowhunting Magazine**, Primedia Enthusiast Publications, 6405 Flank Dr., Harrisburg PA 17112-8200. (717)657-9555. Fax: (717)657-9552. E-mail: bowhunter@cowles.com. Website: http://www.bowhunter.com. Founder/Editor-in-Chief: M.R. James. **Contact:** Richard Cochran, associate publisher/editorial director. **50% freelance written.** Bimonthly magazine (with three special issues) on hunting big and small game with bow and arrow. "We are a special interest publication, produced by bowhunters for bowhunters, covering all aspects of the sport. Material included in each issue is designed to entertain and inform readers, making them better bowhunters." Estab. 1971. Circ. 185,000. **Pays on acceptance.** Publishes ms an average of 1 year after acceptance. Byline given. Kill fee varies. Buys first North American serial and one-time rights. Submit seasonal material 8 months in advance. Accepts queries by mail, e-mail. Reports in 1 month on queries; 5 weeks on mss. Sample copy for $2. Free writer's guidelines.
**Nonfiction:** General interest, how-to, interview/profile, opinion, personal experience, photo feature. "We publish a special 'Big Game' issue each Fall (September) but need all material by mid-March. Another annual publication, *Whitetail Bowhunter*, is staff written or by assignment only. Our latest special issue is the *Gear Guide*, which highlights the latest in equipment. We don't want articles that graphically deal with an animal's death. And, please, no articles written from the animal's viewpoint." **Buys 60 plus mss/year.** Query. Length: 250-2,000 words. **Pays $500 maximum for assigned articles; $100-400 for unsolicited articles.** Sometimes pays expenses of writers on assignment.
**Photos:** Send photos with submission. Reviews 35mm and 2¼ × 2¼ transparencies and 5 × 7 and 8 × 10 prints. Offers $75-250/photo. Captions required. Buys one-time rights.
**Tips:** "A writer must know bowhunting and be willing to share that knowledge. Writers should anticipate *all* questions a reader might ask, then answer them in the article itself or in an appropriate sidebar. Articles should be written with the reader foremost in mind; we won't be impressed by writers seeking to prove how good they are—either as writers or bowhunters. We care about the reader and don't need writers with 'I' trouble. Features are a good bet because most of our material comes from freelancers. The best advice is: Be yourself. Tell your story the same as if sharing the experience around a campfire. Don't try to write like you think a writer writes."

**$ $ BOWHUNTING WORLD**, Ehlert Publishing Group, Suite 600, 601 Lakeshore Parkway, Minnetonka MN 55305-5215. (612)476-2200. Fax: (612)476-8065. E-mail: mike-s@mail.epginc.com. **Contact:** Mike Strandlund, editor.

**70% freelance written.** Monthly magazine for bowhunting and archery enthusiasts who participate in the sport year-round. Estab. 1951. Circ. 130,000. **Pays on acceptance**. Publishes ms an average of 5 months after acceptance. Byline given. Buys first rights and reprint rights. Accepts queries by mail, e-mail; prefers e-mail queries. *No calls, please!* Reports in 3 weeks on queries, 6 weeks on mss. Sample copy for $3 and 9 × 12 SAE with 10 first-class stamps. Writer's and photographers guidelines for SASE.

**Nonfiction:** How-to articles with creative slants on knowledgeable selection and use of bowhunting equipment and bowhunting methods. Articles must emphasize knowledgeable use of archery or hunting equipment, and/or specific bowhunting techniques. Straight hunting adventure narratives and other types of articles now appear only in special issues. Equipment-oriented articles must demonstrate wise and insightful selection and use of archery equipment and other gear related to the archery sports. Some product-review, field-test, equipment how-to and technical pieces will be purchased. We are not interested in articles whose equipment focuses on random mentioning of brands. Technique-oriented articles most sought are those that briefly cover fundamentals and delve into leading-edge bowhunting or recreational archery methods. Primarily focusing on retail archery and tournament coverage." **Buys 60 mss/year**. Query or send complete ms. Length: 1,500-3,000 words. **Pays $350 to over $500.**

**Photos:** "We are seeking cover photos that depict specific behavioral traits of the more common big game animals (scraping whitetails, bugling elk, etc.) and well-equipped bowhunters in action. Must include return postage."

**Tips:** "Writers are strongly advised to adhere to guidelines and become familiar with our format, as our needs are very specific. Writers are urged to query before sending packages. We prefer detailed outlines of six or so article ideas per query. Assignments are made for the next 18 months."

**$ $ PETERSEN'S BOWHUNTING**, Petersen Publishing Company, L.L.C., 6420 Wilshire Blvd., Los Angeles CA 90048-5515. (323)782-2179. Fax: (323)782-2477. Editor: Jay Michael Strangis. **Contact:** Joe Bell, associate editor. **70% freelance written.** Magazine published 8 times/year covering bowhunting. "Very equipment oriented. Our readers are 'superenthusiasts,' therefore our writers must have an advanced knowledge of hunting archery." Circ. 155,000. **Pays on acceptance.** Byline given. Buys all rights. Editorial lead time 6 months. Submit seasonal material 6 months in advance. Accepts queries by mail. Reports in 1 month. Sample copy for #10 SASE. Writer's guidelines free on request.

**Nonfiction:** How-to, humor, interview/profile, new product, opinion, personal experience, photo feature. **Buys 40 mss/year.** Send complete ms. Length: 2,000 words. **Pays $300.**

**Photos:** Send photos with submission. Reviews contact sheets, 35mm transparencies, 5 × 7 prints. Offers $35-250/photo. Captions and model releases required. Buys one-time rights.

**Columns/Departments:** Query. **Pays $200-300.**

**Fillers:** Facts, newsbreaks. Buys 12/year. Length: 150-400 words. **Pays $25-75.**

**Tips:** Feature articles must be supplied in either 3.50 IBM (or compatible) or 3.50 Mac floppy disks.

# Baseball

**$ $ JUNIOR BASEBALL, America's Youth Baseball Magazine**, (formerly *Junior League Baseball*), 2D Publishing, P.O. Box 9099, Canoga Park CA 91309. (818)710-1234. E-mail: dave@juniorbaseball.com. Website: http://www.juniorbaseball.com. **Contact:** Dave Destler, editor. **25% freelance written.** Bimonthly magazine covering youth baseball. "Focused on youth baseball players ages 7 through 17 (including high school) and their parents/coaches. Edited to various reading levels, depending upon age/skill level of feature." Estab. 1996. Circ. 60,000. Pays on publication. Publishes ms an average of 4 months after acceptance. Byline given. Buys all rights. Editorial lead time 3 months. Submit seasonal material 3 months in advance. Accepts simultaneous submissions. Reports in 2 weeks on queries; 1 month on mss. Sample copy for $5 (also online). Writer's guidelines for #10 SASE.

**Nonfiction:** How-to (skills, tips, features, how to play better baseball, etc.), interview/profile (with major league players; only on assignment), personal experience (from coaches' or parents' perspective).When I Was a Kid (a current Major League Baseball player profile); Leagues, Tournaments (spotlighting a particular youth baseball league, organization, event, tournament); Industry (featuring businesses involved in baseball, e.g., how bats are made); Parents Feature (topics of interest to parents of youth ball players), all 1,000-1,500 words. In the Spotlight (news, events, new products), 50-100 words; League Notebook (news, events, new ideas or tips geared to the parent or league volunteer, adult level), 250-500 words; Hot Prospect (written for the 14-and older competitive player. High school baseball is included, and the focus is on improving the finer points of the game to make the high school team, earn a college scholarship, or attract scouts, written to an adult level), 500-1,000 words. **Buys 6 mss/year.** Query. **Pays $50-100.** "No trite first-person articles about your kid." **Buys 8-12 mss/year.** Query. Length: 500-1,500 words. **Pays 10-20¢/word.**

**Photos:** State availability of or send photos with submission. Reviews 35mm transparencies, 3 × 5 prints. Offers $10-100/photo; negotiates payment individually. Captions and identification of subjects required.

**Tips:** "Must be well-versed in baseball! Having a child who is very involved in the sport, or have extensive hands-on experience in coaching baseball, at the youth, high school or higher level. We can always use accurate, authoritative skills information and good photos to accompany is a big advantage! This magazine is read by experts."

# Basketball

⊠ **$ $ $ SLAM**, Petersen Publications, 1115 Broadway, 8th Floor, New York NY 10010. E-mail: annag@harris-pub.com. Website: http://www.slamonline.com. **Contact**: Anna Gebbie, managing editor. **70% freelance written.** Published 8 times/year covering basketball; sports journalism with a hip-hop sensibility targeting ages 13-24. Estab. 1994. Circ. 200,000. Pays on publication. Publishes ms an average of 3 months after acceptance. Byline given. Offers 25% kill fee. Buys all rights. Writer's guidelines free.
**Nonfiction:** Interview/profile, team story. **Buys 150 mss/year.** Query with published clips. Length: 200-3,000 words. **Pays $100-1,000.** Sometimes pays expenses of writers on assignment.
**Photos:** State availability of photos with submission. Negotiates payment individually. Buys one-time rights.

   ▣   The online magazine carries original content not found in the print edition. Contact: Anna Gebbie, online editor.

**Tips:** "Pitch profiles of unknown players; send queries not manuscripts; do not try to fake a hip-hop sensibility. *Never* contact the editor-in-chief. Story meetings are held every 6-7 weeks at which time all submissions are considered."

# Bicycling

⊠ **ADVENTURE CYCLIST**, Adventure Cycling Assn., Box 8308, Missoula MT 59807. (406)721-1776. Fax: (406)721-8754. E-mail: ddambrosio@adu-cycling.org. Website: http://www.adv-cycling.org. **Contact:** Daniel D'Ambrosio, editor. **75% freelance written.** Bicycle touring magazine for Adventure Cycling Association members published 9 times/year. Estab. 1975. Circ. 30,000. Pays on publication. Byline given. Buys first serial rights. Submit seasonal material 3 months in advance. Sample copy and guidelines for 9 × 12 SAE with 4 first-class stamps.
**Nonfiction:** Features include: U.S. or foreign tour accounts; special focus (on tour experience); how-to; humor; interview/profile; photo feature; technical; travel. **Buys 20-25 mss/year.** Query with published clips or send complete ms; include short bio with ms. Length: 800-2,500 words. Pay negotiable.
**Reprints:** Send photocopy of article.
**Photos:** Color transparencies should accompany tour accounts and profiles. Bicycle, scenery, portraits. State availability of photos. Model releases, identification of subjects required.

**$ CRANKMAIL, Cycling in Northeastern Ohio**, P.O. Box 33249, Cleveland OH 44133-0249. Fax: (440)877-0373. E-mail: editor@crankmail.com. Website: http://www.crankmail.com. **Contact:** James Guilford, editor. Monthly magazine covering bicycling in all aspects. "Our publication serves the interests of bicycle enthusiasts . . . established, accomplished adult cyclists. These individuals are interested in reading about the sport of cycling, bicycles as transportation, ecological tie-ins, sports nutrition, the history and future of bicycles and bicycling." Estab. 1977. Circ. 1,000. Pays on publication. Byline given. Not copyrighted. Buys one-time or second serial (reprint) rights. Editorial lead time 1 month. Submit seasonal material 3 months in advance. Sample copy for $1. Writer's guidelines for #10 SASE.
**Nonfiction:** Essays, historical/nostalgic, how-to, humor, interview/profile, personal experience, technical. "No articles encouraging folks to start or get involved in bicycling—our readers are already cyclists." Send complete ms; no queries. Length: 600-1,800 words. **Pays $10 minimum for unsolicited articles.**
**Reprints:** Send typed ms with rights for sale noted and info about when and where it previously appeared.
**Fiction:** Publishes very short novel excerpts.
**Fillers:** Cartoons. **Pays $5-10.**

**$ $ CYCLE CALIFORNIA!**, Advanced Project Management, P.O. Box 189, Mountain View CA 94042. (650)961-2663. Fax: (650)968-9030. E-mail: cycleca@cyclecalifornia.com. Website: http://www.cyclecalifornia.com. **Contact:** Tracy L. Corral, editor/publisher. **75% freelance written.** Magazine published 11 times/year "covering Northern California bicycling events, races, people. Issues (topics) covered include bicycle commuting, bicycle politics, touring, racing, nostalgia, history, anything at all to do with riding a bike." Estab. 1995. Circ. 25,500. Pays on publication. Publishes ms 3 months after acceptance. Byline given. Buys first North American serial rights. Editorial lead time 6 weeks. Submit seasonal material 6 weeks in advance. Accepts queries by mail, e-mail, fax, phone. Accepts simultaneous submissions. Reports in 1 month. Sample copy for 10 × 13 SAE with 3 first-class stamps. Writer's guidelines for #10 SASE.
**Nonfiction:** Historical/nostalgic, interview/profile, opinion, personal experience, technical, travel. Special issue: Bicycle Tour & Travel (January/February). No articles about any sport that doesn't relate to bicycling, no product reviews. **Buys 36 mss/year.** Query with or without published clips. Length: 500-1,500 words. **Pays 3-10¢/word.** Sometimes pays expenses of writers on assignment.
**Photos:** Send photos with submission. Reviews 3 × 5 prints. Negotiates payment individually. Identification of subjects required. Buys one-time rights.
**Columns/Departments:** Buys 2-3 mss/year. Query with published clips. **Pays 3-10¢/word.**

   ▣   The online magazine carries original content not found in the print edition. Contact: Tracy L. Corral, online editor.

**Tips:** "E-mail or call editor with good ideas. While we don't exclude writers from other parts of the country, articles really should reflect a Northern California slant, or be of general interest to bicyclists. We prefer stories written by people who like and use their bikes."

**$ USA CYCLING MAGAZINE**, (formerly *Bike Racing Nation*), One Olympic Plaza, Colorado Springs CO 80909. (719)578-4581. Fax: (719)578-4596. E-mail: media@usacycling.org. Website: http://www.usacycling.org. **Contact:** B.J. Hoeptner, editor. **25% freelance written.** Bimonthly magazine covering reportage and commentary on American bicycle racing, personalities and sports physiology, for USAC licensed cyclists. Estab. 1980. Circ. 52,000. Pays on publication. Publishes ms an average of 2 months after acceptance. Byline given. Accepts queries by mail, e-mail, fax, phone. Reports in 2 weeks. Sample copy for 10×12 SAE with 2 first-class stamps.
  • *USAC Magazine* is looking for longer, more in-depth features (800-1,200 words).
**Nonfiction:** How-to (train, prepare for a bike race), interview/profile, photo feature. No comparative product evaluations. Length: 800-1,200 words. **Pays $50-75/article** depending on type and length of article.
**Reprints:** Send photocopy of article.
**Photos:** State availability of photos. Captions required. Buys one-time rights.
  The online magazine carries original content not found in the print edition. Contact: B.J. Hoeptner, online editor.
**Tips:** "We do not want race reports. We want features from 800-1,200 words on USA Cycling members and their activities. Our focus is on personalities, not opinions or competition."

**$ $ VELONEWS, The Journal of Competitive Cycling**, 1830 55th St., Boulder CO 80301-2700. (303)440-0601. Fax: (303)444-6788. E-mail: vnedit@7dogs.com. Website: http://www.VeloNews.com. **Contact:** John Rezell, senior editor. **40% freelance written.** Monthly tabloid September-February, biweekly March-August covering bicycle racing. Estab. 1972. Circ. 48,000. Pays on publication. Publishes ms an average of 1 month after acceptance. Byline given. Buys one-time worldwide rights. Accepts simultaneous submissions. Reports in 3 weeks.
**Nonfiction:** Freelance opportunities include race coverage, reviews (book and videos), health-and-fitness departments. **Buys 100 mss/year.** Query. Length: 300-1,200 words.
**Reprints:** Send typed ms with rights for sale noted and info about when and where it previously appeared.
**Photos:** State availability of photos. Pays $16.50 for b&w prints. Pays $200 for color used on cover. Captions and identification of subjects required. Buys one-time rights.

## Boating

**$ $ BASS & WALLEYE BOATS, The Magazine of Performance Fishing Boats**, Poole Publications, Inc., 20700 Belshaw Ave., Carson CA 90746. (310)537-6322. Fax: (310)537-8735. E-mail: bassboats@aol.com. Editor: Bruce Smith. **Contact:** Peter D. duPré, managing editor. **50% freelance written.** "*Bass & Walleye Boats* is published 8 times/year for the bass and walleye fisherman/boater. Directed to give priority to the boats, the tech, the how-to, the after-market add-ons and the devices that help anglers enjoy their boating experience." Estab. 1994. Circ. 70,000. **Pays on acceptance.** Publishes ms 3 months after acceptance. Byline given. Offers 25% kill fee. Buys all rights. Editorial lead time 2 months. Submit seasonal material 2 months in advance. Accepts queries by mail, e-mail, fax. Reports "A.S.A.P." Sample copy for $3.95 and 9×12 SAE with 7 first-class stamps. Writer's guidelines free.
  ⚬⚬ Break in by writing—as an expert—on using, modifying and tuning bass and walleye boats/engines for performance fishing use. Writer must be knowledgeable and able to back up document articles with hard sources. Also, your photography skills need to be honed in a marine environment.
**Nonfiction:** General interest, how-to, interview/profile, new product, personal experience, photo feature, technical, travel. Special issues: Annual towing guide and new boats. No fiction. **Buys 120 mss/year.** Query. Length: 1,000-3,000 words. **Pays $300-700.** Sometimes pays expenses of writers on assignment.
**Photos:** State availability of photos with submission. Reviews 2¼×2¼ transparencies and 35mm slides. Negotiates payment individually. Captions and identification of subjects required. Buys one-time rights.
**Columns/Departments:** Product review (consumer report), Quick-fix (how-to), both 750 words, plus photos. **Buys 15/year.** Query. **Pay varies.**
**Tips:** "Write from and for the bass and walleye boaters' perspective."

**$ $ BOATING LIFE**, World Publications Inc., 330 W. Canton Ave., Winter Park FL 32789. (407)628-4802. Fax: (407)628-7061. E-mail: BB2@worldzine.com. Editor: Pierce Hoover. **Contact:** Brett Becker, managing editor. **20-30% freelance written.** Bimonthly. "We are a product-related and lifestyle title. As such, we focus on people, fun, boating skills and technical subjects or product reviews. We demand a higher caliber of writing than has been the norm in the boating industry. In other words, we try not to use established 'boating writers,' and instead prefer qualified generalists who can bring color and excitement to the water." Estab. 1997. Circ. 110,000. **Pays on acceptance.** Publishes ms an average of 4 months after acceptance. Byline given. Offers 50% kill fee. Editorial lead time 4 months. Submit seasonal material 6 months in advance. Accepts queries by mail, e-mail, fax. Accepts simultaneous submissions. Reports in 1 month. Sample copy and writer's guidelines free.
**Nonfiction:** How-to, interview/profile, personal experience, photo feature, technical, travel. **Buys 24-30 mss/year.**

Query with published clips. Length: 800-2,900 words. **Pays $300-750 for assigned articles; $100-500 for unsolicited articles.**

**Photos:** State availability of photos with submission. Reviews transparencies. Offers $50-500/photo. Captions, model releases and identification of subjects required.

**Columns/Departments:** Boat Maintenance, Boat Handling, Boating-related lifestyle (power boat only). **Buys 12 mss/year.** Query with published clips. **Pays $100-500.**

**Fillers:** Anecdotes. **Buys 6/year.** Length: 200-450 words. **Pays $200.**

O→ Break in with 200-500 word travel stories involving great places to take your boat and buying, maintenance and handling tips.

**Tips:** "Our focus is 90 percent fresh water, 10 percent coastal. We avoid straight travelogues and instead favor activity or personality-based stories. The general tone is light and conversational, but all articles should in some way help the reader through the boat buying or owning process, and/or promote some aspect of the "boating lifestyle."

■ **$ $ CANOE & KAYAK MAGAZINE**, Canoe America Associates, 10526 NE 68th St., Suite 3, Kirkland WA 98033. (425)827-6363. Fax: (425)827-1893. E-mail: bryan@canoekayak.com. Website: http://www.canoekayak.com. Editor: Bryan Chitwood. Editor-in-Chief: Jan Nesset. **Contact:** Adem Tepedelen, associate editor. **75% freelance written.** Bimonthly magazine. "*Canoe & Kayak Magazine* is North America's #1 paddlesports resource. Our readers include flatwater and whitewater canoeists and kayakers of all skill levels. We provide comprehensive information on destinations, technique and equipment. Beyond that, we cover canoe and kayak camping, safety, the environment, and the history of boats and sport." Estab. 1972. Circ. 90,000. Pays on publication. Publishes ms an average of 6 months after acceptance. Byline given. Offers 50% kill fee. Buys first North American serial rights or one-time rights. Editorial lead time 4 months. Submit seasonal material 6 months in advance. Accepts queries by mail, e-mail. Reports in 2 months. Sample copy and writer's guidelines for 9 × 12 SAE with 7 first-class stamps.

O→ Break in with good destination or Put-In (news) pieces with excellent photos. "Take a good look at the types of articles we publish before sending us any sort of query."

**Nonfiction:** Historical/nostalgic, how-to (canoe, kayak camp; load boats; paddle whitewater, etc.), personal experience, photo feature, technical, travel. Annuals: Whitewater Paddling; Beginner's Guide; Kayak Touring; Canoe Journal. "No cartoons, poems, stories in which bad judgment is portrayed or 'Me and Molly' articles." **Buys 20 mss/year.** Query with or without published clips or send complete ms. Length: 400-2,500 words. **Pays $25-800 for assigned articles; $25-450 for unsolicited articles.** Sometimes pays the expenses of writers on assignment.

**Photos:** State availability of or send photos with submission. "Good photos help sell a story." Reviews 35mm transparencies and 4 × 6 prints. "Some activities we cover are canoeing, kayaking, canoe fishing, camping, canoe sailing or poling, backpacking (when compatible with the main activity) and occasionally inflatable boats. We are not interested in groups of people in rafts, photos showing disregard for the environment, gasoline-powered, multi-horsepower engines unless appropriate to the discussion, or unskilled persons taking extraordinary risks." Offers $25-350/photo. Captions, model releases and identification of subjects required. Buys one-time rights.

**Columns/Departments:** Put In (environment, conservation, events), 650 words; Destinations (canoe and kayak destinations in US, Canada), 1,500 words; Traditions (essays: traditional paddling), 750 words. **Buys 40 mss/year.** Query with or without published clips or send complete ms. **Pays $175-350.**

**Fillers:** Anecdotes, facts, newsbreaks. **Buys 20/year.** Length: 500-1,000 words. **Pays $5/column inch.**

**Tips:** "Start with Put-In articles (short featurettes), book reviews, or short, unique equipment reviews. Or give us the best, most exciting article we've ever seen—with great photos. Short Strokes is also a good entry forum focusing on short trips on good waterways accessible to lots of people. Focusing more on technique and how-to articles."

**$ $ $ CHESAPEAKE BAY MAGAZINE, Boating at Its Best**, Chesapeake Bay Communications, 1819 Bay Ridge Ave., Annapolis MD 24403. (410)263-2662. Fax: (410)267-6924. E-mail: cbmeditor@aol.com. **Contact:** Tim Sayles, editor. Managing Editor: Jane Meneely. **60% freelance written.** Monthly magazine covering boating and the Chesapeake Bay. "Our readers are boaters. Our writers should know boats and boating. Read the magazine before submitting." Estab. 1972. Circ. 42,000. **Pays within 60 days of acceptance.** Publishes ms 2-12 months after acceptance. Byline given. Buys first North American serial rights. Editorial lead time 1 year. Submit seasonal material 1 year in advance. Accepts queries by mail, e-mail. Accepts simultaneous submissions. Reports in 2 months on queries; 3 months on mss. Sample copy for $5.19 prepaid.

**Nonfiction:** Destinations, boating adventures, how-to, marina reviews, history, nature, environment, lifestyles, personal and institutional profiles, boat-type profiles, boatbuilding, boat restoration, boating anecdotes, boating news. **Buys 30 mss/year.** Query with unedited writing samples. Length: 300-3,000 words. **Pays $100-1,000.** Pays expenses of writers on assignment.

**Photos:** Offers $45-150/photo, $350 day rate for assignment photography. Captions, model releases and identification of subjects required. Buys one-time rights.

**Tips:** "Send us unedited writing samples (not clips) that show the writer can write, not just string words together. We look for well-organized, lucid, lively, intelligent writing."

**$ $ $ CRUISING WORLD**, Cruising World Publications, Inc., Box 3400, Newport RI 02840-0992. (401)847-1588. Website: http://www.cruisingworld.com. **Contact:** Bernadette Bernon, editorial director. **70% freelance written.** Monthly magazine for all those who cruise under sail. Circ. 155,000. **Pays on acceptance.** Publishes ms an average of 8 months after acceptance. Offers variable kill fee, $50-150. Buys first North American periodical rights or first world periodical rights. Accepts queries by mail. Reports in about 2 months. Guidelines free.

**Nonfiction:** Book excerpts, how-to, humor, inspirational, opinion, personal experience. "We are interested in seeing informative articles on the technical and enjoyable aspects of cruising under sail, especially seamanship, navigation and how-to." **Buys 135-140 unsolicited mss/year.** Submit complete ms. Length: 500-3,500 words. **Pays $150-800.**

**Photos:** 35mm slides purchased with accompanying ms. Captions and identification of subjects required. Buys one-time rights.

**Columns/Departments:** People & Food (recipes for preparation aboard sailboats); Shoreline (sailing news, vignettes); Workbench (projects for upgrading your boat). Send complete ms. Length: 150-500 words. **Pays $25-150.**

**Tips:** "Cruising stories should be first-person narratives. In general, authors must be sailors who read the magazine. Color slides always improve a ms's chances of acceptance. Technical articles should be well-illustrated."

**$ $GO BOATING MAGAZINE, America's Family Boating Magazine,** Duncan McIntosh Co., 17782 Cowan, Suite C, Irvine CA 92614. (949)660-6150. Fax: (949)660-6172. Website: http://goboatingmag.com. **Contact:** Eston Ellis, managing editor. **60% freelance written.** Published 6 times/year covering family power boating. Typical reader "owns a power boat between 14-25 feet long and has for 3-9 years. Boat reports that appear in *Go Boating* are designed to give readers a quick look at a new model. They must be lively, entertaining and interesting to our savvy boat-owning readership." Estab. 1997. Circ. 100,000. Pays on publication. Publishes ms an average of 3-6 months after acceptance. Byline given. Buys first North American serial rights. Editorial lead time 3 months. Submit seasonal material 4 months in advance. Accepts simultaneous submissions. Reports in 3 months. Sample copy free. Writer's guidelines for #10 SASE.

**Nonfiction:** General interest, how-to, humor, new product, personal experience, travel. **Buys 10-15 mss/year.** Query. Length: 1,000-1,200 words. **Pays $150-400.** Sometimes pays expenses of writers on assignment.

**Photos:** State availability of photos with submission. Reviews transparencies and prints. Offers $50-250/photo. Model releases and identification of subjects required. Buys one-time rights.

**Columns/Departments: Buys 10 mss/year.** Query. **Pays $150-350.**

**Fillers:** Anecdotes, facts and newsbreaks. **Buys 10/year.** Length: 250-500 words. **Pays $50-100.**

**Tips:** "Every vessel has something about it that makes it stand apart from all the others. Tell us what makes this boat different from all the rest on the market today. Include specifications and builder's address and phone number. See past issues for format."

**HEARTLAND BOATING,** The Waterways Journal, Inc., 319 N. Fourth St., Suite 650, St. Louis MO 63102. (314)241-4310. Fax: (314)241-4207. E-mail: hlboating@socket.com. **Contact:** Nelson Spencer, editor. Estab. 1988. **50% freelance written.** Magazine published 9 times/year during boating season. "*Heartland Boating*'s content is both informative and humorous—describing boating life as the heartland boater knows it. We are boating and enjoying the outdoor, water-oriented way of life. The content reflects the challenge, joy and excitement of our way of life afloat. We are devoted to both power and sail boating enthusiasts throughout middle America; houseboats are included. The focus is on the freshwater inland rivers and lakes of the Heartland, primarily the Tennessee, Cumberland, Ohio, Missouri and Mississippi rivers and the Tennessee-Tombigbee Waterway." Circ. 15,000. Pays on publication. Publishes ms an average of 3 months after acceptance. Byline given. Buys first North American serial and sometimes second serial (reprint) rights. Submit seasonal material 6 months in advance. Accepts simultaneous submissions. Accepts queries by mail. Reports in 4 months. Sample copy for $5. Free writer's guidelines.

**Nonfiction:** General interest, historical/nostalgic, how-to, humor, interview/profile, new product, personal experience, photo feature, technical, travel. Special issue: Houseboats (May). **Buys 20-40 mss/year.** Query with or without published clips. Length: 800-2,000 words. Negotiates payment.

**Reprints:** Send photocopy of article or typed ms and information about where and when it previously appeared. Pays 50% of amount paid for an original article.

**Photos:** Send photos with query. Reviews contact sheets, transparencies. Buys one-time rights.

**Columns/Departments: Buys 50 mss/year.** Query. Negotiates payment.

**$ $LAKELAND BOATING, The Magazine for Great Lakes Boaters,** O'Meara-Brown Publications, 500 Davis St., Suite 1000, Evanston IL 60201-4802. (847)869-5400. Fax: (847)869-5989. E-mail: lbonline@aol.com. Associate Editor: Chad Schegel. **Contact:** Randy Hess, editor. **50% freelance written.** Monthly magazine covering Great Lakes boating. Estab. 1946. Circ. 60,000. Pays on publication. Byline given. Buys first North American serial rights. Reports in 4 months. Sample copy for $5.50 and 9×12 SAE with 6 first-class stamps. Guidelines for #10 SASE.

**Nonfiction:** Book excerpts, historical/nostalgic, how-to, interview/profile, personal experience, photo feature, technical, travel. No inspirational, religious, expose or poetry. Must relate to boating in Great Lakes. **Buys 20-30 mss/year.** Query. Length: 800-3,500 words. **Pays $100-600.**

**Photos:** State availability of photos. Reviews transparencies; prefers 35mm. Captions required. Buys one-time rights.

**Columns/Departments:** Bosun's Locker (technical or how-to pieces on boating), 100-1,000 words. **Buys 40 mss/year.** Query. **Pays $30-100.**

**$ NORTHERN BREEZES, SAILING MAGAZINE,** Northern Breezes, Inc., 245 Brunswick Ave. S., Golden Valley MN 55416. (612)542-9707. Fax: (612)542-8998. E-mail: thomnbreez@aol.com. Managing Editor: Thom Burns. **Contact:** Gloria Peck, editor. **70% freelance written.** Regional monthly sailing magazine for the Upper Midwest. Estab. 1989. Circ. 22,300. Pays on publication. Byline given. Buys first North American serial rights. Editorial lead time 1 month. Submit seasonal material 3 months in advance. Accepts queries by mail, e-mail, fax, phone. Reports in 1 month on queries; 2 months on mss. Sample copy and writer's guidelines free or on website.

**Nonfiction:** Book excerpts, how-to (sailing topics), humor, inspirational, interview/profile, new product, personal experience, photo feature, technical, travel. No boat reviews. **Buys 24 mss/year.** Query with published clips. Length: 300-2,000 words. **Pays $50-150.**

**Reprints:** Accepts previously published submissions.

**Photos:** Send photos with submission. Reviews negatives, 35mm slides, 3×5 or 4×6 prints. Offers no additional payment for photos accepted with ms or negotiates payment individually. Captions required. Buys one-time rights.

**Columns/Departments:** This Old Boat (sailboat), 500-1,000 words; Surveyor's Notebook, 500-800 words. **Buys 8 mss/year.** Query with published clips. **Pays $50-150.**

■ The online magazine carries original content not found in the print edition and includes writer's guidelines. Contact: Thom Burns, online editor.

**Tips:** "Query with a regional connection already in mind."

⭐ **$ $ PACIFIC YACHTING, Western Canada's Premier Boating Magazine**, OP Publishing Ltd., 780 Beatty St., Suite 300, Vancouver, British Columbia V6B 2M1 Canada. (604)606-4644. Fax: (604)687-1925. E-mail: oppubl@istar.ca. Website: http://www.oppub.com. **Contact:** Duart Snow, editor. **90% freelance written.** Monthly magazine covering all aspects of recreational boating on British Columbia coast. "The bulk of our writers and photographers not only come from the local boating community, many of them were long-time PY readers before coming aboard as a contributor. The PY reader buys the magazine to read about new destinations or changes to old haunts on the B.C. coast and to learn the latest about boats and gear." Circ. 14,598. Pays on publication. Publishes ms an average of 6 months after acceptance. Byline given. Buys first North American serial and simultaneous rights. Editorial lead time 4 months. Submit seasonal material 6 months in advance. Accepts queries mail, e-mail, fax. Sample copy for $2 plus postage charged to VISA credit card. Writer's guidelines free.

**Nonfiction:** Historical/nostalgic, how-to, humor, interview/profile, personal experience, travel, cruising and destinations on the B.C. coast. "No articles from writers who are obviously not boaters!" Length: 2,000 words. Query with SAE and IRCs or by e-mail or phone. **Pays $150-500.** Pays expenses of writers on assignment if arranged in advance.

**Photos:** Send sample photos with query. Reviews transparencies, 4×6 prints and slides. Offers no additional payment for photos accepted with ms and $25-300/photo not accepted with ms. Identification of subjects required. Buys one-time rights. Covers: (transparencies): $300.

**Columns/Departments:** Currents (current events, trade and people news, boat gatherings and festivities), 50-250 words. Other departments: Reflections, Cruising, 800-1,000 words. Query. **Pay varies.**

**Tips:** "We strongly encourage queries before submission (written with SAE and IRCs, or by phone or e-mail). While precise nautical information is important, colorful anecdotes bring your cruise to life. Both are important. In other words, our reader wants you to balance important navigation details with first-person observations, blending the practical with the romantic. Write tight, write short, write with the reader in mind, write to inform, write to entertain. Be specific, accurate and historic."

Ⓝ **$ $ $ POWER & MOTORYACHT**, Primedia, 260 Madison Ave., 8th Floor, New York NY 10016. (917)256-2200. Fax: (917)256-2282. E-mail: byrne@primediasi.com. Website: http://www.yachtworld.com. Editor: Richard Thiel. Managing Editor: Kathryn Drury. **Contact:** Diane M. Byrne, senior editor. **20% freelance written.** Consumer publication published monthly covering powerboating. "*Power & Motoryacht* is devoted exclusively to the high-end powerboat market, those boats 24 feet or larger. Every reader owns at least one powerboat in this size range. Our magazine reaches virtually every U.S. owner of a 40-foot or larger powerboat—the only publication that does so. For our readers, boating is not a hobby, it's a lifestyle." Estab. 1985. Circ. 157,000. **Pays on acceptance.** Publishes ms an average of 6 months after acceptance. Byline given. Offers 33% kill fee. Buys first North American serial and electronic rights. Editorial lead time up to 1 year. Submit seasonal material 6 months in advance. Accepts queries by mail, e-mail, fax. *No unsolicited mss.* Accepts simultaneous submissions. Reports in 1 month on queries. Sample copy for 10×12 SASE. Writer's guidelines for #10 SASE or by e-mail.

**Nonfiction:** Book excerpts, how-to (how to fix things, install things, shop for boats and accessories smarter, etc.), humor, interview/profile, personal experience, technical, travel. Coming themes: custom yachts (August, November); maintenance (April); US cruising (December). "Nothing sailing-related! This includes motorsailers!" **Buys 10-15 mss/year.** Query with published clips. *No unsolicited mss.* Length: 800-1,400 words. **Pays $400-1,200.** Sometimes pays expenses of writers on assignment.

**Photos:** State availability of photos with submission. Reviews 4×5 transparencies; "Slides OK, too." Offers no additional payment for photos accepted with ms. Captions and identification of subjects required. Buys one-time rights.

**Tips:** "Writers must be authorities on the subject matter they write about—our readers have an average of 28 years' experience on the water, so they want experts to provide advice and information. Some of our regular feature themes are seamanship (rules of the road and boating protocol techniques); cruising (places readers can take their own boats for a few days' enjoyment); maintenance (tips on upkeep and repair); engines (innovations that improve efficiency and/or lessen environmental impact); sportfishing (fishing news and travel pieces)."

**$ $ POWER BOATING CANADA**, 2585 Skymark Ave., Unit 306, Mississauga, Ontario L4W 4L5 Canada. (905)624-8218. Fax: (905)624-6764. **Contact:** Peter Tasler, editor. **70% freelance written.** Bimonthly magazine covering recreational power boating. "*Power Boating Canada* offers boating destinations, how-to features, boat tests (usually staff written), lifestyle pieces—with a Canadian slant—and appeal to recreational power boaters across the country." Estab. 1984. Circ. 50,000. Pays on publication. Publishes ms an average of 3 months after acceptance. Byline given. Buys first North American serial rights. Editorial lead time 2 months. Submit seasonal material 3 months in advance. Reports in 1 month on queries, 2 months on mss. Sample copy free.

**Nonfiction:** "Any articles related to the sport of power boating, especially boat tests." Historical/nostalgic, how-to, interview/profile, personal experience, travel (boating destinations). No general boating articles or personal anecdotes. **Buys 40-50 mss/year.** Query. Length: 1,200-2,500 words. **Pays $150-300.** Sometimes pays expenses of writers on assignment.

**Reprints:** Send photocopy of article or typed ms with rights for sale noted and information about when and where the article previously appeared.

**Photos:** Send photos with submission. Reviews contact sheets, negatives, transparencies, prints. No additional payment for photos accepted with ms. Captions, identification of subjects required. Buys one-time rights. Pay varies.

**$ $ $SAIL**, 84 State St., Boston MA 02109-2262. (617)720-8600. Fax: (617)723-0912. E-mail: sailmail@channel 1.com. Editor: Patience Wales. **Contact:** Amy Ullrich, managing editor. **50% freelance written.** Works with a small number of new/unpublished writers each year. Monthly magazine "written and edited for everyone who sails—aboard a coastal or bluewater cruiser, trailerable, one-design or offshore racer, or daysailer. How-to and technical articles concentrate on techniques of sailing and aspects of design and construction, boat systems, and gear; the feature section emphasizes the fun and rewards of sailing in a practical and instructive way." Estab. 1970. Circ. 180,000. **Pays on acceptance.** Byline given. Publishes ms an average of 10 months after acceptance. Buys first North American rights. Submit seasonal or special material at least 6 months in advance. Accepts queries by mail, e-mail, fax. Reports in 10 weeks. Writer's guidelines for SASE.

**Nonfiction:** Technical, techniques, how-to, personal experience, distance cruising, destinations. "Generally emphasize the excitement of sail and the human, personal aspect. No logs." Length: 1,500-3,000 words. Examples of shorter features are: vignettes of day sailing, cruising and racing life (at home or abroad, straight or humorous); maritime history; astronomy; marine life; cooking; nautical love; fishing; boat owning, boat building and outfitting; regatta reports. Length: 1,000-1,500 words. Special issues: "Cruising, chartering, fitting-out, special race (e.g., America's Cup), boat show." **Buys 100 mss/year** (freelance and commissioned). Query with SASE. **Pays $200-800.** Sometimes pays the expenses of writers on assignment.

**Reprints:** Send photocopy of article or typed ms with rights for sale noted and information about when and where the article previously appeared. Pays 33-50% of amount paid for an original article.

**Photos:** Offers additional payment for photos. Uses 50-100 ASA transparencies. Identification of subjects, captions and credits required. Pay varies, on publication. Pays $600 if photo is used on the cover.

**Columns/Departments:** Sailing Memories (short essay); Sailing News (cruising, racing, legal, political, environmental). Query. **Pays $25-400.**

**Tips:** "Request an articles specification sheet. We look for unique ways of viewing sailing. Skim old issues of *Sail* for ideas about the types of articles we publish. Always remember that *Sail* is a sailing magazine. Stay away from gloomy articles detailing all the things that went wrong on your boat. Think constructively and write about how to avoid certain problems. You should focus on a theme or choose some aspect of sailing and discuss a personal attitude or new philosophical approach to the subject. Notice that we have certain issues devoted to special themes—for example, chartering, electronics, commissioning, and the like. Stay away from pieces that chronicle your journey in the day-by-day style of a logbook. These are generally dull and uninteresting. Select specific actions or events (preferably sailing events, not shorebound activities), and build your articles around them. Emphasize the sailing."

**$ $SAILING MAGAZINE**, 125 E. Main St., Port Washington WI 53074-0249. (414)284-3494. Fax: (414)284-7764. E-mail: sailing@execpc.com. Website: http://www.sailnet.com/sailing. **Contact:** Gregory O. Jones, editor. Publisher: William F. Schanen, III. Monthly magazine for the experienced sailor. Estab. 1966. Circ. 52,000. Pays on publication. Buys one-time rights. Accepts queries by mail, e-mail, fax. Reports in 2 months.

　　O— "Let us get to know your writing with short pieces for our Splashes section. Query for upcoming theme issues; read the magazine; writing must show the writer loves sailing as much as our readers. We are always looking for fresh stories on new destinations with vibrant writing and top-notch photography. Always looking for short (100-1,500) articles or newsy items."

**Nonfiction:** "Experiences of sailing, cruising and racing or cruising to interesting locations, whether a small lake near you or islands in the Southern Ocean, with first-hand knowledge and tips for our readers. Top-notch photos (transparencies only), with maps, charts, cruising information complete the package. No regatta sports unless there is a story involved." Must be written to AP Stylebook. **Buys 12-15 mss/year.** Length: 750-1,500 words. Must be accompanied by photos, and maps if applicable. **Pays $100-800.**

**Photos:** Color photos (transparencies) purchased with or without accompanying text. Captions required. Pays $50-300.

**Tips:** Prefers text in Word on disk for Mac or to e-mail address. "No attached files, please."

**$ $SAILING WORLD**, Miller Sports Group, LLC, 5 John Clarke Rd., Box 3400, Newport RI 02840-0992. Fax: (401)848-5048. E-mail: editor@sailingworld.com. Website: http://www.sailingworld.com. Editor: John Burnham. **Contact:** Kristan McClintock, managing editor. **40% freelance written.** Monthly magazine emphasizing performance sailing. Estab. 1962. Circ. 62,678. Pays on publication. Publishes ms an average of 4 months after acceptance. Buys first North American and world serial rights. Byline given. Reports in 3 months. Sample copy for $5.

**O→** Break in with short articles and fillers such as regatta news reports from your own area.

**Nonfiction:** How-to for racing and performance-oriented sailors, photo feature, profile, regatta reports and charter. No travelogs. **Buys 5-10 unsolicited mss/year.** Query. Length: 500-1,500 words. **Pays $400 for up to 2,000 words.**

**Tips:** "Send query with outline and include your experience. Prospective contributors should study recent issues of the magazine to determine appropriate subject matter. The emphasis here is on performance sailing: keep in mind that the *Sailing World* readership is relatively educated about the sport. Unless you are dealing with a totally new aspect of sailing, you can and should discuss ideas on an advanced technical level. 'Gee-whiz' impressions from beginning sailors are generally not accepted."

**★ $ $ SEA KAYAKER**, Sea Kayaker, Inc., P.O. Box 17170, Seattle WA 98107-0870. (206)789-1326. Fax: (206)781-1141. E-mail: mail@seakayakermag.com. Website: www.seakayakermag.com. **Contact:** Leslie Forsberg, executive editor. Editor: Christopher Cunningham. **95% freelance written.** Works frequently with new/unpublished writers each year. "*Sea Kayaker* is a bimonthly publication with a worldwide readership that covers all aspects of kayak touring. It is well-known as an important source of continuing education by the most experienced paddlers." Estab. 1984. Circ. 25,000. Pays on publication. Publishes ms an average of 6 months after acceptance. Byline given. Offers 10% kill fee. Buys first North American serial or second serial (reprint) rights. Editorial lead time 4 months. Submit seasonal material 4 months in advance. Accepts queries by mail, e-mail, fax, phone. Reports in 2 months. Sample copy for $5.75. Writer's guidelines for SASE or on website.

**Nonfiction:** Essays, historical, how-to (on making equipment), humor, new product, profile, opinion, personal experience, technical, travel. **Buys 18 mss/year.** Query or send complete ms. Length: 1,500-5,000 words. **Pays 20¢/word for assigned articles; 12¢/word for unassigned articles.**

**Photos:** Send photos with submission. Reviews transparencies and prints. Offers $15-400. Captions and identification of subjects required. Buys one-time rights.

**Columns/Departments:** Technique, Equipment, Do-It-Yourself, Food, Safety, Health, Environment, Book Reviews. Length: 1,000-2,500 words. **Buys 40-45 mss/year.** Query. **Pays 20¢/word for assigned articles; 12¢/word for unassigned articles.**

**Tips:** "We consider unsolicited manuscripts that include a SASE, but we give greater priority to brief descriptions (several paragraphs) of proposed articles accompanied by at least two samples—published or unpublished—of your writing. Enclose a statement as to why you're qualified to write the piece and indicate whether photographs or illustrations are available to accompany the piece."

**$ $ SOUTHERN BOATING MAGAZINE, The South's Largest Boating Magazine**, Southern Boating & Yachting Inc., 1766 Bay Rd., Miami Beach FL 33139. (305)538-0700. Fax: (305)532-8657. E-mail: sboating@icanect.n et. Editor: Skip Allen. Executive Editor: Rick Eyerdam. **Contact:** David Strickland, managing editor. **50% freelance written.** "Upscale monthly yachting magazine focusing on SE U.S., Bahamas, Caribbean and Gulf of Mexico." Estab. 1972. Circ. 35,000. Pays on publication. Publishes ms an average of 2 months after acceptance. Byline given. Buys one-time rights. Editorial lead time 6 weeks. Submit seasonal material 2 months in advance. Accepts queries by mail, e-mail, fax, phone. Sample copy free.

**O→** Break in with destination, how-to and technical articles.

**Nonfiction:** How-to (boat maintenance), travel (boating related and destination pieces). **Buys 100 mss/year.** Query. Length: 600-3,000 words. **Pays $200.**

**Reprints:** Accepts previously published submissions.

**Photos:** State availability of or send photos. Reviews transparencies, prints. Offers $50/photo maximum; negotiates payment individually. Captions, model releases and identification of subjects required. Buys one-time rights.

**Columns/Departments:** Weekend Workshop (how to/maintenance), 600 words; What's New in Electronics (electronics), 1,000 words; Engine Room (new developments), 1,000 words. **Buys 24 mss/year.** Query. **Pays $150.**

**$ $ TRAILER BOATS MAGAZINE**, Poole Publications, Inc., 20700 Belshaw Ave., Carson CA 90746-3510. (310)537-6322. Fax: (310)537-8735. E-mail: tbmeditors@aol.com. **Contact:** Jim Henricks, editor. Managing Editor: Ron Eldridge. **50% freelance written.** Works with a small number of new/unpublished writers each year. Monthly magazine (November/December issue combined) covering legally trailerable power boats and related powerboating activities. Estab. 1971. Circ. 85,000. **Pays on acceptance.** Publishes ms 3 months after acceptance. Byline given. Buys all rights. Editorial lead time 4 months. Submit seasonal material 5 months in advance. Reports in 1 month. Sample copy for 9 × 12 SAE with 7 first-class stamps.

**Nonfiction:** General interest (trailer boating activities); historical (places, events, boats); how-to (repair boats, installation, etc.); humor (almost any power boating-related subject); personal experience; photo feature; profile; technical; and travel (boating travel on water or highways), product evaluations. Annual new boat review. No "How I Spent My Summer Vacation" stories, or stories not directly connected to trailerable boats and related activities. **Buys 70-80 unsolicited mss/year.** Query. Length: 1,000-3,000 words. **Pays $150-1,000.** Sometimes pays expenses of writers on assignment.

**Photos:** Send photos with ms. Reviews transparencies (2¼ × 2¼) and 35mm slides. Captions, model releases and identification of subjects required. Buys one-time rights.

**Columns/Departments:** Over the Transom (funny or strange boating photos). Watersports (boat-related); Seamanship (experienced boaters' tips on navigation, survival, safety etc.); Marine Electronics (what and how to use); Back to Basics (elementary boating tips), all 1,000-1,500 words. **Buys 60-70/year.** Query. **Pays $250-450.** Open to suggestions for new columns/departments.

**Tips:** "Query should contain short general outline of the intended material; what kind of photos; how the photos illustrate the piece. Write with authority, covering the subject with quotes from experts. Frequent mistakes are not knowing the subject matter or the audience. The writer may have a better chance of breaking in at our publication with short articles and fillers if they are typically hard-to-find articles. We do most major features inhouse, but try how-to stories dealing with smaller boats, installation and towing tips, boat trailer repair. Good color photos will win our hearts every time."

**N $ WAVE-LENGTH PADDLING MAGAZINE**, Wave-Length Communications, R.R. 1, Site 17, C-49, Gabriola Island, British Columbia V0R 1X0 Canada. Phone/fax: (250)247-8858. E-mail: awilson@island.net. Website: www.wavelengthmagazine.com. **Contact:** Alan Wilson, editor. **75% freelance written.** Bimonthly magazine covering sea kayaking. "We promote safe paddling, guide paddlers to useful products and services and explore coastal environmental issues." Estab. 1991. Circ. 20,000 plus Internet readers. Pays on publication. Publishes ms an average of 4 months after acceptance. Byline given. Offers 10% kill fee. Buys first North American serial and electronic reprint rights. Editorial lead time 2 months. Submit seasonal material 2 months in advance. Accepts queries by mail, e-mail, phone. Reports in 2 months. Sample copy and writer's guidelines for $2 or on website.

⊶ "Sea kayaking content, even if from a beginner's perspective, is essential. We like a light approach to personal experiences and humor is appreciated. Good detail (with maps and pics) for destinations material. Rarely use fiction/poetry."

**Nonfiction:** Personal experience, trips, advice, book excerpts, how-to (paddle, travel), humor, interview/profile, new product, opinion, technical. **Buys 25 mss/year.** Query. Length: 1,000-2,000 words. **Pays $50-75.** Pays businesses with advertising.

**Photos:** State availability of photos with query. Reviews 4×6 prints. Offers $25/photo; $50 for covers (must be vertical). Captions and identification of subjects required. Buys first and electronic rights. Query.

**Columns/Departments:** Safety, Gear/Accessories, 1,000 words. **Buys 12 mss/year.** Query. **Pays $50.**

**Fiction:** Adventure, humorous. "Unless it has strong paddling aspect, don't bother." Query. Length: 700-1,500 words. **Pays $50.**

**Poetry:** Free verse, light verse. "Has to be paddling focused." Submit maximum 4 poems. Length: 10-25 words. **Pays $10-25.**

**Fillers:** Anecdotes, facts, gags to be illustrated by cartoonist, newsbreaks and short humor. **Buys 8-10/year.** Length: 25-250 words. **Pays $10-25.**

**Tips:** "You must know paddling—although novice paddlers are welcome. A strong environmental or wilderness appreciation component is advisable. We are willing to help refine work with flexible people. E-mail queries preferred."

**$ $ WOODENBOAT MAGAZINE, The Magazine for Wooden Boat Owners, Builders, and Designers**, WoodenBoat Publications, Inc., P.O. Box 78, Brooklin ME 04616. (207)359-4651. Fax: (207)359-8920. E-mail: wbeditor @woodenboat.com. Website: http://www.media4.hypernet.com/~WOODENBOAT/wb.htm. Editor-in-Chief: Jonathan A. Wilson. Senior Editor: Mike O'Brien. Associate Editor: Tom Jackson. **Contact:** Matthew P. Murphy, editor. **50% freelance written.** Works with a small number of new/unpublished writers each year. Bimonthly magazine for wooden boat owners, builders and designers. "We are devoted exclusively to the design, building, care, preservation, and use of wooden boats, both commercial and pleasure, old and new, sail and power. We work to convey quality, integrity and involvement in the creation and care of these craft, to entertain, inform, inspire, and to provide our varied readers with access to individuals who are deeply experienced in the world of wooden boats." Estab. 1974. Circ. 106,000. Pays on publication. Publishes ms an average of 1 year after acceptance. Byline given. Offers variable kill fee. Buys first North American serial rights. Accepts simultaneous submissions. Reports in 3 weeks on queries; 2 months on mss. Sample copy for $4.50. Writer's guidelines for SASE.

**Nonfiction:** Technical (repair, restoration, maintenance, use, design and building wooden boats). No poetry, fiction. **Buys 50 mss/year.** Query with published clips. Length: 1,500-5,000 words. **Pays $200-250/1,000 words.** Sometimes pays expenses of writers on assignment.

**Reprints:** Send tearsheet or photocopy of article or typed ms with rights for sale noted with information about when and where the article previously appeared.

**Photos:** Send photos with query. Negatives must be available. Pays $15-75 for b&w; $25-350 for color. Identification of subjects required. Buys one-time rights.

**Columns/Departments:** On the Waterfront pays for information on wooden boat-related events, projects, boatshop activities, etc. **Buys 25/year.** "We use the same columnists for each issue." Send complete information. Length: 250-1,000 words. **Pays $5-50 for information.**

**Tips:** "We appreciate a detailed, articulate query letter, accompanied by photos, that will give us a clear idea of what the author is proposing. We appreciate samples of previously published work. It is important for a prospective author to become familiar with our magazine first. It is extremely rare for us to make an assignment with a writer with whom we have not worked before. Most work is submitted on speculation. The most common failure is not exploring the subject material in enough depth."

**N $ $ $ YACHTING**, Times Mirror Magazines Inc., 20 E. Elm St., Greenwich CT 06830. (203)625-4480. Fax: (203)625-4481. Publisher: Peter Beckenbach. Editor-in-Chief: Charles Barthold. 50% freelance written. "The magazine is written and edited for experienced, knowledgeable yachtsmen." Estab. 1907. Circ. 130,000. Pays on publication. Byline given. Buys first rights. Submit seasonal material 6 months in advance. Reports in 1 month.

**Nonfiction:** Book excerpts, personal experience, photo feature, travel. No cartoons, fiction, poetry. Query with published clips. Length: 250-2,000 words. Pays $250-1,000. Pays expenses of writers on assignment.

**Photos:** Send photos with submission. Reviews 35mm transparencies. Offers some additional payment for photos accepted with ms. Captions, model releases and identification of subjects required.

**Columns/Departments:** Cruising Yachtsman (stories on cruising; contact Dennis Caprio, senior editor); Yacht Yard (how-to and technical pieces on yachts and their systems; contact Dennis Caprio, senior editor). Buys 30 mss/year. Send complete ms. Length: 750 words maximum. Pays $250-500.

**Tips:** "We require considerable expertise in our writing because our audience is experienced and knowledgeable. Vivid descriptions of quaint anchorages and quainter natives are fine, but our readers want to know how the yachtsmen got there, too. They also want to know how their boats work. *Yachting* is edited for experienced, affluent boatowners—power and sail—who don't have the time nor the inclination to read sub-standard stories. They love carefully crafted stories about places they've never been or a different spin on places they have, meticulously reported pieces on issues that affect their yachting lives, personal accounts of yachting experiences from which they can learn, engaging profiles of people who share their passion for boats, insightful essays that evoke the history and traditions of the sport and compelling photographs of others enjoying the game as much as they do. They love to know what to buy and how things work. They love to be surprised. They don't mind getting their hands dirty or saving a buck here and there, but they're not interested in learning how to make a masthead light out of a mayonnaise jar. If you love what they love and can communicate like a pro (that means meeting deadlines, writing tight, being obsessively accurate and never misspelling a proper name), we'd love to hear from you."

# Football

**N** **$ $ $ $ DAVE CAMPBELL'S TEXAS FOOTBALL**, Host Communications/USA, 4006 Belt Line Rd., Suite 220, Dallas TX 75244. Fax: (972)392-5880. E-mail: dctfe@usasports.com. Website: http://www.texasfootball.com. Editor: Dave Campbell. Managing Editor: David Barron. **95% freelance written.** Consumer publication published annually covering Texas high school, college and NFL football. "*Texas Football* is an annual publication that previews schools, colleges and universities in Texas and the Dallas Cowboys." Estab. 1960. Circ. 160,000. Pays on publication. Byline given. Buys one-time rights. Editorial lead time 2 months. Submit seasonal material 2 months in advance. Accepts queries by mail, e-mail, fax.

**Nonfiction:** Interview/profile, opinion. **Buys 0-5 mss/year.** Query with clips. Length: 13-20″. **Pays $100-2,000.**

**Photos:** State availability of photos. Reviews contact sheets. Offers $45-250/photo. Buys one-time rights.

# Gambling

**$ $ $ $ PLAY THE ODDS**, The Big Dog Press, P.O. Box 55498, Little Rock AR 72215-5498. Phone/fax: (501)228-5237. E-mail: playtheodds@worldnet.att.net. Website: http://home.att.net/~playtheodds/index.html. **Contact:** Tom Raley, editor. Monthly consumer magazine covering gambling. "We cover gambling activities all across the country. We offer tips, reviews, instructions and advice on gaming. We also cover cruise lines since most have casinos on board." Estab. 1997. **Pays on acceptance.** Publishes ms an average of 4 months after acceptance. Buys one-time rights. Accepts simultaneous submissions. Accepts queries by mail. Reports in 3 weeks on queries; 2 months on mss. Sample copy for $2.50. Writer's guidelines for #10 SASE or on website.

   **O─** Break in with short fiction that is fun, entertaining and accurate. Blurbs and short facts about casinos or casino games are also very good.

**Nonfiction:** Primarily dealing with casino gaming, *Play the Odds* also covers horse racing, dog racing, sports wagering and online casinos. Also features service articles on entertainment, lodging, and dining facilities located in or near gaming resorts. **Buys 85-145 mss/year.** Length: 800 words. **Pays $500-1,750.**

**Fiction:** Barbara Stone, fiction editor. Adventure, fantasy (science fantasy), horror, mystery/suspense (cozy, private eye/hardboiled, romantic suspense), science fiction (soft sociological), senior citizen/retirement, sports, westerns (traditional). **Buys 12-20 mss/year.** Length: 600-800 words. **Pays $1,500-3,000.**

**Columns/Departments:** Reviews (shows, games, hotels, casinos, books), up to 300 words; humorous fillers, up to 80 words. **Buys 24-36 reviews/year; 36-60 fillers/year. Pays 50-350.**

   ◼ The online magazine carries original content not found in the print edition and includes writer's guidelines. Contact: Lisa Nimitz.

**Tips:** In nonfiction, the editor advises that a writer present an aspect or area of gaming which is out of the mainstream. In fiction, "we look for fast paced stories with real characters. The stories should be fun, enjoyable and the main character doesn't need to be trying to save the world. Few, if any of us, do that. We do however get in bad situations. You must write what you enjoy writing about. If you don't want to write a story about gambling or a gambler, it will show in your work. If it is something you want, that will also show in your work and we will notice."

## General Interest

**★ $ ALL-STATER SPORTS, America's High School Sports Magazine**, All-Stater Publishing, LLC, 1373 Grandview Ave., Suite 206, Columbus OH 43212. (614)487-1280. Fax: (614)487-1283. E-mail: sstrong@all-statersports. com. Website: http://www.all-statersports.com. **Contact:** Stephanie Strong, managing editor. **80% freelance written.** Quarterly tabloid. "The mission of *All-Stater Sports* is to inform, inspire and recognize today's high school student-athlete. Our audience consists of student-athletes, coaches and athletic directors, but our intention is to speak primarily to student-athletes." Estab. 1995. Circ. 100,000. Pays on publication. Publishes ms an average of 1 month after acceptance. Byline given. Editorial lead time 2 weeks. Submit seasonal material 1 month in advance. Accepts simultaneous submissions. Accepts queries by mail, e-mail, fax. Reports in 1 month. Sample copy $5 for writers only.

○━ Break in with a state championship final coverage or profiles of nationally ranked high school athletes or team.
**Nonfiction:** How-to (training, cross-training, strength building, etc.), humor inspirational, interview/profile, new product, opinion, personal experience, photo feature, technical (sports issues, skill building). **Pays $5-10 cents/published word.** "Profiles writers in our contributor's column, provides extra copies of issue, plugs product, institution, company, etc. All stories will only be printed with photos.
**Reprints:** Send typed ms with rights for sale noted and information about when and where it previously appeared.
**Photos:** State availability of photos with submission. Reviews 5×7 minimum prints. Negotiates payment individually. Model release (if deemed necessary) and identification of subjects required. Buys one-time rights.
**Columns/Departments:** Getting The Edge (sports training/skill building), 1,200 words; Next Step articles about sports in (college sports), 1,200 words; Winning with Heart (overcoming the odds to play high school sports), 1,000 words; In Recognition of Sportsmanship (specific act of sportsmanship in high school sports—real incidents), 1,000 words. Profiles (short articles on outstanding current student athletes). **Buys 10-15 mss/year.** Query. **Pays $5-10 cents/ published word.**
**Fillers:** Anecdotes, facts, gags to be illustrated, newsbreaks, embarrassing sports moments, college signings (300-500 words), short humor. Length: 50-300 words. **Pays $15-30.**
**Tips:** "We are happy to consider any material that would be of interest to high school athletes—even something that is not already included in our issues printed to date. No fiction or poetry. We profile outstanding achievers, but would also like to have human interest stories of accomplishment, satisfaction, sportsmanship, obsessive fans, original coaching methods, team bonding, unusually fine coaches, etc., from non-blue chipper's perspective as well."

**$ $ METRO SPORTS MAGAZINE**, Hebdo Sports Inc., 27 W. 24th St., New York NY 10010. (212)627-7040. Fax: (212)627-7446. E-mail: metrosport@aol.com. Website: http://www.metrosports.com. **Contact:** Angela Garber, assistant editor. **30% freelance written.** Monthly tabloid covering participation sports. "We write about active sports for young professionals: running, cycling, in-line, tennis, skiing, outdoor. The message is 'get out and play.' And here is how, where, when." Estab. 1987. Circ. 160,000. Pays on publication. Publishes ms an average of 2 months after acceptance. Byline given. Buys first North American serial rights. Editorial lead time 3 months. Submit seasonal material 3 months in advance. Accepts queries by mail, e-mail, fax, phone. Accepts simultaneous submissions. Sample copy for $4. Writer's guidelines free.
**Nonfiction:** Book excerpts, exposé, general interest, how-to, humor, inspirational, interview/profile, new product, opinion, personal experience, travel. **Buys 20 mss/year.** Query. Length: 300-1,200 words. **Pays $50-500 for assigned articles. Pays $50-200 for unsolicited articles.**
**Reprints:** Send tearsheet or photocopy of article.
**Photos:** State availability of photos with submission. Reviews transparencies and prints. Offers no additional payment for photos accepted with ms. Buys one-time rights.
**Columns/Departments:** Running (how to, events); Sports Medicine; Equipment (innovations). All 700 words. Query.
**Tips:** "Be aware of active (not TV) sports with East Coast focus."

**$ $ ROCKY MOUNTAIN SPORTS MAGAZINE**, Rocky Mountain Sports, Inc., 1521 Central St., Suite 1C, Denver CO 80211. (303)477-9770. Fax: (303)477-9747. E-mail: Rockyedit@aol.com. Website: www.rockymountainspo rts.com. Publisher: Mary Thorne. **Contact:** Kellee Van Keuren, editor. **50% freelance written.** Monthly magazine of sports in Colorado. "*Rocky* is a magazine for sports-related lifestyles and activities. Our mission is to reflect and inspire the active lifestyle of Rocky Mountain residents." Estab. 1986. Circ. 75,000. Pays on publication. Publishes ms an average of 2 months after acceptance. Byline given. Offers kill fee. Buys second serial (reprint) rights. Editorial lead time 3 months. Submit seasonal material 2 months in advance. Reports in 3 weeks on queries; 2 months on mss. Sample copy and writer's guidelines for #10 SASE.

● The editor says she wants to see mountain outdoor sports writing *only*. No ball sports, hunting, fishing.
**Nonfiction:** Book excerpts, essays, exposé, how-to, humor, inspirational, interview/profile, new product, opinion, personal experience, photo feature, travel. Special issues: Snowboarding (December); Alpine and Nordic (January and February); Running (March); Adventure Travel (April), Triathelon (May); Paddling (July); Mountain Biking (June), Women's Sports (September). No articles on football, baseball, basketball or other sports covered in-depth by newspapers. **Buys 24 mss/year.** Query with published clips. Length: 2,500 words maximum. **Pays $150 minimum.** Also publishes short articles on active outdoor sports, catch-all topics that are seasonably targeted. Query with idea first by mail or e-mail. Sometimes pays expenses of writers on assignment.
**Reprints:** Send photocopy of article and information about when and where the article previously appeared. Pays 20-25% of amount paid for an original article.

**Photos:** State availability of photos with submission. Reviews transparencies and prints. Captions and identification of subjects required. Buys one-time rights.
**Columns/Departments:** Starting Lines (short newsy items); Running, Cycling, Fitness, Nutrition, Sports Medicine, Off the Beaten Path (sports we don't usually cover). **Buys 20 mss/year.** Query. **Pays $25-200.**
**Tips:** "Have a Colorado angle to the story, a catchy cover letter, good clips and demonstrate that you've read and understand our magazine and its readers."

**$ SILENT SPORTS**, Waupaca Publishing Co., P.O. Box 152, Waupaca WI 54981-9990. (715)258-5546. Fax: (715)258-8162. **Contact:** Greg Marr, editor. **75% freelance written.** Eager to work with new/unpublished writers. Monthly magazine on running, cycling, cross-country skiing, canoeing, kayaking, snowshoeing, in-line skating, camping, backpacking and hiking aimed at people in Wisconsin, Minnesota, northern Illinois and portions of Michigan and Iowa. "Not a coffee table magazine. Our readers are participants from rank amateur weekend athletes to highly competitive racers." Estab. 1984. Circ. 10,000. Pays on publication. Publishes ms an average of 3 months after acceptance. Byline given. Offers 20% kill fee. Buys one-time rights. Submit seasonal material 4 months in advance. Reports in 3 months. Sample copy and writer's guidelines for 10×13 SAE with 6 first-class stamps.
  ● The editor needs local angles on in-line skating, recreation bicycling and snowshoeing.
**Nonfiction:** General interest, how-to, interview/profile, opinion, technical, travel. All stories/articles must focus on the Upper Midwest. First-person articles discouraged. **Buys 25 mss/year.** Query. Length: 2,500 words maximum. **Pays $15-100.** Sometimes pays expenses of writers on assignment.
**Reprints:** Send typed ms with rights for sale noted and information about when and where the article previously appeared. Pays 50% of amount paid for an original article.
**Photos:** State availability of photos with submission. Reviews transparencies. Pays $5-15 for b&w story photos; $50 for color covers. Buys one-time rights.
**Tips:** "Where-to-go and personality profiles are areas most open to freelancers. Writers should keep in mind that this is a regional, Midwest-based publication. We want only stories/articles with a focus on our region."

**$ $ $ SPIKE, The Magazine from Finish Line**, Emmis Publishing, One Emmis Plaza, 40 Monument Circle, Suite 100, Indianapolis IN 46204. **Contact:** John Thomas, special projects editor. **100% freelance written.** Quarterly. "*Spike* goes to customers of Finish Line, a chain of more than 300 athletic shoe and apparel stores. Most readers are young males with an interest in sports and pop culture. Writing should be bright, hip and tight." Estab. 1997. Circ. 650,000. Pays on publication. Publishes ms 3 months after acceptance. Byline given. Buys first North American serial rights and one-time rights. Editorial lead time 4 months. Submit seasonal material 6 months in advance. Sample copy for 9×12 SAE and 5 first-class stamps.
**Nonfiction:** General interest, how-to (fitness), interview/profile, new product. *No unsolicited mss.* No first-person essays. **Buys 12-15 mss/year.** Query with published clips. Length: 750-2,000 words. **Pays $250-1,000.** Sometimes pays expenses of writers on assignment.
**Columns/Departments:** Fitness (for ages 15-20); Music (hot new groups); High Tech (games, web pages, etc. that are sports related), all 500-750 words. **Buys 12 mss/year.** Query with published clips. **Pays $50-500.**
**Tips:** "Demonstrated access to and ability to work with top athletes and pop-culture figures is a plus."

**⊠ $ $ $ SPORT**, Petersen Publishing Co., 110 Fifth Ave., 3rd Floor, New York NY 10011. (212)886-3600. Fax: (212)229-4838. E-mail: sport@petersenpub.com. Managing Editor: Steve Gordon. Editor: Norb Garrett. **Contact:** John Roach, executive editor. **80% freelance written.** Monthly magazine "for the active adult sports fan. *Sport* offers profiles of the players and the people behind the scenes in the world of sports. *Sport* magazine is the oldest, largest, monthly sports feature publication reaching over 4.3 million young, active, sports-minded enthusiasts each issue. Not a recap of what happened last week, but previews and predictions of what will happen this month, next month, next year. In-depth profiles, investigative reporting, lively features about the action on and off the field! *Sport* magazine is the complete sports magazine written and edited for the ultimate sports fan!" Estab. 1946. Circ. 1 million. Pays on publication. Publishes ms an average of 2 months after acceptance. Offers ⅓% kill fee. Buys first North American serial and electronic rights. Editorial lead time 6 weeks. Submit seasonal material 6 months in advance. Reports in 2 months.
**Nonfiction:** Book excerpts, exposé, historic/nostalgic, humor, interview/profile, photo feature, travel. "Prefers to see articles on professional, big-time sports: basketball, football, baseball, hockey, some boxing. Articles must be contemporary pieces, not a history of sports or a particular sport." Query with published clips. Length: News briefs, 200-300 words; Departments, 1,400 words; Features, 1,500-3,000 words. **Pays $1/word.**
**Columns/Departments:** Scott Burton, sections editor. Business (how sports affect fans), 800 words; Media (features on top broadcast talent), 1,200 words; Raw Sport (photo-driven look at emerging sports), 400 words. **Buys 40 ms/year.** Query with published clips. **Pays $1/word.**
**Fiction:** Norb Garret, editor. Sports. **Buys 1 ms/year.** Query with published clips. Send complete ms. Length: 1,200-3,600 words. **Pays $1/word.**

**⊠ $ SPORTS ETC, The Northwest's Outdoor Magazine**, Sports Etc, P.O. Box 9272, Seattle WA 98109. (206)286-8566. Fax: (206)286-1330. E-mail: staff@sportsetc.com. Website: http://www.sportsetc.com. **Contact:** Dan Engel, editor. **80% freelance written.** Consumer publication published monthly covering outdoor recreation in the Pacific Northwest. "Writers must have a solid knowledge of sport they are writing about. They must be doers." Estab. 1988. Circ. 40,000. Pays on publication. Publishes ms an average of 6 months after acceptance. Byline given. Buys first rights. Editorial lead time 2 months. Submit seasonal material 4 months in advance. Accepts queries by mail, e-mail, fax. Accepts simultaneous submissions. Sample copy and writer's guidelines free.

**Nonfiction:** Interview/profile, new product, travel. Query with published clips. Length: 750-2,500 words. **Pays $10-50.** Sometimes pays expenses of writers on assignment.

**Reprints:** Accepts previously published submissions.

**Photos:** Send photos with submission. Reviews negatives and transparencies. Captions, model releases and identification of subjects required. Buys all rights.

**Columns/Departments:** Your Health (health and wellness), 750 words. **Buys 10-12 mss/year.** Query with published clips. **Pays $40-50.**

■ The online magazine carries original content not found in the print edition.

**Tips:** "*Sports Etc* is written for the serious Pacific Northwest outdoor recreationalist. The magazine's look, style and editorial content actively engage the reader, delivering insightful perspectives on the sports it has come to be known for—alpine skiing, bicycling, hiking, in-line skating, kayaking, marathons, mountain climbing, Nordic skiing, running and snowboarding. *Sports Etc* magazine wants vivid writing, telling images and original perspectives to produce its smart, entertaining monthly."

**$ $ $ SPORTS ILLUSTRATED**, Time Inc. Magazine Co., Time & Life Bldg., Rockefeller Center, New York NY 10020. (212)522-1212. **Contact:** Myra Gelband. Weekly. "*Sports Illustrated* reports and interprets the world of sport, recreation and active leisure. It previews, analyzes and comments upon major games and events, as well as those noteworthy for character and spirit alone. It features individuals connected to sport and evaluates trends concerning the part sport plays in contemporary life. In addition, the magazine has articles on such subjects as fashion, physical fitness and conservation. Special departments deal with sports equipment, books and statistics." Estab. 1954. Circ. 3,339,000. Query only by mail before submitting.

**◪ $ WINDY CITY SPORTS MAGAZINE**, Windy City Publishing, 1450 W. Randolph, Chicago IL 60607. (312)421-1551. Fax: (312)421-1454. E-mail: wcpublish@aol.com. Website: http://www.windycitysportsmag.com. **Contact:** Jeff Banowetz, editor. **75% freelance written.** Monthly magazine covering amateur, participatory, sports. Estab. 1987. Circ. 100,000 (Chicago and suburbs). Pays on publication. Publishes ms an average of 2 months after acceptance. Byline given. Offers 25% kill fee. Buys first North American serial rights. Editorial lead time 2 months. Submit seasonal material 3 months in advance. Accepts simultaneous submissions. Reports in 1 month on queries, mss. Sample copy, writer's guidelines free.

   **O─** "The easiest way to break into the magazine is through our back page essay. We enjoy creative, funny stories on any of the sports we cover. We are also eager to hear story ideas concerning the sports we cover. Writers with a specific story idea are much more likely to be hired."

**Nonfiction:** Essays (re: sports controversial issues), humor, opinion, personal experience, travel. No articles on professional sports. Special issues: Chicago Marathon (October); Skiing and Snowboarding (November); Winter Sports (December). **Buys 150 mss/year.** Query with clips. Length: 700-2,000 words. **Pays $100-150.** Sometimes pays expenses of writers on assignment.

**Photos:** State availability or send photos with submission. Reviews contact sheets. Buys one-time rights.

**Columns/Departments:** "We run the following columns every month: running, cycling, and in-line skating, all 1,000 words." **Buys 70 mss/year.** Query with published clips. **Pays $100-200.**

**Tips:** "Best way to get assignment: ask for writer's guidelines, editor's schedule and sample copy ($3). *Read magazine!* Query me with story ideas for a column or query on features using editorial schedule. Always try to target Chicago looking Midwest."

**WOMEN'S SPORTS & FITNESS**, Condé Nast Publications, Inc., 4 Times Square, New York NY 10036. **Contact:** Mary Gail Pezzimenti, managing editor. Bimonthly magazine covering sports and fitness from a women's perspective. "A magazine all about participatory sports and spectator sports and fitness issues, we focus on women's involvement and roles in these ever-changing fields." Estab. 1997. Circ. 475,000. **Pays on acceptance.** Byline given. Buys first North American serial and nonexclusive syndication rights. Reports in 2 months.

   **O─** "The best way to break in is to know something we don't: what's the new sport, the new hybrid sport, the new face in emerging sport trends."

**Nonfiction:** "We're interested in emerging sport trends, athletes and attitudes, as well as breaking health and nutrition news." **Buys 35 mss/year.** Query with published clips. Length: 1,000-3,000 words. **Pays $1/word.**

**Columns/Departments:** Active File (fitness, health and nutrition), 300-700 words. **Pays $1/word.** Other departments written by regular columnists.

# Golf

**$ $ CHICAGO DISTRICT GOLFER**, TPG Sports Inc., 1710 Douglas Dr. N., #201, Golden Valley MN 55422. (612)595-0808. Fax: (612)595-0016. E-mail: bob@pgsports.com or rdoyle@cdga.org. Website: http://www.tpgsports. com or http://www.cdga.org. Managing Editor: Bob Fallen. **Contact:** Ryan Doyle, editor [(630)954-2180]. **90% freelance written.** Bimonthly magazine covering golf in Illinois, the official publication of the Chicago District Golf

Association and Golf Association of Illinois. Estab. 1922. Circ. 65,000. Pays on acceptance or publication. Byline given. Buys all rights. Editorial lead time 2 months. Submit seasonal material 3 months in advance. Accepts queries by mail, e-mail. Accepts simultaneous submissions. Sample copy and writer's guidelines free.

**Nonfiction:** Book excerpts, general interest, historical/nostalgic, how-to (golf), humor, interview/profile, new product, opinion, personal experience, photo feature, technical, travel. **Buys 25-35 mss/year**. Query with or without published clips. Length: 500-5,000 words. **Pays $50-500**. Sometimes pays expenses of writers on assignment.

**Reprints:** Accepts previously published submissions.

**Photos:** State availability of photos with submission. Reviews contact sheets. Negotiates payment individually. Captions, identification of subjects required.

**N $ $ $ GOLF CANADA, Official Magazine of the Royal Canadian Golf Association**, RCGA/Laurel Oak Marketing, 1333 Dorval Dr., Oakville, Ontario L6J 4Z3 Canada. (905)849-9700. Fax: (905)845-7040. E-mail: golfcanada@rcga.org. Website: http://www.rcga.org. Managing Editor: Joe Romagnolo. **Contact:** Bill Steinburg, editor. **80% freelance written.** Magazine published 4 times/year April-November covering Canadian golf. "*Golf Canada* is the official magazine of the Royal Canadian Golf Association, published to entertain and enlighten members about RCGA-related activities and to generally support and promote amateur golf in Canada." Estab. 1994. Circ. 135,000. **Pays on acceptance.** Byline given. Offers 100% kill fee. Buys first translation rights and electronic rights (occasionally). Editorial lead time 3 months. Submit seasonal material 6 months in advance. Accepts queries by mail, e-mail, fax, phone. Sample copy free.

**Nonfiction:** Historical/nostalgic, interview/profile, new product, opinion, photo feature, travel. No professional golf-related articles. **Buys 42 mss/year.** Query with published clips. Length: 750-3,000 words. **Pays 50¢/word.** Sometimes pays expenses of writers on assignment.

**Reprints:** Accepts previously published submissions.

**Photos:** State availability of photos with submission. Reviews contact sheets, negatives, transparencies and prints. Negotiates payment individually. Captions required. Buys all rights.

**Columns/Departments:** Guest Column (focus on issues surrounding the Canadian golf community), 700 words. **Buys 4 mss/year.** Query. **Pays 50¢/word.**

**$ $ $ GOLF ILLUSTRATED**, NatCom Inc., 5300 Cityplex Tower, 2448 E. 81st, Tulsa OK 74137. (918)491-6100. Fax: (918)491-9424. Website: www.golfillustrated.com. **Contact:** Mark Chesnut, editor-in-chief. **80% freelance written.** Bimonthly golf magazine. "We cover everything and anything to do with golf, but we're not into the *politics* of the game. Instruction is the primary focus." Estab. 1914. Circ. 300,000. Pays 30 days after acceptance. Publishes ms an average of 3 months after acceptance. Byline given. Offers 20% kill fee. Buys first North American serial rights. Editorial lead time 10 weeks. Submit seasonal material 6 months in advance. Accepts queries by mail. Reports in 2 months. Writer's guidelines free.

**Nonfiction:** How-to (golf instruction), technical, travel (focus on golf) and golf equipment. "No opinion or politics." **Buys 50 mss/year.** Query. Length: 1,200-1,500 words. **Pays $1/word minimum.** Sometimes pays expenses of writers on assignment.

**Photos:** Negotiates payment individually. Identification of subjects required. Buys one-time rights.

**Columns/Departments:** Gallery Shots (short pieces), 200-400 words. **Buys 20 mss/year.** Query. **Pays $50-400.**

■ The online magazine carries original content not found in the print edition.

**Tips:** "Offer a unique perspective; short, sweet queries with SASE are appreciated. *Don't* call every two weeks to find out when your story will be published. Be patient, we get lots of submissions and try our best to respond promptly."

**N $ GOLF NEWS MAGAZINE, Southern California's Premier Golf Magazine Since 1984**, Golf News Magazine, 73-280 El Paseo, Suite 6, Palm Desert CA 92260. (760)836-3700. Fax: (760)836-3703. E-mail: golfnews@aol .com. **Contact:** Dan Poppers, editor/publisher. **70% freelance written.** Monthly magazine covering golf. "Our publication specializes in the creative treatment of the sport of golf, offering a variety of themes and slants as related to golf. If it's good writing and relates to golf, we're interested." Estab. 1984. Circ. 17,000. Pays on publication or **on acceptance.** Publishes ms an average of 2 months after acceptance. Byline given. Offers negotiable kill fee. Buys first rights and makes work-for-hire assignments. Editorial lead time 2 months. Submit seasonal material 2 months in advance. Accepts queries by mail, e-mail, fax. Accepts simultaneous submissions. Reports in 3 weeks on queries; 1 month on mss. Sample copy for $2 and 9×12 SAE with 4 first-class stamps.

**Nonfiction:** Book excerpts, essays, exposé, general interest, historical/nostalgic, how-to, humor, inspirational, interview/profile, opinion, personal experience, photo feature, technical, travel, real estate. "We will consider any topic related to golf that is written well with high standards. **Buys 20 mss/year.** Query with published clips. Length: 300 words. **Pays $25-125.** "Golf equipment is also available as payment."

**Reprints:** Accepts previously published submissions.

**Photos:** State availability of photos with submission. Negotiates payment individually. Identification of subjects required. Buys one-time rights.

**Columns/Departments:** Submit ideas. **Buys 10 mss/year.** Query with published clips. **Pays $25-100.**

**Tips:** "Solid, creative, good, professional writing. Stay away from clichés and the hackneyed. Only good writers need apply. Our guidelines are open—we supply no written guidelines."

**$ $ $ GOLF TIPS, The Game's Most In-Depth Instruction & Equipment Magazine**, Werner Publishing Corp., 12121 Wilshire Blvd., Suite 1200, Los Angeles CA 90025. (310)820-1500. Fax: (310)826-5008. E-mail: editors@ golftipsmag.com. Website: http://www.golftipsmag.com. Senior Editor: Mike Chwasky. Editor: David DeNunzio. Editor at Large: Tom Ferrell. **Contact:** Loren Colin, managing editor. **95% freelance written.** Magazine published 9 times/ year covering golf instruction and equipment. "We provide mostly concise, very clear golf instruction pieces for the serious golfer." Estab. 1986. Pays on publication. Publishes ms an average of 2 months after acceptance. Byline given. Offers 33% kill fee. Buys first rights and second serial (reprint) rights. Editorial lead time 3 months. Submit seasonal material 4 months in advance. Reports in 1 month. Sample copy and writer's guidelines free.
**Nonfiction:** Book excerpts, how-to, interview/profile, new product, photo feature, technical, travel: all golf related. "General golf essays rarely make it." **Buys 125 mss/year.** Send complete ms. Length: 250-2,000 words. **Pays $300-1,000 for assigned articles; $300-800 unsolicited articles.** Occasionally negotiates other forms of payment. Sometimes pays expenses of writers on assignment.
**Reprints:** Accepts previously published submissions.
**Photos:** State availability of photos with submission. Reviews 2×2 transparencies. Negotiates payment individually. Captions and identification of subjects required. Buys all rights.
**Columns/Departments:** Stroke Saver (very clear, concise instruction), 350 words; Lesson Library (book excerpts— usually in a series), 1,000 words; Travel Tips (formated golf travel), 2,500 words. **Buys 40 mss/year.** Query with published clips or send complete ms. **Pays $300-850.**
    ■  The online magazine carries original content not found in the print edition. Contact: Tom Ferrell, online editor.
**Tips:** "Contact a respected PGA Professional and find out if they're interested in being published. A good writer can turn an interview into a decent instruction piece."

**◪ $ $ GOLF TRAVELER, Official Publication of Golf Card International**, Affinity Group, Inc., 2575 Vista del Mar, Ventura CA 93001. Fax: (805)667-4217. Website: http://www.golfcard.com. **Contact:** Valerie Law, editor. **25% freelance written.** Bimonthly magazine "is the membership magazine for the Golf Card, an organization that offers its members reduced or waived greens fees at 3,000 affiliated golf courses in North America." Estab. 1976. Circ. 130,000. **Pays on acceptance.** Byline given. Offers 33% kill fee. Buys first North American serial rights. Editorial lead time 3 months. Submit seasonal material 4-5 months in advance. Accepts simultaneous and previously published submissions. Reports in 1 month. Sample copy for $2.50 plus 9×12 SASE. Writer's guidelines free with SASE.
**Nonfiction:** Book excerpts, essays, how-to, interview/profile, new product, personal experience, photo feature, technical. PGA Orlando Merchandise Show (January-February). No poetry or cartoons. **Buys 25 mss/year.** Query with published clips or send complete ms. Length: 500-2,500 words. **Pays $75-500.** Sometimes pays expenses of writers on assignment.
**Photos:** Send photos with submission. Reviews transparencies. Negotiates payment individually. Model releases and identification of subjects required. Buys one-time rights.
**Tips:** "We're always looking for golf writers who can put together destination features revolving around our affiliated golf courses."

**Ⓝ $ $ THE GOLFER**, Heather & Pine Publishing, 21 E. 40th St., New York NY 10016. (212)696-2484. Fax: (212)696-1678. E-mail: racquet@walrus.com. Editor: H.K. Pickens. Managing Editor: Stephen Weiss. **Contact:** Colin Sheehan, features editor. **40% freelance written.** Bimonthly magazine covering golf. "A sophisticated, controversational tone for a lifestyle-oriented magazine." Estab. 1994. Circ. 253,000. Pays on publication. Publishes ms 2 months after acceptance. Byline given. Offers negotiable kill fee. Buys all rights. Editorial lead time 2 months. Submit seasonal material 4 months in advance. Accepts queries by mail, e-mail, fax. Accepts simultaneous submissions. Sample copy free.
**Nonfiction:** Book excerpts, essays, general interest, historical/nostalgic, how-to, humor, inspirational, interview/profile, new product, opinion, personal experience, photo feature, technical, travel. Send complete ms. Length: 300-2,000 words. **Pays $150-600.**
**Reprints:** Accepts previously published submissions.
**Photos:** Send photos with submission. Reviews any size transparencies. Buys one-time rights.

**$ $ MICHIGAN LINKS**, TPG Sports Inc., 1710 Douglas Dr. N., #201, Golden Valley MN 55422. (612)595-0808. Fax: (612)595-0016. E-mail: bob@tpgsports.com or tbranch@gam.org. Website: http://www.tpgsports.com or http:// www.gam.org. Managing Editor: Bob Fallen. **Contact:** Tonia Branch, editor [(245)553-4200]. **80% freelance written.** Bimonthly magazine covering golf in Michigan, the official publication of the Golf Association of Michigan. Estab. 1997. Circ. 40,000. Pays on acceptance or publication. Byline sometimes given. Buys all rights. Editorial lead time 3 months. Submit seasonal material 3 months in advance. Accepts queries by mail, e-mail. Accepts simultaneous submissions. Sample copy and guidelines free.
**Nonfiction:** Book excerpts, essays, historical/nostalgic, how-to (golf), humor, inspirational, interview/profile, new product, opinion, personal experience, photo feature. **Buys 20-30 mss/year.** Query with or without published clips. Length: 500-5,000 words. **Pays $50-500.** Sometimes pays expenses of writers on assignment.
**Reprints:** Accepts previously published submissions.
**Photos:** State availability of photos with submission. Reviews contact sheets. Negotiates payment individually. Captions, identification of subjects required. Negotiates payment individually. Rights purchased varies.

**$ $ MINNESOTA GOLFER**, TPG Sports Inc., 1710 Douglas Dr. N., #201, Golden Valley MN 55422. (612)595-0808. Fax: (612)595-0016. E-mail: bob pgsports.com or rdoyle@cdga.org. Website: http://www.tpgsports.com or http://www.mngolf.org. Managing Editor: Bob Fallen. **Contact:** Chris Geer, editor [(612)927-4643]. **80% freelance written**. Bimonthly magazine covering golf in Minnesota, the official publication of the Minnesota Golf Association. Estab. 1975. Circ. 72,000. Pays on acceptance or publication. Byline given. Buys all rights. Editorial lead time 3 months. Submit seasonal material 3 months in advance. Accepts queries by mail. Accepts simultaneous submissions. Sample copy and writer's guidelines free.

**Nonfiction:** Book excerpts, essays, historical/nostalgic, how-to (golf), humor, inspirational, interview/profile, new product, opinion, personal experience, photo feature. **Buys 20-30 mss/year**. Query with or without published clips. Length: 500-5,000 words. **Pays $50-500**. Sometimes pays expenses of writers on assignment.

**Reprints:** Accepts previously published submissions.

**Photos:** State availability of photos with submission. Reviews contact sheets. Negotiates payment individually. Captions, identification of subjects required. Negotiates payment individually. Rights purchased varies.

**$ $ VIRGINIA GOLFER**, TPG Sports Inc., 1710 Douglas Dr. N., #201, Golden Valley MN 55422. (612)595-0808. Fax: (612)595-0016. E-mail: bob@tpgsports.com. Website: http://www.tpgsports.com or http://www.vsga.org. Managing Editor: Bob Fallen. **Contact:** Harold Pearson, editor [(804)378-2300]. **80% freelance written**. Bimonthly magazine covering golf in Virginia, the official publication of the Virginia Golf Association. Estab. 1997. Circ. 40,000. Pays on publication. Byline given. Buys all rights. Editorial lead time 2 months. Submit seasonal material 3 months in advance. Accepts queries by mail, e-mail. Accepts simultaneous submissions. Sample copy and writer's guidelines free.

**Nonfiction:** Book excerpts, essays, historical/nostalgic, how-to (golf), humor, inspirational, interview/profile, new product, opinion, personal experience, photo feature, technical (golf equipment). **Buys 30-40 mss/year**. Query with or without published clips or send complete ms. Length: 500-5,000 words. **Pays $50-500**. Sometimes pays expenses of writers on assignment.

**Reprints:** Accepts previously published submissions.

**Photos:** State availability of photos with submission. Reviews contact sheets. Negotiates payment individually. Captions, identification of subjects required. Negotiates payment individually. Rights purchased varies.

**Columns/Departments:** Golf Travel (where to play), Golf Business (what's happening?). Query.

# Guns

**$ $ GUN DIGEST**, DBI Books, Inc., Division of Krause Publications, 700 E. State St., Iola WI 54990. (800)767-6310. Fax: (715)445-4087. **Contact:** Ken Warner, editor-in-chief. **50% freelance written.** Prefers to work with published/established writers but works with a small number of new/unpublished writers each year. Annual journal covering guns and shooting. Estab. 1944. **Pays on acceptance.** Publishes ms an average of 20 months after acceptance. Byline given. Buys all rights. Reports in 1 month.

**Nonfiction: Buys 50 mss/issue.** Query. Length: 500-5,000 words. **Pays $100-600** for text/art package.

**Photos:** State availability of photos with query letter. Reviews 8×10 b&w prints. Payment for photos included in payment for ms. Captions required.

**Tips:** Award of $1,000 to author of best article (juried) in each issue.

**$ $ MUZZLE BLASTS**, National Muzzle Loading Rifle Association, P.O. Box 67, Friendship IN 47021. (812)667-5131. Fax: (812)667-5137. E-mail: nmlra@nmlra.org. Website: http://www.nmlra.org. Editor: Eric A. Bye. **Contact:** Terri Trowbridge, director of publications. **65% freelance written.** Monthly association magazine. "Articles must relate to muzzleloading or the muzzleloading era of American history." Estab. 1939. Circ. 25,000. Pays on publication. Publishes ms an average of 6 months after acceptance. Byline given. Offers $50 kill fee. Buys first North American serial rights, one-time rights and second serial (reprint) rights. Editorial lead time 4 months. Submit seasonal material 6 months in advance. Reports in 1 month on mss. Sample copy and writer's guidelines free.

● *Muzzle Blasts* now accepts manuscripts on 5.25 or 3.5 DOS diskettes in most major word processing programs; they prefer any of the Word Perfect™ formats.

**Nonfiction:** Book excerpts, general interest, historical/nostalgic, how-to, humor, interview/profile, new product, personal experience, photo feature, technical, travel. "No subjects that do not pertain to muzzleloading." **Buys 80 mss/year.** Query. Length: 2,500 words. **Pays $200 minimum for assigned articles; $50 minimum for unsolicited articles.**

**Photos:** Send photos with submission. Reviews 5×7 prints. Negotiates payment individually. Captions and model releases required. Buys one-time rights.

**Columns/Departments: Buys 96 mss/year.** Query. **Pays $50-200.**

**Fiction:** Adventure, historical, humorous. Must pertain to muzzleloading. **Buys 6 mss/year.** Query. Length: 2,500 words. **Pays $50-300.**

**Fillers:** Facts. **Pays $50.**

The online magazine carries original content not found in the print edition.

**Tips:** The National Muzzle Loading Rifle Association also publishes *Muzzle Blasts Online* on the World Wide Web. This electronic magazine is focused primarily for a nonmember audience. Writers and photographers are free to accept or reject this use of their work, and statements regarding this issue can be enclosed with your submission. (No additional payment will be made for use on *Muzzle Blasts Online*. The only time payment will be made for electronic use is when your article is used exclusively on the Web and has not been printed on the paper version of the magazine.) Please contact the NMLRA for writer's guidelines.

**$ $ SHOTGUN NEWS**, Primedia, Box 1790, Peoria IL 61656. (309)679-5408. Fax: (309)679-5476. E-mail: sgnews@aol.com. Website: http://www.shotgunnews.com. **Contact:** Robert W. Hunnicutt, general manager/editor. **95% freelance written.** Tabloid published every 10 days covering firearms, accessories, ammunition and militaria. "The nation's oldest and largest gun sales publication. Provides up-to-date market information for gun trade and consumers." Estab. 1946. Circ. 100,000. **Pays on acceptance.** Publishes ms 3 months after acceptance. Byline given. Buys first North American serial rights. Editorial lead time 1 month. Submit seasonal material 3 months in advance. Reports in 1 month on queries. Sample copy free.

**Nonfiction:** How-to, technical, historical. No political pieces, fiction or poetry. **Buys 50 mss/year.** Query. Length: 1,000-3,000 words. **Pays $200-500 for assigned articles.** Sometimes pays expenses of writers on assignment.

**Photos:** Send photos with submission. Reviews prints. Offers no additional payment for photos accepted with ms. Captions required. Buys one-time rights.

# Hiking/Backpacking

**$ $ $ $ BACKPACKER**, Rodale, 33 E. Minor St., Emmaus PA 18098-0099. (610)967-8296. Fax: (610)967-8181. E-mail: bpeditor@rodalepress.com. Website: http://www.backpacker.com. Executive Editor: Thom Hogan. Managing Editor: Tom Shealey. **Contact:** Jim Gorman, Michele Morris, senior editors. **50% freelance written.** Magazine published 9 times/year covering wilderness travel for backpackers. Estab. 1973. Circ. 280,000. **Pays on acceptance.** Byline given. Buys one-time rights or all rights. Accepts queries by phone, e-mail, fax. Reports in 2 months. Writer's guidelines for #10 SASE.

**Nonfiction:** Essays, exposé, historical/nostalgic, how-to (expedition planner), humor, inspirational, interview/profile, new product, opinion, personal experience, technical, travel. No step-by-step accounts of what you did on your summer vacation—stories that chronicle every rest stop and gulp of water. Query with published clips and SASE. Length: 750-3,000 words. **Pays $400-2,000.** Sometimes pays (pre-determined) expenses of writers on assignment. "What we want are features that let us and the readers 'feel' the place, and experience your wonderment, excitement, disappointment or other emotions encountered 'out there.' If we feel like we've been there after reading your story, you've succeeded."

**Photos:** State availability of photos with submission. Pay varies. Buys one-time rights.

**Columns/Departments:** Signpost, "News From All Over" (adventure, environment, wildlife, trails, techniques, organizations, special interests—well-written, entertaining, short, newsy item), 50-500 words; Body Language (in-the-field health column), 750-1,200 words; Moveable Feast (food-related aspects of wilderness: nutrition, cooking techniques, recipes, products and gear), 500-750 words; Weekend Wilderness (brief but detailed guides to wilderness areas, providing thorough trip-planning information, only enough anecdote to give a hint, then the where/when/hows), 500-750 words; Know How (ranging from beginner to expert focus, written by people with solid expertise, details ways to improve performance, how-to-do-it instructions, information on equipment manufacturers and places readers can go), 750-1,500 words; and Backcountry (personal perspectives, quirky and idiosyncratic, humorous critiques, manifestos and misadventures, interesting angle, lesson, revelation or moral), 750-1,200 words. **Buys 50-75 mss/year.** Query with published clips. **Pays $200-600.** No phone calls regarding story ideas. Written queries only.

**Fillers:** Facts, newsbreaks. **Buys 30/year.** Length: 50-100 words. **Pays $25-100.**

The online magazine carries original content not found in the print edition. Contact: Brian Fiske, online editor.

**Tips:** "Our best advice is to read the publication—most freelancers don't know the magazine at all. The best way to break in is with an article for the Backcountry, Weekend Wilderness or Signpost Department."

**$ $ $ $ OUTSIDE**, Mariah Media Inc., Outside Plaza, 400 Market St., Santa Fe NM 87501. (505)989-7100. Editor: Hal Espen. **Contact:** Sharon Parker, assistant to the editor. **90% freelance written.** "*Outside* is a monthly national magazine for active, educated, upscale adults who love the outdoors and are concerned about its preservation." Estab. 1977. Circ. 500,000. **Pays on acceptance.** Publishes ms an average of 3 months after acceptance. Byline given. Offers 25% kill fee. Buys first North American serial rights. Submit seasonal material 5 months in advance. Reports in 2 months. Sample copy for $5 and 9×12 SAE with 9 first-class stamps. Writer's guidelines for SASE.

● *Outside* won the 1998 National Magazine Award for General Excellence for magazines with circulation of 100,000-400,000.

**Nonfiction:** Book excerpts; essays; reports on the environment; outdoor sports and expeditions; general interest; how-to; humor; inspirational; interview/profile (major figures associated with sports, travel, environment, outdoor); opinion; personal experience (expeditions; trying out new sports); photo feature (outdoor photography); technical (reviews of equipment, how-to); travel (adventure, sports-oriented travel). All should pertain to the outdoors: Bike section; Downhill Skiing; Cross-country Skiing; Adventure Travel. Do not want to see articles about sports that we don't cover (basketball, tennis, golf, etc.). **Buys 40 mss/year.** Query with published clips and SASE. Length: 1,500-4,000 words. **Pays $1/word.** Pays expenses of writers on assignment.

**Photos:** "Do not send photos; if we decide to use a story, we may ask to see the writer's photos." Reviews transparencies. Offers $180/photo minimum. Captions, identification of subjects required. Buys one-time rights.

**Columns/Departments:** Dispatches, contact Kevin Fedanko (news, events, short profiles relevant to outdoors), 200-1,000 words; Destinations, contact Susan Enfield (places to explore, news, and tips for adventure travelers), 250-400 words; Review, contact Eric Hagerman (evaluations of products), 200-1,500 words. **Buys 180 mss/year.** Query with published clips. Length: 200-2,000 words. **Pays $1/word.**

■ The online magazine carries original content not found in the print edition. Contact: Amy Marr, online editor.

**Tips:** "Prospective writers should study the magazine before querying. Look at the magazine for our style, subject matter and standards." The departments are the best areas for freelancers to break in.

## Horse Racing

**$ $ THE BACKSTRETCH**, United Thoroughbred Trainers of America, Inc., P.O. Box 7065, Louisville KY 40257-0065. (800)325-3487. Fax: (502)893-0026. E-mail: uttainc@couriernet.infi.net. Website: http://www.thebackstretch.com. **Contact:** Melissa McIntosh, production manager. **90% freelance written.** Estab. 1962. Circ. 10,000. Uses mostly established turf writers, but works with a few less experienced writers each year. Bimonthly magazine directed chiefly to Thoroughbred trainers but also to owners, fans and others working in or involved with the racing industry. Accepts queries by mail, e-mail, fax, phone. Pays on publication. Publishes ms 3 months after acceptance, often longer. Sample copy on request.
**Nonfiction:** Profiles of trainers, owners, jockeys, horses and other personalities who make up the world of racing; analysis of industry issues; articles on particular tracks or races, veterinary topics; information on legal or business aspects of owning, training or racing horses; and historical perspectives. Opinions should be informed by expertise on the subject treated. Non-commissioned articles are accepted on a speculation basis. Pays on publication. If not suitable, articles are returned only if a SASE is included. Length: 1,500-2,500 words. **Pays $150-450.**
**Reprints:** Occasionally accepts previously published material, especially if it has appeared only in a regional or specialized publication. Send typed ms with rights for sale noted and information about when and where the article previously appeared. Payment negotiable.
**Photos:** It is advisable to include photo illustrations when possible, or these can be arranged for separately.
**Tips:** "If an article is a simultaneous submission, this must be stated and we must be advised if it is accepted elsewhere. Articles should be double spaced and may be submitted by mail, fax or e-mail on 3½-inch disk saved in text or in program compatible with PageMaker 5.0 for Macintosh."

**$ $ THE QUARTER RACING JOURNAL**, American Quarter Horse Association, P.O. Box 32470, Amarillo TX 79120. (806)376-4888. Fax: (806)349-6400. E-mail: aowens@aqha.org. Website: http://www.aqha.com. Executive Editor: Jim Jennings. **Contact:** Amy Owens, editor. **10% freelance written.** Monthly magazine. "The official racing voice of the American Quarter Horse Association. We promote quarter horse racing. Articles include training, breeding, nutrition, sports medicine, health, history, etc." Estab. 1988. Circ. 9,000. **Pays on acceptance.** Publishes ms an average of 3 months after acceptance. Buys first North American serial rights. Submit seasonal material 3 months in advance. Accepts queries by mail, e-mail, fax, phone. Reports in 1 month on queries. Free sample copy and writer's guidelines.
**Nonfiction:** Historical (must be on quarter horses or people associated with them), how-to (training), nutrition, health, breeding and opinion. "We welcome submissions year-round." Special issue: Stallions (December). Query. Length: 700-1,500 words. **Pays $150-300.**
**Reprints:** Send photocopy of article and information about when and where the article previously appeared.
**Photos:** Send photos with submission. Additional payment for photos accepted with ms might be offered. Captions and identification of subjects required.
**Fiction:** Publishes novel excerpts.
**Tips:** "Query first—must be familiar with quarter horse racing and be knowledgeable of the sport. The *Journal* directs its articles to those who own, train and breed racing quarter horses, as well as fans and handicappers. Most open to features covering training, nutrition, health care. Use a knowledgeable source with credentials."

## Hunting & Fishing

**$ $ ALABAMA GAME & FISH**, Game & Fish Publications, Inc., P.O. Box 741, Marietta GA 30061. **Contact:** Jimmy Jacobs, editor. See *Game & Fish Publications*.

**◪ $ $ AMERICAN ANGLER, the Magazine of Fly Fishing & Fly Tying**, Abenaki Publishers, Inc., 160 Benmont Ave., Bennington VT 05201. Fax: (802)447-2471. **Contact:** Art Scheck, editor. **95% freelance written.** Bimonthly magazine covering fly fishing. "*American Angler* is dedicated to giving fly fishers practical information they can use—wherever they fish, whatever they fish for." Estab. 1976. Circ. 58,000. Pays on publication. Publishes ms an average of 6 months after acceptance. Byline given. Buys first North American serial rights (articles) or one-time rights (photos). Editorial lead time over 3 months. Submit seasonal material 5 months in advance. Reluctantly accepts simultaneous submissions, if so noted. Reports in 6 weeks on queries; 2 months on mss. Sample copy for $6. Writer's guidelines for SASE.

**Nonfiction:** Book excerpts (well in advance of publication), essays (a few), how-to (most important), humor, opinion (query first), personal experience ("but tired of the 'me 'n' Joe' stories"), photo feature (seldom), technical. No promotional flack to pay back free trips or freebies, no superficial, broad-brush coverage of subjects. **Buys 45-60 mss/year.** Query with published clips and SASE. Length: 800-2,200 words. **Pays $200-400.**

**Reprints:** Send information about when and where the article previously appeared. Pay negotiable.

**Photos:** Send photos with submission. Reviews contact sheets, transparencies. Offers no additional payment for photos accepted with ms. Captions, identification of subjects required. Acquires one-time rights. "Photographs are important. A fly-tying submission should always include samples of flies to send to our staff photographer, even if photos of the flies are included."

**Columns/Departments:** One-page shorts (problem solvers), 350-750 words. Query with clips. **Pays $100-300.**

**Tips:** "If you are new to this editor, please submit complete queries."

**$ $ AMERICAN HUNTER**, 11250 Waples Mill Rd., Fairfax VA 22030-9400. Fax: (703)267-3971. Editor: John Zent. **Contact:** Bill Rooney, managing editor. For hunters who are members of the National Rifle Association. "*The American Hunter* contains articles dealing with various sport hunting and related activities both at home and abroad. With the encouragment of the sport as a prime game management tool, emphasis is on technique, sportsmanship and safety. In each issue hunting equipment and firearms are evaluated, legislative happenings affecting the sport are reported, lore and legend are retold and the business of the Association is recorded in the Official Journal section." Circ. 1,000,000. **Pays on acceptance** for articles and on publication for photos. Buys first North American serial rights and subsequent reprint rights for NRA publications. Byline given. Reports in 1 month. Writer's guidelines for #10 SASE.

**Nonfiction:** Factual material on all phases of hunting: expository how-to, where-to, and general interest pieces; humor: personal narratives; and semi-technical articles on firearms, wildlife management or hunting. "Subject matter for feature articles falls into five general categories that run in each issue: deer, upland birds, waterfowl, big game and varmints/small game. Special issues: pheasants, whitetail tactics, black bear feed areas, mule deer, duck hunters' transport by land and sea, tech topics to be decided (October 1999); rut strategies, muzzleloader moose and elk, fall turkeys, staying warm, goose talk, long-range muzzleloading (November/December 1998). Not interested in material fishing, camping or firearms legislation." Prefers queries. Length: 1,800-2,000 words. **Pays $250-600.**

**Reprints:** Send typed ms with rights for sale noted and info about when and where it previously appeared.

**Photos:** No additional payment made for photos used with mss. Pays $25 for b&w photos purchased without accompanying mss. Pays $50-175 for color.

**Columns/Departments:** Hunting Guns, Hunting Loads and Public Hunting Grounds. Study back issues for appropriate subject matter and style. Length: 1,200-1,500 words. **Pays $300-350.**

**Tips:** "Although unsolicited manuscripts are welcomed, detailed query letters outlining the proposed topic and approach are appreciated and will save both writers and editors a considerable amount of time. If we like your story idea, you will be contacted by mail or phone and given direction on how we'd like the topic covered. NRA Publications accept all manuscripts and photographs for consideration on a specualtion basis only. Story angles should be narrow, but coverage must have depth. How-to articles are popular with readers and might range from methods for hunting to techniques on making gear used on successful hunts. Where-to articles should contain contacts and information needed to arrange a similar hunt. All submissions are judged on three criteria: story angle (it should be fresh, interesting, and informative); quality of writing (clear and lively—capable of holding the readers' attention throughout); and quality and quantity of accompanying photos (sharpness, reproduceability, and connection to text are most important.)"

**$ $ ARKANSAS SPORTSMAN**, Game & Fish Publications, Inc., P.O. Box 741, Marietta GA 30061. (770)953-9222. **Contact:** Editor. See *Game & Fish Publications.*

**$ BAIT FISHERMAN**, Beaver Pond Publishing, P.O. Box 224, Greenville PA 16125. (724)588-3492. Fax: (724)588-2486. **Contact:** Rich Faler, editor. **80% freelance written.** Bimonthly magazine covering natural bait fishing, fresh and saltwater. "We are slanted exclusively toward bait fishing of all species of fresh and saltwater fish." Estab. 1995. Circ. 5,000. Pays on publication. Publishes ms an average of 6 months after acceptance. Byline given. Buys first rights, one-time rights or second serial (reprint) rights. Editorial lead time 4 months. Submit seasonal material 4-6 months in advance. Accepts simultaneous submissions. Accepts electronic submissions by disk but hard copy preferred. Reports in 2 months on queries; 3 months on mss. Writer's guidelines free.

**Nonfiction:** General interest, how-to (bait collection, presentation, maintenance, etc.), interview/profile, personal experience (with bait fishing-specific slant), travel ("hot spot" locations). **Buys 30-40 mss/year.** Query. Length: 1,000-2,000 words. **Pays $30-100** plus 3 copies.

**Reprints:** Send ms and information about when and where the article previously appeared. Pays 50-70% of amount paid for an original article.

**Photos:** Send photos with submission. Reviews contact sheets, negatives, 35mm transparencies, 5×7 prints (preferred). No additional payment for photos accepted with ms. Captions, identification of subjects required. Buys one-time rights.

**Fillers:** Anecdotes, facts, newsbreaks, bait-specific legislation pieces, how-tos and hints. **Buys 10-20/year.** Length: 50-500 words. **Pays $10-30.**

**Tips:** "Query with detailed description of what you can provide our readers. State availability of photos, graphics and sidebars. We want detailed how-to, where-to and natural history pieces regarding all facets of bait fishing."

**$ $ BUGLE, Journal of Elk and the Hunt**, Rocky Mountain Elk Foundation, 2291 W. Broadway, Missoula MT 59802. (406)523-4570. Fax: (406)523-4550. E-mail: bugle@rmef.org. Website: http://www.rmef.org. Editor: Dan Crockett. **Contact:** Lee Cromrich, editorial assistant; David Stalling, conservation editor; Don Burgess, hunting editor; Jan Brocci, managing editor. **50% freelance written.** Bimonthly magazine covering conservation and hunting. "*Bugle* is the membership publication of the Rocky Mountain Elk Foundation, a nonprofit wildlife conservation group; it also sells on newsstands. Our readers are predominantly hunters, many of them naturalists who care deeply about protecting wildlife habitat. Hunting stories and essays should celebrate the hunting experience, demonstrating respect for wildlife, the land and the hunt. Articles on elk behavior or elk habitat should include personal observations and entertain as well as educate." Estab. 1984. Circ. 195,000. **Pays on acceptance**. Publishes ms 3-9 months after acceptance. Byline given. Offers variable kill fee. Buys one-time rights. Editorial lead time 6 months. Submit seasonal material 6 months in advance. Reports in 1 month on queries; 2 months on mss. Sample copy $5. Writer's guidelines for #10 SASE.

**Nonfiction:** Book excerpts, essays, general interest (elk related), historical/nostalgic, humor, opinion, personal experience, photo feature. No how-to, where-to. **Buys 20 mss/year.** Query with or without published clips, or send complete ms. Length: 1,500-4,500 words. **Pays 20¢/word** and 3 contributor copies; more issues at cost.

**Reprints:** Send typed ms with information about when and where the article previously appeared and rights for sale noted. Pays 75% of amount paid for an original article.

**Columns/Departments:** Situation Ethics, 1,000-2,000 words; Thoughts & Theories, 1,500-4,000 words; Women in the Outdoors, 1,000-2,500 words. Bows & Arrows, 1,500-2,000 words. **Buys 13 mss/year.** Query with or without published clips or send complete ms. **Pays 20¢/word.**

**Fiction:** Adventure, historical, humorous, slice-of-life vignettes, western, novel excerpts. No fiction that doesn't pertain to elk or elk hunting. **Buys 4 mss/year.** Query with or without published clips or send complete ms. Length: 1,500-4,500 words. **Pays 20¢/word.**

**Poetry:** Free verse, haiku, light verse, traditional. **Buys 6 poems/year.** Submit maximum 6 poems.

**Tips:** "Creative queries (250-500 words) that showcase your concept and your style remain the most effective approach. We're hungry for submissions for four specific columns: Situation Ethics, Thoughts & Theories, Bows & Arrows and Women in the Outdoors. Send a SASE for guidelines. We also welcome strong, well-reasoned opinion pieces on topics pertinent to hunting and wildlife conservation, and humorous pieces about elk behavior or encounters with elk (hunting or otherwise)."

**$ $ CALIFORNIA GAME & FISH**, Game & Fish Publications, Inc., Box 741, Marietta GA 30061. **Contact:** Burt Carey, editor. See *Game & Fish Publications.*

**$ $ CANADIAN SPORTFISHING MAGAZINE, Canada's Fishing Authority**, Canadian Sportfishing Productions, 937 Centre Rd., Dept. 2020, Waterdown, Ontario L0R 2H0 Canada. (905)689-1112, ext. 202. Fax: (905)689-2065. E-mail: editor@canadian-sportfishing.com. **Contact:** Matt Nichols, editor. **70% freelance written.** Bimonthly magazine covering sport fishing. Estab. 1988. Circ. 30,000. Pays on publication. Publishes ms an average of 3 months after acceptance. Byline given. Offers 50% kill fee. Buys all rights. Editorial lead time 6 months. Submit seasonal material 8 months in advance. Accepts queries by mail, e-mail, fax. Reports in 2 months on queries; 6 months on mss. Sample copy for $4. Writer's guidelines for #10 SASE.

**Nonfiction:** How-to, humor, new product. **Buys 40 mss/year.** Query. Length: 1,500-4,000 words. **Pays 15¢/word minimum (Canadian funds).** Sometimes pays expenses of writers on assignment.

**Photos:** Send photos with submission. Reviews contact sheets, transparencies and prints. Offers no additional payment for photos accepted with ms. Captions, model releases and identification of subjects required. Buys all rights.

**$ $ DEER & DEER HUNTING**, Krause Publications, 700 E. State St., Iola WI 54990-0001. Fax: (715)445-4087. Editor: Patrick Durkin. Website: http://www.deeranddeerhunting.com. **Contact:** Dan Schmidt, associate editor. **95% freelance written.** Published 9 times/year covering white-tailed deer and deer hunting. "Readers include a cross section of the deer hunting population—individuals who hunt with bow, gun or camera. The editorial content of the magazine focuses on white-tailed deer biology and behavior, management principle and practices, habitat requirements, natural history of deer, hunting techniques, and hunting ethics. We also publish a wide range of 'how-to' articles designed to help hunters locate and get close to deer at all times of the year. The majority of our readership consists of two-season hunters (bow and gun) and approximately one-third camera hunt." Estab. 1977. Circ. 140,000. **Pays on acceptance**. Byline given. Editorial lead time 6 months. Submit seasonal material 6 months in advance. Reports in 3 months. Sample copy for 9 × 12 SASE. Writer's guidelines free.

**Nonfiction:** General interest, how-to, inspirational, photo feature. No "Me and Joe" articles. **Buys 30-50 mss/year.** Query. Length: 750-3,000 words. **Pays $150-525 for assigned articles; $150-325 for unsolicited articles.** Sometimes pays expenses of writers on assignment.

**Photos:** Send photos with submission. Reviews transparencies. Negotiates payment individually. Captions, model releases and identification of subjects required.

**Fiction:** "Mood" deer hunting pieces. **Buys 9 mss/year.** Send complete ms.

**Fillers:** Facts, newsbreaks. **Buys 40-50/year.** Length: 100-500 words. **Pays $15-150.**

**Tips:** "Feature articles dealing with deer biology or behavior should be documented by scientific research (the author or that of others) as opposed to a limited number of personal observations."

**$ $ DISCOVERING AND EXPLORING NEW JERSEY'S FISHING STREAMS AND THE DELAWARE RIVER**, New Jersey Sportsmen's Guides, P.O. Box 100, Somerdale NJ 08083. Fax: (609)665-8656. **Contact:** Steve Perrone, editor. **60-70% freelance written.** Annual magazine covering freshwater stream and river fishing. Estab. 1993. Circ. 4,500. **Pays on acceptance.** Publishes ms an average of 6 months after acceptance. Byline given. Buys first rights and makes work-for-hire assignments. Editorial lead time 6 months. Sample copy for $12.50 postage paid.
**Nonfiction:** How-to fishing and freshwater fishing. **Buys 6-8 mss/year.** Query with published clips. Length: 500-2,000 words. **Pays $75-250.**
**Photos:** State availability of photos with submission. Reviews 4×5 transparencies and prints. Negotiates payment individually. Captions, model releases, identification of subjects required. Buys one-time rights.
**Tips:** "We want queries with published clips of articles describing fishing experiences on New Jersey streams and the Delaware River."

**$ $ $ $ FIELD & STREAM**, 2 Park Ave., New York NY 10016-5695. Editor: Duncan Barnes. **Contact:** David E. Petzal, executive editor. **50% freelance written.** Eager to work with new/unpublished writers. Monthly. "Broad-based service magazine for the hunter and fisherman. Editorial content ranges from very basic how-to stories detailing a useful technique or a device that sportsmen can make, to articles of penetrating depth about national hunting, fishing, and related activities. Also humor and personal essays, nostalgia and 'mood pieces' on the hunting or fishing experience and profiles on outdoor people." Estab. 1895. Circ. 1,790,400. **Pays on acceptance.** Byline given. Buys first rights. Query by mail. Reports in 2 months. Writer's guidelines for #10 SASE.
● Ranked as one of the best markets for freelance writers in *Writer's Yearbook* magazine's annual "Top 100 Markets," January 1999.
**Nonfiction:** Length: 1,500 words for features. Payment varies depending on the quality of work, importance of the article. **Pays $800 and up to $1,000 and more on a sliding scale for major features.** *Field & Stream* also publishes regional sections with feature articles on hunting and fishing in specific areas of the country. The sections are geographically divided into East, Midwest, West and South, and appear 12 months/year. Query: regional articles and ideas by mail to John Merwin, regionals editor. Length: 100-600 words. **Pays $100-400.**
**Photos:** Prefers color slides to b&w. Query first with photos. When photos purchased separately, pays $450 minimum for color. Buys first rights to photos.
**Columns/Departments:** Personal essays suitable for the "Finally . . . " department. Length: 750-800 words.
**Fillers:** Buys short "how it's done" fillers, 75 to 150 words, on unusual or helpful subjects. Also buys short (up to 500 words) pieces on tactics or techniques for specific hunting or fishing situations; short "Field Guide" pieces on natural phenomena as related to hunting and fishing; "Myths and Misconceptions," short pieces debunking a commonly held belief about hunting and fishing; short "Outdoor Basics" and "Sportsman's Projects" articles; and short pieces for the "Up Front" section that run the gamut from natural history to conservation news, anecdotal humor, short tips, and carefully crafted opinion pieces (word length: 25-400).
**Tips:** "Writers are encouraged to submit queries on article ideas. These should be no more than a paragraph or two, and should include a summary of the idea, including the angle you will hang the story on, and a sense of what makes this piece different from all others on the same or a similar subject. Many queries are turned down because we have no idea what the writer is getting at. Be sure that your letter is absolutely clear. We've found that if you can't sum up the point of the article in a sentence or two, the article doesn't have a point. Pieces that depend on writing style, such as humor, mood, and nostalgia or essays often can't be queried and may be submitted in manuscript form. The same is true of short tips. All submissions to *Field & Stream* are on an on-spec basis. Before submitting anything, however, we encourage you to *study*, not simply read, the magazine. Many pieces are rejected because they do not fit the tone or style of the magazine, or fail to match the subject of the article with the overall subject matter of *Field & Stream*. Above all, study the magazine before submitting anything."

**☒ $ $ THE FISHERMAN**, LIF Publishing Corp., 14 Ramsey Rd., Shirley NY 11967-4704. (516)345-5200. Fax: (516)345-5304. Publisher: Fred Golofaro. Associate Publisher: Pete Barrett. Senior Editor: Tim Coleman. 4 regional editions: *Long Island*, *Metropolitan New York*, Tom Melton, editor; *New England*, Tim Coleman, editor; *New Jersey*, Pete Barrett, editor; *Delaware-Maryland-Virginia*, Keith Kaufman, editor. **75% freelance written.** A weekly magazine covering fishing with an emphasis on saltwater. Combined circ. 100,000. Pays on publication. Byline given. Offers variable kill fee. Buys all rights. Articles may be run in one or more regional editions by choice of the editors. Submit seasonal material 2 months in advance. Reports in 6 weeks. Free sample copy and writer's guidelines.
**Nonfiction:** Send submission to regional editor. General interest, historical/nostalgic, how-to, interview/profile, personal experience, photo feature, technical, travel. Special issues: Boat & Motor Buyer's Guide and Winter Workbench (January); Tackle, Trout (March); Inshore Fishing (April); Saltwater Fly, Party Boat, Black Bass (May); Offshore Fishing (June); Surf Fishing (August); Striped Bass (October); Travel (December). "No 'me and Joe' tales. We stress how, where, when, why." **Buys 300 mss/year, each edition.** Length: 1,000-1,500 words. **Pays $110-150.**
**Photos:** Send photos with submission; also buys single color photos for cover use (pays $50-$100). Offers no additional payment for photos accepted with ms. Identification of subjects required.
**Tips:** "Focus on specific how-to and where-to subjects within each region."

**$ $ FLORIDA GAME & FISH**, Game & Fish Publications, Inc., Box 741, Marietta GA 30061. (770)953-9222. **Contact:** Jimmy Jacobs, editor. See *Game & Fish Publications*.

**N: FLYFISHING & TYING JOURNAL, A Compendium for the Complete Fly Fisher**, Frank Amato Publications, P.O. Box 82112, Portland OR 97282. (503)653-8108. Fax: (503)653-2766. E-mail: fap@teleport.com. Website: http://www.amatobooks.com. **Contact:** Les Johnson. **60% freelance written**. Quarterly magazine covering flyfishing and fly tying for both new and veteran anglers. Every issue is seasonally focused: spring, summer, fall and winter. Estab. 1980. Circ. 60,000. Pays on publication. Publishes ms 6 months after acceptance. Byline given. Buys first rights. Editorial lead time 6 months. Submit seasonal material 6 months in advance. Accepts queries by mail, e-mail, fax. Reports in 1 month on queries, 2 months on mss. Writer's guidelines for #10 SASE.
**Nonfiction:** How-to, new product, personal experience, travel. **Buys 55-60 mss/year**. Query. Length: 800-3,000 words. **Pays $200-600**.
**Photos:** State availability of photos with submission. Reviews transparencies. Offers no additional payment for photos accepted with ms. Captions, model releases, identification of subjects required. Buys one-time rights.

**$ $ FLY FISHING IN SALT WATERS**, Hook and Release Publications, Inc., 2001 Western Ave., Suite 210, Seattle WA 98121. (206)443-3273. Fax: (206)443-3293. E-mail: kate@flyfishinsalt.com. Website: http://www.flyfishins alt.com/ffsw. **Contact:** R.P. Van Gytenbeek, managing editor. **90% freelance written**. Bimonthly magazine covering fly fishing in salt waters anywhere in the world. Estab. 1994. Circ. 44,000. Pays on publication. Publishes ms an average of 1 year after acceptance. Byline given. Buys first North American serial rights and electronic rights. Editorial lead time 3 months. Submit seasonal material at least 2 months in advance. Reports in 1 month on queries; 2 months on mss. Sample copy for $3; back issues: $6. Writer's guidelines for #10 SASE.
**Nonfiction:** Book excerpts, essays, historical/nostalgic, how-to, interview/profile, new product, personal experience, photo feature, technical, travel, resource issues (conservation); all on flyfishing. **Buys 40-50 mss/year**. Query with or without published clips. Length: 1,500-2,500 words. **Pays $400-500**.
**Photos:** Send photos with submission. Reviews transparencies (35mm color only). Negotiates payment individually: offers no additional payment for photos accepted with ms; pays $80-300/photo if purchased separately. Captions, identification of subjects required. Buys one-time rights.
**Columns/Departments:** Legends/Reminiscences (history-profiles-nostalgia), 2,000-2,500 words; Resource (conservation issues), 1,000-1,500 words; Fly Tier's Bench (how to tie saltwater flies), 1,000-1,200 words, photos critical; Tackle & Technique (technical how-to), 1,000-1,500 words, photos or illustrations critical; Boating (technical how-to), 2,000-2,500 words. (Other departments are mostly staff written or by assignment only.) **Buys 25-30 mss/year**. Query. **Pays $400-500**.
**Fiction:** Adventure, humorous, mainstream; all dealing with flyfishing. **Buys 2-3 mss/year**. Send complete ms. Length: 2,000-3,000 words. **Pays $500**.
**Fillers:** Most fillers are staff-written.
**Tips:** "Follow up on your inquiry with a phone call."

**$ FUR-FISH-GAME**, 2878 E. Main, Columbus OH 43209-9947. **Contact:** Mitch Cox, editor. **65% freelance written**. Works with a small number of new/unpublished writers each year. Monthly magazine for outdoorsmen of all ages who are interested in hunting, fishing, trapping, dogs, camping, conservation and related topics. Estab. 1900. Circ. 111,000. **Pays on acceptance.** Publishes ms an average of 7 months after acceptance. Byline given. Buys first serial rights or all rights. Reports in 2 months. Sample copy for $1 and 9 × 12 SAE. Writer's guidelines for #10 SASE.
**Nonfiction:** "We are looking for informative, down-to-earth stories about hunting, fishing, trapping, dogs, camping, boating, conservation and related subjects. Nostalgic articles are also used. Many of our stories are 'how-to' and should appeal to small-town and rural readers who are true outdoorsmen. Some recent articles have told how to train a gun dog, catch big-water catfish, outfit a bowhunter and trap late-season muskrat. We also use personal experience stories and an occasional profile, such as an article about an old-time trapper. 'Where-to' stories are used occasionally if they have broad appeal." Query with SASE. Length: 500-3,000 words. **Pays $150 or more** for features depending upon quality, photo support, and importance to magazine. **Short filler stories pay $75-125.**
**Photos:** Send photos with ms. Photos are part of ms package and receive no additional payment. Prefers color prints or transparencies. Prints can be 5 × 7 or 8 × 10. Pays $25 for separate freelance photos. Captions and credits required.
**Tips:** "We are always looking for quality how-to articles about fish, game animals or birds that are popular with everyday outdoorsmen but often overlooked in other publications, such as catfish, bluegill, crappie, squirrel, rabbit, crows, etc. We also use articles on standard seasonal subjects such as deer and pheasant, but like to see a fresh approach or new technique. Instructional trapping articles are useful all year. Articles on gun dogs, ginseng and do-it-yourself projects are also popular with our readers. An assortment of photos and/or sketches greatly enhances any manuscript, and sidebars, where applicable, can also help. No phone queries, please."

**$ $ GAME & FISH PUBLICATIONS, INC.**, 2250 Newmarket Pkwy., Suite 110, Marietta GA 30067. (770)953-9222. Fax: (770)933-9510. **Contact:** Ken Dunwoody, editorial director. Publishes 30 different monthly outdoor magazines, each one covering the fishing and hunting opportunities in a particular state or region (see individual titles and editors). **90% freelance written**. Estab. 1975. Circ. 575,000. Pays 75 days prior to cover date of issue. Publishes ms an average of 7 months after acceptance. Byline given. Offers negotiable kill fee. Buys first North American serial rights. Submit seasonal material at least 8 months in advance. Editors prefer to hold queries until that season's material is assigned. Reports in 3 months on mss. Sample copy for $2.99 and 9 × 12 SASE. Writer's guidelines for #10 SASE.
**Nonfiction:** Prefer queries over unsolicited ms. Article lengths either 1,400 or 2,300 words. Pays separately for articles and accompanying photos. **Manuscripts pay $125-300,** cover photos $250, inside color $75 and b&w $25. Reviews

transparencies and b&w prints. Prefers captions and identification of species/subjects. Buys one-time rights to photos.
**Fiction:** Buys some humor, nostalgia and adventure pertaining to hunting and fishing. **Pays $125-250.** Length 1,100-2,500 words.

**Tips:** "Our readers are experienced anglers and hunters, and we try to provide them with useful, entertaining articles about where, when and how to enjoy the best hunting and fishing in their state or region. We also cover topics concerning game and fish management. Most articles should be aimed at outdoorsmen in one particular state. After familiarizing themselves with our magazine(s), writers should query the appropriate state editor (see individual listings) or send to Ken Dunwoody."

**$ $GEORGIA SPORTSMAN**, Game & Fish Publications, Box 741, Marietta GA 30061. (770)953-9222. **Contact:** Jimmy Jacobs, editor. See *Game & Fish Publications.*

**$ $GREAT PLAINS GAME & FISH**, Game & Fish Publications, Box 741, Marietta GA 30061. (770)953-9222. **Contact:** Nick Gilmore, editor. See *Game & Fish Publications.*

**$ $ILLINOIS GAME & FISH**, Game & Fish Publications, Inc., Box 741, Marietta GA 30061. (770)953-9222. **Contact:** Bill Hartlage, editor. See *Game & Fish Publications.*

**$ $INDIANA GAME & FISH**, Game & Fish Publications, Inc., Box 741, Marietta GA 30061. (770)953-9222. **Contact:** Ken Freel, editor. See *Game & Fish Publications.*

**$ $IOWA GAME & FISH**, Game & Fish Publications, Inc., Box 741, Marietta GA 30061. (770)953-9222. **Contact:** Bill Hartlage, editor. See *Game & Fish Publications.*

**$ $KENTUCKY GAME & FISH**, Game & Fish Publications, Inc., Box 741, Marietta GA 30061. (770)953-9222. **Contact:** Bill Hartlage, editor. See *Game & Fish Publications.*

**$ $LOUISIANA GAME & FISH**, Game & Fish Publications, Inc., Box 741, Marietta GA 30061. (770)953-9222. **Contact:** Editor. See *Game & Fish Publications.*

**$ $THE MAINE SPORTSMAN**, P.O. Box 365, Augusta ME 04330. (207)626-3315. E-mail: ursushpv@mint. net. Website: http://www.mainesportsman.com. **Contact:** Harry Vanderweide, editor. **80% freelance written.** "Eager to work with new/unpublished writers, but because we run over 30 regular columns, it's hard to get into *The Maine Sportsman* as a beginner." Monthly tabloid. Estab. 1972. Circ. 30,000. Pays during month of publication. Buys first rights. Publishes ms 3 months after acceptance. Byline given. Accepts queries by mail, e-mail. Reports in 2 weeks.
**Nonfiction:** "We publish only articles about Maine hunting and fishing activities. Any well-written, researched, knowledgeable article about that subject area is likely to be accepted by us." **Buys 25-40 mss/issue.** Submit complete ms. Length: 200-2,000 words. **Pays $20-300.** Sometimes pays the expenses of writers on assignment.
**Reprints:** Send typed ms with rights for sale. Pays 100% of amount paid for an original article.
**Photos:** "We can have illustrations drawn, but prefer 1-3 b&w photos." Submit photos with accompanying ms. Pays $5-50 for b&w print.

■  The online magazine carries original content not found in the print edition.

**Tips:** "We publish numerous special sections each year and are eager to buy Maine-oriented articles on snowmobiling, ice fishing, boating, salt water and deer hunting. Send articles or queries. You can e-mail us at ursushpv@mint.net."

**$MICHIGAN OUT-OF-DOORS**, P.O. Box 30235, Lansing MI 48909. (517)371-1041. Fax: (517)371-1505. E-mail: mucc@mucc.org. Website: http://www.mucc.org. **Contact:** Dennis C. Knickerbocker, editor. **75% freelance written.** Works with a small number of new/unpublished writers each year. Monthly magazine emphasizing Michigan outdoor recreation, especially hunting and fishing, conservation, nature and environmental affairs. Estab. 1947. Circ. 100,000. **Pays on acceptance.** Publishes ms 6 months after acceptance. Byline given. Buys first North American serial rights. Submit seasonal material 6 months in advance. Accepts phone queries. Reports in 1 month. Sample copy for $2.50. Writer's guidelines free.
**Nonfiction:** Exposé, historical, how-to, informational, interview, nostalgia, personal experience, personal opinion, photo feature, profile. No humor or poetry. "Stories *must* have a Michigan slant unless they treat a subject of universal interest to our readers." Special issues: Archery Deer Hunting (October); Firearm Deer Hunting (November); Cross-country Skiing and Early-ice Lake Fishing (December). **Buys 8 mss/issue.** Send complete ms. Length: 1,000-2,000 words. **Pays $90 minimum for feature stories.** Pays expenses of writers on assignment.
**Photos:** Purchased with or without accompanying ms. Pays $20 minimum for any size b&w glossy prints; $175 maximum for color (for cover). Offers no additional payment for photos accepted with accompanying ms. Buys one-time rights. Captions preferred.
**Tips:** "Top priority is placed on true accounts of personal adventures in the out-of-doors—well-written tales of very unusual incidents encountered while hunting, fishing, camping, hiking, etc. The most rewarding aspect of working with freelancers is playing a part in their development. But it's annoying to respond to queries that never produce a ms."

**$ $ MICHIGAN SPORTSMAN**, Game & Fish Publications, Inc., Box 741, Marietta GA 30061. (770)953-9222. **Contact:** Dennis Schmidt, editor. See *Game & Fish Publications.*

**✪ $ MID WEST OUTDOORS**, Mid West Outdoors, Ltd., 111 Shore Drive, Hinsdale (Burr Ridge) IL 60521-5885. (630)887-7722. Fax: (630)887-1958. E-mail: mwdmagtv30@aol.com. Website: http://www.MidWestOutdoors.com. **Contact:** Gene Laulunen, editor. **100% freelance written.** Monthly tabloid emphasizing fishing, hunting, camping and boating. Estab. 1967. Circ. 45,000. Pays on publication. Buys simultaneous rights. Byline given. Submit seasonal material 2 months in advance. Accepts simultaneous submissions. Reports in 3 weeks. Publishes ms an average of 3 months after acceptance. Sample copy for $1 or on website. Writer's guidelines for #10 SASE or on website.
**Nonfiction:** How-to (fishing, hunting, camping in the Midwest) and where-to-go (fishing, hunting, camping within 500 miles of Chicago). "We do not want to see any articles on 'my first fishing, hunting or camping experiences,' 'cleaning my tackle box,' 'tackle tune-up,' or 'catch and release.' " **Buys 1,800 unsolicited mss/year.** Send complete ms and 1 or 2 photos on 3.5 diskette with ms included. Length: 1,000-1,500 words. **Pays $15-30.**
**Reprints:** Send tearsheet of article.
**Photos:** Offers no additional payment for photos accompanying ms; uses slides and b&w prints. Buys all rights. Captions required.
**Columns/Departments:** Fishing, Hunting. Open to column/department suggestions. Send complete ms. **Pays $25.**
**Tips:** "Break in with a great unknown fishing hole or new technique within 500 miles of Chicago. Where, how, when and why. Know the type of publication you are sending material to."

**$ $ MID-ATLANTIC GAME & FISH**, Game & Fish Publications, Inc., Box 741, Marietta GA 30061. (770)953-9222. **Contact:** Ken Freel, editor. See *Game & Fish Publications.*

**$ $ MINNESOTA SPORTSMAN**, Game & Fish Publications, Inc., Box 741, Marietta GA 30061. (770)953-9222. **Contact:** Dennis Schmidt, editor. See *Game & Fish Publications.*

**$ $ MISSISSIPPI GAME & FISH**, Game & Fish Publications, Inc., Box 741, Marietta GA 30061. (770)953-9222. **Contact:** Editor. See *Game & Fish Publications.*

**$ $ MISSOURI GAME & FISH**, Game & Fish Publications, Inc., Box 741, Marietta GA 30061. (770)953-9222. **Contact:** Editor. See *Game & Fish Publications.*

**$ $ NEW ENGLAND GAME & FISH**, Game & Fish Publications, Inc., Box 741, Marietta GA 30061. (770)953-9222. **Contact:** Steve Carpenteri, editor. See *Game & Fish Publications.*

**$ $ NEW JERSEY LAKE SURVEY FISHING MAPS GUIDE**, New Jersey Sportsmen's Guides, P.O. Box 100, Somerdale NJ 08083. (609)783-1271. (609)665-8350. Fax: (609)665-8656. **Contact:** Steve Perrone, editor. **30-40% freelance written.** Annual magazine covering freshwater lake fishing. *"New Jersey Survey Fishing Maps Guide* is edited for freshwater fishing for trout, bass, perch, catfish and other species. It contains 132 pages and approximately 100 full-page maps of the surveyed lakes that illustrate contours, depths, bottom characteristics, shorelines and vegetation present at each location. The guide includes a 10-page chart which describes over 250 fishing lakes in New Jersey. It also covers trout stocked lakes, fishing tips and 'Bass'n Notes.' " Estab. 1989. Circ. 4,500. **Pays on acceptance**. Publishes ms an average of 6 months after acceptance. Byline given. Buys first rights and makes work-for-hire assignments. Editorial lead time 6 months. Accepts queries by mail, fax. Sample copy for $12.50 postage paid.
**Nonfiction:** How-to fishing, freshwater fishing. Length: 500-2,000 words. **Pays $75-250.**
**Photos:** State availability of photos with submission. Reviews transparencies 4×5 slides or 4×6 prints. Captions, model releases, identification of subjects required. Buys one-time rights.
**Tips:** "We want queries with published clips of articles describing fishing experiences on New Jersey lakes and ponds."

**$ $ NEW YORK GAME & FISH**, Game & Fish Publications, Inc., Box 741, Marietta GA 30061. (770)953-9222. **Contact:** Steve Carpenteri, editor. See *Game & Fish Publications.*

**$ $ NORTH AMERICAN WHITETAIL, The Magazine Devoted to the Serious Trophy Deer Hunter**, Game & Fish Publications, Inc., 2250 Newmarket Pkwy., Suite 110, Marietta GA 30067. (770)953-9222. Fax: (770)933-9510. **Contact:** Gordon Whittington, editor. **70% freelance written.** Magazine published 8 times/year about hunting trophy-class white-tailed deer in North America, primarily the US. "We provide the serious hunter with highly sophisticated information about trophy-class whitetails and how, when and where to hunt them. We are not a general hunting magazine or a magazine for the very occasional deer hunter." Estab. 1982. Circ. 170,000. Pays 75 days prior to cover date of issue. Publishes ms an average of 6 months after acceptance. Byline given. Offers negotiable kill fee. Buys first North American serial rights. Submit seasonal material 10 months in advance. Reports in 3 months on mss. Editor prefers to keep queries on file, without notification, until the article can be assigned or author informs of prior sale. Sample copy for $3 and 9×12 SAE with 7 first-class stamps. Writer's guidelines for #10 SASE.
**Nonfiction:** How-to, interview/profile. **Buys 50 mss/year.** Query. Length: 1,000-3,000 words. **Pays $150-400.**
**Photos:** Send photos with submission. Reviews 2×2 transparencies and 8×10 prints. Offers no additional payment for photos accepted with ms. Captions and identification of subjects required. Buys one-time rights.

**Columns/Departments:** Trails and Tails (nostalgic, humorous or other entertaining styles of deer-hunting material, fictional or nonfictional), 1,400 words. **Buys 8 mss/year.** Send complete ms. **Pays $150.**

**Tips:** "Our articles are written by persons who are deer hunters first, writers second. Our hard-core hunting audience can see through material produced by non-hunters or those with only marginal deer-hunting expertise. We have a continual need for expert profiles/interviews. Study the magazine to see what type of hunting expert it takes to qualify for our use, and look at how those articles have been directed by the writers. Good photography of the interviewee and his hunting results must accompany such pieces."

**$ $ NORTH CAROLINA GAME & FISH**, Game & Fish Publications Inc., Box 741, Marietta GA 30061. (770)953-9222. Fax: (770)933-9510. **Contact:** Steve Walburn, editor. See *Game & Fish Publications.*

**$ $ OHIO GAME & FISH**, Game & Fish Publications, Inc., Box 741, Marietta GA 30061. (770)953-9222. **Contact:** Steve Carpenteri, editor. See *Game & Fish Publications.*

**$ $ OKLAHOMA GAME & FISH**, Game & Fish Publications, Box 741, Marietta GA 30061. (770)953-9222. Fax: (770)933-9510. **Contact:** Nick Gilmore, editor. See *Game & Fish Publications.*

**⬛ $ $ ONTARIO OUT OF DOORS**, Maclean Hunter Publishing Ltd., 777 Bay St., 6th Floor, Toronto, Ontario M5W 1A7 Canada. (416)596-5815. Fax: (416)596-2517. E-mail: jkerr@mhpublishing.com. Website: http://www.fishontario.com. Editor: Burt Myers. **Contact:** John Kerr, managing editor. **90% freelance written.** Magazine published 10 times/year covering the outdoors (hunting, fishing, camping). Estab. 1968. **Pays on acceptance.** Circ. 88,967. Publishes ms an average of 6 months after acceptance. Byline given. Offers 100% kill fee. Buys first and electronic rights. Editorial lead time 6 months. Submit seasonal material 6 months in advance. Accepts queries by mail, fax, phone. Reports in 3 months on queries. Sample copy and writer's guidelines free.
 • Editor notes that *Ontario Out of Doors* needs more articles on camping, boating, recreational vehicles, photography, target shooting and archery as they relate to angling and hunting.

**Nonfiction:** Book excerpts, essays, exposé, how-to and where-to (fishing and hunting), humor, inspirational, interview/profile, new product, opinion, personal experience, photo feature, technical, travel, wildlife management and environmental concerns. "No Me and Joe features or articles written from a women's point of view on how to catch a bass." Special issues: Travel (March); Trout (April). **Buys 100 mss/year.** Query with SASE. Length: 500-2,500 words maximum. **Pays $750 maximum for assigned articles; $700 maximum for unsolicited articles.** Sometimes pays expenses of writers on assignment.

**Photos:** Send photos with submission. Reviews transparencies. Offers no additonal payment for photos accepted with ms except for cover and contents use. Pays $450-750 for covers. Captions required. Buys one-time rights.

**Columns/Departments:** Trips & Tips (travel pieces), 50-150 words; Short News, 50-500 words. **Buys 30-40 mss/year.** Query. **Pays $50-250.**

**Fiction:** Humorous. **Buys 6 mss/year.** Send complete ms. Length: 1,000 words maximum. **Pays $500 maximum.** Occasionally publishes novel excerpts.

**Fillers:** Facts, newsbreaks. **Buys 40/year.** Length: 25-100 words. **Pays $15-50.**

**Tips:** "With the exception of short news stories, it is suggested that writers query prior to submission."

**⬛ $ $ PENNSYLVANIA ANGLER & BOATER**, Pennsylvania Fish and Boat Commission, P.O. Box 67000, Harrisburg PA 17106-7000. (717)657-4520. E-mail: amichaels@fish.state.pa.us. Website: http://www.fish.state.pa.us. **Contact:** Art Michaels, editor. **80% freelance written.** Prefers to work with published/established writers but works with a few unpublished writers every year. Bimonthly magazine covering fishing, boating and related conservation topics in Pennsylvania. Circ. 40,000. Pays 2 months after acceptance. Publishes ms an average of 8 months after acceptance. Byline given. Rights purchased vary. Submit seasonal material 8 months in advance. Reports in 1 month on queries; 2 months on mss. Sample copy for 9×12 SAE with 9 first-class stamps. Guidelines for #10 SASE.

**Nonfiction:** How-to, where-to, technical. No saltwater or hunting material. **Buys 100 mss/year.** Query. Length: 500-3,500 words. **Pays $25-300.**

**Photos:** Send photos with submission. Reviews 35mm and larger transparencies. Offers no additional payment for photos accepted with ms. Captions, model releases and identification of subjects required. Also reviews photos separately. Rights purchased and rates vary.

**Tips:** "Our mainstays are how-tos, where-tos and conservation pieces. Articles are occasionally aimed at novice anglers and boaters, and some material is directed toward the most skilled fishermen and boaters. Most articles cater to people between these extremes."

**$ $ PENNSYLVANIA GAME & FISH**, Game & Fish Publications, Inc., Box 741, Marietta GA 30061. (770)953-9222. **Contact:** Steve Carpenteri, editor. See *Game & Fish Publications.*

**$ $ ROCKY MOUNTAIN GAME & FISH**, Game & Fish Publications, Inc., Box 741, Marietta GA 30061. Fax: (770)933-9510. **Contact:** Burt Carey, editor. See *Game & Fish Publications.*

**⬛ $ $ SAFARI MAGAZINE, The Journal of Big Game Hunting**, Safari Club International, 4800 W. Gates Pass Rd., Tucson AZ 85745. (520)620-1220. Fax: (520)617-0233. E-mail: editorsci@earthlink.net. Website: http://

www.sci-dc.com. Director of Publications/Editor: William R. Quimby. **Contact:** Merrik Bush-Pirkle, manuscripts editor. **90% freelance written.** Bimonthly club journal covering international big game hunting and wildlife conservation. Circ. 30,000. Pays on publication. Publishes ms an average of 18 months after acceptance. Byline given. Buys all rights on story; first rights on photos. Submit seasonal material 1 year in advance. Accepts queries by mail, e-mail. Reports in 2 weeks on queries; 6 weeks on mss. Sample copy for $4. Guidelines for SASE.

> O—¬ Break in with engaging, suspenseful, first-person stories of big-game hunts that involve unique circumstances or unusual regions and animals. Conservation stories should include reputable, known sources in the field, plenty of facts and be supported by scientific data."

**Nonfiction:** Photo feature (wildlife), technical (firearms, hunting techniques, etc.). **Buys 72 mss/year.** Query or send complete ms. Length: 2,000-2,500 words. **Pays $300 for professional writers, lower rates if not professional.**
**Photos:** State availability of photos with query; or send photos with ms. Payment depends on size in magazine. Pays $45 for b&w; $100 color. Captions, model releases, identification of subjects required. Buys first rights.
**Tips:** "Study the magazine. Send complete manuscript and photo package. Make it appeal to knowledgeable, world-traveled big game hunters. Features on conservation contributions from big game hunters around the world are open to freelancers. We have enough stories on first-time African safaris. We need North and South American, European and Asian hunting stories, plus stories dealing with wildlife conservation, especially as it applies to our organization and members."

**$ $SALT WATER SPORTSMAN MAGAZINE**, 263 Summer St., Boston MA 02210. (617)790-5400. Fax: (617)790-5455. E-mail: editor@saltwatersportsman.com. Website: http://www.saltwatersportsman.com. **Contact:** Barry Gibson, editor. **85% freelance written.** Works with a small number of new/unpublished writers each year. Monthly magazine. "*Salt Water Sportsman* is edited for serious marine sport fishermen whose lifestyle includes the pursuit of game fish in US waters and around the world. It provides information on fishing trends, techniques and destinations, both local and international. Each issue reviews offshore and inshore fishing boats, high-tech electronics, innovative tackle, engines and other new products. Coverage also focuses on sound fisheries management and conservation." Circ. 150,000. **Pays on acceptance.** Publishes ms an average of 5 months after acceptance. Byline given. Buys first North American serial rights. Offers 100% kill fee. Submit seasonal material 8 months in advance. Reports in 1 month. Sample copy and writer's guidelines available for SASE.

> • Ranked as one of the best markets for freelance writers in *Writer's Yearbook* magazine's annual "Top 100 Markets," January 1999.

**Nonfiction:** How-to, personal experience, technical, travel (to fishing areas). "Readers want solid how-to, where-to information written in an enjoyable, easy-to-read style. Personal anecdotes help the reader identify with the writer." Prefers new slants and specific information. Query. "It is helpful if the writer states experience in salt water fishing and any previous related articles. We want one, possibly two well-explained ideas per query letter—not merely a listing. Good pictures with query often help sell the idea." **Buys 100 mss/year.** Length: 1,200-2,000 words. **Pays $350 and up.** Also seeking short feature articles (500-1,000 words) on regional hot spots, species, special rigs, fishing methods, etc. **Pays $200-500,** depending on the quality of writing and accompanying photos. Query.
**Reprints:** Occasionally accepts reprints of previously published submissions. Send tearsheet of article. Pays up to 50% of amount paid for an original article.
**Photos:** Purchased with or without accompanying ms. Captions required. Uses color slides. Pays $1,000 minimum for 35mm, 2¼×2¼ or 8×10 transparencies for cover. Offers additional payment for photos accepted with ms.
**Columns/Departments:** Sportsman's Tips (short, how-to tips and techniques on salt water fishing, emphasis is on building, repairing, or reconditioning specific items or gear). Send ms. Length: 100-300 words.
**Tips:** "There are a lot of knowledgeable fishermen/budding writers out there who could be valuable to us with a little coaching. Many don't think they can write a story for us, but they'd be surprised. We work with writers. Shorter articles that get to the point which are accompanied by good, sharp photos are hard for us to turn down. Having to delete unnecessary wordage—conversation, clichés, etc.—that writers feel is mandatory is annoying. Often they don't devote enough attention to specific fishing information."

**$ $SOUTH CAROLINA GAME & FISH**, Game & Fish Publications, Inc., Box 741, Marietta GA 30061. (770)953-9222. **Contact:** Steve Walburn, editor. See *Game & Fish Publications*.

**★ $ $SOUTH CAROLINA WILDLIFE**, P.O. Box 167, Rembert Dennis Bldg., Columbia SC 29202-0167. (803)734-3972. E-mail: scwmed@scdnr.state.sc.us. Editor: John Davis. **Contact:** Linda Renshaw, managing editor. Bimonthly magazine for South Carolinians interested in wildlife and outdoor activities. **75% freelance written.** Estab. 1954. Circ. 60,000. Byline given. **Pays on acceptance.** Publishes ms an average of 6 months after acceptance. Buys first rights. Free sample copy. Reports in 2 months.
**Nonfiction:** Articles on outdoor South Carolina with an emphasis on preserving and protecting our natural resources. "Realize that the topic must be of interest to South Carolinians and that we must be able to justify using it in a publication published by the state department of natural resources—so if it isn't directly about outdoor recreation, a certain plant or animal, it must be somehow related to the environment and conservation. Readers prefer a broad mix of outdoor related topics (articles that illustrate the beauty of South Carolina's outdoors and those that help the reader get more for his/her time, effort, and money spent in outdoor recreation). These two general areas are the ones we most need. Subjects vary a great deal in topic, area and style, but must all have a common ground in the outdoor resources and heritage of South Carolina. Review back issues and query with a one-page outline citing sources, giving ideas for photographs,

explaining justification and giving an example of the first two paragraphs." Does not need any column material. Generally does not seek photographs. The publisher assumes no responsibility for unsolicited material. **Buys 25-30 mss/year.** Length: 1,000-3,000 words. **Pays $200-400** depending upon length and subject matter.

**Tips:** "We need more writers in the outdoor field who take pride in the craft of writing and put a real effort toward originality and preciseness in their work. Query on a topic we haven't recently done. Frequent mistakes made by writers in completing an article are failure to check details and go in-depth on a subject."

**$ $SPORT FISHING, The Magazine of Saltwater Fishing**, 330 W. Canton Ave., Winter Park FL 32789-7061. (407)628-4802. Fax: (407)628-7061. Email: do1@worldzine.com. Managing Editor: Jason Cannon. **Contact:** Doug Olander, editor-in-chief. **60% freelance written.** Magazine covering offshore sport fishing. Estab. 1986. Circ. 150,000. Pays within 6 weeks of acceptance. Byline given. Offers $100 kill fee. Buys first North American serial or one-time rights. Submit seasonal material 5 months in advance. Accepts queries by mail, e-mail, fax. Accepts simultaneous submission. Reports in 2 weeks. Sample copy and writer's guidelines for SASE.

○━ Break in with freelance pieces for the *Out Rigging Tips & Techniques* and *Fish Tales* departments.

**Nonfiction:** How-to (rigging & techniques tips), technical, conservation, travel and where-to (all on sport fishing). **Buys 32-40 mss/year.** Query with or without clips, e-mail preferred; fax, letter acceptable. Length: 1,500-2,500 words. **Pays $150-600.**

**Photos:** Send photos with submission. Reviews transparencies and returns within 1 week. Pays $50-300 inside; $1,000 cover. Identification of subjects required. Buys one-time rights.

**Columns/Departments:** Fish Tales (humorous sport fishing anecdotes); Rigging (how-to rigging for sport fishing); Technique (how-to technique for sport fishing). Length: 800-1,200 words. **Buys 8-24 mss/year.** Send complete ms. **Pays $250 for Fish Tales, $200 for other departments.**

**Tips:** "Don't query unless you are familiar with the magazine; note—*salt water only.* Find a fresh idea or angle to an old idea. We welcome the chance to work with new/unestablished writers who know their stuff—and how to say it."

**$ $ $SPORTS AFIELD**, Hearst Magazines, 250 W. 55th St., New York NY 10019-5201. (212)649-4000. Fax: (212)581-3923. E-mail: saletter@hearst.com. Website: http://www.sportsafield.com. Editor-in-Chief: John Atwood. Features Editor: David Herndon. Editorial Assistant: Monte Burke. **Contact:** Jessica Riback, assistant to editor-in-chief. **50% freelance written.** Magazine for the outdoor enthusiast with special interest in wilderness sports. Covers a wide range of outdoor interests such as: hiking, kayaking, mountain biking, camping, canoeing, fishing, boating, off-road, survival, conservation, tackle, new gear, shooting sports. Published 10 times/year. Estab. 1887. Circ. 450,000. Buys first North American serial rights for features. **Pays on acceptance.** Publishes ms an average of 6 months after acceptance. Byline given. "Our magazine is seasonal and material submitted should be in accordance." Submit seasonal material 9 months in advance. Accepts queries by mail, e-mail, fax. Reports in 2 months. SASE for reply or writer's guidelines.

○━ Break in through the *Reports Afield* or *Almanac* sections. "These sections include newsy material, smaller pieces, useful tidbits of info and more. Familiarize yourself with these sections and go from there!"

**Nonfiction:** "Informative how-to articles with emphasis on product and service and personal experiences with good photos on wilderness sports, camping and environmental issues. We want first-class writing and reporting." **Buys 10-15 unsolicited mss/year.** Length: 500-2,000 words. Query or submit complete ms.

**Columns/Departments:** Almanac (outdoor tips, unusual, how-to and nature items), 200-300 words. Query or submit complete ms.

**Photos:** "For photos without ms, duplicates of 35mm color transparencies preferred."

**Tips:** "Read a recent copy so you know the market you're writing for. Manuscript *must* be available on disk. We are interested in where-to-go and how-to articles. Features based on outdoor products are welcome if they have a fresh slant. We prefer detailed queries first. This saves time and effort on your part as well as ours. If you are sending a finished manuscript, it should be double-spaced and a computer disk should be available if the story is accepted. If you are submitting photos, send only duplicates. Should we want original photos for publication, we will contact the photographer. *Sports Afield* is not responsible for any unsolicited photos or manuscripts."

**$ $TENNESSEE SPORTSMAN**, Game & Fish Publications, Box 741, Marietta GA 30061. (770)953-9222. **Contact:** Steve Walburn, editor. See *Game & Fish Publications*.

**$ $TEXAS SPORTSMAN**, Game & Fish Publications, Inc., Box 741, Marietta GA 30061. (770)953-9222. **Contact:** Nick Gilmore, editor. See *Game & Fish Publications*.

**$ $TIDE MAGAZINE**, Coastal Conservation Association, 220W, 4801 Woodway, Houston TX 77056. (713)626-4222. Fax: (713)961-3801. E-mail: tide@flash.net. **Contact:** Doug Pike, editor. Bimonthly magazine on saltwater fishing and conservation of marine resources. Estab. 1977. Circ. 60,000. Pays on publication. Byline given. Buys one-time rights. Submit seasonal material 6 months in advance. Reports in 1 month.

**Nonfiction:** Essays, exposé, general interest, historical/nostalgic, humor, opinion, personal experience and travel, related to saltwater fishing and Gulf/Atlantic coastal habits. **Buys 30 mss/year.** Query with published clips. Length: 1,200-1,500 words. **Pays $250-350 for ms/photo package.**

**Photos:** Reviews 35mm transparencies and color negs/prints. Offers no additional payment for photos accepted with ms. Captions required. Buys one-time rights. Pays $25 for b&w, $50 for color inside.

⚔ **$ $ TRAPPER & PREDATOR CALLER**, Krause Publications Inc., 700 E. State St., Iola WI 54990. (715)445-2214. Fax: (715)445-4087. E-mail: waitp@krause.com. Website: http://www.trapperpredatorcaller.com. **Contact:** Paul Wait, editor. **90% freelance written.** Monthly tabloid covers trapping, predator calling and muzzleloading. "Our editorial goal is to entertain and educate our readers with national and regional articles that promote trapping." Estab. 1975. Circ. 41,000. Pays on publication. Offers $50 kill fee. Buys first North American serial rights. Submit seasonal material 6 months in advance. Reports in 2 weeks. Free sample copy and writer's guidelines.
**Nonfiction:** How-to, humor, interview/profile, new product, opinion and personal experience. **Buys 60 mss/year.** Query with or without published clips, or send complete ms. Length: 1,200-2,500 words. **Pays $80-250 for assigned articles; $40-200 for unsolicited articles.**
**Photos:** Send photos with submission. Reviews prints. Offers no additional payment for photos accepted with ms. Captions and identification of subjects required. Buys one-time rights.
**Fillers:** Facts, gags to be illustrated, newsbreaks, short humor. **Buys 60/year.** Length: 200-800 words. **Pays $25-80.**
**Tips:** "We are always looking for new ideas and fresh material on trapping, predator calling and black powder hunting."

⚔ **$ $ TURKEY & TURKEY HUNTING**, Krause Publications, 700 E. State St., Iola WI 54990-0001. (715)445-2214, ext. 484. Fax: (715)445-4087. E-mail: lovettb@krause.com. Website: http://www.turkeyandturkeyhunting.com. **Contact:** Brian Lovett, editor. **90% freelance written.** Magazine published 6 times/year (4 spring, 1 fall, 1 winter) covering turkey hunting and turkey biology. "*Turkey & Turkey Hunting* is for serious, experienced turkey hunters." Estab. 1983. Circ. 28,000. **Pays on acceptance.** Publishes ms an average of 1 year after acceptance. Byline given. Offers 50% kill fee. Buys first North American serial rights. Editorial lead time 1 year. Submit seasonal material 1 year in advance. Reports in 2 months. Sample copy and writer's guidelines free.
**Nonfiction:** How-to, personal experience. **Buys 45 mss/year.** Query with published clips. Length: 2,000 words. **Pays $275-300.** Sometimes pays expenses of writers on assignment.
**Photos:** Send photos with submission. Reviews transparencies. Offers $75-300/photo, depending on size. Pays on publication for photos. Buys one-time rights.
**Tips:** "Have a thorough knowledge of turkey hunting and the hunting industry. Send fresh, informative queries, and indicate topics you'd feel comfortable covering on assignment."

**$ $ TURKEY CALL**, Wild Turkey Center, P.O. Box 530, Edgefield SC 29824-0530. (803)637-3106. Fax: (803)637-0034. E-mail: nwtf@gab.net. Editor: Jay Langston. **Contact:** Mary Busbee, publishing assistant. **50-60% freelance written.** Eager to work with new/unpublished writers and photographers. Bimonthly educational magazine for members of the National Wild Turkey Federation. Estab. 1973. Circ. 120,000. Buys one-time rights. Byline given. **Pays on acceptance.** Publishes ms an average of 6 months after acceptance. Reports in 1 month. Queries required. Submit complete package. Wants original mss only. Sample copy for $3 and 9×12 SAE. Writer's guidelines for #10 SASE.
**Nonfiction:** Feature articles dealing with the hunting and management of the American wild turkey. Must be accurate information and must appeal to national readership of turkey hunters and wildlife management experts. No poetry or first-person accounts of unremarkable hunting trips. May use some fiction that educates or entertains in a special way. Length: up 2,500 words. **Pays $100 for short fillers of 600-700 words, $200-500 for features.**
**Reprints:** Send photocopy of article and information about when and where the article previously appeared. Pays 50% of amount paid for an original article.
**Photos:** "We want quality photos submitted with features." Art illustrations also acceptable. "We are using more and more inside color illustrations." For b&w, prefer 8×10 glossies, but accepts 5×7. Transparencies of any size are acceptable. No typical hunter-holding-dead-turkey photos or setups using mounted birds or domestic turkeys. Photos with how-to stories must make the techniques clear (example: how to make a turkey call; how to sculpt or carve a bird in wood). Pays $35 minimum for one-time rights on b&w photos and simple art illustrations; up to $100 for inside color, reproduced any size; $200-400 for covers.
**Tips:** "The writer should simply keep in mind that the audience is 'expert' on wild turkey management, hunting, life history and restoration/conservation history. He/she *must know the subject*. We are buying more third-person, more fiction, more humor—in an attempt to avoid the 'predictability trap' of a single subject magazine."

**$ $ VIRGINIA GAME & FISH**, Game & Fish Publications, Inc., Box 741, Marietta GA 30061. (770)953-9222. **Contact:** Steve Walburn, editor. See *Game & Fish Publications*.

**$ $ WARMWATER FLY FISHING**, Abenaki Publishers, Inc., 160 Benmont Ave., P.O. Box 4100, Bennington VT 05201. (802)447-1518. Website: http://www.flyfishmags.com. **Contact:** John M. Likakis, editor. **95% freelance written.** Bimonthly magazine covering fly fishing for bass, panfish, and other warmwater fish. "*Warmwater Fly Fishing* specializes in how-to, where-to, and when-to stories about fly fishing for warmwater species of fish. The emphasis is on nuts-and-bolts articles that tell the reader about specific techniques, places, equipment, etc." Estab. 1997. Pays on publication. Publishes ms an average of 6 months after acceptance. Byline given. Buys first North American and one-time rights. Editorial lead time 6 months. Submit seasonal material 6 months in advance. Accepts queries by mail, phone. Reports in 6 weeks on queries; 3 months on mss. Sample copy for $4.99. Writer's guidelines for $3 and #10 SASE.
**Nonfiction:** Historical/nostalgic, how-to, technical. No 'Me and Joe' fishing stories, exotic destinations, product reviews or puff pieces. **Buys 70 mss/year.** Query. Length: 1,000-2,500 words. **Pays $250-350.**
**Photos:** Send photos with submission. Reviews transparencies. Offers no additional payment for photos accepted with

ms. "Unless otherwise specified, photos are considered part of the submission." Captions, model releases, identification of subjects required. Buys one-time rights.

**Columns/Departments:** Tech Tackle (innovative rigging); The Deep (fly fishing in deep water); Conservation, Boating, Roots (nostalgia, classic flies); Basic Techniques, Musings (essay); The Tier (tying warmwater flies); all 1,500 words. **Buys 54 mss/year.** Query. **Pays $250-350.**

**Tips:** "Brief but complete query letters detailing what the article intends to cover. Neatness counts! Check your letter carefully for typos, misspellings, proper address and so forth."

**$ $ WASHINGTON-OREGON GAME & FISH**, Game & Fish Publications, Inc., Box 741, Marietta GA 30061. **Contact:** Burt Carey, editor. See *Game & Fish Publications.*

**$ $ WEST VIRGINIA GAME & FISH**, Game & Fish Publications, Inc., Box 741, Marietta GA 30061. (770)953-9222. **Contact:** Ken Freel, editor. See *Game & Fish Publications.*

**$ $ WESTERN OUTDOORS**, 3197-E Airport Loop, Costa Mesa CA 92626. (714)546-4370. Fax: (714)662-3486. E-mail: woutdoors@aol.com. **Contact:** Jack Brown, editor. **60% freelance written.** Works with a small number of new/unpublished writers each year. Emphasizes fishing, boating for California, Oregon, Washington, Baja California, and Alaska. "We are the West's leading authority on fishing techniques, tackle and destinations, and all reports present the latest and most reliable information." Publishes 9 issues/year. Estab. 1961. Circ. 100,000. **Pays on acceptance.** Publishes ms an average of 6 months after acceptance. Buys first North American serial rights. Submit seasonal material 6 months in advance. Accepts queries by mail, e-mail, fax. Reports in 2 weeks. Sample copy free. Writer's guidelines for #10 SASE.

● *Western Outdoors* now emphasizes freshwater and saltwater fishing and boating exclusively. Area of coverage is limited to far west states and Baja California.

**Nonfiction:** Where-to (catch more fish, improve equipment, etc.), how-to informational, photo feature. "We do not accept fiction, poetry." **Buys 36-40 assigned mss/year.** Query with SASE. *No simultaneous queries.* Length: 1,500-2,000 words. **Pays $450-600.**

**Photos:** Purchased with accompanying ms. Captions required. Prefers professional quality 35mm slides. Offers no additional payment for photos accepted with accompanying ms. Pays $350-500 for covers.

**Tips:** "Provide a complete package of photos, map, trip facts and manuscript written according to our news feature format. Excellence of color photo selections make a sale more likely. Include sketches of fishing patterns and techniques to guide our illustrators. Graphics are important. The most frequent mistake made by writers in completing an article for us is that they don't follow our style. Our guidelines are quite clear. One query at a time via mail or e-mail. No phone calls. You can become a regular *Western Outdoors* byliner by submitting professional quality packages of fine writing accompanied by excellent photography. Pros anticipate what is needed, and immediately provide whatever else we request. Furthermore, they meet deadlines!"

**$ $ WESTERN SPORTSMAN**, 2002 Quebec Ave., Suite 201, Saskatoon, Saskatchewan S7K 1W4 Canada. (306)665-6302. Fax: (306)665-6315. E-mail: wsportsman@sk.sympatico.ca. **Contact:** George Gruenefeld, editor. **90% freelance written.** Bimonthly magazine for fishermen, hunters, campers and others interested in outdoor recreation. "Note that our coverage area is Alberta, Saskatchewan and Manitoba." Estab. 1968. Circ. 29,000. Rights purchased vary with author and material. Usually buys first North American serial or second serial (reprint) rights. Byline given. Pays on publication. "We try to include as much information as possible on all subjects in each edition. Therefore, we often publish fishing articles in our winter issues along with a variety of winter stories." Accepts queries by mail, e-mail, fax. Reports in 1 month. Sample copy for $4 and 9×12 SAE with 4 IRCs (US). Free writer's guidelines with SAE and IRC (US).

● *Western Sportsman* now accepts articles and news items relating to British Columbia, Yukon and Northwest Territories hunting and fishing.

**Nonfiction:** "It is necessary that all articles can identify with our coverage area. We are interested in manuscripts from writers who have had an interesting fishing or hunting experience. We also publish other informational pieces as long as they relate to our coverage area. We are more interested in articles which tell about the average guy living on beans, guiding his own boat, stalking his game and generally doing his own thing in our part of Western Canada than a story describing a well-to-do outdoorsman traveling by motorhome, staying at an expensive lodge with guides doing everything for him except catching the fish or shooting the big game animal. The articles that are submitted to us need to be prepared in a knowledgeable way and include more information than the actual fish catch or animal or bird kill. Discuss the terrain, the people involved on the trip, the water or weather conditions, the costs, the planning that went into the trip, the equipment and other data closely associated with the particular event. We're always looking for new writers." **Buys 60 mss/year.** Submit complete ms and SASE or IRCs. Length: 1,800-2,000 words. Payment negotiable.

**Reprints:** Send typed ms with rights for sale noted and information about when and where the article previously appeared.

**Photos:** Photos purchased with ms with no additional payment. Also purchased without ms. Pays $150 for 35mm or larger transparency for front cover.

**$ $ WISCONSIN OUTDOOR JOURNAL**, Krause Publications, 700 E. State St., Iola WI 54990. (715)445-2214, ext. 484. Fax: (715)445-4087. E-mail: lovettb@krause.com. Website: http://www.wisoutdoorjournal.com. **Con-**

tact: Brian Lovett, editor. **90% freelance written.** Magazine published 8 times/year covering Wisconsin hunting, fishing, trapping, wildlife and related issues. "*Wisconsin Outdoor Journal* is for people interested in state-specific hunting, fishing, trapping and wildlife. We mix how-to features with area profiles and state outdoor issues." Estab. 1987. Circ. 26,000. **Pays on acceptance.** Publishes ms an average of 8-12 months after acceptance. Byline given. Offers 50% kill fee. Buys first North American serial rights. Editorial lead time 1 year. Submit seasonal material 1 year in advance. Reports in 2 months. Sample copy and writer's guidelines for SASE.

**Nonfiction:** General interest, historical/nostalgic, how-to. No stories focusing on out-of-state topics; no general recreation (hiking, biking, skiing) features. **Buys 65 mss/year.** Query with published clips. Length: 1,600-2,000 words. **Pays $150-250.** Sometimes pays expenses of writers on assignment.

**Photos:** Send photos with submission. Reviews transparencies. Offers $75-275/photo. Buys one-time rights.

**Columns/Departments:** Wisconsin Field Notes (anecdotes, outdoor news items not extensively covered by newspapers, interesting outdoor occurrences, all relevant to Wisconsin; may include photos), 50-750 words. **Pays $5-75 on publication.** "Include SASE with photos only. Submissions other than photos for Field Notes will not be returned.

**Tips:** "Don't submit personal hunting and fishing stories. Seek fresh, new topics, such as an analysis of long-term outdoor issues."

**$ $ WISCONSIN SPORTSMAN**, Game & Fish Publications, Inc., Box 741, Marietta GA 30061. (770)953-9222. **Contact:** Dennis Schmidt, editor. See *Game & Fish Publications*.

# Martial Arts

**☆ $ $ BLACK BELT**, Rainbow Publications, Inc., 24715 Ave. Rockefeller, Valencia CA 91355. (805)257-4066. Fax: (805)257-3028. E-mail: rainbow@cygnus.rsabbs.com. Website: http://www.blackbeltmag.com. **Contact:** Robert Young, executive editor. **80-90% freelance written.** Works with a small number of new/unpublished writers each year. Monthly magazine emphasizing martial arts for both experienced practitioner and layman. Estab. 1961. Circ. 100,000. Pays on publication. Publishes ms an average of 6-8 months after acceptance. Buys all rights, retains right to republish. Submit seasonal material 6 months in advance. Accepts simultaneous submissions if notified. Accepts queries by mail, e-mail, phone, fax. Reports in 3 weeks.

**Nonfiction:** Exposé, how-to, informational, health/fitness, interview, new product, personal experience, technical, training, travel. "We never use personality profiles." **Buys 8-9 mss/issue.** Query with outline. Length: 1,200 words minimum. **Pays $100-300.**

**Photos:** Very seldom buys photos without accompanying mss. Captions required. Total purchase price for ms includes payment for photos. Model releases required.

**Tips:** "We also publish an annual yearbook and special issues periodically. The yearbook includes our annual 'Black Belt Hall of Fame' inductees."

**☆ $ $ INSIDE KUNG-FU, The Ultimate In Martial Arts Coverage!**, CFW Enterprises, 4201 Vanowen Place, Burbank CA 91505. (818)845-2656. Fax: (818)845-7761. **Contact:** Dave Cater, editor. **90% freelance written.** Monthly magazine for those with "traditional, modern, athletic and intellectual tastes. The magazine slants toward little-known martial arts, and little-known aspects of established martial arts." Estab. 1973. Circ. 125,000. Pays on publication date on magazine cover. Publishes ms an average of 6 months after acceptance. Byline given. Offers 20% kill fee. Buys first North American serial rights. Editorial lead time 6 months. Submit seasonal material 6 months in advance. Accepts simultaneous submissions. Reports in 1 month on queries; 2 months on mss. Sample copy for $2.95 and 9×12 SAE with 5 first-class stamps. Writer's guidelines for #10 SASE.

**Nonfiction:** Book excerpts, essays, exposé (topics relating to the martial arts), general interest, historical/nostalgic, how-to (primarily technical materials), cultural/philosophical, inspirational, interview/profile, new product, personal experience, photo feature, technical, travel. "Articles must be technically or historically accurate." *Inside Kung-Fu* is looking for external-type articles (fighting, weapons, multiple hackers). No "sports coverage, first-person articles or articles which constitute personal aggrandizement." **Buys 120 mss/year.** Query or send complete ms. Length: 1,500-3,000 words (8-10 pages, typewritten and double-spaced). **Pays $125-175.**

**Reprints:** Send tearsheet of article or short story or typed ms with rights for sale noted and information about when and where the article previously appeared. No payment.

**Photos:** State availability or send photos with ms. Reviews contact sheets, negatives, 5×7 or 8×10 color prints. No additional payment for photos. Captions, model release and identification of subjects required. Buys all rights.

**Fiction:** Adventure, historical, humorous, mystery, novel excerpts, suspense. "Fiction must be short (1,000-2,000 words) and relate to the martial arts. We buy very few fiction pieces." Publishes novel excerpts. **Buys 2-3 mss/year.**

**Tips:** "See what interests the writer. May have a better chance of breaking in at our publication with short articles and fillers since smaller pieces allow us to gauge individual ability, but we're flexible—quality writers get published, period. The most frequent mistakes made by writers in completing an article for us are ignoring photo requirements and model releases (always number one—and who knows why? All requirements are spelled out in writer's guidelines)."

**$ KARATE/KUNG FU ILLUSTRATED**, Rainbow Publications, Inc., P.O. Box 918, Santa Clarita CA 91380. (805)257-4066. Fax: (805)257-3028. E-mail: rainbow@rsabbs.com. Website: http://www.blackbeltmag.com. **Contact:**

Douglas Jeffrey, executive editor. **70% freelance written.** Bimonthly. "KKI presents factual historical accounts of the development of the martial arts, along with technical pieces on self-defense. We use only material from which readers can learn." Estab. 1969. Circ. 35,000. Pays on publication. Publishes ms an average of 8 months after acceptance. Byline given. Buys all rights. Editorial lead time 3 months. Submit seasonal material 4 months in advance. Accepts simultaneous submissions. Reports in 2 weeks on queries; 1 month on mss. Sample copy for 9×12 SAE and 5 first-class stamps. Writer's guidelines free.

- *Karate/Kung Fu Illustrated* now publishes "Black Belt for Kids," a separate section currently attached to the main magazine. Query with article ideas for young martial artists.

**Nonfiction:** Book excerpts, general interest (martial arts), historical/nostalgic (martial arts development), how-to (technical articles on specific kicks, punches, etc.), interview/profile (only with *major* martial artist), new products (for annual product review), travel (to Asian countries for martial arts training/research), comparisons of various styles and techniques. "No self-promotional pieces." **Buys 30 mss/year.** Query. Length: 1,000-3,000 words. **Pays $100-200.**

**Reprints:** Send tearsheet, photocopy or typed ms with rights for sale noted and information about when and where the article previously appeared. Pays 75-100% of amount paid for an original article.

**Photos:** Freelancers should send photos with submission. Reviews contact sheets, negatives and 5×7 prints. Offers no additional payment for photos accepted with ms. Captions, model releases and identification of subjects required.

**Columns/Departments:** Traditional Passages (importance of tradition); Counterkicks (letters to the editor). **Buys 12 mss/year.** Query. **Pays $50-100.**

**Fiction:** Publishes novel excerpts.

**Tips:** "You need not be an expert in a specific martial art to write about it. But if you are not an expert, find one and use his knowledge to support your statements. Also, references to well-known books can help lend credence to the work of unknown writers. Inexperienced writers should begin by writing about a subject they know well. For example, if you study karate, start by writing about karate. Don't study karate for one year, then try to break in to a martial arts magazine by writing about Kung fu, because we already have Kung fu practitioners who write about that."

**$ $ MARTIAL ARTS TRAINING,** Rainbow Publications, P.O. Box 918, Santa Clarita CA 91380-9018. (805)257-4066. Fax: (805)257-3028. E-mail: rainbow@rsabbs.com. Website: http://www.blackbeltmag.com. **Contact:** Douglas Jeffrey, executive editor. **65-75% freelance written.** Works with many new/unpublished writers each year. Bimonthly magazine about martial arts training. Estab. 1973. Circ. 35,000. Pays on publication. Publishes ms an average of 6 months after acceptance. Buys all rights. Submit seasonal material 4 months in advance. Reports in 1 month. Writer's guidelines for #10 SASE.

**Nonfiction:** How-to (training related features). **Buys 30-40 unsolicited mss/year.** Query. Length: 1,500-2,500 words. **Pays $125-200.**

**Reprints:** Send tearsheet, photocopy or typed ms of article with rights for sale noted and information about when and where the article previously appeared. Pays 75-100% of amount paid for an original article.

**Photos:** "We prefer color prints. Please include the negatives." Model releases required. Buys all rights.

**Tips:** "I'm looking for how-to, nuts-and-bolts training stories that are martial arts related. Weight training, plyometrics, speed drills, cardiovascular workouts, agility drills, etc. Our magazine covers fitness and conditioning, not the martial arts techniques themselves. We're interested in traditional training and state-of-the-art, cutting edge training."

**$ $ T'AI CHI, Leading International Magazine of T'ai Chi Ch'uan,** Wayfarer Publications, P.O. Box 26156, Los Angeles CA 90026. (323)665-7773. Fax: (323)665-1627. E-mail: taichi@tai-chi.com. Website: http://www. tai-chi.com. **Contact:** Marvin Smalheiser, editor. **90% freelance written.** Bimonthly consumer magazine covering T'ai Chi Ch'uan as a martial art and for health and fitness. "Covers T'ai Chi Ch'uan and other internal martial arts, plus qigong and Chinese health, nutrition and philosophical disciplines. Readers are practitioners or laymen interested in developing skills and insight for self-defense, health and self-improvement." Estab. 1977. Circ. 30,000. Pays on publication. Publishes ms an average of 3 months after acceptance. Byline given. Buys first North American serial rights. Editorial lead time 3 months. Submit seasonal material 6 months in advance. Accepts queries by mail, e-mail, fax. Reports in 3 weeks on queries; 3 months on mss. Sample copy for $3.50. Writer's guidelines for #10 SASE or on website.

**Nonfiction:** Book excerpts, essays, how-to (on T'ai Chi Ch'uan, qigong and related Chinese disciplines), interview, personal experience. "Do not want articles promoting an individual, system or school." **Buys 50-60 mss/year.** Query or send complete ms. Length: 1,200-4,500 words. **Pays $75-500.** Sometimes pays expenses of writers on assignment.

**Photos:** Send photos with submission. Reviews color transparencies and color or b&w 4×6 or 5×7 prints. Offers no additional payment for photos accepted with mss but overall payment takes into consideration the number and quality of photos. Captions, model releases and identification of subjects required. Buys one-time and reprint rights.

**Poetry:** Free verse, light verse, traditional. "No poetry unrelated to our content." **Buys 6 poems/year.** Submit maximum 3 poems. Length: 12-30 lines. **Pays $25-50.**

**Tips:** "Think and write for practitioners and laymen who want information and insight and who are trying to work through problems to improve skills and their health. No promotional material."

# Miscellaneous

**$ $ AMERICAN CHEERLEADER**, Lifestyle Ventures, 250 W. 57th St., Suite 420, New York NY 10107. (212)265-8890. E-mail: editors@americancheerleader.com. Website: http://www.americancheerleader.com. Editorial Director: Julie Davis. Managing Editor: Nayda Rondon. **Contact:** Nayda Rondon, managing editor. **50% freelance written.** Bimonthly magazine covering high school and college cheerleading. Estab. 1995. Circ. 200,000. Pays on publication. Publishes ms 2 months after acceptance. Byline given. Buys all rights. Editorial lead time 4 months. Submit seasonal material 4 months in advance. Reports in 3 weeks on queries; 2 months on mss. Writer's guidelines for #10 SASE.
**Nonfiction:** How-to (cheering techniques, routines, pep songs, etc.), interview/profile (sports personalities), new product, personal experience. **Buys 20 mss/year.** Query with published clips. Length: 750-2,000 words. **Pays $75-200.** Sometimes pays expenses of writers on assignment.
**Photos:** State availability of photos with submission. Reviews transparencies and 5×7 prints. Offers no additional payment for photos accepted with ms. Captions, model releases and identification of subjects required. Buys all rights.

**$ CANADIAN RODEO NEWS**, Canadian Rodeo News, Ltd., #223, 2116 27th Ave. NE, Calgary, Alberta T2E 7A6 Canada. (403)250-7292. Fax: (403)250-6926. E-mail: rodeonews@iul-ccs.com. Website: http://www.rodeocanada.com. **Contact:** Vicki Mowat, editor. **60% freelance written.** Monthly tabloid covering "Canada's professional rodeo (CPRA) personalities and livestock. Read by rodeo participants and fans." Estab. 1964. Circ. 4,800. Pays on publication. Publishes ms an average of 1 month after acceptance. Byline given. Buys first and second serial (reprint) rights. Editorial lead time 1 month. Submit seasonal material 1 month in advance. Accepts simultaneous submissions. Accepts queries by mail, e-mail, fax, phone. Reports in 1 month on queries; 2 months on mss. Sample copy and writer's guidelines free.
**Nonfiction:** General interest, historical/nostalgic, interview/profile. **Buys 70-80 mss/year.** Query. Length: 500-1,200 words. **Pays $30-60.**
**Reprints:** Send photocopy of article or typed ms with rights for sale noted, and information about when and where the article previously appeared. Pays 100% of amount paid for an original article.
**Photos:** Send photos with submission. Reviews 4×6 prints. Offers $15-25/cover photo. Buys one-time rights.
**Tips:** "Best to call first with the story idea to inquire if it is suitable for publication. Readers are very knowledgeable of the sport, so writers need to be as well."

**$ PRIME TIME SPORTS & FITNESS**, GND Prime Time Publishing, P.O. Box 6097, Evanston IL 60204. (847)784-1194. Fax: (847)784-1195. E-mail: dennisdorner@bowldtalk.com. Website: http://www.bowldtalk.com. **Contact:** Dennis A. Dorner, editor. Managing Editor: Steven Ury. **80% freelance written.** Eager to work with new/unpublished writers. Monthly magazine covering seasonal pro sports and racquet and health club sports and fitness. Estab. 1974. Circ. 35,000. Pays on publication. Publishes ms an average of 6 months after acceptance. Byline given. Buys all rights; will assign back to author in 85% of cases. Submit seasonal material 6 months in advance. Accepts queries by mail, e-mail, fax. Accepts simultaneous submissions. Reports in 6 months. Sample copy on request. Writer's guidelines on website.
**Nonfiction:** Book excerpts (fitness and health), exposé (in tennis, fitness, racquetball, health clubs, diets), adult (slightly risqué and racy fitness), how-to (expert instructional pieces on any area of coverage), humor (large market for funny pieces on health clubs and fitness), inspirational (on how diet and exercise combine to bring you a better body, self), interview/profile, new product, opinion (only from recognized sources who know what they are talking about), personal experience (definitely—humor), photo feature (on related subjects); technical (on exercise and sport), travel (related to fitness, tennis camps, etc.), news reports (on racquetball, handball, tennis, running events). Special issues: Swimwear (March); Baseball Preview (April); Summer Fashion (July); Pro Football Preview (August); Aerobic Wear (September); Fall Fashion (October); Ski Issue (November); Workout and Diet Routines (December/January). "We love short articles that get to the point. Nationally oriented big events and national championships. No articles on local only tennis and racquetball tournaments without national appeal." **Buys 150 mss/year.** Length: 2,000 words maximum. **Pays $20-150.** Sometimes pays the expenses of writers on assignment.
**Reprints:** Send tearsheet or photocopy of article or short story or typed ms with rights for sale noted and information about when and where the article or story previously appeared. Pays 20% of amount paid for an original article or story.
**Photos:** Nancy Thomas, photo editor. Specifically looking for fashion photo features. Send photos with ms. Pays $5-75 for b&w prints. Captions, model releases, identification of subjects required. Buys all rights, "but returns 75% of photos to submitter."
**Columns/Departments:** George Thomas, column/department editor. New Products; Fitness Newsletter; Handball Newsletter; Racquetball Newsletter; Tennis Newsletter; News & Capsule Summaries; Fashion Spot (photos of new fitness and bathing suits and ski equipment); related subjects. **Buys 100 mss/year.** Send complete ms. Length: 50-250 words ("more if author has good handle to cover complete columns"). "We want more articles with photos and we are searching for one woman columnist, Diet and Nutrition." **Pays $5-25.**
**Fiction:** Judy Johnson, fiction editor. Erotica (if related to fitness club), fantasy (related to subjects), humorous, religious ("no God-is-my shepherd, but Body-is-God's-temple"), romance (related subjects), novel excerpts. "Upbeat stories are needed." **Buys 20 mss/year.** Send complete ms. Length: 500-2,500 words maximum. **Pays $20-150.**
**Poetry:** Free verse, haiku, light verse, traditional on related subjects. Length: up to 150 words. **Pays $10-25.**
▪ The online magazine contains original content not found in the print edition and includes writer's guidelines.

**Tips:** "Send us articles dealing with court club sports, exercise and nutrition that exemplify an upbeat 'you can do it' attitude. Pro sports previews 3-4 months ahead of their seasons are also needed. Good short fiction or humorous articles can break in. Expert knowledge of any related subject can bring assignments; any area is open. We consider everything as a potential article, but are turned off by credits, past work and degrees. We have a constant demand for well-written articles on instruction, health and trends in both. Other articles needed are professional sports training techniques, fad diets, tennis and fitness resorts, photo features with aerobic routines. A frequent mistake made by writers is in length— articles are too long. When we assign an article, we want it newsy if it's news and opinion if opinion."

**$PRORODEO SPORTS NEWS,** Professional Rodeo Cowboys Association, 101 ProRodeo Dr., Colorado Springs CO 80919. (719)593-8840. Fax: (719)548-4889. E-mail: pasay@prorodeo.com. Website: http://www.prorodeo.com. **Contact:** Paul Asay, editor. **10% freelance written.** Biweekly magazine covering professional rodeo. "Our readers are extremely knowledgeable about the sport of rodeo, and anyone who writes for us should have that same in-depth knowledge." Estab. 1952. Circ. 40,000. Pays on publication. Publishes ms an average of 1 month after acceptance. Byline given. Buys first, one-time rights and makes work-for-hire assignments. Editorial lead time 2 months. Submit seasonal material 2 months in advance. Reports in 2 weeks on queries. Sample copy for #10 SASE. Guidelines free.
**Nonfiction:** Historical/nostalgic, how-to, humor, interview/profile, photo feature, technical. **Buys 20 mss/year.** Query with published clips. Length: 300-1,000 words. **Pays $50-100.** Sometimes pays expenses of writers on assignment.
**Photos:** State availability of photos with submission. Reviews 8×10 prints. Offers $15-85/photo. Identification of subjects required. Buys one-time rights.

**N$$RACQUETBALL MAGAZINE,** United States Racquetball Association, 1685 W. Uintah, Colorado Springs CO 80904. (719)635-5396. Fax: (719)635-0685. E-mail: lmojer@racqmag.com. Website: http://www.racqmag.com. **Contact:** Linda Mojer, director of communications. **20-30% freelance written.** Bimonthly magazine "geared toward a readership of informed, active enthusiasts who seek entertainment, instruction and accurate reporting of events." Estab. 1990. Circ. 45,000. Pays on publication. Publishes ms an average of 2 months after acceptance. Buys one-time rights. Editorial lead time 3 months. Submit seasonal material 3 months in advance. Accepts simultaneous submissions. Reports in 2 months. Sample copy for $4. Writer's guidelines free.
**Nonfiction:** How-to (instructional racquetball tips), humor, interview/profile (personalities who play racquetball). **Buys 2-3 mss/year.** Send complete ms. Length: 1,500-3,000 words. **Pays $100.** Sometimes pays expenses of writers on assignment.
**Reprints:** Send typed ms with rights for sale noted and info about when and where it previously appeared.
**Photos:** Send photos with submission. Reviews 3×5 prints. Negotiates payment individually. Model releases, identification of subjects required. Buys one-time rights.
**Fiction:** Humorous (racquetball related). **Buys 1-2 mss/year.** Send complete ms. Length: 1,500-3,000 words. **Pays $100-250.**

**$RUGBY MAGAZINE,** Rugby Press Limited, 2350 Broadway, New York NY 10024. (212)787-1160. Fax: (212)595-0934. E-mail: rugbymag@aol.com. Website: http://www.inch.com/~rugby. Editor: Ed Hagerty. **Contact:** Christian Averill, managing editor. **75% freelance written.** Monthly tabloid. "*Rugby Magazine* is the journal of record for the sport of rugby in the U.S. Our demographics are among the best in the country." Estab. 1975. Circ. 10,000. Pays on publication. Publishes ms 2 months after acceptance. Byline given. Buys all rights. Editorial lead time 1 month. Submit seasonal material 2 months in advance. Accepts simultaneous submissions. Accepts queries by mail, e-mail, fax, phone. Reports in 2 weeks on queries; 1 months on mss. Sample copy for $3. Writer's guidelines free.
**Nonfiction:** Book excerpts, essays, general interest, historical/nostalgic, how-to, humor, interview/profile, new product, opinion, personal experience, photo feature, technical, travel. **Buys 15 mss/year.** Send complete ms. Length: 600-2,000 words. **Pays $50 minimum.** Pays expenses of writers on assignment.
**Reprints:** Send tearsheet of article or short story or typed ms with rights for sale noted and information about when and where the article or story previously appeared. Pay varies.
**Photos:** Send photos with submission. Reviews negatives, transparencies and prints. Offers no additional payment for photos accepted with ms. Buys all rights.
**Columns/Departments:** Nutrition, athletic nutrition, 900 words; Referees' Corner, 1,200 words; The Zen Rugger (Rugby as Zen), 650 words. **Buys 2-3 mss/year.** Query with published clips. **Pays $50 maximum.**
**Fiction:** Condensed novels, humorous, novel excerpts, slice-of-life vignettes. **Buys 1-3 mss/year.** Query with published clips. Length: 1,000-2,500 words. **Pays $100.**
**Tips:** "Give us a call. Send along your stories or photos; we're happy to take a look. Tournament stories are a good way to get yourself published in *Rugby Magazine*."

**$SKYDIVING,** 1725 N. Lexington Ave., DeLand FL 32724. (904)736-4793. Fax: (904)736-9786. E-mail: editor@skydivingmagazine.com. **Contact:** Sue Clifton, editor. **25% freelance written.** Works with a small number of new/ unpublished writers each year. Monthly tabloid featuring skydiving for sport parachutists, worldwide dealers and equipment manufacturers. "*Skydiving* is a news magazine. Its purpose is to deliver timely, useful and interesting information about the equipment, techniques, events, people and places of parachuting. Our scope is national. *Skydiving*'s audience spans the entire spectrum of jumpers, from first-jump students to veterans with thousands of skydives. Some readers are riggers with a keen interest in the technical aspects of parachutes, while others are weekend 'fun' jumpers who want information to help them make travel plans and equipment purchases." Circ. 14,200. Pays on publication. Publishes ms an average of 3 months after acceptance. Byline given. Buys one-time rights. Accepts simultaneous submissions, if so noted. Reports in 1 month. Sample copy for $2. Writer's guidelines for 9×12 SAE with 4 first-class stamps.

**Nonfiction:** Average issue includes 3 feature articles and 3 columns of technical information. "Send us news and information on how-to, where-to, equipment, techniques, events and outstanding personalities who skydive. We want articles written by people who have a solid knowledge of parachuting." No personal experience or human-interest articles. Query. Length: 500-1,000 words. **Pays $25-100.** Sometimes pays the expenses of writers on assignment.

**Reprints:** Accepts previously published submissions.

**Photos:** State availability of photos. Reviews 5×7 and larger b&w glossy prints. Offers no additional payment for photos accepted with ms. Captions required.

**Fillers:** Newsbreaks. Length: 100-200 words. **Pays $25 minimum.**

**Tips:** "The most frequent mistake made by writers in completing articles for us is that the writer isn't knowledgeable about the sport of parachuting. Articles about events are especially time-sensitive so yours must be submitted quickly. We welcome contributions about equipment. Even short, 'quick look' articles about new products are appropriate for *Skydiving*. If you know of a drop zone or other place that jumpers would like to visit, write an article describing its features and tell them why you liked it and what they can expect to find if they visit it. Avoid first person articles."

## Motor Sports

**$ $BRACKET RACING USA**, McMullen/Argus Publishing, 774 S. Placentia Ave., Placentia CA 92870. (770)442-0376. Fax: (770)410-9253. Website: http://www.cskpub.com. Managing Editor: Debra Wentz. **Contact:** Dale Wilson, editor. Magazine published 8 times/year covering bracket cars and bracket racing. Estab. 1989. Circ. 45,000. Pays on publication. Publishes ms 6 months after acceptance. Byline given. Buys first North American serial rights. Accepts queries by mail, fax, phone. Sample copy for $3 and 9×12 SAE with 5 first-class stamps.

**Nonfiction:** Automotive how-to and technical. **Buys 35 mss/year.** Query by mail only. Length: 500-4,000 words. **Pays $150/page.** Sometimes pays expenses of writers on assignment.

**Photos:** Send photos with submission.

**N $ $RACING MILESTONES**, Trader Publishing Company, 100 W. Plume St., Norfolk VA 23510. (757)664-3552. Fax: (757)640-6363. E-mail: mdowning@traderonline.com. Editor: Mary Scully. **Contact:** Mair Downing, assistant editor. **90% freelance written.** Monthly magazine covering automotive racing—mainly NASCAR. "*Racing Milestones* covers the drivers, tracks and technology in the exciting sport of racing. Race coverage, track profiles, driver profiles and news about collectibles are of interest to our readers." Estab. 1996. Circ. 160,000. Pays on publication. Byline given. Offers negotiable kill fee. Buys first North American serial rights. Editorial lead time 4 months. Submit seasonal material 5 months in advance. Accepts queries by mail, e-mail, fax, phone. Accepts simultaneous submissions. Reports in 6 weeks. Sample copy for $5. Writer's guidelines for #10 SASE.

**Nonfiction:** Historical/nostalgic, interview/profile, photo feature, technical. No fiction, how-to. **Buys 100 mss/year.** Query with published clips. Length: 500-2,000 words. **Pays 20¢/word and up.**

**Photos:** State availability of photos with submission. Negotiates payment individually. Identification of subjects required. Buys one-time rights.

**Columns/Departments:** Victory Lane (hot drivers or up and comers), 800-1,500 words; Behind the Scenes (insider-type stories), 1,000 words; Racer's Edge (car restorations & technical), 1,200 words. **Buys 80 mss/year.** Query with published clips. **Pays 20¢/word and up.**

**Tips:** "Think of new and interesting approaches to racing. We never publish stories that fans can read somewhere else."

**$ $SAND SPORTS MAGAZINE**, Wright Publishing Co. Inc., P.O. Box 2260, Costa Mesa CA 92628. (714)979-2560 ext. 107. Fax: (714)979-3998. **Contact:** Michael Sommer, editor. **20% freelance written.** Bimonthly magazine covering vehicles for off-road and sand dunes. Estab. 1995. Circ. 25,000. Pays on publication. Byline given. Buys first rights and one-time rights. Editorial lead time 3 months. Submit seasonal material 6 months in advance. Sample copy and writer's guidelines free.

**Nonfiction:** How-to technical-mechanical, photo feature, technical. **Buys 20 mss/year.** Query. Length: 1,500 words minimum. **Pays $125-175/page.** Sometimes pays expenses of writers on assignment.

**Photos:** Send photos with submission. Reviews contact sheets, transparencies, 5×7 prints. Negotiates payment individually. Captions, model releases, identification of subjects required. Buys one-time rights.

**$ $STOCK CAR RACING MAGAZINE**, General Media, 65 Parker St., #2, Newburyport MA 01950. (508)463-3789. Fax: (508)463-3250. **Contact:** Dick Berggren, editor. **80% freelance written.** Eager to work with new/ unpublished writers. Monthly magazine for stock car racing fans and competitors. Circ. 400,000. Pays on publication. Publishes ms 3 months after acceptance. Buys all rights. Byline given. Reports in 6 weeks. Guidelines free.

**Nonfiction:** General interest, historical/nostalgic, how-to, humor, interviews, new product, photo features, technical. "Uses nonfiction on stock car drivers, cars and races. We are interested in the story behind the story in stock car racing. We want interesting profiles and colorful, nationally interesting features. We are looking for more technical articles, particularly in the area of street stocks and limited sportsman." Query with or without published clips or submit complete ms. **Buys 50-200 mss/year.** Length: 100-6,000 words. **Pays up to $450.**

**Photos:** State availability of photos. Pays $20 for $8 \times 10$ b&w photos; up to $250 for 35mm or larger transparencies. Captions required.

**Fillers:** Anecdotes, short humor. Buys 100 each year. Pays $35.

**Tips:** "We get more queries than stories. We just don't get as much material as we want to buy. We have more room for stories than ever before. We are an excellent market with 12 issues per year. Virtually all our features are submitted without assignment. An author knows much better what's going on in his backyard than we do. We ask that you write to us before beginning a story theme. If nobody is working on the theme you wish to pursue, we'd be glad to assign it to you if it fits our needs and you are the best person for the job. Judging of material is always a combination of a review of the story and its support illustration. Photography should accompany manuscript on first submission."

## Olympic Sports

**$ INTERNATIONAL GYMNAST,** Paul Ziert & Associates, P.O. Box 721020, Norman OK 73070. Website: http://www.intlgymnast.com. **Contact:** Dwight Normile, editor. **10% freelance written.** Specialty magazine for the gymnastics community published 10 times/year. "Contributing writers must know and understand gymnastics. Most accepted freelance work is fiction." Estab. 1956. Circ. 26,000. Pays on publication. Publishes ms an average of 4 months after acceptance. Byline given. Buys one-time rights. Submit seasonal material 4 months in advance. Reports in 2 weeks on queries; 4 months on mss. Sample copy for $5. Writer's guidelines free.

**Nonfiction:** Humor, interview/profile, opinion, personal experience. **Buys 3 mss/year.** Query with published clips. Length: 1,000-2,500 words. **Pays $15-50 for assigned articles; $15-25 for unsolicited articles.** Pays writers with contributor copies or other premiums at writer's request. Sometimes pays expenses of writers on assignment.

**Photos:** State availability of photos with submission. Reviews negatives, transparencies. Offers $5-50/photo. Captions and identification of subjects required. Buys one-time rights.

**Columns/Departments:** Stretching Out (opinion), 600-1,000 words. **Buys 3 mss/year.** Query with published clips. **Pays $15-25.**

**Fiction:** Humorous, slice-of-life vignettes. **Buys 3 mss/year.** Send ms. Length: 1,000-1,500 words. **Pays $15-25.**

The online magazine carries original content not found in the print edition. Contact: Susan Williams, online editor.

**Tips:** "Please be polite, professional and patient. We use few freelancers, so the chances of being published are slim."

**$ $ OLYMPIAN MAGAZINE,** US Olympic Committee, One Olympic Plaza, Colorado Springs CO 80909. (719)578-4529. Fax: (719)578-4677. E-mail: bob.condron@usoc.org. Website: http://www.olympic-usa.org. **Contact:** Managing Editor. **50% freelance written.** Bimonthly magazine covering olympic sports and athletes. Estab. 1974. Circ. 120,000. Pays on publication. Byline given. Offers 100% kill fee. Free writer's guidelines.

**Nonfiction:** Photo feature, feature/profiles of athletes in Olympic sports. Query by mail or fax. Length: 1,200-2,000 words. **Pays $300.**

**Reprints:** Send photocopy of article. Pay 50% of amount paid for an original article.

**Photos:** State availability of photos with submission. Reviews transparencies and prints. Offers $50-250/photo. Captions, model releases and identification of subjects required. Buys one-time rights.

**USA GYMNASTICS,** 201 S. Capitol Ave., Suite 300, Pan American Plaza, Indianapolis IN 46225. (317)237-5050. Fax: (317)237-5069. E-mail: lpeszek@usa-gymnastics.org. Website: http://www.usa-gymnastics.org. **Contact:** Luan Peszek, editor. **20% freelance written.** Bimonthly magazine covering gymnastics—national and international competitions. Designed to educate readers on fitness, health, safety, technique, current topics, trends and personalities related to the gymnastics/fitness field. Readers are ages 7-18, parents and coaches. Estab. 1981. Circ. 63,000. Pays on publication. Publishes ms an average of 4 months after acceptance. Byline given. Buys all rights. Submit seasonal material 4 months in advance. Accepts queries by e-mail, fax. Accepts simultaneous submissions. Reports in 2 months. Sample copy for $5.

**Nonfiction:** General interest, how-to (related to fitness, health, gymnastics), inspirational, interview/profile, opinion (Open Floor section), photo feature. **Buys 3 mss/year.** Query. Length: 1,500 words maximum. Payment negotiated.

**Reprints:** Accepts previously published submissions. Send photocopy of article.

**Photos:** Send photos with submission. Offers no additional payment for photos accepted with ms. Identification of subjects required. Buys all rights.

**Tips:** "Any articles of interest to gymnasts (men, women and rhythmic gymnastics) coaches, judges and parents, are what we're looking for. This includes nutrition, toning, health, safety, trends, techniques, timing, etc."

## Running

**$ INSIDE TEXAS RUNNING,** 9514 Bristlebrook Dr., Houston TX 77083. (281)498-3208. Fax: (281)879-9980. E-mail: insideTx@aol.com. Website: http://www.RunningNetwork.com/TexasRunning. **Contact:** Joanne Schmidt, editor. **70% freelance written.** Monthly (except June and August) tabloid covering running and running-related events.

"Our audience is made up of Texas runners who may also be interested in cross training." Estab. 1977. Circ. 10,000. **Pays on acceptance.** Publishes ms an average of 2 months after acceptance. Byline given. Buys first rights, one-time rights, second serial (reprint) rights, exclusive Texas and all rights. Submit seasonal material 2 months in advance. Reports in 1 month on mss. Sample copy for $1.50. Writer's guidelines for #10 SASE.

☛ "The best way to break in to our publication is to submit brief (2 or 3 paragraphs) fillers for our 'Texas Roundup' section."

**Nonfiction:** Various topics of interest to runners. No personal experience such as "Why I Love to Run," "How I Ran My First Marathon." Special issues: Fall Race Review (September); Marathon Focus (October); Shoe Review (March); Resource Guide (December). **Buys 20 mss/year.** Send complete ms. Length: 500-1,500 words. **Pays $100 maximum for assigned articles; $50 maximum for unsolicited articles.**

**Reprints:** Send tearsheet, photocopy or typed ms with rights for sale noted and information about when and where the article previously appeared.

**Photos:** Send photos with submission. Offers $25 maximum/photo. Captions required. Buys one-time rights.

■ The online magazine carries original content not found in the print edition.

**Tips:** "Writers should be familiar with the sport and the publication."

**$ $ NEW YORK RUNNER**, New York Road Runners Club, 9 E. 89th St., New York NY 10128. (212)423-2260. Fax: (212)423-0879. E-mail: newyorkrun@nyrrc.org. Website: http://www.nyrrc.org. **Contact:** Lisa Kireta, assistant editor. Bimonthly regional sports magazine covering running, racewalking, nutrition and fitness. Material should be of interest to members of the New York Road Runners Club. Estab. 1958. Circ. 45,000. Pays on publication. Time to publication varies. Byline given. Offers 33% kill fee. Buys first North American serial rights. Submit seasonal material 4 months in advance. Accepts simultaneous submissions. Accepts queries by mail, e-mail, fax. Reports in 2 months. Sample copy for $3. Writer's guidelines for #10 SASE.

☛ Break in through departments *Runner's Diary* (essay); *Footnote* (humor); or *On the Roads* (interesting places to run).

**Nonfiction:** Running and marathon articles. Special issues: N.Y.C. Marathon (submissions in by August 1). No non-running stories. **Buys 25 mss/year.** Query. Length: 750-1,000 words. **Pays $50-250.**

**Reprints:** Send photocopy of article with information about when and where it previously appeared. Pays 25-50% of amount paid for an original article.

**Photos:** Send photos with submission. Reviews 8 × 10 b&w prints. Offers $35-300/photo. Captions, model releases, identification of subjects required. Buys one-time rights.

**Tips:** "Be knowledgeable about the sport of running. Write like a runner."

**N $ $ $ $ RUNNER'S WORLD**, Rodale, 33 E. Minor St., Emmaus PA 18098. (610)967-5171. Deputy Senior Editor: Bob Wischnia. **Contact:** Adam Bean, managing editor. **5% freelance written.** Monthly magazine on running, mainly long-distance running. "The magazine for and about distance running, training, health and fitness, injury precaution, race coverage, personalties of the sport." Estab. 1966. Circ. 500,000. Pays on publication. Publishes ms an average of 6 months after acceptance. Byline given. Buys all rights. Submit seasonal material 6 months in advance. Reports in 2 months. Writer's guidelines for #10 SASE.

☛ Break in through *Women's Running* and *Finish Line* columns.

**Nonfiction:** How-to (train, prevent injuries), interview/profile, personal experience. No "my first marathon" stories. No poetry. **Buys 10 mss/year.** Query. **Pays $1,500-2,000.** Pays expenses of writers on assignment.

**Photos:** State availability of photos with submission. Identification of subjects required. Buys one-time rights.

**Columns/Departments:** Finish Line (personal experience—humor); Women's Running. **Buys 15 mss/year.** Query. **Pays $50 for departments, $300 for essays.**

**N $ $ TRIATHLETE MAGAZINE, The World's Largest Triathlon Magazine**, Triathlon Group of North America, 2037 San Elijo, Cardiff CA 92007. (760)634-4100. Fax: (760)634-4110. E-mail: cgandolfo@triathletemag.com. Website: http://www.triathletemag.com. Editor: T.J. Murphy. **Contact:** Christina Gandolfo, managing editor. **50% freelance written.** Monthly magazine. "In general, articles should appeal to seasoned triathletes, as well as eager newcomers to the sport. Our audience includes everyone from competitive athletes to people considering their first event." Estab. 1983. Circ. 50,000. Pays on publication. Byline given. Buys second serial (reprint) and all rights. Editorial lead time 3 months. Submit seasonal material 6 months in advance. Accepts queries by mail, e-mail. Accepts simultaneous submissions. Sample copy for $5.

**Nonfiction:** How-to, interview/profile, new product, photo feature, technical. "No first-person pieces about your experience in triathlon or my-first-triathlon stories." **Buys 36 mss/year.** Query with published clips. Length: 1,000-3,000 words. **Pays $200-600.** Sometimes pays expenses of writers on assignment.

**Photos:** State availability of photos with submission. Reviews transparencies. Offers $25-200/photo. Buys first North American rights.

■ The online magazine carries original content not found in the print edition. Contact: Ben Blakely, online editor.

**Tips:** "Writers should know the sport and be familiar with the nuances and history. Training-specific articles that focus on new, but scientifically based, methods are good, as are seasonal training pieces."

# Skiing & Snow Sports

$ **AMERICAN SKATING WORLD, Independent Newsmonthly of American Ice Skating**, American Skating World Inc., 1816 Brownsville Rd., Pittsburgh PA 15210-3908. (412)885-7600. Fax: (412)885-7617. E-mail: editorial @americansk8world.com. Website: americansk8world.com. Editor: Robert A. Mock. **Contact:** H. Kermit Jackson, executive editor. **70% freelance written.** Eager to work with new/unpublished writers. Monthly magtab on figure skating. Estab. 1979. Circ. 15,000. Pays following publication. Publishes ms an average of 3 months after acceptance. Byline given. Buys first North American serial rights and occasionally second serial (reprint) rights. Submit seasonal material 3 months in advance. Reports in 3 months. Sample copy and writer's guidelines for $3.50.

● The increased activity and interest in figure skating have increased demands on *American Skating World*'s contributor network. New writers from nontraditional areas (i.e., outside of East Coast, Upper Midwest, California) are particularly welcome.

**Nonfiction:** Competition coverage (both technical and human interest), exposé, historical/nostalgic, how-to (technique in figure skating), humor, inspirational, interview/profile and overview (leading current or past individuals in the field, whether they are skaters, coaches, choreographers, arrangers or parents), new product, opinion, performance coverage (review or human interest), personal experience, photo feature, technical, travel. Also interested in amateur recreational skating (overseen by the Ice Skating Institute); "eligible" competitive skating (overseen by the USFSA, the CFSA and other bodies associated with the Olympics) and professional skating (overseen by the Professional Skaters Association [formerly PSGA]). Rarely accepts fiction. "AP Style Guidelines are the basic style source, but we are not bound by that convention. Short, snappy paragraphs desired." **Buys 150 mss/year.** Send complete ms. "Include phone number; response time longer without it." Length: 600-1,000 words. **Pays $25-100.**

**Reprints:** Occasionally accepts previously published submissions. Send tearsheet of article or typed ms with rights for sale noted and information about when and where the article previously appeared. Pays 50% of amount paid for an original article.

**Photos:** Send photos with query or ms. Reviews transparencies and b&w prints. Pays $5 for b&w; $10 for color. Identification of subjects required. Buys all rights for b&w; one-time rights for color.

**Columns/Departments: Buys 30 mss/year.** Send complete ms. Length: 500-750 words. **Pays $25-50.**

**Fillers:** Clippings, anecdotes. No payment for fillers.

**Tips:** "Event coverage is most open to freelancers; confirm with executive editor to ensure event has not been assigned. We are drawing more extensively from non-U.S. based writers. Questions are welcome; call executive editor EST, 10-4, Monday-Friday."

■ $ $ $ **MOUNTAIN SPORTS & LIVING** (formerly Snow Country), Miller Sports Group, 810 Seventh Ave., 4th Floor, New York NY 10019. (212)636-2700. Fax: (212)636-2730. **Contact:** Perkins Miller, editor. Managing Editor: Abigail Demers. Website: http://www.mountainsportsliving.com. **98% freelance written.** Magazine published 7 times/year focusing on mountain lifestyle and recreation at and around ski resorts. "Because we publish year-round, we cover a broader range of subjects than ski-only publications. Besides skiing, topics include scenic drives, mountain biking, hiking, ski town news, real estate, etc." Estab. 1988. Circ. 465,000. **Pays on acceptance.** Publishes ms an average of 6 months after acceptance. Byline given. Pays 20% kill fee. Editorial lead time 5 months. Submit seasonal material 6 months in advance. Accepts queries by mail, fax. Reports in 1 month. Free writer's guidelines.

○→ Break in with *Mountain Views*, *Mountain Traveler* and *Mountain Sport Health* columns.

**Nonfiction:** General interest, historical/nostalgic, how-to, humor, interview/profile, new product, photo feature, technical and travel. **Buys 70 mss/year.** Query with published clips. Length: 200-2,000 words. **Pays $1/word.** Pays expenses of writers on assignment.

**Photos:** State availability of photos or send photos with submission. Buys one-time rights.

**Columns/Departments:** David Dunbar, executive editor. Feature Travel, 1,000-2,000 words. Mountain Views (short news stories about people, events and issues in mountain towns; also includes an 800-word personality profile that serves as an engaging, three-dimensional portrait of a unique player in mountain-town life); Mountain Traveler (short travel-service pieces packed with useful information and tips for travelers, including restaurant and inn reviews; three short resort profiles; and a first-person *Adventure* story); Mountain Living (4-page *Home* feature depicting an architecturally unique mountain house; a *Business* story that tells readers about people who have created a company in a mountain town; and a *Real Estate* how-to story with a table listing recent mountain-home sales); Mountain Sport (*Personal Trainer*, ski and snowboard fitness instruction; a *Health* article covering the latest topics as they relate to people who play, live or work in the mountains); *What You Wear*, (a roundup of key accessories for mountain-sport enthusiasts); *Gear Tested*, (a review of mountain gear and gadgets); and *Private Lesson*, (a chance to get to know the world's best mountain-sport instructors and learn their best tips.); When and Where (calendar of great mountain-town events); The Last Resort (extraordinary photograph that captures the essence of some aspect of mountain life). **Buys 100 mss/year.** Query with published clips.

**Tips:** "We're always looking for short articles on unique people, events and news in snow country that we may not already know about. We aim to publish travel material that is not regular old press fodder."

Ⓝ $ $ **POWDER, The Skier's Magazine**, Surfer Publications, P.O. Box 1028, Dana Point CA 92629. (949)496-5922. Fax: (949)496-7849. E-mail: powdermag@surferpubs.com. **Contact:** John Bresee, editor. **40% freelance written.** Magazine published 7 times/year covering skiing for expert skiers. Estab. 1972. Circ. 110,000. **Pays on acceptance.** Byline given. Offers 25% kill fee. Buys first North American serial rights. Editorial lead time 3 months. Submit seasonal material 3 months in advance. Reports in 2 months. Sample copy for $8. Writer's guidelines free.

**Photos:** Send photos with submission. Reviews 35mm transparencies. Negotiates payment individually. Identification of subjects required. Buys one-time rights.

**$ $ $ SKI MAGAZINE**, Times Mirror Magazines, 929 Pearl St., Suite 200, Boulder CO 80302. (303)448-7600. Fax: (303)448-7638. Website: http://www.skinet.com. Editor-in-Chief: Andy Bigford. **Contact:** Natalie Kurylko, managing editor. **15% freelance written.** Monthly. "*Ski* is a ski-lifestyle publication written and edited for recreational skiers. Its content is intended to help them ski better (technique), buy better (equipment and skiwear), and introduce them to new experiences, people and adventures." Estab. 1936. Circ. 430,000. **Pays on acceptance.** Publishes ms 3 months after acceptance. Byline given. Offers 15% kill fee. Buys first North American serial rights. Submit seasonal material 8 months in advance. Reports in 1 month. Sample copy for 9×12 SAE with 5 first-class stamps.

**Nonfiction:** Essays, historical/nostalgic, how-to, humor, interview/profile and personal experience. **Buys 5-10 mss/ year.** Send complete ms. Length: 1,000-3,500 words. **Pays $500-1,000 for assigned articles; $300-700 for unsolicited articles.** Pays the expenses of writers on assignment.

**Photos:** Send photos with submission. Offers $75-300/photo. Captions, model releases and identification of subjects required. Buys one-time rights.

**Columns/Departments:** Ski Life (interesting people, events, oddities in skiing), 150-300 words; Going Places (items on new or unique places, deals or services available to skiers); and Take It From Us (special products or services available to skiers that are real values or out of the ordinary), 25-50 words.

**Fillers:** Facts and short humor. **Buys 10/year.** Length: 60-75 words. **Pays $50-75.**

**Tips:** "Writers must have an extensive familiarity with the sport and know what concerns, interests and amuses skiers. Columns are most open to freelancers."

**$ $ $ $ SKIING**, Times Mirror Magazines, Inc., 929 Pearl St., Suite 200, Boulder CO 80302. (303)448-7600. Fax: (303)448-7676. E-mail: holsson@skinet.com. Website: http://www.skinet.com. Editor-in-Chief: Rick Kahl. **Contact:** Helen Olsson, senior executive editor. Magazine published 7 times/year for skiers who deeply love winter, who live for travel, adventure, instruction, gear, and news. "*Skiing*, is the user's guide to winter adventure. It is equal parts jaw-dropping inspiration and practical information, action and utility, attitude and advice. It relates the lifestyles of dedicated skiers and captures their spirit of daring and exploration. Dramatic photography transports readers to spine-tingling mountains with breathtaking immediacy. Reading *Skiing* is almost as much fun as being there." Estab. 1948. Circ. 400,000. Byline given. Offers 40% kill fee. Query. No previously published articles or poetry.

**Nonfiction: Buys 10-15 features** (1,500-2,000 words) and **12-24 short pieces** (100-700 words). **Pays $1,000-2,500/ feature; $175-500/short piece.**

**Columns/Departments: Buys 2-3 articles/year.** Length: 1,000-1,500 words. **Pays $700-1,200.**

The online magazine carries original content not found in the print edition. Contact: Sarah Woodberry, online editor.

**Tips:** "Consider less obvious subjects: smaller ski areas, specific local ski cultures, unknown aspects of popular resorts. Be expressive, not merely descriptive! We want readers to feel the adventure in your writing—to tingle with the excitement of skiing steep powder, of meeting intriguing people, of reaching new goals or achieving dramatic new insights. We want readers to have fun, to see the humor in and the lighter side of skiing and their fellow skiers."

# Tennis

**N $ $ TSL, The Sporting Life**, (formerly *Racquet*) Heather & Pine, Inc., 21 E. 40th St., 13th Floor, New York NY 10016. (212)696-2484. Fax: (212)696-1678. E-mail: racquet@walrus.com. Contact: Stephen Weiss, managing editor. **30% freelance written.** Bimonthly sports/lifestyle magazine. "*TSL* celebrates the lifestyle of the game." Estab. 1978. Circ. 145,000. Pays on publication. Publishes ms an average of 3 months after acceptance. Byline given. Offers negotiable kill fee. Rights purchased negotiable. Submit seasonal material 5 months in advance. Accepts simultaneous submissions. Accepts queries by mail, e-mail, fax. Reports in 1 month. Sample copy for $4.

• *TSL*, formerly *Racquet*, has enlarged its focus from tennis to general sporting lifestyle.

**Nonfiction:** Regular Features: Gear (the best new equipment); TSL Journal (a guide for the sophisticated traveler); Fashion (sporting looks for the season); Essentials (style, travel and trends); Personal Best (health and fitness); Passions (celebrities and the sports they love); Destinations (top sporting resorts around the world); Traditions (the classic sporting events). **Buys 15-20 mss/year.** Query. Length: 1,000-4,000 words. **Pays $200-750 for assigned articles; $100-300 for unsolicited articles.** Sometime pays expenses of writers on assignment.

**Reprints:** Send tearsheet or photocopy of article and information about when and where the article previously appeared.

**Photos:** State availability of photos with submission. Offers no additional payment for photos accepted with ms. Rights negotiable.

**Columns/Departments: Buys 5-10 mss/year.** Query. **Pays $100-300.**

**Fiction:** Publishes novel excerpts.

**Fillers:** Anecdotes, short humor. **Buys 5/year.** Length: 250-750 words. **Pays $50-150.**

**Tips:** "Get a copy, understand how we approach sports, submit article written to style and follow-up. We are always looking for innovative or humorous ideas."

# Water Sports

**$ $ DIVER**, Seagraphic Publications, Ltd., 11780 Hammersmith Way, Suite 230, Richmond, British Columbia V7A 5E3 Canada. (604)274-4333. Fax: (604)274-4366. E-mail: divermag@axio.net. Website: www.divermag.com. Publisher: Peter Vassilopoulos. **Contact:** Stephanie Bold, editor. Magazine published 9 times/year emphasizing scuba diving, ocean science and technology (commercial and military diving) for a well-educated, outdoor-oriented readership. Circ. 17,500. Payment "follows publication." Buys first North American serial rights. Byline given. Travel features considered only August through October for use following year. Accepts queries by mail, e-mail, fax, phone. Reports in up to 3 months. Publishes ms up to 1 year after acceptance. "Articles are subject to being accepted for use in supplement issues on tabloid."

**Nonfiction:** How-to (underwater activities such as photography, etc.), general interest (underwater oriented), humor, historical (shipwrecks, treasure artifacts, archeological), interview (underwater personalities in all spheres—military, sports, scientific or commercial), personal experience (related to diving), photo feature (marine life), technical (related to oceanography, commercial/military diving, etc.), travel (dive resorts). No subjective product reports. **Buys 25 mss/ year. Buys 6 freelance travel items/year.** Submit complete ms. Send SAE with IRCs. Length: 800-1,000 words. **Pays $2.50/column inch.**

**Photos:** "Features are mostly those describing dive sites, experiences, etc. Photo features are reserved more as specials, while almost all articles must be well illustrated with color or b&w prints supplemented by color transparencies." Submit original photo material with accompanying ms. Pays $15 minimum for 5×7 or 8×10 b&w glossy prints; $20 minimum for 35mm color transparencies. Captions and model releases required. Buys one-time rights.

**Columns/Departments:** Book reviews. Submit complete ms. Length: 200 words maximum. No payment.

**Fillers:** Anecdotes, newsbreaks, short humor. **Buys 8-10/year.** Length: 50-150 words. No payment for news items.

**Tips:** "No phone calls about status of manuscript. Write if no response within reasonable time. Only brief, to-the-point correspondence will be answered. Lengthy communications will probably result in return of work unused. Publisher assumes no liability to use material even after lengthy waiting period. Acceptances subject to final and actual use."

**$ THE DIVER**, P.O. Box 28, Saint Petersburg FL 33731-0028. (813)866-9856. Fax: (813)866-9740. E-mail: boxer552 70@aol.com. **Contact:** Bob Taylor, publisher/editor. **50% freelance written.** Magazine published 6 times/year for divers, coaches and officials. Estab. 1978. Circ. 1,500. Pays on publication. Byline given. Submit material at least 2 months in advance. Accepts simultaneous submissions. Accepts queries by mail, e-mail, fax, phone. Reports in 2 weeks on queries; 1 month on mss. Sample copy for 9×12 SAE with 3 first-class stamps.

**Nonfiction:** Interview/profile (of divers, coaches, officials), results, tournament coverage, any stories connected with platform and springboard diving, photo features, technical. **Buys 35 mss/year.** Query. Length: 500-2,500 words. **Pays $25-50.**

**Reprints:** Send tearsheet of article. Pays 50% of amount paid for an original article.

**Photos:** Pays $5-10 for b&w prints. Captions and identification of subjects required. Buys one-time rights.

**Tips:** "We're very receptive to new writers."

**$ $ HOT WATER**, Taylor Publishing Group, 2585 Skymark Ave., Unit 306, Mississauga, Ontario L4W 4L5 Canada. (905)624-8218. Fax: (905)624-6764. **Contact:** Yvan Marston, editor. **50% freelance written.** Quarterly magazine covering personal watercraft market (jet skis, sea-doo's). "Focused on fun-loving watersports enthusiasts, *Hot Water* contains features on new personal watercraft and accessories, places to ride, racing, and profiles on people in the industry. Technical and handling tips are also included." Estab. 1993. Circ. 18,000 Pays on publication. Publishes ms an average of 4 months after acceptance. Byline given. Buys first North American serial rights. Editorial lead time 2 months. Submit seasonal material 3 months in advance. Accepts queries by mail, e-mail, fax, phone. Sample copy and writer's guidelines free.

**Nonfiction:** Historical/nostalgic, how-to (anything technical or handling etc.), humor, interview/profile, personal experience, photo feature, technical, travel. Send complete ms. Length: 1,000-3,000 words. **Pays $300 maximum.** Sometimes pays expenses of writers on assignment.

**Reprints:** Send photocopy of article or typed ms with rights for sale noted and information about when and where the article previously appeared. Pay negotiable.

**Photos:** Send photos with submission. Reviews transparencies, 4×6 prints. Offers no additional payment for photos accepted with ms. Captions, model releases, identification of subjects required.

**Columns/Departments:** Workbench (technical tips); Hot Waterways (riding adventures); all 1,000 words. Buys 6 mss/year. Send complete ms. **Pays $200 maximum.**

**Fillers:** Facts, newsbreaks. Length: 500-1,000 words. **Pays $150 maximum.**

**Tips:** "Make sure your idea has a Canadian angle. If you have a story idea you feel is appropriate, feel free to contact the editor to discuss. Or, if you're familiar with watercraft but need some direction, call the editor who will gladly assign a feature."

**N $ $ IMMERSED MAGAZINE, The International Technical Diving Magazine**, Immersed LLC, FDR Station, P.O. Box 947, New York NY 10150-0947. (201)792-1331. Fax: (212)259-9310. E-mail: bsterner@prodigy.net or immersed@njscuba.com. Website: http://www.immersed.com. **Contact:** Bob Sterner, editor/copublisher. **40% freelance written.** Quarterly magazine covering scuba diving. "Advances on the frontier of scuba diving are covered in theme-oriented issues that examine archeology, biology, history, gear and sciences related to diving. We emphasize training, education and safety." Estab. 1996. Circ. 25,000. Pays on publication. Byline given. Offers kill fee. Buys one-time and electronic rights. Editorial lead time 6 months. Accepts queries by mail, e-mail, fax, phone. Sample copy online at website. Writer's guidelines for #10 SASE.

**Nonfiction:** Historical/nostalgic, how-to, interview/profile, new product, personal experience, photo feature, technical, travel. No poetry, opinion diatribes, axe-grinding exposés. **Buys 30 mss/year.** Query. Length: 500-2,000 words. **Pays $150-250.** Sometimes pays expenses of writers on assignment.

**Photos:** Send photos with submission. Reviews transparencies and prints. Offers no additional payment for photos accepted with ms. Captions required. Buys one-time and promotional website rights.

**Columns/Departments:** Technically Destined (travel), 1,200 words; Rigging for Success (how-to), few words/illustration; Explorer (personality profile), 2,000 words; Tech Spec (product descriptions), 1,000 words; New Products (product press releases), 200 words; Book Review (book review), 800 words. **Buys 12 mss/year.** Query. **Pays $150-250.**

**Fillers:** Newsbreaks. **Pays 35¢/word.**

**Tips:** "Query first with a short, punchy paragraph that describes your story and why it would be of interest to our readers. There's bonus points for citing which feature or department would be most appropriate for your story."

**N $ $ PADDLER MAGAZINE, World's No. I Canoeing, Kayaking and Rafting Magazine**, Paddlesport Publishing, P.O. Box 5450, Steamboat Springs CO 80477-5450. (970)879-1450. Fax: (970)870-1404. E-mail: editor@ aca-paddler.org. Website: http://www.aca-paddler.org/paddler. Editor: Eugene Buchanan. **Contact:** Aaron Bible, associate editor. **70% freelance written.** Consumer publication published bimonthly covering paddle sports. "*Paddler* magazine is written by and for those knowledgeable above river running, flatwater tripping and sea kayaking. Our core audience is the intermediate to advanced paddler, yet we strive to cover the entire range from beginners to experts. Our editorial coverage is divided between whitewater rafting, whitewater kayaking, canoeing and sea kayaking. We strive for balance between the Eastern and Western U.S. paddling scenes and regularly cover international expeditions. We also try to integrate the Canadian paddling community into each publication." Estab. 1991. Circ. 80,000. Pays on publication. Publishes ms an average of 1-6 months after acceptance. Byline given. Buys first North American serial and one-time electronic rights. Editorial lead time 3 months. Submit seasonal material 6 months in advance. Accepts queries by mail, e-mail, fax. Reports in 3-6 months. Sample copy $3 with 8½×11 SASE. Guidelines for #10 SASE.

**Nonfiction:** Book excerpts, essays, general interest, historical/nostalgic, how-to, humor, inspirational, interview/profile, new product, opinion, personal ex-eroemce, photo feature, technical, travel (must be paddlesport related). **Buys 18 mss/ year.** Query. Length: 250-3,000 words. **Pays 10-25¢ for assigned articles; 10-20¢ for unsolicited articles.** Sometimes pays expenses of writers on assignment.

**Photos:** State availability of photos with submission. Reviews contact sheets, negatives and transparencies. Offers $25-250/photo. Buys one-time rights.

**Columns/Departments:** Submissions should include photos or other art. Consider submitting to Departments, especially as a first-time contributor, and be creative. Hotline (timely news and exciting developments relating to the paddling community. Stories should be lively and newsworthy), 150-750 words; Paddle People (unique people involved in the sport and industry leaders), 600-800 words; Destinations (informs paddlers of unique places to paddle), we often follow regional themes and cover all paddling disciplines. Submissions should include map and photo, 800 words; Inn of the Month (a different paddling hotel, lodge or B & B each issue), 500 words; Marketplace (gear reviews, gadgets and new products and is about equipment paddlers use, from boats and paddles to collapsible chairs, bivy sacks and other accessories), 250-800 words; Paddle Tales (short, humorous anecdotes), 75-300 words; Skills (a "How-to" forum for experts to share tricks of the trade, from playboating techniques to cooking in the backcountry), 250-1,000 words. Query. **Pays 10-20¢.**

**Tips:** "We prefer queries, but will look at manuscripts on speculation. No phone queries please. Be familiar with the magazine and offer us unique, exciting ideas. Most positive responses to queries are on spec, but we will occasionally make assignments."

**N SEA MAGAZINE, America's Western Boating Magazine**, Duncan McIntosh Co., 17782 Cowan, Suite C, Irvine CA 92614. (949)660-6150. Fax: (949)660-6172. Website: http://www.seamag.com. Managing editor: Eston Ellis. **70% freelance written.** Monthly magazine covering West Coast power boating. Estab. 1908. Circ. 50,000. Pays on publication. Publishes ms an average of 3 months after acceptance. Byline given. Buys first North American serial rights. Editorial lead time 3 months. Submit seasonal material 5 months in advance. Accepts simultaneous submissions. Reports in 6 weeks on queries.

**Nonfiction:** Exposé, how-to, new product, personal experience, technical, travel. **Buys 36 mss/year.** Query or send complete ms. Length: 300-1,200 words. **Pay varies.** Sometimes pays expenses of writers on assignment.

**Photos:** State availability of photos with submission. Reviews transparencies. Offers $50-250/photo. Captions, model releases and identification of subjects required. Buys one-time rights.

**$ $ SPORT DIVER**, World Publications, 330 W. Canton Ave., Winter Park FL 32789. (407)628-4802. Fax: (407)628-7061. E-mail: gj1@worldzine.com. **Contact:** Gary P. Joyce, editor. **75% freelance written.** Bimonthly magazine covering scuba diving. "We portray the adventure and fun of diving—the reasons we all started diving in the first place." Estab. 1993. Circ. 120,000. Pays on publication, sometimes on acceptance. Byline given. Offers 50% kill fee. Buys first North American serial rights. Editorial lead time 3 months. Submit seasonal material 4 months in advance. Accepts queries by mail, e-mail. Reports in 2 weeks on queries; 3 months on mss. Writer's guidelines for #10 SASE.

**Nonfiction:** Personal experience, travel, diving. No non-diving related articles. **Buys 150 mss/year.** Query with SASE. Length: 800-2,000 words. **Pays $300-500.**

**Photos:** State availability of photos with submission. Reviews transparencies. Offers $50-200/photo. Offers $500 for covers. Captions required. Buys one-time rights.

**Columns/Departments:** Divebriefs (shorts), 150-450 words. Query. **Pays $50-250.**

**Tips:** "Know diving, and even more importantly, know how to write. It's getting much more difficult to break into the market due to a recent series of takeovers."

**$ $ SURFER**, EMAP/Petersen Publications, P.O. Box 1028, Dana Point CA 92629. (949)496-5922. Fax: (949)496-7849. E-mail: surferedit@petersenpub.com. Website: http://www.surfermag.com. **Contact:** Evan Slater, editor. Assistant Editor: Melissa Calvano. **75% freelance written.** Monthly magazine "aimed at experts and beginners with strong emphasis on action surf photography." Estab. 1960. Circ. 110,000. Pays on publication. Byline given. Buys first North American serial rights. Submit seasonal material 6 months in advance. Accepts simultaneous submissions. Reports in 2 months. Sample copy for $3.99 with 9×12 SASE. Writer's guidelines for #10 SASE.

**Nonfiction:** How-to (technique in surfing), humor, inspirational, interview/profile, opinion, personal experience (all surf-related), photo feature (action surf and surf travel), technical (surfboard design), travel (surf exploration and discovery—photos required). **Buys 30-50 mss/year.** Query with or without published clips, or send complete ms. Length: 500-2,500 words. **Pays 25-30¢/word.** Sometimes pays the expenses of writers on assignment.

**Reprints:** Send typed ms with rights for sale noted and information about when and where the article previously appeared. Pays 100% of amount paid for an original article.

**Photos:** Send photos with submission. Reviews 35mm transparencies. Buys 12-24 illustrations/year. Prices vary. Used for columns: Environment, Surf Docs and sometimes features. Send samples with SASE to Art Director. Offers $45-300/photo. Identification of subjects required. Buys one-time and reprint rights.

**Columns/Departments:** Environment (environmental concerns to surfers), 1,000-1,500 words; Surf Stories (personal experiences of surfing), 1,000-1,500 words; Reviews (surf-related movies, books), 500-1,000 words; Sections (humorous surf-related items with b&w photos), 100-500 words. **Buys 25-50 mss/year.** Send complete ms. **Pays 25-30¢/word.**

**Fiction:** Surf-related adventure, fantasy, horror, humorous, science fiction. **Buys 10 mss/year.** Send complete ms. Length: 750-2,000 words. **Pays 25-30¢/word.**

**Tips:** "All sections are open to freelancers but interview/profiles are usually assigned. 'People Who Surf' is a good way to get a foot in the door. Stories must be authoritative, oriented to the hard-core surfer."

**$ $ SWIM MAGAZINE, The Official Magazine of U.S. Masters Swimming**, Sports Publications, Inc., 90 Bell Rock Plaza, Suite 200, Sedona AZ 86351. (520)284-4005. Fax: (520)284-2477. E-mail: swimworld@aol.com. Website: http://www.swimworld.com **Contact:** Dr. Phillip Whitten, editor. **50% freelance written.** Prefers to work with published/selected writers. Bimonthly magazine for adults interested in swimming for fun, fitness and competition. Readers are fitness-oriented adults from varied social and professional backgrounds who share swimming as part of their lifestyle. Readers are well-educated, affluent and range in age from 20-100 with most in the 30-49 age group; about 50% female, 50% male." Estab. 1984. Circ. 46,000. Pays 1 month after publication. Publishes ms an average of 3 months after acceptance. Byline given. Buys all rights. Editorial lead time 3 months. Submit seasonal material 3 months in advance. Accepts simultaneous submissions. Reports in 1 month on queries; 4 months on mss. Sample copy for $5 (prepaid) and 9×12 SAE with 4 first-class stamps. Writer's guidelines for #10 SASE.

**Nonfiction:** Book excerpts, essays, exposé, general health, general interest, historical, how-to (training plans and techniques), humor, inspirational, interview/profile (people associated with fitness and competitive swimming), new product (articles describing new products for fitness and competitive training), personal experience, photo feature, technical, travel. "Articles need to be informative as well as interesting. In addition to fitness and health articles, we are interested in exploring fascinating topics dealing with swimming for the adult reader." **Buys 12-18 mss/year.** Query with or without published clips. Length: 250-2,500 words. **Pays 12¢/word minimum.**

**Photos:** Send photos with ms. Negotiates payment individually. Captions, model releases, identification of subjects required.

**Tips:** "*Always* query first. Writers should be familiar with or an expert in adult fitness and/or adult swimming. Our how-to and profile articles best typify *Swim Magazine*'s style for fitness and competitive swimmers. *Swim Magazine* accepts medical guidelines and exercise physiology articles primarily by M.D.s and Ph.Ds."

**[N] $ $ SWIMMING TECHNIQUE**, Sports Publications, Inc., 90 Bell Rock Plaza, Suite 200, Sedona AZ 86351. (520)284-4005. Fax: (520)284-2477. E-mail: swimworld@aol.com. Website: http://www.swiminfo.com. Managing Editor: Mr. Bob Engram. **Contact:** Dr. Phillip Whitten, editor. **75% freelance written.** Quarterly magazine for professional swim coaches covering swimming techniques. "Covers all aspects of swimming technique and training." Estab. 1963. Circ. 8,000. Pays on publication. Publishes ms an average of 3-4 months after acceptance. Byline given. Buys first and all rights. Editorial lead time 3-4 months. Submit seasonal material 4 months in advance. Reports in 1 month. Sample copy for $5. Writer's guidelines free.

**Nonfiction:** Book excerpts, essays, how-to (swim & technique), interview/profile, opinion, personal experience, technical. **Buys 16-20 mss/year.** Query with published clips. Length: 500-4,000 words. **Pays 12-15¢/word.** Sometimes pays expenses of writers on assignment.

**Reprints:** Accepts previously published submissions.

**Photos:** Send photos with submission. Negotiates payment individually. Captions and identification of subjects required.

Buys all rights.

**Tips:** "Query first—phone call, e-mail, fax."

**$ $ SWIMMING WORLD**, Sports Publications, Inc., 90 Bell Rock Plaza, Suite 200, Sedona AZ 86351. (520)284-4005. Fax: (520)284-2477. E-mail: swimworld@aol.com. **Contact**: Dr. Phillip Whitten, editor-in-chief. Managing Editor: Bob Ingram. **25-50% freelance written.** Monthly magazine. *"Swimming World* is recognized as the authoritative source in the sport of swimming. It publishes articles about all aspects of competitive swimming." Estab. 1959. Circ. 30,000. Pays on publication. Byline given. Kill fee negotiated. Buys all rights. Editorial lead time 2 months. Submit seasonal material 3 months in advance. Accepts simultaneous submissions. Reports in 1 month. Sample copy for $5 and SAE with 4 first-class stamps. Writer's guidelines free.

**Nonfiction:** Book excerpts, essays, exposé, general interest, historical/nostalgic, how-to, humor, inspirational, interview/profile, new product, opinion, personal experience, photo feature, technical, travel. **Buys 30 mss/year.** Query. Length: 300-3,000 words. **Pays $75-400.** Sometimes pays expenses of writers on assignment.

**Photos:** State availability of photos with submission. Reviews prints. Negotiates payment individually. Captions, model releases and identification of subjects required. Buys negotiable rights.

**Columns/Departments: Buys 18 mss/year.** Query with published clips. **Pays $75-200.**

**[N] $ $ WAKE BOARDING MAGAZINE**, World Publications, Inc., 330 W. Canton Ave., Winter Park FL 32789. Fax: (407)628-7061. E-mail: wakeboard@worldzine.com. Editor: Tom James. **Contact:** Tony Smith, managing editor. **10% freelance written.** Consumer publication published 9 times/year covering wakeboarding. *"Wake Boarding Magazine* is the leading publication for wakeboarding in the world. Articles must focus on good riding, first and foremost, the good fun and good times. Covers competition, travel, instruction, personalities and humor." Estab. 1994. Circ. 65,000. Pays on publication. Publishes ms an average of 3 months after acceptance. Byline given. Buys all rights. Editorial lead time 4 months. Submit seasonal material 4 months in advance. Accepts queries by mail, e-mail, phone. Accepts simultaneous submissions. Reports in 1 week on queries; 1 month on mss. Sample copy and guidelines free.

**Nonfiction:** General interest, how-to (wake boarding instruction), humor, interview/profile, new product, photo feature, travel. "No Weekend Wallys having fun on the lake. Serious riders only. Nothing to do with water skiing or barefooting." **Buys 6-8 mss/year.** Send complete ms. Length: 1,000-2,500 words. **Pays $200-500.**

**Photos:** Send photos with submission. Reviews slide transparencies. Negotiates payment individually. Captions and identification of subjects required. Buys all rights.

**Columns/Departments:** Random Notes (events, travel stories), 600-750 words. **Buys 6-8 mss/year.** Send complete ms. **Pays $50-200.**

**Tips:** "Contact us first before presuming article is worthy. What may be cool to you might not fit our readership. Remember, *WBM*'s readership is made up of a lot of teenagers, so buck authority every chance you get."

**$ THE WATER SKIER**, American Water Ski Association, 799 Overlook Dr., Winter Haven FL 33884. (941)324-4341. Fax: (914)325-8259. E-mail: satkinson@usawaterski.org. Website: http://www.usawaterski.org. Publisher and Editor: Greg Nixon. **Contact:** Scott Atkinson, managing editor. **10-20% freelance written.** Magazine published 9 times/year. *"The Water Skier* is USA Water Ski, the national governing body for organized water skiing in the United States. The magazine has a controlled circulation and is available only to USA Water Skis membership, which is made up of 20,000 active competitive water skiers and 10,000 members who are supporting the sport. These supporting members may participate in the sport but they don't compete. The editorial content of the magazine features distinctive and informative writing about the sport of water skiing only." Estab. 1951. Circ. 30,000. Byline given. Offers 30% kill fee. Buys all rights (no exceptions). Editorial lead time 4 months. Submit seasonal material 6 months in advance. Reports in 2 weeks. Sample copy for $1.25. Writer's guidelines for #10 SASE.

○╾ Most open to material for feature articles (query editor with your idea).

**Nonfiction:** Historical/nostalgic (has to pertain to water skiing), interview/profile (call for assignment), new product (boating and water ski equipment), travel (water ski vacation destinations). **Buys 10-15 mss/year.** Query. Length: 1,500-3,000 words. **Pays $100-150 for assigned feature articles.**

**Reprints:** Send photocopy of article. Pay negotiable.

**Photos:** State availability of photos with submission. Reviews contact sheets. Negotiates payment individually. Captions and identification of subjects required. Buys all rights.

**Columns/Departments:** The Water Skier News (small news items about people and events in the sport), 400-500 words. Other topics include safety, training (3-event, barefoot, disabled, show ski, ski race, kneeboard and wakeboard); champions on their way; new products. Query. **Pays $50-100.** Pay for columns negotiated individually with each writer.

▣ The online magazine carries original content not found in the print edition. Contact: Scott Atkinson, online editor.

**Tips:** "Contact the managing editor through a query letter (please no phone calls) with an idea. Avoid instruction, these articles are written by professionals. Concentrate on articles about the people of the sport. We are always looking for the interesting stories about people in the sport. Also, short news features which will make a reader say to himself, 'Hey, I didn't know that.' Keep in mind that the publication is highly specialized about the sport of water skiing."

## Wrestling

**⬛ $WRESTLING WORLD**, Sterling/MacFadden, 233 Park Ave. S., New York NY 10003. (212)780-3500. Fax: (212)780-3555. E-mail: sterlingsports@yahoo.com. **Contact:** Stephen Ciacciarelli, editor. **100% freelance written.** Monthly magazine for professional wrestling fans. "We run profiles of top wrestlers and managers and articles on current topics of interest on the mat scene." Circ. 100,000. **Pays on acceptance.** Byline given. Buys first North American serial rights. Reports in 2 weeks. Sample copy for $4 and SAE with 3 first-class stamps.
   • *Wrestling World* has increased its frequency from a bimonthly to a monthly.
**Nonfiction:** Interview/profile and photo feature. "No general think pieces." **Buys 100 mss/year.** Query with or without published clips or send complete ms. Length: 1,500-2,500 words. **Pays $75-125.**
**Photos:** State availability of photos with submission. Reviews 35mm transparencies and prints. Offers $25-50/photo package. Pays $50-150 for transparencies. Identification of subjects required. Buys one-time rights.
**Tips:** "Anything topical has the best chance of acceptance. Articles on those hard-to-reach wrestlers stand an excellent chance of acceptance."

## TEEN & YOUNG ADULT

Publications in this category are for teens (13-19). Publications for college students are in Career, College & Alumni. Those for younger children are in Juvenile.

**$ $CAMPUS LIFE**, Christianity Today, Inc., 465 Gundersen Dr., Carol Stream IL 60188. (630)260-6200. Fax: (630)260-0114. E-mail: cledit@aol.com. Website: http://www.campuslife.net. **Contact:** Christopher Lutes, editor. **35% freelance written.** Magazine published 9 times/year for the Christian life as it relates to today's teen. "*Campus Life* is a magazine for high-school and early college-age teenagers. Our editorial slant is not overtly religious. The indirect style is intended to create a safety zone with our readers and to reflect our philosophy that God is interested in all of life. Therefore, we publish 'message stories' side by side with general interest, humor, etc." Estab. 1942. Circ. 100,000. **Pays on acceptance.** Publishes ms an average of 5 months after acceptance. Byline given. Offers 50% kill fee. Buys first and one-time rights. Editorial lead time 4 months. Accepts queries by mail, e-mail, fax. Accepts simultaneous submissions. Reports in 5 weeks on queries; 2 months on mss. Sample copy for $3 and 8×10 SAE with 3 first-class stamps. Guidelines for #10 SASE.
**Nonfiction:** Humor, personal experience, photo feature. **Buys 15-20 mss/year.** Query with published clips. Length: 750-1,500 words. **Pays 15-20¢/word minimum.**
**Reprints:** Send tearsheet or photocopy of article or short story or typed ms with rights for sale noted and information about when and where the article or story previously appeared. Pays $50.
**Photos:** State availability of photos with submission. Reviews contact sheets, transparencies, 5×7 prints. Negotiates payment individually. Model release required. Buys one-time rights.
**Fiction:** Buys 1-5 mss/year. Query. Length: 1,000-2,000 words. **Pays 15-20¢/word.**
**Tips:** "The best way to break in to *Campus Life* is through writing first-person or as-told-to first-person stories. We want stories that capture a teen's everyday 'life lesson' experience. A first-person story must be highly descriptive and incorporate fictional technique. While avoiding simplistic religious answers, the story should demonstrate that Christian values or beliefs brought about a change in the young person's life. But query first with theme information telling the way this story would work for our audience."

**N $THE CONQUEROR**, United Pentecostal Church International, 8855 Dunn Rd., Hazelwood MO 63042-2299. (314)837-7300. Fax: (314)837-4503. E-mail: gyouth8855@aol.com. Website: http://www.upci.org/youth. **Contact:** Travis Miller, editor. **80% freelance written.** Literary magazine published bimonthly covering Christian youth. "*The Conqueror* addresses the social, intellectual and spiritual concerns of youth aged 12-21 years from a Christian viewpoint." Estab. 1957. Circ. 6,000. Pays on publication. Publishes ms an average of 4 months after acceptance. No byline. Buys one-time rights. Editorial lead time 4 months. Submit seasonal material 4 months in advance. Accepts queries by mail, e-mail, fax, phone. Accepts simultaneous submissions. Reports in 2 months. Sample copy for 9×12 SAE with 3 first-class stamps. Writer's guidelines free.
**Nonfiction:** Essays, general interest, historical/nostalgic, inspirational, personal experience, religious. **Buys 18 mss/year.** Send complete ms. Length: 250-1,250 words. **Pays $15-30.**
**Reprints:** Accepts previously published submissions.
**Photos:** State availability of photos with submission. Offers no additional payment for photos accepted with ms.
**Columns/Departments:** Time Out for Truth (applying Biblical truth to everyday living), 750 words. **Buys 6-10 mss/year.** Send complete ms. **Pays $30 maximum.**
**Fiction:** Adventure, ethnic, historical, humorous, mainstream, religious, slice-of-life vignettes. **Buys 4-6 mss/year.** Send complete ms. Length: 250-1,250 words. **Pays $15-30.**
**Poetry:** Traditional. **Buys 2-4 poems/year.** Submit maximum 5 poems. **Pays $15.**
**Fillers:** Anecdotes, gags to be illustrated by cartoonist, short humor. **Buys 4/year.** Length: 100 words. **Pays $15.**
**Tips:** "Choose subjects relevant to single youth. Most subjects *are* relevant if properly handled. Today's youth are interested in more than clothes, fashion, careers and dating. Remember our primary objective: inspiration—to portray happy, victorious living through faith in God."

**$ FLORIDA LEADER (for high school students)**, Oxendine Publishing, Inc., P.O. Box 14081, Gainesville FL 32604-2081. (352)373-6907. Fax: (352)373-8120. E-mail: oxendine@compuserve.com. Editor: W.H. "Butch" Oxendine Jr. Managing Editor: Kay Quinn. **Contact:** Teresa Beard, assistant editor. Tri-annual magazine covering high school and pre-college youth. Estab. 1983. Circ. 50,000. Pays on publication. Publishes ms an average of 3 months after acceptance. Buys all rights. Submit seasonal material 4 months in advance. Accepts simultaneous submissions. Accepts queries by mail, e-mail, fax. Reports in 2 months on queries. Sample copy for $3.50 and 8×11 SAE, with 3 first-class stamps. For query response and/or writer's guidelines send #10 SASE.
**Nonfiction:** Practical tips for going to college, student life and leadership development. How-to, new product. "No lengthy individual profiles or articles without primary and secondary sources of attribution." Length: 250-1,000 words. Payment varies. Pays students or first-time writers with contributor's copies.
**Photos:** Send photos with submission. Reviews contact sheets, negatives, transparencies. Offers $50/photo maximum. Captions, model releases, identification of subjects required. Buys all rights.
**Columns/Departments:** College Life, The Lead Role, In Every Issue (quizzes, tips), Florida Forum (features Florida high school students), 250-1,000 words. **Buys 2 mss/year.** Query. **Pays $35-75.**
**Fillers:** Facts, newsbreaks, tips, book reviews. Length: 100-300 words. No payment.
**Tips:** "Read other high school and college publications for current issues, interests. Send manuscripts or outlines for review. All sections open to freelance work. Always looking for lighter, humorous articles as well as features on Florida colleges and universities, careers, jobs. Multi-sourced (5-10) articles are best."

**N $ $ GUIDEPOSTS FOR TEENS**, Guideposts, P.O. Box 638, Chesterton IN 46304. (219)929-4429. Fax: (219)926-3839. E-mail: gp4t@guideposts.org. Editor: Mary Lou Carney. **Contact:** Tanya Dean, managing editor. **90% freelance written.** Bimonthly teen inspirational magazine. "*Guideposts for Teens* is published for teenagers ages 12-18. It is a 48-page, 4-color, value-centered magazine that offers teens advice, humor, and true stories—lots of true stories." Estab. 1998. Circ. 200,000. **Pays on acceptance.** Byline sometimes given. Offers 25% kill fee. Buys first North American serial rights or all rights. Editorial lead time 4 months. Submit seasonal material 6 months in advance. Accepts simultaneous submissions. Reports in 1 month on queries, 2 months on mss. Sample copy for $4.50. Guidelines for #10 SASE.
**Nonfiction:** How-to, humor, inspirational, interview/profile, personal experience, religious. Nothing written from an adult point of view. **Buys 80 mss/year** Query. Length: 700-1,500 words. **Pays $175-500 for assigned articles; $150-400 for unsolicited articles.** Pays expenses of writers on assignment.
**Photos:** State availability of photos with submission. Negotiates payment individually. Identification of subjects required. Buys one-time rights.
**Columns/Departments:** Quiz (teen-relevant topics, teen language), 1,000 words; How-to (strong teen voice/quotes, teen topics), 750-1,000 words; Who's in Charge? (teens who initiate change/develop service projects), 300-500 words; Humor (essays teens can relate to), 750 words; embarassing celebrity moments (celebrity/athlete), 300-500 words. **Buys 40 mss/year.** Query with published clips. **Pays $175-400.**
**Fillers:** Anecdotes, short humor (cartoons, jokes, short humor, quotes). **Buys 20/year.** Length: 100-300 words. **Pays $25-100.**
**Tips:** "We are new and eagerly looking for a number of things: teen how-to pieces, celebrity and embarassing moments for quizzes, humor. Most of all, though, we are about TRUE STORIES in the *Guideposts* tradition. Teens in dangerous, inspiring, miraculous situations. These first-person (ghostwritten) true narratives are the backbone of *GP4T*—and what sets us apart from other publications."

**$ INSIGHT, A Spiritual Lift for Teens**, The Review and Herald Publishing Association, 55 W. Oak Ridge Dr., Hagerstown MD 21740. E-mail: insight@rhpa.org. Website: http://www.insightmagazine.org. **Contact:** Lori Peckham, editor. **80% freelance written.** Weekly magazine covering spiritual life of teenagers. "*Insight* publishes true dramatic stories, interviews, and community and mission service features that relate directly to the lives of Christian teenagers, particularly those with a Seventh-day Adventist background." Estab. 1970. Circ. 20,000. Pays on publication. Publishes ms an average of 4 months after acceptance. Byline given. Offers 50% kill fee. Buys first rights and second serial (reprint) rights. Editorial lead time 3 months. Submit seasonal material 6 months in advance. Accepts queries by mail, e-mail, fax. Reports in 1 month. Sample copy for $2 and #10 SASE. Guidelines for #10 SASE or on website.
**Nonfiction:** How-to (teen relationships and experiences), humor, interview/profile, personal teen experience, photo feature, religious. **Buys 120 mss/year.** Send complete ms. Length: 500-2,000 words. **Pays $25-150 for assigned articles; $25-125 for unsolicited articles.**
**Reprints:** Send typed ms with rights for sale noted and information about when and where the article previously appeared. Pays $50.
**Photos:** State availability of photos with submission. Reviews contact sheets, negatives, transparencies, prints. Negotiates payment individually. Model releases required. Buys one-time rights.
**Columns/Departments:** Big Deal (topic of importance to teens) 1,200-1,700 words; Interviews (Christian culture figures, esp. musicians), 2,000 words; It Happened to Me (1st person teen experiences containing spiritual insights), 1,000 words; On the Edge (dramatic true stories about Christians), 2,000 words; So I Said . . . (true short stories in the 1st person of common, everyday events and experiences that taught the writer something), 300-500 words. Accepting reviews of contemporary Christian music and Christian books for teens. **Buys 80 mss/year.** Send complete ms. **Pays $25-125.**
    • "*Big Deal*" appears in *Insight* every other week, each covering a topic of importance to teens. Each feature

contains: an opening story involving real teens (can be written in first-person), "Scripture Picture" (a sidebar that discusses what the Bible says about the topic) and another sidebar (optional) that adds more perspective and help.
**Tips:** "Skim two months of *Insight*. Write about your teen experiences. Use informed, contemporary style and vocabulary. Become a Christian if you haven't already."

**$ $ $JUMP, For Girls Who Dare to be Real**, Weider, 21100 Erwin St., Woodland Hills CA 91367. Fax: (818)594-0972. E-mail: letters@jumponline.com. Website: http://www.jumponline.com. Editor: Lori Berger. Managing Editor: Maureen Meyers. **Contact:** Jennifer Lin, assistant to the editor-in-chief. **50% freelance written.** Monthly magazine for a female teen market. Estab. 1997. Circ. 300,000. Pays on publication. Publishes ms 4 months after acceptance. Byline given. Offers 33% kill fee. Buys all rights. Editorial lead time 4 months. Submit seasonal material 5 months in advance. Accepts simultaneous submissions. Reports in 1 month.
**Nonfiction:** General interest, how-to, interview/profile, new product, personal experience. Query with published clips. Length: 1,500-2,000 words. **Pays 50¢-$1/word.**
**Columns/Departments:** Busted! (quirky, bizarre and outrageous trends, news, quotes), 6 items, 50 words each; The Dish (food and nutrition for teens), 1,500 words; Jump On . . . In, Music, Sports, Body & Soul (small news and trend items on sports, health, music, etc.), 6 items per page, 75 words each. Query with published clips. **Pays 50¢-$1/word.**
**Tips:** "Writers must read magazine before submitting queries. Will turn away queries that clearly show the writer is not familiar with the content of the magazine."

**$ $KEYNOTER**, Key Club International, 3636 Woodview Trace, Indianapolis IN 46268-3196. **Contact:** Julie A. Carson, executive editor. **65% freelance written.** Works with a small number of new writers each year, but is eager to work with new/unpublished writers willing to adjust their writing styles. Monthly youth magazine (December/January combined issue), distributed to members of Key Club International, a high school service organization for young men and women. Estab. 1946. Circ. 171,000. **Pays on acceptance.** Publishes ms an average of 5 months after acceptance. Byline given. Buys first North American serial rights. Submit seasonal material 7 months in advance. Accepts simultaneous submissions. Reports in 2 months. Sample copy for 65¢ and 8½×11 SAE. Guidelines for SASE.
**Nonfiction:** Book excerpts (included in articles), general interest (for intelligent teen audience), academic, self-help, historical/nostalgic (generally not accepted), how-to (advice on how teens can enhance the quality of lives or communities), humor (accepted if adds to story), interview/profile (rarely purchased, "would have to be on/with an irresistible subject"), new product (affecting teens), photo feature (if subject is right), technical (understandable and interesting to teen audience), travel (must apply to club travel schedule), subjects that entertain and inform teens on topics that relate directly to their lives. "We would also like to receive self-help and school-related nonfiction on leadership, community service, and teen issues. *Please, no first-person confessions, fiction or articles that are written down to our teen readers. No filler, or book, movie or music reviews.*" Buys 10-15 mss/year. Query with SASE. Length: 1,200-1,500 words. **Pays $150-350.** Sometimes pays the expenses of writers on assignment.
**Reprints:** Send tearsheet or photocopy of article and information about when and where the article previously appeared.
**Photos:** State availability of photos. Reviews color contact sheets and negatives. Identification of subjects required. Buys one-time rights. Payment for photos included in payment for ms.
**Tips:** "We want to see articles written with attention to style and detail that will enrich the world of teens. Articles must be thoroughly researched and must draw on interviews with nationally and internationally respected sources. Our readers are 13-18, mature and dedicated to community service. We are very committed to working with good writers, and if we see something we like in a well-written query, we'll try to work it through to publication."

**$LISTEN MAGAZINE**, Review & Herald Publishing Association, 55 W. Oak Ridge Dr., Hagerstown MD 21740. (301)745-3888. Fax: (301)393-4055. E-mail: lsteed@rhpa.org. **Contact:** Lincoln Steed, editor. Assistant Editor: Anita Jacobs. **75% freelance written.** Works with a small number of new/unpublished writers each year. Monthly magazine specializing in drug and alcohol prevention, presenting positive alternatives to various drug and alcohol dependencies. "*Listen* is used in many high school classes and by professionals: medical personnel, counselors, law enforcement officers, educators, youth workers, etc." Circ. 40,000. Buys first rights for use in *Listen*, reprints and associated material. Byline given. **Pays on acceptance.** Publishes ms 6 months after acceptance. Accepts simultaneous submissions if notified. Accepts queries by mail, e-mail, fax, phone. Reports in 2 months. Sample copy for $1 and 9×12 SASE. Guidelines for SASE.
**Nonfiction:** Seeks articles that deal with causes of drug use such as poor self-concept, family relations, social skills or peer pressure. Especially interested in youth-slanted articles or personality interviews encouraging non-alcoholic and non-drug ways of life and showing positive alternatives. Teenage point of view is essential. Popularized medical, legal and educational articles. Also seeks narratives which portray teens dealing with youth conflicts, especially those related to the use of or temptation to use harmful substances. Growth of the main character should be shown. "We don't want typical alcoholic story/skid-row bum, AA stories. We are also being inundated with drunk-driving accident stories. Unless yours is unique, consider another topic." **Buys 30-50 unsolicited mss/year.** Query. Length: 1,000-1,200 words. **Pays 5-10¢/word.** Sometimes pays the expenses of writers on assignment.
**Reprints:** Send photocopy of article or typed ms with rights for sale noted and information about when and where it previously appeared. Pays their regular rates.
**Photos:** Purchased with accompanying ms. Captions required. Color photos preferred, but b&w acceptable.
**Fillers:** Word square/general puzzles are also considered. Pays $15.
**Tips:** "True stories are good, especially if they have a unique angle. Other authoritative articles need a fresh approach.

In query, briefly summarize article idea and logic of why you feel it's good. Make sure you've read the magazine to understand our approach."

**$ $ THE NEW ERA**, 50 E. North Temple, Salt Lake City UT 84150. (801)240-2951. Fax: (801)240-5997. **Contact:** Larry A. Hiller, managing editor. **20% freelance written.** "We work with both established writers and newcomers." Monthly magazine for young people (ages 12-18) of the Church of Jesus Christ of Latter-day Saints (Mormon), their church leaders and teachers. Estab. 1971. Circ. 230,000. **Pays on acceptance.** Publishes ms an average of 1 year after acceptance. Byline given. Buys all rights. Rights reassigned upon written request. Submit seasonal material 1 year in advance. Reports in 2 months. Sample copy for $1.50 and 9×12 SAE with 2 first-class stamps. Guidelines for SASE.
**Nonfiction:** Material that shows how the Church of Jesus Christ of Latter-day Saints is relevant in the lives of young people today. Must capture the excitement of being a young Latter-day Saint. Special interest in the experiences of young Mormons in other countries. No general library research or formula pieces without the *New Era* slant and feel. Uses informational, how-to, personal experience, interview, profile, inspirational, humor. Query preferred. Length: 150-1,200 words. **Pays 3-12¢/word.** Pays expenses of writers on assignment.
**Photos:** Uses b&w photos and transparencies with mss. Payment depends on use, $10-125 per photo. Individual photos used for *Photo of the Month.*
**Columns/Departments:** Bulletin Board (news of young Mormons around the world); How I Know; Scripture Lifeline. **Pays 3-12¢/word.**
**Fiction:** Adventure, relationships, humorous. Must relate to young Mormon audience. **Pays minimum 3¢/word.**
**Poetry:** Traditional forms, blank verse, free verse, light verse, all other forms. Must relate to editorial viewpoint. **Pays 25¢/line minimum.**
**Tips:** "The writer must be able to write from a Mormon point of view. We're especially looking for stories about successful family relationships and personal growth. We anticipate using more staff-produced material. This means freelance quality will have to improve. Try breaking in with a department piece for 'How I Know' or 'Scripture Lifeline.' Well-written, personal expereinces are always in demand."

**$ $ $ REACT, The Magazine That Raises Voices**, Parade Publications, 711 Third Ave., New York NY 10017. (212)450-0900. Fax: (212)450-0978. E-mail: sbyrne@react.com. Website: http://www.react.com. Editor: Lee Kravitz. **Contact:** Susan Byrne, managing editor. **98% freelance written.** "*react* is a weekly news, sports and entertainment magazine for teens." Estab. 1995. Circ. 3,300,000 million. **Pays on acceptance.** Publishes ms an average of 2 months after acceptance. Editorial lead time 2 months. Submit seasonal material 4 months in advance. Accepts queries by mail, fax. Sample copy for 10½×12 SAE and 80¢ postage. Writer's guidelines for #10 SASE.
**Nonfiction:** No articles written for adults from adult points of view. Query with published clips. **Pays $50-1,500.** Pays expenses of writers on assignment.
**Photos:** All photos by assignment only; others purchased from stock houses. Model releases and identification of subjects required. Buys all rights.
**Columns/Departments:** Query with published clips.
The online magazine carries original content not found in the print edition. Contact: Charles Rogers, online editor.
**Tips:** "Before you write, keep in mind: Young Americans in the first throes of teenhood want you to write with clarity and come to them free of any preconceived ideas of who and what they are. When writing for them: Walk their walk. See events through their eyes. Let their world be your world. Let their questions be your questions. Don't talk down. Do not preach. Be as professional and rigorous in reporting as you would be writing for adults. Be honest. They have a built-in phony detector. Report long but write short. Write with style. To put readers at ease, be personal in your writing tone."

**$ $ $ SEVENTEEN**, 850 Third Ave., New York NY 10022. (212)407-9700. Fax: (212)407-9899. Website: http://www.seventeen.com. Editor-in-Chief: Patrice G. Aderoft. **Contact:** Robert Rorke, features editor; Carole Braden, voice; Andrea Chambers, sex and body issues. **50% freelance written.** Works with a small number of new/unpublished writers each year. Monthly. "*Seventeen* is a young women's first fashion and beauty magazine. Tailored for young women in their teens and early twenties, *Seventeen* covers fashion, beauty, health, fitness, food, cars, college, entertainment, fiction, plus crucial personal and global issues." Circ. 2,400,000. Buys one-time rights for nonfiction and fiction by adult writers and. Pays 25% kill fee. **Pays on acceptance.** Publishes ms an average of 6 months after acceptance. Byline given. Reports in up to 3 months. Accepts queries by mail, phone.
○━ Break in with The Who Knew section, which contains shorter items, or *Quiz.*
**Nonfiction:** Articles and features of general interest to young women who are concerned with intimate relationships and how to realize their potential in the world; strong emphasis on topicality and service. Send brief outline and query, including a typical lead paragraph, summing up basic idea of article with clips of previously published works. Length: 1,200-3,000 words. Articles are commissioned after outlines are submitted and approved. Pays the expenses of writers on assignment. **Pays $1/word, occasionally more.**
● Ranked as one of the best markets for freelance writers in *Writer's Yearbook* magazine's annual "Top 100," January 1999.
**Photos:** Georgia Paralemos, art director. Photos usually by assignment only.
**Fiction:** Ben Schrank, fiction editor. Thoughtful, well-written stories on subjects of interest to young women between the ages of 13 and 21. Avoid formula stories—"She's blonde and pretty; I'm not,"—no heavy moralizing or condescen-

sion of any sort. Length: 1,000-3,000 words. Pays $500-1,500. Last year, *Seventeen* published fiction by Joyce Carol Oates and Edna O'Brien. We also have an annual fiction contest.

● Ranked as one of the best markets for fiction writers in *Writer's Digest* magazine's "Fiction 50," June 1999.

▣ The online magazine carries original content not found in the print edition. Contact: Sharon Boone, online editor.

**Tips:** "Writers have to ask themselves whether or not they feel they can find the right tone for a *Seventeen* article—a tone which is empathetic yet never patronizing; lively yet not superficial. Not all writers feel comfortable with, understand or like teenagers. If you don't like them, *Seventeen* is the wrong market for you. An excellent way to break in to the magazine is by contributing ideas for quizzes or the Voice (personal essay) column."

**$ $ SPIRIT, Lectionary-based Weekly for Catholic Teens**, Good Ground Press, 1884 Randolph Ave., St. Paul MN 55105-1700. (612)690-7005. Fax: (612)690-7039. E-mail: jmcsj9@mail.idt.net. **Contact:** Joan Mitchell, CSJ, editor. Managing Editor: Therese Sherlock, CSJ. **50% freelance written.** Weekly newsletter for religious education of Catholic high schoolers. "We want realistic fiction and nonfiction that raises current ethical and religious questions and that deals with conflicts that teens face in multi-racial contexts. The fact we are a religious publication does *not* mean we want pious, moralistic fiction." Estab. 1981. Circ. 26,000. Pays on publication. Publishes ms an average of 3 months after acceptance. Byline given. Buys all rights. Editorial lead time 6 months. Submit seasonal material 6 months in advance. Accepts simultaneous submissions. Accepts queries by mail, e-mail, fax. Reports in 1 month on queries; 6 months on mss. Sample copy and writer's guidelines free.

**Nonfiction:** Interview/profile, personal experience, photo feature (homelessness, illiteracy), religious, Roman Catholic leaders, human interest features, social justice leaders, projects, humanitarians. "No Christian confessional, born-again pieces." Buys 4 mss/year. Query with published clips or send complete ms. Length: 1,000-1,200 words. **Pays $150-250 for assigned articles; $150 for unsolicited articles.**

**Photos:** State availability of photos with submission. Reviews 8×10 prints. Offers $40-80/photo. Identification of subjects required. Buys one-time rights.

**Fiction:** Conflict vignettes. "We want realistic pieces for and about teens—non-pedantic, non-pious. We need good Christmas stories that show spirit of the season, and stories about teen relationship conflicts (boy/girl, parent/teen)." **Buys 10 mss/year.** Query with published clips, or send complete ms. Length: 1,000-1,200 words. **Pays $150-200.**

**Tips:** "Writers must be able to write from and for teen point of view rather than adult or moralistic point of view. In nonfiction, interviewed teens must speak for themselves. Query to receive call for stories, spec sheet, sample issues."

**$ STRAIGHT**, Standard Publishing Co., 8121 Hamilton Ave., Cincinnati OH 45231-2323. (513)931-4050. Fax: (513)931-0950. **Contact:** Heather E. Wallace, editor. **90% freelance written.** Estab. 1950. Weekly magazine (published quarterly) for "teens, age 13-19, from Christian backgrounds who generally receive this publication in their Sunday School classes or through subscriptions." **Pays on acceptance.** Publishes ms an average of 1 year after acceptance. Buys first rights and second serial (reprint) rights. Byline given. Submit seasonal material 9-12 months in advance. Reports in 2 months. Sample copy and writer's guidelines for #10 SAE with 2 first-class stamps. "We use freelance material in every issue. Our theme list is available on a quarterly basis. Writers need only give us their name and address in order to be added to our mailing list."

**Nonfiction:** Religious-oriented topics, teen interest (school, church, family, dating, sports, part-time jobs), humor, inspirational, personal experience. "We want articles that promote Christian values and ideals." No puzzles. Query or submit complete ms. Include Social Security number on ms. "We're buying more short pieces these days; 12 pages fill up much too quickly." Length: 800-1,100 words. **Pays 5-6¢/word.**

**Reprints:** Send tearsheet of article or story or typed ms with rights for sale noted. Pays 5¢/word.

**Fiction:** Adventure, humorous, religious, suspense. "All fiction should have some message for the modern Christian teen. Fiction should deal with all subjects in a forthright manner, without being preachy and without talking down to teens. No tasteless manuscripts that promote anything adverse to the Bible's teachings." Submit complete ms. Length: 900-1,500 words. **Pays 5-6¢/word.**

● Ranked as one of the best markets for fiction writers in *Writer's Digest* magazine's "Fiction 50," June 1999.

**Photos:** Submit photos with ms. Pays $75-125 for color slides. Model releases required. Buys one-time rights.

**Tips:** "Don't be trite. Use unusual settings or problems. Use a lot of illustrations, a good balance of conversation, narration, and action. Style must be clear, fresh—no sermonettes or sickly-sweet fiction. Take a realistic approach to problems. Be willing to submit to editorial policies on doctrine; knowledge of the *Bible* a must. Also, be aware of teens today, and what they do. Language, clothing, and activities included in manuscripts should be contemporary. We are also looking for articles for a monthly feature entitled 'Straight Spotlight,' which is about real teens who are making a difference in their school, community or church. Articles for this feature should be approx. 900 words in length. We would also like a picture of the teen or group of teens to run with the article."

**$ TEEN LIFE**, Gospel Publishing House, 1445 Boonville Ave., Springfield MO 65802-1894. (417)862-2781, ext. 4370. Fax: (417)862-6059. E-mail: teenlife@ag.org. **Contact:** Tammy Bicket, editor. Quarterly magazine of Assemblies of God denomination of Christian fiction and articles for church-oriented teenagers, ages 12-19. Circ. 40,000. **Pays on acceptance.** Publishes ms an average of 15 months after acceptance. Byline given. Buys first North American serial, one-time, simultaneous and second serial (reprint) rights. Submit seasonal material 18 months in advance. Accepts simultaneous and previously published submissions. Send tearsheet or photocopy of article or typed ms with rights for sale noted and information about when and where the article previously appeared. Response time varies. Sample copy for 9 × 12 SAE with 2 first-class stamps.

**Nonfiction:** Interviews with Christian athletes, musicians, missionaries, authors, or others with notable and helpful Christian testimonies or helpful experiences; transcriptions of discussion sessions where a group of teens talk about a particular issue; information on a topic or issue of interest gathered from experts in those fields (i.e., a doctor talks about teens' sexuality, a psychologist talks about dysfunctional families, a police officer talks about the dangers of gangs, etc.). Book excerpts, church history, general interest, how-to (deal with various life problems), humor, inspirational, personal experience, world issues, apologetics, prayer, devotional life, the occult, angels, church. **Buys 25-50 mss/year.** Send complete ms. Length: 500-1,200 words. **Pays 5-8¢/word.**

**Reprints:** Send tearsheet or photocopy of article and information about when and where the article previously appeared. Pays 50% of amount paid for an original article.

**Photos:** Photos purchased with accompanying ms. Pays $35 for 8 × 10 b&w glossy print; $50 for 35mm slide.

**Fiction:** Adventure, humorous, mystery, romance, suspense. **Buys 25-50 mss/year.** Send complete ms. Length: 500-1,200 words. **Pays 3-5¢/word.**

**Tips:** "We need more male-oriented stories or articles and more about life in the city and about people of diverse races. Avoid stereotypes. Avoid clichéd or trite situations with pat Christian answers and easy solutions. Avoid stories or articles without a Christian slant or emphasis, or those with a moral just tacked on at the end."

**N $TODAY'S CHRISTIAN TEEN**, Marketing Partners, Inc., 162 E. Main St., Elverson PA 19520. (610)286-8800. Fax: (610)286-8881. E-mail: tcpubs@mkpt.com. Editor: Jerry Thacker. **Contact:** Elaine Williams, assistant editor. **25% freelance written.** Quarterly magazine covering teen issues from a Biblical perspective. "*Today's Christian Teen* is designed to deal with issues in the life of Christian teenagers from a conservative perspective." Estab. 1990. Circ. 30,000. Pays on publication. Publishes ms an average of 1 year after acceptance. Byline sometimes given. Buys simultaneous rights. Editorial lead time 1 year. Submit seasonal material 1 year in advance. Accepts simultaneous submissions. Query by mail, e-mail, fax. Reports in 1 month on queries; 3 months on mss. Sample copy for 9 × 12 SAE with 4 first-class stamps. Writer's guidelines for #10 SASE.

**Nonfiction:** Inspirational, personal experience, religious. **Buys 6-8 mss/year.** Send complete ms. Length: 800-1,200 words. **Pays $150.**

**Reprints:** Accepts previously published submissions.

**Photos:** Offers no additional payment for photos accepted with ms.

**$ $ $ $TWIST**, Bauer Publishing, 270 Sylvan Ave., Englewood Cliffs NJ 07632. Fax: (201)569-4458. E-mail: twistmail@aol.com. **Contact:** Jeannie Kim or Jena Hofstedt, senior editors. Editor: Lisa Lombardi. Managing Editor: Christine Summer. **20% freelance written.** "Monthly magazine targeting 14-19 year old girls, with an emphasis on using the words, viewpoints and faces of real teenagers. Estab. 1997. Circ. 700,000. **Pays on acceptance.** Publishes ms an average of 3 months after acceptance. Byline given. Offers 20% kill fee. Buys first North American serial rights. Editorial lead time 3 months. Submit seasonal material 4 months in advance. Accepts simultaneous submissions. Reports in 1 month on queries. Writer's guidelines for #10 SASE.

**Nonfiction:** Personal experience (real teens' experiences, preferably in first person), relationships, health, sex, quizzes. "No articles written from an adult point of view about teens—i.e., a mother's or teacher's personal account." **Buys 60 mss/year.** Query with published clips. Length: 100-1,800 words. **Pays minimum $50 for short item; up to $1/word for longer pieces.** Pays expenses of writers on assignment.

**Photos:** State availability of photos with submission. "We generally prefer to provide/shoot our own art." Negotiates payment individually. Model releases and identification of subjects required.

**Columns/Departments:** Pop Life (reviews, short celebrity/media items); Body Buzz (health news/tips), all 75-200 words. **Buys 15 mss/year.** Query with published clips. **Pays minimum $50 for short item; up to $1/word for longer pieces.**

**Tips:** "*Tone* must be conversational, neither condescending to teens nor trying to be too slangy. If possible, send clips that show an ability to write for the teen market. We are in search of real life stories, and writers who can find teens with compelling real-life experiences (who are willing to use their full names and be photographed for the magazine). Please refer to a current issue to see examples of tone and content. No e-mail queries or submissions, please."

**$ $WHAT! A MAGAZINE**, What! Publishers Inc., 108-93 Lombard Ave., Winnipeg, Manitoba R3B 3B1 Canada. (204)985-8160. Fax: (204)943-8991. E-mail: l.malkin@mzci.mb.ca. **Contact:** Leslie Malkin, editor. **60% freelance written.** Magazine covering teen issues published 5 times during the school year. "*What! A Magazine* is distributed to high school students across Canada. We produce a mag that is empowering, interactive and entertaining. We respect the reader—today's teens are smart and creative (and critical)." Estab. 1987. Circ. 200,000. Pays 30 days after publication. Publishes ms an average of 3 months after acceptance. Byline given. Offers negotiable kill fee. Buys first North American serial rights. Editorial lead time 5 months. Submit seasonal material 5 months in advance. Accepts queries by mail, e-mail, fax. Reports in 2 months on queries; 1 month on mss. Sample copy for 9 × 12 SAE with Canadian postage. Writer's guidelines for #10 SAE with Canadian postage.

**Nonfiction:** General interest, humor, interview/profile, issue-oriented features. No cliché teen material. **Buys 6-10 mss/year.** Query with published clips. Length: 700-1,900 words. **Pays $100-500 (Canadian).** Sometimes pays expenses of writers on assignment.

**Photos:** Send photos with submission. Reviews transparencies, 4 × 6 prints. Negotiates payment individually. Identification of subjects required.

**Tips:** "Because *What! A Magazine* is distributed through schools (with the consent of school officials), it's important that each issue find the delicate balance between very cool and very responsible. We target very motivated young women and men. Pitches should stray from cliché and stories should challenge readers with depth, insight and color. All stories must be meaningful to a Canadian readership."

**N $WITH, The Magazine for Radical Christian Youth**, Faith and Life Press, 722 Main St., P.O. Box 347, Newton KS 67114-0347. (316)283-5100. Fax: (316)283-0454. E-mail: deliag@gcmc.org. Editor: Carol Duerksen. 60% freelance written. Magazine for teenagers published 8 times/year. "We are the magazine for Mennonite, Brethren, and Mennonite Brethren youth. Our purpose is to disciple youth within congregations." Circ. 6,100. **Pays on acceptance.** Byline given. Buys one-time rights. Submit seasonal material 6 months in advance. Accepts simultaneous submissions. Accepts queries by mail, fax. Reports in 1 month on queries; 2 months on mss. Sample copy for 9×12 SAE with 4 first-class stamps. Writer's guidelines and theme list for #10 SASE. Additional detailed guidelines for first person stories, how-to articles and/or fiction available for #10 SASE.

**Nonfiction:** Humor, personal experience, religious, how-to, youth. Buys 15 mss/year. Send complete ms. Length: 400-1,800 words. Pays 5¢/word for simultaneous rights; 3¢/word for reprint rights for unsolicited articles. Higher rates for first-person stories and how-to articles written on assignment. (Query on these.)

**Reprints:** Send typed ms with rights for sale noted, including information about when and where the material previously appeared. Pays 60% of amount paid for an original article.

**Photos:** Sometimes pays the expenses of writers on assignment. Send photos with submission. Reviews 8×10 b&w prints. Offers $10-50/photo. Identification of subjects required. Buys one-time rights.

**Fiction:** Humorous, religious, youth, parables. Buys 15 mss/year. Send complete ms. Length: 500-2,000 words. Payment same as nonfiction.

• Ranked as one of the best markets for fiction writers in *Writer's Digest* magazine's "Fiction 50," June 1999.

**Poetry:** Avant-garde, free verse, haiku, light verse, traditional. Buys 0-2 poems. Pays $10-25.

**Tips:** "We're looking for more wholesome humor, not necessarily religious—fiction, nonfiction, cartoons, light verse. Christmas and Easter material has a good chance with us because we receive so little of it."

**$ $YOUNG SALVATIONIST**, The Salvation Army, P.O. Box 269, Alexandria VA 22313-0269. (703)684-5500. Fax: (703)684-5539. E-mail: ys@usn.salvationarmy.org. Website: http://publications.salvationarmyusa.org. **Contact:** Tim Clark, magazine editor. **80% freelance written.** Works with a small number of new/unpublished writers each year. Monthly magazine for high school teens. "Only material with Christian perspective with practical real-life application will be considered." Circ. 48,000. **Pays on acceptance.** Publishes ms an average of 6 months after acceptance. Byline given. Buys first North American serial, first, one-time or second serial (reprint) rights. Submit seasonal material 6 months in advance. Query by mail, e-mail. Reports in 2 months. Sample copy for 9×12 SAE with 3 first-class stamps. Writer's guidelines and theme list for #10 SASE or on website.

⊶ "Our greatest need is for nonfiction pieces based in real life rather than theory or theology. Practical living articles are especially needed. We receive many fiction submissions but few good nonfiction."

**Nonfiction:** Inspirational, how-to, humor, interview/profile, personal experience, photo feature, religious. "Articles should deal with issues of relevance to teens (high school students) today; avoid 'preachiness' or moralizing." **Buys 60 mss/year.** Send complete ms. Length: 1,000-1,500 words. **Pays 15¢/word for first rights.**

**Reprints:** Send tearsheet, photocopy of article or typed ms with rights for sale noted and information about when and where the article previously appeared. Pays 10¢/word for reprints.

**Fiction:** Only a small amount is used. Adventure, fantasy, humorous, religious, romance, science fiction—all from a Christian perspective. **Buys few mss/year. Length: 500-1,200 words. Pays 15¢/word.**

**Tips:** "Study magazine, familiarize yourself with the unique 'Salvationist' perspective of *Young Salvationist*; learn a little about the Salvation Army; media, sports, sex and dating are strongest appeal."

**$ $YOUTH UPDATE**, St. Anthony Messenger Press, 1615 Republic St., Cincinnati OH 45210-1298. (513)241-5615. Fax: (513)241-0399. E-mail: CarolAnn@americancatholic.org. Website: http://www.AmericanCatholic.org. **Contact:** Carol Ann Morrow, editor. **90% freelance written.** Monthly 4-page newsletter of faith life for teenagers, "designed to attract, instruct, guide and challenge Catholics of high school age by applying the Gospel to modern problems/situations." Circ. 24,000. **Pays on acceptance.** Publishes ms an average of 6 months after acceptance. Byline given. Reports in 3 months. Sample copy and writer's guidelines for #10 SASE.

**Nonfiction:** Inspirational, practical self-help, spiritual. "Adults who pay for teen subs want more church-related and curriculum-related topics." **Buys 12 mss/year.** Query or send outline. Length: 2,200-2,300 words. **Pays $350-400.** Sometimes pays expenses of writers on assignment.

▣ The online magazine carries original content not found in the print edition. Contact: Carol Ann Morrow.

**Tips:** "Write for a 15-year-old with a C+ average."

# TRAVEL, CAMPING & TRAILER

Travel magazines give travelers indepth information about destinations, detailing the best places to go, attractions in the area and sites to see—but they also keep them up-to-date about potential negative aspects of these destinations. Publications in this category tell tourists and campers the where-tos and how-tos of travel. This category is extremely competitive, demanding quality writing, background information and professional photography. Each has its own slant. Sample copies should be studied carefully before sending submissions.

**$ AAA GOING PLACES, Magazine for Today's Traveler**, AAA Auto Club South, 1515 N. Westshore Blvd., Tampa FL 33607. (813)289-5923. Fax: (813)289-6245. **Contact:** Phyllis Zeno, editor-in-chief. **50% freelance written.** Bimonthly magazine on auto news, driving trips, cruise travel, tours. Estab. 1982. Circ. 2,000,000. Pays on publication. Publishes ms an average of 6 months after acceptance. Byline given. Buys one-time rights. Submit seasonal material 9 months in advance. Accepts simultaneous submissions. Reports in 2 months. Writer's guidelines for SAE.
**Nonfiction:** Historical/nostalgic, how-to, humor, interview/profile, personal experience, photo feature, travel. Travel stories feature domestic and international destinations with practical information and where to stay, dine and shop, as well as personal anecdotes and historical background; they generally relate to tours currently offered by AAA Travel Agency. Special issues include Cruise Guide and Europe Issue. **Buys 15 mss/year.** Send complete ms. Length: 500-1,500 words. **Pays $15/printed page.**
**Photos:** State availability of photos with submission. Reviews 2×2 transparencies. Offers no additional payment for photos accepted with ms. Captions required.
**Columns/Departments:** AAAway We Go (local attractions in Florida, Georgia or Tennessee).
**Tips:** "We prefer lively, upbeat stories that appeal to a well-traveled, sophisticated audience, bearing in mind that AAA is a conservative company."

**$ $ AAA MIDWEST TRAVELER**, (formerly *The Midwest Motorist*), AAA Auto Club of Missouri, 12901 N. 40 Dr., St. Louis MO 63141. (314)523-7350. Fax: (314)523-6982. E-mail: acmdmk@ibm.net. Editor: Michael J. Right. **Contact:** Deborah M. Klein, managing editor. **80% freelance written.** Bimonthly magazine. "We feature articles on regional and world travel, area history, auto safety, highway and transportation news." Estab. 1971. Circ. 430,000. **Pays on acceptance.** Byline given. Not copyrighted. Buys first North American print serial rights, second serial (reprint) rights. Accepts simultaneous submissions. Reports in 1 month with SASE enclosed. Sample copy or media kit for 12½×9½ SAE with 3 first-class stamps. Writer's guidelines for #10 SASE.
**Nonfiction:** **Buys 40 mss/year.** Query. Length: 2,000 words maximum. **Pays $350 (maximum).**
**Reprints:** Send typed ms with rights for sale noted and information about when and where the article previously appeared. **Pays $150-250.**
**Photos:** State availability of photos with submission. Reviews transparencies. Offers no additional payment for photos accepted with ms. Captions required. Buys one-time rights.
**Tips:** "Editorial schedule set 18 months in advance. Request a copy. Serious writers ask for media kit to help them target their piece. Some stories available throughout the year. Travel destinations and tips are most open to freelancers; auto-related topics handled by staff. Make the story bright and quick to read. We see too many 'Here's a recount of our family vacation' manuscripts. Go easy on first-person accounts."

**$ $ AAA TODAY**, Pro Publishing Service, 378 Whooping Loop, Suite 1272, Altamonte Springs FL 32701. (407)834-6777. Fax: (407)834-3535. E-mail: margcavanaugh@sprintmail.com. **Contact:** Margaret Cavanaugh, managing editor. **50% freelance written.** Bimonthly AAA Club publication magazine covering travel destinations. Estab. 1960. Circ. 550,000. Pays on publication. Publishes ms an average of 6 months after acceptance. Byline given. Offers 25% kill fee. Buys first North American serial rights. Editorial lead time 12 months. Submit seasonal material 1 year in advance. Accepts queries by mail, e-mail, fax. Reports in 2 months. Sample copy and writer's guidelines free.
**Nonfiction:** Travel. **Buys 18 mss/year.** Query with published clips or send complete ms. Length: 500-1,000 words. **Pays $250-400.**
**Photos:** State availability or send photos with submission. Offers $50-200/photo. Captions required. Buys one-time rights.

**★ $ $ $ $ AQUA, The Padi (Professional Assocation of Diving Instructors) Diving Society Magazine**, Islands Publishing Co., P.O. Box 4728, Santa Barbara CA 93140-4728. Fax: (805)569-0349. E-mail: aqua@aquamag.com. **Contact:** Bob Morris, editor-in-chief, or Angela Tripp, managing editor. **90% freelance written with established writers.** Bimonthly magazine covering international travel for scuba diving, snorkeling, kayaking and other water sports enthusiasts. "*Aqua* puts its highest premium on lively storytelling. We avoid the 'been there, done that' treatment by sending our favorite writers to places they've never before visited. We want our readers to discover new destinations and share in waterborne adventures with a sense of awe and wonder that can only be conveyed by facile writers who craft stylish reportage." Estab. 1997. Circ. 125,000. **Pays on acceptance.** Publishes ms 6 months after acceptance. Byline given. Offers 25% kill fee. Buys all rights. Editorial lead time 6 months. Submit seasonal material 6 months in advance. Accepts queries by mail. Reports in 2 months. Sample copy for $6. Writer's guidelines for #10 SASE.
○┰ "Query with good clips, sharp wit, and ideas for our *Flotsam & Jetsam* department that might lead to a longer department assignment and then, if the romance blossoms, a feature assignment. Also considers submissions for *Amphibian at Large*—a singular water adventure or experience, typically from some far-flung or exotic

location, approximately 1,200 words or *Local Dive*—a dossier-type report on a funky bar/restaurant favored by water sports lovers (it can be anywhere in the world, just as long as it's on or near the water and is open to the public)."

**Nonfiction:** General interest, historical/nostalgic, humor, interview/profile, photo feature, travel. No technical articles or gear reviews; no 'my family dive vacation' articles. **Buys 30 feature mss/year.** Query with published clips; feature articles are commissioned. Length: 500-4,000 words. **Pays $250-4,000.** Pays expenses of writers on assignment.

**Photos:** Feature articles are commissioned. Reviews high-quality dupes in 4×5 or 35mm transparency format. Offers $75-350/photo. Model releases, identification of subjects required. Buys one-time rights.

**Columns/Departments:** Local Dive (humorous profile of seedy or colorful watering hole or restaurant on the water), 500 words; Amphibian at Large (short feature piece on a singular and far-flung water-related adventure; i.e., Inner Tubing Balize's Underground Rivers), 1,200-1,500 words; Rhapsody on Blue (A highly personal essay about an epiphany involving the water, i.e. Teaching a boy in the Maldives how to snorkel); Flotsam & Jetsam (snappy 100-500 word pieces about watery subjects—history, exploration, marine archaeology, culture, etc.), 1,200 words; Get-Wet-Aways (service pieces on diving, snorkeling, kayaking, white-water rafting, etc., destinations in the U.S., Mexico, Canada and the Caribbean; basic nuts and bolts information on places that are good for day trips), 500 words. **Buys 50 mss/year.** Query with published clips. **Pays $250-1,500.**

**Tips:** "*Aqua* places a premium on stylish writing. We look for writers with uncommonly good storytelling skills and avoid articles that are overly technical or laden with gear-head jargon. In each issue there are usually four or five feature articles, ranging from 2,000 to 4,000 words. We aim for a lively mix of topics: destination, adventure, and profiles. Most features are staff-generated ideas assigned to a core group of freelance writers, but we welcome proposals with a well-defined focus and point of view. All first-time queries should include recent writing samples and a SASE. Allow at least two months for a response. You may send queries or articles on speculation via e-mail to aqua@aquamag.com (writing samples should follow via regular mail)."

**★☆ $ ARRIVING MAGAZINE, The Ultimate in Transportation**, M.A.K. Publishing, 3431 Cherry Ave., Long Beach CA 90807. (562)492-9394. Fax: (562)492-1345. Website: http://www.makpublishing.com. **Contact:** Julia Armenta, editor. **75% freelance written.** Monthly magazine offering a superlative collection of full-color articles devoted specifically to the big-ticket items in today's transportation marketplace. Estab. 1995. Circulation 20,000. Pays on publication. Buys first North American serial rights. Guidelines for #10 SASE. Accepts unsolicited mss; encourages first time writers. Accepts queries by mail, e-mail, phone, fax.

**Nonfiction:** "The central focus of Arriving is $800,000+ buses/Rvs; however, we also publish articles profiling custom jets, high-end yachts, unique automobiles and other speciality vehicles, as well as reviews of luxury RV resorts, pertinent industry pieces, and a few travel/destination pieces." Query with SASE. **Pays $50-100.**

**Reprints:** Send typed ms with rights for sale noted and information about when and where the article previously appeared.

**Photos:** Include color photos (glossy) or slides with submission. Photos/slides not returned unless other arrangements are made.

**Columns/Departments:** Industry Update; Products of Interest; The Road Less Traveled (focuses on extreme destinations/ultimate travel); The Travel Wonders of the World (past topics have profiled the Concorde and the Shinkansen; future topics include the Chunnel and the Panama Canal); The Ultimate Traveler..

**Tips:** "We are always in need of clean, accurate and intriguing stories profiling celebrity buses."

**★ $ $ ARUBA NIGHTS**, Nights Publications, 1831 Rene Levesque Blvd. W., Montreal, Quebec H3H 1R4 Canada. Fax: (514)931-6273. E-mail: editor@nightspublications.com. Website: www.nightspublications.com. Managing Editor: Zelly Zuskin. **Contact:** Stephen Trotter, editor. **90% freelance written.** Annual magazine covering the Aruban vacation lifestyle experience with an upscale, upbeat touch. Estab. 1988. Circ. 225,000. **Pays on acceptance.** Publishes ms an average of 9 months after acceptance. Byline given. Buys first North American serial and first Caribbean rights. Editorial lead time 1 month. Accepts queries by mail, e-mail, fax. Reports in 2 weeks on queries; 1 month on mss. Sample copy for $5 (make checks payable to "Nights Publications Inc."). Writer's guidelines free.

**Nonfiction:** General interest, historical/nostalgic, how-to features relative to Aruba vacationers, humor, inspirational, interview/profile, eco-tourism, opinion, personal experience, photo feature, travel, Aruban culture, art, activities, entertainment, topics relative to vacationers in Aruba. "No negative pieces or stale rewrites." **Buys 5-10 mss/year.** Submit ms and SASE with Canadian postage or IRC. Length: 250-750 words. **Pays $100-200.**

**Photos:** State availability with submission. Offers $50/photo. Captions, model releases, identification of subjects required. Buys one-time rights.

**Tips:** "Demonstrate your voice in your query letter. Be descriptive, employ vivid metaphors. Focus on individual aspects of the Aruban lifestyle and vacation experience (e.g., art, gambling tips, windsurfing, a colorful local character, a personal experience, etc.), rather than generalized overviews. Provide an angle that will be entertaining to vacationers who are already there. E-mail submissions accepted."

**$ $ ASU TRAVEL GUIDE**, ASU Travel Guide, Inc., 1525 Francisco Blvd. E., San Rafael CA 94901. (415)459-0300. Fax: (415)459-0494. E-mail: chris@asuguide.com. Website: http://www.ASUguide.com. **Contact:** Christopher Gil, managing editor. **80% freelance written.** Quarterly guidebook covering international travel features and travel discounts for well-traveled airline employees. Estab. 1970. Circ. 60,000. Publishes ms an average of 4 months after acceptance. Byline given. Buys first North American serial rights, first and second rights to the same material, and second serial (reprint) rights. Also makes work-for-hire assignments. Submit seasonal material 6 months in advance. Accepts simultaneous submissions. Reports in 1 year. Sample copy available for 6×9 SAE with 5 first-class stamps. Writer's guidelines for #10 SASE.

**Nonfiction:** International travel articles "similar to those run in consumer magazines. Not interested in amateur efforts from inexperienced travelers or personal experience articles that don't give useful information to other travelers." **Buys 16 ms/year.** Destination pieces only; no "Tips On Luggage" articles. Unsolicited mss or queries without SASE will not be acknowledged. No telephone queries. Length: 1,800 words. **Pays $200.**

**Reprints:** Send tearsheet of article with information about when and where the article previously appeared. Pays 100% of amount paid for an original article.

**Photos:** "Interested in clear, high-contrast photos." Reviews 5×7 and 8×10 b&w or color prints. "Payment for photos is included in article price; photos from tourist offices are acceptable."

**Tips:** "Query with samples of travel writing and a list of places you've recently visited. We appreciate clean and simple style. Keep verbs in the active tense and involve the reader in what you write. Avoid 'cute' writing, coined words and stale clichés. The most frequent mistakes made by writers in completing an article for us are: 1) Lazy writing—using words to describe a place that could describe any destination such as 'there is so much to do in (fill in destination) that whole guidebooks have been written about it'; 2) Including fare and tour package information—our readers make arrangements through their own airline."

**$BIG WORLD**, Big World Publishing, P.O. Box 8743-G, Lancaster PA 17604. E-mail: bigworld@bigworld.com. Website: www.bigworld.com. **Contact:** Jim Fortney, editor. **85% freelance written.** Quarterly magazine covering independent travel. "Big World is a magazine for people who like their travel on the cheap and down-to-earth. And not necessarily because they have to—but because they want to. It's for people who prefer to spend their travelling time responsibly discovering, exploring, and learning, in touch with local people and their traditions, and in harmony with the environment. We're looking for casual, first-person narratives that take into account the cultural/sociological/political side of travel." Estab. 1995. Circ. 5,000. Pays on publication. Publishes ms an average of 3 months after acceptance. Byline given. Buys one-time rights. Editorial lead time 2 months. Submit seasonal material 4 months in advance. Accepts queries by mail, e-mail. Reports in 1 months on queries; 2 months on mss. Sample copy for $4. Writer's guidelines for #10 SASE or on website.

**Nonfiction:** New product, opinion, personal experience, photo feature, travel, how-to, tips on transportation bargains and adventuring, overseas work study advice. **Buys 32-40 mss/year.** Length: 500-4,000 words. Query. Pay varies. Sometimes pays with subscriptions.

**Reprints:** Send photocopy of article. Pays 50% of amount paid for original article.

**Photos:** Reviews prints. Negotiates payment individually. Captions required. Buys one-time rights.

**Columns/Departments:** Readers Writes (book reviews by subscribers), 400-500 words; Dispatches (slice of life pieces), 200-800 words; Hostel Intentions, My Town, Bike World, Better Adventuring. Pay varies.

**Tips:** "Take a look at the glossy, fluffy travel mags in the bookstore. They're *not* what we're about. We're *not* looking for romantic getaway pieces or lap-of-luxury bits. Our readers are decidedly downbeat and are looking for similarly-minded on-the-cheap and down-to-earth, first-person articles. Be breezy. Be yourself. First-time writers especially encouraged. You can submit your story to us on paper or 3.5 disc."

**$ $BONAIRE NIGHTS**, Nights Publications, 1831 René Lévesque Blvd. W., Montreal, Quebec H3H 1R4 Canada. Fax: (514)931-6273. E-mail: editor@nightspublications.com. **Contact:** Stephen Trotter, editor. **90% freelance written.** Annual magazine covering Bonaire vacation experience. "Upbeat entertaining lifestyle articles: colorful profiles of locals, eco-tourism; lively features on culture, activities (particularly scuba and snorkeling), special events, historical attractions, how-to features. Audience is North American tourist." Estab. 1993. Circ. 60,000. **Pays on acceptance.** Publishes ms an average of 9 months after acceptance. Byline given. Buys first North American serial rights and first Caribbean rights. Editorial lead time 1 month. Accepts queries by mail, e-mail, fax. Reports in 2 weeks on queries; 1 month on mss. Sample copy for $5 (make check payable to Nights Publications, Inc). Writer's guidelines for #10 SAE.

**Nonfiction:** Lifestyle, general interest, historical/nostalgic, how-to, humor, inspirational, interview/profile, opinion, personal experience, photo feature, travel, local culture, art, activities, especially scuba diving, snorkeling, eco-tourism. **Buys 6-9 mss/year.** Length: 250-750 words. Query or submit ms and SASE with Canadian postage or IRC. **Pays $100-200.**

**Photos:** State availability of photos with submission. Reviews transparencies. Offers $50/slide. Captions, model releases, identification of subjects required. Buys one-time or first rights.

**Tips:** "Demonstrate your voice in your query letter. Focus on the Bonaire lifestyle, what sets it apart from other islands. We want personal experience, not generalized overviews. Be positive and provide an angle that will appeal to vacationers who are already there. Our style is upbeat, friendly, fluid and descriptive."

**N ☆ $ $ $BUON GIORNO, The Onboard Magazine of Costa Cruises**, Onboard Media, 960 Alton Rd., Miami Beach FL 33139. (305)673-0400. Fax: (305)674-9396. **Contact:** Linda Horkitz, editor. **95% freelance written.** "This annual trilingual (English/French/Italian) in-cabin magazine reaches French, Italian and American cruise passengers traveling to various Caribbean port destinations. Articles must appeal to a multinational readership." Estab. 1994. Circ. 43,000. **Pays on acceptance.** Publishes ms an average of 4 months after acceptance. Byline given. Offers 30% kill fee. Buys exclusive first rights for one year and nonexclusive rights to publish in any Onboard Media Publications. Editorial lead time 6 months. Sample copy for 11×14 SAE with $3 postage. Writer's guidelines for #10 SASE.

**Nonfiction:** Features must focus on entire Caribbean region or on specific aspect of cruise line's fleet. General interest, humor, interview/profile of hot artist or writer, photo feature. Does not want politics, sex, religion, shopping information or advertorials. No personal experience. **Buys 4-5 features/year,** plus assigned editorial covering ports of call and numerous fillers. Query with published clips. Length: 400-2,000 words. **Pays $200-1,000** and contributor's copies, negotiable per assignment.

**Reprints:** Accepts previously published submissions if so noted. Send photocopy of article and information about when and where the article previously appeared.

**Photos:** State availability of photos with submission. Negotiates payment individually. Captions, model releases, identification of subjects required. Buys non-exclusive, one-time reprint rights. Photo credit given. Request photographer's guidelines from Bryan Batty, production coordinator; include #10 SASE.

**Fillers:** History, regional culture, food, folklore, local personalities, ecology, arts, natural wonders, lingo/idioms, architecture. **Buys 25/year.** Length: 75-250 words. **Pays from $500** and contributor copies for a group of 10 items.

**Tips:** "Know the port destinations we cover. Know our magazine. Demonstrate your voice in your query letter. Send a selection of published writing samples that reveals your range. The three essential things we look for are: 1) an authoritative voice; 2) intimate knowledge of the subject matter; and 3) original material. Having a clear-cut article in mind is a must. Do not query 'with an idea for an article on Aruba.' Outline your proposal and indicate your angle."

**N ★ CAMPERWAYS, CAMP-ORAMA, CAROLINA RV TRAVELER, SOUTHERN RV, TEXAS RV**, Woodall's, 13975 W. Polo Trail Dr., Lake Forest IL 60045. (800)323-9076. Fax: (847)362-6844. E-mail: bpeterson@woo dallpub.com. Website: http://www.woodalls.com. **Contact:** Brent Peterson. **75% freelance written.** Monthly tabloid covering RV lifestyle. "We're looking for articles of interest to RVers. Lifestyle articles, destinations, technical tips, interesting events and the like make up the bulk of our publications." Circ. 30,000. Pays on publication. Byline given. Offers 50% kill fee. Buys first North American serial rights. Submit seasonal material 4 months in advance. Accepts queries by mail, e-mail. Reports in 3 weeks on queries, 1 month on ms. Sample copy free. Writer's guidelines for #10 SASE.

**Nonfiction:** How-to, humor, inspirational, interview/profile, new product, opinion, personal experience, technical, travel. Special issues: Checkered Flag (relationship between RVs and racing), Northeast Summers (destinations of interest to RVers in the Northeast), Discover RVing (guide to new RVers about how-to get started). No "Camping From Hell" articles. **Buys 1,000 mss/year.** Query with published clips. Length: 500-1,500 words. Pays 10¢/word. Sometimes pays expenses of writers on assignment.

**Photos:** State availability of or send photos with submission. Reviews negatives, 4×5 transparencies, 4×5 prints. Offers $5/photo. Captions, identification of subjects required. Buys one-time rights.

**Columns/Departments:** Gadgets, Gears & Gizmos (new product reviews), 600 words. RV Renovations (how-to building/renovations project), 1,000 words; Stopping Points (campground reviews), 1,000 words. **Buys 100 mss/year.** Query with published clips. Pay negotiable.

**Tips:** "Be an expert in RVing. Make your work readable to a wide variety of readers, from novices to full-timers."

**$ $ CAMPING CANADA'S RV LIFESTYLES**, 2585 Skymark Ave., Unit 306, Mississauga, Ontario L4W 4L5 Canada. (905)624-8218. Fax: (905)624-6764. Website: http://www.rvlifemag.com. Editor: Howard Elmer. **Contact:** Peter Tasler, editorial director. **50% freelance written.** Magazine published 7 times/year (monthly January-June and November). "*Camping Canada's RV Lifestyles* is geared to readers who enjoy travel/camping. Upbeat pieces only. Readers vary from owners of towable campers or motorhomes to young families and entry-level campers (RV only)." Estab. 1971. Circ. 45,000. Pays on publication. Byline given. Buys first North American serial rights. Editorial lead time 2 months. Reports in 1 month on queries; 2 months on mss. Sample copy free.

**Nonfiction:** How-to, personal experience, travel. No inexperienced, unresearched or too general pieces. **Buys 20-30 mss/year.** Query. Length: 1,200-2,000 words. Pay varies. Sometimes pays expenses of writers on assignment.

**Reprints:** Occasionally accepts previously published submissions, if so noted.

**Photos:** Send photos with submission. Offers no additional payment for photos accepted with ms. Buys one-time rights.

**Tips:** "Pieces should be slanted toward RV living. All articles must have an RV slant."

**$ CAMPING TODAY, Official Publication of the Family Campers & RVers**, 126 Hermitage Rd., Butler PA 16001-8509. (724)283-7401. **Contact:** DeWayne Johnston and June Johnston, editors. **30% freelance written.** Prefers to work with published/established writers. Monthly official membership publication of the FCRV, "the largest nonprofit family camping and RV organization in the United States and Canada. Members are heavily oriented toward RV travel, both weekend and extended vacations. Concentration is on member activities in chapters. Group is also interested in conservation and wildlife. The majority of members are retired." Estab. 1983. Circ. 25,000. Pays on publication. Publishes ms an average of 6 months after acceptance. Byline given. Buys one-time rights. Submit seasonal material 3 months in advance. Accepts simultaneous submissions. Reports in 2 months. Sample copy and guidelines for 4 first-class stamps. Writer's guidelines only for #10 SASE.

**Nonfiction:** Travel (interesting places to visit by RV, camping), humor (camping or travel related, please, no "our first campout stories"), interview/profile (interesting campers), new products, technical (RVs related). **Buys 10-15 mss/year.** Send complete ms with photos. Length: 750-2,000 words. **Pays $50-150.**

**Reprints:** Send typed ms with rights for sale noted and information about when and where the article previously appeared. Pays 35-50% of amount paid for an original article.

**Photos:** Send photos with ms. Need b&w or sharp color prints inside (we can make prints from slides) and vertical transparencies for cover. Captions required.

**Tips:** "Freelance material on RV travel, RV maintenance/safety, and items of general camping interest throughout the United States and Canada will receive special attention. Good photos increase your chances."

**★ $ $ CARIBBEAN TRAVEL AND LIFE**, 330 W. Canton Ave., Winter Park FL 32789. (407)628-4802. Fax: (407)628-7061. E-mail: sb3@worldzine.com. Editor-in-Chief: Steve Blount. Managing Editor: Sue Whitney. **Contact:** Jim Bartlett, executive editor. **80% freelance written.** Prefers to work with published/established writers. Magazine covering travel to the Caribbean, Bahamas and Bermuda for sophisticated upscale audience, published 8 times/year. Estab. 1985. Circ. 135,000. **Pays on acceptance.** Publishes ms an average of 2 months after acceptance. Byline given. Offers 25% kill fee. Buys first North American serial rights. Submit seasonal material 4 months in advance. Accepts queries by mail, e-mail. Reports in 2 months. Sample copy for 9 × 12 SAE with 9 first-class stamps. Writer's guidelines for #10 SASE.
- Ranked as one of the best markets for freelance writers in *Writer's Yearbook* magazine's annual "Top 100 Markets," January 1999.

**Nonfiction:** General interest, how-to, interview/profile, culture, personal experience, travel. No guidebook rehashing, superficial destination pieces or critical exposes. **Buys 50-60 mss/year.** Query. Length: 1,150-3,000 words. **Pays $200-2,000 for assigned articles; $100-1,000 for unsolicited articles.**

**Photos:** State availability of photos with submission. Reviews 35mm transparencies and prints. Offers $100-600/photo. Captions and identification of subjects required. Buys one-time rights. **Pays $75-400.**
- Break in through columns and departments.

**Columns/Departments:** Gazette (new, humor); Travel Desk (hotels, cruises, airlines); Day Trip (island excursions); Active Traveler (active, sports-oriented activites); Caribbean Life (people, arts, culture, music); Caribbean Kitchen (restaurants, chefs, food). Query with published clips and SASE. Length: 500-1,250 words. **Pays $250-400.** Buys one-time rights.

**Tips:** "Our only requirements are that the writing be superb, the subject be something unique and interesting, and the writer must know his/her subject. We are NOT interested in stories about the well-known, over-publicized and commonly visited places of the Caribbean. Our readers have likely already 'been there, done that.' We want to guide them to the new, the unusual and the interesting. Please do not call and do not send a complete manuscript unless requested by an editor. E-mail queries OK."

**$ $ CHICAGO TRIBUNE**, Travel Section, 435 N. Michigan Ave., Chicago IL 60611. (312)222-3999. E-mail: rcurwen@tribune.com. **Travel Contact:** Randy Curwen, editor. Weekly Sunday newspaper leisure travel section averaging 22 pages aimed at vacation travelers. Circ. 1,100,000. Pays on publication. Publishes ms an average of 6 weeks after acceptance. Byline given. Buys one-time rights (which includes microfilm, online and CD/ROM usage). Accepts queries by mail, e-mail. Submit seasonal material 2 months in advance. Accepts simultaneous submissions. Reports in 1 month. Sample copy for large SAE with $1.50 postage. Writer's guidelines for #10 SASE.

**Nonfiction:** Essays, general interest, historical/nostalgic, how-to (travel, pack), humor, opinion, personal experience, photo feature, travel. "There will be 16 special issues in the next 18 months." **Buys 150 mss/year.** Send complete ms. Length: 500-2,000 words. **Pays $50-500.**

**Photos:** State availability of photos with submission. Reviews 35mm transparencies, 8 × 10 or 5 × 7 prints. Offers $100/color photo; $25/b&w; $100 for cover. Captions required. Buys one-time rights.

◼ The online magazine carries original content not found in the print edition. Contact: Elise Bittner, online editor.

**Tips:** "Be professional. Use a word processor. Make the reader want to go to the area being written about. Only 1% of manuscripts make it."

**$ $ CHRISTIAN CAMP & CONFERENCE JOURNAL**, Christian Camping International U.S.A., P.O. Box 62189, Colorado Springs CO 80962-2189. (719)260-9400. Fax: (719)260-6398. E-mail: dridings@cciusa.org. Website: http://www.cciusa.org. **Contact:** Dean Ridings, editor. **75% freelance written.** Prefers to work with published/established writers. Bimonthly magazine emphasizing the broad scope of organized camping with emphasis on Christian camping. "All who work in youth camps and adult conferences read our magazine for inspiration and to get practical help in ways to serve in their operations." Estab. 1963. Circ. 7,500. Pays on publication. Publishes ms an average of 4 months after acceptance. Byline given. Rights negotiable. Submit seasonal material queries 6 months in advance. Query by mail, e-mail. Reports in 1 month. Sample copy for $2.25 plus 9 × 12 SASE. Writer's guidelines for #10 SASE.

**Nonfiction:** General interest (trends in organized camping in general, Christian camping in particular); how-to (anything involved with organized camping from motivating staff, to programming, to record keeping, to camper follow-up); inspirational (interested in profiles and practical applications of Scriptural principles to everyday situations in camping); interview (with movers and shakers in Christian camping; submit a list of basic questions first); and opinion (letter to the editor). **Buys 20-30 mss/year.** Query required. Length: 500-3,000 words. **Pays 12¢/word.**

**Reprints:** Send photocopy of article and information about when and where the article previously appeared. Pays 50% of amount paid for an original article.

**Photos:** Send photos with ms. Pays $25-250 for 5 × 7 b&w contact sheet or print; price negotiable for 35mm color transparencies. Rights negotiable.

**Tips:** "The most frequent mistake made by writers is that they send articles unrelated to our readers. Ask for our publication guidelines first. Profiles/interviews are the best bet for freelancers."

⬛ **$ $COAST TO COAST MAGAZINE**, Affinity Group, Inc., 2575 Vista Del Mar Dr., Ventura CA 93001-3920. Fax: (805)667-4217. Website: http://www.coastresorts.com. **Contact:** Valerie Law, editor. **80% freelance written.** Club magazine published 8 times/year for members of Coast to Coast Resorts. "*Coast to Coast* focuses on travel, recreation and good times, with most stories targeted to recreational vehicle owners." Estab. 1982. Circ. 200,000. **Pays on acceptance.** Publishes ms an average of 5 months after acceptance. Byline given. Offers 33% kill fee. Buys first North American serial and electronic rights. Submit seasonal material 5 months in advance. Reports in 1 month on queries; 2 months on mss. Sample copy for $2 and 9×12 SASE.

**Nonfiction:** Book excerpts, essays, general interest, historical/nostalgic, how-to, humor, inspirational, interview/profile, new product, opinion, personal experience, photo feature, technical, travel. No poetry, cartoons. **Buys 50 mss/year.** Query with published clips. Length: 500-2,500 words. **Pays $75-600.**

**Reprints:** Send photocopy of article, information about when and where the article previously appeared. Pays approximately 50% of the amount paid for an original article.

**Photos:** Send photos with submission. Reviews transparencies. Offers $50-600/photo. Identification of subjects required. Buys one-time rights.

**Tips:** "Send published clips with queries, or story ideas will not be considered."

**$ $ $ $CONDÉ NAST TRAVELER**, The Condé Nast Publications, 360 Madison Ave., New York NY 10017. (212)880-8800. Fax: (212)880-2190. Website: www.epicurious.com. Editor: Thomas J. Wallace. **Contact:** Dee Aldrich, managing editor. **75% freelance written.** Monthly. "Our motto, Truth in Travel, sums up our editorial philosophy: to present travel destinations, news and features in a candid, journalistic style. Our writers do not accept complimentary tickets, hotel rooms, gifts, or the like. While our departments present service information in a tipsheet or newsletter manner, our destination stories are literary in tone. Our readers are affluent, well-educated, and sophisticated about travel." Estab. 1987. Circ. 850,000. "Please keep in mind that we very rarely assign stories based on unsolicited queries because (1) our inventory of unused stories (features and departments) is very large, and (2) most story ideas are generated inhouse by the editors, as it is very difficult for outsiders to anticipate the needs of our inventory. To submit story ideas, send a brief (one paragraph) description of the idea(s) to the appropriate editor (by mail or fax). Please do not send clips, résumés, photographs, itineraries, or abridged or full-length manuscripts. Due to our editorial policy, we *do not* purchase completed manuscripts. Telephone calls are not accepted."

▣ The online magazine contains original content not found in the print edition. Contact: Gail Norwood, online editor.

**Tips:** *Condé Nast Traveler* tells us that they are no longer accepting unsolicited submissions. Research this market carefully before submitting your best work.

**$ $CRUISE TRAVEL MAGAZINE**, World Publishing Co., 990 Grove St., Evanston IL 60201-4370. (847)491-6440. Editor: Robert Meyers. **Contact:** Charles Doherty, managing editor. **95% freelance written.** Bimonthly magazine. "This is a consumer-oriented travel publication covering the world of pleasure cruising on large cruise ships (with some coverage of smaller ships), including ports, travel tips, roundups." Estab. 1979. Circ. 175,000. **Pays on acceptance.** Publishes ms an average of 6 months after acceptance. Byline given. Offers 50% kill fee. Buys first North American serial, one-time or second serial (reprint) rights. Accepts simultaneous submissions. Reports in 1 month. Sample copy for $5 postpaid. Writer's guidelines for #10 SASE.

○┯ New writers can break the ice more easily by jotting down and mailing in a list of four to six article ideas that they feel comfortable in developing. Include SASE, home and work telephone numbers for possible contact discussion, and social security number.

**Nonfiction:** General interest, historical/nostalgic, interview/profile, personal experience, photo feature, travel. "No daily cruise 'diary', My First Cruise, etc." **Buys 72 mss/year.** Query with or without published clips, or send complete ms. Length: 500-1,500 words. **Pays $100-400.**

**Reprints:** Send tearsheet or photocopy of article and typed ms with rights for sale noted.

**Photos:** Send photos with submission. Reviews transparencies and prints. "Must be color, 35mm preferred (other format OK); color prints second choice." Offers no additional payment for photos accepted with ms "but pay more for well-illustrated ms." Captions and identification of subjects required. Buys one-time rights.

**Fillers:** "Cruise Views" personal experience. **Buys 6 mss/year.** Length: 300-700 words. **Pays $75-200.**

**Tips:** "Do your homework. Know what we do and what sorts of things we publish. Know the cruise industry—we can't use novices. Good, sharp, bright color photography opens the door fast. We still need good pictures—we are not interested in developing any new contributors who cannot provide color support to manuscripts. Writers should aim for an active, breezy, light, conversational, even "folksy" style; avoid passive voice and pedantic or "stuffy" phrasing. Be informative and descriptive; avoid effusive but empty adjectives (elegant, luxurious, marvelous) unless backed up with descriptitve fact (not just "the elegant hardwood furniture in the main dining room" but rather "the elegant, French Provincial, dark cherrywood furniture . . .)."

**▣ ⬛ $ $CRUISING IN STYLE, The Onboard Magazine of Crystal Cruises**, Onboard Media, Inc., 960 Alton Rd., Miami Beach FL 33139. (305)673-0400. Fax: (305)674-9396. **Contact:** Linda Horkitz, editor. **95% freelance written.** This annual publication reaches guests on board Crystal ships on Caribbean, Panama Canal, Mexican Riviera, Central America, South America and Alaska itineraries. Estab. 1992. Circ. 7,500. **Pays on acceptance.** Publishes ms an average of 4 months after acceptance. Byline given. Offers 30% kill fee. Buys exclusive first rights for 1 year and nonexclusive rights to republish in any Onboard Media Publication. Editorial lead time 6 months. Sample copy for 11 × 14 SAE with $3 postage. Writer's guidelines for #10 SASE.

**Nonfiction:** General interest, humor, interview/profile of hot writer or artist, new product, photo feature. Features must focus on entire Caribbean region or on specific aspect of cruise line's fleet. Does not want politics, sex, religion, shopping information or advertorials. No personal experience. **Buys 5 features/year**, plus assigned editorial covering ports of call and numerous fillers. Query with published clips. Length: 400-2,000 words. **Pays $200-1,000**, negotiable.

**Reprints:** Accepts previously published submissions if so noted. Send photocopy of article and information about when and where the article previously appeared.

**Photos:** State availability of photos with submission. Negotiates payment individually. Captions, model releases, identification of subjects required. Buys non-exclusive, one-time reprint rights. Photo credit given. Request photographer's guidelines from Bryan Batty, production coordinator; include #10 SASE.

**Fillers:** History, regional culture, food, folklore, local personalities, ecology, arts, natural wonders, lingo/idioms, architecture. **Buys 25/year.** Length: 75-250 words. **Pays from $500** for a group of 10 items and contributor copies.

**Tips:** "Know the port destinations we cover. Know our magazine. Demonstrate your voice in your query letter. Send a selection of published writing samples that reveals your range. The three essential things we look for are: 1) an authoritative voice; 2) intimate knowledge of the subject matter; and 3) original material. Having a clear-cut article in mind is a must. Do not query 'with an idea for an article on Aruba.' Outline your proposal and indicate your angle."

**$ $ CURAÇAO NIGHTS**, Nights Publications, 1831 Rene Levesque Blvd. West, Montreal, Quebec H3H 1R4 Canada. (514)931-1987. Fax: (514)931-6273. E-mail: editor@nightspublications.com. **Contact:** Stephen Trotter, editor. Managing Editor: Zelly Zuskin. **90% freelance written.** Annual magazine covering the Curaçao vacation experience. "We are seeking upbeat, entertaining lifestyle articles; colorful profiles of locals; lively features on culture, activities, night life, eco-tourism, special events, gambling; how-to features; humor. Our audience is the North American vacationer." Estab. 1989. Circ. 155,000. **Pays on acceptance.** Publishes ms 9 months after acceptance. Byline given. Buys first North American serial and first Caribbean rights. Editorial lead time 1 month. Accepts queries by mail, e-mail, fax. Reports in 2 weeks on queries; 1 month on mss. Sample copy for $5 (check payable to Nights Publications Inc.). Guidelines free.

**Nonfiction:** General interest, historical/nostalgic, how-to help a vacationer get the most from their vacation, eco-tourism, humor, inspirational, interview/profile, lifestyle, opinion, personal experience, photo feature, travel, local culture, art, activities, night life, topics relative to vacationers in Curaçao. "No negative pieces, generic copy or stale rewrites." **Buys 5-10 mss/year.** Query with published clips and SASE that includes Canadian postage or IRC. Length: 250-750 words. **Pays $100-$200.**

**Photos:** State availability of photos with submission. Reviews transparencies. Offers $50/photo. Captions, model releases, identification of subjects required. Buys one-time rights.

**Tips:** "Demonstrate your voice in your query letter. Focus on individual aspects of the island lifestyle and vacation experience (e.g., art, gambling tips, windsurfing, a colorful local character, a personal experience, etc.), rather than generalized overviews. Provide an angle that will be entertaining to vacationers who are already on island. Our style is upbeat, friendly, fluid and descriptive."

**N ⭐ $ $ $ DESTINATIONS, The Unboard Magazine of Celebrity Cruises**, Onboard Media, Inc. 960 Alton Rd., Miami Beach FL 33139. (305)673-0400. Fax: (305)674-9396. **Contact:** Linda Horkitz, editor. **95% freelance written.** These annual publications reach cruise guests on board Celebrity ships on Caribbean, Mexican Riviera, Alaska, Bermuda and Bahamas itineraries. Estab. 1992. Circ. 130,000. **Pays on acceptance.** Publishes ms an average of 4 months after acceptance. Offers 30% kill fee. Buys first or second serial exclusive rights for 1 year and nonexclusive rights to republish in any Onboard Media Publication. Editorial lead time 6 months. Sample copy free on written request and 11 × 14 SASE with $3 postage. Writer's guidelines for #10 SASE.

**Nonfiction:** Features must focus on entire Caribbean region or on specific aspect of the cruise line's fleet. General interest, humor, interview/profile of photo feature, travel. Does not want politics, sex, religion, shopping information or advertorials. No personal experience. **Buys 9-10 features/year**, plus assigned editorial covering ports of call and numerous fillers. Query with published clips. Length: 400-2,000 words. **Pays $200-1,000** and contributors copies, negotiable per assignment. Sometimes pays expenses of writers on assignment.

**Reprints:** Accepts previously published submissions if so noted. Send photocopy of article and information about when and where the article previously appeared.

**Photos:** State availability of photos with submission. Negotiates payment individually. Captions, model releases, identification of subjects required. Buys non-exclusive, one-time reprint rights. Photo credit given. Request photographer's guidelines from Bryan Batty, production coordinator; include #10 SASE.

**Fillers:** History, regional culture, food, folklore, local personalities, ecology, arts, natural wonders, lingo/idioms, architecture. **Buys 25/year.** Length: 75-250 words. **Pays from $500** for a group of 10 items and contributor copies.

**Tips:** "Know the port destinations we cover. Know our magazine. Demonstrate your voice in your query letter. Send a selection of published writing samples that reveals your range. The three essential things we look for are: 1) an authoritative voice; 2) intimate knowledge of the subject matter; and 3) original material. Having a clear-cut article in mind is a must. Do not query 'with an idea for an article on Aruba.' Outline your proposal and indicate your angle."

⭐ **$ $ $** EXPLORE! The Onboard Magazine of Royal Caribbean International, Onboard Media Inc., 960 Alton Rd., Miami Beach FL 33139. (305)673-0400. Fax: (305)674-9396. **Contact:** Linda Hurleitz, editor. **95% freelance written.** This annual publication reaches cruise guests on board RCI ships on Caribbean, Bahamas, Mexican Riviera, Alaska and Bermuda itineraries. Circ. 715,000. **Pays on acceptance** of material. Publishes ms 4 months after acceptance. Offers 30% kill fee. Buys nonexclusive first rights for 1 year and nonexclusive rights to republish in any Onboard Media publications. Editorial lead time 6 months. Sample copy for 11×14 SAE with 10 first-class stamps. Writer's guidelines for #10 SASE.

**Nonfiction:** Features must focus on entire Caribbean region or on specific aspect of cruise line's fleet. General interest, humor, interview/profile of hot artist or writer, photo feature. Does not want politics, sex, religion, shopping information or advertorials, no personal experience. **Buys 10 features/year,** plus assigned editorial covering ports of call and numerous fillers. Query with published clips. Length: 800-2,000 words. **Pays $400-1,000** and contributor's copies.

**Reprints:** Accepts previously published submissions if so noted. Send photocopy of article and information about when and where the article previously appeared.

**Photos:** State availability of photos with submission. Negotiates payment individually. Captions, model releases, identification of subjects required. Buys non-exclusive, one-time reprint rights. Photo credit given. Request photographer's guidelines from Bryan Batty, production coordinator; include #10 SASE.

**Fillers:** History, regional culture, food, folklore, local personalities, ecology, arts, natural wonders, lingo/idioms, architecture. **Buys 25/year.** Length: 75-250 words. **Pays from $500** for a group of 10 items and contributor copies.

**Tips:** "Know the port destinations we cover. Know our magazine. Demonstrate your voice in your query letter. Send a selection of published writing samples that reveals your range. The three essential things we look for are: 1) an authoritative voice; 2) intimate knowledge of the subject matter; and 3) original material. Having a clear-cut article in mind is a must. Do not query 'with an idea for an article on Aruba.' Outline your proposal and indicate your angle."

**$ $** FAMILY MOTOR COACHING, Official Publication of the Family Motor Coach Association, 8291 Clough Pike, Cincinnati OH 45244-2796. (513)474-3622. Fax: (513)388-5286. E-mail: magazine@fmca.com. Website: http://www.fmca.com. Publishing Director: Pamela Wisby Kay. **Contact:** Robbin Gould, editor. **80% freelance written.** "We prefer that writers be experienced RVers." Monthly magazine emphasizing travel by motorhome, motorhome mechanics, maintenance and other technical information. "*Family Motor Coaching* magazine is edited for the members and prospective members of the Family Motor Coach Association who own or are about to purchase recreational vehicles of the motor coach style and use them exclusively for pleasure. Featured are articles on travel and recreation, association news, meetings, activities, and conventions plus articles on new products. Approximately ⅓ of editorial content is devoted to travel and entertainment, ⅓ to association news, and ⅓ to new products and industry news." Estab. 1963. Circ. 125,000. **Pays on acceptance.** Publishes ms an average of 8 months after acceptance. Buys first North American serial rights. Byline given. Submit seasonal material 2-4 months in advance. Reports in 4 months. Sample copy for $2.50. Writer's guidelines for #10 SASE.

**Nonfiction:** Motorhome travel (various areas of country accessible by motor coach), how-to (do it yourself motor home projects and modifications), bus conversions, humor, interview/profile, new product, technical, nostalgia. **Buys 8-10 mss/issue.** Query with published clips. Length: 1,000-2,000 words. **Pays $100-500.**

**Photos:** State availability of photos with query. Offers no additional payment for b&w contact sheets, 35mm or 2¼×2¼ color transparencies. Captions, photo credits, model releases required. Prefers first North American serial rights but will consider one-time rights on photos only.

**Tips:** "The greatest number of contributions we receive are travel; therefore, that area is the most competitive. However, it also represents the easiest way to break in to our publication. Articles should be written for those traveling by self-contained motor home. The destinations must be accessible to motor home travelers and any peculiar road conditions should be mentioned."

📰 **$ $** FRONTIER MAGAZINE, Adventure Media, 650 S. Orcas St., Suite 103, Seattle WA 98108. (206)762-1922. Fax: (206)762-1886. E-mail: lauras@adventuremedia.com. Editor: Heidi Schuessler. **Contact:** Laura Slavik, managing editor. **60% freelance written.** In-flight magazine published bimonthly covering travel, with special emphasis on the Rocky Mountain states. "*Frontier Magazine* is a sophisticated yet fun-to-read magazine that celebrates the Rocky Mountain lifestyle. It celebrates those attitudes, traditions and issues that define the modern west." Estab. 1998. Circ. 250,000. Pays on publication. Publishes ms an average of 4 months after acceptance. Byline given. Offers 25% kill fee. Buys first North American serial rights. Editorial lead time 4 months. Submit seasonal material 4 months in advance. Accepts queries by mail, e-mail, fax. Reports in 2 months. Sample copy for $2 (shipping and handling). Writer's guidelines for #10 SASE.

**Nonfiction:** Essays, general interest, historical/nostalgic, interview/profile, photo feature, travel, children's stories (8-12 years old). Special issues: Golf guide (June); and Ski guide (November). "We do not accept fiction, religious or how-to articles." **Buys 15 mss/year.** Query with published clips. Length: 300-2,500 words. **Pays 25-30¢/word for assigned articles; $75-600 for unsolicited articles.** Occasionally pays in cash and airline tickets.

**Photos:** State availability of photos with submission. Reviews negatives. Negotiates payment individually. Identification of subjects required. Buys one-time rights.

**Columns/Departments:** Nancy Alton, associate editor. Western Exposure (tourist-oriented events around the route system), 50-500 words; Business along the Divide (interesting or unique businesses), 700 words; and End of the Trail (hotel/restaurant reviews), 700 words. **Buys 30 mss/year.** Query with published clips. **Pays $50-150.**

**Tips:** "Know the airline's route system—we accept stories only from/about these areas. Submit clips with all queries."

**$ $ GO MAGAZINE**, AAA Carolinas, P.O. Box 29600, Charlotte NC 28229-9600. (704)569-7733. Fax: (704)569-7815. E-mail: trcrosby@aaaga.com. Website: www.aaacarolinas.com. **Contact:** Tom Crosby, editor. **10% freelance written.** Bimonthly newspaper covering travel, automotive, safety (traffic) and insurance. "Consumer oriented membership publication providing information on complex or expensive subjects—car buying, vacations, traffic safety problems, etc." Estab. 1928. Circ. 650,000. **Pays on acceptance.** Publishes ms an average of 2 months after acceptance. Buys second serial (reprint) rights, simultaneous rights or makes work-for-hire assignments. Editorial lead time 6 weeks. Submit seasonal material 6 weeks in advance. Accepts queries by mail, fax. Reports in 2 weeks on queries; 2 months on mss. Sample copy for SAE with 4 first-class stamps. Writer's guidelines for #10 SASE.
**Nonfiction:** How-to (fix auto, travel safety, etc.), travel, automotive insurance, traffic safety. Special issues: Canadian Rockies, Alaska, Amelia Island, Pinehurst 1998 Open, Hawaii (November-December 1998); European Tours, Tennessee Places to Visit, North Carolina Skiing, Disney—What's New in 1999, Alaska Cruises, Alaska Vacation Packages (January 1999); Alaska Vacation Packages, Georgia Places to Visit, Cruises in General, Mexico, European Destinations, Caribbean Islands, (February 1999); Disney, Spring Festivals in the Carolinas, Caribbean Islands and Cruises, Spring/European Cruises, European Destinations, (March-April 1999). **Buys 12-14 mss/year.** Query with published clips. Length: 600-900 words. **Pays 15¢/published word.**
**Photos:** Send photos with submission. Offers no additional payment for photos accepted with ms. Buys one-time rights.

**$ $ $ $ GOLF & TRAVEL**, Turnstile Publishing Co., 49 W. 45th St., 6th Floor, New York NY 10036. Fax: (212)536-9888. E-mail: golfntravl@aol.com. **Contact:** Mary Arendt, managing editor. **50% freelance written.** Bimonthly magazine. *Golf & Travel* wants "solid travel writing with a critical eye. No fluff. No common tourist stops unless you've got a unique angle. Destination stories with golf as one of the elements, but not the only element." Estab. 1997. Circ. 160,000. **Pays on acceptance.** Publishes ms an average of 3 months after acceptance. Byline given. Buys first rights or all rights. Editorial lead time 6 months. Submit seasonal material 18 months in advance. Replies only if interested. Sample copy for $3.95 plus postage; (800)678-9717. Writer's guidelines for #10 SASE.
**Nonfiction:** Interview/profile, travel. "No articles about golf courses only; no articles on common golf destinations; no articles written in 'fluff' language." **Buys 30 mss/year.** Query with published clips. Length: 100-2,500 words. **Pays $50-5,000.** Sometimes pays expenses of writers on assignment.
**Columns/Departments:** Starter (golf packages, golf events, golf destination news), 100-150 words; Road & Driver (great road trips with golf along the way), 1,500 words; Urban Outings (places to play golf within city limits), 1,000-1,500 words; Main Course (golf/golf destinations and food/wine), 1,200 words; Fairway Living (destination or issue-related stories about places to live that offer good golf environment), 1,200-1,500 words; Suite Spot (lesser known golf resort), 250 words. Query with published clips. **Pays $50-2,500.**
**Fiction:** Publishes novel excerpts.
**Tips:** "Must be established travel writers with great destination stories in their clips file. Clips must demonstrate unusual angles—off the beaten path. Knowledge of golf extremely helpful. Straight golf writers are not encouraged to query. We do not cover golf instruction, golf equipment or golf teaching aids. We are interested in writers who can combine the two subjects of golf and travel with a third element that is not easily named but has to do with a sophisticated tone, an intelligent attitude, a sensitive eye and, where appropriate, a sense of humor or irony. Magazines whose editorial voice we like include *Town & Country, Men's Journal, Departures, Saveur* and *Smart Money.*"

**$ HEALING RETREATS & SPAS**, 24 E. Cota St., Suite 101, Santa Barbara CA 93101. (805)962-7107. Fax: (805)962-1337. E-mail: walters@grayphics.com. **Editor:** Anthony Carroccio. **Contact:** E.M. Kennedy, managing editor. **90% freelance written.** Bimonthly magazine covering retreats, spas, health and lifestyle issues. "We try to present healing and nurturing *alternatives* for the global community, and provide a bridge between travel, health, and New Age magazine material." Estab. 1996. Circ. 45,000. Pays on publication. Publishes ms within 1 year after acceptance. Byline given. Buys one-time rights. Editorial lead time 6 months. Submit seasonal material 3 months in advance. Accepts queries by mail, e-mail, fax. Reports in 1 month on queries; 2 months on mss. Sample copy for $6.95. Writer's guidelines for #10 SASE.
**Nonfiction:** Book excerpts, general interest, how-to (at-home therapies), inspirational, interview/profile, new product, personal experience, photo feature, travel (spas and retreats only), health alternatives. **Buys 50 mss/year.** Query with published clips. Length: 700-3,000 words. **Pays $25-75.** Pays writers with contributor copies or other premiums if they want 20 or more copies for self-promotion.
**Photos:** Send photos with submission. Reviews transparencies. Offers no additional payment for photos accepted with ms. Captions required. Buys one-time rights.
**Columns/Departments: Buys 40 mss/year.** Send complete ms. **Pays $25-50.**
**Tips:** "Writers can break in with well-written, first-hand knowledge of an alternative health issue or therapy. Even our travel pieces require this type of knowledge. Once a writer proves capable, other assignments can follow."

**$ $ HIGHWAYS, The Official Publication of the Good Sam Club**, TL Enterprises Inc., 2575 Vista Del Mar, Ventura CA 93001. (805)667-4100. Fax: (805)667-4454. E-mail: repstein@tl.com. Website: http://www.goodsamclub.com/highways. **Contact:** Ronald H. Epstein, editor. **40% freelance written.** Monthly magazine (November/December issues combined) covering recreational vehicle lifestyle. "All of our readers—since we're a membership publication—own or have a motorhome, trailer, camper or van conversion. Thus, our stories include road-travel conditions and terms and information about campgrounds and locations. Estab. 1966. Circ. 925,000. **Pays on acceptance.** Publishes ms an average of 6 months after acceptance. Byline given. Offers 50% kill fee. Buys first North American serial and electronic rights. Editorial lead time 15 weeks. Submit seasonal material 5 months in advance. Accepts queries by mail, e-mail, fax. Accepts simultaneous submissions. Reports in 3 weeks on queries; 1 month on mss. Sample copy and writer's guidelines free.

**Nonfiction:** How-to (repair/replace something on an RV); humor; technical; travel; (all RV related). **Buys 15-25 mss/year.** Query or send complete ms. Length: 1,500-2,500 words. **Pays $150-500 for unsolicited articles.**

**Photos:** Send photos with submission. Reviews contact sheets, negatives, transparencies, prints. No additional payment for photos accepted with ms. Captions, model releases, identification of subjects required. Buys one-time rights.

**Columns/Departments:** Beginners (people buying an RV for the first time), 1,200 words; View Points (issue-related, 750 words. Query. **Pays $200-250.**

**Tips:** "Understand RVs and RVing. It's a unique lifestyle and different than typical traveling. Aside from that, we welcome good writers!"

### HISTORIC TRAVELER, The Guide to Great Historic Destinations

- Primedia sold *Historic Traveler* to American Express Publishing, which plans to close the title and fold its subscribers into *Travel & Leisure*.

**\$ \$ INTERNATIONAL LIVING**, Agora Island, Ltd., St. Catherine's Hall, Catherine St., Waterford, Ireland. E-mail: intlliv@compuserve.com. Editorial Director: Jennifer Stevens. **Contact:** Deirdre Gough, assistant editor. **50% freelance written.** Monthly newsletter covering retirement, travel, investment and real estate overseas. "We do not want descriptions of how beautiful places are. We want specifics, recommendations, contacts, prices, names, addresses, phone numbers, etc. We want offbeat locations and off-the-beaten-track spots." Estab. 1981. Circ. 500,000. Pays on publication. Publishes ms an average of 3 months after acceptance. Byline given. Offers 25-50% kill fee. Buys all rights. Editorial lead time 2 months. Submit seasonal material 3 months in advance. Accepts simultaneous submissions. Reports in 2 months. Sample copy for #10 SASE. Writer's guidelines free.

**Nonfiction:** How-to (get a job, buy real estate, get cheap airfares overseas, start a business, etc.), interview/profile (entrepreneur abroad), new product (travel), personal experience, travel, shopping, cruises, etc. No descriptive, run-of-the-mill travel articles. "We produce special issues each year focusing on Asia, Eastern Europe and Latin America." **Buys 100 mss/year.** Send complete ms. Length: 500-2,000 words. **Pays $200-500 for assigned articles; $100-400 for unsolicited articles.**

**Photos:** State availability of photos with submission. Reviews contact sheets, negatives, transparencies or prints. Offers $50/photo. Identification of subjects required. Buys all rights.

**Fillers:** Facts. **Buys 20/year.** Length: 50-250 words. **Pays $25-100.**

**Tips:** "Make recommendations in your articles. We want first-hand accounts. Tell us how to do things: how to catch a cab, order a meal, buy a souvenir, buy property, start a business, etc. *International Living*'s philosophy is that the world is full of opportunities to do whatever you want, whenever you want. We will show you how."

**\$ THE INTERNATIONAL RAILWAY TRAVELER**, Hardy Publishing Co., Inc., Editorial offices: P.O. Box 3747, San Diego CA 92163. (619)260-1332. Fax: (619)296-4220. E-mail: irt.trs@worldnet.att.net. **Contact:** Gena Holle, editor. **100% freelance written.** Monthly newsletter covering rail travel. Estab. 1983. Circ. 3,500. Pays within 3 months of publication date. Byline given. Offers 25% kill fee. Buys first North American serial rights and all electronic rights. Editorial lead time 4 months. Submit seasonal material 6 months in advance. Query for electronic submissions. Reports in 1 month on queries; 2 months on mss. Sample copy for $6. Writer's guidelines for #10 SASE.

**Nonfiction:** Book reviews, general interest, how-to, interview/profile, new product, opinion, personal experience, travel. **Buys 24-30 mss/year.** Query with published clips or send complete ms. Include SASE for return of ms. Length: 800-1,200 words. **Pays 3¢/word.**

**Photos:** Send photos with submission. Include SASE for return of photos. Reviews contact sheets, negatives, transparencies, prints (8×10 preferred; will accept 5×7). Offers $10 b&w; $20 cover photo. Costs of converting slides and negatives to prints are deducted from payment. Captions and identification of subjects required. Buys one-time rights.

**Tips:** "We want factual articles concerning world rail travel which would not appear in the mass-market travel magazines. IRT readers and editors love stories and photos on off-beat train trips as well as more conventional train trips covered in unconventional ways. With IRT, the focus is on the train travel experience, not a blow-by-blow description of the view from the train window. Be sure to include details (prices, passes, schedule info, etc.) for readers who might want to take the trip."

**★ \$ \$ \$ \$ ISLANDS, An International Magazine**, Islands Publishing Company, P.O. Box 4768, Santa Barbara CA 93140-4728. (805)745-7100. Fax: (805)745-7102. E-mail: editorial@islandsmag.com. Website: http://www.islandsmag.com. **Contact:** Joan Tapper, editor. **95% freelance written.** Works with established writers. Bimonthly magazine covering "accessible and once-in-a-lifetime islands from many different perspectives: travel, culture, lifestyle. We ask our authors to give us the essence of the island and do it with literary flair." Estab. 1981. Circ. 200,000. **Pays on acceptance.** Publishes ms an average of 8 months after acceptance. Byline given. Offers 25% kill fee. Buys all rights. Query by mail, e-mail, fax. Reports in 2 months on queries; 6 weeks on ms. Sample copy for $6. Writer's guidelines for #10 SASE or on website.

- Ranked as one of the best markets for freelance writers in *Writer's Yearbook* magazine's annual "Top 100 Markets," January 1999.

**Nonfiction:** General interest, personal experience, photo feature, any island-related material. No service stories. "Each issue contains 5-6 feature articles and 6-7 departments. Any authors who wish to be commissioned should send a detailed proposal for an article, an estimate of costs (if applicable) and samples of previously published work." **Buys 25 feature mss/year.** "The majority of our feature manuscripts are commissioned." Query with published clips or send complete ms. Feature length: 2,000-4,000 words. **Pays $1,000-4,000.** Pays expenses of writers on assignment.

**Photos:** State availability of or send photos with query or ms. Pays $75-300 for 35mm transparencies. "Fine color photography is a special attraction of *Islands*, and we look for superb composition, technical quality and editorial applicability." Label slides with name and address, include captions, and submit in protective plastic sleeves. Identification of subjects required. Buys one-time rights.

**Columns/Departments:** Arts, Profiles, Nature, Sports, Lifestyle, Encounters, Island Hopping featurettes—all island related, 750-1,500 words; Brief Logbook (highly-focused item on some specific aspect of islands), 500 words. **Buys 50 mss/year.** Query with published clips. **Pays $100-700.**

**Tips:** "A freelancer can best break in to our publication with short (500-1,000 word) departments or Logbooks that are highly focused on some aspect of island life, history, people, etc. Stay away from general, sweeping articles. We are always looking for topics for our Islanders and Logbook pieces. We will be using big name writers for major features; will continue to use newcomers and regulars for columns and departments."

**$ $ LEISURE WORLD**, Ontario Motorist Publishing Company, 1253 Ouellette Ave., Box 580, Windsor, Ontario N8X 1J3 Canada. (519)971-3207. Fax: (519)977-1197. E-mail: ompc@ompc.com. Website: http://www.ompc.com. **Contact:** Douglas O'Neil, editor. **20% freelance written.** Bimonthly magazine distributed to members of the Canadian Automobile Association in southwestern and midwestern Ontario, the Niagara Peninsula and the maritime provinces. Editorial content is focused on travel, entertainment and leisure time pursuits of interest to CAA members." Estab. 1988. Circ. 345,000. Pays on publication. Publishes ms an average of 2 months after acceptance. Buys first rights only. Submit seasonal material 4 months in advance. Accepts queries by e-mail. Reports in 2 months. Sample copy for $2. Writer's guidelines for SASE or on website.

**Nonfiction:** Lifestyle, humor, travel. **Buys 20 mss/year.** Send complete ms. Length: 800-1,200 words. **Pays $50-200.**

**Photos:** Reviews slides only. Offers $60/photo. Captions, model releases required. Buys one-time rights.

**Tips:** "We are most interested in travel destination articles that offer a personal, subjective and positive point of view on international (including U.S.) destinations. Good quality color slides are a must."

**$ $ MICHIGAN LIVING**, AAA Michigan, 1 Auto Club Dr., Dearborn MI 48126-2963. (313)336-1506. Fax: (313)336-1344. E-mail: michliving@aol.com **Contact:** Ron Garbinski, editor. **50% freelance written.** Monthly magazine. "*Michigan Living* is edited for the residents of Michigan and contains information about travel and lifestyle activities in Michigan, the U.S. and around the world. Articles also cover automotive developments, highway safety. Regular features include a car care column, a calendar of coming events, restaurant and overnight accomodations reviews and news of special interest to Auto Club members." Estab. 1922. Circ. 1,099,000. Pays on publication. Publishes ms an average of 6 months after acceptance. Buys first North American serial rights. Offers 20% kill fee. Byline given. Submit seasonal material 9 months in advance. Accepts queries by mail, e-mail. Reports in 6 weeks. Free sample copy and writer's guidelines.

● For writers and photographers to reecive a monthly e-mail message sent by *Michigan Living*'s editor, please send your e-mail address to michliving@aol.com.

**Nonfiction:** Travel articles on US and Canadian topics. **Buys few unsolicited mss/year.** Query. Length: 200-1,000 words. **Pays $75-600.**

**Photos:** Photos purchased with accompanying ms. Captions required. Pays $400 for cover photos; $50-400 for color transparencies.

**Tips:** "In addition to descriptions of things to see and do, articles should contain accurate, current information on costs the traveler would encounter on his trip. Items such as lodging, meal and entertainment expenses should be included, not in the form of a balance sheet but as an integral part of the piece. We want the sounds, sights, tastes, smells of a place or experience so one will feel he has been there and knows if he wants to go back. Prefers most travel-related queries via e-mail rather than mail."

**$ $ MOTORHOME**, TL Enterprises, 2575 Vista Del Mar Dr., Ventura CA 93001. (805)667-4100. Fax: (805)667-4484. Website: http://motorhome.tl.com. Editorial Director: Barbara Leonard. **Contact:** Sherry McBride, senior managing editor. **60% freelance written.** Monthly. "*MotorHome* is a magazine for owners and prospective buyers of self-propelled recreational vehicles who are active outdoorsmen and wide-ranging travelers. We cover all aspects of the RV lifestyle; editorial material is both technical and non-technical in nature. Regular features include tests and descriptions of various models of motorhomes and mini-motorhomes, travel adventures and hobbies pursued in such vehicles, objective analysis of equipment and supplies for such vehicles and do-it-yourself articles. Guides within the magazine provide listings of manufacturers, rentals and other sources of equipment and accessories of interest to enthusiasts. Articles must have an RV slant and excellent transparencies accompanying text." Estab. 1968. Circ. 140,000. **Pays on acceptance.** Publishes ms within 1 year of acceptance. Byline given. Offers 33% kill fee. Buys first North American serial and electronic rights. Editorial lead time 4 months. Submit seasonal material 6 months in advance. Query by mail, fax. Reports in 3 weeks on queries; 2 months on mss. Sample copy free. Guidelines for #10 SASE.

○ Break in with *Crossroads* items.

**Nonfiction:** How-to, humor, new product, personal experience, photo feature, technical, travel, profiles, recreation, lifestyle, legislation, all RV related. No diaries of RV trips or negative RV experiences. **Buys 120 mss/year.** Query with or without published clips. Length: 250-2,500 words. **Pays $300-600.**

**Photos:** Send 35mm transparencies with submission. Offers no additional payment for art accepted with ms. Pays $400-600 for covers. Captions, model releases and identification of subjects required. Buys one-time rights.

**Columns/Departments:** Crossroads (offbeat briefs of people, places of interest to travelers), 100-200 words; Keepers (tips, recipes). Query or send complete ms. **Pays $100-200.**

**Tips:** "If a freelancer has an idea for a good article, it's best to send a query and include possible photo locations to illustrate the article. We prefer to assign articles and work with the author in developing a piece suitable to our audience. We are in a specialized field with very enthusiastic readers who appreciate articles by authors who actually enjoy motorhomes. The following areas are most open: Crossroads—brief descriptions of places to see or special events, with one photo/slide, 100-200 words; travel—places to go with a motorhome, where to stay, what to see, etc.; we prefer not to use travel articles where the motorhome is secondary; and How-to—personal projects on author's motorhomes to make travel easier, etc., unique projects, accessories. Also articles on unique personalities, motorhomes, humorous experiences. Be sure to submit appropriate photography (35mm slides) with at least one good motorhome shot to illustrate travel articles. No phone queries, please."

**$ $ $ $ NATIONAL GEOGRAPHIC TRAVELER**, National Geographic Society, 1145 17th St. N.W., Washington DC 20036. Website: http://nationalgeographic.com/traveler. Editor: Keith Bellows. Managing Editor: Paul Martin. **Contact:** Sheila Buckmaster, Steven Knipp or Jonathan Tourtellot, senior editors. **90% freelance written.** Bimonthly magazine. "*National Geographic Traveler* is filled with practical information and detailed maps designed to encourage readers to explore and travel. Features domestic and foreign destinations, photography, the economics of travel, adventure trips, and weekend getaways to help readers plan a variety of excursions. Our writers need to equip our readers with inspiration to travel. We want lively writing—personal anecdotes with telling details, not an A to Z account of a destination." Estab. 1984. Circ. 720,000. **Pays on acceptance.** Publishes ms 8-12 months after acceptance. Byline given. Offers 30% kill fee. Buys one-time rights. Editorial lead time 3-12 months. Submit seasonal material 1 year in advance. Accepts queries by mail. Reports in 4 weeks. Sample copy and writer's guidelines free.

**Nonfiction:** Essays, general interest, historical/nostalgic, how-to, humor, inspirational (destinations), new product (travel oriented), opinion, personal experience, photo feature, travel. "We do not want to see general, impersonal, fact-clogged articles. We do not want to see any articles similar to those we, or our competitors, have run recently." **Buys 80-100 mss/year.** Query with published clips. Length: 750-2,500 words. **Pays $1/word and up.** Pays expenses of writers on assignment.

**Columns/Departments:** Norie Danyliw or Jayne Wise, associate editor; Carolyn Haga, George Stone, assistant editors. Smart Traveler (travel trends, sources, strategies and solutions); Travel Wise (fact-intensive); Metropolis (the best of a city); Without Reservation (unique and special places to stay). **Buys 150-200 mss/year.** Query with published clips. **Pays 50¢/word and up.**

▢ The online magazine carries original content not found in the print edition. Contact: Tom Giovanni, online editor.

**Tips:** "Familiarize yourself with our magazine—not only the types of stories we run, but the types of stories we've run in the past. Formulate a story idea, and then send a detailed query, recent clips and contact information to the editor responsible for the section you'd like to be published in." No unsolicited photographs or mss.

**N $ $ NATURALLY, Nude Recreation Travel**, Events Unlimited, P.O. Box 317, Newfoundland NJ 07435-0317. (973)697-3552. Fax: (973)697-8313. E-mail: naturally@nac.net. Website: http://www.internaturally.com. **Contact:** Bernard Loibl, editor. **90% freelance written.** Quarterly magazine covering nude recreation and travel. "*Naturally* nude recreation looks at why millions of people believe that removing clothes in public is a good idea, and at places specifically created for that purpose—with good humor, but also in earnest. *Naturally* nude recreation takes you to places where your personal freedom is the only agenda, and to places where textile-free living is a serious commitment." Estab. 1981. Circ. 35,000. Pays on publication. Byline given. Buys first rights. Editorial lead time 2 months. Submit seasonal material 2 months in advance. Accepts queries by mail, e-mail, fax, phone. Accepts simultaneous submissions. Sample copy for $9. Writer's guidelines free.

**Nonfiction:** General interest, interview/profile, personal experience, photo feature, travel. **Buys 8-12 mss/year.** Send complete ms. Length: 2 pages. **Pays $70/published page including photos.** Frequent contributors and regular columnists, who develop a following through *Naturally*, are paid from the Frequent Contributors Budget. Payments increase on the basis of frequency of participation

**Reprints:** Accepts previously published submissions.

**Photos:** Send photos with submission. Reviews contact sheets, negatives, transparencies and prints. Offers no additional payment for photos accepted with ms. Buys one-time rights.

**Fillers:** Cheryl Hanenberg, associate editor. Anecdotes, facts, gags to be illustrated by cartoonist, newsbreaks, short humor.

**Tips:** "*Naturally* nude recreation invokes the philosophies of naturism and nudism, but also activities and beliefs in the mainstream that express themselves, barely: spiritual awareness, New Age customs, pagan and religious rites, alternative and fringe lifestyle beliefs, artistic expressions and many individual nude interests. Our higher purpose is simply to help restore our sense of self. Although the term 'nude recreation' may, for some, conjure up visions of sexual frivolities inappropriate for youngsters—because that can also be technically true—these topics are outside the scope of *Naturally* magazine. Here the emphasis is on the many varieties of human beings, of all ages and backgrounds, recreating in their most natural state, at extraordinary places, their reasons for doing so, and the benefits they derive."

**$ $ NEW YORK DAILY NEWS**, Travel Section, 450 W. 33rd St., New York NY 10001. (212)210-1699. Fax: (212)210-2203. **Contact:** Linda Perney, travel editor. **30% freelance written.** Prefers to work with published/established writers. Weekly tabloid. Circ. 1.8 million. Pays on publication. Publishes ms an average of 3 months after acceptance. Byline given. Submit seasonal material 4 months in advance. Reports "as soon as possible."
**Nonfiction:** General interest, historical/nostalgic, travel. Query by mail only. "Most of our articles involve practical trips that the average family can afford—even if it's one you can't afford every year. We rarely run stories for the Armchair Traveler, an exotic and usually expensive trip. We are looking for professional quality work from professional writers who know what they are doing. The pieces have to give information and be entertaining at the same time. No 'How I Spent My Summer Vacation' type articles. No PR hype." **Pays $200.**
**Photos:** "Good pictures always help sell good stories." State availability of photos with ms. Reviews contact sheets and negatives. Captions and identification of subjects required. Buys all rights.

**$ $ NEWSDAY**, 235 Pinelawn Rd., Melville NY 11747. (516)843-2980. Fax: (516)843-2065. E-mail: travel@news day.com. **Contact:** Marjorie Robins, travel editor. **30% freelance written.** General readership of Sunday newspaper travel section. Estab. 1940. Circ. 650,000. Buys all rights for New York area only. **Buys 75 mss/year.** Pays on publication. Simultaneous submissions considered if outside the New York area.
**Nonfiction:** No assignments to freelancers. No query letters. Complete typewritten mss only accepted on spec. All trips must be paid for in full by writer; proof required. Service stories preferred. Destination pieces must be for the current year. Length: 1,200 words maximum. **Pays $75-350.**
**Photos:** Color slides and b&w photos accepted: pays $50-250, depending on size of photo used.

**N: $ $ NORTHEAST OUTDOORS**, Woodall Publications, 13975 W. Polo Trail Dr., Lake Forest IL 60045. (800)323-9078. Fax: (847)362-6844. E-mail: bpeterson@woodallpub.com. Website: http://www.woodalls.com. **Contact:** Brent Peterson, editor. **50% freelance written.** Works with a small number of new/unpublished writers each year. Monthly tabloid covering family camping in the Northeastern US. Estab. 1968. Circ. 30,000. Pays on publication. Publishes ms an average of 4 months after acceptance. Byline given. Offers 50% kill fee. Buys first rights and regional rights. Submit seasonal material 5 months in advance. Accepts queries by mail, e-mail. Reports in 2 weeks. Sample copy for 9×12 SAE with 4 first-class stamps. Writer's guidelines for #10 SASE.
- Break in with regional articles showcasing the RV lifestyle. Local destinations, camp ground news and the like are the best ways to get published.
**Nonfiction:** How-to (camping), new product (company and RV releases only), recreation vehicle and camping experiences in the Northeast, features about private (only) campgrounds and places to visit in the Northeast while RVing, personal experience, photo feature, travel. "No diaries of trips, dog or fishing-only stories, or anything not camping and RV related." Query. Length: 300-1,500 words. **Pays 10¢/word.**
**Reprints:** Send typed ms with rights for sale noted and info about when and where it previously appeared.
**Photos:** Send photos with submission. Reviews contact sheets and 5×7 prints or larger. Captions and identification of subjects required. Pays $5/photo. Buys one-time rights.
**Columns/Departments:** Northeast News (500-1,000 words), Going Places (800-1,000 words). **Pays 10¢/word.**
**Tips:** "We most often need material on private campgrounds and attractions in New England. We are looking for upbeat, first-person stories about where to camp, what to do or see, and how to enjoy camping."

**$ PATHFINDERS, Travel Information for People of Color**, 6424 N. 13th St., Philadelphia PA 19126. (215)927-9950. Fax: (215)927-3359. E-mail: blaktravel@aol.com. Website: http://www.Pathfinderstravel.com. **Contact:** Pamela Thomas, editor-in-chief. **99% freelance written.** Quarterly magazine covering travel for minorities, primarily African-Americans. "We look for lively, original, well-written stories that provide a good sense of place, with useful information and fresh ideas about travel and the travel industry. Our main audience is African-Americans, though we do look for articles relating to other persons of color: Native Americans, Hispanics and Asians." Estab. 1997. Circ. 50,000. Pays on publication. Byline given. Buys first North American serial rights and electronic rights. Reports in 2 months. Sample copy at bookstores (Barnes & Noble, Borders, Waldenbooks) or by e-mail request. Writer's guidelines on website.
- Break in through *Looking Back*, 600-word essay on travel from personal experience that provides a historical perspective.
**Nonfiction:** Essays, historical/nostalgic, how-to, personal experience, photo feature, travel, all vacation travel oriented. **Buys 16-20 mss/year.** Send complete ms. Length: 1,200-1,400 words for cover stories, 1,000-1,200 words features. **Pays $100.**
**Photos:** State availability of photos with submission.
**Columns/Departments:** Chef's Table, Post Cards from Home, 500-600 words. Send complete ms. **Pays $50.**
**Tips:** "We prefer seeing finished articles rather than queries. All articles are submitted on spec. Articles should be saved in either WordPerfect of Microsoft Word, double-spaced and saved as a text-only file. Include a hard copy. E-mail articles are accepted only by request of the editor."

**★ $ $ PORTHOLE MAGAZINE, A View of the Sea and Beyond**, Panoff Publishing, 7100 W. Commercial Blvd., Suite 106, Ft. Lauderdale FL 33319. (954)746-5554. Fax: (954)746-5244. E-mail: portholeed@ppigroup.com. Website: www.porthole.com. **Contact:** Lesley Abravanel, managing editor. **90% freelance written.** Bimonthly magazine. "*Porthole* is a first-of-its-kind, internationally distributed glossy consumer cruise and travel magazine, distributed by Time Warner." Estab. 1994. Circ. 65,000. Pays on publication. Publishes ms an average of 6 months after acceptance. Byline given. Offers 35% kill fee. Buys first international serial rights and second serial (reprint) rights and makes work-for-hire assignments. Editorial lead time 3 months. Submit seasonal material 4 months in advance. Query by mail, e-mail. Accepts simultaneous submissions. Reports in 1 month. Sample copy for 8×11 SAE with $3 postage. Writer's guidelines for #10 SASE.

**Nonfiction:** Essays (your cruise experience), general interest (cruise-related), historical/nostalgic, how-to (i.e., pick a cruise, not get seasick, travel tips), humor, interview/profile (crew on board or industry executives), new product, personal experience, photo features, travel (off-the-beaten path, adventure, ports, destinations, cruises), onboard fashion, spa articles, duty-free shopping, port reviews, ship reviews. No articles on destinations that can't be reached by ship. "Please don't write asking for a cruise so that you can do an article! You must be an experienced cruise writer to do a ship review." **Buys 75 mss/year.** Query with published clips or send letter with complete ms. Length: 400-2,000 words, average 1,100. **Pays 25¢/word average.** Sometimes pays expenses of writers on assignment

**Reprints:** Send photocopy of article or typed ms with rights for sale noted and information about when and where the article previously appeared. Negotiates payment.

**Photos:** Contact: Linda Douthat, creative director. State availability of photos with submission. Reviews transparencies. Negotiates payment individually. Captions, model releases, identification of subjects required. Buys one-time rights.

**Columns/Departments:** "My" Port City (personal accounts of experiences in certain destination), 1,200 words; Beautiful Thing (spa service on board), 700 words; Brass Tacks (travel tips, short bits); Personality Plus (intriguing travel-oriented profiles), 400 words; Fashion File (onboard fashion), 400 words. Also humor, cruise cuisine, shopping, photo essays. **Buys 50 mss/year.** Query with published clips or send letter with complete ms. **Pays 25¢/word.**

**Fillers:** Facts, gags to be illustrated by cartoonist, newsbreaks, short humor. **Buys 30/year.** Length: 25-200 words. **Pays 25¢/word.**

□ The online magazine carries original content not found in the print edition. Contact: Lesley Abravanel, online editor.

**Tips:** "We prefer to be queried via e-mail. Clips are not necessary. Offbeat, original travel stories are preferred. Tie-ins to celebrity culture, pop culture, arts/entertainment, politics, cuisine, architecture, are highly regarded."

**$ $ ST. MAARTEN NIGHTS**, Nights Publications Inc., 1831 Rene Levesque Blvd. West, Montreal, Quebec H3H 1R4 Canada. Fax: (514)931-6273. E-mail: editor@nightspublications.com. Website: http://www.nightspublications.com. Managing Editor: Zelly Zuskin. **Contact:** Stephen Trotter, editor. **90% freelance written.** Annual magazine covering the St. Maarten/St. Martin vacation experience seeking "upbeat entertaining lifestyle articles. Our audience is the North American vacationer." Estab. 1981. Circ. 225,000. **Pays on acceptance.** Publishes ms an average of 9 months after acceptance. Byline given. Buys first North American serial and first Caribbean rights. Editorial lead time 1 month. Accepts queries by mail, e-mail, fax. Reports in 2 weeks on queries; 1 month on mss. Sample copy for $5 (make check payable to Nights Publications Inc.). Writer's guidelines free.

**Nonfiction:** Lifestyle with a lively, upscale touch. General interest, colorful profiles of islanders, historical/nostalgia, how-to (gamble), sailing, humor, inspirational, interview/profile, opinion, ecological (eco-tourism), personal experience, photo feature, travel, local culture, art, activities, entertainment, night life, special events, topics relative to vacationers in St. Maarten/St. Martin. "No negative pieces or stale rewrites or cliché copy." **Buys 8-10 mss/year.** Query with published clips and SASE with Canadian postage or IRC. Length: 250-750 words. **Pays $100-200.**

**Photos:** State availability of photos with submission. Reviews transparencies. Offers $50/photo. Captions, model releases, identification of subjects required. Buys one-time rights.

**Tips:** "Our style is upbeat, friendly, fluid and descriptive. Our magazines cater to tourists who are already at the destination, so ensure your story is of interest to this particular audience. We welcome stories that offer fresh angles to familiar tourist-related topics."

**$ $ TIMES OF THE ISLANDS, The International Magazine of the Turks & Caicos Islands**, Times Publications Ltd., P.O. Box 234, Caribbean Place, Providenciales Turks & Caicos Islands, British West Indies. Fax: (649)941-3402. E-mail: timespub@tciway.tc. Website: www.timespub.tc. **Contact:** Kathy Borsuk, editor. **80% freelance written.** Quarterly magazine covering the Turks & Caicos Islands. "*Times of the Islands* is used by the public and private sector to attract visitors and potential investors/developers to the Islands. It strives to portray the advantages of the Islands and their friendly people. It is also used by tourists, once on-island, to learn about services, activities and accommodations available." Estab. 1988. Circ. 5,500-8,000. Pays on publication. Publishes ms an average of 6 months after acceptance. Byline given. Buys second serial (reprint) rights and publication rights for 6 months with respect to other publications distributed in Caribbean. Editorial lead time 4 months. Submit seasonal material 4 months in advance. Accepts simultaneous submissions. Accepts queries by mail, e-mail, fax. Reports in 6 weeks on queries; 2 months on mss. "Keep in mind, mail to Islands is SLOW. Faxing can speed response time." Sample copy for $4 and postage between Miami and your destination. Writer's guidelines for #10 SASE.

**Nonfiction:** Book excerpts or reviews, essays, general interest (Caribbean art, culture, cooking, crafts), historical/nostalgic, humor, interview/profile (locals), personal experience (trips to the Islands), photo feature, technical (island businesses), travel, nature, ecology, business (offshore finance), watersports. **Buys 30 mss/year.** Query. Length: 500-3,000 words. **Pays $200-600.**

**Reprints:** Send photocopy of article along with information about when and where it previously appeared. Send information about when and where the article previously appeared. Pay varies.

**Photos:** Send photos with submission. Reviews slides, prints or digital photos. Offers no additional payment for photos accepted with ms. Pays $15-100/photo. Identification of subjects required.

**Columns/Departments:** Profiles from Abroad (profiles of T&C Islanders who are doing something outstanding internationally), 500 words. **Buys 4 mss/year.** Query. **Pays $100-200.** On Holiday (unique experiences of visitors to Turks & Caicos), 500-1,500 words. **Buys 4 mss/year.** Query. **Pays $200-300.**

**Fiction:** Adventure (sailing, diving), ethnic (Caribbean), historical (Caribbean), humorous (travel-related), mystery, novel excerpts. **Buys 1 ms/year.** "Would buy 3-4 if available." Query. Length: 1,000-2,000 words. **Pays $250-400.**

**Tips:** "Make sure that the query/article specifically relates to the Turks and Caicos Islands. The theme can be general (ecotourism, for instance), but the manuscript should contain specific and current references to the Islands. We're a high-quality magazine, with a small budget and staff and are very open-minded to ideas (and manuscripts). Writers who have visited the Islands at least once would probably have a better perspective from which to write."

⭐ $ **TRANSITIONS ABROAD**, P.O. Box 1300, Amherst MA 01004-1300. (413)256-3414. Fax: (413)256-0373. E-mail: editor@transitionsabroad.com. Website: http://www.transitionsabroad.com. Editor/Publisher: Clay Hubbs. **Contact**: David Cline, managing editor. **80-90% freelance written.** Eager to work with new/unpublished writers. Magazine resource for low-budget international travel, often with an educational or work component. Focus is on the alternatives to mass tourism. Estab. 1977. Circ. 20,000. Pays on publication. Buys first rights and second (reprint) rights. Byline given. Accepts queries by mail, e-mail, fax. Reports in 1 month. Sample copy for $6.25. Writer's guidelines and topics schedule for #10 SAS, by e-mail or on website.

**Nonfiction:** Lead articles (up to 1,500 words) provide first-hand practical information on independent travel to featured country or region (see topics schedule). Pays $75-150. Also, how to find educational and specialty travel opportunities, practical information (evaluation of courses, special interest and study tours, economy travel), travel (new learning and cultural travel ideas). Foreign travel only. Few destination ("tourist") pieces. *Transitions Abroad* is a resource magazine for independent, educated, and adventurous travelers, not for armchair travelers or those addicted to packaged tours or cruises. Emphasis on information—which must be usable by readers—and on interaction with people in host country. **Buys 20 unsolicited mss/issue.** Query with credentials and SASE. Length: 500-1,500 words. **Pays $25-150.** Include author's bio with submissions.

**Photos:** Send photos with ms. Pays $10-45 for prints (color acceptable, b&w preferred), $125 for covers (b&w only). Photos increase likelihood of acceptance. Buys one-time rights. Captions and ID on photos required.

**Columns/Departments:** Worldwide Travel Bargains (destinations, activities and accomodations for budget travelers—featured in every issue); Tour and Program Notes (new courses or travel programs); Travel Resources (new information and ideas for independent travel); Working Traveler (how to find jobs and what to expect); Activity Vacations (travel opportunities that involve action and learning, usually by direct involvement in host culture); Responsible Travel (information on community-organized tours). **Buys 10/issue.** Send complete ms. Length: 1,000 words maximum. **Pays $20-50.**

**Fillers:** Info Exchange (information, preferably first-hand—having to do with travel, particularly offbeat educational travel and work or study abroad). **Buys 10/issue.** Length: 750 words maximum. **Pays $20.**

**Tips:** "We like nuts and bolts stuff, practical information, especially on how to work, live, and cut costs abroad. Our readers want usable information on planning a travel itinerary. Be specific: names, addresses, current costs. We are very interested in educational and long-stay travel and study abroad for adults and senior citizens. *Overseas Travel Planner* published each year in July provides best information sources on work, study, and independent travel abroad. Each bimonthly issue contains a worldwide directory of educational and specialty travel programs."

⭐ $ $ **TRAVEL AMERICA, The U.S. Vacation Magazine**, World Publishing Co., 990 Grove St., Evanston IL 60201-4370. (847)491-6440. Editor-in-Chief/Associate Publisher: Bob Meyers. **Contact**: Randy Mink, managing editor. **80% freelance written.** Bimonthly magazine covering US vacation travel. Estab. 1985. Circ. 400,000. Byline given. Buys first North American serial rights. Submit seasonal material 6 months in advance. Accepts queries by mail. Reports in 1 month on queries; 6 weeks on ms. Sample copy for $5 and 9×12 SASE with $1.65 postage.

**Nonfiction:** Primarily destination-oriented travel articles and resort/hotel profiles and roundups, but will consider essays, how-to, humor, nostalgia, Americana. "It is best to study current contents and query first." **Buys 60 mss/year.** Average length: 1,000 words. **Pays $125-300.**

**Reprints:** Send typed ms with rights for sale noted. Pay varies.

**Photos:** Top-quality original color slides preferred. Captions required. Buys one-time rights. Prefers photo feature package (ms plus slides), but will purchase slides only to support a work in progress.

**Tips:** "Because we are heavily photo-oriented, superb slides are our foremost concern. The most successful approach is to send 2-3 sheets of slides with the query or complete ms. Include a list of other subjects you can provide as a photo feature package."

⭐ $ $ $ $ **TRAVEL & LEISURE**, American Express Publishing Corp., 1120 Avenue of the Americas, New York NY 10036. (212)382-5600. E-mail: tlquery@travelandleisure.com. Website: http://www.travelandleisure.com. Editor-in-Chief: Nancy Novogrod. Executive Editor: Barbara Peck. Managing Editor: Mark Orwoll. **80% freelance written.** "*Travel & Leisure* is a monthly magazine edited for affluent travelers. It explores the latest resorts, hotels, fashions, foods and drinks." Circ. 960,000. **Pays on acceptance.** Byline given. Offers 25% kill fee. Buys first world rights. Reports in 6 weeks. Sample copy for $5 from (800)888-8728 or P.O. Box 2094, Harlan IA 51537-4094. Writer's guidelines for #10 SASE.

• At press time, American Express Publishing had purchased *Historic Traveler*, and planned to close the title and fold its subscribers into *Travel & Leisure*. Also, remember there is no single editorial contact for *Travel & Leisure*. It is best to find the name of the editor of each section, as appropriate for your submission.

**Nonfiction:** Travel. **Buys 40-50 features** (3,000-5,000 words) **and 200 short pieces** (125-500 words). Query by e-mail preferred. **Pays $4,000-6,000/feature; $100-500/short piece.** Pays the expenses of writers on assignment.

• Ranked as one of the best markets for freelance writers in *Writer's Yearbook* magazine's annual "Top 100 Markets," January 1999.

**Columns/Departments: Buys 125-150 mss.** Length: 1,200-2,500 words. **Pays $1,000-2,500.**

**Photos:** Discourages submission of unsolicited transparencies. Payment varies. Captions required. Buys one-time rights.

**Tips:** "Read the magazine. There are two regional editions: East and West. Short-takes sections (e.g., "T&L Reports" and "Strategies") are best places to start."

**N $ TRAVEL IMPULSE**, Sun Tracker Enterprises Ltd., 9336 117th St., Delta, British Columbia V4C 6B8 Canada. (604)951-3238. Fax: (604)951-8732. E-mail: travimp@ibm.net. **Contact**: Susan M. Boyce, editor/publisher. **95% freelance written.** We work with at least one new writer each issue and are always looking for new voices. "*Travel Impulse* is a quarterly magazine for people who love to travel—in fact, they find travel irresistable. Appeal to their sense of adventure and the playfulness of travel. Many of our readers like to 'pick up and go' at short notice and are looking for inexpensive, unique ways to accomplish that." Estab. 1984. Circ. 1,000. Pays 2 weeks after publication. Publishes ms an average of 6-8 months after acceptance. Byline given. Buys first North American serial rights and second serial (reprint) rights. Editorial lead time 6-8 months. Submit seasonal material 8 months in advance. Accepts queries by mail, e-mail. Reports in 2 months on queries; 4 months on mss. Sample copy for $6. Writer's guidelines for #10 SASE.

**Nonfiction:** Humor, interview/profile, new product (travel gadgets and gear), personal experience, photo feature. No political commentary. **Buys 20-25 mss/year.** Query or send complete ms with Canadian postage or IRCs only. Length: 1,000-1,500 words. **Pays $20-30 for features.**

**Reprints:** Accepts previously published submissions.

**Photos:** State availability of photos with submission or send photocopies. No originals until requested. Reviews 4×6 prints (preferred size). Offers no additional payment for photos accepted with ms, but photos greatly enhance your chances of acceptance. Captions, model releases, identification of subjects required. Buys rights with ms.

**Tips:** "Our readers find travel irresistable. Entice them with unusual destinations and unique ways to travel inexpensively. Show us the playful side of travel."

**N $ TRAVEL SMART**, Communications House, Inc., Dobbs Ferry NY 10522. (914)693-4208. **Contact:** Nancy Dunnan, editor. Covers information on "good-value travel." Monthly newsletter. Estab. 1976. Pays on publication. Buys all rights. Accepts queries by mail. Reports in 6 weeks. Sample copy and writer's guidelines for 9×12 SAE with 3 first-class stamps.

**Nonfiction:** "Interested primarily in bargains or little-known deals on transportation, lodging, food, unusual destinations that are really good values. No destination stories on major Caribbean islands, London, New York, no travelogs, 'my vacation,' poetry, fillers. No photos or illustrations other than maps. Just hard facts. We are not part of 'Rosy fingers of dawn . . .' school." Write for guidelines, then query. Length: 100-1,500 words. **Pays $150 maximum.**

**Tips:** "When you travel, check out small hotels offering good prices, good restaurants, and send us brief rundown (with prices, phone numbers, addresses). Information must be current. Include your phone number with submission, because we sometimes make immediate assignments."

**N ✠ $ TRAVELIN' MAGAZINE, Exploring the Back Roads & By-Ways of the West**, Travelin' Magazine, P.O. Box 23005, Eugene OR 97402. (541)485-8533. Fax: (541)485-8528. E-mail: travelin@teleport.com. Website: http://www.travelin-magazine.com. **Contact:** Finn J. John, editor/publisher. **100% freelance written.** Consumer publication published bimonthly covering travel, chiefly road travel/camping. "Most readers are 45-65 years old, 45% travel in RVs. *Travelin'* gives them ideas for destinations that are little-known, which they would not have discovered without us. We cover the 13 western states, Canada, Alaska and Hawaii." Estab. 1990. Circ. 6,000. Pays on publication. Publishes ms an average of 6 months after acceptance. Byline given. Buys first North American serial rights. Editorial lead time 6 months. Submit seasonal material 6 months in advance. Accepts queries by mail, e-mail (mail preferred). Accepts simultaneous submissions. Reports in 1 month on queries; 2 months on mss. Sample copy and writer's guidelines for #10 SASE or on website.

**Nonfiction:** Humor, personal experience, photo feature, travel. "No articles without photos (other than humor or how-to), no articles about travel outside the western states (AK, WA, OR, CA, NV, AZ, NM, UT, CO, WY, MT, ID, HI and western Canada). **Buys 48 mss/year.** Query or send complete ms. Length: 2,500 words. **Pays $100 average.**

**Photos:** Send photos with submission. Reviews transparencies and 5×7 prints. Offers $10-75/photo. Captions and identification of subjects required. Buys one-time rights.

**Columns/Departments:** Travelin' Light (humor); The Art of Travelin' (how-to), both 800-1,000 words. **Buys 9 mss/year.** Send complete ms. **Pays $2/column inch.**

**Tips:** "We don't care about clips; manuscripts are evaluated on their own merits. Photos are very important. Please request a copy of our writers' guidelines before submitting. We work with a lot of new writers. It's usually a good idea to query first."

▓ **$ $ trips, a travel journal**, 155 Filbert St., Suite 245, Oakland CA 94607. (510)834-3433. Fax: (510)834-2663. E-mail: office@tripsmag.com. Website: http://www.tripsmag.com. **Contact**: Tony Stucker, editor. **90% freelance written.** Bimonthly magazine. "*trips magazine* is the travel journal for younger, active travelers, looking for travel information in an unusual, offbeat, irreverent voice. We are looking for travel articles that would not, or could not, appear anywhere else. We want the exotic, unusual destinations, but we are also looking for traditional sites viewed in unconventional ways. All editorial should be as interesting and entertaining to someone whether they're planning on visiting a destination, have just returned from the destination, or never plan on going there. It should educate and inform, but also entertain. Travel is fun—travel writing should be as well." Estab. 1997. Circ. 40,000. Pays on publication. Publishes ms 3 months after acceptance. Byline given. Buys first North American serial rights. Editorial lead time 6 months. Submit seasonal material 6 months in advance. Accepts simultaneous submissions. Reports in 6 weeks on queries; 3 months on mss. Sample copy for 10×13 SAE with 6 first-class stamps. Writer's guidelines for #10 SASE.

○━ Break in through well-developed, informative or offbeat pieces for our smaller sections, i.e. "tips," "lessons in" and "vice."

**Nonfiction:** Book excerpts, essays, exposé, general interest, how-to, humor, interview/profile, new product, personal experience, photo feature, travel. No "run-of-the-mill travel stories that would appear in Sunday travel sections." **Buys 40 mss/year.** Query with published clips. Length: 450-6,000 words. **Pays $100-1,500.** Sometimes pays expenses of writers on assignment.

**Reprints:** Send photocopy of article and information about when and where the article previously appeared.

**Photos:** State availability of photos with submission. Reviews contact sheets, negatives. Negotiates payment individually. Identification of subjects required. Buys one-time rights.

**Columns/Departments:** "Lessons In . . ." (travel reader service); "Vice" (unusual vices from around the world); "A Travel Journal" (first person essays), all 800-1,000 words. **Buys 30 mss/year.** Query. **Pays $100-500.**

**Tips:** "We want to develop relationships with writers around the world. If you don't have a piece that works now, perhaps a future trip will yield something that's right. E-mail queries OK."

**$ $ VIA**, California State Automobile Assn., 150 Van Ness Ave., San Francisco CA 94102. (415)565-2451. **Contact**: Bruce Anderson, editor. **20% freelance written.** Bimonthly magazine specializing in northern California and the West, with occasional stories on world-wide travel and cruises. Also, traffic safety and motorists' consumer issues. "Our magazine goes to members of the AAA in northern California, Nevada and Utah. Our surveys show they are an upscale audience, well-educated, adventurous and widely traveled. We like our travel stories to be finely crafted, evocative and personal, but we also include nitty gritty details to help readers arrange their own travel to the destinations covered." Estab. 1917. Circ. 2,500,000. **Pays on acceptance.** Byline usually given. Offers 25% kill fee. Buys first rights; occasional work-for-hire assignments. Editorial lead time 2 months. Submit seasonal material 6 months in advance. Usually reports within 2 months on queries. Writer's guidelines for #10 SASE.

**Nonfiction:** Travel. **Buys 15-20 mss/year.** Prefers to see finished mss with SASE from writers new to them. Length: 500-2,000 words. **Pays $150-700.** Pays expenses of writers on assignment, "but assignments are rare except to writers we've already worked with."

**Photos:** State availability of photos with submission. Reviews 35mm and 4×5 transparencies. Offers $50-400/photo. Model releases, identification of subjects required. Buys first-time rights. Not responsible for unsolicited photographs.

**Tips:** "We do not like to receive queries via fax or e-mail unless the writer does not expect a reply. We are looking for beautifully written pieces that evoke a destination. We purchase less than 1% of the material submitted. Send SASE with all queries and mss."

**$ $ $ VOYAGEUR, The Magazine of Carlson Hospitality Worldwide**, Pace Communications, 1301 Carolina St., Greensboro NC 27401. (336)378-6065. Fax: (336)378-8272. Editor: Jaci H. Ponzoni. **Contact**: Sarah Lindsay, senior editor. **90% freelance written.** In room magazine for Radisson hotels and affiliates. "*Voyageur* is an international magazine published quarterly for Carlson Hospitality Worldwide and distributed in the rooms of Radisson Hotels Worldwide, Radisson SAS Hotels, Carlson Cruises Worldwide, and Country Inns & Suites By Carlson throughout North and South America, Europe, Australia, Asia and the Middle East. All travel related stories must be in destinations where Radisson or Country Inns & Suites have hotels." Estab. 1992. Circ. 160,000. **Pays on acceptance.** Publishes ms an average of 2 months after acceptance. Offers 25% kill fee. Buys first North American serial rights. Editorial lead time 4 months. Submit seasonal material 6 months in advance. Reports in 2 months. Sample for $5. Writer's guidelines for #10 SASE.

○━ Break in with a "well thought-out, well-written, well-researched query on a city or area the writer lives in or knows well—one where Carlson has a presence (Raddisson or Country Inns)."

**Nonfiction:** Travel. The *Cover Story* is an authoritative yet personal profile of a destination where Radisson has a major presence, featuring a mix of standard and off-the-beaten path activities and sites including sightseeing, recreation, restaurants, shopping and cultural attractions. Length: 1,000 words including one sidebar, plus At a Glance, a roundup of useful and intriguing facts for travelers. *Our World* brings to life the spectrum of a country's or region's arts and culture, including performing, culinary, visual and folk arts. The successful article combines a timely sample of cultural activities for travelers with a sense of the destination's unique spirit or personality as reflected in the arts. Must be a region where Radisson has a major presence. Length: 1,000 words plus one 200-word sidebar. Query with published clips. **Pays $800-1,000.** Sometimes pays expenses of writers on assignment.

**Photos:** State availability of photos with submission. Reviews contact sheets, transparencies, prints. Negotiates payment individually. Model releases and identification of subjects required. Buys one-time rights.

**Columns/Departments:** In The Bag (place-specific shopping story with cultural context and upscale attitude), 600-800 words and 50-word mini-sidebar; Good Sport (action-oriented, first person focusing on travel involving sports such as biking, kayaking, scuba diving, hiking or sailing), 600-800 words plus 50-word mini-sidebar; Business Wise (insights into conducting business and traveling for business internationally) 350-400 words with 50-word mini-sidebar. **Buys 24 mss/year.** Query with published clips. **Pays $300-700.**

**Tips:** "We look for authoritative, energetic and vivid writing to inform and entertain business and leisure travelers, and we are actively seeking writers with an authentic European, Asian, Latin American or Australian perspective. Travel stories should be authoritative yet personal." .

**$ WESTERN RV NEWS**, 64470 Sylvan Loop, Bend OR 97701. (541)318-8089. Fax: (541)318-0849. E-mail: editor@westernrvnews.com. Website: http://www.westernrvnews.com. **Contact:** Terie Snyder, editor. **75% freelance written.** Monthly magazine for owners of recreational vehicles and those interested in the RV lifestyle. Estab. 1966. Pays on publication. Publishes ms an average of 6 months after acceptance. Byline given. Buys first rights and second serial (reprint) rights. Accepts simultaneous submissions. Accepts queries by mail, e-mail, fax. Reports in 2 months. Sample copy and writer's guidelines for 9 × 12 SAE with 5 first-class stamps. Guidelines for #10 SASE.

**Nonfiction:** How-to (RV oriented, purchasing considerations, maintenance), humor (RV experiences), new product (with ancillary interest to RV lifestyle), personal experiences (varying or unique RV lifestyles) technical (RV systems or hardware), travel. "No articles without an RV slant." **Buys 100 mss/year.** Submit complete ms. Length: 250-1,200 words. **Pays $15-100.**

**Reprints:** Send photocopy of article or typed ms with rights for sale noted and information about when and where the article previously appeared. Pays 60% of *Western RV News* first rights.

**Photos:** Send photos with submission. Accepts b&w or color slides or photos. Can submit on 3.5″ IBM-compatible disk in TIF format. Offers $5/photo. Captions, model releases, identification of subjects required. Buys one-time rights.

**Fillers:** Encourage anecdotes, RV related tips and short humor. Length: 50-250 words. **Pays $5-25.**

**Tips:** "Highlight the RV lifestyle! Western travel articles should include information about the availability of RV sites, dump stations, RV parking and accessibility. Thorough research and a pleasant, informative writing style are paramount. Technical, how-to, and new product writing is also of great interest. Photos enhance the possibility of article acceptance."

# WOMEN'S

Women have an incredible variety of publications available to them. A number of titles in this area have been redesigned to compete in the crowded marketplace. Many have stopped publishing fiction and are focusing more on short, human interest nonfiction articles. Magazines that also use material slanted to women's interests can also be found in the following categories: Business & Finance; Child Care & Parental Guidance; Contemporary Culture; Food & Drink; Gay & Lesbian Interest; Health & Fitness; Hobby & Craft; Home & Garden; Relationships; Religious; Romance & Confession; and Sports.

**$ $ $ BRIDAL GUIDE**, Globe Communications Corp., 3 E. 54th St., 15th Floor, New York NY 10022. (212)838-7733. Fax: (212)308-7165. Editor-in-Chief: Diane Forden. **Contact:** Denise Schipani, managing editor; Laurie Bain Wilson, travel editor for travel features. **50% freelance written.** Prefers to work with experienced/published writers. A bimonthly magazine covering relationships, sexuality, fitness, wedding planning, psychology, finance, travel. **Pays on acceptance.** Accepts queries by e-mail, fax. Reports in 3 months. Sample copy for $4.95 and SASE with 4 first-class stamps. Writer's guidelines available.

● Ranked as one of the best markets for freelance writers in *Writer's Yearbook* magazine's annual "Top 100 Markets," January 1999.

**Nonfiction:** Queries only, accompanied by published clips. "Please do not send queries concerning beauty and fashion, since we produce them in-house. We do not accept personal wedding essays, fiction, or poetry. Address travel queries to travel editor." All correspondence accompanied by an SASE will be answered (response time is within 8 weeks). Length: 1,000-2,000 words. **Pays 50¢/word. Buys 100 mss/year.**

**Photos:** Robin Zachary, art director; Catherine Diaz, associate art director. Photography and illustration submissions should be sent to the art department.

**Columns/Departments:** The only columns written by freelancers cover finance and wedding-planning issues. Welcome queries from men who are engaged or married for Groom with a View essay.

**Tips:** "We are looking for service-oriented, well researched pieces that are journalistically written. Writers we work with use at least three expert sources, such as physicians, book authors, and business people in the appropriate field. Our tone is conversational yet authoritative. Features are also generally filled with real-life anecdotes. We also do features that are completely real-person based—such as roundtables of bridesmaids discussing their experiences, or grooms-to-be talking about their feelings about getting married. In queries, we are looking for a well thought-out idea, the specific angle of focus the writer intends to take, and the sources he or she intends to use. Queries should be brief and snappy—and titles should be supplied to give the editor an even better idea of the direction the writer is going in."

**$ $** **BRIDE AGAIN, The Only Magazine Designed for Second Time Brides**, 1240 N. Jefferson Ave., Suite G, Anaheim CA 92807. (714)632-7000. Fax: (714)632-5405. Website: www.brideagain.com. **Contact:** Beth Reed Ramirez, editor. Quarterly magazine for the encore bride. "*Bride Again* is targeted primarily to women ages 35-45 and secondarily to those 45 and over. They have been married at least once before, and most likely have children from a previous marriage or will be marrying someone with children. They have a career and income of over $45,000 per year, and are more mature and sophisticated than the 26-year-old first-time bride." Estab. 1997. Circ. 125,000. Pays on publication. Byline given. Buys all rights. Does not return mss. Writer's guidelines for #10 SASE.

**Nonfiction:** How-to, humor, inspirational, interview/profile, personal experience. "Topics can be on, but not limited to: remarriage, blending families, becoming a stepmother, combining households, dealing with children in the wedding party, children—his, mine and ours; joint custody, dealing with difficult ex-spouses, real dresses for real women, legal aspects of remarriage, pre- and post-nuptial agreements, alternatives to the wedding veil, unusual wedding and/or honeymoon locations." Special issues: Honeymoon locations: Egypt, Greece, the Seychelles, Mauritius; Remarriage as a widow; Interfaith marriages; Handling extended step families; Having another child together. Send complete ms. *No queries, please.* Length: 1,000 words. **Pays 35¢/word.**

**Photos:** Send photos with submission. Reviews transparencies. Will return photos only if accompanied with SASE. Negotiates payment individually. Buys all rights.

**Columns/Departments:** Finances, Blending Families, Religion, Wedding Plans: Problems & Solutions, Real Life Weddings, Groom's Viewpoint, Unusual Honeymoon Locations, Beauty for Ages 30+/40+/50+, Remarriage, Fashion; all 800-1,000 words. Book reviews (on the feature topics listed above), 250 words. Send complete ms. **Pays 35¢/word.**

**Tips:** "All articles must be specific to encore brides."

**$ $ $ $** **CHATELAINE**, 777 Bay St., #800, Toronto, Ontario M5W 1A7 Canada. (416)596-5000. Fax: (416)596-5516. E-mail: editors@chatelaine.com. Website: http://www.chatelaine.com. **Contact:** Senior Editor, Articles. Monthly magazine. "*Chatelaine* is edited for Canadian women ages 25-49, their changing attitudes and lifestyles. Key editorial ingredients include health, finance, social issues and trends, high profile personalities and politics, as well as fashion, beauty, food and home decor. Regular departments include Health pages, entertainment, Laugh Lines, How-to. **Pays on acceptance.** Byline given. Offers 25-100% kill fee. Buys first and electronic rights. Accepts queries by mail, e-mail, fax. Reports in 2 months on queries. Writer's guidelines for #10 SASE with IRCs.

O⌐ Break in with one-page columns or up-front items.

**Nonfiction:** Seeks "agenda-setting reports on national issues and trends as well as pieces on health, careers, personal finance and other facts of Canadian life." **Buys 50 mss/year.** Query with published clips. Length: 1,000-2,500 words. **Pays $1,000-2,500.** Pays expenses of writers on assignment.

**Columns/Departments:** Length: 500-1,000 words. Query with published clips. **Pays $500-750.**

**Fillers:** **Buys 30/year.** Length: 200-500 words. **Pays $250-350.**

▣ The online magazine carries original content not found in the print edition. Contact: Paula Gignae, online editor.

**$ $** **COMPLETE WOMAN, For All The Women You Are**, Associated Publications, Inc., 875 N. Michigan Ave., Suite 3434, Chicago IL 60611-1901. (312)266-8680. Editor: Bonnie L. Krueger. **Contact:** Lora Wintz, senior editor. **90% freelance written.** Bimonthly. "Manuscripts should be written for today's busy women, in a concise, clear format with useful information. Our readers want to know about the important things: sex, love, relationships, career and self-discovery. Examples of true-life anecdotes, incorporated into articles work well for our readers, who are always interested in how other women are dealing with life's ups and downs." Estab. 1980. Circ. 350,000. Pays 45 days after acceptance. Publishes ms an average of 6 months after acceptance. Byline given. Buys first North American serial, second serial (reprint) or simultaneous rights. Editorial lead time 6 months. Submit seasonal material 5 months in advance. Accepts simultaneous submissions. Accepts queries by mail. Reports in 2 months. Writer's guidelines for #10 SASE.

● The editor reports a need for more relationship stories.

**Nonfiction:** Book excerpts, exposé (of interest to women), general interest, how-to (beauty/diet-related), humor, inspirational, interview/profile (celebrities), new product, personal experience, photo feature, sex, love and relationship advice. "We want self-help articles written for today's woman. Articles that address dating, romance, sexuality and relationships are an integral part of our editorial mix, as well as inspirational and motivational pieces." **Buys 60-100 mss/year.** Query with published clips, or send complete ms. Length: 800-2,000 words. **Pays $160-400.** Sometimes pays expenses of writers on assignment.

**Reprints:** Send tearsheet or photocopy of article or short story or send typed ms with rights for sale noted and information about when and where the article previously appeared.

**Photos:** Photo features with little or no copy should be sent to Gail Mitchell. Send photos with submission. Reviews 2¼ or 35mm transparencies and 5×7 prints. Offers $35-100/photo. Captions, model releases, identification of subjects required. Buys one-time rights.

**Poetry:** Josephine Sharif, associate editor. Free verse, light verse, traditional. **Buys 15-20 poems/year.** Submit maximum 3 poems. Length: 3-10 lines. Pays in contributor's copies.

**Tips:** "Freelance writers should review publication, review writer's guidelines, then submit their articles for review. We're looking for new ways to explore the usual topics, written in a format that will be easy for our readers (24-40+ women) to understand. We also like sidebar information that readers can review quickly before or after reading the article. Our focus is relationship-driven, with an editorial blend of beauty, health and career."

**\$ \$ \$ \$ CONDÉ NAST BRIDE'S**, Condé Nast, 140 E. 45th St., 39th Floor, New York NY 10017. (212)880-2518. Fax: (212)880-8331. E-mail: letters@brides.com. Managing Editor: Sally Kilbridge. Editor-in-Chief: Millie Martini-Bratten. **Contact:** Nancy Mattia, features and travel editor. Bimonthly magazine for the first- and second-time bride, the groom and their families and friends. Circ. 400,000. **Pays on acceptance.** Byline given. Offers 25% kill fee. Buys all rights. Editorial lead time 8 months. Accepts simultaneous submissions. Accepts queries by mail, fax. Reports in 2 months on queries. Writer's guidelines for #10 SASE.

**Nonfiction:** Topic (1) Personal essays on wedding planning, aspects of weddings or marriage. Length: 800 words. Written by brides, grooms, attendants, family members, friends in the first person. The writer's unique experience qualifies them to tell this story. (2)Articles on specific relationship and lifestyle issues. Length: 800 words. Select a specialized topic in the areas of relationships, religion, in-laws, second marriage, finances, careers, health, fitness, nutrition, sex, decorating, or entertaining. Written either by experts (attorneys, doctors, financial planners, marriage counselors, etc) or freelancers who interview and quote experts and real couples. (3) In-depth explorations of relationship and lifestyle issues. Length: 2,000-3,000 words. Well-researched articles on finances, health, sex, wedding and marriage trends. Should include statistics, quotes from experts and real couples, a resolution of the issues raised by each couple. **Buys 100 mss/year.** Query with published clips. Length: 2,000 words. **Pays 50¢-$1/word.** Pays expenses of writers on assignment.

**Columns/Departments:** Length: 750 words. **Buys 100 mss/year.** Query with published clips. **Pays 50¢-$1/word.**

**Tips:** "We look for good, helpful relationship pieces that will help a newlywed couple adjust to marriage. Wedding planning articles are usually written by experts or depend on a lot of interviews with experts. Writers must have a good idea of what we would and would not do: Read the 3 or 4 most current issues. What separates us from the competition is quality—writing, photographs, amount of information."

**\$ \$ \$ \$ COSMOPOLITAN**, The Hearst Corp., 224 W. 57th St., New York NY 10019. (212)649-2000. **Contact:** Ellen Kunes, executive editor. **25% freelance written.** Monthly magazine for 18- to 35-year-old single, married, divorced women—all working. "*Cosmopolitan* is edited for young women for whom beauty, fashion, fitness, career, relationships and personal growth are top priorities. Nutrition, personal finance, home/lifestyle and celebrities are other interests reflected in the editorial lineup." Estab. 1886. Circ. 2,300,100. **Pays on acceptance.** Byline given. Offers 10-15% kill fee. Buys all magazine rights and occasionally negotiates first North American rights. Submit seasonal material 6 months in advance. Reports in 1 week on queries; 3 weeks on mss. Sample copy for $2.95. Writer's guidelines for #10 SASE.

● Ranked as one of the best markets for freelance writers in *Writer's Yearbook* magazine's annual "Top 100 Markets," January 1999.

**Nonfiction:** Book excerpts, how-to, humor, opinion, personal experience and anything of interest to young women. **Buys 350 mss/year.** Query with published clips or send complete ms. Length: 500-3,500 words. **Pays $2,000-3,500 for features; $1,000-1,500 for short pieces.** Pays expenses of writers on assignment.

**Columns/Departments: Buys 45 mss/year.** Length: 750 words. **Pays $650-1,300.**

**Reprints:** Accepts previously published submissions appearing in minor publications. Send tearsheet of article, typed ms with rights for sale noted and information about when and where the article previously appeared. Pays 100% of amount paid for an original article.

● *Cosmopolitan* plans to launch a new spinoff titled *Cosmogirl* for teens. Send SASE for guidelines.

**Tips:** "Combine information with entertainment value, humor and relatability." Needs "information- and emotion- and fun-packed relationship and sex service stories; first-person stories that deal with women's issues; essays from both men and women on topics that most women either relate to or are curious about." This editorial team headed American *Marie Claire* until September 1996.

**\$ COUNTRY WOMAN**, Reiman Publications, P.O. Box 643, Milwaukee WI 53201. (414)423-0100. **Contact:** Kathy Pohl, managing editor. **75-85% written by readers.** Willing to work with new/unpublished writers. Bimonthly magazine. "*Country Woman* is for contemporary rural women of all ages and backgrounds and from all over the U.S. and Canada. It includes a sampling of the diversity that makes up rural women's lives—love of home, family, farm, ranch, community, hobbies, enduring values, humor, attaining new skills and appreciating present, past and future all within the context of the lifestyle that surrounds country living." Estab. 1970. **Pays on acceptance.** Byline given. Buys first North American serial, one-time and second serial (reprint) rights. Submit seasonal material 5 months in advance. Accepts queries by mail. Reports in 2 months on queries; 3 months on mss. Sample copy for $2. Writer's guidelines for #10 SASE.

**Nonfiction:** General interest, historical/nostalgic, how-to (crafts, community projects, decorative, antiquing, etc.), humor, inspirational, interview/profile, personal experience, photo/feature packages profiling interesting country women—all pertaining to a rural woman's interest. Articles must be written in a positive, light and entertaining manner. Query. Length: 1,000 words maximum. **Pays $35-150.**

**Reprints:** Send typed ms with rights for sale noted and information about when and where the material previously appeared. Payment varies.

**Photos:** Send color photos with query or ms. Reviews 35mm or 2¼ transparencies or excellent-quality color prints. Uses only excellent quality color photos. No b&w. "We pay for photo/feature packages." Captions, model releases and identification of subjects required. Buys one-time rights.

**Columns/Departments:** Why Farm Wives Age Fast (humor), I Remember When (nostalgia) and Country Decorating. **Buys 10-12 mss/year** (maximum). Query or send complete ms. Length: 500-1,000 words. **Pays $50-125.**

**Fiction:** Main character *must* be a country woman. All fiction must have a country setting. Fiction must have a positive, upbeat message. Includes fiction in every issue. Would buy more fiction if stories suitable for our audience were sent our way. Send complete ms. Length: 750-1,000 words. **Pays $90-125.**

**Poetry:** Traditional, light verse. "Poetry must have rhythm and rhyme! It must be country-related, positive and upbeat. Always looking for seasonal poetry." **Buys 6-12/year.** Submit 6 poems maximum. Length: 4-24 lines. **Pays $10-25.**

**Tips:** "We have broadened our focus to include 'country' women, not just women on farms and ranches but also women who live in a small town or country home and/or simply have an interest in country-oriented topics. This allows freelancers a wider scope in material. Write as clearly and with as much zest and enthusiasm as possible. We love good quotes, supporting materials (names, places, etc.) and strong leads and closings. Readers relate strongly to where they live and the lifestyle they've chosen. They want to be informed and entertained, and that's just exactly why they subscribe. Readers are busy—not too busy to read—but when they do sit down, they want good writing, reliable information and something that feels like a reward. How-to, humor, personal experience and nostalgia are areas most open to freelancers. Profiles, to a certain degree, are also open. Be accurate and fresh in approach."

**$ $ ESSENCE**, 1500 Broadway, New York NY 10036. (212)642-0600. Fax: (212)921-5173. Website: http://www.essence.com. Editor-in-Chief: Susan L. Taylor. **Contact:** Monique Greenwood, executive editor. Monthly. "*Essence* is the magazine for today's Black women. Edited for career-minded, sophisticated and independent achievers, *Essence*'s editorial is dedicated to helping its readers attain their maximum potential in various lifestyles and roles. The editorial content includes career and educational opportunities; fashion and beauty; investing and money management; health and fitness; parenting; information on home decorating and food; travel; cultural reviews; fiction; and profiles of achievers and celebrities." Estab. 1970. Circ. 1 million. **Pays on acceptance.** Makes assignments on one-time serial rights basis. 3 month lead time. Pays 25% kill fee. Byline given. Submit seasonal material 6 months in advance. Accepts queries by mail, fax. Reports in 2 months. Sample copy for $3.25. Guidelines for #10 SASE.

**Nonfiction:** Buys 200 mss/year. Query only; word length will be given upon assignment. **Pays $500 minimum.** Also publishes novel and nonfiction book excerpts.

**Reprints:** Send tearsheet of article, information about when and where the article previously appeared. Pays 50% of the amount paid for an original article.

**Photos:** Jan de Chabert, creative director. State availability of photos with query. Pays $100 for b&w page; $300 for color page. Captions and model release required. "We particularly would like to see photographs for our travel section that feature Black travelers."

**Columns/Departments:** Query department editors: Lifestyle (food, lifestyle, travel, parenting, consumer information): Beverly Hall Lawrence; Entertainment: Yvette Russell; Health & Fitness: Ziba Kashef. Query only, word length will be given upon assignment. **Pays $100 minimum.**

**Fiction:** Martha Southgate, editor. Publishes novel excerpts.

The online magazine carries original content not found in the print edition. Contact: Taiian Smart-Young, online editor.

**Tips:** "Please note that *Essence* no longer accepts unsolicited mss for fiction, poetry or nonfiction, except for the Brothers, Windows, Back Talk and Interiors columns. So please only send query letters for nonfiction story ideas."

**$ $ $ $ FAMILY CIRCLE MAGAZINE**, Gruner & Jahr, 375 Lexington Ave., New York NY 10017-5514. (212)499-2000. Fax: (212)499-1987. Website: www.familycircle.com. Editor-in-Chief: Susan Ungaro. **Contact:** Nancy Clark, deputy editor. Nancy is sole contact. **80% freelance written.** Magazine published every 3 weeks. "We are a national women's service magazine which covers many stages of a woman's life, along with her everyday concerns about social, family and health issues. Estab. 1932. Circ. 5,000,000. Byline given. Offers 20% kill fee. Buys first North American serial rights or all rights. Editorial lead time 4 months. Submit seasonal material 4 months in advance. Reports in 2 months. Writer's guidelines for #10 SASE.

● Ranked as one of the best markets for freelance writers in *Writer's Yearbook* magazine's annual "Top 100 Markets," January 1999.

**Nonfiction:** Essays, humor, opinion, personal experience. Women's interest subjects such as family and personal relationships, children, physical and mental health, nutrition and self-improvement. "We look for well-written, well-reported stories told through interesting anecdotes and insightful writing. We want well-researched service journalism on all subjects." Special issues: Computers Made Easy (3 times/year). No fiction or poetry. **Buys 200 mss/year.** Query with SASE. "Query should stress the unique aspects of an article and expert sources; we want articles that will help our readers or make a difference in how they live." Length: 1,000-2,500 words. **Pays $1/word.** Pays expenses of writers on assignment.

**Columns/Departments:** Women Who Make a Difference (profiles of volunteers who have made a significant impact on their community), 1,500 words; Profiles in Courage/Love (dramatic narratives about women and families overcoming adversity), 2,000 words; Full Circle (opinion/point of view on current issue/topic of general interest to our readers), 750 words; Humor, 750 words. **Buys 200 mss/year.** Query with published clips and SASE. **Pays $1/word.**

**Tips:** "Query letters should be concise and to the point. Also, writers should keep close tabs on *Family Circle* and other women's magazines to avoid submitting recently run subject matter."

**✖ $ $ $ GLAMOUR**, Condé Nast, 350 Madison Ave., New York NY 10017. (212)880-8225. Fax: (212)880-6663. E-mail: glamour@glamour.com. **Contact:** Kate Westerbeck, editorial business manager. **10% freelance written.** Works with a small number of new/unpublished writers each year. Monthly magazine for college-educated women, 18-35 years old. "*Glamour* is edited for the contemporary American woman, it informs her of the trends, recommends how she can adapt them to her needs, and motivates her to take action. Over half of *Glamour*'s editorial content focuses on fashion, beauty and health, as well as coverage of personal relationships, career, food and entertainment." Estab. 1939. Circ. 2,300,000. **Pays on acceptance.** Offers 25% kill fee. Publishes ms an average of 1 year after acceptance. Buys first North American serial rights. Byline given. Reports in 3 months. Writer's guidelines for #10 SASE.

**Nonfiction:** Mary Hickey, articles editor. "Editorial approach is 'how-to' with articles that are relevant in the areas of careers, current events, health, psychology, interpersonal relationships, etc. We look for queries that are fresh and include a contemporary, timely angle. Fashion, beauty, food and entertainment are all staff-written. We use 1,000-word opinion essays for our Viewpoint section. **Buys 2-3 mss/issue.** Query "with letter that is detailed, well-focused, well-organized, and documented with surveys, statistics and research; personal essays excepted." Short articles and essays (1,500-2,000 words) **pays $1,000 and up;** longer mss (2,500-3,000 words) **pays $1,500 minimum.** Sometimes pays the expenses of writers on assignment.

**Reprints:** Send information about when and where the article previously appeared. Payment varies.

**Tips:** "We're looking for sharply focused ideas by strong writers and are constantly raising our standards. We are interested in getting new writers, and we are approachable, mainly because our range of topics is so broad. We've increased our focus on male-female relationships."

**$ $ $ $ GOOD HOUSEKEEPING**, Hearst Corp., 959 Eighth Ave., New York NY 10019. (212)649-2000. Editor-in-Chief: Ellen Levine. **Contact:** Executive Editor. Prefers to work with published/established writers. Monthly magazine. "*Good Housekeeping* is edited for the 'New Traditionalist.' Articles which focus on food, fitness, beauty, and child care draw upon the resources of the Good Housekeeping Institute. Editorial includes human interest stories, articles that focus on social issues, money management, health news, travel, and 'The Better Way,' an 8-page hard-fact guide to better living." Circ. 5,000,000. **Pays on acceptance.** Buys first North American serial rights. Pays 25% kill fee. Byline given. Submit seasonal material 6 months in advance. Reports in 2 months. For sample copy, call (800)925-0485. Writer's guidelines for #10 SASE.

● Ranked as one of the best markets for freelance writers in *Writer's Yearbook* magazine's annual "Top 100 Markets," January 1999.

**Nonfiction:** Contact: Executive editor. Toni Hope, editor-at-large. Consumer, social issues, dramatic narrative, nutrition, work, relationships, psychology, trends. **Buys 4-6 mss/issue.** Query. Length: 1,500-2,500 words. **Pays $1,500+** on acceptance for full articles from new writers. **Pays $250-350** for local interest and travel pieces of 2,000 words. Pays expenses of writers on assignment.

**Photos:** Scott Yardley, art director. Gail Tolvanen, photo editor. Photos purchased on assignment mostly. Pays $100-350 for b&w; $200-400 for color photos. Query. Model releases required.

**Columns/Departments:** The Better Way, editor: Kristin Godsey (consumer advice, how-to, shopping strategies, money savers, health). Profiles editor: Kathy Powers (inspirational, activist or heroic women), 300-600 words. My Problem and How I Solved It, My Problem editor (as told-to format), 2,000 words. Query. **Pays $1/word** for items 300-600 words.

**Fiction:** Lee Quarfoot, fiction editor. Uses original short fiction and condensations of novels that can appear in one issue. Looks for reader identification. "We get 1,500 unsolicited mss/month. A freelancer's odds are overwhelming, but we do look at all submissions." Send complete mss. Manuscripts will not be returned. Responds only on acceptance. Length: 1,500 words (short-shorts); novel according to merit of material; average 5,000-word short stories. **Pays $1,000** minimum for fiction from new writers.

● Ranked as one of the best markets for fiction writers in *Writer's Digest* magazine's "Fiction 50," June 1998.

**Tips:** "Always send a SASE and clips. We prefer to see a query first. Do not send material on subjects already covered in-house by the Good Housekeeping Institute—these include food, beauty, needlework and crafts."

**$ $ $ $ HARPER'S BAZAAR**, The Hearst Corp., 1700 Broadway, New York, NY 10019. (212)903-5000. Publisher: Jeannette Chang. **Contact:** Eve MacSweeney, features director. "*Harper's Bazaar* is a monthly specialist magazine for women who love fashion and beauty. It is edited for sophisticated women with exceptional taste. *Bazaar* offers ideas in fashion and beauty, and reports on issues and interests relevant to the lives of modern women." Estab. 1867. Circ. 711,000. Pays on publication. Byline given. Offers 25% kill fee. Buys worldwide rights. Reports in 2 months on queries.

**Nonfiction: Buys 36 mss/year.** Query with published clips. Length: 2,000-3,000 words. Payment negotiable.

**Columns/Departments:** Length: 500-700 words. Payment negotiable.

**$ $ INDIANAPOLIS WOMAN MAGAZINE**, Weiss Communications, 6081 E. 82nd St., Suite 401, Indianapolis IN 46290. (317)585-5858. Fax: (317)585-5855. E-mail: jtodd@indianapoliswoman.com. Website: http://www.indianapoliswoman.com. Editor: Joan S. Todd. **Contact:** Krista Hansing, managing editor. **65% freelance written.** Monthly regional women's magazine. "*Indianapolis Woman* aims to capture the spirit of Indianapolis-area women who are committed to maximizing their potential at home, in the community and in the workplace. *IW* strives to provide its readers with information as well as inspiration in a proactive arena." Estab. 1992. Circ. 50,000. Pays on publication. Publishes ms an average of 3-4 months after acceptance. Byline given. Buys first rights. Editorial lead time 4-5 months. Submit seasonal material 4 months in advance. Accepts queries by mail. Accepts simultaneous submissions. Reports in 3 weeks on queries; 1 month on mss. Sample copy online at website. Writer's guidelines for #10 SAE with 1 first-class stamp.

**Nonfiction:** General interest, how-to, inspirational, interview/profile. "No poetry, first-person accounts, book reviews,

cooking reviews, historical pieces, humor, articles about a single organization, building or business." Query with published clips. Length: 2,500-3,000 words. **Pays $100-300.**
**Photos:** State availability of photos with submission. Offers no additional payment for photos accepted with ms. Identification of subjects required. Buys one-time rights.
**Tips:** "Send queries by mail only. Before submitting story ideas, writers are encouraged to read the magazine and understand its mission. In general, articles should focus on Central Indiana women who are making a difference—and current issues of special relevance to women in this area."

**N $ JOYFUL WOMAN**, Joyful Christian Ministries, P.O. Box 90028, Chattanooga TN 37412. (706)866-5522. Fax: (706)866-2432. E-mail: joyfulcmi@aol.com. Website: http://www.joyfulwoman.org. Editor: Joy Rice Martin. **Contact:** Joanna Rice, assistant editor. **10-15% freelance written.** Bimonthly covering Christian women's interests. "For and about Bible-believing women who want God's best." Estab. 1978. Circ. 5,000. Pays on publication. Byline given. Buys one-time rights. Accepts queries by mail, e-mail, fax. Accepts simultaneous submissions. Reports in 6 weeks on queries; 6 months on mss. Sample copy for $3.50. Writer's guidelines for #10 SASE.
**O—** Break in with personal testimonies, articles for women (marriage, child-rearing, etc.) and real-life stories.
**Nonfiction:** How-to, inspirational, interview/profile, personal experience, religious. **Buys 10-12 mss/year.** Query. Length: 500-1,000 words. **Pays $15-30 for unsolicited articles.**
**Reprints:** Accepts previously published submissions.
**Photos:** State availability of photos with submission.

**$ $ $ LADIES' HOME JOURNAL**, Meredith Corporation, 125 Park Ave., 20th Floor, New York NY 10017-5516. (212)557-6600. Fax: (212)455-1313. Publishing Director/Editor-in-Chief: Myrna Blyth. **50% freelance written.** Monthly magazine focusing on issues of concern to women 30-45. They cover a broader range of news and political issues than many other women's magazines. "*Ladies' Home Journal* is for active, empowered women who are evolving in new directions. It addresses informational needs with highly focused features and articles on a variety of topics including beauty and fashion, food and nutrition, health and medicine, home decorating and design, parenting and self-help, personalities and current events." Circ. 5,000,000. **Pays on acceptance.** Offers 25% kill fee. Rights bought vary with submission. Accepts queries by mail. Reports on queries within 3 months with SASE. Writer's guidelines for #10 SASE, Attention: Writer's Guidelines on envelope.
**Nonfiction:** Submissions on the following subjects should be directed to the editor listed for each: investigative reports, news-related features, psychology/relationships/sex (Pam O'Brien, articles editor); medical/health (Elena Rover, health editor); celebrities/entertainment (Melina Gerosa, entertainment editor); travel stories (Karyn Dabaghian, associate editor). Query with published clips. Length: 2,000-3,000 words. **Pays $2,000-4,000.** Pays expenses of writers on assignment.
**Photos:** State availability of photos with submission. Offers variable payment for photos accepted with ms. Captions, model releases and identification of subjects required. Rights bought vary with submission. (*LHJ* arranges for its own photography almost all the time.)
**Columns/Departments:** Query the following editor or box for column ideas. First Person (Karyn Dabaghian, associate editor). **Pays $750-2,000.**
**Fiction:** Shana Aborn, senior editor, books. Only short stories and novels submitted by an agent or publisher will be considered. Buys 12 mss/year. No poetry of any kind.
&#9632; The online magazine carries original content not found in the print edition. Contact: Carolyn Noyes, managing editor.

**$ THE LINK & VISITOR**, Baptist Women's Missionary Society of Ontario and Quebec, 30 Arlington Ave., Toronto, Ontario M6G 3K8 Canada. (416)651-7192. Fax: (416)651-0438. **Contact:** Esther Barnes, editor. **50% freelance written.** "Magazine published 9 times/year designed to help Baptist women grow their world, faith, relationships, creativity, and mission vision-evangelical, egalitarian, Canadian." Estab. 1878. Circ. 4,300. Pays on publication. Publishes ms 6 months after acceptance. Byline given. Buys one-time, second serial (reprint) or simultaneous rights and makes work-for-hire assignments. Editorial lead time 2 months. Submit seasonal material 3 months in advance. Accepts simultaneous submissions. Sample copy for 9×12 SAE with 2 first-class Canadian stamps. Writer's guidelines free.
**Nonfiction:** Inspirational, interview/profile, religious. "Articles must be Biblically literate. No easy answers, American mindset or U.S. focus, retelling of Bible stories, sermons." **Buys 30-35 mss/year.** Send complete ms. Length: 750-2,000 words. **Pays 5¢/word (Canadian).** Sometimes pays expenses of writers on assignment.
**Photos:** State availability of photos with submission. Reviews any prints. Offers no additional payment for photos accepted with ms. Captions required. Buys one-time rights.
**Tips:** "Canadian women writers preferred. Don't send little stories with a moral attached. Show some thought, research, depth of insight. We're looking for material on praise."

**$ $ $ MADEMOISELLE**, Condé Nast, 350 Madison Ave., New York NY 10017. (212)880-8800. **Contact:** Faye Haun, managing editor. **95% freelance written.** Prefers to work with published/established writers. Columns are written by contributing editors Monthly magazine for women age 18-31. "*Mademoiselle* is edited for a woman in her twenties. It focuses on the decade when she is starting out in life as an independent adult and experiencing being on her own for the first time. Editorial offers advice on fashion, beauty, relationships, work and self-discovery." Circ. 1,200,000. Buys first North American serial rights. **Pays on acceptance**; rates vary.
**Nonfiction:** Particular concentration on articles of interest to the intelligent young woman 18-31, including personal

relationships, health, careers, trends, and current social problems. Send entertainment queries to Jeanie Pyun. Query with published clips and SASE. Length: 800-3,000 words. Rates vary.

**Photos:** Cindy Searight, creative director. Commissioned work assigned according to needs. Photos of fashion, beauty, travel. Payment ranges from no-charge to an agreed rate of payment per shot, job series or page rate. Buys all rights. Pays on publication for photos.

**Tips:** "We are looking for timely, well-researched manuscripts that address the particular needs of our readers."

■ **$ $ $ $ McCALL'S**, Gruner & Jahr, 375 Lexington Ave., New York NY 10017-5514. (212)499-2000. Fax: (212)499-1778. Editor: Sally Koslow. **Contact:** Cathy Cavender, executive editor. **90% freelance written.** Monthly. "Our constantly evolving publication carefully and conscientiously serves the needs of the woman reader—concentrating on matters that directly affect her life and offering information and understanding on subjects of personal importance to her." Circ. 4,200,000. **Pays on acceptance.** Publishes ms an average of 6 months after acceptance. Offers 20% kill fee. Byline given. Buys exclusive or First North American rights. Reports in 2 months. Guidelines for SASE.

● Ranked as one of the best markets for freelance writers in *Writer's Yearbook* magazine's annual "Top 100 Markets," January 1999.

**Nonfiction:** The editors are seeking meaningful stories of personal experience, fresh slants for self-help and relationship pieces, and well-researched action-oriented articles and narratives dealing with social problems concerning readers. Topics must have broad appeal, but they must be approached in a fresh, new, you-haven't-read-this-elsewhere way. **Buys 200-300 mss/year,** many in the 1,500-2,000-word length. **Pays $1/word.** These are on subjects of interest to women: health, personal narratives, celebrity biographies and autobiographies, etc. Almost all features on food, fashion, beauty and decorating are staff-written." Sometimes pays expenses of writers on assignment.

**Columns/Departments:** Real Life (stories of women who have lived through or accomplished something extraordinary), 1,800 words; Inspirations (first person stories of women who have changed their lives or accomplished a goal or dream—not stories about overcoming odds), 600 words; Couples (how to make marriages work better), 1,200 words; Consumer Watch (how to spend and save wisely, avoid scams and shop smarter), 600 words; Health Alert, 600 words; Medical Report, 2,000 words; Mind and Body, 1,800 words; Staying Fit, 1,200 words; Prime Time (special bimonthly section featuring articles on health, finance and self-help for readers over 50), 800-1,000 words; Mind & Body (psychological and emotional aspects of good health from overcoming fears to improving one's outlook on life), 1,200 words. Query. **Pays $1/word.**

◪ The online magazine carries original content not found in the print edition. Contact: Rachel Hager, online editor.

**Tips:** "Query first. Articles about food, fashion, beauty, home decorating and travel are staff-written. Read our writer's guidelines and know the type of women we are looking to profile. Use the tone and format of our most recent issues as your guide. Address submissions to executive editor unless otherwise specified. We do make outside assignments for our department categories."

**$ $ $ MODERN BRIDE**, Primedia, 249 W. 17th St., New York NY 10011. (212)462-3472. Fax: (212)367-8342. Website: http://www.modernbride.com. Editor: Stacy Morrison. **Contact:** Lisa Milbrand, associate editor. "*Modern Bride* is designed as the bride-to-be's guide to planning her wedding, honeymoon, and first home or apartment. Issues cover: (1) bridal fashion (including attendants and mother-of-the-bride), travel trousseau and lingerie; (2) home furnishings (tableware, furniture, linens, appliances, housewares, coverings, accessories, etc.); (3) honeymoon travel (covering the United States, Canada, Mexico, the Bahamas, the Caribbean, Europe and Asia). Additional regular features include personal and beauty care, wedding gifts, etiquette, marital relations, financial advice, and shopping information." Estab. 1949. Circ. 406,000. Byline given. **Pays on acceptance.** Offers 25% kill fee. Publishes ms 6 months after acceptance. Editorial lead time 4 months. Buys first periodical rights. Reports in 6 weeks.

**Nonfiction:** Book excerpts, general interest, how-to, personal experience. **Buys 60 mss/year.** Query with published clips. Length: 500-2,000 words. **Pays $600-1,200.**

**Reprints:** Send tearsheet of article or short story. Pays 50% of amount paid for an original article.

**Columns/Departments:** Contact: Geri Bain, editor for travel. Voices and On His Mind (personal experiences of bride and groom).

◪ The online magazine carries original content not found in the print edition. Contact: Nancy Davis, online editor.

■ **$ $ MORE MAGAZINE**, Meredith Corp. (Ladies Home Journal), 125 Park Ave., New York NY 10017. Fax: (212)455-1433. **Contact:** Debra Birnbaum, senior editor. Editor-in-Chief: Myrna Blyth. **90% freelance written.** Bimonthly consumer magazine covering smart, sophisticated 45+ women. Estab. 1998. Circ. 400,000. **Pays on acceptance.** Publishes ms an average of 3 months after acceptance. Byline given. Offers 25% kill fee. Buys first North American serial, first, all rights. Editorial lead time 4 months. Submit seasonal material 6 months in advance. Accepts simultaneous submissions. Reports in 3 months. Writer's guidelines for #10 SASE.

**Nonfiction: Contact:** Debra Birnbaum, senior editor. Essays, exposé, general interest, interview/profile, personal experience, travel. **Buys 50 mss/year.** Query with published clips. Length: 300-3,000 words. Payment depending on writer/story length. Pays expenses of writers on assignment.

**Photos:** State availability of photos with submission. Negotiates payment individually. Captions, model releases and identification of subjects required. Buys all rights.

**Columns/Departments:** Contact: Debra Birnbaum, senior editor. **Buys 20 mss/year.** Query with published clips. **Pays $300.**